FOR SUSAN -

WITH LOVE
+ BEST WISHES,

Eric

CRIME
Extra

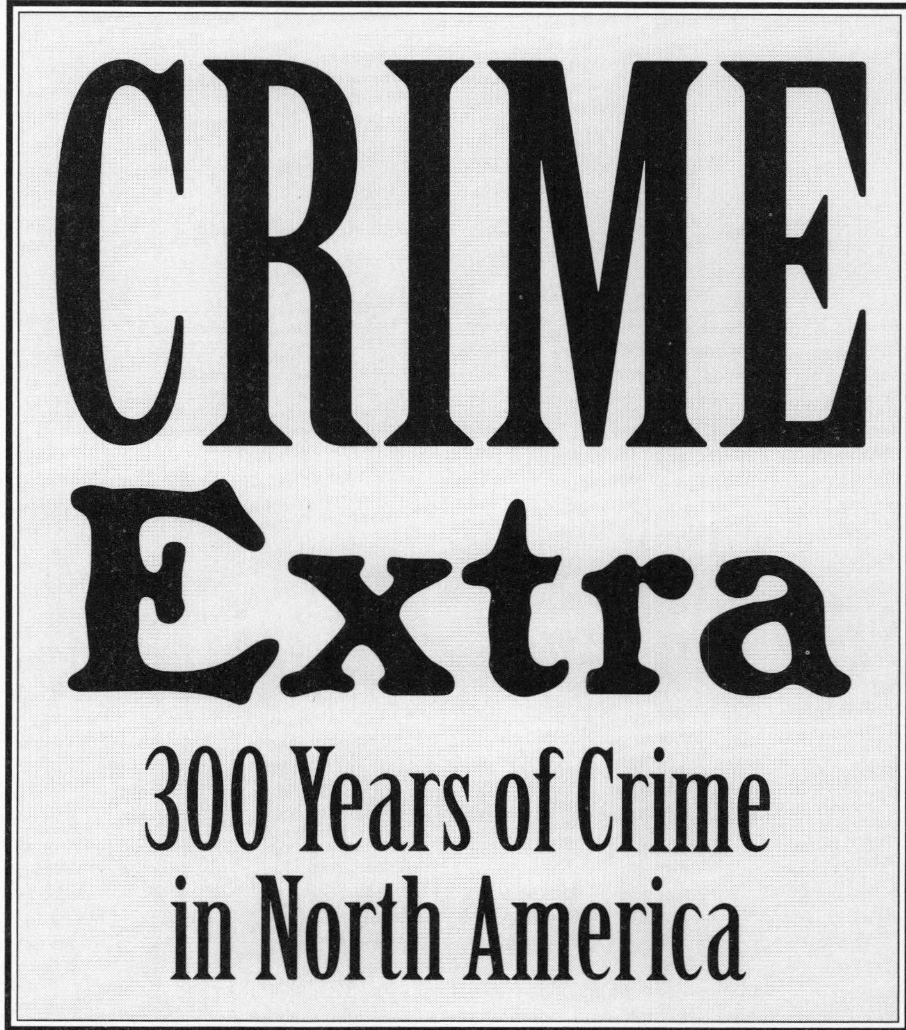

From the Eric C. Caren Collection

CASTLE BOOKS

Published by Castle Books
a division of Book Sales, Inc.
114 Northfield Avenue
Edison, NJ 08837, USA

Compiled by Eric C. Caren
Edited by Julie Saffel

Printed in Spain
ISBN 0-7858-1272-5

Contents

51	October 29-30, 1881	Daily Epitaph	Blow-up of the two previous articles on the "Gunfight at the O.K. Corral," from the Daily Epitaph, due to their historical importance.
52	January 16, 1882	Street and Smith's New York Weekly	"Calamity Jane, The Queen of the Plains"
53	April 20, 1882	The Neosho Times	"Jesse James Assassinated!"
54	April 22, 1882	Frank Leslie's Illustrated Newspaper	Somber portrait of Jesse James, the famed desperado.
55	April 22, 1882	The National Police Gazette	Portrait of Jesse James and illustration of his murder.
56	April 27, 1882	Young Men of America	Coleman and James Younger, brothers and outlaws - An Illustration
57	April 29, 1882	The National Police Gazette	"The Murder of Jesse James - Portraits and Scenes from the Tragedy"
58	May 16, 1882	The Denver Daily Times	"'Doc' Holladay, Man-Killer or an Abused Man, Which?" - An Interview
59	July 21, 1883	The National Police Gazette	Portrait of "The Dodge City 'Peace' Commission" - Including Bat Masterson and Wyatt Earp.
60	September 28, 1883	The Wide Awake Library	"The Life and Trial of Frank James" - An Illustration
61	March 29, 1884	The National Police Gazette	"Ben Thompson's Final Exit"
62	August 21, 1884	Denver Tribune-Republican	"Doc Holliday Again - The Notorious Desperado Shoots a Man at Leadville"
63	May 8, 1886	The Daily Graphic	Sketches from the Haymarket Square Riots in Chicago.
64	August 10, 1887	The Prison Mirror	Cole, Jim, and Robert Younger loan to the "trust fund" to start a prison newspaper. Note their contributions.
65	Late 1880's	The Illustrated Police News	Convict mutiny and Judge Roy Bean's method of holding court - Illustrations
66	August 7, 1890	The New York Herald	The first execution by electric chair.
67	c. October 14, 1890	Harper's Weekly	David C. Hennessy, New Orleans Chief of Police, killed investigating the beginnings of the Mafia.
68	March 28, 1891	Harper's Weekly	Early American Mafia killing in New Orleans - An Illustration
69	October 6, 1892	The Indianapolis News	"The Daltons' Last Raid - Five of the Desperadoes Shot Down by [Coffeyville, KS] Citizens"
70	October 6, 1892	Los Angeles Herald	"The Dalton Boys Dead - Three of the Brothers Died in Their Boots"
71	October 26, 1892	Topeka State Journal	"The Daltons Again - They Will Sue Coffeyville for Damages"
72-73	October 29, 1892	The Illustrated American	"Exeunt the Daltons" - A detailed story of their last raid.
74	July 1, 1893	The Illustrated Police News	"Lizzie Borden Not Guilty" - An Illustration
75	June 16, 1894	The Chicago World	Texas outlaw Bill Dalton goes down with his boots on.
76	February 2, 1895	Harper's Weekly	"The Strike In Brooklyn - Firing at the Mob" - Illustration of the Brooklyn Trolley Strike
77	August 21, 1895	Houston Daily Post	"Wesley Hardin Killed"
78	August 31, 1895	The Illustrated Police News	"Desperado John Wesley Hardin Slain" - An Illustration
79	April 12, 1896	The Sunday Inter Ocean	America's first mass murderer, H.H. Holmes, aka Herman Mudgett.
80	August 28, 1898	The World's Sunday Magazine	Profile of Mrs. Martha Place—a New York murderess.
81	March 20, 1899	The Daily City Item	"First Woman Electrocuted: Mrs. Place Dies in the Death Chair at Sing Sing"; "Death of Owen Kern - Second Victim of Frank Krause's Murderous Assault"
82	June 25, 1899	The New York Herald	An account of a manhunt for the "Hole-In-The-Wall" bandits after their attempt to dynamite a Union Pacific train.
83	September 2, 1900	The Denver Republican	"Notorious 'Butch' Cassidy Said to Have Led Table Rock Train Robbery"
84	February 3, 1901	The New York Herald	"Mrs. Carrie Nation - Terror of Kansas' Saloonkeepers"
85	April 26, 1901	The Denver Times	The horrible execution of "Black Jack" Ketchum—train robber.
86	September 6, 1901	The Buffalo Evening Times - Extra	"President M'Kinley Shot at the Pan-American!"
87	August 7, 1902	The Inter Ocean	"Outlaw [Harry] Tracy Commits Suicide Rather Than Submit to Capture"
88	November 20, 1903	The Cheyenne Daily Leader	U.S. lawman and outlaw Tom Horn is "Hung by the Neck Till Dead".
89	April 17, 1904	The Inter Ocean	The strange career of Pearl Hart, girl bandit.
90	July 11, 1904	The Rocky Mountain News	Hole-In-The-Wall Gang member Harvey Logan commits suicide. Photo of the gang includes Butch Cassidy and the Sundance Kid.
91	September 22, 1904	The Boston Post - Extra	Early anarchism.
92	September 23, 1906	The New York Herald	"Yankee Desperadoes Hold Up the Argentine Republic" - Includes news and photograph of Butch Cassidy, the Sundance Kid, and Kid Curry.
93	March 6, 1908	The Beeville Bee	Pat Garrett, slayer of Billy the Kid and noted outlaw, killed in New Mexico.
94	August 1, 1910	Newark Evening Star	"[Dr. Hawley H.] Crippen and Girl in Cells"
95	May 16, 1911	New-York Tribune	"Standard Oil Company Ordered Dissolved; Reasonable Restraint of Trade Not Unlawful"
96	October 15, 1912	The Boston Post - Extra	"[President Theodore] Roosevelt, Shot by Crank, Makes Speech, Bleeding from Bullet Wound in Breast"
97	September 11, 1919	The Boston Post - Extra	The Boston Police Riots
98	November 18, 1919	Cheyenne State Leader	"Train Bandit [William L.] Carlisle Surrounded"
99	January 16, 1920	Santa Fe New Mexican	"Constitutional Prohibition to be Effective at Midnight"
100	May 13, 1920	The Chicago Evening Post	"Big Jim" Colosimo is rubbed out.
101	May 15, 1920	Los Angeles Evening Herald	Entertainer Fannie Brice's beau, gangster "Nicky" Arnstein surrenders. They both appeared as characters in "Funny Girl" on stage and screen.
102	August 12, 1920	The Cleveland News	Financial wizard Charles Ponzi arrested.
103	September 16, 1920	The Wisconsin News	"Blast Rocks New York!" - Anarchist bomb on Wall Street.
104	September 18, 1920	The New York Times	Wall Street bombing tied to Red Threat—circulars clue to plot.
105	August 1, 1921	Akron Beacon Journal	One of the infamous Hatfield clan of West Virginia is shot.
106	August 3, 1921	The Anaconda Standard	The Black Sox Scandal
107	September 11, 1921	Los Angeles Examiner	Screen actor Roscoe "Fatty" Arbuckle is held for murder.
108	September 22, 1921	The Cleveland News	"Ku Klux Klan Exposed - High Chief Bares All"
109	June 16, 1922	Chicago Daily Tribune	"Seize 3 Klan Night Riders"
110	July 20, 1923	Los Angeles Evening Herald	"Pancho Villa is Slain by Gunmen"

111	February 14, 1924	Oakland Tribune	"Secrecy on Teapot Dome Deal Bared"
112	May 23, 1924	Los Angeles Examiner - Extra	"Kidnapers Hack Boy Dead With Hatchet"
113	June 2, 1924	The Chicago Evening Post	"[Nathan] Leopold and [Richard] Loeb Jailed"
114	September 10, 1924	The Chicago Daily News	"Loeb And Leopold Get Life"
115	October 14, 1924	The Pittsburgh Post	Twenty-Four members of the Blackhand Society, the backbone of the Mafia, held to court in bomb plot.
116	November 11, 1924	The Evansville Courier	"Dion O'Bannion is Murdered: King of Chicago Rum Runners is Victim of Feud"
117	November 25, 1924	The Chicago Evening Post	"Open War on Beer Gangs"
118	January 18, 1925	Chicago Sunday Tribune	"[Johnny] Torrio Given Prison Term"
119	January 27, 1925	Chicago Herald and Examiner	"Plot to Kill Capone and Mrs. Torrio"
120	June 19, 1925	The National Kourier	"Nation's Capital to Witness Giant Klan Parade"
121	July 21, 1925	The Wisconsin News	"[John T.] Scopes is Convicted by 'Ape' Jury" - Anti-evolution trial comes to a close. This trial was the basis for the play "Inherit the Wind" and numerous film adaptations.
122	April 5, 1926	The New Haven Union	"[Gerald] Chapman Pleads for His Life"
123	July 2, 1926	The Chicago Evening Post	"Caponi and Ten Indicted"
124	October 13, 1926	Chicago Herald and Examiner	"Capones Own Amazing Story!"
125	October 15, 1926	The Chicago Evening Post	"[Joe 'Polack'] Saltis Jury Dismissed"
126	October 19, 1926	The Chicago Daily News	"[Earl 'Little Hymie'] Weiss Reprisals Started; One Dead"
127	November 18, 1926	Los Angeles Evening Herald	The Hall - Mills Murder Trial
128	May 19, 1927	Toledo Blade	"Maniac's [Andrew Kehoe] Revenge Sends Forty-Two to Death in Schoolhouse Blast"
129	August 23, 1927	The Boston Herald	"[Nicola] Sacco and [Bartolomeo] Vanzetti are Executed"
130	January 14, 1928	Daily News	The execution of Ruth Snider—the first unofficial photo ever taken in the death chamber.
131	February 29, 1928	The Chicago Daily News	"George Moran Seized in Bomb Drive"
132	February 15, 1929	Daily News - Extra	"7 Massacred in Chicago Beer War" - The St. Valentine's Day Massacre
133	December 23, 1929	The Chicago Daily News	"Jury Calls [Fred] Burke [St. Valentine's Day] Massacre Slayer"
134	May 29, 1930	Chicago Daily Tribune	"Shot Down; Taken for Ride"
135	June 10, 1930	Cleveland Plain Dealer	"Gangsters Slay [Chicago Tribune] Reporter"
136	June 12, 1930	Chicago Herald and Examiner	"'Death Squads' Hunt Killers" - Tribune murder dragnet intensifies.
137	June 21, 1930	Chicago Daily Tribune	Capone distilleries in Cicero raided by prohibition agents.
138	July 1, 1930	Los Angeles Evening Herald	"[George 'Bugs'] Moran Gun Gang Seized Here in Lingle Murder"
139	July 14, 1930	Chicago Herald and Examiner	"Killer [Fred] Burke's Lair Raided"
140	August 11, 1930	Chicago Herald and Examiner	"Moran Ousted in Gang Truce"
141	October 14, 1930	Los Angeles Evening Herald	"L.A. Officers Shoot Down ['Little Jake'] Fleagle, Outlaw Leader"
142	December 12, 1930	Chicago Daily Tribune	"Moran is Found Not Guilty"
143	December 20, 1930	The Chicago Daily News	"[Frank 'The Enforcer'] Nitti Gets 18 Months, $10,000 Fine"
144	February 27, 1931	The Chicago Daily News	"Capone Sentenced to Jail for Contempt"
145	May 9, 1931	Daily News - Extra	"Two Gun" Crowley pleads for his own execution.
146	June 13, 1931	Chicago Daily Tribune	"Indict Capone; 5,000 Counts"
147	October 24, 1931	Los Angeles Examiner	The Infamous Trunk Murders - "Mrs. Judd Surrenders; Confesses Killings"
148	October 24, 1931	Boston Evening American - Extra	"11 Years For 'King' Capone"; Ruth Judd self-defense story professed inconceivable.
149	December 18, 1931	Brooklyn Daily Eagle	Infamous gangster Jack "Legs" Diamond is slain.
150	March 22, 1932	The Cleveland Press	"'Baby-Faced' Coll, Who Dyed His Curls" - A posthumous gangster profile.
151	May 4, 1932	Evening Graphic	"Capone, in Leg Irons, Races to Pen Under Heavy Guard"
152	May 13, 1932	Daily Mirror - Extra	"Lindy's Baby Murdered!"
153	February 16, 1933	Los Angeles Evening Herald and Express - Extra	The attempted assassination of President-elect Franklin D. Roosevelt.
154	June 17, 1933	Los Angeles Evening Herald and Express	"Machine Gunmen Slay 4 Police and Prisoner" - An account of the Kansas City Massacre.
155	July 14, 1933	Quaker City Brevity	"Big White Slave Ring Gets Girls in Phila." - An Exposé
156	July 25, 1933	The Dallas Morning News	"[Brother-in-Crime] Buck Barrow Dying After Gun Battle, but Clyde Escapes"
157	September 7, 1933	Chicago Daily Tribune	"Machine Gun" Jack McGurn found guilty of vagrancy.
158	September 26, 1933	Jackson Daily News	"[George] 'Machine Gun' Kelly Caught"
159	November 27, 1933	Los Angeles Evening Herald and Express - Extra	The John M. Holmes Case - Vigilante mob takes over prison while Governor signals approval.
160	November 30, 1933	Chicago Herald and Examiner	"Verne Miller Found Slain: Worst Outlaw, Once Sheriff, Taken on Ride"
161	January 31, 1934	Chicago Daily Tribune	"Meek [John] Dillinger is Jailed"
162	February 8, 1934	St. Paul Dispatch	"[Edward] Bremer Returns Home; Kidnap Ransom Paid"
163	February 23, 1934	Chicago Daily Tribune	"99 Years for Three Touhys"
164	March 3, 1934	New York World Telegram	"Dillinger Flees Jail With Toy Gun"
165	March 25, 1934	Chicago Sunday Tribune	Chicago's "Most Wanted" presented in mug shot format.
166	April 1, 1934	St. Paul Sunday Pioneer Press	"Dillinger Named as Gunman Here"
167	April 2, 1934	The Dallas Morning News - Extra	"Clyde Barrow, Fleeing, Kills Two Patrolmen"
168	April 5, 1934	El Paso Herald-Post	Photographs of Clyde Barrow and Bonnie Parker.
169	April 22, 1934	Chicago Sunday Tribune	"Dillinger, Archenemy of Society, Another of Crime's Muddleheads" - A Profile
170	April 23, 1934	The St. Paul Daily News	"Trap Closing on Dillinger After Fight Near St. Paul"
171	April 24, 1934	St. Paul Pioneer Press	"Dillinger Gang Believed Hidden Here; One Mobster Shot; Bloody Car Found"
172	April 26, 1934	The Dallas Morning News	"Ray Hamilton Caught 2 Hours After Holdup"
173	April 28, 1934	St. Paul Pioneer Press	"Gunman Believed [George 'Baby Face'] Nelson Wounds Sheriff"
174	May 19, 1934	Chicago Herald and Examiner	"Roosevelt Wars on Gangs!"

175	May 24, 1934	The Dallas Morning News	“Posse Kills Clyde Barrow and Bonnie Parker”
176	July 23, 1934	The Evening Gazette	“Dillinger Died Reaching for Gun”
177	July 23, 1934	Los Angeles Evening Herald and Express - Extra	“Dillinger Led to Death by Girl in Red Dress”
178	August 24, 1934	St. Paul Pioneer Press	“[Dillinger Henchman] Homer Van Meter Killed By Police Here; Woman Friend Leads to Tip-Off”
179	August 25, 1934	Chicago Herald and Examiner	“Order Gunman [George ‘Baby Face’] Nelson Slain: Police Trail Dillinger Aid After Killing”
180	September 21, 1934	The Philadelphia Inquirer	“Lindbergh Kidnapping Case Solved”
181	October 22, 1934	East Liverpool Review	“Search County for Bandit [Charles ‘Pretty Boy’] Floyd; Purvis and U.S. Agents Spread Net”
182	October 22, 1934	East Liverpool Review - Extra	“Floyd Shot Down by Police and Federal Agents”
183	November 29, 1934	Chicago Herald and Examiner	“Dying U.S. Agents Kill ‘Baby Face’ in Battle!”
184	December 14, 1934	The New York Herald Tribune	Albert Fish, the real-life Hannibal Lector.
185	January 17, 1935	The Florida Times-Union	Kate “Ma” Barker and son Fred are slain in gun battle with FBI.
186	January 21, 1935	Chicago Herald and Examiner	“[Alvin] Karpis in Fierce Gun Battle! Escapes With Pal; Woman Shot”
187	January 24, 1935	Chicago Herald and Examiner	“[St. Valentine’s Day] Massacre Confession Puts Capone in Shadow of Chair!”
188	September 10, 1935	The Baltimore News and The Baltimore Post	“[Senator] Huey Long Dies of Bullet Wound”
189	October 24, 1935	Daily Record	“Dutch Schultz Shot Down!”
190	October 24, 1935	Daily News - Extra	“Schultz, 5 Pals Shot”
191	February 15, 1936	Chicago Daily Tribune	“‘Machine Gun’ M’Gurn Slain”
192	April 3, 1936	The Baltimore News-Post - Extra	“Bruno [Hauptmann] Dies, Fails to Talk”
193	May 2, 1936	The St. Paul Daily News	“G-Men Jail Karpis Here After Night Plane Dash”
194	June 8, 1936	Daily News	“[Charles ‘Lucky’] Luciano and 8 Found Guilty”
195	December 17, 1937	San Francisco Chronicle - Extra	“Two Convicts Flee From Alcatraz Isle”
196	May 1, 1939	Chicago Herald and Examiner	“[George ‘Bugs’] Moran and [Frank] Parker Guilty in Forgery; Face Year in Jail”
197	September 15, 1940	Baltimore American	“Hollywood Playboy [Ben Siegel] Linked to Murder Ring”
198	March 20, 1943	Chicago Daily Tribune	“[Frank ‘The Enforcer’] Nitti Kills Himself!”
199	March 5, 1944	Sunday News	Louis “Lepke” Buchalter dies in the chair at Sing Sing.
200	January 28, 1947	Los Angeles Examiner	“Surrender of [Actress] Black Dahlia’s Killer Awaited by Police”
201	June 22, 1947	Los Angeles Examiner	“Hint [Benjamin ‘Bugsy’] Siegel Slain by Own Mob”
202	July 20, 1949	Los Angeles Examiner - Extra	“[Gang Chieftain] Micky Cohen Shot”
203	January 19, 1950	The Boston Herald	“Huge Holdup [the infamous Brink’s robbery] Pinned to Local Gang”
204	January 21, 1950	Chicago Daily News	“Alger Hiss Convicted; Faces Ten Years, Fine”
205	November 2, 1950	The Washington Observer	“Truman Assassination Fails; Guards Shoot Puerto Ricans”
206	March 13, 1951	New York Post	“[Frank] Costello Defies Probe, Move Hinted to Deport Him”
207	March 19, 1951	New Haven Evening Register	“O’Dwyer Questioned on Murder, Inc.”
208	November 18, 1952	Daily Mirror	“U.S. Moves to Bounce [Gaetano ‘Thomas’] Luchese”
209	June 20, 1953	New Haven Journal-Courier	“Rosenbergs [Julius and Ethel] Die in Electric Chair”
210	March 2, 1954	New Haven Journal-Courier	Five congressmen are wounded after four fanatics open fire in House gallery.
211	December 22, 1954	Cleveland Plain Dealer	The local paper reports that Dr. Sam Sheppard is found guilty of murdering his wife. This was the basis for the TV series and movie “The Fugitive”.
212	January 22, 1957	New York Post	The “Mad Bomber” is captured.
213	September 24, 1957	The New York Herald Tribune	“Eisenhower Warns: Peace or Troops, After Mob Riots at Little Rock School”
214	October 25, 1957	New York Post - Extra	“Murder Inc. Boss [Albert Anastasia] Slain”
215	November 15, 1957	New York Post	“The Mob Meets: Cops Seize [Vito Genovese] 65 Hoods - New Killings Feared”
216	January 29, 1958	Los Angeles Evening Herald Express - Extra	Charles Starkweather and his girlfriend are captured after a mass murder spree. They became the models for the motion picture “Natural Born Killers”.
217	April 5, 1958	Los Angeles Evening Herald Express - Extra	“Daughter Kills Lana Turner’s Boy Friend”
218	September 26, 1959	The Macon News	“Mob Kingpin [Little Augie Pisano], Woman Shot to Death in Auto”
219	November 2, 1959	The Cleveland Press	Charles Van Doren reveals that NBC-TV quiz show was fixed.
220	October 10, 1961	New York Post	Police raid headquarters of Brooklyn’s Gallo gang.
221	October 16, 1963	New York Mirror	“[Mobster Joseph] Valachi Sings Here Today”
222	November 23, 1963	The Dallas Morning News	“Kennedy Slain on Dallas Street”
223	March 15, 1964	Sunday News	“Doomed” - Jury sentences Jack Ruby to death in chair.
224	February 22, 1965	Detroit Free Press	“Malcolm X is Slain at Rally in New York”
225	July 30, 1965	Chicago Tribune	“Uphold [James] Hoffa Conviction”
226	June 3, 1966	Chicago Tribune	“Attack Giancana Ruling: Congressmen Study Mobster Law Needs”
227	July 17, 1966	Boston Sunday Advertiser	“[Chicago Police] Name Killer of 8 Nurses”
228	August 3, 1966	The Dallas Morning News	“Last Hours of Charles Whitman” - The University of Texas Tower sniper.
229	November 17, 1966	New York Post	“Why the Jury Freed Dr. Sam [Sheppard]”
230	May 28, 1967	National Informer	“The Boston Strangler’s Perversions”
231	July 25, 1967	The Detroit News	“Snipers Prolong Emergency; Death Toll Climbs to 23”
232	April 5, 1968	The Commercial Appeal	“Dr. King is Slain by Sniper”
233	June 5, 1968	Boston Herald Traveler - Extra	“Bob Kennedy Shot in Calif.”
234	August 10, 1969	The New York Times	“Actress [Sharon Tate] is Among 5 Slain at Home in Beverly Hills”
235	August 11, 1969	New York Post	“Two More Murders, Did Tate Killer Strike Again?”
236	December 8, 1969	The News American	“300 Police Surround Panthers in L.A.; 3 Officers Wounded”
237	January 26, 1970	Midnight	“Hushed Up by Authorities: Names of 9 Hollywood Stars Marked for Death by Sharon Tate’s Murderers”
238	February 16, 1970	The Washington Post	“Chicago 7 Lawyers Face Jail”

239	May 15, 1970	The Militant	"Eyewitness Report of Kent [State University] Massacre"
240	October 14, 1970	Chicago Tribune	"FBI Arrests Angela Davis"
241	March 30, 1971	The Sacramento Union	"Manson Jury Votes Death"
242	May 25, 1971	New York Post	"[Black Panther Chairman Bobby] Seale Charges Dropped"
243	July 1, 1971	New York Post	"New Angle in Shooting of [Joseph] Colombo [Sr.]"
244	May 3, 1972	The New York Times	"Story of Joe Gallo's Murder: 5 in Colombo Gang Implicated"
245	May 16, 1972	The Washington Post	"[Gov. George] Wallace Is Shot, Legs Paralyzed; Suspect Seized at Laurel Rally"
246	October 11, 1973	The New York Times	"Agnew Quits Vice Presidency and Admits Tax Evasion in ' 67; Nixon Consults on Successor"
247	November 18, 1973	The News American	"'I'm Not a Crook,' Nixon Says"
248	March 1, 1974	New York Post	"7 Watergate Indictments"
249	October 16, 1976	New York Post	"Gambino Heir [Carmine Galante]: A Bonanno Man"
250	December 22, 1976	Daily News	"[Rubin 'Hurricane'] Carter, [John] Artis Convicted Again, N.J. Jury Rules They Killed 3 in 1966"
251	January 18, 1977	Daily News	Gary Mark Gilmore becomes the first person to be executed in the United States since the reinstatement, in 1976, of the death penalty after a ten-year hiatus. He dies by firing squad.
252	August 11, 1977	New York Post	Serial killer David Berkowitz, aka "Son of Sam," is caught.
253	July 15, 1979	Daily News	"As [Carmine] Galante Died 20 Mob Bosses Hailed Slaying"
254	March 13, 1980	Chicago Tribune	"[John Wayne] Gacy Found Guilty"
255	December 9, 1980	New York Post - Extra	"John Lennon Shot Dead"
256	March 31, 1981	The Dallas Morning News	"President [Reagan] Shot"
257	November 18, 1986	Daily News	"[Carmine] Persico Gets 39 Yrs. in Jail"
258	December 19, 1987	The New York Times	"[Ivan] Boesky Sentenced to 3 Years in Jail in Insider [Trade] Scandal"
259-260	January 25, 1989	New York Post	Grinning godfather John Gotti outside the Manhattan Supreme Court; "Sobbing [Ted] Bundy Dragged to Chair"
261	March 26, 1990	Newsday	"Social Club Tragedy: Arson Kills 87 in Bronx"
262	July 24, 1991	New York Post	Boxes of body parts are found in mass murderer Jeffrey Dahmer's apartment. Note the unfortunately placed ad for ribs to the left of the article.
263	October 17, 1991	Killeen Daily Herald	Gunman crashes truck into Luby's Cafeteria in Killeen, TX, and kills twenty-two.
264	February 27, 1993	The Washington Post	"At Least 7 Die, 500 Hurt as Explosion Rips Garage Under World Trade Center"
265	April 20, 1995	The Washington Post	"Bomb Kills Dozens in Oklahoma Federal Building"
266	October 4, 1995	Los Angeles Times	"[O.J.] Simpson Not Guilty: Drama Ends 474 Days After Arrest"
267	April 5, 1996	The New York Times	Unabomber Theodore Kaczynski
268	January 12, 1997	New York Post	"Tragic Little Beauty" - The JonBenet Ramsey Murder
269	July 31, 1998	New York Post	"Spot Check: Monica Hands Over Love Dress to FBI for DNA Match"
270	April 20, 1999	Denver Rocky Mountain News - Extra!	"Horror - At Least 21 Wounded as Two Gunmen Open Fire at Columbine High School"

Vol. 9. Numb. 6

The Athenian Mercury:

Saturday, December 31. 1692. Licens'd, E. B.

Quest. 1. IN those remarkable TRYALS of WITCHES publish'd this Week by Mr. Mather, *'tis said that Nineteen Witches have been lately Executed at* New-England, *and that there is an Hundred Witches still in Prison, Committed upon the Accusation of fifty Witches, some of* Boston, *but most about* Salem *and the Towns adjacent: This Relation is very strange and surprizing, I therefore desire your Sentiments of it?*

Answ. You'll find an Answer to this Question in *p.* 48. of the said Book of *Tryals*, in these words:

THE Reverend and Worthy Author having at the Direction of his Excellency the Governour so far obliged the Publick as to give some Account of the Sufferings brought upon the Countrey by Witchcraft, and of the Tryals which have passed upon several Executed for the same:

Upon perusal thereof we find the Matter of Fact and Evidence truly reported, and a Prospect given of the Methods of Conviction used in the Proceedings of the Court of Salem.

Boston, *Octob.* 11. 1692. William Stoughton. Samuel Sewall.

These two Gentlemen who give their Attestation to these *Tryals* published by Mr. *Mather*, being both of 'em Magistrates of known Worth and Integrity, we shall add no more by way of Answer to this Question, but only to acquaint our Readers, that if any thing occurrs in reading which may occasion any doubt or dissatisfaction, We shall be ready if such *Objections* are sent in unto us to give what Explanation we are able, on such *a strange surprizing Subject.*

Quest. 2. *At* Colchester, *where Sir* Charles Lucas *was shot, in the place where he fell, no Grass has grown since that time; there being the perfect shape of a Man's Body, and Grass growing all round it, and between the Sign of the Legs and Arms extended: The Reason of this?*

Answ. This Question, with these immediately following it, were all three sent in the same Hand, and by the same Person, who affirms he's certain of the Truth of 'em all; —— thô we confess *his* being certain makes not *us so*, for things so *strange*, ought to have been better *attested*, than by a *single unknown Affirmation*: However, this of Sir *Charles*, *&c.* if not true, is easily confuted, and does but *disserve* the *Royal Cause* for which that Gentleman dy'd very *bravely*, which needs no *Falshoods* to defend it. If it be true, which may easily be known by any who live about those parts, and if they wou'd inform us thereof, we'd own our selves oblig'd; it can hardly be deny'd, but that 'tis a Confirmation of the *Justice* of the *Cause* in which he suffer'd, and that, as our Histories say, contrary to the *Law of Arms*, he and the rest having *Quarter* promis'd 'em before they yielded.

Quest. 3. *In my Lord* Gainsborough's *Park at* Titchfield *in* Hampshire, *some few years past a Deer was kill'd. After 'twas broke up, the Keeper went to quarter the Heart, and the edge of his Knife grated against something that was hard, which he found to be a Bullet near the middle of the Heart, about which Bullet there was a Callous skin, like Horn, by which 'twas suppos'd that the Deer had been formerly shot, and liv'd several years afterwards: The Reason of this?*

Answ. There are some *singular Cases* of this Nature, which will puzzle all the Anatomists in the World to resolve 'em: There are Instances almost every day both of Men and Beasts, who have liv'd with *Bullets* or *Stakes* lodg'd in their Bodies. The famous *Knife-blade* which lay so long in the *Peasant*, has been sufficiently talk'd of; and we our selves have assurance of a certain *Butcher* that kill'd a Bullock which had been a little lame for a year or two before, and in cutting it up, found between the *Shoulder* and the *Breast*, quite cover'd over with hard flesh, about a *Foot and a half* of an old Hedge-stake, which it seems had been broken off there some years before. But this is nothing to any such substance in the *Nobler parts*, thô even there strange things have been found. —— *Howel* in his Letters, makes mention of a Person who lay for some years languishing of a Disease, which puzzled the *Physicians*, and Death was the only *Cure*, at whose Dissection there was found (as we remember) in the *Left Ventricle* of the Heart, a *Living Serpent*, and the *German Virtuosi* give us Instances much of the same Nature: But neither does this *reach*, for *Violence* from *without* seems more *mortal* than any such Substance bred *within*. To come yet nearer, there are some Surgeons who tell us of *Wounds* in the *Pericardium* which have been cur'd, tho' never any before that we met with in the very substance of the *Heart*; nor can it be easily suppos'd, that the Bullet in the present Case cou'd be lodg'd in any *Vacuity* there, without making a *wound* to get in. The Fact seems to be well enough *Circumstantiated*, and therefore 'tis neither *civil*, nor scarce *reasonable* to deny it; but for the reason and manner how *Nature* cou'd save it self harmless, notwithstanding that *callous substance* wherewith it guarded it self, as is very usual in such Cases, we must ingenuously acknowledge we can't resolve, and here propose it as a *Problem* to the best Professors in the Noble Art of *Chirurgery*, whose Judgments we shan't fail to communicate to the World concerning it.

Quest. 4. *In* Castle-Mallard-Walk *in* New-Forrest *in* Hampshire, *there is an Oak which every* Christmas-day *buds forth leaves as big as those of a Gooseberry, tho' there's no appearance of any Leaf either the day before, or after: The reason of it?*

Answ. We doubt very many Readers will be Infidels in this, as well as in the two former Questions. The Querist wou'd do well to be more particular in this Matter, and 'twou'd be a very pleasing Entertainment to the World, if he, or any other of the Neighbours, cou'd give an exact, and well-attested account, whether this be peculiar to that Oak, or other Oaks or Trees do the same near it? Whether it does this certainly and precisely on *Christmass-day*, and not before or after? In what manner the *Leaves appear*, whether all at once, or by degrees? and how they *go away*, whether they fall off, wither, or creep into the *Bark* again? *Curiosities* worth watching for one 24 hours, which if true, its a wonder how this *Tree* scaped *Reformation* in the last *Age*, when its *superstitious Brother* of *Glastenbury* was cut down by the Souldiers.

Quest. 5. *One that by his daily Labour can procure but just from Hand to Mouth, for the subsistence of himself and Family: Query, Whether or no he be indispensibly bound to give to the Relief of others that are in want; and if he be, in what proportion?*

Answ. That even those who only maintain themselves by *daily labour*, are bound to relieve such as are really *Objects of Charity*, *viz.* such as *wou'd*, and *can't* work for their *Livings*, is very clear from that of the Apostle,

THE LONDON GAZETTE

From Thurſday, May 22, to Monday, May 26, 1701

Place, and intended in 8 or 10 days to go to *Holſtein*. The Duke of *Holſtein-Gottorp* will be going in few days from *Reinbeck* to *Pomeren*, to review the *Swediſh* Forces in that Countrey, which (according to our laſt Advices) are drawing together in two Bodies, the one near *Straelſund*, and the other near *Stettin*; But 'tis ſaid, the Emperor, the King of *Denmark*, and other Princes, have writ in ſuch preſſing Terms to the King of *Sweden* to diſſwade him from cauſing his Forces to make an Inroad into *Saxony*, that 'tis thought this Deſign will be laid aſide.

Hague, May 31. *N. S.* The Count *d'Avaux*, Ambaſſador from *France*, gives out, that he will return home in few days. The Servants Count *Briord*, late Ambaſſador from that Crown, left behind him, will be going towards *Paris* this week, except his Secretary, who is to remain here till farther Orders. General *Coehoorn* was here ſome days ago, and, after having conferred with the Council of State, is returned to the Frontiers. The States have made an Agreement with the Elector Palatine for 7000 Men, and with the Duke of *Mecklenburgh Swerin* for two Regiments, who are all ſhortly expected in theſe Provinces. 'Tis ſaid, the *French* are drawing 16000 Men from the *Rhine* to ſtrengthen their Army on our Frontiers, and they continue to work with great diligence on their Lines, and the new Forts they are making near *Sluyce*. We hear nothing farther of what was reported the laſt week, of an Action between the *Germans* and the *French* in *Italy*.

Paris, June 1. *N. S.* The King has named the Marquis *de Saignelay*, the Marquis *de Denonville*, the Marquis *de Sommery*, and the Chevalier *de Sully*, to be Aids de Camp to the Duke of *Burgundy*, who is to be Generaliſſimo of the *French* Armies in *Flanders*. The Marſhal *de Villeroy* will go from hence in few days to the *Franche Comte*, being appointed to command the *French* Forces on the *Rhine*. The Marſhal *de Tourville* died the 28th paſt; Monſieur *de Chaſteaurenaud* is made Vice-Admiral of *France* in his Place, and is ſucceeded in that of Lieutenant-General at Sea by Monſieur *de Coetlogen*, who commands the Squadron of *French* Men of War

The BIBLE in large Folio for Churches, with ſeveral Thouſand References more than Dr. Scatergood's, by Order of his Grace the Lord Archbiſhop of Canterbury; with the Years before and after Chriſt, according to Primate Uſher's Annals, Reviſed by the Lord Biſhop of Worceſter: With a Chronological Table and Index. Alſo a Table of Scripture Meaſures, Weights, and Coins, and an Appendix, containing the Method of Calculating its Meaſures of Surface; by the Lord Biſhop of Peterborough. The ſaid Book is now ready to be delivered, at very reaſonable Prices, at His Majeſty's Printing-Office in Black-Friers, and at ſeveral Bookſellers in London and Weſtminſter.

Advertiſements.

☞ **This preſent Monday, at 4 afternoon, at Tom's** Coffee-houſe adjoining to Ludgate, will begin the Sale by Auction of the extraordinary Collection of Eccleſiaſtical Hiſtorians and Bibliothecarians, in Gr. Lat. and French, in Page 9. in the Library of a Perſon of QUALITY deceaſed; and to Morrow the Philological Authors and Lexicographers, and on Wedneſday the Byzantine Hiſtorians, &c. in the ſame Catalogue. Catalogues ſold at the Place of Sale.

*** **S. Sanctorii de Statica Medicina Aphoriſmorum** Sectiones ſeptem, cum Commentario Martini Liſter: 1. Agitur de ponderatione inſenſibilis Perſpirationis; 2. De Aere & Aquis; 3. De Cibo & Potu; 4. De Somno & Vigilia; 5. De Exercitio & Quiete; 6. De Venere; 7. De Animi affectibus: In 12° Londini, apud Sam. Smith & Benj. Walford ad Inſignia Principis in Cœmeterio D. Pauli.

☞ **A Choice Collection of Paintings of Italian, and** other eminent Maſters, late belonging to the Rt. Hon. Dorothy Lady Dacres, will be ſold by Auction on Monday the 2d of June next, at the Great Houſe with Twiſted Poſts in Great Queen-ſtreet, where they may be viewed for 4 days before the Sale.

☞ THE Members of the Friendly Society are deſired to take Notice, That on the 28th of April laſt a Fire happened in King-ſtreet, London, which burnt down a Houſe Inſured by the ſaid Society, which with ſeveral Houſes at other Times and Places damnified, the whole Loſs amounts to 373 l. 8 s. 8 d. and the Rate is 8 d. 3 f. per Cent. for Brick, and double for Timber, which is to be paid in Palſgrave-Court without Temple-Bar (by ſuch Members as depoſited but 6 s. 8 d. per Cent.) before the 23d of June next, according to their reſpective Covenants; the whole Loſs being to be paid by the Undertakers within 60 days after the Fire happened, or ſooner upon diſcounting the Intereſt.

LOſt the 25th Inſtant, at or near Garraway's Coffee-houſe in Cornhill, or the Temple Coffee-houſe in Devereux-court, a Three-ſquare turning Seal with 3 Stones, upon one of which (being a Topus) is engraven a Coat of Arms, upon the other (being an Emerald) is a Cypher CDM, on the third (being a Saphyr) is a Cat-amountant with a Garter about it. Whoever brings it to Sir Francis Child at Temple-bar, ſhall have two Guineas Reward.

LOſt the 18th Inſtant, an Ivory Box ſtudded with Gold in Scallop Shells, with a Gold Hinge, and a Scallop Shell ſtudded at bottom. Whoever brings it to Mr. Warner, Goldſmith, without Temple-bar, ſhall have 3 Guineas Reward: Or if Pawn'd, their Money again, and a Guinea.

IT being directed by a Decree of the High Court of Chancery, That Sir Richard Holford Kt. one of the Maſters of the ſaid Court, ſhall ſtate the Debts of Maurice Shelton, late of Barningham in Suffolk, Eſq; deceaſed, and of Henry Shelton, Eſq; deceaſed, in order to the Payment thereen, That Sir Richard Holford hath appointed Creditors to make out their reſpective Debts Firſt day of Trinity Term next, or they'l be fit of the ſaid Decree.

Tavern in Stocks-market, London, is to be re of Mr. Bigley Wilſon on Tower-hill, Mr. Dune, or Mr. Groſvenor in Cannon-ſtreet, Mer-

e, aged about 50, ſhort and well ſet, a thin ong Noſe, little Eyes, with a fawning Scotchway the 13th Inſtant from his Maſter with in Gold. Whoever gives notice of him to ationer, at Furnivals-Inn in Holborn, London, h nded) ſhall have 20 l. per Cent. for ſo much all be recovered.

alias Moore, aged near 40, middle Statured, Complection, a Mole on the ſide of her Noſe, d white Mantua and Petticoat; ſtole from her nſtant, a white Japann'd Mantua lined with d with Silver, and a Petticoat of the ſame; a a green and white enamell'd Dial-Plate, made f Leverpoole, with a Shagrin Caſe with Gold Diamond Ear-rings, and two ſmall Diamond er ſecures the Perſon and Goods if offered to r valued, and gives notice to Mr. Powell, Sta-Court by Grays-Inn, London, ſhall have Ten

d out of the Fields by Nib's-Pound near Hide-Inſtant, a dun Gelding near 15 hands, full e white Rainge down his Face, ſomewhat low Feet ſomething white, a greaſy Heel in the durty-coloured Spot on his near Cheek, all his ver ſecures him, and gives notice to Mr. John over-againſt the Star Inn near Charing-croſs, illiam Frith of Slimbridge in Gloceſterſhire, a Reward, and reaſonable Charges.

London, May 23. This day Capt. *William Kidd*, and three other of the Pirates lately condemned at the Admiralty Seſſions at the *Old-Baily*, were executed at *Execution-Dock.*

Whereas on the 20th of April laſt, there was a Burglary and Robbery committed at the Houſe of John Craige in Little Chelſea, by three or more Perſons, who did in a barbarous and cruel manner give the ſaid John Craige ſeveral mortal Wounds on his Head with a Hammer, of which he is ſince dead; And alſo did wound his Wife, (in Bed with him) ſo that ſhe is in a languiſhing and dangerous condition. His Majeſty being moved therein, is pleaſed to Promiſe His Gracious Pardon to any one of the ſaid Offenders who ſhall firſt diſcover any one or more of his Accomplices, ſo as he or they may be Apprehended and Convicted of the ſame. And a Reward of Fifty Pounds is promiſed to him or her, who ſhall firſt diſcover the ſame before the end of September next enſuing; Which ſaid Sum of Fifty Pounds ſhall be paid upon the Conviction of the ſaid Offender or Offenders, by the Church-wardens of Kenſington and Chelſea, into the Hands of Sir Fran. Child at Temple-bar, for the Diſcoverer.

At the Crown and Thiſtle in Little Chelſea, the Hammer, a Bag, a Pick-Ax, a falſe Key, and a Steel, were left by the ſaid Murderers, where they are to be ſeen by any Perſon in order to the Diſcovery.

Printed by *Edw. Jones*, in the *Savoy*. 1701.

New-England. Numb. 774

The Boston News-Letter.

Published by Authority.

From Monday February 9. to Monday February 16. 1719.

In our Number 771 January 26th we then gave you the Speech of his Excellency Col. Spotswood, *Lieutenant Governour of* Virginia, *to the Assembly there, and having since received some remarkable Proceedings in that Assembly, which was a main cause of that* Speech, *it here follows:*

Virginia On the 20th of *Nov.* 1718 the following Address being brought in by a Member of the House of Burgesses, was immediately put to the Vote, agreed to, and Signed by the Speaker.

To the King's Most Excellent Majesty
The Humble Address of the House of Burgesses.

May it please your Majesty,

E Your Majesty's most Dutiful and Loyal Subjects, the Burgesses of your Ancient Colony of Virginia, *now met in Assembly, having duely Considered several Attempts of your Lieutenant Governour, towards the Subversion of the Constitution of our Government, the depriving us of our Ancient Rights and Privileges, and many Hardships which he daily exercises upon your Majesty's Good Subjects of this Colony, think we should not discharge the Duty we owe to our Soveraign, or the Trust reposed in us by our Constituents, if we any longer forbear to lay them before your Sacred Person.*

And therefore we humbly hope your Majesty will be graciously pleased to receive some Particulars from the Honourable William Byrd, *Esq; whom we have desired to appear in behalf of your Oppressed Subjects of this Colony; being deprived of any other means whereby to make known to your Majesty our Just Grievances, by our Remote Situation; which Misfortune we find greatly increased by being Governed by a Lieutenant Governour, while the Governour in Chief resides in* Great Britain, *to which we attribute many of the Difficulties we now labour under.*

It is with great Comfort we behold your Majesty earnestly imploying your self in the Defence of the Liberties, not only of your own Subjects, but of all Europe; *and cannot doubt that as your Goodness and Mercy are already extended to us in many particulars; so we shall find it's* [illegible] *influences in the Redress of these our Grievances, which we are bound in the most Supplicant manner to implore, in such a way as may be most agreeable to your known Wisdom and Justice.*

By Command of the House of Burgesses

Dan: Mc Carty Speaker.

The next Day being the 21st of *November*, the House, for making out the General Charge mentioned in the foregoing Address, agreed upon the following Articles against the Lieutenant Governour.

I. That he hath by a Misconstruction of our Laws, as much as in them lay, perverted many of them, particularly, That for setling the Titles and bounds of Lands, which makes it a Condition of the Patents, that they are to forfeit them, if they fail Three Years of paying their Quit-Rents, which he hath endeavoured to extend to Lands granted before that Law, which have no such Condition in their Patent or Grant.

II. His Construction of the Law for finishing the Governour's House, whereby he Lavishes away the Country's Money contrary to the intent of the Law, and even beyond what the words of the Law will bear, and hath hitherto refused any Redress therein.

III. That he Endeavoured to Deter the Justices of the Country from Levying the Burgesses Salary setled by Law.

IV. That he hath by provoking Speeches and Messages abused the House of Burgesses, and thrown undeserved Reflections upon them.

Pensilvania, ss.

By WILLIAM KEITH, Esq;
Governour of the Province of *Pensilvania*, &c. In Council.

WHereas the following Proclamation issued in *Virginia*, has been transmitted hither, by his Excellency Col. *Spotswood*, his Majesty's Lieutenant Governour and Commander in Chief over the said Colony: For the better Encouragement therefore, of any Persons within this Government, who shall be generously disposed to follow so good an Example, in their King and Country's Service, I have, by and with the Advice of the Council, directed, And it is hereby Commanded, that the said Proclamation, in the same words as it has been issued, by his Excellency Col. *Spotswood* in *Virginia*, be forthwith published in every County of this Province, and of the Territories upon *Delaware*.

Given at *Philadelphia* the Twenty-fourth Day of *December*, in the Fifth Year of the Reign of our Sovereign Lord King GEORGE. *Annoq; Domini* 1718.

W. KEITH.

Virginia, ss. By His Majesty's Lieutenant Governour and Commander in Chief of the Colony and Dominion of *Virginia*.

A PROCLAMATION, Publishing the Rewards given for Apprehending or Killing of Pirates.

WHereas by an Act of Assembly made at a Session of Assembly begun at the Capitol in *Williamsburgh* the Eleventh Day of *November* in the fifth Year of His Majesty's Reign, Entituled, an Act to encourage the Apprehending and destroying of Pirates; It is amongst other things Enacted, That all & every Person or Persons who from and after the fourteenth Day of *November* in the Year of our Lord one Thousand Seven Hundred and Eighteen, and before the Fourteenth Day of *November*, which shall be in the Year of our Lord one Thousand Seven Hundred and Nineteen, shall take any Pirate or Pirates, on Sea or Land, or in case of Resistance, shall Kill any such Pirate or Pirates, between the Degrees of Thirty four and Thirty nine of Northern Latitude, and within one Hundred Leagues of the Continent of *Virginia*, or within the Provinces of *Virginia* or *North Carolina*, upon the Conviction or making due proof of the killing of all and every such Pirate and Pirates, before the Governour and Council, shall be Entituled to have and receive, out of the Publick Money, in the Hands of the Treasurer of this Colony, the several Rewards following; That is to say, for *Edward Tach*, commonly called Capt. *Tach* or *Black-beard*, one Hundred Pounds; for every other Commander of a Pirate Ship, Sloop or Vessel, Forty Pounds; for every Lieutenant, Master, Quarter Master, Boatswain or Carpenter, Twenty Pounds; for every other Inferiour Officer, Fifteen Pounds; and for every Private Man taken on Board such Ship, Sloop or Vessel Ten Pounds; and that for every Pirate which shall be taken by any Ship Sloop or Vessel belonging to this Colony, or *North Carolina*, within the time aforesaid, in any place whatsoever, the like Rewards shall be paid, according to the quality and condition of such Pirate; Wherefore for the Encouragement of all such Persons, as shall be willing to serve His Majesty and their Country, in so just and Honourable an undertaking, as the suppressing a sort of People, who may be truly called Enemies to Mankind; I have thought fit, with the Advice and Consent of His Majesty's Council, to issue this Proclamation, hereby declaring the said Rewards shall be punctually and justly paid, in Current Money of *Virginia*, according to the Directions of the said Act. And I do order and appoint this Proclamation to be publish'd by the Sheriffs, at the respective Court-houses, and by all Ministers and Readers, in the several Churches and Chappels throughout this Colony.

Given at the Council Chamber at *Williamsburgh* this 25th Day of *November* 1718. In the fifth Year of His Majesty's Reign.

A. SPOTSWOOD.

GOD Save the KING.

New-York, January 26. We have had Winter-like Weather for Three Weeks past, and deep Snows on Tuesday, Wednesday and Thursday last, a great many Persons went from hence upon the Ice Cross Hudsons River to New-Jersey, and returned, the River being fast from the Narrows to Albany (as is supposed.) No Vessels are arrived here from Sea, nor any News that way. Capt. Tannat sails for Bristol assoon as the Ice is gone, Y…rday and the Day before had almost destroyed it, but now it is severe Freezing which will augment it.

They write from Philadelphia, they have the following News from Maryland, viz. That Capt. Hoxton in the Ship Antelope of 500 Tons, belonging to Capt. Hyde of London, coming from

Barbadoes,

New-England. Numb. 776

The Boston News-Letter.

Published by Authority.

From Monday February 23. to Monday March 2. 1719.

Paris, December 8. 1717.

THE Printed Appeal of the Cardinal de Noailles is privately handed about, and makes a great Noise. It bears Date the 3d of April last, and 'tis mentioned therein, that 11 Bishops have adher'd thereto, viz. the Bishop of Chalone Sur Marne, Laon, Auxerre, Macon, Condom, Agen, Bayonne, Dax, St. Malo, Metz, and the late Bishop of Leitoure, amongst whose Papers, 'tis said, a Copy of this Appeal was found. The same has been sent to Rome, and 'tis believed it will exasperate that Court, whom it will be very difficult to perswade that the Cardinal and the other Appealing Bishops did not secretly connive at the publishing of this Appeal. The Parliament has thought fit to issue out an Arrest forbidding the selling of the said Appeal, and ordered the same to be suppressed. On Saturday Night, or rather Sunday Morning, there was a great Tumult before the Hotel of Soissons, where the Ambassador of Sicily gave a great Ball, and 4 Persons were killed on the spot. The same Day there was another Tumult in the House of the Ambassador of Spain, who holds Assemblies, where People game very high, and as the same thing has happened at the Imperial Ambassador's, and that frequent Murders are committed in the Publick Gaming Houses, we hear an Arrest is to come out to forbid these Practices.

Bazil, Decemb. 8. The Abbot of St. Gall departed this Life on the 28th past, near Lindaw on the Lake of Constance, in the 78th Year of his Age.

Venice, Decemb. 10. The Earl of Peterborough having been dismissed by the Cardinal Legate of Bologna, arrived here on the 10th Instant. Letters from Naples advise, that Count Daun had ordered the Pope's Nuncio to depart that City in 24 Hours, and the Kingdom in 48, which Order had been punctually observed. This Week the Duke of Queensbury arrived here. Letters from the Captain General Pisani, give an Account of his being arrived at Corfu with the Fleet, having left Prevess and Voniza well provided with all Necessaries, and that General Schulenbourgh has extended the Contributions beyond Arta.

Paris, Decemb. 11. The Arrest of our Parliament for suppressing the Appeal of the Cardinal Noailles, is made publick, and bears date the 1st of this Month. The Motives of that Suppression are contained in the Speech made by the King's Advocate General, in the Name of the King's Council, importing, That they saw with Grief, that in Contempt of the Declaration of the 7th of October last, which suspends all the Disputes and Contests form'd in the Kingdom, on Occasion of the late Constitution of our most Holy Father the Pope, there are lately spread in this City, many Copies of a Writing, entituled, The Act of Appeal of his Eminence Monseigneur the Cardinal de Noailles, Archbishop of Paris, &c. Printed without the Allowance or Participation of that Prelate. That an Impression made in such Circumstances, could not be other than the Work of Seditious People who employ themselves only in sowing Trouble and Division in the Church, whilst a Prince, more to be respected for his Virtues, and for his Zeal for the Interest of Religion, than for his high Station and high Birth, employs incessantly all his Cares for establishing a Calm. They cannot therefore forbear claiming the Authority of the Court, against a Publication so contrary to the late Declaration of the King; and that in order, to maintain so wise a Law, they believ'd themselves oblig'd to draw up the Conclusions in Writing, which they delivered accordingly, with the Printed Copy of the Appeal. The King's Council being retired, the Court examin'd the said Writing, entituled, An Act of Appeal, of his Eminence Monseigneur the Cardinal de Noailles, Archbishop of Paris, of the 3d of April 1717. to the Pope, better advised, and to a future General Council, from the Constitution of our Holy Father the Pope Clement XI. of the 8th of September 1713. and the King's Declaration of the 7th of October, Register'd in Parliament: And the Matter being put into Deliberation, the Court ordains, that the Copies of the said Print shall be suppress'd, &c. All Persons are forbid selling, publishing or distributing the same, upon the Penalties express'd in the said Declaration of October 7th. And it is ordered that the said Declaration shall be observed and executed in it's full Form and Tenor, &c.

The Partisans of the Bull are not very well pleased with this Arrest, because it confirms People that it is the Genuine Appeal of the Cardinal de Noailles, which some People doubted of before, seeing the Publication of it without the Licence of the Cardinal, and the Contempt of the Edict, forbidding to write or publish in Publick any thing about the Constitution, are the only Motives of this Arrest of the Parliament. That Act of Appeal is very long, and the Cardinal sets forth therein, the pernicious Consequences that all sorts of People draw from the said Constitution, to weaken the most essential Truths of the Christian Faith, and undermine the Foundations of Morality, and declares that he has in vain endeavoured for 3 Years together to obtain from the Pope such Explanations as might prevent these Consequences; concluding, that he finds himself under an unavoidable Necessity to appeal to the Pope, better advised, and the future General Council freely assembled in a safe Place where he or his Deputies may safely appear, from the Constitution Unigenitus, and all other Proceedings made in Consequence thereof.

Rome, Decemb. 11. The Expulsion of our Nuncio from Naples, and the Demands made since by the Imperial Court, embarrass very much the Pontiff, which appears sufficiently by the frequent Congregations that have been lately held; but we do not hear that they are come to any other Resolution, but only to endeavour to pacify the Emperor, who has been perswaded that this Court has not sincerely dealt with him, and has under-hand favoured the designs of King Philip. They complain that the promise made by the Pope upon the Invasion of Sardinia, to recal his Nuncio from Madrid, for having not given him Notice of the Projects of that Court, of which there is a strong Suspicion, if not a clear Evidence, that he was informed, was a gross Imposition upon the Imperial Court, and a new intolerable Provocation, since that Minister continues there, and has not put a stop as it was promised, to the raising of the Tenth Penny Tax on all the Ecclesiastical Revenues, but rather connived at the Continuation thereof; tho' they cannot be ignorant that that Money, which was granted upon pretence of the Defence of Christendom, has been applyed to disturb the Peace of Europe, and assist the Turks against the Christians, by giving a Diversion to the Imperial Forces. They complain on the other hand of the Partiality of the Pope, who readily granted that Tax to the Court of Madrid, whereas he started a World of Difficulties, when the Emperor demanded the like Contribution from the Clergy of Naples and Milan, tho' it was evident, that Supply could not be applyed to any other use but against the Turks, with whom his Imperial Majesty was actually ingag'd in War. They seem perswaded, that the Report we had some time ago of a League between Spain and some Italian Princes, to drive the Imperialists out of Italy, were not groundless, and that the unexpected Defence of the Marquiss de Rubi in Sardinia, having taken up the Spaniards till the fair Season was almost over, the Powers concerned in that League did not think fit to declare themselves, but that this Project is not broke off, but only defer'd to a more favourable Opportunity, in which they are confirmed by the great Preparations of the Court of Madrid, and their Manifestos; in which they alledge some Grievances of the Italian Princes, as one of their Reasons for invading the Imperial Territories.

Hamburgh, Decemb. 14. The King of Poland set out the 1st Instant from Dresden to return into his Kingdom, and has left the Administration of his Electorate to Count Fleming as Statholder thereof, which is very acceptable to the Saxons, that Minister having on all Occasions, given Proofs of his Zeal for the Protestant Religion. Letters from Petersburgh say, that the Czar makes

Septr. 8.1713.

Nov.r 22. 1718. Teach pirata Succiditur.

makes great Preparations of War, and has declared, that if that Peace is concluded this Winter, he will turn all his Forces next Summer against the Ottomans. They add, that he has ordered General Weyde to march with 50000 Men towards Ukrania, in order to besiege Azoph in the beginning of the Campaign, and that in order thereunto, and for the execution of his farther Designs on that side, he has ordered 300 Barks to be got ready at Veronitz with 16 Frigots, which he will send down the Tanais. These Letters say, that that Prince intended suddenly to set out from Petersburgh for Moscow.

Philadelphia, Feb. 12. Our River is still fast at Philadelphia, and some venture over; on Tuesday last ten Oxen coming over from Jersey, eight of them fell in; most of them in the Channel, but all of them are got out again, abundance of People being on the River at the same time. A Sloop from Boston is arrived below at Cohansy, but know not his Name. Outward Bound, Fagan for Bristol, Hardy for Jamaica, Grushee for South Carolina, and several for Barbadoes.

New-York, Feb. 17. No Vessels arrived here since the last Post nor any News. Cleared Out, Jones for Boston and Whippo for Bahemas. Entered Out, Vandyke and Coden for Boston, Tickel for Jamaica and Boyles for Curacoa.

Rhode-Island, February 20. On the 12th Currant arrived here John Jackson from Piscataqua for Connecticut, and Humphry Johnston in a Sloop from North Carolina, bound to Amboy who sailed the next Day, and informs that Governour Spotswood of Virginia fitted out two Sloops, well mann'd with Fifty pickt Men of his Majesty's Men of War lying there, and small Arms, but no great Guns, under the Command of Lieutenant Robert Maynard of his Majesty's Ship Pearl, in pursuit of that Notorious and Arch Pirate Capt. Teach, who made his Escape from Virginia, when some of his Men were taken there; which Pirate Lieutenant Maynard came up with at North Carolina, and when they came in hearing of each other, Teach called to Lieutenant Maynard and told him he was for King GEORGE, desiring him to hoist out his Boat and come aboard, Maynard replyed that he designed to come aboard with his Sloop assoon as he could, and Teach understanding his design, told him that if he would let him alone, he would not meddle with him; Maynard answered that it was him he wanted, and that he would have him dead or alive, else it should cost him his life; whereupon Teach called for a Glass of Wine, and swore Damnation to himself, if he either took or gave Quarters: Then Lieut Maynard told his Men, that now they knew what they had to trust to, and could not escape the Pirates hands if they had a mind; but must either fight and kill or be killed: Teach begun and fired several Great Guns at Maynard's Sloop, which did but little damage, but Maynard rowing nearer Teach's Sloop of Ten Guns, Teach fired some small Guns, loaded with Swan shot, spick Nails and pieces of old Iron, in upon Maynard; which killed six of his Men and wounded ten; upon which Lieutenant Maynard, ordered all the rest of his Men to go down in the Hould, himself, Abraham Demelt of New-York, and a third at the Helm stayed above Deck. Teach seeing so few on the Deck, said to his Men, the Rogues were all killed except two or three, and he would go on board and kill them himself, so drawing nearer, went on board, took hold of the fore sheet and made fast the Sloops; Maynard and Teach themselves two begun the Fight with their Swords, Maynard making a thrust, the point of his Sword went against Teach's Cartridge-Box, and bended it to the Hilt, Teach broke the Guard of it, and wounded Maynard's Fingers but did not disable him, whereupon he Jumpt back, threw away his Sword, and fired his Pistol, which wounded Teach. Demelt struck in between them with his Sword and cut Teach's Face pretty much; in the Interim both Companies ingaged in Maynard's Sloop, one of Maynard's Men being a Highlander, ingaged Teach with his broad Sword, who gave Teach a cut on the Neck, Teach saying well done Lad, the Highlander reply'd, if it be not well done, I'll do it better, with that he gave him a second stroke, which cut off his Head, laying it flat on his Shoulder, Teach's Men being about 20, and three or four Blacks were all killed in the Ingagement, excepting two carried to Virginia: Teach's body was thrown overboard, and his Head put on the top of the Bowsprit.

(How many of Lieut. Maynard's Men were killed in the Action besides the first six, we know not, only his Letter to his Sister in Boston, mentions 35 killed and wounded.)

Outward Bound, Abraham Borden for Barbadoes.

(The Southern Post came so late in, that we could not give you this Paragraph in our last)

Rhode-Island, Feb. 27. Arrived here are Peter Coggeshal from St. Christophers, and James Codine arrived here last Lord's Day from New-York in 17 Hours passage, the like never known before, and bound there again, who informs, that the Dolphin Gally belonging to New-York, Capt. Wells Commander, was taken by the Spaniards, in his passage homeward bound from Jamaica, and made a Prize. Outward bound, Abraham Borden for Barbadoes.

Boston, His Excellency our Governour intends to meet here, the General Assembly of this Province, On Wednesday the 11th of this Instant March, being the Day unto which they were last Prorogued, the 4th of December past.

By Capt. Thomas from Bilboa, who was beat off the Coast to Antigua, we are informed, that there are still a great many Pirates in the West Indies, he met on this Coast Capt. Bull bound hither from Surranam, who was riffled by them of some Rhum and Molasses.

Besides what we gave you in our Last and this, of the taking and killing of Teach the Pirate by Lieut. Maynard, we have this further account of it by a Letter from North Carolina of December 17th to New-York, viz. That on the 17th of November last, Lieut. Maynard of the Pearl Man of War Sail'd from Virginia with two Sloops, and 54 Men under his Command, no Guns, only small Arms, Sword and Pistols, Mr. Hyde Commanded the Little Sloop with 22 Men, and Maynard had 32 in his Sloop, and on the 22d Maynard Engaged Teach at Obercock in North Carolina, he had 21 Men, Nine Guns Mounted, Mr. Hyde was killed, and one more, and Five wounded in the Little Sloop, and having no body aboard to Command them they fell a Stern and did not come up to Assist Lieut. Maynard till the Action was almost over, Maynard shot away Teach's Gibb and Fore-halliards, and put him ashore, then run him aboard, and had 20 Men killed and wounded, Teach Entered Maynards Sloop with Ten Men, and he had 12 stout Men Left, so that they fought it out Sword in hand. Maynard's Men behaved like Hero's, and kill'd all Teach's Men that Entered without any of Maynards dropping, but most of them Cut and Mangled, in the whole he had Eight killed, and Eighteen wounded, Teach fell with Five Shot, and 20 dismal Cuts, and 12 of his Men killed, and Nine made Prisoners, most of them Negro's, all wounded, Teach would never be taken had he not been in such a hole that he could not get away.

Entered Inwards, Richard Thomas Ship Sarah from Bilboa.

Cleared Outwards, Matson for New-London, Parker and Flood for Piscataqua, Richard Pitcher for South Carolina, Richard Langden for North Carolina, Isaac Perkins for Antigua, John Bulkley for Barbadoes and James Blin for Annapolis Royal.

Outward Bound, Joseph Biffel Sloop Prosperity for Annapolis Royal, Endigo Potter Sloop Bonaventure for Virginia, and John Slocum Ship Susannah for London.

On Monday the Second Currant, the Western Post for Connecticut and New-York, &c. setts out here Weekly.

Advertisements.

Boston: Printed by B. Green in Newbury-Street, for John Campbell in Corn Hill. 1719.

THE Post Boy.

The ROYAL EXTRACT; or, the ... never-failing Remedy against the Venereal Disease.

On Tuesday Night last, three Footpads, *viz.* Obrian, Murphey, and Jackson, were seiz'd at a Night-house at Charing-Cross, being charged with robbing a Person both of his Money and Cloaths in the Fields between London and Hampstead. The first hath made his Escape, and the two last (who are Foot-Soldiers) were next day carry'd before William Gore Esq; and by him committed to Newgate.

Our Merchants have Advice, that the Elizabeth (late Capt. Thompson) was taken and plunder'd by the Pyrates on the Coast of Africa.

They write from Bristol, June 18, that the Seneca, Capt. Jones, newly arrived there from Berbadoes, brought Advice, that the Jason Galley, Capt. Plummer, belonging to Bristol, put in at the said Island the 5th of May, by which they received certain Account, that his Majesty's Ship Swallow, Capt. Ogle, had taken by Stratagem on the Coast of Africa three Pyrate Ships, one of which was that of Roberts the great and notorious Pyrate. Their Names were, the Onslow, of above 40 Guns, the Count de Toulose (a Frenchman they had formerly taken) of about 30 Guns, and the other a Dutch Ship of about 20 Guns, supposed to be a new Prize. They had in all 500 Men, 176 of whom are taken, and put into Cape Coast Castle, and those who escaped were pursued; but with what Success we cannot yet learn. The Stratagem was this; Capt. Ogle, in sailing off of Lopas, perceived that two of these Ships were upon the Heel a scrubbing, upon which he acted the Part of a Trader; Roberts being desirous of a Prize, immediately slipt his Cable, and ran out after him; the Swallow ran away, and so decoy'd him out of the Reach of the other Ships hearing the Noise of the Guns; then suddenly tack'd about, and ran out her lower Teer of Guns, and with the first Broadside kill'd Roberts; upon whose dropping the Men were so dishearten'd, that they surrender'd. Afterwards the Man of War hoisted up the King's Colours under Roberts's Black Flag, which had a White Skeleton in it, and so went into Lopas to look after the other two Ships that were upon the Heel: The Pyrates on board seeing the Man of War coming in with a Black Flag uppermost, jump'd for Joy, concluding that Roberts had taken the Man of War; but they soon found the contrary, for the Swallow took them with little Resistance. Roberts was grown near as formidable on this Coast, as the Pyrate England is in the East-Indies, having lately taken 10 Sail of Ships in Whidaw Road, and 'tis believed he had great Riches on Board. He was very severe to his Prisoners, according to the Account of some in this City who have been in his Hands; but one Gillesby, the second Captain, who we hear was once try'd for his Life for attempting an Escape, was very civil to them, and seem'd to act as a Person under Constraint.

Casualties. Drowned accidentally at S. Mary at Lambeth, 1. Excessive Drinking, 1. Hang'd themselves, 2; one (being Lunatick) at S. Botolph without Bishopsgate, and one at S. Giles without Cripplegate. Kill'd, 2; one being blown up by Gunpowder at S. Dunstan in the West, and one by a Fall occasion'd by his Apprentice at Christ-Church in Surrey.

Aged 23. Convulsion 121. Fever 51. Small-Pox 26.
Christned, Males 146. Females 155. In all 301.
Buried, Males 205. Females 216. In all 421.
Increased in the Burials this Week 4.

Yesterday *South-S*... *India* 143... Due *In*... 2 *s.* Premium. *Sou*... and *New* 14½. *Ins*... *Lott. Annuities* 100 ... Disc. *Sword-Blade* ...

The Court of Direct... *That the Transfer Boo*... *taking the Ballot upon* ... *the 19th Instant, wh*... *day, the 23d instant,* ... *from and after which* ... *making the Midsumm*... *Monday the 6th of Au*...

SIR, *Your Vote an*... KILLMISTER, *C*... *Trade a Watchmaker* (... *Aleconners of this Ci*... *ceased; he hath been* ... *served Ward and Pari*... *in Christ's Church Parish, and since 3 Years in St. Mary le Bow; he having had great Losses by Trade, and being in the Seventieth Year of his Age, is uncapable of getting his Livelihood by his Trade, his Sight being much decayed, and his Nerves contracted by much Gilding.* And your Petitioner will ever pray, &c.

Note, *He had the greatest Number of Votes at the last Election of any of the then Candidates, except those who were declared.*

NB. *The Election is on Monday next.*

This Day is publish'd,

|| The PRUDE. A Tale. In two Canto's. Printed at Dublin, and Reprinted at London, for J. Roberts in Warwick-Lane, J. Harrison at the Royal Exchange, A. Dod without Temple-Bar, G. Huddleston in Church-Court against Hungerford-Market, and E. Griffith at Charing-Cross

...ENTS.

TO be disposed of within three Miles of London, about four or five Brace of fine spotted Deer, fit for a Gentleman's Park or Paddock. Enquire at Sue's Coffee-house in Bow-Lane near Cheapside.

MUSICK lately published.

THE most Celebrated Opera's called GRISELDA, FLORIDANTE, and ASTARTUS complete, as they were perform'd at the King's Theatre for the Royal Academy. Also the said Opera's are done for a Flute, the Ariets for a single Flute, and the Duets for two Flutes in a complete manner. Likewise several Curious Pieces for Violins, Flutes, Hautboys, the Harpsichord and Organ, and great Variety of Musick lately come from abroad. Printed for J. Walsh, Servant to his Majesty, at the Harp and Hautboy in Katharine-Street in the Strand, and John and Joseph Hare at the Viol and Flute near the Royal Exchange in Cornhill.

LONDON: Printed for E. *Morphew* near *Stationers-Hall.* 1722.

Numb. 5321.

THE Post-Boy.

From Tuesday August 27. to Thursday August 29. 1723.

Yesterday arrived the Mail due from France.

Lisbon, July 29. N. S.

ONE day last Week, the Lady of Don Alexis de Sousa de Menesez, Count de S. James, was brought to bed of a Son, which is the 26th she has brought into the World, 17 whereof are living. This will seem very strange in Countries where they have a Notion that the Portugueze Women have done Childing whilst young. — The Royal Academy of History met upon the 22d instant, and elected into their Number, Dr. Philip Maciel, Conclavist to the Cardinal d'Acunha at the Election of the present Pope. —The Ships bound for Rio de Janeiro are order'd to be ready by the beginning of Septem

Naples, Aug. 3.
vise, that the Vice
ly Envoy at the C
Dey to go in the q
the United Provin
val of a Dutch Shi
that the Govern
Treaty with the R
Merchant settled a
nate, for their Rat
Conditions for his
Powers in Peace w
the Dey was willin
of Zora, for 60,00
Genoeze formerly g

Naples, Aug. 10.
by Order of the
Kingdom, to disco
of the People again
Merchants of this
merce of the new
have demanded the
vanced; not expe
Merchandizes whic
—— The Marquiss
they are call'd) Son
4th instant, and we
Viceroy, who gives
ring their Residence
designing to return
Possession of their E

Rome, Aug. 10. N
have died suddenly
great number lie sic
rature of the Season
others, has kept his
and his Illness gives
of Conti. —— Th
great deal of Grave
his Physicians have
geon he had sent t
cut him for the Stor

Florence, Aug. 10.
England at the C
thro' this Place, on
had an Audience o
assured, he has obtain'd new Privileges for the English settled at Leghorn.

By the last Letters from New-England we have the following Advices, *viz.*

Rhode-Island, May 22. Two Brothers, Samuel and Abel Chapin, were taken up here, and brought before the Hon. Samuel Granston Esq; the Governor, and his Counsel, for passing a countefeited 5 *l.* Bill of the Province of Massachuset's Bay; and upon Suspicion of their having more of the same sort, they were search'd, and 19 of the said false Bills were found upon Abel. They were both committed to Jail, in order to be farther examin'd.

Boston, June 2. On Thursday last, a Woman of above 50 Years of Age stood in the Pillory, and had her Ear cut off, for aiding and assisting in counterfeiting the small Bills of this Province, and for uttering the same.

We have Advice from the Eastward, that the Indians had last Week kill'd three Englishmen, and carry'd away three more.

A List is printed here, by Authority, of the Names, Ages and Places of Birth, of those Men that were taken by his Majesty's Ship the Greyhound, in the Pyrate Sloop call'd the Ranger, who are now confin'd in his Majesty's Jail in Rhode-Island, to the Number of 30; among which are the following, *viz.* Stephen Mondon Thomas Huggit, and William Jones, of London; William Read, of Londondery; Peter Kews, of Exeter; Thomes Jones, of Flint; James Brinkley, of Suffolk; Joseph Sownd, of Westminster; John Brown, of Leverpool; William Shutfield, of Lancaster; Edward Eaton, of Wrexham; John Brown, of Durham; Eward Lawson, of the Isle of Man; Owen Rice, of South-Wales; John Tomkins, of Glocestershire; John Fitzgerald, of Limrick; Abraham Lacy, and John Waters Quarter-Master, of Devonshire; Thomas Linesker, of Lancashire; Thomas Reeve, of Rutland; John Hinchbard, Doctor, near Edinburgh. The others are Americans, but all of them his Majesty's Subjects.

Paris, Sept. 4. N. S. The King having resolv'd to do the same Honours to the Memory of the late Cardinal Du Bois, as were done in the Reigns of the Kings his Predecessors to the Persons they had honour'd with the same Dignity; a solemn Service was celebrated, upon the 27th of August, in the Metropolitan Church, for the Repose of that Cardinal's Soul, whereat the Cardinal de Noailles, Archbishop of Paris, officiated *in Pontificalibus.* The Parliament, the Chamber of Accounts, and the Court of Aids, who had received the King's Orders upon that Occasion, were present at that Ceremony by Deputation; as were also the University and the City-Companies. —The King has given the Lower Apartment of the Superintendance to the Duke de Bouillon, and the Upper to the Duke of Berwick, who is to come immediately from his Country-Seat.

——'Tis now no longer surprizing, that our Actions are risen from 800 to 1300 lately, in regard the Duke of Orleans is said to be Governor of the India Company, the Duke of Bourbon Sub-Governor, and the Comptroller-General President. They name, beside, 2 Counsellors of State, and 2 Masters of Requests, for Inspectors and Auditors of Accounts; a Secretary, an Under-Secretary, 8 Syndicks, 8 Directors, 8 Registers for the Tobacco, and 8 Merchants. This new Regulation is to appear in Print next Week. — The King has given the forfeited Estate of Monsieur de Talhoet to his Brother Cailhoet, his Father-in-Law having refused it. — The General Assembly of the Clergy of France have withdrawn some Pensions from Members who have employ'd their Pens against the Constitution *Unigenitus*, and conferr'd them upon Jesuites and others who have written in Defence of the said Bull.

By the last Letters from New-England we have the fol-
ers, Samuel and Abel
ught before the Hon.
and his Counsel, for
Province of Massa-
their having more of
d 19 of the said false
vere both committed
l.
a Woman of above
, and had her Ear
nterfeiting the small
g the same.
d, that the Indians
and carry'd away
rity, of the Names,
that were taken by
e Pyrate Sloop call'd
his Majesty's Jail in
among which are the
omas Huggit, and
Read, of Londonder-
es Jones, of Flint;
ownd, of Westmin-
illiam Shutfield, of
ham; John Brown,
Isle of Man; Owen
, of Glocestershire;
m Lacy, and John
hire; Thomas Li-
of Rutland; John
The others are
y's Subjects.

in the Mary, from

ud from S. Christo-
maica. Sailed the
London.
d the Orphan, Ru-
amaica.
Jenny, for Rotter-

he Outward-bound.
rom Virginia; and

Gravesend, Aug. 27. Passed by the George and Elizabeth, and Bootle, from Virginia; John and Isaac from Amsterdam, Mary from Petersburg, Henry from Gotten burg, and Concord from Stockholm.

London, Aug. 29.

The Earl of Essex is so well recover'd, that he is coming to Cashiobury from Bristol.

On Tuesday Morning, Edward Cresset Esq; of Cund in Shropshire, was married at Ormond Chappel to Mrs. James, a young Lady of 20,000 *l.* Fortune.

On Tuesday last, Mr. Riddle, Steward to the Duke of Cleveland, set out for France, to bring over the Body of the Lord Charles Fitz-Roy, his Grace's 2d Son, not the Duke of S. Alban's, (who died lately at Paris of the Small-Pox) in order to its being interr'd in Westminster-Abbey.

—— Martin Esq; is made a Brigadier in the 4th Troop of Horse-Guards.

Numb. 5341.

THE Post-Boy.

From Saturday October 12. to Tuesday October 15. 1723.

On Saturday *arrived One Mail from* Holland.

Constantinople, Sept. 1. N. S.

A New Bassaw is gone to Teflis, with Orders to subdue the Provinces of Erivan, Schirvan, and Ghilan, and some Ports and Places on the Caspian Sea. The Bassaw of Van is order'd to take Tauris, where the King of Persia's Son is; and the Bassaw of Bagdad is appointed to conquer the Provinces that lie contiguous to his Government. Upon the Ottoman Troops entring into Georgia, the Cham or Governor, who is a Greek, fled to the Muscovites; but his Son turning Turk, the Bassaw of Erzerum has made him Governor of the Province. As to the Affairs of Persia, the last Account we had from thence was, that Miriweys had received a Reinforcement of Troops from his own Country, and had taken Casbin, nevertheless his Party daily dwindled; and tho' he has marry'd one of the King of Persia's Daughters, 'twas thought he would not long be able to keep his Ground, because being a rigid Mahometan, he persecutes those of the Sect of Ali, of which most of the Persians are.

Gibraltar, Sept, 20. N. S. Candil, a Barbarian Rover, having sail'd fron … Ship of thirty tw… ing with none bu… Boldness to take… La Rache, on s… pursuing his Crui… of Tetuan, Tang… reaches as far as… Place, hearing o… Civility to write… he would give C… and would even r… as he return'd in… lee are of the 12… French Barque l… made their Escap…

Turin, Sept. 25. … chess-Dowager o… that Violence, a… they went off in… ver, which howe… Royal Highness i… — The Person w… powder is committed Prisoner to the Citadel, for adulterating that which he deliver'd into the King's Magazines; whereupon his Partners and Bail are gone off.

Rhode-Island, July 26. This day 26 of the Pyrates taken by his Majesty's Ship the Greyhound, Capt. Solgard, were executed here, (*whose Names were mention'd in the Account we gave of their Trial and Condemnation, in the* Post-Boy *of* Sept. 5.) Some of them deliver'd what they had to say in Writing, and most of them said something at the Place of Execution, advising all People, young ones especially, to take Warning by their unhappy Fate, and to avoid the Crimes that brought them to it. Their Black Fag, under which they had committed abundance of Pyracies and Murders, was affix'd to one Corner of the Gallows; it had in it the Portraiture of Death, with an Hour-Glass in one Hand, and a Dart in the other striking into a Heart, and three Drops of Blood delineated as falling from it: This Flag they call'd *Old Roger*, and used to say, *They would live and die under it.*

Lublin, Sept. 26. N. S. The Crown-General of Poland sent a Spy some time ago to Oczacow; who being return'd, gives an Account, that fifteen thousand Turks arrived there not long before him; and that while he was there, about twenty thousand Men march'd toward the Frontiers of Persia, to the Relief (as was given out) of Miriweys.

Cracow, Sept. 26. N. S. The Report of a hundred and fifty thousand Turks being march'd to the Frontiers of Persia, under the Command of seven Bassaws, was entirely groundless, and occasion'd only by the Motion of some Infidels toward the Confines of Russia.

Florence, Sept. 28. N. S. The Great Duke having no farther Need of the Syringe, his Physicians begin to entertain some Hope of his Recovery. Mean while, his Royal Highness has thought fit, by the Advice of the Senate and Ministry, to put the Reins of Government into the Hands of the Hereditary Prince of Tuscany his Son, who two days ago gave Audience to the Emperor's General Count Stampa, upon some Affair he is charged with on the part of his Imperial Majesty.

Prague, Oct. 6. N. S. Some People here are so malicious as to insinuate, that the French King will send the Infanta-Queen back to Spain; in which case, they suppose, Don Carlos will return his young Bride, and that perhaps the Princess of the Asturia's must also go home: But these Discourses seem to be the Product of the same Brain, who would persuade us, that the Courts of France and Spain are hatching I know not what dark Designs upon Italy. ——The famous Abbot Strickland has been some days at this Court; whether upon Business, or not, we can't say.

Hanover, Oct. 15. N. S. This day the King of Great Britain arrived at the Ghore from Berlin.

Hamburgh, Oct. 15. N. S. We hear that an Express from Stockholm went thro' this Place two days ago, on his way to Hanover, with Dispatches of great Importance; and among other things, that the Heer Bestuchof had received positive Orders from Petersburg, to notify to the Court of Sweden the Conclusion of the Duke of Holsteyn's Marriage with the Princess of Muscovy. —— Some Advices from Petersburg say, the Emperor of China is lately dead, and his Sons disputing the Succession, as usual in those Countries: But China is a great way off; and we can hardly come at the Truth even at our own Doors.

Paris, Oct. 13. N. S. The Small-Pox continuing to carry off great numbers of People in this City; we are told, it had been resolv'd to follow the Example of England in that Case, and to communicate the Distemper by Insertion, or Inoculation. But it having been judg'd proper to consult some Doctors of Sorbonne concerning the Lawfulness of this Practice, they were divided in their Sentiments, some being for it, and others against it. The Sorbonne hearing it, have condemn'd the Practice in a Body; notwithstanding which, we are confidently assured it will be try'd.

Brussels, Oct. 18. N. S. Our Company's Books for transferring of Stock, are to be open'd upon the 23d instant.

Hague, Oct. 19. N. S. Mr. Haldane, formerly his Bri… …'s newly return'd … part of the King

…he Pyrates taken …pt. Solgard, were …'d in the Account …the Post-Boy of … they had to say …ing at the Place … ones especially, …and to avoid the Black Fag, under of Pyracies and the Gallows; it an Hour-Glass in …ing into a Heart, …s falling from it: to say, *They would*

…n the 19th past, …tine from Barba…s, that the Island …hat Mr. Cox, the late President, who is prosecuted for Mal-Administration, had been on his Trial for several days together, and about seven hundred Depositions had been taken already in relation to that Affair, and many more still remain'd.

They wrote from Rhode-Island, Aug. 2. that on the Monday before, a Sloop was cast away on the West-Side of Montague-Point in Long-Island, and only sixteen Hogsheads of Rum and one Man were saved.

Boston, Aug. 26. On the 23d instant, died the Reverend Dr. Increse Mather, in the 85th Year of his Age, after a Life of many Years Services in England and Ireland, as well as in New-England, and of many Sufferings by a painful Sickness, in which he languish'd a long while before he expir'd. He was born at Dorchester, June 21. 1639, and signalized himself in many Publick Appearances, but especially in the Agency for his Country in the British Court, and as President of Harvard-College. He was Minister of the Old North Church at Boston sixty two Years.

Philadelphia, Aug 22. We have Advice, that the Sloop Robert and James, Robert Bird Master, which came out of South-Carolina in Company with Capt. Slyfield, and was fear'd to be lost in the Storm on the 29th of July, was driven on Shoar twenty Miles to the Southward of Sene Puxon; but the Men were saved, as was also the Cargo, tho' much damaged.

Portsmouth, in *New-England*, Aug. 30. Last Monday Morning, the Indians surprized one Aaron Rawlins and his Family, at Lamprele River, and carry'd them all away, being six in Number. Some time after, they kill'd one Joseph Hain of Quocheca, and two of his Daughters, and took a third; but she made her Escape from them. About the same time, eight Men arm'd at Berwick fell into an Ambuscade of Indians, who kill'd one and wounded another. And yesterday Morning ten Indians were discover'd at

Numb. 5789. 1 ½ d.

THE Post Boy.

From Thursday August 25. to Saturday August 27. 1726.

Hague, Aug. 30. N. S.

'THE Resolution lately taken by their High-Mightinesses, whereby the Generals of our Horse and Foot are authorized to review their respective Troops, instead of Deputies of the Council of State, to whom that Affair was before entrusted, has had a very good Effect, for the Number of our Forces is now complete, whereas the Companies in some Provinces were wont to muster 35 or 40 Men, instead of 50; which was a very notorious Abuse. This wholsome Resolution is owing to the General of Horse Count Hompesch's importunate Representations to their High-Mightinesses Assembly, and to the Council of State; who have made an Addition of 5000 Florins a Year to the Salary of 15000, which each of the Two Generals before enjoy'd, to defray the Expences of their travelling backward and forward, as they must necessarily do in the Business newly committed to their Care.

' On Wednesday last, Count Coningsek, Envoy-Extraordinary of his Imperial Majesty, gave a magnificent Entertainment, follow'd by a Ball, upon Occasion of the present Empress's Birth-day. I am told that all the Foreign Ministers were at it, except the Marquis de Fenelon, Ambassador of France, who is supposed to have absented himself by way of Reprizal, because Count Coningsek did not honour his last Entertainment with his Presence; but Mr. Finch and the Heer Von Meyndershagen were there, together with a great Number of the principal Members of this Republick.

' The many shuffling Tricks play'd by the Danish Commissioners appointed to settle with their High-Mightinesses Envoy the Pretensions on both sides, do not promise either a speedy, or a satisfactory Conclusion of that Affair. But we flatter ourselves, that the Good Offices, which by this State's Accession to the Treaty of Hanover, the Kings of Great Britain and France are engaged to employ, will produce a considerable Change at Copenhagen. The rather, because the ancient Bishop of Frejus has assured Mynheer Hop, our Ambassador at the Court of France, that the Marquis de Chamilly, who is going an Embassy to the Danish Court, has it in his Instructions to press the Ministry there to put an End to all Disputes in relation to that Matter: And we are well assured the British Minister at Copenhagen has received Orders to the same Purpose. Which, join'd to the Complaints made here in their High-Mightinesses Name to Mynheer Gries, the Danish Envoy, may perhaps have in Time a good Effect.

' Mynher Calcoen, nominated Ambassador of this State to the Ottoman Porte, is at last upon the point of his Departure, having actually received his Instructions, and together with them the Sum of 10,000 Florins to defray the Expence of his Journey. Our Company of Turky-Merchants at Amsterdam send a Present to the Grand Seignior upon this Occasion, consisting of the richest Fire-Screens, which they understood by the late Count Goljer would be very acceptable to his Highness.

Falmouth, Aug. 22. This day sailed the Phœnix and Mermaid of this Place, both for Croissick.

Plymouth, Aug. 23. This day arrived the Phœnix for Rhode Island; Elizabeth, of and for Boston, from Amsterdam; and the Diligence of Dublin from Cette, Capt. Roche, for Amsterdam.

Dartmouth, Aug. 23. Came in to-day the Mary from Rotterdam; Abington, Capt. Winter, from Jamaica; Greenoch of Glasgow from Virginia; Pretty Betsy for London, Capt. Galpin, from Virginia, who reports, that 300 Leagues to the Westward he met the Prosperous Nelly from London, in Lat. 49 and 23. bound for Newfoundland.

Deal, Aug. 25. The King's Ships, as *per* last, are still here; also the Dolphin for Cadiz. Came down, and sailed, the Genoa Galley, Capt. Pepe, for Genoa. Arrived the S. George from Hamburgh for Oporto.

Deal, Aug. 26. Remain the King's Ships. Yesterday sailed the Dolphin for Cadiz, S. George for Oporto, and the Charity for the Streights.

Gravesend, Aug. 26. Passed by the Greyhound from Rotterdam, John and Mary from Norway, Medway from Carolina; Ostings, Capt. Ting, from Barbadoes; Mary Yacht from Rotterdam; and the Friends Adventure from Gottenburgh.

Pirates

Bristol, Aug. 20. The following Accounts are come to hand concerning the Murder of Capt Green and his Mate, in the Angola Galley of this Place, in her Passage for Guinea. The Captain having lost several Men by Sickness, shipped some Hands at Barbadoes, who proved to be Pyrates: One of them, called Fly, he made his Boatswain; and being put to Sea on the 27th of May last, by the Instigation of Fly and his Comrades, the whole Crew, (except his Chief Mate and the Doctor) mutiny'd, being 11 in Number, and agreed to murder the Captain, and all that would not consent. When the Hour was come for executing their bloody Design, most of them seemed to be at a stand; whereupon Fly bid them come on, and led them down to the Cabbin-Door, and immediately dispatch'd the Mate; then butcher'd the Captain in a most inhuman manner, leaving him for dead; whilst the Doctor was under a great Consternation, expecting his Fate to be next. Mean while, some of them cry'd out, *Soho! Haloh there! Pray save the Doctor.* Which they did, and brought him upon Deck; but some of the old Rogues said, *D---n him, kill him, Dead Men can tell no Tales*; yet he was not hurt. This being late in the Night, the poor Captain had recover'd a little by Morning, and made shift to crawl up the Gangway upon his Knees, his lower Jaw hanging down upon his Breast, and speechless, making Signs for Mercy; the very Sight of him being so frightful, as shock'd the Spirits of the Murderers themselves. However, Fly said, *D---n him, Let us toss him over-board*, and did accordingly; but he catching hold of something while they were doing it, Fly fetch'd an Ax, and cut off one of his Arms, and so he dropt into the Sea; after which they threw the Mate's Body over. Then they held a Consultation, and made Fly their Commander. In a short time after, they came up with a Sloop of North Carolina, bound for Virginia, which they plunder'd, and put the Doctor on board, who came home in the Dispatch Snow, Capt. Perry. Since which we have an Account from Boston, July 4. that Fly having taken a Sloop bound thither the 3d of June, on board of which was one William Atkinson, a Passenger, and good Navigator, Fly forced him on board. After which, they took a Scooner of Marblehead, and put seven of their best Men in her, leaving Fly only three reputed Pyrates on board, besides forced Hands; so that Atkinson consulted with the rest, and on the 23d of June they found Opportunity to seize and secure Fly and his three Rogues, and bringing the Ship into Boston, deliver'd them safe into the Hands of Justice; and a Court was to be held that very day for trying them. On Tuesday, one John Fisher was committed to Newgate here, charged with having conspired, in Conjunction with other Mariners, on board the Jason Galley of this Place, Capt. Plomer, when at Sea, to carry off the said Ship, and turn Pyrates. On Wednesday Night, one Farmer Young, of Redland, was barbarously murder'd in his Bed, himself only lying in the House; but by whom not yet found out. His Wife and he living a disagreeable Life, and she leaving his Bed for some time, drew a Suspicion that she might be accessary to his Death; and we hear, that she and her Son are both bound over.

London, Aug. 27.

On Thursday Night, his Grace the Duke of Argyll arrived in Town from Scotland, and was yesterday at Kensington to wait on his Majesty.

The same Night, the Lord Walpole and his Lady arrived in Town from Devonshire.

The Lord Cadogan and the Countess of Albemarle are arrived here from Holland.

The Drawing of the Lottery is now fixed to the 19th day of September next.

with when arrived in the U. States; and other parishes must do the same or they will be eat up by them. Many parishes are in that state that the land is worth nothing to the landlord, and I see no remedy except sending the extra population somewhere."

This precious cargo has arrived safely, and will, no doubt, assist in creating a home market for some of our products, at the expense of the native industry of the country.

"The bank trials." This is the title given to the trial of certain well known citizens of Baltimore, for an alleged conspiracy to defraud the bank of the United States. They removed their cases to Harford, and submitted them to the court—after much time spent in examining the witnesses and papers, they were acquitted—the chief judge dissenting from the opinion of his colleagues. Since then, several articles have appeared in the news papers on the subject—but none of them bear the stamp of authority; and will not be noticed by us, though we are anxious for a knowledge of the facts.

The university of Maryland has become an establishment highly honorable and advantageous to the state, as well as the city of Baltimore. The superior talents of the different professors have been most assiduously applied to accomplish the original design of the institution, and, with the perfection of that, to render it profitable to themselves. They have succeeded in the first, but much severe labor is yet necessary to bring about the latter. They had every difficulty to encounter that attends a new establishment, and, as they resolved that it should be a permanent one, if possible, their apparatus and appurtenances are as complete as they could be rendered by the expenditure of time and money, freely given to promote the progress of science and the arts.

The merits of this university are very simply shewn by the increase of its number of students—

In 1820-21 they were only	115
1821-22	247
1822-23	303

The *commencement* took place on the 5th inst. and different degrees were conferred on a considerable number of the students, from many different states—whose general character during the course is highly spoken of, for their orderly conduct in public and private, and steady application to duty.

The Mails. The mail, on its passage between Somersett and Wheeling, has been frequently robbed, and, as it passed through eleven or twelve offices, it seemed difficult to ascertain where the thefts were committed. One person had lost 550 dollars, and several others had been robbed of smaller sums. But an attempt to pass one of the notes stolen, led to the detection of the culprit, who was found to be a person of the name of Yunkin, post-master at a village called Union Town, nine miles west of Zanesville, Ohio. When Yunkin was arrested and committed to prison, he confessed his crime, and wrote a letter to his wife, by which nearly the whole of the money known to have been lost was recovered.

The Congress frigate arrived at Norfolk, some days ago, from a long cruise in the West Indies—officers and crew in fine health; and it has been published in a hundred newspapers that she is to proceed to *Buenos Ayres* to take out our minister, Mr. Rodney, to *Rio Janeiro*. Mr. R. is not our minister at Rio Janeiro, but at Buenos Ayres; and what would we think of a person who should take the land route and proceed from Baltimore to *New York*, that he might arrive at *Philadelphia?* One would suppose that if his destination was Philadelphia, he would think it as well to stop there when passing through it!

The pirates. The account of the total destruction of the pirate La Cata by the British cutter Grecian, is fully confirmed—she was blown up; some of her crew, as they swam ashore, were assailed by the Hyperion, and nearly every one of them killed.

It is stated that a British sloop of war has captured a piratical vessel that had a crew of sixty men, under command of the famous *Lafitte*. He hoisted the bloody flag and refused quarter, and fought until nearly every man was killed or wounded—Lafitte being among the former.

The schooner Pilot, of Norfolk, was lately captured by the pirates off Matanzas—and her crew much abused; but they were put ashore, and the wretches went on a cruise in the prize, and captured and robbed two vessels within *two miles of the Moro* castle, Havana---but, a few days after, the U. S. schooner Jackall fell in with her and made a re-capture, securing, however, only one of the pirates, but several of them were killed in the action, fighting desperately. It is reported that five captures have been made by com. Porter's squadron, which has been very actively employed. Some of the vessels had stopped at *Port Allen*, Thompson's Island, or Key West. They had afforded convoy to many vessels, and the most of the pirates appeared to have retired for the present.

Longevity. Died at Bow, in New Hampshire, on the 6th inst. the venerable *Samuel Welch*, aged one hundred and twelve years and seven months! He was born at Kingston in that state, Sept. 1, 1710, O. S. His father died when aged between 80 and 90—his mother and a sister reached 100 years each. Mr. Welch was much respected by all who knew him—and, says the account, "was the oldest native citizen of New Hampshire. Three, however, have died here at a greater age, viz. Mr. Lovewell, of Dunstable, (father to col. Zaccheus Lovewell, mentioned in Belknap's N. H. vol. ii p. 233), aged 120; William Perkins, of New Market, who died in 1732, aged 116; and Robert Macklin, of Wakefield, who died in 1787, at the age of 115. It may be mentioned in favor of the general salubrity of our climate, that within a century about one hundred persons have lived, in New Hampshire, to the age of a century and upwards. We doubt whether any other state in the union can present so many instances of longevity."

Mr. *Tunis Tiebout*, of New York, lately died at Bellford, Long Island, aged *one hundred and one years*.

Michigan. When intelligence was received of the act of congress to alter the government of this territory, the citizens of Detroit, as if it were spontaneously, assembled, and expressed their gratitude by the firing of cannon, martial music and a parade, and in partaking of a good dinner, in honor of the occasion. They had suffered much inconvenience under the old administration of affairs.

The Albion. We have before noticed this *royal* paper published at New York, ornamented with 'his majesty's' arms at the head of it, for the edification

PUBLISHED DAILY BY
JAMES GORDON BENNETT,
Office in the Clinton Buildings, at the corner of Nassau and Beekman streets.

THE HERALD.

VOLUME II. NEW-YORK, WEDNESDAY, APRIL 13, 1836. NUMBER 30.

☞ THE OFFICE OF THE HERALD IS REMOVED FROM THE CELLAR AT No. 148 NASSAU STREET, TO THE SPACIOUS OFFICE IN THE CLINTON BUILDINGS, CORNER OF NASSAU AND BEEKMAN STREETS.

☞ We have yet to apologize for the slowness of our edition. The steam engine did not work so well yesterday as it ought to have done, considering the plenty of good coal and water it swallowed. As it was, for seven hours the people rolled in and rolled out of our office, buying the Herald as fast as they could be struck off. Probably five thousand persons rushed upon us in a few short hours.

In consequence of the extortion of the newsboys, who have been gouging the public out of their money at the rate of *three, six*, and *ten* cents a copy, we struck yesterday—refused to sell them any papers—and supplied the generous public ourselves at *one cent per copy*.—We shall continue to do so till the news boys promise to behave better.

Persons and families wanting to subscribe to the Herald, had better leave their names at the office.

☞ Advertisements must be handed in not later than five o'clock in the afternoon.

N. B. To-morrow we have several strange disclosures to make, relative to the society in which Ellen Jewett moved. Look out.

STILL FURTHER OF THE TRAGEDY.

REFLECTIONS—WHO IS THE MURDERER?—The denouement of the tragedy of Ellen Jewett continues to agitate the public mind beyond any event that we ever heard of or saw in any city. Yesterday the excitement exceeded anything hitherto known to have sprung out of this awful drama. It is rapidly becoming a doubtful point, notwithstanding the startling circumstances, whether the poor, unfortunate girl was destroyed by the young man now in the custody of the public authorities. It is asked—Is it possible for a youth, hitherto unimpeached and unimpeachable in his character, to have engendered and perpetrated so diabolical an act as the death of Ellen Jewett was? Is it the character of crime to jump at once from the heights of virtue to the depths of vice?

It is true to human nature and to Shakspeare, her master and papil, that villainy does not at once develope itself any more than the poisonous Upas grows in a day, an hour, or during the sun shine of an agreeable afternoon.

The various circumstances indicating the probable guilt of Robinson—can they be explained? Can they be accounted for? Can they not be shown to be naturally growing out of other person's guilt—of a deep laid conspiracy of female rivals—of the vengeance of female wickedness—of the burnings of female revenge? The cloak—the hatchet—the twine—the whitewash on his pantaloons—the traces of blood—all the circumstances accumulating to cover the youth with guilt—may yet be explained on the trial,—a trial which, in deep interest, heart rending pathos, remarkable features, and startling developements, will surpass any trial that ever took place in New York.

One of the most remarkable ideas which have occurred to us, tending to throw a suspicion over the guilt of the unhappy young man, is the probability that Ellen Jewett may have been sent hastily out of existence by one of her own rivals in the same degraded *caste* of society. She was beautiful and accomplished, and accordingly attracted all the attentions of the young and the old—the single and the married—who had been in the habit of visiting such places. Would a young man of intelligence and refinement, barbarously slay a lovely and accomplished female, that adored and idolized him, as he would a wild beast of the forest? Is it natural to suppose that such a fiend-like purpose could emanate from a youth whose countenance is indicative of any thing but villainy? whose former life has been without a stain, except falling a victim to the fascinations of Ellen Jewett? How could a human being possessed of human feelings—a man in any respect, take up the unstained hatchet, and deliberately strike that beauteous alabaster brow, without freezing to the spot in horror at its own atrocity? How could man act so terribly towards lovely woman?

Many minds believe it utterly impossible—utterly beyond nature—utterly incomprehensible. Many of the degraded beings who have seen the superior attractions of Ellen Jewett, could not help feeling a jealousy at her extraordinary success and power. On many occasions Ellen, we are told, received enclosures from her admirers in the South and West, containing bills of $500 and upwards. Money she was supplied with in the greatest abundance. There was no want of cash in her drawers. She was profuse and generous—so were all those who came within the verge of her attractions.

Is it not just as probable that her deplorable end was produced by the enmity of some heartless, malignant rival, living in the same house—and blighted by her superior charms, than that it was caused by the calm and imperturbable Robinson?

It is a horrible thing to convict a man of the greatest of all crimes—of an accumulation of crime without a parallel on record,—except, indeed, it be on the clearest, strongest, and most undoubted evidence. The public ought to pause before it permits itself to criminate a young man of hitherto unblemished reputation. The way of life led at such infamous establishments as Rosina Townsend's, may as likely produce such acts as any private quarrel or jealousy between Ellen and Robinson. The old lady keeps numerous boarders—all young women, more or less agreeable and pretty. None of them, however, could compare with Ellen Jewett. She was the pride of that infamous house, called the City Hotel in Thomas street, and knowingly let out for such purposes by one of our most respectable and pious citizens. She concentrated all attention—she was the flower of that garden of death—she was the Venus of that Paphos of destruction—she was the beautiful ruling spirit of that place of perdition—she gave a refined character to all its amusements—she gave grace to its licentiousness—elegance to its debanchery—and spirit and intelligence to its ignorance and vulgarity.

We do not wish to interfere with the dark but stern current of Justice—but the death of Ellen Jewett is the natural result of a state of society and morals which ought to be reformed altogether in unhappy New York. That horrible tragedy is the legitimate fruit of laxity in our old men—want of principle in many of the married—and unregulated passion in the young. It as naturally springs from our general guilt and corruption as the pestilence does from the waters of death stagnating under an August sun. If the cold-blooded murderer of Ellen Jewett shall be ever fully and legibly discovered, it may as likely be found among her own rivals, and her own sex as among the young men who frequented such infamous places. The deliberate setting fire to a house, has more the character of female vengeance in it than that of the heedless passion of a youth of nineteen.

We do not wish to criminate where no crime ought to be laid—we do not wish to avert the bolt of legal vengeance at white robed innocence. The question now before the public involves more than the guilt of one person—it involves the guilt of a system of society—the wickedness of a state of morals—the atrocity of permitting establishments of such infamy to be erected in every public and fashionable place in our city. *We are all guilty alike*—from the magistrate down to the scavenger—from the leader in society down to its follower. The courts of law have not alone a right to investigate this crime—this red-blood atrocity. The whole community have an interest—the present generation are both court, jury, witnesses, culprit, and executioner. It has sprung from a state of society, that we men, and ye women, also, of this age have permitted to grow up among us, without let or hindrance. Suppose Robinson is guilty—suppose he is tried—suppose he is found guilty—suppose he is carried out to Bellevue, and privately executed accordingly to our bloody law—suppose all this—will that take away the awful guilt of the present age—of this city—of our leaders in society—of our whole frame of morals and manners in permitting such a state of things to exist in a respectable, moral, and Christian city? Beauty and innocence—talent and accomplishment, such as are seldom seen commingled together, gave up its existence when the fatal axe penetrated the alabaster forehead of Ellen Jewett. But had not our morals—our manners—our unprincipled male sex, first inflicted a more fatal blow upon her spotless and innocent soul when she became the first victim of seduction, and gave up, in a moment of love and passion, the only ornaments and value of female character?

ROBINSON'S MINIATURE.—This we saw yesterday, at the Police office. It was found in her possession—and is a circumstance decidedly in his favor. If the refusal to give up his letters and portrait, was one of the causes of the act attributed to him, how came he to forget the purpose of his villany? The portrait is a beautiful piece of art—elegantly enclosed in a green case. The features are beautiful and ruddy—rather more round than oval—with a species of bronze clustering ringlets circling round his forehead. He wears a pointed linen collar, bent about half down his neck.

THE EXAMINATION.—All yesterday morning dense groups of people, men and women, were scattered over the Park, expecting to get a sight of Robinson on his way from Bridewell to the Police office to be examined. The prison was nearly surrounded—every eye turned to the iron gratings, and catching the slightest movement within. This was about eleven o'clock. At that hour, there was a great ignorance professed about the time when the examination should take place, but we suspected that the examination was going on privately at that very moment within the walls of the prison.

Since the above was written, we learn that no examination took place yesterday. Ogden Hoffman, his counsel, put it off a few days. Everything is involved in confusion, excitement, and wonder.

ANOTHER VISIT TO THE SCENE.—What a scene of desolation her room presented after the removal of the lovely remains of the unfortunate! Every thing was in confusion. Fragments of books, dresses, bonnets, paper were strewed around. Beneath an old boot that formerly adorned her beautiful ankle, was found a copy of Lalla Rookh, which had been read and re-read, till it looked like a school book, which had gone through a whole family of young ones. In an old bonnet that once flaunted its feathers over that alabaster brow which the murderer's axe has despoiled, we found a copy of Halleck's poems, every leaf cut and apparently well read. Beneath a fragment of fine velvet, constituting a portion of her winter dress, was discovered Byron's Don Juan and Beppo, in all the elegance of binding that London could afford.

What an air of elegance and intellectual refinement, without the slightest approach to principle and morals, dispersed itself round the apartment!

On turning over one of the linen sheets we found a most elegant octavo volume, in splendid London binding. What could it be? Who would imagine what it was? We turned over the leaves—looked at the title page. It was a recent splendid work of Lady Blessington's entitled the "Flowers of Loveliness," and presenting, on the resemblances of females and flowers to each other.

What a crowd of recollections this singular circumstance brings up to mind!

Lady Blessington! one of the frailest—yet most beautiful—one of the most unprincipled—yet most enchanting women now living in the world!

Lady Blessington and her two sisters, were the daughters of a vintner, who kept a small tavern near or in the city of Cork, Ireland. They were young, beautiful, and served his customers at the counter with glasses of whiskey at a sixpence each drink. Possessed of talents without principle, they started in the career of ambition. They picked up general knowledge as well as they could—they rose step by step, till one of the Miss Power's became Lady Blessington—another Lady Canterbury—and a third, Lady Something-else.

The recent publication of this woman was thus found in the boudoir of the poor unfortunate Ellen Jewett.

In another part of the room we found several receipts for the Albion newspaper, the Mirror—the Lady's Companion; all having been paid in advance, one year, and very recently, too. She was a great patroness of our light city literature, and esteemed highly the Knickerbocker and Monthly.

HER LITERARY CORRESPONDENCE.—This is one of the most interesting remains of the "unfortunate." Her epistolary correspondence possesses interest of the deepest character. Police Justice Lownds, has in his possession about fifty or sixty letters found in her trunk, several written by herself, and others written to her, by persons who admired or pretended to admire her talents and beauty.

Not a fulsome expression nor an unchaste word is from her in any of these letters. They contain apt quotations from the Italian, French, and English poets, on love and friendship, satirizing playfully the little incidents of her life. Her hand writing is uncommonly beautiful—a neat running hand possessing something of the character of Bristow's style, but far superior to her master if he ever taught her. Every letter is written on beautiful embossed paper, green, blue, yellow, and gold edged, as accident might throw in her way. Some of the letters, from the hand writing—disclosures, incidents, and other circumstances are known to be from certain respectable persons in this city—and even married men—at least they are married now. The letters also bear various signatures, such as, "Wandering Willie"—"Roderick Random"—"Frank Rivers," &c. &c. All the letters addressed to Robinson, begin "Dear Frank"—and close with, "To Dear Frank Rivers."

The correspondence like her life is a drama, a jungle—a mingling up of various persons, passages and events. Every one of her correspondents took a name and a character—and supported it as well as he could. She also assumed various characters in her various correspondence, and sustained it with the same good keeping as if it had been a drama.

Among the letters, or on her work table, was found a beautiful Album or Scrap Book—containing choice quotations in prose and poetry, some of which had been, and is in her correspondence—others kept for future application. This pretty little book is also in possession of Justice Lownds.

Among the various letters on love and friendship in the escritoire, there was one, of so remarkable and characteristic a nature, as to identify at once the writer, who was well known last summer to have been connected with certain prints of this city, now going into "the sear and yellow leaf." The one we allude to, is signed "Wandering Willie." The supposed writer has distinguished himself in the South recently, fighting against the Indians, and after a defeat, in rescuing a young lady from the watery grave. The manner he became acquainted with Ellen Jewett, was in an affair which took place at the Police Office, and was reported by him in the following article, which appeared in one of the papers he was connected with at the time, June 1834.

Fruits of Seduction.—A very genteel and pretty young girl, named Ellen Jewett, came before the magistrate a day or two since, to lodge a complaint against a young man, named ———, (son of the gentleman of that name, who is connected with the firm of ——— & ———, Pearl street,) for abusing and brutally kicking her in the Park theatre, on Thursday night. She stated that as she was ascending the stairs leading to the second tier, she dropt, by accident, a $10 bill, and, while looking for the same, she was rudely accosted by Mr. ———, and on her requesting him to desist, he abused and kicked her, and then, taking his friend's arm, they ran down stairs, laughing at what they, no doubt, considered very gentlemanly conduct. An affidavit of the facts were taken, and a warrant issued for the apprehension of Mr. ———, who will have to appear at the Sessions, to answer the charge.

In order to convince our readers of the misery resulting from the villanous artifices of those whose sole aim in life, seems to be the seduction of a young and innocent girl, and then, abandon her to the sneers and insults of the heartless and despicable; we will give a brief sketch of the history of this young girl:—She was born at Massachusetts, and losing her parents at an early age, was placed in a boarding school, a few miles from Boston, at which place, she was first seen by the son of a respectable merchant in Boston, who used to visit the establishment; first engaged her affections, then seduced her, and afterwards prevailed upon her to elope with him to Boston, where he kept her concealed for some time, before she was discovered by her friends, when, at last, her retreat was ascertained by her guardian, he proceeded thither, and on his knees entreated her to return to his protection, and abandon the society of her heartless seducer. She yielded to this request, and legal proceedings were immediately instituted against the betrayer of her innocence; the circumstances attending the seduction and elopement, evinced such a total want of every thing like an honorable disposition on his part, that he was shunned and despised by most of his former friends and acquaintances; to avoid the impending storm, which he saw would soon burst with ten-fold violence on his head, he fled from Boston, few knew where, and has not, we believe, never since returned. His unfortunate victim, although kindly treated by her guardian, was but too soon aware, that to regain her former standing in society, was impossible; and in order to escape from scenes, that only served to remind her, with a soul-harrowing power, of what she was, and what she had been, she came to New York, alone, and unprotected. Here she met with a British officer, named Burke, and he, one evening, through ignorance, tendered a counterfeit $3 bill in payment for some wine, at a party where she was present. A dispute subsequently occurred between them, and he, in order to be revenged, cut to pieces several of her dresses, to the value of $100. She lodged a complaint against him, and he was brought to the police office, and proof being given that he was ignorant of the bill being counterfeit, the complaint was withdrawn on condition that he paid $100, for the dresses that he had cut. This sum was paid, and then the affair ended. Ellen's next appearance at the police office, was under less favorable auspices; she was brought up with some ten or twelve other young girls, from a house that was indicted in Duane street. Her quiet and genteel deportment, procured her dismissal on that occasion, since when she has, we believe, been a constant visiter at the Park Theatre, where she is nightly exposed to insults similar to the one mentioned above. Could her betrayer now see the once fascinating and once innocent inmate of the boarding school from which he seduced her, reduced to the condition we have described, he would, if human, need no further punishment than the remorse which would then gnaw his inmost soul.

The account thus given of her seduction, he procured from Ellen herself, whose bail he became, and whom he escorted from the Police Office. He afterwards corresponded with Ellen, and as well as we can remember, the following is the tenor, or nearly, of one of his letters.

[No date.]

DEAREST ELLEN.—Most lovely and enchanting creature! I shall never forget the moment I saw your fair form in the Police Office. You are fit to be a princess—a very queen. What a prize the villain had who seduced you at the Boarding School! How I should liked to have been in his place! Yet you are as sweet a companion now as ever. Oh! lovely creature, what a form! what a figure! what a fine bust! Your lineaments * * * * rich lips, * * * full bust, * * *. Your mind too, is of the first order. I want to come and see you, and talk to you—I adore to read Byron with you. Did you see the account I gave of you in my paper? How I have served up the immaculate rascal! Oh! such richness as you have in your bosom, sweet Helen. I could almost go the world over in your service—sleep away a whole life on your bosom. *Ma foi*, but I could. What is the reason, Helen, that after a woman falls from virtue she never gets up? I dont know, however, that I am much better than you. When shall I come and see you? Do lovely Helen, say?

Had I never loved so blindly,
Had I never loved so kindly,
Never met or never parted,
I had ne'er been broken hearted.

There's a quotation for you.

I am, your's forever,
WANDERING WILLIE.

TIMES AND SEASONS.

"Truth will prevail."

Vol. V. No. 12.] CITY OF NAUVOO, ILL. JULY, 1, 1844. [Whole No. 96.

Awful assassination of JOSEPH AND HYRUM SMITH!--The pledged faith of the State of Illinois stained with innocent blood by a Mob!

On Monday the 24th inst., after Gov. Ford had sent word, that those eighteen persons demanded on a warrant, among whom were Joseph Smith and Hyrum Smith *should be protected*, by the militia of the State, they in company with some ten or twelve others, started for Carthage. Four miles from that place, they were met by Capt. Dunn, with a company of cavalry, who had an order from the Governor for the "*State Arms*." Gen. Smith endorsed his acceptance of the same, and both parties returned to Nauvoo to obtain said arms. After the arms were obtained, both parties took up the line of march for Carthage, where they arrived about five minutes before twelve o'clock at night. Capt. Dunn nobly acquiting himself, landed us safely at Hamilton's Hotel.

In the morning we saw the Governor, and he *pledged the faith of the State*, that we should be protected. Gen. Smith and his brother Hyrum were arrested by a warrant founded upon the oaths of H. O. Norton and Augustine Spencer for *treason*. Knowing the threats from several persons, that the two Smiths should never leave Carthage *alive*, we all began to be alarmed for their personal safety. The Gov. and Gen. Deming conducted them before the McDonough troops and introduced them as *Gen. Joseph Smith and Gen. Hyrum Smith.*—This manœuvre came near raising a mutiny among the "Carthage Greys," but the Governor quelled it.

In the afternoon, after great exertions on the part of our counsel, we dispensed with an investigation, and voluntarily gave bail for our appearance to the Circuit Court, to answer in the case of abating the Nauvoo Expositor, as a nuisance.

At evening the Justice made out a mittimus, without an investigation, and committed the two Gen. Smiths to prison *until discharged by due course of law*, and they were safely guarded to jail. In the morning the Governor went to the jail and had an interview with these men, and to every appearance all things were explained on both sides.

The constable then went to take these men from the jail, before the Justice for examination, but the jailor refused to let them go, as they were under his direction "*till discharged by due course of law;*" but the Governor's troops, to the amount of one or two hundred, took them to the Court House, when the hearing was continued till Saturday the 29th, and they were remanded to jail. Several of our citizens had permits from the Governor to lodge with them, and visit them in jail. It now began to be rumored by several men, whose names will be forthcoming in time, *that there was nothing against these men, the law could not reach them, but powder and ball would!* The Governor was made acquainted with these facts, but on the morning of the 27th, he disbanded the McDonough troops, and sent them home; took Captain Dunn's company of Cavalry and proceeded to Nauvoo, leaving these two men and three or four friends, to be guarded by *eight men* at the jail; and a company in town of 60 men, 80 or 100 rods from the jail, as a corps in reserve.

About six o'clock in the afternoon the guard was surprised by an armed Mob of from 150 to 250, painted red, black and yellow, which surrounded the jail, forced in—poured a shower of bullets into the room where these unfortunate men were held, "in durance vile," to answer to the laws of Illinois; under the solemn pledge of the faith of the State, by Gov. Ford, *that they should be protected!* but the mob ruled!! They fell as Martyrs amid this tornado of lead, each receiving four bullets! John Taylor was wounded by four bullets in his limbs but not seriously. Thus perishes the hope of law; thus vanishes the plighted faith of the state; thus the blood of innocence stains the constituted authorities of the United States, and thus have two among the most noble martyrs since the slaughter of Abel, sealed the truth of their divine mission, *by being shot by a Mob for their religion!*

Messengers were dispatched to Nauvoo, but did not reach there till morning. The following was one of the letters:

12 o'clock at night, 27th June, }
Carthage, Hamilton's Tavern. }

TO MRS. EMMA SMITH,

AND MAJ. GEN. DUNHAM, &c—

The Governor has just arrived; says all things shall be inquired into, and all right measures taken.

I say to all the citizens of Nauvoo, my brethren, be still, and know that *God reigns. Don't rush out of the city*—don't rush to Carthage; stay at home, and be prepared for an attack from

THE HANGMAN.

"I shall ask for the Abolition of the Penalty of Death until I have the Infallibility of Human Judgment demonstrated to me."....*Lafayette.*

Vol. I.] Boston, (Mass,) Wednesday, August 13, 1845. [*New Series*—No. 20.

Appointment of the time for the execution of Orrin De Wolf.

The friends of suffering humanity have now only a few days more to labor in behalf of Orrin De Wolf. On Tuesday, the 26th inst. the Governor and Council of this Commonwealth will meet in this city for the transaction of executive business. They will then appoint the day and the hour when John W. Lincoln, the Sheriff of Worcester County, shall take Orrin De Wolf from his cell, and hang him up by the neck, until he is dead. Shall this unnecessary and inhuman work be done in this ancient Commonwealth in the year 1845? Is it not full time to discontinue forever this horrid practice? Let all those who do not desire to have De Wolf hung, make great exertions to save his life by circulating petitions immediately asking for a commutation of punishment. Now is the time to work for the prisoner, for him 'who is appointed unto death.' Send petitions to our office. We will forward them to the Executive.

ADDRESS TO THE PEOPLE OF THE STATE OF PENNSYLVANIA.

Fellow-Citizens:—The Philadelphia Society for promoting the Abolition of Capital Punishment, at a meeting held at the County Court House, on June 9th, 1845, directed its Executive Board to issue an address to the people of this State, calling a general convention of the friends of the measure, to be held in this city in November next, to concert a plan for the more speedy accomplishment of the object had in view.

In performing this pleasing duty, the Board would beg leave to remind you that our State has always been conspicuous for a bold and judicious reformation of the defective penal system inherited from our transatlantic progenitors.—That system, originating in the darkness of barbarism, and fostered by centuries of war and violence, has to this time retained the traces, more or less distinct, of its savage and unchristian source. The English law, from which ours is derived, has ever been peculiarly bloody.—The one remedy for all social evils was the gallows. The prison was but a passage from the court-house to the scaffold. To the honor of our Founder be it spoken, among his first exercises of authority in his infant Commonwealth, was the repeal of this Draconic code, in the great majority of the cases to which it applied. By the Great Law enacted at Chester, in 1682, a new system was introduced. That it did not provide for the substitution of a milder punishment than death in all cases, was an error to be pardoned in one who had already done so much for the cause of humanity. As the personal influence of William Penn was gradually lessened, the criminal code of the colony was made to approximate to that of the mother country, until it became almost as sanguinary. But this severity was foreign to the spirit of our institutions, and could not last. The men of the Revolution, actuated by that deep sense of the dignity and value of our common humanity, which they made the corner-stone of our republican liber:y, early applied themselves to the amelioration of the criminal code. The convention which framed the Constitution of 1776, considered the subject so important as to embody in that instrument a declaration of the duty of the legislature to amend the penal laws, so as to render them less sanguinary, and to substitute 'visible punishment of long duration' in penitentiaries for the death-penalty. In 1786 this reform was commenced by the abolition of this penalty in the case of burglary, robbery, and other crimes. By the famous act of 1794, murder was divided into two degrees, and the punishment of death abolished in all cases whatever, except the higher of these two. The same act established the true theory of criminal legislation, in words that should be written on the heart of every Pennsylvanian. We refer to the preamble to the said act, which is as follows:—

'Whereas, the design of punishment is to prevent the commission of crimes, and to repair the injury that has been done thereby to society or the individual, and it hath been found by experience that these objects are better obtained by moderate but certain penalties than by severe and excessive punishment; and, whereas, it is the duty of every government to endeavor to reform rather than exterminate offenders, and the punishment of death ought never to be inflicted when it is not absolutely necesaary to the public safety, therefore, &c.'

Let every man ponder these positions well, and then answer if Capital Punishment is at all admissible into a code which starts from these premises. It is not disciplinary. We hold to the necessity of punishment, because we know that all chastening, though for the present it is not joyous but rather grievous, yet worketh in the end the peaceable fruits of righteousness.—But the death-penalty is not of this character. It cuts off the offender as if utterly incapable of amendment, a fact which no man or body of men can predicate of another, without arrogating to themselves the divine prerogative. It is, therefore, essentially evil in its nature. There can be shown no possible excuse for its infliction, unless it be an absolute and imperative necessity, in order to protect society against repeated crime. But can this necessity be shown? We answer confidently, no! We appeal to the experience of thousands of years of violence and bloodshed, whose only testimony on the subject is, that wrath stirreth up wrath, and violence begets violence. We appeal to the results of the abolition of the death-penalty in regard to other crimes in this country, in Great Britain and the world over. We refer you to the happy effects which have been caused by the same abolition in the case of murder in Tuscany, in Belgium, in Russia, and uniformly wherever the experiment has been tried. The whole history of our race speaks with one voice on this point. The record is true, that the Maker of man will require his blood at the hand of every one that sheddeth it—at the hand of communities as well as individuals—and whether it be shed by the secret dagger or by the sword of the executioner. On whatever people has set up the gallows, or the scaffold in its midst, there has ever rested the curse of blood-guiltiness. Not only has the horrid machinery of destruction entirely failed of the end it was intended to accomplish, but it has itself been a copious fountain of crime, and has stood ready to devour those whom itself had educated to murder, by the lessons of bloodshed and violent revenge.

This, fellow-citizens, is no exaggerated picture, but a solemn reality. Your legislators have already admitted its truth. It would be supererrogatory in us to argue against the moral influence of the gallows, when the idea is, in fact, almost universally abandoned. The act of April 10th, 1834, directs executions to be conducted in private, and provides expressly 'that no person under age shall be allowed on any account to witness the same.' The reason is obvious, and has been given already. We do the deed of blood in secrecy and obscurity, because we know that all its influences are unredeemedly evil.

But the mischief does not stop even here.—The great heart of this community revolts against the infliction of death as a penalty for crime.—Even those who resist the legislative abolition of the death punishment, willingly assist in its practical abrogation in most cases. The difficulty of convicting for capital offences has become notorious to all who have observed the course of justice in our courts. Let a man be indicted for murder, and it is not easy to obtain a jury willing to sit in judgment upon him. The best men on the panel generally refuse to serve, when the violent death of a fellow-being may be the result of their action. In our city, more than thirty jurymen have pleaded conscientious scruples on this subject in a single case. After a jury is empanneled, the awful responsibility connected with a deliberate destroying of the image of God weighs too heavily on all minds to admit of a calm consideration of the evidence.—The slightest testimony which goes to favor the innocence of the prisoner, unconsciously assumes an unnatural importance.—Has not every one noticed the infrequency of convictions in capital cases? And if a conviction is obtained, the appeal to the pardoning power, is instantly made, with a force well nigh irresistible. The crime of the condemned is lost sight of in sympathy for his wretched condition, and judge, jury and prosecutor not unfrequently unite in the recommendation to mercy. Hence comes a too frequent use of the pardoning power, which (however much it may be deplored) any one will be slow to censure, who can place himself for the moment in the painful position of that Executive, on the mere writing of whose signature hang the issues of life and death to a brother man. In view of these facts, we earnestly urge you to unite in promoting the repeal of a law whose very extremity of severity is alone sufficient to render it practically inoperative.

The evil influences of this punishment, just alluded to, have been felt elsewhere as much as in our own State. They have attracted the attention of philanthropists throughout Christendom. The number of offences punished with death has recently been much diminished in Great Britain, on the Continent of Europe, and in several of our sister States. The propriety of an entire abandonment of the penalty is at present undergoing a wide spread discussion in our country. The time cannot be far distant when no gallows will be left standing in all our borders. There is some resistance to this reform from those who have so much fear of innovation as to adhere to an ancient, though acknowledged evil, rather than venture on an untried good.—But the greatest opposition must ever arise from that deep-rooted spirit of malignity, which delights in human suffering, and which believes that it serves God when it can clothe passion with the thin mask of justice. We beg all who have opposed this movement to examine their hearts carefully and ask themselves how far they have mistaken a revengeful impulse for a deduction of reason. Let the subject be fairly examined. Discussion—full, free and impartial discussion—we believe to be all that is necessary to recommend the reform we advocate to the minds of all thinking men. We therefore respectfully suggest to societies for discussion and other public bodies the investigation of the claims which this measure has upon their attention and support. Those who have already arrived at conclusions unfavorable to Capital Punishment, we would urge to renewed and more strenuous efforts for the speedy completion of the good work in which we are engaged, from the consideration that the time for it has evidently come. The public mind is rapidly ripening for the change, and if it is not soon brought about, it will be the fault of our supineness and negligence.

Fellow-citizens, the present is the time for efficient action. Let us come together and consult on the course we should pursue. Hopes are entertained by many that the next Legislature of the Commonwealth will not adjourn without a favorable action on this momentous topic.—We trust that a full representation of our friends from other portions of the State will be present. All who purpose to assist in the deliberations of the convention are requested to annouuce their intention to John Ashton, Jr., Secretary of the Society, No. 30, Market street, at an early date. The meeting will be held on the day previous to that of the American Society for the Abolition of Capital Punishment, at which it is expected that numerous prominent advocates of the measure from other States will be present.'

H. S. Patterson, M. D.,	John Scholefield,
John Bouvier,	John Ashton, Jr.,
Edward Townsend,	Jonah Thompson,
D. S. Skerritt, M. D.,	Jos. Brookfield, M. D.
Benjamin Matthias,	John W. Forney,
J. A. Elkinton, M. D.,	Thomas Ridgway,
William J. Mullen,	Thomas S. Cavender,
Edward A. Penniman,	Thomas Earle,
Daniel L. Miller, Jr.,	Henry Gibbons, M. D.
John B. Ellison,	Wm. F. Kintzing,
Marshall Attmore,	Joseph Sill,
Benjamin C. Bacon,	Jos. McIlhenny,

Thomas L. Kane.

PUBLIC EXECUTIONS

Will speedily be abolished in England, Sir James Graham having given an intimation to that effect on the 8th of May. A recent execution in England caused complant to be made which drew out the intimation above alluded to. The execution was that of T. H. Hocker, a school-master, for the murder of a man named Delarue. The following particulars of the conduct of the man, on the morning of his execution, are very painful;

"The miserable culprit ate a small breakfast of tea and toast, which was supplied to him shortly before 7 o'clock; and after joining the Rev. Ordinary in his devotions, he appeared ready for the moment to arrive which should cut him off from the world.

THE BOSTON HERALD.

J. A. FRENCH, 19 STATE STREET. SATURDAY MORNING, AUGUST 31, 1850. NO. 8482.—PRICE ONE CENT.

THE BOSTON HERALD.
JOHN A. FRENCH,
EDITOR AND PROPRIETOR.

OFFICE NO. 19 STATE STREET.

Five Editions Daily (Sundays Excepted).

Each Edition contains the Latest Intelligence received by Telegraph and the Mails, and all Local News, up to the moment of going to press.

TERMS.—Per week, (payable to the Carriers) SIX CENTS. Per annum (in advance) THREE DOLLARS.

PRICES OF ADVERTISING IN THE HERALD.

[illegible]

Twelve lines are counted as a square, and six lines or less, a half square. Longer advertisements in exact proportion, and all are payable at the time ordered.

THE WEEKLY HERALD.
Is published every SATURDAY MORNING, and contains all the important matter that has appeared in the Daily during the week. Price $1,50 per annum, or three cents single.

All letters must be addressed to the Proprietor. Communicated news, respectfully solicited from all parts of the United States.

SECOND EDITION.

SATURDAY, AUGUST 31—7 A. M.

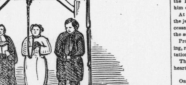

LOVE LAUGHS AT GOLD AS WELL AS LOCKSMITHS. There was an elopement from this city this morning, under rather curious circumstances. A young girl who had for years been engaged to a young mechanic of excellent character, from Vermont, residing here, found a very serious obstacle to her marriage with him in the opposition of her parents. They forbade the bans and insisted upon their daughter's immediate union with another—an acquaintance recently returned from California with gold enough to satisfy half a dozen toiling mechanics. She determined however to marry her old beau—but how, till this event, keep on terms with the wishes of her parents and at the same time escape parental vigilance? She pretended to be ready to submit to the wishes of her parents, allowed their favorite to visit her in the way of courtship, and made arrangements to marry him. In the meantime she had the most perfect understanding with her true betrothed, and agreed to marry him at all events at the first favorable opportunity. After giving themselves up to despair day after day, shedding tears and making protestations of eternal fidelity—that favorable moment arrived last night.

The girl, telling her mother she was going out a moment to a dress maker, to see about her wedding dress, hunted up her Vermont lover, went to a Justice with him, and they were married. The matter was kept entirely secret—the new married pair parted—and the girl went home to receive, as usual, a courting visit from her California aspirant. After passing a portion of the evening with her, he retired, congratulating himself upon the prospect of very soon taking her with him to California. He had been gone an hour, however, than she began to make certain arrangements, which the reader will understand. Whether she slept at all during the night is uncertain, but at early daybreak she stole out of the house without the knowledge of any one in it, joined her young husband, and started north with him, to pass the honey-moon among the hills of Vermont. The whole affair was managed with admirable adroitness, and our word for it, the heroine will make a jewel of a wife.—*Lowell Courier.*

HOW REYNARD WAS CAUGHT.—The Northampton *Courier* gives the following account of how a fox was lately caught in that town, with a hook and line:—

"It appears that Mr. R. Barlow of Warren, was fishing on the bank of a narrow stream, where a tree had been broken off five or six feet from the ground and fallen across an opposite bank. The fox made his appearance at the other end of the fallen tree, and without observing Mr B., who stood below holding the fish line so as to drop across the tree, and while the fox came upon it, by a sudden switch of the line, the end of it passed around the fox's body, and the hook catching formed a noose, and poor fox was caught. He was suffered, however, to go again, his skin being of little value at this season of the year."

TRAGEDY IN NEW YORK. A man named Coates was shot and mortally wounded in New York on Thursday night, by his brother-in-law, Jas. Queen. It appears that Queen was jealous of Coates' conduct with his wife, who was his sister, and sent him an insulting letter about it. Coates sought an interview with his brother-in-law—at which he inflicted some blows upon him—when Queen turned and fired two successive shots with a pistol. The wounded man cannot recover, and the murderer is in jail.

A SINGULAR DREAM QUICKLY VERIFIED. One of our citizens, on Monday night, dreamed twice of being drawn as a juror for the U. S. District Court, which holds its sittings in Boston, and singular to say, on Tuesday forenoon he received information of the fact of his choice to that situation the previous day. Who will say now "dreams go by contraries?"—*Cor. Salem Gazette, 30th.*

CENSUS OF PROVIDENCE. The census of Providence, R. I., is nearly completed, and shows that the present population of that city is not far from 43,062. In 1840, it was 23,172.

QUESTION FOR A DEBATING SOCIETY. Which is the most proud, a girl with her first beau, or a woman with her first baby?

EXECUTION
OF
J. W. WEBSTER!
CONVICTED OF THE MURDER
OF
DR. G. PARKMAN!

SERVICES AT THE JAIL!

THE SCENE AT THE GALLOWS!

Webster's Last Words!

DISPOSAL OF THE BODY,
&c. &c. &c.

The last scene in the great tragedy is over. This morning, on the gallows, John White Webster, recently a Professor in Harvard University, suffered the extreme penalty of the law, for the confessed murder of George Parkman. Sad and most terrible was this last closing scene in the criminal's life—one never to be forgotten by those who witnessed it. But the black curtain of death has fallen on the chief actor in the melancholy drama, and his name and his crimes belong no more to the criticizing tongues of men or the stern judgments of human law. Oblivion will settle darkly over the murderer's grave, and the world, in its ever new and changing scenes of business and excitement, will soon forget the mournful past. All recollection of the disappearance of an old and respected citizen—the surprising arrest of one high in society—the exciting trial—the terrible sentence of a judge—and this day's horrible fulfilment of the law—will ere long be but a vague and passing dream of things that were. Other men and other scenes—new developments of the crime and wickedness of the human heart—will engross the scandal and the judgments of the future; and John White Webster, as he disappears in the great mass of departed humanity, will be forgotten save by a few whom the ties of consanguinity bind to weary years of wretchedness and woe. No pen may picture—no tongue may tell—the misery of that unhappy family. God grant that our city or our State may never thus make desolate another family circle, or plant such a hideous monument of ignominy on another household hearth!

BIOGRAPHY.

John W. Webster was the son of Dr. Redford Webster, once a member of our State Legislature, and a gentleman of considerable wealth and great respectability. John W. was born in this city, about the year 1793. He received a most liberal education, and adopted the profession of medicine, but finally devoted his studies and time to subjects more congenial to his tastes—geology, mineralogy, philosophy and the arts. In 1823, or 24, he travelled in England and Scotland, in company with Professor Sose of Paris; and afterwards went to the Azores.—At the latter place he resided for some considerable time, and on his return home published an interesting and valuable work on the geology of the Azore islands. A valuable collection of minerals, which he had procured in his travels, he sold to Harvard College for eight thousand dollars. He edited, for a time, the Boston Journal of Philosophy and Arts.

In 1827 he was elected Erving Professor of Chemistry, Natural Philosophy, Minerology and Geology, in the University at Cambridge. This honorable post he obtained, it is said, through some peculiar friendship and assistance of Dr. George Parkman. The same year he delivered his first course of lectures before the Medical Class of the University, at the institution in Mason street, in this city, where he succeeded the late celebrated Professor Gorham. Professor Webster's salary was fixed at nineteen hundred dollars per annum. In this position he commenced that awful epoch in his life which has this day closed with his death.

By the decease of his father, in 1834, Professor Webster inherited a fortune of about $40,000, but this has gradually been wasted, until his family are now left with but a comparatively small income. Extravagant in his habits—generous to his family—wishing to maintain a brilliant position in society—he threw his fortune heedlessly away into the vortex of fashionable life. Money went, and debts came; pecuniary troubles accumulated thick and fast; his was not the calculating economy that could avert impending ruin. Old friends became ruthless creditors—poverty and the jail stared him unpityingly in the face—at first he practised fraud, and finally, when disgraceful exposure of some kind must come, he meditated the violent death of his most persecuting creditor. The world knows the rest.

THE CRIME.

The deed of blood, for which the guilty man has suffered, was committed in the afternoon of the 23d day of November last, at the private apartments of Professor Webster, in the Grove street Medical College. Mystery hung over the whereabouts of the murdered man for one week, at the expiration of which time the mangled remains of George Parkman were discovered in places to which no one but Professor Webster had access. That evening, (Nov. 30th,) the Professor was arrested on the charge of murder, at his residence in Cambridge. The thrilling scenes of that night have been so often vividly described, that we have no need to recapitulate them.

On Monday, December 3d, the prisoner was carried before a Justice of the Police Court, where he waived an examination on the charge of murder, and was remanded to jail.

On Wednesday, Dec. 5th, Coroner Pratt, with a jury of inquest, of which Osmyn Brewster was foreman, commenced a careful and lengthy investigation of the case. The verdict of the Jury was terribly concise and definite in its language, and startling in its horrible conclusions, but—as afterwards proved—true to the letter.

On Tuesday, March 19th, Prof. Webster was placed at the bar of the Supreme Court, for trial. No trial ever took place in this or any other country, which excited so much interest. It was the constant theme of the press, and of communities throughout the United States. In our own city, all business seemed palsied, and men waited anxiously to learn the fate of Webster, as if the destiny of a nation depended on the voice of a jury.

On Saturday night, March 30th, at ten minutes past eleven o'clock, the jury were solemnly ushered into the silent but crowded court room. A pin might have been heard to drop upon the floor—every heart seemed to have stopped beating, and the dreadful stillness of breathless expectation was most oppressive to the ear. The word "*Guilty*," as it fell from the quivering lips of the foreman—horrible, startling as it was—gave a melancholy relief to the pent-up and agonizing anxiety of the spectators.—But the prisoner—none could see the misery gnawing at his heart—the utter despair that enveloped his soul—as with bowed head and nerveless limbs, he sank backward into his chair.

On Tuesday, April 2d, Chief Justice Shaw, after some most feeling remarks to the prisoner, passed the full sentence of the law upon Professor Webster, and he was then remanded back to jail, to await his execution at such a time as the Governor might appoint.

Up to a much later date than this, Prof. Webster had most steadfastly denied his guilt, asserting his innocence in the strongest terms. But finally came a confession that he killed Dr. Parkman, coupled with the declaration that it was not a premeditated act. This last assertion, however, had no effect in the quarter it was intended to reach. The Governor and Council weighed the circumstances of the case well, and the sentence of the law was not revoked nor mitigated.

THE CONDEMNED.

For some time after Prof. Webster had received his sentence, he maintained his usual good spirits, partook heartily of the food afforded him by his friends, employed a large portion of his time in reading books on his favorite science, and evidently seemed not to realize the sad truth that he must die a death of ignominy.

But when his fate was sealed by the firm decision of the Governor and Council—when he learned that all the influence of powerful friends, his own protestations, and the beseeching tears of his wife and children were of no avail—then the once strong man bowed down hopelessly to his doom. Then was broken the last fragile thread that Hope had woven in his heart, and he knew that he must die. More recently, the unhappy man has shown signs of contrition, and, if appearances deceive not, he was sincerely endeavoring to make his peace with God.

It has been the frequent remark of those who knew Webster, that, with his knowledge of the most subtle poisons, and his familiarity with the easiest modes of causing death, he would never suffer himself to be hung. But he has not evinced the slightest disposition towards suicide, and the jailor had such complete confidence in the condemned man's declarations and manner, that no guard was placed in his cell, during the last three or four days previous to execution. In fact, it was felt by all, that did Prof. Webster contemplate suicide, it would be in vain to attempt to prevent it. He was therefore left to meet death in such manner as his conscience dictated.

Yesterday, his family visited him at the jail in Leverett street, for the last time, though unconsciously to them so. But the more than usually painful interview must have given them forebodings that the fatal day was rapidly drawing near. They looked upon the animate form of the condemned husband and father, and their hearts told them they would never see him thus again.

DIRECTIONS CONCERNING HIS BODY.

Professor Webster, a few days since, made a request that his body should be disposed of in the following manner. When his body was cut down from the gallows, he desired that it should immediately be carried to the cell lately occupied by him—that it should there remain, unseen by any visiters, until night, when he wished that the corpse might be taken out quietly and secretly, and conveyed to the residence of his family in Cambridge. Furthermore, he wished his body to be placed in a mahogany coffin which he supposed would be furnished by his friends, and not in one of cheap pine, such as is usually furnished by the authorities. The funeral ceremonies, he desired, should take place on Sunday. Thus it will be seen that he coolly deliberated on his approaching dissolution.

CLOSING SCENES YESTERDAY.

The family of Professor Webster remained in his cell until nearly half-past six o'clock, P. M. As they left the prison, a great number of persons were grouped together on the sidewalk, to satisfy a morbid curiosity by gazing on the wretched wife and daughters of the condemned man.

At a little before seven o'clock, Edward D. Sohier, Esq., one of the counsel at Prof. W.'s trial, visited him in his cell, at his own previous request.

At seven o'clock, constable Edward J. Jones and John Leighton, the late clerk of the Jail, entered the Professor's cell, for the purpose of watching him during the night.

At dusk, the first wagon entered the back gate of the jail yard, with the stakes and other fixtures necessary to mark off the ground that was to enclose the scaffold.

Prof. Webster, it is said, passed the night in praying, reading the Scriptures, and in devotional meditation.

This morning, he eat his breakfast with his usual hearty relish, and smoked a cigar.

PREPARATIONS FOR EXECUTION.

On entering the jail yard this morning, a little before 8 o'clock, we found a collection of about 100 persons, of whom one third were constables and police officers.

We found the scaffold erected in the centre of the back jail-yard, in a different position from that occupied by Goode's, but we think, more conspicuously situated.

A clear view of the execution could be witnessed from a dozen houses on Lowell street, and one building at the end of Wall street. The windows of these houses were filled with persons of both sexes, and on the back [illegible] and men and women of all ages. People swarmed upon the tops of buildings, and outside the jail, where no possible view could be obtained, was gathered a motley crowd, eager to hear the first tidings of the fate of Webster.

About a quarter before eight, the carpenters ascended the scaffold, and finished their last duties.

The rope was adjusted on the beam, the noose tied, and all things made ready.

At eight o'clock, nearly two hundred persons had congregated in the jail yard, and were gradually increasing in numbers.

The scaffold was made of unplaned pine joist, and was the same one on which Washington Goode was hung, although yesterday an alteration was made in the trap-door, by which it would fall from the touch of a spring, instead of the cutting of a rope. The arrangement was such as was used on the occasion of Pearson's execution.

At a quarter before nine, Sheriff Eveleth and the jail officers visited the condemned man in his cell. Prof. Webster thanked them for the kindness and attention he had received from them, and after about five minutes interview bid them an affectionate farewell.

At a quarter past nine, the Sheriff, twelve witnesses, members of the press, and a number of public officers, entered the lower corridor of the first prison, and gathered around the cell door.

Dr. Putnam stood at the door of the cell, and offered a most affecting prayer. After this, the assemblage retired to the yard, leaving the Sheriff and his officers, and Dr. Putnam, with the prisoner.

THE GALLOWS SCENE.

At twenty-five minutes before ten o'clock, the Sheriff, with his deputies, the prisoner, and the officiating clergyman, advanced from the prison doors to the scaffold. Professor Webster walked with a firm step to the gallows. He was dressed in deep black, but wore no neck-cloth. He looked in good health, but he appeared reconciled to his fate, although his head was bowed.

The Sheriff read in slow and measured tones, the warrant for the execution of the criminal, amidst the most profound silence of the witnesses in the jail-yard. But from outside the walls were heard the shouts and hootings of the mob.

Prof. Webster behaved in a very firm manner—took his place upon the drop, and stood perfectly quiet. He had a few minutes earnest conversation with Sheriff Eveleth and Rev. Dr. Putnam, which could not be heard by others. The substance of it, however, was to express his thanks to all, for the kindness shown him, and the avowal that *his doom was just.*

He also expressed himself ready to meet his God, and trusted that he died a Christian.

Deputy Sheriff Rugg then put the fatal noose over the head of the unfortunate man, and adjusted it easily around his neck.

The black cap was then drawn over his face by an attendant.

One moment of dreadful silence—the High Sheriff placed his foot upon a spring—the drop fell—and the body of John White Webster was dangling at the end of the hangman's rope!

One spasmodic contraction of the limbs, and the corps swayed to and fro.

In a few minutes after, however, the legs were seen to move suddenly, and the knees quickly drew up. In a moment they fell and no other motion was perceptible.

About ten minutes after ten o'clock, the body was cut down, and removed to the cell lately occupied by the victim of the law.

His body will be disposed of, probably, according to the directions of Prof. Webster, mentioned above.

W. W. KURTZ & CO., Publishers. | ILLUSTRATED EDITION. | SAN FRANCISCO, October, 1856.

PROCESSION OF THE COMMITTEE OF VIGILANCE OF SAN FRANCISCO, IN THE DEMONSTRATION OF AUGUST 18, 1856.

The procession formed in line on Third street, at an early hour on the morning of the 18th of August, and after being reviewed by the Grand Marshal they took up their march though the principal thoroughfares of the city in the following order:

1st. Grand Marshal Doane and Aids.
2d. Col. J. N. Olney and Staff.
3d. Brass band mounted on horseback.
4th. The Light Artillery Battalion, under command of Col. Thomas D. Johns, Lieut. Col. J. F. Curtis and Maj. R. B. Hampton; thirteen pieces.
Company A, Capt. J. Mead Huxley, four bronze six-pounder field pieces; 60 men.
Company B, Capt. Richet, four six-pounder bronze field pieces; 74 men.
Company C, Capt. Behrens, four four-pounder iron guns; 40 men.
Company D (Marine Battery), Capt. J. H. Hasty, two twelve pounder iron guns and two nine pounder iron guns; 64 men.
The Light Artillery Reserve, Lieut. Col. Curtis, two bronze six pounder field pieces; 44 men.
Mounted Detachment of Light artillery Cannoniers; 30 men.
5th. A representation of the Sacramento street Battery or "Fort Gunny Bags"—a large frame work mounted upon wheels,—covered with canvas, which was painted on all sides, to represent the sand-bag fortification thrown up in front of the rooms. There were five port-holes, with the muzzle of the cannon protruding. This was attended by thirty-six men.
6th. The Executive of the Vigilance Committee, to the number of 85 men, mounted, each wearing a badge of white ribbon tied in the lappel of the coat.
7th. Cavalry Companies, Major Frank Baker commanding:
First—The Mounted Light Dragoons, Company A. Capt. Brodt; 125 men, preceded by their band.
Second—Mounted Light Dragoons, Company B, Capt. J. Sewell Read; 125 men.
8th. The Medical Staff, mounted, and wearing yellow badges, and numbering 30 men.
9th. Those connected with the Quartermaster's Department, mounted, with red and blue badges, and numbering 20 men.
10th. The Members of the Vigilance Committee of 1851, with badges, and numbering 90 men. They were preceded by a wagon upon which was constructed a frame work, which was overspread with American flags, and which supported the banner of the Committee; it was full ten feet square, and was a very beautiful affair. Upon one side were the words,—"The Vigilance Committee of San Francisco. Instituted August, 1851." On the reverse side was the following:

"Presented to the Vigilance Committee of San Francisco, by the ladies of Trinity Parish, as a testimonial of their approbation. Do right and fear not. August 9th, 1851."

The wagon was drawn by six spirited grays, and was driven by Orrick Johnson, Esq.
11th. The American Brass Band, on foot.
12th. The Infantry Regiments:

THE FIRST REGIMENT.

The First Regiment embraced the Battalion Citizen's Guard, which is officered as follows: Colonel, J. N. Olney; Lieut. Colonel, J. S. Ellis; Major, Geo. F. Watson; Quartermaster. J. P. H. Wentworth; Adjutant, H. H. Thrall; Commissary, L. S. Wilder; Sergeant Major, R. M. Cox; Quartermaster's Sergeant, H. W. F. Hoffman. The Regimeut was commanded by Major Geo. F. Watson, and was composed of the following companies:
1st. Company A, of the Battalion Citizens' Guard, commanded by Lieut. W. C. Allen, 50 men.
2d. Company C, of the Battalion Citizens' Guard, Capt. H. L. Twiggs, 50 men.
3d. Company B, of the Battalion Citizens' Guard, Capt. A. L. Loring, 50 men.
4th. Company D, of the Battalion Citizens' Guard, Capt. J. V. McElwee, 50 men.
5th. The Executive Guards, Capt. J. M. Taylor, 70 men.
6th. Company Three, Artillery Guards, Capt. Jonathan Gavett, 80 men.
7th. Company Seven, Capt. Geo. H. Hossefross, 100 men.
8th. Company Two, Riflemen, Capt. L. W. Parks, 50 men.

THE SECOND REGIMENT.

The Second Regiment came next, commanded by Col. J. B. Badger, it was composed of
1st. The Vigilant Guards, Capt. W. R. Doty, 75 men.
2d. Company Twelve, Capt. C. G. Bailey, 60 men.
3d. King Guards, Capt. Godfrey, 85 men.
4th. Pioneer Guards, Capt. C. H. Gray, 90 men.
5th. Coleman Guards, Capt. C. R. Bond, 50 men.
6th. Company Ten, commanded by Lieut. J. Wightman, 60 men.
7th. Doane Guards, Capt. George Gates, 68 men.
8th. Company Nine, Capt. J. Wood, 70 men.

THE THIRD REGIMENT.

The Third Regiment, next in the line, was commanded by Col. H. S. Fitch, and was composed of
1st. Company Thirteen, commanded by Lieut. E. J. Smith, 45 men.
2d. Company Fourteen, Capt. W. E. Keyes, 70 men.
3d. Company Fifteen, Washington Guards, Capt. Caleb Clapp, 110 men.
4th. Company Sixteen, Capt. B. S. Bryan, 75 men.
5th. Company Eighteen, Capt. P. W. Shepheard, 75 men.
6th. Company Nineteen, Capt. R. H. Bennett, 50 men.
7th. Company Twenty, American Guards, Capt. S. Gutte, 120 men.
8th. Company Seventeenth, Brigade Rifles, Capt. C. E. S. McDonald, 60 men.

FOURTH REGIMENT.

The Fourth Regiment followed, commanded by Col. F. J. Lippit, and preceded by a band. It was composed of
1st. Company Twenty-Five, Capt. J. Sauffrignon, 130 men.
2d. Company Twenty-Eight, Capt. L. Amand, 125 men.
3d. Arrington Guards, Capt. W. H. Patten, 75 men.
4th. Company Twenty-Seven, Capt. C. H. Gough, 110 men.
5th. Brutus Guards, Capt. J. L. Folger, 50 men.
6th. Company Twenty-One, Capt. S. Meyerback, 60 men.
7th. Company Twenty-Three, Capt. J. F. Little, 85 men.
8th. Company Thirty, Capt. W. O. Smith, 60 men.
9th. A Pistol Company, Capt. E. B. Gibbs, 70 men.
10th. Vigilance Police, Capt. R. B. Wallace, 124 men.
13th. A delegation of 100 horsemen, members of the Committee, without equipments.
14th. Citizens in carriages.
15th. Citizens on foot.

After the procession, a gold medal was presented to Capt. McDonald, of the 17th Rifles, as a token of their estimation of the admirable manner in which the *corps* under his command performed their manœuvres, by Messrs. Hazeltine, James Dow, John Gordon, Samuel Lambert, A. McCorquodale, and several other gentlemen.

A MOSQUE has been erected over the grave of the great patriarch, Noah. A writer remarking upon the fact, says:—I do not remember the exact measurement of the tomb; but if this is his sepulcure, Noah must have been a very tall man, for it seemed to me at a random guess to be about a hundred feet in length. The old man who showed it to us, told me that this was his length as far as the knees, the rest being bent downwards. Over the grave is placed a green cloth—the favorite color of the Mohammedans—and it is visited not only by Moslems, but by Christians.

TWO YOUNG GIRLS have been taken up in Hartford for stealing whalebone, to make fashionable hooped skirts with. Awful depravity?

FRANK LESLIE'S ILLUSTRATED

NEWSPAPER

Entered according to Act of Congress, in the year 1859, by FRANK LESLIE, in the Clerk's Office of the District Court for the Southern District of New York. (Copyrighted March 7, 1859.)

No. 171.—VOL. VII.] NEW YORK, SATURDAY, MARCH 12, 1859. [PRICE 6 CENTS.

NEW TALE!

ADA LEIGH; OR, THE LOVE TEST,

WE desire to call the attention of our readers to the new and deeply interesting tale commenced in our last number, which will be continued from week to week until concluded. The name of the author from whose pen it emanates—PIERCE EGAN, Esq., author of "The Flower of the Flock," "The Snake in the Grass," &c., is of itself a guarantee, that will be found a tale of absorbing interest; and our readers will soon discover for themselves that in accurate delineation of human character, the portrayal of sentiment and the development of a finely constructed plot, ADA LEIGH is a tale that has seldom been surpassed in interest. Let everybody read it. A synopsis of the chapters published in our last is given in this number.

THE WASHINGTON TRAGEDY.

Crime and Bloodshed in the Federal Capital.

SHOOTING OF PHILIP BARTON KEY BY HON. DANIEL E. SICKLES, OF NEW YORK.

(With the only correct Illustrations published; made from sketches by our Special Artist.)

ON the afternoon of Sunday, February 27th, the city of Washington was suddenly thrown into a state of intense excitement on learning

HON. DANIEL E. SICKLES SHOOTING PHILIP BARTON KEY IN PRESIDENT'S SQUARE, WASHINGTON—SCENE OF THE TRAGEDY—FROM A SKETCH MADE ON THE SPOT BY OUR SPECIAL ARTIST.

HARPER'S WEEKLY
A JOURNAL OF CIVILIZATION

VOL. III.—No. 137.] NEW YORK, SATURDAY, AUGUST 13, 1859. [PRICE FIVE CENTS.

OUR SERIALS.

WE commenced in No. 134 a new serial tale, entitled "A Good Fight," by CHARLES READE, author of "Love me Little, Love me Long;" with Illustrations by Tenniel. This exquisite Story is printed *from early proof-sheets* PURCHASED *exclusively by us from the Author.*

In reply to several inquiries, we beg to say that Mr. DICKENS's new serial, "A TALE OF TWO CITIES," was commenced in HARPER'S WEEKLY on May 7, and Mr. CURTIS's delicious Story of American Society, entitled "TRUMPS," on April 9. We can send the back numbers from those dates, or from the beginning of the year, to any person who remits the money.

THE MASSACRE AT MOUNTAIN MEADOWS, UTAH TERRITORY.

[FROM A CORRESPONDENT.]

THE story of so horrible a human butchery as that which occurred at the Mountain Meadows, Utah Territory, in the autumn of 1857, has by this time, no doubt, reached the States; but as no account which I have yet seen can in the slightest degree approximate to a description of the hideous truth, being myself now on the ground, and having an opportunity of communicating with some who were no doubt present on the occasion, I deem it proper to send you a plain and unvarnished statement of the affair as it actually occurred.

A train of Arkansas emigrants, with some few Missourians, said to number forty men, with their families, were on their way to California, through the Territory of Utah, and had reached a series of grassy valleys, by the Mormons called the Mountain Meadows, where they remained several days recruiting their animals. On the night of September 9, not suspecting any danger, as usual they quietly retired to rest, little dreaming of the dreadful fate awaiting and soon to overtake them. On the morning of the 10th, as, with their wives and families, they stood around their camp-fires passing the congratulations of the morning, they were suddenly fired upon from an ambush, and at the first discharge fifteen of the best men are said to have fallen dead or mortally wounded. To seek the shelter of their *corral* was but the work of a moment, but there they found but limited protection.

To enable you to appreciate fully the danger of their position I must give a brief description of the ground. The encampment, which consisted of a number of tents and a *corral* of forty wagons and ambulances, lay on the west bank of, and eight or ten yards distant from, a large spring in a deep ravine running southward; another ravine, also, branching from this, and facing the camp on the southwest; overlooking them on the northwest, and within rifle-shot, rises a large mound commanding the *corral*, upon which parapets of stone, with loopholes, have been built. Yet another ravine, larger and deeper, faces them on the east, which could be entered without exposure from the south and far end. Having crept into these shelters during the darkness of the night, the cowardly assailants fired upon their unsuspecting victims, thus making a beginning to the most brutal butchery ever perpetrated on this continent.

Surrounded by superior numbers, and by an unseen foe, we are told the little party stood a siege within the *corral* of five or seven days, sinking their wagon-wheels in the ground, and during the darkness of night digging trenches, within which to shelter their wives and children. A large spring of cool water bubbled up from the sand a few yards from them, but deep down in the ravine, and so well protected that certain death marked the trail of all who had dared approach it. The wounded were dying of thirst; the burning brow and parched lip marked the delirium of fever; they tossed from side to side with anguish; the sweet sound of the water, as it murmured along its pebbly bed, served but to heighten their keenest suffering. But what all this to the pang of leaving to a cruel fate their helpless children? Some of the little ones, who though too young to remember in after years, tell us that they stood by their parents, and pulled the arrows from their bleeding wounds.

Long had the brave band held together; but the cries of the wounded sufferers must prevail. For the first time, they are (by four Mormons) offered their lives if they will lay down their arms, and gladly they avail themselves of the proffered mercy. Within a few hundred yards of the *corral* faith is broken. Disarmed and helpless, they are fallen upon and massacred in cold blood. The savages, who had been driven to the hills, are again called down to what was denominated the "job," which more than savage brutality had begun.

Women and children are now all that remain. Upon these, some of whom had been violated by the Mormon leaders, the savage expends his hoarded vengeance. By a Mormon who has now escaped the threats of the Church we are told that the helpless children clung around the knees of the savages, offering themselves as slaves; but with fiendish laughter at their cruel tortures, knives were thrust into their bodies, the scalp torn from their heads, and their throats cut from ear to ear.

I am writing no tale of fiction; I wish not to gratify the fancy, but to tell a tale of truth to the reason and to the heart. I speak truths which hereafter legal evidence will fully corroborate. I met this train on the Platte River on my way to Fort Laramie in the spring of 1857, the best and richest one I had ever seen upon the plains. Fortune then beamed upon them with her sweetest smile. With a fine outfit and every comfort around them, they spoke to me exultingly of their prospects in the land of their golden dreams. To-day, as then, I ride by them, but no word of friendly greeting falls upon my ear, no face meets me with a smile of recognition; the empty sockets from their ghastly skulls tell me a tale of horror and of blood. On every side around me for the space of a mile lie the remains of carcasses dismembered by wild beasts; bones, left for nearly two years unburied, bleached in the elements of the mountain wilds, gnawed by the hungry wolf, broken and hardly to be recognized. Garments of babes and little ones, faded and torn, fluttering from each ragged bush, from which the warble of the songster of the desert sounds as mockery. Human hair, once falling in glossy ringlets around childhood's brow or virtue's form, now strewing the plain in masses, matted, and mingling with the musty mould. To-day, in one grave, I have buried the bones and skulls of twelve women and children, pierced with the fatal ball or shattered with the axe. In another the shattered relics of eighteen men, and yet many more await their gloomy resting-place.

Afar from the homes of their childhood, buried in the heart of almost trackless deserts, shut up within never-ending mountain barriers, cut off from all communication with their fellow-men, surrounded by overpowering numbers, harmless citizens of our land of justice and freedom, with their wives and families, as dear to them as our own to us, were coolly, deliberately, and designedly butchered by those professing to be their own countrymen.

I pause to ask one calm, quiet question. Are these facts known in the land where I was born and bred?

I have conversed with the Indians engaged in this massacre. They say that they but obeyed the command of Brigham Young, sent by letter, as soldiers obey the command of their chief; that the Mormons were not only the instigators but the most active participants in the crime; that Mormons led the attack, took possession of the spoil; that much of that spoil still remains with them;

THE SCENE OF THE MOUNTAIN MEADOWS MASSACRE, UTAH TERRITORY.—[FROM A RECENT SKETCH.]

NEW-YORK ILLUSTRATED NEWS.

No. 1.—Vol. I. NEW-YORK, SATURDAY, NOVEMBER 19, 1859. Price Six Cents.

BALTIMORE RIOT—DEATH OF KYLE.

On the 2d inst., the citizens of Baltimore were called upon to poll their votes; on which occasion, from many scenes of violence, with a feeling of regret that such should occur, we present our readers with the following:

Mr. George Kyle and Mr. Barklee Kyle, brothers, having attended a meeting of their party the previous evening, were attacked by a crowd, which assault was caused by a certain Joseph Edwards demanding a number of "reform" tickets, and being refused. One of the assaulters using insulting language, knocked off the hat of Mr. Kyle, who gave the assailant a blow upon the head with a steel cane, which was wrested from him. He was struck several times and knocked down, not, however, until he drew a dagger and stabbed one of his assailants in the breast. He then drew his revolver, and, while upon the ground, discharged three loads, his assailants continuing the assault. During the affair, one of them presented a pistol close to his temple and fired, but he quickly changed his position, and received the ball in the right shoulder. The pistol was so near that its discharge burned him very severely in the face. It was while his brother was upon the ground struggling with a number of assailants, that Barklee Kyle came to his rescue and discharged his revolver. The crowd soon turning upon him, he retreated to the steps of a house on the corner of Quay alley and Light street, and was in the act of entering the same, when he received the fatal wound. He fell instantly, and was shortly afterward picked up by his friends and conveyed to his residence, where he expired at nine o'clock on the same evening, surrounded by themembers and relatives of his family.

THE ELECTION RIOTS AT BALTIMORE—DEATH OF MR. KYLE.

No. 2[illegible].—VOL. IX.] NEW YORK, SATURDAY, DECEMBER 17 1859. [PRICE 6 CENTS.

THE HARPER'S FERRY INSURRECTION.

FROM OUR OWN SPECIAL CORRESPONDENT.

From Baltimore to Charlestown.

SOME men are unfortunate—remarkably so. At Baltimore, on Thursday morning previous to John Brown's execution, there was a crowd of editorial people, a mass of curiosity-seeking people, and a few privileged independents who were secure of a passage to Harper's Ferry. At a quarter past eight A. M. the cars were to leave; crowd wanted tickets; agent politely informed them he had imperative orders not to sell any; the crowd became indignant; at last the President and Superintendent of the Baltimore and Ohio Railroad arrived, we exhibited our letters, friendly and officially, a benignant smile was the answer, and we cried "Saved!" The rest of the crowd were refused, and disappointment dwelt like a cloud upon their countenances. One gentleman was particularly indignant, he was from the interior of the State of New York, he had a certificate from forty-three unknown individuals as to the character of his paper, he stated he was no Abolitionist, he was simply a Republican; the simplicity of that remark drew forth the suggestion that the sooner he was off to his native village the better it would be for his constitutional health and the sacredness of his apparel. Gentleman from interior consequently left in a towering rage. There was a shrill whistle of the engine known to all lovers of music as frightfully like Beaucart's voice, a few puffs of steam, and we were soon rattling along over the rails; at every station we found a body of soldiers drawn up in martial array, the station was crowded with people who seemed to look with solemn interest upon the warlike host which filled the cars, but nearer we came to Harper's Ferry, until the dark tunnel of the bridge clearly denoted we had arrived at the scene of John Brown's insurrection. The place had changed much since our last visit; there were now, besides Captain Moore's troop of Montgomery Guard, two hundred and fifty regular troops of artillery from Point Comfort, under command of Captain Lee. There seemed to be no business in the town, the excitement of the time had absorbed the attention of everybody, and the spirit of inquiry reigned supreme; the exhibition of a Brown pike, the roll of a drum, or the march of the soldiers immediately intensified the excitement. But we had no time to observe or to mingle with them, a special train was waiting for us for Charlestown. A telegraph dispatch from General Taliaferro was presented to us by Captain Barton, United States Army.

"December 1st, 1859, Headquarters at Charlestown.

"This certifies that Dr. A. R——, of Frank Leslie's, is granted permission to visit Charlestown, Virginia, and to remain there unmolested, and all soldiers and citizens are requested to show him every attention. TALIAFERRO, Commander."

Armed with this authority we found every one eager to show every attention. Upon our arrival at Charlestown we visited the General and Staff, and were received with urbanity and courtesy; every request consistent with their duty was granted us, and our comfort was at all times attended to.

Mrs. Brown's Arrival.

The shades of night were gathering over us, there was a solemnity in every soldier's face, Virginia was determined to vindicate the majesty of her law, and every soldier stood ready to perform his portion of the General's commands; but still the announcement that the wife of the condemned was about to arrive to take her last interview with her husband at once changed the scene, the ancient chivalry of Virginia manifested itself at once, and from Governor Wise down to the private in the ranks a feeling of sympathy was shown towards the woman who came to visit her husband. In silence and painful anxiety the soldiers were drawn up into a hollow square commanding the jail, and thus for ten minutes the solid columns waited.

Soon there was heard the sound of approaching cavalry, and then distinctly the Rangers appeared in sight, escorting a carriage which contained Captain Moore and Mrs. Brown. It entered the square—

(Continued on page 39.)

JOHN BROWN'S LAST INTERVIEW WITH HIS WIFE IN THE JAIL AT CHARLESTOWN, VA.

JOHN BROWN ASCENDING THE SCAFFOLD PREPARATORY TO BEING HANGED.—FROM A SKETCH BY OUR SPECIAL ARTIST.

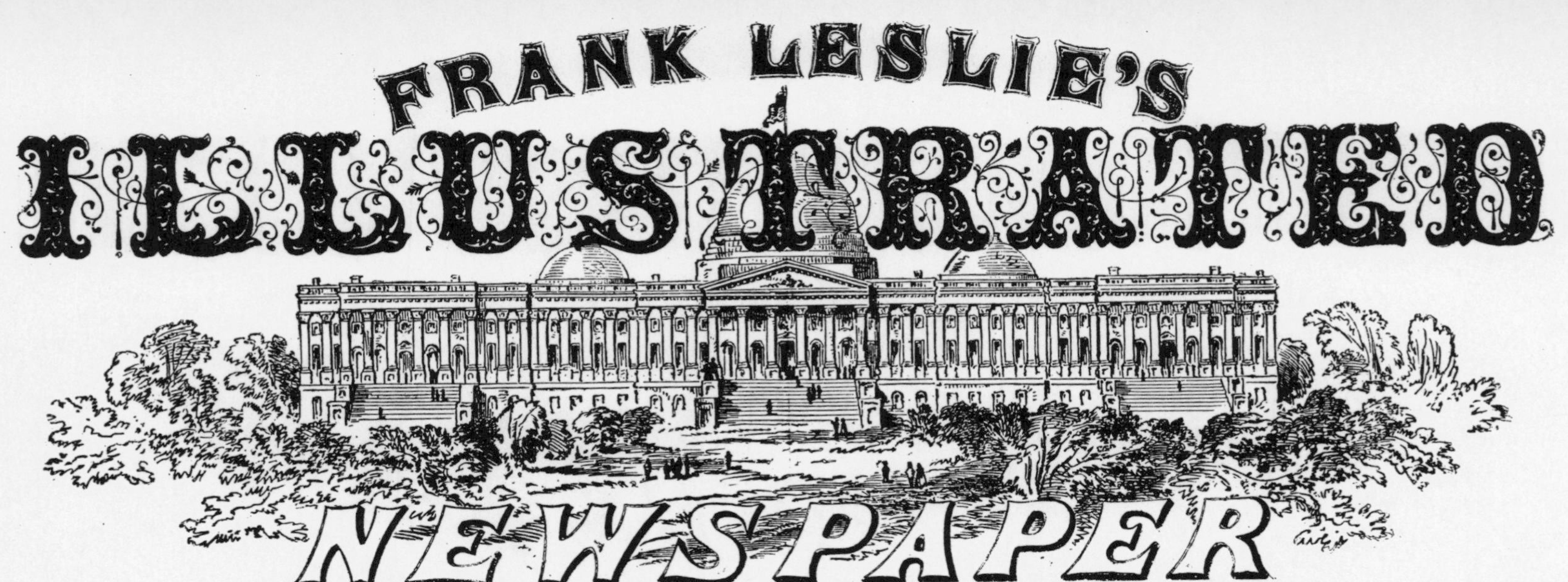

Entered according to Act of Congress in the year 1863, by FRANK LESLIE, in the Clerk's Office of the District Court for the Southern District of New York.

No 415—VOL. XVI.] NEW YORK, SEPTEMBER 12, 1863. [PRICE 8 CENTS.

Our Sketches.

HEADQUARTERS DEPT. OF THE SOUTH,
Morris Island, S. C., Aug. 24, 1863.

Having found it necessary to employ Mr. W. T. CRANE to make sketches of the progressive demolition of Fort Sumter by our batteries, I most cheerfully bear testimony to the general accuracy of his delineations.

Q. A. GILLMORE,
Brig.-Gen. Commanding.

We insert the above high testimony to the fidelity of the sketches which we have given of the operations of our army and navy in the Department of the South, the more readily as it was entirely unsolicited by us.

No reader of FRANK LESLIE'S ILLUSTRATED NEWSPAPER can now indulge any doubt as to the truth of what we occasionally say of the merit of our sketches, as actual living pictures of events passing around us.

We spare no expense in keeping at every important point competent Artists, all of whom could obtain from the Generals on the field similar testimonials. Such we have never sought; but when, amid the cares of so great a campaign, Gen. Gillmore can stop to commend our exertions, it is no vanity on our part to lay it before our readers.

THE LAWRENCE MASSACRE.

THE war has had its terrors. The deep hypocrisy of the Confederate leaders, who, hanging Union men in Tennessee and Missouri as bridgeburners, guerillas, or simply and nakedly as Union men, insulted Heaven and outraged humanity by their mendacious protests against the reprisals occasionally and too seldom made by our kindly-hearted authorities, reaches a climax in the fearful massacre at Lawrence, Kansas.

In atrocity, in bloodthirsty cruelty, in barbarity, rapine and fiendishness it has no parallel in our history. A town entered treacherously by night, nearly 200 of its people butchered without mercy, the city pillaged and fired, such is, in the eyes of the sanctimonious Davis and Beauregard, a part of civilized warfare. When Bishop Lynch chanted his Te Deum to thank the Almighty that civil war had begun, was it to ask the benediction of heaven on scenes like this?

The immediate perpetrator of the frightful massacre was Quantrell, who has, for the last two years, figured in guerilla war, in Missouri, and though often defeated, never captured. His force consisted of 300 picked men from Lafayette, Saline, Clay, Johnson and other border counties of Missouri. It started on the 20th from Middle Fork, Grand river, 15 miles from the Kansas border, and crossed the line near the town of Gardner, reaching Lawrence at four o'clock on the morning of the 21st. He posted a guard around the city and began the work of mur-

THE WAR IN KANSAS—FEARFUL MASSACRE AT LAWRENCE BY QUANTRELL'S GUERILLAS.

THE EVENING TELEGRAPH

DOUBLE SHEET—THREE CENTS.] PHILADELPHIA, SATURDAY, APRIL 15, 1865. [DOUBLE SHEET—THREE CENTS.

DEATH OF THE PRESIDENT.

THE NATIONAL HORROR.

OFFICIAL GAZETTE.

ASSASSINATION OF THE PRESIDENT.

The Wish and an Accomplice the Murderers.

TRAGEDY PLANNED FOR THE FOURTH OF MARCH.

It is Delayed Until Richmond Should be Heard From.

ONE OF THE TWO ESCAPED TO BALTIMORE.

WASHINGTON, April 15, 4·10 A. M.—Major-General Dix, New York.—The President continues insensible, and is sinking.

Secretary Seward remains without change.

Frederick Seward's skull is fractured in two places, besides a severe cut upon the head. The attendant is still alive, but hopeless. Major Seward's wound is not dangerous.

It is now ascertained with reasonable certainty that two assassins were engaged in the horrible crime, J. Wilkes Booth being the one that shot the President. The other is a companion of his, whose name is not known, but whose description is so clear that he can hardly escape.

It appears from a letter found in Booth's trunk, that the murder was planned before the 4th of March, but fell through then, because the accomplice backed out until Richmond could be heard from. Booth and his accomplice were at the livery stable at 6 o'clock last evening, and left there about 10 o'clock, or shortly before that hour.

It would seem that for several days they have been seeking their chance, but for some unknown reason it was not carried into effect until last night.

One of them has evidently made his way to Baltimore. The other has not yet been traced.

EDWIN M. STANTON,
Secretary of War.

DEATH OF THE PRESIDENT.

WASHINGTON, April 15.—Major-General Dix:—Abraham Lincoln died this morning at twenty-two minutes after 7 o'clock.

E. M. STANTON, Secretary of War.

FURTHER PARTICULARS.

The Assassination Last Night While at Ford's Theatre in Washington.

PISTOL BALL PENETRATES THE BRAIN

Mr. Lincoln Dying at Midnight.

FAREWELL OF PRESIDENT'S FAMILY

SAD AND SOLEMN SCENES.

THE ASSASSIN IN HIS PRIVATE BOX.

The Murderer Leaps Upon the Stage and Escapes.

WASHINGTON, April 14.—The President of the United States was shot while attending at Ford's Theatre to-night. It is feared that the wounds are mortal.

President Lincoln and his wife, together with other friends, this evening visited Ford's Theatre for the purpose of witnessing the performance of *The American Cousin*.

It was announced in the papers that General Grant would also be present, but that gentleman instead took the late train of cars for New Jersey.

The theatre was densely crowded, and everybody seemed delighted with the scene before them.

During the third act, and while there was a temporary pause for one of the actors to enter, the sharp report of a pistol was heard, which merely attracted attention, but suggested nothing serious, until a man rushed to the front of the President's box, waving a long dagger in his right hand, and exclaiming, *Sic semper tyrannis!* and immediately leaped from the box, which was of the second tier, to the stage beneath, and ran across to the opposite side, thus making his escape, amid the bewilderment of the audience, from the rear of the theatre, and mounting a horse, fled.

The screams of Mrs. Lincoln first disclosed the fact to the audience that the President had been shot, when all present rose to their feet, rushing towards the stage, many exclaiming, "Hang him! hang him!"

The excitement was of the wildest possible description, and, of course, there was an abrupt termination of the theatrical performance.

There was a rush towards the Presidential box, when cries were heard, "Stand back! Give him air! Has any one stimulants?"

On a hasty examination it was found that the President had been shot through the head, above and back of the temporal bone, and that some of the brain was oozing out.

He was removed to a private house opposite to the theatre, and the Surgeon-General of the army and other surgeons were sent for to attend to his condition.

On an examination of the private box blood was discovered on the back of the cushioned rocking-chair on which the President had been sitting, also on the partition and on the floor. A common single-barrelled pocket pistol was found on the carpet.

A military guard was placed in front of the private residence to which the President had been conveyed. An immense crowd gathered in front of it, all deeply anxious to learn the condition of the President. It had been previously announced that the wound was mortal, but all hoped otherwise.

The shock to the community was terrible.

At midnight the Cabinet, with Messrs. Sumner, Colfax, and Farnsworth, Judge Carter, Governor Oglesby, General Meigs, Colonel Hay, and a few personal friends, with Surgeon-General Barnes, and his medical associates, were around his bedside.

The President in a Dying Condition at Midnight.

The President was in a state of *syncope*, totally insensible, and breathing slowly, the blood oozing from the wound at the back of his head. The surgeons were exhausting every possible effort of medical skill, but all hope was gone.

The parting of his family with the dying President is too sad for description.

The President and Mrs. Lincoln did not start to the theatre till fifteen minutes after 8 o'clock. Speaker Colfax was at the White House at the time, and the President stated to him that he was going, although Mrs. Lincoln had not been well, because the papers had advertised that General Grant and they were to be present, and as General Grant had gone North, he did not wish the audience to be disappointed.

He went with apparent reluctance, and urged Mr. Colfax to go with him; but that gentleman had made other engagements, and with Mr. Ashmun, of Massachusetts, bid him good-bye.

An Attempt to Kill Secretary Seward.

HIS BEDCHAMBER ENTERED BY THE VILLAIN.

Frederick W. and Major Seward Knocked Senseless.

SECRETARY SEWARD STABBED THREE TIMES IN THE NECK.

Terrible Excitement in Washington.

When the excitement at the theatre was at its wildest height, reports were circulated that Secretary Seward had also been assassinated.

On reaching this gentleman's residence, a crowd and a military guard were found at the door, and on entering, it was ascertained that the reports were based upon truth. Everybody there was so excited that scarcely an intelligible account could be gathered, but the facts are substantially as follows:—

About 10 o'clock a man rang the bell, and the call having been answered by a colored servant, he said he had come from Dr. Verdi, Secretary Seward's family physician, with a prescription, at the same time holding in his hand a small piece of folded paper, and saying, in answer to a refusal, that he must see the Secretary, as he was intrusted with a particular direction concerning the medicine.

He still insisted on going up, although repeatedly informed that no one could enter the chamber. The man pushed the servant aside and walked quickly to the Secretary's room, and was there met by Mr. Frederick W. Seward, of whom he demanded to see the Secretary, making the same representation which he did to the servant.

What further passed in the way of colloquy is not known, but the man struck him on the head with a billy, severely injuring the skull, and felling him almost senseless. The assassin then rushed into the chamber and attacked Major Seward, Paymaster in the United States Army, and Mr. Hansell, a messenger of the State Department, and two male nurses, disabling them all. He then rushed upon the Secretary, who was lying in bed in the same room, and inflicted three stabs in the neck, but severing, it is thought and hoped, no arteries.

The assassin then rushed down stairs, mounted his horse at the door, and rode off before an alarm could be sounded, and in the same manner of the assassin of the President. It is believed the injuries of the Secretary are not fatal, nor those of the others, although both the Secretary and the Assistant Secretary are very seriously injured.

Secretaries Stanton and Welles, and other prominent officers of the Government, called at Secretary Seward's house to inquire into his condition, and there heard of the assassination of the President. They proceeded to the house where he was lying, exhibiting, of course, intense anxiety and solicitude.

An immense crowd was gathered in front of the President's House, and a strong guard also stationed there, many persons evidently supposing that he would be brought to his home.

The entire city to-night presents a scene of wild excitement, accompanied by violent expressions of indignation, and the profoundest sorrow. Many shed tears.

The military authorities have despatched mounted patrols in every direction, in order, if possible, to arrest the assassin, while the Metropolitan police are alike vigilant for the same purpose.

The attack, both at the theatre and at Secretary Seward's house, took place at about the same hour (10 o'clock), thus showing a preconcerted plan to assassinate these gentlemen. Some evidences of the guilt of the party who attacked the President are in possession of the police.

Vice-President Johnson is in the city, and his hotel quarters are guarded by troops.

CONDITION OF SECRETARY SEWARD.

Assistant Secretary Seward in a Critical Condition.

WASHINGTON, April 15, 10·30 A. M.—Secretary Seward is in a more comfortable condition at this hour.

Assistant Secretary Seward is in a critical condition.

THE ASSASSINATION.

Further Particulars of the Sad Event.

THE SCHEME AND ITS EXTENT.

The Design to Kill Secretary Stanton Frustrated.

SPUR AND HAT OF THE MURDERER FOUND.

The Excitement in Washington.

[illegible] conversation. The following additional particulars have been obtained:—

The assassin of the President left behind him his hat and a spur. The hat was picked up in the President's box, and has been identified by parties to whom it has been shown, and accurately described as the one belonging to the suspected man by other parties not allowed to see it before describing it.

The spur was dropped on the stage, and that also has been identified as the one procured at a stable where the same man hired a horse in the evening.

Two gentlemen who went to apprise the Secretary of War of the attack on Mr. Lincoln, met at the residence of the former a man muffled in a cloak, who, when accosted by them, hastened away without a word.

It had been the Secretary's intention to accompany Mr. Lincoln, and occupy the same box, but a press of business prevented. It therefore seems evident that the aim of the plotters was to paralyze the country by at once striking down the head and the arm of the country.

As soon as the dreadful event was announced in the streets, Superintendent Richards and his assistants were at work to discover the assassins. In a few moments the telegraph had aroused the whole police force of the city. Mayor Wallach and several members of the city government were soon on the spot. Every measure of precaution was taken to preserve order in the city, and every street was patrolled.

At the request of Mr Richards, General Augur sent horses to mount the police. Every road out of Washington was picketed, and every possible avenue of escape thoroughly guarded. The steamboats about to depart down the Potomac were stopped.

The *Daily Chronicle* says:—As it is suspected that the conspiracy originated in Maryland, the telegraph flashed the mournful news to Baltimore, and all the cavalry was immediately put upon active duty.

Every road was picketed, and every precaution taken to prevent the escape of the assassins. A preliminary examination was made by Mr. Richards and his assistants.

Several persons were called to testify, and the evidence, as elicited before an informal tribunal, and not under oath, was conclusive to this point, that the murderer of the President was John Wilkes Booth.

His hat was found in the private box and identified by several persons who had seen him within the last two days, and the spur which he dropped by accident after he jumped to the stage was identified as one of those which he had obtained from the stable where hired his horse.

This man Booth has played more than once at Ford's Theatre, and is of course acquainted with its exits and entrances, and the facility with which he escaped behind the scenes is easily understood. The person who wounded Secretary Seward left behind him a slouched hat and an old rusty navy revolver.

The chambers were broken loose, as if done by striking. The loads were drawn from the chambers, one being but a rough piece of lead, and the other balls smaller than the chambers, wrapped in paper, as if to keep them from falling out.

THE DYING SCENES.

WASHINGTON, April 15, 11 A. M.—The *Star* extra says:—At twenty minutes past 7 o'clock the President breathed his last, closing his eyes as if falling to sleep, and his countenance assuming an expression of perfect serenity.

There was no indications of pain, and it was not known that he was dead until the gradually decreasing respiration ceased altogether.

The Rev. Dr. Gurley, of the New York Avenue Presbyterian Church, immediately on its being ascertained that life was extinct, knelt at the bedside and offered an impressive prayer, which was responded to by all present.

Dr. Gurley then proceeded to the front parlor where Mrs. Lincoln, Captain Robert Lincoln, Mr. John Hay, the private Secretary, and others were waiting, where he again offered prayer for the consolation of the family. [illegible] taken by Dr. Abbott,

The following minutes [illegible] the President throughout show the condition of [illegible]: [illegible] pulse 44; 11·05 P. M., pulse 45, and growing weaker; 11·10 P. M., pulse 45; 11·15 P. M., pulse 42; 11·20 P. M., pulse 45; respiration 27 to 29; 11·25 P. M., pulse 42; 11·32 P. M., pulse 48 and full; 11·40 P. M., pulse 45; 11·45 P. M., pulse 45, respiration 22; 12·08 P. M., respiration 22; 12·15 P. M., respiration, 21 echmose of both eyes; 12·30 P. M., pulse 54; 12·32 P. M., pulse 60; 12·35 P. M., Pulse 66; 12·40 P. M., pulse 69, right eye much swollen; and echemose; 12·45 P. M., pulse 70, respiration 27; 12·55 P. M., pulse 80, struggling motion of arms; 1 A. M., pulse 86, respiration 30; 1·30 A. M., pulse 95, appearing easier; 1·45 A. M., pulse 86, very quiet, respiration irregular.

Mrs. Lincoln present. 2·10 A. M., Mrs. Lincoln retired with Robert Lincoln to an adjoining room; 2·30 A. M., the President is very quiet, pulse 54, respiration 28.

2·30 A. M., the President very quiet; pulse 54, respiration 28; 2·52 A. M., pulse 48, respiration 30; 3 A. M., visited again by Mrs. Lincoln; 3·25 A. M., respiration 24, and regular; 3·35, P. M., prayer by the Rev. Dr. Gurley; 4 A. M., respiration 26 and regular; 4·15 A. M., pulse 60, respiration 25; 5·50 A. M., respiration 28 and regular sleeping; 6 A. M., pulse failing, respiration 28; 6·30 A. M., still failing and labored breathing; 7 A. M., symptoms of immediate dissolution; 7·22 A. M, death.

Surrounding the death-bed of the President were Secretaries Stanton, Welles, Usher, Attorney-General Speed, Postmaster-General Dennison, M. T. Field, Assistant Secretary of the Treasury; Judge Otto, Assistant Secretary of Interior; General Halleck, General Meigs, Senator Sumner, F. R. Andrews, of New York; Gen. Todd, of Dacotah; John Hay, Private Secretary; Governor Oglesby, of Illinois, General Farnsworth, Mr. and Miss Kenny, Miss Harris, Captain Robert Lincoln, son of the President, and Dr. E. W. Abbott, R. K. Stone, C. D. Gatch, Neal Hall, and Leiberman. Secretary McCulloch remained with the President until about 5 A. M., and Chief Justice Chase, after several hours attendance [illegible] diately after the President's [illegible] Stanton, and held in the room in which the corpse lay. Secretaries Stanton, Welles, and Usher, Postmaster-General Dennison, and Attorney-General Speed, were present.

AFTER THE DECEASE.

The President's body was removed from the private residence, opposite Ford's Theatre, to the Executive mansion, this morning at half-past 9 o'clock, in a hearse, and wrapped in the American flag.

It was escorted by a small guard of cavalry, General Augur and other military officers following on foot.

A dense crowd accompanied the remains to the White House, where a military guard excluded the crowd, allowing none but persons of the household and personal friends of the deceased to enter the premises. Senator Yates and Representative Farnsworth being among the number admitted.

The body is being embalmed, with a view to its removal to Illinois.

Owing to the melancholy event, the Superintendent of Police has caused all places where liquor is sold to be closed during this day and night.

The flags over the departments and throughout the city are at half-mast. Scarcely any business is being transacted anywhere, either on private or public account.

Our citizens, without any preconcerted action whatever, are draping their premises with festoons of mourning.

The bells are tolling. All is sadness. Strong men weep in the streets. The grief is wide-spread, and deep—a strange contrast to the joy so lately manifested over our recent military victories.

This is indeed a day of gloom. Reports prevail that Mr. Frederick W. Seward is dead, but this is not true. Information was, however, obtained by direct inquiry at half-past 10 o'clock that his condition is considered critical. His head is horribly injured.

Secretary Seward suffers intense pain. The gashes made upon his cheek and throat are frightful, but still he is not believed to be in immediate danger, nor in a worse state than his son Frederick.

Major A. H. Seward received two wounds, one in the arm, but no fears are entertained as to his recovery.

Mr. Hansell, an employe of the State Department, who was kindly assisting in nursing Mr. Seward, received a stab in the back. His shoulder-blade prevented the knife or dagger from penetrating far into his body. The prospects are that he will recover.

A report is circulated, and repeated by almost everybody, that Booth was captured fifteen miles this side of Baltimore. If it be true, as asserted that the War Department has received such information, it will doubtless be officially promulgated.

The Government Departments are closed by order and will be draped with the usual emblems of mourning. The roads leading to and from the city are guarded by military, and the utmost circumspection is observed as to all attempting to enter or leave the city.

JOHN WILKES BOOTH.

SKETCH OF THE MURDERER.

John Wilkes Booth was born in Harford county, and not in Baltimore city. He is much addicted to drink, and having lost heavily recently in oil speculations, was supposed to be laboring under temporary insanity. The madness of the act would seem to justify this. He was for some time business agent for his brother Edwin in the West.

He made his first appearance on the stage at the Arch Street Theatre, in this city, some years ago, under the name of John Wilkes, and was considerably liked.

Some time after he made his first appearance as a star at Columbus, Ga., and while there was accidently shot by the manager.

He has been in Washington for some months past, ostensibly for the purpose of organizing an oil company, but really for the purpose of consummating his scheme of wholesale assassination, under the direction of Mosby. There is no doubt that Booth contemplated the act long ago, and only delayed its execution because of some private instructions from Moseby.

Only a month ago he obtained a pass to go to Virginia, ostensibly to buy some land, but really to consult with Moseby and other leaders relative to the murder of Mr. Lincoln and his Cabinet.

He was well acquainted with all the exits and internal arrangements of Ford's Theatre, and kept a horse at livery in a stable immediately in the rear of the theatre.

Booth is a brother of Mrs. John S. Clarke, wife of the celebrated comedian.

Mr. Booth worked hard to have Mr. Ford engage a Mr. C., a Baltimorean engaged at his theatre some time since, and the latter is probably one of his accomplices.

Booth is a very fine-looking man, with black hair and eyes, stately form, and easy carriage.

EFFECT OF THE NEWS

[illegible] ble events that occurred [illegible] night, and the grief of all good men is apparent everywhere at the demise of the President.

No flags were hoisted in this city this morning until the state of the President was known, when they were all placed at half-mast. The people appear perfectly horrified, and the utmost rage is undoubtedly felt towards all known secessionists and Rebel sympathizers.

Easton.

EASTON, April 15.—The announcement of the assassination of President Lincoln has caused the most profound regret. All business is suspended. A man who expressed traitorous sentiments was almost killed by the citizens, and with difficulty was saved from hanging.

Washington.

TEN THOUSAND DOLLARS REWARD FOR THE MURDERERS.

WASHINGTON, April 15.—President Lincoln died this morning at half-past seven o'clock.

Major-General Augur, commanding the Department of Washington, has offered a reward of ten thousand dollars to the party or parties arresting the murderer of the President, and the assassin of the Secretary of State and his son.

This morning at 6 o'clock there was no change in the condition of Secretary Seward. The *Chronicle* says a letter found in J. Wilkes Booth's trunk identifies him as the murderer.

Harrisburg.

HARRISBURG, April 15.—The news of the assassination of the President and the attempted assassination of the Secretary of State was received here with feelings of the most profound regret by all classes of the community.

A mass meeting of the citizens was held at the Court House, and the celebration of the victories, which was to have come off to-day, is ordered to be postponed. All the flags and other decorations intended for the festive display are being draped in the emblems of mourning. The church and other bells of the city are to be tolled at noon, and the citizens have been invited to meet at the Methodist Church at 4 o'clock, to unite with the ministry in religious services proper for the occasion.

Baltimore.

BALTIMORE, April 15.—The feeling here at the horrible crime which has deprived the country of its beloved President is too deep for utterance. Sorrow profound, and rage intense, pervades all loyal hearts. All kindly feelings towards Rebels and Rebel sympathizers has, as it were, been obliterated, and one intense feeling of detestation and abhorrence for all connected with the Rebellion takes its place.

All the flags are at half-mast, and, draped in mourning, denote the public grief, while the bells are tolling mournfully.

NEW YORK, April 15, Noon.—All the places of business are rapidly closing, and the streets are assuming a sombre hue. The various hotels, the New England Rooms, Post Office, Custom House, and other public places are being draped.

The Corn Exchange met, passed suitable resolutions, ordering the building draped, and adjourned.

THIRD EDITION

INAUGURATION OF PRESIDENT JOHNSON.

His Inaugural Address.

WASHINGTON, April 15, Noon.—Andrew Johnson was sworn into office as President by Chief Justice Chase to-day at 11 o'clock. Secretary McCulloch, Atty. [illegible]

President Johnson remarked:—

"The duties are mine—I will perform them, trusting in God."

Installation of Vice-President Johnson.

WASHINGTON, April 15.—At an early hour this morning the Hon. Edwin M. Stanton, Secretary of War, sent an official communication to the Hon. Andrew Johnson, Vice-President, that in consequence of the sudden and unexpected death of the Chief Magistrate, his inauguration should take place as soon as possible, and requesting him to state the place and hour at which the ceremony should be performed.

Mr. Johnson immediately replied that it would be agreeable to him to have the proceedings take place at his rooms in the Kirkwood House, as soon as the arrangements could be perfected.

Chief Justice Chase was informed of the fact, and repaired to the appointed place in company with Secretary McCulloch of Treasury Department, Attorney-General Speed, F. P. Blair, Sr., Hon. M. Blair, Senators Foot of Vermont, Ramsey of Minnesota, Yates of Illinois, Stewart of Nevada, Hall of New Hampshire, and General Farnsworth of Illinois.

At 11 o'clock the oath of office was administered by the Chief Justice of the United States, in his usual solemn and impressive manner.

Mr. Johnson received the kind expressions of the gentlemen by whom he was surrounded in a manner which showed his earnest sense of the great responsibility so suddenly devolved upon him, and made a brief speech, in which he said:—

"The duties of the office are mine; I will perform them. The consequences are with God. Gentlemen, I shall lean upon you. I feel that I shall need your support. I am deeply impressed with the solemnity of the occasion, and the responsibility of the duties of the office I am assuming."

Mr. Johnson appeared to be in remarkably good health, and has a high and realizing sense of the hopes that are centred upon him. His manner was solemn and dignified, and his whole [illegible]

WASHINGTON, April 15.—It is ascertained on the best authority, that Booth, the murderer of the President, has been arrested.

GRANT RETURNS TO WASHINGTON.

LIEUTENANT-GENERAL U. S. GRANT, upon hearing the sad news of the assassination of President LINCOLN, determined to return to Washington as soon as possible. He remained up all last night, suffering great mental agony, and departed for Washington in a special train at 8·15 this morning.

For The Evening Telegraph.

DIRGE.

BY RICHARD COE.

Toll! toll! toll!
On every hand,
Ye bells throughout the land;
Washington's great compeer now lies,
With death-sealed eyes,
And pallid face upturned towards the skies!
Toll! toll! toll!
On every hand,
Ye bells throughout the land!
Toll! toll! toll!
Weep! weep! weep!
On every hand
Ye patriots in the land
Brave Lincoln dead! Great God! and can it be?
"Henceforth there's nothing in mortality
That's serious!" Help us to look to Thee!
Weep! weep! weep!
On every hand,
Ye patriots in the land,
Weep! weep! weep!
Pray! pray! pray!
On every hand,
Ye Christians in the land.
No more his honest face will greet the sun—
His day is finished, and his labor done;
A crown of glory rests his brow upon!
Pray! pray! pray!
On every hand,
Ye Christians in the land;
Pray! pray! pray!

PHILADELPHIA TRADE REPORT.

SATURDAY, April 15.—The "Corn Exchange Association" met this morning, but transacted no business, and adjourned after the adoption of the preamble and resolutions to be found in another column. Business throughout the city was suspended.

—Two Smiths and one Smyth "govern" the New England States. Rhode Island and Vermont have the Smiths, and New Hampshire the Smyth.

THE SENATE AS A COURT OF IMPEACHMENT FOR THE TRIAL OF ANDREW JOHNSON.—Sketched by Theodore R. Davis.—[See First Page.]

VOL. XI. NO. 3319. NEW YORK: SUNDAY, SEPTEMBER 18, 1870. PRICE FIVE CENTS.

MURDER MAP OF NEW YORK.

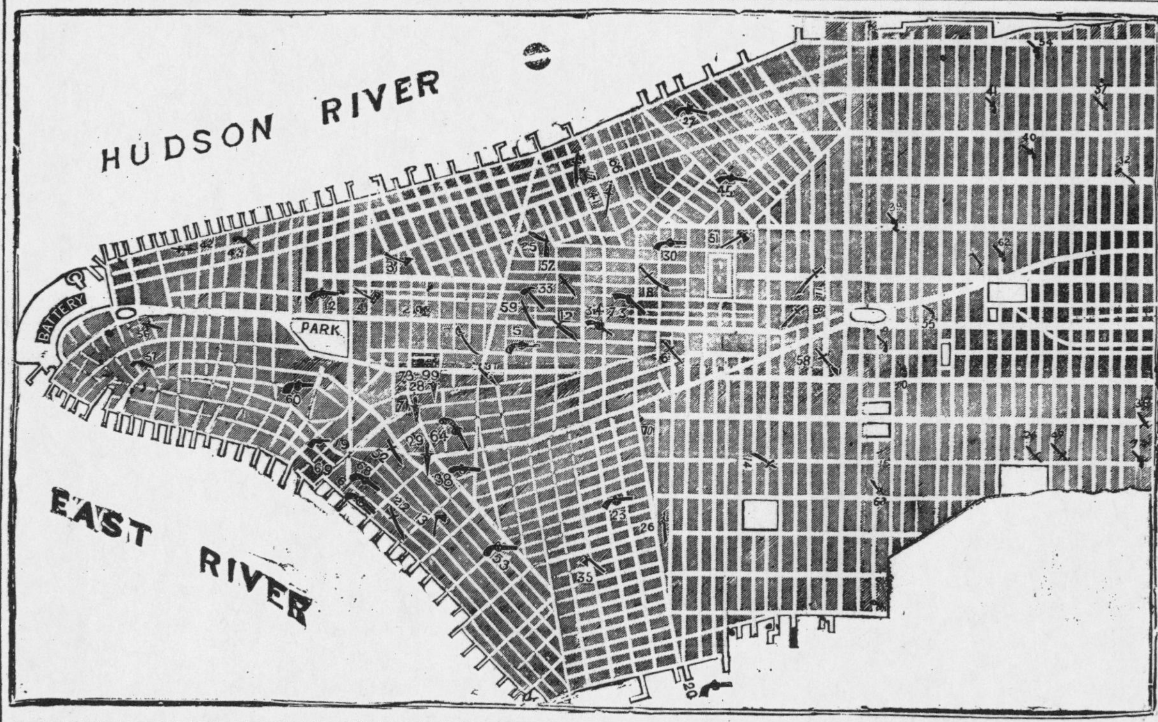

THE MURDER MAP.

The Ways and Means of Murder in the Metropolis.

A BLOOD-RED RECORD.

The Crimes of Two Generations in a Great City.

PISTOL, CLUB, AND DIRK.

Romance and Mystery, Reality and Horror.

CRIMES OF PASSION AND AVARICE, &c. &c., &c.

If every murder ever perpetrated in New York were denoted upon a map of the size presented today by a mark not larger than a grain of wheat it is not too much to say that the bloody *indicia* would blot out the topography of the city. To describe those murders, further, even in the most cursory manner would fill every column in THE WORLD, and for these reasons we merely map and describe, today, first, those mysterious butcheries which may be called the historic murders of New York, and, second, the chief homocidal crimes which have polluted the city within the past ten years. Even within these narrow limits, it will be seen that the map is marked in seventy-eight (78) places, with the indications of death, and to this monstrous list, for the work has gone on while this article was writing, are to be added two more occurring in the past week. Seventy odd murders occurring in a single decade, for the murders prior to 1860 we note are but half dozen in number, is a fearful exhibit and the record darkens when we remember that it is only the known and premeditated butcheries we note. The "found drowned," the "disappeared," the men and women slain in what appears sudden recontres would, if the truth could be but known, dot the city much more thickly than we have already marked it, but, declining to go into conjecture, we have set down only those well ascertained cases in which name, date, locality, and circumstance can be given, the figures on the map denoting the locality and instrument.

1. THE NATHAN MURDER.

First in the list of those crimes which appal, not less by the mystery attending them than by the intrinsic awfulness, comes the murder of Mr. Benjamin Nathan at his residence, No. 12 West Twenty-third street, on the 29th of July, 1870. Mr. Nathan was by birth and family a genuine "old New Yorker," born in the city himself, as was his father, and, if we mistake not, his father before him, and had lived in the city all his life. He was in religion an Israelite, and by avocation a broker. In this calling he had amassed a very handsome fortune, said to have been one of the largest in the city, and in the enjoyment of this affluence, the practice of the charities for which his name was eminent, and in the care and society of his family, bade fair, at the opening of the summer just passed, to live prosperous and respected for many years. With the approach of warm weather he had, like most of our well to do citizens, moved out into the country with his family and only occasionally visited the city upon business. On one of these trips the tragedy connected with his name and localized on the map by the figure 1 occurred. Visiting the city on the 28th of July, 1870, on some business matters which do not appear to have ever been very satisfactorily explained, Mr. Nathan repaired at the close of the day to the residence of a relative and there spent the evening in a social way. On leaving he was desired to stay all night, the argument being that he would be more comfortable than at his own house, which was then in some disorder owing to the absence of the family and the fact that workmen were engaged in repairs, but, declining these friendly solicitations with the remark that his own house was "safe," he departed. Why he should have made this remark about the safety of his mansion does not well appear, since the subject of danger was not mentioned, and it is a curious coincidence that afterwards in the testimony on the inquest it should appear that he had referred some years before to this same topic of safety. Perhaps the theme may have been brought up in the course of conversation, but for all that is known in the evidence the remarks appear isolated, and suggest by that isolation the query whether some vague premonition may not at odd times in his life have crossed the murdered man's brain. Be that as it may, however, Mr. Nathan went to his own house and there retired to rest in a second-story front room, upon which opened a small cabinet, or library, containing an iron safe. Some time after midnight one of his sons, Mr. Washington Nathan, returned home, fastened the front door with all the usual precautions, and repaired to his own room on the third floor, pausing a moment at the door of his father's apartment, which stood open, to see if the old gentleman was awake. Stretched upon his couch the father lay asleep, and turning from the door the young man went to his own room and retired. At 1 o'clock that morning the policeman upon that beat tried the door of No. 12 West Twenty-third street, and found it fast; at some time between 2 and 3 a physician residing on the corner of Twenty-third street and Fifth avenue was aroused by his wife, who had been awakened by a sound apparently from Mr. Nathan's mansion, which just adjoined. Husband and wife then listening, heard several sounds seemingly in that mansion, which resembled the somewhat violent slamming of a door. The sounds ceasing, the couple watched for a few minutes to see if any person issued from the dwelling, and then, dismissing the subject as probably after all but trivial, repaired to rest. Between 4 and 5 the policeman, pacing his beat over again, a second time tried the door of the Nathan mansion and again found it fast. At about 5:30 a newsboy saw a man ascend the "stoop," pick up a piece of paper therefrom, apparently a bank check, and walk away. At 5:45 General Frank Blair, the Democratic candidate for the Vice-Presidency in 1868, rising to close the blinds in his room on the Twenty-third street side of the Fifth Avenue Hotel in order to shut out the light which had disturbed his slumbers, saw a young man, afterwards shown to be Mr. Frederick Nathan, son of the deceased, sitting at a third-story window of Mr. Nathan's mansion, and apparently enjoying the freshness of the early morning air. Leaving the window after a moment or so, the young man was seen moving about in the room, apparently about to dress himself, and with this General Blair, closing his window blinds, saw no more. At 6 the cry of "murder" rang through the street. General Blair, the policeman, and others saw two young men in their night-clothes standing on Mr. Nathan's "stoop," blood on the socks and shirt of one of them, and both uttering that awful cry. On entering the house, outsiders found an iron bar of the shape indicated at 1 upon the map, just inside the door, clotted with blood and hair, and on ascending to the second-story front room discovered the body of Mr. Benjamin Nathan stiff and cold upon the floor, the corpse in the attitude of having fallen in a struggle, the rich carpet soaked for a yard or so in every direction about it with blood, the safe in the cabinet open, papers scattered about the floor, and the dead man's watch and diamond studs gone. When this is said, all is said of the Nathan murder that is now known. Who did the deed, why, how, when, in what manner he or they entered or how left, is a mystery deeper than broods over any murder ever known in the annals of New York. Motive, manner, and murderer are alike buried in obscurity, and all that is known is that in his own house, which he thought so safe, the rich man fell by a bloody, a horrid, a cruel death. The strange character of the instrument used in his murder, the publicity of that neighborhood in which the deed was done, and the utter powerlessness of wealth, which we are all accustomed to think so all-powerful, to prevent or detect the monstrous violence, are salient points in this Twenty-third street tragedy which have wonderfully impressed the public mind. The utmost ingenuity of the whole administration of justice, the extremest power of money, the old adage that murder will out, are all so utterly set at defiance by this deed, that it stands forth so undeniably the first in atrocity and mystery as to justify the bad pre-eminence of 1 upon the map.

2. MARY ROGERS.

By looking to the place denoted by 2 upon the map the reader will see where Mary Rogers, the Beautiful Cigar Girl of New York, whose tragic murder has been woven into fancy by Edgar A. Poe in his murder of Marie Roget, not to speak of lesser *litterateurs*, once resided. Her cigar store, and a store attended by a beautiful girl was a novelty years ago, was on the lot next above the hospital ground, going up Broadway, and now that a street has been cut through that ground the site of the store is occupied by the second large modern store from Thomas street as you face it on Broadway. Taken to Hoboken, on some promised excursion of pleasure, Mary Rogers was brutally murdered, how, or exactly in what manner, was never ascertained; but, if the reader has ever perused Poe's "Marie Roget," he might like in some account of the historical murders of New York to know just where the beautiful cigar-girl crossed the threshhold of her home the last time.

3. HELEN JEWETT.

If the reader will take the trouble to go to the spot represented on the map by the figure 3, he will find before him a fine, new, iron-front store, painted a pure white, and in strong contrast by its clean and stately appearance to the dilapidated rookery next door and the shabby, old-fashioned dwelling, swarming with negroes, which rots just opposite. This store, No. 41 Thomas street, stands on the spot where, up to a brief time since, mouldered the house in which the beautiful Helen Jewett, the very Lais of New York courtesanship, was murdered thirty-four years ago. Look on No. 42, the dwelling opposite, where the inmates sprawl about the door and doze in the sunshine, and in the relics of old-time elegance which peer out of all its dirt and dinginess you will see that the houses of this neighborhood were even fashionable a generation since. Number 41 was in certain circles, in 1836, extremely so. It was the finest establishment of its kind in America, and Helen Jewett, its chief attraction, so amazingly lovely that it is recorded visitors to the city in those days, from all parts of the country, would repair to the house simply to gaze upon the magnificence of that beauty which had extended its reputation over the United States. Robed in the costliest of fabrics and glittering with gems, she whose life was destined to have so terrible an ending in the scene of her triumphs, would sweep through the parlors like a Paphian queen; and there are yet living old New Yorkers who recall from the memories of their "hot youth" the tribute of admiration her appearance on these occasions would produce. Just 23, of a form that was voluptuousness itself, with a skin of silver whiteness, and an eye like melting fire, Helen Jewett might at this time have realized the antique idea of Venus, and in her history could well approve herself from her youth up a veritable devotee of desire. Her real name was Dorcas Dyon, born at Augusta, Maine, in June, 1813, of Welsh parents who had but recently emigrated to the United States. At *eleven* years of age she became too intimate with a lad named Sumner, and soon fell. Sumner was at once sent to sea, and, the secret of his disappearance being unknown, Helen was sent to school and elegantly educated by a wealthy old gentleman of the neighborhood who marked the sprightliness of the poor little Welsh girl. Thus educated and befriended for a respectable life, it seemed as if years of usefulness were opening before little Dorcas, when one day in walking by a grove a stalwart form in sailor's garb stepped out. It was Sumner, and that meeting sealed the girl's fate. Her parents were dead, her patron cast her forth as lost, and her lover having been summoned away by his calling, Helen, as she is henceforth to be known, was forced to face the world. For such beauty it has few frowns, and it was not long before a very wealthy "protector" in Portland became so infatuated with his purchase that he proposed marriage. At this moment a notice of the arrival of Sumner's ship fell under Helen's eye. She wrote to him, they met, the meeting was discovered by her would-be husband, and once more the girl was on the world. It complicated her misfortune that just here Sumner died. His sea life had given him consumption, and, after lingering awhile, he expired in Helen's arms. To the last she never forgot him, and a strange tenderness is recorded in her accent and demeanor whenever an allusion to her early life brought up the memory of the Maine sailor boy. Portland, on her lover's death, becoming insupportable, Helen fled to Boston, and must have arrived there in a state bordering on insanity. She was found fainting in the street by some negroes, who carried her to their hovel and robbed her of her money, jewelry, and clothes. That night a descent was made upon the den for some prior thefts of its inmates, and Helen along with the blacks was brought into the police court. Here a "protector" stood ready immediately on her discharge, and once more the girl entered on a life of shame which bade fair to end as it had in Portland—in honorable marriage. All was arranged between herself and a wealthy broker, when an anonymous note to the prospective husband revealed the past career of his intended wife. Helen then bent her course toward New York, and arrived here when about nineteen. The "town" was taken by storm. The equipment of a queen was put at this modern Nell Gwynn's service, and clad in magnificent raiment, and carrying a letter in her hand—always carrying a letter—the beautiful Helen anticipated on every fine day a generation since the modern song of "Walking down Broadway." One day in these rambles Sumner's successor came. Richard P. Robinson, a youth of but some nineteen, and, though born in the land of steady habits, with the fire of a dozen tropics in his veins, met the "Queen of the Pave," as the old-fashioned slang of the day had it; and, being as handsome for a man as Helen was for a woman, or perhaps (who knows?) resembling Sumner, caught the royal eye. Helen, whose Welsh blood was not the only point in which she resembled Nell Gwynn, instantly conceived for the dashing stripling that affection which a life of simulated passion does not always destroy in a woman of her class. Nell Gwynn is reported to have remained true to her royal lover, the second Charles, to the last, an affection remembered by him on his death-bed in almost his last petition—"Don't let poor Nelly starve;" and certainly Helen Jewett seems to have truly loved "Frank Rivers," as Robinson in her society was known. Out of the very intensity of this feeling it is commonly supposed there arose that tragedy which marks an instrument of death at figure 3 upon our map to-day. Luxuriant as were the charms proffered his acceptance, "Frank" tired of his impetuous beauty. There came a day when virtue asserted its right supremacy over him, as at some time it does over even the most dissolute; when he thought it better to have one chaste woman for his own than all the harlots of Paphos. He desired to marry a virtuous lady, and, as the first step, began that process of "breaking off" which has avenged so many illicit connections on those who have lewdly formed them. Lost in everything else, Helen could not endure to be bankrupt in her love too. Crimination and recrimination followed, and there is a dim intimation of a threat on Helen's part that if Robinson withdrew from her society she would avenge the slight by exposing his acquaintance with her to the young lady he sought to marry. The only date assigned to anything of this kind, however, was November, 1835, and it was not until the 10th of April, 1836, that Helen Jewett was murdered. On Saturday night, the 9th of April, 1836, Helen said she expected "Frank Rivers," there being two persons of that name who visited the house; between 9 and 9:30 there came a man to the door with his face muffled in one of the Spanish cloaks then much worn, and this man the keeper of the bagnio swore was Robinson; Helen accosted him as "Frank," and, still without removing his cloak, the man ascended with her to her room. At eleven the landlady was summoned to bring wine, and through the half-opened door, as she handed the salver in, discerned a man, whose face she could not see, lying on the bed. Helen came to receive the wine, and that was the last ever seen of her alive. At two, Maria Stevens, whose apartment was near Helen's, and who, as the record states, "was kept wakeful by disturbances which to her were not uncommon," heard in Helen's room a deep, sullen blow, which seemed to shudder along the floor. Prompted by that indefinable instinct which so often develops itself in cases of murder, Maria left her room, and stepping across the corridor, listened at Helen's door. Two or three broken sobs, "which," to quote from the record again, "her strange experience told her might proceed from a very ordinary cause," was all she heard, and thinking nothing further of the matter she retired to her own room. Presently the sound of Helen's door gently opening and then softly closing again claimed her attention, and, running to her own door, she saw, as she opened it, a man wrapped in a loose cloak gently making his way down stairs. In one hand, hidden under his cloak, he appeared to have some object, and in the other, which was free, carried the glass lamp ordinarily used in Helen's room. Seeing this much, Maria started to see more, but as she was about to follow the man, the person who was occupying her room that night reached forth his hand and plucked her in, with the order to cease her folly and close the door. This careless demeanor—for the visitor with her had heard the blow, and thus had as much occasion for suspicion as herself—allayed her anxiety, and she soon fell asleep. The man she had seen was, of course, the murderer of Helen Jewett, but Maria had not seen his face, and, while she always avowed that she knew the murderer, is not known to have ever declared it to have been Robinson. Her death before the trial left her testimony unavailable, and for the further circumstances of the case we must rely upon the evidence of others who were asleep at the time the deed was done. About 3 o'clock the keeper of the house was roused to let "her man" in, and after opening the front door, was surprised to find Helen Jewett's lamp burning on the parlor table, and the back door of the house open. Supposing some one in the yard, she called out, but receiving no answer, ascended with the lamp to Helen's room. The door at once opened, and at that moment a stifling volume of smoke rushed forth in the woman's face. Rushing over to Maria Stevens's room, she beat wildly on the door, and aroused the house with her screams. Maria instantly rushed forth, and, in conjunction with the landlady, attempted to enter Helen's room. Again and again the dense, black, pungent smoke drove them away, but as the draught fanned the fire into brightness they were enabled finally to reach the bed. Helen lay dead upon it, a clean, deadly cut in the centre of her forehead, from the part in the hair straight down between the eyes, her body bathed in blood, and the bedding smoking and smouldering beneath her, too thoroughly saturated in gore to blaze. Search was at once given, and in the back yard, jutting on Hudson street, was found a stool close to the fence, as if it had been raised himself up on it to surmount the barrier. Not far off was found a cloak, and close to that again a hatchet. This cloak was sworn to as belonging to Robinson, the hatchet was identified by the porter of the store in which Robinson was employed as belonging there, and one which he had missed the day before the murder. Further than this was the evidence of the women in the house that Robinson was certainly the man who was admitted at nine or half-past, and had retired to Helen's room; and with so much the case against Robinson virtually stands. For him, are the facts that when the police entered the house an unknown man who afterwards escaped was found near the door of Helen's room; that the hatchet was covered with dew, as if it had lain where it was found for hours, and that it had no blood upon it; that the cloak was sworn to by the women of the house; that ill-feeling, produced by rivalry and jealousy, existed toward Helen on the part of those women; and finally that the keeper of a grocery store in Liberty street swore most positively that Robinson was in his store smoking from nine till after ten on the night of the murder, the hours between which he was declared by the women of the bagnio to have entered that house. The result of the trial was a verdict of not guilty; and on his release Robinson, who was looked on with grave suspicion in the community, went to Texas, where he married, became the father of a large family, and some years since died. With some not inconsiderable reason to believe him guilty, the case yet remains a mystery, and if the Nathan tragedy be the most awful, the Helen Jewett murder is the most romantic in the history of New York crime. Novels have been written upon it, one in particular by George W. Matsell, formerly Chief of Police in this city; and on the death, but a few days since, of the venerable Joseph Hoxie, Robinson's old employer, the number of reminiscences evoked of the scene in which a generation since he played a part, amply testify to that strong hold which the murder at No. 41 Thomas street has maintained on the public imagination for thirty-four years. Impure as she was, the strong affections of the unfortunate Helen, her amiable disposition, her surpassing beauty, her accomplishments, her youth, and her terrible ending seem to have made an impression upon her day which has extended down to this a commiseration and allowance that pardon in her fate the faults of the poor Welsh orphan girl.

4. THE COLT MURDER.

Few who have ever entered the up-stairs saloon of Delmonico's restaurant at the corner of Broadway and Chambers street, and seated themselves at the table next the third window from Broadway, on the Chambers street side, would care to be told that they had washed down the *entrees* with claret on the very spot where, at 3:15 in the afternoon of Friday, September the 17th, 1841, murder poured out a redder fluid than any wine. Then and there Samuel Adams was murdered by John C. Colt with such circumstances attending the deed as make it most memorable in that sanguinary book, a few pages of which this article unfolds. John C. Colt, who was born in Hartford, Conn., in 1809, occupied a room on the second floor of the granite building still standing on the northwest corner of Chambers street and Broadway as a teacher of book-keeping, and to this room Samuel Adams, a printer, came on the day above named to urge payment of a bill for publishing a manual of book-keeping some time prior printed by him for Colt. What occurred will be first told from outside. Next to Colt's room, the floor, now thrown into one saloon, then being subdivided into separate apartments, was the writing academy of A. H. Wheeler, a pair of folding doors, ordinarily kept locked, being between the two rooms. At 3:15 on the 17th of September, 1841, Mr. Wheeler and one of his pupils, then busy in the academy, heard from Colt's room a sharp, clashing sound, resembling the striking of foils, which lasted but a moment, and was succeeded by a violent fall. "What's that?" was the exclamation, the old instinct which seems ever to betray murder in its sounds at once awaking. Mr. Wheeler went to Colt's door and listened. All was still. He then tried to look through the keyhole, but the key was in and the slide down. Running his pen through he pushed this to one side, and, in about the centre of the room, saw a man in his shirt sleeves bending down over something and slowly moving his arms as one does in sawing. For ten minutes this continued, the arms sawing, sawing the air, and then the former rose, placed something, what exactly could not be seen, on the table, and returned to the bending posture and the sawing motion. Returning to his own room, the professor found his pupil had listened intently at the folding doors, but heard nothing save one soft sound like a footstep gently slide over the floor. The police were sent for, but in some way failed to appear, and after a while the professor and his pupil went home, leaving in the academy a young man who was temporarily out of a room, having hired Colt's apartment, to have been delivered up that day by Colt, but withheld on the plea of his not being quite ready to move. This young man heard some one come out of the room at dark, lock the door and go away, shortly after returning, unlocking the door and then locking it again. Then came a sound of scrubbing close to the folding door, interspersed with a sound of rinsing a cloth in water. Shortly after the young man fell asleep and slept until 6 the next morning, when he was waked by the sound of nailing up a box in Colt's room. On going to breakfast he perceived a box at the head of the stairs, and on returning the box was gone. Samuel Adams was shortly after missed. Colt, among others, was asked if he had seen him, but said that he had not, expressed surprise at its disappearance, and even called one day at his place of business to ascertain if he had been heard from. Finally suspicion became so strong that an advertisement was issued for any cartman to come forward who might have carried a box from the corner of Chambers street and Broadway on the morning of the 18th of September, 1841. Early in the day a cartman waited on the authorities to say Mr. Colt had engaged him at that time, and that he had carried a box for him to the ship Kalamazoo. The cargo of the vessel was at once discharged, a vile stench before the unlading was half completed warning the officers of the certainty of their search, and almost at the bottom of the cargo the box described by the cartman was found. In it was a decomposing human body, clad only in a shirt, and tied up into small compass by a rope fastened around the neck and thence down about the legs, forcing the knees up upon the trunk and the head down on the chest. The face could not be recognized, but a ring upon the hand was sworn to as belonging to Samuel Adams, and from the testimony of Adams's shoemaker, who measured his foot, and that of his father-in-law, who testified to some private marks on the body, it was sufficiently established that the missing man was found. The forehead and right side of the head were beaten in, and a small hole was found above and behind the left ear. The box was identified as one that had long stood in Colt's room. Colt was at once arrested, and, after some delay, a most exciting trial began, the accused displaying the utmost resolution, except at one awful moment when he fairly broke down. Unknown to him the head was introduced into court, wrapped in a cloth, which one of the testifying physicians held in his lap. It having been decided it was evidence the physician rose from the table where he had been sitting near the prisoner, threw off the cloth, and taking a bloody hatchet which had been found in Colt's sleeping apartment, laid the weapon as close as a bullet in its mould in every gash and orifice the gaping skull contained. Colt hid his face in his hands. The verdict was guilty, and the 18th of November fixed as the day of execution. At 12 o'clock noon, the execution being fixed for 4 P. M., Colt was married to Caroline Henshaw, his mistress, whose testimony on the trial, as she described how he came home to her on the night of the murder, was listened to with absorbing interest, and, as the two were left together for a short time after the ceremony, it became a general impression she supplied the doomed man with a small clasp-knife that had been hidden in her luxuriant hair. However that may be, after she had gone Colt was left to himself to await the fatal hour, and when, shortly before the time, the officers went to lead him forth, he was found dead, the knife sticking in his heart. He had cut a small round hole in his clothes just over the heart, placed the point of the weapon upon it with one hand and with the other driven the steel in with such force that the handle of the knife was broken, though the blade went true. Just as the suicide was discovered, the Tombs was found to be on fire, and out of the confusion of the two occurrences grew a vulgar tradition that John C. Colt was spirited away and some dead body left for appearance sake in his cell. Of the suicide, however, there is as little doubt as the murder; and in a plea to the jury Colt confessed that he had killed Adams, claiming it done in the heat of blood, and that the concealment was an afterthought. Of Adams, the story is told that the night previous to his murder his wife dreamed that she saw him all bloody, and begged him not to go out that day; and, as a further reminiscence, it is reported in the journals of the time that a strange portent, in the shape of a bright star in the firmament at noonday, was visible on the day of the suicide.

5. THE LUTENER MURDER.

About ten o'clock on the morning of Tuesday, the 10th of January, 1854, one of those pushing, driving, "live" business men who give New York its energy was scudding along down town on the east side of Broadway, and had just stepped up from the cross-walk upon the curb on Grand street, when a sound which he took for a pistol shot rang in his ears. For an instant he stopped, the instinct of murder, so to speak, asserting itself, and looked eagerly around, but on every side the street was as it always is, and only remembering that he had an engagement at bank, that day, that business men must be prompt, and that he would be behind time if he delayed at what, after all, was probably nothing, he struck into that shuffling gallop of a walk only to be seen in its perfection when the business men of New York come down town in the morning, and would perhaps never have remembered the shot, and the pause it caused him, had it not been brought to his attention by the announcement that a murder had been committed that morning at No. 458 Broadway. Now 458 Broadway conveyed no very distinct impression, but when it appeared that that number was at the corner of Grand, and that just there he had heard the sound, as he hurried by at 10, the fact rose into importance and was made known. So far as has ever appeared no living soul ever heard that shot save the belated business man, the murderess, and the murdered, if, indeed, it be the case that any man hears that shot which instantly deprives him of life. On the second floor of No. 458, Doctor William R. T. Lutener had his office, and on this Tuesday morning, in the winter of 1854, came down from his residence as usual, entered his office at night, and after a pleasant word to the woman who kept the rooms in order, drew up his chair facing the window, so as to have his back to the door, and in that attitude opened the morning paper and began to read. Having occasion to leave the building the charwoman who had retired from the room when the doctor entered, started on her visit at 9:30 and remained absent for about an hour. At 10, as stated above, the business man heard a shot in passing just under the windows of the office, and at 10:30, when the old woman dropped in the room to see if her employer wanted anything, a terrific scream rang through the building. Before her affrighted eyes was the doctor dead upon the floor, prone upon his face, his hand tenaciously clutching the paper he had been reading, and a bullet hole in the back of his head. He had been shot from behind as he sat reading the paper within thirty minutes of the time the old woman left the building, and he dropped forward dead upon the floor. Shot by whom? The only answer is that this is one of the mysterious murders of New York. Several persons passing up and down the stairs, the building being full of offices, remembered seeing a woman thickly veiled pass into that particular door and out again almost instantly, but beyond this nothing was ever known. Differences having been shown to have existed between Dr. Lutener and a Mr. and Mrs. Hays, living near his residence, suspicion fell on Mrs. Hays, but the murder was, beyond all doubt, shown to have been committed between 9 and 10, and just as fully beyond doubt did Mrs. Hays show by reputable witnesses, that during that time she was transacting some business in Wall street. With this proof, the only thing that seemed a clue, vanished, and the mystery of the murder still remains.

6. THE BURDELL MURDER.

One morning in the winter of 1856-7 a little boy employed by Dr. Harvey Burdell, of No. 31 Bond street, to wait upon him went to the Doctor's door and attempted to enter. Something lay against the door on the inside and prevented his pushing it open at first, and upon a second effort, pushing it more forcibly, the lad saw blood. He gave the alarm instantly, and Dr. Harvey Burdell's body was found lifeless in the room, stabbed with several deep, mortal thrusts, and pricked, one can hardly use an apter term, by over a score of little digs or dabs from a knife or poniard point. There was blood all about the room, in one place a tremendous splash upon the wall, as the knife had evidently struck an artery; blood upon the door and along the sides of the room, as the doctor, bleeding profusely, had been forced up against them; blood upon the stairs outside, and gory finger marks as ensanguined hands had groped down as far as the basement of the dwelling. A chair by a secretary was overturned, and papers strewn about the desk—a counterpart so far of the Nathan murder—and all the internal evidence was that the doctor had been first struck from behind as he sat at his desk; had then risen and fought all around the room until he fell. Being a powerful man, it was argued at the time that his adversary who had grappled with and stabbed him again and again must have been a man of great strength, even conceding that the first blow partly disabled his victim, and yet the many little spiteful stabs, evidently inflicted by a weak, uncertain hand, came in to complicate the question of who did the deed. In the house, which belonged to Dr. Burdell, lived a widow named Cunningham with two daughters, and a young man named Snodgrass and an older man, Eckel, who boarded with Mrs. Cunningham. From certain developments brought out on the inquest an extreme intimacy between Eckel and Mrs. Cunningham was evidenced, and upon this and the farther fact that there were some troubles, pecuniary and other, between Mrs. Cunningham and Dr. Burdell, public opinion soon settled down to the conviction that Eckel did the fatal stabbing, and Mrs. Cunningham, either during the struggle or after its termination, had vented her animosity by venomous—even if futile—"pokes" with a poniard. As a further circumstance, a cobbler swore that on the night of the murder he stopped on the "stoop" of Dr. Burdell's house to tie his shoe, and that a man, whom he identified as Eckel, came to the front door and, partly opening it, roughly ordered him away. But it all came to nothing. The man was dead—murdered—and that was the end of it. What else is to be said of this butchery being more in the nature of circumstance than bearing directly on the main points, who? why? whither? Bloody and awful as the case was, it had yet its titillating side, morsels of the inner life of the house, salacious, dramatic, and humorous, which for days were eagerly devoured by the public. With Eckel as the heavy villain, and Mrs. Cunningham as a managing mamma of a Borgia type, the young man Snodgrass was the light comedian, and the fair Augusta Cunningham the walking lady. While the elders, as the public believed, plotted the deed even down to drugging some punch for the rest of the household, that they might sleep soundly. Snodgrass was pictured forth as now playing "Villikins and his Dinah" upon his banjo, and now reading Byron to the languishing beauty, nothing loth. When the law gave up "beat," Snodgrass and his banjo went to California, Eckel drifted out into business somewhere in the city, and Augusta and Mrs. Cunningham for a time disappeared. But a few months, however, and the whole tragedy was brought into view again. Claiming to have been married to Doctor Burdell, and indeed that she was married at the time claimed to *some* man was sufficiently proven, Mrs. Cunningham announced herself as the mother of a child by the murdered man, and laid claim to his property. The child, however, was proven surreptitious, and then Mrs. C. again disappeared, though up to within a recent date occasionally noticed in the papers as turning up at such and such a place. Eckel figured within a year or so in a prosecution for defrauding the revenue in the matter of a distillery in which he was interested, and not long since died, passing away, it is said, after he had declared that there was something on his mind which he wished and was just about to reveal.

7. THE BURKE MURDER.

On the southeast corner of Broadway and White street stands a store, No. 378, on the second floor of which, some two years and a half after the murder of Dr. Lutener on the second floor of another large building likewise on a southeast corner—Broadway and Grand street—occurred the murder of Bartholomew Burke. This man was the porter of a tailoring establishment carried on some fourteen years since at 378 Broadway, and it so chanced that when on the morning of the 18th of July, 1856, a clerk in the establishment arrived at his place of business, he was surprised to find the store still closed. While wondering at this circumstance as something that had never occurred before in several years, the clerk's eye fell

Continued on Eighth Page.

HARPER'S WEEKLY
A JOURNAL OF CIVILIZATION

Vol. XV.—No. 778.] NEW YORK, SATURDAY, NOVEMBER 25, 1871. [WITH A SUPPLEMENT. PRICE TEN CENTS.

"WHAT ARE YOU LAUGHING AT? TO THE VICTOR BELONG THE SPOILS."

For Sale by all News Dealers.] NEW YORK. [Price 10 Cents.

THE LIFE AND DEATH OF JAMES FISK, Jr.

THE ASSASSINATION.

A Twelfth Night Tragedy.

James Fisk, Jr., is now but a memory.

The career of this eccentric personage has been as brilliant as a rocket—it has terminated in the darkness of death, and, like a rocket, has left but a flash behind, to mark where and what it had been.

It is for us here and now to discuss, by pen and pencil, the details of the shooting of James Fisk, Jr., by Edward S. Stokes.

The tragedy was but the sequel to a farce; the murder was but the culmination—the finale of the tediously disgusting Stokes-Fisk-Mansfield litigation, involving certain correspondence of Fisk with Mansfield; certain pecuniary transactions between them, complicated with the monetary affairs

STOKES ENCOURAGES JOSIE IN COURT.

of Stokes, and indirectly connected, so it has been presumed, with the gigantic operations known formerly as the Erie and the Tammany Rings.

On Saturday, January 6th, 1872, James Fisk, Jr., had, to all appearance, won the suit, and was master of the situation; Judge Brady had given a decision in his favor; he had succeeded in obtaining, so it's said, an indictment against Miss Mansfield and Mr. Stokes on his charge of black-mail; he had, through the lawyers, worried Stokes on the examination, and even moved his former mistress to tears; he was flushed with triumph, and, in the plenitude of his victory, drove, on Saturday afternoon, January 6th, to the Grand Central Hotel, and alighted thereat, for the purpose of visiting some of his lady friends—Mrs. Morse and her daughters.

But at the very moment of might, in the very zenith of glory, in the full flush of life and vigor, the end came.

His former friend, his discomfited enemy, Edward S. Stokes, met him as

HELEN JOSEPHINE MANSFIELD-LAWLOR.

he was ascending the ladies' entrance to the hotel, and then and there shot him.

THE SHOOTING.

While Mr. Fisk was mounting the staircase of the ladies' entrance, before he had reached the third step, his deadly foe, Edward S. Stokes, suddenly made his appearance from his place of concealment, and a shot rang out which struck Fisk in the abdomen, two inches to the right of the naval, and three inches above it, passing downward, backward, and to the left, inflicting a terrible wound. Fisk fell, shouting "Oh!" and immediately scrambled to his feet again, when Stokes again levelled his revolver and fired another shot, the ball passing through and out of Fisk's left arm, without touching the bone. Fisk turned to run, but fell a second time and slid down to the bottom of the stairs, where he was picked up by the crowd, among whom were several of his acquaintances, who had gathered on hearing the report of the pistol, and carried upstairs to rooms 214 and 215, where he was laid upon the bed, and the house physician summoned.

THE ARREST.

Then the alarm was given and the police notified. Stokes did not attemp to leave the hotel. Officer McCadden and Captain Byrne, of the Fifteenth Precinct, came in and arrested him. He said nothing. Captain Byrne said, "Your name is Stokes?" and Stokes bowed, and said, "Yes." The captain said, "Where is the pistol?" and Stokes told the captain where it was.

A crowd had gathered around, and Stokes was taken up-stairs. The

THE LUNCH BEFORE THE MURDER.

mob of men who had rushed from all parts of the hotel, especially from the barber-shop hard-by, in all stages of apron and lather, attempted to follow, but were kept back by two waiters who had been placed at the foot of the main stairs. Another waiter stood guard in the private entrance to the hotel and refused admission to all comers. The crowd in the main hall gave a murmur of disappointment as they saw Stokes being taken away. Men were there in their shirt-sleeves fresh from the billiard-room with cues in their hands; loungers from the street, actors from the theatres, guests of the hotel, thieves from the Eighth Ward, and a swarm of detectives from Police Headquarters were there also.

THE IDENTIFICATION.

Immediately subsequent to his arrest, Captain Byrne, on taking Stokes up-stairs, brought him to the room in which Fisk lay on a lounge, and

STOKES LYING IN WAIT FOR HIS VICTIM.

EDWARD S. STOKES.

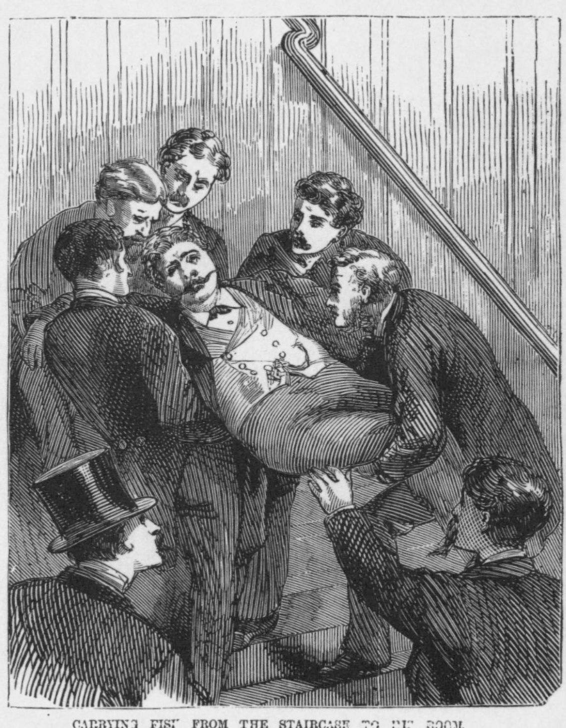

CARRYING FISK FROM THE STAIRCASE TO HIS ROOM.

The Thunderbolt.

Number I. NEW YORK, ALBANY AND TROY, MAY, 1873. Price Ten Cents.

THE REPUBLIC THREATENED!!

THE BEECHER-TILTON SCANDAL

AND THE

BEECHER-BOWEN-COMSTOCK CONSPIRACY.

THE SEAL BROKEN AT LAST.

Woodhull's "Lies" and Theodore Tilton's "True Story."

THE ACCOUNT HORRIBLE AT BEST.

NO "OBSCENITY," BUT GOD'S TRUTH.

The Sexual Ethics of Plymouth Church—A New Revelation—The Brooklyn Saints Torture Saint Paul into a Free-Lover.

The THUNDERBOLT Shatters a Bad Crowd and Ploughs up the Whole Ground.

CHRISTIANITY is the highest word of civilization, and the spirit of Jesus is the true "RELIGION OF HUMANITY." But to-day the "ORTHODOX PULPIT" IS A MENACE TO FORTY MILLIONS OF PEOPLE. To save one powerful preacher from deserved shame its special retainers have raped the goddess of American liberty. And to accomplish this outrage they have resorted to fraud, and have not scrupled at A MONSTROUS CONSPIRACY. 'Tis the purpose of this paper,

THE THUNDERBOLT,

to stun the nation into a knowledge of these crimes. The "Evangelical Church," with its "Young Men's Christian Association," shall no longer cheat the government, browbeat the courts and subsidize the press, with impunity. When a republic is crucified between its priests and its editors, honest patriots should speak out. It is time that theological plotters be thrown upon the defensive, and be made to beg of common-sense a further lease of their own life. THE THUNDERBOLT has power to effect much of this purpose through the very "forbidden fruit" that has tempted the present quacks of conventional piety to become liars, perjurers and law-breakers. By this "forbidden fruit" I mean

THE GREATEST SOCIAL DRAMA

OF MODERN TIMES,

THE BEECHER-TILTON SCANDAL!

This scandal, as reported by Victoria C. Woodhull, is at once a truth and a falsehood; or, as Theodore Tilton has himself explained, a "true story" underlies "the false one." Three months after the Woodhull account had been published, and no one had given the public a direct, authentic denial of it—three months after the country had been insulted in connection with it by the moral and legal fraud of "obscene literature"—I was stung into writing "A FULL ACCOUNT, ANALYSIS AND CRITICISM OF THE BEECHER-TILTON SCANDAL." In that article, (published in the Troy Daily *Press* of February 11th, and since reproduced in other journals), the Woodhull account was given in condensed form, as follows:

"The Beecher-Tilton Scandal Case" is this: Mrs. Woodhull declares there has been a long-continued *liaison* between Mr. Beecher and Mrs. Tilton; that it first came to Mr. Tilton's knowledge through the revelations of one of his children; that he accused Mrs. Tilton of it, and received her acknowledgement of guilt; that he was driven nearly to insanity at the moment, and treated Mrs. Tilton so severely that she miscarried a child, which was considered the offspring of Mr. Beecher. Mr. Tilton kept his grief secret, however, as Mrs. Woodhull asserts, until Mr. Beecher went again to his house, during his absence, and extorted a letter from Mrs. Tilton to the effect that he had never been guilty of the wrong she had acknowledged to her husband. Then Mr. Tilton, doubly outraged, confided his grief to a bosom friend, Mr. Frank Moulton, who went to Beecher's house and forced him, at tne mouth of a pistol, to give up the letter.

This story, in whole or in part, Mrs. Woodhull says, was first revealed to her by Mrs. Paulina Wright Davis, who *received it from Mrs. Tilton*; and then by Mrs. Elizabeth Cady Stanton, who *received it from Mr. Tilton*. The knowledge of it came to Mrs. Woodhull in the early part of 1870, and she refers to an allusion which she made to it in *Woodhull and Claflin's Weekly* at that time. "Subsequently," continues Mrs. Woodhull, "I published a letter in both *World* and *Times*, in which was the following sentence:

"'I know a clergyman of eminence in Brooklyn who lives in concubinage with the wife of another clergyman of equal eminence.'"

Mrs. Woodhull affirms that the day when this letter appeared in the *World*, Mr. Tilton came to her office, No. 44 Broad street, and showing Mrs. Woodhull the letter, asked her whom she meant. "Mr. Tilton," she replied, "I mean you and Mr. Beecher."

According to Mrs. Woodhull's statement, Mr. Tilton then acknowledged that the account was true, and worse than she had heard it. But he said that he was broken-hearted, that his wife was broken-hearted, and that she especially was then in no condition to be dragged before the public. Mr. Tilton took her to see Mrs. Tilton, and both imparted to her the whole story. The same thing was again detailed to her by Mr. Tilton's friend, Mr. Frank Moulton, and finally by Henry Ward Beecher himself.

Mrs. Woodhull's declared purpose in publishing the Beecher-Tilton Scandal was to create a "SOCIAL REVOLUTION." She wished to show that "the foremost minds of the age" had "OUTGROWN THE INSTITUTION OF MARRIAGE," rendering to it only the outward homage of hypocrites, not the adherence of conscience or the practice of life. There is no danger that any "SOCIAL REVOLUTION" will grow to proportions beyond the actual truth and common-sense contained in it. But in one thing Woodhull and Claflin instantly succeeded: they created a

SOCIAL PANIC

THAT TURNED NEW YORK INTO A MOB!

Their scandal, as they have since boasted, was indeed "a bombshell," that carried dismay on every hand—an infernal machine of letters so terrific "that many even feared to read it," while others "cursed and prayed, laughed and cried, as if in the presence of the crack of doom."

THE PLANS OF THIS "SOCIAL REVOLUTION," it seems, were somewhat deeply laid. The issue of *Woodhull and Claflin's Weekly* containing the "bombshell" was dated Nov. 2d, 1872. But, anticipating that some steps might be taken to suppress the entire issue when its contents should become known, the paper was dispatched to its subscribers a week in advance, and, (if the word of its "social revolutionists" can be trusted in anything,) "to the entire list of newspapers in the United States, Canada and Great Britain." Then, on Monday morning the 28th of October, it was put on sale at the Woodhull headquarters. Before night the demand "grew to a rush." During the week it increased to "a crush," needing even the regulation of the police. 'Tis said the sales reached a hundred and fifty thousand copies, and promised two millions. For several days newsmen retailed the paper as high as fifty cents. On the day of its suppression $2.50 was a common price for it. In some instances single copies brought $10, and one extraordinary lover of literature is reported to have invested $40 in a copy. Owners of the paper then leased it to other readers at a dollar a day.

But by Saturday, Nov. 2d, THE GENERAL PANIC OF "GOOD SOCIETY" in New York had so far subsided, that "some steps" were indeed taken—and with a vengeance—to suppress the Beecher-Tilton Scandal. And 'tis these steps alone that make the scandal of sufficient importance to claim the interference of persons in no way connected with it, and to need the unfaltering scrutiny of the public. The "steps," then, were nothing less than a

DARING CONSPIRACY,

not merely against the audacious and hated women, Woodhull and Claflin, but

AGAINST THE

WHOLE PEOPLE OF THE UNITED STATES!

In no other terms will I ever consent to describe that bastard New York monstrosity, begotten of lust, fear and guilt,—the arrest of Woodhull and Claflin for "PUBLISHING OBSCENE LITERATURE."

If I had myself been situated like Theodore Tilton on the day of that arrest, and the darlings of my household had been so cruelly belied as his "true story" claims of his own, I don't know but I could have gone into Broad Street and cut the throats of Woodhulf, Claflin and Blood, with as little compunction as I would shoot a mad dog. But that would have been a business and a risk confined to three or four persons. It would not have been a NATIONAL FRAUD, ENDANGERING EVERY GREAT PRINCIPLE AT THE BOTTOM OF HUMAN LIBERTY. The special friends, however, of Henry Ward Beecher—the skulkers of Plymouth Church and the Young Men's Christian Association—preferred to defouer the laws of their country and the freedom of its people by a gigantic performance of bigotry and chicane. In the shadow of their false pretenses, the Woodhull slanders, however atrocious, have grown comparatively dim and insignificant. The question of the MERE RAKE, WHOM THE MORALIST MIGHT PITY AND FORGIVE, sinks in the question of the CONSPIRATOR AND TRAITOR, WHOM THE PATRIOT MUST HATE.

A law of the United States, passed June 8th, 1872, makes a very proper provision in aid of public morals by branding the transmission of obscene literature through the mails as a misdemeanor. The Act is this:

"No obscene book, pamphlet, picture, print, or other publication of a vulgar or indecent character, or any letter upon the envelop of which, or postal card upon which, scurrilous epithets may have been written or printed, or disloyal devices printed or engrossed, shall be carried in the mail; and any person who shall knowingly deposit, or cause to be deposited, for mailing or delivery, any such obscene publication shall be deemed guilty of a misdemeanor, and on conviction thereof shall for every such offence be fined not more than five hundred dollars, or be imprisoned at hard labor not exceeding one year, or both, at the discretion of the courts."

Whatever sins Woodhull and Claflin had committed in issuing their *Weekly* of Nov. 2d, 1872, THEY HAD CAREFULLY AVOIDED ANY VIOLATION OF THIS STATUTE AGAINST OBSCENE LITERATURE. Their paper contained a harrowing account of seduction—an instance of such diabolical heartlessness that the noted philanthropist, Parker Pillsbury, has since declared that, if its revelations were true, "no matter though Mrs. Woodhull were an imp of hell, she should have a monument of polished Parian marble as high as Trinity steeple, and every father and mother of daughters should be proud to contribute a stone." In addition to that nightmare of horrors, the paper contained several bold articles on social, religious and financial themes, in the midst of which was the Beecher-Tilton Scandal,—a sad, unexpected story of adultery, but differing little in its details from scores of such stories reported in hundreds of newspapers. There is

ONLY ONE TEST OF OBSCENE LITERATURE,—

THE PURPOSE OF THE PUBLICATION:

and any other test a free people should resent, if necessary,

WITH BATTLE AND BLOOD!

Any other test would overturn the Bible, destroy the classics, and exclude physiology from human knowledge. It would insult the grave of every great thinker and poet, from Plato to Shakespeare and Burns. It would steal the bread and meat of letters, and leave only the baby sugar-tits of a Sunday-school library. THE PURPOSE OF OBSCENE LITERATURE IS TO PAMPER LUST; and no fact, no fiction is obscene without this purpose. But the expressed intent of the Woodhull articles was to *destroy* lust; and, whether this intent was real or feigned, the articles were so written as almost to stop the breath and freeze the soul. In a word, they were ghastly, sickening *libels*, if false, but no more *obscene* than a picture of the crucifixion.

Woodhull and Claflin, however, were two women regarded almost as outlaws. They had become feared as "blackmailers," and unfragrantly notorious as "free-lovers." For such reasons, undoubtedly, the special guardians of Mr. Beecher's reputation thought that the worst of means might be good enough to sweep "female nuisances" out of Broad Street. PUBLIC SENTIMENT WAS EXASPERATED, NOT QUITE ENOUGH FOR A DIRECT MOB, BUT AN INDIRECT MOB, SLINKING BEHIND A PRETENCE OF LAW, MIGHT CRUSH ITS VICTIMS WITH SAFETY. In this position, the legal subterfuge was found in the act of Congress passed to punish the venders of obscene prints. Then

MR. ANTHONY J. COMSTOCK,

BACKED BY

THE YOUNG MEN'S CHRISTIAN ASSOCIATION,

stepped up to manage the dangerous FRAUD. Mr. Comstock is generally credited with "good intentions;" and as hell, also, is said to be paved with the same materials, I have never doubted their presence in the man. God seems to have made him partly a fool, in order that the fellow could do a good work as long as he could be kept from getting above his business. The dirty wretches who corrupt young minds by feeding them on licentious books need some little man, by nature a spy and hypocrite, to check their villainous trade. A full-grown, honest soul could neither sell the books nor dodge and lie to catch those who do. In such a dilemma the earth has a Comstock.

Mr. Comstock declares that, in prosecuting Woodhull and Claflin, he has never moved in collusion with Mr. Beecher. In spite of the habit of tongue necessary to his vocation, he probably tells the truth: Mr. Beecher has acted, from the first, through his friends. But one of the affidavits on which the arrest of the two women was procured, was made by one Taliesin William Rees, a clerk in the office of the *Independent:* and that Mr. Henry C. Bowen, the proprietor of that journal, might be trusted to act for Mr. Beecher, (when he could *save himself* by the same industry,) will be quite evident by-and-by to the "gentle reader" of the THUNDERBOLT. Is it not known that the scheme was planned in Mr. Bowen's office—spies being thence dispatched to Woodhull and Claflin to buy papers, and order them sent to certain persons by post? On receipt of the papers, Mr. A. J. Comstock made his complaint before Commissioner Osborn, and the women were arrested. They were in a carriage at the time, and claim to have been hunting up the officials who had come for them.

As the charge against them was

A FRAUD, BORN OF A PLOT,

and as they, if no one else, had brains enough to know it, they naturally supposed it could soon be broken. But in this opinion they measured only the justice of law itself, not the powers of a mob, called "public opinion," which renders American law useless on so many important occasions. THE UNITED STATES GOVERNMENT, HOWEVER, TREATED WOODHULL AND CLAFLIN WITH ENDEARING FAMILIARITY. IT SAT IN THEIR LAP ON THE WAY TO COURT, through the supreme gallantry of Marshall Colfax or Bernhard—one of the two Chesterfields who had them in charge. It then hurried them, not into open court, but into a side room where the "examination" might be *private*. In this "star chamber" they met five persons—District Attorney Noah Davis, "a member of Plymouth Church and a family connection of Mr. Beecher;" Assistant District Attorney Gen. Davies, Commissioner Osborn, and two other gentlemen, one of these being also a member of Plymouth Church. But the "brazen sisters" sent for counsel; and, insisting on being conducted to the proper court-room, their examination was finally held in public. In

THIS EXAMINATION

the prosecuting blunderer, Gen. Davies, let out the secret that Woodhull and Claflin were not merely guilty of "circulating obscene literature," but of a "gross libel" on a "gentleman" WHOSE CHARACTER IT WAS "WELL WORTH THE WHILE OF THE GOVERNMENT OF THE UNITED STATES TO VINDICATE." Interpreted, this lingo meant that a United States Court had been procured to convict, on the pretense of *obscenity*, two women who had *libelled a man*—this man declining to protect himself, except through a conspiracy of his friends and lackeys.

This "holy show" of American jurisprudence took place on Saturday the 2d of Nov., 1872, and was finally adjourned to the ensuing Monday, the prisoners being held to bail in eight thousand dollars each, with two sureties. But when Monday came the Beecher tools of the United States courts *dodged a further examination altogether*. By an unheard-of proceeding, the grand jury had pushed in an indictment which took the case out of Commissioner Osborn's jurisdiction. The motive was evident: Mr. Beecher's General Davies had found that his owner could never be persuaded or dragged into court to pursue Woodhull for her "gross libel," and that the charge of "obscenity" was a most ruinous one to try, if Plymouth Church had any further desire to save its Bible. For by far the most "indecent passage" in *Woodhull and Claflin's Weekly* had been cut out of the divinely inspired book of Deuteronomy. BY THIS INDICTMENT, HOWEVER, THE PRISONERS WERE REMANDED TO JAIL IN UTTER DISGRACE, THE MOB OF PIETY AND FASHION WAS APPEASED, AND THE YOUNG MEN'S CHRISTIAN ASSOCIATION WAS SUSTAINED IN FRAUD!

So much done, it was only necessary to muzzle the New York newspapers, (some of whose editors had strong personal reasons for dreading "black-mailers" if not "free-lovers,") and to bribe or cheat the Associated Press into sending lies by lightning throughout the country. Both feats were performed. A consultation of leading quills *adopted darkness and falsehood as a deliberate policy;* and as for our "country press," that never dares to sneeze unless the metropolitan nose is crammed with snuff. The telegraph even prated about the finding of "immodest cartoons;" and on the 4th of November the credulous public actually supposed that

THE DAYS' DOINGS.

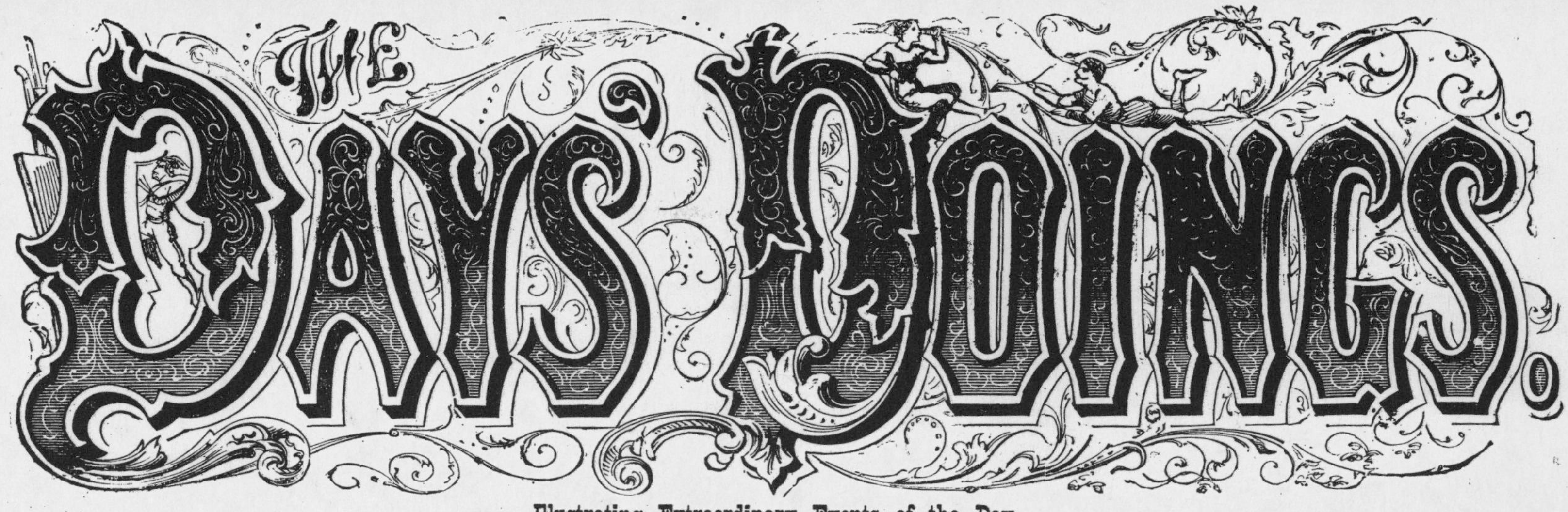

Illustrating Extraordinary Events of the Day.

Entered according to the Act of Congress, in the year 1873, by THE DAYS' DOINGS COMPANY, in the office of the Librarian of Congress, at Washington.

No. 276.—VOL. XI. NEW YORK, SEPTEMBER 8, 1873. {13 WEEKS, $1.00. $4 YEARLY.} PRICE, 10 CENTS.

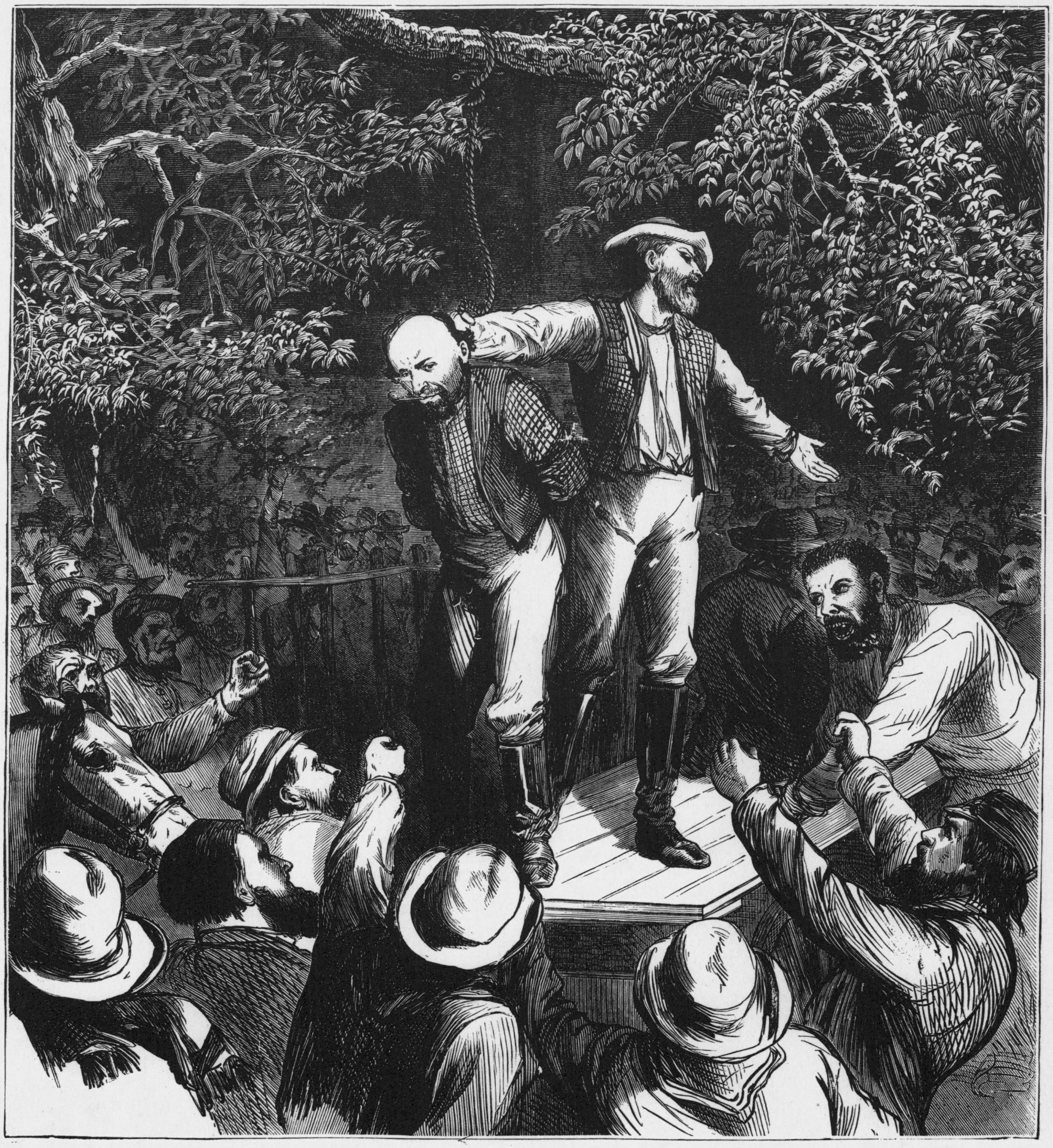

THE "LYNCHING" OF KELLER, THE MURDERER, AT LES CYGNES, KANSAS, AUGUST 20.—SEE NEXT PAGE.

Los Angeles Herald

May 15, 1874

VASQUEZ CAPTURED.

THE ROBBER SEVERELY, BUT NOT FATALLY WOUNDED.

A Party of Los Angeles Men Reap the Honor of the Capture.

Full Account of the Successful Maneuvre Which Placed the Bandit in the Hands of the Law.

If an earthquake had shaken the foundation of our city and swallowed up one-half of our places scarcely more excitement would have ensued than that which followed the announcement of the capture of Vasquez yesterday afternoon.

The City Fathers were in profound deliberation in their rooms, when there was a rush outside the door, a crowd surged about the place, and somebody said, "Vasquez is caught." The Council adjourned *sine die*, without ceremony.

In front of the entrance to the City Prison there was an extremely warlike display. The Sheriff's party, armed with numberless revolvers, Henry rifles, and shooting irons of various descriptions had just arrived, convoying a light spring wagon, in which was lying the man long sought for—the veritable Vasquez.

The wounded bandit was lifted upon the shoulders of four men as he lay on his litter, and borne through the crowd into the jail, where he was placed upon the floor to await medical assistance.

The circumstances of the capture are as follows: For some time past, the authorities have had a spy out observing the movements of the robber and his gang, and by this means secured authentic information of their whereabouts. About 8 o'clock Wednesday night, D. K. Smith came into the city with information which caused the immediate fitting out by Sheriff Rowland of a party to go in pursuit. The party was made up of Under-Sheriff Albert S. Johnson, Major Mitchell, Emil Harris, Officer Hartlee, Sam. Bryant, D. K. Smith, W. E. Rodgers, and G. A. Beers, correspondent for a San Francisco paper. Starting about 1 o'clock yesterday morning, the party left the city and proceeded to the vicinity of Brea Ranch, about ten miles southwest of Los Angeles. Making a halt in Nicholas Cañon, at a place securely sheltered from view of the house where they had reason to expect the presence of their game, they sent out scouts to reconnoitre their position. Major Mitchell, with a field glass, proceeded to a side of the mountain overlooking the house of Greek George, where unobserved he could view all that passed about the premises.

After waiting some time, he saw Vasquez approach the place, dismount and picket his horse, and then go into the house. Another man came out, and taking two horses struck for the woods. Still another came upon the premises and went within. Without waiting for further developments, Mitchell rejoined his party, and they together proceeded to complete their plan of attack. A wood-wagon, coming down the cañon about this time, was seized upon, and the occupants, two Mexicans, compelled to further the plans of the party, as will be seen, in a most valuable manner. The men, after securing their horses, sprang into the wagon-box, and there lay down, so as to be concealed from sight. Thus lodged to their satisfaction, they levelled their revolvers upon the two men on the seat in front, and under threats of instantly shooting them should they make the least sign towards giving an alarm, they drove direct for the house of Greek George.

It was an interesting position, surely—packed like sardines in a box, lying on their backs, with the sun glaring down into their faces, and jolting over the rough road. Their nerves, too, must have been at an interesting tension, as each minute brought them nearer to an expected conflict with men of such known pluck and so thoroughly armed as Vasquez and his gang. Fortunately their plan of procedure was so excellently chosen and executed that their approach was not suspected by the occupants of the house. It was stealing a march worthy of a general in the field. Too much credit cannot be given the managers of the expedition for the wily manner in which they executed this part of the programme. Meanwhile the ostensible wagon load of wood was nearing its point of destination. When within a few yards of the house, the Sheriff's party leaped from their place of concealment and in an instant surrounded the house.

So sudden and so well guarded had been their actions, that they had arrived without raising the least suspicion as to their approach. The house was an ordinary adobe, with a frame kitchen built in the rear. Around this they quickly gathered, and had every avenue of escape cut off. As Rogers approached the door, which was slightly ajar, the inmates for the first time became aware of the presence of the pursuers. A woman within sprang to the half open door and made an effort to close and bar it, but her movement was anticipated and the door forced before she had a chance to make it. [illegible] seated in the . Vasquez, who was took the instant eating his dinner, small single boudarm, and with a small window, not ment through a inches square, and lanhan eighteen feet on the outside. Here upon him by Hartlee, from whom he as met [illegible] the contents of a double-barreled shot gun, and fell to the ground. Quickly recovering, he sprang to his feet, and turning towards the west side of the house, made an effort to fly in that direction; but this time he was confronted by Beers, who lodged a shot in his shoulder from a Henry rifle. Wheeling again, he once more found himself confronted by Hartlee, who had thrown down his gun, and now covered the fugitive with his revolver. He now saw that escape was impossible, and throwing up his hands said, in English, "Don't shoot!" One other shot was fired, as he was in the act of surrendering himself, but it was all done so quickly that no intention to injure their captive is chargeable upon any one of the party. The rest of the inmates of the house were taken without any violence. While some of the party took possession of the house and its occupants, others addressed themselves to caring for the wounded robber. At first it was thought that he was mortally wounded, and this was his own belief, as he expressed it to his captors. Examination, however, showed the wounds not to be so serious as supposed. At the first moment when he gave himself up, Vasquez turned to Hartlee and said, "What's your name?" A remark so singular prompted the inquiry subsequently as to his motive in asking the question, when he said, "I wanted to know the name of a brave man. I am not a coward myself, and I like to know another brave man."

Two of the robber's confederates, inmates of the house, were taken—one a man about forty years of age, and one quite young, not more than eighteen or nineteen years old. They caused no trouble in their capture. Besides the three men, the Sheriff's party captured two horses—one the famous white horse of Vasquez, and one grey belonging to another of the bandits; three Henry rifles, one Spencer rifle, five six-shooters, 400 rounds of ammunition, a villainous looking dirk-knife belonging to Vasquez, and some other arms. Three saddles were also taken, two of them very fine ones, worth probably fifty dollars apiece. The valuable gold watch and chain which was taken from C. E. Miles some time ago, was also recovered. Vasquez said that if he had known Miles was a working man he would not have asked it of him. Probably not. When taken from the pocket of the robber, the watch did not have its own chain attached, but one of heavy silver. Hearing Miles making inquiries after the missing chain, as he lay on the floor in the jail, Vasquez directed one of his attendants to look into a certain pocket and the article was produced.

When first lodged in jail, the bandit expressed some anxiety as to his safety, and had several times to be assured that no further harm would come to him. Dr. Wise was the first physician to attend the wounded man, and proceeded at once to extricate the bullets lodged in various parts of his body. Subsequently Dr. Widney arrived, and attended to bandaging the wounded parts. The man received two buck-shot wounds through the fleshy part of the left arm, between the elbow and shoulder, one through the muscle of the right arm, one in the shoulder, one in the right leg, one in the left nipple, coming out under the arm, and one shot on the left side of the neck. All were flesh wounds, and though severe, will not necessarily prove fatal. The doctors expressed their opinion that with proper treatment he will very soon recover.

It is a great wonder that he was not killed, after standing such a fire as he did, and receiving so many balls. At latest accounts last night he was sleeping, and the doctors interdicted the slightest disturbance to break his rest. He was very weak from loss of blood, but otherwise in as favorable condition as could be expected. It will doubtless be several weeks before he can be removed from his present quarters.

Concerning the general success of the expedition, we will say that it was perfect. Although a part of the bandit's party have succeeded in making their escape, still their power is broken, now that their chief is captured. Doubtless the others will soon find the coils tightening about them, so that they will either leave the country or else they will find themselves taken into custody. At all events, yesterday was a good day for Southern California; a day in which the majesty of the law was vindicated and an effectual check placed upon outlawry in this part of the country forever. Our reports concerning the expedition have been gathered from various members of the Sheriff's party, as we have been able to interview them for a few minutes at a time. But everybody was so excited over the affair that hardly any one was able to give a clear consecutive account of the whole proceeding. Doubtless there are some inaccuracies in our account, but in the main it is correct.

If any should still question whether the real Vasquez has been caught, they may set their doubts to rest without further quibbling. The bandit has been identified by numbers who have the best reason in the world for knowing him, having confronted him at various times as an enemy and as a robber. Besides, he does not pretend to deny his identity, and owns that his bandit days are over and that he is "in for it" finally this time.

The following is a clear and correct summary of the movements of Vasquez since the Rappetto robbery, and of the man who planned and effected his capture. After Major Mitchell's party followed and captured the bandit's camp in Tejunga Cañon, little was known of the real movements of Vasquez until some two weeks ago. A part of the time Major Mitchell was acting independent of Sheriff Rowland, but latterly the Sheriff has known all of Mitchell's operations.

We now leave Mitchell, Morse and others, whose expeditions have already been published, and take up the thread of Sheriff Rowland's plans. His mode of operation was to watch and wait, and so careful and discreet was he that his most intimate friends supposed he was giving the Vasquez matter very little attention.

THIS WAS A MISTAKE.

Rowland had a little bird who told him every movement of the bandit and his gang, and on several nights he has ridden out and reconnoitered the Vasquez camp, but on each occasion the little bird told him not to attempt the capture. This happened so often that he began to suspect the bird might be playing him. This, however, was not true, as the sequel proved—the bird telling the truth in every instance.

FALSE REPORT.

The reports that Vasquez was in the habit of visiting the house of a woman in this city, after nightfall, had no foundation in fact, but if it had been true, Rowland would have captured him, for he knew of the story and the house, and watched the interior of the woman's room night after night. It is safe to say that until to-day Vasquez has not been in this city during the past three months. Vasquez had two men constantly watching the Morse party while in this portion of the State, and no one was more thoroughly posted on the movements of Morse and Cunningham than the bandit. It was Rowland who baffled Vasquez. He was so cool, and apparently indifferent as to whether the robbers were caught or not that the bandit at times really thought he had nothing to fear from him. He was mistaken. Like Prospero's Ariel, Rowland's

LITTLE BIRD

Was obedient to his slightest command, and flew here and there and everywhere, collecting information and delivering it to its master. It told him that for the past two weeks Vasquez and his gang had made their headquarters at the house of Greek George, on the Brea Ranch, ten miles from the city; that Vasquez spent most of his days in the house, but slept at night some distance away in the open air, with his horse always saddled and his Spencer rifle by his side. It gave him an exact diagram of the house, told him in what room Vasquez stopped, in what room his arms were, and the number and quality of those arms. It told him how Vasquez's horse was always kept saddled and ready for traveling in the tall weeds near to a window, through which Vasquez would jump in case of a surprise. It told him on Wednesday night that on Thursday Vasquez would be at the house playing cards, but that he must not leave the city, as he was constantly under the eye of one of Vasquez's spies. Here Rowland's detective shrewdness did him good service. He quietly selected his party, detailed his instructions and continued to walk about the streets in his usual apparently unconcerned manner. In a little time

THE VASQUEZ SPY DISAPPEARED.

His friends supposed he had got drunk and gone to some of the many houses he knew of, to sleep off his whiskey. They knew he was not in jail, for they sought him in that structure. Subsequent events proved that he did not get drunk, nor did he leave town. Rowland had shanghaed him and kept him under close guard, where his friends could not find him, until the party returned with their game from Greek George's house. As Vasquez and his three associates were taken into the jail, the spy—the man who had been sent in to watch Rowland—was also marched into the same edifice. Then it was discovered that Rowland had been watching the spy more closely than the spy had watched him. Vasquez saw that he was trapped, and how it was done. He says

HE WAS BETRAYED,

And assures Sheriff Rowland that but for the treason of some friend he would not have been captured. It will be seen from the facts here detailed that Sheriff Rowland has managed the whole affair in the most masterly manner. He worked carefully and patiently, and from the time Vasquez took up his headquarters at the house of Greek George he has known his every movement. He struck the blow at the right time and in the right manner to secure a successful result. The men he selected were of the true and tried class, and they faithfully performed the dangerous task alloted to them.

VASQUEZ SPEAKS.

This evening, while weak from loss of blood and suffering intense pain, the bandit manifested a disposition to talk with the Sheriff. He told Mr. Rowland that he had been betrayed, and begged for the name of his betrayer. He thanked his captors for their kind treatment, and admitted that they had treated him well, and acknowledged the plan to have been well laid and admirably executed. He assured Sheriff Rowland that he had no hand in the Tres Pinos murder, and says he did not join the party until an hour after it had left the scene of the murder. This is however a little too thin. He says it was his intention to have followed Sheriff Morse back to the vicinity of San Francisco, and capturing ten thousand dollars that he knew of, hasten again to this vicinity and take rest. Sheriff Rowland has interrupted, if not indefinitely postponed the carrying out of this plan. We may add that no woman in any way assisted in the capture. Vasquez says he is too wise to trust his life in the hands of a woman.

Ties for the Spring and Sixth street railroad were being laid on Spring street yesterday.

The sentence of Bernard Newman was yesterday postponed by Judge O'Melveny until June 1st.

Los Angeles Lodge No. 42, F. & A. M., meets to-night for work in the 3d degree. A full attendance is required.

Three drunks were before the Mayor yesterday. One liquidated to the usual extent, one was discharged, and the third was elevated to an honorable membership in the chain-gang.

If you want a nobby suit of clothes, call on F. Adam, Spring street. He has a fine stock of clothes on hand which he makes up to order at the most reasonable terms and in the most stylish manner.

The Coroner's Jury on the case of the woman Rafalia met yesterday, and after hearing evidence, returned a verdict to the effect that the deceased came to her death by bad usage received from her husband. Justice Gray has issued a warrant for the arrest of the wife-beater.

The attention of our readers is directed to the advertisement of Wm. Slaney, which appears in this morning's paper. Mr. Slaney has opened with a full stock of boots and shoes in his store, Main street, opposite Wells, Fargo & Co.'s Express office, and guarantees satisfacttion to all purchasers.

One George Brown was arrested and lodged in the guard yesterday on a charge of grand larceny. He stole a harness valued at $60, and sold it to a pawn broker for $12 50. With the money thus raised he went on a spree, and when arrested had not a cent to bless himself with. The harness so cheaply bought by the honest pawnbroker was immediately resold to a farmer (so it is said), and it is doubtful now whether the property can be recovered.

We notice the arrival in town of Messrs. Tuttle & Lee, the photographers, who have been creating such a furore in Santa Barbara by the excellence of their pictures. They design staying a few months in Los Angeles. We have no doubt our citizens will be glad of the opportunity of securing some of their work. We understand they have taken some fine views of the scenery of Santa Barbara and vicinity, and along the route from there down. They will have them on exhibition in a few days, and will also take views of Los Angeles.

15 Cents.

Pictorial History

OF THE

Beecher-Tilton Scandal.

Its Origin, Progress and Trial, Illustrated with Fifty Engravings from Accurate Sketches.

REV. HENRY WARD BEECHER, THE DEFENDANT IN THE SCANDAL SUIT.

MRS. ELIZABETH R. TILTON.

FRANCIS D. MOULTON, THE MUTUAL FRIEND AND CHAMPION-WITNESS OF AMERICA.

THEODORE TILTON, PLAINTIFF IN THE GREAT SCANDAL SUIT.

THE PRINCIPALS IN THE ACTION.

INDEPENDENT--EXTRA.

Fort Smith, Arkansas, September 3, 1875.

Execution Day!!

[illegible]e Crowd—6 Murderers [illegible]—The Scaffold—De[illegible] the Execution—Brief [Ske]tches of the Convicts and the C[ri]mes for which They Suffered.

[illegible] September 3d, will be long re[illegible] nals as Black Friday. [illegible] who set at defiance [illegible] of God and man were executed in the prison yard of the U. S. Court. In anticipation of such an extraordinary number as six men being hung at once, strangers from abroad have arrived [illegible] day during the past week. Among them we noticed reporters from the St. Louis Times, Mo. Republican, Globe-Democrat, Kansas City Times, and L. R. Gazette. The names of the men hung were W. J. Whittington, James Moore and Daniel Evans, white, S. W. Fooy and Smoker Mankiller, Cherokees, and Edmond Campbell, colored.

The crowd commenced pouring in town early in the morning, and by 10 o'clock every street was crowded. The number present at the execution was estimated at 5000. At 8 o'clock their shackles were removed, and the criminals were carefully washed and neatly dressed. At 9½ o'clock they were escorted to the gallows. The sentences were read and after the termination of religious exercises they shook hands with their friends, the rope were adjusted, the black caps were drawn over their faces, and at precisely five minutes past 11 o'clock,

THE TRAP FELL.

But few convulsive motions were visible, and after a short time the bodies were taken down, coffined and delivered to their friends.

The prisoners were attended through their last moments by Revs. W. A. Sample, S. H. Babcock, Lawrence Symthe and Granade.

Thus terminated an execution of six men, under sentence of one judge, at one term. Two more criminals were sentenced to swing at the same time with these, making eight in all, but one was shot in attempting to escape from his guard, and the other, a young fellow named Snow, has been, on account of his youth, reprieved from death, and will be sent to the penitentiary. This wholesale execution is a fearful comment on the state of affairs in the Indian Territory.

Great credit is due the officers of the U. S. Court for the complete success of all their arrangements in this remarkable affair.

The U. S. court room and jail is in a large brick building formerly a quarter for military purposes. The court rooms are in the upper story and the jail in the basement. The yard or grounds are spacious and surrounded by a stone wall with five gates. In one corner of this wall stands an old pentagon-shaped building, with iron doors and pointed roof, built of solid masonry; it was formerly used as a magazine. The old walls and corner bastions are picturesque with running vines, and the yard shaded by many fine old trees. Here in past days the morning reveille saluted the stars and stripes and the prim martinets of the old school drilled and trained their victims with automatic precision, and the old fort has been lively and interesting in modern days by the successive occupation of Feds and Rebs. Some of the brightest names in our old military galaxy have either resided, served or visited here in the course of military duty, being a favorite point on account of its healthy climate, good water and pleasant society.—Pleased with the fine natural resources and the beauty of the surrounding country, many invested and bought property in the city and vicinity. Our space permits the mention of a few, such as Taylor, Gaines, Arbuckle, Croghan, Bonneville, Belknap, Marcy, McClellan, Johnson, Garnett. The brave old Gen. Bonneville still resides here in his beautiful country residence in full view from the city at an advanced age pretty close to the nineties, hearty and able to prune his grapevines.

THE GALLOWS

in the jail yard in front of and close up to the old magazine is a strong platform about 20 feet square and 12 feet high, with a long trap door in the floor, swung on iron hinges, for the

DEAD FALL.

Over this about 10 feet higher, framed on upright posts and firmly braced, is a long rope-beam with six ropes attached. The 6 convicts were ranged side by side, and were launched into eternity at one drop of the dead-fall. Seven murderers had been before executed on this scaffold.

SKETCH OF CONVICTS EXECUTED TO-DAY.

JAMES MOORE was a fine-looking, square-built athlete, about 6 feet high, weight 170 pounds. His hands were small and delicate in shape, features regular and handsome, expressing firmness and resolution. His age was 28. Born in Johnson county, Missouri, at an early age his parents removed to Grayson county, Texas, where they still reside. James looked as if he could take care of himself in a free fight, and no doubt would have made a very creditable stand up in one. He was connected with a daring band of outlaws in the Indian Territory, and their field of operations reached from the line of Kansas and Missouri into the western counties of Texas. On the night of August 26, 1871, assisted by a "pal" he robbed old crippled farmer Cox of two horses. Cox lived in Washington county, on the line near old Fort Wayne. Moore took the horses while Hunton stood guard. They were promptly followed by citizens to Fort Gibson and thence to Eufaula. Here one of the pursuers took the cars to head them off, while the others continued on the trail on horseback. At Atoka they were seen, when he left the cars and getting assistance they were hotly pursued to the Little Blue near Red River (about a 200 miles run) where they were overtaken, and the wild fun changed into a tragedy, for they fired on the energetic pursuers, killing Spivey on the spot by a ball through the head and dangerously wounding [illegible] the skirmish (which took place [illegible] the night of Sept. 1) however, they lost [illegible] horses and were separated. Hunton the same night steals another horse and solitary and alone retreats back over the same road. This was providential, for he was met and captured on the stolen horse by the party on horseback, about 16 miles from Perryville. He was taken back to Washington county, had a hearing and plead guilty to horse-stealing. His bad luck broke down his spirits and he gave his captors valuable information. He was placed in the U. S. jail at this place, escaped and fled to the Indian country, was pursued and killed by the officers in arresting him. This was the end of Hunton. Moore, although wounded [illegible] getting away. Hunton had told his captors where Moore could be found with a drove of cattle, then on its way from Texas to Missouri, and that Moore's wife was with said drove, and two of his "pals."

After the fight on Blue river Moore made his way to Caddo Station, got on the cars there and went to Eufaula, where he hired a darkey to take him to the camp of the cattle-drover. From here he sent one of his pals, named Nowlen, back to Fort Wayne to find out whether he and Hunton had been suspected; also to make arrangements for selling a drove of cattle! This Nowlen did, arriving at Cincinati, Ark., where he in disguise, passed himself off as owner of said drove, and chaffered for its feeding or sale; but, to his surprise, he was recognized and arrested. While a prisoner, he confessed all their wicked plans, and confirmed Hunton's statement that Moore was hid in his wagon at the camp of the drover. Being tolerably sure of their game-bird, two men here started after him. Moore was found as stated, in the camp of the drover, one mile east of Fort Gibson, near the National Cemetery, on the 10th of September, 1874. When arrested he was lying on his back in a ravine, and was so excited, or scared, that the sweat poured, and he was as wet as if drawn from a river. He begged them not to shoot. He was wounded in the leg, which he said he had received in the fight at Blue river. He thought that the party he fought on the Blue were from Texas, and was under that impression until told differently. Was curious to know how they had found him, and said that if Hunton had blowed on him and others, *he* was not going to tell anything only what concerned himself. He spoke freely afterwards; told of his birth, and the residence of his parents. Ever since a boy he had been a cow-herder in Western Texas, and had fought Indians who had wounded him twice in the same leg. That leg always got hit. If Spivy was killed, he was the eighth white man he had slain—niggers and Indians he did not count. If he ever got out of the scrape, he would go back to his old life; never intended to work for a living, but "would have it, if he had to war on civilization, as long as he [illegible]." When asked why he fired on Spivy and Irwin without giving them warning, he said that "he always done his fighting on the drop." "Some say that a horse-thief can't look a man in the eye; that's all played out; they can look a man square in the eye, and then fight for the horses after stealing them." His captors had his pistol. "He was willing to shoot against any man's rifle with that pistol, at sixty paces."

His "pal" Hunton also gave evidence of an organized band of horse thieves, that had been working their game for three years, giving many names, and what gave weight to his statements is the fact that several of the parties disappeared suddenly on hearing his arrest, and have not been heard of since. He also stated that Moore and his gang intended to

MURDER THE DROVER

after he had crossed the Arkansas river, and to drive the cattle north into Missouri and sell them and divide the proceeds. And it was this information which caused the citizens to take such intense interest in the safe arrival of the drove and the prevention of the foul murder, led them to persevere in the capture of Moore. Of the "pal" Nowlen we hope it is not impertinent to say, that he was introduced to a sheriff from Texas, who was so delighted with Nowlen's acquaintance that he insisted on having his company back home, presented him with a pair of [illegible] and it is said secretly paid his expenses to induce Nowlen to "get up" and go along with him!

Moore had the brazen effrontery to protest his innocence, and said he was 100 miles away from the scene of murder at Blue. Acknowledged that his parents had no control over him, and never went to school but little. Said Hunton was the bravest man he ever knew, was a good shot, but at times was so chicken-hearted as to let a single Indian steal from his herd.

Jim was a good specimen of the frontier outlaw and desperado. He was baptized, and paid respectful attention to spiritual advice.

DANIEL EVANS

was a stout and handsome young man about twenty years old, of light complexion, curly hair and blue eyes, and it is said that he has respectable connections in Missouri, Tennessee and Texas. He was arrested near Eufaula, Creek Nation. He was sentenced to die for killing a young man named Seabolt, near Eufaula, where Evans had a brother residing. His parents live in Bosque county, Texas, about 25 miles from Waco. In November last he started from Denison, Texas, in company with Seabolt, and when they arrived near Eufaula Seabolt was missed, and his body was not found for about a week. It was, however, identified by a pocket-book containing his name, and a patch worn over the left eye. Evans had been seen last in company with the deceased, and was ultimately found in possession of and riding the murdered man's horse, and strange to say, had on the dead man's boots at the time of his arrest, and wore them some time after, and gave the horse to one of his counsel as a fee. His demeanor during his trial and imprisonment, when not engaged in religious exercises, betrayed a gay, careless levity, which was painfully evident when he thanked the judge after hearing his terrible doom—"to be hanged until dead"—and smilingly went back to his cell and joked with his companions about the "jump."

According to his statements he had led a wild and reckless life in the Territory, and associated with outlaws.

"Good people all, I pray give ear,
A woeful story you shall hear.
'Tis of a robber stout as ever,
That bade six true men stand and deliver."
"Re tu re nu ri tooral a."

EVANS' STATEMENTS.

Dan Evans made the following rambling statements to our reporter. We give them as they are for what they may be worth; and for fear they may be the elegant invention of a fertile imagination, we shall not vouch for them. If they should be true in any part or particular, they may be interesting to those who may happen to know any of the facts. If not, we are not responsible. All we can [illegible] to protect his gentle memory from aspersion is, "Peace to his ashes;" here let him lie.

"I suppose I have to jump on the 3d of September. Just one year ago, on the 3d of September, 1874, I was in Bosque county, Texas, and went to a horse-race. There was a bloody fight took place on the ground and several men were killed.

"About 2 years ago I 'rode' with a young man named [illegible], from Mississippi. He was a splendid young fellow, a great dandy and good game. We got into a bad scrape and fight at Fort Belknap. He was shot and killed. I had just time to grab his diamond rings and get away. I sent them to his sister in Mississippi, as I had promised in case of accident to him.

"Sam Perkins was shot here in Ft. Smith. When I first met him he was on foot, ragged and his shoes worn out. I was flush, had 3 horses and plenty of money. I gave him a horse and 'rode' two years, on and off, with him. He was from Missouri. I think he was the bravest young man I ever saw, and had presence of mind. We got into a running fight at Stringtown, Texas; 5 men chased us; Perkins fired and killed 2 men running; he kept the butt of his rifle up at his breast and caught 2 bullets in the wood.

"When Jim Read was killed I was with him, but not in the house. He sat down to dinner and was eating when Morris drew on him and told him he was his prisoner; Jim said all right, and ducked under the table and raised it, throwing the dishes on Morris, and ran to the door, carrying the table on his back as a shield; Morris shot at him twice through the table and hit him twice; I heard the firing, knew what was up, got on Read's horse and sloped. Jim was an awful man; large rewards were offered for him in Texas; he had killed over 40 men in his time; he would kill a man for ten dollars."

Evans also stated that he had assisted in the Watt Grayson robbery over 2 years since in company with Read and Wilder, who was caught and sent to the penitentiary; that Jim Read had went to Watt's 3 times before but was afraid to try it on old Watt; that he (the prisoner) had stuck the burning pine knot to old Watt's feet; that they got $27,000, and that the money was buried in Texas, etc., etc. (Many of our readers may recollect the robbery of old Watt Grayson in the Indian country, when by means of torture the robbers compelled him to disclose the buried hoard and got away with some $30,000. One of the parties was arrested and sent up for 1 year. In order to "get his money back" the old man ought to have a "chance" by special dispensation from high authority, to take this fellow Wilder and choke and splinter him with pine splinters!)

SAMUEL W. FOOY,

Cherokee citizen, nearly white, age 26 years; rather below medium height; fair education. His family reside in the Cherokee Nation, near Webber's Falls. He was condemned partly on circumstantial evidence. Some of the facts are interesting and remarkable, and are as follows: A young white man named John Emmet Naff taught school in Tahlequah, in the Cherokee Nation, for which he received from his employers $250, and started off on a tramp to the Illinois river. Night overtook him at the house of one of Fooy's married sisters, named Mrs. Stevenson. In the morning Naff offered her a $5 bill to pay the fifty cents he owed for his lodging, but she not having change, he promised to leave the money for her at the store by the salt works, and in company with Sam Fooy he started off from the house on foot, and was never more seen.

About a year after a skeleton was discovered under a high bluff on the Illinois river, and said to have been shot in the back of the head, a bullet having been found imbedded therein; and subsequently, an Indian boy, looking around the fatal spot, found a book partially burned, with the name of the missing man written in German, his late residence, and other memoranda, also a quotation in Latin from Horace, book 1, ode 4, which reads thus in English: "Pale death treads with even step the hovels of the poor and the palaces of kings;" and other articles found near identified the remains as the missing schoolmaster.

Only a few weeks after the murder, Fooy confessed the crime to his brother-in-law, but begged him to keep the terrible secret; and he implicated himself by another statement to a young woman, and these facts, although kept from the public for some time, terminated in his conviction. We can only surmise that a terrible remorse preyed on him unceasingly.

"THE PIERCING SHRIEK, THE AGONIZING CRY,"

or the piteous and imploring gaze of the dying victim wrung his heart, and caused him to suffer in mind the torments of the damned, and he found no relief but in revealing the truth to those on whom he might depend for safety. The exhortations and prayers of pious friends have not been in vain, and Sam looks to the end with hope in the Savior of Mankind.

The following is a dream which occurred to Sam Fooy a few days before his execution, also his receipt for curing chills and fever:

SAM FOOY'S DREAM.

"I dreamed that I was on the gallows before a great crowd of people. I was sick and weak and felt like fainting, and I thought I could not face death. Just then a fellow stepped up from the crowd, came right up to me, and said, 'Look here, SAM, don't you be afraid to let them jump you. Jesus is standing under the floor and he will catch you in his arms!' I felt strong, and when the drop came I felt no pain, but fell asleep, and I woke up in a beautiful garden—the most beautiful place I ever saw, with running waters and stars dancing on the waves."

Fooy's Receipt for Curing Chills and Fever and Cough—Take a six-shooter, go into the Cherokee Nation, get into a difficulty, then take a dose of swing in the garrison yard.

EXPERIENCE.

WILLIAM JACKSON WHITTINGTON.

30 years old, born in Reynolds, Taylor county, Georgia; he was raised in Upshur county, Texas; has lived for 5 years past in the Chickasaw Nation, where his mother, wife and two children reside. He was farming for Simon James. There was a vile rum-shop on the Texas side of Red River; Whittington went over there in company with his friend and neighbor, old man Turner, on the Sabbath day, Feb. 7, 1875. Turner had unfortunately about $100 in cash in his pocket. After indulging freely in

BAD WHISKEY!

they started home and nearly arrived when Whittington, instigated by the devil, clubbed the old man from horse and

CUT HIS THROAT!

on the ground, not forgetting in his drunken fury to secure possession of the money. Now it providentially occurred, that old man Turner's son, a brave youth of 18, had ridden forth from home to meet his father, and while crossing a small prairie he saw a man in the distance with two horses in the edge of the timber, the man stooping as if engaged with some object on the ground. As soon as young Turner arrived on the spot he recognized Whittington, who instantly fled, and there on the ground before him laid the

BLEEDING CORPSE OF HIS FATHER!

He immediately gave chase to the murderer, whom he overtook and captured at Red River. Whittington's knife, covered with blood, was found near the body. The money was found with Whittington and identified as Turner's.

Whittington attributed all his errors to whiskey. He was resigned and penitent; said he was never, before, and might never, again, be so well prepared to die, and looked forward with humble Christian hope for his pardon through the Savior.—He was grateful for the attention of ministers and friends; spent much time in writing to his relations; he told our reporter that he was considered a good neighbor when sober, but drunk he was a devil; and would have slain his own brother; when under the influence of liquor he was furious and knew nothing; the whisky den he frequented was kept by a man named Ottery; it was a bad place and murders took place there frequently, a man being killed shortly after he was arrested. As to the murder for which he suffered, it might have occurred just as evidenced—he

DID NOT DENY IT.

SMOKER MANKILLER (INDIAN NAME).

A full-blood Cherokee of medium size, stout and well built; age 19; from Flint District, Cherokee Nation; has wife and one child; his mother, wife and two sisters visited him at the jail; they wept silently and made no noisy demonstration of sorrow; Smoker did not display any emotion; he sat through the interview in gloomy mood and but little was said in subdued voices. He was convicted for killing a white man named William Short, a neighbor, on the 1st day of September, 1874. Short was out hunting when he was met by the

MAN KILLER,

and after pleasant greetings the Cherokee borrowed his gun and

SHOT HIM DEAD!

No cause was assigned for the cruel, bold and treacherous deed. Our Indian brave had openly boasted of it and other evidences made the fact conclusive. There was a little too much of the "Tubbe" in this transaction, and our young would-be hero (?) was promptly arrested and suffered the penalty of the law.

Smoker Mankiller could not speak English, but was educated in Cherokee and could write very well in that language, and furnished our reporter a written statement in Cherokee, covering a sheet of foolscap. This paper we gave to our friend of the St. Louis *Times* as a curiosity. Smoker said he was not guilty of the murder, but was willing and anxious to die and be out of his trouble, but was firmly convinced that his execution was a

JUDGMENT OF GOD

on him for killing a Cherokee Indian who he killed in self defence some time before, but had been tried in the Nation and cleared.

EDMUND CAMPBELL (COLORED).

"Heck" was his nickname. He was born in the Choctaw Nation, about nine miles from Fort Smith, on the old Ring farm. He is 20 years old; can read print; has a wife and two children.

Ed. in company with his brother Frank Butler, and a younger one, went to the house of a colored neighbor named Ross, and, in revenge for some real or fancied wrong or insult, did slay and kill the said Lawson Ross, and a young colored woman, who was shot in the stomach. Ed and Frank were both found guilty of murder and sentenced to die. Frank made a daring and desperate attempt to escape from his guards, and was shot and killed, several weeks since.

Ed had experienced a change of heart, and was resigned to his fate. He claimed to be innocent of the charge, said his life had been sworn away, and complained bitterly of the witnesses who testified against him, "that plenty of niggers will swear to a lie for $10;" "don't think he was a bad man; never drank much whiskey nor played cards." During the interview his features expressed a strange admixture of fury and revenge, and his eyes suffused with tears would flash with excitement as he spoke; didnt want to get out for fear he might kill some of the liars who swore against him; besides he wanted to die and was ready and prepared and thought he would be saved through the blood of the Savior.

LIGHT AT LAST

On the Great Missouri Train Robbery.

KERRY WEAKENS AND CONFESSES ALL.

The James Boys and the Youngers in the Lead.

AN INTERCEPTED LETTER FURNISHES A CLEW.

The St. Louis Police in the Lead District—Down to Bed-Rock.

HOW THE TRAIN WAS ROBBED.

The Gang Dividing the Spoils—$1,200 Apiece.

Now that the excitement and sensational reports incident to the arrest of Bruce Younger and Hobbs Kerry, the supposed Otterville express robbers, have in a measure quieted down, it is but just to give the reading public a detailed statement of the history of the affair, and to place the credit of the arrest where it belongs.

Some weeks previous to the train robbery in question Chief McDonough, of the St. Louis force, had reason to believe that a band of outlaws contemplated a raid on the Granby Bank, and that their headquarters were situated at a place called Coalfield, not far distant from Granby, Newton county, that State. With a view to securing these thieves the Chief sent six picked men into said county to prospect, and gain all the information possible in the matter. After considerable hardship and expense, it was ascertained beyond a doubt that

THE YOUNGER AND JAMES BOYS

were arranging and perfecting plans in Coalfield to rob the Granby Bank by one of those bold dashes which have characterized their previous efforts. For some cause unknown the bank robbery was abandoned, and the officers quietly returned to St. Louis and resumed their regular duties. With the news of the train robbery, the Chief summoned the detail and made a careful review of the facts and incidents as presented at first flash. Becoming satisfied that the robbers of the train were the identical ones who had plotted for the burglarizing of the bank, the officers were started for Granby and Joplin. Hobbs Kerry and those of his ilk who had been in the neighborhood at the first visit of the officers, were absent, and it was learned had not been seen about for a number of days. This was satisfactory evidence, in the light of events, and the "cops" sat themselves down to await the return of the men. On the 26th of July Kerry returned to Granby, and soon succeeded in giving those on the watch additional cause to suspect him. He spent money freely, something rather singular for one of his walk in life, when it was known that he had earned little, and showed a deep interest in the facts relative to

THE TRAIN ROBBERY.

After consultation, it was not deemed advisable to arrest Kerry until some of his companions should put in an appearance, and it was confidently hoped by the Chief that he would be able to corral at least five of the robbers. Kerry remained about Granby in close company with Bruce Younger, for several days. Everything progressed favorably to the cause of the police until July 31, when it became evident that Kerry and Younger had "dropped" on the surveillance of the officers. They conducted themselves in such a manner as to lead to the impression that they intended leaving for some more congenial clime, and it was deemed advisable to make the arrest without delay. The order was executed, and the prisoners, in charge of the officers, arrived in St. Louis on the morning of August 1, being lodged in the Four Courts Calaboose. There they remained in close confinement until the evening of the 3d inst., at which time the Chief proceeded to Sedalia with them. After considerable trouble Kerry was fully identified by Mr. and Mrs. Duvall, living twelve miles from Sedalia, and at whose house he and three others had dined on the Sunday preceding the raid. J. M. Thatcher, agent of the Adams Express Company, and Larry Hagan, of Cincinnati, detective for the Express Company, closely questioned Kerry and importuned him to confess, but he stubbornly denied having anything to do with the robbery, and asserted vehemently in the presence of Mr. and Mrs. Duvall that he had not been in their section of the country for three years, and could prove an alibi by many of the best citizens of Granby. At this juncture, Chief McDonough drew forth from the deep recesses of an inside pocket

AN INTERCEPTED LETTER

of Kerry's, written by himself to one Stapp, a saloon-keeeper at or near Granby, in which reference is made to the proposed raid on the Granby Bank. The letter was captured by the officers in June last, and reads as follows:

COALFIELD, Kansas, June 9.—R. P. Stapp—Sir: I received your letter to-day and was glad to hear from you. Well, Dick, I am in little better spirits than I was when I wrote you before. I have heard from them again yesterday, and they will be here in a day or two, and we are going to do something. But they are very cautious, and are afraid of me and you. They think that it may be that we are fixing some trap to grab them. As it has been tried so often they are afraid of everybody. Charlie says he will fix that all right when they get to see me and talk to me, and it will be all right when we get acquainted with them. We will give them a good talk, and they won't be afraid of us then, but you know it stands them in hand to be careful, for they are not like us. They have to be on the lookout all the time and we don't. Dick, keep up courage, and we will have it some day yet, before long. Charlie and one of

THE "Y" BOYS

will come in a day or two before it takes place, and see you and look into everything. I will bring them right to you, and they will tell you about how it is to be done. So you rest easy, for I will see them about it day after to-morrow. We will all strike out for some place, and it is as liable to be Granby as any other place. So, Dick, if you see Bruce you may tell him it is all knocked in the head; that you got a letter from me, and I was going to the Nation to my brothers. I don't think he will get here any more with us, for I have not heard from him since I wrote to you before; but he will keep everything dark.

I will not have time to let him know about the boys being here. One of the boys that stays with me here got back yesterday, and came right from the boys Monday morning, and rode one of their horses back here. So you know we heard straight news from them, and Bill says they are red hot to do something, and you bet when I get to see them I will convince them that Granby is the best place and the easiest to get at, and they will come sure. Dick, don't you make a track you cannot cover up again, and don't get out of heart, for, as you said, if I can stand it you ought to, for something is bound to turn loose. Charles is getting wild, and so am I, and Bill won't work a damn lick, and is begging us all to go by ourselves. But we want to get them boys with us before we start. Well, Dick, if I had any paper I would write you more, but will have to close. H. KERRY.

To R. P. Stapp.

The reading of the letter was too much for Kerry. He listened attentively to the melodious voice of Chief McDonough as it rang through his cell, and when the conclusion was reached, visibly weakened. He evidently saw that the game was up, and the fact that the letter was in the possession of the officers was proof to his mind that his steps had been closely watched, and that there might be other evidences to follow. After some hesitancy, Kerry concluded to make

A CLEAN BREAST OF THE AFFAIR.

He said that he was a young man, and through Bruce Younger had been led into it, and would have to stand the consequences of his crime. Chief McDonough informed him that no promise of any kind would be made him in the premises; that his statements must be voluntarily made, and without hope of reward. The prisoner, whether with hope of saving himself from a portion of the punishment justly due for his crime, or in sheer desperation, made full confession of his connection with the robbery, and of the part played in it by the several actors engaged. The statement was taken down, sworn and subscribed to, in room No. 48 of the Ives House, Sedalia, August 4. It is as follows:

KERRY'S CONFESSION.

First of all, I left Granby and went to Joplin in the early part of the winter, or latter part of the fall, and there I got acquainted with Bruce Younger. Bruce told me about these boys, and was all the time talking about what they would do about the bank at Granby. The boys came there once while he was there—I mean Bob and Cole Younger, and I refer to Joplin. We stayed there all winter—that is, Bruce and I—and in the spring (May of this year) we went to Coalfield, and there I went to work in a coal bank, holding scrapers. Bruce did not like to work and went to Parli, while I remained and worked eight or nine days. Then I went to work for Scammons, a mile from Coalfield, at Scammon's Switch. I worked there until sometime in June. Don't know when I quit work. Bill Chadwick came. He had been where the Younger boys were, and said they were coming down. We staid there about a week, and as they did not come, Charlie Pitts, who was with me, said we would go up there and see the Younger boys. We got on our horses and started. This was in the latter part of June. We went to Monegaw Springs, but did not find them there, nor had they been there for some time. We then kept on up into Jackson county, and went to Dr. Donyman's, who is a relative of the Youngers. Charlie Pitts went into the house and left me and Bill Chadwick outside. The Younger boys were not there, but on the way back, when we had got within a half mile of Independence, and were riding abreast in a lane, we saw a man riding in the same direction we had come from, in a lane some distance away. When he saw us he turned into a cross lane and went north. We went to the road he had started north on, and saw him riding off, though he turned about frequently to watch us. I had never seen

ONE OF THE YOUNGER BOYS

up to that time in my life. Bill Chadwick said he believed it was Bub Younger—that is, Cole Younger. Charlie Pitts said he did not believe it was, and Bill said he was going to see. He rode some distance toward the man, who, when he got near enough, threw his pistol down on Bill and made him stop. Bill stopped, and the man made him throw up his hands and demanded to know what he wanted and who he was. Bill replied, "It's me, Bill Chadwick." The man then made him come up and tell who that was with him. He told him it was Charlie Pitts, and d'd not name me. He told him to go back and tell Charlie to come up to him. When Bill first went up to the man he said his name was Frank Jones, and said also that he thought he (Bill) was a damned detective, and had a notion to kill him. He told Bill to tell Charlie Pitts to come to him, and to come alone. Charlie went up to where he was. James told him to go to Dick Tyler's, in Jackson county. We started to Dick Tyler's that night, and, as it rained hard, we stopped in a school house all night. Next morning we went to Tyler's and found

COLE YOUNGER AND JESSE JAMES

there. They knew Charlie and Bill, though they did not know me. We stayed there that day, and in the evening started away, the five of us. We rode three or four miles and met Bob Younger and a man named Clem Miller. The four that were at Duvall's house were me, Clem Miller, Cole Younger and Charlie Pitts. I state this to show who was the four. We divided up, three in one gang and four in another. We four went to Mr. Kelly's, a brother-in-law of Cole Younger, and got there at daylight, next morning after our start. We stayed there all day and night, and started out next morning after breakfast. Before we left, Bob Younger and Charlie Pitts came up, they having stayed at the house of a man named Butler. We started out and rode five or six miles. There were me, Cole Younger, Charlie Pitts and Bill Chadwick. Clem Miller and Bob Younger stopped at Kelly's and waited for Frank and Jesse James to come up. After we had ridden five or six miles—we four—the rest caught up.

THE GANG COMPLETE.

We were now eight in number, and all that were directly or indirectly connected with the robbery. I did not know what I was going to do, nor did they; not a particle. Cole Younger, Frank James and Jesse James and Bob Younger did the talking. I judge the James boys were leading the party, because I heard Cole say to them, "You fellows suggested this." He was then talking to Frank and Jesse; "and I am just going with you," he said. We all got on our horses and started four in a crowd. Me and Clem Miller and Cole Younger and Charlie Pitts went together; Bill Chadwick, Bob Younger and Frank and Jesse Jame made the second crowd. We met, I don't know what day it was, at California, on the Missouri Pacific Railroad. It was on the 4th of July, I think. On the 5th it rained very hard and we staid there all day. On the 6th we started back west. We met about two miles from the Laramie bridge, on the east side, about 2 P. M. on Friday, the 7th inst. We staid there until evening, and then Bob Younger, Clem Miller and Charlie Pitts went down to take the watchman at the bridge. Me and Bill Chadwick rode up to the end of the field and tied our horses, and they told us to stay there. This was about fifty yards from where the train was stopped. In about half an hour they brought up the watchman, and I heard him say, "You ain't going to hurt me?" One of the party said, "What do we want to hurt you for; all we want is the money."

STOPPING THE TRAIN.

Probably half an hour elapsed before the train came. I do not know what kind of an obstruction they had before the train, for I did not see it. When the train passed us Bill Chadwick picked up a piece of rail and shoved it under the track. When the cars stopped the shooting commenced. We staid in the rear of the train. I suppose it was an hour before they started off and came down where we were on the bank in the oat field, near the track. There was but one shot fired where we were. As soon as we got together we took to our horses and started off, riding about twenty miles, to a point where we left the road and turned to the right. Clem Miller carried the bag with the money in it part of the time, while Cole Younger and Jesse James also took turns.

DIVIDING THE SPOILS.

About 200 or 300 yards from the road we stopped and divided the money. They tore all the envelopes open and put the money in a pile. Frank James counted it and gave each one his share. They left the envelopes there when they divided, some one carrying off the sack. My share of the money was $1200. After the divide we scattered.

Charlie, Bill and I kept together, and, after riding all day Saturday, forded Grand River in the night at a place where there is a ferry. There I left Charlie and Bill. I went from there to a station on the M., K. and T. Railway, called Montrose, on foot, having turned my horse loose and hid my saddle in the bush at Grand River. From Montrose I went to Fort Scott. I ate supper there, and then went to Parsons by railroad. I staid there over night, and then went to Vinita. From Vinita I went to Granby over the Atlantic and Pacific railroad. I staid in Granby from Monday, July 10, until Saturday, and then went to Joplin. I saw Bruce Younger there, and on Tuesday, July 18, started to the Nation to see my brother. Last Saturday I returned.

BUCKING THE TIGER.

I spent some money at Granby among the boys, I don't remember how much, may be $100. At Joplin I lost $400 bucking faro. I also played poker, and lost $125. When I was arrested I had $20. I lent Dick Stapp $100, and being drunk most of the time spent a great deal of money. Clem Miller lives in Clay county. I give this statement voluntarily, of my own free will, without any hope or promise of clemency.

(Signed) HOBBS KERRY.

Sworn to and subscribed before me, this, the 4th day of August, 1876, in presence of James McDonough and J. M. Thatcher.

N. M. DUVALL, J. P. of Pettis county, Mo.

Witnesses: James McDonough, Chief of Police of St. Louis, and J. M. Thatcher, Agent Adams Express Company, Sedalia, Mo.

BRUCE YOUNGER,

as has been stated, was detained several days in Sedalia, but as no one could identify him as a participant in the train robbery, he was released. The expedition started out before and after the train robbery was in command of Sergt. Boland, who has displayed unquestioned courage and excellent judgment throughout.

A BRAVE BOY.

He Thwarts Three Burglars and Secures their Arrest.

DETROIT, Aug. 7.—The town of Windsor is in a fever of excitement to-day over one of the boldest attempts at robbery which has been made there for several years. The place where the trouble occurred is a banking exchange office kept on Ouillette avenue, near the post-office, by J. W. Holton, who is assisted in the business by his 18-year-old son, John F. Holton. At about 8 o'clock this morning three men, named Robert Webb, William Schweitzer, and John Morgan, drove up to the bank in a buggy, and while Morgan remained outside to hold the horse, Schweitzer and Webb entered for the ostensible purpose of getting a $2 Canadian note changed into American money. Young Holton was alone behind the counter at the time, and while busy at the cash drawer saw the man Webb slipping around the end of the counter with his evil eye fastened upon the safe and its contents. With one bound young Holton was in front of the robber, who pointed a cocked revolver full at his head, and commanded him, if he loved his life, to "show up" immediately. "Never!" cried the plucky youth, and beating up the muzzle of the revolver with his outstretched arm, the bullet intended for his brain dashed harmlessly by and buried itself in the wall. With a cry of baffled fury the robber wheeled and fled out of the door, and leaping into the buggy with his two companions, lashed the horse into a run. There were few persons on the street at that time, but several men who were standing on a corner near by had heard the pistol shot, and seized the horse as he came rushing past. The three robbers leaped from the back of the buggy and fled up Pitt street to Lower Ferry, and thence by Chatham street, Sutton's fruit garden, on the corner of London street and Victoria avenue. A mob of excited citizens followed close upon their heels and fired several ineffectual shots at them as they ran. The fugitives took refuge in a large asparagus bed, and from their place of concealment blazed away at their pursuers as the latter were leaping the fence, but luckily no one was injured, and in a few moments Webb and Morgan had been captured and turned over to the Windsor police, who came tardily up, but in time to put an end to the threats that were made of lynching the prisoners on the spot.

Schweitzer, however, did not propose to yield up his liberty so easily, and leaping the fence at the southwest corner of the garden, he travelled along the street-car track toward Sandwich at the top of his speed. Several citizens on foot and a negro mounted on a horse followed in hot pursuit, and were from time to time made the target of Schweitzer's revolver, whose nerves were either very unsteady or else his aim was atrociously bad, for all his bullets flew wide of their mark. The man upon the horse had not the courage to overtake and seize the flying robber, and finally gave up his saddle to a citizen named Edward Bennett, who galloped a short distance beyond Schweitzer, and leaping to the ground, met him face to face. The desperate and panting thief pointed his empty pistol at the man who had stepped between himself and freedom, but Bennett was not to be intimidated, and after a short, fierce struggle, Schweitzer was secured and conveyed to the police station, where his companions were already confined.

Webb is a fugitive from London, Ont., where a few months ago he was concerned in the shooting of a boy. The sheriff of London had arrived in Windsor this very morning in search of him. Morgan is a well-known Chicago cracksman, and Schweitzer is the identical Potomac ruffian who assaulted Officer Packard on Franklin street several months ago, and has since been living in Windsor to avoid arrest. The fate of these three worthies can easily be guessed at, for the laws of Canada are merciless in regard to such a crime as that committed by them this morning. They may deem themselves especially favored if they escape with less than fifteen years' imprisonment.

A New York paper offers as premiums for its subscribers, an annual cutting of the hair or quarterly vaccination free, and to those who pay three years' subscription in advance a coffin at death, or, when it is preferred, a half a dozen silver plates. There can be no doubt as to the truth of this, for it is printed in a Paris newspaper.

ITEMS OF INTEREST.

—Doing a dun was neatly accomplished in India recently, the debtor handling his case so well as to secure the incarceration of the creditor who did nothing irregular but lay violent hands on himself. "A Brahman of the Brahmans," finding it impossible to collect a claim against a fellow resident of Allahabad, announced that he would sit at his door until the demand should be complied with, "or heaven release him from his sufferings, and so cast the blood of the holy upon the head of the obdurate." Sitting failed to accomplish the desired result, and he desired to live no longer on earth with the stiff-necked, and, seizing a handful of dust from the threshold of his oppressor, he leaped head foremost into the village well. His terrified opponent rushed to the mouth of the well, and, full of the appearance of remorse, implored the man whom he had injured to seize the rope he would cast him, ascend to the surface of the earth, and all would again be well. The holy man availed himself of the rope, was hauled to the mouth of the well, and, instead of being paid his debt, was immediately handed over by his adversary to the police on the charge of attempting to commit suicide.

—The Keokuk Gate City broaches the following proposition for the punishment of the crime against women: "This crime could easily be stopped by law. Let the law provide that every man guilty of rape, or attempted rape, shall, in addition to imprisonment, be unsexed. A penalty of this kind upon the statute books of the State, enforced in every instance where the crime is committed or attempted, will soon make women secure again in their homes, on the street, on the highway, everywhere. The law in its present treatment of crime is foolishly and unphilosophically indifferent to all the disclosures of modern science as to the propagation of crime. We hold it to be the duty of the State to apply the law of natural selection and inheritance to the treatment of social evils. Let the State by its penalties adjust its policy to prevent the propagation as well as the perpetration of crime."

—The Bravo poisoning case which is now occasioning so much excitement in London, is a rich mine for the lawyers, according to Mr. Jehnings. Sir Henry James receives a fee of $500 a day for attending on behalf of Mrs. Bravo. She has also another counsel who receives $100 a day. She also pays the expenses of the counsel who watch the case on behalf of her late "companion," Mrs. Cox, amounting to $375 a day. Dr. Gully's counsel cost him at least $400 a day. Then Mr. Bravo, the stepfather of the deceased, is represented by Mr. Lewis, one of the keenest lawyers in London, and a man who can conduct almost as searching a cross-examination as Judge Fullerton himself. All this is, of course, apart from the expenses of witnesses and other incidental costs of proceedings. If, therefore, they do not succeed in finding out who and what killed Mr. Bravo, it will not be for lack of trouble, time or money.

—A hanging draws well in South Carolina. On the day appointed for hanging Jerry Coleman, at Abbeville, 5000 spectators, black and white, swarmed into the town to see the show. During the morning there was a dance near the jail-yard to the music of a hoarse fiddle, there were several amateur prize-fights, and liquor was on tap everywhere. The jolly spectators were doomed to disappointment. There was no free show; the curtain fell, but not the man; the Governor signed a reprieve.

—Twelve thousand pounds of "C" sugar at ten and one-fourth cents, 10,000 pounds of bacon at eleven and one-fourth cents, 6,000 pounds Rio coffee at twenty-one and one-half cents, and 1,000 pounds half-bright navy tobacco at fifty-five cents passed through Sioux City the other day for the noble red man. The object is to keep the Indians in good trim for murdering soldiers and settlers.

—The trial of Christos Baumbos, the Greek sailor concerned in the Caswell mutiny, took place at Cork recently. The evidence was clear and Mr. Justice Lawson charged directly against the prisoner, but the obstinacy of one juror forced a disagreement. Baumbos was at once placed on trial again, convicted and sentenced to be hanged on the 25th.

—The prisons of Denmark are mostly conducted on the solitary confinement system; yet the prisoners are frequently visited by the officers, whose influence, in theory if not in practice, is exerted to effect reformation of character. The convicts never see each other, and thus are free from contamination.

—William B. Hunt, of Iowa, is the champion rascal. He has a wife and child in nearly every considerable town in the United States east of Kansas. His latest are at Portland, Me. He marries a girl, remains with her for two days, and then leaves. His principal occupation is that of hotel clerk, and he is very handsome.

—The Czar of Russia has abolished public executions, which have hitherto been preceded by an exhibition of the condemned criminal on a black cart with a placard round his neck through the principal streets of the city, besides a parade for ten minutes under the gallows. In future executions will be within the prison walls.

—Mayor Cobb, of Boston, recently gave a position on the police force to a young man who had graduated at Harvard College and the Harvard Medical School The applicant was a practicing physician, but found himself unable to provide the barest necessaries of life for his wife and child.

—Thomas Cox, a 'longshoreman at New Orleans, has saved eleven persons from drowning during the past two years. His latest exploit was the rescue of a woman and two boys who had been upset in a skiff some distance from the shore, and was effected at the imminent peril of his life.

—The Newburyport Herald says the oldest man in the town is ninety-four. He never had a mortgage on his house, never compromised with his creditors, never held public office and stole the funds entrusted to him, and never wrote poetry for the newspapers.

—A Cairo gambler, who recently married a prostitute, released the soiled dove from her allegiance to him, that she might have no hindrance in plying her vocation, on the payment of $30, the other day.

—Fuchs, the murderer of Mr. Simmons, of Derby, Conn., converted a rasp file into a knife, and threatened to cut out the intestines of a fellow convict who had refused him a chew of tobacco.

—There are at this time 1050 convicts boarding at the Tennessee penitentiary. Of these 620 are hired out in various portions of the State, and 430 are hammering away within the walls of the prison.

—An Oakland lunatic carried a butcher-knife around for two hours, offering to kill any one who said he wasn't Moses. Every one said he looked just like Moses.

—"We have plenty of soldiers to whip the Indians."—[General Sheridan. Yes; just so; why don't *you* whip them once or twice for a change?

—The warden of the enlightened Pennsylvania penitentiary is training some model bloodhounds to catch fugitive convicts.

Saint Paul Daily Dispatch.

VOL. IX | ST. PAUL, MONDAY, SEPTEMBER 25, 1876. | NO. 178

Three O'Clock P.M.

By Telegraph

ROBBERS

DEAD AND LIVING

Six of Them Taken

By Dispatch Artists

Third Dead Robber Identified.

The Three Prisoners Recognized

Crowds at the State Capitol.

Detectives' Trip to Faribault.

History of the Younger Family.

All That's Going Worth Knowing

The Dead Robber at the Capitol.

Saturday afternoon, after it was known that a dead bandit, a real flesh and blood villain, that was a member of the most desperate, bloody, and dashing gang of robbers and cut-throats the world ever knew, was in St. Paul, the excitement was intense and hundreds sought access to the State Capitol where Surgeon General Murphy was engaged in embalming the brigand in order to preserve him for identification.

To be relieved of the crowding, impet-

Cole Younger--Captured Near Madelia.

uous mob, in an unguarded moment it was given out that the body would be on exhibition yesterday (Sunday) from 10 A. M. to 4 P. M. in the capitol. This news spread rapidly, and early yesterday morning a crowd began to assemble, so that at 10 o'clock at least two thousand people surrounded the stately red brick barn. In the meantime, it had been decided, after

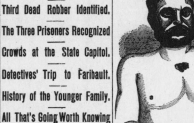

Al Carter--Captured Near Madelia.

a sober second thought and the protest of calm minded citizens, that it was scarcely proper that a dead

ROBBER SHOULD LIE IN STATE.

in the building devoted to making the laws of which the man was a sworn opposer, and it was especially considered improper to hold such a ghastly exhibition on a Sunday, hence the matinee was postponed until to-day, when thousands have looked upon the bloated features of the desperate outlaw.

Texas Jack.

The assembled crowd yesterday consisted of people of all classes, and a large proportion were women and children. It

Bob Younger--Captured Near Madelia.

was eminently a well behaved assemblage, and took its disappointment quietly. While the crowd was the greatest, Mr. J. B. Omolumdro, Texas Jack, sauntered up gay moccasins, a broad trimmed sombrero, and a brilliant silk handkerchief tied carelessly around his neck, his long black locks flowing freely over his shoulders. His costume was evidently new, and was probably the Sunday-go-to-meeting dress which he dons on special occasions when he wishes to produce an effect on the susceptible hearts of fair Indian maidens. As this bright-eyed representative of old Leather Stocking came in sight, walking between two friends, it was whispered around that one of the living bandits was coming, and instantly the innocent and accomplished scout was surrounded by

AN ADMIRING MOB.

The fences were mounted, and even ladies climbed up to the dangerous iron pickets to catch a glimpse of the handsome Indian fighter. The information that the stranger was the famous Texas Jack, however, soon spread, but the curiosity

Charley Pitts--Killed Near Madelia.

was not allayed, as his fame made the public anxious to see him. Jack knew the James brothers, and was to have looked at the body, but when he found that it had been identified as Charley Pitts, he passed quietly away to his hotel.

Identification of the Dead Robber.

By the morning train there arrived Mr. James McDonough, chief of police at St. Louis; a member of the police force of that city; and Mr. C. B. Hunn, superintendent of the U. S. Express Company. These gentlemen came for the purpose of establishing the identity of the robbers. They were satisfied that those killed at Northfield were Bill Chadwell and Clel. Miller, immediately recognizing their photographs.

CHIEF MCDONOUGH

is a straight fleshy gentleman, with a military bearing, a keen eye, and the appearance of a man possessed of the exec-

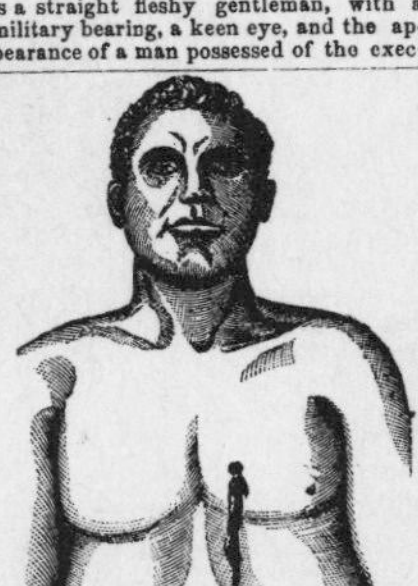

Clell Miller--Killed in Northfield.

utive ability requisite to control and conduct so great a force of men, (over five hundred,) as compose the splendid police force of the city of St. Louis. He had obtained from Hobbs Kerry, one of the gang engaged in the bold raid on the train at Otterville, Mo., July 7th, detailed descriptions of the other members of the gang; and early yesterday morning he visited the capitol to view the body lying there. As soon as he looked upon it he recognized it as

CHARLEY PITTS,

whose real name is George Wells. Every mark was found as detailed by the captured robber, and the Chief was evidently pleased to find that he had succeeded in getting so much very valuable data of one of the members of a gang whose honor is pledged not to "peach" on their comrades. One of the most noticeable peculiarities of Pitts, who is a man of most powerful build,

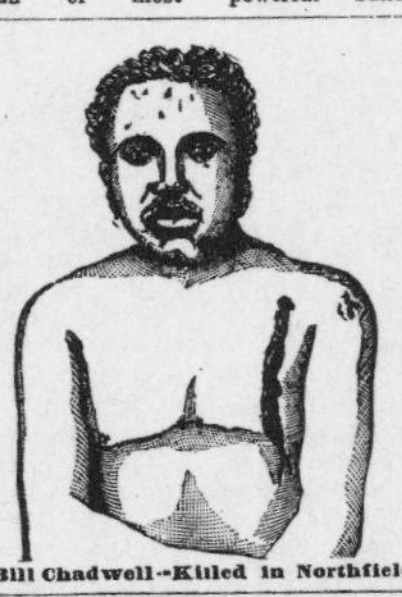

Bill Chadwell--Killed in Northfield.

is his extremely short, thick feet. They require but number 5 boots, and look greatly inadequate to support the ponderous form above. His hands, which are also small and fat, were roughened by work, and covered with black hair, exactly as Kerry had said. From Mr. McDonough it was learned that Pitts is one of the men who are summoned when "dirty work" is on hand. His home is in Texas, and he is known as one of the boldest and most successful horse thieves in the country. His knowledge of horses is so great that the care of the stock of the gang is always confided to him.

Detectives' Trip to Faribault.

Having decided the identity of Pitts, the officers returned to the Merchants hotel, and it was arranged that a special train should be procured to transport them, in company with several officials of this city, and a few well known citizens, to Faribault to interview his

BROTHERS IN CRIME.

was entirely a private arrangement, were Chief McDonough, Mr. Russell and Superintendent Hunn of the United States Express company, all of St. Louis; Mayor Maxfield, Chief King, Capt. Webber, Capt. Macy, Dr. Murphy, Col. John L. Merriam, his son, W. R. Merriam, cashier of the Second National bank, and Master John L., Jr., who was with his father at the time of the Gad's Hill robbery, three years ago; Superintendent Lincoln, who was also a victim of the same raid, Col. Hewitt, R. C. Munger, H. H. Spencer of W. & R. R.; Mr. John Ames, of Northfield; Messrs. Johnston and Yates of Madelia, and several others. At Mendota Junction a train consisting of a sleeping coach and box car joined the expedition, bringing a party of about forty from Minneapolis, among whom were Mayor Ames, Chief Munger, Hon. R. B. Langdon, Charles Prior; Hon. C. A. Gilman of St. Cloud; M. P. Hawkins, W. J. Pence, S. H. Jumper, Jerry Coughlin, H. F. Brown, J. H. Conkey, Ossian Henry, and Thomas King of the P. P. T. The Minneapolis party was accompanied by

A LARGE NUMBER OF LADIES

who desired to look upon the desperate fellows, but who evinced no more curiosity than their male comrades.

The run to Faribault was accomplished at about 4 o'clock. During the ride a most open discussion of the situation of the affair took place, and there was no concealment of the disappointment felt of any of the bandits being taken alive, and the desire was freely expressed that the three

BLOODY BANDITS

would not be permitted to take advantage of the clemency which the laws of Minnesota afford to a self-convicted murderer.

The news that a special train was *en route* had been kept so quiet that on arriving at Faribault no persons were at the depot except the officers of the road and Mr. Case, with several conductors. It had been arranged that only a select few should visit the jail with the detectives, and but eight persons, including the Dispatch representative, were admitted, the remainder of the party separating and seeking a lunch before they interviewed the outlaws.

During the entire day there had been a constant stream of visitors from the adjacent country, who came in all sorts of conveyances, the citizens of Faribault giving way to them and awaiting a quieter time to call on their distinguished guests.

The jail was surrounded by men and women when the chosen delegation arrived, but by an arrangement with Sheriff Barton the crowd was restrained, and the St. Louis gentlemen, Mayor Maxfield, Chief King, Capt. Macy, Dr. Murphy, Messrs. Lincoln and Merriam and representatives of the St. Paul dailies were admitted.

Just here it must be remarked that all were impressed with the apparent

INSECURITY OF THE JAIL

in which these desperate outlaws are incarcerated. The windows are within easy access from the ground, and the building looks as if a strong man could with his shoulder prostrate the walls from the inside.

On reaching the interior it was found that there was but one row of cells in the low one-storied building, perhaps five or six. These were surrounded by a grating of inch iron rods, and the only protection of the blocks of stone that composed the walls, was of sheet iron.

On entering, Bob Younger was found sitting near the corner of the cage, quietly smoking a cigar with a newspaper on his lap. Cole was lying on a pallet at the end of the twenty foot jail outside the cage, with a cigar in his mouth and a daily paper before him. The lazy bandit was bemoaning his lot, and seemed wonderfully comfortable. The third man was lying on a cot, just inside the bars, and was evidently suffering severely from the wounds in his side.

Cole Younger was found to be communicative as usual. Chief King showed him pictures of the two James boys, taken eight years since, and he immediately knew them, but said nobody would recognize them from those pictures now. On looking at his own picture he acknowledged it as one of the best he ever had taken, but when he was shown that of Charley Pitts, he said he knew no man of that name. Chief King said, "But you know this man as Wells," when Cole remarked, "There are Wellses in every part of the country."

At this time Mr. Ames, of Faribault, Cole was asked what part he took in the affair at Northfield. He declined to tell. Mr. A. then said he thought he saw Cole ride a white horse, and was the man that shot the Swede. Cole denied that he shot anybody. Mr. Ames observed this. Ames said that he was the best horseman of the crowd. Younger then said one man was as good a rider as another. He was raised on a saddle, his father having been a herder and stock man, and besides he had served several years in the cavalry. The gentlemen then spoke of the killing of Heywood as a cowardly act. Cole said it was the result of impulse, as they did not intend to kill anybody. Their plan was to accomplish their ends by dash, and boldness, and to go to the robbing while men were frightened. This was denied by the Northfield man, who claimed that they tried hard to kill Manning. Cole said that they did not try to kill him, using his name as if he knew all about it, but fired all around him. Mr. Ames said that could not be true, as shots were found in the railing of the stairs behind which Manning stood. Younger denied this, and said they desired to kill no man, as it would be of no use to them. Ames then said he believed that they had killed a hundred men, when Cole said he had no time to talk with such a man, he had been captured ter than he deserved, that he did not fear death, but hoped to be prepared for a better world. He said he was tired and needed rest. At this an impulsive gentleman standing by said he wished he would soon take his long rest. This seemed offended at this and said it was "of no use to talk to illiterate people, they could not

APPRECIATE A SUBLIME LIFE!"

Cole said he did not ride his fine horse up here, but bought the one he rode of French at Saint Peter. When told by a visitor that they did bad shooting, he said if they could get up at the side of the road he would plug his hat with his left hand at ten rods every time. He said he was the man that took the pistols from the dead man at Northfield, and said he took his handkerchief out of his belt as he took it off. He declined to tell name of dead man, as it was understood none should tell about another dead or alive.

Col. Merriam sat by the side of Cole, and said, "Younger, I am not certain, but I think I have seen you before." "Where was this?" said Cole. The Colonel said it was at Gad's Hill three years ago when the raid was made on the train. This judge and was a member of the legislature, and also to a minister there. He further said that on the day of that raid he and his brother Robert were there and that he preached in the afternoon, commencing at four o'clock.

The Escape of the James Brothers.

[Special Telegram to the Dispatch.]

MANKATO, Minn., 9:30 A. M., Sept. 25.—Sheriff Finch and party returned this morning from their pursuit of the James brothers, considering the chase hopeless. They say the two men are so weak that they are obliged to get on to fences to mount their horses, but they have the advantage of the pursuers in being able to get fresh horses, which the pursuers cannot do. There are still parties out from Sioux City and other places looking for them.

The Younger Family.

From a volume entitled "The Guerrillas of the West; or the True Life, Character and Daring Exploits of the Younger Bros., James Boys and Quantrell;" issued from St. Louis, we gather the following points in the history of the Youngers, two of whom, at least, are now in jail at Faribault. The book is evidently from the pen and brain of

SOME FRIEND OF THE FAMILY

and represents things in their most favorable light for the Youngers.

Col. Henry Younger, the father, was born in Crab Orchard, Ky., moving to Missouri when quite a young man and settling in Jackson county. About 1830 he married, the fruits of the union being a large family of boys and girls, four of the latter being now married to men of standing and wealth in their respective localities. Of the boys living to the age of majority there were Richard, Thomas Coleman, James Henry, John and Robert Ewing Younger.

Col. Younger, in 1858, moved to near Harrisonville, Cass county, Mo. He figured conspicuously in politics, in which he incurred the bitter enmity of men of opposite belief during the Kansas-Nebraska trouble.

Upon the breaking out of the late war, he owned a large livery stable at Harrisonville, was also doing a general merchandising business in the town, and had two large and valuable farms, one of about 600 acres in Jackson county.

Actual hostilities commenced, Colonel Younger espoused the cause of the union, but notwithstanding, so bitter was the feeling against him, that on one of the raids into Missouri in 1861, by the Kansas jayhawkers, lead by Jennison, Col. Younger's livery stable was sacked and property valued at $20,000 run off. In September of the following year, while going to Harrisonville to deposit a large sum of money, he was

WAYLAID AND ASSASSINATED.

To avenge his death the younger boys, under the lead of Cole Younger, became outlaws. To better carry out their plans of revenge the boys joined the famous Missouri guerillas, under the lead of Quantrell, though often engaging in individual enterprises for meteing out vengeance to the slayers of their father.

In 1864 Cole joined the Confederate army, going South with Gen. Price as captain of a company, finally going into Louisiana, where he was when the war closed. Up to this time, it is claimed,

THE BROTHERS HAD KILLED

all the men supposed to have been engaged in the assassination of their father.

The war ended, Cole, with fifteen of his men, including his brother James, went to Mexico, from whence they returned in 1866, settling down on the Harrisonville farm, to repair the ravages and waste caused by the war, the brothers setting themselves vigorously at work.

Soon after their return the Missouri militia and survivors of the Kansas jayhawkers began a

A WAR OF EXTERMINATION

against Quantrell's men, and especially the Younger boys, resulting finally in making the brothers homeless wanderers, since which their career has been one of unexampled crime, perpetrated with a boldness and dash that makes the exploits of Dick Turpin, Jack Shepard, and others of the famous highwaymen of the olden time, sink into significance beside them.

To give even a brief mention of these crimes would occupy more space than we can give to it at this time. Suffice it that bank after bank was robbed, trains of cars halted and the passengers relieved of their valuables, and other deeds of violence committed that made

THEIR NAMES A TERROR

to the country, resulting in large rewards for their capture, dead or alive, the various rewards for Cole alone aggregating $27,500. One of these railroads raids—that at Gad's Hill, Missouri—is especially fresh in the minds of our people from the fact that Hon. John L. Merriam and John F. Lincoln, superintendent of the St. Paul & Sioux City railroad, were among the victims.

It is proper to say that the brothers positively deny any connection with many of the crimes charged to them.

In 1875 a preamble and resolution was introduced into the Missouri Legislature—the preamble reciting the various crimes charged against the brothers, and the resolution

GRANTING THEM AMNESTY

and restoration to citizenship. The movement was ably advocated and resulted in the most exciting debate ever known in that body, at the end of which the resolution was defeated by a small majority. While it was under discussion the brothers abstained from any overt acts against the peace, though compelled to keep in hiding. That effort failing, with heavy rewards for their capture, with almost every man a spy upon their movements, with the whole detective force of the country on the alert for their capture, they have been wanderers, fighting with big odds against them for existence, their career for the present, at least, culminating with their visit to this State, their dash on the Northfield bank with the murder of the lamented Heywood, their chase, capture at Madelia and incarceration in the Rice county jail at Faribault.

Col. Merriam feels sure that Cole was there, judging from his figure, his hair, and particularly by his voice. Mr. Lincoln is also certain that he is one of the men on the train at that time, although he wore a cloth with eye holes over his face. Master Merriam, who was also on the train, is not certain, but thinks he has seen the villain.

Bob Younger was asked if he was in the Gad's Hill raid, but denied it, saying he was in Louisiana at that time, thus contradicting Cole. Bob says he is a novice and has only been in a few scrapes.

While some of the visitors were talking with the boys, Mr. McDonough doubtful. It is felt certain that he is not a Younger, as James was badly wounded in the hip on the 7th of July last, and could not possibly be able to stand a campaign like this at present. There is little doubt but that he is

AL. CARTER,

a Texas desperado, and one that has seldom worked with the gang until lately.

Every point of identification as given by Hobbs Kerry was discovered on the Younger boys, even to the ragged wound on Bob's hand, where the thumb had been torn off and badly attended to.

Dr. Murphy says none are dangerously injured and "are sure to get well unless he doctors them." He made a careful examination and says these are only flesh wounds, so the men can be about in a few days. None of the prisoners are shackled, and as the reporter came out, the last one of the visitors, Cole Younger got up from his bed and walked across the jail as lively as he. They have communicated with each other and it is to be feared that Sheriff Barton does not realize the peril he is in. A fire at one end of Faribault, and a raid of ten determined men would free the desperadoes, and as they are playing baby and working for sympathy it is to be hoped that all attempts at rescue will be prevented.

Lying in State.

Charley Pitts, the dead bandit, still holds his *post mortem* levee at the Capitol. To-day a constant stream of people passed through the gates and gazed on the features of the dead as they were exhibited in all their repulsiveness on a table in the small room on the left as you ascend the stairs in front of the main entrance. The visitors were not by any means confined to the masculine portion of our citizens, but including many ladies of evidently a respectable sphere in life, who commented in audible voices on the appearance of the defunct murderer. Is it not about time that this exhibition was put a stop to, or that at least, if it must go on, be confined to men of mature age, excluding females and children?

Robber Notes.

At Faribault, yesterday, Bob Younger asked the reporter to point out Mike Hoy to him. He said he was curious to see him, and was sure he heard his voice in the crowd. As Mike was not there it is probable that he mistook the voice of Mayor Ames of Minneapolis who led the squad that flushed the camp at Minneopa for him, and who gave the order "keep to the right."

As the reporter left the jail yesterday he encountered an old lady and her daughter who were struggling to get in and demanding that they be allowed to see the "Munger brothers." Their attention was directed to Mr. Russ Munger of this city and Chief Munger of Minneapolis, who happened to be together, but she was not satisfied, as she felt that she ought to find them inside the stone walls

On returning from Faribault yesterday a vote was taken to decide what disposition should be made of the bandits, with the following result: Hang them, 71; not hang them, 6; doubtful, 3. All the ladies voted for hanging except one, who voted to "hang all except Bob."

Just before the train reached St. Paul, a vote of thanks was unanimously passed to Superintendents Lincoln, of the St. Paul and Sioux City, and Prior, of the Chicago, Milwaukee & St. Paul railroads for their generosity and promptness in furnishing every facility in their power to aid in the pursuit of the robbers. The motion was put by Mayor Maxfield and universally endorsed.

The train arrived back at 8 o'clock, satisfied with a trip unexpected but pleasant.

A man from St. Louis, who is thoroughly acquainted with the Youngers and Carter, will arrive to-night and proceed to Faribault with Chief McDonough.

This morning O. H. Whipple, Esq., of Faribault, came up with a requisition for sixty stand of arms, with which a special guard for the jail wherein are the robbers will be armed. The requisition was promptly filled, and parties contemplating the exercise of lynch law might as well understand that such a proceeding will be extremely hazardous after to-night.

The St. Louis chief of police was heard to remark this morning that he only wanted to see Bob Younger. He could not see now in h—ll he could have left Missouri and he not know it. It seems the St. Louis detectives supposed all the time they had these Younger brothers corraled in that State, but it now appears they have been operating in Minnesota for the last six weeks.

A lady and gentleman of Iowa having heard that the dead robber would be on exhibition at the capitol yesterday, came up purposely to see the wonderful show, and failing to get into the capitol, attended church at Dr. Parrott's, perfectly contented to stand the expense and stay in town another day to see Charley Pitts.

THE EASTERN WARS.

The Armistice Ended at Midnight—Servia, Under Guidance of Russians, Prepared for Resumption of Hostilities.

[Special Telegram to the Dispatch.]

LONDON, Sept. 25.—The *Standard's* special from Belgrade Sunday evening says: No news is received of a conclusion of the armistice, yet England's basis for pacification will fall through. The Russians are determined to carry on the war at any cost. The truce, which ends at midnight will be followed by the immediate resumption of hostilities. Preparations were making here this morning for a continuence of war, glaringly at variance with the efforts to make peace.

The Welcome of a Catholic Bishop to His Diocese.

OMAHA, Neb., Sept. 25.—Right Rev. James O'Connor, who was lately consecrated bishop of this Catholic diocese, arrived here Saturday night. All the public Catholic institutions of the city were illuminated, the bells rung and there were many other manifestations of welcome and joy. Bishop O'Connor was yesterday installed in the cathedral. Immense crowds thronged the building and gathered outside. Priests from all parts of the diocese were present. Bishop O'Ryan, of St. Louis, conducted the services.

The river has risen six inches since Saturday. Weather clear and warm.

Spotted Tail Sioux Agree to the Treaty—Hostiles Coming In.

[Special Telegram to the Dispatch.]

FORT LARAMIE, Sept. 25.—The Sioux

SUPPLEMENT TO FRANK LESLIE'S ILLUSTRATED NEWSPAPER

No. 1,124—Vol. XLIV.] NEW YORK, APRIL 14, 1877. [Supplement Gratis.

JUSTICE AT LAST!

EXECUTION OF JOHN D. LEE

FOR COMPLICITY IN THE MOUNTAIN MEADOWS MASSACRE.

THE circumstances of the terrible Utah tragedy of twenty years ago, known as the Mountain Meadows Massacre, are familiar to our readers, as well as the fact of the Mormon elder, John D. Lee having atoned for his complicity in the affair, on March 23d, by his life. The details of this summary, if somewhat tardy, vindication of justice, have been published, with their terribly dramatic accompaniments. The proceedings attending Lee's execution were conducted with appropriate gravity and decorum. It had been determined by the authorities that the execution should take place on the spot where the massacre had occurred, and, accordingly, the prisoner was conveyed, on Wednesday, March 21st, from his prison in Beaver City, the subject of our illustration last week, to the hill-surrounded plain, known as Mountain Meadows. He was in the custody of Marshal Nelson, with an armed guard. The party camped out on Thursday night, and, after making several brief halts along the road, reached Mountain Meadows about ten o'clock, on Friday, the 23d.

Scene of the Massacre.

No more dreary scene can be imagined than those Mountain Meadows. From the point of the massacre to the emigrant-camp measures a distance of about a mile and a half. The meadows are cut up nto deep gullies and covered with sage brush and scrub oak. At the lower part, where the emigrants were encamped, is seen Murderers' Spring, the point where the first acts of the assassins were perpetrated. This spring was twenty years ago on a level with the surrounding country; but it has since been washed until it forms a terrible gulch some twenty feet in depth and eight or ten rods wide.

Coming down to the easterly bank of this ravine is the monument of loose stones erected by Lieutenant Price about thirteen years ago. Some of these stones have slid down the declivity. The ravine monument is oblong in outline and about twenty feet in length, being some three feet high. Under the monument at the time of its erection were placed all the bones that could be obtained on the field; but on removing some of the stones, down to the level of the earth, no trace of bones was dis covered.

JOHN D. LEE, THE MORMON ELDER, SHOT, MARCH 23D, FOR COMPLICITY IN THE MOUNTAIN MEADOWS MASSACRE—TAKEN JUST BEFORE HIS EXECUTION.

Counting the military escort, tne marshal and his deputies, and a few officials, there were probably eighty persons present. A singular feature was the presence of a photographer, who accompanied the solemn band, provided with his camera and paraphernalia, for the purpose of taking pictures of Lee in his last moments, and of the scene of the execution. As soon as the party arrived at the scene of the massacre a halt was called and Lee was ordered to descend from the wagon in which he rode. Before the arrangements for his execution were completed Lee coolly pointed out to Marshal Nelson some points in the vicinity, with a view evidently of showing the movements of the ill-fated people previous to their being so cruelly massacred. The civilians accompanying the officers were still kept back for a time. Some of the soldiers were posted on the adjoining hills to guard against surprise from any quarter.

Concealing the Firing Squad.

The wagons were meanwhile placed in line near the monument and the army blankets fastened over the wheels. Behind this improvised screen the squad of men who had been appointed to shoot Lee were to be stationed. The purpose of this concealment of the firing party was to prevent the men composing it from being seen by any one, there being a reasonable fear that some of the numerous relatives of Lee might wreak vengeance on the heads of his executioners.

The boards of which the coffin was to be formed were next unloaded from a wagon, and the carpenters began to nail them together. It was a rough pine box. While it was being made Lee sat at some distance away with Marshal Nelson, intently watching the scene around him.

The civilians, and those specially invited as witnesses, were allowed to come within the military inclosure. All of the others were allowed to witness the proceedings from a considerable distance east of the ravine. At Murderers' Spring there were only some twenty-five or thirty persons gathered from the neighboring settlements, for the time and place of the shooting had been very sensibly kept private.

Marshal Nelson then read the order and sentence of the Court, directing the Marshal of the Territory to conduct his prisoner from the place where he was confined to the place of execution, and then to see that he was shot to death. The marshal read the order in a clear tone, his words being audible to every one present. As he concluded the reading he asked Lee if he had anything to say before the sentence of the law was carried out. Lee looked up quickly, and noticing Mr. Fennimore, the photographer, in the act of fixing up his canvas preparatory to taking a photograph of the prisoner, pointed with his finger towards him and said: "I wish to

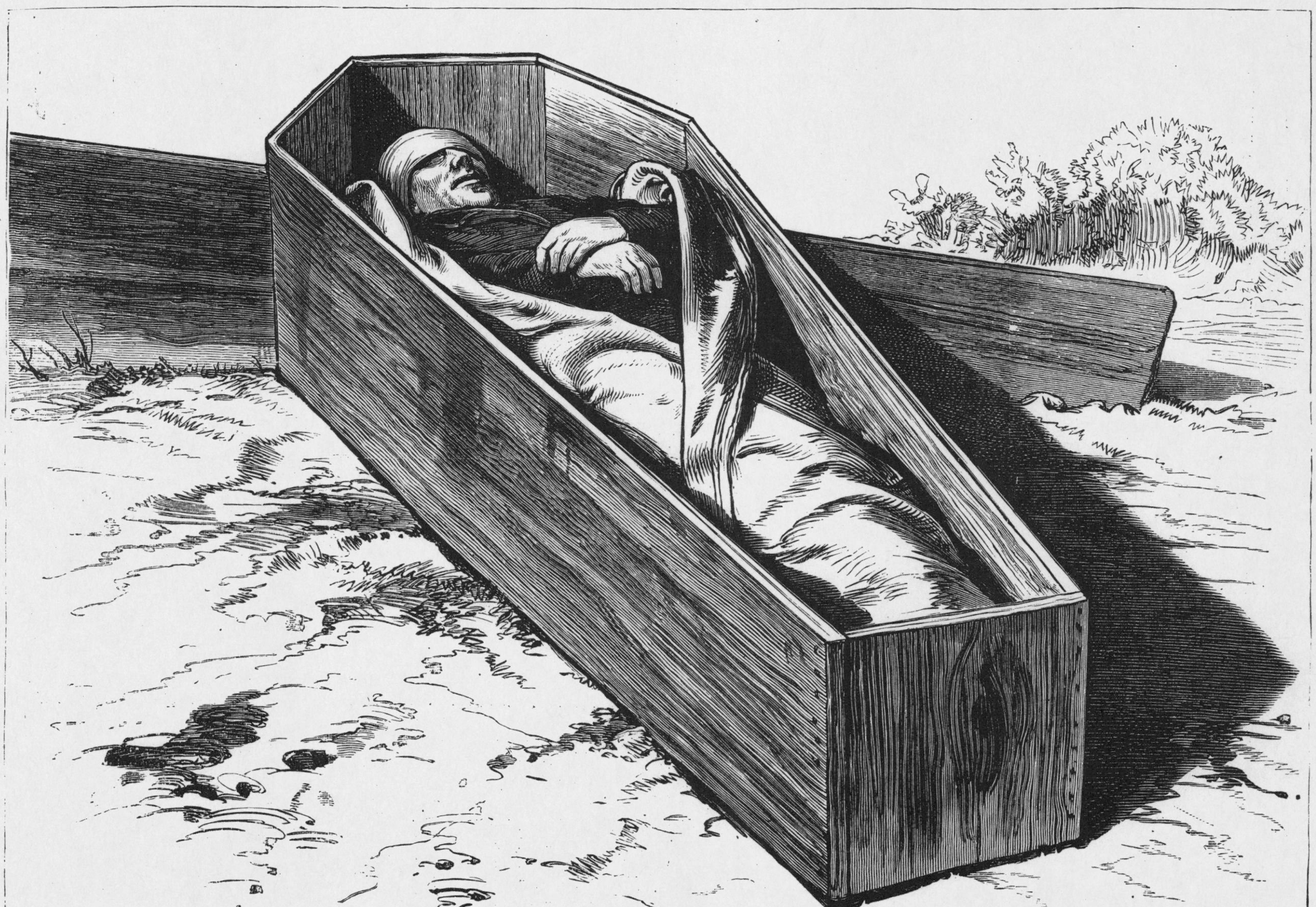

UTAH.—THE MOUNTAIN MEADOWS MASSACRE—THE BODY OF THE MORMON ELDER, JOHN D. LEE, DEPOSITED IN ITS COFFIN IMMEDIATELY AFTER HIS EXECUTION, MARCH 23d.—From a Photograph, Taken Expressly for this Paper, by Fennimore, Beaver City.

DENISON DAILY NEWS.

VOL. V DENISON, TEXAS, SUNDAY MORNING, AUGUST 26, 1877. NO 171

THE DENISON NEWS,

B. C. MURRAY, Proprietor.

TERMS:

Daily—Per mont............	$1 00
" Per week, by carrier,......	25
Weekly—Per annum..........	2 50
Six mor is............	1 50

ADVERTISING RATES:

One inch, first insertion........	1 00
Each subsequent insertion....	50
One-eighth columns, one month..	6 00
Three months............	15 00
One-fourth column, one month....	10 00
Three months............	25 00
Business cards 1½ inch, per month.	3 00

Local notices, 10 cents a line for the first insertion, each subsequent publica tion 7 cents per line

Double column advertisements, one-third extra.

Legal advertisements at legal rates.

Trantient advertisers will be expected to pay in advance.

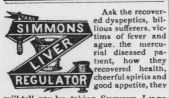

GROCERIES.

JOHN WESLEY HARDIN.

The Big Chief of Texas Desperadoes Captured.

Dallas Daily Commercial.

WHITING, Alabama, August 24.—To-day, as the train was leaving Pensacola, Florida, the sheriff, with a posse, boarded the cars to assist two Texan officials to arrest the notorious John Wesley Hardin, who is said to have committed twenty-seven murders, and for whose body four thousand dollars reward has been offered by an act of the Legislature of Texas. His last murder in Texas was the killing of the sheriff of Comanche county. He has lived in Florida for years as John Swain, and being related to the county officers, has escaped arrest.

About twenty shots were fired in making the arrest. Hardin's companion, named Mann, who had a pistol in his hand, was killed.

Resolutions of the Pennsylvania Democracy.

The Democratic party of Pennsylvania and its delegates in convention assembled, declare the following by resolution:

1st. That the induction of Rutherford B. Hayes into the office of president, notwithstanding the election of Samuel J. Tilden thereto, was a high crime against free government which has not been condoned and will not be forgotten. The spirit of patriotism wnich forebore the contest npon the first offense will resist and punish any attempt at a second.

The Democratic convention reaffirmed and adopted the financial resolutions of the National Democratic platform adopted in St. Louis in 1876.

Gen. Sherman Heard From.

The following has been received at the war department, dated Helena, Montana, August 21st, signed by General W. T. Sherman: "Report my arrival here. Accounts from Indians and General Howard are too confused to make anything out of them. Will ascertain and report at earliest moment."

Pity-Patti.

PARIS, August 24.—Adalina Patti has brought suit for nulity of marriage against the Marquis of Caux. The summons alleges that marriage is null and void, because the priest, Rev. Mr. Plunkett, who performed the ceremony in England, had no license from his Archbishop.

Morton Getting Better.

RICHMOND, Indiana, August 24.—Senator Morton, at midnight, was resting comfortably, and his physicians express the belief that the crisis passed and his gradual recovery is anticipated.

The Daily News' correspondent at Russian headquarters explains the mystification concerning the reported capture of Hainkai pass by the Turks on the 16th inst.

A column of Sblieman pasha's force attempted strenuously to force the pass, reported that they were successful, but, though the column did force its way into the defile, they were there so roughly handled by the Russian artillery, and by the regiment holding the pass, that it was compelled to retire.

An official report upon the condition and treatment of the insane poor in the charitable institutions of Georgia, discloses a revolting state of affairs. The insane and idiotic of both sexes and of all colors are permitted to live together indiscriminately in the alms houses, and idiotic children are born of idiotic mothers, while the sanitary are even

J. WESLEY HARDING.

A Brief Sketch of this Notorious Desperado.

From the Dallas Herald.

His father was a preacher who lived in Southwest Texas. As a boy he was remarkably quiet, and gave no evidence of the terrible passions which, in after life, made him thirst for blood. When about sixteen years of age, and while the State was under military rule, a darkey on his father's place provoked him, and he shot him. For this he was arrested and placed under guard of some soldiers who started to Huntsville with him. As he was only a boy they did not watch him very close, and at night laid down to sleep. Harding arose during the night and killed every one of them. This outlawed him. His next act was the murder of Jack Helm, out of which grew the Sutton and Taylor troubles, Harding siding with the Taylors. His father and brother got mixed up and were taken out and hung in Western Texas.

From this time on he was a desperado of the worst order. Missouri and Kansas became the field of operation, and before he left them he added many more to the death list. In these States there are at present large rewards offered for him. From there he came back to Texas, and kept the border in a state of terrorism. His last murder was the killing of Webb, the deputy sheriff of Brown county, at Comanche. It is estimated that in various sections of the country there is over twenty thousand dollars of rewards offered. Hardin is a young man, about 27 or 28 years of age, five feet eight inches and one-half in height, weighs one hundred and fifty pounds, flaxen hair, blue eyes, and not an unpleasing countenance.

The Murderer of Pirie and Grayson Captured.

About five years ago a Mexican named Segundo Garcia Elisondo attacked a camp of herders near Sherman, in the middle of the night, while they were all asleep. He cut five men on the head with an axe, in a shocking manner, and two of them, John Pirie and Thomas Grayson, of Sherman, were killed; the others finally recovered. The intention of the man was no doubt to murder them all. After he had finished his work he jumped onto his horse and made his escape across the Rio Grande.

It is now believed that one of the desperadoes who raided across the Rio Grande and attacked the jail at Rio Grande City, the other day, is this same Segundo Garcia. As he has been surrendered to the United States authorities, it is quite likely he will suffer the penalty of his horrible crimes.

THE EMPIRE, IT IS PEACE.

If the regular army were as large as the ambition of the military ring would have it, the commander-in-chief might eventually calm the fears of the timid by proclaiming from the capital, "*L'Empire c'est la paix.*"

NOTICE.

To Whom it May Concern.

All persons indebted to the undersigned are hereby notified that if their accounts are not paid within twenty days from this date the claims will be put in the hands of an officer for collection.

R. H. RUE.

Denison, Texas, July 27, 1877.
7-27 3w-d.

In Denison the women quarrel, the men ditto, the girls are homely, the old maids are simply awful, the city don't agree, the editors WON'T agree, they can't get a slaughter house, flour mills, railroads and factories, but they've got tne whooping cough and measles, and—and—oh, well, we should not live in Denison for anything.—*Sherman Exchange.*

Oh, villian, thou liest. The women of Denison neglect their domestic duties to think of sweet things to say to each other. The men get up at night to shake hands. There was never but one homely girl in Denison, and she married a Sherman man as the easiest mode of suicide; the cats all coo like doves, and would not know how to howl "Maria" if they wanted to; the editors are all brothers, sir, twin brothers, who send each other presents every day of beautiful boquets and cord wood and bottled b—r; and we "h-a-v-e" a slaughter-house and four flour mills, and factories, and strikers, and seven churches, and thirty-nine saloons—with back-doors and everything—we mean thirty-nine saloons, and seven churches with back-doors and everything; and then we have A FIRST-CLASS SHOE STORE, at Sherburne's,

St. Louis Globe-Democrat.

VOL. 3—NO. 121. ST. LOUIS, FRIDAY MORNING, APRIL 12, 1878. PRICE FIVE CENTS.

NATIONAL NOTES.

Republican Prospects as Viewed by Secretary McCrary.

What May Be Accomplished in the Coming Campaign.

The Desire and Aim of the Administration.

Gould and Huntington Still Watching the Sinking-Fund Bill.

The House Fixes the Compensation of Pension Agents.

A Universal Opinion that the Bankrupt Law Will be Repealed.

...acres to enter an additional tract of eighty acres adjoining the land embraced in the original entry, or if they or their widows or orphaned children so elect they may surrender the original entry for cancellation and thereupon be entitled to enter 160 acres under the homestead laws elsewhere without the payment of additional fees, and their residence and cultivation under the original entry shall be credited upon the new or additional entry, provided that in every case there shall be at least one year's residence and cultivation required before issuance of patent for second entry. It is also provided that the benefits of this act shall not extend to persons who have sold or in any way attempted to alienate land embraced in their original entries, or to any person who has attempted to alienate his rights under the act of 1872 relative to additional homesteads for soldiers and sailors.

The President and His Party.

WASHINGTON, April 11.—The President does not seem the least disturbed by the action of the recent Republican caucuses. Those nearest him, socially and politically, say there is no probability whatever that he will, as requested by the resolution of Senator Sargent in the caucus last night, rescind the order forbidding participation in political meetings of officials in the executive branch of the civil service, and these friends don't think it probable that any such request will be made by the Congressional committees, though they may confer with the President in political affairs generally in view of the approaching election. They say the President never declines to listen attentively to suggestions, but when he ... as to the rightfulness of a... to it. The Republicans ... greater part, will endeavo... issue with the President, ...

...merce, reported the House bill to prevent the introduction of infectious or contagious diseases. Calendar.

Mr. Plumb, from the Committee on Public Lands, reported a bill for the relief of settlers on public lands. Placed on the calendar.

On motion of Mr. Morrill, the Senate took up and passed the bill to repair and put in operation the Mint at New Orleans.

During the morning hour Mr. Sargent called up his joint resolution on the Chinese question, and urged the necessity of restrictions upon Chinese immigration. Referred to the Committee on Foreign Affairs.

The bill to remove the restrictions on the enlistment of colored men in the army came up during the morning hour, and Mr. Bruce said the colored men wanted all color lines to be abolished, and to be clothed with all the rights of American citizens. They felt capable of paddling their own canoe. They asked no special legislation.

The bill went over without action.

At the expiration of the morning hour consideration was resumed of unfinished business, being the repeal of the bankrupt act.

Mr. Davis, of Illinois, favored amending the present law, if the Senate should reject the bill to repeal it, and said he was authorized to say that Senator Edmunds took the same view.

The bill was then laid aside.

Mr. Eaton, of Connecticut, then called up the resolution of inquiry into the arrest of Benj. Noyes, and detailed the circumstances as he understood them.

After debate, Mr. Eaton's resolution, directing the Judiciary Committee to inquire into the arrest of Benj. Noyes, insurance President, was agreed to, and the Senate proceeded to con...

...shall be filled by wounded or disabled Union soldiers.

The amendment was adopted amid enthusiastic applause and shouts of laughter.

The committee rose and reported the bill. The amendments were concurred in, and the bill passed.

The House then went into Committee of the Whole, Mr. Cox (N. Y.) in the Chair, on the Post Office appropriation bill. As soon as the bill was read by title, the committee again rose, and the House adjourned.

Affairs at Anna.

Special Dispatch to the Globe-Democrat.

ANNA, ILL., April 11.—This morning at about 3 o'clock fire destroyed the large brick house of Mr. D. W. Brown, member of the Board of County Commissioners, situated north and in sight of this town. Nothing of any consequence was saved. No doubt some malicious person is bound to burn up everything belonging to Mr. Brown. He had a house burned last week in the Mississippi Bottom, and a mill a few years ago. The house and contents were insured for some $2,500, which will not cover the loss.

The Commissioners of the Insane Asylum have this week been investigating the scandal case of the Superintendent, but can come to no decision. The investigation will be continued next week, it is said, and something startling is expected.

Southern Illinois is now one immense flower-garden. Strawberries will be ripe in a few days.

BILL, THE BUTCHER.

An Interview with Longley, the Texas Man-Killer.

He Admits Having Murdered Thirty-two Persons.

Says He Hates to Hang, but Isn't Afraid to Die.

The Western Train Robbers Encounter a Plucky Crew,

But, Aided by Kerosene, Accomplish their Purpose.

THE ILLUSTRATED POLICE NEWS.

WILLIAM P. LONGLEY, CHIEF OF TEXAS "MAN-KILLERS," CHARGED WITH THIRTY-TWO MURDERS, HANGED AT GIDDINGS, LEE CO., OCT. 11, FOR THE MURDER OF WILSON ANDERSON.

BILL, THE BUTCHER.

An Interview with Longley, the Texas Man-Killer.

He Admits Having Murdered Thirty-two Persons.

Says He Hates to Hang, but Isn't Afraid to Die.

The Western Train Robbers Encounter a Plucky Crew,

But, Aided by Kerosene, Accomplish their Purpose.

The Blood-Curdling Confessions of an Eastern Assassin.

A Brute Murders His Industrious Wife and Commits Suicide.

The Misery Caused by Bugbee's Extensive Forgeries.

A Record of Rascality and Blood—The Criminal Calendar.

Special Correspondence of the Globe-Democrat.

GALVESTON, TEXAS, April 7.—This afternoon, at 3 o'clock, a correspondent of the GLOBE-DEMOCRAT had a short interview with William P. Longley, the notorious Texas desperado and murderer, who, according to his own account, has killed and murdered thirty-two men at different times within the last seven years.

The interview took place at the jail at Galveston, a strong and substantial brick building near the center of the city, and in one of the dungeons of the lower floor this noted character of the Southwest is now confined under sentence of death. Although incarcerated here, Longley was arrested, tried and condemned in Lee County, Middle Texas, for the deliberate murder of a man while plowing in a field, this being but one of the long list of victims which Longley, according to his own account, has planted.

HIS SENTENCE AFFIRMED.

Longley's death verdict having been affirmed by the Court of Appeals during the late session of that body at Galveston, nothing now remains to complete the stern demands of Justice but the sentencing of the murderer, which will have to be done by the District Court of Lee County. The dungeon occupied by the notorious Texas man-killer is as dark and dismal as any pictured in the pages of romance. A massive iron door from the rear opens into a corridor dimly lighted by rusty iron gratings. At the farther end is the cell of the desperado the strong iron door of which is secured by massive locks, and whose walls are also massive. At the sound of your footsteps, which fall on the brick pavement with an echo that almost startles you as well as the inmates of the neighboring cells, the indistinct outlines of a human figure, like an animal aroused in his lair, emerges from the gloom of the dungeon and approaches the bars

A DESCRIPTION OF LONG

It is Longley. He is rather inclined to ... slim, but well proportioned and not gaunt and "with a lean and hungry look," as was Cassius. The first thing that strikes the beholder is the really handsome physiognomy of the Texas cut-throat. Scarcely yet in his twenty-fourth year, Longley has dark hair, worn rather long and slightly parted at the side; coal black whiskers and beard that shade a fine olive complexion; a nose rather after the Greek model; teeth white and beautiful as a woman's; eyes black as midnight, that seem literally alive with expression, which their possessor seems little inclined to curb or suppress. He looks anything but the cool man-slayer who has undoubtedly sent over thirty of his fellow-men to their long abodes.

Upon the occasion referred to, Longley wore much the same clothes as when first incarcerated—a dark cashmere coat, course hickory shirt, pants of some dark material, and a pistol belt, which the officers have allowed him to retain from the murdering outfit he used to wear.

A TALK WITH THE DESPERADO.

Since he was condemned the Jailor has had orders to allow no stranger to approach the prisoner. A GLOBE-DEMOCRAT correspondent, however, succeeded in being admitted to see him, and the following conversation ensued:

Correspondent. How are you, Longley? I have heard so much of you that I have come to see you.

Longley. That is all right. Glad to see you (smiling).

Cor. I must tell you beforehand that I have come to make up a newspaper article off you. May be you don't want any more said about you in the papers?

Longley. Oh, I don't care much what they say. They've said now about all they could. It don't matter.

Cor. I have myself written a good deal about you.

Longley. Yes, but I don't know that your paper has said anything against me.

Cor. Well, you have not, from your looks, become down-hearted, owing to the serious turn in your case.

Longley (smiling). Oh, I never allow myself to get so under any circumstances.

Cor. Have you anything to say

IN REGARD TO YOUR FATE?

Longley. This much: that I haven't had a fair trial; no trial at all, in fact. They were all my enemies.

Cor. If the worst comes to the worst I suppose you don't care much. I shouldn't think that a man like you, who has "planted" and killed thirty-two men, would be much afraid to die!

Longley. (Here the desperado looked down, and, eyeing the correspondent keenly, said:) No; I don't like to die, but if I have to die I'm not afraid to.

The interview was interrupted by the entrance of the Secretary of the Y. M. C. A., who gave Longley a number of tracts, sang a hymn, prayed, and, after reading a portion of the third chapter of Luke, made an exhortation to the prisoner. During the religious services the condemned desperado leaned his forehead on his left hand against the grating, apparently in deep meditation, at the same time regarding the exhorter with deep attention.

GOOD-BY TO THE DESPERADO.

After the Secretary had taken his departure, Longley asked the correspondent to approach the grating and have a further chat with him. A few words only passed, when the turnkey, presenting himself, intimated the interview must come to an end.

"Good-by, Longley," said the correspondent.

"Good-by, sir," replied the condemned man, offering his hand through the bars.

The correspondent took and shook it, saying, "We may meet again," at the same time regarding the desperado with a significant glance that might have been equivalent to filling out the sentence with "in the shadow of the gallows at Giddings, Lee County."

...cient strength, the Pacific Railroad Committee having already agreed to it. The Senate committee with two dissenting votes, will throw their influence to prevent the measure from going to the Judiciary Committee. Gould and Huntington are determined if possible to incorporate the Blaine amendment.

THE BANKRUPT LAW.

Leaders of both parties in the Senate are of opinion that the bankrupt law will be entirely repealed, save in cases pending.

THE PENSION AGENTS.

It is estimated that the action of the House, to-day, in establishing fixed compensation and allowance to Pension Agents, will effect a saving of $150,000 per annum.

WESTERN ARRIVALS.

Chas. P. Birge, Keokuk, Ia.; N. A. Bryson, wife and son, and Mrs. J. C. Miller, St. Louis.

Sherman and the Syndicate.

NEW YORK, April 11.—The conference at the Sub-Treasury this afternoon, between Secretary Sherman and members of the late syndicate, resulted in the signing of a contract for the sale of $50,000,000 of 4½ per cent bonds.

For the Relief of Settlers.

WASHINGTON, D. C., April 11.—Mr. Plumb, in behalf of the Senate Committee on Public Lands, to-day reported a substitute for two bills heretofore introduced by Messrs. Booth and Ingalls, for the relief of settlers on lands supposed to be within railroad grants...

XLVTH CON[GRESS]

...Pension Agent at Indianapolis; I know it, and I can prove it. "And that's what's the matter with Hanna." [Loud laughter and applause.]

Mr. Smith, of Pennsylvania, moved to increased the amount appropriated for carrying the bill into effect from $96,000 to $130,000. Adopted.

Mr. Powers moved to strike out the section which changes the mode of paying pensions and inserting in lieu thereof a provision fixing the salary of pension agents at $4,000 and alowing them fees for vouchers and actual expenses for rent, clerk hire etc.

Mr. Fort offered a substitute transferring the duties of the pension bureau from the Interior Department to the War Department. Rejected.

A vote was then taken on Mr. Powers' amendment and it was agreed to—112 to 60.

Mr. Marsh offered an amendment providing that Pension Agencies shall be filled by officers of the army and navy on the retired list, who are to receive their full pay while so employed.

Mr. Butler. That is a good opportunity to make Gen. Shields a Pension Agent.

Mr. Powers made the point of order that the amendment would change the existing law, and was not in the interest of economy.

The Chairman overruled the point of order, holding that the amendment was in the interest of economy.

Mr. Foster inquired as to how these officers could give bonds.

Mr. Randall (the Speaker) replied that officers were liable to be court martialed in case of defalcation, and that their education and the life tenure of their commissions was the best bond that could be given.

The amendment was rejected—88 to 99.

Mr. Rice offered a resolution that from and after July, 1878, the offices of Pension Agents

...Lee Ward, of Harrison Township, was horribly burned by her clothing taking fire when she was standing near the stove in her mother's kitchen.

Burned to Death.

DETROIT, MICH., April 11.—Seven stores and five dwellings were destroyed by fire at Cadillac, this State, early this morning. Entire loss about $10,000; very little insurance. Mrs. Blount perished in the flames.

Killed while Hunting.

ERIE, PA., April 11.—Albert Smith, grocer, while hunting snipe on the lake beach, to-day, accidentally shot himself, the charge of shot going through his heart and the ramrod through his head. He leaves a wife and seven children.

Kicked by a Horse.

Special Dispatch to the Globe-Democrat.

GOSHEN, IND., April 11.—A son of Isaac W. Snyder, living in Goshen, was kicked in the face by a horse this evening and fatally injured.

Killed by a Tree.

Special Dispatch to the Globe-Democrat.

MORLEY, O., April 11.—While engaged in cutting a large tree, it fell unexpectedly and killed David Blank. He was a single man, thirty years old, and a resident of Muskegan.

"Good-by, Longley," said the correspondent.

"Good-by, sir," replied the condemned man, offering his hand through the bars.

The correspondent took and shook it, saying, "We may meet again," at the same time regarding the desperado with a significant glance that might have been equivalent to filling out the sentence with "in the shadow of the gallows at Giddings, Lee County."

Another Train Robbery in Texas.

Special Dispatch to the Globe-Democrat.

HOUSTON, TEX., April 11.—Robbers again attacked the Texas and Pacific train last night, about midnight, at Musquite Station, eleven miles east of Dallas. The gang numbered fifteen masked men. The engineer refused at first to stop, when they shot at him. He and the fireman were then arrested, and a battle ensued between the robbers and Conductor Alvord, who ran out and fired on them. All of them then turned and attacked, shooting at him, the bullets passing through the sleeping car. The conductor wounded one, it is thought fatally. He kept on shooting till a Winchester ball from one of the robbers struck him in the arm, breaking it. He then crawled under the car and kept on firing. Express messenger Curley and the armed guard, Gritz, opened fire on the robbers from the express car. One of the villains was wounded, and their leader called for a parley, telling the messenger he should not be hurt if he surrendered. He refused. The thieves talked a few moments, and

Continued on Third Page.

Daily Herald.

THE DAILY HERALD is published every morning, except on Monday, at $10 per annum in advance, postage prepaid; or 25 cents per week delivered in the city.
ADVERTISING RATES: One square (ten lines nonpareil) one time $1 50, each subsequent insertion, 75 cents. Special rates for weekly monthly and yearly advertisers.

DALLAS, TEXAS.

THURSDAY MORNING : : : MAY 16

THE war cloud in Europe darkens once more.

THEY have commenced telegraphing about the health of the new pope already.

WASHINGTON city has a female communist. She delivers speeches "calm in tone" but wildcatish in language.

BROWN BOWEN will be hung at Gonzales to-morrow, the first legal hanging that has occurred in Texas for over a year.

ELIZA PINKSTON should be appointed to something, not necessarily for the benefit of the "something," but as an evidence of good faith.

MINISTER FOSTER gave an official dinner to President Diaz, April 30, and escaped without being lassoed by one of Diaz's noble patriots.

WHAT this country mostly needs at present is an eight-by-seven commission to decide against the delinquent yet wealthy taxpayer.

THE Marshall *Herald* is sad because circus companies do not come to Texas. The saw dust ring and "calico hosses" evidently have a charm for Uncle Bob.

THERE is nothing in the name of Smith is there? The county in this state named after that illustrious individual has no tax collector, any how.

MR. HEWITT'S bill does not take with the army officers. They naturally object to being treated as the Pennsylvania coal corporations treat their miners.

THOSE Munchausen stories in two or three Hubbard organs about the "Hubbard ground swell" were certainly intended for humor, as the governor is an alleged farmer.

THERE is nothing in the report that Conkling, Hayes and Blaine have "made up." Conkling will cologne himself—a gallon of it is sprinkled on his shirt front every morning.

WITHIN the past two or three days people living in Chicago have had a foretaste of what is in store for them after the "coil is shuffled." They have been using furnaces up there to keep warm.

OH, well, there is no use in trying to pound anything like the truth into the Fort Worth *Democrat*, so what is the use in trying to straighten it out on the question of "that letter to a prominent republican in Grimes county?"

DOES the San Antonio *Herald* imagine for a moment that the candidates of the glorious state of Texas are orphans? Else why does it remark, "The people have enough to take care of themselves without supporting candidates."

MR. SHISKIN, the Russian minister at Washington, has asked to be recalled. He says the American newspapers make fun of him, and he can't stand it. He ought to hire Ben Butler as a substitute, and remain awhile to see how it works.

A WASHINGTON special to the Louisville *Courier Journal* says that since the speech of Governor Throckmorton against the reduction of the army and the need of protection on our Mexican frontier, the cabinet has determined to institute a more vigorous policy on the Mexican border.

GRANGER LANG'S visit to Gainsville last week was immediately followed by a copious shower of rain, and now the farmers in that vicinity, who were suffering from drouth, say that Lang is surely the coming man for governor. There is nothing in politics like "fitness" for office.

BISHOP MCCOSKRY has addressed a letter to Bishop Smith, of Kentucky, withdrawing his resignation of March 11, and announcing his purpose to abandon his intended trip to Europe that he may hold himself in readiness to meet all definite charges against him, preferred by responsible parties.

THIS, from the St. Louis *Times*, is the undkindest cut of all at Blaine, of Maine: "The spectacle of James G. Blaine delivering an address at the opening of the Philadelphia exhibition was an eminently fit thing—a played out representative of a played-out party inaugurating a played-out show."

CONGRESSMEN MILLS is opposed to opening the Florida and Louisiana frauds. And Mr. Mills uses some good argument in behalf of his position, too. The question is, will it benefit the country? We think not, for every one is already satisfied that frauds were committed in these states without any investigation.

NOW, this is a nice conundrum to be asked by as good a newspaper as the Chicago *Times*, as if every one couldn't answer it. The *Times* asks: "When Packard ascertains that in the Liverpool consulship there is an uncommonly good chance to knock down with no tell-tale bell-punch in the vicinage, will he hesitate to gather up his carpet-bag and go down to the sea in ships?

ESCAPE OF BASS.

The escape of Sam Bass and his men is certainly anything but gratifying to the law-abiding citizens in the counties in which he has had his rendezvous, and has operated as a highway robber. To say that any one officer or set of officers in pursuit of him are responsible for his escape would be unjust, when the nature of his escape is understood, yet there is a responsibility resting upon this escape which can not be overlooked. When the first robbery, at Allen, was committed it was *then* the duty of the local authorities to have been assisted by the state forces, in at least trying to capture the robbers, for they were evidently unable to cope with them singly. The sheriff of a county generally has from one to half a dozen deputies, who are expected to execute the laws, make arrests, etc., but to summon a promiscuous posse to undertake the capture of dangerous and well armed desperadoes is not always feasible. Bass committed robberies in one county, then another, and took refuge in the wilds of another. Then which of the sheriffs ought to have first attempted his arrest? Some would say, and naturally, too, the sheriff of the county in which he was hid. He, Bass, had six determined followers, all of whom were well mounted and equipped. They took refuge in the wilds of Denton county, where a promiscuous raid was made to no end. The sheriff of Denton county could at almost any time have either killed or captured the robbers before it was too late, if he had have had the proper encouragement from the governor, as well as a warrant for his arrest, which was not forthcoming until after three other robberries had been committed.

Hon. J. W. Throckmorton.

St. Louis Republican: ... on all hands that Governor Throckmorton is one of the ... representatives that Texas ... to congress. He rises ... position of a mere politici... stand on the high plane o... manship and seeks to leg... a district, state, class or ... advance the interest and ... the whole people. With ... gence, liberal views and ... prehension of the needs ... state and of the country ... honestly, earnestly and ... for the success of such me... pear best suited to insure ... the whole nation. This ... the state owes him m... faithful services. But s... more, and should wipe ... tempted stigma which fed... ty sought to fix upon him ... deposed from the office of ... which the people of Texas ... him. The zeal, ability ... views of government poli... in his congressional career ... qualities needed to make ... ernor, and not only his hi... tions as a citizen, but a sec... towards a wronged man sh... him in the executive chair ... socalled reconstruction re... While Governor Throck... earnestly advocated the c... the Texas and Pacific rail... done it more to secure a... way to the Pacific throug... west than on account of it... vantage to northern Texas; and he has shown just as much zeal since he entered congress in efforts for the establishment of an ocean line of steamers from New Orleans and Galveston to Rio and Vera Cruz. He is a democrat, but not a demagogue, and while favoring a wise economy in expenditures, believes the government was created to bless as well as rule the people, and gives his support to such measures of public policy as seem adapted to such a purpose. We are glad to learn that the approaching state convention of Texas is likely to nominate Mr. Throckmorton for the governorship.

A MEMBER of the national democratic executive committee writes that "They are heating the furnaces hot for Hayes in Washington, and our friends are determined to roast all who have been connected with the election frauds in the south. We cannot expect to oust the president, but we can demonstrate the connection of his fraudulency with the conspiracy so that no one can deny or doubt it."

Jay Gould and the Supreme Court.

Philadelphia Sunday Press: A sickening rumor fills the air, and threatens to still further depreciate the value of real estate. Some one has extorted from the administration the secret that Mr. Justice Swayne is to leave the supreme bench, and that Stanley Matthews will go on it. Let's see! Jay Gould contributed seventy-five thousand dollars to the Hayes campaign fund; Stanley Matthews is Jay Gould's attorney; the Pacific railroad bill will fight the new funding act in court; in course of time the case will reach the supreme court, with Stanley on the bench—oh, no! It cannot be!

Out in a Missouri town of nine hundred inhabitants, there are eight hundred members of a total abstinence club, and the habit of winking when ordering a lemonade has afflicted every man but one in the town with a chronic squint. That one is a drunken reprobate who won't reform.

NEW ADVERTISEMENTS.

POST OFFICE DEPARTMENT.

ESCAPE OF BASS.

The escape of Sam Bass and his men is certainly anything but gratifying to the law-abiding citizens in the counties in which he has had his rendezvous, and has operated as a highway robber. To say that any one officer or set of officers in pursuit of him are responsible for his escape would be unjust, when the nature of his escape is understood, yet there is a responsibility resting upon this escape which can not be overlooked. When the first robbery, at Allen, was committed it was *then* the duty of the local authorities to have been assisted by the state forces, in at least trying to capture the robbers, for they were evidently unable to cope with them singly. The sheriff of a county generally has from one to half a dozen deputies, who are expected to execute the laws, make arrests, etc., but to summon a promiscuous posse to undertake the capture of dangerous and well armed desperadoes is not always feasible. Bass committed robberies in one county, then another, and took refuge in the wilds of another. Then which of the sheriffs ought to have first attempted his arrest? Some would say, and naturally, too, the sheriff of the county in which he was hid. He, Bass, had six determined followers, all of whom were well mounted and equipped. They took refuge in the wilds of Denton county, where a promiscuous raid was made to no end. The sheriff of Denton county could at almost any time have either killed or captured the robbers before it was too late, if he had have had the proper encouragement from the governor, as well as a warrant for his arrest, which was not forthcoming until after three other robberries had been committed. It was then that the governor was stimulated "to do something," for popular indignation had become so great that it became an absolute necessity to send state forces to the scene. Major Jones placed the field in the hands of a trusty lieutenant, who deserves credit for the hard and enduring campaign made against the bandits, notwithstanding his failure to capture them. One thing, at least, was accomplished by Major Jones and his co-operators, Bass was driven out of the country. The country in which the state troops have been operating is almost a jungle, and Bass could have been within a hundred yards of his pursuers at different times with impunity. The arrest of twelve or fifteen men who are now lying in jail at Tyler, as accomplices shows that the robbers had aid and abettors in the surrounding country; and taking all these facts into consideration, it was almost impossible to secure their arrest. The governor ought to have acted promptly in the beginning of the disorder; then something might have been accomplished. As the matter now stands it remains for the detectives to learn of Bass' whereabouts, if they do not already know, and to secure his capture by strategy. This method, the detectives claim, is the only one now, by which Sam Bass and his followers can ever be taken.

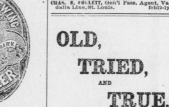

...formed by him.

Sec. 4. No one shall sell or expose for sale any milk, vinegar, molasses, or anything else used for food or drink which is adulterated or which contains impurities injurious to health; and any one violating this section shall be deemed guilty of a misdemeanor, and upon conviction, be fined in any sum not exceeding fifty dollars.

Sec. 5. Any one having an analysis or test made by the City Chemist, shall pay for the same the sum of twenty-five dollars.

Sec. 6. It shall be the duty of the City Chemist to see that all articles shall be of the standard by ordinance to be established.

Sec. 7. The City Chemist shall perform such other duties as may hereafter be required of him in the ordinances establishing the standard of milk, &c., and providing for the inspection by him of any article.

Approved May 10, 1878.
J. B. HEREFORD, City Secretary.
W. L. CABELL, Mayor.
m11-d-10t

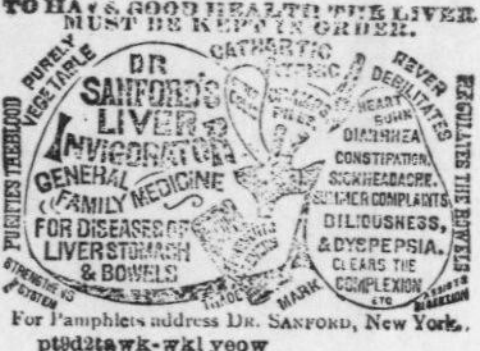

A Woman's Vengeance —Mrs. Townsend's Murderous Onslaught on the Maligner of Her Virtue—A Wretch who Sought Her Daughter's Ruin Foully Slanders Her to Her Husband.

The little town of Corenna, Wright county, Minn., has furnished a sensational tragedy to the current history of the day. The principal actor, or rather actress, was consigned on July 24 to jail at St. Paul for safe keeping. Her name is Jane Townsend, a comely woman apparently about 35 years of age. Her story is that she was married to Marcus Townsend, 60 years of age, the possessor of a fair property, about a year ago. The old man had a daughter, Augusta, 16 years old, who lived with them. The family, she says, lived very happy until this spring, when her husband hired as a farm hand a man named Wm. Dunham, claiming to live in Chicago. Dunham, Mrs. Townsend says, began paying attentions to Augusta soon after his arrival, and a few weeks ago she became satisfied in her own mind that he had accomplished the girl's ruin. She told her husband her fears and asked him to send Dunham away, but he paid no attention to her warning or request. Finally, to separate the two, the girl was sent to a relative on July 4, and she renewed her efforts with her husband to send Dunham off, but without success. Sunday afternoon, while Dunham was absent, she packed up his things and set them out on the steps, and when he returned showed him what she had done and told him to take them and leave. Dunham laughed at her order and told her that she instead of him would have to go away. She asked him what he meant and he referred her to her husband. She sought her husband then out in the field and asked him what Dunham meant, and was told that Dunham said she had been untrue to him. In answer to her question if he believed the charge, he replied affirmatively. She protested her innocence on her knees and asked her husband to say he believed her, but he would not. Filled with frenzy she rushed back to the house where she had left Dunham. As she came up she saw him sitting on the steps. Going toward him she saw two axes, and as quick as thought she picked up one double blade and hurled it at Dunham, but without effect. Then Dunham started toward her and she picked up the other axe, and as he approached struck him a terrible blow, the blade entering his neck just below the left ear, cutting a fearful gash. She then delivered herself up, and was brought to St. Paul to await the result of Dunham's injuries, who was alive at last accounts, though not expected to recover.

The above is the substance of the woman's story, told in sentences broken by sobs and fits of crying. She says she was perfectly conscious of what she was doing when she

THE LAST RAID OF SAM BASS, THE TEXAS TRAIN ROBBER—HE IS BETRAYED BY JIM MURPHY, THE "HERO SPY," AND RECEIVES HIS DEATH WOUND AT ROUND ROCK.

HON. JOSEPH H. ACKLEN, OF LOUISIANA, MEMBER OF CONGRESS, CONCERNED IN THE WIDOW GODFREY AFFAIR AT WASHINGTON, D. C.

JOHN FRANCIS, OF FAIR GROVE, TUSCOLA COUNTY, MICH., MISSING SINCE JUNE 21—A REWARD OF $100 FOR INFORMATION REGARDING HIM.

SIR CAPEL FITZGERALD, THE ENGLISH BARONET, IN CUSTODY FOR STEALING THE JEWELS OF MRS. SUSAN STEVENS, HIS PARAMOUR.

DEADLY AFFRAY AT NASHVILLE, TENN.—A STREET ENCOUNTER IN WHICH SAMUEL H. HICKS AND JONES F. BAXTER WERE KILLED AND TWO OTHERS WOUNDED.

THE BRAVERY OF A BOY IN MONROE COUNTY, MO.—HE JUMPS INTO A WELL TO RESCUE A DROWNING CHILD AND BOTH ARE DRAWN TO THE SURFACE.

THE LAST OF LONGLEY—EXECUTION OF "BILL" LONGLEY, THE "MAN KILLER," AT GIDDINGS, TEXAS—See Page 6.

1—The desperado on the eve of the hanging. 2—A narrow escape—hanged as a horse thief, but cut down and resuscitated. 3—Fatal duel on horseback, on the prairie. 4 Assassination of Wilson Anderson, the crime which brought him to the gallows. 5—Acknowledging on the scaffold the justice of his doom.

THE PEOPLE.

EXTRA.

VOL. IX. INDIANAPOLIS, INDIANA, JANUARY 29, 1879. NO. 14

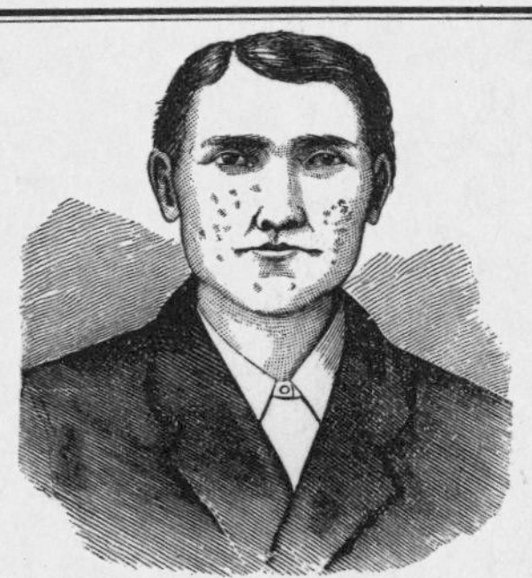

JOHN ACHEY.

From The People of July [illegible] 1878.

A Deliberate Murder!

One Gambler Kills Another at Chapin & Gore's In Broad Daylight.

THE MURDER.

On Tuesday afternoon July 16th, 1878 shortly after 2 o'clock, a cool and deliberate murder was perpetrated in this city at Chapin & Gore's, on North Illinois street, John H. Achey premeditatedly killing George Leggett—both parties being well known gamblers by profession and old residents of the city. The news spread like wild fire throughout the city, but, strangely enough, neither the Sun nor the News, afternoon papers which are issued between 3 and 4 o'clock, had a line about the murder, kindly leaving the interesting and tragic affair for the morning papers to announce—thereby showing what magnificent specimens of afternoon papers we have with us.

It seems that about the hour named, Achey walked into Chapin & Gore's with a pistol partially concealed up one of his coat sleeves, evidently looking for some one. He soon espied his game in the person of George Leggett, who was standing in the rear portion of the room. Achey approached Leggett and calling out "George, I am now ready for you, draw your gun!" attracted Leggett's attention, who turned around only to receive a ball from Achey's pistol in his abdomen. Leggett first ran to the rear, but subsequently started out front and passing by Achey, threw up the latter's hand which held the pistol—Achey having previously fired a second shot which failed in taking effect. It is said that he attempted to fire several more shots, but his pistol would not go off. Leggett ran into Cady's shoe store, falling on the threshold, remarking "I've got my death shot." He was [illegible] up, placed in a hack and taken to the [illegible]tute, where the physicians pronounced his wound fatal, when he was taken to his residence on North Illinois street, and died in ten minutes after he had reached it.

At the time of the firing there was a general stampede of those assembled at Chapin & Gore's—many supposing that a promiscuous fight was about to ensue, and for a while the doors were completely blockaded by struggling and perspiring humanity. In the midst of the excitement Achey walked out and down Washington street. In front of Hogshire's shoe store he was arrested by Taylor Edwards. It is stated that at first he drew his pistol on the officer, but he was soon disarmed and gave no further trouble.

THE CAUSE OF THE MURDER.

The Sentinel gives the following account of an interview between its reporter and the murderer, which took place in the station house shortly after the shooting:

Reporter—Why did you shoot Leggett?

Achey—Because he stole $875 from me, and has been carrying a gun for me for some days past, and I knew that he intended to kill me the first chance he got.

Reporter—Do you know that he is dead?

Achey—Yes, I heard so. He brought it on himself; and when I shot I shot to kill; he deserved all he got. If I had it to do over I would do just what I have done. I am not sorry.

Reporter—How did he steal your money?

Achey—Some weeks ago Leggett and I started a faro bank in the Occidental hotel. Ed Brown was connected with the bank. On June 27 I took my wife to the Opera House, and on returning was informed that a man from Cincinnati who they called "Doc" had won about $600 from the bank during my absence. Leggett then asked me to play a game of poker with him and "Doc," and I did so. While we were playing Leggett sent out and got some whisky and I took a drink. I played with them until I lost $225 when I saw the game was not square, and I got up from the table and told them so. I afterward found out that Leggett, Brown and the man they called "Doc" were in partners for the purpose of fleecing me and that "Doc" had been telegraphed to come here for that purpose. Their winning the $825 from me broke me and left me without a cent. Why, on Sunday I did not have anything to eat, and I met Leggett in front of the St. Cloud hotel the morning and asked him to give me $25, and I would [illegible] and never bother him any more. He just laughed at me. While we were talking he took a pistol from his pants pocket and placed it in his coat pocket, and pointing at me called me all the harsh names he could think of. I then went to my room and got my pistol, an improved Smith & Wesson, which I purchased a few days since just on purpose to kill him with, and came down in town to find him. I saw him enter Chapin & Gore's, and followed him in. When I had advanced within eight or ten feet of him I said, "George, I am fixed for you; pull your gun;" but I had mine out and shot before he could get his hand to his. I shot both times to kill, and was determined when I went into the saloon that he should kill me or I kill him. I am not sorry for what I have done. I went before the shooting and took several drinks to brace myself up for the work.

GEORGE LEGGETT.

THE MURDERER,

John Achey, is a son of Henry Achey, an old citizen of Indianapolis—the man who gave rise to the saying, "He kept tavern like h—ll—like Henry Achey." This originated we believe, when Henry kept the old Galt House at Cincinnati. John is a professional sporting man—being a third or fourth rate gambler. A short time since he got hold of two or three thousand dollars from his mother's estate, and, as he says, opened a faro bank with Leggett. Whether the latter plucked him or not is not known. There is no doubt but that Achey looked upon himself as a victim who had been taken in and done for in a set up game by Leggett. He worried over it and talked about it almost constantly. He is about 46 years of age, and of late years has been quite dissipated, and particularly so within the past few weeks. He is an uncle of the McDowel girls, who have lately taken to the stage—one of them, Kate, making her appearance a few months since in this city with considerable credit in Evangeline. One of his brothers has just concluded a term in the penitentiary, and another, some years since, was killed in a row in a saloon on Illinois street. The murderer lately married a cook at his sister's, who is said to have received $500 for consenting to the nuptials, and is again represented as a very respectable woman. Achey is said to have told his wife on last Monday as she was going to the country, and a friend, Jack Bernard, that he intended to kill Leggett, saying to the former that when she returned he would be in jail for murder. John Achey is a man of medium height, dark complected, smooth faced, showing marked traces of small pox

THE VICTIM.

George Leggett was a member of a very respectable family, living at Edinburgh, Franklin county, this State—his father being one of the oldest farmers of the county named. One of his sisters is the wife of the Hon. T. E Knightly, formerly a State Representative and now assistant sergeant-at-arms of the House of Representatives at Washington. Another sister is the wife of Homer Frost, formerly a railroad conductor, now of Louisville, Ky. Some years since the deceased married Miss Lucy Dare, of Harrison, Ohio. He has one son about eight years of age. He is represented as having been worth from forty to fifty thousand dollars, and outside of his profession a man of generous impulses and honorable in his dealings. He was about the age of his murderer and of large and fine physical proportions. He was what might be termed a first-class gambler, and very successful. He is said to have engaged in legitimate business at several different times, but could never succeed therein. He was greatly esteemed by his friends and acquaintances. He was gentlemanly in his deportment and a man of sober habits.

ACHEY PLEADS GUILTY.

A few hours after the murder Achey was taken before Mayor Cavin, and when the indictment was read to him, and he was asked to plead thereto he replied, "I guess that is [illegible]; I plead guilty." He manifested but little if any concern for the dead, rather leading one to believe that he took pride in what he had done. He told officers Steinhaur and Shea as they were taking him to jail that they never "would get to hang him, for he would commit suicide."

One of the papers was mistaken in the statement that George Legget won all, or nearly all his money in gambling. He was left a considerable inheritance by his father.

When the coroner with his jury went to jail to take the testimony of Achey, the murderer of Leggett, he refused to say anything, having been posted by Hoffman, the murderer of Jesse Noble, to keep his mouth shut. He has already said enough to hang him, if hanging isn't played out in Marion county.

LOUIS GUETIG.

MOLLIE McGLEW.

From The People of Sept. 21st, 1878.

Another Fearful Murder.

Louis Guetig Kills Mollie McGlew.

ALL FOR LOVE.

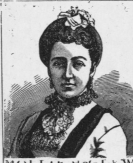

About 9 o'clock on Thursday night, September 19th, 1878, a most fiendish and brutal murder occurred at the Spencer House, corner of Illinois and Louisiana streets, in which Mollie McGlew, formerly a waiting girl in the house, was the victim, and Louis Guetig, a nephew of the proprietor, Henry Guetig, and his adopted son, the ruthless murderer. It was a cold-blooded, merciless affair, and, apparently, as causeless as brutal.

It seems that Guetig, who has not yet reached his majority, had been paying attentions to his victim for two years or more, and at one time was engaged to marry her. But of late he became quite dissipated, and preferred the company of dissolute women, when Mollie resolved that she would not trust her happiness in his hands. She afterward left the house and broke off the engagement. Since she left the Spencer young Guetig has several times threatened to take her life, and on Thursday night, as stated, accomplished the hellish deed. He had been drinking freely during the day, playing pool, etc., and had got his blood up to fever heat, until, as [illegible] his own assertion, he [illegible] was about as good a time to kill her as any. [illegible] between 8 and 9 o'clock he met his victim on the street, in company with a companion, Anna McLaughlin. He asked Mollie to go to the Spencer House with him to see his mother. She at first refused, but subsequently, at his earnest solicitation, and being afraid of him, accompanied him. They had got into the yard adjoining the laundry when he again asked her to go in and see his mother. She again declined, and some words passed between them, and he pulled out his pistol and commenced to fire at her. He had told a man on the sidewalk that he intended "to kill the d—d b—h!" His first ball missed Mollie and [illegible] the cheek of her companion, Annie McLaughlin. Mollie fell on her knees and implored him "for God's sake not to kill me!" He fired again, the ball almost tearing off two fingers of her left hand, and, entering the face under the left eye, passed through the lobe of the ear, taking a piece of the ear with it. The poor girl again begged piteously for mercy, but her frantic appeals were in vain; the brutal wretch fired again, exclaiming, "G—d d—n you, ain't you dead yet?" the third ball passing entirely through the neck, severing the jugular vein. He fired two other shots, one of which took effect in the thigh of Kate Collins, a dining room girl. The fifth shot was fired directly in the face of the already dying girl. The third shot is thought to have done the fatal work, the poor girl bleeding to death in a very short time. The murderer, after emptying all the chambers of his revolver, put it against his breast and pulled the trigger. The remains were taken to the undertaking establishment of Russell & Lee, where they still are.

The deceased is represented as being a brunette, quite good looking, tall and well proportioned, about 20 years of age. The Sentinel reporter, shortly after the murder, picked up her pocketbook, containing one ten, a five and a one dollar bill and a collar, with a slip of paper containing the address, "Miss Froseman, 37 Indiana avenue," and a paper of needles. One of the dead girl's slippers was also picked up close to where she had plead for mercy and received her death wound.

A Journal reporter interviewed young Guetig in the station house shortly after the murder. He said:

"Well, I suppose Mary is dead, and as I killed her I might as well tell all about it now as any other time. When Mary McGlew first came to the Spencer House, nearly five years ago, I met her and liked her very much, and I have been going with her all the time since then until a short time ago, when she went back on me. Ragsdale, the other clerk at the house, was the cause of this, because he lied to her like the devil about me and got her to promise to go with him about six weeks ago. This made me sick, and I had spasms for awhile. I told her that I would die if she did not go with me. Finally, after she had told me several times that she would not have any more to do with me, I concluded to kill her. Last Friday I wrote two notes and sent them to her at the house of Addie McLaughlin, No. 208 South West street. The first of these notes was asking her to let me know whether or not I should come down that evening, and the second was to let her know that I should be satisfied to let all of our difficulties drop there if she would agree to go with me. I told the boy to offer her the first note, and to give her the second after she had read the first. She refused to accept either of them, and when the boy returned and told me I felt very badly. I went on and got full of beer then and have kept full ever since. I intended to kill her last Friday evening if she had let me come down to call on her, and borrowed two revolvers to do the job with. But I couldn't make it work then, so I took the guns back where I got them. I haven't had a good chance since then, until last night, to do the job. Night before last I borrowed a revolver of a butcher whose name I won't tell representing to him that I was going to a dance. This evening I met Addie McLaughlin and Mary on South street, and thought I would kill her then, but Addie caught my wrist after I had my revolver in my hand, and made me promise not to shoot. That was about six o'clock, and about nine o'clock I met them at the Spencer House. Katie Collins was standing near them also. I walked up to where they were standing, drew my revolver and asked Mary if she would promise to go with me right along and she said she would. But I knew she was just saying that because she was afraid I was going to kill her. My adopted mother put her head out of the window and told me not to quarrel, and Ragsdale [illegible] me to come away, but I wanted to talk to Mary and wouldn't go. I don't believe I would have killed her just then if Katie Collins hadn't made such a d—d noise, yelling that I was going to kill Mary. Just then Mary moved as if she was going to step away, and I let her have it. I don't know how many shots I fired. I meant to save one for myself and finish my life, too. I fired the last shot with the revolver right against her face. Then she began to kick. God! I can see her kicking there just as plain as I can see you right in front of me. Then I placed the pistol to my heart and pulled the trigger, but the shots were all gone. I am sorry they were.

"I dont want any penitentiary business in mine for this, now. I ought to hang for it, and I want to. I want to be buried beside Mary, though; I want to see my mother, and then I don't give a d—n what comes. I want to die. I am in earnest about it. I am very sorry, indeed, that I shot Addie McLaughlin and Katie Collins, because I have nothing in the world against them, and they have always treated me right. I hope their wounds are not at all serious. Well, I guess I have told you about all I know, or want to tell you about this affair."

The deceased is represented as having been a very worthy girl—a strict Catholic. Her father is dead and her mother lives at Paris, Ill. She lost her life because she would not associate with a dissolute and vile young man. The wounds of Addie McLaughlin and Katie Collins are not thought to be serious. The murderer is so ready and willing to hang that we think he should be accommodated as soon as possible.

THE GALLOWS.

A. Drop partly sprung. B. Bolts supporting drop. C, Lever operating bolts. D, Ropes connecting drop with springs. E E to accelerate motion.

WM. MERRICK.

MRS. MERRICK.

From The People of Sept 28th 1879.

THE LATEST AND WORST.

Another Terrible Murder Brought to Light.

On Monday September 23, 1878, the city was all agog with the story of another and more atrocious murder than any of the appalling list that now darkens the history of Indianapolis. Three young men named William Palmer, and Joseph and Samuel Sponce [illegible] ported that whilst out upon a fishing excursion they had found the remains of a human being, lying in the woods near the Morris street bridge over Eagle creek. The coroner was at once summoned and with several other persons, accompanied the young men to the place, where guided by the stench, they reached a log, from behind which a human hand protruded.

After repeated efforts the log was displaced and a sickening spectacle met their eyes—the nude and discolored bodies of a woman and a babe, to which she had just given birth, wedged between her limbs.

The bodies were at once removed to Russell & Lee's undertaking establishment. The woman appeared young and of medium size; her hair was of a reddish brown; her upper teeth perfect, though the most of the lower ones were gone. The babe was a well developed male infant, with the umbilical cord nearly seven inches in length. Notwithstanding the horrible stench, a throng of persons with a strange taste for the horrible, crowded and jostled each other to look upon the bodies.

There appeared but slight evidence for the police to work upon to discover the brutal villain who committed this foul deed. There were wagon tracks in the sand and a rusty knife found near by. With the slightest possible clue they went to work, however, energetically and systematically, and within twenty hours arrested the man whom they had every reason to suspect to be the murder. This is William Merrick, owner of the Southside livery stable, and husband and father of the unfortunate woman and child.

The readers of The People will remember that in July last, we published the bastardy case of Julia A. Paul against William Merrick, which was compromised by marriage. Julia Paul was the daughter of a wealthy farmer of Morgan county. She was an intelligent and well educated girl, modest and reserved in manner, but at a very early age had an unfortunate misunderstanding with her parents and left home, and they have never been reconciled to each other. After leaving her parents Miss Paul supported herself by teaching school and teaching music, boarding in respectable families. At one time she boarded at Maywood with Dr. Sample Loftin, the present Democratic candidate for county treasurer. Her last engagement as a teacher was at Sunnyside.

By practicing economy Miss Paul had accumulated the sum of $450. About three years ago Julia Paul met her fate in the person of William Merrick, to whom she became engaged to be married. He seduced her and put off the marriage from time to time, and borrowed her money, which has never been paid. In October, 1877, she brought suit against him to recover her money; but soothed by his protestations and entreaties she withdrew the suit and lived with him during the winter. In July she sued him for bastardy, and finding the suit going against him Merrick consented to marry her openly, threating however to kill her. They were married on the 16th of July, but Merrick continued to keep a girl named Jessie Batchelor in his house whom his wife and others believed to be his mistress. Mr. and Mrs. Merrick separated soon after their marriage and she brought suit for divorce and alimony. Again Merrick made overtures for peace, dismissing the girl Batchelor, and in an evil hour she again relente. From this time there was little peace between them, though Mrs. Merrick tried in every way to conciliate the brute; her strange infatuation and devotion to him are attested by all who know them. He frequently cursed and taunted her, once telling her he would marry a black-haired girl before October. Mrs. Merrick told officers Beltz and Splann that she feared she would be murdered.

The last few days before her disappearance Merrick treated her more kindly, and on the fatal day—Saturday, the 14th—Mrs. Merrick told Mrs. Kissler, a neighbor, with great exultation, that "Will had asked her to ride." Though she was hourly expecting to be confined, Mrs. Kissler advised her to fix up in her best and go, and "may be all would yet come right." She then got into the buggy and went with him and never returned.

These facts having been hunted out by the police it was not difficult to form a conclusive chain of circumstantial evidence against Merrick, of which the following are the chief points: The dress and shawl worn by Mrs. Merrick upon the occasion of her leaving home were found and identified by Mrs. Kissler, who had assisted her to dress, and they were stained with blood. The carriage cushion and robe and Merrick's pantaloons were also full of blood. Dan Stepp, a boy employed at Merrick's stable, testified that on the afternoon of the 14th Merrick took his wife away in a buggy and told them all not to wait for him, that he would groom the horse himself. He returned at a late hour alone. John Fisck, a farmer, living near the locality of the murder, heard the screams of a woman coming from woods about 9 o'clock that night; got out of bed and dressed and went to the spot, where he found a man standing [illegible] ground in great agony. The man said she was drunk and was "just screaming because she could." Mr. Christian Lentz and wife then drove up, and Mr. Lentz and himself then assisted the woman into the buggy. They then went away, but Flack afterwards heard the woman screaming again. Both Flack and Lentz identified Merrick as the man.

A saloon-keeper on Indiana avenue, named William Hindel, states that on the afternoon of the 14th Merrick drove up to his saloon with a woman in the buggy. He went in and got whisky for himself and a glass of wine, he said, for his wife. Before taking it to her Hindel saw him empty a powder into it, and thought it strange at the time. Late that night Merrick returned for more whisky, and was alone.

These facts, in connection with the confused and contradictory statements of Merrick, seem to fasten his guilt beyond doubt. When questioned as to the mysterious disappearance of his wife he states that whilst riding with her they met a colored mid-wife, named Lucy, and his wife got out and went with her to stay until she was over her trouble, but he did not know where the woman lives, nor what her last name is.

There are various theories in regard to the murder. The child was evidently born whilst the mother was in her death agonies. At first the supposition was that having given her something to cause immediate labor, Merrick caused her death by malpractice, the womb being nearly torn from the body. It is now more generally conceded to have been poison, Merrick having bought strychnine the day previous to the murder, he said to kill rats. She must have been in one of her last convulsions at the time she was put into the buggy by Flack and Lentz, and the babe was probably born a minute after.

Merrick is a notoriously bad man. Fifteen years ago he was tried for murder at Connersville, and defended by Judge Logan. He then made a narrow escape for his life. He has since been arrested once or twice for stealing, and is a long-suspected resurrectionist. He is a medium sized man, neither particularly bad nor good looking. His hatred for the woman forced to be his wife was intense. It is little less than a phenomenon what strange attraction such a man could have for a person of Julia Paul's character and attainments that she should so persistently hold to him when she knew that such a course would only bring her misery and infamy, and her steps take hold on death.

Merrick lives in great terror of lynching. Like all other low and brutal creatures he is a coward. This is, in its details, the most shocking and revolting murder ever known to have been committed in this city.

Charles Broich, a druggist on South Meridian street, testified before the coroner's jury that on Thursday or Friday, September 12 or 13, he sold Merrick ten cents' worth of strychnine. He told Broich that he wanted it to kill dogs with. It is stated that the presence of strychnine has been detected in the stomach of the murdered woman.

The suspicion that Merrick had accomplices in committing his foul deed was strengthened by a colored wagon driver named Hiram Peters, who stated on last Thursday that he saw three men about midnight on the 14th washing their hands in the river near the spot where the murder had been committed. They were talking very earnestly in low tones.

If any doubts existed as to Merrick's guilt, they must have been dissipated by his behavior when confronted with William Hindel and Maurice Polsner on last Thursday. The former keeps the saloon at which place Merrick bought wine for his wife on the day of her disappearance. Mr. Polsner was in the saloon at the time, and both saw Merrick when he put the powder in her wine. When he saw these gentlemen enter his cell with Coroner Wishard, he became so nervous that he could scarcely stand, cringing and trembling and casting the most appealing glances at his attorney.

Merrick has made over his property to Jessie Batchelor, or Harmison, as it is found that is her real name. The girl it seems is really Merrick's neice. She came here from Kansas to go to school, and acknowledges that she has been living in adultery with her uncle, but denies all knowledge of the murder. Merrick says he made his property over to her because he got it from her mother.

The following are the circumstances of the murder at Connersville, for which Merrick was tried fifteen years ago, as told by a gen-

Continued on third page.

MORNING
LAS VEGAS GAZETTE.

VOL. 2. LAS VEGAS, N. M., MONDAY, DECEMBER 27, 1880. NO. 140.

EXTRA.

"THE KID."

At Last the Leaders of the Portales Gang Are Rounded up by Garrett and Party.

Billy "The Kid," Rudabaugh, Wilson and Pickett Now in the Vegas Jail,

Having Surrendered at Stinking Springs.

Story of the Search and Capture.

The greatest excitement prevailed yesterday afternoon when the news was noised abroad that Pat Garrett and Frank Stewart had arrived in town bringing with them Billy "the Kid," the notorious outlaw and three of his gang. People stood on the muddy street corners and in hotel offices and saloons talking of the great event. The excitement and interest can scarcely be imagined for days our people have been highly expectant to learn news from the parties in search of the desperadoes who have been depredating the Pecos and White Oaks country and when it was found that the nucleus of the band was captured they were at first dazed by the astonishing news of the success of the brave, determined men. Astonishment gave way to joy when the real truth was known. Groups of people flocked to the jail and hung around the corners straining their necks to catch a glimpse of Sheriff Garrett, Frank Stewart and the brave fellows who had brought in the outlaws. But they went quietly from the jail to the corral and from there to the National House where the half-starved, tired men sought to escape the scrutinizing gaze of the scores of hero woshipers.

A little after 4 o'clock yesterday afternoon a two-mule wagon hauling four or five men besides the driver, with three men on horseback came at a good gait up the old Santa Fe trail. They kept on past the plaza and drew up at the jail. The few who were on the streets followed the little cavalcade, but their curiosity was only slightly satisfied, for without any ceremony the crowd was quickly within the jail.

The announcement was made that the party comprised Billy "the Kid," captain of the gang that has been making its headquarters at Las Portales; Dave Rudabaugh, his desperate lieutenant who killed Lopez the jailer in this city the first of last April; Billy Wilson, the slick young fellow who has been passing counterfeit money, and Tom Pickett, the expoliceman of Vegas who was reported to have been killed in Sumner one week ago. News of their arrival ran like wildfire about town and everyone was on the *qui vive* for particulars of the capture.

A representative of the GAZETTE sought out Sheriff Garrett and had a short talk with him, but this modest man who has little to say, but is always ready for action, turned him over to Mr. M. S. Bazil, whom he said knew all the particulars.

Accompanying Mr. Bazil to the residence of Mr. T. W. Garrard the GAZETTE map was told the story of this last successful campaign.

After the affair at Jim Greathouse's ranch, the details of which were published in the GAZETTE a few days ago, "the Kid" and his few remaining followers thought it about time to leave the country. They went to the ranch of T. Z. Yerby and hung around there and the ranch of Mr. Bazil for some days, making frequent visits to Ft Sumner.

While they were rusticating about fifteen or twenty miles from here a Mexican living on Buffalo Arroyo, named Lojino Anala, came into Sumner, while a few of Garrett's party were there. It was thought by some that it would not be wise to allow him to go out again as it was intended to keep all news of the whereabouts of the party in search of the outlaws from them. A few suggested that he be detained till after the party set out, but he was finally permitted to go on his way. On the road home near Alamo Gordo Lojino met Bob Campbell, who was formerly employed by Mr. Bazil, and told him that Garrett and five men were already at Sumner and that more men were expected there, Campbell straightway rode off to find "the Kid's" gang and meeting them on the road, they fell back and secreted themselves. Two or three days later, Garrett's party left Sumner and Bob Campbell learning of this went to Bazil's ranche and hired a Mexican boy, about 16 years old, to take a note to Yerby's ranche telling the gang that the coast was all clear. The crowd were then making arrangements to leave the country but were anxious to get supplies and so they would venture into Sumner. Charley Bowder, who was recently so clamorous for a vindication from the charge of being a desperado, that was made against him in the GAZETTE, had been enticed by "the Kid" to join him. It is thought by many that the latter, who has a faculty for making friends with everybody, attracted Charley to him. They had both been concerned in the Lincoln county war and Charley knowing there was a U. S. warrant out for his arrest for a murder committed in Lincoln made arrangements to skip the country with them. On the 19th, Tom O'Foliard and Tom Pickett, "the Kid" and Rudabaugh, and Charley Bowdre and Billy Wilson, riding two and two, came into Sumner just about dark. Garrett and his men had returned and when the six came around the northeast corner of the hospital building, Garrett, who was in advance, ordered them to halt. O'Foliard and Pickett were in front and the former reached for his six-shooter but was not quick enough for Garrett who fired first, bringing down O'Foliard The other five put spurs to their horses and rode away under cover of a heavy fire from the attacking party. It was thought that Pickett was shot, as pools of blood were discovered, but this was a mistake, only O'Foliard being shot, besides one horse. The night was so foggy that the others got away safely. They made Bazil's, and Rudabaugh's horse was found to be badly shot through the entrails, and it is a wonder that it did not die on the way. Rudabaugh and one of the others doubled up and they made off as fast as they could.

Tom O'Foliard lived only two hours after being shot.

Word was brought to Garrett at Sumner that the croud were hanging around Bazil's and Yerby's ranch and Wednesday night sixteen men under command of Garrett set out for Bazil's, ten miles east of Sumner. They arrived there about midnight and learned that "the Kid" Rudabaugh, Wilson, Pickett and Bowdre had been there during the afternoon but had ridden away again. About three or four inches of snow was on the ground, and the moon being out it was easy to follow their trail. Following it up at about 3 o'clock they came to an old deserted house at Stinking Springs four miles away near the junction of the Cañunditas and Alamosa where they found the men. They divided into several parties and keeping guard on the house lay down to wait till daybreak.

The house is built of stone with a door and window on one side. It is situated about six or seven steps from the arroyo, on the top of a hill.

Just at daybreak Charlie Bowdre came to the door and stepped out. He had on a hat like what "the Kid" has been wearing, and he was mistaken for him. "The Kid" had repeatedly given out that he would never surrender, even though a six-shooter were placed to his head, that it wasn't thought worth while to give him a chance to surrender. Someone fired and Bowdre staggered and then bracing himself up for a moment against the door-post stepped into the house. He told his companions that he was badly wounded and could not assist them any and wanted to go out, and calling to the men outside the situation was explained. Bowdre stepped out again and started forward to give himself up when he reeled a little and said: "I wish —," and while making an effort to express his desire, he fell dead close by where one of the beseigers was lying concealed.

Quiet prevailed all day, the besiegers determined to stay until they carried away the outlaws dead or alive. The outlaws had two horses in the house with them and about 4 o'clock were discovered trying to drag in a third. They had his head and shoulders just inside the door when Garrett brought it down and it fell on the door step blocking up the entrance to the house. Two other horses were tied outside the house and the besiegers amused themselves by shooting at their halters and succeeded in cutting them loose. The intention of the gang was to get the third horse inside the house and then all four were to make a break on horseback. But they were forced to give up this plan as the body of the dead horse was a blockade against them. A consultation was held and Rudabaugh, Wilson and Pickett voted to surrender much to the disgust of "the Kid," who kicked and kicked, but it was of no avail. He branded the others as cowards but was unable to dissuade them from their project to surrender.

Finally, some of the attacking party saw a rag being twirled about the end of a stick stuck through the door which was mistrusted to be a flag of truce. Remembering the fate of poor Carlyle at Greathouse's, Garrett said that two could play at that game and let the crowd inside amuse themselves by waving the stick. He called out to them to know what they wanted when Rudabaugh announced that they wanted to surrender. They had not counted on such an easy capture and felt that the desperadoes were playing some game. But in response to the call "come out then." Rudabaugh advanced and talked with Garrett and some of the men.

He offered to surrender conditionally, provided the party would take them to Santa Fe, and everything being arranged, he returned to the house again. A short time only elapsed before they all filed out and gave themselves up.

They were mounted with some of their captors and the party moved on to Bazil's house, sending back a team for the guns and outfit of the gang which they had left in the house.

The two horses which had been stabled in the house belonged to "the Kid" and Billy Wilson and the former made a present of his to Frank Stewart. "The Kid's" animal is a beautiful bay mare, which he has always [illegible] to take him out of a tight place, and has shared his love in common with his guns. Stewart now has the pleasure of owning the fleetest horse in the territory, for it is said by many who have a good opportunity for judging that there is not another such animal in the territory.

Among the attacking party was Lojino, the Mexican, who had given information of Garrett's presence in Sumner, and whom the latter captured and forced to take part in the search for the outlaws.

The party spent the night at Bazil's, where Rudabaugh and "the Kid" were chained together. The body of Bowdre was taken to the house and it was found that he had been shot through the right breast the ball coming out in the neck.

Just after sunrise Friday morning the party set out for Sumner, with the body of Bowdre, and leaving that came on towards Vegas with a guard of nine men keeping watch over the prisoners, who were placed in Mr. Bazil's wagon. They reached Gerhardt's ranche about 10 o'clock that night and remained all night setting out the next morning again. Arriving at Puerta de Luna Saturday night about sundown they stopped long enough to change horses and chain Pickett and Wilson together, who until that time had not been bound. Here four of the guards left them and the rest traveled all night, and on the way the lock fastening the chain binding Wilson and Pickett was broken, but a sharp lookout was kept on them. They took breakfact at Mr. Hayes's yesterday morning about 10 o'clock and then came right through, arriving at the jail late in the afternoon as has been stated.

Besides Pat Gurrett and Frank Stewart, in the party who brought the gang into Vegas, there were J. N. East and F. W. Emory of the Panhandle and Barney Mason.

Garrett and some of his men guarded the prisoners carefully at the jail, it being their intention to take "the Kid" and Billy Wilson to Santa Fe to-day, as they are wanted for counfeiting as well as for other crimes. Rudabaugh and Pickett will be kept in our jail.

The party was intending to slip out of the country the morning that they were attacked so that the pursuing party were none too soon in coming up with them.

Billy "the Kid" explains that they thought that the besiegers were stronger than what they really were, and that it would have been certain death to have attempted to get away "Life is sweet if it is behind prison bars" exclaimed Billy. But "the Kid" will have enough of it to sour him, it we mistake not.

The campaign has been a credit to the brave fellows who have participated in it, and we congratulate Sheriff Garrett and all of his men for the successful issue of their round-up.

—The five hundred dollars reward for the [illegible] gang is not sufficient to pay Stewart, Garrett and party fo the work they havedone. It would be the proper thing and advisable for the citizens of Las Vegas to head subscriptions with a sum at least more adeqlate to the services rendered.

ASSASSINATION.

A. M. Conklin of the Socorro Sun Most Foully Murdered by one Baca.

Great Excitement Throughout the Territory and Justice Demanded.

A Probable Conflict at Socorro Between the Friends of the Parties.

Saturday the citizens of Las Vegas were startled and horrified by a telegraphic dispatch from Socorro stating that A. M. Conklin editor of the Socorro *Sun* had been shot through the heart and instantly killed by a Mexican while in attendance at a Christmas eve entertainment at the Methodist church of that city. The public excitement at once became great and the slightest particulars of the terrible event were eagerly sought after. A special to the *Gazette*, yesterday evening gives the particulars of the assassination

Two causes for the foul deed are stated in the dispatch. The immediate cause of the terrible deed was a reproof administsred by Mr. Conklin to the perpetrator, Jacabo Baca, in the church. Deceased was appointed usher at the Christmas tree entertainment. Jacabo Baca with several others came in and behaved in a disorderly manner and conducted themselves rudely towards ladies in the audience. Mr. Conklin at once quieted the disturbers giving them to understand that nothing improper would be alowed. Baca became very angry at the reproof and evidently nursed his vengeance and murderous intent until the close of the meeting. As the audience passed out, Mr. Conklin and wife also started home. On stepping out of the door he was seized on either side by two men while Baca fired two shots at his breast from a large six shooter. Both balls took effect one passing directly through the heart. He died almost instantly and without speaking. His wife fainted from the excitement and was carried into the church and the spectators were horrified by the violent death. Amid the excitement the murderers fled away to a place of safety under the protection of friends. The excitement in Socorro is intense and there are prospects of a bloody contest. The miners are gathering in from the mountains fully armed and determined to bring the offender to speedy justice. Saturday a large number of men came up from San Marcial equipped with Winchester rifles to see if the law and justice can be openly defied. Baca is a prominent citizen of Socorro and has held several important offices No justice of the peace can be found to issue a warrant for his arrest and this bold murderer is allowed to stalk under the protection of friends.

The deceased was a bold and fearless writer and it is said incurred the displeasure of the assassin while the Santa Fe correspondent of the GAZETTE last winter in reporting the proceedings of the Territorial legislature. Last winter, he criticised severely the abuses of civil trusts and boldly expressed his sentiments in favor of education and progressive measures. This malice has been cherished and but awaited this small provocation to put the hellish design into effect.

A M. Conklin was an upright man, a warm hearted friend and an affectionate husband. He was a careful writer, not aiming to give offense, but not fearing to express his honest conviction on all questions of public concern. He was exercising a power for good in this Territory. His paper, the Socorro Sun, is well established and his future prospects vere bright. Deceased came to this Territory on the 7th day of June 1876, the morning tnat Dugi and Barela were hanging on the well pump in the plaza. He accepted a position on the GAZETTE editorial staff and aided in establishing the Daily Gazette, working off and preserving the first paper from the press. He continued doing able duty for the Gazette until the meeting of the legislature in January when he went to Santa Fe as special correspondent. He crossed the mountains to Santa Fe on foot and wrote up his trip in a series of interesting letters. Last spring he went to Albuquerque and established a weekly paper and afterwards removed to Socorro where he had an open field and every prospect of success. Previous to coming to New Mexico he was connected with the Indianapolis Sentinel. He was, daring as he was, one of the brave volunteers who carried his musket with Sherman from Atlanta to the sea. He leaves a wife in deep affliction at his lost. His death was a foul and treacherous murder which demands that every power of the Territory should be brought into requisition to bring the perpetrators of it to justice. They must face the law for this thing.

Christmas Shootings

AT SANTA FE.

Passengers on the up train from Santa Fe yesterday, brought the news, that a shooting affair had taken place in that city on Christmas eveuing. The particulars of the affair appears to be about as follows:

Several men it seems, had engaged in a drunken row of some kind, when one of them drew his pistol and fired a shot at the other two who were a few feet distant. The ball missed its mark however, and took effect in the forehead of a German, who was in no way engaged in the affair. Another man was wounded but whether seriously or not, could not be ascertained.

AT WALLACE

early yesterday morning a breakman by the name of Whitney was shot through the body by Conductor Jim. Curery. At last accounts Whitney was not dead; the wound is thought to be fatal. A dispatch was sent to Bernalillo for a physician to attend the wounded man Whitney has the reputation of being a very quarrelsome man, and Curry was considered justifiable in the act. No feeling is evinced by the people at Wallace against Curry and he was not arrested as Whitney had followed him arround and tried to pick a fight with him. Curry is a freight Conductor on she A. T. & S. F. road and is favorably known in Las Vegas.

—They need a little Las Vegas justice in Socorro. This town has had some violent deeds, but it has established an enviable reputation for meting out justice to offender, Las Vegas has let but few guilty men escape. The remedy has been fearful, but the disease has been desperate Crime has not gone unpunished Criminals will learn to give Las Vegas a wide berth for when she calls them she is liable to get them.

DAILY GAZETTE

TUESDAY, DECEMBER 28, 1880.

HALT!

The Sheriff Orders out a Posse to Prevent Rudabaugh's Removal to Santa Fe.

Garrett Declares That He Has Given His Word and Rudabaugh Shall Go.

The Sheriff's Party Stop the Mail Train.

There were rumors about town on Sunday night that the party that had been captured at Stinking Springs would be taken from the jail and lynched. Pat Garrett, Stewart and the other captors put a stop to all this by standing guard over them themselves. Everything was, therefore, quiet; but the rage and hate of some of the people was at boiling point when it was made known that it was the intention of the party to take "the Kid," Wilson, Rudabaugh and Pickett to Santa Fe. Sheriff Romero remonstrated, saying that Rudabaugh should not go as he was wanted here on a warrant for killing Jailer Lopez "That makes no difference," said Stewart, "we gave all four our word that we would take them to Santa Fe, and go they shall."

Finding that no amount of persuasion would avail, Sheriff Romero telegraphed Gov. Wallace for an order restraining the party from removing the prisoners. Not receiving word before the time arrived to start for the train, the sheriff sent his deputies every which way commanding the attendance of various citizens at the depot, and he himself personally summonsed members of his posse.

All four of the captured men were taken to the depot and carefully boarded while the southbound train was side-tracked. The sheriff and a posse of thirty-five men was on hand, and made a formal demand for Rudabaugh. "We won't give him up and if you want him, you've got to come and take him," said Garrett.

The sheriff stationed a party to guard the switch and still another party covered the cab of the locomotive with Winchesters. While all these preliminaries were being arranged, men were gathering about the train and there was a bristling of Winchesters and a hump on the hip of many men that plainly showed that they had on shooting irons. Both platforms of the coach in which the prisoners were temporarily jailed were crowded with additional guards impressed into service by the Garrett-Stewart party.

The critical point was reached when Garrett exclaimed "if you wanted the men so badly why didn't you go out and take them." And then when something was said about taking them then, Frank Stewart said: "As soon as the first shot is fired we'll unloose every man and arm him." From the determined manner of the man they all knew that he meant every word that he said.

Within the railway jail, the guard were in readiness for action and six-shooters and Winchesters were seen resting on the window sills ready for action, and the first shot fired would have been a signal for the discharge of a whole broadside from the little battery. Rudabaugh was settled comfortably in one of the seats calmly puffing away at a cigar.

"Aren't you at all alarmed," was asked of "the Kid?"

"No! we knew to whom we were surrendering when we gave ourselves up. They gave us their word and they'll keep it: they will see us through," was the response.

Chief Engineer Robinson came upon the scene and demanded that the train be allowed to proceed. "Are you aware that you are detaining the U. S. mail?" he enquired. And Trainmaster Rogers declared that if the train was not released he would arm all the railroad men and take it out.

Detective J. F. Morley, a special officer of the post office department, jumped into the cab with a pair of six-shooters on, and told the engineer to let her go. But a conference had just concluded its labors, a compromise being effected by which it was agreed that the sheriff and two men should go to Santa Fe with the party and then if the governor agreed to let them bring back Rudabaugh they would return to Vegas with him.

He discharged the rest of his posse and they dispersed with a whoop, paling over a pile of boards which was taken by the crowd to be the signal for the opening of hostilities. A little puff went up from the locomotive and the train rolled on towards the south.

It certainly looked squally at one time but for all that there were men willing to give odds that no conflict would come off. Chief Engineer Robinson declared that he would arrest the sheriff and every man concerned in delaying the train but no arrests have yet been made.

THE KID.

Interview With Billy Bonney The Best Known Man in New Mexico.

With its accustomed enterprise the GAZETTE was the first paper to give the story of the capture of Billy Bonney, who has risen to notoriety under the *sobriquet* of "the Kid," Billy Wilson Dave Rudabaugh and Tom Pickett. Just at this time everything of interest about the men is especially interesting and after damning the party in general and "the Kid" in particular, through the columns of this paper we considered it the correct thing to give them a show.

Through the kindness of Sheriff Romero, a representative of the GAZETTE was admitted to the jail yesterday morning.

Mike Cosgrove, the obliging mail contractor, who has often met the boys while on business down the Pecos, had just gone in with four large bundles. The doors at the entrance stood open and a large crowd straining their necks to get a glimpse of the prisoners, who stood in the passage-way like children waiting for a Christmas tree distribution. One by one the bundles were unpacked disclosing a good suit of clothes for each man Mr. Cosgrove remarked that he wanted "to see the boys go away in style.

Billy "the Kid" and Billy Wilson who were shackled together stood patiently up while a blacksmith took off their shackles and bracelets to allow them an opportunity to make a change of clothing. Both prisoners watched the operation which was to set them free for a short while, but Wilson scarcely raised his eyes and spoke but once or twice to his compadre. Bonney, on the other hand, was light and chipper and was very communicative, laughing, joking and chatting with the by-standers.

"You appear to take it easy" the reporter said.

"Yes! What's the use of looking on the gloomy side of everything. The laugh's on me this time," he said. Then looking about the placita, he asked, "is the jail at Santa Fe any better than this?"

This seemed to trouble him considerably, for, as he explained "this is a terrible place to put a fellow in." He put the same question to every one who came near him and when he learned that there was nothing better in store for him, he shugged his shoulders and said something about putting up with what he had to.

He was the attraction of the show, and as he stood there, lightly kicking the toes of his boots on the stone pave ment to keep his feet warm, one would scarcely mistrust that he was he hero of the "Forty Thieves" romance which this paper has been running in serial form for six weeks or more.

"There was a big crowd gazing at me wasn't there," he exclaimed, and then smilingly continued "well, perhaps some of them will think me half man now; everyone seems to think I was some kind of an animal."

He did look human, indeed, but there was nothing very mannish about him in appearance, for he looked and acted a mere boy. He is about five feet, eight or nine inches tall, slightly built and lithe, weighing about 140; a frank open countenance, looking like a school boy, with the traditional silky fuzz on his upper lip; clear blue eyes, with a roguish snap about them; light hair and complexion. He is, in all, quite a handsome looking fellow, the only imperfection being two prominent front teeth slightly protruding like squirrel's teeth, and he has agreeable and winning ways.

A cloud came over his face when he made some allusions to his being made the hero of fabulous yarns, and something like indignation was expressed when he said that our Extra misrepresented him in saying that he called his associates cowards. "I never said any such a thing," he pouted "I know they ain't cowards."

Billy Wilson was glum and sober, but from underneath his broad-brimmed hat, we saw a face that had a by no means bad look. He is light complexioned, light haired, bluish-gray eyes, is a little stouter than Bonny, and far quieter. He appeared ashamed and not in very good spirits.

A final stroke of the hammer cut the last rivet on the bracelets, and they clanked on the pavement as they fell.

Bonney straightened up and and then rubbing his wrists, where the sharp edged irons had chafed him, said:

"I don't suppose you fellows would believe it but this is the first time I ever had bracelets on. But many another better fellow has had them on too."

With Wilson he walked towards the little hole in the wall to the place, which is no "sell" on a place of confinement. Just before entering he turned and looked back and exclaimed: "They say, a fool for luck, and a poor man for children'—Garrett takes them all in."

We saw him again at the depot when the crowd presented a really warlike appearance. Standing by the car, out of one of the windows of which he was leaning, he talked freely with us of the whole affair.

"I don't blame you for writing of me as you have. You had to believe others stories; but then I don't know as any one would believe anything good of me anyway." he said. "I wasn't the leader of any gang—I was for Billy all the time. About that Portales business, I owned the ranche with Charlie Bowdre. I took it up and was holding it because I knew that sometime a stage line would run by there and I wanted to keep it for a station. But, I found that there were certain men who wouldn't let me live in the country and so I was going to leave. We had all our grub in the house when they took us in, and we were going to a place about six miles away in the morning to cook it and then 'light' out. I haven't stolen any stock. I made my living by gambling but that was the only way I could live. They wouldn't let me settle down; if they had I wouldn't be here to-day," and he held up his right arm on which was the bracelet. "Chisum got me into all this trouble and then wouldn't he p me out. I went up to Lincoln to stand my trial on the warrant that was out for me, but the territory took a change of venue to Dona Ana, and I knew that I had no show, and so I skinned out.' When I went up to White Oaks the last time, I went there to consult with a lawyer, who had sent for me to come up. But I knew I couldn't stay there either."

The conversation then drifted to the question of the final round-up of the party. Billy's story is the same as that given in our Extra, issued at midnight on Sunday

"If it hadn't been for the dead horse in the doorway I wouldn't be here. I would have ridden out on my bay mare and taken my chances of escaping" said he. "But I couldn't ride out over that, for she would have jumped back, and I would have got it in the head. We could have staid in the house but there wouldn't have been anything gained by that for they would have starved us out. I thought it was better to come out and get a good square meal—don't you?"

The prospects of a fight exhiliarated him, and he bitterly bemeaned being chained. "If I only had my Winchester, I'd lick the whole crowd" was his confident comment on the strength of the attacking party. He sighed and sighed again for a chance to take a hand in the fight and the burden of his desire was to be set free to fight on the side of his captors as soon as he should smell powder.

As the train rolled out, he lifted his hat and invited us to call and see him in Santa Fe, calling out *adios*.

The Yankees' Christmas.

Again the New England Club laughed defiance to all old women's saws, by sitting down to a Christmas dinner with thirteen plates. The dinner was served in the Exchange dining rooms, in Deacon Sanford's best style. Great preparations had been made and the bill of fare was quite elaborate. Ample justice was done by the members who have already gained such notoriety as epicures. We doubt if a better dinner was ever spread anywhere else in the territory, which was voiced by the following:

Resolved: That, whereas we had reason to compliment Deacon Sanford and his assistants for the way in which they had previously served us, therefore, resolved that they have gone 'one better.'

After the banquet was over an adjournment was taken to the president's quarters where the evening was spent at whist and general jollity.

The following were in attendance at the dinner:

J. S. Pishon, C. F. Allen, M. Seamans, C. A. Rathbun, A. N. Houghton, A. A. Keen, F. W. Barton, L. V. Marks, Edgar Smith, Edmond Grover, H. C. Baldwin, H. A. Wise, George F. Canis.

—It is reported that brakeman Whitney, who was shot by conductor Curry, cannot possibly recover. He says that he does not blame Curry in the least for shooting him.

Las Vegas Daily Gazette Extra

Las Vegas, March 23, 2 P. M.

MURDER

James H. Curry, a Railroad Man Shot by Joe Ebright.

The Dastardly Deed Committed This Forenoon in a Low Den.

"Bertha's Parlor" the Scene, and Her "Pimp" the Author.

Our city has been the scene of another disgraceful shooting affair. Early this forenoon a rumor ran like wildfire through the streets that a man had been killed in a low-lived den on the east side. The excitement was great and every available vehicle on the west side was impressed into service carrying men to the scene of the murder. Men gathered in groups on the street corners and gravitated towards a small frame building in Center St., where the killing was made. There were numerous reports current as to the cause of the shooting but every one was united in saying that it was a cold blooded murder.

The murder was committed in a disreputable house on the south side of Centre St., just east of Maitland & Co. store, known as "Bertha's Parlor. James H. Curry, a freight conductor being shot and almost instantly killed by Joe Ebright, the barkeeper.

J. C. Caldwell, "Curly" as he is commonly called, a hackman was sitting in his carriage nearly opposite the house when the shooting took place and was a witness to the whole affair. "Curly" saw Curry walk down the street and enter the saloon, the door being wide open. Soon after there were loud words inside and a woman came to a door leading from the back part of the house into the saloon. Curry was seen to wave a six-shooter above his head when the woman ran back again. A man was in the saloon at the time drinking beer and when this gun play was made, he dashed outside and ran down the alley at the west side of the building, where he finished his potations.

Curry immediately after came to the door, placed his six-shooter in the right pocket of his coat, and turned back to the bar. He braced himself up against the bar, resting on his left arm, his right arm hanging at his side. Loud words passed between Curry and the barkeeper, in which some reference to money was made, and finally Ebright quickly pulled out an English "Bull-dog" pistol from under the bar, brought it down on Curry. Just as the former covered him, the latter drew back a step, the finger of the left hand still resting on the bar, and then Ebright fired. The ball struck Curry in the middle of the forehead, passing out behind the left ear, and the victim fell to the floor, dead. He was bespattered with brains and the blood oozed out into a little pool about the body of the unfortunate man. The report of the shot brought men quickly to the house but it was found that interment was all that was required for Curry.

Ebright promptly gave himself up, and after being carefully guarded in Judge Steele's office for a short while was sent to jail in a hack.

Wm. Steele, as justice of the peace and acting coroner, immediately ordered an inquest, and a jury of as good men as could be found was impanelled, who after sitting on the body returned the following verdict:

CORONER'S VERDICT.

TERRITORY OF NEW MEXICO, }
COUNTY OF SAN MIGUEL. } ss

We, the underigned justice of the peace and jury, who sat upon the inquest held this 23d day of March, 1881, on the body of James H. Curry, found in a house in east Las Vegas, in said county and Territory, and in precinct number 21, do find that the deceased came to his death by reason of a pistol shot fired from a pistol called a British bull-dog, calibre number 44, the same being in the hands of Joseph Ebright, and that said shooting and killing on the part of Joseph Ebright was done in self-defense. Given under our hands and seals this 23d day of March, 1881.

(Signed) WM. STEEL,
Justice of the Peace, Foreman.
J. W. LEWELLING,
A. G. STARK,
R. H. HOPPER
C. A. RATHBUN,
W. G. WARD,
I. M. TALBOTT,

While the inquest was in session there were heard rumors that a lynching was certain to follow. A large number of railroad men were in the streets, and their opinions were positive that prompt justice should be meted out to the murderer. The report of the jury was a surprise to many, for the first reports had all tended to show that the shooting was entirely unprovoked. No one, not even the friends of the dead man, has aught to say against the men who sat on the coroner's jury, for each and all are highly respected citizens, and the testimony that they had to consider certainly enabled them to form a better opinion than those who were excited by the news of the bloody affair.

Mr. Brightwell, with Maitland & Co., was standing on the sidewalk in front of the store. He stated that he saw Curry a short time before the shooting took place quarreling with a "soiled dove" at the door of a house of prostitution just above. Curry appeared to be drunk, and after a while he was ordered away. The "soiled dove" testified at the inquest that she "fired him out" of the house. It is stated by other people that Curry was rather promiscuous in swinging about with a full-cocked six-shooter.

Whether or not the man was drunk is not known, several testifying that he was, and others putting in counter evidence. It is reported that Curry was robbed last night in "Bertha's Parlor" of something like $75, but no proof of this has thus far has been educed. The theory is advanced by the friends of the victim that he went to the saloon to recover his money, supposed to have been stolen from him.

Till about noon the body of Curry was lying near where it fell, his friends not being able to find any room suitable for laying him out in. At last Rev. Mr. Murphy kindly offered Conductor Hornberger the use of a room over Stark's store, where the body could be kept till it was decided whether it should be buried here or sent east. Curry is survived by a daughter in Illinois whom it was considered proper to communicate with before any disposition was made of her father's remains.

Curry was a native of South Carolina, and about 42 years of age. He was a small man, about 5 ft. 6 1-2 inches tall, weighing 130 or 140 pounds. He has railroaded for many years, having run ten or twelve years in Texas, which accounts for his having been called "Texas" Curry, by which name he was generally known. He had been married but his wife died about eight or ten year ago. An only daughter, seventeen or eighteen years of age, has resided for some time on a farm near Quincy, Ill. She is said to be a highly accomplished young lady having recently graduated from a High School or Seminary in Illinois. Curry was well liked by all the railroad men who knew him, and is spoken of as generous to a fault. He has been on the A. T. & S. F. R. R. for three years, and for a year or more on the Southern division. He has been running from Vegas to Glorieta hill for some months. He was a hard drinker but has not borne a hard character. He was very economical and is supposed to have been worth some $4,000.

Ebright, who did the killing, is a hard character. A little less than two months ago he came to Vegas from Colorado with a woman called Bertha, equally as bad as himself.

They rented a store on Railroad Avenue, opposite the commission house of Browne & Manzanares representing that they intended running a cigar shop. It was soon apparent that it was one of the lowest houses of prostitution in the city, and they had to go. They opened the place spoken of, and there is no knowing what bad deeds may have been committed there, for in one way and another the place has gained a bad name. They sought to entice people to their "hell-hole" by sending out elaborate invitations, soliciting people to call at "Bertha's Parlor House." The cards of invitation bore the legend "wine and pleasure" which covered a multitude of crimes in that brothel.

Both man and woman are said to have a bad character, but we have no means of finding out their record at present. Ebright is still in jail, having requested that he be kept under guard, alleging that he fears violence.

DAILY GAZETTE

WEDNESDAY. APRIL 20, 1881

GAZETTE GLEANINGS.

BORN—To the wife of J. S. Duncan, April 19th, a son, twelve pound weight.

Borlan & Williams yesterday commenced the foundation for a new adobe wall for Mr. Fraley.

Close & Patterson are renovating their dance hall and putting in a new bar, furniture etc. They intend to keep up with the prosperity of the city.

Within the last few days a very important strike of mineral has been made. The exact locality of the find is not known, but it is said to be very rich. A number of gentlemen in this city are interested in the new strikes.

The Kansas City *Star* in commenting on the doings of Eugene Moise, who recently made himself so notorious in Las Vegas, states that he has borne a bad reputation in that city. His relatives and friends, who enjoy a high reputation, are reported to be greatly grieved by the actions of the young "blood."

The work of excavating the cellar for O. L. Houghton's new building on Center St. on the east side is being rushed ahead. Donohue, the contractor for the stone work and John B. Wootten, contractor of the carpenter work will commence operations as soon as everything is ready for them. The building must be ready for occupancy by June 10th.

Charles Patton, the man who was implicated in the robbery of Reilly last week, was brought before Judge Steel yesterday for trial. He was bound over in $1,000 to await the action of the grand jury and went to jail in default of bail. He was brought back from Pueblo where Officer Jilson was just in time to nab him.

The directors of the New Mexico & Southern Pacific R R. at their first meeting held in Santa Fe on Monday elected a board of directors and officers. The stock holders of the Rio Grande, Mexico & Pacific R. R. and the Rio Grande & Mexico extension companies
consolidat
company
consolidat
of directo
the only c
that Thor
dropped.

Sho
Special to th
Pueblo,
fray took
Saturday.
and a man
principals
quarrel a
shots we
in the
the town.
the lungs
er. Mast
started th
cape ther
As yet no
capture hi
been in th
[There we
on the stre
Bat Mast
Dodge Ci
were rep
The abo
ceived at
the *Puebl*
an inquiry
had happ
were unab
graph but
from that

A

Will Wi
placed co
since a yo
mons by n
tumwa, Ia
ed and "br
with whor
Iowa. I
circumsta
his room t
tended an
comfortab
spirits. S
mons who
health, it i
belonging
$300. Be
funds he r
erything o[f value he could manage to] walk off with. He is supposed to have left on the east bound express, and telegrams were sent out in the hopes of securing his detention at Nickerson, Ks.

Rev. Monjeau, of Kansas City, accompanied by Messrs. Strickler and Barnes, arrived on yesterday's train from the east. Mr. Monjeau brought considerable machinery with him for testing ores, which he will take to the White Oaks with him. The party will start to-day.

SAN MARCIAL'S BURNING.

Full Particulars with Amount of Losses.

Special to the Gazette.

San Marcial, April 19.—At two minutes past six o'clock this evening a wild cry of fire was heard and at six twenty the entire row of buildings west of the depot building, 22 in number, were in ashes. Simultaneous with the cry, great volumes of smoke issued from the rear of Lockwood's billiard hall. Within two minutes from the first cry the entire building was in flames. A furious gale prevailed and the flames swept across the street setting fire to Fred Geisler's new saloon and residence. So rapidly did the flames sweep that scarcely anything was saved. Many persons had barely time to escape. The unfortunates and their estimated losses are as follows: L. M. Speare, store, dwelling and four other buildings, $6,000, small insurance. Lockwood's billiard hall, $5,000, small insurance. F. Geisler, saloon and residence, $1,600, no insurance. Mrs. L. Eaton, lodging house and news stand, total loss, no insurance. "Gem" saloon, owned by Speare, total loss. Colorado Restaurant, owned by Chas. Hand, $600. Chris. Davis, bar and liquors, $700, no insurance. Burbridge, barber shop and building, total loss. Pat's "Way Up" saloon, total loss. Adams Express office, saved only the books and safe. Cook's saloon, total loss. Alex. Rogers, store room, hay, grain and provisions, $1,000. Concannon's saloon and boarding house, total loss, $5,000. Schwingle's wholesale store, nothing saved but a few pieces of furniture belonging to Mrs. Mitchell, now in Las Vegas. Holmes' lodging house, in the rear of Geisler's saloon a total loss. Immediately in the rear of Spear's store was a small frame building in which Mr. Spear had stored a thousand pounds of giant powder. this building as by a miracle is left standing unburned. Many of the saloonists and storekeepers had just received a new invoice of stock, not yet opened. The town will be rebuilt as speedily as possible. The origin of the fire as yet remains a mystery.

Joe Stokes.

[...] years of age, 5 ft. 9 in. tall, and weighed 165 pounds.

After Stoke's release from jail at this place he went south and took up with a disreputable character near El Paso and was aiming to make a new start by stealing cattle. A number of men from El Paso learnining of his depradations visited his retreat and took him and another man and hung them. Thus it seems that Stokes has met with a violent death at last.

Mrs. J. H. Mitchell of San Marcial arrived on yesterday's train.

Shooting at Dodge City.

Special to the Gazette.

Pueblo, April 19.—A shooting affray took place at Dodge City last Saturday. Bat Masterson, Peacock and a man named Updraff were the principals. The cause was a private quarrel and whisky. Over twenty shots were fired in the streets in the business part of the town. Updraff was shot through the lungs but possibly he may recover. Masterson and his party, who started the row, were allowed to escape thereby avoiding prosecution. As yet no efforts have been made to capture him. It is said that he has been in this city since the shooting.

[There were numerours rumos current on the streets last night stating that Bat Masterson had been killed in Dodge City. Numerous other men were reported killed or wounded. The above special despatch was received at a late hour last night from the *Pueblo Chieftain* in response to an inquiry from this office as to what had happened in Dodge City. We were unable to reach Dodge by telegraph but presume this is the latest from that place.—ED]

PERSONAL.

L. C. Roberts came up from Santa Fe yesterday.

O. Newell, of the Trinidad *News*, paid the GAZETTE office a pleasant call yesterday.

Doc. Webster of the Nogal mines left yesterday with shipments for his camp in that district.

Mr. and Mrs. Lockwood will start for New York City to-day. They will make that city their future home.

The floor is being put down in Hopper Bros. new store. The boys are becoming very nervous to get to the front.

J. E. Bass of Pueblo, Colorado, came in on yesterday's train. He will take a look at the country and likely make this his future home.

Fletcher A. Blake, of White Oaks, and family arrived on yesterday from Topeka. Mr. Blake will start to the White Oaks in a few days.

M. Friedman, a traveling agent for one of the principal liquor firms of Denver left on yesterday's train for the north. He did a good business while here.

W. P. Tuttle and D. H. Law of Chicago, Ill., have just returned from an extensive trip to the White Oaks, Mogollons and other mineral districts of the south.

Judge Lee and family of Cimarron came down on yesterdays train. They will make this city their future home. They will be heartily welcomed by the people of Las Vegas.

Whitehead, the talented correspondent of the Kansas City *Journal*, is now on his way back from a trip through California. He will write up New Mexico and his letters are certain to prove very interesting.

Thos. Goin, of Lockhart & Co.'s mills near Hermit's peak came in yesterday. He reports the mills running at a lively rate and turning out large amounts of lumber. He also says that trout fishing is excellent. Large numbers being caught daily.

Mr. F. C. Burchard, paying teller of the First National Bank of Denver, who has been spending several weeks of his vacation in Las Vegas journeyed south yesterday en route to San [...] He will spend several [...]e Golden Gate and then [...]e by the upper trans-con[...]oute. Mr. Burchard made [...]ds in Las Vegas who will welcome him again to the [...] of New Mexico.

[T]he Well Meeting.

[...]ht a goodly number of citi[...]t the St. Nicholas dining [...] purpose of considering [...]ty of continuing the work [...]l now being dug at Pader[...]. Geo. Hubbs. The meet[...]lled to order and Col. G. [...]d elected chairman, and [W]. G. Koogler and Frank [...] secretaries.

[...]hard stated the object of [...]g to be the obtaining of [...]he road to the White Oaks. [...]bbs stated that the well at [...] has been sunk to the depth [...]t a cost of $400. That there [...]dication of water at the [...]e. He estimates the prob[...]f sinking 90 feet further at [...]is amount to include the [...]f a team for the purpose of [...]ter to work with. The [...]tion of land whereon the [...]ated has been secured.

[...] M. Whiteman and Rev. [...] made some very applica[...]s on the subject and urged [...]ance to Las Vegas of carry[...] work to completion.

[...]190 has already been raised [...]ption.

[...]ion, the Chair appointed [W]hiteman, Robt. Hopper [...] Chas. Blanchard, as a com[...]wait upon the business men [...]as, to raise money in aid of [...]rise.

[...]on the meeting adjourned [...] the St. Nicholas Hotel Fri[...]or the purpose of consider[...]ort of the committee.

[...] New Tomatoes.

[...]ili Colorado and Celery at [...] & Boffa's. 4-20tf.

[W]ay Down Prices.

[...]sche offers great induce[...] boots and shoes, ties and [...]ationery and wall paper, [...] and edgings. My prices are the lowest ever named in Las Vegas.

Corn for sale at
C. E. WESCHE'S.—3-26-tf.

To the Public.

I am prepared to sell boots and shoes in job lots at a bargain. Goods forwarded to all points of the A. T. & S. F railroad. C. E. WESCHE, Las Vegas, N. M.

You Must Not Stay Away

from Bramm's because he has just received fresh cigars, imported and domestic; all kinds of wines and whisky so old that it reminds you of the revolution when you drink it. 3-23-tf.

Grand Masquerade at Concert Hall.

Thursday evening April 21. Masks can be obtained free at the hall.
4-19-3t. CHAS. E. TOFT.

The Man Who Talks.

Has been to the Centre Street Bakery and got some of that nice pickled tongue. 4-19-4t

Beautiful stock of pocket books at the New York Clothing House. 4-8-1m

The Man Who Laughs

Has just finished one of the five cent pies at the Centre Street bakery. 4194

C. R. Browning pays the highest cash price for county warrants. 4-8-tf

Wines and liquors of the best quality, and of the best brand at wholesale or retail at M. Heise's, south side of the plaza, Las Vegas, N. M. 353-tf

Cauliflower at
4-19-4t MARCELLINO & BOFFA'S.

A Man Without Brains

Should go to the Centre Street Bakery and get some of those "fresh fried brains." 4-19-4t

Special Class in Spanish

At the Las Vegas College from 7 to 8 p. m. Apply at College.

SilK neckwear, the largest stock in Las Vegas, at the Boston Clothing House.

Boys clothing, a fine selection of the latest spring styles for all ages, has just been received at the Boston Clothing House. 4-19-tf

Dress your boys with a nice summer suit at the Boston Clothing House. 4-19-tf

Crisp Celery

at Marcellino & Boffa's. 4-19-4t

Hurry Up

If you want to buy a store and lot in the center of the business portion of East Las Vegas to be sold at a bargain. Apply at Hartwell's Grocery Store. 4-7tf.

Corn meal for sale at
C. E. WESCHE'S.—3-26tf.

Seventy-Five Men.

Seventy-five men, tie makers and teamsters are wanted immediately. Apply to Eugenio Romero's tie camp at San Geronimo. 4-8-tf

Do you want something fine in the liquor and cigar line? Go to C. E. Wesche's. His sherry, port, claret, gin, his whiskys and cigars are magnificent.

Pie plant at
4-19-4t MARCELLINO & BOFFA'S.

The New York Clothing Store has received the finest line of goods, better quality and style than any other house in town. 4-8-1m

The freshest, neatest and most complete stock of summer suits are now to be found at the Boston Clothing House.

California canned fruits at
4-19-2t HOPPER & BROS.

Strawberries at
4-19-4t MARCELLINO & BOFFA'S.

Charles Rathbun, of the Chicago Shoe Store, has filled his new building full to overflowing with new goods, such as boots, shoes, hats caps, and the largest and finest stock of furnishing goods in the city is to be found at this place. C. E. Burt's celebrated shoes, and Burt & Packard's elegant make of shoes are to be found among his stock. Go there if you want something nice. 4-19-3t

California canned fruits just received at 4-19-2t HOPPER BROS.

A large number of the very best brands of cigars just received at Maitland & Co's. 4-19-4t

New Potatoes at
4-19-4t MARCELLINO & BOFFA'S.

Silver Plated Ware and Clocks.

T. Rutenbeck has just received a fine stock of silver plated ware and a number of fine fancy clocks suitable for wedding presents. He has also just opened a nice lot of gold and silver filigree jewelry. 4-16-1w.

I have just received a new line of gents linen collars, Balbrigan and British socks, suspenders, shirts and underware and have marked the goods at once at bottom prices.
C. E. WESCHE,
Plaza, Las Vegas, N. M.

J. D. Wolf having purchased A. Austin's interest in the Exchange saloon, will be glad to have his friends call and see him at his new place of business where he will be pleased to wait upon them with the best brands of liquors, wines and cigars, also two finely furnished club rooms are kept in connection with the saloon. Free lunch at all hours. 4-16-1w

For gold and silver filigree jewelry, fine plated ware and fancy clocks go to
4-16-1w T. RUTENBECK'S.

15 cents vs. 5 cents.

Why pay fifteen cents a glass for beer when you can get just as good for five at BRAMM'S.—3-23-tf.

Garfield pie at the Center Street Bakery, call around and try it.-4-14-4t

Buy a "hammock" at the New York Clothing House. 5-8-1m

—Go to M. Heise, on the south side of the plaza for fine wines, liquors and gars. 253-tf

Neat line of boys spring clothing at the New York Clothing Store.

Cabbages just received at Marcellino & Boffa's 4-14-4t.

Bath House.

Davis' American Steam Laundry and Bath house is the best place in Las Vegas to get a good warm or cold bath. Shower baths also. Central Las Vegas. 4-10-1w.

Entire new spring stock at the New York Clothing Store. 4-8-1m

Strawberries at
4-14-4t MARCELLINO & BOFFA'S.

Wanted-For Sale-For Rent-Lost.

FOR SALE.—The property on Zion Hill known as the Foster House. This property consists of two corner lots with a good two story frame building. Terms reasonable. Enquire of I. W. Foster. 4-19-1m

FOR SALE—Fine stock ranch, good range, plenty of running water, has a good house and corral. Will be sold for cash, or cattle taken in exchange. Apply to C. R. Browning, East Las Vegas. 3-13tf.

FOR SALE--Dry cows and calves. Also sheep. Address C. W. Lewis, Albuquerque, N. M.

LIME FOR SALE.—By Moore & Huff, at the Hot Springs. Leave orders at Herbert & Co's drug store, on the plaza.

FURNISHED ROOMS TO RENT.—Apply to Mrs. Judge Hubbell, opposite GAZETTE office. 3-30-tf

FOR RENT.—A double store room until recently occupied by T. Romero & Son west side of the plaza, Dold's block. Apply to A. Dold. 3-29-tf

FOR RENT.—Sewing Machines, new and old at Allison's. 157-tf.

FOR SALE—Five head of horses, three carriages and three sets of harness. Will be sold for cash or on time with approved security. Enquire at the office of Calvin Fisk, east Las Vegas. 4-10tf.

FOR SALE—Horses, mules, buggies, etc., at the livery stable, in east Las Vegas of
4-8-tf J. S. DUNCAN.

LOST.—A cameo ring. Initials and "1875" engraved within. Liberal reward upon leaving at First National Bank. 4-19-3

WANTED.—To buy a good sheep ranche with plenty of range and permanent water, with or without sheep. Address "Range," GAZETTE office. 4-20-2t

WANTED.—Job of building fences around yards. Address P. W., Postoffice box 156. 4-20-1

WANTED.—Sixteen Stonemasons by M. G. Donahue who will pay $4.00 per day; all workmen to be on hand by the 27th. Apply at Houghton's hardware store. 4-19-tf

WANTED.—Two or three number one planing mill bench hands. None but first-class need apply. At Wootten's planing mill.

WANTED.—A small house with three or more rooms. Inquire at this office.
4-16-1w

CAUTION.—The public is warned against purchasing a certificate of deposit given by Browne & Manzanares, No. 16,124, and for the sum of $100, as it is in improper hands and payment has been stopped.
3-29-1m D. D. MATHERSON.

Holbrook's tobacco is the best.

SANTA FE DAILY NEW MEXICAN.

VOLUME X.---NUMBER 53. SANTA FE, NEW MEXICO, TUESDAY MORNING, MAY 3, 1881. PRICE 5 CENTS

THE KID'S ESCAPE!

Full Details of His Escape From Jail at Lincoln.

The Shooting of His Guards With Their Own Weapons.

Desperation Unto Death, with the Coolness of a Turpin.

His Threats of Revenge Upon Sheriff Garrett and Others.

General Alarm Throughout the Country,

Mingled With Sorrow For the Dead Guards.

The Steamer Thomas Corwin to Leave San Francisco in a Short Time,

For the Arctic, to Search for the Jeanette and the Missing Whalers.

The Tide of Immigration, Still Flowing to this Country.

The Particulars of the "Kid's" Escape.

Special Correspondence of the NEW MEXICAN.
FORT STANTON, N. M.,
April 30, 1881.

EDITOR NEW MEXICAN:

The particulars of the escape of the notorious "Billy the Kid," are about as follows: Robert Ollinger and J. M. Bell were the two guards. The former had just gone to his supper, and Bell was sitting down on the floor, when "Kid" approached him, talking in his pleasant way. Quick as lightning he jumped and struck Bell with his handcuffs, fracturing the skull. He immediately snatched Bell's revolver and shot him through the breast. Ollinger, hearing the shot, ran from the house where he was eating supper (about seventy-five vards away) and just as he entered a small gate at the end of the house where "Kid" was confined, the latter, being in an upper story window, said, "Look out Bob," and immediately after fired a charge of buckshot into him, killing him instantly. "Kid" then went and made a man, who was in the corral of the house, saddle a horse for him; which being done, he jumped on and rode away, saying, "Adios, boys!" He has repeatedly threatened different men's lives since his arrest, and every person believes that he will put his threats into effect. The day before he escaped he said: "People thought me bad before; but if ever I should get free, I'll let them know what bad means."

Bound for the Arctic.

Washington, May 2.—The secretary of the treasury transmitted to San Francisco, to-day, the orders which are to govern the actions of Captain Hooper, of the Thomas Corwin, in his approaching cruise to the Arctic. The Corwin is to sail within a few days. The instructions given to her able and gallant commander are, like those under which he cruised last summer, most liberal and elastic. Nominally the Corwin goes to the Arctic to prevent frauds on the revenue, practically, she goes to discover the whereabouts of the Jeanette, and, if possible, of the Wallaston, and the Vigilant, to rescue their crews and bring them home. It is with this view that Secretary Windom confers upon the commander discretion and personal power. It is for this that the Corwin has been strengthened and improved, within and without, and furnished with double supplies of everything usually found in a ship's stores. She is in perfect condition, and is in fact much better fitted to battle with the ice than was the costly Roger, nee Mary and Helen. The Corwin's crew are picked men, and most of them have served in similar expeditions. Her commander, Charles L. Hooper, a young and enthusiastic skilled mariner, possesses the confidence of the treasury department to an unlimited extent. He achieved more in that icy region last summer than any of his predecessors. He is instructed this year to sail for Behring's Straits, stopping on the way at the stations on the coast, and the islands, and and from thence into the Arctic. He is to use every means in his power to find the missing vessels, and in the attempt is to be guided only by his own judgment. It is believed that he will find them, if they are to be found. The race between the Corwin and the Rogers, on this errand of mercy, will be an exciting one. Capt. Hooper believes that the whalers will never be see again.

Foreign Gold.

New York, May 2.—The steamer Rheim, recently arrived, brought over

"The Sick Man."

Constantinople, May 2.—An imperial irade, authorizing the Porte to accept the proposed solution of the Greek frontier question has been issued, and an official notice of the fact, for communication to the ambassadors of the powers, is being prepared. It is now pretty generally accepted that the reason for the sultan's zeal concerning the inquiry into the death of Abdul Aziz, is that a serious conspiracy was organizing against himself, in view of which he possibly thinks that an exemplary punishment of the assassins will furnish a salutary example. The sultan's two brothers, Ealam Mahomed Pasha and Noury Pasha, who are under arrest, are suspected of having been deeply implicated in both cases.

Constantinople, May 2.—It will be remembered that the vast treasure which Abdul Aziz amassed, mysteriously pisappeared after his decease, and that the ministry then in power, gave out that it had been used for war expenditures. Recent inquiry, however, tends to show considerable part was appropriated by high officials, and others connected with the palace. Noury and Mahmond have began to incriminate each other. Noury, for example, accuses Mahmond of having caused a female slave to be disemboweled to discover whether she had swallowed a valuable diamond which was missing from the treasury. During the examination of Fahri Bey, the chamberlain of Abdul Aziz, who is accused of an active share in the murder, although his victim had formerly conferred great benefits on him, the Sultan became very much excited, and declared that he could hardly refrain from taking vengeance on him with his own hands. On hearing this the chief nunuch beat Fahri with his fists, until the Sultan ordered him to desist.

Tea Culture.

Chicago, May 2.—The Inter Ocean's Washington correspondent says that the pet sheme of the commissioner of agriculture is now in a fair way of fruition, unless the official axe sends Mr. Le Duc's head into the basket. Meantime a venerable gentleman named Henry A. Middleton, living about twenty miles from Charleston, S. C. believes with the commissioner that the tea plant can be successfully cultivated in the United States. No money has been appropriated for the purchase of any land on which to establish a tea farm, but Mr. Middleton has leased to the commissioner a tract of 200 acres on his estate, for twenty years, in consideration of the sum of $100. A suitable building for carrying out the experiment will be constructed, and a Mr. John Jackson, whoha: been engaged in tea culture in India for sixteen years, will have charge of the plantation.

About 17,500 plants will be sent downthis spring, and thecommissioner avers that in three years he will have as fine a crop of tea as ever was raised in the world.

The Evangelists.

New York, May 2.—The Tribune says: Ira D. Sankey, the singing Evangelist, was present, yesterday afternoon, at the gospel services held in Lennox hall. He is looking well, though somewhat wearied. It is expected that Moody will be present at the Cooper union services, next Sunday, and continue to aid in the meetings during the summer. Sankey yesterday described his work on the Pacific coast as follows: "From the time we left here, until our return, it is just seven months, and the Lord has seemed to be with us in all our journeys and labors. We are greatly satisfied with our work on the Pacific coast."

Ireland's Reign of Terror.

London, May 2.—Accounts from the west of Ireland represent the state of affairs there as becoming very serious. A number of outrages of various degrees of atrocity are reported. Bands of men promenade the country and terrorize the inhabitants, unchecked. The Times says: It has been our painful duty to record, during the past two or three weeks, repeated acts of outrage in west and south Ireland, scarcely inferior in atrocity to those which awakened the national conscience four months ago. To-day's record of agrarain crime is more serious than at any time since January.

Abyssinia's King Not Dead.

Suez, Egypt, May 2.—The reports of the death of the king of Abyssinia are unfounded. Herr Gohard Rohlfs has just reached here from his mission on behalf of the German emperor to King John. He says that he met with a cordial reception. King John charged him to negotiate peace between Abyssinia and Egypt. Herr Rohlfs accepted the mission, provided that Germany sanctions it. He will start for Europe to-morrow, but will return to Egypt if the peace mission is approved. He says that he believes Abyssinia will declare war unless a definite treaty is accorded.

Decisive Engagement Expected.

Paris, May 2.—The Kroumers who were dislodged from the Rockpon sea-coast, are believed to have entrenched themselves on the heights near Sediabdallat. Three columns of troops are converging thither to cut off their retreat, and a decisive engagement is expected. All the mountains are alive with Arabs, armed with flint-lock guns, each man carrying thirty charges. It is impossible to calculate their numbers, as they appear behind every rock and tree.

Perished in the Flames.

New Providence, Pa., May 2.—The house of David Reese, near here, was burned this morning. While Mr. Reese and his son were endeavoring to preserve some effects from burning, the building suddenly collapsed and both were burned to death. Mrs. Reese was also severely burned.

Ingersoll.

New York, May 2.—Ingersoll lectured at the Academy of Music last evening, on the great infidels. The academy was not crowded. The ticket scalpers had secured a large number of the best tickets, but had to sell many of them at the regular

Denouncing Gorham.

New York, May 2.—The Times editorially says: Whatever has induced the republicans to select that gentleman, (Gorham), as their candidate for the secretaryship of the senate, there are very much stronger motives why he should be dropped. He is no more competent than any one of a hundred who might be named. It is understood that he represents in some undefined manner, jointly with Riddleberger, the wishes of Senator Mahone, but we do not understand that Senator Mahone makes his co-operation with the republicans conditional on the retention of Gorham. Even if he did, that would be no reason for adhering to Gorham, for under the existing circumstances, the republicans can much better afford to lose the aid of Mahone than they can afford to continue in so conspicuous a position as the supporters of the most prominent apoligest of the star route frauds. Whatever else Gorham may be, this is the character in which he is now, by his own choice, most generally recognized throughout the country, and no possible claim to consideration that he may possess can outweigh the scandal of this fact.

Brigands.

Constantinople, May 2.—The retreat of the brigands who captured Mr. Suter, the Englishman, and demand a ransom for him, has been cut off on the land side by the Turkish troops, and by sea by the gun-boats. A Turkish gun-boat recently chased a bark, which was believed to have been manned by the brigands, and having several times vainly summoned her to stop, sunk her. It is feared that Mr. Suter was on board the bark.

Doing Colorado.

Denver, May 2.—The second division of the Colorado and California excursion party, from Boston and Philadelphia, arrived in Denver at 7 o'clock yesterday morning, and after breakfasting left on the Rio Grande road for Maulton. They will visit the "Garden of the Gods" to-day, the grand cañon to-morrow, and go to Black Hawk and Georgetown on Wednesday. The party numbers about one hundred, nearly evenly divided between Philadelphians and Bostonians.

Emigrants.

London, May 2.—The Cunard line steamers, Scythia and Malta, which sailed from Liverpool Saturday last, for New York, took out more than 1,000 emigrants, a large number of them being Swedes. The Cunard company have arranged for dispatching four vessels to America the first of next week, all of which are expected to be filled with emigrants.

Counterfeiters.

Wilkesbarre, Pa., May 2.—Charles Moohen, of Pittsburg, was arrested here for passing counterfeit trade dollars. He was committed to jail this evening in default of $3,000 bail. There is a gang of counterfeiters in this city, of which he was leader, and other arrests will soon follow.

Revolution.

Havana, May 2.—There is probably a revolution going on in Santa Domingo. A Spanish mail steamer was not allowed to enter the port of the capital, under a pretext of the unhealthfulness of the crew. It was noticed that there was much unwonted commotion among the people on shore.

Another Strike.

New York, May 2.—The bakers have instituted a strike for an increase of wages or a reduction of hours. They paraded down town one thousand strong, and afterwards assembled at Irving hall, where addresses were made.

Through a Bridge.

Patterson, N. J., May 2.—An engine and tender on the Mount Clair and Greenwood Lake railway, yesterday afternoon, crashed through the trestle work at Kingswood. Engineer Skully and fireman John Marker were killed.

Burned.

St. Thomas, Ontario, May 2.—The Canada Southern's freight shed was burned this morning. The building was 150 feet long, and contained a large quantity of goods. The loss is between $50,000 and $100,000.

Referred to the Sultan.

Constantinople, May 2.—The bey of Tunis has telegraphed the Porte that he will not treat with the French, or any other government making proposals to him, to the Porte.

Warning.

Paris, May 2.—It is rumored that Abdul Kadir has written a warning to the French to prepare for a serious uprising in Algiers.

The Suez Canal Obstructed.

Port Said, Egypt, May 2.—A steamer is aground in the Suez canal and all the traffic is stopped.

An Increase Demanded.

Toronto, May 2.—The brakeman on the Grand Trunk line demand an increase of wages or they will strike.

Another Brigadier Gone.

New York, May 2.—General John S. Preston died at Columbia, S. C., yesterday.

Fillibustering.

The solons of the Illinois legislature have begun to ape congress in the methods of endeavoring to defeat or carry measures which come up for consideration. The Inter-Ocean thus describes the most important of the recent contests:

A fight over the apportionment question was the event in the Illinois house of representatives. It was forced upon the republicans by the democrats, and was conducted after the manner employed in the last congress, with equally successful results. The democrats refrained from voting on the senate resolution, and the greater part of the day was wasted in roll-calls and calls of the house, the former showing no quorum and the latter a quorum. At last the house

THE KID'S ESCAPE!

Full Details of His Escape From Jail at Lincoln.

The Shooting of His Guards With Their Own Weapons.

Desperation Unto Death, with the Coolness of a Turpin.

His Threats of Revenge Upon Sheriff Garrett and Others.

General Alarm Throughout the Country,

Mingled With Sorrow For the Dead Guards.

The Steamer Thomas Corwin to Leave San Francisco in a Short Time,

For the Arctic, to Search for the Jeanette and the Missing Whalers.

The Tide of Immigration, Still Flowing to this Country.

The Particulars of the "Kid's" Escape.

Special Correspondence of the NEW MEXICAN.
FORT STANTON, N. M.,
April 30, 1881.

EDITOR NEW MEXICAN:

The particulars of the escape of the notorious "Billy the Kid," are about as follows: Robert Ollinger and J. M. Bell were the two guards. The former had just gone to his supper, and Bell was sitting down on the floor, when "Kid" approached him, talking in his pleasant way. Quick as lightning he jumped and struck Bell with his handcuffs, fracturing the skull. He immediately snatched Bell's revolver and shot him through the breast. Ollinger, hearing the shot, ran from the house where he was eating supper (about seventy-five vards away) and just as he entered a small gate at the end of the house where "Kid" was confined, the latter, being in an upper story window, said, "Look out Bob," and immediately after fired a charge of buckshot into him, killing him instantly. "Kid" then went and made a man, who was in the corral of the house, saddle a horse for him; which being done, he jumped on and rode away, saying, "Adios, boys!" He has repeatedly threatened different men's lives since his arrest, and every person believes that he will put his threats into effect. The day before he escaped he said: "People thought me bad before; but if ever I should get free, I'll let them know what bad means."

since 1877 has been in high favor in the Contract Office. A. S. Patrick, of Omaha, is Brown's partner, and Patrick is backed by ex Governor Thayer, of Wyoming. Brown & Patrick were given the route from Rock Creek to Fort Custer at the rate of $12,000 per annum, which was increased by General Brady to $90,000. Brown's intimacy with the Contract Office secured the additional $78,000.

Chase Andrews was also a postoffice clerk, and was discharged by Postmaster General Tyner when he became head of the department. Mr. Andrews is a deacon in one of the Presbyterian churches in Washington.

In addition to the money given to these large contractors, who made their bids through straw agents, it is

reaching the common goal. There is plenty of room in New Mexico for any number of fine towns, and consequently no cause for injurious rivalry. So neighbors, Santa Fe will give you a healthy competition, but will aim at you no abuse nor black eyes.

PRESIDENT GARFIELD

The Murderous Attack on His Life This Morning.

LINCOLN'S MURDER RECALLED.

Why Was the Cowardly Attempt Made?

As we are writing these lines there is doubt as to whether the President's wounds are mortal. There is no one in the country who will not wish that he may survive.

The full particulars of the attempted assassination are not yet at hand. But from all that can be gathered there is reason to believe that the crime was the work of a lunatic and had no political significance whatever.

President Lincoln was slain at a moment when, to all appearance, he was about to enter upon the enjoyment of the fruits of the great work which he had done so much to accomplish. President Garfield has been struck down almost at the threshold of his term of office.

It would be idle at this moment to speculate upon the political consequences which are likely to result from this crime. That they will be grave and far-reaching there can be no doubt.

On the contrary, he was the lawfully chosen ruler of a great nation of freemen. No one had suffered injury at his hands.

But this morning, as he was about to leave Washington to rejoin his wife, who has for some time been in very delicate health, he was shot down by an assassin. A more cruel fate could not have been his had he been the Czar.

America is not Russia.

President Garfield was not a despotic tyrant, who had earned the hatred of men whom he had oppressed and wronged.

Nor was he the head of a system of autocratic government, in which freedom of speech and of action was liable at any moment to be punished as a crime worthy of death.

On our news pages we give all the information respecting the attempted assassination that has been obtained up to this moment.

The President may die; it is said at this moment that his death is inevitable. The universal sympathy of the people of the nation will be extended to his wife, who has been thus stricken with a terrible calamity.

President Garfield came to the Presidency at a comparatively very young age, as he will not reach his fiftieth year until the 19th of November next. His father died almost as soon as he was born, and there were three children older than he. His mother's struggles during their infancy have often been told of late and they form one of the most touching chapters of American biography. How her youngest son strove for an education amidst his rough surroundings has also been told. When but a mere boy he started to learn the carpenter's trade, but finding that he could earn more money by driving mules on the Ohio and Erie canals he took to that when seventeen years of age and soon rose to the position of boatman. He then conceived a scheme to ship as a sailor on the lakes, but a fever which he contracted by dint of hard work and poor living put an end to that.

In the spring of 1849, when he was not quite eighteen, his mother gave him a few dollars which she had saved for the purpose by pinching economy, and told him he could now realize his ambition of learning something more than the district school could teach. He went to Geauga Academy, an obscure institution in a country village not far from Orange, and being too poor to pay the $1.50 a week, which was the price asked for board, he took a few cooking utensils and a stock of provisions, and, hiring a room in an old unpainted farmhouse, boarded himself. From the day he left home for the academy he never had a dollar which he did not earn. He soon found employment with the carpenters of the village, and by working mornings and evenings and Saturdays he earned enough to pay his way. The summer vacation enabled him to save something towards the fall term, and in the ensuing winter he taught a district school. Thus he kept on for several years, teaching in the winter, working at the bench in summer and attending the academy during the fall and spring terms.

When he was twenty-three years old he felt that he had got all the education out of the country academy which it was capable of giving, and resolved to go to college. He was confident that he could enter the junior class, and so have only two years to complete the college course, and he calculated that he had saved by his teaching and carpenter work about half enough money to pay his expenses. How to get the rest of the sum needed was a problem. A kind hearted gentleman, many years his senior, who has ever since been one of his closest friends, loaned him the amount. So scrupulous was the young man about the payment of the debt that he got his life insured and placed the policy in his creditor's hands. "If I live," he said, "I shall pay you, and if I die you will suffer no loss." The debt was repaid soon after he graduated. He went to Williams College in the fall of 1854, and, as he had anticipated, passed the examination for the junior class. Two years later he graduated, and bore off the metaphysical honor.

PRESIDENT JAMES A. GARFIELD.

THE SHOOTING.

PRESIDENT GARFIELD'S HOME AT MENTOR, OHIO.

TAKING THE PRESIDENT TO THE WHITE HOUSE.

THE ATTEMPTED ASSASSINATION OF PRESIDENT GARFIELD THIS MORNING AT THE BALTIMORE AND POTOMAC DEPOT, WASHINGTON.

[FROM TELEGRAPHIC AND OTHER SKETCHES BY OUR SPECIAL ARTISTS.]

SANTA FE DAILY NEW MEXICAN.

VOLUME X.—NUMBER 118. SANTA FE, NEW MEXICO, TUESDAY MORNING, JULY 19, 1881. PRICE 5 CENTS

HUNTED DOWN.

"Billy the Kid" Falls a Victim to the Unerring Aim of Sheriff Pat Garrett,

Of Lincoln County, N. M., Who has Followed Him Ever Since His Escape;

Full Details of How the Noted Desperado Met His Death;

Shot Through the Heart, but Dies with His Boots Off.

The President has his Back Scratched, and Rolls Over, Crossing his Legs.

It is Proposed to Move Him to the Seashore,

Making the Trip by Water, As he Could Not Stand it By Rail for Some Time.

The Grand Jury Discharged And Guiteau Will Not Even Be Indicted Until Fall;

All the Star Route Cases also Go Over.

A Shocking Murder in Rio Arriba County, N. M.

The Death of "Billy the Kid."

Special Dispatch to the New Mexican.

Las Vegas, N. M., July 18.—The full particulars of the shooting of "Billy the Kid," at Ft. Sumner, about half past twelve o'clock on Saturday morning, were brought to this city early this morning by Mr. Cosgrove, the mail contractor, who was in the immediate vicinity at the time. It is a well known fact that Pat Garrett, the sheriff of Lincoln county, has been on his track ever since his escape from jail last May, and also that for some time past the "Kid" has been living near the fort disguised as a Mexican. On Friday, Garrett, knowing that the "Kid" was near, threatened violence to two or three Mexicans unless they divulged the whereabouts of the "Kid." The ruse having the desired effect, about midnight Garrett entered the room of one Pete Maxwell, a large stock owner, living at Ft. Sumner, to inquire if he knew anything of the "Kid," leaving two men to guard the door while he was inside. He had not been in Maxwell's room over twenty minutes when the "Kid" came along, greeting the two Mexicans and passed on into Maxwell's room. He was in his stocking feet and had his knife in his hand; from which fact it is supposed that he came there for the purpose of getting some meat, not suspecting the presence of Sheriff Garrett. When inside he discovered the form of Garrett, crouched down at the head of the bed, and asked Maxwell who was there, at the same time drawing his revolver. Maxwell did not answer, but whispered to Garrett, saying: "That's him." Billy again asked who it was but received no answer from Maxwell, that individual moving toward the foot of the bed, suspecting hot times. Billy then stepped a little to one side and the light of the moon shining very strongly through the window enabled Garrett to recognize the "Kid" to a certainty; whereupon he fired immediately, the ball passing through his heart. "The Kid" fell backwards, dead, his knife in one hand and revolver in the other, and never spoke after he fell. Garrett then shot at him again, but being in a great state of excitement missed him. It is supposed that Billy thought him a friend of his or of Maxwell's, and therefore did not endeavor to protect himself any better than he did, as had he suspected the presence of Garrett he would certainly have riddled him with bullets.

The Censors, Under the Land Bill.

London, July 18.—In the House of Commons to-day Mr. Gladstone announced the names of the censors under the land bill. They are: Sergeant O'Hagar, Edward Falconer Litton, (liberal) member of parliament, and John Vernon. The homeruler received the last name with prolonged groans. O'Donnell will divide the House on each name. Vernon is Lord Pembroke's agent and is well known in Ireland.

Murder in Rio Arriba County—A Guilty Wife and Her Paramour—The [illegible] Unearthed.

Special Correspondence of the New Mexican.

BLOOMFIELD, Rio Arriba county, N. M., July 16, 1881

A terrible murder has just been committed on the Animas river, Rio Arriba county, New Mexico, about twenty miles above Farmington. A family named Lewis moved into this country this spring from Canon City, Colo. They were accompanied by a man named T. H. Jennings. It seems that an undue intimacy has for a long time been existing between Mrs. Lewis and Jennings. Between the two a plan was arranged, by which the husband, Lewis, should be murdered and the guilty pair go back to Missouri, and be married. The plan was carried into execution on Friday, the 8th, instant. Lewis was killed by Jennings, his body hid in the bushes during the day time, and buried at night in a hole along side of an irrigating ditch and the water run over the ground in order to eradicate all signs of the crime. The absence of Lewis was noticed and Sheriff Blancett at once set to work to investigate the matter. With a skill equal to that of an experienced detective he managed to find the body, and fix the murder on Jennings. A party was formed to lynch Jennings, but by the great influence possessed by Haines and Sheriff Blancett this was prevented. Jennings, upon the assurance of these gentlemen that he should not be lynched, made a full confession, stating that the woman was the cause of the entire matter, and that upon a promise of marriage from her he committed the deed. After the coroners inquest, an examination was held before Captain Haines, justice of the peace, at which the woman also confessed to being implicated in the murder. Both of the prisoners were committed, and will be taken to Tierra Amarilla to be placed in jail. Sheriff Blancett will safely deliver these guilty parties to the proper authorities; and now comes the question, will they escape from the jail and evade their just dues?

All the parties in the case seem to have stood well, socially, in Cañon City, and to be possessed of considerable property. Three little children are thrown on the hands of the public by the death of their father, and the crime of their mother.

SUBSCRIBER.

The President has his Back Scratched.

New York, July 18.—The Herald's Washington special says: Dr. Bliss, on being intervied to-day said: "There was rather a funny thing happened to-day. We were dressing the Presidents wound with antizeptics dressing, which is done twice a day, and had him turned over on his side. I was bathing him with alcohol and pretty soon the President said: 'Doctor, scratch my back.' I began rubbing him up and down along the back bone with my hand, and said: 'Now when you feel that I have rubbed enough just say so.' I continued for some time, but the President said nothing. Pretty soon I called for a hair brush and used that instead of my hand. I then rubbed for a long time and his back was rather red. 'Now,' I said, in a laughing way: 'Now don't hesitate to speak out if you want me to stop.' He did not make any reply, but after a while he said, with a sort of a sigh: 'Well, Doctor, there is an end to all things; you can stop.' We all burst out laughing at this; he liked it so much that he hated to have me stop. He gains every day. To-day he rolled himself over in his bed and crossed his legs. We are going to talk about sitting up and going out. He said to me to-day, having heard that the Cabinet officers went down the river on the steamer Despatch on Saturday; 'Doctor, when do you think I can go out on the Despatch?'

"'Are you a good sailor, Mr. President?' said I.

"'I always have been and I guess I am now,' he replied.'

"'Well,' I answered, 'we will consider matters. I think you will be able to go out that way before you can go on a railroad.'"

As the Doctor went out one of the gentlemen connected with the White House, said: "I think that he will be sitting up inside of ten days."

Others predicted that by this time next week he would be able to get out of bed. The amount of solid food that the President is eating and his returning strength seem to justify these predictions.

A Stalwart of the Stalwarts.

Albany, July 18.—In the joint convention to-day, Tuthill said, that as to Conkling's resignation leaving the Senate democratic, so did Blaine's, or Kirkwood's, or Windom's, or Garfield's, but no action of the republican legislatures of Maine, Iowa, Minnesota, or Ohio would undertake to overthrow the time honored usage of all parties. Individual preferences were submitted to the arbitrament of a caucus, and harmony resulted, as it would have done here, and one of common fairness would have avoided the disclosures of the past few weeks. He scathingly alluded to the facts of the bribery indicted by the legislature, and said that if two men were indicted for a State's prison offence, it was time to adjourn when members are indicted for a State's prison offence. When irgular caucuses were resorted to, where this contest has so completely debauched certain participants and they have become so low and degraded as to be willing to allow themselves to be used as step ladder sneaks and transom peeping pimps, in order to give a locus of truth and currency to a weak innovation and base slander against an honest citizen, why not adjourn? he asked. Could they not trust the governor to fill the vacancy again, if necessary after reason resumed sway? If not could they not trust the people? Were they afraid to trust Conkling to go before the people? Were they afraid to trust him in Indiana and New York, when these States were essential to Garfield's election, and did he not vote carry the banner to victory and might to bask resplendent? He would vote for the stainless citizen, the matchless orator, the illustrious statesman, under whose wise and skillful leadership the republicans of New York had gained so many victories. He voted for Conkling.

The New York Election and the Speakership.

Chicago, July 18.—The Inter-Ocean's Washington special says: The news of the election of Warren Miller to the Senate to succeed Platt was not unexpected to the supporters of the administration. There is considerable speculation as to the effect which the choice of these gentlemen, who are members of the next House, to be senators, will have upon election of a Speaker and the other officers of the House. After the election of last fall the membership of the House was as follows: Total number of representatives, 293; republicans, 147; democrats 136; greenbackers, 9; independents, 1. The independent is J. Hyatt Smith, of Brooklyn, who will vote for the republican candidate for Speaker. Frye was elected a Senator to succeed Blaine and the vacancy there has not been filled. There are, or will be, four vacancies in New York, three of which were filled by republicans, viz: Morton, Miller and Lapham. No election has been ordered in the sixth district, wherein a vacancy was caused by the death of Fernando Wood. If, as is assured, the successors to Miller and Lapham cannot be elected and qualified in time to take their seats in December next. The greenbackers will hold the balance of power. The democrats here profess great confidence in their ability to elect a successor to Morton, notwithstanding the fact that the loss of one vote would be seriously felt by the republicans. The democrats, however, are believed to be reckoning without their host, in placing any reliance on the greenbackers' vote. It is hardly possible for the greenbackers to unite upon any candidate of their own for the speakership and the four Missouri greenbackers, Hazeltine, Rice, Ford and Burroughs, have announced their intentions of voting with the republicans.

Thinking of Moving the President to Long Branch.

New York, July 18.—A Washington special says: The intense weariness of the President with his confinement, which finds expression in almost every conversation with his friends and attendants, and the anxiety of Dr. Boynton to secure for Mrs. Garfield a change of scene and air has led to a discussion of the ways and means to make a movement without danger. Dr. Bliss says that the motion of a railway train might be dangerous, even for a month yet, while the danger of a train, the noise, crowds, etc., render that mode of travel out of the question for many weeks. Colonel Rockwell proposes, first to take the President to Old Point Comfort on the steamer Despatch. Should this prove of benefit after a few days there, to take advantage of the first calm weather and run around to Long Branch. The President is in favor of a seaside resort and longs for the sea voyage. Mrs. Garfield has taken a strong dislike to the White House. She says that every hour in it has been replete with care, illness and danger. She believes that if the President should recover quickly if once out of its influences. If his improvement continues at its present rate, the surgeons say that there is no reason why the President should not spend the first week of August at Long Branch.

Every effort will be made to keep from the President the knowledge of his mother's illness, as the shock might be injurious to him at present.

The New Ute Agency.

Washington, July 18.—J. J. Russell, the chairman of the Ute commission, arrived in Washington this morning and later in the day presented his report to Secretary Kirkwood, in which he stated that the commission had selected the lands and proposed to locate the Uncompaghre Utes in the Green and White rivers, in Utah, and that they proposed to erect a temporary agency building there and have the agency removed to that point as soon as possible.

By this arrangement the Uintahs, White River and Uncompaghre Utes will be placed side by side, immediately adjoining the Uintah river. Russell also states in his report that it would be necessary before the removal of the Uncompaghre to have a military force of at least 150 men stationed at the point indicated for the agency building, as well as a small force for the winter at the Uintah agency. Secretary Kirkwood at once transmitted a copy of this report to the Secretary of War, accompanied by a letter, in which he requested Secretary Lincoln to issue such instructions to the military commandants as may be necessary to carry into effect the views and wishes of the commission respecting the location of the troops at the new agency and at the Uintah reservation.

Extremely Weak, but Out of Danger.

Washington, July 18; Executive Mansion, 7:30 p. m.—The President has passed a very comfortable day. Dr. Boynton, in a conversation this afternoon, expressed the opinion that the critical period had passed, and that the President, although extremely weak, is now out of danger. Continuing he said: "There is no doubt that he will gain strength daily now and there is every reason to hope for his ultimate recovery."

Major Crump, stewart of the Mansion, and one of the night attendants upon the President says: "If the President continues as well during the next week as he has been for the past few days, he will in, my opinion, be able to sit up and eat his meals by next Sunday."

Major Swain, who is almost constantly with the President, said this afternoon that he was progressing finely. In reply to a question about Mrs. Garfield's health he said: "Oh, Mrs. Garfield is gitting along nicely; she spends most of the time at her husband's bedside.

The Potato and Tobacco Crops.

Washington, July 18.—The following reports, showing the condition, acreage, etc., of the potatoes and tobacco throughout the country, on July 1st, were issued to-day from the bureau of agriculture to-day:

Potatoes: There has been an increase of two per cent. in the area in potatoes throughout the whole country [illegible] 1880. The increase is general [illegible] sections. The States of New York and Michigan, report an increase of five per cent., Missouri an increase of six, and Ohio a decrease of two. The condition of the crop is reported to be very high. Insect injuries are reported in many localities, but the damage will be slight.

Tobacco: The acreage in tobacco is largely in excess of that of last year, particularly in Maryland, Virginia and Kentucky, but in view of the large decrease in 1880 in these States, owing to the scarcity of plants, it is not greater this year than in 1879, the year in which the area was given for the census of 1880. The condition of the crops i reported higher than at the same time last year.

Posting Drs. Hamilton and Agnew.

Washington, July 18.—The following telegram was sent by the attending surgeons to the consulting surgeons to-night:

Executive Mansion, 7 p. m.

Dr. Frank H. Hamilton and Dr. H. Agnew, New York:

Shortly after our dispatch of yesterday the President received an hypodemic injection of one-eighth of a grain of sulphate of morphia. He slept well during the night and this morning at 8:30, had a pulse of 88; temperature, 98.6; respiration, 18. This day, however, was not quite so comfortable as was yesterday. A slight gastric disturbance was noted towards noon, in consequence of which the quantity of nourishment administered was temporarily diminished. This was followed by rather more afternoon fever than he had yesterday, but the difference was not great and is thought to be merely a temporary fluctuation. At 1 p. m., to-day his pulse was 98; temperature, 98.5; respiration 18. At 7 p. m., his pulse was 102; temperature 100.7; respiration, 21

Signed) D. W. BLISS,
J. K. BARNES,
J. J. WOODWARD,
ROBT. REYBURN.

Freights Via Cape Horn.

New York, July 18.—The prevailing feature in the freight market via Cape Horn is dullness, without any outward signs of improvement. Both the A. J. Fullen and B. J. Cheney are well advanced and with pleasant weather ought to get away this week. Rates are firmly maintained and there is no sign whatever of weakness, notwithstanding the dullness of the market. Tonnage is still scarce, but there are several vessels pointing this way and some of the lines will no doubt secure them. The only charters to note are the ships Armenia, for the Van Vlick line, and the St. Lucie, with a cargo of coal to Pichilinque, on a government account, at $9.34 per ton.

Markets as a general thing remain quiet.

Wheat is dull and heavy and a half a cent lower.

Pork and lard are nominal.

Sugars are moderately active but prices are weak, and in some cases lower.

Hides are in limited demand, but firm.

Mustard seeds are in better demand, with sales of 150 pounds of California [illegible] from 3¾@4; now held at 4¼ @4½

[illegible] is nominal and dull.

Denver Locals.

Denver, July 18.—The Alvord House was to-day attached by Daniels, Fisher & Co. and Kilpatrick & Brown. The former's claim amounts to about $5,000 and the latter's to $3,000. Ireland, the junior partner, went East on Saturday, and the creditors suspected something crooked.

Ice has risen from twenty-five to fifty cents per hundred. Ireland was the proprietor of the Archer ice house and it has been attached for his debts. The only two other ice houses are the Crystal Lake, containing about 10,000 tons, and another with 2,000 tons. The Crystal Lake raised the price and the smaller company followed suit.

The county commissioners have increased the number of, and rearranged the voting precincts of this county.

Mayor Sopris has announced his intentention to not be a candidate for re-election.

Sitting Up By Sunday.

Washington, July 18.—To-day Crump said to the President that he believed that he would be sitting up to his breakfast next Sunday.

"Do you really think so?" asked the President.

"I do, indeed," replied Crump.

"I would not be surprised, myself, judging from the way I feel now," said the Bresident.

Doctors Bliss and Reyburn left the White House together about 9 o'clock to-night. Dr. Bliss replied when asked about the President: "He is doing splendidly and that covers everything. He is decidedly better than at any time yet. His fever came on later this evening than at any previous day. He has a good appetite and relishes his food. He is gaining some strength and beginning to be able to move himself about. He is cheerful and getting well."

The Highest Hopes Realized.

Washington. July 18.—To-day Dr. Bliss pressed on the President's stomach, along where the ball is believed to have passed, and started a flow of pus. The doctors say that at least a wine glass full of pus started, which is an indication that the wound is open all along the track of the ball and that it will begin healing from the inside. All the surgeons said to-night that their highest hopes of the President's case have been realized up to to-night and their confidence of his recovery is greater than ever before. Only one eighth of a grain of morphine is given every twenty-four hours now. The fever to-day has been very slight and the President rests well, sleeping most of the night.

Destructive Tornado.

Chicago, July 18.—The loss by the cyclone at; New Ulm, Minn., is estimated at $250,000. The track of the tornado is forty miles, long by one mile wide, and a full list of the killed and wounded is not yet obtainable. About a dozen lives are now known to have been lost.

One Advantage of the English Railway System.

London, July 18.—The Standard in an editorial says: The robbery on the railway train in America, an account of which is published to-day, although by no means an uncommon occurrence, happens to afford us an opportunity to reply to some American strictures upon the danger of the English plan of separate compartments. American cars seem specially made to invite this kind of outrage, while with the English system, such a wholesale raid is impossible. In any case, one carriage could alone be robbed before the passengers and officials could organize a resistance. As there is no example of such an event in our railway history, we may assume that the difficulty and danger is so great as to deter even the most daring criminals, and the actual danger of murder and robbery is far less on English lines than on American.

Taking Solid Food.

Washington, July 18; Executive Mansion, 9 a. m.—The President's progress towards convalescence, noted in the official bulletins of Saturday steadily continues. He feels greatly refreshed by the restful, unbroken sleep which he had last night and which was assisted by an agreeable change in the weather. His pulse is gradually lessening, it now being 88, with a normal temperature and respiration. He will receive for breakfast some beefsteak, toast, mint juice and poached eggs, the latter on a little oat meal cooked to a jelly. It is deemed best by the surgeons to give him solid, substantial food in the morning, discontinuing it at one o'clock, after which only liquid nourishment is administered.

Doctored Races.

Chicago, July 18.—The Times says: There is a shrewd suspicion abroad that the time at the Pittsburg races during the past week has been doctored in one or two instances for sensational purposes. The management is said not to be of a class to inspire the utmost confidence. The track is not known to be specially fast and when it was given out that Maud S. had lowered her record there, it was thought rather startling. Now comes the news that Mattie Hunter paced a mile there yesterday in 2:12¾, or 2¼ seconds lower than her record, and the fastest ever paced except Sleepy Tom's 2:12¼. This will be likely to cast a shadow of doubt over the alledged performance of Maud S.

Treasury Notes.

Washington, July 18.—Secretary Windom has gone to Deer Park to remain several days.

The Treasury Department to-day ordered the transfer of $5,104,466 in gold bullion from the New York assay office to the Philadelphia mint, to be coined into eagles and half eagles. This makes about $10,000,000 in bullion similarly transferred during the present month.

The Secretary of the Treasury has directed the redemption of the coupon five per cent bonds embraced in the 103d call, now outstanding, with interest to the date of their presentation.

Will Not Acknowledge His Defeat.

New York, July 18.- The Tribune says of Conkling, who arrived in town yesterday: Conkling declared that he was not beaten and that a final determined effort must be made to adjourn the legislature without electing a successor, "but at all hazards," said he, "Mr. Lapham must be prevented from reaping the reward of his perfidy by an election to the Senate." Conkling referred to Senator-elect Miller in a snearing way, according to his friends, while he did not notice his late supporter, Speaker Sharpe.

The War in Passenger Rates.

New York, July 18.—The war among the competing roads leading westward still continues, and to-day the scalpers are selling tickets to Chicago for $9. Persons purchasing tickets to points further west than Chicago do not find it an easy matter to obtain a reduction on the old rates. There appears to be no war on prices within this State. The greatest reduction is being made on tickets to Chicago. Many persons are taking advantage of this war, and are spending their vacations in the western cities.

Trouble With the Mexican Authorities at Guaymas.

San Francisco. July 18.—A Guaymas dispatch, via. Tucson, says: The federal judge here has refused permission to Sam Brannan to have his lands surveyed, and his engineers have gone to the City of Mexico. Brannan has appealed to the federal government, and will soon return to San Francisco to await developments. The railroad has resumed track laying, and has plenty of ties now, but only enough steel rails to get within seven miles of Hermosillo

Official Bulletin.

Washington, July 18; Executive Mansion, 7 p. m.—The President has had a little more fever this afternoon, which is regarded as merely a temporary fluctuation.

At 1 p. m. his pulse was 89; temperature, 98.5; respiration, 18. At present his pulse is 102; temperatere, 100.7; respiration, 21.

(Signed.) D. W. BLISS,
J. K. BARNES,
J. J. WOODWARD,
ROBT. REYBURN.

The Grand Jury Discharged.

Washington, July 18.—District Attorney Corkhill to-day read to the grand jury a note signed by the President's physicians, saying that while progressing well, his recovery is not certain. Then on Corkill's motion the jury were discharged until September 12th, so that nothing will be done with Guiteau until the fall. The adjournment carries the star route cases over also.

Paying out the Fishery Award.

Gloucester, Mass., July 18.—Secretary of State Blaine is paying out the money received from Great Britain on account of the unlawful interference with the American fishery fleet at New Foundland.

A Consolidation Effected.

New York, July 18.—A meeting of the stock holders of the Louisville, New Albany & Chicago Railroad, was held this afternoon for the purpose of voting upon the proposed consolidation with the Chicago & Indianapolis Railroad. Those interested refused to make known the result of the meeting, but it was learned from another source that the consolidation was effected.

Perished in the Flames.

San Francisco, July 18.—The hotel at Nimpew, Bath county, belonging to County Assessor McClennan, was this morning. Edward Morris and Wm. McIntosh perished in the flames, and a portion of the assessor's records were burned. The loss is $3,000. Mr. McClennan and family escaped with but slight injuries.

The Anglo-French Commission.

London, July 18.—In the House of Commons to-day the under secretary of state for foreign affairs said that the Anglo-French commissioners are now sitting in London in regard to the Newfoundland coast and that the action of the French commandant on that coast is now the subject of communications between the two governments.

A Two Years' Fight With a Fire.

Wilkesbarro, Pa., July 18.—After two years' labor the fire in the Stanton shaft, this city, has been subdued. The work of repairing the immense destruction caused by the water and fire is now being pushed vigorously.

Adjourned After Two Ballots.

Albany, July 18.—After two ballots, the stalwarts remaining unbroken, the convention adjourned.

Dead.

Washington, July 18.—Lieut. Colonel Nathaniel Michler died at Saratoga Springs yesterday.

HENRY O. FLIPPER,

THE COLORED OFFICER, ACCUSED OF DEFRAUDING THE UNITED STATES GOVERNMENT.

BLANCHE DOUGLAS,

THE NEW YORK CYPRIAN AND MISTRESS OF WALTER MALLEY, OF NEW HAVEN, CONN.

The Fort Smith Murderers.

Fort Smith, Ark., on September 9th, was the scene of the hanging of six murderers, three white men and three Indians.

Pat McGowan was of slender build, about five feet eight inches. He was thirty-five years of age; was born in Ireland but raised in this country from infancy; served in the Union army in the 12th Illinois Cavalry; was mustered out and went to live in Rockford, Ill. Thence he went to Cedar Falls, Iowa, where he worked at the wagon-making business. He left there in 1870, going through Kansas and the Territory to Texas; thence he drifted back to the Chickasaw country, where he married a white woman and took a lease on 360 acres of land, which he cultivated for a time with Latta. Falling out with Latta, he bought him out, and Latta left threatening McGowan's life. Shortly afterward McGowan, smarting under what he deemed to be dangerous to his life, followed Latta and shot him. He never denied the charge, and never ran away to avoid the deputies.

George W. Padgett is a heavy-set, fair complexioned man of twenty-three years of age. He was born in Smith county, Texas. He murdered Wm. H. Stephens in July, 1880, on the Salt Fork of the Arkansas river, about thirty miles south of Caldwell, Kansas. Stephens was a Texan and had charge of the herd. The difficulty arose about a few head of cattle that Padgett charged Stephens with having stolen in Texas. Padgett refused to "cut them out" of the herd for Stephens' share, and here a quarrel arose and Padgett shot him dead.

William T. Brown was born in Davis county, Missouri, and is twenty-seven years old. He has lived in the Chickasaw country for the last few years, and at the time of the murder was engaged in supplying the Quartermaster at Fort Sill with hay for the cavalry. He killed Ralph C. Tate, who was from Texas.

The two Creek Indian boys, Amos and Abler Manley, murdered a man named MacVeigh. They are respectively nineteen and seventeen years of age, and present the pure features of the uneducated Indian, wild and defiant. The murder they are charged with was bloody and brutal. They came to MacVeigh's house on a cold night in December last, and asked for a lodging. MacVeigh made a good, warm fire for them and placed a pallet near the fire for their use. Toward morning they arose and killed MacVeigh and mangled his hired man, Barnett, almost cutting his head off with an ax and completely severing his wrist. These boys had two trials. The first, early in May, the jury failed to agree, standing eleven for conviction and one for acquittal; the second trial the jury brought in their verdict of guilty in less than one hour. It has never transpired why these boys should have done this horrible deed.

Tulwaharjo is a full-blooded Seminole Indian, and is fifty-six years of age. He was one of a party of Indians under command of Charley Bowlegs (who was a son of the famous Billy Bowlegs, of Florida war fame), who murdered Scott Davis, a white man married to a Chickasaw woman, and also for the murder of Joseph Bateman, a white man who had leased under Davis. These murders were committed in May, 1879, and were outrageously cruel and cowardly. Davis was ambuscaded in a lonely place and shot, and was buried in a hollow tree. Bateman was fired upon while plowing in his field

A HUNTER'S DISCOVERY.

THE MANGLED CORPSE OF A BEAUTIFUL WOMAN FOUND IN A SWAMP; FREEPORT, L. I.

THE FORT SMITH, ARK., MURDERERS.

1—GEO. W. PADGETT. 2—WILLIAM T. BROWN. 3—PATRICK MC GOWAN. 4—ABLER MANLY. 5—TULWAHARJO. 6—AMOS MANLY.

Lieut. Flipper.

On the morning of August 13, the people of the pleasant garrison of Fort Davis, Texas, were thrown into a state of wild excitement by a rumor to the effect that Lieutenant H. O. Flipper of the Tenth cavalry (the only colored officer in the army), had been detected in an attempt to defraud the government of nearly $4,000. For several months Lieutenant Flipper has been Acting Commissary of Subsistence of that post, and a few days ago, Colonel Shafter, the commanding officer, received a telegram from the Commissary at San Antonio, stating that Lieutenant Flipper's funds had not been received, and requesting Colonel Shafter to investigate the affair. Colonel Shafter questioned Lieutenant Flipper, who stated that he had sent the funds by mail on the 9th of July, but that he had kept no record of them, and as no one had witnessed the mailing, he could not prove that he had done so. This was looked upon as a very gross piece of carelessness on the part of Lieutenant Flipper, but no one regarded it as anything more. On the following evening some of the officers thought that Lieutenant Flipper might be contemplating a flight into Mexico, so the commanding officer required him immediately to turn over his funds to another officer and relieved him from duty as acting commissary of subsistence.

The commanding officer determined to have Lieutenant Flipper's quarters searched for the missing checks. He accordingly placed him in arrest and began the search of his quarters.

The A. C. S. and the Adjutant repaired to Lieutenant Flipper's quarters, where the search began. Soon they were seen returning to the office with Lieut. F.'s cartridge belt and pistol. They reported the finding of over $300 lying around loose in different places. Much new woman's clothing in trunks, several patterns, and any amount of jewelry, a large diamond stud (afterward found to be paste), an elegant gold locket and neck chain, a woman's gold watch and chain, bracelets, four handsome finger rings, a man's gold watch and chain, and smaller articles. As the woman's clothes were found in Lieut. Flipper's room and closet, the Colonel meant to have Lucy Smith, a colored cook of Mr. Flipper's, searched.

During this the Colonel directed his orderly to take Lucy to his office, and he would question her as to whether the jewelry, etc., belonged to her, and if Mr. Flipper

THE FIVE CENT

WIDE AWAKE LIBRARY

Entered according to Act of Congress, in the year 1881, by FRANK TOUSEY, in the office of the Librarian of Congress, at Washington, D. C.

Entered at the Post Office at New York, N. Y., as Second Class Matter.

No. 457. {COMPLETE.} FRANK TOUSEY, PUBLISHER, 20 ROSE STREET, N. Y. NEW YORK, October 10, 1881. ISSUED EVERY MONDAY. {PRICE 5 CENTS.} Vol. I

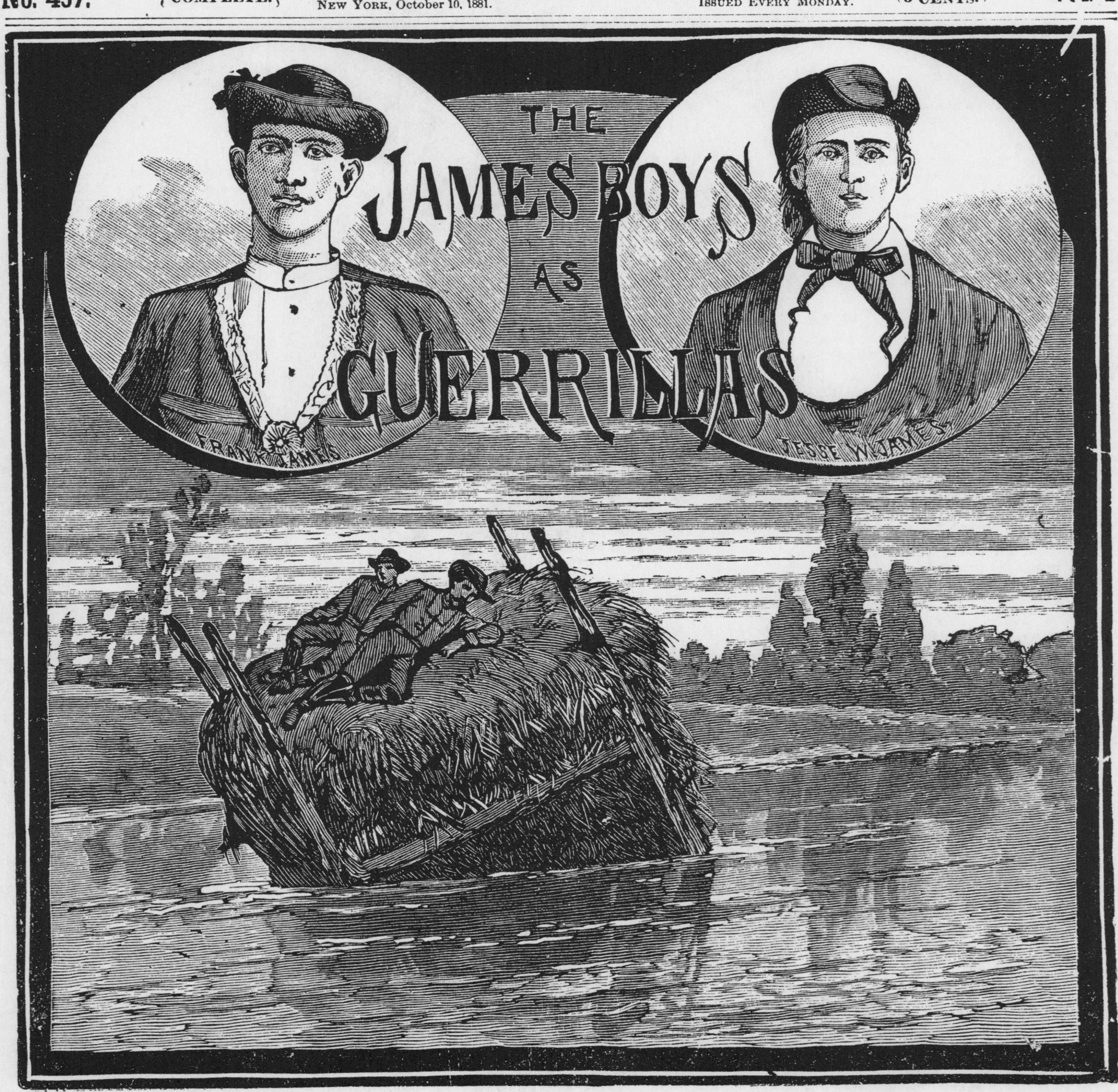

DAILY EPITAPH

Saturday Morning:...... Oct. 29, 1881

LOCAL SPLINTERS.

THE nipping weather of the last two days has made fire an indispensable luxury, and stove dealers are rushed with orders in consequence.

THE publication of the testimony in the case now before the Coroner's Jury, has crowded out our usual batch of news from our sister city of the plains.

THE walls of the store of P. W. Smith are rapidly rising from the earth, skyward. It will be an ornament to the city as well as a convenience to the owner.

Miss Nellie Cashman, Treasurer of Wolf Tone Branch of the Irish National Land League, forwarded to the executive authorities of the League, last night, the sum of $200.

M. CALISHER furnishes a very readable column of news in to-day's EPITAPH. It will well repay a careful perusal, as he offers great inducements to purchasers. He has a large and well selected stock of goods just opened at 525, 527, and 529 Allen street.

Miss Cashman has information that Tucson is the only town in Arizona that has not contributed funds in aid of the Irish National Land League. This is strange, when the fact is known that there are over 1,000 Irish-Americans in that city. Is it possible that the tropical heat of the ancient and honorable pueblo has burned the patriotism all out of the breasts of the sons of the Emerald Isle, resident there?

LOCAL PERSONALS.

MR. ARTHUR LAING came in from Bisbee yesterday.

MR. C. S. ABBOTT left for California yesterday morning. His absence will be but temporary as he has large interests here to look after.

MR. J. W. POWELL, who has been spending a few days in Tombstone, took his departure for New York last evening. He expressed himself well pleased with the mines of Tombstone. He is well qualified to speak from long experience in the silver mines of Nevada, and his favorable opinion will go far with our Eastern friends.

MR. BAKER, correspondent of the San Francisco Journal of Commerce, takes his leave of Tombstone this morning. While here, he went through the Grand Central and Tombstone Companies' mines, and expressed himself as surprised at the extent and richness of them. His report from this place to his journal will be entirely favorable.

UNCLAIMED telegrams: Miss Ella Sheldon, Martin Alarcon, Mrs. Mary Spencer, Wm. McDonald, Thos. Ogden, W T. O'Brien.

Justice's Court.

A. J. FELTER, J. P.

The Territory vs. Charles Ewing and John McGinness, arraigned for grand larceny, yesterday, plead not guilty. By consent of counsel, the case was continued until Monday the 31st inst., at 10 o'clock. These are the parties alleged to have stolen the mules and horses of L. Gruff, of this city, on the 24th of August last. Mr. Gruff had a man especially deputized to follow the thieves, which he did to El Paso, Texas, where he found the animals—fourteen in number, eleven mules and three horses—with these men, whom he arrested. He brought the whole outfit back to Tombstone, lodging the prisoners in jail.

Cochise County Records.

The following instruments were filed for record in the County Recorder's office yesterday:

DEEDS OF MINES.

J H Allman to C H Brooks, the Belgic, Huachuca Mountains; $50.

W Thomas to M Stuart, the Cactus, Tombstone district; $50.

DEEDS OF REAL ESTATE.

J West to T H Corrigan, lot 18, block 34, in Tombstone; $500.

T Anderson to J Locker, lot 13, block 33, in Tombstone; $800.

MILL SITE.

R E Gray, the Gladstone, Cochise district.

LOCATION NOTICES.

E W Stevens et al, Comet A, Dos Cabezas district.

E W Stevens et al., Comet B, Dos Cabezas district.

APPOINTMENT OF AGENT.

Ingersoll Consolidated Mining Company to H W Massey.

TRANSFER OF CONTRACT.

J M Armstrong to J Hunter.

POWER OF ATTORNEY.

J Liggett to A W Say.

J Hunter to A Hopkins.

Hotel Arrivals Yesterday.

AT THE GRAND.

J Reney, San Simon; J H Collins, Contention; William Reney and wife, Contention.

AT THE COSMOPOLITAN.

N. Henderson, Tucson; George R. King, El Paso; Mrs Watson, San Francisco; E H. Allen, El Paso; J B Watson, D W Wheeler, W H Savage, Tucson; W H Taylor, San Francisco.

Passenger Departures.

BY SANDY BOB'S STAGE.

Judge Dibble, S Rosenblat, S B Hastings, T M Pearlman, J Roach, G W Jones, J Ames, J Kendall, G Harkins, H Stewart, J Bugby, C S Abbott, Charles Peterson.

BY KINNEAR'S LINE.

E F Morehouse, J W Powell, Mrs. Dell Rhodes.

The One I Love.

He came home last night singing an old familiar song, the one I love so well, and dropping into an easy chair with more than his usual grace, and taking me on his lap presented me with a kiss and the loveliest set of jewelry I ever saw. Oh, it was just too sweet! I think they call it Filigree, and it was made in the extensive manufactory of S. H. Lucas & Co., Santa Fe, New Mexico. He has everything unique and pretty. Everybody should call at the popular store of P. Heitzelman for a few days, and examine the beauties. They are just too lovely.

OFFICERS and members of Solomon Lodge, U. D., F. and A. M., are hereby notified that there will be a meeting at their hall this (Saturday) evening, October 29. Visiting brethren are cordially invited.
W. A. HARWOOD, W. M.
C. D. REPPY, Sec.

CORONER'S INQUEST.

Investigation into the Cause of the Recent Killing.

Following is a verbatim copy of the testimony given before the Coroner's Jury in relation to the killing of the McLowry brothers and Clanton, up to the time of adjournment last evening. At the rate of progress made yesterday, the investigation is liable to last for a week.

The Coroner's Jury

was composed of the following citizens: T. F. Hudson, D. Calisher, M. Garrett, S. B. Comstock, J. W. Conwell, J. C. Davis, Thomas Moses, C. D. Reppy, F. Hafford, George H. Haskell, M. S. Goodrich.

The Testimony.

J. H. Behan, Sheriff of Cochise county, sworn, testified as follows: I was present on Fremont street when the shooting occurred; know all the parties participating in that affair. I slept late the day of the shooting; got up about 1 or half-past in the afternoon; went to the barber shop to get shaved; while there heard some one say there was liable to be trouble between Clanton and the Earp boys. Told the barber to hurry up, as I wanted to get out to arrest and disarm the party. I meant all of them, every one that had arms except the officers. Going out, crossed the street to Hafford's corner and asked Marshal Earp what was the excitement. He said, "There are a lot of—I think he said —s—s of b—s who want to make a fight." Said to him: "You had better disarm them." He said he would not do it, and if they wanted a fight they could have it. I said: "It is your duty as a peace officer to stop this thing." Told him I was going to arrest and disarm the cow-boys, meaning McLowry and any others that had arms or showed a disposition to make trouble. Walked to corner of Fourth and Fremont streets; met Frank McLowry holding a horse; told him to give up his arms. He said he would not unless the other people were disarmed also. Think he referred to Holliday and the Earps. Said also that he had done nothing and did not want to make a fight. I looked down Fremont street and saw the Clanton brothers with Tom McLowry. I said to Frank, "Come on with me," and we went together to where the parties who were killed and Ike Clanton were standing. I said: "I will arrest you all. Go up to the Sheriff's office and lay down your arms." Frank McLowry demurred to going, saying that the Earps should be arrested as well. About that time saw Marshal Earp, Doc Holliday, Wyatt Earp and Morgan Earp coming down the street. Expecting there would be trouble if they met, I walked towards them and ordered them back as I was there to disarm the party. Appealed to them several times not to go any further, but they passed on. When they got to the party of cow-boys they drew their guns and said, "You s—s of b—s, you have been looking for a fight, you can have it now." Some one, I think Marshal Earp, said, "Throw up your hands, we are going to disarm you." Then the fight began, some 25 or 30 shots being fired. Could not count them; they sounded like a bunch of firecrackers to me. Could not count them. Before firing commenced I kept telling all parties to put up their arms, not to shoot. Heard Billy Clanton say, "Don't shoot me, I don't want to fight," or something to that effect. Afterwards saw Billy Clanton shooting while lying on the ground, his gun resting on his knee. Before the shooting Tom McLowry said, "I have nothing," and threw his coat open to show he was unarmed. The order to throw up their hands, this remark of McLowry's and the shooting were almost simultaneous. After the fight was over Wyatt Earp said to me, "You have deceived me; you told me you had disarmed them." Told him I had said nothing of the kind, and repeated my conversation with the other party before the fight. Found before the fight that Ike Clanton was unarmed, he told me they were "Just getting ready to leave town." Frank McLowry and William Clanton were the only two of the party that I knew to be armed. Frank McLowry had a horse, think Bill Clanton had one, am not sure. There were six of us standing around. Clanton said there were four in their party. Cannot say who shot first, think a nickle-plated pistol was the first to go off; it was on Earp's side. There was also a shot gun, Holliday had it; was putting it under his coat to conceal it when they came down the street. Don't know whether the shot-gun was fired. First saw Billy Clanton shoot, then Frank McLowry who was on north side Fremont street almost opposite Fly's. Did not see Tom McLowry fall, watched Frank most of the time. Fight commenced on a vacant space between Fly's and the next house west. This is on south side of Fremont street between Fourth and Fifth. Am satisfied that two of Clanton's party were unarmed at the time of shooting, viz., Ike Clanton and Tom McLowry. The Earp party and the McLowrys were violating a city ordinance when I went to disarm them; thought there would be trouble, and went to disarm them for that reason. No one but McLowry refused to give up their arms: did not tell the Earp party that I had disarmed the other party; did not tell them there would be trouble if they went down, but said I would not allow trouble if I could help it; Frank McLowry did not have his pistol drawn when Marshal Earp told him to throw up his hands. Considered the Clanton party under arrest when I left them, before meeting the Earp party; nothing was said to lead me to believe the Earps were acting in an official capacity. After the fight was over, heard Wyatt Earp say, "We won't have to disarm that party;" think Virgil Earp said the same thing. During my conversation with the boys, Ike Clanton said he was going out of town, but Frank McLowry said he was not, as he was on business. [A juror asked witness if he considered a party under arrest when he refused to give up his arms. Mr. Behan replied, "Certainly not."]

WILLIAM CLAIBORNE

On being sworn testified as follows: Was present at the shooting; know the parties engaged in it. They were, Frank McLowry, Tom McLowry, Billy Clanton, and Ike Clanton, Doc Holliday and three Earp brothers; don't know their names except Morgan. Was standing with Mr. Behan, the McLowrys and Clantons when shooting commenced. The day it happened went to Dr. Gillingham's with Ike Clanton to get his head dressed. After that I walked up Fourth street and met Bill Clanton and Frank McLowry. Bill said, "Were is Ike? I want to get him and go home; I don't want to fight anyone." He then asked me to go to Behan's stable with him. We went to the stable and got his (Bill's) horse, after which we passed through Benson's corral. Bill said he wanted to go to some other corral to get his brother's horse. Just then we met Ike and the McLowry boys. Bill said, "Ike, I want you to get your horse and come home." Ike told him he would "go directly." At this time the sheriff came up and commenced talking to the boys. Didn't hear what he said. Soon after Behan turned his back and walked up the street, and next thing I saw was Doc Holliday, Morgan Earp, and his two brothers. Marshal Earp says, "You s—s of b—s, you have been looking for a fight and now you can have it." Earp then said, "Throw up your hands," which Bill Clanton, Ike Clanton, and Frank McLowry did. Tom McLowry caught hold of the side of his coat and said, "I haven't got anything." At that instant the shooting commenced by Doc Holliday and Morgan Earp. The first shot took Tom McLowry which was fired by Doc Holliday. The next by Morgan Earp struck Billy Clanton while his hands were up above his head. After firing commenced, Bill Clanton said, "Don't shoot me, I don't want to fight." That is the last I saw of Bill alive. Then Behan put me in the photograph gallery out of the way. Next I saw the dead bodies in the presence of the coroner's jury and identified them under oath. Had known them all for about four years. Don't know whether Bill heard any of the conversation on the part of the Sheriff or not. He was talking to me about fifteen minutes while the Sheriff was talking to the others. When the Earp party came up they had their pistols in their hands. Saw Bill Clanton draw his pistol after he was shot down. Frank McLowry drew his pistol after the Earps had fired about six shots. Am sure the first two shots were fired by Morgan Earp and Holliday. At the first shot, Tom McLowry staggered back a little. Don't think he fell. He had no weapon of any kind. Think there were about 16 shots fired before I left. Was struck myself through the leg by a bullet. Ike left after seven or eight shots; did not see what he was doing while he was there; think the Sheriff had been with the boys about twenty minutes; he asked me if I was one of the party, and I told him no; said they were doing the same thing; they said no also. The distance between the parties was not over four feet when the shooting commenced; think Doc Holliday fired the first shot, with a nickel-plated six-shooter; don't think I saw a shot-gun in the fight; think there were about 28 or 30 shots altogether. While I was talking to the Clantons, they spoke of going home and said nothing of fighting. The McLowrys had been in town about three-quarters of an hour when the trouble commenced; saw the other two Earps firing before Bill and Frank commenced shooting.

C. H. LIGHT

Testified: Saw part of the shooting between the Earps and Doc Holliday, and the McLowrys and Clantons; know the Earps and Doc Holliday since the shooting. While being shaved that afternoon the barber told me there was likely to be trouble between the Earps and Doc Holliday, and the cow-boys; saw the Earps just pass down street with their guns; then went towards my house, corner Third and Tough Nut streets; was in the house when the shooting commenced; heard two shots an instant apart; going to the window saw a man reel and fall at corner of Fremont and Third streets. Don't know who the man was. Looked up Fremont street and saw a man standing with a horse. There appeared to be two men firing at the man. He appeared to be struck. Saw him fire at the man lowest down on Fremont street; his shot seemed to take effect, as the man fired at turned partly round. Next saw a man leaning against the side of the house slide to the ground apparently wounded; his head and shoulders rested against the house; he rested his pistol across his leg and fired two shots; tried to fire a third, but was too weak; the shot went into the air. At this time, there was a tall man with gray clothes and a broad hat standing about the middle of the street in the direction of the man leaning against the house. There was another party firing down the street toward where the man lay; this man fired only three shots; a few more shots were fired by parties on this side of the street. Saw no one fall on the north side of the street; my view was obscured. Next a tall man, dressed in black, appeared with a rifle in his hand and said, take that pistol away from that man (the man on the ground), or he would kill him; this man with the rifle was not a participant in the fight. Whole thing occupied about 15 or 20 seconds. Think there were about six parties firing and no more, four in the middle of the street, one on the south side, and one with the horse. Recognized the man with the gray clothes as Holliday. Must have been 25 or 30 shots fired. I was probably 130 or 140 feet away. Saw no shot-gun; think first two shots were pistols; may have heard report of shot-gun afterwards, but cannot be positive. Saw the man who fell on the street lying there during the fight; did not see him shoot. There was not time between first two shots for a man to draw his pistol. Heard two shots before I got to the window.

WM. A. CUDDY

on being sworn said: I was standing at the postoffice when Mr. Dillon told me there was some trouble between the Earps and the cow-boys, then Mr. Page told me the cow-boys were down at Fly's house. Walked down there and saw Sheriff Behan and four farmers. As I approached saw one of them, Bill Clanton, put his hand on his pistol as if in fear of some one, then recognizing me he withdrew his hand. Heard Behan say, "I won't have any fighting, you must give up your arms or leave town at once." Ike Clanton answered, "There will be no trouble with us, Johnny, we are going to leave town now." I walked off and got as far as the dance-house on Allen street, when shooting began. Looking towards where I had left the Sheriff and the party I saw Ike Clanton exit through the back door of the house next Fly's, in a minute he passed me and went into the dance-house on Allen street. Went back and heard the Sheriff say to Wyatt Earp, "I will have to arrest you now." Earp replied, "Nobody could arrest me now." Mr. Coonstock said, "There is no hurry in arresting these men just now; he did right in killing them and the public will uphold him." Then Wyatt said, "You bet we did right, we had to do it. And you threw us, Johnny; you told us they were disarmed." Behan denied that he said they were disarmed. Heard Behan say, "He was not afraid to arrest Earp if he wanted to." Earp said, "As soon as the excitement was over he was willing to be arrested." To my knowledge there was but two men present besides the Clantons. When I left the Sheriff and boys were in a group together. Saw one of them armed, don't know if the others were armed or not; think not. Witness did not identify Mr. Claiborn as having been there.

At this point inquest was adjourned until 10 o'clock this morning.

Notice to Tax Payers.

The members of the Board of Common Council will sit as a Board of Equalization on the 27th, 28th, 29th and 31st days of October, 1881, to equalize the assessment of property for fiscal year 1882. All application for reduction of assessment must be made in writing and filed with the Clerk of the Board on or before the 29th day of October, 1881.

By order of the Board.

S. B. CHAPIN, Clerk.

WINTER underwear, of every conceivable kind, at Glover's.

A. COHN & BRO., corner of Fifth and Allen streets, have the largest and most complete stock of Tobacco and Cigars to be found in Tombstone. They keep the finest as well as common brands, and sell wholesale and retail.

IF you don't see what you want, ask for it, at Glover's.

Attention, Ladies.

Go to the Boot and Shoe Store, 505 Allen street, between Fifth and Sixth, for your shoes, as it is the only place to get a good fit at a reasonable price.

THE latest style overcoats at Glover's.

THE largest variety of infants' and children's shoes can be found at the Boot and Shoe Store, 505 Allen street, between Fifth and Sixth.

SEE the news from Glover's in to-day's EPITAPH.

WATER SUPPLY.

A City Located Two Years Ago Upon a Waterless Mesa,

That Has Now Copious Streams Flowing Through Its Streets,

With No Fears of a Future Dearth of the Aqueous Fluid.

About the first question asked by people abroad in relation to the resources, surroundings and facilities for building up a city at Tombstone is, "What is your water supply?" This is a very natural and proper inquiry, for without an abundance of water, no matter what the other resources may be, there can be no extensive and prosperous growth. In order that our numerous readers abroad may fully realize and understand what has been done in the line of water supply, we will take a retrospective glance at the place upon the discovery of the mines by the Schieffelin brothers in the beginning of 1878.

At that time the mesa east of the San Pedro was as waterless as the desert of Sahara, with the exception of a few springs that burst out near the base of the Dragoon mountains, twelve miles to the northeast, the nearest spring being eight miles away. It was not known, even, that water could be had by digging for it, and the chances seemed all against such a proposition; however, like the boy hunting the woodchuck, it was a necessity; therefore, these pioneers prospected around and decided to try the experiment in the canyon about two miles below town. The formation there being granite was favorable for finding it if it existed in the country. Besides, there were some scattering walnut trees, that in this country are considered an indication of water at some depth, it often, however, being found far below the surface. Fortunately for the camp, it was here found at a depth of fifteen or twenty feet and seemingly in large quantities. This settled the

FATE OF TOMBSTONE,

and from that day a feeling of gladness filled the hearts of the prospectors, for they knew that should the mines develop as rich as they hoped and believed, there would be no difficulty in supplying the necessary population and machinery to unearth the hidden treasure however great it might be. At first, the domestic supply was packed in upon burros, and afterwards hauled upon wagons in huge tanks holding from 500 to 2,000 gallons, and sold to the consumers at so many cents per gallon, commencing at 5 cents and gradually falling in price, as competition increased, to 1 cent, the ruling rates until the present time.

THE FIRST WATER COMPANY.

formed to bring a regular supply through pipes into town was a Boston incorporation. The company purchased the Sycamore Springs near the Dragoon Mountains, and constructed a large reservoir around them for the storage of the water. They laid a line of iron pipe, three-inch bore, from the storage reservoir to their distributing reservoir situated upon the hill near the Empire mine, overlooking the town. This pipe-line is nearly nine miles in length. This first step met the immediate demand, but the rapid growth of the city and multiplication of steam hoisting works created a still further demand which has been met by the

TOMBSTONE W. M. & L. CO.,

a San Francisco company, organized for the purpose of supplying water to the city, and the further purpose of milling and lumbering—that is, supplying fuel for domestic and mining purposes—the company owning a large tract of valuable timber at the base of the Dragoon mountains.

SEAT OF OPERATIONS.

The seat of operations of this company is the wells above described, situated about two miles below Tombstone, on the stage road to Contention. The promoter of this enterprise was Mr. W. K. Leveredge, a San Francisco gentleman who came to Tombstone some time about May last. With a keen perception, he immediately saw the necessity for an increased water supply, that mills might be erected at the mines and citizens be supplied at a reduced cost. He examined the wells at Watervale and satisfied himself that there must be a large underground flow; the drainage of the watershed west of the Sulphur Spring Valley. He at once made arrangements with Mr. Henry Fuller, who owned one of the best wells in the canyon, and returned to San Francisco and laid the matter before George M. Blake and D. H. Alderson, two capitalists, and enlisted them in the enterprise. This was the inception of the scheme that has just been successfully completed and put in operation.

THE FIRST STEP.

This was to deepen and increase the size of the well to test the capacity of the water-bearing strata. Not to interfere with the well in use they sunk another sixteen feet below, of the dimensions of ten by seventeen, which they sunk to a total depth of thirty-nine feet, having twenty-seven feet of water, which came in at the last at the rate of 6,000 gallons per hour. A steam pump was used in sinking the well, and the water from it was run into the canyon made quite a brook. In addition to the square shaft, or well, they drove a tunnel southeast, four by six feet and twenty-five feet long. They have also another tunnel northwest, the same dimensions, nineteen feet long. This gives with the well—the water standing twenty-seven feet in the well—a storage capacity of 40,000 gallons underground, where, of course, it keeps perfectly cool. This is the present water supply, but, according to pumping tests, is equivalent to 140,000 gallons in the twenty-four hours.

THE WORKS.

The water from this well is forced by a Worthington duplex steam pump, through a 6 inch pipe, a distance of 8,251 feet into the reservoir on Comstock hill, below town, the elevation above the well being 387 feet. Each cylinder of the pump is 10 inches in diameter with a 12 inch stroke and, being double acting, or duplex, it keeps a steady flow of water with no perceptible pulsation whatever. The boiler is 48 inches in diameter, 16 feet long, with forty 3½-inch tubes. The consumption of wood is about one cord per day, the pump at present being run only about 10 hours. This pump is to be relieved by one of double its capacity as soon as it is completed, it having been ordered some time ago. The present pump will remain to supply any contingency that may arise from damage to the working pump. The building is 32x35 feet, built of adobe, with a cement roof, thus being entirely fire-proof. The pump sets in a pit 12 feet below the surface of the ground, the pit or room being 12x18 feet in dimensions, heavily timbered and planked around the sides. The pipe from the reservoir, as before stated, is 6 inches in diameter, of ¼-inch boiler iron, double riveted, made in sections of 28 feet, and was manufactured at Marysville, California.

THE RESERVOIR AND MAIN.

The reservoir is situated on Comstock hill, about one mile below town, at an altitude of seventy-four feet above the level at the intersection of Fremont and Fourth streets. It is built of one-quarter inch boiler iron, and is thirty-five feet in diameter by fourteen feet eight inches high, having a capacity of 110,000 gallons. It sets in a groove cut in the solid rock, and has a concrete and cement bottom about six inches thick. From the reservoir into the town the pipe is only four inches in diameter, thus giving the advantage of two inches in the supply pipe in case a fire should make an extra demand on the reservoir. The main from the well to the reservoir is in an air line, as is also that from the reservoir to the intersection of Second and Fremont, where it makes an obtuse angle and then runs straight up Fremont to Eighth street, where it turns to Allen and down Allen to Third and across Third to intersect with the main again. At every cross street intermediate between Third and Eighth a two-inch pipe connects the Fremont and Allen streets lines of main. There are also branches from Fremont down Fourth and Fifth streets to Bruce and from Allen to Tough Nut. There are twelve fire plugs distributed at convenient points along Allen and Fremont streets, where hose can be attached for fire purposes.

CONCLUSION.

Our citizens already begin to feel the effect of this new enterprise. All houses having pipe service have a reduction of 50 per cent in the price of water, which is no small item to even the smallest consumer; and to hotels, restaurants, boarding-houses, and bar-rooms it amounts to a very large item in the course of a year. With this ample supply it becomes practicable to sprinkle the streets, and in case of fire there is no fear of shortage of water; and with a pressure of 74 feet from the reservoir the attachment of hose to the fire-plugs will dispense with the use of the fire-engine except outside the limits of the plugs.

This company are deserving the support of every consumer of water within the city, for the reasons that their property will be protected from fire in the future; that our streets will be sprinkled; and, last but not least, that they have broken a monopoly that refused to put in fire-plugs after they had been ready on the ground, because the City Council paved the way for healthy competition in the water business, by granting the right of way for pipes to this company. The effects upon the future growth of the city cannot but be of the most beneficial characters for the reason it makes possible many industrial pursuits that before were barred to our people, notably the milling of the ore at or near the mines.

THEY are always selling out, but not for cost, at Glover's.

ALL kinds of repairing in gents' and ladies' boots and shoes neatly and cheaply done at the Boot and Shoe Store, 505 Allen street, between Fifth and Sixth.

THE very lowest prices at Glover's.

Carpets! Carpets!

J. Lenoir has received from New York a large invoice of Brussels, tapestry, three-ply and ingrain carpets of the latest patterns, all of which he desires parties desiring carpets to call and examine before purchasing elsewhere.

A GREAT Indian war at Glover's.

Wall Paper.

Those intending to rehabilitate their houses by supplying fresh wall paper will do well to call and examine the large stock just received from New York by J. Lenoir. It is of the latest patterns and exquisite coloring.

Occidental Chop House.

From this date onward, to the advent of hot weather again, the proprietor of the Occidental Chop House will keep a supply of fresh California Salmon and Eastern Oysters, which, in addition to the other elaborate bill of fare, will be served in the best style and the lowest price possible. Remember that there is now a private dining room for ladies and their escorts, and where they will be genteelly served. Give me a call.
A. PETRO, Proprietor.

Union Market.

Messrs. Baur & Kehoe, having contracted with Mr. Frink of Sulphur Spring Valley for 600 head of prime American beef cattle, take pleasure in announcing to their patrons and the public that from this time forward they will be able to supply them with meat of a superior quality to any ever before seen in this Territory.

P. W. Smith is sole agent for the celebrated Amazon Whisky and St. Louis Robstock Beer.

MEN's heavy brogans at $1.75 per pair at the Boot and Shoe Store, 505 Allen street between Fifth and Sixth.

DAILY EPITAPH

Sunday Morning ....Oct. 30, 1881

LOCAL SPLINTERS.

Recorder Wallace fined one lonesome d. d. $5 yesterday.

The Coroner's inquest completed its labors last evening and was discharged.

The Justices' courts have all been running at full blast for the last week, doing a large amount of petty criminal business.

Remember the elegant French dinner at the Rockaway Restaurant to-day. All the delicacies of the season will adorn the table.

At the Occidental chop house there was a fine display of turkey, lobsters and fresh Eastern oysters in the shell, last evening. Those who feed at the Occidental to-day will fare sumptuously.

There is no reason for any idle men in the country at this time. The New Mexico & Sonora Railroad Company have posters for 250 track-layers to work on the road from Benson to Contention.

Tombstone M. & M. Co. shipped 4 bars of bullion last night per Wells, Fargo & Co's express. Weight, 831 pounds; value, $11,653.

The Palace Restaurant on Allen street, near Sixth, is one of the neatest and most comfortable places in town. You can always find there the choicest viands cooked in the most approved style.

The jewelry store of Mr. Schmeding has been under a state of repairs during the last week, but is rapidly approaching completion. It is safe to say that when finished it will be the handsomest room in Arizona. The wall and ceiling paper received yesterday, is something perfectly elegant, in fact, "too, too. The floor is to be covered with oil-cloth to correspond with the elegance of the walls and ceiling.

LOCAL PERSONALS.

J. G. Manning, civil and topographical engineer, now in the employ of the Atchison, Topeka & Santa Fe road, writes from Crittenden, that the grading up the Barbacomari is rapidly progressing.

Col. Stanford, of Tucson, is in the city. He will probably remain two or three months. He is one of the attorneys for Field & Sanford, in the celebrated Gilded Age mining suits.

Meeting of the City Council.

The City Council met in special session yesterday afternoon. A complaint against City Marshal V. W. Earp having been entered, he was suspended, and James Flynn appointed to temporarily fill the office.

Hotel Arrivals Yesterday.

AT THE GRAND.

A Mooser, Sacramento; E Brown, P S Woods, U. S. A., F Coblentz, San Francisco; A Fanbery, Bodie; J Smith, Contention; J Webster, E Brown, Sacramento.

AT THE COSMOPOLITAN.

Mrs Marks, Yorkville; Jas Burnett, Charleston; F. Baggot, M Rhodes, San Francisco; F Galvin, Contention; J Silt, Phil; S Hunt, Bisbee; A P Green, Tucson; F Renshaw, Benson.

Passenger Departures.

BY SANDY BOB'S STAGE.

M Wilson, W Turner, E S Baker, W S Williams, J Lenoir, F Rhode, J McGowan, G Dill M Taylor, M Stearns and wife.

BY KINNEAR'S LINE.

L Goodman, F Calvin.

Justice's Court.

A. J. FELTER, J. P.

The Territory vs. Richard McMahon, arrested on complaint of John C. Bracy for threatening his life. For lack of evidence the defendant was discharged.

G. W. Jones, arrested on complaint of Miss Nellie Cashman for intention to leave the Territory with intent to defraud his creditors. Tried by jury and defendant found guilty. He gave bonds pending motion for new trial.

Church Notice.

There will be divine services in the Methodist church, Seventh and Fremont, on October 30, as follows: Preaching at 11 o'clock a. m.; subject, "Security of Believers."

Sunday school at 2 o'clock p. m. This school is fully equipped with an efficient corps of officers, who will take pleasure in attending to the comfort and instruction of all children committed to their care. We are in need of a few more faithful teachers. Come and help us in this blessed work. Visitors always welcome.

Preaching at 7 o'clock p. m. Subject, "Marriage." Young people are especially invited. All are welcome.

Rev. J. P. McIntyre, Pastor.

Cochise County Records.

The following instruments were filed for record in the County Recorder's office yesterday:

DEEDS OF MINES.

A. H. Prattet al to W White—the Stonewall; $1.

A W Say to J Liggett—½ Stonewall, $1.

DEEDS OF REAL ESTATE.

G Tribolet to S Tribolet—Bisbee Brewery; $967.

J B Jennings to J P Broad—lot 20, bl'ck 21, Tombstone; $250.

AGREEMENT.

A Beasley et als with J B Smith—to sell the Nellie James and Salinas mines.

APPOINTMENT OF AGENT.

S S Water Co. to A W Johnson.

POWER OF ATTORNEY.

B J Marks et al to H Hollenstien.
Lucy Farnsworth to J M Wiggins.
May Christy to J M Moran.

BILL OF SALE.

Ida West to T H Corrigan—furniture; $800.

BONDS.

W Williams et al to H L Hart—¾ Revenue mine; $24,000.

Justice's Court.

BEFORE JUSTICE SPICER.

In the case of Wyatt Earp, Morgan Earp, V. W. Earp and J. H. Holliday, charged with the murder of William Clanton, Thomas and Frank McLowry, on complaint filed by Isaac Clanton, the defendants Wyatt Earp and J. H. Holliday were refused bail as a matter of right. Said defendants were admitted to bail on showing by affidavit in the sum of $10,000 each, to appear for examination at 10 o'clock, Monday morning. Defendants gave bail, with sureties justifying in $20,000 in each case.

Pickled Pigs Feet' and Lambs' Tongues, at H. E. Hills & Co's.

WEEKLY MINING REPORT

An Exceedingly Quiet Week in Mining Circles.

Huachuca Letter.

We introduce our mining report to-day with an interesting letter from a much neglected mineral country; a country that is destined ere long to attract both energy and capital, which, from all reports, will be amply repaid for all outlays. The Huachuca mountains are the most prominent land-mark in Cochise county, and offer every facility for profitable mining, there being an abundance of wood and water and easy of access from every side. The Atchison, Topeka & Santa Fe Railroad passes up the Barbacomari valley, near the north end of the range, which will give transportation almost to their doors. This is a matter of great importance, from the fact that there are extensive copper mines that, when developed, will demand cheap rates for coke and copper. There are also carbonate deposits, both rich and extensive, which will make a like demand. Our correspondent says:

Editor Epitaph:—In accordance with your suggestions I will submit a few points about the western slope of the Huachuca Mountains at the further end of Tanner's Canyon. This part of the country has been slighted thus far by capitalists, owing possibly to its remoteness and inducements on the eastern slope. The Huachucas have been cried down as base, and by many condemned in a wholesale manner, simply because their interests are elsewhere, but the time is coming when their true merit will be recognized and the former unjust prejudices will change to just praise.

A first-class wagon road leads from Charleston to Tanner's Canyon on this side, the lowest depression in the range as viewed from Tombstone, into which picturesque and romantic canyon one drives several miles and then crosses by a good trail, horseback, to the west side, passing Hayes & Tanner's sawmill near the summit, where lumber is prepared for the Harshaw market. On the descending slope are some promising properties, and at the foot and in the heart of the deep canyon is a four-stamp quartz mill in fine running order, and which has lately tested some of the various ores with flattering results, using copper plates to catch the free gold which is quite plentiful in the iron pyrites with which the numberless ledges are well seamed. Wood and water are both abundant and plentiful, lessening the expense of milling materially, and high hopes are entertained of this now comparatively lonely locality soon budding into a very promising mining camp. And why not? The ledges are strong and well defined, running generally north and south with a pitch west, and although some blankets are found, the indications of true fissure veins are very apparent, and when work has been done by the prospectors to any extent, the claims promise well and offer great inducements to capital to take hold and continue the development. Some limited development is going on, but not in a manner to show much results, one way or the other. Limited funds means limited work, and one can not expect to pay as he goes in this more than in any other business. Capital must be invested judiciously and the risk taken, and as a minimum risk the Huachucas offer superior inducements.

In conclusion, I beg leave to differ from those holding the opinion that the ores can not be successfully milled, as experience teaches the contrary where the mines and mill are consolidated so that the tailings will not be lost to the former. After the drift is through the pan and the settler, the greatest percentage possible is had, as the sulphurets can not be worked in any other way more economically.

I shall be glad to furnish information at any time to any one before returning to the mountains the middle of next week.

Very truly yours,
George Whitwell Parsons.

Tombstone M. & M Co.

No. 2 shaft West Side, the vein has increased to 4½ feet, all of one fine quality. The drift is in north on the ledge 30 feet. Are working only 9 men, including surface men, and taking out 36 tons of ore per week, which goes forward to the mill. This ore is all extracted in the legitimate way of development by running the drift upon the vein. Counting the ore at $50 per ton (a very low estimate for this ledge) the product is $1800 per week, less mining expenses, $252; which leaves a balance of net ore value at the mine of $1528. Body of ore in Tough Nut on 200 level getting superficially larger and thicker as the development proceeds. It is of the regular uniform Tough Nut ore, running about $60 to the ton. Work in the old mine east of the northwest shaft, shows the ore body going down to the level of the northwest workings. The Combination continues to yield its accustomed amount of ore. The developments for the last month have been more favorable than for any preceding period in the history of the mines, and there are more good ore bodies exposed at any former period. The mills are working at their full capacity and will make a good monthly showing.

Contention.

Are still drifting north on 212 level, all in good ore. On 312 north drift same ore body as above and equally rich. Sinking winze on 312 down from 312 to connect with 400. Full size of winze in rich ore. Still drifting on 400 and raising to connect with 312. Making from 35 to 40 feet in the various drifts per week. There is no change on 600 level, where crosscutting still goes on. Are passing through a kindly ledge matter, which indicates that ore will be found at an early day. The stopes are all looking well, and show a plenty of rich ore everywhere. The mill is running smoothly, and up to its full capacity. The bullion output will be short, owing to the break in the engine in the early part of the month, which caused a stoppage of one whole week. However, with the surplus in the treasury, we anticipate no suspension of dividends for the month. We expect to record the payment of $900,000 in dividends the current year

Head Center.

There have been no new developments for the past week. Prospecting on the first and second levels is being pushed ahead with good results. Taking out the usual amount of ore, which goes forward to the mill. The mill has been working steadily during the month. Have just completed a new cage, that is as fine a specimen of forging and workmanship as can be turned out anywhere. The safety cage is a half circle, made of three-sixteenths boiler plate, opening in the center, one-half dropping down upon either side to form a platform for landing long timbers upon the cage. When closed, the joint is only just perceptible. It reflects great credit upon the maker, as it is one of those jobs of piece work sandwiched in between tool sharpening.

Grand Central.

New shaft down 35 feet below 300 level. The rock is harder, slower progress being the result. Cross-cut on 300 level in 10 feet. Drifting south on 200. Old shaft down 94 below the 500 level. Will put in station on 690 this week, when cross-cutting will be commenced to prospect this level. An important point will be settled this week, and that is, whether the same level in the various mines on the Contention lode will develop water. Head Center struck a heavy flow near or at 500 feet; Grand Central is 87 feet higher; therefore the 600 level will be equivalent to a little more in the Head Center. If no water is struck about this point it will be conclusive evidence that the water veins in the fissure are controlled by the nature of the formation and vary in depth accordingly. This is fairly demonstrated already in Silver Belt, which struck water at about 187 feet. The difference in altitude between Head Center and Silver Belt is not over 25 or 30 feet.

In the stopes there is no material change. There is plenty of ore in sight and of a good quality. The mill is running satisfactorily and the out-put will be up to last month. The new ore house will be raised this week and finished as rapidly as possible.

San Diego.

During the month have added 10 feet to the depth of the shaft. Drifted south on the ledge 12 feet at the 266 ft. level, and have cross-cut 12 feet to the east at the same level. The cross-cut is still in porphyry which is heavily stained and contains iron pyrites in great abundance. No work has been done during the month at the 130 ft. level, although both drifts show a strong ledge of low grade quartz. The north drift has been run but 40 ft., improving in appearance and richness with every foot of advance.

Prompter.

Down 200 feet in shaft No. 3. Put in station on Monday last and are cross-cutting the vein. In 15 feet, cutting for the hanging wall. It is all medium grade ore, assaying from $40 to $60 per ton. It is all being saved for the mill. Sinking continues at the rate of about 2 feet a day. Grading for hoisting works, which will be erected as soon as it arrives from Chicago, where built.

Horseshoe.

Drift on 220 level in 45 feet. The rock which is porphyry and talc, works well and good headway is being made. The strike of the Emily and other veins is in a direction toward this location. The formation is all that could be desired, in fact, so identical with the entire central and eastern system of ledges and deposits that at any point almost there is a liability to meet an ore body.

Ruby.

Down 100 feet. Cross-cut at 50 feet; in 8 feet; all ledge matter, with 18 inches of high grade ore. Cross-cutting at 100 feet, drifting to the vein. Have to run between 15 and 20 feet. Started work on shaft No. 2, on Monday last and are down 13 feet. Sinking on the vein, the whole size of shaft in ledge matter with some fine ore.

Mesa Consolidated.

Down 133 feet. The increase in size of boulders indicates the near approach to bedrock. There has been more quartz in the debris for the last week, and the fine earth has a more mineralized appearance. Assays will be made from it to test the question as to whether it carries silver or not.

Silver Belt.

Still crosscutting to the west. The rock is harder than some feet back. The drift is in 120 feet. The country is a mixture of lime, porphyry, black spar and talc. It is more kindly in appearance than for some feet back.

Vizina.

There is really nothing new to report from this mine. Everything runs along so smoothly from week to week that what was written one week ago would answer for this week. The usual progress was made and the ore bodies all yield as heretofore.

Huachuca Water Company.

From Mr. L. J. Gird, engineer of the works, it is learned that the rip-rap for the reservoir has been completed, and the whole work will soon be finished. It will not take long to lay the pipe when it arrives. The catchment reservoir was the heaviest work on the line.

BISBEE.

Atlanta.

Work was started up on this mine last week. A tunnel was started on the west end, to cut the big croppings near the Copper Queen. The prospects are considered first-class.

Golden Gate.

A shaft was started in the iron-cap that crosses this location on the 4th instant, and has been sunk to a depth of 14 feet. At 4 feet a vein of carbonate ore 2 inches thick came in, and at the bottom it had widened to over two feet. This promises to be a rich mine.

TUCSON SMALL TALK.

Star.

The Board of Supervisors will meet on Tuesday, November 1st.

The District Court will open in Tombstone November 14th,

Carlito Meyer, the young son of Judge Meyer, is ill with typhoid fever.

D. H. Ming has been appointed Public Administrator of Graham county.

Solon M. Allis is on his way back from the East.

The Fleishman-Meyer wedding comes off next Monday night.

The Cochise Board of Supervisors seem disposed to take their own time in bringing their settlement with Pima county to a focus.

Robert Bible, who is charged with killing Stiles, his step-father in Pinal county, is transferred to Tucson, on a change of venue, and is now in jail here. He was formerly a pupil in a school taught by Mr. George A. Clum, and now the friends of George are inquiring how far he becomes accessory before the fact in Bible's offense, he being in some measure responsible for Bible's moral training. 'Tis all proper enough "to teach the young idea how to shoot," but not in this particular scriptural way.

A. Cohn & Bro., corner of Fifth and Allen streets, have the largest and most complete stock of Tobacco and Cigars to be found in Tombstone. They keep the finest as well as common brands, and sell wholesale and retail.

CORONER'S INQUEST.

Conclusion of the Evidence, with the Verdict of the Jury.

At 10 o'clock yesterday morning the examination of witnesses before the Coroner's Jury was continued.

First witness called was

P. H. FALLEHY,

who testified as follows: After the shooting commenced, saw Holliday in the middle of the street, and the youngest of the Earps about three feet from the sidewalk; he was firing at a man behind a horse; Holliday was also firing at the same man; Holliday was also firing at a man who had run by him to the opposite side of the street. Then I saw the man who held the horse let go the bridle and keep staggering until he fell, his back within a few feet of a house; had a pistol in his hand, but I did not see it go off; did not see the other two Earps at this time; went and offered to pick up the wounded man; he did not speak, though his lips moved; picked up a revolver laying about three feet from him and placed it by his side; this was on the north side of Fremont street. Next saw Doc Holliday running towards where the man was lying; had his pistol in his hand; he said, "The son of a b—— has hit me—I mean to kill him." Holliday did not shoot after saying this; did not see a shot-gun there; don't know who fired the first shot.

MRS. MARTHA KING,

sworn, said: I was standing in Bauer's butcher shop before the fight began; looking out saw all the parties and heard a man with a horse say to another man, "If you want to find us, you will find us just below here." Next, saw Holliday and the Earps coming down the street. Holliday had a gun. I heard the man on the outside say to Holliday, "Let them have it," and Holliday said, "All right." That is all I know.

R. F. COLMAN

testified. I saw the arrest of Ike Clanton before the shooting. Marshal Earp went up behind him and grabbed his gun, then there was a scuffle, and Clanton fell. Did not see Earp hit him. Saw Earp have a six-shooter, but don't know if he took it from Clanton or not. He then took Clanton to the police court. After the trial was over, Earp offered Clanton his rifle, but Clanton did not take it. Heard Clanton say all he wanted was four feet of gronnd. Soon after I was standing in front of the O. K. Corral, and saw the two Clantons and two McLowrys in a stall in Dunbar's corral in conversation. Soon after they all came over toward the O. K. Corral. Billy Clanton was on horseback and Frank McLowry was leading his horse. As they passed me, Billy Clanton said, "Where is the West End Corral?" Told him where it was. They passed through the corral and I walked up Allen street. Met Sheriff opposite Headquarters Saloon and said to him; "You should disarm those men; they are up to mischief." Soon after met Marshal Earp and told him the same thing. After this met the Clantons and McLowrys opposite Ely's, on Fremont street. Sheriff Behan was talking to them. One of them said, "You need not be afraid of us, Johnny; we will make no trouble." Billy Clanton had his horse with him. I turned and walked up Fremont street. I met the Earps and Doc Holliday opposite Bauer's meat market. Just as they passed me, Johnny Behan said, "Hold on, boys, I don't want you to go any further." Don't think they made any reply, but passed on down till they were opposite where the Clanton party was standing. Never heard one of the Earp party say throw up your hands or give up your arms. Just then two shots were fired as quick as that [clapping his hands quickly], and then the shooting became general. After the first two shots Ike Clanton ran through Fly's house; think there were two shots fired at him. After the first two shots, Tom McLowry ran down Fremont street and fell; saw Billy Clanton fire two or three shots while in a crouching position; saw one of the shots hit Morgan Earp, who stumbled or fell; jumping up again, he commenced firing. At this time saw Frank McLowry advancing toward Holliday and saying "I've got you now," firing a shot at the same time. That shot struck Holliday on the hip. Frank passed on across the street and fell. Billy Clanton, after being struck, bent down in a stooping position and fired two shots, one of which struck Marshal Earp. Wyatt and Morgan Earp were still firing at Billy Clanton until he fell still holding his pistol. After the shooting was over, heard Behan say to Wyatt Earp, "I shall have to arrest you." Wyatt said, "I won't be arrested now; you have deceived me, Johnny; you said they were disarmed. I am here to answer for what I have done." Saw Billy Clanton with his hand on his pistol, which was in the scabbard; his right hand was on his left hip. This was after the first two shots; could not swear how many of the Clantons were armed: don't think Ike was armed. Don't think there was anybody with the Marshal when he arrested Ike Clanton. Believe the report I gave the Epitaph was about correct. Can't say that I saw a shotgun in the hands of either party. Think Billy Clanton was not hit before he commenced firing. Believe the parties were about 10 or 12 feet apart when shooting commenced.

JOSEPH ISAAC CLANTON

sworn, said: My name is Joseph I. Clanton, am cattle dealer by occupation; reside in Cochise county; am brother to William Clanton who was killed; saw the whole affair. Night before the shooting went into the Occidental Chop house to get lunch. While there Doc Holliday came in and commenced abusing me; had his hand on his gun all the time and called me a d—d son of a b—. Told me to get my gun out. I told him that I had no gun. Looking around I saw Morgan Earp sitting on the bar with his hand on his gun. Doc Holliday still kept abusing me until I went out. Virg. Earp, Wyatt Earp and Morgan Earp were all around. They told me if I wanted a fight to turn myself loose. All had their hands on their guns while they were talking. Holliday said, "You son of a b—, go and arm yourself." Then I went off and did heel myself. Came back soon and played poker with Virg. Earp, Tom McLowry and others. Virg. had his gun on his lap all the time. At daylight we quit. About 8 o'clock in the morning I went and got my Winchester, expecting to meet Doc Holliday on the street, but never saw him until Virg. and Morg. Earp slipped up behind me and knocked me down with a six-shooter. Soon after I met my brother William; he asked me to go out of town. We went to the corral where my team was. There we met Sheriff Behan. He said he would have to arrest us and take our arms off. I told him that we were going out of town right away. He then told Billy to come up to his office and put off his arms. Billy told him he was just leaving town, but if the Sheriff would disarm the Earps he would lay his aside. Just at that time I saw Doc Holliday and the Earps approaching. The Sheriff stepped out to meet them, and said, "I have these parties in my charge and don't want any trouble." They went right by. I advanced two or three steps from the crowd and met Wyatt Earp at the corner of the building. He stuck his six-shooter at me and said, "Throw up your hands." The Marshal also said to the other boys, "Thow up your hands." Tom opened his coat and said, "I have no arms. "They said, "You son of a b—h, you want to make a fight." At the same instant Doc Holliday and Morg. Earp shot; Morg shot Bill Clanton, and I don't know which of the boys Holliday shot; saw Virg Earp shooting at the same time. I pushed Wyatt Earp around the corner of the house and jumped into the gallery; as I jumped saw Bill Clanton falling; ran through the photograph gallery and got away. When ordered to hold up our hands, we all held them up, except Tom, who held open his coat to show that he was unarmed. There was nothing between the Earps and the boys that were killed. The Earps and myself had a transaction which made them down on me; they don't like me. There were no threats made against the Earps by any of the boys that were killed. The boys expected no attack until just before they got ready to leave town. I had no arms when ordered to throw up my hands; the Marshal had taken my Winchester and six-shooter; had not seen Frank and Billy McLowry for two days previous to their coming in town; never spoke to them about fighting the Earps; don't know whether the Earp party had a shot-gun or not. Virg. and Doc. were about six feet from the McLowrys and Morg. Earp when they commenced shooting; did not see the McLowrys or my brother shoot. The boys were not sent for by anyone that day; they came in at the request of Major Frink. Behan saw the Earps coming before we did; he told us to stay there. After the Sheriff left I would not stay, only the Sheriff told us to. Behan was with us long enough to say what I have before stated.

Verdict.

The following is the verdict of the Coroner's Jury:

We, the undersigned, a jury of inquest, summoned by the Coroner of the county aforesaid, to determine whose the bodies are, submitted to our inspection, and under what circumstances they came to death, after viewing the bodies and hearing such testimony as has been submitted to us, find, first, that the persons' names were, William Clanton, aged 19 years, Frank McLowry, aged 29 years, and Tom McLowry, aged 25 years, nativity unknown, and that they came to their death in the town of Tombstone, in said county, on the 26th day of October, 1881, from the effects of pistol and gunshot wounds inflicted by Virgil Earp, Wyatt Earp, Morgan Earp, and one Holliday, commonly called Doc Holliday. (Signed,) Thomas Moses. T. F. Hudson, D. Calisher, M. Garrett, S. B. Comstock, J. W. Conwell, J. C. Davis, C. D. Reppy, F. Hafford, George H. Haskell, M. S. Goodrich.

CITY ITEMS.

Thurber's Deep Sea Codfish and Mess Mackerel, at H. E. Hills & Co's.

Catholic Church.

Services will be held at the Catholic church on Sunday, October 30th. First mass at 7:30 a. m.; High-Mass with music at 10 o'clock a. m.; Sunday-school at 3 p. m.; evening service, with music at 7:30 o'clock.

Monday, October 31st—All Saints' vigil fast. Tuesday, November 1st—Holy Day of Obligation: morning service the same as on Sunday; evening vesper of the dead at 7 o'clock. Wednesday, November 2d—All Souls' Day: High Requiem Mass, with music, for the souls in Purgatory, at 9 a. m.; vespers of the dead at 7 o'clock p. m. Every day mass at 7 o'clock a. m.

Justice, charity, piety and gratitude command us to observe these days.

The One I Love.

He came home last night singing an old familiar song, the one I love so well, and dropping into an easy chair with more than his usual grace, and taking me on his lap presented me with a kiss and the loveliest set of jewelry I ever saw. Oh, it was just too sweet! I think they call it Filigree, and it was made in the extensive manufactury of S. H. Lucas & Co., Santa Fe, New Mexico. He has everything unique and pretty. Everybody should call at the popular store of P. Heitzelman for five days, and examine the beauties. They are just too lovely.

Chow-chow, Picalilli, plain and mixed Pickles, in pints, quarts, kegs and barrels, at H. E. Hills & Co's.

Men's nailed mining shoes at $2, at the Boot and Shoe Store, 505 Allen street, between Fifth and Sixth.

Everybody's goods at everybody's prices, at Glover's.

Delmonico Lodging House.

Mrs. T. J. Cunningham, a sister of Miss Nellie Cashman, has rented the Vickers' building on Fremont street, between Fourth and Fifth, and has repainted and fitted up the rooms for a lodging house. The beds and furniture are all new and will be kept cleanly and in the best of style. This is one of the most pleasant and desirable houses in the city and we bespeak for the lady a liberal patronage.

The latest news at Glover's.

Notice to Tax Payers.

The members of the Board of Common Council will sit as a Board of Equilazation on the 27th, 28th, 29th and 31st days of October, 1881, to equalize the assessment of property for fiscal year 1882.

All application for reduction of assessment must be made in writing and filed with the Clerk of the Board on or before the 29th day of October, 1881.

By order of the Board.

S. B. Chapin, Clerk.

Winter underwear, of every conceivable kind, at Glover's.

If you don't see what you want, ask for it, at Glover's.

Attention, Ladies.

Go to the Boot and Shoe Store, 505 Allen street, between Fifth and Sixth, for your shoes, as it is the only place to get a good fit at a reasonable price.

The latest style overcoats at Glover's.

The largest variety of infants' and children's shoes can be found at the Boot and Shoe Store, 505 Allen street, between Fifth and Sixth.

See the news from Glover's in to day's Epitaph.

They are always selling out, but not for cost, at Glover's.

All kinds of repairing in gents' and ladies' boots and shoes neatly and cheaply done at the Boot and Shoe Store, 505 Allen street, between Fifth and Sixth.

The very lowest prices at Glover's.

Carpets! Carpets!

J. Lenoir has received from New York a large invoice of Brussels, tapestry, three-ply and ingrain carpets of the latest patterns, all of which he desires parties desiring carpets to call and examine before purchasing elsewhere.

A great Indian war at Glover's.

Wall Paper.

Those intending to rehabilitate their houses by supplying fresh wall paper will do well to call and examine the large stock just received from New York by J. Lenoir. It is of the latest patterns and exquisite coloring.

Occidental Chop House.

From this date onward, to the advent of hot weather again, the proprietor of the Occidental Chop House will keep a supply of fresh California Salmon and Eastern Oysters, which, in addition to the other elaborate bill of fare, will be served in the best style and the lowest price possible. Remember that there is now a private dining room for ladies and their escorts, and where they will be genteelly served. Give me a call. A. Petro, Proprietor.

Union Market.

Messrs. Baur & Kehoe, having contracted with Mr. Frink of Sulphur Spring Valley for 600 head of prime American beef cattle, take pleasure in announcing to their patrons and the public that from this time forward they will be able to supply them with meat of a superior quality to any ever before seen in this Territory.

P. W. Smith is sole agent for the celebrated Amazon Whisky and St. Louis Robstock Beer.

Men's heavy brogans at $1.75 per pair at the Boot and Shoe Store, 505 Allen street between Fifth and Sixth.

NOTICE.

Notice.

ALL PERSONS ARE HEREBY CAUTioned against purchasing any fractional interests of the Alps mine, as such fractional interests are indebted to me. Parties owning such interests are requested to call and settle them before the 3rd day of July, or legal proceedings will be commenced against them. Sal purchasers wil. be held responsible GEO. RUTLEDGE.

Notice.

CAME INTO MY CORRAL, SAN PEDRO river, near Boston Mill, a chestnut sorrel horse, with saddle marks and white spot on forehead; branded on left hip P, with a wave stroke across the P. F. A. ABBOTT.

WANTED.

Situation Wanted.

A FIRST-CLASS WOMAN, WHO UNDERstands her business thoroughly, wants a situation to do chamber work or wait upon a table. Apply at Cosmopolitan, room No. 1.

WANTED—First-class plumber and gas-fitter. Apply at 305 Fifth street.

WANTED—A good wheelwright, at Graf & Schoenholzer, corner Third and Fremont streets.

Girls Wanted.

THE UNDERSIGNED, HAVING RECENTly opened a concert hall in Globe, is desirous of obtaining the services of six respectable girls to wait upon customers. Salary ten ($10) dollars per week and expenses. Apply immediately to A. OHLIO, Proprietor. Globe, A. T., October 18, 1881.

FOR RENT

FOR RENT—Furnished rooms, double and single; nicest rooms in Tombstone; northwest corner Third and Fremont streets.

FOR RENT—A nice cabin, 12x14, on Bruce street, near Fourth. For particulars, apply at Bourland's Cigar Store.

FOR RENT—A large room, 20x40, next door to the Epitaph office. Apply to W. A. EASTMAN, on the premises.

FOR RENT—Furnished rooms, on Fourth st., near the Presbyterian Church. Rooms well ventilated, and finest of spring beds, carpets, etc. Inquire at Fonck's furniture store on Fremont street, opposite postoffice.

FOR SALE.

For Sale at a Bargain.

A HOUSE OF TWO ROOMS AND CELLAR, nicely furnished, on Fifth street. For particulars inquire at Alhambra Saloon of J. H. LADD.

FOR SALE—A first-class Restaurant, with building and fixtures; doing the best business in town; a bargain if taken by November 1. Apply to J. V. Vickers, Real Estate agent.

FOR SALE OR RENT CHEAP—A house 12x36, three rooms, chicken house, etc., south side Fremont street, between Eighth and Ninth. Apply to McKean & Knight, store corner Sixth and Allen streets.

FOR SALE—One-half interest in three Mining Claims, situated in Tombstone Mining District, close to town, and all in a group, at a bargain. Inquire at Milliken & King's Saloon, 432 Allen street.

FOR SALE—At a great bargain—furniture of three rooms, including brussels and 3 ply carpets, two chamber sets, cook stove, etc. All nearly new. Apply at 7[illegible] Fremont st. Price $250.

Chance for a Good Bargain.

FOR SALE—On account of departure, one Self-regulating Incubator machine, for hatching chickens. Inquire at 523 Allen street.

Notice.

NOTICE IS HEREBY GIVEN THAT THE Belle Isle mine, in Mule Mountains, Warren District, running parallel above the Copper Queen and Atlanta mines, is owned by Geo. W. Atkins and A. B. Res. [illegible] is given not to negotiate with others for the purchase of same. GEO. W. ATKINS.

Notice.

ALL PERSONS INDEBTED TO ANDERSON & Schmidt are hereby notified to call at office of N. D. Anderson, 424 Fremont street, and settle same, and thereby save costs of legal proceedings. ANDERSON & SCHMIDT.

Notice.

ALL PARTIES ARE CAUTIONED AGAINST buying from R. Campbell, or others, 20 feet of the ground occupied by the New Orleans Restaurant and Saloon, and adjoining the adobe house, No. 217, on Fourth street, as I am the owner. J. MANAUDAS. Tombstone, September 24, 1881.

W. S. MURRAY. M. B. CLAPP

CLAPP & MURRAY,

GENERAL

INSURANCE AGENCY

508 Allen Street.

COMBINED ASSETS

of Companies represented,

$75,000,000!

FRENCH RESTAURANT,

Main Street Contention City.

BOARD AND LODGING, BEST ACCOMMOdations, at lowest rates.

L. LARRIEU, Proprietor.

BARNETT & BLOCK

General Forwarding and Commission Merchants, Willcox, and Benson, Arizona.

WE offer the Best Terms on Contracts for shipment of freight and other freight to any part of Arizona or Mexico. Prompt attention given to all orders

$100 Reward!

STOLEN FROM CAMP THOMAS ON THE 17th inst, one buckboard painted gray, back left hand wheel is dished, one part of double trees is cracked and bound with a piece of leather; one large gray horse, very large, formerly belonged to Jas. Lee of Tucson; two black mares, one black mule, half circle on left shoulder; deep bay mare with white face.

Above reward will be paid on returning property to A. M. Franklin & Co., Camp Thomas or Safford, or A. E. Jacobs, with M. Calisher, Tombstone.

CALIFORNIA TIN SHOP,

205 FOURTH STREET | W. FESENFELD, Manager.

PLUMBING, TIN, COPPER,

—AND—

Sheet-Iron Work and Tin Roofing.

Better work and lower prices than any other shop in Tombstone. Pumps and pump work a specialty. Sole agents for Gipsy Queen Range—the best and cheapest stove in Arizona. A full assortment of everything sold in a First-Class Tin Shop always on hand or made to order.

☞ Call before Purchasing Elsewhere—205 Fourth St.

HOTELS AND RESTAURANTS.

RUSS HOUSE,

CORNER OF FIFTH AND TOUGH NUT STREETS.

Tombstone, Arizona.

UNDER A NEW MANAGEMENT.

MISS NELLIE CASHMAN and MR. JOSEPH PASCHOLY HAVING taken charge of this new and popular house, beg to announce to their friends and the traveling public that it is their determination to run it first class in every respect. Their knowledge of "how to keep a hotel," will be their endeavor to maintain that reputation. Call and be convinced.

U. S. HOUSE.

112 Allen Street.

J. B. Soolary & Co., Props.

HAVE ALWAYS ON THEIR TABLE ALL THE MARKET AFFORDS. BOARD PER WEEK $8. Single Meals, 50c. Also, Finest Liquors and Cigars always on hand.

112 Allen Street, below Fourth.

THE COSMOPOLITAN,

ALLEN STREET, TOMBSTONE A. T.

Headquarters for All Stage Companies.

C. BILICKE, Proprietor.

BOOTS AND SHOES.

Pioneer Boot and Shoe Store

The only exclusive Boot and Shoe House in Tombstone, has on hand

A COMPLETE ASSORTMENT OF

BOOTS AND SHOES!

LADIES', MISSES' AND CHILDREN'S

SLIPPERS & SANDALS.

In fact, everything belonging to a First-Class

BOOT AND SHOE STORE.

Fine Ladies' Shoes and Slippers

MADE TO ORDER ON SHORT NOTICE.

Repairing Neatly Done.

POSITIVELY ONE PRICE | GIVE US A CALL.

H. KAYSER & CO.

505 ALLEN STREET, Between Fifth and Sixth.

HAWKINS, BOARMAN & CO.,

WHOLESALE DEALERS IN

WINES, LIQUORS, OILS AND CIGARS,

No. 116 Fourth St.

Have a complete stock of WINES, LIQUORS, OILS and CIGARS of the Finest Brands, which they offer to the public at prices to suit the times.

We will confine ourselves EXCLUSIVELY to the Wholesale Business and trust to this fact, and the good quality and reasonable prices of our goods to obtain a fair share of patronage from the merchants and families of this community.

HAWKINS, BOARMAN & CO.

116 Fourth Street, between Allen and Toughnut.

DAILY EPITAPH

(Tombstone, AZ)

Saturday, October 29, 1881

CORONER'S INQUEST.

Investigation into the Cause of the Recent Killing.

Following is a verbatim copy of the testimony given before the Coroner's Jury in relation to the killing of the McLowry brothers and Clanton, up to the time of adjournment last evening. At the rate of progress made yesterday, the investigation is liable to last for a week.

The Coroner's Jury

was composed of the following citizens: T.F. Hudson, D. Calisher, M. Garrett, S. B. Comstock, J.W. Conwell, J.C. Davis, Thomas Moses, C.D. Reppy, F. Hafford, George H. Haskell, M.S. Goodrich.

The Testimony.

J. H. Behan, Sheriff of Cochise county, sworn, testified as follows: I was present on Fremont street when the shooting occurred; know all the parties participating in that affair. I slept late the day of the shooting; got up about 1 or half-past in the afternoon; went to the barber shop to get shaved; while there heard someone say there was liable to be trouble between Clanton and the Earp boys. Told the barber to hurry up, as I wanted to get out and arrest and disarm the party. I meant all of them, every one that had arms except the officers. Going out, crossed the street to Hafford's corner and asked Marshal Earp what was the excitement. He said, "There was a lot of — I think he said s—s of b—s who wanted to make a fight." Said to him: "You had better disarm them." He said he would not do it, and if they wanted a fight they could have it. I said: "It is your duty as a peace officer to stop this thing." Told him I was going to arrest and disarm the cow-boys, meaning McLowry and any others that had arms or showed a disposition to make trouble. Walked to corner of Fourth and Fremont streets; met Frank McLowry holding a horse; told him to give up his arms. He said he would not unless the other people were disarmed also. Think he referred to Holliday and the Earps. Said also that he had done nothing and did not want to make a fight. I looked down Fremont street and saw the Clanton brothers with Tom McLowry. I said to Frank, "Come on with me," and we went together to where the parties who were killed and Ike Clanton were standing. I said: "I will arrest you all. Go up to the Sheriff's office and lay down your arms." Frank McLowry demurred to going, saying that the Earps should be arrested as well. About that time saw Marshall Earp, Doc Holliday, Wyatt Earp and Morgan Earp coming down the street. Expecting there would be trouble if they met, I walked towards them and ordered them back as I was there to disarm the party. Appealed to them several times not to go any further, but they passed on. When they got to the party of cow-boys they drew their guns and said, "You s—s of b—s, you have been looking for a fight, you can have it now." Someone, I think Marshall Earp, said, "Throw up your hands, we are going to disarm you." Then the fight began, some 25 or 30 shots being fired. Could not count them; they sounded like a bunch of firecrackers to me. Could not count them. Before firing commanced [*sic*] I kept telling all parties to put up their arms, not to shoot. Heard Billy Clanton say, "Don't shoot me, I don't want to fight," or something to that effect. Afterwards saw Billy Clanton shooting while lying on the ground, his gun resting on his knee. Before the shooting Tom McLowry said, "I have nothing," and threw his coat open to show he was unarmed. The order to throw up their hands, this remark of McLowry's and the shooting were almost simultaneous. After the fight was over Wyatt Earp said to me, "You have deceived me; you told me you had disarmed them." Told him I had said nothing of the kind, and repeated my conversation with the other party before the fight. Found before the fight that Ike Clanton was unarmed, he told me they were "Just getting ready to leave town." Frank McLowry and William Clanton were the only two of the party that I knew to be armed. Frank McLowry had a horse, think Bill Clanton had one, am not sure. There were six of us standing around. Clanton said there were four in their party. Cannot say who shot first, think a nickel-plated pistol was the first to go off; it was on Earp's side. There was also a shot gun, Holliday had it; was putting it under his coat to conceal it when they came down the street. Don't know whether the shot gun was fired. First saw Billy Clanton shoot, then Frank McLowry who was on north side Fremont street almost opposite Fly's. Did not see Tom McLowry fall, watched Frank most of the time. Fight commenced on a vacant space between Fly's and the next house west. This is on south side of Fremont street between Fourth and Fifth. Am satisfied that two of Clanton's party were unarmed at the time of the shooting, viz., Ike Clanton and Tom McLowry. Clanton and the McLowry's were violating a city ordinauce [*sic*] when I went to disarm them; thought there would be trouble, and went to disarm them for that reason. No one but McLowry refused to give up their arms: did not tell the Earp party that I had disarmed the other party; did not tell them there would be trouble if they went down, but said I would not allow trouble if I could help it; Frank McLowry did not have his pistol drawn when Marshal Earp told him to throw up his hands. Considered the Clanton party under arrest when I left them before meeting the Earp party; nothing was said to lead me to believe the Earps were acting in an official capacity. After the fight was over, heard Wyatt Earp say, "We won't have to disarm that party;" think Virgil Earp said the same thing. During my conversation with the boys, Ike Clanton said he was going out of town, but Frank McLowry said he was not, as he was on business. [A juror asked witness if he considered a party under arrest when he refused to give up his arms. Mr. Behan replied, "Certainly not."]

WILLIAM CLAIBORNE

On being sworn testified as follows: Was present at the shooting; knew the parties engaged in it. They were, Frank McLowry, Tom McLowry, Billy Clanton and Ike Clanton, Doc Holliday and three Earp brothers; don't know their names except Morgan.

Was standing with Mr. Behan, the McLowrys and Clantons when shooting commenced. The day it happened went to Dr. Gillingham's with Ike Clanton to get his head dressed. After that I walked up Fourth street and met Bill Clanton and Frank McLowry. Bill said, "Were [*sic*] is Ike? I want to get him and go home; I don't want to fight anyone." He then asked me to go to Behan's stable with him. We went to the stable and got his (Bill's) horse, after which we passed through Benson's corral. Bill said he wanted to go to some other corral to get his brother's horse. Just then we met with Ike and the McLowry boys. Bill said, "Ike, I want you to get your horse and come home." Ike told him he would "go directly." It [*sic*] this time the sheriff came up and commenced talking to the boys. Didn't hear what he said. Soon after, Behan turned his back and walked up the street, and next thing I saw was Doc Holliday, Morgan Earp, and his two brothers. Marshal Earp says, "You s—s of b—s, you have been looking for a fight and you can have it now." Earp then said, "throw up your hands," which Bill Clanton, Ike Clanton, and Frank McLowry did. Tom McLowry caught hold of the side of his coat and said, "I haven't got anything." At that instant the shooting commenced by Doc Holliday and Morgan Earp. The first shot struck Tom McLowry which was fired by Doc Holliday. The next by Morgan Earp struck Billy Clanton while his hands were up above his head. After firing commenced, Bill Clanton said, "Don't shoot me, I don't want to fight." That is the last I saw of Bill alive. Then Behan put me in the photograph gallery out of the way. Next I saw the dead bodies in the presence of the coroner's jury and identified them under oath. Had known them all for about four years. Don't know whether Bill heard any of the conversation on the part of the Sheriff or not. He was talking to me about fifteen minutes while the Sheriff was talking to the others. When the Earp party came up they had their pistols in their hands. Saw Bill Clanton draw his pistol after he was shot down. Frank McLowry drew his pistol after the Earps had fired about six shots. Am sure the first two shots were fired by Morgan Earp and Holliday. At the first shot, Tom McLowry staggered back a little. Don't think he fell. He had no weapon of any kind. Think there were about 16 shots before I left. Was struck myself through the leg by a bullet. Ike left after seven or eight shots; did not see what he was doing while he was there; think the Sheriff had been with the boys about twenty minutes; he asked me if I was one of the party; and I told him no; he asked the boys the same thing; they said no also. The distance between the parties was not over four feet when the shooting commenced; think Doc Holliday fired the first shot, with a nickel-plated six-shooter; don't think I saw a shot-gun in the fight; think there were about 28 or 80 shots altogether. While I was talking to the Clantons, they spoke of going home and said nothing of fighting. The McLowrys had been in town about three-quarters of an hour when the trouble commenced; saw the other two Earps firing before Bill and Frank commenced shooting.

C.H. LIGHT

Testified: Saw part of the shooting between the Earps and Doc Holliday, and the McLowrys and Clantons; knew the Earps and Doc Holliday since the shooting. While being shaved that afternoon the barber told me there was likely to be trouble between the Earps and Doc Holliday, and the cow-boys; saw the Earps just pass down [*sic*] street with their guns; then went towards my house, corner Third and Tough Nut streets; was in the house when the shooting commenced; heard two shots an instant apart; going to the window saw a man reel and fall at corner of Fremont and Third streets. Don't know who the man was. Looked up Fremont street and saw a man standing with a horse. There appeared to be two men firing at the man. He appeared to be struck. Saw him fire at the man lowest down on Fremont street; his shot seemed to take effect, as the man fired at turned partly round. Next saw a man leaning against the side of the house slide to the ground apparently wounded; his head and shoulders rested against the house; he rested his pistol against his leg and fired two shots; tried to fire a third, but was too weak; the shot went into the air. At this time, there was a tall man with gray clothes and a broad hat standing about the middle of the street in the direction of the man leaning against the house. There was another party firing down the street toward where the man lay; this man fired only three shots; a few more shots were fired by parties on this side of the street. Saw no one fall on the north side of the street; my view was obscured. Next a tall man, dressed in black, appeared with a rifle in his hand and said, take that pistol away from that man (the man on the ground), or he would kill him; this man with the rifle was not a participant in the fight. Whole thing occupied about 15 or 20 seconds. Think there were about six parties firing and no more, four in the middle of the street, one on the south side, and one with the horse. Recognized the man with the gray clothes as Holliday. Must have been 25 or 30 shots fired. I was probably 130 or 140 feet away. Saw no shot-gun; think first two shots were pistols; may have heard report of shot-gun afterwards, but cannot be positive. Saw the man who fell on the street lying there during the fight; did not see him shoot. There was not time between first 2 shots for a man to draw his pistol. Heard two shots before I got to the window.

W.M. A. CUDDY

on being sworn said: I was standing at the postoffice when Mr. Dillon told me there was some trouble between the Earps and the cow-boys, then Mr. Page told me the cow-boys were down at Fly's house. Walked down there and saw Sheriff Behan and four farmers. As I approached saw one of them, Bill Clanton, put his hand on his pistol as if in fear of someone, then recognizing me he withdrew his hand. Heard Behan say, "I won't have any fighting, you must give me your arms or leave town at once." Ike Clanton answered, "There will be no trouble with us, Johnny, we are going to leave town now." I walked off and got as far as the dance-house on Allen street, when shooting began. Looking towards where I had left the Sheriff and the party I saw Ike Clanton exit through the back door of [*sic*] house next to Fly's, in a minute he passed me and went into the dance-house on Allen street. Went back and heard the Sheriff say to Wyatt Earp, "I will have to arrest you now." Earp replied, "Nobody could arrest me now." Mr. Comstock said, "There is no hurry in arresting these men just now; he did right in killing them and the public will uphold him." Then Wyatt said, "You bet we did right, we had to do it. And you threw us, Johnny; you told us they were disarmed." Behan denied that he said they were disarmed. Heard Behan say, "He was not afraid to arrest Earp if he wanted to." Earp said, "As soon as the excitement was over he was willing to be arrested." To my knowledge there was but two men present besides the Clantons. When I left the Sheriff and boys were in a group together. Saw one of them armed, don't know if the others were armed or not; think not. Witness did not identify Mr. Claiborne as having been there.

At this point inquest was adjourned until 10 o'clock this morning.

DAILY EPITAPH

(Tombstone, AZ)

Sunday, October 30, 1881

CORONER'S INQUEST.

Conclusion of the Evidence, with the Verdict of the Jury.

At 10 o'clock yesterday morning the examination of witnesses before the Coroner's Jury was continued.

First witness called was

P.H. FALLEHY,

who testified as follows: After the shooting commenced, saw Holliday in the middle of the street, and the youngest of the Earps about three feet from the sidewalk; he was firing at a man behind a horse; Holliday was also firing at the same man; Holliday was also firing at a man who had run by him to the opposite side of the street. Then I saw the man who held the horse let go the bridle and keep staggering until he fell, his back within a few feet of a house; had a pistol in his hand, but I did not see it go off; did not see the other two Earps at this time; went and offered to pick up the wounded man; he did not speak, though his lips moved; picked up a revolver laying about three feet from him and placed it at this side; this was on the north side of Fremont Street. Next saw Doc Holliday running towards where the man was lying; had his pistol in his hand; he said, "The son of a b— has hit me— I mean to kill him." Holliday did not shoot after saying this; did not see a shot-gun there; don't know who fired the first shot.

MRS. MARTHA KING,

sworn, said: I was standing in Bauer's butcher shop before the fight began; looking out saw all the parties and heard a man with a horse say to another man, "If you want to find us, you will find us just below here." Next, saw Holliday and the Earps coming down the street. Holliday had a gun. I heard the man on the outside say to Holliday, "Let them have it, " and Holliday said, "All right." That is all I know.

R.F. COLMAN

testified. I saw the arrest of Ike Clanton before the shooting. Marshal Earp went up behind him and grabbed his gun, then there was a scuffle, and Clanton fell. Did not see Earp hit him. Saw Earp have a six-shooter, but don't know if he took it from Clanton or not. Did not see Earp hit him. He then took Clanton to the police court. After the trial was over, Earp offered Clanton his rifle, but Clanton did not take it. Heard Clanton say all he wanted was four feet of ground. Soon after I was standing in front of the O.K. Corral, and saw the two Clantons and two McLowrys in a stall in Dunbar's Corral in conversation. Soon after they all came over toward the O.K. Corral. Billy Clanton was on horseback and Frank McLowry was leading his horse. As they passed me, Billy Clanton said, "Where is the West End Corral?" Told him where it was. They passed through the corral and I walked up Allen street. Met Sheriff opposite Headquarters Saloon and said to him; "You should disarm those men; they are up to mischief." Soon after met Marshal Earp and told him the same thing. After this met the Clantons and McLowrys opposite Ely's, on Fremont street. Sheriff Behan was talking to them. One of them said, "You need not be afraid of us, Johnny; we will make no trouble." Billy Clanton had his horse with him. I turned and walked up Fremont street. I met the Earps and Doc Holliday opposite Bauer's meat market. Just as they passed me, Johnny Behan said, "Hold on boys, I don't want you to go any further." Don't think they made any reply, but passed on down till they were opposite where the Clanton party was standing. Never heard one of the Earp party say throw up your hands or give up your arms. Just then two shots were fired as quick as that [clapping his hands quickly], and then the shooting became general. After the first two shots Ike Clanton ran through Fly's house; think there were two shots fired at him. After the first two shots, Tom McLowry ran down Fremont street and fell; saw Billy Clanton fire two or three shots while in a crouching position; saw one of the shots hit Morgan Earp, who stumbled or fell; jumping up again, he commenced firing. At this time saw Frank McLowry advancing toward Holliday and saying, "I've got you now," firing a shot at the same time. That shot struck Holliday on the hip. Frank passed on across the street and fell. Billy Clanton, after being struck, bent down in a stooping position and fired two shots, one of which struck Marshal Earp. Wyatt and Morgan Earp were still firing at Billy Clanton until he fell still holding his pistol. After the shooting was over, hear Behan say to Wyatt Earp, "I shall have to arrest you." Wyatt said, "I won't be arrested now; you have deceived me, Johnny; you said they were disarmed. I am here to answer for what I have done." Saw Billy Clanton with his hand on his pistol, which was in the scabbard; his right hand was on his left hip. This was after the first two shots; could not swear how many of the Clantons were armed; don't think Ike was armed. Don't think there was anybody with the Marshal when he arrested Ike Clanton. Believe the report I gave to the *Epitaph* was about correct. Can't say I saw a shotgun in the hands of either party. Think Billy Clanton was not hit before he commenced firing. Believe the parties were about 10 or 12 feet apart when shooting commenced.

JOSEPH ISAAC CLANTON

Sworn, said; My name is Joseph I. Clanton, am cattle dealer by occupation; reside in Cochise county; am brother to William Clanton who was killed; saw the whole affair. Night before the shooting went into the Occidental Chop house to get lunch. While there Doc Holliday came in and commenced abusing me; had his hand on his gun all the time and called me a d—d son of a b—. Told me to get my gun out. I told him I had no gun. Looking around I saw Morgan Earp sitting on the bar with his hand on his gun. Doc Holliday still kept on abusing me until I went out. Virg. Earp, Wyatt Earp and Morgan Earp were all around. They told me if I wanted a fight to turn myself loose. All had their hands on their guns while they were talking. Holliday said, "You son of a b—, go and arm yourself." Then I went off and did heel myself. Came back soon and played poker with Virg. Earp, Tom McLowry and others. Virg. had his gun on his lap all the time. At daylight we quit. About 8 o'clock in the morning I went and got my Winchester, expecting to meet Doc Holliday on the street, but never met him until Virg. And Morg. Earp slipped up behind me and knocked me down with a six-shooter. Soon after I met my brother William; he asked me to go out of town. We went to the corral where my team was. There we met Sheriff Behan. He said he would have to arrest us and take our arms off. I told him that we were going out of town right away. He then told Billy to come up to his office and put off his arms. Billy told him he was just leaving town, but if the Sheriff would disarm the Earps he would lay his aside. Just at that time I saw Doc Holliday and the Earps approaching. The Sheriff stepped out to meet them, and said, "I have these parties in my charge and don't want any trouble." They went right by. I advanced two or three steps from the crowd and met Wyatt Earp at the corner of the building. He stuck his six-shooter at me and said, "Throw up your hands." Tom opened his coat and said, "I have no arms." They said, "You son of a b—h, you want to make a fight." At the same instant Doc Holliday and Morg. Earp shot; Morg. shot bill Clanton, and I don't know which of the boys Holliday shot; saw Virg. Earp shooting at the same time. I pushed Wyatt Earp around the corner of the house and jumped into the gallery; as I jumped saw Bill Clanton falling; ran through the photograph gallery and got away. When ordered to hold up our hands, we all held them up, except Tom, who held open his coat to show that he was unarmed. There was nothing between the Earps and the boys that were killed. The Earps and myself had a transaction which made them down on me; they don't like me. There was no threats made against the Earps by any of the boys that were killed. The boys expected no attack until just before they got ready to leave town. I had no arms when ordered to throw up my hands; the Marshal had taken my Winchester and six-shooter; had not seen Frank and Billy McLowry for two days previous to their coming in town; never spoke to them about fighting the Earps; don't know whether the Earp party had a shot-gun or not. Virg. And Doc were about six feet from the McLowrys and Morg about three and a half from Willie when they commenced shooting; did not see the McLowrys or my brother shoot. The boys were not sent for by anyone that day; they came in at the request of Major Frink. Behan saw the Earps coming before we did; he told us to stay there. After the Sheriff left I would not stay, only the Sheriff told us to. Behan was with us long enough to say what I have before stated.

Verdict.

The following is the verdict of the Coroner's Jury:

We, the undersigned, a jury of inquest, summoned by the Coroner of the county aforesaid, to determine whose the bodies are, submitted to our inspection, and under what circumstances they came to death. after [*sic*] viewing the bodies and hearing such testimony as hath been submitted to us, find, first, that the persons' names were, William Clanton, aged 19 years, Frank McLowry, aged 29 years, and Tom McLowry, aged 25 years, nativity unknown, and that they came to their death in the town of Tombstone, in said county, on the 26th day of October, 1881, from the effects of pistol and gunshot wounds inflicted by Virgil Earp, Wyatt Earp, Morgan Earp, and one Holliday, commonly called Doc Holliday. (Signed,) Thomas Moses. T.F. Hudson. D. Calisher, M. Garrett, S.B. Comstock, J.W. Conwell, J.C. Davis, C.D. Reppy, F. Hafford, George H. Haskell, M.S. Goodrich.

STREET AND SMITH'S

NEW YORK WEEKLY

A JOURNAL OF USEFUL KNOWLEDGE, ROMANCE, AMUSEMENT, &C.

Entered According to Act of Congress, in the Year 1882, by Street & Smith, in the Office of the Librarian of Congress, Washington, D. C.——Entered at the Post Office New York, N. Y., as Second Class Matter.

Vol. 37. FRANCIS S. STREET } OFFICE No. 31 Rose St., P. O. Box 2734 New York. New York, January 16, 1882. Three Dollars Per Year. Two Copies Five Dollars. { FRANCIS S. SMITH No. 10.

Calamity Jane,

THE QUEEN of the PLAINS.

A Tale of Daring Deeds by a Brave Woman's Hands.

By RECKLESS RALPH.

"If you are men, stay outside a little while, and let him die in peace! If you are beasts, come in, and I'll die with him! But some of you will travel the same road!"

INTRODUCTORY.

It's not my fault, good folks—I mean you that are to read what I'm writing for the NEW YORK WEEKLY—if I make a fool of myself, and put up a bad job on you. Just you blame STREET AND SMITH, for they heard I was clean shavin's on shoving a wild goose-quill, and sent me an offer. There was *coin* in it, easier made than by rifle and trap, too, and I couldn't say no, without its going against the grain.

One thing you can bet on and win every time. I know who and what I write about. I don't take my characters out of lyin' books or pick 'em up in the theaters and circusses. The book of Nature has been my study for five-and-twenty years, and there you'll find the lesson every time.

I'm on a new trail to me; if it isn't just as smooth as an otter-slide, make a little allowance till I get used to the game.

RECKLESS RALPH.

CHAPTER I.

They had him cornered. Worse than that, they had him down. And, bitter luck for him, he was never going to get up again. *He* knew it, and *they* knew it, and it made them a little easier on him than they would have been, for he'd fought game, hadn't tried to skulk or run, and only went down when his body was chock-full of lead, and his Winchester was empty. Then he dropped right in front of his cabin, grit to the last, and *his* gal, or *a* gal, as handsome as ever smiled perdition to man, ran out, and bending down, with a screech that rung for miles through hills and gulches, carried him inside and laid him down on a pile of wolf skins. And she was at the door when the vigilantes closed up in front, and she said, while her eyes almost flashed fire:

"If you are *men*, stay outside a little while, and let him die in peace! If you are *beasts*, come in, and *I'll* die with him! But some of you will travel the same road!"

She held a cocked revolver in each hand as she spoke.

The door was open, and they could look right in and see that he was at his last gasp, unable to raise hand or foot, just able to speak to her in low, whispering tones.

Her eyes told at a glance that she meant all she said, or a little more, and, without taking any vote on it, the vigilantes just nodded *yes*. And she went back and knelt down over him, and listened while he talked, the blood once in awhile gushing out between his lips and almost choking him.

What he said, none of them that looked through that open door could hear, but, all at once, she shrieked out:

"*Not* my father? Who, then, are you? Oh! who and where is *my* father? Why did not mother tell me this before she died?"

He was all choked up, but he tried to speak louder, and those who were outside heard him say, "papers hid," and the rest was so low spoken that they lost it.

He didn't last but a little longer, but in his dying agony he rose half up, and raising his hand, as if appealing to God, cried out:

"Men, this girl is as free from crime as the angels in heaven! So was her sainted mother! Harm not a hair of her head, breathe not a word of insult, do her no wrong! If you do, the curse of a dying man fall upon and blast you as lightning blasts all it smites!"

He fell back so dead he never quivered. And the girl stood over him, her face white as winter's snow, her figure stiff and rigid, yet not a tear falling from her eyes. But no statue ever cut, could speak grief plainer than did her face and form.

The armed men stood still, awe-struck and silent. Yet they were rough and hardened, used to many a scene of violence, accustomed to seeing men shot, and cut, and hung, almost every week of their lives, in the mines where they dwelt.

Finally, the leader of the party, gently, as if he was asking a favor, spoke up and said:

"Miss, we'd a hard job afore us, but we had to do it. He wouldn't surrender, and six of our boys lay dead or dyin' behind us. Will you let us bury him decent, for your sake?—for we owe him no grudge now."

As if waking from a dream, she looked up. The captain was doubtful if she had heard him, and he said the same words over, as near as he could.

She bent down and closed the glassy eyes with hands as smooth and white as her face.

Then she rose up, and said:

"Yes. You have killed a brave man, who has been more than a father in kindness to me. Never in all his life did dark look or word from him cast a shadow in my path. He was good to my mother while she lived—dying, she had no word to speak against him. Yes; hide your work under the green sod—hide all you *can* of it. But when you look on his dead face, ask yourselves if you ever can forget *James Morrison*—'Mountain Jim'—and how alone against a score of you he battled and he died!"

The men made no reply. There was something so grand, yet so quiet, in her grief, that every one bowed down his head and felt ashamed that he had helped to bring sadness on one so young and so beautiful.

And they went in silently, with bared heads, and lifted the giant form of the dreaded outlaw up carefully on the robe which lay beneath him, and carrying it out, laid it upon a great flat rock at the foot of a little waterfall, close by the cabin, where ferns, and wild-flowers, and trailing vines abounded—a fitting bier for the brave dead.

And then, with a miner's pick and shovels, found in front of the cabin, they dug by turns, until a deep grave was ready. And then they asked the beautiful girl if there was anything she wished done before they wrapped him up and laid him down in the deep and narrow pit.

"Yes; bury him as he would have been buried had not misfortune driven him from rank and place well earned, and honors bravely won," was her reply.

She went inside the cabin, and came out in a few seconds with a splendid sword and belt, a pair of silver spurs, and a plumed hat, such as is worn by officers of high rank in the army.

"Place them upon his body when you lay it there, as emblems of his better life. Then fire three volleys above his form—it is all I shall ever ask of any of you."

It was a strange request, but those men were softened down, and did all she asked.

Then one of the roughest of them all, after the grave had been filled and covered with sod, asked the captain if they shouldn't "go through" the cabin and see what plunder they could find.

"No," said the captain of the band—"no, we have done enough here; we will leave her in peace. Most of us have wives and daughters of our own. Don't you forget it!"

And in single file they turned away and marched down the shadowy gulch, along the leaping, foaming little brooklet till they came to the place where they had surprised the outlaw, and called on him to surrender.

A deer which he had freshly skinned hung on a stout limb, just over a pool whence he had dashed water on the opened carcass with a wooden scoop.

Beyond, where they had grouped when they opened fire on him, six of their band lay, four dead, two others so near it, that while the party dug graves for the first the others stiffened out, and were ready for the *one* grave, and the *one* burial of all.

"It's a sad tale we'll have to tell when we're back to Long's Peak!" said the leader. "But there's *this* for comfort, Mountain Jim is dead!"

After all the vigilantes, as those men were called in the early days of gold discovery, had left the valley or gulch in the mountains, in which had occurred the tragedy so briefly described in the foregoing pages, the young girl who had borne her sad part in it, followed their footsteps to the place where the battle had begun, and where they had buried their dead.

"Murderers!" she muttered, as she passed the grave. "You sought your fate and found it. There were twenty-six, twenty left, and each one is a marked man, for the hereafter. They have gone—gone to boast of killing *one* man, who never sinned till he was driven to desperation and made an outlaw, by men far worse than he! And I—am alone. I will not stay here. They are merciful to me just now; they did not search the cabin, as they might have done—on second thought most like will do. I will secure my mother's jewels, and the money she left for me. *His* gold I will hide where none but myself or heirs of his, if I ever find them, will discover it. That done, I will go first to my dear mother's grave; then I will go to seek the papers that he spoke of in his last breath. I fear it will be a vain search, his words were so faint and broken. But I will try to find them. Till I do, I shall never know my true father's name—if he be dead or living.

Slowly she retraced her steps to the lonely cabin. Entering it, shuddering as she saw the blood stains there, she busied herself for an hour in gathering up his treasures and his arms.

Going up above the waterfall, by simply moving a stone, which he had laid over a funnel-shaped aperture in the rock, the water which before poured over in a broad sheet, rushed noisily down out of sight, coming out again in the bed of the former stream several rods below. And with the water-curtain thus lifted, a cavern large enough for a man to walk into and stand erect in, and several yards deep, was revealed.

Into this she carried several heavy bags of gold, his rifle, pistols, and knife, and a box of ammunition.

Covering all with robes that he had prepared, she left them, and going up overhead by a rocky path, leaving no sign, she slid the broad stone into its former place, and again the water rushed in a white cascade full over the cavern's mouth, hiding it from view.

This done, she entered the cabin and remained there but a few moments. When she came out her appearance was changed. Before she had been plainly but neatly clad in calico, made up in simple style, well-fitting her fine and shapely figure.

Now she had her long curls tucked up under a cap of fur. She wore a tunic, or short hunting-coat, of fringed buckskin; wide pantaloons, fringed and beaded, of the same material. She carried a light repeating-rifle, and in her belt two revolvers, a hunting-knife, and hatchet. A large pack, looking too heavy for her to carry, was strapped to her back, and a pouch of ammunition hung at her side. She looked like a very handsome, well-armed hunter-boy of sixteen or eighteen years.

Stepping outside the cabin, she cast one long, sad, wistful look upon the weird and mystic beauty of the place. On her right a lofty mountain, faced with rocks, half-hidden in luxuriant forest growth. In front the narrow valley, shaded with giant trees, made bright by the swift-rushing stream, lovely in its carpet of varied hue—grass, ferns, and flowers.

NEOSHO TIMES.

The only Democratic Newspaper in Newton County

PUBLISHED EVERY THURSDAY BY
SEVIER & STOCKTON
PROPRIETORS.

RATES OF SUBSCRIPTION.
One copy, one year........................$1 00

The Neosho Times.

VOLUME 13. CITY OF NEOSHO, MISSOURI, APRIL 20, 1882. NUMBER 24.

Job Printing

The Job Printing Department of THE TIMES is now under the supervision of competent and skillful workmen, and our facilities being the best in the west enable us to turn out the best work

—AT—

Lowest Prices

JESSE JAMES

ASSASSINATED!

Having Greatly Reduced Our Stock by our great Clearance Sale, we have remodeled and refitted our commodious store rooms and purchased one of the largest, choicest and most varied stocks ever bought in the Southwest, and are now ready to offer bargains in all the departments enumerated below:

IN THE DRESS GOODS DEPARTMENT

We have all the newest, latest and most desirable styles out from the finest silk to the cheapest calico.

IN DRESS TRIMMINGS we have EVERYTHING any one COULD DESIRE

WE MAKE A SPECIALTY in LADIDES', MISSES', CHILDREN'S,

Men's and Boys' Shoes, and we assure you that you will be pleased in this line of Goods and the Prices.

OUR CLOTHING AND HAT DEPARTMENT

Is immense, and by looking through this department you will be convinced of the fact that neither man nor boy can fail to be suited in style, make and price.

CARPET DEPARTMENT!

We have an elegant line of Carpets which we still offer to close at Cost.

OUR NOTION DEPARTMENT

IS COMPLETE IN EVERY LINE.

In conclusion we will say, that it is no longer necessary to send abroad for anything you may need in our line for we assure you we have everything you may need. We cordially invite every one to call and examine our stock and be convinced of the facts we have stated. Yours,

Entered according to Act of Congress, in the year 1882, by Mrs. Frank Leslie, in the Office of the Librarian of Congress at Washington.—Entered at the Post Office, New York, N.Y., as Second-class Matter.

No. 1,387.—Vol. LIV. NEW YORK—FOR THE WEEK ENDING APRIL 22, 1882. [Price 10 Cents. $4.00 Yearly. 13 Weeks, $1.00.

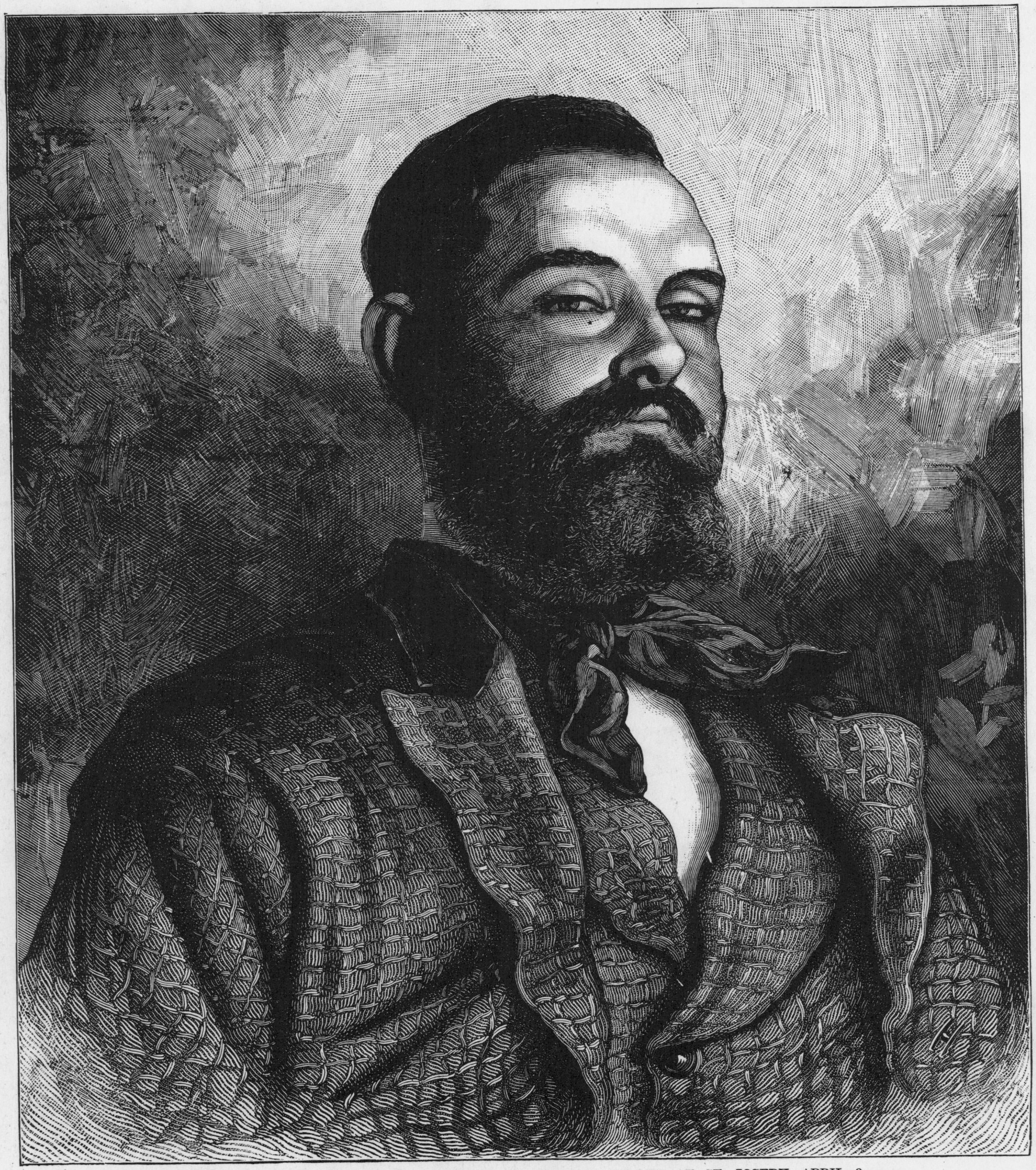

MISSOURI.—JESSE JAMES, THE NOTORIOUS DESPERADO, KILLED AT ST. JOSEPH, APRIL 3d.
From a Photo. by Alex. Lozo.—See Page 135.

A ROW IN THE RING.

AN ELOPING WIFE JOINS A CIRCUS WITH HER LOVER, AND THE SHOW IS RAIDED IN TEXAS BY THE FURIOUS HUSBAND AND HIS COW-BOY FRIENDS, WHO CARRY OFF THE FAIR EQUESTRIENNE.

JESSE JAMES, THE BANDIT.

KILLED BY HIS PAL, BOB FORD, ON THE 3D INST., AT ST. JOSEPH, MO.

[From a Portrait taken expressly for the POLICE GAZETTE.]

JESSE JAMES' MURDER.

BOB FORD, THE BANDIT'S FRIEND, TREACHEROUSLY SLAYS HIM IN HIS OWN HOUSE, AT ST. JOSEPH, MO.

A TRUE STORY, by D. W. Stevens, begins in this number.

LOOK OUT FOR A GREAT DETECTIVE STORY!

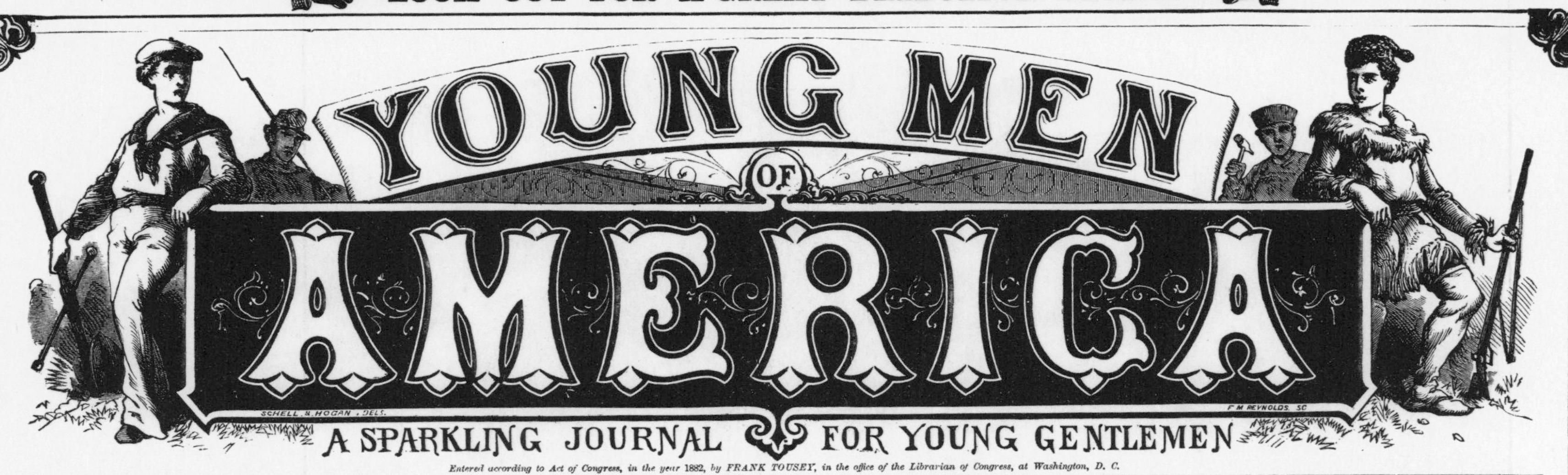

Entered according to Act of Congress, in the year 1882, by FRANK TOUSEY, in the office of the Librarian of Congress, at Washington, D. C.

ENTERED AT THE POST OFFICE AT NEW YORK, N. Y., AS SECOND CLASS MATTER.

Vol. V. | FRANK TOUSEY, Nos. 34 & 36 North Moore St. | NEW YORK, APRIL 27, 1882. | $2.50 PER ANNUM, IN ADVANCE, $1.25 FOR SIX MONTHS. | No. 242

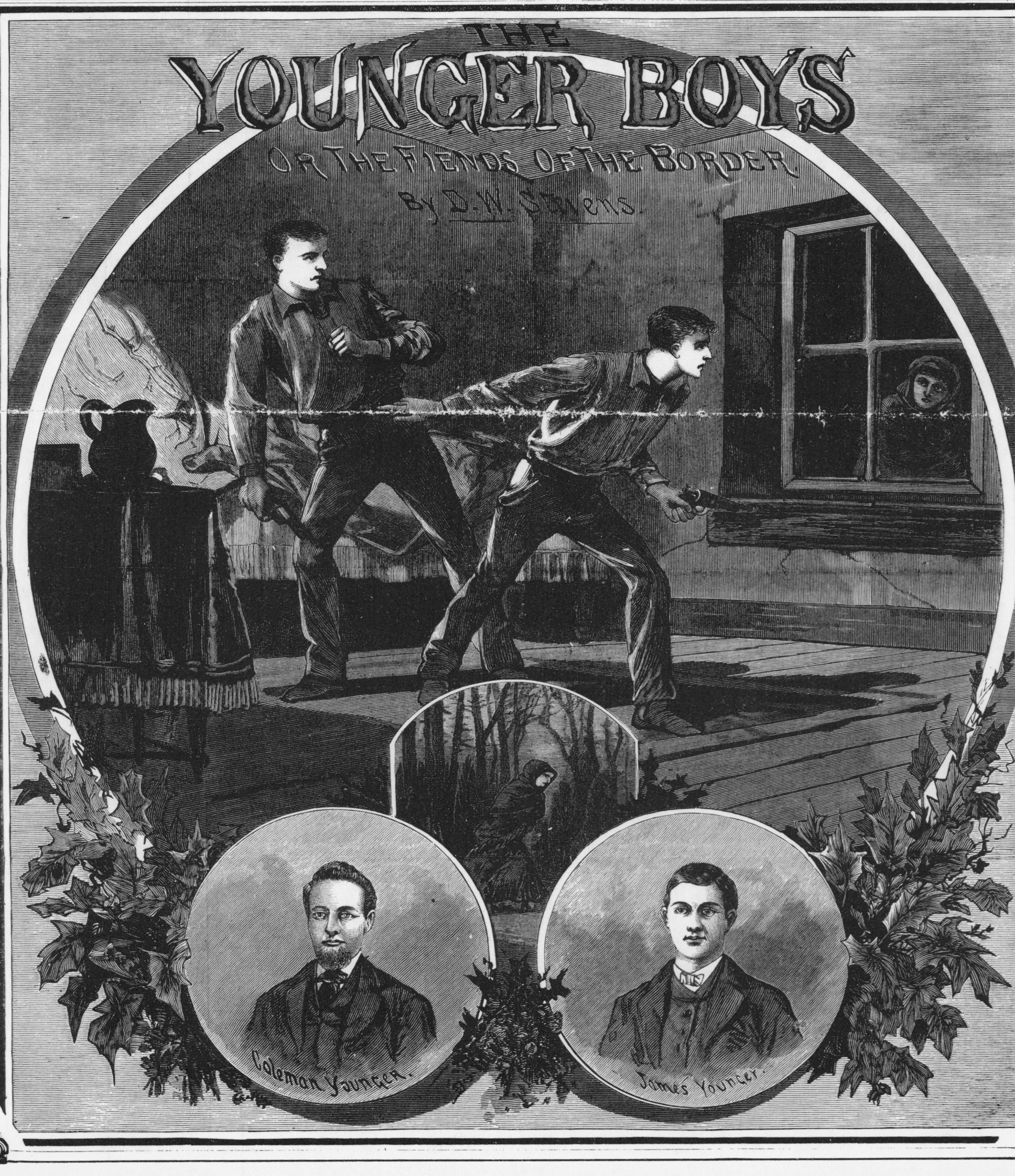

THE YOUNGER BOYS

OR THE FIENDS OF THE BORDER

By D. W. Stevens

Coleman Younger.

James Younger.

THE MURDER OF JESSE JAMES.

PORTRAITS AND SCENES FROM THE TRAGEDY—FROM SPECIAL PHOTOGRAPHS FOR AND SKETCHES BY POLICE GAZETTE ARTISTS ON THE SPOT.

The Denver Times.

DENVER, COLORADO.

Harness—DENVER MF'G. CO. 10-tf

Saddles—DENVER MF'G. CO. 10-tf

Our soda water the best, SCHOLTZ & HANUS. 6-tf

F. R. Eastman & Co., fashionable Hatters. 31-tf

Ross & BEHYMER, undertaking and embalming. No. 542 Larimer street, Denver, Colo. 22-tf

Manitou soda water, at SCHOLTZ & HANUS. 6-tf

New styles of hats received to-day by F. R. EASTMAN & CO. 13-7t

The Radiant Grate, the best grate made, for sale at BACON & SON'S. 18-tf

Purchasers to the amount of $1.00 or more at JOSLIN'S receive a handsome souvenir. 9-tf

A large assortment of marble mantels and grates at bottom prices. GEORGE TRITCH & CO. 20-tf

J. N. AMMEN & CO., City Laundry, offer special rates on collars and cuffs left at their office, 428 Larimer and 264 15th. The work will be first-class. mtu&w-tf

That car-load of marbleized iron and slate mantels at BACON & SON'S were bought cheap, are of the latest styles, are nice in variety, and are all for sale at low prices. 18-tf

Elgin Watches.

Elgin, Howard and Waltham watches, wholesale and retail, at GOTTESLEBEN'S. tu th&s

Announcements.

The Athletic club of the Broadway hose company will meet to-morrow evening.

Lawrence Barrett in "Yorick's Love" at the Tabor Grand opera house to-night.

Meeting of Colorado commandery No. 1, K. T., this evening. Work on the order of K. T.

The regular monthly meeting of the board of managers of the Orphan's Home association will be held to-morrow (Wednesday) p. m. at three o'clock at the house of Mrs. Governor Evans.

The prayer meeting of the Presbyterian church in East Denver will be held on Wednesday at 7:45 p. m. at the residence of Rev. E. P. Wells, No. 710 Lawrence street. All are cordially invited.

Personal.

F. H. Conant, Esq., editor of the Leadville Herald, is in the city.

Mr. George Williams, a prominent lumber merchant of Leadville, is in the city.

Geo. L. Hodges, Esq., a prominent Leadville attorney, arrived here this morning.

John L. Dormer is down from Central, attending the races, and is registered at the American.

H. D. DaBella, agent for John Robinson's Big Show, is in the city, and holds forth at the American.

W. T. Hays, western passenger agent of the Michigan Central railroad, is sojourning at the American.

C. S. Cooper, Esq., an ex-alderman of Leadville, came down yesterday and is stopping at the St. James.

The wife and family of Capt. Lindsay, of the South Park railroad, have gone to Washington, D. C., to spend a few weeks.

S. T. Armstrong, secretary of the Mining Exposition association, returned last evening, from a trip to Las Vegas and the Hot Springs.

Notes About Town.

The new street car stables are looming up rapidly.

It is probable that Australia will have an exhibit at the mining exposition.

The stone cutters are still striking. There is no fear that it will be a "long strike."

The lithograph pictures of Lawrence Barrett are remarkably fine pieces of work.

About the only persons who occupy boxes at the Tabor Grand are newspaper men.

The obsequies of the late John H. Clark will be conducted by the Jefferson and Jackson club.

Every hack and express wagon in the city is in service this week, conveying people to the races.

Wall & Witter have received a fine lot of Norman horses. This breed of horses find a ready sale in Denver.

Real estate predictions are being realized. There has been a steady advance in prices since the first of the year.

The first excursion of the season will take place next Sunday to Idaho Springs. It will be given by the Denver Turn Verein and Sangerbund.

All of the city police should be uniformed. They make a sorry looking lot when walking in squads—some in uniform and some in nondescript apparel.

The agents of theatrical combinations linger longer in Denver than they do in any other western city. There are many attractions for them here.

Seventeenth street, between Holladay and Blake, has been reduced to a lower grade than the sidewalks. Holladay street, near 17th, is now being improved.

Marshal Clayton visited the several fire headquarters yesterday afternoon accompanied by Colonel E. P. Richardson, ex-chief of the Manchester, N. H., department.

The mud which was left in 17th street, near the depot track, when the pool of water evaporated has begun to crack into cakes. It looks like cakes of painted paraffine.

An approaching marriage is that of Dr. Drury, the popular young dentist, to Miss Lou Hawley. Their many friends will wish them joy in advance of the ceremony.

The law firm of Whitcher & Austin has been dissolved. They were attorneys for Sawyer, who sued Lawyer Naylor. The dissolution was brought about by this suit.

A crazy man undressed himself in the Union depot yesterday despite the screams and protests from the ladies in the waiting room. He was locked up in the county jail.

Rolla, the bright ten-year old son of Captain H. H. Shepperd, died yesterday. He was a fine boy, and everybody who knew him loved him and will grieve with his father at his loss.

Big Ike, the famous Colorado trotter, was to have taken part in a big race at Cincinnati on Friday, but postponement was necessitated on account of rain. He is entered to trot in an important 2:30 race at Dayton, Ohio, to-day.

A man who raises a disturbance of any kind at a theatre should be promptly thrown out. The officer in the gallery of the opera house should have made an example of the rude fellow who last night nearly spoiled a scene by his boisterous manner.

Yesterday morning Mr. George E. King, the general business agent for Messrs. Hallack & Howard, was married to Miss Josephine Clise. The ceremony was performed by Rev. Reuben Jeffrey, at the residence of the bride's father, Mr. J. D. Clise, No. 302 Twentieth street.

At a regular meeting of the Chaffee Light artillery, held at their company headquarters last evening Dr. Ambrose L. Everett was unanimously elected to the position of first assistant surgeon with the rank of captain, as prescribed in section 6, article 4 of the laws governing the national guard of the state of Colorado. This completes their organization as a four gun battery.

"DOC" HOLLADAY.

MAN-KILLER, OR AN ABUSED MAN, WHICH?

Arrest of an Alleged Arizona Outlaw and Assassin—A Story With Two Sides.

Last evening about nine o'clock a scene occurred on the corner of 15th and Lawrence which for a moment caused the blood of the bystanders to stand still. The usual gang of corner gossippers were grouped around the electric lamp post, when they were startled out of all the proprieties of life by the stern command: "Doc. Holladay, hold up your hands or you are a dead man!" From the instantaneous scattering it might have been imagined that there were several Doc. Holladays in the vicinity. When the panic subsided sufficiently to permit investigation it was found that there was little cause for alarm except on the part of one man,—a well built, daring looking man, who stood in the full glare of the brilliant light, while not three feet away stood another, covering him with a pair of Colts 44s, backed by an air of determination and a pair of eyes which gave emphasis to the air. Before the crowd had fully recovered from its astonishment Deputy Sheriff Linton stepped up and in a moment a pair of darbies were slipped over Holladay's wrists, and in another instant the party were moving off down Lawrence street to the sheriff's office.

The story is a brief one but highly sensational. The man who wielded the artillery with such immediate effect was Perry Mallen, an officer of Los Angeles, California, and to the desire of capturing a noted criminal was added the incentive for personal revenge. Seven years ago Mr. Mallen in company with a young man named White was at St. George, Utah. The two young men came west together, and were bound by ties of association and friendship that in the course of years had ripened into absolute affection. At the time stated, last night's prisoner, Holladay, was dealing faro at St. George's. One night Mallen and White strolled into the saloon and became engaged in the game. In a few minutes a dispute arose between Holladay and White, and angry words were exchanged. Through the efforts of Mallen a fight was prevented, and White induced to leave the saloon. The next day the partners again went to the saloon. As White stepped into the saloon Holladay stepped from behind the door, and without a word of warning, shot poor White, continuing to shoot into the prostrate body until life was extinct. Surrounded, as he was, by a crowd of desperadoes, Mallen could do nothing, but from that moment devoted himself to revenge with a ferrency which has been maintained with a persistence almost unparalleled even in the annals of the border vendetta. Nothing was done to Holladay, murder in those days being of too common occurrence to attract more than passing notice, but very soon after the murderer left the country. For a long time Mallen lost track of his man, but finally he heard of him as the leader of a band of cattle thieves and desperadoes operating above Yuma, on the Colorado river. A sheriff's posse of six started from Yuma, of which Mallen was a member, and encountered the gang. But there were twenty-five of the desperadoes, and in the fight three of the sheriff's posse were killed, and Mallen himself severely wounded. Holladay seemed to recognize the presence of a Nemesis, for soon afterward he dispersed his gang, and disappeared from the vicinity. But Mallen followed close upon his tracks. To Los Angeles, to Fort Dodge, to Arizona and other points in the Southwest, he followed his quarry with the persistence of a hound, but only once did he come upon him, which was six weeks ago, when in an encounter a second comrade of Mallen was shot dead by his side. Holladay was at this time heading for his old haunts near Fort Dodge. Mallen was hot upon his trail, and at Pueblo saw his man in a variety theatre. Before an officer could be procured he had disappeared. At a venture Mallen came to Denver with the result above stated. The record of the desperado is as villainous as that of the worst of his class. No fewer than twenty-five men have fallen by his hand, most of them murdered without provocation and in the most cold-blooded manner. At every point of his sojourn his record has been stained with blood.

Four weeks ago, while running from Mallen, Holladay was at Albuquerque with the infamous Earp gang, who had taken refuge in New Mexico from the pursuit of the officers of Arizona. There it seems that the party separated. It will be remembered that the Earp brothers returned to Arizona and were both shot. Holladay and Wyatt Earp quarrelled in Albuquerque, one of the gang named Tipton accompanying Holladay to Arizona by a different route. A week ago last Monday, Wyatt Earp, while returning from a visit to his wounded brother at Colton, California, was ambushed near Hooker's, Arizona, and killed. A day or two previous Holladay and Tipton were attacked and the latter killed, Holladay with his usual luck escaping, but only to fall into the hands of Mallen.

The capture of Holladay disposes of four of the seven who were at Albuquerque, one of the worst gangs of desperadoes which has ever disgraced humanity.

The above is substantially the story told by this man Mallen, and also by the Albuquerque News, which gives the latter portion of the narrative, referring to the alleged shooting of Wyatt Earp and Tipton. It was evident that something lay beneath all this matter, and accordingly a TIMES reporter was detailed to see the prisoner and get his statement of the affairs which have led to his arrest. Certain outside intelligence bearing on the case came to the knowledge of the reporter, who was therefrom enabled to put leading questions to the prisoner.

When Mr. Holladay came out of his cell the reporter was surprised to find, instead of the typical western ruffian, a delicate, gentlemanly man, apparently weighing not more than one hundred and thirty pounds, perhaps thirty-five years of age, with a prematurely gray head, and a heavy sandy mustache. He was evidently laboring under suppressed excitement, resulting from an anticipation of personal danger. At the slightest noise at the window near which he sat, he started and cast a quick, anxious glance in that direction, showing that he felt unsafe, even when protected by the bars of a prison.

He had determined to say nothing, but he was satisfied that a representative of the TIMES desired his statement he at once became communicative.

He said that the entire difficulty arose primarily from political differences. Cochise county, of which Tombstone is the county seat, was created while General Fremont was governor of the territory, and consequently the governor had the appointment of the county officers. Wyatt Earp, who at that time, kept a large saloon in Tombstone, was an applicant for the appointment of sheriff. J. H. Behan was also an applicant. The governor appointed Behan, who had agreed with Earp that whichever received the appointment should appoint the other under sheriff, an agreement which he ignored after receiving the appointment. This caused a coolness between the two men. This coolness grew into absolute hostility, owing to the fact that Earp became an active partisan of the United States marshal, in his efforts to suppress lawlessness, while Behan took the side of the cowboys, who were responsible for the majority of the acts of lawlessness which have made the very name of Arizona a terror. The "Curly Bill" mentioned by Mallen was a most notorious character, and was wanted by the United States for a number of outrages, among which were the killing of the marshal of El Paso and the shooting of lieutenant Butler, a son of Gen. B. F. Butler, during an attempted robbery of a stage coach. (This fact is well remembered in the west but does not argue well for the associations of the alleged officer Mallen, even if his story be true.) The enmity of the marshal's force rendered the outlaws desperate, and they determined to run the Earp boys and their adherents out of the country. The respectable business men of the town supported the Earps and Mr. Holladay, but they were in the minority, and it was impossible to maintain themselves. The Epitaph was bold and outspoken in its denunciation of the sheriff and his adherents, but the cowboys threatened to kill C. D. Reppy, the editor of the paper, and actually attempted to assassinate Wm. Clum, the president of the company of the Epitaph company by attacking the stage in which he was a passenger. This statement of Mr. Holladay's is confirmed by a letter from Mr. Reppy to his brother Mr. George Reppy, of this city, which also states that on account of this situation the paper has been sold and will be turned into a Democratic sheet. Mr. Gage, superintendent of a prominent mining company, was also a warm supporter of the Earp party, and he was compelled to leave the country on account of the threats to take his life. Last fall the two parties came together and three of the cow boys were killed. This, Mr. Holladay states, was the only fight that he has been in. This spring the entire party became convinced that their only hope of safety lay in flight, and accordingly early in April they started and were soon afterward followed by a party of cowboys, headed by the sheriff. At the ranch of Mr. Hooker, the reputed cattle king of Arizona, they were hospitably treated and promised protection if they desired to remain. They pushed on, however, and eventually reached New Mexico and the railroads. Holladay went to Kansas for a few days, while the remainder waited in New Mexico and southern Colorado. Four or five days ago, while Holladay was in Tom Kemp's theatre in Pueblo, an acquaintance came in and told him that there was a man outside who was inquiring for him. Holladay stepped out and says he saw this man Mallen for the first time in his life. Mallen said to him that he (Holladay) had saved his (Mallen's) life in Santa Fe at one time, and that he desired to return the favor; that a man named Stilwell was in Pueblo who had announced a determination to shoot Holladay on sight. Holladay replied that it could not be possible that he had ever saved Mallen's life as he had never been in Santa Fe in his life, but thanked him for his information, and saw nothing more of him until he arrived here. After Mallen left Pueblo, a barkeeper told Holladay that Mallen had represented to him that he was going into the cattle business in the vicinity, and upon the strength of an eighteen thousand check, had borrowed ten dollars, promising to pay it in the morning, but went off forgetting the trifling circumstance. This convinced Holladay that his new acquaintance was not of much account, so when he found him in Denver he did not recognize him. Mr. Holladay thinks that Mallen is some crank who wanted to get his name in the papers as a great detective. He says he was never a member of the cowboy gang who never handle their pistols so awkwardly as Mallen did his last night, and either lived some time in Tombstone or obtained his meagre array of facts from the papers.

He says there is not a word of truth in the statement that Wyatt Earp and Tipton were killed. They left Pueblo the day before himself and are now in Gunnison, where they will remain, unless it becomes necessary to put more space between themselves and the cowboys. Mr. Holladay evidently thinks it necessary, for he was about to move to Montana.

Holladay is well known in this city, and names a number of well-known men as references. He lived here several years ago, and has a large number of friends, who are interesting themselves in his behalf. He says that the only object of his arrest now is to get him down to Arizona in order to murder him, but he does not believe that Governor Tritte will give a requisition for him.

When he lived here Holladay had a difficulty with a gambler, and cut him. His former antagonist is now one of his best friends. He is strongly of the impression that the cowboys would not hesitate to follow him up here if they thought they could succeed in taking his life without being caught. It is safe to assert that he will not be long here after his release, which will doubtless take place as soon as the necessary papers can be made out, as Holladay laughs at the idea of any reward being offered for him. As to the story about killing White, he says it is a pure fiction invented by Mallen for the purpose of obtaining a little brief notoriety as a fighter, as he was never in Utah in his life, and has not the remotest idea where St. George's is.

Mr. Holladay's story, corroborated as it is by Mr. Reppy's letter, is plausible, and is certainly told with an air of candor and straightforwardness that carries conviction. It will not be surprising if it turns out that the matter grows out of the Arizona troubles, and that Mallen's story was made up to give him an excuse for making the arrest, and for giving him tone as a seven-years' avenger of a friend's death.

The Book Sale Continues.

There has never been anything in Denver to compare with the present book sale at PAUL STRICKLER & CO.'S, 419 Larimer street. The variety is inexhaustible. All the leading authors of fiction are represented in sets or single numbers, lives of eminent men, works of mythology and theology, poetry, history and medical works of the most noted authors and best authority. A complete line of Catholic works and general goods, together with an immense assortment of standard and classic books. There are 30,000 pieces of music, which comprise the latest and most popular airs, both instrumental and vocal. This music is selling for less than it cost to publish it and is consequently going very rapidly. Taking everything into consideration this is a wonderful opportunity to stock your library and music racks with the best productions at a very small cost. Sales commence at 2 and 7 p. m. 1t

Theodore and Hattie Price in their unique and interesting entertainment at the First Baptist church, on 18th street, between Curtis and Champa street, on Tuesday night, May 16th. The most enjoyable entertainment of the kind ever given in Denver. Repeated by special request. Admission, 50 cents; children, 15 cents. 13-3t

Genuine Iron Ute water, at SCHOLTZ & HANUS. 6-tf

LOCAL NOTICES.

Advertisements in this department will be charged fifteen cents per line for first insertion and ten cents per line for each subsequent insertion.

MILLS, Insurance, 357 Arapahoe street. 14-tfs

ALGER, Optician, 390 Lawrence. 26-tfs

GANO & THOMAS, furniture, 437 Larimer. 11-tfs

DR. J. J. BURNS, dentist, 250 15th street. 25-tf

Buy furniture at GANO & THOMAS'S. 11-tfs

For silk wraps and ulsters go to DANIELS & FISHER'S. 15-6ts

$4.00 will buy a French Penang suit at DANIELS & FISHER'S. 15-6ts

Remnants of table linen very cheap at DANIELS & FISHER'S. 15-6ts

Stone, cement and tar sidewalks, good and cheap, put down by P. T. HUGHES, 432 Lawrence. 2-tfs

E. J. LOPER'S pure cider vinegar, pickles sauer-kraut and russet cider, Denver, Colo. f9-6ms

Big bargains those $10, $15 and $20 suits at DANIELS & FISHER'S. 15-6ts

Gents' fine neckwear and fancy shirts at DANIELS & FISHER'S. 15-6ts

Soiled napkins at half-price all this week at DANIELS & FISHER'S. 15-6ts

Headquarters for novelties in ladies' neckwear is at DANIELS & FISHER'S. 15-6ts

Kid, dog-skin, chamois and buck-skin driving gloves at DANIELS & FISHER'S. 15-6ts

Black nun's veilings, a full assortment and prices low, at DANIELS & FISHER'S. 15-6ts

New styles in gingham and Foulard suits just opened at DANIELS & FISHER'S. 15-6ts

Gents' fine balbriggan underwear in plain and fancy colors, at DANIELS & FISHER'S. 15-6ts

Job lot of watered ribbons, all widths and the new shades, at DANIELS & FISHER'S. 15-6ts

Extra drive, 27 inch, all wool serge, new shades, 50 cents per yard at DANIELS & FISHER'S. 15-6ts

All of the new shades of plain and fancy dress goods at bottom prices. DANIELS & FISHER. 15-6ts

Every lady wishing perfect fitting gloves should go to DANIELS & FISHER'S. 15-6ts

A handsome and elegant line of Foulard silk suits just opened at DANIELS & FISHER'S. 15-6ts

Heavy, medium and light weight underwear for ladies and gents at DANIELS & FISHER'S. 15-6ts

Opening this week for the races. Special line of ladies' summer suits at DANIELS & FISHER'S. 15-6ts

Now is the time to secure a bargain; soiled quilts at half the regular price, at DANIELS & FISHER'S. 15-6ts

A new line of parasols, bought expressly for race week, now on exhibition at DANIELS & FISHERS. 15-6ts

Complete assortment of dress trimmings and buttons. All the late novelties at DANIELS & FISHER'S. 15-6ts

Everything requisite for art embroidery and home decoration can be found at DANIELS & FISHER'S. 15-6ts

Ladies' hand bags and pocket books. DANIELS & FISHER have just opened a line of novelties in the above goods. 15-6ts

At our job counter in the hosiery department one can always find bargains at half price. DANIELS & FISHER. 15-6ts

Zephyr and ginghams at the dress goods department, 200 styles to select from, colors fast. DANIELS & FISHER. 15-6ts

Use the Stewart coal, as it is the best in market. GOODBRIDGE & MARFELL, 263 17th street. 5tfs

The season for Lisle thread and silk gloves is at hand. DANIELS & FISHER have an endless variety for the ladies to select from. 15-6ts

Bargains in black and colored Rhadamas. We will offer our stock of these goods at very low prices for this week. DANIELS & FISHER. 15-6ts

Those new boulevard parasols at DANIELS & FISHER'S are too lovely for description. To understand their full glory you must see them. 15-6ts

We are now showing our importation of foreign cotton dress goods, many patterns of which are exclusive and can be had only of us. DANIELS & FISHER. 15-6ts

DR. R. F. PRICE, 250 15th street. *Female diseases* specialty. Ladies out of health find prompt relief. Fifteen years practice; three years in Denver. References. 10-6ms

Beautify your homes by ordering one of our Champion iron fences. The cheapest, most durable and ornamental fence in the market. GUSTAV WINTER, 287 17th street. 13-1ms

Do not forget that when you want any French stamping done go to DANIELS & FISHER'S, for they do the best work and have a larger and newer variety of patterns to select from than any other house. 15-6ts

Notice This.

$4.00 Penang suits.
$8.00 White suits.
Our $5.00 jackets. DANIELS & FISHER. 15-6ts

No matter what the mouth's disease—
How foul the breath or teeth's decay—
With SOZODONT on all we seize,
And swiftly sweep it far away,
Leaving the gums pure, firm and white,
And the dull teeth as ivory white.
tuths&ws

"Perry Park" Summer Resort

Will be open to receive guests June 1st. The Park is situated 40 miles from Denver—two hours' ride on the D. & R. G. road. It comprises the grandest and most beautiful mountain scenery in the state, also mineral springs, and is a most desirable place for parties wishing to spend the summer in the country. For particulars address: P. R. RICKARD, Perry Park, Larkspur, Colo. 29-tfs

Tabor Grand Opera House

ONE WEEK

COMMENCING

Monday, May 15.

GRAND SATURDAY MATINEE

THE EMINENT TRAGEDIAN,

LAWRENCE BARRETT!

SUPPORTED BY

Company of Unusual Excellence.

MONDAY EVENING, MAY 15—Bulwer's Master Play, in Five Acts……RICHELIEU.

TUESDAY EVENING, MAY 16—Mr. W. D. Howell's Translation and Adaptation from the Spanish of Estebanez, entitled……YORICK'S LOVE.

WEDNESDAY EVENING, MAY 17—Shakespeare's Tragedy, in Five Acts……HAMLET.

THURSDAY EVENING, MAY 18—Shakespeare's Tragedy, in Five Acts……OTHELLO.

FRIDAY EVENING, MAY 19—Grand Double Bill—Shakespeare's Great Play, THE MERCHANT OF VENICE, and Robertson's Comedy, in Three Acts……DAVID GARRICK.

SATURDAY MATINEE—Bulwer's Love Story, ……LADY OF LYONS.

SATURDAY EVENING, MAY 20—Shakespeare's Historical Tragedy, in Six Acts……JULIUS CÆSAR.

PRICES.

Parquette and Dress Circle……$1 50
Balcony……1 00
Family Circle……50

MATINEE PRICES.

Parquette and Dress Circle……75c
Balcony……50c

Seats now on sale.

Monday, May 22,

Mitchel's Pleasure Party in

"OUR GOBLINS"

LOCAL ADVERTISEMENTS.

Advertisements under this head reduced to eight cents per line for first insertion and five cents per line each additional insertion.

WANTED.

WANTED—A girl to do general housework. None but first class need apply, at 460 California street. 16-tf

WANTED—Girl for general housework. At 29 Grant avenue. 16-2*

WANTED—A good brick moulder. Apply to GEORGE ANSTEE, No. 28 15th street, North Side. 16-2*

WANTED—A young man well acquainted with city to drive delivery wagon. 416 Welton. 1t

WANTED—Girl for general housework. No. 200 Broadway. 10-5

WANTED—Good canvassers to sell sewing machines, 389 Lawrence street. 4-tf

WANTED—Watchmaker at once. Must have best of references. C. W. LITTLE, 324 and 326 15th street, city. 4-tf

WANTED—Inventors having good patents or desiring to secure patents for their inventions should call at Room 2, No. 409 Larimer, Denver, Colo. 28-tf

TO RENT.

TO RENT—3 good houses, $15, $20, $20. SPRAGUE, 440½ Larimer St. 16-3t*

TO RENT—A furnished house, with bath, or three or four rooms with privilege of housekeeping. Apply 374 Lawrence street. 9-tf

TO RENT—Store and basement in Windsor block; store and basement at 17th and Larimer; store and basement on Blake street; suite of offices in Duff block, corner of 18th and Larimer. Apply to JAMES DUFF, 456 Larimer street. 8-tf

TO RENT—Three fine 10 room houses, furnace, gas, bath, etc. Good location. MORGAN, FRENCH & CO., 293½ 16th street. 2tf

FOR SALE.

FOR SALE—Several neat houses; owners must sell. This means business. SPRAGUE, 440½ Larimer St. 16-5t*

FOR SALE—200 feet picket and rough board fence, to be seen 484 Arapahoe. 10 6t

FOR SALE—Four hundred and eighty acres, only half a mile east of the projected Circle railroad, in small or large lots to suit. RUFUS CLARK. my4-1m*

FOR SALE—All the personal property belonging to the estate of the late Caroline J. Wolff, consisting of household furniture, etc., will be sold at auction at the late residence, Ashland avenue North Denver, on Saturday, May 13. Sale commencing at two o'clock p. m. E. A. WOLFF, Administrator. 3-10t

FOR SALE—The cheapest place in West Denver. A nice 5-room furnished house with large grounds, shrubbery, grass, trees, good well, barn, and everything to make a pleasant home. Inquire at A. B. ULLERY'S law office, 265½ 11th street, near Lindell hotel. 2-12t

FOR SALE—Pure, sweet cream in quantities to suit. P. O. Box 2445. 4-tf

FOR SALE—New and second-hand wagons at NOVELTY CARRIAGE WORKS, Blake and 14th. 24-tf

FOR SALE—An account against the Denver Cooperative Supply association. W. J. HARTINGTON, President. 9-tf

FOR SALE—Three of the best building lots in Denver, 12, 13 and 14, block 37, H. C. Brown's addition. F. J. B. CRANE. 24 tf

FOR SALE—At the TIMES office, cards "To Rent," "For Sale," "Furnished Rooms," etc.

LOST.

LOST—On Saturday evening, black Scotch shepherd dog (collie), long sleek hair, jet black, nose white below eyes white streak in forehead, both fore feet tipped with white, full brush tail also tipped with white, white breast. Extremely bright animal, amiable and playful. Answers to name of "Bret." Will pay liberal reward for his return to 534 Stout street, or for information where he may be found. FRANK HALL. 15-3t

PERSONAL.

PERSONAL—The leading candy and fruit house, STANDLEY'S, 434 Larimer st. Root beer, meat, soda water, cigars by the box, Wheeling Stogies; broken candy, 20 c. per pound. f10-tf

TO LOAN.

TO LOAN—Money, at low interest on good real estate security, in sums of $1,000 to $5,000. J. M. BERKEY & CO., 271 15th st. 19-tf

TO LOAN—Money to loan. MORGAN, FRENCH & CO., 29½ 16th street. 19-tf

FINANCIAL.

FINANCIAL—Invest $100 or upwards in Able Consolidated Mining company's 8 per cent coupon bonds. An investment in mining stock without any risk whatever. Capital and interest absolutely safe. Report on mine and full particulars at company's office, Room 15, Tabor block, Denver, Col. 7-3m

TAKEN UP.

TAKEN UP—By the subscriber, living on Ashley Bros.' ranch, in Douglas county, Colorado, five dark brown mules and one bay horse pony, all except one mule branded thus: U T on left shoulder. The remaining mule branded thus: [brand] on left shoulder. All the mules are badly harness-marked. Came here 12th of May, afternoon. Last mentioned mule had hobbles on. Owner requested to call and prove property, pay charges and take them away. WILLIAM ASHLEY. May 13th, 1882. 16-5t

STAGES.

STAGES leave Georgetown daily for New Dillon, Frisco, and all points in Summit county. S. W. NOTT, Proprietor. a15-1m*

WM. H. ARMSBY & CO

New Departure!

Which Will You Have?

LOOK

AT THE

OLD PRICES

AND

AT THE NEW!

IF YOU PREFER THE

New Prices, Buy of Us,

IF

THE OLD, BUY ELSEWHERE.

BURT & MEARS'S

Men's Hand-Sewed Work

THE BEST MADE IN AMERICA.

	Formerly.	Now.
Double-Soled Opera Boots	$12.00	$10.50
Single-Soled Opera Boots	11.00	9.50
Double-Soled Button Shoes	9.00	8.00
Single-Soled Button Shoes	8.00	7.00
Men's Fine Calf Button Shoes	7.00	6.00
Men's Calf Button Shoes	6.00	5.00
Men's Calf Button Shoes	4.50	3.50
Women's French Kid Button	7.00	5.50
Women's Curacoa Kid Button	4.50	3.50
Women's Curacoa Kid Button	3.00	2.50
Women's Pebbled Goat Button	3.25	2.75
Women's Pebbled Grain Button	2.50	2.00
Women's Pebbled Grain Button	2.25	1.75
Women's Pebbled Grain Button	2.00	1.50
Women's India Kid Button	2.25	1.75
Women's India Kid Button	1.75	1.50
Women's Pebbled Grain Polish	2.00	1.50
Women's Kid or Goat Slippers	1.50	1.00
Misses' Pebbled Grain Polish	1.75	1.25
Children's Shoes	1.50	1.00
Children's Shoes	1.00	.75

We are now receiving our Spring Stock, all of which we offer at above prices.

WM. H. ARMSBY & CO

397 Larimer Street, Denver.

DANIELS & FISHER

HO! FOR THE RACES!

WE HAVE JUST RECEIVED PER EXPRESS

Special Novelties for Race Week.

Parasols, elegant novelties,

Kid Gloves, Lace Fichus & Collars,

SILK HANDKERCHIFFS, BEAUTIFUL LINE OF FANS.

Summer Suits for the Races.

DANIELS & FISHER

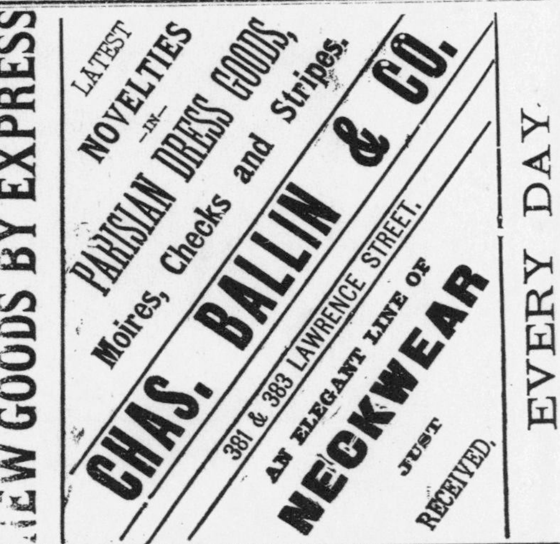

A HANDSOME SOUVENIR!

SEE THE PARASOLS.

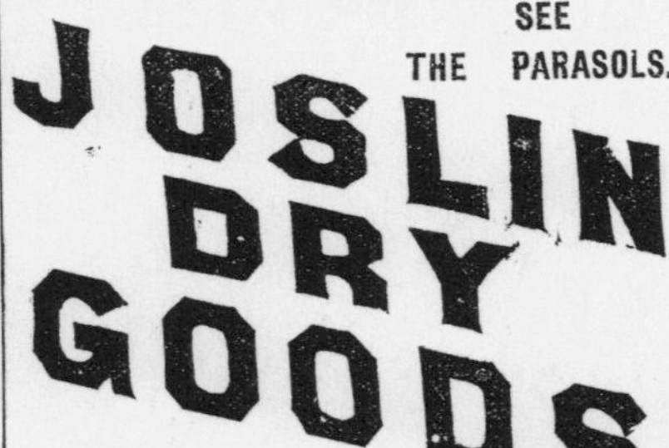

LADIES PURCHASING GOODS TO THE AMOUNT OF $1.00 OR OVER RECEIVE A HANDSOME PLAQUE TO THE AMOUNT OF $5.00 OR OVER A PAIR.

SEE Our Silks.

Come and See Our New Goods.

BUY ONLY THE CELEBRATED

Jewett's Refrigerator.

Chandeliers, Lamps, Water Coolers.

Queensware and Silverware.

S. L. HOLZMAN, 15th and Lawrence.

CHINA AND GLASSWARE.

THE LADIES

—OF—

EVANS CHAPEL

Will give a

Japanese Tea

—AT THE—

Tabor Grand Opera House

ASSEMBLY ROOMS

Under the Post-Office. Entrance on 16th St.

TUESDAY, May 16, 5 to 10 P. M.

Each purchaser of a ticket will receive a genuine Japanese cup and saucer.

A plain tea will be served to all ticket holders, with extra charge, from 5 to 8 P. M.

Ladies in attendance will be dressed in Japanese costume.

Orchestral music during the evening.

Children (under 12), tickets entitling to ice-cream and cake, 50c.

Tickets for sale by Chamberlin & Co., 212 15th street; Stone & Co., 372 Larimer street; E. A. Tunnel & Co., 372 Curtis street; and Welch Bros., corner Champa and 16th streets. 16-13-15&16

THE PIANO TUNER.

A. WEHRLE.

Has removed his business to 432 Champa street. He has the highest testimonials from some of the most celebrated manufacturers as a tuner and repairer of pianos and organs. Tuning, $2.00. Satisfaction guaranteed.

TRUSTEE'S SALE—PUBLIC NOTICE.—Whereas, the St. Louis Gold Mining company, a corporation duly organized under the laws of the state of Colorado, by its deed of trust duly executed, dated and made the 15th day of December, A. D. 1880, duly recorded in Book 77, page 15, in the office of the recorder of Gilpin county and state of Colorado, conveyed to Cyrus H. Burnham and Jacob C. Van Blarcom, of St. Louis, Missouri, in their own right, all the real estate situate in Gilpin county and state of Colorado, known and described as follows, to-wit: The property known as the Gold Hill claim, situate on Quartz Hill, Nevada district, together with all the machinery and buildings situate on said claim, or pertaining thereto, which conveyance was in trust to secure the payment of certain bonds of said company and coupons representing interest thereon, all which will fully appear by reference to said conveyance; and whereas default has been made by said company therein, whereby also all of said bonds and coupons have become due; and whereas Jacob C. Van Blarcom, one of the trustees, has failed to act in said deed of trust: now, therefore, I, Cyrus H. Burnham, the remaining trustee, at the request of sundry holders of said bonds, will sell and dispose of the said premises, property and premises, and all the right, title and interest of said company, at public auction, at the front door of the court house, in the city of Denver, in the county of Arapahoe and state of Colorado, in front of the postoffice in said city, on THE 17TH DAY OF JUNE, A. D. 1882, between the hours of ten o'clock a. m. and five o'clock p. m. of said day, to the highest bidder for cash, for the purposes in said deed of trust set forth.

DENVER, COLO., May 16, 1882. CYRUS H. BURNHAM, Trustee. m16-lm

LEGAL NOTICE.—In the matter of the estate of Mary Olive Lane, a minor. Notice of application for order to sell real estate. In pursuance of an order made by the county court of Arapahoe county, in the state of Colorado, all persons concerned, that on THURSDAY, THE 8TH DAY OF JUNE, A. D. 1882, at the opening of court on that day, or as soon thereafter as counsel can be heard, I shall apply to the county court of said county of Arapahoe, at the court house in the city of Denver, for an order to sell the real estate of said minor, to-wit: Lots 30, 31 and 32, in block 5, in Brown's addition to Denver, for the purpose of support, maintenance and education of said minor, as by reason of the guardianship may be required. JOHN M. LANE, General Guardian of the Estate of Mary Olive Lane. WM. H. MILLS, Attorney. May 15th, 1882. m16 dtjune 8

SAUL STERN,

WHO BECAME AN EXPERT FORGER TO SATISFY HIS MISTRESS' DEMANDS; NEW YORK CITY

MRS. CARRIE FROST,

WHO SHOOK HER SANCTIMONIOUS HUBBY AND ELOPED WITH MAJOR POWELL; BROOKLYN, N. Y.

WILLIAM J. POWELL,

DEMOCRATIC POLITICIAN WHO ELOPED WITH THE WIFE OF HIS PIOUS FRIEND FROST.

Dodge City's Sensation.

The Luke Short affair in Dodge city, Kansas, has created much excitement in that section of the country. The main factor in the affair was Luke Short, a Texan, well known as one of the most fearless men in the Lone Star State. He fought a duel some years ago at Tombstone, Arizona, with one Storms, the fighter of the "Slopers," who had been imported to kill him. Storms himself, however, was killed in the duel, and Short became the "cock of the walk." His recent trouble in Dodge city grew out of a shooting scrape, in which no one was hurt. He gave bonds in $2,000 for his appearance and was released, but was rearrested on the following day and ordered by an armed mob to leave the city. Attorneys who came to defend him were prohibited by the authorities from stepping off the train.

Thus matters were looking very blue for our friend, when a number of his friends from different sections—chiefly sheriffs and marshals—came to Dodge city to dictate the terms of a treaty on the basis of Luke Short's return to his place of business in Dodge city without danger of future molestation. After some trouble the "peace commissioners," as they have been termed, accomplished the object of their mission, and quiet once more reigns where for several weeks war and rumors of war were the all absorbing topic.

All the members of the commission, whose portraits we publish in a group, are frontiersmen of tried capacity. The following is a brief but eloquent sketch of each of them, reported as sent to us by Harry E. Gryden, the able Dodge city reporter of the Associated Press, and an occasional correspondent of the POLICE GAZETTE:

"Bat Masterson, of whom so much has been written, arrived from the West prepared for any emergency and with a shotgun under his arm, on the next train after Short had returned. His record of having killed 26 men and being 27 years of age, is rather exaggerated. He has been sheriff of Ford county, in which Dodge city is situated, and has occupied positions as marshal of a number of rough border towns. All his killings were done in the discharge of his official duties, and he has never even been tried for an offence.

"Wyatt Earp, of California, is the celebrity who about two years ago went on the warpath at Tombstone, Arizona, against a mob of desperadoes who had assassinated his brother, Morgan Earp. In the terrible encounter which ensued he killed not less than eight of the assassins. Wyatt has been Marshal of Dodge city, Kan., and Tombstone, Ariz., and other frontier towns.

"M. F. McLean has an Arizona and Rio Grande record for wiping out Mexican ruffians, and came from Lower California to see that his friend Luke Short could 'stay in town' to attend to his business. He is cool and clear-headed. The great ability which he displayed in managing a fight has obtained for him the sobriquet of 'The General.'

"Charles Bassett was the first sheriff of Ford county, with his headquarters at Dodge city, being twice elected to that office, and succeeded by Bat Masterson. In those days men appeared always well armed, but he astonished the natives by taking post at the court house door, when the district court was in session, and disarming all persons desiring to enter. Of the small party that attended court he gathered no less than forty-two six-shooters and only killed one man (*sic*). He is now engaged in business in Kansas city, but came to Dodge to see if his friend Luke Short could take his regular meals without being molested.

"Neal Brown was formerly a marshal of Dodge city, and is a wonderful snap shot with both hands at once, with a cool and determined head in a fight. He came from his cattle ranch, forty miles south of here, to look out for Luke Short's interests.

"W. H. Harris is Short's business partner, and acted as manager of the commission.

"W. F. Petillon was secretary of the peace commission, and as such was instrumental in restoring law and order to Dodge city.

"Since their object in view was accomplished, all, with the exception of the two principals, Harris and Short, have left, and peace hovers like a white winged dove over the late turbulent city.

THE DODGE CITY "PEACE COMMISSION."

A GROUP OF PROMINENT FRONTIERSMEN WHO RESTORED QUIET IN A TROUBLED COMMUNITY.

No. 1 LUKE SHORT. No. 2—BAT MASTERSON. No. 3.—WYATT EARP. No. 4.—M. F. McLEAN. No. 5.—CHARLES BASSETT. No. 6.—NEAL BROWN. No. 7.—W. H. HARRIS. No. 8.—W. F. PETILLON.

Saved from Death.

A thrilling spectacle was witnessed by a large number of persons on Monday, July 2, in the neighborhood of No. 121 West Eleventh street. Miss Susie Staver, who resides at the above locality with her mother and sister, while suffering under a spell of mental derangement, made her way to the roof of the house, and was about to throw herself over the parapet, when she was discovered by her mother and sister. The women had just time to grab the wou'd-be suicide by the arms and hold on to her until their screams attracted the attention of neighbors, who succeeded in rescuing the girl from her perilous position.

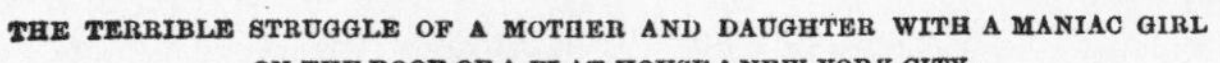

SAVED FROM DEATH.

THE TERRIBLE STRUGGLE OF A MOTHER AND DAUGHTER WITH A MANIAC GIRL ON THE ROOF OF A FLAT HOUSE; NEW YORK CITY.

MURDER AND SUICIDE.

THE TRAGIC DEATH OF MISS FANNY SEAMAN AT THE HANDS OF HER BROTHER, AND SUICIDE OF THE MURDERER, AT THROGG'S NECK, N. Y.

THE WIDE AWAKE LIBRARY--Special Number.

PRICE] SEPTEMBER 28, 1883. [10 CENTS.

THE LIFE AND TRIAL

BEN THOMPSON'S FINAL EXIT.

THE LAST ACT OF A FIERCE AND DESPERATE CAREER, AS PERFORMED IN A SAN ANTONIO, TEXAS, TEMPLE OF THE WILD AND UNTRAMMELED DRAMA.

BEN THOMPSON'S DEATH.

The Noted Ex-Marshal of San Antonio, Texas, Dies at Last With His Boots On.

[With Illustration and Portrait.]

Ben Thompson and Ning Fisher were shot dead in the Vaudeville theatre Tuesday night, March 11. Joe Foster was shot in the leg, and will probably die of hemorrhage. Thompson and Fisher had been drinking together, and entered the theatre in company. They met Foster in the dress circle, and some words followed, when shortly after shots were exchanged. The dress circle was quickly cleared, the occupants jumping into the parquet below and through the side windows into the street. Before the theatre was fairly cleared of its occupants 1,500 persons on the outside were clamoring at the closed doors for admittance. Shortly after the shooting Thompson's brother appeared on the scene, but was promptly arrested.

The remains of the two victims were taken in charge by a host of friends, and the obsequies have been ordered on the grandest scale, regardless of expense. The theatre where the affray occurred was the scene last year of the killing by Thompson of Jack Harris, who was the proprietor of the place. Fisher and Thompson were probably the two most desperate and widely known men in Texas. They have each killed a large number of men.

Thompson possessed a wide reputation as a man-killer. He had frequently threatened to take San Antonia, and the San Antonia police were determined he should not. His desperate ferocity when roused, his fearless disregard of his own and other lives, and his fatal proficiency in the use of the revolvers were too well known to fail in acting as a warning to the employees of a house whose former owner had been killed some months ago. From the moment of his entrance to the theatre he was a doomed man.

Fisher was the younger man, but the greater desperado. He was originally from Goliad county, and his baptismal name was John King. His murders were innumerable. He was for years the captain of the celebrated Breeton gang, and in every town on the Rio Grande his name was a terror.

It is the irony of fate that men of such reputation for personal prowess as these two desperadoes should have been shot to death with not one life to render up in exchange for their own. Foster was accidentally shot by one of his own party.

TRIBUNE-REPUBLICAN.

THURSDAY, AUGUST 21, 1884.

THE OFFICIAL PAPER OF THE COUNTY.

PUBLISHED BY

THE REPUBLICAN PUBLISHING CO.

Entered at Denver (Colorado) Postoffice for transmission through the mails as second-class matter.

RATES OF SUBSCRIPTION.

BY CARRIER—ALL PARTS OF THE CITY.

DAILY—(Seven Issues) per week	$ 25
DAILY—(Seven Issues) per month	1 00
DAILY—(Seven Issues) per year	12 00

BY MAIL—IN ADVANCE—POSTAGE PREPAID.

DAILY—(Seven Issues) one year	$10 00
DAILY—(Seven Issues) six months	5 00
DAILY—(Seven Issues) three months	2 50
DAILY—(Seven Issues) one month	1 00
SUNDAY EDITION—One year	2 50
WEEKLY—One year	2 00
WEEKLY—Six months	1 00

All letters and remittances should be addressed to The Republican Publishing Co. Drafts, Checks and Postoffice Orders must be made payable to the order of the company.

The TRIBUNE-REPUBLICAN has double the Circulation of any other newspaper in Colorado.

REPUBLICAN NATIONAL TICKET.

For President,
JAMES G. BLAINE of Maine.
For Vice-President,
JOHN A. LOGAN of Illinois.

Indications for Colorado to-day are: Cooler, partly cloudy weather and local showers.

Republican State Convention.

HEADQUARTERS REPUBLICAN STATE CENTRAL COMMITTEE,
DENVER, August 5, 1884.

In pursuance of the action of the Republican State Central Committee, a convention of the Republican party of Colorado is hereby called, to meet in Colorado Springs, September 10, at 11 a. m., to nominate candidates for the offices to be filled at the State election, to be held on Tuesday, the fourth day of next November, as follows:

Three Presidential electors, one Representative in Congress, one Governor, one Lieutenant-Governor, Secretary of State, State Treasurer, Auditor of State, Superintendent of Public Instruction, two Regents of the University for full term, and one to fill the vacancy, one Attorney-General, a Chairman of the State Central Committee, and to transact such other business as may properly come before the convention.

The various counties of the State will be entitled to representation in the convention, as follows:

Arapahoe	59	Hinsdale	3
Bent	3	Jefferson	9
Boulder	13	Larimer	11
Chaffee	13	Lake	35
Costella	6	Las Animas	9
Conejos	7	La Plata	7
Clear Creek	13	Mesa	5
Custer	11	Montrose	4
Delta	3	Ouray	5
Dolores	3	Park	8
Douglas	3	Pitkin	4
Eagle	6	Pueblo	17
Elbert	3	Rio Grande	6
El Paso	14	Routt	2
Fremont	9	Saguache	8
Garfield	3	San Miguel	4
Gilpin	11	San Juan	6
Grand	3	Summit	9
Gunnison	19	Weld	9
Huerfano	6		

Each county delegation is requested to select a suitable person to act as a member of the State Central Committee and report name and post-office address to the convention.

J. B. CHAFFEE,
Chairman.
SYLVESTOR NICHOLS,
Secretary.

THE NEWS OF THE DAY.

The Silver and Lead Market.

SILVER is quoted in New York at $1.10⅛ per ounce.

LEAD is quoted dull at $3.55 per 100 pounds in New York.

Domestic.

MR. HENDRICKS announces his formal acceptance in a brief letter.

BOULDER is to have a new bank, to be called the Boulder National Bank.

FRANK HURD has been renominated for Congress in the Tenth Ohio District.

THE seventh annual meeting of the American Bar Association at Saratoga is largely attended.

WARNER & MERRITT, fruit importers of Philadelphia, have assigned. Liabilities, $500,000.

A DISEASE which affects the eyes of the cattle, resulting in blindness, is reported from Boulder.

THE Democrats of New Mexico have nominated Antonio Joseph of Taos Conty fer delegate to Congress.

THE presence of pleuro-pneumonia in Illinois has been established by the officials of the Department of Agriculture.

The Michigan Democrats have affected a fusion with the Greenbackers and divided the nominations on their state ticket.

ALEXANDER GRAVES has been nominated for Congress by those Democrats who did not bolt in the fifth Missouri District.

THE authorities of Pueblo and South Pueblo prevented a hard-glove fight between Tom Walling and Bryan Campbell.

GOVERNOR KNOTT of Kentucky has pardoned the two prisoners who stood by their guards in the recent outbreak in the Penitentiary.

AN Indian, inspired by a cheap publication, attempted to kill Agent McGillicuddy of the Pine Ridge Agency. The culprit is under arrest.

OUT of a bunch of fifty-four head of high-grade cattle from Missouri which were turned loose near Montrose, thirty-one have died of Texas fever.

ONE hundred men are hunting for David Avery near Vienna, Illinois, who burned his wheat stacks to prevent a constable's levy and shot his neighbor.

A FIRE in Central Pueblo burned Gallagher's galvanized cornice manufactory and a building in the rear of it. An adjoining building was damaged. Loss, $6,000, partly insured.

THE Missouri Greenbackers have nominated Nicholas Ford of Buchanan County for Governor, and make no other nominations. It is understood that the remainder of the ticket is to be named by the Republicans.

Foreign.

A NEW iron-clad for the Chinese navy has been launched at Stettin, Germany.

CLEMENTS R. MARKHAM of the Royal Geographical Society condemns American journalism for its accusations of murder and cannibalism against the Greely party, and says decency should have suggested silence.

Local.

THE city is overrun by petty thieves.

THE Passenger Agents returned to the city.

THE Seventh Ward Blaine and Logan Club held a ratification.

GOVERNOR GRANT pardoned three men from the penitentiary.

The Criminal Court was in session. A number of criminal trials were set.

MR. CLEVELAND speaks of morality as if he knew something about it. His assurance is refreshing.

GROVER has evidently reformed since that little affair in Buffalo nine years ago. He says he has faith in God.

MR. BENJAMIN BUTLER gave it out very cold that he would not write his letter of acceptance until Mr. Grover Cleveland had written his; but Cleveland was so long about his epistolary work that Ben was forced to send his out first. Twenty-four hours after Benjamin's had appeared, Grover sent out his. It is plain that Cleveland was afraid to give Ben a chance to dissect his "greatest effort." We have read his letter and we can assert that he had good reason to be afraid. A less skillful critic than Butler could readily tear it in pieces.

The anti-Hill Conspirators will resort to every political trick that is known. We caution the voter to carefully examine his ballot before depositing it. Stickers have been printed bearing the names of anti-Hill delegates. The scheme is to paste them on Hill tickets and by smart work palm them off on men who desire to vote for Hill delegates. Be watchful.

IT IS Bill Smith against the city.

CLEVELAND says nothing on the coinage question. He is an anti-silver man, and he dared not express his convictions.

HILL stood with the Republicans of Denver when they asked for the nomination of Blaine. Mr. Routt was against them.

IF the men of character—the men who bear the burdens of the municipal management of the city, will devote to-day to the primaries, Denver will be relieved of Bill Smith.

AS BETWEEN Mr. Hill and Mr. Routt the people of Arapahoe County ought not to question which would the more ably represent Colorado in the United States Senate.

GO TO the polls early and do not turn away without voting simply because Mr. Routt's and Bill Smith's bummers are trying to keep decent men away from the voting window.

EVEN an incompetent Mayor can aspire to a higher office; but Mayor Routt has no right to use the paid employes of the city, to round up the criminal element of the city to elect his delegates.

DO NOT be deceived. If Routt carries the primaries to-day, Teller and Elbert will not be candidates for the Senate. If Hill carries them, they will be candidates and Routt will not. This is the situation in a nutshell.

THE *Times* says Routt and Teller "understand each other perfectly." Of course they do, otherwise Mr. Routt would not be spending his money to carry the primaries. He has Teller's assurance that he will not be a candidate against him.

THE Routt candidates for delegates in the Eighth Ward have signed a compact, agreeing to support Charles W. Smith, proprietor of the Washington Beer Hall, on Larimer street, for the Legislature. Routt for the Senate and Smith for the Legislature! A strong team, surely.

TO-DAY'S primaries will decide a more important question than whether Senator Hill or Mayor Routt is to be elected, and that question is whether the reputable citizens are to prevail over the bummer element. Mayor Routt and Bill Smith have rallied the bummer element. Will the citizens rally!

MR. HILL is honest, able and industrious. He has made by all odds the most useful Senator Colorado has had. He may well be proud of his record, and the people of Colorado may well be proud of him. He has earned a re-election, and the Republicans of the State will make a mistake if they do not grant it to him.

IN another column we print the names of the gentlemen wh m the friends of Mr. Hill have decided to support for delegates, in the several wards. We print them that voters may know before they go to the polls which tickets favor Mr. Hill, and that they may be enabled to detect the tricks of the "combination."

THE gentlemen who are candidates for delegates to the County Convention in the Eighth Ward have agreed to vote as a unit in case they shall be elected, and further, to vote for no man who is not favorable to Mr. Routt for the United States Senate. Does this mean Routt or Teller? The weak hirelings of Mr. Teller will probably tell you that it means Teller. They will not stop lying to-day.

ALL day long yesterday the pavement in front of Routt's headquarters on Lawrence street was crowded with bummers and strikers. Every reputable citizen whose business made it necessary for him to push through them was disgusted. Hundreds of men will vote against Routt to-day because of the tactics he and his man Bill Smith are employing to carry the primaries.

MR. O. H. ROTHACKER, editor of the *Opinion*, is one of the managers of Mr. Routt's campaign. He makes the assertion that Mr. Routt has in his possession a letter from Henry M. Teller, in which the latter declares that if Routt can carry the primaries to-day, he (Teller) will not be a candidate against him in the Senatorial contest. This makes Teller a candidate only upon the contingency of Routt's failure to-day.

Mr. Rothacker will not deny that he has said this. He has as good as said it in his paper, and he has openly said it to the editor of the Boulder *Herald*.

Mayor Routt has said that this is *his* fight; that if he wins to-day he is to be the man; that his arrangements with Mr. Teller and Judge Elbert are satisfactory to him, and that if they were not he would not be in the contest.

Mr. Teller is to be a candidate only upon condition that Routt shall fail to-day. He has not denied this. He cannot deny it, though he is willing that his friends shall say that he is *now* in the race, if by so saying they can help Routt. He has frequently said that he does not care to be a candidate if there is any other man who can beat Hill. Until Routt can demonstrate his strength in Arapahoe County, Teller is entirely out of the race. If Routt loses to-day, we think it highly probable that Mr. Teller will then declare his candidacy.

This is the true inwardness of the "combination," the petty prevarication of the *Times* to the contrary notwithstanding.

IT WOULD not be to Colorado's credit to send John L. Routt to the United States Senate, and it would not be to her advantage, because he could be of no use there. Nature did not cut him out for a statesman, and if Colorado should send him among statesmen they would not be long in discovering that it was not his fitness for the office which won it for him.

The people of Colorado know this already. The people of Denver know to their sorrow that Mr. Routt is not the right kind of man for high office. Whatever the opinion of him may have been before they elected him to be their Mayor, there is no questioning the unanimity of their opinion since that inauspicious event.

Mr. Routt has made a lamentable failure as Mayor; he would make a dismal failure as Senator, and the State would be the loser. Routt has nothing to lose.

IF THE Routt ticket is elected it will result in the choice of a legislature of unpledged men—of representative, honest and good men, who will win at the polls because of good character, and who will make thoroughly capable legislators—who will wear no man's collar, and who will vote for the best man for Senator when that question shall come up.—*Times of Yesterday.*

"Mr. Teller is not in position to make a canvass, owing to the fact that he is a member of the President's Cabinet. He will take no active part in the contest in Arapahoe County for the reason above given and for the additional reason that both Ex-Governor Routt and Senator Hill, who are residents of the county, are candidates. It is, however, no breach of confidence to say that his interest in this contest lies in the success of Mr. Routt, and that he is in sympathy with that gentleman in the local contest."—*Times of Saturday.*

The first paragraph is a flimsy lie. The second one is as near the truth as the *Times* dare go. The reader will naturally ask why Mr. Routt should spend $20,000 to carry the primaries to-day if the men who are to be elected to the legislature from this County are not to vote for him for the Senate? They will also ask why Mr. Teller should be interested in having Governor Routt get these votes if he himself would like to have them? The disguise is too thin.

THE *Opinion*, Mr. Routt's personal organ, on Saturday defined the Senatorial situation. We know that its definition is correct and we ask Republicans who are in doubt as to what the fight means to read it. The *Opinion* said:

"It became evident some time ago that neither Chaffee nor Teller could carry this County against Hill, and, at the same time, it became equally evident that Routt was the only man here who could make a warm fight. In an interview published in the East some time ago, Secretary Teller was quite frank in stating his position. He said that he did not want to go to the Senate, but that he wanted to defeat Senator Hill, and would assist any man whom he thought could accomplish the object. Chaffee intended to make the fight at first, but his financial losses and his palpable unpopularity with the great masses of respectable people in the State deferred him. Elbert was talked of, but not seriously, as he lacked the elements of strength which were necessary. This forced the matter to a point wnen it became evident that Routt was the only man in the County they could rely on for the struggle. When the matter was proposed to Routt, however, he showed at once and distinctly that he would not be trifled with. He told them that he must have the absolute assurance that he should have the entire field, and that none of the three were to enter afterwards. He had a large number of influential friends who would help him, but who declined utterly to have anything to do with the contest if it meant Chaffee or Teller. These friends insisted upon the clearest satisfaction on this point, and would not be content with anything else. There was some delay in this by reason of the absence of Secretary Teller, but when he returned on Tuesday of this week he gave the requisite assurance that he would not be in the race at any event, and on the day following Routt's candidacy was formally announced.

Since the publication of the foregoing Mr. Rothacker, editor of the *Opinion*, has openly stated that Mr. Routt has Mr. Teller's assurance, in black and white, that he will not be in the race.

THE Teller-Routt organ, the *Times*, in its issue of yesterday devotes all of its editorial space and much of its local space to an attempt to prove that, though Mr. Teller would like to see Mr. Routt succeed in his race for the Senate, yet Mr. Teller himself is in the race. This is a somewhat paradoxical problem and sensible persons will not waste much time in trying to solve it, and they certainly will not accept the solution which the *Times* has furnished.

If our esteemed cotemporary really desired to convince its readers that Mr. Teller is in the race, and that he doesn't want to see Mr. Routt succeed, it should have gotten Mr. Teller to write a formal card saying so. Possibly it would have done so had Mr. Teller been willing to do his part; but he was not; so the *Times* had to content itself with saying that Mr. Teller had certified the correctness of Routt's statement that it is his (Routt's) understanding that Mr. Teller is in the Senatorial race, and that Mr. Teller had not written a note withdrawing in Mr. Routt's favor.

This is a roundabout way of making a point, and the *Times* doubtless thought that so much circumlocution would deceive people. If it thought so it was mistaken.

In the first place it has never been alleged that Mr. Teller has withdrawn in Mr. Routt's favor, and Mr. Teller cannot evade the issue by resorting to lawyers' trickery. No, he has not withdrawn in Routt's favor; he has simply agreed to give him a chance to demonstrate his claim that he can beat Hill. If Mr. Routt can carry the primaries to-day, Teller will be satisfied that the Mayor's claim is well based and will give him a clear field and his aid.

Ah, no, the trick will not work, and if we are right in our estimate of the tendencies of our people, the fact that the anti-Hill combination has resorted to trickery on the eve of the primaries will lose it many votes. We say honestly and sincerely that the *Times's* many articles on the question of Mr. Teller's candidacy are nothing more than political roorbacks. The fact that they were printed on the eve of the election, and not till then, is proof of it.

GROVER CLEVELAND'S letter of acceptance has been given to the public. It is only one-sixth as long as Mr. Blaine's, and it cannot be compared with it for merit. Mr. Cleveland probably thought he was making a ten-strike when he confined his letter to one thousand words; and there is no doubt that its brevity is highly appreciated by those who have read it. If it wer
few people would read it to t
score, Mr. Cleveland was wi
short. The reading public n
forgiven him if he had wri
letter.

The texture of Mr. Clevela
of fine quality. It is coarse
is why Mr. Cleveland is stu
be any who doubt that he i
them to carefully read his let
and find the proof.

Cleveland makes a very go
his epistle, and if he could h
a logical end, we believe that
have made friends for him
with the proposition that a
cepting a nomination should
than to endorse the platform
is to stand, except to make re
known truths" relating to th
Government. But he doesn'
takes up and discusses supe
questions of minor importa
cording to the rule which h
should not be discussed eith
superficially. He speaks in a
the dignity of American labo
word about the necessity of r
dignity by protecting it aga
competition of Europe. He
laboring classes constitute t
our population," but ignore
which the laboring classes
tariff that their rights ma
He indirectly opposes the p
tuary laws; but says not a wo
can shipping. The plain infe
believes beer to be more
prosperity than commerce.

The letter is not worthy of
been nominated for the Pr
United States. It is weak
tempt at sophistry. It is w
State paper. The fact that C
fused to discuss the leading i
Protection, and tried to hide h
upon it by taking up questio
significant beside it, will hurt
Free-Traders and Protectionis
is no doubt that the former w
We expected more from Gr
He could not have done less.

AMERICANS IN M

Causes of Bad Feeling on t Natives.

As bearing on recent trou
in Mexico, the following rem
spondent of the Newark *Adve*
cial moment: The recent
Rev. A. W. Greenman, an
sionary, and his assistant,
Torres, by a mob of religious
laya, a large city at th
the Mexican National rail
suggestive of priestly m
country. An American rail
estant Missionary produce t
upon the average Romish priest in this country that a red flag does upon the bulls in the arena at Madrid. The Mexican priests are not deficient in cunning and in strong powers of observation (many an ignorant man possesses those faculties), hence they early saw that if the Americans built railroads down into this country, and introduced the light of civilization to this benighted people, the priestly power would wane. Hence they have fought and continue to fight with equal vigor both railways and missionaries. I am informed by a very intelligent American, who has been here several years and understands the language and people of the country thoroughly, that he has positive evidence that priests in small towns along the line of the Mexican Central Railroad have directly incited their parishioners to place obstructions upon the tracks of that road in order to derail the trains. A holy crusade, truly, is this which is being secretly preached by some of the intolerant bigots among the Mexican clergy. This same informant tells me that not only has he positive evidence of the above described efforts to ruin the property of Americans in this country and destroy lives, but also that he heard in Celaya, on the evening after the mob attacked Mr. Greenman in his home, a priest blessing as he walked through the streets some of the would-be murderers for the share which they took in that holy work.

Many of the contemptible little provincial sheets, none of which circulate more than 200 to 300 copies each issue, indulge in their regular weekly fling at the "gringoes," the "primos," and all that sort of thing, but their petty spite and harmless hatred is rarely re-echoed by the press of the capital, and fall quite unnoticed by most Americans, who, if they chance to read it, merely smile and say: "Poor fools!" The men who are in power seem to be friendly to both Americans personally and the American government. If they are not, they studiously conceal their real sentiments. Therefore we are enabled to dwell together in peace and harmony, at least outwardly. No doubt there are some Americans here who provoke the Mexican greatly. There is a class of Americans who have left their country's good, and who come to this country to make money by gambling and other disreputable devices. There are also many railroad men, laborers, engineers, mechanics, etc., who are not always very courteous in their language to Mexicans, especially to the peon class, and it is these Americans who are the cause of much ill-feeling against us. A very sensible editorial appeared in one of the leading daily papers (Mexican) yesterday, in which, after citing the case of an American rough who refused to pay his bill at a restaurant, and abused both the restaurant keeper and the country, using very foul language, the editor remarks that "we did not invite such fellows to come here: they would do better to stay

---

DOC HOLLIDAY AGAIN.

The Notorious Desperado Shoots a Man at Leadville.

On Tuesday last Doc Holliday, who is well known in Denver and Leadville among the sporting fraternity, shot and seriously wounded a man named Allen in a saloon in Leadville. The difficulty grew out of a debt for $5 which Holliday owed Allen, and which the latter made several unsuccessful efforts to collect. Allen was a bartender in what is known as the Monarch Saloon, which is on Harrison avenue, and on Tuesday, having heard that Holliday was in a saloon kept by a man named Hyman a few doors below the Monarch, he went into that place to see him. Some of his friends advised him not to go, but he did not heed their warning. It appears that he had annoyed Holliday somewhat by his efforts to collect the debt, and it was also claimed that he had made threats of personal violence toward Holliday. However this may be, when Holliday saw Allen come into the saloon he pulled his gun, which was a 44-calibre single-action Colt, and fired. The firit shot missed Allen, and Holliday fired again after Allen had fallen down in an attempt to get out of the saloon. The second shot took effect in Allen's arm. Holliday was then disarmed and taken to jail, and Allen was at once removed to his room. The wound is not considered fatal, but it may result in the loss of the wounded man's arm. Holliday will be remembered as a man who was reported to have been connected with the Erb difficulties in Tombstone, which occurred about two years and a half ago. He is the same man who was arrested in this city in an effort to remove him to Arizona, but the Governor refused to order his release into the hands of the Arizona authorities.

THE CORNER WHERE THE FIGHTING OCCURRED.

SUPERINTENDENT FREDERICK EBERSOLD.

INSPECTOR JOHN BONFIELD.

EX-SUPERINTENDENT AUSTIN J. DOYLE.

THE MOB SEEKING SHELTER IN THE SALOONS.

LAKE ST
PLATFORM
SIDEWALK
WHERE THE BOMB FELL
ALLEY
LINE of POLICE
ALLEY
DESPLAINES ST
The bomb was thrown from here
RANDOLPH ST
The crowd stood in front of Platform

MAP OF THE LOCALITY.

THE EXPLODING BOMB.

SACKING ROSENFIELD'S DRUG STORE.

THE POLICE FORMING IN FRONT OF THE DESPLAINES STREET STATION HOUSE.

SCENES DURING THE RIOTS IN CHICAGO.

[FROM SKETCHES BY LEDERER.]

The Prison Mirror.

Vol. 1. No. 1. Stillwater, Minn. Wednesday, Aug, 10th. 1887. Price 5 Cts.

OUR MOTTO: - - - - - "GOD HELPS THOSE WHO HELP THEMSELVES."

PRISON OFFICIALS.

—:o:—

—:{ Inspectors. }:—

E. G. BUTTS, - - - - - - - - - - Stillwater.
JOHN F. NORRISH, - - - - - Hastings.
LIBERTY HALL, - - - - - - - Glencoe.

—:o:—

—: Resident Officers. :—

H. G. STORDOCK. - - - - - - - - - - Warden.
J. A. WESTBY, - - - - - Deputy Warden.
JOHN COVER, - - - Ass't. Dep'ty. Wrd'n.
FRANK BERRY, - - - - - - - - - - - - Clerk.
H. E. BENNER, - - - - - - - - - - - Steward.
W. H. PRATT, - - - - - - - - - - Physician.
F. H. HALL, - - - - - - - Hospital Steward.
GEORGE P. DODD, - - - - - - Storekeeper.
W. J. MATHEWS, - Protestant Chaplain.
M. E. MURPHY, - - - - Catholic Chaplain.
MRS. SARAH McNEAL, - - - - - Matron.

SALUTATORY.

"The Prison Mirror" casts its first reflections upon the world.

And sheds a ray of light upon the lives of those behind the bars.

Its Founders, Its Mission, And Its Management.

It is with no little pride and plearure that we present to you, kind reader, this our initiave number of THE PRISON MIRROR, believing as we do, that the introduction of the printing press into the great penal institutions of our land, is the first important step taken toward solving the great problem of true prison reform. With this our maiden issue, of THE MIRROR is born a new innovation into the heretofore dark, dreary, monotonous existence of those whom fate hath led downward to the narrow confines of a prison cell and branded as social outcasts; upon the darkened lives of such, it shall be the one great mission of THE MIRROR to reflect a glad ray of hope to light and encourage them upward toward a higher and nobler life, to banish from their hearts the midnight gloom of prejudice, envy and malice, and in their bosoms reflect the cheering light of reason, truth and love.

It shall be the untiring mission of the "MIRROR" to encourage prison literary talent, and to instruct, assist, encourage, and entertain all those within our midst, and to scatter words of warning upon the unwary pathway of those in the outside world, whose reckless footsteps may be leading them hitherward. In thus, sending forth to the world this humble little sheet, we trust and pray that it is destined to become the corner stone of the great pedestal whereon shall stand the living statue of truth, bearing aloft, the flaming torch of mercy, justice and reason; and from the sands of this tiny brooklet there may be gathered many brilliant gems of truth to forever decorate the soverign heads of honor, manhood and right. It shall be our earnest endeavor to bury meloncholy, estrangement, and enmity in the vast region of the past, and to sow in the hearts of our readers the golden seeds of charity, hope and love.

This, we believe is the only printed sheet now in existence, organized, published, edited and sent forth to the world by prisoners, confined within the walls of a penitentiary.

In thus extending to us the privelege of publishing and sending forth to the world THE PRISON MIRROR, our Warden, Mr. H. G. Stordock, has, we feel, extended to us a most elevating and beneficial privelege, which we trust, will be most fully appreciated and honored by each and every prisoner within our midst.

The great success which has thus far attended our little enterprize has already been far in excess of the most lofty dreams of its foundes; which fact we owe to the great kindness, encouragement, and assistance of Warden Stordock, Deputy Warden, Jacob Wesby, Ass't Deputy Warden, John Cover, and our "rustling" outside business manager, and treasurer, Mr. Geo. P. Dodd, Prison Store Keeper, and to the officers of the prison, in general, to whom, one and all, we return our most earnest thanks, and deepest gratitude. We also appreciate most highly, the many kind words of encouragement which has been extended toward us, by the "boys."

THE PRISON MIRROR, will be issued on Wednesday of each week, and will contain continuous contributions upon all general subjects, sketches, words of wisdom, jokes, poetry etc., from the pens of our comrads in prison; also a general budget of prison news, and possibilities, and realities, never before offered to the public; also a general report of the financial condition of the prison; prison statistics, etc., of interest and value to the taxpayers of the State, the public, and the fireside; it will contain each week, words of warning to the young, from the pens of those who know whereof they speak, in verification of that great scriptural truth "the way of the transgressor is hard." THE MIRROR will be moral in tone, instructive, and entertaining, and should find a place in every home, and at every fireside: its management will be without official interference, and soley in charge of the managing editor, who will use his every endeavor to maintain it a credit to the "boys," and an honor to the Warden.

The entire profits of THE MIRROR, above the running expences, will be devoted soley to the purchase of books and periodicals for the prison library, thus being a part and parcel thereof in accordance with the following agreement of its foundres viz:—

AGREEMENT OF THE SHARE HOLDERS OF THE PRISON MIRROR.

July, 11, 1887.

H. G. STORDOCK, Warden.

We the undersigned do hereby voluntarily loan to the "trust fund" for the purpose of starting a prison paper, under the management of Lew. P. Shoonmaker, the following sums opposite our respective names, said sums to be replaced to our several credits with interest thereon, at the rate of three per cent per month, from the first earnings of said paper, and when full amount of said loan with due interest thereon is so refunded and paid to our private accounts in prison office, our claims upon the stock, material and shares of said paper shall cease, and said stock, material and shares of said paper, become the property of the prison library, and a part and parcel thereof; and the net profits of said paper shall be devoted exclusively to the prison library, in the purchase of such books and periodicals as the Warden may select; and we hereby pray that you will accept this, and consider the same an order to pay the said respective sums opposite our names, to the treasurer of said paper, Mr. Geo. P. Dodd, and charge the same to our several accounts.

SIGNED

Lew P. Schoonmaker.............$20,00.
Coleman Younger.................$20,00.
James Younger,...................$20.00.
Robert Younger....................$10,00.
John Gilbert,.......................$10.00.
Frank P. Landers,................$20,00.
Lloyd Porter........................$10,00.
Walter E. Nutt,....................$10,00.
William Riley,.......................$20,00.
George Anderson,..................$10,00.
William Hohl,........................$10.00.
James Craig,.........................$10,00.
James Irwin,..........................$10,00.
Jacob Bird,.............................$10,00.
Charles Hickling,....................$10,00.

Our exchanges will be distributed gratuously to the inmates of this institution; which feature of our enterprise, will alone, be most highly appreciated by our unfortunate fellowmen, in-as-much as they will thus be provided with an unceasing flow of pure, fresh, entertaining and instructive literature, thus keeping them educated and informed with the steady advance and progress of the great outside world, and thus be prepared, when the hour of their restoration to freedom shall dawn, to meet the glad era, upon an equal footing with the world, and we trust, regain and maintain the position of honorable upright men and useful citizens; and we feel and trust that the great press of America, and especially of Minnesota will not permit us to want for exchanges to fulfill this part of our mission.

In thus sending forth our tiny sheet to our mothers, fathers, sisters, homes and friends, and the world at large, we present thereto a model gem of minature literature, born and sustained under difficulties, but which we are fain to say will prove a boon and a blessing to our brethern in prison, our homes and humanity, believing, as is indicated by the motto of THE MIRROR that "God helps those who help themselves."

With the above remarks by way of introduction, and most earnestly soliciting the kindly assistance and support of our readers, we most humbly submit to their kindly encouragement, the future success of THE PRISON MIRROR.

We Wish He Was Rich.

In reply to a Postal Card making inquiries as to THE MIRROR etc. Warden Stordock vouchsafed the following reply.

STILLWATER, MINN., July, 27th, 1887.

N. J. GORSUCH ESQ.,

WESTMINISTER, MD.

DEAR SIR:—The subscription price of our PRISON MIRROR Will be $1,00. per. year. It will be issued Aug., 10th, and every week thereafter. The profits to go to prison library. It will be an interesting paper because it will contain a financiel statement every month, of receipts and expenditures, so that all can figure out just what it costs. Another feature will be the weekly population, new arrivals, discharged either by full time served, commutations or pardons. Also short articles written by convicts. We hope to receive your subscription.

Yours etc.,

H. G. Stordock.

To the above, the following reply was received.

WESTMINSTER, MD., Aug., 2nd, 1887.

H. G. STORDOCK, Warden.

DEAR SIR:—Please find inclosed $1,00. to pay for paper to be published by the unfortunates of your prison. Please convey to them my best wishes and my approval of their noble enterprise, and if I was a rich man would subscribe for one hundred copies.

Yours very truly,

N. J. Gorsuch.

STASTISTICS OF POPULATION,

Of The Minnesoto State Prison For The fiscal year ending July 31st. 1887.

Entire population, July, 31st. 1886	387.
RECIEVED DURING THE YEAR.	
State Courts.	202.
U. S. District Court	003.
U. S. Army	003.
Total number in prison during the year	595.
DISCHARGED DURING THE YEAR.	
On expiration of sentence, less good time	145.
On expiration of sentence as commuted	021.
Pardoned by Governor	007.
Pardoned by President	001.
Commuted by military authorities	001.
Transferred to Insane Hospital	003.
Died	005.
Total	183.
POPULATION.	
Population August, 1st. 1887	412.
Population August 1st. 1886	387.
Increase during the year	025.
COLOR.	
White	393.
Colored	019.
Total	412.
SEX.	
Males	405.
Females	007.
Total	412.
COMMITTED BY	
State Courts	399.
U. S. District Court	005.
U. S. Army	008.
Total	412.

To the Public.

The PRISON MIRROR is now before you. If it shall prove a failure then the blame must all rest on me. If it shall be a success then all the credit must be given to the boys who have done all the work. It was necessary to have my consent before the experiment could be tried, and therefore I am responsible for the venture. I hope and believe that a generous public will give the MIRROR all the encouragement that it shall deserve, and as it does not cost the State anything and only the prison library can be benefited, the people will, I feel sure, bid it "God-speed." The one feature of the MIRROR that ought to be of value to all tax payers will be the financiel statement of the receipts and expenditures of the prison. August 1st. is the beginning of this ficial year. We make monthly statements of expenses, and the first issue in September will contain expenses from all sources for the month of August. We collect pay for convict labor quarterly, so that the receipts will be given only once each quarter. The receipts from visitors (our only fund for library) will be given each month. If the local papers will reproduce from the MIRROR, every tax payer in Minnesota can at the end of the year know just as much about the management of the prison as the officers of the institution. This prison belongs to the people and they have a right to know how their money is expended. Encourage our little enterprise if you can, criticise us if you must, but please do it kindly and fairly.

H. G. STORDOCK, Warden.

Contributions.

We have been handed some excellent contributions from the pen's of our prison breathern, which will appear in our columns next week, and, from time to time as space permits.

"FIVE MINUTES TO GO BACK TO YOUR CELLS."

CONVICT MUTINY IN THE UNITED STATES JAIL AT FORT SMITH, ARK.—MARSHAL CRUMP, WITH A BEAD DRAWN ON THE MUTINEERS BY THE PRISON GUARDS, TIMES THE EXECUTION OF HIS ORDER TO "FIRE."

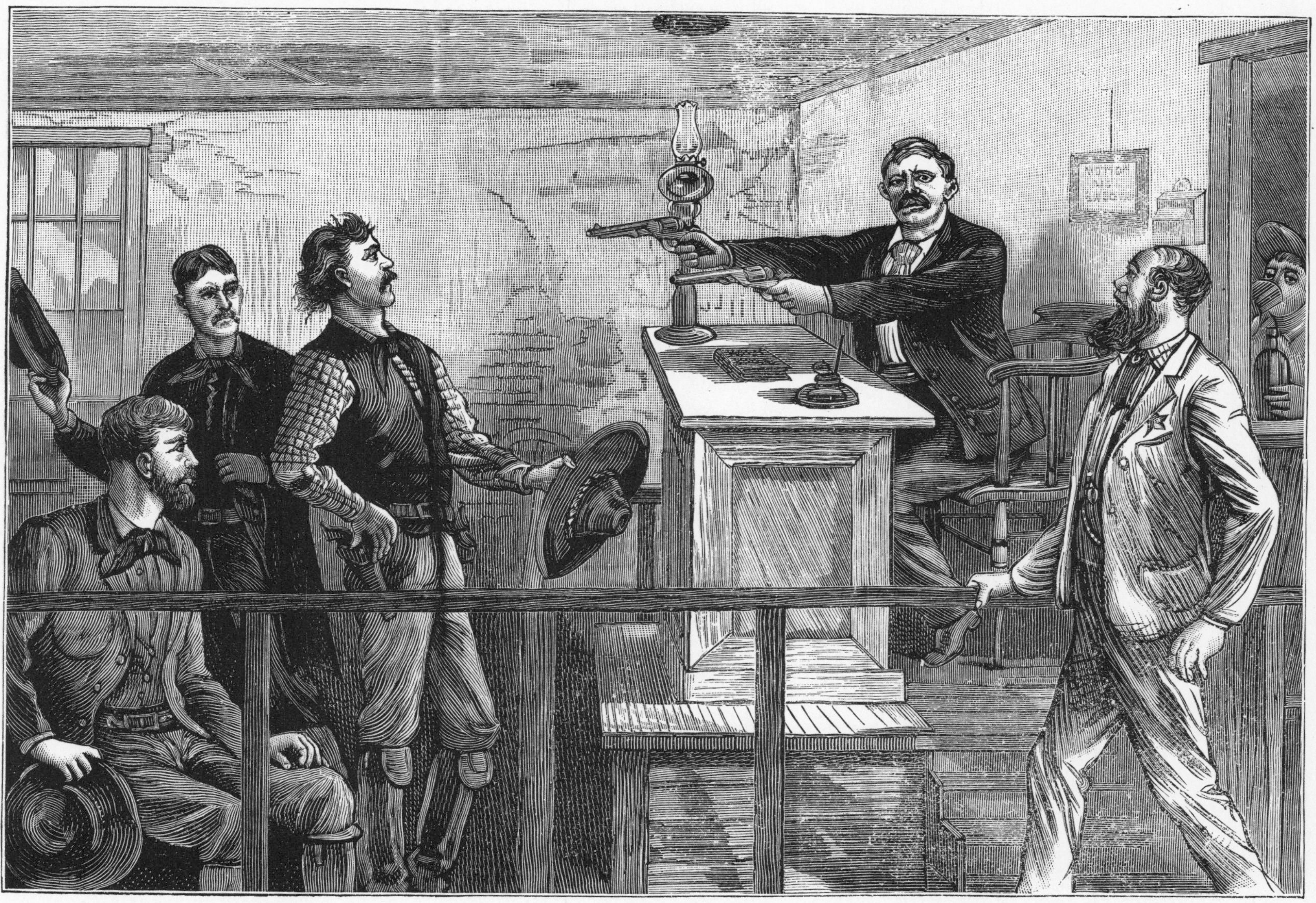

"I WILL HAVE A TRIAL OR AN INQUEST."

JUDGE BEAN OF PECOS VALLEY, TEX., HOLDING COURT—HIS METHODS WITH A DEFIANT LITIGANT—"GO AHEAD, CONSTABLE, AND OPEN COURT."

KEMMLER'S DEATH BY TORTURE.

Twice the Current Was Sent Through the Murderer's Quivering Frame.

BREATHED AFTER THE FIRST SHOCK.

Doctors Pronounced Him Dead and Then to Their Horror Discovered Their Mistake.

WITNESSES FAINT AND SICK

Terror Added to the Scene by the Burning of Parts of the Body.

DISAGREEMENT OF SCIENTISTS

Not Satisfied that the New Method of Execution Is a Success.

THE HERALD'S EYE WITNESS.

[BY TELEGRAPH TO THE HERALD.]

AUBURN, N. Y., August 6, 1890.—The killing of Kemmler to-day marks, I fear, the beginning and the end of electrocution, and it wreaths in shame the agents of the great Empire State who, entrusted with the terrific responsibility of killing a man as a man was never killed before, brought to the task imperfect machinery and turned an execution into a horror.

William Kemmler is dead, indeed, but at what a price? He has paid a double penance to the law which in his ignorance and beastliness he had outraged, a penance for his crime and a penance for his childlike trust in men who by their carelessness have brought shame upon the great State whose servants they are.

The scene of Kemmler's execution was too horrible to picture. He died the death of Freel, the lineman, who was slowly roasted to death in the sight of thousands.

Men accustomed to every form of suffering grew faint as the awful spectacle was unfolded before their eyes. Those who stood the sight were filled with awe as they saw the effects of this most potent of fluids which is only partly understood by those who have studied it most faithfully, as it slowly, all

KEMMLER.

too slowly, disintegrated the fibre and tissues of the body through which it passed.

The heaving of a chest which it had been promised would be stilled in instant peace as soon as the circuit was completed, the foaming of the mouth, the bloody sweat, the writhing shoulders and all the other signs of life.

THE ODOR OF BURNING FLESH.

Horrible as these were they were made infinitely more horrible by the premature removal of the electrodes and the subsequent replacing of them for not seconds but minutes, until the room was filled with the odor of burning flesh and strong men fainted and fell like logs upon the floor.

And all this done in the name of science.

It would be strange, indeed, if this execution had been anything else than what it was—a shameful thing. There has been no feature connected with the punishment of William Kemmler that was not shameful. The instruments were stolen in the first place. They were admittedly imperfect. But though the makers offered under pressure to build the State a machine that could be relied upon, they were told that they were merely making a hue and cry to save themselves.

The events of to-day prove either that the dynamos were faulty or that the interested company had bribed some one to make them seem so.

Yesterday, with fourteen months behind him in which to complete his preparations, the Warden had the execution room moved and the newly repaired voltmetre put in a place where those conducting the execution could not see it or know whether it was registering 2,000 or 200 volts.

And the doctors were told before it was known that the facts had better be suppressed that the machine was only registering from 700 to 1,300 volts, when 1,800 were needed.

AN INQUIRY NEEDED.

Nothing but a legislative inquiry will bring out the truth. And those who were present say that in the interests of humanity it is to be hoped that one will be had before another poor wretch is put on the official grill.

Kemmler went to the slaughter like a big boy, trusting and hopeful, leaving ill will to none and with no apparent fear of what was coming. He chided his executioners for their nervousness and did everything in his power to help them make a good job of it.

Not a cloud flecked the morning sky as he sauntered into the chamber of death, adjusting his cravat as he went. Without the prison walls a vast crowd was collected and the windows of the death chamber were closely watched.

The ivy on the great gray walls was filled with twittering sparrows, the St. Bernard barked in its kennel. The rifle and lariat armed guards mounted to their wonted places on the prison parapets, and the prisoners were turned out at seven just as usual.

It was not until little District Attorney Quimby, of Buffalo, came tottering down the steps, his face purpling and every fibre in his being trembling, and whispered, "It is over," that people knew the end had come.

The doctors sitting in a semi-circle about the room saw the quiet fellow enter, accompanied by the Warden.

SHAVED HIS HEAD.

A monk's spot had been raggedly cut on the crown of Kemmler's head in order to make a place for the sponge of the upper electro, and the death warrant had been read and the new brown trousers and vest and spotless shirt put on and the minister had prayed and read the Scriptures, while Kemmler said "Amen" to everything.

When Kemmler sat down in that chair that has so quickly earned the title of the chair of death the morning sun streamed in the window and kissed the floor. It touched with light the face, stupid perhaps, but placid. It was the faces around about that were the hue of ashes. It was the Warden of the prison who could scarcely find the hands to work with.

The story of the drama that followed is told below by an eye witness. Of the parts played by the various actors let them speak for themselves. Nine minutes, that seemed an hour, got by at last, and the deed was done.

It was not until an hour after that the body was cold enough to put under the shining scalpels of the post-mortem inquisitors. The doctors came out of the prison determined to be discrete and silent, but honest indignation soon overmastered them and it was not long before they were talking of the horrors that they had seen.

DIVIDING THE BODY.

The autopsy was made very carefully, and the doctors made it thorough. They could not have any legal disputes as to whether the man was dead nor as to the cause of death, so Dr. Jenkins took the chest and abdominal region and Dr. Daniels the brain and head and spinal cord, and with deft fingers dissected them while the others looked on.

They found a splendid specimen of physical manhood. They found to their surprise a brain that weighed forty-five ounces, the exact normal weight. When they came to remove the skull they found that in the small blood vessels between the brain and the skull all the blood was like charcoal. It was not burned to ashes, but all the fluid had been evaporated. The skull itself was badly burned.

But it was at the base of the spinal cord, where the other electrode touched, that the burning was most terrible. The examination of the spinal cord showed negative results. The doctors could find no trace of the current which had passed through it.

Across the forehead and nose where the straps had pressed were slight discolorations. The burned spot on the back was four inches in circum-

TILLIE ZEIGLER (Kemmler's victim).

ference. The blood retained its fluidity during the autopsy, showing very slight tendency to coagulation. The water in both sponges had evaporated. The doctors helped themselves generously to interesting parts of the dead man's body, and then the inquest, so far as it could be carried on without the use of microscope and the finer analysis, was finished.

Kemmler was ready for his bed in the prison cemetery and the quick consuming of his remains by quicklime which the law imposes.

The people of Auburn are very grateful to-night that at last Kemmler is dead.

IN THE DEATH CHAIR.

Kemmler at the Moment of Receiving the Fatal Shocks of Electricity in the Auburn Prison, in Pursuance of the Law.

THE HERALD'S OWN WITNESS.

A TERRIBLE SCENE WHICH HE SAW IN THE EXECUTION ROOM.

[BY TELEGRAPH TO THE HERALD.]

AUBURN, N. Y., August 6, 1890.—I am a reporter of the HERALD and, so far as I know, the only special newspaper representative who saw this most grievous failure. I will try to relate a plain and simple tale, giving all the details so far as I was able to see them. I need not say that I was stricken with horror at what I saw, but I did not forget my duty nor permit my eyes to stray from the ghastly drama that was enacted in that room of death.

The first arrivals within the prison yard were the chaplain of the prison and Rev. W. E. Houghton, Kemmler's spiritual adviser. They came in at five o'clock. Before that time there had been some ringing at the bell, but no one was admitted.

Dr. Houghton and the chaplain went to the Warden's office for a minute and then were escorted to the lower floor and along the familiar passage which they had trod so often together to Kemmler's cell. They found the condemned man awake and talking with his guards, McNaughton and Donlon. McNaughton had remained after the end of his watch, midnight, that he might see the prisoner in the morning and bid him farewell. He had refused to be present at the execution.

Kemmler had an inkling of the approximate time set for the execution last night, yet he slept through that night as he had through all the nights just preceding it, as calmly and as peacefully as a healthy man might sleep who had no sword of Damocles hanging over his head.

KEMMLER DRESSED HIMSELF.

Dr. Houghton and the chaplain found him awake when they went in and arraying himself in the new suit of clothing which the Warden had furnished him. There were a pair of trousers of mixed yellow pattern and woollen material, a light sack coat of dark gray and a vest of the same pattern. Under

KEMMLER IN HIS CELL. (From a photograph taken for the HERALD by Mrs. Durston.)

these he wore his striped drawers and a white linen shirt and brown mixed socks. His shoes were neatly polished, around his neck was a low standing collar such as he had learned to affect since he became an inmate of the prison and become accustomed to civilized attire; about that was a narrow linen tie with little white squares with black checks. This was tied in a neat bow. In fact Kemmler's appearance was quite spruce and natty.

The coat hid from immediate view a peculiarity in the trousers—a semi-oval opening cut in the back from the waistband half way down the seat for the purpose of giving free access to the electrode in the back of the chair when he should be placed in it.

Dr. Houghton and the chaplain remained with the condemned man until the time he was called to meet his death. They prayed with him and talked to him particularly of the promises of the Saviour.

Kemmler listened attentively to all they said and reiterated in his plain way his faith in the Bible lessons which he had been taught. He seemed inclined to take a rather light view of the situation, and he laughed and joked about little things—such things as he could comprehend, and they were very little and very few. He was by far the most unconcerned member of the party.

In the meantime the witnesses were gathering in the warden's office upstairs. Dr. Fell was one of the first to arrive and he busied himself with the preparation in the inner room of some microscope slides, with which he proposed to make tests of the blood, skin, &c., after death and before the autopsy.

JENKINS TO WIELD THE KNIFE.

Dr. Daniels came in a little later with a bundle of surgical instruments under his arm. He had been up until two o'clock in a consultation of physicians over the programme for the autopsy, in which no agreement had been reached. Some of the physicians had held out that Dr. Jenkins, of New York, in view of his long experience with subjects who died of electric shocks, ought to do the work of the surgeon, while Dr. Southwick, who feels a personal responsibility for the electric method of punishment, and some others were anxious that Dr. Daniels, of Buffalo, should wield the surgeon's knife.

The matter was undetermined when the conference broke up. In fact, it was not determined when the physicians assembled at the prison this morning, and there was not a final determination until the execution had taken place and the autopsy was about to be held, when the claims of Dr. Jenkins were recognized.

Dr. Southwick came in with Dr. Daniels, and one after another the other witnesses followed until almost the full number had gathered. Still some of the most important of the experts were not in sight, and Warden Durston, appearing on the scene, became anxious about them. At twenty-three minutes past six he came down the hall and asked where Dr. Spitzka was. The reply was that the Doctor had not arrived. The correspondent of one of the press associations was then asked for, and he, too, was not to be found.

"These people ought to remember," said the warden, "that we have got a great big place and a thousand men to handle here, and we must act promptly and be on time. I'll not wait much longer."

Almost as he spoke the press representative was seen coming in the gate, and a few minutes later Dr. Spitzka came hurrying up the walk a bag of instruments in his hands.

"It's not my fault," said the doctor. "I was waiting for the others, and they are still at break fast."

INTO THE EXECUTION ROOM.

"Time's up," said the Warden a minute later, and turning around without further ceremony he started toward the back hallway of the prison, the witnesses following him. The door to a flight of narrow stairs running next the inner wall was opened by a turnkey and the little procession passed in. There was no identification of any of them further than the presentation at the gate of the little card, which read:—

Admit........
CHARLES F. DURSTON, Agent and Warden.

There was no order of precedence. They went down the stairs helter-skelter without much conversation, but with very little restraint. At the bottom of the stairs the Warden threw open a little door and ushered the party, to their great astonishment, directly into the execution room. Then they learned for the first time that the location of the electric chair had been changed. It was changed probably for two reasons—that Kemmler might not see the lever thrown to turn the current into his body, and that the witnesses might be in ignorance of the identity of the man who controlled the lever. Mr. Durston says to-day that the identity of that man never will be known.

So the electric chair was taken out of the room where the volt metre and the lever and the incandescent lights and the other paraphernalia of the apparatus were placed and put in a room which was free of any of the other furniture of the experiment.

This was the corner room below the clerk's office, in the first bend of the wall beyond the main entrance to the prison.

It was illuminated by two windows about five feet from the floor. One of these faced the street and the other, just across the corner of the wall from it, faced down the yard. The first was hung with a green curtain to keep out prying glances. Each of them was screened, but in spite of the smallness of the room and the way in which it was enclosed, at no time was the heat in it oppressive, either during the execution or during the autopsy.

THE WARDEN READING THE DEATH WARRANT.

At the right of the main door of the room, the one through which the witnesses entered, was the electric chair. It faced the windows, but it could not be seen easily in their dim light, so three of the gas jets in the two fixtures that hung from the ceiling were lighted, and they cast a dim yellow light over the scene.

THE CHAIR OF DEATH.

The chair has never been properly described—that is, it has been changed so often that no description of it published heretofore was in any great degree accurate. It was fashioned like a square, high backed, easy chair. The seat was of perforated wood. The arms were about two inches broad. Across the back of the chair, between a point a few inches from the top and a point about midway between the top and bottom were three wooden braces, to the upper two of which was fastened a cushion of hard rubber, three inches thick at the top and shaved off toward the bottom to about one-half that thickness. Midway between these and the seat of the chair, at a point where the arms joined the back, was another brace—a broad board. In front of it was stretched a heavy cotton band, to which was attached one of the electrodes of the dynamo. This electrode consisted of a cup of rubber, within which was another cup of metal, to which was attached a sponge. This apparatus was attached firmly to a wooden button, behind which was a spiral spring resting against the broad board. Running up from the top of the chair was a "figure four" framework of heavy wood, through the point of which passed the wire to the second electrode. This wire was twisted into a heavy spiral immediately below the frame, and attached to this spiral was a cup similar to the one at the base of the chair.

Two wooden clamps held this frame in place or when released permitted it to be moved up or down. The wire which was attached to it ran to a button on the ceiling, whence it was carried to the doorway and through the door frame into the next room. The wire to the other electrode ran to the floor, protected by a piece of wooden moulding, and along the wall to the doorway, where it passed into the next room.

STRAPS THAT HELD HIM.

The straps on the chair were arranged so as to go around Kemmler's chest in two diagonal directions, across his legs and around each of his limbs. They were broad leather straps, capable of resisting any ordinary pressure and certainly beyond the strength of any struggling man.

GOING TO THE DEATH CHAMBER.

Along one side of the room ran a long bench. On the other end of the room were placed chairs to accommodate all of the witnesses. Not all of them were present, and one of them who came, District Attorney George Quinby, of Buffalo, left the room before the affair had been carried to its conclusion, in spite of the Warden's determination that no one should leave the building or even the execution chamber until Kemmler was dead and the certificate of death had been signed.

District Attorney Quinby is not a very robust man, and the scenes in the death chamber were too much for his nerves. He told the Warden he must go out before the affair was half over, and when he got into the upper hallway he fainted.

He was the only member of the party who gave way completely, although several of the witnesses were prostrated for a brief spell in the chamber during the execution.

When the door had been locked upon the party the Warden asked them to seat themselves, and then he quickly set about his preparations. There was a low murmur of conversation while Mr. Durston looked at the straps and walked for a minute into the next room to see that the electricians were in place. While this interval was passing Dr. Jenkins, of New York; Dr. Balch and Dr. Shrady came hurriedly in. They had delayed over their breakfast at the hotel, and as they took their seats Dr. Balch entered into an animated conversation with Dr. Spitzka about their tardiness and about Dr. Spitzka's failure to wait for them.

DECIDING ON THE CURRENT.

The conversation was broken by the Warden, who walked over to where Dr. Spitzka and Dr. McDonald sat side by side and said:—

"How long shall I have the current on? You shall say whether it shall be fifteen seconds or three or five."

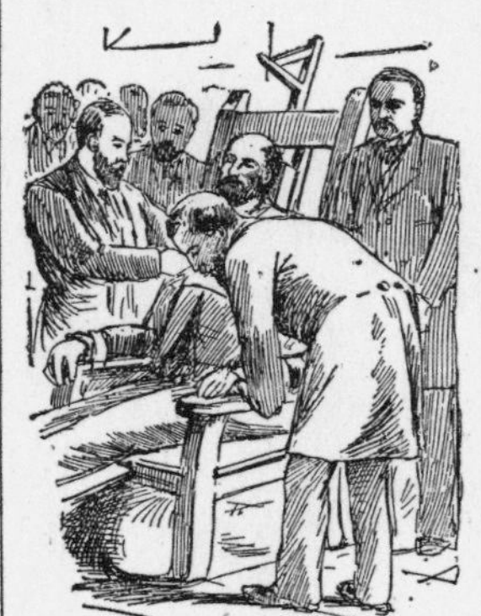

YES, HE IS DEAD.

"Fifteen seconds," Dr. Spitzka promptly replied.

"That's a long time," said the Warden.

"Will you say, Doctor?" said Dr. Spitzka, turning to his colleague. "You have had more to do with these things than I have.'

"Well, I have left the matter entirely to you," said the Warden. "How much time do you say?"

"Well, say ten seconds at least," replied Dr. McDonald.

"All right," was the Warden's laconic answer, and he turned sharply around and went into the next room.

During his absence Dr. Spitka said:—"Has any gentleman here a stop watch?" Sheriff Conway, of Troy, tendered one, but at that moment Dr. McDonald produced one from his waistcoat pocket and Dr. Spitka declined the Sheriff's offer, with thanks.

There was a hum of conversation about the room. The party had hardly got quite settled down. No one was looking for the near approach of a climax. But Warden Durston is a man of deeds, not of words. He had left the room after his consultation with the two doctors to go direct to the cell where Kemmler was confined.

He said, "Good morning, Bill," as he went in, and the prisoner replied pleasantly, "Good morning."

READING THE WARRANT.

Without further preliminaries the Warden took from his pocket the death warrant.

Kemmler stood quietly through the reading, his spiritual advisers standing on either side of him. When it was over the Warden said, "Come."

Kemmler turned and said "Goodby" to his keeper, McNaughton, and to his other keeper, Donlon. Then he shook hands with the chaplain and Dr. Houghton, saying "Goodby" to each in an animated, cheerful tone.

He might have been going out for a quiet walk for all his voice showed. Coming back up the corridor he stepped in behind the Warden and the little procession started out. It walked in upon the assemblage in the execution room in the most unconventional way. The door opened and in walked the Warden, behind him Kemmler, without a falter in his walk or a bit of hesitancy in his demeanor. His face was quite characterless, its only expression being that which it took from a full heavy black beard cut round and parted in the middle. His manner was calmer than that of the Warden, which is always nervous and bustling.

The two ministers were quiet and apparently unmoved. Both of them had witnessed executions before, and Dr. Houghton had been the witness of several autopsies.

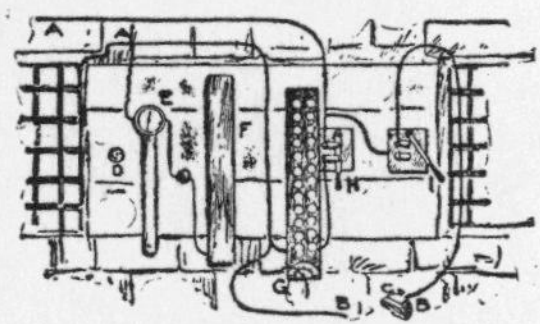

AA—Dynamo wire. BB—Wires to connect with Kemmler's head and base of spine. C—Cap goes on top of Kemmler's head. D—Signal button to dynamo room. E—Voltmetre register. F—Resistance box. G—Lamp board and register. H—Lamp switch. I—Main switch, by handle of which executioner will connect current.

THE SWITCH BOARD.

Kemmler stopped as the Warden stopped and glanced rather curiously about the room. His beard gave to his face a quizzical, half amused expression, which was ghastly under the conditions. Only his eyes were restless. They wandered about a little, but they returned regularly to the calm face of the Warden, in whom he had put his strength for the final test. It was a confidence in the Warden's assurances rather than a firm faith in his hereafter that buoyed him up and carried him through his experience in the execution room. Whenever he showed a disposition to move about in the chair the Warden would encourage him with assurances that it was all right, and they seemed quite enough for him.

SAT DOWN FOR A MOMENT.

"Give me a chair, will you," said the Warden, as he stepped in front of the semi-circle of witnesses. A chair was handed him from the circle and he placed it nearly beside the execution chair and Kemmler sat down in it. He leaned forward a little as he did, his elbows partly resting on his knees. The prison clock at this time marked thirty-four minutes past six.

"Now, gentlemen," said Warden Durston, looking about the room, "this is William Kemmler. I have just read the death warrant to him and told him that he has got to die and if he has anything to say he will say it."

The little prisoner had looked up once or twice during this speech. He was thoroughly composed and evidently prepared for this little act in the drama. When the Warden stopped he began in a monotonous, thin voice to recite what he had evidently committed to memory in preparation for the event. Doubtless he knew that his words would go down in history, and he had his lesson well learned. He addressed his audience in a commonplace way and without hesitation.

KEMMLER'S LAST SPEECH.

What he said was not particularly significant, except as it cast some doubts on the security of his religious convictions rather than in a blind faith in what he terms "luck." These are his words:—

"Well, gentlemen, I wish everyone good luck in this world, and I think I am going to a good place, and the papers have been saying a lot of stuff that isn't so. That's all I have to say."

And so with a parting shot at what he was good enough to refer to not long ago as "those d——d

DR. A. P. SOUTHWICK (father of the Electrical Execution law).

reporters," William Kemmler took his leave of earth. The quiet demeanor of the man as he entered had made a strong impression on those in the room. His self-possession after his oratorical effort simply amazed them. He got up out of his chair as though he were anxious to try the experiment, not as though he courted death, but as though he was thoroughly prepared for it. Turning his back to the Warden and his profile to the spectators, he drew off his coat, which he handed to Mr. Durston. Then he began to unbutton his waistcoat, but the warden told him not to do that and so he calmly buttoned it up again. Afterward he unfastened the two lower buttons and they remained unfastened to the end. The Warden took the coat and laid it on the table at the side of the room. Then he turned back and examined the opening in Kemmler's trousers. The shirt was in the way and Warden Durston pulled it through and cut it off.

Kemmler calmly adjusted his necktie and as calmly sat down in the electric chair.

ASSISTED IN THE WORK.

The moment he was in the chair and had settled back so that his head rested against the rubber cushion he raised his arms and held them bowed so that they would not interfere with the work of the Warden and his assistant, George Vieling.

"Don't hurry about this matter, be perfectly cool," the Warden had said as Kemmler was removing his coat, and Kemmler was undoubtedly the coolest man in the room.

Warden Durston caught hold of the straps on the right and Deputy Vieling of those on the left and they began quickly to adjust them. There was no delay. Kemmler constantly encouraged the workers at the straps with "Take your time; don't be in a hurry; do it well; be sure everything is all right." He did not speak with any nervous apprehension.

Warden Durston leaned over, drawing the h...

THE PARISH PRISON, WHERE THE ACCUSED ASSASSINS ARE CONFINED.

DAVID C. HENNESSY, LATE CHIEF OF POLICE.

ANTONIO SCAFFIDI.

JOSEPH P. MACHECA.

A. BAGNETTO.

JOHN MATRANGA.

PIETRO MASTERO.

TOM DUFFY.—(THE NEWSBOY WHO SHOT ONE OF THE ASSASSINS.)

SUPPOSED LEADERS AND INSTRUMENTS OF "THE MAFIA."

⁎ Where Hennessy stood when first fired at.

A. Mastero's Shanty, in which the Assassins lay in wait. **B.** Wagon Gateway from which they emerged. **C.** Shed under which they stood when firing.

THE SCENE OF THE SHOOTING, SHOWING THE UPPER AND LOWER SIDES OF GIROD STREET.

"THE MAFIA" IN NEW ORLEANS.—[SEE PAGE 874.]

HARPER'S WEEKLY
A JOURNAL OF CIVILIZATION

Vol. XXXV.—No. 1788. NEW YORK, SATURDAY, MARCH 28, 1891. TEN CENTS A COPY, INCLUDING SUPPLEMENT.

THE KILLING OF SIX OF THE ITALIANS IN THE YARD OF THE PARISH PRISON IN NEW ORLEANS.
From a Sketch by Charles Graham.—[See Page 226.]

4 O'Clock THE INDIANAPOLIS NEWS 4 O'Clock

VOL. XXIII—NO. 37. WHOLE NO. 7,312.

INDIANAPOLIS, THURSDAY EVENING, OCTOBER 6, 1892.

PRICE TWO CENTS. PER YEAR IN ADVANCE, $5.

THE DALTONS' LAST RAID

FIVE OF THE DESPERADOES SHOT DOWN BY CITIZENS.

But Four of the Latter Are Killed and Others Mortally Wounded — The Desperate Encounter at Coffeyville, Kas., Yesterday.

COFFEYVILLE, Kas., October 6.—The notorious Dalton gang of highway robbers, murderers and general desperadoes was virtually wiped out yesterday, but not until four citizens of this place yielded up their lives in the work of extermination. Six of the gang rode into the town this morning and robbed the two banks of the place. Their raid had become known to the officers of the law, and when the bandits attempted to escape they were attacked by the marshal's posse. In the battle which ensued four of the desperadoes were killed outright, and one was so badly wounded that he is sure to die. The other escaped, but is being hotly pursued. Of the attacking party four were killed, one was fatally and two were seriously wounded. The dead are:

BOB DALTON.

BOB DALTON, desperado, shot through the head.

GRANT DALTON, desperado, shot through the heart.

EMMETT DALTON, desperado, shot through the left side.

FATALLY WOUNDED.

JOSEPH EVANS, desperado, shot through the head.

JOHN MOORE ["Texas Jack"], desperado, shot through the head.

T. C. CONNELLY, city marshal, shot through the body.

L. M. BALDWIN, bank clerk, shot through the head.

G. W. CUBINE, merchant, shot through the heart.

C. J. BROWN, shoemaker, shot through the body.

The wounded are:

THOMAS G. AYRES, cashier of the First National Bank, shot through the groin; can not live.

T. A. REYNOLDS, of the attacking party, shot in the right breast; not considered necessarily dangerous.

LAIS DEITZ, another of the attacking party, shot in the right side; seriously but not fatally hurt.

It was 9 o'clock in the morning when the Dalton gang rode into town. The bandits came in two squads of three each, and, passing through unfrequented streets, all rendezvoused in the alley in the rear of the First National Bank. They quickly tied their horses and, without losing a moment's time, proceeded to the attack on the banks. Robert Dalton, the principal leader of the gang, and Emmett Dalton, his brother, went to the First National Bank, the other four, under the leadership of "Texas Jack" or John Moore, going to the private bank of C. M. Condon & Co.

While the marshal was collecting his forces the bandits, all ignorant of the trap that was being laid for them, were proceeding deliberately with their work of robbing the banks. "Texas Jack's" band had entered Condon's bank, and, with their Winchesters leveled at Cashier Ball and Teller Carpenter, had ordered them to throw up their hands. Then "Texas Jack" searched them for weapons while the other three desperadoes kept them covered with their rifles. Finding them to be unarmed, Cashier Bell was ordered to open the safe. The cashier explained that the safe's door was controlled by a time lock, and that it could not by any means, short of dynamite, be opened before its time was up, which would be 10 o'clock, or in about twenty minutes. "We'll wait," said the leader, and he sat down at the cashier's desk. "How about the money-drawers?" he asked. Then he jumped from his seat, walked to the desks of the paying and receiving tellers, and, taking the money, amounting in all to less than $500, dumped it into a flour-sack, with which he was supplied, and again sat down while the time-lock slowly ticked off the seconds and the hands of the clock tardily moved toward the hour of 10.

Bob and Emmett Dalton, in the meantime, were having better luck at the First National Bank. When they entered the bank they found within Cashier Ayers, his son, Robert Ayers and Teller W. H. Shepherd. None of them was armed, and, with leveled revolvers, the brother bandits easily intimidated them. Albert Ayers and Teller Shepherd were kept under the muzzle of Emmett Dalton's revolver while Bob Dalton forced Cashier Ayers to strip the safe, vault and cash-drawers of all money contained in them and place it in a sack which had been brought along for that purpose. Fearing to leave them behind, lest they should give the alarm before the bandits should be able to mount their horses and escape, the desperadoes marched the officers of the bank out of the door, in front of them, keeping them under guard while they made their escape.

The party made its appearance at the door of the bank just as liveryman Spears and his companions of the marshal's posse took their positions in the square. When the Dalton brothers saw the armed men in the square they appreciated their peril on the instant and, leaving the bank officers on the steps of the building, ran for their horses. As soon as they reached the sidewalk Spears's rifle came to position. An instant later it spoke, and Bob Dalton, the notorious leader of the gang, fell in his tracks dead. There was not a quiver of a muscle after he fell. The bullet had struck him in the right temple and plowed through his brain and passed out just above the left eye. Emmett Dalton had the start of his brother, and before Spears could draw a bead on him he had dodged behind a corner of the bank and was making time in the direction of the alley in which the bandits had tied their horses.

The shot which dropped Bob Dalton aroused "Texas Jack's" band in Condon's bank, who were patiently waiting for the time-lock of the safe to be sprung with the hour of 10. Running to the windows of the bank, they saw their leader prostrate on the ground. Raising their rifles to their shoulders they fired one volley out of the windows. Two men fell at the crack of the guns. Cashier Ayers fell on the steps of his bank, shot through the groin. Shoemaker Brown, of the attacking party in the square, was shot through the body. He was quickly removed to his shop, but died just as he was carried in.

The firing attracted the attention of Marshal Connelly, who, with the men he had collected, ran hurriedly to the scene of the conflict. After firing the volley from the windows of the bank, the bandits, appreciating that their only safety lay in flight, attempted to escape. They ran from the door of the bank, firing as they fled. The marshal's posse in the square, without organization of any kind, fired at the fleeing bandits, each man for himself. Spears's trusty Winchester spoke twice more in quick succession before the others of the posse could take aim, and Joseph Evans and "Texas Jack" fell dead, both shot through the head, making three dead bandits to his credit. In the general fusillade Grant Dalton, one of the surviving members of "Texas Jack's" squad, Marshal Connelly, George Cubine and L. M. Baldwin, one of Condon's clerks, who was out collecting when the attack was made, were mortally wounded and died on the field.

The bodies of Bob Dalton, leader of the gang; Grant Dalton, his brother; Joe Evans and John Moore, known as "Texas Jack," lie in the courthouse. Across the street the bodies of City Marshal Connelly, George Cubine, a merchant, and Charles Brown, a shoemaker, were laid out. They were finally taken to their homes. In an improvised hospital Thomas T. Ayers, cashier of the First National Bank, lies at the point of death. Thomas A. Reynolds and Louis Deitz are badly wounded, but they will recover.

Emmett Dalton's Account of It.

COFFEYVILLE, Kas., October 6.—Emmett Dalton made the following ante-mortem statement last night: "October 1, I met the boys south of Tulsa. Bob said he could discount the James boys' work and go up and rob both Coffeyville banks in one day. I told them that I did not want any of it at all. He said I had better go along and help and get some of the money and leave the country; that if I stayed around here I was sure to get caught or killed by myself. The morning of October 3 we saddled up north of Tulsa, in the Osage Nation, and rode twenty miles toward Coffeyville and talked the matter over. I went out of love for my brothers, for I knew that the authorities would get after me anyhow and I would have no money to get out of the country. We camped at the head of Hickory creek at Limber hill, about twelve miles from Coffeyville, the night of October 4. That night we saddled up and rode to the bottoms of Onion creek, on the Davis farm. This morning I asked them how they were going to do the business. Bob said we would ride in about 9:30 o'clock in the morning. He said there would not be many people in town so early and not many would be in. He said he wanted me along, because I was quick on foot. He said that I would go to the First National and let the boys go to the Condons. He said we would ride in and hitch at the old Condon building. People would not see us until we got right into the banks. All five horses belonged to Bob. I am a full cousin to Bob and Cole Younger. My mother was a sister of Cole Younger's father."

Dalton confessed that the gang was responsible for the Red Rock, Wharton and other train robberies in the Indian Territory which had been credited to them. The story of a hidden treasure, he said, was nonsense. "If there had been a hidden treasure," he said, "we would all have been alive to-day. It was because we were all 'broke' that we planned the Coffeyville raid. We were being hard pressed by the officers down in the Territory when Bob decided that we would have to get out of the country."

Marshal Connelly Came From Indiana.

Special to The Indianapolis News.

ROCKVILLE, October 6. — City Marshal Connelly, killed in the fight with the Daltons at Coffeyville, Kas., was a native of this county and had been until a few years ago. His brother is a Rockville merchant, and many other relatives live at Bloomingdale and Annapolis.

The History of the Daltons.

There were five boys and three girls in the Dalton family. Of the boys, two are engaged in farming—one in Oklahoma, where the mother of the family lives, and one near Coffeyville, where three of the brothers met their death yesterday. The Daltons were second cousins of the noted James boys, who defied the law in Missouri for so many years, and through them were related to the Youngers, who are now serving life terms of imprisonment in the penitentiary in Minnesota. Bob Dalton was the first of the boys to enter on a career of crime. While he was scarcely more than a boy he became a cattle thief and did a thriving business, driving off cattle from Cherokee Strip herds and taking them across the Indian Territory into Colorado, where he would sell them. He was joined soon after he entered the business by his brother, Grant Dalton. Their depredations became so frequent and troublesome that the cattle men organized to drive them from the Strip. A posse of cowboys was formed for that purpose and gave the Daltons a hard chase, finally losing them in the wilds of New Mexico. The next heard of the Daltons was in California, where they took to train and stage robbery. While robbing stages there one of the passengers was killed in the attack. This spurred on the extraordinary efforts to effect the capture of the gang, and Grant Dalton was finally captured. While being taken to a place for safe-keeping he was rescued by the other members of the gang, the whole party finally escaping after being chased in California and through a good part of Arizona.

In the spring of 1889 the gang turned up again in the Indian Territory, when Oklahoma was opened to settlement, the Dalton boys securing a choice claim for their mother near Hennessey, where she still lives, supported by one of her sons. At the time of the opening Bob Dalton was a United States marshal, being selected on account of his peculiar fitness to deal with desperate characters. After the opening he returned to his life of outlawry, and he and Grant were then joined by their brother Emmett, the youngest of the brothers. They were at that time also joined by "Texas Jack," and soon gathered about them several desperate characters. It was then that the most successful period of the Daltons' career, from their stand-point, began. Their attention was first directed to the robbing of express trains, and they perpetrated many successful "hold-ups," the most noted of which are the robberies of the Santa Fe, at Wharton and Red Rock, the Missouri Pacific, at Adair, and the Frisco, near Vinita.

The Wharton robbery was perhaps the most dramatic of all. The robbers went to Wharton on horseback, and entering the station there asked the operator if the train was on time. He replied that he would inquire, and was about to do so when one of the band, fearing the operator had recognized them, shot the operator dead on the spot without a word of warning. When the train arrived it was held up in regulation manner. After the pursuit of the robbers which followed, outlaw Bryant was captured at Enid, by Deputy United States Marshal Short, known throughout the entire country as a brave officer. Short placed his captive in a baggage car of a Santa Fe train to take him to Guthrie. He had disarmed him, placed his brace of revolvers on a convenient trunk, and had put the desperado in irons. When the train reached Adair Short disembarked to send a telegraphic message. When he re-entered the car Bryant had secured one of his weapons, and, holding it in his manacled hands, fired, mortally wounding Short. The officer, however, had strength to seize his Winchester, and pumped four bullets into Bryant's body, expiring as he pulled the trigger the last time.

There were no fatalities attending the Red Rock robbery, but the Adair robbery resulted in the death of two men. The express car was guarded on that occasion, and a hot fight between the guards and robbers occurred. The place where the train was held up was in the midst of the town. One stray bullet passed into the room of a physician, and, striking the physician in the head, killed him instantly. Another physician, who heard the firing and had run in its direction, was also shot and killed. The last train robbery by the gang was that of the Frisco, near Vinita.

The amounts secured by the robbers in their various raids will probably never be known. It was very great, however, and has been estimated at $200,000. After the Frisco robbery the Daltons seemed to have diverted their attention to the robbery of banks. They rode into El Reno one day and attacked the only bank in town. The only person in the bank at the time was the wife of the president, who fainted at the first sight of the ugly revolvers. The bandits leisurely took all the money in sight, and, remounting their horses, road away. This raid netted them $10,000, which was such a severe loss to the bank that it was forced into liquidation.

Barn Burning Near Gosport.

Special to The Indianapolis News.

GOSPORT, October 6.—The barn of Henry Peters, occupied by the J. L. Rumbarger Live Stock Company, was destroyed by fire this morning, with all its contents, consisting of hay, sulkies and one horse. Loss, $2,500. Insurance on barn and contents, $3,000.

LORD TENNYSON IS DEAD.

ENGLAND'S POET LAUREATE PASSED AWAY TO-DAY.

Surrounded By His Family, the End Comes Peacefully — His Principal Works, and When They Were Written.

Tennyson:

ENGLAND, OCTOBER 6, 1892.

I.

We of the New World clasp hands with the Old
In newer fervor and with firmer hold
And nobler fellowship,
O master-singer, with the finger-tip
Of Death laid thus on thy melodious lip.

II.

All ages thou hast honored with thine art,
And ages yet unborn thou wilt be part
Of all songs pure and true
Thine now the universal homage due
From Old and New World—aye, and still THE NEW.

—[James Whitcomb Riley.

LONDON, October 6.—Lord Tennyson died at 1:35 o'clock this morning. His passing away was calm and peaceful. Sir Andrew Clarke, who attended the poet in his last hours, said, in an interview just after leaving the death-chamber, that Lord Tennyson's death was beautiful. "In all my experience," said the eminent physician, "I never witnessed anything more glorious." There were no artificial lights in the chamber. All was darkness, except for the silver lights of the full moon which fell upon the bed and played across the features of the dying poet like the halo in one of Rembrandt's pictures. Hallam Tennyson, the poet's son, said: "The end was beautiful, calm and painless. He passed away as if in sleep. The watchers could hardly distinguish the final moment."

LORD TENNYSON.

Twice during the night the dying man smiled upon those around his bedside, indicating that he was conscious and recognized them, but he was too feeble to speak. Lady Tennyson bears her affliction with a fair degree of fortitude, but is nearly prostrated by grief and fatigue. Soon after the poet's death, the sky, which had been clear, became overcast, and the light of the moon was obscured. Shortly afterward rain fell heavily, and the scene contrasted strongly with that which had illumined the parting hours of the great poet.

Throughout his illness Lord Tennyson showed grateful appreciation of every kindness and attention extended to him; until he became too feeble to speak, he frequently thanked the doctors and nurses, as well as the members of the household who ministered to his wants. When the Queen's telegrams of inquiry as to the sick man's condition were received Hallam Tennyson read them to his father, who listened with evident pleasure. About 10:30 o'clock last evening the dying man swallowed with apparent difficulty some brandy and milk given to him by the physicians. This was the last nourishment he was able to receive. Thereafter he gradually grew weaker until the heart ceased to beat.

Yesterday morning Tennyson was turned at his request to face the light. After looking at the window for several minutes he spoke of the brilliancy of the sunshine and the clearness of the air. Early in the afternoon he slept lightly. He awoke in full consciousness. He asked for his favorite copy of Shakespeare, turned the leaves until he found "Cymbeline" and gazed at one page for several minutes, moving his lips as if reading to himself. The watchers waited in silence for him to speak, but he finally laid down the volume without having uttered a word, and, with his fingers still between the leaves, he fell asleep. The book was not removed. Late in the evening the moon rose with unusual splendor and flooded the death chamber with light. Tennyson watched it through the curtainless window with his hand still resting between the leaves of "Cymbeline," and thus he died.

The space reserved for Tennyson in Westminster Abbey is just to the left of Browning.

Tennyson's Life and Works.

Alfred Tennyson, Baron, D.C.L., F.R.S., Poet Laureate of England, third son of the Rev. George Clayton Tennyson, L.L. D., was born at Somersby, his father's parsonage, near Homcastle in Lincolnshire, England, August 6, 1809. Dr. Tennyson, whose father was George Tennyson, of Bayon Manor, a lawyer of wealth, was descended from the Plantagenets through the Norman family of D'Eyncourt. He was rector of Somersby and Enderby and vicar of Great Grimsby, and his wife was the daughter of the vicar of Louth. His father was a man of fine and powerful character, and considerable attainments. His mother was "a sweet and gentle and most imaginative woman." It is not remarkable that three of the sons of these parents should have turned out poets.

Lord Tennyson's early education was conducted partly at home and partly at a village school. He showed, when very young, a thoughtful and imaginative vein. His first verses were written on a slate when he was only a child, and while still in early youth he wrote, at his grandfather's request, an elegy on the death of his grandmother. The next heard from the young poet he is pouring forth verses under the inspiration of the sound of the sea, of which he was passionately fond. Together with his elder brother Charles he was sent in due time to South Grammar School, and it was in that town that the publication of his first literary venture was arranged. It was not a single-handed one, being shared by Charles. "Poems of Two Brothers" was purchased by Messrs. Simpkin and Marshall, of London, in 1827, but it was only many years afterward that the book attracted notice by reason of the world-wide fame acquired by one of the authors.

In 1828 the "two brothers" joined their elder brother, Frederick, at Trinity College, Cambridge. Here Alfred Tennyson formed important friendships, notably that which was eventually to be connected with one of his greatest works. Arthur Henry Hallman, who was also entered at Trinity in 1828, must be reckoned as the most considerable of those who influenced Tennyson's life when a young man, although he was a year and a half the great poet's junior. In 1829 Tennyson was awarded the chancellor's medal for the poem in blank verse entitled "Timbuctoo." A year later he published his first volume of poems, "Chiefly Lyrical." "Mariana" was the only famous poem in this volume, but in a revised and enlarged edition issued in 1833 were ound the "May Queen," the "Lotus Eater," "The Lady of Shalott," "A Dream of Fair Women," "Oenone," and others that are still well-known. But this volume attracted comparatively little attention and nothing but fugitive bits from his pen appeared until 1842, when he published "English Idyls and Other Poems." He preserved in this new volume all that he cared to have live of his efforts in earlier publications and included in them some of the works which gave him place in the first rank of living poets, notably "The Day Dream," "Ulysses," "Locksley Hall," "St. Simeon's Stylites," "The Two Voices," "The Talking Oak" and "Mort d'Arthur." One of his next great efforts was "The Princess, a Medley," in blank verse, with its theme the proper sphere of women, published in 1847.

In 1850 there appeared anonymously what was probably the purest and finest poem of that period, Tennyson's "In Memoriam," a series of 129 brief poems all wrought together in grand pathetic tribute to the memory of the poet's college friend and companion, Arthur Halam, who died in Vienna in 1833. For seventeen years Tennyson had borne the sacred grief of his friend's death, during which time he composed the elegies contained in the volume "In Memoriam."

November 21, 1850, Tennyson was appointed to the honorary place of poet laureate of England, succeeding Wordsworth. Of the poems written in that capacity there have been few that have been considered by critics as works which are to take rank with others of his poems, notably the "Ode on the Death of the Duke of Wellington" and the "Charge of the Light Brigade at Balaklava." Both of these were included in his volume entitled "Maud and Other Poems," published in 1855. "Maud" was described as being "so monotonous," both in narrative treatment and metrical construction and in its characters and incidents, and variance concerning it. Whatever adverse criticism might have been evoked over "Maud" was lost sight of and forgotten through the universally applauded "Idyls of the King," four stories in blank verse published in 1859 under the titles "Enid," "Vivien," "Elaine" and "Guinevere," drawn from the legends of King Arthur. Tennyson had begun in these a series of epic poems which he continued in various volumes of verse published during the next fifteen years, entitled in the order of their publication: "The Holy Grail," "Gareth and Lynette," "Pelleas and Ettarre," "The Last Tournament" and "The Passing of Arthur." These works did not include all Tennyson's productions during this period. In 1864 the poem which has since become familiar to nearly the whole of Christendom, "Enoch Arden," was published, along with other compositions, including "Tea Dreams, an Idyl," which had been written originally for Macmillan's Magazine, and for which Tennyson received £10, or $50, a line, which at that time, at least, was the greatest sum ever paid a poet for one of his works. "Enoch Arden" met with a wide popularity, as much the result of the peculiarity of the plot as from its literary merit.

He was elected a member of the Royal Society in 1865, and refused a baronetcy in the same year, the offer being repeated in 1868. In the latter year a few new poems appeared in magazines, and in 1869 "Lucretius" came out in Macmillan's and "The Holy Grail and Other Poems" as a separate volume announced as completing the "Idyls." "The Window, or the Songs of the Wrens," with music by Sullivan, followed in 1870, and the next three years were marked by a further completion of the Arthurian cycle of poems, "The Last Tournament" appearing in the Contemporary Review, and "Gareth and Lynette" in a volume with a reprint of "The Last Tournament."

Tennyson turned his attention toward the dramatic art first in 1870, when he wrote "The Window, or the Songs of the Wrens," which was set to music by Sir Arthur Sullivan. In 1875 he wrote "Queen Mary," a drama, and his last effort in the dramatic line was "The Foresters," which was first presented in London a few months ago. The former works of the Poet Laureate were unsuccessful, but in "The Foresters" he scored a success which put him in the first rank with contemporaneous dramatists. While there were many parts which received severe criticism, yet there were unmistakable Tennysonian passages and lines that received the highest compliment.

The residence of Lord Tennyson has been on the Isle of Wight for several years, near Freshwater Gate. He owned there a commodious stone house, with a pleasant library, where he spent the most of his hours of literary work, surrounded by his books. Until 1851 he had lived in various places, principally in London, but in that year he was married to Emily, daughter of Henry Sellwood, and his removal to the Isle of Wight followed almost immediately. He owned a home in Petersfield, Hampshire, another in Aldworth, Haslemere, Surrey, and a fourth in London.

Tennyson was always careless of his dress—careless to a degree not far removed from untidiness. He was to be met about his house wearing a soft slouch hat, a suit the worse for wear, long, straggling locks and an unkempt beard, while he was rarely without a short, black pipe in his mouth.

He was created a peer by Queen Victoria early in 1884, in consideration of his distinguished services. March 11 of that year he took his seat in the House of Lords, but he has since attended it very rarely.

Tennyson's Income and Peculiarities.

NEW YORK, October 6.—The Tribune's London special says: It is understood that Tennyson received a handsome income from the copyright of his works. When Strahan & Co. became his publishers, they paid him £5,000 down for his books then in existence, with a seperate account for his new works. This contract ran for five years, and Strahan's books show that in that time they paid him an aggregate sum of £31,000. His next publishers were King & Co., who undertook to pay him £40,000 for his copyrights, with a separate account for his new works.

Tennyson at one time made a practice of running up to London at least once a year and roaming about, as far as possible, unrecognized, but no one could pass him by without turning to look at one of the strangest figures that ever trod the streets of modern London. A tall, round-shouldered man, growing stout these later years, he always walked with a stick and gave the impression he was not entirely free from gout. A long beard covered his face, and he looked through a pair of large spectacles upon the world, which, on the whole, he was rather inclined to despise. In supplement of his spectacles there dangled a cross, a somewhat shabby looking tweed dustcoat, a pair of gold-rimmed eye-glasses. The tweed dustcoat, in color a musty red, was evidently an acquaintance for many years, and grown too tight for him across the chest, over which it was, nevertheless, determinedly buttoned. Dark trousers, with gaiters over thick-soled boots, and a broad-brimmed felt hat, probably older by some years than the tweed dustcoat, completed the dress of the Poet Laureate when seen sturdily plodding across Regents Park. Tennyson took the best possible means of preventing his memoirs from being written, keeping no record of his correspondence, much less building up a diary. "I will take good care," he said to a friend a year or two ago, "that they shall not, when I am dead, rip me up like a pig."

Tributes of the London Editors.

LONDON, October 6.—All the evening dailies contain leaders on Tennyson. The St. James Gazette says that "Tennyson embodied all that is best in the Victorian age. Some might have soared higher and touched deeper, but none knocked at so many hearts."

The Pall Mall Gazette says that the civilized world considered Tennyson's name immortal long before he died. It thinks that the next poet laureate will be Swinburne. Such an appointment, despite Gladstone's prejudice against Swinburne, would be a fine instance of a great man's magnanimity, the paper adds.

The Evening News and Post regards Tennyson as the Mendelssohn of poets.

The Globe says that the verdict of posterity will always be that Tennyson was the greatest singer of the Victorian age.

Judge Dewitt C. Dawkins.

JACKSONVILLE, Fla., October 6.—Judge Dewitt C. Dawkins, a thirty-third degree Mason and grand secretary of Florida Grand Lodge, died at his home here yesterday aged sixty-three years. He has been grand secretary for twenty-eight years, and was also inspector-general in the order of A. and A. S. R., of America, and a lawyer of ability and reputation.

SUPPOSED TO BE CHOLERA.

A Suspicious Case Being Investigated in New York City.

NEW YORK, October 6.—Dr. Koertes, of No. 233 East Eighty-fifth street, at a late hour last night reported a supposed case of cholera to the police of the Eighty-eighth street station. The patient is James Finley, twenty-seven years old, of No. 229 East Eighty-fifth street. The case is being investigated by the health board.

Rev. Dr. Warner's Call.

BRIDGEPORT, Conn., October 6.—The Rev. Beverly E. Warner, of this city, has received a call to Trinity Episcopal church, of New Orleans. Trinity parish is one of the largest and richest in the South.

THE BALTIMORE COUNCIL

IMPORTANT MATTERS CONSIDERED BY EPISCOPAL COUNCIL.

The Proceedings of To-day—Proposed Changes Referred to Committees—The Women's Auxiliary.

BALTIMORE, October 6.—This is the second day of the great national council of the Protestant Episcopal church of the United States. The clerical and lay delegates met this morning in Emmanuel church, which was crowded. The house of bishops assembled an hour later in the parish house, Bishop Neely, of Maine, temporarily presiding over the latter body, and the Rev. Morgan Dix, of New York, over the house of deputies. The proceedings of both bodies were preceded by brief devotional exercises. At the last general convention, held in New York in 1889, the committee on hymnal was instructed to revise its work and report at the Baltimore convention. Deep interest is attached to this report, because the first committee rejected a number of hymns which had become endeared to the membership of the church by long usage. The committee, with the addition of new members, has restored a few of the hymns and rejected some twenty which, for more than a hundred years, have been favorites with the clergy and laity. Joseph Packard, a member of the commission on the revision of the common book of prayer, says the report is ready for presentation. In this revision the committee aimed to follow the text of the standard prayerbook of 1884 and the sealed prayerbook of the Church of England of 1549. Changes in the lessons from the Scriptures are reported by the committee.

A movement has been inaugurated among the delegates to the house of bishops looking to a division of the diocese of Michigan and the creation of an independent diocese for the upper peninsula of that State. The movement is actively fathered by the Rev. G. Mott Williams, formerly dean of All Saints' cathedral of Milwaukee, and upon whose shoulders it is expected that the new bishopric would fall in the event of its being created.

The house of bishops always sits behind closed doors and gives out the result of their deliberations at the close of the day's session. In the house of deputies Dean Hoffman, of New York, announced that he had eleven new canons on ordination. They were referred to the committee on canons. The Rev. Dr. Richmond, of Newark, had a number of amended canons, which were also referred. The Rev. Dr. Huntingdon, of New York, offered a resolution which had for its object the incorporation into the constitution of the church the four points known as the Lambeth doctrine of church unity. It was referred to the committee on resolutions.

The Women's National Auxiliary.

BALTIMORE, October 6.—Prominent women from nearly every State in the Union are participating to-day in the triennial general meeting of the Women's National Auxiliary to the Board of Missions of the Episcopal church. Prior to the convention the delegates attended the celebration of the holy communion at St. Paul's church, Rt. Rev. Wm. Paret, bishop of Maryland, being the officiating divine. After the service the delegates marched in procession to Hazzard's Hall, where the convention was called to order by Mrs. Helen Sioussat, president of the Maryland branch of the Women's Auxiliary, and who was chosen as permanent chairman. After a roll-call by dioceses and addresses of welcome a lengthy report of the work accomplished by the auxiliary during the past three years was presented by Julia C. Emery, of New York city. After a brief recess for lunch the report was discussed at length, the speakers, including Mrs. Brewer, of Montana; Miss Sibyl Carter, of White Earth, Minn.; Mrs. Pott, of Shanghai; Mrs. Gardner, of Tokio, and Miss Mailes, of Osaka. The report was adopted.

A WARM WINTER COMING.

At Least All the "Signs" Indicate Its Probable Mildness.

SCRANTON, Pa., October 6.—"I saw more signs to-day of a late fall and a mild winter," said an old Lackawanna valley weather prophet yesterday. "I have lived eighty-six years and I have never before seen dandelion blossoms in this region on the 1st of October, except three years ago, when we had a very warm fall and uncommonly mild winter. Goldenrod all over the upper Lehigh plateau are as fresh and bright as they were three weeks ago. I never saw the blossoms so yellow and beautiful on the 1st day of October before. Mountain ashberries are two weeks later in getting real red than they generally are, and that is a sure indication of an open winter. There has been no frost to change the color of the forest leaves; chestnut burrs still cling to the nuts, and acorns have not dropped from the trees yet. This is a good sign of a warm winter.

"Then the grasshoppers are another sure sign of a late fall. They are as lively as they were in August. I caught three to-day, and they yielded 'molasses,' as freely as they did in midsummer. When there is going to be a cool fall and a hard winter, you can't coax a grasshopper to spit out molasses after the 1st of September. Crickets are thicker than they were six weeks ago, and that's another unfailing indication of an open winter. Tree toads have sung after nightfall two weeks longer than they did in 1891. They are good prophets and they tell me that heavy overcoats will be a drug in the market next winter. Bullfrogs croak in the ponds at night with a good deal more energy than they generally do at this time of the fall, and that means a long, pleasant autumn and a winter without snow. All the indications go to show that people will have to pay about 300 per cent. more for their ice next summer than they gave this year."

MISS DREXEL'S ENGAGEMENT.

The Daughter of the Banker Will Marry a Philadelphia Man.

PHILADELPHIA, October 6.—The official announcement was made yesterday of an engagement of more than ordinary interest. It was that of Dr. Charles B. Penrose, of Philadelphia, to Miss Kate Drexel, of New York. They are both widely known, and the announcement of their engagement will attract much attention. Miss Drexel is a daughter of the late Joseph R. Drexel, one of three brothers forming the Drexel banking firm, which has a reputation that is world-wide. Few young men in Philadelphia are better known than Dr. Penrose. He is a son of Dr. R. M. Penrose, and a nephew of Judge Penrose. In personal appearance he is unusually tall and distinguished-looking, with the air and presence of a Spanish cavalier of the olden days.

THE HANGMAN'S HARVEST DAY.

Two Men and Two Women To Be Executed In South Carolina.

COLUMBIA, S. C., October 6.—To-morrow will be harvest day for the hangman in South Carolina. Two murderers and two murderesses will leave this world by the rope route. A fifth, Gus Deering, an Edgefield negro, who killed a fellow-workman, had his sentence commuted yesterday to life imprisonment. Governor Tilman has decided to let the law take its course in the case of Mildrey Brown, a thirteen-year-old colored girl who poisoned a white infant in Spartanburg. By refusing to interfere in the case of John Williams, a negro, who killed Mayor Henneman, of Spartanburg, the Governor has prevented a lynching, as a secret committee had made all arrangements to kill him the moment mercy was extended. Amanda Tribble, a colored woman of Newberry, will hang for the murder of her offspring. The other prospective victim of the hangman's noose is a white man named William Wilson, of Anderson, who murdered his wife about a year ago.

BAD WRECKS REPORTED.

Several Killed on the Northern Pacific—Senator Peffer's Son Killed.

WINNIPEG, October 6.—A serious accident is reported to have occurred on the Northern Pacific railway between here and Minneapolis, an express colliding with a freight train. It is said that the two firemen, the engineer of the freight train, and two, if not more, passengers on the express were killed, and the engineer of the express is not expected to live. It is also said that twelve men were taken out of the debris more or less injured.

A Missouri Pacific Wreck.

COUNCIL GROVE, Kas., October 6.—A freight train on the Missouri Pacific road met with a bad accident about sixty miles west of this place early this morning, caused by going through a burning bridge. The engineer, a son of Senator Peffer, and Clint Howard, fireman, were both instantly killed. Charles Hart, another fireman, was also badly injured. After the accident occurred the wreck took fire, burning up thirteen cars of grain.

MR. RUNK'S SUICIDE.

A Leading Business Man of Philadelphia Kills Himself.

PHILADELPHIA, October 6.—William M. Runk, of the large dry-goods firm of Darlington, Runk & Co., and a director in the Penn Mutual Life Insurance Company, committed suicide last night. Mr. Runk carried life insurance to the amount of $525,000.

HE USED THE FIRM'S MONEY.

It now develops that Mr. Runk committed suicide because he used $80,000 of the firm's money in stock speculation.

MET A HORRIBLE DEATH.

An Electric Light Man Instantly Killed—His Body Left Dangling.

SPRINGFIELD, Mass., October 6.—Peter Bertheume, an electric light lineman, while repairing the wires this morning, was killed by a shock of two hundred volts. His foot caught in the wires as he fell, and the dead body dangled half an hour fifty feet above the street. The fire department was called out to take the body down.

THE WEATHER BULLETIN.

WASHINGTON, October 6.—Forecast until 8 p. m. Friday: For Indiana—Fair; warmer; southwesterly winds.

THE LOCAL FORECAST.

For Indianapolis and Vicinity—Fair to-day and to-morrow; slowly rising temperature.

LOCAL TEMPERATURE.

7 a. m. ...... 42 | 2 p. m. 63

The Weather in Other Cities.

Observations taken by the United States Weather Bureau at 7 a. m. to-day:

Boston, fair, temp. 44°.
New York city, fair, temp. 48°.
Washington, fair, temp. 42°.
Jacksonville, fair, temp. 66°.
Pittsburg, fair, temp. 38°.
Cleveland, fair, temp. 42°.
Cincinnati, fair, temp. 40°.
Louisville, fair, temp. 44°.
Chicago, cloudy, temp. 44°.
St. Louis, fair, temp. 50°.
Kansas City, fair, temp. 56°.
Omaha, fair, temp. 58°.
St. Paul, cloudy, temp. 46°.
Bismarck, cloudy, temp. 56°.

Resented a Cheer for Harrison.

Special to The Indianapolis News.

LAPEL, October 6.—The Hon. W. D. Bynum spoke here last night to an audience of one thousand. Dr. J. Rollis Moore, a life-long Republican of the ultra type, introduced the speaker, and made known that he had become a Democrat. The Anderson drum corps paraded the streets, yelling for Cleveland, and when Murry Ingalls, son of the postmaster, hurrahed for Harrison the drum-major knocked him down. Ingalls watched his chance, and when the drum-major went to strap on the drum he floored him with a boulder. The town was wild with drunkenness.

Robbed of Diamonds and Money.

BUFFALO, October 6.—W. A. Meyer, of Milwaukee, a delegate to the real-estate convention, who with his wife occupies rooms at the Iroquois Hotel, was the victim Tuesday night of a clever sneak thief, who stole from his rooms $1,000 worth of diamonds and $250 in money.

Street Railway Strike in Memphis.

MEMPHIS, Tenn., October 6.—The conductors and motormen of the Citizens' Street Railway struck this morning for an increase in wages. Few cars are running, but the company expects to have its lines in full operation to-morrow with non-union men.

A Fireman Suspended.

Sam Null, the tower watchman, was to go on duty at 11 o'clock to-day. President Hawkins of the Board of Public Safety, says Null was found on the streets in an intoxicated condition, and was suspended from duty.

A Victim Every Month.

Special to The Indianapolis News.

ROCKVILLE, October 6.—David Blackwell was instantly killed at Rosedale yesterday afternoon in mine No. 6, by falling slate. The Rosedale mines claim a victim every month.

TO-DAY'S BRIEF NEWS.

Natural gas been struck near Mattoon, Ill.

The condition of Mrs. Harrison continues unchanged.

John L. Sullivan denies that he ever said he was drugged at the time of his fight with Corbett.

The rumors of a serious accident to Edwin Booth, the actor, are unfounded. He is as well as usual.

The whaleback steamer, Wetmore, which went ashore on the Oregon coast last month, yesterday was got off.

Near Branden, Miss., two negroes who had robbed a store and assaulted the clerks were taken from jail and lynched.

President Hubbel, of the Des Moines, Northern & Western railroad, decided yesterday to reinstate the discharged engineers in their old positions.

Charles Nellman, dealer in spices at 204 West street, New York, assigned to-day to William H. Fischer, with preferences for $9,000 to Annette Nellman.

While repairing some machinery at St. Joseph, Mo., Frank E. Welton, of Troy, Kas., had one side of his face and chin torn off by catching his whiskers in a belt.

At a meeting of granite manufacturers of Boston it was decided to offer the cutters the same terms as those offered by the manufacturers of Barre and Quincy.

Monte Cochonous, an elevator boy, employed in Wilson Bros.' shirt factory at Chicago, fell out of the elevator and through an open window in the seventh story to the pavement. He was killed instantly.

DELAMATER CONVICTED.

THE MEADVILLE (PA.) BANKER FOUND GUILTY.

The Other Defendants Acquitted—The Man Whom Governor Pattison Defeated Is In Deep Trouble.

MEADVILLE, Pa., October 6.—The jury in the embezzlement cases against the Delamaters returned a verdict this morning of guilty as to the Hon. George Wallace Delamater, and not guilty as to the other defendants. The jury stood ten for conviction and two for acquittal upon the first ballot. Tuesday night Mr. Delamater received the verdict without flinching. The defense will apply for a new trial and will also question the legality of the act of 1889.

The defendant was a State Senator for many years and the Republican candidate for Governor in 1890, when he was defeated by Robert E. Pattison, the present incumbent. The embezzlement charges were the outgrowth of the failure of the Delamater Banking Company.

FATAL FIRE IN MICHIGAN.

Three Men Killed By the Falling of a Building.

HOWELL, Mich., October 6.—A fire here yesterday destroyed an entire block of buildings. While a number of persons were engaged in removing goods from a store an explosion occurred. The walls of the building collapsed and many persons were buried in the ruins. F. G. Hickey is missing and is supposed to be dead under the debris. A man named Isaacs was so badly injured that he can not survive. Last night two bodies were taken out of the ruins. One of them was that of F. J. Henrich, the other Darwin Wines, a prominent builder. Both bodies were badly charred and mutilated, being almost unrecognizable.

A Big Fire in New York.

NEW YORK, October 6.—The Kinney cigarette factory, at Tenth avenue and Twenty-second street, was almost totally destroyed by fire at 5 o'clock this morning. Estimated loss, $150,000.

The greater part of the building, which was four stories high, was completely gutted, the dry tobacco with which the place was filled rendering the efforts of the firemen almost futile. Two of the firemen were injured by falling timbers. The loss is fully covered by insurance.

Another Fatal Fire.

BROOKLYN, N. Y., October 6.—Mrs. Josephine Groll and her two children were badly burned by the explosion of a kerosene lamp in the apartment of Mrs. Groll, No. 11 Kossuth Place, this city, last evening. One of the children died at the hospital last evening. Charles Basch, who had run to the aid of the woman and her children, was also badly burned about the hands.

ELECTIONS IN THE SOUTH.

Georgia Is Democratic by 70,000—Florida by About 27,000.

ATLANTA, Ga., October 6.—Returns from seventy-five counties out of a total of 137 give the Democratic ticket a majority of over thirty thousand. There seems to be no possible doubt that this majority will reach fifty thousand when the vote of all the counties is in. The third partyites will probably carry six or eight counties for the Legislature, and it is estimated that their strength will be about twenty members of the House out of 175. Following is the ticket elected:

Governor—W. J. Northen.
Secretary of State—Philip Cook.
Controller—Gen. William A. Wright.
Treasurer—R. U. Hardeman.
Attorney-General—Joseph M. Terrell.

Reports from many places say that the negroes openly voted the Democratic ticket. Governor Northen's official majority is now placed at 70,555, from the latest returns.

The Result in Florida.

JACKSONVILLE, Fla., October 6.—Mitchell (Dem.) is elected Governor by fully 27,000 majority. Only one county (Baker) gave a majority against him. The Legislature will be solidly Democratic in both branches.

CUTS THE GIRLS' SUSPENDERS.

A Camden (N. J.) Man Who Is Causing Much Annoyance.

CAMDEN, N. J., October 6.—Twenty determined young men of this city have banded themselves together for the avowed purpose of capturing "Jack the Suspender Slasher," who, for two weeks or more, has been causing terror among numerous members of the fair sex whom he has met in the twilight or dark in unfrequented places. The slasher has a weakness for dividing the suspenders of such young ladies as wear these masculine articles with a knife as keen as a razor, the division being generally made across the shoulders. Of course the young ladies do not depend upon the suspenders to support any portion of their lower apparel, and consequently those attacked have, in this regard, been spared considerable embarrassment, but nevertheless, they have been scared and shocked, and in two or three instances severe fits of hysteria have resulted from the molestations of the unknown slasher. Besides the young men in question the entire police force is on the lookout for the miscreant.

ATTACHED FOR A DEBT.

Mrs. Paran Stevens's Horses and Carriages Seized By the Sheriff.

BOSTON, October 6.—A Newport (R. I.) special to the Herald says that F. P. Garretson, a grocer, sent a sheriff last night to the residence of Mrs. Paran Stevens and seized her horses and carriages for debt, and in the event of the fact that Mrs. Stevens is in Boston, where her mother lies dead, the action of the tradesman will be severely censured.

The Typefounders' Trust.

NEW YORK, October 6.—A company has been incorporated under the laws of New Jersey to be called "The American Typefounders' Company." Its object is to control all the type-foundries in the country. The capital stock is $9,000,000. George Bruce & Sons' Company, the largest concern in the business, is strongly opposed to the trust.

Taking the Trotters South.

NEW YORK, October 4.—Charles Marvin has started for Lexington with Miller & Sibley's stable to fill engagements at Lexington, Nashville and Columbia. He has taken Sunol and Arion with him. He hopes to lower the record with Sunol, and with Arion he expects to wipe out all three-year-old records.

Big Lien.

Special to The Indianapolis News.

JEFFERSONVILLE, October 6.—The Phoenix Bridge Company has filed a lien for $201,335.55 against the Jeffersonville and Louisville Bridge Company.

LOS ANGELES HERALD.

VOL. XXXVIII.—NO. 178. TEN PAGES. THURSDAY MORNING, OCTOBER 6, 1892. TEN PAGES. PRICE FIVE CENTS.

THE DALTON BOYS DEAD.

Three of the Brothers Died in Their Boots.

They Came to Grief in Making Their Last Raid.

Two Other Members of the Gang of Desperadoes Killed.

Only One Escaped—A Daring Double Bank Robbery at Coffeyville, Kansas, That Cost No Less Than Ten Lives.

By the Associated Press.

COFFEYVILLE, Kan., Oct. 5.—The Dalton gang has been exterminated—wiped off the face of the earth; caught like rats in a trap. They were today shot down, but not until four citizens of this place had yielded up their lives in the work of extermination.

Six of the gang rode into town this morning and robbed two banks of the place. Their raid had become known to the officers of the law, and when the bandits attempted to escape they were attacked by the marshal's posse.

In the battle which ensued four of the desperadoes were killed outright, and one so badly wounded that he has since died. The sixth escaped, but is being hotly pursued.

Of the attacking party, four were killed, and one fatally and two seriously wounded.

The dead are: Bob Dalton, desperado; Grattan Dalton, desperado; Emmett Dalton, desperado; Joseph Evans, desperado; John Moore, alias Texas Jack, desperado; T. C. Connelly, city marshal; L. M. Baldwin, a bank clerk; G. W. Cubine, a merchant; C. J. Brown, a shoemaker.

The wounded are: Thomas G. Ayres, cashier of the First National bank, shot through the groin and cannot live; T. A. Reynolds, wounded in the right breast; Lais Detz, shot in the right side.

THE RAID LONG ANTICIPATED.

It was rumored a month ago that the Dalton gang were contemplating a raid upon the banks of the city. Arrangements were made to give them a warm reception, but excitement finally died away, and the street patrol was given up.

About 10 o'clock this morning the gang rode into town. They came in two squads of three each, and passing through unfrequent streets, rendezvoused in an alley in the rear of the First National bank.

Robert Dalton, the notorious leader, and Emmett, his brother, went to the first national bank, the other four, under the leadership of Texas Jack, or John Moore, going to the private bank of C. M. Congdon & Co. In the meantime the alarm was given. The Dalton brothers were born and bred in this vicinity and had been recognized.

HOW THE BANKS WERE HELD UP.

City Marshal Conneily was quickly notified and began collecting a posse. While the marshal was assembling his forces the bandits, all ignorant of the trap, were proceeding deliberately with the work of robbing the banks. Texas Jack's band entered Congdon's bank, and with Winchesters leveled at Cashier Ball and Teller Carpenter, demanded that the safe be opened. The cashier explained that the door of the safe was controlled by a time lock and could not be opened for about twenty minutes, or at 10 o'clock. "We'll wait," said the leader, and he sat down at the cashier's desk, first gathering up the money in the cash drawer.

BOB AND EMMETT'S WORK.

Bob and Emmett Dalton in the meanwhile were having better luck at the First National bank. When they entered the bank they found Cashier Ayres, his son, Albert Ayres and Teller W. H. Shepherd. None of them were armed, and with leveled revolvers the brother bandits easily intimidated them. Albert Ayres and Teller Shepherd were kept under the muzzle of Emmett Dalton's revolver, while Bob Dalton forced Cashier Ayres to strip the safe vault and cash drawers of all the money, and place it in a sack.

Fearing to leave them behind, lest they should give the alarm too soon, the desperadoes marched the officers of the bank out of the door, with the intention of keeping them under guard while they made their escape. The party made their appearance at the door just as Liveryman Spears and others of the marshal's posse took a position in the square.

When the Dalton brothers saw armed men in the square they appreciated their peril in an instant, and leaving the bank officers on the steps of the bank building, ran for their horses.

BOB DALTON BITES THE DUST.

As soon as they reached the sidewalk Spears' rifle quickly came into position. An instant later it spoke, and Bob Dalton, the notorious leader of the notorious gang, fell dead.

Emmett Dalton had the start of his brother, and before Spears could draw a bead on him, had dodged behind the corner of the bank and was making time in the direction of the alley where the horses were tied.

The shot which dropped Bob Dalton aroused Texas Jack's band in Congdon's bank. Running to the windows, they saw their leader prostrate on the ground. Raising their rifles they fired one volley out of the window. Cashier Ayres fell on the steps of the bank, shot through the groin. Shoemaker Brown, of the attacking party in the square, was shot through the body and died in a few minutes.

The firing attracted the attention of Marshal Connelly, who was collecting more men for his posse, and with those he had already gathered, he ran hurriedly to the scene of the conflict.

After firing a volley from the windows, the bandits, appreciating that their only safety was in flight, attempted to escape. They ran from the door of the bank, firing as they fled. The marshal's posse in the square, without organization of any kind, fired at the fleeing bandits, each man for himself.

SPEARS' TRIED WINCHESTER

spoke twice more in quick succession before the others of the posse could take aim, and Joseph Evans and Texas Jack fell dead, both shot through the head, making three dead bandits to his credit.

In the general fusillade, Grattan Dalton, one of the two surviving members of Texas Jack's squad, Marshal Connelly, L. M. Baldwin and George Cubine were mortally hit and died on the field. Allie Ogee, the only survivor of the band, succeeded in escaping to the alley where the horses were tied, and mounting the swiftest of the lot fled south, in the direction of Indian Territory.

EMMETT DALTON BROUGHT DOWN.

Emmett Dalton, who escaped from the First National, had already reached the alley in safety, but had some trouble in getting mounted. Several of the posse quickly mounted and pursued the escaping bandits. Emmett Dalton's horse was no match for the fresher animals of his pursuers. They closed on him; he turned suddenly in his saddle and fired upon his would-be captors. The latter answered with a volley, and Emmett toppled from his horse, hard hit. He was brought back to town, and died late this afternoon. He made an ante-mortem statement, confessing various crimes committed by the gang.

ALL THE MONEY RECOVERED.

After the battle was over search was made for the money the bandits had secured from the banks. It was found in the sacks where it had been placed by the robbers. One sack was found under the body of Bob Dalton, who had fallen dead on it while escaping from the First National bank. The other was tightly clenched in Texas Jack's hand.

BODIES OF THE DEAD MEN.

The bodies of those of the attacking party who were killed were removed to their respective homes, while the bodies of the dead bandits were allowed to remain where they had fallen until the arrival of the coroner from Independence, who ordered them removed to the court house, where he held an inquest, the jury returning a verdict in accordance with the facts.

During the time the bodies remained in the square they were viewed by hundreds of people from this and surrounding towns, who having heard of the tragedy, came in swarms to inspect the scene.

The excitement was of a most intense character, and the fate of Allie Ogee, should he be captured, has been determined by universal consent. He will be hanged by the people.

DIED WITH THEIR BOOTS ON.

Among other topics which attracted universal comment were the fulfillment of the prophesy that the Daltons would "die with their boots on;" the peculiar fate which decreed that they should die by the hands of their old friends in the vicinity of their place of birth, and the excellent marksmanship of Liveryman Spears, who with three shots sent death to as many bandits.

THE DALTONS' HISTORY.

The Daltons were a numerous family; there were five boys and three girls. Of the boys two engaged in farming, one in Oklahoma, where their mother lives, and one near Coffeyville, where three of the brothers met their death today. The Daltons were second cousins to the noted James boys, and through them related to the Youngers, now serving life terms of imprisonment in the penitentiary of Minnesota for train and bank robberies.

Bob became a cattle thief when a mere boy, and was soon joined by his brother Grattan. They were finally run out of the country, and the next heard of them was in California, where they took to train and stage robbing. After exciting experiences there they returned to Indian Territory, in the spring of 1889, when Oklahoma was opened to settlement, securing a homestead for their mother, where she still lives. At the time of the opening of Oklahoma, Bob Dalton was a United States deputy marshal, being selected on account of peculiar fitness to deal with desperate characters.

After the opening he returned to his life of outlawry, and he and Grattan were joined by their brother Emmett, the youngest of the brothers, Texas Jack and others of desperate character. From this time their record as robbers of express trains and the perpetrators of other outrages is fresh in the public mind.

EMMETT DALTON NOT DEAD YET.

Later—Emmett Dalton is not dead. He is slowly dying in a room in a hotel here, and his death is expected at any moment. Indignation against the robbers was so intense this afternoon that the citizens wanted to lynch the dying bandit. To prevent this the coroner gave out the statement that he was already dead.

Up to 11 o'clock tonight, Allie Ogee was not captured.

THEY HAD NO HIDDEN TREASURE.

Late tonight an Associated Press representative had a talk with Emmett Dalton. He declared that the stories of their hidden treasure are all nonsense. "If we had had hidden treasure," he said, "we would all be alive tonight. It was because we were all broke that we planned the Coffeyville raid. We were being hard pressed by the officers down in the territory, and Bob decided that we would have to get out of the country. He planned the robbery about two weeks ago, while we were camped in the Osage country. We tried to persuade him not to try it. He called us cowards—that settled it; we started."

It was with great difficulty that the bandit told the story, as he was suffering terribly from wounds in the side. The physician says he cannot possibly recover.

Cashier Ayres is resting easier tonight.

The Garfield Park Trouble.

CHICAGO, Oct. 5.—Master in Chancery Barber today decided to recommend an injunction in the suit brought by the Garfield Park club, to restrain the city of Chicago from interfering with the racing.

THE FINAL ENGAGEMENT.

A Desperate Battle Fought in Venezuela.

Six Hundred Men Left Dead on the Field.

Many High Government Officials Made Prisoners.

The Revolutionists' Triumph Complete. General Crespo Expected to Enter Caracas Today—Foreigners in Jeopardy.

By the Associated Press.

NEW YORK, Oct. 5.—A World La Guayra, Venezuela, cable, dated October 5th, says:

A desperate battle has just taken place at Los Teques. Six hundred men were killed, and many high government officials captured. Crespo struck another decisive blow, which, following upon his previous successes since the revolution began in last March, means victory for the Crespists. Los Teques is but ten miles from Caracas, and Crespo has announced his determination to enter the capital tomorrow.

From details received here, the fight was a most bloody one, 600 men being left dead on the field of battle. Considering the size of the contending armies, this indicates serious fighting. The government forces were routed. Crespo had 14,000 men, including 6000 brought by General Colino.

The revolutionist general possessed twelve pieces of artillery and had the assistance of several Americans, besides General Widener, a German, and General Betalli, an Italian.

General Pulido, uncle of the acting president, was in command of the government forces, numbering 6000, and went to Los Teques, to repel Crespo's advance. This defeat robs the acting president of his army. All the government officials at Los Teques, and those accompanying the presidential army, are reported prisoners in Crespo's camp.

Crespo has made a formal demand for the surrender of the capital. He has backed up his demand with the announcement that he intends to enter Caracus tomorrow at the head of the regolutionary army.

La Guayra is still in the hands of the government, but cannot hold out against the victorious Crespists if Caracas opens its gates.

Foreigners are now in jeopardy. It may be impossible to control the murderously inclined populace and the ruffian element of the soldiery.

Americans may, however, feel somewhat secure, as the Chicago is close in port, ready to protect Uncle Sam's subjects.

RUMORS AT THE STATE DEPARTMENT.

WASHINGTON, Oct. 5.—It was rumored about the state department this afternoon that news had been received from Venezuela to the effect that a disturbance had again broken out, and that the state of affairs was so serious as to require the continuance on the coast of Admiral Walker's fleet. Nothing can be learned from the officials of the department, and the advices received indicate a sudden change in the situation, as a cablegram received yesterday from Admiral Walker stated that everything was quiet.

LATEST ADVICES BY STEAMER.

NEW YORK, Oct. 5.—The steamship Venezuela arrived from La Guayra this afternoon. According to the news she brings, the long struggle in Venezuela is nearing the end and will result in the overthrow of the government, which made such a persistent fight. Colino had joined forces with Crespo, and they were advancing on Caracas. Crespo has possession of every city and stronghold except Las Pegues, Maracaibo and Caracus. At Las Pegues the revolutionists expected to fight the decisive battle. It is the best fortified place the government troops hold, and General Palido is there with 6000 soldiers. On the 28th ult. there was a battle between the revolutionists and government troops at Macuto, in which the revolutionists were defeated.

When the Venezuela left La Guayra, the 19th ultimo, the revolutionists were looking along the coast for the steamer South Partland, which sailed from New York some time ago with a cargo of arms.

Apparently no effort was being made to get hold of the six political refugees seized by General Urdaneta on board the steamer Caracas in the harbor of Puerto Cabello several weeks ago.

Neither Admiral Walker nor Minister Scruggs knows just where the six men now are. The government does not know where the refugees are. The man who seized them is now in opposition to the government. Reports are current, however, that the six refugees are having a hard time in the dungeons of Fort San Carlos, at Maracaibo. Their friends say they are being very badly treated, in addition to being half starved.

From accounts given by passengers of the Venezuela, it appears that the captain of the Spanish gunboat Jorge Juanis is running things to suit himself in the harbor and city of La Guayra. The captain, it seems, gives protection to everp foreigner who needs it, and, as the result, is highly popular with the foreign element in La Guayra. The officers of ships speak of him in terms of unstinted praise. The Spaniard took it upon himself, among other things, to protect American ships from many petty annoyances thrust upon them by the customs authorities.

When the Venezvla arrived in La Guayra there was trouble about landing. The customs authorities refused to allow the ship to land unless she deposited her register in the custom house. Captain Hopkins refused to give up the register, but turned it over to the American consul. Then, with the captain of the Spanish gunboat on board, Captain Hopkins pulled into the breakwater. The Spaniard then suggested that the captein should call for help from the American men-of-war. A signal was run up and hardly had it got to the peak when a boat dropped into the water from the Chicago, and 35 marines tumbled into it. The marines soon had possession of the Venezula's deck, and there was no further trouble.

WEAVER GROWING BOLD.

He Will Speak at Pulaski, Regardless of Consequences.

NASHVILLE, Tenn., Oct. 5.—Gen. Jas. B. Weaver, the People's party candidate for president, has an appointment to speak Saturday at Pulaski, in this state, where he was in command during the war, and where it is charged he was cruel and tyrannical. An attempt was made to have him withdraw the appointment, but failed. A meeting has been held to adopt measures to secure him a respectful hearing, but some conservative citizens fear trouble. Every effort is being made to avoid it.

Springer Taken to Task.

BOSTON, Oct. 5.—S. N. D. North, secretary of the National Association of Wool Manufacturers, has written a letter to Hon. William M. Springer of Illinois, charging him with misuse of wool statistics. He sent a copy of the letter to the Illinois State Journal of Springfield.

GEORGIA HEARD FROM.

SHE ROLLS UP AN OLD-FASHIONED DEMOCRATIC VICTORY.

The State Ticket Elected by About 50,000 Majority—The Populist Vote a Mere Bagatelle, and the Republican Nil.

ATLANTA, Ga., Oct. 5.—Georgia today elected a governor and other state officers and a full general assembly. Two full tickets were in the field, the straight Democratic and People's party. The Republicans have simply a national electoral ticket and will throw the state vote to the People's party.

The Democratic ticket was headed by Hon. W. J. Northen for governor, and the People's party by Hon. W. L. Peck. The day opened beautifully, and reports from every part of the state pronounce the vote the heaviest in many years.

Returns from 75 counties out of a total of 137 give the Democratic ticket a majority of more than 30,000. There seems little doubt that the majority will reach 50,000 when the vote of all the counties is in. The third party will probably carry six to eight counties for the legislature, and their strength will be about 20 members of the house, out of 175. The third party leaders concede not less than 30,000 Democratic majority at 11 p. m.

COLUMBUS, Ga., Oct. 5.—The election in this district passed off quietly. In this county the Democratic majority will be between 12,000 and 15,000. A vast majority of the intelligent negroes cast a Democratic ballot. Marion county, where the third party was considered very strong, has given a handsome Democratic majority. Reports from various counties in the fourth district show a Democratic majority. Muscogee gives over 12,000 Democratic majority. The Democrats are firing cannon and ringing bells, and are jubilant generally. The state is safe for the Democrats by about 40,000 majority.

SAVANNAH, Ga., Oct. 5.—The total vote of this county is 3250, of which the third party polled only 200. Governor Northen and the entire state ticket have 3000 majority. The colored Republicans repudiated the deal with the third party by the leaders, and openly voted the straight Democratic ticket.

INDIAN VOTERS.

Sisseton Bucks Show Their Aptness for Politics.

SISSETON, Oct. 5.—The Indian voters on this reservation, to the number of about 400 were initiated into the politics of their native land yesterday, a council being held at which they considered their future course in the field of politics. Rev. Charles Crawford, Senator Pettigrew, Major Dickler, and a number of chiefs spoke. The council was really called by the Republican county committee. It is surprising to see how apt the Indians are proving. An examination of affairs developed the fact that schemes are on foot that would do credit to the most experienced politicians.

AFTER THIRTEEN YEARS.

The Last Chapter in the Celebrated Sharon Case.

SAN FRANCISCO, Oct. 5.—After dragging through the courts over 13 years, the Sharon case was finally settled today, when the supreme court of the state dismissed the appeal that had been taken by Sarah Althea Terry from the judgment rendered by the late Judge McShafter in August, 1890, which judgment was the granting of the petition of Sharon's executors that the alleged marriage contract between William Sharon and Sarah Althea Hill be declared a forgery.

Not Going to Fuse.

YANKTON, S. D., Oct. 5.—The Democratic state central committee has forwarded to the secretary of state, as required by law, certificates of the nominations made by the Democratic state convention. This settles the question of fusion in South Dakota. The state is believed to be surely Republican.

Ordered to Redondo.

SAN DIEGO, Oct. 5.—Orders have been received instructing the commanders of the cruisers Charleston and Baltimore to sail Friday morning for Redondo. The four days' drill which had been planned for the local company of naval reserves must be deferred.

Florida Election Returns.

JACKSONVILLE, Fla., Oct. 5.—Completed county returns came in slowly and there is nothing to warrant a change in last evening's figures.

A Short Stop.

Uncle Si—Bless Moses! Dar comes dat ole mule runnin away wid little Abraham!

Abraham—Oh! Fodder! Fodder! Stop us, fodder!

Mule—Who said fodder?—Smith & Gray's Monthly.

THE DALTONS AGAIN.

THEY WILL SUE COFFEYVILLE FOR DAMAGES.

EMMET DALTON GETTING WELL.

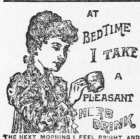

Will Dalton Claims That His Brothers Had $900 of Their Own Money When They Went to Coffeyville, and That It Was Taken From Their Dead Bodies by the Citizens —Will Bring Suit.

COFFEYVILLE, Kan., Oct. 26.—A new feature in the Dalton affair is promised, and a most unique one it is. Will Dalton is contemplating suing the city for damages, alleging as a cause of action that while the bodies of the dead bandits were in charge of the city unauthorized persons were allowed to rifle the pockets and abstract money and valuables, which have not yet been turned over to William or the family.

Will was interviewed in regard to the matter and acknowledged that there was a strong probablity of such an action being begun, claiming, however, that one of the ablest attorneys in the state was backing and instigating the suit on a contingent fee.

Will said that he knows one of the citizens robbed the bodies of the $900 which Emmet claims they had before coming into Coffeyville. This is in all probability the sheerest nonsense, as no one else seems to know anything about it. The chances are that it is only a bluff game, played in order to force those who took the articles from the bandits' pockets and are keeping them as relics to return them.

William is not very popular here as it is, and such a move as this and statements like he made yesterday morning when he said: "The boys were wrong in trying to rob the banks, but were right when they shot the men who were trying to kill them" are calculated to make him even less so.

Emmet is still improving and will undoubtedly recover. His cell is brightened by bouquets of beautiful flowers sent him by foolish women and he is having what many people think an easy time when it is considered that three widows and one poor old mother mourn their husbands and son by reason of the Dalton raid. William declares that there will be no danger of Emmet's conviction and that there will be plenty of money for his defense is certain. Will's actions and words and his bank account are all interesting straws to watch when considering the question of his being a silent partner in the late firm of "Dalton Brothers, bandits and outlaws," whose business cards should have borne the inscription, "Train and bank robbing a specialty."

LOOKS DARK FOR ROBINSON.

The Testimony in the Sedalia Tragedy Points to the Negro.

SEDALIA, Mo., Oct. 26.—The coroner's jury was yesterday in session with closed doors all day taking testimony in the murder case of Miss Johanna Scholman, the young German girl who was assassinated on Sunday night, and adjourned without finishing. Much damaging testimony against the negro prisoner, Dick Robinson, was elicited and it is believed the crime will be fixed upon him.

Killed Without Warning.

DALLAS, Tex., Oct. 26.—Dr. H. Jones, a prominent physician of Dallas, Tex., shot and killed W. G. Vial at ex-Confederate headquarters of the Dallas fair without a moment's warning, for committing an assault on his (Jones') wife. The tragedy took place in the presence of a great crowd of prominent ex-Confederate soldiers.

COMMENTS OF THE PRESS.

What English Papers Have to Say on Mrs. Harrison's Death.

LONDON, Oct. 26.—The Chronicle says: "Very great sympathy with President Harrison will be felt everywhere. Mrs. Harrison was the counterpart of her husband, whose private character is most respected even by his political enemies."

The News eulogizes the deceased lady and praises her courage in going to Washington when she knew her illness was fatal, adding:

"She had won the renown of the American nation by her worth of character and devotion to her husband."

The Graphic condoling with President Harrison says: "We think his success is partly due to his wife's counsel and inspirations. Her death comes at a peculiarly cruel moment."

The Times says: "The death of Mrs. Harrison is of more than ordinary importance, inasmuch as her husband's success may in a very large degree be ascribed in her. Wide in her culture, catholic in her tastes and ideas, she broadened her wide circle of friends with her advancing years. Her death will cause genuine and widespread sorrow."

Switchmen Preparing for a Big Strike.

BUFFALO, N. Y., Oct. 26.—The switchmen of the country are preparing for a monster strike next May, expecting to cripple the world's fair business of the railroads and force them to concede the demands of the employes. "The Buffalo strike and the lesser ones which have occurred this year," said Secretary Joseph Heimeri of the switchmen's union, "are but preludes to the great strike of 1893. It will be a strike the like of which has never been seen and will extend all over the country. The railroads will be making enormous profits. The public would not want the world's fair injured and a clamor would arise. The plans are all made for a giant uprising and the demands this fall are to test the attitude of the railroads toward us. The Buffalo switchmen are biding their time until next spring and then the uprising will be national, great profits made in the manufacture of woolen goods and hats by the present tariff. He says the offer is to stand for thirty days. He will prepare a certified check for $10,000, payable to Crisp's order as a forfeit.

REGISTRATION LAW VOID.

The Indiana Supreme Court Declares the Law Unconstitutional.

INDIANAPOLIS, Ind., Oct. 26.—The supreme court yesterday rendered a decision declaring unconstitutional the registration feature of the election law. The grounds upon which the law is held to be a violation of the constitution is that it is class legislation.

Close Will Be Pulled Off.

TOPEKA, Kan., Oct. 26.—At a secret meeting of the Populist and Democratic congressional committees of the First district held Sunday at Topeka it was definitely decided that Fred Close, the Populist nominee, should be pulled off the track a day or two before the election.

Political Notes.

The registration of Chicago is reported to reach 260,006, nearly 100,000 over four years ago.

The Republicans and People's partyites of Saline county, Missouri, have fused on county officers.

Alabama politics are at fever heat and are likely to grow hotter still. Captain Kolb, who was rotten egged at Beraen, has had the ringleaders in the assault arrested, but it is feared a mob will take them from the officers.

SIGNAL SERVICE REPORT.

It Shows That Great Good Has Arisen From Speedy Communication.

WASHINGTON, Oct. 26.—General A. W. Greeley, chief signal officer, in his annual report to the secretary of war dwells at great length upon the value to the country of the 900 miles of telegraph lines which have been successfully maintained in operation during the year by the signal corps. As an instance he cites the use of the Fort McKinney line during the cattle war in Wyoming, and of the line between Fort Brown and Ringgold, Tex., during the Garza trouble. The latter line it is proposed to extend from Fort Ringgold to Pena, on the Mexican National railway.

With an eye to the demands of modern warfare, special attention has been given to the equipment of field or flying telegraph trains for army operations away from the permant telegraph lines of the country. The field telegraph kit, wherewith a moving line can keep in communication with its brigade or division commander has been satisfactorily developed. For the first time since the war the signal corps constructed field telegraph line for the use of the Mexican boundary commission, between Separ, N. M., and the "Corner," a distance of forty-two miles. Twelve miles of wire were run the first day in eight hours. In seventeen days the command unloaded the material, erected and maintained the line in an unfavorable country until it was no longer required and dismantled and shipped it; all with untrained help for the officers. The heliograph has been perfected so that messages may be sent by its light beam distances ranging from sixty to 100 miles.

The obvious advantage arising from concerted action in harbor defense, insured through reliable and instant communication between the more important forts and harbor defenses, has led General Greely to submit a special estimate to initiate a system of military cables and connecting lines in New York, Boston and San Francisco.

A simple system of whistle signals based on the service code has been devised for the transmission of orders to troops in the extended, or open formation, and is now under consideration by the major general commanding.

In conclusion General Greely speaks encouragingly of the growing interest in signal work manifested by the militia of the United States, and he suggests that the militia act be amended so as to permit signal stores to be issued to the state guards upon requisitions as part of their allotments.

W. C. T. U. Convention.

DENVER, Col., Oct. 26.—The vanguard of the delegates to the W. C. T. U. convention, which will begin its labors in this city Friday, arrived yesterday. In an unostentatious manner Miss Francis E. Willard, president of the temperance hosts, and Private Secretary Miss Anna Gordon, Lady Henry Somerset, a peeress of England and leader of the thousands who battle against intemperance in Great Britain, and Mrs. Rastell, the corresponding secretary of the national W. C. T. U. and head of the Union Signal, allighted from the Union Pacific train at 7:30 yesterday morning. Through some misunderstanding none of the ladies appointed to welcome delegates at the depot were present and after arranging for their baggage the visitors entered a hack and were driven to the Brown hotel.

Kansas Journalist Dead.

HARPER, Kan., Oct. 26.—L. A. Hoffman, editor of the Harper Advocate, died here of paralysis early yesterday morning, aged 57 years. Mr. Hoffman was one of the early newspaper men of Kansas, having moved from Pennsylvania to Doniphan county in 1857. He worked in the Free Soil Democrat office for Jim Lane and had spent forty years in the newspaper business. The Advocate will in all probability be continued by his sons.

A Colored Man Suicides.

KANSAS CITY, Mo., Oct. 26.—Despondent over his inability to control his appetite for drink and suffering from ill health, Ed. Overton a colored man 27 years old, yesterday afternoon bade his friends goodby and taking a cheap revolver placed it against his breast and sent a bullet into his heart and fell to the floor a corpse.

A. O. U. W. Reunion.

SALINA, Kan., Oct. 26.—Representatives from all the Ancient Order of United Workmen lodges comprised in the Fifteenth district celebrated their twenty-fourth anniversary here yesterday. The grand lodge officers were present and made addresses. The meeting closed with a reception.

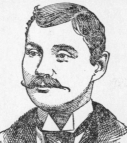

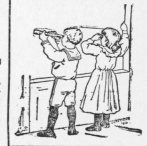

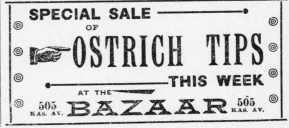

MARSHAL C. T. CONNELLY.
Killed by the bandits.

EXEUNT THE DALTONS.

The notorious band of outlaws attempt a daylight robbery of two Coffeyville, Kan., Banks, and are shot dead.

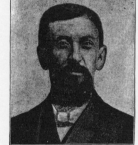

THE killing of the notorious Dalton band of outlaws at Coffeyville, Kan., is one of the most sensational stories of the day, and outdoes anything that has occurred for many years past in the wild and woolly West.

The Dalton gang was very notorious in the Southwest. For many years it had been a terror to train hands and express messengers.

Bob, Grant, and Emmett Dalton were brothers, and were born in Coffeyville. Early in life they developed a weakness for crime and became the terrors of the community. They began their villainous career by stealing sixteen or seventeen horses from the Osage reservation. For several years previous to this raid they had been serving as deputy marshals for the United States Court of the Western District of Arkansas. In November, 1889, Frank Dalton, the oldest of the brothers, was killed in a fight with some desperate criminals in the Cherokee Nation, but before he received his death wound he killed two of the outlaws. After Frank's death Grattan and Robert Dalton served the Fort Smith court as deputy marshals for some time. Afterward Robert became attached to the Wichita court, and then became chief of police of the Osage Nation. He lost the latter position by taking whiskey into the nation, and then for a while he acted with the Fort Smith deputies, his younger brother Emm t also joining the service. In June, 1890, the three brothers ıade their last trip for the government, and a few week later made their initial raid in the Osage territory. After th.. they rounded up and drove off twenty-five or thirty horses from near Claramore, I. T. The owners overtook the thieves at Baxter Springs, where they were attempting to dispose of another bun.h of horses. There was a hot chase, and Grant Dalton was captured, but was released later, there being no evidence against him.

In the meantime Bob and Emmett had gone to California, and when Grant got out of jail he joined them there. On February 6, 1891, two armed men attempted unsuccessfully to rob a train near Alila, Cal., and in the fight the fireman of the train was mortally wounded. Grant Dalton was arrested, charged with the crime, and large rewards were offered for the capture of Bob and Emmett, but in vain.

The two younger brothers made their way back to the Indian territory, where in May, 1891, they, assisted by several other men, robbed the Wells Fargo Express on the Santa Fé road at Wharton, and since then all train and bank robberies which have occured in the Southwest have been laid to their charge.

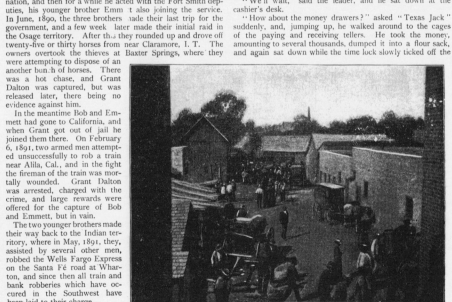

In the early forenoon of October 5 six men wearing broad-brimmed hats, mounted on magnificent horses, carrying Winchesters on their shoulders, and with belts well filled with cartridges, rode into Coffeyville and went straight into the business portion of the town. They turned their horses into an alley and stopped immediately in front of the city jail, where they dismounted and tied their animals to a fence. Four of the gang, guided by "Texas Jack," proceeded to Congdon's bank, and two—Robert, the leader, and Emmett—went to the First National.

In the meanwhile the news had spread that the Daltons were in town, and before they had entered the banks the city marshal, C. T. Connelly, was at work hunting up a posse to capture or kill them.

His first recruit was John Klaehr—whom all Coffeyville calls "Jim Spears," because it isn't his name—the keeper of a livery stable and a dead shot.

While the marshal was collecting his forces the bandits, all ignorant of the trap that was being laid for them, were proceeding deliberately with their work of robbing the banks. "Texas Jack's" band had entered Congdon's bank, and with their rifles levelled at Cashier Ball and Teller Carpenter had ordered them to throw up their hands. Then "Texas Jack" searched them for weapons while the other three desperadoes kept them covered with their rifles. Finding them to be unarmed Cashier Ball was ordered to open the safe. The cashier explained that the safe's door was controlled by a time lock, and that it could not by any means short of dynamite be opened before its time was up, which would be ten o'clock, or in about twenty minutes.

"We'll wait," said the leader, and he sat down at the cashier's desk.

"How about the money drawers?" asked "Texas Jack" suddenly, and, jumping up, he walked around to the cages of the paying and receiving tellers. He took the money, amounting to several thousands, dumped it into a flour sack, and again sat down while the time lock slowly ticked off the

THE ALLEY AFTER THE FIGHT.

Reduced to the Popular Price. THE NINETEENTH CENTURY C Price 10 Cents.

THE ILLUSTRATED AMERICAN

VOL. XII. No. 11
Whole Number 141

A Weekly News-Magazine

For Week Ending October 29, 1892

CONTENTS.

ENTERED AT POST OFFICE AS SECOND-CLASS MATTER.

Price 10 Cents.

NEW YORK'S GREETING TO COLUMBUS.

seconds and the hands of the clock tardily moved toward the hour of ten.

Bob and Emmett Dalton in the meanwhile were having better luck at the First National bank. When they entered the bank they found there Cashier Ayers, his son, Albert Ayers, and Teller W. H. Shepherd. None of them was armed, and with levelled revolvers the brother bandits easily intimidated them. Albert Ayers and Teller Shepherd were kept under the muzzles of Emmett Dalton's revolvers, while Bob Dalton forced Cashier Ayers to strip the safe vault and cash drawers of all the money contained in them and place it in a sack.

FENCE TO WHICH THE OUTLAWS TIED THEIR HORSES WHEN THEY ARRIVED IN TOWN.

Fearing to leave them behind lest they should give the alarm before the bandits could mount their horses and escape, the desperadoes marched the officers of the bank out of the door with the intention of keeping them under guard while they made their escape. The party made its appearance at

THE C. M. CONGDON & CO. BANK, SHOWING BULLET HOLES IN THE WINDOWS.

the door of the bank just as "Jim Spears" and his companions of the marshal's posse took their positions in the square. When the Dalton brothers saw the armed men in the square they appreciated their peril on the instant, and leaving the bank's officers on the steps of the bank building ran for their horses.

But they had no sooner reached th: sidewalk than "Jim Spears's" rifle came to position. An instant later he had pulled the trigger and Bob Dalton fell dead.

Emmett Dalton had the start of his brother, and before "Spears" could draw a bead on him he dodged behind a corner of the bank and ran towards the alley where the bandits had tied their horses.

The shot which dropped Bob Dalton aroused "Texas Jack's" band in Congdon's bank, who were patiently waiting for the time lock of the safe to be sprung with the hour of ten. Running to the windows of the bank they saw their leader prostrate on the ground. Raising their rifles to their shoulders they fired one volley out of the windows. Mr. Ayers fell on the steps of his bank, shot through the groin. C. J. Brown, a shoemaker, of the attacking party in the square, was shot through the body. He was removed to his shop, but died on the way.

The firing attracted the attention of Marshal Connelly, who, collecting more men for his posse, and with the few which he had already gathered, ran to the scene of the conflict. After firing their volley from the windows of the bank, the bandits, appreciating that their only safety lay in flight, attempted to escape. They ran from the door of the bank, firing as they fled. The marshal's posse in the square, without organization of any kind, fired at the fleeing desperadoes, each man for himself. "Spears's" trusty rifle spoke twice more in quick succession before the others of the posse could take aim, and Joseph Evans and "Texas Jack" fell dead, both shot through the head, making three dead bandits to the credit of the liveryman. A general fusillade followed. Grant Dalton, one of the two surviving members of the gang, was killed, and so were Connelly, George Cubine, and L. M. Baldwin.

One of the desperadoes, whose name is not known, succeeded in escaping. Emmett Dalton managed to reach the alley in safety, but had some trouble in getting mounted, and the unknown had already made his escape before Emmett got fairly started. Several of the posse pursued the escaping bandits. Emmett Dalton's horse was no match for the fresher animals of his pursuers. As his pursuers closed on him he turned suddenly in his saddle and fired upon his would-be captors. The latter answered with a volley and Emmett toppled from his horse hard hit. All the money robbed from the banks was recovered to the last cent.

Emmett Dalton made an ante-mortem statement in which he explains how it happened that the gang conspired to raid their native city. He gave as the principal cause of the raid that the gang was "hard broke," and that Bob Dalton aspired to outshine the James boys.

The photographs which accompany this article were taken by photographer Glass, of Coffeyville.

JOHN KLAEHR, ALIAS JIM SPEARS.

Each time his trusty rifle spoke a bandit fell.

C. M. CONGDON & CO.'S BANK AFTER THE ROBBERY.

This bank was visited by four of the bandits, guided by "Texas Jack."

THE COFFEYVILLE JAIL,

Where the bodies of the Daltons were conveyed after the fight. Upon the stone in front Emmett Dalton rested, after first being shot.

THE ILLUSTRATED POLICE NEWS
LAW-COURTS AND WEEKLY RECORD

LIZZIE BORDEN NOT GUILTY.

VOL. 54—NO. 1393. FOR THE WEEK ENDING SATURDAY, JULY 1, 1893. PRICE TEN CENTS.

LIZZIE BORDEN ACQUITTED.

"NOT GUILTY," THE JURY AT NEW BEDFORD, MASS., JUNE 20, DECIDED ON FIRST BALLOT—"THE LIBERATED PRISONER FELL INTO HER SEAT AS IF SHOT WHEN THE VERDICT WAS ANNOUNCED."

THE CHICAGO WORLD.

FOURTH YEAR.—NO. 15. CHICAGO, ILL., SATURDAY, JUNE 16, 1894. PRICE 5 CENTS.

A GAMBLING HELL.

Hot Springs, Ark., the Most Notorious Bunco Town On the Continent.

Here Highway Robbery Is Legalized and Plucked Victims Dare Not Squeal.

Three Hundred Blacklegs and Gamblers Thrive and Wax Fat in a Population of About 16,000.

Hot Springs, Ark., June 13.—This city is really and truly the gambler's paradise. Here everything in that line is "protected." In that regard this a high tariff city with free trade. There are thirteen gambling-houses in this city—ominous for the bettor. Of this number eight are of the "brace" variety, being so-called because the dealer pulls two cards instead of one when he sees that he is about to loose a large stake. These games are "protected" by the payment of a sum monthly to the usual middleman who stands between them and some occult power or hidden force. There are about three hundred gamblers in this city, including the steerers and bunco men. The city has a population of about 8,000, with about an equal number of visitors. This shows a large percentage of the gambling element. The middleman receives a percentage of the profits of each gaming-house for and in consideration of his statesmanship in "fixing things dead to rights." He also receives 50 per cent of the stealings of the bunco men, and if the buncoist gets in jail he must fix things to get him out. The business is reduced to a system.

When a man is robbed of, say, $500, the buncoists hand the money to the middleman, not necessarily for restoration, but as guarantee of good faith. If the victim makes a "roar" he is given back a small portion. If nothing is heard from him in three or four days, the middleman takes his lion's share and the remaining half is divided among the buncoists. If a buncoist attempts to do business without first making a treaty with the middleman he is arrested after beating his first victim, and usually gets a long term in jail. If he attempts to hold back the middleman's half he likewise comes to grief, for the middleman must also be protected and has spotters on the streets. These buncoists have their signals, by which a confederate may know that a "sucker is on the string."

When a bunco thief starts toward Happy Hollow with a stranger or a Boston clergyman he signals to a confederate in waiting. When they have arrived at the cave in the glen, the favorite promenading spot, they find a game in full blast. The confederate, with his pasteboard layout, had cut across the hill. These fellows carry an assortment to please—faro layout, dice boxes, shells, three cards for monte and all the latest devices known to gambling and swindling. Another class haunt the hotels. These are mainly "steerers" for brace faro banks. They receive 5 per cent of the victim's losses.

There is still another class at the hotels, often boarders, who do not associate with the well-known gamblers, nor do they visit the gambling houses. These are the card sharpers. They cultivate acquaintances for the purpose of getting up a social game. They carry their own cards and shears to cut them with, so that they may prepare a deck for poker or for faro. They affect the airs of business men and repudiate the idea of even visiting a gaming-house, yet they are even more adroit thieves than the professional brace dealer. Private faro banks exist in some of the hotels, and visitors are usually robbed of large sums. As a rule, they are the most interested in keeping the matter quiet. Very few men wish to proclaim that they have been fools or that they are impoverished.

Steering or roping is one of the chief industries of the town. It enters into almost everything. The physicians have cappers, to whom they pay from 25 to 50 per cent and tax the sick victim accordingly. The keeper of the bathhouse has steerers out on the streets, and he pays a per cent to the doctor or hotel-keeper who sends him a customer. The drug stores have cappers, and there are even cappers for the sale of bathing towels. The shops which sell antique curios (especially manufactured for tourists) also give commissions. As the visitor is here for only two or three weeks they endeavor to make his stay interesting and the nervous man will not soon forget it.

The gaming evil has given the city a bad reputation. Were the gaming-houses closed and the gamblers and their adjuncts, the bunco men, made to leave the city and the main away, there would be a greater number of health-seekers here every season.

MRS. PAT ROONEY DEAD.

The Famous Chimpanzee of Cincinnati Follows Her Husband to the Monkey Heaven.

Mrs. Rooney, widow of Pat Rooney, was found dead in her cage at the Zoological gardens in Cincinnati the other morning. Consumption carried her off, as it did her husband three months ago. They were the finest chimpanzees ever in captivity and were all but human. They ate at a table, sitting on chairs and using dishes, knives, forks and spoons like human beings and had often been declared the missing link.

Since Pat's death Mrs. Rooney had been melancholy and would spend nearly all her time gazing earnestly at the stuffed form of her husband that stood near by. A month ago she had consumption developed and all efforts so save her life proved futile. Professor Garner, who studied the chimpanzee from a cage in the African forests, visited Mrs. Rooney last week and declared she could not live long. Mrs. Rooney's skin will be mounted and placed alongside the stuffed form of her late husband.

JUDGE BONNEY'S DEFEAT.

A reader of the World writes to the editor as follows: "I have noticed in the paper various theories as to the recent political revolution in the Fourth Illinois judicial district. There is, however, one cause for Judge Bonney's defeat which I have seen no mention—that is the intervention of the A. P. A., a non-political organization, the A. P. A., which indorsed Mr. Carter and urged all its members to vote for him."

FELL ASLEEP ON THE RAILROAD TRACK.

William Christman, while walking home from Freeport, Ill., sat down on the railroad track and fell asleep. A freight train came along, struck him on the shoulder and hurled him several feet. He was picked up and taken to Freeport and afterward brought home.

SPIRITUALIST LEADER DIES.

Mrs. Minerva Merrick Orchardson, aged 84 and wealthy, died at Quincy, Ill. She has been the head of the spiritualistic colony here for years. A year ago she married Prof. Charles Orchardson of Chicago, who came here with the noted spook priestess, Vera Ava, now sojourning in Joliet.

JERRY SIMPSON CONVALESCENT.

Congressman Jerry Simpson, of Kansas, who was taken to Berkley Springs, Va., seriously ill is reported as mending rapidly. His wife writes he will soon be able to attend to his duties

THE THRILLING DEATH OF BILL DALTON NEAR ELK, I. T.

RUDELY SNATCHED

From His Bride's Side While Congratulations Were Yet Exchanged.

Charles Lamb's Wedding to Miss Davis Is Followed by Prompt Arrest.

This Gallant Groom Fondled Others Besides Clara and Loved Minnie Neubert Not Wisely but Too Well.

Charles Lamb a handsome looking blonde conductor with fine chop siders and a delicately curled mustache that would be the delight of a tenor singer, is in deep trouble. He has just embarked on the matrimonial seas, and his frail bark is having tough weather. His troubles began literally, one might say, at the altar.

Lamb was married Wednesday to Miss Clara Davis. The wedding had just been solemnized and the two score invited guests and friends of the happy couple had scarcely concluded their congratulations, when an unfeeling policeman stepped in and said that he wanted the groom—and he wanted him right then. This took place at Burnside, a suburb of Chicago.

There's a little story in it, and of course another woman. Without another woman a story of this sort would necessarily be ridiculously flat. Miss Minni Neubert is the other woman, and, with the assistance of her mother, Mrs. Kate Neubert, caused the rumpus. They succeeded in separating the wedded pair before the groom's tip to the minister had had time to grow cold in the dominie's pocket.

The warrant sworn out by Mrs. Neubert, whose home is in Kensington, avenue, charges Mr. Lamb with assaulting her daughter. According to Minnie's tale of woe, Lamb had been keeping her company for a year or more, and matters had progressed in such fine style that their marriage seemed only a question of a little while; in short, that Lamb had offered to make Minnie "his'n" forever and had been promptly accepted.

While this appeared to be the case and there seemed to be no possible way of escape that glad day when their hearts should be glued together and beat as one there was no friction between Miss Neubert and her adored one. In fact, it is not of record that Mrs. Neubert placed large obstacles in the roadway of the couple.

But trouble brewed fast. Another charmer appeared. She is the young woman who until yesterday was Miss Clara Davis and later in the day secured the position coveted by Minnie. Their courtship must have been less boisterous, for no one knew that they were to be married until Sunday when Charles hunted his old flame and told her of his decision to make Miss Davis his bride. There was some exclamations of surprise; then a course of tears, a collapse upon the part of the jilted one and then followed threats of revenge. The couple finally parted in friendliness, at least so it seemed to Lamb, but here is where he knew not of woman's craftiness. Wednesday morning Minnie appeared at Charles' boarding house. She pleaded for her old love and sought by all sorts of artifices to kindle the dead embers. The appeal fell flat. It was then that dire revenge entered her little cabalistic head. She swore a warrant for assault on Lamb and it was served as related above.

Just what the nature of the assault was Miss Minnie didn't say, but she avers Mrs. Lamb will be interested in its recital.

CHASED THROUGH A CHURCH.

Father of a Girl, With a Big Revolver, Makes It Hot for Janitor Neile.

George L. Bellows, a Chicago printer, chased Willis Nelle, an assistant janitor at the Moody church, on Chicago avenue, through several rooms of the church Wednesday with a revolver. Although Bellows told the assistant janitor several times that he intended to shoot him and during the chase was in range frequently he did not fire a shot. Neile ran into the apartments of Head Janitor R. R. Aitchison, on the third floor.

Mr. Aitchison then took a hand in the affair and called upon Bellows for an explanation. The party adjourned to another room, to which Mrs. Bellows and her daughter Nannie, 15 years old, who had accompanied Bellows to the church, were admitted. The parents of the girl accused Nelle of planning to elope with her. He denied the charge and the girl also said it was untrue. Then Mr. and Mrs. Bellows wanted to know where Nelle was last Thursday night, upon which occasion their daughter was away from home until a late hour. He satisfied them that he was at home sick, where he had been for a week. He also explained the buying of a new hymn book for the girl by saying he had accidentally broken the cover of her book and she insisted upon his buying her a new one. Then Mr. and Mrs. Bellows and Miss Bellows gathered up the revolver and returned to their home.

HE WANTED AN OFFICE.

And if You Will Carefully Read This You'll Learn What He Got.

Washington, June 15.—Mark Twain's story of the man who went to Washington as an applicant for a foreign mission and gradually abated his demands until he would have taken a janitorship if he could have got it is not nearly so pitiful as the case of A. C. Chewing, who was picked up senseless from hunger in the Smithsonian grounds a few nights ago.

Chewing came from Virginia six weeks before in the hope of obtaining a government situation. His money became exhausted, he was forced to leave his boarding house, and when he was picked up unconscious by a policeman he had eaten nothing for four days. It is to the credit of the people of Washington, who are not commonly credited with much sympathy for unfortunates like Chewing, that they have raised a comfortable sum of money and sent him back to his wife and children in Virginia, who, it turns out, were also starving.

The moral of the incident is plain. Any man who can make a bare living at anything else should shun the idea of getting a "political job" as he would pestilence. The best of these positions, even after they are secured, are neither permanent nor comfortable. The pursuit of them, in nine cases out of ten, results in disappointment and misery.

OUTLAWS ARE DEFEATED.

Officers in the Indian Territory Prevent a Wholesale Robbery by Timely Arrival.

Wagoner, I. T., June 15.—A battle took place the other day between a band of outlaws and deputy marshals at Claremoon, thirty miles northwest of here. Four armed men rode into town and hitched their horses in the rear of George Eaton's store. Two of the men were identified as horse thieves whom the authorities had long been hunting, and a posse of officers immediately placed them under arrest and started with them to the jail.

When about half way the two remaining bandits opened fire upon them with Winchester rifles, which was warmly returned by the marshals, driving the outlaws to their ponies and out of town. The firing was kept up by the officers as long as the bandits remained within range. One of the horses was riddled with bullets and his rider wounded, it is thought fatally, but he made his escape into the brush. Close investigation brought to light the fact that there was a big robbery on foot and has led to the arrest of eight or nine men of this place who it is thought were implicated with them.

BROOKLYN'S HAIR CLIPPER.

Six Inches Cut Off Mary Zimmerman's Braid in an Elevated Railroad Station.

The hair clipper has reappeared in Brooklyn, N. Y., and has clipped off part of a braid of pretty 14-year-old Mary Zimmerman. She went down town on an elevated train to attend a class at the Young Women's Christian association. Her glossy brown hair was shorn while she was on the platform of the Bridge street station. She thus describes how the clipper did his work.

"As I entered the gate at the station I felt a slight tug on my hair, which was closely braided and tied with a ribbon. I turned around in time to see a man who was close behind step back a pace and then move off quickly. It was not until I called at a friend's house that I discovered that my hair had been cut through about five or six inches from the end."

AFTER SUNKEN TREASURE.

A. Bauman, a capitalist of Johannesburg, South Africa, is floating an enterprise to recover $1,500,000 in sunken treasure. The gold is contained in two iron safes which went down with the ship Birkenhead off the African coast forty years ago.

MADE A BIG HAUL.

Newell B. Parsons, aged 24, and a society leader at Saginaw, Mich., has been convicted of stealing railroad bonds valued at $463,000, which he sent to Grand Rapids for safe keeping. The bonds were recovered.

BACK TO VATERLAND

Hundreds of Uncle Sam's Foreign Born Citizens Disgusted With This Country.

Hard Times and Labor Unions, They Claim, Have Forced Them Out of Good Jobs

Scandinavians, Italians and Germans Are the Nationalities Most Affected—Low Rates an Inducement.

Our foreign born citizens are going back home. Since the 1st of March a tidal-wave of homesickness and discontent seems to have swept over the Scandinavian, Italian and German residents of Chicago. In some neighborhoods entire families are packing up their belongings and taking passage for the fatherland.

It is remarked that a large proportion of these emigrants belong to the higher class of artisans—carpenters, iron-workers and molders—and in perhaps half of the cases they have sold out all their possessions and are taking the money that remains after their tickets are procured to the old country, where it is their expressed intention to remain the rest of their days.

Among the Italians the lowest classes are remaining in America, principally for the reason that they cannot get enough money ahead to take them away.

Wednesday one of the waiting-room of Dearborn station was crowded with several hundreds of these emigrants and their baggage. They had all taken passage on a steamer leaving New York the last of the week, and a jollier crowd of travelers it would have been hard to find. They seemed wonderfully pleased at the prospect of getting out of the United States. Many of them had been in the country but a few years, and they had undergone a marvelous change from the shawl-headed stolid, practically penniless condition in which they arrived. All of them were neatly dressed, and by the number of bundles, valises and band boxes which they carried it was evident that they were far from being dependent on charity.

There were a great many different reasons assigned for leaving the country. First and foremost, all the men complained of hard times and of inability to obtain employment at living wages. One or two men said they could not get along with the labor unions, and cited several instances in which they had been forced out of jobs by the walking delegates. It had made them so disgusted that they concluded to go back to Norway.

"You see," said a brawny Swedish carpenter, "we can't make a living here and it is much cheaper for us to go home, especially when the rates of travel are so low. One dollar in Scandinavia will go as far as four here. Besides that, times are better all over Europe than they are in this country and we can probably secure employment at good wages."

The agents of the various steamship lines tell a convincing story of the emigration spirit. It was the general consensus of opinion among them that fully four times as many emigrants had left so far this spring as in any previous year. Among these the largest number are Scandinavians, but there are also many Italians, Germans, Poles and a few Scotchmen.

MAUD RUBLE'S MURDER.

Dr. Brown Is Formally Arraigned and Sam Payne, a Negro, Is Also Arrested.

Omaha, Neb., June 14.—Dr. William P. Brown who was arrested charged with the murder of pretty Maude Ruble has been arraigned. Little light has been thrown on the mysterious case. Yesterday, however, Samuel Payne, a negro who had occupied the house where the body was found up to within a few days of its discovery, and whose wife was found in possession of the girl's jewelry, was captured in [illegible]tic, Iowa, and brought to Omaha. Payne fled from the city the night the girl's body was found. The day following Dr. Brown, with whom Miss Ruble had kept company, was arrested.

Payne says he met Brown on the street one night and the doctor handed him a bundle, remarking, "Here's a present for you." On opening it he found the Ruble rings. He will be subjected to a rigid cross-examination and the police are sure he will give the details of the murder. Their theory is that Brown murdered the girl in a fit of anger when she demanded that he fulfill his promise of marriage and then employed Payne to assist him in concealing the body. The defense claims that the body found is not that of Maude Ruble; that she is alive and well, and that she has absented herself in this manner to secure notoriety to enable her to go on the stage, for which she had a passion.

A POPULIST MURDERER.

Peyton G. Bowman, Leader of Kolb's Alabama Campaign, Shoots Down Eugene Jeffries.

Birmingham, Ala., June 14.—Eugene Jeffries, the mayor's son was murdered in cold blood yesterday by Peyton G. Bowman, the leader of Kolb's populist campaign in this state. Late in the afternoon while Bowman was drinking and talking in a loud voice in the saloon ex-Mayor Jeffries entered when, it is said, Bowman made an insulting remark to him. Jeffries replied by saying Bowman had had a confederate deserter for a law partner. The lie was passed, when Bowman struck Jeffries twice, knocking him down. Colonel Jeffries is an old and inoffensive man, small in size and feeble. Friends separated them, and Jeffries went his way.

When Eugene Jeffries, a mere stripling, heard of the insult to his father, it is said, he expressed his intention to have Bowman apologize About 8 o'clock young Jeffries entered the saloon Just as he put his head through the folding doors Bowman snatched out a pistol and fired at him. The ball entered the boy's neck, breaking it, and he died instantly.

Bowman surrendered, and was hurried off to jail. Immediately a great crowd of indignant citizens began gathering at the scene. Threats of lynching were freely indulged in, but it is not thought the threats will be put into execution. One story is that Bowman's brother held Jeffries while Bowman shot him. Bowman claims that Jeffries was armed, but this is denied. Excitement is intense, the general opinion being that it was a cold-blooded murder. The effect of the murder on Kolb's campaign will be most disastrous.

AMERICAN RAILWAY UNION CONVENTION.

Several hundred delegates are in attendance at the first quadrennial convention of the American railway Union now in session in Chicago. In his opening address President Eugene V. Debs paid his respects to the Pullman corporation in no uncertain tones. He then promised that the strike of the employes at Pullman would occupy the attention of the convention, and it is reported that these words mean no less than the tying up of Pullman cars on all railway lines. The union then proceeded to business, and passed a resolution denouncing the Tawney bill now before congress on the compulsory arbitration of labor troubles. The union will be in session several days.

IS THE STRIKE ENDED?

The miners' representatives and the operators assembled in Columbus, Ohio, and agreed upon a scale of wages for the miners in all sections of the United States. Some of the miners appear to be satisfied with it and some do not. Whether the arrangement wil actually end the strike cannot be foretold at this writing.

GOT $400,000 FOR KEEPING SOBER.

George Crocker, the youngest son of the California millionaire, has just been paid $400,000, the amount promised him in case he should keep sober for five years. Another $400,000 will be paid him if he keeps sober during the next five years. At that rate George will never land in the poor house.

BROKE HIS JAWBONE.

Perry Watkins, a colored pugilist of fame local to Jacksonville, Fla., is in the hands of the police for breaking the jawbone of Tom Reddick in a set-to. Watkins swears that the affair was a friendly scrap for points. Reddick will think differently till he can chew again.

A LAD MURDERED FROM AMBUSH.

Frank Richards, an 18-year-old lad of Mauckport, Ind., was shot from ambush and killed while returning home from church recently. The bullet hit young Richards behind the ear, killing him almost instantly. No cause is known for the attack, and no clue to the murderer.

TOO HOT FOR GROVER.

Washington, June 14.—Since the warm weather set in President Cleveland has been considerably indisposed and constantly under the doctor's care He is allowed no exercise and receives no callers. Mrs. Cleveland and the babies are at Buzzard's Bay, Mass.

THE SOLDIER BOYS WERE DRUNK.

The Canadian government has satisfactorily explained the incident of hauling down the stars and stripes at St. Thomas, Ont., on the queen's birthday, by stating that the militiamen were drunk and will be properly dealt with.

AVENGED HER HONOR

Alexander McKillop, Betrayer of Miss Keatley, Is Murdered by Her Father and Brother.

Had Scornfully Refused to Right the Wrong and They Took His Life.

Shocking Sequel to an Illicit Love Between a Gay Girl Cashier and a Street Car Conductor.

Alexander McKillop, a conductor for the Chicago City railway was murdered almost in front of his home on Wabash avenue shortly after midnight Tuesday. At first the shooting of the man was wrapped up in considerable mystery, and it was thought that footpads had done the deed. Subsequent developments however reveal quite a different story. The shooting occurred in front of the Haven school building on Wabash avenue near Fifteenth street.

When the detectives began investigating they did not have any trouble in finding a clew. They found that McKillop had boarded at 1536 Wabash avenue. He drew his month's wages Monday and in the evening left to go to Hyde Park. Shortly after he left two men called at the boarding house and asked to see McKillop. They were told that he was out. At 10 o'clock another man came and asked Mrs. Johnson, the colored woman, who occupies the basement at 1536, if McKillop had reutrned. He was answered, no. Shortly before 11 o'clock the first man came back. When asked what he wanted with McKillop, he answered: "That's all right. I'll wait till I see him."

McKillop came in about 11:20 and went out to the dining-room. He was eating when the door-bell rang. McKillop went to the door. Officer Rogers heard him make some laughing remark, and then he went away. That was the last time he was seen alive by any of the boarders. McKinley, who keeps the boarding house in Wabash aveneue, told the police that McKillop had compromised Miss Emily Keatley of 7840 Emerald avenue, and that her father and brother had insisted upon his marrying her. McKillop had said he would rather commit suicide than marry the girl. It was on this information that the real facts in the case were found out. The Keatleys were arrested and Orlando Keatley the son confessed.

According to his confession, McKillop had been acquainted with Miss Keatley for some time. The marriage of the two was opposed by the members of the family, but Mrs. Keatley finally consented to it. The wedding was set for several dates, but McKillop steadily failed to appear. It was set finally for last Saturday, but McKillop again remained away. The father and the son had in the meantime found out the relations existing between McKillop and Miss Keatley and they decided upon radical measures. They told McKillop that he must marry the girl. He refused. Then they planned his death.

They called again and again at the boarding house in Wabash avenue Monday night. They knew that McKillop was not working. When he saw them at the door he was evidently not frightened, for he joked with them and left a few moments later. They had gone but a few steps when the father and son turned on McKillop. The exclamation, "Then die, you cur," was heard. Five shots were fired, some by both men. Two of them took effect and death came almost instantly.

From persons who saw part of the tragedy it was ascertained that after McKillop had fallen and lay with his face to the ground one of the men struck a match, turned over the body and examined it to make sure that death had ensued. After the shooting the father held the small crowd that had come up at bay. Then both the men escaped.

The son, Orlando Keatley, is a lawyer, 28 years old. His father, Calvin F. Keatley, is an old resident in good circumstances.

GIVES BIRTH TO TRIPLETS.

Mrs. Jerry Brown, of Broadland, Ill., six miles north of Newman, gave birth Monday to three children, two girls and a boy. The girls weighed eight pounds each, while the boy tipped the beam at seven pounds. All are alive and doing well.

DIED FOR LOVE.

Benjamin F. Cox, a prominent young Boston man loved Laura Wheelwright, and the day she was married to a young Englishman, who came over after her, Benjamin took a sip of cold paison and died.

BILL DALTON DEAD.

The Notorious Western Bandit at Last Goes Down With His Boots On.

Surrounded by a Sheriff's Posse Near Elk, I. T., He Is Killed While Trying to Escape.

An Interesting Sketch of the World's Most Famous Bandit and Outlaw—One of Ten Brothers.

Ardmore, I. T., June 14.—There's no doubt of it this time, Bill Dalton is dead, and he died with his boots on, and a six shooter in his hands. The encounter was brief but it was telling while it lasted. It occurred near Elk a few miles from here.

Ever since the famous Longview, Texas, bank robbery which occurred May 23 last special posses and United States marshals have been on the chase for the notorious bandits, who of course were said to be no others than the Dalton gang. The details of that robbery are still fresh in mind.

On the morning of May 23, a man carrying a rifle concealed under his coat handed this note to President Clemmens of the Longview bank:

"This will introduce to you Charles Speckleneyer, who wants some money and is going to have it. B. and F."

It was written in pencil legibly on the back of a printed postal. The bank president thought it a subscription to some charity, and started to ask for particulars, when the stranger pointed his rifle at him, and told him to hold up his hands. The other man rushed into the side wire door and grabbed the cash. Tom Clemmens, cashier, and other bank officials also were ordered to hold up their hands. The robbers hurriedly emptied the tills and then went into the vaults, securing $2,000.

While this was going on two confederates were in the rear alley shooting at every one who appeared. They were soon being fired upon by City Marshal Muckleroy and Deputy Marshal Will Stevens. The firing made the robbers in the bank nervous, and they hurried the bank officers out and told them to run. This was done to save their lives. Bullets flew thick and fast, and the bank men hastened around the corner with several shots flying after them. George Buckingham, who was shooting at the robbers in the alley, was shot and killed. While he was lying on the ground the robbers shot at him several times. City Marshal Muckleroy, who was shooting at another robber, received a ball in the abdomen. The robbers rode rapidly out of town shooting their rifles and displaying their money. That was the last seen of them.

Some days ago, however, word was brought to the marshals that a band of desperadoes had come in the country near Elk, and were making their headquarters with a man named Houston Wallace. When the Longview bank robbery occurred it was learned that the horses ridden by the men were stolen near Elk, also the last heard of their trail on their return from the raid they were going in the direction of this place.

Saturday morning Houston Wallace came to town, accompanied by two women. He had an unusual amount of money, and bought a wagon load of provisions, suitable for traveling with complete camp outfit. He visited the hardware store and laid in an enormous quantity of ammunition. Deputy Marshal T. Lindsey was suspicious that something was wrong, as Wallace is a man of very small means. After loading his wagon, Wallace had a large box put on from the express office. Deputy Lindsey resolved to search the outfit, and did so, finding three gallons of whisky. The large amount of ammunition and the various purchases further aroused his suspicion, and he resolved to go to Wallace's place, thinking the bank robbers were there.

The man and two women were held under arrest by Commissioner Gibbons on the whisky charge, while Deputy Lindsey secured a posse of Deputies Denton, Letherman, Booker, Reynolds, Hart, Freeman and E. W. Roberts, to raid Wallace's place. They left Ardmore Saturday night, riding by a circuitous route, and reaching Wallace's place about daylight the next morning. The house was quickly surrounded, but a woman had seen the deputies, and gave the alarm.

Dalton rushed to a rear window and leaped out, but was ordered to halt by Deputy Hart, who commanded him to stop three times. Dalton refused, and pulled his pistol, when Hart fired, striking Dalton in the left side. Dalton fell, and expired in a few moments.

Another of the band was seen at a window but escaped into a thicket near the house, where pursuit was useless.

The house was then entered and searched and over 150 letters besides numerous rolls of crisp bank bills were found.

There is not the least possibility of a doubt as to the identity of Dalton, as letters were found in his trunk, and the woman in the house with him proved to be his wife, Mrs.

Bill Dalton as He Looked Last Fall.

Dalton seems very much affected over the death of her husband, but says she always expected him to meet his death as he did. Dalton was married in California. He leaves his widow with two small girls, one of whom is a cripple.

The working up of the case and the execution reflects great credit on Deputy Lindsey, who had charge from beginning to end. The officers reached town with the body of Dalton about 6 o'clock in the evening. The streets leading to the undertaker's was thronged with an eager crowd trying to get a glimpse of the most noted outlaw in this country since the time of the James boys. The body was embalmed, to await officials from Longview, who had been wired to come. A sum of money was found in Dalton's trunk, along with a corn sack, such as is usually used by banks. The officers refuse to talk until the other two are captured. They are well-known as hard characters, and the marshals expect to effect their capture.

The body of the noted bandit was viewed at the undertaker's establishment where it was embalmed for shipment to San Fran-

TWENTY-ONE ILLUSTRATIONS OF THE BROOKLYN STRIKE IN THIS NUMBER.

HARPER'S WEEKLY

A JOURNAL OF CIVILIZATION

Vol. XXXIX.—No. 1989.

NEW YORK, SATURDAY, FEBRUARY 2, 1895.

TEN CENTS A COPY. FOUR DOLLARS A YEAR.

THE STRIKE IN BROOKLYN—FIRING AT THE MOB.—Drawn by T. Dart Walker

A Detail of the Seventh Regiment escorting Car filled with Newspaper Men on Gates Avenue, Evening of January 21st.

NO TRACE OF THE NEGRO.

Disappearance of Deputy Brown's Murderer Still a Mystery.

TOBACCO OF MONTGOMERY COUNTY

Will Be Made Into Cigars at Willis. Burglars Entered Many Houses at Lexington—Suicided.

Wharton, Texas, August 20.—(Special Correspondence.)—A veil of mystery seems to hang over the recent tragedy as to what has been the fate of the murderer of Deputy Sheriff Brown. That strip of the county in which the search for the escape has been going on is the most remote and inaccessible portion of this section. The larger part of the territory is covered with heavy timber, reinforced by thick and impenetrable undergrowth. As to local happenings a long time transpires before the matter became public property. Grave doubts are now entertained by a very large body of people as to the truth of the report that the negro escaped from the custody of the posse who had him last in charge. But people who seem to know show a very firm disinclination to discuss the whole affair and maintain that the "negro escaped." Today Constable Heartt tells The Post reporter that he is certain that the negro who committed the murder was not an escaped convict, but had been at work several days prior to the tragedy in and about town, and that he decamped suddenly from this locality about the time the murder took place. He has other matters bearing upon the subject, which he refused to let The Post representative publish.

This morning Mr. W. M. James, who has been near the scene of action and who was present with the posse when the negro was in their possession yesterday morning, tells the reporter substantially the following story:

"There were about twelve or fifteen men in the party who had the prisoner in charge; they had a rope or a chain around his neck, I think chain, for there was also a padlock on it. He was fully questioned by different men of the posse, and he was induced to confess to the killing, which he did voluntary, saying in brief that while the deputy was in advance horseback, he (the prisoner) having a pistol concealed in his bosom, took a favorable opportunity and shot the deputy in the back; the first shot disabled him; he fired twice with the pistol and taking the dead man's gun, fired once again into the body. He told where he hid the gun, etc."

James says that he lingered only about ten or fifteen minutes with the posse and firmly maintains that he does not know what became of the prisoner after he left.

Sheriff Rich returned from Spanish Camp last evening and brought the two negroes arrested at that point by M. S. Anderson, and supposed to be two of the escaped convicts.

This morning Adam Howard, a colored man, brought in a negro who confesses to being one of the escapes from the State farm in Matagorda county.

Sheriff Rich has gone down in the lower precinct to the scene of the recent tragedy.

At 5 p. m. Sheriff Rich returned from the lower precinct, where he went this morning, as indicated above, in search of some traces of the murderer. The sheriff says though he interrogated several parties no one can furnish him the least information as to what has become of the escape. All affirm that the prisoner escaped. There are, however several rumors afloat, the last one—which is given the most credence—is that the negro is alive and under a strong guard, hidden away and that tonight the crowd will meet and take a vote on the disposition to be made of him—whether he will hang or be brought to the county seat and placed safely in jail to await the action of the courts.

W.F.L.

Montgomery County Tobacco.

Willis, Texas, August 19.—Contractor Leslie has resumed work on the brick tobacco warehouse for T. W. Smith, after a suspension of work of two weeks on account of being out of brick. The building will be ready for business in thirty days. It is rumored there is a project on foot by which this building will be converted into a large cigar factory. It is the object of those interested to form a joint stock company with sufficient capital to buy up all of last year's crop of tobacco here and employ about twenty cigarmakers, putting out 50,000 cigars per month. The demand for Willis cigars has increased to such an extent that it is impossible for Blohm Brothers to fill the orders. The fact that these men have never had a salesman on [illegible]

barrel and started to charr it on the inside; when he dropped the fire into it the gas exploded, the flames leaping out and completely enveloping the sailor's body, burning his breast, left arm and mouth severely before assistance could reach here. The injuries are not dangerous, but painful and precludes the possibility of his working for some time. Elfstone's home is in Galveston, where he has a family, and he had only shipped with the Perkins yesterday, having came from Galveston on the Annie Root.

PREACHERS. SUSPENDED.

Investigating Committee Deem a Trial Necessary.

Galveston, Texas, August 20.—The committee appointed by Bishop J. C. Keener to investigate the reports in circulation in reference to Rev. E. H. Harmon and Rev. W. Wimberly has been in session for two days and concluded its inquiries at 10:30 o'clock tonight. The committee was careful and thorough in its investigation. More than a score of witnesses were examined, and information was sought from all available sources. After considering the case fully the committee rendered the following decision:

"We, the committee appointed by Bishop J. C. Keener to investigate the rumors and reports seriously affecting the moral and religious characters of Rev. E. H. Harmon, presiding elder of the Brenham district, and Rev. W. Wimberly, preacher in charge of Brenham station, have made thorough inquiry into these matters, and from the evidence before us we deem a trial necessary. Therefore, in due time, bills of charges and specifications will be formulated and copies of the same will be furnished the accused in time to allow them ample opportunity for the preparation of their defense." Signed by G. C. Rankin, O. T. Hotchkiss, C. A. Lamar.

As a result of this decision the gentlemen accused are suspended from the ministry until their cases are finally disposed of by the Texas annual conference which meets in Brenham, Texas, on the 4th day of next December.

Seth Ward,
Chairman Committee.

Anti-Class Resolutions.

Halletsville, Texas, August 20.—The Negro Anti-Class Legislation club of Lavaca county at their meeting here Saturday passed the following resolutions, which were handed to your correspondent for publication in The Post:

1. That we, the members of the Colored Men's conference, will not support any party or any candidate who aspires for representative or any office where the powers invested in him for control of the same and will not give equal representation to the negroes as a race as that of any other race.

2. That if any party or candidate uses the slightest attempt of discrimination against the negroes politically as a race that we as members of the Anti-Class Legislation organization will not support such party or candidate.

3. That it shall be the object of this conference to use every effort to secure recognition for negroes of Lavaca county.

W. J. Stephens, Chairman.
W. W. Scott, Secretary.

Corpus Christi Cullings.

Corpus Christi, Texas, August 20.—Engineer Ripley of Galveston arrived at Aransas Pass yesterday and will proceed at once to make a survey of the old channel and the jetty work now under construction.

Another new quarry has been opened seven miles this side of Laredo, making four quarries in all now being operated.

Contractor Clarke says from now on twenty-five carloads of rock will arrive here daily.

A few nights ago a Mexican woman on the bluff had trunk robbed of $130 in money, diamonds valued at $300 and all her wearing apparel. The empty trunk was found next day in the Arrayo. No clue to the robbers.

Major James Moore of Hondo City left here yesterday morning for Hebbvonville, where he will receive 1000 head of cattle purchased for himself and John Merriman from Ed Corkill.

Cuero's New Compress.

Cuero, Texas, August 20.—An event of no small value to the commercial importance of Cuero transpired yesterday evening when the new compress began to press the fleecy. A crowd of citizens interested in the city's growth assembled, and at 4 o'clock the lever was pulled. The press worked as though many a bale had gone the same way before. The compress was built entirely by local capital and is complete in every detail. The visitors were regaled by the management with barbacued meats, drinkables, etc. This scores another success for Cuero's enterprising citizens.

Today is the ninth anniversary of the great storm of 1886, which devastated this section to such an alarming extent.

The many friends of The Post and Mr. C. S. E. Holland read with pleasure the announcement that he had assumed his former relations with the paper. He is a [illegible]

WESLEY HARDIN KILLED.

Another of the Few Bad Men Laid Low in a Saloon.

HE WAS SHOT BY A CONSTABLE

Whose Life He Had Threatened and Who Acted in Self-Defense—Hardin's Record of Crime.

[illegible] arrested him a few nights before. One word brought on another and it ended by his telling Sellman to get out in the middle of the street and he would come soon and come "a smoking."

Sellman waited for him several hours but he did not come out. Then Sellman went into the saloon with a friend and stepping up to the bar near Hardin they both watched one another through the mirror in front. After Sellman had taken his drink he says Hardin reached for his gun and he pulled his own and turned loose. The first shot crashed through Hardin's brain and killed him instantly. He received two more shots while falling to the floor. He had a gun in each hip pocket but did not get a chance to pull either. Thus ended the career of the man who has for several months been feared by the public in general.

Constable Sellman is an old officer and has a record as a killer of smugglers and thieves. Some years ago he fought a band of cattle thieves in Dona Ana county, New Mexico, and killed two and captured the rest, four in all. He killed Bass Outlaw in this city a year ago. Outlaw was a deputy United States marshal and had come to Texas in such a hurry that he had neglected to bring his right name along, and in an emergency picked up the one he died under in Western Texas. Outlaw was killed by Sellman in self-defense a few seconds after the former had killed Ranger M. C. Kittridge.

Wes Hardin, as he was familiarly known over Southwest Texas, was easily the most noted of the living Texas desperadoes. Hardin's early career was spent in De Witt county, and he was a terror in that section in the 70's, or until he was sent to the penitentiary. He was sentenced to fifteen years, but got a time allowance for good conduct, which enabled him to secure his discharge eighteen months earlier than would have been the case had he been compelled to serve out his full time.

After spending some time in Cuero and afterwards at Gonzales, where he nearly got into trouble in the excitement of the county election last year, he came to El Paso about three months ago. On his way out here he stopped in San Antonio and renewed many old acquaintances of former days. During his stay in San Antonio he was sober and quiet, but there was the same dare-devil look in his eyes and the same old restless spirit burning inside of him, which indicated to his old acquaintances that he would soon break out again. He was a prominent figure around the vicinity of Main Plaza and Soledad street for several days.

Soon after his arrival here he became the leading figure in a case where in it was attempted to induce a fugitive from American justice to come back to this side of the Rio Bravo, and which resulted in the killing of the fugitive on the bridge that connects El Paso with Juarez. Hardin, however, could not long restrain his old propensity to drink and gamble, and when in his cups was very quarrelsome and threatening.

One night shortly after his arrival he made a losing of $75 against a crap game in one of the gambling houses. Being exasperated at his loss he pulled his pistol and compelled the dealer to hand him the money back. He then walked out to the middle of the room, flourishing his pistol and declared if any — — didn't like his style, let him say so and "get out in the road."

On another occasion, in a poker game with four men, he lost a big pot and compelled the winner to give it back to him.

Nearly everybody got out of his way when he was in an ugly mood, and this led him to believe he was cock of the walk and bore a charmed life.

Hardin was the son of a Methodist preacher, and was born in Trinity county, being 45 years of age at the time of his death. He was sent to the penitentiary

In 1868 John Wesley Hardin entered upon his career of crime and bloodshed at the early age of 17. At that time originated the Taylor-Sutton feud; his nerve and daring soon placed him at the head of the Taylor faction, and between the years of 1868 and 1874 forty or more of the Sutton faction were extirminated, sixteen deaths being laid at Hardin's door. Two years after the conception of the feud Hardin became the leader of seventeen desperadoes, who terrorized and controlled the town of Comanche at intervals, for two years or more openly defying law and order. The gang did not confine their operations to the town of Comanche alone, but roamed over the counties of Comanche, Gonzales and DeWitt, stealing cattle, demanding supplies at the points of their pistols, and for excitement exterminating all stray members of the Sutton crowd who came across their paths.

In February of 1874 while Hardin and his crowd were carcusing in a saloon at Comanche Deputy Sheriff Webb of Brown county rode up and entered the saloon by the back door. Seeing himself outnumbered he attempted to pass through, but was accosted by Hardin, who demanded to know if he had a warrant for any of his (Hardin's) crowd and if he expected to execute it.

Upon Webb replying in the affirmative Hardin drew his gun and Webb gamely gave up his life in defense of his duty. This aroused public indignation to such a pitch that Hardin became an outlaw and a price was set on his head. Shortly before this time he killed Captain Jack Helm, a man of note in his day, who was in command of a Ranger company which wherever it went in Southern Texas left a trail of blood behind it.

Helm got into a dispute with a 14-year-old boy, of whose father he was the murderer. While Helm was in the act of stabbing the boy with a knife Hardin's pistol cracked and Helm turned up his toes. The Rangers took after him and run him near Yorktown, but Hardin killed three of his pursuers and escaped.

After the killing of Deputy Sheriff Webb Hardin's band dwindled to a mere handful and owing to vigilance of the Rangers the leader was forced to seek safety in flight. Going to Jacksonville, Fla., in 1876 he entered the butcher business under the assumed name of Swain. In six month's time his whereabouts became known to detectives, who had been on his trail. Becoming uneasy, the fugitive started for his old haunts in Texas and was captured and brought back to Comanche, tried for the killing of Webb, receiving a sentence of twenty-five years penal servitude. Seventeen years of this was served before being pardoned by the governor.

During his confinement he applied his leisure hours to the study of law and upon his release was admitted to the bar at Pecos. He came to this city last October in the capacity of attorney for J. P. Miller, who was to be tried on the charge of conspiracy against the life of Sheriff Bud Frazier of that place.

His next move was to send word to a local saloon man that he wanted to be his partner and he, thinking discretion the better part of valor, gave him a half interest next day. Going to a local wholesale liquor house he ordered all the wet goods he thought necessary and had it charged. The liquor house not only charged this, but told him the store was at his disposition whenever he wanted it. He published a card to the effect that while he was in the saloon he would see that belligerents had a fair deal and no dead sure thing would go ' 'he knew of it. In consequence the saloon was given a wide berth and soon closed for want of patronage.

Hardin was well connected and has many relatives in all parts of the State. Three hundred and sixty pages of closely written manuscript was found in his trunk today, which purports to be a history of his life. The police refuse to allow any one to read it, and will hold it until the arrival of relatives, who will reach here tomorrow. Joe Hardin, a brother of John Wesley, was lynched in Comanche in 1874, principally because he was a brother of the latter,

from Lampasas county in 1876 for the killing of the sheriff of Comanche county, who was attempting to arrest him. He was released in 1894, and stood his last trial for murder in Cuero in the same year. The jury failed to agree at the trial, and as it was an old case in which it was difficult to secure testimony, the case was subsequently dismissed.

In his personal appearance John Wesley Hardin was as typical a Texas desperado of the earliest type as was ever portrayed in the dime novel. He was of medium weight, nearly six feet tall, straight as an arrow and light complexioned, with an eye as keen as a hawk. As an expert shot he was the peer of either King Fisher or Ben Thompson in their palmiest days.

He could shoot as quickly and aim as straight as either of them. It was almost sure death for anyone who was in front of his gun when Hardin drew a bead.

Seventeen scalps are said to have dangled from his belt and it is likely that the number of human lives that he has taken will exceed that number.

Louis Dreyfous, formerly a San Antonio gambler, was dealing monte once at Cuero in the early days of Hardin's career. Hardin walked up to the table where Dreyfous sat. He wore two pistols and a very boyish look. Dreyfous had heard of Hardin's exploits but did not know him by sight and did not recognize Hardin when the latter walked up to where the game was being dealt. Hardin asked for a "lay out," but Dreyfous remarked that he was too fresh and did not need so many sixshooters.

Hardin laughed his peculiar laugh and the men about the table began to fall back. Dreyfous asked what was the matter, when one of the players whispered in his left ear, "Why, you blasted idiot, that is Wes Hardin." Dreyfous ran out of the room as fast as his legs could carry him and has never been seen since in that vicinity.

Fortunately for him Hardin considered Dreyfous' ignorance as a good joke, called for a fresh dealer and the game proceeded until Hardin "busted" the game.

Hardin had a National reputation as a desperado and the news of his tragic taking off is being sent all over the world by the enterprising newspaper correspondents.

RELIGIOUS.

Meeting at Georgetown.

Georgetown, Texas, August 20.—The three meetings held at the old fair grounds Sunday by the First Baptist church were well attended and much interest manifested. The singing, conducted by Val C. Hart of Galveston is a feature He has organized a splendid choir and they succeed in making the woods ring with harmonious melody. The grounds are well shaded and watered with cool springs. About two dozen families occupy tents on the grounds and others are expected to join them this week.

Rev. Isaac Sellers, the pastor, who is a splendid outdoor speaker, is doing every thing in his power to make the meeting a grand success.

Fifteen Accessions.

Caldwell, Texas, August 20.—Rev. A. S. Blackwood has just returned from Cook's Point, where he has been engaged for the past ten days in conducting a camp meeting. He reports fifteen accessions to the Methodist church, twenty-five reclamations and more than forty who expressed their intention to lead a better life. He will begin next Friday a camp meeting on the Yegua in Lee county.

Religious News.

Comanche—The Baptists are holding a protracted meeting near Whattville under the auspices of Rev. T. S. Bomar.

Comanche—The third quarterly conference of the Comanche Methodist church met in this city today.

Palestine—A big Methodist camp meeting is going on at Brushy creek, sixteen vW*S2fafiaokr fd..eGfi Pa,fl(z miles north of this city. Presiding Elder [illegible]

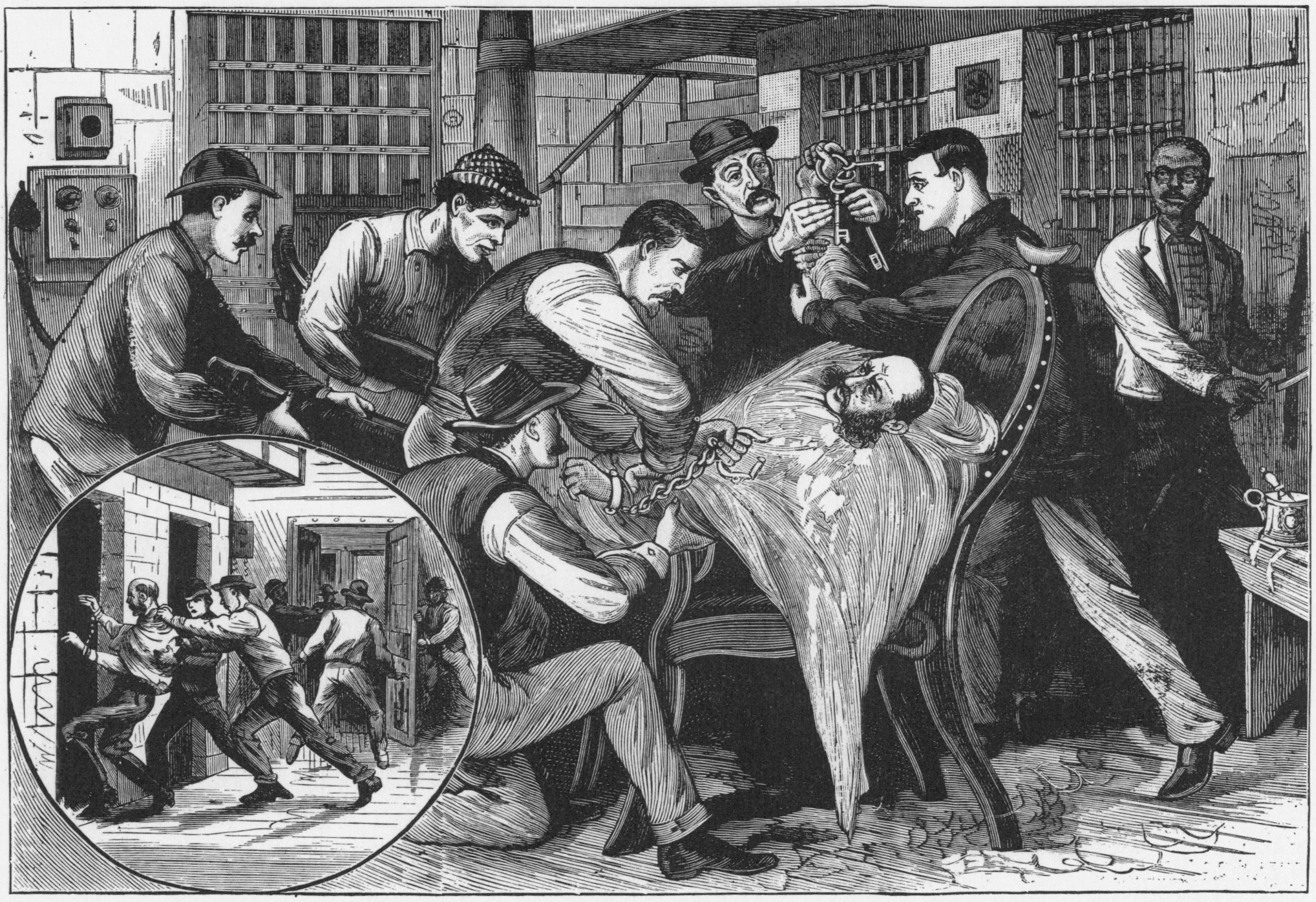

HANDCUFFED THE TURNKEY IN THE JAIL BARBER SHOP.

SIX PRISONERS FREE THEMSELVES IN A DARING MANNER AT TOLEDO, O., AUG. 17—HOW THEY SECURED THE JAIL KEYS AND LOCKED TURNKEY MOSHER IN A CELL.

DESPERADO JOHN WESLEY HARDIN SLAIN.

THE MOST NOTED OF TEXAS MAN-KILLERS SLAIN AT EL PASO, AUG. 19, BY CONSTABLE JOHN SELLMAN—HOW THE KING OF SOUTHWESTERN MAN-KILLERS HAS FINALLY FALLEN A VICTIM TO VIOLENCE.

The Sunday Inter Ocean.

VOL. XXV., NO. 19. CHICAGO, SUNDAY, APRIL 12, 1896.—FORTY-FOUR PAGES. PRICE FIVE CENTS.

THE CONFESSION OF H. H. HOLMES

Murderer Whose Crimes Have Shocked the Civilized World Speaks.

HIS VICTIMS NUMBER TWENTY-SEVEN

Standing Within the Shadow of the Gallows, This Monster Avows He Tells the Truth.

BELIEVES HIMSELF TO BE A MORAL DEGENERATE

With the Nicest Regard to Details and with Apparent Candor He Narrates a Story of Self-Incrimination.

In the following columns The Inter Ocean presents the confession of H. H. Holmes. The narrative of this man's acts as given to the public by the press in fragments from time to time, as developments have permitted, has been the criminal sensation of the age. Heretofore Holmes has maintained the silence of a desperate, defiant criminal, and all facts regarding his career have been dug from the graves of his victims or sifted from the ashes found in his extemporized crematories. Now, however, the man has spoken, and such a gory flood of self-accusation has never before been let loose in a land of schools and churches.

This remarkable statement was secured from the condemned criminal by the New York Journal, and by special arrangement with that paper is published simultaneously in The Inter Ocean. The authenticity of the confession is assured by the following fac simile statement of Holmes himself:

The following statement was written by me in Philadelphia Co Prison for the Journal of N.Y. as a true & accurate confession in all particulars. It is the only confession of my fearful crimes I have ever made or will make. I write it fully appreciating all the horrors it contains & how it condemns me before the world.
Signed H H Holmes
April 9th 1896

Wherever blanks occur in the confession names have been omitted pending investigation by the proper legal authorities in each case.

This article was copyrighted April 10, 1896, by the Morning Journal Association of New York. Any unauthorized publication of the whole or part of this matter will be made the subject of vigorous legal prosecution.

Philadelphia County Prison, April 8.—"During the past few months the desire has been repeatedly expressed that I make a detailed confession of all the grave crimes that have, with such marvelous skill, been traced out and brought home to me. I have been tried for murder, convicted and sentenced; the first step of my execution upon May 7, namely, the reading of my death warrant, has been carried out, and it now seems a fitting time, if ever, to make known the details of the twenty-seven murders, of which it would be useless for me longer to say that I am not guilty.

"In the face of the overwhelming amount of proof that has been brought together, not only in one, but in every case, and because in this confession I speak only of cases that have been thus investigated, and of no other, I trust it will not give rise to a supposition that I am still guilty of other murders, the facts of which I am withholding. To those inclined to think thus, I will say that the detectives have gone over my entire life. Hardly a day or an act has escaped their closest scrutiny, and to judge that I am guilty of more than these cases, which they have traced out, is to cast discredit upon their work. So marvelous has been the success of these men into whose hands the proving of my guilt was given, that, as I look back over their year's work, it seems almost impossible that men gifted with only human intelligence could have been so skillful, and I feel that I can here call attention to what the prosecution at the close of my trial was denied, the pleasure of stating concerning their ability, though no word of mine can fittingly express what the world at large owes to these impartial and untiring representatives, and more especially to Assistant District Attorney Barlow and Detective Frank Geyer, for it is principally owing to their unerring judgment, skill, and perseverance, that in a few days I am to be placed beyond the power of committing other, and, perhaps, if possible, more horrible wrongs. Surely justice, if always attended by such servants as these, could no longer, in the sense of making a mistake, be appropriately portrayed as being blind.

"I am moved to make this confession for a variety of reasons, but among them are not those of bravado or desire to parade my wrong-doings before the public gaze, and he who reads the following lines will, I beg, make a distinction between such motives and a determination upon my part to enter plainly and minutely into the details of each case without favor toward myself; and, having done so, I have chosen to make it public by publishing it in The Inter Ocean.

"A word as to the motives or causes that have led to the commission of these many crimes, and I will proceed to the most difficult and distasteful task of my life, the setting forth in all its horrid nakedness the narrative of the premeditated killing of many human beings, and the unsuccessful attempt to take the lives of others, thus branding myself as the most detestable criminal of modern times; a task so hard and distasteful that beside it the certainty that in a few days I am to be hanged by the neck until I am dead, seems but a pastime.

"Acquired homicidal mania—no cause, save the occasional opportunity for pecuniary gain, occasioned my crimes, and, in advancing this theory, at this time, I do not do so with the expectation of a mitigation of public condemnation, or that it will in any way read in my favor. Had this been my intention, I should have considered it at the time of my trial, and had it used as my defense.

"All criminologists who have examined me here seem to be unanimous in the opinion they have formed, that while I was committing crime, these abnormal symptoms were not present, but that they commenced to develop after my arrest. Two years ago I was thoroughly examined by four men of marked ability, and by them pronounced as being both mentally and physically a normal and healthy man. Today I have every attribute of a degenerate; a moral idiot.

"Is it possible that the crimes, instead of being the result of these abnormal conditions, are in themselves the occasion of the degeneracy?

"Even at the time of my arrest in 1894, no defects were noticeable, under the searching Bertillon system of measurements to which I was subjected; but later, and more noticeably within the last few months, these defects have increased with startling rapidity, as is made known to me by each succeeding examination, until I have become thankful that I am no longer allowed a mirror with which to note my rapidly deteriorating condition. Nature, ever kind, provides in this, as in the primary forms of insanity, where the sufferer believes himself always sane, that unless called to his attention, he does not notice his infirmity, nor suffer therefrom.

"The principal defects that have thus far developed, and which are all established signs of degeneracy, are a decided prominence upon one side of my head and a corresponding diminution upon the other side; a marked deficiency of one side of my nose and of one ear, together with an abnormal increase of each upon the opposite side; a difference of one and one-half inches in the length of my arms and an equal shortening of one leg from knee to heel; also a most malevolent distortion of one side of my face, and one eye, so marked and terrible that in writing of it for publication Hall Caine, the novelist, although I wore a beard at the time to conceal it as best I could, described that side of my face as marked by a deep line of crime, and as being that of the devil. So apparent were these peculiarities that an expert criminologist in the employ of the United States government, who had never previously seen me, said, within thirty seconds after entering my cell: "I know you are guilty."

"Would it not, then, be the height of folly for me to die without speaking, if only for the purpose of justifying the scientific deductions, and accrediting what is due to those to whom society owes so much for bringing me to justice, and also making it easy for them to convict certain ones alluded to herein, whom at the present time they can do little more than suspect, in consequence of their frantic efforts during the last summer to shield themselves at my expense?

"The first taking of human life was a torturing thought. This, it will be understood, was before my constant wrong-doing. I had become wholly deaf to the promptings of conscience; for, prior to this, I beg to be believed in stating that I had never sinned so heavily, either by thought or deed. Later, like the man-eating tiger of the tropics, whose appetite for blood has once been aroused, I roamed about the world, seeking whom I could destroy.

"Think of the list that follows—men and women, young girls and innocent children, blotted out by one monster's hand, and you, my reader of a tender and delicate nature, will do well to read no further, for I shall in no way spare myself, and he who reads to the end, if he be charitable, will say, in the words of the district attorney, when the evidence of all these many crimes had been collected and placed before him by his trusty assistants, 'God help such a man!' If uncharitable, or only just, will he not rather say, 'May he be utterly damned,' and is it not almost sufficient to cause one to doubt the wisdom of Providence that such a man should have so long been allowed to live? If so, I earnestly pray that this condemnation and censure may not extend to those whose only crime has been that they knew and trusted, aye, in some instances, loved me, and who today are more deserving of the world's compassion than censure.

"Dr. Russell was a tenant in the Chicago building recently renamed Castle. During a controversy concerning the non-payment of rent due me I struck him to the floor with a heavy chair, and he, with one cry for help, ending in a groan of anguish, ceased to breathe. The quarrel and death occurred in a small outer office, and, as soon as I realized that my blow had been a fatal one, and I had recovered somewhat from the horror of having still another victim's blood upon my hands, I was forced to look about for some safe means of concealing the crime. I locked the doors of the office, and my first intention was to dispose of the body to a Chicago medical college, from one of whose officers I had previously obtained dissecting material, as they believed, but in reality to be used in insurance work.

"I found it difficult, if not impossible, to thus dispose of the body, and I was directed to call upon a person to whom I sold bodies, and whose name I withhold, but which I have confided to parties in whom I have confidence. To him I sold this man's body, as well as others at later dates. In short, be it understood that in each instance, when the manner of the disposal of their remains is not otherwise specified, it will be understood that they were turned over to him, he paying me from $25 to $45 for each body; and right easily could he, during the recent investigations, have gone from room to room in the building, when each was more or less gruesomely familiar to him. It is not necessary for me to add that the efforts of his friends to shield

HERMAN MUDGETT (H. H. HOLMES.)
(The arch fiend, murderer of more than a score of men, women, and children, convicted for the killing of Benjamin F. Pitzel. Condemned to pay the penalty of death May 7 next.)

him, when it became evident that he had talked too freely for his own safety, should not have saved him from being compelled to turn over the remains of these persons for decent burial, or to point out the various places where they were sold.

Mrs. Julia Connor.

"The killing of Mrs. Julia Connor was, to a certain extent, due to a criminal operation performed by —— and —— who were cognizant of and partly responsible for both the operation and the death. A reference to almost any newspaper of August, 1895, will give the minute details. The horrors of this case were worked out by the detectives, therefore making it unnecessary to repeat it here. The death of Pearl, her little daughter, was caused by poison; —— and —— were equally responsible for its administration, although it was at my instigation that it was done. I believed the child was old enough to remember her mother's sickness and death. The other parties wished at first to place the child in the care of their aged parents, who lived south of the city, but were overruled by my opposition. Owing to the suddenness of Mrs. Connor's death, a certain note of considerable value, well secured by property south of the "Castle," was uncollectable, and at the time of my death it will be sent to such of her relatives as it may appear have the greater right to receive it.

Charles Cole.

"The next case is that of Charles Cole, a Southern speculator. After considerable correspondence, this man came to Chicago, and I enticed him into the 'Castle,' where, while I was engaging him in conversation, —— struck him a most vicious blow on the head with a piece of gas pipe. So heavy was the blow that it not only caused his death without a groan and hardly a movement, but it crushed his skull to such an extent that his body was almost useless, to ——. This was the first instance in which I know of this confederate having committed murder, though in several other instances he was fully as guilty as myself, and if possible more heartless and bloodthirsty, and I have no doubt he is still engaged in the same nefarious work.

"Lizzie" the Seventh Victim.

"A domestic, named 'Lizzie,' was the seventh victim. She for a time worked in the 'Castle' restaurant and I soon learned that —— was paying her too close attention, and, fearing lest it should progress so far that it would necessitate his leaving my employ, I thought it wise to end the life of the girl. This I did by calling her to my office and suffocating her in a vault, of which so much has since been printed. She was the first victim that died there. Before her death I compelled her to write letters to her relatives and to state that she had left Chicago for a Western state, and should not return. A few months ago the prosecution, believing from certain letters purporting to have been written by her that she was alive, showed me its willingness to give me a fair trial by having this publicly known, she being a witness that I could have used to great advantage in the Pitzel case.

Miss Emeline Cigrande.

"Soon after this Miss Emeline Cigrande was sent to me by a Chicago firm to fill the vacancy of stenographer. She had formerly been employed at Dwight, Ill., where she had become acquainted with a man who visited her from time to time while she was in my employ. She was finally engaged to him, and the day was set for their wedding. This attachment was particularly obnoxious to me, both because Miss Cigrande had become almost indispensable to me in my office work, and because she had become my mistress, as well as stenographer. I endeavored upon several occasions to take the life of the young man, and, failing, I finally resolved that I would kill her instead, and upon the day of their wedding, even after cards had been sent out announcing that it had occurred, she came to my office to bid me good-by. While there I asked her to step inside the vault for some papers for me. There I detained her, telling her that if she would write her husband that at the last moment she had known that it would be impossible to live happily with him and consequently had left Chicago in such a way that search for her would be useless, I would take her to a distant city and live openly with her as my wife. She was very willing to do this, and prepared to leave the vault on completing the letter, only to find that the door would never again be opened until she had ceased to suffer the tortures of a slow and lingering death.

He Loses Three Victims.

"Here follows an unsuccessful attempt to commit a triple murder for the $90 that —— would have given me for the bodies of the intended victims, who were three young women, working in my restaurant upon Milwaukee avenue, Chicago. That these women lived to tell of their experience to the police last summer is due to my foolishly trying to chloroform all of them at one and the same time. By their combined strength they overpowered me and ran screaming into the street, clad only in their night robes. To this attempt to kill could very justly be added my attempt to take the lives of Mrs. Pitzel and two of her children at a later date, thus increasing the total of my victims, as it was no fault of mine that they escaped.

Anna Van Tassaud.

"My next attempt was carried out with more caution. The victim was a very beautiful young woman named Anna Van Tassaud, whom I induced to come into my fruit and confectionery store, and, when she was once with me, I compelled her to live there for a time, threatening her with death if she appeared before my customers. A little later I killed her by administering ferrocyanide of potassium. The location of this store was such that it would have been hazardous to have sent out a large box containing a body, and I therefore buried her remains in the store basement, and from day to day during the investigations at the 'Castle' I expected to hear that excavations had been made there as well.

Robert Latimer.

"Robert Latimer, a man who had for some years been in my employ as a janitor, was my next victim. Several years previous, before I had ever taken human life, he had known of certain insurance work I had engaged in, and when, in after years, he sought to extort money from me, his own death and the sale of his body was the recompense meted out to him. I confined him within the secret room and slowly starved him to death. Of this room and its secret gas supply and muffled windows and doors, sufficient has already been printed. Finally, needing its use for another victim, and because his pleadings had become almost unbearable, I ended his life. The partial excavation in the walls of this room found by the police was caused by Latimer's endeavoring to escape by tearing away the solid brick and mortar with his unaided fingers.

Miss Anna Betts.

"The succeeding case was that of Miss Anna Betts and was caused by my purposely substituting a poisonous drug in a prescription that had been sent to my drugstore to be compounded. I believed that, as it was known that I was a physician, I should be called in to witness her death, and as she lived very near the store. This was not the case, however, as the regular physician was in attendance at the time. The prescription, still on file at the Castle Drug Store, should be considered by the authorities if they are still inclined to attribute this death to causes that reflect on Miss Betts' moral character.

Miss Gertrude Connor.

"The death of Miss Gertrude Connor of Muscatine, Iowa, though not the next in order of occurrence, is so similar to the last that the description of one suffices for both, save in this respect: Miss Connor left Chicago immediately, but did not die until she had reached her home in Muscatine. Perhaps these two cases show more plainly than any other the light regard I had for the lives of my fellow beings.

Warner Reduced to Ashes.

"The next death was that of a man named Warner, the originator of the Warner's Glass-Bending Company, and there again I realized a very large sum of money, which, prior to his death, had been deposited in two Chicago banks, nearly all of which I secured by means of two checks made out and properly signed by him for a small sum each. To these I later added the word 'thousand' and the necessary ciphers, and, by passing them through the bank where I had a regular open account, I promptly realized the money, save a small amount not covered by the checks, in the Park National Bank, northwest corner of Washington and Dearborn streets, in that city.

"It will be remembered that the remains of a large kiln made of fire brick were found in a basement. It had been built under Mr. Warner's supervision for the purpose of exhibiting his patents. It was so arranged that in less than a minute after turning on a jet of crude oil, atomized with steam, the entire kiln would be filled with a colorless flame, so intensely hot that iron would be melted therein. It was into this kiln that I induced Mr. Warner to go with me, under the pretense of my wishing certain minute explanations of the process, and then, stepping outside, as he believed, to get some tools, I closed the door and turned on both the oil and steam to their full extent. In a short time not even the bones of my victim remained. The coat found underneath the kiln was the one he took off before going therein.

Mr. Rogers, a Chicago Banker.

"In 1891 I associated myself in business with a young Englishman, who, by his own admission, had been guilty of all other forms of wrong doing save murder, and presumably of that as well, to manipulate certain real estate securities we held, so as to have them secure us a good commercial rating. It was an easy matter for him, and he was equally able to interest certain English capitalists in certain patents, so that it seemed that in the near future our greatest concern would be how to dispose of the money that seemed about to be showered upon us. By an unforeseen occurrence our rating was destroyed, and it became necessary to at once raise a large sum, and this was done by enticing a wealthy Chicago banker named Rogers from a Wisconsin town, in such a manner that he could have left no intelligence with whom his business was to be. To bring him to the 'Castle' and into the secret room, under the pretense that our patents were there, was easy, much more so than to force him to sign checks, and drafts for $70,000, which he had prepared. At first he refused to do so, stating that his liberty that we offered him in exchange would be useless to him without his money, and that he was too old to hope to make another fortune. Finally, by alternately starving him, and nauseating him with the gas, I made him sign the securities, all of which were converted into money, and by ——s' skill as a forger, in such a manner as to leave no trace of their having passed through our hands, I waited with much curiosity to see what proposition —— would advance for the disposal of our prisoner, as I well knew that he, no more than I, contemplated giving him his liberty. Evidently —— waited with equal expectancy for me to suggest what should be done, and I finally made preparation to allow him to leave the building, thus forcing —— to suggest that he be killed. I would consent to this only upon the condition that he should administer the chloroform and leave me to dispose of the body as part of the work. In this way I was enabled to keep —— in ignorance of my dealings with ——.

"That evening this large sum of money was divided between us.

This Victim's Name Is Forgot.

"The next case is that of a woman whose name has passed from my memory, who came to the Castle restaurant to board. —— was conducting the restaurant at the time, and immediately became very much infatuated with the woman, who, he heard, was a widow, and wealthy. —— was married and his wife occasionally came to the restaurant when this boarder was there, which did not

MINNIE WILLIAMS.
(One of Holmes' victims, who was murdered for her property in Fort Worth, Texas.)

tend to decrease a family quarrel which for quite a time had threatened the —— family with disruption. Finally he came to me for advice, and I was very willing to have him in my power, that I could later use him if need be. I suggested that he live with the woman in the 'Castle' for a time, and later, if this life became unpleasant to him, we would kill her and divide her wealth. Although —— showed no disposition to spare me in the recent investigations, and also deserved death for this and other crimes, it is but fair to say that at first he was not willing to enter into this arrangement, and would probably today not be guilty of murder but for my influence. As I had anticipated, he soon tired of the 'Castle' life, and suggested that it was time to take his companion's life. This was done by my administering chloroform while he controlled her violent struggles. The name of this woman was given to the authorities by ——'s father.

"I can well judge of his anxiety and concern when his parents unwittingly opened up such a dangerous topic. It was the body of this woman within the long, coffin-shaped box that was taken into the 'Castle' late in 1893, of which —— told the police. Is it to be wondered at that he should have remembered it?

The Williams Sisters.

"In order that these deaths may be more fully understood, it is necessary for me to state that what has been said by Miss Williams' Southern relatives regarding her pure and Christian life should be believed; also that prior to her meeting me in 1893 she was a virtuous woman, thus rendering truthful the statement of Charles Goldthwaite of Boston, that he had never known her otherwise than as an intimate friend of his wife's, and that in June, 1893, he did not wire her a considerable sum of money to Chicago, in response to a demand for the same from her; that she was not temporarily insane at a hotel opposite the Pullman building, Chicago, May 20 to 23, 1893; was not a little later secluded in the Baptist Hospital in Chicago, under the name of Mrs. Williams; was not still later in a retreat at Milwaukee, and that she did not kill her sister and threaten to kill her nurse, who had her in charge at No. 1220 Wrightwood avenue, Chicago. All these statements it gives me a certain amount of satisfaction to retract, thereby undoing, so far as I can, these additional wrongs I have heaped upon her name.

"I first met Miss Williams in New York, in 1888, where she knew me as Edward Hatch, and later under the same name in Denver, as has been testified to by certain young women who recognized my photograph. Early in 1893 I was again introduced to her as H. H. Holmes. She had applied for a position as a stenographer. Soon after entering my employ I induced her to give me $2,500 in money and to transfer to me by deed much Southern real

THE HOLMES CASTLE AT SIXTY-THIRD AND WALLACE STREETS.
(Built and arranged for a human slaughter-house. Most of the Chicago murders committed by Holmes were done in this building. Since the arrest of Holmes it has been remodeled.)

estate, and a little later to live with me as my wife; all this being easily accomplished, owing to her innocent and childlike nature, she hardly knowing right from wrong in such matters. Thereafter I succeeded in securing two checks from her for $25 each, and I also learned that she had a sister, Nannie, in Texas, who was heir to some property. I induced Miss Williams to have her come to Chicago on a visit. Upon her arrival I met her at the depot and took her to the 'Castle,' telling her Miss Williams was there. It was an easy matter to force her to assign to me all she possessed. After that she was immediately killed, in order that no one in or about the 'Castle' should know of her having been there, save ——, who burned her clothing. It was the footprint of Nannie Williams, as was later demonstrated, by that most astute lawyer and detective, Mr. Capps of Fort Worth, that was found upon the painted surface of the vault door. It was made during her violent struggle before her death. It was also easy to give to Miss Williams a delayed letter, stating that her sister's proposed visit had been given up, and also by intercepting later letters and substituting others to keep her from learning that her sister had left the South.

Her Day of Doom Arrives.

"Having secured all the money and property Miss Williams had, it was time that she was killed. Owing to a fire that occurred in the 'Castle,' I was unable to resort to the usual method in taking her life, and, after some delay, I took her to Momence, Ill., about Nov. 15, 1892, registering at a hotel near the postoffice, under an assumed name, but as man and wife. My intention was to quickly kill in some sure manner, but a freight wreck that occurred on the outskirts of the town the day following my arrival there, which, out of curiosity, I visited, brought me into contact with a passenger conductor, Peck, who knew me, and I therefore abandoned my plans, but later returned and took the girl eight miles east of Momence on a freight line little used, ended her life with poison, and buried her body in the basement of the house spoken of at about the time of the Irvington discoveries in 1895.

"It was a great wonder that the body was not found at that time, if the detectives in reality went to that location. Nothing would, at the present time, give me so much satisfaction as to know that her body had been properly buried. I would be willing to give up the few remaining days I have to live if by so doing this would be accomplished. Because of her spotless life, before she knew me, because of the large amount of money I defrauded her of, because I killed her sister and her brother, and because, not being satisfied with all this, I endeavored, after my arrest, to blacken her good name by charging her with the death of her sister, and later with the instigation of the murder of the two Pitzel children; endeavoring to have it believed that her motive for so doing was to afford an avenue of escape for herself, if ever she should be apprehended for her sister's death, by pointing to me as a wholesale murderer, and therefore presumably guilty of her sister's death as well; for all these reasons, this is, without exception, the saddest and most heinous of my crimes.

Another Name He Can't Recall.

"A man who came to Chicago to attend the Columbian Exposition, but whose name I cannot recall, was my next victim. The local authorities can, if they choose, learn the name by inquiries made of the Hartford Insurance Company, of a Mr. Lasher of the Stock Exchange building, of T. D. Duncomb of the Metropolitan building, all of Chicago; of a sash and door manufacturing company opposite the Deering (Ill.) station, or of F. L. Jones, a notary public at Indianapolis. At some one of these places I have named either his name, or handwriting, may have been preserved, thus affording a clew for identification by his friends. I determined to use this man in my various business dealings, and did so for a time, until I found that he had not the ability I had at first thought he was possessed of, and I therefore decided to kill him. This was done.

"After Miss Williams' death I found among her papers an insurance policy made in her favor, by her brother, Baldwin Williams of Leadville, Colo. I therefore went to that city in 1894. A little later, the assignment of the policy, to which I had forged Miss Williams' name, to John Maxwell of Leadville, the administrator of the Williams estate, was honored, and the money was paid. Both in this instance, and in that of the $1,000 check given by D. Tolman, and checks aggregating $2,500 by J. R. Hitt & Co. of Chicago, inasmuch as the indorsement are forgeries, the Wiliams heirs can now recover these amounts, although it will be an undeserved hardship on those who have once advanced the money upon them.

Benjamin F. Pitzel.

"So much has already been printed, even in South Africa, where the Pitzel case was recently given considerable prominence in local papers, regarding this case that there is little for me to tell, save the actual manner in which his death was brought about.

"It will be understood that from the first hour of our acquaintance, even before I knew he had a family who would later afford me additional victims for the gratification of my bloodthirstiness, I intended to kill him, and all my subsequent care of him, as well as my apparent trust in him, by placing in his name large amounts of property, was simply to gain the confidence of him and his family, so that when the time was ripe they would the more readily fall into my hands.

"It seems almost incredible now, as I look back, that I expected to have experienced sufficient satisfaction in witnessing their death to pay me for even the physical exertion that I had put forth in their behalf during those seven long years, to say nothing of the amount of money I had expended for their welfare over and above what I could have expected to receive from his comparatively small life insurance. Yet, so it is, and it furnishes a very striking illustration of the vagaries in which this human mind will, under certain circumstances, indulge, vagaries in comparison with which the seeking of buried treasure

EMALINE G. CIGRABD.
(Was employed by Holmes as a stenographer in his office in the "castle." Disappeared in December, 1892.)

at the rainbow's end, the delusions of the exponent of perpetual motion, or the dreams of the hasheesh fiend are sanity itself.

"Pitzel left his home for the last time late in July, 1894. We journeyed together to New York, and later to Philadelphia, where the fatal house on Callow Hill street, in which he met his death in September, was hired. Then came my writing to him the discouraging letters, purporting to be from his wife, causing him to resort to drink, then the waiting from day to day until I should be sure to find him in a drunken stupor at midday. This was an easy matter, as I was well acquainted with his habits, and so sure was I of finding him thus incapacitated that, when the day came on which it was convenient for me to kill him, even before I went to his house I packed my trunk and made other arrangements to leave Philadelphia in a hurried flight immediately after his death. After thus preparing, I went to the house, quietly unlocked the door, and stole noiselessly within. In the

True Stories About New York ON PAGES 21, 22, 23, 24, 25, 26, 27, 28, 29 and 30. In other words, on every page of this section. No need to go outside the great metropolis for real interesting stories of to-day

The World's SUNDAY MAGAZINE

Notable Contributors to THIS SUNDAY WORLD MAGAZINE: Max Nordau, Mrs. Jefferson Davis, Liane de Pougy, Dr. Hausman, Mrs. Phebe Crabbe, Mayor Van Wyck's Niece, Countess de Chauvanne, Charles Frohman, George Cary Eggleston.

PAGES 21 TO 30. NEW YORK, SUNDAY, AUGUST 28, 1898. PAGES 21 TO 30.

MRS. MARTHA PLACE. The First American Woman to Be in Imminent Danger of Death in the Electric Chair. Studied for The World BY MAX NORDAU.

The Greatest Psycho-Criminol-

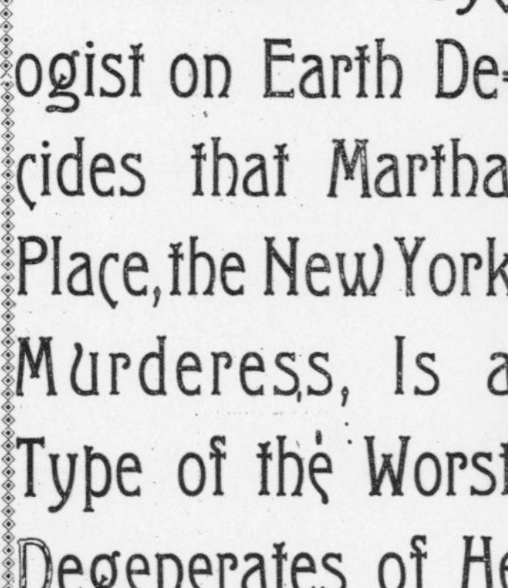

ogist on Earth Decides that Martha Place, the New York Murderess, Is a Type of the Worst Degenerates of Her Sex.

THE CRIME OF MARTHA PLACE—A SHORT REVIEW.

OF THE WOWEN CRIMINALS, MRS. NACK AND OTHER RECENT WOMEN MONSTERS WHOSE HORRIBLE DEEDS HAVE SHOCKED NEW YORK, MRS. MARTHA PLACE IS MOST REMARKABLE. IF THE SENTENCE OF THE COURT HAD NOT BEEN STAYED BY AN APPEAL SHE WOULD HAVE BEEN EXECUTED THIS COMING WEEK.

NEVER DID A WOMAN STAND IN SUCH IMMINENT DANGER OF BEING KILLED IN THE ELECTRIC CHAIR. ONE OTHER ONLY—MARIA BARBERI—WAS SENTENCED TO DIE BY ELECTRICITY, BUT THERE WAS A DEFINITE UNDERSTANDING ON THE PART OF THE JUDGE WHO PASSED SENTENCE UPON HER THAT SHE WOULD NOT BE EXECUTED. WHEN MRS. MART HA PLACE WAS SENTENCED TO DIE DURING THE WEEK OF AUG. 29 THE JUDGE WHO CONDEMNED HER HAD NO REASON TO BELIEVE THAT SHE WOULD NOT DIE IN THE ELECTRIC CHAIR IN SING SING PRISON.

MRS. PLACE MURDERED HER STEPDAUGHTER, IDA PLACE, IN HER HOME, AT NO. 598 HANCOCK STREET, BROOKLYN, ON FEB. 7 LAST. A HORRIBLE JEALOUSY OF THE VICTIM PROMPTED THE CRIME. CARBOLIC ACID WAS FIRST THROWN IN THE YOUNG GIRL'S FACE, AND THEN SHE WAS SMOTHERED. WHEN HER HUSBAND CAME HOME MRS. PLACE ATTACKED HIM WITH AN AXE, AND HE LAY AT THE POINT OF DEATH FOR WEEKS, BUT FINALLY RECOVERED.

WHEN MRS. PLACE WAS ON TRIAL SHE SHOWED ABSOLUTELY NO CONCERN. SHE SAT MOTIONLESS FOR HOURS, NOW AND THEN CHATTING WITH HER COUNSEL IN THE MOST UNTROUBLED MANNER. SHE SEEMED TO EXERT NO SELF-CONTROL TO MAINTAIN HER ATTITUDE OF INDIFFERENCE. THE BLOODY EXHIBITS OF THE PROSECUTION MOVED HER NOT IN THE LEAST.

WHEN SHE WAS CONVICTED OF MURDER IN THE FIRST DEGREE SHE DID NOT EVEN PALE. BROUGHT BEFORE JUDGE HURD FOR SENTENCE, SHE SMILED UPON HIM. SHE WALKED OUT OF COURT WITH A FIRM STEP.

SHE WAS AN ENIGMA THAT NO ONE WHO SAW HER COULD SOLVE.

SINCE THE MURDERESS WAS TAKEN TO SING SING TO PREPARE FOR DEATH SHE HAS BEEN CHEERFUL AND CONTENT. NEITHER HER PAST NOR HER FUTURE TROUBLES HER. SHE PASSES HER TIME IN KNITTING SLIPPERS, AND THE COLOR OF THE YARN CONCERNS HER MORE THAN HER FATE.

In these three portraits of degenerate women, sent to The World by Max Nordau, Mrs. Place is compared to two famous European Murderesses.—Note the points of resemblance in weakness of chins, foreheads, eyes and mouths.

An incendiary (6), whose nose, mouth, chin, cheekbones and ear are of the type represented by Mrs. Place.

An Italian woman (5) who poisoned her daughter-in-law from jealousy—a pronounced criminal type.

THE widely-known case of the Brooklyn murderess, Martha Place, the account of which in the New York World I have followed with the greatest attention, has naturally excited exceptional interest in America. It has aroused my critical faculties by its unusual features and deserves a thorough study from the standpoint of criminal psychology.

A murder committed by a woman alone, without the co-operation of an accomplice, accomplished by physical force and at one blow or stab, belongs to the class of the greatest rarities.

The share of women in the whole field of criminality is in any case a restricted one. In Europe, according to Hausner, who has made the most thorough investigation of the subject, only 16 per cent. of all the crimes are committed by women.

In other words, although there are practically as many women as men in the region covered, there are more than six crimes committed by men to one which is the work of a woman.

Crimes of women against the person, such as murder, homicide and bodily injury, take a scarcely noticeable place even in the comparatively small number of female crimes. They are almost entirely limited to child-murder, which is naturally the typical crime of women against the person.

Leaving this out, scarcely anything remains except the crimes which are in one way or another connected with the passion of love, such as assaults on seducers, on unfaithful lovers, on rivals—crimes which spring from rejected or wounded love, jealousy or revenge. Murders or murderous assaults from self-interest or with the motive of robbery are scarcely ever undertaken by woman alone. Her role in such crimes is only that of assistant to a man.

She may be the inspiration of the deed, she may sketch out the plan; but the material execution takes place by the heavier and more brutal hand of man.

In all cases of murder (except infanticide) committed by women alone without the assistance of men, the means employed by them in fully ninety-eight cases out of one hundred is poison.

All criminologists designate poisoning as the crime of women par excellence. And this has been so in all ages. Euripides puts the word into the mouth of Medea: "Poisoning is the crime in which women excel." In more recent times, the downfall of the Marquise de Brinvilliers, of the woman Lagrange and others are so well known by the general public as to call for no detailed study by criminologists.

Mrs. Place did not make use of poison. She strangled her stepdaughter with her own hands, or smothered her under pillows. She tried to split her husband's skull with a hatchet. In so doing she differentiated herself completely from the typical murderess.

"EXHIBITS MANY OF THE TRAITS OF THE BORN CRIMINAL."

The study of the entire crime of Mrs. Martha Place proves beyond a doubt that we have in her an abnormal being, anatomically and physically, who exhibits many of the traits of the born criminal.

Let us go on to study the physical indications of Mrs. Place. This study will necessarily be incomplete, because I have to work with very limited documents. I have only before me the pictures which the New York World has printed of her head (full face and profile), of the palm of her right hand and of her ear. Anthropological measurements seem not to have been taken. In any case I have seen none given.

Moreover I must note that the anatomical peculiarities of a criminal must be accepted only with many precautions and restrictions as elements in the investigation of a given case. The great significance of such peculiarities comes out only in a mass of statistics.

It is clear that one is logically justified in designating the criminal as a degenerate sub-species of man, when it is established that out of one hundred criminals investigated at least eighty-eight exhibit most or all of the known symptoms of physical degeneration.

It may well happen, however, that in a given single case the marks of degeneration may not be clear, or may consist in internal anomalies—for example, of the brain—which we cannot verify in a living subject, or which transcend our limited knowledge for the present. The absence of otherwise perceptible marks of degeneration would in such a case by no means lead to the conclusion that we are not dealing with a born criminal.

Finally, we have to remember that woman in general exhibits the marks of degeneration less often in proportion than man. This is apparently explained by the fact that woman is less differentiated than man; that she comes nearer to the type of the genus. Woman is, anatomically and physically, a human being that has remained in a primary stage of racial development, and in the childish stage (before the appearance of the beard, the full development of the larynx and so on), is capable of close comparison with the masculine type.

As woman tends normally to differentiate less widely from the primitive type of the human race than man, so in her morbid development she remains nearer to it than man. The absence of the signs of degeneration also means less in a woman than it does in a man.

Therefore their presence is much more significant, since the morbid tendencies in the woman must be much stronger than they would be in a man, in order that they may overcome the natural inclination of the woman to approximate to the type and produce anatomical irregularities.

In the case of Mrs. Place a number of peculiarities occur which are recognized and classified as elements of the physiognomy of the born criminal.

There is first, the whole character of the face, which may be described as masculine. It is entirely deficient in womanly softness and sweetness. The lines are hard, sharp, angular. The shape of the bones in the face is coarse; the facial muscles are tense.

"THE FACE, WHICH MAY BE DESCRIBED AS MASCULINE."

Now, a masculine appearance is a characteristic recognized by all criminologists as belonging to female offenders. Salsotto has investigated 130 female murderers, a number of whom were infanticides and therefore did not belong to the category of born criminals; nevertheless he remarked in fourteen, or over 10 per cent., a masculine physiognomy.

Lombroso and Pasini had sixty-one murderesses before them, of whom nine, or 14.7 per cent., showed the same.

Take the accompanying portrait of Mrs. Place (1) (on page 22), on that shows her to advantage, at a time when she had not approached her crime, and when she was no doubt invited by the photographer to look friendly and pleasant. Would you not think you had the face of a clean-shaven man before you?

And do not think that it is the mannish hat and necktie that produce this impression. It is the head. It is the face.

Compare the picture with the next portrait (2) (on page 22), one of a woman criminal, a Russian prostitute, observed by Dr. Tarnowsky.

This woman wears no man's hat or tie; but she, too, looks like a man dressed as a woman. Each of her features differs from those of Mrs. Place; but the resemblance of the whole is none the less striking.

The eyes of the Russian woman have a wild look; those of Mrs. Place affect a mild expression; but both have the same masculine character which links them to each other.

Now to consider the details. Mrs. Place's nose is long and sharp. Mingazzini, Tarnowski, Lombroso and others give a striking length of nose as an element of female criminal physiognomy.

Mingazzini, for example, finds in his criminals, as the typical length of the nose, 48.9 millimetres, while the normal length of the noses of Italian women not criminals is 36.53 millimetres.

The eyes of Mrs. Place seem to have struck all observers. The portraits in The World cannot, of course, give their expression accurately. I must rely on the personal impression which they made on those who have seen them. The reporter of The World in the court-room describes them as "small gray eyes," as "cold eyes," which yet "suggest frightful passions and an ungovernable temper."

Mrs. Harriet Hubbard Ayer remarks on the "brilliancy" of these eyes, and says further that they are "keen, intense, suggesting a little the eye of the owl or the cat. * * * I have seen women lunatics with eyes like Margaret Place's.

"ABNORMAL EAR THAT IS VERY RARE AMONG WOMEN."

All that is characteristic. An impression is made on each observer of the fixity of the criminal's eyes, their expression, their hardness and grayness; and all compare them to the eyes of wild beasts.

Joly speaks, like Mrs. Ayer, of "cat's eyes," while Lombroso mentions the impression of "the glassy stare of tiger's eyes."

But the ear of Mrs. Place is especially remarkable. "Abnormal ears are particularly rare among women." Ranke establishes this, and fortifies his conclusions with many figures.

Laycock shows, in an investigation still noteworthy (Medical Times, March 22, 1862), that the absolute and relative size of the lobe and helix (outer convolution) of the ear are distinct signs of active impulses in women.

Roncoroni, Nacke, Kurella, Lombroso, all point out that anomalies in the female ear occur almost exclusively in the weak-minded and the criminal, and very frequently in them.

rMs. Place's ear hows a whole series of gross anomalies. It is half as large again as the normal female ear. The helix is twice as broad as usual. The anthelix comes out over the level of the helix, like a wild beast's ear, and its upper end, which in the normal divides into two branches (crura), here remains undivided and has the shape of a single solid roll.

The lobulus again is monstrously long and wide, and shows instead of the normal two slight depressions between the antitragus and the lower border a single large depression.

That is the typical criminal ear, and indeed the ear of the violent, rough criminal with the lowest instincts.

The hand contributes as decisively to our view, being exceptionally broad and having short fingers. The lines of the palm are manifestly only sketched in.

If the picture in the New York World included these details we should probably be able to observe a strikingly irregular running of the lines.

The crookedness of the little finger I am unable to explain since I do not know whether it is not the result of some earlier injury, with the appearance of a scar affecting the tissues and muscles. There is certainly nothing to be seen in the picture which could confirm such a theory; but if it is a congenital malformation, then it is to be considered as a mark of degeneration, not of the strongest, it is true, but still leaving no doubt as to its nature.

Notice the accompanying pictures. Compare the portrait of Mrs. Place with 5 and 6.

No. 5 is the likeness of an Italian woman of thirty-five years, who poisoned her daughter-in-law. The motive for this crime was not given; apparently it was jealousy of the younger woman, who contested with her the first place in their common household.

The crime shows, as will be noticed, a certain similarity to that of Mrs. Place. The faces also are convincingly similar.

Take the hat and veil away from Mrs. Place's portrait, turn the head to three-quarter face, and you will have the likeness of the Italian woman before you.

The resemblance to portrait No. 6, that of an incendiary, is less striking, but still it exists. Nose, mouth, chin, cheek-bones, the large, plump ear, have kindred characteristics. One can at least speak of a family likeness between these three features.

Again, the likeness of another incendiary through revenge is significantly like the profile of Mrs. Place.

It would be an easy task to bring together dozens of pictures of female criminals who all remind one of the portrait of Mrs. Place. But the three proofs given above are sufficient to show that Mrs. Place has the declared physiognomy of a criminal.

Even more easily studied than her physical appearance, for any one who has nothing more than the newspaper reports to go by, is her psychology.

The motive of the crime is transparent. It was jealousy of the place which the unlucky stepdaughter had taken in the heart, as in the household, of her husband.

It was the hatred of an aging woman for a blooming girl, of an ugly scarecrow for beauty, of the unrefined rough person, formerly a servant, for the well-brought up, educated young lady, who could not forget the social difference between herself and the former maid-servant who had become her stepmother.

"IT WAS THE HATRED OF AN AGING WOMAN FOR A BLOOMING GIRL."

No feeling is stronger or more intense in criminal or even ordinary female natures than hatred toward more favored persons of their own sex. This feeling is at the bottom of most of the murders committed by women against adults.

If Mrs. Place affirms that she was provoked by the unfortunate Ida, if she speaks of injuries done to her by the girl, one need not go far to discover that these are inventions and lies. It is much more likely that the murderess easily imagined persecutions, and took all the words and deeds of her stepdaughter and her husband

Continued on Page 22.

THE advertiser who keeps at it constantly usually gets there first and stays at the top.

The Daily City Item.

THE business man who fails to advertise does not experience the pleasure of being in the procession.

22ND YEAR—NO. 6,563. ALLENTOWN, PA., MONDAY, MARCH 20, 1899. TEN CENTS A WEEK

FIRST WOMAN ELECTROCUTED

MRS. PLACE DIES IN THE DEATH CHAIR AT SING SING.

Aguinaldo in a Fury.

More Lessons Given the Filipinos by our Troops.

AN ALABAMA TORNADO.

First Exchange of Civilities Since the War Began.

SING SING, March 20.—Mrs. Place was electrocuted this morning. The procession started for the death chamber at 10.45 and the electrocution was immediate. Two shocks were employed. Although the prisoner was somewhat hysterical through the night, she recovered her nerve this morning and was still brave at the critical moment. She was accompanied to the chair by her old pastor, Dr. Cole, of Yonkers, who stood by her side offering spiritual consolation to the last. Only two newspaper men were present in accordance with the edict of the Governor. Dr. Jennie Griffin, of Troy, a well known physician, was also present at the request of the Governor. The other witnesses were principally physicians and professional men.

Attack on Iloilo Repulsed.

ILOILO, March 20.—This afternoon General Miller reports that the insurgents attacked Iloilo and the outlying village of Jaro, but were repulsed with a loss of two hundred killed and wounded.

Colonel Duboce, with a battalion of the First California Infantry, will go to Negros Island to-morrow to join Colonel Smith. Insurgent emissaries from the island of Panay are reported agitating Negros.

The members of the United States Philippine Commission, with the exception of Colonel Denby, who has not yet arrived, held their first meeting to-day.

General Wheaton's brigade, which defeated and drove the enemy fifteen miles yesterday, has returned to its position near Pasig. The lines are quiet.

Aguinaldo in Furious Mood.

MANILA, March 20.—Aguinaldo is taking extreme measures to suppress signs calculated to cause a cessation of hostilities. Twelve adherents of his plan of independence, residents of Manila, were condemned to death because they wrote advising surrender, and all loyal Filipinos have been called upon to perform national service in despatching the enemy. Friday last General Lagarda visited Malolos for the purpose of advising Aguinaldo to quit. He argued with the insurgent leader and attempted to convince him of the folly of his persistence in the face of overwhelming odds. Aguinaldo was furious at the advice. He ordered Lagarda to be executed immediately. The unfortunate general was promptly decapitated.

Saluted Each Other's Flags.

GIBRALTAR, March 20.—As the Spanish squadron under command of Admiral Camara was leaving Gibraltar Bay yesterday it met near Algesiras the United States cruiser, Raleigh, which was returning home from Manila. The Raleigh hoisted the Spanish flag and the Spanish Admiral replied by hoisting the Stars and Stripes. This was the first act of international courtesy between the United States and Spain since the outbreak of the war.

Tornado in Alabama.

BIRMINGHAM, March 20.—Latest advices estimate that fifty buildings in Alabama were blown to pieces.

BISMARCK, Ala., March 20.—A terrific wind storm accompanied the rain and hail that passed through the extensive plantation of Samuel Curry in Chilton county last night. Eleven tenements were demolished. Two negro boys were killed. Seventeen other negroes were injured.

General Henry's Denial.

WASHINGTON, March 20.—General Henry, commanding the United States forces in Porto Rico, cabled the War Department this morning a positive denial of interviews published a week ago crediting him with saying there were chances for an uprising on the island.

Two Bodies Found in the Windsor's Ruins.

NEW YORK, March 20.—Workmen at the Windsor Hotel this morning found two bodies in the ruins. They had no marks of identification and were burned to a crisp. Near the last body a hand and forearm were also found. There was a gold ring on one finger, with a stone missing.

Winter Again in England.

LONDON, March 20.—Winter has returned to the British Isles. There was a heavy fall of snow in London and snow storms swept the Mildands and North country. Outdoor work is at a standstill. Storms raged in the North Sea.

A Sentry Fired On.

PARIS, March 20.—The *Journal* to-day says that a sentinel, stationed at Beaumott Tower near Toulon, was fired on yesterday evening, the bullet penetrating his cap. The sentry replied to the shot, but his assailant fled. An inquiry will be instituted.

Many Soldiers Exhausted.

MANILA, March 20.—Inability of the Commissary train to keep up with the advance led to considerable suffering. Many men were completely exhausted and fell in the ranks. They were strung along a line of almost six miles. Numbers are returning to camp on artillery ambulances which are always close up to the lines.

Train Wrecked.

BUFFALO, March 20.—The Lake Shore & Southwestern limited was wrecked at West Seneca this morning, due to ice clogging a switch. Engineer Shattuck was killed. Brakeman Roberts was severely injured. The passengers were badly shaken but none were hurt.

An Officer Used Up.

Special Officer Daniel B. Geary, of Hefel's Casino, is suffering greatly from the effects of a bad beating he received on Saturday at the hands of a gang of toughs. While the performance was going on at the casino on Saturday evening, "Bully" Young began to raise a disturbance. He refused to leave and Officer Geary arrested him. He wanted to hand him over to the policeman at Sixth and Hamilton streets and started out with his man. At Sixth and Union streets the officer was tripped by Wilson Fenstermacher, who had just arrived in town from the West and who left on the next convenient train after the assault. After Mr. Geary was on the pavement four friends of Young began to do him up. In the scuffle Geary was bit behind the ear with his own billy, received a kick under the right eye, causing a deep cut, a bruise on the forehead from a heel of a shoe and a split left ear. He was rolled in the mud in the street and was bedecked from head to foot. Young got away during the melee. Mr. Geary was taken to Dr. C. H. Martin's office, where his injuries were dressed. They are not dangerous but are painful. Mr. Geary was about again yesterday. Peter McMullen was later locked up as one of the assailants.

McMullen had a hearing before the Mayor, but Mr. Geary could not identify him as one of his assailants. The prisoner claimed he assisted the officer. He was turned over to Constable Schrunk, who had a warrant for him. Alderman Haines heard the case and discharged him. Mr. Geary says his assailants were Young and the Fenstermacher brothers. All have left town, it is believed. Warrants are hanging over their heads.

Numerous people have inquired whether Mr. Geary was dead. The report was spread over all sections of the town. The officer is improving and the law will be fully applied to the culprits.

PERSONALS.

Samuel Lichten is expected home to-morrow from his six weeks' stay in Jamaica for the benefit of his health. He writes that he is much improved.

W. H. Miller, who came here a year ago from Columbia as storekeeper of the P. & R. R. W. Co. at the East Penn Junction, has been appointed to a similar position at Port Reading, N. J. He will leave to-morrow to take charge.

Dr. Clemens supplied St. John's Reformed pulpit at Bangor last evening, the regular pastor having been absent. Subject, "Christ's Advice to an Unconverted Minister," St. John 3:7. The doctor was listened to with rapt attention and the attendance was good.

F. P. Hunsicker, E. H. Mullen, Francis M. Berkemeyer, Emanuel Reinhard, H. W. Smith, Ed Diefenderfer, Preston Diefenderfer, Geo. Haldeman, Guy P. Erdman, E. B. Blank, Charles E. Searle, Dr. F. B. Scheirer, Chas. Addis and H. Kepp, the degree team of Livingston Castle, drove to Pleasant Corner on Saturday and in the evening installed 27 new members at a boom session of Jordan Castle, increasing the membership to 56. An enjoyable banquet followed at the hotel. The Castle will celebrate its first anniversary on April 29, when another boom session will be held.

Died of Cancer.

Agnes Kern died this morning at the home of her mother, Mrs. Hannah L. Kern, No. 410 North Seventh street, after a long illness from cancer. She was forty-three years old and leaves two sons. She was an employe of Boney & Berger's shoe factory. The funeral will be held on Thursday. Rev. G. W. Richards will hold the services. Deceased was a member of Salem Reformed Church and of the Bible Class of the Sunday School.

Letter Carriers' Meeting.

Letter carriers from Allentown, Bethlehem, South Bethlehem, Phillipsburg and Easton to the number of thirty-five met in this city yesterday and discussed matters of mutual interest. The question of attending the United States Carriers' Association meeting at Scranton was considered, and it was decided that as many as possible of the Lehigh Valley Association shall attend. All the local carriers will attend if possible.

Another Death from Diphtheria.

A two-year-old son of Lycurgus W. Strock, of West Bethlehem, died Friday night of diphtheria. This is the third death in that family from this disease within four weeks.

Guild Meeting.

Miss Ruth A. Hersh, of 124 North Ninth street, will entertain the Guild of St. John's Reformed Church to-morrow evening.

Cars off the Tracks.

In shifting yesterday forenoon at the East Penn Junction, two cars jumped the track, delaying traffic until they could be replaced.

Finished Their Work.

The County Auditors on Saturday finished their work of auditing the county's accounts.

LICENSE APPLICATIONS.

Clerk Kreitz Has Received 294 in All.

18 ARE FOR NEW STANDS.

Seven Are from Allentown—Three Wholesalers Want New Licenses in the First Ward, Catasauqua.

Clerk of Quarter Sessions Kreitz has received the applications for liquor licenses for the April term of Court. There are 294 in all, 18 of which are new ones. The number is as follows:

RETAIL.

Allentown—	
First Ward	10
Second "	13
Third "	6
Fourth "	9
Fifth "	14
Sixth "	13
Seventh "	3
Eighth "	4
Ninth "	7
Tenth "	2
West Bethlehem—	
First Ward	4
Second Ward	8
Third Ward	1
Catasauqua—	
First Ward	6
Second Ward	6
Coopersburg	3
Fountain Hill	3
Coplay	4
Macungie	2
Emaus	6
Slatington	12
Hanover	10
Heidelberg	5
Lowhill	3
Lower Milford	4
Lynn	8
Lower Macungie	9
Salisbury	11
Upper Saucon	7
North Whitehall	12
Upper Milford	6
South Whitehall	16
Upper Macungie	10
Weisenburg	6
Whitehall	18
Washington	7
Total	263

WHOLESALE.

Allentown—	
Second Ward	2
Third Ward	1
Fourth Ward	3
Slatington	3
Catasauqua—	
First Ward	3
Second Ward	1
Whitehall	3
Emaus	1
Weisenburg	1
Total	18

BREWERS

Allentown—Second Ward, 1; Third Ward, 2; Sixth Ward, 1; Catasauqua—First Ward, 1; total, 5. Total, 285.

DISTILLERS.

Heidelberg—Lewis B. Reitz.
Lynn—Jesse Weaver, Henry Weaver.
Lowhill—M. A. and F. P. George.

BOTTLERS.

Allentown—Frederick Horlacher.
Catasauqua—August Hobl.
Hanover—Goundie, Moll & Co.
Salisbury—James B. Smith, Jos. F. Gorman.

With the distillers and bottlers, the total number of applicants is 294.

The applicants for new licenses are: Retail—Granville Gernert at 155 Hamilton street; W. J. Trexler at 17 South Seventh street; Christian H. Sefing at 148 North Seventh street; Joseph F. Martz at Sixth and Court streets, Henry H. Detweiler at 402 North Seventh street; Joseph Fisher at 819 Allen street; Charles Gruele at Fifth and Turner streets; Samuel J. Kohler, Howertown road and Mulberry street, Catasauqua; Levi Tice, West Bethlehem; Samuel J. Guth, Coplay; Wm. B. Croman and Nathan F. Newhard, South Allentown; John Herman, Second and Bridge, West Catasauqua; Alvin E. Fogel, near Coplay.

Neff and Best Have Moved.

Neff & Best, the stove, tinware and roofing slate dealers have moved from 428 North Tenth street to 34 North Seventh street, lately occupied by the Lehigh Valley Furnishing Co. They now have a most eligible site for their building and large and convenient room for manufacturing, storage and for transacting their business. Neff & Best have a full and choice line of heaters and ranges, refrigerators and ice boxes, wickless oil stoves, combination coal and gas ranges, etc.

Viewers' Meeting.

Walter J. Grim, J. W. Crader and J. H. Birchall, viewers on the opening of Thirteenth street from Gordon street to the city limits met on the grounds this morning and adjourned to meet on Thursday at 10 A. M. in the City Engineer's office to hear testimony. The lands to be taken belong to John and Lewis Nonnemacher, G. W. Seagraves, Reuben Helfrich and the West End Improvement Co.

An Imposter.

Some time in January a gentleman came to town and called on all teachers of the schools and kindergartens, representing himself to be an agent for the firm, "Self Culture," Werner & Co., Akron, Ohio. His smooth and oily tongue won him many subscribers. As an inducement also he gave the *Ladies' Home Journal* at club rates, making altogether for the year, the two magazines for $1.50. He gave a receipt for the money but without the firm's name stamped thereon. After a delay of a month or more, one of the victims wrote to the firm and received the following letter. It may be of interest to many in this city who were swindled:

AKRON, Ohio, March 17th, 1899.

DEAR MADAM:—We beg to acknowledge the receipt of your favor of the 1st inst., which, however, only came to hand just after the writer had left the city on a business trip, which accounts for our delay in replying to the same. We sincerely regret that you have been victimized by Mr. O. H. Maynard, whoever he may be, as we are wholly unacquainted with any such man. As you are the tenth or twelfth person who has written us in the same way, we have for three or four weeks been doing our best to locate this person, but so far without success. We have never heard of the man nor can we address him in any way, as of course we do not hear from people whose subscriptions he has taken until some two or three weeks after they have given the order and in the meantime he has departed for parts unkown. We hope that we may in some way get hold of him in a very short time and shall do our best to protect your interests in the matter. Of course these things may happen in spite of all that we can do and it only goes to prove that one should be very careful in subscribing for any periodical or book to be sure that the one who represents it has authority to do so. We hope that we may very soon give you some information in the matter and in the meantime remain, Yours very truly,

SELF CULTURE MAGAZINE.

To-night's Band Concert.

This evening the first concert of the series will be given by the Allentown Band, Martin Klingler, Musical Director, assisted by Madame Emma Suelke, soprano, and Frank D. Hartman, accompanist. The following is the program:

Overture—"The Italian in Algiers"....Rossini
Gems from Opera—"El Capitan"......Sousa
Baritone Solo—Fantasia "Bonnie Scotland" [Lax
Howard Hass.
Soprano Solo—"Nymphs and Fawns" ..... [Bemberg
Madame Emma Suelke.
a Intermezzo—From "Pagliacci".......... Leoncavallo
b Entr'acte et Valse—"Coppelia" from Delibes Ballet..............Tobani
Overture—Zu dem Festspiele "Des Wandrer's Ziel" (The Traveller's Aim)........Suppe
Descriptive Fantasie—"Cavalry Charge".... Luders

SYNOPSIS: Morning of the Battle; Infantry is heard approaching with fifes and drums; Cavalry in the distance, coming nearer and nearer until they charge upon the Enemy; Cavalry, Infantry and Artillery in the Melee of Battle; Defeat of the Enemy, pursued in the distance by the Cavalry.

Caprice—"Bewitching Beauty" (Beaute enchantresse) ....Laurendeau
Soprano Solo—"May Morning"........Denza
Madame Emma Suelke.
Humoristique Fantasie—"The Colored Wedding"....................Laurendeau

SYNOPSIS: Introduction, strains from Mendelssohn's Wedding March, more humorous than classical in the interpretation; The Wedding Party proceeds on its way to the parsonage; At the Parson's, the Ceremony; The fatal words "I will"; The kiss and words of advice; Return home; The festivities begin; Finale, "Nigger nebber die."

Ballet Music and Soldiers' March—From "William Tell"..................Rossini
Star Spangled Banner..................

Services for Railroad Men.

Several hundred railroad men took advantage of the second service in their interest in Bethany U. E. Church last evening. The program rendered was a very interesting one. It included selections by the choir, solos, select readings and prayer by Rev. C. L. Oswald and an entertaining talk by Philip Larve, of Easton, an engineer of the Lehigh Valley Railroad. The services were under the auspices of the Y. W. C. U.

BASKET BALL.

The Allentown Y. M. C. A. Juniors, who defeated the Reading Reserves in Allentown by 3 to 0, played them again at Reading on Saturday night and were defeated this time by 20 to 12. They will get another chance at them soon. It was a good game in which Newhard, of Allentown, excelled. The Allentown players were Powell and Newhard, attacks; Schultz, centre; Williams and Dietz, defense; Acker, sub., and Ziegenfus.

Arbor Days in Pennsylvania.

Governor Stone issued a proclamation designating April 7 and 28 as Arbor days.

DEATH OF OWEN KERN.

THE SECOND VICTIM OF FRANK KRAUSE'S MURDEROUS ASSAULT.

LINGERED FOR FIFTEEN DAYS

An Operation Performed on Saturday Afternoon by Dr. Estes.

FUNERAL SET FOR THURSDAY.

Sketch of Mr. Kern—New Charge Preferred Against and Served on Krause—His Early Trial Likely—The Hearing.

Owen Kern is dead. These words spread from mouth to mouth yesterday and brought expressions of sorrow and regret, wherever uttered. So much sympathy has been excited for him by the violent and unprovoked murderous assault made by his hostler, Frank Krause, on that fateful evening of Friday, March 3d, that there was the deepest interest stirred up in his case. No one deserved death, less in such a manner, was the general comment, when the fatal effect of the bullet was heard. Coupled with the expressions of regret over the death of Mr. Kern was uttered the hope that his murderer and the murderer of Maggie Guth would find a speedy and ignominious end on the gallows, a fate that he so richly deserved. The death of Mr. Kern removes one of the props on which it is believed that Krause leaned for a defence in his case of the homicide of Maggie Guth. It is very likely that had Mr. Kern survived his injuries, Krause would have defended his killing of Miss Guth on the ground of accident in an endeavor to shoot Mr. and Mrs. Kern for interfering between them. If that was Krause's intention Mr. Kern's death leaves no such recourse for him. It leaves to him only the alternative of pleading guilty to a double murder and throwing himself upon the mercy of the Court. His is a gallows offence. His plea of being intoxicated and hence irresponsible from drink is untenable in law. There are no traces of insanity in the family and Krause had at no time in his life met with an accident that might affect his mind. The shooting was simply the outcome of a vicious spirit and ugly temper, frenzied with jealousy and piqued by crossed love.

Death relieved Mr. Kern from his pains and tribulations just before the midnight hour was struck on Saturday night, heralding the coming of the holy Sabbath day of rest and communion with God. He sank gradually until the weakness of the flesh overcame the strength of the spirit and he sank into eternal rest.

Mr. Kern died as the result of a bullet wound in the right chest, inflicted by his hostler, Frank Krause, on Friday evening, March 3d, at his hotel in Cedarville. The details of the horrible crime are still so fresh in the minds of the people that they need but be briefly referred to at this time. Krause was enamored of Mr. Kern's servant girl, Miss Maggie Guth, who had been at the hotel since last fall. Warned by Mrs. Kern and others of Krause's true character, that of a gay Lothario, who had already ruined three girls in the community, she did not reciprocate his affections, which nettled the young man and preyed upon his mind. On the Friday evening in question when Krause had finished his chores, he called Miss Guth out of the kitchen to the pump, and Mrs. Kern soon heard them quarreling. Harry Grim, who was passing the hotel at the time, also heard hot words between the two. Mrs. Kern besought them to cease and finding her efforts futile she called her husband from the barroom, who told Krause that he should be ashamed of himself to harrass and annoy Miss Guth as he did. Krause drew his 32-calibre revolver and fired five shots at the three. His aim was good, although it was dark (about 7 P. M.). Miss Guth was shot in the right thumb, left breast and right breast. She died in a few minutes, after being helped to a lounge in the sitting room. Mrs. Kern was shot in the left arm, the bullet lodging in the shoulder joint. It is not a serious wound and Mrs. Kern is recovering nicely

OWEN A. KERN, WHO DIED SATURDAY FROM BULLET WOUND INFLICTED BY FRANK KRAUSE.

from its effects. Mr. Kern was shot in the right chest, the bullet entering two inches below the collar bone and near the breast bone. It took an inward and downward course, cutting the lung and severing important blood vessels.

Krause fled to the home of his brother, Henry, near F. T. Dorney's bakery, where he was arrested by Detectives Keck and Haines, his brother having meanwhile disarmed him. Krause was very much intoxicated when arrested, though those at the hotel just before the murder was committed say that he was sober then. Krause was quickly railroaded to jail, where he has been since. The funeral of Miss Guth was held on the 9th inst.

Drs. A. P. Fetherolf, of this city, and A. N. Miller, of East Texas, attended Mr. Kern. They at once recognized the gravity of the wound. He was given the best of medical attention and he was carefully nursed by his relatives, who took turns in watching by his bedside and attending to his wants. By the eleventh day the doctors saw the beginning of the end. Mr. Kern had a powerful physique, a strong constitution and a grim determination to live. All these operated in his favor and prolonged his life beyond a point at which men of frailer fibre would have succumbed. The right lung, wounded and bleeding, failed to perform its functions, thus throwing double duty upon the left lung. It bore the strain until it too became affected and collapsed. The clogging of the lungs with bloody matter accumulated in the chest cavity caused labored breathing and made the patient restless and uneasy.

MISS MAGGIE GUTH, FIRST VICTIM OF FRANK KRAUSE'S MURDEROUS REVOLVER—PICTURE REPRODUCED FROM TINTYPE.

(Continued on fifth page)

URGED TO CONTINUE.

Pressing Appeal to Rev. G. W. Richards.

BY SALEM'S CONSISTORY.

The Popular Pastor of Salem Reformed Church Receives an Urgent Petition to Remain Here.

The consistory of Salem Reformed Church has adopted and it was endorsed yesterday by a rising vote of the entire congregation at both morning and evening services, and by every department of the Sunday School, a strong appeal to Rev. G. W. Richards to remain as their pastor. It was read at both services. It recites that the members and officers of the church appreciate the honor of his election to the professorship of church history in the Seminary, and while not desiring to be insubordinate, they ask his attention to the united prayers of a most devoted people. Continuing it says:

"We are now, more than ever, convinced that you are peculiarly adapted to carry on the work of the congregation, which, you well know, represents nearly 2500 souls. The circumstances, which have developed since your election and resignation, could not be forseen then, but they are of such a nature as seen now that, we believe, they would warrant a reconsideration of your resignation, even in the mind of the church at large. We feel assured that no one could unite all the members into a harmonious body as you can, should you remain in our midst. You have shown yourself, thus far, a most acceptable leader of the people. They have followed you gladly and profitably. You have not only gained the affection of your congregation, but you have won the esteem of the people in this community. We have heard many good men during the past months. They adorn the Reformed ministry, and we are proud of them. Yet we are the more convinced you alone can successfully guide the congregation, according to the plans you laid before us in part, before your election. We refer to the extension of Reformed interests in this city by building mission churches. It is the unanimous feeling of the people, men, women and children, that an effort should be made to have you reconsider your resignation; and it is their earnest prayer that you would kindly do so and continue as pastor among us."

The congregation would assist him in any way possible to bear his weighty responsibilities and would enable him take a long rest in Europe during the spring and summer.

Interesting Meeting.

Announcements were made yesterday of two meetings to be held next Thursday which will afford opportunities for hearing one of the most prominent Christian workers of the State. Charles E. Hurlburt, at one time State Secretary of the Y. M. C. A. and now superintendent of the Pennsylvania Bible Institute and Director of the African Inland Mission, will speak on Thursday afternoon at 3.30 in Bethany U. E. Church, Sixth and Oak streets, and in the evening in the Y. M. C. A. Hall at 7.30. These meetings should become generally known, and all persons interested in Christian work should attend. The meetings will interest all and especially young men.

An Eye Removed.

Jacob S. Herman, residing near Santee's Mills near Bethlehem, has been suffering for a long time with detachment of the retina and malignant glaucoma and it was found necessary to remove the left eye to save his life. Dr. G. T. Fox performed the operation assisted by Drs. Hearne and Stout, of Bethlehem.

The Hospital.

The new hospital building at Seventeenth and Chew streets is to be completed within six weeks. The plasterers will finish their part of the work this week. A porte cochere is being erected along the Chew street front at the main entrance.

Good Shows Coming.

Among the attractions to be seen at the Academy of Music during April are these: Sousa's opera, "The Bride Elect," on the 6th; "The Geisha" again, on the 10th, and "The Little Minister," on the 14th.

Will Move to Town.

A. P. Anthony, of Rittersville, will retire from the butcher business and move to town into a house on North Madison street, which he has bought from J. A. Wieder for $1800.

Mr. Wagner's Successor.

Elizabeth Farreschlader will succeed Jacob Wagner at the Hotel Arlington at Fifth and Allen streets.

Mission Service.

The Girls' Mission Band of St. John's Reformed Church will hold a mission service on Wednesday evening in the chapel, to which the public is invited.

A Cocking Main.

A cocking main between local sports is on the tapis for to-night. Those who are in it expect to have an ample return for their $1 admission fee.

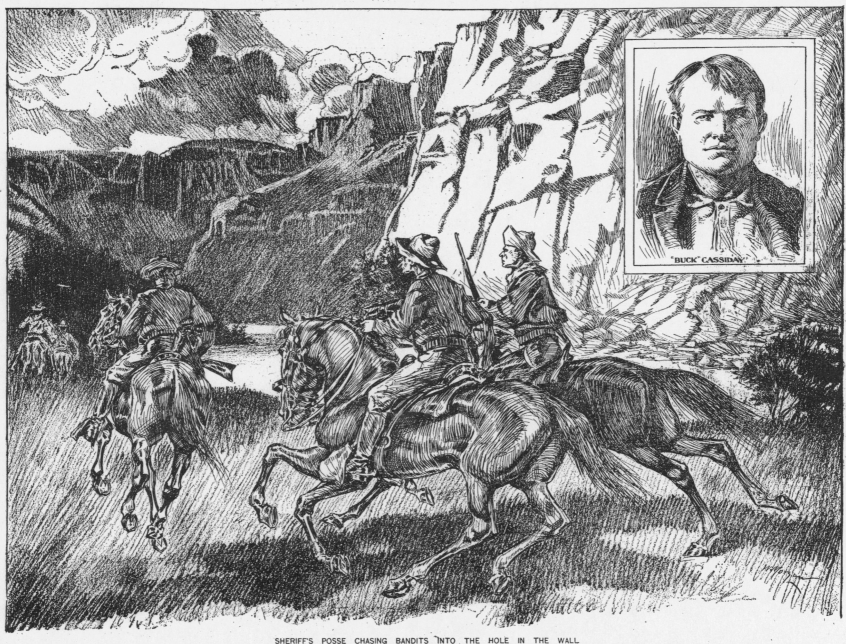

"BUCK" CASSIDAY.

SHERIFF'S POSSE CHASING BANDITS INTO THE HOLE IN THE WALL

"HOLE-IN-THE-WALL" BANDITS.

A Remarkable Chase Through Western States for the Men Whose Latest Escapade Was to Dynamite a Union Pacific Train.

NOT even the stirring annals of Missouri and the Cherokee Strip, where train robbing and flight were reduced to a fine art, can furnish the tale of such a man hunt as that which has just been led zigzagging across sandy plains, swollen streams, through precipitous canyons and over rugged mountainous ranges in Wyoming.

Three men, desperate and daring, with a price of thousands of dollars on the head of each, have been the quarry. More than five hundred men have been the pursuers—sheriffs and deputies, marshals and deputies, cowboys and prospectors, and old Indian fighters, picked men from the State and federal troops, and even Shoshone Indians, all crack shots and all eager for the reward or for a fight that would stir the blood. Aiding them have been bloodhounds trained to follow human fugitives. For almost four hundred miles the chase was led, until, separated from their friends and surrounded by their enemies, George and "Tom" Roberts and George Currie, leaders of the notorious "Hole-in-the-Wall" band, sought a final refuge in the Owl Creek Mountains, near the Shoshone.

The story of the hunt is a tale of the frontier, of lawless men who have lived long in the crags and become like eagles, shunning mankind, except when they swooped down upon some country bank to rob it at the point of pistol, or rode out on the range to gather in the cattle or horses of other men.

Their Refuge Once a Great Lake.

Five States have known the exploits of the "Hole-in-the-Wall" band. From the Black Hills of Dakota to the "Robbers' Roost," in Utah; from Central Montana to Central Colorado, for years the bold outlaws, about fifty in number, have plundered cattle raisers, settlers, banks and post offices. Their refuge deserves well to rank with the wonders that have been gathered by nature in the Yellowstone Park region.

The "Hole-in-the-Wall" is about fifty miles south of Buffalo, Wyo., and eighty miles northwest of Casper. It is the outlet to a great basin, about twenty miles wide and thirty miles long. Here once was a lake hemmed in by the Big Horn Mountains and a high ridge that runs almost parallel with them.

On the outside of this ridge is a huge cliff, between five and six hundred feet high, and extending almost its whole length. Except for one break it is almost impassable. The "Hole" was made by the water from the lake, which overflowed, and in centuries cut out a channel for itself to form the Powder River. Buffalo Creek and its two forks now water the valley and find an outlet through the "Hole."

In the narrow gorge only two horses can pass abreast, and the robbers have always been able to hide themselves in the valley or the Big Horn mountains beyond before their pursuers could pass the narrow entrance.

Posses have followed bold members of the band time and time again to the "Hole-in-the Wall" but when they reached that narrow gorge lost the trial and had to turn back. Men who had something to conceal, however, have been certain of a cordial reception, fresh horses and aid in concealment until the hunt was ended.

Dynamiting Train Their Climax.

It was only when the leaders of the band [illegible] it a climax on their feats by attacking the Fast Mail on the Union Pacific Railroad that they found enemies determined to follow them through their retreat and drive them out. Less desperate men would have hesitated long to undertake this task, for all frontier bandits know the government never forgives one who tampers with its mails and railways, and express companies will hunt to the death those who interfere with the safety of their business.

The bandits' deed will live long in the memories of Western railroad men. It was early on the morning of June 2 that they stopped the first section of the westbound Fast Mail half a mile east of the Wilcox Creek bridge, compelled the engine driver to take the mail and express cars across the bridge, blew up the structure with dynamite, and then shattered the express car and safe with a charge of that explosive, only to find less than $3,000 to reward them.

There were six men in the daring band. They stopped the train with red and white emergency signals, and cowed the conductor and train hands with pistols. After taking the money from the express company's safe they separated, three leaving no trace of their movements, the other three striking for the refuge that had proved their salvation more than once.

Boldly Rode Through City.

They had camped nearby while awaiting the train, and fleet horses were ready for them when they had obtained their booty. Straight across the plain they rode, heading for the bluffs of the Platte River, east of Casper. A posse taking the trail next morning felt that capture would be easy, for they knew the men could cross the swollen Platte River and reach the rugged mountains only over the bridge at Casper, seventy miles from the scene of the robbery, where railway men, United States marshals and deputy sheriffs were perparing for the hunt.

None of those who were in the chase could believe the bandits would dare enter this city, and the bridge was left unguarded. On the second day, however, the men, after stealing fresh horses at a ranch, turned abruptly to the west, and in the middle of the night rode through the city, crossed the bridge over the swollen river, obtained supplies from friends and were well on their way to the Big Horn Mountains when their pursuers followed their trail across the bridge.

Sheriff Killed by Fugitives.

Westward across the plain the chase led, the bandits, with horses tired from their long ride, the pursuers with fresh ones furnished in Casper. The bandits kept always to the high ridges, and, armed with powerful field glasses, could see for ten miles behind the ten men on their trail—one riding directly over the tracks of their horses, the others spread out to prevent surprise.

Thus they led away for sixty miles, until in the heart of the mountains, near the head of Teapot Creek, they stopped for rest for themselves and horses. They had little time to sleep, however, for soon the trailing posse entered the narrow canyon. The leader was stopped with a shot that pierced the heart of his horse. Another horse was killed as a second pursuer rode up. Though half a mile away, the robbers' aim was deadly. The posse fought the robbers Indian fashion for hours, driving them away from their horses and forcing them to take to the rocks. The task was costly, however, for while closing in on them the head of the posse, Sheriff Joseph Hazen, of Converse county, was killed by a bullet.

Dared Not Enter the "Hole."

Crippled by their losses, the posse could not guard the outlaws, and that night they crept away, stole horses from a ranch near by and rode off northeast across the hills, toward the "Hole-in-the-Wall." A herder at the K. T. ranch, near the entrance, was met by them two days later, and he told them the posse had cut in ahead of them, and that the ranch and the "Hole" were guarded.

They dared not enter their old retreat, but friends gave them horses and food. Then, making a wide detour, they went down the Powder River and struck off across a trail that led around the great cliff wall.

They found time for rest and recuperation on the solitary E. K. Mountain, which raises its ragged sides above the "Hole in the Wall" valley. Bloodhounds trailed them there, and scores of men surrounded them, penning them in canyons time after time.

The news of the killing of Sheriff Hazen had spread throughout the State. The Governor had offered $3,000 reward for each of them, and the railway and express companies had proffered an equal amount.

Troopers had been sent from Fort McKinney to the north; picked militiamen had been equipped as cowboys, and the United States Marshal and the sheriffs had gathered the crack shots and fearless characters of the whole region to aid in the chase.

Escape Again from Posse.

From rock to rock and gully to gully they fought against great odds for a week, the pursuers constantly closing in, avoiding a charge in their desire to take the men alive. Then one morning the posse closed in on the retreat from which they had fought the night before, only to find that the desperate little band had escaped again.

Bloodhounds took up the trail again, crossing west through the "Hole-in-the-Wall" valley and the Big Horn Mountains, then southwest toward the Shoshone Indian reservation, and finally into the heart of the Owl Creek Mountains, where they again took a stand. Persons who had met them in their flight said they had five fine horses, two carrying supplies and ammunition. They stole fresh animals from the Indian reservation in their flight, but no animal could stand such a chase against the fresh relays of the determined men behind.

In the Owl Creek Mountains it was three against four hundred—desperation matched against skill and a fortune for the man who might pot them. With bloodhounds and Indian trailers about them, and keen eyes watching for any movement, they could do little else than try to sell life dearly, according to the laws of men of their stripe.

The three men are worthy of their calling. Cherokee blood runs in the veins of the Roberts brothers, and the mixture has made them hate white men. Currie was formerly a cowboy, but turned cattle thief four years ago, and he and the Roberts brothers by their fierceness and daring became leaders of the "Hole-in-the-Wall" band.

The end of this trio, however, does not mean the end of the band. There are still fearless desperadoes to be hunted out of the "Hole." "Buck" Cassiday, known from Canada to Mexico and "blood enemy" of Colonel Jay L. Torrey, of the Second Rough Riders, will be their leader.

The authorities of the West have declared war on these men. In three years they have robbed the Post Office at Powderville, Mont., and killed the Postmaster; robbed the bank at Belle Fouche, S. D., and the one at Montpelier, Idaho, and robbed stores extending south to Fort Bridger, Utah, besides innumerable ranches and sheep camps. They have ambushed posses who have followed them and stopped pursuit. Now, however, it is declared they will be hunted out, even if bloodhounds and troops must be employed.

SCIENTIST ALLEGES PROOF OF IMMORTALITY.

Says He Has Talked with Dead Friends Through Spiritualist Mediums, and Gives His Theories of Life and Death.

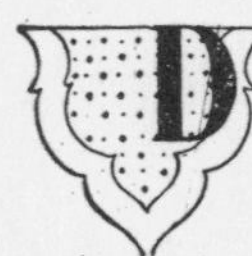

DR. PAUL GIBIER has made no little stir in the world by declaring that he has absolute proof of immortality. In explanation of his views he gives the following interview setting forth his reasons for his belief:—

"Do you believe that the soul of the higher self of man survives the dissolution of the body?" he was asked.

"I do not believe, I know that the intellectual principle of man survives the death of the body."

"You have stated that we can have material proof of this; can you tell me in what way it may be had?"

"It can be had in several ways, namely, through hypnotism, hypno-magnetism, and psychic experiment, and, I need not add, that some of the best known scientists of the age have accepted as proof the evidence deduced from these same sources. One of the simplest yet one of the most powerful proofs that intelligence exists apart from matter may be found in the sort of an experiment where subjects under the influence of an operator become, at certain states, seers, and see objects and persons invisible to those in a normal state—things and persons which sometimes leave an impression upon a photographic plate. When in this state I have known a subject to converse with an invisible being, some one I had known in the body, a fact with which the subject was in nowise acquainted. The person on this occasion told me things, through the subject, which left me no chance to doubt—things which I did not know myself and which, for that reason, could not have come from my sub-conscious mind. The psychic appearance of the person seen was real to the subject and the conversation was in a language which I could not hear, but which sounded very real to the subject, who seemed astonished that I could not see the apparently solid body of the person with whom he was conversing.

"Following the person just referred to came a gentleman whom the subject said he could not speak with because the man was sobbing so violently. I had also known this person in life, and I could not believe that he had reason for such grief after death, and I began to doubt the powers of the subject until he suddenly pointed to a photograph which hung on the wall and said:—'That is the man.' Then the subject said, with a shudder:—'He is sorrow personified.' Later I learned, to my regret, that the gentleman in question, who, by the way, had been a very distinguished scientist, had really done in life that which would produce such a state of mind or soul as that described by the subject."

"Can you give the name of the person?"

"No, he was too well known a character.

"I have made many experiments in my own laboratory under test conditions which have proven to me and to my associates to a mathematical certainty that the conscience of man survives the death of the body, but I do not care to give the details of the experiments to the public just at this time. Then there are the experiments which come under the head of hypnotic and hypno-magnetic, with which nearly every enlightened person is familiar. I have known of crimes which have been committed through hypnotism, and I assure you that the person in whose mind the crime is committed is much more to be pitied than the actual instrument or victim."

Here Dr. Gibier was asked to give an explanation—the why and wherefore of these phenomena—an explanation which might be readily comprehended by the person of average intelligence, and one which, owing to his position in the scientific world and profound method of thought, would be accepted as incontrovertible fact.

He referred to what he had already written in the following words:—

"Casting aside the power of attraction which binds us to earth, and while leaving our planet, we will, with the mind's eye, make a cursory examination of its surface. First, we will take a portion of the substance of which it is formed and endeavor to discern its component parts. In a word, we will start from the atom and with gigantic strides scale the immensity which leads to the macrocosm.

"Returning to our planetisphere, we will seek the epitome of the universe, or so called marcrocosm, and in studying its anatomy and physiology compare it with that of its model. While making our titanic excursion through the boundless realms of Ether we shall pause for a moment and seek the third principle, the true being, which, with matter and energy, constitutes the animated universe. This principle in man, which is the proof of his independence and continuance outside of matter, will be the chief object of our work."

After dealing with the periodical cataclysm the Doctor takes up the study of the macrocosm, and shows that through philosophical analysis and the atomic theory "matter is something which we can touch and see, but that it is formed of parts that have materially no existence." In other words, matter loses, as it were, its materiality and is merged into energy.

After claiming that even if man were composed alone of matter and energy, "he is immortal and even eternal, for although matter and force may be transformed they remain anatomically the same for all time," Dr. Gibier holds that neither matter nor energy has intelligence, and, since this is true, there must be a third element, and it must be coexistent with matter. To this element he gives the name of intelligence, or soul.

In this connection Dr. Gibier says:—"Science, when it so decides, will be able to study the third consititution element of the macrocosm (which is found again in the microcosm). Just at present it studies the two other elements—matter and energy—which it will be able to understand far better than before."

He continued:—"We have, so far, proven that just as is the macrocosm, so is man made up of the three fundamental parts—matter (the body), energy (the soul), intelligence (the spirit). Each one of these parts may be considered under several different aspects, which would make as many subdivisions, but we will defer entering into the details of a more complicated system of hyperphysics.

"When true death occurs, the spirit is the first to leave the body, leaving it in a more or less rapid way, according to the manner of death. At the same time a certain part of the energy is dissipated, and, in a gradual way, re-enters the great common storehouse of universal energy. Another part of this force remains bound to the spirit, without which it would probably return to universal intelligence, just as the matter of the body and a certain quantity of its energy return to the ambient matter and energy. But it is later that this force definitely leaves the body, providing it (the body) has not been destroyed by fire or through any other destructive cause immediately after death.

"In other terms, intellectual secession occurs first, and the animic follows gradually, more or less rapidy, according to the manner of death and degree of temperature. It is, so to speak, the successive cellular death. Life, the anima, leaves the cells one by one, and the being of the new life is only definitely constituted when the animic force which permeated the various cells and globules has left them to join once more the spirit toward which it tends, in virtue of a law analogous to the attractions which we observe, but whose nature at present is equally unknown to us."

The animic force, which Dr. Gibier and many other scientists say resembles electricity, or a white light, is the force through which spirits manifest themselves to those of us who still live in the matter. The person who is mediumistic and through whom the disembodied entity sometimes returns to the earth plane has usually more of this animic force than persons lacking the mediumistic quality. At séances where spirits are said to appear and materialize they are held to do so by absorbing or taking on, in addition to their own, the animic force of the medium, which has been exteriorized by the medium for that purpose.

PART 2

THE DENVER REPUBLICAN.

PAGES 11-20

REPUBLICAN, Vol. XXII, No. 245.
TRIBUNE, Vol. XXXIV, No. 245.

30 PAGES. DENVER, COLORADO, SUNDAY MORNING, SEPTEMBER 2, 1900. 30 PAGES. PRICE FIVE CENTS

NOTORIOUS "BUTCH" CASSIDAY SAID TO HAVE LED TABLE ROCK TRAIN ROBBERY

CHEYENNE, Wyo., Sept. 1.—(Special.)—Deputy Sheriff Robert Guy returned to Rock Springs to-night from chase of the Table Rock train robbers. He says Sheriff Swanzon and Marshal Hadsell's posses are hot on the trail of the bandits who were heading for the Brown's Park and Powder Springs country. The officers found the place where the outlaws had breakfasted this morning, the ashes of the camp fire being hot, pieces of masks worn by the robbers were found in the camp. Deputy Guy believes the robbers cannot escape, but fears they may ambush the officers.

Fresh horses are being hurried south to the posses together with fresh provisions for the officers and grain for their mounts. General Manager Dickinson is at Rock Springs and is personally directing the manhunt. The government has offered a reward of $1,000 each for the outlaws. The rewards for the five men now aggregate $10,000.

CHEYENNE, Wyo., Sept. 1.—(Special.)—The opinion is growing here that the men who held up and robbed the Union Pacific express train at Table Rock Wednesday were members of the "Butch" Cassiday gang and that the notorious "Butch" himself was leader of the party. This belief has been strengthened by developments of the past 24 hours. A ranchman has reached the railroad from the Brown's park country with the information that he saw "Butch" Cassiday in that section two weeks ago in company with four other men. All were well armed and mounted on good horses and were riding in the direction of Spring mountain, a known rendezvous for robbers and cattle thieves. Not satisfying himself with a first glance, the ranchman took another look through a field glass and was convinced that the leader of the party was none other than the famous bank and train robber.

Postal Clerk Pruitt, who was in charge of the mail car, cut loose from the balance of the train with the baggage car Wednesday night, has returned to Cheyenne. He says that he was lined up with the trainmen while three robbers were dynamiting the express car. The robber on guard stood close to him and talked freely. Among other things, he said:

Bandit's Ruminations.

"Don't know how we will fare here, but we did pretty well at Wilcox. We got a little short of money and come down here to get some more. This ain't the train we wanted. That one went through a week ago and carried a lot of government gold, but the man who was a goin' to stop her backed out when he see two cars of bums on board, thinkin' as how they was officers. We'd have done well on that train. But bein' here and needin' money, we thought we'd better tackle this one, as we are pretty sure she's got money in the safe. We don't want to kill anybody, but we might do it just the same. We really ought to have killed that engineer in the Wilcox affair, but let him off with a rap on the head. If we ever come across him again and he acts that way we'll have to let him have it. There's no use in anybody acting smart with us. I wish those fellers would get a move on, for we want to get away from here. We gave it to old man Hazen on Tea Pot creek because he followed us, and if anyone follows us this time we'll give 'em the same dose. We ain't a skeered much, as we know roads in this country that they don't and any way if they got close we can give it to 'em."

The denials of officers of the Pacific Express company to the contrary notwithstanding, it is believed the robbers secured many thousands of dollars from the safes of the wrecked baggage car. While the robbers were at work in the car it was noticed they stooped over frequently and picked up articles from the floor, which they hurriedly thrust into their pockets. When the car reached Green River three $20 gold pieces were found on the floor, indicating that a sack of gold coin had been broken open and its contents scattered by the explosion. Then too, when the robbers ran away from the car, it required two men to carry the sack of plunder and load it on a horse.

Chief Canada of the Union Pacific force of detectives has gone to the scene of the hold-up to direct the movements of the special officers of the company at work on the case. Bloodhounds will be brought into use, and if the posses fail to run the robbers down the dogs will be started out at once.

Dickinson Denies Loss.

The express car which was dynamited will be repaired in the Omaha shops and will be taken east in a few days. It will be necessary to build new sides and an entire new roof.

It is reported that the packages which Express Messenger Woodcock threw behind a pile of trunks contained $6,000, instead of $600, as at first reported.

The following self-explanatory telegram was received in Denver yesterday from General Manager Dickinson of the Union Pacific:

"ROCK SPRINGS, Wyo., Sept. 1, 1900.—Answering your telegram, robbers secured three money packages of $24, $5 and $3.40, aggregating $50.40, and two packages cheap jewelry. Damage to car by explosion, about $2,000. Contents of car also considerably damaged by explosion. E. Dickinson."

EXTERIOR OF WRECKED CAR.

Showing How It Was Torn by Dynamite Used by the Wyoming Train Robbers.

AN ODD EXPERIENCE.

A School of Herring Chased by a Monkey Fish.

M. H. Shaw of Boston was telling the other evening at the Murray Hill hotel of an experience he had some time ago at New Harbor, Maine, says the New York Tribune. "The last time I was there," said Mr. Shaw, "was in the summer of 1884. In those days the railroad stopped short at Portsmouth, N. H., 12 miles distant, and the balance of the journey you made by coach. It is one of the most attractive places I have ever visited. But I knew it in its stage coach days, and prejudice has kept me from returning since the railroad reached out and touched it. It was in this summer that I witnessed one of the most remarkable sights it has ever been my luck to see. York harbor is a beautiful circular bay, into one end of which the river runs. Behind the bluff the river forms a small harbor, and then it decreases rapidly in size as you proceed inland. Two miles above the harbor it is scarcely more than a creek. One evening after supper I had taken a couple of young ladies for a row. Dusk found us about a mile from the hotel on our way home. As I was rowing, my back was to the stream. Suddenly the girl steering cried out, 'Gracious me, what's that?'

"Turning I saw in the gloaming what seemed a wall of phosphorescent water, some two feet high. It was running toward us, and, thinking it must be a tidal wave, or something of that kind, I grabbed for the oars. There was no time to reach the shore, so I held the boat head on to the advancing wave, at the same time warning my companions to sit perfectly still. In a second it struck out, and it struck us hard. Fish in twos and threes began to jump into the boat, and the frightened girls, screaming, jumped on the thwarts. I implored them to sit down and to keep perfectly still, for the boat rocked fearfully and we were in imminent danger of upsetting. The river was covered with fish from bank to bank, like a gigantic sardine box, and if we had ever gone over among them knowledge of swimming would not have been of the slightest use. The girls finally quieted down, and we were able to watch the spectacle without fear. It was the strangest of sights. Down the stream to the bay the river seemed a mass of living, leaping quicksilver. The head of the line was 100 yards beyond us, a moving, living line of light. Fish by the score jumped into the boat, and kept us busy pitching them out. I thrust my oar down into the water, and you could feel their bodies leaping against its entire length. Finally, however, the stream cleared enough for me to row again, and we returned to our hotel.

"The explanation of the phenomenon was comparatively simple," Mr. Shaw went on. "Herring have a deadly enemy called, I think, monkey fish. They hunt them in schools and destroy the herring by hundreds. When the monkey fish gets after them the herring run for it, as their only means of escape. A school of herring had been chased into the outer harbor. The monkey fish blocked their way back to the sea. Then the herring found the way into the river, and the whole frightened school tore through and up the stream in their wild effort to escape. They died there by thousands. The next morning the pilot in front of the Marshall House was silvered with their bodies, and both shores of the river for miles presented a similar appearance. Farmers all over the country came there and took the fish away by the carload to use as fertilizers. But there were fish enough to have fertilized New England, and presently they began to decay. The people stood it for a day or two, but by that time they smelt to high heaven, and every one that could fled as from the bubonic plague. I coudn't, and had too stay through. It was an awful experience. The water in the river ran like glue, and so impregnated the water of the outer bay that bathing for a while was out of the question. You ate, drank, slept and cursed fish. Fish were in the clear weather and in the storm. The summer of 1884 at York Harbor has since been known as the stale fish summer. To give you an idea of how bad it was, a French poodle fell off a float on the river side, and he had to be sent out of the state. That's an actual fact, for he was sent to Portsmouth."

McJigger—I see Mr. Barnpaws, the circus man, was married the other day. That was something of a comedown for him.

Thingumbob—Why so?

McJigger—The wedding was nothing but a one-ring performance. — Philadelphia Press.

SHOULD STICK TO SIMPLE FOOD.

The American Business Man's Pace Demands Easily Digested Dishes.

"There was in the old days far less wear and tear upon the nerves; and, under such conditions digestion was more completely performed," writes Mrs. S. T. Rorer of "Why I Am Opposed to Pies," in the Ladies' Home Journal. "The mothers of to-day must look more carefully to the building of their bodies and brains than their mothers and grandmothers did. Indeed, at the pace at which we Americans are going we use our brains at full speed nearly all the time. What man can build brain and brawn on pies, layer cakes or preserves, or any other mass of material which from its very complexity requires labor and time for digestion, drawing the blood from the brain into the stomach during his working hours? Observe those who eat their complex foods carelessly and hastily, and you will see at a glance the conditions that necessitate a complete rest every now and then, or an early nervous breakdown.

"In my close observation in the last twenty years I find very few people in our common struggle for existence who can for any length of time eat carelessly of complex foods. At 40 or 50 a man may perhaps have accumulated wealth, but not health; and of what earthly use is the first without the second? Many persons in the generation gone before have eaten pies at least once a day, but they have not had meat three times a day, nor have they rushed at our pace. They gave more time to the digestion of the pie. People who recommend these rich foods rarely know anything of their complex conditions, and still less of the complexity of digestion."

No Repose for Them.

Two old jokes met in the next world.

"Well, well," said the Mother-in-Law Joke, "are you dead at last?"

"Yes," replied the Cook-and-Policeman Joke, "as dead as you. Of course, we are liable to be resurrected any moment."—Philadelphia Bulletin.

TENTING ON THE BEACH AT CAPE NOME--- THOUSANDS OF DISAPPOINTED GOLD SEEKERS

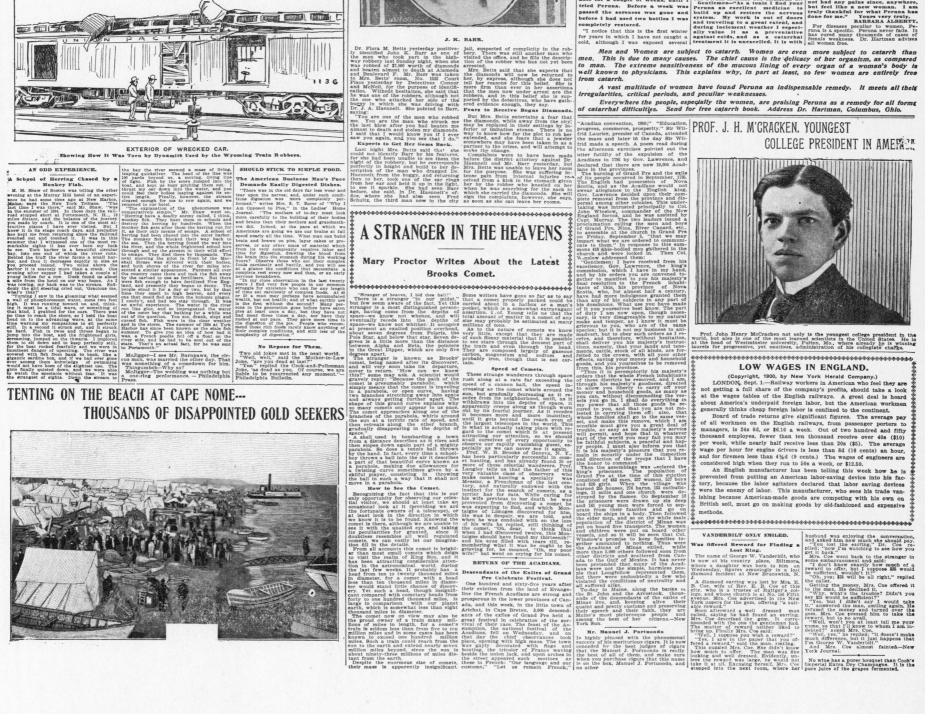

"YOU ARE ONE," SAYS MRS. BETTS

Victim of Diamond Robbers Positively Identifies J. K. Barr as One of Her Assailants—She Expects to Get Her Gems Back, but Fears Bogus Stones Will Replace the Genuine.

J. K. BARR.

A STRANGER IN THE HEAVENS

Mary Proctor Writes About the Latest Brooks Comet.

THREE FAIR AMERICAN LADIES Who Use PERUNA

MISS J. WILSON GAIRE. MISS IDA HARNED. MISS BARBARA ALBERTY.

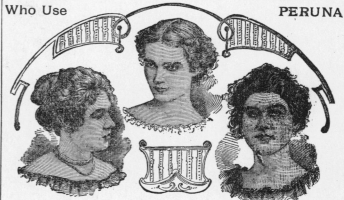

PROF. J. H. M'CRACKEN, YOUNGEST COLLEGE PRESIDENT IN AMERICA

Prof. John Henry McCracken not only is the youngest college president in the world, but also is one of the most learned scientists in the United States. He is at the head of Westminster university, Fulton, Mo., where already he is winning laurels for progressive, yet cautious, administration of his collegiate charges.

LOW WAGES IN ENGLAND.

(Copyright, 1900, by New York Herald Company.)

LONDON, Sept. 1.—Railway workers in American who feel they are not getting a full share of the company's profits, should take a look at the wages tables of the English railways. A great deal is heard about America's underpaid foreign labor, but the American workmen generally thinks cheap foreign labor is confined to the continent.

Board of trade returns give significant figures. The average pay of all workmen on the English railways, from passenger porters to managers, is 24s 8d, or $6.16 a week. Out of two hundred and fifty thousand employes, fewer than ten thousand receive over 40s ($10) per week, while nearly half receive less than 20s ($5). The average wage per hour for engine drivers is less than 8d (16 cents) an hour, and for firemen less than 4½d (9 cents.) The wages of engineers are considered high when they run to 50s a week, or $12.50.

An English manufacturer has been telling this week how he is prevented from putting an American labor-saving device into his factory, because the labor agitators declared that labor saving devices were the enemy of labor. This manufacturer, who sees his trade vanishing because American-made goods are competing with his own on British soil, must go on making goods by old-fashioned and expensive methods.

VANDERBILT ONLY SMILED.

Was Offered Reward for Finding a Lost Ring.

MRS. CARRIE NATION—TERROR of KANSAS' SALOONKEEPERS

MRS NATION FROM A SKETCH MADE IN WICHITA

THE COUNTY JAIL X SHOWS MRS NATION'S CELL

MRS NATION FROM A PHOTO TAKEN TWENTY YEARS AGO

DAVID NATION

NEW LEADER OF THE WOMEN OF THE "BLEEDING STATE," WHO IS NOW CONDUCTING A GREAT CRUSADE AGAINST THE LIQUOR TRAFFIC, AND HAS RAISED AN ISSUE IN THE WEST WHICH SHE THREATENS TO CARRY INTO THE EFFETE EAST.

MRS NATION AND HER COMPANIONS WRECKING A SALOON

ONCE more the State of Kansas is in the throes of a violent temperance feud. Again it is the women who have assumed the aggressive and lead in violent measures that has divided the sentiment of the entire State to a point of menace to public safety. Mrs. Carrie Nation, of Medicine Lodge, is the determined upholder of the law which became a statute in 1881, but which has since fallen into disrepute owing to general apathy and the interest of liquor men. At the head of a small but fearless band of anti-liquor champions Mrs. Nation has started on a career of general saloon wrecking which threatens to make all precedents of former years pale into insignificance. Already half a dozen saloons have been demolished, blood has flowed, and the reign of terror promises to continue with increased fury.

The personality of the leader of the anti-drink crusaders is interesting. Mrs. Nation is a woman with a history. Born in a fighting district of Kentucky about half a century ago, she inherited the stubborn and aggressive qualities of her frontier forefathers, and from early womanhood has been identified with reform movements in various parts of the Southwest.

Twenty-five years ago Mrs. Nation was the wife of Dr. Loyds, of Holden, Mo. After a year of married life the doctor died of delirium tremens. Over the grave of her husband the young woman took a solemn oath that the remainder of her life would be spent in combating the demon rum and saving young men from the fate which befell her husband. How far she has succeeded is a question in dispute, but one thing is certain—she is quite the most celebrated character in the whole West at the present time, and the outcome of her warfare is a matter of grave speculation.

After ten years of widowhood Mrs. Loyds married David Nation, her present husband and co-worker in the prohibition field, and for a time the pair resided at Richmond, Texas. There Mrs. Nation made herself felt widely in the community, being identified with several reform projects, among others the negro suffrage question. Mr. Jefferson McLemore, secretary of the Texas Democratic Executive Committee, is authority for the fact that the "storm and stress" period of the Nations in Richmond kept that part of the Lone Star State in a ferment. Mr. Nation was the editor of a Richmond local paper and also kept a hotel. He, as well as his wife, was a strong negro sympathizer. As it was just after the reconstruction times, when the feeling between the white and colored races was particularly bitter, the feud threatened bloodshed.

In the national campaign of 1884 David Nation placed in the hands of the republican campaign managers some printed matter which, it is alleged, reflected strongly upon that district of Texas in which he resided. The result was that when these strictures were disseminated and the author became known a lynching bee was narrowly averted. As the antagonism to the Nations grew more violent, the aggressive pair thought it to best to retreat, and, shaking the dust of Texas from their feet, they took refuge in Kansas. The latter expedient was decided upon only after Mr. Nation had been set upon by a party of young men of Richmond and given a severe beating. Mrs. Nation pronounced a curse upon every man implicated in the assault, and, curious as it may seem, every member of that party is now dead, some dying by violence.

Mrs. Nation's strong anti-rum sentiments found in Kansas a fertile field for aggressive operations. The law of 1881 providing a penalty for selling, giving away or harboring any intoxicating liquor was practically a dead letter. Many amendments to the original statute were passed by the Legislature, but the local option element found ways to evade the law, and it has been practically inoperative for years.

Mrs. Nation resolved to see that the law was enforced, and, failing to move the State or local municipal powers to the accomplishment of this big task, took retribution into her own hands and began the career of saloon wrecking that has made her the terror of the State.

It was fully ten years ago that Mrs. Nation made her first raid on a saloon. She made havoc of the finest barroom of Medicine Lodge, where she was living at the time. For this offence she was arrested and locked up for days. She was released when the fury of the anti-saloon element became a public menace, and, though disseminating her violent theories in various parts of the State, she refrained from actual assault till about two years ago, when she broke forth again and wrecked two saloons in the town of Kiowa. Even then she escaped punishment, growing bolder with each raid and gathering about her votaries of her prohibition gospel. Thence into the larger towns Mrs. Nation carried her conquest, and late in December last swooped down upon Wichita.

Few who saw the kindly featured woman of mature years who came into the town on that eventful day attired in black silk and a bonnet of forgotten vogue realized her mission. Wandering up Douglas avenue she picked out the handsomest wine room in town, which happened to be the Carey Annex. Gathering an armful of stones in a rear alley, the reformer made her descent upon the café, smashing glassware, mirrors and other fixtures, ending by throwing a rock through a painting of the nude valued at $1,000. For the assault Mrs. Nation was arrested and held in jail, where, it is alleged, she was not altogether kindly treated.

A smallpox quarantine was placed on the jail, and Mrs. Nation could not get out, even on bail. After some legal difficulties, however, the prisoner, assisted by her husband, who is a wealthy farmer of Medicine Lodge, was released by order of the Supreme Court of Kansas. Her trial was set down on the calendar, but some days previous to that event the charges against the crusader were dismissed by County Attorney Conley, who expressed in his petition the belief that Mrs. Nation was insane. The sudden termination to the proceedings seemed to be a grave disappointment to Mrs. Nation, who chose to become a martyr to the cause, affirming repeatedly that she would gladly give up her life, if need be, to the accomplishment of the enforcing of the State prohibition law.

The saloon men, fearing another onslaught, hired guards to watch their doors. Their precautions, however, were vain. Having pledged twenty or more members of the Woman's Christian Temperance Union, who met at their headquarters in the Sedgwick block, Mrs. Nation delivered her ultimatum.

"I am here for the purpose of getting revenge on this town for keeping me in smallpox quarantine for twenty days when there was no smallpox in that jail," said the intrepid crusader. "I must have revenge. It will do the cause good. Women, you who have signed the pledge, I want you to follow me and we will wreck every saloon in Wichita!"

Only three sympathizers were fearless enough to follow their leader to a point of violence. These were Mrs. Lucy Wilhoite, a local charity worker; Mrs. Julia Evans, wife of a well known physician of the city, and Mrs. Kate Abbot, a temperance advocate. Arming themselves with stones, bricks and cudgels, Mrs. Nation carrying a hatchet, the quartet went forth on their mission of vengeance. The saloon of James Burns sustained the first onslaught. Plate glass windows, expensive fixtures and bottles of liquor were reduced to chaos. No effort was made to restrain the women, mirrors, pictures and glassware being pounded into hopeless wreckage. Leaving the place with the air of conquerors, the women proceeded to the saloon of John Herrigg, which was treated in somewhat the same manner, the keeper drawing a revolver and standing guard over the stock room, where thousands of dollars' worth of liquor was kept. A detachment of police arrived, taking the crusaders to the station, but Chief of Police G. T. Cubbon did not hold them, taking their promise not to raid any more wine rooms. In the neighborhood of the wrecked saloons the women mingled with the thousands who were gathered there, and, mounting a box, Mrs. Nation addressed the people.

"Men of Wichita," said the speaker, "I tell you it is the right hand of God that has struck you. I will never leave this town till every saloon in the place is closed."

The crowd did not receive the remarks with temperate spirit, and the crusader was obliged to take flight. The timely arrival of the police saved the temperance advocate from rough handling. That night Mrs. Nation was arrested on a warrant charging her with malicious destruction of property, the Sheriff having something of a battle with his prisoner, afterward retaliating for her violence by placing her on a diet of bread and water.

It was while in her cell that Mrs. Nation gave a statement to a correspondent for the Herald. "I am only started on this saloon work," said the champion of prohibition. "I may be stoned, mobbed, even tarred and feathered, but that will have no effect, so long as there is breath in my body. I have secured the aid of rich and influential people, and I will do the rest. I intend to raid every saloon in the State. The law is on my side. I have been repeatedly arrested, but always released. The laws of Kansas do not recognize saloons, and that is why we shall wreck them. Wichita is the Sodom of Kansas, and I will direct my crusade from this place. I am willing to die martyr to this cause, if need be; but if I am killed by the saloon ruffians it will cause the greatest revolution for temperance ever known in this country."

When Mrs. Nation was released again every saloon proprietor closed his place and stood guard before it. Many threats of violence are heard, and there is belief that the leader will be killed if she persists in her violent policy. Although the local papers treat the matter lightly, some expressing the belief that the crusader is insane, it is generally conceded that the most bitter liquor war ever known in Kansas is now under way and bloodshed may result.

MRS. NATION MAY MOVE ON NEW YORK WITHIN NEXT THREE MONTHS.

Mrs. Nation has made no definite plans concerning her future movements in the work of driving the saloons out of the rest of the United States. She is uncertain how long she will be engaged in perfecting her plans and driving the saloons from Kansas. She says that she has received assurances of help which lead her to believe that she can finish her work there and move on New York city within the next three months.

"Before I move on the Eastern States," she said, "I must necessarily perfect the organization of my standing army of women. They will be recruited from every State and county of the Union. After I save the young men of my own State from ruin and death I will move on New York city. That place is the Sodom of America. By its example it causes many smaller cities in the country to go wrong. If it can be reformed, and I have no doubt it can, we will have finished our hardest task. Other cities will capitulate without a contest. In fact, I believe when we drive the saloons from New York the other cities will accept our terms and we will have our victory won. We will maintain the headquarters of our organization, which will be known as 'Mothers' and Sisters' Aid Society,' in Kansas, and as long as the order lives we will prevent the sale of liquor in the United States."

"I have just received word from God," concluded Mrs. Nation, "that He expected me to stay in Topeka until I had saved Kansas from the liquor curse. He told me that Kansas was on the verge of a temperance revival, and that I was to start it in Topeka."

A CAUTIOUS ANSWER.

"Where is Josiar?" asked Mrs. Corntossel, uneasily.

"Well," answered her husband, as he proceeded to fill his pipe, "I won't say fur certain. If the ice is as strong as he thinks it is he's gone skatin', an' if it ain't he's gone swimmin'."—Washington Star.

Is New York "a City without a Face"? Views of Ernest Crosby, W. Dean Howells and Frederick Dielman

Mr. Crosby's Severe Strictures on New York as a City Without Art and Literature Elicit Sharp Rejoinders.

THAT supremacy in the realm of art and literature which New York regards as peculiarly her own is questioned by Ernest H. Crosby. He says that New York has little literature and art, and, taken all in all, "is a city without a face." He wonders what there would be in this city worth picking up and preserving in a museum should the metropolis be visited by some calamity such as overwhelmed some of the Greek and Roman cities.

William Dean Howells comments upon Mr. Crosby's view of New York as a literary centre, and Frederick Dielman, president of the American Academy of Design, combats the opinions of American art which Mr. Crosby expresses.

"When I say that New York is a city without a face," said Mr. Crosby the other evening, "I mean that she is lacking in individuality. The city has no definite plan, and it has no distinctive life. When you visit the smaller Italian cities you find a square in the centre, and you notice that the streets are laid out with regard to some definite plan. There are many American cities which excel New York in this respect.

"This city reminds me of a jellyfish—all arms and stomach. New York is always reaching out. Everything is based on money.

"The people have not time to live. They rush hither and thither in mad haste. They suffer from nervous exhaustion. There is no time to think of literature and art. Everything is considered by the amount of money which it will bring. If a man has a lot, with a frontage of twenty-five feet, he calculates not upon the kind of a building which will harmonize with its architectural surroundings, but upon the kind which will return the largest amount of money on the investment.

"It is an age of hideous skyscrapers. It may be that in time this condition will be remedied, and that New York will work out its own artistic salvation. The city is filled with houses of brown stone which have no artistic beauty. In the architecture of New York there is scarcely anything distinctively American, and little which is artistic. If the whole city were destroyed, as were some of the cities of ancient times, I wonder what there would be worth picking up and placing in a museum. Perhaps some of the fragments of the City Hall would be regarded as of sufficient interest.

"There is in New York," continued Mr. Crosby, "very little art which is distinctively American. There is an art colony here, but it is exceedingly small in proportion to the population. The young men who study art go abroad, learn foreign methods, and return to put those methods in practice here. There are few works of art in this city which are not foreign. Take, for instance, the Metropolitan Museum of Art. Practically everything there has been brought from other countries.

"This country lacks the artistic impulse. An artist is one who can convince others of the beauty which is around them. In old Athens there was an amphitheatre so large that nearly the entire population of the city could go there to see the dramas and tragedies of the times. Every one was intensely interested in dramatic art. When an Italian painter completed his picture of the Madonna the work of art was borne in triumph to the cathedral, followed by cheering thousands.

"In musical art the city of New York has accomplished comparatively little. Whatever there is good of music is so given that only the wealthy may hear it. In the cities of the Old World there is an opportunity for all classes of society to know and to appreciate good music. It is very strange, with the large German immigration which this country has had, that the German love of music has not more deeply affected the people. It looks as though after the first generation the Germans lose their interest in music.

"New York," concluded Mr. Crosby, "is by no means a literary centre. That is, in the sense of being the home of literary men. It is true that the magazines are published here, and that there are many great publishing houses. The men who write the books and the magazine articles are not New Yorkers. When I think of literary New York, the only names which have a high place in literature are those of Mark Twain and William Dean Howells. E. C. Stedman is a distinguished poet and critic, and the poems of Richard Watson Gilder must not be forgotten.

"Beyond these, I can think of no others. If we go back to the New York of forty or fifty years ago, the names of many authors who have won a distinguished place in literature may be mentioned. There were N. P. Willis, Bayard Taylor, Washington Irving, James Fenimore Cooper, Edgar Allan Poe, Fitz-Greene Halleck, Walt Whitman and William Cullen Bryant. I can think, of course, of many men in the present day who write well and acceptably. Yet there is no such literary centre in New York as there was many years ago.

"I do not mean this to be a pessimistic view. I think when this age of money making is past that the people will have more time to think and to read. The tendency of the present age must stop; it cannot go on. When the people think less of money getting and wealth is more equably distributed, I think that the change will come."

Why Mr. Howells Disagrees with Mr. Crosby—New York the Great Mart for Literary Wares

William Dean Howells was much interested in Mr. Crosby's view that this city had no literature.

"In saying that literature in this city," said he, "is represented by Mark Twain and myself Mr. Crosby does not do justice to the writers of New York. The city naturally attracts men from all parts of the country. Here is a literary mart. I am not in favor of centralization as far as literature is concerned. I believe in individuality.

"I should not advise a young author to come to New York. The transplanting process may injure the roots. In New York writing is not recognized as a profession. I mean by that, it does not have the same standing as law and medicine and even as commerce. Here in New York the people do not read books, they read about them. If the writers depended upon New York alone they would not find much recognition.

"Throughout the country there is much more interest in literature than there is here. Yet, for all that, the metropolis is the market for literary wares. Here are the great publishing houses and the magazines. This is the place for those who have something to sell, no matter what it may be. I do not know but what it is better as it is.

"Yet there are New York authors who are distinctly the products of this city. There is Edmund Clarence Stedman, poet and critic. High on the list I would place Stephen Crane. He certainly was typical of New York in his style. He did much work which had the flavor of the metropolis. I would also mention Cahen, who has written stories of Hebrew life full of sweetness and charm. You may call them east side stories, yet they are more than that. What more thoroughly represents the spirit of New York than the stories of Brander Matthews? There is so much in these days of a high standard that we do not give credit for what there is.

"The people expect more than they did fifty years ago. The works of some of the poets and writers of the period of which Mr. Crosby speaks would not attract as much attention now as they did then. You speak of Edgar Allan Poe. His name and his fame are great, yet it cannot be said that he is distinctly American.

"There are some young men in Chicago who are doing more to develop a distinctively American literature than is being done here in New York. I think I might mention Henry B. Fuller, Hamlin Garland, William Payne and George Ade. I read 'Artie' with much pleasure, and I have followed Ade's fables in slang. Slangy? Yes, intentionally so, yet they contain some real philosophy. They are original and they are intensely American.

"Then there are some of the young Chicago newspaper writers who have produced poems prettily expressed. I have read some of the work of Samuel E. Kiser with interest, and I think that 'Mr. Dooley' is amusing."

Mr. Dielman Defends New York as an Art Centre and a City of Architectural Individuality.

Frederick Dielman, president of the National Academy of Design and a representative American artist, does not agree with the views of Mr. Crosby concerning the lack of originality in American art.

"Mr. Crosby," said he, "would hardly have been so bold as to have made such an assertion at a time, for instance, when there was a collection of American paintings before the public such as those of Thomas B. Clarke and William T. Evans. The work of Lafarge, Winslow Homer and Thayer, of Inness, Wyant and Martin, is distinctively American. Lafarge is conceded to be in certain departments of art at the head, and I fail to see in what respects he is not American. I do not see where the peculiar excellence of his work in design and color, which may be studied in church decorations in this city, fails to be personal and American.

"The work of these men and of many others has a personal quality, and it is American because they were Americans.

"But we may go further back for evidence of the influence of American character, not only on our own art, but on the art of the world. More than a century ago Benjamin West, an American by birth, and whose youth and early manhood were passed in Philadelphia and New York, revolutionized a higher branch of art by freeing it from the trammels of convention, for which service he is justly styled the father of modern historical painting, and since his day there have been many others who, in portrait, in genre and in landscape painting have done work which, if not always to be classed as great art, is nevertheless distinctively American.

"The trouble is that American art cannot be seen in its entirety and properly estimated, because there exists no representative collection. The nucleus of such a representation is held by the National Academy of Design, which, as I may remind you, is now calling upon the public for assistance in its endeavor to make that collection truly national and to give it a worthy home in a permanent building. Mr. Crosby's strictures emphasize the need of such an institution.

"The strongest men in this country are not imitators. At the recent Exposition in Paris it was said by competent foreign critics that the collection from the United States had distinctive American qualities.

"And is New York the art centre of the country? Without question she is becoming more than that. It is a tendency of men who are the ablest in art to gravitate toward this city. Another tendency appears in the fact that New York is becoming the financial centre of the world, as I am told.

"Unquestionably patronage is a necessary element for the full development of the art of the country. Hence in time the art products of all countries will find their greatest market in the metropolis.

"Only this morning a delegation from a Western city called upon me to ask information to guide them in making arrangements for the decoration of a public building in their city. They wished to have American subjects treated by American artists. If there were no such thing as American art why should they have come here? Why could they not have decided to employ an Italian decorator and not have given any consideration to American artists?

"It is said that Americans go to Europe to study art, and then imitate only European style. There are some American artists who have expatriated themselves, but this tendency is disappearing. It is the duty of every student of art to familiarize himself with the best work which has been done. Therefore he goes to Europe.

"Was Rubens any the less a Belgian artist because he went to Italy to study? Surely Michael Angelo was individual in his work, yet he could not have existed without the antique. The study of foreign art by young American artists no more renders them incapable of developing a national art than the study of the antique made the artists of the Renaissance incapable of producing art peculiar to their times and countries."

Mr. Dielman held the view that there were many things of American origin in New York which would be well worth picking up in after ages.

"There is the Washington statue, in Union square, or the Farragut, for instance," he said. "We need not be ashamed to have anybody see those as representing American art.

"There are many unsightly buildings in New York," said Mr. Dielman, "but there are also many beautiful ones. The country and especially this city have undergone periods of abominable taste. Mr. Crosby speaks of the brown stone fronts as unsightly. They are the relics of a period of forty and fifty years ago, when there was a fad for brown stone, and cannot be charged against this day and generation. The worst features of that craze appear in brown stone imitations of cast iron. Yet, I must say that some of the more recent attempts of the architects to produce something new and striking make one appreciate our dignified, if monotonous, rows of brown stone.

"Certainly Mr. Crosby would not like to have New York look like some of the Italian cities of which he speaks. In so doing he would defeat his own contention. Does he see nothing individual in the skyscrapers? To me the lower part of New York, irregular and ragged as is the sky line, is very interesting. There are different ideals.

"In Paris the avenues are broad and the buildings not high, yet nobody would assert that Florence and Venice are not picturesque and individual, although one can scarcely raise an umbrella in the narrow streets. We will yet evolve new and artistic forms from our present conditions. Mr. Crosby must remember that a complete national art or a complete national character is not evolved in a day."

The Denver Times

EST'D 1872. LAST EDITION—12 PAGES. DENVER, COLORADO, FRIDAY, APRIL 26, 1901. WEATHER—SHOWERS, COLDER 5 CENTS.

HIS HEAD SEVERED!

WHO GAVE 2 O'CLOCK ORDERS?

Adams Says Armstrong Did.

"I suppose the chief of police gave those orders. He has been trying to keep the business within bounds. Of course the fire and police board knows very well that the board cannot conflict with the law. If the people want the saloons open after midnight all they have to do is to have the city council pass an ordinance to that effect and we will obey it. We are here to execute the laws and for nothing else."—President Adams of the fire and police board.

ARMSTRONG SAYS HE DIDN'T.

"The fire and police board has taken no official action allowing the saloons to run till 2 o'clock in the morning, but there is an understanding between the board and myself that the saloons may run their back rooms till 2 a. m. As I understand the matter, the board is doing this merely temporarily. It is intended to take up the matter in the near future and come to a definite conclusion as to how long the saloons can operate. Until I receive further orders, or have my present ones countermanded, I shall allow the saloons to be open till 2 a. m."—Statement from Chief of Police Armstrong this morning.

THOMAS SAYS NEITHER CAN.

"There is a city ordinance compelling the saloons to close at midnight. The fire and police board cannot interfere with this ordinance by orders allowing the saloons to keep open any longer. Therefore, I shall ignore such orders, as I have been doing. Any saloonkeeper who is brought before me and against whom it is proven that he kept open after midnight, I shall fine. I have been doing this for the last two years that I have been in office and shall continue to do so. The fire and police board has no power whatever in the matter. The only way for the saloons to keep open after midnight would be a repeal of the present city ordinance and the passage of another."—Statement of Police Judge W. J. Thomas.

TOWN WIDE OPEN

No Attention Is Paid to Midnight Closing Order, and Bunco Steerers Jostle Each Other Along Seventeenth Street.

Women Filled Up Winerooms Until Almost Dawn—No Attention Paid to Police.

This was 12-o'clock-day with the fire and police board.

After a heart-to-heart talk with the other members this morning, and a telephone message from Governor Orman, President Adams introduced a resolution to the effect that the laws should be enforced.

"On and after Saturday night, the 27th inst.," resolved the president, "at 12 o'clock midnight all saloons in the city shall be closed and remain closed until 5 o'clock Monday morning. And every night thereafter the closing hour shall be 12 o'clock, and the chief of police is hereby instructed to see that this order is rigorously enforced."

It was further decreed that all winerooms in the city should be suppressed and that women should not be allowed in any portion of any saloon, "and there shall be no exceptions to this order."

Probably had anyone met the two members of the fire and police board, John T. Bottom and President Adams, who have been wrestling with three mighty forces the last week—public sentiment, the law and politics—and had inquired of them: "Watchmen, how goes the night?" they would have answered: "Far from well, brother, far from well."

For there are said to have been many sleepless hours for both and much thinking and a few conferences and finally the expressed conclusion:

"Well, we're up against it!"

About the first business the board transacted at its morning meeting was the adoption of the Adams resolution admitting the victory for the people and the defeat of the rounders.

Governor Said His Say.

When Governor Orman was seen at noon he said he had little to add to what he had already said on the subject of saloon closing. He had been in conference with the members of the fire and police board over the telephone and it was understood they were to adopt a resolution on the lines of the original agreement made in his office at the time the board was appointed.

"I understood that the agreement made at that time when I had the members of the board in conference was to the effect that the law was to be obeyed in every particular. The board has agreed to adopt a resolution along those lines, and I suppose it has been adopted by this time. The law is to govern. I do not approve of any other policy."

The governor seems determined that the board shall live up to the law and the ordinances with respect to saloons closing promptly at 12 o'clock every night in the week, and closing at midnight Saturday night to remain closed until 5 o'clock Monday morning.

WIDE OPEN LAST NIGHT.

"The fire and police board did not issue the order yesterday that the saloons and sporting houses should close at midnight," said Chief Armstrong this morning.

The dives of the lower district kept up their orgies until 4 o'clock this morning. Con Keleher's place was a scene of merry-making and ribaldry. Confidence men, bunco steerers and all the representatives of the criminal classes who rely on the pull of their leader to prevent the police from running them out of town, gathered to celebrate.

The places run by Pat Hickey, Billy Rogers and others were thronged with members of the "liberal" element, who rejoiced in the turn affairs had taken. The promptness with which the denizens of Market street and habitues of the questionable blocks and saloons of the lower section took advantage of their victory was not surprising. It is not the first time that these same classes have followed a victory with demonstration in the past two years. They are proud of their ability to override the decent element and trample under foot the plans of law-abiding citizens to have a better city, rid of dangerous and desperate characters.

Brazen street walkers were plying their vocation through the early hours of the evening and as long as pedestrians were abroad on the street. In the redlight district a display was made by throwing everything wide open as well as the saloons. Window screens were thrown aside and the glamour and glare of vice was exposed to the open streets.

Bunco Men at Work.

Confidence men operated in the business center of the city with no attempt at concealment, seemingly confident of their power to defy the decent people of the city. Bunco steerers lent their presence and influence to make the celebration a success in numbers and noise. If the fire and police board could conveniently stretch the limit a couple of hours they considered it a right to exercise the same prerogative over the members of that august body and extended the limit as much more. So the lower district was awake and keeping everybody else awake until 4 o'clock this morning. They closed in time to open again at 5 o'clock.

Lou Blonger's gang of crooks was openly operating under the nose of the police. They boldly pounced upon their prey in the security of police protection from one end of Seventeenth street to the other. Under one of the chiefs of the gang several new recruits, young men all of them, were being introduced to the haunts of the professionals and taught the lesson of how easy it is to commit crime in Denver. They did not desist from their operations with the termination of night. They were active again this morning.

Hall Must Move On.

"Jack" Hall, the notorious politician, is an apt illustration of how the mighty sometimes fall. There was a time when Hall had pull and influence sufficient to make the police department bow down to him. But that time is past. For years Hall has been known as a professional bondsman, becoming surety for women arrested for soliciting. In this way Hall made from $5 to $10 on each case. Chief Armstrong has refused bond offered by him and instructed him to move on.

SHE HELPED CROWE

Woman Aided Him in the Cudahy Kidnaping.

TRIAL OF JIM CALLAHAN

Identified as One of the Participants in the Preparations for the Kidnaping—Renting of the Old Outhouse.

Omaha, April 26.—(Associated Press.)—James Callahan is a different looking man now than the James Callahan arrested two months ago charged with the kidnaping of Eddie Cudahy. He appears in court well dressed, his hair carefully combed and clean shaven, with the exception of a mustache, which has grown out so much during his confinement as to deceive the average witness.

B. K. Munshaw, who lives near the Melrose hill house, was the first witness called this morning on the trial of James Callahan in the Cudahy kidnaping case. He identified the picture of Crowe as that of a man who came to his house about three weeks before the kidnaping and wanted to know who owned the Schneiderwind house.

Munshaw said he told him, and the man came back later and said he had rented it and paid $1 down and would pay the balance when he moved in the following Monday.

Munshaw testified that he saw Crowe there on the day before the kidnaping and talked with him again, and the latter said he would move in the next Monday.

Munshaw added that on the night of the kidnaping the dogs barked late in the evening, and he went out by the well and saw a buggy or spring wagon drive past and draw up to the steps of the Schneiderwind house. He was down hill from there, and the parties were outlined against the sky. The night was dark, but he could see the outlines. He saw what he thought was two men go up the steps and into the house, and he thought the parties were moving in some of their goods.

Accompanied by a Woman.

Crowe, Munshaw testified, was accompanied by a woman when he called the first time in a buggy and inquired about the house.

Detective Savage was recalled. He testified that he talked with Callahan at Fourteenth and Douglas about three weeks before he was arrested. Callahan claimed that he was going to work switching for the Chicago, St. Paul, M. & O. road on the following morning. They talked about Pat Crowe and the kidnaping, and that Callahan expressed his belief in Crowe's innocence and said that he had taken Crowe with him to his sister's house and introduced Crowe to her as Mr. Johnson. This, Callahan said, was just after the Northwestern train robbery, when Mrs. Kelly was living in Council Bluffs.

Savage testified that later Callahan admitted to the chief of police that he had introduced Crowe to his sister as Johnson. He testified that Callahan said he could not turn up, and that he would not if he could.

George Wittum identified Callahan as a man who passed by his house on the day before the kidnaping, between 12 and 1 o'clock. He said he and his wife both watched the man while he traveled 200 or 300 feet, and until he passed out of sight.

THE TIMES DOES THINGS.

The Times exclusively told how Con Keleher had beaten the fire and police board into submission. Yesterday no other paper published the statement of Governor Orman that the board had broken its pledge to him.

The defalcation of James Secrist, banker of South Side Camp No. 71, Woodmen of the World, was exclusively told in The Times yesterday.

The election of George J. Gould as chairman of the Denver & Rio Grande board and E. H. Harriman and Winslow S. Pierce as directors, was told in The Times. The Times was the noly paper in the United States that previously announced that George J. Gould would be elected.

Harry Corson Clarke had his ears boxed by Bessie Blix Paxton, who quit his company and returned to Denver. The Times alone had the story.

The advent of David May, Dennis Sullivan and W. H. James into the Beaumont oil fields was another Times exclusive yesterday.

The Times told exclusively of the meeting of Pugilist Sharkey with Dr. Crandall of the naval recruiting station, his first referee.

The Times was the only paper which told yesterday of the organization of thieves and pickpockets to loot the crowds that greet President McKinley on his tour.

Guide Goff's story of the Roosevelt hunt was published exclusively in The Times yesterday.

Interest of prominent citizens in a plan to organize a stock company to bore for oil near Denver was another exclusive.

The Times was the only Denver paper which told that "Black Jack" was being taken from Santa Fe to Clayton via Trinidad under heavy guard, on the day of his removal.

And there were more yesterday and will be every day. It's a way The Times has of doing things.

WILL VISIT CREEK

President McKinley Will See Colorado Gold Camp.

SPRINGS WILL DIVIDE TIME

President Will Not Be Able to Extend His Visit to Denver, and Committees Are Arranging Program Accordingly.

President McKinley will visit Cripple Creek. The committee of the Colorado Springs chamber of commerce which has charge of the two-days' visit allotted to Colorado Springs in the itinerary has divided time with the Cripple Creek district. For the second day the committee has arranged so that the presidential party will leave Colorado Springs for Cripple Creek at 9 a. m. and leave Cripple Creek at 3:15 p. m. on Wednesday, June 9.

The party will probably be taken one way over the Colorado Springs & Cripple Creek District railway and the other way over the Midland Terminal and Colorado Midland roads, which will allow the president to see practically the entire district.

A telegram from Presidential Secretary Cortelyou to Chairman Charles J. Hughes of the committee to receive President McKinley announces that the program arranged for Denver, for a stop of four hours, cannot be changed. The committee is accordingly arranging details of provisional program to make the best possible use of the short stop to be made in Denver.

CHINESE TROOPS APPROACH

Pekin, April 26.—(Associated Press.)—The Chinese regulars who retired beyond the great wall have reappeared at another point within the international area. Strong representations have been made to the Chinese plenipotentiaries in regard to the necessity for their immediate retirement. The French force is in readiness to renew the operations, but it has been ordered to await the result of the imperial edict.

A PUBLIC HEARING

Fire and Police Board Will Discuss Billboards.

SIDETRACK SALOON QUESTION

One Subject Getting Too Hot for Comfort and Those Who Oppose Billboards Will Be Given a Chance.

The fire and police board will tomorrow morning at 11 o'clock give a hearing to all those citizens who are opposed to the billboards.

If the board room is not large enough to hold the indignant ones, adjournment will be taken to the council chamber.

The Curran Billposting company has applied for a renewal of its license, and in view of the many complaints received the last few days the board has decided to listen to the public before granting the renewal. The company has been cited to appear and show cause why its license should not be cancelled.

Mrs. M. G. Fries, who built a new frame barn last week and awoke the other morning to find it plastered with tobacco advertisements, will appear and ask the board to refuse the company a license, and J. T. Hanley of Eleventh and Broadway, who has been opposed to the billboards for some time and has threatened to take the law into his own hands if the board does not do something, will also be a witness, and any others who have reason to be opposed to the billboard as it is now handled are asked to appear and state their grievances.

CONTROVERSY DECIDED.

Washington, April 26.—Secretary of the Interior Hitchcock yesterday decided in favor of the Kern Oil company and the Gray Eagle Oil company in the two cases instituted against them separately by C. W. Clarke in the Kern river oil district, California. Clarke is the Forest lien land selector in each case and the two companies named are the mineral claimants in oil land litigation which has attracted great attention in California.

HELD UP A TRAIN

The Robbers Get Only About $350, However.

LEFT A $1,000 PACKAGE

The Safe Resisted the Attempts of the Robbers to Open It—Officers Looking for the Bandits, Who Escaped.

Macon, Ga., April 26.—(Associated Press.)—The express car of the Central of Georgia railroad was robbed between 12:50 and 1:50 o'clock this morning by two men who boarded the train at Macon. The car was going through from Atlanta to Savannah. Some time after the train pulled out of Macon the two men, who had secreted themselves in some way, entered the express car and confronted Express Messenger J. N. White. They seized and bound him hand and foot and threw a sack over his head. They then went through his packages and secured about $350, but left a $1,000 package lying on the floor. The safe resisted their attempts to open it. When the train reached the village of Gordon, twenty miles from Macon, the robbers dropped off. The messenger was uninjured when discovered by the conductor. Detectives and company officers are now scouring the country. The men are supposed to be two suspicious characters who were seen hanging about the Union depot for two days. Two nights ago Messenger White observed two men closely watching his car in the station and ordered them away.

Anaconda, Mont., April 26.—(Associated Press.)—A most audacious robbery was committed here early today by two burglars, who secured $10,000 in gold. The burglars entered the Alaska saloon by forcing the main street door. Bodily picking up a 300-pound safe, they loaded it onto an expres wagon. Driving outside the city limits, they broke the safe open and secured $10,000 in gold. Putting the broken safe back into the wagon, they started the horse toward the city and made good their escape. There is no clew.

GENERAL LUDLOW VERY ILL

Attack of Grip and Localized Congestion Which Developed Into Tuberculosis.

Manila, April 26.—(Associated Press.)—Owing to his illness, the appointment of Brigadier General William Ludlow to be military governor of the department of the Visayas has been revoked. A board of surgeons has made an examination and reports that General Ludlow suffered from an attack of grip and localized congestion, which has developed into a dangerous case of tuberculosis. General Ludlow will return to the United States by the first transport.

ONE APPOINTMENT TODAY.

The mayor this morning appointed Benjamin Sutherland chief at the city shops and then closed up the appointment and application book for the day.

SPEER "LAUGHS LAST."

What did I tell you? I knew you'd get it! Haw! Haw! Haw! Haw! He-e-e-e! Ha-a-a-w!

MISS LEWIS' EVIDENCE REMAINS UNSHAKEN

Former Fiancee of Sam Strong Is Cool Under Cross-Examination.

Miss Nellie Lewis was on the stand again this morning in the Strong damage case, in Judge Palmer's court. She submitted to a terrible cross-examination at the hands of Attorney Waldron. But Miss Lewis, it must be conceded, held her own with the shrewd attorney and was never much baffled by his keen questions.

The plaintiffs were present in court, including "the Honorable Mr. Colbourn," so drastically flayed by Attorney Waldron yesterday.

There was a good attendance of spectators and prominent members of the bar attracted by the unusual interest of the case.

Sam Strong was there, quiet and alert. He watched the girl whom he had formerly loved, and who had secured a judgment against him for breach of promise. Sometimes Strong whispered to one of his attorneys. Occasionally he wrote a note and handed it to one of the lawyers. He rarely took his eyes off Miss Lewis, however. Miss Lewis had plenty to do to parry Attorney Waldron's thrusts, but she took an occasional glance at Strong.

Miss Lewis was cool and calm. She thought over her answers and kept Mr. Waldron often repeating his questions. She wore a black silk dress, with pink ribbon at her throat, and a spreading white hat, with lace and chiffon trimming. Her black hair was drawn down over her ears.

Mr. Waldron went over the story of the trip of Strong and Miss Lewis from Colorado Springs to Victor and the things Strong had told Miss Lewis. Miss Lewis did not remember some things that Mr. Waldron wanted to know.

"Why don't you remember?" demanded the attorney.

"Because this case doesn't concern me," was the reply.

"Why doesn't it concern you?"

"Because it isn't any of my concern."

"Do you mean to say you don't care whether Sam Strong wins or loses this case?"

"It is none of my business."

"Do you mean to say that this case does not concern you any more than if Sam Strong was not in it?"

"I don't know."

"Will you say that you would be equally pleased whether Sam Strong wins or loses this case?"

"I don't understand what you mean."

"I mean have you any more interest in this case than if the defendant were an entire stranger to you?"

"I can't say."

Miss Lewis finally rewarded the infinite labors of Attorney Waldron by stating that she didn't care which way the case went.

Mr. Waldron attempted to get particulars more in detail on the ride from Victor to Colorado Springs.

"Who did the driving?" asked the attorney.

"Sam Strong," was the reply.

"Why, didn't you say he was sick?"

"Yes, he was."

"Then why did he do the driving?"

"I don't know."

"Do you mean to say you let a sick man drive all the way?"

"He wanted to drive and I didn't pay any attention to who was to do the driving."

"Wasn't that a fast trip?"

"Sam Strong said it was the quickest trip ever made between Cripple Creek and Colorado Springs."

"Yes, but I want to get at what you know. Wasn't it down hill?"

"I don't know."

Cripple Creek Up Hill.

"Don't you know that Cripple Creek is 2,000 or 3,000 feet higher than Colorado Springs?"

"I never thought about it. Since you say so, I believe it is."

"Then it was down hill that morning?"

"If it was down hill any time, it must have been down hill that morning."

"What was Strong doing during the drive?"

"He was sick. He was smoking and vomiting."

Mr. Waldron spent the next ten minutes trying to get Miss Lewis to say how many cigars Strong smoked, how many times he vomited and what proportion of the time was allotted to each occupation. But, after parrying questions for a time, Miss Lewis settled it by saying:

"I don't remember and I don't intend to say."

Miss Lewis was aroused to brisk replies when Mr. Waldron touched on her motives for appearing in the case.

"If Sam Strong had never married, would you have appeared in this case?"

"I don't know."

"If Sam Strong had never got married,

Continued on Page Seven.

"Black Jack" Ketchum's Execution at Clayton This Afternoon a Scene of Awful Horror.

The Rope Broke, but the Fall Was So Great That Train Robber's Head Was Jerked Off.

Clayton, N. M., April 26.—The execution of "Black Jack" Ketchum this afternoon was one of the most horrible ever witnessed in the country.

The rope broke, but the fall was so great that the train robber's head was jerked off.

A cry of horror arose from those who witnessed the terrible scene, and one man fainted away.

Ketchum had eaten a hearty meal, taking forty minutes to finish it, and chatting and joking all the time with those about him.

It was 1 o'clock when Sheriff Garcia told him to get ready. He complied at once and at 1:17 the party mounted the scaffold.

It took but four minutes to finish the scaffold details.

He became nervous and said "Let 'er go."

At 1:21 the trap was sprung.

The body rebounded once and then, to the horror of all those about, it was seen that the fall had been too great and that the head was severed from the body.

Clayton, N. M., April 26.—(Special.)—Thomas Ketchum, alias Black Jack, spent the morning talking to friends, his attorney and newspaper representatives. He said to his attorney:

"Tell Harrington I'll meet him in hell soon."

After eating a hearty dinner he was told to prepare himself for death. The death warrant was read to him early this morning. The priest went into the cell just before the start for the scaffold was made and accompanied Tom on his death march.

At 1 p. m. he began the march to the scaffold after having his last request for music complied with. He had given his attorney direction for disposing of his effects.

With Sheriff Garcia on his right, Harry Lewis of Trinidad on his left, and accompanied by Detective Chambers of Denver, Tom marched coolly and calmly to the gallows. Going up the stairs leading to the noose he kept his eyes on the ground. He stepped firmly on the trap door and his legs and arms were pinioned. Then he asked for the black cap, which he put on. For some reason it was taken off and Tom shook hands with the sheriff and several deputies. Then the cap was adjusted again. By this time he was getting nervous.

He finally became impatient at the delay and said:

"Let 'er go, boys."

"Not quite ready," replied the officers.

Then when they were ready he again shook hands with them and said:

"Let 'er go, boys; let 'er go."

Sheriff Garcia then, at 1:21 p. m., cut the rope and Black Jack's body shot down.

The fall severed his head frim his body. He alighted on his feet and his headless trunk stood for an instant upright, then swayed and fell, and great streams of blood shot out of the severed neck.

The head remaining in black-cap, rolled to one side and the rope, released, flew high in the air. No physician was needed to tell that life was extinct.

There was a small stockade, but the people could look through the cracks. Quite a crowd was present to witness the horrible spectacle.

Thirty minutes before the drop fell Tom said he would meet Captain Forrest, counsel for the Wells-Fargo Express company, and District Attorney J. Leahy, who prosecuted him, and W. H. Reno, the Colorado & Southern detective, in hell, also, inside of a year.

Black Jack said he wrote a letter to "the boys" and smuggled it out of Santa Fe penitentiary, telling them to send these parties after him soon. Says they are "marked." Expressed himself very bitterly against those who were engaged in prosecuting him. Says Judge Mills, Leahy and others were bought by the railroad and express companies. He retained his nerve to the last and died game like he said he would. He failed to make the speech promised, but included all he had to say in his statement to his lawyer.

He said he would advise all the boys not to steal sheep, cattle or horses, but if they must steal, to rob a bank or railroad train. He said he began his career of crime in 1897, and never had murdered anybody. The priest attending was Father Dean of Trinidad. The head was sewed on and the body prepared for burial by E. J. Sibort of Trinidad. Thus closes the history of one of New Mexico's greatest bandits. His remains will be buried here.

HE HAD NO FEAR OF DEATH

Clayton, N. M., April 26.—(Special.)—Ketchum passed a quiet night and ate a hearty breakfast. He took a bath and put on a new suit of clothes this morning. Sheriff Garcia bought them. Twenty deputies were on guard last night. A priest from Trinidad was with him from midnight till dawn. In an interview with John R. Guyer, his attorney, yesterday, he asked him to

Continued on Page Seven.

KETCHUM CONFESSES TO TRAIN ROBBERY

Clayton, N. M., April 26.—(Special.)—"Black Jack" Ketchum this morning made a full confession of the crime for which others were punished. Following is his message to the president as given out at 10 a. m.:

To His Excellency, the President of the United States, Washington:

Sir—Being now at the town of Clayton, N. M., awaiting my execution, which is set for this day, and realizing the importance to the liberty of other men and the duty which I conceive to be incumbent upon myself, standing in the presence of death, where no human aid can reach me, I desire to communicate to you by means of this letter some facts which I deem would be of interest to people through their president and perhaps be the means of liberating innocent men.

There are now three men in the Santa Fe penitentiary serving sentences for the robbery of the United States mail at Stein's Pass, Ariz., in 1897, viz: Leonard Albertson, Walter Huffman and Bill Waterman. They are as innocent of the crime as unborn babes.

The names of the men who committed the crime are Dave Atkins, Ed Bullin, Will Carver, Sam Ketchum, Broncho Bill and myself. I have given to my attorney in Clayton means by which articles taken in said robbery may be found where we hid them, and also the names of witnesses who live in that vicinity, who will testify that myself and gang were in that neighborhood both immediately before and after the robbery.

The fact that these men are innocent and others suffering, impels me to make this confession. While you cannot help me and while I realize that all efforts to secure to me a commutation of my sentence have signally failed, I wish to do this much in the interest of these innocent men, who, as far as I know, never committed a crime in their lives.

I make this statement, fully realizing that my end is fast approaching and that I must very soon meet my Maker. Very respectfully, your servant,

T. E. KETCHUM.

5 O'Clock

THE BUFFALO EVENING TIMES

Last Edition

[THE ONLY DEMOCRATIC EVENING NEWSPAPER IN BUFFALO OR WESTERN NEW YORK WHICH IS A MEMBER OF THE ASSOCIATED PRESS.]

VOL. XXXV—NO. 153. FRIDAY EVENING, SEPTEMBER 6, 1901. ON TRAINS TWO CENTS. ONE CENT.

EXTRA!

PRESIDENT M'KINLEY SHOT AT THE PAN-AMERICAN!

RECEPTION TO THE PRESIDENT

Royally Welcomed at Niagara Falls After a Trip Over the Gorge Road---Returns to Buffalo.

A public reception to President McKinley is in progress in the Temple of Music, Exposition grounds, this afternoon, beginning at 4 o'clock.

"The Exposition seems more beautiful in the morning, even, than in the evening," remarked President McKinley this morning at the railroad gate, just before his special train started for the Falls, and just after he had been driven across the grounds.

The President's visit to the Exposition this morning was unofficial. There was a crowd of loyal Americans at the Lincoln Parkway gate at 8:40 o'clock when the President and his party drove into the grounds. The horses sped along rapidly and the President was whisked past the waiting crowds at a rate that gave those in waiting only a glimpse of a smiling face and an uplifted hat.

The President's carriage was escorted by a platoon of mounted police. Behind him was a carriage full of detectives, and, following that, several carriages containing invited guests and members of the diplomatic corps, who were to accompany him on his trip to Niagara Falls.

The escort of military officers, detailed to accompany the President, followed the party in automobile, the entire line making a rather imposing impression. Among the military officers were: Brig.-Gen. S. M. Welch, Major M. B. Butler, Mayor of Niagara Falls, and commander of the 1st Battalion, National Guard; Lieut.-Col. Chapin, representing Major-Gen. Roe; Captains White, Pagan and Chapin, and Lieut. William H. Hicks of the 65th Regiment, and Capt. Walter Grant King of the 4th Brigade staff.

The dew was still on the grass, glistening brightly, and the flowers in the various gardens, refreshed by a night of rest, were holding up their gaily colored heads, and nodding in the morning breezes, as if in salute to the Nation's chieftain. The Exposition looked its prettiest and the absence of the crowds of yesterday gave the President an opportunity to study and admire its artistic charms.

The drive to the Railroad Gate was made without interruption, and the special train left the grounds promptly at 9 o'clock on the schedule to the minute.

Reception to the President.

George K. Birge and other prominent citizens will give a reception to President McKinley at the Mission Building, near the Stadium, on the Exposition grounds, this afternoon at 3 o'clock.

PRESIDENT M'KINLEY WELCOMED AT THE FALLS

PRIVACY WILL BE A MARKED FEATURE OF HIS STAY IN THAT CITY.

Special to THE TIMES.

NIAGARA FALLS, Sept. 6.—President McKinley, his escort and the members of the legations arrived here on time to the minute this morning on their way to Lewiston, it being just 9:35 o'clock when the big engine No. 890 with a train of five handsome coaches poked its nose into the Falls Street Station.

Very few knew the exact time of the arrival of the train and there were not over 200 people about the depot. Those who were there made no demonstration as the train drew up, but all wandered up and down the cars in hopes of catching a glimpse of the Chief Executive. The last coach soon became the center of attraction and just as the train started up after a half-minute stop the President stepped to one of the windows in the center of the rear coach. In a second every hat was lifted in a respectful salute, which was returned with a smile. At the North End station the same was repeated and then the special wound its way around the Lewiston branch and was soon lost in the distance.

Many of the business houses of the city are decorated in honor of President's day. All arrangements are with a view of the utmost privacy for the President and the private dining-room at the International has been screened off.

The return of President McKinley and party from Lewiston to this city was exactly on schedule time, the private car of Mr. Morgan of the Gorge Road arriving at Second and Main Streets at exactly 11:15. This car carried the President and Mrs. McKinley and a score of diplomats, while another which followed closely, contained the balance of party. A long line of carriages was in waiting and the party entered and, headed by Col. Welch of the 65th Regiment and staff, proceeded to the International Hotel. Mrs. McKinley had signified her desire to go to the hotel as soon as possible to enjoy rest and relief from the burning sun. A crowd surrounded the hotel as the carriages drove up, and there was a ringing cheer as the First Lady of the Land was escorted through the long corridor to the suite that had been reserved and guarded at all entrances by police. The party then resumed the drive, passing through the park and around Goat Island, returning to the hotel at 12:10 for luncheon. The President's carriage and the second containing Secret Service men, drove into the Hotel Park in the rear, while the balance went to the front. At 12:30 luncheon was served in the private dining room. The ladies' parlor, the white parlor and two of the prettiest rooms on the ground floor were magnificently decorated with Turkish tapestries and draperies, the whole ornamentation representing in value over $10,000. After luncheon the party go to the Power House and at 2:15 take a special train for Buffalo.

DIED.

WATERBURY—Thursday, September 5, 1901, Sarah A., widow of Francis N. Waterbury, mother of Frank and Harry Waterbury. Funeral services from the residence of her son, No. 471 West Ferry Street, Saturday, September 7th, at 3:30 P. M. Interment at Noroton, Conn.

ROBINSON—In this city, September 5, 1901, Catharine L., widow of the late Capt. William D. Robinson, aged 81 years and 4 months. The funeral will take place from the residence of John J. Hynes, No. 838 Auburn Avenue, Monday morning at 8:30 o'clock, and from the Chapel of the Blessed Sacrament at 9:30 o'clock. Friends are invited to attend. Detroit, Mich., Chicago, Ill., and Cleveland, O., papers please copy. Flowers gratefully declined. 6t7

HANLEY—In this city, September 5, 1901, Edward P., son of Julia and the late James Hanley, aged 2 years and 5 months. The funeral will take place from the family residence, No. 684 Fulton Street, on Saturday afternoon at 2 o'clock. Friends and acquaintances are respectfully invited to attend.

WEBER—In this city, September 5, 1901, Rosinna, wife of the late Michael G. Weber, aged 85 years, 5 months and 23 days. Funeral will take place from the family residence, No 380 Spring Street on Monday morning at 8:30 o'clock and from St. Mary's Church at 9 o'clock. Friends and acquaintances are respectfully invited to attend. Flowers gratefully declined.

BATAVIA CARRIERS

FREE DELIVERY IS TO BE ESTABLISHED AND TWO NEW MEN APPOINTED.

Special to THE TIMES.

WASHINGTON, Sept. 6.—Additional rural free delivery services will be established November 1st next as follows: Batavia, Genesee County, with two carriers, Burt Radley and John D. Forward; length of routes, 47 3-4 miles; area covered, 30 square miles; population served, 1,142.

VICE-PRESIDENT ROOSEVELT

Guest of U. S. Senator Proctor—Made a Speech at the Vermont State Fair.

By Associated Press.

BURLINGTON, Vt., Sept. 6.—Vice-President Theodore Roosevelt arrived in this city Thursday afternoon by special train from Proctor, where he was the guest of U. S. Senator Redfield Proctor at luncheon, after speaking at the State fair at Rutland this morning.

AT THE ELLICOTT CLUB

The following guests registered at the Ellicott Club today: Arthur Burtis, Pay Director, U. S. Navy; Ethelbert Watts, U. S. Consul, Jamaica, W. I.; J. A. McKay, Chicago; S. B. Roby, Rochester; C. M. Warner, Syracuse; W. H. Suntun, New York; J. Falkner, Saranac Lake, N. Y.

HE STOLE DESSERT.

Leslie Perrine was fined $15 by Judge Murphy in the Police Court today for stealing potatoes from Harlem Bros.' grocery store.

BRIEFS BY WIRE.

NEW YORK, Sept. 6.—The Shamrock did not go out for a spin this forenoon owing to fog and light winds.

SYRACUSE, N. Y., Sept. 6.—The entries for the horse show of the State Fair which have closed are 500 in number.

Special to THE TIMES.

PAN-AMERICAN GROUNDS, SEPT. 6, 4.25 P. M.—PRESIDENT M'KINLEY WAS SHOT TWICE IN THE STOMACH AT THE TEMPLE OF MUSIC. HE FELL AND WAS TAKEN TO THE EXPOSITION HOSPITAL.

STRIKERS REJECT LATEST OFFER

Positive Statement Made That All Negotiations Between Contending Parties Had Come to an End.

PITTSBURG, Sept. 6.—IN STEEL CORPORATION CIRCLES IN PITTSBURG TODAY IT WAS POSITIVELY ANNOUNCED THAT THE LAST OFFER MADE BY THE BIG STEEL COMBINATION HAD BEEN REJECTED BY THE AMALGAMATED BOARD, AND THAT ALL NEGOTIATIONS WERE ENDED.

EXECUTIVE COMMITTEE OF THE ASSOCIATION MEETS

SIX MILLS OUT OF 15 STARTED THIS MORNING

OUT OF TOWN MEMBERS ORDERED TO PITTSBURG

THE STEEL CORPORATION WILL NOT CONFER AGAIN

FLYING AFTER THE FLYER

BICYCLE RACKS ABOLISHED

SHAKE-UP OF POLICE

Capt. Regan Goes Back to the First Precinct, Taylor Goes to the Third and Killeen to the Thirteenth.

A meeting of the full Board of Police Commissioners was held this morning, when sweeping changes were made in the location of inspectors and captains. Mayor Diehl and Commissioners Rupp and Cooper attended.

The changes decided upon go into effect at 6 o'clock this evening. There is one exception. Capt. Notter will remain in charge of No. 13 Police Station until Capt. Killeen reports for duty next Monday morning.

Capt. Regan under the new dispensation takes command of No. 1. Capt. Taylor going to the Third Precinct. Following is a complete list of the changes:

Inspector Martin 1st to 2d Precinct.
Inspector Donovan, 2d to 1st Precinct.
Capt. Burfiend, 13th to 4th Precinct.
Capt. Regan, 4th to 1st Precinct.
Capt. Killeen, 2d to 13th Precinct.
Capt. Taylor, 1st to 3d Precinct.
Special Caney, 13th to 10th Precinct.
Capt. Notter, 13th to 5th Precinct.
Sergt. Given, 8th to 3d Precinct.

The transfer of Capt. Regan to No. 1 has been in contemplation by the Commissioners for some time. Capt. Killeen, who goes from No. 3 to the Thirteenth Precinct, has had a bitter warfare made against him for some time by persons determined to oust him. Capt. Taylor's new position will be little different from the one he has held.

Not in a long time have changes in the police force been made of such sweeping and widespread importance. The purpose, no doubt, is to benefit the service. The present season is especially trying to the police authorities, who have problems presented to them daily which are difficult of solution.

SWINDLED

E. B. CARLTON OF FLORIDA CLEVERLY FLEECED IN TONAWANDA.

E. B. Carlton of Arcadia, Fla., has complained to the police of Tonawanda and Buffalo that he has been swindled out of $600 by a sharper who gave the name of G. B. Lovering. The trick was carried out in Tonawanda.

Mr. Carlton came here with maps of property he had for sale in Florida. He met the confidence man, he says, at the Union Station in Tonawanda and the fellow represented he was anxious to buy. He actually paid $100 down on the deal. Afterwards he assumed to make another payment amounting to $600 or $700. Mr. Carlton put his own good currency on top of this bunch and the Tonawanda man put a rubber band around one end of the bundle. In trying to put a band on the other end he dropped the package. Mr. Carlton put the bundle in his packet and boarded a train for home.

He soon discovered, he says, that the package in his pocket was of paper, cut out the size of bills. There was a good $1 bill on the top and another on the bottom. He got off the train and is now trying to find the man who basely deceived him. He gave a deed of the property in Florida and has notified the recorder in the county where the real estate is situated, not to put the deed on record.

ATTEMPTED SUICIDE!

James Hurley took a dose of "rough on rats" at the Unique Hotel at an early hour this morning. Medical aid was promptly summoned and his condition was reported as favorable this afternoon. This is said to be the second attempt at self destruction within a week.

BUFFALO CLEARING HOUSE.

Clearing for week ending September 5th, $5,067,774.50; balances, $978,193.78; clearings for corresponding week last year, $4,718,511.76; balances, $749,915.32.

TOO LATE TO CLASSIFY.

KING EDWARD A SICK MAN

By Associated Press.

LONDON, SEPT. 6.—THOUGH KING EDWARD IS CONSCIENTIOUSLY SUBMITTING TO THE LIGHT, WATER AND MASSAGE "CURE" AT HOMBURG, HIS HEART TROUBLE, THE CANDID FRIEND, A WEEKLY PAPER, SAYS, FROM WHICH HE HAS SUFFERED SINCE AND BEFORE HIS ACCESSION, SHOWS NO IMPROVEMENT.

PAN-AMERICAN COMMISSIONERS.

By Associated Press.

TORONTO, Sept. 6.—Executive Commissioners of Pan-American Exposition arrived in city this morning. Civic reception committee met visitors at wharf, afterwards being driven round city and taken to Exhibition grounds. Luncheon was served, A. E. Ames, president Board of Trade, presiding.

LICENSES UNSETTLED.

BOY AND THE TILL.

"The Only Paper in Chicago that dares to print the News."

The Inter Ocean.

"The Only Paper in Chicago that dares to print the News."

VOL. XXXI., NO. 136. CHICAGO, THURSDAY MORNING, AUGUST 7, 1902. PRICE—TWO CENTS.

OUTLAW TRACY COMMITS SUICIDE RATHER THAN SUBMIT TO CAPTURE

With Leg Broken, Surrounded, and Unable to Stanch Bleeding Artery, Bandit Sends Bullet Into His Brain.

DRIVEN TO BAY AT LAST BY SMALL POSSE OF CITIZENS

Uses Farmer and Horse as Shield in Final Stand on Farm Near Fellowes, Wash.—Dispute Over $5,600 Reward—Crowds View Remains.

Special Dispatch to The Inter Ocean.

SPOKANE, Wash., Aug. 6.—Harry Tracy is dead. The most talked of desperado of recent times has ended one of the most sensational man hunts in the history of the West and the entire country, with a bullet sent into his brain by his own hand. He had boasted that he would never be taken alive, and he kept his word. Discovered in a barn near Fellowes, a station on the Washington Central, fifty miles west of Spokane, last night, he made a dash for liberty. A bullet fractured his right leg, but he escaped into a wheat field, where after an unsuccessful attempt to stay the flow of blood from a severed artery, he ended the long chase of nearly two months by blowing out his brains.

Scores of peace officers have spent weeks and thousands of dollars in chasing the escaped convict over the states of Oregon and Washington since his escape from prison, June 9, but none of them was "in at the death," and the big reward is likely to be divided between outsiders.

Sheriff Arrives Too Late.

After baffling the officers of two states, after a wonderful flight of nearly 400 miles across Oregon and Washington, Tracy was hunted down by four citizens of the little farming town of Creston, and a single deputy sheriff. Sheriff Gardner and posse arrived in time to guard the wheat field through the night, but the work had already been done.

The men that will share the reward are: C. A. Straub, constable; Dr. E. C. Lanter, Maurice Smith, attorney; J. J. Morrison, railway section foreman, and Frank Lillengren.

These men, armed to the teeth, set out from Creston yesterday afternoon about 2 o'clock. They were working on the information of the Goldfinch youth, who had been forcibly made the companion of the Oregon convict for over twenty-four hours at the ranch of L. B. Eddy, about three miles south from Fellowes.

The party made all possible haste in getting to the ranch. When within a few hundred yards of the farm they encountered Farmer Eddy mowing in one of his fields. While engaging him in conversation they saw a man issuing from the barn door.

"Is that Tracy?" asked one of the party.

"It surely is," replied Eddy.

The party separated, Canter and Smith accompanying Eddy in the direction of the barn, while the other two men swung around to the other side. Two of the man hunters stepped behind the barn on a slight eminence, from which they could watch everything that went on, and Eddy continued on up to the door. Tracy came from the barn again and began helping his host unhitch the horses. He carried no rifle, although he had his revolvers in place.

The fugitive finally saw the men carrying rifles and turning sharply to Eddy, said:

"Who are those men?"

"I don't see any men," said Eddy.

Tracy pointed out the two men on the hill. Eddy informed his companion who the men were, and the outlaw made a leap for the barn door. The pursuers, stepping a bit closer, commanded, "Hold up your hands."

Last Stand for Liberty.

The outlaw jumped behind Eddy and placed first the farmer and then his horse between himself and the pursuers. He commanded the farmer to lead his horse to the barn and remaining under cover moved toward shelter. When near the stable he broke and dashed inside. He quickly reappeared, rifle in hand, and started on the run.

Turning on the two men nearest him the desperado fired two shots, but without his usual luck, neither bullet taking effect. Without waiting for further fighting Tracy made a dash down the valley leading south from the barn and headed for the brush.

In an instant the man-hunters were off in pursuit, firing as they ran. Coming to a rock, Tracy dodged behind it, and resting his gun began a fusillade. Eight shots in all were fired by the outlaw, not one hitting its mark. He then bolted for a wheat field close by. At the edge of the field he stumbled, falling on his face, and crawled into the grain on his hands and knees.

It was growing dark and the pursuers not daring to move in closer decided to surround the place and wait for daylight.

In the meantime, Sheriff Gardner, with Policemen Stauffer and Gemmerim of Spokane, Jack O'Farrell of Davenport, and other re-enforcements had arrived on the scene, and they went into camp around the field during the night.

End of Long Chase.

Shortly after Tracy disappeared a shot was heard from the direction of the wheat field. No investigation was made, however, until this morning.

As soon as dawn came an entrance was made into the wheat field. Tracy's dead body was found lying amid the grain, with his face turned toward the sky. His left hand, thrown over his head, held a revolver, which had inflicted the death wound. The thumb of his hand was on the trigger of the pistol. His right hand, thrown across the lower part of his body, firmly grasped the barrel of the famous rifle.

Death was inflicted by a revolver held close to the forehead. The top of his head was badly shattered.

Two bullet wounds on the left leg showed the cause of the man's despondency. One shot had broken the leg between the ankle and the knee. The other cut the tibial artery, which of itself was sufficient cause for death.

It is believed that both of these wounds were received after the convict left the shelter of the rock and made his break for the wheat field. The murderer had taken a strap and buckled it tightly around his leg in an attempt to stop the bleeding. Despite this the bleeding continued until he probably realized his hopeless condition and ended the struggle.

He was dressed in blue overalls, a white shirt, and wore no coat or vest. He wore a bicycle cap and a pair of rough shoes. He had one rifle and two revolvers.

Dispute Over Reward.

Sheriff Gardner of Lincoln county and his assistants arrived on the scene in time to help in the final discovery of the remains and it is stated that the sheriff maintained that he and his deputies were entitled to at least a share of the booty. This was disputed by the Creston party, the members of which maintain that they did the work, and to them belongs the reward. Finally Sheriff Gardner was allowed to take the body with the understanding that he recommend that the reward be paid to the men from Creston.

The body, effects, and the horses of the notorious man were taken in charge by Sheriff Gardner, and taken direct to Davenport, where they will be kept pending the decision of the final disposition of Tracy's body.

Reports come from Davenport that wild excitement prevails. Stores are closed and people are crowding around to get a sight of the outlaw. A heavy guard is kept around the morgue where the body is kept, as well as around the corpse itself, to prevent relic hunters from tearing the clothing to pieces and carrying away souvenirs.

Two Days at Eddy Ranch.

For two days and as many nights Tracy held the family of Farmer L. B. Eddy under subjection. Here again he showed the qualities of nerve and coolheadedness, but these very qualities brought about his downfall. Had he not allowed G. E. Goldfinch, the 18-year-old boy, to leave the ranch when he did the story today might be different, but the outlaw had too much faith in estimating the terror his words of warning would give to the lad.

The story of the exploits of the famous bandit at the Eddy ranch are given by the boy, who was his servant for over a day. It was Sunday afternoon that Goldfinch was riding a horse across the prairie not far from the Eddy farm. He noticed a strange man camped not far from where he passed. To all appearances the stranger was just having his supper, but young Goldfinch paid no attention to him, not seeing anything unusual in his actions. Just as the boy was going by the camper called out, asking him to have some supper. With the reply that he had finished his supper, Goldfinch did not even slacken the pace of his horse, and passed the stranger. It was then that an imperative command from the stranger brought Goldfinch to a sudden stop. He was ordered to come back. This order the boy obeyed. With his usual ceremony, he soon made himself known. He inquired the way to the nearest farm and was directed to the Eddy place. Tracy at this time still had two horses. One he rode, the other, the boy says, was loaded with groceries, meat, sugar, coffee, and bedding.

"You go ahead and tell them I am coming," commanded the outlaw.

Goldfinch readily complied and started ahead to announce the coming of the guest. Tracy, however, kept close on the heels of the lad, evidently not intending to give him a chance to give warning.

On the way to the house Tracy noticed a rope trailing from his pack animal. "That's leaving a bad mark," said the outlaw, and stopped to gather in the trailing coils. He then went on his way to the Eddy ranch. Arriving there Goldfinch performed the service allotted to him and soon told the family who the visitor was.

The night passed without any special happenings, so far as the lad relates. In the morning Tracy first made his toilet. A bath and a shave were included in his morning make-up, the farmer and his men having provided soap, towels, and water.

Assists Farmer in Work.

When the men started for their work Tracy discovered they were constructing an overhead rack in the barn for the fall crop. The outlaw decided to make himself useful, and, divesting himself of his rifle and one of his revolvers, labored with the other men during most of the morning. He kept one revolver, however, in the holster by his side ready for instant use. During the day the outlaw wanted his other weapons, which had been left with his bedding and traveling outfit. He sent Goldfinch after the weapons and proudly passed them around to the awe-stricken workmen. They were allowed to handle the weapons and inspect them, but it is said they took care not to have the muzzles of the guns pointing toward the outlaw.

Tracy all this time had a revolver himself and left no opening for the farmers to get the drop on him. That the outlaw stood in no fear of Eddy and his men attempting to take advantage of the opening was vouched for by himself, he having remarked to the farmer: "I am not afraid of you." During

(Continued on Second Page.)

HARRY TRACY.

(Famous outlaw, who, wounded to death and surrounded in a wheat field, blew out his brains rather than surrender.)

MANY ARE DEAD IN TRAIN COLLISION

Eight Bodies Are Taken from Wreck on St. Paul.

SIGNAL IS IGNORED

Conductor and Engineer Fail to Heed Warning.

Flood in Colorado Throws Cars from Track, but 300 Tourists Escape Injury.

Special Dispatch to The Inter Ocean.

MARSHALLTOWN, Iowa, Aug. 6.—Two engineers and many laborers were killed this afternoon in a collision on the Chicago, Milwaukee & St. Paul road, two miles west of Rhodes, this county, between a fast freight and a work train. It is not known how many were killed, but eight bodies had been recovered up to 3 o'clock. Seventy-eight laborers were on the work train. The freight met the work train going at full speed on a reverse curve.

It appears that the work train, in charge of Conductor Craig, started west from Rhodes against east-bound freight train No. 92 without orders, notwithstanding the fact that the block signal stood against the work train, and the further fact that the telegraph operator informed Conductor Craig that No. 92 had left Collins, the next station west.

Officers Are Surprised.

The officers of the road are utterly unable to account for the act of the conductor and engineer of the work train in leaving Rhodes station in the face of a regular scheduled train past due, and with the block signal standing in the danger position against them.

The dead and injured were taken to Collins station. Surgeons from different parts of the line were immediately taken to the scene of the accident by special trains and everything possible was done for the relief of the injured.

Flood Causes a Wreck.

FLORENCE, Colo., Aug. 5.—A Rio Grande special passenger train from the East, bound to California and carrying 300 tourists, was ditched just east of Florence, near Swallows. The wreck was caused by the train being struck by a wall of water eight feet high coming down Peck creek, caused by the heavy rains in the mountains south of here yesterday afternoon. The brakeman saw the torrent when it was only a short distance from the train. He rushed through the eight coaches and told the passengers on the two rear cars to hurry to the front of the train. Just as the last tourist left the rear coach the water struck the cars and, breaking the coupling pins, hurled them into the air and landed them forty feet from the track.

The trucks were knocked off the day coach, which, after striking the ground, went down fifteen feet into the mud. The sleeper was thrown against the farmhouse of J. G. Roberts, which was occupied by himself, wife, and three children. The coach formed a wall and turned the water from the house, thus saving the building from going into the river and also the lives of its occupants.

The engine was badly damaged by the water, but managed to pull the cars remaining on the track some distance from the flood, and they are now occupied by the tourists and trainmen. A wrecking train was ordered from Salida and the passengers were cared for as well as possible under the conditions. No one is reported injured.

5,000 PERSONS GO FISHING.

Large Crowd Seeks the Finny Tribe at Bloomington.

Special Dispatch to The Inter Ocean.

BLOOMINGTON, Ill., Aug. 6.—Five thousand persons participated today in the third annual fish day, and it was a great success, due to perfect weather and extraordinary good luck of the seekers of the finny tribe at the Miller park lake. There were no time restrictions as in the past, and the public was allowed twenty-four hours for the enjoyment of the sport.

The experienced fishermen were on hand soon after midnight last night, and were rewarded with excellent luck. After daylight the crowds grew larger and until evening there were thousands of people around the banks. The noise and confusion as usual put a quietus on the luck, and but few fish were caught during the day. Tonight with smaller numbers of fishermen the luck returned. Midnight wound up the sport.

$182,000 FOR ILLINOIS RIVER.

Estimate Submitted for Improvement During 1904.

WASHINGTON, D. C., Aug. 6.—Major J. H. Willard has submitted his annual report on the improvement of the Illinois river. He makes an estimate of $182,000 to be expended during the fiscal year, which will complete the project. No estimate is made for funds for the construction of the Illinois and Mississippi canal, of which the Illinois river is a part.

INDEX TO THE NEWS.

UNITED STATES MAY AID BRITISH SHIP

Quito Threatened with Seizure by Colombia.

APPEAL NECESSARY

No Steps Would Be Taken Unless Asked.

Captain of the Gunboat Ranger Instructed to Then Act as in the Case of an American Vessel.

Special Dispatch to The Inter Ocean.

WASHINGTON, D. C., Aug. 6.—The United States may yet be called upon to interfere with affairs in Colombia. The threatened seizure of a British ship by the Governor of Panama might result in this government taking a hand in the trouble.

Several days ago the Governor of Panama requested Commander Potter of the United States gunboat Ranger to leave the harbor and go in search for the Colombian warship Boyaca, which was supposed to be in distress either through a breakdown of her machinery or from having fallen in with one of the revolutionary vessels. Permission was granted from here for the Ranger to do so. But yesterday Commander Potter reported that he would not go to sea because of the appearance off the harbor of a revolutionary ship.

Today he cabled that he had been informed that the Governor of Panama contemplated seizing the British vessel Quito, and, there being no British warship at Panama, he asked for instructions as to what course to pursue.

An Appeal Would Be Necessary.

The presumption at the Navy Department is that the appearance of the revolutionary vessel off the harbor alarmed the government authorities, and, having no ship at hand to meet her, they proposed to press the Quito into service, possibly for the purpose of arming her and sending her out to meet the insurgent vessel.

When the property of one nation is threatened in this fashion, in the absence of a warship of that particular country, it is customary for a warship of a friendly nation, when appealed to, to protect the property of the country requesting aid. But it is not proper for a warship of one country to proffer protection unless formally requested to do so.

Instructions to this effect were immediately sent to Commander Potter, and if the British Consul at Panama should appeal to the Ranger for assistance to prevent the seizing of the Quito, Commander Potter will be expected to adopt the same method to prevent seizure which he would if the Quito were an American ship.

Fear Situation Is Critical.

The situation is considered critical if Commander Potter's information as to the contemplated action of the authorities should prove to be correct.

BURLINGTON TRAIN HELD UP BY SIX MEN AND EXPRESS CAR LOOTED

Wounded Robber Killed by Comrades and Body Thrown Into Ditch Beside the Railroad.

SAFE WRECKED AND SIX BAGS OF MONEY TAKEN

Deed Committed in Carroll County and Band Is Supposed to Have Escaped Into Mississippi River Bottoms.

Special Dispatch to The Inter Ocean.

MOUNT CARROLL, Ill., Aug. 6.—Hundreds of men are tonight searching the country in this vicinity for the gang of robbers who held up the north-bound Burlington limited train last night at Marcus, five miles from Savanna. The country is heavily timbered in the hills, while in the Mississippi river swamps thick underbrush and tall grass make excellent hiding places. There are many ways by which they could escape into Iowa or Wisconsin, and there is little chance of their immediate capture.

The deed was done quickly, the trainmen and passengers making no defense. Six sacks of money, valued at about $2,000, were secured. The passengers were not molested.

There was no way of telegraphing news of the hold-up, and a flagman walked back and gave the alarm. A special train of citizens and several policemen at once proceeded to the scene, but, as the track runs along the Mississippi and the country is well adapted to a successful flight, the robbers easily escaped. The work was evidently that of experts, as they went at it coolly and methodically.

The train attacked is one of the finest in the world and usually carried considerable money, which must have been known by the highwaymen.

Many View Remains.

Hundreds of people from the surrounding country visited Savanna today to see if they could recognize the dead robber. Many of the visitors were police officers from Iowa and Illinois. So far the body has not been identified. It is still at the undertaking establishment, where it will remain for a few days, in the hopes that it may be identified. If the identity of the dead robber can be established it will be an important factor in determining the other bandits.

The wounds on the dead man and the testimony given at the inquest this evening by Engineer John E. Mooney, who pulled the train that was held up, strengthens the theory that the robber was killed by his companions. After the deed had been committed and Mooney was on the engine ready to obey the orders of the robbers, a shot was fired near the engine. He heard a man say, "What did you shoot me for?" There was a scuffling on the ground, and the next moment the body of one of the robbers was placed in the gangway. Mooney was then ordered to get off the engine. He said this one shot was all he heard. When the body was found in the morning there were three wounds, one in the breast just above the right nipple, the ball lodging just beneath the skin in the back. One finger was also shot off. Those two wounds were probably made by the same bullet, and fired by one of the robbers, who mistook the man for one of the trainmen. The other bullet entered the right eye and came out the back of the head. This bullet was undoubtedly fired by the robbers after the man had been placed on the engine, and when they discovered the seriousness of the first wound, knowing the man would be a burden to them and fearing he would expose them for leaving him, they killed their companion in crime to avoid detection.

The dead robber was a man of fine appearance, perhaps 30 years of age. He was dark complexioned, had sideburns and a mustache, and wore an air of considerable refinement. His hair and eyes were jet black. He was well dressed and wore blue overalls and a blue jacket. In his pocket was found an Iowa Central mileage credential from Grinnell to Gilmap, Iowa, issued in the name of A. L. Jacobs. All the men were dressed exactly alike.

Story of Engineer Mooney.

The principal witness at the inquest was Engineer John E. Mooney, who said:

"While nearing the south switch at Marcus, I saw a trainman's lantern being swung across the track. Thinking we were to go on a siding I slowed down. When near the switch saw a man holding the switch bar and the switch was partly thrown. If I had not stopped the train it would have been wrecked. As the train came to a standstill several men jumped on the engine. I saw revolvers pointed at me in every direction I looked. I saw we were in for it. One of the robbers, a heavy-set fellow, who would weigh about 180 pounds, said if the fireman and I would do exactly as told we would not be harmed. Otherwise we had better prepare to meet our fate. In the meantime the express, baggage, and buffet cars had been cut off from the train, and one of the robbers said: 'Pull up the track until I tell you to stop.' After I had gone perhaps a mile I was ordered to stop. The robbers then told the fireman and myself to get off and go with them. All this time they had a revolver at each of our heads. They marched us to the rear of the baggage car, where they had taken the express messenger. We remained there under guard of two of the men while the others blew open the safe. I think they used four charges of dynamite, two of which sounded like earthquakes. The express messenger said to the robbers that it was impossible to blow open that safe. One of them said: 'We will show you.' When the last explosion occurred we heard the money jingling down. One of the guards said: 'I told you we would open it.'

"The car was set on fire by the explosion and the fireman was told by the robbers to put it out. They marched us to the engine and I was ordered into the cab.

"Soon after I heard a shot fired, and a man said: 'What did you shoot me for?' I heard a scuffling of the men, and the next moment the body of one of the robbers was laid in the gangway. I was told to get off and out of the way. Before leaving the engine I cut off the air, hoping to prevent the men from starting the engine. They called to me when I was a short distance away and told me to come back. I started down the track as fast as I could run. I had had enough of them.

Escape of Robbers.

"However, the men soon discovered what was wrong, and in a moment I heard the engine going up the track. Part of the gang, if not all of them, were railroad men, and one was a good engineer, as was shown by the way the engine was handled. Some time after the robbers had left I found my engine several miles up the track. It was dead, but the throttle was open. The boiler was empty and the fire was out. I am of the opinion the men stayed on the engine until it stopped, then took across the country. The first thing I did when I arrived at the engine was to look in the firebox, as I thought the robbers had made away with their wounded companion and thought, perhaps, they had burned his body.

"The only shot I heard was that fired near the engine. The robbers did not appear to be the least excited and were cool and deliberate."

The residents of this vicinity who are familiar with the surroundings are of the opinion the robbers are now in hiding on some one of the numerous islands in the Mississippi river. There are scores of these islands between Clinton and Savanna, some of which are thousands of acres in extent, and are covered with an almost impenetrable growth of willows and underbrush. The robbers could have easily escaped to the islands in a boat, and could secrete themselves so securely that were a thorough hunt to be made on the islands they could not be located for months. Three strange men were in Savanna a few days before the robbery, and the man who was shot was shaved by a barber there a day or two ago.

Arrest of a Suspect.

City Marshal Parker and Policemen Bill Horn and Doty of Savanna brought in a suspect whom they arrested near Hanover this evening, but he will admit nothing so far. He went to a farmhouse this afternoon and presented a revolver to the head of the owner's wife and demanded something to eat. She complied with his request and he ate ravenously. Soon thereafter the officers appeared and she related her story, with the result that they followed him and overtook and arrested him.

Byle Lives in Joliet.

JOLIET, Ill., Aug. 6.—William Byle, Adams express messenger, who killed the main robber, is a Joliet man. His family lives at 406 Webster street. One son is employed by the express company, two daughters, Grace and Cora, are teachers in Joliet public schools.

MINISTER TO HAVANA SAYS WIFE IS INSULTED

Mr. Squiers Complains to the Cuban Authorities and Has Two Policemen Discharged.

Special Cable Dispatch to The Inter Ocean.

HAVANA, Aug. 6.—Mr. Squiers, the American Minister, has complained to Senor Tamayo, Secretary of the government, that Mrs. Squiers was insulted by a police officer. He said that Mrs. Squiers had driven to the Hotel Inglaterra in a hired carriage, with her own footman on the box, to visit the wife of the French Minister. As the carriage stopped at the curb in front of the hotel a policeman, who was subsequently joined by two other officers, ordered the coachman to drive off and told the footman to come off the box. When told that the wife of the American Minister was in the carriage the policeman shrugged his shoulders and reiterated his order that the carriage drive off and the footman get off the box. Mr. Squiers said that if the policeman had acted in accordance with any municipal ordinance he would respect it, but that as the wife of a Minister Mrs. Squiers should not have been treated as she was. The matter was referred to the ayuntamiento, which directed the mayor to apologize in its name. The chief of police has explained to Mr. Squiers that the municipal ordinances forbid carriages stopping at the curb in front of the Hotel Inglaterra, and that it was also forbidden for two persons to sit on the box of a hired carriage. Nevertheless, three policemen have been suspended and two discharged for their behavior toward the Minister's wife.

FIGHT FOR LOVE OF A GIRL.

Two Society Youths of St. Louis Said to Have Waged Desperate Battle.

Special Dispatch to The Inter Ocean.

ST. LOUIS, Mo., Aug. 6.—Two young men prominent in society are said to have fought seven bloody rounds with gloves Tuesday night in the parlor of the L. Scharff residence, 4371 Lindell boulevard. According to rumor, Lionel Kalisch, living on Delmar boulevard, near Sarah street, was the victor, and his opponent was young Alvin Moss of 4100 West Pine boulevard. The fight is said to have been for the hand of a society girl. According to reports of the fray which have leaked out, Moss went down and out in the seventh round, and both were badly battered and weakened by the desperate contest. The principals had

HIS LAST APPEAL.
Today Tom Horn will be summoned to appear before the great supreme court of another world.

The Cheyenne Daily Leader.

THE PIONEER NEWSPAPER OF WYOMING.----Established in 1867.

WYOMING WEATHER.
Washington, Nov. 19.—Forecast for Wyoming: Partly cloudy and warmer Friday and Saturday.

VOL. XXXVII. NUMBER 88 | CHEYENNE, WYOMING, FRIDAY MORNING, NOVEMBER 20, 1903. | PRICE FIVE CENTS

HUNG BY THE NECK TILL DEAD

Horn's Neck Was Broken in an Instant, and He Died Without a Struggle

Horn Dies as He Lived, a Man of Blood and Iron Nerve, and Goes to the Scaffold Unflinchingly--Made No Confession

At 11:07 o'clock this morning Tom Horn was hanged, his neck being broken instantly. On the scaffold he gave an exhibition of nerve that has never been surpassed in criminal annals and his dauntless bearing made the hanging a less gruesome circumstance than was expected.

There were thirty-five witnesses to the execution. At the request of the condemned man Charles and Frank Irwin sang a typical cowboy melody just before he was led to the scaffold and then mounted the platform to tell him good-bye.

The spectatoors were admitted to the jail at 10:55 o'clock. They beheld Horn lying back on the cot in his cell as cool and unconcerned as though idling away spare moments. As the spectators filed in he turne his head and looked at them curiously, once or twice nodding as he recognized an acquaintance. He was smoking and the puffs of smoke left his lips at regular intervals, while occasionally he removed the cigar from his mouth and regarded it meditatively. He was dressed in a red striped shirt with low collar, a corduroy vest, black trousers and gaiters.

Deputy Sheriff Proctor walked to the side of the scaffold and dumped the binding straps and the black cap on floor in plain sight of Horn. The straps were hung on the railing where they could be reached handily and the condemned man was led forth. He stood waiting as the bolts of his cell door were swung back with a rasping clang and then stepped forth with a firm tread, walking to the side of the gallows between two men. At his request the Irwin boys struck up their song, and while their tones filled the room Horn stood leaning cerelessly on the railing of the gangway regarding the crowd below. Once or twice he turned away, but not from nervousness or a desire to hide emotion.

The Irwins then bade him good-bye, Charles Irwin saying in a husky voice:

"Be game, Tom."

"I want to say good-bye," was the answer. "A man can die but once and as well first as last."

Irwin asked: "Tom, did you make a confession to that preacher that you killed Willie Nickell?"

"No," was the answer in a loud, clear voice.

The binding of the prisoner then began. As Deputy Sheriff Proctor placed the straps about his wrists and thighs he moved his body so as to facilitate the work, in the meanwhile chatting with those about him and laughing once or twice at his own quips.

He was then led to the scaffold, walking firmly and regarding the gallows frame, noose and trap with curiosity.

At 11:04 o'clock the noose was placed over his head, and as it touched the top of his head Horn bent forward in order that Deputy Proctor might adjust the rope without difficulty. His knees and ankles were then bound. Once or twice the prisoner was jerked slightly, and, turning to the deputy, he said in a jesting tone:

"You fellows ought to have a handle on me."

When the noose was adjusted Dr. G. C. Rafter read a short extract from an Episcopal prayer book, Horn meanwhile standing stiffly erect and with his eyes on the onlookers below. Not a sign did he give that he feared death and involuntarily a murmur of admiration arose from the sheriffs who had witnessed other hangings. Once he moved his head as though the rope bothered him and it was readjusted.

As the prayer was finished Deputy Proctor, who had been standing with the black cap over his shoulder, dropped it over the head of the condemned man, shutting out from his eyes forever the light of day. As the cap obscured his features Horn could be seen smiling. The cap was placed at 11:06 o'clock.

"Are you ready, Tom?" asked Proctor.

"Yes," came clearly through the meshes of the cap and at a signal two men lifted him upon the trap. Instantly there was a slight click and water commenced to pour from the balance tank into a flat pan in front of the gallows.

As motionless as stone Horn stood waiting for the fall, his figure drawn to its full height and his hands clinched tightly. No shiver shook him, nor did he make any sound. The next thirty-five seconds probably were the longest that any of those who witnessed the execution will ever pass. It seemed as though the trap would never fall and in the tense expectancy the stillness was that of death. Suddenly there was a thud as a bolt slid back, and like a stone the form of the murderer shot through the trap and stopped with a jerk at the end of the rope. There it swayed from side to side without muscular motion, the head and shoulders projecting through the trap. Death had been instantaneous.

Immediately the spectators were ordered from the building and the attending physicians stepped forward and awaited to pronounce life extinct. The body was permitted to hang for several minutes and was then cut down and delivered into the hands of Sheriff Sperry of Boulder, Colo., who will take them there for interment at the expense of the dead man's brother, Charles Horn.

Those who had expected to see Horn break down, or even express the slightest emotion, were disappointed. He treated the whole execution as a joke and met death with Spartan fortitude. Even after the black cap had been placed and he staod waiting to be lifted to the trap, he turned to one of the men beside him and said:

"I understand you're married now?"

"Yes," was the answer.

"Well, treat her right and I hope you live happily," said Horn in a jesting tone.

As he was being lifted to the trap he said to the man beside him:

"Aint getting nervous, are you?" and laughed audibly.

After the hanging a communication which Horn spent the morning in writing was handed to Charles Irwin, at his request. Its contents have not been made public.

Throughout the execution was conducted with the regularity of clockwork and was perfect from a hangman's standpoint.

At 9 o'clock the number of militiamen guarding the jail was greatly increased and thereafter until the hanging was over a complete cordon surrounded the court house square and held back the growing crowd of spectators. As early as half-past eight the first morbid curiosity seekers gathered and, although knowing they could see nothing, seemed content to stand in the chilly air and speculate on the condemned man's probable actions when the moment of death came. The windows of the court house were watched for the slightest sign of what was passing within and trivial incidents were magnified into important occurrances, regardless of the fact that they had nothing to do with the execution.

In the corridor of the court house those who were to witness the execution stood and talked as though the occasion were an ordinary one, and they had no expectation of being confronted by a morbid spectacle within a few minutes. The name of the condemned man was scarcely mentioned, an instinctive delicacy seming to intentively teach that this would be bad taste. An expectant eye of all was kept on the door of the sheriff's office in expectation of the notification that the spectators were to file in and take their places.

John C. Coble, Horn's closest friend, was not present. Early in the morning he was admitted to the condemned cell and bade Horn good-bye. Horn informed him that he would hand a written statement to Chas. Irwin when the march to the gallows was ended. Coble's last words to Horn were an admonition to tell all that he knew and from that time until Rev. G. C. Rafter gave him final spiritual consolation he wrote constantly on his statement to Irwin. He was calm and the strength of his nerve remained unshaken during this time.

At 9:45 o'clock the final preliminary test of the gallows occurred. The machinery worked without a hitch and the trap fell thirty-five seconds after the weight was placed upon it. For some time before the execution the death wagon to which the remains were to be transferred stood near the court house and attracted much attention.

HORN'S HISTORY.

Story of the Life of the Cattle Detective.

Tom Horn was born in Franklin county, Mo., thirty-three years ago tomorrow. He was one of a good sized family of children and the son of a farmer in ordinary circumstances.

TOM HORN
Who Was Hanged for the Murder of Willie Nickell in 1901 This Morning.

While he was yet a boy his father became a fugitive from justice through forging the name of his brother to notes for a large amount and at an early age Tom was thrown on his own resources. The southwest then was the Mecca of all of an adventurous spirit and thither young Horn made his way. For a time he made his living driving bull teams and gradually drifted westward into Texas and New Mexico, acquiring the name of a bad man as he went. He is known to have killed an officer in the Mexican army in a dispute over the affections of a woman and often boasted of the fact, one of the occasions being that of his celebrated confession to Joe LeFors.

Killed Two Herders.

In New Mexico they say that Horn was responsible for the death of two Mexican sheepherders and that this was the first occasion on which he received money for committing murder. The herders were found dead at their camp and, while the crime was never directly traced to Horn, there was little doubt in the minds of the authorities that he was the guilty man. He was long suspected but never arrested and to this day the identity of the murderer remains a mystery.

Brave Indian Fighter.

While in New Mexico Horn became attached to the government scouts and on many occasions gave proof of iron nerve and great courage. It is said that in one fight he was the means of preventing a posse of scouts from being annihilated by a gang of mixed Mexicans and Indians. The posse was ambushed and when the fire of the enemy raked their ranks all fled save Horn. He held his ground and with great rapidity poured shot after shot into the outlaws, every shot bringing down a man. His bravery so awed the enemy that they failed to take advantage of the opportunity to pursue the disorganized posse. While Horn held them at bay the posse recovered its nerve and came to his rescue, routing the Indians and Mexicans with great slaughter.

Friend of Gen. Miles.

While in the scouting service Horn frequently worked with Col. W. F. Cody (Buffalo Bill) and they became fast friends. He also frequently met Gen. Nelson A. Miles, then in command of the department of Texas, and the general grew to admire his courage, often speaking of Horn's dauntless spirit and coolness in trying positions.

Horn is believed to have come to Wyoming first with a herd of Texas steers, at that time trailed through because there was no railroad. This he has denied, also that he was one of the forty Texans imported to take part in the celebrated cattlemen's invasion of 1892, although this is reported to have been a fact.

Reached Wyoming in 1894.

According to his own story Horn first came to Wyoming in 1894 and within a short time accepted a position as a cattle detective. His duties were to ride the range and see that as little rustling as possible was done by confirmed cattle thieves and small ranchmen. He first became conspicuous in the same year that he claimed to have reached the state through his suspected connection with the murders of William Powell and William Lewis. Powell and Lewis were small ranchmen operating about forty-five miles north of Cheyenne, and both were suspected of rustling. Both were assassinated within a short time and there were reasons to believe that Horn did the killing. For months attempts were made to work up a case against him and not until he told Joe LeFors last January that he was guilty did the truth come out.

Went to the War.

In 1898 Horn enlisted in the government pack train service and went to Cuba during the Spanish-American unpleasantness. There he was attacked by fever and when he returned to the state was a mere shadow of his former self. For weeks it was thought that he could not survive but the salubrious Wyoming air and the kind ministration of friends pulled him through and in a short time after beginning to improve he had regained his splendid physique.

Killed Prospectors.

In 1898 a Union Pacific train was held up at Wilcox and robbed of a large amount of money. Among the men who took the trail of the robbers was Horn, and one day he returned with a claim for $4,00 of the $10,000 offered for the five robbers, dead or alive. He claimed to have killed two of the bandits and buried them where the killing occurred. He was not believed and to prove his story it is said that he lead officers to the spot and disinterred his victims. Instead of train robbers they were harmless prospectors whom Horn had shot from ambush without warning. Horn used to tell the story of his "funny mistake" and seemed in no wise concerned that he had murdered two innocent men. He was never arrested for this crime and the truth of the story has been doubted.

SHERIFF E. J. SMALLEY
Who Arrested Horn.

Two More Murders.

In 1900 Matt Rash and Isham Dart, small ranchmen of the Brown's Hole county, Colorado, were foully assassinated with a short interval between the crimes. As in the cases of Powell and Lewis, Dart and Rash were suspected of rustling and it was claimed that they had been put out of the way at the instigation of large owners of cattle. Horn was in the Brown's Hole country at the time and was known to have eaten supper with Dart, who was a negro, the night before the ranchman was killed.

In Hostile Country.

Few people in Northern Colorado knew Horn by sight and while posses were scouring the country for the murderer he rode unmolested back into Wyoming. At Dixon, a small settlement, he stopped for a drink and entered a saloon in which one of the posses was imbibing refreshments. None there knew him and his appearance was not given particular notice. Before many minutes, however, he became engaged in a quarrel with one of the posse and they started to settle their difficulty with knives. Horn was terribly wounded in the fight, receiving a slash in the back of the neck that disfigured him for life, but in the end cut his antagonist to ribbons and, having had his wound dressed, continued his journey. The scar resulting from this wound was that which attracted so much attention during his trial for the murder of Willie Nickell.

His Last Murder.

After his return from Colorado Horn became a cattle detective for the Iron Mountain Ranch company, owning ranches at Bosler, Albany county, and Iron Mountain, Laramie county.

On the morning of July 18, 1901, Willie Nickell, a 14-year-old boy, was shot in the back and killed near his father's ranch in the Iron Mountain district. He was shot twice, and after he had fallen the murderer placed a small stone in such a position that it supported his head in a peculiar manner.

Kels P. Nickell, father of the murdered boy, was not liked by his neighbors, having brought sheep into a cattle country, and as Willie wore his father's hat and rode the old man's horse when shot, immediately the conclusion was reached that he was killed by mistake, the murderer intending to assassinate Nickell, Sr.

Authorities at Sea.

Horn was in the vicinity of Iron Mountain a day or two before the killing and at once was suspected. He had disappeared, however, and his whereabouts could not be ascertained. Matters were complicated by the fact that the Nickell family and the Miller family, living on adjoining ranches, were enemies and members of both families had made threats to kill. So the Millers were suspected of having committed the murder, also, and the authorities were at sea.

Kels Nickell Shot.

Three weeks after the murder of his boy Kels P. Nickell was shot as he went about his chores early in the morning. One bullet shattered his left elbow and another passed through his thigh, but he escaped by running for his cabin while his would-be assassin clipped the grass beneath his feet with bullets. Nickell fell exhausted into his own door and was placed in a wagon and brought to St. John's hospital at Cheyenne, arriving after nightfall and suffering intensely during the trip.

Nickell Accuses Millers.

While his wounds were being dressed Nickell made the statement that the men who tried to kill him were Jim Miller and one of his sons. This made the case against the Millers stronger and Jim Miller and his son Victor, a lad of 16 years, were arrested on a charge of murdering Willie Nickell. A mob met the train that brought them to Cheyenne, but no violence was attempted.

A coroner's jury was empanelled to inquire into the death of Willie Nickell and met in the court room of the county court house. While the inquest was in session disguised men attacked the sheep on the Nickell ranch and clubbed several hundred to death. The sheepherder was so badly frightened that he left the country and the true facts of the attack never became known.

Millers Released.

Before the coroners' jury the Millers, father and son, proved an absolute alibi by the testimony of members of their family and of Miss Glendolene Myrtle Kimmell, a schoolteacher who boarded with them. The murder was known to have been committed at 7 o'clock in the morning because the shots were heard. Miss Kimmell and the Miller family swore that Jim and Victor Miller were eating breakfast at 7 o'clock and that neither went near where the body was found that day. This exonerated the prisoners and they were given their liberty.

The coroners' jury desired to obtain the testimony of Tom Horn, but his whereabouts were still unknown and the jury was compelled to adjourn without deciding upon a verdict.

Horn's Bold Front.

The authorities continued to work on the case and in a short time a second session of the coroners' jury was held. By this time Horn had turned up at the Bosler ranch of the Iron Mountain Ranch company and readily consented to testify. He told a straightforward story of his whereabouts at the time of the killing and there being no direct evidence against he he could not be arrested. Again the coroners' jury adjourned without reaching a verdict.

Horn seemed to think that the suspicion connecting him with the murder had been allayed and during the next three months frequently visited Cheyenne and engaged in protracted carousals. When drunk he had a habit of boasting of his prowess and was prone to claim to have committed every murder of which he had heard. Few people took his boasting seriously but in the end the habit proved his undoing.

Detective Joe Lafors.

In the meantime Deputy United States Mashal Joe Lafors had been retained by the county to investigate the murder of Willie Nickell. He soon reached the conclusion that Horn was the guilty man and worked indefatigably to bring him to justice. The county commissioners offered a reward of $1,000 for the arrest and conviction of the murderer and others worked on the case also, but Lafors was the only man wiith his mind on the truth.

In December Lafors wrote to a friend in Montana instructing him to offer Horn a profitable position as a cattle detective. This was done and Horn came to Cheyenne to arrange details with Lafors.

Horn Confesses.

On January 12th, 1902, Horn, who had been drinking, went to the office of the United States marshal wiith Lafors and there the wily detective by artful questioning wormed from the cattle detective a confession that hee murdered Willie Nickell and a partial confession that he killed Lewis and Powell in 1894. Concealed in an adjoining room were Deputy Sheriff Les Snow and Stenographer Charles Ohnhaus, who overheard the entire conversation, Ohnhaus making a full stenographic report. The following day Horn was arrested by Sheriff Smalley and Under Sheriff Proctor as he sat in the lobby of the Intèr Ocean hotel.

Horn Found Guilty.

Horn's employers and friends immediately rallied to his cause and employed the ablest legal talent of the state to defend him. In February his preliminary hearing was held and after he had pleaded not guilty the startling evidence of Lafors, Ohnhaus and Snow came out. His trial was set for the May term of court.

When the preliminary call of the May docket of the district court occurred, Horn's trial was postponed at the request of the attorneys. On October 10, 1902, the trial was begun and on October 24, the thirteenth day of the trial, the jury brought in a verdict of guilty of murder in the first degree. A few days later Judge Scott sentenced Horn to be hanged on January 9, 1903.

Fighting for Life.

The attorneys for the condemned man carried the case to the supreme court, an indefinite stay of execution being secured. In October, 1903, the supreme court sustained the verdict of the district court and sentenced Horn to be hanged November 30.

Then the fight for Horn's life was transferred to the governor. Horn's attorneys presented an affidavit made by Glendolene Myrtle Kimmell, the school teacher who had oprven an alibi for the Millers, in which she swore that Victor Miller had confessed to ehr that he had killed Willie Nickell, that he had confessed to the fact to his father and that Jim Miller frequently had confessed to her that Victor Miller had confessed to him. Another affidavit was that Ollie Whitman, who swore that Victor Miller confessed to him that he killed Willie Nickell. There were many other affidavits having more or less connection with the crime. In rebuttal of these affidavits Prosecuting Attorney W. R. Stoll presented other affidavits, also affidavits making stronger the evidence of Horn's guilt. On November 15 Governor Chatterton refused to interfere and the doom of the condemned man was sealed.

During all of the time that Horn was in jail reports were rife that his friends intended to storm the jail and release him. The prisoner was planning to escape contantly and the ingenious plans that he formulated were marvels of cunning. Once, in August, 1903, he actually managed to overpower his jailer, witih the aid of Jim Mccloud, a prisoner charged with post office robbery, and both men gained the streets of Cheyenne. They were recaptured within a few hundred yards of the jail, Horn being roughly handled by his captors. On this occasion Horn gave an exhibition of his murderous nature, deliberately trying to shoot Under Sheriff Proctor after he had been overpowered and was helpless.

Horn's case was given more newspaper notoriety than any other in the history of the Rocky Mountain region. His reputation became national and hundreds of columns of matter concerning him were published. Special correspondents were sent by metropolitan journals to report his trial and his name became a byword in criminal annals. His execution will hailed with satisfaction by thousands of people who never saw him and never heard of him prior to the murder of Willie Nickell.

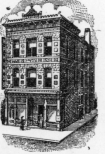

RECIPROCITY BILL PASSED BY AN OVERWHELMING VOTE

After Four Days' Discussion, the House Passes the Cuban Bill as It Came From the Committee, by a Vote of 335 to 21—The House Proceedings

Washington, Nov. 19.—The house today by a rising vote of 335 to 21 passed the bill to make effective the Cuban reciprocity treaty. The dissenting votes were about equally divided between Republicans and Democrats, but there was no record vote, the minority having too few votes to order the yeas and nays.

The Democrats, under the leadership of Mr. Williams, sought to the last to secure amendments to the bill in accordance with the action of the Democratic caucus, but were defeated steadily. Mr. Williams made the final effort when he tried to have the bill recommitted to the ways and means committee with instructions to amend, but a point of order under the special rule providing for a vote on the bill without intervening motion, was sustained.

The Speaker Applauded.

Mr. Cannon received the applause of the Democratic side when he entertained the appeal from his ruling made by Mr. Williams, the speaker saying he preferred to err, if he erred at all, in giving the house the right to express its will. The appeal was tabled by a strict party vote.

The debate, begun Monday, was continued to within a few minutes of 4 o'clock, the time appointed to take a vote on the final passage of the bill. Mr. Williams closed the debate for his side, and made an arraignment of the Republican policy of protection. Mr. McCall, Republican of Massachusetts, made the closing speech on the Republican side. The announcement of the passage of the bill caused only a slight demonstration.

Mr. Clellan, mayor-elect of New York, occupied the speaker's chair for a while today as chairman of the committee of the whole house.

Mr. Hepburn's Speech.

In the discussion of the measure Mr. Hepburn of Iowa declared that there was nothing in the bill that differed one iota from the established policy of the Republicans. He believed in protection as advocated by the Republican party, but there was no sanctity or sacredness in schedules, and he cited the number of times tthey had been changed. He reviewed the history of tariff legislation, comparing the balances in favor of this country under Republican policies with those under Democratic control. This country is no longer a debtor, he said, and the Republicans had changed all this.

Mr. Sulzer, Democrat of New York, said he would vote for the bill, as it was a little step in the right direction.

Mr. Watson, Republican of Indiana, one of the new members on the ways and means committee, favored the bill.

Williams and Payne Spar.

Mr. Williams, Democrat of Mississippi, leader of the minority, answering a statement on the Republican side that the Democrats forced the talking on this bill, said he had offered to have a vote on the minority amendment and then vote on the bill without debate.

Replying to Mr. Watson, Mr. Williams said:

"Protection is a system of taxation whereby many are robbed in order that a few may be hot housed by legislation into artificial prosperity."

Mr. Williams charged that the Republicans did not dare to enter on tariff revision for fear it would open the doors to too extended a revision. The Republicans had a majority in the house and senate and a "very large majority in the White house." Some of the pledges of prosperity of the majority were already collapsing. The people, he said, were beginning to find that their laws were keeping in power not only monopolies, but public cheats. Mr. Williams in supporting his contention for an amendment to the treaty, said that it would take only a few weeks to secure.

Mr. Payne replied.

"The gentleman is trying to help the sugar trust by his amendment."

"Well," responded Mr. Williams, "if I am, the Lord knows I am unconscious of it. But I will say the length it would take will depend upon the care and strenuosity brought into action at the other end of the avenue. If you could just half way approximate the celerity that has lately actuated this administration in connection with the new born republic of Panama you would have it back here in three days."

"But the mind of all the mighty czars in another place have not operated on this Panama business yet and they have operated on this treaty," said Mr. Payne.

"They will operate quickly in some way or other," said Mr. Williams, "providing the trust is not hurt. They are waiting for us."

Debate Closed.

Just before 4 o'clock Mr. Payne of New York said he did not care to talk further, and Mr. Williams moved to recommit the bill to the ways and means committee with instructions in the line of amendments proposed.

The speaker ruled the motion to be out of order. Mr. Williams appealed from the decision of the chair and asked to be heard on the point of order. Mr. Payne raised a point of order, but the speaker entertained the appeal, saying that he preferred to err, if at all, in giving the house the right to express its will, although it had previously expresed itself otherwise. Mr. Williams said his motion was not dilatory, but was made because the majority had endeavored persistently to prevent a vote on the amendments.

Voting Begins.

Mr. Payne moved to lay the appeal on the table, and the motion was carried by a vote of 193 to 165, a strict party alignment.

On the passage of the bill an attempt was made to secure a yea and nay vote, but only twenty-three members seconded the demand, an insufficient number.

Wm. Alden Smith, Republican of Michigan, demanded a division, and on a rising vote the yeas were 335 and the nays twenty-one. This passed the bill.

It was agreed that when the house adjourned tomorrow it meet on Tuesday next. The house at 4:38 adjourned.

The Inter Ocean. Magazine.

VOLUME XXXIII. CHICAGO, SUNDAY MORNING, APRIL 17, 1904. NUMBER 24.

CHICAGO GIRL BOOTBLACK AS AN ARIZONA BANDIT

Release of Pearl Hart from Prison Reveals Some Strange Things in Life of the Only Woman Who Ever Held Up a Stage Coach.

THERE is scarcely a person in America that does not know of Pearl Hart, the only woman bandit who ever held up a stagecoach, but until this story is seen none will know that she is a Chicago product.

Pearl Hart got her first bandit training in Chicago. She committed her first theft here, and when she left this city it was to plunge into the wild life of the Southwest with a Chicago man whom she led at will.

Pearl Hart is now in Kansas City, Kan., where she owns a cigar store. She does not try to hide her name. She is trading upon her notoriety. She has told but one man aside from her partner in crime whence she came. That one man is Francis Reno, who until recently was a United States deputy marshal in Arizona, the scene of the young woman's exploits.

Not many years ago Pearl Hart, dressed as a boy, was shining shoes in the down town district of Chicago. Her sister, a year younger than herself, was with her. These two young girls, then in their early teens, slept in the box cars out along State street, in the Wabash avenue livery barns, in lofts, or wherever they could sneak in unnoticed. In Chicago Pearl was arrested for the first time. It was here she was first sentenced for crime. Still, her history during the time she was here has always remained until now a blank.

This notorious young woman first sprang into public attention in May, 1899, when she held up the Globe, Ari., stage. Until recently, when she was paroled, she has been serving time in the penitentiary at Yuma Ari. She confessed her crime to Francis Reno, and at the same time gave to him the entire history of her strange career, a great part of which was spent in this city.

Always Went Dressed in Men's Clothes

Pearl Hart is a little woman, and, dressed in male attire, she appeared very small. At the time of her arrest after the stage holdup she tipped the scales at 101 pounds, but even though she was small she had the nerve of an old outlaw, and was all dare-devil. At first she was naturally a tramp. When she was 13 years of age she ran away from her home in Lindsay, Ont., taking with her her sister. The two, dressed as boys, made their way by boat to Buffalo, N. Y., where they worked for a while in a factory where children were employed. After the sisters had been in Buffalo for about two months their parents got track of and finally recovered them.

Two years later the two girls again ran away from home. That time they came to Chicago. Pearl, the elder of the two, had the features of a boy, and, dressed as she was in boy clothes, was enabled to conceal her sex. The two sisters went to work as bootblacks. They worked first in the south end of the business district, and later, as they grew acquainted with the other bootblacks, roved all over the downtown district.

One evening Pearl Hart saw a wagon load of watermelons standing near the corner of State and Harrison streets. Several of the melons had been taken from the wagon, and were piled upon the sidewalk. When no one was looking she stole one of the melons and ran down Harrison street with the heavy load. Before she had gone a block a policeman caught her, and both she and her sister were taken to the Harrison street police station.

Climbed from Window and Ran Away

After the two girls were arrested and sentenced to a boys' school their sex was discovered, and they were sent to the reform school for girls. Pearl was only a young girl, but she had been roving too long to content herself with life at the school. She and her sister had been locked up for almost three months and were apparently unusually tractable. Then one morning the matron awoke to find them gone. The two girls had made a rope of two sheets and a night gown and had lowered themselves from a window.

Pearl's sister climbed down first and without accident. Pearl followed, but being the heavier of the two she got a fall that knocked out her breath. Instead of tying the nightgown at the lower end of the rope she had tied one sleeve to the bed. Her weight ripped off the sleeve and she fell ten feet to the ground. This slight accident did not prevent her, however, from discarding her dress until she could scale the high wire-bound fence and help her sister over.

When the sisters escaped they hastened away from Chicago as soon as they could secure two suits of boy's clothes. They made their way over the Northern Pacific railroad to Helena, Mont., and later to Victoria B. C.

The two girls remained in Victoria for three months and then slowly made their way back to Chicago, the round trip being the most remarkable ever made by two girls their age. When they arrived here the younger one became ill and soon grew homesick. As soon as she regained her strength Pearl took her back to Canada.

Became a Tramp; Crossed the Continent

By this time the elder of the two girls had become a confirmed tramp in everything except appearance. The long journey twice across the country had given her strength and a dare-devil disposition. Her parents knew she would not long remain at home unless she was placed under restraint. They sent her to a boarding school near Montreal, where it was supposed she would be closely guarded. She was closely guarded, too, but she found a way to elude her watchers. She met a man who lived in the town where the school was located, a Harry Bordeman, and before she had been at the school four months she eloped with him.

At that time Pearl Hart was 16 years old. She and Boardeman came directly to Chicago, but she remained here but a short time. Following a quarrel one day she disappeared. She went directly to Trinidad, Col., but later came back to Chicago and patched up the quarrel with Boardeman. They remained here during the year of the World's Fair, after which another quarrel again sent her flying to the West. She returned to Trinidad and later went to Phoenix, Ari. She had not been in Phoenix a week when she met Boardeman at a boarding house. A reconciliation followed and the two lived together until the beginning of the Spanish-American war, when Boardeman enlisted in McCord's regiment and left the territory.

When Boardeman left his wife she again donned men's clothes and went to Mammoth, Ari., where she hired as cook in a mining camp on the banks of the Gila river. Soon after she went to Mammoth the largest mine there shut down, leaving her without work. She had saved a little money, about $10, and with this she determined to pay her way to Globe, Ari. She found two Mormon boys who were going by wagon to Globe and she paid them $8 to allow her to ride with them.

Became Acquainted with Chicago Cobbler

When the Mormon lads left Mammoth they had beside Pearl Hart another passenger, a former Chicago shoemaker, who had for sometime been prospecting for gold in Arizona. Pearl looked the part of a young cow puncher and the cobbler, who said his name was Joe, soon struck up an acquaintance with the young woman.

It is sixty miles from Mammoth to Globe, and the trip was made slowly. In the evening of the last day of the trip the party camped three miles from the latter place, and while they were there the Globe stage, containing several passengers, passed the camp. A hold-up did not suggest itself to Pearl at the time, but later the memory of the passing stage drew her into her one big crime and finally landed her in the penitentiary.

The next morning the party reached the mining camp and Pearl went to work as a cook and office "boy" in a sort of hotel. Before she had been there a week, Joe, her companion on the trip, went to her and told her he had a good mining claim not far distant. She was out of money, and declared she wished to return to Canada. The Chicago prospector's glowing picture of the claim led Pearl to believe the two could dig up enough gold in a short time to pay her way back to Canada, and she went with him. Several days' work failed to develop any trace of color in the dirt on the claim, and she grew disgusted with both her condition and her new friend.

She then thought of the Globe stage. She proposed a "stick-up" to her companion. The business was entirely new to him, and he strongly objected, but the young woman bandit insisted, until he finally gave in. She had a brace of pretty six-shooters and she could handle them with the greatest skill. She showed the ex-cobbler how well she could shoot and then cooked up detailed plans for carrying out the robbery.

Planned the Hold-Up; Carried It Out

Pearl Hart and the prospector left the mining claim and rode over the mountains until they struck the Globe trail. At a bend in the trail the two concealed themselves behind a big rock. The stage was due at that point during the day, but on account of the tortuous path the stage must travel the driver at this point could not see the roadway twenty feet ahead of his horses.

The two stage robbers waited for three hours before they heard the rattling coach. One was then concealed on one side of the road, the other on the opposite side. Just as the lead team got between Pearl and the prospector she leaped from her hiding place and, leveling one revolver at the driver's head and the other at the window of the stage door, yelled for the driver and passengers to throw up their hands.

The driver and the three passengers—two white men and a Chinaman—heeded the command. Pearl then ordered the prospector to keep a bead on the driver. She ordered the passengers out of the stage and took their firearms from them. When she was sure they had no weapons left she searched them all. From one white man she secured $390, from the other $36, and from the Chinaman $5. The driver had $8 in his pocket, but this she returned to him, with the remark that he had earned his money carrying the three cowards across the hills.

When she was certain she had stolen all the money she gave each one of the passengers a dollar, and, at the point of two six-shooters, forced them to go on down the road. When they were out of sight the young woman bandit led the way into the mouth of a canyon and, by a circuitous route, she and her companion made their way back to their horses. They then rode through a long box canyon, where this notorious young woman had the one great fright of her life. She afterward confessed to a creepy feeling after the robbery, but a hideous noise in the box canyon was more terrifying to her. As she rode on, however, she discovered that the noise was merely the croaking of millions of frogs.

Surprised and Taken to Jail at Tucson

After riding for a mile or two the young woman turned her horse into a transverse canyon, which soon led them to an abandoned trail. She and the prospector, now become a desperado, rode to a point near Cane Springs. There they came across a mountain lion. The young woman, who could shoot as straight as a sharpshooter, quickly mounted her horse and chased the animal for two miles. The prospector followed her until she gave up the chase. They then rode on until they came within six miles of Mammoth. There the prospector and his horse fell into a river and both were nearly drowned.

About eight miles from Mammoth they lay down in some bushes to sleep during the rest of the night, expecting to hide in the hills during the next day. That day the prospector's tobacco appetite and Pearl's appetite for food caused the man to ride to Mammoth to secure tobacco and food. For several days after that they drifted down through the mountains until they came within twenty miles of Benson. They camped there one day—they did most of their traveling by night—and both were asleep when they were surprised by Sheriff Truman of Pinal county and captured. Preceding the capture the young woman desperado was awakened by shouting and the firing of guns, and when she jumped to her feet she looked into the muzzles of two ugly Winchesters.

From their camping place Pearl Hart and the prospector were taken to Benson, and then to Florence, where she was separated from her bandit companion and taken to Tucson, where she was lodged in jail. But she did not like the jail, and she did not intend to remain there if there was any way of getting out. She did escape, but was recaptured twelve days later at Deming, N. M. She had again donned men's clothes to aid her in escaping. She was then taken back to Tucson.

She was aided in her escape by a man who had but one day to serve in the jail. This man was regarded as a deadly enemy by Pearl Hart before he aided her in escaping. After that she regarded him as a friend. While in the jail the young woman bandit made a pet of a young wild cat. She kept the animal in her cell most of the time, but occasionally it roamed out into the corridor and visited the cells of the other prisoners. One day it entered the cell of the short term prisoner. He picked up the cat and held it above his head, and the animal bit the prisoner's hand, badly lacerating it. With a howl of rage and pain he threw the cat to the steel floor of the cell and killed it.

For hours Pearl sat in her cell cursing the man who had killed her pet, but later, when he had an opportunity to speak to the young woman he told her he would get her out. He was a trusted prisoner, and the next day he climbed to the top floor of the jail and cut a hole nine inches wide and twelve inches long through a grated window. Through this window Pearl Hart escaped.

As an instance of the nerve of Pearl Hart Mr. Reno tells of an incident in her cell. The day he secured the confession from her, which was some time before she was brought to trial, he took several photographs of her. The wild cat was lying on the cot in the cell at the time. Once the cat got in the woman's way and she lifted it up to drop it on the floor. As soon as she took hold of the animal it sank its teeth through her thumb. With a string of oaths that would shame the worst bad man that ever traveled the sands of Arizona she grabbed the cat by the neck and halfway beat it to death.

Sent to Yuma Prison for Term of Five Years

When Pearl Hart was brought to trial she was convicted and sentenced to the Yuma penitentiary for five years.

And that is the kind of a woman that grew out of the little girl who used to shine shoes in the heart of Chicago. She is the only woman stage robber in the history of the country. She is now about 32 years old and has two children, who live with their grandmother in Toledo, Ohio. She has quit the trail herself, after leading one of the strangest lives ever led by a woman.

The prospector, Joe, who aided in the stage hold-up, has always been able to conceal his identity. He was sentenced to the penitentiary for thirty years under the name of Joe Boots. This name came to him in a singular way. When he and Pearl were arrested he refused to talk. The officers could learn nothing about him. Sheriff Truman went to the young woman to attempt to learn the man's name. At the time she was pulling on one of her high boots.

"What's that man's name?" asked the sheriff.

"Joe," said Pearl.

"Joe how much?" asked the sheriff.

"Why, Joe Boots," said Pearl.

He was indicted under that name, and under it was sentenced to the penitentiary for thirty years. Boots, or whatever his name may be, made a wonderful escape from the penitentiary afterward, but was recaptured. While working with a gang of convicts he made a break for liberty. An alarm was sounded, and the lookouts turned a gatling gun upon him. Nearly a thousand shots were fired at the fleeing convict, but he escaped unhurt. He was never recaptured.

PEARL HART, GIRL BANDIT.

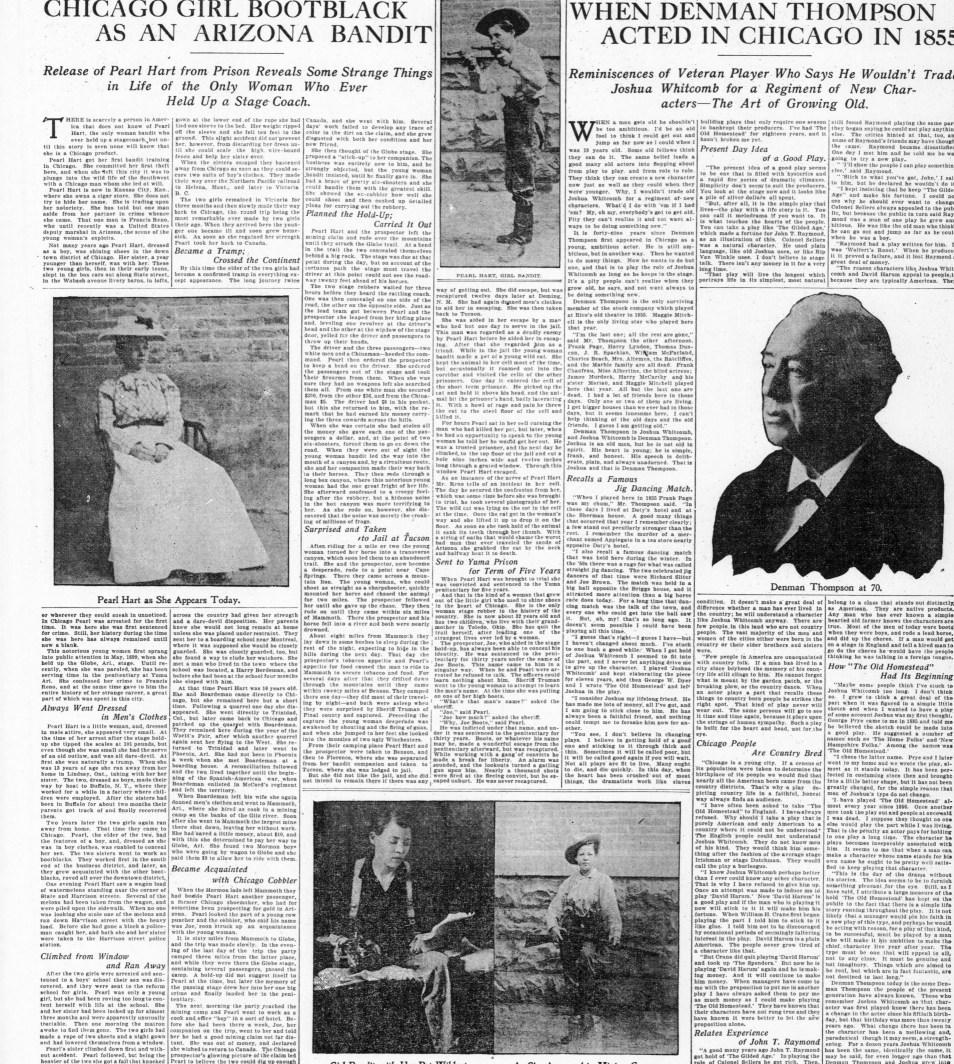

Pearl Hart as She Appears Today.

Girl Bandit with Her Pet Wildcat. As She Appeared in Mining Camps.

WHEN DENMAN THOMPSON ACTED IN CHICAGO IN 1855

Reminiscences of Veteran Player Who Says He Wouldn't Trade Joshua Whitcomb for a Regiment of New Characters—The Art of Growing Old.

WHEN a man gets old he shouldn't be too ambitious. I'd be an old fool to think I could get out and jump as far now as I could when I was 18 years old. Some old fellows think they can do it. The same belief leads a good many old actors into flopping about from play to play and from role to role. They think they can create a new character now just as well as they could when they were younger. Why, I wouldn't trade old Joshua Whitcomb for a regiment of new characters. What'd I do with 'em if I had 'em? My, oh my, everybody's got to get old. Pity they can't realize it and not want always to be doing something new."

It is forty-nine years since Denman Thompson first appeared in Chicago as a young, ambitious actor. He is still ambitious, but in another way. Then he wanted to do many things. Now he wants to do but one, and that is to play the role of Joshua Whitcomb as long as he keeps to the stage. It's a pity people can't realize when they grow old, he says, and not want always to be doing something new.

Denman Thompson is the only surviving member of the stock company which played at Rice's old theater in 1855. Maggie Mitchell is the only living star who played here that year.

"I'm the last one; all the rest are gone," said Mr. Thompson the other afternoon. Frank Page, Harry Lyndon, Thomas Duncan, J. R. Spacklan, William McFarland, Charles Beach, Mrs. Altemus, the Ratcliffes, and the Marble family are all dead. Frank Chanfrau, Miss Albertine, the blind actress; James Murdock, Harry McCarthy and his sister Marian, and Maggie Mitchell played here that year. All but the last one are dead. I had a lot of friends here in those days. Only one or two of them are living. I get bigger houses than we ever had in those days, but it seems lonesome here. I can't help thinking of the old days and the old friends. I guess I am getting old."

Denman Thompson is Joshua Whitcomb, and Joshua Whitcomb is Denman Thompson. Joshua is an old man, but he is not old in spirit. His heart is young; he is simple, frank, and honest. His speech is deliberate, plain, and always unadorned. That is Joshua and that is Denman Thompson.

Recalls a Famous Jig Dancing Match.

"When I played here in 1855 Frank Page was my chum," Mr. Thompson said. "In those days I lived at Doty's hotel and at the Sherman house. A good many things that occurred that year I remember clearly; a few stand out peculiarly stronger than the rest. I remember the murder of a merchant named Applegate in a tea store nearly opposite Doty's hotel.

"I also recall a famous dancing match that was held here during the winter. In the '50s there was a rage for what was called straight jig dancing. The two celebrated jig dancers of that time were Richard Sliter and Joe Brown. The match was held in a big hall opposite the Briggs house, and it attracted more attention than a big horse race does today. For a long time that dancing match was the talk of the town, and every one who could get into the hall saw it. But, oh, my! that's so long ago. It doesn't seem possible I could have been playing all this time.

"I guess that's right—I guess I have—but I haven't changed about much. I've stuck to one bush a good while. When I got hold of Joshua Whitcomb I seemed to fit into the part, and I never let anything drive me to give up the character. I played 'Joshua Whitcomb' and kept elaborating the piece for eleven years, and then George W. Dyer and I wrote 'The Old Homestead' and left Joshua in the play.

"I consider Joshua my lifelong friend. He has made me lots of money, all I've got, and I am going to stick close to him. He has always been a faithful friend, and nothing could tempt me to forsake him now for another.

"You see, I don't believe in changing plays. I believe in getting hold of a good one and sticking to it through thick and thin. Sometimes it will be called poor, but it will be called good again if you will wait. Not all plays are fit to live. Many ought to die, and die quickly. In this day, when the heart has been crushed out of most things, the dramatists work like slaves building plays that only require one season to bankrupt their producers. I've had 'The Old Homestead' for eighteen years, and it hasn't broken me yet.

Present Day Idea of a Good Play.

"The present idea of a good play seems to be one that is filled with hysterics and a rapid fire series of dramatic climaxes. Simplicity don't seem to suit the producers. You look at the stage now and it looks like a pile of silver dollars all spent.

"But, after all, it is the simple play that lives—the play with a life story in it. You can call it melodrama if you want to. It is what touches the hearts of the people. You can take a play like 'The Gilded Age,' which made a fortune for John T. Raymond, as an illustration of this. Colonel Sellers was a natural character. He used plain language, like old Joshua uses, or like Rip Van Winkle uses. I don't believe in stage talk. There isn't any money in it for a very long time.

"That play will live the longest which portrays life in its simplest, most natural condition. It doesn't make a great deal of difference whether a man has ever lived in the country; he will understand a character like Joshua Whitcomb anyway. There are few people in this land who are not country people. The vast majority of the men and women of the cities either were born in the country or their elder brothers and sisters were.

"Few people in America are unacquainted with country folk. If a man has lived in a city since boyhood the memory of his country life still clings to him. He cannot forget what is meant by the garden patch, or the breaking plow, or the country dance. When an actor plays a part that recalls these things to country born people he strikes the right spot. That kind of play never will wear out. The same persons will go to see it time and time again, because it plays upon the strings of human sympathy. Such a play is built for the heart and head, not for the eye.

Chicago People Are Country Bred

"Chicago is a young city. If a census of its population were taken to determine the birthplace of its people we would find that nearly all the American born came from the country districts. That's why a play depicting country life in a faithful, honest way always finds an audience.

"I have often been asked to take "The Old Homestead" to England. I have always refused. Why should I take a play that is purely American and only American to a country where it could not be understood? The English people could not understand Joshua Whitcomb. They do not know men of his kind. They would think him something after the fashion of the average stage Irishman or stage Dutchman. They would call the play a burlesgue.

"I know Joshua Whitcomb perhaps better than I ever could know any other character. That is why I have refused to give him up. Once an attempt was made to induce me to play 'David Harum.' Now 'David Harum' is a good play and if the man who is playing it now will stick to it it will make him his fortune. When William H. Crane first began playing the part I told him to stick to it like glue. I told him not to be discouraged by occasional periods of seemingly faltering interest in the play. David Harum is a plain American. The people never grow tired of a character like that.

"But Crane did quit playing 'David Harum' and took up 'The Spenders.' But now he is playing 'David Harum' again and he is making money. And it will continue to make him money. When managers have come to me with the proposition to put me in another play I have always asked them to pay me as much money as I could make playing 'The Old Homestead.' They have known that their characters have not rung true and they have known it were better to let the new proposition alone.

Relates Experience of John T. Raymond

"A good many years ago John T. Raymond got hold of 'The Gilded Age.' In playing the role of Colonel Sellers he got rich. Then, after years passed by and the theater goers still found Raymond playing the same part, they began saying he could not play anything else. The critics hinted at that, too, and some of Raymond's friends may have thought the same. Raymond became dissatisfied. One day I met him and he told me he was going to try a new play.

"'I'll show the people I can play something else,' said Raymond.

"'Stick to what you've got, John,' I said to him, but he declared he wouldn't do it.

"I kept insisting that he keep "The Gilded Age" and make his fortune. I could not see why he should ever want to change. Colonel Sellers always appealed to the public, but because the public in turn said Raymond was a man of one play he grew ambitious. He was like the old man who thinks he can go out and jump as far as he could when he was a boy.

"Raymond had a play written for him. It was 'Wolfert's Roost.' When he produced it it proved a failure, and it lost Raymond a great deal of money.

"The reason characters like Joshua Whitcomb and David Harum appeal to people is because they are typically American. They belong to a class that stands out distinctly as American. They are native products. Any man who has ever known a simple hearted old farmer knows the characters are true. Most of the men of today wore boots when they were boys, and rode a lead horse, and did up the chores. If a man would get on a stage in England and tell a hired man to go do the chores he would have the people thinking he was talking in a foreign tongue.

How "The Old Homestead" Had Its Beginning

"Maybe some people think I've stuck to Joshua Whitcomb too long. I don't think so. I grew to think a great deal of the part when it was figured in a simple little sketch and when I wanted to have a play of some account Joshua was my first thought. George Prye came to me in 1885 and told me he believed the sketch could be made into a good play. He suggested a number of names such as 'The Home Folks' and 'New Hampshire Folks.' Among the names was 'The Old Homestead.'

"I chose the latter name. Prye and I later went to my home and we wrote the play, almost as it stands today. It has been perfected in costuming since then and brought into a little better shape, but it has not been greatly changed, for the simple reason that men of Joshua's type do not change.

'I have played 'The Old Homestead' almost every year since 1886. Once another man took the play out and people at once said I was dead. I suppose they thought no one else would play the part while I was living. That is the penalty an actor pays for holding to one play a long time. The character he plays becomes inseparably associated with him. It seems to me that when a man can make a character whose name stands for his own name he ought to be pretty well satisfied to keep playing that character.

"This is the day of the drama without its stories. The idea seems to be to furnish something pleasant for the eye. Still, as I have said, I attribute a large measure of the hold 'The Old Homestead' has kept on the public to the fact that there is a simple life story running throughout the play. It is not likely that a manager would pin his faith in a new play of this type, and perhaps he would be acting with reason, for a play of that kind, to be successful, must be played by a man who will make it his ambition to make the chief character live year after year. The type must be one that will appeal to all, not to any class. It must be genuine and not imaginary. Things which are aimed to be real, but which are in fact fantastic, are not destined to last long."

Denman Thompson today is the same Denman Thompson the people of the present generation have always known. Those who remember Joshua Whitcomb as that character was first played know there has been a change in the actor since his fiftieth birthday, but that birthday was more than twenty years ago. What change there has been in the character has been a mellowing and, paradoxical though it may seem, a strengthening. For a dozen years Joshua Whitcomb has been the same, identically the same, it may be said, for even longer ago than that Denman Thompson and Joshua grew into each other.

Denman Thompson at 70.

ROCKY MOUNTAIN THE NEWS

VOL. XLV: NO. 193. DENVER, COLORADO, MONDAY, JULY 11, 1904.—10 PAGES.—PRICE 5 CENTS. ESTABLISHED 1859.

MOST NOTORIOUS BANDIT AND TRAIN ROBBER OF THE WORLD IS BURIED IN THE MOUNTAINS

THE OLD HOLE-IN-THE-WALL GANG OF OUTLAWS.

This choice collection of train robbers appears in the photograph in the following order: Harry Longbaugh, alias the Sundance Kid, express and train robber, whose body is worth $10,000 to his captors; Harvey Logan, alias Kid Curry; George Ceirsie, who is still in the saddle, although badly wanted; Elza Lay; George Parker, alias Butch Cassidy.

EAST ASKS FOR MORE

Indications That New Yorkers Will Insist on Hill's Choice of Man to Run Campaign.

CHAIRMAN JONES SAYS PARKER MUST BE SEEN

National Committee Suggests Taggart of Indiana as National Chairman but Nothing Decided Till Meeting in Gotham.

ST. LOUIS, July 10.—The Democratic national committee, new in its make-up, met at 2:30 o'clock this morning and again at 4 o'clock this afternoon, with the avowed intention on behalf of the supporters of Taggart of Indiana of electing him chairman. The early morning meeting was not fully attended and the object aimed at was not accomplished. It was pointed out by Mr. Mack of New York that it would be discourteous to take any action until Mr. Parker, as the candidate, was consulted. The Taggart men, while not having enough to elect, still suggested that Mr. Hill, Mr. Sheehan and Mr. Belmont, the candidate's friends, were still here, and adopted a resolution that they be invited to meet the committee this afternoon. When afternoon came there were three new complications in the way of electing. Chairman Jones of the old committee boldly asserted that such action as contemplated would be unprecedented and, in fact, illegal. It also turned out that at a late hour the convention adopted a resolution authorizing Chairman Jones of the old committee to call the new commitee together in New York city at such time as he might suggest.

Then the other thing was that Senator Hill and Mr. Sheehan left for New York at noon, and could not, therefore, attend the meeting.

Chairman Jones' Statement.

Senator James K. Jones, the retiring chairman of the national committee, made this statement to the Associated Press:

"The national convention, by specific instruction, last night authorized me to call the first meeting of the new committee in New York city. Until I call it the new committee cannot organize and meetings they have held are unauthorized. Now let me say, forcibly, if need be, that, acting under the convention authority, I shall call the national committee to meet in New York city at such time as Judge Parker shall designate, for before I call it I shall consult him. It would be an unprecedented thing for the new committee to organize without consultation with the candidate. Such a thing was never heard of."

Just after the afternoon session began, Mr. Taggart, who was presiding, was asked to retire so that he need not be embarrassed.

August Belmont of New York was called into the room and asked to give Judge Parker's views. He said he could not do so.

(Continued on Page 6—1st Col.)

NOT TOO COARSE FOR P. C. KNOX

W. B. Childers Charged With Serious Offense of Aiding a Monopoly but Attorney General Forgave Him.

(By News Leased Wire.)

WASHINGTON, July 10.—One of the most sensational cases in the department of justice came to light here today, when it became known that William B. Childers, United States district attorney for the territory of New Mexico, was appointed in the closing days of the second Cleveland administration upon the recommendation of powerful magnates, and who was retained in office through the same influences by President McKinley and President Roosevelt, was charged with acting as an attorney for the Colorado Fuel and Iron company, of which Paul Morton, secretary of the navy department, is a director, in a suit in which that corporation was sued in the courts of New Mexico for violating the Sherman anti-trust law.

Never before in the history of the government has an officer of the United States, whose sworn duty it is to prosecute violators of the anti-Sherman trust law, not only failed to perform his duty, but actually gone into open court and boldly appeared as a champion of a trust, and as counsel for the defendant in a suit brought to punish violators of the Sherman law. In the judgment of many persons here, the case has no parallel in the history of the department of justice.

William B. Childers of Albuquerque, N. M., was appointed United States district attorney for the territory of New Mexico in the last month of the second Cleveland administration. Childers was indorsed for the position by persons influential in Southwestern industrial circles. Among his backers were the of-

(Continued on Page 3—2nd Col.)

TRAGIC CONFESSION BEFORE DEATH

Durango Man Tells of Trying to Kill His Family by Putting in Stove Dynamite Sticks With the Fuel.

Special to The News.

DURANGO, Colo., July 10.—Isaac E. Covert, who last Wednesday was frightfully injured by an explosion of dynamite in a cook stove at his home, died this morning at 1:45 o'clock. On his death bed he confessed that he had placed the dynamite in the stove intentionally in the hope that the explosion would not only kill himself, but his wife and seven children.

Covert lived with his family on a farm six miles out of Durango. He was highly respected and an industrious man. His family consists of seven children, ranging in age from an infant to a boy 18 years old. For the past few years Mr. Covert had brooded over the fact that his children were not receiving the schooling he thought they should have.

He arose early Wednesday morning to go after some horses. On returning to the house at breakfast time he placed in the stove a pan supposedly containing chips, but mixed with these chips were three sticks of giant powder a quantity of black powder and a box of giant caps. His wife was serving breakfast from the stove at the time, and his children were all in the house. The explosion which followed fatally injured Mr. Covert, inflicted severe cuts and burns about Mrs. Covert's face and eyes, and slightly injured one boy, Freddy Covert. Mr. and Mrs. Covert were taken to the hospital in Durango. Mrs. Covert will recover, but will probably lose the sight of one eye.

Until shortly before the death of Mr. Covert, when he made his confession, everyone thought he had placed the explosives in the stove by mistake.

DOMINATE PORT ARTHUR

Japanese Batteries Are Strongly Entrenched So as to Command All Parts of the Fortress.

LOSSES IN THE RECENT NAVAL ENGAGEMENTS

Chinese Say More Than 800 Dead Russians Were Carried Into Port Arthur After a Recent Engagement.

CHE FOO, July 10, 5 p. m.—A fair wind brought a fleet of junks from Port Arthur today, carrying both Chinese and Europeans. Reports which they bring of conditions at Port Arthur are contradictory, but they all say that a Japanese division from the northward is entrenching seven miles from the marine camp, while another division from the eastward is fighting continuously and with the aid of the fleet is endeavoring to gain a position commanding the town and the naval basis.

A Russian says that the Japanese occupied the summit of Takushan mountain, which is about three miles from Port Arthur, on the night of July 6, with a mounted battery of artillery.

On July 7 the Russian cruiser Novik and four gunboats went out under protection of the guns on Golden hill and shelled a Japanese battery, which was surrounded and captured finally by the Russian infantry.

The fighting to the eastward of Port Arthur has been very heavy since July 4. The Japanese ships along the shore are shelling the Russian position in the hills. The smoke from the artillery on the hills around Port Arthur is seen almost continuously. Dead and wounded are being brought in at all hours and many private houses have been turned into hospitals. Only skirmishes have occurred to the northward. The main Japanese force is ten miles away, but Japanese scouts have been seen in the vicinity of Marine camp, which commands the principal pass to the hills directly back of Port Arthur. On the nights of July 2, 3 and 4 the Japanese fleet bombarded the roads from the south of the town. The forts were not damaged. No further night attacks have been made since July 4.

(Continued on Page 3—4th Col.)

CAPTAIN OF THE HOLE-IN-THE-WALL GANG LED RIO GRANDE RAILWAY HOLDUPS

Harvey Logan, Who Broke Jail in Tennessee, Killed Himself When Cornered by Posse in Colorado.

Defied Officers of the Law Only to Die a Suicide to Escape Capture in Recent Fight Near Rifle.

To the determination of one woman the police are indebted for the death of the most desperate train robber in the world. After the Rio Grande train robbery at Parachute Mrs. Larson saw a stranger trying to steal one of her horses. She called her two boys to her aid, after remonstrating with the trespasser, and they started in pursuit, armed with carbines. On their way they met the posse that was searching for the train robbers and invoked their assistance. This act was the undoing of Harvey Logan, the bandit king, as the following story recites:

Logan was one of the most desperate bandits that ever infested the West or the country. Among his last robberies was the Denver & Rio Grande train.

On June 7, the westbound passenger train on the Denver & Rio Grande railroad was held up at Parachute, Colo. The robbers, three in number, blew the safe in the express car, rifled it, and then detached the express car from the train and escaped. Posses were organized at once and gave chase. The robbers were well mounted, but their horses had run down, and they abandoned them June 8. On the same day they stole three horses from Ranchman Bandy, near Rifle, Colo. Bandy organized a posse of young farmers and followed the three men, coming up with them between Rifle and New Castle on the afternoon of June 9.

The robbers showed fight and shot at the posse, nearly wounding one of the young men in the posse. Their fire was returned, and one of the robbers fell from his horse, seeing which one of his companions shouted out to him: "Tom, are you hurt?" The wounded robber answered: "Yes; I am all in, and I will end it right here!" saying which he drew a revolver and shot himself through the head.

Addresses found on the body of the dead robber caused inquiries to be made in Texas, where he was identified as Tap Duncan of Knickerbocker, Tex. Further investigation indicated who his companions were, and it was for a time accepted that the identification was reliable until officials of Pinkerton's National Detective agency at Chicago identified the photograph of the dead robber as being that of Harvey Logan, alias Kid Curry, alias Bob Nevilles, alias Tom Jones, alias Nelson, alias Whelan, the leader of the West and Southwest gang of train robbers, who escaped from the county jail at Knoxville, Tenn., on June 27, 1903, after having received a sentence of twenty years in the penitentiary for participating in the Great Northern Express robbery, which occurred at Wagner, Mont., July 3, 1901. In this robbery Logan was assisted by Ben Kilpatrick, who is serving fifteen years for it in the Ohio penitentiary. The third man in this robbery, O. C. Hanks, alias Deaf Charley, was shot and killed while resisting arrest at San Antonio, Tex., April 16, 1902.

Notwithstanding the identification by the Texas officers and others, William A. Pinkerton sent Assistant Superintendent Spence to Knoxville with the photograph of the dead man, and it was identified there by a dozen persons as Harvey Logan. Mr. Spence had previously identified the picture. He had attended Logan's trial and was with him more or less for a period of two weeks before his conviction, and he declared there could be no mistake and that it was Harvey Logan beyond a doubt.

Harvey Logan was a member of the famous "Wild Bunch" band of outlaws. They robbed the Butte County bank, Belle Fourche, S. D., in 1897; in June, 1899, they held up a Union Pacific train at Wilcox, Wyo.; in August, 1900, they robbed another Union Pacific train at Tipton, Wyo., and in the following month they robbed the First National bank of Winnemucca, Nev., of $32,640; in July, 1901, they held up the Great Northern Express at Wagner, Mont., and secured about $35,000. The Pinkertons were put on the trail of the gang in 1897, and since that time eleven of the fourteen members have either been killed or arrested and sent to prison.

Logan was pursued through Montana, Wyoming, Colorado, New Mexico, Kansas, Arkansas and Texas. Finally the chase grew so hot that Logan went to Tennessee, where he was arrested in November, 1901. The charge brought him into the jurisdiction of the United States court, and he was tried and sentenced to twenty years' imprisonment. Fearing that an attempt would be made to help Logan to escape, the Pinkertons recommended that he be guarded night and day by specially chosen men. Notwith-

(Continued on Page 6—2nd Col.)

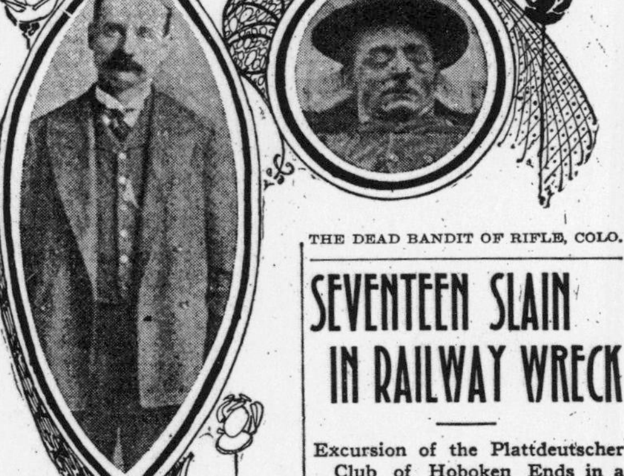

HARVEY LOGAN. From a Photograph Taken in 1900.

THE DEAD BANDIT OF RIFLE, COLO.

MAY SEND FLEET TO FORCE SULTAN

United States Said to Have Made Final Demand for Fair Play for American Teachers and Professional Men.

VIENNA, July 10.—A dispatch from Constantinople says that American Minister Leishman handed a note to the porte declaring that unless a prompt settlement of the school question was arranged a United States fleet would appear in Turkish waters. The sultan ordered the grand vizier to comply with the American minister's demands.

The American demands upon the sultan are for privileges to schools and colleges conducted by American teachers equal to those given to foreign teachers; for permission for American professional men to practice on even terms with foreigners, and for the direct access of the American minister to the sultan in the transaction of business.

ST. PETERSBURG, July 10.—While the Baltic fleet on its way to the Far East is not likely to be able to get coal at French ports, it is understood that the contractors will send out coal from these ports to meet the fleet beyond territorial waters.

SEVENTEEN SLAIN IN RAILWAY WRECK

Excursion of the Plattdeutscher Club of Hoboken Ends in a Horrible Accident and Loss of Life.

NEW YORK, July 10.—Seventeen persons were killed and about fifty injured in a collision which occurred at Midvale, N. J., just before noon today, when a regular passenger train on the Greenwood Lake branch of the Erie railroad ran into an excursion train that had stopped to take water. All the dead and injured lived in Hoboken, Jersey City and New York.

The accident is believed to have resulted from a tower operator having lowered his signal too soon.

The train which was run into was a special carrying members of the First Plattdeutscher association of Hoboken on their annual outing, and had 800 passengers. It consisted of twelve cars and two engines. The first engine had taken water and the train had moved up and stopped with the second engine beside the tank, when the regular train drew near. The flagman of the special signaled the engineer of the oncoming train, but owing to a curve in the road, his flag was not seen until too late. It is claimed that the engineer of the regular train had slowed down to about ten miles an hour before he crashed into the special, but his engine tore through the rear car the greater part of its length and drove the forward end of that car into the car ahead. The killed and injured were in these two cars.

The wreckage did not catch fire and the work of taking out the dead and maimed was accomplished quickly.

The passengers from the uninjured coaches ran back and joined in the work and the residents of Midvale, many of whom had heard the crash, assisted them.

While physicians were being sent for women of Midvale brought bandages and other articles that could be used in caring for the injured.

An engine and cars were sent from Little Falls to the scene of the wreck

(Continued on Page 8—3rd Col.)

WILLIAM B. CHILDERS,
United States District Attorney, Who Is Accused of Acting for the Colorado Fuel and Iron Company.

WATCH THE 78,234 INCREASE

The circulation of The Sunday News yesterday was 78,234 copies, of which a little over 44,000 was confined to the city of Denver and its suburbs. The sales on the streets, at newsstands and by the railroad news agencies were the greatest in the history of The News. The number of copies going to outside cities and towns also broke all records.

The circulation increase of The News and The Times together during the past week continued to exceed 300 daily, of which an average of about 160 daily was in Denver, The Times leading The News in its local gain by a considerable majority. Outside the city The News continues to rule favorite.

Where a large portion of this subscription gain, in Denver at least, comes from may be judged from the following facts: The evening Post has instructed its solicitors to offer to deliver that paper absolutely free for an indefinite period to anybody who will agree not to discontinue it, and if such an offer fails to effect a discontinuance the evening Post's carriers are instructed to continue to deliver the paper at all hazards.

Anybody wishing to verify this statement can do so at the city subscription department of The News and The Times.

In like manner the management of The News and The Times will be glad to offer those interested conclusive evidence of the great increase in the circulations of these papers during the past month throughout Colorado and adjoining states. For example, in one day last week forty-five new subscriptions to The News were received from Albuquerque, N. M., and on the following day twenty-seven from Las Vegas. On every rural mail route in Colorado reference to any carrier will disclose that an average of not less than five copies of The News and The Times are taken as against one copy of all other daily papers combined.

The Sunday News printed yesterday 100 columns of advertising, or about three-fifths of its normal advertising patronage. It will be seen by this that the boycott is still quite effective.

Elsewhere in this issue is printed a "News-Times Shopping Directory" for the convenience of purchasers.

The News and The Times Want the Small Ads of the People. They Guarantee All Such the Greatest Circulation Ever Attained in the West

Another FREE Magazine With Next Sunday's Post. Big Hit Last Sunday

EXTRA   The Boston Post EXTRA

TWELVE PAGES—ONE CENT | THURSDAY, SEPTEMBER 22, 1904 | TWELVE PAGES—ONE CENT

BLEW UP ELECTRIC

CAR EARLY LAST EVENING IN MELROSE

WITH DYNAMITE

MELROSE, Sept. 21.—An outward bound Boston electric car, well loaded with people, was blown to pieces by dynamite at 8 o'clock near corner of Wyoming and Main streets

SCENE AT THE MOMENT OF THE EXPLOSION

NINE DEAD 41 INJURED

CAUSE OF THE ACCIDENT

A FIFTY-POUND BOX OF DYNAMITE FELL FROM AN EXPRESS WAGON IN FRONT OF THE ELECTRIC CAR. IN THE DARK, THE MOTORMAN FAILED TO DISCOVER THE PERIL IN TIME TO STOP.

LIST OF THE DEAD

DR. MALCOLM E. M'LENNAN, Melrose Highlands.

E. B. HAYNES, Fairmount street, Melrose.

WINFIELD ROWE, Saugus, motorman.

E. A. STOWE, 848 East Fifth street, Boston

DR. FRED D. MARSHALL, Danvers.

MRS. ADA CROUCH, Fullerton stre[et], Stoneham

MISS LOUISE TEACKLES of Lyndon st[reet], Malden.

MRS. EDWARD HAYNES of Fairm[ount] street, Melrose.

LITTLE GIRL, three years old, thought to be daughter of Mrs. Haynes.

LIST OF INJURED

EDWIN A. WATERHOUSE, 19 Rowe street, Melrose. Face cut and ankle fractured. One foot amputated.

THOMAS BIGWOOD, Chelsea. Slight.

JOHN M. MILLER, 40 Charles street, Lynn. Slight.

CHARLES E. BUTTERFIELD, 102 Broadway, Chelsea. Slight.

SARAH E. BARRETT, 3 Winter place, Malden. Slight.

ANN BARRETT, 3 Winter place, Malden. Slight.

J. D. PATTEN, Melrose Highlands. Both ankles injured, scalp wounds; left foot amputated.

GEORGE H. ANDREWS, 216 Grove street, Melrose. Compound fracture left leg; foot amputated at ankle.

EDITH FURLONG, colored, Sanford street, Melrose. Slight.

REBECCA F. WALLACE, Short street, Malden. Slight.

BLANCHE SHANNON, Malden. Slight.

FRANK BURNHAM, Maple street, Melrose. Slight.

MARTHA LEE, colored, Wyoming. Scalp and breast wound.

C. B. SHAW, 154 Clifton street, Malden. Slight.

HENRY BOWES, Pleasant street, Melrose. Slight.

J. M. EDWARDS, Jr., 15 Francis street, Malden. Face cut.

MRS. JOHN CONWAY, Gibbons street, Melrose. Both legs broken below knee. May die.

GEORGE P. HARRIS, Elmwood place, Malden. Slight.

Continued on Page 5—Fifth Column

(For detailed story of the explosion, illustrations, experiences of survivors, etc., see Pages 2, 3, 4, 5, 12.)

MAGAZINE SECTION. **THE NEW YORK HERALD.** PART I. PAGES 1 TO 8.

NEW YORK, SUNDAY, SEPTEMBER 23, 1906.— PRICE FIVE CENTS.

[illegible] ROMANTIC EXPLOITS OF [illegible] WESTERN TRAIN ROBBERS IN [illegible] AMERICA

HARRY LONGBOUGH

ETTA PLACE LONGBOUGH

FOUR leisurely horsemen just after ten o'clock one morning early in last March appeared in the public square of Villa Mercedes, in the province of San Luis, which occupies a central position in the Argentine Republic. Three of the men, it was noticed by those members of the population who were not too sleepy to notice anything at all, were of about medium height, well knit, bronzed and athletic. The fourth was shorter and of slender physique, with delicate hands and feet, with the flush of youth upon cheek ...

...en unconcernedly pulled up ... small hotel that occupies ... square and ordered drinks ...r, who emerged lazily in ... bidding. Having disposed ... ment and handed back ... to the dull witted ... [illegible] ... Nacion Argentina and ... the Bank of Terrapoca of ... The three stalwart mem... tossed their bridle reins ... ller companion and entered ...

...our of the day in Villa Mer... in most other inland towns of the Argentine Republic, there is very little doing in the way of business activity, and upon the particular occasion in question a solitary clerk was in charge. This individual, casually glancing up from the ledger spread out before him, was intensely surprised to find himself gazing with rapt concentration into the frowning muzzle of a large revolver pointed directly at him by one of his visitors, who accompanied the operation with a sharp reminder that death would instantly follow any outcry or attempt at resistance. Meanwhile the two comrades of the man behind the gun had vaulted over the counter and were rapidly but systematically gathering up all the cash and securities exposed to their view. They had not completed their task when the manager of the bank, having perceived from the outside an apparent access of business to the institution of which he was the Villa Mercedes head, stepped in to take personal charge of whatever transaction might be in progress.

He was promptly shot in the head by one of the intruders, all three of whom, with drawn weapons, backed out through the open door and sprang upon their horses, the whole quartet galloping out of town before the residents had fairly awakened from their accustomed state of somnolence. In a few moments the entire township was ablaze with excitement, but the marauders had made good their escape and all efforts to overtake them were futile.

HARVEY LOGAN IN HIS WORKING CLOTHES

Twenty Thousand Dollars in One Haul.

During the few preceding months there had been two or three similar attacks in various sections of the Argentine, and this final assault, obviously manoeuvred by the same band that had taken part in the previous outrages, served to stir the authorities of the Southern republic. They found among the documents in their possession—and which had been in their possession for a long time back—a notification from the Pinkerton National Detective Agency, through a representative visiting the Argentine, that in the year 1901 a band of North American train and bank robbers had landed in Buenos Ayres and had taken up a permanent residence in the remote interior. This gang consisted of Harry Longbaugh, alias "the Sundance Kid," Mrs. Harry Longbaugh and George Parker, alias "Butch" Cassidy, who were subsequently joined by Harvey Logan, alias "Kid" Curry. These were the four persons engaged in the Villa Mercedes affair, which netted them between $15,000 and $20,000. The description of three of them as issued in Spanish by the Southern police from memoranda furnished by the Pinkertons is as follows:—

Nombre—Cassidy, alias James Ryan, alias Santiago Ryan.
Nacionalidad—Norte Americano.
Ocupacion—Gaucho.
Edad—33 años.
Altura—5 pies con 9 pulgadas, ó sea 1 metro, 75 centimetros.
Peso—165 libras, 75 kilos.
Cuerpo—Mediano; complexion, claro.
Color del Pelo—Rubio claro; ojos azules.
Bigote—Colorido claro, si es que no lo ha afeitado.
Observaciones—Dos cicatrices atras de la cabeza, cicatrice chico debajo del ojo izquierdo, verruga chica color café en la pierna, ras de la pierna, y debajo de la rodilla.
Nombre—Longbaugh, alias Harry A. Place.
Nacionalidad—Sueco Norte Americano.
Ocupacion—Gaucho.
Edad—35 años.
Altura—5 pies con 10 pulgadas, ó 1 metro, ...ímetros.
...165 á 175 libras ó sea 75 a 79 kilos.
...azules gris; cuerpo, bien desarrollado.
...—Mediano.
...actualmente tiene, de color café natural colorido.
...Tipo griego; nariz, mas bien

Color del Pelo—Color café ó marron natural; es posible que lo; se peina estilo pompadour.
Tiene las peinas muy apartadas se debe esto probablemente por andar mucho á caballo.
Nombre—Mrs. Longbaugh, alias Mrs. Harry A. Place, esposa del que antecede.
Nacionalidad—Norte Americana.
Edad—26 años; peso, 110 libras (50 kilos).
Altura—5 pies con 5 pulgadas, ó sea 1 metro, 67 centimetros.
Complexion—Mediana; ojos azules ó gris.
Pelo—Mediano oscuro.
Fisonomia—Regular.

Etta Longbaugh Aids Robbers.

It was Etta Longbaugh, wife of Harry Longbaugh, who, dressed in masculine attire, held the horses of herself and her companions in front of the Villa Mercedes branch of the bank of Terrapoca while it was being robbed by her husband and his mates, just as she had held their horses upon other occasions when similar raids were made in the Argentine.

Mr. and Mrs. Longbaugh and George Parker sailed from this country directly for Buenos Ayres. After reaching Buenos Ayres they took passage on a coastwise steamer to the port of Bahia Blanca, still further south. From this place they shipped upon a semi-monthly river steamboat to an inland point called Rawson, thence striking out across country mounted on mules. They had already purchased extensive pasture lands to the southward some seventy-five miles from the small village of Cholulo, where their nearest white neighbors were situated. When they reached their destination the party had travelled in all some seventy-four days from New York—thirty-nine days to Buenos Ayres, twenty days more to Rawson and fifteen days from that interior hamlet to their ranch, which is in the province of Chibute, or Chubut, in the Department of the Sixteenth of October.

The capital required for this investment, together with the no inconsiderable amount demanded for travelling expenses on the journey of twelve thousand miles, had been derived from sundry train and bank robberies in the western part of the United States, the bold and daring character of which will be described later.

LEFT TO RIGHT HARRY LONGBOUGH, SUNDANCE KID' BILL CARVER (DEAD) BEN KILPATRICK (DOING 15 YEARS) HARVEY LOGAN ALIAS KID CURRY, GEORGE PARKER, ALIAS BUTCH CASSIDY.

It is apparent that Longbaugh, the leader of what is left of one of the most noted bands of robbers in this country, intended, when framing up the trip to South America, to abandon the life of outlawry and become a legitimate rancher, together with the man and woman who accompanied him. The ranch upon which the little party settled occupies a high tableland in the Indian country of the South, and from its surface there is a perfect view of the country for twenty miles or more in every direction. The spot is inaccessible in the extreme, and if any attempt were made to dislodge or capture the "Americanos" it might require the services of a full regiment of soldiery and would undoubtedly end in much loss of life, owing to the naturally defensive quality of the position.

Even then it is extremely doubtful if their capture might be effected, for there is reason to believe that the northern bandits have acquired a very thorough knowledge of the country they have chosen to honor with their presence. They began operations upon their elevated tableland by erecting living quarters, and proceeded in due course to stock the ranch with sheep, horses and cattle. According to such information as may be gleaned from the Indians (for white men have not considered it a healthful proposition to invade the Longbaugh-Parker-Logan territory), there are between five hundred and one thousand head of domestic animals now upon the ranch.

It is supposed that Longbaugh and his friends miscalculated in the matter of how far their funds would go and found they could not swing the ranching proposition upon their original capital. In this emergency they went back to first principles and took up the series of exploits the most recent of which to be recorded took place in Villa Mercedes.

LAURA BULLION.

The stuff of which the three men and their woman consort are made may be gathered from the fact that as the crow flies the Villa Mercedes is approximately four hundred miles from the ranch which they make their home. The actual journey must have been fully half again as long, owing to the rough and circuitous route necessarily followed both going and coming. But the members of the band had been accustomed to much sterner feats of horsemanship and endurance in North America, and they quite probably looked upon the Villa Mercedes undertaking as a mere incident of ordinary life.

Once before two of the men, in playful mood, presumably Logan and Parker, were travelling in the mountains in a stage coach, the only other occupants of which were the driver and one passenger. In the course of conversation they learned that their fellow voyager had with him a trunk containing a large sum of money in gold. At a convenient place where the coach was traversing the edge of a deep ravine the two Americans pitched the driver and passenger headlong into the abyss below, rifled the trunk of its golden contents and rode off upon the backs of the coach horses, escaping unmolested to their distant plateau. Although their identity was more than suspected and their location had been made known to the authorities through the Pinkertons, no visible attempt was ever made to overtake and punish the ostensible ranchers.

HARVEY LOGAN

A certain romantic interest is thrown about this little coterie of desperadoes by reason of the presence among them of Etta Longbaugh, the intrepid wife of the leader. She is but twenty-six years of age, with graceful, girlish figure, dark, flashing eyes, regular features, brilliant white teeth and a mass of wavy dark hair. She can shoot with the rapidity and precision of a professional marksman, handling rifle and revolver with equal deftness. She wears masculine attire almost invariably and rides astride of her horse quite as well and with fully as much fortitude as her male associates. Where she originally found Longbaugh, or where he found her, is not an item of police history, but the Pinkertons would probably pay any one who could identify her and furnish her pedigree.

It is known, however, that she went with Longbaugh when he left this port upon his long journey to the Argentine. There is a belief that Etta in her youth was a Western cowgirl known as Etta Place, and that Longbaugh met her and induced her to run away with him during one of his hold-up raids in this country some years ago.

It is altogether probable that Longbaugh and the rapidly diminishing remnant of his outlaw gang in America were induced to emigrate to southern climes by the uncomfortable pressure of the net that the Pinkertons, together with [illegible] police, sheriffs and United States [illegible] of the Western States, had been [illegible] about their quarry, slowly but sur[ely, for] eight or ten years.

It is one of the special provinces o[f the] Pinkerton agency to safeguard the i[nter]ests of express and railway companies [and] of banking institutions that are membe[rs] of the American Bankers' Association. In this capacity they are constantly in pursuit of the various classes of criminals whose aim it is in one way or another to rob express cars and banks. The most dangerous, as well as the most difficult, to capture of all grades and conditions of looters are the "stick-up" gangs, composed of men fearless to the point of desperation, to whom bloodshed is a matter of not the slightest consequence, while they value their own lives as nothing at all.

For a number of years the section of Wyoming known as the "Hole in the Wall" was infested with men of this description. From horse thieving, cattle rustling and similar pursuits they turned their attention to holding up railway trains and banking houses in small towns scattered all over the West, and they gradually formed themselves into various bands or mobs, which consisted of the following:—

First Leader—"Tom" Ketcham, alias "Black Jack," hanged at Clayton, N. M., April 26, 1901, for killing Sheriff Edward Farr, of Whalenburg, N. M., who was attempting to arrest him. "Black Jack" was the original leader of this entire band of "hold-ups."

Second Leader—George S. Curry, alias "Flat Nose George," was killed April 17, 1900, by a sheriff's posse about seventy miles east of Thompsons, Utah, while resisting arrest. He was concerned in the robbery of a Union Pacific train at Wilcox, Wyo., June 2, 1899.

Third Leader—William Carver, alias "Bill" Carver, was killed April 2, 1901, while resisting arrest in Texas for murder at Sonora, that State.

Fourth Leader—Harvey Logan, alias Harvey Curry, alias "Kid" Curry, arrested near Knoxville, Tenn., December 13, 1901. Subsequently convicted and sentenced to twenty years' imprisonment for uttering altered national bank notes stolen from the Great Northern Express Company on the Great Northern Railway July 3, 1901, by train robbers who forced their way into the express car by using dynamite, overpowed the messenger, blew open the safe and stole therefrom upward of forty-five thousand dollars in unsigned national bank notes.

Logan's Daring Escape.

Knowing Logan's desperate character, the Pinkertons recommended to the Great Northern Express Company that a night and day watch be placed over the prisoner in the Knox county jail to prevent his escape until he was delivered to the Columbus (Ohio) State Prison, to which institution he had been sentenced.

On Saturday, June 27, 1903, Logan made a daring flight, through the gross carelessness of the jailer and special guards. He had been confined in a separate corridor under these guards. One of their number, Irwin, left his revolvers in a basket at one end of the corridor and went to the other end, directly in front of Logan's cell door, to look out of the window. While the guard was at the window Logan stealthily lassoed him with a wire he had unwound from an old broom, and which he fastened in a noose to the end of the broomstick. Casting the noose over the guard's head, Logan pulled him off his feet and drew him to the cell door, at the same time threatening to choke Irwin to death if he made an outcry. The guard submitted.

With the same broomstick and another wire hook Logan pulled the guard's two revolvers in to him and then called Jailer Bell to give him some medicine. Logan having been under the doctor's care, Mell responded, and as he entered the corridor the bandit covered him with the pistols, demanding his own release. To this the jailer consented, and Logan walked ou[t] of the jail, defying every one in his pat[h] went to a stable in the rear of the buildi[ng]

(CONTINUED ON SECOND PAGE.

The Beeville Bee.

VOL. XXII. $1.50 Per Year. BEEVILLE, BEE COUNTY, TEXAS, FRIDAY, MARCH 6, 1908. Established May 13, 1886 NO. 46.

PAT GARRETT KILLED.

Noted West Texas Character and Slayer of Bad Man Slain—Was Friend of Roosevelt.

El Paso, Texas, Feb. 29.—Pat Garrett, slayer of "Billy the Kid," the noted outlaw and cattle rustler, sheriff in New Mexico in the days when he had to take his life in his hands to leave his home, former collector of customs at El Paso and personal friend of President Roosevelt, was killed today at Las Cruces, N. M. Wayne Brazel, a cattleman with whom Garrett had had a dispute for several months, surrendered himself.

Both men were coming to Las Cruces from their ranches, Garrett in a buggy with another man, and Brazel riding on horseback with a friend. Brazel overtook Garrett. Brazel says Garrett reached for a shotgun. The shooting was four miles out from Las Cruces, and Brazel rode into town and surrendered.

Garrett went to New Mexico in the 70s from Kentucky and located first at Carlsbad, where he was elected sheriff of Lincoln county on a platform to suppress cattle rustlers. His life was repeatedly threatened, but he succeeded in suppressing the criminals, and in doing so killed "Billy the Kid," one of the west's most desperate outlaws and leader of a band of rustlers. Later he was elected sheriff at Las Cruces, where he killed several men in the discharge of his duties.

Garrett's bravery attracted the attention of President Roosevelt, who appointed him customs collector at El Paso in December, 1901. In 1905, during the reunion of rough riders at San Antonio, President Roosevelt invited Garrett to meet him there, and he dined with the president at the fair grouds, but the president refused to re-appoint Garrett.

Pat Garrett came to Texas from Kentucky, and first settled at Uvalde, then moved to the Pecos country and was elected sheriff of Lincoln county in 1878, when he began his war on the cattle rustlers. He had a blind daughter, Elizabeth, who graduated from the state school for the blind about three years ago at Austin.

With regard to Pat Garrett, Emerson Hough, in his "The Story of the Outlaw," has the following to say:

Patrick Floyd Garrett, better known as Pat Garrett, was a southerner by birth. He was born in Chambers county, Alabama, June 5, 1850. In 1856 his parents moved to Claiborne Parish, Louisiana, where his father was a large land owner and among the bitter opponents of the new regime which followed the civil war. When young Garrett's father died the large estates dwindled under bad management, and when within a short time the mother followed her husband to the grave, the family resources, affected by the war, became involved, although the two Garrett plantations embraced nearly 3000 acres of rich Louisiana soil. On January 25, 1869, Pat Garrett, a tall and slender youth of 18, set out to seek his fortunes in the wild west, with no resources but such as lay within his brain and body.

He went to Lancaster in Dallas county, Texas. A big ranch owner in southern Texas wanted men and Pat Garrett packed up and went home with him. The world was new to him, however, and he went off with the northbound cows, like many another youngster of his time. His herd was made up at Eagle Lake, and he only accompanied the drive as far as Denison. There he began to get uneasy, hearing of the delights of the still wilder life of the buffalo hunters on the great plains which lay to the west, in the Panhandle of Texas. For three winters, 1875 to 1877, he was in and out between the buffalo range and the settlements, by this time well wedded to the frontier life.

In the fall of 1877 he went west once more, and this time kept on going west. With two hardy companions he pushed on entirely across the wild and unknown Panhandle country, leaving the wagons near what was known as the "Yellow Houses," and never returning to them. His blankets, personal belongings, etc., he never saw again. He and his friends had their heavy Sharp's rifles, plenty of powder and lead, and their reloading tools, and they had nothing else. Their beds they made of their saddle blankets and their food they killed from the wild herds. For their love of adventure they rode on across an unknown country, until finally they arrived at the little Mexican settlement of Fort Sumner, on the Pecos river, in the month of February, 1878.

Pat and his friends were hungry, but all the cash they could find was just $1.50 between them. They gave it to Pat and sent him over to the store to see about eating. He asked about meals and they told him 50 cents per meal. This would permit them to eat but once. He concluded to buy $1.50 worth of flour and bacon, which would last for two or three meals. He joined his friends and they went into camp on the river bank, where they cooked and ate, perfectly happy and careless about the future.

As they finished their breakfast they saw up the river the dust of a cattle herd, and noted that a party were working a herd, cutting out cattle for some purpose or other.

"Go up there and get a job," said Pat to one of the boys. The latter did go up, but came back reporting that the boss did not want any help.

"Well, he's got to have help," said Pat. So saying he arose and started up stream himself.

Garrett was at that time, as has been said, of very great height, six feet four and one-half inches, and very slender. Unable to get trousers long enough for his legs, he had pieced down his best pair with about three feet of buffalo leggins with the hair out. Gaunt, dusty and unshaven, he looked hard, and when he approached the herd owner and asked for work the other was as much alarmed as pleased. He declined again, but Pat firmly told him that he had come to go to work and was sorry, but it could not be helped. Something in the quiet voice of Garrett seemed to arrest the attention of the cowman. "What can you do, lengthy?" he asked.

"Ride anything with hair and rope better than anything you've got here," answered Garrett, casting a critical eye at the other men.

The cowman hesitated a moment and then said, "Get in." Pat got in. He stayed in. Two years later he was still at Fort Sumner and married.

Garrett moved down from Fort Sumner soon after his marriage and settled a mile east of what is now the flourishing town of Roswell, at a spring on the bank of the Hondo, and in the middle of what was then the virgin plains. Here he picked up land until he had in all more than 1250 acres. If he owned it now he would be worth a half million dollars.

In the month of December, 1901, President Theodore Roosevelt, who had heard of Garrett, met him and liked him, and without any ado or consultation, appointed him collector of customs at El Paso, Texas. Here for the past four years Garrett made a popular collector and a fearless one.

Possibly the event in the life of Garrett for which he will be longest remembered is the killing of the famous and notorious outlaw known as "Billy the Kid," which occurred at Fort Sumner after the Kid had escaped from prison a few days before the date set for his execution. Garrett being at that time a United States deputy marshall and sheriff-elect, and having, only a short time before, placed the Kid under arrest.

Accompanied by two deputies Pat Garrett went to Fort Sumner, and on a bright moonlight night entered the town, making his way to the residence of Pete Maxwell, as he knew that the Kid was somewhere in the neighborhood. Unaware of the fact that the Kid was in bed in a house just opposite. Garrett placed his two deputies outside of Maxwell's house and entered. He realized that when he met the man he was pursuing that one or the other was to die.

He was sitting at the bedside in the house talking to Maxwell, when the Kid, in his stocking feet, crossed the street to obtain some meat from Maxwell and entered the room. The desperado had noted the men outside the house, but did not suspect anything. On entering he perceived Garrett, but did not recognize him in the dark, although had the deputy marshal been standing his great height would have betrayed him. The Kid, however, motioned toward Garrett 'with a self-cocking .41 which he carried in his hand, as he asked Maxwell who was his guest.

Just at this instant, according to Garrett's own story of the affair, it flashed over his mind that he had to shoot and shoot at once, and that his shot must go to the mark.

"Just as he spoke," said Garrett in relating the incident, I dropped over to the left and rather down, going after my gun with my right hand as I did so. I had caught him just about the heart. His pistol, already pointed toward me, went off as he fell but he fired high. As I sprang up I fired once more, but did not hit him, and did not need to, for he was dead. I don't know that he ever knew who killed him. He could not see me in the darkness."

Parkhurst On Prohibition.

New York, Feb. 29.—Dr. Charles H. Parkhurst, pastor of the Madison Square Presbyterian church, who, as president of the Society for the Prevention of Crime, a few years ago made the charge of partnership between the police of this city and criminals, that led to a legislative investigation of the department, authorized a formal interview last night in which be advocated the passage of law only so stringent as will appeal to the average sentiment of the community. He would legalize the sale of liquor on certain hours on the Sabbath, he said, if the community demands this practice. On the theory that only laws backed by popular will could be enforced and that unenforced laws led to a degeneracy of morals, Dr. Parkhurst's interview was on the question prohibition by statute. He said:

"While I will not say prohibition by statute is impossible, I do know that no prohibitory statute enacted in the past has actually prohibited traffic in liquor. "I believe in the passage of laws so stringent as to be sure of the indorsement of the average sentiment of the community. If you enact laws beyond that point your statute will not be enforced, and a statute that is not enforced is a great deal worse than no statute at all.

"The degeneracy of morals in our country is due to a considerable extent to the fact that the legislation has been above the country's moral sentiment. The only straight road toward prohibition is to enact restriction of the laws only so rigid that their unequivocal enforcement will be assured. People have to be led on to better things by short steps."

No Delay For Aransas Pass.

Washington, Feb. 28—Prof. Paust of Philadelphia, lost his suit in the district court here to restrain the secretary of war, General McKenzie and Contractor Pigon from prosecuting the deep water work at Aransas Pass, Paust claiming patent right in the single jetty system being used. Justice Gould refused the injunction on the ground that it was an indirect attempt to sue the federal government without the consent of congress. Paust has appealed the case.

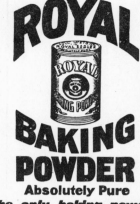

SECOND EDITION

Newark Evening Star

AND NEWARK ADVERTISER

SECOND EDITION

ESTABLISHED 1832. ONE CENT. NEWARK N. J., MONDAY, AUGUST 1, 1910.—14 PAGES. FAIR TONIGHT; TUESDAY PARTLY CLOUDY.

DEEP MYSTERY IN MURDER OF MAN NEAR BELLEVILLE

Well-dressed Man, Believed to Be New Yorker, Killed for Revenge.

IDENTITY OF VICTIM NOT YET DISCOVERED

Scene of Crime, Secluded Spot, Was Carefully Chosen by His Enemies.

Italian policemen from every section of Essex county today spread out in a hunt among the Italian tenements and shacks in Nutley, Bloomfield, Montclair, the Oranges and in this city for a clew to the murderer or the identity of the man, plainly an Italian, who was shot and stabbed to death in the lonely section of Franklin street, between Magnolia street and Marion place, in the Silver Lake section of Belleville.

All agreed that the victim, who was better dressed than the average, was murdred in revenge, possibly the betrayal of a secret of some society. Money and valuables on the body were left undisturbed. There was evidence that the body had been dragged some distance, probalby from a spot near the Silver Lake depot of the Erie railroad.

Many of the detectives proceeded today on the theory that this spot has been hit upon by members of various murderous societies as ideal for their peculiar crimes. They recalled that five years ago the body of a man riddled with bullets was found in the canal near there and not less than six mon thsago two men were found stabbing a third in the desolate spot.

Many Officers in Hunt.

The Italian policemen working on the murder are Louis Bonnello, of Belleville; Adubato, of this city, and Cozzens, of Montclair. Other officers in the case are Chief Wiemer, of the prosecutor's office; Chief Flynn, of Belleville, and Detective Thomas Meyers, of the prosecutor's office.

An arrest that looked as though it might be fruitful petered out today. Patrolman Ambrose Francis remembered that on Sunday morning, shortly before the body of the murdered man [illegible] found, James Crino, 28 years old, [illegible] Oliver street, ran up to him in Belmont avenue and asked protection from Americao Cirestofino, 35 years old, of 44 Heckel street. He told the policeman that Cirestofino wanted to kill him. Cirestofino got away at that time, but both men were later locked up by Patrolman Louis Bonnello, the only Italian member of the Belleville police force. Both men were put through a severe questioning by Chief Wiemer, of the prosecutor's office, and Chief Flynn, of Belleville, and it was agreed that they knew nothing of the murder.

The searchlight of the automobile of Dr. Lester R. Davis, of 58 Elizabeth avenue, revealed the body of the murdered man, when the doctor was returning from a sick call shortly after 1 o'clock yesterday morning. Dr. Davis jumped from his machine, saw at a glance that life was extinct and that the body was still warm. He then called Chanceman William Keefe, of the Belleville police force. Chanceman Keefe fired a shot which brought Patrolman Francis. Then in turn came Chief Flynn, County Physician William H. McKenzie and Chief Weimer, of the prosecutor's detectives.

Dr. McKenzie's autopsy showed that a bullet had passed through the body from the back and that there was a stab wound about four inches from the bullet wound. The knife thrust had been made by a circular bladed knife, evidently while the victim was prostrate. Neither wound would have caused death.

Detectives at work today said that Charles Alsworth, of Franklin street, Bloomfield, near the scene of the crime, no doubt heard the shot and saw the murderers. Alsworth's story is that he was about to retire at 1:15 o'clock yesterday morning when he heard a shot and heard loud voices. He looked from the window, and saw two men hurrying by. They were talking excitedly It was so dark, he said, he could not see their faces.

Believe Victim Was New Yorker.

In their hunt for a clew today the police questioned the crew of the Erie train, which got into Silver Lake at 12:30 o'clock yesterday morning. It is the last train in and the police are of the opinion that it is more than likely that the victim is a New York man and that he was lured to the spot where he was done to death.

The belief is that the victim is from New York. His hat has a New York label. He was about 35 years old and had dark hair, eyes and mustache. He weighed about 150 pounds and was five feet eight inches tall. His clothing was of good quality and of dark blue, and he wore a silk shirt and patent leather shoes. The initials "S. C." were in his hat, and the initial "S." was on a gold signet ring he wore. Cash amounting to $4.22 was found in one of his pockets.

"It is my belief," said Chief Flynn today, "after a careful investigation of all the circumstances, that the victim was lured to the spot where he was murdered and that it is more than likely that he was brought from some other city, possibly on that late Erie train. He does not live in this neighborhood. He is so well dressed that I am sure he was a man of means. He may have been a gang leader who betrayed a secret or he may have refused to accede to the demand of some secret society. It is plain that his body was dragged some feet in an effort to hide it, but evidently the murderers were scared off before they got it in a spot off the road. They might have been scared off by the light of an automobile or someone approaching on foot."

ENRAGED FIREMAN SHOOTS CAPTAIN, SLAYS ANOTHER

Insane Over Discharge He Fires at Companions, Then Kills Family.

SAN DIEGO, Cal., Aug. 1.—Bert S. Durham, a former fireman, mortally wounded Captain Sampsell, of the fire department; killed a second and seriously wounded a third near a firebox, where he sent in a false alarm in an insane fit of revenge early today.

Nursing an old grudge against Captain Sampsell, under whom he had worked as an engineer and on whose complaint he had been discharged from the service for insubordination, Durham early today sent in a false alarm from the outskirts of the city. When Captain Sampsell and his engineer drove up Durham opened fire on his former workmates with a revolver.

At the first shot Driver Don Grant fell from his seat dead with a bullet in the head. At the second shot Hoseman Guy Elliott pitched to the ground with a bullet through the stomach. Durham then leveled his revolver at Sampsell and fired twice, both bullets piercing Sampsell's lungs.

Two more shots fired at other members of the crew went wild. Durham drew another revolver and covered his retreat as he started to run from Assistant Chief Snedecor, who had driven up in answer to the fire alarm. As he disappeared in the darkness Durham shouted back to the chief:

"Tell my wife I am going to kill myself."

The victims of the shooting were rushed to St. Joseph's Hospital in one of the hose wagons.

Operations were performed on Sampsell and Elliott. The surgeons say Sampsell suffered a severe hemorrhage, and they hold out no hopes of his recovery. Elliott has a chance.

Within half an hour after the shooting a score of police officers and deputy sheriffs were on the scene in automobiles and had begun a man-hunt. Owing to the darkness Durham reached home and slew his family and then fled again.

During his service in the department, which terminated several months ago, Durham had a reputation for being quarrelsome. Firemen with whom he worked thought him insane.

BOY IS HELD AS ASSAILANT OF AN UNCONSCIOUS MAN

Crowd Identifies Latter, a Boy, Captured After Midnight Chase. Injured Man Unconscious.

Held for an assault on an elderly man, George Powers, 18 years old, of 134 South street, was arrested in the small hours of this morning and arraigned before Judge Hahn in the First Criminal Court. He was held to await the outcome of the injuries received by the assaulted man, John Reilly, who, it is said, lives in Montclair, and is at present in the City Hospital in an unconscious condition.

John Reilly, jr., 25 years old, of 51 Clinton street, the injured man's son, was also held as a material witness.

Just what caused the quarrel between the two men the police refuse to tell, claiming that they do not know. Patrolman Dauber, who arrested Powers, says that he was on Mechanic street when he noticed two men running toward him. He caled to them to stop, but they paid no heed and kept on their way. He gave chase and succeeded in landing Powers. Powers said he was on his way home.

The policeman took him back along the way he had come, and at Market street he saw a crowd collected in front of 228. A man was lying on the pavement, and when the crowd saw Powers in the custody of the officer they cried:

Crowd Cries "hat's He."

"That's the man that cut him.'"

Reilly, jr., who was by the side of his father, identied the prisoner also. The injured man wyas taken to the hospital in an unconscious state, and up to a late hour today had remained so. Reilly, jr., resfused to make any statement as to the nature of the quarrel. Powers is reticient.

MOBS ATTACK CARS; BURNING PREVENTED.

Gov. Hannon Unable to Settle Columbus, O., Strike.

COLUMBUS, O., Aug. 1.—Governor Harmon has so far failed to settle the street car strike.

The company offered to take the union men back as individuals if they will discard their union button. This the strikers refuse to do. They demand recognition of their union. Two Leonard avenue cars were attacked by mobs today and had to be abandoned.

The police stopped an attempt to burn the cars.

Troops again are patrolling the streets and few people are riding in the cars.

MARK TWAIN'S IMAGE ON CALF.

ALBURTIS, Pa., Aug. 1.—Almost at the same moment that Mark Twain died a calf was born near here with a figure in the field of white that encircles its body closely resembling the bust of the peer of American humorists. Scores or persons have visited W. F. Walker's farm to see the curiosity.

EX-GOV. STOKES MAY BE LEADER OF REPUBLICANS

Trenton Hears Rumor That He Is Mysterious "Big Man" Mentioned.

ACTIVE CANDIDATE FOR UNITED STATES SENATOR

Nothing in His Statement to Indicate Second Term Gubernatorial Ambitions.

[Special to the Newark Star.]

STATE HOUSE, TRENTON, Aug. 1.—There has been considerable speculation in Republican circles for the last two weeks as to the identity of the "Big Man whose name as a candidate has not been mentioned," and there are many who now believe that the name will be Edward Casper Stokes, who was elected to the office six years ago by the largest majority ever given any candidate for that office in this State, and who is now an aspirant for the Republican primary indorsement for United States Senator.

The former Governor's name as a candidate for a second term is used without knowledge on his part, for he has repeatedly stated his attitude on the gubernatorial situation and reiterates that he is very much in earnest in the senatorial race.

Anxious for Senatorship.

"I entered the contest for the primary indorsement for election as United States Senator in good faith," said former Governor Stokes today, "and the outcome is in the hands of the Republican voters of the State. My intention was announced coincident with the circulation of the necessary nominating petitions and will be filed as required by law."

The fact that the Stokes nominating petitions have not been filed occasioned some comment at Sea Girt last Thursday, and started the rumor that he had been induced by the leaders to withdraw from the senatorial contest and enter the open list for the gubernatorial nomination.

One of the reasons advanced for the desire to see the former governor again the nominee is his well-known ability as a campaigner.

Such a man was admitted to be absolutely necessary, in view of the fact which the Republicans accept as almost certain that President Woodrow Wilson, of Princeton University, will be the Democratic nominee.

Will Surely File Petition.

The former governor says there was no foundation whatever for the supposition that he would not file his petition. The law requires a petition signed by 1,000 voters and verified in the manner provided for all nominating petitions to be filed with the secretary of state in ample time to permit that officer to transmit copies of the petitions to the several county clerks at least twenty days prior to the primary elections.

In Cumberland, his home county, the voters' petition had more than one thousand signers within a brief period after it was issued, and the filing of that one document would have caused the name of Edward Casper Stokes for United States Senator to appear on every Republican ballot to be used in the primary election on September 13.

Preferring to have a more general expression of sentiment, Mr. Stokes or his friends have circulated petitions in other sections of the State, and within a short time, or some time within the next twenty days, the Stokes petition containing several, instead of one thousand names, will be filed.

Wednesday, August 24, is the last day for the county clerk to receive the petition or a copy thereof from the secretary of state, but the law is silent as to when the petition shall be filed. The Stokes petition will be filed in ample time and will be the only regular petition seeking indorsement.

May Be Only Candidate.

That means that unless the Progressives name a new candidate for indorsement, Stokes will be alone in the field and consequently receive a very large vote.

In the meantime it is expected that he will tour the State in his own behalf and probably have some nice things to say about the prominent Republican candidate he hopes to see nominated and elected Governor.

This will unquestionably make the Cumberland statesman appear as the man of destiny before the Republican convention, no matter how he may plead for Vivian M. Lewis, for whom he is known to have a very high regard, or for any of the other Republican aspirants such as Senators Wakelee or Frelinghuysen.

Such a course would have the harmonizing effect of removing at least one of the candidates for Senator John Kean's seat in Congress and it would give the party a candidate known from Sussex to Cape May, with an executive and legislative experience of about twenty years, and the prestige of carrying the State primaries on their first trial, as well as the one best equipped to meet his Democratic opponents. That is the way some of the Republican leaders summarize the situation.

BURNED PLAYING WITH FIRE, CHILD MAY DIE.

Trying to kindle a bonfire while her mother was out washing, little Josephine Brunt, colored, 5 years old, of 20 Seventh avenue, was severely burned about the body, in the rear of her home today.

Desk Sergeant Thomas Purcell, of the Second Precinct, summoned the ambulance and had the child taken to the City Hospital.

DR. CRIPPEN, ENGLISH INSPECTOR WHO CAUGHT HIM, AND DIAGRAM OF CHASE

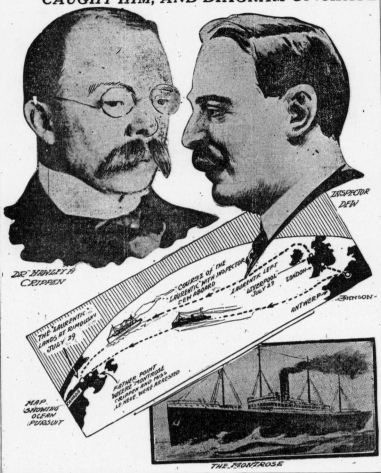

INSPECTOR DEW

DR. HAWLEY H. CRIPPEN

COURSE OF THE LAURENTIC WITH INSPECTOR DEW ABOARD

LAURENTIC LEFT LIVERPOOL JULY 23

LONDON

ANTWERP

THE LAURENTIC LANDS AT RIMOUSKI JULY 29

FATHER POINT WHERE MONTROSE CRIPPEN AND MISS LE NEVE WERE ARRESTED

MAP SHOWING OCEAN PURSUIT

THE MONTROSE

JOHNSON

2 KILLED, 16 HURT IN DESTRUCTION OF ENTIRE TRAIN

Engine and Three Cars Plunge Through Blazing Trestle. Others Burn.

AUGUSTA, Ga., Aug. 1.—Passenger train No. 2, of the Charleston and Western Carolina railroad, ran into a burning trestle about a mile and a half from Woodlawn, S. C., yesterday, resulting in the total destruction of the train, the death of Engineer Hank Taylor and Fireman Dunbar, colored, of Augusta, and slight injury to sixteen passengers.

When the train was entering a reverse curve Baggagemaster George Box directed the attention of Conductor W. B. Verdery to a large volume of smoke, which he believed to be coming from the trestle, then a mile distant.

Verdery watched the smoke until the train had rounded the curve, when he saw that the trestle was on fire. Immediately he gave the danger signal, ran from the baggage car to the first-class passenger coach and applied the emergency brake, but already the engine had run into the trestle and plunged through on into the little creek below, pulling with it the tender, baggage car and the front of one of the passenger coaches.

Whole Train in Flames.

The coach tilting from the wreckage to the road-bed above formed a flue through which the flames from the trestle debris were carried to the train proper and in less than five minutes the entire train was aflame.

Engineer Taylor and Fireman Dunbar went down with the engine and were caught under the tender. Both bodies are still in the wreckage.

Baggagemaster Box also went down with his car, but succeeded in escaping from the fire with slight injuries.

Mail Clerk Bloom, of Spartanburg, did not leave his car and was seriously, though not fatally, injured.

None of the passengers was injured beyond minor cuts and bruises. Relief trains were sent out from Augusta and all the passengers brought here.

B. & O. FLYER WRECKED, ENGINEER FATALLY HURT.

PARKERSBURG, W. Va., Aug. 1.—The New York express, a fast Baltimore and Ohio railroad train running between New York and St. Louis, was wrecked yesterday afternoon near Eatons Station, eighteen miles east of this city, when the engine struck a large rock which had rolled down on the track.

The train was running forty miles an hour at the time, and the engine was overturned and rolled over a high embankment. Engineer John Murray, of Grafton, stuck to his post and was probably fatally hurt. Fireman Adams, of Clarksburg, was very severely injured. Five passenger coaches loaded with people remained on the track and not a passenger was hurt.

FEARS FELT FOR MAN MISSING THREE DAYS.

Trouble Over Legacy Impaired William Sutcliffe's Mind.

It was stated today at the home of William Sutcliff, 82 Garden street, the man who wandered from his home on Saturday, that the police have not located him as yet.

Sutcliff is an epileptic and his mind was weakened from worry over the settlement of an estate.

A week ago he came home from a walk wet to the skin. He told his sister that he had accidentally fallen into the Passaic river and was fished out by a "German" man.

On Saturday he told his sister, Miss Eliza Sutcliff, who keeps house for himself, three brothers and two sisters, that he was certain the man downstairs, a Mr. Lee, would shoot him. He was advised to see Mr. Lee to have it "out with him," which he did, and had a satisfactory interview, to which his sister was listening, without his knowledge. When asked about the result of the talk he said he thought Mr. Lee "was off his trolley." He then went out, and has not been seen since. It is feared by his family that he had gone to the meadows, and then during one of his fits died.

When last seen he wore a dark suit of clothes, black shoes and black derby hat. He is about 5 feet 11 inches tall, has dark auburn hair and is 40 years old.

HUNDREDS IN WRECK ON D. & H., ONE WILL DIE.

SCHENECTADY, N. Y., Aug. 1.—A Delaware and Hudson passenger train containing between 300 and 400 persons was ditched at about 9:30 o'clock last night about twelve miles north of this city by wreckers. The entire train, consisting of four coaches and baggage cars, left the tracks, but with the exception of the firemen, Frederick Schermerhorn, 27 years old, of this city, who is believed to have been fatally hurt, none was dangerously injured.

Among the more seriously injured are:

George Lemp, Schenectady, cut about the head; not serious.

John Silvo, New York City, broken ribs and internal injuries.

B. R. Gaige, Schenectady, baggageman, badly bruised and cut about the hands and arms.

WRECK VICTIM BURNS IN SIGHT OF COMPANIONS.

YOUNGSTOWN, O., Aug. 1.—Escaping uninjured from the wreck of his freight train, which collided with another freight at Lowellville yesterday, Conductor Charles A. Williams was unable to free himself from the wreckage and was burned to death before the eyes of a number of men who were unable to help him.

With the exception of Williams the crews of both trains escaped without injury. The dead man was 30 years old and lived at McKees Rocks, Pa.

TORONTO WINS MORNING GAME.

[Special to the Newark Star.]

TORONTO, Aug. 1.—Toronto defeated Baltimore here this morning, 10 to 3.

"PLEASE FIND MY WIFE AND BABIES OR LET ME DIE"

Appeal of Distracted Husband Whose Alleged Insane Wife Disappeared With Children.

After she had refused to take medicine prescribed by a physician to ward off an impending case of dementia, to which she has been subject, Mrs. Mary Polan, with her three young children, the baby in a go-cart, left her home and husband at 264 Prince street yesterday afternoon at 1 o'clock, and has not been seen since. Her husband Samuel Polan, is able neither to sleep nor eat, and begge dthe police of the Fourth Precinct today to find his wife, or else let him die.

For several days Mrs. Polan acted queerly. Polan remembered that once before, shortly after Mrs. Polan had undergone an operation, she acted the same way. She refused to eat at mealtimes; she would caress her children with an overdue show of affection, and when her husband called in a doctor she flew into a rage. She cried at intervals after the doctor had left, leaving a vial of medicine for her to take. Her husband tried to persuade her to take the medicine, but she steadfastly refused to touch it.

After the noonday meal yesterday Mrs. Polan suggested that she take the children for a walk. Polan agreed. thinking that the fresh air would do his wife good. Four o'clock came and the wife and children were not yet home; 5 o'clock, and Polan began to worry. After supper time, when he had walked the streets for several hours without success, the distracted man ran to the Fourth precinct station and told the desk sergeant of his troubles. The sergeant tried to reassure him, but as the night dragged on and his wife and children did not return, Polan's anxiety increased to a dread of what might have happened to his wife and babies.

KING ALFONSO TO VISIT ENGLAND AND FRANCE.

SAN SEBASTIAN, Spain, Aug. 1.—King Alfonso and Queen Victoria left today to pay a visit to the royal family in England. They will stop on the way at Rambouillet, France, to visit President Fallieres.

JESTED ABOUT DEATH; ENGIN EKILLED HIM.

CLEVELAND, O., Aug. 1.—With a jest at death on his lips, Michael Cosmo, 20 years old, stepped in front of a yard engine here yesterday afternoon and was instantly killed.

Cosmo had just been telling three girl friends that he had made application to join the army and asked them if they would weep for him when he was in a soldier's grave. Waving them good-by, he turned to cross the freight yard when he was struck by the engine and instantly killed.

CRIPPEN AND GIRL IN CELLS

Inspector Dew Lands His Prisoners at Quebec.

BOTH NEAR COLLAPSE AFTER ARREST SUNDAY

Neither Expected to Make Objections to Early Return to England.

QUEBEC, Que., Aug. 1.—Canadian justice moved swiftly today in the case of Dr. Hawley H. Crippen and Ethel Clare Le Neve, who, charged with "guilty knowledge of an abominable crime," fled from the other side of the Atlantic only to be caught in a box-trap before they could put foot on the soil of the dominion.

The steamer Montrose upon which the fugitives were arrested while the vessel was still 160 miles from this port yesterday, arrived at her pier here at 1:35 o'clock this morning.

The prisoners were hastened through an enormous crowd of curious ones to the provincial jail, where they were placed in separate cells for the night. Here they got a few hours' sleep, the best rest which they have had since they fled from London on July 9, shortly before detectives found in the cellar in the Crippen home the bits of human flesh which, the authorities have tried to establish, once went to make up the body of Belle Elmore, Crippen's lawful wife. Today both prisoners appeared refreshed.

Justice Moves Swiftly.

As soon as the arrests were made the local court authorities were notified and Judge Panet Angers arranged to hold court at 10:30 o'clock this morning. The accused were held under the law pertaining to fugitives who are suspected of connection with a crime, and the court proceedings were arranged to be conducted expeditiously.

It is hoped that Crippen and his typist can be sent back to London on the steamer Royal George, which will sail on Thursday. However, under the fugitive offending act the prisoners have a right to remain here fifteen days before their departure. This period affords them opportunity to seek release through habeas corpus proceedings. Crippen also may exercise his right as an American citizen to appeal to the American consul here and so make sure that his rights are not infringed. It is doubtful if Crippen avails himself of either chance for delay.

Crowd Gathers at Dock.

It was known that the steamer with the prisoners and their captors aboard would be due here soon after midnight, and early in the evening crowds began to gather at the pier. As the night advanced the crowd grew greater until the police found that they had a big job on their hands to restrain the curious ones and so permit the landing of Inspector Dew and his prisoners.

When the steamer was sighted down the harbor the excitement was intense and the police, who up to that time had used moral suasion, assumed a more determined attitude, finally pushing back the throng from the gangway in no more gentle manner than the circumstances necessitated.

When the boat swung into her pier Crippen was stil in cabin No. 8, where he was confined yesterday. With him was Detective Denis. Miss Le Neve was under the close watch of Chief McCarthy in cabin No. 5. Throughout the night Inspector Dew had passed from one cabin to the other, not for one moment relaxing the watch on the prisoners, who had slipped through his fingers once before.

Prisoners Are Haggard.

A half hour before the landing the prisoners were told that they were nearing Quebec. Both, who had been under the greatest strain for hours, showed increased restlessness. Crippen, who had been attempting to read a novel, tossed the book aside and dropped his head in his hands in a disparing attitude.

At the same time Miss Le Neve, in her quarters in another part of the vessel, fell on her knees and gazed out of the porthole into the blackness of the night. Suddenly she turned back into her room and was seized with a fit of nervous coughing.

The bells that indicated that the steamer was being reduced to half speed, stopped and backed, sounded through the ship, and the prisoners looked anxiously toward their captors, as though realizing that they had reached the shore that had refused them a refuge, but wondering what the next hour would bring them.

Preparations to Disembark.

At 1:30 o'clock Captain Kendall came down from the bridge and notified Inspector Dew that in a few minutes his passengers would be taken ashore. Dew notified McCarthy and Denis. Presently Denis emerged from the cabin door with Crippen, whom he held firmly by the arm as they passed not up the main companionway to the afterdeck, where the gangplank way was fixed, but by a side passage, passing both main cabins in a roundabout direction in a less conspicuous path.

Crippen, his face white as death, walked with a shambling gait. As they passed the stateroom which the doctor had formerly occupied with Miss Le Neve the door of that room swung

New-York Tribune.

Vol. LXXI....No. 23,557. To-day, fair. To-morrow, probably fair; west winds. NEW-YORK, TUESDAY, MAY 16, 1911.—SIXTEEN PAGES. PRICE ONE CENT In City of New York, Jersey City and Hoboken. ELSEWHERE TWO CENTS.

STANDARD OIL COMPANY ORDERED DISSOLVED; REASONABLE RESTRAINT OF TRADE NOT UNLAWFUL

United States Supreme Court Gives Standard Oil Six Months in Which to Reorganize.

OPINION BY CHIEF JUSTICE

The Great Corporation Held To Be a Monopoly Within the Letter and the Spirit of the Sherman Anti-Trust Law.

APPLIES "RULE OF REASON"

No Precise Definition of the Statute Given—Justice Harlan Would Be More Drastic—American Tobacco Case Not Decided.

BIG AUDIENCE IN COURT

Well Known Men See End of Momentous Legal Battle—New "Rule of Reasonableness" Welcomed by Business Men.

VITAL POINTS IN STANDARD OIL DECISION

The United States Supreme Court holds:

That the Standard Oil Company is a monopoly in restraint of trade.

That the corporation must be dissolved within six months.

Corporations whose contracts are "not unreasonably restrictive of competition" are not affected.

Other great corporations whose acts may be called into question will be dealt with according to the merits of their particular cases.

The court was unanimous as to the main features of the decision, Justice Harlan dissenting only as to a limitation of the application of the Sherman anti-trust law.

[From The Tribune Bureau.]

Washington, May 15.—The Supreme Court of the United States, by a practically unanimous decision, to-day declared the Standard Oil Company to be a combination in restraint of trade within the meaning of the anti-trust law, and ordered its dissolution within six months. This applies to the Standard Oil Company of New Jersey and thirty-three other corporations, having an aggregate capital of $110,000,000. The court declares that the anti-trust law is clearly intended to prevent monopolies; that the history of this company, the course of its projectors and the results of their acts clearly establish a purpose to monopolize the trade in petroleum, which monopoly is equally clearly a violation of the intent of the statute.

The opinion, which was handed down by Chief Justice White and is regarded as remarkable for the succinctness and the clarity of its reasoning, makes obvious the view of the court that the purpose of the law is to prevent monopoly and indicates that wherever it may be shown that such monopoly exists the court will hold that the statute has been violated.

The Chief Justice rejects the contention of the government that the statute prohibits every case within its letter and language, and holds that in each case presented the judgment of the court must be called into play to determine, first, whether the particular act comes within the prohibition of the statute, and secondly, whether such act causes it to be a restraint within the intendment of the act. Chief Justice White expressly states that the statute is not intended to limit its own scope by precise definition, but that, by defining ulterior boundaries, it does purpose to fix a standard which cannot be transgressed with impunity, thus leaving it to the court to enforce the public policy embodied in the statute and to exercise its judgment in the case of each particular act brought before it.

Justice Harlan Takes More Drastic View.

Justice Harlan subscribed to the decision of the court in so far as it applied to the Standard Oil Company, thus making the decision in this case unanimous, but he dissented from the conclusion of the majority that a restraint of trade must be shown to be "undue" in order to come within the purview of the statute, and objected to the extent by which the remainder of the court was guided by the common law in this respect. It was asserted by Justice Harlan that for fifteen years the trusts had sought to have this limitation imposed by legislative amendment, and that they now sought such limitation by judicial determination, whereas, in his opinion, it was the intent of the statute to prohibit all restraint of trade, whether "undue" or otherwise.

Gives No Precise Definition of the Law.

The expectation of the Attorney General and of other high legal authorities in the government that the court would refrain from imposing any limitation on its further determination of the law by that "precise definition" which would clearly mark the limits to which restraint might be carried without subjecting its authors to penalty was fully met. The decision, in the opinion of able lawyers, makes it clear that whenever the Supreme Court shall determine, in the light of the facts presented, that there has been a successful attempt to create a monopoly, it will adjudge the result to be a violation of the anti-trust law, but that beyond that the opinion does not go, and that the efforts of those who would achieve that end without rendering themselves liable will be attended with as great difficulty in the future as in the past. On the other hand, it is contended that the opinion will serve to relieve from anxiety those whose business operations may to some extent assume the appearance of an effort to create a monopoly, but who may be able to show an entire absence of such intent, and that the restraint achieved is only reasonable.

Standard Oil Purposed to Create a Monopoly.

In the case of the Standard Oil Company, the court declares the purpose to create a monopoly to have been so obvious that no unprejudiced person can review its history "without being irresistibly driven to the conclusion that the very genius for commercial development and organization, which it would seem was manifested from the beginning, begot an intent and purpose to exclude others which was frequently manifested by acts and dealings wholly inconsistent with the theory that they were made with the single conception of advancing the development of business power by usual methods, but which, on the contrary, necessarily involved the intent to drive others from the field and to exclude them from their right to trade and thus accomplish the mastery which was the end in view."

Meeting the contention that dissolution of the trust must work inordinate injury to property, the court points out that the stockholders are not restrained from making "normal and lawful contracts," but are restrained from seeking by any device whatever, directly or indirectly, to recreate "the illegal combination which the decree dissolved."

Washington, May 15.—Announcing the opinion of the United States Supreme Court in the Standard Oil case, Chief Justice White reviewed the preliminary proceedings in the case in the Circuit Court of the United States for the Eastern District of Missouri. He restated the essential points in the bill of the government asking for the dissolution of the Standard Oil Company and the answer questioning the jurisdiction of the court and denying the claims of the government. He dismissed the objection to the jurisdiction in a few words by holding that it was not well founded.

He then came to the arguments as to the law and the facts in the case, saying that out of the "jungle" of law and facts both sides were agreed on only one thing, and that was that the determination of the controversy rested on the proper construction and application of the first and second sections of the anti-trust act. The first section reads as follows:

> Every contract, combination, in the form of trust or otherwise, or conspiracy, in restraint of trade or commerce among the sceveral states, or with foreign nations, is hereby declared to be illegal.

The second section reads:

> Every person [which subsequently was explained in the statute to include corporations] who shall monopolize or attempt to monopolize or combine or conspire with any other person or persons to monopolize

THE JUSTICES OF THE UNITED STATES SUPREME COURT.

Top row (left to right), Associate Justices Van Devanter, Lurton, Hughes and Lamar; seated, Associate Justices Holmes and Harlan; Chief Justice White, who delivered the opinion in the Standard Oil case; Associate Justices McKenna and Day.

(Photograph copyright, 1911, by Clinedinst, Washington.)

GET WOMAN WITH DIAMONDS IN TEETH

Secret Service Sleuths Say She Is Leader of Gang of Counterfeiters.

FURNISHED THE FUNDS

Five Had Planned to Go to Alaska and Make $5 Notes, Detectives Allege—To Be Arraigned To-day.

Richard H. Taylor, who took charge of the Secret Service men for the United States when Mayor Gaynor "borrowed" William J. Flynn, summoned some of his most trusted sleuths about six weeks ago and told them to keep their eyes on a band of five, four men and a woman, who he had reason to suppose thought the scarcity of $5 bills ought to be relieved.

"Her name's Cleo," he told them, "and her husband is James Glevard," putting the woman first, with due gallantry. "She has gold plates on her incisors, and there's a real diamond in each plate."

That item digested, and armed with descriptions of the husband of the jewelled teeth, and the other men, the Secret Service men went to work in their quiet way. They couldn't lose Cleo. When she smiled they knew about it, and a block or so of intervening space made no difference.

According to the detectives, Michael Kasbsiek, an engraver, was friendly with a pair of Montenegrins, Marko Pazowich and Sam Pekovich, and the three decided to become wholesale manufacturers of 10-kronen notes in competition with the Austrian government, which maintains a monopoly in that industry, as well as in the sale of cigarettes. But after a while they decided that the Indian $5-bills made by Uncle Sam would be easier to duplicate, the detectives said.

"The nerve of 'em," commented one operative.

But even the manufacture of money requires capital, and the three had none. Entered, somewhat reluctantly, the Glenards, Mrs. Cleo, of the diamond studded teeth, being a capitalist. She pawned some of the jewels not set in portions of herself, according to the Secret Service men, and supplied the cash. Kasbsiek, they say, produced a good stone and got $500—in money made by the Bureau of Engraving and Printing, not by himself. No bills have been made or passed as yet.

That work was done here, and then the party moved to Hoboken, for a reason the Secret Service men didn't attempt to explain. Thence they decided to go to Alaska to make and dispose of their $5-bills, that being the result of a short stay in Hoboken. They were off to Chicago yesterday, according to the detectives, when the five were arrested.

John A. Shields, United States Commissioner, will look into Cleo's radiant mouth to-day, when she and the others will be arraigned.

DANGER OF FOREST FIRES

Dix, in Proclamation, Asks Co-operation of People.

Albany, May 15.—Fearing the danger to the state's forests because of the long dry period, Governor Dix to-night issued a proclamation to the people of the state urging their co-operation in preventing forest fires. "The Governor points out that dead wood and soil are like tinder at times and in a single moment a camp fire may get beyond control and inflict irreparable injury and loss.

He calls upon parents of children who take their outings in the public parks and forest preserves "to inculcate them with a sense of responsibility, and to point out the dangers of a destructive conflagration from a match carelessly used, or a neglected camp fire," and urges upon all visitors to the Adirondacks and Catskills to "find an added pleasure in doing their utmost to guard the parks and forests from destruction."

HAMMOND 'ASKS' COURT'S AID

Seeks Postponement of Sully Hearing to Allow Him to Act as Ambassador.

Washington, May 15.—John Hays Hammond to-day petitioned the Supreme Court of the District of Columbia to postpone the further hearing of the $1,600,000 damage suit of Daniel J. Sully against him until next November.

Mr. Hammond informed the court that his mission as Special Ambassador of the United States to the coronation of King George of England would necessitate his departure by May 27. The petition will be argued Wednesday. This is the first time Mr. Hammond's special mission has been called to the attention of the court.

FREES BOY ON ASSAULT CHARGE.

The case of Samuel Hakeman, the elderly real estate operator, of No. 69 West street, who caused the arrest of Edward L. West, on a charge of felonious assault and robbery, was up before Magistrate Breen in the West Side Court, yesterday afternoon. Four witnesses testified that four young men had attacked Hakeman, but that West was not one of them. Magistrate Breen discharged the boy for lack of evidence.

SECOND HOFFSTOT TRIAL OPENS.

Pittsburg, May 15.—Frank N. Hoffstot, the millionaire banker and car manufacturer, was placed on trial here to-day, on a charge of bribery, growing out of the councilmanic graft investigation. He was tried on a charge of conspiracy last week and the jury disagreed.

OSBORNE MAY RESIGN TO-DAY.

Auburn, N. Y., May 15.—It is expected that Thomas M. Osborne, Forest, Fish and Game Commissioner, to-morrow will personally tender his resignation to Governor Dix. Mr. Osborne, who has been ill here for three weeks, left here for Albany this afternoon. He expects to sail for Europe next week.

JAPAN AND SPAIN MAKE PACT.

Madrid, May 15.—A treaty between Japan and Spain was signed here to-day by Garcia Prieto, Spanish Minister of Foreign Affairs, and M. Arakawa, the Japanese Minister.

HUNDRED HURT IN RIOT

Striking Michigan Furniture Workers Clash with Police.

Grand Rapids, Mich., May 15.—Nearly one hundred persons were injured, several probably fatally, to-night, when a mob of nearly two thousand striking furniture workers and sympathizers clashed with the police. The riot is still in progress. Many shots have been fired.

BELLEVUE ALIENIST HURT

Dr. Gregory Falls Downstairs and Two Ribs Are Broken.

Dr. Menas S. Gregory, the alienist in charge of the psychopathic ward at Bellevue Hospital, fell downstairs in the altoholic pavilion last night. His spine was injured, two ribs were broken and his body was bruised. He is confined to his room under the care of Drs. Carlyle and Smith, visiting surgeons.

John Norton and Patrick Callahan, ambulance drivers, were watching Dr. Gregory's Boston bull terrier, a $600 prize dog, chase a cat in the Bellevue yard when the dog cornered the cat under the alcoholic pavilion. They said they saw Dr. Gregory come out of the pavilion to get after the dog and cat and separate them.

He did not appear for a few minutes and they went over and found him stretched out unconscious at the foot of the stairs.

PILOT BOAT FORCED TO SEA

Five Bermudians Off Scotland Lightship Six Days from Home.

After having been lost at sea for six days, her crew of five men supposedly without food, Bermudian Pilot Boat 2 was picked up late yesterday, five miles southwest of Scotland Light by New York Pilot Boat 5. A wireless dispatch received last night from Pilot Boat 5 said all the Bermudians were well.

Details are lacking as to the cause of the little sloop rigged vessel being forced practically seven hundred miles from her island home. The first news that she was missing was contained in a wireless dispatch from the steamer Bermudian on Sunday night. Vessels were asked to keep a sharp lookout for her.

R. I. NATIONAL COMMITTEE

Republicans Appoint Ex-Congressman Sheffield Successor to Gen. Brayton.

Providence, May 15.—A successor to the late General Charles A. Brayton, as Republican National Committeeman from Rhode Inland, was appointed to-day. Ex-Congressman William P. Sheffield, of Newport, was chosen for the place by the State Central Committee.

Mr. Sheffield was elected to Congress in 1908 and served until last year, when he was was defeated by Representative O'Shaughnessay, a Dewocrat.

BLACK HAND MAN SENTENCED

Threatened to Kill Ex-Governor Draper and Blow Up Plant.

Worcester, Mass., May 15.—For sending Black Hand letters to ex-Governor Eben S. Draper and to officials of the Draper Company, of Hopedale, Frank H. Costello, of Milford, was sentenced in the Criminal Court to-day to from five to seven years in state prison. Costello had previously pleaded guilty to sending letters to the former Governor threatening to kill him and to blow up the plant unless the wages of the employes were raised.

TURKISH RAILWAY PROJECT

Parliament Sends American Syndicate's Plan to Committee.

Constantinople, May 15.—The railway project for the construction of an extensive system in Asiatic Turkey by an Awerican syndicate under Dr. Chester, was presented to Parliament to-day. It was referred to committee without debate.

TROUBLE DUG FROM MOSQUE

Governor of Jerusalem Recalled—Was Mobbed Because of Excavation.

Constantinople, Maf 15.—The Governor of Jerusalem has been recalled on account of the trouble which has arisen over the operations of an English expedition acused of having excavated beneath the Mosque of Omar.

This expedition was under the leadership of Captain Montagu Parker, a brother of the Earl of Morley. After it had become known that the mosue qhad been profaned and relics removed the Governor was mobbed by natives.

DEATH SHOWS HIDDEN STORE

Man Had $3,400 in Bank and Copper Deposit of $29.50 a Ton.

Benjamin Curley, seventy-five years old, who had lived in a furnished room at No. 675 Second avenue since November, in the home of Mrs. David Nelson, was found dead there last night. Though believed to be poor, he had a bank book showing deposits of $3,400 in the Fourth National Bank and a letter from E. E. Burlingame, an assayer of Denver, in which that man said that copper sent him by Curley had assayed at $29.50 to the ton. Receipts for dues in the International Association of Machinists were also found.

Curley was ill not long ago and went to Bellevue Hospital for a month, returning again to his room. There was nothing serious the matter. He was found dead last night, and Dr. Biram, of Bellevue Hospital, did not know the cause. The Coroner will try to find out. No one knows of any relatives of the man.

HUGGED, ASKS DIVORCE

Wife Says Loving Husband Broke Two of Her Ribs.

[By Telegraph to The Tribune.]

Okaton, S. D., May 15.—Charging cruelty in that she had to submit to hugs until her health became permanently impaired, Mrs. Winifred Ingalls has brought suit for divorce against Nicholas Ingalls. In her petition Mrs. Ingalls says:

"Nicholas, before he went to work and whenever he returned, would throw his arms about my waist, pressing me until the breath almost left my body. At one time he forced me to submit to a bear hug that resulted in the fracturing of two ribs, while at another time the hugging was so severe that circulation was stopped and my nose bled, the blood spurting over his clothing."

Not only does Mrs. Ingalls object to the bear hugs and the crushing of bones, but she also objects to being smothered with kisses. Ingalls admits the hugging and kissing, but adds that the treatment was most tender and affectionate, and that the breaking of ribs and gushing of blood from her nostrils was due to tight lacing.

DOCTOR'S AUTO KILLS BOY

Chauffeur Rushes Victim to the Hospital—Later Is Arrested.

William Godilstein, two and one-half years old, of No. 1053 Prospect avenue, The Bronx, died in Lebanon Hospital last night shortly after being run over by an automobile, operated by James Calville, chauffeur for Dr. Alexander Goldman, of No. 1709 Fulton avenue.

The accident occurred in front of the child's home. Without waiting for the arrival of the boy's parents the chauffeur hurried him to the hospital, where he was attended by Dr. Langdon.

Calville was arrested later in the evening by Patrolman Smallman of the Morrisania police station, on the technical charge of operating an automobile without a license.

SIBERIAN OIL WELL ON FIRE.

Uralsk, Asiatic Russia, My 15.—An oil gusher of 60,000 barrels capacity daily in the region of the Kirghiz Steppe caught fire and to-day is blazing furiously.

WALL STREET CROWDS CHEER THE DECISION

Without Regard to Effect on the Standard Oil Co., Brokers Rejoice When Suspense Ends.

NEWS TICKERS IN DEMAND

Luncheons Wait Court's Recess, Market Is Neglected, then Men Linger Until Night to Learn Full Details.

Wall Street spent the day yesterday, as has been the custom on "decision Mondays" for several months past, hanging over the tickers and praying that the long awaited decisions in the trust cases would be handed down at last, and although it was not until 4:05 o'clock that the first intimation was received that the Standard Oil decision would be rendered, the crowds around the tickers in the various brokerage offices at that hour were as large as at any time during the day.

The announcement brought a cheer that echoed in the tower of the Singer Building, so great was the delight of the waiting thousands of bankers, brokers and speculators that the uncertainty that had been hanging over the market like a black cloud was about to be swept away.

Nobody seemed to care particularly what the decision would be. What was wanted was an ending of the uncertainty that for so many weary weeks had oppressed business in the Street, and whether or not it was favorable or unfavorable to the Standard Oil Company appeared to make little difference to the crowds around the tickers.

From the moment that the court assembled at noon until a recess was taken at 2 o'clock space around the tickers was at a premium. Nobody thought of luncheon, except perhaps the clerks, who had orders not to leave their offices until it was known whether or not the trust cases would be handed down, and as the various justices read their opinions the interest grew.

Wall Street Remembers Hunger.

When it was announced at 2 o'clock, however, that the court had taken a recess for half an hour for luncheon, Wall Street suddenly remembered that it was hungry, and there was a rush for the nearest restaurants, where between mouthfuls the prospects of the decisions being handed down by one or more of the remaining justices was the principal subject of conversation.

Nobody who had any interest in the trust decisions tarried over his luncheon, and long before the court reassembled crowds again surrounded the tickers. The market itself was neglected. No one seemed to care whether prices went up or down, and trading was at such a low ebb that the stock tickers were silent for minutes at a time.

All interest was centred in the news tickers. The stock market was temporarily forgotten, and when the announcement "market closed" came over the tickers nobody paid any attention. Justice Harlan and Chief Justice White were still to be heard from, and everybody was hoping against hope that they would hand down the anxiously awaited decisions.

Groans at Prospect of Delay.

When it was announced that Justice Harlan was handing down opinions in several minor cases a groan went up, which deepened when the ticker stated that Chief Justice White would give a hearing on several motions before him.

This was taken to mean that he would

Continued on third page.

TOBACCO DECISION NEXT

It May Be Governed by New Rule of Reasonableness.

Washington, May 15.—Many persons expected that the decision of the United States Supreme Court in the dissolution suit against the American Tobacco Company would be handed down immediately after that in the Standard Oil case to-day. This was not done, however, but the opinion is expected on May 29, the last decision day of the court until next October.

The opinion of the court to-day was construed to mean that the tobacco case, like every other case in which restraints of trade are alleged, must be subjected to the new test of reasonableness of the restraint, as laid down in the Standard Oil decision.

Ever since the decree in the Standard Oil case in the lower court was announced, hope has been expressed by the "business world" that the law would be modified so as not to interfere with what was designated as honest business. To-night that section of the opinion calling for the use of the "rule of reason" in applying the law is regarded in many quarters as an answer to the prayers of the "business world."

RENO DIVORCES OPEN

Judges Rule Against Practice of Sealing Papers.

[By Telegraph to The Tribune.]

Reno, Nev., May 15.—Judges Oren and Moran, of the 2d Judicial District, entered an order here to-day forbidding the further sealing of complaints in all civil actions. The new ruling is the answer of the court to County Clerk Fogg, who asked specifically what attitude he should adopt in reference to divorce complaints.

The local press has waged a bitter fight against the custom of concealing divorce papers within a sealed envelope, contending that the practice opened the way to fraud upon the defendants in the suits. The decision says that the records must be left open both before the case is heard and afterward.

USED LOADED GUN IN PLAY

Girl Shoots Chum While Pretending To Be an Actress.

Hackensack, N. J., May 15.—Singing and waving in her hand a small revolver, Miss Josie Ackerson, of Allendale, aimed the supposedly empty gun at the breast of her chum, Kitty Austin, and pulled the trigger. For a few minutes Miss Austin did not realize that she had been shot. Then blood began to trickle through her waist.

Miss Ackerson, who is the seventeen-year-old daughter of Charles R. Ackerson, a contractor became hysterical. The sight of the blood on her friend's waist caused her to lapse into unconsciousness, and for three hours Dr. Rodman worked over her before she was revived. Meanwhile, the wounded girl, who is a daughter of Frank Austin, a local commission merchant, was hurried to the General Hospital, in Paterson. Her condition is not considered serious.

The girls were portraying the scenes of an impromptu play when the accident happened. Twice Miss Ackerson pointed the revolver at her own breast and pulled the trigger. She did not know that her brother William had put two or three cartridges in the weapon a few days ago, and Miss Austin was shot when the trigger was pulled a third time

THE BAHAMAS AND CANADA.

Ottawa, May 15.—In the Commons to-day George E. Foster inquired of the government as to the status of the application of the Bahama Islands for annexation.

"There have been no negotiations," replied Finance Minister W. S. Fielding. "We are cognizant of the request, and it is probable the Prime Minister will discuss it with the Colonial Office while in London."

EXTRA

EIGHTEEN PAGES—ONE CENT Established 1831 TUESDAY, OCTOBER 15, 1912**** Copyright, 1912, by Post Publishing Co. EIGHTEEN PAGES—ONE CENT

ROOSEVELT, SHOT BY CRANK, MAKES SPEECH, BLEEDING FROM BULLET WOUND IN BREAST

Manuscript About Wilson in Pocket Breaks Force of Missile—Would-Be Assassin Barely Escapes Lynching at Hands of Milwaukee Crowd—Colonel Insists Upon Shaving on Way to Chicago Hosptial and Talks Politics to Surgeons—Doctors Declare Wound Is Not Serious—Shooter Is John Schrenk of New York

MRS. ROOSEVELT AT THEATRE WHEN TOLD

NEW YORK, Oct. 14.—Mrs. Theodore Roosevelt was attending a musical comedy at a Broadway theatre tonight at the time the attempt was being made upon her husband's life in Milwaukee.

The news was broken to her as she sat in a box with a party of friends at the theatre.

In fear that the announcement of the attempted assassination might be made from the stage and be an unnecessarily great shock to the colonel's wife, George W. Perkins, chairman of the executive committee of the National Progressive party, who was among the first to receive the news, had despatched a messenger to Mrs. Roosevelt.

IMMEDIATELY LEFT THEATRE

Although assurances were given in the first dispatches that the colonel had not been seriously wounded, Mrs. Roosevelt was alarmed and immediately left the theatre, driving to the headquarters of the National Progressive committee in the Hotel Manhattan.

Here she waited anxiously further details from Milwaukee. She was considerably relieved by the early bulletins reporting that the colonel had been so slightly wounded that he was able to proceed with the scheduled speech for the evening.

She was alarmed again later, however, when the wires told of the removal of the colonel to a hospital and doubt among his physicians as to the seriousness of the wound. Mrs. Roosevelt had not been able to decide, as these reports came in, whether to leave tonight for Milwaukee or not.

Mr. Perkins said that announcement of Mrs. Roosevelt's intentions would be made later. As to how Mrs. Roosevelt had received the news, Mr. Perkins only said:

"Just as such a strong woman as Mrs. Roosevelt is would receive it."

GREAT BLOW TO TAFT

President Taft and Governor Wilson were among others to be quickly advised of the attempted assassination of Colonel Roosevelt. The President was in attendance at a banquet which the Mayor of the city was giving tonight to the President, the members of his cabinet, 600 naval officers and several distinguished citizens, when the news was communicated to him. It was evident that the report fell upon the President's ears as a great blow.

He was in a conversation with Mayor Gaynor at the time and after hearing the news he sat silent for some minutes. He declined at first to make any statement, being apparently reluctant to credit the report. Later, as the news was confirmed, the President said to the newspaper men:

"I am very sorry to learn of the assault upon Colonel Roosevelt, and I am glad to learn that no harm was done."

At the time the President made this statement the bulletins from Milwaukee gave the assurance that Colonel Roosevelt had sustained practically no injury.

Insists Upon Shaving Before Taking Rest

ROOSEVELT SPECIAL TRAIN, SOUTH MILWAUKEE, Wis., Oct. 15.—Before Colonel Roosevelt would lie down he insisted on shaving himself, and did so despite the protests of the surgeons who accompanied him.

The train started on a slow run.

It was planned to get to Chicago somewhere near morning, although the run could be made in less than two hours in an emergency.

The train is expected to reach Chicago at 5 o'clock, but if the patient is sleeping he will not be disturbed until 6 o'clock.

The colonel's bullet-pierced coat and blood-soaked waistcoat were brought into the press car. The following pieced memoranda were in the coat:

"Wilson's record as Governor."

"Wilson's attitude toward trusts."

"LaFollette."

"Wilson's report on record of immigration 10 years ago as compared with the present."

ALL WILL DEPLORE ATTACK ON COLONEL

BY CHARLES S. BIRD

Progressive Candidate for Governor

"The Progressives of Massachusetts greatly deplore the attempt made on the life of our great leader. It is cause for deep and heartfelt rejoicing from all Americans, without distinction of party, that it was not more serious, and they will join with us in our expressions of sympathy to the wife and family of Colonel Roosevelt following the cruel attempt on his life."

HOPES ROOSEVELT IS NOT BADLY INJURED

BY RICHARD T. MACLAURIN

President of Massachusetts Institute of Technology

"Until I learn more about the attempt to assassinate Colonel Roosevelt I will not comment on the affair. It seems almost incredible and I hope Mr. Roosevelt escaped without serious injury."

Now Isn't It a Wonder

How the Post Leads in Display Advertising all Boston Papers with Daily and Sunday Editions?

WEEK ENDING OCTOBER 13, 1912

	AGATE LINES
Post	140,570
Globe	120,452
American	113,552
Herald	85,075

Both Sunday and Daily Display Included

HIGH TIDE TODAY

A. M. 2:21 P. M. 2:38

Portland 12m., Gloucester 30m., Newport 3h. 44m. earlier.

SUN Rises 5:57 Sets 5:03 MOON 5 days old Sets 8:06 p. m.

289th day of year; 23d day of autumn. Day 11h. 6m. long; day's decrease 4h. 11m. Venus sets 6:11 p. m., Jupiter sets 7:32 p. m., Saturn rises 6:58 p. m.

Light auto lamps tonight at 5:33.

TODAY'S ANNIVERSARIES, ETC.

General Gage arrived in Boston from England and inaugurated military rule, 1768.

United States frigate President captured British packet Swallow, 1812.

Party of 60 left Boston on a journey which ended in founding of Hartford, Windsor and Weathersfield, Conn., 1634.

FAIR

Forecast for Boston and vicinity—Fair Tuesday and Wednesday, not much change in temperature; moderate westerly winds.

WASHINGTON, Oct. 14.—Forecast for New England: Fair Tuesday and Wednesday; moderate west winds.

YESTERDAY'S TEMPERATURE

Reported by Thompson's Spa.

	'11	'12		'11	'12
3 a. m.	46	54	3 p. m.	62	64
6 a. m.	46	54	6 p. m.	59	59
9 a. m.	49	56	9 p. m.	54	54
12 m.	62	60	12 mid.	52	51

Average temperature yesterday, 56 14-24.
Average one year ago yesterday, 53 12-24.

COLONEL THEODORE ROOSEVELT, FROM HIS LATEST STUDIO PHOTOGRAPH, TAKEN SINCE HIS NOMINATION BY THE PROGRESSIVE CONVENTION IN CHICAGO. (Photo Copyright by Moffet, Chicago.)

MILWAUKEE, Wis., Oct. 14.—Colonel Theodore Roosevelt was shot and slightly wounded tonight as he was leaving the Gilpatrick Hotel for the Auditorium to make a speech. The wound was superficial and the Colonel went on to the hall and began his speech after he had seen his assailant arrested and taken to the police station.

Henry F. Cochems seized the man, who refused to give his name, and held him until policemen came up. A mob surged around the prisoner, who apparently is mentally upset on the subject of Colonel Roosevelt's running for another term as President. The man admitted firing the shot, declaring that "any man looking for a third term ought to be shot."

SPIRIT OF McKINLEY IN DREAM

In notes found in the man's pockets at the police station were statements that the man had been visited in a dream by the spirit of William McKinley, who had said, indicating Colonel Roosevelt, "This is my murderer; avenge my death."

Also in his pocket was a copy of the Colonel's itinerary, written on a sheet of note paper taken from the Bismarck Hotel and cafe, Nashville, Tenn.

The would-be assassin is 5 ft. 5 in. in height, weighs 170 lbs., light complexion, bald and fairly well dressed.

HAD PROCLAMATION

A written proclamation found in the clothing of the man reads:

"Sept. 15, 1912.

"Sept. 15, 1901, 1:30 a. m. In a dream I saw President McKinley set up in a monk's attire, in whom I recognized Theodore Roosevelt. The President said, 'This is my murderer, avenge my death.'

"Sept. 12, 1912, 1:30 a. m. While writing a poem someone tapped me on the shoulder and said, 'Let not a murderer take the presidential chair. Avenge my death.'

"I could plainly see Mr. McKinley's features.

"Before the Almighty God I swear this above writing is nothing but the truth."

Another note found in the man's pocket read:

"So long as Japan could rise to the greatest power of

Continued on Page 3—3d Column

Ludendorff Story on Page 9 Today

The Boston Post

EXTRA

EIGHTEEN PAGES—TWO CENTS Established 1831 THURSDAY SEPTEMBER 11 1919 Copyrighted, 1919, by Post Publishing Co. EIGHTEEN PAGES—TWO CENTS

TROOPS PATROL CITY AS RIOTING FLAMES UP ANEW; LITTLE LOOTING

State Guard, Consisting of Infantry Regiments, Cavalry Troops and Machine Gun Battalion, Nearly 7000 in All, Take Charge of Situation in Response to Mayor's Proclamation—Man Killed in Howard Street During Riot and Woman Shot on Washington Street—Guards Fire Into Rioting Crowds in South Boston—Volunteer Police on Duty

APPEAL TO CITIZENS BY MAYOR PETERS

In the performance of the duty which the law places on me to preserve peace in the situation created by the existing police strike, I need the co-operation of every good citizen. I urge upon every inhabitant of Boston, men and women, to do what they can to help; to be patient under such small inconveniences as cannot be avoided; to keep calm and in good temper; to avoid unnecessary crowding and loitering on the streets, or any other action which may create confusion or excitement and thereby add to the difficulties of those charged with the preservation of the peace.

I and the others charged with the duty of keeping order have ample forces at our disposal, and we are ready to meet anything which we can now foresee. But for full success in our task we need to have the entire community behind us.

The success of a community in dealing with such a crisis as now confronts Boston depends on the character of its citizens.

If the men and women of Boston will be true to themselves the situation will be met in a way worthy of the great tradition of our city and of our Commonwealth, which makes our government a government of laws and not of men.

If you see a crowd and join it unnecessarily, you are hindering, not helping.

ANDREW J. PETERS, Mayor.

INTENT UPON ONE DUTY NOW

Mayor Says Restoration of Order to Come First

ADJUSTMENT OF STRIKE ISSUES COMES LATER

Puts Responsibility for Riots Up to Curtis

"The restoration of law and order will be my first duty," said Mayor Peters last night. "After that is done,

Continued on Page 6—Seventh Col.

POLICE MAKING ARREST AFTER INTERMITTENT RIOTING IN SCOLLAY SQUARE. Sergeants reinforced with special volunteer officers are shown arresting a man who they allege was hurling stones at them. Drawn revolvers were necessary to keep the crowd at bay while they brought the man to a patrol.

Superintendent Crowley Warns Women to Keep Off Streets After Nightfall

Central Labor Union to Discuss General Strike at Meeting to Be Held Today

HIGHLIGHTS OF DAY'S AND NIGHT'S DOINGS

State guardsmen called out by Mayor Peters and additional troops ordered to report by Governor Coolidge.

First trooper of the State cavalry to be injured was Private Carl Mead, who was hit on the head with a bottle wrapped in a newspaper.

State guard cavalry successfully charged a rioting mob in Scollay square late yesterday afternoon, also ran their horses through side streets, dispersing the fleeing rioters.

Former Mayor Curley harangued hundreds of men and boys on Washington street late yesterday afternoon, attacking Mayor Peters' administration of city affairs.

Boston public libraries closed their doors at six o'clock last night because of the strike.

Howling mob of men and boys held at bay by officers with drawn revolvers in Scollay square all the afternoon.

Several volunteer officers, including Harvard men, more or less seriously injured by missiles and manhandling yesterday afternoon. One of the Harvard students hurled bodily through the window of a shoe store on Washington street near Adams square.

Millions of dollars worth of riot, theft and burglary insurance placed by Boston business firms during the day.

Unprecedented sale of all sorts of firearms to business men to be used in arming guards and for home defence.

Thousands of feet of lumber used to barricade show windows.

Announced last evening that 53 of the Metropolitan police refused duty in Boston and were suspended for disobedience.

The number of private guards about business buildings and banks increased during the day.

Several machine guns of latest model were brought to Boston last night and prepared for instant use. One located in Scollay square. Machine guns were also placed in all police stations, ready for instant use.

Mayor Peters put the responsibility for the lack of police protection up to the Governor and Police Commissioner Curtis in a statement issued last night.

Casualties up to a late hour last night included one man dead, a woman shot, a guardsman hit with a bottle and knocked from his horse and numerous volunteer policemen injured by missiles, as well as injuries from accidental shootings.

State guardsmen fire into crowd at C street and Broadway, South Boston.

Boston's second night without police protection was not as riotous as the first night, but there was great disorder in different sections of the city, particularly in the West End, or between Scollay and Bowdoin squares.

Many of them mounted, had the difficult task of keeping the mobs under partial control, and the wanton destruction of property that characterized Tuesday night was not repeated. While the West End was the scene of the principal trouble in the city proper, there was rioting in South Boston, culminating in firing upon the mob by guardsmen. The shooting took place at C street and Broadway. Several people were wounded.

The presence of State guardsmen,

KILLED IN HOWARD STREET

The killing of an unidentified man by a bullet from a West End rioter's gun, the wounding of several civilians by shots fired in frequent clashes between

Continued on Page 6—Column One

UNIONS TOLD TO GET READY

Action on a General Strike Tonight —Ask Carmen and Phone Workers First

"I cannot answer that until we get to Boston."

Queried as to general strike plans in support of the Boston Policemen's Union, Michael J. O'Donnell, president of the Boston Central Labor Union, made the above response to a Post reporter in Greenfield last night. Mr. O'Donnell is attending the sessions of the 34th annual convention of the State branch of the American Federation of Labor.

Mr. O'Donnell and P. Harry Jennings, business agent of the Central Labor Union, gave out a signal state-

Continued on Page 6—Fourth Col.

BALTIMORE WELCOMES CARDINAL MERCIER

BALTIMORE, Md., Sept. 10.—Cardinal Mercier, primate of Belgium, was welcomed to Baltimore this afternoon by a throng which filled the streets from the railroad station to the residence of Cardinal Gibbons, whose guest he will be until next Wednesday.

Yesterday's Baseball Results

AMERICAN LEAGUE

Cleveland 3, New York 0, 1st game.
Cleveland 3, New York 2, 2d game.
Philadelphia 6, Detroit 5.
Boston-St. Louis—Rain.
Chicago-Washington—Rain.

NATIONAL LEAGUE

New York 7, Chicago 1.
Cincinnati 2, Philadelphia 0.
St. Louis 11, Brooklyn 8.
Boston-Pittsburg—Rain.

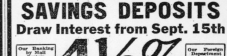

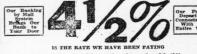

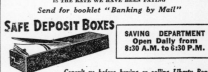

HIGH TIDE TODAY

12:53 A. M.

SUN Rises 6:15. Sets 7:03. MOON Rises at 7:36 p. m. Light all vehicles tonight at 7:33.

TODAY'S ANNIVERSARIES, ETC.

Henry Hudson entered river named after him, 1609.

Battle of Delhi, wherein British defeated French and Mahratta, 1803.

Allies sought billion dollar war loan in United States, 1915.

One year ago today—British advance near to Cambrai and St. Quentin.—Germans counter attack Franco-Americans and suffer heavy losses.—French repulse six German attacks in region of Laffaux.

SHOWERS

Forecast for Boston and vicinity—Showers Thursday and probably Friday; moderate easterly winds.

Pressure is low from the upper Mississippi Valley eastward, and showers were general over this area.

It is considerably cooler in the Middle Atlantic States.

Unsettled showery weather will continue Thursday and Friday in New England and the Middle Atlantic States.

BUYS ARMY BLANKETS

Two thousand army blankets have been purchased in Baltimore by City Manager Bingham of Waltham, to be placed on sale the latter part of next week at $4.65 each.

FELLOW CITIZENS

As citizens of Massachusetts we have volunteered our services for the safeguarding of Boston—its capital—in the serious emergency caused by the determination of its police to abandon its protection.

We have entered upon this service in no spirit of hostility to the members of the police force individually or collectively, but because, in the absence of its appointed and sworn defenders, means must be adopted for the protection of life and property.

Far more importantly, however, we are convinced that the real issue now is whether organized, properly constituted, democratic government, representing all the people, shall be sustained and perpetuated, or whether any element, no matter what, shall assume control of the destinies not merely of our city but, inevitably, of the republic itself.

We, therefore, urge all citizens who share our convictions and who believe that our democratic form of government should be upheld, to join with us by immediately tendering their services for volunteer police duty to William H. Pierce, Superintendent of Police, Retired, Room B, third floor, Boston Chamber of Commerce.

EARL C. BULLOCK,
GODFREY L. CABOT,
JEREMIAH CAMPBELL
SUMNER CLEMENT,
JOHN FEDERKIEWICZ
HENRY M. FENTON,
EDWARD C. FITZGERALD,
JAMES J. FITZGERALD,
FRANCIS E. FROTHINGHAM,
WOLF GOLDSTEIN,
PAUL L. HACKEL,
EDWIN H. HALL,
GEORGE A. HARPER,
HUNTINGTON R. HARDWICK,
PERCY D. HAUGHTON,
BARTLETT H. HAYES,
FREEMAN HINCKLEY,
JOSHUA B. HOLDEN,
CHARLES J. HUBBARD,
BRONISLAS A. JEZIERSKI,
GEORGE S. KEYES,
W. KORYTKOWSKI,
FREDERICK A. LAMB,
BRONISLAS LUTECKI,
WILLARD B. LUTHER,
BRENTON H. MacCURDY,
JOHN J. McGOVERN,
GEORGE VON L. MEYER,
J. J. MORRISEY,
GEORGE A. MORIARTY,
JOHN J. MURPHY,
K. NAWROCKI,
FRANCIS PEABODY,
GEORGE F. PONTESSE,
THOMAS H. RATIGAN,
JOHN C. ROCK,
JOHN ROMASZKIEWICZ,
BERNARD J. ROTHWELL,
JAMES S. RUSSELL,
PAUL D. RUST,
DANIEL M. SHARKEY,
DANIEL L. SMITH,
DANIEL H. SUGHRUE,
HUGH G. TIERNEY,
JOHN B. VARIAKOJIS,
ROMAN J. VASILIANSKAS,
JOSEPH L. WALSH,
SAMUEL H. WOLCOTT.

MOVIE MAGNATES PROBABLY ARE GRINDING THEIR TEETH IN CHAGRIN OVER REALIZATION THAT BILL CARLISLE IS NOT AVAILABLE FOR A "BLOOD-AND-THUNDER" PICTURE

ONE YEAR AGO
Pay of the French soldiers raised 10 cents a day.
United States troops crossed Belgium border north of Verdun.

"WYOMING'S GREATEST NEWSPAPER"

CHEYENNE STATE LEADER

THE WEATHER
WYOMING — Forecast: Fair Tuesday and Wednesday, probably becoming unsettled northwest portion Wednesday.

VOL. 56. NO. 262. CHEYENNE, WYOMING. TUESDAY, NOVEMBER, 18, 1919. PRICE FIVE CENTS

TRAIN BANDIT CARLISLE SURROUNDED

PRESIDENT SERVES NOTICE THAT HE WILL POCKET TREATY IF RESERVATIONS CUMBER RATIFICATION

Republican Foes of League of Nations Determined to Stand Pat and Indications of Deadlock Loom Large at Washington.

WASHINGTON, Nov. 17.—On the eve of a final vote on the peace treaty President Wilson gave the senate to understand today that unless it modified the reservations already adopted he would take the treaty back to the White House and lock it up in his desk.

The first effect of the warning was to stiffen the lines on both sides of the senate fight. Then compromise proposals of many kinds were thrown out by the democrats in a final effort to break into the majority program. They found the treaty's republican friends, all of whom had voted for the reservations, disposed to listen but to promise nothing and tonight the life of the treaty seemed to hang on a slender thread.

A decision one way or the other is planned for Wednesday, and under the cloture rule the leaders say it cannot be delayed beyond Thursday or Friday. Tomorrow the senate will remain in session until it has cleared away all proposed reservations, leaving nothing to do but to act upon the ratification resolution itself.

The president's determination was made known at a White House conference with Democratic Leader Hitchcock, who declared afterward President Wilson never would have an opportunity to pocket the treaty because his supporters in the senate would vote down any ratification resolution which contained the unacceptable reservations. The senate leader reiterated his belief that once such a resolution was defeated there would be a compromise that will keep the treaty alive.

Hope of such development had a setback later in the day, however, when a number of the mild reservation republicans agreed to vote with Republican Leader Lodge against any substitute resolution of ratification if the first one had been rejected. Vice-President Marshall has indicated that he will rule an alternate proposal in order and the democrats have counted on help from the mild reservationists to sustain that ruling. How many republicans will be bound by today's contrary decision remained uncertain tonight.

SLAVERS FINED $3,000 FOR VIOLATING MANN ACT

RIVERTON MAN AND THERMOPOLIS WOMAN HEAVILY MULCTED IN FEDERAL COURT FOR TRAFFIC IN IMMORAL WOMEN.

Henry C. Goldberger and Grace Gilmore, who were doubly indicted by the federal grand jury Friday on 32 counts for violation of the white slave traffic, and who were arraigned before Judge John A. Riner in the United States district court Saturday and entered a plea of not guilty, reversed their plea when brought into court yesterday for trial.

Upon pleading guilty they were fined by Judge Riner $1,500 each.

Both defendants were named in two indictments, one charging them on two counts and the other on 30 counts with furnishing money for the transportation of girls from Denver to Thermopolis and Greybull, the specific instances cited occurring at different times during the last few months.

Goldberger makes his home at Riverton, but spends much time in Thermopolis. Grace Gilmore is proprietress of the Hot Springs hotel in the restricted district in Thermopolis, and is also proprietress of a house in Greybull.

NEW COLORADO STRIKE CALLED ON GROUND OF DISCRIMINATION

DENVER, Nov. 17.—J. G. Welborn, president of the Colorado Fuel & Iron company, tonight denied that union men were being discriminated against at the mines of the corporation. He said men were being re-hired following the strike without questioning regarding union affiliation. They are required to sign a card, he admitted, pledging their support to the Rockefeller industrial plan for settlement of all differences with their employer. Mr. Welborn said he doubted if Johnson's strike order would be obeyed.

Turn to Page 4 No. 3.

FOE OF LEAGUE SENT ON HIS WAY BY MEMBERS OF AMERICAN LEGION

ORTONVILLE, Minn., Nov. 17.—Ernest Lundeen, former representative in congress from the Fifth district, who was scheduled to speak at a local theater tonight against the league of nations, was taken from the stage by members of the local post of the American Legion and escorted out of town.

A large crowd had gathered at the local opera house to hear Lundeen's speech. Just as he started to talk Sheriff John Gowan of Big Stone county and a number of members of the local Legion post rushed upon the stage, surrounded Lundeen and marched him out of the hall.

They went directly to the railroad depot where a freight was just getting under way, unlocked a refrigerator car, pushed Lundeen in and locked the door.

The next stop of the freight was scheduled to be Montevideo, Minn., about 40 miles from here.

APPLETON, Minn., Nov. 17.—Ernest Lundeen, former congressman from Minnesota, who was locked in a refrigerator car at Ortonville, about 20 miles from here, tonight, arrived here shortly before 11 p. m. Members of the train crew who heard his shouts released him and permitted him to ride in the caboose.

YOU SAID IT, C. P.

PEACE TREATY RATIFICATION
SETTLEMENT OF STRIKES
REDUCE H.C.L.
R.R. SETTLEMENT
ELIMINATION OF PROFITEERS
DEPORTATION OF UNDESIRABLE ALIENS
LABOR AND EMPLOYERS TRUCE
GOSH- WOULDN'T IT BE A GLORIOUS THANKSGIVING IF I COULD BAG TH' WHOLE FLOCK WITH ONE SHOT!
C.P.
Bushnell '19

LIQUOR INTERESTS GET TWO HARD JOLTS IN ATTACKS ON WAR-TIME AND VOLSTEAD PROHIBITION STATUTES

Federal Judge Carpenter of Chicago Holds That Both Acts are Constitutional and Peoria Judge Concurs

CHICAGO, Nov. 17.—The liquor interests were given another set-back today when Judge George Carpenter handed down a decision in the United States district court which held that the war-time prohibition act and the Volstead constitutional enforcement act were constitutional. Judge Carpenter announced that Judge Louis Fitzhenry of Peoria, Ill., has concurred in the decision.

In making his ruling Judge Carpenter denied the suit for an injunction brought by Attorney Levy Mayer, representing Hannah & Hogg, wholesale liquor dealers, to restrain United States District Attorney C. L. Cline and Julius Smietinka, collector of internal revenue, from enforcing the dry act and the enforcement law.

Under the fifth amendment to the constitution, which declares that legislation restricting personal liberties of individuals may be passed if the community as a whole is benefited, Judge Carpenter held that congress was empowered to pass the two acts involved in the case.

He held the acts constitutional because "demobiliation of industries mobilized by the war is not yet complete and the country is still in a state of war, regardless of General Pershing's statement that army demobilization was complete and despite the president's veto of the Volstead act indicating that the war was over."

Judge Fitzhenry is expected to hand down his decision at Peoria tomorrow.

JAIL-BREAKERS WHO SLEW SHERIFF'S SON TAKEN BY PURSUERS

SIOUX CITY, Ia., Nov. 17.—William Convey, Harry Smith, James O'Keef, Lee Barrington, and W. Cullon, the five desperadoes who early Friday night shot their way out of the Plymouth county jail at LeMars, Ia., mortally wounding William Maxwell and also wounding his father, Sheriff Hugh Maxwell, were captured today and tonight are under guard of six deputies in the Woodbury county jail here.

The men were taken by a posse at Maurice, Ia., and brought in automobiles to Sioux City. They imprisoned themselves in a barn five miles from LeMars after their escape, where they remained for 48 hours. Two are suffering from frozen feet and all are in an exhausted condition from hunger and cold. They crawled from their hiding place early today and started for Maurice. Although heavily armed they made no resistance when pressed by their captors.

MOVING PICTURES MAY BE WITNESSES FOR PANDOLFO IN HIS TRIAL

CHICAGO, Nov. 17—Testimony for the defense will take about two weeks in the trial of 13 officials of the Pan Motor company of St. Cloud, Minn., charged with misuse of the mails, attorneys said tonight. The prosecution has introduced its evidence.

More evidence tending to show that moving pictures of the plant taken last spring were authentic records of the actual conditions were introduced by Senator Brower, attorney for the defense, today. Judge Landis last week ruled out the pictures as testimony on the ground that they might be colored to favor the defendants.

R. H. Moth, works engineer for the Pan plant, was the man who testified that he was present at the taking of part of the pictures and that only normal and actual conditions were photographed.

The costs of the buildings of the plant were put at from $650,000 to $700,000 by the witness. He said that when the plant has been completely finished according to the building plans it would be capable of turning out from 350 to 450 cars per day.

LAST CREDIT OFFERING IN STATE LEADER'S SALESMANSHIP CLUB TO BE ANNOUNCED SOON

The Banner Period in the State Leader's Salesmanship Club, which closed at ten o'clock last Saturday night, was a success and the next published list will show great gains made by the Club members throughout the territory.

The next list of members and their credits will be tabulated and published Wednesday or Thursday. It is estimated that the period just closed will show a greater gain in Club credits than the first period did.

Only a little more than a week remains before the final end of the State Leader's Salesmanship Club, and every remaining hour should be put to a good advantage by the Club members who are working for the big prizes.

It is necessary for Club members to turn in at least one subscription each week during the last two weeks of the campaign. One subscription this week and one next week is necessary in order to qualify for one of the prizes.

The judges who officiate at the close will be governed by this rule.

The credit offer of the State Leader's Salesmanship Club will be announced on Thursday, November 20th and this will last until the close of the campaign.

Receipts for subscriptions received last Saturday will be mailed today. In case there is any error in subscription totals, Club members are requested to notify the management at once.

FUGITIVE TRAIN BANDIT REPORTED ABOUT TO BE CAPTURED OR KILLED BY POSSEMEN NEAR WAMSUTTER

Bloodhounds Trail Spectacular Criminal to Point Where He Obtained Warm Clothing, Rifle and Abundance of Ammunition.

RAWLINS, Wyo., Nov. 18.—At a late hour last night William L. Carlisle, the train bandit who escaped from the Wyoming penitentiary Saturday afternoon, was reported virtually surrounded by possemen near Wamsutter, 40 miles west of here in the desolate Red Desert. News of his capture or death resisting capture momentarily is expected.

Bloodhounds brought here from Green River Sunday were used today in trailing the fugitive from Latham, a station between this place and Wamsutter, where Carlisle secured a sheepherder's clothing, a repeating rifle and half a hundred rounds of ammunition. That the man obtained this outfit was established by a shirt he left at Latham. The garment bears Carlisle's penitentiary number—2354.

Deputy Warden Pickett is leading the pursuers of the fugitive. If Carlisle resists capture the possemen have instructions to shoot without parley. Union Pacific special agents are assisting the penitentiary employes.

An interest feature of the situation here is that public sympathy appears to be with the bandit, scores of expressions of the hope that he makes good his escape having been voiced openly since news of his get-away became public.

The most daring of scenario mixers in even the most melodramatic offerings of film fiction has presumed on pubic credulity by presenting an episode so improbable as Carlisle's escape from the state prison. Such a proceeding if incorporated in a celluloid drama would be branded as preposterously impossible. Truth is, in this case, indeed stranger than fiction.

Carlisle, who during the three and one-half years of his imprisonment as punishment for train robbery, has been a model of good behavior and his supposed regeneration recently was rewarded by commutation of his sentence of life imprisonment to an indeterminate sentence of from 25 to 50 years. He was considered throughly trustworthy and was permitted a considerable measure of freedom within the prison walls. Among his duties was that of assisting in packing for shipment shirts manufactured by the convicts.

The penitentiary shirt factory is not operated on Saturday afternoons, the convicts on that day enjoying a week-end half-holiday, but a gang of packers works in the factory Saturday afternoons. Last Saturday this crew consisted of Carlisle and the following: LeRoy Martin, sent up from Hot Springs county; Blinkey McCarthy, sent up from Platte county; Fred Hart, sent up from Natrona county; and Jim Howell, serving a life term for the murder of James Besler, turnkey of the Carbon county jail, two years ago. It was the task of these men to pack shirts into several cases and place the cases on a truck for transportation to the depot.

Assumably in accordance with a pre-arranged plan, Carlisle curled his gaunt length up in the largest of the packing boxes and the

Turn to Page 4 No. 2.

SOME UNUSUAL HAPPENINGS IN DAY'S NEWS RUN

POSSEMAN SLAIN BY FRIENDS, NOT BY RED

CENTRALIA, Wash., Nov. 17.—John Haney, Tenino posseman, who was slain in the hunt of I. W. W. murder suspects in the Honnaford Valley last Saturday afternoon, died from the fire of his own comrades through an accidental brush between the separated parties, it was learned tonight when the body of the deputy was brought here.

CURIOSITY AT FIRE, LURES 8 TO DEATH

HAYS, Kans., Nov. 17.—Curiosity prompted by a desire to be near a spectacular blaze of four oil tanks lured eight persons to their death today and resulted in serious injury to 26 persons, three of whom may die, and the less serious injury of scores of others.

A crowd of several hundred persons gathered about the fire when three of the huge tanks exploded.

BEAUTIFUL LOG HOUSE CONSUMED BY FLAMES

The residence of I. M. Conness, near Encampment, was recently burned while Mr. Conness was away in behalf of good roads.

The home, which was built over 35 years ago, was one of the most beautiful log houses in the entire region. So perfect was the workmanship in two rooms in particular that an Eastern architect who was in the house last summer made the statement that he knew of no more beautiful work in logs anywhere in the country.

Not only was the building and its household contents a total loss, but the flames also consumed many very valuable documents and souvenirs.

INDUSTRY OF BADGER UNCOVERS RICH MINE

WHEATLAND, Wyo., Nov. 17.—The industry of a badger three years ago was the beginning of a series of events which are culminating in the establishment of an asbestos mining plant on the headwaters of Blue Grass creek, forty miles southwest of here, from which asbestos soon will be moving to the railroad at Bosler.

Three years ago the attention of C. Z. Goodrich was attracted by a fibrous substance which a badger had thrown up in excavating a burrow. He had the stuff examined by a mineralogist, who pronounced it asbestos of a fair grade. Goodrich prospected in the vicinity of the badger hole and uncovered the deposit from which the asbestos came. The Omaha Asbestos company has taken a lease on the deposit and will pay $30,000 a year for the privilege of removing asbestos therefrom. The company now is installing a mining plant which will give employment to 50 men.

BRAGGED THAT HE COULD GET AWAY ANY TIME

"I can get out of this place any time I want to. I'm staying here because I want to—not because I have to.'

Smilingly badgering the state board of charities and reforms, William L. Carlisle, the now fugitive convict, cooly made the foregoing statement during a recent inspection of the state prison by the board.

The board smiled back, believing the west's most famous prisoner to be merely expressing his well-known penchant for braggadocio. In the light of Saturday's developments, however, it appears that Carlisle spoke prophetically—at least insofar as his reference to his ability to get away was concerned.

Carlisle's statement was made on the occasion of the board's first visit to the penitentiary after it had commuted his sentence of life imprisonment to a term of from 25 to 50 years.

CARLISLE'S CAREER OF OUTLAWRY

Feb. 9, 1916—Held up Union Pacific train No. 19, near Rock Springs.
Apr. 4, 1916—Held up Union Pacific Overland Limited near Cheyenne.
Apr. 21, 1916—Held up Union Pacific train No. 21 near Hanna.
Apr. 22, 1916—Captured 30 miles from scene of last robbery.
May 8, 1916—Placed on trial at Cheyenne for train robbery, a capital offense.
May 10, 1916—Convicted of train robbery, without capital punishment.
May 11, 1916—Sentenced to life imprisonment in state penitentiary at Rawlins.
Sept. 8, 1919—Sentence commuted to from 25 to 50 years.
Nov. 15, 1919—Escaped concealed in packing case.

Well, the Bolsheviki Have Already Invaded the U. S. Finish Our War First.

SANTA FE NEW MEXICAN

56 YEARS OF LEADERSHIP
VOLUME 56, NO. 289.

Full Leased Wire Service of THE ASSOCIATED PRESS

SANTA FE, NEW MEXICO, FRIDAY, JANUARY 16, 1920

Daily, by carriers or mail, 70c a month. Single copies 5c.

Constitutional Prohibition to Be Effective at Midnight

RED PERIL AT GATES OF ASIA

Great Britain Alarmed; Bolsheviki Menace Indian Frontier

KOLCHAK ARMY IN UTTER ROUT

(By Leased Wire to New Mexican.)

London, Jan. 16.—Attention of the British people is fixed on the Near East where recent Bolshevik successes have carried the red Russian armies almost up to the threshold of India, Persia, Mesopotamia, and Asiatic Turkey. Cabinet members and chiefs of the British army and navy are today in Paris, and are conferring with Premier Lloyd George on military and naval matters in connection, it is believed, with conditions in southwestern Asia.

Apprehension was aroused by the issuance of a statement yesterday pointing out the situation that has arisen through the collapse of General Denikine's army in southern Russia and Bolsheviki penetration of Trans-Caspia. Not only was it admitted the menace from a Russian bolsheviki invasion of the near east was very real but it was pointed out internal conditions in Persia, Turkey and Afghanistan were threatening.

While there is a possibility the bolsheviki may launch an overwhelming attack against the statement issued yesterday showed the greatest pre-occupation of officialdom was the debacle of Denikine's armies and the rapid advance of the soviet forces toward the Persian and Afghan frontiers.

Admiral Kolchak's army in Siberia seems to have been completely defeated if not dispersed. The reds are today far east of Krasnoyarsk and are moving nearer Irkutsk.

ODESSA OCCUPIED BY BOLSHEVIKI, IS REPORT

Paris, Jan. 16. (Havas.)—Odessa, the chief port of Russia on the Black Sea, has been occupied by the Bolsheviki, according to newspaper dispatches received there.

BRITISH BRASS COLLARS ARRIVE IN PARIS

Paris, Jan. 16. (Havis)—Winston Churchill, British secretary of war; Walter Hume Long, first lord of the admiralty; Field Marshal Sir Henry Wilson, chief of the imperial staff and Baron Beatty, commander of the grand fleet, arrived in Paris today from London.

According to the newspapers they have come to confer with Premier Lloyd George and the French government on measures to be taken to check bolsheviki propaganda among the Moslem population of Asia.

MORE HELL IN HAITI.

Washington, Jan. 16.—United States marines and Haitien gendarmeries yesterday repelled an attack on Port Au Prince, the Haitien capital, by a force of 300 bandits, more than one-half of whom were killed, wounded or captured after being pursued outside the city.

The Weather

38 was the highest and 26 the lowest temperature here yesterday which was a cloudy forenoon with light snow flurries, the afternoon was clear and it was clear during the night. The average relative humidity for the day was 86 per cent and the highest velocity of the wind was 28 miles per hour from the north. The lowest temperature during the night was 22 degrees and it was 29 at 6 o'clock this morning.

Weather Forecast for Santa Fe and vicinity: Partly cloudy, possibly with snow tonight or Saturday; comewhat warmer tonight.

For New Mexico: Fair south, snow north portion tonight or Saturday; warmer tonight.

MORALE OF U. S. NAVY ALL SHOT TO PIECES ADMIRAL SIMS SAYS; A LIVELY WITNESS

Fuss Over Decorations Has Made It Worse, Officer Declares

BAD BREAK BY DANIELS and BOARD

Navy Officers Should Be Permitted to Write Criticisms

(By Leased Wire to New Mexican.)

Washington, Jan. 16.—Rear Admiral William S. Sims, whose letter to Secretary Daniels recently, declining the distinguished service medal awarded him, precipitated the controversy over the award of naval war time honors, was the first witness on the list of those to appear before the senate subcommittee today, according to an announcement by Chairman Hale.

On taking the stand Admiral Sims said he had received a reply to his letter to Mr. Daniels criticising the methods of making the naval awards; that the reply was personal and simply said no final action on the awards had been made.

Admiral Sims said some newspapers had been mistaken in ascribing personal motives to some of those who had criticised the awards and in assuming that advantage was taken of the incident to make a personal attack on the secretary.

"Nothing could be further from the truth," he said, adding that in probably the nearly unanimous opinion of officers of the navy, "certain mistakes were made in the awards which involved not only the question of justice, but the morale of the fighting force."

"Our navy," said Admiral Sims, lacks constructive criticism from the public—and necessarily so because our naval officers are forbidden to publish anything without the permission of, and usually censorship by the department. This is, to say the least, a singular regulation to be enforced in a democratic form of government and the inevitable result is that the American public know less about naval matters than the public of any other considerable martime power because the officers of the latter are permitted, under certain regulations, when not on duty, to publish any articles in criticism or suggestion which in their judgment will be of benefit to their service or their country. A similar permission granted to American naval officers would not only be of great benefit to the public and the navy, but the navy cannot attain its maximum efficiency without it."

Referring to the case of Commander David Worth Bagley, brother-in-law of Secretary Daniels, whose recommendation for a navy cross was changed by the secretary to a distinguished service medal, Admiral Sims said Commander Bagley was one of the most capable young officers in the service. The admiral read a letter he wrote to Commander Bagley congratulating him on his conduct when his ship, the destroyer Jacob Jones, was sunk by a submarine, and then presented a letter from Mr. Daniels asking the admiral what recommendation he had made for medals for Commander Bagley and other officers of the Jacob Jones.

Admiral Sims said he replied that in cases where commanders of destroyers won actions against submarines special distinctions were recommended, but that he did not recommend any special distinctions in cases where "the action resulted in defeat."

Declaring that he had read statements in the press that he had recommended every officer on his staff for a D. S. M., the witness said he had recommended only 19 officers for that decoration out of 202 on his staff. He characterized the services of these officers as of "paramount importance" and reviewed their records to show why he recommended them for decoration.

"Whatever of recognition praise or credit I may have gotten out of this war belongs to the officers of my staff" he declared. "I only claim the credit for building the machine and picking the right men."

MEDALS A PROLIFIC SOURCE OF TROUBLE

Admiral Sims said medals are only a source of trouble and the service in general would be glad if all could be withdrawn and the government call it square."

"Unfortunate and unnecessary" controversy, he said, had arisen because "a policy defined by the secretary had not been written into instructions to the Knight medal award board as he and other officers had urged.

He had recommended, he added, three out of 80,000 for medals of honor, "and all got something else," the only honor medal awarded going to Lieutenant Isaacs, captured by a submarine after the sinking of the transport President Lincoln.

General decoration of officers who

(Continued on page 3.)

TIGER OF FRANCE LICKED

Defeat for Presidency Means Clemenceau Is to Retire

PREMIER BACKS POINCARE

(By Leased Wire to New Mexican.)

Paris, Jan. 16.—(By The Associated Press)—Premier Georges Clemenceau went down to defeat at the hands of his countrymen today in a caucus of the senate and chamber of deputies to chose a candidate for the presidency of the republic.

M. Clemenceau thereupon announced his withdrawal from the contest and asked his supporters to cast their votes for the re-election of President Poincare.

Senators and deputies, after the caucus in which Paul Deschanel, president of the chamber, led the premier by 14 votes, generally expressed the opinion that votes mean the elimination from public life of the Father of Victory, Premier Clemenceau being neither a senator nor a deputy.

M. Clemenceau's friends already are searching for another candidate, as Poincare is reported to have refused to accede to the demand of a deputation of senators and deputies that he be a candidate for reelection. He is said to have renewed emphatically the expression of his determination not to be a candidate.

Never before in the history of presidential elections in France has a plenary caucus been attended by such a large number of deputies and senators, 821 out of 924 being present. Heretofore it has been the custom to call a caucus only of the parties of the left, but today M. Deschanel stands as the chosen candidate both of the chamber and senate—all the parties. Neither Premier Clemenceau nor M. Deschanel were present at the caucus but former Premier Briand, Andre Lefevre and Edouard Herriot, the latter, the new president of the radical party, were conspicuous in marshalling the Deschanel forces, while Georges Mandel, formerly Premier Clemenceau's confidential secretary, and Edouard Ignace were canvassing on behalf of M. Clemenceau. Those presiding at the voting table were fairly swamped by the venerable senators and young deputies anxious to cast their votes before the polling closed at 4 o'clock.

A few bets were recorded with M. Clemenceau the pronounced favorite.

JAPS NOW READY TO RETURN SHANTUNG

Tokio, Thursday, Jan. 15.—(By the Associated Press.—The Japanese government, according to the newspapers today, sent instructions last evening to Yukichi Obata, the minister to China, to notify the Peking government that Japan, having succeeded to Germany's rights in Shantung on January 10 by virtue of the treaty of peace, was now ready to negotiate at any time for their return.

TWO JAPANESE ARE SLAIN IN MEXICO

Nogales, Ariz., Jan. 16.—Reports of the recent murder of two Japanese employed at a mine at San Xavier, Sonora, were confirmed today by American mining men who arrived at the border. One of the men killed was a servant in the home of W. C. Laughlin, president of the W. C. Laughlin Mining company. It is said that the Japanese were shot from ambush while they were out hunting. Francis J. Dyer, American consul at Nogales, Sonora, received a report of the facts in the case from American sources.

Pershing Eulogizes the Public School

Ogden, Utah, Jan. 16.—General Pershing and party arrived in Ogden this morning in the midst of a rain and snow storm. He gave an address to thousands of school children and others who assembled in a park, despite the weather conditions, in which he paid tribute to the public school. He stated that many of the qualities which made the American soldier the best in the world were gained from the public schools. He departed at 11:10 o'clock for Salt Lake City.

SOVIET "ENVOY" IN WASHINGTON OFFICE

S. NUORTEVA, SECRETARY of the RUSSIAN SOVIET REPUBLIC and LUDWIG C.A.K. MARTENS SELF STYLED SOVIET AMBASSADOR to the U.S ©UNDERWOOD

Photograph of "Ambassador" Martens and his secretary, taken recently in the Russian Soviet headquarters in the Lafayette Hotel, Washington, D. C., immediately after they had been served with subpoenas to appear before the subcommittee of the Senate Foreign Relations Committee.

Straw Fight on Straw Vote by Rah-Rah Boys

(By Leased Wire to New Mexican.)

Washington, Jan. 16.—Deductions to be drawn from recent voting of college students and faculties on peace treaty issues were disputed today in the senate, Senator Hitchcock of Nebraska, administration leader, in presenting the latest results characterizing them as "amazing" in the sentiment for unqualified ratification expressed. About 40 per cent of the ballots were cast for ratification without reservations, he said.

"This shows a sentiment for uncompromised ratification much stronger than I had supposed," said Mr. Hitchcock.

Senator Smoot, republican, Utah, replied that he could see no reason for jubilation by Mr. Hitchcock over the college vote, saying:

"If it had been taken one month after the treaty reached here, 90 per cent would have been for unqualified ratification. Now, after being informed the vote is reduced from 90 to 40 per cent for the treaty as it stands."

IRISH PROTEST FIRST COMPLAINT RECEIVED AT FIRST MEETING OF NATIONS' LEAGUE

Paris, Jan. 16.—Representatives of France, Great Britain, Italy, Greece, Belgium, Spain, Japan and Brazil, members of the council of the league of nations, met in the "clock room" of the French foreign office at 10 o'clock this morning for the first meeting in the history of the league.

The council organized at 10:30 o'clock by electing Leon Bourgois, chairman, and confirming the choice of Sir Eric Drummond of Great Britain as general secretary. The first official act of the council was the appointment of a commission to trace upon the spot the frontiers of the territory of the Sarre Basin.

IRISH PROTEST.

The council received the first formal protest almost before it came into being with today's initial sessions. The protest was from "The Envoys of the Elected Government of the Irish Republic" against the "unreal English simulacrum of a league of peace."

NEW TRAFFIC MAN FOR THE CENTRAL

Willard, Jan. 16.—A. P. Ogier, who for the past two years has been the local agent for the Santa Fe, has resigned his position and will take the position as traffic manager for the New Mexican Central with headquarters at Santa Fe. Mr. Ogier has had a wide experience in railroad work and is said to be a live wire along these lines.

DE KOVEN DEAD.

Chicago, Jan. 16.—Reginald De Koven, American operatic composer and conductor, died here early today of apoplexy.

URGENT APPEAL TO AMERICAN PEOPLE TO AID VICTIMS OF QUAKE IN MEXICO

Thousands in Pressing Need of Succor, Says Commerce Chamber

(By Leased Wire to New Mexican.)

Mexico City, Jan. 16.—The American Chamber of Commerce of Mexico has directed appeal to the American people, through the Associated Press, for the immediate relief of victims of the recent earthquake and volcanic eruptions in the states of Vera Cruz and Puebla.

"So great is the suffering of the survivors, says the appeal, and so urgent is their need that the American Chamber of Commerce has organized a relief committee with George T. Summerlin, charge at the American embassy in Mexico City, as honorary chairman to collect money for medicine, blankets and clothing for direct distribution to the needy.

"Entire villages have disappeared and numberless lives have been lost and the chamber now apepals to the people of the United States to join their fellow Americans here in the work of relief for the sick, hungry and home less thousands who must be helped. The need is great. This is an opportunity to help Mexico in a practical way and serve humanity."

Over $100,000 Worth of Hooch Stolen Today

(By Leased Wire to New Mexican.)

Chicago, Jan. 16.—Spectacular robberies marked the early hours of prohibition eve here. In one, six masked men bound the yardmaster and watchman of a railroad, drove six trainmen into a shanty and took between $75,000 and $100,000 worth of whisky from two box cars.

In the other, several men held a watchman for the Coca Cola company at bay with revolvers and rolled four barrels of alcohol from a warehouse to a waiting automobile truck. Their booty was valued at $5,000.

AMERICAN WOMAN TELLS OF TORTURE BY MEXICANS IN PARRAL

San Antonio, Texas, Jan. 16.—Miss Anita Whatley told the senate subcommittee investigating Mexican affairs today how revolutionists in Parral threatened her with death because she was unable to deliver to them money she did not have .

The revolutionists appeared at her home one night in Parral, demanded money from her mother and then turned their attention to her and her sister. She stood against the wall for execution. She told them there was no money. The order to cut her foot to see if that would compel obedience was carried out but her repeated denial appeared to convince the Mexicans. The property has been destroyed by the Mexicans.

U. S. FIRST NATION TO BAN BOOZE IN FUNDAMENTAL LAW

Drastic Powers Conferred Upon Government for Complete Wiping Out of Traffic in and Consumption of Any Liquor Containing Half of One Per Cent or More of Alcohol; Possession of Liquor in Home, if Purchased Prior to Tonight, Permitted; Doctors Cannot Prescribe More Than Pint a Month for One Person

Constitutional prohibition, effective at midnight tonight, and the enforcement legislation enacted by Congress, make the following provisions:

Declare unlawful the manufacture or sale of any beverage containing one-half of one per cent or more of alcohol.

Declares places where liquor is sold in violation of law to be common nuisances, abatable as such.

Search and seizure powers given prohibition enforcement officers, except for the search of private dwellings unless used for the unlawful sale of intoxicants or in part as places of business.

Liquor seized to be destroyed, vehicles and other property to be sold and proceeds paid into United States treasury.

Advertising of liquor by any method prohibited.

Permit manufacture at home for personal use of non-intoxicating ciders and fruit juices. While "non-intoxicating" is not defined specifically, the term "intoxicating" is construed by law to mean one-half of one per cent or more of alcohol.

Permit manufacture of alcoholic liquors for sacramental and medicinal uses, under restrictions.

Permit manufacture of alcohol for industrial and scientific uses.

Permit possession of liquor in home if purchased before prohibition became effective.

Physicians prohibited from prescribing alcoholic liquor for patient unless in good faith they believe it will afford relief from ailment. Not more than one pint can be prescribed in any month for one person.

Complete records of sales, including names of persons obtaining liquors, required of manufacturers and druggists.

Various penalties for violation fixed, the most severe being $2,000 fine and two years' imprisonment.

LAST SAD RITES AT MIDNIGHT TONIGHT.

Washington, Jan. 16. — Constitutional prohibition becomes effective at midnight tonight.

From 12:01 a. m., the "manufacture, sale or transportation of intoxicating liquors within, the importation thereof into, or the exportation thereof from the United States and all territory subject to the jurisdiction thereof for beverage purposes" is prohibited by the eighteenth amendment to the constitution, and the United States becomes the first nation of the world to make such a provision part of its basic law. Congress has defined intoxicating liquor as any beverage containing one-half of one per cent, or more, of alcohol.

Actually, the advent of constitutional prohibition will make little difference in the daily life of the people of this country, as they have been living under the nationwide wartime ban on alcoholic drinks since last July. There have been eager hopes entertained by the thirsty, by distillers and by speculators holding large quantities of whiskey for higher prices, that war-time prohibition would be lifted before today in accordance with the recommendation of President Wilson to congress, but congress refused to do so and the arid spell now about to begin under authority of the nation's constitution, which prohibitionists declare will continue in effect for all time inasmuch as it could be revoked only in the same manner in which it came into existence, will permit no opportunity for the replenishment of private cellars or the unloading of investment stocks. There are two cases pending in the supreme court, however, attacking constitutional prohibition, one by the state of Rhode Island. the other on behalf of the Retail Liquor Dealers' association of New Jersey.

Thousands of gallons of whiskey remain in bonded warehouses with no chance to be sold at prevailing high prices. The liquor can be taken out only for medicinal and scientific uses with the bureau of internal revenue exerting extreme precautions to see that none of it is used in violation of the law. During the last two months, many owners of alcoholic liquors, foreseeing no opportunity for sale in this country have endeavored to rush the surplus to other countries. Lack of shipping space prevented more than a fraction being exported. Cuba and the Bahamas have received most of what was sent abroad. There were 70,000,000 gallons on hand when war time prohibition went into effect. The amount exported is not known but is probably less than 20,000,000 gallons.

Attacks on constitutional prohibition began in several states, apparently are now viewed with alarm by the reform forces. After the supreme court upheld the constitutionality of war time prohibition and the measures to enforce it, Wayne B. Wheeler, general counsel of the Anti-Saloon League of America, announced that the only question left on which the wets could make a fight was whether prohibition was a proper subject for constitutional action and whether the amendment had been adopted legally. He contended there was no doubt on the subject. New Jersey officials, who searched state department records of ratification of the amendment, announced they had found no variations in language which would warrant attacking it.

REVENUE BUREAU HAS ENFORCEMENT JOB.

Enforcement of constitutional prohibition was lodged by congress with the bureau of internal revenue, which for years has been in close touch with distilling and brewing interests in the collection of excise taxes and active in running down "moonshiners." Evidence collected by the bureau will be used in prosecution by the department of justice.

Commissioner Roper has established an entirely separate division in the bureau of internal revenue for the enforcement of prohibition, headed by John F. Kramer of Mansfield, Ohio, as prohibition commissioner for the United States. He will have under him nine federal supervisors in charge of as many districts, a director in each state and a mobile force which can be shifted from place to place as conditions demand.

Mr. Roper has made plain, however, that enforcement of prohibition depends largely on local sentiment and has appealed to citizens of the United States to give their cooperation to upholding the laws of the country. Federal forces, he said, would be used to reinforce local efforts, and where any state officer failed in his duty, his constitutents would be informed.

Approximately $500,000,000 in taxes has been collected annually on alcoholic beverages, which now will have to be obtained by the government in some other way.

Prohibition sentiment, culminating in the epoch-making amendment to the constitution, has been growing steadily in this country since 1808, according to records compiled by the board of temperance of the Methodist Episcopal church. At that time, a demand for moderation in the use of ardent spirits arose, followed ten years later by an even broader movement for abstinence from ardent spirits and for moderation in the use of malt liquors. This in turn gave way, in 1840, to sentiment for abstinence from all alcoholic beverages.

Agitation for abolition of the practice of licensing the sale of liquors did not come until 1847, resulting four years later in the enactment of prohibition laws in Maine, the first state to put prohibition into effect. Kansas was second in 1880 and North Dakota third in 1889. Meanwhile the movement had grown to such proportions that a national prohibition party was formed at a convention in Chicago, September 1, 1869.

Women, always in the forefront of the activity to stop the sale of alcoholic drinks, organized for a concerted fight after the Famous Women's Crusade, 1873-74. Their association was later to become known throughout the world by the name of the Women's

(Continued on page 3)

JUMPS TO DEATH FROM CITY HALL

EVERYDAY SONGS
Find Beauty in Life's Commonplace
By Edgar Guest, in The Post Every Day

THE CHICAGO EVENING POST

THIRTY-FIRST YEAR — THURSDAY, MAY 13, 1920. — PRICE TWO CENTS

SEES COLOSIMO SLAYER FLEE CAFE

DESCRIPTION IS GIVEN BY VISITOR HERE

Still bewildered by a jumble of clues suggesting a dozen motives for the murder of "Big Jim" Colosimo, police department heads, employing every available detective, today grasped at two theories as the most plausible developed in three days and nights of mystifying search.

One idea is that Frank Razzina, escaped convict, slipped back to the old levee to take his vengeance on Colosimo, whose testimony had much to do with sending him to prison for a life sentence.

The other deals with Colosimo's domestic affairs, complicated by the recent divorce from the wife who had risen from obscurity with him and his marriage less than a month after to the youthful and pretty girl who had charmed him as a singer in his glittering resort. It involves a musician, fellow entertainer of Colosimo's bride when she was poor, whose unrequited passion might have urged him to slay his triumphant rival.

Eyewitness Tells Story.

Either of these men may have been the one described to the police today in the most startling eyewitness story presented thus far. It was related to detectives of the South Clark street station by Arthur Rockhill of New York, who is staying at the Y. M. C. A. hotel on South Wabash avenue.

Rockhill was walking on State street, near 8th street, late Tuesday afternoon shortly after the hour when Colosimo was shot down at the ornate entrance to his brilliant restaurant, when he saw a man hastening toward him. The man was so nervous he staggered, and when close to Rockhill he fell to his knees near a garbage can. Rockhill hurried to help him.

As the man arose a nickel-plated revolver fell from his pocket.

"You ought to be careful," Rockhill said. "That might go off."

"Oh," the man replied. "It went off once today. I've just bumped off that Dago ———— ————, the big stiff."

At that a man ran across the street and took charge of the man.

"You keep your mouth shut about this," the newcomer warned Rockhill.

Redouble Search for Pair.

Rockhill's story served to redouble the search for Razzina, who has been reported back in his old haunts since escaping the asylum for the criminal insane, and for Arthur Fabbri, the violinist who helped Dale Winter when she was penniless, who introduced her to Colosimo and whose actions indicated he hoped to be more than just a friend to the pretty singer.

Either Razzina or Fabbri might be described as Rockhill described the man he encountered, according to information gathered by the police. In general the descriptions given by Rockhill and by Joe Gabiel, porter at the cafe, who saw a man nervously pacing the entrance to the place just before the murder, are close likenesses.

They give the appearance of the supposed murderer as dandified in dress, of medium height and weight, 25 to 30 years old, rosy-cheeked and dark-haired. Such a man is all the police thus far have been able to evolve as the object of their intensive search.

Ex-Wife Clue Dies Out.

Altho the half dozen other misty clues have not been entirely abandoned, they were overshadowed today in the concentrated search for Razzina and Fabbri. The possibility that the first Mrs. Colosimo, Victoria Moresco, instigated the murder particularly lost credence.

Mrs. Colosimo was located in southern California, apparently making no secret of her whereabouts. She had been reported in the loop at the hour of the murder, and the first search, prompted by reports of her furtive appearance here when she was supposed to be in the west, was directed toward finding her.

Her whereabout was revealed in a telegram to Michael Potzin, a business associate of Colosimo's, in a telegram from his wife, who is in Los Angeles. Mrs. Potzin said Mrs. Victoria Colosimo was in Long Beach preparing to take a trip to Santa Catalina island.

Then she talked freely to Associated Press correspondents. She will return to Chicago at once, she said, to contest for the Colosimo estate. She said she did not believe her former husband's marriage to Miss Winter was valid in Illinois, because they were married in Indiana less than a year after the divorce.

Denies "Third Person" Story.

Mrs. Colosimo, who has been visiting relatives in California, stoutly denied that her rumored relation with a third person has caused the separation, or needed any defense.

As an important sidelight on the mysterious chain of events that led to Colosimo's murder is the impression of great change in the man gained by his friends since his marriage to Miss Winter.

"I can't imagine how a man could change more," said Detective Sergeant Anthony Gentile today. "I knew Jim for ten years, and I never passed his place when he did not give me the cheeriest kind of greeting. But lately it all changed. I saw him Saturday night, and he said, 'Hello, Jim.' At first he didn't appear to see me. Then he stuck out his hand, but it was limp—the old, warm grip was gone.

"I'm certain something was preying on his mind. His appointment to meet some one at the cafe at the hour he was killed, the gun in his pocket and the nervous farewell he gave his wife all show he knew he was going to meet trouble."

Linked With Enright?

Colosimo's murder may be connected with the sayings of "Moss" Enright ...

NEWEST PICTURE OF COLOSIMO'S WIDOW-BRIDE

This is one of the latest photographs of Mrs. Dale Winter Colosimo, the youthful cafe entertainer, whose marriage to "Big Jim" was only a month old when her husband was assassinated in his South Wabash avenue cafe, the center of Chicago's night life.

ARRESTS SEEN AS RESULT OF BOOZE SEIZURE

Arrests were expected today as the result of a raid yesterday by federal prohibition agents on the Sibley Warehouse and Storage company, 325 North Clark street, in which fifteen barrels of whisky, valued at $35,000, were confiscated.

According to Maj. A. V. Dalrymple, federal prohibition director for the central states, the permits on which the liquor was to have been transported were forged. Attorney George Remus is the notary public whose name appears on the alleged forged permits.

Offer to Help.

The discovery of the liquor came about unexpectedly. Two government agents were loitering near the warehouse when the liquor was being loaded on trucks.

They noticed the men who were doing the loading seemed to have trouble lifting the barrels, and offered to help.

Sensing that the barrels contained liquor, they took down the address to which they were being sent. The name of the person who was to receive the liquor is Angelo Provenzano. His address was given as 3433 Fullerton avenue, which turned out to be a vacant house.

In a garage at the rear of the house, however, the government men said they found forty permit blanks in a small iron box.

Maj. Dalrymple said he believed a consignment of fifteen barrels of liquor was delivered to the same house two months ago.

He said Reisus would be charged with violation of the federal prohibition law in warrants that would be asked for his arrest.

Drivers Are Arrested.

The two express drivers who were loading the liquor on the truck were arrested by the agents.

They are Sam Albrecht and Charles Harris. They denied having any knowledge of the alleged forged permits.

France Can Eat White Bread by Next August

PARIS, May 13.—France will again enjoy the luxury of white bread next August, in the opinion of M. Thoumyre, undersecretary for food, who announced at a banquet early this week that this year's crop promises to be exceptionally large. Large quantities of wheat are being imported into France, the minister said.

PITTSBURG RAIL WALKOUT FAILS TO MATERIALIZE

BULLETIN.

PITTSBURG, May 13.—Six hundred shopmen, yardmen and trainmen of the Pittsburg and Lake Erie railroad who have been on strike at the important terminal at Dickson Run, Pa., returned to work today, it was announced at the general offices of the company. It is the most important break in the strikers' ranks since the strike was called a month ago.

PITTSBURG, May 13.—Canvass of the offices of the Pennsylvania, Baltimore & Ohio, and Pittsburg and Lake Erie railroads this morning developed that freight and passenger movement was going on as usual, and so far as was known there had been no attempt on the part of the engineers and firemen to walk out.

Officials of the Brotherhood of Locomotive Firemen and Enginemen are in the city today, it was said, to investigate the origin of the strike report.

Special representatives of the brotherhood were sent from Cleveland during the night to make the investigation, it was learned.

"Efforts to retrieve a lost cause will end with a stampede have failed," G. C. Davis, vice chairman of the Pennsylvania Lines East, of the Brotherhood of Railroad Trainmen, said today regarding the predicted strike of engineers and firemen. "It would be odd if the engineers, who very largely have resisted the strike to date, should go out now," he concluded.

A. J. Lovell, vice president of the Brotherhood of Locomotive Firemen and Enginemen, said that, from all reports he could gather this morning, not a single new man has joined the strikers on any railroad in the Pittsburg district. Other brotherhood officials gave the same report.

Committee Recommends Hunt for Siam Post

WASHINGTON, May 13.—Confirmation of former Governor Hunt of Arizona to be American minister to Siam was recommended today by the senate foreign relations committee by a vote of 11 to 4. Four Republicans and seven Democrats supported the nomination and four Republicans opposed it. The vote was delayed pending inquiry into the charges that Gov. Hunt had expressed sympathy with the I. W. W.

Vinci Squirms Under O'Brien's Verbal Attack

James C. O'Brien, who is known in gangland as the "hanging prosecutor," today made his final argument to force the alleged confession of James Vinci before the jury in Judge Sabath's court.

He derided the claim of the defense that the repudiated confession was obtained by duress, and said the "lurking knowledge of murder which preyed on the murderer's conscience," made it impossible for the shifty eyed chauffeur to remain silent.

If Mr. O'Brien wins his point and the confession goes to the jury it is considered likely that Vinci will go to the gallows—and if Vinci goes to the gallows it is probable that "Big Tim" Murphy, "Dago Mike" Carrozzo, and Vincenzo Cosmano will follow him.

Causes Prisoner to Squirm.

As the "hanging prosecutor" spoke he stood beside Vinci and looked him square in the eyes. When he used the terms "confessed murderer" and "cold-blooded slayer" and demanded the death penalty the prisoner squirmed and twisted in his chair and looked appealingly at his attorney, James J. Barbour. O'Brien scored his opponent, Barbour, time after time for the latter's bitter attack on State's Attorney Hoyne and his staff yesterday. He branded the actions of the attorney for the defense as "childish" and accused him of "playing to the gallery."

"Forty per cent of what Mr. Barbour said yesterday was citations from the law which, in no way, affect this case, and the other 60 per cent was spleen vented against State's Attorney Hoyne and his assistants," O'Brien said.

Calls Her a Manikin.

"Barbour reminded me of a little boy or an imitation manikin, hopping about at the end of a string for the amusement of an admiring crowd.

"Mr. Barbour tells you that an hour before this defendant confessed, he started to make a statement, and then said, 'Oh, ———, I won't say any more!'" the prosecutor continued. "This indicates that there was more to be said.

"It was the lurking knowledge of murder that forced the confession, for murder will out. No human breast can contain the knowledge of a cold-blooded murder. It was Vinci's conscience, Vinci's God, that broke him down—not the state's attorney."

Becker Trial Cited.

In making his argument Mr. O'Brien cited the famous Becker murder trial in New York as an example to justify the state's attorney's office in promising immunity to some persons connected with the crime in order to convict those "higher up." He said this was what State's Attorney Hoyne had done in promising immunity to Vinci in return for a confession.

Mr. O'Brien declared that Vinci had only driven the "death car" from which the shot that killed "Moss" Enright was fired and that Murphy, Corazzo and Cosmano were the "higher ups" in the murder. This, he said, justified State's Attorney Hoyne.

At the conclusion of the argument Judge Sabath is expected to rule on whether the confession may be read to the jury or not.

ALEX TWIRLER IN FINAL GAME WITH DODGERS

THE LINE-UP.

Cubs.	Dodgers.
Flack, rf.	Olson, 2b.
Hollocher, ss.	Johnston, 3b.
Paskert, cf.	Ward, ss.
Barber, 1b.	Wheat, lf.
Robertson, lf.	Myers, cf.
Deal, 3b.	Konetchy, 1b.
Terry, 2b.	Neis, rf.
Killefer, c.	Krueger, c.
Alexander, p.	Pfeffer, p.

Umpires—Klem and Emslie.

By Malcolm MacLean.

Grover Alexander got his long-delayed chance to do a little slabbing this afternoon. He was on the Cubs' practice, taking his regular turn, and the fans believed he had an excellent chance to bring his string of straight victories up to six, with the Dodgers as the victims.

During the first two days Brooklyn had Mamaux or Marquard in mind as probable twirler, but as the series now consists of today's game only the visiting club figures on sending its best to the mound. This will be Pfeffer, the giant right hander, formerly an ensign at the pier.

These few days of rest have been welcomed by the crippled Cubs and they now are in better shape to give battle than they were last week. As soon as the warm days come—if they ever do appear—things will be even brighter.

Mitchell is sort of up against it regarding his pitching staff, needing another regular. Perhaps Tuck Turner, recruit from Bloomington, may be the fellow for the job as soon as he gets in his best form. He made a great reputation in the minors.

There is the usual chatter of a possible trade with Dodgers, who are overstupplied with star pitchers, but the Cubs don't seem to have any swapping material the visitors could use. Cash is seldom used these days in securing ball players.

Swim by Meters.

Olympic trials for swimmers to be held here July 17 and 18 will be conducted in strict Olympic fashion ... contests will be measured in m[illegible]

Sales Exhaust Supply of Army Frozen Beef

WASHINGTON, May 13.—The army surplus of frozen beef probably will be exhausted thru sales to the public by the end of this week. Since April 13 daily sales have averaged 500,000 pounds, the price having been maintained at 10½ cents per pound.

"COL." SEYMOUR FREED, BUT HELEN STILL IS MISSING

"Col." Eugene Edward Seymour was on hand this morning to defend himself before Judge Stewart in the Clark street court. He is accused by his divorced wife, Helen O'Leary, 2845 Abbott court, 20 years old, of abduction, a mystic eye, a haunting charm and a riotous trip to Milwaukee with his reluctant sweetheart.

The "colonel's" iron-gray hair lay in a perfect marcel, and he flashed a dawn-pink carnation to those who would gaze.

Helen Is Still Missing.

Helen, who swore out a warrant against him last Monday, disappeared the same night, and has not been seen since. So all the "colonel" had to do today was to swing himself forward on his wooden legs and hear his case dismissed.

"The whole thing is preposterous," said the "colonel." "I never hypnotized the girl. I love her, and she loved me. This whole thing is trumped up by those who wish to thwart our affection."

But Helen's father, Thomas O'Leary, a substantial citizen, with no thought o' fine mystic, thinks otherwise.

Wants Affair Hushed Up.

"Mystic, nothing," said Mr. O'Leary. "The attraction is a purely material one, perfectly natural between a man of his years and experience and my little girl. We want the whole thing hushed up and Helen to come home. We've no idea where she is—she just vanished—and we want to forget this whole horrible thing and have her home wit us again. And to hasten that day, we are letting the case go by default.

"She's the best little girl in the world—and all we ask of anyone is that Helen will come back to her mother and me."

If you see her, tell her that.

B'nai B'rith Against Using Bibles in Schools

CLEVELAND, May 13.—The Independent Order of B'nai B'rith, in convention here yesterday, advocated the establishment of orphanges in Europe for Jewish war orphans, establishment of a B'nai B'rith lyceum bureau and increased contributions to charitable organizations. Use of the bible in public schools was opposed. It was voted to increase contributions to the B'nai B'rith Educational league, the Leo N. Levi Memorial hospital in [illegible] Denver Tuberculosis sanitar[illegible] rious Jewish orphanages. [illegible] of the lyceum bureau p[illegible] eliminate relig[illegible] prejudic[illegible]

19 BARRACKS DESTROYED IN IRISH RAIDS

BULLETIN.

DUBLIN, May 13.—At least nineteen police barracks in various parts of Ireland were wiped out in the course of widespread destruction of public property and other activities by bands of armed and masked men in various parts of Ireland last night. Five income tax customs offices also were raided and papers found in them burned.

LONDON, May 13.—Reports of an unusual number of activities by armed and masked men in various sections of Ireland were received in London today. The reports began trickling in early in the morning and, by noon, had reached the proportions of an avalanche. As at Easter time, many police barracks were attacked.

Most of the barracks which were the object of attack were not occupied by the regular police force, which had been sent to the larger centers.

Income tax offices also were again attacked and many documents were destroyed. A notable instance of such attacks was a raid upon an income tax office in the heart of Belfast.

At the Irish office it was said at midafternoon that that office was without advices concerning the events mentioned in the reports.

French and Law Confer.

Meanwhile Viscount French, the viceroy, was in London for a conference with Andrew Bonar Law, the government leader in the house of commons, regarding the policy to be pursued with a view to the restoration of order in Ireland.

The reports of the demonstrations followed closely the announcement made by Mr. Bonar Law in the house of commons that Gen. Sir Nevil MacReady, military commander of Ireland, was inaugurating new plans thru which it was expected conditions shortly would be improved.

Police Barracks Attacked.

DUBLIN, May 13.—Two hundred men besieged the Hollyford police barracks in County Tipperary for four hours early Wednesday morning, using rifles and bombs. A part of the building was set on fire, but the ten officers defending the place withdrew to another section of the sructure and continued their resistance. The attackers eventually retired. No casualties were reported.

DE GROAT SAYS "NOT GUILTY" IN TATE MURDER

Edward DeGroat, alias Eddie James, alleged murderer of William Tate, 1701 Crilly court, who was killed Aug. 3, 1917, while in his home, entered a plea of not guilty today before Judge Scanlan in the Criminal court. The jury, which had been selected yesterday, was sworn in, and Assistant State's Attorney John Cashen outlined the case of the prosecution.

DeGroat is said to have been an admirer of Mrs. Tate, and urged her to leave her husband. Upon her refusal, DeGroat became enraged and said he would kill Mr. and Mrs. Tate and himself, it is charged.

He went to the home, in which he had previously lived as a roomer, awoke Tate and his wife from sleep and while Mrs. Tate ran for assistance, is said to have shot the husband and escaped.

DeGroat was arrested in California and brought back to Chicago.

Lieut. Ferrari Flies from Shanghai to Tsingtao

SHANGHAI, May 9 (Delayed).—(By the Associated Press.)—Lieut. Ferrari, first of the airmen in the Rome-Tokyo flight to reach Shanghai, flew today from this city to Tsingtao. He will proceed to his objective by way of Peking, Mukden, in southern Manchuria, and Seoul, Korea. Lieut. Masiero, the second of the Italian airmen in the flight, who crashed recently at Canton, came to Shanghai by steamer. He is obtaining a new machine and will follow Wednesday along the route taken by Lieut. Farrari.

Advocate Farm Industrial Colonies for Prisoners

NEW YORK, May 13.—Farm industrial colonies for prisoners were advocated today by speakers attending the annual meeting and conference of the national committee on prison and prison labor. The convention will last three days. Wardens from many of the largest prisons in the country are in attendance.

Miners Discuss Wages with Secretary Wilson

WASHINGTON, May 13.—Reresentatives of anthracite miners met again in conference today with Secretary Wilson but adjourned without making public any of the results of the discussions. Mr. Wilson was expected to meet the committee of operators later, after which he planned to call the miners again into conference.

Odds on Resolute.

The Resolute is a 2-to-1 favorite in the betting to win from the Vanitie in the trial cup races which begin May 21. Vanitie money has been slow in coming to the surface.

Another Bowl.

Work has already begun on the University of Washington's stadium, which will rival Yale's famous bowl in seating capacity and arrangement. It will seat 60,000 [illegible]

German Ships Barred from Foreign Trading

BERLIN, May 13.—Orders have been given by the German government that German ships will not be allowed to ply any longer between foreign ports, as all tonnage is required in domestic commerce, says a Hamburg dispatch to the Boersen Courier.

Horner Chosen Head of Illinois Grain Dealers

DECATUR, Ill., May 12.—Fred G. Horner, Lawrenceville, was re-elected president of the Illinois Grain Dealers' association in the closing sessions of the twenty-seventh annual convention here yesterday.

Three More Cities Gain in Population Figures

WASHINGTON, May 13.—Census figures given out today include:

Camden, N. J., 116,309, an increase of 21,771, or 23 per cent.

Concord, N. H., 22,167, an increase of 670, or 3.1 per cent.

Parsons, Kan., 16,028, an increase of 3,565 or 23.6 per cent.

Two Women Burned to Death in Hospital Fire

OTTAWA, May 13.—Two woman patients were burned to death in a fire which damaged the Doctor Hagar Maternity hospital here today.

JUMPS TO DEATH FROM CITY HALL

A man identified by a card in his pocket as Tom Wilton, a member of the garage employes' union, jumped from an upper story of the city hall into LaSalle street this afternoon and was instantly killed. Ald. A. J. Cermak saw the man fall, but could not say from which story he had jumped.

STRIKE OUT GERMAN PEACE NEGOTIATION

WASHINGTON, May 13.—The provision in the Republican peace resolution requesting the President to open negotiations with Germany for a separate treaty was stricken out today on motion of Senator Lodge of Massachusetts, the Republican leader.

SOCIALISTS NOMINATE DEBS

NEW YORK, May 13.—Eugene V. Debs, federal convict N 2253, was nominated by acclamation for the presidency of [illegible] United States at the Socialist party's national convention here [illegible]

BRITONS PLAN SPECIAL COURT FOR IRISH CASES

LONDON, May 13.—The British government has decide[illegible] ate a special judicial body to examine the cases of Irishmen under arrest, it was announced in the house of commons [illegible] Andrew Bonar Law, the government leader.

AMERICAN LEAGUE

Sox-New York game postponed; wet grounds.
Cleveland-Boston game postponed; rain.
St. Louis-Philadelphia game postponed; wet grounds.
Detroit-Washington game postponed; wet grounds.

READY FOR HUGE CELEBRATION ON 'LINK' TOMORROW

A mammoth parade with more than 8,000 automobiles, a fortune of fresh flowers, numerous bands and fireworks in profusion will be features of Chicago's celebration tomorrow in honor of the opening of the new "boulevard link" and the mayor's fiftieth birthday.

Mayor Thompson has declared a part holiday. The city hall will be closed fro m3 o'clock on, with the usual exception of the departments of police, fire, electricit yand public health.

The parade has been arranged by Aludermen J. P. Garner and Henry J. Kramer. It will begin at 4 o'clock from Monore street and Michigan avenue and will proceed to the new bridge, across which a red, white and blue ribbon will be tied. Mayor Thompson will cut the ribbon and the parade will then move across the bridge and north on Michigan avenue.

Mayor, Faherty in First Car.

In the first car will be Mayor Thompson and Michael J. Faherty, president of the board of local improvements. Following them will be the mayor's cabinet and members of the city council. State and county officials will be next in the line of march. Gov. Lowden and his family are expected to take part in the parade.

Bridge Operators' union, local 184, will lead a delegation of sixty machines containing bridge operators. The Medina Motor club will follow with decorated cars and a floral float with the Shriners' emblem in flowers six feet high.

The Chicago Motor club with 1,000 cars, the Illinois Motor club with 750 cars, the Chicago Auto club with 500 cars and the Avendale Motor club with 250 cars will comprise the next division of the parade. Among these clubs will be a number of bands calliopes and artistic floats.

Following these will come the Chicago Automobile Trade association with 1,000 cars and two floats, the Sinclair Oil company, with a fleet of 100 white painted cars, and the Standard Oil company with 250 cars, a band of 100 pieces, and two floral floats.

Property Owners in Line.

Property owners involved in the opening of the link will have 1,000 cars in the parade. Employes of the state, county and city will follow in 700 cars. Six hundred cars carrying the ward committeemen and other city politicians will be next, followed by the Big Bill Boosters' club of the 23d ward in 250 cars.

A floral float representing the boulevard linking the north and south sides, valued at $3,000, contributed by the Fleischman Floral company, will be one of the features of the parade. The Allied Floral association of wholesale and retail florists has appropriated $2,000 for a float and decorations for 250 cars.

The general public will follow this division. All cars will park in Grant park.

Park Bond Issue to Voters in November

Voters will have the opportunity next November of approving or rejecting a bond issue of $1,000,000 for the extension of Lincoln park to Montrose boulevard. The commissioners have authorized the bond issue and plan ultimately to extend the park to Devon avenue. The zoo is to receive an addition [illegible] pygmy hippo, the gift of Willian [illegible] ley Jr., commissioner of the [illegible] supporters [illegible] were attacked by adherents of the opposition.

CARRANZA HOLDS BACK REBEL HORDE

BULLETIN.

BROWNSVILLE, Texas, May 13.—There are further indications today that Gen. Rafael Colonga, Carranza commander at Piedras Negias, the Mexican town near the border, would surrender that city to revoluntionists.

Gen. Calunga declares he will turn the city over to responsible revolutionary forces, but says that he would defend the town against small bands of rebels who might launch an attack.

United States army border planes were in the air early today in an effort to locate rebel forces reported near Matamoros.

VERA CRUZ, May 13.—(By the Associated Press.)—Furious fighting between rebel troops and forces commanded by President Venustiano Carranza occurred yesterday at Hacienda Tamariz, on the Mexican National railroad north of San Marcos, state of Puebla, according to dispatches received here. The area of the battle field is reported to be approximately five square miles. President Carranza is said in wireless messages from Mexico City to have personally directed the operations of his troops for eight hours on Tuesday.

Terrific storms have swept the mountain region where the struggle is going on and telegraphic communication has been interrupted in the immediate vicinity of the scene of battle. It is known, however, that heavy rebel re-enforcements have been sent to San Marcos by rebel chieftains, artillery being rushed forward to force the surrender of the troops still loyal to the president.

Gen. Guadaloupe Sanchez has gone to Esperanza with his personal staff and five trainloads of troops to co-operate in what is believed to be the decisive action of the rebellion. Esperanza is about forty miles southeast of San Marcos. A correspondent of the newspaper El Dictatem is with the rebel forces in the battle zone, but up unt[illegible] an early hour this morning nothing ha[illegible] been heard from him. This silence, however, was probably due to the break in the telegraphic line in the state of Puebla.

Carranzistas Slay Rebel Captain.

YUMA, Ariz., May 13.—Capt. Carter G. Calles, a nephew of Gen. P. Elias Calles, was shot and killed at his doorway i[illegible] San Luis P. Sonora, a small garriso[illegible] town twenty-five miles below the inte[illegible] national border, early today, accordi[illegible] to a telephone message received here day and later corroborated.

According to the message, a for[illegible] lieutenan[illegible] of the Carranza forces took charge of all arms and muni[illegible] at San Luis and announced that he the place for the Carranza regime small detachment of troops comm[illegible] by Capt. Calles had been aligned the Sonora revolutionists.

Tampico Is Quiet.

EL PASO, Texas, May 13.—[illegible] quiet [illegible] county hospital [illegible] he had been [illegible] commission [illegible] wife, after eating a heavy [illegible] Thanksgiving day, he refused to take of food.

CANTU GENERAL JOINS REBELS

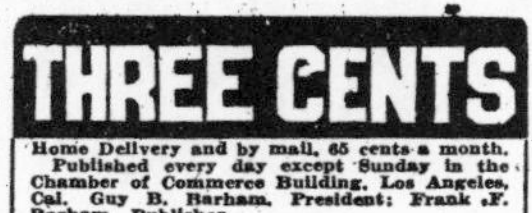
THREE CENTS
Home Delivery and by mail, 65 cents a month. Published every day except Sunday in the Chamber of Commerce Building, Los Angeles, Cal. Guy B. Barham, President; Frank F. Barham, Publisher.

LOS ANGELES
EVENING HERALD
AN INDEPENDENT NEWSPAPER

Reg. U. S. Pat. Off. The Evening Herald Grows Just Like Los Angeles

LATEST NEWS

VOL. XLV. Entered as second-class matter Nov. 2, 1911, at the post-office at Los Angeles, Cal., under act of March 3, 1879. SATURDAY, MAY 15, 1920 THREE CENTS NO. 168

$5,000,000 CROOK GIVES UP

Execute Woman for Treason

CARRANZA IS ONCE MORE REPORTED CAPTIVE

Obregonistas Claim President Has Been Taken by Revolutionists

By United Press

AGUA PRIETA, Sonora, May 15.—Revolutionary leaders this morning were attempting to verify or trace to its source a report received during the night that Carranza had surrendered. Many leaders are inclined to give the report credence.

By International News Service

WASHINGTON, May 15.—Neither the state department nor the revolutionary agency here had confirmation today of reports that President Carranza has surrendered. The revolutionary agency had such a report, which reached New York from Nogales, but no credence was given it.

WASHINGTON, May 15.—The state department received word today, it is reported, that the southern half of Lower California has declared for the Mexican revolution.

This caused much comment here, for Gov. Estuban Cantu, who six weeks ago let it be known that he favored Carranza, is now in a position of peril and may be forced to defend the territory still left under his control.

Cantu, who has always maintained a sort of independent government in Lower California, has been on closest terms with the United States officials.

COMPLICATIONS LOOM

Any change which would remove Cantu from power might be fraught with serious American complications.

The territory under Cantu's control is the richest revenue producing district of Northern Mexico. At Tia Juana and Mexicali the gambling concessions net large sums daily and covetous eyes have long been cast upon these sources of governmental income.

The report today says that Gen. Manuel Mezta, who has been one of Cantu's officers, has turned against him and declared for Obregon.

HOPES FOR GOVERNORSHIP

It is thought that Mezta may have hopes of being made governor and succeeding to Cantu's power and revenues.

Cantu, on the other hand, is in so separated a position that he has little [illegible] from troops in Mexico proper, [illegible] would have to come by sea [illegible] across 500 miles of desert before [illegible] could attack him.

[illegible] therefore, he can conquer the [illegible] under Mezta, he might declare [illegible] California an independent gov-

CONTINUED ON PAGE TWO

BLUEBEARD IN NEW MURDER QUIZ; OFF TO PRISON

Bigamist Slayer Suspected of Killing Widow of Canadian Army Officer

On the eve of his departure for San Quentin prison late today to begin serving a life sentence for the slaying of one of the nine wives he has confessed killing, the name of "Bluebeard" Joseph Gillam was linked with another murder mystery today. A dispatch from Toronto, Canada, reported that he was suspected of having slain the widow of a young Canadian army officer there after having inveigled her into a marriage with him.

The Toronto police found a trunk believed to have belonged to the slayer of the woman, and in it was a bloodstained weapon which probably had been used to commit the crime.

TO VISIT JAIL

Lee Lucas of Clearwater was scheduled to visit the county jail today to determine whether "Bluebeard" Gillam was the man who stopped at a ranch house near Muroc, in Kern county, where Lucas was employed about a year ago and asked information as to the most direct road to Barstow or Needles. Lucas naw believes the man may have been transporting the dead body of a slain wife in the car.

The man's actions were suspicious, Lucas said, and so he took particular note of the stranger's appearance. He declares that pictures of Gillam which he has seen resemble the mysterious stranger.

When the automobile was stopped, Lucas said, the engine was kept running. The side curtains of the car were in place. The man said he had a sick wife in the rear of the car but would not permit Lucas to look behind the curtains.

HURRIES AWAY

Because of the woman's supposed illness, Lucas invited the stranger to remain over night at the ranch, where she could receive some care. The man declined the invitation and hurried away.

Since Gillam was remtved from his cell in the county hospital late yesterday he has been in terror of possible violence at the hands of the prisoners in the county jail, who had made threats that he would suffer violence if he was taken to the county jail. He also is fearful of being poisoned and can hardly be induced to eat.

The wife slayer and bigamist showed that he has a "yellow streak" when he was notified late yesterday that he was to be taken to the county jail. He trembled like a man stricken with ague and begged for assurances that he would be protected after his re-

(CONTINUED ON PAGE FIVE)

Hunt Alleged Slayer After Gun Battle

By International News Service

LOS ALTOS, Cal., May 15.—Sheriffs' posses early today were searching the orchard districts for H. Sims, fugitive from justice, who escaped last evening when cornered in an orchard after a gun battle with officers.

Sims is wanted in Oklahoma City on the charge of having blown up his home with dynamite, killing his two children and injuring his wife. He escaped from the Oklahoma jail.

Sims is believed to have been wounded in the exchange of shots with officers late yesterday.

Bill Pertica Slated To Oppose Beavers At Local Park Today

Bill Pertica, with six consecutive wins to his credit, will tackle the Beavers at Washington park this afternoon in an effort to even up the series for the Angels. The count stands 2 to 1 in favor of Portland.

Pertica has been pitching high class ball for the Seraphs.

Rudy Kallio and Sutherland were the twirlers McCredie told to warm up.

BEAVERS—	ANGELS—
Blue, 1b.	Killefer, cf.
Wisterzil, 3b.	McAuley, ss.
Maisel, cf.	K. Crandall, 2b.
Schaller, lf.	Griggs, 1b.
Siglin, 2b.	Crawford, rf.
Cox, rf.	Lapan, c.
Koehler, c.	Ellis, lf.
Kingdon, ss.	Niehoff, 3b.
Kallio, p.	Pertica, p.

Woman Kills Her Sister and Self

By United Press

WEISER, Idaho, May 15.—Fearing her sister, Mrs. Louise Taber, a divorcee, would marry again and force a division of joint property, Mrs. Tolla Johnson shot Mrs. Taber today, killing her instantly. She then summoned several neighbors and informed them of the murder. She turned as if to leave the room and as she stood in the doorway she turned the revolver to her temple and sent a bullet into her brain, dying instantly. The family is prominent in this section.

Athlete Dies as He Finishes Race

By United Press

WALLA WALLA, Wash., May 15.—Toppling over just as he crossed the finish line after running the 220-yard dash, Peter Pongen, 19-year-old freshman at the Walla Walla high school, lived only a few minutes late yesterday. He was a contestant in the interclass games. Pongen was gassed while fighting in France and his heart was affected.

INDIANA SOCIETY TO DANCE

An old fashioned box social will be the feature of the regular monthly entertainment and dance of the Indiana State society to be held at the Fraternal Brotherhood building, 845 South Figueroa street, Tuesday evening. All Hoosiers and their friends are invited.

SPY CHEERS FRANCE AS SHE DIES

Shouts Innocence and with Eyes Uncovered Calmly Faces Firing Squad

PARIS, May 15.—Shouting her innocence and cheering for France, Alice Aubert, convicted as a traitor, faced a firing squad and was shot to death at the execution grounds in Vincennes this morning.

She met her fate calmly and declared to the end that she was being made the victim of a conspiracy.

Three men, also convicted as traitors in the recent war, went to their death at her side.

FOUND GUILTY

Alice Aubert was found guilty of having carried on treasonable dealings with the German forces occupying Northern France during the middle stages of the late war.

The scene at the execution grounds this morning was impressive. The woman marched out with a firm step and took her place before the firing squad. She asked that she be not blindfolded, talking calmly with those in charge of the execution.

DENIES GUILT

As the rifles of the firing squad were brought into position for the fatal volley the woman squared her shoulders, threw back her head and cried:

"I am innocent! Vive la France!"

While the sound of her voice still echoed, the crash of the lethal volley came and she crumpled in a heap.

Proposes Sales Tax on Sugar Dealers

By International News Service

WASHINGTON, May 15.—As a measure of protection against excessive prices, Representative Steenerson of Minnesota this afternoon introduced a bill in the house providing a sales tax of 2 cents a pound upon sugar when the manufacturer or importer has not listed with the federal trade commission his stocks of sugar and his schedule of prices.

Forced Purchases to Get Sugar Barred

By International News Service

CHICAGO, May 15.—The practice of merchants in forcing customers to buy other articles in order to obtain sugar has been forbidden by Attorney General Palmer, according to an order from Washington to Federal District Attorney Clyne, ordering him to institute prosecution of all such merchants.

FIND WOMAN GUILTY

SAN DIEGO, May 15.—The jury in the case of Mrs. Pansy L. Stewart, charged with robbing the San Miguel schoolhouse Feb. 4, returned a verdict of guilty of second degree burglary. The penalty is not less than five years.

L.A. Artists to Play in 'Ingomar'

Mrs. Roberts-Kamm to Appear as Parthenia in 'Ingomar' for Children's Benefit

Sponsored by leaders in exclusive social circles, "Ingomar" will be put on at Philharmonic Auditorium, formerly Clune's, at Fifth and Olive streets, Thursday, May 27, with the beautiful social favorite, Mrs. Roberts-Kamm, in the role of "Parthenia," a lovely Grecian maiden.

The production is to be given for the benefit of the Home for Crippled Children, which was recently moved into the old Singleton place in Palm drive.

R. D. MacLean will appear in the leading role.

Mr. MacLean's wife, known in private life as Odette Tyler and to the public as Mrs. R. D. Shepherd, is directing.

President and Mrs. Wilson sponsored the beautiful and unique affair, and members of Washington's smart set, with a sprinkling of brilliant New York society folk, were patronesses.

The production to be offered here promises to surpass that given during war times and a cast culled from most notable figures in the dramatic world will offer their services.

In the cast are such well known folk as William Courtleigh, Wallace Reid, Lawson Butt, Casson Ferguson, Irving Cummings, James O. Barrows, Emmitt King, George Darrell, Dwight Crittenden, Hardee Kirkland, Edward McWade, Nelson McDowell, Benson North, Jack Livingston and Miss Anne Schaffer. Mrs. Roberts-Kamm is the only non-professional in the cast.

The affair is under the auspices of W. A. Clark jr. and Mrs. R. D. Shepherd.

PEACE MEASURE VOTE UP TODAY IN SENATE

By International News Service

WASHINGTON, May 15.—By unanimous agreement the senate will vote on the amended Knox peace resolution at 4 o'clock this afternoon. Passage of the measure by a "comfortable majority" is predicted by the Republican leaders.

Elimination from it by Senator Lodge of Massachusetts, the Republican leader, of a request that President Wilson negotiate a separate treaty with Germany, solidified Republican support with the exception of Senator McCumber of North Dakota, "mildest of the mild reservationists."

A number of Democratic senators opposed to the President's attitude on the peace treaty and the League of Nations have signified their intention of voting for the resolution.

Following its expected passage by the senate the measure will be sent to the house and there formally referred to the house foreign affairs committee. Republican leaders of the lower house are planning to force a vote on it by the end of next week.

ARNSTEIN, HUNTED IN U.S., BOWS WAY PAST POLICE PARADE

NEW YORK, May 15.—After five months of being hunted by the authorities, "Nicky" Arnstein, the "master crook" who engineered the wholesale bond thefts amounting to $5,000,000 from Wall street brokers, today motored past the assembled forces of Gotham's police review, tipped his hat to high police officials, circled the court house twice and was not recognized until he voluntarily gave himself into custody.

With Arnstein was his actress wife, Fannie Brice. They entered the office of the district attorney at 10:30 o'clock and, after he had surrendered, he posed for photographs.

PROMISES TO TALK

He refused to make any statement other than to say

"I'll do all my talking lated."

To this his wife added the somewhat enigmatical statement that she "is the happiest woman in the world."

Arnstein arrived from Pittsburg, where he had been hiding, at 9 a. m. and motored to Ninetieth street, where he met his wife. Accompanied by William J. Fallon, attorney, the party motored down Fifth avenue and passed through long lines of policemen gathered for their annual parade.

SALUTES OFFICIALS

As the automobile swung past Union Square, Arnstein tipped his hat to high police officials gathered in a grandstand erected to witness the parade.

The automobile was driven twice around the court house without Arnstein being recognized.

The first official to recognize Arnstein was William Hanna, clerk of courts. The news spread rapidly and a large crowd gathered while Arnstein and his wife posed for pictures.

Arnstein refused to say anything

(CONTINUED ON PAGE FIVE.)

LATEST NEWS

CLASH LOOMS OVER WATER RATE INCREASE

A clash between members of the city council and the public service commission loomed today over the commission's decision to increase water rates in Los Angeles. Members of the council say they must be "shown" what is to be done with the increased revenue.

L. A. COURT TEST ON SUGAR PROFITS HINTED

A federal court jury may be called upon in a test suit to determine if local dealers in sugar who exceed the profit margin of 1 cent for wholesale and 2 cents for retailers shall be prosecuted as profiters.

TRADE LEADERS URGE PEACE WITH RESERVATIONS

SAN FRANCISCO, May 15.—Urging immediate adoption of a treaty of peace "safeguarding every fundamental principle of the government of the United States," the committee of the national foreign trades convention today submitted its report.

BANDITS ELUDE OFFICERS IN GUN FIGHT

Two automobile thieves fought a running gun fight with Detectives Barnes and Hawtrey of the police flying squadron at dawn today when the officers found them in a stolen automobile at Santa Fe avenue and Sacramento street.

The two men leaped from the speeding automobile and escaped from the police. The automobile crashed into a fence and was damaged. It is the property of F. G. Mayers of the Security building.

While searching for Mayers' car Hawtrey and Barnes ran across the thieves and commanded them to halt. The thieves answered with a fusillade of shots.

For more than two blocks the officers attempted to overtake the

(CONTINUED ON PAGE FIVE)

SLAIN ROBBER'S $50,000 LOOT IS SOUGHT

With the clearing away of mystery surrounding the identity of the "silk glove" bandit, who was slain the night of April 2, last, by James Stuchberry, a private watchman of the Windsor patrol, at the home of P. J. Fellater in Windsor Square, search for $50,000 in loot believed to have been hidden by the bandit was launched today.

According to Los Angeles and Long Beach detectives, who have been working on the case, the slain bandit's real name was Emanuel Smith, but he was known in the Utah penitentiary, from which he escaped on Oct. 15, last, as Frank Johnson. He had been sentenced the preceding February for burglary.

Finger prints assisted in the identi-

(CONTINUED ON PAGE FIVE)

BEST SPORTS MARKETS COMICS CITY NEWS
IT'S IN THE NEWS

THE CLEVELAND NEWS

HOME Edition

EXCLUSIVE ASSOCIATED PRESS DISPATCHES

VOL. 79.—NO. 225. Published on six days of the week by the Cleveland Company, Cleveland, O. Entered as second class matter at Cleveland postoffice under the act of March 3, 1879. CLEVELAND, THURSDAY. AUGUST 12, 1920. PRICE THREE CENTS

PONZI ARRESTED; RECEIVER ASKED

ALLY SPLIT ON RUSS HINTS WAR

ENGLAND HURRIES TO PARLEY WITH FRANCE ON WRANGEL ACTION

Conference of Chieftians Called in Effort to Prevent Break; Britain Alarmed by Blow at Soviet Government.

BULLETIN.

PARIS, Aug. 12.—Advices from the eastern theater of war indicate that a grand battle for Warsaw will be precipitated along the whole Polish battle line today, it was announced at the foreign office.

The daily soviet war office communique had not been received by wireless from Moscow up to 1:30 o'clock this afternoon.

Exclusive Dispatch to THE NEWS by Associated Press.

LONDON, Aug. 12.—Great Britain has been notified officially of the recognition by France of the government of Gen. Baron Wrangel as the de facto government of South Russia, and the question is being discussed between the two governments.

Something akin to consternation is evinced by evening newspapers over the French action, which is characterized as contrary to British ideas and a menace to entente relations.

Meanwhile, King George, who was to leave for Scotland tomorrow, has postponed his trip, owing to the situation.

Conference Called.

It was unofficially reported this afternoon that Premier Lloyd George and Earl Curzon, the secretary for foreign affairs, plan to meet Premier Millerand at Boulogne Sunday to discuss the recognition of Gen. Wrangel.

Premier Lloyd George last evening notified Leo Kameneff, soviet emissary here, that the Polish government had just informed the British premier that up to 9 p. m. Tuesday Poland had not received a reply from the Moscow government to the message of Poland expressing a willingness to send delegates to the armistice and peace conference at Minsk.

Poland informed the British prime minister that the Polish officer commanding the sector beyond Siedloe had just announced that the Russian peace delegation had arrived in that sector and, not finding the Polish delegates, had stated that it would wait until 3 o'clock Wednesday.

Rush Delegates.

Poland further stated she was notifying the soviet authorities that she was prepared to start her armistice and peace delegation for the scene Wednesday night.

Lloyd George told M. Kameneff he trusted he would expedite the passage of the Polish delegates to Minsk. The premier called attention to the refusals of the Russian wireless service to accept messages for the soviet government from Waraw, as reported by the Poles, and said this raised a justifiable suspicion, and that it was not conducive to a prompt and peaceful solution of the crisis.

BRITAIN WORRIED BY FRENCH MOVE AGAINST SOVIETS

LONDON, Aug. 12.—War clouds again loomed ominously on the horizon today. A cabinet council was summoned to consider the decision of France to sever all relations with the soviet government of Russia and to throw French support to the defacto government established by Gen. Wrangel, the anti-Bolshevik leader, in southern Russia.

A wave of alarm has swept Great Britain as a result of the unexpected decision of France in breaking away from Premier Lloyd George's policy of conciliation.

The British labor council, which is vigorously opposing and all war measures against soviet Russia, was hastily called into secret session to consider action in view of the new French attitude.

Premier Lloyd George, who has been making tremendous efforts to restore peace in the east and prevent a new war from sweeping Europe, was plainly anxious. It was announced at the premier's official residence at No. 10 Downing st., just before noon, that no French note relative to France's new Russian policy had yet been received from Paris.

The line-up of the powers is described as follows:

GREAT BRITAIN—Demands a free and independent Poland, but is willing to make concessions to the soviet government at Moscow.

FRANCE—Hostile to the soviet government and will support the de-facto government of Gen. Wrangel by force of arms.

ITALY—Opposed to war or blockade against Russia.

UNITED STATES — Demands a free and independent Poland and is hostile to recognition of the soviet government.

JAPAN—Attitude unknown, but has recently effected an armistice with the Russian Bolsheviki in Siberia.

GERMANY—Future German atti-

Continued on 2d Page, 1st Column

STOLEN STOCK FOUND IN REAL ESTATE OFFICE

Telephone Worker Discovers Valuables Taken Saturday Night at Lakewood.

Two thousand dollars' worth of stock, stolen from the home of Herman Schmitt, 16711 Lake ave., Saturday night, was found Thursday hidden behind the bell box of a telephone in an abandoned real estate office on Riverside rd., one block south of Madison ave.

The discovery was made by Norman Kelly, a lineman for the Cleveland Telephone Company, who went to the office, a one-room, one-story frame structure, to remove the telephone. The office had been used by Maerkle & Co., real estate dealers.

When Kelly attempted to open the door, he discovered there was someone on the inside holding it. He ran across the street and telephoned Lakewood police. As he was returning a man ran out of the door and disappeared in the Rocky river valley.

When Kelly removed the bell box from the wall, the stock, in an envelope fell out. Indications were the stock had been hidden in the box Wednesday. Lakewood police took the stock and learned it belonged to Schmitt.

Schmitt surprised burglars in his home Saturday night. They fled when he entered at 10:30 o'clock. A safe and desks had been ransacked and papers were scattered about the floor. Schmitt did not know the stock was missing until it was turned over to him by Lakewood police.

Cloth valued at $1,000 was stolen from the tailor shop of David Grunzweig, 1277 E. 105th st., Wednesday night, he reported to police Thursday. The thieves entered through a rear window. Several bolts of cloth were taken.

Police believe the thieves used a motor car to cart the loot away. The back door was open when Grunzweig opened the store in the morning.

The News is the only afternoon paper in the city carrying Associated Press dispatches.

Take Down Clothes Line for Thunder Showers Are Due

"Take down the clothesline and set out the rubber plant," is Weather Forecaster Emery's word to Cleveland housewifes for Thursday night.

Thundershowers are on the way.

"I don't say that definitely," says Emery. "But the weather conditions are of the sort that thunderstorms grow from, and there will probably be one by early evening. There may be more rain Friday."

Temperature readings for Thursday follow:

12 midnight	70	7 a. m.	66
1 a. m.	70	8 a. m.	69
2 a. m.	69	9 a. m.	72
3 a. m.	69	10 a. m.	77
4 a. m.	68	11 a. m.	78
5 a. m.	67	12 noon	78
6 a. m.	67	1 p. m.	79

4 ARRESTED; CHARGE $1,000 CAR ROBBERIES

CINCINNATI, Aug. 12.—Four men were arrested, seven automobiles are held by the police and $1,000 worth of merchandise, a negro was recovered in an automobile chase in the exclusive Avondale district last night.

An automobile driven at a high speed into a dead-end street excited the suspicion of a private policeman. Overtaking the abandoned car, filled with merchandise, a negro was pressed into service by police as guard and a search began. In the meantime another auto carrying four men approached. They were captured.

The men confessed to looting freight cars, police said, and declared at the home of one of the quartet five automobiles, all laden with fabrics, were found.

MOTHER OF MANNIX PRAYS TO SEE HIM

DUBLIN, Aug. 12.—"My son is a man of peace, he wouldn't hurt a fly," was the comment of Mrs. Mannix, eighty-nine years old, the mother of Archbishop Daniel J. Mannix, of Melbourne, Australia, now in England under surveillance. "I hope that God will spare him and induce the English officials to let him come home to me. I am too old to make the trip to England to see him."

The press associaton wires have carried nothing further concerning Bishop Mannix since he was conducted to London after being taken forcibly from the liner Baltic and landed at Penzance, England.

PHONE PARTY SEES WASHINGTON SYSTEM

That a telephone switchboard system of the sort used in Cleveland may give speedy and efficient service was the discovery of members of the telephone committee of city council who spent Thursday in Washington, D. C., the second stop on their inspection tour.

In Washington the same system employed in Cleveland is used, but the committee was able to find Washingtonians to indorse it.

The party, which is headed by Perry D. Caldwell, chairman of the committee, and includes technical and legal advisers and representatives of civic organizations, will proceed to Norfolk, Va., where an automatic system is used. The findings there will be compared with observations at Lima, where the tourists stopped Wednesday. Automatic boards are used in Lima.

EXPRESS FIRM ACTS FOR BOOST IN RATES

WASHINGTON, Aug. 12.—Application for permission to file supplementary requests for increased express rates to cover the labor board increased wage award for employes was filed today with the interstate commerce commission by the American Railway Express Company.

The company estimated the total increased salaries due to the award to be $43,800,805. The original estimate of the increase was $30,000,000.

BEAT ATTEMPT TO BLOCK SUFF VOTE

NASHVILLE, Tenn., Aug. 12.—Suffragists in the lower house of the Tennessee legislature today won another point in the fight for ratification of the federal suffrage amendment, a joint resolution which would have prohibited action of any kind on ratification being tabled by a viva voce vote.

Girl Collapses on Dance Floor, Dies

CANTON, Aug. 12.—Kathryn Jean Smith, seventeen, of Canton, died in Aultman hospital yesterday, one hour after she had fallen in a faint in the dancing pavilion at Myers Lake Park. Miss Smith had danced two sets while her mother watched her from the side of the ball. Death was pronounced due to hemorrhage of the lungs.

LA FOLLETTE MAY HEAD NEW LIBERAL PARTY

Wisconsin Senator to Write Own Platform.

By Carl D. Ruth.

NEWS BUREAU, 420 COLORADO BLDG.

WASHINGTON, Aug. 12.—Another new political party under the leadership of Senator Robert M. LaFollette of Wisconsin to be known as the Liberal party seems assured from developments in the last few days. The new organization will be dominated absolutely by the senator from Wisconsin.

He will accept the nomination, it is now asserted by those engineering the movement, upon a platform which he will write.

Plans were matured at a conference in New York a few days ago in which some of the elements that figure in the Farmer-Labor party at Chicago participated. The movement, it is confidently asserted, will have the support of the Scripps-McCrae newspapers, including a Cleveland afternoon paper and certain other press organizations.

It will have other advantages in the way of publicity in the support of certain magazines and other periodicals. It will also be well financed, its sponsors say.

GRAVEYARD REMOVAL PLAN LEADS TO FIGHT

Organizations at Odds on Proposal for Abandoning Erie Street Cemetery.

Abandonment of the Erie street cemetery is being pronposed again.

This time it is the city plan commission that is taking up the question.

Richard Harburger, secretary of the commission, said Thursday the commission will pay $500 to the Clevelander who submits the best suggestion on "The Future Use of the Erie Street Cemetery."

The Erie Street Removal Association is urging the cemetery be abandoned, while the Pioneer Memorial Association is fighting the proposal, Harburger said.

"More than 3,000 bodies already have been disinterred," Harburger said.

"The cemetery is in the heart of the downtown business district and is of use no longer as a cemetery. It sands in the way of the extension of Carnegie ave."

Calls "Burglar" Yells Efforts to Shorten Life

ELYRIA, O., Aug. 12.—Asserting that attempts to shorten his life were made by their crying at various times of the night that burglars were in the house and further that he was not given proper care,

Allen Sanders, eighty-three, retired Murray Ridge farmer, has sued W. R. and Ella Morgan to recover his $15,000 farm which he had agreed to turn over to the defendants for nurse, board and room until his death.

Free Social Disease Clinic Opened for City

A free clinic for the diagnosis and treatment of social diseases is to be established in Fairview Park hospital, Health Commissioner Rockwood said Thursday.

It will be opened August 16, with Dr. H. H. Ward in charge. The clinic will be open three evenings a week from 5 to 7 o'clock and Saturday afternoons.

"There has been a great increase in the number of people seeking treatment," Rockwood said. "This is not due to any alarming spread of the disease, but because the war service educated the people to the benefit of proper treatment."

'Money Wizard,' Wife

CHARLES PONZI MINUS "THE SMILE"

BABE SAYS HE'LL BE BACK SURE IN TODAY'S LINEUP

Ruth's Injured Knee Much Improved; No Bones Broken Nor Ligaments Torn.

Babe Ruth, the Yanks' slugging demon, intends to play in Thursday's game.

Dr. M. H. Castle, physician of the Cleveland baseball club, announced the Bambino would be out in uniform this afternoon and would endeavor to return to the lineup.

Ruth singled in the first inning of Wednesday's game and took second when Speaker momentarily fumbled his hit. In sliding into the sack, however, he wrenched his right knee. He limped when he arose and the game several times was held up for a few minutes during the inning while Babe tested out his leg. At the end of the Yanks' half, however, Babe decided to quit and was carried from the field.

Upon first examination it was feared he would be out of the game for an extended period, but detailed investigation revealed no broken bones nor torn ligaments. The injury was painful, but not necessarily serious. The pain had subsided to such an extent Ruth was determined to be back in the game Thursday and Dr. Castle, after his investigation Thursday morning, offered no objections.

INNOCENT, 2 SERVE 15 MONTHS FOR HOLDUP

NEW YORK, Aug. 12.—Two Croatians, serving eight to sixteen years in Sing Sing for alleged partnership in the holdup of a sailors' boarding-house here more than a year ago, are innocent, and legal machinery has been started to effect their release, Assistant District Attorney Bohan, who prosecuted them, announced today.

The men, behind prison bars for fifteen monhs, are Frank Pezzulich and Frank Sgelirrach. Confessions of three men arrested in Milwaukee early this year have exonerated them, Bohan said. Tony Blazoik, Frank Fratar and John de Franza, the Milwaukee trio, were brought here later. Two of them were convicted, but Blazoik jumped bail and is a fugitive.

U. S. HORSEMAN DIES SUDDENLY IN ENGLAND

Exclusive Dispatch to THE NEWS by Associated Press.

LONDON, Aug. 12.—Walter Winans, widely known American resident of London, collapsed and died while driving his horse, Henrietta Guy, in a race at Parsloes Park this afternoon.

Winans called out for his horse to be stopped, but before this could be done he fell off the sulky. He was dead when picked up.

ARRAIGN "THE CRANK" IN COUGHLIN MYSTERY

PHILADELPHIA, Aug. 12.—August Pascol, or Pasquale, "the crank" in the Baby Coughlin kidnaping case, will be arraigned on a formal charge before Justice of the Peace Clark in Norristown today.

He was taken to Norristown from this city this morning, after a "wild goose" chase yesterday to Egg Harbor and New Gretna, N. J., where Pascol said the Coughlin baby might be found.

CANADIAN STAR LEADS IN EARLY GOLF PLAY

Edgar Finishes First Round With Two Over Par; Columbus Man Second With 76.

Exclusive Dispatch to THE NEWS by Associated Press.

TOLEDO, O., Aug. 12.—Douglas Edgar, Canadian open champion, today led the early finishers in the first 18-hole round for the national open golf championship at Inverness with 38-35-73, two over par. This equalled his first qualifying round score and was eight better than his score of yesterday.

George Sargent, of Columbus, formerly champion, scored 76 today, one better than his pair of 77s made in qualifying, while M. J. Brady, runner-up to Hagen last year, took 77 today. Charles Thom, of New York, required 79 and Alex Ross, of Detroit, a former champion, 80.

Under lowering skies that threatened rain a large gallery followed Chick Evans, former champion, and Bob McDonald, of Chicago. The mist disturbed Evans' putting and with a few misses, including one of two feet on the ninth green, he required 38 strokes for the first nine. McDonald took 36. Edgar's card:

Out	5	5	3	4	5	4	4	3	5—38	
In	3	3	5	3	4	4	4	5	4—35	—73

Bobby Jones, of Atlanta, was off his game on the first nine, taking forty strokes. His putting was so atrocious at times that he displayed temper by throwing his club.

Jack Burke, who was second in the qualifying rounds with 146, took 75 for his first round.

James Barnes, of St. Louis, playing with Harry Vardon, scored 37 to the Briton's 38 on the first half.

Scores of the morning round:

Douglas Edgar, Atlanta, 38-35—73; Jack Burk, St. Paul, 37-38—75; George Sargent, Columbus, 39-37—76; E. F. Loeffler, Pittsburg, 36-40—76; M. J. Brady, Detroit, 40-37—77; William Kidd, Minneapolis, 40-37—77; Gil Nichols, New York, 40-37—77; Charles Hall, Birmingham, 40-37—77; Alex Cunningham, St. Joseph, Mo., 38-41—79; Charles Thom, New York, 39-40—79 (*)Harrison Johnston, Toledo, 39-41—80; Alex Ross, Detroit, 42-38—80; (*)John G. Anderson, New York, 40-42—82; Tom Kennett, Chicago, 40-42—82; J. J. O'Brien, Pittsburg, 41-41—82; Peter O'Hara, New York, 42-42—84.

LOCOMOTIVE BLAMED FOR BENZINE BLAZE

Fire destroyed twenty-four barrels of benzine at the Canfield Oil Company, E. 52d st. and the Wheeling & Lake Erie railroad, shortly before noon Thursday.

The benzine was in a large tank. It is believed sparks from the railroad started the blaze. The loss is $425.

Bergdoll Awaits Fate.

NEW YORK, Aug. 12.—The government was expected to conclude its case today against Erwin Rudolph Bergdoll, wealthy Philadelphian, who is being court-martialed on Governors island for desertion in evading the draft. It was considered possible that the defense also would rest its case.

Associated Ad Clubs Vote on New Chieftain

Twelve members of the executive committee of the Associated Advertising Clubs of the World met in Cleveland Thursday to consider the choice of a new president.

Charles A. Otis, head of Otis & Co., Cuyahoga building, who was named at the recent Indianapolis convention, has declared himself unable to assume the duties. The twelve, all of whom are vice presidents, met with Otis and Charles W. Mears, president of the Cleveland Advertising Club, at the club's headquarters in Hotel Statler.

Otis' successor was to be named late in the day.

KING OF HIGH FINANC UNABLE TO PAY; BAN IN BOSTON WIPED OU

Head of Syndicate Forestalls Action by Police; Declares Funds Drained; Wife Collapses as Her Idols Crash.

BULLETIN.

BOSTON, Aug. 12.—Bank Commissioner Allen announced this afternoon that the capital of the Hanover Trust Company probably had been completely wiped out. The bank was closed by the commissioner yesterday. Charles Ponzi had been a director up to yesterday.

BOSTON, Aug. 12.—Charles Ponzi, "money king," today surrendered to the United States marshal.

Ponzi was accompanied to the federal building by his counsel, Daniel H. Coakley, and United States District Attorney Gallagher.

Gallagher said that Ponzi had surrendered because he felt himself unable to carry out promises he had made for the redemption of his notes tomorrow.

Later Ponzi was formally placed under arrest by the federal authorities, charged with using the mails to defraud. Bail was fixed at $25,000.

At the time Ponzi gave himself up a hearing was being held before Judge Bennett, of the municipal court, sitting in chambers, on a police application for the arrest of the financier. The hearing was secret.

Seek Receivership.

A creditor's petition asking for appointment of a receiver for Ponzi was filed in the federal [illegible] day.

Mrs. Ponzi's condition was reported as pitiable. A physician is attending her. Some time prior to her husband's surrender she entirely collapsed.

Armed men guarded the Ponzi mansion in Lexington for hours before the surrender came. It was reported these men were detectives, put there to make certain Ponzi did not flee.

Displays Revolver.

Meanwhile, Ponzi paced his veranda, his hand clutching a revolver.

Ponzi today claimed a "bank oligarchy" was against him. He told reporters he would face the music and had no intention of fleeing the country.

He declared that he was going to prove he was "on the level" and added that his prison past had nothing to do with the present.

He seemed fearful that some attempt was to be made on his life, keeping his pistol handy at all times. Ponzi was informed that a fast automobile containing two men was loitering about the entrance to his grounds, apparently intent on following him if he left the house. He made no comment.

Seek Word of Warrant.

Ponzi expressed the fear he would be arrested on some technical violation of law and be deported by the same method.

Ponzi's attorneys were conce[rned] too, for they visited the courts [and] requested that they be notified i[f any] person applies for a warrant for P[onzi.] They said they would apply in fe[deral] court for a petition for a receive[r for] Ponzi's securities company.

TWO MEN HELD AS ROBBERS IN $35,000 THEFT

Witnesses Identify Suspects as Bandits in Bergman Diamond Gem Crime.

Two men were being held by police on Thursday for the sensational robbery of the jewelry store of Sol Bergman, 1969 E. 9th st., Tuesday morning. Two clerks were severely beaten in the raid and the loss was estimated at $35,000.

According to Detective Captain Matowitz three witnesses believe they recognize the pair as two of the three men who committed the robbery. However, he added, no one was positive in his identification.

The two men will be brought before other witnesses, Matowitz declared. He expressed himself as confident that police would be able to establish their conection with the holdup.

Bergman's store was raided as hundreds of people were passing to work. According to Frank Schuck and Jerome Susskind, the two clerks in the establishment, they were confronted by two men with guns shortly after they opened the place. The robbers ordered them to put up their hands, they said. After the two complied, the bandits gathered quantities of diamonds into a handbag. They beat the clerks over the head with their revolvers and dashed out the door.

Spectators in the street nearby said a machine, with engine running, was waiting for them. The two got into the car and it raced down Chestnut ave. to E. 11th st., down E. 11th st. to Payne ave. and disappeared out Payne ave.

Police said Thursday that the proprietor of the store, Sol Bergman, now claims the bandits' loot amounted to $50,000 instead of $35,000 as at first reported.

Held in Car Thefts.

Mrs. Francis Babvitch and George Podyed were bound over to the federal grand jury Thursday by Commissioner Maguire on charges of receiving stolen property. Federal authorities said $8,000 worth of clothing stolen from New York Central box cars was found in their homes. Mrs. Babvitch lives at 2144 Thames ave. and Podyed at 14927 Sylvia ave.

Employer of "Bianco" Thinks Ponzi Same M[an]

CHICAGO, Aug. 12.—Luiga Zar[rossi], an Italian whose tobacco business [w]as forced into bankruptcy in Montreal in 1907 through the defalcations of a bookkeeper, "Joseph Bianco" was located here today. Zarrossi declared that from what he had heard of the case of Charles Ponzi, the Boston banker, he believes Ponzi and "Bianco" may be the same man.

"In 1907 I fell ill and left my business to my manager, Anthony Russo," said Zarrossi. "When I recovered my business was wrecked. Papers were found which Russo said were forged. I was exonerated of any blame by the court, and Bianco was in prison. I went back to Italy.

"I remember Bianco and he seems to tally with this man Ponzi. Bianco was of small stature, about 5 feet 6 inches.

"If Ponzi is Bianco, his statement I forged anything or was involved in any criminal way while in Montreal is untrue."

Zarrossi has been in Chicago eleven years, most of which time he has been in the liquor business.

THE WEATHER

THE NEWS BAROMETER

Showers and thunder storms are probable Thursday night and Friday. Cooler Friday. Moderate variable winds, becoming west to north on Friday.

(Sea level) 11 a. m. 29.95

Urge Emerson Seek Common Plea Po[st]

Freinds of Congressman Emer[son] are urging him to run for comm[on] pleas judge and have volunteered [to] circulate petitions for the 2,500 s[ig]natures necessary to get his name [on] the non-partisan judicial ballot.

Only three Republicans sou[ght] party nominations for the four pla[ces] to be filled. If Emerson files, it [will] give the Republicans four condida[tes] on the non-partisan judicial bal[lot.] Should he be elected it probab[ly] would be necessary for him to resi[gn] from congress early in January.

DON'T MISS "THE BLACK SHEEP" By the Author of "The Woman Hater" IN FRIDAY'S NEWS

$6,000 GEM ROBBERY REVEALED

5 O'CLOCK

The Evening Wisconsin, Est. 1847
The Milwaukee Daily News, Est. 1885

MILWAUKEE, THURSDAY, [illegible]EMBER 16, 1920

PRICE 2 CENTS EVERYWHERE

BLAST ROCKS NEW YORK!

[illegible]day

...e 1,000,000 to 1.
...assenger Service.
...Week to Live.
...iers and Heroes.

By Arthur Brisbane

In Wall street the betting is 5 to 1 on Harding. The question is, What generous soul is putting up the one without the slightest chance of getting it back?

The issue in this election is the war League of Nations, which would take from the United States the independence that it won in 1776 and hand it back to a group of foreign nations controlled by England.

That the people of the United States will not vote to give up their independence is a 1,000,000 to 1, not a 5 to 1 bet.

Thanks to Mr. Burleson, government ownership of passenger service has begun in a small way, it is true, but in the right place. Contracts have been let to a Chicago firm and flying cars with wicker chairs, inclosed in glass and steel, will carry passengers as well as mail, and the United States will be the owner of the transportation.

As soon as the thing is a success "private ownership" will step in and kindly explain that the government is not able to do anything well. It is to be hoped that those soon to be in charge of the government will have the energy, once started, to keep on.

The most weak-kneed thing ever heard of was done by the Democratic administration, handing back railroads to private owners, after spending billions of the people's money rebuilding and re-equipping the roads and paying the highest profit to the private owners.

Mayor MacSwiney has gone without food for thirty-four days. His mental courage and interest in the fight that he is making may keep him alive ten days more. He probably cannot live longer than that.

He probably will die in the course of the coming week if England's attitude does not change. Meanwhile, the Irish correspondent of the London Times, owned by the son of an Irishwoman, says that if MacSwiney dies it will make it impossible for the Irish and English difficulty to be successfully arranged or compromised.

That, undoubtedly, is true. Every Irishman feels toward MacSwiney how as though he were his own son or brother. When he dies every Irishman will feel that he has been murdered.

The harm that will be done to England, and to English representatives in Ireland, should MacSwiney die, is clear to everybody. What good England hopes to achieve by allowing him to die is not clear here. There must exist an undercurrent of hatred in England, not understood in this country.

"News," so called, from Russia, tells of serious rioting against the Bolshevik government at Petrograd and "six of the Bolshevist commissioners" drowned. This is a variation in news of that kind. Usually Lenin kills Trotsky, or Trotsky kills Lenin. Neither has done that for some months.

Another kind of news, representing facts more closely, says the Russians are getting together an army of four and three-quarter millions and that Gen. Wrangle, who was supposed to restore ancient conditions and force payment of Russian bonds, has again been kicked out of the place where he most recently was.

All of this does not affect the United States much, as long as we keep our men out of Siberia and our country out of the League of Nations.

But when you read about that Russian army of four and three-quarter millions, you understand how glad other countries would be if they could trap old Uncle Sam in the League of Nations, and make it his business to take care of that Bolshevik crowd and finance that war.

..wo more flying men in the government mail service are killed, ...ed to death. This fills with hor... ...hose that learned to read quite ...ily about death in war.

Friends of the dead flyers have the satisfaction of knowing that they were soldiers and heroes in the truest sense, men fighting to achieve progress for all time, not fighting against other men, in quarrels to be renewed indefinitely.

Every tunnel built, almost every great building, means one to a hundred workmen's deaths. Perhaps an occasional dramatic death, in the flying service, will cause the public to appreciate the heroes of industry ...lled every week in blast furnaces, ...nels, railroad construction, with ...ands playing and no newspapers ...ise them.

...t Milwaukee

...'s Slogan.
"Milwauk... Have a $10,000,000 ...Dock."
Tomorr... Slogan.
"Milwaukee ...is Nation in T...king."

$6,000 GEM ROBBERY EXPOSED

Two Upper East Side Homes Entered; Posed as Meter Inspector.

Information now in the hands of Shorewood police and deputy sheriffs, points plainly that the "screen burglar," who has successfully looted more than a score of homes during the last month, is working with a "set of books" which contain valuable data, pertaining to homes which will be entered.

The homes entered on the upper East Side a month ago are: A. L. Frisch, 555 Wahl av., and Byron H. Abert, 936 Shepard av. The amount of jewelry taken from both is placed at $3,000 each.

Entrance to the homes were made by the ruse that the robber was connected with the Electric company and wanted to inspect the meters.

HOME IS GUARDED.

As a result of this discovery a Frederick av. home, one of the most exclusive residential streets in the city, is being carefully guarded by authorities on the theory that it is marked for a visit by the robber within the next 24 hours.

The clew which the investigators have obtained comes in the form of a scrap of paper bearing a name and address on Frederick av., which they refuse to give out. The scrap of paper was found in the eave trough of the A. E. Jackson home, 1547 Farwell av., an hour after that home had been visited by the robber early today.

The attempt to loot the Jackson home was unsuccessful. Members of the family, awakened by a loud crash of breaking wood, ran out on the porch of the home and saw a man fleeing across the yard in the dark.

Searching the yard, Mr. Jackson discovered a box standing near the corner of the porch. The top of the box had been broken by the robber, evidently while letting himself down from the roof of the porch.

POLICE FIND PAPER.

Police of Shorewood were called to the scene and the investigation of the ground and roof of the porch resulted in the finding of the paper.

Outside of the name and address

(Turn to Page 9, Column 4)

DOUBLE FUNERAL FOR BROTHER AND SISTER

PORTAGE, Wis.—James Sweaney, aged 75, and his sister, Miss Elizabeth Sweaney, aged 65, died a few hours apart on their farm in Fort Winnebago, near here. Both had been ill for several weeks of erysipelas. A double funeral was held yesterday from St. Mary's church in Portage, the Rev. J. J. Nicholas being assisted in the service by the Rev. Thomas Cosgrove of Fond du Lac and the Rev. McCarthy of Briggsville. The brother and sister had lived together for a great many years on the farm near Portage.

BOSTON STORE TO CLOSE FOR A. L. STONE FUNERAL

The Boston store will be closed all day Friday in tribute to its late vice president, Abraham L. Stone, who will be buried in Chicago tomorrow. Mr. Stone died Wednesday, after an illness of several weeks. He was a brother of Nat Stone, head of the Herzfeld-Phillipson company, which own the Boston store. The late Mr Stone was vice president and treasurer of the company, with which his son, Stanley, is also identified. Mr. Stone was 62 years old and was born in St. Louis.

"The Great Redeemer" Is Viewed by Clergymen

"The Great Redeemer," a photoplay with religious motive as its reason for existence, was viewed today at a private exhibition at the Strand theater.

The audience was composed of about 200 Milwaukee ministers, their wives, Christian Scientists, and leading exponents of the Catholic faith who had been invited by Manager Frank Cook to view the film and give their opinions of it. By this "acid test" Mr. Cook will determine whether or not he will book the photoplay for the Strand. Written criticisms will be sent by the guests to their host, Mr. Cook.

Maurice Tourneur is the producer of "The Great Redeemer;" Marjorie Daw and House Peters play the leading roles. The photoplay is founded on a story by H. H. Van Loan and released through Metro.

THINK BRENNER LEAPED TO DEATH

That Herbert Brenner, 19 year old chauffeur, who left a bundle of clothing and a note, in which he expressed his intention of ending his life, at the foot of Cherry st. bridge, actually leaped to his death in the river, was practically established today.

Mrs. Sarah Stein, 55 years old, 673 East Water st., reported to the police that early Tuesday morning, as she was returning from the public market at Fifth and Poplar sts., she saw a young man, coatless and hatless, standing at the north end of the bridge. A moment after she first caught sight of him, the man shouted, "Shoot me, shoot me," and leaped into the water, according to Mrs. Stein.

"I ran to the spot, but could see nothing of him. Meantime, I had cried out for help and a number of persons came running up. Then we discovered the bundle of clothing and cap, with the note, at the end of the bridge, just at the spot where I had seen the fellow standing. I was about 200 feet away when he leaped into the water."

If Brenner's body is in the water it probably has been carried out into the lake by the strong current, police say. Brenner was awaiting trial on a charge of operating an automobile without the owner's consent. Friends say he brooded over this fact.

LOST WILL COPY BRINGS HUSBAND $30,000 LOSS

The admission of a copy of the lost will of the late Anna K. Binder to probate today by County Judge M. S. Sheridan resulted in the loss of a $30,000 estate to Joseph Binder, widower and second husband of Mrs. Binder, and a distribution of the estate among her brothers, sisters, nieces and nephews.

At the time of her death, June 1, 1920, no will was found. There being no children, the estate according to probate law would go to her second husband, Joseph. A sister of Mrs. Binder objected, producing what was purported to be a copy of a lost will.

The lost will provided that the estate be divided between Charles F. Kargl, 553 Reed st.; Joseph Kargl, 552 Reed st., and Mrs. Mary Vogel, 553 Reed st., brothers and sister of the deceased. No provision was made for the widower, Joseph. A number of bequests were made to nieces and nephews.

MERRILL'S POPULATION REPORTED DECREASED

WASHINGTON—The 1920 population of Merrill was announced today as 8,068, a decrease of 7.1 per cent since 1910 or 621.

Richland Center, Wis., gained 28.5 per cent, having a population of 3,409.

RENT QUIZ TO COVER COUNTY

Bender Says Check Will Be Kept on Operations of All Landlords.

The rent bureau plans to investigate profits of all landlords in the county, it was announced today by Administrator Walter H. Bender, who has returned from a conference with the railroad rate commission at Madison.

Mr. Bender said that he was convinced that heretofore the bureau has only been scratching the surface and that, while relief has been granted in many cases, the great majority of tenants fear to make complaint because of the landlord's power to force them to move.

This condition has been unfair to the honest landlord, Mr. Bender pointed out, because scores of those who have been collecting exorbitant rents have thus far been unmolested.

REVIEW ALL PROFITS.

"We expect to have on file within a short time a card index system including every landlord in our county," said Mr. Bender, "together with the profits he is realizing. "We shall compile our lists from the office of the tax commissioner, the building inspector and other sources.

"All rents and profits will be reviewed and we will initiate action without a complaint from the tenant in those cases where the rents appear exorbitant.

"Scores of persons have been coming into the office to seek advice on purely hypothetical cases. They have refused to give the name of the landlord and put in a formal complaint. A close study of the situation has convinced me that we have been traveling only around the edges of the siuation and that something further ought to be done. We have had our hands full with the present staff but expect to increase it.

PROTECTION TO LANDLORDS.

"It should be understood that the rent bureau does not intend to adopt an inquisitorial and drastic attitude toward the landlords. The information we desire is not very detailed and can be easily given. We intend to protect the honest landlord as well as compel reductions where raises have been exorbitant.

"It is not fair that scores of landlords should be pursuing an equitable policy and others permitted to go on collecting excessive sums.

"Every landlord in our files will have to give us notification of proposed raises and each case will be reviewed. We feel that this in itself will make

(Turn to Page 9, Column 3)

PERCIVAL ROBERTS JR. REPORTED ASHORE

MACKINAW CITY, Mich. — The steamer Percival Roberts, Jr. of the Pittsburgh Steamship company, from Lake Superior to Lake Michigan with cargo of ore, is ashore on the north side of Round island. The wrecking tug Favorite is pulling on the stranded vessel. The small barge Snyder and consort are ashore on the south side of Mackinac island. Strong westerly winds, rain and fog when vessels went ashore.

OPEN FIGHT TO OBTAIN BAIL FOR CHAS. ROWAN

A fight to obtain bail for Charles Rowan, held for trial in federal court on a charge of using the mails to defraud, has been opened by his attorneys. Judge Geiger refused to grant Rowan bail when he was recaptured after jumping a bond of $10,000. A writ of habeas corpus, returnable next Wednesday, has been obtained at which time arguments will be heard. Rowan is charged with having obtained $100,000 from persons to whom he sold rabbits and guinea pigs on presentation that he would buy their offspring. This he failed to do, it is alleged.

30 DEAD, 200 HURT AT MORGAN'S OFFICE

NEW YORK—A mysterious explosion, disastrous in its effect, occurred at noon today in Wall st., killing 30 persons and injuring approximately 200.

Office workers were just hurrying into the street for their noon day meal when a jet of black smoke and flame rose from the center of the world's great street of finance.

MORGAN'S SON NEAR DEATH IN BLAST

JUNIUS SPENCER MORGAN.

THOMAS W. LAMONT.

HENRY W. DAVISON.

Above is shown Junius Spencer Morgan, son of the noted financier, who was in the Morgan firm's offices when the explosion occurred and was cut by flying glass.

Below are Thomas W. Lamont and Henry W. Davison, members of the firm. Both were in the office when it was wrecked by the explosion, but escaped injury.

Then came a blast. A moment later scores of men, women and children were lying, blood-covered on the pavements.

Two minutes later nearly all the exchanges had closed. Men had turned from barter to an errand or mercy.

While the police toiled for hours seeking the dead and injured, trained investigators were trying in vain to determine definitely whether the explosion had occurred from a bomb dropped in front of the office of J. P. Morgan & Co. or whether an automobile dashing into a wagon loaded with explosives had taken its toll.

Police announce they have found enough evidence to justify belief that the Morgan explosion was caused by a huge T. N. T. bomb, timed to explode at 12:01 p. m.

COLLISION THEORY.

Frank Francisco, one of the most able investigators of the department of justice, declared after arriving on the scene that it was his opinion that not a bomb plot but a collision had been responsible for the blast which rocked skyscrapers, tore the fronts from office buildings for blocks around and scattered deadly missiles in all directions.

The wall of the Morgan building on the Wall st. side is pitted with holes as if it had been bombarded by light caliber artillery.

Word reached here that William J. Flynn, chief of the United States secret service, was speeding to New York upon a special train to take charge of the federal end of the investigation.

The Broad st. hospital announced at 2 o'clock that it had treated nearly 200 people, mostly men, for injuries due to the explosion.

GIRLS AMONG DEAD.

According to a clerk in the Morgan offices at the time of the explosion three men and one girl employe of the Morgan house were killed. A number of the employes of the Equitable Trust company were injured and have been taken to the Broad st. hospital.

FIND WRECKED AUTO.

The first thing that occupied the attention of the investigators were wrecks of a truck and automobile at the spot from which the blast was believed to have come. From the wreckage were taken a New Jersey automobile license whose reported number corresponded with that issued to Dunham Beedon, a Newark pharmacist, who was reported this morning to have come to Wall Street on business.

Beedon later was found safe in an accountant's office at 52 Wall street. He said he had parked his car, which contained no explosive, in front of the building and behind another machine. He added that he knew no more of the explosion.

Federal investigators, soon to be headed by William J. Flynn, chief of the department of justice bureau of investigation, summoned from Washington, centered their attention on these wrecks.

Some advanced the theory that the automobile had collided with a powder wagon, and the Du Pont company was asked to find out whether any of its vehicles had been in the vicinity at the time.

Other investigators sought to run down reports that a bomb had been exploded in front of the Morgan building.

HOLD TO BOMB THEORY.

Assistant District Attorney Tally after visiting the scene, announced his belief that the explosion could not have been due to an accident.

He announced that his staff would question all witnesses of

(Turn to Page 2, Column 1.)

BIG NEWS

Two series of games starting today in the National and American leagues probably will decide definitely the two teams that will meet in the World's Series. These games will be between the New York and Chicago teams, American league, and the Brooklyn and Cincinnati teams, National league. By special arrangement, THE WISCONSIN NEWS will carry the stories of these two important series play by play as they are made. This extraordinary news service starts today in the Sporting Extra editions. This is a reading "treat" no one can afford to miss.

"All the News That's Fit to Print."

The New York Times.

THE WEATHER
Fair and warmer today; Sunday, fair; moderate to fresh west winds.
For weather report see next to last page.

VOL. LXX...No. 22,883. NEW YORK, SATURDAY, SEPTEMBER 18, 1920. TWO CENTS In Greater New York | THREE CENTS Within 200 Miles | FOUR CENTS Elsewhere

SEEK OWNER OF TRUCK THAT CARRIED BOMB TO WALL STREET; FISCHER, WHO SENT WARNINGS, UNDER ARREST IN CANADA; RED THREATS MAILED NEAR SCENE JUST BEFORE EXPLOSION

COX IN CALIFORNIA PORTRAYS HARDING AS A REACTIONARY

Says He Was Nominated and Is Sponsored by Group Whom Johnson Fought in 1912.

HITS "CHAMELEON" POLICY

Asserts Rival Reversed Himself in a Day to Meet Gov. Stephens on Oriental Question.

PLEDGES AID TO CALIFORNIA

Promises Full Co-operation When Question of Japanese Settlers Comes Up in Washington.

Special to The New York Times.

SAN FRANCISCO, Sept. 17.—Governor Cox invaded the home State of Senator Hiram W. Johnson today, talked progress in Government and the League of Nations, promised to co-operate with California when the question of Japanese exclusion should come before the Federal Government, and went in detail into his charge that Senator Harding was actually nominated in the room of a Chicago hotel by the same group of reactionary leaders whom Johnson assailed so bitterly in 1912.

Tonight Governor Cox spoke in the great convention hall where he was nominated by the Democratic National Convention last July. He was given a noisy and prolonged demonstration. He plunged first into a comparison of the scenes which had marked his selection "as a result of the unfettered and free expression of the delegates," and asserted that he went into the campaign a free man. The people of San Francisco who watched the convention, Governor Cox said, knew that to be the fact.

And then the Governor took the crowd over the ground at the Republican Convention in Chicago, quoting from a statement which he said Colonel George Harvey made "more in pride than in caution" an hour after Harvey's return to New York following the Republican Convention. It was in Colonel Harvey's room at Chicago, Governor Cox told the people, that Senators Smoot, Brandegee, Lodge and others whom he termed the "Senate oligarchy" cast Wood and Lowden and Johnson aside, and selected their own reactionary candidate.

"Custodians" for Harding.

"The small group of men that made the nomination," said Governor Cox, "has been the custodian of the candidate, sponsored and censored his spoken word and outlined his whole course. In grateful recognition Senator Harding, in his speech of acceptance, promises a plural government in contradiction to the conscience and personal responsibility of the President himself.

"The performance at Marion throughout the weeks has been the greatest political farce in the history of the country. Certain types of men are sent for, and as they leave the front porch prepared interviews are handed to the press. Everything works with mechanical precision. The hand of the masters is supreme, and the one objective is to deceive the public as to what is actually going on behind the scenes."

Taking up the Japanese question, Governor Cox charged that Senator Harding had altered his convictions on that, as well as on the League of Nations and other issues, to satisfy a delegation which came to him from California headed by Governor Stephens. Senator Harding's final statement was quite different from advance copies of his proposed address.

Says Harding Has Chameleon Policy.

"It all promises to the country a chameleon policy," said the Governor. Of his own position, Governor Cox said:

"If California does not desire her lands to come into the possession of Orientals, she may expect, in consequence with the established Democratic principle, the genuine co-operation of the National Government in the working out of a plan whereby she excludes the Oriental settler. There is nothing evasive about this."

Prior to speaking here, Governor Cox made an address to 5,000 people in the public plaza at Sacramento, the home of Senator Johnson.

In his address at San Francisco Governor Cox said in part:

"You can well imagine how deeply my emotions are stirred as I come into this great auditorium. Here it was that our platform was written and leadership in this campaign was established. It would seem fitting that the circumstances attendant upon this convention be recalled in order that a contrast based upon actual fact might be made in the public mind as between the San Francisco and the Chicago convention."

Continued on Page Seven.

Bomb on Genoa Exchange, But Causes No Casualties

LONDON, Sept. 17.—A time bomb was exploded at the Stock Exchange in Genoa today, says a dispatch to Exchange Telegraph from Genoa.

Some damage was done, but there were no casualties.

The authors of the outrage were not apprehended.

BOTH LOWDEN MEN LEAD IN ILLINOIS

Error of 6,463 Votes Puts Small Behind Lieutenant Governor Oglesby.

McKINLEY'S MARGIN GAINS

But Official Canvass Will Probably Be Needed to Decide the Winners.

Special to The New York Times.

CHICAGO, Sept. 17.—The result of Wednesday's voting in the Republican primary is still in doubt, and it will probably require an official canvass to determine the successful candidates for the gubernatorial and senatorial nominations. John G. Oglesby, the Lowden candidate for Governor, jumped into the lead today over Len Small, in the incomplete election returns.

An error of 6,463 votes was discovered by the City News Bureau in its totals for Small in the Thirty-second Ward, and reduced his city lead by that much.

Representative William B. McKinley, another Lowden candidate, increased his margin for Senator over Governor Frank L. Smith.

Returns from 5,372 out of 5,737 precincts in the State, including all except 97 precincts down-State and 268 in Cook County, give for Governor: Oglesby, 349,795; Small, 345,649. Oglesby's lead, 4,146.

Oglesby's managers assert that official figures will give him 10,000 plurality. Small's managers make similar claims for him.

Small issued a statement that he had won by more than 30,000, stating that "false reports to the contrary are being circulated for the purpose of encouraging the stealing of votes from me and the falsifying of returns."

Returns from 5,330 precincts, including all except 139 precincts down-State and 268 in Cook County, give for Senator: McKinley, 344,391; Smith, 329,824. McKinley's lead, 14,574.

On Attorney General, the latest figures indicate that Edward J. Brundage, anti-Thompson candidate, has a plurality of about 7,500 in the entire State.

The General Assembly remains Republican and dry. There will be no chance for a revocation of the State search and seizure law or amending it to increase the alcoholic content of beverages to more than half of 1 per cent.

Action by the City Council of Chicago to take from Mayor Thompson the power to control the Police Department in connection with election returns was urged today by James Sullivan, Chief Clerk of the Election Commissioners' office. Plans are under way to call a special meeting of the Council to pass an ordinance to be put into effect before Election Day.

CHICAGO, Sept. 17.—Final revision of returns on the Republican ballot in the Congressional primaries outside of Cook County today showed the successful aspirants were as follows:

10th District—Carl R. Chindblom.
11th District—Ira C. Copley.
14th District—William J. Graham.
16th District—Clifford Ireland.
17th District—Frank H. Funk.
18th District—Joseph G. Cannon.
19th District—Allen F. Moore.
21st District—Loren E. Wheeler.
22d District—William A. Rodenberg.

Of the five Democratic contests for Congressional nominations, only one, that in the Tenth District, was settled tonight. John H. Haderlein was nominated to oppose Representative Chindblom in November.

MACSWINEY 'VERY LOW,' SAYS LATEST BULLETIN

Prisoner Rallies in the Afternoon and Then Relapses—He Is Still Conscious.

LONDON, Sept. 17.—The condition of Lord Mayor MacSwiney of Cork was described as very low in the Irish Self-Determination League's bulletin issued tonight. The bulletin says: "Lord Mayor MacSwiney is very low indeed. He is suffering from severe pains in the head. He is still conscious."

An earlier bulletin said:

"Mrs. MacSwiney, who was with the Lord Mayor all afternoon, said he rallied in the early part of the afternoon but later collapsed again. She reported he was conscious, but very exhausted and in great pain."

MacSwiney passed a somewhat better night and had a little sleep, said a bulletin issued at 10 o'clock this morning by the Irish Self-Determination League.

In his report to the Home Office, the physician at Brixton Prison declared there was no change in the Lord Mayor's condition except that a gradual deterioration was noticeable daily.

FISCHER CALLED INSANE

Hamilton, Ont., Doctors Recommend Sending Him to Asylum.

HEARD "MESSAGE FROM AIR"

Deportation Warrant Asked For —Prisoner Held to Await Our Demand.

WARNED FIVE FRIENDS

Sent Post Cards to Three Here and Predicted Explosion Verbally Before Leaving City.

Special to The New York Times.

HAMILTON, Ont., Sept. 17.—Edwin P. Fischer, the New Yorker who sent post cards to New York friends warning them of an impending catastrophe in Wall Street, is under arrest here. He was placed in custody at the request of his brother-in-law, Robert A. Pope, also of New York and formerly a resident of Hamilton, who has been in this city lately as a landscape gardener for a syndicate laying out a model residential site. Pope based his action on the ground that Fischer is mentally irresponsible and wants him committed to a sanitarium. Several Hamilton doctors have testified that Fischer is mentally unfit to be at large.

H. S. Sweeney, Canadian Immigration Agent here, applied tonight for an order for the deportation of Fischer to the United States. The reason given in the application is that Fischer is illegally in Canada, having previously been confined in a sanitarium for mental diseases in the United States.

No request for extradition has yet been made by New York or United States authorities, but that may come with the officer now on the way to Hamilton. Pending this officer's arrival the charge against Fischer will remain as that of insanity.

In the meantime he is held in the Barton Street Jail here, awaiting the arrival of a detective from New York, who is on his way here in the hope of taking him back as a witness before the Grand Jury. There may be a hot legal battle over the disposition of Fischer, his brother-in-law and his friends desiring that he be sent to a sanitarium or asylum, while the New York authorities want him in that city as soon as possible.

Strangely enough, both Fischer and Pope are in accord on one thing. They believe that Fischer received messages "through the air" warning him of a plot for the explosion in Wall Street. Pope heard last night of Fischer's eccentric actions in a Toronto hotel and his reported threats against millionaires. He motored to Toronto in search of Fischer, found that he had gone to Niagara Falls and followed him there. He persuaded Fischer to come to this city, where both have a number of friends, and had him placed in custody.

"I am convinced," said Mr. Pope today, "that my brother-in-law while in his abnormal mental condition received impressions communicated from the minds of men who were plotting the outrage. On the other hand, in view of the unrest prevalent in the world today, it is just likely that a man in that condition would predict such a disaster to the financial centre of the continent, and a coincidence is possible."

Fischer, himself, when taken before a lunacy commission, consisting of Magistrate Jelfs and Drs. McGillivray and Rosebrough, immediately after his arrest, declared his belief in the theory advanced by Pope.

"I don't know where the message came from—through the air, I guess. I have lived a life of hopefulness and unselfishness. I have never held a grudge against any one, and have always tried to do good to everybody. For this reason I think that God has perhaps given me a power that has not been given to those who lead selfish lives.

"I know when anything awful is going to happen. I know that something terrible is happening right now, because I have that same pain across my forehead which came before the Wall Street explosion."

Magistrate Jelfs asked:

"How did you know exactly when the explosion was going to be?"

"I know," Fischer answered, "because Wall Street is the centre of evil in the world. There is the Stock Exchange. My brother-in-law got in with a firm there. They gave him a buy-and-sell agreement and took all his money. That cost him $15,000. There are stockbrokers there who change their books every three months—get rid of the old books and the old customers."

The two physicians on the commission agreed that Fischer was not responsible. They examined him privately as well as at the hearing. Dr. McGillivray says that Fischer appeared to have an antipathy to J. Pierpont Morgan and President Wilson; this he thought was of recent origin and entirely the product of his present mental derangement.

This evening Pope conferred with his legal advisers, T. H. Sloane, and Vincent Paul Creighton and William L. Buchanan, two special agents from Buffalo, representing the United States Department of Justice and Charles Arien, a

Continued on Page Two.

Ex-Service Men Organize To Seek Punishment of Reds

William J. Burns, head of the Burns Detective Agency, last night at his home, 42 West Seventy-second Street, issued the following statement:

"Today I was approached by a group of ex-service men of various former divisions of the United States Army wanting to employ my services to run down the perpetrators of yesterday's dastardly bomb outrage.

"They expressed their deep and intense indignation at the fact that several of their former comrades were killed and injured. They also pointed out that this outrage was apparently not aimed at any individual or group of individuals, but at organized government, and recalled that the Reds have frequently denounced our form of government and declared their intention of bringing about a revolution by terrorism.

"These former soldiers further told me they had raised among themselves $526 as a starter for a reward for the apprehension of those responsible for this outrage, and stated they were determined to increase this sum through contributions from the thousands of ex-service men throughout the country."

Mr. Burns said that he expected to confer with the men today, when he will make known his decision.

PALMER COMES HERE TO DIRECT INQUIRY

Attorney General Accompanied by F. P. Garvan, Who Investigated Enemy Aliens.

"TERRORIST" PLOT IS SEEN

Federal Officials Believe Explosion Was Work of Anarchists —Experts Coming.

Special to The New York Times.

WASHINGTON, Sept. 17.—Attorney General A. Mitchell Palmer and Francis P. Garvan, assistant Attorney General in charge of the Government's anti-radical campaign, left Washington for New York City today to direct the main investigation of the explosion in Wall Street. They were to confer with William J. Flynn, head of the department's Bureau of Investigation, regarding the evidence so far obtained.

Chief Flynn has made preliminary reports to the Department of Justice and officials here are abreast of the evidence so far uncovered by him. The Government officials here are convinced that the explosion was caused by an unusually powerful time bomb deliberately placed at Broad and Wall Streets by an anarchistic group.

They are satisfied that the bomb was hauled to the vicinity of the United States Sub-Treasury and the Morgan bank on a wagon, splintered fragments of which were found after the tragedy, and that the infernal machine was timed for explosion at noon. This wagon, which was not a "red" vehicle as at first reported, was drawn by a horse which was killed in the explosion, but there is no evidence indicating that those who were responsible for placing the wagon and its load of danger at the designated spot were injured by the bomb.

Believed an "Act of Terrorism."

All the evidence that has been gathered by Flynn and operatives working with him in New York City has been rather carefully sifted and has convinced Government officials that the bomb was exploded as an "act of general terrorism," believed to have been aimed against the Federal Government as well as against American capital.

There is no evidence, however, it was asserted today, to show that this explosion was to be accompanied at this time by any widespread series of similar acts in other cities. Reports to the Department of Justice show that extra precautions have been taken in various parts of the country for the protection of Federal structures and financial institutions. No extra guards, so far as Federal officials will admit, have yet been placed around Government buildings in Washington, but instructions have been given to Government watchmen, guards and to the police in the nation's capital to be especially on the alert.

As a result of the developments there is every indication that there will be an early roundup of anarchists and "Reds." It was pointed out that the only Federal law violated in the explosion of the bomb was that which provides punishment for injury to public property—the Sub-Treasury being Government property—and it was indicated that the Federal Government's investigation will deal chiefly with the extent to which radicals were implicated.

One official, when asked whether any "Red" or anarchistic literature had been discovered in the vicinity of Broad and Wall Street, replied:

"I hope you will not press that question."

Explosive experts were assigned by the United States Bureau of Mines today to

Continued on Page Two.

CIRCULARS CLUE TO PLOT

Show That Explosion Was the Work of Anarchists, Says Flynn.

LIKE BOMB ATTACKS IN 1919

Demand to Free Political Prisoners, Signed "American Anarchist Fighters."

PALMER ORDERS PUBLICITY

Threats Dropped in Mail Box by Men Who Planted Explosive, Investigator Asserts.

Evidence that has convinced Government investigators that the explosion in Wall Street was caused by a bomb planted by the same group of anarchists who perpetrated the bomb outrages of June, 1919, was made public in New York late last night by William J. Flynn, Chief of the Bureau of Investigation, Department of Justice.

This evidence was in the form of five rough sheets of paper on which had been printed in red ink:

> Remember
> We will not tolerate
> any longer.
> Free the political
> prisoners or it will be
> sure death for all of you.
> American Anarchist Fighters.

Some of the words in this warning were misspelled. The misspelling is not given because it varied on the different sheets.

These circulars, which Chief Flynn referred to as a "challenge to the American Government," were found by a letter carrier in a mailbox at the southwest corner of Cedar Street and Broadway, about two and one-half blocks, or four minutes' walk, from the spot where the bomb exploded, at 11:58 A. M. on Thursday. They were turned over to Chief Flynn by Chief Post Office Inspector Cochran and were made public by order of United States Attorney General A. Mitchell Palmer, who arrived from Washington last night to take charge of the investigation by the Federal Government.

"It will be recalled," Chief Flynn said, "that the circulars in connection with the bomb outrages of June, 1919, were similarly misspelled, and similarly printed by single rubber-typed stamps. It also will be remembered that those bombs pitted walls as did this one.

Found Just Before Explosion.

"The letter carrier had opened that box at Cedar Street at 11:30 and had found it empty. When he found the five circulars stuffed into it, without wrapping of any sort, at 11:58 he went on to Church Street. He heard a noise which he later learned was the explosion. He turned the circulars over to Mr. Cochran.

"This makes the plan of the bombers fairly clear. They left the wagon with the horse attached in Wall Street, having set the timing device a few moments ahead. They didn't want to take a chance of mailing them. They didn't want to throw them into the street. As they walked away from the scene of their crime, which resulted in the death of so many innocent and law-abiding citizens, they stuffed them in the box. Three minutes later their bomb had exploded.

"There is no doubt at all in my mind that this is about what happened. The fact that the box was empty when the letter carrier visited it at 11:30 and that the circulars were in it at 11:58, so close to the time of the explosion, and so close to the scene of it, carries conviction.

"This is one of the most important clues we have, but, of course, the identification of the horse and wagon that carried the infernal machine to Wall Street is paramount. If we can identify that we should have clear sailing.

"The witnesses thus far examined have told us that the horse was facing east, which is against traffic regulations. However, terrorists would be in a hurry under the circumstances, and probably wouldn't care much about traffic regulations.

"No clockwork has been found—and it shouldn't be expected that any would be left. No metal parts were found in the débris left by the bombs of June 2, 1919, either. But we are reasonably sure that a time device was used. A fuse would have smoked. Some one might have smelled it. The clock arrangement would be safest.

"You might add as an expression of my personal opinion that the bomb was not directed at Mr. Morgan, any member of the Morgan firm, or any other individual. It was planted in the financial heart of America as a defiance against the American people and the American Government. That is my opinion.

"The other circulars we have found have been signed simply 'anarchist fighters.' You may see from these copies that they have added 'American' to their title now.

"The printing indicates that the work

Continued on Page Three.

Horseshoes a Clue to the Explosion Truck; Give Lead That May Identify the Owner

HACKENSACK, N. J., Sept. 17.—The horseshoes found on the shattered animal when examined after the Wall Street explosion may furnish the clue to the identity of the driver of the truck believed to have carried the bomb. Detectives are reported to have found a blacksmith who had partly identified the shoes found on the dead horse.

This information was furnished today by Colonel William Mead, chief clerk for J. P. Morgan & Co. He lives at 52 Euclid Avenue, Hackensack.

"We feel that the explosion was premeditated and that a deliberate attempt was made to destroy the building of J. P. Morgan & Co. and to kill and injure as many people as possible. Cast iron slugs and other evidences of a bomb have been found. The most likely story of the explosion is that a red wagon drawn by a horse stopped on the left side of the curb facing east on Wall Street and directly in the centre of the Morgan Building. A man most likely then set the large bomb in the wagon to explode at 12 o'clock noon and then walked away.

"We have found parts of the wagon and shoes of the horse. These shoes are expected to aid materially in solving the mystery attending the tragedy, for we have found the blacksmith who shod the horse and who claims to know the man who owns the animal."

PATRIOTIC SPIRIT STIRS WALL STREET

Noonday Crowds Turn from Murder Scenes to Observe Constitution Day.

VOW JUSTICE TO ASSASSINS

Brig. Gen. Nicholson Denounces Outrage and Calls for Plotters' Deaths.

Noon and the murder hour had come again to Wall Street and, at the spot where enemies of America twenty-four hours before had slain and maimed, this is what happened:

At the base of Washington's statue on the Sub-Treasury steps, maybe twenty feet from the jagged mark of the bomb, a tall soldier, with a single silver star on each shoulder, was standing at the salute. Down Broad Street to the point where the street seemed to touch the sky, thousands and thousands were standing with bared heads. East and west through Wall Street and north into Nassau Street were other thousands.

Welling in thousand-throated chorus up between the skyscraper cathedrals of commerce, pocked by the assassins' work, the last bars of "America" were going—the preliminary to the observance by the Sons of the American Revolution of the 133d anniversary of the adoption of the Constitution of the United States.

The anthem ended. A silence, complete, significant, was on the great throng. The Brigadier General, William J. Nicholson, turned and faced them. Alluding to Constitution Day and what it should mean, the overseas leader of the 79th Division told of the rights and responsibilities of freemen in such a country as America. The greatest trouble in this country, he told them, is that people think more about their responsibilities. Then he seemed to stretch himself taller. And leaning forward in his earnestness he said:

Nicholson Denounces Outrage.

"Yesterday one of the greatest outrages ever committed against society was perpetrated on the very spot on which we stand. Are we, as American citizens, going to close our eyes to things like that? I say no, a thousand times no!"

"No!" came the mighty response and cheering started. The speaker checked them at once and continued:

"If a crime really has been committed it is the duty of every man here to take a solemn oath to do all he can to bring these vampires to justice. No man who would take part in such a crime has any right in any community, not even in his own. Those who would do such a thing should be killed every time they show their heads. They should be killed like a snake!"

Swelling, rising, thrilling came the answer, a sound so great it could almost be seen. The answer was "Yes!"

The speaker ended. A man sprang up in his place. Waving his hands he began "The Star-Spangled Banner," and again the vast harmonization of thousands rang out.

"O'er the land of the free and the home of the brave!" came the anthem's close and from the base of the statue came the roll of a drummer and the shrill notes of a fifer, both in Revolutionary costume. Two hundred Sons of the American Revolution fell in back of General Oliver B. Bridgman and Colonel Louis Annin Ames and marched off—leaving the spirt of '76 where the day before had been the spirit of hate.

That was the climax and the contrast of the day after in Wall Street, a street which made valiant efforts to get back to normal and almost succeeded, although from early to late hundreds of thousands filtered through the canyon to see the effects of the explosion.

Working throughout the night, city and private laborers managed to clear the streets of débris. Thirty big acetylene arcs, at strategic points, threw powerful beams on the toilers carrying

Continued on Page Three.

CITY-WIDE SEARCH FOR TRUCK OWNER

200 Detectives Canvass Farrier Shops for Clue to Identity of Bomb Driver.

WAGON YELLOW, NOT RED

Story Vehicle Was Dynamite Delivery Cart Discredited —Time Bomb Theory.

Failure of anybody yesterday to admit ownership of the horse and truck blown up in the Wall Street explosion convinced detectives, operatives of the Department of Justice and Secret Service agents that the blast was due to a time bomb placed in the vehicle by radicals. Evidence of that belief was presented in the attitude of officials of the Detective Bureau, who early yesterday morning established a miniature museum at Police Headquarters, where the remnants of the horse's harness, as well as shattered pieces of the vehicle recovered by the police soon after the explosion, were placed on exhibition in the hope that somebody would come forward to identify them.

If the motive for the explosion ever is discovered, detectives said yesterday, it is more than likely it will be through the identity of the owner of the vehicle. They pointed out that, unlike most of the bomb outrages in this city, the police in this case have something to work on to establish the identity of the perpetrators through the possession of the pieces of harness and the twisted mass of axles and other parts of the truck as well as the head and hoofs of the dead horse, which recently had been shod.

200 Detectives Engaged in Canvass.

More than two hundred detectives yesterday continued the canvass of stables and horseshoeing establishments in the five boroughs which was started by Captain John Coughlin, Acting Inspector in charge of the Detective Bureau, less than an hour after the explosion. Each detective was instructed to notify Inspector Coughlin by telephone if he obtained information which might establish the identity of the owner of the horse and wagon. A special force of detectives was assigned to handle reports from detectives assigned to the work as well as those from Captains who, under an order from Chief Inspector Lahey Thursday afternoon, instructed the uniformed men under them to aid the detectives in the quest.

That the ownership of the horse and wagon was considered the most promising clew of the police and Government officials engaged in the investigation was evidenced by the fact that agents of the department, on instructions from William J. Flynn, former Deputy Police Commissioner and head of the United States Secret Service, visited many farriers and stables in different parts of the city, and it was said that in most instances the Government agents acted on mysterious tips and anonymous letters received by Chief Flynn at his office during the day.

Clew in Horse's Hoof.

It was learned at Police Headquarters yesterday that expert horsemen in the Police Department had been called on to aid the detectives in establishing the identity of the owner of the vehicle. These policemen were called on to decide whether it would be possible for a person to identify the head of the horse, which is being preserved by the police. It was said that all of the horsemen said that the owner of the animal would have no trouble in identifying it as the head was the one part of the body not affected by the blast. These policemen, it is understood, measured the head and estimated the probable height of the animal.

Farriers in the Police Department as well as policemen who were horseshoers before they joined the force, were called in to aid in running down the owner through the shoes taken from the

Continued on Page Two.

DEATH LIST MOUNTS TO 33

All Investigators Are Now Convinced Bomb Caused Disaster.

ACCIDENT IS ELIMINATED

$20,000 Reward Offered for Criminal and $500 for Owner of Truck.

GRAND JURY BEGINS INQUIRY

Palmer and Garvan Here to Direct Federal Investigation —First Funerals Today.

All competent investigating authorities yesterday reached the conviction that Thursday's disaster in Wall Street was a willfully criminal bomb explosion.

With the whole weight of expert opinion solidly against any hypothesis of accident, the entire energy of Government agents, the District Attorney's office and the police was directed to tracing the horse and wagon on which they are virtually certain the infernal contrivance stood before the new Assay Office.

Colonel William C. Mead of 52 Euclid Avenue, Hackensack, N. J., chief clerk for J. P. Morgan & Co., whose banking house shared with the new Assay Office the greater brunt of the terrific detonation, announced last night that the man who shod the horse had been found. Colonel Mead said this blacksmith asserted he knew the owner of the horse. The Colonel did not amplify this information, and in official circles there was impressive reticence regarding it.

The authorities did not even verify the discovery of evidence of such profound importance, though throughout their first full day of investigation they frankly had regarded the identity of the vehicle's ownership as the pivotal point upon which must hinge any successful effort to find and punish the guilty.

$20,500 Rewards Offered.

So much emphasis was laid upon the need for finding out who owned the horse and wagon, who drove it, and from where it had come, that the Board of Estimate, at a special meeting called by Mayor Hylan after offering a reward of $10,000 for the arrest and conviction of the single criminal or the conspirators involved, proffered an additional $500 to any one who could solve that question of ownership. The Preferred Accident Insurance Company offered another $10,000 for identification and conviction, making a total of $20,500 to stimulate the hunt.

The conclusion that the explosion was a piece of calculated, cunningly planned and deftly executed wholesale murder rested upon the results of three lines of investigation—study of the aftermath by men with wide knowledge of explosives and their behavior, autopsies by skilled pathologists on the bodies of many victims, and the elimination by the Fire Department's Bureau of Combustibles of any tenable belief in an accident connected with the lawful transport of explosive.

Minute consideration of the iron slugs, the bits of curved, caplike metal, the scars on buildings, the hole under the spot where stood the wagon, the nature and direction and force of the blast, the heat and light accompanying the detonation and other technical minutiae left no doubt in informed minds that a bomb did the deadly work.

Experts Reconstruct Bomb.

British experts long familiar with air raids in London and elsewhere went further and reconstructed by deduction a powerful torpedo-like bomb, loaded with TNT and equipped with detonator and time device, very similar except for the time device to the aerial torpedoes which wrought such havoc abroad. There appeared to be no foundation for published reports that clockwork was found near the Sub-Treasury.

The autopsies and examination of the wounds of many injured in the hospitals removed the last trace of doubt from the minds of such men as Dr. Charles Norris, the city's chief medical examiner, and Dr. Otto H. Schultze, District Attorney Swann's medical expert. They reached the conclusion that only missiles incorporated, shrapnel fashion, in a device deliberately constructed to kill could have inflicted such injuries.

The Fire Department's careful inquiry led to a report that all explosives lawfully in the city were accounted for and neither unavoidable accident nor criminal carelessness longer could be taken into consideration. At the same time it developed that the DuPont "powder" wagons, the reported presence of which in the vicinity caused such confusion, in reality were trucks carrying non-explosive by-products. They, too, are accounted for.

Flynn Convinced It Was Bomb.

Heeding the opinions of these various experts and weighing all evidence gathered by his own men and the police, William J. Flynn, former head of the Secret Service and now Chief of the Department of Justice Bureau of Investigation, announced that he too was converted definitely to belief in a criminal outrage.

Neither Mr. Flynn nor his subordinates, the police nor the District Attor-

June Daily Circulation 32,087

AKRON BEACON JOURNAL.

FINAL EDITION

FIFTY-FIRST YEAR | No. 205 | AKRON, OHIO, MONDAY EVENING, AUGUST 1, 1921. | (SIXTEEN PAGES) | PRICE TWO CENTS

SID HATFIELD AND CHAMBERS SHOT

World News Quickly Told

CRUSHED BY TRUCK
SANDUSKY, O., Aug. 1. — Jay W. Garrison, 33, Pennsylvania car inspector, was run down by a heavy truck loaded with sand in front of St. Mary's Catholic church this morning. His head was crushed off by a wheel.

FALL PROVES FATAL
GALION, O., Aug. 1. — Joshua Summers, 69, is dead of injuries sustained when he fell from the hay loft of his barn, a distance of 20 feet.

TO CREATE FIVE CARDINALS
ROME, Aug. 1. — A consistory will be held at the Vatican in October when five new cardinals probably will be created, including one American, it was learned in Vatican circles today.

MAY AID RUSSIA
LONDON, Aug. 1. — It is highly probable that the supreme council will take up the Russian famine situation when it meets. Premier Lloyd George announced in the house of commons this afternoon. Questioned about reports that Poland and Rumania were massing troops on the Russian frontiers the premier said he was not aware of any exceptional concentration.

AMERICANS FINISH THIRD
COWES, Eng., Aug. 1. — The Americans finished third in the yacht race for the British-American cup at the Cowes regatta today. The British Thrift Poll was first, the Fly, also British, was second, and the American boat Sheila, third. The craft were of the six meter class.

MOTOR CAR OVERTURNS
MADISONVILLE, Ky., Aug. 1. — Frank Daves, 21, of Milan, Tenn., was killed, and Adair Stum, 20, son of a local banker, was probably fatally hurt when Stum's auto was overturned near this city.

REVOLT ADDS TERRORS
PARIS, Aug. 1. — A revolutionary uprising has added fresh terrors to the terrible famine and plague situation in Russia, but the government troops are crushing the rebels, said a [illegible]

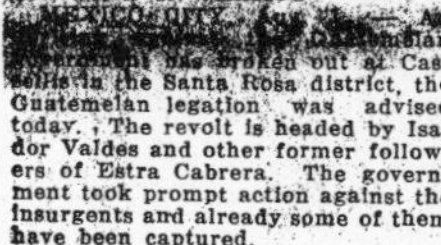

UPRISING IN MEXICO
[illegible] the Santa Rosa district, the Guatemalan legation was advised today. The revolt is headed by Isaac Valdes and other former followers of Estra Cabrera. The government took prompt action against the insurgents and already some of them have been captured.

HOOVER GETS REPLY FROM MAXIM GORKY

WASHINGTON, Aug. 1.—Secretary of Commerce Hoover today received a reply from Maxim Gorky to his recent communication setting forth the terms upon which American relief would be furnished to famine stricken Russia.

The reply, which came by way of Riga and London, now is being considered, Secretary Hoover stated. No details were made public, but it is believed to be an acceptance of the conditions imposed by Hoover that American prisoners in Russia must be released before American famine relief would be forthcoming.

Sale Of Illicit Liquor Has Made This Woman Rich, Declares McGuire

When Anna Schaaf, 46, 706 Home av., is arraigned for having liquor in her possession and a still for manufacturing whisky, a charge upon which she was arrested Saturday night, Lieut. McGuire head of the vice squad declared today he would cite her case as an example of the profit to be derived in the manufacture of illicit liquor.

The lieutenant said today that the woman was arrested eight months ago on a similar charge and because of her destitute circumstances was released by the court. He now says an investigation revealed that she owns three lots and a $12,000 brick house. Citing her case as the results of leniency by court judges, the lieutenant indicated that he would plead for the maximum penalty for the defendant.

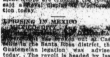

OHIO WEATHER

COLUMBUS, Aug. 1. — Showers tonight and Tuesday; not much change in temperature.

The temperature Monday morning at 9 o'clock was 68. Sunday the highest temperature was 72 and the lowest 55.

Atlantic city, clear	64	66
Boston, pt. cloudy	68	78
Chicago, pt. cloudy	68	72
Cleveland, pt. cloudy	67	70
Cincinnati, clear	80	80
Detroit, pt. cloudy	70	72
Duluth, pt. cloudy	68	76
Jacksonville, cloudy	88	92
Knoxville, cloudy	76	92
Memphis, rain	78	86
Montgomery, clear	94	98
New Orleans, clear	86	96
New York, clear	78	86
Pittsburg, pt. cloudy	68	80
Toledo, clear	70	72
Washington, clear	80	92
Galveston, clear	82	88
Los Angeles, clear	72	74
San Francisco, pt. cloudy	60	64
Portland, clear	80	82

SUMMIT CO. PEOPLE INJURED IN STORM WHICH SWEPT CAMP

Wife of Major Johnston Struck By Falling Pole—Many Narrow Escapes

BARBERTON CROWD HIT

Mrs. Joseph J. Johnston, wife of Major Johnston of the First Cav. O. N. G., suffered painful injuries Saturday night during the terrific storm which wrecked buildings and tents at Camp Perry on Lake Erie where the National Guard soldiers are encamped.

Details of the injury to Mrs. Johnston were lacking but it was stated that the pole which was guying wires leading to other poles snapped when the strain became too great and fell just as Mrs. Johnston was hurrying past to gain shelter. It was reported that although painful her injuries were not serious.

Elnora, the 10-year-old daughter of Major and Mrs. H. A. Rodenbaugh of Barberton, became confused by the storm and wandered into the lake, the while crying for help but being unable to see her way because of the storm and total darkness.

Mrs. Rodenbaugh, hearing her daughter's cries followed for a distance of 100 feet into the lake. the water being four feet deep in places and was aided in her search for her child by a photographic flashlight which some one on shore had the presence of mind to use. The child and her mother were enabled to reach shore and safety by this light.

Scantily Clothed.

During this time Major Rodenbaugh was occupied at the hospital assisting in caring for the injured and nervous people. Tents in the camp were blown down and clothing of the occupants was scattered and drenched by the storm which blew at the rate of 60 miles an hour.

Automobiles which were parked in the open lost their tops, and some of the interior fittings and many Akron and Barberton folks who lost their belongings in the wrecked conditions of the camp following Saturday night's storm, came home in scant attire, some wearing bathing suits and others attired in pajamas.

The storm broke over West Hill in Akron shortly before 2 o'clock Sunday morning, and confined the damage to felling trees. This kept the forces of the service department busy all day Sunday and Monday. Some telephone wires were dislocated and the trouble crews worked all day Sunday and all Sunday night to make repairs. The force of the storm shattered a heavy plate glass window of the north court room on the third floor of the court house.

NO WORD RECEIVED FROM SINN FEINERS

LONDON, Aug. 1.—The Irish settlement still is pending and no move will be made by the British government until the Sinn Fein at Dublin takes decisive action.

Premier Lloyd George declared this afternoon in statement in the house of commons:

"The Sinn Fein has not yet replied to the government's terms. Consequently I am unable to make a statement at this time."

NEW POLITICAL CRISIS THREATENS IN PORTUGAL

LONDON, Aug. 1.— The Portuguese legation anxiously awaited word from Lisbon today regarding the new political crisis in the Portuguese capital.

According to a dispatch to the Daily Mail from the Spanish-Portuguese frontier the Lisbon garrison was suddenly called out to picket the streets, while cannon were planted to sweep the public squares. The cabinet met to discuss the situation.

GERMANY SENDS HELP TO RUSSIAN VICTIMS

By FRANK E. MASON.

BERLIN, Aug. 1.—The German Red Cross has heeded Russia's cry for help. Announcement was made today that a ship is being loaded with medical supplies with which to fight the Russian cholera plague. It will be sent to Petrograd. A number of German doctors are going with the medicine to cooperate with the Russian Red Cross.

The Petrograd correspondent of the German newspaper says: "The discipline of the workers has broken down, but there is practically no work because there is no raw materials, no iron, no coal, no nails for building and no tools. In Petrograd the ration of bread is one pound daily. The people are supposed to get a quarter of a pound of sugar monthly and some times they get a pound of dried fish. Speculators are profiteering in the little stocks of butter, coffee, lard, shoes, clothing and other necessities that are on hand.

"Seventy-five per cent. of the factories are idle. The workmen are fleeing from the country in search of food."

AMERICAN COIN HELD AT HIGH PREMIUM BY LATIN-AMERICAN FOLK

Belgian, German and Other Traders Have Forced U. S. Out of Business

WASHINGTON, Aug. 1.— The American dollar is at such a premium in Latin-American and South American countries that Belgians, Germans and other foreign traders, through ability to quote goods at lower prices, have forced virtually a suspension of American selling campaigns in countries to the south.

Cable reports of American consuls in principal South American capitals to Secretary of Commerce Hoover today added more uncertainty to an already complex exchange and foreign trade problem as it affects American business here.

Sell 50 Per Cent. Cheaper.

Consuls told of Germans quoting a wide range of goods, and commodities in South America at 50 per cent. below the price quoted by American firms. The Germans, they said, are gaining a monopoly in the South American market through their ability to ship cheaply priced goods and often goods inferior to American commodities in quality.

Although Argentina's commercial situation was reported by Consul Freely at Buenos Aires to be improved, Argentine imports from the United States continue to show a marked decline.

Argentina Selling Grain.

Argentina, however, is selling grains heavily to Europe. Argentina is buying only necessities from the United States. Many American houses there have liquidated their affairs and quit the field until exchange conditions improve, Consul Freely declared.

American consuls generally advised Secretary Hoover to discourage American selling campaign while conditions in the field remain chaotic financially.

JUDGE PARDEE WILL TALK TO LIONS' CLUB

Judge L. S. Pardee of the municipal court will be the principal speaker at the meeting of the Lions' club to be held Tuesday noon at the Y. W. C. A. His subject will be "Amusing Incidents of Police Judge Life." Plans for the club picnic to be held at Sandy lake will be completed at the meeting.

CHARGED WITH LARCENY.

Maglisca Sebastian and Felici Nori, 342 Turner st., charged with grand larceny and accused of stealing a tire were arraigned in police court this morning. They were arrested by Deputy Sheriff Scott Ingerton at Springfield lake, Sunday.

Thugs From Other States Come To Ohio To Commit Crimes

By FRANK H. WARD
Beacon Journal Bureau,
145 E. State st.

COLUMBUS, Aug. 1. — Crooks and thugs in other states come into Ohio to commit crimes and do not worry whether they'll be caught or not because they know they'll get "soft treatment" from the courts and, in prison, if they are convicted.

This was the declaration today of Senator A. E. Culbert, Fremont, chairman of the senate committee investigating the Ohio penitentiary.

Calls Courts Chicken Hearted

"I have talked with 50 prisoners, probably 40 of whom were from other states," said Senator Culbert. "They all tell the same story. I have seen judges who were so chicken hearted that they almost shed tears when they sentenced a prisoner; I have heard the jurists tell the prisoner to be good and they'll sign a recommendation for parole in a few years.

"These judges should have talked to the men something like this: 'I am putting you away for a long, long time, where you no longer will be a menace to society.'"

Senator Culbert believes that the Norwood law, fathered by Senator Frank K. Norwood, his republican colleague on the committee will have a wholesome effect. It permits the trial judge to fix the minimum sentence for a crime, and this sentence must be served before a pardon can be granted.

Easy to Get Out of Pen

Now, prisoners automatically come up for parole after they have been in prison for one year and, if they are first timers, they generally get out; if not the first year, the second.

Between June 8 and July 1, 126 convicts were granted paroles from the penitentiary by the state board of clemency, which was legislated out of office June 30, and succeeded in its functions by Dr. Howard S. MacAyeal, director of public welfare.

At the June 8th meeting the clemency board, recognizing the number of prisoners whose homes are in other states, ordered 23 of the 60 men released to leave Ohio forever, on penalty of being returned to prison; at the June 30th meeting, nearly 40 were ordered to leave the state.

Privileges of Free Citizens

Testimony before the committee showed that an "honor gang" of prisoners, assigned to work at the state brick plant near Junction

(Continued on P[illegible])

GUNS OF WARCRAFT BOOM SALUTES AS PLYMOUTH F[illegible]

President Aboard Modern [illegible]flower Sails Up Port W[illegible] Pilgrim Fathers Di[illegible] Ages Ago

SCHOOL GIRLS ON DOCK

PLYMOUTH, Mass., Aug. 1.— Three centuries after the pilgrim fathers sailed into Plymouth harbor and laid the foundations of the American nation, President Harding came today to this national shrine to pay his tribute to the nation's founders and the principles which they laid down for the nation's building.

The president, aboard the modern Mayflower, and sailing the same course which Miles Standish and his fellow pioneers followed in the historic Mayflower, entered the sunlit Cape Cod amidst a great patriotic display.

The presidential yacht steamed across Cape Cod bay in the wake of the Pennsylvania, flagship of the Atlantic fleet, and dropped anchor in Plymouth harbor at 9:15 a. m.

Patriotic Fever Aroused.

The pilgrim fathers caused small excitement to a few scattered Indians when they came to Plymouth, but President Harding, escorted by two big battleships from the Atlantic fleet and a division of destroyers, with big guns booming in salute, aroused the greatest patriotic fever in the bosoms of thousands gathered here to commemorate the memories of their courageous forefathers.

This old New England town is in gala array, waiting to do honor to the nation's chief when he landed within a stone's throw of the famed Plymouth Rock, where the pilgrims are reputed to have first set foot.

President Harding's first act upon setting foot in Plymouth is to urge the children of America to carry on these principles which brought success to the Pilgrims in their long struggle against great odds to found Plymouth colony. Thirty-five nervously excited school girls of New Bedford were waiting upon the dock for the presi-

(Continued on Page Twelve.)

N. O. T. CAN CHARGE FIVE-CENT FARE UNTIL OCTOBER 1

The N. O. T. has a legal right to charge a five cent cash fare on the city lines until October 1 under a temporary franchise granted by the city council last June, according to a ruling Monday by City Law Director Henry Hagelbarger in reply to an inquiry by Councilman Gus Kasch.

The ordinance was duly passed by the city council, and is effective, he said. Hagelbarger also ruled that it was within the province of the city council to pass such an ordinance to increase street car fares in the city as an emergency measure.

Under the regular 25-year franchise with the city, the N. O. T. shall charge a ticket fare of 25 rides for $1, or 6 for 25 cents. The emergency ordinance was first passed a year ago, and has been renewed at the end of every three month period for a like duration.

MAIL POUCH STOLEN; CLERK BEING SOUGHT

CLEVELAND, O., Aug. 1.—A mail pouch believed to contain upwards of $5,000 in currency and jewels, was stolen early this morning from postal sub-station E.

Postal authorities are seeking a clerk who left the station at 4 o'clock without reporting off duty. He had not returned to his home at 9:45 this morning. The robbery was not discovered until the day force reported for duty.

"NEVER AGAIN" READ SIGN CARRIED BY WORKERS IN GERMAN PEACE PARADE

BERLIN, Aug. 1.—"Never again," now is the slogan of Germany. A monster pacifist demonstration was held here Sunday commemorating the seventh anniversary of the outbreak of the World war and marchers carried numerous banners with such inscriptions:

"No more war" and "peace for all time."

The sentiment of the demonstrators was reflected in the editorial comment of the newspapers today.

HEARING OF M'GANNON PLEA AGAIN DELAYED

CLEVELAND, O., Aug. 1. — Trial of ex-Judge William H. McGannon, and others charged with contempt of court and obstructing justice, was postponed until September 19, by Judge Homer G. Powell. The absence of D. T. Anderson of Youngstown, Cartwright's chief counsel, who is taking a vacation in Canada, caused the postponement.

OPEN SHOP ISSUE ON PENNSY ROAD BROUGHT TO FRONT

Railway Labor Board Orders New Elections Representatives For Employes

[illegible]RDER SETS ASIDE VOTE

CHICAGO, Aug. 1. — The issue of the open shop as it affects employes of the Pennsylvania railway, was brought sharply to the front today by the action of the U. S. Railway Labor board in ordering new elections of representatives of employes of the road and prescribing the manner of voting.

The order sets aside elections already held and overrules the contention of officials of the railway that their employers' representative shall be chosen without regard for union affiliations. Conferences to be held before August 12 will determine the method of holding the new elections.

Deny Rights of Board

Officials of the Pennsylvania railway frankly stated at the recent hearings of the labor board that they would deal with their employes according to their own plans, virtually denying the right of the board to interfere. This attitude of the decision issued by the board, is called "quibbling" and "almost treasonable." The board expressed impatience with "quibbling" over technicalities and declared that at a time when the nation is slowly and painfully progressing through the condition of industrial depression, unemployment and unrest, it is almost treasonable for any employe stubbornly to haggle over unessentials at the risk of social chaos.

The Pennsylvania in ostensible compliance with an order of the board for conferences with its employes on new rules, had held a general election, votes were cast for individuals only and the names of the various labor organizations among the Pennsylvania employes did not appear on the ballot.

Rules Put Into Effect.

Rules negotiated by representatives related have been effective.

The board sets aside the election and these rules and orders a new election at which the employes may vote for representatives of the labor organizations if they desire. The representatives chosen at the new election are to be given recognition by the board in new conferences.

No statements of their attitude toward the board has come from Pennsylvania officials.

CARNIVAL MAN IS HELD AS GAMBLER; VICTIM COMPLAINS

A new phase of gambling at the carnival grounds near Brittain bridge on the Akron-Canton-E. Market st. rd. led to the arrest of George Edgar, 32, on a charge of operating a game of chance. He was arrested by deputy sheriffs late Saturday night following a complaint to the sheriff's office by a man who said he was a victim in the game. The deputies confiscated $23 which they say they found in play.

An exposure by publication of a story concerning the gambling methods in the games for money resulted in a temporary cessation last week. This activity started but a few days, it is declared. Edgar is to be arraigned in police court before Police Judge Pardee.

Summit Lake Is Polluted From at Least 10 Sources

The pollution in Summit lake, which makes the waters unfit for bathing, comes from at least ten different sources, according to tests of the waters of incoming streams completed Monday. Each of the ten samples collected last week from such streams showed the same pollution as is contained in the lake.

What action will be taken by the health department in its campaign to clean up the lake could not be determined Monday by the health officials. The next move in the campaign will not be made until after a detailed report is submitted by the city chemist's office. The report Monday was verbal.

According to the report, the contamination in the lake is being furnished by the waste deposits of the South End factories and other industrial plants in the vicinity of the lake. Small streams flowing into the lake from other sources are equally contaminated, while the waters in the swamp lands near the lake are also polluted, the tests indicate.

Drinking Of Iodine Fails To Prove Fatal

Mrs. Hazel Worrell, 40, 253 Fuller st., is recovering from the effects of drinking iodine in an attempt to end her life at 2 o'clock Saturday afternoon, following a quarrel in domestic differences with her husband. She was taken to the City hospital, where her condition today is reported as good. Detective Will McDonnell and Patrolman G. Stewart investigated.

Prosperity Wave Hits Pittsburg And Youngstown As Steel Plant Stacks Begin Belching Smoke

WALTER C. MERRITT.

PITTSBURG, Pa., Aug. 1.— Prosperity is returning to the great Pittsburg and Youngstown industrial districts. There is a noticeable revival in business in most lines.

Within the last ten days several thousand men have gone back to work largely in the allied steel industries, several thousand more resumed work today and indications are that thousands more will be given employment within the next two weeks.

Invariably the men who are going back to mills and mines are doing so at reduced wages, generally ten to 15 per cent. below what they formerly received, and in some instances at reductions of 20 per cent., but the hysteria over wage cuts and the open shop has died out. Men want work and they are glad to accept steady employment even at reduced wages.

Steel plants and steel working industries are booking large orders and the whole atmosphere is more optimistic and cheerful. There is a renewal of confidence among workers and business men.

The independent steel mills have reduced wages to almost pre-war scales. U. S. Steel is expected to get down to the independents basis shortly.

Price cuts in steel products are

(Continued on Page Twelve)

WHITE PLAGUE DRIVE LAUNCHED BY MEMBERS OF CATHOLIC ORDER

Declared Concentrated Localized Activity Is Most Efficient Preventive

SAN FRANCISCO, Cal., Aug. 1.— A comprehensive and sustained attack by 800,000 men and their families on the white plague was launched today at the international convention of the Knights of Columbus. Under the chairmanship of Dr. E. W. Buckley, of St. Paul, supreme physician of the K. of C., the Knights throughout the United States and Canada will initiate and maintain an informal campaign against tuberculosis to be supported by local aid in the maintenance of beds in sanitoriums and the rendering of local aid to consumptives.

Will Concentrate Work.

"After an exhaustive research and consultation with noted experts on tuberculosis," Dr. Buckley reported, "the Knights of Columbus anti-tuberculosis committee has concluded that the concentrated localized activity is the most efficient preventive against the spread of tuberculosis.

With Dr. Buckley on the committee are Dr. James T. McMahon of New Haven, Conn., Dr. William F. Lawler of Lansing, Mich., and James O'Toole of Pittsburg.

Plan to Form School.

K. of C. educators from all parts of the country met today to formulate final plans for the K. of C. correspondent school system. The Knights, it was announced plan the largest correspondence school in the United States to augment their free night school system numbering 132 units and serving 150,000 former service men and women.

Approximately 2,000 delegates are here today to attend the convention.

Man Is Charged With Making False Report Of Hold-up

John H. McKee, Palmer's hotel, was placed under arrest by Lieut. McAllister, Sergeant Fetherson and Patrolman B. Ward for making a false report of a hold-up and robbery. McKee told the police that he was enticed into a rear room of a soft drink parlor at High st. and Steiner av. and robbed of a diamond ring worth $250 and $45 in money. This report the police say was proved to be fictitious and McKee was locked up in the city prison.

HUGHES REJECTS PLAN TO PUT PANAMA-COSTA RICAN ROW UP TO COURT

WASHINGTON, Aug. 1.—The suggestion of Panama that the Panama-Costa Rican boundary dispute be referred to the permanent court at The Hague for arbitration has been rejected by Secretary Hughes.

Supreme Council May Aid Famine Victims In Russia

PARIS, Aug. 1.—The inter allied supreme council will meet on Aug. 8 and probably will be in session two or three weeks, according to the newspaper Bon Soir today. The meeting will be in Paris instead of Boulogne.

Opinion was expressed by Bon Soir that the allied statesmen would discuss Russian relief along with the Upper Silesian issue and the Greco-Turk war. It was intimated unofficially at the foreign office, however, that France will decline to discuss Russia, believing that Russian relief is a question for individual action.

WORLD WAR SOLDIERS STAND VIGIL ALL NIGHT OVER VETERAN'S BODY

CANTON, O., Aug. 1.—A guard of overseas soldiers stood lonely vigil all last night and until 11 o'clock today in Westlawn cemetery, over the body of Corporal Walter Griffith, who was killed in the battle of the Marne.

Then the trustees of the cemetery announced that they had placed a ban on all Sunday funerals at the big cemetery and that Griffith's body could not be buried that day.

The American Legion immediately got into action, asking for a rescinding of the order so far as military funerals are concerned, for it is the only one day that the former soldiers can attend the last rites of their departed buddies. But the cemetery officials were adamant, so the funeral was held, there were services at the grave and then a guard was posted on the flower and flag bedecked casket under a canopy until this morning when interment was made.

J. L. SLOAN, WELL KNOWN AKRON RESTAURANT MAN VICTIM OF INFLUENZA

J. Lambert Sloan, 45 years old, proprietor of Sloan's restaurant, 213 E. Market st., died yesterday afternoon at his home, 92 N. Forge st., after having been ill for four days from influenza.

Funeral services will be held tomorrow morning at 9 o'clock at the residence. The body will be taken to Titusville, Pa., his former home, for burial.

Mr. Sloan is survived by his widow, Mrs. Rosa Sloan, and his mother, two brothers and three sisters, who live in Titusville.

Mr. Sloan came to Akron about five years ago and since that time was engaged in the restaurant business.

BEACON EMPLOYES WILL HOLD PICNIC

Beacon Journal employes and members of their families will hold their annual picnic and outing tomorrow afternoon and evening at Summit Beach park. A program of sports and entertainments has been arranged.

People Of Erin Will Depend On Reserve Strength To Win Freedom At Peace Parleys

By SEUMAS MacMANUS

Seumas MacManus

NEW YORK, Aug. 1. — The amount of reserve strength still left in the Irish people will be the determining factor in the peace conference. If they feel they can go forward with the fight for even another six months they can compel worth while terms from England. For England and England's ministers are today in more desperate straits than they have known in a hundred years—if we except their utterly desperate condition just before America entered the war. Chiefly because of the marvelous (we might say miraculous) fight that the little Irish republican army has made, England's power in Europe, in Asia, in all corners of the world, is paralyzed—and her vast schemes for after-the-war aggrandisement have all proved futile. Pole, Persian, Turk and Arab flout her. And among the bigger powers at the diplomatic table she, with her hands tied by little Ireland, can no longer bully and browbeat so that she is moving heaven and earth to defer the diplomatic game and mark time, till she is again in position to domineer and dominate the board.

This is one compelling reason for the amazing climb-down of Lloyd George, who a few short weeks ago loved to tell the world that "we have the Irish murder-gang by the throat, and there will be no let-up till we strangle it." But by one of his most recent utterances in the House of Commons Lloyd George, making his astounding right-obout-face, not only forgot to call De-Valera the "chief of the murder gang"—but actually made many of the old hard-shell Tories gasp by politely terming the same murder chief "The chieftain of the overwhelming majority of the Irish nation!"—and he was wiring to the

(Continued on Page Two.)

CENTRAL FIGURES IN MATEWAN CASE DIE IN GUN FIGHT

Called To Welch, W. Va., For Trial Both Become Targets For P. E. Lively

DRAWS PISTOL QUICKLY

WELCH, W. Va., Aug. 1.— Sid Hatfield and Ed. Chambers, two of the principal defendants in the great murder trial at Williamson, W. Va., several months ago for the battle at Matewan, W. Va., a year ago, were both shot and killed just before noon here today by P. E. Lively.

The two men were here to face trial for the shooting up of the town of Mohawk, W. Va. An argument ensued and Hatfield attempted to shoot Lively but the latter was too quick on the draw and beat Hatfield to it.

Detective Lively and four others were arrested following the shooting.

Welch is county seat of McDowell county and is the stronghold of the Baldwin-Felts detective agency, which provides mine guards for many workings in this part of the state.

Lively was the Baldwin-Felts "under cover" man who ran a restaurant for a long time in Matewan and acted as a spy in the meetings of the United Mine workers. He was the principal witness for the state at the trial in Williamson.

From the time of the trial at Williamson bad blood had existed between Hatfield and Lively.

MAN SHOT IN HIP BLAMES ROBBERS, STORY IS DOUBTED

Says He Ran When He Was Ordered To Give Over His Money

The motive that prompted the firing of a bullet which found its mark in the hip of Will Dotson, 28, 151 Spring st., and passed through his body is to be established by the detectives investigating the mysterious circumstances surrounding the shooting which occurred shortly after midnight Saturday.

Dotson is in the Peoples hospital to which he was taken in the police emergency patrol at 6 o'clock Sunday morning. The wounding of the man was not reported until then. The first story concerning the shooting was to the effect that Dotson, with $12 in his pocket was stopped by two highwaymen on North st., near Furnace st. He ran when they ordered him to hand over his money and as he did so was shot.

This story, detectives believe is an attempt to shield the real person who held the weapon and who is supposed to be either a woman who was jealous or a friend of Dotson's with whom he quarreled in a game of dice.

GIRL'S TIP BELIEVED TO HAVE SAVED PAY ROLL OF OHIO FIRM

CLEVELAND, Aug. 1.—Arrests of nine men, all aliens, in a raid on an alleged robbers den in E. Fourth st., on a tip furnished by a young waitress, is believed by police to have frustrated a plot to seize the payroll of the Ohio Quarries Co. at Amherst, near Elyria, this morning.

Eleven automatic pistols and two automobiles, were also seized by the police.

The girl heard three men plotting a payroll robbery in a downtown eating place Saturday. According to her story, the concern was named, and the robbery was to have been staged at noon today. The anticipated loot was named as $24,000.

Word has been sent to nearby towns, and an effort will be made to identify the men held as participants in recent crimes.

BUILDING STRIKE ENDS; 30,000 BACK AT WORK

NEW YORK, Aug. 1. — The building trade strike called July 1, and which has affected close to 30,000 workers ended today. both sides having agreed to arbitrate. Union workers quit following their refusal to grant the contractors' demand for a 25 per cent. wage reduction.

PATROLMAN INJURED

Robert Miller, motorcycle patrolman, was seriously injured at noon today when the handle bars of his machine refused to turn and he crashed into a telephone post near the Firestone. He was taken to City hospital in the police emergency. Examination showed that his leg had been badly crushed and that he probably had been internally injured.

COPPER AND SILVER
Copper—
Spot and near by 12c
Later ....12¼c@12½c
Bar Silver—Domestic..........99¼c

WEATHER FORECAST
Today, fair.

More Butte News in the Standard Than in Any Other Paper

The Anaconda Standard.

THE WORLD'S NEWS.
The Standard carries the most extensive telegraph service in Montana.
Full Associated Press.
Universal Service.
Special leased wire.

VOL. XXXII.—No. 334. ANACONDA, MONTANA, WEDNESDAY MORNING, AUGUST 3, 1921. PRICE FIVE CENTS.

FORMER WHITE SOX PLAYERS FOUND NOT GUILTY

Decision of Jury on Conspiracy Charge Is Reached on the First Ballot

BALL PLAYERS FREED BY JURY IN CONSPIRACY CASE

CHARLES RISBERG

ARNOLD GANDIL

OSCAR FELSCH

BUCK WEAVER

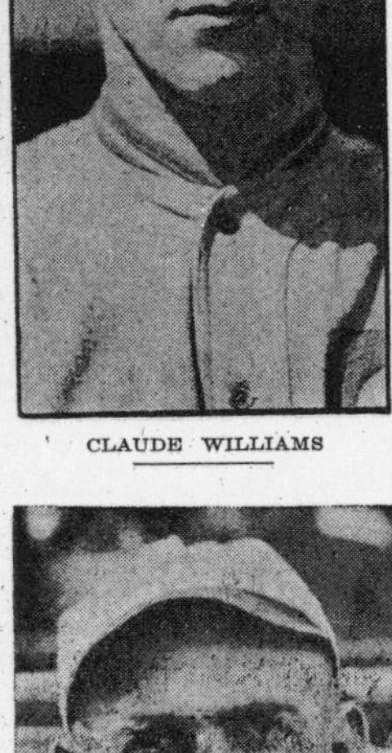
CLAUDE WILLIAMS

EDDIE CICOTTE

JOE JACKSON

ENRICO CARUSO FAMOUS TENOR DIES IN ITALY

Golden Voice, Which Has Charmed Thousands in Every Nation of the World, Is Stilled by Death.

NONE TO TAKE HIS PLACE

Passing of Acknowledged King of the Opera Leaves Vacancy Which Can Not Be Filled. Wide World Mourns.

FUNERAL TODAY.

By the Associated Press.
LONDON, Aug. 3.—The burial of Caruso will take place today (Wednesday) amid national mourning at the Church of Santa Maria Gracia in Naples, according to the Daily Mail.

By the Associated Press.
NAPLES, Italy, Aug. 2.—Enrico Caruso died today. The great singer, whose ultimate recovery had been hoped for under the benign influences of his own Italy, passed away at 9 o'clock this morning at the Hotel Vesuvius in this city. He had been brought here hurriedly from Sorrento, on the Bay of Naples, where less than a week ago he avowed his returning strength and expressed the conviction that he would sing again as in the old days.

He had been able to visit the famous sanctuary of Our Lady of Pompeii, giving thank offerings for his recovery.

He went also to the wonderful island of Capri, where he attended a luncheon in his honor, but soon afterward unfavorable symptoms, in the form of a high fever, manifested

(Continued on Page 2, Column 1.)

COMPLETE REST IN WHITE MOUNTAINS HARDING PROGRAM

By the Associated Press.
LANCASTER, N. H., Aug. 2.—President Harrison came into the White mountains of Northern New Hampshire today for the first real vacation since his inauguration. At a little lodge high above the reach of the heat wave and four miles removed from the nearest telephone, the president and Mrs. Harding with a party of close friends will be guests for the remainder of this week at least, and longer if public affairs permit. Complete rest, with perhaps some golf, fishing and mountain climbing mixed, will occupy their first attention.

The house selected by the president for his vacation is the country home of Secretary Weeks of the war department. It stands on the very summit of Mount Prospect, 2,000 feet above the sea level, with only wooded slopes about it. A private drive, closed with a substantial wooden gate at the base of the mountain, winds up to the little clearing that contains the lodge.

LUMBER INDUSTRY SLOWLY IMPROVES

By the Associated Press.
EUGENE, Ore., Aug. 2.—Sixty-five per cent of all lumber mills and 50 per cent of all logging camps of the Pacific Northwest are working, employing about the same percentage of mill hands and loggers, according to a survey read at a meeting of district No. 1, Loyal Legion of Loggers and Lumbermen, here. Since the ending of the marine strike lumber has begun to move, and mills which suspended because of the strike are reopening. Predictions were that the industry would improve slowly and that 70 to 75 per cent of the mills would be working full time by Christmas. Wage survey presented showed that food scales were not discussed, but a food for a family of five should cost $1.45 a day.

RYAN IS CHARGED WITH INSTIGATING RUSSIAN REVOLT

Senator France Makes Accusation Against Red Cross Commissioner.

By the Associated Press.
RIGA, Aug. 2.—Prior to his departure for Berlin last night, Senator Joseph I. France of Maryland personally accused Dr. Edward W. Ryan, American Red Cross commissioner in the Baltic states, of having instigated the revolt at Kronstadt last winter.

The doctor had expressed his opinion of the senator's credence in what Dr. Ryan termed bolshevik reports and of the senator's dealings with the bolsheviki in general.

When questioned today concerning the incident, Dr. Ryan said:

"The charge is ridiculous. The senator must have been raving."

Mr. France is said to have declared that he would renew his charge on the floor of the United States senate.

It is understood that Senator France invited Dr. Ryan to his room and abruptly made his accusation and added that the bolshevik foreign office had promised to furnish him proof of the charge.

Dr. Ryan has been engaged in Red Cross and other relief work in various parts of Europe since early in the war. His home is in Scranton, Pa.

The mutiny in Kronstadt began early in February, 1921, when soviet sailors in the Baltic revolted and seized the city, which was held for about 15 days, when it was surrendered to the soviet forces. All officers and civilian leaders of the revolt who were captured were executed.

CANON CITY, COL., SUFFERING FROM DAMAGE BY FLOOD

By the Associated Press.
PUEBLO, Col., Aug. 2.—Heavy property damage was done in Canon City tonight when heavy rains in the mountains sent the waters of the Arkansas river and its tributaries to the flood stage. Parts of the city are under two to four feet of water. Several thrilling escapes from the flood were reported, but apparently no loss of life has resulted.

Grape creek and Sand creek, tributaries of the Arkansas, poured volumes of water into the river, flooded celery lands and cellars in residence sections. Automobile campers were forced to flee from City park when the park was inundated with three feet of water.

Efforts to communicate with Portland, Col., 18 miles east of Canon City in the path of the flood, failed tonight.

Local police are preparing to warn inhabitants of the lowlands here in case a repetition of the June 3 flood appears possible. Although the Canon City flood is said to be the worst in years, city officials believe the flood will spread out before it reaches here and eliminate the danger. The river is narrow at Canon City, where it emerges from the Royal gorge.

OLIVER APPOINTED.

HELENA, Aug. 2.—The appointment of John Oliver of Ekalaka, former state senator, to be deputy state examiner, in charge of municipal accounting, is announced by L. Q. Skelton, state examiner.

KNIGHTS TO START GREAT SCHOOL FOR FORMER SOLDIERS

The Largest Correspondence School in United States Is Plan Outlined.

By the Associated Press.
SAN FRANCISCO, Aug. 2.—A decision to establish what it terms "the largest correspondence school in the United States," which shall be devoted exclusively to the education and general welfare of former service men, and announcement that the order had increased by 87,660 since last year, made up the outstanding features today of the opening session of the Knights of Columbus thirty-ninth annual supreme convention. Supreme Secretary William J. McGinley outlined the correspondence system, which will have its headquarters in the order's new building in New Haven, Conn.

(Continued on Page 10, Column 1.)

BOGUS OATH OF K. C. DENOUNCED BY SUPREME KNIGHT

By the Associated Press.
SAN FRANCISCO, Aug. 2.—Opposition to religious prejudice is the keynote of the Knights of Columbus annual convention opening here today, sounded in the preconvention address of Supreme Knight James A. Flaherty. Mr. Flaherty denounced what he termed "professional purveyors of prejudice" whom he charged with seeking to divide American citizens into classes and to create suspicion and distrust.

Mr. Flaherty's address drew attention to the widespread circulation of an oath attributed to the fourth degree members of the Knights of Columbus, which was characterized as a "vile invention."

"This oath," he declared, "is impossible and ridiculous on its face, but is now being circulated by millions of copies through the country bearing the imprint of the Congressional Record, because by accident it appeared as an exhibit in the proceedings of congress.

"For the first time in the history of the Knights of Columbus, at this convention, we take occasion to ask press and public to make known as widely as possible the real obligation taken by all Knights of Columbus:

The Genuine Oath.

"'I swear to support the constitution of the United States. I pledge myself fully on my duties as a citizen and to conscientiously perform such duties entirely in the interest of my country and regardless of all personal consequences. I pledge myself to do all in my power to preserve the integrity and purity of the ballot and to promote reverence and respect for law and order. I promise to practice my religion openly and consistently, but without ostentation, and to so conduct myself in public affairs as to reflect nothing but credit upon our holy church to the end that she may flourish and our country prosper to the greater honor and glory of God.'"

COST OF SCHOOL CENSUS CAUSES LIVELY DEBATE

One Board Member in Favor of Paying Five Cents Per Name.

Whether or not Clerk O. G. Wood shall let a contract for the taking of the school census this fall and how much shall be allowed as expense money for each name collected was the subject of a lengthy debate at last night's meeting of the school board. One of the board members insisted that the clerk and his clerical force should personally attend to the gathering and compiling of the names in addition to their regular duties.

"There aren't to be any rakeoffs as long as I am a member of the board," he declared at one point.

This remark was made when the question arose as to what should be a fair amount to allow the clerk for expense money. The law stipulates that a maximum of 10 cents a name may be allowed, but that the school board has the privilege of allowing a designated amount to the school clerk, who in turn may employ such help as necessary.

Favors Five Cents.

Trustee Lindsay was in favor of setting the maximum at 5 cents a name and requiring that all work be handled through the clerk's office.

He declared that other clerks had been allowed as high as 8 cents a name and that all actual expenses was allowed them as compensation for their work. Trustees Fulton and Baldwin said that many hours of overtime had been put in by the clerks and that the few dollars left over had been paid them for their extra work.

The necessity of securing a correct census of all the children in the district was urged by all but one member of the board. When the failure

(Continued on page 10, Section A)

FULL MEETING OF DAIL EIREANN TO DISCUSS PROPOSAL

By the Associated Press.
LONDON, Aug. 2.—There will be no sectional meeting of the Dail Eireann to consider the British porposals for an Irish peace conference, and these proposals will only be considered by a full meeting of that body, according to advices received tonight by the Westminster Gazette.

The Dail Eireann is making no direct application to the British or the Irish government for the release of its imprisoned members, it was said, but will follow the procedure of issuing notices for convening the meeting to all members including those in custody. These notices will be addressed to the prisoners where they are held, and it will then be for the authorities to decide whether the prisoners are released. It is anticipated that this will be promptly done.

Eamonn de Valera, leader of the Irish republicans, has informally submitted to all available members of the Irish republican parliament the peace proposals of Prime Minister Lloyd George, it is declared by the Daily Sketch. When the members of the parliaments are summoned to debate the prime minister's sugestions, the newspaper says, the session will probably be secret. It is expected to last for several days.

SENATOR WALSH ON WAY TO STOCKHOLM

WASHINGTON, Aug. 2.—Senator Walsh of Montana left tonight for New York and sails tomorrow for Stockholm, Sweden, to attend the annual meeting of the interparliamentary union, commencing Aug. 16, the first session since work was interrupted by the war. The interparliamentary union is an association for the promotion of peace, dating from 1888, membership in which is restricted to members of the highest legislative body of the nations of the world. It was on its initiative that the second Hague conference was called. The American group at the forthcoming session consists of Senators Walsh, McKinley, Sterling and Robinson and Representatives Montague, Brooks and Britain and former Representative Slayden. The party sails on the George Washington and lands at Bremen, proceeding by way of Berlin. They expect to be absent about a month.

CROWD CHEERS JURY VERDICT IN COURTROOM

Bailiffs Vainly Try to Restore Order Then Join in Demonstration Staged by the Throng of Spectators.

JUDGE SAYS VERDICT JUST

Defense Counsel Calls Decision "Complete Vindication of the Most Mistreated Ball Players in History."

By the Associated Press.
CHICAGO, Aug. 2.—The seven former Chicago White Sox baseball players and two others on trial for alleged conspiracy to defraud the public through throwing of the 1919 world's series games tonight were found not guilty by a jury.

The verdict was reached after 2 hours and 47 minutes deliberation, but was not returned until 40 minutes later, Judge Hugo M. Friend being out of court when the decision was reached. The jury took only one ballot.

The defendants were:

Buck Weaver, third baseman; Oscar Felsch, outfielder; Charles Risberg, shortstop; Arnold Gandil, first baseman; Claude Williams, and Eddie Cicotte, pitchers; Joe Jackson, outfielder—all former White Sox players—and Carl Zork of St. Louis, and David Zelcer of Des Moines.

Announcement of the verdict was greeted by cheers from the several hundred persons who remained in court for the finel 2decisions and shouts of "hooray for the clean sox."

Judge Friend congratulated the jury, saying he thought it was a just verdict.

Eddie Cicotte was the first of the defendants to reach the jurors. He grabbed William Barrett by both hands, shouting his thanks.

Joe Jackson, Claude Williams and

(Continued on Page 10, Column 1.)

WESTERN FARMERS UNDULY CURTAILED BY RESERVE BOARD

By the Associated Press.
WASHINGTON, Aug. 2.—Policies of the federal reserve board during the past 18 months or more were attacked today before a joint congressional commission by John Skelton Williams, former comptroller of the currency, who charged that the board had displayed undue favoritism in lending to New York banking groups, while southern and western borrowers were unduly curtailed. There was "abundant ground for complaints of discrimination by farmers generally," he added.

In December, 1919, Mr. Williams said, one New York state banking institution, which he described as "known for speculative activities," borrowed $130,000,000 through the New York Federal Reserve bank. No law was broken, he said, but several other New York banks, "in hard and in good times," were allowed to hold out large amounts of reserve loans while western and southern borrowers were being pressed to reduce loans.

JAPS GRADUALLY GAINING CONTROL HAWAIIAN ISLAND

Finance Trip to Washington of Delegates of Union Men to Urge Opposition to Admission Chinese Coolies.

By the Associated Press.
WASHINGTON, Aug. 2.—Representatives of organized labor in Hawaii, sent to Washington to oppose legislation under which Chinese collies would be admitted to Hawaii to help relieve the agricultural labor shortage, testified before the house immigration committee today that their expenses had been paid by Japanese.

Wilmot C. Hilton, who came here with George W. Wright, president of the Central Labor union of Honolulu, when questioned by Representative Free, republican, California, declared that Japanese merchants on the island had contributed $1,500 so that they might personally oppose admission of Chinese, and that he had split it "fifty-fifty" with Wright.

Samuel Gompers, president of the American Federation of Labor, was present when Mr. Free developed that the Japanese Chamber of Commerce of Honolulu, acting on a request for help, decided it would be "unwise" for the organization to contribute, but that individual members could do so. Earlier in the day, Mr. Gompers told the committee that the federation, with which the Central Labor union of Honolulu is affiliated, would not issue union charters requested by Japanese labor groups in this country.

Throughtout the long hearings on pending relief legislation, spokesmen for the sugar planters of Hawaii have asserted that the Japanese gradually were gaining business control on the island, and that they were secretly opposing temporary lifting of American immigration laws which would permit a flow of labor needed to meet shortage in time to save future crops. Delegate Kalanianole, sponsor of the bill before the committee, declared in a statement tonight that control of Hawaii had been Japan's objective for many years.

RUM-RUNNING CONSPIRACY INVOLVES PROMINENT MEN

It Is Believed by Officers That Mystery of Phantom Ships Bobbing Up Here and There Is Solved.

By the Associated Press.
NEW YORK, Aug. 2.—Federal officials claimed tonight to have evidence of a rum-running conspiracy involving prominent persons in various cities along the Atlantic seaboard, which would go far toward clearing up the mystery of phantom ships for several months reported bobbing up outside the three-mile limit.

This claim was made after the liquor-laden schooner Henry L. Marshall had been seized off Atlantic City and brought into this port with four of her crew by the coast guard cutter Seneca. Her captain and mate escaped in a swift motorboat.

Federal agents declined to reveal the nature of the evidence at their command, but intimated that more than one vessel was engaged in landing liquor along the coast from Maine to Florida. Firm belief was expressed that these were the lightless crafts which mariners had declared on reaching port had been sighted at sea, but had refused to answer signals.

No specific complaint thus far has been lodged against the schooner Marshall, which with her cargo of more than 1,500 cases of liquor, is being held by armed guards pending further investigation. Her cook and three seamen are being detained as material witnesses.

Captain Aaron L. Gamble of the Seneca has made an official report of the seizure to Collector of Customs Aldridge. United States Attorney Hayward also has been called into conference.

Although the schooner was outside the three-mile limit and was flying the British flag when she was seized, federal officials asserted they were justified in taking charge of her by the evidence of conspiracy in their possession.

CALIFORNIA FORECAST
Los Angeles and Vicinity—Sunday, fair, except cloudy or foggy near the coast in the morning; moderate westerly winds.
San Francisco and Vicinity—Sunday, generally foggy or cloudy; moderate westerly winds.

COAST TEMPERATURES (Mean)

Los Angeles	68	San Francisco	59
Portland	66	Seattle	58
Sacramento	66	Spokane	50
San Diego	67	Salt Lake	59

CHARACTER QUALITY — AMERICA FIRST! — ENTERPRISE ACCURACY

Los Angeles Examiner

AN AMERICAN PAPER FOR THE AMERICAN PEOPLE — THE GREAT NEWSPAPER OF THE GREAT SOUTHWEST

SUNDAY EXAMINER 10c PER COPY
Daily and Sunday, Delivered by Carrier, $1.05 a Month

VOL. XVIII—NO. 274 Official Forecast—*Fair* See Old Home Weather, First Column, Want Ads. LOS ANGELES, SUNDAY, SEPTEMBER 11, 1921

ARBUCKLE HELD FOR MURDER!

250 Dead, New Estimate in Big Flood

Today

Magna Charta Day.
Rockefeller and Louis XI.
For Health to Europe.
Society Mule Race.

—By Arthur Brisbane—

Cotton "crossed 22 cents" on Thursday, although it didn't stay there. And the North has been forced to realize what Southern prosperity would mean, Southern prosperity being a decent price for cotton.

The moment cotton began to go up, optimism awoke in Wall Street's Stock Exchange and cheerfulness cropped up in New York's big banks.

No man can be happy with a desperately sick brother. No part of the country can be happy, or healthy, with another part desperately sick through no fault of its own.

Dr. Nicholas Murray Butler thinks we ought to celebrate, with all other English speaking nations, the signing of Magna Charta. Mr. McSweeney, for the Knights of Columbus, objects.

"Magna Charta is such a fellow that he will have no sovereign," said Sir Edward Coke in Parliament three hundred years ago. "Such a fellow" might reasonably be celebrated here, were it not for the fact that we have built up in various trust offices, certain taxing "sovereigns" that would make old King John of the Thirteenth Century look feeble.

Magna Charta gave the English trial by jury and certain rights, especially for the barons of England. The little people didn't amount to much then—and don't now. It guaranteed that justice should be neither sold, denied or delayed. In England, at least, they don't delay justice. We do delay it here.

We shall have a Magna Charta celebration of our own some day but not for a while. Meanwhile, the Fourth of July is a good enough celebration. We got rid of one sovereign then, even though we have built up a thousand abler sovereigns to tax and direct us.

Twenty-three communities have voted to change the name of a highway to "Rockefeller highway" in honor of John D. Rockefeller. Those recalling the bitterness of ancient attacks may wonder at this.

But the young, now living, may see in many cities statues of John D. Rockefeller and Louis XI side by side. Underneath will be written "The Deliverers."

Louis XI delivered France from confusion of weights, measures and money and from the power and exalations of innumerable petty barons and great dukes. When he settled Charles the Fool Hardy, Duke of Burgundy, it was a great day for France.

John D. Rockefeller will be remembered for his wise, scientific, educational and health benefactions, but especially for having delivered the people from the foolish idea that competition is necessary and big business in itself harmful.

Louis XI thought he was working for himself. John D. Rockefeller, probably in his youth, also thought he was working for himself. History will show that they worked, more wisely than either knew, for the benefit of everybody.

American doctors are sending patients to Europe "to take two pints of good beer every day for a year, that being essential to their health."

That sounds strange to all earnest prohibitionists. Yet the great American railroad man, E. H. Harriman, when his health failed, was ordered by the best doctors his money could find, to drink beer for his health, and was told that if he had taken light wine and beer in moderation all his life, easing the strain, releasing the belt from the driving wheel of his mind, occasionally, he

(Continued on Page 4, Columns 3-4)

MAY ALLISON SAID TO BE SECRET BRIDE

Prisoner at Santa Ana Claims He Wed Girl Bearing Star's Name There Two Years Ago

RECORDS REVEAL CEREMONY

William Stephenson Groom's Name; Ceremony Performed in Office of Atty. Clyde Bishop

"I am May Allison's husband."

From the prisoner's dock in the courtroom of Judge Cox at Santa Ana yesterday, a man known as R. W. Lyhne made the statement.

Lyhne was under arrest charged with passing worthless checks. He was bound over to the Superior Court for trial.

His statement started an investigation which revealed that a May Allison, giving her age as 23 and her residence as Los Angeles, was licensed to wed a William Stephenson, 45, of Philadelphia, at Santa Ana on December 1, 1919.

MISS ALLISON ABSENT

They were married, it was learned, by the Rev. J. A. Stevenson, pastor of the First Presbyterian Church, in the law offices of Clyde Bishop.

Revelation of the secret marriage started a maelstrom of speculation in Hollywood's motion picture colony.

Miss May Allison, the star, could not be found. A maid at her home, 813 Camden Drive, said she went away Friday and would be gone a week. Her destination could not be learned.

But her friends were emphatic in asserting she was not the May Allison of the Santa Ana marriage. It has been only a few months, they pointed out, since she had denied reports she was married.

They were likewise firm in declaring that, even if she was married, there was no likelihood that the man known in the courts as Lyhne was Stephenson or had ever been known by that name.

Their belief was strengthened when Attorney Bishop, after visiting the man called Lyhne, announced the prisoner was not the man who went through a marriage ceremony in his office.

The Rev. Stevenson also visited the prisoner in the Orange County jail. "He bears some resemblance to the man I joined in marriage with Miss Allison," said the minister, "but I cannot tell. I really don't believe he is the man."

FRIEND'S POSITIVE DENIAL

One of the cinema star's friends who wished to remain anonymous made this statement:

"I have known May Allison a long, long time. She has told me she was never married, and I have every reason in the world to believe her.

"I don't know the man named Stephenson. I am sure the May Allison with whom he was married is not the May Allison recently with Metro.

"And as to this man Lyhne, I am positive he is in no way related to Miss Allison, the star."

Lyhne was arrested in Santa Ana August 13. He was taken to jail, removed to the Orange County Hospital for observation and escaped. He was rearrested in Los Angeles a few days ago.

President Harding on Holiday at Atlantic City

ATLANTIC CITY, N. J., Sept. 11.—President Harding and party arrived here at 12:30 o'clock this morning for a stay of several days. The President and Mrs. Harding motored here from Washington, leaving the Capital at 2 p. m., yesterday, with a two-hour stop at Philadelphia for dinner.

Pershing Will Award French Hero U.S. Medal

WASHINGTON, Sept. 10.

GENERAL PERSHING, acting at the direction of President Harding, will sail Wednesday for Paris, where, on October 2, he will award the medal of honor voted by Congress to the unknown soldier of France whose body was placed in the Arch of Triumph.

The General probably will be accompanied by a high naval officer, who will also participate in the ceremonies. Secretary Weeks, in announcing General Pershing's mission, said:

"The French Government has announced its intention of signalizing by appropriate military ceremonies the action of Congress as another evidence of the historic relations which have always prevailed between the two republics."

JEALOUS MAN IN DOUBLE SLAYING

Spurned by Widow, Willard Jenks Shoots Her, Then Drives Wildly Home and Ends Life

Believed to have been spurned after he had made violent love to her for nearly a year, Willard E. Jenks, 30, of El Monte, last night shot and instantly killed Mrs. May Blachley, 28, in Pasadena, and after a frantic motor ride to his home at 717 Hoyt street, El Monte, accompanied by his 9-year-old daughter, he fired a bullet into his own brain, according to reports received here from the Pasadena police department.

The first part of the tragedy was enacted at the home of Mr. and Mrs. Cyril Bennett, 235 Elm street, in one of Pasadena's exclusive residence sections, where Mrs. Blachley was engaged in caring for the Bennetts' two small children during their absence for the evening.

Jenks' body was still warm when found in the upper room of a water tank building in the rear of his home after a posse of Pasadena and El Monte officers had surrounded the building. None heard the shot with which it is said he ended his life.

"Jenks drove up in front of the house about 8 o'clock," said Miss Ida Goodell, who was in another room of the house, "and came into the house, to see Mrs. Blachley. I heard their voices raised in what seemed to be an argument, and heard Mrs. Blachley cry out, 'Don't you dare do that.'

"An instant later two shots rang out. Jenks ran from the house, hurried into his car, and drove rapidly away.

"I rushed into the room. Mrs. Blachley was lying on the floor, bullet wounds through her chest and heart. I called Dr. T. A. Williams, but life had passed before he arrived.

Jenks' 9-year-old daughter Mildred, who accompanied him on the trip to Pasadena and on the wild ride back, said her father had repeatedly told her, after leaving the Bennett home, that he had not shot Mrs. Blachley.

"And he was driving, oh, so fast," the little girl said. "I asked him two or three times not to drive so fast, but he didn't seem to hear me."

Reports by friends of Mrs. Blachley to Pasadena police declared that her husband had died less than a year ago, and that Jenks, a friend of both Mr. and Mrs. Blachley, had taken the body back to Cherokee, Iowa, for burial.

A little later, it was said, Mrs. Blachley gave birth to a baby, which survives her.

Coal Miners' Pay Cut Set Aside in Colorado

WALSENBURG, Colo., Sept. 10.—(By the Associated Press.)—The Colorado State Industrial Commission today set aside a wage reduction inaugurated in coal mines of the Colorado Fuel and Iron Company in Huerfano and Las Animas counties and placed the old wage scale in effect pending further investigation of the controversy which has tied up many mines for more than a week.

TROOPS TAKE CONTROL AT SAN ANTONIO

Heavy Life Loss From Texas Storm Caused by Residents Refusing to Heed Police Warning

THOUSAND HOMES SMASHED

Soldiers Drag 500 Out of Water and Begin Relief Work; Forty Bodies Have Been Recovered

SAN ANTONIO, Texas, Sept. 10.—(By Associated Press.)—Thirty-six persons are known to have been killed and hundreds injured in flood waters which swept down on this city early today. Police estimates, however, place the total death list as high as 250. The property damage will run into the millions.

SAN ANTONIO, Texas, Sept. 10.—(By Universal Service.)—As San Antonio settled down in darkness tonight following a day of floods thirty-five bodies had been recovered and the estimated dead was placed at seventy-five.

The estimate was made by Mayor O. B. Black and military authorities. The property damage was placed at $12,000,000.

The city is dark because the water which overflowed from San Antonio River early this morning wrecked the lighting plant.

But darkness is not the worst of the city's discomforts. The waterworks and the sewer systems are also out of commission and it is feared this will cause an epidemic of sickness to follow in the wake of the flood.

SEMI-MARTIAL LAW

Semi-martial law prevails here tonight. The city is being patrolled by troops from Camp Travis and Fort Sam Houston.

The business district and the Mexican quarter were the worst hit. In the business district, water ran from 10 to 15 feet deep when the flood was at its highest.

A citizens committee, aided by the military forces, is caring for the thousands of homeless tonight at army kitchens. Military authorities and the citizens have provided tents, food and medical supplies for the unfortunate.

Telephone lines are out of commission and most of its streets in and leading to the down town section are impassable because of the chaos wrought by the waters.

Most of the bodies recovered up to the time that darkness fell tonight are those of women and children—helpless victims of the deluge as it swept everything before it in a two-mile strip in the western part of the city.

1000 HOMES SMASHED

In that part of the city occupied largely by Mexicans, more than 1000 homes were smashed to bits like they were cardboard by the wall of water that swept down on them. Tonight more than 5000 persons made homeless in the devastated area are being sheltered in tents provided by military authorities.

At the same time approximately twenty blocks of downtown stores are almost a total loss from the twelve feet of water which swept into the business district, filling basements where stores of merchandise were kept and converting the entire district into a mass of muck and ruin.

Much of the property loss than resulted from the cloudburst and storm was unavoidable. Around the loss of life, however, can be written another story.

It was the old, old case of people refusing to be warned.

Last night, two hours before the flood waters swept upon the city, police officers sent out from central headquarters went from house to house in the Mexican district notifying residents there that the entire district was al-

(Continued on Page 4, Column 2)

SCREEN BEAUTY DEATH VICTIM

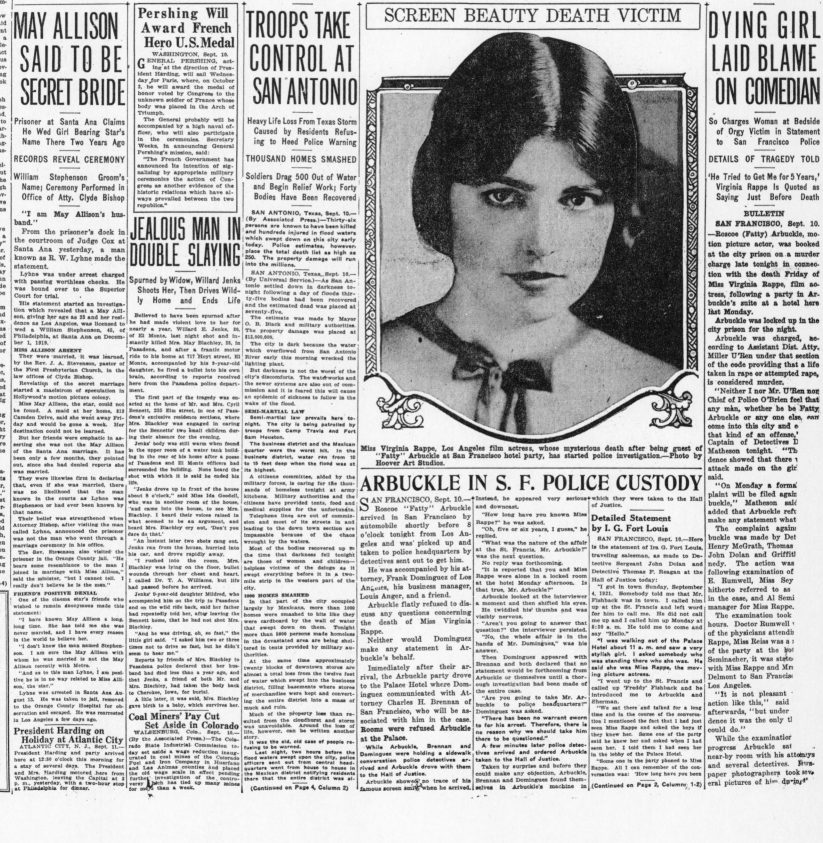

Miss Virginia Rappe, Los Angeles film actress, whose mysterious death after being guest of "Fatty" Arbuckle at San Francisco hotel party, has started police investigation.—Photo by Hoover Art Studios.

ARBUCKLE IN S. F. POLICE CUSTODY

SAN FRANCISCO, Sept. 10.—Roscoe "Fatty" Arbuckle arrived in San Francisco by automobile shortly before 8 o'clock tonight from Los Angeles and was picked up and taken to police headquarters by detectives sent out to get him.

He was accompanied by his attorney, Frank Dominguez of Los Angeles, his business manager, Louis Anger, and a friend.

Arbuckle flatly refused to discuss any questions concerning the death of Miss Virginia Rappe.

Neither would Dominguez make any statement in Arbuckle's behalf.

Immediately after their arrival, the Arbuckle party drove to the Palace Hotel where Dominguez communicated with Attorney Charles H. Brennan of San Francisco, who will be associated with him in the case. **Rooms were refused Arbuckle at the Palace.**

While Arbuckle, Brennan and Dominguez were holding a sidewalk conversation police detectives arrived and Arbuckle drove with them to the Hall of Justice.

Arbuckle showed no trace of his famous screen smile when he arrived. Instead, he appeared very serious and downcast.

"How long have you known Miss Rappe?" he was asked.

"Oh, five or six years, I guess," he replied.

"What was the nature of the affair at the St. Francis, Mr. Arbuckle?" was the next question.

No reply was forthcoming.

"It is reported that you and Miss Rappe were alone in a locked room at the hotel Monday afternoon. Is that true, Mr. Arbuckle?"

Arbuckle looked at the interviewer a moment and then shifted his eyes.

He twiddled his thumbs and was visibly nervous.

"Aren't you going to answer that question?" the interviewer persisted.

"No, the whole affair is in the hands of Mr. Dominguez," was his answer.

Then Dominguez appeared with Brennan and both declared that no statement would be forthcoming from Arbuckle or themselves until a thorough investigation had been made of the entire case.

"Are you going to take Mr. Arbuckle to police headquarters?" Dominguez was asked.

"There has been no warrant sworn to for his arrest. Therefore, there is no reason why we should take him there to be questioned."

A few minutes later police detectives arrived and ordered Arbuckle taken to the Hall of Justice.

Taken by surprise and before they could make any objection, Arbuckle, Brennan and Dominguez found themselves in Arbuckle's machine in which they were taken to the Hall of Justice.

Detailed Statement by I. G. Fort Louis

SAN FRANCISCO, Sept. 10.—Here is the statement of Ira G. Fort Louis, traveling salesman, as made to Detective Sergeant John Dolan and Detective Thomas F. Reagan at the Hall of Justice today:

"I got in town Sunday, September 4, 1921. Somebody told me that Mr. Fishback was in town. I called him up at the St. Francis and left word for him to call me. He did not call me up and I called him up Monday at 8:30 a. m. He told me to come and say "Hello."

"I was walking out of the Palace Hotel about 11 a. m. and saw a very stylish girl. I asked somebody who was standing there who she was. He said she was Miss Rappe, the moving picture actress.

"I went up to the St. Francis and called up 'Freddy' Fishback and he introduced me to Arbuckle and Sherman.

"We sat there and talked for a long time and in the course of the conversation I mentioned the fact that I had just seen Miss Rappe and asked the boys if they knew her. Some one of the party said he knew her and asked when I had seen her. I told them I had seen her in the lobby of the Palace Hotel.

"Some one in the party phoned to Miss Rappe. All I can remember of the conversation was: 'How long have you been

(Continued on Page 2, Columns 1-2)

DYING GIRL LAID BLAME ON COMEDIAN

So Charges Woman at Bedside of Orgy Victim in Statement to San Francisco Police

DETAILS OF TRAGEDY TOLD

'He Tried to Get Me for 5 Years,' Virginia Rappe Is Quoted as Saying Just Before Death

BULLETIN

SAN FRANCISCO, Sept. 10.—Roscoe (Fatty) Arbuckle, motion picture actor, was booked at the city prison on a murder charge late tonight in connection with the death Friday of Miss Virginia Rappe, film actress, following a party in Arbuckle's suite at a hotel here last Monday.

Arbuckle was locked up in the city prison for the night.

Arbuckle was charged, according to Assistant Dist. Atty. Miller U'Ren under that section of the code providing that a life taken in rape or attempted rape, is considered murder.

"Neither I nor Mr. U'Ren nor Chief of Police O'Brien feel that any man, whether he be Fatty Arbuckle or any one else, can come into this city and c[illegible] that kind of an offense,' Captain of Detectives D[illegible] Matheson tonight. "Th[illegible] dence showed that there [illegible] attack made on the gir[illegible] said.

"On Monday a forma[illegible] plaint will be filed agai[illegible] buckle," Matheson sai[illegible] added that Arbuckle ref[illegible] make any statement what[illegible]

The complaint agains[illegible] buckle was made by Det[illegible] Henry McGrath, Thomas [illegible] John Dolan and Griffit[illegible] nedy. The action was [illegible] following examination of [illegible] E. Rumwell, Miss Sey[illegible] hitherto referred to as [illegible] in the case, and Al Semi[illegible] manager for Miss Rappe.

The examination took [illegible] hours. Doctor Rumwell [illegible] of the physicians attendi[illegible] Rappe, Miss Reiss was a [illegible] of the party at the hot[illegible] Seminacher, it was state[illegible] with Miss Rappe and Mr[illegible] Delmont to San Francis[illegible] Los Angeles.

"It is not pleasant [illegible] action like this," said [illegible] afterwards, "but under [illegible] dence it was the only t[illegible] could do."

While the examinatio[illegible] progress Arbuckle sa[illegible] near-by room with his attorneys and several detectives. Newspaper photographers took several pictures of him during [illegible]

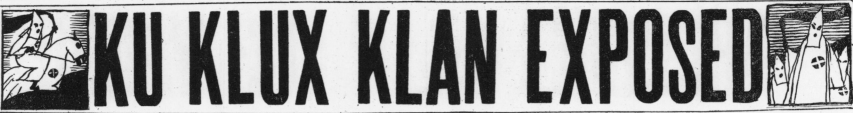

STOCKS
PAGES 21 AND 22

THE CLEVELAND NEWS

FIRST BASEBALL

VOL. 80.—NO. 265. Published on six days of the week by the Cleveland Company, Cleveland, O. Entered as second class matter at Cleveland postoffice under the act of March 3, 1879. CLEVELAND, THURSDAY, SEPTEMBER 22, 1921. PRICE TWO CENTS

KU KLUX KLAN EXPOSED

"TODAY" ON PAGE 13 TODAY

GRAND GOBLIN RISKS DEATH TO EXPOSE KU KLUX SECRETS

FOLLOWING a threat on his life, C. Anderson Wright, who has been a member of the headquarters staff of the Invisible Empire of the Ku Klux Klan, has resigned from that organization.

Much has been published about the Ku Klux Klan, but little has been told.

Through the first-hand information of Wright, who up until now has been a faithful member of the Invisible Empire, readers of The Cleveland News and The Sunday News-Leader will be told the whole story of this mystic, secret organization whose tentacles reach into every phase of the nation's life and every part of the country as it is known only to a very few persons actually at the head of the order.

With the signature on his resignation hardly dry, Wright began preparing for an astounding expose.

His first article, beginning in The News today, goes right down to the actual operation of the Klan and deals specifically with a plot to drive the Jews out of America.

Ex-Grand Goblin Wright will tell of the national scope of the Ku Klux Klan and how these schemes would, if carried out, affect the entire United States.

Mr. Wright is a well-known figure in aeronautics, being honorary member of more than thirty foreign national aero clubs and having received citations and diplomas from sixteen foreign nations for war work.

He is president of the Mississippi Valley Aviation Clubs Association, a reserve military aviator in the inactive federal air service, was officer in charge during the war and later publisher of "Tale Spins," the national aircraft magazine.

Originally founded in the reconstruction days following the Civil war to "maintain white supremacy," the revamped organization, with brutality in many instances, seeks to hamper all progress within the United States of all foreign-born citizens, all Catholics and all Jews.

Nor is there any hampering influence to prevent the extension of their secret antagonism to any group or movement at any time.

Already more than 700,000 members blindly follow the initiative of the "Imperial Wizard." His word is law and his demands are followed without a moment's pause. Secretly or openly, depending upon the atmosphere at the scene of attack, the Klan does its will.

The state and city chapters of the Klan have committed countless outrages and personal spite has in many instances been the only traceable purpose of beatings, application of tar and feathers and the "riding out of town" of citizens whose greatest fault was the accident of their birthplace or their religious belief.

The growing menace has now extended to forty states and is constantly progressing, largely through the eloquence of solicitors who are very generously paid for their efforts in obtaining memberships.

The vital weakness of this theory of lawless order is but emphasized by the new strength of organization. A protest, national in scope, gives promise of soon banishing forever the white mask, flowing gown and flaming cross of the Klan.

VETERANS HERE OPEN KLAN WAR

Legion Members Back Council, While Labor Joins in Fight.

An organized campaign to stamp out the Ku Klux Klan in Cleveland was launched Thursday by World war veterans and members of organized labor, adding their strength to the stand already taken by the city council.

Every legitimate means of fighting the Klan will be used by the Cleveland Federation of Labor, Secretary John G. Owens announced. The federation, he said, has gone on record by a unanimous vote as "definitely opposed to the organization, its secrecy, and the references to it as the 'Invisible Empire.'"

Legion Men Take Stand.

A resolution, similar to the one unanimously adopted by city council several weeks ago, was passed by a caucus of Cleveland delegates to the American L[illegible] state convention, opening in Toledo Monday. The resolution, introduced by Attorney T. A. Ryan, chairman of the committee of delegates, follows:

WHEREAS, there is in existence in the United States and in the state of Ohio an organization under the name and style of the Ku Klux Klan; and

WHEREAS, one of the declared objects of this organization is the disenfranchisement of the negro, an object which is in direct violation of the constitution of the United States, and it is well known that the said organization has for its object the furtherance of propaganda tending to foment religious and racial prejudice and to create dissension among the people of the United States; and

WHEREAS, it is the desire of the American Legion of Ohio that the unification of the nation affected during the world war would remain as one of the great benefits of the conflict;

NOW THEREFORE BE IT RESOLVED by the American Legion of the state of Ohio, in convention assembled at Toledo, O., that we, the delegates representing the entire membership of the organization in the state condemn the formation of any organization wose purpose is to breed religious or racial strife or destroy the unity of the American people; and

BE IT FURTHER RESOLVED that we particularly condemn and hereby go on record as being opposed to the organization known as the Ku Klux Klan.

BE IT FURTHER RESOLVED that the state adjutant be and is hereby directed to transmit a copy of this resolution to the President of the United States, the attorney general of the United States, the United States Senators from Ohio and the national commander of the American Legion.

Copies of it will be sent to the

Continued on 2d Page, 2d Column.

Harding to Get Debs Findings Next Week

WASHINGTON, Sept. 22.—Attorney General Daugherty announced today that his recommendations on the appeal for a pardon for Eugene V. Debs, Socialist leader now in the Atlanta penitentiary, probably will be sent to the President next week.

The recommendations now are ready for the President, the attorney general said, although he refused to disclose their nature.

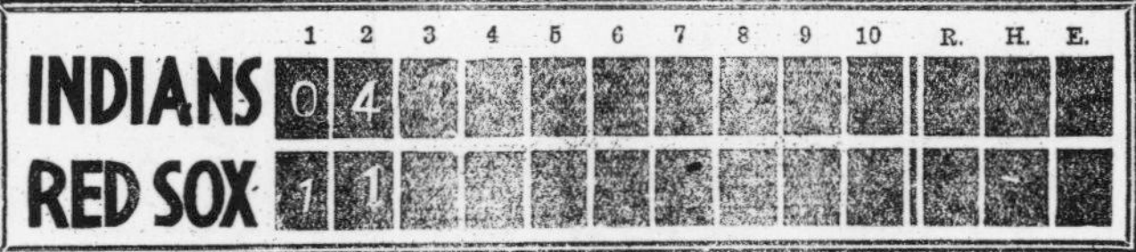

	1	2	3	4	5	6	7	8	9	10	R.	H.	E.
INDIANS	0	4											
RED SOX	1	1											

Sothoron-O'Neill; Russell-Walters

Head of Ku Klux, and Ceremonials

Taking Oath to the KU-KLUX-KLAN amidst the Georgia Pines. The American Flag and the Fiery Cross are always inseparable symbols of the Klan at all ceremonies.

KU-KLUX-KLAN During a Weird Ceremony on Top of Stone Mountain, near Atlanta. Note Fiery Cross' Symbol of Order.

WILLIAM J. SIMMONS, Imperial Wizard.

UP TO SOTHORON TO TRIM BOSTON IN LAST BATTLE

By Wilbur Wood.

BOSTON, Sept. 22.—With an opportunity to regain first place in the American League providing they defeated the Boston Red Sox here this afternoon and the Detroit Tigers trimmed New York, the Cleveland Indians took the field confident of victory.

Allan Bothoron was on the mound for the Indians and was opposed by Russell.

FIRST INNING

CLEVELAND—Jamieson rolled to McInnis. Wamby fanned. Wood walked. Smith doubled to center, Wood stopping at third. Russell threw out Gardner. No runs, one hit, no errors.

BOSTON—Leibold got all the way to second when his roller was fumbled by Wamby. Foster sacrificed, O'Neill to Johnston. Pratt singled to center, scoring Leibold. McInnis sacrificed, O'Neill to Johnston. O'Neill was hit on the finger by a foul tip bu tstayed in the game. Collins struck out. One run, one hit, one error.

OTHER GAMES

AMERICAN LEAGUE

Detroit at New York—		R.	H.	E.
Det...	0 . . . .—	.	.	.
N. Y..	0 . . . .—	.	.	.

Ehmke-Bassler; Shawkey-Schang.

First Game

St. Louis at Philadelphia—		R.	H.	E.
St. L..	200000300 . . .—	5	10	1
Phil...	000000000 . . .—	0	6	2

Davis-Severeid; Moore-Myatt.

Second Game

St. Louis at Philadelphia—		R.	H.	E.
St. L..	0 . . . .—	.	.	.
Phil..	0 . . . .—	.	.	.

Bayne-Severeid; Naylor-Perkins.

NATIONAL LEAGUE

First Game

Brooklyn at Pittsburg—		R.	R.	E.
Bklyn.	000010000 . . .—	1	7	3
Pitts..	00000003* . . .—	3	4	1

Grimes-Miller; Glazner-Gooch.

AMERICAN ASSOCIATION

First Game

Kansas City at Columbus—		R.	H.	E.
K. C..	0000 . . . .—	.	.	.
Col..	0124 . . . .—	.	.	.

Lambert-Skiff; Danforth-Hartley.

Happenings in the realty world appear every day in the real estate column on the financial page.

WILSON LOSES PURSE

JERSEY CITY, N. J., Sept. 22.—The New Jersey boxing commission today decided to deprive Johnny Wilson, middleweight champion of $35,000 he was to have received for his Labor Day bout with Bryan Downey, of Cleveland. Wilson was accused of failing to put forth his best efforts in the contest, and found guilty by the commission.

STAUFFER, MARSHAL?

WASHINGTON, Sept. 22.—That G. A. Stauffer of Ottawa will be appointed United States marshal at Cleveland was an indication today following the visit of Senator Willis at the White House. In that event, Major Fanning may be appointed his assistant.

WORLD'S SERIES GAMES TO BEGIN ON OCTOBER 5

With Winners in Doubt, First Game Will Be Played in National League City.

CHICAGO, Sept. 22.—(By A. P.)—The world's series will start October 5, it was decided today, the first game being played on the home grounds of the National League team.

In the event Pittsburg or Cleveland should finish first two series games will be played in the National League city, the next two in the American League town, and so on. Both New York teams are at present leading the leagues.

The details of the series were arranged today at a meeting of the league presidents with Judge Kenesaw M. Landis, baseball commissioner.

President John Heydler, of the Nationals, won the toss and the first game for his league.

Leslie O'Connor, secretary to Judge Landis, tossed the coin and Ban Johnson, president of the American League, called "heads." It fell "tails."

The commissioner and the league presidents fixed the prices for the series at from $1 to $6.

If one or both New York teams win the prices will be $1 in the bleachers, $3 for unreserved seats in the upper grand stand, $5 for lower grand stand reservations and $6 in the boxes.

In the event Cleveland wins, boxes will be $6, reservations $4 and $5, pavilion seats $2 and general admission $1.

Minutes sail by like the galleons of old, each with its cargo of silver and gold. Some of these minutes are headed for you; mark that you signal them out of the blue. Let them not sail past your port on the coast, lest they be wrecked and their cargoes be lost.

THE WEATHER

THE NEWS BAROMETER. (Sea level) 11 a. m. 30.00

Fair tonight and Friday. Slightly cooler Friday. Fresh and strong southwest winds.

High Chief Bares All

Driving Out of Jews, Catholics and Foreign Born One Aim of "Money-Making" Scheme, Charge.

CHAPTERS TO COME:

THE WAR ON THE CATHOLICS.
NIGHT RIDERS OF THE AIR.
THE $7,000,000 AIR GRAB.
WHERE $20,000,000 GOES.
$3,500,000 FOR DIRTY RIVER WATER.
THE PLOT AGAINST MASONRY.
PLANNED THEFT OF 5,000 PLANES.

And many other chapters, to be printed exclusively in The Cleveland News and The Cleveland Sunday News-Leader.

BY C. ANDERSON WRIGHT

Former Grand Goblin, King Kleagle, Invisible Empire, Ku Klux Klan, and Chief of Staff, Invisible Planet, Knights of the Air.

The Ku Klux Klan is all a mere money-making scheme.

The Ku Klux Klan, going into a locality, ascertains local conditions.

It finds the local prejudice, whatever that may be.

In the Middle West the Ku Klux Klan is aimed at the Negro and the Socialist.

In the South the prejudice is against the Negro.

In the West the yellow peril forms the basis of the Ku Klux operations.

In the East it finds there is a certain prejudice against the Jew and Catholic. In this first article I will deal specifically with the Jewish question. I will deal with the opposition to the Catholics in another article.

It must be borne in mind that what the Ku Klux Klan is trying to do to the Jews in New York city it is trying to do to the Jews wherever they are found.

The Invisible Empire of the Ku Klux Klan plans to drive Jews out of New York.

This is their talking, their selling point, their argument in their drive for membership here.

There are more Jews in New York than any other city in America.

The high officials of the Ku Klux Klan, believing there are more Jew haters in New York than elsewhere, aim to get them into the invisible empire.

After the first class had been initiated into the Ku Klux Klan in New York city last February, Grand Goblin Lloyd P. Hooper received his instructions from the propagation department, which is run on a commercial basis by E. Y. Clarke and Mrs. Elizabeth Tyler. These instructions were in turn passed along to the king kleagles in command of states and the kleagles under them in charge of cities and towns, and then on to the acting klan officers, or direct to the individual klansmen in places where the klan was not well organized.

THE ANTI-JEW PLOT

These instructions were, in exact wording, as follows:

"The Jew patronizes only the Jew, unless it is impossible to do so. Therefore, we, the only real Americans (klansmen), must, by the same methods, protect ourselves and practice by actual application the teachings of klannishness. With the policy faithfully adhered to, it will not be long before the Jew will be forced out of business by our practice of his own business methods, for when the time comes when klansmen trade only with klansmen, then the days of the Jews' success in business will be numbered and the Invisible Empire can drive them from the shores of our own America."

The actual working of this plan was the elaborate publication of a list of every klansman and his occupation, with imperial instructions that whenever possible klansmen would trade only with klansmen and hire only members of the invisible empire as employees.

This actual application of klannishness, preached at great length and which would eventually have caused great havoc among commercial establishments in New York city and elsewhere, has never as yet been carried into effect.

WANT HUGE FUNDS

The reason is this: The klan intends to accumulate a fund so large that failure will be impossible.

A large fund is deemed necessary to establish klansmen

Continued on 2d Page, 1st Column.

LAST MAIL

Chicago Daily Tribune

THE WORLD'S GREATEST NEWSPAPER

VOLUME LXXXI—NO. 143 [COPYRIGHT 1922 BY THE CHICAGO TRIBUNE] FRIDAY, JUNE 16, 1922.—32 PAGES THIS PAPER CONSISTS OF TWO SECTIONS—SECTION ONE. * PRICE TWO CENTS IN CHICAGO AND SUBURBS: ELSEWHERE THREE CENTS

SEIZE 3 KLAN NIGHT RIDERS

MAYOR'S VIEWS ON RECRUITING AIRED AT TRIAL

Reporter Tells of Complaints to U. S.

BY PHILIP KINSLEY.

Complaints made to the federal authorities in 1917 concerning the alleged disloyal utterances of Mayor William Hale Thompson at that time were made a subject of examination yesterday in THE TRIBUNE-Mayor Thompson libel trial in Judge Wilson's court.

Thomas Kennedy, teacher of English in the Carnegie Institute of Technology in Pittsburgh, former city hall reporter for the Chicago Evening Journal, was the witness who introduced this subject. Although married, in 1917 he left his work and his family and enlisted in the army, where he served a year in the air service.

Testifies to Interviews.

In common with other afternoon newspaper men, Mr. Kennedy had various interviews with the mayor during the spring of 1917, he said. Part of the direct examination by Attorney Weymouth Kirkland for THE TRIBUNE threw new light on these interviews. Telling of an interview with the mayor about April 15, 1917, concerning the great increase in the number of men at the marriage license window, the witness said:

"Some one asked the mayor if he had heard about the line of people who were waiting to get marriage licenses, three or four hundred couples sometimes in line those days, waiting to get marriage licenses, a very unusual number; some one of us had just come from there watching the spectacle and watching the soldiers who were there pinning yellow ribbons on some of the men getting licenses. We told the mayor the circumstances and asked him what he thought about it.

Quotes Mayor on "Yellow Ribbons."

Q.—What did he say? A.—He said, "I don't know that the fact those men are getting marriage licenses at this time proves they are cowards. I don't favor pinning yellow ribbons on them, either, or bothering them in any way."

Q.—Was anything else said? A.—Some one of the group who had been there a few minutes previously told the mayor that not one in a hundred of these men when interviewed expressed any desire or willingness to fight for this country, and asked him what he thought about that. I suppose, having in mind his statement that he didn't believe the fact they were there proved they were cowards, and my recollection is that the mayor said, "Why, I think that proves conclusively that the people of this country don't want to send an army to Europe," or "That the citizens of this country don't want to send an army to Europe," something like that.

Recalls Statement on Invasion.

Q.—Do you recall whether he said anything about invasion? A.—He said he thought the people of this country were all of them willing, or practically all of them willing to do anything necessary to repel any invasion or defend this country if it were invaded, but that he did not—I think he went on to say that he himself did not favor sending anybody abroad or sending American soldiers to fight in any other country.

Q.—Go ahead. A.—A few days after that was the anniversary of Paul Revere's ride—something of that sort—any way, some revolutionary holiday was more or less being celebrated, and the mayor was asked whether or not he was willing to take part in a plan to stimulate recruiting, a special recruiting drive on that day. He thought about it a little bit and then he said: "I don't think much of the idea." Then, on being asked further, "Are you planning to take a part in the recruiting campaign?" he said: "What is the matter with letting the federal government do it?" or something like that. "Isn't it up to the federal government?"

Tells Stand on Recruiting.

Q.—Before we get to the Joffre incident, did you ever have an interview with him one day concerning some naval lieutenant who wanted assistance from him? A.—Yes, sir. This naval lieutenant—I think his name was Stevens—came in to see the mayor.

Q.—What did the mayor say about it, anyway? A.—It developed that the mayor said—this is just as I remember it, and I think the mayor told me himself—the mayor said to him: "I told him I was busy, too busy to aid any plan for recruiting; that the mayor of Chicago had too many things to do to take part in that, and I suggested to him that he enlist the aid"—he mentioned the name of a prominent yachtsman in Chicago, the name of some former commodore of the Chi-

(Continued on page 4, column 1.)

NEWS SUMMARY

LOCAL.

"Klan will open cell doors for us," is boast of three men held for threatening doctor.

Mrs. James W. Thorne, testifying at Mader trial, testifies she paid $1,400 to avert Drake hotel strike.

Blind girl "marvel" really has some vision, declares University of Wisconsin professor.

Cashier of Grant Park Trust and Savings bank testifies in Small trial that in his reports for his institution he did not recognize "Grant Park Bank" as a banking institution.

Witness in TRIBUNE-Mayor Thompson libel suit tells of complaints made to federal authorities in 1917 about the mayor's utterances in connection with the war.

WASHINGTON.

Ship subsidy bill, urgently demanded by President, jeopardized by prohibition issue raised by government's sale of liquor on shipping board ships; threatens to force big fight and may prevent merchant marine relief.

Republicans of senate finance committee refuse to reconsider high tariff rate on aluminum, which has been criticized both within and without the party.

Secretary Hoover gets assurances of coöperation on coal price restriction in harmonious conference with representatives of operators and retailers.

State department gets hopeful reports from Cuba and Gen. Crowder.

Consolidation of the Illinois Central and Seaboard Air Line with other lines into the Illinois Central-Seaboard system opposed today by C. H. Markham, president, and C. R. Capps, vice president, at a hearing before the interstate commerce commission.

President Harding's leadership facing acid test in both houses of congress in the struggle over the tariff, soldiers' bonus, ship subsidy, and liquor questions.

Senator McCormick ... amendment to naval bill to increase ... for Great Lakes Naval Tr... station to $350,000 defeated in se... vote of 37 to 17.

DOMESTIC.

Secretary of War Weeks hits at reformers, "blocs," and congressmen generally, and says recent constitutional amendments show U. S. heading away from ancient safeguards.

Associated Advertising clubs elect Louis Holland of Kansas City president. Indorse government reports of newspaper circulation.

American Federation of Labor indorses the coal strike and loudly cheers announcement that 1,000,000 railroad workers are going to strike.

Dr. Boynton of Chicago loses in test vote at Baptist Northern convention.

Charters as temples denied Midwest oases by imperial council at Shrine conclave.

Walter S. Ward, wealthy baker, rearrested in blackmail slaying case and charged with first degree murder.

Bentonite, a clay like substance, is said to have been used successfully in dissolving the ink from old newspapers, leaving the paper in a perfectly clean condition.

Next Monday, when Mars will be only 42,000,000 miles from the earth, Sig. Marconi on his yacht at sea will try to pick up wireless messages from that planet.

FOREIGN.

Hullinger says Communism is dead in Russia. Greed among officials and wild speculation among people now rules.

SPORTING.

Sox winning streak nipped after six straight, when Athletics win, 10 to 8. Cubs kept idle by rain in Boston.

Suzanne Lenglen announces she will disregard father's prohibition and will play in Wimbledon international tennis tourney in order to meet Mrs. Molla Mallory, but "doubts Mrs. Mallory will reach finals."

North Shore and Army polo teams play at former's field here today.

Athletes from all over country arrive for preliminaries in annual national collegiate meet on Stagg field this afternoon.

Public clamor for a Wills-Dempsey fight in evidence when Brennan and Willard are advanced by promoters as prospective matches for the champion.

EDITORIALS.

Sea Control and Prohibition; La Follette Proposes a Revolution; The City Hall Sugar Bowl.

MARKETS.

"Bear drive" sends stocks down again; high grade investment bonds advance sharply; London bank rate cut from 4 to 3½ per cent.

Illinois Bell Telephone company plans to increase its capital stock from $50,000,000 to $60,000,000 and is considering selling the new stock to patrons and employés.

July wheat hits new low on present downturn, wheat's net losses being 1⅛ @2⅝c; corn off ¾@1⅝c, oats ⅝@1⅛c, and rye ⅝@1⅛c lower.

Choice cattle in good demand at strong prices; other kinds weak to 25c lower; hogs close firm after early break; lambs hit new low mark.

ON THE HIGH SEAS

[Copyright: 1922: By The Chicago Tribune.]

MRS. ROBBINS TO BE ARRESTED IN FATAL CAR SKID

(Picture on back page.)

Kenosha, Wis., June 15.—[Special.]—When Mrs. Mary Robbins, 623 Cornelia avenue, Chicago, is discharged from St. Catherine's hospital here tomorrow, she will be taken into custody on a manslaughter charge growing out of an automobile accident in which Deputy Sheriff Jacob Keul was killed Sunday night at Liberty Corners, seventeen miles west of Kenosha.

Mrs. Robbins, who was driving the car, owned by Norman Weiss, general manager of the Calumet Refrigerator company, Chicago, is the divorced wife of Cutler B. Robbins, son of George B. Robbins, former president of the Armour Car company.

Weiss, who was in the rear seat of the car in which Mrs. Robbins, Mrs. Neil Curry, and Deputy Sheriff Keul were riding when it turned turtle, was released on bonds today after he had been arraigned on a manslaughter charge.

MAN KILLED BY GRIZZLY AFTER TERRIFIC FIGHT

Livingston, Mont., June 15.—Yellowstone park rangers are trailing a huge grizzly bear that recently killed and partly devoured Joseph Duret, 60, an old time Montana trapper. Duret's body was found yesterday on Slough creek, near the park, with an arm and a leg partly chewed off. Signs indicated the bear had been caught in one of Duret's traps, but had broken loose when the trapper came by on his rounds.

Horace M. Albright, superintendent of the park, said there were evidences of a terrific battle, and a rifle, clawed and chewed, was found near the broken trap. One shot had been fired from the rifle and a bloody trail showed that the man had crept a mile and a half after receiving his injuries.

BLOW UP HOUSES TO STOP BLAZE ON LONG ISLAND

New York, June 15.—Fire raging over Arverne, a Long Island bungalow colony on the edge of Greater New York, is reported to have destroyed more than seventy homes tonight and several persons are said to have been injured.

Fire fighters are attempting to check the flames by dynamiting houses in the path of the conflagration.

Hundreds Hear Speakers at 'Stepladder' Meeting

(Picture on back page.)

Hundreds of loop employés crowded the arcade and La Salle street adjacent to the Central Y. M. C. A. yesterday as the first of the series of summer "stepladder" meetings was held at noon. Bishop Thomas Nicholson, the Rev. Howard Agnew Johnston, president of the Chicago Church federation, and the Rev. Ernest A. Bell were speakers.

BLIND "MARVEL" SEES, IS REPORT

Girl Self-Deluded, Is Expert's Belief.

An explanation of the unusual senses developed by Miss Willetta Huggins, 17 year old deaf and blind girl, an inmate of the Wisconsin School for the Blind, is given in the current issue of the American Medical Journal by Prof. Joseph Jastrow of the department of psychology of the University of Wisconsin.

WILLETTA HUGGINS.

In a recent demonstration before the Chicago Medical society Miss Huggins apparently distinguished colors by the sense of smell, told what was spoken to her by means of a wooden rod, one end of which she held and the other end of which was placed against the head of the speaker, and "read" newspaper headlines by the sense of touch.

Can See in Part.

"The reason Miss Huggins is accredited with these unusual senses is through the conviction that her sight and hearing are useless," Prof. Jastrow says, and explains that those conducting such experiments usually have "the will to believe" and are credulous at the beginning.

Instead of distinguishing colors by smell, Prof. Jastrow says Miss Huggins was able to tell them through the remnant of sight which she retains. There probably is no intention to deceive on her part, he explains, as serting the case may be one of self-deception. Instead of actually smelling colors, he contends that Miss Huggins sees them through the slit of vision she still has. To prove this he asserts that the tests failed in a dark room, and adds that dyes used for wool, silk, and cotton are very different for the same colors. He asserts that Miss Huggins is able to see under a blindfold in the same manner.

Hears Without Rod.

He states that Miss Huggins was able to distinguish sounds when the wooden rod was not in contact with the head of the speaker.

"Noiseless Bullet" Fells Cafe Man on South Side

Wabash avenue police last evening sought to learn the source of a "noiseless bullet" which seriously wounded James Costello, 4040 Grand boulevard, cafe owner, as he was walking near East Forty-second and State streets. Neither the victim nor persons nearby heard the shot. Costello was taken to Wesley hospital by Albert Capona, 6832 Sheridan road, where the bullet was extracted from his chest.

EX-"SUB" CHASER BURNS AND SINKS; WOMAN INJURED

Key West, Fla., June 15.—Former submarine chaser No. 205, owned by E. T. Sulzer of Brooklyn, N. Y., was burned to the water's edge and sank today off Sand Key. Mrs. Sulzer, who with her husband and a party of friends was aboard, was slightly burned.

The guests and crew included Mr. and Mrs. Sulzer, Otis Burrell, Forest Cooper and George Pine of Miami, Frank Baziler and William Carey of Key West, Wallace Stuart and Walter Dewoiser of Northboro, Mass., Larry Johnston and William Nelson of Boulder, Colo., and Clyde Earle of Jacksonville. They were taken off by the schooner Champion.

The vessel, which left here early today after putting into Key West for fuel, was enroute from Miami to Matanzas, Cuba. The fire, believed to have originated from a short circuit, was discovered when the boat was thirteen miles from Key West.

Monument to a Hog Is Dedicated in Ohio Town

Middletown, O., June 15.—Hundreds of stock breeders from all over the country gathered at Blue Ball, near here, today to witness the unveiling of a monument to a hog, the first of the Poland China strain. The monument marks the site of the home of W. C. Hankinson, now dead, who in 1875 wrote the first hog pedigree which established the Poland China strain. Miss Irene Hankinson, a granddaughter, unveiled the monument.

THE WEATHER

FRIDAY, JUNE 16, 1922.

Chicago and vicinity—Partly cloudy Friday and Saturday, with possibly a local thundershower; slightly warmer Friday; moderate to fresh southwest to west winds.

Illinois—Partly cloudy Friday and Saturday, possibly local thundershowers in north portion; not so warm Saturday in west portion.

Indiana—Partly cloudy Friday and Saturday; continued warm.

Lower Michigan and Upper Michigan—Unsettled Friday and Saturday, probably showers; not much change in temperature.

Upper Lakes — Moderate to fresh easterly winds on Superior and southeast to south winds on Michigan, and Huron; showers Friday and possibly Saturday.

Lower Lakes—Moderate easterly winds; partly cloudy and somewhat unsettled Friday and probably Saturday.

Wisconsin—Showers Friday, warmer in east portion; Saturday generally fair and cooler, preceded by showers in east portion.

Missouri—Generally fair Friday and probably Saturday; not so warm Saturday.

Minnesota—Showers Friday, slightly cooler in west and south portions; Saturday probably fair.

Iowa—Unsettled Friday, probably showers in east portion; Saturday probably; fair not so warm Saturday, and in extreme west portion Friday.

North Dakota—Unsettled Friday, possibly showers; Saturday generally fair; not much change in temperature.

South Dakota—Unsettled Friday, possibly showers; cooler in east portion; Saturday generally fair.

Nebraska—Fair Friday and probably Saturday; not so warm Friday.

Kansas—Partly cloudy Friday and probably Saturday; not so warm Friday.

Montana—Generally fair Friday and probably Saturday; warmer Friday in southwest portion.

Wyoming—Fair Friday and probably Saturday; warmer Saturday, and in west portion Friday.

ASSAILANTS OF MORRIS DOCTOR ARE ARRESTED

Ku Klux to Open Jail, Their Boast.

(Pictures on back page.)

"The klan is powerful, it will not let us stay in jail or suffer for what we've done—the klan has too much influence for that; it will get us out of trouble, come to our rescue."

This early yesterday, according to detectives, was the optimistic statement of three members of the Ku Klux Klan who were arrested for speeding on their return early in the morning from Morris, Ill., where they confessed they made a fiasco of the attempted chastisement of Dr. William A. Muttera.

Klan Fails Them.

But late last night the "powerful" klan had done nothing for them, the three were still in custody, and they were told by Maj. Albert L. Denman, head of the highway police, that they will be arraigned this morning on charges of speeding, carrying concealed weapons, and of disfiguring their automobile license plates to escape detection.

Herbert Pascolini, 25 years old, 3745 Maple Square avenue; A. R. Umbach, 27, 1929 Orchard street, and William W. Newman, 29, 1737 Otto street, were the three arrested. Four highway motorcycle policemen took them into custody following a chase after their speeding machine in [illegible] about 4 o'clock in the morning.

When their car finally was brought to a stop the license plates were found to be smeared with grease so as to affect a change in the numbers. In the car were two loaded revolvers, a blackjack and a cat-o-nine-tails.

They were taken to the detective bureau, where they were questioned and soon began to unfold their story.

Visit to Doctor.

They declared their night visit to Morris was the last of four recent night trips there, during each of which they failed in attempts to mistreat Dr. Muttera, a chiropractor, whom they accused of having attacked young girls.

The physician, in Morris, denied their charges, stating their attacks had nothing to do with his treatment of young women. He said it was an attempt to drive him out of business.

"About six weeks ago I began receiving letters signed 'Ku Klux Klan,' ordering me to quit my chiropractic practice, and leave Morris, under threats of being horse whipped or otherwise mistreated if I failed to comply.

"I notified the local authorities and they made investigations, but failed to disclose the identity of the letter writer. Late last night, as I was leaving a dance, I was trailed by an automobile containing three men. Just as I reached my home the automobile drew up to the curb and the three leaped out. They attempted to drag me into the car, but I fought them off and got safely into the house.

Calls Them Paid Agents.

"Their stories concerning my mistreatment of girls are false. They are the paid agents of some one who is trying to put me out of business."

Pascolini and Umbach, at the detective bureau, asserted Newman is an official of the Ku Klux Klan. They admitted they went to Morris to flog the doctor because he "abused" a young girl. They could not, however, give the identity of the girl nor the nature of the alleged "abuse." They stated also it was their fourth unsuccessful attempt to "reach" the doctor and mistreat him.

Detectives Search Home.

Following these admissions detectives searched the home of Newman, where they found a letter from Phillip H. Kohl of Morris and a receipt showing Newman to be a member of the Klan.

The letter from Kohl, signed "fraternally yours," stated:

"This party with whom you left a note last Tuesday evidently is not much afraid. Maybe you had better write him a stiff one on the regular letterhead. Tell him the next time you will call on him in person when he is not looking. He is too fresh and needs the 'proper remedy' to keep him from doing what he has done and no doubt is still doing."

Receipt for $10.

The receipt showing Newman to be a member of the Ku Klux Klan read:

"This is to certify that William W. Newman has donated $10 to the propagating fund of the Knights of the Ku Klux Klan, Inc., and the same is accepted as such and as the full sum of 'Klectokon,' entitling him to be received on the acceptance of his petition under the laws, regulations, and

(Continued on page 6, column 3.)

Mrs. Thorne Bares 'Holdup' at Mader Trial

(Picture on back page.)

Mrs. Narcissa Niblack Thorne, wife of James Ward Thorne, former vice-president of Montgomery, Ward & Co., called by Assistant State's Attorney Hobart P. Young, as a witness in the trial of Fred [Frenchy] Mader, president of the Chicago Building Trades Council, yesterday declared that only by the payment of $1,400 was a strike averted during the construction of the Drake hotel.

Mader, together with Orrington C. Foster, an architect, in charge of the erection of the hotel, are charged with conspiracy to hinder the construction of the building. Foster was granted a separate trial by Judge William A. Dever, who has not as yet fixed the date of Foster's hearing.

How the Trouble Arose.

In response to questioning by Mr. Young, Mrs. Thorne asserted that trouble with the labor leader arose over the furnishing, under contract, by the Women's Exchange, a charitable organization, of which Mrs. Thorne is vice president, of 2,000 lamps, which were made by exchange members and consequently were not union products.

Excerpts from Mrs. Thorne's testimony follow:

Q.—In November, 1920, did you have a conversation, with Mr. Foster, in regard to the lamps furnished the Drake hotel? A.—Yes.

Q.—What was said? A.—He told me the lamps made by the exchange were not union made and that the union would call a strike on the grounds that it was unfair to union labor. Then Mr. Foster brought the lamps to me and I tried to find a way to rectify the matter. I said I would have the lamps rewired at my own expense. A few days later I went to the construction camp, where I met Mr. Foster, John Drake, and Mrs. Drake. I also met Mr. Mader and I told him I wanted to get a union man to put in the rods.

Could Not Pay Fine.

Mrs. Thorne declared that inasmuch as the Women's Exchange was a charitable organization it could not pay a fine, but that she would be willing to have any necessary changes made by union men.

Mrs. Thorne identified a receipt given her by Hinkle & Best company, the firm inserting the required rods in the lamps, showing that she had paid them $1,418. In answer to Mr. Young's question Mrs. Thorne asserted that she had paid the money from her personal funds and had not been authorized by the Women's Exchange.

"The indictment in this case charges that it was money belonging to the Women's Exchange," declared Attorney Charles Erbstein, counsel for Mader, which precipitated a verbal tilt between opposing counsel.

Erbstein Ready to Fight.

"Just because she is Mrs. Thorne she is not entitled to more consideration than any one else," shouted Mr. Erbstein, declaring that he "would go the limit to protect himself and his client."

"Rail on. Rail on," replied Mr. Young.

"Yes, and if you persist in those remarks," interrupted Attorney Erbstein, "I'll knock you over."

"Try it now," challenged Mr. Young, as Erbstein advanced threateningly towards him. At this juncture Judge Dever intervened, warning the lawyers that they were "not going to make a beer garden out of the courtroom."

"Where did you get the $1,418?" asked Mr. Erbstein, in continuing the cross-examination.

"From my husband," answered Mrs. Thorne.

"Was your personal bank account depleted?"

Mrs. Thorne, plainly uncomfortable at the turn the questioning was taking, replied that she "couldn't just remember."

CONGRESS DRYS FROWN ON SHIP SUBSIDY BILL

Ocean Liners' Bars May Wreck Fleet.

[BY A STAFF CORRESPONDENT.]

Wasihngton, D. C., June 15.—[Special.]—The ship subsidy bill, urgently demanded by President Harding before congress adjourns, was confronted today with the predicted formidable opposition, jeopardizing its passage as a result of complications growing out of the sale of liquor on American ships.

Middle western Republicans, never more than lukewarm toward the subsidy, if not openly opposed to it, gave clear indications of their intention of supporting an amendment to the subsidy bill to keep liquor off American ships.

Such an amendment was offered by Representative Bankhead [Ala.], Democrat. It probably will be taken up by the merchant marine committee tomorrow and indications are that it will be rejected. Efforts are being made to prevail upon the rules committee to report an airtight rule that will bar all amendments and prevent the consideration of such a proposal as the Bankhead amendment on the floor. If such a rule is reported, a bitter fight may be expected in the house.

Leaders Are in Quandary.

The situation is a perplexing one for leaders. If they yield to "dry" demands and agree to a prohibition amendment in order to assure passage of the subsidy the value of the measure to many ship owners would be destroyed. Many of them believe that a subsidy which denied them the right to sell liquor to their passengers would be little better than no subsidy at all. On the other hand, if "dry" amendments are voted down, the bill will have a difficult passage through both houses. A careful canvass is being made of votes in the house in an effort to ascertain whether the subsidy can command a majority without a "dry" amendment.

Subsidy advocates conceded that the Busch letter denouncing the sale of liquor on American ships has seriously affected their prospects of success. Some of them estimate that the disclosure of the sale of liquor on American ships has cost them from 15 to 50 votes unless a "dry" amendment is accepted.

May Postpone Subsidy Bill.

It is known that Republican leaders who were reluctant to press the subsidy bill, but were about ready to support the administration program, are now planning to urge Mr. Harding to agree to postponement of the measure until next winter. These members take the position that the bill may be defeated if it is brought up now and that it would be better for administration prestige to delay it.

The attitude of many Republican drys was voiced in the house by Representative Cooper [Ohio]. Mr. Cooper declared his opposition to any rule that would bar amendments banning liquor on American shops. In a speech to the house he vigorously arraigned the shipping board's policy of permitting the sale of liquor on American vessels.

"The continuation of the present policy, in my opinion, justifies the charge that 'Uncle Sam is engaged in bootlegging,'" said Mr. Cooper. "Our government cannot afford to permit this condition to continue and the shipping board has no more right to permit liquor to be sold on government owned ships operated under the American flag than the moonshiner and bootlegger at home has to dispense his whisky and raisin jack."

Both Sides Rap Wayne B. Wheeler.

The shipping board's policy was also strongly condemned in the senate. Senator King [Utah], Democrat, declared Chairman Lasker ought to be removed, while Senator Caraway [Ark.], Democrat, characterized the subsidy as "a $100,000,000 bill to enable people to run floating saloons."

Both joined in criticizing Wayne B. Wheeler, anti-saloon league spokesman, who issued a statement yesterday denouncing A. A. Busch for exposing the sale of liquor on American ships. Senator King called attention to the fact that Wheeler advocates prohibition for Americans in China, but added that he countenances the sale of liquor on board American vessels beyond the three mile limit.

"The attorney general says he will hold by the opinion rendered by former Assistant Attorney General Frierson until the courts decree otherwise," Senator Caraway said. "Mr. Lasker says he will hold by the opinion of a lawyer whose name sounds so much like beer that I can't pronounce it until the courts hold otherwise. Mr. Haynes says that between the two he is not going to do anything and Mr. Wheeler, the guardian of prohibition

ARREST 'FATHER' OF 57 GIRLS

Reg. U. S. Patent Office. Copyright, 1923, by Evening Herald Publishing Company

The Evening Herald Grows Just Like Los Angeles

BOX SCORE AND COMPLETE MARKETS EDITION

VOL. XLVIII THREE CENTS FRIDAY, JULY 20, 1923 THREE CENTS Hotels and Trains Five Cents NO. 224

Francisco Villa, Slain Rebel

Mexican bandit chieftain, who for years terrorized the border and for whom the United States sent an expeditionary force after a raid across the line, who was shot and killed near his ranch at Canutillo, state of Durango, by assassins today. At the time of his assassination he had but a handful of faithful bodyguards about him, and several of these were slain.

PANCHO VILLA IS SLAIN BY GUNMEN

Blighted Romance in 'Death Hoax' of Flier

ANTI-SALOON LEAGUE HEAD INDICTED IN N. Y.

By International News Service

NEW YORK, July 20.—William H. Anderson, superintendent of the Anti-Saloon league of New York, was indicted by the grand jury here today on two counts of grand larceny and one of forgery.

The indictments were filed with Judge John F. McIntyre of general sessions.

The charge grew out of the alleged misuse of $24,700 of the Anti-Saloon league's funds.

O. B. Phillips, a former collector for the Anti-Saloon league, was the principal complaining witness before the jury.

'FORCED TO SPLIT'

Phillips told how he solicited funds, under Anderson's direction, being paid a commission on all money he secured toward the support of the league.

Anderson, he charged, forced him to "split" these commissions.

The forgery count involves the alleged altering of the league's books in connection with the Phillips activities. The charge reads that "Anderson caused a false entry to be made involving $4400, the entry being changed from 'salary' to 'hotel and expenses' under the account of Phillips."

PLEADS NOT GUILTY

Word that Anderson had been indicted spread quickly and crowds gathered about the court building. It was necessary for police reserves to maintain order.

Anderson had been notified of his indictment some time previous to the actual return, and arrived in

(CONTINUED ON PAGE ELEVEN)

Patrol Docks to Prevent Violence In English Strike

LONDON, July 20.—Policemen, equipped for riot service, were on duty in the dock districts of British port cities today to prevent violence by dock strikers. The situation is serious.

Government officials are making an inquiry to ascertain the source of strike funds and to learn if they are coming from communists.

Some of the workers have returned, but most of them are still holding out.

The food shortage has improved slightly, owing to the decision of the market workers to return to their posts on condition they are not asked to handle merchandise passing through the hands of strikebreakers.

U. S. Marshal for Arizona Confirms Retirement Report

PHOENIX, Ariz., July 20.—Semi-official reports that T. J. Sparkes, United States marshal for Arizona, has been retired from office have been confirmed by Mr. Sparkes, who is attending the session of the federal court in Prescott, Ariz.

George Mauk of Phoenix, former secretary of the Arizona state fair commission, is understood to have received notice of his appointment to succeed Mr. Sparkes. Mr. Mauk is in California and expected to return here Monday.

Mr. Sparkes was made marshal on the recommendation of United States Senator Ralph Cameron and had served approximately 17 months of his four-year term.

Puts Fire Hydrant In Front of Home For Parking Space

ALAMEDA, July 20.—J. J. Searle had trouble finding parking space for his auto in front of his home. He bought an old discarded fire hydrant and planted it near his curb. Now he isn't troubled any more.

BIG BATTLE AFTER MEX. CHIEFTAIN MURDER

President Obregon Orders Troops Rushed to Scene of Fighting

MEXICO CITY, July 20.—Pancho Villa, famous Mexican rebel leader and bandit chieftain, was shot down and killed by assassins early today while motoring from Villa's big ranch at Canutillo, state of Durango, Mexico, to Parral.

Slain at the same time with Villa was Col. Miguel Trillo, formerly Villa's chief of staff and more recently his secretary and chief of Villa's bodyguard. Three other armed guards of Villa were killed by the assassins.

President Obregon has been officially informed of Villa's assassination, but made no statement, although the secretary of war has been instructed to rush troops to the scene.

REPORTS DIFFER

According to reports from Parral and Chihuahua City Villa was shot dead in his auto by Colonel Trillo and the latter was then slain by some of Villa's guards after a fight in which a number of Villa's friends and foes were slain.

According to reports to the government, Villa, Colonel Trillo and three guards were waylaid en route to Parral by a force of 20 mounted men, who killed the entire Villa party. The report to the government from the Chihuahua police said the slayers might have been former followers of Villa who had turned against him, but that this was not certain.

The shooting of Villa and Trillo was followed by a pitched battle between the assassins who were reinforced and considerable numbers of former soldiers of Villa who remained faithful to their chief.

The Villa forces were driven back

(CONTINUED ON PAGE TEN)

Hollywood Country Club Threatened by Big Fire in Hills

A big brush and grass fire in the hills near the Hollywood Country club was reported late this afternoon to be threatening that fashionable establishment with destruction.

In response to urgent appeals 40 Los Angeles firemen, with apparatus for fighting the flames, were rushed to the scene under command of Capt. T. H. Lane.

Telephone reports were that the fire had gained great headway, fanned by a breeze off the ocean, and that not only the clubhouse, but a number of fine homes in the countryside were in the path of the flames if they were not checked.

FEAR 4 COAST SHIPS MAY BE LOST

SAN FRANCISCO, July 20.—Four sailing vessels from whom reports have been anxiously awaited for days by mariners, have been listed as overdue in official bulletins, and apprehension is felt for their safety.

The barkentine Conqueror, 1221 tons, Captain James A. Hearsy, is 41 days out of Los Angeles harbor. The vessel headed for Puget sound. Captain Hearsy is accompanied by his wife and a crew of 10.

The schooner Annie M. Campbell, Captain Foss, and a crew of 11 is three weeks overdue from New Britain, South Sea islands, for San Francisco. She cleared three months ago.

The barkentine Monterey, Captain Dennecke, cleared from Port Natal, South Africa, for Puget sound 128 days ago and has not been sighted since. She is only eight days overdue.

The barkentine Alta, which sailed from San Francisco Feb. 20 for Bellingham, has not been heard from since. She is believed lost. Captain Charles Sexon, his wife and their two small children and a crew of 14 were aboard the vessel when she sailed.

MRS. LETZ WINS

CHICAGO, July 20.—Mrs. Fred C. Letz jr. defeated Miss Edith Cummings 1 up at 22 holes in the finals of the women's Western Golf association city of Chicago tournament here today.

PICK PONDER TO TWIRL FOURTH

Right Hander Opposes League Leaders at Local Park; Angels Score One in First

Douglas McWeeny went to the firing line for the league-leading Seals in the fourth game of their series against the Angels at Washington park this afternoon.

Elmer Ponder was on the mound for the locals.

McWeeny got away to a bad start, the Angels finding him for three hits in the initial frame which netted one run.

FIRST INNING

SEALS—Kelly popped to Ponder. Valla flied to Hood. Mulligan out, McAuley to Griggs. NO RUNS.

ANGELS—Smith singled to left. Krug singled to center, Smith going to third. Krug took second on the throw to third. Twombly grounded to Ellison, who touched first and then tagged Krug out off second in a rundown play. Griggs doubled to left, scoring Smith. Hood fanned. ONE RUN, THREE HITS, NO ERRORS.

SECOND INNING

SEALS—Hendryx flied to Twombly. Ellison hit the ball over the leftfield fence for a home run. Kilduff flied to Hood. Walsh fouled to Smith. ONE RUN. ONE HIT. NO ERRORS.

ANGELS—McCabe singled to left. McAuley singled to left. Byler fanned. Ponder fanned. McCabe scored and McAuley took third when Yelle overthrew third trying to catch McCabe off the base. Smith fanned. ONE RUN. TWO HITS. ONE ERROR.

THIRD INNING

SEALS—Yelle flied to Twombly. McWeeny fanned. Kelly fanned. NO RUNS.

ANGELS—Krug flied to Hendryx. Twombly out at first on a missed third strike, Yelle to Ellison. Griggs doubled to center. Hood fanned. NO RUNS. ONE HIT. NO ERRORS.

FOURTH INNING

SEALS—Valla flied to Hood. Mulligan singled infield. Hendryx fouled to Griggs. Ellison tripled to center, scoring Mulligan. Kilduff popped to McAuley. ONE RUN. TWO HITS. NO ERRORS.

ANGELS—McCabe fanned. McAuley walked. Byler flied to Hendryx. Ponder fanned. NO RUNS.

FIFTH INNING

SEALS—Walsh walked. Walsh stole second and took third on Byler's wild throw. Yelle sent a sacrifice fly to McCabe, Walsh scoring. McWeeny out, Ponder to Griggs. Kelly popped to Byler. ONE RUN. NO HITS. ONE ERROR.

ANGELS—Smith out, Mulligan to Ellison. Krugg flied to Hendryx. Twombly singled infield. Twombly out stealing, Yelle to Kilduff. NO RUNS. ONE HIT.

SIXTH INNING

SEALS—Valla out, Smith to Griggs. Mulligan hit the ball over the leftfield fence for a home run. Hendrix out, Smith to Griggs. Ellison out, Smith to Griggs. ONE RUN. ONE HIT. NO ERRORS.

ANGELS—Griggs hit the apple over the centerfield fence for a home run. Hood fouled to Yelle. McCabe flied to Kelly. McAuley flied to Kelly. ONE RUN. ONE HIT. NO ERRORS.

SEVENTH INNING

SEALS—Kilduff safe at first on McAuley's bad throw. Walsh flied to Hood. Yelle fanned. Kilduff stole second. McWeeny fanned. NO RUNS. NO HITS. ONE ERROR.

ANGELS—Byler singled to center. Ponder forced Byler at second, Ellison to Mulligan. Smith singled to center. Krug fouled to Ellison. Twombly popped to Ellison. NO RUNS. TWO HITS.

Today's Score

—:o:—

Seals 7, Angels 4

SEALS—	Ab	R	H	Po	A	E
Kelly, lf...	5	0	1	2	0	0
Valla, cf...	4	0	0	0	0	0
Mulligan, ss	5	2	2	2	2	0
Hendryx, rf.	4	1	1	3	0	0
Ellison, 1b.	3	1	2	11	1	0
Kilduff, 2b.	4	1	1	1	0	0
Walsh, 3b..	3	2	1	0	0	0
Yelle, c....	4	0	0	8	3	1
M'Weeney,p	4	0	1	0	0	0
	0	0	0	0	0	0
	0	0	0	0	0	0
	0	0	0	0	0	0
	0	0	0	0	0	0
Totals....	36	7	9	27	6	1

ANGELS—	Ab	R	H	Po	A	E
Smith, 3b..	5	1	2	1	4	0
Krug, 2b...	5	0	1	1	0	0
Twombly,rf	4	0	1	4	0	0
Griggs, 1b.	4	1	3	10	0	0
Hood, cf...	4	1	1	4	0	0
McCabe, lf.	4	1	1	0	0	0
McAuley, ss	3	0	2	1	2	1
Byler, c...	4	0	1	5	0	1
Ponder, p..	4	0	0	1	2	0
	0	0	0	0	0	0
	0	0	0	0	0	0
	0	0	0	0	0	0
	0	0	0	0	0	0
Totals....	37	4	12	27	8	2

San Francisco- 010 111 003—7
Los Angeles - -110 001 010—4

Baseball Results

NATIONAL LEAGUE

At Boston—		R.	H.	E.
Pittsburg	0 0 0 0 1 0 2 2 0	5	9	2
Boston	2 0 0 1 0 2 3 0 x	8	11	0

Batteries: Hamilton, Bagby, Kunz and Gooch; Genewich and O'Neill.

At New York—		R.	H.	E.
St. Louis	0 3 1 4 0 1 0 0 0	9	12	1
New York	1 0 0 1 0 6 0 0 2	10	14	2

Batteries—Stuart, Clemens and Ainsmith; Scott, Ryan and Snyder.

At Brooklyn—		R.	H.	E.
Cincinnati	3 0 0 1 0 0 6 1 0	11	15	1
Brooklyn	0 0 1 0 0 0 0 0 3	4	14	5

Batteries—Rixie and Hargrave; Reuther, Schrieber and Taylor, DeberrY.

At Philadelphia—		R.	H.	E.
Chicago	0 0 0 0 0 0 0 0 0	0	5	1
Philadelphia	0 0 0 0 0 0 0 0 1	1	6	0

Batteries—Kaufmann and O'Farrell; Mitchell and Wilson.

AMERICAN LEAGUE

At Chicago—		R.	H.	E.
Boston	0 2 0 0 0 2 1 0 0	5	11	3
Chicago	3 0 1 0 0 0 0 0 0	4	7	0

Batteries—Piercy and Picinich, Walters; T Blankenship, Leverett and Schalk, Graham.

At Cleveland—		R.	H.	E
Washington	0 0 5 0 0 0 7 0	12	12	
Cleveland	0 0 0 0 3 0 0 0 2	5	12	

Batteries—Zachary and Ruel; Uhle, Boone Shaute and O'Neil.

EASTERNER SEIZED IN SPLENDOR HERE AS MANN ACT VIOLATOR

Indicted for the alleged illegal transportation of one of his 57 adopted daughters from Sabot, Va., to Pittsburg, Dr. Helon B. Allen, who conducted a girls' school at Sabot, was today arrested by department of justice investigators at 1941½ Argyle avenue, where he was living in near-oriental splendor with two other adopted daughters, and a housekeeper, who, he admitted, were brought here from the east in February.

Allen was arrested under the alias of Preston H. Drake by Investigator Meehan and Police Detective Jack Trainor. The two girls, Myrtle Allen, 19 years, and May Cruze, 17 years, were to be held by the juvenile authorities, while the housekeeper, Mrs. Helen Cruze, 29 years old, was expected to be held as a material witness.

CLOSED HIS SCHOOL

Following Allen's indictment for the alleged violation of the Mann act in taking Gladith Allen from Sabot to Pittsburg, there was such a plethora of unpleasant publicity that the doctor closed his school, located on a 900-acre plantation, changed his name and came west with the three women. He expected to enter motion pictures as a producer, he said.

Mrs. Allen, the doctor's wife, went to New York city with seven of the young women, where she is now, fully cognizant of her husband's presence in California with two young and beautiful, dark-haired, sparkling-eyed girls and Mrs. Cruze.

Allen, a man of means and apparent culture, attended the University of Michigan for several years and later was graduated from another institution, he said.

HIS STORY

It was while traveling with his wife in the southern states 14 years ago that he claimed to have been impressed with poverty-stricken conditions and lack of advantages afforded the children in the moun-

(CONTINUED ON PAGE ELEVEN)

LOVE ROW IN 'DEATH HOAX' OF FLIER

That Jack B. Gregory, aviator, did not fly to Sacramento but drove there in his little red speedster, and that he himself sent the telegrams to his sweetheart in Fullerton detailing his own "death" by a 1600-foot plunge into a rocky canyon near Lake Tahoe, was the belief expressed today by pretty Miss Sarah Stewart of 546 West Wilshire avenue, Fullerton, who was to become Gregory's bride next Monday.

When Gregory left her Tuesday, Miss Stewart said, he expressed the fear that he would not see her again. When she asked him what he meant by that, Gregory replied that he had "a fearful hunch that he was going to be killed in a fall."

HAD NO QUARREL

"We have not had a single quarrel in the five months we have been engaged," said Miss Stewart today.

Her half-formed idea that Gregory himself sent the telegrams signed "Harry Turner," Miss Stewart admitted, is based on the fact that she and her friends have been unable to obtain any details of the

(CONTINUED ON PAGE ELEVEN)

The Weather
Oakland and Vicinity—Fair tonight; Friday probably rain; moderate winds, becoming southerly.

Exclusive Associated Press Service

Oakland Tribune

United Press
International News Service

VOLUME C—THREE CENTS—SUNDAY—TEN CENTS. OAKLAND, CALIFORNIA, THURSDAY EVENING, FEBRUARY 14, 1924 28 PAGES

NO. 45.

SECRECY ON TEAPOT DOME DEAL BARED

No Legal Authority Is Sought

McKEAN SAYS ALAMEDA IS LESS COSTLY

SPECIAL BY WIRE TO THE TRIBUNE

WASHINGTON, Feb. 14.—Establishment of the Alameda naval base would be "a great deal cheaper" than the heavy expenditures that would be involved in dredging and maintaining a deep channel and making other necessary improvements at Mare Island, the House Naval committee was told today by Admiral McKean, commandant of the Mare Island navy yard.

Answering Representative Logan, North Carolina, McKean said that the Mare Island, or any other channel, could be deepened if sufficient money were expended. It was his belief, though, that the Alameda Naval Base could be established at 25 per cent less cost than would be consumed by necessary improvements at Mare Island. The saving at Alameda, he added, would be very much in favor of that station.

"Do you really think Congress would authorize keeping up Mare Island," asked Logan, "if you had this base at Alameda?"

McKean answered: "I hope it would."

The existing navy yard, he said, if the supply station were moved from there, could be made more efficient for repair and upkeep of vessels of not over 30-foot draft.

FAILS TO AGREE WITH ADMIRAL ROBINSON'S VIEW.

The witness was asked by Logan whether he agreed with the view credited to Admiral Robinson, chief of the Bureau of Engineering, that if Pearl Harbor were extensively developed the Pacific Coast would be amply protected.

"I don't agree," replied McKean, "and I don't think that's what he meant."

He agreed that if any new information were developed on the naval base situation that might tend to show Alameda is not the best available location, he would investigate along the lines suggested. He added that he had made very careful investigation of all data now available, all of which convinced him Alameda is the best location.

McKean pointed out that the only San Francisco bay dry dock capable of handling a battleship is at Hunters Point. He added that even if there were such facilities at Mare Island, a battleship could not get up there.

WOULD NOT VIOLATE SPIRIT OF TREATIES.

The Alameda base would violate neither the letter nor the spirit of the arms conference treaties, he said, and in replying to Chairman Butler, Pennsylvania, who wanted to know whether such a development would promote amicable conditions between this and other nations, he stated, "Friendship is based on nothing but respect, and respect between nations is like that between individuals."

Butler complained about the additional overhead that would result from establishment of the Alameda base. McKean said this would be justified because it would bring a reduction in the Mare Island overhead, and in the long run would prove an economy.

Butler thought it might be advisable to establish a supply base and operate it from Mare Island.

Mexicali Is Termed "Sink of Iniquity"

BY ASSOCIATED PRESS LEASED WIRE TO TRIBUNE

LOS ANGELES, Feb. 14.—Mexicali, the Mexican town facing Calexico, California, across the American-Mexican border, 230 miles south of here, is a "sink of iniquity," whose evil influence permeates the entire Imperiral Valley, according to a statement made here today by Lucien Wheeler of the United States department of justice investigation bureau who just returned from a trip of investigation at the border.

Wheeler said he was preparing a report for the department at Washington in which he would recommend that the border be closed between Calexico and Mexicali every evening at 7 or 8 o'clock to prevent Americans pourirng into this "pot of vice."

German Village Boasts No Death Since May, '22

BY ASSOCIATED PRESS LEASED WIRE TO TRIBUNE

KANIGSHOFEN, Baden, Feb 14.—The village of Althausen near here, claims the non-death record of Germany, there not having been a funeral since May 23, 1922.

There are some 400 residents of Althausen, the eldest of whom is 87, and still on the job every day as the village cobbler.

WIDESPREAD WAR LOOMS ON RHINE

Six Killed in Uprising Against Separatists; Police Mobbed.

BY ASSOCIATED PRESS LEASED WIRE TO TRIBUNE

AMSTERDAM, Feb. 14.—Reports from Pirmazens, Kaiserlauten and other centers in the Palatinate state that the disorders are continuing and it is feared a general uprising against the Separatists will break out. The French are remaining neutral, the advices state, but stopped traffic at the bridge over the Rhine near Ludwigshafen to prevent Germans from the non-occupied zone coming into support the Palatinate population.

BY ASSOCIATED PRESS LEASED WIRE TO TRIBUNE

BERLIN, Feb. 14.—Six Separatists were killed at Baduerkheim, a town of 7000 inhabitants, in an anti-Separatist outbreak similar to that at Pirmazens. The Separatists refused to evacuate the town and the inhabitants stormed the quarters.

BY UNITED PRESS LEASED WIRE TO TRIBUNE

COLOGNE, Feb. 14.—One man was killed and eight wounded when Communists attacked safety police at Stettin during the night. Communists from Solingen and Bruhl, in the British zone, taking advantage of the anti-Separatist disturbances throughout the Rhineland, attacked a detachment of safety police from Cologne.

(An official French report says the Communists numbered 5000.)

An unconfirmed report says the Rhineland commission has decided to place Pirmazens, where many were killed in an anti-Separatist uprising Wednesday, under martial law.

Former German officers, Nationalist partisans, are reported to have arrived in the Rhineland from Heidelburg, for the purpose of leading a campaign against the Separatists. The German police are said to be not interfering.

Pulitzer Sued For Divorce in Paris

PARIS, Feb. 14.—Mrs. Ralph Pulitzer, wife of the millionaire publisher of the New York Morning and Evening World, has filed suit for divorce in the Seine tribunal, it was learned this afternoon from an authoritative source. Previously it had been understood that a joint petition had been filed for mutual divorce.

Under the French laws, divorce actions are kept secret upon the request of counsel representing the interested parties.

Pulitzer, who is a son of the late Joseph Pulitzer of New York and St. Louis, was married to Miss Fredericka Vanderbilt Webb of New York in New York on October 14, 1905.

Prussian Prisons Reduce Rations

BY ASSOCIATED PRESS LEASED WIRE TO TRIBUNE

BERLIN, Feb. 14.—The inmates of Prussian prisons have been put on reduced rations to save expense. They now get only 125 grams of meat weekly, saccharine is substituted for sugar, and baths are provided only once in four weeks. Clean linen is issued fortnightly. Berlin newspapers denounce this saving and contend prisoners will leave the jails worse than when they entered.

'COUNT HELD' FOR FRAUD IN S. F. CHARITY

SAN FRANCISCO, Feb. 14.—Trapped by officers of the Department of Justice just as he was making final preparations for a bazaar and ball designed to aid the starving "children of Hungary," a man giving the name of Richard Gruber and posing as a Hungarian count, was taken into custody early today. Federal officials say that he is an imposter and that he has been defrauding the public in the United States and in South American Republics for two years, collecting large sums of money from the charitably inclined and pocketing it for his own purposes.

After first getting on his trail several days ago the officers discovered that while he was making his headquarters at the Fairmont and was nattily and even jauntily attired, he was in reality living in a garret room at 1915 Franklin street. Moreover, it is said that he is engaged to marry a wealthy San Francisco girl; who is ignorant of his alleged unlawful operations.

ALL PREPARATIONS MADE FOR BAZAAR.

All preparations had been made for the bazaar, musical and grand ball, which was to have taken place at the Fairmont Hotel on Wednesday next for the benefit of the starving "children of Hungary." Tickets have been on sale at Sherman, Clay & Co., and huge posters had been displayed around the city advertising the affair as being under the auspices of the Hungarian Child Relief Association. Dr. Gruber advertised that he had two depositories for the money, the Anglo-London National Bank and the Crocker National Bank. Federal officers say that in one of these banks he had deposited $5 and withdrawn $2.50. He had only a few cents in his pocket when he was taken into custody.

Among the patronesses mentioned as sponsoring the benefit entertainment for next Wednesday, were:

Miss Estelle Carpenter, Miss May Sinsheimer, Mrs. M. S. Koshland, Mrs. A. W. Scott, Mrs. G. A. McGowan and Judge and Mrs. Daniel C. Deasy. The musical features of the entertainment were to be Guyla Ormay, noted Hungarian Orchestra conductor of the city.

"TIPS" CAME FROM HUNGARIAN COLONY.

According to officers of the Department of Justice, Dr. Gruber has been in San Francisco about eight months. He is said to have come to America two years ago from Buenos Aires, where Hungarian benefits were also staged. He is known, the officials say, to have given benefits in New York and Salt Lake City. There is a Hungarian colony in San Francisco of about 5000 persons and it was from one of these that the officers were tipped off to the alleged fraudulent operations of the accused, who signs himself Dr. Richard Gruber Gilady, chairman executive board of the Hungarian Children's Relief Association.

A number of dodgers have been printed advertising the work of Dr. Gruber, the first sentence of a long appeal reading: "uffering little children are knocking at the door of your heart. Can you refuse to hear their piteous cry for help?" These documents bear the stamp: "Authorized by Secree Royal Hungarian government" dated May 3, 1921. Other documents indicated the accused's connection with the Hungarian Children's Sanitarium Association of Hungary.

Dr. Gruber is debonair and even dapper in appearance, looks the foreign count and has an air of respectability and wealth.

Richardson on Tour Of Valley Roads

BY UNITED PRESS LEASED WIRE TO TRIBUNE

EL CENTRO, Feb. 14.—Continuing their investigation of Imperial valley highways, Governor Friend W. Richardson and State Highway Commissioner M. P. Edwards today toured the north-end section, visiting Brawley, Westmoreland and other points. Tonight the party will be entertained at Indio, and go on into Los Angeles tomorrow. The governor was the guest of honor at a reception here last night.

Probe Planned Of Underground Currents Here

By Special Wire to The TRIBUNE

WASHINGTON, Feb. 14.—Nothing of any particular consequence having been discovered in California of late, Representative John E. Raker proposes that an expeditionary force be sent out there by the geological survey in search of "underground currents."

Raker has introduced a bill in the House to authorize such an undertaking, and he proposes that $50,000 be appropriated for the work.

DAWES PERFECTS REPARATION PLAN

General Shows How Germany Can Pay Allies and Rebuild Self.

By CARL D. GROAT,
United Press Staff Correspondent.

BERLIN, Feb. 14.—General Charles G. Dawes and his committee of international experts were on their way to Paris today, convinced they have found a plan whereby the Allies can collect reparations and Germany can be rehabilitated financially.

The plan, Daws believes, will be satisfactory to both France and Germany if viewed from a strictly business viewpoint. It will enable the Allies to get reparations, presupposing that Germany is allowed economic control of the Rhur and Rhineland.

Under the plan outlined by Daws' committee, the maximum amount obtainable as reparations will depend upon the extent to which the world absorbs German products. Some of the features are:

1—New gold-backed currency, supplanting land mortgages now backed by the rentenmark, must be introduced in Germany.

2—A total circulation of five billions of marks must be provided, although temporarily a smaller sum, possibly three billion, will suffice.

3—This currency must be backed by 50 percent gold or the equivalent.

4—The German budget must be balanced; according to the experts this should not prove difficult. Germany probably can manage it herself through readjusted taxation, but if she doesn't, she must be helped by outside loans. It is believed a large part of the stock of the new bank could be subscribed in America.

5—Germany must be freed of restrictions now hampering production.

The experts told the United Press it was silly to try to name a concrete maximum sum for reparations, but insisted it would be possible to ascertain what the minimum will be under the new plans. The maximum will be determined as Germany's foreign trade develops. In other words, if the world absorbs a lot of "made in Germany" goods, then there will be more reparations.

Uncle Sam to Close Herrin Rum Joints

BY UNITED PRESS LEASED WIRE TO TRIBUNE

CHICAGO, Feb. 14.—The federal government today took a hand in the troublesome situation in Williamson county, Illinois, where "dry" Ku Klux Klan and "wet" anti-Klan forces have been at war for supremacy.

Attorney Cavanaugh of the Washington office of the prohibition department, left here for Herrin, center of the booze war, armed with affidavits to close 123 liquor establishments in Williamson county.

Meeting Called On Foreign Debtors

BY ASSOCIATED PRESS LEASED WIRE TO TRIBUNE

WASHINGTON, Feb. 14.—Secretary Mellon today called the debt funding committee to meet Monday, when the whole question of policy with respect to future dealings with the foreign debtors will be considered.

PUBLISHER BARES GIFT BY SINCLAIR

BY ASSOCIATED PRESS LEASED WIRE TO TRIBUNE

WASHINGTON, Feb. 14.—E. C. Finney, assistant secretary of the interior, testified before the oil committee today that his recollection was that Secretary Fall told him a short time before the Teapot Dome lease was announced that arrangemnts had been made with Harry Sinclair to give some land in the reserve to John C. Shaffer, the publisher.

BY ASSOCIATED PRESS LEASED WIRE TO TRIBUNE

WASHINGTON, Feb. 14.—John C. Shaffer, publisher of the Chicago Evening Post and a number of other papers, was questioned by the oil committee today about a reputed grant to him of a one-eighth interest in the Pioneer Oil Company, a Standard subsidiary "for services rendered."

Senator Walsh, Democrat, Montana, produced what he said was a record of proceedings of directors of the Pioneer company making such a grant.

Shaffer said he never heard of these proceedings. He did hold an eighth interest in the company, however, he said, but had sold it.

Asked what "service" he had rendered the witness replied "none." He added that he had had land adjoining Teapot Dome.

Shaffer said his payment from the Pioneer Company came out of the $1,000 000 paid that company by the Sinclair interests.

"The Pioneer people felt we had a common interest in the Teapot holdings in case the Dome ever was thrown open to the public," he continued. "They made the proposal to give it to me. I gave up nothing. It was their idea.'

Shaffer testified that Secretary Fall told him in March, 1921, that he was going to lease Teapot Dome to Harry F. Sinclair.

(The Teapot Dome lease was signed by Fall and Secretary Denby on April 7, 1922).

A letter to Assistant Secretary Finney from Shaffer dated April 19, 1922, was put into the record. In it the publisher said he had "a personal interest in this dealing and added:

"Secretary Fall has arranged with Mr. Sinclair for some acreage for me personally."

Just before the letter was read the witness had testified he had no interest in the Sinclair lease.

Asked if his memory now was refreshed, he said that back in 1917 he had applied for land on Teapot and later had been promised 200 acres by Fall.

"Was it your opinion that anybody could go to Secretary Fall and demand a share in the Sinclair leas or money for it?" he was asked.

"I think so," Shaffer replied.

"He could distribute the interest around just as he saw fit?"

"I thhink so."

The publisher said under questioning that it was his understanding the land on which he filed in 1917 was not at that time open to leasing.

Asked if it was on the basis of that sort of a claim that he "made a demand" on Fall for some of the Dome, he replied:

"No, not at all. I made no demand. I just urged that I get it."

When he was asked if the policy of his papers was involved in the deal, Shaffer replied:

"The support of my newspapers was never mentioned or promised. I don't even know what position they took on the proposition."

Jessie Reed to Wed Russell G. Colt

BY ASSOCIATED PRESS LEASED WIRE TO TRIBUNE

CHICAGO, Feb. 14. — The engagement of Jessie Reed, Follies star, and Russell Griswold Colt, divorced husband of Ethel Barrymore, was announced today by Edward Rosenbaum, show manager, who said he made the announcement on behalf of Miss Reed. Miss Reed and Dan Caswell, son of a wealthy Cleveland family, were divorced a year ago, Caswell charging neglect. Colt and Miss Barrymore were married in 1909 and had three children. They were divorced in 1921, Miss Barrymore charging cruelty.

Vanderlip Quiz On Harding Slur Held Up for Day

BY INTERNATIONAL NEWS LEASED WIRE TO TRIBUNE

WASHINGTON, Feb. 14.—Frank A. Vanderlip, New York financier, who made sensational insinuations concerning the sale of the Marion Star by the late President Harding, did not get a chance today to tell the Senate oil investigating committee what lay behind his veiled charges.

Vanderlip sat all day in the committee room, listening to sensational testimony offered by John C. Shaffer, western newspaper owner; E. C. Finney, assistant secretary of the interior under Fall, an others, and then was informed by the committee it would be impossible to hear him until tomorrow. He was instructed to stay in Washington.

BY ASSOCIATED PRESS LEASED WIRE TO TRIBUNE

COLUMBUS, Ohio, Feb. 14.—Minority stockholders of the Marion Star of which Mrs. Harding is one, offered to buy back the newspaper from Roy D. Moore and Louis H. Brush, after the death of Mr. Harding, at the prcie for which it was purchased, Hoke Donithen, Ohio, manager of the Coolidge campaign said here today.

SAN JOSE FIRE RUINS BUILDING

Business Firms and Leading Cafe Suffer Loss in $30,000 Blaze.

SAN JOSE, Feb. 14.—Fire of unknown origin practically destroyed the Smout building at 63 West Santa Clara street at 7 o'clock this morning, doing damage estimated at more than $30,000, which is only partly insured. Half a dozen business firms with offices in the building suffered losses, the Goodfellows Restaurant, one of the most pretentious in the city, being the heaviest loser. To keep the fire confined the firemen fought one of the most desperate battles in years.

The fire when discovered had gained such headway it had burned through the roof of the building in several places. The smoke blowing down onto the street attracted the attention of pedestrians who turned in the alarm. Practically every piece of fire apparaus in the city was called to fight the blaze, the heat from which cracked windows across the street and crisped wall paper on the opposite side of the firewalls dividing the building from these adjoining.

The building isowned by Alec Hart. Others who lose in the fire were Jorgensen & Thomy, contractors; Megna and Newell, contractors; Henry A. Gabriel, attorney; The Santa Clara Contractors' association; all of whom had offices on the second floor, and the Hawkins Realty Co. and Goodfellows Restaurant occupying the first floor.

Klondiker Secures Russ Mine Rights

BY ASSOCIATED PRESS LEASED WIRE TO TRIBUNE

MOSCOW, Feb. 14.—A relatively small placer gold mining concession in the Amur region, operated by James Vint of Seattle, Washington, under an agreement with the old Far East Republic, has been ratified by the federal council of council of commissars. Thus Vint, who is an old Klondiker, is the first American to secure a Far East Russian concession.

European Dies at 120; Leaves Son 17

BY ASSOCIATED PRESS LEASED WIRE TO TRIBUNE

VIENNA, Feb. 14.—Yussuf Maca Mahomettan is dead at Yagoubitza, Jugo-Slavia, at the age of 120, according to a Belgrade despatch. Yussuf married thrice and one of his surviving sons is only 17 years old. Being a true follower of the prophet, he neither drank nor smoked. His only beverage was Turkish coffee, which he consumed in vast quantities.

SECRET SIGNING OF LEASE FOR TEAPOT DOME RESERVE IS REVEALED BY ASSISTANT

(By Associated Press Leased Wire to TRIBUNE.)

WASHINGTON, Feb. 14.—A subpoena for Edward B. McLean, publisher of the Washington Post, was issued today by the Senate oil committee. The immediate presence here of the publisher will be required.

(By Associated Press Leased Wire to TRIBUNE.)

WASHINGTON, Feb. 14.—E. C. Finney, assistant secretary of the interior, testifying today before the Senate oil committee, said he disagreed with Oscar Sutro, counsel for the Standard Oil Company of California, a previous witness, who held there was no legal authority for the leases made by A. B. Fall while secretary of the interior.

The witness could not recall all the circumstances, but said he would not deny Sutro's testimony as to their talk about the reasons for not asking Attorney-General Daugherty for an opinion on the validity of the deals

"My superior having decided upon a policy," Finney said, "it wasn't up to me."

Asked directly why Attorney-General Daugherty was not asked for an opinion, Finney said the secretary did not regard it as necessary. Finney said the Teapot Dome contract was handled "very largely" by Secretary Fall.

Fall left Washington for his New Mexico ranch immediately after signing the Teapot Dome lease, Finney testified. He could not say where it was signed.

Before leaving, he said, Fall locked the lease up in his desk and it remained there until he returned.

Asked if he was "suspicious," Finney said:

"I thought then, and hope now, Fall was an absolutely honest man."

Finney testified that Fall instructed him to issue a statement denying that leases had been entered into a week after Teapot actually had been leased to Sinclair.

FALL WIRED FOR FINNEY TO SIGN.

Explaining how he came to sign the Doheny-Pearl Harbor contract, Finney said Fall was in New Mexico and wired him to sign after the secretary had studied the summary of the bids sent to him at his home.

The real reason why the Teapot lease announcement was held up, Finney said was because Fall did not want it made public until the Doheny lease to the California reserve had been signed.

Finney disclosed that the question as to the legality of the leasing program never was referred to the Interior Department solicitors. He said he was very certain the program was legal.

He said the lease negotiations were conducted in the "manner of private negotiations' and added "I would not have handled them that way. It impressed me as a wrong way.'

There was no dispute as to facts, Finney said, but there was one of law. Fall did not ask as to that, he testified, adding that he then and now believed Fll's action was wrong.

DISPUTE AS TO FACTS WAS ONLY ISSUE.

In dismissing the proceedings to recover sections 36 and 16 in California from the Standard Oil company of California, Finney said, Fall had asked department

(Continued on Page 8, Col. 3)

$1,000,000 SLUSH FUND IS AIRED

Wilson and Harding Officials Involved as Recipients of Thousands.

By PAUL R. MALLON
(United Press Staff Correspondent.)

WASHINGTON, Feb. 14.—Reports of a $1,000,000 "slush fund" raised by oil interests, provided the senate oil scandal investigators with another startling "lead" today as they prepared to run down gossip which dragged the name of the late President Harding into the affair.

The $1,000,000 "slush fund," according to gossip about the committee room, was provided by oil men interested in the leases for the uses of government officials. A man close to the Harding administration, though not officially connected with it, was reported to the committee to have drawn more than $200,000 from the fund at one time.

Harry F. Sinclair, now on his way home from Europe, will be subpenaed the minute he lands and will be questioned about the slush fund.

Edward L. Doheny, lessee of the California reserves, will be recalled for further questioning concerning "influence" wielded with government officials in connection with oil deals.

An important cabinet member of the Wilson administration was mentioned to the committee today as recipient of hundreds of thousands of Doheny money.

Woman Ends Life; Leaves $2 For Gas

BY ASSOCIATED PRESS LEASED WIRE TO TRIBUNE

NEW ORLEANS, Feb. 14.—Police are attempting to establish the identity of a young woman who ended her life in a rooming house, leaving a note which stated she was enclosing $90 for her burial expenses and $2 for the gas consumed in asphyxiating herself.

The woman told the proprietor of the lodging house that her name was Lillian Leone and that her home was in Nashville, Tenn. Scraps of paper found in her room indicated she had purchased an automobile in San Francisco. A torn envelope pieced together bore the name of Mrs. Lucille Burke, 996 Valencia street, San Francisco.

U. S. Consul General To Ecuador Is Ill

BY ASSOCIATED PRESS LEASED WIRE TO TRIBUNE

GUAYAQUIL, Ecuador, Feb. 14.—Dr. Frederic W. Goding, American consul general here, is seriously ill.

Golden Opportunities

An echo of the Spoilers and of the gold rush of twenty years comes down to us in an advertisement under "Business Opportunities" in The TRIBUNE of February 5, 1906:

"EXTRACT FROM A NOME LETTER: 'Was surprised at the amount of coarse gold and nuggets—things coming our way at last—sell only $5000 of the treasury stock.' This mine is backed by responsible parties, be wise and buy some of the stock. Call at — 18th St." The prospect of sudden wealth still attracts us but we have learned to be content with the surer investments of the type listed under "Business Opportunities" last evening and today.

At that, more fortunes have been made in gold camps out of ham and egg counters (at $1.50 a plate) than out of gravel banks or quartz lodes. Are you investing? Have you considered today's offers?

Another Tong Tragedy by De Bra In Sunday's Tribune

WILBUR ASSAILS NAVY WEAKNESS

CALIFORNIA WEATHER FORECAST
Los Angeles and vicinity—Fair and moderate temperatures today.
San Francisco and vicinity—Generally cloudy today; moderate westerly winds.
COAST TEMPERATURES (Mean)

LOS ANGELES	60	San Francisco	55
Portland	61	Seattle	56
Sacramento	64	Salt Lake	72
San Diego	61		

CHARACTER QUALITY AMERICA FIRST! ENTERPRISE ACCURACY
Los Angeles Examiner
AN AMERICAN PAPER FOR THE AMERICAN PEOPLE — THE GREAT NEWSPAPER OF THE GREAT SOUTHWEST
Reg. U.S. Pat. Off.

LATEST NEWS EXTRA

VOL. XXI—NO. 164 Official Forecast--Fair — For complete weather reports see Page 6, Part II. — LOS ANGELES, FRIDAY, MAY 23, 1924 — Copyright, 1924, by The Los Angeles Examiner — ★★★★ — PRICE FIVE CENTS

KIDNAPERS HACK BOY DEAD WITH HATCHET

Today

Wall Street Better Again
How Publicity Hurts
Used Cars for Europe
Rye—500 Gallons an Hour

By Arthur Brisbane

STOCKS crept upward a little farther today. Speculators are getting over the dreadful thought that paying a few hundreds of millions to soldiers may ruin the United States—a country that so easily found thousands of millions for patriot-grafters.

Washington predicts that Mr. Coolidge will sign the tax bill. That will cheer everybody in Wall Street except the financial dozen that consider it most un-American and dangerous to let the people know how much income tax they have been paying.

IF INCOME tax returns were made public it is clear that many prosperous gentlemen would be considerably worried. Perhaps they are afraid to have the public know how generous and conscientious they are and how fully they pay their income tax.

At all events, you know that they are worried and that they object to publicity when you find so many of them anxious to see the proposed tax bill changed, sacrificing the great tax saving that it would give them rather than have the publicity clause go through.

WHEN the automobile arrived old-fashioned carriages, victorias, broughams, etc., became worthless here and a market was found for them in South America, where they did not give up horses and carriages so easily.

Lately the American problem has been "how to get rid of second-band automobiles." Europe, it seems, will help solve that problem.

A company formed to ship second-hand cars to Europe sends over bargains by the shipload. Money is not as plentiful there as it is here. The "used car," at a whittled-down price, is attractive.

Unloading of used cars abroad will be a good thing for Europe, which needs economy, and a good thing for the United States, where millions need "a bigger or better car."

PROHIBITION in America spells profit elsewhere, especially in Scotland and the British West Indies. The Lord Chief Justice of the Bahamas, Sir Sydney Nettleton, arrives with the information that Bahaman citizens on Hog Island intend to supply the United States' demand for rye whisky.

Englishmen don't care for it; they like smoky Scotch. Nevertheless they have built on Hog Island a distillery that will turn out 500 gallons of rye whisky an hour. They will sell it on English soil, and it will be the job of law abiding American bootleggers to put it within reach of whisky drinking Americans.

THE ROYAL DUTCH SHELL COMPANY of Amsterdam, powerful and efficient, abandoned efforts to invade the United States oil territory and sells its California oil fields to American interests. The Dutch Shell got thirty millions for its oil wells, probably didn't lose anything and will invest the money in Russian oil fields.

When you go against private oil concerns in the United States you come in contact with REAL competition. Our friends from Amsterdam should have tried old Uncle Sam. That would have been easier. Getting oil away from him is like taking a stick of peppermint candy from a sick child.

IN 1923 fires cost the United States more than $500,000,000. Of this wasteful loss, at least $350,000,000 could have been prevented and saved by ordinary precautions.

This is a wasteful country from every point of view. Rust needlessly wastes hundreds of millions a year. Carelessness of property owners, encouraged by reckless competition among gigantically profitable fire insurance companies, costs the country other hundreds of millions. One of these days we shall not be so rich, perhaps, and shall have to economize. It will not be easy to learn.

MOST important news, to the greatest number of people, is the description of President Coolidge sitting in an air-tight chamber, breathing in chlorine gas and air mixed, to cure his cold. British doctors laugh at the "cure." But that isn't important. They also laughed at Jenner when he talked about preventing smallpox by vaccination. They wouldn't laugh now at that idea.

If the chlorine gas treatment does what it may reasonably be expected to do, there will be an inhaling room in every school, big business building and hotel. The time saved by curing colds in a few hours would make up for the loss caused by fire and rust.

FIFTY FACE ARREST IN BLAST PLOT

Dynamiting of L. A. Aqueduct Laid to Group of Farmers; Suspects Names Are Known

Approximately fifty people face arrest for the bombing of the Los Angeles Aqueduct. Some of the suspects are said to be prominent in the agricultural life of the district about Bishop. Evidence gathered yesterday by investigators in the Owens Valley country gave such important leads that it is believed the first arrests will be made soon.

Some of the dynamiters are said to be known. Their names are being withheld pending the checking of information against other members of the gang which touched off three boxes of dynamite early Wednesday morning in a spillway of the water system near Lone Pine.

It has been demonstrated that the explosion was the result of a highly organized and efficiently carried out conspiracy. At least forty people are believed to have been active participants in the dynamiting. Many others were involved in the plot, it is believed.

A Los Angeles lawyer slipped into a prominent but precarious place in the investigation yesterday when word reached the District Attorney's office that the attorney, not named, had made the statement that his "clients would blow up the aqueduct as often as necessary to gain justice in the Owens Valley."

Cites Discontent

The lawyer, it was said, represents several property owners in Owens Valley, where dissatisfaction is said to have existed for years because of the fact that water flows through their territory on its way to Los Angeles consumption when Owens Valley lands are more or less arid.

According to information given to the District Attorney's office, the attorney left his offices yesterday and was reported on his way to Inyo County.

In the absence of District Attorney Asa Keyes, the latter's secretary, Harold Davis, immediately took steps to get in touch with Jack Dymond, investigator now in Owens Valley, to inform him of this late sensational turn of the investigation and have him develop all facts possible.

Investigators reported last night that they had encountered an attitude of general indifference in their probe of the dynamiting among residents of Bishop and the surrounding territory. The general opinion was summed up in the statement of

(Continued on Page 3, Column 1)

Canada's Richest Man Will Wed U. S. Countess

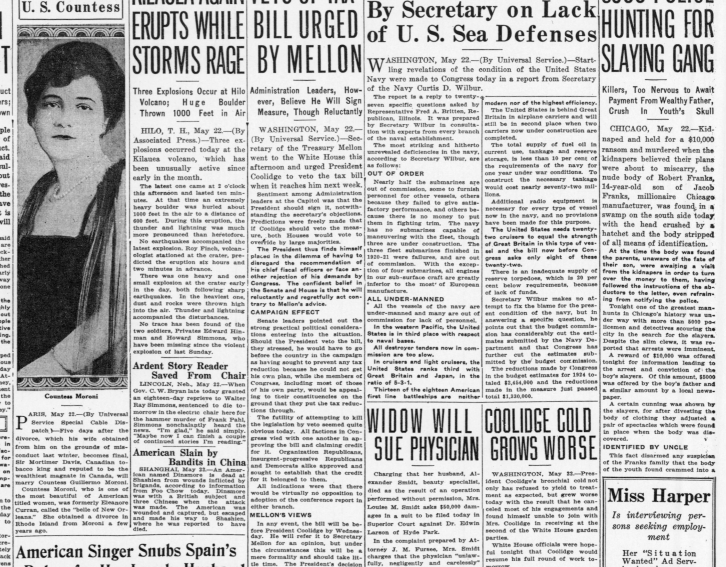

Countess Moroni

PARIS, May 22.—(By Universal Service Special Cable Dispatch.)—Five days after the divorce, which his wife obtained from him on the grounds of misconduct last winter, becomes final, Sir Mortimer Davis, Canadian tobacco king and reputed to be the wealthiest magnate in Canada, will marry Countess Guiliermo Moroni.

Countess Moroni, who is one of the most beautiful of American titled women, was formerly Eleanore Curran, called the "belle of New Orleans." She obtained a divorce in Rhode Island from Moroni a few years ago.

KILAUEA AGAIN ERUPTS WHILE STORMS RAGE

Three Explosions Occur at Hilo Volcano; Huge Boulder Thrown 1000 Feet in Air

HILO, T. H., May 22.—(By Associated Press.)—Three explosions occurred today at the Kilauea volcano, which has been unusually active since early in the month.

The latest one came at 2 o'clock this afternoon and lasted ten minutes. At that time an extremely heavy boulder was hurled about 1000 feet in the air to a distance of 600 feet. During this eruption, the thunder and lightning was much more pronounced than heretofore.

No earthquakes accompanied the latest explosion. Roy Finch, volcanologist stationed at the crater, predicted the eruption six hours and two minutes in advance.

There was one heavy and one small explosion at the crater early in the day, both following sharp earthquakes. In the heaviest one, dust and rocks were thrown high into the air. Thunder and lightning accompanied the disturbances.

No trace has been found of the two soldiers, Privates Edward Hinman and Howard Simmons, who have been missing since the violent explosion of last Sunday.

Ardent Story Reader Saved From Chair

LINCOLN, Neb., May 22.—When Gov. C. W. Bryan late today granted an eighteen-day reprieve to Walter Ray Simmons, sentenced to die tomorrow in the electric chair here for the hammer murder of Frank Pahl, Simmons nonchalantly heard the news. "I'm glad," he said simply. "Maybe now I can finish a couple of continued stories I'm reading."

American Slain by Bandits in China

SHANGHAI, May 22.—An American named Dinsmore is dead at Shashien from wounds inflicted by brigands, according to information from Foo Chow today. Dinsmore was with a British subject and three Chinese when the attack was made. The American was wounded and captured, but escaped and made his way to Shashien, where he was reported to have died.

American Singer Snubs Spain's Rulers for Her Lonely Husband

MADRID, May 22.—(By Universal Service Special Cable.)—For the first time a royal command has been disobeyed, and by an American woman.

Through the agency of Ambassador Alexander P. Moore, Mrs. Arthur J. Willson of Philadelphia, a society woman who is noted as an amateur singer of Spanish and Russian songs, received a command to sing before the King and Queen of Spain at the big reception the Ambassador is giving to their majesties at the Madrid Embassy, May 24.

Simultaneously, however, Mrs. Willson received a cable from her husband in America, saying in substance: "Come home. I am lonely."

Without hesitating Mrs. Willson chose hubby before royalty. She is sailing Saturday.

VETO OF TAX BILL URGED BY MELLON

Administration Leaders, However, Believe He Will Sign Measure, Though Reluctantly

WASHINGTON, May 22.—(By Universal Service.)—Secretary of the Treasury Mellon went to the White House this afternoon and urged President Coolidge to veto the tax bill when it reaches him next week.

Sentiment among Administration leaders at the Capitol was that the President should sign it, notwithstanding the secretary's objections. Predictions were freely made that if Coolidge should veto the measure, both Houses would vote to override by large majorities.

The President thus finds himself placed in the dilemma of having to disregard the recommendation of his chief fiscal officers or face another rejection of his demands by Congress. The confident belief in the Senate and House is that he will reluctantly and regretfully act contrary to Mellon's advice.

CAMPAIGN EFFECT

Senate leaders pointed out the strong practical political considerations entering into the situation. Should the President veto the bill, they stressed, he would have to go before the country in the campaign as having sought to prevent any tax reduction because he could not get his own plan, while the members of Congress, including most of those of his own party, would be appealing to their constituencies on the ground that they put the tax reductions through.

The futility of attempting to kill the legislation by veto seemed quite obvious today. All factions in Congress vied with one another in approving the bill and claiming credit for it. Organization Republicans, insurgent-progressive Republicans and Democrats alike approved and sought to establish that the credit for it belonged to them.

All indications were that there would be virtually no opposition to adoption of the conference report in either branch.

MELLON'S VIEWS

In any event, the bill will be before President Coolidge by Wednesday. He will refer it to Secretary Mellon for an opinion, but under the circumstances this will be a mere formality and should take little time. The President's decision may be known by the end of the week.

Secretary Mellon's strong views in opposition to the bill were outlined at the Treasury early in the day. Later he went to the White House and was closeted with the President for half an hour. When he came out he told newspaper correspondents that he had repeated to the executive what he had said to the correspondents this morning.

The secretary regards the bill as

(Continued on Page 2, Column 2)

Startling Report Made By Secretary on Lack of U. S. Sea Defenses

WASHINGTON, May 22.—(By Universal Service.)—Startling revelations of the condition of the United States Navy were made to Congress today in a report from Secretary of the Navy Curtis D. Wilbur.

The report is a reply to twenty-seven specific questions asked by Representative Fred A. Britten, Republican, Illinois. It was prepared by Secretary Wilbur in consultation with experts from every branch of the naval establishment.

The most striking and hitherto unrevealed deficiencies in the navy, according to Secretary Wilbur, are as follows:

OUT OF ORDER

Nearly half the submarines are out of commission, some to furnish personnel for other vessels, others because they failed to give satisfactory performance, and others because there is no money to put them in fighting trim. The navy has no submarines capable of maneuvering with the fleet, though three are under construction. The three fleet submarines finished in 1920-21 were failures, and are out of commission. With the exception of four submarines, all engines in our sub-surface craft are greatly inferior to the most of European manufacture.

ALL UNDER-MANNED

All the vessels of the navy are under-manned and many are out of commission for lack of personnel.

In the western Pacific, the United States is in third place with respect to naval bases.

All destroyer tenders now in commission are too slow.

In cruisers and light cruisers, the United States ranks third with Great Britain and Japan, in the ratio of 5-3-1.

Thirteen of the eighteen American first line battleships are neither modern nor of the highest efficiency.

The United States is behind Great Britain in airplane carriers and will still be in second place when two carriers now under construction are completed.

The total supply of fuel oil in current use, tankage and reserve storage, is less than 10 per cent of the requirements of the navy for one year under war conditions. To construct the necessary tankage would cost nearly seventy-two millions.

Additional radio equipment is necessary for every type of vessel now in the navy, and no provisions have been made for this purpose.

The United States needs twenty-two cruisers to equal the strength of Great Britain in this type of vessel and the bill now before Congress asks only eight of these twenty-two.

There is an inadequate supply of reserve torpedoes, which is 20 per cent below requirements, because of lack of funds.

Secretary Wilbur makes no attempt to fix the blame for the present condition of the navy, but in answering a specifrc question, he points out that the budget commission has considerably cut the estimates submitted by the Navy Department and that Congress has further cut the estimates submitted by the budget commission.

The reductions made by Congress in the budget estimates for 1924 totaled $2,454,000 and the reductions made in the measure just passed total $1,330,000.

WIDOW WILL SUE PHYSICIAN

Charging that her husband, Alexander Smidt, beauty specialist, died as the result of an operation performed without permission, Mrs. Louise M. Smidt asks $50,000 damages in a suit to be filed today in Superior Court against Dr. Edwin Larson of Hyde Park.

In the complaint prepared by Attorney J. M. Fursee, Mrs. Smidt charges that the physician "unlawfully, negligently and carelessly" performed a major operation upon her husband on May 15.

The beauty specialist was a patient at Doctor Larson's sanitarium in Hyde Park, the complaint alleges, when the asserted operation took place.

The suit is being brought by Mrs. Smidt and her three minor children, Louise Alice Smidt, Katherine Smidt and Olga Smidt.

Mrs. Smidt conducts a beauty parlor at 822 West Seventh street and resides at 6841 Fifth avenue.

COOLIDGE COLD GROWS WORSE

WASHINGTON, May 22.—President Coolidge's bronchial cold not only has refused to yield to treatment as expected, but grew worse today with the result that he canceled most of his engagements and found himself unable to join with Mrs. Coolidge in receiving at the second of the White House garden parties.

White House officials were hopeful tonight that Coolidge would resume his full round of work tomorrow.

Indian, Aged 110, Dies at Conejo Reservation

SAN DEIGO, May 22.—Juan de la Cruz Pipo, said to be 110 years old, is dead at the Conejo Indian Reservation near Alpine, San Diego County, according to word sent here today. One of his two sons said that Juan never ate flesh of domestic animals or vegetables such as grown by white men and always arose at 4:30 a. m. and took a bath in a cold stream.

5000 POLICE HUNTING FOR SLAYING GANG

Killers, Too Nervous to Await Payment From Wealthy Father, Crush In Youth's Skull

CHICAGO, May 22.—Kidnaped and held for a $10,000 ransom and murdered when the kidnapers believed their plans were about to miscarry, the nude body of Robert Franks, 14-year-old son of Jacob Franks, millionaire Chicago manufacturer, was found in a swamp on the south side today with the head crushed by a hatchet and the body stripped of all means of identification.

At the time the body was found the parents, unaware of the fate of their son, were awaiting a visit from the kidnapers in order to turn over the money to them, having followed the instructions of the abductors to the letter, even refraining from notifying the police.

Tonight one of the greatest manhunts in Chicago's history was under way with more than 5000 policemen and detectives scouring the city in the search for the slayers. Despite the slim clews, it was reported that arrests were imminent.

A reward of $10,000 was offered tonight for information leading to the arrest and conviction of the boy's slayers. Of this amount, $5000 was offered by the boy's father and a similar amount by a local newspaper.

A certain cunning was shown by the slayers, for after divesting the body of clothing they adjusted a pair of spectacles which were found in place when the body was discovered.

IDENTIFIED BY UNCLE

This fact disarmed any suspicion of the Franks family that the body of the youth found crammed into a

MARKET EDITION

THE CHICAGO EVENING POST

THIRTY-FIFTH YEAR.—OFFICIAL NEWSPAPER OF CITY OF CHICAGO * MONDAY, JUNE 2, 1924. * PRICE THREE CENTS

LEOPOLD AND LOEB JAILED

SUPREME COURT ORDERS RELEASE OF GROSSMAN

Chicago Saloon Man, Jailed by 2 Judges, Gets Habeas Corpus Writ.

WASHINGTON, June 2.—Philip Grossman of Chicago, recently committed to the Chicago House of Correction upon orders of Judges Carpenter and Wilkerson after President Coolidge had pardoned him, was today granted a writ of habeas corpus by the Supreme court.

Grossman's sentence by former Judge Landis for contempt of court in connection with a violation of a prohibition padlock injunction was commuted by President Coolidge after the Supreme court had refused to review his case.

Taking the position that the President's power of executive clemency did not extend to such contempt cases, Judges Carpenter and Wilkerson ordered Grossman's arrest and commitment.

Up at October Term.

The highest court in October next will go into the merits of the controversy as to the authority of the President to exercise executive clemency in cases where persons are held to be in contempt of court.

Grossman applied to the court for release on a writ of habeas corpus, contending Judges Carpenter, Wilkerson and Cliffe, composing the federal District court at Chicago, were disqualified from passing on such a writ.

Justice McKenna, in announcing the granting of the writ of habeas corpus, said a rule would be issued returnable Oct. 6. next, and pending final disposition of the case Grossman would be released on furnishing bail of $5,000.

HISTORY OF CASE

On a contempt charge involving the violation of an injunction against the continued sale of whisky, Grossman, whose place of business was at West Madison and Halsted streets, was sentenced by former Judge Landis to a year in the bridewell on July 28, 1922.

The case was immediately appealed. All the higher courts ruled against the defendant, however, and on March 1, 1923, commitment papers were issued ordering the saloon-keepr confined at once.

Political influence, apparently, was brought to bear, and for some reason the order was pigeon-holed. Grossman was never taken into custody, and his name appeared on President Coolidge's pardon list of last Christmas.

It was only when this pardon was served on the warden of the bridewell that the public discovered for the first time that Grossman had never been locked up.

Taken to Cell.

He was again sentenced last month by Judges Carpenter and Wilkerson, who ruled President Coolidge had exceeded his authority in granting a pardon. The court ordered Marshal Levy to ignore the pardon and seize Grossman forthwith. He was accordingly taken to a cell in the bridewell.

So widespread was the feeling over the affair after the President's pardon was made public that it assumed national proportions. Ex-Judge Landis appeared before a senatorial investigating committee in Washington and testified that he was at a loss to know how Grossman had escaped punishment.

Groom U. S. Dirigible for Flight Into Canada

LAKEHURST, N. J., June 2.—The navy dirigible, Shenandoah, is being groomed today for her long flight tomorrow to Albany and Buffalo, where she will cross the Canadian border for the first time. The flight is to be made in connection with the celebration of the founding of Albany, where the Shenandoah will circle slowly while Assistant Secretary of the Navy Roosevelt is expected to inaugurate speechmaking from a dirigible with the use of a loud speaker. The Shenandoah will pass over Williamsport, Scranton and Philadelphia on the return trip.

Portugal to Send Select Team to Olympic Games

LISBON, June 2.—Portugal will send a small but highly selected representation to the Olympic games in Paris. A government appropriation has been supplemented by private donations, and teams are now in training.

Fencing is given first place in Portugal's hopes, but swimming, rowing, wrestling, discus throwing and weight lifting entries also will be made, and a rifle team selected from among her many good marksmen.

Ex-Governor Morrow to Speak at Ebenezer Church

Former Governor Edwin P. Morrow will address the Sons and Daughters of Kentucky at the Ebenezer Baptist church, 45th street and Vincennes avenue, tomorrow night. His topic will be "Industrial Conditions of the ..." Rev. C. H. Clark, D. D., is ... church.

COURTROOM SCENE AS FRANK SLAYERS SEEK FREEDOM ON WRIT

Post photo.

Scenes in Chief Justice Caverly's courtroom in the Criminal court today when Nathan E. Leopold Jr. and Richard Loeb, confessed murderers of Robert Franks, were arraigned on writs of habeas corpus. In the top picture, from left to right, are Attorney Clarence Darrow, Attorney Benjamin Bachrach, Loeb, Leopold, Chief of Detectives Hughes and State's Attorney Crowe. In the lower picture, showing a group of spectators, are, from left to right, Forman Loeb, Richard's brother; Attorney Bachrach, Nathan Leopold Sr. and Jacob M. Loeb, Richard's uncle.

LIGHT VOTE TO BE CAST FOR JUDGES TODAY, PREDICTION

Heroic Efforts of Both Parties to Interest the Voters Seen Failure.

Today's Election

Polls open from 6 a. m. to 4 p. m. Candidates to be elected: Justice of the Supreme court, 7th district, which includes Cook, Lake, Dupage, Will and Kankakee counties.

Judge of the Circuit court, Cook county (to fill vacancy).

Judge of the Superior court, Cook county (to fill vacancy).

Three associate judges of the Municipal court, Chicago.

Bond issue proposals: $10,000,000 for widening and double-decking of South Water street. $1,000,000 for completion of Roosevelt road, bridge and viaduct. $5,000,000 for remodeling of Fine Arts building in Jackson park into convention hall with capacity of 20,000 attendance (in south park district only). $1,000,000 for widening of south park boulevard (in south park district only).

Despite heroic efforts of Republican and Democratic party workers, indications were that a comparatively light vote would be cast today in the judicial election. Polling places were deserted during the early hours and the apathy of the voters was apparent. Ward and precinct workers, however, were ordered to remain on the job and use every effort to get as many voters to the polls as possible.

This apathy prevailed despite the importance of today's election, in which five of the seven members of the Illinois Supreme court are to be chosen. The estimated vote was set at about 300,000, or about 30 per cent of the registered vote. The bond issue proposals were expected to increase the turn out slightly.

Four Downstate Districts Vote.

While Cook county was sharing its suffrage with Lake, Will, Dupage and Kankakee counties, in choosing between Superior Court Judge Frederick R. De Young, Republican, and Angus R. Shannon, Democrat, for the Supreme court from the 7th district, voters in four of the six downstate districts will select four justices.

Three associate judges of the Municipal court were to be elected today.

Continued on Next Page.

Bullets Drive Off Thieves Who Try to Rob O'Brien Garage

Burglars who tried to rob the garage of former Assistant State's Attorney James O'Brien, 3446 West Adams street, today were interrupted by Acting Lieutenant Al Hoffman and his "flivver" squad, who fired twelve shots at them before they made their escape down an alley.

The thieves were discovered by Mrs. O'Brien, who called the police. They had entered the garage by breaking a window, and were removing one of the O'Brien automobiles when the police opened fire.

Deputy Superintendent of Police John Alcock, whose home is near the O'Brien residence, heard the shots and joined in the chase after the burglars, one of whom was believed wounded.

PAN-AMERICAN HIGHWAY BODY READY FOR WORK

They Will Be Received by Coolidge and Hughes Today.

WASHINGTON, June 2.—Members of the Pan-American Highway commission, comprising more than thirty engineers and public officials from nineteen countries of Latin America, assembled today for a three weeks' conference under the auspices of the highway education board.

After two days here, given over principally to entertainment of the delegates and meetings with high officials of the government, the commission will begin a tour of inspection which will take it into at least eight states.

Engagements with President Coolidge and Secretary Hughes and a luncheon at the Pan-American union, given in their honor by Dr. L. S. Rowe, the director general, formed the main points of today's program.

Arriving at Raleigh, N. C., Wednesday, the commission will spend a week in that state, where conditions for road building are similar to those in many Latin-American countries. The remainder of the itinerary includes Lexington, Ky.; Cincinnati; Wilmington; Chicago, Peoria, Aurora and Springfield, Ill.; St. Paul, Minneapolis, Hibbing, St. Cloud and Duluth, Minn.; Madison and Milwaukee, Wis.; Ann Arbor, Mich., and Cleveland.

Dates for the concluding lap of the trip, which will probably be thru New York, Pennsylvania and New Jersey, are being arranged.

Rejects Bids for Patrol Boats.

WASHINGTON, June 2.—Rejection of all bids for construction of twenty-five patrol boats for use in chasing rum-runners on the Pacific coast, was announced today by coast guard headquarters.

HOUSE VOTES TO ADJOURN AT 7 P. M. NEXT SATURDAY

WASHINGTON, June 2.—The house today adopted a resolution calling for sine die adjournment of congress at 7 p. m. next Saturday. Senate concurrence is required.

A proposal for a recess for a month or six weeks, and a return to consider a definitely outlined program was being discussed meantime by members of the senate farm bloc and some progressives. It was expected the suggestion would be introduced in the senate as a substitute for the adjournment resolution.

Scant encouragement was given at first to the recess proposal. Both the Republican and Democratic senate leaders were said to be convinced that a non-partisan majority was in favor of adjournment.

Vote Is 221 to 157.

The adjournment resolution was adopted in the house by a vote of 221 to 157.

The opposition came chiefly from Democrats, Republican insurgents and other Republicans from the middle and far west who have been demanding action on farm, reclamation and railroad legislation.

A "sincere hope" that some form of farm relief legislation could be passed before adjournment was voiced by Representative Longworth, after Representative Rubey, one of the chief supporters of the McNary-Haugen bill, had remarked its defeat appeared probable.

Congress of No Value.

Declaring he would not seek to block adjournment, Representative Garrett said he was certain no "good public service can be rendered by keeping congress in session so that the Republican party can wander around in the wilderness, accomplishing nothing, or something worse.

"The responsibility for putting thru legislation rests with the Republican majority, where it belongs and the minority should not attempt to usurp that responsibility when it is without power to force its will."

Despite the stand taken by their leader, more than half of the Democrats present voted to keep congress in session.

Majority Wants Adjournment.

Mr. Longworth in presenting his resolution said "a large majority feels we are ready to adjourn, and we ought to adjourn." He announced there would be a vote later in the day on the postal salaries bill and tomorrow on the McNary-Haugen farm relief measure.

A delegation representing farmers of the west and northwest conferred today with the Republican leaders in an effort to agree on some substitute for the McNary-Haugen bill. One suggestion was the scope of the bill be limited to wheat and either hogs or cattle. No definite decision was reached.

Here's Party Line-up.

Fifty-nine Republicans, ninety-five Democrats, one Farmer-Labor, one Socialist and one Independent opposed adjournment, while 136 Republicans and eighty-five Democrats supported the resolution.

Man Under Influence of Moonshine Stabs Woman and Her Son

Charles Patchik, 3258 South Paulina street, stabbed and seriously wounded Mrs. Mary Cunningham of 3123 Archer avenue, and her son, Alphonse Tyler at 35th street and Archer avenue last night. The police say Patchik had been drinking.

Both victims were taken to the county hospital. Tyler, it was said, probably would die.

According to the story told Brighton Park police, Patchik had quarreled with young Tyler. When Mrs. Cunningham attempted to interfere, Patchik drew a knife and stabbed her, then turned on the son, driving the knife into his body several times.

Patchik then fled to his home where police surrounded him. He surrendered after a struggle and was locked up in a cell at the Brighton Park station.

Coolidge to Act on Tax Bill Today or Tomorrow

WASHINGTON, June 2.—President Coolidge probably will dispose of the tax bill, awaiting his signature, today or tomorrow. He has virtually completed his study of the measure along with the report sent to him on Saturday by Secretary Mellon. The President had another conference today with Secretary Mellon for the purpose of clearing up several of the points arising from the measure.

U. S. Supreme Court Rules for Ford Company

WASHINGTON, June 2.—The Ford Motor company was declared by the Supreme court today not to have infringed the Harmatta patent for electric welding of thin sheets of iron and steel, owned by the Thomson Spot Welder company. The federal courts in Michigan had declared the patent invalid but that decision had been reversed by the Circuit Court of Appeals.

Metro-Goldwyn-Mayer to Spend 15 Million in '24-'25

LOS ANGELES, June 2.—The newly merged Metro-Goldwyn-Mayer corporation will expend at least $15,000,000 in the production of half a hundred film plays during the coming year, according to a detailed statement of plans made public today by Louis B. Mayer, chief executive of the motion picture concern.

FRANKS SLAYERS PUT IN JAIL ON ORDER OF COURT

Leopold and Loeb Taken from Crowe and Given to Sheriff's Custody.

Nathan E. Leopold Jr. and his chum, Richard Loeb, millionaires' sons, will be charged formally with the murder of 14-year-old Robert Franks and kidnaping for ransom in the Municipal court by 4 o'clock this afternoon, State's Attorney Crowe promised Chief Justice Caverly today after the court had continued habeas corpus writs for the two until Friday.

The continuation of the writs automatically placed both boys in the custody of Sheriff Hoffman until the formal charges are filed.

Both charges carry the death penalty.

Inquest Is Reopened.

Immediately following the hearing in court both boys were bundled into an automobile and under the guard of a picked group of deputy sheriff, aided by the police, were rushed to the inquest which was reopened by Coroner Wolff at Furth's undertaking rooms, 942 East 47th street.

A crowd of between 400 and 500 persons had gathered outside the place and the police had to hurl themselves upon them several times before they could force a lane large enough to get the prisoners inside. Even then the crowd refused to move and pushed about trying to peep in the windows to get a glimpse of the youths.

The writs were filed by Attorneys Clarence Darrow and Benjamin Bachrach, and asked that the boys be taken out of the custody of the state's attorney and the police, who were holding them without legal right. The ruling of the court was the first skirmish won by the defense.

"I am not asking the release of the prisoners," Attorney Darrow said, "but merely that their attorneys, Mr. Bachrach and myself, be allowed to consult with them, in accordance with their constitutional rights.

"We were denied this right yesterday, and, in the meantime, these youths, neither of whom is more than 19 years old, are being made to incriminate themselves by making repeated statements to the police and pointing out supposed places."

Crowe to File Charges.

"I realize these boys have rights and if the court will give me until 2 o'clock I will turn the prisoners over to their attorneys for as long a conference as they may want," State's Attorney Crowe replied.

"That is an extraordinary request," said Mr. Darrow. "The state's attorney is violating the constitutional rights of the prisoners and asks the court to aid him. I want to protest against any delay that will result in forcing the boys to testify at the inquest."

Then, upon the promise of the state's attorney to place the formal charges against the men, the court continued the hearing.

Talk with Relatives.

When the boys were brought into court they were allowed to talk for a few moments with their relatives. Nathan Leopold Sr., a multi-millionaire paper-box manufacturer, was present, and Loeb's uncle, Jacob Loeb, former president of the school board, was also there.

Loeb's father, Albert H. Loeb, vice president of Sears, Roebuck & Co., has been confined by illness to his bed for several days.

While the officials at the inquest were waiting for the appearance of the boys, Deputy Coroner Charles Fitzner scurried around the neighborhood and secured six men to serve on the jury.

Those choosen are B. G. Stobo, 6714 Merrill avenue; William Dining, 953 East 47th street; Able Wolf, 1001 East 47th street; Ira Lowenstein, 921 47th street; Neils Werner, 917 East 47th street, and James Lite, 921 East 47th street.

Sidetrack Other Cases.

Mr. Crowe announced he had ordered Thomas Marshall, the indictment expert of his office, to prepare an indictment to be presented to the grand jury tomorrow, when it is formally sworn in. He said all other matters would be sidetracked to give a clear track to the voting of the true bill.

The inquest was continued by Deputy Fitzner until June 27 and on motion of Mr. Crowe and without objection of Mr. Darrow or Mr. Bachrach. No testimony was heard and the boys were again placed in automobiles and started for the county jail, where, according to the court order, they must be held, without bail.

A stop was made on the way for luncheon, so each escaped a meal on prison fare.

Quiz Another Boy.

While these proceedings were going on, Assistant State's Attorney Joseph Savage, back in the Criminal court building, was questioning John Levinson, 9 years old, a son of Attorney Salmon Levinson, 4049 Lake Park avenue.

The boy said Loeb, whom he knew, stopped him at 49th street and Prairie avenue, May 21, the day of the murder and talked to him for a short time. This, according to Mr. Savage, bears out the statement of the two that they had no especial victim in mind and were planning to kidnap any wealthy

Continued on Next Page.

LAST-MINUTE NEWS

NATIONAL LEAGUE

		R	H	E
Boston (at New York)	000			
New York	010			

McNamara-O'Neil, Boston; Ryan-Snyder, New York.

		R	H	E
St. Louis (at Pittsburg)	000			
Pittsburg	000			

Dyer-Gonzales, St. Louis; Kremer-Gooch, Pittsburg.

AMERICAN LEAGUE

		R	H	E
Washington (at Phila.)	10			
Philadelphia	00			

Johnson-Ruel, Washington; Heimach-Perkins, Philadelphia.

SENATE VOTES TONIGHT ON CHILD LABOR AMENDMENT

WASHINGTON, June 2.—The senate agreed today to vote at 9 o'clock tonight on the child labor constitutional amendment, which already has passed the house.

70-YEAR-OLD MAN, DESPONDENT, SHOOTS HIMSELF

Walter H. Stacy, 70 years old, 206 North Kolin avenue, attempted suicide by shooting himself while in his home today. He was taken to the county hospital. According to the police, he was despondent over the death of his wife, which occurred several months ago.

EVANSTON MAN FOUND DEAD IN TRAIN AT LOUISVILLE

LOUISVILLE, June 2.—S. Wood Beal of Evanston, prominent lumber expert, was found dead in a sleeping car berth today when the train arrived here.

RACE RESULTS (BELMONT)

First—Turf, 7-1; Chrysalis, 6-5; Wilbur C. Whitehead, 3-5.
Second—Decisive, 10-1; Peccant, 1-2; Regalia, 6-5.
Third—Klondyke, 3-5; Banter, 5-2; Prince Hamlet, 4-5.

RACE RESULTS (THORNCLIFFE)

First—Spanish Name, 8.50; Effort, 2.65; Battleman, 2.60.
Second—Shue, 21.10; Thornyway, 4.50; Amber Fly, 8.75.

RACE RESULTS (CONNAUGHT PARK)

First—Kirkfield, 15.25; Mary Dear, 3.15; Elm, 2.90.
Second—Top Notch, 3.10; Aunt Lin, 6.35; Gay Kap, 2.85.

RACE RESULTS (KEMPTON)

First—Dardanella, 4.00; Swim, 2.35; Jack Reeves, out.

Writes Death Note About Plot; Kills Self, Child, by Gas

Suffering from a nervous breakdown, Mrs. Alice Kilender turned on the gas in her home at 1309 Rosedale avenue today, killing herself and her 11-year-old daughter, Dorothy.

A note found in the room read as follows

"The one who is hid and plotted against us is responsible for this act. To my friends and good fellows, goodby. I clear my conscience."

It was unsigned.

Andrew Kilender, husband and father of the victims, and head of the A. Kilender & Co. furniture store at 126 South Clinton street, found the two dead when he awakened this morning. He slept in a distant bedroom of the home.

A pulmotor squad called to the scene sought for hours to revive the mother and daughter, but in vain.

According to Mrs. Charles Edman, 1244 Rosedale avenue, a sister of the dead woman, Mrs. Kilender had just returned yesterday from a trip to New York, and had seemed overwrought by the trip, on which her husband and daughter accompanied her.

Five years ago Mrs. Kilender suffered a general breakdown, due to overexcitement.

Will Hear More Witnesses for Senator Mayfield

WASHINGTON, June 2.—Counsel for George E. B. Peddy, contesting the seat of Senator Mayfield (Dem., Texas), told the senate elections committee today they had concluded testimony on the issue of alleged misuse of funds, and were ready to make a final argument. Arguments were delayed, however, pending a further hearing of witnesses for Senator Mayfield at an afternoon session of the committee. An effort will be made to finish the hearings by the end of the week.

British Modify Attitude on Mosul, Envoy States

CONSTANTINOPLE, June 2.—(By the Associated Press.)—Sir Percy Cox, British high commissioner for Mesopotamia, today informed Fethi Bey, speaker of the Turkish assembly and head of the Turkish delegation which has been negotiating with a British delegation regarding the Mosul district, that he had modified the attitude it had taken in demanding complete rendition of the disputed territory.

Bill to Abolish Rail Labor Board to Be Shelved

WASHINGTON, June 2.—House supporters of the Barkley bill to abolish the railroad labor board today abandoned their fight to enact the measure into law at this session of congress.

SHRINERS TREKE INTO KANSAS CITY BY TRAINSFUL

Nobles Cross Hot Sands to Pitch Tents for Annual Convention.

KANSAS CITY, June 2.—(By the Associated Press.)—They're here—and more are trekking across hot desert sands to the shrine mecca in the heart of America.

Members of the Ancient Arabic Order of Nobles of the Mystic Shrine, gathering here today for the fiftieth annual session and golden jubilee tomorrow, Wednesday and Thursday, represent every point of the compass. They are here from Aloha, Honolulu; from Calgary, Canada; from New England and the south; from the plains of Texas and the sunny slopes of sunkist California.

Thousands already had arrived early today and at shrine headquarters in Convention hall it was predicted 20,000 will have pitched their tents on the oasis by nightfall.

Medinah Temple Arrives.

Among the temples already registered are Medinah, Chicago; Egypt, Tampa, Fla.; Mecca, New York City; Aleppo, Boston; Osman, St. Paul, and Hadi, Evansville, Ind.

At one period today, twenty special trains arrived at the Union station within forty minutes. The terminal engineer piloting the incoming caravans into their retreat all wore the shrine fez over their headlights and carried the crescent and scimitar over the steaming breasts of their hugh boilers. Each train bore a new temple, new colors, new enthusiasm.

A bedlam of flashing colors, blatant music and hilarious greetings—that's the Union station.

Thousands Line Streets.

And along the brilliantly bedecked thorofares other thousands thronged today and watched the impromptu parades, heard the band concerts, and applauded their approval.

Among the early arrivals today was the noblest noble of them all—Conrad V. Dykeman, the imperial potentate of shrinedom. His arrival at the Union station was the signal for a rousing demonstration.

War Condemned at Meet of Northern Baptists

MILWAUKEE, June 2.—War as a method of settling international disputes was condemned in a resolution adopted at the Northern Baptist convention at noon here today.

SPORTS ON PAGE 25

THE CHICAGO DAILY NEWS.

10th EDITION THE CLOSE IN STOCKS AND GRAINS.

TWO CENTS—OUTSIDE CHICAGO AND SUBURBS 3 CENTS 49TH YEAR—218. COPYRIGHT 1924 BY THE CHICAGO DAILY NEWS CO. WEDNESDAY, SEPTEMBER 10, 1924. ★ HOME EDITION ON SALE EVERYWHERE IN CHICAGO AT OR BEFORE 5 O'CLOCK

LOEB AND LEOPOLD GET LIFE

JUDGE SCORES CRIME, DECLARES BOYS SANE IN 'MERCY SENTENCE'

"No Mitigating Circumstance," Caverly Asserts, Branding Murder as a "Crime of Singular Atrocity"; Says "Humanity" Dictates Decision.

Ninety-Nine Years Added for Kidnaping as Means of Circumventing Future Hope of Parole—Boys Show Little Interest as Caverly Speaks Fateful Words.

THE FATEFUL WORDS.

"In No. 33623, indictment for murder, the sentence of the court is that you, Nathan F. Leopold, Jr., be confined in the penitentiary at Joliet for the term of your natural life. The court finds that your age is 19.

"In No. 33623, indictment for murder, the sentence of the court is that you, Richard Loeb, be confined in the penitentiary at Joliet for the term of your natural life. The court finds your age is 18.

"In 33624, kidnaping for ransom, it is the sentence of the court that you, Nathan F. Leopold, Jr., be confined in the penitentiary at Joliet for the term of ninety-nine years. The court finds your age is 19.

"In 33624, kidnaping for ransom, the sentence of the court is that you, Richard Loeb, be confined in the penitentiary at Joliet for the term of ninety-nine years."

ANALYSIS OF DECISION.

Judge John R. Caverly spared the lives of Richard Loeb and Nathan Leopold, Jr., to-day by sentencing them to prison, "each of you for the rest of his natural life," with the recommendation that they never be paroled.

He could find "no mitigating circumstances" in the kidnaping and murder of 14-year-old Bobby Franks," he said, as he pronounced the fate of the two wealthy, college-trained boys, but "in accordance with the progress of criminal law all over the world" and "the dictates of enlightened humanity," he saved them from death on the gallows.

Life imprisonment for the murder, was his decree; ninety-nine years for the kidnaping for ransom.

Builds Barrier to Parole.

How those sentences will run under the Illinois parole law isn't easily reckoned, disagreeing lawyers said. State's Attorney Crowe said he thought the boys would be eligible for parole in twenty years; others figured on thirty, thirty-five and fifty years. But if Judge Caverly's pronouncement is heeded Loeb and Leopold will not leave the gray walls of Joliet until they die, for the judge recommends that they never be admitted to parole.

"In the case of such atrocious crimes," he said, "it is entirely within the discretion of the department of public welfare never to admit these defendants to parole. To such policy the court urges them strictly to adhere."

Guards stood at the judge's side as he pronounced sentence in "the murder case of the century." Others, a small army in all, guarded the murderers, watched the crowd inside the room, did sentry duty at the doors, in the hallways and in an iron cordon all about the building and the jail, lest some of the hundreds of "cranks" who had written threatening letters should try to do violence.

Quick Trip to Joliet Planned.

And as soon as the two boys—happy now, and smiling—had been led back to their cells the patrols outside the jail were doubled while Sheriff Hoffman made plans to hurry his prisoners down to Joliet to begin their double life terms. He would have them in the penitentiary before night, he said, for safety's sake.

Afternoon found the boys still in the jail, though, with the wreckage of a banquet of steak and onions beside them. Clerk Passmore had held up the papers in the case for the state's attorney's scrutiny, "so that there will be no slip," and it seemed possible that the trip to Joliet might be put off until to-morrow.

Loeb and Leopold laughed about it.

"We don't care when we go," said Leopold. "To-morrow or next week is all right with us. We've got plenty of time."

Packed into the brief hour of the last act of the Franks tragedy was drama of the richest kind—tense, colorful, trying. The interest of the outside world, focused for the moment on that dingy little room, could almost be felt. The two hundred-odd spectators breathed excitedly, stood tense and still.

Carries Verdicts in Bundle.

The judge took his seat promptly at the appointed hour, carrying in his hand a great bundle of papers—the verdict and copies of the verdict.

"Richard Loeb and Nathan Leopold,

[Continued on Third Page.]

TEXT OF CAVERLY'S DECISION.

The text of Judge Caverly's decision follows:

"The state of Illinois vs. Leopold and Loeb.

"In view of the profound and unusual interest that this case has aroused, not only in this community, but in the entire country and even beyond its boundaries, the court feels it his duty to state the reasons which have led him to the determination he has reached.

"It is not an uncommon thing that pleas of guilty are entered in criminal cases, but almost without exception in the past such pleas have been the result of a virtual agreement between the defendant and the state's attorney, whereby, in consideration of the pleas, the state's attorney consents to recommend to the court a sentence deemed appropriate by him, and in the absence of special reasons to the contrary it is the practice of the court to follow such recommendations.

Different in This Case.

"In the present case the situation is a different one. A plea of guilty has been entered by the defense without a previous understanding with the prosecution and without any knowledge whatever on its part. Moreover, the plea of guilty did not in this particular case, as it usually does, render the task of the prosecution easier by substituting admission of guilt for a possibly difficult and uncertain chain of proof.

"Here the state was in possession not only of the essential substantiating facts, but also of voluntary confessions on the part of the defendants. The plea of guilty, therefore, does not make a special case in favor of the defendants.

"Since both of the cases, that, namely, of murder and that of kidnaping for ransom, were of a character which invested the court with discretion as to the extent of the punishment, it became his duty under the statute to examine witnesses as to the aggravation and mitigation of the offense. This duty has been fully met. By consent of counsel for the state and for the defendants the testimony in the murder case has been accepted as equally applicable to the case of kidnaping for ransom. In addition a prima facie case was made out of the kidnaping case as well.

"The testimony introduced, both by the prosecution and the defense, has been as detailed and elaborate as though the case had been tried before a jury. It has been given the widest publicity, and the public is so fully familiar with all its phases that it would serve no useful purpose to restate or analyze the evidence.

No Insanity Defense.

"By pleading guilty the defendants have admitted legal responsibility for their acts, the testimony has satisfied the court that the case is not one in which it would have been possible to set up successfully the defense of insanity, as insanity is defined and understood by the established law of this state for the purpose of administration of criminal justice.

"The court, however, feels impelled to dwell briefly on the mass of data produced as to the physical, mental and moral condition of the two defendants.

"They have been shown in essential respects to be abnormal; had they been normal they would not have committed the crime. It is beyond the province of this court, as it is beyond the capacity of human science in its present state of development, to predicate ultimate responsibility for human acts.

Abnormality Is Not Considered.

"At the same time the court is willing to recognize that the careful analysis made of the life history of the defendants and of their present mental, emotional and ethical condition has been of extreme interest and is a valuable contribution to criminology. And yet the court feels strongly that similar analysis made of other persons accused of crime would probably reveal similar or different abnormalities. The value of such tests seems to lie in their applicability to crime and criminals in general. Since they concern the broad questions of human responsibility and legal punishment and are in no wise peculiar to these individual defendants, they may be deserving of legislative but not of judicial consideration. For th... regular ... conviction

[Continued on Third Page.]

PARENTS LOSE FIGHT ON HARPER TRANSFER

Court Upholds School Officials, but Says Plaintiffs May Get Added Hearing.

M'ANDREW RULE ON TEST

Prospective victory changed to defeat to-day for parents of former grade pupils at the Harper school, 6500 South Wood street, when Judge Harry M. Fisher denied an injunction asked by them to restrain the board of education from changing the school to a junior high.

The decision was a surprise to the parents. Judge Fisher was sitting for the first time in the case, having had it left to him on call of Judge George Fred Rush, who had indicated that he would grant the petition filed by Attorney A. W. F. Siebel for the parents.

However, Attorney Frank S. Righeimer, for the board, asked a continuance to study amendments to the petition filed by Attorney Siebel and Judge Rush left on his vacation before the final decision was due.

Parents Hopeful for Retrial.

Judge Fisher left only one ray of hope to the parents. At the close of the session he granted Attorney Siebel permission to take the matter before a master in chancery. The counsel announced that the parents would renew the fight there to have planning their children cross traffic-loaded streets to get to schools farther away than the Harper school had been.

At one other point the parents gained some consolation in the verdict. Judge Fisher said that, although he believed that the approval of junior high school came only after careful and mature deliberation by the board and was fair to the children, he would suggest that the board reopen the matter and see if something couldn't be done to end the controversy.

The decision was made, Judge Fisher said, on the fact that in his opinion the parents had failed to show that the action of the board in changing the nature of the school was arbitrary in any way or different from the situation with other schools in the city.

Only one demonstration marred the proceedings. While one school official was testifying a voice from the crowded courtroom, full of parents, was raised in protest. The judge promptly announced that any further outbreak would result in the clearing of the courtroom of all spectators.

Coroner Fears Arrangement.

Judge Fisher denied the bill in spite of an affidavit signed by Coroner Wolff, stating that the traffic arteries which the children would have to cross to reach other schools would be a constant menace to their safety, and asserting that he had warned Superintendent McAndrew that fatal results were almost sure to follow.

The parents also filed an affidavit signed by 235 of them showing that 743 pupils in the school district were affected by the situation and are out in school because of overcrowded conditions in the feeder schools to which they were ordered transferred.

The parents, after the court session, announced that they would hold a mass meeting and plan a further campaign at the Harper school during the afternoon.

Declaring that $50,000 worth of junior high equipment installed in the Harper school would be wasted should the petition for an injunction be granted, Attorney Frank S. Righeimer appeared with a twenty-five-page answer to the injunction plea.

Granting of the injunction would be a body blow to the junior high school system, the answer asseverates, and asserts also that $100,000,000 would be necessary to build enough schools where no hazard would exist.

The future action will take place before Master in Chancery Ninian H. Welch. Attorney Siebel said that he would see Mr. Welch immediately in an effort to have an early hearing on the proposition.

Heckle Wight on Statement.

The interruption by the crowd came when Ambrose B. Wight, assistant sup-

[Continued on Third Page.]

BE CROSS-WORD PUZZLER

Everybody Else Is Becoming One, So Why Not Go Along?

Anyway the Craze Is Good Fun and It's So-o-o Educational!

Cross-word puzzling, first seizing upon Chicago as a fad, is now an institution, and is fast becoming a happy mania.

And just what is cross-word puzzling? Well, it's a game—a game which turns every player into an amateur Sherlock Holmes, solving mysteries of words—the most fascinating of all mysteries.

It started as an amusement feature in the east. New York literary and artistic celebrities took it up and made it a rage. As a book it skyrocketed to best-seller heights in a month. And now it's sweeping the country.

No doubt you've heard otherwise sane persons mumble absent-mindedly, "What's a four-letter word meaning satyr?" Probably you've heard tales of a children's pastime disrupting pleasantly the households of their elders.

Or if a man's late for work these days the cross-word puzzle is the probable dire reason. If a beefsteak broils not wisely but too well, blame the helpless cross-word puzzle. If the children of school age—well, hysteria is a mild term.

What a Cross-Word Puzzle Is.

So far so good. But precisely what is this most absorbing of pastimes?

A cross-word puzzle is no more nor less than a rectangular arrangement of black and white squares. The white squares are to be filled with letters. The letters, properly arranged, become words. And from the words—if they're right—comes the puzzle.

It's easy. That's why it's so much amusement.

It's fascinating. That's why business and households are being neglected. It's educational. That's why we mothers are giving their children cross-word puzzles instead of story books. And that also is why dictionaries and books of synonyms are being more generally consulted now than ever before.

And it's fun.

The First Problem.

The Daily News, in order to keep step with this newest American rage, has been publishing one puzzle each week, on the Saturday children's page. The pace has quickened, however, and to satisfy the requests made in many letters from readers The Daily News begins publication to-day of cross-word puzzle No. 1, The Daily News series. It, together with directions and a few useful hints, will be found on page 10.

Get out your dictionaries and pencils, you puzzle hounds—and don't forget your erasers.

And go to it!

BAY STATERS ARE DINED

Massachusetts Chamber of Commerce Feted by Chicagoans.

New England took over the Hotel LaSalle in a manner of speaking this noon when 125 members of the Massachusetts state chamber of commerce were entertained at a New England boiled dinner by the Chicago Association of Commerce at its first autumn Wednesday luncheon.

Samuel H. Thompson, vice-president of the eastern business men, talked about the rising influence of New England in the business affairs of the nation, following an address of welcome by W. R. Dawes, president of the Chicago group. The first lunch of the season brought out a big crowd.

Maj.-Gen. Harry C. Hale, commander of the 6th corps area, U. S. A., another speaker, told the audience that Defense day, Sept. 12, will be an appeal to civic efficiency rather than an overt expression of militarism. His explanation brought large applause.

WEATHER INDICATIONS.

The official weather forecast for the thirty-six hours ending to-morrow at 7 p. m. is as follows:

Chicago and vicinity—Unsettled to-night and Thursday; probably showers beginning late to-night; continued cool; winds mostly moderate southeasterly.

Hourly temperatures since 3 p. m. yesterday.

Hour	Temp.
[illegible]	53
[illegible]	52
[illegible]	52
[illegible]	50
[illegible]	50
[illegible]	52
[illegible]	56
[illegible]	56
[illegible]	56
[illegible]	55
[illegible]	55
[illegible]	55

ARMORED FLEET TO TAKE KILLERS AWAY

Motorcycle Corps to Clear Path for Sheriff and Prisoners on Joliet Dash.

LEOPOLD SHEDS TEARS

Nathan Leopold, Jr., and Richard Loeb paced their quarters in the county jail for the last time at noon to-day, just before an armored police caravan was to whisk them away to Joliet penitentiary to begin their sentence of imprisonment for life.

Plans for the getaway to Joliet were made in record time and the boys would have begun their term shortly after noon had the mittimus been ready. Only official red tape gave the youthful murderers a few extra hours in Chicago.

Sheriff Peter M. Hoffman said he would lead the heavily armed cavalcade which is lining up for Joliet. Capt. George Weidling of the county highway police will accompany him, as will two deputy sheriffs, David Edfeldt and Samuel Anoreno. Warden Wesley Westbrook may go along.

A fleet of motorcycle policemen, heavily armed, will clear the way for the prison car. The trip is expected to be run in fast time.

Can Choose Last Meal Here.

Sheriff Hoffman told his prisoners they could have anything they wanted for their last meal under his supervision—the last meal they'll ever eat, very probably, in Chicago.

"Dickie" and "Babe" agreed on a steak—and the sheriff himself is authority for the statement that it was two inches thick. A battery of side dishes made the farewell lunch something of a banquet. Both boys asked for chocolate eclairs for dessert.

"I suppose this is the last square meal we'll ever eat," Loeb said.

The boys showed very little emotion as they talked over the situation with Judge Caverly's decision, but immediately afterward they snapped—just a little. A deputy sheriff noticed it first, as they were being led back to the bullpen directly after the zero hour in court.

"Look!" he whispered. "Look! Leopold's crying!"

And for almost the first time during the long travail the imperturbable and supercilious Leopold was seen with tears in his eyes. As he himself might have said, his lachrymal glands were at last functioning.

Loeb, too, had finally cracked under the three-month strain and he was puckering his face to restrain his emotion. Later they explained the final weakening just a little shamefacedly.

Extra Sentence Breaks Them.

The ninety-nine year sentence was what did it, they agreed. Life imprisonment they could stand, and life imprisonment they were steeled against, but when Judge Caverly sonorously announced the penalty for the kidnaping charge, they snapped.

"Ninety-nine years was the straw that broke the camel's back in this story," said Leopold afterward.

As soon as they realized clearly that the shadow of the gallows was finally removed from their thoughts and dreams both boys naturally enough underwent a sharp reaction. They smiled. They laughed. They almost giggled.

"As happy as two school boys," commented Sheriff Hoffman. "I've never seen anything like it. They act as if they were free."

Leopold seemed to have little difficulty in living up to his famed reputation for complete nonchalance. Perhaps it was merely a gesture—the supreme gesture of his life—but at any rate, fronting the iron-faced judge, he didn't bat an eye.

Loeb Plainly Flustered.

Loeb, on the other hand, couldn't quite achieve his companion's imperturbable coldness. He gulped three or four times as Judge Caverly intoned his fate, continually wet his lips and

[Continued on Third Page.]

5,000 JAM STREETS AT JAIL

Big Crowd Hoped to Get Glimpse of Franks Slayers.

Bomb Fanatics, Evidently Awed by Show of Force, Absent.

More than 5,000 persons, packed in the streets around the Criminal court building, behind lines of foot, motorcycle and mounted policemen, made a North Clark street holiday of Judge Caverly's pronouncement of sentence on Nathan Leopold, Jr., and Richard Loeb this morning.

For the 5,000 the "kick" in the situation was in being within sight of the fateful scene, and then, unexpectedly, the chance that they might glimpse the sentenced boys as Sheriff Hoffman hustled them from the jail into a fast automobile to take them to Joliet prison.

No fanatics came with bombs. All those who have written letters threatening destruction of Judge Caverly if his verdict did not suit them were absent or cowed by the display of force.

Altogether it was such a crowd as might gather on any Clark street corner, from the river to Chicago avenue, mostly men with nothing else to do, a few women, truck drivers stopping for a moment, and employes of neighboring concerns perched in windows and on top of buildings.

Poses as "Mrs. Leopold."

Once a frail, gray-haired woman dressed in a black gown of a fashion of twenty-five years old got to the door of the building.

"I must see either Judge Caverly or Mr. Leopold; I'm Mrs. Leopold," she said.

A bailiff, knowing that Mrs. Leopold has been dead several years, took her kindly by the arm and told her that it was impossible for her to see Mr. Leopold or Judge Caverly.

"Well, all right," she said without protest, and went away.

When the Wrigley building clock had passed 9:30, the hour when Judge Caverly was to go to the bench, half of those in the street took their watches in their hands and figured the minutes until the verdict might come. Ten minutes passed. Then a deputy sheriff popped out the door and passed the word to the group of officers guarding the entrance. A county motorcycle policeman cupped his hands and shouted to a friend across the street:

"Rest o' natural life."

News Runs Through Crowd.

"Yeah, it's life," some one shouted down the line, and in a twinkling the news had gone around the block.

If any one was dissatisfied he kept it to himself. The crowd went to pieces as quietly as it had gathered and half the 5,000 had started away when the others sniffed new excitement in the hasty gathering of policemen around the Dearborn street entrance to the jail. Sightseers flowed into the block before the barred windows, but the police were there first, with every possible precaution taken against disturbance while young "Babe" and "Dick" were to start for prison.

Elbow to elbow, policemen stood in two lines from the jail door to the curb and it seemed plain to the least experienced observer of street events that something was to happen. But time passed while Sheriff Hoffman was arranging the commitment papers, and most of the crowd gave it up.

Guard Placed Early.

The authorities who arranged the elaborate guard of the Criminal court neighborhood were satisfied they had done well. They regarded it possible that some overwrought person might attempt violence unless the show of authority was overwhelming.

The guard was established at 7 o'clock, which was before the most enthusiastic outdoor fan arrived. When Judge Caverly arrived with an escort of riflemen, the forces were so well disposed that, seemingly, they could have handled a national invasion.

Chief of Detectives Michael Hughes, who directed the protective arrangements in accordance with Judge Caverly's wishes, brought along seven detective bureau zone squads, each with a high-powered car parked in front of the bu... an instant.

ANOTHER RESULT OF MODERN TRANSPORTATION.

LATE BASEBALL SCORES.

SCORE OF THE NATIONAL LEAGUE—AT CHICAGO.

	1	2	3	4	5	6	7	8	9
Cincinnati	6	0							
Chicago (Cubs)	0	0							

Batteries—Donohue-Wingo, Cincinnati; Jacobs-O'Farrell, Cubs.

SCORE OF THE AMERICAN LEAGUE—AT DETROIT.

	1	2	3	4	5	6	7	8	9
Chicago (White Sox)	0	0							
Detroit	1	1							

Batteries—Thurston-Crouse, White Sox; Collins-Bassler, Detroit.

AMERICAN LEAGUE.

At Philadelphia—First game. Final: Washington, 1; Philadelphia, 2.

Batteries—Zachary-Ruel, Washington; Gray-Perkins, Philadelphia.

At Philadelphia—Second game, 2d: Washington, 5; Philadelphia, 1.

Batteries—Mogridge-Ruel, Washington; Heimach-Perkins, Philadelphia.

Cleveland and St. Louis had no games scheduled.

At Boston—New York-Boston game postponed; rain.

NATIONAL LEAGUE.

At New York—First game. Final score: Boston, 1; New York, 22.

Batteries—Cooney-Gibson, Boston; Barnes-Gowdy, New York.

At New York—2nd game. End of 1st inning: Boston, 0; New York, 2.

Batteries—Genewich-Gibson, Boston; McQuillan-Gowdy, New York.

At Brooklyn—End of 5th inning: Philadelphia, 1; Brooklyn, 4.

Batteries—Betts-Wilson, Philadelphia; Ehrhardt-Deberry, Brooklyn.

Pittsburgh (at St. Louis)....

St. Louis....

RESULTS OF TO-DAY'S RACES.

AT AURORA, ILL.

FIRST—Phyllis Gentry, 8-1, won; Sorline, 6-5; Glory, 4-1.

SECOND—May Buddy, 5-1, won; Boot Black, 2-1; Miss Fortune, 2-1.

HURRY 40,000 TROOPS TO CHINESE WAR LINE

Peking Authorities Strengthen Force Battling to Capture Shanghai.

CHANG TO RUSH TO AID

BY JAMES L. BUTTS.

SPECIAL CABLE
To The Chicago Daily News Foreign Service. Copyright, 1924, by The Chicago Daily News Co.

Shanghai, China, Sept. 10.—Desultory fighting continued throughout this afternoon along the whole front. Owing to the continued rain an opportunity was given for bringing up reserves and ammunition both by the troops attempting to capture Shanghai and by those defending it.

An unconfirmed report has been received that Gen. Chang Tso-lin has planned to land two divisions in the Shanghai area, possibly from Hangchow bay. This report has spread among the Chekiang forces and has aided in strengthening their morale, which, however, has been good from the start and their deportment continues excellent.

Desertion Report Confirmed.

In the meanwhile a fairly authentic report has been received that two divisions of 20,000 troops, rushed by the Christian general, Feng Yu-hsiang, to Nanking, are being sent to the Quinsan-Liuho fronts.

A visit to a point just east of Taihu lake shows that the Chekiang troops are highly optimistic and are slowly advancing.

The reports that two battalions of Kiangsu troops had deserted and joined the Chekiang troops has been confirmed.

It is reported on apparently good authority that 200 young women from the colleges and schools in Soochow have enlisted and volunteered to proceed to Shanghai to organize propaganda for enlisting their sisters on behalf of their native province. This has caused Gen. Ho Feng-lin to issue an order to arrest all suspicious women and to counteract the movement in the Shanghai institutions.

Red Cross Signs Barred.

The abuse of the Red Cross emblem has led to the issue of a general order to search all craft on the rivers carrying such signs.

The tremendous influx of refugees is creating alarm among the Chekiang officials, who suspect that spies are working within the protected settlements. Short shrift is giving to suspects arrested on Chinese territory. Twenty were executed to-day at Lungwha where it was said that they were caught bearing arms and bombs for an attack upon the arsenal, which is poorly protected.

The settlement defense units are mounting guards to-night.

Chinese Civil War Spreads.

Shanghai, China, Sept. 10.—China's civil war has spread to a new sector, Chuchow, 190 miles southwest of here. The new fighting front was revoted by the movement of the troops of Rafaun. Sun Chuan-fang, a supporter of Tsao Kun and the Peking government, Fukien province northward, where

[Continued on Third Page.]

Mi... large aud... Pat—... "An' what d... "Not guilty."—London Tit-Bits.

SMALL'S BANK STOCK BARED

Attorney Says Interest Money Bought Ridgely Securities.

Special to The Chicago Daily News.

Springfield, Ill., Sept. 10.—Money collected from interest on Chicago packers' notes was used by Gov. Len Small to purchase stock in the Ridgely Farmers' bank in this city, Assistant Attorney-General Floyd Britton declared before Master in Chancery Briggle to-day in his closing argument in the civil suits against the governor. The late Senator Edward C. Curtis, he said, was simply a financial agent for the governor and received as his share of interest only what the governor gave him.

Britton, in discussing the purchase of stock by Small and Curtis in the Ridgely Farmers' bank said that Small used $275,000 to purchase stock and that money was replaced in the state treasury from interest on packers' notes. He said that exhibits in the case had shown conclusively that interest derived from state funds was used by Small and not by Curtis, and that "Small gave Curtis little of the money derived from interest on packers' notes."

Statements made by the governor while on the witness stand in his own behalf relative to financial transactions between him and Curtis were branded by Britton "as ingenious and without legal weight."

In support of his argument that Curtis received only a small portion of interest alleged to have been collected, Britton said that the records in the case showed that Curtis owed Small large sums of money on various occasions.

Britton will be followed by Assistant Attorney-General Boord, and at the conclusion of his argument a recess will be taken to next Monday morning, when Attorney Werner W. Schroeder, counsel for the governor, will begin his closing argument.

GOODRICH ON WITNESS STAND

Indiana Ex-Governor and Others Say Smith Was Sane.

Additonal testimony that Delavan Smith, wealthy newspaper publisher, was sane when he made his will cutting off sixteen cousins was given today before Judge Claire C. Edwards at Waukegan, where the relatives of the late millionaire are trying to break the will.

James G. Goodrich, former governor of Indiana; Carl Lieber director of conservation in the Hoosier state, and Charles H. Hammond, a Chicago attorney, were the principal witnesses. Each testified that in his opinion Mr. Smith was entirely normal when he signed the will. Former Governor Goodrich declared that he had known Mr. Smith for several years and talked with him four months after the signing of the document. At that time, Mr. Goodrich said, Mr. Smith was normal.

GIRL, 15, SEIZED IN HOLDUPS

One Wears Overalls as They Order Second Victim to "Beat It."

[By The Associated Press.]

Edwardsville, Ill., Sept. 10.—Two 15-year-old girls, one attired in overalls and a sweater, the other wearing regular feminine attire, were in jail here today, having been arrested last night on charges of having committed two holdups. They were arrested as they were ordering their second victim "to beat it home." The girls gave their names as Olga Endruizzi and Margaret McMullen, both of Gillespie, Ill. One of the girls carried a revolver with which the victims were held up to-day, while the other girl searched his ..., according to the police report ...

GOOD MORNING!
The ZR-3 stays up on gas
Which some men try in vain, alas!

The Pittsburgh Post

GOOD MORNING!
Tune in, my children, and you will, maybe,
Catch a broadcast hail from the ZR-3.

82ND YEAR—NO. 268. TUESDAY MORNING, OCTOBER 14, 1924. TWO CENTS A COPY.

BLACK HAND BROKEN HERE

MORE U. S. MARINES LAND AS DEFENDERS QUIT SHANGHAI

ZR-3 Nearing Bermuda After Passing by Azores

ARMED TROOPS AND REFUGEES POURING INTO DESERTED CITY

Foreign Section in Peril After Chiefs Flee on Tokio Ship.

LU WILL HELP CHANG, BELIEF

By JOHN POWELL.
(Copyright, 1924, by the Chicago Tribune.)

SHANGHAI, Oct. 13.—The United States and other foreign powers landed more marines for the defense of the foreign settlements this afternoon and tonight, in view of the continued unsettled conditions following the departure of Generals Lu Yung Hsiang and Ho Feng-Lin, commanders of the Chekiang troops, this morning.

Following the example of Lu and Ho all generals commanding the front Chekiang lines also deserted and sought safety either in the foreign areas or on outward bound ships. As a result about 30,000 armed soldiers on the local fronts have begun flocking in the direction of the foreign settlements.

REFUGEES FLOCK IN.

In addition to this the remaining population of the countryside for a radius of 30 miles also is flocking into Shanghai and congestion is approaching the danger point, making necessary the landing of more marines for the protection of life and property. It

(Continued on Page Two, Col. Three.)

Student Located In Kansas City to Start Home Soon

MEADVILLE, Pa., Oct. 13.—Information reaching Meadville friends from Kansas City, Mo., this afternoon was that Arthur James, Allegheny College freshman, who disappeared from Meadville Octover 1, and who was located at the General Hospital in Kansas City October 7, had been discharged from the hospital and was expected to start immediately for his home in Pittsburgh. The information did not state whether James had thrown any light on his mysterious disappearance.

Until a few days ago he could not remember anything after being in school September 30. His friends here still believe he was the vcitim of upper classmen.

It is expected that he will reach Pittsburgh Wednesday or Thursday.

AMHERST INVITES COOLIDGE

AMHERST, Mass., Oct. 13.—President Coolidge and other distinguished alumni of Amherst College, have been invited as special guests for his inauguration of George Daniel Olds as ninth president of the college, November 14. Others are Frederick H. Gillett, '74, speaker of the House; Harlan F. Stone, '94, attorney general of the United States; Arthur P. Rugg, '83, chief justice of the supreme court of Massachusetts, and Governor Cox of Massachusetts.

ONE ENGINE DOWN, BIG SHIP GOES ON WITH OTHER THREE

"All Well" Despite Slight Mishap; Men Lounge About Writing Letters As Titanic Craft Flies Toward America

LOOMING STORM MAY ADD SPEED; TIME OF LANDING NOW DOUBTFUL

BY THE ASSOCIATED PRESS.

BOSTON, Oct. 13.—(By the Associated Press.)—The dirigible ZR-3, en route from Germany to the United States, passed over Flore's Island, the most westerly of the Azores group, at about 6:30 eastern standard time, according to a message from the ZR-3, picked up by the Chatham, Mass., station of the Radio Corporation of America tonight.

The message, sent to Hamburg, Germany, was not timed, but was picked up by Chatham at about 6:30 p. m. The island is in latitude 39 degrees 25 minutes, north; longitude 31 degrees 12 minutes, west.

ONE ENGINE GOES DOWN.

The ZR-3 was talking with Hamburg, the operator reported. Earlier, at 1:30 a message was sent indicating that the ship had sighted Pico Island, in the Azores. The message indicated that the giant air cruiser had encountered some slight engine trouble but that she was proceeding satisfactorialy with three engines running.

It was estimated that there was a difference of three hours and one minute between the American eastern standard time and that at Flores. Thus at the time the messages was dispatched stating that the ship was passing Flores Island, the hour aboard the dirigible was 9:31 p. m., according to the estimate.

In conversation with Hamburg, it was reported that the crew had become habituated to life on board the

(Continued on Page, Two, Col. Four.)

Watching the ZR-3

CHATHAM, Mass., Oct. 13.—(By the United News)—ZR-3 passed over Flores Island, western tip of Azores group, about 6:30 p. m., Eastern Standard time, according to message from ZR-3 to Hamburg, picked up by Station WCC here.

WASHINGTON, Oct. 13.—(By The Associated Press)—A message from the air cruiser ZR-3 received at the navy department tonight, reported her position at 3 o'clock Eastern Standard time this afternoon as 130 miles west of Fayal course (Azores) and added that all was well.

BERLIN, Oct. 13.—(By The Associated Press)—The giant dirigible ZR-3 reached the Azores Islands at noon, Greenwich Meridian time, according to a wireless message received here.

DEAD MAN'S DIVORCE VACATED

PHILADELPHIA, Oct. 13.—The superior court today vacated the divorce granted the late J. H. Fleming, of Media, Delaware county, from his first wife. The divorce, on grounds of malicious desertion was attacked in a lower court when a letter said to have revealed fraud, was introduced. The lower tribunal, however, refused to annul the decree as Fleming had married again. Today's action automatically awards the first wife one-half of Fleming's estate.

GERMAN PRIZE WINNERS NAMED

BERLIN, Oct. 13—The German winners of the peace klan award offered by Edward A. Filene, of Boston, were announced today. The first prize of $5,000 is divided between Dr. Eduard David of Darmstadt, Socialist Reichstag member and former minister of the interior, and Dr. Wilhelm Ricker, of Boln, near Munich. The second prize of $1,000 went to Dr. Gustav Jodleder, of Berlin. The third prize was divided among 35 contestants, each receiving $100.

1,000 Drug Containers Are Seized in Raid On Third Avenue Chinese

Three Alleged Gunmen Arrested by Raiding Squad.

MANAGER LEAPS OUT WINDOW

One thousand empty "toys"—containers for opium and other "hop"—were found when two Federal narcotic agents and two city detectives raided a building at 521 Third avenue, in which the Hip Sing Tong has its headquarters.

Three Chinese, alleged gunmen, who refused to give their names, were captured and locked in the Center avenue police station on the charge of "suspicious person." Yyalock Yunck, a Chinese, said to be manager of the building raided, escaped through a window when the raiders broke in.

The raiding party was made up of Frank Ferris and William Duffy, narcotic agents, and David Corbett and Edward Harkins, city detectives assigned to narcotic investigations.

The four men broke down the door to gain entrance to the building. Their information was that the place was being used as an opium den. The 1,000 toys were found in a satchel. Several pistols and other weapons were found in the place. The three alleged gunmen arrested refused to answer any questions put to them by the police.

Police say the three were brought here from Chicago or New York when the tong war broke out afresh last Thursday when Lee Sam, a Hip Sing, was shot to death by the On Yong Tong killer.

Pittsburgh's Chinatown has been quiet since the killing last Thursday, but there is war in the air and surrounding communities are being watched closely.

Word came from Uniontown that the police of that city are looking for five Chinese gunmen who left Pittsburgh early yesterday morning headed for Uniontown. Pittsburgh police sent out word of the trip and asked that they be headed off.

The mission of the five is supposed to be the fomenting of tong war spirit among the Chinese of towns throughout Western Pennsylvania. The five are believed to be in hiding in the homes of friends in Uniontown.

NORTHSIDE BOY IS KILLED BY TRUCK; RUNS IN PATH OF CAR

Former Sharpsburg Councilman Struck By Machine.

WOMAN HURT IN ACCIDENT

Leroy Camp, 8 years old, of 21 Superior avenue, Northside, was killed instantly when he ran from behind a street car in California avenue, near Island avenue, into the path of a truck at 7:45 o'clock last night. George W. Brooks, Negro, of 246 Maple avenue, Ben Avon, driver of the truck, was turned over to the coroner and released on $1,000 bail, pending an inquest.

WOMAN INJURED.

Two persons were injured by automobiles yesterday and several others had narrow escapes. Mrs. Catherine Michaels, 40 years old, of East street, was taken to the Allegheny General Hospital after receiving body bruises when struck by a machine in East Ohio street, near East street. J. H. Mackall, 40 years old, West Diamond street, was arrested charged with reckless driving.

Fred W. Pilgrim, 53 years old, Clifton avenue, Sharpsburg, a former Sharpsburg councilman, suffered several fractured ribs and lacerations on the face yesterday when he was struck by an automobile, driven by Howard Nesbitt, Butler street, in North Canal street, Sharpsburg. Pilgrim was taken to St. Francis Hospital and Nesbitt is being held by the police to await the result of the victim's injuries.

When two automobiles ran into a wagon he was driving at the south end of the Tenth street bridge yesterday, Jacob Rectenwald, 56 years old, a grocer, of Mountain street, old St. Clair borough, was thrown to the street and escaped with slight injuries. Police are looking for the occupants of the two cars.

Mrs. John Fitzpatrick, Carson street, and Fred Roamer, Carrick, narrowly escaped injury yesterday when the automobiles they were driving, collided at South Twenty-fourth and Carson streets. Roamer was driving a truck. The machines were damaged.

A truck of the Liberty Transfer Company, driven by Patrick Flaherity, was damaged $25 when it caught fire in Smithfield street, near Carson street, yesterday.

Monte Carlo's New Low Limit Bars Old Women's Wee Stakes

PARIS, Oct. 13.—(Chicago Tribune Foreign News Service.)—A new regulation in the Monte Carlo Casino, doubling the minimum stakes for roulette threatens to destroy the livelihood of hundreds of old women who have been one of the sights of the Riviera. These genteel, poor women—every third one of whom is pointed out as a former "friend" of King Edward or the former kaiser—eke out their incomes by 30 or 40 francs daily, won by cautious playing at 25 cents a shot. The new regulation establishes a minimum stake in the public rooms at $1.

"PERFECT LOVER" IS FREE TO WED MRS. HALL-QUEST

Mrs. Hart's Divorce Follows Pitt Professor's.

IS AWARDED $200 MONTHLY

BY THE ASSOCIATED PRESS.

CINCINNATI, Oct. 13.—Frederick William Hart, former major in the British army, was free tonight to marry Mrs. Shirley Knox Hall-Quest, divorced wife of Dr. Alfred Lawrence Hall-Quest, dean of the extension department of the University of Pittsburgh, in the realm of "perfect love."

Mrs. Rosamond Hart of Cincinnati was granted a divorce from her husband here today just seven days after Mrs. Hall-Quest was released by her husband, in order that she might marry Hart. Dr. Hall-Quest was granted his divorce in Chicago where he made every effort to conceal from publicity the name of his wife's associate.

GETS $200 MONTHLY.

The hearing was brief, Judge Charles Hoffman granted Mrs. Hart a divorce on the grounds of extreme cruelty. He approved a contract entered into by Hart whereby Mrs. Hart received $5,000 in cash and a monthly allowance of $200 during the remainder of her life. She likewise was given possession of furniture and effects located in the Hart apartment here which adjoined that formerly occupied by the Hall-Quests. This contract will automatically become void should Mrs. Hart marry again.

Hart was not in court. He left Chicago last night, ostensibly for Cincinnati. Judge Hoffman said although he had granted the divorce he would not draw the formal decree until tomorrow.

During the hearing the name of Mrs. Hall-Quest was frequently mentioned as the "other woman" in the unusual triangle.

Walter Locke, attorney for Mrs. Hart, took the stand and told of a conversation she had with Hart.

COULDN'T BE RECONCILED.

"He was discussing what he was able to do for Mrs. Hart's support," he said. "He admitted to me he was living in Chicago with Mrs. Hall-Quest. He said he would live with her whether he was divorced or not. I asked him whether there was not

(Continued on Page Two, Col. Three.)

FLIER GOES 36,555 FEET HIGH

PARIS, Oct. 13.—The world's airplane altitude record of 11.145 meters (36,555 feet), made by the French aviator Sadi Lecointe, in October, 1923, was eclipsed at Villacoublay, Friday by the French aviator Callizo, who set the mark at 12,066 meters, it was announced today, after an official examination of the altitude instruments on Callizo's machine. The aviator had been training for three years in an endeavor to break the record.

Prisoner Perishes As Lock-Up Burns

Boy's Cries Unheeded Until Too Late; Another May Die.

SPECIAL TO THE PITTSBURGH POST.

PHILIPSBURG, Pa., Oct. 13.—A fire of incendiary origin this morning in the local municipal building caused the death of one police prisoner and another is in the hospital and may not recover. Frederick Beam, 20 years old, of Woodland, is dead; Walter Ralston, aged 18, of Kylertown, may not recover.

This morning when the smoke from the burning building was smothering them they called for help, but it was presumed they had again become noisy, and no attention was paid to their cries. Later, when smoke began to issue from the lockup, an effort was made to save the prisoners.

In Beam's case they were too late, but Ralston had put his head in his blanket, and at the hospital it was found that there still was some life in him.

Shenandoah Ready For Flight Today

To Leave San Diego For Journey Up Pacific Coast.

BY THE ASSOCIATED PRESS.

SAN DIEGO, Cal., Oct. 13.—Refueled and reprovisioned, girders damaged in landing here repaired, and fresh helium wating in tanks to be injected into her gas bags, the navy dirigible Shenandoah is swinging at her North island anchor mast tonight ready for the start at 7:30 o'clock tomorrow morning on her voyage up the Pacific coast.

Waiting aboard for all hands are wool and fur-lined flying suits and wool-lined arctic boots for the upper air, even over southern California, carries a penetrating chill.

Each of the suits is "wired" for connection to electric plugs. If the wearer feels cold he may back up to the wall, "plug in" and warm up.

Provisions taken on consisted mainly of sandwiches, wrapped in oiled papers, and beans.

TWO KILLED IN TRAIN CRASH

NEW MILFORD, Pa., Oct. 13.—The engineer and fireman of a pusher engine at the rear of a freight train, were killed, and three persons injured early today when passenger train No. 14 of the Lackawanna railroad, running through a heavy fog, crashed into the freight one mile west of here. Failure of the engineer of the passenger train to see the home signal protecting the freight, due to the fog, is believed to have caused the accident. The dead are Michael Kelly, 40 years old, and Roy Osterhout, 33, both of Halstead, Pa.

24 MEMBERS HELD TO COURT IN BOMB PLOT IN EAST END

Two Others Flee to Canada Following Wide Clean-Up On Black Hand By Police

REIGN OF TERROR IN DISTRICT SUBSIDES WITH CAPTURES

The backbone of the Mafiá — the Blackhand Society—is in the county jail. For there 24 Italians implicated in the bombing of the home of Anthony Bernerdino, 7232 Kelly street, were taken yesterday to answer a common charge of conspiracy.

With the apprehension of the gang, complete except for two alleged members who have fled to Canada, police expect to halt the systematic extortion of large amounts of money from Italian citizens, and dissipate the clouds of fear and terror which the Mafia caused to hang over them. Already three recent victims of the terrorists have advanced to police their desire of assisting in the trailing and prosecution of the members. Several Italian women have expressed the hope that the Mafia will be crushed for all times, and have offered their help.

For the first time in history, it is thought, police and detectives have pierced into the furthermost secrets of the order, which, brought from the bandit-infested hills of Sicily years ago—has since exercised a death-dealing and ruthless power over many of the hard working in the Italian colonies. Federal officials and county detectives also are pursuing the chase.

CHIEF IS JAILED.

The 23 were given hearings in the Frankstown Avenue police station yesterday, and held for court. To Dominick Capubito, 27-year-old Calabrian, Magistrate R. E. Smith gave the privilege of answering to a higher court for his chieftaincy of the society. In addition to the common charge, he must face others of extortion, a charge against morals, and violation of the Snyder act. Capubito has been in this country three years, coming here from Gizzeria, in Calabria. In that short period he has worked himself up to the head of the organization.

The age and position of the members range from young to old. Some have been implicated in other crimes, John and Joseph Gigliotti, father and son, having been mentioned in the murder trial of Phillip Germano, Homewood avenue merchant, who was slain in his store. Joseph was acquitted of the shooting. They have been re-arrested, and are held without bail, as is Capubito and Antonio Rocco.

FORMER HEAD SLAIN.

Germano was formerly head of the society, and previous to his reign, which was said to be one of ruthless oppression. Joseph Mino was the leader. Mino, Christmas Eve, 1922, was found dead in a sewer on the Lincoln road. His body had been

(Continued on Page Two, Col. Five.)

Ex-Kaiser's Murder Is Attempted

BY WORLD NEWS SERVICE.

NEW YORK, Oct. 13.—An attempt to murder the former kaiser at his Doorn, Holland, retreat has been made by a German, according to a dispatch broadcast from Neuen, Germany, and picked up tonight by the wireless of the World News Service.

The message declared the local police believe the would-be assassin was one of a gang of conspirators whose chief aim is Wilhelm's death. The man carried two sets of Passports, one forged and the other in good order.

IACOVELLI MURDER TRIAL OPENS

Michael Iacovelli was placed on trial before Judge John C. Haymaker in criminal court yesterday on a charge of having shot and killed his brother-in-law, Joseph Dimilo, of 1910 Fifth avenue, at Fifth avenue and Logan streets, April 13. Assistant District Attorney Benjamin Lencher is prosecuting the case. Attorney Peter M. Cancelliere is representing the prisoner.

In a statement, said to have been made to police before his death, Dimilo said Iacovelli had called him vile names and then shot him. He said Iacovelli always had been unfriendly to him and had persuaded Iacovelli's sister, who was Dimilo's wife, to leave him. The cash will be resumed today.

CAR DISTRIBUTION RULING UPHELD

WASHINGTON, Oct. 13.—The application of the New River and other coal companies in West Virginia for a review of a decision rendered last term in which the supreme court sustained the order of the interstate commerce commission regulating the distribution of cars among coal mines, was refused today by the supreme court.

WOMEN 92 YEARS OLDS DIES

FRANKLIN, Pa., Oct. 13.—Mrs. Anna Jane Adams, one of Venango county's oldest residents and who formerly lived on the farm where the State institution at Polk is located, died this morning. She was in her Ninety-second year.

ST. LOUIS CAPITALIST DIES

ST. LOUIS, Oct. 13.—Charles C. Sutter, 66 years old, retired capitalist, and a member of the United States shipping board during the Wilson administration, died here yesterday.

Enough Poison to Kill 25 In Family Cider; One Dead

SPECIAL TO THE PITTSBURGH POST.

MARIETTA, O., Oct. 13.—Enough poison to kill 25 persons was found in four ounces of cider which killed George West and poisoned other members of his family, Saturday, it developed today, in the analysis by Marietta College chemists. Sheriff Link Yarnell expects to make an arrest soon.

West drank cider at the home of his mother-in-law, Mrs. Ellen Chandler, at Warner, near Marietta, Saturday, and died a short time later. Other members of the family drank also. Prosecuting Attorney Everett Folger found that four kegs of cider at the Chandler home had been poisoned.

SEVEN BADLY BURNED IN OIL TANKS BLAZE

BY THE ASSOCIATED PRESS.

DALLAS, Tex., Oct. 13.—Seven men, including six firemen, were burned seriously and others were reported injured in a fire which was sweeping a number of oil tanks here of the Clayco Company. Two tanks, which have a capacity of 1,000 barrels, exploded.

The explosion rocked houses for blocks around the plant. A match accidentally dropped in waste oil is said to have started the blaze, which almost immediately appeared to be beyond control.

Dry Navy Sweeps Rum Row, Taking 13 Ships; One Has Record Cargo

Sagatind's Crew Had Merry Time, Now Nursing Wounds.

WILL CONFISCATE FOREIGN CRAFT

BY THE UNITED NEWS.

NEW YORK, Oct. 13.—Thirty derelict Russian and Scandinavian sailors, picked up in dockside groggeries in Antwerp to man a steamship for a cruise along America's Atlantic rum row, are enjoying their first spell of peace since they signed on for the awful cruise.

Their ship, the Norwegian steamer Sagatind, lies behind the shelter of Sandy Hook and the injured men among the crew are receiving attention for a gruesome assortment of leg, arm and jaw fractures and other hurts of a less serious nature incurred in light hearted brawling along her decks as the boat and all hands lurched along the liquor horizon. It was a great cruise while it lasted, with 100,000 dozen bottles of whisky and other spirits in the hold and in every other place that afforded stowage and with every man his own commanding officer.

LARGEST SHIP CAPTURED.

The Sagatind was only one of 13 vessels picked up in the latest raid of the coast guard and revenue services between Gloucester, Mass., and the Jersey shore, but she was the largest fish ever hauled up in the wide sweeping net of the prohibition navies.

New London, Conn., reported the capture of two tugs, three schooners and a launch, but the schooners and

(Continued on Page Two, Col. Three.)

THE EVANSVILLE COURIER

VOL. 73—No. 299 FINAL EDITION EVANSVILLE, INDIANA, TUESDAY MORNING, NOVEMBER 11, 1924. SIXTEEN PAGES PRICE THREE

DION O'BANNION IS MURDERED

DEATH OF LODGE WILL CAUSE NEW SENATE CHANGES

Selection of G. O. P. Floor Leader to Succeed Veteran Statesman Faces Party

WASHINGTON IN MOURNING

President Coolidge Appoints Personal Representatives to Attend Funeral Rites

WASHINGTON, D. C., Nov. 10.—Grief at the death of Henry Cabot Lodge was voiced in Washington today by public men and friends of the Massachusetts senator.

President Coolidge in a formal statement spoke of him as "one of the great men of our time," while members of the cabinet and colleagues in congress, in expressing regret at his passing, referred to his attainments and to his long career in the senate and house.

Arrangements were at once made by Mr. Coolidge to be represented at the funeral, he requesting Secretaries Hughes and Weeks and Captain Adolphus Andrews, his naval aide, to attend in that capacity. At the same time officials of the senate and house made plans for delegations to represent those bodies officially at the services.

Senate Representatives

The senate committee, designated by Senator Cummins of Iowa, president pro tem, was announced as follows:

Walsh, Massachusetts; Curtis, Kansas; Borah, Idaho; Swanson, Virginia; McLean, Connecticut; Smoot, Utah; Ashurst, Arizona; Pittman, Nevada; Sterling, South Dakota; Underwood, Alabama; Wadsworth, New York; Fernald, Maine; Watson, Indiana; Gerry, Rhode Island; Hale, Maine; Moses, New Hampshire; Spencer, Missouri; Ball, Delaware; Edge, New Jersey; Keyes, New Hampshire; Pepper and Reed, Pennsylvania; Copeland, New York; Edwards, New Jersey; Greene and Dale, Vermont.

The committee to represent the house at the funeral was not completed tonight and therefore any announcement concerning it was withheld.

Historic memories cluster around the desk which Senator Lodge occupied on the floor of the senate, for former distinguished sons of Massachusetts, Charles Sumner and George Frisbie Hoar, had occupied it and unauthenticated report is that it one time it was used by Daniel Webster.

When the senate vacated the chamber now occupied by the supreme court and moved to its present quarters in the new wing of the capitol, the desks including that which Senator Lodge used and which had long seen service were retained. As new states were admitted into the union and new senators entered the chamber, desks of the same style were constructed for them.

These relics are highly cherished by the senate and it has been the unbroken rule, so far as the memory of the oldest senate employes goes, to refuse permission for the removal of any of them.

While duplicates are in storage available to replace any that might be in need of repairs it would require the consent of the committee on rules which has charge of the property of the senate, to take any of them out of the capitol. [illegible] the committee has consistently refused to sanction all suggestions that the senate part with any of its heirlooms.

Although the passing of the veteran leader is recognized as requiring a new appraisal of conditions which will confront the senate upon its convening for the short term next month, because of the absence from Washington of many republican spokesmen at the capitol, definite plans for a reorganization of the republican forces there are expected to be delayed for a longer period than might otherwise be the case.

In the determination of questions surrounding the problem of leadership in the senate, however, President Coolidge, through the mandate given him at the election of last week, will have an opportunity to exert the dominant power. Any ad-

(Continued on Page Two)

KENTUCKIANS ARE INJURED IN CRASH

Inspection Party's Car and Coal Train Collide Near Bardsville

CINCINNATI, O., Nov. 10.—C. M. Mitchell, general superintendent of the Southern Railway system, was under the care of physicians at Christ hospital, Cincinnati today, following a collision of a gasoline propelled inspection car with a loaded coal train near Bardsville, Ky., last Saturday.

Mr. Mitchell suffered a fractured [illegible] and numerous painful bruises when he jumped from the car which in addition to Mr. Mitchell, was carrying seven passengers, three of whom were more or less seriously hurt when they leaped from the car.

Mr. Mitchell and Mrs. Norman Naylor of Burnside, Ky., were brought to Cincinnati late Saturday night, it was learned. Two others, Miss Alice Bronson and Mrs. Charles Wesley, both of Cumberland Falls, Ky., were treated elsewhere.

The party was on an informal inspection of the Southern Railway system when Mr. Mitchell noticed the coal train bearing down on them. He gave the alarm and the party leaped [illegible]

Recount Shows 400 Decrease in Brookhart Lead

Des Moines, Ia., Nov. 10.

SENATOR SMITH W. BROOKHART'S unofficial majority over his democratic opponent for the United States senate in Tuesday's election had dwindled from 1,025 to 674 when more than half of the election boards in Iowa's 99 counties completed their official canvass of the vote late today. Returns from these official surveys are not expected to be completed until late this week.

The loss and gain for each candidate had fluctuated widely on the reports so far received. In fifty counties the result was a gain of 96 votes for Senator Brookhart while his loss totalled 200 votes. Steck, his opponent, had gained 470 and lost 223.

U. S. HARVESTS SMALLEST CORN CROP SINCE 1913

Merchantable Quality of Grain Is Lowest in 30 Years, Report Shows

WASHINGTON, D. C., Nov. 10.—The smallest corn crop since 1913 was the reward of American farmers this year who planted the fifth largest acreage to that crop in the history of farming. Not only was the harvest substantially below those of the last four years but the merchantable quality of this year's crop is the lowest in 30 years, with the exception of 1917.

Preliminary estimates of production, issued today by the department of agriculture, placed the crop at 2,477,538,000 bushels, the acreage at 105,604,000, or 1.4 per cent more than last year, and the merchantable quality of the crop as 63.2 per cent. Corn production during the last four years has averaged more than 3,000,000,000 bushels.

Potato Crop Better

The white potato crop, estimated at 454,119,000 bushels, is slightly larger than the big crops of 1917 and 1922, yields in northern states running far above earlier expectations because in some regions the crop escaped frost and continued growing far into October. Per capita production this year is 4.09 bushels compared with an average of 3.76 bushels per capita during the last 20 years.

There will be an ample supply of good potatoes at moderate prices, government officials declare, and because of low prices in some western states some good potatoes will be fed to live stock. There are indications that some of the crop in those states will not be even harvested. The average yield was 121.0 bushels per acre compared with 99.1 bushels the ten-year average.

Sweet Potatoes Damaged

Drought in important southern producing states greatly reduced the sweet potato crop, which is estimated at 75,620,000 bushels, or about 25,000,000 bushels below the average of the last five years, and the smallest crop since 1916.

Tobacco production is 261,000,000 pounds less than last year, with a crop of 1,213,975,000 pounds, estimated. Bright tobacco shows a decrease of 115,000,000 pounds, cigar types 63,000,000 pounds, and Maryland and eastern Ohio export types 1,617,000 pounds. Quality of the crop in New England is good in Pennsylvania, not so good in the Miami valley of Ohio, and poor in Wisconsin.

Quality in Kentucky is uncertain as yet and will depend upon rains during the curing season. Maryland exports suffered some from frost. Bright tobacco in the main producing regions is slightly better in quality than last year, though still low.

Corn production averaged 23.5 bushels per acre this year as compared with 29.8 bushels last year and 27.6 bushels the ten-year average. Over most of the corn belt weather during October was very favorable for maturing and drying the crop. Sections not frosted made material gains over earlier expectations and an increase of about 19,000,000 bushels in the total crop over last month resulted.

Favorable weather improved the quality of the crop much more than seemed probable. Much corn that was frosted in Iowa, the largest producing state, and other states had dried out with a minimum of souring and moulding, though much of the frosted corn is chaffy, shrivelled and loose on the cob.

Protest Disallowed

A protest by Wallace Henry Rich that his property would be damaged to the extent of $500 by the opening of the Koehler road in Pigeon township was disallowed by the county commissioners yesterday when they ordered the road opened. Viewers appointed to report on the road declared that the benefits would exceed the damages. The road was voted a public utility some time ago.

THE WEATHER

HOURLY TEMPERATURES YESTERDAY

2 a.m...42	8 a.m...42	2 p.m...71
4 a.m...40	10 a.m...55	4 p.m...72
6 a.m...39	12 noon..61	6 p.m...66

Highest temperature yesterday ...72
Lowest temperature yesterday ...39
River stage at 7 a. m. ....8.5 feet

Local record for year ago yesterday:
Highest temperature 64; lowest temperature 37. Precipitation 1 in. River at 7 a. m. 8.6 ft.

Sunrise yesterday ....6:26 a. m.
Sunset Yesterday ....4:42 p. m.
Sunrise today ....6:27 a. m.
Sunset today ....4:41 p. m.

INDIANA—Rain Tuesday; continued warm; Wednesday cloudy and colder.

ILLINOIS—Rain Tuesday, colder at night; Wednesday partly cloudy and colder.

KENTUCKY—Unsettled, probably

ANNUAL MEETING OF MEDICAL ASS'N CONVENES TODAY

Eminent Physicians Will Give Lectures and Hold Clinics in City

BANQUET SET FOR TONIGHT

More Than 100 Doctors Are Expected to Attend O. V. M. A. Sessions

The annual meeting of the Ohio Valley Medical association convenes at the Y. M. C. A. this morning for a two-day session. Many applications have been received from persons desiring to have their ailments diagnosed at the free clinics that will be held during the sessions. Dr. Curran Pope, medical director of the Pope sanitarium of Louisville, will be in charge of the neural syphilitic clinic this morning and Dr. T. L. Higginbotham of Louisville, will be in charge of a clinic of [illegible]. Three applications have been received for the clinic on diagnosis of urolic troubles, under direction of Dr. N. E. Eisendrath of Chicago.

100 Visiting Physicians

More than 100 visiting physicians are expected to be present for the meeting and many had arrived last night.

All preparations for both an instructive and entertaining meeting have been completed, Dr. Sydney J. Eichel, chairman of the arrangements committee, said last night.

The high point on the program will be the banquet tonight at 7:30 o'clock in the Hotel McCurdy, when an address will be given by Dr. Oskar Frankl, professor of the University of Vienna, who is conducting a series of thirty lectures for local physicians at Evansville college. "The future of the Doctor of Medicine" will be the subject of an address by Dr. Leon L. Solomon of Louisville, president of the association. A talk on "Service" will be made by Dr. G. A. Hendon of Louisville, professor of surgery in the University of Louisville; and Dr. A. E. Sterne of Indianapolis, professor of nervous and mental diseases, in the Indiana university school of medicine, will discuss the question of personal responsibility.

Address of Welcome

An address of welcome by Mayor Elmendorf will open the first session this morning at 9 o'clock. Dr. Solomon will give the response. Reports of committees and appointments of committees will follow.

Dr. M. Ravdin, visiting rhino-otolaryngologist at the Deaconess hospital, will read a paper on pupillary reaction as an aid to diagnosis.

(Continued on Page Two)

GUARDS CALLED TO QUELL RACE RIOTS

White Laborers and Farmers Clash With Negroes at Harrodsburg, Ky.

HARRODSBURG, Ky., Nov. 10.—After a night of disorder, quiet had been restored tonight in the construction camp that flank the site of Dix river dam, a huge hydro-electric project under construction on Dix river near here. Arrival of detachments of Kentucky national guardsmen brought to an end clashes between white construction workers and farmers on one side and negro workers at the dam which followed the slaying of Edward Winkle, 21, white worker, by a negro laborer Sunday night.

Sheriff W. Kennedy of Mercer county tonight said the situation no longer was tense and further trouble was not expected.

Laborers Clash

Clashes followed rapidly Sunday night and early today resulting in a general exodus of negroes from the labor camps.

Quiet was restored when 35 members of Troop A, 54th Machine gun squadron, national guard, arrived in motor trucks and assumed charge of the situation. Nearly 300 of the 700 negroes employed on the dam and driven from the camp returned after arrival of the troops.

They came wandering back to the camp in groups of a half a dozen or more.

All showed traces of exposure. Many were without shoes, none were fully dressed and a number were without trousers.

Law Protects Negroes

About 250 of the negroes, following their flight, were corraled by authorities at Burgin where they spent the night under the protection of deputy sheriffs and citizens of the village.

The negroes were harbored in an abandoned rock quarry where they huddled around a bonfire. Deputy sheriffs stationed around the quarry permitted none to leave. They were taken back to the dam this afternoon.

Baldwin and His Cabinet

Top: NEVILLE CHAMBERLAIN, COL. L. S. AMERY & SIR W. JOYNSON-HICKS (Below) WINSTON CHURCHILL, SIR SAMUEL HOARE & VISCOUNT CAVE

British Head Names Final Cabinet Roll

LONDON, Nov. 10.—(By A. P.)—Premier Baldwin completed his new cabinet today by appointing Viscount Peel as first commissioner of works and public buildings and Viscount Cecil as chancellor of the Duchy of Lancaster.

King George called a meeting of the privy council today and parliament was further prorogued from November 18 to December 2. This postponement was made to enable the new ministers to become acquainted with their departments before the meeting of the new parliament. When parliament does reassemble, many days will be spent in swearing in the members and electing a speaker and other officials.

Perform Formality

Only when the formalities have been completed will the king formally open parliament with a state ceremony. With the completion of the cabinet today Premier Baldwin will call the ministers together in council Wednesday morning to discuss general lines of policy.

The addition of Viscount Cecil to the cabinet is considered of importance owing to his deep interest in the league of nations. It is also regarded as showing that the new government's policy with regard to the league will remain unchanged.

Expect Other Appointments

The remaining government appointments are expected to be announced tomorrow. They will have no special interest, as it is understood Mr. Baldwin has decided to reappoint as under secretaries the men who held these posts in his previous administration.

Premier Baldwin

No Authority to Place License Plates on Sale

The office of the Evansville Auto club was swamped with inquiries about the new 1925 automobile license plates yesterday afternoon, following a statement by the local Scripps paper that the plates would be put on sale Wednesday.

O. L. Keeler, secretary of the Evansville Auto club, said last night there was no basis for the report. "We have not been authorized by the secretary of state to place the plates on sale," he said. "Ordinarily that is about December 12 or 15. Not until then or until after we have our instructions from Indianapolis will the plates be put on sale."

Klan Will Parade In Grand Rapids Despite Mayor's Plea

GRAND RAPIDS, Mich., Nov. 10.—In spite of pleas of Mayor Swarthout, to call off a parade scheduled for tomorrow because it was Armistice day, state leaders of the Ku Klux Klan announced late today that 20,000 members of the klan would parade tomorrow in connection with a state klonvocation. The mayor told the klan committee the day was set aside for reverence to the men who died on the battle fields of France.

Klan leaders, after conferring with the city attorneys who ruled a permit was not needed for the parade, announced the parade would be held.

SIMPLE RITES TO MARK BURIAL OF SENATOR LODGE

Services to Be Held From Christ Church at Cambridge at Noon Tomorrow

BOSTON, Nov. 10.—Senator Henry Cabot Lodge, who in life was a figure apart from the mass of the national legislative leaders among whom he moved with distinction, will have funeral services in which old associations will be maintained to the end and in which his simplicity of tastes will be preserved. The services at Christ church, Cambridge, on Wednesday noon with Bishop Lawrence, his schoolmate and college classmate, officiating will be nearly those of the man whom friends of a life-time mourn than the United States senator who has passed after a notable career.

Although it was suggested by Governor Cox that the bier be taken to the capitol on Beacon Hill to lie in state the senator's family decided to make no change from the home on Deacon street, of Dr. Sturgis Bigelow, his boyhood chum, where the body has rested since a few hours after death last night. Dr. Bigelow himself, is seriously ill, and cannot attend the funeral, but the thought that it was there the senator would choose to lie within a block of his father's home prompted the decision.

Representatives to Attend

With word that provision should be made for the president's official representatives, Secretary Hughes, Secretary Weeks and Captain Andrews, his naval aide, for Governor Cox and various delegations, the family felt that opportunity for the tributes these delegations seek to show may still be afforded in Christ church, with its limited seating capacity of 420 at the same time that the senator's personal associates are present.

Among the attendants at the services will be delegations from the national senate and house of representatives from both branches of the Massachusetts legislature; committees representing the town of Nahant, which Senator Lodge had served as moderator for years; of the Massachusetts' historical socie-

(Continued on Page Two)

CITY TO OBSERVE ARMISTICE WITH VARIED PROGRAM

Patriotic Meeting to Be Held in Coliseum at 2 O'clock This Afternoon

DANCE SLATED TONIGHT

Mrs. John W. Spencer, Sr. to Preside at Celebration—Legion Officers to Speak

Although there will be no general observance of Armistice Day in Evansville, school children and several patriotic organizations will stage programs remindful of that momentous day six years ago when the last gun of the World war boomed and hostilities ceased.

Principal features of the day's program will be a patriotic meeting starting at two o'clock this afternoon in the Coliseum and a dance tonight at the same place under auspices of the American Legion posts of the city. The afternoon meeting is to be staged by the Service Star Legion.

Whistle to Blow

The water works whistle will blow at 11:11 o'clock this morning, the exact time of the signing of the Armistice six years ago, Mayor William H. Elmendorf, announced yesterday.

An elaborate patriotic program will be presented at the Coliseum this afternoon, Mrs. James M. Hitch, president of the Service Star legion announced. Mrs. John W. Spencer sr., will preside at the meeting.

The program, as announced by Mrs. Charles G. Schulz, chairman of the committee on arrangements, follows:

Addresses by Art O. Lillicrap, commander of the Disabled Veterans of the World War; W. D. Daniels, commander of Henry W. Lawton post, Veterans of Foreign Wars; Mrs. J. J. Schulz; A. W. Epperson, former commander of Everett Burdette post, American Legion.

Patriotic readings by Mrs. H. F. McCool.

Singing of the new service song, "Little Gold Star Mother of Mine," by Mrs. J. M. Humphreys. The song, written by Bernard F. Avery, disabled war veteran, was first heard in a legion gathering when it was sung at the state auxiliary convention.

Mrs. Bayard Goodge will sing patriotic songs and lead the audience in community singing.

Public Invited

Those in charge of the affair have invited the public to attend.

The dance tonight will be in charge of Funkhouser post of the American Legion. Every ex-service man in the city has been invited to participate in the affair.

All banks and the majority of the offices at the courthouse will be closed in observance of Armistice day. Business establishments of the city will not observe the day, according to plans last night.

At 11:05 o'clock this morning school bells will ring as a signal for pupils to leave their class rooms for the school grounds, where they will stage a short program. The children will stand at attention while the flag is raised at 11:11 o'clock, following which they will sing "The Star Spangled Banner."

Mrs. Rose to Speak

Mrs. B. S. Rose, prominent Evansville woman, will be the principal speaker at the Armistice day celebration of the American Legion auxiliary at Poseyville this afternoon. Mrs. Rose is district chairman of the legion auxiliary. One of the features of the program will be the unveiling of a bronze tablet in the library of that city. The program proper will be held in the Methodist church.

Local Men Leave For Cincinnati to Attend Convention

Mayor William H. Elmendorf, Secretary J. S. Johnson of the Chamber of Commerce, William Burkert of the Manufacturers' association, S. L. May and Lachlan McCleay, secretary of the Mississippi Valley Improvement association, left last night for Cincinnati where they will attend the annual convention of the Ohio Valley Improvement association which starts today. McCleay will invite those present at the convention to attend the annual meeting of the Mississippi Valley association, scheduled to take place in Evansville November 20, 21 and 22.

Thanksgiving Baskets

Thanksgiving baskets will be sent out by the Salvation Army this year, in keeping with their usual custom. Adt. Charles Crismier announced yesterday. Enough food will be contained in each basket to last the family for several days. No drive for funds to be used in filling the baskets will be made, but contributions may be sent to the workers. Kettles for the Christmas fund of the Army will be placed on the streets December 1.

Fascist Chief To Duel With Italian Patriot

Rome, Nov. 10.

GENERAL PEPPINO GARABALDI, grandson of the Italian patriot, today named Deputies Bencivenga and Cimarra to act as his seconds in a duel with Dr. Italo Balbo, commander in chief of the Fascist national militia, who on Friday sent a challenge to Garabaldi. Balbo's seconds are Deputy Barnaba and General Gualtieri.

The seconds met today to discuss arrangements for the duel, but the central committee of the Free Italy organization still objects to Garabaldi's taking part in the combat.

The challenge was an outgrowth of a protest made by Garabaldi against an attack by Fascist militiamen on unarmed former Italian soldiers in Rome during the celebration of the anniversary of the armistice with Austria.

HILL'S DEFENSE TAKES STAND IN LIQUOR HEARING

Prosecution Claims Congressman Served Booze Containing 11 Per Cent Alcohol

BALTIMORE, Md., Nov. 10.—After placing only two witnesses on the stand, the government at last this afternoon closed its case against John Philip Hill, and defense testimony was begun in the congressman's trial in federal district court on indictments charging violation of the Volstead act through the manufacture and possession of wine and cider of more than one-half of one per cent alcoholic content.

George F. Beyer and Richard Ryan, government chemists, testified for the prosecution. Beyer said he was sent to Mr. Hill's home here in September 1923, to take samples of the congressman's home-made grape juice for analysis. The question "was certain liquor in a five gallon keg at Mr. Hill's home?" was put to the witness by District Attorney Amos W. W. Woodcock, was objected to by defense counsel. Mr. Beyer then testified that the beverage he tested contained "around 11 per cent" of alcohol by volume.

Defense Opens

Ryan testified that the cider made this fall by Mr. Hill contained 2.75 per cent alcohol. The defense opened its case by putting Dr. John McGinity, a pharmacist, on the witness stand. Dr. McGinity was asked if he had attended the "party given recently by Mr. Hill, at which the congressman furnished his cider to several hundred guests." The doctor replied that he had.

"Did anybody get drunk?" asked defense counsel.

District Attorney Woodcock objected to the question, which he said was "irrelevant."

"The question," he said, "is one of the alcoholic content of the cider."

Judge Morris A. Soper, presiding, then asked Mr. Woodcock if it was his understanding of the law that "any beverage containing over one-half of one per cent is forbidden."

The district attorney replied that it was, and the defense took issue with him, and the jury was dismissed until tomorrow morning while the point was argued. Judge Soper asked Mr. Woodcock if it were not his understanding of the prohibition act, that congress in referring to cider and fruit juices meant the word "intoxicating" to mean intoxicating in fact, without reference to the one-half of one per cent alcoholic limit placed on other drinks.

Woodcock Differs

Mr. Woodcock replied that this was not his understanding of the law, and said the government had the right to seize fruit juices with no alcohol in them if they suspected that they would be converted into intoxicating beverages. He cited the fact that prohibition agents may seize sugar if they think it is going to be used for manufacture of liquor. Arthur W. Machen of defense counsel then read a quotation from a decision by Judge Augustus Hand of New York, issuing an injunction against a New York district attorney, unnamed, to restrain him from interfering in the business of a New York manufacturer of sweet apple cider. In his complaint, on which the junction was issued, the manufacturer had declared that it was practically impossible to manufacture a sweet cider, the alcoholic content of which would not occasionally go above one-half of one per cent even at the moment of manufacture, Mr. Machen said.

Argue Meaning

Court adjourned until tomorrow, with opposing attorneys still arguing the exact meaning of the word "intoxicating" as used in the Volstead act.

Wilbur Formally Signs Order for ZR-3 for Navy

WASHINGTON, D. C., Nov. 10.—An order formally accepting the ZR-3 German built zeppelin, on behalf of the American government was signed today by Secretary Wilbur.

The action was taken upon approval by the secretary of the report of the special board of inspection and survey which examined the air cruiser at her Lakehurst hangar.

Organization of a trained American crew to take charge of the ship has practically been completed and arrangements are under way for a series of test flights.

Bank Clearings

Bank clearings in Evansville banks totalled $528,067.52 yesterday. The

KING OF CHIC[...] RUM RUNNE[...] VICTIM OF [...]

Three Unidentified M[...] in Waiting Auto A[...] ing Shots

POLICE HOLD S[...]

Detectives Search fo[...] of Underworld Cha[...] Believed Implic[...]

CHICAGO, Nov. 10.—[...] nion, Chicago gangster [...] termed "king of the be[...]" was shot and killed tod[...] quiet respectability of [...] shop by three unidentifi[...]

Tonight the Miller [...] Herschie, Max, and Davi[...] enemies of O'Bannion, w[...] after satisfying investi[...] had no connection with [...] Herschie is the owner [...] ing and dyeing plant [...] twice bombed some tim[...] an attempt had been m[...] lives of Herschie and M[...] of a downtown theater.

Accused Twice

O'Bannion was accuse[...] instances, but the assa[...] was the only one to reach [...] this only reached the s[...] police court arraignment [...] Miller is a prominent box[...] in the middle west.

Orders were dispatche[...] diately after the shootin[...] arrest of Earl Weiss, Joh[...] "Yankee" Schwartz and [...] Dan" McCarty, all of [...] been involved in hi-jacking [...] running scandals in th[...] years and all of whom [...] arrested in connection [...] slayings. O'Bannion wa[...] among his plants and blo[...] north side shop shortly [...] when three men entere[...] rear of the place wa[...] Critchfield, negro porter, [...] ante room Victor Young [...] and Vincent Glavin, book[...]

Meets Callers

O'Bannion greeted his [...] a "hello boys." Then, [...] Critchfield, who was [...] custody tonight for quest[...] four walked over to a co[...] room and conversed in [...] tones. This continued fo[...] being cut short by the s[...] firing of three revolvers, [...]

O'Bannion fell into a be[...] dead.

The trio fled, runnin[...] three blocks to a wai[...] mobile. Many pedestrian[...] men running and later w[...] describe them, but none [...] to stop them, as the rep[...] shots was not heard in [...] The police tonight state[...] was their belief that O'B[...] shot as the result of an [...] feud.

Pursues Killers

It was developed later [...] Loftis, employed as a ch[...] O'Bannion, had comman[...] passing automobile and [...] pursuit of the killers. [...] hours after the murder [...] returned to the shop or [...] whereabouts.

Mrs. Harding M[...] Only Slight [...]

MARION, O., Nov. 10.—[...] ence Kling Harding is no [...] night and "her condition [...] about the same," a brief [...] sued by her physician, D[...] Sawyer tonight said. T[...] follows:

"Mrs. Harding had a f[...] fortable day. She has [...] the gain which was pr[...] morning, but her conditio[...] about the same."

This morning's bulletin [...] had rested comfortably [...] and that her general con[...] slightly improved. Her o[...] spirit, according to Dr. S[...] fled and she is critically [...] Harding is suffering fro[...] kidney trouble with compli[...] many years' duration.

Women Order Ducks, but Eat—Just Food

Eleven women thoroughly enjoyed a duck dinner at the Shrine mosque last night for it was said to be a delicious dinner.

Eleven other women who had ordered their special banquet several days early to be served in a private dining room, had neither duck dinner nor private dining room in which to eat what was left for them.

It was a case of the first one to arrive getting the "best of the bargain."

A club of well known Evansville month at the Mosque failed to make reservations until Monday morning, and were told by the manager that they would have to eat in the general dining room downstairs.

The person who made the reservation was not to be present for the dinner, and she failed to inform the president or others of the club that they would not have their usual room on the second floor. The others came and as usual took their places in the private dining room.

A 75-cent dinner is regularly served the members of the club [...] that goes with it, they looked a bit puzzled. And when the salad proved to be a tinted apple, very lovely and very unusual—said one, "Isn't this a lovely dinner? You don't suppose, do you, that the boy made a mistake, and we are eating some one else's food?" And they all laughed merrily and passed on to their discussion of Edna St. Vincent Millay as the most charming of the modern poets.

And then, just as the dessert was coming in, the manager appeared at the door.

"Is this the Press club?"

[...] pened seemed to take possession of each of the eleven women.

"Yes?" with a questioning inflection.

"Ladies, you have eaten the wrong dinner. You were not to be in this room at all."

No one was to blame at all, the manager said, for the boy at the door had expected the club members to go to their usual place, and the women themselves had not known they were to do otherwise, but—eleven women who had expected a usual dinner had a feast of duck, and eleven other women who

XX EDITION

THE CHICAGO EVENING POST

XX EDITION

THIRTY-FIFTH YEAR.—OFFICIAL NEWSPAPER OF CITY OF CHICAGO * TUESDAY, NOVEMBER 25, 1924. * PRICE THREE CENTS

OPEN WAR ON BEER GANGS

TRAIL OF SINISTER STAINS FOUND IN FURNACE MYSTERY

Body of Mrs. Sheatsley May Be Exhumed; Missing Poison Found.

COLUMBUS, Ohio, Nov. 25.—Convinced that Mrs. Clarence V. Sheatsley, wife of the pastor of Christ Evangelical Lutheran church, whose partially cremated body was found in the furnace of the parsonage in Bexley, Nov. 17, was either murdered and cast into the furnace or that she committed suicide and was placed there by some one who sought to cover up the act, County Prosecutor John R. King today centered his investigation upon these theories.

Possibility that the body of Mrs. C. V. Sheatsley may be exhumed was indicated here today following a conference late last night between county authorities and Edwin Abbott, an undertaker, who removed Mrs. Sheatsley's remains from the furnace.

Just where his quest would lead him today was not disclosed by the prosecutor, other than that he would interview a woman at Lithopolis, twelve miles from here, who, the prosecutor said, had lunch with the Sheatsley family on the day of the tragedy.

Minute search of the Sheatsley home by investigators yesterday brought forth what Mr. King termed as "important discoveries," tending to show, he said, that the pastor's wife was a victim of murder.

Sinister Stains.

Brownish crimson stains, which chemical analysis may prove human blood, Mr. King said, were found on a number of articles, including a table covering, unearthed in a crumpled condition in an upstairs closet, on a pair of blue trousers, on a rug, on a burlap sack found in a vacant lot about 100 feet from the house and on the asbestos covering of a heat conduit directly above the furnace door.

Another find which Mr. King said he considers significant was an upturned fruit jar containing about half an ounce of crimson fluid, which Chemist C. F. Long said closely resembles human blood.

Red Finger Prints.

The lid was found in the fruit storage-room adjacent to the furnace-room. Bits of tissue, such as might have been torn from the body of a human was taken in several places, Mr. King announced. Red finger prints on a clothes shute door in the cellar were found by Detective Harry Carson.

Rev. Mr. Sheatsley, who, with his four children, is at Paris, Ohio, visiting relatives, in a telephone conversation said the stains were "probably rabbit blood," he having shot several while hunting on Saturday before the tragedy.

The minister, when informed that a bottle of poisonous acid, which authorities said was missing on the night of the tragedy from the medicine cabinet, had been found in the cabinet yesterday, said he was glad that it had been located.

Rev. Mr. Sheatsley believes his wife committed suicide by casting herself into the furnace after becoming violently insane, according to a statement he made to Mr. King last Wednesday.

Guinea Pig Experiment.

Chemist Long, seeking to verify his conclusion that Mrs. Sheatsley was dead when her body was placed in the furnace, yesterday experimented with two guinea pigs. Death was caused by carbon-monoxide fumes, Long said he believed. He will analyze blood taken from their lungs in an effort to determine this positively.

Mr. Abbott told County Prosecutor John P. King that a portion of Mrs. Sheatsley's skull was broken. He indicated, however, that this might have been caused by the intense heat of the furnace.

In Long's report to Prosecutor King on blood taken from the lungs of Mrs. Sheatsley said that there was no trace of carbon-monoxide poisoning. The woman, he said, did not breathe after being placed in the furnace.

Von Nathusius to Be Freed Today or Tomorrow

PARIS, Nov. 25.—The release of Gen. von Nathusius, the German officer sentenced by court-martial at Lille last week to a year's imprisonment on conviction of having confiscated French property during the war, will be effected as soon as President Demergue signs the pardon decree decided upon by the government. This is expected to occur by this evening, or tomorrow at the latest.

Mexican Minister Quits.

MEXICO CITY, Nov. 25.—Bernardo Gastelum has resigned as minister of public instruction.

Special Notice to Our Readers and Advertisers

Thursday is Thanksgiving Day—and The Chicago Evening Post will not publish on that day—therefore the RADIO MAGAZINE will be published tomorrow, Wednesday (Nov. 26), instead of Thursday (Nov. 27). The same will apply to Christmas and New Year's (both falling on Thursdays), the RADIO MAGAZINE being published on Wednesday preceding.

Small Calls on Citizens to Give Thanks for 1924

SPRINGFIELD, Ill., Nov. 25.—Calling upon citizens to give thanks in their churches and homes, Gov. Small today issued his annual Thanksgiving proclamation.

"As the year of 1924 nears its close," the proclamation said, "a survey of conditions in the United States and especially in the state of Illinois must give us renewed confidence in the future.

"Abundant crops have been garnered by our people, there is a marked improvement in industrial and commercial lines, unemployment is vanishing, health conditions were never better and our people are looking forward with trust and confidence to a happy and prosperous year."

30 NEW SCHOOLS TO BE AUTHORIZED BY SCHOOL BOARD

20 Million to Be Spent; Seats for 40,000 Planned.

Construction of fourteen new elementary and sixteen junior high schools, costing approximately $20,000,000 will be authorized by the board of education when it meets tomorrow.

The schools will provide seats for approximately 40,000 pupils, and will do away with most of the portable schools now in use in the territories which they will serve.

The program provides for the purchase of sites for the buildings except in a few instances where "branch" schools now in existance will be replaced by the new buildings.

Get Bids After Dec. 7.

Beginning Dec. 7, it was learned, the architectural forces under the direction of Supervising Architect Edgar A. Martin, will prepare the plans and let the bids at the rate of one building a week. The new schools do not include the nine made public several weeks ago.

The construction will be paid for out of the school buildings fund which is apart from the educational fund, and involves no added expense to the taxpayers.

Elementary Schools Planned.

The fourteen elementary schools follow:

At 114th street and Stewart avenue; seating capacity, 816, plus kindergarten.

Purchase of site and erection of school seating 1,104, plus kindergarten, in vicinity of 63d street, 67th street, Ashland and Western avenues.

Purchase of site and erection of school seating 816 and kinergarten, in vicinity of Crawford, Kenton, 55th and 63d streets, seating 816, plus kindergarten.

Completion of condemnation proceedings and erection of school in vicinity of Belmont, Fullerton, Major and Narragansett avenues, seating 816, plus kindergarten.

School at LeMoyne and LeClaire avenues, seating 816, plus qindergarten.

School at 52d and Rockwell streets, seating 1,104 plus kindergarten.

Purchase of site and construction of school in vicinity of Austin and Cicero avenues, 47th and 55th streets.

Purchase of site and construction of school in vicinity of Avondale, Montrose, Long and Meade avenues, seating 816 plus kindergarten.

School at Henderson and Keeler avenues, seating 816 plus kindergarten.

School at 84th street and Phillips avenue, seating 816 plus kindergarten.

School at 62d street and Linder avenue, seating 816 plus kindergarten.

School at Byron and New England avenues, seating 624 plus sixty in kindergarten.

School at 80th street and Chappel avenue, seating 624 plus sixty in kindergarten.

School at Granville and Fairfield avenues, seating 816 and kindergarten.

The junior high school program contemplates:

Purchase of property bounded by 81st, 83d, Essex and Yates avenues, for future use.

Purchase of site and construction of building seating 4,000 in vicinity of Kinzie street, Western avenue, Division street and Milwaukee avenue.

Extension of the Phillips Junior-Senior high building, so a junior high group of 2,500 can be housed in addition to a senior high school with an enrollment of 1,000.

Purchase of site and construction of building seating 2,500 in vicinity of Madison street, Blue Island avenue, 16th street and Ogden avenue.

Purchase of site and construction of building seating 2,200 in vicinity of Jackson, Rockwell, Leavitt and the Burlington tracks.

Purchase of site and construction of building setaing 3,000 in vicinity of Milwaukee avenue, Oakley, Sacramento and Humboldt boulevards.

Purchase of site and construction of building, seating 2,200, in vicinity of 47th street, Cottag eGrove avenue, 59th street and Stewart avenue.

Extension of present site and construction of building, seating 1,500, near Cornelia and La Vergne avenues.

Purchase of site and construction of building, seating 1,500, in vicinity of Logan boulevard, River street, North and Milwaukee avenues.

Construction of building, seating 2,800, at Leland and Kimball avenues.

Purchase of site and construction of building, seating 1,800, in territory south and east of Ogden avenue to the river.

Erection of junior high unit of junior-senior high, seating 2,200 at Archer and California high schools.

Purchase of site and erection of junior high unit, seating 1,800, in vicinity of Wentwort havenue, 39th street, Ashland avenue and near-by areas not served by other schools.

Construction of building seating 2,500, at Winnemac park.

Purchase of site and erection of building, seating 1,300 pupils, in vicinity of Kinzie, Racine, River and Campbell avenue.

Erection of building, seating 1,800, near 77th street and Ingleside avenue.

Erection of building near North Shore and Greenview avenues, seating 1,800.

The buildings are all of the unit type of construction evolved by Supervising Architect Edgar A. Martin. Under the new construction methods made possible, it is expected to rush them to completion within a year, instead of taking two years to erect a building, as was the custim under the old conditions.

U. S., CITY, STATE, UNITE TO BREAK UP BOOZE GANGS

O'Bannion Jury Probes Killing of Tancl in Beer War.

City, state and federal officials joined hands today to conduct an intensive investigation into beer and booze running and conditions in the underworld which have caused two murders and numerous shootings in the last month.

While Coroner Wolf was conducting the O'Bannion jury over the ground where Eddie Tancl was killed Sunday morning, Maj. Percy B. Owen, federal prohibition director, announced he would be glad to co-operate with the city and state officials in a grand clean-up on beer and booze and dry up the wet spots here.

A conference with Assistant State's Attorney Joseph P. Savage was arranged for later in the day.

The county grand jury which held an extra session last night at the request of State's Attorney Crowe today returned indictments formally charging Myles O'Donnell, who is recovering from a wound at St. Anthony's hospital, and his fugitive companion, James Doherty, with the Tancl slaying.

Witnesses in both the Tancl and O'Bannion murders were recalled to the state's attorney's office for further questioning, and Herschie Miller was called to learn why the charges against O'Bannion were dropped when the latter shot his brother David in the lobby of the La Salle theater several months ago.

Preacher on Jury.

When O'Bannion was slain, Coroner Wolff summoned half a dozen well-known citizens to conduct the probe. Among them was Rev. Elmer L. Williams. After Tancl's death the same jury was ordered to report on his killing.

The jury has plans in mind which may assist materially in the drive. What these suggestions are Rev. Mr. Williams, foreman, declined to say today. The inquest, he said, probably would be continued in deference to the grand jury probe.

Sleuths on Trail.

Other agencies also took up the fight. The Chicago Crime commission was to meet today to discuss the situation. Law enforcement officials of the city and county were to appear.

Meanwhile State's Attorney Crowe's men made flying visits to Burnham, Burr Oak, Steger, Blue Island and Cicero. Everything was quiet. Resorts were dark, curtains drawn. The "dry" saloons were dry. The prosecutor's detectives planned to revisit these places again today.

IDENTIFIES GEMS OF VICTIM AT VALANIS TRIAL

Gowns, jewelry and silverware found in the possession of Anna and Anthony Valanis, William Lydon and Lucille Marshall, youthful defendants in a murder trial before Chief Justice Hopkins of the Criminal court, were identified today by Miss Jennie Sandusky, 821 Garfield court, as being the property of the victim, Mrs. Bessie Gansaler, who was found strangled to death at her home, 217 South Irving avenue, last April.

The quartet has pleaded guilty to the killing.

Keen questioning on the part of Assistant State's Attorney Michael Romano failed to shake the woman's testimony.

The property, it was shown, had been taken from the murdered woman by her slayers after they had gone to her apartment to collect the money from her they thought due them.

EXPECT TO FILL FORBES TRIAL JURY BOX TODAY

A jury for the trial of Charles R. Forbes, former director of the United States veterans' bureau, and John W. Thompson, millionaire contractor of St. Louis, will be selected by tonight, it was expected in Judge Carpenter's federal court today.

Forbes and Thompson are charged with having cheated the government in the matter of war supplies.

The veniremen were questioned today by Special Assistant Attorney General Ralph F. Potter and by Defense Attorney Elwood Godman. Peremptory challenges were frely exercised.

Mrs. Helen Votaw, sister of the late President Harding, may be one of the government's principal witnesses, it was learned today.

WITNESS AGAINST FORBES

Mrs. Carolyn Votaw, sister of the late President Harding, who will be one of the principal witnesses for the government at the trial of Col. Charles H. Forbes and J. W. Thompson.

COMPLETE NEW FEDERAL BUDGET

Coolidge and Lord Keep It Under $1,800,000,000

WASHINGTON, Nov. 25.—Despite last-minute additions to meet the wishes of cabinet officials, the national budget for the next fiscal year as completed today at a conference between President Coolidge and Budget Director Lord limits the ordinary expenditures of the government to a figure well under the $1,800,000,000 total fixed by President Coolidge in his talk last June to government fiscal officers.

Mr. Lord declined to reveal the precise total or discuss details of the budget, but he said previous expectations of the governmental economies possible had been more than realized.

For one thing, the original estimate of the cost of the soldier bonus law had proved too high. The small number of applications for the insurance bonus permitted a reduction in the annual fund allowed for amortization purposes, while additional cuts were made in the estimated cost of administration of the bonus law.

THOUSANDS AT CARDINAL LOGUE FUNERAL SERVICE

Armagh in Mourning as Primate Is Laid to Rest.

ARMAGH, Ireland, Nov. 25.—(By the Associated Press.)—This was a city of mourning today, the occasion being the funeral of Cardinal Michael Logue, primate of all Ireland, who died last Wednesday.

Despite a heavy rain, thousands came here to attend the obsequies. The crowds would have been larger had it not been for a railway mishap which held up many hundreds at Kady station. Virtually all of Ireland was represented, the mourners coming from Dublin, Belfast, Derry and other outlying points.

The burial was preceded by the celebration of a pontifical mass in St. Patrick's cathedral. The cathedral was draped in black and white, while the pillars along the approach to the edifice were also encased in somber wrappings. Almost everyone wore a mourning symbol, and so great was the desire to attend the services that many had to be content with kneeling on the long tier of steps leading to the central aisle.

There were 600 priests at the ceremonies. The Free State government was represented by Governor General Timothy Healy, Kevin O'Higgins, minister for home affairs, and Desmond Fitzgerald, minister for foreign affairs.

At Dundalk, with which the dead primate was closely associated for forty years, business was entirely suspended for two hours.

CHARGES HEARD IMPEACHING JUDGE

Subjudiciary Committee Sits on Baker Case.

PARKERSBURG, W. Va., Nov. 25.—A "cross section" of the impeachment charges against Judge William E. Baker of the United States District court in the northern district of West Virginia, and of his reply to these charges, rather than an effort to hear complete evidence on either side, is the aim of a subcommittee of the house of representatives, parties to the case were informed by the committee before its hearings opened here today.

The subcommittee of the judiciary committee of the house which will conduct the hearing is headed by Representative L. C. Dyer of Missouri. The committee secretary today notified United States District Attorney T. A. Brown, who preferred the formal charges against Judge Baker, of the committee's wish to hear only a "cross section" of the case at the present time and proposed that today be given over to evidence bearing on the charges and tomorrow to the defense of Judge Baker.

At Mr. Brown's office it was indicated that today's evidence probably would be devoted to only two of the thirty-three charges. The first charge is that Judge Baker was responsible for falsification of the court records in a prohibition case in 1922, while the second deals with the disposition of 800 quarts of bonded liquor. The district attorney charges that John J. Koontz, a deputy United States marshal, had stated that half of the liquor was taken to Elkins, home town of Judge Baker, and that the remainder was left with C. E. Brown, United States marshal. Koontz is also alleged to have said that the deputy received some of the liquor and gave some of it to friends.

Other charges alleged that Judge Baker had on several occasions appeared in public under the influence of liquor, and incompetence.

When the district attorney's charges were filed in the house of representatives that body directed its judiciary committee to investigate and determine whether the matter was one in which it should exercise its powers of impeachment, and the present hearing by the subcommittee is held under that direction.

Paris Wants a Mayor Like Other Big Cities

PARIS, Nov. 25.—Paris wants a mayor like the other cities have, "a real governing city hall symbol of communal autonomy," according to resolutions adopted unanimously today by seventy-five city councillors. They added that they were desirous that the capital of France be placed on an equal footing, so far as city government is concerned, with provincial towns. Paris is the only city in Europe which is unable to boast a mayor or burgomaster at the head of the city's affairs.

FAHY AND MURRAY FOUND GUILTY IN RONDOUT ROBBERY

Jury in Mail Holdup Case Out 4 Hours; Frees McComb.

Like a schoolboy whose plans went awry, William Fahy, former "ace" of the government postal inspectors, awoke in the county jail today still bewildered. He was found guilty of participation in the $3,000,000 Rondout mail robbery at 1:45 o'clock this morning in Judge Cliffe's court. The jury was out four hours.

The attitude of James Murray, former west side politician, also found guilty, was in direct contrast to that of Fahy. Becoming increasingly sulky as the defendants waited thru the night for the return of the jury, he broke into furious cursing when the verdict was read. Walter McComb, the third defendant, who was freed by the jury, lost no time in leaving the courtroom and the federal building.

New Trial Asked.

Closing arguments in the long trial were begun early yesterday evening. At 8:30 Judge Cliffe instructed the jury, which immediately filed out. Then came the long tense wait, which proved the most strenuous part of the trial for all concerned. As a matter of course, the defense attorneys moved for a new trial and Judge Cliffe set next Saturday as the day for argument on the motions.

Fahy and Murray were found guilty on eleven counts for robbing the mails, for which they can be sentenced to serve a total of 162 years in prison. Government attorneys predicted long sentences for both as well as the other members of the Rondout robbery band, who are: Brent Glasscock, alleged leader, the four Newton brothers and Herbert Holliday, all of whom confessed and aided the government in the trial.

Just what the compensation will be for the confessed members of the gang for their help to the prosecution was a matter of interested speculation today.

Glasscock, the chief government witness, was the only member of the crew to make a statement after the verdict. "They should have taken my word about McComb in the first place; he didn't have anything to do with it. I'm wondering now what we get for setting the government on the right track."

Used Tear Bombs.

The Rondout robbery was considered by authorities the most daring in history. On the night of June 12, a Chicago, Milwaukee and St. Paul mail train bearing heavy shipments of money and securities was stopped near the little hamlet of Rondout, Ill., by a bandit gang. Mail clerks barricaded the doors of their cars, but the bandits forced them out with tear bombs and systematically removed all the valuable mail sacks.

One slip during the robbery, however, proved the bandits' downfall. One of their number disobeyed instructions and was shot. It was thru the arrest of this wounded man in a Chicago flat by Capt. William Shoemaker and a squad from the detective bureau that the entire gang was rounded up.

Medical Students Flee Boarding-house Fire Clad in Nighties

Thirty medical students fled to the street in scanty attire early today when fire spread thru the three-story rooming-house at 3661 South Michigan avenue. Firemen estimated the damage caused by the blaze to be $1,000.

According to Battalion Chief John J. Lynch of the 10th battalion, the fire started in the basement from a defective flue. The blaze was controlled soon after the arrival of firemen who answered the first alarm.

The rooming-house, a brick structure, is leased by John C. Seeberg, a medical student, who in turn rents rooms to other students of medical schools in the vicinity.

Descriptions of New Hard Roads Given Out

SPRINGFIELD, Ill., Nov. 25.—Description of proposed hard-road work to be offered for bids Dec. 17 in the third road letting under the $100,000,000 bond issue were announced here this morning by the department of public works and buildings. Thirty-six sections, aggregating 202 miles, seventy-one miles of heavy grading and eight large bridges are included.

Section Meetings Today's Program of Physicians

NEW ORLEANS, Nov. 25.—Activities of the Southern Medical association in annual convention here today will be devoted to section meetings, the next general session of the convention being scheduled for Thursday, the closing day.

Fascisti in Convention.

ROME, Nov. 25.—A congress of fascist corporations, attended by 3,000 delegates representing 2,000 organized workers, opened here yesterday.

Police Sergeant Hit by Motorcycle of Park Policemen

Police Sergeant Michael O'Malley, assigned to the Chicago avenue station, was seriously injured early today when he was struck by a motorcycle driven by C. D. Schmidt, Lincoln park motorcycle policeman.

The accident occurred at Oak street and Michigan avenue as the police sergeant was crossing Oak street, and the motorcycle policeman was in pursuit of a speeding automobile.

Sergt. O'Malley was taken to the Passavant hospital, suffering from a broken leg and a possible skull fracture. He lives at 4342 North Tripp avenue.

ZR-3 ON WAY TO WASHINGTON FOR ITS CHRISTENING

Dirigible to Be Named "Los Angeles" by Mrs. Coolidge.

BULLETIN.

BALTIMORE, Nov. 25.—(By the Associated Press.)—Flying so low that the humming of her motors could be heard, the ZR-3 passed over Baltimore for Washington at 11:41.

LAKEHURST, N. J., Nov. 25.—The German-built dirigible ZR-3 took the air at 9:05 a. m. at the naval air station today and headed southwest for Bolling field, Washington, where she will be christened "Los Angeles" by Mrs. Calvin Coolidge this afternoon.

Naval officers asserted the ZR-3 would have little trouble making what will be her first flight in the United States.

Taken from the hangar shortly after 8 o'clock, the ZR-3 was carried to a point several hundred feet from the huge mooring mast here and with 350 men clinging to her landing ropes was held to the ground until the take-off.

The line of flight to the capital carries her over Trenton, N. J., Philadelphia, Wilmington, Delaware and Baltimore, with her arrival at Bolling field scheduled for about 2 o'clock this afternoon. The ship is due back here between 7 and 8 o'clock tonight.

Forty-two Men Aboard.

The crew of the ZR-3 today numbered forty-two men, including eleven of the German crew which brought her here and two American navy officers who also made the transatlantic flight. Commander J. H. Klein Jr., acting commandant at the naval air station, was in command.

Lieutenant Commander Sidney M. Kraus, who with Commander Klein made the trip from Germany in the ZR-3, today was her engineering officer.

Two photographers, one representing the navy and another a news reel corporation, also were aboard.

Early this morning a trap containing thirty-three homing pigeons was fastened to the nose of the huge airship. The pigeons will be released by Mrs. Coolidge as part of the christening ceremonies today, and their return here will be hailed as a symbolic completion of the naming of the giant airship.

Flight of Interest.

Because today's flight represented her first trip under American guidance and because of the substitution of helium for hydrogen with which the ZR-3 was inflated for her trip across the Atlantic, officers here were intensely interested in her handling. Observers reported the ship in her preliminary movements seemed unusually graceful and docile to her handlers.

She was "walked out" of the hangar in about forty-five minutes, a shorter time than ever was needed for the Shenandoah, and floated lightly, apparently amply supported by the helium, whose lifting power is not considered as great as that of hydrogen. With the rising of the sun, the heat expanded the gas and she became even more responsive to the breeze.

Bolling Field in Readiness.

WASHINGTON, Nov. 25.—Bolling field lay in trim dress today for the christening there by Mrs. Coolidge of the dirigible ZR-3 as the Los Angeles.

The air field had been put in readiness for a capacity throng to witness the gala scene of christening of the great air liner. Sparkling toy balloons whose strings will slip from the fingers of the sponsor also carry a flavor of the airship's exclusion by prior agreement from the ways of warfare.

The ceremony was scheduled for 3 o'clock. A crew of 300 men from the navy-yard here and the air station were ready to give a hand in hauling the big ship to earth.

Immediately after the ZR-3 is landed, the christening will take place. At the moment Mrs. Coolidge releases the pigeons the navy-yard battery will fire a national salute of twenty-one guns and the navy band will play "The Star-Spangled Banner."

Nearly all of official Washington, members of diplomatic corps, high ranking army and navy officers prepared to go to the field for the ceremony, and among the guests to have places were the four world flyers, headed by Lieut. Lowell H. Smith, who arrived here yesterday to make a final report of their exploit.

Write to THE POST. Express your ideas in the paper read by thinking people.

SEEK PERMIT TO START BACK TODAY WITH LEO KORETZ

Crowe's Aids Eager to Return to Chicago with Swindler.

An attempt to cut all red tape and brush aside all legal delays in order that Leo Koretz, arch swindler, who was captured at Halifax, can be started back to Chicago at once will be made today in the Canadian courts.

Assistant State's Attorneys John Sbarbaro and William McSwiggin, who were sent to Nova Scotia to handle the details preliminary to bringing Koretz back here to stand trial, announced when reached by long-distance telephone, they would make every effort to block delays.

Mr. Sbarbaro said he would go into court today and ask that in view of the fact that Koretz had waived extradition and that he had admitted the authorities here have a prima facie case against him, the courts in Canada waive the clause in the Canadian law which provides for a fifteen-day continuance of all extradition cases.

Anxious to Get Back.

"Papers will arrive from Ottawa today," said Mr. Sbarbaro. "We plan to take the first train for Chicago, the courts approving. Koretz is anxious to get back and has helped us in every way but confessing his guilt."

The return of Koretz, it is expected, will precipitate a battle between the federal and state authorities as to who shall prosecute him first.

Federal authorities urge they have a much stronger case against the alleged swindler than the state courts, and that justice, as laid down by the federal statute is much stronger and surer.

At the same time State's Attorney Crowe is loath to allow the prosecution to go out of his hands and will bend every effort to retain the prosecution.

It is possible under the federal law for a district court judge to issue a writ of habeas corpus for Koretz and thus force the state to turn him over to the government. The district attorney's office, however, has not yet indicated it would take this step.

The capture of Koretz, according to evidence disclosed last night, came just in the nick of time. He was ready, it was said, to move on, a jump ahead of his pursuers. For this, according to his captors, he had provided a swift power schooner, well found and ready for instant departure.

Koretz Planned Flight.

Incidentally, it was learned Koretz had three exits planned. There were: Flight to Central America, the scene of his Bayano River Trust company, which caused all of his trouble.

Retreat up the North Atlantic coast to Labrador and beyond.

Suicide by means of an automatic pistol he carried with him always and which was found in his pocket when arrested.

Koretz was postponing one of these moves as a last resort. It became known yesterday he had been for many years a sufferer from diabetes and it was thru this disease that he was traced.

Prosecutor Sbarbaro revealed that as early as five months ago Koretz had been traced to Montreal, under the name of Lou Keyte, the alias he assumed in Nova Scotia, where he had gone to be treated with insulin. Koretz spent several weeks there in a sanitarium and left only a jump ahead of his pursuers.

Beard Shaved Off.

Yesterday the swindler called for a barber and asked that the beard grown in the seclusion of a New York apartment in the early days of his flight, be shaved off. His request was granted but he was not allowed to handle the razor himself for fear he might choose suicide.

In wires yesterday to State's Attorney Crowe, his assistants stated they already had taken possession of Koretz's lodge, Pinehurst, valued at $34,000, and would move soon to take possession of his bank accounts amounting to well over $100,000.

Even at that, Koretz's creditors, who have received a 5 per cent dividend from the Chicago Title and Trust company, the receiver appointed for the Bayano "bubble," may have to content themselves with this sum.

George N. Murdock, special solicitor for the internal revenue department, made preparations to impound a fund of $400,000 in the hands of the receivers, for $753,000 Koretz owes the government for back income tax. And ordinary taxes take precedence over all other debts.

Cranks His Auto While in Gear; Fatally Crushed

EL DORADO, Ark., Nov. 25.—Gus A. Nollie, aged farmer, whose home was near here, died today from injuries sustained recently when run over by his own automobile. Nollie who came to El Dorado to obtain medicine for his wife, cranked his automobile while the machine was in gear and incurred a broken hip and other injuries.

Twenty-five Years for Bandit

OMAHA, Nov. 25.—Jay Graham, harvest hand of Fort Smith, Ark., held up an oil station in Council Bluffs, was captured an hour later, pleaded guilty and was sentenced to twenty-five years in the pe[illegible]

10 CENTS PAY NO MORE

Chicago Sunday Tribune

THE WORLD'S GREATEST NEWSPAPER

LAST MAIL

VOLUME LXXXIV.—NO. 3 [REG. U.S.PAT. OFFICE: COPYRIGHT 1925 BY THE CHICAGO TRIBUNE.] JANUARY 18, 1925. * SEVEN CENTS IN CHICAGO AND 40 MILE RADIUS | TEN CENTS ELSEWHERE.

TORRIO GIVEN PRISON TERM

WAGE EARNERS' SAVINGS BOOM STOCK MARKET

New Economic Era Seen in Buying.

BY ARTHUR SEARS HENNING.

Washington, D. C., Jan. 17.—[Special.]—The stock market boom that has developed since the presidential election and still shows no signs of subsiding is regarded by economic authorities as the most extraordinary financial phenomenon in our history.

The fact that there was no profit taking during the first two months of the boom on a scale sufficient to produce a general setback is accepted as an indication that the bulk of the public buying has been for investment rather than speculation.

Never before has there appeared to be so enormous a volume of savings seeking investment. Specially significant are the indications that the investments of wage earners are growing by leaps and bounds. The workers are buying corporation stocks with savings increased by the higher wages prevailing during and since the war and, according to some commentators, still further increased by the radical reduction of the expenditures of the working class on drink under the prohibition régime.

Economic Revolution Seen.

Wage earners are now receiving a rapidly increasing percentage of the total volume of dividends paid out annually, while the percentage of dividends received by the rich is decreasing. Herein is noted a trend of corporation ownership from the rich few to the many of meager means, a trend denoting an economic revolution, thinks Prof. T. N. Carver, head of the economics department of Harvard university.

"The only economic revolution in the world that amounts to a hill of beans," he says, "is taking place in this country right now.

"Members of the federal reserve board are inclined to believe that the United States may now be entering upon an era of investment by persons of small means that will bring about very striking shifts in the ownership of the great corporations during the next few years."

It was expected by the board when the unusual activity began that New York member banks would be rediscounting in an increased volume to finance the borrowings which professional traders are accustomed to make in periods of stock market activity. The rediscount demand failed, however, to develop in any volume approaching a normal ratio to the volume of sales.

Purchases Are Outright.

This, coupled with the heavy movement of remittances to New York, as disclosed by the clearing house operations of the federal reserve system, has been taken as an indication that persons from all sections of the country are actually making outright purchases of securities. Remittances to pay in full for securities purchased provided the New York banks with ample funds to meet loan demands, making recourse to the federal reserve bank unnecessary. These circumstances have satisfied the board that the stock market boom has been due to the purchase of securities for investment rather than professional speculation.

The tendency toward wider distribution of corporation stocks is shown by the increase in the number of stockholders in the country from 4,400,000 in 1900 to 14,400,000 in 1923, while the average number of $100 shares per stockholder decreased from 140 to 50.

$1,000 to $5,000 Men Buying.

Great significance attaches to the large increase in the amount and the proportion of the total dividends received by the class with incomes of $1,000 to $5,000. This class includes the overwhelming majority of the wage earners of the country.

In 1917 the dividends reported by this class amounted to 9.5 per cent of the total, and in 1918 to 14.1 per cent of all dividends reported. There was a slight decline in 1919 and a small gain in 1920, followed by a spectacular advance to 22.7 in 1921. There was a decline in 1922 from the high point of the preceding year, but the amount of dividends received approximated half a billion dollars, which was higher than for any year with the exception of 1921.

The proportion of the total dividends received by the classes with incomes from $5,000 to $20,000 remained relatively stable from 1917 to 1922. Starting at 25.8 per cent in 1917, the first year for which comparable figures are available, it advanced to 31.5 per cent in 1920 and declined to 29.1 per cent in 1922.

It is evident, therefore, that the

[Continued on page 4, column 2.]

NEWS SUMMARY

LOCAL.

Johnny Torrio and four others, two of them ex-policemen, get jail terms in Sieben brewery beer running case.

Report to miners' union chiefs charges locomotive engineers' coal mine evicts union miners.

Scientists of Chicago and vicinity prepare for observations of eclipse next Saturday.

Gov. Small starts contemplated job shakeup by appointing Hugh Willis securities supervisor of the state industrial commission.

Sanitary board sending delegation to Washington to answer charges made before senate committee.

Steam railways ask state commerce commission for permission to increase suburban fares 20 per cent.

Census bureau report shows that Chicago hasn't reduced taxes or cost of crime.

WASHINGTON.

Coolidge advises idealism; says United States newspapers are best in world in address to editors.

Boom in stock market traced to multitude of investments by wage earners; called financial phenomenon.

Flood of Canadian real beer overwhelming near-beer business, Anheuser attorney protests to Coolidge.

Denatured alcohol biggest problem of dry law enforcement forces, Couzens' senate committee is told.

House stands by Coolidge farm commission in passing $159,000,000 deficiency appropriation bill.

Hoover says United States is eliminating waste in economic system at rate of $600,000,000 a year.

Ray Stannard Baker named authorized biographer of Woodrow Wilson in accordance with dead president's wish.

Senator McCormick [Rep., Ill.] makes strong plea for treaty confirming Cuba's claim to Isle of Pines.

Signing of recent Paris debt agreement by United States envoys worries senators and copy of agreement from state department is asked.

DOMESTIC.

Grand Duke Boris, brother of claimant to Russian throne, lands in New York "for a good time;" denies his visit is political.

State to ask life term for girl who killed mother; coroner's jury holds her guilty.

Air committee told of huge new mail plane with seven times capacity of those now in use.

Daniel G. Reid, multimillionaire tin plate king, dies in New York of pneumonia.

Two of Means' alleged "fixers" to testify for Uncle Sam in trial this week.

FOREIGN.

Chinese pirates hold British ship three days while robbing passengers.

Soviet envoy to London says Russia will not curb communist activities to gain American recognition, which he expects soon.

Premier Mussolini agrees to drop plural vote scheme as Italian parliament passes his new electoral law.

New German chancellor calls Republicans' distrust of him unfair; says he will work with all parties.

More U. S. gunboats arrive at Shanghai to guard foreigners endangered by Chinese civil war.

British so slow on debt settlement with France because of present poor condition of French finances.

SPORTING.

Tex Rickard goes ahead with plans for two Dempsey fights during summer.

Johnny Dundee runs out on Paris promoters, claims Bennie Leonard's title and sails for United States.

American coaches say Nurmi is greatest runner of all times.

Field of seventy-seven riders to compete today in Norge club ski tourney at Cary, Ill.

Charley Hollocher, star shortstop, is gaining health and says he'll be back with Cubs in spring.

EDITORIALS.

How It Must Look to Hungry Europe; A new Revolt Against Coal; Diplomatic Cigaret Butts; Kellogg for Secretary of State; The Commuter's Ticket.

MARKETS.

May wheat closes above $1.88, leading other grains, all of which close week strong.

Stock market ends decline; prices advance sharply with short covering.

Good butcher hogs sell at high prices despite realizing sales.

FEATURES.

Part 2—Automobile news; Farm and Garden.

Part 5—Magazine section: "Shelled," by Carl Clausen; "Literature and the Schoolmarm," by H. L. Mencken; "Mud Pies and Maple Sugar," by George M. Cohan; "The Amazing Crime," by Henry C. Rowland.

Picture section—Twelve pages of rotogravure news pictures and sketches in "Parlor Tricks," by W. E. Hill.

Comics—Eight pages of comics in colors.

THERE MUST BE SOME REASON

Real Beer Too Near for Near Beer to Sell

Washington, D. C., Jan. 17.—[Special.]—Charging that lax enforcement of the prohibition laws was driving his company out of business, Attorney Lawrence Eades, general counsel for the Anheuser-Busch Brewing company, manufacturers of near-beer, called at the white house today and appealed for relief from what he termed unfair competition.

He charged that within the last few months Canadian brewers had shipped in so much real beer carrying an alcoholic content of from six to eight per cent that the market for legitimate near-beer had almost disappeared.

Tells His Story to Slemp.

"Our company will be driven out of business," he told C. Bascom Slemp, secretary to the President, "unless illegitimate sales are curbed. The Canadian brewers are even advertising the merits of Canadian near-beer, large quantities of which are coming into this country."

Attorney Eades was referred to commissioner of internal revenue where he again told his story. When he left he told friends the government had promised to investigate. At the office of Prohibition Commissioner Haynes it was said that it was virtually impossible for real beer to be shipped into this country from Canada as near-beer and that if Canadian beer had come into this country it had been smuggled in.

Haynes Exit Looms.

Officials close to the administration cited this case as an instance of the sort of thing which is said to have caused the President to make up his mind to remove Commissioner Haynes within the next two months. Too much attention, it is held, has been paid to the toter of hip liquor and not enough to stopping the flow of liquor at the source.

Officials close to the President said today that there was little doubt but that Commissioner Haynes would have to go, regardless of whether the Crampton bill creating a separate bureau for the prohibition unit, passes congress or not. The commissioner, however, told newspapermen today that he had no knowledge of any intention on the part of the President to oust him.

Scofflaw Gets 2 1-2 Years in Prison and $3,000 Fine

Peoria, Ill., Jan. 17.—A sentence of two years and a half in jail and the federal penitentiary and a fine of $3,000, the stiffest bootleg penalty ever dealt out in federal court here, was given Alex McCarren. More than ninety defendants have been sentenced to jail and fines of more than $45,000 imposed during the present term of court.

THE WEATHER

SUNDAY, JANUARY 18, 1925.

Chicago and Vicinity—Partly cloudy Sunday; not much change in temperature; gentle to moderate shifting winds.

Illinois—Partly cloudy Sunday; rising temperature in northwest portion.

Indiana—Mostly cloudy Sunday; not much change in temperature.

Lower Michigan—Mostly cloudy Sunday, probably light snow Sunday; not so cold in northeast portion.

Upper Michigan—Unsettled Sunday, probably light snow.

Wisconsin—Partly cloudy Sunday, probably light snow in northeast portion.

Missouri—Partly cloudy Sunday.

Iowa—Mostly fair Sunday; warmer in east central portion.

Minnesota—Partly cloudy Sunday, probably light snow in northeast portion.

North Dakota—Partly cloudy Sunday.

South Dakota—Mostly fair Sunday.

Nebraska—Generally fair Sunday.

Kansas—Generally fair Sunday.

Lake Michigan—Gentle to moderate shifting winds; mostly cloudy Sunday, probably light snow.

Montana—Mostly cloudy Sunday, probably snow west of the Divide; not much change in temperature.

Wyoming—Mostly fair Sunday; rising temperature in southwest portion.

GENERAL FORECAST.

Some snow is indicated within the next twenty-four hours for most of the upper lake region and portions of Minnesota and Wisconsin; otherwise, mostly fair weather will prevail in this forecast district through Sunday. A new cold wave is developing over Alaska, and may advance into the northwestern states early next week.

ADVICE TO SHIPPERS.

Protect shipments originating in or passing through Chicago to reach destination within the next thirty-six hours from temperatures as follows: North and northwest, zero to 10 above; west, 5 to 10 above; south and east, 15 to 20.

ALCOHOL WORTH $500,000 SEIZED BY U. S. AGENTS

St. Paul, Minn., Jan. 17.—Three carloads of alcohol, said to be valued at $500,000, and which was alleged to have been taken secretly from a Philadelphia distillery, were seized here tonight by the federal prohibition agents from Minneapolis.

New York Bankers to Loan Poland $50,000,000, Report

WARSAW, Jan. 17.—[By Associated Press.]—A loan to Poland of $50,000,000 by American banking interests is said to have been successfully negotiated. The newspaper reports mention the names of Lee Higginson & Co., Callaway Fish & Co., Spencer Trask & Co., and White Weld & Co., all of New York, as participants in the loan. On Dec. 30 last, the Polish president issued a decree authorizing the cabinet to negotiate a loan up to $60,000,000.

Student Goes to Prison for Attempted Extortion

Peoria, Ill., Jan. 17.—Theodore Markstty, 23, former Bradley college student here, who confessed to attempting extortion of $5,000 from Mrs. David Proctor, prominent Peoria society woman, on threat of harm to her daughter, Edna Dean Proctor, a freshman at the University of Wisconsin, today was sentenced to from one to twenty years at hard labor in prison.

Pirates Hold Ship 3 Days to Hunt Loot

HONGKONG, Jan. 17.—[United Press.]—The British steamer Hong Hwa, which sailed for Singapore three days ago, put back into port here today with an amazing story of piracy on the high seas. All the steamer's passengers were penniless and the safe had been rifled, yet those aboard were otherwise unharmed.

Officers of the Hong Hwa reported that for three days the vessel had been in the possession of Chinese pirates. The latter embarked with the rest of the passengers, without exciting suspicion.

Overpower the Crew.

When the steamer was a short way out, the pirates gathered, rushed the bridge, and overpowered the captain and crew. A volley was fired during the attack on the bridge, but no one was hurt. The British officers were for the most part at breakfast and were surrounded and made prisoners. The first thing the pirates did was to demolish the steamer's wireless. Then they forced the officers to navigate the ship for three days on the high seas, keeping out of touch with land or other vessels.

Systematically Rob Passengers.

The pirates systematically robbed the passengers, who were kept prisoners and forced, when their turn came, to give up all their valuables. The robbers took their time, working for a day at opening the steamer's safe.

Finally, when they possessed all the money on board, they ordered the Hong Hwa to land them with their booty.

Father and Son Are Found Dead; Son Believed Slayer

St. Louis, Mo., Jan. 17.—August Geiger, 70, retired bookbinder, and his son, August Jr., 38, automobile tire designer, were found dead today in their three room cottage here. Police believe the son killed the father while suffering from mental aberration, then killed himself by asphyxiation.

J. R. Drexel Jr. Weds Louisville Magazine Artist

New York, Jan. 17.—John R. Drexel Jr., son of John R. Drexel of New York and Philadelphia, was married today to Miss Jane Barbour of Louisville, Ky., a magazine writer and artist. Mr. Drexel's first wife, Elizabeth Thompson Drexel, obtained a final decree of divorce in Reno on Dec. 12.

South Africa to Return to Gold Standard on July 1

Ottawa, Jan. 17. — [By Associated Press.]—The department of trade and commerce was informed today that South Africa would return to the gold standard on July 1.

FOUR OTHERS, TWO EX-COPS, SENTENCED, TOO

Judge Says Crime Ring Exists.

Johnny Torrio, theoretical chief of Chicago's underworld, two of his vice lieutenants, and two former policemen yesterday went up against federal law and were sent to jail. Six truck drivers, accused with them of looting the Sieben brewery last May, were fined $500 each.

Dean O'Banion, slain gangster, and the defendants facing Federal Judge Adam C. Cliffe were bitterly assailed by Judge Cliffe and District Attorney Olson as "outlaw gunmen."

Two Defendants Missing.

Louie Alterie, O'Banion gang gunman now in refuge in Colorado, and George Frank, two other defendants, didn't show up. Their cases were continued until Monday. Two others in the raid are dead beside O'Banion, one of them Johnny Phillips, who died under fire of a policeman. Twenty-two brewery officials and employés were freed.

Torrio was sentenced to nine months in the Du Page county jail and fined $5,000.

All the defendants were given a stay of execution for ten days to arrange their affairs.

O'Donnell Gets Eight Months.

Edward O'Donnell was sent to Kane county jail for eight months and fined $2,000 for his part in the brewery robbery. Nick Juffra, already under a two year sentence, tied in legal tape, got six months in De Kalb county jail and a fine of $2,000. The former policemen, Joseph Warszynski and Joseph J. Sonnefeld, who were on guard at the brewery at the time, changed their pleas to guilty and drew down three months in jail.

The truck drivers who were fined $500 each are Richard Wilson, George J. Murphy, George Wells, Edward McDermott, Arthur Barrett, and Jack Heiman.

"These are the type of men who put the courts to shame," Judge Cliffe said in passing sentence. "We might as well close the courts as let them go unpunished.

Slain by Former Pals.

"Dean O'Banion and John Torrio were chief conspirators in this case, but O'Banion, as well as another defendant, were murdered in cold blood by criminals of their own class since their indictment, and no further attention need be paid them by enforcement officers."

"These are outlaw gunmen who ought to have been prosecuted by state authorities years ago for robbery, murder, or other crimes," District Attorney Olson said. "But they were allowed to pursue their criminal careers. It remained for the federal government to give them their first experience behind prison bars, and that had to be done on a common liquor charge.

"State authorities tried to release these outlaws by issuing habeas corpus writs from three different courts on the morning of their arrest, but Chief of Police Collins turned the defendants over to the United States attorney fifteen minutes before the writs were served."

Find Beer Running in Progress.

The Sieben brewery at 1470 Larrabee street was raided by police squads on the morning of May 19. They found four truckloads of beer in the yard and another truck loading at the platform. Thirty-four men were arrested, including Torrio and O'Banion.

"O'Banion was the chief conspirator and actually in charge," the court was told. "Torrio is the principal living defendant and O'Donnell was in charge of the brewery and gave orders to the others."

Recommendation of the district attorney that charges against Bernard F. Sieben, owner of the brewery, and twenty-one other defendants be dismissed, was accepted by the court. These were freed: John Novak, George Dickinson, William Mann, George R. Jacobs, Steve Cook, Daniel J. O'Connor, Phillip Reis, Martin Johnson, Warren Scherer, Albert Johnson, Robert Jacobs, August Suhr, John Burns, William C. Smith, Joseph Smith, John King, Guy T. Littlejohn, Frank Chuse, Charles Hurts, George Mack, and Joseph White.

Tell of Woman's Threats at Her Trial for Killing

Rock Island, Ill., Jan. 17.—"If Frank has any more children by his wife I'll kill them, and him and his wife, too," is one of the many threats state witnesses today attributed to Mrs. Mayme Gale Herman, on trial for the murder of Frank Andrews last September. Mrs. Herman is charged with having fatally stabbed Andrews when he announced his intention of ending their love.

Duke Boris in U. S. for Fun; Bars Politics

New York, Jan. 17.—Boris Vladimirovitch, grand duke of Russia and second in line of succession to the Russian throne should the Romanoffs ever regain the government, arrived on the Olympic today for a "jolly good time" in the United States. He was accompanied by the grand duchess and a family party.

The duke entered port with a reputation among his fellow passengers as a "good mixer" and a "regular fellow," largely as a result of his part as peacemaker in an altercation which closed a party given aboard ship in his honor last Thursday night, New Year's eve by the Russian calendar.

At least two other male guests got discolored eyes. The story was that the party, organized by Col. J. L. O'Connor, D. S. O., who is coming here for British oil interests on a mission to Mexico, and William H. Halligan, an actor and vaudeville booker, started at 10 o'clock Thursday night and broke up at 5 Friday morning, after a heavy consumption of champagne.

Duke Quells Disturbance.

A toast was proposed to Halligan, and the party, with one exception, se to drink it. The exception, who said he was Alexander Grows of Miami, Fla., but who appeared on the passenger list as "A. Gross," remained seated. Halligan and Grows engaged in an altercation, which ended when the actor was struck by a champagne bottle across his forehead. The grand duke intervened, quelled the trouble and sent Halligan to the ship's doctor.

The grand duke this morning held an informal reception for newspaper men in his cabin, a small one and plainly furnished in contrast to the quarters occupied by his sister-in-law, the Grand Duchess Cyril, wife of the man who recently proclaimed himself heir to the Romanoff throne, when she came here a few weeks ago.

Recalls His Earlier Jaunt.

The grand duke flashed ready and witty answers to an avalanche of questions. There was no financial or political significance to his visit, he said. "Just here on my own hook," he said. The phrase was a cutback to his American visit of twenty-four years ago, he said, a visit which brought him much publicity, notably on the occasion when he drank champagne from a chorus girl's slipper in Chicago.

He personally had no aspiration to the Russian throne, he said, adding that he supported the claim of his brother, his elder by more than a year. The "thinking Russians," he thought, desired the return of monarchical government.

Smiles at La Guardia Alarm.

When told of Representative La Guardia's recent statement in congress that the grand duke should be questioned as to whether he intended to attempt an overthrow of the American government, the grand duke replied:

"Ah, then I would be emperor of this great America! How charming."

"I'm here for a good time, that's all," he concluded. "I hope I get invited to some good shooting, some golf, and, O, many other things. I love fun."

His mother-in-law, his titled secretary, and his wife's niece, Natalie, 8 years old, who accompanied them, arrived second class for "purposes of economy."

Man Shoots Wife and Boarder, Kills Self

Everett, Mass., Jan. 17.—Three persons were dead tonight as a result of a triple shooting in the kitchen of the home of Frank Ferranti here this afternoon. The dead are Frank Ferranti, his wife Frances, and their boarder, Paul Lombardi.

Neighbors, hearing the shots, entered the kitchen, where they found Mrs. Ferranti and Lombardi dead and Ferranti dying of a bullet wound in his right temple, a revolver clutched in one hand.

COOLIDGE URGES PRESS TO PATH OF HIGH IDEALS

Calls U. S. Papers Best in World.

Washington, D. C., Jan. 17.—The pathway to success in American journalism lies in the avoidance of propaganda, the separation of news policies from business motives, and continued appeal to the idealism of the American people, President Coolidge declared tonight in speaking to the American Society of Newspaper Editors.

PRESIDENT COOLIDGE. [Walinger Photo.]

Avoiding for the most part reference to governmental problems, Mr. Coolidge talked shop with the editors, speaking from the viewpoint of one not in the newspaper business, as was his predecessor, but as one who has watched the growth and development of the American press. This growth, he declared, had given the United States "the best newspapers in the world."

No Fear of Capitalism.

Mr. Coolidge made it plain that he entertains no fears as to the influences of what is sometimes called a "capitalistic press."

"Some people feel concerned about the commercialism of the press," he said. "They note that great newspapers are great business enterprises earning large profits and controlled by men of wealth. So they fear that in such control the press may tend to support the private interests of those who own the papers, rather than the general interest of the whole people.

"It seems to me, however, that the real test is not whether the newspapers are controlled by men of wealth, but whether they are sincerely trying to serve the public interests. There will be little occasion to worry about who owns a newspaper so long as its attitudes on public questions are such as to promote the general welfare."

Keep Idealism Alive.

Advising the editors as to their greatest opportunity for aiding the government, the President said he unhesitatingly placed it in the direction of keeping alive American idealism.

"It is only those who do not understand our people, who believe that our national life is entirely absorbed by material motives," he added. "We make no concealment of the fact that we want wealth, but there are many other things that we want very much more. We want peace and honor, and that charity which is so strong an element of all civilization.

"The chief ideal of the American people is idealism. I cannot repeat too often that America is a nation of idealism. I cannot repeat too often that America is a nation of idealists. That is the only motive to which they ever give any strong and lasting reaction. No newspaper can be a success which fails to appeal to that element of our national life. It is in this direction that the public press can lend its strongest support to our government.

"I could not truly criticize the vast importance of the counting room, but my ultimate faith I would place in the high idealism of the editorial room of the American newspaper."

Unhampered Press Needed.

A public press unhampered is a true instrument under a republic for true representation and sound and logical interpretation of the truth, he contended.

"The public press under an autocracy is necessarily a true agency of propaganda," he continued. "Under a free government it must be the very reverse. Propaganda seeks to present a part of the facts, to distort their relations, and to force conclusions which could not be drawn from a complete and candid survey of all the facts.

"This has become one of the dangers of the present day. The great difficulty in combating unfair propaganda, or even in recognizing it, arises from the fact that at the present time we confront so many new and technical problems that it is an enormous task to keep ourselves accurately informed concerning them. In this respect you gentlemen of the press face the same perplexities that are encountered by legislators and government administrators.

Must Rely on Experts.

"Whoever deals with current public questions is compelled to rely greatly upon the information and judgments of experts and specialists. Unfortunately, not all experts are to be trusted.

Today

Shooting It Out.
The Bootleg Boss.
Fear and Brutality.
Week-End Fliers.

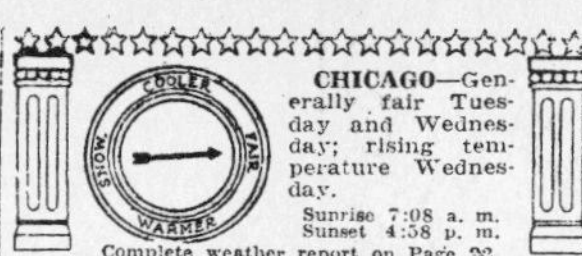

CHICAGO—Generally fair Tuesday and Wednesday; rising temperature Wednesday.
Sunrise 7:08 a. m.
Sunset 4:58 p. m.
Complete weather report on Page 26.

HERALD CHICAGO AND EXAMINER

FINAL EDITION

44th YEAR No. 224 — Registered U. S. Patent Office. Copyright, 1925, Herald and Examiner — Telephone Main 5000 — TUESDAY, JANUARY 27, 1925. — C*** — TWO PARTS — PRICE 3 CE[NTS]

PLOT TO KILL CAPONE AND MRS. TORRI[O]

Coolidge Urges Slashing of U. S. Payrolls

CAR LINES VALUED AT $162,843,584

—By Arthur Brisbane—

(Copyright, 1925, by Star Company.)

FOR a picture of civilization in 1925, study events in Herrin, Ill., when S. Glenn Young, engaged in "cleaning up bootleggers" for the Ku Klux Klan, and Ora Thomas, sheriff, once jailed for bootlegging, decided to "shoot it out."

They shot it out in a cigar store; both were killed, and two others in the store were killed.

The widow of Young, who had locked up more than 125 bootleggers, and who now lies in an undertaker's shop, dressed in the purple robe of a "kleagle," says: "My husband played the game straight."

He certainly played it to the end, and "shot it out" to a bitter finish.

MRS. YOUNG, the widow, represents in her way our peculiar civilization of klan, anti-klan, bootleg and prohibition. She is totally blind. Somebody, trying to kill her husband, shot out her eyes. This interesting incident of our civilization will seem queer to people that read about it ten thousand years hence.

One venerable citizen yesterday uttered this new complaint:

"Once in a while, in my business, I have to ask a favor from a political boss. In old days the boss was somebody that had grown up with the community, somebody that understood the people, often an Irishman.

"Now, when I want to see the boss, it's a young bootlegger, often scarcely able to speak English. Bootlegging brings in so much ready money that the bootleggers have crowded out the old-time bosses."

IN Washington an aged Negro barber, E. C. Washington, seeing the sun going out during the eclipse, decided that it meant the end of the world, ran amuck, razor in hand, and slashed one man before he was overpowered. He acted quite naturally.

Fear takes men back to the animal condition and makes animals of them.

You see it in war, when horrible brutalities often disgrace both sides.

Fear has more to do with fighting than courage. You see what fear does in shipwreck, causing men to trample down women and children fighting for the lifeboats.

It is perfectly natural that the ancient Negro, frightened by the world's coming to an end, should instinctively feel that he wanted to cut somebody with his razor. That's what fear does.

The strange thing is that anybody should be worried about the world end. The same thing would happen to everybody, and nobody, except, perhaps, the real estate owner, would have cause for especial protest.

FRENCH fliers on their way to Lake Tchad in the Sudan landed at Colomb Bechar in the Sahara Desert promptly on time, reaching their first stopping place at 3:20 Sunday afternoon.

While this country, where flying machines were invented, wishes it had flying machines and does nothing. European countries manufacture them and use them. British companies make three round trips a day between Paris and London, carrying passengers. The round trip costs $60 and the journey takes three hours. It used to mean a train from London to the English channel, then the steamboat across the channel, then a train from the channel to Paris. Now it means one short, straight flight.

The French and British governments subsidize commercial flying as they should do, and as this country should do. They encourage aircraft manufacturers, that they may have plants ready and able to turn out machines in case of emergency.

THIS country will fly eventually, after having watched and waited for Europe and Japan to teach us.

The day is coming when Winter resorts, Summer resorts and mountain resorts will look up into the sky every Friday afternoon to see the week-enders come flying from the big cities. The father in New York, Boston, Detroit, Chicago, will send his family to a warm place in Winter, a cool place in Summer, and distance won't matter. To fly a thousand miles to spend a week-end and fly back again for business on Monday will be no more than going now from New York to Atlantic City or from Milwaukee to Oconomowoc.

A GREAT change is coming in transportation. Henry Ford starts it with his steamships, that leave the heart of this continent, starting from the River Rouge in the Great Lakes region, stopping to unload at seaports all along the [coa]st and around on the Gulf of [Me]xico. [illegible] these ships will [illegible] freight of [illegible] will be [illegible] distribu[tion] [illegible] future will [illegible] passenger

PRESIDENT ASKS NEW SAVING OF $62,000,000

Predicts Era of Increasing Prosperity for Nation if Program of Economy Is Carried Out by Bureau Heads.

HINTS NEW TAX CUT NEAR

Expenditures Down $2,004,000,000 in 4 Years; Debt Reduced $3,198,000,000, He Says; Speech on Radio

By Universal Service.

WASHINGTON, Jan. 26.—The now familiar economy theme, with a plea for still further cuts in government expenditures, was the keynote of President Coolidge's speech before the semiannual meeting of the business organization of the government tonight.

The meeting, which was attended by the heads of all branches of the government service which have a hand in the spending of the people's money, was broadcast by stations WCAP and WEAF, the first time one of the government's business meetings has been sent on the air. The President said:

"So far as it is within my power, I propose to continue my efforts for economy in federal expenditures. What we have done must be considered only the beginning."

He pointed out that expenditures for the fiscal year 1921 reached $5,538,000,000, while those for the present year will probably be kept within $3,534,000,000, a reduction of $2,004,000,000 in four years.

The President asked officials to keep down the government costs for the present year within the three billion dollar limit. On the basis of present estimates, this will require a cut of about $62,000,000 by the end of June.

Results Answer Critics.

During the same four years, he continued, there has been a reduction in the public debt of approximately $3,198,000,000. This has resulted in a reduction of the annual interest on the debt from $999,000,000 to $865,000,000, a saving of $134,000,000 each year.

Tax reductions therefore have amounted to about $2,000,000,000 yearly, according to the President.

"If the practice of economy is not popular, the results of it are viewed with tremendous satisfaction," he said. "Let those who are inclined to scoff at it, those who are inclined to refer to it as cheese paring, look at the results it has accomplished. They will find there an answer which is complete and overwhelming.

"No longer are the funds appropriated by Congress regarded as the minimum amount to be expended. Every dollar that is saved by careful administration adds to the amount by which taxes may be reduced in the future.

"It is practical economy which I have in mind and which we must practice. I had rather talk of saving pennies, and save them, than

Turn to Page 2, Column 2.

Mellon Insists All Nations Pay Uncle Sam

By Universal Service.

WASHINGTON, Jan. 26.

SECRETARY OF THE TREASURY MELLON is firmly opposed to any proposal involving cancellation of France's debt to the United States or of any other debts growing out of the war. It was said for Secretary Mellon at the Treasury Department today that his policy as a member of the debt commission will be to insist upon payment by the nations which are indebted to the United States. Treasury officials are awaiting France's next move, which they believe will come from M. Emile Daeshner, the new French ambassador.

(Other news of the debt situation on Page 2.)

THREE HEROES DIE IN CAISSON

Suffocate Trying to Rescue Mate; Fifth Workman Braves Gas and Recovers Bodies.

COLUMBUS, O., Jan. 26.—A gas-filled shaft, forty-seven feet deep, within a caisson of the new American Insurance Union Building here, claimed the lives of four men today, three of the victims going to their doom as heroes.

A fifth man who went to the rescue of his pals in the shaft came through unscathed and a few hours later a movement was started intended to fittingly reward him.

The dead are: C. R. Bowen, 22, Greenwood, Ind.; Jack Smith, New York; John C. McCarthy, 48, New York, and John Peterson, 22, Columbus. All were steamfitters.

It is believed Bowen was in the shaft fitting pipes when he was overcome and fell to the bottom. The others climbed down to rescue him but failed to come back.

All was quiet within the tube and workmen gathered. Ambulances and physicians were summoned.

Suddenly a huge crane swung high into the air from another part of the excavation. Dangling from its steel cable was William V. ("Big Bill") Martin, a structural steel worker. Fellow workmen remonstrated. Three had gone down and had not come back, they told him.

"Big Bill" snapped his fingers and signaled the crane engineer. Some one handed him a gas mask and he was dropped into the shaft.

Minutes seemed like hours to the watchers. The cable jerked. The crane moved upward and out came the limp form of a man, a rope around his waist.

Three more bodies followed.

The cable jerked again. Out came "Big Bill." He clung to the cable desperately. His face was ashen white. The gas mask was gone.

The bosses said that "Big Bill" found the four dead men at the bottom of the shaft and that he had reported that he worked as fast as he could in getting them out. He took off his mask when it hampered him, he said.

Dr. Sun Yat Sen Has Cancer; Case Hopeless

PEKING, Jan. 26.—(AP)—An operation performed on Dr. Sun Yat Sen, head of the so-called South China government, revealed that he is suffering from cancer of the liver. His case is hopeless, physicians say.

EXPERTS URGE CITY TAKE OVER STREET CARS

Duplication of Properties Would Cost at Least $176,500,000, Report Says.

BIG EARNINGS INCREASE

Aldermen Will Discuss Figures in Detail at Session Today.

BY JOHN W. DIENHART.

The three engineers retained by the city to appraise the Chicago Surface Lines reported yesterday that the bankers' demand for $162,843,584.07 for the system is not excessive.

They said the price is the "present fair value of these properties for the purpose of purchase by the city."

If the city, however, were to pay only the amount of money actually put into the system, the price would be $141,773,000, Maj. R. F. Kelker, the city's representative on the board, reported.

Hold Duplication Costly.

William J. Hagenah, representing the bankers, and Gen. William B. Parsons, selected as the "neutral" member, said this figure should be $167,180,727.

The value of the lines, on the basis of reproduction at present prices, less depreciation, is $176,500,000, Maj. Kelker added. Mr. Hagenah said the sum would be from $204,308,669 to $245,621,621. Gen. Parsons did not mention any figure, but said his estimate would be even greater than Mr. Hagenah's.

The engineers agreed that the average market value of the lines' securities during their eighteen years of operation has been $129,395,777, as against the average capital account, or purchase price, of $131,614,872.

Rapid Earnings Increase.

Concerning the earnings, the report said the gross receipts jumped from $18,823,094 in 1908 to about $58,015,000 for the present fiscal period.

After deducting all operating expenses, including contributions to the renewal fund, taxes, the payment of 55 per cent of the net divisible receipts into the city's traction fund and payment of 5 per cent on the bonded debt, the net earnings have jumped from $1,280,143 in 1908 to $1,337,648 for the last year.

The average net earnings during the last four years has been $1,635,383.

The future growth of passengers may be expected to jump from 824,000,000 this year to 1,354,000,000 twenty years hence.

"Assuming that the properties shall be operated efficiently, the present and prospective net earnings warrant the city, in our opinion, in making the purchase at the ordinance purchase price," the report noted.

Realty Worth $8,937,277.

The engineers also agreed that the $20,000,000 of valuation allowed by the Illinois Public Utilities Commission on November 5, 1920, for "going value" is a fair figure and should be sustained. It is included in the proposed sale price.

The physical condition of the properties is "excellent," the report continued. It pointed out that a maintenance fund of $19,000,000 exists. This also is included in the purchase price.

The companies' real estate is worth $8,937,277. This includes thirteen parcels of real estate not used for railroad operation.

The committee on local transportation will meet again today to study the report.

Mayor Dever declined to comment on the findings. He said he was opposed to having the appraisal committee appointed, but that the committee decided on such a course to determine what a fair price should be.

British Plane to Speed Mile in 12 Seconds

Herald and Examiner-Universal Special Cable.

LONDON, Jan. 26.

BRITAIN is secretly building a seaplane with a speed of five miles per minute to compete for the Schneider cup, the Daily Express says. The machine is said to be stream-lined from end to end, with the engine let into the fusilage.

ZERO WAVE TO END TOMORROW

Relief Promised From Cold Which Rode Into Chicago on Gale-Driven Snowstorm.

[Picture on Back Page.]

The snow storm that whirled over the city intermittently earlier yesterday was intensified into blizzard proportions shortly before midnight and raged through the night, sending the mercury further downward and hindering traffic.

The cold wave from the west will continue today, according to Forecaster C. A. Donnel of the weather bureau. No relief is in sight until tomorrow.

His prediction yesterday was for temperatures ranging from zero to 5 above by early morning, if the wind remains at north-northwest. Should the wind change, and blow from the west, he added, temperatures considerably lower might be expected, for the west is in the grip of a below-zero cold wave.

Should the wind come from directly north, the temperature may only reach ten above. By this afternoon, according to observations, the mercury will read fifteen, and by tomorrow afternoon the temperature probably will reach normal—thirty. Higher temperatures may be expected by the end of the week.

Traffic Slowed Up.

Yesterday's storm, which brought high winds, and a half-inch snowfall, was influenced by the Alaska storm, parts of which have spread to various parts of the country, particularly to the northeastern states, where a below-zero storm raged several days ago.

There has been considerable deficiency in the amount of snowfall this Winter. With the warm wave of the last several days, and the thaw, the storm was felt more keenly than ordinarily. Slippery rails slowed up street car and elevated traffic, and icy walks added to the dangers of pedestrians and motorists.

Blizzard Down State.

PANA, Ill., Jan. 26.—Pana and central Illinois are in the grip of a severe blizzard tonight with mercury two below zero, a drop of 34 degrees in ten hours. Heavy snow is falling, which is expected to protect the wheat crop.

Booth Tarkington Beats $500,000 Damage Suit

LOS ANGELES, Jan. 26.—Booth Tarkington, author, defeated a $500,000 damage suit against him here today without even appearing in court. He was sued by Miss Maud Greenwood, of Palestine, Texas, who alleged he had stolen her plot for one of his film works. The Superior Court threw out the case.

Barnard Senior Leaps to Death From Eighth Story

NEW YORK, Jan. 26.—Helen E. Vosburgh, 23, brilliant Barnard College senior and daughter of a wealthy Norwalk, Conn., judge, leaped to her death today from an eighth-story window in Brooks Hall as fellow students, on their way to classes, cried warnings to her not to leap.

Verses by a Nine-Year-Old Poetess, in next Sunday's HERALD AND EXAMINER. Circulation Over

ACTORS OPEN NATION-WIDE FIGHT ON RADIO

Equity Union's Move to Protect Spoken Drama Includes Plan to Curb Movies.

BRADY CHAMPIONS CAUSE

"Air Raids" and Films Have Ousted Legitimate Play in 34 States, He Asserts.

NEW YORK, Jan. 26.—The Actors' Equity Association launched a movement this evening to organize the entire theatrical industry to resist radio, compete with moving pictures and safeguard the stage as a national institution.

Resolutions were adopted unanimously at a mass meeting in the Forty-eighth St. Theater, representing all branches of the drama, by which committees are to be appointed to form a central body with country-wide authority.

The resolutions outlined the most ambitious program for theatrical development ever attempted. While radio was the chief subject, united action is to be taken toward the abolition of censorship, the repeal of the tax on tickets and the legalizing of children's acting and the creation of a propaganda department for the spoken play.

The restoration of one-night stands, the doubling of the number of stock companies and the increasing of traveling tent and repertoire productions is included.

Brady Backs Move.

William A. Brady, the bitterest foe of radio among managers, rose from a sick bed to speak. He asserted that since the actors' strike, he had become a champion of Equity and proclaimed his pride in it.

"I've heard people here say that radio helps the stage, but let me tell you that the night John McCormack went on the air, Marcus Leow's chain of theaters played to 40 per cent reduced receipts. I know that the Longacre Square was deserted on election night as a result of the 'air raid.'

"In Washington the Sterling bill is pending which will permit radio to broadcast any play, book, music, or other form of entertainment without paying a penny to the owners. My own booking agent tells me that in Massachusetts and Connecticut 90 per cent of the theaters don't want spoken plays of any kind. Texas, Alabama, Georgia, Colorado, Tennessee, Washington, Montana, the Dakotas and other states, thirty-four in all, are virtually closed to the spoken play. And they call me an alarmist for raising my voice!"

Gene Buck, leader of the composers, authors and publishers, said: "There are 540 broadcasting stations now and in ten years there will be only fifty-four and later perhaps only ten, but they will cover the country. This is the most important problem facing the theater.

Envisages Dire Future.

"What is to prevent the Radio Corporation of America from organizing the greatest dramatic company on earth and relaying plays over every station every night? Or they could pay Paul Whiteman $25,000 a week to give a nightly concert, and hook up every home, dance hall and motion picture theater in

Turn to Page 2, Column 4.

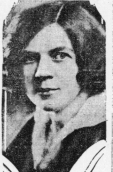

Vanishes

ETHEL LEGINSKA, only woman orchestra leader in the world, who disappeared in New York last night when her secretary left her a moment to call a cab.

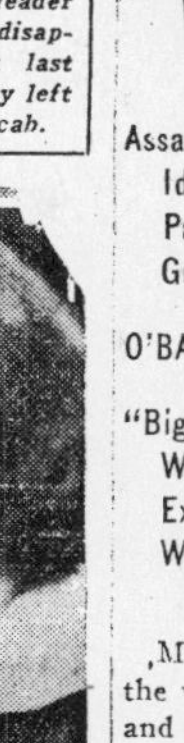

ETHEL LEGINSKA PIANIST, LOST

Famous Musician Vanishes While Crowd Waits at Theater; Amnesia Feared.

NEW YORK, Jan. 26.—Ethel Leginska, orchestral director, concert pianist and composer, mysteriously vanished tonight.

While a capacity audience waited in Carnegie Hall, where she was to give a recital, her first appearance here since February 20, 1923, she dropped from sight.

With Lucile Oliver, her secretary, Miss Leginska left her studio apartment at 7:40 p. m.

She waited while Miss Oliver went for a cab. Returning, the secretary found Miss Leginska gone.

After a hasty search, Miss Oliver rushed to Carnegie Hall. Miss Leginska had not arrived. At 8:15 p. m., the time for the recital to begin, she was still missing. The excited managers telephoned police.

Substitute Takes Place.

The audience was informed that Miss Leginska had been delayed. Later the management offered to refund admission money, but most of the audience decided to remain, when Mieczyslaw Inunz, pianist, volunteered to substitute.

To relieve anxious friends in the audience, announcement was made that Miss Leginska had been delayd by traffic.

Meanwhile Miss Oliver and police were canvassing the city. Hospitals were checked, her haunts were visited, but she was not found.

Friends said Miss Leginska had become nervous as the time for her recital approached. This worry mounted when at practice she split two finger tips. This might have brought on amnesia.

Famous for Temperament.

Since her first appearance here in 1912 Miss Leginska has been internationally recognized as an interpreter of Chopin. She is almost as famous for eccentricities, which have earned her the soubriquet, "The Tempestuous English Pianist." She strove for boyishness in looks and helped to introduce the fashion of bobbed hair.

She was divorced in 1918 from Roy Emerson Whittern, composer, by whom she had a son, Cedric, now 16.

DEATH TRA[P] SET BY GANG TO SILENCE WITNESSE[S]

Assassins, Desperate in Fear [of] Identification, Seek to L[ure] Pair to Lonely Spot; Pol[ice] Guard Doubled at Hospi[tal]

O'BANION PAL IS ARREST[ED]

"Big" Moran Indentified by [a] Witness of Shooting; Wa[r of] Extermination Expec[ted;] White Slavery Cause H[ ]

[Picture on Back Page.]

Mrs. John Torrio, wife [of] the wounded underworld ru[ler], and his chief lieutenant, "Sc[ar]face Al" Capone, have b[een] marked for immediate de[ath] in the war of exterminati[on] now raging in gangland, [it] was learned by the police la[st] night.

A bold attempt to lure both within range of gangmen's bullets was made last evening. It will be followed by other attempts, Captain of Detectives John Stege has been informed.

While the police were striving to avert this new danger, George Moran, pal of the slain Dean O'Banion, and known as a gangster and friend of "Tommy" O'Connor, who had been seized earlier in the day, was identified at the Detective bureau as one of the men who shot Torrio.

He was picked out from a group of twelve men by Peter Vezert, [a]n eye witness to the shooti[ng.] Moran strenuously denied he was party to the attempt to kill Torr[io.]

Pledge Immediate Death.

Mrs. Torrio must die, Torrio's [ri]vals have decreed, because she saw the would-be assassins of her husband last Saturday and knows their identity.

Fear that her feminine impulses might lead her to betray the gunmen, if she sees them in police custody, has added to the determination to "get her immediately," according to the police.

A mysterious telephone cal[l] sought twice last evening t[o lure] Mrs. Torrio from the Jacks[on Park] Hospital, where her husband [is fight]ing for life, to a lonely spot [at Sev]enty-third st. and Stony Isla[nd av.]

A girl's voice called first [on the] telephone. She announced [herself] as "long distance" and said [Cleve]land was calling Mrs. Joh[n Tor]rio." The call was connec[ted to] Mrs. Torrio's room, adjoin[ing that] of her husband. She answ[ered and] the girl caller yielded the [phone] to a man. He gave a na[me] Mrs. Torrio did not recogn[ize.]

"I'm in Cleveland now," t[he man] said, "but I'm leaving for [ ] at 10:45 tonight. Now, lis[ten care]fully. This is important, an[d so is] Capone.

Lays Plan to Trap H[im.]

"There's a man within a [ ] the hospital right now w[ho has] some information that mu[st reach] Johnny right away. It's [ ] to him. You and Al go to [the cor]ner of Seventy-third st. a[nd Stony] Island av. in half an h[our and] you'll find this fellow wait[ing. Don't] fail."

Frightened, Mrs. Torri[o told her] husband and then Cap[t.] McCauey of the Woodl[awn station.] An investigation proved t[he call was] local, not long distance. [Capt. Mc]Cauley deemed the fact [import]ant he called Capt. Steg[e. The in]formation dovetailed wi[th informa]tion of the death plot t[o] come to the detective [ ] ordered Mrs. Torrio [ ] rushed to the bureau [under] guard.

Mrs. Torrio, Miss C[ ] sister of Johnny; Al [ ]

Turn to Page 10, C[olumn]

TRY OUR SCRAM[BLED COM]ICS. Prize[s] [illegible]

BUCKET OF WATER TO PLAY SOLOMON TO RIVAL MOTHERS

PHILADELPHIA, Jan. 26.—A bucket of water will be used in court tomorrow to determine whether a 3-year-old boy belongs to Mrs. Russell Earl Steinling of Girard Manor or to Mrs. Martha Silknitter, laundress, and [illegible] of them claim him, and by [illegible] as both.

Miss Mary Steinling suggested that a bucket of water be brought, and that if the child were Russell Steinling he would immediately attempt to sit in it, as Russell had a penchant for such informal immersions in mud puddles.

The court agreed to the test.

PRETTY GIRLS TO HELP WIN BUNDESEN TO OYSTER DIET

BALTIMORE, Jan. 26.—When Health Commissioner Bundesen of Chicago arrives in Baltimore tomorrow morning to begin [his] investigation of [illegible] invitation [illegible] will be tendered an "oyster breakfast," with pretty chorus girls serving the maligned bivalves. The Maryland governor confer[illegible]

THE NATIONAL KOURIER

"Put Americans on Guard."—George Washington.

VOLUME 4, NUMBER 31 | Office of Publication, 315-317 G Street N. W., Washington, D. C. | WASHINGTON, D. C., FRIDAY, JUNE 19, 1925. | Entered as Second-Class Matter, Post Office, Washington, D. C. | PRICE FIVE CENTS

NATION'S CAPITAL TO WITNESS GIANT KLAN PARADE

Mayor Curley of Boston Heads Crusade of Intolerance

PROTESTANTS OF HUB CITY ROUTED FROM BOSTON HALLS

Department Heads, Including Crawley, Glynn, Mahoney, Casey and Mickelajowski, Lead Raids Ordered by Roman Catholic Official.

CLINTON OFFICIALS TO GO TO GOVERNOR

Continued Physical Assaults On Protestants to Be Protested by City Head; Newspapers Begin to Ask Questions.

(By Staff Correspondent.)

Boston, Mass., June 15.—With the declaration of Fire Commissioner Glynn, backed by Mayor Curley, Roman Catholic, that "he would condemn any hall in which the Klan attempted to meet, and the city officials of Clinton declaring that they are going to the Governor in an attempt to stop the brutal assaults being made on Klansmen, the riot of intolerance on the part of Roman Catholics and other foreigners in Massachusetts continues here today.

If the rulings of Fire Commissioner Glynn, in his effort to thwart the Ku Klux Klan are carried out by hotels, it will be necessary to close their parlors or keep employes stationed to see that not more than three guests congregate in any of the large and spacious parlors provided by the leading hotels. Neither could a man and wife and two small children occupy the same hotel room, unless a fire escape ran directly out of that room, if the hotels diligently carry out the commands of Fire Commissioner Glynn in finding a "law" whereby he can estop Klansmen from organizing in Boston.

Police Rout Americans.

On two occasions last week, Fire Inspector Glynn, Superintendent Crawley, Building Inspector Mahoney, and about twenty fire inspectors and police officers, acting under the orders of Mayor Curley, broke up two Klan meetings in different halls. The show of intolerance now being made in Boston, is almost beyond the belief of American citizens. The names of the officials already mentioned, however, will give the reader an inkling of from just where the attack is being made.

The pretext being made that the halls from which the Klansmen were ejected were not complying with the fire laws is but a reflection on the city administration if the charge made is true. But as one citizen pointed out, the fire inspectors seem to get to no halls except those in which Klansmen are meeting.

"Why," said one Bostonian, "did the squad sent out by Mayor Curley, cease operations when the Klansmen were routed. Hundreds of other meetings were going on in all parts of the town, including those of the Knights of Columbus and other Irish and papal organizations. Isn't it absurd to assume that the only halls in town which should be condemned are those which Klansmen happen to rent for their meetings? Where is this squad on nights on which the Klan does not meet, or at least on nights when it meets and the police know nothing about it? Is it supposed to look for

(Continued on page two.)

Mexico Starts Fight Against Pulque Drinking

Federal Health Department To Educate People On Intemperance Evil.

(Special to The Kourier.)

Mexico City, Mexico, June 15.—The Federal Department of Health has launched a campaign of education of the Mexican people calculated to convince them of the detrimental and injurious effects of intoxicating liquors. Quantities of pamphlets and circulars will be distributed by government agencies throughout the republic, in which the injurious effects of alcohol will be emphasized. Pulque is the national drink in Mexico and according to official investigations of the pulque traffic this city alone consumes 132,000 gallons daily. In Pachuca, capital of the state of Hidalgo, consumption runs to 33,000 gallons and Puebla, second city in Mexico, consumes 20,000 gallons. Five million pesos of annual Federal taxes levied against the producers of the drink has not visibly reduced production.

PASTOR PRAISES ORDER FOR CHRISTIAN SUPPORT

Falmouth, Ky., June 15.—Pendleton Klan No. 12 conducted the dedication exercises of the Methodist Church at Caddo, Ky. About 500 Klansmen in equipment participated in the exercises.

Pendleton Klan also contributed the sum of $150 toward paying off the debt on this church. The pastor of the church in an eloquent address, praised the Klan, and thanked Pendleton Klan for their participation and substantial donation.

Negro's Anti-Klan Bill Is Killed In Illinois

Springfield, Ill., June 15.—The house killed an anti-Ku Klux Klan bill sponsored by Representative William E. King, negro, Chicago. The vote was taken following arguments against the bill and an impassioned plea for it by King.

Although it was subjected to bitter attacks from every angle not a word was spoken in defense of the Klan. All the arguments against the bill were based on the policy involved. Even some who opposed the bill scored the organization.

THREATS FAIL TO HALT PARADE IN NEW JERSEY

Klansmen From Scene of Alien Riots Are in Line of March.

OPEN AIR MEET HELD

Middlesex County Has First Celebration of Summer Season.

(Special to The Kourier.)

Spottswood, N. J., June 15. Cheers greeted the Perth Amboy delegation of Klansmen as they swung along the line of march in the long parade given here by the Middlesex County organization. The South Amboy delegation also were greeted with applause. It was at these two places riots occurred, in which aliens viciously attacked and beat Americans. Undaunted, however, the two local units have grown and responded to the appeal of Americanism. At South Amboy was the "church riot" when Roman Catholics attacked the church and afterward attacked those who were in attendance at what they termed "a Klan meeting." The riots at Perth Amboy, more than a year ago, will long be remembered as one of the worst in the county. At that time it was necessary for Masons to remove their Masonic pins and rings to save themselves from brutal attacks by Roman Catholics and other alien mobs. Many Klansmen were beaten unconscious the first night of the riot.

All Towns Represented.

All of the towns in this county were represented in the parade as were a number of Klan units from the surrounding counties. The parade was a part of the first open celebration for this season. The meeting was attended by a crowd estimated at approximately 12,000 Klansmen. The parade was led by the Burlington County Klan Band.

Preceding the parade, addresses were delivered by officials of the organization in New Jersey. The celebration was closed with a brilliant display of fireworks. During the event refreshments were served on the grounds. Amplifiers carried the words of the speakers to all parts of large grounds in which the meeting was held.

The meeting was held on a tract of land embracing about twelve acres. A smaller tract in connection with that used for the meeting, was held open for parking purposes.

Pay No Attention to Threats.

In the face of open threats from the enemy that the Klan dare not parade in this county. Despite the many threats, however, there was no trouble of any kind. This probably was due to the fact that Klansmen appeared in greater numbers than usually and it has always been an outstanding feature of the alien attacks that they will never attack without having an advantage of about ten to one or more.

Kansas Busy Filling National Bread Basket

(Special to The Kourier.)

Kansas City, June 15.—Wheat harvest is under way in Kansas.

The whir of reapers and binders was heard in fields of Southwestern Kansas today, presaging the swelling chorus to come when the gathering of the state's contribution to the national bread basket gets into full swing the middle of this month.

The harvest march northward through the state is not expected to end until the last week in June, when the extreme northern counties are cleared of their crops.

Gas Filling Stations Wear Out Paper Money As Well As Pocketbooks

Gasoline filling stations are one of the two great causes for the life of paper currency decreasing from a year to seven months since the close of the war, a survey by the United States bureau of efficiency has developed.

The ever increasing number of automobiles causes more money to be spent on gasoline and oil and thus to be handled by greasy, dirty hands that discolors the bills and weakens their tensile strength, officials say. This leads to their early discard. The second great reason is that a dollar's purchasing power has dropped to about 60 cents and people carry about twice the number of bills on their persons they did previously. This subjects more bills to folding and frequent handling.

California Pastor Sticks to Post

Priest's Act Forces Widow Into Hysteria at Funeral

Appears at Home and Demands Roman Services for Man Who Died a Protestant; Threat to Call Police Necessary to Halt Disgrace.

(Special to The Kourier.)

Toronto, Ont., June 15.—Much sympathy today is felt for the widow of Peter Minchelli, an Italian who gave his life to save a fellow workman, and who has just been buried here. Mrs. Minchelli was forced into a most harrowing scene at the funeral of her husband, who was a Methodist, when a Roman Catholic priest came to the home during the funeral services and insisted that the deceased was a Roman Catholic. It was necessary that friends threaten to call the police before the priest would leave the house. The sorrowing widow was completely overcome by the added distress caused by the priest. The three Minchelli children attended the Baptist Sunday School, the faith which Mrs. Minchelli professes. At one time the whole family were Roman Catholics and this brought an uninvited visit from Roman Catholic sisters immediately after the death of Mr. Minchelli. It was explained to them that the family were no longer Roman Catholics. This did not, however, deter the priest from intruding at the time of the funeral service.

Nuns Are Insistent.

At the time of the visit of the nuns, they insisted that the husband be given a Roman Catholic funeral. Mrs. Minchelli explained that they were not members of the Roman Church and that Rev. D. R. Gualoeri, of the Elm Street Methodist church, was to have charge of the funeral services. Rev. Gualoeri was just opening the services when the priest arrived.

The priest went immediately to the side of the casket and turned and spoke to the widow.

"Your husband," he said, "is a Catholic and must have a Catholic funeral."

"No," replied the sorrowing woman, "my husband was a Methodist. He left the Catholic church some time ago."

"But you are a Catholic," said the priest.

"No, not now," she replied. "I feel I have done better."

"But your children are Catholics. They were baptized in the church."

"That is true, they were baptized in the Catholic church, but they now attend the Baptist Sunday school. Won't you please leave? This is distressing."

Refuses to Leave.

The priest, who was accompanied by a man who said he was from the "Children's Aid Society," then became abusive and with Mrs. Minchelli bordering on hysteria, friends requested that he leave. This he refused to do and a friend of the Minchelli family threatened to call the police that the funeral might proceed. With bitter words, the Roman Catholic priest withdrew.

The services were then resumed and the deceased, who was electrocuted when falling in high voltage wires while saving another's life, was given a Protestant burial.

JEW OBJECTS TO JUNIORS GIFT TO PUBLIC SCHOOL

Wants Kendallville, Indiana, to Return Falg to American Boys.

(Special to The Kourier.)

Kendallville, Ind., June 15.—Recent attempts by a non-resident of Kendallville to force a public school to return an American flag presented to the school by the Junior Klan has ended in defeat for the non-resident, a Jew who formerly lived in Kendallville. A number of Jews and Roman Catholics living in this city were much disturbed over the gift to the school but could not muster up courage to demand that the gift be returned.

It was for this reason that an outside party was called in. The efforts of the Jew were without avail and the flag is still in its accustomed place where first hung upon being presented. Just why this man believes that he has a right to dictate to the local schools is not quite clear to patriotic residents and taxpayers.

Many harsh words have been spoken of the Juniors by alien-minded persons but these are not noticed. The boys are continuing their building of their organization and are thriving. Harsh words have no effect on them.

THE OLDEST NEWSPAPER

What is the oldest newspaper in the United States? The Philadelphia North American until its purchase by Cyrus H. K. Curtis and its combination with the Public Ledger held that distinction. The Chambersburg Weekly Repository now claims the honor. It has had a continuous existence since 1790.

SPELL-BINDER TALKS TO 2,000 AT CHATHAM

National Lecturer of Wide Reputation Induces Many to Become Americans.

(Special to The Kourier.)

Chatham, Ill., June 15.—Chatham Klan No. 131 accompanied by the Ku Klux Kazoo and the local drum and bugle corps, held a monstrous parade at Loami, Illinois, last Thursday night, June 4th. The parade, which was several blocks long, consisted of Klansmen, Klanswomen and Juniors.

This was the first appearance of the season for the Klan in this section, and was well received by the public. In addition to the parade a public speaking was held in the city park.

A national lecturer of wide reputation delivered an address on Americanism. The crowd, estimated at about two thousand, was held spellbound by Mr. Moore for almost two hours. Application cards were passed throughout the crowd and a great many were signed and turned in.

GIVES $2,000,000 MORE TO DUKE UNIVERSITY

(Special to The Kourier.)

Durham, N. C., June 15.—An additional gift of $2,000,000 by James B. Duke, tobacco magnate, to Duke University, was announced today by President R. P. Few, of the institution. The gift increases the building fund previously created by Mr. Duke to $8,000,000.

To Examine Aliens in Their Own Lands Before Leaving

(Special to The Kourier.)

New York, June 15.—Recent discussion and agitation to conduct the physical examination of those seeking admission into the United States as immigrants in their own country before leaving for America, is now under consideration by the British government. It is argued that much hardships to the immigrants may thus be avoided as well as useless expense saved to both the interested countries.

The negotiations are the result of a visit of the official American commission consisting of Court Dubois, chief of the State Department visa office; R. C. White, assistant Secretary of Labor, and Dr. J. W. Kerr, assistant chief of the public health service, who came abroad for the purpose of preparing a report on the question.

These American representatives have just returned from the Irish Free State, where, it is understood the new system is likely to be tried out first.

The free state government, it is reliably stated, has agreed to the American suggestion, but under a provision of the Anglo-Irish treaty which would make a consent of the British government necessary. This, of course, would be required in the case of emigrants from Great Britain and Northern Ireland.

Though negotiations with the British government still are in an informal stage, it is said the foreign office already has taken the position that if the government agrees to physical examination being held here, then there must be no question about successful applicants being admitted to America once they have obtained the United States visa here.

The American plan, as at present contemplated, provides that, before obtaining the United States visa the prospective emigrant should undergo a physical examination in his country similar to that now given on arrival at Ellis Island. However, as the visa is good four months from date of issue, it would be necessary for the emigrant to have another, though minor, examination just before sailing, to make sure he or she had not contracted any illness or disease, or suffered any serious injury during the interval.

After completing its work here, the American commission probably will go to the continent for a similar investigation there.

DELIVERS HIS LECTURE AFTER ASSAULTED IN ANAHEIM STREET

Los Angeles Dailies Carry Big Headlines Covering Affair; Klan Continues to Have Substantial Growth.

SECOND RECALL OF CITY HEADS PREDICTED

Hostile Crowd Surrounds Church Which Is Packed to Hear Pastor; Police Arrest Man Delivering Bills.

(Special to The Kourier.)

Anaheim, Calif., June 15.—It is confidently predicted here that as soon as it is legally possible to take the steps, that a recall of city officials will be attempted in this city. This will be the second such occurrence to take place in Anaheim, the first now being regretted by many citizens who now declare that they were not well informed on city affairs when they took part in the former recall. At that time men were recalled from office who had been very active against the bootlegging element here.

Since the recall, however, a Protestant minister, known to be active against the Roman Catholic influence in politics, has been physically assaulted and many other things have taken place which has not been to the liking of the better class of citizens. Also, during this time, due to the moves made against the Protestant organization, its ranks have grown to much greater numbers.

Reporters Flock to City.

The assault on Rev. Leon L. Myers, the day before he was to deliver a lecture, believed by Roman Catholics to be one in which he would give certain facts about the city which would not reflect to the credit of the Roman machine, brought many reporters here from larger cities. The Los Angeles dailies carried large headlines on the story.

In a circular distributed about the city, announcing the lecture of Rev. Myers, the following questions were asked: "Will a Rome controlled administration enforce the law?" and "Is Anaheim now controlled by Rome?" The following day Rev. Myers was assaulted by a man whom it was declared was about to be appointed to the police department. It was also declared that he was a friend to another potential appointee of the department who had not long before lost a high priced automobile by it being confiscated while carrying illicit liquor.

Police Hold Worker.

When the bills were being distributed one of the workers were held by the police and taken to the police station. No charge was placed against him and he was turned loose without the circulars he had left when taken in tow by the police.

When the present chief of police, Charles B. Nichols, was appointed, it was stated that he would make a good officer and had held the office of sheriff in Cattaragus county, N. Y. During his lecture, which was held despite the physical assault on the preceding day, Rev. Myers read a newspaper account of the sentencing of a Charles B. Nichols, of New York, to the penitentiary for grand larceny some years before that. The speaker declared the men to be the same persons. The article stated that the courthouse from which the Nichols was sentenced had been "in keeping for three years."

Ugly Crowd Gathers.

On the night of the lecture, despite the fact that many rumors of violence had been persistent, there was no interference, although a crowd, quite apparently hostile, gathered near the church.

During all of this time the Klan has been growing steadily in numbers. The organization is gaining an excellent footing here as in other parts of California.

200,000 Aliens Smuggled Into U. S. Unlawfully

Ellis Island officials last week estimated that more than 330,000 aliens lawfully entered the country during the first nine months' operation of the Selective Immigration Law, although only 140,000 were admitted under quota provisions.

The large number of exemptions allowed under the Johnson law caused the excess immigration, officials explained. At least 200,000 other aliens are believed to have been smuggled into the country.

With twenty-three days before the end of the fiscal year and with many quotas nearly filled, immigration inspectors expect a rush of aliens this week. The Italian liner Conte Rosso, the Columbus of the North German Lloyd and the Cunarder Aquitania, which docked Saturday, brought 1,000 aliens, most of whom had been examined by nightfall. Five hundred others are detained on Ellis Island pending further examination and appeal.

Oklahoma Bishop Mesmerizes Cash From Protestants With Which to Fight Americanism

(Special to The Kourier.)

Oklahoma City, June 15.—The program of the Catholic hierarchy concerning the spiritual annexation of Oklahoma to Rome, of which there has been much evidence since the first of this year, is outlined in a recent letter of Bishop Kelley and published in the official organ of the diocese. Citizens of Oklahoma are indebted to the bishop for so much of his plans as he chooses to make public.

"A million dollars wisely expended here," says the bishop, "and in a few years the seeds would be sprouted. Soon after the sprouts would be above the ground, Catholic education would flourish, a native priesthood would be an assured fact; neat churches and schools would dot the land; our colored brethren would be increased by thousands; missionaries would be wherever a remnant of the Indians could be found; the faith would have hundreds of new apologists; the diocese would have a modest Cathedral;" etc., etc.

Important, it seems, is the plan to extend "Catholic education." Although public schools now "dot the land," and Oklahoma spends millions every year for education, the subject is treated as if the state were a wilderness of ignorance and a school were a curiosity. This is official acknowledgement of the fact that the Roman church does not recognize public schools, and as much may prove to be of some enlightenment to many Protestants who have permitted themselves to be deluded and deceived on this point.

There appears sufficient evidence that the bishop already has at his command the necessary million dollars, if not much more, for the purposes of promotion and publicity. This is to say nothing of the three or four millions which is to be invested in church and school and hospital buildings now in course of construction or soon to be built in this state.

Meanwhile, since the Protestants are in a large majority, the good bishop goes on collecting Protestant money to further his plans for building up a competitive system of religious teaching and education, calculated to overthrow Protestantism and public schools. None seem so blind as those who are too busy to see.

UNIT AT ALBERT LEA PURCHASES A NEW KLAVERN

Six Thousand Attend Dedicatory Ceremonies—Long Parade Is Cheered.

(Special to The Kourier.)

Albert Lea, Minn., June 15.—Meetings are now being held in the newly dedicated Klavern of the Klan for which the dedication services were recently held. The services were in charge of a local minister. The Klavern was recently purchased by the Freeborn County Klan and was the center of a large celebration held here on Memorial Day. Approximately six thousand Klansmen and Klanswomen attended the celebration from Southern Minnesota.

During the day a number of addresses were delivered by brilliant speakers and the principal address was by the Imperial Representative of this state. The Albert Lea Klan orchestra furnished music during the day. The dedication ceremony took place in the evening. This was followed by a parade through the principal streets of the city. Thousands of spectators packed the line of march. The marchers wore their visors up.

Following the parade, the K-Uno degree was exemplified in full form by the crack St. Paul team and real credit is due them for the efficient manner in which the work was done. The Women of the Klan initiated a large class of candidates in an adjoining Klavern at the same time.

KLANSMEN AID AUTHORITIES IN SEARCH FOR MEN

Terrorizing of Virginia Family Results In Scouring County.

(Special to The Kourier.)

Fraconia, Va., June 15.—Klansmen are today receiving much praise for their cooperation with the local officials here in the attempt to run down the person or persons who are terrorizing the family of Norman Gill, a farmer living near here. Friday night approximately one hundred Klansmen joined with the authorities and continued an all night search, beating the bush for miles in all directions. To this date, however, the culprits have not been apprehended.

Despite the fact that Mrs. Gill has been attacked by having red pepper thrown in her face; stones have been hurled at an eight-year-old daughter and an attempt made to burn the house, it was stated that Fairfax county authorities were "taking the incident lightly." This, however, could not be confirmed.

It is also stated that a note has now been received by the Gill family with orders to move from the county. Gill says he has no enemies and believes the work that of an escaped lunatic. A strange white man has been seen in the vicinity and it is believed possible that it is he who has committed the depredations.

Cowardly Rowdies Attack Protestant Jersey Youth on Suspicion of Being Klansman

Mob of Alleged Roman Catholics Knock 17-Year-Old Boy to Ground, Breaking His Nose and Brutally Kicking Him When He Lay Senseless.

(Special to The Kourier.)

New Brunswick, N. J., June 15.—Feeling runs high in New Brunswick because of a dastardly assault made on Albert Lindemann, a 17-year-old high school student, Protestant, while walking quietly with a boy companion, through the streets of the city. Foes of the Klan attacked him, knocking him to the ground, breaking his nose, and hitting and bruising him all over his body. The young man's sole offense, as given by the cowardly assailants themselves, was that his father was suspected of being a member of the Protestant American organization, the Knights of the Ku Klux Klan.

In the company of his young friend the pair were walking quietly down the street when they were halted and accused by a crowd of rowdies alleged to be Roman Catholics of being Klansmen. They paid no attention to veiled threats that were made, but proceeded on about their business. On their return the Lindemann boy was stopped by the same crowd which showed its proficiency in the use of vile language by applying all sorts of indecent epithets to him. The boy's denial that he was a member of the Klan did not stay the fury of the zealots.

They proceeded to attack him, breaking his nose and knocking him to the ground and hitting him and kicking him, bruising his body in many places. This boy is not a member of the Knights of the Ku Klux Klan. Many times this un-American crowd have passed his home, abusing him and his parents with vile names and accusing them of being Klansmen.

The affair is an aftermath of decoration night when several uniformed Klansmen appeared outside the city limits at the cemetery and held funeral services for their departed brethren. After the services were concluded, several men in uniforms of officers of New Brunswick appeared on the scene, which is out of the city's jurisdiction, and blocked the road with their cars and proceeded to question those who remained on the grounds. Some civilians tore the cross down and the officers helped to trample it out, but it was well made and the more they trampled the better it burned. Suffice to say most of the uniformed men were not of the Protestant faith as well as the men that accompanied them.

Feeling runs high in the community that Protestants must be disturbed when holding services over the graves of their departed brethren. No Klansman or Protestant has ever entered a Roman Catholic cemetery and disturbed religious services. They hold the dead as sacred and more than that they are too broad-minded, high thinking Americans to lower themselves to such a disgrace.

AUGUST 8 SET FOR MAMMOTH PROCESSION IN WASHINGTON

Many Notables Will Take Part In and Witness March of Americans — Permit Has Been Granted.

COMMITTEES BUSY ON MANY ARRANGEMENTS

Further Details Are Promised In Next Few Days—Growth of Klan In District of Columbia Has Been Very Rapid.

Washington, D. C., June 15.—That one of the largest parades ever held in the Nation's capital was learned today when it was announced the Ku Klux Klan will stage a procession here on August 8 in which from 175,000 to 200,000 Klansmen will take part. A permit for this parade, it was announced by a representative of the Klan, has been granted and preparations are now under way to hold a spectacular procession on the date named.

Details concerning the big event were not made public at this time although it was stated that a number of committees were at work on the many different arrangements necessary for such a great undertaking. Klansmen from many states will be in the procession, it was stated. Large delegations from all nearby states will find a place in the line, as well as smaller delegations from states farther removed.

The event will be the first of its kind to be held in Washington, although Klansmen in uniform have appeared in public in this city. Great headway by the organization is being made in the District of Columbia and its membership here has grown very fast.

It is expected that many notable Klansmen and Klanswomen high in the organization will be present to take part in and witness the long procession of Americans. It was promised that further details concerning the affair would be made public within the next week or ten days.

TO PROSECUTE BOOTLEGGERS UNDER OLD LAW

Measure Passed by Congress In 1886 Is Effectively Used at Tacoma.

(Special to The Kourier.)

Tacoma, Wash., June 15.—Federal agents have dug up a section of the revised Federal statutes which covers an act of Congress passed in 1886, and which it would seem is destined to bring ruin and desolation to the bootleggers of rum and narcotics, who heretofore have been getting rich through their illegal traffic. The digging up of this old measure of the Federal Government is hailed with delight by the officials and with consternation by the fraternity of bootleggers who have been plying their trade with but little or no attention to the possible consequences of their disregard for the law.

"Thirty-four-fifty," which in a day almost, has attained wide prominence, means section 3450 of the revised Federal statutes and covers an act passed by Congress in 1886. It refers to the transportation of articles that have not paid an internal revenue tax and provides that the vehicle used for such transportation shall be confiscated.

The Volstead law has a somewhat similar provision, but Federal prosecutors here found that forfeitures under it were not successful owing to conditional sales of automobiles.

So the Government attorneys decided to use the power provided by section 3450 and they have been employing it with great effect. Every few weeks the United States marshal holds an auction sale of automobiles confiscated because they were hauling liquor on which no Federal tax was paid. In several cases a jury has found the operator of a rum carrier innocent, but his car has been libeled under section 3450 and ordered sold.

Wallace Mount, assistant United States district attorney, says that the Government has obtained the forfeiture of every automobile or truck libeled under section 3450 in this district.

Members Invited to Privileges of Swimming Hole

Bloomington, Ill., Unit Also Extends Courtesies to Protestant Churches.

(Special to The Kourier.)

Bloomington, Ill., June 15.—Klansmen have a fine swimming pool here that was dedicated June 3 and is now being utilized by Protestant churches for baptismal purposes as well as a most convenient and splendid swimming pool for members of the local unit. On the occasion of the dedication 26 young men and women were baptized.

A large 80-foot electric cross illuminated the scene. Several hundred persons were present to witness the ceremonies.

The local organization does not want to be selfish with their pool and extends an invitation to any visiting Klansman to partake of its joys. Identification is all that is required.

BADGER EDUCATOR DISAPPEARS IN LONDON, FEAR FOUL PLAY

2 cents In Milwaukee County PAY NO MORE

WISCONSIN NEWS

HOME EDITION

TWO FIRST PAGES, TWO PAGES OF FICTION AND COMICS

The Evening Wisconsin, Est. 1847; The Milwaukee Daily News, Est. 1885; The Evening Sentinel, Est. 1917.

MILWAUKEE, TUESDAY, JULY 21, 1925

TELEPHONE BROADWAY 4800.

Daily Milwaukee and County, 2 cents a copy; by carrier 12 cents a week; elsewhere 3 cents.

SCOPES IS CONVICTED BY 'APE' JURY

PROFESSOR CARRIED $3,000 IN POCKET

Wife and Daughter of Normal Professor Get Aid of Scotland Yard.

Prof. Joseph Victor Collins of the state normal school at Stevens Point, Wis., is missing in London and grave fears are entertained for his safety, according to cablegrams received by The Wisconsin News over Associated Press and International News Service wires today.

Scotland Yard issued today a description of Prof. Collins, who disappeared last night, the Associated Press says. It adds: "His wife and daughter, who are here, express great anxiety because he carried a large amount of money in travelers' checks. Prof. Collins had just returned from Scotland and never reached his hotel in London."

Prof. Collins, who is 66 years old, has been a teacher of mathematics in the State Normal school at Stevens Point, Wis., since 1894.

The International News Service cablegram differs in details:

"Prof. Collins disappeared while en route to King's Cross railway station to make inquiries about a train for Edinburgh, where he was going to attend a conference of the World Federation of Educational Associations," the International News cable says.

"He had $3,000 in checks and money with him as well as return tickets to the United States, and Mrs. Collins and her daughter fear he may have met foul play."

ARCHBISHOP MESSMER IS ENJOYING TRIP

Archbishop Sebastian G. Messmer is well and is enjoying his trip abroad, according to a cablegram received from Rome today by Msgr. Bernard Traudt, head of the diocese during the prelate's absence. The archbishop will return to Milwaukee in September after a visit to Goldach, Switzerland, where he was born.

YOUTH KILLED ON ROLLER COASTER

HAMMOND, Ind.—(By A. P.)—Dale Good, 21, Gary, Ind., was instantly killed last night at an amusement park here when he was thrown from the front seat of a roller coaster as it reached the top of a glide. The car passed over him while Charles Milbourne, his companion, attempted to save him.

Gets Robbery Warrant in Slugging

Charging that he had been slugged and robbed in an automobile at the wheel of which sat a woman, Albert Otto, a Chicago salesman, today swore to a warrant charging a West Side man with assault and robbery.

Otto alleges that he and the man named in the warrant had gone automobile riding yesterday. At Sycamore and Third sts. they met the woman, Otto said.

After visiting a roadhouse and riding about in the city and county, Otto claims that the machine was crossing Oklahoma av., when he was suddenly struck with a hammer on the head and chest. The woman, at the wheel of the car, drove on as her companion robbed Otto of his watch and $8 in cash, Otto said. Then they put him out of the car.

Otto made his way to the Bay View station where he was questioned by Acting Detectives John McGarvey and John McCarthy. He was later treated at Emergency hospital.

PROBE DEATH OF BOY BELIEVED BERRY VICTIM

Dr. E. L. Miloslavich, coroner's pathologist, today was making a microscopical examination of the stomach contents of 4 year old Joseph Kaczkowski, who died after a short illness yesterday in the home of his parents at 1636 Third av. The examination was to be made to determine if green chokecherries may have been responsible.

In the meantime, Angeline and Ralph Weinstock, the children of a neighbor living at 1642 Third av., are ill with symptoms similar to those developed by the Kaczkowski boy and which resulted in his death. The condition of the Weinstock children, however, is considered not serious.

HAD BERRIES SUNDAY.

Coroner Henry Grundman who investigated the death, declared today that he had been informed that the dead boy had in his possession on Sunday a quantity of green choke cherries, taken from a tree in the yard. It is thought that he ate some.

The boy appeared ill when he was put to bed Sunday night. At 11 a. m. yesterday he was seized with a violent convulsion and was dead when Dr. S. A. Baranowski reached him.

ZOO GETS WHYDAH AND MYNAH—THEY'RE BIRDS

The Sakabuli Whydah and the Hill Mynah are the latest additions in the bird family at the Washington Park zoo. They were the gifts of Miss Lenore Cawker to the Washington Park Zoological society.

The Whydah—of Africa—resembles a canary and is noted for its tail feathers, which usually measure a foot in length. Its plumage is jet black in color.

The Hill Mynah, whose home is in India, has all the characteristics of a very small crow. It has yellow head wattles.

MINE WAGE FIGHT SETTLEMENT IS NEAR

LONDON—(By A. P.)—The dispute between the miners and the mine owners centering on wages and working hours appears to be approaching a settlement, some going so far as to say the deadlock may end today.

Great pressure is being exerted upon the miners and mine owners to induce them to get together for a discussion of their differences and to negotiate new agreements.

BRITISH STEAMER IN PERIL ON REEF

MANILA—(By A. P.)—The British steamship Egremont Castle is aground on Pubbataha reef in the Sulu sea and is leaking badly. The vessel grounded because the reef light was not burning. Salvage tugs have been dispatched to her assistance but it is feared that she will be a total wreck. The ship has a cargo of sugar and is bound for New York.

Risk Head Sees Fine Business Outlook

PREDICTS DIVIDEND INCREASE

Northwestern Mutual Company Agents Told of Gains in Surplus.

All things considered, the business outlook in this country was never built upon a firmer foundation or with brighter prospects than it is today.

This encouraging declaration was made here today by W. D. Van Dyke, president, Northwestern Mutual Life Insurance company, at the forty-ninth annual gathering of the association of agents of the company, attended by about one thousand representatives of the firm from all sections of the country.

INCREASE IN DIVIDEND.

In affirmation of this belief, Mr. Van Dyke announced for 1926 an increase in the regular dividend scale for policy holders amounting to 6.7 per cent over that of 1925, indicative of the healthy growth of the company, which has its home offices in Milwaukee.

Touching on the general business outlook, Mr. Van Dyke said:

"The general business outlook indicates continued improvement in response to the growing feeling of confidence and the increase in the buying power of the public. Steady, continuous growth is more to be desired than spasmodic, rapid progress which too often results in violent reaction.

"Easy money, augmented by a reduction in federal taxes, has furnished an additional surplus to an already overabundance of capital for investment, and the emphatic commendation of economy and thrift by our government itself is the highest indorsement of life insurance."

EMPLOYES GIVE PLAY.

The morning session closed with an address on "Building a Complete Program" by Robert R. Reid, Chicago.

This afternoon home office employes present a two-act play, "The Wife Speaks for Herself," while papers by C. S. Beck, Ohio, on "Lump Sum Settlements," and on

(Turn to Page 2, Column 8.)

PURSUIT PLANES HOP OFF FOR SECOND TRIP

OMAHA, Neb.—(By A. P.)—Commanded by Maj. Thomas G. Lanphier, six army pursuit planes, accompanied by a huge Curtiss N. B. S. 4 bomber, hopped off from Jarvis Offutt field, Fort Crook, for Cheyenne, Wyo., at 9 a. m. today.

Today's hopoff marked the beginning of the second day's flight of a test to determine the military value of the air mail route. The six planes left Selfridge field, Mount Clemens, Mich., Monday morning and will journey to San Francisco, arriving there Thursday.

THE WEATHER

TEMPERATURES.

1 a. m.	69	7 a. m.	67
2 a. m.	68	8 a. m.	69
3 a. m.	66	9 a. m.	72
4 a. m.	65	10 a. m.	73
5 a. m.	64	11 a. m.	74
6 a. m.	65	12 noon	76

FORECAST.

Milwaukee and Vicinity—Fair tonight and Wednesday. Not much change in temperature. Moderate northerly winds.

Wisconsin — Fair tonight and Wednesday. Not much change in temperature.

Sunrise, 4:32 a. m.; sunset, 7:25 p. m.

Light vehicle lamps at 7:55 p. m.

SIX HURT AS AUTOS CRASH

Man's Skull Fractured in Head-on Collision; Two Children Escape.

Harry Gross, 29, 1239 Twenty-second st., is at Emergency hospital with a skull fracture and five other persons are nursing bruises and other injuries as the result of a head-on collision between two light, closed cars on the Grand av. viaduct at 11:30 o'clock last night.

Gross was riding with Francis Joseppi, Fond du Lac, and George Ramsdell, 85, 235 Ninth st. Joseppi suffered a fractured arm and Ramsdell was cut about the face.

Mr. and Mrs. Francis Cannon, 141 Cedar st., Wauwatosa, and their two children, a girl, 13, and a boy, 8, and Nathan Ransohoff, Cincinnati, were riding in the other car. Mr. and Mrs. Cannon and Ransohoff were cut and bruised, but the children, asleep on the rear seat, escaped injury. Both cars were badly wrecked.

Harry A. Benfeldt, clubman and ice cream manufacturer, injured with two women companions in an automobile accident on the Port Washington road, near Donges Bay yesterday, was still at Columbia hospital today. His condition, however, is reported improved. The women, Mabel McPherson and Marguerite Burns, are also at Columbia. A report that a fourth person, a man, was in the car when it left the road and crashed into a pole, is being investigated.

FRENCH EVACUATE AS GERMANS FIGHT

BOCHUM, Germany—(By A. P.)—A free-for-all fist fight here last night between monarchists and Republicans was the only untoward incident accompanying the French evacuation of this section of the Ruhr.

The mayor of Bochum had issued a proclamation saying the town would be considered free of French troops at midnight. However, the German proprietor of the railway station hotel hoisted the monarchist colors above his establishment at 9 o'clock. Large crowds assembled around the place and monarchists and Republicans began to fight. It was necessary to summon police and the proprietor was compelled to furl his flag.

TWO HOMES DAMAGED AS FIRE RAZES BARN

Two homes were damaged when fire destroyed a barn on Scott st. between First and Second avs., yesterday afternoon. The homes were those of R. D. Wolfe, 433 Scott st., and Mrs. George Wusler, in the rear of 456 Second av.

The fire started in the hay loft of the barn, located in the rear of 450 Second av. Sparks set fire to the roofs of the two homes.

IDENTIFY LABORER KILLED BY TRAIN

GREEN BAY, Wis.—(By A. P.)—The laborer killed here Monday by a passenger train was identified as William P. Maltzou of St. James, Minn. A fellow worker recognized the remains.

4 BURN TO DEATH IN DALLAS BLAZE

DALLAS—(By A. P.)—Four men were burned to death and five others suffered injuries in a fire which destroyed a two story frame rooming house here early this morning.

GUILTY IN 'APE' TRIAL

JOHN T. SCOPES.

MOTHER BEATS 'STAR GAZING' SON IN COURT

An attack by Mrs. William A. Kimpel on her son, Carl, principal figure in the "star gazing" divorce action and numerous damage suits, just outside the court room of Judge Gustav Gehrz yesterday afforded spectators unexpected thrills, and resulted in the mother, crying and hysterical, being taken before the court and warned of contempt.

"It appears I am the guilty party and my son is the innocent one," she managed to say between sobs, after Judge Gehrz had warned her to control her emotions.

Kimpel had been ordered by the court to pay $9 a week temporary alimony for the support of his wife and three children with the provision that he be allowed to visit his children within a month if he made regular payments. He was leaving the court room when the attack occurred. The mother rushed at her son and struck him several times with her open hand before officers quieted her.

HOLD SUSPECT IN QUARRY STABBING

John Savizch, an employe at a stone quarry near Ives, a village four miles north of Racine, was being held in the county jail in the latter city today pending the outcome of stab wounds he is alleged to have inflicted on Myron Novakovish, 35, in the dining hall of the quarry camp late yesterday.

Novakovish is in a critical condition at St. Mary's hospital in Racine. Savizch was arrested by the Racine county sheriffs. He denied he made the assault.

CHINESE CUT OFF FOOD FOR AMERICAN BOAT

PEKIN—(By A. P.)—Advices from Canton say that food supplies have been cut off from the American gunboat stationed at Woochow, as well as from the British residents. It is added that the British consul at Woochow has advised all British subjects to leave because of the strict boycott against them.

CHARGE 2 MEN KIDNAPED PAIR OF GIRLS

A "sweetheart kidnaping" episode that occurred Sunday night at a lonely point on the Green Tree road resulted in the bringing of serious charges today against Fred Schiffman, 34, relief Whitefish Bay police officer, and A. C. Kupper, 35, the alleged "kidnapers."

A warrant sworn out by Dist. Atty. Eugene Wengert charges Officer Schiffman with an offense punishable by a thirty year prison term. Kupper is already under arrest on another serious charge.

On Sunday night, Clarence McGuire, 27, and Harry Seeman, 25, both living at a downtown hostelry, took two girls employed at the hotel for an auto ride. They had stopped their car at the side of the Green Tree rd. when, it is alleged, Schiffman and Kupper, who had parked their car about a block away, approached.

According to McGuire and Seeman, Schiffman made known that he was a police officer, flashing his badge and then ordered them all out of the car. After they had alighted, the men alleged, Schiffman ordered them to drive away in their car, remarking:

"We'll take care of the girls."

The officer and his companion then led the girls to their machine and after they had entered, drove farther out on the Green Tree rd., it is alleged, where the girls were mistreated.

BOY, 13, KILLS SELF AFTER STEALING $10

ST. LOUIS, Mo.—(By A. P.)—Fear of punishment for the theft of $10 from his father, caused 13 year old Jesse Mallory to commit suicide here last night. Death was due to an overdose of medicine. The boy's grandmother, Mrs. Anna Mallory said he denied taking the money, but later admited it and said he would commit suicide. The matter was not taken seriously until he collapsed an hour later; he died in a hospital.

DEFENSE AGREES TO VERDICT AFTER SETBACKS

COURTROOM, DAYTON, Tenn.—(By the Associated Press)—A verdict of "guilty" was returned in the Scopes case at 11:29 a. m. The case was given to a Rhea county jury at 11:20 a. m. The jury returned to the court room at 11:28.

Scopes was summoned before the bar. Judge Raulston told him of his conviction by the jury and read a copy of the statute to him. The judge then fixed the fine at $100. Bond was fixed at $500, pending an appeal. "Have you anything to say, Mr. Scopes?" asked the judge. "Your honor, I have been convicted of violating an unjust statute," replied Scopes. "Any action other than I have pursued would be in violation of my idea of academic freedom." The judge repeated the fine of $100.

By **WILLIAM K. HUTCHINSON,**
International News Service Staff Correspondent.

COURT HOUSE, DAYTON, Tenn.—Attorneys for John Thomas Scopes, young high school professor, today entered an agreement in open court to have their client found guilty by the jury in the anti-evolution trial.

The agreement came after presiding Judge John T. Raulston barred all the defense's religious witnesses from the stand, excluded their scientists and expunged the testimony given yesterday by William Jennings Bryan. It virtually ended the case, as opposing attorneys waived their summing up speeches. The judge instructed the jury to bring in a verdict.

The decision wiped out the last vestige of the Scopes defense, because it barred all religious testimony from the trial. With their scientists excluded last week, the Scopes attorneys closed their case and the jury was called in to wind up the trial.

"Our defense witnesses are excluded, we are denied the right to cross examine the state's witnesses," said Dudley Field Malone. "There is no need of going on, so we close our case."

An exception to the order was taken immediately by defense counsel. Darrow told the court the testimony was germane to the defense contention that the Bible cannot be interpreted literally.

DARROW BAITS BRYAN.

That brought Bryan to his feet, holding his fan. He addressed the court with great seriousness.

"I fully agree with the court that the testimony taken yesterday was not legitimate or proper," said Bryan. "I was not in a position to raise an objection myself nor was I willing to have it raised for me without ascertaining my willingness to be cross examined."

Then, turning to the court, Bryan asked: "You expunged the questions as well as the answers?"

"Yes," replied Judge Raulston.

"I shall make a statement to the press, giving them a list of questions, which I would have asked defense counsel if they had taken the witness stand as they said they would," Bryan added.

"Go out on the lawn and make that speech," said Darrow. "I object to the speech."

COURT FEARS ERROR.

Bryan charged the defense with "hiding behind a screen of the law."

"I object to that," Darrow shouted.

"We are willing to meet Mr. Bryan for further discussion of this sub-

(Turn to Page 2, Column 1)

Ford's Bid for 200 Ships Favored

WASHINGTON—(By A. P.)—Acceptance of Henry Ford's bid of $1,706,000 for the two hundred shipping board vessels, set aside for scrapping, has been recommended to the board by President Palmer of the Fleet corporation.

Indications are that the board will approve the recommendation. Its general counsel has held the procedure of the Fleet corporation in conducting the proposed sale to be legal, although the Boston Iron and Metal Co., of Baltimore, protested it was irregular.

BID WAS REJECTED.

The Baltimore company was the highest bidder when the original tenders were opened June 30, its offer being $1,370,000, but this bid was rejected by the board after President Palmer had urged its acceptance and new offers were called for to be opened July 16. The Baltimore company then withdrew its offer, claiming that only the original bidders should be permitted to submit new offers. Henry Ford was not among those submitting tenders when the bids were opened June 30.

It is the intention of Mr. Ford to scrap most of the two hundred ships but he will retain some for conversion to Diesel engine propulsion in salt water transportation. He also will use some of the engines and other equipment in his own manufacturing operations.

CALLES' ECONOMIES SAVE 19 MILLION

MEXICO CITY—(By A. P.)—It is announced more than $19,000,000 has been saved by economies in President Calles' 1925 budget. $9,000,000 in the war department alone.

"Change lays not her hand upon truth" —*Swinburne (Born April 5, 1837)*

The Weather

Forecast for Southern New England: Mostly cloudy and slightly colder tonight; Tuesday fair and colder; fresh northwest and north winds.

The New Haven Union

HOME EDITION
LATEST NEWS

VOL. 145—NO. 95 | Entered as Second-Class Matter at Post Office at New Haven, Conn., under the Act of 1879. | NEW HAVEN, CONN., MONDAY, APRIL 5, 1926 | Full Leased Wire Service of United Press. Founded in 1871 by Alexander Troup. | PRICE TWO CENTS

CHAPMAN PLEADS FOR HIS LIFE

Local Child Killed, 15 Hurt In Auto Crashes

AUTHORITIES SEEK "CUT IN" AUTOMOBILIST

Major Accident Occurs Near Wallingford—Five in Hospital Here as Result of Week-End Accidents

MOST OF VICTIMS ARE CHILDREN

Tragedy stalked in the paths of New Haven motorists yesterday when one child was killed and 15 persons hurt in automobile accidents in the city and suburbs.

The major accident occurred at 3 o'clock yesterday afternoon, one mile past Wallingford in the direction of Meriden when a truck driven by Luca Villani, of 171 Franklin street, overturned, after an unidentified machine had cut in on it. Evelyn Villani's 22-month-old daughter was killed and 10 persons were injured.

Another accident occurred on Derby avenue near Central avenue, when the car in which three men were driving became caught in the trolley tracks.

Two children were hurt in automobile accidents earlier in the day.

The injured are:

Luca Villani, left hand sprained.

Mrs. Teresa Villani, right arm wrenched.

Mrs. Angeline Vergardi, possible fracture of the skull and concussion of the brain.

Celia, Josephine, Eva, Angelo, children of Villani.

Lucy Vergadi, five, injury to breast.

John Vergadi, eight, and Catherine nine, bruises, all of 171 Franklin street.

Frank Aguila, also of 171 Franklin street, bruises.

The injured are Andrew Tonnee, 19, of Griffin avenue, Shelton and Samuel Faigen, 5, of 495 Columbus avenue, Emily Mongillo, 5, of 256 Cedar street, Louis Oragietti, 22, of Corona, Long Island, and Primo Lanzel, 18, of Foley avenue, Shelton received slight injuries but were released from the hospital after receiving treatment.

The Villani party set out about 3 o'clock yesterday intending to visit relatives in Meriden. When they were one mile west of Wallingford, a closed machine cut in on the Villani truck, forcing it from the road. The truck overturned and pinned the eleven people underneath and two-year-old Evelyn was killed at once.

The operator of the closed car sped away from the accident without stopping to ascertain the injury, and his identity has not been learned as yet.

Mrs. Villani sits in her home today rocking back and forth moaning the loss of her child. When she is questioned, she answers incoherently. Her eyes were red from tears, and she clutched at her arm which was hurt.

The rest of the family were gathered around the room chattering hysterically, but Mrs. Villani ignores them and keeps up a continual rocking while she mutters, "She was a good girl—she was a good girl, she never cry."

Tonaci was taken to St. Raphael's hospital shortly before 1 o'clock this morning suffering from a fractured right arm sustained when the automobile in which he was riding turned over on Derby avenue, near Central avenue. Oragietti and Lanzel also passengers in the automobile, were shaken up and Oragietti sustained a cut on his cheek that required four stitches to close, but their injuries were not serious and they were released from the hospital after being treated.

The little Faigen lad was rushed to the New Haven hospital yesterday afternoon suffering from a possible fracture of the skull sustained when he was struck by the automobile operated by Gaetano Visconte, 29, of 276 Oak street. His condition is not considered critical, however, it was stated by hospital authorities this morning.

The lad was sitting in his father's car on Oak street near Temple when he suddenly left the car and stepped directly in the path of the machine.

The Mongillo girl was struck yesterday afternoon by the automobile of Bernard Clario, 24, of 39 Washington avenue, when she stepped out from behind two parked cars on Frank street and directly in the path of the automobile. She was taken to the New Haven hospital but was later released.

DOTY FINED

For driving an automobile while under the influence of liquor, William H. Doty, 40, 37 Putnam street, was fined $100 and given a 30-day suspended jail sentence in city court this morning.

He was arrested on Whalley avenue on March 31 by Policeman James F. Shalvey.

CLASSIFIED READERS get the biggest and best bargains.

Butler on Eve of Trial Starts Series In Union

General Butler In Marine Uniform Just Before He Accepted the Invitation To Clean Up Philadelphia. Observe The Fighting Face.

Fighting Marine's Fascinating Revelation of Philadelphia's Crime and Intrigue Begins Today—A Thrilling, True Account of His Battle

Smashing Crime and Vice

By SMEDLEY D. BUTLER
Former Director of the Department of Public Safety, Philadelphia, Pa.
INSTALMENT —1.

It hurt to be dismissed—hurt with with a sharpness that will last the rest of my life.

The sensation was not, however, one of humiliation or wounded pride, as it would have been had I been summarily fired for dereliction of duty. The sensation was one of bitter disappointment and futile anger at being deprived of the opportunity to continue the war, just when the first big engagement was imminent; just when the two forces had finally come face to face and the true issue had been definitely disclosed—the naked and raw issue of impartiality in law enforcement; the issue of equal treatment of rich and poor, powerful and weak.

At that critical period I was dismissed without cause or reason from my post of Director of Public Safety of Philadelphia by the Mayor of that city, W. Freeland Kendrick.

For two years the great forces of privilege and impartiality had been manouvering, innumerable small skirmishes and a few large engagements had taken place and the forces of impartiality had become more expert in the art of enforcement warfare through experience and study.

Now they were about to grapple in a life and death struggle, a struggle that might not have resulted in immediate physical victory for impartiality, but which, at least, would have once and for all expelled every traitor from the army and put distinctive uniforms on the combatants of both sides.

The Mayor of Philadelphia had taken an oath before God Almighty as Commander-in-Chief of the Army of Fair Play, but for two years had failed to appear at its head. The responsibility which was his, and which he accepted in pre-campaign and post-election pledges, he passed on to me. Mayor Kendrick thus dodged all responsibility and sat on the fence, ready to jump to either side.

He never wore the uniform of this army of impartiality of his and never aided it in any but disinterested ways. It is true he never interfered in small scraps, beyond admonitions to caution. but it is equally true that he never used his influence towards the success of any of its movements.

While he had been uold in his public avowals of support he had artfully and cleverly allowed those carefully worded utterances to be his sole contribution to the cause of law enforcement.

He, who had been elected to lead, and who had in a pompous inaugural address publicly sworn to do so, rode comfortably miles in the rear of his firing line, and only took that risk in order to restrain his first line troops, less they injure social, political and financial friends among the enemy. So far as impartial law enforcement is concerned, he is a strong pacifist.

I was his subordinate, commander of the front line troops, and the only one of these troops who trusted him. To be sure, there were many times when I doubted him. But even now, I cannot understand how he expected to advance politically, as he often the strong and the rich against the weak and the poor in an issue so vital.

Neither Army was deceived by these tactics—only the people who had elected and who trusted him were deceived.

The truth, therefore, MUST be told.

The cause of honest, vigorous and impartial law enforcement, like any other worthy cause, is more important than any individual advocating or combatting it. The citizens cannot and do not know the treatment to which an honest public official particularly a police official, is subjected.

To tell of my experiences in Philadelphia, as Director of Public Safety during the past two years may help the public more clearly to understand the difficulties that confront and beset honest men in public office.

If, through the medium of these articles, the public can be made to understand and to become more free to give its support to such officials, then the cause will have been advanced and the effort will be really worth while. While law enforcement is a vital and outstanding issue of the day, the position of the enforcement official is a lonely one, unless the public openly and actively supports the official.

I want to tell the "constructive" story of the Philadelphia effort, of the fight, of the progress made and of the lessons learned. Necessarily I will be forced to relate the unpleasant experiences as well; to tell of the efforts of high and trusted officials to interfere with my efforts, of the means used to have me favor certain privileged interests—interests privileged because of their social, financial or political power and influence.

Because this story would not be complete without such references, and the cause would not be aided materially without them, I shall include them.

I will not accept any payment for this work.

I want to help the movement for decency in Philadelphia, and through the double means of this story and the possible proceeds from its sale, I believe I can do so.

If my share of the income is sufficient, therefore, I will assign it to a Trust Fund for use in protecting honest policemen and police officials who, because they persist in carrying out their sworn oaths of office, are harassed and

(Continued on Page Seven)

COURT UPHOLDS TENANTS' RIGHT TO HAVE HEAT

Judge Picket Sets Precedent By Confirming Fine on West Haven Woman Landlord

CITES LACK OF CARE IN FINDING

Any doubt as to whether under the laws of the state tenants of apartment houses are entitled to sufficient heat during the winter months was set at rest by a finding handed down by Judge Walter M. Pickett of the court of common pleas this morning. He confirmed a fine imposed upon Mrs. Rosina Coppola, who owns an apartment house at 178 Campbell avenue, West Haven. She was heavily fined in the West Haven town court $25 on the charge of failure to supply insufficient heat on the premises.

The charge was brought in the West Haven court upon information lodged by tenants in the house, and upon the fine being imposed. Mrs. Coppola immediately tok an appeal to the common pleas court, the appeal coming before Judge Pickett at the closing of the March term of the court immediately preceding the opening of the April term this morning.

In the course of his summary of the case Judge Pickett did not stress the terms "wilfully and intentionally" as they appear in the statute, but based his decision on the lack of care shown by the apartment house owner in the matter of obtaining a regular heat supply for the tenants.

Following the hearing of some probation cases left over from the March term Judge Pickett caused the March term to be closed without date, resigning his set on the bench to Judge John R. Booth for the opening of the April term.

BROTHER WITNESS

Joseph Rosenberg on Stand in Will Hearing

Hearings on the petition for probate on the will of the late Attorney Sidney Rosenberg were resumed this morning with the time being consumed in an effort to have Joseph Rosenberg, a brother tell of the actions of the late attorney before he was found frozen o death in an automobile in Orange three months ago.

No testimony was given, but Rosenberg admitted that his brother spoke to him about the provisions of h s will but said that he was not informed what the provisions were.

EASTER PARADE

Cloudless Spring Day Brings Gay Crowd to Streets

Despite the high north winds and except for a chilly tank in the air and a gusty wind the weather was all that could be desired for Easter Day as there was not a cloud in the skies and the Easter paraders enjoyed the promenade to their heart's delight.

The streets were crowded with gaily gowned women.

The colors certainly were along brilliant lines, gray being the popular color.

Suits are to appear after a three years rebuff although it was too cold yesterday to see many.

Hats are small, those were yesterday's favorites.

Coats were of two types, dressy and atilored. Skirts are short, very short in fact judging from yesterday's parade. All with this will be a social week filled with gay events.

EASTER HUNT

Boys and Girls at White House Today

WASHINGTON, D. C., April 5. — Outside the White House gates early this morning there gathered an eager crowd of boys and girls to attend the annual Easter egg-rolling, the great event of the year for Washington's children.

The egg-rolling is for children only. Guards at the gates let no adult pass unless bringing a child.

HEINBURGE HELD

The case of Wiliam C. Heinburge, 41 years old, of 87 Fulton, charged with passing a standing trolley car, was continued in the City court this morning until April 7.

Heinburge was arrested yesterday morning by Policeman James Brennan on Grand avenue.

Looking Gerald Chapman In The Eye

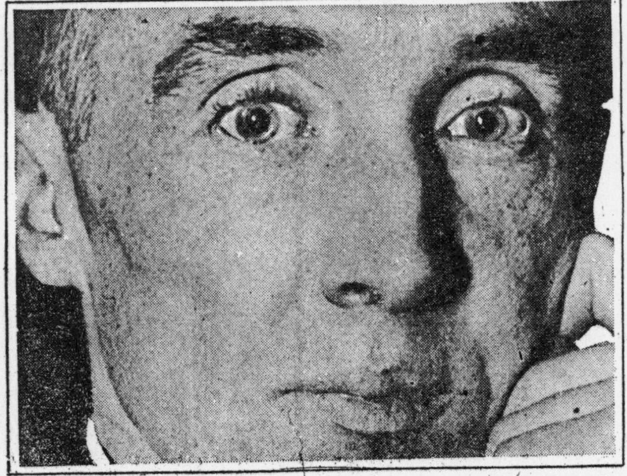

Between midnight tonight and 1 oclock Tuesday morning, the American continent's most notorious bandit will hang in the State Prison at Wethersfield, Conn. As the time of death nears the suave "gentleman burglar" retains his callous calm.

ALDERMEN FACE BIG BOND PLAN

New City Hall Bond Project, Police Station Site and Other Matters Up

It is expected that Mayor John B. Tower's plan for issuing of $350,000 in bonds for the purchase of the Orange street property in connection with the new City hall plans will be approved when the board of aldermen meets tonight at 8 o'clock.

Should all the members of the board be present tonight the consensus of opinion is that the vote will stand 25 to 10 in favor of the plan.

An emergency measure will be presented by Mayor Tower, asking the adoption of a proposal that the city enter into an agreement with the state highway department making possible the immediate rebuilding of the eastern approach to the Tomlinson bridge.

There will be a discussion over a petition which has been presented to the board questioning the legality of the source of money obtained by the board of police commissioners for the purchase of the site for the new Fair Haven police station at Blatchley avenue and Woolsey street. The petition was presented by residents of Fair Haven who are opposed to the new station.

Maps have been prepared by the city engineer's office, which call for the elimination of at least two bad curves on Forbes avenue between the Grannis Corner drug store and Fulton street.

Parts of the Kendall property on Forbes avenue and the Grannis property may be taken for the straightening of the highway.

President John K. Punderford of the Connecticut Co. announced that he ies ready to proceed with double-tracking of the Forbes avenue car line. Eventually the trolley to the east shore will be rerouted through Forbes avenue and over the Tomlinson bridge.

It is evident that the city will take up the matter of paving Forbes avenue. The roadway has been in such a bad condition that most travel has been diverted through Farren avenue over the Ferry street bridge by way of Chapel street.

Mayor Tower, Director of Public Works Michael D. McGovern and City Engineer Nettleton have held a conference with the state highway department officials in Hartford, with the result that $50,000 has been made available for the paving.

A lively debate is expected to result when an unfavorabel report from the committee on legislation is made on Alderman John Murphy's petition to reduce the working hours of city laborers from nine hours to eight hours per day.

Because some of the members of the board of compensation are ill, the report on the matter of widening Elm street will not be made. If the widening is accomplished, property owners will lose nearly half a million dollars, is has been estimated.

It is expected that an unfavorable report will be made on the petition for more space for the public market. It is proposed that the market be extended from South Orange street to Meadow street.

Mayor Tower will not ask the board to give him authority to appoint a city recreation commission, as he has not yet completed the desired data.

Noted Critic Defies Ban On Magazine

Mencken Will Sell Mercury in Boston and Face Arrest

By United Press

BOSTON, April 5, — Henry L. Mencken, editor of the American Mercury, will turn newsboy here this afternoon to prove the authorities had no right to prohibit sale of the alleged immoral April number of his magazine.

Following a conference with his lawyers, Mencken notified the Rev. J. Frank Chase, secretary of the Watch and Ward Society, that he would sell a copy of the banned magazine at Park and Tremont streets at 2 p. m.

Chase, through whose efforts the magazine was barred, told Mencken he would be at "the scene of the crime" at that hour.

As soon as Mencken receives the half dollar in exchange for the Mercury he will be arrested as the first step in his fight to test the validity of the suppression. He will be accompanied by Arthur Garfield Hays, counsel of the American Civil Liberties Union, when he keeps his appointment with the police.

Mencken's magazine was ousted from Boston newsstands last week on complaint of the Watch and Ward Society, whose leaders charged than an article entitled "Hatrack" was immoral and not fit to be read.

"This case is entirely malicious." Mencken told the United Press. "We allege and can prove that the Rev. J. Frank Chase has been after us for the past six months. We have attacked him in the Mercury.

"We don't want to go to jail but we will if we have to. The Mercury is published by intelligent people and anyone who has read it knows it is not an indecent magazine.

"Chase is neglecting his real function which is to suppress smutty and indecent magazines. We contend that no magazine is indecent unless it is lewd and lascivious. The complaint which was filed against the news vendor who was arrested for selling the Mercury does not claim this. The complaint claims that the 'Hatrack' story was an attack upon a Methodist revivalist meeting."

Yale Professor Given $10 Fine

Wilbur W. Swingle, 35, of 625 Orange street, a professor at Yale University, was arraigned before Judge Sheridan T. Whitaker in the city court this morning on charges of violation of traffic code 17 which pertains to parking on a restricted side of the street and operating a motor vehicle without a license.

He was fined $10 for operating without a license and received a suspended judgment on the traffic code violation charge.

POLITICAL AXE HITS POLICEMEN

Four Members of Motorcycle Squad Displaced By G. O. P. Appointees

The political axe is out again in the police department.

Four members of the motorcycle squad were dropped and their places filled by Republican appointees.

The men dropped are Robert Connolly of Station 3, Edward Gannon of Station 6, James Coughlin of Station 3, and John Lynch of Station 4. James Dinan formerly on the squad is now in the Detective bureau.

Their places will be taken by Stanley Cudgma, Larry Buckmiller, Paul Ward, Arthur J. Bode, and J. P. Robbins.

The new appointees to the squad will not, however, be put on the road until later in the month when increased motor vehicle travel will warrant it.

In addition, five old members of the squad, Charles P. Stratton, Eddie J. Cooke, William A. Frank, Edward J. Rice and James J. Coogan will be assigned to road duty later in the month.

Ten members of the squad, 3 from Station 2, 3 from Station 3, 2 from Station 4, 1 from Station 5, and 1 from Station 6, went on regular road duty yesterday afternoon. They are Richard Hunihan, 2, Lawrence Lee, 2, William B. Fisher, 2, William D. Hallisey 3, Lawrence Mooney, 3, John Alexander 3 John J. McHugh 4, Joseph Sullivan, 4, Charles Loughrain, 5, and Hugh McGuire, 6.

NOT REGISTERED

Peter Weed, 19, of 400 Forest street Allingtown, was fined $25 when he was arraigned in the city court this morning on a charge of driving an unregistered motor vehicle.

He was arrested on Dixwell avenue late Saturday night by Policeman John Lynch of the Dixwell avenue station.

GIRLIGAGS

GIRLIGAGS — "Knocking the girls' bare knees seems to be entirely unnecessary," says frivolous Flo, "since a great many of them do their own knocking."

BANDIT APPEARS IN PERSON FOR FINAL HEARING

State Board of Pardons Considers His Application for Commutation of Death Sentence

SCHEDULED TO HANG TONIGHT

WETHERSFIELD PRISON, HARTFORD, Conn., April 5.—(U. P.)—Gerald Chapman sat before the Board of Pardons today, and, while all around him were tense with nervousness, he joined with his attorneys in the final effort to prevent the state from hanging him.

If the effort fails, Chapman will hang here soon after midnight tonight.

Yet with the gallows less than half a day away, this man who never had been known to lose his nerve, carelessly read a newspaper while he waited for the hearing to open. Then he drew himself up in a chair beside his lawyers and resumed the role of director of his own defense which he had first taken up at the trial.

The appearance of Chapman was sudden. When the prison board went into session the previous announcement that Chapman would not be allowed to appear, still stood.

Then after the meeting had been in progress a few minutes word came out that plans had been changed completely and the board would hear Chapman in person.

Guards immediately went to the bandit's cell not far from the conference room and brught him to the meeting. The doors f the meeting room wre bolted behind him, guards and state police with rifles paced the corridor outside, and then the man who has amazed the country with his banditry settled back, ready o make his final plea that life in prison be his punishment instead of execution.

As Judge Frederick J. Groehl, his chief counsel, argued, Chapman wrote notes to him—notes which at times indicated that although death was at the moment reaching out for him, he retained a clear sense of logic, reason and knowledge of the law.

Often he engaged in whispered conferences with others of his legal staff.

Not for a moment did he betray nervousness. His face was pale, but it seemed more the pallor of long confinement away from the sunshine, than the pallor of approaching death. In his cheeks there was a little touch of color. His hand was steady; in fact steadier than the hands of half of the men who sat with him in that final judgment.

Capman was called to the hearing on the demand of his lawyer after it had first been announced he must remain in his cell.

With two armed guards behind him, but not manacled, he walked unconcernedly into the conference room. He was motioned to a chair and seated himself without speaking a word; then picking up a newspaper he began perusing it.

When the pardon board met Judge Frederick J. Groehl, the bandit's chief counsel, immediately called attention to the fact that Chapman was absent and demanded the prisoner be produced.

"Granted," announced Governor Trumbull, of Connecticut, who was presiding.

Guards immediately left to bring Chapman in. When he appeared in the corridor he was not handcuffed. He seemed very pale despite a slight flush in his cheeks.

Two state police stood in the conference room, armed, in addition to the prison guards.

Chapman was led to a seat where he settled back in a chair and picked up a newspaper, beginning to read it as if nothing was happening which might interest him.

Judge Groehl then began his argument for commutation of sentence. As Groehl talked Chapman dropped his paper and sat, resting his chin in his hands, listening to what was being said.

The lawyer devoted much time to the difficulty he had experienced in getting witnesses to testify and intimated that intimidation had been encountered.

Chapman was given his opportunity to make a statement on his own behalf after his lawyers had finished.

He placed great emphasis on the dying statement of Policeman John Skelly of New Britain, whom Chapman is alleged to have killed, that "Shean got me." Shean was Walter Shean, alleged confederate of Chapman, who was one of the state's chief witnesses against the bandit.

Just then Chapman leaned forward and pressed a note into Groehl's hand. Groehl stopped and carefuly read it.

"Oh, yes," Groehl said, resuming. "I am reminded of another case." And then he told of a case in the law books o fa man who three times was reprieved and finally proven innocent.

He drew the parallel between this case and that of Chapman.

But when the hearing began he was all attention. He followed closely each word Judge Groehl uttered in his behaf ond soon was engaged in writing hasty notes, sometimes to one of the other attorneys and sometimes interrupting Groehl with them.

"This man was doomed before his trial," Groehl told the pardon board. He charged the jury was prejudiced against Chapman.

(Continued on Page 1, Second Section)

XXX EDITION

THE CHICAGO EVENING POST

THIRTY-SEVENTH YEAR.—OFFICIAL NEWSPAPER OF CITY OF CHICAGO * FRIDAY, JULY 2, 1926. * PRICE THREE CENTS

CAPONI AND TEN INDICTED

JUNIOR MOOSE TO INITIATE MAYOR DEVER AND SMALL

Ceremony Tomorrow Night to Be Feature of Annual Meeting.

They may, in the words of the old song, be "hangin' Danney Dever in the mornin'" but they're "riding" Mayor Dever tomorrow afternoon. And Gov. Small, as well.

His Honor and His Excellency are going to "ride the goat" at the Coliseum, when they are initiated into the junior auxiliary of the Loyal Order of Moose by 250 children, ranging in ages from 2 to 16 years. It will be the feature of the third day's session of the thirty-eighth annual meeting of the supreme council of the world, Loyal Order of Moose.

The "big kid" doings will begin at 4 p. m., with the presentation of a pageant representative of child life at Mooseheart, the home for children of deceased members which the order maintains on the Lincoln highway near Aurora, thirty-five miles west of Chicago. In the pageant Mayor Dever will represent the children of Chicago, Gov. Small the children of Illinois and Grand Regent Brandon the children of the Mooseheart legion.

Children's Band Will Play.

Secretary of Labor James J. Davis, the builder of the Loyal Order of Moose, will represent the children of the United States. A children's band will provide the music.

Today was given over chiefly to business sessions and ritualistic contests. The latter were conducted by the Women's legion in the Hotel Sherman. Teams from many cities competed, including Newport, R. I.; Hammond, Detroit, Toledo, Indianapolis, Maplewood, Mo.; Clinton, Iowa; Fond du Lac, Wis.; Grand Rapids, Mich.; Rochester, N. Y.; Pittsburg and Webster City, Iowa.

In addition, there was an individual contest with forty-six entrants.

Twelve hundred women had registered at headquarters on the mezzanine of the Hotel Sherman today.

The Supreme council held a second session in the Auditorium theater today and the Supreme lodge met in the Sherman.

Tonight at 6:30 o'clock the Mooseheart Alumni association will hold a banquet in the Sherman, followed by a grand ball at Guyon's Paradise.

Discuss Building Program.

A $1,500,000 building program for Moose homes in various parts of the country was discussed today at the Supreme lodge meeting. Secretary Davis, speaking at the meeting, introduced a motto, which he said had been prepared by R. H. Brandon.

The motto read:

Better hands by work, better bodies by play, better minds by study, better souls by prayer—this is the heart of Mooseheart.

The "Birth of Chicago" pageant was presented again in Grant park this afternoon. The performance last night was interrupted by the rain. Indians from several reservations are here to help portray the rise of a great metropolis from the ashes of a humble outpost stockade. The pageant is being given in Soldiers' field stadium.

Preparations were being completed today for the great parade which, with a patriotic and civic celebration, will conclude the convention next Monday.

Kills Self in Rear of Friend's Undertaking Shop

Frank Kamin, 513 Eugenie street, today carried out his threat to commit suicide. His body, a revolver clutched in his right hand, was found in the rear of the undertaking establishment of Leo M. Brieske at 3037 Lincoln avenue. Kamin yesterday had sent Brieske, a friend, a letter telling of his plans and asking the undertaker to care for his body. Kamin, according to police, had been despondent because of illness and also the death of his wife.

Indian Trailers Join Hunt for Lost Child

PARK RAPIDS, Minn., June 2.—(AP)—Indians from the White Earth reservation, known as expert trailers, were recruited last night to join 800 citizens in a lantern and torchlight search for Esther Bittman, 4-year-old girl. The child was lost Wednesday in the woods near here. Footprints of a child were found in the field of an abandoned farm two and one-half miles from her home at Two Inlets. The road to the farm is an old trail from Two Inlets to Osage in Becker county.

New Quakes Rock Island of Sumatra

PADANG, Sumatra, July 2.—(AP)—New earth shocks have occurred in central Sumatra, where at least 200 persons are reported to have been killed in Tuesday's quake. The damage to property will be enormous, dispatches say, running into millions of guilders.

Motion to Censure British Government Is Defeated

LONDON, July 2.—(AP)—A Labor motion, equivalent to a vote of censure on the Baldwin government for its handling of the coal strike, was defeated in the house of commons today. The motion was rejected by the overwhelming vote of 356 to 95.

Caponi Brothers and 9 Others Are Indicted by Vote Fraud Jury

Al and Ralph Caponi, Earl "Hymie" Weiss, John J. Ludein, president of the village of Stickney, and Arthur Rench, chief of police of that village, are among the eleven persons named in five indictments returned today before Chief Justice Thomas J. Lynch by the special grand jury. They are charged with conspiracy to suborn perjury, and others are charged with assault in connection with terrorism in Cicero polling places. Bonds for the Caponis were set at $5,000.

"We take pleasure in returning the indictments," James A. Williams, foreman of the special jury, said. "We have made no written report. We have only combed the matters under investigation, and from what we have learned, believed that the work should be continued to its conclusion. We feel there is ample work for the next special grand jury, and possibly for even another one."

Others Are Named.

Others named in the indictments are Frank Foster, alleged notorious gangster and gootlegger; John O. Williams, manager of the Harlem Inn; Frank Kramer and Mack Priesopak, charged with assault with intent to murder; James West and John Doe, known as "Bulldog," charged with kidnaping Joseph Gavoni from the 21st precinct of the 21st ward, 2346 West 26th street, and holding him prisoner in a saloon for three hours on primary day.

Al, "Scarface," Caponi, is being sought by the police because of his alleged connection with the murder of Assistant State's Attorney William H. McSwiggin. Priesopak is in the bridewell hospital. He was shot by Policeman William Zeigert of the west park force in a fight at the 14th precinct polling place of the 21st ward, 2105 South Western avenue, on primary day.

Dudein and Rench, the Caponis and Williams are named in one indictment. Most interesting testimony given the inquiring body, it was reported in connection with Stickney politics. The vice interests, it is said, threatened to "bring in Italians" when assured of opposition in the primary by a reform element. On voting day some twenty men, witnesses are reported to have said, appeared in the village and cast ballots.

Too Many Votes Cast.

Then they "drove around the cemetery, turned their hats around and voted again, and then again," it was said. The result was that 114 more votes were cast in Stickney than the registry of votes called for, according to evidence.

Village officials, when charged by citizens with failure to drive out the gang, are reported to have declared they were afraid for their families and lives.

Weiss and Foster are named in connection with Foster's attempt to vote under an assumed name in the polling place at 752 North Wells street, the 22d precinct of the 42d ward. Weiss, who drew a revolver during the altercation, is charged with assault to inflict body injury, Foster with illegal voting.

Chief Justice Lynch thanked the jurors, informing them that special State's Attorney Charles M. McDonald already had petitioned for another special jury, which would be impaneled July 6. Attorneys James C. O'Brien and Lloyd Heth, assistants to Former Judge McDonald, also were in court when the jury made its report. The jury was discharged following submission of the indictments.

$7,000 TRAIN RIDE TAKEN TO ATTEND SCIENCE MEETING

Mystery of Mrs. McCormick's Dash from New York Explained.

Mrs. Cyrus McCormick Jr. made her now famous $7,000-plus dash in a special train from New York to Chicago to get here in time to attend the annual meeting of the Bicknel Young Student association, composed of students of Mr. Young, an authorized lecturer of the Christian Scientist church.

This was authoritatively stated today by an official spokesman for Mr. Young. The association is composed of about fifteen students of Mr. Young and Mrs. McCormick has been a member for some years.

Began at 11 O'Clock.

The annual meeting started at 11 a. m. Tuesday in the Masonic hall at Dearborn street and Walton place. Luncheon was served and the meeting lasted well into the afternoon. It was not revealed who the other persons at the meeting besides Mr. Young and Mrs. McCormick were or what business was transacted.

Mrs. McCormick, accompanied by her husband, landed in New York on aboat from Europe Monday too late to catch any scheduled train which would bring her to Chicago in time for the meeting.

She immediately chartered a special train on the Pennsylvania railroad which rushed her to Chicago in record time. To charter the train she had to buy 125 full-fare tickets and pay some extra fees which totaled over $7,000, while if she had waited for the next regular fast train the trip would have cost her approximately $56.30 for railroad fare.

Only Few Minutes Late.

The trai nreached Chicago shortly before 11 a. m., and Mrs. McCormick immediately took a cab and drove to the Drake hotel, a block from the hall where the meeting was held. The cab went a roundabout way and in her efforts to dodge reporters, Mrs. McCormick was delayed, but she got to the Bicknel Young Student association meeting only a little time after it had convened and stayed until it was ended.

Mr. Young's spokesman said the meeting was the only reason he knew why Mrs. McCormick was in such a hurry to reach Chicago.

Mrs. McCormick today kept to her policy of silence and refused to make any statement concerning her dash from New York to Chicago.

Sister Takes Stand for Durkin

THORO PROBE OF AIMEE'S KIDNAPING STORY IS ORDERED

Grand Jury Is to Investigate; U. S. May Sift Mail Fraud Charge.

LOS ANGELES, July 2.—(AP)—A grand jury investigation of her abduction story instead of a wildly demonstrative throng of 50,000 persons that greeted her a week ago, awaits Aimee Semple McPherson on her return here today from Douglas, Ariz.

The crux of the evangelist's mysterious case was reached yesterday when postoffice inspectors revealed that a letter carrying what was designed to be substantial proof that the pastor was still alive had been tampered with in an apparent attempt to cover up the fact that the communication was delivered before and not after thousands of dollars in donations and pledges had been made at a memorial service for the then missing religious leader. The Angelus temple congregation still thought at the time of the service that their leader had gone to her death May 18, the victim of the surf at Ocean Park.

Plan Complete Probe.

Closely following the postal official's revelation, the county grand jury called before it Herman Cline, chief of Los Angeles detectives; Joe Ryan, deputy district attorney, who have been working on the case, and District Attorney Asa Keyes. Their appearance was followed by the announcement that the inquisitorial body was going to make a complete investigation of all phases of the case.

"The grand jury desires to be satisfied that the public may be given the facts to which they are entitled," said William H. Carter, foreman of the jury. "The grand jury wants the most exhaustive investigation and a full report will be made when the investigation is completed."

"While the county inquisitors were starting their investigation, it was disclosed that J. Edwin Simpson, deputy United States attorney, that because the letter in question also contained a demand for $500,000 ransom for the return of the evangelist, the McPherson case also probably would come to the attention of the federal grand jury.

Charges Mail Fraud Plot.

"We have become deeply interested in this case," Simpson said, "because it is apparent that a deliberate attempt was made to use the United States mails to defraud."

According to postoffice inspectors, the letter addressed to Mrs. Minnie Kennedy, the evangelist's mother, was delivered special delivery Saturday, June 19, the day before the memorial service. It contained what was described as a lock of Mrs. McPherson's hair and partial answers to questions propounded by Mrs. Kennedy to test the authenticity of a claim that her daughter was being held by kidnapers.

Mrs. Kennedy declared in Douglas last night that 12 stamps on the envelope had been tampered with, adding "but we think nothing about it; the letter was received by her Monday.

Mrs. McPherson and her mother left Douglas last night and are due to arrive here today. They arrived in Douglas from Los Angeles Thursday to aid in the search for a shack in which the evangelist said she was confined by kidnapers prior to her escape to Agua Prieta, Mexico. The search was unsuccessful.

Hit by Mayor's Story.

TUCSON, Ariz., July 2.—(AP)—Ernest Boubion, mayor of Agua Prieta, in a statement printed by the Arizona Daily Star here today, tells of his investigation of Mrs. Aimee Semple McPherson's story of her kidnaping after she appeared at his town on the morning of June 23 in a state of exhaustion.

Boubion was one of the first to talk to the Los Angeles evangelist and says he offered her food and aided her to reach Douglas, Ariz., where her identity was established. He said that Mrs. McPherson had alighted from an automobile a short distance from Agua Prieta and walked into the town.

Boubion said he instructed his chief of police to start the investigation the morning following the appearance of the evangelist. The inquiry showed that a woman had alighted from an automobile and went to a shack about four miles from Agua Prieta. She then returned to the car. The same tracks reappeared at the side of the road two miles from town and went to a slaughter-house a mile from Agua Prieta, where they were lost, the report stated.

Her Car Guarded.

The mayor said the tracks indicated they had been made the afternoon of June 22. He said a search covering a large desert area failed to reveal similar tracks.

When Mrs. McPherson passed thru here early this morning guards were stationed at the doors of her car. The conductor agreed to give her a copy of the Boubion's report.

Chicago looks to THE POST for its autor·bile news and views.

RESOLUTIONS IN SENATE TO BLOCK SEATING OF VARE

Huge Primary Expenses Are Cited Against the Candidate.

WASHINGTON, July 2.—(AP)—While the senate campaign investigating committee continues its pursuit of elusive details of the $3,000,000 Pennsylvania Republican primary, agitation is mounting in the senate for action before adjournment on resolutions which proponents say would prevent the seating of Representative Vare, the successful senatorial candidate in that contest.

Senator La Follette of Wisconsin, the insurgent Republican member of the committee, is the author of one of these resolutions, which already has been submitted to another committee for consideration, and Senator Neely (Dem., W. Va.) is the sponsor of another. Both would establish a rule designed to bar from the senate any candidate whose primary and election campaigns cost him and his supporters more than $10,000 to $25,000, according to the number of votes involved.

His Expenses Enormous.

Representative Vare's primary campaign has been shown to have cost something like twenty-five times the maximum set in the pending resolutions. His personal expenditures alone exceeded $70,000, and Senator Norris (Rep., Neb.) disclosed yesterday that he had indorsed the candidacy of his Democratic opponent, William B. Wilson, who told the investigating committee he spent less than $89 for the Pennsylvania senate seat.

Meantime the committee again has accelerated its pace, with its attention directed particularly toward the operations of the Anti-Saloon league and the reports of attempted purchases of support for Vare during the primary campaign. These subjects and others, including further inquiry into the activities of the Association Against the Prohibition Amendment, occupied it thru three sessions yesterday and last night.

Bribe Offer Disclosed.

Senator Pepper, who, with Gov. Pinchot, was defeated by Vare for the senatorial nomination, testified that Frank K. O'Connor, Philadelphia magistrate who ran against Vare's candidate for the seat he now holds in the house, told him he had been offered $75,000 to go over to the Vare organization.

This testimony flatly contradicted statements made to the committee earlier in the day by O'Connor, who reiterated his denial of the assertions of three Philadelphia Public Ledger reporters that he had ever told them or anyone else that Albert N. Greenfield, wealthy supporter of the representative, and Vare himself had offered $75,000 or $150,000 to change his course.

Pepper Gives More Facts.

Telling of a visit by O'Connor to his home during the campaign, Senator Pepper said the magistrate "even simulated how Vare and Greenfield approached him," and added that "this thing is so clear in my mind that it is as if it happened yesterday."

Senator Reed (Dem., Mo.), chairman of the committee, conducted the examination of most of the day's witnesses, who included, besides Pepper and O'Connor, Joseph A. Tatro, who was dismissed from the federal prohibition service, and who now is a special agent for the Pennsylvania alcohol permit board; Wayne B. Wheeler, general counsel of the Anti-Saloon league, and Charles S. Wood, national campaign manager for the Association Against the Prohibition Amendment. Questioning of Wood was turned over to Senator King (Dem., Utah), a dry member of the committee.

Three Miami, Fla., Banks Are Forced to Close Their Doors

MIAMI, Fla., July 2.—(AP)—Three Miami financial institutions, the Bank of Coconut Grove, the Bank of Buena Vista and the Bank of Little River, suspended operations here today. Outstanding loans on which they could not deliver were given by directors as reasons for suspension of activities.

BREEN CLEARED BY PROBE OF PENSION FUND PAYMENTS

W. F. Dodd Holds Evidence Insufficient for Action Before Bar.

Questionable conduct figured thruout the settlement of numerous claims made by widows of policemen and firemen during the regime of Mayor Thompson, according to a report made today by Attorney W. F. Dodd to Corporation Counsel Busch.

Mr. Dodd, who was appointed special counsel for the city to investigate the advisability of making charges against James Breen, who was first assistant corporation counsel under Thompson, informed Mr. Busch that altho questionable conduct figured in the various cases investigated by him he did not consider the evidence sufficent to prosecute Breen before the Chicago Bar association.

However, Dodd informed the corporation counsel the charges filed with the bar association would remain there for the time being. He said he intended to investigate certain definite angles before he makes a final report and recommendation.

Widows, Orphans, Robbed.

Dodd takes up specific cases in which it is claimed widows and orphans were robbed by city officials. He analyzed the evidence which was presented to him and in each instance explains his reasons for doubting the necessary evidence was forthcoming if the Bar association should go into the matter.

This is the second time Breen has been vindicated on the same ground. When the city council committee, of which Ald. Albert is chairman, investigated the scandal in connection with the pension funds, State's Attorney Crowe was appealed to by the aldermen to begin a criminal prosecution against Breen. The prosecutor, however, decided there was no evidence which would warrant a grand jury investigation and the matter was dropped.

George Silkes, who was secretary of the pension board, as well as the members appointed by Mayor Dever, however, insisted on further investigation. The result was that Busch appointed Dodd as special counsel with directions to make a thoro investigation.

Breen frequently denied having any part in any of the graft which Ald. Albert's committee found had prevailed during the Thompson administration.

Rhode Island Textile Mills to Shut Down

PROVIDENCE, R. I., July 2.—(AP)—Comparatively few looms and spindles in Rhode Island's textile mills will be in operation next week as a result of shutdowns for periods ranigng from one to four weeks. Announcement that approximately 2,000 operatives in the Pawtucket valley will be made idle by the closing of mills in that section was made today.

Latonia Scratches

Second—Mary Beverly, Cynthia Gray, Junior's Nurse, Secrecy, Niani Beach, Poly Angle.
Third—Lady Stone.
Fourth—Mr. Kirkwood, Undergrowth, Bunthorne, Aurous, Brumfield, Busy Day, Dolly S.
Seventh—You Are, Big Money, Barrister, Vivandiere, Ethel K., Smacker, Lord Meise.

Akron Scratches

First—Theoden, Broadway Rose, Roseberry, Napan, Millie G., Rivulet, Dora Lutz, Dan E. Stewart.
Second—Harry M. Stevens, Hindoostan, Farewell, Tapsv, Duke of Ridgeview, Billy Walz.
Seventh—Tease, Mary G.

Windsor Scratches

First—Ima Vamp, Lillian L.
Third—Rock Sugar, Powder, Charlie.
Sixth—Donges, Desert Gold, Denizen, Faenza, Camouflage, Delusive, Who Knows Me, Labelle.

Fairmount Scratches

First—Bonny Castle.
Second—Shining Gold, The Count.
Seventh—Willies Maid.

Celebrates Her Ninety-third Birthday.

MINONK, Ill., July 2.—Mrs. Gretje Oltman of Clayton township celebrated her ninety-third birthday Tuesday. She was born in Germany and came to Am·ica with her husband in 1867.

TRACK PROMOTERS PLAN LEGAL PLEA TO ALLOW WAGERS

Homewood Track to Open Tomorrow, Says Sweitzer.

The new Washington park race track at Homewood is scheduled to open tomorrow, but State's Attorney Crowe is determined that there shall be no open betting at the thirty-one-day meeting. Crowe has marshalled ninety deputies in his office and has given them instructions for their first day's drive against the certificate system of betting which the Homewood officials figure on using.

With the gathering of the army of deputies the war between Crowe and Robert Sweitzer, president of the jockey club, has reached a climax.

Sweitzer and his associates issued the following statement today:

To Open Tomorrow.

"We will open the track tomorrow and we are going to have a high class brand of racing; as high as there is in America. Our attorneys tell us that our plans are within the law. We have no desire to violate the law and, if we think necessary, we will go into court today and let the courts decide the merits of this case.

"I have been told that Mr. Crowe has stated that he would ignore any court injunction that we might get out restraining him from interfering with our opening tomorrow. The state's attorney, by saying that, takes on the power of the Supreme court and the sheriff, which powers are not given him by the statutes.

"We are only seeking the good will of the people. The Aurora plan has met with favor thruout the state and is apparently legal thruout the state and no public official has tried to stop them."

There has been considerable doubt

Continued on Page 6.

DEPUTIES GOT TAXI RECEIPTS TO "PAD" EXPENSES

DES MOINES, July 2.—(AP)—An investigation into an alleged conspiracy on the part of two deputies of United States Marshal Roy Gault of the southern district of Iowa, to defraud the government thru expense accounts padding has been completed by two department of justice agents.

The checkup of records is reported to have involved two deputy marshals who were alleged to have been aided by two outsiders in procuring fake taxi receipts and other false items which were included in expense vouchers for trips made in handling federal prisoners. The money involved in the inquiry would not exceed $500.

A report of the investigation will go to Washington at once and action is expected to be taken there by the first of next week.

FATHER ASKS HIS SON BE JAILED FOR STEALING

William Michaelson, 1454 Melrose street, appeared today in the Town hall court before Judge Harry F. Hamlin as the sole witness against his son, Theodore, 18 years old, charged with larceny.

The father related how the boy recently, rifled his pockets of $14 while he was asleep and stole the key to the family garage, taking out the automobile which he wrecked.

"What do you want done with him?" Judge Hamlin asked the father.

"I want him put away until he5s 21," Michaelson said. "His mother and I can do nothing with him."

Theodore, who said he had spent the $14 on gasoline for the automobile, was sentenced to six months in the house of correction.

Senate Adopts Resolution Regarding Civil Service

WASHINGTON, July 2.—(AP)—A joint resolution offered by Senator Heflin (Dem., Ala.) directing the civil service commission in reducing the force of civil service employes to make the separations from states which have an excess quota was passed last night by the senate and sent to the house. It would also direct the commission to separate no employe from a state in arrears of its quota except from cause.

Radio Aerial Helping Growth of Tomatoes

NOTTINGHAM, England, July 2.—(AP)—That vegetables can be grown by wireless energy is the claim of an amateur gardener of West Bridgeford. He says he noticed that tomato and cucumber plants were drawing energy from his aerial and making wonderful headway. Plants eighteen feet long are said by him to have yielded thirty-five cucumbers, some two feet long.

Write to THE POST. Express your ideas in the paper read by thinking people.

Taxi Driver Stabbed in Abdomen Traps 2 Assailants in Cab

Converting his taxicab into a temporary "prison," Michael Argondis, 4630 North Racine avenue, today locked inside two men who had stabbed him, commandeered another taxi and returned with a squad of police who arrested his assailants.

The prisoners were Edmund Platt, 2125 North Clark street, and John Edwards, 548 North Dearborn street. The stabbing occurred at State street and Delaware place during a dispute over a fare. Argondis was seriously stabbed in the abdomen and on the face.

Altho weak from loss of blood, Argondis heroically locked Edwards and Platt inside the cab and raced to the Chicago avenue station. With the bluecoats he was back again within a few minutes. Platt and Edwards were ready to break the taxicab windows to escape when nabbed. Argondis was taken to the Henrotin hospital.

MOOSE WOMEN PROVE EQUALITY BY KEEPING SECRET

Mooseheart Legion Holds Sessions Behind Locked Doors; Men Barred.

By Ione Quinby.

Men for years have puffed out their chests and strutted with pride because they considered themselves superior to women.

And what was this superiority? Lend your ears, oh, men and women readers and I'll tell you. They thought because they were men they could keep a secret, and they thought because women wer women, that women couldn't. Well, this morning at the first ritualistic meting of the Mooseheart legion of the Loyal Order of Moose, at the Hotel Sherman, all of this part of men's fancied superiority was knocked into a cocked hat.

Women proved by putting themselves behind locked doors, that they too could know something and not reveal it. The legion part of the Moose order is the women's auxiliary and represnts close to 60,000 thruout the country. Thousands of the members are in Chicago this week to attend the annual convention and they aren't letting outsiders or men Moose, either, into ·ings of their own particular section.

Represent 1,400 Lodges.

The women, here from all over the country, and one from Honolulu, represent 1,400 lodgesf o the legion. A large portion of these lodges sent representatives or delegates into the huge Louis XVI. room of the hotel today to take part in the ritualistic contest.

To those who are unitiated, in even the appearance o the Moose's locked horns, I want to explain that the ritualistic contest has to do with the reciting the ritual of the legion. The lodge representative who recite it (and one of them told me it is quite lengthy and t akes about a month to learn, if one concentrates), are doing it with three prives in view. The virst prize for the lodge that knows its ritual best is $300. The second is $200 and the third $100. The money, of course, will go into the lucky lodge's coffers to be spent on Moosehaven, the haven of aged Moose members near Jacksonville, Fla.

Andrews Sails Tuesday to Get British Dry Aid

NEW YORK, July 2.—(AP)—Lincoln C. Andrews, assistant secretary of the treasury in charge of prohibition enforcement, will head a commission sailing for England on the Aquitania Tuesday to seek closer British co-operation in enforcing prohibition regulations.

Test Student Killed by Shock at Electric Plant

SCHENECTADY, N. Y., July 2.—(AP)—R. E. Porter, test student at the General Electric company plant, was almost instantly killed by coming in contact with a 1,250-volt collector ring of an inductor motor today. Porter came here last week from Kansas City. He is survived by his widow.

Bishop Muldoon Doing Well After Operation

ST. LOUIS, June 2.—(AP)—Continued improvement was reported today in the condition of Bishop P. J. Muldoon of Rockford, Ill., who was operated upon for appendicities at St. John's hospital here Wednesday.

Twenty-five Years for Slayer.

PETERSBURG, Ill., July 2.—(AP)—Alfred Bradley, 19, who stabbed his former friend, John Tice to death last Janary, was found guilty of murder and sentenced to twenty-five years' imprisonment by a jury at 2:30 o'clock this morning.

Man, 72, Leaps to Death.

DANVILLE, Ill., July 2.—Despondent because of ill health, John Wendt, 72, leaped from an upper story of St. Elizabeth's hospital to his death last night.

LUCILLE DENIES HE THREATENED TO KILL POLICE

Girl of 17 Testifies in Effort to Save Life of Slayer.

Her boyish bob accentuating her youth and giving her the appearance of being the kid brother of Martin Durkin, 17-year-old Lucille Durkin, the gunman's sister, took the witness stand in Judge Miller's court today to try to save her brother from the gallows.

Lucille made altogether too pretty and bewitching a picture, in a trim frock of blue heather with a sau·y flare, as she told of her faith in Marty and contradicted the damaging statements made by Betty Werner, his jilted flame.

She told of her motor trip to California in 1925 with Matry, Betty and her own mother, Mrs. Hattie Durkin. But it was not true, she insisted, that her brother had warned them the police were after him, that, should any officer of the law try to stop him, he would shoot his way out.

"What Marty really did," she lisped, "was that if bandits or holdup men stopped us, he would shoot, and we should lie down on the bottom of the car. He carried a good deal of money with him, and he had a gun in the car. But he was not afraid of the police—only of highwaymen."

After the shooting of Federal Agent Edwin C. Shanahan, she testified, she had seen Marty on the street and talked to him.

Saw Bill of Sale.

She had seen, she said, a bill of sale for the Packard sedan her brother was accused of stealing.

Cross-examined by Assistant State's Attorney Romano, Lucille denied Marty had ever used an alias, at least, so far as her own knowledge went. She had never inquired into his occupation, and didn't know the nature of his business, she said. Only that he was generous and often gave her money.

Durkin lost an important decision, when Judge Miller turned thumbs down on the motion of the defense attorney that the transcript of Harlow George's testimony at the coroner's inquest be introduced in evidence.

George, regarded as an important defense witness, has been absent since the beginning of the trial, and his mysterious disappearance especially worried Durkin today.

Was An Eye-Witness

It was George, a former companion of Durkin who tipped off the federal officers to his whereabouts. George also was an eye-witness to the shooting—or so he testified before the inquest jury. And, according to his statements at that time, it was Shanahan, not Marty, who fired the first shot in the gun duel.

Prosecutor Romano suggested that if the defense wanted this testimony it would be advisable to procure the witness and to get it at first hand, and Judge Miller was inclined to agree with this.

The day's first witness was Sam R. Merchant of 5602 South Racine avenue, Betty Werner's grandfather and the father-in-law of Harlow George.

It was his opinion, he declared on the stand, that Betty's reputation for truth and veracity was none too good. He testified to having seen a bill of sale for Durkin's Packard car.

Argument Over Car.

There had been some trouble between Betty and George over the sale of this car, he said. George, he said, maintained it was a "hot," or stolen car. It was to settle the argument, he testified, that Durkin produced the bill of sale.

Another witness was Mrs. Blanche Golz, Betty's aunt, who also expressed her doubts as to the girl's reputation for truth telling.

It was suggested by Romano that she might possibly be jealous of her niece because of the fine feathers of the latter, but this the woman denied emphatically.

On Stand Next Week.

Durkin probably will not take the stand until next Tuesday.

A slight possibility that he might be called late today was voiced by McGarry, providing that all other defense witnesses had completed their story. If not, court will adjourn until Tuesday over the holiday week-end.

N. Y. "L," Subway Men, Threaten Walkout July

NEW YORK, July 2.—(AP)—A labo cloud today cast a shadow on th Fourth of July holiday prospects o thousands of New Yorkers. Motor men and switchmen of the Interbor ough Rapid Transit and subway line have fixed midnight Monday for walkout if the company fails to ac favorably on their ultimatum th wages be increased.

John A. Foster Resigns.

NEW YORK, July 2.—The resigna tion of John A. Foster, former fed eral prohibition administrator of th New York district, and at present s pervisor of alcohol control at Was ington, D. C., was announced tod

READ 'THE MIRACLE'—TODAY'S TRUE STORY—PAGE 20

Automobile Market
A list of the best "buys" in used cars every day in the classified section.

HERALD CHICAGO AND EXAMINER

FINAL EDITION

46th YEAR No. 133 | Registered U. S. Patent Office Copyright, 1926, Herald and Examiner | Telephone Main 5000 | WEDNESDAY, OCTOBER 13, 1926. | C*** | TWO PARTS. | PRICE 3 CENTS

CAPONE'S OWN AMAZING STORY!

REGISTRATION FALLS OFF BY 188,000; TAKE KLAN DRAGON FROM PRISON TODAY

Today

The Bootleg Tong.
He Did Not Believe Them.
New-Old Kind of Death.

—By Arthur Brisbane—

(Copyright, 1926, by Star Company.)

WE used to wonder at Chinese tongs, their murderous feuds, their unwillingness to enter courts, their Chinese home-made "justice" in this land.

Now the Chinese wonder at us, as our bootleggers—Chicago holding the championship—show how a tong should be run for efficiency.

In the latest alcoholic tong exploit there figured two machine guns, public streets swept with bullets, two killed, three wounded. More killings will come within a week, the police say, for the O'Banion gang, having lost two men, will demand double blood pay.

While the bootleg tongs fight it out police cars dash through the streets, catching nobody. No fault of the police. They cannot guess what bootlegger is preparing his machine gun for his enemies.

The bootleg barrage was laid down directly in front of the Holy Name Cathedral, and close to the home of Mr. Rockefeller's daughter—nothing lacking, in romance or audacity.

COLUMBUS DAY is over, and you could probably count on your fingers those in your circle that thought as much as two minutes about Columbus.

His achievement can be summed up in a few words:

"He did not believe those that said it could not be done."

He ran the usual course, rendered service to the world, was put in jail for his pains, and as much as possible of the credit was taken by Isabella and others that deserved NO credit. This continent was not even named for its discoverer.

Yes, others came here before Columbus, but that means nothing. A steam engine was exhibited more than two thousand years ago in the Serapeion, at Alexandria. That does not hurt the inventor that makes the practical success.

Columbus was followed by practical success. Look at Chicago, Seattle, New York, Boston, San Diego, and respect Columbus.

IN the best known Japanese suicide, the gentleman, opening the wall of his abdomen with a sharp knife, disembowels himself, showing no sign of pain. That takes courage.

Giichi Kitawaza of Tokyo, disappointed in love, tried a new way, and ate himself to death. With his hard-hearted, adored one across the table from him, he deliberately stuffed himself with rice, curry, eggs, pouring down whisky and a worse drink, sake. Soon he was unconscious and in a few hours dead.

Let us remember, for our good, that what Mr. Kitawaza did in a few hours nine-tenths of us do in about half a normal lifetime. Too much eating or wrong eating or both kill the great majority. Senator Copeland, who is also a doctor, says "half of what we eat keeps us alive, the other half keeps the doctors alive."

SECRETARY MELLON, whose management has cleared away seven thousand millions of our national debt, says Mussolini's government is no longer a one-man machine.

Mr. Mellon sees in Mussolini, with whom he has had long conversations, not merely "one of the world's most vigorous personalities," but a sound organization builder. Mr. Mellon has proved that he knows something about organization. Ask his business competitors.

He says "Mussolini's organization is sound and there should be time enough for him to build strongly. He is a young man yet."

Mr. Mellon added a parenthesis: "That is, of course, if they stop throwing bombs at him."

That is the big IF, but courage counts, even against bombs; it discourages and intimidates the bomb thrower, and prolongs life. Mussolini has courage.

THINKING does make it so, sometimes. Mrs. Victoria Irsyebisk, 30, of Detroit, consulted a fortune teller, who said, "You will die a suicide." The woman, brooding over the prediction, killed herself with poison. The fortune teller will go to prison, if caught.

The unhappy woman's fate, fortunately rare, reminds you that thousands live, and fail, victims of some harmful suggestion.

Let a man get it into his head that he amounts to nothing and he WILL amount to nothing, usually. Conceit is bad, often destructive, but absence of all confidence in yourself is fatal.

It's the old golden mean—not

Turn to Page 7, Column 1.

STEPHENSON SELLS OUT TO FOES, REPORT

Chief of Counsel Is Ousted; Editor Before Jury 2 Hours; 'Steve' Comes Up Thursday

Forces Seeking to Bare Corruption Fear 'Double Cross'; Women Hold Vital Clues

By Sam Blair,
Herald and Examiner Staff Correspondent.

INDIANAPOLIS, Oct. 12.—Surrounded by a heavy guard, D. C. Stephenson, former klan czar and political dictator of Indiana, is expected to be taken from Michigan City penitentiary Wednesday night and rushed by motor to Indianapolis, where he will appear before the grand jury Thursday morning at 9 o'clock.

Hopes, however, that the man who is now serving a life sentence for murder will make good his promise to lay bare Indiana's "political rottenness" were considerably dampened today by a series of peculiar developments which indicate he has sold out to the very interests he was to "expose."

The first of these developments came in a telegram signed with Stephenson's name and presumably sent from the penitentiary.

Switches Attorneys

It was addressed to Tom Miller, Muncie lawyer, recently employed by Stephenson to arrange for an appeal from the murder conviction and to disseminate, for public edification, the documents supposed to rip the fabric of the state's corrupt politics wide open.

The telegram read: **"Stop all publicity; put Kiplinger back on list."**

John I. Kiplinger, attorney of Rushville, Ind., and chief counsel for Stephenson during his trial a year ago, telephoned Miller and explained the telegram meant he had been re-retained to represent Stephenson.

"I don't regard that telegram as genuine," Miller responded.

Kiplinger thereupon hurried to Michigan City. Accompanied by L. G. Julian of Evansville, one of Stephenson's intimates, he was given an immediate interview with the prisoner. Later another telegram

Turn to Page 4. Column 2.

THE WEATHER

WEDNESDAY, OCTOBER 13, 1926.

Sunrise, 6 a. m.; sunset, 5:13 p. m. Moon sets, 9:56 p. m.

Chicago and Vicinity—Generally fair Wednesday and Thursday; somewhat warmer by Thursday; moderate variable winds.

Illinois — Generally fair Wednesday and Thursday; rising temperature Thursday, and in northwest portion Wednesday.

COOLER / FAIR / WARMER / RAIN

TEMPERATURES IN CHICAGO

MAXIMUM, NOON 67
MINIMUM, 1 A. M. 55

3 a. m..57	12 noon..67	9 p. m..54
4 a. m..57	1 p. m..64	Unofficial
5 a. m..59	2 p. m..63	10 p. m..53
6 a. m..59	3 p. m..57	11 p. m..53
7 a. m..60	4 p. m..58	12 mid't..52
8 a. m..61	5 p. m..57	1 a. m..51
9 a. m..63	6 p. m..57	2 a. m..50
10 a. m..64	7 p. m..55	
11 a. m..65	8 p. m..54	

Mean temperature for twenty-four hours ended at 7 p. m., Tuesday, 61; normal for day, 56. Deficiency since January 1, 191 degrees.

Barometer, 7 a. m., 29.94; 7 p. m., 30.02. Precipitation, .39 of an inch. Excess since January 1, 3.02 inches.

Official Weather Table on Page 27.

The Classified Ads Begin on Page 27. Read Them for What You Want.

May Rule Britain

Princess Beatrice.

RUMOR MARRIES WALES AGAIN!

LONDON, Oct. 12.—Reports that the Prince of Wales is to marry the Infanta Beatrice of Spain have been revived.

This is in spite of an official and formal denial issued tonight from York House. It was pointed out in the denial that the report was published here two weeks ago and promptly denied then.

The renovation of Marlborough House has been resumed, and this is regarded as the strongest indication that the rumor is founded on fact. The Spanish princess has been a frequent visitor at Buckingham Palace.

Ye Queene Daunces at Ye Gillies Balle

LONDON, Oct. 12. — (AP) — King George was a smiling spectator when Queen Mary took the floor at the annual "Gillies ball" and led off the opening reel with one of the higher officials of their Balmoral castle. The Queen finished the dance, but sat out most of the others—which did not include a modern dance and not even a little bit of jazz.

Lady Cathcart Writes 'Very Modern' Novel

LONDON, Oct. 12.—(By Universal.)—Vera, Countess of Cathcart, whose detention at Ellis Island caused a stir last year, has completed a new novel, according to the Daily Sketch. The book is shortly to be published and is entitled "It Came to Pass." It is described as "very modern."

ONLY 876,509 QUALIFY FOR NOVEMBER VOTE

G. O. P. Split, Ballot Frauds, Blamed; Hailed as Good Omen for Brennan Ticket

Final vote registration figures last night showed a loss of 188,386 over the 1924 total, a loss attributed in some quarters to factional fighting in the Republican party, and by others to public reaction to the recent vote fraud exposé.

The registration total was 876,508 against a total of 1,064,895 for 1924.

"The loss is startling," said Judge Daniel Trude, who contested the Republican nomination for Assistant State's Attorney Joseph P. Savage for county judge on a charge of fraud. "It shows many persons have become convinced that it is useless to vote, because the state's attorney has neglected to prosecute the vote fraud cases."

Whatever the reason for the loss, despite the fact that population is greater, impartial observers said the Democratic party—particularly the wet element backing Brennan—will profit by it.

Democratic leaders said the loss was due in part to the Illinois G. O. P.'s divided stand on the prohibition question.

A total of 461,679 citizens registered yesterday. This, with the October 2 registration, brought the figure for this year to 876,509.

The registration total this year and that in 1924 follow:

W.	1926.	1924.	W.	1926.	1924.
1..	14665	17099	26..	11333	12937
2..	22785	27566	27..	17082	20215
3..	23856	33516	28..	16375	21650
4..	22453	28403	29..	22398	26651
5..	21149	29140	30..	28083	31263
6..	20471	28111	31..	8889	9245
7..	23869	28941	32..	10351	12277
8..	22402	25571	33..	10931	13128
9..	14942	18367	34..	11905	14403
10..	11953	13263	35..	13071	17190
11..	11608	13875	36..	14823	17997
12..	19328	17875	37..	28720	33995
13..	9597	10327	38..	13931	17815
14..	16232	18871	39..	24056	28941
15..	27577	29472	40..	21990	30383
16..	16788	20392	41..	26485	29319
17..	16757	22771	42..	12983	19090
18..	20723	23426	43..	12549	17012
19..	24795	29264	44..	14264	19878
20..	14363	13045	45..	14952	17749
21..	12588	13715	46..	14871	21373
22..	12927	14152	47..	20350	26336
23..	16970	18663	48..	17339	24448
24..	13442	13664	49..	25957	35185
25..	10562	14632	50..	20118	25216
Total				876509	1064895

The total for October 2, the first day of registration, was 414,830. Yesterday's figures were 461,679.

Moffett Will Fly Dirigible to Detroit

LAKEHURST, N. J., Oct. 12.—Flight of the navy dirigible Los Angeles to the Ford airport at Dearborn, Mich., today was postponed until tomorrow because of unfavorable weather conditions.

WASHINGTON, Oct. 12.—Rear Admiral William A. Moffett, chief of naval aeronautics, will make the flight to Detroit with the Los Angeles, it was announced today.

MARIE SAILS FOR U. S. WITH FIFTY TRUNKS

'Visit Will Realize My Fondest Dreams,' Writes the Queen in Message to America.

Queen Marie sailed from France yesterday for America on the Leviathan with her royal retinue and fifty trunks of personal attire. On the eve of her departure she wrote as follows about her approaching visit:

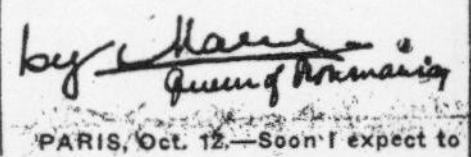

PARIS, Oct. 12.—Soon I expect to realize my dream of coming to America.

I feel I am coming to a country full of friends.

Now, more than ever, I am looking forward to America, and what great joy I find in that looking forward—so much joy that I hope it will not end in disappointment on either side.

I shall do all I can that it shall not be a disappointment. I want you to feel that I come to you all, to be able to go everywhere.

I believe women have a peculiarly keen intuition about people, and know whom to trust and whom not to. As I look back over a lifetime of none-too-guarded speech and action, I find I have been taken advantage of very rarely.

I am misquoted, misunderstood sometimes. But I would rather have that happen than set a padlock upon my lips and a ball-and-chain upon my feet. I trust people, believe in them, and am more than ready to think them sincere, and I want others to treat me likewise.

All Effort Counts

If we are wise we do not kick too hard against inevitable things, things that just are without our being able to avert or alter them. But we do look back sometimes to learn, so that we may more wisely look forward, taking lessons from the past.

If we are good as well as wise, we will become kinder as our wisdom deepens. For if knowledge increases sorrow, it also increases understanding of others' sorrow and the desire to help, strengthen and forgive.

God has a work, a place, for each of us on earth.

Cites Own Spirits

Things usually look better or worse than they are. The prim young woman, the studious-looking youth, must not always be taken at their face value.

On the other hand, the audacious girl and the boy who thinks himself "a devil" are often quite mild in spirit and straight as a string morally.

When I was young, I was most daring. I did things just for the fun of it, to let off steam, to try my muscles, my powers of resistance, perhaps my powers of exciting admiration, but always for the sheer joy of living and nothing more.

Remembering my own tempestuousness, I am perhaps now too lenient toward youth's audacities.

News of Queen Marie's departure for America on Page 5.

San Francisco Arms Against Mad Slayers

SAN FRANCISCO, Oct. 12.—Every San Francisco police officer was ordered on duty today in an effort to trap the pair of maniac desperadoes who last night murdered three men and wounded five others in a carnival of crime. They are thought to be the same pair who killed two men Saturday night and wounded several others in a similar outbreak.

Peace! Pleads Cicero Czar; Invites Foes to Meet and End War

By Patricia Dougherty.
(Copyright, 1926, by Herald and Examiner.)
Reproduction in Whole or in Part Strictly Prohibited.

WHILE Chicago police were "looking for" Alphonse ("Scarface Al") Capone last night, to get his version of the machine gunning that sent "Hymie" Weiss to a slab in Sbarbaro's morgue, "the King of Cicero" sat in his room at the Hawthorne Inn and told me his story of Chicago's reign of terror.

The man whose name has echoed through every bloody chapter of the city's barbaric battle over rum and its profits broke his long silence to tell the story in all its gruesome detail, and throughout the recital ran a strange undertone.

A Prayer for Peace

It was a passionate denunciation of the "butchery" that has horrified the nation, and a pleading prayer for peace.

"I've got a boy," he said, handing me a photograph of a beautiful child of 7.

"I love that kid more than anything in the world, and next to him I love his mother, and then my own mother and my sisters and brothers. I don't want to die. Especially I don't want to die in the street, punctured with machine gun fire. That's the reason I've asked for peace.

Begs Shooting Cease

"I've begged those fellows to put away their pistols and talk sense to me. They've all got families, too; most of them are kids and they haven't any children, but they've got mothers and sisters.

"What makes them so crazy to end up on a slab in a

Alphonse Capone.

Turn to Page 2, Column 3.

U. S. FOES MAR WILSON SLAB

GENEVA, Oct. 12.—(AP)—Criticism of the United States was contained in a placard today found pasted on the marble slab in the wall of the League of Nations Building that commemorates the memory of Woodrow Wilson as founder of the league.

The placard read: "In considering him as the founder of the league of nations, President Wilson should be considered in a personal sense and not as President of the United States. The American people have done nothing to deserve that their President should be designated as the founder of the league.

The placard was written in English and its authorship is not known. League officials removed it.

Nicotine and Swear Words Bars to Debate

BALDWIN, Kan., Oct. 12.—(AP)—Students who swear or smoke cannot participate in oratorical contests at Baker University here, for which the will of Albert Lumpkin of Fort Worth, Tex., provided gold prizes.

RAIDERS STEAL $2,000,000 GEM

CHANTILLY, France, Oct. 12.—(AP)—The famous rose diamond known as "the Grand Conde," and valued at more than $2,000,000, was the most precious of a number of priceless treasures stolen this morning from the chateau of the Duc D'Aumale, a national museum of France.

A band of thieves scaled the high walls of the castle grounds with the aid of two ladders, crossed a moat and climbed to the famous "room of gems."

The rose diamond, heart-shaped, an inch long and more than a half-inch wide, was once owned by Prince De Conde, Louis II of Bourbon.

Husband and Wife Killed by Same Car

George S. Manner, 68, of 548 Elmwood av., Evanston, died last night at the St. Francis Hospital from injuries suffered Saturday when he and his wife were struck by an automobile at Ridge blvd. and Seward av. Mrs. Manner died a few hours after the accident.

WEISS' AIDS ACCUSED OF SHOOTING HIM

Eyewitness Names Pellar and Jacobs; They Deny It; Police Seek 40 Gangster Chiefs

Saltis Trial's Fate in Doubt; Deneen Denies Threats; Shotguns for Flivver Squads

Out of eyewitness' accounts of the slaying of Earl ("Hymie") Weiss and an aid in the beer and alcohol gang war there was evolved last night a theory of a "triple cross" suggested by the testimony of Charles E. McKibben, 730 N. State st., at the double inquest yesterday.

He asserted his conviction that two members of the Weiss-Vincent ("Schemer") Drucci combine shot Weiss to death, and in their flight were wounded by machine gun bullets from the "second floor front" of 740 N. State st. by the two hidden machine gunners.

Sleuths Divided

Sam Pellar, Weiss bodyguard, and Ben Jacobs, Twentieth Ward politician, who said he drove Attorney W. W. O'Brien, who was wounded in the gang ambush, to the Holy Name Cathedral corner, were identified by McKibben as the two men who fired round after round of revolver bullets at Weiss.

The "triple-cross" theory had its supporters and its doubters among police investigating the murder of Weiss, his henchman, Patrick Murray, and the wounding of Attorney O'Brien, Pellar and Jacobs.

Other developments during the day were:

1. **Reports that spies from one of the powerful gangs have had the home of United States Senator Deneen under surveillance and were under orders to assassinate any liquor graft informers who might visit him.**

2. While police were reported to have drawn up a list of forty prominent gangsters to be arrested, and supposedly were

BOYS TIPSY, GIRLS SMOKING, CHARGE AT SCHOOL GRID GAME

MADISON, Wis., Oct. 12.—(AP)—Charges that Madison High School students were intoxicated on the streets of Richland Center October 2, when they accompanied the football team to a game, were being investigated today by Volney G. Barnes, principal of the Madison High School.

The charges were made by H. S. Bonar, principal of the Richland Center High School, and citizens of Richland Center.

Mr. Bonar declared that one of his instructors and several citizens have reported the case to him.

"They told me that girls and boys smoked cigarets, both on the football grounds and on the main street," Mr. Bonar declared. "Others were drinking. I am told that one boy was so drunk that he was ill and his companions were hurrying around to find medicine for him when a Richland Center man told them to get him out of sight or he would have them arrested."

XXX EDITION

THE CHICAGO EVENING POST

XXX EDITION

THIRTY-SEVENTH YEAR.—OFFICIAL NEWSPAPER OF CITY OF CHICAGO * FRIDAY, OCTOBER 15, 1926. * PRICE THREE CENTS

SALTIS JURY DISMISSED

DISMISSES SALTIS JURY ON MOTION OF PROSECUTION

Judge Orders New Trial in Murder Cases Started Oct. 20.

The jury which on Wednesday started the trial of "Polack Joe" Saltis and his lieutenant, Frank ("Lefty") Koncil, charged with the murder of John ("Mitters") Foley, today was dismissed by Judge Harry B. Miller on the motion of the state, because, evidence disclosed, there was a man in the box alleged to be insane.

The motion for the dismissal was made by Special Assistant State's Attorney Lloyd Heth as the result yesterday of the testimony of Dr. William Krohn, alienist, that John Riley, 5224 Warner avenue, one of the jurors, was a victim of "circular insanity." The defense, represented by Attorney Frank McDonnell, agreed to the procedure.

Following the dismissal of tht jurors a hoe fight developed between Mr. Heth and Mr. McDonnell. Heth refused to accede to the request of the defense lawyer to have the case continued indefinitely, or ten days he asked in a later request, but insisted a new jury be selected immediately.

State Wins Victory.

Judge Miller upheld the state and ordered the lawyers to start picking the new jury next Wednesday. An other panel of 100 men will be called for that date.

The jury was brought from its quarters in the Alexandria hotel. The jurors knew something was up, but, as they have had no newspapers and no one had been allowed to communicate with hem, they had no way of knowing that one of their number had been declared insane.

Riley, the unfortunate juror, came into court smokin ga cigaret. Earlier, Bailiffs Nathan Blond and Walter Koehler had notified Judge Miller that last night Riley ha dbecome uncontrollable and they were forced to strap him to his bed with sheets. They said he had tried to hurl the dishes at them when they brought hi mhis dinner.

One of the bailiffs tapped Riley on the shoulder and told him it was against court ruels to smoke.

"All right, thank you," he replied in a loud voice.

Faces Mind Test.

Judge Miller outlined the situation t othe others and then assigned Deputy Sheriff John Stefanou to take Riley to the psychopathic hospital for observation. The other jurymen were allowed to go to their homes.

When the jury had filed out and the attorney asked the court's pleasure as to the next proceedings, Attorney McDonnell made his request for a continuance for twenty days,

"Mr. O'Brien (W. W. O'Brien who was wounded in the shooting melee in front of Schofield's floral shop in which two other also were wounded and "Hymie" Weiss and Paddy Murray killed) will be out of the hospital in that time and I am not prepared to go on with the case without him," he said.

Mr. Heth reminided the court McDonald had announced just after the shooting that he would carry on.

State Is Ready.

"A long continuance in this matter would result in the collopse of the state's case," the prosecutor said. "We have our witnesses in police custody—for their own safety—and they are becomni gimpatient. They want to go home.

"One f our witnesses, a Mrs. Brown, was threatened with having her home bomber and her child kidnaped. Another, Jack Dunn, was threatened with death and was offered a bribe. Two of our witnesses have disappeared supposedly sent awy with money in their pockets."

Attorney McDonnell, pparently angered, lossed a torrent of bitter denunciation of the special prosecutors and their methods. He termed them "inhuman" an daccused them of "trying their case in the newspapers. He said the state was arousing a spirit of mob violence against the defendants.

He cotniued along this line and in lengthy argument against immediate trial declared that the gangsters who shot and killed Weiss and Murray really believed Murray to be him.

His argument was overruled, however, and the court set next Wednesday for the selection of the new jury.

The new "gang squads" put to work yesterday by Chief Collins had little to do last night. The squads in zone D, under Capt. Frank Mitchell, raided a poolroom at 1225 South Kedzie avenue and arrested ten men. They were taken to the detective bureau and probably will be charged with disorderly conduct.

Meanwhile, it was learned, a new gang chieftain has taken over the reins dropped by Weiss. He is, the police say, George Moran, a tough gangster and a deadly foe of Alphonse Caponi, better known as Scarface Brown, leader in Cicero and Chicago Heights vice and booze rings. Moran, it is said, is known to the Cicero gangsters as "The Devil."

Laurel Scratches

First—Sealady, Romany, Merry Monarch, Candymaker, Steelribs, Meridian Hill.

Second—Trajanus, Allumeur Jr., ...achenee Belle, Flint, ... Golden Volt. ...ition, Eda C.

Police Chase and Halt "L" Train to Seize Two Bandits

Racing thru city streets at sixty miles an hour, a detective bureau squad early today overtook a speeding loopbound elevated train, flagged it at the Indiana avenue station and nabbed two alleged bandits, one a pretty young woman, bobbed-haired and blond, who had a short time before held up a taxicab chauffeur, according to his complaint.

They gave their names as Albert Weisbaum and Jean Hunter, 23 years old, and their addresses as the Sheridan Plaza hotel. Miss Hunter is from Peoria.

The couple had been driven to 56th street and South Spauling avenue by Elmer Sach, 125 Clyde avenue, Evanston, a Yellow cab chauffeur.

Robs Driver of $6.

There, according to his story, they robbed him of $6. Their efforts to steal his cab was frustrated when Sach temporarily put it out of commission. Weisbaum and Miss Hunter then jumped into another cab, and Sach, after waiting a moment, followed. The trail led to the elevated road at 63d and Loomis street where Sach saw the couple board a northbound train.

Sach ran downstairs, met Policeman William Ward and followed the disappearing train. A few blocks ahead they saw Sergt. Michael Con-

(Continued on Next Page.)

FUNERAL OF WEISS, SLAIN GANGSTER, LACKS IN POMP

"Hymie" Denied Last Rites of Church; Only Few Hundred Attend.

By Paul T. Gilbert.

The little mortuary chapel at 708 North Wells street—the scene of Dean O'Banion's funeral when Chicago's gangster feud was new—was packed wit hsuffocation this morning as the last rites of Earl (Hymie) Weiss were observed by those nearest and dearest to the slain gunman.

No black-robed priest was there to murmur prayers for the dead. The muted tones of harp and violin, breathing an Ave Maria, seemed to accentuate the silence that was broken only by the convulsive sobs og Hymie's mother, his sister, his two brothers, and the tall, star-eyed Polish girl he is reputed to have married recently.

Hymie, gangster and beer racketeer, successor to the suave and oily O'Banion, was shot down by machine-gun fire late Monday near William F. Schofield's flower shop, where O'Banion was slain, and the police have not as yet located the murderers.

Funeral Is Unimpressive.

The funeral was perhaps the least impressive in the long succession of bootleggers' funerals that have marked gang warfare in Chicago.

To be sure, the mourners filled every available square foot of space in the tiny chapel and overflowed even into the morgue. An idle crowd, numbering only a few hundred—not enough to dela ytraffic—gathered at the doorway.

Passengers in passing surface cars and automobiles paused a moment to glance at the scene, but it meant little to them—only another bootlegger gone; only another phaase of Volsteadism.

Down the street were parked eight or ten cars laden with floral offerings. There were elaborate baskets of golden chrysanthemums and autumn leaves. A wreath of roses with a ribbon bearing the words "My son." A vacant chair done in American beauty roses. A floral arch embracing a clock bordered with white carnations, the hands set at the hour of 4—the hour at which the Thompson machine gun, nested in the upper window of a rooming-house, poured forth its deadly hail. A rather modest floral piece from "the boys" to "Our pal." Another from "Uncle Joe and family." An open book—"the last chapter."

No Broken Pillars.

But a conspicuous absence of any broken columns, gates ajar, portraits wreathed in flowers or snow-white doves.

Uniformed police, guarding the entrance, held back the curiosity seekers and admitted only the immediate friends of the slain ganster. Plainclothes men mingld with th crowd, but onbody was frisked for guns.

No politicians or public office holders were observed ether inside or outside the chapel. Only a few of "the boys"—George Moran, Vincent Drucci, Eddie Vogle, "Potatoes" Kaufman, Sa mFinkelstein, Maxie Eisen, Leo ("Nebo") Weiss (no relative of Hymie)—all known to the police.

The silver-mounted bronze cacket was lighted by two tall candles which threw over its floral blanket the shadow of the cross from a mosaic crucifix above.

Mrs. O'Banion Is Mourner.

Seated wtih the immediate family was the widow of Dean O'Banian, whom Hymie had once served as lieutenant.

Only Eisen and Kaufman were recognized among the pallbearers. There had been a last minute shift i nthe list, it was whispered, "Dapper Dan" McCarthy, Moran, Drucci and others having objections apparently to exposing themselves to a battery of cameras.

Broker Plunges to Death in Loop

LEADERS OF GUN WAR ON GANGSTERS

Post photo.

Six of the seven zone commanders armed with sawed-off shotguns who have been placed in command of "gang squads" by Chief of Police Collins. Left to right are shown Capts. Dennis Carroll, John Stege, James Allman, Frank Matchett, John Egan and Charles McGurn. The responsibility of ridding Chicago of gangsters and machine-guns slayers has been placed in their hands by the chief.

GIANT DIRIGIBLE REACHES DETROIT; MOORED SAFELY

DETROIT, Oct. 15.—(AP)—The navy's great airship, the Los Angeles, arrived at the Ford airport at Dearborn, near here, at 3:28 a. m. today and was anchored safely to the mooring tower two and one-half hours later.

The big Zeppelin completed the trip from the airport at Lakehurst, N. J., to Dearborn, the objective of the ill-fated Shenandoah, in slightly more than sixteen hours. Weather conditions encountered along the route were generally good and the ship functioned well, according to members of the crew.

Thousands of persons waited all night for the arrival of the ship at the airport and cheered as the big gray hulk hove into sight. Altho the airport, which is fenced off, was not thrown open to the public until after the ship was moored, crowds gathered at the inclosure and witnessed the arrival and mooring operations from the outside.

Moored to Tower.

Lieut. Z. W. Hicks of the Lakehurst airport was in charge of the landing crew detailed to receive the Los Angeles. The ship hovered about the mooring mast more than two hours. Finally lines were caught and the great dirigible drawn gently down by means of a traveling mooring groove. The landing tower is the newest of its kind, the invention of Herbert Thaden of Detroit, and the Los Angeles was the first large ship attached to it.

Lieutenant Commander C. E. Rosendahl, in charge of the ship, was the first to clamber down the ladder to the ground. He was quickly followed by Admiral Moffett and others of the personnel.

After greetings by members of the landing crew and officials at the airport, they were whisked off to quarters prepared for them for a little rest preparatory to an official welcome to be extended later by city authorities and others.

Most of the men showed signs of fatigue, having been on watch since their departure from Lakehurst.

Trip Without Mishap.

The trip, which marked the first inland voyage of the Los Angeles, was without serious mishap. Casting off from the naval airport at Lakehurst at 11:05 a. m. Thursday morning, the ship maintained a speed of better than fifty miles per hour over Pennsylvania. As it entered the dangerous pocket territory of Ohio the ship was piloted close to the ground. Altho no particularly serious winds were encountered in the district, Commander Rosendahl, who was also second in command of the Shenandoah, took every precaution on his second venture.

Speed was reduced to a minimum over the treacherous stretch where the Shenandoah was destroyed and Lieutenant Commander Zachary Lansdowne and a number of the crew killed. The ship was jockeyed about considerably to avoid air pockets and head winds, descending sometimes as low as 1,500 feet from the earth and ascending again as the elements dictated.

Several times during the journey

(Continued on Next Page.)

Urges Flavor for Postage Stamp to Aid Mail Business

WASHINGTON, Oct. 15.—(AP)—Postoffice department officials scratched their heads today in wonder and amazement over the latest voluntary suggestion to boom their business.

It came in a letter from the "always willing-to-help manager" of a trade magazine who expressed enthusiastic approval of Uncle Sam's stamp except the sticky gum on the back. "It's the same flavor we have had ever since the civil war days," the letter complains. "It is bad-tasting.

"I want you to put some flavoring extract in the paste. Have some peppermint, sarsaparilla, and other nice-tasting flavors. It will help sell stamps. People will feel a longing for a little flavor and they will go in and buy a stamp and write a letter to mother."

$30,000 FIRE IN WAREHOUSE OF STATUARY FIRM

Damage estimated at $30,000 to the stock of the Deprate Statuary company was caused early today by fire in a four-story brick building at 527 South Peoria street.

A 2-11 alarm was sounded. The blaze, of undetermined origin, was confined to the second and third floors.

The statuary concern's warehouse occupies the second floor, and G. Daprato, president of the company, asserted more damage was done by water and smoke than by fire.

Fairmount Scratches

First—Sir Lawnfal, Head Cover, Ramble, Pangold, Joe Paton, Climax.
Second—Pat Field.
Third—Note o' Love, Better Luck, Judge Dailey, Turner, Yoo Hoo, Spats, Miss Freyer, High Joy, Wishtonwish, Star Purse.
Fifth—Senator Norris.
Sixth—Bob Spalding, Fanny de Coursey, Catesby, Ormesvale.
Seventh—Watchful, Nell Maxim.

Latonia Scratches

First—Blue Granite, Wayward, Marvin.
Second—Magnus, Benito, Croatan, Pippin.
Third—Antiquarian, Amir, Disciple.
Fourth—Equity, Zero Hour, Welcome.
Sixth—Peach, My Pet, Jessie Belle.
Seventh—Grand King, Iraq, Six-Sixty, Anona.

Aurora Scratches

First—Leontes, Countess Claridge, Bad Luck, Brown Betty, Rugby.
Second—Jedburgh Abbey, Marius, Ring, Emancipation, Pines Emblem.
Third—Billy Brush, Bonnie Lizzie, Barthelmess, Tailteann.
Sixth—Transplant, Pompous.
Seventh—Kingscourt II.
Weather clear; track good.

Akron Scratches

First—Illinois King, Richard Murray, Flora.
Second—Green Briar, Black Sand.
Fourth—Serbian, Polly May, Theoden, Perfect Ripper.

Beulah Park Scratches

Second—Huzzas.
Fourth—Clever Seth.

U. S. YOUTHS SEND LOVE LETTERS TO PRINCESS ILEANA

S. S. LEVIATHAN, Oct. 15.—(AP)—Mrs. Woodrow Wilson's birthday celebration on the Leviathan today was of special interest because of the fact that both Queen Marie and Princess Ileana will have birthdays during their American tour and both of them are speculating as to where they will be on their natal day.

Marie's birthday will be Oct. 29, when she will be 51 years old. She probably will be on a train that day proceeding to the Pacific coast. Princess Ileana's eighteenth birthday will occur Jan. 5.

American youths are writing ardent letters to Princess Ileana. Jealousy of other suitors and self praise have found their way into the missive of at least one young man in the United States who has proposed marriage.

Princess Reads Letters.

While Queen Marie in her suite listens in on the radio or reads as the Leviathan shapes her course for New York the pretty 18-year-old princess pores over letters received in Paris and brought on board the liner by her to kill dull moments during the voyage.

"Don't pay any attention to other Americans seeking the hand of your Highness," said one letter. "They are no good. I am the man for you."

There is one good American on board the Leviathan who has a good lead on the letter writers ashore. He already has captivated Ileana and also her mother.

"Is the queen nicer than you?" asked the young man of Ileana, and after the princess had assured him she was, she arranged a visit for him to the royal suite to meet the woman who is considered the handsomest of all the handsome queens. When he emerged from the drawing room the boy, like a true courtier, maintained silence as to what the queen said to him and he to her. But he volunteered stoutly, "the queen is all right." And, as if showing that Marie had been pleased with the visit, he carried in his hand a bouquet of roses, orchids and other flowers she had given him.

He's 4 Years Old.

The lad is Sidney Heller of New Rochelle, N. Y. He is 4 years old. He told Ileana before the visit was arranged that he wanted to see ex-

(Continued on Next Page.)

Togo, Famous Japanese Naval Hero, Gravely Ill

TOKYO, Oct. 15.—(AP)—Japan's greatest naval fighting man, Admiral Count Heihachiro Togo, outstanding figure of the Russian-Japanese war, is bed-ridden as the result of a nervous trouble. Because of his advanced age, 79, his physicians are somewhat anxious. It was Admiral Togo's strategy which out-maneuvered and defeated the Russian fleet in their spectacular engagement in the Sea of Japan May 27, 1905, which was the turning point of the war.

Pickpockets Frisk Mexican Lawyer, Judge, on Jail Visit

MEXICO CITY, Oct. 15.—(AP)—The light fingered gentry of Mexico ply their trade even behind prison walls, and apparently they show no discrimination between ordinary persons and Criminal court judges and lawyers.

Prisoner pickpockets inside the famous Belem prison, Mexico's principal penitentiary, have taken the watches of Judge Pino Camara of the criminal bench and Gonzales Pastor, counsel for an alleged murderer, while they were on their way thru the prison yard to the hospital to question the lawyer's client.

At all times the judge and the lawyer were in plain view of the warders. They discovered the loss of their time pieces before they left the prison and notified the head warder. An extensive search failed to find the watches.

POLICE KILL MAN WHO, AS ALLEGED, PLANNED MURDER

Firing in the dark, with nothing but the clicking of a revolver hammer to guide them, two policemen last night shot and killed an alleged maniac in the building at 808 West Roosevelt road.

Lucales Corrales, a roomer at that address, saw a figure creeping up the fire escape and notified the Maxwell street police that a burglar was entering the house. When Policemen Dennis Parkerson and Alfred Huntington responded and trapped the man in a dark attic room, he attempted to shoot them, snapping the hammer of his revolver several times in a vain effort to make it explode.

The police believe the dead man, Henry Castillo, a Mexican, living in the house, was insane and intended to kill his roommate, Abraham Chagolla.

Wreck in Which 30 Lost Lives Laid to High Speed

WASHINGTON, Oct. 15.—(AP)—Excessive speed was the cause of the passenger train wreck on the Denver and Rio Grande Western near Waco, Colo., Sept. 5, in which thirty persons were killed and fifty-four injured, the safety bureau of the Interstate Commerce Commission reported today. Several cars were thrown into a river when the train was derailed. The train was being operated by G. M. Lillin, a foreman of equipment, who had taken the throttle over from the regular engineer.

Anti-British Strike at Canton, China, Is Ended

CANTON, Oct. 15.—(AP)—South China's anti-British strike is at an end, at least officially, and the gates of Shameen, the foreign quarter of Canton, were reopened today after being closed for sixteen months. Altho the anti-British boycott has been declared off also, Chinese merchants still are refusing to handle British goods. Strike pickets have been withdrawn and Chinese servants of foreigners are allowed to resume their duties. Similar action was recently ordered at northern ports.

Harry Feder Dies in an 8-Floor Leap in Conway Building

Harry Feder plunged eight floors down the courtway of the Conway building to instant death today.

Feder, a second mortgage broker living at 1383 Greenleaf avenue, with offices in room 1142 of the huge skyscraper at Washington and Clark streets, was in his place of business alone shortly before noon.

He either fell or leaped from the eleventh floor courtway window and his body smashed on the heavy wire grating protecting the glass skylight in the court three floors above the street level.

He struck the grating with terrific force so that his body was badly smashed, but the wire held, and he did not plunge down thru the glass to the main floor, where hundreds of persons were hurrying about their business.

S. Weinberg, Feder's father-in-law and a business associate, identified the body. Weinberg could give no explanation and said that Feder had seemed in good health and spirits, and this morning had gone to buy some theater tickets.

Marks on the window ledge led police to conclude Feder had crawled out the window and jumped, and the authorities considered it a case of suicide.

BISHOP HUGHES IS IGNORED BY DRYS IN PICKING SMITH

Anti-Saloon League Facing Split in Ranks Over Candidate.

By Joel David Wolfsohn.

The Anti-Saloon League of Illinois in its indorsement of candidates, including that of Col. Frank L. Smith for United States senator, did not receive the advice of its president, Bishop Edwin Holt Hughes.

This became known today when it was learned that Bishop Hughes was attending a religious conference in Pawhuska, Okla., and probably would not be back before Monday or Tuesday. His views on the situation in Illinois are unknown, and it is believed here that he is not aware of the impending revolt, first evidences of which were seen yesterday.

Churches May Revolt.

The league is now in the embarrassing position, it was pointed out today, of having, to put it mildly, antagonized the hand that feeds it—the church. And the cleft, indicated by the "friendly call" of yesterday, was said today to be rapidly developing in a split which might result in a loss of church support to the league, predicted to be a disastrous situation.

Bishop Hughes is conceded to be one of the biggest influences in the local dry league. It was reported that telegrams from friends and league supporters to the bishop have failed to elicit any reply on the vital question of indorsement of senatorial candidates.

"Was Bishop Hughes present when the indorsements were made?" Dr. George Safford, the league's superintendent, was asked in a telephone interview today. He replied in the negative.

Hangs Up Receiver.

"Then the recommendations were made without his knowledge?" And to this question the superintendent replied by hanging up the receiver and terminating the conversation.

The league's indorsements as made public last night were for Col. Frank L. Smith, Richard Yates and Henry R. Rathboe for congressman at large and for various downstate representatives. Recommendations for membership in the state legislature also were made.

HOWARD P. SAVAGE IS NOMINATED FOR CHIEF OF LEGION

PHILADELPHIA, Oct. 15.—(AP)—Col. J. Monroe Johnson, Marion, S. C.; Howard P. Savage, Chicago, Thomas A. Lee, Topeka, Kan, and Jay Williams of Aberdeen, S. D., were nominated today for national commander of the American legion. The first ballot for national commander resulted in no choice. The vote was: Johnson, 488; Savage, 485; Lee, 29, and Williams, 18. Nevessary to a choice, 519.

Man Crushed to Death.

EAST ST. LOUIS, Ill., Oct. 15.—Arley Overturf, 40, was fatally injured late Thursday while returning from the Fairmont race track when he jumped from his automobile, which had stalled on the interurban tracks, and was crushred between his machine and a trolley car.

SUBPOENA FRIENDS OF FORMER DRAGON IN INDIANA PROBE

Grand Jury Recalls Adams for Further Questioning.

INDIANAPOLIS, Oct. 15.—(AP)—The grand jury investigating alleged corruption in Indiana politics today summoned for the second time Thomas H. Adams, publisher of the Vincennes Commercial. Adams' charges that high officeholders bargained corruptly for political support with D. C. Stephenson, former grand dragon of the Ku Klux Klan, culminated in the grand jury probe.

The publisher wa[illegible] called last Tuesday [illegible] gation was started [illegible] was issued calling hi[illegible] today.

William H. Remy, [illegible] Attorney General Gilli[illegible] cial assistant in the i[illegible] pressed the hope that [illegible] a 23-year-old girl who [illegible] been a confidante of Stephenson, could also be brought in to testify. She has been missing from her home here since last Friday.

Apparently having gained little information from Stephenson himself when the ex-klan leader was brought from the state prison Wednesday, officials turned their attention today to persons who were close to him before he was convicted of murdering Madge Oberholtzer and sent to prison for life. Subpoenas were issued for several of Stephenson's friends.

Seek to Locate Evidence.

Adams has alleged that Stephenson has concealed somewhere information that will substantiate every allegation of graft made. Remy and his colleagues declared they were making every effort to locate such evidence.

Strenuous efforts were made yesterday to interest Senator Reed, Democrat, of Missouri, in the Indiana situation to the extent of having him bring his senatorial investigating committee here for a hearing. At Joplin, Mo., last night Senator Reed declined to say whether the committee would enter the Hoosier state. He did say, however, that at a meeting to be held in Chicago Monday the committee would consider any suggestions regarding conditions in other states, and will take such action as facts seem to warrant.

Adams' charges having brought him into conflict with the Republican state committee, he issued several statements yesterday in one of which he called upon State Chairman Clyde Walb to resign. He also asked Walb to join in a request for the Reed committee to investigate Indiana conditions, but the state chairman replied that he considers the grand jury investigating sufficient.

Photographer is Quizzed

Yesterday's session of the grand jury was concluded with the appearance of Mr. and Mrs. C. M. Hull of Anderson, Ind., where Hull is a photographer. Hull recently was quoted as saying that he had photographed a number of important documents for Stephenson and that among them was a check for $2,500 payable to Gov. Ed Jackson.

Another witness was Floyd Christian, Noblesville attorney, who was one of defense counsel at Stephenson's murder trial. Before testifying Christian said he had seen in Stephenson's cell a check for $5,000 payable to Gov. Jackson. The governor denied receiving any financial support from Stephenson.

Man Who Fired Last Shot in Custer Massacre Dies

NEWTON, Mass., Oct. 15.—(AP)—The man who believed he fired the first and last shot in the Custer massacre on the Little Big Horn died at his home here last night. He was John Ryan, 81, civil war veteran, former captain of police here. Ryan was a sergeant under Maj. Reno at Custer's last stand and after the massacre had charge of the squad which buried the famous general and forty-five other dead.

Two More Yank Women Get Divorces in Paris

PARIS, Oct. 15.—(AP)—[illegible] crees involving two Am[illegible] were registered today. [illegible] granted Edith Blackb[illegible] from William Fessenden [illegible] address was given as [illegible] des Capucines, Paris, [illegible] to Lillian Garland Wilso[illegible] George Wilson of No. [illegible] Maistre, Paris. No American addresses or other details [illegible] ceedings were given.

Tory Party Organizer to Be Governor of Bengal

LONDON, Oct. 15.—(AP)—Lieut. Col. F. S. Jackson, chairman of the conservative party organization, has been appointed governor of Bengal, India. He will succeed the Earl of Lytton, whose term expires in March next. Col. Jackson at one time was a fa[illegible] cricket player.

SPORTS ON PAGE 27

THE CHICAGO DAILY NEWS

HOME EDITION

51ST YEAR—250. COPYRIGHT 1926 BY THE CHICAGO DAILY NEWS INC. TUESDAY, OCTOBER 19, 1926.—FIFTY-TWO PAGES. ON SALE EVERYWHERE IN CHICAGO AT OR BEFORE 5 O'CLOCK | OUTSIDE CHICAGO AND SUBURBS 3 CENTS | TWO CENTS

WEISS REPRISALS STARTED; ONE DEAD

QUEEN PAYS WHITE HOUSE VISIT TO-DAY

CHICAGO'S NEW $20,000,000 RIVER BOULEVARD TO BE OPENED TO-MORROW

BIRD'S-EYE VIEW OF NEW WACKER DRIVE TAKEN FROM TOP OF BUILDING NEAR WESTERN TERMINUS OF THOROUGHFARE.

[Photograph by Cliff Thompson, staff photographer.]

DANO NAMED AS MAN WHO TRAILED O'BRIEN

Slain Bootlegger Identified with Gunman in Court Before Shooting.

ATTORNEY AFTER HIS FEE

Much advertised reprisals for the shooting of "Little Hymie" Weiss, Patrick Murray, Attorney W. W. O'Brien and others in the State street machine gunning were on the way to-day as the coroner's jury was tallying the first score.

John Dano, Bellwood bootlegger, whose sudden taking off two days ago was seemingly without a motive, to-day was made a link in the Weiss case by witnesses who were positive in their identification. He may have been innocent of any part in the shooting. But, like other principals now in morgues and hospitals, he picked the wrong hour for showing his face north of the river. And before Mr. Weiss' body was very cold Dano was dead.

Dano, in company with one Red Kosone, a gunman, from New York, had entered Judge Harry B. Miller's courtroom on the day of the shooting soon after a jury had been selected to try Joe Saltis and Frank Koncil for the murder of "Mitters" Foley.

Follow O'Brien from Court.

Attorney O'Brien had left the room. Before any one could warn him the two gunmen followed him. After them marched Ralph Sheldon.

It was learned to-day that Mr. O'Brien's mission into North State street, euphemistically described in his own statements as a journey to meet his wife, was really peaceable enough. He had been informed by his clients that his contingent fee was ready and that it would be paid him at an office over Schofield's flower shop in State street. The attorney had never met Mr. Weiss and, as it turned out, his acquaintance with Mr. Weiss was brief.

What became of Messrs. Dano, Kosone and Sheldon is not told in the information given to the police. Officials would like to find out whether they were the occupants of the car which drove southward in State street and paused only long enough to shoot Mr. Weiss before the machine gun was turned on.

Weiss' Friends Strike Swiftly.

The friend of Weiss and "Schemer" Drucci, George Moran, Frank McErlane and Saltis did not bother to investigate Mr. Dano's motives for trailing Mr. O'Brien out of the courtroom. Little Hymie was buried on Friday. On Sunday night Mr. Dano's body was found near Franklin Park. He had been taken for a ride and shot five times.

Drucci and Vincent McErlane were arrested for questioning in connection with this new development. But they had alibis and waited in their cells

[Continued on Fifth Page.]

CAPITAL TURNS OUT TO WELCOME MARIE

Sovereign Sees Mount Vernon Before Afternoon Calls on Coolidges.

THRILLED BY WELCOME

BY LEROY T. VERNON.

Special Dispatch from a Staff Correspondent.

Washington, D. C., Oct. 19.—Historic Pennsylvania avenue added another star to its glory as a pathway of the celebrated into the heart of America when Marie, queen of Roumania, rode into the national capital last night.

Beneath the scintillation of the bright lights there glowed from the faces of thousands of Washingtonians who lined the curb from the union station to the Roumanian legation a welcome cordial and sincere. Queen Marie and her children bowed and bobbed about in their official limousines trying to make adequate responses to their reception.

No more sightseer in Washington ever before registered such sheer delight at being here as did Queen Marie. Her vivacious spontaneity captured everybody. Apparently she wished to see more than to be seen. Prince Nicholas, her son, peered in a dignified, but none the less constant, way from the windows of his car, directly behind that of his mother. Princess Ileana, the "baby" of the Roumanian dynastic family, totally unconscious of the presence of her corpulent and richly caparisoned military aid, plastered her face to the window of her car with all the eagerness of a simple child who was afraid it might miss seeing something worth while. Personally, it was an informal and exuberant entrance which Queen Marie and her children made in Washington.

Royal Party Dines Late.

Many persons in Washington missed their dinners to do honor to the Roumanian queen, the second reigning queen to visit the national capital, the first having been Elizabeth of Belgium, who came with her consort, Albert, just after the war to thank America for what it had done for Belgium. Incidentally, Queen Marie did not get her own dinner until 8:30 o'clock last night, when she dined at the Roumanian legation with the members of her entourage, the legation staff and a few official and unofficial Americans who will assist in entertaining her during her stay in America. Certainly, her appetite should have been amply whetted, not only by the delay but by the success of her debut here.

Cordiality of a sincere type, rather than enthusiastic cheering, greeted Queen Marie as she emerged from her private car. Swathed in a gray fur coat, with a close-fitting, high-crowned turban which so closely matched her hair as to leave even women in doubt as to where the one began and the other left off, and radiating her regal personality so famous throughout Europe, she tripped gayly down the station platform to the president's room in the union station. She was escorted by Assistant Secretary of State J. Butler Wright, who greeted her in New York on behalf of the government.

Responding to the cheers and hand-

[Continued on Third Page.]

HELP FOR BUSINESS IS ANDREWS POLICY

Dry Chief Says Force Will Encourage Legitimate Alcohol Dealers.

Brig.-Gen. Lincoln C. Andrews, dry chief of the United States, announced a new policy of "co-operation with business" in the prohibition regime here to-day.

Henceforth the federal prohibition forces will count it as much a duty to encourage legitimate alcohol business, he declared, as to block violation of the dry law.

It was on a mission of that kind of co-operation that the general was in the city. He was guest of honor at the convention of the Barbers' Supply Dealers' association, which he congratulated as "an organization of square shooters." Also he took advantage of the visit to confer with officials of the National Association of Retail Druggists, whose headquarters are here.

Explaining the new policy of busi-

[Continued on Fifth Page.]

DEBS IS BETTER, BUT CONDITION IS CRITICAL

Socialist Leader Making Brave but Almost Hopeless Fight for Life, Says Physician.

While Eugene V. Debs, socialist leader, was reported "slightly better" to-day, physicians attending him at the Lindlahr sanitarium, Elmhurst, had virtually abandoned hope of his recovery because of his physical condition and his age. Mr. Debs, who will be 71 years old next month, is suffering from inflammation of the heart muscles.

"His condition to-day is slightly better," Dr. O. H. Wiseman said, "but is critical.

"Mr. Debs is a superhuman sort of a man. He is remaining alive mostly by sheer will power. I have seen him 'come back' before and he may do it again, but the chances are almost certainly against it."

Mr. Debs' wife and his brother, Theodore, are maintaining almost constant watch at the bedside.

Dr. Wiseman said that Mr. Debs went to the sanitarium about a month ago, suffering from a nervous breakdown, accentuated by kidney trouble.

INDIANA GRAND JURY CONTINUES KLAN QUIZ

Stephenson's Attorney in Murder Trial Is Summoned as Witness.

Indianapolis, Ind., Oct. 19.—(AP)—A week of investigation by the Marion county grand jury into allegations of corruption among high state, county and city officials apparently has unearthed information which warrants continuation of the inquiry, for the jurors were summoned again to-day to hear the evidence of several witnesses who have been subpœnaed.

The jury started delving into Indiana political affairs a week ago after Thomas H. Adams, publisher of the Vincennes Commercial, had for several days made sweeping charges against officials who he declared had been corrupted by D. C. Stephenson, former grand dragon of the Ku-Klux Klan.

Stephenson's Attorney Called.

Among the witnesses waiting to be called was John H. Kiplinger, attorney of Rushville, counsel for Stephenson at the ex-Klan leader's trial for the murder of Madge Oberholtzer. Stephenson is now serving a life sentence for that crime.

Adams has declared that, if permitted by prison officials, Stephenson would produce documentary evidence which would corroborate the corruption charges. A possibility that some such evidence came before the grand jury was seen yesterday when Miss Mildred Meade, 23 years old, a confidante of Stephenson, carried into the jury room a safety deposit box from a local bank. Miss Meade was interrogated for an hour and a half.

May Call Former Secretary.

Fred Butler, Stephenson's former secretary, is another witness under subpœna. He may be called to-day. William H. Sheaff, deputy prosecutor, said a number of other witnesses are to be called before the grand jury returns a report.

A group of republican editors meeting here yesterday declared that "the Indiana Republican Editorial association never, at any time, nor does it now approve of a probe prompted by a desire on the part of Mr. Adams * * * to seek revenge for alleged personal grievances in which the association is not in any way interested."

When Adams, who is chairman of the editorial association's executive committee, first made public his charges of alleged corruption he asserted he and his associates constituted a "probe committee" of the association.

FIND ALL THAT TICKS IN NIGHT NOT BOMBS

Police and Beauty Shop Proprietor Unable to Blame Plumber Either.

"That can't possibly be the leaky kitchen faucet," Mrs. Rose concluded as she lay in bed last night, cold sweat prickling her forehead.

And still it continued with monotonous reiteration its "tick, tick, tick," and then Mrs. Rose remembered.

Her home is in the rear of her beauty shop at 4317 West Taylor street and the sleepless one had heard rumors and she had read newspaper accounts of certain inconsiderate actions toward beauty shops in the dark hours near midnight.

"Something must be done—even if I am a woman," she ventured to herself in a voice she didn't recognize.

Palsied, she arose.

No, it wasn't the faucet. Plumbers for once had done their duty. But the ominous "tick, tick, tick" continued its deadly detonations——

That was it—a time bomb. Short-distance records were broken in Mrs. Rose's flight to the telephone. And automobile records were equaled in the response of a flivver squad.

Police and Mrs. Rose located the ticking of the "bomb" between the walls next the kitchen. They dug, but the elusive bomb was not there. Moreover, in the manner of Edgar Allan Poe, the ticking had ceased.

"It was cold last night," commented the police this morning. "And some furnaces were heated up to capacity for the first time. Heat has a way of expanding and contracting wall paper and other wall materials."

That was Sergt. Edward Hanley's only remark as he viewed the work of plasterers in the apartment back of the beauty shop.

ATTEMPT BELIEVED MADE TO POISON 70 CHILDREN

Somerset, Ky., Oct. 19.—(AP)—An apparent effort to poison seventy pupils of the Short Creek school near here is being investigated to-day by parents and school officials. Mrs. Bertha Mize, teacher, arriving at the school yesterday, discovered that several window panes had been broken and the door was open. When she lifted the top from a water cooler she was almost strangled by puffs of gas.

Further investigation revealed that the water in the cooler had been impregnated with sulphuric acid.

The Short Creek neighborhood is a farming and timbering community. Residents of the section can offer no reason for a wholesale attack on their children.

JOHN G. SHEDD BETTER FOLLOWING OPERATION

Improvement in the condition of John G. Shedd, chairman of the board of Marshall Field & Co., was reported to-day at St. Luke's hospital, where he underwent an operation for appendicitis last Friday. Mr. Shedd passed a restful night, and was said to be in "very good condition" this morning.

GIRL, 13, CROSSED IN LOVE, KILLS SELF BY SHOOTING

Uniontown, Pa., Oct. 19.—(AP)—Maternal opposition to a love affair with a boy a few years her senior was believed to have led Mildred Burrie, 13, to end her life by shooting here last night. The girl, with a bullet wound in her forehead, was found dead by her stepfather.

O'BRIEN HURLS LIE AT SAFFORD IN QUIZ

Pastor-Backer of Magill Tells of Meeting Anti-Saloon League Official.

BULLETIN.

Investigation of the political situation in Indiana was decided upon today by the senate campaign funds committee.

BY PAUL R. LEACH.

The Rev. Robert E. O'Brien, pastor of the West Pullman Methodist Episcopal church, one of the original sponsors of the independent republican senatorial candidacy of Hugh S. Magill, passed the lie directly to the Anti-Saloon League of Illinois and America to-day in testifying before Senator James A. Reed's slush fund committee at the federal building.

Dr. George B. Safford, superintendent of the Illinois league, and F. Scott McBride, general superintendent of the national organization, testified yesterday that O'Brien had boasted to them that he had $400,000 "which was available and would be spent" on Magill's campaign.

The Rev. Mr. O'Brien's statement to-day was that Safford told him that he understood O'Brien had $400,000 to spend.

"I did not want to expose my ignorance," the Rev. Mr. O'Brien said, "for it was news to me, so I said, 'What of it?'

Calls Statement False.

"Did you make the statement," Senator Reed asked, "that if you could not elect Magill you could at least elect George Brennan?"

"That is absolutely false," Mr. O'Brien cried.

"Was there anything said," Reed asked, "about 'holes in the law?' That is a leading question, but there has been testimony to that effect. Dr. Safford said yesterday that O'Brien had talked of 'holes in the law.'"

"Dr. Safford told me," the witness said, "that no individual could spend that amount of money, but that organization could. I said that if such were the case the Anti-Saloon league ought to be acquainted with it. It was thus my understanding that if an individual could not spend the money the Anti-Saloon league could spend it.

"I had this idea from Dr. Safford for he told me they had no money—that they were spending it all on electing a dry United States senator."

"Did they tell you anything about Julius Rosenwald as a contributor?" Senator Reed asked.

"Dr. Safford said they had never been able to get a cent out of Mr. Rosenwald," Mr. O'Brien replied.

Magill Is Excused.

Hugh S. Magill, independent republican candidate for United States senator, to-day had to be excused from appearance before Mr. Reed until to-morrow. He was in Springfield fighting for his place on the Nov. 2 ballot, which has been challenged.

Mr. Magill is wanted by Senator Reed to explain allegations made yesterday by George B. Safford, superintendent of the Anti-Saloon League of Illinois, and F. Scott McBride, general superintendent of the Anti-Saloon League of America, that the Rev. Mr. O'Brien had told them a fund of $400,000 had been raised for Magill's campaign.

The second failure of Clement Studebaker Jr. to appear before the committee has excited some comment in political groups. Mr. Studebaker, president of the Illinois Power and Light corporation, of which Senator

[Continued on Fifth Page.]

BRITISH PRESS JEERS AT U. S. WELCOME TO MARIE

Also Expects Next to Hear Roar of Heavy Artillery in Gang War "on Chicago Front."

BY JOHN GUNTHER.

SPECIAL CABLE

To The Chicago Daily News Foreign Service. Copyright 1926, The Chicago Daily News, Inc.

London, England, Oct. 19.—America looms large in British headlines.

The queen of Roumania's entrance into New York and her first interviews with hard-boiled newspaper men are provoking big type in the news columns here.

The Evening Standard says:

"We have not yet heard that by some marvel of engineering the statue of liberty which guards New York harbor has been made to curtsey as Queen Marie passed. But nothing else seems likely to show how the republic can adore a regular royal queen."

Give Much Space to Queen.

Every London paper carries a story of the queen's arrival almost as detailed as those in America. And even if they are printed under headlines like "America's hysteria of queen worship" they seem to indicate a certain amount of interest in royalty here.

More important is the apparent editorial theory whereby every American crime is now big news in England. A New York kidnaping, a New Jersey post robbery, and to-day the Chicago factory robbery have been prominently displayed. Last week Chicago's machine gun killing received the top headline on successive days in most London newspapers.

The Daily Telegraph prints the following editorial this morning:

Pictures Hectic Life in U. S.

"We begin to have our doubts about the United States. Other countries can put up a rousing crime now and then. Our own effete society produces an occasional gunman, native or imported, but American style is much more romantic. The average day of a citizen of the United States would seem to include assorted varieties of battle, murder and sudden death.

"The American gunman has gone far beyond pistols. He works with machine guns and armored cars and we daily expect to hear of heavy artillery in action on the Chicago front."

The long editorial concludes:

"We find it very hard to imagine, however, that anywhere in America can real life be so preposterously like the most preposterous film."

IN THE DAILY NEWS TO-DAY

HOLD UP OWNER AND THREE GIRLS, GET $15,000 FURS

Three bandits held up the Uptown Fur shop, 1135 Wilson avenue, this morning and stole seventy fur coats valued at between $15,000 and $20,000.

The trio entered through a rear door and held up John Balales, the proprietor, and three woman employes. While one of the men covered the proprietor and one of the women, the remaining bandit piled the coats into a gray sedan in the rear of the store.

The employes held up were Rose Chesley, 2904 North Francisco avenue; Ann Anderson, 4620 Magnolia street, and Mary Vignes, 5104 Sheridan road.

GROOM QUITS, BRIDE WEEPS AND CHARITY GETS THE FEAST

Milwaukee, Wis., Oct. 19.—(AP)—A "runaway" bridegroom to-day is speeding toward Pittsburgh. His Milwaukee "bride that was to be" is suffering from a nervous breakdown.

A wedding feast that was to have fed 400 persons has been turned over to charity.

Sophie Ogloff is heartbroken at the sudden disapearance of her intended husband, Harry Gerson. Yesterday when Gerson was at the Ogloff home preparing for the ceremony he received a telephone call. He left the house and did not return.

Will Rogers in a Burst of Gratitude to Royalty

Special to The Chicago Daily News.

Spartanburg, S. C., Oct. 19.—Welcome to Queen Marie. Bless her heart. America will always owe her a debt of gratitude for running "Peaches" and Aimee McPherson back among the want ads. Yours for credit where credit is due.

WILL ROGERS.

SONIA: Her Search for Adventure. By VIDA HURST

Here begins the story of the experiences in Chicago of Sonia March, a young girl who came to the city to live untrammeled by conventions, to be mistress of her own fate and happy in her complete freedom of choice and action. Its vivid pictures of life and the remarkable knowledge shown by the author of the thoughts and emotions of eager, inexperienced young girls, give the story absorbing interest.

"Sonia, maybe, dancing in a silver gown, with an emerald ring on her hand."

INSTALLMENT 1.

AS MRS. MAINE opened the door Sonia and Joe Carter sprang apart. But not quickly enough! She had seen him kissing Sonia!

It was, as Mrs. Maine said, disgusting. Seventeen years old and alone in the room where the girls had left their coats, with no light!

Sidney Maine was giving a farewell party to the senior class of the Muncie high school, which Mrs. Maine, relating the episode, was careful to explain was the reason for Sonia's presence.

Every one knew that Sidney Maine liked Sonia. But every one knew, too, that Sonia went too far for one whose social position was not secure. Her father was a grocery clerk, her mother a dressmaker. Even so, Sonia might have made the grade had she been more circumspect. But Muncie mothers distrusted her. And not without reason. It had been rumored that she not only smoked but she dangled cigarettes, loosely, from her lips; without holding them.

"She's wild," the mothers had concluded.

And no one challenged the statement. Least of all, Sonia, who faced Sidney's mother now, head high, green eyes blazing in her white face.

"Do you think this is any way for young people to act?" Mrs. Maine gulped, fumbling for her poise and the electric switch at the same time. As a matter of fact, she was much more embarrassed than either of the others. Joe Carter was shamefaced, but grinning.

"Aw, Mrs. Maine, we didn't mean any harm. Did we, Sonia?"

But the girl, tossing her head a trifle higher, refused to answer. Without a word of apology or explanation, she seized her coat and left the house.

* * *

Sonia stalked through the summer street swiftly. Joe Carter, rather tardily gallant, had to run to catch her.

"My gosh, Sonia, this is no way to act. We hadn't done anything

She faced him, stormily.

"Do you think I'd stay in that awful house after that? Having her think things. . . ."

She flung away as he attempted to take her arm.

"Leave me alone. Don't."

"Well, but Sonia . . . my gosh . . . this is awful. It isn't my fault she opened the door."

"Your fault the light was off," she said, darkly.

"You looked so tantalizing. And you hadn't forgotten your handkerchief, you know. I saw you stick it down your neck before you missed it. You wanted me to come after you. Didn't you?"

The girl said nothing but her pace slowed to his. His hand crept down her arm.

"You wanted me to kiss you, didn't you, Sonia? Are you sorry I did?"

"No," she answered.

* * *

Hand in hand they walked through the poignant sweetness of the night. The dim lanterns of the stars glowed above them. There was a young moon hanging, crescent-shaped, detached Sonia caught her breath.

"Isn't it wonderful?"

"You are wonderful," the boy murmured, awkwardly.

"No, I mean the night—life—everything! It's like what the minister said in the baccalaureate sermon! We are standing on the threshhold of life. And what does it hold for us? I wish I knew."

"Better take it as it comes. And not worry over the future. It holds a devil of a lot of work for yours truly. I'm going into the garage with dad next week. Overalls and grease for me. And I like it!"

"But wouldn't you like to know?" she persisted, dreamily. "Wouldn't you like to look in a glass and see the next few years unroll before you? I would! See, maybe, Sonia, dancing in a silver gown, with an emerald ring on her hand. I like emeralds, Joe, better than diamonds. And my hands aren't bad."

She sent them, like frail messengers, to his lips for a kiss.

"Sonia, when you talk like that you seem like somebody else. I'm half afraid of you. Why are you so different from other girls?"

"How could I be like them?" she asked frankly. "I've never had any of the things they're used to. Think how miserable I'd be if I tried to imitate them. I have had to be myself, Joe, and live in my own world. While they go away to summer camps or to places up north where it's cool I have been at home washing dishes!"

"I know, and it's a darned shame."

"Oh, I wasn't asking for pity. I don't want that from anybody."

She drew herself proudly erect.

"I am seeing visions while I wash the dishes, you know. And I have my own ideas and plans for the future. No one need be sorry for me."

* * *

They had reached her door now. As if by common consent, they drew closer together and lowered their voices

"I'll bet your ideas are pretty grand, aren't they?"

"It will take a whole lot of money to carry them out. I can tell you that."

He said wistfully: "I suppose that lets me out. You don't see a little bungalow down across from the garage in that kind of dream!"

She slid her hand into his.

"I'm afraid not, Joe. No bungalows in my dreams. But I like you an awful lot."

"You liked to kiss me?" he asked timidly, hopefully.

Sonia laughed.

"I think I might have, but in the grand uproar that followed I was too stunned to notice whether I liked it or not."

He put both arms about her slender young body.

"Sonia, kiss me again."

But she drew away.

"A kiss," said Sonia, with infinite

[Continued on Sixteenth Page.]

WEATHER INDICATIONS.

The official weather forecast for the thirty-six hours ending to-morrow at 7 p. m. is as follows:

Chicago and vicinity—Mostly cloudy to-night and Wednesday, with probably showers; slightly warmer to-night; moderate variable winds.

Hourly temperatures since 3 p. m. yesterday were:

3 p. m.	49	2 a. m.	47
4 p. m.	47	3 a. m.	46
5 p. m.	49	4 a. m.	46
6 p. m.	49	5 a. m.	46
7 p. m.	48	6 a. m.	43
8 p. m.	48	7 a. m.	42
9 p. m.	48	8 a. m.	41
10 p. m.	48	9 a. m.	43
11 p. m.	48	10 a. m.	44
12 midnight	47	11 a. m.	44
1 a. m.	47		

Sunrise to-day, 6:07; sunset to-day, 5:01; moon sets 5:08 a. m. to-morrow.

BLIZZARD GRIPS MIDWEST

Suicide Vow Kept by Sterling

SPORTS AND RACES

LEXINGTON RESULTS

First race, claiming, $800, futurity course—George Groom (Smith), won; The Runt (Hooper), second; Estin (Craver), third. Time, 1:13. Kublai Kahn, Blue Granite, Coral Reef and Harlan also ran.

Second race, maiden 2-year-olds, claiming, $800, futurity course—Clover Club (McCoy), won; Joy of Life (Smith), second; Live Let Live (Ralls), third. Time, 1:14 1-5. Rothwell, Gotham, Thistle Peggy and Ranchlass also ran.

Third race, claiming, $800, one mile and a quarter—Grand King (Dubois), won; Saar (Heupel), second; Chittagong (McElroy), third. Time, 2:13. Long Champs, Eight Sixty and Deceitful also ran.

Fourth race, the Savoy hotel purse, 2-year-old fillies, allowances, $800, futurity course—Mary Jane (Morris), won; Attica (Smith), second; Acirma (Ryan), third. Time, 1:13. Fannie May, Duenna and Damara also ran.

Fifth race, the Big Sandy purse, 3-year-olds,

(CONTINUED ON THIRD SPORT PAGE)

NIGHT EDITION

THREE CENTS

LOS ANGELES EVENING HERALD

AN INDEPENDENT NEWSPAPER

The Evening Herald Grows Just Like Los Angeles

VOL. LII THREE CENTS Hotels and Trains Five Cents THURSDAY, NOVEMBER 18, 1926 Hotels and Trains Five Cents THREE CENTS NO. 15

SAW MRS. HALL AT DEATH LANE SWEARS 'PIG WOMAN'

MRS. GIBSON FROM BED IN COURTROOM IDENTIFIES THREE

COURTHOUSE, SOMERVILLE, N. J., Nov. 18.—Defying death to make the trip, Mrs. Jane Gibson, "pig woman" and star witness for the state in the Hall-Mills murder trial, today came to the courthouse here on a stretcher and identified Mrs. Frances Stevens Hall, widow of the slain Edward W. Hall, and her two brothers, Willie and Henry Stevens, as the trio she had seen quarreling with Dr. Hall and his sweetheart, Mrs. Eleanor Mills, on the Phillips farm the night of the murder.

Over and over Mrs. Gibson identified the Stevenses as those she had seen at the murder scene, and, when her testimony was concluded, she suddenly raised herself from her bed and, pointing to Mrs. Hall, exclaimed:

"I have told the truth here today, so help me God!"

As Mrs. Gibson made this dramatic statement, Mrs. Hall turned a deathly hue.

The other two defendants sat like images.

The jury had been withdrawn at the time and did not hear the statement. They had been instructed to leave the room in order that Mrs. Gibson could be carried out on a stretcher.

The state will rest its case by noon tomorrow unless the unforeseen happens, Prosecutor Alexander Simpson announced this afternoon.

Brought 30 miles in a hospital ambulance and laid on a little white bed before the jury box, Mrs. Gibson, pain-wracked but determined that those who have been randing her "as a liar for four years" shall be refuted, told a story with which the state hopes to prove the guilt of the aristocratic Stevens family.

HIGHLIGHTS OF STORY

She spoke in a voice that was scarcely audible.

But she swore that:

She saw Mrs. Frances Stevens Hall, Henry Stevens, Willie Stevens and Henry de la Bruyere Carpender at the murder scene the night of the killing. Each in turn stood before her in the courtroom and was identified.

She heard some one shout "Explain those letters."

She heard a man curse.

She heard one shot, then, later, three more.

Then, she said, a woman screamed "Oh, Henry, very easy."

"She screamed like a screech owl," she testified.

And next she said she had seen Mrs. Hall, kneeling.

She charged she had been ordered by a defense detective to "keep her mouth shut."

At times it seemed her testimony might become incoherent. When asked once about money she mumbled of $100 and two mules. She became confused as to the date of her wedding. She could not remember if she had been married more than once. She muttered of "what people would think of a pig woman running around."

MAY CALL MOTHER

At those times, a physician and a nurse would hover over her and the examination would halt for a moment, but Mrs. Gibson, steeled for her ordeal by the thought that it was the moment for which she had waited four years, would wave them aside and the testimony would go on.

Surrounded by detectives, her mother sat listening in the courtroom while rumors went around that the mother might herself be called to impeach the daughter's testimony.

The defendants sat showing intense interest and Mrs. Hall at times paled to a ghastly hue.

While hundreds milled for vantage points in the corridor and other hundreds crowded outside the courthouse, the sick woman within told

(CONTINUED ON PAGE EIGHTEEN)

Ordeal Fails to Injure 'Pig Woman'

By International News Service

SOMERVILLE, N. J., Nov. 18.—Mrs. Jane Gibson withstood the ordeal of a trip in an ambulance from Jersey City and the three hours' testifying before the jury in the Hall-Mills case today in a remarkably good manner, considering her weakened physical condition.

During her cross-examination her temperature rose to 102.4, but after her ordeal in court was over it dropped to 100.

She seemed tired and relieved as she was taken out of the court room, put back in the white ambulance and driven back to Jersey City with two nurses and a doctor in attendance.

Storm Signals Are Flown on Coast; Rain Falls in S. F.

SAN FRANCISCO, Nov. 18.—Storm signals were being hung up along the northern California coast today following the announcement by the weather bureau that a storm located 1400 miles off the coast is working shoreward.

A light rain fell in San Francisco this afternoon. Rain and unsettled weather for the San Francisco bay region tonight with unsettled weather tomorrow is the forecast announced today.

2 Ticket Scalpers Are Ejected From Naval Academy

ANNAPOLIS, Md., Nov. 18.—Two New York ticket scalpers were ejected from Annapolis academy today after seeking to buy tickets for the Army-Navy football game from midshipmen.

The two scalpers sought to buy tickets for from $5 to $40.

Commander Jonas H. Ingram, athletic director, sent two midshipmen to the men with tickets. The scalpers bought them for $40 apiece.

Sheriff Re-Elected On Absentees Votes

SANTA ROSA, Cal., Nov. 18.—E. Douglas Bills, veteran Santa Rosa deputy sheriff, today was declared Sonoma county sheriff on the strength of seven ballots cast by absent voters Nov. 2 and opened, according to state law, by the county supervisors.

All seven votes were cast for Bills, giving him a four-vote edge over Mike Flohr, Petaluma police chief.

BARE POISON PLEDGE OF CAL. POET

SAN FRANCISCO, Nov. 18.—The body of George Sterling, 57, California poet laureate, defeated by life whose beauty he had caught more fully than most, lay ready for burial today.

Sterling, torn in body from protracted ill health, swallowed poison in his rooms at the Bohemian club yesterday, choosing the same method to attain death as that taken by his wife eight years earlier.

Friends today said his death was fulfillment of a promise often made by the poet himself. He frequently discussed suicide and always carried a small phial of poison, they said.

Search of the famed poet's quarters did not disclose a farewell message. On a small invalid table beside his bed, where his body was found, were scraps of torn manuscripts and papers some bearing fragments of writing.

CALLS DEATH FRIEND

Two such fragments read:

"Until all friendship ends in death, the friend of friends"——; "Deeper in the darkness can I peer, than most, yet find the darkness still beyond."

On this table, littered with charred papers and ashes of others, which Sterling had completel; burnt prior to his going, were other fragments containing words in a woman's handwriting.

"A little depressed—," "—general delivery—" and "—two weeks lost—" was all detectives could decipher from them, and whether they would, if complete, have shown a vivid love in the life of the poet was left, probably for all time, a matter of conjecture.

But the two phrases in Sterling's handwriting were construed by friends of his as perhaps containing a note of prophecy.

'BEST WAY OUT'

"Sterling often said that suicide is the best way out for poets," Gouverneur Morris, author, declared today.

"I have often heard Sterling discuss suicide," said Morris, "although I do not remember his ever threatening to do the same thing, but on more than one occasion he has told me of the manner in which his wife ended her life.

"He thought of suicide as many intelligent men think of it—as an expedient that some day might use-

(CONTINUED ON PAGE NINETEEN)

Tragic Verse Lives After Sterling Dies

In the tragic lines of George Sterling, whose colorful life ended in San Francisco yesterday, flowed the bitter-sweet charm of Edgar Allen Poe, literary critics in Los Angeles agreed today.

Between each rhyming line, akin only to a despairing and yet ecstatic refrain, was told the story of a candle burning at both ends in order that "a wonderful light would be thrown," critics pointed out.

Poems by George Sterling, representative of a dying classical age in America, follow:

A MOOD

I am grown weary of permitted things
And weary of the care-emburdened age—
Of any dusty lore of any priest and sage
To which no memory of Arcadia clings;
For subtly in my blood at evening sings
A madness of the faun—of choric rage
That makes all earth and sky seem but a cage
In which this spirit pines with cheated wings.

Rather by dusk for Lilith would I wait
And for a moment's rapture welcome death,
Knowing that I had baffled Time and Fate,
And feeling on my lips, that died with day
As sense and soul were gathered to a breath,
The immortal, deadly lips that kissing slay.

TO EDGAR ALLEN POE

Time, who but jests with sword and sovereignty,
Confirming these as phantoms in his gloom
Or bubbles that his arid hours consume,
Shall mold an undeparting light of thee—
A star whereby futurity shall see
How Song's eventual majesties illume,
Beyond Augustan pomp or battle-doom,
Her annals of abiding heraldry.

Time, tho' his mordant ages gnaw the crag,
Shall blot no hue from thy seraphic wings
Or vex thy crown and choral glories won,
Albeit the solvents of Oblivion drag
To dust the sundered sepulchre of kings,
In desolation splendid with the sun.

DIRGE

(From "Lilith," which H. L. Mencken said was Sterling's greatest).

O lay her gently where the lark is nesting
And winged things are glad!
Tears end, and now begins the time of resting
For her heart was sad.

Give roses, but a fairer bloom is taken.
Strew lilies—she was one,
Gone in her silence to a place forsaken
By roses and the sun.

Deep is her slumber at the last of sorrow,
Of twilight and the rain.
Her eyes have closed forever on tomorrow
And on tomorrow's pain.

IN THE MARKET PLACE
(Rev. 18; 10-13)

In Babylon, high Babylon,
What gear is bought and sold?
All merchandise beneath the sun

(CONTINUED ON PAGE NINETEEN)

RAILROADS AND WIRES TIED UP BY SNOWSTORM

CHICAGO, Nov. 18.—Midwinter blizzards swept virtually the entire middle west today, crippling wire communications and delaying railroad schedules.

At least three persons have been killed in Chicago alone by the storm.

Snow fell over a wide area in a half dozen states and in many places reached a depth of four inches. At Peoria, Ill., it was seven inches.

Temperatures fell during the night and were still on the downward trend today. Winds of extreme velocity whipped the snow into huge banks at many points.

The weather forecast offered no relief within the next 48 hours. Subfreezing temperatures were anticipated.

WEATHER UNSETTLED

"The weather will be unsettled over most of the district Thursday and Friday, with rain or snow in the upper and middle Mississippi valley and Indiana," the forecaster said.

The toll of lives taken directly by the storm in Chicago mounted to three today when Albert Wendell, teamster, was killed with his horses as he blindly drove his team into a fallen high voltage wire.

Vernon Smith, 45, switchman, was killed by a passenger train, he apparently failed to see, and an unidentified woman was struck today by a street car while shielding the rain from her face.

8 INCHES OF SNOW

Eight inches of snow fell at Springfield, 6 at Pana, and at Kewanee the wind, snow and sleet developed into a big storm.

All November snow records were broken at Peoria.

Traffic was reported tied up in some parts of the Dakotas and Minnesota.

A fall of 5½ inches of snow in St. Louis, Mo., set a new record for the date, while Alton, Ill., also reported a tieup.

SPRINGFIELD, Ill., Nov. 18.—With a record November snow covering the ground, Springfield and central Illinois continued today to be bombarded by swirling flakes, while the thermometer hovered below the freezing point. Depth of the snow was reported at 7.9 inches today by the United States weather bureau and drifts several feet deep were delaying traffic.

LATEST NEWS

MANY DIE IN NEW MEX. BATTLE

NOGALES, Ariz., Nov. 18.—Nineteen Mexican federals and 90 Yaqui Indians were killed in the battle of Las Arenas in which federal troops succeeded in dislodging the rebels in their mountain stronghold, according to official reports made public today.

The Indians were caught between a cross-fire while fighting their way through a mountain pass, and were prevented from reorganizing on the eastern side of the mountains by aviators using bombs and machine guns.

FLOOD CONTROL IS PROBED BY GRAND JURY

The county grand jury is conducting a secret investigation of the $35,000,000 county flood control program and the office of Flood Control Engineer J. W. Reagan, according to well authenticated reports circulated today at the courthouse.

The inquiry was instituted very quietly and neither the members of the grand jury nor of District Attorney Keyes' staff would even admit that it was under way, but it became known that the jurymen questioned several witnesses Tuesday on flood control matters.

Whether the investigation is general in scope or relates only to charges of inefficiency made against Reagan by the Los Angeles Municipal league was not known.

With the report of the grand jury investigation, it was learned also that the first act of the board of supervisors when it reorganizes on

(CONTINUED ON PAGE NINETEEN)

QUEEN LEAVES FOR RUMANIA WEDNESDAY

ABOARD QUEEN MARIE'S SPECIAL TRAIN (at Louisville Ky.), Nov. 18.—Queen Marie of Rumania will leave tonight for New York city, canceling all engagements in her American itinerary, it was officially announced today. Her majesty expects to arrive in New York about Saturday to await quietly the sailing of the liner Berengaria next Wednesday.

"My heart is heavy," said her majesty with tears in her eyes. "I have heard unfortunate news. I must go home. I am a soldier and duty takes precedence."

It was the queen's former intention to sail aboard the White Star liner Majestic Dec. 11, but recently she received two undecipherable code messages which puzzled, then frightened her. When she received a message from her daughter, Queen Marie of Serbia, stating that the king was better today, she cabled

(CONTINUED ON PAGE NINETEEN)

The Weather
FOR TOLEDO AND VICINITY: Mostly cloudy and unsettled tonight and Friday; slightly warmer Friday.
Coldest town in U. S. Wednesday night
Duluth, Minn.................36 degrees
Warmest town in U. S. Wednesday
Phoenix, Arizona.........100 degrees

TOLEDO BLADE

HOME EDITION

The Blade Is the Only Evening Newspaper in Toledo Receiving the Associated Press News Dispatches

Vol. 78—No. 119 FORTY-FOUR PAGES TOLEDO, OHIO, THURSDAY, MAY 19, 1927 ★ ★ ★ ★ TWO CENTS

MANIAC'S REVENGE SENDS FORTY-TWO TO DEATH IN SCHOOLHOUSE BLAST

VILLAGERS TURN TO PRAYER AFTER SCHOOL TRAGEDY

Every Family Feels Tragic Blow of Mad Man's Terrible Revenge.

BY MARGRETE DANEY
Of the Blade Staff.

Bath, Mich., May 19—Bleeding and torn, this little tragedy-swept Michigan town Thursday prayed for its many injured while it made plans to bury its youthful dead.

Like fingerprints from the hand of death, wreaths and sprays were tacked on the doors of many homes in Bath and surrounding territory.

Behind closed doors and darkened windows women and men cried out the heartbreak of cheated parenthood. Or sat and stared through a daze of unbelief.

Never to hear the happy voice that said "goodbye" for the last time Wednesday morning. Never to hear again those dancing steps leading from home to the nearby school.

In the center of the town it stands, the Bath Consolidated school where more than 35 school children and a few teachers lost their lives and an equal number were injured following a dynamite explosion, caused by a maniac Wednesday morning.

Pride of Town.

Yesterday it was the pride of the town. Today it stands—a death trap that claimed two-score lives. A tomb where other bodies may be still held.

Ropes marked it off Wednesday evening when thousands of people from Lansing, Leslie, Jackson and other Michigan towns circled this monument to dead students—this wrecked pile of brick and stone and wood.

There were few people from Bath near the school Wednesday night. The tragedy was too new, too horrible—too intimate.

There were too many children from Bath homes for the parents to care to see how it happened.

* * *

Grim reminders of the horror greeted the eye everywhere. Bedclothing, blankets and sheets were stretched out on piles of wood or the ground, showing the imprint of tiny forms.

Buckets with rags soaking, showed that first aid had been given the little victims by those who rushed to their rescue.

Coats and caps, shoes and hose were strewn about the yard. One room torn completely open at the end, showed coats and hats neatly hung in the cloak room, and a row of lunch baskets above.

"Whoever touches this studies at his own risk," was written in the jaunty hand of a sixth grader in his book. Its torn message greeted the tear filled eye.

The blood-stained coat and hat of a little girl who arrived late for class, but tragically in time for the explosion, was hung from the limb of a tree. A catcher's mitt was flung on the ground.

* * *

How the hills and the forests about Bath must have rung with the cries of pain from the victims and the

Continued on Page Two, Second Col.

TRUCK CRUSHES BOY TO DEATH

Lad Is 32nd Auto Victim of Year; Run Down While at Play.

Death claimed its 32nd automobile victim of the year Thursday when William Horn, 10, of 2687 Monroe street, a pupil in the fourth grade of St. Ann's school, Forest avenue and West Bancroft street, was crushed under the wheels of a heavy truck near the school.

The boy died in Mercy hospital at 10:15 A. M., a half hour after he was run down by a truck of the M. & H. Transport Service Co., 3403 Detroit avenue, driven by John Weirica, Jr., 2432 Ayres avenue.

Mr. Weirica said that he was driving in Forest avenue when six or seven children ran in front of his machine. He told police he applied his brakes and thought he had missed hitting the children.

A piercing scream and shouts of children to "back off the body" were the first indications the driver said he had hit anyone.

He backed his truck. The right rear wheel had been resting on the boy's chest.

The Medical Service bureau called Clegg's ambulance which took the boy to Mercy hospital where he died 10 minutes later.

Children at the school said that they had been playing "pump-pump-pull-away" and that Billy had slipped in a mud puddle, falling into the street and under the truck wheel.

Mr. Weirica gave himself up to police. He is being held for investigation. The accident was witnessed by J. C. Berkebile, 3131 Broadway.

The Horn boy lived with his grandmother, Mrs. Barbara Raab.

The boy's mother and stepfather, Mr. and Mrs. D. J. McGinness, live at 2639 Monroe street.

Last Minute News

NEW AIR MAIL ROUTE OPENS

Louisville, May 19 (AP)—The airplane Cincinnati with a five-plane escort took off from Bowman field Thursday on the beginning of its first trip over the Louisville-Cincinnati-Cleveland air route.

FLOOD FUND REACHES $12,772,254

Special to the Blade.

Washington, May 19—The Red Cross flood relief fund reached $12,772,254 Thursday.

FORMER COLLEGE HEAD DIES

Special to the Blade.

Chester, Pa., May 19—Dr. Joseph Swain, 69-year-old president emeritus of Swarthmore college, died in a private infirmary in Swarthmore Thursday.

SOVIET NOTE DELIVERED IN LONDON

London, May 19 (AP)—Soviet Russia's note of protest against the British raid on the Soviet house in London was received at the foreign office and laid before the cabinet in Downing street Thursday.

19 DROWN AS BARGE SINKS

Kiev, Russia, May 19 (AP)—Nineteen peasants were drowned Thursday in the capsizing of a milk barge in the Dnieper river. Five others were saved.

LOCUSTS DESTROY GRAIN

Astrakhan, Russia, May 19 (AP)—Grain areas estimated at 125,000 acres have been devastated by a plague of locusts in Astrakhan, Kalmuck and Caucasus provinces.

ROOSEVELT SUFFERS INFECTION

Oyster Bay, N. Y., May 19 (AP)—An infected right foot, neglected the last six months while he attended to pressing business, forced Colonel Theodore Roosevelt, Jr., to bed at his home Thursday.

HORSE TRAINER IS KILLED

Akron, May 19 (AP)—William G. Matthews, 60, horse trainer at Northampton race track, was killed when struck by a hit-skip driver on the state road near the stables.

TWO VIEWS OF WR... SCHOOL—BEFORE AND AFTER BLAST

A before and after picture of the scene of Michigan's greatest tragedy is shown here. The top view was taken shortly after the fine two-story brick structure was completed. The lower shows the ruins brought about by the maniacal twist of a farmer's mind. Rescue workers are shown searching for bodies in the remains of the building, twisted and shattered by an explosion of dynamite.

REAGAN MURDER CLUES TANGLED

Police Follow Winding Trail Into Western Pennsylvania.

Cleveland, May 19 (AP)—Investigation into the unsolved murder of Elizabeth Reagan, 27-year-old butterfly divorcee here last Saturday night, has extended into Pennsylvania. Parts of western Pennsylvania have been visited by Cleveland detectives, who traced movements of men acquintances of the girl.

A Butler, Pa., friend of the girl appeared of his own volition before Cleveland authorities to clear himself of suspicion, when he learned police had gained possession of letters he had written Miss Reagan. He is a traveling salesman and said he had several "dates" with the girl.

On the night she was murdered, however, he said he was in Ashtabula, Ohio. Police went there Thursday to check upon his movements. Pittsburgh and New Castle also were visited by detectives from here, while out of the state, tracing her admirers' movements.

Additional bloodstains were discovered by detectives late yesterday on the inner doorknob of the waitresses' apartment, when they again visited the scene of the killing. The stains indicated, detectives said, that the slayer opened the door with bloody hands.

Spain, Portugal Shaken by Quake

Lisbon, Portugal, May 19 — This city and suburbs were shaken by earthquake shocks early Thursday. No damage or casualties were reported.

Madrid, May 19—A slight earthquake shock was felt at La Carolina early Thursday. Windows were broken and walls were shaken down, but so far as known no persons were injured. People fled from their homes in panic.

Crazed Man Bore Grudge Against Life in General

Campaign of Ruthless Destruction Carried On by Farmer Who Dynamited Bath School Building; Destroyed Trees.

BY WALTER W. SCHRAMM
of the Blade Staff

Bath, Mich., May 19 — Complete destruction of everything connected with his life apparently was the aim of Andrew Kehoe who, crazed by the loss of his farm, dynamited the Bath Consolidated schoolhouse Wednesday after burying his wife in the ruins of his home and barns.

With an ax in his hands, Kehoe went over his entire farm in the last few days and girdled every tree so that when the leaves die this fall, new ones never will appear. And there were two beauty spots in this little village—the Consolidated school building and the Kehoe farm.

Even after he had wrecked his home and killed his wife, the crazed farmer's intention of ruthless destruction did not waver. Before touching off the dynamite that hurled more than two score little souls into eternity, Kehoe called the superintendent of schools, E. E. Huyck into his machine and at the same time the cache of explosives in the school let go, a bushel basket full of dynamite in Kehoe's car blew the two men to atoms.

Blown to Bits

A wide path was beaten through thick clover off the road opposite the school by curious throngs who tramped more than 100 yards through the field to see where pieces of the automobile and little bits of the two bodies were scattered over a half acre.

That the man had been planning the deed for some time is evident Several days ago, a huge, rudely painted sign appeared on his well-kept lawn. It said: "Criminals are Made—Not Born." Probably the same night he painted the sign, he planted more dymamite in the basement of the school building.

What pains he took to get everything in order to accomplish his plan! Wires were arranged as neatly and with as much care as if he had expected the job to be examined by a master. He felt, it is believed, he had a legitimate grudge against the community and, painful as it would be, he must exact his just dues.

A month ago, Andrew Kehoe was a highly-respected and popular citizen of Bath. As has been said, he was treasurer of the school board, he took an active interest in all civic affairs, his judgment and advice were sought on every hand. To all intent he was prosperous. Visitors to Bath were shown first the school

Continued on Page Two, Third Col.

Striking Scenes of School Tragedy

The Blade Today Presents a

FULL PAGE OF PICTURES

of the havoc wrought by Michigan's maniac.

By Blade Photographers

N. C. Hauger, using an airplane, Russell Van Horn, Walter Schramm and Margrete Daney, using an automobile, brought back for Blade readers details of this tremendous story.

Turn to Page 30

HOUSE OF DAVID SECRETS BARED

Witness Describes Group Marriages Ordered by Purnell.

St. Joseph, Mich., May 19 (AP)—Group marriages were ordered for girl members of the House of David colony when a federal white slave investigation was threatened, according to Mrs. Ruth Swanson of South Orange, N. J., a witness in the dissolution proceedings against the cult here.

More than 50 girls were quickly assembled, when word of the proposed inquiry was received, Mrs. Swanson, a former member of the colony testified Wednesday. Benjamin Purnell, head of the colony ordered the marriages, she said, and told the girls their husbands would have to live with them, "if it became necessary." The witness then explained that celibacy was one of the tenets of the faith.

The girls were called into a room and told to pick out a husband, the witness said, preferably someone they liked, among a group of men colonists. If a choice made was not mutually agreeable they were given permission to pick again, she testified.

C. L. Swanson, an electrician and husband of Mrs. Swanson, told of installing an electrical alarm system in Purnell's headquarters building to be used in event of raids.

Slicker Weather to Be Continued

Continued showers with cooler weather is promised for Thursday by Weather Forecaster Currier.

A total of .73 of an inch of rail fell during the heavy showers Wednesday night. The lowest point the mercury reached during the night was 47 degrees and it was up to 50 at 8 A. M. Thursday.

The wind during the night reached a velocity of 36 miles an hour.

BODY OF MADMAN'S WIFE IS FOUND IN DEBRIS NEAR HOME

Injured Pupils Crowd Hospitals After Huge Dynamite Cache Is Exploded.

BY WALTER W. SCHRAMM
of the Blade Staff

Bath, Mich., May 19—Finding the body of Mrs. Andrew Kehoe, wife of the demented farmer who dynamited the Bath Consolidated schoolhouse Wednesday morning, raised the death toll to 42 and cleared the remaining mystery connected with the tragedy.

Her body, horribly mangled, was found in the ruins of the barn on the Kehoe farm, a short distance from the village. Her skull had been crushed, which led officers to believe that Kehoe, in his madness, clubbed his wife before he hurled her into the barn and set off the dynamite that ruined the barn and house.

BATH AWAKENS TO TRAGEDY

There were no classes at the Bath schoolhouse Thursday.

With one out of every four children in the village dead and more injured and dying, Bath just began to realize Thursday morning the awfulness of the tragedy. There is not a home in the village that has not lost a child, relative or friend.

While thousands from surrounding cities viewed the wreckage which took a toll of 42 lives Wednesday morning, residents of the village remained in their homes, too stricken with grief even to go near the mass of debris which once was the pride of the town.

RELATIVES SEARCH RUINS

Thursday morning, however, instead of hurrying children off to school, mothers and fathers ventured forth to claim the coats and hats and little treasures so dear to their children who were hurled into eternity by a crazed farmer. The farmer, Andrew Kehoe, had planted enough dynamite in the building to wreck the entire town. Kehoe, who was treasurer of the school board, blew himself to atoms, together with Emory E. Huyck, superintendent of schools. Bits of their bodies still are lying in a field of clover.

36 PUPILS DEAD

Of the 42 who were killed, 36 were pupils of the school. About 40 others were injured, some so seriously that little hope is held for their recovery. The injured are being cared for in Lansing hospitals, about 10 miles south of here

GROUP FUNERAL PLANNED.

While plans for a group funeral of 36 children are under way, details of the grim tragedy are being told over and over to an endless line of curious visitors.

The general belief is that Kehoe became crazed several days ago when a mortgage on his farm was foreclosed by his wife's aunt, who resides in Lansing. He had been opposed to the building of the school. His taxes became much heavier and he blamed that for failure to make both ends meet at his model farm.

STEALS AND BUYS DYNAMITE.

He stole some dynamite from a construction camp, bought some and borrowed more. Every bit of it—more than 600 pounds, was planted in the basement of the school and in his home and buildings on the farm.

Conflicting stories are told of the explosion in the car that sent Kehoe and the superintendent of schools to their deaths. Some say that Kehoe fired a rifle into a bushel of dynamite and immediately after touching off the dynamite in the basement of the school, while others insist, on account of the wiring, that the two charges were linked together.

SETTING OF DEATH SCENE.

The setting immediately before the catastrophe was this: Kehoe was sitting in his car; Superintendent Huyck was standing by the machine, talking to Kehoe; Glenn O. Smith, village postmaster, and Nelson McFarran were talking a few feet away.

The blast came from the machine—Kehoe and Mr. Huyck were blown to bits. McFarran was killed outright and Smith was injured fatally.

On account of examinations, there were not as many pupils in the school as there generally are. Many escaped death because they had been excused from taking the tests at the end of the semester. But the plant of dynamite which really did the most damage was placed under the rooms occupied by little children of the lower grades. More than 500 pounds of dynamite, planted in

Continued and Page Two, Third and Fourth Columns.

FAMOUS STORY SERIES
See Page 16
FUNNY POEM SERIES
See Page 16

THE BOSTON HERALD

PARTLY CLOUDY
Boston and Vicinity—Partly cloudy, probably showers today; Wednesday cloudy, cooler.
New England—Cloudy, probably showers today; Wednesday cloudy, cooler.
Full report on page 2.

VOL. CLXII, NO. 54 — TUESDAY MORNING, AUGUST 23, 1927—TWENTY-SIX PAGES — * * * * — TWO CENTS

SACCO AND VANZETTI ARE EXECUTED

RUSSIAN HATE NOW DIRECTED AGAINST BRITAIN

Chamberlain's Face Butt of Every Cartoon in Defense Week

WAR PARTY INCITES ILLITERATE MASSES

Proletariat Hoarding Food in Anticipation of Coming War

This is the sixth of a series of daily articles on Russia by Robert Choate, Washington correspondent of The Boston Herald. Mr. Choate went to Russia to investigate conditions at first hand. For fear that his stories might be censored, he wrote nothing until he had returned to Berlin. He has treated the whole subject in a spirit of impartial inquiry. These articles will answer in an authoritative way the scores of questions which Americans have been asking in regard to the economic, industrial, military and social conditions of Russia.

By ROBERT CHOATE

BERLIN, Aug. 15—During the middle of July defence week was staged in Moscow. For six days the proletariat paraded through the streets. On Sunday a military demonstration was staged before 300,000 people.

Russian hate is concentrated against England.

In July, after the Arcos raid and the severance of relations, the feeling was especially bitter. Poor Austen Chamberlain's elongated British face was made the butt of every Russian cartoon and poster. His top hat and monocle, his clenched fist dripping the blood of war, were caricatured from one end of Russia to the other as the embodiment of the war-like spirit of capitalistic nations.

PREPARING FOR WAR

Russia is preparing for war. With what nation it proves impossible to tell. In Moscow toward the end of July it was impossible to buy flour, sugar or salt in the stores. The proletariat were hoarding it.

Without understanding a little of the Russian temperament one would wholly fail to grasp the effect of the communist war propaganda on the Russian masses. For seven years the Russian people have been told by their leaders that the capitalist nations of Europe were about to descend on them in allied ranks to reduce the workers to slavery and the peasants to serfs.

In a country where the press serves only to preach the views of the ruling party, where the voice of opposition or even ridicule is muffled by a rifle shot, it proves comparatively easy to put across this hokum.

There has arisen in Russia today as there arose in Germany before the war, and probably will arise in Italy under Mussolini, a war party which has talked so much, made so many promises, so fired the imagination of illiterate people, that to carry on it must precipitate a struggle.

SOLDIERS TAUGHT TO SING ON MARCH

The British severance of relations, the assassination of the soviet ambassador in Poland, gave communist officials the ready excuse they had long been looking for, the means of inciting an ever deeper nationalist feeling with which to unite the discordant elements within the union.

An American in Moscow jokingly remarked that if singing were fighting the Russian army should make Chaliapin its

(Continued on Page Fifteen, Column 3)

Chaplin's Wife Gets Divorce, $625,000 and Care of Children

Income from $200,000 Trust Fund Provided for Latter

TO PAY PRINCIPAL WHEN YOUNGER IS 35

Court Approves Settlement—No Sensational Evidence Introduced

LOS ANGELES, Aug. 22 (AP)—Lita Grey Chaplin was granted an interlocutory decree of divorce from Charles Spencer Chaplin at a brief court session here today after the film comedian had agreed to pay his wife $625,000 as a property settlement and grant her permanent custody of their two small sons. Chaplin was not present.

A property settlement reached out of court was announced by Edwin E. McMurray, chief of counsel for the suing wife, and Mrs. Chaplin told instances of her husband's cruelty from the witness stand. A few corroborative witnesses were sworn, testified briefly and the decree was granted. A year must elapse before the final decree is awarded.

TRUST FUND FOR CHILDREN

The agreement between Chaplin and his wife provides for the creation of a trust fund of $200,000, the income to be paid Mrs. Chaplin for the support and education of the children. The principal is to go to the children when the younger attains the age of 35.

The trust fund is in addition to the $625,000 Chaplin agreed to pay Mrs. Chaplin.

It was understood that Chaplin also agreed to pay $10,000 as expenses of his wife during their separation; $22,000 as receiver's costs and fees; $2100 court costs and $1000 a month for the support, maintenance and education of the children for a period of five years pending setting up of the trust fund.

Mrs. Chaplin will receive $375,000 of the total award at once in cash, reliable reports said, the remainder to be paid her over a period of three years, as follows:

On Sept. 1, 1928, $100,000; Sept. 1, 1929, $100,000, and on Sept. 1, 1930, the balance of $50,000.

Within 15 seconds after Judge Walter Guerin had completed reading a temporary ruling barring certain testimony, Atty. McMurray had announced reaching of the settlement and Mrs. Chaplin was on her way to the stand. Rapidly and with finality she answered the questions which Atty. McMurray put to her.

Neglect of herself and the children, absence from home at night and cruelty which forced her to leave the film comedian were the burden of her testimony.

NO SENSATIONAL TESTIMONY

Not a word was mentioned of the sensational charges which she hurled at the screen jester in her divorce complaint.

Gavin McNab, chief of Chaplin's quintet of legal advisers, dramatically came to the comedian's defense in a five-minute display of oratory. He pictured Chaplin as a dutiful husband and father and as a man whose purse was the object of attack.

"Who steals my purse steals trash," McNab quoted from Shakespeare in drawing a parallel, "but he that filches from me my good name robs me of that which not enriches him and makes me poor indeed."

Mrs. Chaplin came into court with her mother, Mrs. Lillian Spicer.

She was smartly attired in black silk, dark hat and big white fur choker.

The plaintiff testified that she left her husband on advice of physicians when her condition was "hysterical" because of cruelty. During the four months she remained away from him, Chaplin called on her about once a week. During that time he took her to dinner twice.

"Did he take you out at all?" Atty. McMurray asked.

"Very seldom and then he would say that he was taking me out for appearances sake only. He used to say that to me even before I left him."

Poetess Arrested as Sacco Parader

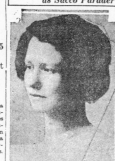

Edna St. Vincent Millay

154 PARADERS ARE ARRESTED

Edna St. Vincent Millay, Poetess, Among Those Taken Into Custody

COMMIT HAPGOOD FOR OBSERVATION

DAY'S DEVELOPMENTS IN SACCO INQUIRY

Gov. Fuller tells defense counsel at 11:03 P. M. that he will not interfere with execution in any way.

Defense counsel appeals in vain to Chief Justice Taft and Justices Stone and Holmes of U. S. supreme court, Judge Sisk of superior court, Judge Lowell in federal court and Judge Anderson in circuit court of appeals.

One hundred and fifty-four pickets arrested in front of State House.

Arthur D. Hill, chief of defense counsel, somewhere in Maine after futile trip to Isle au Haut, off Rockland.

Mrs. Sacco and Miss Vanzetti visit prison three times and then talk with Governor for hour.

William G. Thompson and other lawyers made last-minute appeal to Governor.

Between noontime and 6 P. M. yesterday, police on guard in front of the State House broke up eight "death watch" demonstrations and arrested 154 men and women pickets carrying placards or marching in silent protest against the execution of Sacco and Vanzetti. One of the women was Edna St. Vincent Millay, poetess, Pulitzer prize winner, and author of the text of "The King's Henchman," an American opera.

Those arrested ranged from youths and young women in their 'teens to persons 75 years old. They included persons of various nationalities and occupations.

Four between 11 and 17 years of age, were also among the pickets taken in custody. Among the persons arrested who are more or less well known were: John Howard Lawson, dramatist; John Dos Passos, writer, Miss Ellen Hayes, former professor at Wellesley; Miss Louise Brown, also of Wellesley; Clarina Michelson, writer, arrested twice during the day; Alfred Baker Lewis, organizer of the Socialist party; Margaret Hatfield, daughter of Charles E. Hatfield, treasurer of Middlesex country; Lola Ridge: Powers Hapgood, labor worker;

(Continued on Page Three, Column 3)

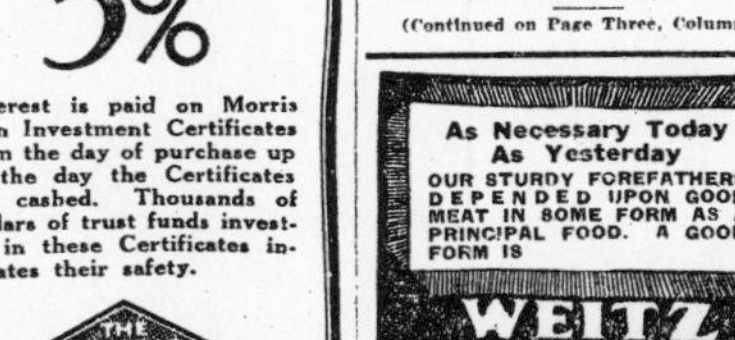

Flier Coins New Word---'Avigate'

Lt. Maitland Suggests Its Use in Referring to Piloting in Air

[Special Dispatch to The Herald]

WASHINGTON, Aug. 22—The suggestion that the word "avigation" be used in connection with aeronautics has been made by Lt. Lester J. Maitland, who piloted an army plane in the first successful non-stop flight from California to Hawaii. The idea has found favor with officers of the navy bureau of aeronautics. Lt. Maitland suggested that "we use the term 'avigation' for the directing or operating of air craft from one place to another."

The combination of the Latin roots, avis (bird) and agere (to drive) is etymologically correct, the bureau officers argued, and the word will serve to differentiate navigation from avigation, which are two different arts. It is not too much to believe, officers of the bureau said, "that in years to come a skilled navigator may be entirely useless in an airplane, while 'avigators' will be in great demand for long distance commercial flying."

30 DUCKED AS FLOORING OF PIER FALLS THROUGH

Victims Had Just Been Landed by Launch at Oak Bluffs

[Special Dispatch to The Herald]

OAK BLUFFS, Aug. 22—Thirty passengers of the excursion launch Marion, running between this town and Falmouth, received an unexpected ducking late this afternoon when the flooring of the pier at which the Marion landed fell through and dropped them into Oak Bluffs harbor. Fortunately, it was low tide at the time.

The Marion, which puts out from this town each afternoon on excursions to the mainland or to the lightship in the sound, had just deposited its last passenger when the pier fell apart. Practically the whole party fell into the harbor, all escaping with a ducking and shaking up except two elderly women, who suffered from the shock and from bruises where their bodies came into contact with the woodwork of the pier.

The clothing of all those who fell in was badly damaged by the salt water and the mud at the bottom of the harbor. The police are investigating the cause of the accident tonight.

TRUCK RUNS OVER WOMAN IN LYNN

Mrs. Rita Vient, 20, of 61 Commercial street, Lynn, is at the Lynn Hospital suffering from a possible fracture of the skull and probable internal injuries as the result of being run over by a motor truck at Summer and Pleasant streets, Lynn, last night. Her name is on the danger list.

With a companion, Miss Mary Bernard of 7 La Grange terrace, Lynn, Mrs. Vient started across the street while the signal tower showed the red and yellow lights for pedestrians to cross. When the two women were part way across, according to one version, the lights were changed for vehicular traffic to move, and before the two could gain the sidewalk they were run down by a truck that had been started in motion.

Both the forward and the rear wheels of the truck, operated by Peter Chopaf of East Ware, N. H., passed over Mrs. Vient. Miss Bernard received a glancing blow from a mudguard which threw her onto the sidewalk, but her injuries were not serious enough to necessitate going to the hospital.

FALL RIVER BOAT TRAIN HELD UP AT SANDWICH

SANDWICH, Aug. 22 (AP)—The Hyannis to Fall River boat train of the New York, New Haven & Hartford Railroad was held up near here for several hours tonight when the rear wheels of the tender were derailed.

Fifty passengers bound for New York via the Fall River boat connection were transferred from the train and transported to their destination by busses.

RICHARD BARTHELMESS AND ACTRESS TO WED

NEW YORK, Aug. 22 (AP)—The New York Herald-Tribune will say tomorrow that Richard Barthelmess, film star, and Katherine Wilson, Broadway actress, will be married this fall.

Barthelmess, the former husband of Mary Hay, dancer, is now in New York but will return to Hollywood this week. The couple have known each other for more than three years and after their marriage will live on the Pacific coast.

WITNESSES OF ELECTROCUTION

Top row, left—Surgeon-General Frank P. Williams of the Massachusetts National Guard, and Warden William Hendry. Bottom row, left—Medical-Examiner Magrath and Sheriff Samuel H. Capen of Norfolk County.

2 SCHOOLBOYS LEAD GOLF FIELD

Homans and Finlay with 71 and 72 Show Way in U. S. Amateur

OUIMET AND JONES TAKE 75 STROKES

By W. E. MULLINS

MINNEAPOLIS, Minn., Aug. 22—While the giants of the field were engaged in a keen struggle for the distinction of producing the best score in the first round of the 36-hole qualifying test for the amateur championship today at Minikahda, three unheralded youngsters stole their thunder, with the result that three new names are at the head of the list.

Gene Homans of Englewood, who starts his college career at Princeton in the Fall, holed the course in 71 shots in the closing hours of this very exciting day and is leading the field by a single putt. Out of the 160-odd golfers who teed off today, he was the only one who succeeded in beating par.

Philips Finlay, the 19-year-old Exeter boy, who enters Harvard next month, put through a rather spectacular 72 with none but his caddy, his partner and a handful of admirers looking on. From a place of obscurity in the golfing field these school boys have leaped up into the clouds.

PAIR HAVE MET BEFORE

The battle between them for the medal is only a resumption of rivalry between them. Already this season they have come to grips at match play and Finlay was the victory. They were the finalists in the recent national interscholastic championship and the title went to Exeter after a furious engagement.

Next to the two school boys came Don Carrick of Toronto, the current amateur champion and native of Canada and a heavyweight boxer of considerable reputation up home. Playing with Francis Ouimet, just as he did two years ago at Oakmont, Carrick came home in 35 shots over the tougher of the two nine holes and his 73 landed him in third place.

Locked in a tie for fourth place came five of the golfers from whom such achievements are expected. They are Harrison Johnston of this club, who knocked them dead in two rounds in the last open; George Rotan ,the Texan; Max Marston, Clarke Corkran and

(Continued on Page Thirteen, Column 1)

Gov. Fuller for 13 Gruelling Hours Hears Final Appeals

Does Not Leave State House Until After One of Trio Is Executed

WIFE AND SISTER OF DOOMED MEN PLEAD

By THOMAS CARENS

Gov. Fuller did not leave the State House until 12:13 o'clock this morning. Madeiros had already been dead four minutes. Sacco had entered the death chamber. Vanzetti was awaiting the final summons. But the Governor had no knowledge of what was taking place at Charlestown, less than two miles away. His responsibility had ended at midnight.

HAS NO STATEMENT

He had no statement. There was no comment to make on the 13 gruelling hours during which from behind his big desk he had listened to the last despairing pleas for the lives of three men. The world had known for more than an hour before the death march began that the Governor of Massachusetts had intervened for the last time.

All day long men and women had gone in and out of the white doors leading to the private office. Lawyers, editors, writers, poets, laborers, society women—they had come with their arguments, their criticisms, their appeals for mercy. But all left without hope. Each told the same story—the Governor had been courteous, but inflexible in his purpose.

The first of the petitioners were in the Governor's office before he arrived at 10:40 in the morning. The last came through the white doors at one minute before midnight.

Most pitiful of all the Governor's visitors were the two women most keenly affected by the executions. Mrs. Rose Sacco, who became a widow in the first 19 minutes of today, and Miss Luigia Vanzetti, sister of the third man to die, arrived at the State House at 9 o'clock. They had not intended to come. They knew in their hearts they would fail. But as the long day wore on, and one by one the avenues of possible escape were closed, they determined to take the chance of desperation.

ENTRANCE OF WOMEN IS DRAMATIC ONE

Their entrance was dramatic in the extreme. A messenger had been sent to meet them at the entrance to the State House. As they stepped from the elevator Mrs. Sacco was in the lead, and with her eyes straight ahead and with firm step she walked through the reception room toward the inner office. A few feet behind came Miss Vanzetti, obviously bewildered, and hesitating be-

(Continued on Page Six, Column 5)

7000 AT SACCO PEABODY RALLY

Socialist Mayor Bakeman, Lewis and Another Address Crowd

NEW MAN REPLACES OUSTED POLICE HEAD

More than 7000 persons crowded into Peabody square, Peabody, last night at a Sacco-Vanzetti protest meeting sponsored by Mayor Robert A. Bakeman, Socialist mayor of Peabody, who was one of the three speakers.

Interest in the meeting had been stirred to fever heat earlier in the day by the action of Mayor Bakeman in ousting Deputy Chief Edward A. Callahan of the Lynn police from his temporary office of chief of the Peabody police. He was lent to Peabody six months ago to readjust the Peabody police force, and it is said that his ousting yesterday was a result of his arrest of Alfred Baker Lewis, noted Socialist orator, last Friday while Lewis was delivering an address in Peabody in behalf of Sacco and Vanzetti.

PERCHED ON ROOFTOPS

In addition to filling the square, the crowd last night overflowed into Chestnut and Lowell street and to the veranda of the city hall, and many persons were perched on rooftops in the vicinity. Deputy Chief Callahan did not appear at the meeting, but 20 state policemen and about 75 regular and special local policemen were on guard. It was noted that the regular police made no effort to clear the traffic jam on Lowell street, the main highway between Lowell and Peabody, and the thoroughfare was blocked from 8 until 9:30 P. M., the duration of the meeting.

There was no excitement, even when a young man in the crowd set off a three-inch firecracker, and the applause given the three speakers came from about 50 persons. It seemed that

(Continued on Page Five, Column 2.)

MARCH TO CHAIR CALMLY AFTER MADEIROS DIES

"Good-by Wife and Children, Farewell Mother," Sacco Moans

'LONG LIVE ANARCHY,' HIS PARTING SHOT

"I Wish to Say That I Am Innocent," Vanzetti Cries Out

In the half hour just after midnight this morning, Nicola Sacco, Stoughton shoe worker, and Bartolomeo Vanzetti, Plymouth fish peddler, died in the electric chair in the state prison at Charlestown, for the murder of Frederick Parmenter, a South Braintree paymaster, and his guard, Alexander Berardelli, in April, 1920.

Preceding them by 10 minutes was Celestino Madeiros, whose case had been linked closely with that of the two others. He was found guilty of killing a Wrentham bank cashier in November, 1924.

The three men were executed in almost exactly 24 minutes. All went to their deaths calmly, Madeiros being pronounced dead at 12:09 A. M., Sacco at 12:19 A. M. and Vanzetti at 12:26 A. M.

"LONG LIVE ANARCHY"

Sacco died with a cry of "Long live anarchy!" on his lips, but his compatriot, Vanzetti, went to his death with forgiveness for those who were sending him to his death and a protestation of his innocence. Madeiros died without a murmur.

The execution marked the second time within six months that three men had died in the electric chair at Charlestown. Like the first, there was not a falter from the time that Warden Hendry went to the death cells a minute after midnight until 26 minutes later, when Vanzetti had been pronounced dead.

GO TO DEATHS CALMLY

None of the men showed a sign of fear. None of them at any time was in danger of collapse. They walked into the death chamber with heads erect and with firm step. All of them died without embracing the Catholic faith in which they had been raised.

Just a minute before midnight, Chaplain Murphy, who had endeavored to persuade the three to allow him to administer the last rites of the church entered the warden's office. "Good evening, gentlemen," he said. "I guess I will go home." With those words he left the prison.

It was only a few minutes after midnight, when the warden, Deputy Warden Hogsett and two guards went to the cell of Madeiros, whose confession sought to save the lives of Sacco and Vanzetti. Madeiros was sleeping, as he had been all the evening.

The warden aroused him, and with a guard on either side, the condemned man entered the death chamber. He seemed to be in a sort of stupor, with no expression on his face. Officially it was 12:02:47 when he walked into the room. The straps were adjusted quickly and Madeiros died without speaking a word. At 12:09:35 he was pronounced dead.

"FAREWELL MY WIFE," SACCO CRIES IN CHAIR

Less than two minutes later, at 12:11:12 A. M., Sacco was led into the chamber between the same two guards who had escorted Madeiros. Sacco was very pale. He was silent as he walked across the room, but as he seated himself in the death chair and the guards

(Continued on Page Six, Column 1)

BIG LEAGUE RESULTS

NATIONAL LEAGUE

Boston 5, Chicago 3.
St. Louis 1, Philadelphia 0.
Only games scheduled.

AMERICAN LEAGUE

Cleveland 9, New York 4.
Detroit 4, Washington 2 (first game.
Detroit 7, Washington 3 (second game).
Chicago 6, Philadelphia 3.
Boston-St. Louis game, played Sunday.

Average net paid circulation of THE NEWS, Dec., 1927:
Sunday, 1,357,556
Daily, 1,193,297

DAILY  NEWS

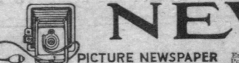

FINAL EDITION

Copyright, 1928, by News Syndicate Co., Inc. Reg. U. S. Pat. Off.

NEW YORK'S PICTURE NEWSPAPER

Entered as 2nd class matter Post Office, New York, N. Y.

Vol. 9. No. 174 28 Pages ** New York, Saturday, January 14, 1928 2 Cents IN CITY LIMITS | 3 CENTS Elsewhere

CROWDS Follow Ruth and Judd to GRAVE

Story on Page 3

(© 1928 by Pacific & Atlantic Photos)

WHEN RUTH PAID HER DEBT TO THE STATE!—The only unofficial photo ever taken within the death chamber, this most remarkable, exclusive picture shows closeup of Ruth Snyder in death chair at Sing Sing as lethal current surged through her body at 11:06 Thursday night. Its first publication in yesterday's EXTRA edition of THE NEWS was the most talked-of feat in history of journalism. Ruth's body is seen straightened within its confining gyves, her helmeted head, face masked, hands clutching, and electrode strapped to her right leg with stocking down. Autopsy table on which body was removed is beside chair.

—Story on page 3.

Fliers Up 37 Hours at 11 o'Clock Despite Accidents to Plane—Page 2

SPORTS ON PAGE 25 THE CHICAGO DAILY NEWS HOME EDITION.

53D YEAR—51. COPYRIGHT 1928 BY THE CHICAGO DAILY NEWS INC. WEDNESDAY, FEBRUARY 29, 1928—FORTY-EIGHT PAGES. ON SALE EVERYWHERE IN CHICAGO AT OR BEFORE 5 O'CLOCK—THREE CENTS

GEORGE MORAN SEIZED IN BOMB DRIVE

Four Marines Killed, 9 Wounded, in Nicaragua Skirmish

EMMERSON TO RUN ON OWN RECORD

Will Wage Personal Campaign, but Not One of Personalities, He Says.

A BUSINESS MAN FIRST

BY FRANK A. SMOTHERS.
Special Dispatch from a Staff Correspondent.

Springfield, Ill., Feb. 29.—Louis L. Emmerson, the country banker, secretary of state and candidate for governor, means to win his race on a personal basis. Which is to say that he doesn't intend to wage a campaign of personalities. He doesn't intend to talk personalities against his rival for the republican nomination, Gov. Len Small, nor does he intend to talk against the men backing Small—in Cook county or elsewhere.

What he does intend to do is convince the voting public of Illinois that he, Louis Emmerson, can give the state better government for less money than it has had to pay under the regime now in power. He intends to run positively as himself, not negatively as a mere attacker of somebody else.

That much and a good deal more about his place and aims in public life he said in the course of an informal interview during a motor trip from Peoria to Springfield and back to Springfield.

The man who plans thus to go into the governor's office on the "personal basis" is a person both genial and shrewd. He is tall, with a noticeably determined chin, and large, steady hands. A rugged gentleman, despite his thinness, he wears clothing of the "conservative cut," creased to perfection. His shoes are black and they shine. And through all his talk, his appearance and his clothing there is the stamp of the country banker in him, but also of the seasoned man of affairs and the attentive traveler of the world.

Grandfather Came Here in 1817.

Here, in brief, is a sketch of his life. The facts were set forth by Mr. Emmerson himself during the interview.

His grandfather came to Illinois in 1817 and the family has been here ever since. Mr. Emmerson himself was born in Albion, Ill., and lived there through most of his boyhood, a normal Illinois small-town boyhood with a fair amount of work in it.

The boyhood also had a tailor-made suit in it at one time, but, as Mr. Emmerson recalled, with twinkles in his eyes, the suit was ruined very early in its career by the family cow, which insisted upon kicking a half-filled milk pail into the air above his head while he was milking her.

At 16 he became a business man. He began clerking in a hardware store at Albion. Shortly after the age of 20 he went to Mount Vernon, Ill., which remains his home today.

[Continued on Seventh Page.]

PERMANENT PADLOCKS SNAPPED ON 4 PLACES

Permanent injunctions padlocking four of the thirty-four cafes and drug stores charged with violating the prohibition law were granted today by Federal Judge Walter C. Lindley. The places ordered padlocked are those of George Graham, 95th street and California avenue; James Belcastro, 6336 Cottage Grove avenue; J. Merch, Oak Forest, and Jack Harrison, 54 South Water street, Aurora.

Others up for hearing included those of John Hogan, 1110 West Madison street, where William Skidmore, professional bondsman, was listed as the property owner; Jack Sullivan, 448 North State street; Joseph Daniels, 918 North Wells street, where Lawrence C. O'Brien, well-known politician, is listed as property owner, and Patrick Skinners, 815 North Clark street.

The drug store of Mathew McAny, 901 East 55th street, where University of Chicago students are alleged to have purchased gin that resulted in the death of one of them, was permitted to operate, where it was proved that the place had changed hands. Several continuances to March 8 and 9 were granted by Judge Lindley.

WEATHER INDICATIONS.

The official weather forecast for the thirty-six hours ending tomorrow at 7 p.m. is as follows:

Chicago and vicinity—Cloudy and somewhat unsettled tonight and Thursday; colder; lowest temperature tonight about 24; fresh to strong shifting winds, mostly northwest.

Hourly temperatures since 3 p. m. yesterday are:

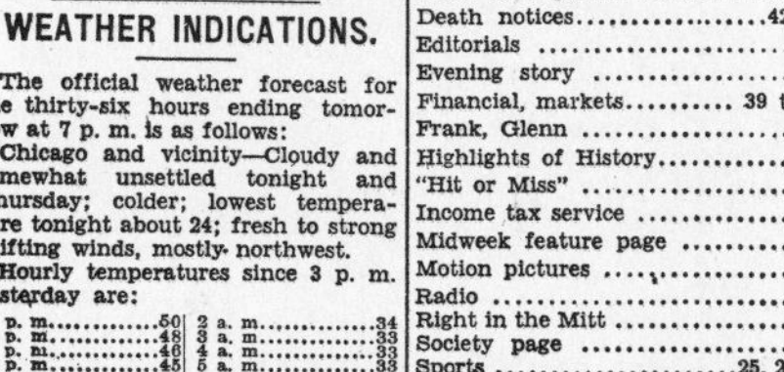

CROWD SEES WOMAN DIE UNDER "L" TRAIN

Tragedy Follows All-Night Search by Husband After Disappearance.

Mrs. Catharine Brewder, 5048 Dakin street, jumped or fell to her death in front of a Chicago & North Shore electric train shortly before 7 o'clock this morning in plain view of a score or more persons on the Sheridan road elevated platform awaiting trains to carry them to work.

She was instantly killed, her body being mangled beneath the wheels of the train before it could be stopped.

Mrs. Brewder's death ended an all-night search for her by her husband, John J. Brewder, and the police, following her mysterious disappearance last evening when she left presumably to go to the home of Miss Annie Wilson, 1022 Byron street, a sister. She never reached the Wilson home.

Had Been in Ill Health.

Mrs. Brewder was 50 years old and mother of four children. She had not been in good health recently, her husband said, and had also been considerably worried by the condition of another sister, Mrs. Florence Ranske of 1328 Fletcher street.

Investigation by the police failed to disclose where she spent the night after she had left her daughter, Catharine, 18 years old, who had accompanied her to Irv— Park boulevard and Leclaire avenue, where she boarded a car shortly after 8 o'clock last evening.

Says She Plunged Before Train.

Benjamin Wickhan of Waukegan, motorman of the train, said that the woman plunged directly in front of his train and that he had no opportunity to avoid hitting her. A number of the persons who were on the platform and were horror stricken by the woman's tragic death, were unable to enlighten the police as to whether she had thrown herself into the path of the onrushing train or had accidentally fallen to her death.

She was last seen standing at the edge of the platform and then, almost as the train was abreast of her, plunged to the tracks.

Mrs. Brewder is survived in addition to her daughter, Catherine, by a son, John, 19 years old; Marjorie, 15 years old, a student at the Carl Schurz high school, and George, 13 years old.

Search Began at Midnight.

Search for Mrs. Brewder was begun shortly before midnight when the husband called up Miss Wilson to inquire whether Mrs. Brewden wanted him to drive over to get her. He was surprised when he was informed that she had not been there and that Miss Wilson had not seen or heard from Mrs. Brewden. He next communicated with Mrs. Ranske, who also said she had not heard from Mrs. Brewder.

LINDBERGH TO ALBANY TO TALK OF AVIATION

Curtiss Field, N. Y., Feb. 29.—(AP)—Col. Charles A. Lindbergh took off at 10:10 o'clock today for Albany, where he will address the state legislature on a proposed state program for the development of aviation.

Earlier in the forenoon F. Trubee Davison, assistant secretary of war, and Lieut. Lester J. Maitland, San Francisco-to-Honolulu flyer, left the field in an army transport plane for Albany.

In taking off over frozen ruts at Curtiss field the shock absorber cord of the tail skid of Lindbergh's plane broke, rendering the tail skid useless, but Lindbergh declined to let this hinder him. He craned out of the pilot's seat, glanced back at the dragging tail skid and then gave his engine the gun, making a graceful ascent.

Aviators on the field expressed admiration for the maneuver, saying that less skillful handling might easily have permitted the tail to drop to the earth again before the plane left the ground, resulting in a possible smashed rudder or more serious damage.

IN THE DAILY NEWS TODAY

HE CAN'T HELP BUT NOTICE IT

U. S. INDICTS FIVE IN TRAIN HOLDUP

Grand Jury Names Cleaver, Donovan and Others as Robbers.

A blanket indictment charging five men with the $133,000 Evergreen Park railway mail robbery of Saturday was returned by the federal grand jury today before Judge Adam C. Cliffe. The men named in the indictment are Charles Cleaver, William Donovan, Frank Meccia, alias Bozo, Virgil Litsinger, alias Bill Collins, and William Jackson. The last named has not been mentioned in connection with the robbery before.

Judge Cliffe fixed the bonds of the men at $100,000 each. The case was presented to the jury by Assistant District Attorney John E. Northup, who told the court that while he did not know the individual parts the men played in the robbery he had definite information that all of them participated.

To make bond the five indicted men will have to put up $500,000 in cash or Liberty bonds, or furnish bonds of $2,000,000 in real estaate. Attaches of the court deemed this impossible for the accused men.

The true bills were voted, it is said, on the confession of Mrs. Cleaver, wife of one of the accused men. In her confession, which she repeated to the jury, she is said to have told how the robbery plot was hatched in the Cleaver home, where police recovered $17,125 of the loot.

Act to Forestall Writs.

Mrs. Cleaver, Mrs. William Donovan, in custody of the government, and other witnesses in the case were rushed before the grand jury last night when Assistant United States District Attorney Northup was warned that lawyers for the prisoners were to appear before Judge Evans in United States Circuit Court of Appeals at the opening of court this morning in an effort to obtain their freedom.

Mrs. Cleaver first made her confession, during the afternoon to Sergt. Michael Naughton of the detective bureau and Postal Inspector F. N. Davis.

"We won't kill any one if we can help it, but if they start shooting shoot back, because we might as well be killed as to be caught," were the final instructions of her husband to his confederates, police say Mrs. Cleaver told them and federal officials.

According to police Mrs. Cleaver said the six men met at her home about Feb. 20 to discuss plans for the robbery. Besides her husband, Donovan and Meccia there were three others present whose names police assert she said she did not know. The band met again Friday, the night before the robbery, at Evergreen Park.

[Continued on Third Page.]

FEAR GIRL, 14, SEIZED BY KIDNAPER GANG

"Phone Voice" Tells Mother of Men in Car; Strangers Quiz Neighbor.

Two swarthy young men, who watched the Stichberry home at 3221 West Flournoy street from an automobile last night, were hunted by the police today in connection with the mysterious disappearance of Jeanette Stichberry, 14-year-old schoolgirl, missing since Monday night.

The police believe the girl was kidnaped.

Louis Sacci, 3311 Flournoy street, tried for contributing to the delinquency of a minor a year ago on Jeanette's parents' complaint, was found by the police today. He said he had been ill and in bed since Sunday. A physician substantiated his story.

Saw Suspicious Strangers.

Mrs. Blanche Tolan, 3326 Flournoy street, told the police of the swarthy young men.

"I was on my way to the store," she said, "when these two men jumped out of an automobile. 'Where does Jeanette Stichberry live?' one asked. I told him I didn't know. My little boy was with me and said, 'Yes, mother, sure you do.' I started to hurry on. One of them said, 'Pretty smart, ain't you? I've a good mind to give you a bust in the nose.' When I came back from the store their car was still parked near the Stichberry home."

Described as being unusually pretty, Jeanette, clad in a pink and white house dress and slippers, left her home shortly before 8 o'clock that night to go to a neighboring store to buy ice cream. She has not been seen since by her relatives.

Mrs. Alice Stichberry, the girl's mother, received a telephone message last night, indicating Jeanette had been kidnaped.

Mysterious Caller Cut Off.

"I saw your little girl forced into an automobile last night," the voice, believed to be that of a man, had informed the nearly frantic mother when there was a rasping sound and then the connection was broken.

She said she became so excited that she could not tell whether it was a man or a woman talking. Frank Stichberry, the father, immediately informed the police of the incident.

"I feel sure that she is being held against her will, as she was unusually attached to her home life," Stichberry said. "She had only 15 cents with her when she left the house and was only wearing a house dress and soft slippers when she went to the store to get ice cream. I believe that the person who telephoned my wife probably wanted to communicate with us about her when he was disconnected, I believe she was kidnaped."

Returned Home Week Ago.

Jeanette, who had been making plans to celebrate her fifteenth birth-

[Continued on Third Page.]

BLUNDERING BEN? NO, FEBRUARY 29

It's Singer's Fifth Birthday and Only 13th for Mother of Two.

BY JUNE PROVINES.

Miss Gladys Billiekin, 5821 Winthrop avenue, will celebrate her fifth birthday anniversary this evening by making her debut in a song recital at Kimball hall.

Mrs. Carl Latham, 1118 Sheridan road, Evanston, wife of an attorney with offices in the loop, will observe her thirteenth birthday anniversary by going to the theater (in a new birthday motor car) with her husband, her two daughters and their husbands.

Gloria Foryere Collins, 5649 North Artesian avenue, is giving a party to a group of her friends, with games and ice cream and cake, on the occasion of her first birthday anniversary today.

Victims of Calendar.

This all sounds like an installment of the Blundering Ben serial, but there are no inaccuracies in the above news items. Nor is Miss Billiekin a child prodigy, in curls and sash, Mrs. Latham the world's youngest mother, or the Collins child advanced for her years. They are, all of them, leap-year babies, and today they have a birthday to celebrate for the first time in four years.

There are many other persons in Chicago who, being victims of a calendar originated by one Lillio Ghiraldi, whose brother introduced it to Pope Gregory III., according to one version, have a birthday today for the first time in four years. The other version is that astronomers of Julius Cæsar started it going in 46 B. C. by setting the solar year at 365 days six hours.

Mother and Daughter Celebrate.

Mrs. Florence Dow and her daughter Flo, whose Chicago residence is at 7049 Parnell avenue, both have birthdays today, the mother celebrating her seventh and the daughter her second. Mrs. Samuel Straus, 84 years old today, is observing her twentieth birthday anniversary. Mrs. Straus had an eight-year interval between birthdays once, as there was no leap year between 1896 and 1904.

Sidney Shaw, 8-year-old son of Mr. and Mrs. H. H. Shaw, 5[illegible] East 72d street, is having a party today, as is 4-year-old Gloria Foryere Shaw, who doesn't yet understand why she was named Foryere.

William P. McEvoy Jr., grandson of the late Roger Sullivan, is studying at Notre Dame, and his birthday box from his family, containing four years' worth of parents, was to be opened there.

REED TELLS OF IMMUNITY OFFER

Declares Confession of Bombing Was Obtained by Coercion.

JURY IS BARRED OUT

Hiram Reed took the witness stand at his trial at Ottawa today to convince the court that his confession to dynamiting the Pleasant Valley schoolhouse was obtained under coercion and through misrepresentation of the state's attorney.

The bushy haired young farmer might have been talking in his own home, so unperturbed was he. Stepping slowly to the witness chair, he did not glance at his former sweetheart, Miss Iola Bradford, who was nearly killed when the school stove exploded. She, however, stared coldly at him as he testified.

Hiram's mother, Mrs. Thomas Reed, glanced defiantly at the girl and then turned her attention to her son. She did not appear to be under as great a strain as when Iola told her story a few days ago.

Tells of Signing Confession.

"When you signed that confession the morning of Dec. 2 what did the state's attorney tell you?" asked Attorney George Sprenger.

"He said that if I married Iola Bradford she could not testify against me," young Reed replied quietly.

The defense attorney then turned his attention to the much discussed immunity clause.

The clause reads: "If I marry Iola Bradford before the next grand jury meets, this confession will not be used against me."

The defense holds that State's Attorney Russell O. Hanson, after obtaining the confession, called a special session of the grand jury and obtained the indictment against the young man, accused of attempting to avoid fatherhood and marriage with the young teacher by placing the dynamite.

Reed testified that he would not sign the confession until the state's attorney put the immunity clause in it.

"What did you understand when you signed that statement?" asked Sprenger.

"I understood I would be free of all charges, permitted to marry the girl and there would be no publicity."

Jury Is Barred Out.

The jury did not hear any of the testimony, which was for the purpose of permitting Judge Frank Hayes to decide as to the admissibility of the confession.

Defense counsel then led Reed to describe the time he spent in the county jail, starting with 11 o'clock the night after the explosion at the school, Dec. 1.

He said he received no food or refreshment until 6 o'clock the next morning and when he signed the confession he was fatigued, thirsty and hungry. Reed said he had been out until 2:30 the previous morning, shucked corn all day and then was subjected to six hours of continuous questioning.

The defendant testified he finally told the state's attorney to write down what he pleased. He said Hanson told him that it would be better for him and all concerned to make the confession.

When the state's attorney came to writing "dynamite" into the confession, he asked Reed how much he used. Reed replied he did not know because he did not put dynamite into the stove. After conferring with oth-

[Continued on Third Page.]

War or No War, Draft Business Is Good Side-Line for Policemen

BY ROBERT J. CASEY.
SPECIAL CORRESPONDENCE
Of The Chicago Daily News Foreign Service.
Copyright, 1928, The Chicago Daily News, Inc.

Hongkong, Dec. 29.—Since the war has moved away from Kiukiang there is great suffering among the police. Their plight is pitiable, for there is no longer need for troops in Hankow, or at any rate there wasn't last night.

True, Kiukiang sends no fewer troops to the front now than it did when there was a front to send them to, but, on the other hand, the prospective soldiers are not so likely to pay for exemption from the draft as they were when the draft seemed so imminent—and permanent.

Kong Phoy, said by some to be the brains of the police department, sat by his empty rice bowl and considered the situation. His salary would never support him in the style to which a policeman should be accustomed—one reason was that he didn't seem likely to get a salary. As against that the percentage of illiterates among the coolie classes was quite high. They probably hadn't heard that the war was temporarily over.

Why Hesitate, Indeed?

Why, then, should he fail in his patriotic duty of impressing troops just because there happened to be no market for them after impressment? He couldn't see any very good answer to that.

So Officer Kong went out into the market place and he laid a heavily patriotic hand on the shoulder of Seng Choy.

"You are chosen for the splendid duty of military service," he announced t. Mr. Seng. Mr. Seng, being an ignorant coolie, failed to show proper appreciation.

"I am sick," he replied. "I should not do very well fighting for the liberties of this glorious land, if any. I shall have to step back in favor of one more worthy."

Maybe We Can Fix It——

"Don't let sickness worry you," admonished the gendarme cheerfully. "You would be sick very shortly after

[Continued on Fourth Page.]

SANDINISTS AMBUSH PACK-TRAIN PATROL

Well-Directed Machine Gun Fire Takes Toll of Little U. S. Force.

BY JULIAN F. HAAS.
SPECIAL RADIO
To The Chicago Daily News Foreign Service.
Copyright, 1928, The Chicago Daily News, Inc.

Managua, Nicaragua, Feb. 29.—Four American marines were killed and nine wounded, one seriously, in a conflict between a marine patrol and Sandinists yesterday afternoon, it is officially announced by the headquarters here of Gen. Logan Feland, commander of the marines in Nicaragua.

The skirmish occurred near Daraily, halfway between Yali and Condega, while an empty pack train under command of Lieut. Edward O'Day was returning to the base at Estali.

Patrol Was Ambushed.

According to headquarters the patrol was ambushed and the casualties were the result of a well-directed machine-gun fire from the hidden Sandinists. The names of the marines killed or wounded and other details of the affair are lacking.

There were thirty-six marines and ninety pack animals with Lieut. O'Day, comprising a part of Maj. Pierce's ox-cart train, which has been trekking into the battle area with supplies for six months for the marines.

Reports Routed by Planes.

Airplanes yesterday sighted the bandits and reports are that they were routed with bombs and machine guns. Though hit many times by return fire, the planes reached their base successfully.

16 STATES HAVE "WORSE" MARRIAGES THAN ILLINOIS

Despite allegations that Cook county runs a divorce mill, married couples in Illinois have a better chance of making their marital bliss permanent than do couples in sixteen other states in the nation.

This was discovered today by comparing figures compiled by Thomas C. Wallace, clerk of the Circuit court, with those of the federal census bureau.

Mr. Wallace noted, while making his daily report on the number of divorce cases, that only one state in the union had a larger number of divorces than Illinois. Texas claims the record with 15,120 for 1925, while Illinois follows with 13,882.

Fears that marriage might be in a precarious position in Illinois were set at rest, however, by referring to the federal trade census, which shows that Illinois has only 1.95 divorces to every 1,000 of population. There are sixteen other states with higher divorce records than that of Illinois, if considered on the basis of population.

It is an even break between the chance for marriage and the chance for divorce in Illinois as compared with other states. Sixteen states have a higher marriage record per 1,000 population than Illinois. The record in this state is 4.61.

Nevada, not Illinois, should be shunned as a menace to the marriage state, the report indicates. In Nevada 13.98 divorces are granted per 1,000 of population. But even Nevada has its advantages, for while it ranks first in the number of divorces it also ranks first in the number of marriages with 34.69 marriages per 1,000 persons.

$325,000,000 FLOOD BILL APPROVED BY SENATORS

Washington, D. C., Feb. 29.—(AP)—A Mississippi flood control bill, carrying a total of $325,000,000, all to be paid out of federal funds, was approved today by the senate commerce committee.

GANG CHIEF AND 4 OTHERS HELD

Hint Charges in Blasts at Officials' Homes and Ravenswood Job.

EX-AID OF O'BANION

George Moran, once a pal of Dion O'Banion and an heir to the leadership of the north side "alky" mob of the late Hymie Weiss and "Schemer" Drucci, was seized with three other men and a woman in raids early today and held in what may be an attempt to run down the bombers who hurled explosives at the homes of City Comptroller Charles C. Fitzmorris, Dr. William H. Reid, former smoke inspector, and Assistant State's Attorney John S. Sbarbaro.

The police were extremely mysterious as to the reason the five were held. They were hurriedly booked on charges of robbery, disorderly conduct and vagrancy. and reports spread that the robbery charge involved the recent $80,000 looting of the Ravenswood National bank.

Bombing Link Looms.

But when officials of the bank said they had received no notification from the police as to the seizure of any suspects in the case, the second report came out that the bombing of the homes of the three politicians—presumably in connection with protection for gambling dives—was at the bottom of the arrests.

The bank-robbery charge, it was believed, was a subterfuge under which the prisoners could be held in custody until further investigation in the bombings is made. The five are due to go before Judge John H. Lyle in Grand Crossing court tomorrow morning for arraignment, and it is pointed out that Judge Lyle is noted for the huge bonds he usually fixes in such cases.

Known as Gunman.

Moran is known as a fearless gunman and one of the leaders of the north side gang that he served in under the leadership of O'Banion, Weiss and Drucci, all of whom were killed. Since their deaths he has allied himself with Jack Zuta, head of the combine that controlled the gambling privileges in his old north side territory.

Moran is the only one of the north side leaders, it is said, who has remained in the city since the upheaval in gambling and vice circles that grew out of the political and gang warfare over syndicate privileges. Zuta and Barney Bertsche, another ally, both fled, as did Al Capone, chief of the rival syndicate.

Seized in Dawn Raid.

Sergt. Dan Healy and a squad of detectives rounded up the four men and woman early this morning. Besides Moran they gave these names:

James Clark, 3806 North Francisco avenue, said to be an official of a teamsters' organization.

George Deaur, 1836 North Long avenue.

Adam Sklodowski, 1111 North Mozart street, owner of a drug store at 3000 South 52d avenue, Cicero.

The identity of the woman prisoner was not divulged.

Deputy Commissioner William E. O'Connor and Lieut. John Norton were questioning the five at the bureau.

"We'll book them for bank robbery at once," was all Lieut. Norton would say. "They'll be booked before they can be 'sprung' on writs."

JOBLESS MAN RETURNS $52,000 HE PICKS UP

New York, Feb. 29.—(AP)—Jobless for several weeks, Alexander Lubowsky, 40-year-old painter, found a sack containing $52,000 lying in a gutter in Brooklyn and returned it to its owners.

Today he has a first class reputation for honesty, still no job, and no definite prospect of a reward.

Lubowsky is married and has two children, a daughter, 19, who works in a needle factory and is the only member of the family employed, and a son, 10, who goes to school.

CHILD FALLS 20 FEET; 180 EGGS SAVE LIFE

Burlington, Wis., Feb. 29.—(AP)—Eggs probably saved the life of 6-year-old Valieta Vos here when she fell though a skylight of a store and landed twenty feet below in a box filled with fifteen dozen eggs.

Will Finds Arkansaw Perfect in One Prod

Special to The Chicago Daily News.

Camden, Ark., Feb. 29.—Say know this little city has a six dollar plant where they m[illegible] ping paper out of post oak jack trees? Arkansaw ha[illegible] derful improvements in but I doubt if I coul[illegible] wife out of the state [illegible] twenty years ago W

rage net paid circulation THE NEWS, Jan., 1929:
Sunday, 1,581,237
Daily, 1,255,101

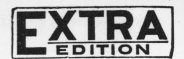

DAILY NEWS
Copyright, 1929: by News Syndicate Co., Inc. Reg. U. S. Pat. Off.
NEW YORK'S PICTURE NEWSPAPER
Entered as 2nd class matter Post Office, New York, N. Y.

EXTRA EDITION

Vol. 10. No. 201 64 Pages New York, Friday, February 15, 1929 2 Cents IN CITY LIMITS | 3 CENTS Elsewhere

7 MASSACRED IN CHICAGO BEER WAR

Story on Page 2

(By A. P.; A. T. & T. transmission)

The room of death. Against that white wall of a garage in Chicago, seven men were lined up yesterday and sprayed with bullets from rival gangsters' machine guns. They're lying where they fell. Six were killed instantly. Seventh died three hours later.

(By A. P.; A. T. & T. transmission)

Horror-stricken crowds struggle to get better view as bodies of six victims of Chicago gangsters are carried from the garage on Chicago's north side after they had been shot down. Seventh victim, who died later, already had been removed in police ambulance.

GANG KILLERS GET SEVEN.—Four men, two of them in police uniforms, turned machine guns on seven Moran-O'Banion gangsters in Chicago garage yesterday and got their men in most cold-blooded slaughter in history of Chicago gang warfare.—*Story on page 2.*

ACCUSES HUBBY AS HOSPITAL GRAFTER.—Thomas Howell, assistant superintendent of New York hospital, was accused yesterday of taking commissions from dealers in hospital goods in return for buying supplies, by estranged wife, Mrs. Sylvia Howell (above). Information secured exclusively by THE NEWS says Supreme court investigation will follow sensational graft charges.

—*Story on page 9.*

I. R. T. Ready for 7-Cent Fare Monday

PAGE THREE

COMPLETE WANT ADS

THE CHICAGO DAILY NEWS

FINAL MARKETS

54TH YEAR—306. COPYRIGHT 1929 BY THE CHICAGO DAILY NEWS INC. MONDAY, DECEMBER 23, 1929.—FORTY PAGES. THREE CENTS

JURY CALLS BURKE MASSACRE SLAYER

Aldermen Balk at $3,000,000 Loan for Teachers' Pay

TODAY'S RACE RESULTS

AT JEFFERSON PARK, NEW ORLEANS, LA.

First—Paddoed, $6.20; Coreopsis, $15.20; Upsedaisy, $3.80.

LATE NEWS BULLETINS

PANTAGES ATTORNEYS SEEK RELEASE ON BONDS.

Los Angeles, Cal., Dec. 23.—(UP)—Attorneys for Alexander Pantages, who is in the county jail here pending an appeal from his conviction on charges of assaulting 17-year-old Eunice Pringle, today petitioned Superior Judge Charles Fricke to release Pantages on bond.

SOVIET AND CHINA END WAR; RECALL BORDER TROOPS

Chinese Eastern Railway Status Is Restored; Parley Jan. 25.

Moscow, U. S. S. R., Dec. 23.—(AP)—Moscow and Mukden have made their peace and have signed a protocol fixing future relationship between the soviet Russian government and the Manchurian Chinese provincial government.

A foreign commissariat announcement says the soviet plenipotentiary, M. Simonovsky, and Tsai Yun-shen, the Chinese representative of the Mukden government, signed at Khabarovsk, Siberia, a protocol which restores the status quo ante on the disputed Chinese Eastern railway and immediately restores consular and commercial organizations in the two countries.

Formal resumption of relations will not be arranged until a further conference is held Jan. 25, but meanwhile all troops will be withdrawn from the Russian and Manchurian borders, all persons arrested in connection with the railway dispute will be released, and white Russians will be disarmed and deported by the Chinese.

New Manager Leaves Soon.

The new Russian general manager of the railway and his assistants will leave soon for Harbin to assume their duties in connection with the joint operation of the railroad as outlined in the Peking-Mukden agreements of 1924.

The protocol, it appears, ends a six-month chapter of violent conflict between China and Russia, growing out of Chinese seizure of the Chinese Eastern railway, which traverses Manchuria. Last spring, the Russians, unable to regain the road to a mutual management scheme, sent troops to the border and recently completely routed the Chinese and took possession of western Manchuria.

The Moscow newspaper Izvestia today asserted that the adjustment of the Russo-Chinese conflict was a "triumph for the soviet's peaceful policy over the adventurous policy of Chinese militarists and the imperialistic powers."

Settlement Pleases Stimson.

Washington, D. C., Dec. 23.—(AP)—Secretary Stimson indicated his pleasure over the settlement of the Chinese-soviet difficulties.

Mr. Stimson declined to comment beyond the fact that reports from Moscow clearly indicated that the long-standing problem had been settled, adding that he was pleased by the outcome.

SNOW FLURRIES GIVE CITY NEW ERMINE COAT

Snow flurries early this morning adorned Chicago and the suburbs with a fresh coat of white for the yuletide season, while the weather bureau indicated that the mild temperature would probably prolong to greet Kris Kringle upon his arrival tomorrow night.

Snow began falling in the Chicago area last night and was reported to be general throughout the middle west. While leaden skies were predicted for tonight and tomorrow the fall of snow was not expected to be heavy.

"It will be just enough to give Chicago a new raiment of white for Christmas," said C. A. Donnel, weather forecaster, this morning.

"No immediate change in temperature is indicated in the weather reports we have received."

At St. Paul, Minn., it was 4 below zero, but in the middle west temperatures ranged higher, from 12 above at Omaha to 30 at Milwaukee. Chicago readings were in the 20's early today.

FLOATING WHITE BLOOMS AWE VISITING AFRICANS

New York, Dec. 23.—(AP)—As the Mauretania came up the bay through a snowstorm today two African natives stood on deck, rigid and suspicious, flinching fearfully as white flakes lighted on their faces and clothing.

"We've never seen floating white blossoms like these," they muttered to their interpreter. "What will they do to us?"

Dressed in European clothes, but wearing fezzes, Riano, a gun boy and Masai warrior, and Mulia, a member of the Akawba tribe, have come over to work in a motion picture in Hollywood.

CREW IN LAKE CRIB BARES STORM'S HORROR

Five Miles Out, Men Were in Panic as Ice Bottled Them Up.

A tale of watery horror hardly to be matched in the memory of old sailors of the great lakes was told today by the icebound crew of the five-mile crib when the tug Fred A. Britten, Patrick Cullnan master, bucked through with Christmas turkeys and other welcome provisions.

John G. Beuckman, keeper of the crib, and his five famished assistants whooped with delight and relief as the tug fought its way through three inches of ice to the bottled-up conical cribhouse of stone. Then, as the turkeys and provisions were unloaded, they gathered round and told of the nightmare of a sixty-six-mile gale and a tomb of sheeted ice.

Lights Go Out.

The freezing water clogged the chimney, so that there was no vent. Cinders and fine ashes from boiler and cookstove were blown wildly over everything, sugar, flour, food, furniture, linen. The light in the tower went out. The fire in the boiler went. The stove fire went out. The men tried to relight a fire but the air was sucked out of the structure so rapidly that no fire would burn.

The place became almost a vacuum. Beuckman and his companions assert. It was impossible to keep a cigarette going. It became difficult to breathe. The men feared they would suffocate.

One of the men smashed one of the windows to let air in. This was of little use. Water washed in through the opening. Ice rapidly covered the breach. Ice was rapidly forming all about the place, bottling it up.

The men became nearly frantic. "I was frightened some myself," said Beuckman, who has been at the crib twelve years.

"I gave the men trivial little jobs to do, just to keep them occupied and quiet their nerves.

"We had a flashlight. That was the only light in the whole place. We were trapped like rats in a caulked barrel."

Cuts Ice from Window.

When the gale had somewhat abated Beuckman took a hatchet and chopped away the ice from rung after rung of the eighty-six-foot tower, climbing as he chopped. Then he relighted the beacon.

"It was the worst storm I ever saw," said Beuckman.

"Same here," said Capt. Cullnan, who has been operating tugs on the Chicago lake front since the five-mile crib was built in 1896.

FIRE AND YULE CALLS OVERLOAD LOOP PHONES

Crippled telephone service on five loop telephone exchanges was experienced today as the result of increased Christmas trade traffic and repair work on the State exchange, which was paralyzed last week by a fire that put 8,500 telephones out of commission.

"Service is not yet quite up to normal on account of the fire and a heavier than usual Christmas traffic," said D. J. Christensen, traffic manager of the Dearborn exchange. "The Harrison, Dearborn, Wabash, Franklin and Randolph exchanges are taking care of part of the service for the State exchange. This makes service a little slow at times, but the delay won't last long, for repairs on the crippled exchange are almost completed. The peak of the load was between the hours of 9 and 11 a. m. today, when patrons may have experienced some inconvenience in getting their numbers."

GIRL, 12, DROPS DOLLS TO LEARN AVIATION

Los Angeles, Cal., Dec. 23.—(AP)—Twelve-year-old Pretto Bell, Los Angeles schoolgirl, is learning to fly. She gave up her dolls three years ago to play with airplanes. After importuning her parents, Mr. and Mrs. Dan Bell of Beverly Hills, for a long time to permit her to take flying lessons, she is today perhaps the youngest aviation student in the country.

Too young to take up actual flying instruction under department of commerce regulations, she is enrolled in the ground school of the Curtiss-Wright flying service and after two years, when she becomes 14, will, by special dispensation, begin flight training.

SANTA SEEKS AIDS TO STEM LOSS OF FAITH

Must Find Way to Reach Hundreds of Homes at Last Minute.

APPEALS PILE UP

Santa Claus, who works hard all year getting his toys and candy assembled and his reindeers shod, only to be paid in Christmas week by the loss of faith of many of his young followers, was head over heels in work today, figuring out his annual task of reaching the hundreds of homes where he has no official representative.

He had a bunch of letters to take care of, more than 3,000 of them, and several hundred more pouring in today at the office of John T. McGrath, assistant postmaster, who, with his assistant, Harry P. Reidy, acts as downtown agent of S. Claus, Inc. The letters are addressed to Santa Claus, North Pole.

Broke Leg, Family Told.

The missives were appeals of children, some of which come from poverty-stricken homes. One daddy, presumably out of work or sick, has told the children that Santa Claus broke his leg, and wouldn't make the rounds this year.

"Please, Dear Santa," writes Walter, aged 7, "I can't believe it. Why will you not come to us and you will always come to people wich don't need it so much. This looks funny to me."

Santa Claus, through his agents, McGrath and Reidy, has to find some one to restore this doubting Thomas' faith, for the youngster goes on to explain: "Some boys said there was no Santa Claus, that daddy was Satna Claus, but I don't believe them. Now if you can come, Santa, I want mittens and my sister wants a doll."

More querulous thoughts, from 6-year-old Marion: "If you got 30,000 why don't you put our name in first? De Santa wer are all praying that you should bring us some toys. The little boy Steve, he is four, yrs old, he hangs his stocking every night. Ma hollers on him but he says no i won't be in bed until Santa brings me a big dumping truck. She was going to spank him but he started to cry, so please come to us, Santa."

Their Daddy Is Gone.

Milton and Richard don't know where their daddy is, but can't Santa get them high top boots, a fire engine that can be sat in, pencil, tablets and candy?

Alice, living on the outskirts, writes in a big round hand to tell St. Nick, that she has no mama and lives with other people and that she would like some toys. "I only got a doll and she is sick. Her head is almost off."

Other thousands of missives, some of them from obvious "chisselers," others from rich and well-off children, and the residue of pathetic appeals from destitute childhood, whose faith in the fat man in the red suit is suffering because they have been let down before, are piled up in the assistant postmaster's office, waiting for responsible agents of S. Claus to take care of them. Cases with a face value of destitution are given applicants with the instructions that they investigate cases themselves and act accordingly.

Everybody knows that S. Claus is terribly rushed this week, and the wise guys will tell you he can't get down a chimney, but if enough believers come to his rescue he will save a host of little children who in their "second floor rears" are verging on the brink of disillusionment.

MERRY YULE FOR MAILMAN?

W. Sorensen, who finds going tough, what with all the Christmas cards and gifts going through the mails He was snapped in the 1100 block in Monroe street. [By a staff photographer.]

INDIAN "REDS" FAIL IN PLOT TO KILL VICEROY

Gesture That Might Have Brought War May Be Forgotten.

BY CONSTANTINE BROWN.

SPECIAL CABLE

To The Chicago Daily News Foreign Service. Copyright, 1929, The Chicago Daily News, Inc.

London, England, Dec. 23.—Had Lord Irwin, viceroy of India, lingered only three minutes longer over the last cup of tea at dinner on the train which was bringing him back to Delhi after a successful visit to the Indian princes, the British empire might have faced a civil war on its hands.

Indian extremists had cleverly arranged a miniature Sarajevo murder with incalculable consequences to the peace of the British empire. They set off a bomb on the tracks over which the viceroy's train passed. The viceroy, however, escaped unhurt, and the India office hopes that the attempt will now have no further consequences as far as India is concerned.

On Way to Conference.

Lord Irwin was hurrying back to the capital to meet Mahatma Ghandi and four other Indian leaders. During the last few years Indian nationalists have avoided public meetings with British officials. Since the labor government announced its intention of giving India home rule, however, Ghandi and his followers have relented and decided to have conversations with the English viceroy on the eve of the meeting of the congress, which will decide whether or not a general boycott will start Dec. 31.

News of the proposed conversations disturbed Indian revolutionaries, who decided to prevent the meeting at any price. Hence the bomb in the viceroy's dining car.

Although Mahatma Ghandi, Pundit Moti Lal Nehru, head of the extremists, and V. J. Patel, president of the lower chamber of parliament, the three stars of the nationalist movement, immediately wrote a letter to the viceroy expressing their abhorrence of this outrage, it is possible that the criminal attempt may have serious consequences.

See Hand of Moscow.

It was only last week that the soviet ambassador presented his credentials to the prince of Wales. From that moment on, Russia was expected to keep the pledges given to Foreign Minister Arthur Henderson that

[Continued on Second Page.]

Markets at a Glance

NEW YORK—Stocks weak; bonds irregular; curb weak; foreign exchanges irregular; cotton higher; sugar steady; coffee higher.

CHICAGO—Wheat steady; corn easy; cattle strong; hogs higher; stocks irregular.

MORRIS WINS POINT IN DIVORCE ACTION

Chicagoan Defeats Effort of Actress Wife to Obtain Huge Allowance.

Paris, France, Dec. 23.—(UP)—Col. Nelson Morris of Chicago won a preliminary victory today in the suit for divorce brought by Jane Aubert, his actress wife.

The Versailles court refused the demand of Miss Aubert for a huge allowance pending a verdict in her suit and granted her 25,000 francs a month ($975). The court ignored the vehement pleas of Joseph Paul Boncour, the wife's attorney, for a larger allowance.

Paul Boncour, socialist deputy who has attained international fame at Geneva and The Hague rather than in the divorce court, revealed on his return to Paris that Miss Aubert had "just begun to fight."

"It was a hard fight at Versailles," he said. "We expected more, since the sum is hardly in keeping with Morris' known fortune. He is determined to oppose the divorce, but Miss Aubert has made up her mind and you know what that means.

"He objects to her continuing her career. She prefers the stage to a husband. He should know better than to insist when a woman decides she no longer loves.

"Mlle. Aubert will seek a court order ejecting him from her country house at Le Vesinet."

Morris, whose spectacular efforts to force his wife to leave the stage furnished Paris amusement, is starting damage suits against the theater owner booking her and the theatrical publicity agent who is plastering her pictures around Paris.

POLA AND PRINCE HAPPY; HE SAYS IT WILL LAST

Paris, France, Dec. 23.—(UP)—Prince Serge Midvani said today he believes his reconciliation with Pola Negri, the motion picture actress, was complete and permanent.

Although the actress indicated to the court Saturday that she merely wished to delay strengthening her divorce petition, until the reconciliation is complete, the prince said:

"We were reconciled before we decided to go before the judge. We only went to the reconciliation court because it was necessary in order to withdraw papers. Henceforth, we will be very happy. I love her more every hour and we are going to have a real honeymoon at St. Moritz."

WEATHER INDICATIONS.

(Dec. 23, 1929.)

Chicago and vicinity—Mostly unsettled tonight and Tuesday; no decided change in temperature; lowest tonight between 15 and 20 degrees above zero; gentle to moderate shifting winds.

Hourly temperatures since 3 p. m. yesterday are:

3 p. m.	[illegible]	3 a. m.	[illegible]
4 p. m.	[illegible]	4 a. m.	[illegible]
5 p. m.	[illegible]	5 a. m.	[illegible]
6 p. m.	[illegible]	6 a. m.	[illegible]
7 p. m.	[illegible]	7 a. m.	[illegible]
8 p. m.	[illegible]	8 a. m.	[illegible]
9 p. m.	[illegible]	9 a. m.	[illegible]
10 p. m.	[illegible]	10 a. m.	[illegible]
11 p. m.	[illegible]	11 a. m.	[illegible]
12 midnight	[illegible]	12 noon	[illegible]
1 a. m.	[illegible]	1 p. m.	[illegible]
2 a. m.	[illegible]	2 p. m.	[illegible]

Sunrise today, 7:16 a. m.; sunset today, 4:23 p. m. Moon rises at 1:02 a. m. Tuesday.

DEMAND PLEDGE OF BANKERS TO BUY WARRANTS

Plan Is Vetoed by Committee Unless Secured by Signatures.

COUNCIL MEETS TODAY

The city council finance committee today refused to recommend to the council the school board's request for a $3,000,000 loan with which pay rolls for the city's 13,000 teachers could be met.

The council was to meet within a few hours after the finance committee's unanimous refusal of the loan. The citizens' committee, headed by Silas H. Strawn, will have to produce pledges that $3,000,000 in tax anticipation warrants will be taken by banks and other firms, council leaders said, before the council will approve the school board borrowing the $3,000,000 from the $10,000,000 in cash which the city has.

H. Wallace Caldwell, president of the board of education, who has been striving to get the cash so that the teachers might receive a pay check before Christmas, said he doubted if he would appear in person before the council.

"I doubt if I have enough pep left to go before the council," he said. "I've been working on this for three days and I'm worn out."

The finance committee called in Bert Keefe, deputy city treasurer, to ask him about the financial status of the city.

Enough for City Pay Roll.

Keefe said there was enough cash on hand to meet January pay rolls, but whether the February pay rolls can be met will depend on the bankers' willingness to buy tax-anticipation warrants.

Ald. John S. Clark, chairman of the finance committee, explained the finance committee's refusal.

"The understanding," he said, "was that the citizens' committee was going to get capitalists to put up $3,000,000, taking tax receipts, and turn the money into the treasury so the city could advance the cash to the schools without depleting our own funds.

"No one paid any taxes in advance except George F. Harding. A number of corporations that we thought were going to make the tax advances failed to produce."

The plan under consideration was to have the city lend the school board the $2,934,557 necessary to meet the pay roll, taking as security interim certificates. Leaders in the city council agreed to do this, providing the bankers would purchase a similar amount of 1928 tax anticipation warrants, so that there would be no depletion of cash in the city treasury.

Strawn was hopeful that the bankers would consent to this plan, but a definite answer was to be received from them later in the afternoon.

Board Passes Resolution.

Confident that this plan would work out, the board at a morning session

[Continued on Fourth Page.]

U. P. PASSENGER TRAINS CRASH IN KANSAS; 4 HURT

Gorham, Kas., Dec. 23.—(AP)—Three trainmen and a woman passenger was injured severely and several other trainmen bruised today when Union Pacific passenger train number 21, west bound from Kansas City, sideswiped the locomotive of passenger train number 128 eastbound, from Los Angeles.

The westbound train, traveling at high speed, hurled the engine of the eastbound train fifty feet and it came to rest in a wheatfield.

HELEN WILLS IS BRIDE TODAY IN SIMPLE RITE

Only Six Guests Will See Her Become Broker's Wife; "Obey" Omitted.

Berkeley, Cal., Dec. 23.—(AP)—Extremely simple ceremonies will mark the wedding here today of Helen Wills, women's tennis champion, and Frederick S. Moody Jr., San Francisco stock broker.

In picturesque little St. Clement's chapel at the foot of the Berkeley hills the Rev. Lindley H. Miller will read the Episcopalian marriage service. Besides Dr. Miller and the bride and bridegroom, only six persons will be present.

They are the bride's parents, Dr. and Mrs. C. A. Wills; the bridegroom's parents, Mr. and Mrs. Frederick S Moody, and Mr. and Mrs. Corbett Moody, the bridegroom's brother and sister-in-law.

Obey Is Left Out.

Dr. Miller arrived here last night after a hurried trip from the east, where he had gone to attend the funeral of his mother. The new Episcopalian marriage service which he will read does not make the bride promise to obey her husband nor does it require the groom to promise to endow his bride with all his worldly goods.

As revised two years ago, the service requires the bride to "love, comfort and honor" her husband and "keep him in sickness and in health, forsaking all others."

Reports are that the tennis champion and her husband will depart aboard the yacht Galatea immediately after the service, but the honeymoon plans are carefully guarded.

Tennis as Usual.

Apparently not a bit perturbed by her coming nuptials, Miss Wills spent yesterday on the courts of the Berkeley Tennis club. In the afternoon she rested and last night an informal family gathering took place at the Wills home.

Telegrams of congratulations from all over the world continue to pour in to the Wills home, which is filled with flowers sent by friends.

Aside from the flowers almost the only sign of the wedding preparations yesterday was that afforded by several trunks packed with the trosseau purchased by the tennis champion when she was abroad recently.

LONE BANDIT RAIDS CAFE; GETS $1,653 IN LOOT

A bandit wearing a black mask staged a one-man holdup of the H. & H. restaurant at 7 East Congress street this morning, got $1,653 in loot and made his getaway while Christmas shopping crowds hurried along the sidewalk.

The robber, armed, entered at about 10 a. m., and herded a cook, waiter and porter into the basement. He kept Harry Snitovsky, manager, covered until he had looted the cash register of $638 and taken an $800 diamond ring, $150 stickpin and $65 wrist watch from him. Then he forced Snitovsky into a rear room and dashed out to where a confederate waited in a motor car at the curb. The two sped away.

Another bandit got $20 for Christmas buying when he entered the Buddy Squirrel nut shop at 116 South Dearborn street, in the heart of the loop, and held up Miss Gwendolyn Weeks, manager, at 11 a. m. today.

LUEDER SETS DEADLINE FOR CITY'S YULE MAIL

Postmaster Arthur C. Lueder announced today that all local mail deposited today or early tomorrow morning will be delivered before Christmas.

According to Mr. Lueder, a full force of employes working from 7 o'clock yesterday morning until midnight enabled the postoffice to be ready for the last-minute rush of mail. Special delivery service only will be given on Christmas day, it was announced.

Christmas Through 1930!

I desire to share in The Daily News Christmas plan of aiding the Sixty Neediest Families in all Chicago throughout the year to come. Please list my gift as follows:

$.........., as a single contribution. Check enclosed.

$.......... per month for twelve months, monthly notice to be sent me by The Daily News.

Name ....

Street No. ....

City and State ....

(Note: Fill out, clip and mail to Sixty Neediest Families, care The Daily News, 400 Madison street, Chicago. Make checks payable to Sixty Neediest Families.)

GUNS OF BANDIT CALLED WEAPONS THAT SHOT SEVEN

Solution of Clark Street Killing Complete, Jury Hears.

PRESS HUNT FOR KILLER

A coroner's jury today named Fred Burke, hair-trigger chief of a band of journeyman killers, kidnapers and bank bandits, as one of the slayers in the St. Valentine's day massacre.

The jury based its verdict on testimony of Lieut.-Col. Calvin H. Goddard, ballistics expert, that two machine guns found in Burke's St. Joseph (Mich.) hideout were the same guns used in the slaying of seven Moran men in a North Clark street garage last February.

The coroner's jury verdict places the official stamp on the belief of authorities that the massacre has been solved. The verdict recommends that Burke be held to the grand jury for the murder of two of the massacre victims.

The suggestion that bullets from Burke's machine guns be compared with those found in the massacre victims, was made to Coroner Herman N. Bundesen by The Daily News.

Final Link in Evidence.

Police Commissioner William F. Russell, Deputy Commissioner John Stege, Coroner Herman N. Bundesen, Pat Roche, the state's attorney's chief investigator, and Assistant State's Attorney Harry S. Ditchburne said they believed Goddard's testimony was the final link in the chain tying Burke to the massacre of the Moran men in a North Clark street garage last February.

Three witnesses, they pointed out, have already identified Burke as one of the firing squad. Goddard's testimony, they said, gives that testimony complete corroboration.

Gives Findings to Jury.

Lieut.-Col. Goddard, as quiet and unobtrusive as a country clergyman, took his place before the coroner's jury of business and professional men. Coroner Bundesen called the inquest to order. Present were a handful of officials—the police commissioner, Deputy Stege, Assistant State's Attorney Ditchburne, Pat Roche and a dozen newspaper men.

The ballistics expert cleared his throat and read his report of a comparison of shells and bullets fired from Burke's guns with the bullets taken from the bodies of the massacre victims and the shells found in the shambles of the North Clark street garage.

His microscopic studies revealed that both Burke guns had been used in the massacre, Lieut.-Col. Goddard said.

James Clark, one massacre victim,

[Continued on Fourth Page.]

FRENCH FLYERS CRASH IN INDIA; SAVED BY LEAPS

Paris, France, Dec. 23.—(AP)—The French aviators, Le Brix and Rossi, who are making a flight from Paris to French Indo-China, have come to grief in India. A telegram from Le Brix today said that their airplane had been wrecked but both the aviators were safe. They jumped with parachutes and Rossi was slightly injured.

Le Brix's message was dated Hlaingbwe, Burma. It read: "We had to jump with parachutes during the night over the mountains near Moulmein on account of bad weather. Rossi slightly hurt, but Le Brix uninjured. Airplane and mail destroyed.

"(Signed) LE BRIX."

Le Brix is one of the best known of French airmen, and was the companion of Dieudonne Coste on a flight around the world two years ago.

IN THE DAILY NEWS TODAY

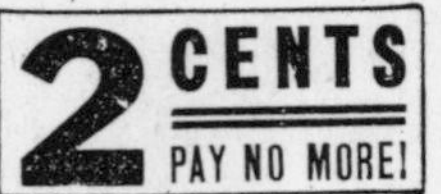
2 CENTS PAY NO MORE!

Chicago Daily Tribune

THE WORLD'S GREATEST NEWSPAPER

FINAL EDITION

VOLUME LXXXIX.—NO. 128 C [REG. U. S. PAT. OFFICE: COPYRIGHT 1930 BY THE CHICAGO TRIBUNE.] THURSDAY, MAY 29, 1930.—34 PAGES THIS PAPER CONSISTS OF TWO SECTIONS—SECTION ONE * * * PRICE TWO CENTS IN CHICAGO AND SUBURBS ELSEWHERE THREE CENTS

SHOT DOWN; TAKEN FOR RIDE

MEMBERS VOTE 3 WEEK RECESS OF LEGISLATURE

More Time Granted Strawn Group.

BY PARKE BROWN.
[Chicago Tribune Press Service.]
(Picture on back page.)

Springfield, Ill., May 28.—[Special.]—After working about five normal legislative days since it was convened May 12, the special session of the Illinois general assembly recessed today until June 17.

This delay was agreed on at a conference between Gov. Louis L. Emmerson and house leaders after it was learned that the Strawn committee will not be ready to go ahead with the bills for the financial relief of the local governments of Cook county next week and that Gov. Emmerson will not be here the next week.

The interval will give an opportunity for compliance with the demands of many legislators that Chicago and the other governmental subdivisions seeking financial rescue formally get behind the bills for their assistance instead of leaving them backed by the unofficial Strawn committee alone.

Conferences Are Held.

There was some criticism of the delay. Conferences of both the Cook county delegation and the down state bloc were held. The latter, eager to dispose of the proposed revenue amendment, voted to insist that amendments be taken up the first day after reconvening and the Chicago men were equally insistent on prompt action.

With the decks cleared by the recess program, the house gave its farewell hours to listening to a defense of the Cook county reassessment by Harry S. Cutmore, who carried it out, and William H. Malone, chairman of the state tax commission, who ordered it.

Members responsible for calling the two men here had admitted their intention to cross-examine them about reputed inequalities in the reassessment and the reduction of loop property valuations, but Speaker Shanahan and Minority Leader Igoe seized the opportunity to get at the basic facts of the Chicago situation.

Want Another Special Session.

This hearing came to a climax with a motion by Igoe that a committee be appointed to urge Gov. Emmerson to issue another session call that would permit the enactment of legislation to carry out the Fairweather plan of replacing the present boards of assessment and review in Cook county with a single appointive assessor.

With only a minority present, Igoe's motion was passed by acclamation and a committee, including Igoe, Elmer J. Schnackenberg, Mrs. Rena Elrod, F. W. Lewis, and Roger F. Little, was named. Four of them were on hand and went to the governor's office.

Gov. Emmerson said he told the callers that he considered the Fairweather plan outside the category of emergency business to which special sessions are limited. He suggested, he said, that it would be proper for the regular session of the new assembly next January to consider it.

Sixteen amendments to the constitutional resolution were introduced in the house. Members said they would have additional proposals later.

INDORSE RELIEF BILLS

A majority of the city council yesterday signed a telegram sent to David E. Shanahan, speaker of the state house of representatives, in which they indorsed the bills presented to the special session of the legislature by the Strawn citizens' committee to obtain financial relief for the city. Ald. John S. Clark [30th], chairman of the finance committee, and Ald. Oscar F. Nelson [46th], Mayor Thompson's floor leader in the council, were among the 29 who signed. The telegram said:

"We indorse in principle the bills presented to the general assembly by the citizens' committee for financial relief to the city. We are making this individual expression because the city council does not meet until June 4. At that time the city council will take formal action approving these bills."

J. Pierpont Morgan Has Examination of His Eyes

Baltimore, Md., May 28.—(AP)—John Pierpont Morgan, head of the banking house of J. P. Morgan & Co., was a visitor today at Wilmer Opthalmological institute of Johns Hopkins hospital. He returned to New York after having his eyes examined by Dr. William H. Wilmer. It was said to have been one of a number of periodical visits to the institution, to which he gave $100,000 in 1928.

NEWS SUMMARY of The Tribune

[And Historical Scrap Book.]
Thursday, May 29, 1930.

Plane Crashes Descending to Field; Couple Killed

Pinele, Mont., May 28.—(AP)—Dr. A. S. Sherill and Miss A. Lindquist, both of Bellefourche, S. D., were killed late today when an airplane crashed near here in the darkness.

Average net paid circulation of THE CHICAGO TRIBUNE April, 1930:
Daily - - - - 846,108
Sunday - - 1,116,031

REVEAL CHURCH REPORT FLAYING SMITH BACKERS

Dr. Wilson Assails Pope as Meddler.

(Picture on back page.)

Washington, D. C., May 28.—[Special.]—The supporters of former Gov. Al Smith when he ran for President were characterized as "Jews, Catholics, foreigners, and wets," banded in "the worst combination ever got together to scuttle the ship of state," in a report approved by the Methodist board of temperance, prohibition, and public morals on Dec. 4, 1928.

Deets Pickett, the church board's research secretary, testified today before the senate's lobby committee that the Methodist board had so approved the report. He said the report had been made by Dr. Clarence True Wilson, general secretary of the board. The report was a confidential summary of his own activities in that position.

Dr. Wilson's Other Charges.

In addition to assailing Al Smith's followers Dr. Wilson's report:

1. Accused the pope of meddling in the election.

2. Attacked Smith as the defender of saloons, brothels, and gambling halls.

3. Asserted that President Hoover was pledged to make every government official in his administration and every employé in the federal service, including the army and navy, teetotalers.

4. Denounced the department of justice during the Coolidge administration for "stalling" on Volstead enforcement.

5. Sharply criticized Dr. Henry Van Dyke, noted Presbyterian divine, scholar, and Princeton university professor, for deploring the entry of the church into politics and referring to former Assistant Attorney General Mabel Willebrandt as a "female firebrand."

Text of Wilson's Report.

Commenting upon his election activities, Dr. Wilson said:

"We went up against the worst combination that ever fought together in the United States; an effort to corral all the foreigners to get the united voice of one great thoroughly organized church which for the first time gave its sisters, its nuns, its religious orders the right to register and voted them almost to a man, and especially to the last woman.

"Then the entire group of wets, the thirsty and those whose cupidity wanted a continuance of the bootleg trade; an effort to make the Jews believe that they had something in common with the Catholics in the contest and with the aid of one or two distinguished rabbis, who tried to whip them as a race into line back of the marching column for Al Smith, and then that carefully created class known as 'tolerants' who wanted to be so broad that they were glad to vote against their own and denounce their own leaders in order to show how very liberal and tolerant they were."

Reference to "Tolerants."

Senator Glass and Joseph T. Robinson were named in this reference to "tolerants," the letter saying:

"I think some of the leaders of this group will be spending the balance of their lives trying to explain away their speeches in the last campaign, the Carter Glasses, the Robinsons, etc.

"We went up against that combination with only the haphazard support of the newspapers that dared not offend the other side, but the churches of the country and the women instinctively felt that this was their cause and thoroughly did they turn the tide."

In commenting on President Hoover's victory, Dr. Wilson's report read:

"It is a happy circumstance that the government is to fall into the hands of a consistent Quaker and a Methodist Vice President.

Schemes of the Wets.

"It was very interesting to watch the schemes of the wets and the nullifiers as they sought to bow the preacher out of politics and bring in all the trusted wet advocates of the church that has taken no part in politics or religion, but got the consent of its pope for all sisters of charity, all nurses, all the inmates of nunneries to register and to vote with the expectation that they would make it unanimous for a son of the church and a ruler of Tammany Hall and a man whose unbroken advocacy of the saloon, the brothel and the gambling hall cannot be questioned by any act of his in thirty years."

Replying to the charge that if congressmen would vote as they drink,

(Continued on page 2, column 4.)

TRYING TO SLIP BY

U.S. SENATE

THE BIG RUSH TO GET THE TREATY PAST THE SENATE BLOCKADE

NAVAL TREATY

ATTEMPT TO HIDE THE TRUE FACTS SURROUNDING THE LONDON NEGOTIATIONS

Director Quits in Goodman Theater Row

(Picture on back page.)

Dissension that has split the management of the Kenneth Sawyer Goodman Memorial theater for months on the question as to whether it should be conducted for profit or for art, reached its denouement last night in the resignation of Thomas Wood Stevens, director of the theater since its foundation five years ago.

With him resigned, or threatened to resign, the majority of the company, including two stage directors, B. Iden Payne and Whitford Kane; a scenery designer, Leslie Marzolf, the lighting expert, Arvid Crandall, and the leading man, Neal Caldwell. There was hardly a corporal's guard left, back stage or front, after the mutineers had called the roll.

Box Office Keeps Control.

But the box office, it appears, has triumphed over art. Mr. Stevens and his followers represented the cultural or little theater uplift ideal, as opposed to the business views of such men as Robert B. Harshe, director of the Art institute, and Charles Worcester, chairman of the institute's committee supervising the theater.

Mr. Stevens will be succeeded by Hubert Osborne, who joined the company this years as stage director. Mr. Osborne takes charge in the midst of a campaign to raise $120,000 by public subscription. It is known that the Goodman theater has been losing money on its productions because of scant patronage.

Stevens Explains Position.

In a letter to Mr. Harshe supplementing that containing his resignation Mr. Stevens said:

"I am writing to make quite clear my position with regard to the theater's policy for next year. I am sorry if this is a disappointment to you and to Mr. Goodman, but I feel I am hopelessly in disagreement with the theater committee. I believe that the Goodman should be a true art theater, and that it should devote itself to really important plays, not otherwise to be seen in Chicago, and to new plays with some emphasis on vital experiment. . . ."

The theater committee with which Mr. Stevens differed includes, besides William O. Goodman, who built the theater in memory of his son, Mr. Worcester, chairman; Walter B. Smith Arthur T. Aldis, Walter S. Brewster, and Percy B. Eckhart.

Harshe Issues Statement.

None of these would discuss the resignation last night. The only statement came from Mr. Harshe, who said:

"We greatly regret Mr. Steven's resignation; his five years' work at the Goodman represents a distinguished achievement. We have full faith in Mr. Osborne's power to carry on and develop that work. He will be in authority over the repertory company and will direct its policy."

The members of the company who indorsed Mr. Steven's action besides Caldwell, Payne, Kane, Marzolf, and Crandall, are: Roman A. Bohnen, Bernard Ostertag, Bess Kathryn Johnson, Elizabeth Hooker Parsons, Ellen Root, Charles Schlesinger, Mary Agnes Doyle, Dorothy Raymond, Harry Mervis, Harriet A. Wapp, Lawrence Paquin, George Storm, Francis Brownlow, and Gordon W. Ray.

THE WEATHER

THURSDAY, MAY 29, 1930

[Daylight saving time.]

Sunrise, 5:19; sunset, 8:15. Moon sets at 10:31 p. m. today. Uranus and Mercury are morning stars; Venus, Neptune, and Jupiter are evening stars.

Chicago and vicinity—Generally fair Thursday and probably Friday; not quite so cool; gentle to moderate winds, mostly northeast to southeast.

Illinois — Mostly fair Thursday, except unsettled and cooler in extreme south portion, with showers or thunderstorms; partly cloudy to cloudy Friday, possibly showers in south portion, slightly warmer in north and central portions.

TRIBUNE BAROMETER.

CLOUDY FAIR VERY DRY RAIN STORMY

TEMPERATURES IN CHICAGO

MAXIMUM, NOON....51
MINIMUM, 6 A. M....44

3 a. m.	47	Noon	51	8 p. m.	48
4 a. m.	46	1 p. m.	50	9 p. m.	46
5 a. m.	45	2 p. m.	50	10 p. m.	46
6 a. m.	44	3 p. m.	50	Unofficial—	
7 a. m.	44	4 p. m.	48	11 p. m.	47
8 a. m.	45	5 p. m.	48	Midnight	47
9 a. m.	46	6 p. m.	48	1 a. m.	47
10 a. m.	47	7 p. m.	48	2 a. m.	46
11 a. m.	48				

For 24 hours ended at 8 p. m. May 28:

Mean temperature, 48 degrees; normal, 62; excess since Jan. 1, 438.

Precipitation, none; deficiency since Jan. 1, 1.67 inches.

Barometer, 8 a. m., 30.09; 8 p. m., 30.13.

Highest wind velocity, 23 miles an hour from the north at 5:47 a. m.

[Official weather table on page 26.]

FAMILY SHARES $1,000,000 ESTATE OF JOHN POWERS

The will of the late John Powers, member of the city council for 38 years, was filed for probate yesterday before Edward S. Scheffler, assistant to Probate Judge Henry Horner. The bulk of the estate, estimated to total $1,000,000, is left to his widow, Mrs. Franc Lawler Powers, a son, John F. Powers, and other relatives.

The will sets up two trust funds of $150,000 each, the income of which will be paid to his son and Miss Janith Mary Lawler, a step-daughter. Another trust fund of $10,000 was left for Kelly Powers, a grandson, who will receive the principal of a $150,000 trust fund upon the death of his father, John F. Powers. The Little Sisters of the Poor, Throop and Harrison streets, were bequeathed $20,000.

Mr. Powers died at his home at 6038 Sheridan road May 19 at the age of 78.

Robs Actress of Gems on Santa Fe Train

BY GEORGE SHAFFER.
[Chicago Tribune Press Service.]
(Picture on back page.)

Los Angeles, Cal., May 28.—[Special.]—Several passengers on The Chief, crack train of the Santa Fé railroad, were held up tonight soon after it had pulled out of Los Angeles starting on its fast run to Chicago.

From first reports one daring robber went through the sleeping coaches just before the train reached Pasadena and held up several prominent men and women.

According to railway special agents, the bandit, who worked alone, obtained rings and cash totaling $11,075 from three individuals.

Works as Train Creeps.

He was described as a tall young man of sandy complexion and wore a handkerchief drawn tightly over the lower portion of his face.

First to be held up was Marian Nixon, who in real life is Mrs. Edward Hillman, wife of a well known Chicago merchant. He noted Miss Nixon's four and one-fourth karat diamond, famous throughout Hollywood as one of the finest engagement rings worn in the motion picture colony.

After forcing the actress to hand over this ring he called for another of her rings. This one, Miss Nixon said, was valued at $4,000. From Mr. Hillman the bandit got $400 in cash.

Mrs. Jolson Visited.

Robert G. Lehman, Detroit business man, also was robbed, but reported that the bandit was satisfied with his ready cash, totaling $175.

Next the bandit entered the drawing room of Ruby Keeler, actress wife of Al Jolson, but she reported he got nothing.

Victim Tossed Into Auto; Nab One Gangster

(Picture on back page.)

A motor car loaded with gunmen apparently bent on a mission of vengeance late last night made a foray into a quiet residential neighborhood—at Berwyn and Ashland avenues—on the north side, shot and probably fatally wounded their victim, dragged him into the car, and sped away. But they did not escape unscathed. One of their number, presumably the man who did the shooting, was torn from the running board of the fleeing car by policemen and early this morning was being questioned.

The prisoner is Sam Hunt, 27 years old, who first gave his address as 1035 South Wabash avenue and later said he lived at the Hotel Harmonia, 3000 Indiana avenue. The identity of the gang victim was not learned, but the police said they expected to find his body before long.

See Echo of Indictments.

In seeking a motive for the shooting the police turned first to the indictment of Ralph Capone by a federal grand jury yesterday on charges of violating the prohibition law. Hunt, they said, has been arrested in the past with men believed to be identified with the Capone liquor interests, and detectives saw in the assassins' raid a possibility that the gang was taking revenge on an informer.

The police also said they would investigate a possibility that the shooting might be an outgrowth of the recovery of $1,000,000 worth of jewelry and the arrest of six alleged members of a gem theft ring in New York.

The attack occurred about 11:30 o'clock. Three young men towing an automobile south in an alley between Ashland avenue and Clark street, just north of Berwyn avenue, were startled by a fusillade of shots from the darkness beyond the mouth of the alley south of Berwyn avenue. They heard a man scream and the roar of a powerful automobile motor.

Find Wounded Man.

A moment later a flashily dressed man carrying a golf bag appeared under the street light at the mouth of the alley, looked hastily east and west in Berwyn avenue and ran back into the shadows of the alley. The three young men were Cletus O'Rourke, 1321 Ardmore avenue; Carl Peterson, 4913 North Clark street, and Carl Boyke, 5749 Ridge avenue.

Boyke, bolder than his companions, ran across the street and into the alley. Seventy-five feet from the street, lying against the wall of a building, was the body of a man. Boyke stooped and saw that one side of his face had been blown away by a shotgun charge.

"Help me. They got me. I'm dying," mumbled the victim.

Boyke had turned to go for a policeman when the roar of an automobile engine was heard again and the headlights of a car flashed in the alley to the south. It was the assassins' car returning. Boyke concealed himself behind the corner of a building and watched.

Victim Pushed Into Auto.

The car stopped as it came abreast of the moaning victim. Boyke said there seemed to be four men in the machine. One of them stepped out and with the help of his fellows inside the car pushed the wounded man into the tonneau.

"We told you we'd get you, and we did," the gangster remarked as he clambered back into the machine and kicked at the prostrate victim. As the car started slowly out of the alley the man whom Boyke and his companions had seen with the golf bag ran up and leaped on the running board.

It was at this moment that Joseph

(Continued on page 2, column 2.)

U. S. INDICTS 300 UNDER JONES 5 AND 10 RUM LAW

Name Ralph Capone in Air Booze Plot.

The May federal grand jury completed its work yesterday, returning 100 indictments, naming more than 200 defendants who are charged with liquor violations under the Jones 5 and 10 law. About fifty true bills against another 100 Jones law defendants had been previously reported, making a total of more than 300 persons indicted under the Jones law during the month. This is a record for this district.

Ralph J. Capone and eight of his associates were named in two of the indictments returned before Federal Judge Woodward. They are charged with conspiracy to "commit divers offenses against the United States," including the running of "large quantities" of liquor from Canada to Cicero by airplanes. The true bills against Capone and his employés also contain Jones law counts. Most of the other Jones law charges name obscure offenders.

Raids Reveal Plane Inquiry.

The Capone indictments follow an investigation begun several months ago by special prohibition agents under Alexander Jamie. The investigation was first made public with the raiding of Ralph Capone's two Cicero cabarets, the Montmartre and the Cotton club. At that time the federal investigators disclosed that the gang had used airplanes to bring booze from Windsor since last August, and it was estimated that $1,400,000 worth of liquor was so transported.

The conspiracy count of the indictment charges that the defendants "transported and caused to be transported 500 cases of whisky from Windsor to Cicero by airplanes," but Assistant United States Attorney Victor La Rue explained that this quantity would be sufficient to prove an overt act.

Eight Capone Aids Named.

Those indicted besides Capone are Percy Haller, manager of the Cotton club; Benny Compton, Jack Keeler, Harry McRae, Robert Kinney, Art Goldie, John Doe (a person known only as Rasputin), and John Doe (a person known only as Logan). All were attachés of the Cicero cabarets.

Besides the conspiracy count, there are charges of possessing liquor at the cabarets, selling liquor, and maintaining a nuisance. The maximum penalty for conspiracy is two years' imprisonment and a fine of $10,000. The maximum penalties for the Jones law violations, sale and transportation of liquor, are five years in prison and a fine of $10,000.

Investigate Plane Owners.

Federal agents disclosed that the investigation is not finished and that there is a possibility of bringing action against several alleged members of the gang, including the pilots and owners of the airplanes. The planes were said to have been owned by a Detroit rum syndicate, which is under investigation there now.

Capone and the other defendants are at liberty in bond on the liquor charges. Capone faces a possible sentence of twenty-two years in prison and a fine of $40,000 on his recent conviction of income tax fraud.

Indict "West Side" Frankie Pope.

Other indictments returned yesterday included that of "West Side" Frankie Pope, charged with conspiracy in connection with others to violate the dry laws. Pope is now serving a prison term for violation of the Harrison anti-narcotic law.

One true bill named John W. Sheridan, wealthy real estate operator, in connection with the seizure of a still on a farm he owned near the Higgins road.

Two physicians were indicted under the Jones law on charges of selling liquor. They are Dr. Martin H. Fash, 2258 Madison street, and Dr. Carl Furness, 2527 East 73d street.

A south side gang, allegedly headed by John Bernardi, was indicted as the result of raids on two Calumet Park stills. Bernardi, who is in the cheese importing business, is alleged to have sold sugar for use in the operation of stills.

U. S. INDICTS RONGETTI

The federal grand jury yesterday returned a true bill against Dr. Amante Rongetti, who has been in the state courts many times on charges of abortion, murder and manslaughter. The indictment charges unlawful selling and prescribing of narcotics. There are 31 counts.

The true bill sets forth that Ron-

WEATHER Cloudy today and Wednesday

CLEVELAND PLAIN DEALER

FINAL EDITION

89TH YEAR Published every day by The Plain Dealer Publishing Company. Entered as Second Class Matter at the Cleveland Postoffice under the act of 1879. 30 PAGES CLEVELAND, TUESDAY MORNING, JUNE 10, 1930 PRICE THREE CENTS NO. 161

GANGSTERS SLAY REPORTER

ST. LOUIS LOSES; THIS IS 6TH CITY

Official Census Figures for Western Metropolis Put Population at 817,334.

CIVIC GROUPS HAD HOPED TO REGAIN OLD RATING

Drift to Suburbs Held Down Growth as It Did Here.

Cleveland will be the sixth city of the United States for the decade between 1930 and 1940.

That was determined late yesterday with the official announcement of the 1930 census figures for St. Louis, which had threatened to push Cleveland into seventh ranking. The St. Louis figure, as announced in Associated Press dispatches, is 817,334. Cleveland's 1930 figure is 901,482.

Los Angeles already has pushed Cleveland out of her standing as fifth city, which she held from 1920 to 1930.

Except for the undetermined ranking of Detroit and Los Angeles, both candidates for fourth place, the standing of the principal American cities apparently is:

NEW YORK, first (unannounced).
CHICAGO, second (unannounced).
PHILADELPHIA, third (unannounced).
DETROIT, fourth (unannounced), or
LOS ANGELES, fourth, 1,231,730.
CLEVELAND, sixth, 901,482.
ST. LOUIS, seventh, 817,334.
BALTIMORE, eighth, 790,000.
BOSTON, ninth, 780,851.

St. Louis civic organizations have been hoping for weeks that the Missouri city would pass Cleveland and regain the ranking it held prior to 1920. The St. Louis Chamber of Commerce and other civic bodies had estimated that the city would exceed the 900,000 mark.

But like other large cities, with the notable exception of Los Angeles, which gained 655,057 over 1920 for an increase of 115 per cent., St. Louis fell below its expected population.

St. Louis had a gain of only 44,437 for the last decade, in comparison with Cleveland's gain of slightly more than 100,000. After Cleveland's figure was announced St. Louis enumerators redoubled their efforts to list every possible resident.

Just as the drift of population to the suburbs held down Cleveland's 1930 total, a similar drift held down St. Louis' figure, dispatches said. Limits of St. Louis have not been changed since 1875, the dispatches related.

The combined population of St. Louis City and St. Louis County, which are separate, is expected to exceed 1,000,000, dispatches relate, while the population of the St. Louis metropolitan area, including St. Clair and Madison Counties in Illinois, containing the city of East St. Louis is expected to exceed 1,250,000.

SEIZES SARDINES SUPPLY

U. S. Charges Packers Contracted to Fix Prices.

WASHINGTON, June 9.—(AP)—Announcing an investigation had disclosed that the packers of Norwegian sardines had contracted to fix prices and regulate that business, the Department of Justice made known today that it had ordered seized 5,000 cases of Norwegian sardines in New York City.

Customs agents made the seizure at the warehouse of Charles Bjelland & Co., New York City, for alleged conspiracy in restraint of trade.

SPORTS

Miller and Morgan Star as Indians Beat Nats, 5-4.

Mrs. Tyler's 85 Is Low in Tourney.

Sharkey, in Angry Mood, Flails 2 Sparring Mates.

For details, see sport pages.

OLD LOVES BOB UP TO BOTHER CAROL

King Expected to Call for Mme. Lupescu if Helene Doesn't Join Him.

(Copyright, 1930, Universal Service, Inc.)

BUKHAREST, June 9.—King Carol, who today solidified his position on the throne which he captured within a brief 36 hours, has begun a battle to lay the specter of the past and bring about a reconciliation with Princess Helene, the former wife he hopes to make queen.

Love for his son, a passionate desire to have Michael, is the motivating reason. A reconciliation with Helene means an annulment of their divorce and his restoration as the head of the royal family, for only as the head of the family can he be sure of his rights over Michael.

King's Past Troubles Him.

Three other women of King Carol's past and present came forward tonight to trouble the mind of him who is trying desperately to occupy himself with kingly affairs and matters of state.

From only one of the women did the new king receive any consolation; that from his mother, Queen Marie. An exchange of telegrams between mother and son today indicated Marie is reconciled to her son's accession to the throne and that Carol is all-forgiving toward the "mother queen of the Balkans."

Princess Helene, however, is reported still to resolutely refuse a reconciliation with the husband who deserted her, their son, Michael, and a throne for the fascinating red-haired Mme. Lupescu.

Reports have it that Mme. Lupescu is not entirely out of the picture.

(Continued on Page 6, Column 1)

BANQUET BAR STORY A LIE, SAYS COOPER

Governor States He Knows That Schorr Served No Liquor to G. O. P. Delegates.

7,500 SPEAKEASIES IN CITY, ARTICLE REPORTS

2,500 Are Beer Flats Run by Women, It Is Alleged.

BY RALPH J. DONALDSON.

The charge made by Walter Liggett in the July issue of Plain Talk, on sale yesterday, that Commerce Director Edward Schorr, personal friend and campaign backer of Gov. Myers Y. Cooper, served liquor to delegates at the recent banquet of the Ohio League of Republican Clubs at Columbus was branded a "deliberate and malicious falsehood" by Gov. Cooper last night.

"Mr. Schorr had a headquarters for the Cincinnati delegation where cigars and cigarets and red carnations were passed around, but there was not one drop of liquor," Gov. Cooper said. "I know the article is untrue because I was up in that room myself."

Liggett said that Schorr "thoughtfully had caused a portable bar to be set up in a suite of rooms at the Deshler-Wallick Hotel where he acted as host while a corps of capable bartenders dispensed spirituous liquors to all comers."

"Col. Schorr," the article continued, "had instructed an attendant to

(Continued on Page 9, Column 1)

EX-OFFICIALS ARRESTED

Former Dominican Cabinet Members Thrown Into Jail.

SANTO DOMINGO, Dominican Republic, June 9.—(AP)—Two officers who served in the cabinet of former President Horatio Vasquez, Angel Maria Soler, former minister of foreign affairs, and Martin Moya, former finance minister, were arrested and imprisoned today.

The reason was not given. The political stiuation appears to be quiet.

NEWS SUMMARY

Cleveland Plain Dealer.

Tuesday, June 10, 1930.

HOOVER SIGNS PENSIONS BILL

WASHINGTON, June 9.—(AP)—President Hoover today signed a bill increasing the pensions of Civil War veterans.

The bill increases to $75 monthly the pension of veterans who formerly received $65. Those receiving $72 and $90 will receive $100 under the bill. Widows of veterans who formerly had to be 75 to get a $40 monthly pension now may get it at the age of 70.

It was said at the White House that the president regards the bill as an old age pension measure and not objectionable as was the Spanish-American War veterans' pension bill which he recently vetoed.

ADMITS RIGHT OF INDIANS TO RULE SELVES

Simon Report, However, Says Country Is Not at Present in Condition for Dominion Status.

CITES COMPLEXITIES OF RACES AND RELIGION

Stresses Need of Co-Operation Between Hindus and Moslems.

(Plain Dealer Cable)

LONDON, June 9.—India at the moment is not prepared for independence or self-government, but prospects of the status of a British dominion for the strife-ridden country some generations hence must be admitted.

This is the dominant note in the first volume of the report of the Indian statutory commission, popularly known as the Simon commission, which was presented to the House of Commons tonight and which will be made public tomorrow.

Main points outlined in the report as bearing upon the future of India and its place in the British Empire are:

1—A national spirit must be engendered in the polyglot population of more than 300,000,000 people, which now compose the most heterogeneous country in the world;

Castes Must Co-Operate.

2—A method must be found to establish co-operation among the many castes of the Hindu religion; castes which now serve to render that co-operation impossible;

3—Self-government will be possible only when a means is devised to bring about co-operation between Hindu and Moslem, and while some Moslems have joined the Nationalist independence campaign, their number and force are negligible;

4—Education of the masses is vitally necessary in India, with a population mostly of uneducated agrarians and politics the province only of the highly educated;

Small Group Backs Gandhi.

5—Mahatma Gandhi's independence campaign is backed by only a comparatively small group of natives, a group, however, which is at the moment the most aggressive and powerful of all Indian organizations;

6—India would be unable to preserve home rule without an Indian army, which is non-existent at

(Continued on Page 12, Column 7)

HANRATTY O. K.'S ONLY 2 TRACKS

Sheriff Edward J. Hanratty, having reflected for 24 hours on inferences that might be drawn from his statement Sunday that "apparently the public is satisfied" with racing with betting, yesterday considerably clarified his position by saying:

"While I believe that the public wants racing at Thistle Down and Randall, that does not mean that other race courses in the county may open with betting. No, sir! They're off the map. They can't start.

"And as for the dogs—" He waved his hand. "They can't run, not any place in Cuyahoga County."

He was asked if he intended to permit betting at the North Randall course. He shrugged his shoulders.

Won't Discuss Randall Bets.

"I don't believe I want to say anything about that," he said. "But you can say this: Regardless of all the criticisms that have come my way since the Thistle Down course opened, I still believe that the public wants racing at that course and at Randall.

"Both courses have beautiful plants, and they can't run unless there is betting. I believe that no

(Continued on Page 16, Column 3)

MUSIC TO SOOTHE VETS

Organ to Be Used as Test in Treating Nervous Ailments.

WASHINGTON, June 9.—(AP)—An experiment in the use of organ music in the treatment of nervous conditions is to be launched at the Northampton (Mass.) Neuropsychiatric Veterans Hospital, and its sponsors are seeking President Hoover's participation.

A delegation of veterans came here today to ask the president to dedicate the $10,000 pipe organ at the hospital June 18. They believe the soothing effect of organ notes will aid in bridging memory lapses.

Pictorial Story of Reporter's Death

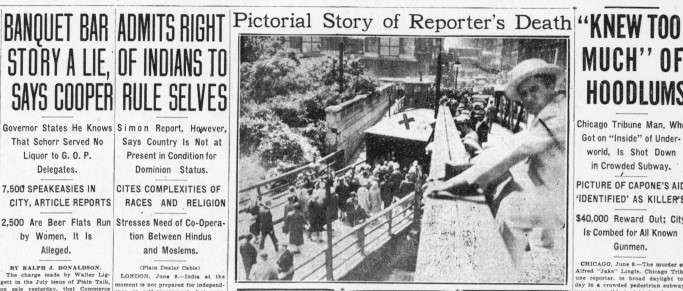

"X" marks spot in pedestrians' subway where Alfred Lingle was killed in Chicago. Photo looking down Randolph Street from bridge over Illinois Central tracks with Michigan Boulevard in the background.

LEFT, BELOW—The murdered reporter.

CENTER—John J. (Boss) McLaughlin, said to have had a grudge against Lingle, shortly after arrest for questioning.

RIGHT—Coroner Herman Bundeson with gun thrown away by killer.

All photos telephotoed to the Plain Dealer by Pacific and Atlantic Photos, Inc.

LATE NEWS BULLETINS.

Tongman Is Slain

MINNEAPOLIS, June 9.—(AP)—Reprecussions of recent tong war slayings in New York and Chicago, echoed in Minneapolis today with the death of Woo Sam, Chinese laundryman and a Hip Sing.

Dry Officer Slain.

ALTURUS, Cal., June 9.—(AP)—Albert Brown, federal prohibition officer, was killed, and Robert Davis, fellow officer, wounded at Indian Springs today when they attempted to arrest an unidentified man on a charge of selling liquor at a gasoline filling station.

WICKERSHAM HITS HARSH DRY LAWS

Would Educate U. S. to Temperance Instead of Using Prisons.

(Plain Dealer Special)

BOSTON, June 9.—In an unexpected departure from his prepared address, George W. Wickersham, chairman of President Hoover's law enforcement commission, tonight astounded 5,000 social workers in the Boston Garden by declaring, in effect, for modification of existing federal laws for enforcement of the prohibition amendment.

With measured deliberation, Wickersham asserted, in substance, that the English system of promoting temperance by education and restriction of liquor sales is far more effective than the American method of absolute prohibition with harsh penalties for violation.

In his first public statement on the prohibition controversy, the Hoover appointee indicated belief that enforcement today has failed because too much stress has been placed on constantly increasing penalties and too little on education in the benefits of temperance.

His audience, quick to grasp significance of such an important contribution to the prohibition discussion

(Continued on Page 11, Column 1)

Named for Civil Service Board.

WASHINGTON, June 9. — (AP) — Thomas E. Campbell, former governor of Arizona, today was nominated by President Hoover to the Civil Service Commission, succeeding William C. Deming, resigned.

CLEVELAND GETS SHRINE '31 SESSION

(Plain Dealer Special)

TORONTO, June 9.—Cleveland will be the next convention city of the Ancient Arabic Order, Nobles of the Mystic Shrine, with Chicago welcoming the annual huge imperial council session in 1932, on recommendation of the imperial divan which is composed of the imperial potentate and his officers.

Rochester, home of next year's imperial potentate, Esten Fletcher, was the logical location but facilities there are lacking for handling such a big assembly and Cleveland was decided upon owing to its centrality, accommodations and as the hub of Ohio Shrine endeavor.

This decision was reached today at one of the opening business meetings.

Cleveland temples are here in full force. Fred A. Dickson, director of Al Koran temple, and his fellow nobles were elated over the divan's decision.

E. W. Besaw of Rameses Temple and president of the Firestone Tire & Rubber Co. of Canada and a party of fellow Shriners and officials of the Firestone Co. arrived from Akron, O., and Hamilton, Ont., today in the Firestone trimotor plane.

YOUTH SHOT AS HE HUNTS GOLF BALLS

Gravely Wounded by Country Club Guard, Who Says He Was Attacked.

John Mencini, 19, of 15340 Yorick Avenue N. E., an amateur golfer and pupil at Collinwood High School, was shot and perhaps fatally wounded late yesterday by a private policeman at the Country Club golf course as he was trying to pick up a golf ball that had gone into a small creek near the eleventh tee, according to police.

At East End Hospital this morning Mencini was reported in critical condition. Hospital attaches said a bullet had entered his body through the back and had penetrated the right lung, remaining in his body.

Among pupils at Collinwood High School, where Mencini has been taking part junior and part senior studies, he has a reputation as an amateur boxer and has played foot-

(Continued on Page 11, Column 3)

JOHN MENCINI

Congress to Pass Tariff It Doesn't Like, Says Rogers

(Plain Dealer Special)

WASHINGTON, June 9.—In spite of the "Crusaders" in society, enforcement is making headway here in Washington. Mrs. McLean has announced the fact that there will be no drinks served to guests at her home at breakfast, but lunch will be early.

Seven hundred legislators here have done what no other 700 men in the world could have done. They have succeeded in making a tariff bill that no one in the 700 thinks is any good, and yet they will pass it.

Yours,

WILL ROGERS.

"KNEW TOO MUCH" OF HOODLUMS

Chicago Tribune Man, Who Got on "Inside" of Underworld, Is Shot Down in Crowded Subway.

PICTURE OF CAPONE'S AID 'IDENTIFIED' AS KILLER'S

$40,000 Reward Out; City Is Combed for All Known Gunmen.

CHICAGO, June 9.—The murder of Alfred "Jake" Lingle, Chicago Tribune reporter, in broad daylight today in a crowded pedestrian subway was responsible tonight for the most intensive man hunt Chicago has known for months.

Lingle, who was reputed to know more of the inside of gangland's activities than any other Chicago reporter, was shot down in the Michigan Avenue subway as he was on his way to the Illinois Central Station.

Developments tonight included:

REWARD of $25,000 offered by the Chicago Tribune; a second reward of $10,000 offered by the Chicago Press Club, and a reward of $5,000 by the Chicago Evening Post for information leading to the arrest and conviction of Lingle's slayer or slayers.

IDENTIFICATION by two witnesses of a picture of Sam Hunt, Capone racketeer and gunman, as the man who fired the fatal shot.

AN ORDER by Police Commissioner W. F. Russell that every known gangster, including Hunt, be brought to detective headquarters for questioning.

RAIDS throughout underworld haunts in which quantities of weapons were seized and several of the city's most notorious gangsters were captured.

AN ORDER that John J. ("Boss") McLaughlin, former state senator, be asked to give his version of a dispute he is said to have had recently with Lingle concerning the opening of a gambling house. McLaughlin was taken into custody tonight.

Sam Hunt, for whom search was made, was the gangster who was pulled last week from the running board of a supposed confederate's car after he is believed to have shot down an enemy.

Four witnesses testified they saw and talked to a wounded man who afterward was thrust into a sedan and spirited away. Hunt was arrested, but the wounded man never was found and it was necessary to let the gunman go.

Lingle today had talked with two

(Continued on Page 5, Column 5)

39TH 1930 GANG KILLING VIEWED AS "DYNAMITE"

CHICAGO, June 9.—(NANA)—The 39th gang killing of 1930 attributed to mobs with headquarters in Chicago was an unlucky one—unlucky, at least, for gangland.

That was the sentiment here today as the city began to flame more than it has in a decade—shocked by the super-boldness of gangdom in murdering a newspaper reporter.

And, if the smoldering embers that were fanned by the slaying of Alfred ("Jake") Lingle do not die down too quickly, the bullets that sent the reporter to his death may also write the knell of Chicago gangdom.

Chicago's reputation as a crime center had been caused principally by the gang war back and forth between undesirable citizens. Hoodlums never have dared to fight back against the upperworld until this afternoon.

Friend of Police Head.

Lingle was the close personal friend of Police Commissioner William F. Russell and of Detective Chief John Stege. He also had been an intimate of "Scarface Al" Capone, whose trail he crossed many times in his undercover investigations of gangland for the Chicago Tribune.

Once before since liquor profits began to enrich Chicago hoodlums the city thought it had been aroused by the killing of "a respectable citizen." Young Billy McSwiggin, ace of the state's attorney's office with a record as "the hanging prosecutor," was machine-gunned to his death along with two gangsters in April, 1926. There were investigations and inquiries, statements and threats to gangland, ultimata and shouts.

Then it began to be spread about the city that McSwiggin had not been the target of the killers. He had

(Continued on Page 2, Column 5)

All Chicago Celebrates Census Gain of 672,048

50th YEAR No. 27 — Registered in U. S. Patent Office — C★★★ — THURSDAY, JUNE 12, 1930 — Telephone Randolph 2121 — TWO PARTS. — PRICE 3 CENTS

'DEATH SQUADS' HUNT KILLERS

Today

Mr. Mulrooney's Luncheon.
Mr. Kahn Is Not Worried.
$500 Per Killing.
Welcome to Brazil.

—BY ARTHUR BRISBANE—

JAMES W. GERARD, formerly ambassador to Germany, organized a luncheon yesterday for Commissioner Mulrooney, the newly appointed head of New York's police. Everybody was there, including Otto H. Kahn. He says grand opera by radio is coming, but it will not interfere with the Metropolitan Opera, always needed to create great reputations.

Also, according to Mr. Kahn, who studies this earth and its doings "from Paris to Peking, and from Peking to Rome," there is nothing to worry us.

When the British have temporary hard times they sit still, play a little golf, don't do much.

In America we can't sit still. We have to do something. When stocks refuse to go up we sell them and force them to go down.

After a dull period it will occur to Americans that they have the United States back of them and they will recover their balance.

Commissioner Mulrooney, a real policeman, discourses interestingly on crime. He says:

"In a murder case you must have one of two things—an eye-witness or a confession.

"With gangsters well organized, witnesses are afraid to testify. The killers do not confess."

The modern killer runs little risk. For $500 he hires a boy 16 or 17 years old; the boy does the shooting, not even knowing the name of the man "put on the spot," or why he is killed.

Racketeers, according to Commissioner Mulrooney, would vanish if citizens would do their part. As a rule they prefer being blackmailed to defending themselves.

Racketeers and gangsters are miserable cowards, except "when ganged up and armed. A real man could take a chair and beat up half a dozen of them."

Young criminals should be segregated, not confined with older criminals, who teach them all they know.

Capital punishment does no good. "Send the gangster caught carrying a gun, thus proving his intention or willingness to commit murder, to some place just inside the arctic circle, where he will do useful hard work for the rest of his life, and you will get results that no electric chair could give."

Commissioner Mulrooney's job, protecting property and life in the world's biggest, richest city, is "a business in itself." He has under him 19,000 men and a department that spends $60,000,000 a year.

He is an able citizen.

President-elect Julio Prestes de Albuquerque of Brazil, coming to visit us, will be welcome everywhere. As head of Brazil's government, he represents a gigantic empire, magnificently typical of wealth and greatness in America.

Larger than the United States, with one water power much more powerful than Niagara, a soil of fertility indescribable, diamond mines whose blue-white products surpass all others, and, most important, an intelligent, patriotic, hard-working people, our guest from Brazil speaks for a nation of whose friendship this country may be proud.

What will be the future of a nation sixty-five times as big as England, its soil sixty-five times as fertile, with one magnificent plateau, 1,000 to 3,000 feet high, seven times as big as France, and a river so wide you can sail out of sight of land, on fresh water? Brazil, rich, powerful, progressive, for national defense relies largely on airships, sure sign of intelligence.

Brazil's military flying school, with a field in the suburbs of Rio de Janeiro, is one of the finest in the world.

Chicago is proud and says, "I not only WILL, but I DID." Chicago's population in the new census is 3,373,753, an increase of 672,048 in ten years.

Second among the cities of the nation, Chicago starts on its fourth million. Everybody in Chicago, north, south, west or out on the lake, is sure that New York will be passed and forgotten before long.

To prove it, ticker tape and confetti in showers came from windows all over downtown Chicago yesterday.

Wall street continued its sorrow festival yesterday, stocks dropping, bears using unpleasant rumors in their battle against prices. One rumor concerned a big bank, another dealt with an imaginary attack on the life of the President. Results achieved by so much lying were not great, a few stocks dropping from 1 to 8 points.

Grover Alexander, famous baseball pitcher, is "unconditionally released" by the Philadelphia National League club. It means that his day is done.

He has been playing baseball

Turn to Page 4, Column 1.

3,373,753 Here; 10-Year Increase Nation's Greatest

Official Figures Found Above Estimate.

GAIN OF 24 PCT.

Growth Rate Near 3 Times That of New York.

(Pictures on Page 3 and Picture Page.)

Chicago—metropolis of 3,373,753 residents!

That is the city's official 1930 population, announced by the federal census supervisors yesterday. It was made public by Col. Robert Isham Randolph, president of the Association of Commerce, at the Census Day luncheon in the Hotel La Salle, which climaxed Chicago's city-wide celebration of its record-breaking population gain since the 1920 census.

GAIN LARGEST IN U. S.

This increase within the city limits of 672,048 residents over the 1920 census count of 2,701,705, is not only the largest gain in any ten-year census period in the city's history. **It is numerically the biggest gain shown in the 1930 census by any American city. It assures Chicago its rank of second American city. And it may be the basis of a challenge of Berlin's right to rank next to London and New York as third largest city in the world.**

Chicago's official population figure confirms the check-up printed exclusively by The Herald and Examiner more than a month ago, in which it was conservatively stated on the basis of incomplete returns that the count would exceed 3,350,000.

That is within less than 1 per cent of the actual figure announced yesterday.

ABSENTEES BOOST TOTAL.

The slight increase shown in the final figure came through the enumeration of additional persons missed in the original count.

Significantly focusing world-wide attention on Chicago's meteoric rise, since its first federal census in 1840 counted but 4,479 inhabitants, the new population figure represents a gain of 24.8 per cent during the last decade.

New York's increase since 1920 has been 530,000—only 9 per cent. Steadily gaining ground on America's largest city, Chicago has doubled its population in the last thirty years.

And the city's figure, of course,

Turn to Page 3, Column 2.

Directory of Features

Bandits Rule Hotel for Hour; Menace and Rob Guests

Herd Victims in Lobby; Compel Manager to Open Safe.

Holding possession of the Garfield Arms Hotel for almost an hour, four bandits escaped with more than $1,000 loot early today after terrorizing fifteen guests.

The Garfield Arms, an apartment hotel, is at 3256 Maypole av., a short distance from Garfield Park.

The bandits surprised half a dozen persons in the lobby shortly after midnight. Herding them with the night clerk up against a wall, they waited for others who live at the hotel to come in.

SEARCH GUESTS.

One gunman stood at the entrance, signaling each time a newcomer appeared. When the crowd was deemed profitable enough, the gunmen searched all the victims, took their valuables, and then ordered the clerk, Melville Eberhardt, to open the safe. He protested that only the manager knew the combination.

Two of the gunmen forced from him the apartment number of the manager, Thomas D. Lawlor, on the second floor. They led Eberhardt to the apartment, entered, and compelled the manager and a guest, Forrest Corlette, to accompany them downstairs in night clothes.

LOOT SAFE.

Then with guns at his back the manager swung open the safe doors, giving the bandits access to $400 in addition to the loot they had taken from the hotel guests. The robbers ordered their victims, one of whom was a woman, into the hotel office and locked the door.

Police squads made a hurried investigation and then raced to the Graemere, Alcazar and other hotels of the Garfield Park district to protect them from further raids by the bandit gang.

Miss Helen Jones, the woman victim of the holdup, collapsed after the robbers left.

He Passes Up Light; Evanston Apologizes

Evanston police apologized last night for arresting a motorist accused of disregarding a red light. For the driver produced a police courtesy card identifying him as G. De Pasta, Greek consul general, and reminded the officers that his office exempts him from such arrests. The officers let him go and he left a note, they say, demanding a written apology from the police chief.

45 DEAD AFTER TANKER AND LINER COLLIDE

19 Seamen Go Down With Pinthis in Blazing Brine; Steamer Limps Into Port

BOSTON, June 11.—(AP)—The Boston Herald quotes Capt. Charles M. Lyons, federal steamboat inspector, as saying that Capt. Archibald Brooks of the Fairfax was guilty of gross negligence after ramming the Pinthis.

BOSTON, June 11.—(AP)—Dull red flames on the Atlantic tonight burned a memorial across a murky sky to the tragedy of the steamers Fairfax and Pinthis, which sent forty-five men and women to death by fire and water a few minutes after the ships collided.

COLLIDE IN FOG.

Last night in a heavy fog the Merchants & Miners liner Fairfax, bearing a holiday crowd to Norfolk and Baltimore, crashed into the Fall River oil tanker Pinthis in Massachusetts Bay, off Scituate, Mass.

In a minute blazing oil erupted from the tanker and showered the Fairfax and sea around. The Pinthis, fatally stricken, sank quickly, carrying down all her crew of nineteen, leaving the Fairfax ablaze.

The Pinthis was loaded with 504,000 gallons of high test gasoline. The sea still blazed tonight.

A score of persons aboard the Fairfax were burned, one of them fatally and five others probably fatally, but the stricken vessel and the remainder of its 140 passengers and crew were saved.

Panic threatened, but officers and men quieted the milling crowd.

WIRELESS DISABLED.

The fire melted the wireless antennae so no message could be sent immediately.

A marine cast himself into the sea of fire in a vain effort to save a woman who leaped over the rails.

Two other marines and John Popp, chief radio operator aboard the U. S. S. Childs, scaled the mast to repair the broken antennae.

A graphic eyewitness story of the disaster is printed on Page 5, Col. 1.

Birmingham Refuses City Hall to De Priest

BIRMINGHAM, Ala., June 11.—(AP)—J. M. Jones Jr., president of the Birmingham city commission, said today Oscar De Priest, Negro congressman from Illinois, would not be permitted to use the municipal auditorium for a scheduled address on July 17.

House Grants Funds for 2 Soldier Homes

WASHINGTON, June 11.—(I. N. S.)—The House today passed bills authorizing establishment of two soldier homes in the north Pacific and southern states at a cost of $2,000,000 each.

SENATORS VOTE TODAY ON PACT DEFI BY HOOVER

Committee to Make Final Demand for Secret Notes; Threaten Ratification Tieup

BY KENNETH CLARK,
Herald and Examiner-Universal Staff Correspondent.

WASHINGTON, June 11.—The Senate foreign relations committee will adopt the resolution asserting its full rights to the secret London naval treaty documents withheld by President Hoover.

A vote is scheduled tomorrow. Copies of the resolution will be sent to the White House and to Secretary of State Stimson.

Senator Shipstead of Minnesota declared treaty consideration should be held up until President Hoover gives the committee the secret correspondence.

SECRET NOTES VITAL.

There are instances, Shipstead declared, in which notes concerning a treaty were the deciding factor in its ratification or rejection.

Chairman Borah indicated the committee will take no further action on the treaty until a reply is received from President Hoover.

Committee members feel that the papers, containing the history of the London negotiations, are essential if the Senate is to understand the treaty before giving its consent to ratification.

UPHOLDS SENATE RIGHTS.

A subcommittee met this afternoon to whip the resolution into shape. Two major policies were enunciated in the resolution.

First. It was set forth the Senate's right, under the Constitution, to have all treaty correspondence.

Second. It declared that upon the Senate and President jointly, and not the Executive alone, rested the responsibility to determine whether treaty documents should be made public.

In other words, it is a clear cut reaffirmation of the Senate's constitutional duty to share co-ordinately in treaty making.

Coste Honored Over Byrd and Eckener

PARIS, June 11.—(AP)—Dieudonne Coste, French aviator, today was awarded the International Aeronautic Federation's medal for the year's most noteworthy achievement. The names of Admiral Byrd and Dr. Hugo Eckener were considered for the honor.

British Launch 3 Submarines in Day

BARROW-IN-FURNESS, England, June 11.—(AP)—Three submarines for the British admiralty—the Regulus, Regent and Rover—were launched at one shipyard today.

THE WEATHER

THURSDAY, JUNE 12, 1930.

Sun rises 5:14 a. m.; sun sets 8:26 p. m.; moon rises 10:17 p. m.

Chicago and Vicinity—Today showers followed by partly cloudy. Tomorrow partly cloudy and warmer, probably followed by showers; fresh southerly winds.

Illinois and Vicinity—Today cloudy, with showers in north portion and somewhat warmer in afternoon; tomorrow partly cloudy and warmer, followed by showers in north portion.

TEMPERATURES IN CHICAGO

HIGHEST, 1:30 P. M. 78
LOWEST, 6 A. M. 58

3 a. m. . 63	12 noon . . 76	9 p. m. . 65
4 a. m. . 62	1 p. m. . 77	10 p. m. . 64
5 a. m. . 60	2 p. m. . 77	Unofficial:
6 a. m. . 58	3 p. m. . 75	11 p. m. . 63
7 a. m. . 60	4 p. m. . 73	Midnight . . 62
8 a. m. . 64	5 p. m. . 71	1 a. m. . 61
9 a. m. . 69	6 p. m. . 68	2 a. m. . 60
10 a. m. . 72	7 p. m. . 67	
11 a. m. . 76	8 p. m. . 65	

Mean temperature for twenty-four hours ended 8 p. m., 63: normal for day, 66; excess since January 1, 2.6 degrees.

Barometer: 8 a. m., 30.04; 8 p. m., 30.04.

Deficiency of precipitation since January 1, 2.08 inches.

Official weather report on Page 27.

'Dry' British Embassy Restocked With Liquor!

WASHINGTON, June 11.—Thirsty diplomats at the British embassy smiled today. A truckload of rare liquor, the first to arrive since the former ambassador, Sir Esme Howard, forbade its importation for the embassy, was delivered at the back door.

Whisky, brandy, champagne and other wines and liquors were in the shipment. And there's more coming.

For some time the new burglar-proof cellars have been ready for filling, but since the edict of Sir Esme a year ago they have been empty. Sir Ronald Lindsay, the present ambassador, indicated some time ago that he would not keep the embassy on the dry basis.

Recently he ordered new supplies from England. They arrived on the British freighter, Manchester Exporter, and arrangements were immediately made to have the liquor delivered safely. Washington police convoyed it to the embassy.

Police Give Words and Gestures When City Wants Action

MISERABLE INEFFICIENCY of the Chicago police department is demonstrated before the world. The average citizen believes the department is corrupt.

Murder will not out if public officials entrusted with enforcement of the law busy themselves blotting out the trail of tribute leading from gangland, instead of identifying the footprints.

Bootlegging, gambling, prostitution pay for police protection and get lagniappe in indifference to gang murders incident to carrying on those criminal activities. Honest investigation of many a recent murder might have concentrated attention on important links in the chain of graft that binds politics and the police to crime.

After every fresh gang murder, committed with a disregard of law and order that would shock a border town of desperadoes, the police set out in full cry on innumerable false trails. There is a great running round in circles; vigorous proclamation; thundering threats of punishment.

All words! All gestures! Nothing comes of it. Quickly the crime is shadowed into forgetfulness by a new murder in the spotlight.

Citizens' committees that have come forward to take a hand in cleaning up Chicago have been feeble expressions of rising public anger. The Crime Commission appears to be mainly engaged in compiling statistics. The "Secret Six" appears to be only an effective title for a moving picture.

Chicago is disgusted with its headless, footless city administration, so streaked with rottenness that honest men in it, thinking of their daily bread, keep their mouths shut and their eyes closed.

With an optimism that has deserved a better reward, Chicago has allowed its faithless, weak, inefficient public servants to go forward promising better things. They have been traitors to the city that made them and gave them the chance to leave behind them respected memories instead of stolen estates.

There must be some men in this city, either in public office or in private life, who have sufficient character to be above graft—men of sufficient courage and high enough sense of civic duty to put the work of rescuing this city above the business of making money.

If there are no such men, Chicago is in a bad way, indeed. If we are without capable leadership we must turn to the governor of this state and cry for help. Gang rule, with its concomitant murder in the public streets, must be ruthlessly stamped out if it takes the establishment of martial law to do it.

If there are any honest officials in this city let them show it now by seeing to it that a sincere, efficient investigation of the Lingle murder is pushed to the limit. Let them see to it that there is no smothering of evidence; no covering up of clues.

The Herald and Examiner has added $25,000 to the $30,000 already offered by the Tribune and the Evening Post as a reward in this case.

Chicago wants to know the truth about this murder. An explanation is whispered in the underworld and in police circles.

The slain man has been described as an intimate of the chief of police and an intimate of notorious gangsters.

Why was he murdered?

Is this another "McSwiggin mystery"?

ARREST 640, BUT GET NO GANG CHIEFS IN DRAGNET

Lid Clamped Tight on City; Keepers of Resorts Flee Before Police Get Around

Russell Insists Conscience Is Clear; Refuses to Quit; Predicts Results Very Soon

$55,100 Rewards!

Total rewards of $55,100 for arrest and conviction of the murderer of Afred Lingle, Tribune reporter, had been offered up to yesterday. The latest offer of $100 came yesterday from the Press Club of Birmingham, Ala. The others are $25,000 from The Herald and Examiner; $25,000 from the Chicago Tribune; $5,000 from the Chicago Evening Post.

Any one having any information concerning Lingle's assassin should phone the City Editor of The Herald and Examiner, Randolph 2121.

The murder of Alfred ("Jake") Lingle, a reporter for the Chicago Tribune, which took place Monday, was followed yesterday, some forty-eight hours later, by a series of spectacular police activities of the sort which Chicago has been taught—through many lessons—to expect in such cases.

Raid everything.

Arrest everybody who might be guilty of this or other crimes.

Charge them with "disorderly conduct" if nothing else will stand up.

Make a showing.

EXECUTION SQUADS.

Six "execution squads," each commanded by a lieutenant who has a record for killing men, were sent forth as a special expedition. All regular squads, of course, were also taking a hand.

Technically, squad leaders were instructed to bring hoodlums in to be viewed by witnesses, but their increased armament and the "killer" records of the commanders were significant.

Police Commissioner William F. Russell and Deputy Commissioner John Stege, as is customary, were issuing statements to the general effect that the forces of government had been challenged, that the challenge had been accepted, that the crime would be punished.

As was done after the St. [...]tine's Day massacre, after [...]der of Assistant State's [...] McSwiggin, after the Di[...]ion killing and a score [...] cases, the police overw[...] patrol wagons last ni[...] in a motley throng o[...] characters, known or[...]

By midnight 640 h[...] up at the de[...] other stat[...] offici[...]

[...]S

goo[...]Marion and Lake
N[...] OAK PARK
Broadway and Fifth
GARY

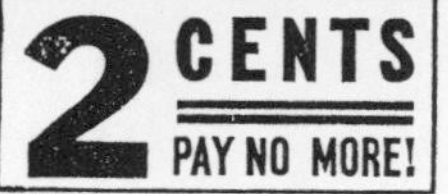
2 CENTS PAY NO MORE!

Chicago  Daily Tribune

THE WORLD'S GREATEST NEWSPAPER

FINAL EDITION

VOLUME LXXXIX.—NO. 148 C [REG. U.S. PAT. OFFICE: COPYRIGHT 1930 BY THE CHICAGO TRIBUNE.] SATURDAY, JUNE 21, 1930.—26 PAGES THIS PAPER CONSISTS OF TWO SECTIONS—SECTION ONE ** PRICE TWO CENTS IN CHICAGO AND SUBURBS ELSEWHERE THREE CENTS

U.S. WRECKS 24 CICERO STILLS

FINISH ILLINOIS WATERWAY BY 1933, U. S. PLAN

State Not Worried by Blaine Rider.

Completion of the Illinois waterway by April 1, 1933, under the federal government, was looked for yesterday by the state division of waterways, the date of the opening being now estimated at two years later than was expected two years ago. The action of the senate in Washington on the rivers and harbors bill, which carries an appropriation of $7,500,000 to finish the project between Lockport and Utica, was taken by the authorities as assurance that the government will take over the undertaking at an early date.

Work by the state has been closed down, except for some dredging, as the $20,000,000 which Illinois is spending of its own money was insufficient to finish the job.

Summer's Delay Seen.

The state officials figure that when the government takes hold, it will require some time to let the first contracts, which might cause a summer's delay this year, and that the program will be carried out in the two working seasons of 1931 and 1932. The state has the work of building the bridges.

State officials expressed the opinion that the Blaine amendment in the senate, limiting the amount of diversion from Lake Michigan for the waterway to the maximum amount set forth in the Supreme court decision, pending further action from congress, will not affect navigability in the early years of the waterway. As they view it, under the greatest restriction, the waterway would have a diversion of 3,200 cubic second feet in 1938, which would be five years after the route has been in operation. By that time the development of transportation, they declare, will lead congress to provide the diversion deemed necessary by the secretary of war in the report he is to submit by 1938.

Restrictions by Court.

The Supreme court decree allows a diversion of 6,500 cubic second feet until 1935, and after that 5,000 cubic feet until 1938, when it is to be cut to 1,500 feet, plus pumpage for Chicago's domestic needs, which amounts to about 1,700 cubic feet. As the officials see it, one of the most important phases of the waterway item is that congress, when the bill is passed, will have given official recognition to the waterway project for the first time.

7½ MILLION FOR WORK

[Chicago Tribune Press Service.]

Washington, D. C., June 20.—[Special.]—Without a record vote the senate today passed the rivers and harbors bill, carrying total authorizations of upward of 125 million dollars, including $7,500,000 for federal completion of the Illinois waterway.

The bill will be in the hands of President Hoover early next week, prompt concurrence in senate amendments to the original house bill by the house being assured. It is taken for granted that the President will sign the bill, inasmuch as it incorporates authorizations for carrying out the inland waterway developments program which he has advocated.

Expended Over Period of Years.

Supporters of the measure insist that it need not interfere with the administration's financial program, inasmuch as the money will be expended over a period of years and only as allotted by the chief of engineers of the war department from lump sum annual appropriations.

The rivers and harbors bill includes authorizations for scores of projects in all sections of the country. By means of the Illinois waterway provision it makes possible completion of the lakes to the gulf waterway. It adopts a nine foot project for the upper Mississippi where the depth is at present six feet, a six foot project in the Missouri river up to Sioux City, and a nine foot project on the Tennessee river from its mouth to Knoxville. It authorizes deepening of the connecting channels in the great lakes and transfer of the New York state barge canal from the state of New York to the federal government if the state approves it.

Senator A. H. Vandenberg [Rep., Mich.], who was active in yesterday's successful move by representatives of lake states to restrict water diversion at Chicago through the Blaine amendment, expressed his opposition to the entire bill just before it was passed. No other voice was heard when the nays were called for by Vice President Curtis.

"The bill came to the senate from

(Continued on page 4, column 6.)

NEWS SUMMARY
of The Tribune
[And Historical Scrap Book.]
Saturday, June 21, 1930.

Average net paid circulation of THE CHICAGO TRIBUNE May, 1930:

Daily 835,053
Sunday . . 1,096,066

MELLON COMES TO DEFENSE OF THE NEW TARIFF

Insists It Will Aid Better Business.

[Chicago Tribune Press Service.]

Washington, D. C., June 20.—[Special.]—Secretary of the Treasury Andrew W. Mellon today issued a defense of the new Hawley-Smoot tariff law. Instead of injuring business, retarding business recovery or ruining foreign trade, Mr. Mellon, as the financial authority of the administration, asserted that it makes a "definite contribution to business stability."

Elimination of the uncertainties of the last 15 months while the tariff bill was pending and the promise of a more businesslike revision in the future through the amended flexible provisions are the factors in Mr. Mellon's opinion which will aid business recovery.

Say Gloomy Prophecies Fail.

"It seems to me that fears and criticisms have been greatly exaggerated," said Mr. Mellon. "Whenever a new protective tariff law has been enacted gloomy prophecies have been made. They have failed to materialize as far back as I can remember, and my memory goes back many years. The rates in the bill as it passed the house a year ago were higher than in the bill recently signed by the President. Yet business at that time did not take alarm. There seems to be no reason why it should now. I know of no industry that is seriously hurt, while those industries which needed additional protection and received it are benefited.

"I have canvassed the situation with the secretary of commerce, and the notion that this law is going to destroy our foreign trade, expressed in some quarters, is certainly without foundation. The United States will continue to buy a vast quantity of foreign products and to sell the products of its farms, mines, and factories all over the world. In so far as imports are concerned, foreign nations that do business with us would do well to remember that the all important factor is the maintenance of the high purchasing power and standard of living of the American people."

Predicts Early Adjustment.

Secretary Mellon insisted that industries should be able to adjust themselves to the new law without difficulty. He denied that there is such a marked increase in the level of industrial rates as critics of the bill would have the country believe. He expressed particular approval of the flexible provisions.

"The enactment of this measure brings to an end fifteen months of uncertainty," said Mr. Mellon. "American industries know now where they stand and will, I am confident, adjust themselves without difficulty to new conditions.

"There seems to be an impression that the new bill makes a sweeping revision upward of existing rates. While it is true that there is a sharp increase in rates applicable to the agricultural schedule, generally speaking, other rates cannot be said to have been advanced sufficiently to alter substantially our existing economic position. In fact, only a comparatively few of the major items have been changed.

"I do not mean to imply that the bill is free from defects. No tariff bill is. But this measure at least by its own terms provides the means whereby inequalities and errors may be adjusted.

Praises Flexible Provisions.

"I look upon the flexible provisions as highly important. I believe that they offer the opportunity not only to correct errors and to adjust rates to meet new and changing conditions, but that they lay a foundation for a businesslike method of tariff revision, free from the pull of sectional and political interests that seem to make by the legislative body almost impossible a scientific and well balanced revision possible.

"If these provisions are intelligently and courageously applied, they should go a long way toward making another legislative revision of the tariff unnecessary for many years to come."

Watson Defends Tariff.

Senator James E. Watson [Rep., Ind.], majority leader of the senate, defended the new law in a radio speech tonight.

"The law just passed was held in the senate almost nine months and it is now but four months and a half until the election occurs this fall," said Senator Watson.

"Whether or not four months will

(Continued on page 2, column 5.)

WOULDN'T IT SURPRISE—

The Gangsters and Hoodlums if—

The New Chief should go after them hard?

ALERT BOY RIDES WITH POLICE AND SPOTS A GUNMAN

The alertness of a 15 year old boy, William Maloney, brought about the capture yesterday of a St. Louis gunman an hour after he had slugged and robbed Leo Breskin, 74 year old haberdasher, in his store at 3509 West North avenue.

Living next door at 3507 West North avenue, William witnessed the robbery and found Breskin unconscious from a blow of a pistol butt after the gunman fled with $50. When a flivver squad composed of Detectives Curran, Mulvey and McMahon arrived from Austin station William climbed into their car.

They had cruised the neighborhood for many blocks when at Kedzie and Chicago avenues William spied the fugitive. The police captured and disarmed him. At the Austin station he confessed 15 previous robberies. He was booked as Leslie Moore Combs. He said he came here recently from St. Louis.

ALL OVER WITH MORROW NOW, M'BRIDE SAYS

Minneapolis, Minn., June 20.—(AP)—F. Scott McBride, general superintendent of the Anti-Saloon League of America, declared here today that Dwight W. Morrow has sacrificed his political future by winning the Republican nomination for senator in New Jersey on a wet platform.

Dr. McBride said the ambassador's stand on the prohibition question "takes away his last chance for the Presidency." Dr. McBride added:

"Mr. Morrow will be merely another wet from New Jersey if he is elected. So far not one dry vote in the house has been lost and nominations for the senate represent a net gain of one dry vote, even though New Jersey again sends a wet to the senate."

SUMMER DEBUT TODAY TO BRING RISE IN MERCURY

Summer begins officially today, the longest day of the year. The solstice occurs at 10:54 o'clock tonight, Chicago daylight saving time, when the sun reaches the northernmost extremity of its six months' swing in the northern hemisphere, and turns back southward.

The sun rises today at 5:24 a. m. and sets at 8:40 p. m., making 15 hours and 16 minutes of sunshine.

The forecast for today was fair and somewhat warmer, with the temperature reaching a probable maximum of 86 degrees. This is about six degrees above the normal maximum for this time of the year, according to Forecaster W. P. Day.

O. K. M'Nider Over Protest by Brookhart

[Chicago Tribune Press Service.]

Washington, D. C., June 20.—[Special.]—Hanford MacNider, former assistant secretary of war, was today confirmed by the senate as minister to Canada over the protest of Senator Smith Wildman Brookhart [Rep., Ia.], who climaxed a bitter attack on MacNider by charging the latter had turned recent American Legion conventions into "drunken revels."

Except for a spirited defense of MacNider's personal habits and his devotion to the interests of ex-service men by Senator Daniel Steck [Dem., Ia.], Brookhart's attack left the senate unmoved and his was the only dissenting voice when MacNider's appointment was approved without a record vote.

"Too many Legion conventions have been just drunken revels," shouted Brookhart, "and I've seen this man MacNider leading those revels, and I am opposed to sending him anywhere to represent the United States."

Steck Leaps to Defense.

"I cannot let that last statement go by unchallenged," declared Steck in one of the few speeches he has made during his nearly six years in the senate. "I care nothing about the political differences between my colleague and Mr. MacNider, but I can't overlook such statements when I know what he has done for veterans.

"When the senator, my colleague, says Hanford MacNider is a drunkard he is either ill advised or he doesn't know what he is talking about. Years ago Mr. MacNider did take a drink occasionally, but for the last four years, since he came into political life, he has been a teetotaler."

Brookhart candidly admitted that his attack on MacNider was the outgrowth of a personal as well as a political feud which reached its greatest height when MacNider and his father, a prominent Iowa banker, led the fight which resulted in the ousting of Brookhart from the senate in 1926.

Calls Him Soldiers' Enemy.

"The younger MacNider was the chief lobbyist against me among senators at that time," asserted Brookhart. "He is the worst enemy that soldiers ever had. He represents the cement trust and the chain farming evil. I don't know why he was appointed, unless it was to reward him for his work in the campaign. He has succeeded in making the American Legion a partisan and political organization."

Reading from some of MacNider's speeches criticizing senate radicals in general and himself in particular, Brookhart came on one in which MacNider complained that in spite of his constant opposition to the administration Brookhart was allowed to control federal patronage in Iowa.

"That," said Brookhart, "refers to young American Legion members who I succeeded in getting appointed as United States marshals in Iowa, any one of whom would make a better minister to Canada than this man MacNider."

THE WEATHER

SATURDAY, JUNE 21, 1930.

[Daylight saving time.]

Sunrise, 5:14; sunset, 8:28. Moon rises at 2:12 a. m. Sunday. Uranus, Mars, and Mercury are morning stars. Venus and Neptune are evening stars.

Chicago and vicinity—Generally fair and slightly warmer Saturday; probably followed by showers at night or on Sunday; gentle variable winds Saturday.

Illinois—Mostly fair Saturday; Sunday increasing cloudiness, probably showers in north and central portions, cooler in northwest and central portions Sunday.

TRIBUNE BAROMETER.

TEMPERATURES IN CHICAGO

MAXIMUM, 11 A. M. 80
MINIMUM, 5 A. M. 64

3 a. m.	65	Noon	78	8 p. m.	71
4 a. m.	65	1 p. m.	74	9 p. m.	74
5 a. m.	64	2 p. m.	73	10 p. m.	74
6 a. m.	64	3 p. m.	75	Unofficial—	
7 a. m.	64	4 p. m.	75	11 p. m.	73
8 a. m.	66	5 p. m.	76	Midnight	73
9 a. m.	73	6 p. m.	74	1 a. m.	72
10 a. m.	77	7 p. m.	73	2 a. m.	72
11 a. m.	80				

For 24 hours ended at 8 p. m. June 20.

Mean temperature, 72 degrees; normal, 69; excess since Jan. 1, 444.

Precipitation, none; deficiency since Jan. 1, 2.64 inches.

Barometer, 8 a. m., 30.01; 8 p. m., 29.94.

Highest wind velocity, 9 miles an hour from the east at 12:24 p. m.

[Official weather table on page 20.]

Wife, 17, Says Old Photo Led Her to Wed Man, 70

Superior Judge Williams yesterday granted leave to Mrs. Lottie Gut, 17 years old, 4921 South Wood street, to file a cross bill to her husband's suit for divorce. She testified she married Cazimir Gut, 70 years old, on Feb. 3, 1927, without seeing him previously. Her mother, she said, had shown her Gut's picture, but she later found out that the picture had been taken when he was young. She left him the day after their marriage. A few days ago her husband filed suit for divorce, charging desertion.

Eats Hearty Meal, Puffs Cigar on 104th Birthday

Cleveland, O., June 20.—(AP)—Patrick Vizzard celebrated his 104th birthday anniversary at his home here today by eating a hearty meal and smoking a black cigar. Vizzard was born in Ireland and came to the United States when 30 years old.

Girl, 4, Gives Clew to 'Tape Bandit' Gang

Louise Patterson, who has a keen memory for a 4 year old, told Detective Sergeants Fred Wirsing and William O'Neil a story yesterday which, they said, had helped them a long way towards solution of two of the major house robberies of last winter.

Early in the evening on Jan. 6 five bandits strode past a maid into the home of Charles M. Richter, millionaire magazine publisher of 1418 Lake Shore drive, subdued the family and servants with pistols and soft words, and gathered up $23,742 in jewelry. Before departing they bound and gagged all members of the household with tape.

Three weeks later a band of four housebreakers posing as interior decorators persuaded a servant to admit them to the home of Stuart Templeton, a lawyer living at 1388 North Green Bay road, Lake Forest. The Templetons being away, the robbers ransacked the house at leisure and took approximately $5,000 in loot. Again tape was used to bind and gag the servants.

Woman Gives Bandit Clew.

Information as to the "tape" bandits came to the police four weeks ago from Louise's mother, Mrs. Kathleen Patterson, at that time a county jail prisoner. She had been returned here from Victory, Ky., with Ray Miller, a former convict, to whom she had turned over the $18,000 inheritance of her husband, Merton Patterson, former marine and father of Louise.

"Ask Harry Lewis about the Richter and Templeton jobs," the erring wife hinted to Sergt. Wirsing. Questioned further, she admitted a grudge against Lewis, who had spurned her to marry another woman, but she would go no further in implicating him in the robberies.

As a matter of routine, Sergts. Wirsing and O'Connell investigated Lewis, a handsome man of 26 years, found him living with his bride at the Hermine hotel, 4101 Kenmore avenue, and took him in custody for questioning.

Denies Knowledge of Robberies.

"Sure, I knew Mrs. Patterson, and she's given me this rap because I wouldn't marry her," Lewis asserted. "I've had all my teeth kicked out by Oregon state police trying to connect me with a big mail robbery out there. You can kick me around, too, but I don't know a thing about these jobs you speak of."

To the sergeants Mrs. Patterson's hint began to appear dubious. Since the gunmen in both robberies had been masked, they decided it would be useless to have the victims confront Lewis. But before releasing him they decided to consult 4 year old Louise in his presence.

Yesterday, therefore, they took the prisoner to the Lincoln hotel, 1812 Lincoln avenue, where Louise and her mother have been staying.

Child Tells of Game.

"Yes, I remember Mr. Lewis," piped Louise. "He used to call on mother real often. He used to bring other men in and they would play a game of 'prisoners.'"

"What game is that?" asked O'Neil.

"Well, Mr. Lewis would tie another man's hands behind his back with tape. Then he would paste tape across the other man's mouth. Then he'd say to him, 'Now, tug hard and see if the tape holds.'"

Louise wriggled in her chair and compressed her lips, illustrating the game. "But the other men couldn't get free, so Mr. Lewis would take off the tape and say, 'We win.'"

All this was related to Police Chief Lester Tiffany of Lake Forest, who put Lewis in the village jail on a warrant charging robbery and larceny. Warrants were also taken out against Fred Ramsey, Willim Heeney, and Lester Gillis, reputed "playmates" of Lewis in the "game" Louise remembered so vividly.

PEACE MAKING COP LOSES HIS GUN IN HOLDUP

While off duty and strolling in plain clothes yesterday morning Policeman Patrick Duggan of the Hudson avenue station encountered at Hamlin and Eddy streets three men who apparently were having a quarrel.

"Say, what's going on here?" asked Policeman Duggan.

"Merely a stickup," replied one of the men, pointing a pistol at the policeman. "I'll frisk you, too, since you have insisted upon joining the party." Duggan, who was going to his home at 3800 Eddy street, surrendered his service revolver, and the other two, Jack Rose, 3735 Irving Park boulevard, and James Ward, 3757 Patterson, each gave up a small amount of money.

The bandit climbed into a nearby automobile, but, unable to start it, fled on foot. Acting Commissioner of Police Alcock said he will scan the report on the policeman's conduct before taking any action.

DRYS FIND ALKY PLANTS PAYING $30,000 A DAY

Capone Vats Hidden in Bungalows.

Boss Racketeer Slain

Yesterday's raids on the Capone syndicate's distilleries in Cicero followed the discovery of the body of Lorenzo Juliano, boss racketeer and Capone henchman, who had been taken for a ride and slain.

(Pictures on back page.)

Twelve Cicero alcohol distilleries, believed to have been operated by the Capone booze syndicate, were raided late yesterday by twenty prohibition agents under Assistant Administrator George Hurlburt.

Yesterday's cleanup brought the total of stills raided in Cicero in the last week to twenty-four. The average capacity of the twenty-four plants was 250 gallons a day, which would mean a daily output of 6,000 gallons, worth $30,000, according to Hurlburt. The monthly revenue to the booze syndicate on this basis would be $900,000.

Stills in Bungalows.

Only two prisoners were taken in the raids yesterday and early last evening, but six had been apprehended on the previous raids, and the agents said they would connect several others in the development of a conspiracy case. All of the twenty-four distilleries were found in bungalows.

The most elaborate plant was found at 3414 South 58th avenue, a 750 gallon recooker, which was used to refine first run alky made in the smaller stills. The recooker had a double column 24 inches in diameter and 15 feet in height. It was equipped with an electric blower designed to force the alcohol fumes upward, so they would not be smelled by dry snoopers.

The apparatus also included a 600 gallon receiving tank, which supplied the crude alky for the refining process an electric motor and an oil burner. There were 260 gallons of the finished product, which tested 190 proof, as chemically pure as the government standard.

Two Stills; Two Prisoners.

The two prisoners were seized at 3404 South 58th avenue, where two 100 gallon stills were found. The prisoners are Louis Nassatta and Joe Falsetto. A 150 gallon preheater and sixty gallons of alky were found at this address, together with three large concrete vats filled with mash.

At 1438 South 51st avenue, the raiders destroyed a 500 gallon distillery and eight 750 gallon vats of mash. At 3405 59th avenue a 200 gallon still, a 250 gallon preheater, and 20,000 gallons of mash were destroyed.

The raiders destroyed two 300 gallon stills at 3710 South 59th avenue. This bungalow also housed a 350 gallon preheater, 150 gallons of alcohol and 7,500 gallons of mash. The agents were still working at an early hour this morning and had not reported on all the addresses at which they were directed to make raids.

The lawns about the bungalows raided were well kept and the buildings in a good state of repair, and lace curtains at the windows added to the appearance of domesticity. However, nothing except the distilling apparatus was found inside.

Oak Park Seizure.

Oak Park police yesterday arrested three men and seized 1,338 bottles of bourbon, Scotch whisky, imported gin and Barcardi rum. They captured an automobile in an alley at Pleasant street and South boulevard and arrested James Matthews, who gave his address as Daytona Beach, Fla. The car was loaded with liquor. Later they seized another car in a garage at 110 South Grove avenue, where the remainder of the liquor was stored. Jesse Warren, who admitted driving this car from Florida, was arrested. V. A. Howard of 932 Pleasant street, admitted having rented the garage but denied ownership of any part of the liquor. All three were turned over to prohibition authorities.

THE JULIANO MURDER

Back of the murder of Lorenzo Juliano, whose body was found yesterday in an automobile near 123d street and California avenue, there was a story of bombings, murders, blackmail, and the business of making and selling alcohol. Juliano had been beaten to death.

Juliano was rated as the boss of racketeers in the southern part of the county by virtue of his affiliation with Al Capone. Juliano was a Sicilian of 23 years' residence in this county,

LIERS UP 483 HOURS; TALK ON RADIO

'al. Drys Indorse Gov. Young

NIGHT EDITION

NATIONAL LEAGUE

At Pittsburg—

		R.	H.	E.
Boston	0 0 0 0 0 0 1 1 1	3	11	2
Pittsburg	0 3 1 0 0 0 1 3 x	8	11	3

Batteries—Brandt, Cunningham and Gowdy, Cronin; French and Hemsley.

At Chicago—

		R.	H.	E.
New York	0 2 0 2 2 0 1 0 0	7	13	1
Chicago	2 0 0 0 3 0 0 0 0	5	8	1

Batteries—Fitzgimmons and Hogan; Bush, Osborne, Teachout and Hartnett.

At St. Louis—

		R.	H.	E.
Brooklyn	2 0 0 0 1 0 1 0 3	7	11	4
St. Louis	3 0 11 0 1 0 0 0 x	15	17	1

Batterie[illegible] Dudley, Elliott, Luque and Lopez, Picinich; H[illegible] and Wilson.
Only gam[illegible]eduled.

AMERICAN LEAGUE

At Boston—

		R.	H.	E.
Cleveland	0 1 0 0 0 0 0 0 0	1	3	2
Boston	0 0 2 0 0 0 0 1 x	3	11	1

Batteries—Harder and Myatt; Gaston and Berry.

At Philadelphia—(game called, rain)—

		R.	H.	E.
Detroit	0 0 0 0 1	1	1	0
Philadelphia	0 4 0 0 x	4	4	0

Batteries—Hogsett and Rensa, Desautels; Grove and Cochrane.

Detroit at Philadelphia second game postponed, rain.
St. Louis at Washington postponed, rain.
Chicago at New York postponed, rain.

EASTERN BALL SCORES

Reg. U. S. Pat. Office. Copyright, 1929, by Evening Herald Publishing Company

The Evening Herald Grows Just Like Los Angeles

L. LV THREE CENTS Hotels and Trains Five Cents — TUESDAY, JULY 1, 1930 — Hotels and Trains Five Cents THREE CENTS NO. 207

MORAN GUN GANG SEIZED HERE IN LINGLE MURDER

'Five Gentlemen From Chicago'

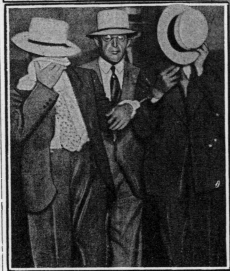

Upper photo shows five alleged Chicago gangsters arrested in Los Angeles today in connection with investigation of the slaying of Alfred Lingle, Chicago reporter. Left to right, Marvin Hart, George Davis, Frank Foreman, alias Frank Foster; Frank Fisher and Herman Walter. Foreman is said to have furnished the gun with which Lingle was killed. The lower photo shows two of the alleged gangsters, handcuffed together and holding hankie and hat over their faces on way to the identification bureau with a guard. At left is George Davis; at right, Frank Foreman.

'TIC' JURY 'EADLOCKED 'IGHTS FOR VERDICT

A jury of six men and six women late today was reported deadlocked over the fate of [illegible]o Sanhuber, charged with the murder eight years ago of [illegible]y Fred Oesterreich.

[illegible]ur hours after the jury had [illegible]ed at noon to deliberate on Sa[illegible]uber's fate, no inkling of the [illegible]ess of the balloting came from [illegible]uarded jury room.

[illegible], jury, which has sat in [illegible] Carlos S. Hardy's court for [illegible]st two weeks listening to the [illegible] weird testimony ever unfolded [illegible]os Angeles courtroom, retired [illegible]egin deliberations after Judge [illegible]rdy had spent 45 minutes in[illegible]ucting the talesmen in the [illegible]estions of fact and of law in[illegible]ol[illegible]d in the case.

JURORS LOCKED UP

[illegible]ore settling down to what [illegible]xpected to be a long-drawn [illegible]rument, the jurors were taken [illegible]ch by Bailiff Charles Bryant, [illegible]ere locked in the jury room [illegible] his afternoon.

[illegible]e the jurors were deliberat[illegible]nhuber and his wife, Mrs. [illegible]a Klein, sat chatting in the [illegible]nte-room, the door of which [illegible]ked, inasmuch as the attic [illegible] was in custody. The meek [illegible]fendant twitched nervously [illegible]vals, but smiled at those [illegible]pproached his miniature

[illegible] Refroir and James Lou[illegible]lternate jurors who were [illegible] when Judge Hardy read [illegible]uctions, both declared they [illegible]ave voted Sanhuber guilty [illegible]d degree murder.

[illegible]oth thought his confession [illegible]rand jury was the truth," [illegible]rnate jurors said. "We [illegible]lieve h[illegible] repudiation of the

([illegible]NUED ON PAGE FIFTEEN)

BILLIE DOVE, FILM BEAUTY, DIVORCES DIRECTOR MATE

Dark-eyed Billie Dove, oftimes called "the most beautiful girl in the films" and known in private life as Lillian Bohny Willat, was today granted a divorce from her director husband, Irvin Willat, by Superior Judge Harry R. Archbald on grounds of cruelty.

The court also issued an order restoring to Miss Dove her maiden name, Lillian Bohny.

Questioned by her attorney, Neil McCarthy, the beautiful screen star declared she married Willat on Oct.

(CONTINUED ON PAGE TWENTY)

Stock Prices Fall Under Selling Wave After Early Rally

By International News Service

NEW YORK, July 1.—A wave of profit-taking and professional selling in the last half-hour today wiped out the effects of the day's rally in the speculative leaders, and forced prices of a hundred or more representative stocks from 2 to 4½ points below the level of yesterday's close. Buying demand evaporated as soon as short-covering had been completed, and values faded when stocks were forced on the market in the final selling wave.

RED SOX DOWN INDIANS TO EVEN SERIES

By International News Service

FENWAY PARK, BOSTON, July 1.—The Red Sox evened up the series with the Cleveland Indians this afternoon by winning the second game of the series, 3 to 1.

It was a pitching duel between Milton Gaston and Mel Harder,

(CONTINUED ON PAGE SIXTEEN)

DRY LEAGUE INDORSES YOUNG

Governor C. C. Young was indorsed for re-election today by the board of directors of the California Anti-Saloon league after an all-day meeting in the Los Angeles Chamber of Commerce building.

No other candidacies had been taken up late this afternoon. Dr. Arthur H. Briggs, state superintendent, said that a statement was being prepared explaining the board's action on the governorship.

The board had under consideration three propositions regarding the governorship, one of them was to indorse Governor Young, another to indorse District Attorney Buron Fitts and the third to make no indorsement at all.

George B. Bush, Southern California manager of Fitts' campaign, talked with members of the board before the meeting. He said that he hoped that if any recommendation is made it would be given to Fitts, but thought that the wisest move was to express no choice.

None of the other candidates was

(CONTINUED ON PAGE FOURTEEN)

Stars 6, Oaks 5

OAKS—	Ab	R	H	Po	A	E
Uhalt, lf	5	1	2	1	0	0
Martin, cf	5	1	2	4	0	0
Vergez, 3b	4	0	2	0	4	0
Lombardi, c	5	0	0	8	0	0
Fenton, 1b	4	0	0	9	0	0
Dean, 2b	4	1	1	2	3	1
Griffin, rf	4	1	2	0	0	0
Devivrons, ss	3	0	1	0	2	1
Olsen, ss	0	0	0	0	1	0
McEvoy, p	3	1	1	0	0	0
McQuaid, p	0	0	0	0	0	0
Arlett	0	0	0	0	0	0
Read	1	0	1	0	0	0
Pearson	0	0	0	0	0	0
Totals	38	5	12	24	10	2

STARS—	Ab	R	H	Po	A	E
Hill, lf	4	1	1	2	0	2
Lee, ss	4	1	1	6	4	0
Brannan, 2b	3	1	3	1	2	1
Barbee, rf	3	1	1	0	0	0
Carlyle, cf	3	1	0	3	0	0
Heath, 1b	3	0	1	10	1	0
Bassler, c	3	0	1	3	0	0
Green, 3b	4	0	0	2	5	1
Shellenbck, p	1	0	0	0	0	0
Page, p	3	1	1	0	2	0
Totals	31	6	9	27	14	2

Oakland	102 200 000	5
Hollywood	300 200 10x	6

Hollywood continued its winning streak by taking the measure of Oakland in the opening game of their series at Wrigley field today,

(CONTINUED ON PAGE SIXTEEN)

GIRL, 5 MEN NABBED IN ROUNDUP OF SUSPECTS

Frank Foreman, alias Frank Foster, "keeper of the arsenal" for the George "Bugs" Moran gang of the Chicago northside and who is said by Chicago detectives to have furnished the pistol with which Alfred "Jake" Lingle, Chicago newspaper man, was murdered last June 9, was arrested in Los Angeles today.

Simultaneously police announced that four other known Chicago gangsters were arrested at the same time Foster was apprehended; that Foster's wife, who was going under the name of Mrs. Frank Bowman, also is held in custody in belief she is a member of the same gang; and that they expect to arrest the slayer of Lingle in Los Angeles some time in the next few hours.

PLACED UNDER ARREST

Those under arrest are:

Foreman or Foster, 32, known also as Foss and Bowman, asserted leader of the gang in the western invasion, who is held on suspicion of murder.

George Davis, 35, asserted to be Foster's bodyguard and chauffeur, who was identified half an hour after his arrest as a fugitive from Chicago where he is wanted on a charge of assault to commit murder.

Marvin Hart, 35, Frank Fisher, 36, and Herman A. Walter, 31, all of whom are said by Chicago officers to be members of the Moran gang, who have not yet been booked, but who will be held, the detectives said, on suspicion of murder.

TRACE DEATH GUN

Mrs. Foreman, held in "technical custody," also had not been booked and officers had not determined what charges will be preferred against her.

Late today Mrs. Foreman was escorted to the district attorney's for questioning. She told interviewers she and her husband came

(CONTINUED ON PAGE FIFTEEN)

BROADCAST MESSAGE TO U. S. FROM PLANE

SKY HARBOR AIRPORT, CHICAGO, July 1.—Radio and aviation joined hands today with the result that the entire nation was able to hear the voices of John and Kenneth Hunter and the roar of the motor of their endurance plane, City of Chicago, as they drew close to the end of their twentieth day in the air.

At 6:40 p. m., central standard time, the brothers had been aloft 483 hours, or 63 hours beyond the St. Louis Robin's time of 420 hours and 21 minutes.

The broadcast was accomplished shortly before noon when a bombing plane equipped with a short wave transmitter flew over the City of Chicago and lowered a microphone to the endurance ship. The words of the Hunter brothers were sent out over the stations of the Columbia Broadcasting System. An effort to repeat the broadcast is scheduled to be made at 5:30 o'clock this evening, central standard time, if the City of Chicago is still in the air.

STAY UP IN AIR

"We'll stay up as long as we can," John and Kenneth declared in their radio talks.

Irene Hunter replied to her brothers' greetings. Her words also were broadcast over the network.

Following a few danger-laden hours this morning, when a heavy fog surrounded their plane, the Hunters continued their flight under weather conditions that were generally favorable. The fog, coupled with a drizzle, presented the greatest peril the Sparta, Ill., miners have faced since they left the earth. They were forced to fly with a ceiling of 200 feet for a time.

The Chicago is in none too good shape, even thought its motor still drones away with never a break.

BOLTS LOOSENED

Constant vibration has loosened bolts near the motor and Kenneth had to crawl out on the "cat walk" and tighten some of them.

Ordinarily an airplane's motor is inspected after every 50 hours of service and overhauled after every 200 hours. For more than 470 hours

(CONTINUED ON PA[illegible]FTEEN)

HERALD CHICAGO AND EXAMINER

50th YEAR No. 84 Registered in U. S. Patent Office C★★★ MONDAY, JULY 14, 1930 Telephone Randolph 2121 TWO PARTS PRICE 3 CENTS

KILLER BURKE'S LAIR RAIDED

Today

Too Close to Fifth Avenue.
Abraham Cahan's Birthday.
An Army of Danger.
Fourteen to One and Fifty to One.

—BY ARTHUR BRISBANE—

(© 1930, by King Features Syndicate, Inc.)

NEW YORK'S respectability was shaken, figuratively and literally, at 4 o'clock last Saturday morning. A racketeer bomb exploded on the window sill of a fine dwelling house at 26 W. Fifty-third st., a few doors west of Fifth avenue, one block south of the town residence of John D. Rockefeller Jr.

The bombed residence is occupied by a night club, and police say the bomb was a warning to the club that it must divide profits with the racketeers. This first bomb was not planned to kill, merely to serve notice.

An English lady, in 1916, when she could no longer get the right dog biscuit for her chow, said: "The war has ceased to be a joke." New York says gang war ceases to be a joke when it reaches Fifth avenue.

New York's police believe that the racketeers are moving from Chicago to New York because of increased Chicago police activity. New York police act, with gangsters, less ruthlessly than they do in Chicago.

A Chicago beer seller "tipped" the police that racketeers were to visit him. The police hid in his beer flat and when the racketeers appeared shot them dead.

Learning that gangsters were to raid a payroll of a big laundry, New York's police hid and arrested instead of killing the five gangsters.

Visiting gangsters should not, however, count on too much police gentleness in New York. Mayor Walker's new chief, Mulrooney, knows criminals, and how to discourage them. If shooting at sight is necessary, there will be plenty of it.

Abraham Cahan, editor and creator of the Jewish Daily Forward, received many congratulations yesterday on his 70th birthday. One came from Snowden, British Chancellor of the Exchequer, another from Adolph S. Ochs, editor of a different type.

Mr. Cahan, a brilliant writer and absolutely sincere, has spent his life teaching men and women to think for themselves. No work on earth is more important.

Many columns are printed about fighting armies in China and possibilities of other wars among human beings. But more important to the human race, perhaps, is the extraordinary migration of rats reported under way in eastern Siberia.

Rats carry fleas, fleas carry diseases most dangerous and fatal to men—bubonic plague, typhus and the pneumonic plague, contracted merely by inhaling the breath of its victims and able to strike down those that attend the victim's funeral.

Rats every year destroy $200,000,000 worth of property in the United States. But that is nothing compared with the harm that an invasion of an eastern plague might do in a few weeks.

If governments would spend on the destruction of rats and mosquitoes one-tenth the amount they spent on the last war, this would be a better, safer world.

W. J. Bryan made a good guess when he suggested sixteen to one as the ratio for gold and silver. The Bureau of Mines shows that, theoretically, it should be only fourteen to one.

During the past 437 years the world has produced 14,000,000,000 ounces of silver, only 1,000,000,000 ounces of gold. That amount of silver would make a cube 114½ feet square.

Mexico leads the world in silver production with 40 per cent of the total. The United States comes next.

Relatively gold production has increased more rapidly than silver production. Nevertheless, because the nations have demonetized silver, gold is now worth fifty times as much per ounce as silver, although silver is only fourteen times more plentiful.

Bryan could make another good "Cross of Gold" speech on that.

Oscar Bodenhausen, traveling salesman, saved his dimes for twenty years in the savings bank and now begins a six months' tour of the world. The dimes will pay for it.

One good idea properly developed, twenty years ago, might have enabled Mr. Bodenhausen to travel around the world forever.

However, thrift is important. He who saved money, and has it ready, will have power to develop his own idea if he ever gets one. Without the savings his idea might die with him.

In a small Louisiana town, several children having died of infantile paralysis within a few days, the local authorities forbid all public gatherings.

And wisely the ban includes theaters, churches and assemblies of every kind. In old days in time of plague the mob hurried to the churches in search of miraculous protection and the plague was made worse.

Senators Decide Navy Pact's Fate at Hoover Camp

Must Wait Till Fall or Take Norris Reservation.

S O S CALLS OUT

Summon Absentee Administration Lieutenants.

BY FRASER EDWARDS.
Herald and Examiner-Universal Staff Correspondent.

WASHINGTON, July 13.—The London naval treaty today stood at the crossroads in the Senate. Its fate probably will be decided by the end of this week.

Ratification or rejection hinges upon the disposition of the Norris reservation.

The attitude of the administration on this reservation, which provides that the United States shall not be bound by any secret agreement, may be determined by the week-end conferences between the President and his new leaders at the Rapidan retreat.

The conferees today were Senators Smoot, Allen, Vandenberg, Hebert and Thomas of Idaho.

SENATE SITUATION.

The situation which confronts the President and his cohorts in the Senate is unconditional surrender on the Norris reservation or a postponement of action until Fall.

It is significant that Senator Reed of Pennsylvania, American delegate to the London conference who drew the issue on the Norris reservation, was not one of the Republican leaders called into conference with the President.

On the other hand, Senator Vandenberg took the view there would be nothing objectionable in the Norris reservation, if the preamble was eliminated. And Vandenberg was called to the Rapidan.

Another Republican senator called to the Rapidan was Senator Henry J. Allen of Kansas, who has assumed to speak for the administration.

SPECULATE AT SELECTIONS.

It was a matter of much speculation why Reed, Senator Watson of Indiana, Republican floor leader, and Senator Borah of Idaho, chairman of the foreign relations committee, were ignored by the President.

Senator Moses of New Hampshire declared that twenty-three senators now in Washington would vote against the treaty if the Norris reservation is rejected.

S O S CALLS SENT.

The administration, greatly perturbed over the situation, has sent out S O S calls to all absent Republican senators.

So critical is the administration's situation that Senator Dale of Vermont failed to make the trip to Chicago to attend the meeting of the campaign funds committee, which reopened its inquiry into the McCormick-Deneen primary fight.

Reed probably will open his defense of the treaty in the Senate tomorrow.

Directory of Features

Doyle Sends Wife 'Private Message'; Meeting Breaks Up

LONDON, July 13.—(AP)—The receipt of what purports to be a direct message from the late Sir Arthur Conan Doyle was claimed tonight by a woman clairvoyant at a memorial meeting for him. The message was accepted as genuine by Lady Doyle.

Its substance was not made public, but on hearing it the novelist's widow exclaimed: "I am perfectly convinced the message is from my husband."

Before it was delivered, the meeting, organized in Albert Hall by spiritualist societies of London, had broken up in confusion.

50 LEAVE AUDIENCE.

During the delivery by Mrs. Estelle Roberts, a salaried clairvoyant employed by the Marylebone Spiritualist Association, of alleged messages from five spirits about forty or fifty persons in various parts of the hall suddenly rose and started for the doors. The noise and disturbance caused by their departure bothered Mrs. Roberts.

"I can't go on with all these people walking out," she announced from the platform.

A tumult of conversation and excited calls broke out, and the meeting came to a sudden and unexpected end.

Mrs. Roberts, turning away from the audience, which numbered fully 10,000, walked over to Lady Doyle, who was seated on the platform beside an empty chair symbolizing the presence of the late creator of Sherlock Holmes.

"I HAVE A MESSAGE."

"I have a message from Sir Arthur," she said.

Lady Doyle stood up, greatly interested.

"The message is this," said Mrs. Roberts: "'Tell Mary——'" At this point the pealing of the pipe organ drowned out the rest of the message.

Mary is the name of Sir Arthur's first daughter.

Lady Doyle refused to make the rest of it public. She said, however, "It is a happy message; one that is cheering and encouraging."

Great interest had been roused by the meeting, for there had been a long discussion in advance of alleged plans made by Sir Arthur before his death to guarantee the genuineness of any messages he might be able to send to his family.

Pray for Clear Skies as Rain Kills Stock

MEXICO CITY, July 13.—(AP)—While the inhabitants of the village of Coatepec, in the federal district, were assembled in the plaza praying for relief from recent heavy rains a cloudburst today flooded the village, killed all the live stock and destroyed crops and homes.

BOSTON BLUE LAW PINCH HITS TO BEAT CUBS!

Calls Game in Ninth When Bruins Take Lead; McCarthy Will Get Heydler's Ruling

BY WAYNE K. OTTO.

BOSTON, July 13.—Strict enforcement of the new Massachusetts Sunday amusement law, which specifies that baseball play must cease at 6 o'clock, today resulted in a bitter controversy between the Cubs and the Braves over the result of the second game of a double header.

Police, swarming on the field sharply at 6 o'clock, stopped play in the last half of the ninth, when the score was Cubs, 4; Boston, 3. Boston had been leading, 3 to 0, at the end of the eighth inning.

CUBS STAGE RALLY.

The Cubs had staged a four-run rally to take the lead and the Braves had gotten men on second and third with one out when the game was stopped.

The official scorer immediately credited the game to Boston, applying the rule which declared the game reverted back to the last even inning because it terminated in less than the regulation time.

The last even inning was the eighth, in which Boston led 3 to 0. The Braves had won the first game, 2 to 1.

UMPIRE'S DECISION.

Later Umpire Scott decreed that under the new National League ruling, which states every inning must be finished, the game had not been officially finished and he would withhold decision until he had conferred with John Heydler, league president.

Boston claims to have won the game, 3 to 0, while Manager McCarthy of the Cubs insists it should be played off or played out from the point where it was stopped.

Heydler, in a long distance telephone conversation, said he would await a report on the agreement the umpires and managers had entered into before the second game was started.

He also evidenced keen interest on the "stalling" tactics of the Braves. Reports that it took twenty-one minutes to play the last one and one-third innings drew special attention from Heydler, who said the average time for an ordinary inning is twelve minutes.

M'CARTHY FILES PROTEST.

The abrupt and unsatisfactory ending climaxed twenty-five minutes of stalling, that may or may

Turn to Page 20, Column 5.

Church Padlocked for Dry Violation

JERSEY CITY, N. J., July 13.—(AP)—A building taken over by the congregation of the St. Paul Negro Baptist Church as a place of worship has been padlocked because of a liquor law violation by a former tenant. The congregation spent $2,000 in redecorating and refurnishing the building and was to have dedicated the church Saturday.

Hoover Periled by Woman's Wild Automobile Drive

Careening Car Crashes Into White House Motor Procession.

WASHINGTON, July 13.—(AP)—Careening past President Hoover's automobile and one occupied by secret service men, a car driven by a woman today crashed into the third car returning from the presidential lodge in Virginia. No one was injured.

The accident occurred near Falls Church, Va., about eight miles from the capital.

Lawrence Richey, secretary to the President; Capt. Joel T. Boone, White House physician; Mrs. Boone and their young daughter, Suzanne, and Mrs. Stark McMillan of Palo Alto, Cal., were in the White House car.

WOMAN DRIVER.

The other machine was driven by Mrs. Carolyn Stonebeach of New York. She was accompanied by her husband, her mother, Mr. Beach's mother and their young child.

No charges were preferred, Mr. Richey holding the accident was an incident of travel on crowded roads.

Pushing their way through dense traffic from the camp, about 125 miles from Washington, the presidential party was nearing home when the car driven by Mrs. Beach apparently got beyond control, Mr. Richey said.

HOOVER ESCAPES.

It cut from side to side as Mr. Hoover's machine, the first in line, passed, barely avoided the secret service car, which always trails the President closely, and then plunged head on into the side of the third car. Both machines were damaged.

President Hoover immediately ordered his car to stop and while Mrs. Hoover remained in it, he and Senators Allen of Kansas and Thomas of Idaho, who were riding in the first car, went back to assure themselves no one was hurt.

The occupants of the damaged car transferred to the personal automobile of Mrs. Hoover, which was trailing, driven by a chauffeur, and all came directly to the White House.

Last week-end a woman motorist dashed past the Hoover motorcade from behind, the first time such a stunt ever occurred.

The President does not use a motorcycle escort on his trips to the Virginia lodge.

Runs Beneath Gates; Train Kills Girl, 9

Running under the gates after a freight train passed, Marion Kickta, 9, of 212 Parkview road, Riverside, was killed yesterday by a Burlington passenger train at the Common road crossing. The girl's body was identified at a morgue by her father, Michael, employe of the Chicago Art Institute.

Excursionist Shot in Fight for Deck Chair

BEAR MOUNTAIN, N. Y., July 13.—(AP)—Joseph Zec, 28, of New York, was shot tonight on the excursion steamer Clermont by John Filomena, 30, also of New York, during an argument over a deck chair. Police rescued Filomena when the 2,000 aboard the boat attempted to lynch him.

THE WEATHER

MONDAY, JULY 14.

Sun rises 5:26 a. m.; sun sets 8:23 p. m. Moon rises 10:53 p. m., July 14.

Chicago and Vicinity—Today generally fair and continued cool; winds mostly moderate north to northeast. Tomorrow fair and slightly warmer.

Illinois—Today generally fair, somewhat cooler in extreme south portion. Tomorrow generally fair, slightly warmer in west and north portions.

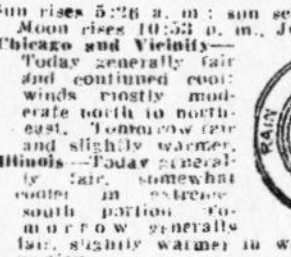

TEMPERATURES IN CHICAGO

HIGHEST, 8 P. M. (JULY 12).....94
LOWEST, 5 P. M. (JULY 13).....63

3 a. m. . 80	12 noon . . 65	9 p. m. . 63
4 a. m. . 77	1 p. m. . 64	10 p. m. . 62
5 a. m. . 76	2 p. m. . 64	Unofficial:
6 a. m. . 75	3 p. m. . 65	11 p. m. . 61
7 a. m. . 75	4 p. m. . 64	12 mnt. . 60
8 a. m. . 71	5 p. m. . 63	1 a. m. . 60
9 a. m. . 69	6 p. m. . 64	2 a. m. . 59
10 a. m. . 69	7 p. m. . 65	
11 a. m. . 67	8 p. m. . 66	

Mean temperature for twenty-four hours ended at 8 p. m. 78; normal for day 77; excess since January 1, 489 degrees. Barometer, 8 a. m., 29.78; 8 p. m., 29.91. Precipitation for twenty-four hours ended at 8 p. m., .01 inch; deficiency since January 1, 2.56 inches.

Official Weather Report on Page 21.

$25,000,000 TO SPEED START ON TRACTION WORK

Insull Employs Bankers as Syndicate Guides; Move to Keep Referendum Pledge

A significant step in Chicago's traction problem was announced yesterday by Samuel Insull.

Halsey, Stuart & Co., investment brokers, have been asked to guide the formation of a syndicate to raise $25,000,000 for rehabilitating the city's transportation system, Mr. Insull revealed.

AVERTS LEGAL TANGLE.

The step, it is further explained in the announcement, is being taken with a view toward hastening the consummation of pledges contained in the new traction ordinance, averting legal difficulties which must arise from the consolidation of properties.

It is hoped, Mr. Insull stated, that by raising the money through bankers, the work may be carried on immediately, thus providing work for the unemployed and creating confidence in the new transit system.

Alderman Joseph McDonough today will ask the local transportation committee for the approval of an ordinance authorizing the existing surface and elevated lines companies to spend "not to exceed $12,000,000" on an immediate building program.

LARGER LIMIT REPORTED.

However, it was reported yesterday that the companies will meet today with Alderman McDonough to discuss the proposal of increasing the $12,000,000 limit to at least $30,000,000.

Permission of the federal court will be necessary to the expenditure of any funds by the surface lines, since they are now in receivership. It is by no means certain that this consent will be quickly granted.

The "L" company, however, must clear no such obstacles and will proceed to build extensions to its loop and outlying platforms.

Mr. Insull stated that Halsey, Stuart & Co. also have been requested to become consolidation managers for the lines, and a plan has already been suggested.

Robert Ridgway, chief engineer of the New York City transit board, today will confer with Alderman McDonough and Attorney Walter L. Fisher on the matter of his appointment as consultant on subway plans.

Fight Lumber Fire as 10,000 Look On

A spectacular fire swept the Advance Window Frame Company plant at Division and Kilbourn sts. early today, causing a loss estimated at $100,000. More than 10,000 persons watched the firemen battle the flames that transformed the brick building into a roaring furnace.

Heavy smoke stifled the firemen, while the intense heat from stored lumber made it impossible for them to get close. They kept stubbornly at their task lest other industrial plants in the neighborhood be burned.

Deputy Fire Marshal Daniel J. Carmody announced that a searching investigation of the origin of the blaze would be made.

Airman Escapes From Tiger Jungle; Chum Left to Die

RANGOON, Burma, July 13.—(AP)—The tiger-haunted jungles of southern Burma have surrendered Jimmie Matthews, one of two British airmen lost for ten days on a flight from England to Australia.

His companion, Eric Hook, severely injured in their plane crash, is still missing.

After days of wandering through dense forests and swampy, malarial valleys, Matthews yesterday reached Prome, 160 miles north of Rangoon.

RESCUERS SEEK HOOK.

He said he had been forced to leave Hook behind. Sick and desperate, Hook had urged him to go on alone, chancing being left to die in the jungle. Matthews struggled on until he was picked up by natives.

A rescue party was sent from Padaung to find Hook, who, Matthews said, was dying.

The two aviators left London June 20 in an attempt to beat Bert Hinkler's record for the England-Australia flight.

CRASH IN JUNGLE.

According to Matthews' story, their plane crashed on the eastern slopes of the Arakan Yoma Range while they were crossing to the valley of the Irawadi.

The spot where they crashed was swampy and wild and infested with tigers and other jungle beasts. To the north was a region inhabited by hill tribes, known to the Burmese as "demon worshipers."

Hook and Matthews had only a small supply of food and very little drinking water.

STUMBLE ON FOR WEEK.

Hampered by Hook's injuries, they stumbled down the steep slopes of the range, following for seven days a mountain stream. Many times Matthews picked up his injured comrade and carried him, but as Hook grew weaker, he gave in to Hook's request and went on alone to seek help.

Hunt Youth After Shooting at Party

Brighton Park police yesterday began a search for William Hughes, 3640 S. Paulina st., accused of shooting another youth in the leg following a drinking party Saturday night. The victim, Walter Jedlowski, 19, of 3758 S. Honore st., named Hughes as his assailant.

Yacht Rum Suspect Dies From Wounds

OSSINING, N. Y., July 13.—Philip Pescitello of Detroit, shot Wednesday when state troopers and federal agents arrested twenty-two men unloading liquor from a yacht in the Hudson at Scarborough, died today.

Aguinaldo Weds; Cousin Officiates

MANILA, July 14.—(AP)—Gen. Emilio Aguinaldo today married Miss Maria Agoncillo, 40. The wedding was performed by Father P. Aguinaldo, cousin of the general.

Girl and Outlaw's Aid Seized; Police Surround Hideout

Posse Lies in Wait for Desperado at Resort.

SLAYER FLEES

Slips Through Fingers of Village Police Chief.

Fifteen Chicago detectives, reinforced by Michigan state police and deputy sheriffs, yesterday raided a cottage in the woods of central Michigan, known to have been for three months the hiding place of Fred Burke, murderer, bank robber and one of the most "wanted" men in police history.

Burke apparently had slipped away only an hour before the raid. But two important personages were seized in the place.

Blonde Seized

One is a blonde girl who has been living at the cottage where Burke has been hiding.

The other may show the way for the ultimate capture of Burke and probably will provide solution for the most recent gang killing, that of Thomas Bonner.

He is William H. Smith—a name which Burke sometimes adopted as an alias—and he operates a malt and hops shop at 818 Division av., Grand Rapids.

He is supposed to have been Burke's companion in the hide-out. His capture was regarded as highly significant. With his grudgingly-given agreement he was rushed to Chicago for questioning. Chief of Detectives John Norton began questioning Smith when the party arrived here at 1:45 this morning.

The girl, who is pretty, identified herself as Caroline Burkle and said she worked in a Grand Rapids department store. Beyond making the admission that she is 20 years old, she would tell nothing.

Forest Lair Raided

The cottage raided is in a forest-sheltered spot on the edge of Hess Lake, a mile from the village of Newaygo and about forty miles north of Grand Rapids.

Within the officers found two rifles of .30-.30 caliber, some ammunition and a quantity of beer, wine and alcohol.

That Burke departed shortly before the arrival of the raiding force was established by the police chief of Newaygo. About noon yesterday a man, whom he recognized as an occupant for the last three months of the Hess Lake cottage, asked where he could cross the route of a bus line to Muskegon. He was told that the nearest point was Casnovia, twenty miles away. The man obtained auto transportation immediately to Casnovia.

Identifies Outlaw

When shown photographs of Burke the chief became excited. He shouted:

"That's the man. And I've seen him almost every day for three months and just a little while ago I let him slip through my fingers."

Officials at Casnovia and Muskegon were notified at once to be on the alert for the fugitive.

Smith drove up to the cottage at the hour of his capture in a Cadillac automobile, which police declare they can identify as Burke's. The engine numbers had been tampered with and, most important of all, the car bore the Illinois license number 1-052-358.

This is significant. The number was issued for a Packard car owned by Philip R. McDonnell, a Chicago druggist living at 501 W. Seventy-ninth st.

McDonnell, alleged to be Burke's

Thinking Things Over With Calvin Coolidge

BY CALVIN COOLIDGE.

NORTHAMPTON, Mass., July 13.—The economic progress not only of our own country but of the world at large has been retarded by three factors of uncertainty—the German bond issue, the tariff revision and the long session of the Congress. All of these have now been removed.

Business can stand anything better than uncertainty. A bad situation it can write off and then start anew, but when confronted by the unknown it can only remain inactive. The universal oversubscription to the German loan was most encouraging. It shows the financial world has confidence in the Young plan and in the credit stability of Germany.

It was also a gratifying illustration of a broad desire to restore Germany and, on our part, of a continuing purpose to help Europe. The worst and the best are now fairly well known about the tariff. The Congress will cease from troubling for a period of five months.

International finance and domestic legislation have reached a more certain position. Certainty is the basis of business confidence.

CAT WORTH $5,000 —WHEN IT'S SHOT!

LEXINGTON, Ky., July 13.—(AP)—A dentist who shot a tomcat which disturbed his slumbers with nocturnal aries on the back fence has been made defendant in a $5,000 damage suit brought by the pet's spinster owner.

Miss Mary Brent Hutchcraft charges that her neighbor, Dr. W. W. Aylor, inflicted on "Jerry" a "severe and dangerous wound," resulting in great trouble to his owner.

Accompanying the damage suit was a petition for a restraining order to prevent the dentist from further molesting Jerry.

GRABS EXTORTION MONEY; SEIZED

Charles A. Peck, a grain broker with offices at 323 S. La Salle st., dropped a package of money on the Seventh st. bridge to the outer drive last night, as directed in an extortion letter. Otto Tanis of 4447 Ellis av. picked it up. Sergts. Harry Miller and Harry Lang arrested Tanis. The package, a decoy, contained $1 instead of the $500 demanded.

Mr. Peck, who lives at 1020 E. Forty-eighth st., received two threatening letters last week. Each was a demand for $500 and contained a threat that the broker and his family would be "done away with."

Tanis is being held at the detective bureau.

HERALD CHICAGO AND EXAMINER

FINAL

50th YEAR No. 78 Registered in U. S. Patent Office C★★★★ MONDAY, AUGUST 11, 1930 Telephone Randolph 2121 TWO PARTS. PRICE 3 CENTS

MORAN OUSTED IN GANG TRUCE

Today

The Ten-Month Year. Shocking Air Disaster. Keep Your Mainspring. One White, One Black Kid.

—BY ARTHUR BRISBANE—

(© 1930, by King Features Syndicate, Inc.)

THE IMPORTANT thing in this land is business, and the fact that Ford is on the front page oftener than Lindbergh proves it. Mr. Ford's newest idea is "the ten-month year," every workman to have two full months to rest in Summer, which is the worst season for factory work.

To carry out that program all ten months' workers must learn how to save. But squirrels do it, hoarding nuts; red Indians did it, drying pemmican. American labor would learn to do it.

At first the factory might withhold one-sixth of the wages, distributing the amount, plus interest, in weekly installments during the two months' holiday. Or possibly, NOT probably, employers might add one-sixth to the usual wages for vacation distribution.

There is involved in the plan this question, "How would two months' leisure affect the minds of workers?"

The cloak and suit industry, one of the biggest in the nation, has long compelled workers to take off several months without pay each year, sometimes almost half the year.

The men and women are driven hard during the working season, then compelled to be idle.

The result, according to some employers, is communism, anarchism, class hatred and similar by-products of idleness.

It would be wise somehow to supply weekly incomes during the two months' vacation. Then, with Tom Thumb golf, motoring, swimming, radio, etc., there would be little dangerous thinking.

The average mortal thinks only when compelled to, rarely when he has an assured income. Study the sons of rich men if you doubt it.

Yesterday's newspapers reported a most shocking airplane disaster. In threatening weather a pilot in Chicago took two girls up for a sightseeing ride.

They were last seen, with lightning flashing about their plane, headed for an enormous gas tank in the thick of the city. The plane plunged through the tank roof, made of steel, carrying the doomed passengers down through the gas chamber into a forty-foot well filled with water at the bottom of the tank.

Flying, and especially carrying passengers under any but safe conditions, should be strictly regulated by law, with severe punishment for recklessness.

Dr. Thomas, president of Rutgers University, advises 200,000 young men and women about to enter American colleges to "leave their conceit at home." The doctor's advice is sound, if properly understood, but it is not to be taken literally. What we call "conceit" is half-developed ambition.

To tell a young man to leave at home the driving power of conceit would be like telling a watch to leave its mainspring at home. You need conceit, which means belief in yourself, to keep you going. "Conceit is not the way to popularity, least of all on a college campus," says the doctor.

On the other hand, popularity on a college campus is of no great importance later in life.

When young Bonaparte sulked in corners, at French military school, despising comrades that laughed at his Corsican accent, he was not popular. But later, as Emperor, he made some of them marshals and had others shot.

"Courage lost, everything lost, better thou wert never born," says Goethe, who had plenty of conceit always and stands third among the great writers of the world.

Conceit is a form of mental courage. The wise young man or woman does not parade it, but clings to it until cold reality and failure wipe it out.

New York City enjoys another of the prize fights that pay profits to politicians.

A small Cuban Negro, "Kid" Chocolate, weighing ten pounds less than his white British opponent, "Kid" Berg, was declared loser.

Thirty-five thousand intellectual Americans paid $150,000 to see the battle and started separate fights of their own, arguing about the decision. Those that bet on the Negro, hitherto undefeated, thought they had been cheated, which was probable. There will be another fight between the two "Kids," more betting, more arguing, and perhaps cheating, and unboubted 35,000 more intelligent Americans will pay $15[illegible] again.

Hoover Will Lend $342,000,000 to Drought Victims

Co-Operatives Are Promised Big Fund.

LAYS AID PLANS

Promised Rains May Lessen Task.

BY FULTON LEWIS,

Herald and Examiner-Universal Staff Correspondent.

WASHINGTON, Aug. 10.—With the weather bureau holding out its first hope for general rains, President Hoover today completed the groundwork of his plan for extending relief to the nation's drought-stricken area.

Working in the seclusion of his Rapidan camp, the President devoted the entire day to that work.

Details of setting the machinery in motion await issuance of the Agriculture Department's special report from all county agents in the affected areas tomorrow, and the conference with the governors of the drought states on Thursday.

DETAILS OF PLAN.

In general, according to word reaching here from the Rapidan camp, the President's plan provides:

FIRST—Organization of emergency associations in the drought-swept counties through which the farm board can advance long term credits to farmers for purchase of feed and food. The board has $342,000,000 upon which it can uraw for this purpose.

SECOND—Setting up of a transportation board to direct the activities of the railroads in conveying feed, food and water to the affected regions. The roads already have started to file reduced rates.

THIRD—An effective organization to prevent food profiteering, with the Department of Justice taking a hand where the interstate movement is involved.

With the exception of Governor Weaver of Nebraska, all of the twelve governors has notified the White House today that they will be in Washington on Thursday. At that time the President will suggest that each appoint a "rehabilitation commissioner" to have charge of the work in his state.

EXPECT RAINS SOON.

Meanwhile the weather bureau for the first time was optimistic for early relief in drought conditions throughout the area, particularly in the Middle West.

But even general rains at this stage would not lessen the gigantic relief task facing the government.

Details of the "railroad administration" to be set up will be worked out tomorrow at a conference with A. P. Thom, general counsel of the Association of Railway Executives.

Directory of Features

35,000 HEAR EMMERSON AT GUARD REVIEW

Illinois Proud of Its Militia, Says Governor; Pays High Tribute to Dead Heroes

BY LIEUT. WM. WESTLAKE,

Herald and Examiner-Universal Staff Correspondent.

CAMP GRANT, Ill., Aug. 10.—Before a crowd of 35,000 at Bell Bowl today Governor Emmerson, commander-in-chief of the Illinois National Guard, praised the militiamen for service to the state and nation.

The governor said:

"This is the best encampment, judged from the standpoint of training and numbers of officers and enlisted men, in the history of the Thirty-third Division. My inspection of the division this morning makes me prouder than ever to be its commander."

The governor lauded Adj. Gen. Carlos E. Black for transforming the camp grounds into the most beautiful national guard grounds anywhere.

PRAISES GUARD MORALE.

To Maj. Gen. Roy D. Keehn, commanding general of the division, he gave praise because of the guard's high morale.

The governor declared:

"Illinois is proud of you, just as it is proud of its record in every hour of need, when the nation, to protect itself, has called on its men to rally round the flag.

"Perhaps no one, not connected with the national guard, realized the sacrifices which you must make in order to serve the state and to keep up the framework of the national defense."

The United States is not a militaristic nation, Governor Emmerson explained, but to perpetuate principles of human liberty it is necessary to train its boys and men in the essentials of national defense.

Governor Emmerson paid high tribute to Illinois world war veterans, saying:

"We honor them here today, and especially those who never returned. Let us consecrate ourselves to the perpetuation of the ideals for which they fought."

CHIPPERFIELD SPEAKS.

Col. B. M. Chipperfield, judge advocate of the state guard staff, introduced the governor. He declared that under the leadership of Gen. Keehn, the National Guard has reached its highest standard. He added:

"You have the largest national guard in the United States and it is no idle boast to say the best. Your progress in training has met with the approval of the governor, your officers and those of the United States Army."

Today was "Visitors' Day" at the camp. The program included military exhibitions.

Convicts Save 4, One a Police Chief, and Return to Cells

Universal Service.

OSSINING, N. Y., Aug. 10.—Faced with the opportunity to save four lives, a Sing Sing official broke a hard and fast rule today and permitted four convicts to go outside the prison walls. They rescued four persons from a sinking boat.

Most of the 2,200 prisoners were in the yard. The atmosphere was tense until the four convicts were back with those they had saved.

The rescued were Chief of Police J. D. Rosa of the New York Central Railroad Lines, of Chappaqua, and wife; her brother, Albert Graff of Chappaqua, and wife.

The hero prisoners were Irving Brown, Joseph Oates, Anthony Triano and David Weller, all short-term convicts. They belong to the prison fire department.

On Sergeant of the Guard Alfred Mollitore rested the decision of whether the lives should be saved. Possibly he was guided by the fact that two men were drowned three years ago because convicts were not allowed to rescue them.

As the guards trained machine guns on the men massed in the yard the four slipped through a gate in the fence that separates the prison from the Hudson River.

As hundreds of convicts at the fence watched the four ran toward the water. Two jumped in and the other two, using their hooks, helped to keep the rapidly filling rowboat from sinking.

Note in Bottle Tells of Lake Ship Adrift

Floating in a bottle, a note was found on the lake shore at Gary yesterday. It read: "S.O.S. Emma Press. Drifting in Lake Michigan ten miles north of Gary. We lost our rudder. August 9, 5 p. m. John Young." The Empress could not be identified in Chicago yachting circles. Michigan City coastguardsmen could not locate the vessel.

Norman Thomas Seeks House Seat

NEW YORK, Aug. 10.—Norman Thomas, guiding genius of the Socialist Party, threw his hat in the political ring again today. He will seek the Socialist nomination for Congress in the sixth district in Brooklyn. Thomas will run on a platform of unemployment relief and national referendum on prohibition.

Thinking Things Over With Calvin Coolidge

BY CALVIN COOLIDGE.

NORTHAMPTON, Mass., Aug. 10.—Good health is one of our chief national assets. Yet, in spite of all the progress that has been made in the science of hygiene, the yearly losses in this country from the ravages of disease run into many hundreds of millions of dollars.

The discouraging feature of the situation is that much of this is needless. With the present knowledge of medicine, surgery and dentistry, and the possibilities of preventive measures, oftentimes illness is only personal carelessness.

People give altogether too little attention to their health. They neglect to get sufficient fresh air and exercise. They are not careful enough of their diet. They overstrain their physical and nervous systems with disastrous results.

Because illness makes us a liability to ourselves, our family and our community, we all have a personal obligation to keep well. To neglect the health is one of the most wasteful things a person can do. It is a violation of a moral duty. While both state and national agencies are alert to preserve health, the real success of all their efforts lies in the vigilance of the individual. If we should all think and try to live healthful lives we would greatly increase the power of the nation.

Copyright, McClure Newspaper Syndicate.

Hoover Is 56; Cuts Cake; King Felicitates Him

ORANGE, Va., Aug. 10.—Amid the quietness of his mountain camp, President Hoover today observed his fifty-sixth birthday in simple fashion.

The occasion was marked only by a birthday cake with fifty-six candles at dinner and the presentation of gifts to the President by Mrs. Hoover and other week-end guests.

President Hoover received a message from King George. It read:

"It is with great pleasure, Mr. President, that I offer you on the occasion of your birthday my warmest felicitations, together with my sincere good wishes for your continued health and happiness."

PLANES COLLIDE IN AIR; ONE DEAD

TERRE HAUTE, Ind., Aug. 10.—One pilot was killed and another fatally injured in an airplane collision at Davis Garden, just south of this city.

Bernard Allen of Terre Haute and Arthur Foulkes, also a resident here, were two of five contestants in a race. Several hundred feet up Allen's ship rose directly under that of Foulkes and brushed the upper wing against Foulkes' landing gear.

Allen's plane sped just ahead of Foulkes' ship, executed a complete loop and crashed nose-down into the cockpit of the other plane.

The planes came down a tangle of wreckage. Allen was killed instantly. Foulkes, unconscious, was hurried to a hospital here. Surgeons said he could not survive.

Women Ask Total Disarming of World

WASHINGTON, Aug. 10.—(Universal.)—Calling for "total and universal disarmament," the American section of the Women's International League for Peace and Freedom today mailed petitions to its membership.

Speedboat Hits Buoy; Sinks; Youth Killed

LAKEVILLE, Minn., Aug. 10.—(AP)—Herbert MacLaughlin, 18, of Watertown, S. D., was killed today when a speedboat he was piloting on Lake Marion, near here, struck a buoy at a turn and sank.

Snow in New York Breaks 'Hot' Spell!

PLATTSBURGH, N. Y., Aug. 10.—(AP)—It snowed in the eastern Adirondacks tonight. Travelers from Elizabethtown reported a snow flurry lasting several minutes between Lewis and Rock.

Girl, 11, Killed When Gunmen Fight Duel

NEW YORK, Aug. 10.—(AP)—A school girl, 11, was killed today by a stray bullet when two gunmen emptied their weapons at each other and then fled.

THE WEATHER

MONDAY, AUGUST 11, 1930.

Sun rises 5:34 a. m.; sun sets 7:56 p. m. Moon rises 9:19 p. m. August 11.

Chicago and Vicinity—Fair and continued cool today; gentle northwest winds. Tomorrow fair and slightly warmer.

Illinois—Fair and continued cool today. Tomorrow fair with slowly rising temperature.

TEMPERATURES IN CHICAGO

MAXIMUM, 8 P. M. (Aug. 9) 72
MINIMUM, 5 A. M. 61

3 a. m.	70	12 noon	70	10 p. m.	67
4 a. m.	69	1 p. m.	71	11 p. m.	67
5 a. m.	69	2 p. m.	70	Unofficial.	
6 a. m.	68	3 p. m.	70	11 p. m.	67
7 a. m.	68	4 p. m.	71	Midnight	66
8 a. m.	67	5 p. m.	69	1 a. m.	65
9 a. m.	69	6 p. m.	69	2 a. m.	65
10 a. m.	70	7 p. m.	68		
11 a. m.	70	8 p. m.	68		

Mean temperature for twenty-four hours ended at 8 p. m., 70; normal for day, 72; excess in temperature since January 1, 506 degrees.

Barometer, 8 a. m., 30.13; 8 p. m., 30.14. Deficiency of precipitation since January 1, 3.50 inches.

Other Weather Reports on Page 25.

TOKYO FLIERS FORCED DOWN AT VANCOUVER

Clogged Air Line Ends Hop for White Horse Soon After Departure From Tacoma

VANCOUVER, B. C., Aug. 10. (AP)—Bob Wark and Edward L. Brown, Seattle aviators, were forced down here today on the first leg of their flight from Tacoma to Tokyo.

Two main gas lines became "airbound" and the fliers were forced to bring their biplane to a quick landing.

With the exception of the gas lines, the motor and ship functioned perfectly, the fliers said. They said they would take off tomorrow morning for White Horse.

(Picture on Page 2.)

TACOMA, Wash., Aug. 10.—(AP)—The Pacific Era, Fokker biplane with Robert Wark and Eddie Brown, young Seattle aviators, as co-pilots, soared off the runway at Tacoma field at 10:33 a. m., Chicago time, today on the first leg of a scheduled four-stop flight to Tokyo.

Just before the takeoff the fliers were advised ideal weather prevailed along the entire route of the first leg, scheduled to end at White Horse, Yukon Territory, 1,200 miles north of Tacoma, tonight.

Wark said he would land his big red Fokker biplane at Hazelton, B. C., if unfavorable weather should be encountered.

Wark said he expected to negotiate the distance in about twelve hours.

With Wark at the controls the Pacific Era had little difficulty in getting off the ground, despite its load of 400 gallons of gasoline.

From White Horse the pilots expect to reach Tokyo via Fairbanks and Nome, Alaska, and Petropavlovsk, Siberia. From White Horse to Fairbanks is about 800 miles; Nome is 500 miles farther on, and the distance from Nome to Petropavlovsk is about 1,400 miles.

Wark said he planned only brief stops for refueling and rest. The fliers expected to negotiate the entire distance in five or six days.

[Robert Wark's own story of the flight will be found on Page 2.]

Lindbergh to Attend Institute of Politics

WILLIAMSTOWN, Mass., Aug. 10.—(AP)—Col. Charles A. Lindbergh plans to attend a session of the Institute of Politics here this week, it was announced today by Edward P. Warner, chairman of the round table on "The Political Aspects of Aerial Navigation." Mrs. Lindbergh is expected to attend the conference.

Shot Dead in Street Row; Onlooker Hurt

In a street quarrel with an unidentified man late last night, Sam Siciliano, 1006 Cambridge st., was shot to death. One assassin's bullets struck Joe R. Breader, 1403 Larrabee st., a pedestrian, in the foot. He was taken to the Henrotin Hospital. Siciliano was a laundry worker.

BURGLARS LOOT M'CULLOCHS' HOME

The residence of Attorney Frank H. McCulloch and of his wife, Mrs. Catherine Waugh McCulloch, at 2236 Orrington av., Evanston, was burglarized last night during the absence of the couple.

The thieves obtained a brooch worth $1,000, pendants purchased during a tour of India and most of Mr. and Mrs. McCulloch's apparel.

An hour later a fire alarm was sounded from the residence of Walter A. Uphoff, 635 Judson av. Firemen found the house had been ransacked, after which the thieves had fired the house. Damage was confined to one room. Mr. Uphoff and his family were away.

Newberry Given North Side Vice Rule by Capone

Lingle and Zuta Slayings Clear Way for Peace.

SPLIT RACKETS

Hoodlums Look to Happy Days; 'All for Al' Now.

George ("Bugs") Moran has abdicated as ruler of the North Side gangsters, leaving the throne to his one-time aid, Teddy Newberry—as a result of a long series of involved machinations and murders, including the assassinations of Alfred ("Jake") Lingle, Tribune reporter, and Jack Zuta, trafficker in vice and booze and gambling.

This was learned yesterday by officers investigating the Lingle-Zuta killings.

Capone Comes Back

Newberry has taken up his new dominion, with headquarters at the Lantern Cafe, Broadway and Waveland av., with the backing of the notorious "Scarface Al" Capone, now back in Chicago apparently with a stronger grip than ever upon the underworld.

With the enthronement of Newberry this word was passed along through the ranks of liquor traffickers, gamblers, vice purveyors and racketeers:

"The 'heat' is off the Lingle killing. It was just another one of those things. Happy days are here again."

Gangs Make Peace

First definite negotiations for the new arrangement were made a week ago last Friday night—almost at the hour of Zuta's death—when Capone and other gangsters held a truce meeting in Cicero.

The final touches for the agreement, according to the investigators, were made a few days later when Capone summoned the faithful to a good-will jollification at the Lexington Hotel.

Zuta was dead. Moran, his forces decimated by deaths and desertions, had left Chicago indefinitely, sojourning for the time in Minnesota. Perhaps, investigators say, the Capone council decided Moran might be permitted to handle some of his minor rackets as a portion of the cleaners and dyers "organization," but that was to be judged by his future attitude.

Divide Rackets

As for the Aiellos, allies of Moran and Zuta, they would retain their Sicilian dominance, but labor in the consolidated Capone vineyard. Their willingness to do this was signified months ago when Capone returned from his sojourn in a Pennsylvania penitentiary.

Thus gangland, having eliminated two troublesome attaches, both of whom had begun to show too

Girl and 2 Women Stricken by Poison in Suicide Soda

Three women were stricken last night in a strange case of bichloride of mercury poisoning at the Graves Nut Shop, 3145 Logan blvd.

A young girl entered the shop and asked for a pineapple soda. She took only a swallow of it and left the store.

FEARS DRINK IS BAD.

Mrs. Hope Dwelly, 50, of 3056 Logan blvd., the waitress who had served the girl, observed that she had taken but a small portion of the soda. Thinking it had not been made properly, she called the manager, Mrs. Anna Graves.

Mrs. Graves and the waitress both drank of the soda, pronounced it satisfactory and dismissed the matter.

A few moments later, both suffered serious headaches and finally collapsed. Dr. Benjamin Milton of 3040 Logan blvd., was called.

He tested the remainder of the drink and stated that it contained a large amount of bichloride of mercury. The women were given antidotes.

A short distance away, West Park Policeman Joseph Bjestian saw a girl lying on the steps of the Logan monument in the center of Logan Park. She was taken unconscious to the Belmont Hospital, where it was learned that she was the girl who had been served the soda.

IDENTIFY GIRL BUYER.

She was identified as Miss Agnes Orlikowski, 19, of 2532 N. Mozart st., the daughter of Policeman Barney Orlikowski of the Shakespeare av. station.

Police believed that the girl, despondent for some reason, had attempted to take her life and had put poison tablets in the drink.

National Auto Race Head Killed by Car

STERLING, Ill., Aug. 10.—(AP)—Trying to keep spectators from pushing onto the track, Robert Whalen, president of the National Automobile Racing Association, was instantly killed here today by a swerving racing car. Mrs. Whalen witnessed the accident.

U. S. Agent Slain in Texas Border Fight

LAFERIA, Tex., Aug. 10.—(AP)—Burt Ellis, 35, United States customs officer, and Margarito Rodriguez, a Mexican, were killed and another Mexican probably fatally wounded as the result of a new outbreak of border gun fighting here.

Captain Disappears From Ship at Sea

BOSTON, Aug. 10.—(AP)—The steamer San Gil docked here today without her captain, Leslie E. Large of London and Boston, who disappeared on the early morning of August 1 while the steamer was en route from Havana, Cuba, to Castilla, Honduras.

FOILED BANDITS KILL FATHER; WOUND SON

A father was killed and his son wounded by Negro bandits last night when they attempted to save their cousin from a holdup.

John Standwick, 50, of 130 Swan st., the father, and his son, Stephen, 21, were walking past an alley near Forty-seventh st. and the Rock Island tracks when they saw their cousin, David Chalko, 53, with his hands in the air.

They advanced into the alley and the Negroes ran.

Under the railroad tracks, the bandits turned and fired. Standwick, the elder, fell, mortally wounded in the abdomen and head. Steve was struck in the thigh.

Style Contest Prize Winners!

Names of winners in the Marion Davies Style Contest, which attracted nation-wide interest, are announced on page 6 of this issue of the Herald and Examiner. Included are the winners' prize letters and much pithy and illuminating discussion of modern fashions.

Generals Die in Bed *Great War Story Starts in The Herald and Examiner* **Next Sunday**

FIND MISSING GIRL DROWNED

NIGHT EDITION

LOS ANGELES EVENING HERALD — AN INDEPENDENT NEWSPAPER

Reg. U. S. Pat. Office. Copyright, 1929, by Evening Herald Publishing Company

The Evening Herald Grows Just Like Los Angeles

VOL. LV — THREE CENTS — Two Sections Section A — TUESDAY, OCTOBER 14, 1930 — Hotels and Trains Five Cents — THREE CENTS — NO. 297

LATEST NEWS

WOMAN IN CAT-E'R CUTTING CREATES SCENE

After creating a sensation in Municipal Judge Ellis A. Eagan's court late today by crying hysterically and shouting that she "would take her case to the supreme court," Mrs. Martha Peterson, accused of cutting the ears of a cat because it cast a curse upon her, was taken to the psychopathic ward of the General hospital for observation. Her trial was continued pending an alienists' report on her sanity.

HOOVER CONFERS WITH N. Y. STOCK HEADS

WASHINGTON, Oc. 14.—Richard Whitney, president, and Allen Lindley, vice president, of the New York Stock exchange, were visitors at the White House on Sunday night, and discussed the present situation with President Hoover, it was learned today. It was learned that the President and the stock exchange officers discussed the matter of short selling on the exchange.

Last of Julian Cases Dismissed

L.A. OFFICERS SHOOT DOWN FLEAGLE, OUTLAW LEADER

LAST MAN OF 'WOLF PACK' IN MURDERS TRAPPED

By EUGENE COUGHLIN

His gun pumping a futile rain of bullets and his lips twisted in a defiant snarl, "Little Jake" Fleagle, leader and lone survivor of the notorious Fleagle "wolf pack" of western bandits and killers, was captured and wounded, probably fatally, at Branson, Mo., today.

Fleagle was surprised on the railway station platform of the little town, nestling in the Ozark mountains, and elected to "shoot it out" with peace officers, heavily armed and prepared for the savage gun battle.

The outlaw fell with a bullet in his abdomen—a bullet fired by Detective Lieutenant Harry Wilde of Los Angeles.

OPERATE ON BANDIT

And while Dr. J. G. Mitchell of Branson was performing an operation to save the bandit's life so that the state may claim it, dispatches revealed that Los Angeles officers had run Fleagle to earth after five months of patient and persistent detective work.

With Wilde when the chase ended were Detective Lieutenant Chester Lloyd and Postal Inspector Edward Cline of Los Angeles.

The trio led the most formidable posse of officers ever assembled to trap a lone criminal. All told, 23 detectives, deputy sheriffs, postal inspectors and private investigators were in the party that brought the outlaw to bay.

FACES HANGING

If Fleagle survives his wound, he can expect the same fate meted out to his brother, Ralph Fleagle, and two other members of the pack of killers. They were hanged at Canon City, Colo., last July for the most cold-blooded murders since the James and Younger gangs rode wild—the robbery of the First National bank at Lamar, Colo., on May 22, 1928, and its attendant killings.

They killed the bank president,

(CONTINUED ON PAGE EIGHTEEN)

Last of 'Wolf Pack' Snared

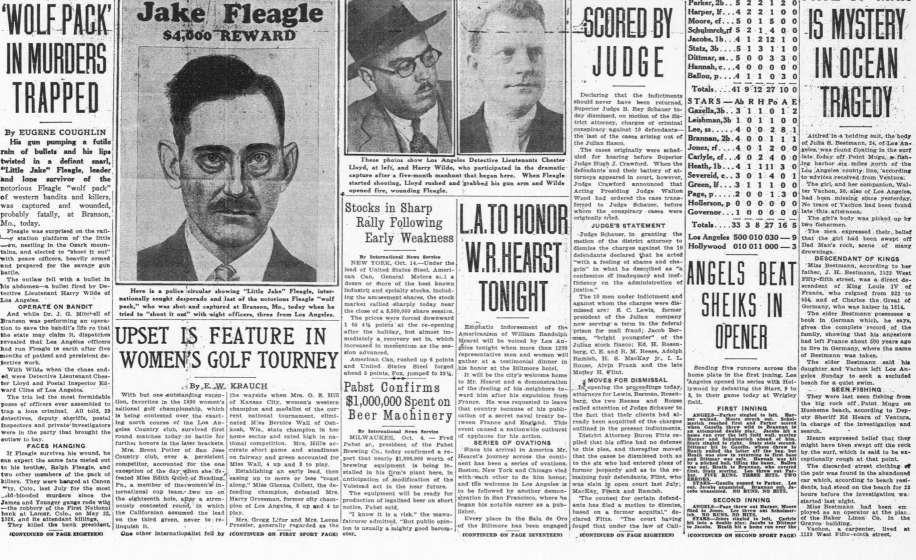

Here is a police circular showing "Little Jake" Fleagle, internationally sought desperado and last of the notorious Fleagle "wolf pack," who was shot and captured at Branson, Mo., today when he tried to "shoot it out" with eight officers, three from Los Angeles.

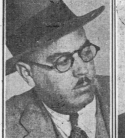

These photos show Los Angeles Detective Lieutenants Chester Lloyd, at left, and Harry Wilde, who participated in the dramatic capture after a five-month manhunt that began here. When Fleagle started shooting, Lloyd rushed and grabbed his gun arm and Wilde opened fire, wounding Fleagle.

UPSET IS FEATURE IN WOMEN'S GOLF TOURNEY

By E. W. KRAUCH

With but one outstanding exception, favorites in the 1930 women's national golf championship, which is being contested over the exacting north course of the Los Angeles Country club, survived first round matches today to battle for further honors in the later brackets.

Mrs. Brent Potter of San Jose Country club, ever a persistent competitor, accounted for the one exception of the day when she defeated Miss Edith Quier of Reading, Pa., a member of the women's international cup team, two up on the eighteenth hole, after a strenuously contested round, in which the Californian assumed the lead on the third green, never to relinquish it.

One other internationalist fell by the wayside when Mrs. O. S. Hill of Kansas City, women's western champion and medalist of the current national tournament, eliminated Miss Bernice Wall of Oshkosh, Wis., state champion in her home sector and rated high in national competition. Mrs. Hill's accurate short game and steadiness on fairway and green accounted for Miss Wall, 4 up and 3 to play.

Establishing an early lead, then easing up to more or less "coast along," Miss Glenna Collett, the defending champion, defeated Mrs. Harry Grossman, former city champion of Los Angeles, 6 up and 4 to play.

Mrs. Gregg L:fur and Mrs. Leona Pressler, generally regarded as the

(CONTINUED ON FIRST SPORT PAGE)

Stocks in Sharp Rally Following Early Weakness

By International News Service

NEW YORK, Oct. 14.—Under the lead of United States Steel, American Can, General Motors and a dozen or more of the best known industril and spcialty stocks, including the amusement shares, the stock market rallied sharply today near the close of a 3,500,000 share session.

The prices were forced downward 1 to 4½ points at the re-opening after the holiday, but almost immediately a recovery set in, which increased in momentum as the session advanced.

American Can, rushed up 6 points and United States Steel forged ahead 5 points, Fox, jumped to 39¼.

Pabst Confirms $1,000,000 Spent on Beer Machinery

By International News Service

MILWAUKEE, Oct. 4. — Fred Pabst sr., president of the Pabst Brewing Co., today confirmed a report that nearly $1,000,000 worth of brewing equipment is being installed in his firm's plant here, in anticipation of modification of the Volstead act in the near future.

The equipment will be ready for production of legalized beer on short notice, Pabst said.

"I know it is a risk," the manufatcurer admitted. "But public opinion is usually a mighty good barometer.

L.A. TO HONOR W. R. HEARST TONIGHT

Emphatic indorsement of the Americanism of William Randolph Hearst will be voiced by Los Angeles tonight when more than 1290 representative men and women will gather at a testimonial dinner in his honor at the Biltmore hotel.

It will be the city's welcome home to Mr. Hearst and a demonstration of the feeling of his neighbors toward him after his expulsion from France. He was requested to leave that country because of his publication of a secret naval treaty between France and England. This event caused a nationwide outburst of applause for his action.

SERIES OF OVATIONS

Since his arrival in America Mr. Hearst's journey across the continent has been a series of ovations. Boston, New York and Chicago vied with each other to do him honor, and the welcome in Los Angeles is to be followed by another demonstration in San Francisco, where he began his notable career as a publisher.

Every place in the Sala de Oro of the Biltmore has been engaged

(CONTINUED ON PAGE SEVENTEEN)

INDICTMENTS SCORED BY JUDGE

Declaring that the indictments should never have been returned, Superior Judge B. Rey Schauer today dismissed, on motion of the district attorney, charges of criminal conspiracy against 10 defendants—the last of the cases arising out of the Julian fiasco.

The cases originally were scheduled for hearing before Superior Judge Hugh J. Crawford. When the defendants and their battery of attorneys appeared in court, however, Judge Crawford announced that Acting Presiding Judge Walton Wood had ordered the case transferred to Judge Schauer, before whom the conspiracy cases were originally tried.

JUDGE'S STATEMENT

Judge Schauer, in granting the motion of the district attorney to dismiss the charges against the 10 defendants declared that he acted "with a feeling of shame and chagrin" in what he described as "a confession of inadequacy and inefficiency on the administration of justice."

The 10 men under indictment and against whom the charges were dismissed are: S. C. Lewis, former president of the Julian company now serving a term in the federal prison for mail fraud; Jacob Berman, "bright youngster" of the Julian stock fiasco; Ed. H. Rosenberg, C. E. and R. M. Reese, Adolph Ramish, H. S. MacKay jr., I. L. Rouse, Alvin Frank and the late Motley H. Flint.

MOVES FOR DISMISSAL

In opening the proceedings today, attorneys for Lewis, Berman, Rosenberg, the two Reeses and Rouse called attention of Judge Schauer to the fact that their clients had already been acquitted of the charges outlined in the present indictments.

District Attorney Buron Fitts replied that his office had no defense to this plea, and thereafter moved that the cases be dismissed both as to the six who had entered pleas of former jeopardy and as to the remaining four defendants, Flint, who was slain in open court last July; MacKay, Frank and Ramish.

"The counsel for certain defendants has filed a motion to dismiss, based on a former acquital," declared Fitts. "The court having found that under the law of Cali-

(CONTINUED ON PAGE EIGHTEEN)

Stars Box Score

ANGELS—	Ab	R	H	Po	A	E
Parker, 2b..	5	2	2	1	2	0
Harper, lf...	4	2	2	1	0	0
Moore, cf...	5	0	1	5	0	0
Schulmrch,rf	5	2	1	4	0	0
Jacobs, 1b...	4	1	2	12	1	0
Statz, 3b....	5	1	3	1	1	0
Dittmar, ss..	5	0	0	3	3	0
Hannah, c...	4	0	0	0	0	0
Ballou, p....	4	1	1	0	3	0
Totals....	41	9	12	27	10	0

STARS—	Ab	R	H	Po	A	E
Gazella,3b..	3	1	1	0	1	2
Leishman,3b	1	0	1	1	0	0
Lee, ss.....	4	0	0	2	8	1
Brannan, 2b.	4	0	0	1	1	1
Jones, rf....	4	0	1	2	0	0
Carlyle, cf...	4	0	2	4	0	0
Heath, 1b....	4	1	1	11	3	0
Severeid, c...	3	0	1	4	0	1
Green, lf....	3	1	1	1	0	0
Page, p.....	2	0	0	1	3	0
Hollerson, p	0	0	0	0	0	0
Governor...	1	0	0	0	0	0
Totals....	33	3	8	27	16	5

Los Angeles 500 010 030 — 9
Hollywood 010 011 000 — 3

ANGELS BEAT SHEIKS IN OPENER

Sending five runners across the home plate in the first inning, Los Angeles opened its series with Hollywood by defeating the Stars, 9 to 3, in their game today at Wrigley field.

FIRST INNING

ANGELS—Parker singled to left. Harper walked. Moore struck out. Schulmerich reached first and Parker scored when Gazella threw wild to Brannan in an attempted double play. Jacobs hit a home run over the left field wall, scoring Harper and Schulmerich ahead of him. Statz singled to right. Statz stole second. Dittmar hit to Gazella, whose throw to Heath pulled the latter off the bag, but Heath was slow in returning to first base and Dittmar was safe. Hannah was hit by a pitched ball, filling the bases. Ballou was out, Heath to Brannan, who covered first, Statz scoring. Lee threw out Parker. FIVE RUNS, THREE HITS, TWO ERRORS.

STARS—Gazella popped to Parker. Lee out, Jacobs unassisted. Brannan out, Jacobs unassisted. NO RUNS, NO HITS.

SECOND INNING

ANGELS—Page threw out Harper. Moore flied to Jones. Lee threw out Schulmerich. NO RUNS, NO HITS.

STARS—Jones singled to left. Carlyle hit into a double play, Jacobs to Dittmar to Jacobs. Heath hit a home run over the

(CONTINUED ON SECOND SPORT PAGE)

FATE OF MAN IS MYSTERY IN OCEAN TRAGEDY

Attired in a batding suit, the body of Julia S. Bestmann, 24, of Los Angeles, was found floating in the surf late today off Point Mugu, a fishing harbor six miles north of the Los Angeles county line, according to advices received from Ventura.

The girl, and her companion, Walter Vachon, 30, also of Los Angeles, had been missing since yesterday. No trace of Vachon had been found late this afternoon.

The girl's body was picked up by two fishermen.

The men expressed their belief that the girl had been swept off Dad Man's rock, scene of many drownings.

DESCENDANT OF KINGS

Miss Bestmann, according to her father, J. H. Bestmann, 1522 West Fifty-fifth street, was a direct descendent of King Louis IV of France, who reigned from 922 to 954, and of Charles the Great of Germany, who was kaiser in 1814.

The elder Bestmann possesses o book in German which, he says, gives the complete record of the family, showing that his ancestors had left France about 500 years ago to live in Germany, where the name of Bestmann was taken.

The elder Bestmann said his daughter and Vachon left Los Angeles Sunday to seek a secluded beach for a quiet swim.

SEEN FISHING

They were last seen fishing from the big rock off Point Mugu on Hueneme beach, according to Deputy Sheriff Ed Hearn of Ventura, in charge of the investigation and search.

Hearn expressed belief that they might have been swept off the rock by the surf, which is said to be exceptionally rough at that point.

The discarded street clothing of the pair was found in the abandoned car which, according to beach residents, had stood on the beach for 23 hours before the investigation was started last night.

Miss Bestmann had been employed as an operator at the plant of the Baker Linen Co. in the Grayco building.

Vachon, a carpenter, lived at 1129 West Fifty-ninth street.

Average net paid circulation of THE CHICAGO TRIBUNE, November, 1930, in excess of
Daily - - - 815,000
Sunday - - 1,080,000

Chicago Daily Tribune

THE WORLD'S GREATEST NEWSPAPER

VOLUME LXXXIX.—NO. 297 [REG. U. S. PAT. OFFICE: COPYRIGHT 1930 BY THE CHICAGO TRIBUNE.] FRIDAY, DECEMBER 12, 1930.—42 PAGES THIS PAPER CONSISTS OF TWO SECTIONS—SECTION ONE PRICE TWO CENTS IN CHICAGO AND SUBURBS ELSEWHERE THREE CENTS

MORAN IS FOUND NOT GUILTY

SENATE VOTES 118 MILLIONS TO SPEED U. S. WORK

But Tell President How to Spend It.

BY ARTHUR CRAWFORD.
[Chicago Tribune Press Service.]

Washington, D. C., Dec. 11.—[Special.]—President Hoover's emergency construction bill was passed today by the senate, but only after the last vestige of the broad discretionary authority originally requested for him had been eliminated.

The bill was passed without a record vote and without opposition, although its consideration again was made the excuse for attacks upon the President. Amendments which were approved ran the total amount up to 118 million dollars, an increase of $8,000,000 over the total in the bill as passed by the house.

The elimination of a section giving discretionary authority to the executive was construed as a direct slap at President Hoover. The action was taken on the motion of Senator Joseph T. Robinson [Dem., Ark.], minority leader, after Senators William E. Borah [Rep., Idaho] and George W. Norris [Rep., Neb.] had raised questions about the provision.

Projects Already Authorized.

Under the terms of the bill as originally introduced in the house on the recommendation of President Hoover and the budget bureau, the President was given blanket authority to spend 150 million dollars for various highway and construction projects already authorized by law, but for which sufficient appropriations were lacking. The house appropriations committee, to meet objections of the Democrats, cut the total to 110 millions and provided for the appropriation of this money for specified purposes. The only authority given to the President was in a clause which stated that "the sums herein appropriated shall be available interchangeably for expenditure on the objects named in this act upon order of the President stating the amounts and the appropriations from which such interchanges are to be made." It was this provision which was eliminated by the senate.

Senator Borah asked Senator Wesley L. Jones [Rep., Wash.], chairman of the appropriations committee who was in charge of the bill, if this discretionary provision was not such as to make it a lump sum appropriation. Senator Jones said this probably was true, but that he did not think the President would take advantage of the authority given him.

Norris Raises Objection.

"Isn't it true that the President might transfer the entire amount to any one item in the bill?" asked Senator Norris.

Senator Jones replied in the affirmative, whereupon Senator Norris said no provision ever has been incorporated in a law heretofore.

Senator Robinson said it was "a most unusual provision," and that he "fails to see the necessity for the granting of any such broad power to the President."

Amendments added in the senate included one by Senator T. L. Oddie [Rep., Nev.] for the appropriation of $5,000,000 for roads on the public domain and on Indian and other federal reservations and one by Senator Carl Hayden [Dem., Ariz.] for $3,000,000 for highways in national forests. Senator Jones consented to the acceptance of both of these items so they might be considered by conferees of the senate and house in adjusting the differences in the senate and house bills.

Include 80 Million for Loans.

Appropriations included in the original 110 million dollars included $80,000,000 for loans to the states for highway construction to be repaid over a five year period by deductions from federal aid contributions, $22,500,000 to the army engineers for river and harbor improvements, $3,000,000 to the army engineers for flood control work on the Mississippi, $3,000,000 to the department of agriculture for forest roads and trails and $1,500,000 to the department of the interior for roads in national parks. The river and harbor item will also make possible allotment of $1,200,000 for the Illinois waterway.

Under a senate amendment the money will be available within limit as to date instead of only for use between Jan. 1 and June 30, 1931, as in the house bill.

The senate adopted an amendment by Senator James Couzens [Rep., Mich] giving preference work done under federal contracts to laborers or mechanics residing at least 90 days within a district, city or state and also

(Continued on page 4, column 4.)

NEWS SUMMARY of The Tribune

[And Historical Scrap Book.]
Friday, December 12, 1930.

LOCAL.

"Bugs" Moran is acquitted of vagrancy charge.

Chicago and Alton railroad is sold to Baltimore and Ohio for $73,000,000 at Wilmington auction.

Fund for jobless is boosted above $2,000,000 mark; chairman sees end of drive within a week.

Chicago Art theater to give performance for benefit of Good Fellow fund.

Sheets answers critics of highway financial policy and explains status of bond issue system.

Four more indicted by grand jury in probe of bail bond situation.

Northup refuses to apologize to Judge Williams in sanitary district case; plans appeal to McGoorty.

M. S. Szymczak and Michael L. Igoe proposed as possible Democratic candidates for mayor.

Guard William Lenhardt in cell at county jail as hour for his execution nears.

Council orders ordinances for street extensions as prod for rail terminal action.

State Representative O'Brien, on stand at his income tax trial, tells value of political favors in his trucking business.

WASHINGTON.

Senate votes 118 millions to speed United States work, but tells President how to spend it.

New labor secretary says his first big task will be to rid Chicago and other big cities of gangsters by deportation.

Controversy over world court protocol turns to problem of special session of senate.

Prohibition Director Woodcock frowns on interference by dry agents in holiday merrymaking.

Admiral Pratt tells committee the danger of delaying navy building in advance of arms parleys.

Senate is expected to pass 44 hour week for postal employés.

Open revolt in senate against President spreads to 17 Republicans.

DOMESTIC.

Girl goes on stand to tell of love affair with major charged with slaying wife.

Industry must solve consumption as it has production, Glenn Frank says.

Einstein, overwhelmed by riotous welcome, shies at interviews; sticks to ship.

New York City bank with fifty-nine branches is closed.

FOREIGN.

Germany orders withdrawal of war film, "All Quiet on the Western Front."

Winston Churchill, Conservative leader, attacks parley on India, declaring dominion status would mean fall of British empire.

President Machado put Cuba under martial law as student riots dot island.

Illinois Supreme court refuses to rehear grain "gambling" case.

SPORTS.

New York's three charity productions lead to exchange of glares.

Fifty dollar tickets for Army-Navy game still priced at $50.

Maroons play Cornell five in opening game.

Major and minor leagues split; see baseball war.

Griffith meets Stribling in Stadium ring tonight.

EDITORIALS.

The President and the Senate: The League and Its Court: British Force in India: Crooked Pavements for Straight Streets.

FINANCE, COMMERCE.

Smart rally brings aid to declining Chicago stocks.

Southern railway declares dividends aggregating $5.65 per share.

Scrutator says 99.5 per cent of advertised goods are as represented.

New York stocks creak and slide, but later recoil.

Weakness of stock market depresses all grains.

Price slashing is in vogue in all branches of live stock.

Banks loosen money bags for Christmas buying as credit demand expands.

Doctor Slain in Stairway to Office; Woman Gives Up

Sulphur Springs, Tex., Dec. 11.—(AP)—Dr. R. M. Payne, 50, was shot and killed as he entered a stairway leading to his office in a downtown building today. Mrs. Lydia Skidmore, about 40, surrendered to officers.

After the shooting Mrs. Skidmore walked across the street to the sheriff's office. She handed officers a shot gun. One charge had been fired. She refused to make a statement and was released under $5,000 bond. Both parties were lifelong residents of this section. Mrs. Skidmore was a widow and Dr. Payne, a dentist, had a wife and several children.

CHRISTMAS SHOPPING IN WILMINGTON, ILL.

GRANDCHILDREN OF HOOVER MAKE DEBUT IN TALKIES

Washington, D. C., Dec. 11.—(AP)—Two new moving picture actors today made their debuts on the south lawn at the White House.

They were Herbert Hoover III. and Peggy Ann, grandchildren of the President.

They demonstrated to their own satisfaction that the new bicycles they found upon their arrival early this week were very good.

Asked by their grandmother what they wanted Santa Claus to bring them for Christmas, Herbert Hoover III. replied he wanted an engine.

"Do you want a big engine or a little engine?" he was asked.

"A big one," was the quick reply.

He also expressed a desire for a policeman's uniform with a badge and a large stick.

Missouri U. Ends Taboo on Smoking by Either Sex

Columbia, Mo., Dec. 11.—(AP)—No longer will the student with a cigaret or pipe have to dodge the professors as he enters the University of Missouri administrative building. Signs prohibiting smoking have been ordered down by President Walter Williams upon his finding there is no rule against it. The university does not discriminate between men and women smokers, but co-eds have not made it a practive to smoke in corridors of university buildings.

2 Brothers Are Dead from Drinking Varnish Remover

Indianapolis, Ind., Dec. 11. — [Special.]—Varnish remover was blamed tonight for the death of two men who drank a quantity of it and died. They were Charles Payne, 46, and Bruce Hampshire, 56, brothers-in-law, who died shortly after they were admitted to the city hospital.

THE WEATHER

FRIDAY, DECEMBER 12, 1930.

Chicago and vicinity—Mostly cloudy Friday; somewhat colder; winds mostly moderate west to northwest.

Illinois—Generally fair Friday, except mostly cloudy in extreme north portion; somewhat colder.

Indiana—Fair in south, mostly cloudy in north portion Friday; colder.

Lower Michigan—Cloudy Friday, probably occasional snow; somewhat colder.

Upper Michigan—Cloudy Friday, probably occasional snow; somewhat colder.

Wisconsin—Cloudy to partly cloudy Friday; somewhat colder in southeast portion.

Missouri—Generally fair Friday; somewhat colder in east portion.

Iowa—Mostly fair Friday; slightly colder tonight in extreme southeast portion.

Minnesota—Friday mostly fair.

North Dakota and South Dakota—Mostly fair Friday; no decided change in temperature.

Nebraska—Probably fair Friday: no decided change in temperature.

Kansas—Fair Friday; little change in temperature.

Ohio—Friday partly cloudy, slightly colder in east portion; probably light rain or snow along the lake.

Upper great lakes—Winds mostly moderate to fresh southwest to northwest; cloudy Friday, probably occasional snow.

Lower great lakes—Winds mostly moderate to fresh southwest to west; mostly cloudy Friday, probably occasional rain or snow.

Doak's First Task: Deport Big Gangsters

[Chicago Tribune Press Service.]

Washington, D. C., Dec. 11.—[Special.]—As his first major act after taking office, Secretary of Labor William N. Doak, today announced a nation-wide campaign to rid Chicago and other big cities of deportable gangsters. He said a thorough investigation had been initiated into the personal history of the leading underworld figures of the country with a view to their deportation wherever possible, under the law.

"We are going into the gangster problem with all the resources at our command," Secretary Doak said. "We are going to ask congress for additional funds enabling the department to increase its staff of investigators. We also intend to obtain funds if possible to increase our deportation machinery so that delays of this nature will be cut to a minimum."

Deportation Only Way.

The new cabinet member declared that the life stories of several "big shots" in Chicago's crime centers were being scrutinized to determine the advisability of setting in motion machinery to deport them. He emphasized that deportation could only be accomplished through due process of law.

"We intend to make every effort to deport all deportable criminals," Mr. Doak said. "In some cases aliens who have made millions by crime have been able to stave off deportation proceedings for long periods. We are going after funds so we can wage a successful campaign against this class of criminal."

Scans "Public Enemies" List.

Called upon to reveal the names of some of those against whom action will be taken, Mr. Doak stated that the law required the observance of the utmost secrecy regarding the proceedings and for that reason he was not at liberty to disclose the names of gang leaders under investigation.

He intimated, however, that the list of Chicago's "public enemies," recently made public, included several names which the department was tracing.

THIS PAIR FREED FROM JAILHOUSE BY SIZE 13½ FEET

Macon, Ga., Dec. 11. — (AP) — Jesse Glenn and Walter Banks, Negroes, wear number 13½ shoes, and that's why they are not in jail.

They were held in the stockade for a minor offense until they asked the superintendent for shoes. The superintendent took one look at their feet and appealed to the mayor.

"We can't work them barefoot," said the mayor, "and we can't find shoes big enough to fit them."

So they were released. In the space reserved for "remarks" in the release order, the mayor wrote "13½ shoes."

TWO BOYS KILLED AS AUTO HITS FIVE IN SCHOOL BAND

Two boys were killed and three other children, all members of a school band, were slightly injured last night when they were run down by an automobile in St. Charles road at 50th avenue, Bellwood.

The dead were Gerald Felkner, 10 years old, and Frank Veces, 13, both of Bellwood. Their injured companions are Irene McCleary, 13; Joseph Joura, also 13, and Frank Behrendt, 12, all of Bellwood. The latter were given first aid at the Josyln clinic in Maywood.

The children had been rehearsing in the band of the Sunnyside school, St. Charles and Wolff roads, and were returning home with two other young musicians at the time of the accident. As they were walking in the west side of the road, the machine of Frank Beukema, 53 years old, 2248 West 2d street, a decorator, bore down upon them from behind. Two of the group leaped to safety. The others were struck. Beukema was held by Bellwood police. He said he did not see the children until it was too late.

GIRLS! WANT TO BUY AN OFFICER? ITALY "SELLS" 'EM

TURIN, Italy, Dec. 11.—(AP)—American girls who want to marry Italian officers would better pick generals. It costs less. No officer may marry without his commander's consent, and the commander doesn't consent until shown the bride is bringing her husband a substantial "dot."

There is a regular scale of prices, running inversely to the officer's rank. "Shavetails" are offered at $600; a girl needs $400 to marry a captain, and she gets a general free.

It's all based on the officer's wage scale and what is considered his ability to provide for a wife.

Gallery Girl Invites Him to Shoot; He Kills Self

Long Beach, Cal., Dec. 11.—(AP)—Oscar E. Mayhugh, 53, was lounging in front of a shooting gallery on the Pike today.

"Want to shoot, mister?" the girl attendant in the gallery asked.

"I believe I will, he answered. He took a gun, fired once at the target and then swung the weapon around and sent two bullets through his head. He died an hour later.

Shoes Worth $300 Stolen, but All for Left Foot

Indianapolis, Ind., Dec. 11. — [Special.]—A thief stole shoes valued at $300 today from J. B. Novotony, Chicago salesman. But they were samples and all for the left foot.

Henry Ford and Wife Will Spend Night at White House

Washington, D. C., Dec. 11.—(AP)—Mr. and Mrs. Henry Ford will be dinner and overnight guests at the White House on Monday.

ALTON RAILWAY SOLD ON BLOCK FOR 73 MILLION

Baltimore and Ohio Is Purchaser.

From its mightiest locomotive to its last stray tool box, the Chicago and Alton railroad, a carrier operating between Chicago, St. Louis, and Kansas City since 1861, was knocked down at public auction yesterday to an eastern road, the Baltimore and Ohio, for a cash sum of $23,000,000 and other considerations bringing the total price to approximately $73,000,000.

On the instant of 2 p. m., Herbert A. Lundahl, master in chancery for Federal Judge Carpenter of Chicago, stood up in the south doorway of the red brick depot at Wilmington, a few miles south of Joliet, and began reading the foreclosure decree of the United States District court in which the auction was ordered.

Grouped before him in the stuffy little waiting room were some sixty officials and attorneys, representing both railroads and the owners of defaulted bonds, who had journeyed down to Wilmington to witness the auction.

Townfolk Watch Auction.

It was Wilmington's big, historic day and a delegation of the townsfolk, mostly old men and housewives, appeared at the station to see the railroad and financial moguls from the city transfer the road they had known from childhood to a foreign company. There was something in the atmosphere of the proceedings, in the solemn reading of the documents and the earnest attention of all that gave the auction the atmosphere of a religious rather than a financial event.

Something of the pervading spirit was expressed by the wife of a Baltimore and Ohio official who, when the sale was over and the crowd dispersed, laughed nervously and remarked to a friend:

"I never felt so strange in my life. It was exactly like attending a funeral. I was waiting for the auctioneer to close by saying, 'May the Alton rest in peace.'"

Special Train Carries Party.

The auction special, a train made up of the president's private car, the general manager's car, two coaches and a diner, pulled out of the Chicago Union station at 11:35 a. m., five minutes behind the Alton limited, the first de luxe train in the west and the pride of the Alton road. Aboard the special were 75 persons, five-sixths of them attorneys, whose duty was to supervise the Alton's legal obsequies.

For an hour before train time the president of the Alton, William G. Bierd, was at the station gate, attending the journey comforts of his party, from the highest Baltimore and Ohio official to the least stenographer. To each he extended an invitation to dine aboard the train as the Alton's guest.

Bierd an Active Host.

As the special clicked over the switches and crossings on the city's southwestern limits, Mr. Bierd was moving from car to car, introducing New York, Baltimore, and Chicago attorneys to one another and presenting the chief personalities of the party to the newspaper men. The train was rolling over the prairie west of Willow Springs when the Alton president finally concluded his duties as host and took a chair.

He chose a seat near the glassed rear door of his own car, affording a view of the country spread on either side in the noon sunshine.

In the staterooms ahead typists were clicking out copies of the legal forms to be used and attorneys were in consultation over the final rules

(Continued on page 8, column 2.)

Girl Tells of Love Affair with Major

Kansas City, Mo., Dec. 11.—[Special.]—Plans for a honeymoon with Miss Grace Brandon a few months after his wife had died, from what the government declares was poison by his hand, were read as testimony against Maj. Charles A. Shepard, late today. They were in letters written to Miss Brandon, who sat in the witness stand and identified them between sobs.

Mrs. Shepard died in June, 1929. The letters were written between July and October the same year, and described one proposed honeymoon to Canada and Niagara Falls.

Miss Brandon gave the thrill-seekers an emotional scene this morning, weeping almost immediately after taking the stand. She was asked by L. E. Wyman, first assistant United States district attorney, to "tell the court in your own words just what conversation you had with Maj. Shepard concerning his wife and their relations."

Tears Interrupt First Answer.

She hesitated a minute, as if struggling to begin, and then the tears started to her eyes and she made no answer. After regaining her composure, Miss Brandon said:

"He said he and his wife had not been getting along well the last five years. That they kept up congenial appearances at social functions because of his rank in the army."

All week the spectators have waited for the testimony of the girl in the case, curious for the airing on the stand of the love affair between the army major and the stenographer he met in a San Antonio boarding house while he was stationed at Brooks field.

Tells of Meeting Major.

She met Maj. Shepard about the first of November, 1928, she said. She was introduced to him as the other boarders were.

"Did Maj. Shepard ask you to go out with him?"

"He did. He asked me how I would like to go out with a major, as well as with the lieutenants. I told him 'Sure, I would.'"

"Did you know Maj. Shepard was married?" came the question.

"Yes, I did know it. I asked him whether his wife objected."

Spectators never learned whether the major said the wife did or didn't, for the questions continued then about the relationship between the army man and Miss Brandon.

Received Many Presents.

A veritable tide of presents from Maj. Shepard were enumerated by Miss Brandon as follows: A bracelet, toilet set, gold ring, canary, check for $10 to $15 to buy ice skates, necklace, diamond in platinum setting, crystal bead necklace, pearl necklace, another bracelet, $1,500 coupé, mesh bag, another pearl necklace, string of Japanese pearls, fitted week-end bag, silver fox fur piece, diamond dinner ring, cedar chest filled with lingerie, two dresses, and numerous books.

Love Letter Before Wife Died.

A letter written by Shepard on March 13, 1930, showed the major had vowed his love months before Mrs. Shepard's death.

"It will be two years in November, dear—do you still remember when and where we pledged our first love—do you still remember the first sweet kiss you gave me—I was so happy that night to feel those dear arms around my neck—and how often they have been there since, each time more precious than the previous time.

"Sweetheart, when I opened the door of my room, the first thing I saw was your dear face in your picture smiling at me, as much as to say, 'I love you Charlie.' I picked it up, kissed those lips and cried like a child. Oh, sweetheart, I do love you, please, please, forgive."

A postscript acknowledged a letter from Miss Brandon for which Shepard had waited impatiently.

"When I saw the opening words, 'My darling sweetheart,'" Shepard

(Continued on page 2, column 5.)

GANGSTER IS ACQUITTED IN VAGRANT CASE

'Bugs' and Detective Near Blows.

BULLETIN.

George "Bugs" Moran was found not guilty of vagrancy by a jury in Waukegan at 8:15 last night.

The Waukegan jury trying George (Bugs) Moran on charges of vagrancy was reported last night to stand 10 to 2 for acquital, after taking several ballots. The two jurors in the minority were reported to be weakening in their stand and court attachés predicted that the gangster would be found not guilty on the final ballot.

At 8 o'clock the jurors sent word to Judge Persons that they wished to read the testimony concerning drinking at the Cassidy resort at Bluff Lake, where Moran was arrested. The state's attorney had argued that if Moran were shown to be a patron of a place where liquor was sold, he was a vagrant under the law. The judge consulted with attorneys about permitting the jurors to read the evidence they requested.

Report U. S. Agents Waiting.

The last day of the trial in the Lake county court room of Judge Perry L. Persons was tumultuous. There were several sensational developments. Moran, who ruled over the north side gangsters until the St. Valentine's day massacre of 1929 removed his chief aids, maintained his smiling, confident demeanor, despite reports that a number of federal agents were waiting in the courtroom to arrest him on charges of violating the income tax laws.

In and out of the courtroom fun and fisticuffs continued to lend a holiday air to the case. Moran furnished most of the excitement in the court corridor when he engaged in an altercation with Edward J. Hargrave, head of a private detective agency, whose operatives arrested the gangster in Lake county on the vagrancy charge. The two men were separated before they came to blows.

Moran Aid Is Seized.

Other developments of the day included the seizure by federal agents of Benjamin H. Kornack, one of Moran's associates in the cleaning and dyeing business, after he left the witness stand. Kornack was ordered to produce all the books and records of the Central Cleaners and Dyers association, of which Moran is vice president. He promised to bring the records before the federal grand jury today.

Capt. John Stege, former chief of detectives, another witness, noticed a Moran gangster loitering about the corridor and arrested him after a chase. He was identified as Mike Douvich, alias Doorman, and booked on a charge of vagrancy. Stege declared that Douvich was a known gangster and a member of the Moran gang for eight years.

When told of the arrest, Moran said: "We'll see whether he can get away with that."

Advises "Bugs" to Leave.

In closing arguments Attorney Richard I. Gavin, representing Moran, turned to the gangster and said:

"Every one's against you in this state. You'd better leave. Their prejudice will never give you a chance."

Mrs. Lucille Moran, the defendant's wife, burst into tears at these words. Moran lost his smile for the first time.

State's Attorney A. V. Smith told the jury in his closing argument that Moran was a "bloodthirsty tiger who should be treated as all dangerous animals are treated."

Prosecutor Sidney Block, summing up the evidence to the jury, stressed the fact that Moran was not a vagrant in the sense that he was without money or without a job. The defendant should be found guilty under the vagrancy statute, he declared, because the evidence showed he had been a "thief and burglar since 1910."

Assailed by Prosecutor.

"He said he was a business man," the prosecutor remarked. "What a business man he was! Every time he registered at a hotel it was under an alias. He served time in prison. He was convicted of burglary and robbery."

In the cross-examination of Moran on the witness stand by State's Attorney Smith at the morning session furnished the crowd with a number of thrills and laughs. The prosecutor began by questioning the gangster about his connection with the cleaning and dyeing industry and asked:

"Isn't it true that you elbowed your

Normal Buying Unlocks Gate to Normal Times

Prosperity could be brought back in a lot of different ways—for a while. A big war might do it. Or a big subsidy of some kind by the government. Or the discovery of gold or platinum in everybody's back yard.

The most effective way of bringing back good times, however, is based on no such sensational contingencies. Moreover, the one workable way is the solid, common sense way. We refer to normal buying for normal needs.

There is no magic formula or quick remedy for current ills. The present lull in business has been on for now more than a year. Time has been given its chance to patch up what it could. It is now up to people themselves to see that the ball starts rolling. Practically all that is needed now is the resumption of normal buying on the part of everybody whose income hasn't been materially affected. Such action will provide jobs for those who now can't buy normally. Then, when the jobless are back in jobs, prosperity again will rule.

Chicago Tribune
THE WORLD'S GREATEST NEWSPAPER

This Issue Includes the Saturday PHOTOGRAVURE SECTION

THE CHICAGO DAILY NEWS

BLUE STREAK

55TH YEAR—302. SATURDAY, DECEMBER 20, 1930.—TWENTY-SIX PAGES [and 8 pages of PHOTOGRAVURE] THREE CENTS

NITTI GETS 18 MONTHS, $10,000 FINE

APPLE-SELLING A RACKET? NOT WITH THESE VETS

They're Bona Fide ex-Service Men and Have Slim Profits.

ONE IS A REAL HERO

BY GENE MORGAN.

All quiet on the vets' apple-selling front. Just the lull before the noon-hour rush, maybe. Here's a lady who wants an apple. No, she doesn't. She just squints curiously at the apple box on the curb through her glasses and shakes her head. Wonder what she keeps looking for? Does she think a fellow's a freak just because he's selling apples?

"Look here, young man," says the lady decisively. "You don't look much like a veteran to me. And if you aren't what you claim to be it's a shame to impose on the public."

The lady whisks away in Randolph street, her head in the air and piously confident that she has done her duty toward solving the problem of unemployed ex-soldiers.

People Suspicious of Rackets.

"She think's it's a racket," confides the apple salesman in the frayed brown overcoat. "That's the trouble nowadays. People suspect everything's a racket. Well, here's my army discharge paper. But I can't open it to everybody who stops to buy an apple. And I can't explain that the American Legion is running this apple business and won't let anybody in unless he's got credentials. Tell 'em, mister, that this ain't a racket. That we're all ex-service men and are giving full value with every apple. Sure, here it is on my discharge paper. Eight months overseas. Two major engagements. Got gassed, too. No, mister, you've got to take the change. This is business, not charity."

A racket? Standing all day from 7 a. m. until late at night, offering big, red, juicy apples to the passing crowds at a nickel apiece. Then going home with the slim profits to a wife and little ones, one of them sick, perhaps. Facing eviction notices and bills. Then up early to be back at the stand and hoping to sell at least a couple of boxes before the chill sundown.

He Pawns Medal to Start.

A racket? Tom McManus, who's selling the ruddy pommes near Randolph and State, would never be taken for a racketeer. In the first place, his overcoat must be five years old and his shoes aren't seaworthy. Nor has he enjoyed a swell hotel massage and haircut. Yet Tom knows his firearms. Both as a British Tommy and an American doughboy he served the allies well. And now—

Well, for one thing, he's got his Mons medal back. Perhaps you know what that is, a trinket worn by only the first hundred thousand of Kitchener's armies in France. McManus was one of the first to enlist in England and served as a member of the Black Watch in the fiercest fighting of the first years of the war. Then he was invalided home. Got to America somehow and shortly afterward this country got into the mess. Enter also Private Thomas McNamara, a member of an ambulance unit of the 33d division.

When Tom heard about the chance to sell apples under the Legion's auspices he tried to dig up the $2.15 necessary for the initial box. Then he hocked his Mons medal and reported at the apple depot at 8 South Wells street. That set him up in business, and soon he was able to show a small profit and reclaim his precious medal.

"Of course he didn't really need to borrow on his medal," explained Capt. Oliver J. Sheehy, who with Glen Suthers is in charge of veterans' apple selling for the American Legion, "we would have trusted him with the box. But then, these aren't ordinary street-

(Continued on Fifth Page.)

EGBERT VAN ALSTYNE, SONG WRITER, DIVORCED

Egbert Van Alstyne, veteran song writer, composer of "Memories" and "Afraid to Go Home in the Dark," was divorced by Mabelle Van Alstyne, 536 Oakdale avenue, on grounds of desertion, in the Circuit court of Judge Daniel P. Trude today. Van Alstyne did not contest the divorce. She received a property settlement said to be in excess of $100,000.

U. S. ENVOY TO HOLLAND DEAD

Gerrit J. Diekema.

[The Associated Press.]

TWO CHILDREN PERISH, MOTHER INJURED, IN FIRE

Blast and Flames Raze Three Stores and Sweep Home in Rear.

Mrs. Dora Israelson, mother of two small boys who were burned to death early this morning when fire following an explosion swept their home in the rear of a one-story building at 3649-59 North Kedzie avenue, was near death at the Martha Washington hospital today. The children were Jerome, 5 years old, and his brother, Homer, 4.

The structure, which houses three other shops besides a notion store owned by the Israelsons, was virtually destroyed by the explosion, which blew off the roof of the entire building, and the flames that followed. Deputy Chief Fire Marshal Daniel J. Carmody expressed the opinion that the blast was caused by a collection of gas between the ceiling and the roof.

Mrs. Israelson was dragged from the flames by Jacob Kraitsek, 3649 North Kedzie avenue, owner of a tailor shop in the same building. Awakened by the blast he rushed into the Israelson's living quarters, picked up Mrs. Israelson and battled his way through the fire to the street.

As he stumbled into the arms of firemen two other neighbors, Ralph Ballou, 3818 North Troy street, and Frank Larkey, attempted to rush into the structure to save the Israelson children. The flames, however, had turned the structure into a blazing furnace and they were driven back gasping for breath.

The father, Irving Iraelson, was away at a lodge meeting at the time

EX-POLICEMAN DROPS DEAD AT HIS OLD CORNER

Cornelius Buttimer, 57 years old, a retired south park policeman since 1921, when he lost his right leg as the result of an automobile accident, dropped dead this morning in the Peoples Trust and Savings Bank, 32 North Michigan avenue. It was on the corner on which the bank stands that for eleven years Policeman Buttimer was a familiar figure as he directed traffic.

Relatives feared to inform his wife, Mary, of the death, as she is in a hospital with both legs fractured as the result of being struck by an automobile six weeks ago.

ATTACKED 14 YEARS AGO BY DOG; SUES FOR $10,000

Morris, Ill., Dec. 20.—(AP)—Fourteen years ago two bull dogs allegedly belonging to W. A. Southcomb of near here attacked Grinnell Oswood, then 7 years old, and not only fearfully bit and lacerated his face but chewed off his right ear.

Suit was started immediately, but for lack of prosecution the case was dropped.

Today, having passed his twenty-first birthday anniversary, Oswood entered suit against Southcomb for $10,000 damages.

45 DIE IN ICY SEA AS SHIPS CRASH; 40 ARE RESCUED

Four Survivors Make Way to Shore in Boat and Tell of Fog's Horror.

VESSEL PICKS UP 36

Copenhagen, Denmark, Dec. 20.—(AP)—Four members of the crew of the steamer Oberon, which sank last night in the icy Cattegat with the loss of forty-five lives after a collision with the steamer Arcturus, arrived here today on the rescue ship Hengist with the first story of the wreck.

The Arcturus, standing by after the crash, saved thirty-six persons, four passengers and thirty-two crew members, many of whom are seriously injured. The fog was so thick at the time that it was impossible to see two yards ahead. The Arcturus had a bad hole in its hull and is proceeding to port.

The ships, both of Finnish registry, came together in a heavy fog with a terrific crash, the four survivors said.

The four sailors, without even kicking off their shoes, slipped into the water astern and found it so cold that they were almost paralized.

Climb Into Loose Boat.

In the muck and dark they banged into a boat which apparently had broken loose. In they climbed, unlashed the one oar in the boat and sculled away as quickly as they could. From time to time they saw people in the water, some of them without even life belts, but they quickly lost these indistinct figures in the fog.

The Oberon was sinking fast and as the water closed over it the boilers went up in a great blast. There was strong suction as the ship went down.

The four sailors and the skipper of the Hengist said they could hear the screams of those who were fighting for their lives in the freezing water but the fog was so thick they could not see the people. Once or twice they narrowly missed running down some of those struggling in the sea.

The seamen thought none of the Oberon's boats got away, but there was a report that one boatload of ten persons was able to get clear before the ship went down. What became of it was not learned.

The tragedy was heightened by the fact that the captains of the two steamers were brothers, Eris Hjelt commanding the Oberon and Ossi Hjelt the Arcturus.

Noted Briton Believed Lost.

The famous British cricketer, J. W. H. T. Douglas, and his father, were believed to have been among those who lost their lives.

Among the passengers rescued was the English girl, Phyllis Tipping, a secretary at the American consulate at Helsingfors.

The Danish steamer Garm picked up several bodies in the vicinity of the crash and was bringing them here. The Hengist reported that the captain of the foundered vessel had been taken aboard his brother's ship with his first and second mates.

Five Danish seaplanes were ready for a flight to Laso island to aid in searching for survivors as soon as the fog lifted.

17 Rescued in Freighter Crash.

Yarmouth, England, Dec. 20.—(AP)—Seventeen men, comprising the crew of the Aberdeen freighter Glen Derry, were brought into this port today by the freighter Hedworth, which rammed the Glen Derry and sank it during the night in a heavy fog.

Ships Collide in Black Sea.

Constanza, Roumania, Dec. 20.—(AP)—A severe storm in the Black sea continues to tie up and endanger shipping. A collision between the German steamer Olympus and a Roumania steamer is reported. Both vessels were considerably damaged.

Senate Must Have Time to Denounce, Says Will

Special to The Chicago Daily News.

Hollywood, Cal., Dec. 20.—The senate has been in session almost a month and only yesterday passed the very bills that President Hoover suggested in the first hour that it met. It could have passed them in the second hour. But no, that wouldn't give the senators a chance to denounce. A foreigner reading the Congressional Record would say that the president of the United States was elected solely for the purpose of giving Senators somebody to call a horse thief, and the stupid part about it is they have played right into the president's hands, for there is nothing the people believe in any more than some one the senate is denouncing. Six months like that and Hoover would be re-elected by acclamation. WILL ROGERS.

PASS THROUGH CHICAGO

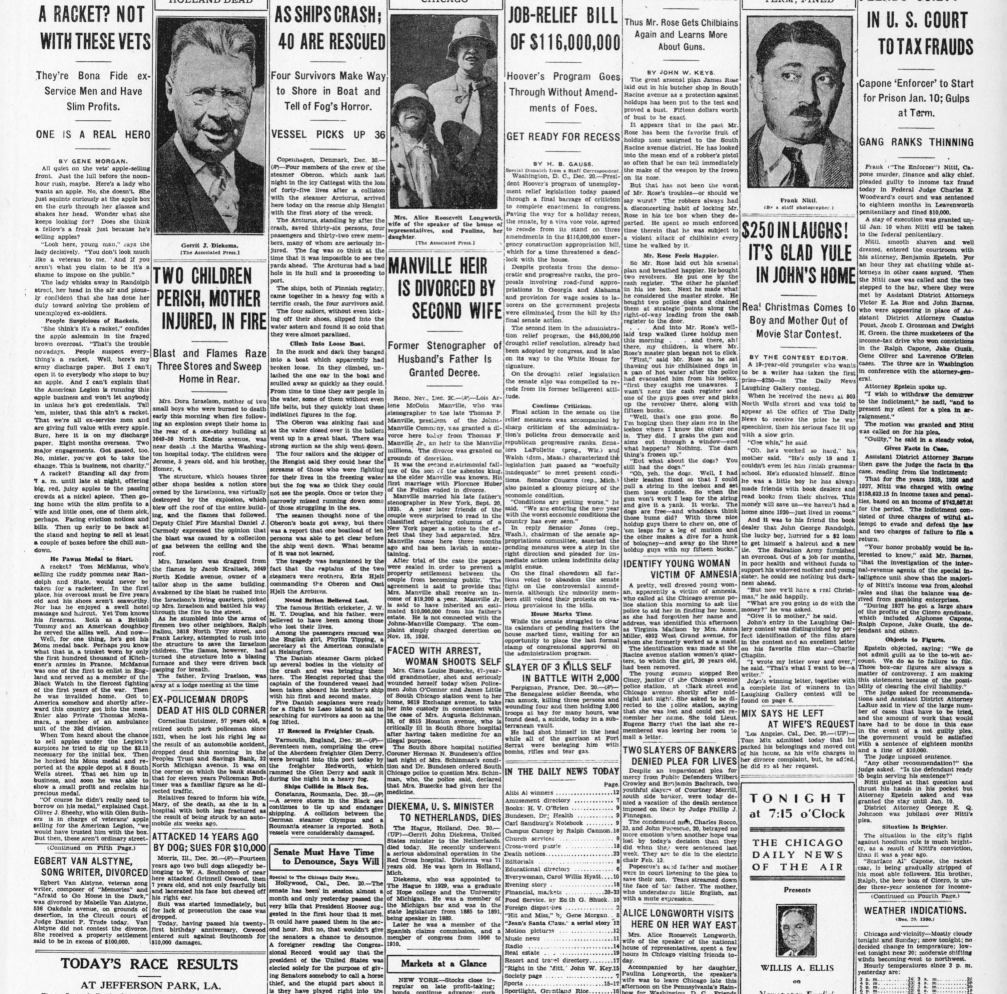

Mrs. Alice Roosevelt Longworth, wife of the speaker of the house of representatives, and Paulina, her daughter.

[The Associated Press.]

MANVILLE HEIR IS DIVORCED BY SECOND WIFE

Former Stenographer of Husband's Father Is Granted Decree.

Reno, Nev., Dec. 20.—(AP)—Lois Arlene McCoin Manville, who was stenographer to the late Thomas F. Manville, president of the Johns-Manville Company, was granted a divorce here today from Thomas F. Manville Jr., an heir to the Manville millions. The divorce was granted on grounds of desertion.

It was the second matrimonial failure of the son of the asbestos king, as the elder Manville was known. His first marriage with Florence Huber of the Follies ended in divorce.

Manville married his late father's stenographer in New York, Sept. 20, 1925. A year later friends of the couple were surprised to read in the classified advertising columns of a New York paper a notice to the effect that they had separated. Mrs. Manville came here three months ago and has been lavish in entertaining.

After trial of the case the papers were sealed in order to prevent a property settlement between the couple from becoming public. The agreement is said to provide that Mrs. Manville shall receive an income of $19,200 a year. Manville Jr. is said to have inherited an estimated $10,000,000 from his father's estate. He is not connected with the Johns-Manville Company. The complaint simply charged desertion on Nov. 15, 1926.

FACED WITH ARREST, WOMAN SHOOTS SELF

Mrs. Clara Louise Busecke, 47-year-old grandmother, shot and seriously wounded herself today when Policemen John O'Connor and James Little of South Chicago station went to her home, 9619 Exchange avenue, to take her into custody in connection with the case of Mrs. Augusta Schinman, 38, of 8515 Houston avenue, who is critically ill in South Shore hospital after having taken medicine for an illegal purpose.

The South Shore hospital notified Coroner Herman N. Bundesen's office last night of Mrs. Schinman's condition and Dr. Bundesen ordered South Chicago police to question Mrs. Schinman, who, the police said, declared that Mrs. Busecke had given her the medicine.

DIEKEMA, U. S. MINISTER TO NETHERLANDS, DIES

The Hague, Holland, Dec. 20.—(UP)—Gerrit John Diekema, United States minister to the Netherlands, died today. He recently underwent a serious abdominal operation in the Red Cross hospital. Diekema was 71 years old. He was born in Holland, Mich.

Diekema, who was appointed to The Hague in 1929, was a graduate of Hope college and the University of Michigan. He was a member of the Michigan bar and was in the state legislature from 1885 to 1891, being speaker in 1889.

Later he was a member of the Spanish claims commission, and a member of congress from 1906 to 1910.

Markets at a Glance

NEW YORK—Stocks close irregular on late profit-taking; bonds continue advance; curb stocks gain moderately; foreign exchange declines; rubber futures sag to new lows on movement; cotton futures advance 8 to 12 points.

CHICAGO—Wheat steady; corn weak; stocks quiet and steady.

SENATE PASSES JOB-RELIEF BILL OF $116,000,000

Hoover's Program Goes Through Without Amendments of Foes.

GET READY FOR RECESS

BY H. B. GAUSS.

Special Dispatch from a Staff Correspondent.

Washington, D. C., Dec. 20.—President Hoover's program of unemployment relief legislation today passed through a final barrage of criticism to complete enactment in congress. Paving the way for a holiday recess, the senate, by a viva voce vote, agreed to recede from its stand on three amendments in the $116,000,000 emergency construction appropriation bill, which for a time threatened a deadlock with the house.

Despite protests from the democratic and progressive ranks, the proposals involving road-fund appropriations in Georgia and Alabama and provision for wage scales to laborers on the government projects were eliminated from the bill by the final senate action.

The second item in the administration relief program, the $45,000,000 drought relief resolution, already had been adopted by congress, and is also on its way to the White House for signature.

On the drought relief legislation the senate also was compelled to recede from its former belligerent attitude.

Continue Criticism.

Final action in the senate on the relief measures was accompanied by sharp criticism of the administration's policies from democratic and republican progressive ranks. Senators LaFollette (prog., Wis.) and Walsh (dem., Mass.) characterized the legislation just passed as "woefully inadequate" to meet present conditions. Senator Couzens (rep., Mich.) also painted a gloomy picture of the economic condition.

"Conditions are getting worse," he said. "We are entering the new year with the worst economic conditions the country has ever seen."

In reply Senator Jones (rep., Wash.), chairman of the senate appropriations committee, asserted the pending measures were a step in the right direction and pleaded for immediate action unless indefinite delay might ensue.

On the final showdown all factions voted to abandon the senate fight on the controversial amendments, although the minority members still voiced their protests on various provisions in the bills.

House Marks Time.

While the senate struggled to clear its calendars of pending matters the house marked time, waiting for an opportunity to place the last formal stamp of congressional approval on the administration program.

SLAYER OF 3 KILLS SELF IN BATTLE WITH 2,000

Perpignan, France, Dec. 20.—(AP)—The Senegalese soldier Seenda, who ran amuck, killing three persons and wounding four and then holding 2,000 troops at bay for many hours, was found dead, a suicide, today in a subterranean vault.

He had shot himself in the head while all of the garrison at Fort Serrat were besieging him with bombs, rifles and tear gas.

IN THE DAILY NEWS TODAY

BANDIT TRAP WORKS SWELL—FOR ROBBERS

Thus Mr. Rose Gets Chilblains Again and Learns More About Guns.

BY JOHN W. KEYS.

The great arsenal plan James Rose laid out in his butcher shop in South Racine avenue as a protection against holdups has been put to the test and proved a bust. Fifteen dollars worth of bust to be exact.

It appears that in the past Mr. Rose has been the favorite fruit of holdup men assigned to the South Racine avenue district. He has looked into the mean end of a robber's pistol so often that he can tell immediately the make of the weapon by the frown on its nose.

But that has not been the worst of Mr. Rose's troubles—or should we say wurst? The robbers always had a disconcerting habit of locking Mr. Rose in his ice box when they departed. He spent so much enforced time therein that he was subject to a violent attack of chilblains every time he walked by it.

Mr. Rose Feels Happier.

So Mr. Rose laid out his arsenal plan and breathed happier. He bought two revolvers. He put one by the cash register. The other he planted in his ice box. Next he made what he considered the master stroke. He bought two police dogs and chained them at strategic points along the right-of-way leading from the cash register to the door.

. . . And into Mr. Rose's well-laid trap walked three holdup men this morning . . . and there, ah! there, my children, is where Mr. Rose's master plan began not to click.

"First," said Mr. Rose as he sat thawing out his chilblained dogs in a pan of hot water after the police had evacuated him from his icebox, "first they caught me unawares. I wasn't near the cash register and one of the guys goes over and picks up the revolver there, along with fifteen bucks.

"Well, that's one gun gone. So I'm hoping then they slam me in the icebox where I know the other one is. They did. I grabs the gun and aims out through a window—and what happens? Nothing. The darn thing's frozen up."

"But what about the dogs? You still had the dogs."

"Oh, yeh, the dogs. Well, I had their leashes fixed so that I could pull a string in the icebox and set them loose outside. So when the gun won't work I leap for the string and give it a yank. It works. The dogs are free—and whaddaya think those bums did? With three nice holdup guys there to chew on, one of 'em leaps for a leg of mutton and the other makes a dive for a hunk of bologney—and away go the three holdup guys with my fifteen bucks."

IDENTIFY YOUNG WOMAN VICTIM OF AMNESIA

A pretty, well dressed young woman, apparently a victim of amnesia, who called at the Chicago avenue police station this morning to ask the police to aid her in finding her home, as she had forgotten her name and address, was identified this afternoon as Virginia Madison by Mrs. Anna Miller, 4932 West Grand avenue, for whom she formerly worked as a maid.

The identification was made at the Racine avenue station women's quarters, to which the girl, 20 years old, had been removed.

The young woman stopped Reo Cincy, janitor of the Chicago avenue police station, at Clark street and Chicago avenue shortly after midnight last night. She asked to be directed to the police station, saying that she was lost and could not remember her name. She told Lieut. Eugene Barry that the last she remembered was leaving her room to mail a letter.

TWO SLAYERS OF BANKERS DENIED PLEA FOR LIVES

Despite an impassioned plea for mercy from Public Defenders Wilbert Crowley and Benjamin Bachrach, two youthful slayers of Courtney Merrill, south side banker, were today denied a vacation of the death sentence imposed on them by Judge Phillip J. Finnegan.

The condemned men, Charles Rocco, 23, and John Popescue, 20, betrayed no more emotion when another hope was lost by today's decision than they did when they were sentenced last week. They are to die in the electric chair Feb. 13.

Popescue's aged father and mother were in court listening to the plea to save their son. Tears streamed down the face of the father. The mother, who understands little English, sat with a mute expression.

ALICE LONGWORTH VISITS HERE ON HER WAY EAST

Mrs. Alice Roosevelt Longworth, wife of the speaker of the national house of representatives, spent a few hours in Chicago visiting friends today.

Accompanied by her daughter, Paulina Longworth, the speaker's wife was to leave Chicago late this afternoon on the Pennsylvania's Rainbow for Washington, D. C. Friends said Mrs. Longworth visited with Mrs. Ruth Hanna McCormick, congresswoman at large, during the early afternoon.

Mrs. Longworth and her daughter were registered at the Blackstone hotel.

GETS 18 MONTHS' TERM; FINED

Frank Nitti.

[By a staff photographer.]

$250 IN LAUGHS! IT'S GLAD YULE IN JOHN'S HOME

Real Christmas Comes to Boy and Mother Out of Movie Star Contest.

BY THE CONTEST EDITOR.

A 19-year-old youngster who wants to be a writer has taken the first prize—$250—in The Daily News Laughing Gallery contest.

When he received the news at 903 North Wells street and was told to appear at the office of The Daily News to receive the prize he was speechless, then his serious face lit up with a slow grin.

"Gee whiz," he said.

"Oh, he's worked so hard," his mother said. "He's only 19 and I couldn't even let him finish grammar school. He's educated himself. Since he was a little boy he has always made friends with book dealers and read books from their shelves. This money will save us—we haven't had a home since 1920—just lived in rooms."

And it was to his friend the book dealer that John George Randolph, the lucky boy, hurried for a $2 loan to get himself a haircut and a new tie. The Salvation Army furnished an overcoat. Out of a job for months, in poor health and without funds to support his widowed mother and young sister, he could see nothing but darkness ahead.

"But now we'll have a real Christmas," he said happily.

"What are you going to do with the money?" he was asked.

"Give it to mother," he said.

John's entry in the Laughing Gallery contest was distinguished by perfect identification of the film stars in the contest and an excellent letter on his favorite film star—Charlie Chaplin.

"I wrote my letter over and over," he said. "That's what I want to be—a writer."

John's winning letter, together with a complete list of winners in the Laughing Gallery contest will be found on page 6.

MIX SAYS HE LEFT AT WIFE'S REQUEST

Los Angeles, Cal., Dec. 20.—(UP)—Tom Mix admitted today that he packed his belongings and moved out of his house, as his wife charges in her divorce complaint, but, he added, he did so at her request.

PLEADS GUILTY IN U. S. COURT TO TAX FRAUDS

Capone 'Enforcer' to Start for Prison Jan. 10; Gulps at Term.

GANG RANKS THINNING

Frank ("The Enforcer") Nitti, Capone murder, finance and alky chief, pleaded guilty to income tax fraud today in Federal Judge Charles E. Woodward's court and was sentenced to eighteen months in Leavenworth penitentiary and fined $10,000.

A stay of execution was granted until Jan. 10 when Nitti will be taken to the federal penitentiary.

Nitti, smooth shaven and well dressed, entered the courtroom with his attorney, Benjamin Epstein. For an hour they sat chatting while attorneys in other cases argued. Then the Nitti case was called and the two stepped to the bar, where they were met by Assistant District Attorneys Victor E. La Rue and John Barnes, who were appearing in place of Assistant District Attorneys Cassius Poust, Jacob I. Grossman and Dwight H. Green, the three musketeers of the income-tax drive who won convictions in the Ralph Capone, Jake Guzik, Gene Oliver and Lawrence O'Brien cases. The three are in Washington in conference with the attorney-general.

Attorney Epstein spoke up.

"I wish to withdraw the demurrer to the indictment," he sadi, "and to present my client for a plea in arraignment."

The motion was granted and Nitti was called on for his plea.

"Guilty," he said in a steady voice.

Gives Facts in Case.

Assistant District Attorney Barnes then gave the judge the facts in the case, reading from the indictment:

That for the years 1925, 1926 and 1927, Nitti was charged with owing $158,823.15 in income taxes and penalties, based on an income of $742,887.81 for the period. The indictment consisted of three charges of wilful attempt to evade and defeat the law and two charges of failure to file a return.

"Your honor probably would be interested to know," said Mr. Barnes, "that the investigation of the internal-revenue agents of the special intelligence unit show that the majority of Nitti's income was from alcohol sales and that the balance was derived from gambling enterprises.

"During 1927 he got a large share of the profits of the Cicero syndicate, which included Alphonse Capone, Ralph Capone, Jake Guzik, the defendant and others.

Objects to Figures.

Epstein objected, saying: "We do not admit guilt as to the to-wit account. We do as to failure to file. Those box-car figures are always a matter of controversy. I am making this statement because of the possibility of clearing the civil liability."

The judge asked for recommendations and Assistant District Attorney LaRue said in view of the large number of cases that have to be tried, and the amount of work that would have had to be done in this case in the event of a not guilty plea, the government would be satisfied with a sentence of eighteen months and a fine of $10,000.

The judge imposed sentence.

"Any other recommendation?" the judge asked. "Is the defendant ready to begin serving his sentence?"

Nitti gulped at that question and thrust his hands in his pocket but Attorney Epstein asked and was granted the stay until Jan. 10.

District Attorney George E. Q. Johnson was jubilant over Nitti's plea.

Situation Is Brighter.

The situation in the city's fight against hoodlum rule is much brighter, as a result of Nitti's conviction, than it was a year ago.

"Scarface Al" Capone, the racket czar, is being gradually stripped of his most able followers. His brother, Ralph, the beer boss of Cicero, is under three-year sentence for income-

(Continued on Fourth Page.)

WEATHER INDICATIONS.

(Dec. 20, 1930.)

Chicago and vicinity—Mostly cloudy tonight and Sunday; snow tonight; no decided change in temperature; lowest tonight near 20; moderate shifting winds becoming west to northwest.

Hourly temperatures since 3 p. m. yesterday are:

3 p. m.	34	3 a. m.	22
4 p. m.	33	4 a. m.	20
5 p. m.	32	5 a. m.	20
6 p. m.	32	6 a. m.	19
7 p. m.	32	7 a. m.	19
8 p. m.	32	8 a. m.	20
9 p. m.	32	9 a. m.	22
10 p. m.	[illegible]	10 a. m.	26
11 p. m.	27	11 a. m.	32
12 midnight	26	12 noon	35
1 a. m.	25	1 p. m.	37
2 a. m.	24	2 p. m.	37

Sunrise, 7:14; sunset, 4:21; moon rises at 3:01 a. m. Sunday.

(Detailed weather chart on page 6.)

TODAY'S RACE RESULTS

AT JEFFERSON PARK, LA.

First—Gertrude Reade, $14; Nervator, $3.60; Fast Life, $9.20.

AT HAVANA, CUBA

First—Chantry, 3-1; Jane Rinehart, 3-1; Sweet Lacruse, 3-1.

Second—Fairy Man, 20-1; Trappy, 31-; Aristocrat, 3-5.

COMPLETE WANT ADS

THE CHICAGO DAILY NEWS

FINAL MARKETS

56TH YEAR—49. COPYRIGHT 1931 BY THE CHICAGO DAILY NEWS INC. FRIDAY, FEBRUARY 27, 1931.—FORTY-EIGHT PAGES. THREE CENTS

CAPONE SENTENCED TO JAIL FOR CONTEMPT

Senate Enacts Vet Loan Bill Despite Veto

Overrides President's Objection by Vote of 76 to 17.

HINES READY TO ACT

Washington, D. C., Feb. 27.—(AP)—The veterans' loan bill was enacted into law today over the veto of President Hoover. The senate voted 76 to 17 to override the presidential opposition. This action, coupled with a similar decision yesterday by the house, put the law into immediate effect.

The act authorizes world-war veterans to borrow up to half the face value of their adjusted compensation certificates—an estimated average of $500 being made available to each of the 3,498,000 ex-service men who hold the insurance.

As in the house, the senate flouted the veto with little ceremony. With a two-thirds vote required, the house count was 328 to 79.

Sixteen republicans and one democrat in the senate voted to sustain the veto. Thirty-six republicans refused to support Mr. Hoover's veto and joined in passing the measure.

Loans to Start at Once.

Veterans Administrator Hines was at the White House when the senate acted. As he left he said the bureau could make the first loan under the bill within five minutes.

At the veterans' bureau some ex-soldiers were in line to apply hours before the vote.

Although Gen. Hines has not given an official opinion on the question, it was said at his office the "accepted opinion" was that the certificates would have to be two years old before being eligible for loans, as under regulations governing loans heretofore. This would affect numbers of holders.

Word of the new law went forth quickly to the fifty-four regional offices of the bureau, so applications could be accepted at once.

Checks for the loans will be mailed as rapidly as possible, with the first expected to be on their way tonight or tomorrow to applicants whose requests for loans were mailed in. After the rush starts, however, checks will be issued from within ten to twenty days of receipt of loan requests.

Vandenberg Defends Bill.

Senator Vandenberg, one of the administration stalwarts, opened the debate with a plea to disregard the veto He dissented with the president "with the greatest reluctance," but argued that "the facts are the same as when the senate voted 72 to 12 to pass this legislation."

"This bill is a sane solution to the perplexing question which some have proposed to answer with a $3,000,000,000 or $4,000,000,000 program," the Michigan senator said.

Vandenberg said the bill's loan proposal was satisfactory when the larger

(Continued on Third Page.)

GIVES BOND IN WIFE'S SUIT

Sir Charles L. Ross; Lady Ross. [Bain newsphotos.]

WARD LEADER'S HOME BOMBED; FAMILY PERILED

Enmity Stirred Up in Aldermanic Fight Hinted as Cause of Blast.

An aftermath of possible enmity stirred up in the 14th ward aldermanic campaign during last Tuesday's election was seen by the police as the motive for the bombing early today of the home of William Dunworth at 9030 South May street.

Several members of the family including a 17-month-old baby were endangered by the blast, which caused damage estimated at $1,000, tearing away the front porch and shattering all the windows in the building.

The bomb was the second of the night, a smaller black-powder blast having been exploded an hour earlier at the rear of a soft drink parlor at 4177 South Halsted street. The place was closed and the damage done was two smashed windows.

The explosion at the Dunworth home shook up Mrs. Dunworth and her baby daughter, Mary, and jolted another daugh r, Helen, 14, and Mrs Mary McDonald, who lives with her son-in-law, from their beds in a front bedroom.

Dunworth, formerly a cigar and cigarette wholesaler, was campaign manager for his brother-in-law, Cormac McDonald, 616 West 44th street, who was defeated as a candidate for alderman in the ward.

NAB TWO IN BURGLARY; ONE SHOT BY POLICE

Two youthful alleged burglars were captured by police early today after one of them had been shot in the side and seriously wounded. The wounded youth, who identified himself as Alex Frederick, 1361 South Homan avenue, was removed to the bridewell hospital. His companion, seized, gave the name of John Caduto, 2828 Lexington street.

The shooting took place at 1908 West Roosevelt road, where the youths are alleged to have broken into a butcher shop. Motorcycle Policeman Frank Kinsella, noticing the boys in the rear of the shop, called on them to halt and when they continued to run opened fire.

BARONET MAKES BOND IN SUIT WITH WIFE

Washington, D. C., Feb. 27.—(AP)—Sir Charles L. Ross, wealthy Scottish baronet, today was released on $60,000 bond in a suit for maintenance brought by his wife, Lady Patricia Ross.

After spending the night in the custody of officers in default of the $100,000 bond originally set upon request of his wife's attorneys to prevent him from leaving the court's jurisdiction, Sir Charles today succeeded in getting the figure reduced. It was signed by a surety company.

TODAY'S RACE RESULTS

AT NEW ORLEANS, LA.

First—Marabou, won; Florence May; Vladimir.

AT MIAMI, FLA.

First—Chuckling, $8.20; Fourth Ward, $3.10; Pat. Callahan, $2.60

Second—Siberia, $6.10; Maligned, $8.30; My Purchase, $2.90.

Third—Caterer, $15.40; Politen, $3.60; Pourboire, $2.90.

AT HAVANA, CUBA

First—Choice Caller, 2-1; Howee, 8-5; Cerveza, 6-5.

Second—Pere Noel, 2-1; Dinard, 2-1; Miss Evat, 8-5.

DEFENSE POUNDS DOCTOR'S THEORY IN DRAVES CASE

State's Witness Insists Attack Caused Death of Gary Girl.

CROWD PACKS COURT

BY GUY HOUSLEY.

Special Dispatch from a Staff Correspondent.

Valparaiso, Ind., Feb. 27.—In large measure the fate of Virgil Kirkland, Gary high-school football star, on trial for the gin-party death of Arlene Draves, appeared today to rest on the testimony of Dr. James D. Burcham, Lake county coroner's physician.

Throughout the morning session of court Defense Attorney Ronald Oldham of Chicago pounded away at the young physician, proppounded hypothetical questions and even threatened impeachment of his testimony. Dr. Burcham, however, stoutly defended his statement that the girl's death was caused by mistreatment other than a blow on the head.

"Death was due to shock and hemorrhage," maintained Dr. Burcham.

"This is the crux of the case," John Crumpacker, attorney for the defense, asserted.

Defense Scores Point.

Unruffled by Attorney Oldham's repeated questioning, Dr. Burcham maintained his stand. However, the defense scored a point by gaining an admission that the blow on the head which Miss Draves suffered caused a slow clot that resulted in a condition which might have been mistaken for the "dizzy drunkenness" mentioned in Kirkland's confession.

"Could slow dying from a clot forming on the brain be mistaken for drunkenness?" Attorney Oldham asked.

"Yes, sir, I grant you that," was the reply.

"The condition may even have fooled a doctor?"

"Yes, sir."

Attorney Oldham's hypothetical question set up the picture of the gin party at the home of David Thompson on the night of Nov. 30 and assumed the hypothesis that Miss Daves fell out of a chair while sitting on the porch and struck her head on the floor.

"Such a thing could have happened," Dr. Burcham said.

"The question demands an answer, yes or no, that it could have caused death," snapped Oldham.

"I didn't say it could cause death."

"Well, could it, doctor?"

"Such a thing is possible."

State Backs Doctor.

The defense openly declared during recess that it was tearing down the structure of the state's case and after an open threat in court to impeach Dr. Burcham's testimony asserted that it would put witnesses on the stand to disprove his statements. The state, however, stood by its guns and declared itself satisfied with the crucial witness as to the cause of the girl's death.

Today decorum ruled in the courtroom. Extra bailiffs guarded every door and after space roped off for the families of the defendont and victim had been occupied the doors were opened long enough to permit filling the remainder of the seats. Several hundreds thronged the corridors but failed to gain admission.

Behind the guard rail sat only the attorneys and representatives of the press, as compared to the Roman holiday experienced yesterday.

Judge Rebukes Audience.

Only once during the morning session was there a demonstration. Several spectators laughed at a clash between Oldham and Dr. Burcham. Judge Grant Crumpacker immediately rapped for order and said:

"This is not a show nor a political meeting. Demonstrations will not be countenanced in this court and any one making such a demonstration falls under contempt of court. Repeated offenses will result in the courtroom being cleaed. This is a public trial and we hope to conduct it as such. There must be no inteference from the spectators."

Then he ordered the bailiffs sprinkled through the crowd to hale before him any person violating his order.

"If necessary," he said, "I will send them to jail."

Judge Crumpacker, after hearing an hour's argument for and against admission of Kirkland's confession declared that the state must show conspiracy to gain its point and to date no conspiracy had been proved.

250 DEAD IN STORM THAT SWEPT FIJI ISLES

Suva, Fiji Islands, Feb. 27.—(AP)—Terrific winds swept the Fiji islands for more than twenty-four hours last week-end and at least 250 persons were dead, hundreds were injured and thousands homeless today. The death toll included at last five Europeans.

"KING OF JAZZ" ASKS DIVORCE

Mrs. Whiteman; Paul Whiteman. [Photograph of Mr. Whiteman by a staff photographer.]

PAUL WHITEMAN ASKS DIVORCE IN 'FRIENDLY' SUIT

She's Wonderful, but Marriage Is Failure, Says Jazz King Here.

A suit for divorce in which Paul Whiteman, the "king of jazz," now playing an engagement with his orchestra in a south side cafe, charges his wife, Vanda Hoff, with desertion was filed today by Attorney Benjamin F. Kanne in the Superior court.

The action is absolutely "friendly," asserted the rotund orchestra leader at the Flamingo hotel a short time later. His wife was here recently when returning to New York after a visit to a sick relative in California. The matter was thoroughly discussed and agreed upon at that time, said Mr. Whiteman.

"There is no venom in this action whatsoever," said the jazz king. "I think she's wonderful. We have been practically separated for three years, and actually for two. We tried married life on the road for seven years, and found it's no go. It certainly was no place to bring up a baby.

"I'll have the boy, Paul Jr., three months out of the year. His mother was very generous about that. He will be with me when I'm not playing one-night stands. Mrs. Whiteman will receive $600 a week."

The divorce is the third in the life of the musician. He was first married in 1908 to Nellie Stack of Denver, and separated in 1914. The second was to a "Jimmie Smith" in 1922, with divorce following in the same year.

$300,000 IN RUM SEIZED ON WINDJAMMER

Port Arthur, Tex., Feb. 27.—(AP)—Liquor valued at $300,000 was seized by customs officers who raided the sailing ship Seahawk here last night.

BLIND AD LEADS HIM TO ROLE IN BANK ROBBERY

Deal May Net Him $5,000, Chicagoan Says on Return from Canada.

'TWAS A "THRILLER"

BY STERLING NORTH.

As colorful an action story as any fiction concerning northwest mounted police, bank robbers, or the brave man who foiled the plot has been written in actual life by Fred P. Granger, 4716 Sheridan road, who has just returned from Weyburn, Sask.

Answering a blind ad in a Chicago paper of Jan. 22 for a "strong, alert man to go to Canada," Granger got in touch with a man who said he was Tom Porter, a heavyset, black-headed, broad-shouldered personage.

"Can you drive a truck?" asked Porter.

"I've had experience driving a truck in the army," said Granger.

First gaining assurance that it was not a liquor truck, Granger left for Canada with his new employer, who promised him $7.50 a day and expenses. They took a North Western train the evening of Wednesday, Jan. 28, and arrived in Weyburn, Sask., on Friday afternoon.

"We're driving back a liquor truck," said Porter as they reached Weyburn, the little town of 6,000 population, seventy-five miles north of the border.

This contradiction about the character of the truck was quickly squared with the facts, however, when Porter said it was not a liquor truck at all.

Porter Reveals His Plans.

But when safe in a hotel room across from the Weyburn branch of the Bank of Montreal, however, Porter revealed his real plans.

"There's your plant," he said pointing across to the bank.

"Where?"

"The bank. There's over ten grand in that joint. We'll split fifty-fifty, and there are only two clerks and no flatties on the street between 11 and 1."

"Walking over to the writing desk, he drew a diagram of the bank, showed me the layout of the vaults, the cashier's windows and the doors," Granger related on returning today. "Then he ripped up the map and tossed it aside. Later those ripped bits of paper helped to send Tom Laing, alias Tom Porter, to the penitentiary at Prince Albert for three years on a sentence from Judge James Graham of Weyburn.

Gets in Touch with Police.

"After he left my room I sent a note to the royal Canadian mounted police and got in touch with Detective Sergeant Metcalf.

"The final plans were made for Tuesday, Feb. 3, for 12:15. 'I'll telephone the teller and get him out of the cage,' said Laing at our final meeting previous to the robbery. 'You go in the door at exactly 12:15, snap the Yale lock behind you, pretend to be writing a check until the phone rings, cover the teller and the boy as the teller steps out of his cage to answer the phone, bang the receiver to let me know everything has gone all right, lock the two in the vault, scoop up the swag, and I'll be waiting around the corner with the car.'

"He gave me a businesslike .38 to do the business."

"But seven northwest mounted were planted at strategic points watching the car," he continued. "The faked bank robbery went through without a hitch. I filled the suitcase that was supposed to take the money with magazines on home canning, jumped into the car that was parked around the corner with motor racing, put the gun in the back of Tom Laing's neck and kept him still till the mounted police closed in."

Laing was convicted on Granger's evidence on the attempted bank robbery and is to stand trial on several other charges. The standard award of the Canadian Bankers' Association of $5,000 for information leading to the arrest of bank robbers will be forthcoming to Granger.

Warm Spell Doesn't Help Needy Appetites, Says Will

Special to The Chicago Daily News.

Beverly Hills, Cal., Feb. 27.—The stock market is picking up. That makes the rich boys feel a little better. Appropriations bills for government expenditures have been passed. Business in general in the last four or five weeks looks better. But all that has nothing to do with the folks whom the Red Cross has to feed. United States Steel may go to 1,001, Auburn to 1,000,000, but that doesn't bring one biscuit to a poor Negro family of fifteen in Arkansas who haven't got a chance to get a penny in money till their few bales of cotton are sold next fall. That some places haven't reached their Red Cross quota doesn't seem possible. Just because it's getting warm doesn't lessen these folks' appetites any. WILL ROGERS.

ON FILE AT ROGUES' GALLERY

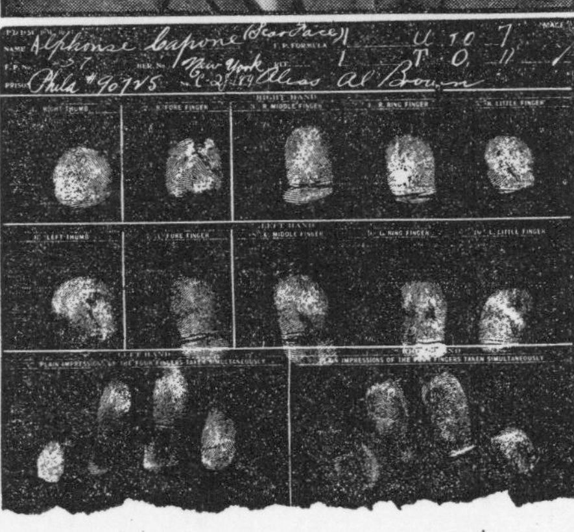

Pictures of Alphonse ("Scarface Al") Capone made at the bureau of identification here after his arrest recently on vagrancy charge. Finger prints of the jailbird and brothelkeeper and boss of rackets. Not since 1925 had Capone suffered the indignity of being "mugged" and finger-printed for the rogues' gallery. Capone drew a six months' sentence on a contempt charge in federal court today.

CHAPLIN FINDS SHAW A RIVAL FUNMAKER

Comedian Writes of Meeting with Playwright; Calls His Humor "Amazing."

BY CHARLIE CHAPLIN.

London, England, Feb. 27.—(NANA)—My meeting with Bernard Shaw, an event I had so long looked forward to, was delightful. We had the friendliest talk, which I hope will be resumed soon again.

For many years it has been my desire to meet Mr. Shaw. There were so many things that I wished to say to him I scarcely remember where I began in our conversation. For one thing I asked him whether he was going to the United States to make a talkie. Mr. Shaw laughed and said:

"But you know I have already made talkies in England. They came down to me at my home and recorded my voice on my own lawn. As for going to the United States—well, no, I am too old for that. In fact the strain of it would be far too great. Besides I am very busy in England and I am working every day."

Mr. Shaw's sense of fun amazed me. He really sees the funny side of things and we have a lot in common. I enjoyed his talk far more than words can say. We exchanged lots of stories of a humorous vein.

SHOPKEEPER MISTAKES CHARLIE FOR A BANDIT

London, England, Feb. 27.—(AP)—The constant pursuit of Charlie Chaplin by London street crowds led to his being mistaken for a holdup man.

He was walking down Westminister Bridge road with two companions, revisiting the scenes of his impoverished youth, when some one spotted him and a crowd gathered. Chaplin and his companions ducked into a candy shop.

Mrs. Powell, the elderly proprietor, feared they intended a holdup when they rushed in and closed the door. She insisted that the door be opened.

"I was almost hysterical," she said, "but when the little man asked for some nougat I wrapped up a shilling's worth. He paid me and walked quietly out. As the three left one of them said, 'You have lost a big order.'

"Then I saw the crowd outside and some one told me that the little man was Charlie Chaplin. I have sent him a letter of apology."

Markets at a Glance

NEW YORK—Stocks irregular. Bonds irregular. Curb stocks quiet and mixed. Call money holds at 1½ per cent. Foreign exchange mixed. Cotton lower. Rubber firm.

CHICAGO — Wheat steady. corn lower. Stocks mixed.

DOAK ORDERS DEPORTATION OF 'MOPS' VOLPE

Public Enemy No. 2 to Be Sent Back to Italy by U. S. Decree.

Tony ("Mops") Volpe, lieutenant of "Scarface Al" Capone and public enemy No. 2, today was ordered deported to Italy by Secretary of Labor Doak.

The order, issued at Washington, D. C., follows a series of hearings here at which it was shown that Volpe had technically violated the immigration laws of the United States by making a trip to Cuba and return.

John Elliott Byrne, Volpe's counsel, announced he would seek a writ of habeas corpus as soon as the warrant arrives here from Washington, probably within a week.

Volpe is 40 years old and lives at 1500 North Menard avenue with his wife and two children.

In 1925 Volpe was found guilty of counterfeiting war savings stamps and sentenced to the penitentiary. He has since been active in the Capone murder division—so active that at one time the north side gang, headed then by "Little Hymie" Weiss, offered to make peace if Volpe was "put on the spot" so they might square accounts with him.

Volpe is at liberty in bonds of $10,000 in the deportation proceedings and $10,000 on a public enemy vagrancy charge.

U. S. MISSIONARIES FLEE TO HANKOW, CHINA

Hankow, China, Feb. 27.—(AP)—American missionaires at Kikungshan, Honan province, 100 miles north of Hankow, were evacuating to this city today as a result of encroachments by communists following withdrawal of government troops.

IN THE DAILY NEWS TODAY

GANG CHIEFTAIN GLUM AT RULING OF U. S. JUDGE

Plans Appeal of 6-Month Term in Cell; Crowd Mills Around.

AFFIDAVIT IS ASSAILED

"Scarface Al" Capone, jailbird and brothelkeeper and public enemy No. 1, was found guilty of contempt of court today by Federal Judge James H. Wilkerson and sentenced to six months in the Cook county jail.

Judge Wilkerson overruled a motion for a new trial and an arrest of judgment. He ordered the district attorney to prepare a formal order and announced that it would be entered Monday.

Capone's lawyers, however, were granted leave to appeal the case to the United States Court of Appeals. The judge granted them thirty days to file a bill of exceptions and allowed the $5,000 bond which Capone had posted for his appearance in the contempt case to stand for the appeal. Capone will be at liberty until the case is settled by the higher courts.

Capone had been leaning forward, looking glummer and glummer as the judge's review of the testimony gave little indication of hope. When sentence was pronounced he slumped back in his chair and his jaw dropped.

Crowd Mills Around.

As the crowd milled around the gang chief following the decision he rose slowly from his chair at the counsel table and, staring straight ahead, pulled up his trousers. He appeared wrathful rather than sad over the prospect of six months in jail. The gum which he had previously been chewing placidly he now ground furiously; that was the only visible effect of the verdict.

"Anything to say?" he was asked.

"No, nothing," he answered.

A moment later, however, as he was shouldering his way out of the courtroom surrounded by his police guard, he gave vent to one remark:

"We'll get another court to overrule this court."

Case Ends Suddenly.

The case came to an end with a suddenness that surprised observers, although the judge during the time of Assistant District Attorney Jacob I. Grossman's closing argument had given indication that he planned to find Capone guilty.

Attorney Epstein in his closing argument found the going rocky what with the judge's interruptions to demand that he stick to essentials. He finally ended with, "Well, that's all I have to say."

Mr. Grossman spoke for a moment, asserting there was no foundation in fact for Epstein's declaration that the district attorney's office had regarded the Capone appearance as of no major importance.

Judge Begins Review.

The judge picked up his papers and began a review of the case.

"There was submitted an affidavit executed in Florida and sent by the respondent [Capone] to Chicago, signed by a physician named Phillips [Dr. Kenneth Phillips of Miami] and a lawyer."

The judge proceeded to read from the affidavit which set forth that Capone had been out of bed only ten days after a serious illness and that he was too weak to come to Chicago at that time.

"The affidavit," the judge continued, "was sent to Chicago with a letter presumably written by Capone. There was nothing to show he did not understand the affidavit. On the contrary he adopted the allegations in the affidavit.

"The testimony of Dr. Phillips must be considered in the light of the telegram which he sent to Dr. Omens (he told Dr. Omens that Capone was not seriously ill). We won't consider

(Continued on Fourth Page.)

WEATHER INDICATIONS.

(Feb. 27. 1931)

Chicago and vicinity—Mostly unsettled tonight and Saturday; some rain probable; slightly warmer tonight; lowest temperature near 40; moderate to fresh southerly winds, probably shifting on Saturday.

Hourly temperatures since 3 p. m. yesterday are:

3 p. m.	39	3 a. m.	34
4 p. m.	37	4 a. m.	34
5 p. m.	36	5 a. m.	35
6 p. m.	35	6 a. m.	34
7 p. m.	35	7 a. m.	34
8 p. m.	35	8 a. m.	35
9 p. m.	35	9 a. m.	38
10 p. m.	34	10 a. m.	42
11 p. m.	36	11 a. m.	44
12 midnight	35	12 noon	47
1 a. m.	35	1 p. m.	49
2 a. m.	34	2 p. m.	51

Sunrise, 6:29; sunset, 5:37; moon sets at 4:13 a. m. Saturday.

(Detailed weather chart on page 6.)

The net paid circulation for APRIL exceeded
Daily - - 1,320,000
Sunday, 1,780,000

DAILY NEWS

Copyright, 1931, by News Syndicate Co., Inc. Reg. U. S. Pat. Off. NEW YORK'S PICTURE NEWSPAPER Entered as 2nd class matter. Post Office, New York, N. Y.

Vol. 12. No. 272 40 Pages New York, Saturday, May 9, 1931★ 2 Cents IN CITY LIMITS | 3 CENTS Elsewhere

CROWLEY PLEADS 'KILL ME QUICK!'

Story on Page 2

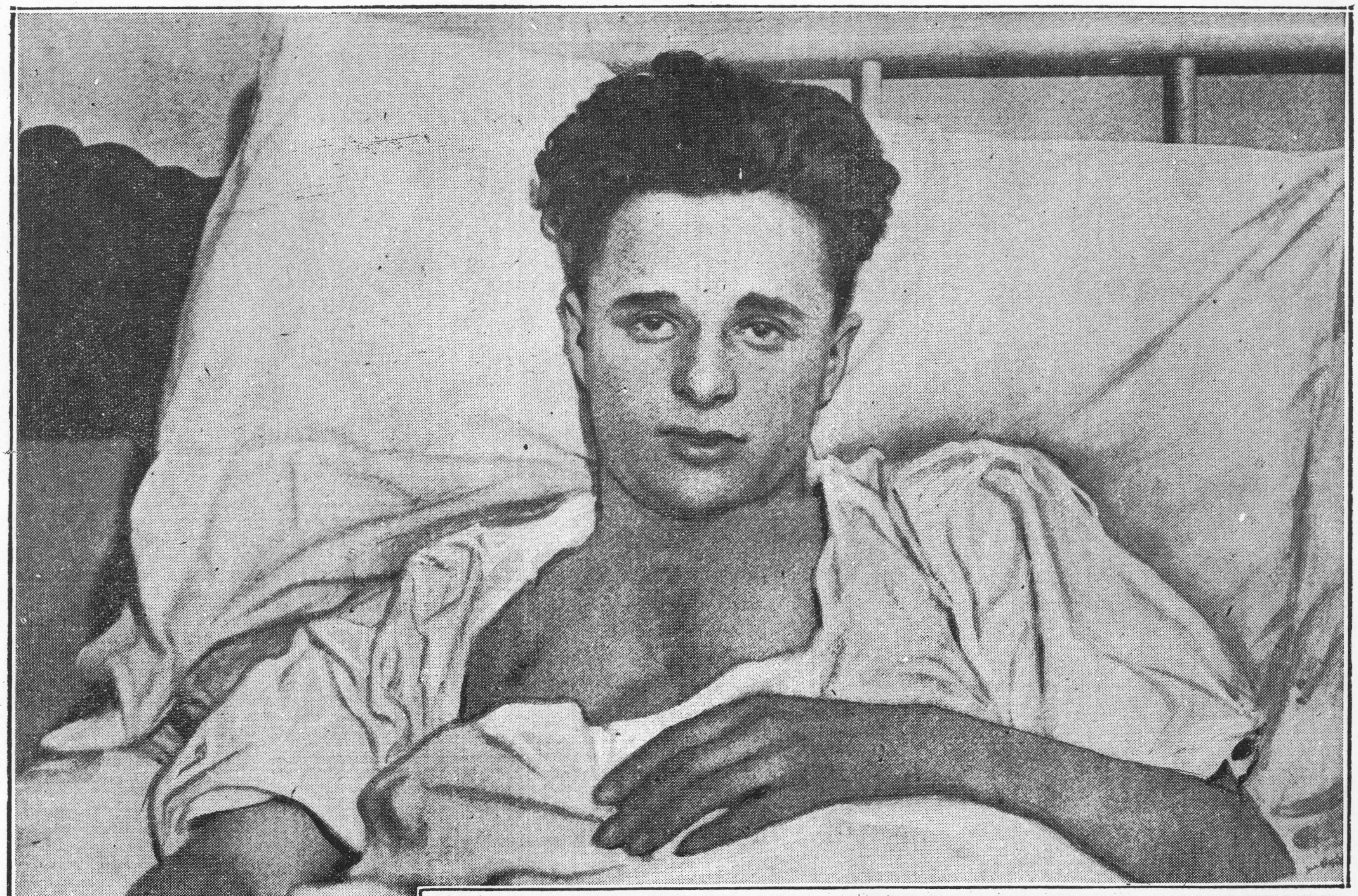

(NEWS photos)

With his shooting hand all wrapped up in bandages and useless, Francis (Two Gun) Crowley, cop killer, lay in Bellevue hospital yesterday crying: "Aw, I know I'm going to burn and I want to get it over with—right away. What's the use of fooling around with a trial?"

Rudolph Duringer, handcuffed, shows detectives in Yonkers where he tossed Virginia Brannen's body.

W-H-I-Z-Z!—Speedy justice got going in Bronx and Nassau yesterday. Francis Crowley was indicted for murder of Patrolman Frederick Hirsch, and Rudolph Duringer was indicted for killing Virginia Brannen. Helen Walsh, Crowley Sweetheart was held as witness.

—Story p. 2; other pics. p. 19.

Bennett Hiding Family After Gang Threats

PAGE TWO

2 CENTS PAY NO MORE!

Chicago Daily Tribune

THE WORLD'S GREATEST NEWSPAPER

FINAL EDITION

VOLUME LXXXX.—NO. 141 C [REG. U. S. PAT. OFFICE: COPYRIGHT 1931 BY THE CHICAGO TRIBUNE.] SATURDAY, JUNE 13, 1931.—28 PAGES THIS PAPER CONSISTS OF TWO SECTIONS—SECTION ONE ** PRICE TWO CENTS IN CHICAGO AND SUBURBS ELSEWHERE THREE CENTS

INDICT CAPONE; 5,000 COUNTS

WOMAN JURORS BILL DEFEATED BY SINGLE VOTE

Ends Old Battle for Present Session.

BY PERCY WOOD.
[Chicago Tribune Press Service.]

Springfield, Ill., June 12.—[Special.]—Lack of one vote prevented passage of the women's jury bill in the house today. It required 77 to go over and obtained 76, opponents tallying 46 votes against it.

J. J. McVICKER.

This ended, for the session, the struggle to allow women equal rights to men to sit in judgment upon others. The bill was introduced a month ago by James J. McVicker [Rep., Chicago], long a jury commissioner, immediately after the Illinois Supreme court had knocked from the statute books the law passed in 1929. The preceding assembly passed the same bill, subject to a referendum vote, which won last November, but in so doing was delegating unconstitutional powers to the voters, the court held.

The new bill, on third reading today, was championed first by its sponsor, Mr. McVicker. "Twenty-one states already have the law in effect," he said, "giving women full rights as citizens." His new measure had the support of every woman's organization in Illinois, he told the members as he importuned them to repass it in its present form, without a referendum.

Doubts Constitutionality.

R. J. Branson [Rep., Centralia] was immediately hostile. He opposed taking women from their homes and into the jury box, and questioned the constitutionality of the bill, even without a referendum.

Matching him in vehemence but aligned on the other side was Howard L. Doyle [Dem., Decatur], one of the few downstaters who eventually voted for the bill. He contended that since women already have suffrage they should be given the grant as jurywomen.

Mrs. Anna Wilmarth Ickes [Rep., Hubbard Woods], declared that the women of the state were glad to assume the duties of citizenship and were fully qualified for the responsibility.

Truman A. Snell [Dem., Carlinville], long an opponent of the legislation, delivered the major speech of the controversy. His plea was that the jury box is no place for a woman —the testimony in many cases being so vile as to put to shame any woman who would listen to it. The high point in chivalry, as the assemblymen could bestow it, he said, would be to protect them from such verbal contamination.

Keep 'Em at Home, Says Snell.

Instead of legislating to take women from their homes and put them into a service which might require their sitting all night debating in a stuffy jury room, the members would better vote laws to keep them at home and with their children, said Mr. Snell.

Miss Josephine Perry [Rep., Chicago] answered Snell by saying that women already serve in every capacity in court save upon the jury and observed that the most objectionable testimony ever heard in a Chicago court was given before a woman judge—Mary Bartelme. As far as night service is concerned, women frequently work all night long counting ballots at election time, she said.

CHAIN STORE TAX PASSED

Springfield, Ill., June 12.—[Special.]—Chain stores will be put under a tax in Illinois if a bill passed by the house today is voted upon favorably by the senate. The bill, introduced Feb. 3 by Anthony Pintozzi [Dem. Chicago], went through the house today by a vote of 135 to 0.

The bill requires any person operating and owning more than three business establishments or stores known as chain stores, in the retail of food products, meats, groceries, drugs, tobacco, wearing apparel, furniture hardware or manufactured products, to procure a license.

The fee of $25 for the first three stores and $1,000 for each additional store shall be paid each year to the department of trade and commerce. The act is to take effect Oct. 1.

Violation is a misdemeanor punishable by a fine and not less than $1,000 nor more than $5,000.

NEWS SUMMARY of The Tribune

[And Historical Scrap Book.]
Saturday, June 13, 1931.

LOCAL.

U. S. grand jury indicts Al Capone and 68 henchmen in $200,000,000 beer syndicate. Page 1.

Police get aid of detective chief and conduct a successful man hunt; suspect trailed to his lair. Page 1.

More Chicagoans are driving to work in downtown district than did so in 1929, traffic survey shows. Page 1.

Three agencies launch inquiry into three bombings in three days on west side and in Oak Park. Page 2.

School board plan revealed to spend a total of $81,000,000 on sites and buildings in two years. Page 3.

Court contest precipitated when father cuts off two sons in will and bequeaths estate to fiancée. Page 3.

Hundred answer call to "Progressive Republican" conference; prepare to launch slate. Page 4.

Merger formed by Central Trust and Bank of Republic announces officials of new bank and basis of exchange of stocks. Page 5.

Death notices, obituaries. Page 14.

DOMESTIC.

Second love diary of Starr Faithfull found; police hint it holds key to her murder. Page 1.

Lack of one vote prevents passage of the women's jury bill in the Illinois house. Page 1.

Miss Rhea Munroe will be married today, overcoming legal tangle. Page 1.

Dry navy seizes rum ship and $100,000 cargo in gun battle. Page 2.

Eva Le Gallienne is burned when heater explodes. Page 3.

Member of the million dollar Rondout train robbery gang killed trying to steal five tires. Page 5.

Senate leaders plan to speed action next week on reapportionment and tax relief bills. Page 6.

Socially prominent eastern girl picked up on hiking escapade after 10 days' disappearance. Page 9.

WASHINGTON.

Senator James Hamilton Lewis suggests short platform to win for Democrats. Page 4.

Young Republicans wind up rally with resolution calling Hoover as great as Lincoln. Page 4.

President gags navy on his economy move. Adams told White House will do all talking. Page 7.

FOREIGN.

New riots over emergency tax decrees grip Germany; police fire on communists and kill three. Page 3.

Pope replies to Fascist regret over violence. Page 8.

Paul Doumer will be inaugurated as president of France today to succeed Gaston Doumergue. Page 8.

SPORTS.

Cubs win third in a row from Phillies, 7 to 4. Page 19.

One hundred members of Slovak Union Sokol swell entry for Chicagoland Sports Congress. Page 19.

Gehrig hits tenth home run as Yankees beat Sox, 11 to 2. Page 19.

Jamestown and Twenty Grand race for $60,000 Belmont prize today. Page 19.

Braves defeat Cardinals, 7 to 5, for third straight victory. Page 19.

Risque, Hertz filly, wins Amazon purse by neck. Page 20.

EDITORIALS.

A Lesson in Demagogy; Dedicating the Harding Tomb; The Driver Bill; This Nutty World. Page 10.

BOOKS.

Writing on Dorothy Parker's new book of poems, Fanny Butcher tells how she regards ocean voyage, which she is taking. Page 12.

Prince von Bulow, from grave, strikes at ex-kaiser in first of four books; reviewed by Bernadotte Schmitt of the University of Chicago. Page 12.

FINANCE, COMMERCE.

Chicago stock prices hold steady in quiet day of trading. Page 22.

Scrutator explains new Illinois law which reduces time required in foreclosing mortgages. Page 23.

Railroad shares again are feature of trading on stock exchange. Page 23.

Survey tells how stock market weakness tends to slow up business expansion. Page 23.

Railway officials agree on details of consolidation plan. Page 23.

Wheat prices advance to end five day decline. Page 25.

Want Ad index. Page 25.

Average daily net paid circulation of THE CHICAGO TRIBUNE

February, 1931, *in excess of* **795,000**

March, 1931, *in excess of* **805,000**

April, 1931, *in excess of* **815,000**

May, 1931, *in excess of* **820,000**

Find Starr's Second Love Diary

POLICE HINT IT YIELDS KEY TO GIRL'S MURDER

Take New Trail in Hunt for Slayers.

BY TOM PETTEY.
[Chicago Tribune Press Service.]
(Pictures on back page.)

New York, June 12.—[Special.]—A second and more complete diary chronicling the life and love adventures of Starr Faithfull, Greenwich Village beauty, who died mysteriously in the Long Beach surf, was found today when detectives raided the Faithfull apartment in the absence of the family.

The discovery was declared by Inspector Harold R. King of the Nassau county police to be of "overwhelming" importance. The inspector and two detectives immediately chartered an airplane and flew to Riverhead, L. I., where District Attorney Elvin N. Edwards had gone for the week end at the adjournment of the Nassau county grand jury investigation until Tuesday.

In the jury room at Mineola nineteen witnesses had told almost every detail known of the life and last hours of Starr Faithfull to the jurors, who were asked to return indictments against two men identified only as "John and Richard Doe."

Diary Gives New Impetus.

Nothing in the day's testimony had developed to strengthen the murder case and the investigators were struggling with a mass of circumstantial evidence when the new and more conclusive information of Starr's affairs with wealthy and influential men came to light in the second diary.

Little information was permitted to be given out concerning the new book. It was revealed, however, that it was up to date and contained specific names and accounts of meetings with persons only vaguely mentioned in the original diary. The find was not made public until just before midnight.

Upon his return from a conference with Mr. Edwards Inspector King declared the new information tended to strengthen the theory that Miss Faithfull had been murdered. He added, however, that he did not expect an immediate arrest.

Stepfather Is Excited.

Stanley E. Faithfull, the dead girl's stepfather, who tried to keep detectives from removing the first diary from Starr's bedroom, was asked to night to explain the secreting of the second diary, the existence of which has been strongly suspected for several days.

Faithfull refused to discuss the diary, but talked mysteriously of dread surprises to come.

"Something important," he said. "something tremendously important, and something I've been hoping could be avoided is going to take place at Mineola in the morning. I can't tell you any more about it now."

While the Faithfull family was in Mineola courthouse awaiting a call before the jurors detectives entered their Manhattan flat to conduct a further search for the supplemental diary. The detectives were unable to obtain entrance and left, apparently to await the return of the family.

Later Hunt Successful.

Later two of them returned and entered the apartment, although it has not been made clear just how they got inside. Soon afterwards things began to happen and the Faithfull murder mystery took on new life.

During the day an assorted lot of witnesses, including all members of the Faithfull family, the divorced father of Starr, taxi drivers, pier attendants, persons from a midtown office building, a Boston society man, and two Manhattan artists who knew the slain girl well passed in and out of the grand jury room.

Four of them believe they saw Starr shortly before her death, either last Thursday or Friday afternoon. Three witnesses were drawn from the first diary.

Sylvia Elizabeth "Tucker" Faithfull, the little sister who liked parties, too, and whose stories have been strangely conflicting, spent an hour before the jury.

Meanwhile the cremation of Starr Faithfull, postponed at the last moment yesterday, was being completed.

Story of Girl in Taxi.

The elements of the story told by four witnesses before they appeared in the Mineola courtroom, pieced to-

(Continued on page 6, column 1.)

ON HER WAY TO BE REMAPPED UNLESS THERE'S A SLIP-UP

Copyright, 1931, by The Chicago Tribune.

Rhea Munroe Weds Today by Judge's Help

Greenwich, Conn., June 12.—[Special.]—Because Charles Arthur Moore Jr. was forgetful during the first part of this week, it appeared for some hours today that his marriage to Miss Rhea Logan Munroe, daughter of Charles Andrews Munroe, Chicago and New York utilities magnate, would not take place tomorrow.

The Connecticut law provides that application for a marriage license must be made five days before the ceremony is read. It was not until Thursday that Mr. Moore went for his license and was informed firmly but politely that he and Miss Munroe might be married next Tuesday and no earlier.

Judge Comes to Rescue.

But the Moore-Munroe wedding bells will ring out tomorrow in Christ Episcopal church. Probate Judge William G. Rungee, after a long conference this evening with the prospective bride and bridegroom, their parents, friends, relatives, and counsel, decided that, in view of the fact that 3,500 invitations had been sent out and that numerous social functions had been planned, it would be in line with public policy to waive the five day clause.

It was so ordered and the much needed license was issued by Town Clerk Henry P. Crawford, who went to the Probate court chambers to accommodate the anxious couple with the precious paper.

Judge Rungee had been appealed to much earlier, but was reluctant to grant the waiver. He said that he disliked to stretch the provisions of the law to fit this case and appealed to the attorney general of the state for advice. The state's attorney's office informed him that it was proper to waive the law under the circumstances.

Point to Many Tangles.

Meanwhile Ralph E. Brush, counsel for Mr. Moore, had pointed out to the jurist the lack of public policy involved if 3,500 socially prominent persons had to be informed that the wedding would be held on Tuesday instead of Saturday or to be told that the post-wedding parties would have to be pre-wedding parties.

With the obstacles all removed it is authoritatively stated tonight that Mr. Moore and Miss Munroe will be married by the Rt. Rev. E. C. Acheson, bishop of Connecticut, at 4 p. m. tomorrow. The bride's sister, Mrs. Herbert Lloyd, will be the matron of honor. Miss Edith Behr, daughter of the Benjamin Leslie Behrs of Chicago, will be the maid of honor. Henry S. Moore is to be the best man.

A reception will be held following the ceremony at Inverness, the summer home of the bride's parents.

GEN. ASHBURN RIDES BOAT BEARING NAME; OPENS BARGE SERVICE

St. Louis, Mo., June 12.—(AP)—Two oil burning towboats pushing five well laden barges left St. Louis late today for Peoria, Ill., to inaugurate the new barge service in the long planned lakes to the gulf waterway.

One of the towboats, the Gen. Ashburn, carried its namesake, Maj. Gen. T. Q. Ashburn. Secretary of War Hurley was expected to board the boat somewhere up the river. The other towboat was the Wynoka.

The tows will reach Peoria Monday noon, landing at the new barge terminal, which will be dedicated by the secretary of war, Maj. Gen. Ashburn, Congressman Hull, and others.

The cargo of the boats on the initial trip was composed of nearly all water borne goods, pineapples that came through the Panama canal from Hawaii, coffee that was shipped from South America, and sugar refined in Louisiana, besides a number of carloads of merchandise from St. Louis merchants.

BANDITS KIDNAP SPANIEL AFTER ROBBING COUPLE

Charcoal, a coal black spaniel, was taken for a bandit ride early this morning. The dog was in the automobile of R. C. Garlick, a sales manager, and his daughter, Mary Anne, when four robbers held them up in front of the Garlick home at 5480 Hyde Park boulevard.

The robbers boarded the car and forced Garlick to drive to 47th street and Wabash avenue. There they took $30, a $600 ring, and a $45 watch from him and $50 in jewelry from his daughter and drove away in the car. Charcoal was taken along.

"Charcoal's a fighter," said Miss Garlick later. "Maybe those robbers will be sorry they kidnaped him."

Monkey Bites Small Child; Is Placed in Dog Pound

Jim, a performing monkey, belonging to Nick Capo, 2808 Normal avenue, was in the dog pound last night after it had bitten a 3 year old boy. The boy, Robert Schroeder, 1506 East 55th street, had attempted to play with the monkey as it danced to the tunes from Capo's organ. The monkey is to be examined for possible rabies infection.

Robbers Bind 2 in Radio Store; Escape with $145

Two bandits last night tied M. B. Robinson, 4355 Drake avenue, manager, and Sol Bloom, 423 East 62d street, his assistant, with shoe laces and tape in the radio store at 3822 West 26th street. They then took $145 from the till and two radios and fled.

Auto Traffic in Loop Gains 4% in 2 Years

More Chicagoans are driving their automobiles to work at present than did so during the boom times two years ago, it was shown by the preliminary figures from a recent traffic survey of the downtown area, released yesterday by Leslie J. Sorenson, city traffic engineer.

The traffic survey, made by the police on May 26, showed, however, that the number of taxicabs entering the downtown district has fallen off 21 per cent from the volume of 1929, and that the number of service vehicles and trucks has fallen off 7 per cent.

Count Shows 4 Per Cent Increase.

The survey was made on all streets entering the area bounded by the river on the north and west and Harrison street on the south. The police counted 145,939 vehicles from 7 a. m. to 7 p. m., an increase of 4 per cent over the 139,891 counted on a similar occasion in 1929.

Passenger vehicular traffic increased 15 per cent, the figures being 101,831 this year and 88,489 in 1929.

Comparative figures for five principal entrances to the 'loop, for all vehicles, are as follows:

	1931.	1929.
Michigan ave. bridge		
[upper level]	21,760	21,926
[lower level]	4,803	6,494
La Salle st. bridge	11,579	5,466
Washington st. bridge	9,725	9,254
Jackson blvd. bridge	7,338	7,445
Michigan at Harrison st.	11,184	11,208

Await Wabash Ave. Figures.

The decrease in traffic over the link bridge, Mr. Sorenson pointed out, is explained by the completion of the Wabash avenue bridge, figures for which have not yet been totaled, and the widening of North La Salle street, with the consequent increase of traffic over that artery.

The traffic count, when completed, will include all persons entering the downtown district. Figures on pedestrians, collected by the police, are still being arranged, and the surface lines, elevated company and railroads are preparing statistics on their traffic on the day of the count, which will be furnished to the city.

Baby Swallows a Safety Pin; Dies After Operation

St. Louis, Mo., June 12.—(AP)—Swallowing a safety pin while his mother was dressing him after a bath proved fatal today to Donald Lee Moore, 2 year old son of Mr. and Mrs. Clyde Moore of Evansville, Ind. The child died at Barnes hospital here this afternoon after operation the preceding day failed to remove the pin. An autopsy revealed the pin had punctured the esophagus and penetrated into the right pleural cavity. A verdict of accident was returned by a coroner's jury.

Police Trail Suspect Right Into His Lair

(Picture on back page.)

Policeman Thomas Meagher, in charge of long distance calls at the detective bureau, put a telephone receiver to his ear yesterday afternoon in response to the operator's report that a call had come in from Fond du Lac, Wis.

"This is Chief of Police Silgen of Fond du Lac," said an excited voice on the wire. "We have a tip for you on which you can arrest Albert Jennings, escaped from the Boise, Idaho, state penitentiary, and wanted for forgery and other crimes in Idaho, Wisconsin and Illinois."

"Yes, yes," said Policeman Meagher.

Calls Wife from Chicago.

"He called his wife in this town from a telephone in Chicago," went on the voice. "Our force is alert and we had ordered the telephone company to trace any calls to the woman. They obeyed us and found that the number was Triangle 6699."

"It's a swell tip," said Policeman Meagher, with interest. "We'll get right on it."

But the policeman found there were difficulties in tracing the number. The telephone company reported that it was an unpublished number concerning which no information could be given out.

Detectives Await Word.

Policeman Meagher pleaded with the company officials to no avail. He conferred with Chief of Detectives John Norton. Chief Norton began to put pressure on the officials and Policeman Meagher ordered a squad of detectives posted at 79th street and Cottage Grove avenue, beside the substation of the Triangle exchange.

The men in the squad car waited tensely. They had been notified that Jennings was a desperate character and they made ready with machine guns and tear bombs. Meanwhile, Chief Norton succeeded in obtaining the desired information from the telephone company.

Over the radio came the measured accents of the police announcer.

End of the Man Hunt.

"Go to 830 East 75th street for Triangle 6699," the voice said.

The squad car roared into 75th street and halted in front of No. 830 East.

It was the Grand Crossing police station.

Inside the detectives found Jennings in a cell. He had been captured three days before and had telephoned his wife in Fond Du Lac from the pay telephone in the station.

VOTE TO FORBID FIREWORKS SALE ON COUNTY ROADS

The public service committee of the board of county commissioners yesterday approved a resolution to prohibit the sale of fireworks in Cook county outside of Chicago. The action was taken at the request of the city council.

The sale of fireworks in Chicago has been prohibited for a number of years, but because they have been sold outside the city limits, the city act has been virtually nullified. Since the county board has no jurisdiction in the country towns and villages the ban will apply only to the sale of fireworks along the highways.

THE WEATHER

SATURDAY, JUNE 13, 1931.

Sunrise, 5:14; sunset, 8:26. Moon rises at 3:14 a. m. on Sunday. Venus, Mercury, and Saturn are morning stars. Jupiter and Mars are evening stars.

Chicago and vicinity—Cloudy, becoming fair, not so warm Saturday; moderate winds, mostly west to northwest; Sunday partly cloudy.

Illinois—Becoming fair, slightly warmer in extreme northwest portion Saturday; Sunday mostly fair, slightly warmer in north portion.

TRIBUNE BAROMETER.

TEMPERATURES IN CHICAGO

MAXIMUM, 3:30 P. M. 87
MINIMUM, 2 A. M. 69

3 a. m.	72	Noon	83	8 p. m.	74
4 a. m.	71	1 p. m.	84	9 p. m.	74
5 a. m.	71	2 p. m.	86	10 p. m.	74
6 a. m.	70	3:30 p. m.	87	Unofficial—	
7 a. m.	71	4 p. m.	86	11 p. m.	72
8 a. m.	73	5 p. m.	85	Midnight	71
9 a. m.	76	6 p. m.	84	1 a. m.	70
10 a. m.	79	7 p. m.	80	2 a. m.	69
11 a. m.	82				

For 24 hours ended 8 p. m. June 12: Mean temperature, 78; normal, 66; excess since Jan. 1, 506 degrees.

Precipitation, trace; deficiency since Jan. 1, .60 of an inch.

Barometer—8 a. m., 29.92; 8 p. m., 29.83.

Highest wind velocity 20 miles an hour from the south at 1:25 p. m.

[Official weather table on page 14.]

U. S. JURY HITS $200,000,000 BEER COMBINE

Gang Chief Named with 68 Aids.

BY CHESLY MANLY.
(Pictures on back page.)

The federal government yesterday delivered another smashing blow at the Capone gang with the indictment of Al Capone himself and 68 of his followers in a $20,000,000 a year beer combine.

The evidence of dry law violation piled up against Capone and his men constitutes the greatest prohibition conspiracy case on record, according to federal agents. The indictment tells the story of the rise of a gigantic industry with total receipts of $200,000,000 for the ten years beginning in 1921 and with hundreds of trucks convoyed by gunmen ready to shoot it out with dry agents as they moved through the loop.

5,000 Offenses Charged.

The true bill alleges 5,000 separate offenses, 4,000 of which consisted in the transportation of beer trucks with their loads of 32 barrels each.

During the ten year period covered by the alleged conspiracy the gang had an average of ten breweries in operation all the time, according to federal investigators. Each brewery had a capacity of 100 barrels of beer a day and the standard Capone price is $55 a barrel, so that the daily gross receipts would be $55,000.

Back of the indictment is the story of an intensive investigation, led by Eliot Ness of the special prohibition agents, of telephone wire tapping, wild night rides in pursuit of beer convoys, near gun battles, threats of death, and offers of bribes as high as $50,000.

Second Indictment.

The indictment, returned by the grand jury before Federal Judge John P. Barnes, follows another one returned last Friday charging Capone with income tax evasion. The new charge adds the possibility of two years in the penitentiary and a $10,000 fine to the possible maximum of 32 years' imprisonment and an $80,000 fine which Capone faces if he is convicted under the income tax indictment.

Capone already is under sentence of six months in jail for contempt of federal court and is awaiting the outcome of an appeal in this case. He is to be arraigned at 2 p. m. Tuesday before Federal Judge James H. Wilkerson on the income tax indictment, and the federal prosecutors will ask an early trial.

Gang in Financial Straits.

Yesterday's indictment, say the federal men, not only represents the first time the "big shots" of a gang have ever been hit by liquor law charges in Chicago but virtually assures the undoing of Capone.

His gang is said to be almost insolvent, due to the wrecking of his huge breweries by raiders, the large amounts paid for protection, the high bonds required of his gangsters in the federal courts, and the business depression.

United States Attorney George E. Q. Johnson permitted the $50-

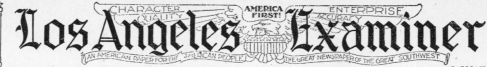

CALIFORNIA FORECAST
Los Angeles and Vicinity—Fair Saturday and Sunday; moderate temperature.
San Francisco and Vicinity—Fair and mild Saturday and Sunday.
MEAN TEMPERATURES
Los Angeles... 63 New York... 58
San Francisco... 61 Chicago... 67
San Diego... 63 Detroit... 66
Seattle... 47 Boston... 58
Portland... 51 Washington... 58
Omaha... 66 Atlanta... 71

CHARACTER QUALITY — AMERICA FIRST! — ENTERPRISE ACCURACY

Los Angeles Examiner

AN AMERICAN PAPER FOR THE AMERICAN PEOPLE — THE GREAT NEWSPAPER OF THE GREAT SOUTHWEST
Reg. U.S. Pat. Off.

FINAL AND COMPLETE

VOL. XXVIII—NO. 317 | Copyright, 1931, by Los Angeles Examiner | Two Sections—Part One | LOS ANGELES, SATURDAY, OCTOBER 24, 1931 | S | For Complete Weather Reports, See Page 7, Part II. | PRICE FIVE CENTS

MRS. JUDD SURRENDERS; CONFESSES KILLINGS

Today

Laval, of Many Races
Idaho and France
Fine Titles, Fine Names
Venus' Birthplace

By Arthur Brisbane

An official dinner at the White House enabled some American newspaper men to study and admire the French visitor, Premier Laval, "close up." There were Ogden Reid, who owns the New York Herald-Tribune, Gannett and Paul Block, each owning many newspapers, Frank Kellogg from Chicago, and others.

Laval, officially announced as "the president of the council of ministers of France," walked slowly around the White House reception room in which guests stood, in a row, shaking hands with each. Marshal Petain, called by General Pershing "the greatest soldier that France produced in the war," followed.

Last came President Hoover, shaking hands with all his guests, then walking to the dining room, with Laval beside him.

The President looked weary, and no wonder. A White House official of long experience said:

"I have seen seven Presidents and not one ever worked as resident Hoover works."

Premier Laval and Senator Borah, side by side, with an interpreter translating what each said, formed an interesting contrast, as far apart as the buckwheat cakes of Idaho from the *bouillabaisse* of Marseilles.

Newspaper reporters who write "You see in Laval's face his French peasant ancestry" would change the description on closer inspection.

You see in the face traces of many nations that have sailed the Mediterranean for five thousand years, coming in over the Pyrenees, the Alps and down from the North and East.

Who sees only "peasant ancestry" in the face of Laval would see only a peasant woman in the Mona Lisa face.

Laval's eye is as penetrating as a steel drill, and his face tells nothing of what he thinks. His smile, reflecting the sunshine of the *Midi*, tells nothing. Don't play poker with him.

He is exactly the height of Vice President Curtis, whose head comes as high as President Hoover's shoulders. But Laval is perhaps an inch or two taller than Napoleon the first, more securely powerful than Napoleon, and he will have no Waterloo or St. Helena.

The democratic Laval had about a the following gentlemen with resounding names: Marquis de Chambrun, Duc de Broglie, Major Gen. Count de Chambrun, Marquis de Grasse, Marquis de Rochambeau, and Duc de Noailles.

Perhaps Mr. Laval has heard of a certain weakness for titles in this proud democratic country.

The French thought they were rid of titles in the revolution, but they were not. Such things stick, for if you have nothing else to distinguish you, a title is convenient. When a strong-lunged servant roars out "MARQUIS DE ROCHAMBEAU," democracy is impressed.

If Premier Laval went to China he would taste birds-nest soup, or shark's fins, and look pleased. Arriving here, he tasted ice water for the first time, and remarked that it was "a good cure for a Frenchman." He didn't say WHAT it would cure.

If his grandmother in the little Auvergne village near Clermont-Ferrand could have seen little "Pierre" with that glass of water, she would have dashed it at him to save him from destruction, mixing some claret with the water, or at least a few drops of *fleur d'oranger*.

It would have amazed sincere prohibitionists to see Laval, with the energy of ten dynamos, the French Marshal Petain, straight as an arrow at 75, and the others, NOT raised on ice water, or ginger p, who have drunk French red ne all their lives, and show no bad effects.

Long ago, Disraeli, British statesman, whose ancestors came out of Aria, and who made Victoria Empress of India, Disraeli, to whom Bismarck referred admiringly as "The Old Jew," went to Berlin.

He came back bringing "peace with honor," casually picking up and adding the useful island of Cyprus, one of the largest in the Mediterranean, to Britain's possessions

Now the inhabitants of Cyprus are in rebellion, demanding the right to leave Britain and join with Greece. Britain sends airships with soldiers and that rebellion will be squelched. There is just enough reality to remind you how easily big empires can go to pieces.

A really interesting spot on earth is that island of Cyprus, with its 350,000 inhabitants.

Alexander the Great quarreled about it, St. Paul and St. Mark preached on it, Richard the Lion-Hearted was married on it and Aphroulte, goddess of love, is supposed to have been born of its sea foam.

The present row is prosaic, having to do with an unpopular tariff.

We shall see a real flyer when Gen. Italo Balbo flies here from Rome to represent Mussolini with a squadron of 24 Italian sea planes on a trip round the world.

General Balbo, only 35 years old, is Mussolini's air minister and a real flyer.

When he soars above Washing-

(Continued on Page 4, Column 5)

LAVAL, HOOVER CONFER; BORAH ASSAILS PACT

Senator Raps Security Treaty Proposal; Capital Doubts Conference Will Be Success

President and Premier Reveal Parley Solely to Expedite Recovery From Depression

By William P. Flythe
Universal Service

WASHINGTON, Oct. 23.—President Hoover and Premier Laval of France, flanked by their advisers, opened their momentous international conference at the White House tonight after a day of preliminaries marked by a blast from Senator William E. Borah of Idaho against any security pact and any extension of the moratorium.

There was an atmosphere of grave doubt that agreement can be reached on any of the important points at issue.

As the conference proceeded and in order to clarify the situation, the White House issued the following statement:

"Both the President and Premier Laval wish it made clear that the conversations upon which they are engaged are solely in respect of such policies as each of the two Governments can develop to expedite recovery from the world economic depression. There is no remote basis whatever for statements as to 'demands,' 'terms of settlement' or any other like discussions.

Frank Exposition

"Happily there are no controversies to be settled between France and America. None such exist.

Borah's frank exposition of his viewpoint on international problems came at a remarkable conference held in the foreign relations committee room at the Capitol. Before him were the correspondents of the French newspapers who came over with Laval and the Washington correspondents.

A security pact, or an alliance with the United States to side with France in case of attack, appeared to be the obstacle on which no accord can be reached. In turn this may prevent an understanding on armaments war debts, and moratorium extension.

It was officially stated, before the President and the Premier went into the meeting, that public expectation is too high and that it will be physicall impossible to arrive at any definite agreements at this time.

Major Importance

The meeting in the White House is of major importance. All of the widely divergent views of the two Governments will be explored

For the most the talks will be conducted in French. Undersecretary of the Treasury Ogden Mills has been called in to act as interpreter for the President and also to give expert financial advice on the extension of the debt moratorium and the gold question. Secretary of State Stimson was called in as America's expert on armaments and the other diplomatic questions. M. Laval was accompanied by Jacques Bizot, French financial expert. Secre-

(Continued on Page 11, Cols. 2-4)

100 MARGIN SEEN FOR MACDONALD

LONDON, Saturday, Oct. 24.—(Universal Service Special Cable.)—An election forecast published in this morning's Daily Telegraph gives the National Government a majority of 100 votes over Laborite-Liberal opposition. The Government: Conservatives, 320; Liberal-Nationalists, 25; Labor-Nationalists, 9. The opposition: Laborites, 209; Liberals, 45.

SEAHAM, England, Oct. 23.—(AP)—Prime Minister MacDonald, returning to his constituency today from a tour of the midlands, said the National Government's election campaign was proceeding splendidly, and started his final drive in a series of four meetings.

Japan Refuses to Set Date for Troops' Recall

Reply Balks Efforts of U. S. and League to Settle Dispute With China

BY GEORGE W. HINMAN JR.
Universal Service Special Cable

GENEVA, Oct. 23.—The Japanese Government today refused to set a date for withdrawal of troops from Manchuria, balking the efforts of the council of the League of Nations and the United States to settle the China-Japanese dispute.

In a series of counter-proposals to the council's resolutions recommending direct negotiations to evacuate Manchuria and Chinese methods for guaranteeing security of Japanese lives, rights and property, Japan so juggled the council's recommendations as to make withdrawal of troops dependent on preliminary negotiations.

Stand Unchanged

Tokyo's answer to the council's recommendations did not swerve from the original Japanese stand—that Japan must be convinced of the efficiency of Chinese guarantees of security and must be assured that Japanese treaty rights will be recognized before troops are withdrawn.

China's acceptance of the League's recommendations was based on the beginning of the withdrawal of Japanese troops simultaneously with the beginning of direct negotiations.

The Japanese counter-proposals further recommended immediate China-Japanese negotiations to arrange details of the evacuation when a date is set, the communication of results of negotiations to the council and the convoking of the council to examine the situation at the discretion of the president, instead of on November 16.

Italian Monarchs Wed 35 Years Today

ROME, Oct. 23.—(AP)—King Victor Emmanuel and Queen Elena, who in thirty-one years on the throne have had the longest reign in modern Italy, celebrate their thirty-fifth wedding anniversary tomorrow at San Rossore. Already telegrams of congratulation have begun to arrive from rulers and heads of governments in almost every corner of the globe.

Pauline Lord Sued for Divorce in Reno

RENO, Oct. 23.—(AP)—Pauline Lord, actress star of many stage productions, including "Strange Interlude," was sued for divorce today by Owen B. Winters, advertising man. They were married in Elkton, Md., April 27, 1929.

12 Inches of Snow Fall in Idaho Area

BOISE, Ida., Oct. 23.—(AP)—Twelve inches of snow fell yesterday at Atlanta in the Boise watershed and snow was still falling, the Forest Service here was advised.

Hoover Does Finger Talk

BY ARTHUR "BUGS" BAER.

President Hoover and Premier Laval had a nice friendly chat with gestures.

Mr. Laval adenoids no English. Mons. Hoover nasals no French.

Everything was going fine until Mons. Hoover tried to order an egg.

They used signs for everything. When Herbert rubbed his thumb and forefinger together that meant war debts.

When Laval turned his pockets inside out it signified no checkee, no laundry.

Mr. Hoover held his nose and that was an inquiry about business conditions. Mons. Laval responded graphically by doing the dying swan while the interpreter played the piccolo.

The concensus of opinion on the gold standard resulted in that good old pantomime, London bridge is falling down.

Then Mr. Mellon arrived and they played shadowgraphs on the wall. Mons. Laval pinned the tail on the donkey and they wound up with an international banquet of bird seed and animal crackers.

(On Page 9 Linguist "Bugs" springs an eloquent answer to critics of his doughnutting policy.)

TRADE REVIVAL CLOSE AT HAND, SCHWAB SAYS

Declares Nation Will Be More Prosperous Than Ever; Other Steel Men Say Worst Is Past

NEW YORK, Oct. 23.—(AP)—Belief in slow, but sure revival of business throughout the United States was the keynote sounded today at the annual fall meeting of the American Iron and Steel Institute.

While leaders of the industry, headed by Charles M. Schwab, president of the institute, did not attempt to gloss over or evade the fact that the country has been in a "real depression," they were generally of the opinion that the worst had been seen and that there were indications of a betterment all along the line.

Mr. Schwab recalled that during his career he had seen a number of serious depressions weathered with the result that the country always emerged more prosperous than before.

"And," he added, "history will repeat itself."

Sentiment Better

"Fear has been lessened," he said, in expressing his belief that better times were ahead. **"There will be no collapse. The sources of credit have been mobilized and we shall pull through. I have seen us pull through too many crises to be overwhelmed by the situation of the past months."**

Other speakers believed President Hoover's credit corporation had generally strengthened the hand of business and, although the steel industry was admittedly "in the dumps" just at present, the outlook was not viewed as discouraging.

Sentiment was **"a little better,"** Eugene Grace, president of Bethlehem Steel told the meeting, **with some consumers already showing signs of taking more interest in their steel requirements. The recent slight gain in commodity prices was looked upon as hopeful.**

Calles' Daughter and Mate in U. S.

SAN ANTONIO, Tex., Oct. 23.—Dr. Joseph J. Eller of New York and his bride, the former Artemisa Calles, left by plane this afternoon for Dallas and will fly on to New York tomorrow. The couple arrived by plane yesterday following their marriage at the home in Mexico City of the bride's father, former President Elias Calles.

Hollywood Man Shot Dead At Tulare

TULARE, Calif., Oct. 24—(AP)—In a pistol duel with Traffic Officer L. Hans Kober, a man identified as Bert Coulter, 25, Hollywood, was shot and killed yesterday. A coroner's jury returned a verdict of "justifiable homicide" when it was shown the youth started firing when Kober signaled him to stop.

Duce Seeks Better Bread for Italy

ROME, Oct. 23.—(AP)—Premier Mussolini is taking an interest in a widespread complaint that the bread here isn't all it should be. As a result, breads of all nations are to be gathered to show bakers and their customers how good bread can be.

Dirigible Los Angeles Will Fly to Atlanta

LAKEHURST, N. J., Oct. 23.—The Navy dirigible Los Angeles will make a flight to Atlanta on Monday, according to present plans. After a short cruise today, it returned about 5 p. m. and was safely berthed in its new hangar.

PARAGUAY REVOLT QUELLED, 3 SLAIN

BUENOS AIRES, Oct. 23.—(Universal Service Special Cable.)—A mob of communists tonight stormed the Presidential palace at Asuncion, capital of Paraguay, allegedly bent on assassinating President Jose Patricio Guggiari, Asuncion dispatches stated.

Three reds were killed by police who beat back the attack, the advices added.

The disorders were reported still in progress at a late hour tonight and several additional deaths are believed to have occurred.

The Government issued a communique declaring the situation well in hand, however.

Slew Two Women in Self Defense She Says; Packed Bodies Unaided; Hand Wounded, Bullet Extracted

Bares Quarrel Before Tragedy; 'Victims Attacked Me'

OWN STORY

Suffered From Pain and Hunger While a Fugitive

Weak and suffering from the pain of her wounded hand and the exhaustion of her four days in hiding, Mrs. Ruth Judd last night told her own story of the double killing in Phoenix Friday night, October 16, that was discovered when two trunks and a suitcase yielded their ghastly secrets in a Los Angeles baggage room.

She told it to her husband and his attorney, Judge Louis P. Russill, as a stenographer took down her broken words. Here it is, as gathered from those who heard it.

Three in House
Suddenly Miss Samuelson Became Enraged

"The three of us were in the house together. I was talking to Miss Samuelson, and we were discussing Miss LeRoi.

"Suddenly Miss Samuelson became infuriated at me. It seemed that she thought I was going to say something about Miss LeRoi.

"Everything happened so fast after that that I have difficulty in remembering details of what occurred. In her rage Miss Samuelson left the room and came back immediately.

"I saw that she had a gun in her hand. She was rushing toward me. I was petrified with fear.

"Before I could do anything, or even scream, she fired.

We Fought
Finally I Got My Hand on on the Gun

"The bullet hit me in the hand. It stung dreadfully. The blood came. I lunged toward her and grabbed her. We wrestled around, and both of us fell to the floor. The gun fell from her hand, and it was there, between us.

"We fought desperately. Finally I managed to get my hand on the gun and shot her. I couldn't see what Miss LeRoi was doing while this was going on. It all happened so quick.

"The first thing I knew after I shot was that Miss LeRoi was pounding me over the head with an ironing board. I tried to dodge her blows, but couldn't. I was getting weak and weaker. Then I shot her, too.

"I shot to save my life. Miss Samuelson plainly meant to kill me when she fired at me. Miss LeRoi was doing her best to kill me with the board.

Terrified
I Hid in Unoccupied House All the Time

"I put the bodies into the trunks and came to Los Angeles by train. The first thing I did here was to try and reach my brother.

"I had some difficulty in getting in touch with him, and

(Continued on Page 2, Columns 7-8)

'End of the Trail'

DOCTOR JUDD AND HIS WIFE, RUTH, just after she had surrendered and confessed killing Hedvig Samuelson and Agnes LeRoi in Arizona and bringing their corpses to Los Angeles as railroad baggage. Note Mrs. Judd's wounded hand, from which a bullet was extracted.—Examiner photo.

Bulk of Morrow Estate Bequeathed to His Widow

ENGLEWOOD, N. J., Oct. 23.—(AP)—Senator Dwight W. Morrow left his entire estate, with the exception of $1,130,000 in specific bequests, to his widow.

The will was filed for probate today at Hackensack, N. J., and made public here. It made no provision for any of his children and created no trusts.

No estimate of the value of the estate was made public, but it is said to amount to several million dollars.

The Senator died in his sleep of a cerebral hemorrhage October 5 at the age of 58. His will named his widow, Mrs. Elizabeth Cutter Morrow, joint executor with the Bankers' Trust Company of New York.

In making Mrs. Morrow residuary legatee with no provision for his children, the will explained that Senator Morrow had "every confidence in her that she will provide for herself and my children for the best interests of all concerned."

The will made it explicit that the bequest to her was free of all restrictions.

While it was said at the Morrow home that it had been decided not to make public the value of the estate, there seems to be a fairly general agreement that the total is probably about $20,000,000.

Bequests of $50,000 each were made to Senator Morrow's sisters and his brother. They are Mrs. Agnes M. Scandrett, Miss Alice Morrow, Mrs. Hilda M. McIlvaine and General Jay J. Morrow.

Two sisters of Mrs. Morrow and her mother were left $25,000 each. They are Mrs. Annie E. Cutter, Mrs. Edith Cutter Yates and Miss Annie S. Cutter.

Claims Samuelson Girl Shot Her First; 'We Fought'

'DISGUISED'

Dyed Dress and Hid in Vacant House, She Reveals

PHOENIX, Ariz., Oct. 24.—Sheriff J. R. McFadden of Maricopa County, is leaving here this morning at nine o'clock, bearing extradition papers signed by Gov. George W. P. Hunt, for Mrs. Winnie Ruth Judd. He will drive through in his car, arriving in Los Angeles Saturday night.

County Attorney Lloyd J. Andrews, in Los Angeles, gave these instructions to McFadden in a telephone call tonight. The pair plan a fight to return Ruth Judd here immediately.

Wounded and on the verge of collapse after four days of eluding the pursuit of hundreds of officers, Ruth Judd, arrested last night in downtown Los Angeles, confessed that she had shot and killed both Hedvig Samuelson and Agnes LeRoi, the Phoenix trunk murder victims. She said she had been hiding in a vacant house.

Story Interrupted
Arrival of Police Breaks Her Narrative

The woman surrendered to her husband, Dr. William C. Judd, only after the pain of the gunshot wound in her hand—a wound, she declares, that was inflicted by Miss Samuelson — had driven her almost to madness.

She told her story to Judge Louis P. Russill, Doctor Judd's attorney, who repeated it to police officers in her presence. It was a story which she broke off abruptly at the sudden arrival of the police, who placed her formally under arrest.

Hiding Place
Says Vacant House Here Was Her Refuge

That Mrs. Judd's claim of self-defense and her custody will be the center of a strenuous battle was indicated last night. Police declared that her story is "full of holes." Her attorneys plunged into a bitter wrangle with the authorities, charging the use of third degree methods and fighting vigorously against her immediate extradition to Arizona.

Mrs. Judd's story, as repeated by Judge Russill, was that she had killed both women in self-defense, after Miss Samuelson had attacked and wounded her in a rage over something that Miss Samuelson

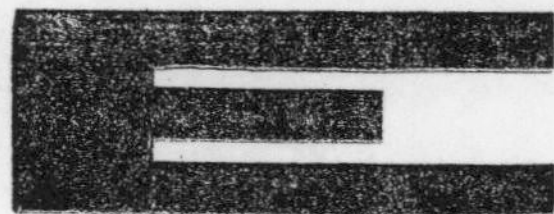

EXTRA

BOSTON EVENING AMERICAN

A HOME PAPER FOR PEOPLE WHO THINK

VOL. 28—No. 181 Published Daily by N. E. Newspaper Pub. Co. Entered as 2d Class Matter at Boston P. O. BOSTON, SATURDAY, OCTOBER 24, 1931 2 CENTS ZONE PRICE 3 CENTS

CAMBRIDGE EDITION

WEATHER

Partly cloudy, probably with light showers late tonight and Sunday morning; not much change in temperature; moderate south to west winds.

High tide, 9:48 a. m.; 10:07 p.m. Sun rises, 9:48; sets, 4:50.

The American is the only Boston daily paper using Universal Service and International News Service.

Texans Tackle Harvard on Fast Dry Field

11 YEARS FOR 'KING' CAPONE

Today

Laval, of Many Races
Idaho and France
Fine Titles, Fine Names
Venus' Birthplace

By Arthur Brisbane

AN OFFICIAL dinner at the White House enabled some American newspaper men to study and admire the French visitor, Premier Laval, "close up." There were Ogden Reid, who owns the New York Herald-Tribune, Gannett and Paul Block, each owning many newspapers: Frank Kellogg from Chicago and others.

Laval, officially announced as "the President of the Council of Ministers of France," walked slowly around the White House reception room in which the guests stood in a row, shaking hands with each. Marshal Petain, called by Gen. Pershing "the greatest soldier that France produced in the war," followed.

Last came President Hoover, shaking hands with all his guests, then walking to the dining room with Laval beside him.

The President looked weary, and no wonder. A White House official of long experience said: **"I have seen seven Presidents, and not one ever worked as President Hoover works."**

Premier Laval and Senator Borah, side by side, with an interpreter translating what each said, formed an interesting contrast, as far apart as the buckwheat cakes of Idaho from the *Bouillabaise* of Marseilles.

Newspaper reporters who write, "You see in Laval's face his French peasant ancestry," would change the description on closer inspection.

You see in the face traces of many nations that have sailed the Mediterranean for 5000 years, coming in over the Pyrenees, the Alps and down from the North and East.

Who sees only "peasant ancestry" in the face of Laval, would see only a peasant woman in the Mona Lisa face.

Laval's eye is as penetrating as a steel drill, and his face tells nothing of what he thinks. His smile, reflecting the sunshine of the *Midi*, tells nothing. Don't play poker with him.

He is exactly the height of Vice-President Curtis, whose head comes as high as President Hoover's shoulders. But Laval is perhaps an inch or two taller than Napoleon the First, more securely powerful than Napoleon, and he will have no Waterloo or St. Helena.

The democratic Laval had about him the following gentlemen with resounding names: Marquis De Chambrun, Duc De Broglie, Maj.-Gen. Count De Chambrun, Marquis De Grasse, Marquis De Rochambeau and Duc De Noailles.

Perhaps Mr. Laval has heard of a certain weakness for titles in this proud democratic country.

The French thought they were rid of titles in the Revolution, but they were not. Such things stick, for if you have nothing else to distinguish you, a title is convenient. When a strong lunged servant roars out "MARQUIS DE ROCHAMBEAU" democracy is impressed.

If Premier Laval went to China he would taste birdsnest soup, or shark's fins, and look pleased. Arriving here he tasted ice-water, for the first time, and remarked that it was "a good cure for a Frenchman." He didn't say WHAT it would cure.

If his grandmother in the little Auvergne village near Clermontferrand could have seen little "Pierre" with that glass of water she would have dashed at him to save him from destruction, mixing some claret with the water, or at least a few drops of *fleur d'oranger*.

It would have amazed sincere prohibitionists to see Laval, with the energy of ten dynamos, the French Marshal Petain, straight as an arrow at 75, and the others, NOT raised on ice water, or ginger pop, who have drunk French red wine all their lives, and show no bad effects.

Long ago, Disraeli, British statesman, whose ancestors came out of Asia, and who made Victoria Empress of India, Disraeli to whom Bismarck referred admiringly as "the old Jew," went to Berlin.

He came back bringing "peace with honor," casually picking up and adding the useful Island of Cyprus, one of the largest in the Mediterranean, to Britain's possessions.

Now the inhabitants of Cyprus are in rebellion, demanding the right to leave Britain and join with Greece. Britain sends airships with soldiers, and that rebellion will be squelched. There is just enough reality to remind you how easily big empires can go to pieces.

A really interesting spot on earth is that Island of Cyprus, with its 350,000 inhabitants.

Alexander the Great quarreled about it, St. Paul and St. Mark preached on it, Richard the Lion-Hearted was married on it, and Aphrodite, Goddess of Love,

Continued on Page 2, Column 4

"TIGRESS" CAGED BY LAW

Mrs. Winnie Ruth Judd, confessed slayer of two women, is shown shortly after her surrender in Los Angeles. Mrs. Judd is holding up her hand, which she says was wounded when one of the women shot at her before she slew them, assertedly in self defence. The photo was sent to the Boston Evening American from Los Angeles by International Newsreel telephoto.)

WOMAN LYING TO SAVE SELF, POLICE SAY

Doubt Mrs. Judd's Confession; Prosecutor Says She Shot Self to Prove Defense

Phoenix, Ariz., Oct. 24—Branding as "inconceivable" the self-defense story of Mrs. Winnie Ruth Judd, confessed slayer of two women, as told the police in Los Angeles, Deputy County Attorney G. A. Rodgers charged the woman had made "one fatal error in her story." That, he said, was in regard to the wound in her left hand.

Mrs. Judd's attorneys today announced they had obtained from her a letter that explained in detail the relations of the women. It will be produced at the trial to substantiate her declaration of "self-justification."

Atty. Rodgers said three witnesses would testify that Mrs. Judd carried her right arm in bandages last Saturday and Sunday. The slaying of Miss Hedvig Samuelson and Mrs. Agnes Ann Le Roi was done here Friday night, Oct. 16.

SAID SHE WAS BURNED

"The wound in Mrs. Judd's left hand, for which she was treated in Los Angeles last night, was self-inflicted," Rodgers charged. "She apparently forgot which hand she bandaged when she was

Continued on Page 5, Column 1

TEXANS BUCK HARVARD ON FAST FIELD

First Game in 30 Years Is Expected to Be Sensation of the Season

By BILL GRIMES

Accompanied by its university band, a 16-piece cowboy outfit and approximately 1000 Lone Star Staters, the University of Texas eleven makes its first bid in 30 years for international honors, against Harvard this afternoon in the Stadium.

The field is fast and dry and the game is expected to be one of the most thrilling to be played in the Stadium this season.

The Texans will be in the minority as regards numbers, but are confident that they will display as much, if not more, real enthusiasm as Harvard. The Lone Star State delegation is predicting that the Longhorns will furnish a surprise such as Harvard sprung at West Point. They point to the fact that the University of Texas is the Southwestern Conference titleholder.

Continued on Page 10, Column 3

Balances and Receipts

Washington, Oct. 24—Today's Treasury balance, $327,895,697; U. S. customs receipts, $24,565,479.

OFF TO PRISON TONIGHT

"Scarface Al" Capone, sentenced in U. S. court at Chicago today to 10 years in prison at Leavenworth, Kan., and one year in the county jail, must go to prison at once, Federal Judge Wilkerson ruled. He ordered the notorious gangster to be taken from Chicago to prison tonight. Capone was also fined $50,000. Here he is in court. (I. N. R. photo.)

SCARFACE AL ALSO IS FINED $50,000

Underworld Chief Calm at the Climax of Government's Long Battle

Federal Building, Chicago, Oct. 24—Federal Judge James H. Wilkerson today sentenced Al Capone, king of gangdom, to 11 years imprisonment for evasion of the income tax laws.

Capone also was fined $50,000 and ordered to pay the costs of his prosecution.

Judge Wilkerson ordered the marshal to take Capone to Leavenworth penitentiary tonight and the gang chief was taken to the U. S. marshal's office to wait until that time in a small cell-like room.

IN FINE PURPLE

Capone, standing before the bench, his hands behind his back, accepted the sentence stoically. His pendulous lips twitched a bit and his fingers clencvhed tightly as the judge read the somewhat complicated sentence.

The defendant was attired in a dark purple pinch-back suit and lavender tie. The indixe finger of his right hand was bandaged. His swarthy face was quite solemn as he stood there, listening to the ominous words of the judge.

"IT'S ALL OVER"

Capone appeared stunned by the verdict. He stood before the judge, watching him intently after the sentence was read, his hands behind his back.

After an application for a writ of supersedeas had been denied and Capone apparently realized he soon would be on his way to prison, the bulky gang chief walked over to his attotrneys, shook their hands and said:

"I guess it's all over."

Capone yet faces the possibility that he may be prosecuted, with his bodyguard, Phil D'Andrea, who toted a pistol into Federal Court October 10. D'Andrea has been cited for contempt. The case, after various continuances, comes up next Tuesday.

Capone had been convicted on three felony counts in the indictment—count 1, 5 and 3. He had

Continued on Page 5, Column 4

BELDEN, HEAD OF LIBRARY, DEAD

Picture on Page 5

Charles F. D. Belden, director of the Boston Public Library and former president of the American Library Association, died early this morning at the Pittsfield Hospital at Pittsfield.

He was advised by his physician early this week to go to Lenox for a rest. Three days ago he became suddenly ill and was taken to the hospital.

He was 61. His death is believed to have been due to heart trouble.

14 YEARS IN CHARGE

He had been director of the Boston Public Library since 1917. He lived in Eliot st., Jamaica Plain, and had a summer place at Martha's Vineyard.

His death was a shock to his associates, to many public officials, and to countless friends in Boston and throughout the country. He was widely known in his field.

He was a graduate of Harvard.

Continued on Page 5, Column 3

Girl and Man Killed in Crash; One Hurt

Wallingford, Ct., Oct. 24 (AP)—A girl and a man were killed today when their automobile crashed into a truck near here. Miss Adele Klemas of Hartford died shortly after being admitted to the Meriden Hospital. Several hours later, Philip Bressler, 25, of New York, died at the same hospital.

The driver of the machine, Louis Sargeant, 25, 115 Clairmont pl., Elmira, N. Y., was severely injured. A charge of manslaughter was lodged against him at the hospital.

FUMES KILL 1; 3 STRICKEN

Danvers, Oct. 24—One woman is dead, another is dying, and two children are ill, all victims of mysterious poison fumes intheir home at 59 Lawrence st. today.

The woman killed was Mrs. Lillian A. Pitman, 72 years old. Her daughter, Mrs. Eva Hamilton, 43, is dying at the Hunt Memorial Hospital.

The two girls who were overcome and are being treated at the hospital are Olive Hamilton, 17, and Dorothy Hamilton, 20 years old. The victims were found unconscious in the kitchen and living room by Mrs. Hamilton's youngest child, Austin, 15.

He rushed to the home of Mrs. Earl Warman, nctx door, and asked her to investigate.

Firemen were forced to work in relays to romev the victims.

Dr. John Moriarty pronounced Mrs. Pitman dead and ordered the others to the hospital.

Emergency calls were sent to the Beverly Gas Co., but after an investigation it was declared no illuminating gas fumes could be found in the house.

Safe-Crackers Fire at Man in Bedford

Bedford, Oct. 24—Two shots were fired at a B. & M. engineer on his way to work by safebreakers, who broke into the Middlesex Coal & Grain Company's office and blew the door from the safe.

The engineer, Frank Freeman, told police he could not see his assailants because of a heavy mist. The safebreakers were unable to force the inner safe, but got $8 from a desk.

Good News

In the Day's News

(Further details elsewhere in this edition.)

LADIES' GARMENT Manufacturing Co. of Minneapolis has added 200 workers to its payroll.

CHAMPION ANIMAL Food Co. of Minneapolis has jumped its payroll from $85,000 to $125,000.

JARMAN SHOE Co., Nashville, Tenn., now has more than 1200 workers on its payroll, a., output of 6750 pairs daily and is putting on more help.

ELECTRIC output of New England Power Assn., index of business activity, for past month is up 11 per cent over total for year ago.

AMERICAN ZINC reports earnings for September and first nine months of 1931 well above those for like 1930 period.

FEDERAL Motor Truck retires $625,000 notes without borrowing, leaving $1,000,000 in cash and securities in reserve.

OWENS-ILLINOIS Glass Co. is recalling workers and laying plans for expansion.

FULL TIME employment for winter indicated at Corona plant, now on overtime basis.

Rain Is Put Off to Tonight; Sunday Fair

Boston's first big football Saturday of the season found the weather man warming it up slightly with a southwest wind for the throngs making their way toward the Stadium and Fenway Park, many of them from Texas and Michigan, here to root for the "longhorn eleven" and Marquette against Harvard and Boston College.

Sunday is predicted fair, with possible light showers during tonight.

TWO TUFTS BOYS PUT OFF TEAM

Two members of the Tufts freshman football team were barred from participating in today's game with Andover pending investigation of a night of revelry on the Boxboro-Acton road which resulted in the arrest of 18 fraternity initiates.

Ben Carlyn, star center, and Rafael Parlade, Cuban lineman, who were among the group arraigned in Concord district court charged with malicious destruction of property and disturbing the peace, were replaced by substitutes.

In the meantime, Dean Frank Wren probed reports that the 18 freshmen, all of whom pleaded not guilty, were inspired by seniors to bring a cow and a pig back to the campus as part of their obligation to Thelta Delta Chi, the fraternity to which they sought membership.

According to reports on the Tufts campus today the 18 were taken in a truck to Boxboro at 9:30 p. m. Thursday and marooned there without money and under oath not to accept rides back to college.

It was the customary "forced hike" which all candidates to the fraternity must undergo. But with this proviso—that they should bring back one cow and one pig to serve as sleeping companions for two seniors.

It was while seeking these animals that a farmer's fence was damaged and the boys were arrested.

Graf Over South Atlantic

Fernando do Noranha Island Oct. 24 (AP)—The Graf Zeppelin on the way back to Germany from Pernambuco, passed over this island, 125 miles off Brazil, today.

In Today's American

THE WEATHER
By U. S. Weather Bureau
PARTLY CLOUDY TONIGHT AND TOMORROW: MODERATE TEMPERATURE
Temperature, 12 M. ... 40
Year ago (clear) ... 40
Mean average 10 years, same date ... 35
Complete Report on Page 21

BROOKLYN DAILY EAGLE

WALL STREET CLOSING PRICES ★★★★

91st YEAR—No. 349 M I ★ NEW YORK CITY, FRIDAY, DECEMBER 18, 1931 ★ 42 PAGES THREE CENTS

DIAMOND IS SLAIN AFTER ACQUITTAL

DOYLE UPHELD IN DEFIANCE OF SEABURY PROBE

Appellate Court O.K's Justice Dore's Purging Former Horse Doctor of Contempt—Seabury to Appeal Decision

Dr. William F. Doyle gained the upper hand over Samuel Seabury for the first time today and Seabury promptly announced he will attempt to carry the fight to the Court of Appeals.

The Manhattan Appellate Division, in a unanimous decision and without opinion, sustained the contention of the $2,000,000 horse doctor that he had purged himself of contempt of the Hofstadter Committee in denying he had bribed any public officials

The Appellate Division upheld the findings of Supreme Court Justice Dore, who had ruled in favor of Doyle in the latter's six months battle to keep the secrets of his fee splits and zoning victories safe from the Hofstadter probers.

Seabury to Fight

As soon as Seabury was informed at the headquarters of the Hofstadter Committee of the Doyle victory, he announced he would ask the Appellate Division at the January term for the right to appeal to the Court of Appeals at Albany.

The principal issue before the court was Seabury's contention that Doyle had "perjured, not purged" himself before the committee when he denied having bribed officials or politicians out of the proceeds of his Board of Standards and Appeals fees.

Second Major Reversal

The Doyle legal battery argued that perjury had not been proved and that, even if it had, Doyle had obeyed the court order when he answered questions.

Seabury's principal victory in the Doyle case was the confining of the erstwhile horse doctor to jail for 18 days as a defiant witness.

The defeat was the second major reversal suffered by Seabury this week. Clarence J. Shearn, Appellate Division referee, recently cleared 12 of the 14 Women's Court lawyers whose disbarment Seabury sought.

Sherwood Case Put Over

Hearing on Seabury's application to have the missing Russell T. Sherwood fined $170,000 for failure to heed the published call of the probers was today put over until

Please Turn to Page 2

WHAT A GIFT!

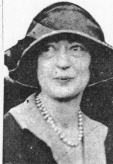

Washington, Dec. 18 (AP)—Edward B. McLean, publisher of the Washington Post, was cited for contempt of court today for sending a daintily wrapped Christmas box to his home containing a summons for his estranged wife to appear in a Latvian Court as a defendant in divorce proceedings.

Lamont Calls Reich Credits In U. S. Heavy

Cumbersome, but Do Not Endanger Banks, He Informs Senators

Washington, Dec. 18 (AP)—A member of J. P. Morgan & Co. said today there had been a cumbersome amount of German short term credit in this country, but that it did not endanger American banks.

He was Thomas W. Lamont, testifying before the Senate Finance Committee. He said probably 90 percent of American banks engaged in the process.

"The largest holding of such credits by any one bank is $70,000,000, and that institution is so large that it is not a matter of danger or even of comment," he added.

Lamont told how his company had handled $300,000,000 of loans for France and $208,250,000 for Germany. He added that all but $131,000,000 of the French loans had been repaid.

House Vote Due Tonight

As the committee recessed for lunch the House took up the moratorium measure with the expectation of ratifying it before adjournment, which may be deferred until late tonight.

"The banks are not loaded up with German bonds to the extent the people believe," stated Lamont.

"Yes," interrupted Senator Gore, Democrat, Oklahoma, "it is Tom, Dick and Harry who have taken the losses."

"It is true that upon the great investing public has fallen the brunt of the declines and not upon the banks," Lamont replied.

Lamont had said the first German issue bore 7 and the second 5½ percent interest.

He told the committee he was "a little mortified" to tell of the small commission that firm had received from floating foreign bonds in this country.

"I am afraid it will make the sympathy and pity of the committee too much," he said.

Lamont enumerated numerous bond issues the firm handled for Argentina, Canada, Austria and Belgium. The committee was making the study at the request of

Please Turn to Page 2

Rich Woman Is Freed By Kansas City Gang; Fail to Get Ransom

Mrs. Donnelly and Chauffeur Left at Bridge by Kidnapers—Tells How She Fought and Screamed as Cars Streamed By

Kansas City, Dec. 18 (AP)—Nervous but unharmed after almost 36 hours in the "filthy" rendezvous of three kidnapers, Mrs. Nelly Donnelly, wealthy founder of a Kansas City garment company, and George Blair, her Negro chauffeur, were freed by their captors early today.

FREED

Mrs. Nelly Donnelly

They were released from a motorcar near the Kansas Ave. bridge on the Kansas side of the city and soon were back at the Donnelly home. Their return marked the end of a period of anxious waiting by her husband, Paul Donnelly, and his attorneys, who were at a loss as to how to get in touch with the abductors for the delivery of $75,000 in ransom, demanded under a threat of death to Blair and blindness for the woman.

Anonymous Call

James A. Reed, neighbor and counsel to Donnelly, said today no ransom had been paid for the release of his wife, Mrs. Nelly Donnelly.

"We did not arrange the matter. It happened. That is all."

He was referring to the most heavily insured woman in Kansas City. Mrs. Donnelly carries life insurance of approximately $750,000, much of which is in favor of her company and her employes.

"It's wonderful," said Reed, who had spent a sleepless night. "Now

Please Turn to Page 18

BEFORE GANGLAND 'RUBBED HIM OUT'

Jack (Legs) Diamond, right, with his counsel, Daniel A. Prior, shown yesterday after his acquittal in Troy of kidnaping.

Tipsy After Party, Trapped In Albany Room

One Holds 'Legs' Down on Bed as the Other Pumps Lead Into Him

Eagle Bureau, Capitol Building.

Albany, Dec. 18—Cornered like a rat in his own bedroom, Jack (Legs) Diamond was shot and killed in a lodging house here at 4:45 a.m. today.

While one of two men who had followed the slightly intoxicated gangster from a speakeasy where he had been celebrating his kidnaping acquittal yesterday held him on the bed, the other pumped three bullets into his head.

"Oh, hell, that's enough!" Mrs. Laura Woods, proprietor of the rooming house, heard one of them exclaim after the third shot.

She looked out of a front window in time to see two men climb into a motorcar and speed away.

Carefully Planned

The murder gun and a flashlight, carefully wrapped in a handkerchief, found on a vacant lot a block away, are the only tangible clues in the hands of the police.

They were investigating a report current in New York City that two gunmen had been hired by a Manhattan gambler to "get" Diamond.

The motive, according to this report, was that the gambler suspected the racketeer of being involved in a plot to extort $25,000 from him.

Several New York City detectives attended the kidnaping trial but the State took no special precautions to guard Diamond in the courtroom.

A brief investigation convinced the authorities that the killing was a carefully planned underworld crime. They were not notified of the shooting until two hours after it occurred.

Meanwhile, newspapers and press associations in Albany received long distance telephone inquiries from unidentified persons in Chicago, Cleveland and New York City, asking if it were true that Diamond had been shot.

Three former Diamond gangsters, who attended his trial and the subsequent celebration tour of speakeasies are being sought in New York City.

Near State Capitol

The lodging house in which the shooting occurred is at 67 Dove St., not far from the State Capitol. Diamond had the front room on the second floor. His sister-in-law, Mrs. Eddie Diamond, and her 5-year-old son had engaged a rear room on the same floor but were not in the house when the shooting occurred.

So far as the police have been able to learn, Diamond, after his acquittal in Troy yesterday, came to Albany with his wife, his sister-in-law, Daniel Prior, his counsel, and Mrs. Prior.

The celebration began in a speakeasy on Broadway. Who the celebrators were other than "Legs," his wife and his sister-in-law the police have not learned. Diamond left about midnight to continue the celebration in another speakeasy on Pembroke St. Mrs. Diamond remained at the Broadway place and was there when notified of the shooting.

Fired From Front

Diamond's chauffeur said he drove her to the Dove St. house after she had been told her husband had been wounded.

Contrary to earlier reports, all three of the bullets that tore through Diamond's head had been fired from the front and slightly to one side. The first report was that one of the bullets had been fired into the back of his skull.

He was befuddled with liquor and unsteady on his feet when he summoned a taxicab to go to his lodging house.

come, in somewhere around 4:30 a.m. She did not hear his assailants

Please Turn to Page 3

Market Rises Wildly in Big Bull Recovery

Auburn Up 15, Steel 5 and Others as Much—Bonds, Wheat Move Up

A wild rally carried leading stocks up from three to 15 points today. It was accompanied by an equally large advance in bonds and good gains in the grain market. Starting, with much uncertainty, prices rose steadily and gained momentum which reached a peak in the last hour.

Auburn led the market up with an advance of about 15 points to 140 in the late trading. United States Steel was up over five points from the early low of 36 and American Telephone rallied from 113¼ to above 120.

Similar movements were seen in other sections of the list, with railroad shares upward as a body and utilities following. Active bear covering and belated investment buying was evident in the rise.

An assuring statement by Thomas W. Lamont in Washington to the Senate Finance Committee to the effect that German short term credits were no menace to American banking, higher prices for copper and the meeting of rail men here to discuss rail wage cuts tended to help the markets upward.

Stock Table on Page 39

Leaders Pledge Quick Passage Of Moratorium

Chiefs of Both Parties at Hoover Breakfast—McFadden Is Snubbed

Eagle Bureau, Colorado Building.

Washington, Dec. 18—President Hoover breakfasted this morning with Republican and Democratic House leaders and received the following assurances:

1. The debt moratorium bill will be taken up by the House today and passed before adjournment tomorrow night.

2. The farm loan bank legislation will be passed before the holiday recess Tuesday.

3. The reconstruction finance corporation legislation will be taken up immediately after the holidays.

As the White House sees it, these pledges given by the leaders of the two parties are absolutely without qualification. The President, it was authoritatively asserted, was given to understand that there would be no hitches. No "ifs," "ands" or "buts" accompanied the pledges, it was stated.

Those at the breakfast were Speaker Garner, Republican Floor Leader Snell, James W. Collier, chairman of the Ways and Means Committee; Henry B. Steagall, chairman of the Banking and Currency Committee; Charles R. Crisp,

Please Turn to Page 3

2 Scientists to Get Rewards for Labors

Washington, Dec. 18 (AP)—Two scientists will be honored tonight by the Smithsonian Institution.

Dr. Andrew E. Douglass of Tucson, Ariz., and Dr. Ernst Antevs of the University of Stockholm will receive awards of $2,500 each.

Dr. Douglass developed the "tree-ring" method of prehistoric chronology. Dr. Antevs worked out a similar chronology based on the annual layers of clay left in the wake of melting glaciers.

Browning Wins Divorce Fight

Manhattan Supreme Court Justice Walsh today decided in favor of Edward West (Daddy) Browning, in the suit for divorce brought by Mrs. Frances Heenan Browning. The decision was made before summation by attorneys.

Further Details on Page 2

Roosevelt to Hear Crowley Plea Jan. 11

Albany, Dec. 18 (AP)—A clemency hearing for Francis (two-gun) Crowley, 20-year-old New York hoodlum, sentenced to be executed, will be held before Governor Roosevelt Jan. 11.

Crowley's electrocution is set for Jan. 21. Crowley was convicted of murdering a Nassau County policeman.

5 Million Home Aid Is Voted; Berry Objects

Prial, Speaking for Controller, Voices His Fear of Scandal

The $5,000,000 home relief resolution the Board of Estimate has been considering three weeks was passed this afternoon after a discussion lasting two hours.

This appropriation is in addition to the $15,000,000 unemployment fund the city already has voted and is to be used exclusively for destitute and needy families not eligible for the benefits of the other appropriation.

Considerable surprise was registered when Deputy Controller Prial stated that, on orders of Controller Berry, he would vote against the resolution.

Berry Fears Scandal

Prial said that Berry believed that "at best home relief plans presented a danger because of scandals in the past in the distribution of public money."

He said Berry also told him to state that he was in sympathy with the needy, but that he believed some restrictions should be placed on the expenditure of this money.

At the word "scandal" Mayor Walker interrupted and stated vehemently that there never had been

Please Turn to Page 2

U. S. Warning Sent to Japan On Manchuria

Nanking Ousts Student Rioters—Tokio Plans New Bandit Campaign

Washington, Dec. 18 (AP)—A new expression of concern over the Manchurian situation, in friendly but positive terms, has been communicated to Japan by the American Government.

Ambassador Forbes in Tokio, on instructions of Secretary Stimson, has again emphasized to the Japanese Foreign Office American solicitude that obligations under the Nine-Power and Kellogg-Briand treaties be respected.

Readiness to show correspondence on Manchuria to the Senate was indicated this afternoon by Stimson. The Senate has asked it.

The Secretary indicated, however, there were some documents he would be unable to give the Senate for publication and would have to show them to individual Senators in confidence.

Nanking Expels Students

Nanking, Dec. 18 (AP)—The government moved today, with troops, to terminate the student demonstrations which have bordered on a reign of terror here for more than two weeks.

Without advance notice but with sharp precision large units of soldiers were sent out to round up the students, who were then escorted to waiting trains which immediately left for the youths' homes in north China cities and Shanghai.

As a result of the cleanup the capital breathed easier this afternoon and the belief was expressed

Please Turn to Page 2

Asks Jury Quiz On Short Sales

Washington, Dec. 18 (AP)—Investigation by both the Administration and the Senate into short selling operations on the Stock Exchanges was asked today by Senator Thomas, Democrat, of Oklahoma.

He blamed the declines in prices of securities on "bear raids" in the market brought about through selling stocks short.

One resolution would have the Senate request President Hoover to direct Attorney General Mitchell to summon a grand jury to inquire into short sales.

German Woman Flier Reported Missing

Basra, Irak, Dec. 18 (AP)—Fraulein Elli Beinhorn, German woman flier, was reported missing today somewhere in Irak or Persia.

She left Bagdad yesterday and has not been heard from since. Radio inquiries were made over all the territory she planned to cover but they failed to bring forth any information.

Winston Churchill Rests Comfortably

Winston Churchill, British statesman, spent a very comfortable night, it was reported this morning at Lenox Hill Hospital, Manhattan, where he is recovering from injuries received last Sunday when he was struck by a taxicab. Mr. Churchill slept soundly through the night.

THE EAGLE INDEX

S. B. Chapin Jr. Injured by Car

Simeon B. Chapin Jr., socially prominent member of the brokerage and banking firm of S. B. Chapin & Co., 111 Broadway, Manhattan, was injured critically by an automobile shortly before 1:30 o'clock this morning at 74th St. and Park Avenue.

The operator of the automobile, Louis Slater of 600 W. 111th St., took the injured man to Lenox Hill Hospital, where it was found he was suffering from a fracture of the skull and a compound fracture of the left leg.

Jury at Odds In Ewald Case

The jury in the Federal Court, Manhattan, deadlocked over the fate of former Magistrate George F. Ewald and three others, resumed deliberation this afternoon after being taken to a hotel for lunch.

The jurors debated all night without reaching a decision on the alleged guilt of Ewald, Dr. Francis M. Schirp, Harry C. Cotter and Frank E. Mitterlechner, accused of fraudulent promotion of stock in the Cotter Butte Mines Company.

Laval Defeated In Chamber Vote

Paris, Dec. 18 (AP)—Premier Laval's government was defeated by a vote of 292 to 281 in the Chamber of Deputies today but a question of confidence was not involved. The vote was on the Government's motion to set a date for closing of debate on unemployment.

Duce Gets New Publicity Agent

Rome, Dec. 18 (AP)—Lando Ferretti, chief of the Government Press Bureau and as such the most powerful factor in the direction of news in Italy, was reported to have resigned today, and it was said the announcement would be made after tomorrow's cabinet meeting.

Gaetano Polverelli, editor of Premier Mussolini's newspaper, Popolo D'Italia, a member of the Chamber of Deputies, was said to be in line to succeed him. The change was described as merely an item in the Premier's policy of a periodical turnover.

Smuts Warns Party To Prepare for Vote

Johannesburg, S. A., Dec. 18 (AP)—Gen. Jan. Christian Smuts, former South African Prime Minister, warned the South African party to prepare for an early general election.

He launched another vigorous attack against remaining on the gold standard.

HOOVER HOST TO GANNETT

Washington, Dec. 18 (AP)—Frank E. Gannett, Rochester, N. Y., newspaper publisher, was a luncheon guest of President Hoover today at the White House

Schoolboy's Death Laid To Classroom Prank

East Orange, N. J., Dec. 18 (AP)—Earl McQuillan, 15, of 19 Eaton Place, a freshman at the East Orange High School, died today in Orange Memorial Hospital of blood poisoning which physicians said resulted from an intestinal injury received when he sat upon a pencil in school, Dec. 11.

John Mecker, 13, of 105 N. Arlington Ave., a classmate, was holding the pencil on the seat at the time, according to police. School authorities and police, however, decided the injury was accidental.

John McQuillan, father of the dead boy, said: "I hope his death will be a lesson to all boys and that it will teach them the seriousness of such pranks."

Needy Cases Benefit From Eagle Dinner

Entire Proceeds of Employes' Fete at Guild Contributed to Fund—Dealers Donate Food and Prizes

By JANE CORBY

All promises of a good time were fulfilled at The Eagle's annual "50 Neediest Cases" party last night, held by Eagle employes at the Home Guild. The festivities began with a six-course duck dinner at 6 o'clock and continued with dancing and games, with substantial rewards for the winners. Through the courtesy of many manufacturers and retailers all proceeds of the affair are to be turned over to the Neediest Cases Fund.

Everything at the party was donated, from the services of the orchestra, Addy Amor and his Villanovans, to the last item in the menu. Mr. Amor's 10-piece collegiate orchestra, which had its origin in Villanova College, Philadelphia, is well known on the radio and is a feature at the Hotel Piccadilly Sunday nights. The piano was loaned by the Lester Company. Thanks are also due the Silver Key Orchestra for their services.

Hoffman's Beverages were sold at their booth and the proceeds donated to the cause.

Groceries as Prizes

The feature prizes included 25 baskets of groceries donated by the

Please Turn to Page 19

Contributions Today

J. F. C.	$100.00
A Friend	30.00
H. F. Quinn	25.00
W. C. Taggard	25.00
S. M. M.	10.00
In Memory of J. A. H	10.00
Thomas L. Driscoll	10.00
Mme. Gertrude	10.00
Mrs. Edward J. Aylward	10.00
Anonymous	10.00
Fred A. Thor	5.00
Mrs. Agnes B. Kellogg	5.00
Miss E. W.	5.00
In Memary of Frences Wells Speck—Alpha Kappa Sorority	5.00
Vivien P. Gallagher	5.00
Henry Siedenburg	5.00
Henry E. Sloan	5.00
C. E. Edwards	5.00
R. P. Forshaw	5.00
A. Adelaide Bahrenburg	4.00
A Friend	3.00
In Memory of E. M. B	3.00
Grace Boeckel	2.50
A Friend	2.00
G. M. Jr.	2.00
A Friend	2.00
R. E. Stacy	2.00
Emeline B. Kendall	1.00
M. A. M.	1.00
Mrs. E. L. Kane	1.00
Mrs. M. K. H.	1.00
Mari	1.00
Today's total	$310.50
Total	$8,084.74

British Bar Gandhi From Cairo Visit

On Board the Steamship Pilsna, Dec. 18 (AP)—Mahatma Gandhi, bound from Europe back to India, had planned to get off at an Egyptian port, pay a visit to Cairo and then rejoin this ship later on. The authorities, however, refused him permission to leave the vessel.

A similar attempt to go to Cairo, to which he was invited, was blocked by the British authorities last Summer.

Benefit Review Tonight

The 105th Artillery review for the 50 Neediest Cases takes place at the armory, 171 Clermont Ave., this evening. See Page 19.

Pola Negri Facing Crisis in 72 Hours

Santa Monica, Cal., Dec. 18 (AP)—A rising temperature marked the condition of Pola Negri, film actress, today, but her physicians were not alarmed.

They said it was a reaction to an operation for removal of an intestinal obstruction she underwent Wednesday.

A crisis is expected within 72 hours.

Coast Guard Speeds Woman To Her Dying Father's Side

Mrs. John J. Mealey was at the bedside of her dying father, George Mancuso of 1080 78th St., today through the good offices of the United States Coast Guard and the Massachusetts State police.

On Monday afternoon Mrs. Mealey, who was with her husband on Nantucket Island, received word that her father had suffered a stroke and was seriously ill. She appealed to authorities for aid in getting off the island. A Coast Guard patrol rushed her and Mr. Mealey through the four-hour trip from Nantucket to Woods Hole.

There State troopers met them and drove them to New Bedford, where they caught a train for New York. They arrived home yesterday, where Mrs. Mealey's mother, three sisters and brothers awaited her.

Mr. Mancuso is a retired importer. It was said that he was "very low" today.

Christmas CHURCH NUMBER

ALL of Brooklyn's churches will celebrate Christmas with their most beautiful services of the year. And the Christmas Church Number of The Eagle, out tomorrow, will publish complete details of special programs and sermons for the guidance of its readers. This is an annual editorial feature and the largest newspaper church section in the entire country.

TOMORROW in Saturday's EAGLE

The Cleveland Press

SECTION TWO | TUESDAY, MARCH 22, 1932 | WANT ADS—COMIC PAGE

JOHN W. LOVE

The operators and the miners both have their stabilizing plans, but neither would sell more coal than the railroads and factories can burn.

THE war in coal fields has moved north, into both the hard and the soft.

The anthracite fields are swept by an "outlaw" organization which threatens the remaining financial strength of the United Mine Workers. The southern Ohio revolt is more "regular" unionwise, but has been conducted with the same show of violence as in the eastern Pennsylvania fields.

The strikers in the Hocking field are fighting over some of the forgotten battleground of the 1890s' when miners were thrust back into dollar-a-day miseries. When business returned they had generated enough pressure to put over the practice of interstate wage agreements. These came to an end with the great growth of southern West Virginia, and the present chaos is the result.

Coal operators, some of them as hard up as the coal miners, have been trying to organize regional sales agencies which would get for them something of the same benefit they used to have from interstate wage agreements in the days when the union really stabilized wages.

The miners have their own stabilizing plan: Strike until the price of coal gets high enough to pay to mine. This is cruder, but it has worked, tho never in times like these.

Unless the state is willing to guarantee that no family will starve, perhaps it would be just as well to move the troops into the Hocking field for the summer.

* * *

Cushion of Credit

UNDER a nation organized either for complete Fascism or complete Communism, it would be possible for a government to transfer idle coal miners to other parts of the country, where they would work at something the government was managing to keep running.

In our individualism we can only feed the dependent or threaten them.

Yet Russia is finding it very hard to marshal its industrial workers in any kind of efficiency. A single plant inclines to have too many or too few. The consequence is waste, whether in the form of delay or underproduction or overproduction.

The McKee people are completing Magnitgorsk, the great steel works that the Russians intend to rival our Homestead or our Gary. It was necessary for the Russians to utilize private credit to some degree, but within the country they hoped to get along without credit. Yet they run into the lack of something which probably represents, under Communism, what credit is to a capitalism.

They are unable to keep their industries marching together. Some get ahead, others behind. They need a cushion between them. This cushion in a capitalistic society is what we call credit.

* * *

Magnitogorsk

THE first iron was poured at Magnitogorsk the other day, and by the end of spring the Russians hope to have at their Urals plant a daily capacity of 2000 tons of pig a day.

These are furnaces of the best American practice. The Cleveland engineers were somewhat skeptical of the ability of the Russians to take over, intact, a complete system of pig iron production on the highest volume that any American plant has attained.

"You must walk," said the McKee people, "before you can run."

"Run, hell!" said the Russians, or words to that effect, "we must fly."

* * *

More Deflation

PRESIDENT PALMER of the Real Estate Board calls for the suspension of all capital outlays by the county and all the political subdivisions within it the next couple of years.

Whether or not such extreme economy should occur, the wild wave of cancellation of public construction now sweeping the country is the biggest threat to the whole reconstruction program. It is deflation in its crudest form.

It is the admission that the 1930 campaign to maintain prosperity, encouraged by President Hoover and partcipated in by newspapers and civic organizations, was badly timed and completely ineffective.

An estimated billion dollars' worth of public work has stopped. We witness one of the most complete collapses of public confidence in itself that this country has ever seen. Once more we have swung from one extreme to the other.

CHICAGO GUNMAN SHOT

CHICAGO, March 22—A man who said he was George Schaia was probably fatally wounded today when detectives sought to arrest him, three other men and two women as holdup suspects.

URGES CAPITAL SHARE PROFITS WITH WORKERS

Jesuit Economist Warns Chamber of Possible Wealth Conscription

By EUGENE A. KELLY

A profit-sharing plan for labor and building up of reserve funds against old age and unemployment were commended to consideration of capital today by the Rev. Dr. Edmund A. Walsh in a talk before the Cleveland Chamber of Commerce at Hotel Statler.

"Share your profits with the workingman. If you do not, it is inescapable that the government will conscript your wealth or the mob will confiscate it," said the Jesuit economist as his prescription for the ills of a world threatened with Communism.

Dr. Walsh, diplomat and educator, is the foremost Catholic commentator on Soviet Russia. He spoke last night in Severance Hall under auspices of the Newman Club of Western Reserve University and Case School of Applied Science.

Predicts Future Disaster

"To achieve this co-operation with labor is the present task of industry," he said. "If it is not accomplished, disaster is inevitable. Catholic philosophy holds that no crime is committed by a man who steals a loaf of bread from another man's superfluous supply to prevent starvation. How shall we escape the appalling consequences if 7,000,000 men faced with starvation follow that natural law?"

Opposed Recognition

Regent of Georgetown University's School of Foreign Service and former member of a relief commission to Russia, Dr. Walsh opposed recognition of the present Russian government by citing these arguments:

"The Soviet regime is the only foreign power which has set up bureaus in the principal cities of the United States with the avowed purpose of destroying our form of government.

"On Dec. 13, 1917, Lenin and Trotzky were empowered by the Soviet of People's Commissars to distribute $1,000,000 among ambassadors in all the countries of the world, whether at peace or in alliance with Russia, to further world revolution.

"Soviet Russia is actively and militantly opposed to the Bill of Rights and the Constitution of the United States, which guarantees us a republican form of government; it fulminates against all forms of democracy in favor of a limited group, the so-called proletariat.

"Bayoneted Convention"

"A constitutional form of government in Russia was assassinated by the dictatorship of Lenin on Jan. 19, 1918, when he dispersed 700 delegates to the constitutional convention he had promised the Russian people and bayoneted to death two sick delegates as a final thrust at democracy.

"American citizens and all others who become members of the Communist Party agree to follow the decisions of the 'world Soviet,' with headquarters in Moscow, as their highest command"—the speaker quoted from literature distributed to new members of the party in America.

"Moscow claims jurisdiction over American citizens superior to the Constitution of the United States, the laws of the state of Ohio, or the ordinances of the city of Cleveland. Communists transfer their political allegiance to a foreign power militantly hostile, and agree to take orders from Joseph Stalin and his 'Mongolian satraps'."

Hits at Borah

The speaker went on to say that "If England or Italy should so interfere in the internal affairs of this country, their ambassadors would be ordered out tomorrow. Senator William E. Borah libeled the intelligence of the people, and suffered an extraordinary lapse of memory, in urging immediate recognition of Communist Russia. He uses curious logic for a man under oath to defend the Constitution."

Newton D. Baker, chairman, presented the educator as "an American who knows the most, and has thought the most about the Russian experiment, of any of our countrymen. No one in America compares with him in the accuracy and depth of his knowledge about Russia." William J. Towell, Newman Club president, introduced Baker.

Debunking the "Big Shots"—No. 2

"Baby-Faced" Coll, Who Dyed His Curls

"Beat Rap" in Murder of Child in Street

Mowed Down by Rival Gang Guns as His Guards Fled

They had wealth. They had power. They lived like feudal barons. They controlled elections. They dictated administrations. There was a certain glamor about the tales told of them. Their names became famous. Yet— What manner of men are they—the ones that still are living? What kind of men were they—the ones who died "on the spot"? Are they "big shots," lions of adventure or rats of stealth? This series gives a view of the gangsters that did not appear in the running account of their heyday activities.

By JAMES P. KIRBY

THE lights always seem softer after midnight.

The glasses glisten, reflecting the sparkling silver on the white table linen. Obsequious waiters glide about with their trays.

The string orchestra maintains the tempo of the dance. It is more mellow than the jazz of another era.

The shaded lights are more kindly to the feminine faces. The lines about the mouth seem to disappear. Even the telltale tracery about the eyes seems to become blended with the shadows.

Ice clinks merrily in tall glasses. The "set-ups" are always deftly being replaced. The fumes of alcohol become more noticeable. And so do the effects.

Thus, thru the early morning hours, Vincent Coll sat in the night clubs, night after night, with his girl. A personable young man, was Coll, until he spoke.

The baby-faced Coll, youngest and most ruthless of the younger generation of New York mobsters, undeniably had an air. And, in the night clubs he frequented, Coll was at his best.

True, this bearing in a police lineup disappeared in the cold, harsh light of dawn. Singular, how different a gangster looks in a lineup.

The shiny lapels of the dinner jacket appear somewhat incongruous at that hour; the unshaven faces appear unkempt, and dinner clothes somehow show the wrinkles more, after having been slept in.

But on a morgue slab they again appear to be different. It was so with Coll. . . .

* * *

FOUR-YEAR-OLD Michael Vengalli was playing in September, 1931, with other children on the only playground children know, in the upper East Side of New York City—the sidewalks.

People passed in both directions. A heavily-curtained auto sped thru the street, disregarded by the children. There came the sharp rat-tat-tat of a machine gun thru the curtains. Little Michael Vengalli fell dead. The car sped on.

In a moment there was chaos. Screaming mothers ran from tenements to pick up their children. People swarmed about the little form even as police sirens screeched the approach of the law.

Policemen and reporters swarmed about. Suspects were rounded up, taken to headquarters, and released. Pictures were shown, hundreds of them. They were the small, square pictures of known gangsters. There are thousands of them on file.

Witnesses feared to talk. They feared to identify anyone. The city became incensed at the wanton slaughter of a child. It was established that the machine-gun bullets were aimed at someone else. The little Michael happened to get in the way.

Detectives scurried thru the haunts of known gangsters and brought them in. They were placed in the lineups, and released. Vincent Coll and his mob became the objective of the detectives.

* * *

FOR weeks they searched the city for the gangster whose operations in the beer racket were believed to have laid the foundation for the shooting that ended with the child's murder.

Coll was arrested on the night of Oct. 4, in a raid on his hotel in the Bronx, which had been under surveillance for some time. Seized with him at the time were five other men and two women, all identified as being members of his mob.

The same night, New York City detectives and state troopers surrounded a house in Averill Park, N. Y.

The house was known for some time as a rendezvous for the Coll mob. Mrs. Agnes De Lucca drove up to the house. She had learned earlier of Coll's arrest, while she was in Troy. She was arrested when she neared the house.

She disclosed that Joseph Redden, brother-in-law of Coll, was alone at home. Others, she said, were at a movie in Troy. Detectives forced an entrance. Redden opened fire with a shotgun but missed. He was quickly overpowered. Secreted about the house, in strategic places, the detectives found shotguns, revolvers and ammunition.

The weapons were confiscated. The detectives put out the lights and waited. Shortly a sedan drove up. Coll's sister, her 13-year-old son, and several of Coll's henchmen entered. Without turning on the lights they stirred up the embers on the fireplace.

"Throw them up," came the gruff command of a detective, out of the darkness.

The two gunmen opened fire immediately. They emptied their revolvers and the shooting stopped. A detective snapped on the lights. As he did so, Coll's sister entered from another room, swinging a chair at the detective's head. The fight was short. All were placed under arrest.

* * *

COLL was brought to New York City with the others. The baby-faced gangster was found to have dyed his wavy hair to a dark black. He also had grown a mustache, and was wearing horn-rimmed glasses as a further disguise.

Coll's trial was sensational. He was acquitted. Witnesses somehow developed considerable reluctance about testifying. The identification was incomplete.

Other charges of robbery, carrying concealed weapons, etc., remained undisposed of. Bail for Coll was fixed at $60,000. Somehow he raised it and was released.

Women attracted Coll. Like Diamond, whose mob he fought over the liquor racket, he was vain. Shortly after his release, he married.

The "heat was on," however, and Coll and the mob found the going tough. Detectives showed up unexpectedly and disconcertingly.

On an afternoon in January of this year, he stepped into a phone booth. A detective was in the next booth. The detective got the number Coll called. It was to a rendezvous in the Bronx.

"Tell the boys to be ready for tonight," Coll said into the 'phone.

Coll and two of his retainers were taken into custody. A raid on the Bronx flat resulted in the arrest of two others and Coll's wife.

Search of Coll at headquarters revealed that he had the funds for the mob.

Coll, the racketeer and gangster, who laid claim to recognition as a big shot, had only $150 on his person.

* * *

ALTHO Coll already was at large under $60,000 bail, before the party had left the station house for police headquarters, a professional bondsman appeared with Coll's lawyer.

New charges of conspiracy were placed against Coll and the other members of the mob. He was again released on bail to await trial.

Coll never traveled without his bodyguard. Like the other gangsters, he expected trouble at any minute. Nor was he disappointed.

On the afternoon of Feb. 8 he stepped into a telephone booth in a drug store. He made a number of calls and was in the booth for more than 10 minutes. His bodyguard remained on watch outside.

Suddenly, a man walked into the store. The bodyguard walked out. Under his arm, in plain sight of customers and clerks in the store, the man carried a submachine gun.

"Keep cool and you won't get hurt," the man cautioned everyone.

Then he walked to the telephone booth. He stood outside, raised the machine gun and began to fire. The bullets crashed thru the flimsy wood and glass.

The killer walked out, carrying the smoking weapon.

Coll's body toppled out of the booth to the floor.

* * *

FROM testimony of witnesses to the killing, detectives were convinced that Coll was killed with the connivance of his own bodyguard.

Coll's bride arrived on the scene within a few moments. When police arrived, search of the body disclosed that he was unarmed. The gangster had $110 in his pockets, and the picture of another woman.

The word of Coll's passing spread rapidly. Thereupon, the stories of his double-crossing of his partners and even of members of his own mob were revived.

Coll was alleged to have had a bitter hatred of "Dutch Schultz" Flegenheimer over the division of the beer business in the Bronx.

Within a week previous to the killing, Coll escaped when rival gangsters opened up on a gathering of his henchmen in a Bronx flat. He was expected to have been present, but had not appeared.

Three of Coll's followers were killed by the bullets of the attacking mob. Two men and a woman were injured.

They put Coll on a slab in Bellevue Hospital.

The baby-faced gangster had been paid off.

Vincent Coll, New York City's baby-faced gangster, muscleman and beer racketeer, dyed his wavy hair brown in a vain effort to elude police. Coll, shown in the upper picture, "got his" in a telephone booth when his own bodyguard conveniently stepped out of the way for a rival mobster with a machine gun. Hunted for months as the killer of a 4-year-old child on an upper East Side street, Coll was acquitted when witnesses failed to complete the identification. Below, Coll is shown in a lineup at police headquarters with members of his mob. From left to right, they are: Dominick Ordino, Mike Basile, Pasquale Del Greco, Frank Giordana and Coll.

TOMORROW: The greatest "sure thing" gambler of his time, Arnold Rothstein.

HEYWOOD BROUN

Terseness is the twin of accuracy and not its stepfather. My chief complaint against the world is that people have an insufficient capacity for excitement.

IT was my intention not to mention the epoch-making controversy between Dr. Sirovich and the dramatic critics again. It seems to me that the show is ended. The Congressman isn't funny any more, and none of my best friends are Siroviches.

But it was my peculiar fortune yesterday to find myself on a luncheon program in association with the good doctor. In fact, he was the guest of honor. In his speech, which ranged from the validity of the Christian, the Jewish and the Buddhist religions to newspaper reviews and widows' pensions, Dr. Sirovich mentioned the wisecrack. He could hardly have avoided it.

This was an omnibus address, in which nothing was neglected. Even the humblest of God's creatures and Dr. Sirovich himself got his line of credit. Oh, well, in the case of the autobiographical aspects of the address, make it 20 or 30 lines.

* * *

The Wisecrack

THE record is less than complete unless it contains the information that this servant of the people has done all that he has done without, hope or even desire for compensation.

But next to the subject of Sirovich the speech was chiefly concerned with the wisecrack. This, I gathered, is the lowest, the most malicious and the most depraved form of human expression.

It seemed to be the doctor's notion that the pithy and blighting sentence is a recent invention never known in the world before the advent of Broadway columnists and newspaper reviewers.

But I disagree utterly. The epigrammatic form of criticism is ancient, honorable and exceedingly effective. In this matter I have no ax to grind, for, unfortunately, I have no skill in paragraphic utterance. There are those who can wheel like a polo pony and cover in a single sentence the views which I cannot state in less than 800 words.

In the Commentaries of the great Roman chieftain, which I studied grudgingly in school, it is distinctly set down that upon a certain occasion "Caesar said, not unwittily." This was probably not the world's first wisecrack, but it was a timid effort in that direction. I cannot remember the gag, but it is my impression that it was less successful than many later efforts.

Still it must be said for Caesar that he tried. Others have continued the practice. In recent years Dr. Freud has sanctified this form of expression by pointing out that the wisecrack is a direct contribution from the unconscious mind and generally represents the inspired kernel of the individual's whole life of experience.

* * *

Chance to Be Set

IF you say to any acquaintance, "Tell me quickly in a thousand words what you think of this or that," he is almost certain to wander off into platitudes and extraneous opinion. In a single sentence he will be both more eloquent and truthful.

Even in the case of a Dr. Sirovich speech I feel that the first two hours are by far the best.

And so I think that all critics of the stage, our government and the world in which we live should be encouraged to be pithy. A good slogan is worth a thousand sermons.

It is held, most erroneously, that truncated expression must be insincere and exhibitionistic.

Easter Music

The Press will publish the Easter music programs of Greater Cleveland churches in its editions of Saturday, March 26. Bring or mail such programs to the Easter Music Editor of The Press not later than Thursday night. Information should be given in the following order: Denomination, name and location of the church, name of the pastor and choirmaster and the detailed program.

50,000 DOGS HERE

H. K. Ferry Estimates Canine Population on Expected Registration

Cuyahoga county's dog population is in excess of 50,000, a survey being made by the Cuyahoga County Society for the Prevention of Cruelty to Animals shows.

To date this year 44,500 dogs have been registered and licensed by the county. H. K. Ferry, chief dog warden, said the registration will pass the 50,000 mark. Licenses for male dogs over three months of age cost $2, and for females $4.

ECLIPSE OF SUN AUG. 31 WILL BE THE LAST VISIBLE IN UNITED STATES FOR NEARLY HALF CENTURY

Case Observers Will Make Movies of Event

Phenomena in Early Days Roused Terror

By DAVID DIETZ
Scripps-Howard Science Editor

AN eclipse of the sun on Aug. 13 will be the last opportunity to see an eclipse in the United States for almost half a century. The next solar eclipse visible in the United States will take place in 1979.

The Warner & Swasey Observatory of Case School of Applied Science is organizing and expedition to observe the eclipse of Aug. 31, Dr. J. J. Nassau, director, announced today.

The eclipse will be 87 per cent total in Cleveland. It will be total in a narrow band extending across New England and eastern Canada. Cities in the belt of totality include Montreal, Concord, N. H.; Portland, Me.; Salem, Mass., and Provincetown, Mass. Boston is just a few miles outside the band of totality.

In Cleveland, the eclipse will begin at 2:14 p. m. At that time, the moon will just come in line with the edge of the sun. Gradually, as the moon moves across the face of the sun, less and less of the sun will remain in sight.

The eclipse will reach its maximum for Cleveland at 3:27 p. m. when only a narrow crescent of sun will remain in view. Eighty-seven per cent of the sun will be obscured. Then gradually the sun will come back to view, the eclipse ending at 4:34 p. m.

Clevelands who journey to Canada or New England will see the marvelous spectacle of a total eclipse.

* * *

FEW occurrences are more impressive or dramatic than a total eclipse of the sun. The whole visible earth and sky form the setting for the spectacle, while the actors are the moon and that great blazing monarch of our solar system, the sun.

In the early days of civilization, eclipses were regarded with panic and terror. Many thought that they heralded war and pestilence and even the end of the world.

Slowly, as the eclipse begins, the disk of the moon is seen blotting out the sun. When only a narrow crescent of the sun still remains in sight, the landscape begins to take an unusual and almost terrifying appearance. This is because the light from the edge of the sun is not only fainter, but has a different color value from the light of the whole disk.

Two or three minutes before the eclipse becomes total, the moon's shadow comes sweeping over the landscape from the west with awe-inspiring swiftness.

Suddenly the eclipse becomes total. The whole sky is dark. The brighter stars appear in the sky. Around the disk of the moon can be seen a rim of red fire. This is the chromosphere of the sun. Great tongues of crimson fire, the solar prominences, can be seen extending from the chromosphere. Surrounding the fiery chromosphere can be seen a great silvery halo, the corona of the sun.

* * *

THE Case expedition will make its headquarters near Douglas Mill, Me., Dr. Nassau announced today. The same location also will be used by an expedition from the Perkins Observatory of Ohio Wesleyan University. This expedition will be headed by Dr. Harlan T. Stetson.

The two expeditions will supplement and assist each other, Dr. Nassau said today.

The Case expedition will be unusually well equipped.

"A four-inch lens has been loaned us by J. W. Fecker of Pittsburgh," Dr. Nassau said today. "The Warner & Swasey Co. is loaning us a complete mounting and driving clock. This lens and mounting will constitute a camera 14 feet long.

"Dr. D. C. Miller is loaning us a chronometer. Other apparatus will come from our observatory."

The program outlined by Dr. Nassau includes exact timing of the eclipse, photographing of it with the 14-foot camera, photographing the corona with special instruments, the making of radio tests during the eclipse, and the making of a motion picture of the eclipse.

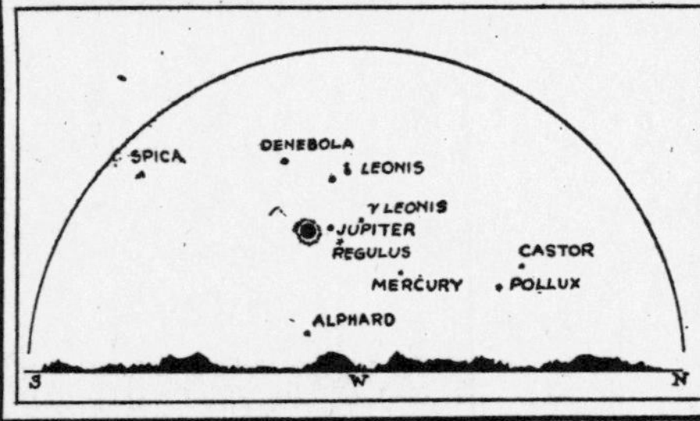

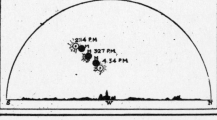

Diagram at the left shows how the eclipse will appear in the region of totality. The center diagram shows the way in which the eclipse is caused.

Diagram at the right shows how the eclipse will appear in Cleveland. The diagrams were prepared at the Warner & Swasey Observatory of Case School of Applied Science.

Tot Hunger Stirs Pity Of Father Coughlin. Story on P. 3

EVENING GRAPHIC

Vol. 8. No. 2349 NEW YORK, WEDNESDAY, MAY 4, 1932 2 Cents In City LIMITS | 3 CENTS Elsewhere

CAPONE, IN LEG IRONS, RACES TO PEN UNDER HEAVY GUARD

—STORY ON PAGE 2—

 (Telephoto from Chicago to The GRAPHIC)

CAPONE LEAVES FOR ATLANTA—Weeping and ranting at the "injustice" of his sentence, Al Capone, for seven years overlord of America's underworld, bade farewell to his family and started on his way to Atlanta where he will serve a sentence of ten years. He's shown in telephoto received from Chicago, in auto in which he was taken to train

SPEEDBOAT QUEEN HERE—En route to Italy where she will compete in the international regatta on Lake Garda, Loretta Turnbull, who hails from California and is regarded as America's premier woman speedboat driver, arrived here accompanied by her brothers. She is shown looking at plans of her boat with brothers Rupert and Raymond

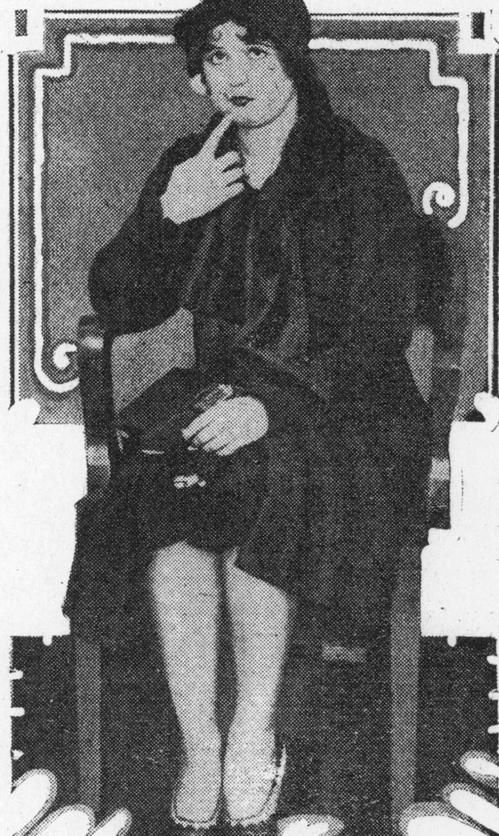

BOOP-BOOP-A-DOOP WORTH $250,000—Helen Kane, who rose to fame on the stage through her boop-boop-a-doop interpolation of songs, has filed suit for $250,000 damages and a permanent injunction to restrain film company from producing animated cartoon creation, "Betty Boop"

Woman Killed, Public Defender Missing

—STORY ON PAGE 3—

DAILY MIRROR

EXTRA
MUrray Hill 2-1000

Copyright, 1932, Daily Mirror, Inc. Registered U. S. Patent Office.

Entered as second class matter Post Office, New York, N. Y.

Vol. VIII. No. 279 *** New York, Friday, May 13, 1932 2 cents IN CITY LIMITS | 3 CENTS Elsewhere

LINDY'S BABY MURDERED!

Baby Charles A. Lindbergh, Jr., was foully murdered! The body of the missing infant was found yesterday in the woods at Mt. Rose, N. J., near the Lindberghs' Hopewell estate, on Sourland Mountain. All hopes that the report of the finding of the body might be proved untrue were crushed by an official announcement by Gov. A. Harry Moore, of New Jersey, who said: "It is true. The body of little Charlie Lindbergh has been found."

(See Page 2 for Detailed Story)

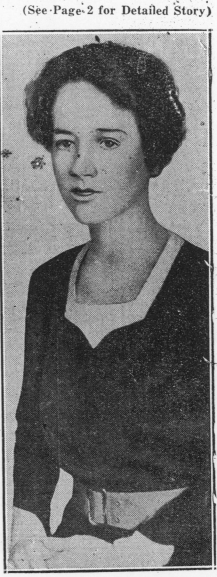

A bereaved father, Lindy, mourns...

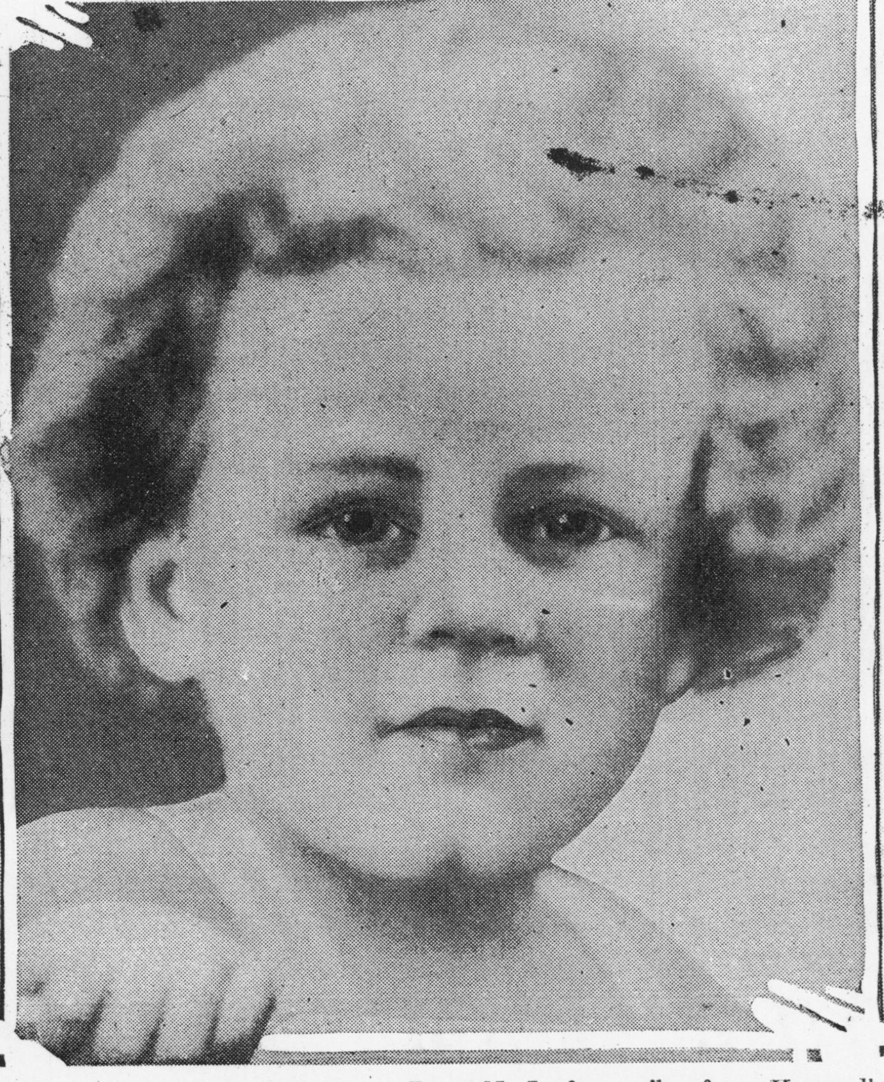
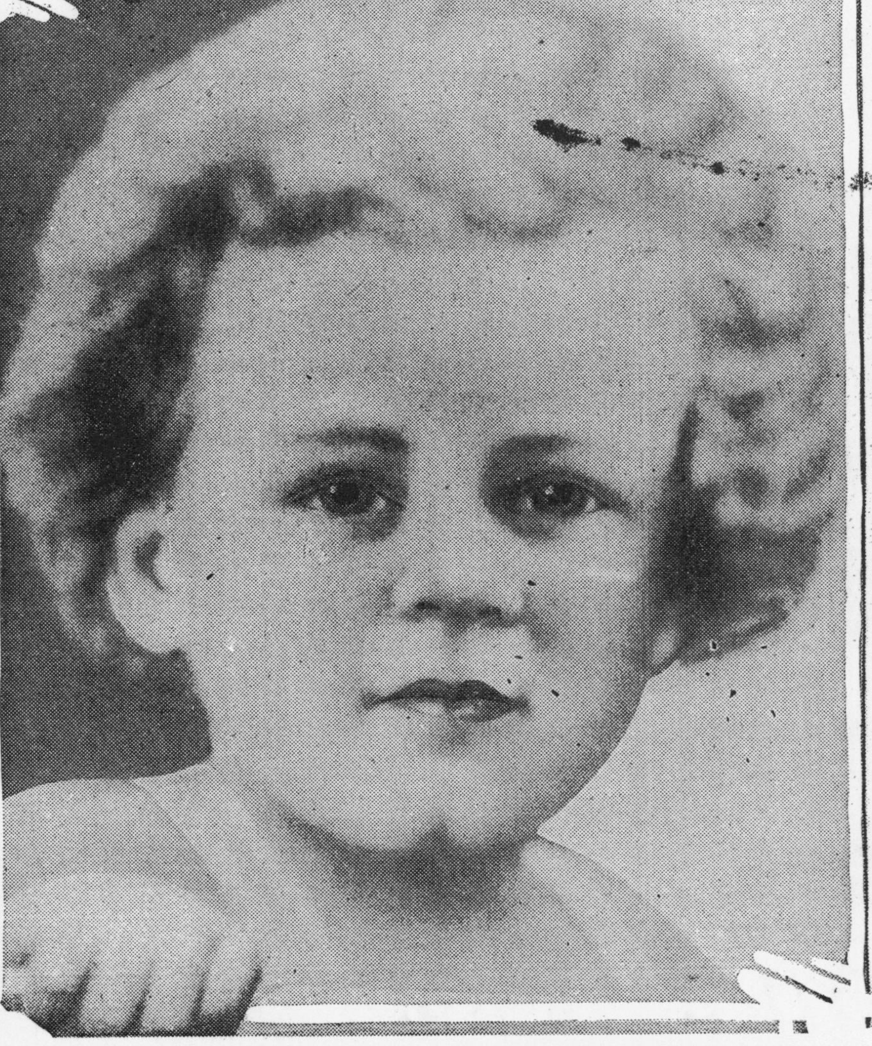

his baby, found dead at Mount Rose, N. J., four miles from Hopewell.

Anne collapsed completely.

DRY REPEAL WINS IN SENATE

Only Los Angeles Newspaper With All Leading News Services — Associated Press, International News, United Press, Dow-Jones

Reg. U. S. Pat. Office. Copyright, 1933, by Evening Herald Publishing Company
The Evening Herald and Express Grows Just Like Los Angeles

NIGHT EDITION

VOL. LXII THREE CENTS Hotels and Trains Five Cents THURSDAY, FEBRUARY 16, 1933 Two Sections Section A THREE CENTS NO. 280

ROOSEVELT'S ASSAILANT IS ANARCHIST FROM L. A.

SUBMISSION TO STATES IS PASSED 63 TO 23

Action on Anti-Prohibition Resolution to Be Taken at Once in House

By Associated Press

WASHINGTON, Feb. 16.—With five votes to spare, the senate this afternoon dispatched to the house with its indorsement the Blaine resolution for prohibition repeal, containing a protection for dry states from liquor importations.

The count was 63 to 23, and at once Speaker Garner reiterated the other congressional branch on Monday would speed the resolution to the states for ratification by convention. It does not go to the White House. Thirty-six states must call conventions and approve it within seven years to change the 13-year-old national dry law.

Advocates of the legislation were exultant over the margin by which the required two-thirds vote was exceeded in the tensely expectant and crowded senate chamber.

The roll call showed 33 Democrats and 29 Republicans and the lone Farmer-Labor member favoring submission, with 14 Republicans and nine Democrats opposed.

VOTE FOR REPEAL

The final roll call for passage of the repeal resolution follows:

Democrats for:

Ashurst, Bailey, Bankhead, Barkley, Black, Bratton, Bulkley, Bulow, Byrnes, Clark, Connally, Coolidge, Dill, Fletcher, Harrison, Hayden, Hull, Kendrick, King, Lewis, McKellar, Neely, Pittman, Reynolds, Robinson of Arkansas, Russell, Smith, Swanson, Trammell, Tydings, Wagner, Walsh of Massachusetts and Walsh of Montana—33.

Republicans for:

Austin, Barbour, Bingham, Blaine, Couzens, Cutting, Davis, Frazier, Glenn, Grammer, Hale, Hastings, Hebert, Johnson, Kean, Keyes, LaFollette, McNary, Metcalf, Moses, Nye, Oddie, Patterson, Reed, Shortridge, Vandenberg, Walcott, Watson and White—29.

Farmer Labor for:

Shipstead—1.

Democrats against:

Caraway, Costigan, Glass, Gore, Logan, McGill, Sheppard, Stephens and Thomas of Oklahoma—9.

Republicans against:

Borah, Brookhart, Capper, Dale, Dickinson, Goldsborough, Hatfield, Norbeck, Norris, Robinson

(CONTINUED ON PAGE SEVEN)

Mrs. Roosevelt Saved From Being Struck by Train

By Associated Press

ITHACA, N. Y., Feb. 16.—Mrs. Franklin D. Roosevelt today was saved from injury or death when a policeman escorted her out of the way of an oncoming string of railroad cars that had come within 20 feet of her at the Lehigh Valley station this morning.

She had just alighted from her special train and was standing on one of the tracks with members of her party and with Mayor Herman Bergholtz and Miss Flora Rose, director of Cornell university's college of home economics. Neither Mrs. Roosevelt nor any of the other members of the party noticed the string of cars being backed in their direction until Motorcycle Policeman Edward J. Moore took Mrs. Roosevelt's arm and moved her off the tracks.

Banking Support Is Thrown in Market To Check Decline

By International News Service

NEW YORK, Feb. 16.—Banking support was thrown into the stock market to check the decline this afternoon after heavy selling in which European speculators were reported prominent, drove the list down to new lows for the year.

The support accorded pivotal issues steadied the list and brought about a mild recovery, but this was nullified by an outburst of liquidation in the oils.

Closing prices were: United States Steel common 26⅝, off ¼; Steel preferred 57⅞, off ⅝; American Telephone 100⅝, off ¼; General Electric 13, off ⅝; General Motors 12¼, ex-dividend unchanged; Standard Oil of New Jersey 24⅜, off 1; Atchison 39½, off 2; Southern Pacific 15½, off ⅛.

75 in Alleged Rum Ring Indicted; Set Profit at 6 Million

By Associated Press

CHICAGO, Feb. 16.—Seventy-five members of an alleged liquor ring were indicted by the federal grand jury today.

The indictments charged them with gathering $6,000,000 in profits from 60 stills from 1929 to 1932. Joseph Peskin, reputed "corn sugar king," headed the list of defendants.

Jacob Berman Ill In Federal Prison

By United Press

LEAVENWORTH, Kan., Feb. 16.—Jacob Berman, alias Jack Bennett, one of the central figures in the Julian Petroleum case, was reported ill today in the federal prison hospital here. At the warden's office it was said Berman's illness was due to indigestion.

RECORD OF ASSASSIN HERE TOLD

Bankbook Reveals Giuseppe Zangara Lived in L. A.; Activities Being Traced

United States government secret service agents checking at the former residence in Paterson, N. J., of Guiseppe Zangara, the black-browed little Italian anarchist who last night attempted to assassinate President-elect Roosevelt in Miami, discovered today that Zangara resided in Los Angeles for a time in 1931.

The secret service agents made this discovery through a bankbook Zangara left with his uncle, Vincent Cafaro, with whom Zangara lived in Paterson.

ENTRIES IN BOOK

The book, a safety account passbook of the Security-First National bank of Los Angeles, showed an initial deposit of $150 on Sept. 8, 1931. On Oct. 13, the book showed a withdrawal of $50 and the account was canceled with the withdrawal of the balance, $100, on Oct. 22.

Los Angeles government agents and police, launching an immediate investigation to determine the extent of Zangara's suspected anarchist activities in this city, learned through officials of the downtown bank branch where angara kept his account that he had given his address in this city as 425 Park Front walk, about four blocks east of San Pedro street and Forty-ninth street.

Walter A. Wentz, of 4019 Wade avenue, Venice, owner of an 11-room rooming house on Park Front walk, said he was actively managing the place in September and October of 1931 and remembered Zangara.

MET ON LINER

Wentz said Mrs. Ruth May Rice of New York city, a friend of Mr. and Mrs. Wentz, became acquainted with Zangara while both were passengers on the liner Virginia en route to Los Angeles harbor from the Atlantic coast in August or September of 1931.

Upon arrival of the Virginia, Mrs. Rice sent Zangara to the Wentz rooming house and he remained there two weeks before moving to take a room with Paul Cenci, a Los Angeles tailor he had met, Wentz said. Wentz said all he remembered of Zangara was that he said he was a contracting bricklayer. Wentz is now renting his rooming house to Mrs. Arno Wolf, who resides there.

'DRIVE' ON THEN

Invstigation by the Los Angeles police was led by Capt. William Hynes, head of the police "Red squad, who declared it was significant that at the time Zangara was in Los Angeles there was an especially vigorous membership drive on foot in this city by an anarchist organization.

"It is extremely probable that Zangara at that time was a special agent detailed here from eastern anarchist headquarters," Captain Hynes declared. "The money he de-

(CONTINUED ON PAGE TEN)

Telephoto shows Giuseppe Zangara, 33, diminutive asserted anarchist formerly of Los Angeles, in custody of Sheriff Dan Hardie, at left, and a policeman at the Miami jail after he attempted to assassinate President-elect Franklin D. Roosevelt and wounded five persons. The officer holds Zangara's gun with which he fired six shots into the crowd at a Miami park. Most of his clothing was torn off by infuriated bystanders and the rest by police when they searched him.

This dramatic picture shows Anton Cermak, Chicago's mayor, in center, being assisted to Mr. Roosevelt's car immediately after Cermak was shot and critically wounded by Zangara. The man at left in the white suit is L. L. Lee, Miami city manager, holding Cermak's arm. At right is W. W. Woods, Democratic committeeman.—Telephotos by International News photo service.

ASSASSIN TELLS OF PLAN TO KILL HOOVER; CERMAK HOLDS OWN

MIAMI, Fla., Feb. 16.—Anarchism—fostered by a burning hatred of "presidents and kings" and "the rich and powerful"—today was blamed for the attempt to assassinate President-elect Roosevelt and the shooting of five persons in the midst of a crowd of 20,000 in Bay Front park last night.

The assassin, Giuseppe Zangara, admitted his hatred of all officials. Secret service men called him just "a plain anarchist" and back-tracking over his 10-year stay in this country, found evidence of previous anarchistic utterances by the diminutive swarthy Italian.

DOCTORS MORE HOPEFUL FOR RECOVERY OF MAYOR CERMAK

Mayor Anton Cermak, the most prominent of the assassin's victims, was battling for his life in Jackson Memorial hospital and as the day wore on physicians grew more hopeful of his recovery. The mayor fell asleep at 3 o'clock and a bulletin issued at 4:30 p. m. said he was still resting quietly and no unfavorable developments had arisen. The condition of the other most seriously wounded victim, Mrs. Joseph Gill, was still critical, despite a blood transfusion.

Meanwhile Mr. Roosevelt was speeding by train to New York, having departed at 10:15 after visiting the three men and two women who received the bullets intended for him.

Tracing back over the history of Zangara secret service men found he had wandered from the Atlantic coast to the Pacific coast in the past two years and once resided in Los Angeles. However, no evidence of crime on his part was found.

SWIFT JUSTICE LOOMS FOR HATER OF ALL OFFICIALS

The law acted swiftly to bring the hater of all officials to justice when County Solicitor Charles A. Morehead filed four counts of "assault with intent to commit murder" against him. Actual trial of the gunman may be started tomorrow morning. Each of the four charges carries a maximum of 20 years in state prison, so that life imprisonment or a total of 80 years behind the bars, is possible. If either Mayor Cermak or Mrs. Gill should die murder charges would be filed. Florida has the death penalty for murder.

In addition to Cermak and Mrs. Gill the other bullet victims are: William Sinnott, New York detective, Russell Caldwell of Miami and Miss Margaret Kruis of Newark. All are on the road to recovery.

Far from showing any contrition at his deed, Zangara said stolidly:

"I am sorry I didn't kill Roosevelt. I like Roosevelt personally, but I don't like Presidents."

Zangara also said he first intended to kill President Hoover, but on learning that Mr. Roosevelt was coming to Miami decided to wait for him.

Although there was no recurrence of the mob spirit which prompted the crowds to shout "Lynch him!" immediately after the shooting, Zangara was kept under heavy guard in a cell high up in Dade county jail.

A woman's bravery and presence of mind was credited with saving the President-elect from the bullets, although he did not learn of it until just prior to his departure. The woman was Mrs.

(CONTINUED ON PAGE TEN)

U. S. TURNS DOWN STABILIZED MONEY

Only Los Angeles Newspaper With All Leading News Services—Associated Press, International News, United Press, Dow-Jones

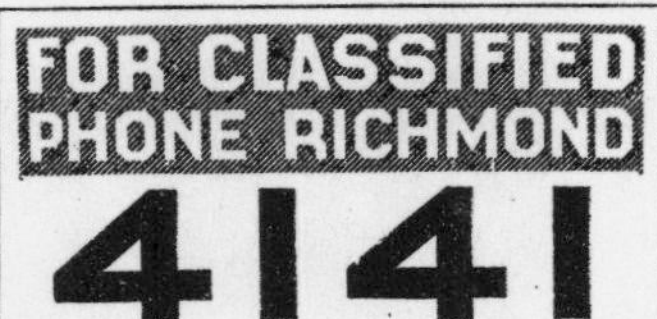

Reg. U. S. Pat. Office. Copyright, 1933, by Evening Herald Publishing Company
The Evening Herald and Express Grows Just Like Los Angeles

VOL. LXIII THREE CENTS Hotels and Trains Five Cents SATURDAY, JUNE 17, 1933 Two Sections Section A THREE CENTS NO. 72

MACHINE GUNMEN SLAY 4 POLICE AND PRISONER

Bare Attic Door Clue in Lamson Case

STATE FINDS PUZZLING EVIDENCE IN HOME

Prosecution Reveals Stains Found on Trapdoor High Above Hall Floor

By United Press

SAN JOSE, June 17.—Bloodstains on a trap door leading to an attic in the campus home of David Lamson were revealed by the state today as a new and puzzling bit of evidence connected with the mysterious death of Mrs. Allene Lamson.

Police were at a loss to explain how the stains were made, some 13 or 14 feet above the floor of the hall outside the bathroom door. They expressed the theory the attic was intended as a hiding place for blod-stained clthing and the murder weapon.

Tarle G. Hamilton, undersheriff, said he believed the stains were made by human fingers.

STATE'S 'BIG GUNS'

Marking time today the state wheeled into line the remaining two of its four big guns to fire at Lamson when the preliminary hearing of the handsome Stanford university publishing house executive is resumed Monday morning.

Lamson literally reeled in his chair as the first two of the prosecution's "big berthas" — Undersheriff Hamilton and Deputy Sheriff John Moore—poured round after round of high explosives into his story that he found the nude body of Mrs. Lamson, with head bludgeoned, in the tub of their Stanford campus bungalow on Memorial day.

CHEMIST TO TESTIFY

And the same ordeal is in prospect again for Lamson before the preliminary, being held in the tiny courtroom of Justice of the Peace Grandin Miller, is concluded.

The next heavy blasts will come from Deputy Sheriff Howard Buffington and Dr. Frederick Proescher, county chemist.

Then the state's case will be complete, except for some comparatively minor witnesses, and As-

(CONTINUED ON PAGE FIVE)

PRICE FIXING IS ACCEPTED BY U. S. OIL PRODUCERS

Production Control by President Also Approved in Code of Industry

CHICAGO, June 17.—Representatives of more than 40 crude oil producing companies that supply 95 per cent of the nation's oil today adopted a proposal allowing the President of the United States to fix maximum and minimum prices.

The proposal comprises a section of a code being drafted by independent and large oil producers as demanded by the federal government in the national industry recovery act to set up "fair practices regulations" for all industries.

An allotment plan for the oil industry under which production would be limited also was agreed upon.

PROVISIONS TOLD

Provisions of this agreement follow:

Production—Provides that production plus imports and withdrawals from storage will be restricted to approximately the current domestic demand, plus export demand.. The amount will be determined and allocated by the President, ample provision being made for protection of stripper wells.

Drilling—Provision is made for continuation of wild catting but there is no need for such discoveries at the present time, it was stated. Production should be so limited from new pools as to discourage wild-catting. No drilling would be allowed without first getting the President's permission. When a new discovery is made no further drilling in that pool area would be permitted until plans for development are approved by the President.

RIGHTS OF LABOR

The code would also put the industry on record as recognizing the right of labor to organize and bargain collectively.

Adoption of the price fixing section came after heated debate, during which the proposal was con-

(CONTINUED ON PAGE FIVE)

Disappears

Helen Lee Worthing, blonde former Follies beauty and ex-wife of Dr. Eugene Nelson in a "Desdemona and Othello" romance, disappeared from a train somewhere between Los Angeles and Pasadena, it was revealed today. Police feared that she might have leaped from the train to death.

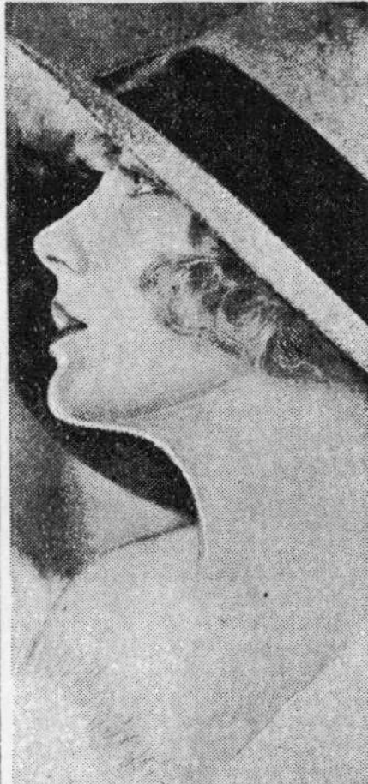

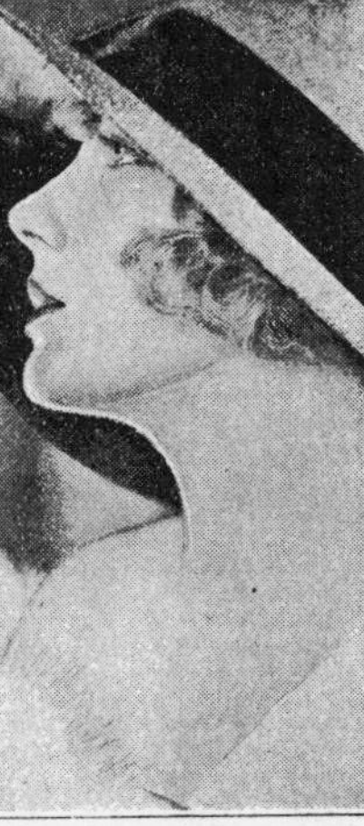

Eastern Scores

NATIONAL LEAGUE

At Cincinnati— R. H. E.
St. Louis ....5 0 2 2 0 1 0 5 2—17 23 0
Cincinnati ...0 1 0 0 0 0 1 0 0— 2 5 2
Batteries—Carleton and Wilson, O'Farrell; Lucas, Stout, Frey, Quinn and Lombardi.

At Pittsburgh— R. H. E.
Chicago .....1 0 0 1 0 0 0 1 0— 3 14 0
Pittsburgh ...0 1 0 0 0 2 0 1 x— 4 10 1
Batteries—Malone and Hartnett; Swetonic and Grace.

At New York (first game)— R. H. E.
Brooklyn ....0 0 0 1 1 0 5 0 0— 7 9 1
New York ...4 0 0 0 1 1 2 0 x— 8 15 1
Batteries—Carroll, Shaute, Heimach, Beck and Lopez, Outen; Hubbell, Clark, Bell and Mancuso.

At Philadelphia (first game)— R. H. E.
Boston ......0 0 0 0 5 1 0 4 1—11 20 0
Philadelphia..0 0 0 0 0 2 1 0 0— 3 11 2
Batteries—Frankhouse and Hogan; Holley, Pickrel, Liska and Davis, Todd.

At Philadel. (2nd, 10 innings)— R. H. E.
Boston ....1 0 0 0 0 0 0 0 1 0 1— 3 12 1
Philadelph..1 1 0 0 0 0 0 0 0 0— 2 7 1
Batteries—Starr, Mangum, Cantwell and Spohrer; A. Moore and Davis.

AMERICAN LEAGUE

At Boston (first game)— R. H. E.
Philadelphia..4 2 0 0 0 0 2 7 0—15 16 0
Boston .....0 1 0 0 1 0 0 1 0— 3 7 1
Batteries—Earnshaw and Cockrane; Andrews, Kline, Welch and Gooch.

At Boston (2nd; called, rain)— R. H. E.
Philadelphia..0 2 2 0 0 0 0 1 — 5 6 1
Boston ......1 0 2 0 1 1 0 2 — 7 11 1
Batteries—Cain, Grove and Cochrane; Rhodes and Gooch.

At Chicago— R. H. E.
New York ..0 1 0 2 2 2 1 0 0— 8 14 0
Chicago .....0 0 0 0 0 2 0 1 0— 3 7 0
Batteries—Brown and Dickey; Jones, Heving and Grube.

At St. Louis— R. H. E.
Washington...0 0 0 2 0 1 0 0 7—10 12 0
St. Louis ....0 0 0 0 0 1 2 0 0— 3 6 1
Batteries—Whitehill, Russell and Sewell, Berg; Wells, Gray and Shea.

At Cleveland (10 innings)— R. H. E.
Detroit ....0 0 0 2 0 0 0 0 0 0— 2 7 1
Cleveland ..0 0 2 0 0 0 0 0 0 1— 3 9 0
Batteries—Bridges and Hayworth; Ferrell and Spencer.

HELEN LEE WORTHING MISSING

Ex-Follies Beauty, Former Wife of Colored Doctor, Disappears

Missing from a Santa Fe train which she boarded at Los Angeles Thursday to go to New York, Helen Lee Worthing, former blonde Follies beauty and former wife of Dr. Eugene C. Nelson, Los Angeles colored physician, was sought by police today in a new climax of her strange "Desdemona and Othello" career with Dr. Nelson.

According to Special Agent Fred Phillips of the Santa Fe railroad, Miss Worthing left the train somewhere between the Los Angeles and Pasadena stations, and it was feared she may have leaped from a car platform to her death.

NELSON PRESENT

Dr. Nelson, Phillips said, saw Miss Worthing off at the local station.

At Pasadena, where the train stopped 35 minutes later, the one-time Follies dancer was missing, but her baggage was still in her compartment, Phillips said.

Officers from Los Angeles and Pasadena began searching the arroyos along the railroad right-of-way on the theory Miss Worthing may have leaped or fallen into one of the numerous narrow gulches near the tracks.

Dr. Nelson was notified of his ex-wife's disappearance today when Agent Phillips made his report to police.

UNDER TREATMENT

Miss Worthing had been under treatment at the Santa Monica Rest Home for some time. She had been suffering from a nervous disorder.

Miss Worthing obtained a divorce from Dr. Nelson on May 25, 1932, but November 18, last, Dr. Nelson obtained an annulment which superseded the divorce decree.

On Nov. 29, last, Miss Worthing was before Judge Thomas C. Gould on an insanity complaint which resulted in her being committed to the rest home in the custody of Dr. Nelson. The physician at that time pledged himself to be responsible for the girl who had once been the "toast of Broadway."

EIGHTEENTH OPERATION

QUINCY, Mass., June 17.—(U.P.)—Ivan Mills, a sign painter, recently underwent his eighteenth operation in 20 years.

FIXING RATE ON DOLLAR OPPOSED

Control of Markets Only to Prevent Drastic Fluctuations Is Urged

By International News Serivce

WASHINGTON, June 17.—President Roosevelt has decided to refuse France any hearing on a new debt settlement until that nation pays up the $19,000,000 on which it defaulted last December, International News Service learned tonight on high authority.

By United Press

WASHINGTON, June 17.—Money stabilization proposals made to the United States last night by representatives of the world economic conference "are not acceptable" to the United States, Undersecretary of Treasury Acheson explained today.

It was stated at the treasury that the suggestion made by the delegates in reference to money stabilization were too crystalized to meet with the approval of the American government.

By stating the stabilization proposal was too crystallized, Atcheson, apparently meant that the United States was not in favor of

(CONTINUED ON PAGE FIVE)

COAST GUARD HUNTS MATTERN, MISSING

By United Press

NOME, Alaska, June 17.—Hope for the safety of James Mattern, round-the-world flier, believed down somewhere in the remote Behring sea area, had not been abandoned by airmen today.

Because of dense fogs and clouds, an organized search for the Texas aviator, who left Khabarovsk, Siberia, for Nome Wednesday, appeared unlikely for several days. Two coast guard cutters searched in Behring sea, however.

Airmen here believed Mattern landed on one of the Aleutian chain of islands or on an island in the Behring sea. They said he could live in safety with natives for weeks before establishing communication with the outside world.

Angels Box Score

DUCKS—	AB	R	H	O	A	E
Reeves, 2b..	5	0	2	5	4	0
Mulligan, 3b	4	0	2	0	3	0
Blackerby, rf	4	1	1	2	0	0
Oana, cf....	4	0	1	2	0	0
Keesey, 1b..	4	0	0	9	2	0
Moore, lf...	4	1	2	0	0	0
Sankey, ss..	3	0	0	1	4	0
Palmisano, c	4	1	1	6	0	0
Bowman, p.	4	1	2	2	1	0
Totals....	36	4	11	27	14	0

ANGELS—	AB	R	H	O	A	E
Statz, cf.....	4	1	3	3	0	0
Reese, 2b....	4	0	0	3	4	0
Stainback, rf.	4	0	0	5	0	1
Gudat, lf....	4	0	2	2	0	0
Oglesby, 1b.	4	0	1	9	2	0
Lillard, 3b...	4	0	0	1	2	0
Mohler, ss..	3	0	0	1	1	0
McMullin, c..	3	0	0	3	1	0
Nelson, p...	3	1	1	0	2	0
Gazella.....	1	0	0	0	0	0
Totals....	34	2	7	27	12	1

Portland..	002 001 001	— 4
Los Angeles	000 020 000	— 2

BEAVERS DEFEAT L. A. 4-2 IN 5TH GAME

At Sacramento— R. H. E.
REDS 1 0 1
SOLONS 0 0 0
Batteries—Pillette and Fitzpatrice; Bryan and Woodall.

At Oakland— R. H. E.
STARS 0 0 0 0 3
OAKS 1 0 0 0 0
Batteries—Page and Bassler; Walsh and Veltman.

At San Francisco— R. H. E.
INDIANS 0 0 0
SEALS 0 0 5
Batteries—Page and Cox; Henderson and McIsaac.

Portland collected the fifth game of the series at Wrigley Field today when they defeated Los Angeles by a score of 4 to 2.

FIRST INNING

BEAVERS—Reeves flied to Statz. Mulligan beat out an infield hit to Mohler. Blackerby forced Mulligan at second, Oglesby to Mohler. Oana flied to Stainback. NO RUNS, ONE HIT.

ANGELS—Statz singled infield. Bowman threw out Reese. Stainback safe on a fielder's choice and Statz was run down between second and third, Sankey to Mulligan to Reeves. Gudat forced Sainback at second, Sankey to Reeves. NO RUNS, ONE HIT.

SECOND INNING

BEAVERS—Mohler threw out Keesey. Reese threw out Moore. Reese threw out Sankey. NO RUNS, NO HITS.

ANGELS—Reeves threw out Oglesby. Sankey threw out Lillard. Mulligan threw out Mohler. NO RUNS, NO HITS.

THIRD INNING

BEAVERS—Palmisano singled to right. Bowman doubled to center. Reeves fanned. Mulligan singled to left, scoring Palmisano. Blackerby flied to Stainback. Bowman scoring and Mulligan going to second after the catch. Oana fouled to McMullen. TWO RUNS, THREE HITS.

ANGELS—McMullen fanned. Reeves threw out Nelson. Statz doubled off the left field wall. Reese fouled to Palmisano, who reached into the boxes to get the ball. NO RUNS, ONE HIT.

FOURTH INNING

BEAVERS—Keesey flied to Stainback. Reese threw out Moore. Nelson tossed out Sankey. NO RUNS, NO HITS.

ANGELS—Sankey threw out Stainback. Gudat beat out an infield hit. Oglesby beat out an infield hit. Gudat and Oglesby worked a double steal as Lillard

(CONTINUED ON PAGE ELEVEN)

KANSAS CITY CROWD SEES GANG SHOOT 7 AT UNION STATION

By Associated Press

KANSAS CITY, June 17.—Blazing machine guns turned Kansas City's Union station plaza into a scene of horror today as seven officers and a prisoner were ambushed, five of them killed outright and two others wounded in a brief burst of fire. Hundreds of terror-stricken travelers witnessed the massacre.

The wholesale killing was staged in an effort to release or slay Frank Nash, notorious Oklahoma train robber and killer, being returned to the federal prison at Leavenworth, where he escaped three years ago.

When the murderous rattle of machine gun slugs ceased, Nash, the Oklahoma desperado, was crumpled dead in an automobile he had entered the moment of the attack. Lifeless about him were:

Raymond J. Caffrey, special agent of the United States bureau of investigation.

Otto Reed, chief of police at McAlester, Okla.

Frank Hermanson, Kansas City detective.

W. J. Grooms, Kansas City detective.

TWO OTHERS WOUNDED

The wounded were F. G. Lackey special agent at Oklahoma City of the bureau of investigation, whose condition is considered critical, and R. E. Vetterli, agent in charge of the Kansas City bureau of investigation, who returned the fire of his assailants as they drove away.

Lackey was shot three times in the back. Vetterli suffered a slight wound in the left arm.

Nash, a member of the Al Spencer gang which terrorized northeast Oklahoma 10 years ago, was arrested by agents of the bureau of investigation, department of justice, at Hot Springs, Ark., yesterday after a long and relentless search. An early theory that the gunmen entered to "rub out" Nash for fear he might have information against them was discarded later today.

One theory was that Nash was killed by one of the officers after the shooting started. Another theory was that Nash was killed by the gangsters bullets.

SURVIVOR'S STORY

"I don't believe they intended to kill Nash," Vetterli said in recounting the details of the slaughter, apparently staged by four men armed with machine guns, who had hidden themselves near the officers' car and calmly waited for them to group themselves about the automobile.

"We went to the station to meet the officers who were bringing Nash back from Hot Springs," Vetterli continued.

"Raymond Caffrey and I drove to the station in his car. The two Kansas City detectives, Hermanson and Grooms, drove to the station in their car. We met the train and started over to Caffrey's car, headed south on the station drive across from the east door of the station.

EIGHT IN GROUP

"There were eight of us, including Nash, and seven officers. We were to enter Caffrey's car and the Kansas City detectives were to follow us to Leavenworth in their car.

"I was standing at the rear and west side of Caffrey's car. In the back seat were Lackey and Smith, the agents from Oklahoma, and Otto Reed, chief of police at McAlester, who came up with the prisoner.

"Caffrey was to drive. Nash had sat in the driver's seat temporarily until the car was loaded and then he was to move over into the other front seat which was folded up to allow the three men to enter the rear seat.

"Caffrey stood on the pavement beside Nash on the east side of the car waiting for Nash to slide over into the folding front seat. Hermanson and Grooms were standing on the west side of the car and toward the front.

HEARS COMMAND

"Suddenly I heard a man say, 'Put 'em up, up, up.'

"I looked and saw a man blazing away with a machine gun from near the southwest corner of the car. He seemed to be standing on something—perhaps the running board of a car. I don't know exactly, but he was very close to us.

"I crouched under the murderous fire. I believe there were other machine guns working, too. Hermanson and Grooms fell to the pavement in front of me, their bodies riddled. The windshield of Caffrey's car was splintering. The men inside of it were powerless before the red fire from the rattling guns.

"I fell to the pavement. I felt a stinging pain in my left arm. When the firing ceased—and it was all over in a flash—I leveled a pump gun at the escaping car, which

(CONTINUED ON PAGE FOUR)

PHILADELPHIA'S LARGEST WEEKLY TABLOID NEWSPAPER

QUAKER CITY
BREVITY
5¢ 5¢

VOL. I. — No. 16 PHILADELPHIA, JULY 14, 1933 FIVE CENTS

BIG WHITE SLAVE RING GETS GIRLS IN PHILA.

Men Caught Taking Cabaret Beauty To Peddle Her Honor

The white slave octopus, that every year has crushed the lives and souls of hundreds of girls in Pennsylvania and nearby states, was caught in a net flung out last week by federal agents and the police of several states. The steel bars of two county jails are clamped down on its tentacles.

Three men and three women are under arrest. Police have a list of girls and a list of the houses that belong to the white slave chain.

One man and two women are in a Connecticut jail, awaiting trial. Two men and a woman are being held in another jail. They represent, officials believe, every part of the vicious chain of bawdy houses extending over the entire Atlantic seaboard.

Pennsylvania is dotted with these houses, where townsfolk and transients satisfy their lust. A few of the houses are "independents," most of them belong to a chain.

The chain houses get their women from New York and upstate Pennsylvania. The girls are recruited there from the ranks of those who have fallen, and those who are willing to fall because it is the last way left for them to make a living. They are sent to one of the houses in the chain for a couple of weeks, then new girls supplant them there and they are carried on to another house. They are transferred several times, then they are laid off for a few weeks of rest.

One of these unfortunates, bound for the Old Colony tea room in Wallingford, Conn., from a house in Philadelphia, conducted by a notorious madam, was picked off the road in Stamford last week by an alert Stamford policeman. Her arrest was the blow that broke open the chain.

The girl gave her name as Madeline Rutledge, 25, of 118 W. 76th street, a night club entertainer and dancer who worked under the name of Patsy Yorke while there was work, and was willing to turn to anything to keep from starving. She was in an automobile with Nicola Romeri, 28, of 172 Williams avenue, Brooklyn, and

Continued on Page Twelve

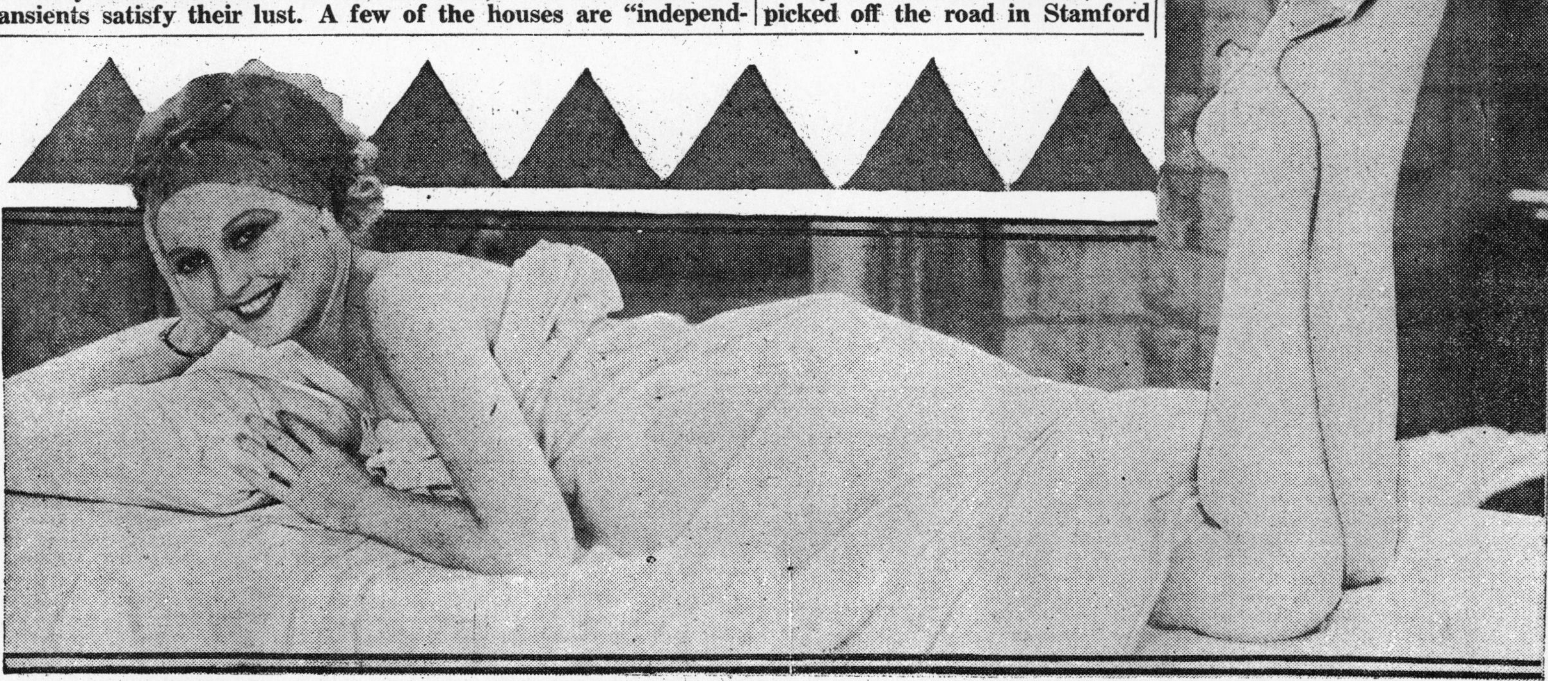

Thelma Todd, shown here in a fetching pose at a masseur's establishment, has almost convinced us that the newspaper business is the bunk. With hands like ours, we ought to make a fortune rolling ham like this. Thelma's slender figure, the envy and despair of a million movie fans, is the result of hours spent in steam rooms, etc., under the care of Sylvia, Hollywood's famous weight reducer.

CONSOLATION indiscreetly pressed upon us, when we are suffering under affliction, only serves to increase our pain, and to render our grief more poignant. —Rousseau.

The Dallas Morning News

Section One
General News

48TH YEAR NO. 298 (AP)—Associated Press. (UP)—United Press. (NANA)—North American Newspaper Alliance. DALLAS, TEXAS, TUESDAY, JULY 25, 1933—SIXTEEN PAGES Oldest Business Institution in Texas—Founded in Galveston April 11, 1842—Established in Dallas October 1, 1885. 5c PER COPY

Buck Barrow Dying After Gun Battle, but Clyde Escapes

French Want No Indefinite Parley Delay

Sentiment for Reconvening of World Conference Grows With Adoption of Report

Currency Worries

Paris Group Still Is Concerned Over Stabilization Moves

LONDON, July 24 (AP).—Sentiment favoring the reconvening of the world economic conference after the recess which begins Thursday increased Monday as the monetary commission adopted its report for submission to the final plenary sitting.

The French delegation was reliably reported to be anxious that the parley should not adjourn indefinitely and Georges Bonnet, French Finance Minister, is understood to have made this clear in submitting, as reported, the document ontlining the work of the monetary group.

At a meeting of the steering committee which also was held Monday. James M. Cox of Ohio supported a move for the formation of a permanent executive body which could reassemble the congress, but which could not disband it without first calling for a plenary session to give this authorization.

The French still greatly are concerned over the currency stabilization and this feeling apparently is the basis of their desire to reopen the deliberations after a long holiday.

May Break Away From Franc.

Some members of the British and Dominions delegations expect to see British currency unhooked from the French franc after the recess begins and the possibility of this development is causing some concern among the Paris group.

Several important delegates from the Dominions probably will remain a short time after the parley disbands for private conversations with members of the British Government in the hope of forming a sterling bloc whose currencies would not be hitched either to gold or to the dollar.

American silver experts virtually have completed a supplementary agreement among silver producing nations to allot to each its portion of the 35,000,000 ounces which silver-holding countries will be allowed to put on the market annually.

New Draft of Wheat Accord.

The wheat negotiators worked out a new draft for an accord which they will ask importing States to accept as their contribution to the scheme for acreage restriction.

Cox and Bonnet, who engaged in a sharp struggle for the chairmanship for the monetary commission with the American as winner, exchanged cordial tributes at the closing session of that body, both expressing themselves as determined to press on in the endeavor to solve the world's economic problems.

"We shall continue the attack along

See PARLEY on Page 8.

When Post Completed His World Flight

—Associated Press Photo.

Surrounded by cheering thousands, Wiley Post is shown being assisted from the cockpit of his plane, the Winnie Mae, at Floyd Bennett Field, Long Island, midnight, July 22, at the completion of his remarkable solo flight around the world. Post is wearing a handkerchief tied around his forehead. Mrs. Post and Harold Gatty are shown in the lower photo. Gatty was a companion of Post on the previous flight around the world.

Her Escort Killed, 19-Year Old Girl Is Attacked and Slain

Man's Body Found Near Parked Car, Her's in Pasture Fifty Feet Away, Both Shot

From the Austin Bureau of The News.

FORT WORTH, Texas, July 24.—Attacked Sunday night by an unidentified man and later slain, the body of Geneva Cantrell, 19, of Muskogee, Ok., was found Monday near Twelfth street and Samuels avenue. Near-by was the body of her escort, A. S. Michael, 33, an electrician, evidently murdered before the girl was attacked by a man who sneaked up behind the parked auto in which the couple was sitting.

Three brothers of Michael identified his body. The girl was identified by her finger prints. She was arrested five days ago on a vagrancy charge and later released.

The bodies were found Monday by a man who telephoned the police but cut himself off without giving his name.

Michael's body was lying a few feet from the abandoned car, his pockets inside out and a pistol shell under it.

On the running board was a crumpled silk chimse. In the bottom of the car was a girl's shoe, a handkerchief, a box of snuff and a girl's Panama hat. In the front seat was a woman's purse containing a few pennies. The inside of the car was blood spattered.

The body of the girl was fifty feet from the car, in a pasture. Near it was the other stocking, rolled into a wad and bloodsoaked. She had been attacked and shot through the back of the head.

Michael last seen Sunday at 5 p. m. when he left the home of his brother, H. W. Michael who had loaned him his automobile.

The bullet was extracted from the dead man's skull, and may help to identify the pistol from which the shots were fired.

The girl last was seen at 9:30 p. m. Sunday by Inez Jones, a friend, at Second and Houston streets.

Detectives believe they were slain shortly before midnight Sunday.

Mrs. Burt Michael, the slain man's mother, is in a critical condition at the home of a daughter in Cleburne. She recently was injured in an automobile wreck.

Chicago Gunman Kills Officer in Courtroom Fight

Breaks From Guard and Races Toward Freedom Before Shot Down

CHICAGO, Ill., July 24 (AP).—A killer broke awa yfrom his guard in the Criminal Courts Building Monday, shot Policeman John Sevick dead and raced down the corridor toward freedom.

As bullets thudded against the door of the courtroom the audience and attaches ducked in panic from the line of fire, a baliff snatched the fallen policeman's pistol and ran after the fugitive. He shot the gunman, John Scheck, twice in the back, but Scheck ran on down the courthouse stairs.

On the floor below a clerk accosted Scheck. The gunman wheeled, leveled his pistol and pulled the trigger. It clicked harmlessly. He slumped to the floor. The bailiff's shots had taken effect. Physicians said he probably would die.

Carl Grundhoefer, codefendant with Scheck on charges of robbery and murder, had sprinted from the bullpen with Scheck but was unarmed. He gave himself up, protesting his 21-year-old companion had forced him to run.

Sevick, 32, was fifth of the Chicago force to die on duty in the last month.

Policeman Shot in Heart.

He had jumped to his feet as Bailiff Jack Kavanagh reached into the courtroom with the warning cry: "Look out! There's a man coming with a gun!" The officer let the fleeing pair pass from the room and then sent four bullets after them. They chunked into plaster walls and door.

Scheck, desperate, turned to face the policeman's gun and fired twice, both bullets entering the officer's heart.

The weapon had been smuggled to Scheck probably a few moments before his sensational break. In violation of criminal court rules, eight persons had visited him in the bullpen

See GUNMAN on Page 8.

Hitch-Hiker Survives Swim Through Rapids Below Niagara Falls

—Associated Press Photo.

Carried into the whirlpool rapids in the lower Niagara River at Niagara Falls, N. Y., while attempting to swim to the Canadian shore, William Kondrat, 18, of Chatham, N. J., swam the entire length of the rapids and through the whirlpool to safety and in doing so, accomplished a feat that has never been duplicated and which has cost the lives of several noted swimmers who attempted to conquer the dangerous rapids in the past. Kondrat had hitchhiked to see the falls, and had entered the river above the rapids for a swim without knowledge of the powerful currents and eddies.

Outlaw's Wife Jailed, Second Woman Injured

Located in Hideout in Woods, With Arsenal of Machine Guns, Automatics and Revolvers

Flee in Stolen Car

Posses in Airplanes and Armored Autos Pursue Escaping Trio

DEXTER, Iowa, July 24 (AP).—Clyde Barrow, notorious Texas outlaw, Monday fought a machine gun battle with police in a wooded hideaway and at night was dodging over Western Iowa with a network of men in airplanes, armored cars, motorcycles and automobiles, all connected by wireless, hot in pursuit.

Fleeing with him in a stolen automobile was a man identified as Jack Sherman and a woman, both of them believed badly wounded. They had hidden out near here in Wild West fashion for a week with an arsenal of two machine guns, thirty-four automatic pistols and five revolvers.

The machine gun battle brought about the capture of Marvin (Buck) Barrow, brother of Clyde, and Marvin's wife. The Barrows are wanted for four murders and wounding three policemen.

The chase for the Barrows began after a waiter in a restaurant reported one of the men had daily purchased five dinners and taken the meals into the woods. A farmer also informed authorities of finding blood-stained bandages near their camp.

The gun battle took place at the outlaws' barricade behind a fallen tree when a posse approached. Clyde Barrow and the other two escaped the posse by wading a stream and creeping through a corn field to a farm owned by Valley Fellers. Marvin Barrow was wounded so badly he was not expected to live.

Airplane Leads Hunt.

Park A. Findley, chief of the State bureau of investigation, and Adjutant General Charles Grahl of the Iowa National Guard led the hunt from an airplane. They soared low over highways to direct the several hundred men in the search.

The State Department's station at Des Moines kept the wireless equipped cars constantly advised of the trend of the hunt. United States Marshal Fred Hird and several men with rifles and Federal Investigator O. C. Dewey of Des Moines joined in the intensified search.

At the Fellers farm Clyde Barrow lined Fellers, his son Marvel and an employe against the barn. With Fellers' car he and his companions fled to Polk City, thirty-eight miles east and just outside Des Moines. There they held up an oil station attendant, took his car and doubled back forty miles to Guthrie Center.

Spotted by Findley, a posse of 200 men surrounded the fleeing trio.

They slipped away and later were reported 100 miles north of here in Southern Kossuth County. Last re-

See BARROW on Page 8.

Little Girl Is Electrocuted At Play by Touching Fence Energized by Broken Wire

While playing about a neighboring house during a visit at the home of her grandparents, Barbara Jean Shuford, 6, was electrocuted Monday afternoon when she laid her hands on a wire netting fence, charged by an electric light wire that had accidentally fallen on it.

Barbara Jean was the only child of Mr. and Mrs. J. M. Shuford and with her parents was visiting at the home of her grandparents, Mr. and Mrs. E. G. Shuford, 5427 Lindsley. The electrocution occurred at the home of Mr. and Mrs. W. J. Moorman, 5401 Lindsley, at Fairview, East Dallas.

Barbara Jean lived most of her life in Dallas, but recently she and her parents have been making their home temporarily at Waco where Mr. Shuford is now employed.

Children Alarmed.

Apparently there were no witnesses to the accident. Mrs. Moorman was the first to reach her after children had called her attention to the victim.

"Look at Barbara Jean," shouted Mrs. Moorman's daughter, Wanda, 6, to another small girl. "She's lying real still and won't move."

Looking outside Mrs. Moorman immediately saw that something was

See ELECTROCUTION on Page 8.

Post 'Disgusted' With Time Record, But Praises Luck

World Air Girdler Recounts Some of Obstacles of Epic Voyage

BY WILEY POST.

(Copyright, 1933, by the North American Newspaper Alliance, Inc.) World rights reserved.)

NEW YORK, July 24.—Now that it's over and I am back where I started from, the chief idea in my mind is that I am disgusted with my flight. I realize, of course, that I have broken the record of eight days, fifteen hours and fifty-one minutes which Harold Gatty and I made together two years ago, but I had expected to break it by a much wider margin, and I am disappointed.

I should have made this flight a month earlier. Then I would have escaped some of the fogs and stormy weather which I have had almost ever since I left New York on my trip around the world, as a matter of fact, until well along on the last leg of the flight, I had had only three hours of good weather all the way.

That was one hour going into Moscow, and two hours going out of Moscow. The bad weather began five minutes after I left Floyd Bennett Field and it dogged me all the way. On this last day it started out as bad as ever. Half way from Fairbanks to Edmonton, where I was flying the Canadian Rockies, I had to fly blind for three hours at 20,000 feet. The mountains there have an elevation of 15,000 feet.

Ice Forms On Wings.

While I was up at that extreme height, ice began to form on my wings. It got heavy enough so that I mushed down some. It cleared up the last half of the way into Edmonton, and then it was plain sailing until between Toronto and New York. There I encountered considerable smoky haze, and I also had to fly around two thunderstorms.

There was a kick in getting back to the old field here and meeting my wife and friends, but there was no thrill to the flight coming in. I was so disappointed with my record that I actually thought one time of sitting down and coming on in Sunday.

I couldn't realize then that I was coming home. After I had got out of the bad weather on this last leg the going was so smooth that I flew mechanically and I kept going to

See POST on Page 8.

Mollisons Finish Hop to New York In Another Plane

Jim, Injured in Sunday Crash, Is Carried From Ship to Waiting Car

NE WYORK, July 24 (UP).—Jim and Amy Mollison ended their long trans-Atlantic flight from Wales to the United States at 5:10 p. m. (Dallas time) Monday night when they reached Floyd Bennett Field as passengers in an amphibian plane.

Their own ship, the black and orange biplane Seafarer, was wrecked Sunday night in a swamp at Bridgeport, Conn. With Jim's face and head heavily bandaged, they came to New York with Ralph Wickford at the controls of another plane.

Four other planes escorted the Mollisons to Floyd Bennett Field, one of them piloted by America's aerial speed king, Frank Hawks.

The big plane came down from the north across Jamaica Bay, where the seaplanes of Gen. Italo Balbo's fleet are at anchorage. It swept up the long concrete runway while 10,000 persons cheered, throwing their hats into the air.

Police Flank Plane.

Motorcycle police flanked the big plane as it trundled up the runway. It reached a halt and Jimmie Mollison, smiling through a mass of bandages, popped out carrying baggage. The famous Amy remained in the cabin.

It became apparent at once that neither Jim nor Amy was in condition to walk. Policemen carried Mollison from the plane. When Amy emerged, seh was given a pack-saddle escort. A woman broke through the police lines and thrust a bouquet of flowers into her hands.

Mrs. Mollison managed to walk to a waiting automobile but Jim had to be

See MOLLISONS on Page 8.

Torrential Rains Wash Out Crops, Hamper Traffic

Eastern Part of Texas Hardest Hit as Rivers Go on Rampage

(By the Associated Press.)

General rains which ranged from a trace to thirteen inches seriously handicapped traffic and washed out crops in some parts of Texas, aided crops in others and resulted in lower temperatures generally over the week-end.

A wide strip of East Texas, extending roughly from the northern edge of the oil field southeast ward to the coast at Beaumont, had the heaviest fall. The gauges at Beaumont showed 13.05 inches of rain from 7 a. m. Saturday until noon Monday.

In the vicinity of Center, in extreme East Texas, thousands of acres of bottom land were under water, rivers went on a rampage, highways were blocked in Shelby and Panola Counties and trains were delayed. Several bridges were washed away and automobiles careened into the swirling water but no one was hurt.

Heaviest in Marshall Area.

The Marshall section experienced the greatest rain fall in the last few days that can be remembered during July, a total of 5.21 inches having

See RAINS on Page 8.

Union Laborers At Film Studios To Go on Strike

Producers Charged With Breaking Agreement, So Walkout Ordered

HOLLYWOOD, Cal., July 24 (AP).—Every union laborer employed in the motion picture studios of Hollywood was today ordered to walk out on strike at midnight Monday.

The strike order was issued gy Richard L. Green, international representative of the International Alliance of Stage Employes and Motion Picture Machine Operators of the United States and Canada.

The strike was called on the grounds that the motion picture producers had violated a union agreement wherein they promised not to employ nonunion help. Green said the producers had employed nonunion men to replace the striking sound technicians who went out on strike at midnight Saturday.

Dallas Not to Feel Strike.

If the studio walkout is protracted, the effect will not be felt by local theaters for at least ten weeks, it was said Monday night by leading Dallas film distributors and exhibitors. The theater owners said they are better stocked than usual with completed pictures due to the fact that this is the height of the film selling season and the studios are several weeks ahead of schedule. Films on hand include some of the major releases for the early season.

It is estimated that completed motion pictures by leading producers which have not yet been shown in Dallas number between fifty and sixty. With the Melba closed, there are only four first run theaters in Dallas. During the next sixty days the Palace will require eight pictures, the Majestic eight, the Old Mill sixteen and the Capitol sixteen.

Local theater managers expressed their chief concern over what may happen after the labor difficulties are settled in Hollywood. If production is delayed as much as two weeks before settlement is reached the studios may be forced to make "quickies" to meet their release schedules. "Quickies," as the name implies, are hastily produced pictures sometimes inferior in quality. Local film row, however, expects production to resume in Hollywood before serious damage is done.

Lufkin Man Electrocuted.

LUFKIN, Texas, July 24 (AP).—Delbert Reed, 36-year-old operator of a garage and filling station, was killed Sunday night when he turned on an electric light while standing in water at his place of business. He died thirty minutes after the shock.

Touhy and Three Of Gang Charged With Kidnaping

Four Men Are Viewed by Millionaire Brewer Hamm in Chicago

MILWAUKEE, July 24 (AP).—Roger Touhy and three members of his Chicago gang were charged in Federal warrants Monday with the $100,000 kidnaping of William Hamm Jr., millionaire St. Paul, Minn., brewer.

Milwaukee police and United States marshals were dispatched immediately to Elkhorn, Wis., where the four men are held. They are to be brought to Milwaukee and placed in the county jail pending removal proceedings to St. Paul.

Melvin H. Purvis, chief of the United States Bureau of Investigation at Chicago, said the warrants named the prisoners specifically for the Hamm kidnaping. United States Commissioner Floyd Jenkins and officials of the District Attorney's office would not discuss the exact nature of the charges.

Purvis would not discuss persistent reports that Hamm had positively identified Touhy and the other three or that money found in their possession had been traced by serial numbers as the ransom paid for Hamm's release.

He admitted, however, that the St. Paul brewer viewed the four men in the offices of the United States Bureau of Investigation at Chicago Sunday night.

On Trial for Kidnaping.

KANSAS CITY, Mo., July 24 (AP).—With his life at stake, Walter McGee went on trial in Criminal Court here Monday for the kidnaping of Miss Mary McElroy, daughter of the City Manager, for whose release her father paid abductors $30,000.

Clean House, Grain Trade Told or U. S. Will Do It for You

Speculators Have No Divine Right to Handle Farm Goods, Says Peek

WASHINGTON, July 24 (AP).—In a warning to put its house in order or the Government would reform grain market practices, the farm administration informed the grain trade Monday that it did not recognize that the present trading regime "has any divine right to handle the farmer's products."

George N. Peek, chief administrator of the farm act, issued the warning at a conference of representatives of the grain industry shortly before they took steps to explore the possibilities of establishing a code of competition under which stringent regulations covering commodity marketing would be established.

Peek and other administrators, aroused over the recent sharp rise and fall in wheat, corn and other grain prices, expressed the intention of taking the initiative in reforming grain marketing practices unless the exchanges obtain results by mutual agreement.

Committees representing grain exchanges, terminal elevators and country elevators opened the effort to draft

See GRAIN on Page 8.

Mutilated Body Of Missing Boy Is Found in Bay

SAN DIEGO, Cal., July 24 (AP).—The body of Dalbert Aposhian, 7, badly mutilated, was found floating in San Diego Bay Monday. The boy, missing a week, had been attracked, tortured and beaten to death, County Autopsy Surgeon Frank E. Toomey said.

He was reported missing by his parents, Mr. and Mrs. George W. Aposhian, last Wednesday. They said he had left their store with a young friend, Jackie Confar, to go to the zoo and he last saw Dalbert playing across the street at 5 p. m. Tuesday.

Police said the slaying was similar in many respects to the unsolved killing of Virginia Brooks, 11, here in 1931.

The girl disappeared while en route to school. A shepherd found her body, mutilated and tied in a sack, on isolated Camp Kearney mesa.

Wife of Kidnaped Oklahoman Takes Charge of Affairs

Police Guard Removed to Make Contact With Abductors Easier

OKLAHOMA CITY, Ok., July 24 (AP).—Serene, brown-eyed Bernice Urschel laid business-like plans Monday to free her husband, independent of the horde of police and Federal operatives who have hunted the oil man and his kidnapers since he was snatched from a quiet bridge game late Saturday night.

"I am interested only in the safe return of Mr. Urschel," she said, through her spokesman, "and not in what happens to the kidnapers after his return."

Monday night, however, the only thing the slight widow of Tom B. Slick, king of oil wildcatters, had from the machine gunners who held Charles F. Urschel, trustee for the many millions left by Slick, was complete silence.

A police guard was removed from the brick mansion of the Urschels during the day in order that any contact with the abductors might be faciliated, and Mrs. Urschel selected Arthur Seeligson, another Slick estate trustee, to take charge of the entire case upon his arrival Tuesday by train from North Carolina.

"We will co-operate with the Federal and other officials but we are ready to make a contact with the kidnapers ourselves," said E. E. Kirkpatrick, spokesman for Mrs. Urschel. "If I could make a contact right now I would do it in spite of everything."

Mrs. Urschel directed every move Monday. She slept soundly Sunday night, although her 16-year-old daughter Betty Slick, paced the floor in her lighted room.

Weather

NEW ORLEANS, La., July 24 (AP).—Government weather forecast for Tuesday:

East Texas: Partly cloudy, probably thundershowers in southeast portion; light to moderate variable winds on the coast.

West Texas: Generally fair; warmer in north portion.

Louisiana: Partly cloudy, local thundershowers in east portion; light to moderate southerly winds on the coast.

Arkansas: Partly cloudy, showers in east portion.

Oklahoma: Partly cloudy; warmer in west portion.

Dallas Temperatures.

Temperatures in Dallas Monday, July 24, and for the same date last year, as reported by the United States Weather Bureau, follow:

	1933.	1932.		1933.	1932.
Midnight	75	80	Noon	82	89
2 a. m.	74	77	2 p. m.	85	93
4 a. m.	74	76	4 p. m.	84	94
6 a. m.	74	74	6 p. m.	83	85
7 a. m.	74	75	7 p. m.	82	83
10 a. m.	78	81			

Maximum temperautre July 25 last year 95 degrees, minimum 74 degrees. Rainfall for 24 hours ending 7 p. m., .03 inches. Total precipitation so far this year 20.43 inches.

Full weather report on Page 7, Section II.

PRETENSE.

TOMORROW when I go to shop,
I'll buy a painted mask,
The brightest one on any shelf;
And then when people ask

Where you have gone, I'll be so gay
No one will ever guess
That now and then I catch my breath
In sudden loneliness.

And heads will nod, and lips will say,
Once you were out of sight,
Forgetting was an easy thing. . . .
And I'll pretend they're right.

—Helen Welshimer, in Good Housekeeping.

Bad Weather Delays Balbo's Start Home

NEW YORK, July 24 (AP).—Because of unfavorable weather Gen. Italo Balbo Monday postponed until Tuesday the take-off of his twenty-four-plane armada on its return journey to Italy.

The General left the field to return to his hotel in New York City after waiting some four hours in the hope that fog conditions along the East Coast would improve.

The motors of the twenty-four Italian planes were covered and naval boats were sent out to bring in the crews of the airships.

Baby Member of James Band Dies Mourning Runaway Son

DENVER, Colo., July 24 (AP).—Alexander Adair, whose early life of crime was followed by thirty years as a mission evangelist, died in a hospital without realizing his one remaining ambition—to see his son, who had run away after a break with his father, and to effect a reconciliation.

Until he suffered a paralytic stroke two months ago Adair worked actively at the Volunteers of America Mission he founded here thirty years ago. Unable to speak distinctly because of the stroke, he has laid on his hospital bed hoping his son, Jesse, named for Jesse James, bandit leader and once Alexander Adair's chieftain, would return to his father.

"I don't know what their trouble was about, but the boy went away years ago and has refused since to return to his father or aid him," said Col. George Duquette, acting head of the mission.

Adair was born June 29, 1850, at Zanesville, Ohio, and ran away at 11 to see the Wild West that his father, a noted jurist, often told him about.

Young Alexander ran into an older brother, Marvin, who also had left home in boyhood, and who persuaded Alexander to join the James gang.

In sermons at his mission, Adair often told how his early days included participation in a Muncie, Ind., train robbery and other escapades as the baby member of the James gang.

Adair was converted at Emporia, Kan., after he had been released from prison and had gone there to live. After he came to Denver, thirty years ago, he established a mission and married one of the mission workers. She died some years ago. They had only one child.

Vendor Loser as Policeman's Horse Eats His Confections

SAN FRANCISCO, Cal., July 24 (AP).—Lee Mock, vendor of Oriental confections, stood at a street corner Monday, awaiting a street car.

Lee's basket was at his feet. It contained candied cocoanut, golden limes, li chi, with paper-thin shells and quartered melons.

As Lee pondered and watched for his street car, a traffic patrolman's horse, hitched near by muzzled into the basket and ate the candied cocoanut.

Next went the golden limes and the quartered melons. The crunching of the li chi nuts awakened Lee, but it was too late.

The horse sighed and went to sleep.

Lee has no recourse, for city statutes say a policeman's horse is not liable for damages inflicted while on duty.

2 CENTS PAY NO MORE!

Chicago Daily Tribune

THE WORLD'S GREATEST NEWSPAPER

FINAL ★★

VOLUME XCII.—NO. 214 C (REG. U. S. PAT. OFFICE: COPYRIGHT 1933 BY THE CHICAGO TRIBUNE.) THURSDAY, SEPTEMBER 7, 1933.—30 PAGES THIS PAPER CONSISTS OF TWO SECTIONS—SECTION ONE PRICE TWO CENTS IN CHICAGO AND SUBURBS ELSEWHERE THREE CENTS

FIND GOLFER M'GURN GUILTY

ASK 50 MILLION U. S. EASY MONEY FOR PORT HERE

Engineer Outlines Harbor Plans.

BY WALTER FITZMAURICE.

Aroused over the abundance of federal easy money allotted to the east, the south, and the far west for public works while Chicago and the central states receive a comparative pittance, the Chicago regional port committee is sponsoring a project designed to get some of the federal millions out of Washington for the aid of jobless workers and tax burdened business of this area.

The project was announced yesterday by Maj. Rufus W. Putnam, executive secretary of the port committee. In its barest outline the project calls for allotment of 50 millions of federal funds to improve navigation on the drainage canal and the Sag channel of the Chicago sanitary district, thus diverting marine traffic from Chicago's busy loop district to the Calumet industrial area, where engineers contend it belongs.

Would Give Jobs for 7,000.

Completion of this long considered improvement, Maj. Putnam pointed out, would provide the last essential link to join the great lakes water routes to the inland waterways, on which routes the government has already spent 800 million dollars. Moreover, he pointed out, the project would create jobs over a five year period for an estimated 7,000 workers, more than half the 50 millions estimated for the work being figured for wages.

Within the next week, Maj. Putnam said, the port committee will call together representatives of the four state and local agencies concerned in waterway questions to line up solid support for the project. The agencies involved and the subjects of their interests are: Chicago city council, bridge construction; Chicago sanitary district, canal right of way; Cook county board, bridge abutments and bridge maintenance, and state highway commission, bridge maintenance.

If previous conflicting interests of the city and sanitary district can be reconciled, Maj. Putnam said, the project should be ready for submission to the public works administrator, Secretary of the Interior Ickes, within a month. Thereupon, he said, the port committee and local authorities will have provided a test of Mr. Ickes' claim that the federal government is disposed to be generous with hard pressed Chicagoland if the authorities here will only submit plans.

Details on Cost of Project.

Members of the port committee are William R. Dawes, Chicago, chairman; John T. Pirie, Floyd L. Bateman, and E. M. Antrim, also of Chicago, and Col. Walter J. Riley, East Chicago, Ind. At their behest Maj. Putnam has set up a schedule of cost on the project, as follows:

1. Widening of the Sag channel from 60 to 250 feet for a distance of twenty miles between Lake Calumet and the Sag canal's junction with the main drainage canal, $20,000,000.

2. Purchase of privately owned right of way for a distance of eight miles along the Little Calumet river between Lake Calumet and the outer Calumet harbor on Lake Michigan, widening of the Little Calumet to 250 feet, and reconstruction of 37 fixed bridges in the Sag channel, $22,500,000.

3. Improving of Lake Calumet harbor facilities for use of grain storage, steel, and other heavy industries of Calumet district, $2,500,000.

4. Reconstruction of ten low bridges along 13 miles of main canal from Lockport to Cicero avenue, $2,500,000.

5. Purchasing privately owned right of way and widening of Grand Calumet river from Sag canal to Indiana Harbor, Ind., $2,500,000.

Approved by Army Engineers.

No great federal generosity is entailed, Maj. Putnam contended, in approving item 1, the $20,000,000 Sag channel widening, as army engineers approved this project once before. Nor could he see any cause of federal hesitancy in allowing the $2,500,000 Lake Calumet improvement, a project he regards as a normal federal function.

There will be real federal generosity displayed, however, he conceded, if the government consents to purchase private right of way and to pay for reconstruction of the 47 bridges in the project. Even here he could see no inconsistency in the government undertaking the job, for it is because of requirement of federal engineers for a 34 foot clearance above the canal that the bridges must be changed.

Were it not for the inability of the

[Continued on page 6, column 3.]

NEWS SUMMARY of The Tribune

[And Historical Scrap Book.]

Thursday, September 7, 1933.

LOCAL.

Machine Gun Jack McGurn convicted of vagrancy; gets 6 months. Page 1.

Chicago port commission asks $50,000,000 of U. S. easy money for Chicago harbor development under public works program. Page 1.

New York governor orders extradition of Attorney Aaron Sapiro to stand trial in Chicago on racket charges. Page 1.

School economy program will provide 6,000 more high school seats in schools 46 to 50. Page 3.

Nude girl's death leap off yacht described by business men and other girls of party. Page 3.

New York state to take spotlight at Fair tomorrow; Gov. Lehman to head official party. Page 4.

Mother Cabrini, a Chicago resident before her death in 1917, may be made saint; Catholic church tribunal takes testimony in traditional rite. Page 5.

Double barreled drive on tax waste and county's antiquated revenue system launched by Mayor Kelly. Page 7.

Aeronautical officials ready to start search for two missing balloons which left Glenview Saturday in Bennett trophy race. Page 11.

Death notices, obituaries. Page 14.

Radio programs. Page 14.

News of society. Page 15.

CUBAN SITUATION.

American marines land in Havana; guard hotel, refuge of United States citizens. Page 1.

More warships on way to Cuba; Roosevelt sends Secretary of Navy Swanson to Havana on cruiser Indianapolis. Page 1.

WASHINGTON.

Gen. Johnson decides to rely on Blue Eagle to bring Henry Ford into NRA lineup. Page 7.

After meeting with President Roosevelt coal code labor clause is adjusted; unions made stronger by Johnson decision. Page 7.

Senator Van Nuys visits capital to push Indiana's plea for federal public works funds. Page 13.

DOMESTIC.

Claire Windsor tells of 7 a. m. raid on her bungalow when she and young broker visited Agua Caliente. Page 1.

Erie railroad official puts blame on engineer for wreck in which 14 died and scores were injured. Page 2.

TRIBUNE survey in east indicates travel to Chicago Fair increase with cooler weather. Page 4.

Grand jury inquiry resumed into "bank crisis" at Detroit. Page 8.

Orthodox Jews in United States ordered to boycott German goods. Page 9.

FOREIGN.

Viscount Grey of Fallodon, foreign minister when Britain entered war, is dead. Page 1.

Norman Davis, United States ambassador at large, explains Roosevelt arms policy to Great Britain. Page 8.

Thousands of persons called out to fight British forest fires. Page 10.

Samuel Insull extradition papers sent out of Athens to be photographed; case delayed another week. Page 11.

John Cudahy, new U. S. ambassador to Poland, presents credentials to President Moscicki. Page 11.

SPORTS.

Cubs win, 4-3; check Boston Braves' rally in ninth. Page 19

Pirates fail to gain; divide double header with Giants. Page 19.

Sharkey arrives to train for bout with Levinsky. Page 19.

Tuffy Griffith is knocked out by Tony Shucco. Page 19.

Senators beat Sox, 3 to 1, with 39 year old rookie pitching. Page 19.

Teralice wins by a nose in stretch drive. Page 20.

Bonzani runs 65 yards for touchdown in Bears' practice. Page 21.

Parker, Lott lose, Vines wins in title tennis. Page 21.

EDITORIALS.

Unemployment in the Building Trades; The Triumph of Tyranny; Problem in Conduct; The Busy Propagandists; Cuban Questions. Page 12.

FINANCE, COMMERCE.

Refiners raise crude oil and gasoline prices in western fields. Page 22.

Bankers urge Roosevelt delay putting deposit plan into effect. Page 23.

U. S. experts favor new law to base bank capital on deposits. Page 23.

Kansas governor predicts disaster for bank deposit guarantee. Page 23.

Stocks rally nearly wipes out early losses. Page 23.

Grains seesaw as traders await NRA results; wheat makes gain. Page 23.

Realty dealers told details of their NRA code. Page 24.

Want Ad Index. Page 16.

Average net paid circulation of THE CHICAGO TRIBUNE August, 1933 DAILY in excess of 800,000

GETS 6 MONTHS IN JAIL UNDER NEW VAG LAW

Freed on Cash Bond of $10,000.

(Picture on Back Page.)

Machine Gun Jack McGurn, who was the principal gunbearer for Alphonse Capone when that fat gangster was boss of the Chicago underworld, was found guilty of vagrancy under the new criminal reputation law by a jury in the Felony court last night. The jury was out just 19 minutes.

Judge Thomas A. Green, who presided at the trial, denied a motion for a new trial and immediately sentenced McGurn to six months in the Bridewell, the maximum punishment under the law's provisions.

Attorney Benjamin Feldman, who conducted the defense, gave notice of appeal and requested that his client be freed on bonds while this was pending.

"He can get out," said Judge Green, "only if the $10,000 is furnished instanter."

Bondsman Halts March to Cell.

No one appeared at the moment, and McGurn was being led out to the Bridewell when Robert R. Marcus described as a professional bondsman, stepped up and presented the required sum in cash. A stay of mittimus was then issued, and McGurn, refusing to comment, left the courtroom.

Machine Gun Jack had been arrested Aug. 27 at the Olympia Fields Country club while he was competing under his real name, Vincent Gebhardi, for the Western Open golf championship. The police officers encountered him while he was finishing the sixth hole. He was one under par at that spot, but their presence rattled him and he made an 11 on the eighth hole. The officers permitted him to finish the 18 holes before he was actually taken into custody.

His Country Club Tone.

From the time McGurn first appeared in court yesterday morning until the end of the trial he maintained a sturdy country club attitude. He wore a blue sports coat with pearl buttons, gray flannel slacks impeccably pressed, and shiny white and black shoes. Although the day was hot and the jurors, attorneys, and court attachés all took advantage of permission to shed their coats, he stuck with his, conveying the subtle impression that he disapproved of such informality. The trial lasted until 9:30 p. m.

Altogether eleven witnesses, ten of them members of the Chicago police force, testified that McGurn was well known as a gangster and hoodlum and had no known legitimate means of support. The defense produced five witnesses who testified that they knew him as a good fellow and a good golfer and as one greatly maligned by current reports.

Had Played with Judge Green.

One of the strange facts brought out during the questioning was that McGurn and Judge Green, who was presiding at his trial, had once played a part of a round of golf in the same foursome. Judge Green aided in bringing it out himself. As Attorney Feldman was trying to frame an acceptable question to show that the game had been played, the judge halted him and said:

"I know what you are driving at. I was playing once at the Evergreen public fee course with the manager and the professional. A fourth man joined and was introduced to me. That man was McGurn. It was purely a coincidence and it might happen to any one on a golf course."

Later, not in the hearing of the jury, the judge said that only a few holes had been played when he realized the identity of his new companion and that he then withdrew from the game.

Override Delay Motions.

The dapper defendant, who had never before been convicted of a crime in the state courts, began to suffer in the machinery of the law early in the morning. When the case was called Attorney Feldman presented several motions. One was to quash. Another was to do something else of a technical nature. A third was a demand for a change of venue.

"All motions overruled," said the judge. "The one for a change of venue should have been filed yesterday."

A jury trial was then requested. Some difficulty was encountered in finding a venire, so busy were all the courts in the Criminal Court building

[Continued on page 6, column 6.]

U. S. Marines on Guard in Havana

A FEW OF THE INTERESTING THINGS CHICAGO CAN SHOW YOU

The Hall of Religions attracts enormous crowds.

And so does its rival, the Hall of Science.

You can see sky ride, air ride, boat ride, and lake ride.

You can see an antarctic ship and a modern submarine.

You can usually see some visiting celebrity.

You can see Jane Faunts at the Streets of Paris.

You can see motion pictures being made at "Hollywood."

You can see dashing cowboys riding at a rodeo.

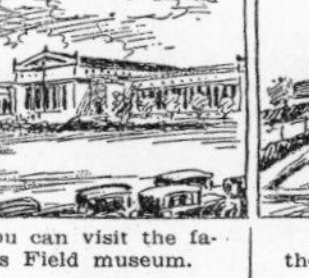

You can see a section of old Belgium.

You can see the Wings of a Century.

You can see a wonderful art exhibit at the Art Institute.

You can see Chicago's wonderful retail stores.

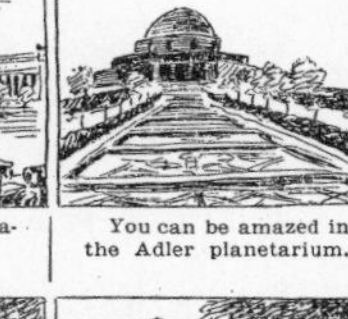

You can see quaint gardens at the Horticultural building.

You can see the fascinating Enchanted island.

You can visit the famous Field museum.

You can be amazed in the Adler planetarium.

You can study ocean fish in the Shedd aquarium.

You can see tires made and automobiles assembled.

You can visit Lincoln park and the Chicago Historical building.

In Jackson park you can see the Rosenwald Industrial museum.

Orders Sapiro Extradited for Racket Trial

(Picture on Back Page.)

Gov. Herbert H. Lehman of New York yesterday granted the extradition of Attorney Aaron Sapiro to Illinois to stand trial in Chicago with 23 other men on charges of conspiracy to control the laundry industry here by racketeering methods. Sapiro, nationally known as a professional organizer, is one of the six leading defendants in the case. The five others are Al Capone, Murray Humphries, Dr. Benjamin M. Squires, Ald. Oscar F. Nelson, and Attorney Morris I. Kaplan.

Announcement of the New York governor's action was made at Albany last night by Charles Poletti, executive counsel. Sapiro is now in New York City, and Illinois authorities announced last night that, assisted by New York agencies, they would take steps to compel his return to Chicago at once.

Two Extradition Hearings.

Two separate extradition hearings were required. The first ended in failure because of a faulty indictment. As a result Sapiro and the others were reindicted. Gov. Lehman's action yesterday was based on the new indictment.

The first indictment was returned on July 27. It charged Sapiro, Capone, and the others with conspiracy to stifle the laundry industry by bombings, sluggings, acid throwings, strikes, and intimidations. Only a month before this Sapiro had resigned as counselor for the Chicago Laundry Owners' association.

Action for Return Begun.

Sapiro was in New York at the time. He asserted that he had worked for the best interests of the Chicago laundry industry. He also intimated he would not return voluntarily to face trial. Accordingly, extradition proceedings were begun, with First Assistant State's Attorney Grover C. Niemeyer representing Cook county.

The New Yorker testified in his own behalf before Gov. Lehman, and helped prove that he was in New York on May 30, one of the dates cited in the alleged conspiracy. On that proof Gov. Lehman refused extradition. Then, on Aug. 18, the second indictment was returned, with the May 30 date eliminated.

GUNMAN SLAIN IN FLIGHT FROM 2 DETECTIVES

A gunman identified as Edwin Harris, 25 years old, was shot and killed by two policemen at 5th avenue and Independence boulevard last night when he and another man tried to escape after being caught in a stolen automobile. The second man got away.

The pair were sighted at Crawford and 5th avenues by Detectives Frank Krueger and William Gibbons of the stolen automobile detail and trailed to Independence boulevard and 5th avenue, where they were forced to stop for a red light. The detectives walked up to Krueger with guns drawn.

"Put up your hands, we're policemen," he ordered.

"Go to hell," returned the driver. Then he backed up his car, almost running over Gibbons, and the next instant proceeded forward. The fugitive car was wrecked in a crash with three other autos and the detectives opened fire as the two occupants fled on foot, killing Harris.

A loaded revolver was found in Harris' pocket. The car had been stolen Aug. 29 from A. Saxton, 116 South Springfield avenue.

MERCURY RISES TO 95°, HOTTEST SINCE JULY 30

(Picture on back page.)

Yesterday was Chicago's hottest day since July 30, the mercury climbing to a high of 94 at the Federal court building at 4 p. m. At the University of Chicago, where the official records formerly were kept, the highest mark was 95.

The hottest Sept. 6 on record here was in 1922, when a mark of 96 was attained.

Forecaster W. P. Day said that today would be unsettled and considerably cooler, due to a shift in the wind from the west and southwest to the north tonight. Showers are expected tomorrow.

21 Young Athletes Drown as Typhoon Capsizes Boat

TOKIO, Sept. 6.—(AP)—The death toll of the recent typhoon in southern Corea and western Japan mounted today to 49, of whom 21 were young athletes en route to a track meet. They drowned when the motor boat in which they were crossing Lake Hachiro near Akita capsized in the high wind.

Viscount Grey Dies; British Leader in War

(Picture on Back Page.)

CHRISTON BANK, England, Sept. 7 [Thursday].—(AP)—Viscount Grey of Fallodon, former British foreign secretary and ambassador to Washington died today at the age of 71. Death came at 6:05 a. m. The viscount had been in a coma since Monday, when he suffered a relapse.

LED BRITAIN INTO WAR.

Viscount Grey of Fallodon will go down in history as the man who, as British foreign secretary under Premier Asquith in 1914, led Great Britain into what soon developed into the world war. It was Grey who convinced the British nation that to fail to go to war with Germany in behalf of Belgium would be unworthy and cowardly.

Four months before the European crisis arose it had been said of Grey that if it ever became necessary for him to take such a step he would do it with the calm deliberation of a man about to sip a cup of tea. So it proved.

When Grey—then Sir Edward—made the decision which brought England into the mêlée it was with the laconic observation, "The neutrality of Belgium must be preserved."

Inspired Entente Cordiale.

Indirectly Viscount Grey also had other responsibility for the extent of the war, for it was he who was instrumental in the formation of the entente cordiale with France in 1907 and the entente with Russia that same year which caused these three nations to take up cudgels against their common foe.

Not that Viscount Grey—he acquired the viscountcy in 1916—did not try valiantly to avert the war. He had long been known for his pronouncements for peace and had advocated some sort of peace league through the efforts of which international strife might be abolished. But even he must have made those speeches with his fingers crossed, for he was a consistent advocate of a larger British navy.

In speaking of his diplomatic efforts to bring peace out of the 1914 crisis he said:

"All efforts to avoid war failed because you cannot have peace without

[Continued on page 8, column 4.]

Actress' Home Raided; Read Was Her Guest

BY GEORGE SHAFFER.

Los Angeles, Cal., Sept. 6.—[Special.]—Details of a pleasure trip to Agua Caliente on which Alfred C. Read Jr., wealthy young broker, accompanied Claire Windsor, movie actress, and during which four detectives broke into Miss Windsor's bungalow at 7 o'clock in the morning, were related on the witness stand by the actress today. She testified in the $100,000 alienation of affections suit filed against her by Mrs. Marian Young Read.

"We went across the border and had dinner," Miss Windsor said. "During the meal Al became ill and I accompanied him to my bungalow and got him to lie down for a while on the bed.

"After a while others joined us. Al felt better and we left the bungalow, returning about midnight.

"Grace Read was staying with me in my bungalow and she retired to her room. The other man left and pretty soon Al left."

Read Not There at 7 A. M.

"What time was that?" demanded Attorney C. Ray Robinson, representing Mrs. Read.

"I don't just know," Miss Windsor replied.

"Was it 1 o'clock?" Robinson pressed.

"I can't say exactly as to the time," Miss Windsor answered.

"Well, was Read there at 7 o'clock the next morning?" Robinson asked.

Miss Windsor flushed. Her eyes snapped and in an almost hysterical voice she replied:

"No, he was not, but four detectives walked in on me at that hour."

Robinson did not pursue the line of questioning further.

"Eternal Love" Cools.

Earlier Miss Windsor had declared on the stand that the "eternal love" that Read pledged her lasted slightly under three months.

Her testimony was given as she interpreted and explained lovelorn passages in a sheaf of letters presented for the perusal of herself and the jury, five of whom were women.

The packed courtroom evidenced great eagerness to hear Claire's tender messages, but Read's were a trifle too apologetic in tone. There was a stir of evident discontent when Read, in letters sent from Hollywood, where he was enjoying life with film social groups, began to evade answers to the beauty's letters entreating the broker to hurry to her side in, successively, Philadelphia, Washington, Cleveland, and Chicago.

"Accident" Prevents Visit.

Read wrote Claire, in answer to fervent wires inviting his presence in Chicago on Christmas day, 1931, and again on New Year's eve, saying that he had been seriously injured in an airplane crack-up in Oakland. According to Mrs. Read's attorneys, Read was living with his wife at the time in Oakland and had had no crack-up. But Claire, in Chicago, didn't know that.

Ray Robinson of Merced, Cal., attorney for the plaintiff, brought slight furrows in the white brow of the poised defendant, smart in linen suit with abbreviated sleeves, polka

[Continued on page 8, column 1.]

THE WEATHER

THURSDAY, SEPTEMBER 7, 1933.

[Daylight Saving Time.]

Sunrise, 6:22; sunset, 7:14. Moon rises at 8:35 p. m. today. Venus, Jupiter, and Mars are evening stars. Saturn is an evening luminary, visible in the southeast after dark.

Chicago and vicinity—Mostly cloudy and slightly cooler Thursday; Friday unsettled, probably followed by showers and cooler; gentle shifting winds Thursday.

Illinois—Fair and continued warm Thursday; Friday unsettled.

TRIBUNE BAROMETER.

RAIN CLOUDY STORMY FAIR VERY DRY

TEMPERATURES IN CHICAGO

MAXIMUM, 4 P. M. 94

MINIMUM, 6 A. M. 71

3 a. m....72	Noon 89	8 p. m....88
4 a. m....72	1 p. m....90	9 p. m....85
5 a. m....72	2 p. m....91	10 p. m....83
6 a. m....71	3 p. m....93	Unofficial—
7 a. m....71	4 p. m....94	11 p. m....83
8 a. m....72	5 p. m....94	Midnight ..83
9 a. m....77	6 p. m....92	1 a. m....82
10 a. m....83	7 p. m....90	2 a. m....82
11 a. m....86		

For 24 hours ended at 8 p. m. Sept. 6.

Mean temperature, 82 degrees; normal, 68 degrees; excess since Jan. 1, 888 degrees; excess for September, 51 degrees.

Precipitation, none; deficiency since Jan. 1, .80 of an inch; deficiency for September, .53 of an inch.

Barometer, 8 a. m., 29.94; 8 p. m., 29.85. Highest wind velocity, 17 miles an hour from the southwest at 10:44 a. m.

[Official weather table on page 26.]

AMERICANS IN CUBAN CITY ASK FOR PROTECTION

Take Refuge in Hotel; Fear for Lives.

(Pictures on Back Page.)

HAVANA, Cuba, Sept. 7 [Thursday].—United States marines early this morning disembarked from the destroyer McFarland and boarded waiting automobiles which took them to the National hotel, where they now are on guard.

One hundred and fifty American families took refuge at the hotel in fear of violence should the United States decide on intervention.

Cubans Unaware of It.

Few citizens in Havana at the moment were aware the marines had set foot on Cuban soil protecting Americans.

Ambassador Welles was reported to be arranging with Wilbur P. Taylor, the hotel manager, to lodge other Americans, believing their lives in danger.

Cuban soldiers are guarding foreign banks.

The situation generally is tense—like awaiting a powder keg to blow up momentarily.

[Other news from Cuba on page 2.]

NAVY SECRETARY EN ROUTE

BY JOHN BOETTIGER.

[Chicago Tribune Press Service.]

Washington, D. C., Sept. 6.—[Special.]—Secretary of the Navy Claude Swanson was steaming at full speed for Havana, Cuba, tonight, nearly 1,000 marines were assembling at Quantico for possible duty in Cuba, and more American warships were under orders to proceed to that island.

Secretary Swanson boarded the cruiser Indianapolis that was anchored off the naval academy at Annapolis. The ship soon left.

Other warships en route to Cuba included the battleship Mississippi, the cruiser Richmond, and several lighter craft.

The situation admittedly was tense, although up to the present no direct attacks or threats of attacks had been made on American citizens or American property in Cuba.

Roosevelt Takes Charge.

President Roosevelt, assuming full charge, conferred with various officials during the day, including Secretary Swanson, just before the cabinet member left to board the cruiser Indianapolis for Havana.

It was insisted at the White House that Mr. Swanson was not being ordered to Havana, but was stopping at the Cuban capital on a previously planned cruise to the west coast through the Panama canal.

It was plain, however, that with a dozen or more war craft either in Cuban harbors or hurrying there Secretary Swanson's presence there would be important. The President stated plainly today that he regards armed intervention by the United States in the Cuban imbroglio as absolutely the last resort. He indicated that the uncertainty of just what kind of government eventually may be set up in Cuba made it impossible to forecast what will be done by the United States in the future. If there is any honorable way for the United States to avoid it, however, no forcible entry into the island will be ordered.

Statement by Swanson.

Before leaving Washington, Secretary Swanson issued this statement:

"A wholly erroneous interpretation has been given to my trip. This trip to the west coast was planned, as every one knows, a month ago. No one at that time expected a second revolution in Cuba.

"I had told Ambassador Welles, when the trip was first planned, that I would drop in and visit with him in Havana if I could. During my conversation with the President today he told me he saw no reason why I should not carry out the original plans for the trip.

"I have not been ordered to Havana.

"I am carrying no instructions to Ambassador Welles or any one else. The Cuban situation will continue to be handled from Washington by the President."

Explains to Cuba's Neighbors.

At the close of the day Mr. Roosevelt called in the diplomatic representatives of four South American coun-

MISSISSIPPI'S LARGEST DAILY NEWSPAPER

JACKSON DAILY NEWS

PUBLISHED EVERY DAY DURING THE YEAR

FORTIETH YEAR | LEASED WIRE REPORTS | JACKSON, MISS., TUESDAY, SEPTEMBER 26, 1933 | NEA SERVICE | STATE EDITION

"MACHINE GUN" KELLY CAUGHT

The Low-Down On The Higher-Ups

By FREDERICK SULLENS

The Goodyear interests have picked Arizona as the state in which to grow the "best cotton," according to a press dispatch yesterday. The Goodyear interests merely mean that the Arizona type of cotton is best suited to the manufacture of automobile tires. The Mississippi delta continues to grow the finest cotton in the world, and will continue to do so for the sufficient reason that no other terrain in the world is so admirably adapted to cotton growing.

• • •

The sporting pages of the daily papers lost one of their brightest lights in the death last night of Ring Lardner. Second only to Grantland Rice, he was perhaps the nation's foremost authority on nearly every form of sport. In some respects he was far more entertaining than Rice because of a vein of brilliant humor that ran through his writings. Lardner was true to tradition. He insisted on having a typewriter swung across his bed and was pounding away while the breath of life was leaving his body.

• • •

Soviet Russia built the biggest balloon in the world to send up into the stratosphere. It actually rose to a height of 10 feet and then quit. That's like most of Russia's experiments.

• • •

Gosh, but love is getting precious. A Los Angeles court ordered Claire Windsor to pay $75,000 for alienating the affections of a husband, and now comes a story from New York about Mrs. Helen Vogel Stern, social registerite, bringing a suit against Mrs. Ruth Erlanger Nathan for stealing the love of the former's husband, a wealthy turfman. Mrs. Stern asks $4,000,000 damages, which would indicate that hubby was a very valuable possession.

• • •

Doggone the wimmen, anyway! A Texas woman proposes to President Roosevelt a household code wherein it is provided that the husband or some other member of the family must dry the supper dishes; that wives must be taken out to dinner one night each week, and to the movies twice each week; that the wife must have 10 per cent of the pay check for personal expenses, and be allowed to sleep late two mornings each week. Now is the time of all times for President Roosevelt to show himself a real hero by putting an emphatic stamp of disapproval on the plan.

• • •

A report comes from Washington that Gen. Hugh Johnson's Blue Eagle laid a couple of eggs last week, but both of the darned things were hard-boiled.

• • •

Of course, we folks down in Dixie would like to see 20-cent cotton, and we wouldn't kick a bit against 30-cent cotton, but just now the prospect of 12-cent cotton looks mighty good. No use in being hoggish.

• • •

On December 15th, European nations will owe us $50,000,000 on war debts, not including interest or sums on which default has been made. Watch us try to get it and again fall down on the job.

• • •

Canon Chase is appealing to prohibitionists to test the constitutionality of elections held on the 18th amendment during the past few months. Canon Chase and his crowd will get the same sort of cold comfort in the courts that they got at the polls. Whether they be right or wrong, the people have expressed themselves on this subject in no uncertain terms.

• • •

Some calamity howlers are predicting that this nation has a hard and bitter winter ahead. It is just as easy to predict that business and economic conditions will be distinctly better during the coming winter. One guess is as good as another, and all guessing is foolish.

• • •

Regardless of what the thermometer registers, this is autumn. Leaves are falling from some of the deciduous trees, and the goldenrod is in full bloom by the roadsides. A more infallible sign is the new autumn frocks, some of them furtrimmed, you see on Capitol street.

• • •

Sam Gordon, scholarly son of Israel, has a just grievance against President Roosevelt and Secretary Wallace. At least, he thinks he has, which is the same thing insofar as he is concerned. Sam says that the scheme to slaughter about 2,100,000 pounds of hog meat in Mississippi in order to get it off the market, is all wet; that he doesn't own any hog meat, and he doesn't eat hog meat. "Where do I come in?" asks Sam. The answer is, you don't.

• • •

Gen. Johnson says the paradox of bursting warehouses and starving multitudes must be solved. It certainly must. The picture of people starving to death in a land of plenty is utterly ridiculous. Surely, there is sufficient common sense somewhere to find a solution.

• • •

"Cast your bread upon the waters and it will return after many days." Two years ago a man left the restaurant at a Tupelo hotel without paying his 30-cent meal check. He was penniless. The other day that man returned, paid the 30 cents, and then rented a room in the hotel to sleep with an easy conscience.

MEXICO SPEEDS AID TO STORM RAVAGED ZONE; 5,000 KILLED

Hurricane Turns Tampico Into Shambles; Area Still Isolated

MEXICO, D. F., Sept. 26—Mexico's resources were mobilized today to aid the storm stricken and flooded city of Tampico, where estimates placed the number of dead or injured as high as 5,000 and thousands were left homeless. Enormous property damage was reported.

Two relief trains, carrying battalions of infantrymen to aid in reconstruction work and food and medical supplies, were en route to the oil port.

But parts of the city were under 14 feet of water and railroad tracks in the area were flooded or washed away, so it was problematical when they could arrive. A squadron of military airplanes was ordered to leave at dawn. Meanwhile, Tampico was virtually isolated from the outside world, along with its scenes of death and destruction.

Although more than two days have passed since the hurricane struck with all its fury, the city was without communication facilities except by means of wireless from ships in the harbor. Officials reported the damage there and in other parts of the nation was "catastrophic."

General Eduardo Vasconcelos, secretary of the interior, who planned to fly to Tampico to direct relief work, said the number of dead "can not be stated exactly," but the military chief of the district reported by wireless that three-fourths of Tampico had been destroyed with many victims.

Unofficial reports set the death toll at from 200 to 5,000. Dispatches by round-about means said the wind, of 125-mile an hour velocity, levelled the Civil hospital, railroad station, and customs house and that nearly every structure was destroyed or unroofed.

It was feared that hundreds had been buried alive in the ruins. The flood waters of the Panuco and Tamesi rivers added their terrors to those of the hurricane.

Tampico was placed under martial law. Its harbor was closed to shipping. If airplane could not get through to its flooded airport, it was believed days might elapse before relief could reach the city. Today the possibility of disease, it was thought here might hold new dangers.

In the entire Tampico district, as far west as 175 miles, the storm spread death and destruction. The city to Cardenas, in San Luis Potosi, reported that at least 30 drowned as the result of the collapse of a railroad dam.

It was feared that many more had been trapped by a sea of water and mud which swept the city, destroying many houses.

Two trains were reported to have been completely covered by water between Tampico and Cardenas. The National Railways officials estimated that damage to their destroyed or flooded property would amount to $1,000,000 or more.

Crops suffered throughout the northeastern and central parts of the country, where torrential rains fell until midnight.

Heavy damage was done in the oil fields, according to reports reaching here by way of San Luis Potosi. A number of refineries and other buildings were completely wiped out.

Throughout the rest of Mexico heavy losses were reported because of continuing rains.

DODSON TRIAL IN DELTA DUE NEXT MONDAY

Venire of 100 Requested By State to Pick Jury; Witnesses Sought

INDIANOLA, Sept. 26—(Special) Elbedeen Dodson and his sister Frances will go to trial in circuit court here next Monday on a charge of slaying Wheeler Brown, Merigold druggist.

The trial jury will be drawn from a special venire of 100 granted today at the request of District Attorney P. A. Jordan.

Defense counsel, Elmore and Shands, of Cleveland, and F. E. Everett, of Indianola, vigorously protested the state's motion for a special venire.

The brother and sister were again in the courtroom Tuesday morning, the latter displaying none of the nervousness noted Monday when she was arraigned.

Temporary delay in getting to the Dodson case was caused by failure of a number of important witnesses for the state to appear Monday.

T. B. Ends Career Of Ring Lardner, Famous Humorist

All U. S. Mourns Passing Of Noted Newspaperman and Author

NEW YORK, Sept. 26—Ring Lardner, who once noted that there wasn't much difference between his native Niles, Mich., and his adopted New York because both begin with an "N," has lost his long fight against tuberculosis.

The lean, six-foot humorist who made you and me know Al, and who became a ranking figure of American literature, died suddenly at his East Hampton, Long Island, home last night in the 48th year of an active, interesting life.

For 10 years Ringgold Wilmer Lardner had fought the disease. During those years, with the spectre drawing steadily closer, his humor flowed on, bringing laughs to the faces of those who saw on the stage "Elmer the Great," and then "June Moon," and to other tens of thousands who read his "Story of a Wonder Man," "Love Nest," and other stories.

Heart disease, complicated by other ailments, was given by his doctors as the immediate cause of death.

Only in the last few years has Lardner's typewriter gone on short hours. His doctors ordered him to the Southwest, and he remained there many months. When he returned to New York several months ago he was reported much better.

Lardner was born in Niles, Mich., March 6, 1885. As he put it, he was born during "Have-a-Baby-Week." In comparing Niles and New York later he said there was little advantage either way, as the New York Central tracks ran through both places.

WEATHER

WASHINGTON, Sept. 26—Forecast for Mississippi — Partly cloudy tonight and Wednesday; probably showers in extreme north portion tonight. Light to moderate southeast to south winds on the coast.

SHOWERS

Louisiana—Partly cloudy tonight; Wednesday mostly cloudy. Light to moderate southeast to south winds on the coast.

Alabama—Generally fair tonight and Wednesday. Light to moderate easterly to southerly winds on the coast.

Arkansas—Occasional showers tonight and Wednesday; cooler in extreme northwest portion tonight and in north portion Wednesday.

WEATHER SUMMARY

The area of high pressure still remains along the Atlantic coast, but the western area of low pressure is divided and centers over the Great Lakes region and over west Texas. The higher pressure area of cool weather is centered over South Dakota. The temperatures are high over the eastern states, but there are freezing temperatures over the northwest.

A minimum temperature of 18 degrees was reached at Calgary, Can. During the past 24 hours, rain has fallen in the northern states and in southern Texas. The weather is generally clear over the southern states.

LOCAL OBSERVATIONS
(Hourly Temperatures)

Monday, September 25

3 p. m.	93
4 p. m.	92
5 p. m.	90
6 p. m.	86
7 p. m.	80
8 p. m.	78
9 p. m.	79
10 p. m.	77
11 p. m.	76
12 midnight	75

Tuesday, September 26

1 a. m.	75
2 a. m.	74
3 a. m.	73
4 a. m.	71
5 a. m.	71
6 a. m.	70
7 a. m.	73
8 a. m.	83
9 a. m.	84
10 a. m.	86
River gauge, ft.	2.1
Rainfall past 24 hours	.0

River Bulletin
(Stages in Feet)

Stations	Flood Stage	Present Stage	24-hour Change
Mississippi—			
Memphis	33	5.3	0.1 fall
Helena	44	6.9	0.1 fall
Arkansas City	48	8.0	0.5 fall
Vicksburg	45	7.6	0.2 fall
Natchez	46	9.0	0.9 fall
New Orleans	22	3.0	Sta.

Byrd-men Off On New Antarctic Venture

Rear Admiral Richard E. Byrd's second great expedition into the Antarctic was in the final stages of organization when these pictures were taken at Boston. At upper left you see Chief Pilot Harold June and Admiral Byrd as they discussed last-minute details for the two-year exploration trip. At right is the Bear of Oakland, former U. S. Coast Guard cutter which became famous for rescue work in the far north. The Bear will be the party's base ship, and is pictured as it was brought to drydock in Boston for minor repairs.* Below is one of two aircraft to be used for flights about the southern continent, and over the pole. This is a huge twin-motored Curtiss Condor capable of carrying men, instruments, supplies, and sled-dogs.

Rumors of U. S. Custodianship Stir Havana; Army Augmented

NEW RECOVERY PLANS STUDIED AT HYDE PARK

President Carries Manifold Program to Old Home For Study

WASHINGTON, Sept. 26—President Roosevelt turns homeward today to develop in the quiet of his Hyde Park residence new invigoration of the government's manifold recovery efforts.

Ways to expand credit and lift farm prices topped the chores scheduled for even more intensive study by Mr. Roosevelt after three crowded weeks spent canvassing every phase of the federal push toward economic settlement.

These tasks have received the president's earnest attention from the hour of his return to the White House after Labor Day from a brief yachting holiday. New orders seeking to boost farm incomes and aid NRA industries have been issued rapidly, and demands for currency inflation apparently rejected for the present.

Newest developments in an intensive credit-expansion program was a promise given the president by steel executives to submit competitive bids on a 700,000 tonnage order for steel rails. Mr. Roosevelt planned to advance the $25,000,000 or more needed by the carriers to buy the rails—provided the prices are low enough.

The steel purchase was the subject of another in a plea for 1926 money and price levels presented by a farm group headed by Edward A. O'Neal, president of the Farm Bureau Federation.

Already the president has initiated numerous federal moves aimed at higher farm prices and easier credit. Prominent in the new steps of recent weeks were:

A program for spending $75,000,000 or more on surplus farm and staple products for distribution to the needy.

A concerted effort to expand credit, joined in by the Federal Reserve Board, the Reconstruction Corporation, the Farm Credit Administration, the Home Owners' Loan Corporation, and the Public Works Administration. The drive included offers to advance millions to banks for industrial loans, to relieve banks of slow farm and city mortgages, to open and strengthen closed and restricted banks, to spend faster the $1,600,000,000 of allocated Public Works money.

NO CONFIRMATION

Cuba Tense at Reported Change in Attitude of Washington

HAVANA, Sept. 26—Cuban military forces were strengthened today as rumors reached the government of a change in the American policy toward Cuba and of plans for another revolt.

Simultaneously there were authentic reports that negotiations between opposing factions and the Ramon Grau San Martin regime had approached no closer toward a solution of problems which threatened to end the life of the two-weeks-old government.

A rumor, not confirmed in responsible quarters, was circulated that some sort of custodianship for Cuba was planned by the Washington administration and created a tense atmosphere here.

Colonel Fulgencia Basista's army was increased by the addition of a civil guard of 2,000 members of the Caribbean army, a student organization.

These youths did guard duty in small interior towns. Regular troops were being concentrated in provincial capitals.

All "suspicious" automobiles entering or leaving Havana early today were being searched. Soldiers helped police on duty at stations throughout Havana. No official explanation was given for these steps.

The provincial governor at Santiago was forced by revolutionaries to resign. Workers on the Consolidated railroad at Antilla threatened to destroy the road if demands for back wages were not met. In several places strikes continued, there was inceasing industrial unrest, and talk of a general strike was widespread.

These and scattered reports gave rise to a belief in some quarters that a new revolutionary movement was being formed.

President Grau San Martin, it was learned authoritatively considered issuing two new decrees—one demanding the immediate return to the proper owners of all sugar mills seized by striking workers, and the other setting a time limit of 72 hours for the 500-odd officers in the National Hotel to return to their posts, or consider themselves ousted.

Meanwhile, seven Americans were in refuge at the Puerto Padre Yacht Club in Chaparra, while an American destroyer stood by in the bay. The Americans are mainly officials of a sugar mill and have been in a storm center of industrial unrest.

Juan Blas Hernandez, veteran revolutionary leader against former President Machado, arrived in the capital, and denied reports he had tried to revolt against the government.

SPEED SOUGHT FOR HIGHWAY WORK IN STATE

Commission Opens Bids on Lauderdale Job; Kenna Seeks Aides

As bids were opened here Tuesday by the State Highway Commission on the third project in its $10,000,000 national recovery highway program, the highway department's director, E. D. Kenna, was in Montgomery conferring with federal road officials about speeding up the program.

All Mississippi projects are cleared through the bureau's Montgomery office after approval by the federal engineer, F. A. Davis, stationed here. It was understood Mr. Kenna would request additional engineer assistance for Mr. Davis here to facilitate movement of state projects.

The commission received bids today on bridges and construction work for 7.05 miles of the Topton-Lauderdale road in Lauderdale county at an estimated cost of $153,000. The project is expected to provide work for 600 men and involves grading, drainage work and construction of two railroad overpasses.

MARKETS

New Orleans Cotton

NEW ORLEANS, Sept. 26—The cotton market opened active but somewhat easier today. Liverpool cables were slightly lower than due and today was first notice day for October deliveries. The notices here called for 19,500 bales and New York notices were announced at 40,000 bales. As a result of the tenders, the start was lower, first trades in October showing losses of ten points and that month soon dropped to 9.73 down 12 points net. December started six points lower and did not break below that decline, ruling at 10.06.

Later the market rallied on reports that the notices were being stopped, October advancing to 9.86, up 13 points from the early low and one point above yesterday's close. December recovered 8 points to 10.14, up 2 points net.

Near the end of the first hour the market held steady near the highs.

KILLER IS TRAPPED IN MEMPHIS HOUSE; GIVES UP MEEKLY

Immediate Trial at Oklahoma City Indicated For Bad Man

OKLAHOMA CITY, Sept. 26—J. Edgar Hoover, director of the United States Bureau of Investigation, advised federal authorities here today by telephone from Washington of the capture in Memphis, Tenn., of George Kelly, widely hunted as one of the Charles F. Urschel kidnapers, and his wife Kathryn.

Asked whether Kelly and his wife will be brought to Oklahoma City immediately for trial in the Urschel case, R. H. Colvin, head of the Federal Bureau of Investigation here said: "It's too soon to talk about that now."

Information that led to the capture reached Department of Justice agents here last midnight, Colvin said. The information was telegraphed to federal agents at St. Louis and Birmingham, he said, and raiding squads were organized at both bureaus. They rushed to Memphis in planes, and, assisted by Memphis officers, made the arrests.

Joseph B. Keenan, assistant United States attorney-general, said the Kellys would be brought here immediately for trial.

"We'll go to trial with them as soon as we finish with the other defendants, perhaps Friday of this week," Keenan said. "Witnesses already are here. Everything is ready. We'll start as soon as the jury has brought in its verdict."

Trial of the other 10 defendants in the Urschel case was resumed today.

Wife, Two Others Caught In Daylight Raid; Bandit Confesses Identity

MEMPHIS, Tenn., Sept. 26—George E. "Machine Gun" Kelly, desperado of the Southwest, sought in connection with the Kansas City massacre, and on kidnaping and robbery charges, surrendered peacefully to officers who surprised him asleep in a rooming house here early today.

After talking with W. A. Roper, a department of justice operative, Police Chief Will D. Lee announced that there was no question about the identity of the prisoner as Kelly.

Arrested with the outlaw were a woman Lee said was his wife, Kathryn Kelly, 29, and two men described as J. R. Tichnor, 30, and S. E. Travis, 26.

Kelly's capture was effected by a group of officers who surrounded the house in which he and the others were sleeping.

Detective Sergeant W. J. Raney said Kelly met them at the door of the home with a pistol.

"Drop that gun, Kelly," Raney told him.

Kelly peacefully put up the gun and surrendered.

"I have been waiting for you all night," Raney quoted him as saying.

"Well, we are here," was Raney's answer.

At the police station, Police Chief Lee said Kelly admitted his identity but refused to talk.

"Chief," he was quoted as saying, "I'm not talking about anything."

Later, smiling broadly and smoking one cigaret after another, Kelly remained defiant in another interview with police.

As Chief Lee walked into his cell, he demanded:

"Who are you?"

"I'm Chief Lee," was the reply.

"Give me a light, then," was Kelly's response.

Noticing the fugitive's yellow hair, Lee asked:

"When did you dye your hair?"

"That's been there for a long time," Kelly answered.

Chief Lee said Chicago police think Kelly and another man were among the machine gun bandits who held up a Federal Reserve bank in Chicago September 22 and escaped with $500,000. The bandits shot down a policeman and made their escape in a dense smoke screen.

At the time of the Chicago robbery, a feverish hunt was being staged in other sections, especially for Kelly. Officers alleged that he had threatened the families of prosecutors, a witness and the victim of the Charles Urschel kidnaping trial.

Kelly had been identified as a member of the kidnaping gang who had extorted $200,000 from the oil man's family. A number of other accused kidnapers are on trial in Oklahoma City.

Arriving at the police station, Department of Justice Agent Roper immediately telephoned the arrest to J. E. Hoover, chief of the Bureau of Identification, in Washington.

The capture, he reported, was made in a bungalow known as the home of Tichnor.

"We found him in bed," Roper said, "and he was captured without a struggle."

A cordon of police surrounded the home about 6 a. m. One group of officers made their way through the front entrance. Another group slipped down in the hallway, facing Kelly's closed door, with a sawed-off shotgun held straight in front of him.

Suddenly the door swung open. There stood Kelly with a revolver in his hand. The shotgun, however, was pointed straight at him.

"Drop it, Kelly," Sergeant Rainey said.

Kelly's gun dropped to the floor, and his hands pointed to the ceiling.

"I have been waiting for you all night," Kelly said.

"Well, here we are," Rainey said, smiling.

CONNER NEEDS 9 PLEDGES TO BRING SESSION

Governor Hints at Special Session Call This Week; 16 Out in Senate

Governor Mile Conner needs but nine pledges from 63 Mississippi legislators who have failed to answer in his "poll" for a constitutional convention, he said today in revealing the first official tabulation of the standings.

Broadly hinting that he expects to issue the special session call within the next few days, the governor revealed figures showing that 66 House members have pledged their votes for the constitutional convention; 27 have refused to sign the pledge and 47 have not yet reported. A House majority, needed, would be 71.

In the Senate 21 have pledged votes for the bill, 12 have refused to sign and 16 have failed to report.

Thus of the 189 members of the two houses, 87 have "voted" for the bill in the letter poll, only 39 have refused to sign and 63 have not yet answered.

In making public the first official count of answers, the governor insisted that he "has not talked to any members of the legislature about this since I sent out the letters," excepting only those who came to his office and asked to discuss the matter.

"If they don't hurry and call the constitutional convention," he warned, "and change the requirement that property owners must pay all taxes before they can vote or hold office, there will be still fewer qualified electors after January 1, when taxes are again due, and there are likely will be many vacancies in public office."

HAMBONE'S MEDITATIONS

By J. P. Alley

TOM'S CHILLUNS ALL GITS UP SOON DESE MAWNIN'S, SO'S TO SEE WHICH UN GITS TO WEAH DE SHOES TO SCHOOL!
9-26

CONNER ASKS COTTON FARM AID BY BANKS

Executive Urges Institutions to "Stand By" as New Plan Looms

Governor Mike Conner today called upon Mississippi banks and bankers to make "liberal" loans to cotton growers, in order that they may hold cotton until the government has put into effect its proposed plan to loan a stated amount per pound to those who cut acreage in 1934.

"I think banks of the state should be very liberal in extending loans to enable growers to hold their cotton until the government loan plan is formulated and in operation and I urge this policy on the banks," the governor said.

FIRST LYNCHING MOB PHOTOS

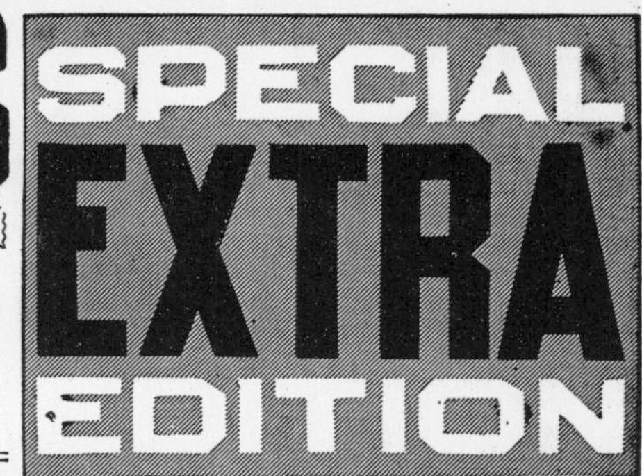

NIGHT FINAL

Only Los Angeles Newspaper With All Leading News Services—Associated Press, International News, United Press, Dow-Jones

Reg. U. S. Pat. Office. Copyright, 1933, by Evening Herald Publishing Company
The Evening Herald and Express Grows Just Like Los Angeles

VOL. LXIII THREE CENTS Hotels and Trains Five Cents MONDAY, NOVEMBER 27, 1933 Two Sections Section A THREE CENTS NO. 211

ROLPH PARDON, PRAISE OF LYNCHERS STIRS ROW

'GOOD JOB' AT SAN JOSE, IS VERDICT OF EXECUTIVE

Issues Statement in Which He Denounces Kidnapers and Defends Citizens

By International News Service

NEW YORK, Nov. 27.—A telegraphed demand to President Roosevelt to state whether he agreed with Governor Rolph of California in the latter's pro-lynching statement was sent today to the White House by William L. Patterson, secretary of the International Labor Defense. The wire asked the President immediately to denounce Rolph's action.

By International News Service

SACRAMENTO, Nov. 27.—**If any persons are arrested and convicted in connection with the San Jose lynchings they will be pardoned.**

In this striking fashion Governor James Rolph jr. today made his position clear on what his attitude would be toward those who lynched Jack Holmes and Thomas H. Thurmond. His statement follows:

"If anyone is arrested for this 'good job' I'll pardon him.

"It was the only way to give a lesson to the country. This kidnaping has terrorized other states

(CONTINUED ON PAGE TEN)

Herald-Express Special Features

VIGILANTES DRAGGING HOLMES FROM JAIL

Picture by International News Photo Service, rushed here by United Air Lines

This photo shows John Holmes, indicated by arrow, being dragged from jail by the mob which last night lynched him and Thomas Thurmond for the kidnap-murder of Brooke Hart. Sneering and kicking, Holmes fought desperately till the last.

PROTEST AND LAUD MOB HANGING OF 2 HART KIDNAPERS

(For other photos of lynching see Page Three.)

SAN JOSE, Nov. 27.—The vigilantes had marched again and "Cocky" John M. Holmes and cringing Thomas H. Thurmond, kidnapers and murderers of young Brooke L. Hart, had swung on two trees in a public park after San Jose's "red night."

But, similar to the days of the San Francisco vigilantes, there was a swinging of the pendulum late today—the forces of "law and order" were rallying, charges of "excited hoodlums" were being flung at some of the leaders of the mob, men and women were violently taking sides as to whether Holmes and Thurmond should have been brought to trial by due process in the courts or whether the mob had done a "good job," as affirmed by the governor of California, James Rolph jr.

The controversy developed two things.

One was that there was an organized "vigilance committee" composed of about 500 men of good standing who participated in the actual hangings.

The other was that the original crowd that began showering rocks on the jail and started the great surge for the kidnapers was largely composed of a rough element, some of whom had been drinking.

The "vigilantes" really took the matter in hand in the last hour after a mob had surged about the jail for many hours, occasionally making attacks and constantly showering the prison with rocks.

When the "vigilantes" took hold, the mob followed and the storming of the jail and the lynching of the prisoners quickly followed.

A crowd of 10,000 persons, including hundreds of women and children, watched the lynching—women, men and even children kicked and struck at the kidnapers as they were dragged to their doom, and a blonde girl led the grim mob.

The authorities had been warned that it was coming—they had been told that the city had gone mad, that women were clutching their children to their breasts in fear of other kidnapings and urging their men folks to "go get them."

So, when the mob stormed at the prison doors, the officers had turned down their guns, let their machine gun remain silent and depended on tear bombs to repulse the waves of attackers that stormed the jail.

Eight persons were sent to hospitals from injuries suffered

(CONTINUED ON PAGE TWELVE)

LOUIS B. MAYER WIRES DENIAL OF FOX CHARGE TO SENATORS

Emphatic denial that he had ever caused department of justice records to be changed in connection with the Fox-Loew theater property merger, as was charged on the witness stand before the senate banking committee in Washington by William Fox, former theater magnate, was made in a telegram sent to the committee by Louis B. Mayer, vice president of Metro-Goldwyn-Mayer.

The telegram, which Mr. Mayer

(CONTINUED ON PAGE THIRTEEN)

Hunt Banker's Son; Kidnaping Feared

SAN DIEGO, Cal., Nov. 27.—Feared to have been the victim of a kidnaping plot, Walter Butts, 16, son of a wealthy Calexico, Cal., banker, today was sought by San Diego police at the request of Sheriff George L. Campbell of El Centro. Butts disappeared from his Calexico home shortly before dark Saturday.

EYE-WITNESS TELLS OF MOB LYNCHING HART'S SLAYERS

By HARVEY WING

Copyright, 1933, by United Press

SAN JOSE, Cal., Nov. 27.—I saw a wild mob lynch Thomas H. Thurmond and John M. Holmes here last night.

The mob took them from the county jail after the body of Brooke Hart had been found in San Francisco bay. Thurmond and Holmes

(CONTINUED ON PAGE THIRTEEN)

53d YEAR No. 173 — Registered in U. S. Patent Office. — C★★★ x — THURSDAY, NOVEMBER 30, 1933 — Telephone Randolph 2121 — FIVE SECTIONS. — PRICE 3 CENTS

VERNE MILLER FOUND SLAIN

Today

See the Alamo.
And Randolph Field.
San Antonio's Fine City.
Sunshine Stays All Winter.

—BY ARTHUR BRISBANE—

(© 1933, by King Features Syndicate, Inc.)

SAN ANTONIO, Tex., Nov. 29. —This is San Antonio, "where the sunshine spends the Winter," according to the citizens. This is the place to learn about Texas, biggest state in the Union, in which you could lose two or three little European kingdoms. This is the state which with intanse cultivation could feed the entire population of the earth and have plenty left over.

And this is a beautiful growing city, active in commerce, cheerful with its skyscrapers, modern methods, and old-fashioned Texas Americans.

Young college men, imitating Oxford, who vote "under no circumstances," should visit the great Randolph flying field at the edge of San Antonio, where real fighters of the future are educated, and the old fort of the Alamo, a sacred shrine, dedicated to the memory of brave men that gave up their lives to the last man for their country, and gave Texas to the United States.

Somebody ought to tell the story of the Alamo to those pale and wan college boys. It would make them shiver and crawl under their little cottage cots.

There were 4,000 of the enemy outside the fort. About 121 Texans left alive inside. It was not possible to win, but it was still possible to fight for your country. Col. Travis drew a line on the floor of the old chapel inside the fort, invited those in favor of fighting until death to cross the line with him. Every man crossed the line, every man was killed. James Bowie, lying sick and wounded in a little cot in the confessional room, on the left of the chapel entrance, demanded that his cot be carried across the line. He could not rise from his cot, but he could still fight on his back and killed two or three of the enemy before they succeeded in killing him. He was quick with knife or pistol. David Crockett of Tennessee, killed there, was found with dead enemies around him. Texas has adopted him.

Col. Travis was shot as he stood on the wall cheering his men. As he fell, one of the enemy bayoneted him, and, as he did so, Travis, dying, killed the man with the bayonet, making good his statement that he would make a "victory worse to the enemy than a defeat."

You should visit the little chapel of the Alamo fort, see the portraits of old Americans, who believed in fighting and created this country. And you should visit Randolph flying field, where American army officers teach young Americans how to fly and fight in the air.

On the Randolph flying field American army officers and the courageous young boys are eager to fly and, if their country needs them, to fight and die flying. After you have seen the Alamo shrine, sacred to those dead long ago, and the flying field, that trains young Americans of today, you know this country need not worry about attack from east or west, if it will give to *real* young Americans the fighting machinery that they need.

Gen. Charles H. Danforth, who commands the three army units out here, and Lieut. Col. F. L. Martin, who commands Randolph Field, use 300 one-engine biplanes, teaching young men from West Point, Annapolis and all over the country how to fly. Not everybody can learn. The elimination process is severe, but necessary and just, and young men told to go home, because they can never learn army flying, are disappointed but not bitter.

All say that they had their fair chance, no favoritism.

It is in the faces of those young men, keen eyes, well-shaped heads, strong chins, simple courage, and in the experience and patient teaching of the United States army officers that you see this country's safety.

When the United States is able to send into the air ten thousand such men as pilots in pursuit planes and bombing planes, kept constantly up to date, this country will not need to worry about any "attack," and the entire equipment would cost less than three or four of the old-fashioned battleships that are now only airplane targets.

A couple of the hundreds of millions that the R. F. C. is so liberally dispensing would do the work. The men are here and ready.

Come here some day through the air, by comfortable railroad train or in your automobile, see these air fields that belong to you and 123,000,000 other Americans and you will be proud of your investment.

See San Antonio and become acquainted with one of the country's most energetic and beautiful cities.

Life starts early in the day here in the West. You get off your Southern Pacific train at Randolph Field, in the "pitch darkness," and find Gen. Danforth, Lieut. Col. Martin and the general's brilliant young flying aid, Lieut. P. W. Douglass Jr., all at the station, all having "been up a long time." It is still dark and continues dark as you eat breakfast at Gen. Danforth's house and become acquainted with the generally interesting ninety-pound police dog.

You are told, "Don't get up from your chair suddenly or try to go through any door, because he

Turn to Page 4, Column 1.

Whole Nazi Church Cabinet Resigns in Dispute Over Bible

Bishop Mueller to Appoint New Group.

'KEEP GOSPEL'

Assures U. S. Reich Will Stand by Testament.

BERLIN, Nov. 29.—(AP)—The whole Reich church cabinet, governing body of all Protestant groups in Germany, resigned tonight in a crashing climax to the bitter church controversy over strict adherence to the letter of the Bible.

The resignations, including that of Bishop Joaquin Hossenfelder, who withdrew from his official position yesterday under pressure from the cabinet, were accepted by Reichsbishop Ludwig Mueller.

Picking New Cabinet

The Reichsbishop will appoint a new cabinet, and asked the present members to stay until a new group is formed.

Bishop Mueller instructed the Associated Press to "tell American churchgoers that in the new Evangelical church the gospel will naturally remain as a foundation on which the message of Christ will rest."

He declined to discuss the situation further, beyond saying that Bishop Hossenfelder would remain a bishop.

The new upset in the church is paralleled by another source of strife in German religion.

This is the growth of the "Germanic faith movement," which would substitute Germanic legend for Christianity.

Rests on Christianity

Reichsbishop Mueller during the Luther exercises at Eisenach hurled at his Germanic cult rivals that "the state of Adolf Hitler rests upon the rock of a positive Christianity."

The "German Christians" are apparently finding it easier to be a Lenin than a Kerenski—that the offer of an abridged Bible and of a Christianity cleansed of Jewish influence merely encourages the further step of scrapping Christianity altogether.

Unity Is Aim

Dr. Ernst Bergmann even said National Socialism and Christianity are incompatible. He said:

"Germany's aim must be: One people, one reich, one religion, one church. The 'one religion' can be only a Nordic-Germanic one. The National Socialist revolution must be a heathenish Germanic one."

(Details of the complication in the German religious war in the substitution of German legends for the religion of the Bible, will be found on Page 11.)

Directory of Features

Chicago Hostess Heroine as Plane Falls in Icy Lake

Stands Neck-Deep in Water to Supervise Rescue of Nine Passengers.

WINDSOR, Ont., Nov. 29.—(AP)—Climbing from the submerged cabin of a large airplane which crashed in Lake St. Clair, nine passengers and a crew of three sat on top of the wings of the ship until rescuers broke their way through ice and brought them safely ashore tonight.

The plane, an American Airways craft, piloted by Dean Smith of Summit, N. J., was forced down by engine trouble.

Landing was made on the thin sheet of ice covering the lake, near Peche Island, close to the Canadian shore.

WINGS HOLD UP PLANE.

The body of the plane crashed through the ice, but the wings prevented it from going to the bottom in some thirty feet of water.

Miss Kathleen Smith of the Kenrose Hotel, 6417 Kenwood av., Chicago, hostess of the plane, calmly opened the door of the cabin and assisted the nine passengers to climb through the struts of the machine to a place of comparitive safety atop the wings.

STANDS IN ICE WATER.

By the time all were out, she was standing in ice-cold water up to her neck, but her passengers were safe. She climbed up beside them.

While the stranded party waited for rescuers to reach them, a vacuum bottle partly filled with hot soup came floating to the surface from the cabin of the plane, and was salvaged. The soup was portioned out among them.

LIST OF PASSENGERS.

Passengers on the plane were Mrs. I. O. Cole and her son, James L., Rochester, N. Y.; R. H. Brown, Detroit; Charles E. White Jr., 321 N. Euclid av., Oak Park, Ill., passenger agent for the American Airways; T. K. Thalon, Gross Pointe Park, Mich.; Mrs. H. L. Pratt, Newton Centre, Mass.; R. H. Pearsall, Elgin, Ill.; Fred A. Holtz, Elkhart, Ind.; George E. Conde, Flint, Mich.

Smith, the pilot, said he had bucked a heavy headwind all the way from Buffalo and his gasoline was running low. Engine trouble added to his difficulties and he sought a landing place.

The passengers praised Smith for the careful way in which he "pancaked" his machine in the dark. The also praised the hostess, who had been with the company only six weeks. It was necessary to break a channel to the stranded plane and for twenty minutes passengers and crew watched the battle with the ice until boats reached the side of the plane.

Envoy McDowell's Wife Is Dead Here

Mrs. Mary Lee McDowell, wife of William Wallace McDowell of Butte, Mont., recently named American minister to the Irish Free State, died yesterday in the Presbyterian Hospital following an operation. McDowell is a former Chicagoan.

ALDRICH URGES WIDE REFORMS FOR BANKING

Chase National Head Recommends Officers Barred From Pools; Asks Loan Report

By Arthur Hachten,
Herald and Examiner-Universal Staff Correspondent.

WASHINGTON, Nov. 29.—Sweeping legislative reforms for the banking world, including a prohibition against bank officers participating in stock market pools or syndicates, were recommended before the Senate banking committee today by President Winthrop W. Aldrich of the Chase National Bank.

Looming as a new champion of ethics for bankers and leader of a "new deal" in Wall street as successor to J. P. Morgan and others whose word has been law to the "street," Aldrich bluntly charged that "indefensible transactions were indeed entered into in the period of the speculative mania" that collapsed in 1929.

He lashed the practice of Albert H. Wiggin, former Chase bank president, in participating through his Shermar Corporation in stock market syndicates financed by the Chase bank while Wiggin was in charge. Other officers of the Chase bank, as well as of other banks, had been revealed as participating in stock market "pools."

LAUDS GLASS ACT.

Lauding the objective of the Glass-Steagall act to divorce completely commercial banks from investment affiliates, Aldrich contended the law needs many changes to separate commercial banking from the investment banking business.

An amendment requiring bank officers and employes to report to the institution's board of directors all personal loans above some nominal minimum related to the size of their salary was among Aldrich's far-reaching proposals.

Present laws require loans made by bank officers from another bank to be reported, but Aldrich pointed out the door was wide open for loans from investment bankers, brokers and others.

ASKS PROHIBITION.

Executive officers and directors of the twelve federal reserve banks should be prohibited from participating in stock market pools or syndicates, Aldrich said.

Aldrich's experience as a bank official began at the end of 1929, when he became president of the Equitable Trust Company. When the Equitable merged with the Chase National Bank, making it the largest bank in America at the time, Aldrich became president. He was elected chairman of its executive board last January, when Wiggin retired. Aldrich is a son-in-law of John D. Rockefeller Jr., largest stockholder in the Chase bank.

(A summary of the banking reforms urged by Aldrich will be found in financial section.)

Bullitt Sails for Post at Moscow

NEW YORK, Nov. 29.—(I.N.S.)—William C. Bullitt, first American ambassador to the Soviet republic, sailed for Russia today on the President Harding of the United States line to present his credentials at Moscow.

Fleming Appointed Traction Receiver

Harvey B. Fleming was appointed receiver for the South Side surface lines yesterday by Federal Judge James H. Wilkerson to succeed the late Edward N. Hurley.

WORST OUTLAW, ONCE SHERIFF, TAKEN ON RIDE

Renegade Beaten to Death; Bound Body Tossed in Ditch on Outskirts of Detroit

(Picture on Back Page.)

Verne Miller, the nation's most hunted outlaw, was found murdered yesterday on the outskirts of Detroit—less than a month after he had shot his way out of a government agents' trap here.

Despite the raging Detroit gang war, in which three gang leaders have been slain since Sunday, authorities believe Miller was "bumped off" by his friends because he demanded that they protect him from the government's relentless search.

BODY LEFT IN DITCH.

His body, nude, strapped and bound, and wrapped in two blankets, was found in a roadside ditch in the northern part of Detroit. He had evidentally been dumped from an automobile in typical gangland "ride" fashion.

But examination disclosed that he had not been shot. Instead, his skull had been crushed.

Authorities established that the body had been placed in the ditch yesterday morning, but said Miller had been dead twenty-four hours when the body was found.

Investigation disclosed that he had been dividing his time between Chicago and Detroit hideouts recently, traveling between cities by automobile and plane.

WANTED FOR ROBBERIES.

Miller was wanted by the government here for the loop mail robbery of September 22, when the robbers shot Policeman Miles Cunningham to death, and for the previous loop mail robbery of last December, when $250,000 loot was obtained.

But more important, in the eyes of the government, was the charge that Miller fired the machine gun in the Kansas City massacre of last June, when four officers were killed with their prisoner, Frank Nash, in a vain attempt by Harvey Bailey's Oklahoma kidnapers to free their comrade, Nash. Miller also was wanted in the Urschel kidnaping and a score of other abductions.

PRICE ON HEAD.

With a price of $10,000 on his head, dead or alive, and a government order that he must be captured outstanding, Miller was the "hottest" or most dangerous criminal to shield in the country. Six men already are under indictment for having aided him and almost at the same time his body was found two Chicago women, Bobby Moore and Vivian Gibson, were being sentenced to a year and a day in prison for helping him in his escape here.

Hence, authorities assert, Miller's friends decided that the safest course was to kill him, since he would undoubtedly have killed them had they refused to aid him.

(An account of Verne Miller's criminal career appears on Page 2)

Joan Crawford Ill in East, Says Paper

WATERBURY, Conn., Nov. 29.—(AP)—The Waterbury Republican says that Joan Crawford, motion picture actress, is in a private sanitarium at Cromwell. The newspaper reports that Miss Crawford, said to be using an assumed name, has been seen by a Waterbury nurse in Glenarch Sanitarium, which has few patients.

THE WEATHER

THURSDAY, NOVEMBER 30, 1933.

Sun rises 6:58; sun sets 4:20; moon sets 6:52 a. m. tomorrow.

CHICAGO AND VICINITY—Today, generally fair with moderate temperature, moderate westerly winds. Tomorrow unsettled and somewhat colder.

ILLINOIS—Today generally fair. Tomorrow unsettled; somewhat colder in north and central portions. Tomorrow unsettled, followed by colder in north portion.

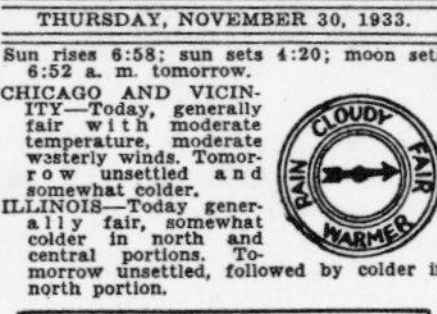

TEMPERATURES IN CHICAGO

HIGHEST, 1:10 P. M. 64
LOWEST, 1:30 P. M. 39

3 a. m.	45	12 noon	65	9 p. m.	60
4 a. m.	47	1 p. m.	64	Unofficial:	
5 a. m.	49	2 p. m.	64	10 p. m.	60
6 a. m.	52	3 p. m.	63	11 p. m.	60
7 a. m.	56	4 p. m.	64	Midnight	59
8 a. m.	58	5 p. m.	64	1 a. m.	59
9 a. m.	60	6 p. m.	64	2 a. m.	58
10 a. m.	62	7 p. m.	64		
11 a. m.	64	8 p. m.	64		

Mean temperature for twenty-four hours ended 7 p. m. 52; normal for the day, 34; deficiency since November 1, 75 degrees; excess since January 1, 863 degrees.

Barometer: 7 a. m. 29.93; 7 p. m. 29.82.

Precipitation for twenty-four hours, .03 inch; deficiency since November 1, 1.72 inches; since January 1, .24 inch.

Air route and other forecasts on Page 16.

Subway Crowd Separates Young Honeymoon Couple

NEW YORK, Nov. 29.—(I.N.S.)—Mr. and Mrs. Edmund Kenny, 22 and 20, respectively, married in Lawrence, Mass., last Sunday, came here on a wedding trip.

Mrs. Kenny decided to visit her aunt, Mrs. Anna Vanis in Brooklyn, so they boarded a subway train in the rush hour.

As the train pulled into the first Brooklyn station a crowd surged for the doors. Mrs. Kenny was swept outside while her husband struggled to keep his footing.

Before Kenny could hop out the doors slid shut and the train pulled out. He managed to get out at the next station and, not knowing the address of Mrs. Vanis, sought the nearest police station.

"I've lost my wife," he told Lieut. Joseph Glassman.

"That," mused the lieutenant, "may be a tragedy or a blessing—"

"But we were just married Sunday," pleaded Kenny.

Glassman promptly made a few telephone calls, located Mrs. Kenny at another police station where she had gone in search of her husband, and sent the pair to their aunt's in a police car.

The Kennys are going home to Lawrence in a couple of days, and don't plan to visit here soon.

Dr. Alice Wynekoop Indicted; Named Slayer of Son's Wife; Expects to Die Before Trial

Speedy Hearing Ordered by Judge Sullivan.

LIST 12 COUNTS

Grand Jurors Give All Possible Causes of Death.

The Great Wynekoop Murder Mystery was submitted yesterday to the mercy of two courts—

By the grand jury, returning an indictment charging Dr. Alice Wynekoop with murder, to the Criminal Court of Cook County.

By Dr. Alice, to Death, the court she believes will take her fate out of the hands of her earthly judges.

"I REALIZE THAT I MAY FACE THE HIGHEST COURT OF ALL," SHE SAID, AS SHE LAY ILL IN THE COUNTY JAIL. "SO I HAVE TOLD THE TRUTH."

12 Counts Listed

The murder indictment returned before Chief Justice Philip Sullivan by the grand jury contains twelve counts—none of them charging manslaughter—and Dr. Wynekoop will be prosecuted for the murder of her daughter-in-law, Rheta Wynekoop,—or for nothing.

As the first step toward a speedy trial, Judge Sullivan set the case on call for Monday, when Dr. Wynekoop will be arraigned, and will be called upon to enter her plea after the indictment is read to her.

At that time, the case will be assigned to a trial judge and a day will be set for preliminary motions, so that the case will probably go to trial in the early part of January.

Delay Action on Earle

The grand jury took no action against Dr. Wynekoop's son, Earle, husband of the dead girl, but Assistant State's Attorney Charles S. Dougherty indicated that he is not satisfied with his alibi, even though it helps to strengthen the case against his mother.

Half a dozen investigators were at work checking the alibi, and Dougherty made it plain that the son, held on a warrant charging accessory before the fact.

Frank Tyrrell, attorney for the Wynekoops, said he will demand Earle's unconditional release when a writ of habeas corpus comes up before Judge David tomorrow. The lawyer said he will base his demand on the grand jury's failure to act against Earle and the inability of police to shake the son's alibi.

Neighbor on Stand

The only grand jury witness not connected with the official staff handling the case was Dr. Wynekoop's neighbor, Mrs. Vera Duncan, who lives next door to the Wynekoop home at 3408 W. Monroe st., the last person except her slayer to see Rheta alive.

The twelve counts of the indictment charged murder by a bullet wound, murder by chloroform poisoning and all the various combi-

Turn to Page 8, Column 3.

FIVE SECTIONS

This edition of The Herald and Examiner consists of five parts—four news sections and a special Christmas Toy Supplement. BE SURE TO GET THEM ALL.

U. S. TO ADMIT ALIEN LIQUORS IN TRADE DEAL

Markets for Surplus Products Demanded in Exchange; J. H. Choate Head of Board

Illinois will have no liquor control law when repeal becomes effective as a result of the adjournment of the Assembly yesterday. Governor Horner expressed disappointment. Story on Page 10.

WASHINGTON, Nov. 29.—(AP)—The United States will give foreign countries a market for their liquors in exchange for a place to sell surplus farm and industrial products.

Such reciprocal trade agreements are now in process of negotiation with several nations.

Government officials made this known today at a hearing on a code for importers. This code would give the federal alcohol control administration authority to limit the volume and origin of wine and spirits imports on a quota basis.

NAMES LIQUOR BOARD.

Hastening the administration's plan to be in complete control of the liquor situation on December 5 — the repeal date — President Roosevelt at Warm Springs named the five members of the federal alcohol control administration that will supervise the industry until Congress can enact permanent legislation.

Joseph H. Choate Jr., New York attorney, and son of a former ambassador to Great Britain, was appointed federal administrator, to sit with a board of government officials including W. A. Tarver of the Justice Department, Edward G. Lowry Jr. of the Treasury, W. L. Thorpe of the Commerce Department and Harris E. Willingham of the Agricultural Department.

INITIATIVE UP TO LIQUOR.

The board will hold its organizing meeting here Friday to prepare for supervising the distilling and other branches of the liquor industry.

The President expects the liquor industry to take the initiative, with the federal government exercising

Turn to Page 10, Column 1.

Lindberghs Plan West African Hop

PORTO PRAIA, Cape Verde Islands, Nov. 29.—(AP)—Col. Charles A. Lindbergh was said by the governor's adjutant tonight to be planning a flight either to Bathurst, the capital of Gambia, or Portuguese Guinea, both on the west African coast. An erroneous report published in Paris last night said they had left Porto Praia.

40,000 Get Jobs Within Ten Days in Chicago Area

New CWA Projects Approved; 25,867 Men to Work Here; Others in Cook County.

As a Thanksgiving offering, officials of the civil works administration yesterday approved new projects which will give employment to 40,000 in Chicago and Cook County.

Half of the required number of workers will be taken from the ranks of the unemployed who are not on relief rolls. The other 20,000 will come from those listed with the emergency relief.

Because of the necessity for getting materials and tools, the men probably will not be put to work for about ten days, Dr. M. H. Bickham, in charge of county CWA, said.

25,867 IN CITY.

The work to be done calls for 25,867 on city projects, more than 9,000 on forest preserve activities and the others in the Lincoln and South Park districts.

The city will be given the following men:

Bureau of parks 5,831
Department of sewers 184
Building repair department. 301
Street Department—
Relaying brick pavement. 11,551
Laying asphalt 8,000

Landscaping, fixing drains and otherwise reconditioning the forest preserves will be the duty of 9,200 workers assigned to the forest preserve commissioners. The work will be mainly in the north section through the Skokie Valley to Palos Park.

1,800 IN SOUTH PARKS.

About 1,800 men will work in the South Parks, and 2,500 will be assigned to the Lincoln Park board for setting in order the new north section of Lincoln Park.

The CWA yesterday also approved five projects for Chicago Heights requiring services of 253 men.

Registration of all unemployed will be resumed tomorrow in the forty-one city stations and the fifteen offices in the county.

John D. Is Better, but Gains Slowly

TARRYTOWN, N. Y., Nov. 29.—(AP)—Improvement was noted tonight in the condition of John D. Rockefeller Sr., who is recovering from an attack of the grippe. Unless he shows a decided improvement tomorrow, however, he will not be allowed to see any one except members of the family, for his physicians have prescribed quiet.

Sir Arthur Currie Dies of Pneumonia

MONTREAL, Quebec, Nov. 30.—(AP)—Sir Arthur Currie, 57, commander in chief of the Canadian corps in France and principal and vice chancellor of McGill University since 1920, died of pneumonia here early today.

BOY KILLS AND GETS LIFE IN 24 HOURS

GRAND RAPIDS, Mich., Nov. 29.—(AP)—William L. Crandell, 15-year-old schoolboy, who told police he killed Mrs. William Brewer, 68, during a struggle which followed his attempt to rob her of enough money "to buy himself some shirts," was sentenced to life imprisonment tonight.

Crandell was arrested, arraigned and sentenced less than twenty-four hours after Mrs. Brewer had staggered from her kitchen suffering from fatal bullet wounds and saying that a masked intruder had shot her.

The boy was traced through a truancy card which fell from his pocket into the Brewer yard as he fled from the house.

Crandell expressed no remorse for the slaying.

FIDDLE TAKES NAZI PRINCE FROM CELL

KLAGENFURT, Austria, Nov. 29.—(AP)—The youthful Nazi, Prince Bernhard von Sachsen-Meiningen, has fiddled his way out of jail into the Winter rigors of Chancellor Dollfuss' new concentration camp.

The prince was clapped into the Klagenfurt jail on October 21, when authorities declared him and his pretty 22-year-old wife, Princess Margot, guilty of conspiracy.

Then Prince Bernhard kept asking the jailer to send to his nearby romantic Carinthian castle for his violin. Requests for the fiddle were rejected.

Why, persisted the prisoner, was not a German prince allowed even to play a fiddle in jail?

And so the 5-foot chancellor has ordered the prince sent to the concentration camp.

2 CENTS PAY NO MORE!

Chicago Daily Tribune

THE WORLD'S GREATEST NEWSPAPER

FINAL ★★

VOLUME XCIII.—NO. 27 C [REG. U. S. PAT. OFFICE. COPYRIGHT 1934 BY THE CHICAGO TRIBUNE.] WEDNESDAY, JANUARY 31, 1934.—34 PAGES THIS PAPER CONSISTS OF TWO SECTIONS—SECTION ONE PRICE TWO CENTS IN CHICAGO AND SUBURBS ELSEWHERE THREE CENTS

MEEK DILLINGER IS JAILED

GOLD BILL MADE LAW; PRESIDENT SIGNS MEASURE

Expect Dollar Cut Today.

BY JOHN BOETTIGER.
[Chicago Tribune Press Service.]
(Picture on Back Page.)

Washington, D. C., Jan. 30.—[Special.]—President Roosevelt signed the gold bill at 3:50 o'clock this afternoon and remarked with a smile that it was the nicest birthday present he had ever had.

The bill gives him and his secretary of the treasury, Henry Morgenthau Jr., the most extraordinary control over the fate of the American dollar which any administration ever possessed.

First, it permits the President to fix the value of the dollar at anywhere between 50 and 60 per cent of its old gold standard valuation. Second, it provides a huge fund of 2 billion dollars which Mr. Morgenthau may use secretly to sustain the valuation set by the President.

Will Be Historic Date.

One way or another, this 52d birthday of the President seems destined to be well marked in the nation's history. Advocates of the gold bill before the congress called it the key to a steady and managed prosperity. Opponents saw it heading the country into a dark abyss.

Besides giving the extraordinary powers for manipulation of the dollar, the new law removes gold from circulation as coin of the realm, and while the law is limited to three years of operation, it is deemed certain that never again will Americans be passing out "eagles" or "double eagles" as Christmas presents. The law requires that henceforth all monetary gold shall be held by the treasury of the United States in the form of bullion.

Profit for Government.

The signing of the bill also provided a considerable present for Uncle Sam, for automatically all the gold coin and bullion owned by the twelve federal reserve banks became the property of the government, and with it went a clear profit of at least 2 billion 686 million dollars, as soon as devaluation is accomplished.

Here again there is a difference of opinion among commentators on the bill. Supporters of the new law refer to the huge gain of the treasury as a "profit," but opponents have labeled it "larceny," for not only do the federal reserve banks lose the profit on their gold, but citizens who reckoned their dollars as backed by the one time "permanent" value of gold, and those who invested in government bonds, also will suffer the loss in value rising out of a devaluation of the dollar.

Devaluation Comes Next.

The President is expected to issue promptly a proclamation devaluing the dollar to 60 per cent of its gold standard value. Secretary of the Treasury Morgenthau tonight discouraged reports that the devaluation would be announced tomorrow, but he and his aids were moving at breakneck speed, engaging in the most stupendous transactions by telegraph, all in a general aim to accomplish that aim at once.

The best information was that the dollar would be ready for the operating table tomorrow, and that the President would not hesitate any longer to apply the knife of devaluation.

The President summoned his monetary experts to a conference tomorrow afternoon and it was expected that the gold proclamation would be issued following that session.

Black Does It Gracefully.

The turning over of the ownership to the vast stores of gold held by the federal reserve banks was done gracefully by Eugene Black, governor of the federal reserve board.

Present with other officials when the President, for the benefit of news photographers, poised his pen over the bill which he had already signed ten minutes before, Gov. Black remarked good-naturedly:

"The caption for this picture is the governor of the federal reserve bank compelling the President of the United States to sign the gold bill."

There has been considerable public confusion concerning the prospective devaluation of the dollar. Many citizens have inquired whether paper dollars will now be worth only 60 cents; assuming that the devaluation will be that proportion, and whether when they tender it for groceries they will buy only 60 cents' worth at current prices.

Alteration Made in Advance.

The treasury has replied that so far as the public generally is concerned in its daily transactions there will be

[Continued on page 6, column 1.]

NEWS SUMMARY of The Tribune

(And Historical Scrap Book.)

Wednesday, January 31, 1934.

LOCAL.

John Dillinger, desperado, locked up in Indiana jail after airplane trip to Chicago from Arizona. Page 1.

State frees McFadden in Touhy gang trial, but he's rearrested on Wisconsin charge; prosecution completes Factor kidnaping evidence. Page 2.

Emergency relief commission, heeding federal appeal, decides to continue on the job in helping to carry on CWA activities. Page 5.

Motor car developments of future will be more rapid than in past, says Olds Motor works president. Page 8.

Unsuccessful offer is revealed of Walter J. Cummings to form syndicate to control unified Chicago car lines. Page 8.

State wins right to present additional "plot" evidence in racket trial; list of 41 "co-plotters" introduced. Page 9.

Citizens' committee on public expenditures discloses city and school budgets face $26,000,000 deficits. Page 10.

Physicians attending Melvin A. Traylor trace illness to unusual germ as he improves. Page 11.

Mayor Kelly tells how World's Fair regained for Chicago the respect of the world. Page 15.

News of society. Page 17.

Radio programs. Page 18.

Death notices, obituaries. Page 18.

DOMESTIC.

State assembly passes liquor control bill after 11 weeks' bickering when house votes 105 to 30 for it. Page 1.

Secretary of Labor Perkins advocates shorter hours, higher wages before United Mine Workers. Page 6.

Infra red rays disclose what Spanish inquisition censors blotted out. Page 15.

Cleveland to default Thursday on 1¾ millions due on bonds. Page 16.

PRESIDENT'S BIRTHDAY.

More than 6,000 parties held in honor of President's birthday. Page 1

Chicago joins nation in honoring President Roosevelt on his 52d birthday. Page 3.

WASHINGTON.

Cut in valuation of dollar expected today as President Roosevelt signs gold bill. Page 1.

House votes big navy bill; 102 ships are added. Page 1.

Senator La Follette charges Morgan interests fight St. Lawrence treaty and calls power the chief issue. Page 6.

Foreign lands owe U. S. nearly 12¾ billions; 622 millions overdue; only Finland pays up. Page 12.

FOREIGN.

Greek minister of interior seeks further information on Insull's physical condition; residence permit expires today. Page 4.

Forty-four men marooned from Byrd flagship battle for life as antarctic ice front continues to crumble. Page 5.

Germany rewards Chancellor Hitler on anniversary of ascension to power by making him sovereign of all German states. Page 7.

Nazi birthday marked in Austria by stench bomb explosions and students' demonstrations. Page 7.

Fail to find soviet Russian stratosphere balloon after flight. Page 11.

TRIBUNE WIDER MARKET DRIVE

Premier Bennett of Canada says trade reciprocity with U. S. is still in state of "exploration." Page 11.

SPORTS.

Blackhawks win from Ottawa sextet, 2 to 0. Page 23.

Boys' races start Silver Skates tonight. Page 23.

English squash racquets team defeats Chicago stars, 6-1. Page 23.

Order decision in Savoldi-Londos match tonight. Page 23.

Bears raise $25,000 for coast charities in three games. Page 23.

Stagg, visiting in Chicago, compares Big Ten and coast football. Page 25.

Sixteen thousand cheer Shore as Bruins win, 2-1; Americans beat Maroons. Page 26.

EDITORIALS.

Gen. Johnson's Elephantine Pets; Dillinger and His Gangsters; Business Opening for Ambassador Bingham. Page 14.

FINANCE, COMMERCE.

Lammot du Pont assails economic experiments of United States. Page 27.

Pecora ordered to draft stock exchange regulation bill. Page 27.

United States Steel corporation halves deficit in 1933. Page 27.

Heaviest rush of buying in seven months drives stocks up. Page 27.

Packers make peace with government over processing bids. Page 30.

Want Ad index. Page 31.

Average net paid circulation December, 1933
THE CHICAGO TRIBUNE
DAILY in excess of 785,000

6,000 PARTIES HELD IN HONOR OF ROOSEVELT

Celebrate Birthday All Over U. S.

The text of President Roosevelt's birthday address and his plea for support in the fight against infantile paralysis will be found on page 3.

(Picture on Back Page.)

The 52d birthday of President Roosevelt was celebrated throughout the country last night at innumerable dinners, balls, musicals, and speech-making parties. One rather careful estimate placed the number of birthday dinners at six thousand. In New York there were 200 celebrations, including a ball at the Waldorf-Astoria attended by 6,000 persons.

In Chicago there were three big birthday assemblages and dozens of neighborhood parties of varying types and sizes. Donations of funds, large and small, to the Warm Springs foundation for crippled children featured the celebration parties and birthday cakes everywhere marked the good wishes to the President.

Detroit's celebrations garnered a fund of approximately $100,000 for Warm Springs. How much was given in Chicago will not be known until today.

In Milwaukee 10,000 persons attended a celebration in the Auditorium. A huge 700 pound cake was cut.

From Washington late in the evening the President made a speech of thanks, broadcast throughout the country.

HAPPIEST HE'S KNOWN

[Chicago Tribune Press Service.]

Washington, D. C., Jan. 30.—[Special.]—Toward midnight tonight Franklin D. Roosevelt summed up his 52d birthday with the simple statement that it was the happiest he had ever known.

As he spoke these words from the White House his wife and daughter, standing before thousands in the ballroom of the Shoreham hotel, silently listened. They, too, smiled satisfaction. And the crowds of Washington celebrated, jammed together, smiled with the Roosevelts when the President's voice said:

"No man has ever had a finer birthday remembrance from his friends and fellows than you have given me tonight."

Dance Only in Name.

This Washington ball was, for the first crowded hours, a dance in name only. Everybody wanted to get a squint at everybody else, so everybody pushed into the main lobby and stared.

The Morgenthaus were merry; the Hulls looked happy; Director of the Budget Lew Douglas smiled a wide smile.

Some of the small fry—and there were many at this public party—tarried overly long on the stairs hopeful of a flash from the cameras.

Mrs. Roosevelt was due at 10:30. She was delayed. The crowd grew restive.

Mrs. Wilson a Guest.

Up the corridor came Mrs. Woodrow Wilson, in black satin with diamonds and the inevitable orchids. With her, Mrs. James Hamilton Lewis, wife of Chicago's Democratic senator; the French ambassador and the German, Isabella Greenway, the lovely lady who comes to congress from Arizona, and Daisy Harriman, with the perfect poise.

Very sedate, down the aisle, comes a big man. Quietly he steps on the platform and asks that the photographers ask him to stand. Can it be? Yes, it is Brig. Gen. Johnson of NRA fame. He has put on dancing school manners with his evening clothes.

The elderly gentlemen in gold lace—most of them reserve colonels—scurry up the hall as fast as they can. There is much arranging and rearranging, so that each has his right position. Then the revolving door swings, and Mrs. Roosevelt is blown into the room. Her gown is pale peach. There are emeralds somewhere. Again the door swings and Daughter Anna, dazzling in flame colored satin, is swept in. Then a party of women friends follow.

Wife Cuts the Cake.

Mrs. Roosevelt starts to walk into the lobby. But, no, the committee must carry out orders. There is a huddle, many orders, and at the last the procession proceeds into the main ballroom, where they stand at attention while President Roosevelt's speech

[Continued on page 3, column 4.]

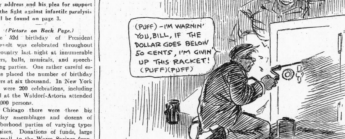

Illinois Liquor Bill Passes

SKETCHES OF THE NEWS

RECALL TO GERMANY
BILL HOHENZOLLERN
HOPE SPRINGS ETERNAL
BUZZ
GRAFTER
WHEREVER THERE'S HONEY
(PUFF)—I'M WARNIN' YOU, BILL, IF THE DOLLAR GOES BELOW 50 CENTS, I'M GIVIN' UP THIS RACKET! (PUFF) (PUFF)

BENJAMIN PUTS HIS PANHANDLING ON A HIGH PLANE

Benjamin Sullivan, 36 years old, 1130 East 81st place, may beg for his food, but he is particular what is offered him, he demonstrated last night in two south side restaurants.

Sullivan first objected to the bowl of soup which was offered him in the Iowa restaurant, 1404 East 63d street, owned by Mrs. C. J. Bransfield. His objections were couched in such terms that he was ejected. Outside, he threw a brick which smashed the plate glass window and a large neon sign, and fled.

A short time later Sullivan entered Mother's restaurant, 1043 East 63d street, and again asked for food. Given a bowl of chicken soup, he threw it on the floor and demanded chicken. He was ordered to leave and Lieut. Walter Storms of the Woodlawn police station, who had been eating in the restaurant, seized him outside just as he was picking up a brick from the gutter.

Miss Ellen Bransfield, daughter of Mrs. Bransfield, identified the prisoner as the man who smashed her mother's window and he was booked on a charge of malicious mischief.

COLD WAVE DUE TO RETIRE TODAY; 40° IS PREDICTED

The first cold wave of 1934, which sent temperatures below zero during the last two days, will retire today before southwest winds expected to lift the mercury to 40 degrees, according to the forecast of C. A. Donnel, government meteorologist. The temperature rose steadily yesterday from 2 below zero at 8 a. m. to 21 degrees above at 9 p. m.

More than 100 fire alarms, most of them traced to overheated furnaces, kept firemen busy yesterday. The worst blaze of the day caused $8,000 damage to frame dwellings from 2001 to 2009 South Racine avenue before it was extinguished. Seven families were driven to the street and Mrs. Margaret Folken, 81 years old, who lived at 2007, was slightly burned before she was rescued from her blazing bed by firemen.

A dozen University of Chicago students were driven from their quarters at 5558 Ellis avenue by a fire which caused damage of $4,000.

Swallows Nickel; Slap Gets It—With Interest

Hollister, Cal., Jan. 30.—(AP)—William Dunlop, 4 years old, literally declared a 20 per cent dividend here today as he was forced to cough up a 5 cent piece he had swallowed. The boy's father held him by the heels, patted him between the shoulders, and out flew a nickel—and a penny.

Big Navy Bill Passes House; Add 102 Ships

Washington, D. C., Jan. 30.—(AP)—The house voted today a naval strength which far surpasses the cold statistics of the bill.

It debated, passed and sent to the senate the Vinson treaty navy bill calling for 102 new fighting ships, to bring the numerical strength of the United States navy up to 240 ships by 1939 at an estimated cost of 570 millions. But behind these statistics was a fighting strength vastly augmented by the improvements in warfare designed since 1919.

Tremendous cruising range, higher speed, longer, more accurate and more deadly guns and keener mechanical eyes for scouting units have been designed for the navy since the world war ended and naval treaties trimmed fleets.

Effectiveness Tells Story.

Numerically the number of fighting ships, when the navy reaches its treaty strength, will be less than half that of the navy in the fall of 1919, 240 compared with 559 ships then listed as "fit for service." The increase in effectiveness is another story.

Naval officials decline, for obvious reasons, to discuss the speed and cruising range of the new ships, either on the ways, or to be put there under the Vinson treaty measure.

In this broadened cruising range of United States ships is found a partial answer to one of the navy strategy problems—lack of naval bases except in the remote Pacific.

The new ships have "blister" hull construction, double hulls, with oil to take up the concussion of under water explosions that ordinarily crumple plates.

Plan New Aircraft Carrier.

In the air the treaty navy will both augment its offense and defense, build a fifth aircraft carrier to float a new swarm of planes and, on the defensive side, equip itself with anti-aircraft large caliber machine guns of new design and highly improved accuracy.

The 1,184 airplanes the Vinson bill would add to the fleet would be radically different craft from those of world war days.

Passage of the bill by the house today sent the measure to the senate where the naval committee already had approved its companion bill. Senator Robinson of Arkansas, the Democratic leader, said the senate would begin consideration of it Thursday.

The house debate brought frequent avowals of a desire for peace and action designed to take some of the profits out of war, but not even a roll call was demanded.

4 LIONS PUNISH THE SLAYER OF TROUPE LIONESS

Cleveland, O., Jan. 30.—(AP)—Sammy, the 400 pound lion with jungle manners, who yesterday killed a lioness, was taken over the bumps by four of his tawny colleagues in Clyde Beatty's animal training act today.

Beatty put Sammy in the cage today and then brought in a correctional squad of four husky lions named Nero Jr., Brutus, Leo, and King. They went to work on Sammy with considerable enjoyment.

Leo slid a long, white tooth along Sammy's shank. Nero pulled a heavy paw across Sammy's mane. Two other lions growled and looked disapprovingly at the killer. Sammy drooped a bit, tried to get out of the cage and finally took refuge in a corner.

There was a tussle and Sammy indicated he had had enough. Beatty opened the door to the runway. That seems to be the way lions are trained.

GUM MACHINE, MACHINE GUN CONFUSE POLICE

Cal Hoff, telephone operator at the Waukegan police station, had just finished reading an account of John Dillinger's airplane trip yesterday when in an excited message from a telegraph operator at the North Western railroad station he thought he heard the words "machine gun" and "slugs."

He sprang to action. In a jiffy three squads of police and deputy sheriffs were speeding to the railroad station, a few blocks away. Dashing into the station they demanded of Floyd Dixon, the telegraph operator: "Where are the machine gunners?"

"Machine gunners?" queried Dixon. "What I said was that two kids were putting slugs in a gum machine. I grabbed one, but they got away."

48 U. S. PLANES HOP FOR SECRET HAWAIIAN TESTS

[Copyright: 1934: By the New York Times.]

HONOLULU, T. H., Jan. 30.—The largest air force ever to operate from Pearl harbor left today under secret orders for ten days of advanced base operations in which the army and navy air corps are taking part.

Forty-eight patrol planes, including the squadron which flew here from San Francisco early this month, departed at intervals between 5 a. m. and noon for a station on the outlying islands. They will operate there until the final day of the maneuvers, which will culminate in tests to include troops, submarines and surface ships. The sea craft left Pearl harbor Sunday and yesterday.

House Votes for Code at Last, 105-30

BY PERCY WOOD.
[Chicago Tribune Press Service.]

Springfield, Ill., Jan. 30.—[Special.]—In a last minute burst of speed, the Illinois liquor control bill passed the house tonight by a vote of 105 to 30. A few minutes later appropriations for the administration of the measure, totaling $481,000, had been approved and sent to the senate, where enactment seemed certain.

Gov. Horner's signature will make the key bill a law by Thursday, or Friday at the latest. He announced tonight that he would sign it as soon as its 25,000 words had been engrossed and laid on his desk.

"While it is not a perfect measure," said the governor, "it is undoubtedly the best that could be obtained with so many divergent views on the subject."

This divergence of opinion kept the general assembly in session the better part of eleven weeks in the attempt to draw a law which would satisfactorily regulate the manufacture, sale and use of post-repeal beverages.

Repeal Beats Legislators.

The Dec. 5 celebration found the legislature barely started on its big job; New Year's eve passed with both houses in a wrangle and only today, with February pushing hard against the calendar, was it possible to secure passage of a measure by the two-thirds constitutional majority necessary for immediate enactment.

For a time during the roll call it appeared that this would not be possible. Last Thursday recess was taken until today because the bill was six votes short of success. This evening it tallied 58 votes on first roll call, 85 on the call of absentees and then, vote by vote, it gained an "aye" here and there and was lifted, finally, over the 102 vote barrier which meant victory.

Thirty Republicans—25 from downstate and 5 from Chicago—composed the opposition. These "die-hards" fought hard last week and harder today, even though some of their colleagues fell by the wayside and didn't attend for the final vote.

Republican Saves It.

Therefore many considered it ironic that a Republican, Representative Thomas J. Stack of Peoria, should have cast the 102d vote. He entered the chamber a little late to find his minority brethren storming at Speaker Roe and demanding that the vote be announced.

The count stood at 101 at the time and the Republicans were trying to force another recess while the Democrats waited for another hard riding "Sheridan" to cast the final vote.

But Mr. Stack did the trick. His deep bass "aye" carried from the rear of the hall to the ears of Clerk Charles P. Cahey. Mr. Cahey jabbed at the tally sheet with his pencil and the bill had passed. Three other superfluous votes were added just to give weight.

Hold Train for Vote.

Appropriation bills came next. They were passed in a hurry while the evening train was kept waiting fifteen minutes to accommodate the Chicago members.

The finance bills appropriate $293,000 to the department of finance for the expenses of administering the measure until July 1, 1935; $160,000 to the Illinois liquor commission, created by the

[Continued on page 4, column 1.]

THE WEATHER

WEDNESDAY, JANUARY 31, 1934.

Sunrise, 7:04; sunset, 5:03. Moon rises at 6:15 p. m. today. Jupiter is a morning star; Venus, Mars, and Saturn are evening stars.

Chicago and vicinity—Generally fair and warmer, fresh to strong southwest winds Wednesday; Thursday unsettled, probably some rain or snow with somewhat colder by night.

Illinois—Generally fair and warmer Wednesday; rain probable Wednesday night or Thursday, warmer in extreme south, colder in extreme northwest portion Thursday.

TRIBUNE BAROMETER.

TEMPERATURES IN CHICAGO

MAXIMUM, 11 P. M. 23
MINIMUM, 6 A. M. .... —2
[Maximum a year ago, 44; minimum, 19.]

3 a. m.	0	Noon	10	8 p. m.	20
4 a. m.	—1	1 p. m.	11	9 p. m.	21
5 a. m.	—1	2 p. m.	13	Unofficial—	
6 a. m.	—2	3 p. m.	14	10 p. m.	22
7 a. m.	—2	4 p. m.	16	11 p. m.	23
8 a. m.	—2	5 p. m.	17	Midnight	23
9 a. m.	0	6 p. m.	18	1 a. m.	23
10 a. m.	3	7 p. m.	19	2 a. m.	24
11 a. m.	7				

For 24 hours ended at 7 p. m. Jan. 30:
Mean temperature, 8 degrees; normal, 24 degrees; excess for January, 259 degrees.
Precipitation, none; deficiency for January, 1.01 inches.
Barometer—7 a. m., 30.40; 7 p. m., 30.06.
Highest wind velocity, 22 miles an hour from the northwest at 9:10 p. m.

[Official weather table on page 28.]

HELD IN INDIANA AFTER AIRPLANE HOP TO CHICAGO

He Denies Killing of Policeman.

John Dillinger, notorious criminal whose banditry and other depredations caused the state of Indiana to mobilize its National Guard several months ago, was tightly locked behind the bars of the Lake county jail at Crown Point last night. There he is to await trial on an indictment charging him with the murder of Policeman William Patrick O'Malley in a holdup of the First National bank of East Chicago on Jan. 15.

The outlaw arrived at 7:35 p. m., approximately 26 hours after four Indiana law enforcement officials had carried him, screaming and fighting, aboard an American Airways plane at Tucson, Ariz., where he and three others of his gang had been arrested last Thursday.

Manacled and meek, Dillinger was swiftly transported across more than 2,000 miles of American scenery to Chicago. At 6:10 p. m. he and his guards swept down, in a plane that had left St. Louis two hours before, upon the Chicago airport at 63d street and Cicero avenue.

120 Policemen on Guard.

Prepared for him at the airport was a reception such as had never been accorded a criminal in Chicago. Sixty Chicago policemen were stationed there with no other orders than to see that nothing untoward happened to him or to the law's majesty on the field. Thirty-two more Chicago policemen, clad in bullet proof vests and carrying machine guns, rifles, shotguns, and pistols, were waiting, with 29 policemen from the northern Indiana cities, to guard him on the last lap of his journey—the thirty miles from the airport to Crown Point.

Thus, in all, the official welcoming party for John Dillinger, paroled ex-convict, numbered more than 120 men.

Pulled Out of Plane.

Events moved swiftly at the airport. The plane roared down and taxied to its appointed berth. A fourth of the police detail crowded about it, flares lighting their faces and their bared heads. Camera flashlights boomed as a shivering Dillinger was half lifted, half dragged, to the ground.

A medium smallish, slim man with thinning light brown hair, he blinked in the glare, set his face in expression of patient resignation, briefly and uninformingly answered a few questions put to him and was bundled into one of 13 automobiles in a cortége that was waiting.

Beside him as he rode out toward Indiana justice sat Lieut. Frank Reynolds of the Chicago police. The lieutenant's orders were direct and simple. They had been given by Capt. John Stege, who for weeks had led a Chicago search for the Dillinger gang.

"If any effort is made to raid the caravan and release Dillinger," said the captain, "or if he makes a break at escape, kill him at once."

Neither contingency developed. Without incident the thirteen carloads of guards safely conducted Dillinger to the custody of Lake county's woman sheriff, Mrs. Lillian Holley.

Poses with Prosecutor.

Hardly had the iron doors clanged behind him when the outlaw, no longer glum and morose, but rather smiling and alert, posed for pictures with his principal guards and Prosecutor Robert G. Estill, who is to ask a jury of Lake county residents to send him to the electric chair for the O'Malley murder.

Next, with an air that demonstrated him to be as mild a mannered man as ever shot up a bank, he submitted to general interviewing. Gone were the snarls with which he had greeted the Arizona police. His talk was full of praise, even for the Chicago policemen whom he had described in Tucson as "the dumbest in the world." There were verbal bouquets for the "nice fellows" who had accompanied him on the plane trip and an admission: "I like Mr. Estill and Mrs. Holley seems like a fine lady."

Denies Killing Policeman.

As for the Dillinger career—well, yes, it had had its bad points, but it hadn't included the killing of O'Malley, according to Dillinger.

"Why, they can't hold me for that," said the outlaw. "When that job was pulled I was in Florida. Never had anything to do with the East Chicago stickup."

From point to point, as the questions were thrown at random by a dozen interviewers, the most notorious criminal of his day went on with his answers.

"I was just an unfortunate boy,"

Minnesota Weather

Mostly cloudy tonight and Friday; possibly light snow in east; slowly rising temperature.

St. Paul Dispatch

General telegraph, Northwest and local news.

Editorial page and its daily features.

VOL. 66. NO. 129. 20 PAGES Exclusive Service of the Associated Press. ST. PAUL, MINN., THURSDAY, FEBRUARY 8, 1934. c☆☆ TWO CENTS IN ST. PAUL.

BREMER RETURNS HOME; KIDNAP RANSOM PAID

The National Whirligig

News Behind The News

WASHINGTON

WORKERS can't understand how the NRA is their friend when they're thrown out of jobs by NRA orders to suspend production.

A big lumber concern in Washington State was forced to close several weeks ago. The workers threatened violence until the management proved that shutdown orders came from the "code authority." Then the workers kicked. Business organizations protested. The senators protested. The newspapers protested. Nothing doing. Voluntary relief committees had to be organized to feed the workers who must be idle till late in February.

Meanwhile a Soviet ship arrived from Vladivostok with a cargo of lumber which undersold American lumber in the Seattle market—thanks to high prices ordered by code authority. Local communists hailed their comrades, gave them a dinner and all hands saluted the red flag and pledged allegiance to Moscow.

Idleness in lumber mills in Texas has raised a similar howl against the NRA.

A LOT of water has gone over the dam since the status of the proposed new food, drug and cosmetics bill was discussed last in this column.

A powerful lobby is tearing the measure to ribbons bit by bit. Unless the White House takes a hand a feeble bill will be reported out of committee and probably will never reach a final vote.

The first few bites that the pain-and-paint lobby took were anticipated by the Food and Drug administration, which seems to be standing alone in the fight for the bill. All legislation is a matter of compromise. But those bites have only served to increase the lobby's appetite.

IN THE original Tugwell bill it was provided that drugs and foodstuffs must have an intemization of their contents printed on the label. As rewritten by Senator Copeland, who will steer the bill if it ever gets out of committee, the provision affecting drugs was eliminated. This was done on the complaint that patented formulas would be revealed to chiseling competitors.

The bill has detoured far from the road that Prof. Tugwell mapped and it's a real issue with him. If he doesn't get some strong White House backing soon insiders shouldn't be surprised if he resigned and went back to his classrooms.

THE HOUSE Progressive bloc, which functioned so valiantly under Florella LaGuardia in the Seventy-

(Please Turn to Page 2, Col. 3.)

RIOTING ENDED AS DOUMERGUE REACHES PARIS

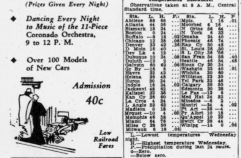

Premier-designate Cheered Wildly Whenever He Appears in Streets.

BEGINS WORK ON CABINET

Officials Admit France on Verge of Revolution; Death Toll Now 12.

(Pictures on Page 1, Section 2.)

Paris, Feb. 8.—(AP)—Premier-designate Gaston Doumergue, whose new cabinet may be formed by tonight, seemed today to have ended Paris' two days of rioting and terror.

The 71-year-old former president and France's new man-of-the-hour took only fifteen minutes after his arrival today to tell President Albert Lebrun what he meant to do.

Then he immediately started to carry out his program.

He was given the quarters at the foreign office once occupied by the beloved late Aristide Briand, many times premier of France.

There Doumergue received party

CALL IT "DOO-MAYERG"

Paris, Feb. 8.—(AP)—Gaston Doumergue, new premier of France, pronounces his last name in two syllables: "Doo-Mayerg."

leaders and the men he wanted to place in his ministry.

Wherever he passed, he was cheered wildly.

His route was a veritable triumphal procession as he went from the Elysee palace to make the traditional calls on the presidents of the senate and chamber.

Then he conferred with Daladier.

On all sides it was freely admitted that France was close to civil war

(Please Turn to Page 2, Col. 1.)

BREMER FAMILY STAGES HAPPY REUNION

The Edward G. Bremer family had a happy reunion today. Released by kidnapers after 21 days of fearful captivity, the St. Paul banker (left) returned to his wife and 8-year-old daughter, Betty, (together on the right) whom he had not seen since the morning of January 17, when he left his colonial home at 92 North Mississippi River boulevard to take Betty to school.

Bank Chief Released at Rochester

Abduction Victim, Severely Beaten and Exhausted, Ordered to Bed by Physician, Who Says Patient Is Extremely Nervous; Is Wearing Full Beard When He Appears at Father's Home in St. Paul.

THREE MEN IN SMALL CAR FREE CAPTIVE; WALTER MAGEE ACTS AS CONTACT M

(FURTHER DETAILS AND PICTURES ON PAGES 3, 4 AND

E. G. Bremer, 37-year-old St. Paul banker, return safely to St. Paul early today on payment of an undi closed amount of ransom reported to be the full $200,00 demanded by kidnapers who had held him 21 days sin January 17.

The president of the Commercial State bank, tire nervous and showing painful evidence of ill treatment b his abductors, was released about 8 P. M. Wednesday a Rocheser, 85 miles south of here. Three men release him from a small coupe.

Mr. Bremer bore marks of having been beaten about the hea and face, and he had a full growth of beard. He appeared at th home of Adolf Bremer, his father and president of Schmidt's Brewery shortly after midnight. The home is at 855 West Seventh street.

WALTER MAGEE DELIVERS RANSOM.

Walter Magee, wealthy contractor friend of the family, was intermediary who delivered the ransom. Full details of the deliv were not disclosed though it was learned that Magee had taken fr the pocket of a small coupe at the contact spot, a note from t kidnapers, standing with his back to the curb while reading t communication. The car now is in the garage at the Adolf Brem home.

After replacing the note in the pocket of the car, Magee the set two "bundles of money" on the seat. It was presumed the ranson was wrapped in two large cardboard suitboxes tied with heavy cord in accordance with the gang's earlier instructions.

It was not revealed where the payment was made or what the instructions were. In view of the family's earlier statements, that they were ready and eager to pay the full ransom the view was taken in some quarters that the entire $200,000 was turned over to the captors.

One source of information said that a note enclosed with the ransom money read:

"To the parties holding Edward:

"I have done my part and kept my word 100 per cent. as I said I would. This money is not marked and you have the full amount asked for. Now, boys, I am counting on your honor.

"Release Edward and tell him to come to my house first.

"(Signed) Adolf Bremer."

Unconfirmed reports were that the full $200,000 ransom was paid Wednesday. The elder Bremer is said to have dispatched the money, $85,000 of which was in $5 bills, and the remainder in $1 bills.

U. S. AGENTS TAKE CHARGE.

Reporters were not permitted to talk to Mr. Bremer immediate because of the activity of the federal men and the fatigued conditio of the kidnap victim.

Mr. Bremer, on revealing his experiences to friends, told of ho he realized he was being kidnaped and tried to escape.

When his car was stopped at Goodrich and Lexington ave. one of the kidnapers climbed in the front seat with him with a in his hand. Mr. Bremer opened the door on his left and trie get out.

As he did this, another of the kidnapers met him on the side of the car and pushed him back into the seat, climbing in be him.

Mr. Bremer was struck on the head by both men at about same time, he believes. He does not remember being transfe from his own car into the automobile of the kidnapers.

The next thing he recalls was that he was being taken som where in an automobile. He had a bandage over his eyes so that he couldn't see and he says he has no idea how many men were in the car with them.

Mr. Bremer expressed the belief that there must have been or twelve men in the gang, basing his opinion on the number voices he heard in the place where he was being held a captive.

The room in which he was kept was dark. His eyes were not bandaged. During the entire time that he was held, two men sat back of him at all times.

He was warned not to attempt to look around.

"One look and we'll blow your damned brains out, Bremer re lated he was told.

GUARDS WORKED IN RELAYS.

The guards worked in relays. Two men would remain with him for a while and then they would be relieved. From their conversation and the number of changes made in the guards, Mr. Bremer believes there were ten or twelve men involved in watching him.

One close friend of the Bremer family, who declined to permit his name to be used, said:

"He (E. G. Bremer) put up a hell of a battle (with the kidnapers). The blood in his car was not all his. He has a leg injury that he got when he stuck his foot out so they couldn't close the door. It seems they got the door closed and his leg may have a very bad bruise or worse. He was treated well enough while they had him, considering all the circumstances.

"Both he and his father were in bed this morning and under the care of a doctor and a nurse. He is suffering from the shoc

(Please Turn to Page 4, Col. 2.)

SENATE COMMITTEE O. K.'S PROBE INTO POWER RATES

Washington, Feb. 8.—(AP)—The Senate Interstate Commerce committee approved today the Norris bill proposing a power commission investigation to determine rates charged all consumers of electrical energy by private and municipal corporations.

Senator Norris, Repulican of Nebraska, estimated the cost of the inquiry at between $300,000 and $300,-000 and to come out of public works funds.

MERCURY HITS 1 ABOVE IN COLD WAVE HERE

The temperature sank to 1 degree above zero early today in St. Paul as colder weather moved into the Midwest. Rice Lake, Wis., reported a minimum of 18 below, while northeastern Michigan had 30 below at some points.

Slowly rising temperature is forecast for St. Paul, with light snow possible tonight and Friday.

THE WEATHER

St. Paul Forecast.

Mostly cloudy tonight and Friday, possibly light snow; slowly rising temperature.

St. Paul Temperatures.

Low. last night	0	10 A. M.	3
6 A. M.	1	11 A. M.	6
7 A. M.	1	12 M.	9
8 A. M.	2	1 P. M.	11
9 A. M.	2		

A Year Ago Today.

Highest ......—10 | Lowest ......—28

Precipitation.

Amount during 24 hours ending at 7 A. M. .... .01

Relative Humidity.

7 A. M. ....75 | Noon 47

Wind velocity—7 A. M., 10 miles per hour.

Temperatures Elsewhere.

Observations taken at 8 A. M., Central Standard time.

Sta.	L.	H.	P.	Sta.	L.	H.	P.
Abilene	58	66	...	Mpls.	1	16	.01
Atlanta	44	56	...	Moorhed	6	16	....
Bismark	18	24	...	N Orlns	56	64	...
Boston	0	24	...	N York	6	32	...
Buffalo	—8	18	.02	Omaha	24	40	...
Chicago	12	28	.06	Phoenix	46	74	...
Denver	32	42	.36	Rap Cy	30	48	...
D Moin	16	40	...	St. Louis	28	50	...
Dev Lk	4	12	...	S L City	36	56	...
Dubuque	10	24	.08	San Fran	54	58	.40
Duluth	—12	2	...	Seattle	46	54	.48
Galvstn	60	62	.06	Sioux Cy	20	34	...
Gr By	—16	8	...	Washgtn	22	40	.01
Havre	22	42	...	Wichita	30	60	...
Helena	36	48	...	Williston	22	30	...
Huron	20	34	...	Yel Park	32	46	...
Indpls	16	34	.02	Calgary	30	50	...
Jacksnvl	48	62	...	Edmontn	20	28	...
Kalispel	32	36	...	Le Pas	—12	6	...
Kan Cy	26	60	...	Med Hat	34	52	...
La Cros	4	24	...	Minedos	—8	2	...
L Angls	52	62	...	Montrl	—24	4	.02
Madison	0	18	...	Pt Art	—28	—4	...
Mrquet	—10	4	.02	Pr Albrt	10	18	...
Memphis	46	58	...	Qu'Appel	10	22	...
Miami	64	76	...	Swift Cr	28	44	...
Miles C	28	50	...	Winipg	—14	0	.06
Milwauk	6	18	.06				

L.—Lowest temperatures Wednesday night.
H.—Highest temperature Wednesday.
P.—Precipitation during last 24 hours.
0—Zero.
—Below zero.

Automobile Interiors More Beautiful And Durable Than Ever, Show Reveals

Mohair, Broadcloth and Whipcord Most Popular Materials for Upholstery but Weaves Are Just as New as Cars; Chronium, Stainless Steel and Silver Plate Used for Fittings.

Mohair, broadcloth and whipcord are the choice of automobile manufacturers for upholstery this year, in the order named, as evidenced at the St. Paul Automobile show in the Auditorium.

But the weaves are just as new as the cars. Material manufacturers have been experimenting for some months to get a longer wearing material and a still more beautiful fabric, and they have succeeded.

Interior metal fittings are chromium plated, stainless steel or silver plate, in the order named. Many of them are exquisite reproduction of hand-tooled fittings and some are tipped with onyx or ivory compositions.

Colorful, yet subdued, is the interior of all of the models on display this week in the Auditorium. Delicate tints of color enliven the interiors of the cars and yet are so designed as to harmonize with any frock.

Lighting effects in the new cars are subdued yet sufficient for any reasonable purpose. The trend for interior lighting is toward the indirect method but as yet no manufacturer has achieved this goal in production.

Practically all the open models, including those which are convertible, have leather upholstery. This is not genuine leather but so clever an imitation that few persons can detect the difference.

The upholstery for each car, given as standard, is: Chevrolet, whipcord and mohair; Ford, mohair, bedford cord and broadcloth; Hupmobile, mohair and broadcloth; Buick, broadcloth, Bedford cord and mohair; Cadillac, whipcord and broadcloth; Oldsmobile, whipcord and mohair; Graham, mohair; Pierce Arrow, broadcloth; La Salle, whipcord and broadcloth; Pontiac, mohair; Packard, silk and wool broadcloth; Nash, mohair and broadcloth; Terraplane, whipcord and broadcloth; Dodge, whipcord and mohair and Studebaker, broadcloth and mohair.

Gould's 50-piece banjo band will be the feature of tonight's program in honor of Minneapolis day. Dancing will be until midnight. Judges in the dancing contest tonight are Frank Gordon of Vanity Fair, St. Paul, and Jack Malerich of the Leamington hotel, Minneapolis.

DR. NIPPERT REVEALS CONTACT WITH GANG

Bottle Hurled Through Glass Jan. 20 Called Attention to Notes.

First contact between kidnapers of Edward G. Bremer and the victim's family was made through Dr. H. T. Nippert, the physician disclosed today.

Dr. Nippert, Bremer family physician, received three notes, at least one from the kidnaped man, the morning of January 20, three days after the banker was abducted.

The gray-haired physician's attention was called to the contact notes, all in a large envelope which was slipped under the front door of his home, 706 Lincoln avenue, by a bottle hurled through the door and a telephone call.

Breaking of the front door by an 8-ounce dentifrice bottle was reported shortly after it occurred, although Dr. Nippert denied any notes were found.

In the large envelope were three smaller ones—one addressed to Dr. Nippert, one to Walter Magee, the contact man, and the third to Adolf Bremer, the kidnaped man's father.

Dr. Nippert's story concerning the note incident was substantially the same as he told when queried about

(Please Turn to Page 4, Col. 1.)

FATHER OF BREMER EXPRESSES THANKS

Parent of Kidnap Victim Hopes Other Families Will Be Spared Such Agony.

Thankfulness for the return of his eldest son, held 21 days by kidnapers who demanded $200,000 ransom, was expressed today by the happy father of Edward G. Bremer, banker.

His statement said:

"I am so happy to tell you that my boy is back at last after his terrible experience. The hideous hours of suspense have been almost unbearable for all of us.

"I greatly appreciate the personal interest of the President and the Governor and the splendid co-operation of the press."

(Please Turn to Page 3, Col. 1.)

MAYOR NONCOMMITTAL

Mayor Mahoney refused today to make any comment regarding the return of Edward G. Bremer, kidnaped banker.

"I don't want to say anything about it until I know more about it," he said. "I don't know anything about it at all."

OWATONNA MAN'S CAR USED TO DELIVER RANSOM

A small coupe, owned by E. J. Petronik of Owatonna, was reported to have been used for delivering the ransom money for the release of Edward B. Bremer, St. Paul banker seized January 17 for $200,000.

Reports were that Walter Magee, wealthy contractor friend of the banker, drove the automobile when he turned the ransom over to the gang.

The coupe was reported to have both side windows soaped and a rear window slightly opened. The windshield was not soaped.

Petronik could not be reached immediately for confirmation.

Kidnaping Menace Worse Than Rule Under Tyrant, Olson Says

A threat of life under conditions "worse than under the rule of a tyrant" unless police and citizens "crush the menace of kidnaping" was emphasized today by Governor Olson as he announced his calling a conference of law enforcement officials at his office at 10 A. M. Saturday.

Governor Olson, calling the conference in connection with the Edward Bremer kidnaping, said that after this meeting contact will be made with federal agencies to obtain "united action" between Minnesota and the federal government. Governor Olson's statement said:

"All law enforcing agencies and all law-abiding citizens must join together to crush the menace of kidnaping. Unless that is done it will grow to such an extent that no one will be safe and we will live under

(Please Turn to Page 4, Col. 6.)

2 CENTS PAY NO MORE!

Chicago Daily Tribune

THE WORLD'S GREATEST NEWSPAPER

FINAL ★★

VOLUME XCIII.—NO. 47 C [REG. U. S. PAT. OFFICE. COPYRIGHT 1934 BY THE CHICAGO TRIBUNE.] FRIDAY, FEBRUARY 23, 1934.—32 PAGES THIS PAPER CONSISTS OF THREE SECTIONS—SECTION ONE PRICE TWO CENTS IN CHICAGO AND SUBURBS ELSEWHERE THREE CENTS

99 YEARS FOR THREE TOUHYS

JOHNSON'S NRA LABOR FIGURES ARE QUESTIONED

Fail to Agree with Miss Perkins'.

BY ARTHUR SEARS HENNING.
[Chicago Tribune Press Service.]

Washington, D. C., Feb. 22.—[Special.]—Gen. Hugh S. Johnson, NRA administrator, is now under fire from two fresh quarters.

The senate has adopted a resolution demanding information on the extent to which the NRA under his administration is being dominated by big business.

Secretary of Labor Perkins has issued a report on reëmployment which raises the question of the accuracy of Gen. Johnson's claims of the number of jobs the NRA has provided.

About the first of the year the NRA estimated "that some 4 million workers have been restored to gainful employment" as a result of the adoption of the codes of fair competition and of the President's reëmployment agreement. By the end of January Gen. Johnson had shaded the claim to 3 million men.

Below Johnson's Estimate.

But now comes Miss Perkins with her January report on employment, in which she estimates only 2 million more persons employed in industry than last March, not to mention last July, when the NRA was established.

The defense of Gen. Johnson is that his reports are more comprehensive than Miss Perkins', that his figures of 3 millions reëmployed are based on the returns from the questionnaires sent to 800,000 employers.

Miss Perkins' report shows that more than two-thirds of those reëmployed got their jobs directly or indirectly from the government. Of 6,555,000 persons returned to work only 2 million were employed by private industry.

Figures on Employment.

The figures are:

Civil works	3,800,000
Private industry	2,000,000
Civilian conservation corps	330,000
Public works	265,000
State road projects	160,000

Both employment and pay roll totals declined in January, though not as much as usual at this season, Miss Perkins says.

"Factory employment decreased by 1.1 per cent and factory pay rolls declined by .8 per cent in January," Secretary Perkins said. "The employment index fell from 70.1 per cent of the 1926 average to 69.3 in January. The pay roll index fell from 49.8 to 49.4. These decreases, it is estimated, represent a release of 70,000 employés from gainful employment in manufacturing industries, and a falling off of $883,000 in weekly pay rolls.

"Marked Seasonal Declines."

"Employment in the nonmanufacturing industries was characterized by marked seasonal declines. Despite a significant increase in anthracite mining and gains in the hotel, telephone and telegraph, power and light, and laundry industries, the large decrease in quarrying, nonmetallic mining, and building construction, coupled with an expected decrease in the retail trade group, reflecting the release of employés engaged for the Christmas trade, resulted in the total employment in the nonmanufacturing fields falling off considerably. The combined decline in employment in the manufacturing and nonmanufacturing industries is estimated to have aggregated approximately 500,000 wage earners and the combined fall in weekly pay rolls approximately $5,400,000.

"The January decline is smaller than is usual at this time of the year, when shutdowns for inventories and repairs are customary. The average decrease in factory employment in January over the last ten years has been 1.4 per cent. The pay roll decline over the same period has averaged 4.6 per cent."

Claims Are Punctured.

Miss Perkins' statistics punctured Gen. Johnson's claim that the decline of employment which began in October would be found to have been reversed in January.

Gen. Johnson claims that the NRA has restored 3 billion dollars of purchasing power. Miss Perkins says that weekly pay roll totals in industry have gained 55 millions since March. Since July, however, when the NRA was established weekly pay roll totals have gone up only 21 millions, indicating an increased purchasing power of 630 millions a little

[Continued on page 6, column 2.]

NEWS SUMMARY

of The Tribune
[And Historical Scrap Book.]

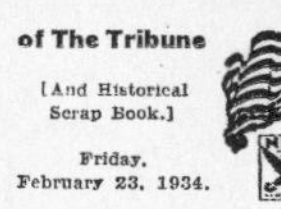

Friday, February 23, 1934.

Average net paid circulation
January 1934
THE CHICAGO TRIBUNE
DAILY in excess of 785,000

FAIR BILLS PASS; READY TO BEGIN 5 MILLION BOOM

Jobs to Be Provided for Thousands.

BY EARL MULLIN.

Preparations for the expansion and perfection of this year's greater World's Fair swung to full speed ahead yesterday following word from Springfield of the unanimous passage by the house of enabling legislation for the 1934 A Century of Progress. The legislation now needs only Gov. Horner's signature to become law and signal the launching of a substantial boom on the lake front.

Within a week, once the governor has signed the bills, the Fair grounds, silent and almost deserted since last November when the 1933 Exposition closed its gates, will become a scene of widespread activity, with 7,500 men working on projects involving the expenditure of more than $5,000,000.

Jobs for Additional Thousands.

Additional thousands will be provided with employment outside of Chicago in manufacturing pursuits and construction projects traceable directly to rehabilitation and expansion of the Fair. It is estimated that for each man employed on Fair projects in Chicago an additional 10 to 15 men will be employed elsewhere.

Rufus C. Dawes, president of the Exposition, and Maj. Lenox R. Lohr, general manager, were in Nashville on their way back to Chicago to take immediate charge of activities after a vacation in the south. Both expressed gratification at the rapid favorable action of the legislature, and promised a thorough, high speed campaign assuring that the 1934 Fair will be complete in the most minute detail when the gates open on June 1.

Lohr Thanks Legislature.

"The legislators are to be commended," Maj. Lohr said, "on the speed with which they passed the enabling acts. I can now promise that the Exposition officials will, in turn, do their part in carrying on in the same speedy manner in the preparation of the Fair. We have more or less rested during the winter, but that is past. We will give Chicago a real Exposition."

Work on contracts totaling $5,200,000, all of which have been contingent on the passing of the legislation, can now get under way. Pending exhibition contracts total $3,200,000 and concessions contracts amount to $2,000,000. At present the Exposition, which unofficial observers last year described as the most international in character of all world fairs, shapes up as a $40,000,000 show. Last year the estimated cost of the production amounted to $37,000,000.

Building Space All Used.

There now is no more space available for additional buildings. All has been contracted for or covered by existing buildings. Approximately 15 per cent of the space in exhibit buildings remains unrented, but several hundred applications are pending. Within a week, Fair officials said yesterday, all of this space will be sold.

Not only does the start of new activity at the Fair presage one of the largest single steps toward economic rejuvenation in Chicago, Fair officials pointed out, but it means a large item in national recovery.

Construction will especially benefit workers in other parts of the country. Large industrial exhibits will need fabricated steel and lumber, shipping service will entail increased employment, and skilled craftsmen will be put at work preparing buildings and exhibitions. The increased employment will be felt throughout the country.

$1,000,000 Ford Exhibit.

Typical of the industrial exhibits which will be important contributing factors in this economic rise is the Ford exhibit and building. This exhibit, on which work will be started within a week, is situated on the old site of Camp Whistler. One hundred tons of steel for the framework already have been contracted for. The estimated cost of the building is $1,000,000.

The General Motors exhibit, contracted for last week, calls for the expenditure of another $1,000,000 for redecorating, landscaping, and the installation of working models. This year's appropriation makes a total of $3,000,000 which the company has spent for participation in A Century of Progress Exposition.

Aside from the Ford exhibit the next largest single unit of construction at the Fair comprises the erection of ten

[Continued on page 8, column 1.]

THE FELLOW WHO STARTED ALL OUR TROUBLES

BLAZE DAMAGES CONVENT HOME OF HOSPITAL NUNS

First last night attacked the convent next door to the John B. Murphy hospital, 620 Belmont avenue, in which Catholic nuns who serve as nurses in the hospital reside. An overwarm heating boiler exploded and sent flames and smoke shooting up through the three floors of the building, which is at 628 Belmont avenue.

Six sisters, including Sister Julia, head of the convent, were asleep. They hurriedly dressed and ran to the hospital to quiet the patients there.

Damage of approximately $2,000 was caused by the flames, which burned a quantity of medical supplies and linens. The fire was confined chiefly to the basement, but some damage was also done to rooms on the first floor.

EATS $5 BILL OFFERED HIM IN NEW DEAL TALK

Denver, Colo., Feb. 22.—(AP)—Deloss Walker, speaker for the national recovery crusade, was explaining to high school pupils here that money doesn't do you any good unless you spend it.

With a flourish Walker pulled a $5 bill from his pocket.

"I'll give this to anybody who'll eat it," he cried.

"I'll eat it!" Harlan Stone, 16, a student, cried right back, and he did.

Walker, somewhat surprised, then explained that if Stone had spent the money for fried chicken it would have been better for his stomach, and in addition would have helped to relieve an overburdened poultry market.

Mallorca to Send 4 Yanks Into "Exile" for 4 Months

MADRID, Feb. 22.—(AP)—Four Americans who were pardoned early this month, after being sentenced to jail for assaulting a civil guard, will be banished from Mallorca for four months only, it was learned tonight in official circles. The four—Mr. and Mrs. Clinton B. Lockwood of West Springfield, Mass.; Roger F. Meade of New York, and Edmund A. Blodgett of Stamford, Conn.—planned to leave Mallorca as soon as their bail has been refunded and to remain in France until the termination of their exile period. The pardons were issued on condition that they leave the Balearics.

Huge Reservoir Bursts in Canary Islands; 8 Drowned

LAS PALMAS, Canary Islands, Feb. 22.—(AP)—Eight persons drowned and great property damage resulted today when a huge reservoir burst. Many inhabitants sought refuge from the waters by climbing trees.

Pu-Yi Declines to Have More than One Wife

(Picture on page 3)

HSINKING [Changchun], Manchukuo, Feb. 22.—(AP)—When Henry Pu-yi drops his civil title of "Mr. Chief Executive" March 1 and becomes emperor of the new Manchurian empire, his wife, Mrs. Elizabeth Pu-yi, will automatically be raised from the position of a commoner to full queenhood.

She is the daughter of a Manchu business man named Jung Yuang, now head of a Manchukuo investment concern here. Little is known to the outside world about her, for it is the tradition and practice in the orient for women in the ruling circles to stay discreetly in the background.

Described as "Manchu Beauty."

Ten years after his dethronement as emperor of all China, Pu-yi selected the present Mrs. Pu-yi as his bride from a group of photographs of "marriageable young ladies" submitted to him by his advisers. She was then described as a "Manchu beauty."

Later, in accordance with Chinese imperial custom, the youthful Manchu nobleman acquired two additional "unofficial wives" or concubines. In the course of time he got rid of these extra wives, largely at the instance of his "No. 1 wife."

It was announced today that when Pu-yi becomes emperor he will lead a "strictly monogamous life," even dispensing with the time honored eunuchs, who have always been employed in all Chinese imperial households to protect the women of the ruler.

Leads Secluded Life.

In her earlier days in Peiping Mrs. Pu-yi received part of her education from two American women, Miss Miriam Ingram and Miss Isabel Ingram, daughters of a Congregational missionary of Philadelphia, from whom she learned English, history, and something about western life. She was described then as modern in her ideas and tastes.

Mrs. Pu-yi has never been seen in public since her husband became chief executive. She leads a secluded, lonely life. The authorities declare that she is in delicate health, never receives visitors, and never appears in public.

In any case, she will not participate in the ceremony March 1.

No Heir to Throne.

The fact that Mr. and Mrs. Pu-yi have no children—especially no male children—has given Manchukuo and Japanese authorities considerable anxiety. When asked how the question of succession would be settled, they told questioners:

"Constitutional means will be found for providing an heir in case the emperor's present wife does not present him with one."

Nab 40 as Plotters.

[Copyright: 1934: By the New York Times.]

MUKDEN, Feb. 22.—Forty Chinese and Russians have been arrested at Harbin accused of plotting to blow up the Sungari river bridge of the Chinese Eastern railway and commit other outrages on March 1 to bring discredit on the Manchukuo government on the day of Henry Pu-yi's enthronement. Official hints make it plain that soviet instigation is suspected.

Fearing other plots engineered from Nanking and Moscow may interfere with the enthronement program, the police and military are taking strict precautions throughout the country. In the new capital their forces have been tripled and strangers are investigated. Even resident newspaper men who are to attend the ceremony have been questioned as to their intentions and attitude.

THE WEATHER

FRIDAY, FEBRUARY 23, 1934.

Sunrise, 6:34; sunset, 5:33. Moon sets at 4:04 a. m. tomorrow. Venus is a morning star.

Chicago and vicinity—Partly cloudy, possibly a snow flurry Friday, followed by colder at night; Saturday generally fair and cold; moderate winds, mostly northwest.

Illinois—Generally fair Friday, followed by colder at night; Saturday probably fair and cold.

TRIBUNE BAROMETER. (SNOW · CLOUDY · FAIR · VERY DRY · STORMY)

TEMPERATURES IN CHICAGO

MAXIMUM, 11 A. M. 23
MINIMUM, 2 A. M. 11

3 a. m. 23	Noon 23	8 p. m. 19
4 a. m. 21	1 p. m. 23	9 p. m. 16
5 a. m. 19	2 p. m. 23	Unofficial—
6 a. m. 18	3 p. m. 22	10 p. m. 15
7 a. m. 18	4 p. m. 22	11 p. m. 14
8 a. m. 18	5 p. m. 21	Midnight ..13
9 a. m. 18	6 p. m. 20	1 a. m. 12
10 a. m. 20	7 p. m. 20	2 a. m. 11
11 a. m. 23		

For 24 hours ended at 7 p. m. Feb. 22:

Mean temperature, 26 degrees; normal, 28 degrees; excess for February, 8 degrees; excess since Jan. 1, 274 degrees.

Precipitation, .02 of an inch; deficiency for February, 1.31 inches; deficiency since Jan. 1, 2.37 inches.

Barometer, 7 a. m., 30.12; 7 p. m., 30.16.

Highest wind velocity, 18 miles an hour from the northwest at 11:32 a. m.

[Official weather table on page 16.]

Prince George Gets Title of "Hail, Mighty Elephant"

KING WILLIAM'S TOWN, South Africa, Feb. 22.—(AP)—To his other titles Prince George tonight was able to add that conferred today by representatives of 600,000 natives in this territory—"Ngangedlovu," or "Hail, Mighty Elephant." Three thousand natives flocked into town as the prince, in the course of his South African tour, attended his first important native gathering.

GANG LEADER MADE ILL, PALS SHAKEN BY VERDICT

Found Guilty on 1st Ballot of Factor Kidnaping.

BY WILLARD EDWARDS.

(Pictures on Back Page.)

Ninety-nine years in the penitentiary was the penalty meted out by a jury early this morning for each of three Touhy gangsters charged with the kidnaping last July 1 of John Factor, wealthy speculator.

Roger Touhy, noted as the merciless leader of the Touhy gang, became ill when the verdict of the jury was read at 12:30 a. m. Gagging and coughing, his handkerchief held to his face, the gangster who once defied the Capone syndicate was assisted from the courtroom of Judge Michael Feinberg.

Jurors Watch Exit.

Solemnly the twelve jurors watched him and his co-defendants, Albert Kator and Gus Schaefer, make their exit. Schaefer was white faced. Kator, known as a cold-blooded gunman and killer, managed a last scornful grimace as he followed his companions.

Less than four hours had been required by the jury to decide upon the guilt of the gangsters. The remainder of the six hours they were in their jury room was occupied by deliberation over the proper penalty. Six of the jurors wished to send the defendants to the electric chair. The 99 year sentence was a compromise.

Write Finis for Gang.

The jury had written finis to the so-called terrible Touhys of the northwest side. Of the once mighty gang which controled all the territory north of Irving Park boulevard in Cook county only two remain at liberty. They are Charles (Ice Wagon) Connors and Ludwig Schmidt.

Hopeless and despairing were the three gangsters in their cells after the verdict had been read. The curly haired Roger Touhy lay stretched on a cot, groaning. Kator and Schaefer snarled feebly at reporters.

Encouraged by Delay.

The returning of the verdict came dramatically. Reports had spread early through the courtroom that the jury had decided upon a guilty verdict, but as the hours sped on with no message from the jury room William Scott Stewart, defense attorney, and his clients took heart.

A crowd gathered. The courtroom swarmed with the curious. Fifteen squads of police mobilized for action. The fifth floor of the Criminal court building, upon which Judge Feinberg's courtroom is located, was cut off by police from the rest of the building. The judge ordered that the defendants be manacled to their guards. There was an air of tense expectancy.

Stewart Is Downcast.

Prosecutor Wilbert F. Crowley, who headed the prosecution; Marshall Kearney, his assistant, and State's Attorney Courtney gathered in the judge's chambers. Outside in the corridor Defense Attorney Stewart talked disconsolately with friends of the Touhy family.

Hope lingered in Stewart despite all the reports from the jury room until at 11:45 p. m. the jurors sent the following significant message to the judge:

"Is 99 years the strongest sentence which can be imposed be-

HERE'S RECORD OF GRIM FATE OF KIDNAPERS

Police and court records show that death or prison has been the lot of kidnapers in more than 90 per cent of the major abduction cases since 1931. Here are the names of these kidnapers and what happened to them:

Charles Y. Abernathy, Negro. Sentenced to 10 years in prison at St. Louis in 1931 for kidnaping Adolphus Busch Orthwein, 13 years old, of the famous family of brewers.

Martin Depew and William Werner, sentenced to life, and **Charles Mele**, sentenced to 35 years early in 1932 at Kansas City for kidnaping the then Mrs. Nell Q. Donnelly, now the wife of former United States Senator James A. Reed.

William Thomas and John Pingera. Sentenced to life imprisonment in Chicago in May, 1932, for kidnaping Dr. Max Gecht.

James W. Betson, Claude Evans, Arlos Stoops, and Cecil Menninger, 25 years each; **Raymond Stoops**, 15 years; **Dwight Bartlett**, 7 years, and **Joseph H. Pursifull and Homer Massey**, 5 years each, at Peoria, for kidnaping Dr. James W. Parker.

Walter McGee, sentenced to electric chair, and his brother, **George McGee**, sentenced to life imprisonment, at Kansas City, in July, 1933, for kidnaping Miss Mary McElroy and collecting $30,000 ransom.

Henry Jennings, shot to death in San Francisco last August while kidnaping William F. Wood, cousin of late President Taft.

Randolph E. Norvell, Percy Fitzgerald, and Mrs. Lillian Chessen, life terms; **Michael Musila**, 20 years, and **Charles Chessen** and **Christ Gitcho**, 5 years each, at Edwardsville, Ill., in October, 1933, for kidnaping August Luer, Alton banker.

Harvey Bailey, Albert Bates, George [Machine Gun] Kelly and **Kelly's** wife, **Kathryn**, and **Mr. and Mrs. R. G. Shannon**; sentenced to life terms at Oklahoma City in October, 1933, for kidnaping Charles F. Urschel.

John M. Holmes and Thomas H. Thurmond, lynched and hanged at San Jose last Nov. 26 by mob for kidnaping and murder of Brooke L. Hart.

Willie Sharkey, Touhy gangster, committed suicide last Dec. 1 in St. Paul jail after his acquittal with others of the gang in the William Hamm kidnaping.

Theodore [Handsome Jack] Klutas, central Illinois kidnaping gang leader, slain by police in hideout in Bellwood on Jan. 6, this year.

Frank B. Souder and Gail Swolley, members of Klutas gang, sentenced to life in Chicago on Jan. 23, this year, for kidnaping James Hackett, Blue Island gambler.

Verne Sankey, hanged himself in a cell at Sioux Falls, S. D., on Feb. 8, this year, while awaiting trial for kidnaping Charles Boettcher of Denver.

Gordon Alcorn, sentenced to life the next day after he pleaded guilty to Boettcher kidnaping.

Charles Mayo, hanged himself yesterday in Chicago police cell after confessing attempt to kidnap E. P. Adler, publisher, of Davenport, Ia.

GOOD NEWS

Today's Tribune should be checked by thrifty housewives who want to save money on their week-end food shopping. Paul Potter has a helpful article on Page 19. On Pages 18, 19, 20, and 21 are food and grocery advertisements which merit your careful attention.

Tune in W-G-N at 2:00 this afternoon for Mary Meade's interesting Food Tips.

World Telegram

SPORTS
LATEST RACING
PRICE THREE CENTS.

Local Forecast:—Cloudy with occasional rain tonight and tomorrow; warmer tonight.

VOL. 66.—NO. 206.—IN TWO SECTIONS—SECTION ONE. NEW YORK, SATURDAY, MARCH 3, 1934. Entered as second-class matter, Post Office, New York, N. Y. * *** ***

DILLINGER FLEES JAIL WITH TOY GUN

MOTHER, CHILD KILLED BY FIRE IN TENEMENT

Three Other Boys Rescued by Passersby from Flat in Second Ave.

ANOTHER FAMILY FLEES

Fatalities Raise Total Resulting from Blazes to 15 in Two Weeks.

Fire Situation.

Mother and child die in east side tenement fire, bringing total fire deaths in two weeks to fifteen.

Tenement House Commissioner Post announces withdrawal of moratorium on violations in effect since 1929, and drafting of new multiple dwelling law.

Legal department reorganized to prosecute violations rigorously.

Mayor La Guardia blames courts for blocking demolition of fire trap tenements.

In the third serious tenement fire in the city in two weeks a mother and the smallest of her four sons were burned to death today when flames swept through a third floor flat at 1,109 Second Ave., between 58th and 59th Sts. The deaths brought the tenement fire fatalties for the two weeks to fifteen, eight persons having perished at 40 E. Seventh St. and five as a result of a fire at 169 Carroll St., Brooklyn.

Tenement House Commissioner Langdon W. Post, active recently in attempts to enforce fire regulations, arrived at the scene of today's fire before firemen had completed their work and made a personal inspection of the old four-story building.

Dozen Violations.

Mr. Post revealed there had been twelve fire violations against the building a year ago which had been dismissed by the former administration as having been complied with. He ordered a reinspection o fthe building for other possible violations.

The victims today were Mrs. Margaret Callas, 38, and her son, John, 3. John's brothers, August, 11, James, 10, and George, 7, were rescued by men who found them all but suffocated in the apartment.

Husband at Work.

Spiros Callas, head of the family, left home about 5 o'clock, about two hours before the fire was discovered, and was in his restaurant around the corner, at 301 E. 59th St., when fire apparatus arrived. He had to be restrained from rushing into the burning building.

Another family, living on the fourth floor, escaped to the roof and to an adjoining building. The father, Joseph Nicholas, was awak-

(Continued on Page Four.)

DROWNS DURING QUAKE

Boy Falls Into Well While Fleeing Chile Shocks.

By the Associated Press.

OSORNO, Chile, March 3.—Freak casualties marked recent earthquakes here.

A boy, fleeing in panic, fell into a well and drowned. A woman living next door to a disinfecting plant was asphyxiated by gases formed from chemicals mixed by the quake. A frightened woman jumped from a window and was gravely hurt.

World-Telegram Index

Mayor Orders Interne to Tell of Failure to Aid a Mother

La Guardia Calls Doctor and Hospital Head to City Hall—Physician Accused of Putting Woman Out of Ambulance on Way to Hospital.

Mayor La Guardia, angered today when he was told that Dr. Robert Warren, interne at the Long Island College Hospital, had ordered a woman removed from an ambulance to a taxicab half an hour before she gave birth to twins at the Cumberland St. Hospital, ordered the interne and his superior, Acting Superintendent Bernard McDermott, to City Hall on thirty minutes' notice.

There they were questioned for nearly two hours by Irving Ben Cooper, special counsel to the Commissioner of Accounts, who sent a transcript of the testimony to Commissioner of Hospitals S. S. Goldwater for consideration.

A report on the incident was taken to City Hall by Carmine Manfredi, unemployed, of 160 Luqueer St., in the Red Hook section of Brooklyn.

Manfredi's wife, Blanche, 24, mother of a 21-month-old child, had received prenatal care at Cumberland St. Hospital and planned to go there to bear an expected child.

Yesterday she was taken ill and asked her sister to summon an ambulance. One was sent from Long Island Hospital. The interne agreed, according to Mrs. Manfredi, to take her to the Cumberland St. Hospital and helped her into the ambulance.

At Court St. and Atlantic Ave., however, he decided the case was not an emergency one and told Mrs. Manfredi and her sister to continue the trip in a taxi.

The ambulance drew up beside a cab, but neither of the women had taxi fare. They saw a neighbor, Mrs. Lily Buomatta, pass by and borrowed $1. Mrs. Manfredi was rushed into the delivery room at the hospital, where twins were born almost immediately.

The Mayor, on hearing the story, called Mr. McDermott on the

(Continued on Page Two.)

POST LAUNCHES FIRE TRAP WAR

Will End Moratorium on Violations and Ask for New Housing Law.

Langdon W. Post, Tenement House Commissioner, moved vigorously today to check the growing toll of tenement house fires.

He withdrew, effective immediately, the moratorium on certain violations which has been in effect since 1929 and declared he would after next week a new multiple dwellings bill aimed at the prompt elimination of fire-traps.

Meanwhile Mayor La Guardia commented caustically on the court decisions whereby demolition of old law tenements was blocked. He said the Second Ave. building should have been razed thirty years ago.

Blames Courts.

"The courts," he asserted, "gave these poor defenseless people the constitutional right to be burned to death. The Legislature called these fire-traps illegal and condemned them, but the courts gave the people the constitutional right to live in them and be burned to death. And we have to respect the courts."

The violations no longer condoned under the moratorium are expected to have a widespread effect. Among things owners now must do, Mr. Post declared, is to build fire resistant ceilings, abolish cooking in apartment hotels unless protected by a sprinkler system and construct staircases leading from the top floor to the roof.

The Commissioner revealed that in scores of tenements only a rope leads from the top floor to the roof.

Post's Statement.

Commenting on the Second Ave. fire, Mr. Post said:—

"It's the same old story of the fire-trap, and there are 67,000 just like it in the city."

Mr. Post revealed he had appointed as Second Deputy Commissioner David A. Ostreicher, who would reorganize the legal division of the department and start a rigorous campaign of prosecuting for violations.

A delegation of the Lower East Side Public Housing Conference presented a demand to the Mayor for slum clearance, model housing at reasonable rentals, strict enforcement of laws and revision of the Multiple Dwellings Law to eliminate the fire-trap.

AMERICAN KILLED IN PERU.

By the Associated Press.

LIMA, Peru, March 3.—The newspaper El Comercio reported today that one American was killed and another critically injured in an oil well explosion at Talara yesterday. J. L. Stauft, 36, died, and A. B. Farmer, 29, lies in a serious condition in the hospital.

DR. DEAN GUILTY; GETS LIFE TERM

Woman Physician Sobs Over Conviction in Poison Highball Murder.

By the Associated Press.

GREENWOOD, Miss., March 3.—Dr. Sarah Ruth Dean, 36-year-old baby specialist, today was convicted of the alleged poison whisky highball death of Dr. John Preston Kennedy, 41. The jury fixed her punishment at life imprisonment at hard labor. It had deliberated thirteen hours and fifty-two minutes.

Tries to Smile.

Obviously shocked, the woman heard the verdict with her hands clenched in her lap. She tried to smile as she arose to go to a waiting room, but broke into sobs. She was followed by women relatives and her attorneys.

Half an hour later, however, she was composed and smiling as she returned for sentence.

Allowed to Go Home.

"The jury has found you guilty of murder and fixed your punishment," Judge Davis said gravely. "It now becomes my duty to sentence you to spend the rest of your natural life at hard labor in the State penitentiary."

The Judge asked if she had anything to say. The smile suddenly gone from her lips, Dr. Dean looked at her attorneys, then shook her head, keeping silent.

"You are under a $10,000 bond, so I am going to let you go home until 2 o'clock," the Judge said. Deputies stepped forward to claim the prisoner.

Widow Rejoices.

As the defendant turned away, Mrs. Bessie Barry Kennedy, widow of the dead surgeon, who charged Dr. Dean with breaking up her home, came into the court room and flung her arms around the neck of District Attorney Arthur Jordan.

"It's the happiest moment of my life," said Dr. Barney Kennedy, brother of the dead man.

Members of the Kennedy family shook hands with the jurors.

VISCOUNT ADARE TO WED

Miss Nancy L. Yuille, of New York, To Be His Bride.

Special to the World-Telegram.

PALM BEACH, Fla., March 3.—Viscount Richard Adare, 46, of London, guest of Charles A. Munn at Villa Amada, and Miss Nancy L. Yuille, of 14 E. 69th St., New York, will be married on Wednesday in Palm Beach, it was announced today.

Miss Yuille is visiting her sister, Mrs. Wolcott Blair, here.

LATEST RACING RESULTS

NEW ORLEANS—1ST—TADCASTER, 4.00, 2.80, 2.20, first; CANTERON, 9.00, 10.00, second; CAPPOQUIN, 10.80, third.

OAKLAWN—1ST—MATURE, DIAN, CORIDA.

HIALEAH—2ND—NEW PIN, 7.90, 5.60, 5.20, 1st; ARBITRARY, 4.90, 4.60, 2nd; UP AND UP, 7.00, 3rd. No scratches.

HIALEAH—3RD—ONE CHANCE 24.40, 11.50, 6.60, 1st; AUNT FLOR 22.40, 9.90, 2nd; KINDACORN, 4.00, 3rd. No scratches.

(Charts on Page 18)

'FRAMED!' CRIES MAN IN HOUSE MAYOR RAIDED

Court Sets Hearing for Monday and Asks for Attendance of Prosecutor's Aid.

DEFENSE WANTS GEOGHAN

Attorney Calls Proceedings "Outrageous" and Asks for District Attorney.

Christian Klosset, whose home was personally raided by Mayor La Guardia Thursday on an anonymous tip that it was a disorderly house, was arraigned in Gates Ave. Court today on a charge of bookmaking.

Klosset and his wife protested that the case was a "frame-up." Defense Counsel John J. Riordan called it "an outrageous proceeding" and said:—

"This man is the subject of persecution as a result of an anonymous letter and people as high as the Mayor of the City of New York have joined hands in this persecution."

Magistrate Gaspar J. Liota fixed bond at $500 and set the hearing for Monday, saying he wanted an Assistant District Attorney to be present.

Wants Geoghan at Hearing.

"I think the District Attorney should be represented here," said Mr. Riordan. "I feel sure that before this is over, the District Attorney will have on his hands an investigation to which he will have to give careful attention."

Plainclotheman Stewart Donnelly alleges that he and Plainclothesman Thomas O'Brien called to see Klosset at his home, 807 Quincy St., Brooklyn, yesterday. The telephone rang. Donnelly alleged, and he heard a man placing a horse race bet with Klosset, so he snatched the telephone. Another call came, he charges, and he answered the phone, accepted a horse race bet from "Mike" and then arrested Klosset.

Mr. and Mrs. Klosset said they had no idea who made the calls. Mrs. Klosset said she had a maid and two guests to testify in her husband's behalf. She said that she tried to trace the calls as soon as they were made, but failed, and so had her telephone disconnected.

Klossets Talk About Raid.

After the hearing, Mr. and Mrs. Klosset talked about the Mayor's personal raid with Chief Inspector Lewis Valentine. They said that Mr. Klosset was lying on a couch downstairs and her husband was resting in bed upstairs when Mayor La Guardia aroused them and without revealing his identity demanded:—

"Are you man and wife? Are you really married?"

"Of course we are," Mrs. Klosset said she replied. The Mayor, she says, then demanded:—

"Well, why do you sleep down here while he sleeps up there? Why don't you both sleep in the same bed?"

She said that Inspector Valentine found a bottle of dark liquid in the icebox and triumphantly announced, "We are told you sell liquor here." The liquid, however, was prune juice.

J.E. HOOVER REJECTS MEDAL

Justice Department Agents' Head Declines Flag Assn. Honor.

By the Associated Press.

WASHINGTON, March 3.—J. Edgar Hoover, chief of the Justice Department's Bureau of Investigation, has declined a medal, awarded him as the person doing the most toward law enforcement in the capital.

He advised the United States Flag Assn., which offered the medal, that it would be against the policy of the department for him to accept.

ASK LUTHER TO BE 'HITLER'

Jews Prepare for German Chancellor's "Trial" at Garden.

Dr. Hans Luther, German Ambassador to the United States, was invited today by the American Jewish Congress to take the part of Hitler at the coming "trial" of the Chancellor in Madison Square Garden next Wednesday.

Samuel Seabury will present the indictment of Hitlerism by civilization. Invited witnesses will include Alfred E. Smth, Mayor La Guardia and Aldermanic President Bernard S. Deutsch.

DIES IN FALL OFF TRAIN.

By the Associated Press.

NEW BRUNSWICK, N. J., March 3.—The body of Howard Trainor, 50, of 91 Nichol Ave., a night supervisor of passenger traffic for the Pullman Co., was found today along the tracks of the Pennsylvania Railroad in Stelton. William H. Jaquie, coroner, of Highland Park, said Trainor had been pushed off the train or had fallen off.

WOMAN JAILER AND FUGITIVE

Sheriff Lillian Holley.

John Dillinger.

Woman Sees Escort Slain by Gunman in Riverside Dr.

Intruder Raps on Parked Car, Growls "Stick 'Em Up" and Fires—Man Falls Dead Against Friend of Childhood Days—Her Screams Summon Aid.

In the dawn mist today Mrs. Lillian Dawson, 29, 62 E. 127th St., attractive divorcee, sat in the front seat of a sedan parked at a secluded spot on Riverside Dr., and in paralyzed horror saw her best friend, a man she had known since childhood, shot to death without warning.

The man, Joseph Arbona, 36, of Bridgeport, Conn., slumped over against her, a bullet through his skull, while the gunman, who had rapped on the window of the sedan and then pushed a .45 automatic against Arbona's mouth and fired, slipped away in the fog to his own car parked a few feet away with the engine running.

Became Lost on Ride.

"I got through work at 9 o'clock last night," Mrs. Dawson told police.

"I am a telephone operator. I met Mr. Arbona at 9:40 at 125th St. and Lenox Ave. I got into his car, and we drove to the Valencia restaurant at 116th St. and Lenox Ave. and had coffee. Then we said we'd ride to Washington Bridge, but we got lost and we rode for several hours.

"Finally we got back to the Drive and we were sitting under an arc light. He was on my left side. I was turned, facing him. We were talking about his eventual return to Spain, to his home town in Spain.

Stick 'em up, Buddy"

"I noticed another car drive up. A man got out. He walked toward us. I believe there were two other men in the car. This man came to the window and he said, 'Stick 'em up, buddy.' Mr. Arbona said, 'Oh! Oh!'

"And then the shot came. I jumped out into the road and waved my hat. The first car, with two people in it, wouldn't stop. Then three boys came and I said, 'Hold-up! Help me get this man to a hospital.'

"They went to get a policeman and the policeman drove Mr. Arbona to the hospital.

"As for myself, I met my husband, Harry Dawson, eight years ago in Newark. We couldn't get along, so we separated three years ago. I thought he was in Newark, but I am told he is in Oklahoma. He is a metal lath worker."

Three young men on their way home from a basketball game heard

(Continued on Page Four.)

REPORT PARIS SEEKS U. S. DEBT SOLUTION

Early Discussion by Doumergue Cabinet Expected.

By the Associated Press.

PARIS, March 3.—The Doumergue government today was reported seriously considering how the question of debts owed the United States may be settled.

It was thought likely that the entire matter may be discussed by the Cabinet as soon as pressing domestic questions can be settled.

Both the Foreign Office and the Ministry of Finance are eager for the debts to be settled either by some kind of symbolic payment or a payment after negotiations. The attitude of the rest of the Ministry, however, is undetermined.

MISS INGALLS AT DAYTONA

Woman Flier, Thought Missing, Continues Flight Southward.

By the Associated Press.

DAYTONA BEACH, March 3.—Laura Ingalls, New York woman flier for whom fears were expressed after she took off from Charleston, S. C., yesterday for Jacksonville en route for South America, stopped at the airport here at 10 A. M. today, gassed up and flew on southward, airport officials reported. Later she flew on to Miami.

POLICE CAPTAINS SHIFTED.

Police Captain Brooks Gulgar was transferred today from the Central Park station to New Drop, S. I.; Captain George Rennsaeler was transferred from New Drop to Queensborough Bridge precinct, and Captain John Hammil from the Queensborough Bridge precinct to the Greenwich St. station.

RINGLINGS SUIT FILED.

By the Associated Press.

SARASOTA, Fla., March 3.—Suit for divorce from Emily Ringling, his second wife, was filed in Circuit Court here today by an attorney for John Ringling, circus magnate.

HOSTAGES SEIZED BY BANK ROBBER, RELEASED LATER

Hunted by Many Posses in Three States After Breaking Out of "Escape-proof" Indiana Institution Headed by Woman Sheriff.

GUARD COWED BY WOODEN PISTOL

Notorious Desperado Is Accompanied by Negro Slayer in His Flight—Fugitives Reported Seen 15 Miles from Chicago.

By the United Press.

CROWN POINT, Ind., March 3.—John Dillinger, one of the most dangerous desperadoes ever to terrorize the Middle West, made an amazing escape from the county jail today with the aid of a wooden pistol. A huge police force was immediately mobilized to recapture him under orders to shoot to kill.

The man who was known as Public Enemy No. 1 in Chicago, fled in an automobile owned by the countys' woman sheriff, Mrs. Lillian Holley. He carried with him two hostages and a Negro murderer.

Armed with two machine guns and a pistol, Dillinger headed north out of Crown Point. Within an hour three States were spreading a net in which they hoped to trap the desperate fugitive.

Hostages Freed in Illinois.

Soon after the escape, carried out in defiance of the extra guards posted by the woman sheriff, the car carrying Dillinger and a Negro accomplice was sighted near Peotone, Ill., east of here.

Ernest Blunt, the guard who was intimidated by Dillinger's makeshift imitation of a gun and who was taken with the desperado in the sheriff's car, was thrown out of the car near Peotone and was found by Ed Rust, a farmer. With him was the night mechanic at the Main St. garage from which Dillinger and his accomplice stole the sheriff's car.

The two immediately joined a hurriedly organized posse and started in pursuit of the desperado.

Takes Jail Keys With Him

In Indiana, Illinois and Michigan highways were patrolled and the entire populace was looking for the bad man who escaped from one of the heaviest guards ever placed over a criminal.

Officers and posses throughout this immediate territory led the search for the desperado with orders to shoot to kill on sight. Authorities recognized the fact that Dillinger, with his armament, is ready to kill any person who stands in his way.

The city of Crown Point was thrown into confusion by the escape. Dillinger walked out of the jail at 9:30 A. M., carrying the jail keys away, having locked up the woman sheriff who had boasted he would never escape, and her deputies, before entering a nearby garage. They also had secured real weapons after overpowering a guard with a fake pistol, officials said.

Garage Held Up

In the garage he and John Youngblood, the Negro murderer, trained their guns on attendants.

"One move out of you," snarled the Midwest's most notorious bad man, "and I'll blow your heads off!"

With Dillinger and Youngblood was Blunt, apparently taken along as a hostage.

They forced Ed Saager, a mechanic, to get behind the wheel of the woman Sheriff's car. They piled into the back seat, Dillinger still menacing the other garage employes with one of his machine guns.

"Let's get out of here!" he commanded.

Saager backed the car from the garage into the street and roared away northward.

The city was stunned by the recklessness of the man who, when

(Continued on Page Two.)

INSULL MUST LEAVE, SAYS GREEK MINISTER

Orders Immediate Expulsion as Grace Expires.

By the United Press.

ATHENS, March 3.—Foreign Minister James Maximos today notified the Ministry of Interior that Samuel Insull must be made to leave Greece at once.

Insull's fifteen-day period of grace, granted him as an extension of a previous expulsion order because of ill health, expires today.

Insull has been isolated at his hotel and has denied himself to visitors on the plea that he is gravely ill. He must seek refuge in some other country or return to the United States to face trial.

"IT'S A BOY!" DAD DIES

Young Father Slips, Fractures Skull Celebrating Birth.

By the Associated Press.

WHEELING, W. Va., March 3.—"It's a boy!" a beaming nurse told John Ward, 32, in a hospital here.

Overcome with joy, Ward capered about the corridor. He slipped, fell to the floor, and fractured his skull. A few hours later, before he had even seen his new son, he died.

Mother and son were "doing nicely." Mrs. Ward had not been informed of her husband's death.

LINER CAUGHT IN ICE

Providence-New York Steamer Trapped in Sound.

By the Associated Press.

NEW LONDON, March 3.—The steamship Lexington, operating on the Providence-New York run, was caught in heavy ice on Long Island Sound today, five miles west of the Cornfield Lightship. A lighthouse tender went to her assistance.

ARIZONA TO MOBILIZE

State Guard to Bar Water Encroachment by California.

By the Associated Press.

PHOENIX, Ariz., March 3.—Governor B. B. Moeur announced today he would call out national guardsmen to protect this State's rights from encroachment on the Parker Diversion Dam on the Colorado River. Governor Moeur plans to accompany the troops into the field.

The Weather.

(Official United States Forecast.)

New York and metropolitan area: Cloudy with occasional rain tonight and tomorrow; warmer tonight, moderate southwest to south winds.

Lowest temperature expected tonight:—50.

New Jersey:—Cloudy, probably occasional rain tonight and tomorrow; somewhat warmer tomorrow.

Connecticut:—Cloudy, probably occasional rain tonight and tomorrow; mild temperature tomorrow.

Seaboard:—Light southerly winds are general except fresh from Delaware Breakwater to Nantucket.

TODAY'S TEMPERATURES.

Midnight	38	8 A. M.	44
1 A. M.	37	9 A. M.	41
2 A. M.	38	10 A. M.	41
3 A. M.	40	11 A. M.	45
4 A. M.	42	12 Noon	45
5 A. M.	42	1 P. M.	46
6 A. M.	43	2 P. M.	48
7 A. M.	44		

Highest and lowest temperatures a year ago:—42-34.

Additional weather data on page 2.

Chicago Sunday Tribune

March 25, 1934

W A N T E D

IF YOU SEE ANY OF THESE FUGITIVES, NOTIFY THE NEAREST POLICE OFFICER

WANTED FOR MURDER.
SYDNEY RANDALL; age 26 yrs.; height 5 ft. 9 in.; weight 140; blue eyes; light brown hair; sometimes works as a radio mechanic. His girl friend had this picture of him in her room.

WANTED FOR MURDER—KILLING A POLICEMAN.
STANLEY GRACYAS, alias Stanley Mike; age 30 yrs.; height 5 ft. 7 in.; weight 155 lbs.; dark brown hair.

WANTED FOR KIDNAPING.
FRANK (PORKY) DILLON; age 38 yrs.; height 5 ft. $9\frac{1}{2}$ in.; weight 178 lbs.; gray eyes; dark hair.

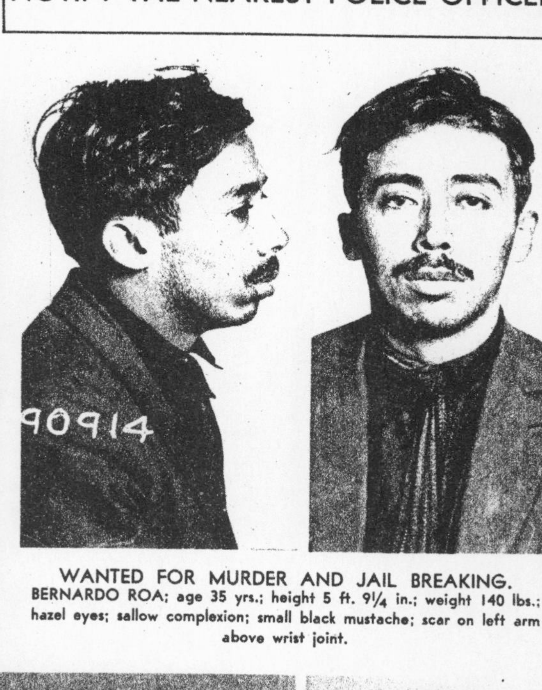

WANTED FOR MURDER AND JAIL BREAKING.
BERNARDO ROA; age 35 yrs.; height 5 ft. $9\frac{1}{4}$ in.; weight 140 lbs.; hazel eyes; sallow complexion; small black mustache; scar on left arm above wrist joint.

WANTED FOR KILLING A POLICEMAN.
WILLIAM NEVERASKI; age 28 yrs.; height 5 ft. $9\frac{1}{2}$ in.; weight 196 lbs.; hazel eyes; medium chestnut hair; tattoo: dagger piercing heart right forearm; mole under left lobe.

WANTED FOR MURDER AND JAIL BREAKING.
TOMMIE O'CONNOR; age 43 yrs.; height 5 ft. $7\frac{1}{4}$; weight 136 lbs.; medium chestnut hair; hazel and greenish blue eyes; scar left ring finger; mole on left wrist; scar above left ear; scar over left eyebrow.

WANTED FOR MURDER—KILLING A POLICEMAN.
HYMAN SINNENBERG; age 23 yrs.; 5 ft. 5 in.; weight 145 lbs.; medium chestnut hair; gray blue eyes; both hands burned on palms and rear.

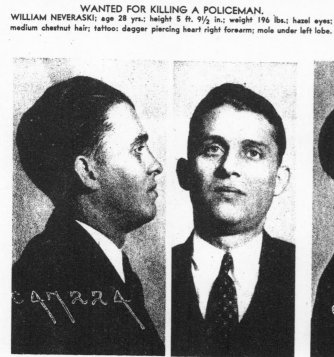

WANTED FOR MURDER.
FRANK NEFF; age 31 yrs.; height 5 ft. $7\frac{3}{4}$ in.; weight 130; dark chestnut hair; blue eyes; vertical scar on left side of chin; tattoo: dagger piercing heart on right arm.

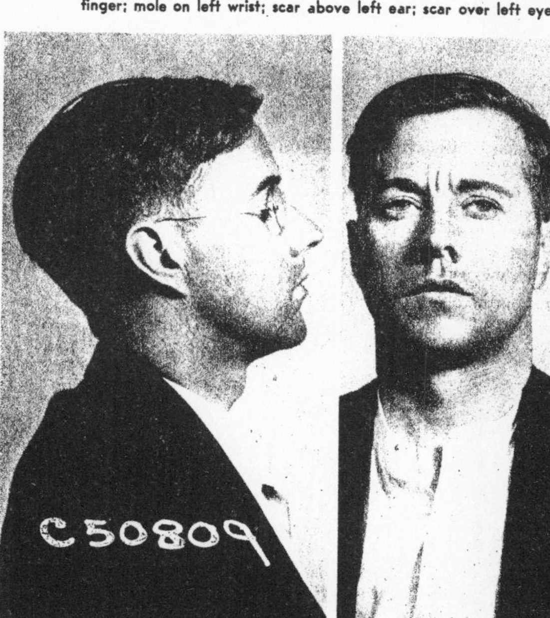

WANTED FOR MURDER.
MATHEW BREEN; age 30 yrs.; height 5 ft. $7\frac{1}{2}$ in.; weight 152 lbs.; blue eyes; dark hair; scar on left side of forehead; scar over eyebrows.

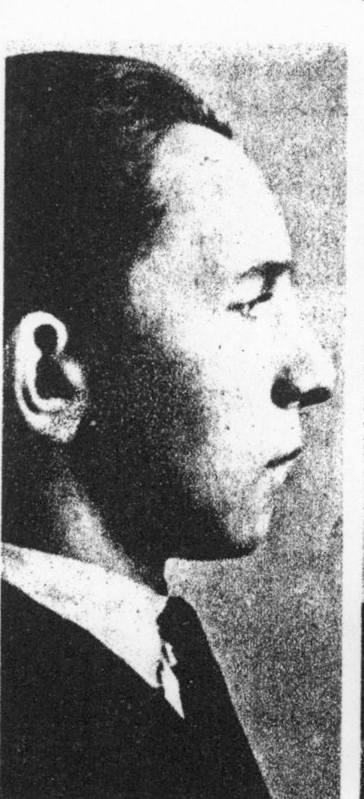

WANTED FOR MURDER AND ROBBERY.
WASIL J. MELENCHUCK, alias William J. Marks, alias Richard W. Strong; age 31 yrs.; height 5 ft. 8 in.; weight 165 lbs.; dark hair; brown eyes; scar near center left eyebrow; tattoo: dagger piercing flesh left forearm.

Weather
Rain east, possibly west today; warmer.
Detailed Weather on Page 4, Sec. 1.

St. Paul Sunday Pioneer Press

SUNDAY EDITION OF THE ST. PAUL DISPATCH

Telegraph
Local News
Editorial Page
Financial
Call of the Open

VOL. 81. NO. 91. | Associated Press News Service. | ST. PAUL, MINN., SUNDAY, APRIL 1, 1934. | Final City Edition. | PRICE TEN CENTS IN ST. PAUL

DILLINGER NAMED AS GUNMAN HERE

Six Found Slain in Ransacked Home

DARES POLICE BY RETURN TO SCENE OF BATTLE, DRIVING SAME AUTO USED IN ESCAPE

Boy Sees Desperado Who Fled in Hail of Bullets Get Out of Car Near Apartment House; Fingerprints and Photograph Give Clues to Identity; Pal Believed to Be John Hamilton.

MONEY PAID FOR NEW AUTO SOUGHT IN BELIEF IT MAY BE RANSOM CASH

Definite information that one of the two men who fled from an apartment at 93 South Lexington avenue Saturday morning after a gun battle with Department of Justice agents and a city detective is John Dillinger, notorious desperado, was given the Pioneer Press from a reliable source Saturday night.

The second man is believed to be John Hamilton, Dillinger's chief lieutenant.

A short time before this information was received one of the escaped gunmen, believed to be Dillinger, with cool insolence and complete disregard of police and Federal men who swarmed about the building, drove back to the apartment house. This daring was cited by police as characteristic of Dillinger.

Neither Thomas E. Dahill, St. Paul police chief, nor Werner Hanni, Department of Justice agent in charge here, would confirm the report that one of the men had been positively identified as Dillinger, but from other sources word came which left little or no doubt as to the information.

Fingerprints found in the apartment and on one of the automobiles left behind by the gunmen were said to have checked with those on file as Dillinger's. Bertillon pictures also were used in establishing the identification.

In addition, a photograph found in the apartment was believed to have been of Dillinger and one cherished by him. It was of a young man about 20 years old, in sailor's uniform, and the face bore a strong resemblance to the desperado.

Two persons observed a man believed to have been one of the escaped gunmen who brazenly returned to the apartment shortly after 2 P. M., less than four hours after the suspects had shot their way out. One was Charles Coffey, 14-year-old son of Daniel Coffey, proprietor of the building.

SAME CAR, BOY ASSERTS.

The boy told officers it was the same man and that his car was the same large green Hudson sedan in which the gunner and a man and woman companion made their escape earlier in the day after shooting their way from the place.

J. P. Burke who lives at the apartment building, also identified the man who returned.

"I saw the man as well as the boys. The Department of Justice men were carrying a bunch of grips from the building. When I saw them I yelled that the man had just jumped into his car and sped around the corner."

The apartment is less than a block from the place where Edward G. Bremer was kidnaped for $200,000 ransom January 17.

Hanni, his officers and a number of St. Paul police who were in the place left immediately in cars, driving southward on Lexington avenue, the direction young Coffey told the officers the car had gone.

WALKS TOWARD APARTMENT.

A checkup with other witnesses about the place showed that the man drove his sedan up in front of the residence of Dr. W. H. Hengstler, 1120 Lincoln avenue, less than a block from the apartment, parked it and started to walk eastward on Lincoln avenue toward the apartment.

Observing a group of Department of Justice agents carrying clothing and household goods from the building to their autos, the man turned around, sauntered back to his car and stopped. Then he reached down, petted a chow dog, property of the Hengstler family, and walked toward the Hengstler front door.

Changing his mind, he sauntered out to his auto said: "Hello, boys," to the group of youths walking past, got in and drove eastward on Lincoln avenue.

Stopping for the arterial highway at Lexington, within a few feet of the Department of Justice cars, he gazed quietly at them, started his car, turned southward on Lexington avenue and sped away.

Information that authorities are satisfied that the two escaped gunmen are Dillinger and Hamilton was substantiated when Chicago police announced, according to the Associated Press, that they had been warned by St. Paul police that these two outlaws might be on the way to Illinois from here. Hamilton was partially identified by a description given by Mrs. Coffey, wife of the apartment proprietor.

Chief Dahill also disclosed that the identification numbers on both captured machines guns have been filed off. The numbers of the guns stolen by Dillinger from the jail at Crown Point, Ind., are known and the natural resource of Dillinger would be to file them off.

Seek Clue in Gun Numbers.

Chief Dahill said that the guns taken here will be subjected to a heat and chemical process which ordinarily is successful in revealing numbers of automobile engines that are mutilated or ground off. If the numbers can be brought out by this process, it will provide an important link in proving the identity of the two desperate gunmen here.

Hanni gave orders to proprietors of the apartment and others not to answer questions by newspapers or others but to refer all questions to him. He refused to answer any questions. His agents, assisted by police, removed from the place all clothing and household materials that might belong to the occupants or have fingerprints on them. These, with two submachine guns and other firearms found in the apartment, were taken to the headquarters of the Department of Justice in the Federal building.

The small coupe which the desperadoes abandoned in their flight was hauled to the Public Safety building where fingerprint expert began a minute study of its entire interior and exterior for print

Other steps being taken by the officers were:

A check was being made on all persons having any dealings with the autos used by the gang.

Officers were making arrangements to trace and impound $1,700 in $5, $10 and $20 bills paid by members of the gang Friday for the new Hudson car in which they escaped. These were to be checked against lists of kidnap ransom funds and bank robbery loot in various crimes.

Search was instituted in St. Paul for another mysterious auto. Police squads were ordered by radio to pick up the car and occupants and were warned to use care because the occupants "are heavily armed and will shoot on sight." This was broadcast a second time after the second appearance of the Hudson sedan at the Lexington avenue apartment. The car was described as a Ford sedan bearing 1934 Minnesota license, B413-975.

At the office of the secretary of state, it was said these plates

(Please Turn to Page 2, Col. 4.)

GANGSTERS AND GETAWAY SCENES

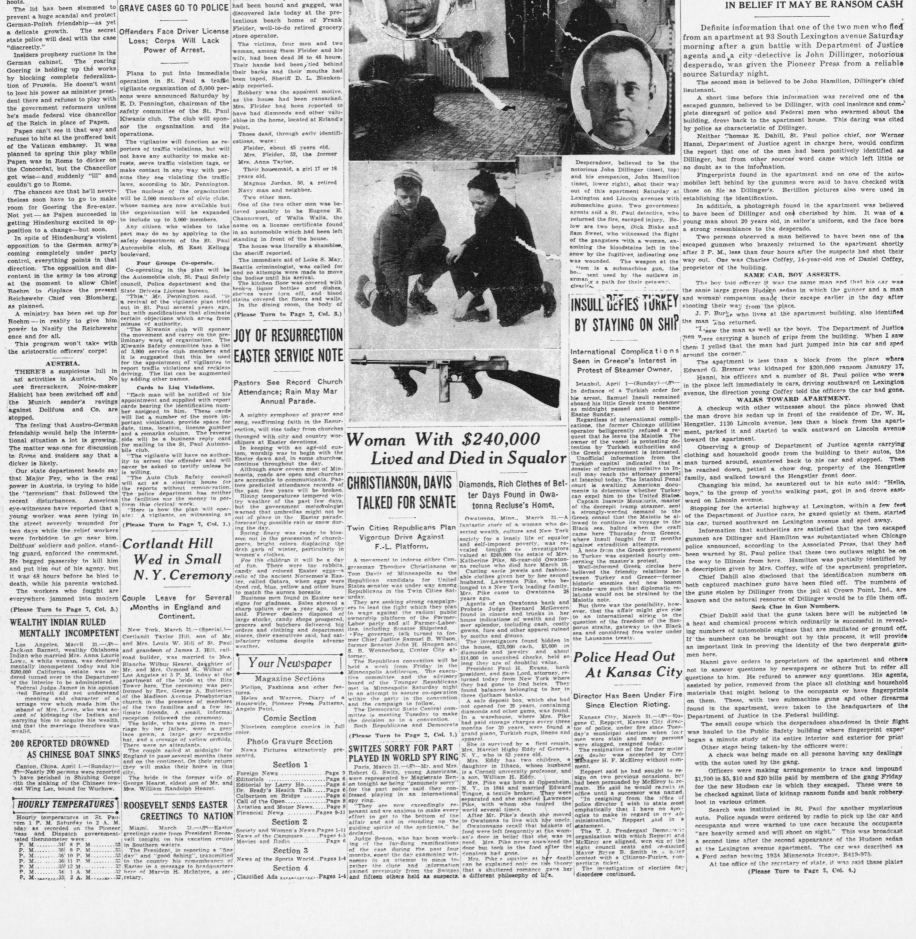

Desperadoes, believed to be the notorious John Dillinger (inset, top) and his companion, John Hamilton (inset, lower right), shot their way out of this apartment Saturday at Lexington and Lincoln avenues with submachine guns. Two government agents and a St. Paul detective, who returned the fire, escaped injury. Below are two boys, Dick Blake and Sam Sweet, who witnessed the flight of the gangsters with a woman, examining the bloodstains left in the snow by the fugitives, indicating one was wounded. The weapon at the bottom is a submachine gun, the armament used by the outlaws in clearing a path for their getaway.

The World In Review

News Behind the News.

GERMANY.

A $20,000,000 subsidy has gone from the German government exchequer to Henschel & Son, locomotive builders, for construction of super high-speed steam airplane engines. The type originated in the air ministry, has been handed over to Henschel for experimentation, and, according to insiders, is nearing perfection.

The Johannistal factory is guarded like a mint. Recently a Polish colonel was arrested there for espionage and several highly placed Germans were found in cahoots.

The lid has been slammed to prevent a huge scandal and protect German-Polish friendship—as yet a delicate growth. The secret state police will deal with the case "discreetly."

Insiders prophesy ructions in the German cabinet. The roaring Goering is holding up the works by blocking complete federalization of Prussia. He doesn't want to lose his power as minister president there and refuses to play with the government reformers unless he's made federal vice chancellor of the Reich in place of Papen.

Papen can't see it that way and refuses to bite at the proffered bait of the Vatican embassy. It was planned to spring this play while Papen was in Rome to dicker on the Concordat, but the Chancellor got wise—and suddenly "ill" and couldn't go to Rome.

The chances are that he'll nevertheless soon have to go to make room for Goering the fire-eater. Not yet—as Papen succeeded in getting Hindenburg excited in opposition to a change—but soon.

In spite of Hindenburg's violent opposition to the German army's coming completely under party control, everything points in that direction. The opposition and discontent in the army is too strong at the moment to allow Chief Roehm to displace the present Reichswehr Chief von Blomberg, as planned.

A ministry has been set up for Roehm—in reality to give him power to Nazify the Reichswehr once and for all.

This program won't take with the aristocratic officers' corps!

AUSTRIA.

THERE'S a suspicious lull in Nazi activities in Austria. No more firecrackers. Noise-maker Habicht has been switched off and the Munich sender's ravings against Dollfuss and Co. are stopped.

The feeling that Austro-German friendship would help the international situation a lot is growing. The matter was one for discussion in Rome and insiders say that a dicker is likely.

Our state department heads say that Major Fey, who is the real power in Austria, is trying to hide the "terrorism" that followed the recent disturbances. American eye-witnesses have reported that a young worker was seen lying in the street severely wounded for two days while the relief workers were forbidden to go near him. Dollfuss' soldiers and police, standing guard, enforced the command. He begged passersby to kill him and put him out of his agony, but it was 48 hours before he bled to death, while his parents watched.

The workers who fought are everywhere jammed into modern

(Please Turn to Page 7, Col. 5.)

WEALTHY INDIAN RULED MENTALLY INCOMPETENT

Los Angeles, March 31.—(AP)—Jackson Barnett, wealthy Oklahoma Indian who married Mrs. Anna Laurie Lowe, a white woman, was declared mentally incompetent today and his $890,000 California estate was ordered turned over to the Department of the Interior to be administered.

Federal Judge James in his opinion said Barnett did not understand the meaning and character of a marriage vow which made him the husband of Mrs. Lowe, who was accused of kidnaping the Indian and marrying him to acquire his wealth, and that the marriage therefore was invalid.

200 REPORTED DROWNED AS CHINESE BOAT SINKS

Canton, China, April 1.—(Sunday)—(AP)—Nearly 200 persons were reported to have perished in Shiuhing Gorge with the sinking of the Chinese towboat Wing Lee, bound for Wuchow.

HOURLY TEMPERATURES

Hourly temperatures in St. Paul from 1 P. M. Saturday to 2 A. M. today as recorded on the Pioneer Press and Dispatch government-tested thermometer were:

P. M.	34	8 P. M.	33
P. M.	36	9 P. M.	33
P. M.	36	10 P. M.	33
P. M.	36	11 P. M.	33
P. M.	35	12 M.	32
P. M.	34	1 A. M.	33
P. M.	33	2 A. M.	32

5,000 TRAFFIC VIGILANTES TO OPERATE HERE

Kiwanis Club Sponsors Organization Which Will Report Violations.

GRAVE CASES GO TO POLICE

Offenders Face Driver License Loss; Corps Will Lack Power of Arrest.

Plans to put into immediate operation in St. Paul a traffic vigilante organization of 5,000 persons were announced Saturday by E. D. Pennington, chairman of the safety committee of the St. Paul Kiwanis club. The club will sponsor the organization and its operations.

The vigilantes will function as reporters of traffic violations, but will not have any authority to make arrests, serve traffic violation tags, or make contact in any way with persons they see violating the traffic laws, according to Mr. Pennington.

The nucleus of the organization will be 3,000 members of civic clubs, whose names are now available but the organization will be expanded to include up to 5,000 members.

Any citizen who wishes to take part may do so by applying to the safety department of the St. Paul Automobile club, 85 East Kellogg boulevard.

Four Groups Co-operate.

Co-operating in the plan will be the Automobile club, St. Paul Safety council, Police department and the State Drivers License bureau.

"This," Mr. Pennington said, "is a revival of the vigilante plan tried out in St. Paul several years ago, but with modifications that eliminate certain objections which arose from misuse of authority.

"The Kiwanis club will sponsor the movement and carry on the preliminary work of organization. The Kiwanis Safety committee has a list of 3,000 service club members and it is suggested that this be used for the appointment of vigilantes to report traffic violations and reckless driving. The list can be augmented by adding other names.

Cards to List Violations.

"Each man will be notified of his appointment and supplied with report cards bearing the identification number assigned to him. These cards will list a number of the more important violations, provide space for date, time, location, license number and a remarks column. The reverse side will be a business reply card for mailing to the St. Paul Automobile club.

"The vigilante will have no authority to arrest the offender and will never be asked to testify unless he is willing.

"The Auto Club Safety council will act as a clearing house for the reports without remuneration. The police department has neither the facilities nor the money to perform this clerical work.

"Here is how the plan will operate: A vigilante, on witnessing an

(Please Turn to Page 7, Col. 1.)

Cortlandt Hill Wed in Small N. Y. Ceremony

Couple Leave for Several Months in England and Continent.

New York, March 31.—(Special.)—Cortlandt Taylor Hill, son of Mr. and Mrs. Louis W. Hill of St. Paul and grandson of James J. Hill, railroad builder, was married to Mrs. Blanche Wilbur Hearst, daughter of Mr. and Mrs. Ormond K. Wilbur of Los Angeles at 5 P. M. today at the apartment of the bride at the Ritz Tower here. The ceremony was performed by Rev. George A. Buttericks of the Madison Avenue Presbyterian church in the presence of members of the two families and a few intimate friends. A small, informal reception followed the ceremony.

The bride, who was given in marriage by her father, wore a grey lace gown, a large grey organdie hat, and a corsage of yellow orchids. There were no attendants.

The couple sailed at midnight for England to pass several months there and on the continent. On their return they will make their home in this city.

The bride is the former wife of George Hearst, eldest son of Mr. and Mrs. William Randolph Hearst.

ROOSEVELT SENDS EASTER GREETINGS TO NATION

Miami, March 31.—(AP)—Easter greetings came from President Roosevelt tonight on his vacation cruise in Southern waters.

The President, in reporting a "fine day" and "good fishing," transmitted to the country his remembrance of Easter in a message to headquarters here of Marvin H. McIntyre, a secretary.

Victims Tied, Gagged and Shot to Death

Pretentious House of Well-to-Do Bremerton, Wash., Couple Ransacked.

Bremerton, Wash., March 31.—(AP)—A grim tragedy, the shooting to death of six persons after they had been bound and gagged, was discovered late today at the pretentious beach home of Frank Fleider, well-to-do retired grocery store operator.

The victims, four men and two women, among them Fleider and his wife, had been dead 36 to 48 hours. Their hands had been tied behind their backs and their mouths had been taped, Sheriff D. L. Blankenship reported.

Robbery was the apparent motive, as the house had been ransacked. Mrs. Fleider had been reported to have had diamonds and other valuables in the home, located at Erland's Point.

Those dead, through early identifications, were:

Fleider, about 45 years old.

Mrs. Fleider, 32, the former Mrs. Anna Taylor.

Their housemaid, a girl 17 or 18 years old.

Magnus Jordan, 50, a retired Navy man and neighbor.

Two other men.

One of the two other men was believed possibly to be Eugene E. Channowort, of Walla Walla, the name on a license certificate found in an automobile which had been left standing in front of the house.

The house was literally a shambles, the sheriff reported.

The immediate aid of Luke S. May, Seattle criminologist, was called for and no attempts were made to move the bodies until his arrival.

The kitchen floor was covered with broken liquor bottles and dishes, shelves were torn off, and blood stains covered the floors and walls.

In the dining room, the body of

(Please Turn to Page 2, Col. 3.)

JOY OF RESURRECTION EASTER SERVICE NOTE

Pastors See Record Church Attendance; Rain May Mar Annual Parade.

A mighty symphony of prayer and song, reaffirming faith in the Resurrection, will rise today from churches thronged with city and country worshipers at Easter devotions.

In keeping with an age-old custom, worship was to begin with the Easter dawn and, in some churches, continue throughout the day.

Although snow covers most of Minnesota, roads are open and churches are accessible to communicants. Pastors predicted attendance records of the past few years will be broken.

Rising temperatures tempered wintry weather of the past few days, but the government meteorologist warned that umbrellas might not be out of place in the Easter parade, forecasting possible rain or snow during the day.

Spring finery was ready to blossom out in the procession of churchgoers, bright colors displacing the drab garb of winter, particularly in women's clothes.

For the children it will be a day of fun. There were toy rabbits, candy and colored Easter eggs—a relic of the ancient Norsemen's Easter, called Ostara, when eggs were dyed red, blue, yellow and other hues to match the aurora borealis.

Business men found in Easter new signs for gladness. Sales showed a sharp upturn over a year ago, they said. Flower dealers disposed of large stocks, candy shops prospered, grocers and butchers delivered big orders and clothing and department stores, their executives said, had satisfactory volume despite adverse weather.

Your Newspaper

Woman With $240,000 Lived and Died in Squalor

CHRISTIANSON, DAVIS TALKED FOR SENATE

Twin Cities Republicans Plan Vigorous Drive Against F.-L. Platform.

A movement to indorse either Congressman Theodore Christianson or Tom Davis of Minneapolis as the Republican candidate for United States senator was under way among Republicans in the Twin Cities Saturday.

They are seeking strong campaigners to lead the fight which they plan to wage against the radical public ownership platform of the Farmer-Labor party and all Farmer-Laborites, including Senator Shipstead.

For governor, talk turned to former Chief Justice Samuel B. Wilson, former Senator John H. Hougen and S. B. Wennerberg, Center City attorney.

The Republican convention will be held a week from Friday in the Minneapolis Auditorium. The executive committee and the advisory board of the Younger Republicans met in Minneapolis Saturday night in an attempt to assure co-operation within the party in the convention and the campaign to follow.

The Democratic State Central committee is meeting Tuesday to make the decision as to a convention.

Both Republicans and Democrats

(Please Turn to Page 2, Col. 1.)

SWITZES SORRY FOR PART PLAYED IN WORLD SPY RING

Paris, March 31.—(AP)—Mr. and Mrs. Robert G. Switz, young Americans, were represented by Magistrate Benon tonight as being "genuinely sorry" for the part police said they confessed playing in an international spy ring.

"They are now exceedingly repentant and are anxious to make every effort to get to the bottom of the affair and aid in rounding up the guiding spirits of the syndicate," he declared.

Judge Benon, who has been working of the far-flung ramifications of the case during the past four months, spent the day examining witnesses in an attempt to piece together the clues and information received previously from the Switzes and fifteen others held as suspects.

Diamonds, Rich Clothes of Better Days Found in Owatonna Recluse's Home.

Owatonna, Minn., March 31.—A fantastic story of a woman who deserted wealth, culture and New York society for a lonely life of squalor and self-imposed poverty, was revealed tonight as investigators valued at $240,000 the estate of Mrs. Katherine Pike, 80-year-old Owatonna recluse who died here March 10.

Casting aside jewels and fashionable clothes given her by her second husband, Lawrence Pike, who belonged to a New York leading family, Mrs. Pike came to Owatonna 28 years ago.

Agents of an Owatonna bank and Probate Judge Bernard McGovern found in closets and trunks in her house indications of wealth and former splendor, including cash, costly gowns, furs and other apparel ruined by moths and disuse.

The investigators found hidden in the house, $23,000 cash, $3,000 in diamonds and jewelry and about $14,000 in uncashed checks, held so long they are of doubtful value.

President Paul H. Evans, bank president, and Sam Lord, attorney, returned today from New York where they had gone to find heirs. They found balances belonging to her in three Gotham banks.

A safe deposit box, which she had not opened for 29 years, containing diamonds and other gems, was found. In a warehouse, where Mrs. Pike had paid storage charges every three months for 30 years, were found a grand piano, Turkish rugs, linens and apparel.

She is survived by a first cousin, Mrs. Harriet Higby Eddy of Geneva, N. Y., who is 83 years old.

Mrs. Eddy has two children, a daughter in Ithaca, whose husband is a Cornell university professor, and a son, William H. Eddy.

Mrs. Pike was born at Oppenheim, N. Y., in 1846 and married Edward Tingue, a textile broker. They were separated and she married Lawrence Pike, with whom she toured the world several times.

After Mr. Pike's death she moved to Owatonna to live with her uncle. Owatonnans recall that baskets of food were left frequently at the woman's door in belief that she was in need. Mrs. Pike never answered the door but took in the food after the donaters had gone.

Mrs. Pike's squalor at her death can be explained only on the theory that a shattered romance gave her a different philosophy of life.

INSULL DEFIES TURKEY BY STAYING ON SHIP

International Complications Seen in Greece's Interest in Protest of Steamer Owner.

Istanbul, April 1—(Sunday)—(AP)—In defiance of a Turkish order for his arrest, Samuel Insull remained aboard his little Greek tramp steamer as midnight passed and it became Easter Sunday.

Regardless of international complications, the former Chicago utilities operator belligerently refused a request that he leave the Maiotis. The owner of the vessel is protesting detention by Turkish authorities and the Greek government is interested.

Unofficial information from the Turkish capital indicated that a dossier of information relative to Insull may reach the attorney general at Istanbul today. The Istanbul Penal court is awaiting American documents to determine whether Turkey can expel him to the United States.

Captain Ioannis Mousouris, master of the decrepit tramp steamer, sent a strongly-worded demand to the Greek consul that the Maiotis be allowed to continue its voyage to the Black sea, halted when the craft came here Thursday from Greece, where Insull fought for 17 months against extradition attempts.

A note from the Greek government to Turkey was expected hourly concerning the master's protest.

Well-informed Greek circles here believed the friendly relations between Turkey and Greece—former historic enemies and now bosom friends—are such that diplomatic relations would not be strained by the Maiotis note.

But there was the possibility, however, that the affair might give rise to an international airing to the question of the freedom of the Bosporus straits, gateway to the Black sea and considered free water under the Lausanne treaty.

Police Head Out At Kansas City

Director Has Been Under Fire Since Election Rioting.

Kansas City, March 31.—(AP)—Eugene C. Reppert, Kansas City director of police, under fire since Tuesday's municipal election when four men were slain and many persons were slugged, resigned today.

The resignation of the former motor car dealer was accepted by City Manager H. F. McElroy without comment.

Reppert said he had sought to resign on two previous occasions, but had been persuaded by McElroy to remain. He said he would remain in office until a successor was named.

"In resigning from the office of police director I wish to state most emphatically that I have no apologies to make in regard to my administration," Reppert said in a statement.

The T. J. Pendergast Democratic organization with which Reppert and McElroy are aligned, won six of the eight council seats and re-elected Mayor Bryce B. Smith in a bitter contest with a Citizens-Fusion, nonpartisan ticket.

The investigation of election day disorders continued.

EXTRA **The Dallas Morning News** EXTRA

49TH YEAR NO. 184 (AP)—Associated Press. (UP)—United Press. (NANA)—North American Newspaper Alliance. DALLAS, TEXAS, MONDAY, APRIL 2, 1934—FOURTEEN PAGES Oldest Business Institution in Texas—Founded in Galveston April 11, 1842.—Established in Dallas October 1, 1885. 5c PER COPY.

Clyde Barrow, Fleeing, Kills Two Patrolmen

Insull Ashore, To Be Turned Over to U. S.

Former Utilities King Taken From Floating Refuge to Hear Edict of Turkish Court

Action Protested

Through Pouring Rain Fugitive Is Escorted by Maritime Police

ISTANBUL, Turkey, April 1 (AP).—Bewildered Samuel Insull, virtually a prisoner of the Turkish Government, will be told Monday that he is to be turned over to American authorities for extradition.

A decision of the Turkish Cabinet to hand him over was communicated Sunday night to the Governor General of Istanbul, who will inform the former Chicago financier. After notification he will be placed formally under arrest.

Removed from the Greek freighter Maiotis, his floating haven for the last fifteen days, Insull heard a Turkish court declare the offense of which he is accused a common crime and was escorted to a room in a modest hotel for the night.

The final scenes of Insull's long fight to escape American authorities who seek him on embezzlement charges, flashed in kaleidoscopic fashion across the most significant Easter Sunday of the 74-year-old man's life.

It was generally conceded that he had reached the end of his rope.

Cabinet Makes Up Mind.

The Turkish Cabinet, sitting at Ankara, the capital, wasted no time in making up its mind to grant a request from Washington for his extradition when word was flashed from Istanbul that the court had found Turkish law would uphold the action.

Insull's last request of the authorities was for permission to send telegrams. This was granted. Authorities ordered him left alone for the night in his hotel room in the old city of Istanbul.

Insull himself did not know his own status when he left the court and was taken to the hotel.

"What is my legal position?" he asked.

"We can not tell you anything until Monday," officials answered.

Insull had asked to be allowed to

See INSULL on Page 5.

Retired Pastor Dies At End of Services

BALTIMORE, April 1 (AP).—As the Easter festival service ended in the Church of the Ascension and the Prince of Peace, the Rev. Robert Kell, retired Protestant Episcopal rector, collapsed and was dead before aid reached him.

Only a few minutes earlier, the Rev. Mr. Kell, assisting the Rev. Robert E. Browning, had read from an epistle "for ye are dead, and your life is hid with Christ in God. When Christ who is your light shall appear then shall ye also be with Him in glory."

The Weather

NEW ORLEANS, La., April 1 (AP).—Government weather forecast:

East Texas (including Dallas and vicinity): Monday cloudy, probably thundershowers in east portion.

West Texas: Monday fair.

Arkansas: Monday partly cloudy, cooler.

Oklahoma: Monday partly cloudy.

Louisiana: Monday unsettled, probably thundershowers, cooler in northwest portion.

Dallas Temperatures.

Temperatures in Dallas Sunday April 1, 1934, and for the same date last year, as reported by the United States Weather Bureau, follow:

	1934.	1933.		1934.	1933.
Midnight	65	62	Noon......	70	74
2 a. m....	62	62	2 p. m....	73	77
4 a. m....	59	59	4 p. m....	78	80
6 a. m....	60	58	6 p. m....	79	80
8 a. m....	60	58	7 p. m....	74	79
10 a. m....	67	69			

Maximum temperature April 2, last year, 71 degrees; minimum, 48 degrees. Total precipitation so far this year, 6.24 inches.

RENDEZVOUS.

FOR just a brief while every day,
I steal away from duty
And leave the indoor tasks undone,
To keep a tryst with beauty:
Bird-song and lily-bell,
Music thin and sweet;
Sun-gold and starry bloom
Flash about my feet;
Cool mist, with crystal beads
Gleaming everywhere;
Wild-plum and pink-thorne
Hanging on the air.
Swiftly, then, I can return
To tread the rounds of duty—
Since for one fleet half-breath I stood
Hand-in-hand with beauty.
—Mary S. Fitzgerald, in Progressive Farmer.

Convicted Felon, Luke Trammell, Caught on Farm

House Dean Dies

EDWARD W. POU.

Edward W. Pou, 70, Of North Carolina, Claimed by Death

Was Oldest Member in Point of Service in National House

WASHINGTON, April 1 (AP).—The Dean of the House—Rep. Edward W. Pou, 70, of Smithfield, N. C.—died Sunday of a heart attack following a siege of influenza.

Pou was chairman of the powerful House Rules Committee, which formulates the legislative program of the party in power. He also held this post during the administrations of Woodrow Wilson, who was his close friend.

Funeral services will be held at a joint session of the House and Senate at 1 p. m. Monday in the House chamber. Burial will be at Smithfield, the boyhood home of the veteran legislator, beside the grave of Ensign Edward Smith Pou, naval aviator son who was killed in action during the World War.

Entered Congress in 1900.

The quiet spoken but courageous North Carolinian came to Congress in 1900 and had served continually since from the Fourth District. He was a leader in the democratic party for many years and handled many of President Wilson's war time legislative proposals.

Twice Pou sacrificed his prerogative of seniority for the speakership because of his health. He stepped aside for the election of John N. Garner, now Vice President, as speaker in 1931, and again for Speaker Rainey in 1933.

Pou suffered an attack of influenza

See POU on Page 2.

Spring Business Saved When Auto Dispute Settled

Removes Curtailment in Major Industries, Says National City Bank

NEW YORK, April 1 (AP).—Peaceful settlement of the threatened strike in the automobile industry has saved spring business from a severe setback, the National City Bank of New York says in its monthly review of business conditions.

"The settlement accomplished by President Roosevelt," the survey asserts, "is a very important achievement. It removes the danger of enforced curtailment of automobile operations, which would cause curtailment in other industries; and if the formula upon which the settlement was reached works in one major industry it will probably work in others, wherever controversy over similar issues may arise. Thus the danger of a series of great strikes over questions of union jurisdiction appears to be averted."

Business Improves.

The survey finds that business generally continued to improve in March, but that the gains were more irregular and at a slower pace than in February.

Building lines showed a pronounced improvement during the month, the bank notes, and cotton mills continued busy. The coal industry gave more support to general business than for some time, owing to the prevalence of abnormally cold weather, and retail figures showed the broadest gains in several years.

The bank states that the request of the Government that industry pay

See BANK SURVEY on Page 2.

Officers Surround Him in Barn Near Coleman and Fugitive Gives Up Without Resistance

Begs Not to Shoot

Taken to Stephenville for Questioning Concerning Car Theft

COLEMAN, Texas, April 1 (AP).—Luke Trammell, convicted burglar who escaped from the King County jail at Guthrie, Texas, last Tuesday night, was captured twenty-five miles south of Coleman Sunday at a farmhouse where he was hiding. He surrendered without resistance when a party of officers from Coleman surrounded the house.

The party of officers was led by Sheriff Frank Mills, Deputies H. T. Obar and Mace Blanton and Police Chief Carroll Land.

The officers took Trammell to Stephenville for questioning concerning the theft of an automobile stolen from Dublin, which was found Saturday, abandoned on a farm south of Coleman near the place where Trammell's mother lives. He was captured at the home of a relative.

Begs Not to Be Shot.

As the officers drew up before the house in two automobiles, they saw Trammell run from the house to a barn, to hide. They surrounded the barn and ordered him to come out. He complied, holding his hands aloft and begging them not to shoot him.

Trammell had escaped from the Guthrie jail after slugging Jailer Sam Rogers, when he went to Trammell's cell with food. Rogers was struck on the head with an iron bar.

The prisoner had been convicted the previous day of the burglary of a store at Dumont, King County, in which a safe was broken open and

See TRAMMELL on Page 2.

Securities Act Again Under Fire Of U. S. Chamber

Claim Is Made Proposed Law Harmful to Industry of the Nation

WASHINGTON, April 1 (AP).—The Chamber of Commerce of the United States Sunday renewed its attack on the truth in securities act, adding its voice again to what has become a virtually unanimous assault on the law by major organized business and industrial groups.

In a special report drafted by a committee of experts, the chamber said the act, designed to protect investors by giving them full information about securities, had practically stopped the issuance of high grade corporate issues.

The act was condemned in a general way because, the committee contended, it imposed liabilities on persons who might be in no way to blame for errors.

Earlier this week similar opinion was expressed by the National Automobile Chamber of Commerce, and previously the American Bar Association had demanded revision.

The consumers goods and capital

See SECURITIES on Page 2.

Dallas Girl Slated for Stardom

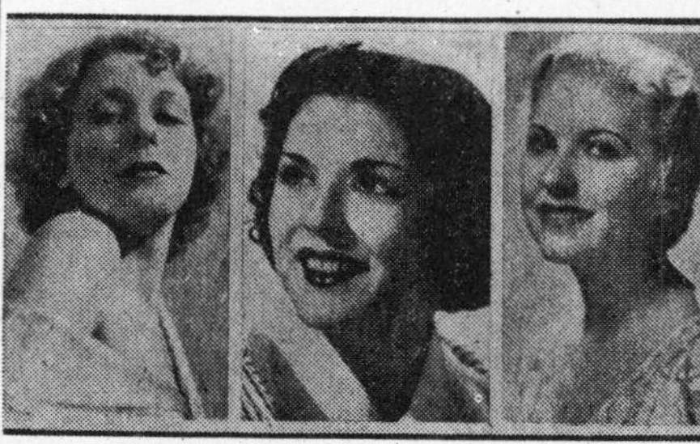

—Associated Press Photo.

Jacqueline Wells (left) of Dallas was one of the three lucky thirteen young motion picture actresses who were selected out of a field of thirty-eight nominees by the Western Association of Motion Picture Advertisers at Hollywood recently as the ones most likely to reach stardom. The others are Jean Gale (center), San Francisco, and Lucille Lund, Buckley, Wash.

Easter Is Celebrated World Over in Song, Service and Festivity

Churches Jammed and Fashionable Display Finery on Streets

(By the Associated Press.)

All the creeds of Christendom joined Sunday in hallelujahs for the risen Lord as they celebrated Easter in song, service and festivities.

In Jerusalem where Christ made His triumphal entry, thousands of Christians from over the globe knelt in adoration at His tomb. Temple bells rang out paens of praise calling the faithful to worship.

A beneficent sun shone down on the city that cradled Christianity to bathe in bright light the colorful parades of the pilgrims. Mohammedans flocked to the Mosque of Omar to pray before the sacred stone as a prelude to a pilgrimage to one of their holy places, the site of the Tomb of Moses. Christian and pagan brushed shoulders without disorders.

Rome, the city that nurtured the

See EASTER on Page 2.

Guggenheim Trust 10th Year Awards Cover Wide Range

Forty Fellowships Include Theater, Arts, Sciences, Literature

NEW YORK, April 1 (AP).—Six artists, nine authors, two composers of music, two workers in the arts of the theater and twenty-one scholars studying in as many different fields of knowledge were announced Sunday as winners of the tenth annual fellowship awards of the John Simon Guggenheim Memorial Foundation.

The fellowships, normally $2,000, are adjusted to meet the needs of the individual fellows. Periods for which the fellowships are granted vary with the necessities of the work. The recipients this year will work in four Continents and in the islands of the East and West Indies.

Trustees of the foundation said these awards bring the total grants of the foundation to more than $1,200,000, and the total number of fellowships to 577. Another series of grants to Latin-American scholars will be made next June.

Former United States Senator and Mrs. Simon Guggenheim established the foundation in 1925 as a memorial to a son. Heretofore the fellowships have been granted only for work abroad, but this year provision is made to permit some fellows to work in the United States.

Theatrical Fellowships.

The theatrical fellowships were awarded to:

Miss Angna Enters of New York, a

See AWARDS on Page 2.

Frenchmen to Fight Duel With Pistols

CARCASSONNE, France, April 1. (AP).—Pistols at twenty paces were decided upon in principle Sunday for a duel between Deputy Jean Mistler, Minister of Commerce in the Daladier Cabinet, and Roger de Tour, Royalist sympathizer.

Seconds were arranging details for the encounter, which is the outcome of a political dispute in a cafe Saturday night. Witnesses said De Tour struck Mistler as the latter was putting on his overcoat.

Cards were immediately exchanged and seconds, one of whom is the Mayor of Carcassonne, were designated. The time and place of the meeting have not been decided.

Card Dealer Is Held After Six Persons Killed

Detained After Taking Blood-Stained Suit to Tailor in Bremerton

BREMERTON, Wash, April 1 (AP).—A roundup of all persons who might be able to shed some light on the brutal slayings of two women and four men in the summer colony home of Mr. and Mrs. Frank Flieder at Erlander's Point, was started by authorities Sunday. Their deaths, believed to have occurred Thursday night, were discovered late Saturday.

Among those held was a man named Murphy, described by police as a card dealer. Authorities emphasized, however, no one was now directly under suspicion.

Attention was called to Murphy when Isadore Laschbin, Bremerton tailor, reported to Sheriff D. L. Blankenship of Kitesap County that Murphy had brought a blood-stained suit to his shop Friday for cleaning, explaining he had a hemorrhage. Laschbin, who was also questioned, reported the incident to police after he had read of the slayings.

Blankenship and Luke S. May, Seattle detective chief and well known criminologist, declined to discuss details of their investigations for the present.

Shots Discharged Into Prone Body, Witnesses Relate

Dallas Couple, Driving, Hear Report, Return to Road and See Tall Man Firing Shotgun

Miss Being Chased

Get Away and Assailants Turn Car Into Highway, Speeds to Dallas

The experience of being eyewitness to the fatal shooting Sunday of State Highway Patrolmen E. B. Wheeler and H. D. Murphy near Grapevine, Tarrant County, and of being threatened with pursuit by the slayers was related by Mrs. Fred A. Giggal of Dallas upon her return from the scene of the double killing.

Mrs. Giggal and her husband, of 4226 Prescott, were taking a Sunday afternoon drive on the Northwest highway to Rhome. The couple, with Mr. Giggal at the wheel, had noticed two highway patrolmen turn up a dirt side road, and as they passed the road, saw a black sedan parked there. Mr. and Mrs. Giggal had hardly driven by the road when they heard a volley of shots.

See Men on Ground.

Mr. Giggal immediately slowed down and turned back, trying to see through a screen of trees. As he got to the entrance of the dirt road, he and his wife saw the two patrolmen stretched out on the ground with the

See EYEWITNESS on Page 2.

Minnesota Police Hold Eight Men In Dillinger Hunt

Believed Bandit, Eluding St. Paul Officers, Was Planning Robbery

ST. PAUL, Minn., April 1 (AP).—Underworld haunts were combed Sunday for clues to the outlaw killer, John Dillinger, and his gangster pal, John Hamilton, as Department of Justice agents questioned eight men in custody.

Theorizing the men who masked their flight from an apartment house Saturday behind a curtain of submachine gunfire when surprised by authorities, were still in town and ready to carry out a planned bank robbery, investigators sought the fugitives' trial in Twin City hoodlums' hideouts.

Clarence Colton, acquitted in the Third Northwestern National Bank robbery in Minneapolis and killing of two policemen several years ago, was one of those held, together with hi. brother Doc Colton, alias Devol.

Police believed Dillinger had gathered the remnants of other gangs, and, with his new mob, planned a bank robbery in the Twin Cities. Examination of the apartment indicated the gang was ready for a robbery, police said, and orders were issued for all officers to be on the alert for the next two days particularly.

A check of hospitals and physicians on the chance they might have treated the woman who fled with the desperadoes, also was made. She was wounded by a shot from the gun of Detective Henry Cummings as she and one of the men scuttled down the rear stairway of their third floor apartment.

Killed

E. B. WHEELER.

E. B. Wheeler of Fort Worth was one of the two State highway patrolmen killed Sunday by Clyde Barrow.

Freed by Bandit

MRS. CAM GUNTER.

Woman Hostage Of Bandit Tells Story of Capture

Stopping to Offer Aid, Loses Her Auto and Taken to Houston

HOUSTON, Texas, April 1 (AP).—Mrs. Cam Gunter of Mexia was forced to accompany a man identified as Raymond Hamilton, notorious desperado, more than 175 miles Saturday and Saturday night as a result of her desire to be of assistance to an ill-fated motorist.

The attractive 27-year-old brunette told of the kidnaping and the all-night ride after she was freed here shortly before 9:30 a. m. Sunday. She said she was treated courteously and that the desperado left her $30 to have her car fixed up. The automobile had been badly used, she explained.

Mrs. Gunter said she left her home in Mexia about 9:30 o'clock Saturday morning and drove her husband, an oil gauger, downtown. She then drove to Thelma to get her 4-year-old son,

See HOSTAGE on Page 2.

Bandit Shoots Officers Down On Side Road

Parked Near Grapevine, Robber and Woman Companion Fire as Officers Approach Car

Flee Toward Dallas

Believed to Be Waiting for Hamilton When Killings Occurred

FORT WORTH, Texas, April 1 (AP).—Gunfire pouring from an automobile believed occupied by Clyde Barrow, Texas' public enemy No. 1, and a red-haired woman companion, possibly Bonnie Parker, almost instantly killed two State Highway Patrol officers Sunday afternoon near Grapevine.

Detective A. C. Howerton of the homicide squad of the Fort Worth police department said there was no doubt the killer was Clyde Barrow.

The officers, E. B. Wheeler and H. D. Murphy, both of Fort Worth, were shot down as they approached the car parked on a side road.

Barrow and the cigar-smoking Bonnie Parker had been there since midmorning, officers believed, awaiting the arrival of Raymond Hamilton, freed recently from a prison farm under a barrage thought laid down by Barrow and whose latest exploit was the single-handed hold-up of a bank in West yesterday.

Fled Toward Dallas.

The direction in which the death car headed after the fusillade that cost the lives of the two officers was not immediately determined, though it was thought to have gone toward Grapevine or Dallas.

State Motorcycle Patrol Officers Polk Ivy, Wheeler and Murphy were riding on Highway 114 between Grapevine and Rhome. Ivy, who was several hundred yards in advance of the other two officers, noticed a black Ford sedan with yellow wire wheels parked on a side road fifty yards from the highway five miles northwest of Grapevine.

He thought nothing of it, however, until having gone a quarter of a mile he glanced back and saw that Wheeler and Murphy were not following him. Turning back he discovered them lying near their motorcycles at the spot where the car had been parked. Wheeler was dead and Murphy dying from buckshot wounds. Their pistols still were in their holsters, indicating that as they drew near the machine the deadly fire from within began.

An ambulance was summoned but

See CLYDE BARROW on Page 2.

Slaying of Pair Is Attributed to Clyde and Bonnie

Chief Deputy Checks Descriptions and Opines Hamilton Not Present

Belief that the killer of the two highway patrolmen was Clyde Barrow, noted desperado, accompanied by Bonnie Parker, was expressed Sunday night by Chief Deputy Sheriff Bill Decker. Mr. Decker was called to the scene of the shooting a few minutes after it happened and checked all angles of it.

"The car which Patrolmen Murphy and Wheeler approached just before they were shot by its occupants had been seen there since 11 o'clock Sunday morning," Mr. Decker said. "If Raymond Hamilton let out his prisoner, Mrs. Cam Gunter, at Houston at 9:15 o'clock Sunday morning, he couldn't have been at Grapevine two hours later, particularly by back roads. It doubtless was Clyde Barrow and Bonnie Parker."

The possibility also was suggested that Barrow had been waiting for Hamilton, whom he freed recently from the State prison farm near Huntsville. The deputy did not believe Barrow took part in the West bank robbery Saturday.

Mr. Decker also did not believe the killer had driven on to Dallas. Although the car was reported headed for this city, he thought Barrow had turned north soon after passing through Grapevine.

Late descriptions of the pair seen in the car tallied more nearly with Barrow and his woman than with Hamilton. The man was said to be about five feet six inches, weighing around 140 pounds, dressed in dark tan riding pants and blue shirt. His companion also was dressed in riding pants, which gave rise to reports there were two men in the car. It was a woman, however, wearing brown riding pants and a brown blouse, Dallas police were informed.

News Behind the News

By PAUL MALLON (Copyright, 1934, by Paul Mallon)

Mr. Hull Is Not a Mr. Milquetoast; It's Unsafe to Step on His Toes

Perseverance.

WASHINGTON, April 1.—The mild demeanor of State Secretary Hull is deceiving.

Behind it he hides the heart of a Canadian Northwest policeman. He always gets his man.

This time the man is none other than President Roosevelt's own special foreign trade adviser, George Peek. When Mr. Peek's appointment was announced it was generally assumed around the State Department that Mr. Hull's influence on that subject was on the wane. Mr. Peek was supposed to be the big influence on foreign trade, overriding the executive commercial policy committee started by Mr. Hull.

Mr. Hull said nothing, but was annoyed. A week ago the White House gave out an executive order formally installing Mr. Peek and giving him $100,000 to work with.

The laugh was on Mr. Hull—but not for long.

Retribution.

Two days after Mr. Roosevelt left on his fishing trip Mr. Hull's State Department made public a supplemental executive order the President had signed before he left.

Why its announcement was delayed forty-eight hours was not explained, but the fact is that by that time Mr. Roosevelt was out on the Astor yacht, out of reach of Mr. Peek and everyone else.

This supplemental order specifically instructed Mr. Peek not to interfere with the executive policy committee. It did not say directly, but clearly implied that Mr. Peek was also not to interfere with Mr. Hull, and gave Mr. Hull the right to name a representative on the policy committee.

The inner departmental circlers nudged each other and allowed that many influential persons have found it distinctly unprofitable to step on Mr. Hull's toes. He is decidedly not a Mr. Milquetoast.

NRA.

Those on the inside at the NRA are talking among themselves about the radical changes which have been quietly going on within the organization.

For instance, W. Averill Harriman has virtually taken the entire routine off General Johnson during the last few weeks. He appears to be running the show since he was made first assistant administrator.

One job General Johnson has taken on recently is the writing of office orders. They are supposed to be more secret than a Supreme Court decision. If anyone is caught disclosing an order outside the organization it constitutes grounds for dismissal.

Lately the orders have been more picturesquely worded than when they were written by Executive Director Alvin Brown.

Opposition.

These and other signs have led to considerable discussion as to the future of the NRA. Some wise boys are saying the outfit will grow less and less important. They expect that a compliance drive will be started soon by the legal division. The show will then center around technical individual cases of enforcement. Any broad further curtailment of hours seems to be out of the question.

The tendency of the administration is to temporize with the existing setup and await developments in hopes that more reforms may be forced later.

But industry is getting its back up. It is organizing quite effectively backstage against the Wagner Labor Board bill. Three of the largest industries have sent letters to all stockholders urging them to campaign actively against the measure.

They will probably be able to block it for this session.

Regrets.

The White House crowd took the defeat on the veterans' pay restoration bill very hard. Their advance information was to the effect that the Senate would save them by sustaining the veto.

It is rather important politically, but not financially.

When the figures are all in June 30 you will find that Mr. Roosevelt's budget estimate of this year's deficit will be just about half what he thought it would be. He has been unable to spend money as fast as he estimated.

The condition of the Treasury will not be as seriously affected by the $228,000,000 additional expense of the veterans' pay restorations.

That is only a drop in a $7,000,000,000 budget bucket.

Hitler.

The inner group at the State Department believes it is going to be a long time before anyone gets any money out of Berlin.

Germany's gold reserves, according to their calculations, are only 8 per cent of her total currency outstanding. Her gold position is so bad she can not pay for current foreign purchases and has slapped an embargo on cotton, wool, etc.

Hitler's diplomats have been sounding us out on a proposition whereby they would pay in kind for their domestic purchases. That means we would have to buy in Germany as much as they buy here.

We will not fall for that one.

Trick.

There is more than a desire for reform behind this democratic movement for revision of the electoral college system.

If they succeed, the Republicans may never get back in the White House.

The constitutional amendment approved by Mr. Roosevelt the other day provides that the electoral vote of each State be split in accordance with the popular vote. For instance, Hoover carried Pennsylvania last year with a total vote of 1,453,540, against Roosevelt's 1,295,948, and thus won the whole block of thirty-six electoral votes.

Under the proposed amendment, Pennsylvania's electoral vote would have been split, about twenty for Hoover and sixteen for Roosevelt.

It would mean that the Democrats would get electoral votes out of their minority representation in normally Republican States, but would lose little in their stronghold, the solid South, where Republican voting is nil.

El Paso Herald-Post

Home Edition

THREE CENTS IN EL PASO
FIVE CENTS OUTSIDE EL PASO

SIXTEEN PAGES

Weather Forecast: F[illegible] and tomorrow; not much change in tem perature

VOL. LIV. NO. 82 — EL PASO, TEXAS, THURSDAY, APRIL 5, 1934

WOMEN VOTERS ATTACK REGAN FOR STAND ON CHILD LABOR

LONG REBUKED AFTER THREAT TO HIT LAWYER

Senator Tells Huey Nation Gives Him Little Respect

ROW AT HEARING

'Kingfish' Offers to Fight Attorney Outside Over Racetrack Charge

By Associated Press

WASHINGTON, April 5.—Antagonism between Huey Long and administration leadership burst forth in the senate today with Pat Harrison of Mississippi saying "the opinion of the senator from Louisiana is less respected by the membership of this body as a whole and by the country than that of any other senator here."

The two outspoken legislators had been in several lesser disputes a while before at a senate finance committee hearing on the confirmation of D. D. Moore as internal revenue collector in Louisiana, opposed by Long. Long charges Moore is linked with Louisiana racetrack promoters.

Edward Rightor, Moore's attorney, was invited by Long to "go outside" after Rightor had said of Jefferson race track in Louisiana "that's your track, senator." Long called that statement an "infamous falsehood."

Replies to Speech

The exchanges between the Louisiana senator and Harrison, who heads the finance committee, pertained to conduct of the hearing.

Again a crowd was on hand, many of whom went to the senate floor later and heard Long in a speech calling for heavier taxes on the wealthy.

Then Harrison undertook a reply to a speech yesterday by Long, blaming the Democratic leadership for "helping the Hoover administration to send the country to hell."

"A surplusage speech," Harrison termed Long's earlier address.

"I shall offer no defense of what this side of the aisle did during the Hoover administration. It needs no defense on the part of good Democrats and I am sure the country appreciates the fact when men charged with a high responsibility here attempt to cooperate in trying to bring the country back to economic normalcy.

Huey Interrupts

"Of course the leader on this side of the aisle (Robinson of Arkansas) needs no eulogy from me because what is in my heart, and my estimate of him and his labors and services here is shared by every member of the senate on both sides of the aisle, with possibly one exception."

Here Long interrupted:

"In speaking of the leadership I had more particularly in mind, as well as anybody else, the senator from Mississippi. I was not speaking only of the senator from Arkansas. When I speak of the leadership, I think the senator knows I certainly had him in mind for the tax policy he had pursued. He need make no defense of anyone else; let him take care of himself."

Rebuked

"I am glad," Harrison replied, "the senator looks on me as included in the leadership, but if others care no more about his estimate of me than I care about it, it makes no difference because in my opinion the opinion of the senator from Louisiana is less respected by the membership of this body as a whole and by the country than that of any other senator here."

PLANE CRASH VICTIM ALIVE IN JUNGLE

Engineer Found With Four Dead; Ship Crashed March 10

By United Press

CALI, Colombia, April 5.—Indians reported today the finding in the jungles of Newton C. Marshall, American mining engineer, sole survivor of a passenger plane that crashed on the banks of the Sipi river in Colombia three weeks ago.

The plane, the Von Khorn of the Scadta line (Colombian-German air Transport Co.) left Buenaventura on the Pacific coast of Colombia March 10, for Medellin, in the interior. Five persons were aboard.

"Stop It!"

Only two days old was this rental ad in the Herald-Post when the advertiser ordered it stopped:

EAST side duplex, beautiful new, modern 4 room, tile bath, tiffany walls, hardwood floors, electric refrigeration, gas range, stone garage, water paid, lovely yard. 4302 Chester. E1542.

Because it had found a tenant for the place advertised. "Very well pleased with the results of my ad," said the advertiser.

Now is the time to fill that vacancy of yours. And the most effective place to advertise it is in the Herald-Post where your ad will reach more than 3 out of every 4 English reading El Paso families for only one cost to you. A very small cost, too . . .

Only 2c a Word

Just Call

Main 4380

Desperado and Cigar-Smoking Pal

Clyde Barrow and his cigar smoking woman companion, Bonnie Parker, was hunted by hundreds of police today, following the slaying of two state highway motorcycle police near Dallas, Sunday. They were shot to death when they investigated a car parked near the highway. Barrow first drew the attention of police when he was held in Dallas in connection with chicken theft.

CALLES GRAVELY ILL OF MALARIA

Former Mexico President Is Stricken After Visit to Tropical States

By United Press

MEXICO CITY, April 5.—Plutarco Elias Calles, Mexico's foremost statesman, was gravely ill of malaria today at his Cuernavaca home.

Recently he paid a visit to the tropical states of Tabasco and Campeche. Malaria, from which he had suffered, recurred and he was ordered to bed.

Calles is former president of Mexico.

WIRT'S SUPPORTERS CALLED 'JACKASSES'

Committee Named to Investigate Revolt Charges

WASHINGTON, April 5.—Champions of Dr. William Wirt's "red plot" charges were denounced today as "intellectual jackasses" by Rep. George Foulkes, Dem. Mich., leading defender of the "brain trust" in congress.

A committee of five was named to investigate the charge of Dr. William Wirt, Gary, Ind., that administration brain trusters are planning a revolution.

WOMAN WHIPS JACK DEMPSEY

Wife of Wrestler Attacks Ex-Champ After He Hits Husband on Chin

By Associated Press

ALEXANDRIA, La., April 5.—Jack Dempsey lost a ring battle here last night. Worse than that, he was forced into ignominous retreat from the scene of contest. It all happened as the ex-heavy champion was refereeing a heavyweight wrestling match and the 95 pound wife of one of the participants climbed into the rope square and took a hand in the proceedings.

Dempsey lost his shirt and a good deal of hair.

Mrs. Johnny Plummer, whose husband was tying up with Bruce Noland in the feature of a mat card, gave the fans the unexpected extra thrill when she challenged the former pugilistic king and won at least a temporary victory.

Mrs. Plummer Rises

It all started when Dempsey warned Plummer that he would not allow any kicking of Noland when the latter was on the floor. One thing led to another and Referee Dempsey closed the argument by delivering three quick upper-cuts to the chin, which ended the evening's entertainment for Plummer.

But not for Mrs. Plummer. She was through the ropes from her ringside seat in a second and going after Dempsey's shirt and his hair before anybody could do anything about it.

Lots of Excitement

Dempsey retreated as far as the ropes would allow and stood there for a while, proving he could still take it, without raising a hand in defense. When Mrs. Plummer really got organized, however, Dempsey slipped through the ropes and retreated into the crowd.

By that time, Promoter Mike Mule was in the ring trying to make everyone listen to reason, but when Mrs. Plummer turned her attention to him, he quickly pinned her arms behind her and held them thus while Dempsey slipped back into the ring and raised Noland's arm in token of victory by default on a foul.

There was lots of excitement, but really very little damage to anyone.

SENATE BANS HIKE IN INCOME TAXES

Refuses to Increase Levy on Small Incomes

By Associated Press

WASHINGTON, April 5. — The senate today rejected a proposal to increase from four to six per cent the existing normal income tax and to levy surtaxes ranging from six to 71 per cent as against an existing range of one to 59 per cent.

By this action the senate retained the less severe finance committtee schedule for a flat four per cent normal rate and surtaxes ranging from five to 59 per cent.

The committee surtaxes run through 29 brackets as compared with 28 in the house bill and begin the five per cent on net incomes between $4000 and $6000 and reach 59 per cent on those over $1,000,000.

U. S. OFFICER'S CONTRACT WITH CELIA UPHELD

Inspector Says Locke Acted Properly in Villa Case

SIGNED VOLUNTARILY

Mystery Woman Again Asks Movie Manager for $500 For 'Information'

T. A. Arnold, inspector in charge of the plant quarantine bureau, said today that a thorough investigation showed that Clarence M. Locke, plant quarantine inspector at the bridge, acted properly in signing a contract as manager for Celia Villa.

"I talked with the girl in Las Cruces yesterday and she said she signed the contract voluntarily," said Mr. Arnold.

Miss Villa, daughter of Gen Francisco (Pancho) Villa, spurned a Metro - Goldwyn - Mayer publicity tour contract to take her chances with Mr. Locke as her manager.

Mr. Locke is trying to get her a job in Hollywood.

The woman who asked Metro-Goldwyn-Mayer for $500 in return for revealing the whereabouts of Miss Villa is still trying to collect the $500.

She appeared at the Plaza theater Monday and told E. B. Coleman, M.-G.-M. representative, that Celia, who had signed a contract with Coleman, would be at the El Paso courthouse at 11:45 a. m. Monday.

Miss Villa, after signing the contract, had left El Paso and Mr. Coleman could not find her.

He waited at the courthouse for nearly an hour. At that time, Celia was in the Las Cruces courthouse, where her cousin, Fermin Torres, was taking out guardianship papers.

Mr. Coleman left in disgust when Celia did not return. He was informed that she had signed a previous contract with Clarence M. Locke, plant quarantine inspector at the bridge.

John Paxton, Plaza theater, today had received a letter from the "mystery" woman asking him to send the $50 0to a Las Cruces address. The letter was unsigned.

FLOOD DEATHS GROW TO 40

11 More Bodies Are Found In Oklahoma Ruins; Million Damage

By THE ASSOCIATED PRESS

Texas entered into the nation's flood picture today with four victims, as 11 bodies were recovered in a western Oklahoma flood in which nearly a score may have perished.

Recovery of the 11 bodies brought flood deaths to 40.

As was the case in the Oklahoma flood which centered around Elk City and Hammon, the southwest Texas deaths near Menard occurred when a stream, usually shallow, became a torrent because of heavy rains.

C. P. Smith district FERA engineer, reported the Oklahoma flood damage at $625,000.

It was estimated that damage of several millions dollars was done in northern and western Wisconsin by rain and melting snow.

Seven channel projects on the upper Mississippi were endangered today when the river reached a high stage and continued its rise.

Storms in Ohio caused damage estimated at $100,000. A man was killed by lightning at Canton.

In Kansas, the rains continued but were less serious. Farmers expected their crops to benefit.

Snow held up highway and air traffic in the Rocky Mountains region and lay as deep as 15 inches in places in the Dakota hills.

In the east, 10 families near Hartford, Conn., abandoned their homes when the Connecticut river rose more than two feet above flood stage.

MACHINE GUNNERS ROUTED FROM BANK

Two Employes Battle Bandits And Foil Robbery

By United Press

BISHOP, Texas, April 5—Two machine gun bandits were routed in a gun battle at the First State bank here today by Cashier William A. Harlan and his assistant, Leon Hagan.

No one was injured.

The bandits held the trigger down on their machine gun while the two bankers emptied their two automatics.

Where Six Were Brutally Slain at House Party

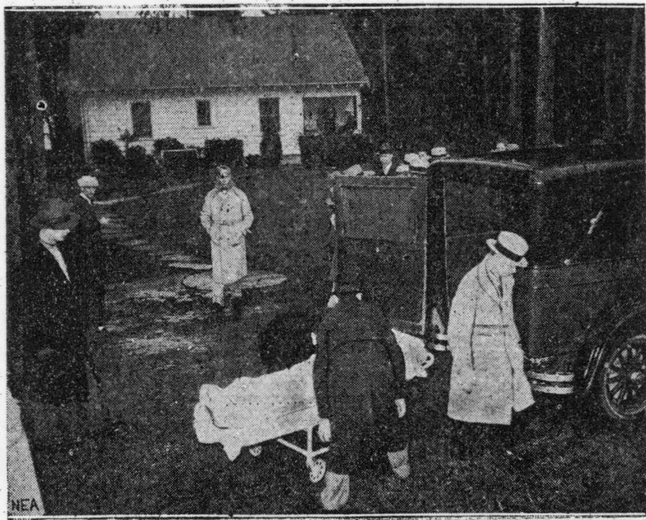

Above is the scene of the Pacific northwest's most gruesome murder—the home of Frank Fileder, near Bremerton, Wash., where Fileder, his wife and four guests were blindfolded, bound, then beaten to death. Photo shows exterior of the murder house, with authorities removing one of the victim's bodies.

Below, a corner of the blood-drenched house—a closet where the body of Fred Balsom was found in pools of blood. Police are mystified.

TURNER ATTACKS EDITOR PERRY

Board President Charges That Publisher Seeks Control Of School Affairs

Dr. George Turner, school board president, asserted today that a faction opposing him on the school board is trying to give control of the board to Wallace Perry, Herald-Post editor, and a group of school teachers.

Dr. Turner said:

"It appears from editorials published in the Herald-Post that Mr. Perry has forgotten about Dr. E. J. Cummins running for election to the school board and has taken out after me. He seems to have taken a lot for granted and shaped a background and attitude for me to suit his own purpose.

"The background of my candidacy a year ago was no faction or group as Mr. Perry pointed out. I was requested to run by a number of prominent citizens for the sole purpose if elected to use my best judgment in helping to work out for El Paso a nine months' term of school with the small amount of money which every one knew would be available and to keep if possible the school system on a cash basis for the general good of the teachers, taxpayers and all concerned.

"Product of Imagination"

"The statement that I was supported and elected by a group of teachers playing politics for the purpose of favoring them through my actions on the board is a product of Mr. Perry's imagination.

"The only reference made to 'Hughey and anti-Hughey politics' was when the candidates got together for the first time. This was in Mr. Harwell's office. Mr. Harwell, Mr. Covington, Mr. Wilcox, Mr. Roy Hoard, Mr. Robert Price and others were present and discussing Mr. Hughey when I arrived.

"After listening for a few minutes, I said these words: "If the purpose of organizing this ticket is to oust Mr. Hughey and put a new man at the head of the school system who is unfamiliar with its organization and operation at a time when drastic reductions must be made, I thank you for the compliment of asking me to run with you, but I have plenty of work to do and will be going."

Says Perry Changed

"Speaking of some one changing. How about Mr. Perry?

"Just what is back of his supporting Mrs. Burnett?

"He couldn't know anything of her value on the board as compared with Dr. Cummins because he has spoken long and well of Dr. Cummins and admits he did not know Mrs. Burnett until the time of her announcement. Just what does Mr. Perry want to do, anyway?

"Does he want to control the school board himself through teacher group politics at the expense of public school disruption? Judging from previous editorials and his attitude toward the advancement of the school system this would seem to be the case.

"The Herald-Post bitterly opposed

(Continued on Page 9)

He's 'Yes' and 'No' Man, Cummins Replies to Critics

School Trustee Denies He Is 'Yes Man' for Dr. George Turner, President of Board

Dr. E. J. Cummins, candidate for election to the school board, answered "yes" and "no" today when asked if he is "yes man" for Dr. George Turner, board president, as charged by a group of teachers.

Dr. Cummins said:

"If they mean that I vote with Dr. Turner on a question I think is right, then I am 'yes man.' If they mean when I vote against him, then I am his 'no man.'

Dr. Cummins replied to a statement attributed to Mrs. Burnett that Mrs. Susan Buck, Bowie High school teacher, was saved from dismissal by Joseph G. Bennis, C. K. Jameson, and Roland Harwell, board members assertedly composing the "anti-Hughey" faction.

"If those three members favored Mrs. Buck, then the implication is that C. C. Covington, Harvey Wilcox and I opposed her," said Dr. Cummins.

"If that is true, then the vote of Dr. Turner, board president, was necessary in case of a tie, and Dr. Turner is the one who must have 'saved' her.

"As a matter of fact, Mrs. Buck's rating is such that there never was any discussion as to whether she should be retained."

Mrs. Burnett's Children Sick

Mrs. T. R. Burnett, candidate for election to the school board, lost interest in the campaign today when her two children became ill.

She spent the day conferring with physicians about the health of her children. It is believed they have the measles.

Mrs. Burnett said she is sure she will win a place on the board in the voting Saturday.

Dr. E. J. Cummins, her opponent, predicted victory for himself.

TEMPERATURES

City			City		
Chicago	44	40	New York	48	34
Denver	38	30	Phoenix	76	46
EL PASO	68	44	Roswell	70	36
Kansas City	68	54	San Antonio	78	58
Los Angeles	74	54	Seattle	60	46

Solicitation of Fund For Mrs. Buck Charged

Friends of Mrs. Susan Buck, president of the El Paso Teachers' Assn., are collecting 10 cents each from school teachers to buy Mrs. Buck a present, Dr. E. J. Cummins, candidate for reelection to the school board, and Dr. George Tur-

(Continued on page 16)

Criticize State Senator For Opposing Texas Amendment

URGE SEX EDUCATION

Speaker Says Adolescents Should Be Told About Origin of Life

League of Women Voters members today criticized State Sen. Ken M. Regan for voting against Texas ratification of the child labor amendment.

"When he comes up for re-election we'll put him on the spot by making him put his name on the dotted line for or against the child labor amendment," members said at the league's citizenship school at the College of Mines today.

Mrs. W. P. Hobby, Houston, charged that eastern manufacturers are fostering paid propaganda in Texas to defeat state ratification.

"They know the amendment will be ratified unless they can get farmers excited about some misconception," she said.

"They are telling the farmers that children won't be permitted to milk a cow until they are 18 years old, if the amendment is ratified. The amendment excepts farm labor of children.

"That line of attack against it is contemptible, ridiculous."

She advised the league to request every candidate in the next election to answer a questionnaire about his views on child labor and the amendment.

Sex Education Advocated By Dr. Joseph M. Roth

Shildren today develop into adolescence faster than in previous generations because of oversexed stimulation in modern life, Dr. Joseph M. Roth, College of Mines psychology professor, told the League of Women Voters citizenship school today.

Dr. Roth blamed "the type of news some newspapers carry, the type of moving pictures, risque literature and irregularities in actual life" for the serious problem of too early adolescence.

"The need for sex education starts with the child in his cradle," he said. "Clement of Alexandria said: 'No one should be ashamed to name what God was not ashamed to create.'"

He warned mothers that chaildren know more about sex than "many of the foolish people who do not care to discuss the subject."

Should Answer Questions

Questions of children about sex never should be disregarded, he warned. They should be answered as fully as the age, interest and capacity to the child to understand permits, he said.

He advised gradual education of children in sex matters, beginning with illustrations from animal life.

"Puppy love which often begins between eight and 10 years of age, is an essential preparation for future love and the great work of married life," Dr. Roth said.

"The child who is teased and ridiculed about puppy love may become surreptitious. He will not seek advice from the parent when he needs it, because of lost confidence in the parent."

Appeal to Courage

He advised parents to appeal to manliness, courage and heroism in boys and the motherhood instinct in girls of growing years, to keep them from mis-steps.

"Adolescence is a dream time," he said. "It is unfortunate that some parents goad their adolescent children into activity by poking fun at their dreams. Their dreams and ideals should be encouraged."

He advised hobbies for children, such as scoutcraft, or stamp collecting, athletics for boys and less strenuous exercise for girls.

The dangers of social disease should be impressed upon youth, but this must be convincing, or parents had better leave such negative sex education phases to their ministers or physicians, he advised.

Discuss Dress

Dr. Roth advocated sex instruction in high schools and colleges, especially in connection with biology courses.

During a discussion following his talk, women members of the audience asked Dr. Roth what can be done about immodest dress on bathing beaches.

"Ideas of what is modest change with age and decade," Dr. Roth replied. "In Japan, it is immodest for a woman to appear in a drawing room without long sleeves, yet the same women see nothing immodest in going nude on the beach. Customs and the norm set ideas of modesty. Uncovering the body is not a sign of immodesty, where we are accustomed to it."

Speaker Says E. P. Lacks Public Health Nurses

El Paso always will have a high infant death rate because of its great percentage of foreign population, poor sanitation, economic conditions, and excessive child bearing among some classes, Mrs. Lois Huffaker told the League of Women Voters citizenship school today.

She said El Paso has only one public health nurse to each 11,200 persons, whereas one to each 2500 population is the ideal.

Harvard Student Follows Freudian Impulse and Socks Sea Serpent

EDITOR'S NOTE: Coast-guards and fishermen saw Thomas G. Ratcliffe, Harvard junior and member of a prominent St. Louis family, seize an oar and strike at an object in Vineyard Sound yesterday. Ratcliffe thus became perhaps the first person ever to engage in actual combat with a sea serpent—if sea serpent it was—although Jonah is said to have gotten in some infighting with a whale. In the following article, Ratcliffe tells of the "Freudian impulse" which led him to wallop the monster.

By THOMAS G. RATCLIFFE
(Written for U. P.)

PENZANCE POINT, Mass., April 5.—Eric Warbasse and I took the outboard about 3 p. m. yesterday afternoon and made a complete circle of great harbor. I had bet Eric he could not start the motor but he did and I lost five cents. We headed for the hole.

On the way I saw an object and thought it was the body of William Hulten, who was drowned a week ago. I said to Eric, "That must be the boy's body." We started for it and then I saw that it was a serpent. It was by the spindle near the rock and not far from the steamer wharf.

When I saw the thing close up my first thought was of Loch Ness, but I said to Eric, "There is no Scotch mist here." Remembering the days when knighthood was in flower, I socked it on the head. The head was not defined from the body but tapered to a snub nose. When we got to within 10 feet of the monster, we noticed for the first time a tail out of the water about 20 feet away.

Eric cut the motor and we came alongside just a foot or two away. It looked like a gigantic eel head and was six inches out of the water.

After it was struck, it slowly slipped down under the water, apparently arching its body, though it had never been completely out of the water. It slipped alongside the boat for probably 15 seconds and we had ample time to see the monster. I did not strike it again because by that time I had realized what I had done.

As the tail came slowly along I noticed that it tapered to a point and appeared to carry a fin. The body did not lash or writhe and the beast simply sounded, like a submarine or a whale. We followed slowly on the surface in the direction the monster was headed into Great Head but nothing more was seen of it.

The center of the body was about three feet in diameter; it was quite large and about 30 feet in length.

I don't know why I hit it—just a Freudian impulse, I suppose—but I bashed it hard. Then when I saw it move I decided that discretion would have been the better part of valor but the snake, or monster, or whatever you want to call it, seemed perfectly bored with the situation, and remembering Harvard indifference, it simply pushed off.

Graphic Section

Chicago Sunday Tribune

WORLD'S GREATEST NEWSPAPER

Camera News Review

April 22, 1934

DILLINGER, ARCHENEMY OF SOCIETY, ANOTHER OF CRIME'S MUDDLEHEADS

Like the James Boys and Gerald Chapman, the Desperado of the Wooden Pistol Must Pay in the End

By Joseph U. Dugan

SCARRED by many gunshot wounds, a broken old man said just before his death in 1915 on a little farm in Excelsior Springs, Mo.: "God alone knows what my brother and I suffered. We starved almost to death with our pockets stuffed with money. Many times we had to lie, badly wounded, for weeks in the woods without medical attention. Always we were hunted like the wolves of the prairie."

His name was Frank James His brother, Jesse, had been shot to death in 1882 by Bob Ford, a member of the James boys' gang, who turned traitor in order to collect the $30,000 reward offered for Jesse, dead or alive. Thus ended the career of the most notorious American criminal of the 19th century.

Let's turn the crimsoned pages of criminal history to the chronicle of an event which occurred within grim gray walls of the prison at Wethersfield, Conn., shortly after midnight on the morning of April 6, 1926. A little group of official witnesses sat muted, staring fixedly at the scaffold and the empty noose before them. Through a small door came a guard. Behind him marched the figure of a prisoner. The executioners were mercifully quick in placing a black hood over his head and fastening the noose about his neck. A few seconds later the trap was sprung. The hooded figure dangled lifeless at the rope's end.

His name was Gerald Chapman, police killer, bank robber, jail breaker—most notorious criminal of the period covering the first quarter of the 20th century.

So much for prelude. We come now to the present and a parallel, the much sung but unhallowed subject of this story. His name is John Dillinger. His account with society, as these words are written, remains unpaid. When it is closed, he will be dead.

Like Jesse James and his infamous companions in crime, the three Younger brothers, Jim, Bob, and Cole, and the lesser members of the gang; like Gerald Chapman and scores of other criminals whose accounts have been settled, John Dillinger has been living through a hell of numbered days. In spite of his melodramatic exploits, his fabled courage and cleverness, Dillinger, like his predecessors, is, in the language of the street, both a sucker and a sap. An obvious fact, which leads to an important question: Why Dillinger?

Psychiatrists offer complex theories and deductions They classify Dillinger as a perverse personality of the anti-social type. Sociologists point with solemn conviction to the influence of his early environment and associations. Another school of thought blames political corruption, lax officials, and deplores the absence in this country of swift, sure punishment as a deterrent of crime.

All of these theories, in greater or lesser degree, may be applied truthfully in solving the riddle presented by this amazing criminal personality In the last analysis our social system must share in the blame. Most certainly officials of the state of Indiana must accept a share of responsibility for crimes committed by Dillinger and his murderous gang following the bandit's unbelievable escape from the Crown Point jail.

The boldness and cold bloodedness of Dillinger's crimes may be compared justly with those of Jesse James and his gang. It must be remembered, however, that the James and Younger gangs came into existence during the civil war. Jesse, Frank, and the Younger brothers were arch sympathizers with the cause of the south. Their early ventures in crime were committed under the sincere, if mistaken, guise of patriotism. As members of Quantrell's guerilla band of rebels operating against union forces in Missouri and Kansas, the James boys and the others learned the tactics which proved so successful in their subsequent criminal careers. None of these bandits had the advantage of more than rudimentary education.

John Dillinger was born in 1902 in Mooresville, a rural village of Morgan county, Indiana, the home county also of the present governor of the state, Paul V. McNutt. At the time of John's birth his father, John W Dillinger, of good Quaker stock, was a substantial farmer of the community. The first tragedy in the family, a fact significant to sociologists, was the death of John's mother when he was but three years old Only recently, in making a pathetic plea against the public attitude toward his son, Dillinger's father said: "John had no mother." Soon after the death of his wife, Dillinger senior moved to Indianapolis, where he conducted a grocery on the west side of the city. Here Dillinger grew up in city slum surroundings. He was 13 years old and had completed grammar school when his father, now remarried and with a family increased by another son, decided to return to Mooresville.

Dillinger entered the Mooresville High school. He was a normal, typical boy. He played baseball on the school nine and helped his father in the grocery the elder Dillinger had acquired in Mooresville. On Sunday the youth was a regular attendant at the Quaker church of the community. But even the wholesome atmosphere of rural villages has its taint of vice, or rather its opportunities for wrong doing. In Dillinger's own words, spoken to newspaper reporters after his capture in Tucson, Ariz.:

"I was just an unfortunate boy. I got drunk ten years ago back in Mooresville. I held up a grocery. I got $550 and then I got caught. They gave me ten to twenty in Michigan City prison. Only a year ago they let me out."

Dillinger's version of his first misstep was not entirely accurate. If, as it has been contended, the initial crime is an important indication of future conduct, the details of this first law violation may be interesting here.

According to the record, Dillinger and another village youth, Ed Singleton, were frequenters of the Mooresville pool hall. Score two for sociology. The year was 1924. Dillinger and Singleton laid plans to waylay and rob a village merchant, Frank Morgan, who then was 65 years old. That night they assaulted Morgan, striking him with a lead pipe and robbing him of his wallet. Morgan recognized his assailants and their arrest followed almost immediately. Singleton, however, bargained with the prosecutor. He pleaded guilty and turned state's evidence. In return he was given a light sentence. Dillinger was sent to the Pendleton reformatory to serve from ten to twenty years.

Whatever sense of fair play he possessed had been violated. He entered prison with his mind embittered against the law and all who uphold it. This bitterness today has increased a thousandfold.

At Pendleton Dillinger was an unruly prisoner. He quickly became a bosom pal of the more vicious of the youthful convicts and was an apt pupil at learning the secrets and habits of young men hardened to criminal pursuits. Twice Dillinger attempted to escape. After the second try, he was transferred to the state penitentiary at Michigan City.

(Continued on Page Three)

JOHN DILLINGER

That federal operatives and the police of every city in the country are closing the net around the reorganized Dillinger gang is indicated by late developments in the nation-wide man hunt. Evelyn Frechetti, red-haired beauty and Dillinger's latest girl friend, was seized less than two weeks ago in Chicago. At the same time authorities at St. Paul, where Dillinger recently escaped from a police trap, announced a new roll call of the gang. Pictures of some of these men appear on page three. They are:

Alvin Karpis, Oklahoma outlaw, named by Attorney General Cummings as a suspect in the Bremer kidnaping case; Fred Barker, another Oklahoman and a Bremer case suspect; "Doc" Barker, brother of Fred; Tommy Carroll, St. Paul bank robber and machine gunner; John Hamilton, Dillinger's chief ally; Homer Van Meter, another of Dillinger's right-hand men; George ("Baby Face") Nelson, Chicago gunman; and Volney Davis, another suspect in the Bremer kidnaping.

In addition to the Frechetti girl, another woman is said to be a member of the gang. She is Beth Green, "wife" of Eugene Green, gangster slain by St. Paul police.

Today

(This column contains the personal views of a great commentator. His ideas do not necessarily coincide with the editorial ideas of The Daily News.)

Average Life To Be 100. Produce More, or Less? Vengeance Is Mine. Insult To Mules.

BY ARTHUR BRISBANE

THE American College of Physicians heard Dr. Meakins of Montreal promise that within 50 years any man willing to "use his intelligence and will power" may live 100 years. Fifty years ago the average human being was through with life at 40. Today's average is beyond 60. Dr. Meakins' promise of "a century of vital, energetic life for every member of the human race" is encouraging. The wise would want to be guaranteed to the "vital, energetic" part. Nothing sadder than to live merely for the sake of living.

Doumergue, prime minister, possessing the aggressive energy in old age that distinguished so many Frenchmen, says that France must have more allies, or more weapons. Allies being uncertain, he will rely on weapons. He says that French conditions are improving, gold again flowing to the Bank of France, and **he intends to help improvement by reducing the cost of living.**

Mussolini, with the same idea, makes products cheaper, urges greater production to let the people live more cheaply.

Here we have the other plan making everything dearer, cutting down production, plowing crops underground, paying farmers for not planting, instead of paying them for their crops, as in olden times, buying "farrow" sows, with little, unborn pigs inside them, and killing them to get rid of the pig crops.

The future will tell whether prosperity is based most securely on energy, work, full production, or on restriction of production, artificial increase of living costs.

Some think our plan will work no better than a plan for making water flow uphill. Events will show. It might have been simpler to organize and encourage production and distribution, at best prices obtainable. There would be no surplus, if everybody had all he needs. DEFECTIVE, COSTLY DISTRIBUTION is the real trouble.

"Vengeance is mine; I will repay, saith the Lord." Fred Lockhart, in the Shreveport (La.) jail waiting to be executed for his brutal murder of a 16-year-old girl, escaped a lynching mob of 4,000 only because in Shreveport the prison is on the upper floor of a skyscraper. He knows that the words above, from the 12th chapter of Romans, are true.

About 20 years ago Lockhart, under another name, was driving the car that carried Leo Frank from a Georgian prison, surrounded by a mob, that lynched him.

Vengeance has taken some time to catch up with him, but it has "caught up."

Convicts pulling cotton planting machines in Arkansas, taking the place of mules, have been released from that work. It was not hard, but the governor decided that convicts doing the work of mules represented in some way an insult to man, made in the image of his Creator.

If mules could talk, and were informed as to the character and crimes of the convicts, they might consider it an insult to honest mules.

In Tibet, women carry heavy loads on their heads over Himalayan mountain passes 20,000 feet high, where climbing Englishmen carry oxygen tanks. In China women carry bricks and mortar on their backs up hills too steep for horses. Two of those women could do easily the pulling work done by six Arkansas convicts.

"We are entering a period of sunspot activity." Astronomers, watching giant, mysterious "spots" moving over the sun's surface, seek exact knowledge as to their effect on the earth's climate. In one of these spots now visible, 16,000 miles in diameter, our earth could be lost and hidden.

Such spots affect the earth's heat supply, as clouds do, when passing before the sun. They produce also electrical storms, rains, tornadoes Some day men will know the exact

(Continued On Page 2, Col. 1.)

VOTE City Election Tuesday VOTE

THE ST. PAUL DAILY NEWS

Complete Wire Reports Of United Press, The Greatest World-Wide News Service

VOL. 35, NO. 54 — ST. PAUL, MINN., MONDAY, APRIL 23, 1934 — WEATHER: Fair and colder tonight; Tuesday fair with slowly rising temperature — PRICE TWO CENTS

TRAP CLOSING ON DILLINGER AFTER FIGHT NEAR ST. PAUL

POLICE IN SWARMS PURSUE TRIO THAT BATTLED WITH DEPUTY AT ST. PAUL PARK

All squads still on duty in St. Paul at 1:20 p. m. today were instructed to guard banks in their districts against the possibility of a holdup by the Dillinger mob.

With an army of federal, state, county and city police patrolling every road between St. Paul, Stillwater, Hastings and Prescott, Wis., John Dillinger and two of his mobsters were believed trapped in a gigantic net today.

Fleeing to his St. Paul hideouts after a midnight gun battle with federal officers and local officers at Mercer, Wis., the fugitive Indiana desperado and his companions engaged in a gun battle at noon today with a Dakota county sheriff's deputy who recognized the license plate numbers on a Ford V-8 coupe.

Dillinger's two companions were tentatively identified as Tommy Carroll, St. Paul's home-town member of the Dillinger gang, and John Hamilton, veteran Dillinger lieutenant.

Police In Hot Purspit.

The gunfight took place near St. Paul Pork.

Fleeing, after a barrage of machine-gun slugs had been fired at the deputies' car, the gunmen were pursued by the deputies and by two St. Paul squads who responded to a telephoned call for aid,

With half the St. Paul police detective squad already out of the city on a mysterious trip in connection with the Dillinger case, the city was practically stripped of police protection, as squad after squad was dispatched to the St. Paul Park-Afton area, and seven Minneapolis squads, equipped with submachine guns and rifles, were dispatched to the police headquarters at 10th and Minnesota sts.

Most of these squads, too, were soon dispatched to the St. Paul Park battlefront, and two held in reserve at the police station.

Flee Through Afton.

From Ramsey, Washington and Dakota counties squads of sheriffs' deputies were called in to aid in patrolling the area in which the three mobsters were believed trapped, and from the offices of the bureau of investigation United States department of justice, several of the few remaining agents were dispatched.

Last reports, telephone to police headquarters from a point near St. Paul Park, stated that the gangsters' car had fled through Afton closely pursued by three squads.

The three gunmen were riding in a black Ford V-8 coupe with Wisconsin license No. B 92-683.

When the bandits fled from Mercer broadcasts were sounded for three cars believed used: a Packard sedan, Wisconsin license 3111; a black V-8 Ford coupe, Wisconsin license 166-529, and a Ford coach, Wisconsin license 92-652.

It is believed that during the night the gangsters switched the license plates from the coach to the coupe.

T. H. Mattimore, cashier of the Farmers-Terminal bank at Newport

(Continued On Page 2, Col. 4.)

Schall Ducks Direct Defi By Mrs. F. R.

Ignores White House Bid To Repeat Charges On Furniture Plant.

By United Press.

WASHINGTON, April 23.—Mrs. Franklin D. Roosevelt today invited Sen. Thomas B. Schall, Republican, Minnesota, to the White House to challenge a statement he made concerning the Reedsville, W. Va., farm factory and the Val-Kill Furniture factory at Hyde Park, N. Y.

Schall did not appear after Mrs. Roosevelt waited two hours.

The President's wife has a financial interest in the Hyde Park factory, and has been active in sponsoring the Reedsville project.

Her denial of Schall's statement was made when the senator did not appear at the White House after Mrs. Roosevelt said he promised to see her.

"The denunciation," Schall's statement said, "of Dr. Wirt because he labeled Mrs. Roosevelt's attempt to build a furniture factory at Reedsville with $25,000,000 of the taxpayers' money, a communistic enterprise, is interesting in view of recent developments in connection

(Continued on Page 2, Col. 4.)

—VOTE TUESDAY—

HEFFELFINGER GIVES UP TO STAND TRIAL

W. R. Heffelfinger, for whom an attachment was issued in Ramsey county court last week when he failed to appear for a civil suit trial, today surrendered to Sheriff George Moeller.

He was taken before Judge R. D. O'Brien, who had issued the attachment, and was released on his own recognizance.

The civil suit, which is an action by stockholders of the United Oxide Co. to recover some ore leases in Cuba from Heffelfinger, is expected to go to trial within a few days.

GETS $100 FOR DIME

Miss Nancy Brown, 271 Maria ave., pictured above, is making a buy that looks like $100 for two nickels. But the catch on the sale Joe Osborne is making, is that the $100 is in stage money. Every person who attends the election night party of the St. Paul Junior Association at the municipal Auditorium Tuesday night will receive $100 worth of the stage money for his 25-cent admission ticket. The money can be used in the Auditorium to play the many games of chance to be set up. In addition to that form of entertainment, there will be dancing, a wrestling match between Abe Kashey and George Kuba, and a movie featuring Bobbie Jones. Loud speakers will broadcast the election returns, and winning candidates will be introduced.

Only 24 Hours Remain To Enter City Bridge Tourney; Valuable Prizes Offered

Bridge players who want an opportunity to annex one of the seven silver cups and the many other prizes to be awarded in the St. Paul contract bridge title tournament have only a little more than 24 hours to get into the running.

For entries for the tournament, which starts later thi. week, will close at 6 p. m. Tuesday. Entries may be made at The Daily News, at the St. Paul Athletic club, which is jointly sponsoring the event, at Field-Schlick's, or by mail on the form printed below. The coupon should be sent to The Daily News.

The contest is open to any bridge player, whether a resident of St. Paul or not, and many of the best players of St. Paul and nearby cities and communities already have entered.

A charge of 50 cents a person is made to cover the cost of cards, duplicate boards and other expenses. The charge also will admit those eliminated in the earlier rounds, as spectators to the later

(Continued On Page 2, Col. 5.)

Both Camps Confident In Hot City Race

Final Pleas To Be Made Tonight Over Air For Rivals In Campaign For Mayoralty.

Both sides in the hotly contested mayoralty campaign, which will be determined by the voters of St. Paul Tuesday, today predicted victory.

"Mark H. Gehan will be elected mayor by a good majority," was the prediction of Walter Fosness, chairman, Gehan-for-mayor volunteer committee, and an almost identical prediction was made by Charles Gerber, secretary of the mayor's volunteer committee.

In a brief statement at noon today, Mr. Gehan expressed himself as "absolutely confident of a favorable result."

Meantime, the campaign promises to end tonight with the customary display of verbal fireworks, both at meetings and on the air.

Candidates and their supporters were busy today rallying their respective followers for Tuesday's big battle of ballots, which will determine whether St. Paul shall be governed the next two years by independent officials or by a group carrying the Farmer-Labor banner and committed by their state platform to establishment of a "co-operative commonwealth."

Among the latest developments were:

Announcement that the final appeal for Mark H. Gehan for mayor will be made by former Mayor Gerhard J. Bundlie at 10:35 p. m. over radio station KSTP.

Announcement that the mayor will make his final personal appeal over radio station KSTP at 9:45 p. m., to be followed at

(Continued On Page 7, Col. 1.)

—VOTE TUESDAY—

Two Held Up

Burglary, Attempted Safe-Cracking Also Reported Here.

Two holdups, a burglary and an attempted safe cracking were reported to police over Sunday.

Ed J. Engman, 676½ Selby ave., was held up early Sunday on Selby ave., between Grotto and St. Albans sts., by three young bandits. The trio forced him to drive to near Rice st. and county road B, where they left him, taking his car and $5.

F. P. Koch, 1151 Reaney st., operator of a Dale-Phalen streetcar, was held up early today by a bandit at Denny and Forest sts. and robbed of $35.85 in cash and tokens.

Burglars who broke into the Minnesota Box Co., 327 Forest st., ransacked the place, smashing the dial off the safe, but obtained no loot.

Returning to his apartment after 20 days in a hospital, W. E. Wolf, 395 Dayton ave., discovered Sunday that a thief had gained entrance, and stolen $150 in cash contained in a $15 bag.

DILLINGER, EIGHT GANGSTERS ESCAPE TRAP IN WISCONSIN; 3 DIE IN ALL-NIGHT BATTLE

Carroll Was In Gun Fight, Federals Say

St. Paul Gunman Helped Dillinger Escape In Rhinelander Battle.

By United Press.

WASHINGTON, April 23.—John Dillinger and three members of his gang were definitely identified today as the gunmen who shot themselves out of a federal trap in northern Wisconsin.

The gangsters who escaped, according to Attorney General Homer S. Cummings, were John Dillinger, Tom Carroll, St. Paul gunman; Homer Van Meter and John Hamilton.

The three persons who were killed were one department of justice agent, W. Carter Baun; a CCC worker and a constable.

Three others were wounded, including a department of justice agent, Jay G. Newman, and two CCC workers.

—VOTE TUESDAY—

May Rescind $270,000 Deal

Sanitary Trustees Act On Engineers' Fee.

Trustees of the Minneapolis-St. Paul sanitary district were to meet today for final action on the much discussed $270,000 contract with Chicago engineers to supervise the $18,000,000 sewer project.

Voted last week by a majority of only one ballot, the plan to engage out-of-town engineers immediately elicited a barrage of criticism. Since all seven trustees of the sanitary district must sign the engineers' contract to make it effective, there was a possibility today that the necessary unanimity could not be obtained.

Meanwhile, PWA officials in Washington today said public works administration authority will prevent exorbitant fees for engineering service. They declined, however, to comment on the reasonableness of a $270,000 fee for the Chicago firm of Consoer, Townsend, Older & Quinlan.

By United Press.

EAGLE RIVER, Wis., April 23 Elusive John Dillinger and eight of his gangsters escaped again today from a federal trap after three gun battles in which reports of several officers placed the dead at two and the wounded at four persons.

Three women members of the gang were coptured. Sheriff Thomas McGregor, holding them in jail at Ironwood, Mich., refused to disclose their names.

Hundreds of federal agents, police from a half dozen cities and hastily deputized possemen converged on the lake-dotted wilderness of the Lac de Flambeau Indian reservation, hoping to trap the Indiana outlaw and his confederates in this region of but few roads.

Dead Placed At Three.

Undersheriff D. A. McGregor, brother of the sheriff, placed the number of dead at three and the wounded at eight.

Casualties, so far as could be learned, through federal censorship:

Dead:

W. Carter Baum, federal agent, Chicago.

Eugene Boiseneau, CCC worker, Mellen, Wis.

Wounded:

Carl Christiansen, constable, Spider Lake, Wis.

John Hoffman, city employe, Ironwood, Mich.

John Morris, CCC worker.

J. C. Newman, federal agent.

The series of bloody battles which turned a resort known as Little Bohemia lodge into a shambles before daybreak began at 10 p. m. Sunday.

Escape of Dillinger and his associates was made possible by unwitting interference with ambush plans by Boiseneau and two CCC companions, John Hoffman and John Morris.

Innocent Man Slain.

Just as the federal agents and deputy sheriffs had surrounded the lodge and prepared to enter, the trio of conservation corps workers walked out and entered their motor car.

When they refused to answer challenges of agents who thought they might be members of the gang the besieging force loosed upon them a fusillade of machine gun fire. Boiseneau was killed and his companions wounded as their car crashed out of control into a tree.

Returning to the lodge, the beseigers met such a withering fire from windows and doors of the resort that they retreated to the woods. Baum was fatally wounded in the sally and Carl Christiansen, constable of Spider Lake, critically wounded by a half dozen bullets.

Quarry Gets Away.

At 2:30 a. m., after summoning aid from Eagle River, the law forces attacked again. Machine guns flamed on both sides and several raiders fell as bullets ricocheted through the dark forest. Again the agents retired.

The third raid, at dawn, was made

(Continued on Page 2, Col. 3.)

TEMPERATURES

Hour	6	7	8	9	10	11	12	1	2
Temperature	46	45	43	43	42	43	44	45	43

Lowest last night, 44; a year ago today, highest, 74; lowest, 43.
Relative Humidity—7 a. m., 60 per cent.
Wind Velocity—7 a. m., 22 miles per hour.

(Further Weather News, Page 15.)

PERSONALITIES IN TODAY'S NEWS SPOTLIGHT

Another famous war ace has gone west. He is **WILLIAM THAW II,** commander of the Lafayette escadrille, who died in Pittsburgh after a week's illness of pneumonia . . . Safely back at Miami today is **LAURA INGALLS,** aviatrix who crossed the Andes alone and completed a 16,000-mile air tour of Central and South America . . . Science is willed the body of **DOLORES,** world famous model, a figure of glamour in the art world, who is dying in London . . . Newlyweds are **LOUIS F. SWIFT, JR.,** and **ELIZABETH CHASE.** The packing magnate and his bride will make their home in Ft. Worth, Tex. . . . Defying a death threat **MME. ERNESTINE SCHUMANN-HEINK,** 72-year-old grand opera star, sang at a concert held in New York by the Nonsectarian Anti-Nazi league . . . No more wedding bells for **JOAN CRAWFORD,** picture star, whose divorce decree from Douglas Fairbanks, Jr., becomes final May 13. Her name has been linked of late with that of Franchot Tone, but Joan says careers and matrimony do not mix.

FLAPPER FANNY SAYS:

REG. U. S. PAT. OFF.

Girls pensive before marriage are usually ex-pens've after marriage.

Minnesota Weather
Fair and cool today; Wednesday cloudy, possibly showers.
Detailed report on Page 16.

St. Paul Pioneer Press

Common Cause
Lion and lamb stand against the red dragon—Digest of the Minnesota Press on the Editorial Page.

VOL. 81. NO. 114. Full Leased Wire Service of the Associated Press. ST. PAUL, MINN., TUESDAY, APRIL 24, 1934. Complete Service of The United Press. c PRICE THREE CENTS IN ST. PAUL

DILLINGER GANG BELIEVED HIDDEN HERE; ONE MOBSTER SHOT; BLOODY CAR FOUND

EVERY ONE VOTE TODAY IS PLEA OF CANDIDATES

...ehan and Mahoney Urge Representative Ballot Significant of Citizens' Choice.

POLLING HOURS 6:30 TO 8

Junior Association in 'Last Night Move' to Get Out City Polls Record.

Bringing their campaigns to a close with a final barrage of addresses at numerous meetings and over the radio Monday night, candidates for city offices prepared to await the verdict of the voters in today's election.

Confident of success, leaders of both the Labor and Independent factions appealed to all citizens to cast their votes as an assurance that the final count will be representative of the will of the majority.

A campaign to get out the vote carried on under direction of the St. Paul Junior Association of Commerce culminated Monday night with the distribution of thousands of tags urging citizens to vote which were hung on door knobs throughout the city. Posters and cards were placed in automobiles parked in the downtown district.

New Filing Plan Issue.

Besides voting for mayor and councilmen, comptroller and minor officers, citizens will be asked to vote on an amendment to the city charter which would eliminate the present provision for the filing of 50 petitions for candidates for city offices. The proposed amendment provides for filing by the candidate with payment of a $10 filing fee.

All polling places will open at 6:30 A. M. and close at 8 P. M. Records in the office of the city clerk show that 129,630 persons are registered and eligible to vote.

In an appeal for a representative vote, Mark H. Gehan, candidate for mayor, said:

"I want to urge all citizens of St. Paul to go to the polls. It is important that you cast your vote. A government can be properly representative only when all citizens take part in its selection.

"Only about 55 per cent of the eligible voters take part in the average election in this country. It is conceivable that under these circumstances 30 per cent of the eligible voters of a city may select the officials and determine policies which affect vitally all the people. The idea of letting a small minority run our government seems repugnant to most of us, yet we contribute to that condition when we fail to go to the polls and vote.

"Ordinary Citizen" Should Vote.

"The persons who have public jobs or some special interest in the expenditures of a city usually vote, while too often the ordinary citizen, who expects nothing from his officials but good city government, neglects his franchise. The man who pays the bills too often does not vote. Many of us do a lot of complaining about the acts of our officials but do not take the trouble to vote on election day.

"No duty is so important as that of voting. Unless the great bulk of our citizens go to the polls our officials have no way of knowing what the people want. Governments pretty largely represent the people who put them into office. If all the people would vote, the trend of our governmental action would be considerably different than it is now when officials usually are

(Please Turn to Page 5, Col. 1.)

COOL WEATHER PREDICTED FOR CITY AND STATE

Fair and rather cool weather is predicted for St. Paul and the rest of the state for today, by the government weather bureau.

Increasing cloudiness followed possibly by showers in the west portion of Minnesota is forecast for Wednesday.

HOURLY TEMPERATURES

Hourly temperatures in St. Paul from 1 P. M. Monday to 7 A. M. today as recorded on the Pioneer Press and Dispatch government tested thermometer were:

1 P. M.	43	8 P. M.	42
2 P. M.	43	9 P. M.	41
3 P. M.	43	10 P. M.	40
4 P. M.	45	11 P. M.	37
5 P. M.	43	12 M.	34
6 P. M.	44	1 A. M.	33
7 P. M.	44	2 A. M.	33

LITTLE BOHEMIA, BLOODY ESCAPE CAR AND RESORT MEN

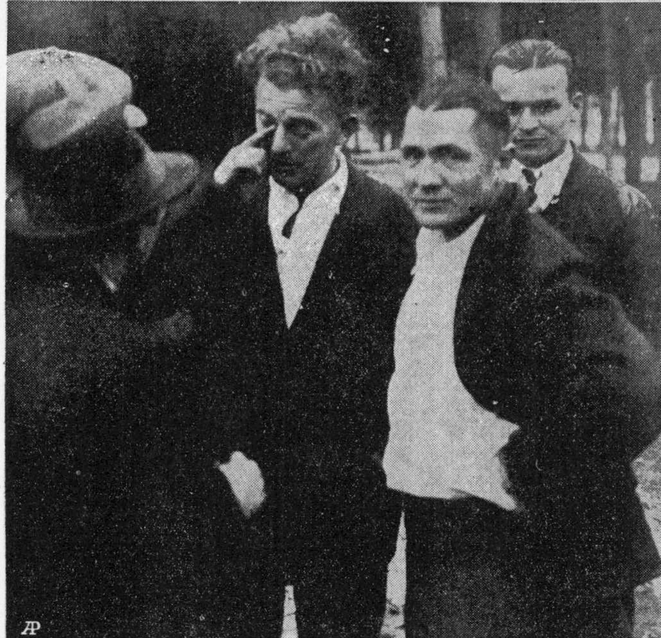

Here are scenes and some of the principals in the Federal government's latest skirmish with John Dillinger, the killer, who came back to St. Paul for refuge following a gun fight Sunday night near Mercer, Wis.

Left above is the Little Bohemia resort, which Dillinger and his gang seized Friday and from which they fled Sunday night.

The bullet-pierced and blood-stained auto is the one abandoned near St. Paul after the gangsters battled a police detail near Hastings. The heavy bloodstain, with the light mark in the center showing where bullet emerged, indicates one of the men was wounded.

The two men in the foreground of the lower picture are Frank Traube (with his hand to his face) and Emil Wanatka (hands on hips) who were virtual prisoners while the gangsters occupied the Little Bohemia camp. Wanatka is the proprietor.

'Kept My Mouth Shut So Dillinger Gang Wouldn't Hurt Me,' Resort Owner Says

Tells of Losing $18 to Fugitive in One Poker Game and Later Winning $28.

By EMIL WANATKA.
(Owner of Little Bohemia Resort.)

Manitowish, Wis., April 23.—(AP)—John Dillinger had been here at Little Bohemia only about four hours when I recognized him. I had seen his picture in the newspapers many times. After supper, Dillinger and four of his gang invited me to play cards with them.

We sat there playing two-bit limit poker when I suddenly recognized his features. I was frightened. I knew I should not do anything that would cause Dillinger and his pals to hurt me so I kept my mouth shut. I played along and lost $16 or $18. Dillinger won. It was a gentlemanly game and Dillinger enjoys cards. He is a good player. The women played rhummy.

Last Friday afternoon one man and a woman came here and asked for accommodations. I showed them the rooms and they said more people were coming. About two hours later another car came. There were three

(Please Turn to Page 3, Col. 3.)

HIRING CONSULTANTS ON SEWER UP FRIDAY

Sanitary Trustees Vote Down Motion to Reconsider Employing Chicago Concern.

Trustees of the Minneapolis-St. Paul Sanitary district will consider at 2 P. M. Friday a contract with the engineering firm of Consoer, Townsend, Older & Quinlan of Chicago, which a majority of the trustees have voted to employ as consultants on the Twin Cities sewage disposal project.

This was determined Monday after a motion to reconsider the employment of this concern was defeated by the same vote which failed to defeat the original employment. The motion was made by Sidney Benson of Minneapolis and supported by A. G. Bastis and W. J. Meagher of Minneapolis. It was opposed by Mayor Mahoney, Commissioner Clyde R. May, H. P. Keller, St. Paul members of the board, and R. A. Olson of Duluth, the member named by Governor Olson.

Judge J. C. Rockwood of the Minneapolis Taxpayers league appeared before the trustees and urged them to give more study to the employment of consulting engineers and to determine more closely the scope of employment before signing with the Chicago firm.

The Engineers club of St. Paul sent a communication to the trustees urging that in any contract the trustees might have with an out-of-town engineering concern safeguards be written to insure the employment of as many local engineers as possible.

The trustees also received a communication from Alexander Potter

(Please Turn to Page 5, Col. 5.)

KANSAS CITIAN NAMED LIQUOR CONTROL HEAD

Washington, April 23.—(AP)—Arthur J. Mellott of Kansas City was named by Secretary Morgenthau today to head the government's liquor control campaign.

Mellott will be a deputy commissioner of internal revenue. He will direct tax collecting on liquor as well as efforts to prevent illicit liquor operations.

The Treasury's force for such work will be increased May 10 by the transfer of approximately 750 men from the Justice department's old prohibition unit. Mellott will take office May 2.

AAA SHELVES PLAN TO CUT DAIRY OUTPUT

Abandons 165-Million-Dollar Program Including 12 Million for Minnesota.

By J. R. WIGGINS.
(Pioneer Press Staff Correspondent.)

Washington, April 23—Dairy production control plans, calling for payment of more than twelve million dollars in benefits to Minnesota farmers alone, were shelved today by the AAA as the result of opposition within the industry.

Admitting that its proposal to reduce milk ouptut by 10 per cent, through 165 million dollars in benefit payments and disease eradication, did not have support sufficient to assure its success, the administration announced that it "will not undertake a benefit payment dairy production control program for the present".

The dairy plan is the only one of the seven curtailment schemes formulated by the government so far to be refused by a group of farm producers. Its rejection leaves the largest single farm industry, the returns from which represent one-fourth of the earnings of American agriculture, outside the operation of the Agricultural Adjustment act, except for milk marketing agreements in 21 milk sheds controlling probably less than 10 per cent of the whole milk output.

The effectiveness of this aid to even a small minority of the industry will be impaired by the failure to control milk production as a whole, it is feared.

The opposition to the dairy plan was led by the National Co-operative Milk Producers federation whose spokesmen voiced dissent from the

(Please Turn to Page 5, Col. 3.)

Gangsters Split in Flight After Shooting Out of Trap

Three Women Seized at Wisconsin Hideout Refuse to Talk to Agents.

(Copyright by Associated Press.)

Mercer, Wis., April 23.—(AP)—John Dillinger, with hate in his heart and murder on his trigger finger, was at large tonight, grim posses hard on his heels after he had blazed his way out of a police trap leaving two dead and four wounded.

He vanished out of a beleaguered Wisconsin resort Sunday night, with his quick shooting first lieutenant, John Hamilton, and five of his outlaw band, after he had taken possession of the place and mounted a machine gun to repel invaders.

Tonight, this north woods section was in the grip of a blizzard, with hard driving snow hampering the government men and local officers in their relentless pursuit of clues to the arch criminal.

Apparently the Dillinger gang split after the deadly gun battle, but there was no letup in the search for the outlaw whose exploits have become fabled.

The latest victims of the Dillinger hunt were:

W. Carter Baum, Federal agent from Chicago, shot dead by an outlaw.

Eugene Boisoneau of Mellen, Wis., killed mistakenly, by the officers.

Carl C. Christensen, constable of Spider Lake, Wis., wounded probably fatally by Baum's assassin.

John Hoffman of Mercer, wounded while riding with Boisoneau.

John Morris, Civilian Conservation camp officer, shot three times, riding with Boisoneau.

J. C. Newman, Federal agent, slightly wounded.

A tip telephoned to the Chicago Bureau of Investigation of the Justice department brought the government men swooping down on the timberland retreat which the Dillinger mob had taken over by force Friday. There were seven of his band, including Hamilton, escaped convict; Tommy Carroll, St. Paul bank robber; Homer Van Meter, George (Baby Face) Nelson, others unidentified and three girls.

Emil Wanatka, proprietor of the Little Bohemia resort on Spider lake, recognized Dillinger when his gang arrived and registered, but "why should I try to take him?" he remarked. "I played cards with him every day. Say, he had a roll of money big enough to choke a cow."

Wanatka said he and his two employes were virtual prisoners. A machine gun was installed on the roof. Some one was always on guard.

The Federal men, reinforced with local officers, began surrounding the resort Sunday night.

About 10 P. M., three men, having regaled themselves with beer, walked out of the Little Bohemia and stepped into their automobile. The officers commanded them to halt. They failed to hear the order because, they said, the radio in the car was on.

Watchdogs began barking. The machine gun on the roof let loose a deadly blast. The officers fired back, and in the cross fire Boisoneau, one of the trio who had stopped in for drinks, was killed. Morris wounded and Hoffman hurt as he fled into the woods. He was captured and taken with the others to a

(Please Turn to Page 3, Col. 1.)

Latest Moves On Dillinger And His Flight

Following is a chronological summary of events in the latest effort to capture John Dillinger and members of his gang:

FRIDAY—Dillinger and three companions, identified as John Hamilton, Homer Van Meter and Tommy Carroll, seized by force the Little Bohemia camp, a summer resort nine miles northeast of Mercer, Wis., in the heart of wild forest country. Here they "partied" until Sunday night.

SUNDAY NIGHT—Federal agents, assisted by peace officers, attempted to raid the resort. Dillinger and his followers fled through a rear door as the raiders mistook another party for the gangsters. A government agent and a CCC worker were killed. Two of the latter's companions and a Department of Justice agent and a constable were wounded.

MONDAY, 11:35 A. M.—Three of the fleeing desperadoes, one of them possibly Dillinger himself, appeared in the St. Paul vicinity, and escaped after a gun battle with deputy sheriffs between Hastings and St. Paul Park.

MONDAY, 1 P. M.—The gang stole an automobile from a South St. Paul man, forcing the man, his wife and a year-and-a-half-old baby out of the car near South St. Paul.

MONDAY, 1:30 P. M.—A blood-soaked coupe, which had been stolen at Mercer, and was used by the gangsters in the gun fight near St. Paul, was found on Highway 53, five miles south of the St. Paul city limits, near the point where the South St. Paul man was robbed of his car. Blood stains and the position of bullet holes in the car left

(Please Turn to Page 2, Col. 2.)

Today's Editorials

Page 6.

Vote Today
The duty of every citizen, also the invaluable right.

Dillinger's New Escape
Let everyone co-operate with the authorities in finding him out.

The Dixie Differential
Southern industry argues for lower wage scales than their Northern rivals.

Relief from the Drouth
Sun spots may usher in a new long wet cycle of years.

Spain Wants to Trade
We should accommodate her.

Cop's Bullet Hits Fugitive At Hastings

Truck Gets Between Fleeing Auto and Officers' Machine on Spiral Bridge, Blocking Pursuit After Exchange of Shots; Police Look for Body or Appeal to Doctor for Clues; Banks Get Extra Guards.

REPORTS HAVE BAND'S LEADER IN TAXI AND CLYDE BARROW NEAR ST. PAUL

John Dillinger, America's most treacherous and wanton killer, apparently had returned to St. Paul for refuge Monday, and either one or more of his companions is wounded.

Evidence that one or more of the gangsters was shot when in their flight to St. Paul from a Northern Wisconsin gun battle with Federal men they ran into a Dakota county police detail at Hastings, was obtained Monday afternoon with the recovery of an automobile abandoned by the gang.

The car, blood-soaked and bullet-riddled, was found on Highway No. 53, five miles south of the St. Paul city limits. This is near the point where the fleeing desperadoes, after their gun fight with three Dakota county deputies and a Hastings policeman, stole a car from a South St. Paul man.

Dillinger's Hair Dyed Bright Red

Mercer, Wis., April 23.—(AP)—John Dillinger's hair has been dyed a bright red, it was said by Emil Wanatka, resort proprietor who was forced to give accommodations to the fugitive and his companions for three days. Dillinger's hair, before artificially colored, was light brown. It has grown some since it was dyed, with the result it is darkening at the roots, Wanatka said.

The seat of the abandoned car, a coupe, was blood soaked, and at least one bullet had entered the rear of the machine at a point where it could not miss one of the three occupants.

MOBSTER MAY STILL CARRY BULLET.

This bullet was from a 30-30 rifle in the hands of Fred McArdle, Hastings policeman. Search of the car failed to reveal the slug, and, unless the wounded gangster has found medical assistance, it probably is still in his body.

The evidence that one of the gang was hit increased the hopes of Department of Justice operatives and police of capturing or gaining some clue to the fugitives. It was believed certain, if one of the gangsters is killed, his body will be found, or if he is wounded, an effort will be made by his pals to get medical assistance.

While there were numerous reports up to an early hour today that the gang had been sighted in or near St. Paul, the encounter with the Dakota county officers was the last definite clue to the whereabouts of the gang, whose escape from a resort they took by force near Mercer, Wis., three days before resulted in the killing Sunday night of a Federal man and a CCC worker, and the wounding of four other men.

BELIEVED IN HIDEOUT IN ST. PAUL.

Dillinger and his henchmen, who found refuge here once before only to flee after a gun battle with Department of Justice agents in an apartment March 31, apparently had reached a hideout in their dash through St. Paul streets following the clash with the Dakota county detail.

Meanwhile the Dakota county pursuers disclosed that a slow-moving cattle truck and an official auto that was outdistanced served to block the capture of the gangsters as they approached St. Paul.

But if these factors prevented the capture of Dillinger, they also probably saved the lives of some of the four officers who tried to capture the outlaws.

"We were stationed at the bridge at Hastings," Patrolman McArdle said. "We saw the Ford coupe coming up to the spiral bridge and we jumped into Joe Heinen's car. There were Joe, Norman Deiter and Larry Dunn, (all Dakota county deputies), and myself.

"Just as we were going to cut this coupe off at the bridge, a cattle truck pulled in front of us, the coupe got on the bridge, and we couldn't pass the truck until after we got across the bridge. Then the coupe was way up ahead and going fast.

"We took out after them, and we were nearly up to St. Paul Park before we could begin shooting. They began shooting back. I guess there were at least fifteen or 20 shots fired from each car. One of the bullets hit our car in the wood framework above the windshield, and just above Joe Heinen's head.

"At St. Paul Park, they turned off east, and took to the hill roads over toward Cottage Grove. We kept after them and did some more shooting, but they got away from us on those roads. We went as fast as we could on those roads but they outdistanced us. So we finally lost them.

"Joe was awful lucky. If the bullet had been three inches lower it would have hit him right in the head."

The belief that Dillinger has accomplices in the Twin Cities was

(Please Turn to Page 2, Col. 1.)

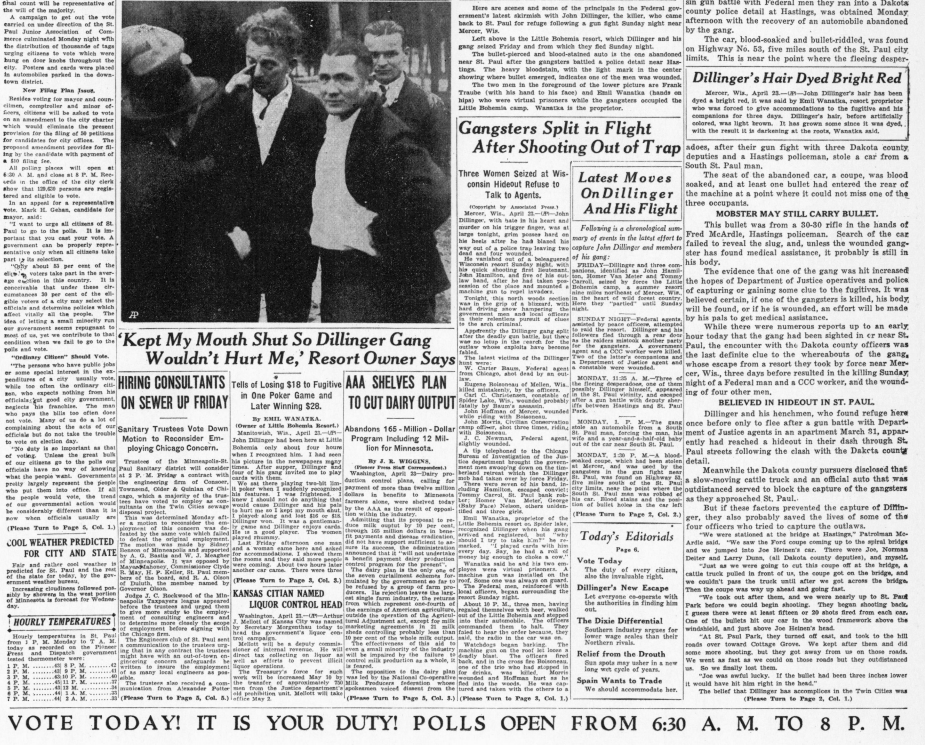

VOTE TODAY! IT IS YOUR DUTY! POLLS OPEN FROM 6:30 A. M. TO 8 P. M.

NONE but an author knows an author's cares,
Or fancy's fondness for the child she bears.
—Cowper.

The Dallas Morning News

Section One General News

49TH YEAR NO. 208 (AP)—Associated Press. (UP)—United Press. (NANA)—North American Newspaper Alliance. DALLAS, TEXAS, THURSDAY, APRIL 26, 1934—TWENTY PAGES Oldest Business Institution in Texas—Founded in Galveston April 11, 1842.—Established in Dallas October 1, 1885. 5c PER COPY

Ray Hamilton Caught 2 Hours After Holdup

Asia's Dominance Japan's Aim, Says Chinese Spokesman

Nine-Power Treaty Signatories to Be Sounded Out on Appeal From Nipponese Fiat

London Worried

Officials in Washington Concerned, but Reticent Over Possibilities

GENEVA, April 25 (AP).—Indications that China will sound out the United States and other signatories of the nine-power treaty to determine whether an appeal against Japan would have their support or would merely result in another Japanese diplomatic victory were given Wednesday night.

A charge that Japan seeks to dominate Asia and the Pacific was made by Chi Tsai-Hu, Chinese Minister to Switzerland, who even drew a picture of Japan dreaming of world supremacy.

To support this he cited from an alleged memorandum of the late Premier Guiichi Tanaka, which declared "to conquer the entire world, conquest of China is essential."

Wants Chinese Market.

Japan, Chi Tsai-Hu asserted, objects to China's markets being opened indiscriminately to foreign nations, insisting that Tokio wishes to keep a privileged situation to herself.

Alluding to Japan's objections to League of Nations assistance for China, the Minister said China sought aid from Geneva because she wished to develop her national resources and increase purchasing power, which would absorb goods from other nations and contribute to a solution of the economic crisis.

"Japan's policies, he asserted, violate

See JAPAN on Page 2.

Weather Report

NEW ORLEANS, La., April 25 (AP).—Government weather forecast:

East Texas (including Dallas and vicinity): Generally fair Thursday; Friday partly cloudy to cloudy, cooler in north portion.

West Texas: Partly cloudy to cloudy, cooler in the Panhandle Thursday; Friday partly cloudy, cooler in north and east portions.

Louisiana: Generally fair Thursday; Friday partly cloudy.

Arkansas: Increasing cloudiness, warmer Thursday; Friday partly cloudy to cloudy and somewhat unsettled.

Oklahoma: Mostly cloudy and unsettled, cooler in northwest portion Thursday; Friday partly cloudy to cloudy, cooler in east portion.

Dallas Temperatures.

Temperatures in Dallas Wednesday, April 25, 1934, and for same date last year, as reported by United States Weather Bureau, follow:

	1934.	1933.		1934.	1933.
Midnight	67	66	Noon	63	74
2 a. m.	67	63	2 p. m.	67	77
4 a. m.	65	63	4 p. m.	70	75
6 a. m.	65	62	6 p. m.	72	65
7 a. m.	64	63	7 p. m.	72	59
10 a. m.	62	71			

Maximum temperature April 26 last year 84 degrees, minimum 60 degrees. Rainfall for 24 hours ending 7 p. m. Wednesday .03 inch. Total precipitation so far this year 9.79 inches.

Full weather report on Page 7, Section II.

WILD FOWL IN FLIGHT.

ALONG the mauve and silver sky
With golden memories in the west,
You stream, scarce beating as you fly,
To some far land addressed,
Linked like a kite tail in the air,
Or silken ladder moving there.

I should not waste with wondering
This moment of your stately flight;
How, without lapse or blundering,
You steer by day, by night,
As poets of an earlier time
Have marveled in exalted rime;

But I should ask you if I could,
Do you forget your breeding ground,
The hearty spice of Northern wood,
When the long trail, southbound,
Ends in some marsh with dipping moss
Where lazy herons flap across?

Or, marching northward overhead
When spring has set her signals there,
Flout the warm lavish land that spread
Her best and did not spare?
Fly on! The beckoning signs tell true:
Worlds left behind are naught to you.

—Jeannie Pendleton Hall, in the Lantern.

Newspaper Heads Urged to Protect Freedom of Press

Increasing Vigilance Is Sought at New York Meeting of Publishers

NEW YORK, April 25 (AP).—The American Newspaper Publishers' Association unanimously adopted on Wednesday a resolution urging its members to be increasingly vigilant to protect the principles of the freedom of the press from impairment.

The resolution, watched closely in view of the fight waged by an A. N. P. A. committee for a free press clause in the daily newspaper code, avoided any criticism of NRA or Government officials.

Its passage without a dissenting voice came several hours after Howard Davis, president of the association and chairman of its code committee, said the daily press had a good code under which to operate, one which is concise, clear and specific.

In his opening address, Davis, business manager of the New York Herald Tribune, said the constitutinoal guaranty of the freedom of the press remained unimpaired.

The resolution was introduced by the chairman of the freedom of the press committee, Col. Robert R. McCormick of the Chicago Tribune, who criticized the recovery administration in his argument for it. It read:

"Whereas, The freedom of the press

See PRESS on Page 2.

Posseman Tells Story of Taking Pair of Bandits

Hamilton and His Pal Stuck Hands in Air at First Commnad

Special to The News.

SHERMAN, Texas, April 25.—The story of how the capture of Raymond Hamilton, widely wanted Southwestern desperado, and T. R. Brooks of Wichita Falls, was affected was told here Wednesday evening by Dr. John T. Nall, local optometrist and arms instructor on the police department. Dr. Nall was one of the four men who assisted in the capture of the two desperadoes who robbed the Lewisville bank Wednesday, and who were caught at Howe, ten miles south of Sherman.

Dr. Nall5s story follows:

"The Sheriff's department was notified by telephone from Gunter that the bandits were headed toward Sherman, driving fast and reckless. In the party leaving here were Deputy Sheriff Collier Yuery and Deputy Sheriff Roy McDaniel, men under the regime of Sheriff J. Benton Davis and myself. We left here shortly after 4. We received notice that Hamilton was cutting through toward Van Alstyne, going east out of Gunter. We drove to Howe and Van Alstyne and returning we recognized the car, on the Dallas-Sherman highway.

"McDaniel was driving our car. When he recognized Hamilton's car, he turned around as fast as he could and gave chase. It was a sweet one, too. Just as soon as we got in shooting range of the car, which was on the outskirts of Howe, they wheeled and tried to pass us. aFiling to pass us, Roy McDaniel swung his car and blocked them.

"I covered the desperadoes, with Yuery following me with his gun. Seeing that they were covered, they brought their car to a stop. Hamilton and Brooks, with Hamilton at the wheel, had their hands in the air.

See CAPTURE on Page 3.

Girl, 6, Kidnaped, Held for $15,000

TUCSON, Ariz., April 25 (AP).—June Robles, 6-year-old daughter of Mr. and Mrs. Fernando Robles, and granddaughter of Bernabe Robles, one of Pima County's wealthiest citizens, was kidnaped as she was returning home from school here Wednesday afternoon and held for $15,000 ransom, police reported.

Income Boost Holds Up Agreement on Tax Bill

WASHINGTON, April 25 (UP).—Senate and House conferees Wednesday night agreed on all provisions of the new tax bill except the Senate amendment for a 10 per cent increase on all income tax payments on 1934 income.

Bank Robbery Leads to Bandit's Capture

—News Staff Photo.

The top panel shows Assistant Cashier E. R. Wolters of the First National Bank at Lewisville, which was robbed by Raymond Hamilton Wednesday. Lower panel shows the bank with crowd. In the inset is Hamilton, who was caught two hours after the robbery.

Skirts of Woman Cannon Defense, Attorney Claims

Counsel Equally Vigorous in Holding Bishop Being Persecuted

WASHINGTON, April 25 (AP).—Disagreeing in the usual vigorous manner of opposing counsel, prosecution and defense attorneys alternately told a jury Wednesday that Bishop James Cannon Jr. was hiding "behind a woman's skirts," and that the churchman and Ada L. Burroughs were being persecuted.

The case probably will go to the jury Thursday.

In presenting the Government's summary of evidence to substantiate its charges tha tthe bishop and his former secretary conspired to violate the corrupt practices act, John J. Wilson, the prosecutor, said Cannon had spent for his personal use money that was contributed to the 1928 campaign against Alfred E. Smith.

"He talks to you about tin boxes

See CANNON on Page 2.

Spanish Cabinet Quits After Row With President

MADRID, April 25 (AP).—The declaration of a nation-wide state of alarm and recurrent reports that President Niceto Alcala Zamora would quit were sensational sequels Wednesday night to the resignation of Premier Alejandro Lerroux's Government.

High ministerial sources said the executive conferred with close friends of the administration about the advisability of resigning in view of the tense political and strike situation, which the President apparently believes can not be solved merely by a Cabinet shake-up.

A break with Alcala Zamora over his congressional message on a political amnesty law, which Lerroux interpreted as an implied lack of confidence in his Cabinet, led to the Government's resignation.

Rafael Alonso, Interior Minister in the resigned Cabinet, declared the state of alarm—similar to martial law.

Bulk of Navy's Strength Moved Through Panama

COLON, Canal Zone, April 25 (AP).—As the United States Navy fleet of 111 vessels completed its forty-eight-hour transit through the Panama Canal Wednesday it was learned that war-like conditions obtaining during the movement were made necessary by fears that attempts might be made to interfere with the maneuver.

Authorities received information from the army intelligence service several months ago that a conspiracy seemed in progress to thwart the swift passage of the flotilla through the locks.

Consequently heavy guards of soldiers patrolled the locks during the transit and a smaller force will remain indefinitely, it was said, to supplant guards stationed at the vital parts of the canal late in March.

Hitherto the locks have been without protection and anybody has been able to approach them day or night.

In view of the reported plot, naval

See FLEET on Page 2.

Twenty New Ships To Start Navy's Race for Parity

First of 95 Modern Vessels to Be Laid Down in Four Months

WASHINGTON, April 25 (AP).—Within four months, the administration expects to start building twenty of the ninety-five ships needed to give the United States a fleet second to no other navy in the world.

President Roosevelt let it be known Wednesday that the $1,500,000,000 appropriation bill he will submit to Congress shortly would provide money for initial construction in the treaty navy program.

The bill, said Chairman Vinson (Dem.), Georgia, of the House Naval Committee, will carry about $40,000,000 for the first year's work on six submarines of 1,300 tons, twelve destroyers of 1,500 tons and two destroyer leaders of 1,850 tons.

"We expect to spend actually only about $37,000,000 the first year," Vin-

See NEW SHIPS on Page 2.

Long-Sought Thug And His Latest Pal Surrender Mildly

Woman Associate Of Hamilton in Jail at Amarillo

Held Three Days While Officers Lie in Wait for Bandit to Appear

Mary O'Dare, former companion of Raymond Hamilton and alleged partner of his in the robbery of the West, McLennan County, bank, was arrested Monday at Amarillo by Special Investigator M. L. Miller of District Attorney Robert L. Hurt's staff, Hurt was informed Wednesday night.

Miller telephoned Hurt of the arrest immediately after he and other officers at Amarillo learned of Hamilton's arrest. They had arrested her Monday but kept the arrest secret in the hope of catching Hamilton if he returned to Amarillo to join her.

Expected Bank Robbery.

"Miller said the officers he was with at Amarillo knew Hamilton was preparing to rob a bank, but they didn't know where," Hurt quoted. "Miller said they knew Hamilton would attempt to rejoin Mary O'Dare immediately after the robbery."

Hurt said Miller, Special Investigator Denver Seale, Ranger Capt. D. E. Hamer and Rangers Jim Shown and W. R. Todd had been waiting at Amarillo for more than a week to "put Hamilton on the spot." He said they had the co-operation of Detective Chief Clark Caine and the chief of

See O'DARE on Page 2.

Prosecutor Hurt Wants Hamilton Tried Here First

Convinced County Jury Would Assess Death in Bank Robbery

Immediate indictment and trial of Raymond Hamilton for his part in the Lancaster and Grand Prairie bank robberies will be asked, District Attorney Robert L. Hurt said, and the jury that tries him will be urged to assess the death penalty.

"Hamilton already has 263 years of prison sentences against him," Hurt said. "We believe he deserves the death penalty and that a Dallas County jury will give it to him.

"He was in the Lancaster robbery and the Grand Prairie robbery, and in either case a jury should give him death as punishment.

"With so many years of imprisonment assessed against him, Hamilton didn't stay in prison long, and we don't think it would do any good to give him any more prison terms.

"He deserves the death penalty and if Denton County will let us try him first, we will do all in our power to see that he gets it."

Assistant District Attorney Winter R. King of Dallas County left for Denton immediately after the report Hamilton was being transferred there, and was instructed by Hurt to request the Denton County prosecutors to permit trial of Hamilton in Dallas first.

Farley to Stay Out Of Tammany Dispute

WASHINGTON, April 25 (AP).—Postmaster General Farley, national and New York State chairman of the Democratic party, told reporters Wednesday that neither he nor the Roosevelt administration would take any hand in the selection of the a successor to John F. Curry, as leader of Tammany Hall.

Lewisville Bank Robbed of $1,000 and Officers, Immediately on Trail, Do Quick Work

Guilt Is Admitted

Stolen Currency and Silver Found in Car When Arrests Made

Less than two hours after Raymond Hamilton held up the First National Bank at Lewisville in Denton County, for nearly $1,000 Wednesday, the long-sought desperado and escaped convict was captured on the Dallas-Sherman highway, seven miles south of Sherman in Grayson County.

A posse of officers and citizens halted Hamilton and his sole companion, T. R. Brooks, 21, Wichita Falls, as they raced through the town of Howe in a small sedan. All currency and silver stolen from the bank were found in the car. Although armed with automatic pistols, neither man offered any fight when cornered by the posse.

Admitting his identity, Hamilton and his partner were taken under heavy guard to Sherman, where they were kept overnight. They will probably be brought Thursday to either Denton or Dallas, where charges will be filed.

Howard Gunter, a citizen living at Gunter, Collin County, who joined the chase, lost his life in an accident near Sherman while driving Hamilton's stolen car from Howe.

Captured After Chase.

The capture came as the climax to a forty-mile, neck-and-neck race between Hamilton and Constable D. H. Street of Lewisville, who was driven in a new small car by State Legislator T. B. Hyder of Lewisville. The 27-year-old legislator, who urged a $25,000 dead-or-alive reward by the State for gunmen at the recent special session at Austin, was unarmed.

While Street and Hyder were chasing the bandits through Little Elm, Frisco, Celina and Gunter to a junction with the Dallas-Sherman highway at Howe, scores of peace officers and private citizens in five counties were conducting one of the most determined cross-country manhunts on record. This was possible due to the quick wit of President M. H. Milliken of the Lewisville bank, who at once telephoned Dallas peace officers. They in turn had Police Radio Station KVP broadcast news of the robbery and a description of the bandits' car.

Sheriffs, Constables, deputies, State highway patrolmen and private citizens, ignoring county lines, scoured the countryside as a result. Thus, the posse at Howe, co-operating with the Dallas police radio, was able to make the first major catch of a criminal under the recently worked out agreement between officers in twenty-two North Texas counties.

The Lewisville bank, which proved to be Hamilton's Jonah, was merely living up to its old reputation. Held up only once before, back in 1915, its victimizers then also were caught in a few hours and their criminal careers ended.

Teammate of Barrow.

Hamilton for a long time was a teammate of the even more notorious Clyde Barrow of Dallas. North Texas

See HAMILTON on Page 2.

Levelland Bank Robbed of $2,500 By Four Bandits

Gang Escapes Toward New Mexico in Auto With Texas License

LEVELLAND, Hockley Co., Texas, April 25 (AP).—Four armed bandits swooped down to this little Hockley County town shortly after 2 p. m. Wednesday and robbed the First National Bank of Levelland of about $2,500. Rounding up all employes and customers in the bank, and locking them in the vault, the bandits worked quickly and were soon speeding westward toward the New Mexico State line.

The gang escaped in a V-8 Ford thought to be bearing a Texas license plate.

Bandits Wave Pistols.

Two men appeared in the front door of the bank and announced it was being held up, waving pistols in the faces of customers and employes and ordering them to the rear of the building. Two or three men were thought to have stood guard on the outside of the building.

All officers of the bank, including John Doyle, president; Harry Mann, vice president, and Mrs. Irene Ellis, cashier, were shoved into the vault along with at least eight or nine patrons. As they were being forced into the vault, one of the men robbed sev-

See LEVELLAND on Page 2.

News Behind the News

By PAUL MALLON (Copyright, 1934, by Paul Mallon)

Pig Poundage Problem Is Getting Weighty for AAA Men.

Pig Food.

WASHINGTON, April 25.—The three little pigs and all their kin are no joke to the big brain men in the AAA.

There is some talk now that the Government may send out reducing machines or masseurs to make the pigs of the country keep their figures within reason. At any rate, the pig poundage problem is getting weighty.

The AAA has now loaned the farmers 45c a bushel on approximately 262,000,000 bushels of last year's corn. This hog-fattening food has been put under seal in corncribs on farms. The loan contracts provide that the farmers shall pay the Government back Aug. 1.

But pig-caviar is now selling for about 46c a bushel in an unsatisfactory market.

The market would be revived if the sealed surplus were released either to the public or the dieting pigs Aug. 1 or any time. What to do?

Borrowing Trouble.

The AAA is saying nothing about it yet. It's master mentalities are beginning to appreciate, however, that they have worked themselves into something like the mess of Mr. Hoover's farm board.

The farmers have on hand, unsealed, about 570,000,000 bushels, which will provide the curtailed diet of the pigs until Aug. 1. Then, this year's corn crop will be available.

Half the insiders are inclined to do what Brazil did with her surplus coffee not long ago. They would make bonfires out of it, or toss it in the ocean—anything to keep it away from the pigs. It would cost the Government around $117,000,000 but that probably would be the cheapest way out.

It only goes to show the trouble you get into when you start regimentation of the girth of pigs. Also what happens when the Government starts lending money to its citizens.

Prosperity.

The new corn-hog checks have just started going out to Midwestern producers. That means strong stimulation of purchasing power in that section during the next few months.

These payments are for acreage curtailment and have nothing to do with the loans on last year's crop.

The only connection is that the farmers who got the loans last year agreed in their contracts to curtail their acreage this year.

Worry.

The House leaders fumed when a conservative press association recently carried a yarn indicating Mr. Roosevelt might get some new leaders for the next session of Congress.

What hurt was that the story was true, despite all the denials and confusion subsequently stirred up.

The story was inspired by persons very close to the White House. For some weeks they have been groaning backstage about the clumsiness with which the House has handled administration business.

The leaders know where the story came from and one was so worried he went to the White House to ascertain how he stood. When he came away he appeared somewhat glum, at least not exactly happy.

Results.

As usual, the leaders tried to blame the story entirely on the newspapers, as if any newsman would sit around and dream such stuff. Regardless of how the White House itself feels, there is a considerable portion of the inside administration crowd dissatisfied with the way congressional affairs have been going.

There probably will be no change in leadership. The Roosevelt forces hardly will go to the extent of conducting an open reorganization. The immediate effect will be to stimulate White House support in the House. That result was first noticeable in the rejection of the McLead bank deposit bill. The House leaders phenagled thirty-eight Democrats sponsoring the bill into changing their position before the roll was called. The switches blocked the measure .

It shows what the existing House leadership can do when it really sets its mind to its business.

Notes.

An organized movement against the American Legion lobby has been started in New York as a result of the veterans' restorations. As a matter of fact, the work of the legion lobby on the inside was to restrain the House veterans' bloc, which wanted to grant even larger restorations. The legion did not have to do much lobbying on that bill.

The congressional leaders could not even catch any fish during their foray at Hoover's camp on the Rapidan. The only one who caught a fish worth mentioning was Representative McRenyolds The consensus was that the Hoover camp fish are all Republicans, who have not heard about the change in Government management.

Minnesota Weather
Partly cloudy today, cooler tonight; Sunday unsettled.
Detailed report on Page 16.

St. Paul Pioneer Press

War
Women can stop it, declares the granddaughter of General Grant in an article in the Sunday Magazine.

VOL. 81. NO. 118. | Full Leased Wire Service of the Associated Press. | ST. PAUL, MINN., SATURDAY, APRIL 28, 1934. | Complete Service of The United Press. c | PRICE THREE CENTS IN ST. PAUL

GUNMAN BELIEVED NELSON WOUNDS SHERIFF

U. S. ATTACKS OWN GLECKMAN CASE WITNESS

Testimony Different From That Before Grand Jury, Government Says.

PARTNERSHIP PLAN TOLD

Defendant Unaware Name Was on Firm Books, Dry Cleaner States.

Attacking one of its own witnesses a moment after he took the stand Friday in the income tax evasion case against Leon Gleckman, the Federal government charged that his testimony in the trial differed from statements he made before the grand jury which indicted Gleckman.

The witness was David Bunin, president of the University Cleaners & Dyers. Gleckman formerly was financially interested in this concern. The government claims he was a partner, and was attempting to establish this through Bunin's testimony.

Bunin claimed Gleckman was merely interested through loans he had made to Bunin.

Before Bunin had answered more than a half dozen questions after being called to the stand, Norman T. Morrison of the prosecution rose and addressed Federal Judge M. M. Joyce who is hearing the case.

"I claim surprise and ask leave to cross-examine this witness, your honor," Mr. Morrison said. "The testimony he now gives is in conflict with his previous statements before the grand jury and to revenue agents."

Mr. Morrison, with a long barrage of questions, forced from Bunin admissions that Gleckman was listed on the books of the company as a partner from the time he made loans to Bunin in 1926 until the partnership was dissolved in 1929. When the partnership ended, it was said, the concern was incorporated and Gleckman man given one-third of the capital stock of the new corporation, as equivalent to his $4,000 share of the partnership, plus his share of a gain in the valuation of the equipment. The $4,000 worth of stock also included a partnership share of profits of the University Cleaners & Dyers for certain years, and there was deducted from this amount a partnership share of a loss suffered in one year's business.

Mr. Morrison also obtained from Bunin identification of two income tax returns made by Bunin for the company, in which it was listed as a partnership, with Gleckman as one partner.

In his testimony, however, Bunin repeatedly insisted that he made Gleckman a partner on the books without Gleckman's knowledge, consent, or signature on a partnership agreement. This was done, he testified—

(Please Turn to Page 2, Col. 1.)

Publishers Urge 3-Cent Pieces

Coinage Would Aid Business, Treasury Told.

New York, April 27.—(AP)—Coinage and distribution of 3-cent pieces was urged on the secretary of the Treasury by the American Newspaper Publishers association today.

The need for an intermediate coin between the 1-cent piece and the nickel has been recognized by many lines of business and now is becoming increasingly urgent, the association said.

"Millions of daily newspapers are sold at 3 cents and a 3-cent coin would simplify the purchase of newspapers and be a convenience to the buying public," a resolution adopted by the A. N. P. A. said.

The resolution pointed out that postage stamps now are sold for 3 cents and that many stores price their goods at such intermediate figures that a 3-cent coin would facilitate business operations.

CLOUDY, COLDER TONIGHT, FORECAST FOR ST. PAUL

Partly cloudy today followed by colder again tonight is the weather predicted for St. Paul and the rest of Minnesota in the government forecast. Sunday will be unsettled, the forecast stated.

Temperatures here Friday ranged from 27 to 52 degrees above zero.

HOURLY TEMPERATURES

Hourly temperatures in St. Paul from 1 P. M. Friday to 2 A. M. today as recorded on the Pioneer Press and Dispatch government tested thermometer were:

1 P. M.	46	8 P. M.	46
2 P. M.	46	9 P. M.	46
3 P. M.	48	10 P. M.	44
4 P. M.	51	11 P. M.	44
5 P. M.	52	12 M.	44
6 P. M.	51	1 A. M.	43
7 P. M.	52	2 A. M.	43

Flees Prison

RANDOL NORVELL.

2 CONVICTS CRAWL IN SEWER TO ESCAPE

Kidnaper of Illinois Banker and Burglar Flee From Prison.

Chester, Ill., April 27.—(AP)—Two convicts, one of them Randol Norvell, supposed "brains" of the sensational kidnaping of August Luer, 77-year-old Alton banker, last July 10, crawled through a sewer of the Southern Illinois prison at Menard, near here, shortly before sundown today and escaped.

Nearly 300 officers, armed with rifles and machine guns and aided by searchlights, formed a posse and beat the brush along the Mississippi river for the convicts.

James O'Connell, serving an indeterminate sentence from Effingham for burglary, fled with Norvell, prison officials announced. O'Connell was received at the prison in April, 1933. The officials also said the plot apparently followed weeks of planning.

Several hours after the escape, Warden J. E. Raegan said he had reports one of the fleeing fugitives had been seen on the Missouri side of the river. The report sent additional men into the search, augmenting the original 200 who went out from the prison when the first alarm was spread.

Norvell, described as a "model prisoner," was working in the prison machine shop with 150 other prisoners, the warden said. Removing bars from a tunnel used to house water and heat pipes, the abductor and O'Connell crawled through the narrow chamber to the prison yard.

There they removed the cover from a sewer and crawled about 40 yards to the outlet in the Mississippi river. It was not known by officials if they were met there by accomplices, but the general opinion was they were unaided.

It was more than two hours before the escape became known outside the prison. Scores of guards were hunting the men in the vicinity before townspeople knew they were free.

Luer, wealthy 77-year-old banker and meat packer, was taken from his home by a woman and two men. He was released six days later near Collinsville, Ill. A part of the time the banker, in ill health, was locked in a concrete cellar. During his entire captivity he was blindfolded with adhesive tape and forced to undergo other hardships.

Solution to the abduction began to unravel July 18 with the arrest of Percy M. Fitzgerald. The cleanup of the band of six alleged abductors followed. They were convicted in September.

Fitzgerald and Mrs. Lillian Chesson received life sentences. Others convicted were Mike Musiala, twenty years, and Christ Nicola Gitcho and Charles Chesson, five years each.

PHYSICIAN PUNISHED FOR HITLER 'INSULT'

Bad Salzufen, Germany, April 27—(AP)—A physician named Engeland was arrested today for making a derogatory remark about Chancellor Hitler and led through the streets with a placard around his neck inscribed: "I am a scoundrel; I have insulted the leader."

Japs Charge Nations 'Endanger East Asia Peace' by China Aid

Tell U. S. and Britain Tokio "Cannot Remain Indifferent."

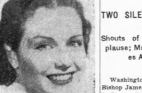

Tokio, April 28—(Saturday)—(AP)—An official statement of Japan's China policy, asserting that Japan "cannot remain indifferent" to the efforts of foreign powers to aid China has been furnished to the American and British ambassadors here.

The statement was delivered to Joseph C. Grew and Sir Francis Lindley, American and British ambassadors, respectively, after they had requested Foreign Minister Kioki Hiroto for an authoritative translation of the "hands off China" declaration of the foreign ofice of April 17.

The official statement, which was revealed here today follows the main lines of the earlier declaration but contains what diplomatic circles regarded as more conciliatory language.

Certain foreign efforts to help China, the new declaration says "endanger the peace of East Asia." Japan, however, it continues, has no intention of violating China's sovereignty and integrity; desires the unification of China; suports the open door equal opportunity policies and has no invention of infringing upon existing treaties.

The foreign office characterized Minister Hirota's statement, which was delivered to the ambassador Thursday night, as "the only official" statement of China policy, thereby disclaiming Hirota's responsibility for earlier statements.

It was confirmed from reliable sources that the foreign minister had not intended that the declaration of April 17 be published, although it was based on instructions which Hirota signed and dispatched to Akira Ariyoshi, Japan minister to China.

DAVIS GIVES GLOOMY ARMS PICTURE TO F. R.

Washington, April 27.—(AP)—A discouraging report on world disarmament possibilities was given President Roosevelt today by Norman H. Davis, chief American delegate to the Disarmament conference, at a meeting in the White House which was also attended by Secretary Hull.

Davis, who has just returned from Europe where he conferred with Sir John Simon, British foreign minister, and other European officials especially interested in disarmament questions, told reporters after the meeting that he had no immediate plans for returning to Geneva.

The President, Hull and Davis, all refrained from any official comment on the meeting but it was learned from authoritative sources that the ambassador-at-large had presented a dark picture of the present European situation to the President.

Spurns Films

MISS JUNE GRABINER.

Hollywood was astounded when Miss June Grabiner, daughter of Harry Grabiner, vice president of the Chicago White Sox baseball club, rejected the offer of a studio to give her a movie part. Here she is in a photo made at Paramount studios when she had a film test. A studio executive met her in Hollywood and invited her to have the preliminary test.

2 BLOWS AT SEWAGE ADVICE PLAN BALKED

Moves to Halt Chicago Firm or Limit Work Voted Down by Board.

Two attempts to prevent engaging $270,000 worth or engineering advice and supervision on the eighteen million dollar Twin Cities sewage disposal project or to cut down the extent of consultant service, were defeated Friday afternoon when trustees of the Minneapolis-St. Paul Sanitary district met here.

One was a motion by Sidney Benson, Minneapolis member, to halt preliminary work by the Chicago firm which has been chosen for the consulting work until a site has been selected for the treatment plant.

Inasmuch as five of the sanitary board's seven members must agree on the treatment plant's location and as the three Minneapolis members

(Please Turn to Page 7, Col. 4.)

KIDNAPED FOR $15,000

Kidnaped as she was walking from school in Tucson, Arizona, Wednesday, June Robles, 6 years old, daughter of a wealthy pioneer Arizona family, was being held for $15,000 ransom Friday night. It was indicated the family would meet the demand. Meanwhile, 1,000 quick-shooting cowboys, ranchers, policemen, sheriffs and volunteers halted their search for the child while negotiations for her return were underway.

BISHOP CANNON AND SECRETARY WIN ACQUITTAL

'Hug Away,' Churchman Tells Woman Admirer and She Does.

TWO SILENT ON VERDICT

Shouts of 'Quiet' Halt Applause; Mrs. Cannon Brushes Away Tears.

Washington, April 27.—(AP)—Bishop James Cannon Jr. and Ada L. Burroughs are innocent of concealing campaign contributions in 1928, when the churchman opposed Alfred E. Smith for president, a jury decided today in the District of Columbia Supreme court.

After three hours of deliberations, during which the jury took four ballots, it brought to the bishop, sitting tensely forward on the edge of his chair, and Miss Burroughs, standing stiffly and grasping a table, an acquittal on both counts of the indictment against them.

Cannon smiled and settled back into his chair. Miss Burroughs stood for a moment, still staring across the counsel table into the face of the jury foreman, then the tension in her body dropped away and she sat down.

Brushes Tears Away.

Mrs. Cannon moved away from the crowd which thronged about her husband and Miss Burroughs, and wiped away the tears.

"What do you think of that verdict, Mrs. Cannon?" a reporter asked.

"It was what we expected, of course," she said.

As his friends and newspaper men crowded about his chair in the courtroom, the bishop waved aside immediate comment. He said that later "after I take a nap" he would have a statement.

Miss Burroughs too preferred to remain silent but she smiled when women pushed through the crowd to shake her hand or touch her arm and congratulate her.

A few handclaps rippled through the hum of voices but sharp shouts of "quiet" from marshals halted this.

A woman spectator, Ada L. Piercy, formerly of Parkersburg, W. Va., now of Washington, fought her way through the crowd surrounding the bishop to exclaim:

"Bishop, I said I'd hug you if you were acquitted."

Told to "Hug Away."

"Hug away," the bishop said smiling.

She did.

"We still love you, we know you're not a criminal," she said. "It is a victory for Protestantism."

The courtroom, the seating capaci-

(Please Turn to Page 7, Col. 5.)

$2,290,000 GRANTED TO STATE FOR RELIEF

May Allotment Nearly Three Times All Public Funds Spent Last Year.

By J. R. WIGGINS.
(Pioneer Press Staff Correspondent.)

Washington, April 27.—Minnesota has been allotted $2,290,262 in Federal emergency relief funds for May, nearly three times as much as was spent for direct relief purposes from all public funds in the same month last year, Federal Administrator Hopkins announced here today.

If all the funds ear-marked for the state today are paid out during May, at the end of the next month the FERA will have spent for relief purposes in Minnesota during the first five months of 1934 within two million dollars of all relief expenditures in the state from public funds of all kinds for all twelve months of 1933.

The peak of relief spending in Minnesota in 1933 was not reached until November when it climbed to $1,035,000. The Civil Works Administration program was inaugurated November 16 and seventeen million dollars poured into Minnesota for civil work payrolls up to April 1 when the CWA stopped.

The April and May direct relief allotments, accordingly, are the first months offering a comparison between this year and last. The April outlay for direct relief from all public funds last year was $684,250 and this year the FERA alone contributed $2,249,000.

The more than seven million dollars appropriated to the state to June 1 this year carried through direct relief costs into October last year.

Today's $2,290,262 allotment is distributed as follows: Transient relief, $39,823; running expenses for national re-employment service offices, $19,969; student aid, $30,480; general relief, $2,200,000.

U PROFESSOR NAMED HISTORICAL GROUP HEAD

Columbia, Mo., April 27.—(AP)—Lester B. Shippee, University of Minnesota professor, was elected president of the Mississippi Valley Historical association at its annual meeting here today. Mrs. C. S. Paine of Lincoln, Neb., was re-elected secretary-treasurer.

Members voted to hold the 1935 meeting in Cincinnati next April.

Bullets Halt Officer's Pursuit of Car Stolen By Dillinger Mobster

Battle Near Solon Springs, Wis., Staged as Hundred Men Circle Swamp to Capture Fugitive Thought Tommy Carroll; Posses Ready to Close in Near Lac du Flambeau; Van Meter Named in Holdup.

GRAND JURY REPORT EXPECTED TODAY; VIDLER MAY BE BROUGHT HERE FOR TRIAL

Wounding of another peace officer marked the search for members of the John Dillinger gang Friday night as the manhunt again centered on the Minnesota-Wisconsin north woods and on the roads leading from there to St. Paul.

Al Johnson, a special deputy and one of the hundreds of local police and deputized volunteers who are aiding Federal Department of Justice men in the case, was cut by flying glass near Solon Springs, Wis., when he was fired on after he attempted to halt a speeding car believed to contain George (Baby Face) Nelson, quick-shooting Dillinger henchman.

While Nelson apparently had eluded or was lying back from the hundreds of guns awaiting his effort to get out of the north woods region, another member of the gang, believed to be Tommy Carroll of St. Paul, was said to cornered in a four-mile square swamp near Lac du Flambeau, Wis.

MANY REPORTS ON OTHER MOBSTERS.

Other Dillinger outlaws were reported at half a dozen points over the United States, and the far-flung case produced these additional developments:

Homer Van Meter, one of the Dillinger gangsters who fled from Federal agents in a gun battle at a Northern Wisconsin hideout Sunday night was identified as one of five bandits who robbed a Chicago suburb bank of $6,000 in cash shortly before noon Friday.

A Federal grand jury here heard testimony against persons accused of harboring the Dillinger mobsters in St. Paul and aiding in their escape from an apartment here March 31, and was expected to return secret indictments today.

Charges were placed against William E. Vidler, former convict arrested in Chicago with nearly $3,000 of the Edward G. Bremer kidnaping ransom in his possession, and several unnamed persons, and indications were that Vidler will be brought to St. Paul for trial. Dillinger's associates are named as the Bremer kidnapers.

Disclosure that Van Meter was the man who, with Dillinger, fled from the St. Paul apartment March 31.

Return to Beth Green, reputed wife of Eugene Green, Dillinger gangster slain by Federal men here of $4,000 found in a safety deposit box.

Johnson was on duty on Highway 53, eight miles east of Solon Springs when he spotted a car answering the description of one that Nelson stole at Lac du Flambeau. He followed the speeding car, a Plymouth coupe bearing Wisconsin license 5970, but shots broke the window of his machine. Severely cut on the face and one hand by the flying glass, he was forced to give up the pursuit.

The deputy said there were two men in the car, but he did not get a close enough look to be able to identfy them.

The search for Nelson, turning the focal point of the hunt for Dillinger gangsters back to the north woods and the highways by which they might attempt to find refuge in the Twin Cities, followed the disclosure that Nelson had been hiding for three days in the shack of an Indian near Lac du Flambeau, only 40 miles from the scene of the gun battle near Mercer, Wis., Sunday night in which two men were killed and four were wounded.

Nelson Killed Agent.

Federal operatives were particularly anxious to catch Nelson—a five-foot-six gangster with a face like a child—because it was he, they say, who killed W. Carter Baum, Department of Justice agent Sunday night.

While Associated Press dispatches told of the hunt for Nelson and the attack on the special deputy, a United Press message said that the man cornered in a swamp was believed to be Tommy Carroll.

The gangster being sought in the swamp was first sighted late Friday afternoon by B. Lee of Powell, who has a home on the Flambeau river. He said that the gangster was armed and fled into the brush. An engineer on the North Western railway, tracks of which cut across a section of the lowland where the desperado was believed trapped, reported that he saw a man who answered the gangster's description jump off a freight train and go into the woods.

Plan to Close in Today.

The possemen planned to huddle along crudely established picket lines all night and when reinforced in the morning close in on the suspect.

Deputy Sheriff William Yeschet, who operates the Crawling Stone lodge in the vicinity and had spent the entire day hunting through the swamplands and forest, returned to Lac du Flambeau Friday night to report that the searchers believed they were near victory.

"We are convinced," Yeschet said, "that Nelson has escaped, probably to St. Paul. But in searching for Nelson, we found out that an-

(Please Turn to Page 2, Col. 3.)

In Bremer Case

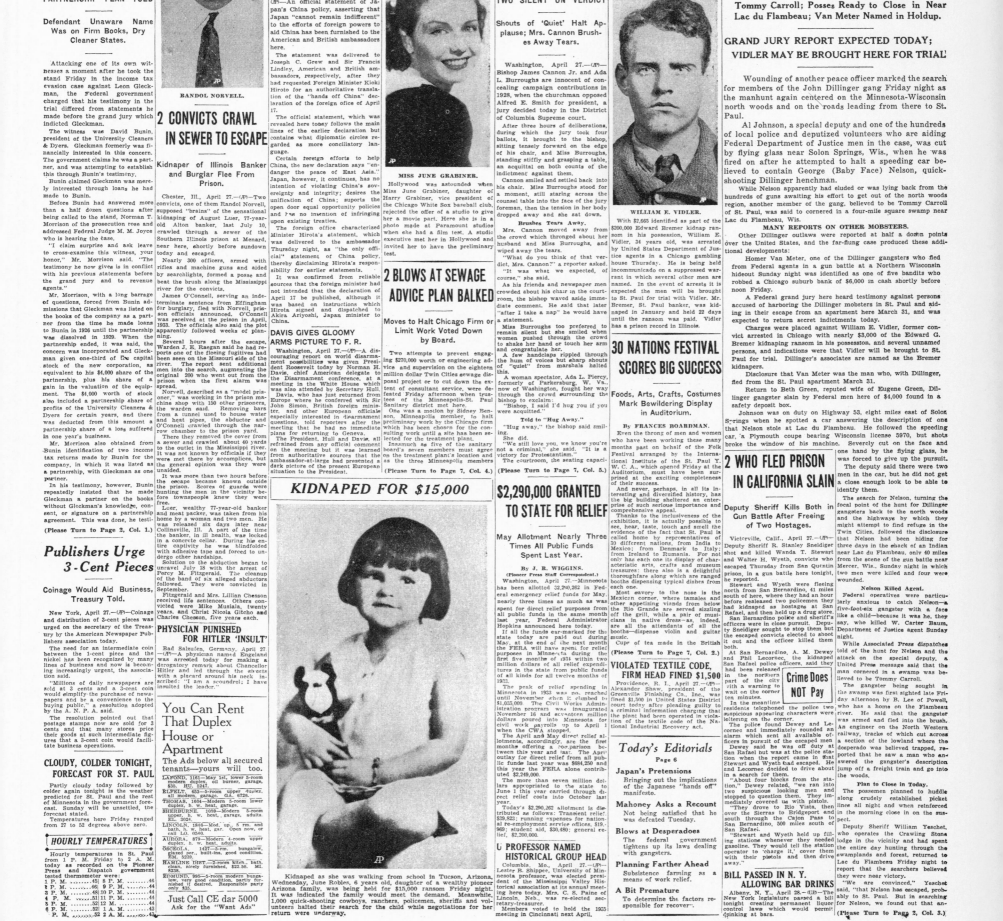

WILLIAM E. VIDLER.

With $2,665 identified as part of the $200,000 Edward Bremer kidnap ransom in his possession, William E. Vidler, 34 years old, was arrested by United States Department of Justice agents in a Chicago gambling house Thursday. He is being held incommunicado on a suppressed warrant in which several other men are named. In the event of arrests it is expected the men will be brought to St. Paul for trial with Vidler. Mr. Bremer, St. Paul banker, was kidnaped in January and held 22 days until the ransom was paid. Vidler has a prison record in Illinois.

30 NATIONS FESTIVAL SCORES BIG SUCCESS

Foods, Arts, Crafts, Costumes Mark Bewildering Display in Auditorium.

By FRANCES BOARDMAN.

Even the throng of men and women who have been working these many months past on behalf of the Folk Festival arranged by the International Institute of the St. Paul Y. W. C. A., which opened Friday at the Auditorium, must have been surprised at the exciting completeness of their success.

And never, perhaps, in all its interesting and diversified history, has the big building sheltered an enterprise of such serious importance and comprehensive appeal.

Thanks to the inclusiveness of the exhibition, it is actually possible to see, hear, taste, touch and smell the evidence of the fact that St. Paul is called home by representatives of 30 different nations, from India to Mexico; from Denmark to Italy; from Ireland to Rumania. For not only has each one its display of characteristic arts, crafts and museum treasures: there also is a delightful thoroughfare along which are ranged booths dispensing typical dishes from each one.

Most savory to the nose is the Mexican corner, where tamales and other appetizing viands from below the Rio Grande are served sizzling off the grill, while a pair of musicians in native dress—as, indeed, are all the attendants of all the booths—dispense violin and guitar music.

Cups of tea made in the British

(Please Turn to Page 7, Col. 2.)

VIOLATED TEXTILE CODE, FIRM HEAD FINED $1,500

Providence, R. I., April 27.—(AP)—Alexander Shaw, president of the Greenville Finishing Co., Inc., was fined $1,500 in United States District court today after pleading guilty to a criminal information charging that the plant had been operated in violation of the textile code of the National Industrial Recovery act.

Today's Editorials

2 WHO FLED PRISON IN CALIFORNIA SLAIN

Deputy Sheriff Kills Both in Gun Battle After Freeing of Two Hostages.

Victorville, Calif., April 27.—(AP)—Deputy Sheriff R. Stanley Sneidiger shot and killed Wanda T. Stewart and Walter H. Wyeth, convicts who escaped Thursday from San Quentin prison, in a gun battle here tonight, he reported.

Stewart and Wyeth were fleeing north from San Bernardino, 41 miles south of here, where they had an hour before realeased two policemen they had kidnaped as hostages at San Rafael, and then held up a drug store.

San Bernardino police and sheriff's officers were in close pursuit. Deputy Sneidiger sought to stop them but the escaped convicts elected to shoot it out and the officer killed them both.

At San Bernardino, A. M. Dewey and Phil Lecornec, the kidnaped San Rafael police officers, said they had been released in the northern part of the city with a warning to wait on the corner ten minutes.

Crime Does NOT Pay

In the meantime residents telephoned the police two suspicious appearing characters were loitering on the corner.

The police found Dewey and Lecornec and immediately sounded an alarm which sent all available officers in pursuit of the escaped men

Dewey said he was off duty at San Rafael but was at the police station when the report came in that Stewart and Wyeth had escaped. He and Lecornec decided to drive about in a search for them.

"About four blocks from the station," Dewey related, "we ran into two suspicious looking men and stopped to question them. They immediately covered us with pistols.

"They drove to Rio Vista, then over the Sierras to Bridgeport and south through the Cajon Pass to San Bernardino, 500 miles south of San Rafael.

"Stewart and Wyeth held up filling stations whenever they needed gasoline. They would tell the station operator to 'charge it,' cover them with their pistols and then drive away."

BILL PASSED IN N. Y. ALLOWING BAR DRINKS

Albany, N. Y., April 28.—(UP)—The New York legislature passed a bill tonight creating permanent liquor control laws which would permit drinking at bars.

Complete Baseball and Race Results

Turn to Sports Pages

NRA MEMBER U.S. WE DO OUR PART

Herald and Examiner
Chicago

2 CENTS
METROPOLITAN EDITION

54TH YEAR No. 6 Registered in U. S. Patent Office. TWO PARTS. C★ ...RDAY, MAY 19, 1934 TWO CENTS IN CHICAGO AND SUBURBS ELSEWHERE THREE CENTS

ROOSEVELT WARS ON GANGS!

Council Votes Higher Taxicab Rates

BRITISH GIVE JAPANESE 'GO AHEAD' SIGN IN CHINA CRISIS

Refuses to Use Force Against Tokyo's Encroachments; Ready for Air Fleet Race

LEAVES U. S. 'HOLDING BAG'

Sir John Simon Pronounces Policy; Sir Stafford Cripps Assails Vacillating Stand

Herald and Examiner-Universal Special Cable.

LONDON, May 18.—(U.S.)—Great Britain is neither pledged to nor contemplating the use of force in warding off further Japanese encroachments on Chinese territory.

Sir John Simon, foreign secretary, bluntly indicated this in the House of Commons today, in a discussion with Sir Stafford Cripps.

PREPARED FOR AIR RACE.

A second salient declaration of British policy emerged from the debate when Stanley Baldwin, lord president of council, assured the House that, if British fears of failure of the disarmament conference are realized, Britain is prepared to enter an arms race by building an air fleet **"as big as any in the world."**

Sir Stafford Cripps, solicitor-general in the first MacDonald Labor government, started the debate by intimating Britain is preparing to allow the United States and Russia to hold the bag, in the face of Japan's "hands off China" warning to the world.

URGES CO-OPERATION.

He charged the British government's "vacillation" and weak far eastern policy was encouraging Japan's plans to snatch another slice of territory from China. The United States and Russia are arming because of the danger from Japan, and Britain is allowing her to violate the nine-power treaty, the Laborite leader said.

He urged Britain's co-operation in the Far East with the United States, Russia and the league of nations against a "German-Japanese" combination that is hastening the world to the brink of war.

Sir John coolly reiterated that Britain would insist on "due observance" of the nine-power treaty. Then he declared the treaty bound Britain to respect China's territorial integrity, but did not commit her to the use of force in protecting China. He said:

"The United States has done for the world great public service, but there is no good in pretending not to observe the limitations in which the United States is likely to act in the course of the Geneva disarmament discussions.

"The American declaration answering the British draft convention was a very valuable one, but it would be absurd to pretend it encouraged us to believe America would take full part in economic sanctions or join in 'pool security.'

"We have exhausted the time when we can usefully express ourselves in sincere platitudes, and are right up against the hard facts of the situation.

"There is no use talking about sanctions unless we are certain they would be effective. Sanctions cannot be effective unless the United States actively co-operates. We acknowledge with gratitude the contributions the United States has been able to make toward improvement of international affairs. It is a matter of great regret, however, that the United States is not prepared to join the league."

He added that it was not a matter with which anybody should be reproached.

Johnson 'Guards' NRA in Publicity

WASHINGTON, May 18.—(I.N.S.) Further efforts to remove the spotlight of publicity from the national recovery "gold fish bowl" were in progress today as Recovery Administrator Johnson placed a permanent cordon of guards about the NRA duplicating division. Under the new order, all employes of the Commerce Building are required to present passes before being allowed admittance or egress from the section.

Report Stalin Will Take Trotzky Back

GENEVA, May 18.—(I.N.S.)—A rumor that Josef Stalin, Russian dictator, has taken steps to heal his breach with Leon Trotzky and hopes to persuade the latter to take over the leadership of the Red army was circulated in league circles tonight. Threat of a Far Eastern war lent color to the report.

Turn to Page 2, Column 1.

Shape $6,000,000 Relief Monthly for Drought's Victims

Federal Agencies Will Unite Forces.

BUYING CATTLE

4,000 Families to Move in South Dakota.

WASHINGTON, May 18.—(A.P.)—More money and food for the drought-stricken, plus removal to better farms of from 3,000 to 4,000 South Dakotans, were phases of the relief program that took definite shape in conferences today.

Federal relief forces will head for the sun-parched areas of the Dakotas, Minnesota and Wisconsin next week to prevent undue suffering.

The emergency relief, farm and farm credit administrations, the Department of Agriculture and the surplus relief corporation joined hands with state and local officials in working out the relief program.

Harry L. Hopkins, the relief director, said the program could be spread to any area as soon as a serious situation developed.

DETAILS PLANS MADE.

The program will proceed along these lines:

The Surplus Relief Corporation will buy cattle in the dry area.

The bureau of animal industry will examine every cow in the area and confiscate any pay for every one found with tuberculosis.

The relief administration will supply funds to buy food for farmers and to provide seed for forage crops. It also will supply funds for deepening wells and digging new ones.

The farm credit administration will relax its rules regarding loans already made or which can be made.

From 3,000 to 4,000 farm families may be moved in South Dakota from farms which have proved insufficient for a decent living to some of the 4,000 farms now owned by the state.

INCREASE CATTLE BUYING.

Hopkins said the cattle purchasing program of the farm agency would be many times larger than the purchases made in recent months for it by the Surplus Relief Corporation.

He added that within three weeks all surplus cattle would be taken out of the drought area.

The program of the relief organization will cost about $6,000,000 a month in the four states until the drought is broken, Hopkins said. Besides feeding people who are unable to pay for food Hopkins said work programs would be carried out to provide these people with needed funds.

INSECTS CREATE HAVOC.

Department of Agriculture officials, meanwhile, received new reports of insect outbreaks, which they called the "inevitable aftermath" of the drought.

Dr. C. J. Drake, state entomologist of Iowa, and Walter W. McLaughlin, director of agriculture for Illinois, told Rexford G. Tugwell, acting Secretary of Agriculture, and Senator Murphy, Iowa Democrat, that the threat of crop damage

Insull Considers Darrow as Chief Trial Attorney

Famous Lawyer, at 77, May Return to Courtroom for Big Battle.

Clarence Darrow may defend Samuel Insull.

Persistent reports that the 77-year-old master courtroom strategist would be counsel for the 74-year-old master organizer drew from Samuel Insull Jr. the following comment yesterday:

"My father and I have reached no decision. We are considering all available attorneys. To that extent, we are considering Clarence Darrow."

Mr. Darrow last night was in Washington, where, as chairman of the national recovery review board, only a few days ago he presented a report assailing Gen. Hugh Johnson's administration of the NRA and charged monopolies in eight major industries were crushing small firms.

If he comes out of retirement to defend Insull against federal charges of mail fraud and bankruptcy law evasion, and against state charges of embezzlement, it will be his first appearance in a major case since the famous Massie case in Honolulu.

For fifty-six years Darrow has been a practicing lawyer, and defender in more famous trials than any other attorney in the country.

Accuses Harriman of False Entries

NEW YORK, May 18.—(AP)—Testimony that J. W. Harriman signed duplicate tickets for alleged false entries in the books of the Harriman National Bank & Trust Company and told other officers that **"I stand behind anything I told you boys to do"** was offered to a federal jury today by Arnold Colombo, cashier of the bank of which Harriman was president.

Doumergue Wins Confidence Vote

PARIS, May 18.—(AP)—Premier Doumergue again smashed through his opposition today, winning a heavy vote of confidence in the Chamber of Deputies on his refusal to enter into an immediate discussion of interpellations on the government's drastic economy decrees. Confidence was voted 360 against 205.

Lion Starts to See Paris; Mauls Volunteer Samson

PARIS, May 18.—(AP)—A soldier who tried to play Samson with a runaway circus lion was badly scratched and mauled for his heroism today.

The lion, bored with life in a menagerie on the outskirts of Paris, decided to see the sights.

He pulled up the planks in the bottom of his cage and headed for the bright lights of the French capital.

The soldier, attached to the air service, tried to capture the sightseer single-handed, instead he went to a hospital.

The soldier cornered the lion in an angle in an old fortification.

The lion took a swipe at him. He kicked the lion.

Thereupon, the king of beasts bit the soldier in the shoulder and clawed him about the head.

It was just about this time that the lion's trainer arrived. He got the fugitive into a portable cage, while the whole neighborhood scurried for shelter.

CITY COUNCIL APPLAUDS PLAN OF FEALTY OATH

Commends School Board; Resolution Orders Municipal Employes Pledge Loyalty

By unanimous vote, the city council yesterday commended President James B. McCahey and the board of education for their proposal to require all teachers in Chicago public schools to take an oath of allegiance to the Constitution of the United States and the state of Illinois.

At the same time the council requested city department heads to administer an identical oath to all municipal employes.

ADOPTS RESOLUTION.

The action was taken through adoption of a resolution offered by Alderman J. M. Arvey, president pro tem of the aldermanic body. Arvey was inspired to put the council on record in support of the school board, he said, by a situation existing in New York where 700 school teachers signed a petition urging Governor Lehman to veto a bill requiring instructors to swear fealty to their government.

The resolution was as follows:

"Whereas, President James B. McCahey and members of the Board of Education of the city of Chicago have announced they will promulgate a rule requiring all teachers in the public schools to take an oath of allegiance to the Constitution of the United States and the State of Illinois; and

"Whereas, it is a well-known fact that there are at work in this and other states certain un-American influences aimed particularly at the teaching forces; and

"CHICAGO TEACHERS LOYAL."

Whereas, Chicago's teachers have given a demonstration of loyalty to their duty, their city, their state and the best traditions of the American govern-

Turn to Page 4, Column 3.

Hamilton Resigns Rail Union Post

CLEVELAND, O., May 18.—(AP)—Resignation of W. V. Hamilton of Knoxville, Tenn., as director and vice president of the Brotherhood of Railroad Trainmen because of illness was announced today by A. F. Whitney, president. Hamilton, a director since 1924, will be succeeded by E. E. Oster of Louisville, for many years chairman of the brotherhood on the Louisville & Nashville Railroad.

Capone Aid Goes to Leavenworth

Hymie ("Loud Mouth") Levin, former Capone collector, surrendered late yesterday and within two hours was en route to Leavenworth to serve an eighteen months' sentence for failure to report on a million dollars of income. With sixteen other federal prisoners, Levin was shipped to the penitentiary in a special barred car.

Operators Given 25-Cent Mile in 6½-Year Permit

Mayor's Signature Expected Today; Crowe Changes Ballot to Make It Unanimous.

Increased taxicab rates for Chicago were authorized yesterday by the city council. At the same time, the aldermen gave existing companies a six and a half years franchise. Heretofore the companies operated by license.

The vote was unanimous and came after Alderman James B. Bowler, chairman of the local transportation committee, declared the measure provided the solution **"for one of the most vexing of municipal problems."**

CROWE CHANGES VOTE.

Alderman Dorsey R. Crowe voted against the ordinance on roll call, but later changed to the affirmative **"rather than vote alone in the negative."** Aldermen John Grealis and Henry Sonnenschein were absent.

Mayor Kelly is expected to sign the ordinance today. It will be effective upon acceptance by the companies. They requested higher rates several weeks ago.

NEW RATES.

The new rates are:

For the first one-third of a mile or fraction thereof, 15 cents.

For each additional two-thirds of a mile or fraction thereof, 10 cents.

For each additional person of the age of 12 years or more, 5 cents.

For each three minutes of waiting time or fraction thereof, 10 cents.

Present rates are: Yellow Cab Company, 10 cents for the first two-thirds mile, 10 cents for each additional two-thirds; Checker Cab Company, 5 cents for the first one-third, 5 cents for each additional one-third. Neither company charges for extra passengers, nor do any of the independent companies.

Thus the new schedule provides a rate of 25 cents for the first mile, exclusive of the charge for extra passengers. This is an increase of 5 cents over the present Yellow and 10 cents more than the present Checker rates.

WAIT KELLY'S SIGNATURE.

Officials of the major cab companies said last night they would not put the new rates into effect until Mayor Kelly signs the new ordinance and they have duly accepted it. They pointed out it may also require several weeks' time to effect the necessary readjustment of cab meters.

Pond and Sabelli Visit De Valera

DUBLIN, May 18.—(I.N.S.)—Cesare Sabelli and George R. Pond, ocean fliers forced down at Lahinch Tuesday, visited President De Valera at Government House today. They expect to continue their flight to Rome Saturday.

U. S. Marshals for Illinois Named

WASHINGTON, May 18.—(U.S.)—President Roosevelt today nominated William Ryan to be United States marshal for the eastern district of Illinois. R. Kenneth Kerr was nominated for marshal of the southern district.

THE WEATHER

CHICAGO AND VICINITY—Some prospect of a shower by night; not much change in temperature. Outlook for Sunday: Partly cloudy, some probability of showers.

LOWER LAKES — Moderate shifting winds; partly cloudy.

UPPER LAKES—Partly cloudy, probably some local showers.

ILLINOIS—Generally fair, except possibly local showers in extreme north portion; slightly cooler in extreme northwest.

INDIANA—Generally fair, not much change in temperature.

LOWER MICHIGAN — Possibly local showers; somewhat warmer in south portion.

WISCONSIN—Some probability of local showers, slightly warmer in extreme east; cooler in southwest.

IOWA—Generally fair; cooler in north portion.

MRS. DOUBLEDAY AND M'CORMICK TO SETTLE SUIT

$1,500,000 Love Action Reported Closed for $100,000; 68 Letters to Be Returned

For a consideration reliably reported at approximately $100,000, Mrs. Rhoda Tanner Doubleday of New York has agreed to dismiss her $1,500,000 breach of promise suit against Harold F. McCormick, Chicago millionaire.

John P. Wilson of Wilson & McIlvane, attorneys representing Mr. McCormick, and Henry K. Urion of Urion, Drucker, Bishop & Boutell, Chicago attorneys for the comely New York divorcee, confirmed last night the reports that a settlement was reached while Mrs. Doubleday was in Chicago last month.

RETURNS 68 LETTERS.

They refused to discuss the amount for which Mrs. Doubleday, who is in her thirties, had agreed to drop the action and give up the sixty-eight letters which Mr. McCormick had written her, according to her lawyers, during a courtship extending over more than a year, in 1932 and early 1933.

Mr. McCormick was out of town last night, but from other sources it was learned that the sum of approximately $100,000 includes the fees for Mrs. Doubleday's attorneys both here and in New York and Santa Barbara, Cal.

SOCIETY DISAPPOINTED.

The decision to settle with Mrs. Doubleday, who in 1925 divorced Felix Doubleday, New York publisher, means that Chicago society will never learn what was in the McCormick love notes. Their presentation in court has been eagerly awaited by society folk whose interest in the harvester millionaire's loves was whetted by his short-lived marriage to Madame Ganna Walska, following his divorce by the late Edith Rockefeller McCormick.

News of the settlement had been carefully suppressed. Several days ago Henry A. Uterhart and A. M. Schaffer, Mrs. Doubleday's attorneys in New York, asked the Chicago lawyers to submit their fees. Mr. Wilson and Mr. Urion indicated last night they may appear in court early next week for the formal final chapter, when the court will be asked for leave to withdraw the suit.

MARRIAGE FORECAST.

Marriage of Mr. McCormick and the comely New York divorcee, who spends much of her time at Santa Barbara, Cal., had been forecast by society columns as far back as the Summer of 1932. At that time Mr. McCormick, asked to confirm the rumors, had gallantly but non-committally said:

"Ask Mrs. Doubleday."

Mrs. Doubleday, however, said of the rumor:

"Absurd."

Besides declaring that he would neither affirm nor deny the report, Mr. McCormick at the same time declared that:

"Mrs. Doubleday is the most charming woman I have ever known. She is very fascinating."

Three House Members Ill With Amoebic Dysentery

WASHINGTON, May 18.—(AP)—Three House members and the House sergeant-at-arms are receiving daily treatment at Naval Hospital here for amoebic dysentery.

They are Representatives McKeown of Oklahoma, Lehr of Michigan and Hess of Ohio, and Kenneth Romney, the sergeant-at-arms. Mrs. McKeown and Mrs. Lehr also are being treated.

Romney said today all of them stopped in Chicago last October when bankruptcy receivership practices were being investigated for the House judiciary committee. Hess, he said, was in a Cincinnati hospital for seven weeks after contracting the disease at Chicago. Recently he spent two weeks in Naval Hospital.

The others were less seriously affected. The present course of injections will be continued three more weeks. Romney said they might effect a permanent cure or that it might be necessary to be treated every six months for a year or two.

President Signs Seven Bills Aimed at Crime's Reign

Demands Citizens' Support in New Crusade.

TEETH IN LAW

Kidnaping Will Become Federal Offense After Week.

WASHINGTON, May 18.—President Roosevelt today signed seven anti-crime bills designed to put teeth in the federal search for John Dillinger and other public enemies.

At the same time he issued a militant statement saying the Department of Justice is going after every criminal, "big and little."

The President asked all citizens to support the government's drive on crime, adding that the extermination of gangsters will be difficult as long as the public looks with tolerance upon known criminals.

The measures provide federal penalties for offenses heretofore curbed only by state law.

CHALLENGE RENEWED.

The text of the President's statement follows:

"These laws are a renewed challenge on the part of the federal government to interstate crime. They are also complementary to the broader program designed to curb the evil-doer of whatever class.

"In enacting them, the Congress has provided additional equipment for the Department of Justice to aid local authorities.

"Lacking these new weapons, the department already has tracked down many major outlaws and its vigilance has spread fear in the underworld.

CONFIDENT OF RESULTS.

"With additional resources, I am confident that it will make still greater inroads upon organized crime.

"I regard this action today as an event of the first importance. So far as the federal government is concerned, there will be no relenting.

"But there is one thing more. Law enforcement and gangster

Scour Dillinger's Chicago Haunts After Bank Raid

Ground Forces Take Up Search; Airplane Abandons Quest in $30,000 Haul.

As darkness compelled an airplane crew to abandon its scanning of Michigan highways, ground forces were searching the Chicago area for John Dillinger last night in belief he led the gang which yesterday morning robbed a Flint, Mich., bank of $30,000 to $100,000.

The bank was a branch of the Citizens' Commercial & Savings Bank.

Five men and a woman comprised the holdup party. The leader was positively identified by Kirk Roland, a patron, as Dillinger.

RECOGNIZES SCAR.

"I knew the scar on his face," it was declared by Roland, a druggist who had come to the bank to get $3,000 cash to handle checks for customers employed at the main Chevrolet plant.

"I was standing at the teller's cage when I felt a gun muzzle in my back. I turned and saw it was a machine gun.

"The man who held it was John Dillinger. Another bandit tripped me and I fell on my face. Dillinger poked the gun in my back, saying:

"'If I feel your muscles move, I'll let you have it!'"

Meanwhile, with seven other customers and four employes forced to lie on the floor, one of the gunmen vaulted the cashier's cage and scooped up the money, delivered a short time before for the motor company pay day.

ALARM TOO LATE.

An alarm button was pushed as the men ran out, but they had roared far down Route M-21, leading to Grand Rapids, before police arrived.

A short time later all state highway cruisers were notified that a state plane crew had sighted what was believed to be one of the bandit cars near Holly, fifteen miles south of Flint; but no further word of the car was received.

Society Girl Wed to Hobart Henley

BEVERLY HILLS, Cal., May 18.—In a simple ceremony at the home of the bride's parents, Miss Dorothy March, former New Orleans society belle, today became the bride of Hobart Henley, motion picture director. After a honeymoon in Hawaii the couple will go to Henley's Belair estate.

THE vanity of human life is like a river, constantly passing away, and yet constantly coming on. —Pope.

The Dallas Morning News

Section One General News

49TH YEAR NO. 236 (AP)—Associated Press. (UP)—United Press. (NANA)—North American Newspaper Alliance. DALLAS, TEXAS, THURSDAY, MAY 24, 1934—TWENTY PAGES Oldest Business Institution in Texas—Founded in Galveston April 11, 1842.—Established in Dallas October 1, 1885. 5c PER COPY

Posse Kills Clyde Barrow and Bonnie Parker

Manchukuan Farm Villages Wrecked By Japanese Bombs

Chinese Sources Claim 1,000 Dead as Planes Drop Explosives on Twenty Towns

Fires Still Raging

Refusal of Settlers to Give Up Arms Alleged Cause of Reprisals

SHANGHAI, May 24 (Thursday) (AP).—Reports that Japanese military airplanes had destroyed twenty farm villages in Southeast Manchukuo, killing 1,000 persons and injuring hundreds of others, reached here Thursday from Peiping.

The reports, not confirmed from other sources, were that Chinese farmers in Manchuria refused to give up their arms on demand of the Japanese Army and that the bombing of their homes resulted.

The bombing was said to have occurred Wednesday and many villages were reported still burning from incendiary bombs.

The efforts of Japanese troops to clear out opposition elements in the Japanese-sponsored Empire of Manchukuo have given rise to reports of numerous clashes with Chinese.

Communication with the territory involved is extremely difficult and the interpretations placed upon activities of the troops and of citizens and irregular Chinese forces vary with the source of the reports.

Attention has been called several times by the Soviet Union to allegations that Japanese military planes are active in Manchukuo and several months ago charges were made that they were flying over the Russian border.

Japanese sources at that time denied that Russian territory had been trespassed upon and said only a few planes were in Manchukuo.

Relief Is Promised For Drouth Sections

KANSAS CITY, Mo., May 23 (AP).—Promising that Texas would receive a substantial amount for relief purposes, particularly in the drouth-stricken Panhandle counties, Federal relief administration Harry L. Hopkins said Wednesday a definite agreement with the Texas relief delegation would be drafted Thursday morning.

The Weather

NEW ORLEANS, La., May 23 (AP).—Government weather forecast:

East Texas (including Dallas and vicinity): Partly cloudy to cloudy, thunderstorms in northwest portion Thursday; Friday partly cloudy.

West Texas: Partly cloudy Thursday and Friday.

Arkansas: Cloudy and unsettled Thursday and Friday.

Oklahoma: Cloudy and unsettled Thursday and Friday.

Louisiana: Partly cloudy Thursday; Friday cloudy and unsettled.

Dallas Temperatures.

Temperatures in Dallas Wednesday, May 23, 1934, and for same date last year, as reported by United States Weather Bureau, follow:

	1934.	1933.		1934.	1933.
Midnight	76	78	Noon	86	84
2 a. m.	74	75	2 p. m.	87	87
4 a. m.	72	75	4 p. m.	89	90
6 a. m.	70	74	6 p. m.	86	88
8 a. m.	72	74	7 p. m.	84	86
10 a. m.	80	81			

Maximum temperature May 24 last year 81 degrees, minimum 65 degrees. Total precipitation so far this year 10.38 inches.

Full weather report on Page 11, Section II.

BIRD SANCTUARY.

THIS is a spot where God might choose to rest
And look upon the beauty He has made;
The sunlight filtering through the leafy shade;
The mourning dove contented on her nest;
The tanager in scarlet raiment dressed—
A flash of lightning in the dewy glade—
The oriole in rainbow hues arrayed;
And bluebird with a pink rose at his breast.

The yellowhammer beats his brave tattoo;
The bobolink calls from the underbrush;
The mocking bird sings songs forever new;
The jaunty waxwing and the timid thrush.
Yes, God might choose to come and rest Him here,
For He and His high heaven seem very near.

—Fitzhugh L. Minnigerode in New York Times.

Salutatorian at Rusk Not Only Gets Diplomo, But Check for $11,600

RUSK, Texas, May 23 (AP).—Graduation was a big event for Ruth Moseley. In addition to being class salutatorian and receiving her diploma, she received a share of an $11,600 oil lease check. She and her brothers, orphans, shared the check.

Dr. E. M. Moseley, her guardian, took advantage of Rusk's infant oil boom to cash in.

Dillinger's Girl And Doctor Aiding Him Get 2 Years

Another Woman in Conspiracy Also Convicted and Third Acquitted

ST. PAUL, Minn., May 23 (AP).—The law won two more associates of desperado John Dillinger Wednesday, while the outlaw himself roamed free, outside its clutches.

A Federal Court jury convicted Evelyn Frechette, his sweetheart, and Dr. Clayton May, Minneapolis physician, of conspiracy to hide the fugitive, and sentenced each to a prison term of two years and to pay a fine of $1,000.

Mrs. Augusta Salt, in whose apartment Dr. May was alleged to have treated Dillinger after he was wounded in escaping March 31 from an apartment where he lived with Miss Frechette, was acquitted.

Mrs. Beth Green, indicted with the three whose case was concluded Wednesday, was sentenced to fifteen months in prison. She pleaded guilty several days before the trial started.

Granted Week's Stay.

Miss Frechette and Dr. May were granted a week's stay of execution and their attorneys announced an appeal would be taken to the circuit court of appeals.

The half Indian girl, who was ar-

See DILLINGER on Page 4.

New Australian Flight Mark Set By Plucky Girl

Jean Batten Makes Trip From England After Two Attempts Fail

PORT DARWIN, Northern Australia, May 23 (AP).—Petite Jean Batten, who refused to quit trying after two failures, Wednesday made a new aviation record for women by completing a flight from England to Australia in 14 days, 23 hours and 25 minutes.

The 24-year-old New Zealand girl brought her old Wooden Moth plane, which has been in use for nearly five years, down at 3 p. m. to cut four and a half days off the previous woman's record, set by Amy Johnson, wife of Capt. James A. Mollison.

"I had an adventurous trip" she said upon her arrival, "the weather was frightful throughout—where can I get a cup of tea?"

Battled Headwinds.

On the last stage of her trip, across the Timor Sea, headwinds blew her plane miles south of the course, she said, but she managed to battle

See FLIGHT on Page 4.

America's Silver Plan Blocks Hope For Gold Return

(Copyright, 1934, by the Associated Press.)

LONDON, May 23.—British financial leaders were pictured in well-informed quarters Wednesday as being highly alarmed by the prospect that President Roosevelt's silver monetization program will blast their hopes for the return of Great Britain to the gold standard in the near future.

Despite the nonchalant attitude they assumed toward the American President's message, financial circles were pictured as being thrown into gloom.

"Financial leaders here have been hoping for some time that President Roosevelt would head off the silverites, so there would be no further steps in the direction of world-wide bimetallism," said a well-informed observer.

Forestalls Return to Gold.

"Roosevelt's capitulation to the silverites will only give new impetus to

See SILVER on Page 4.

Leading Principals in Slaying of Outlaws

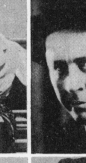

Here are some of those who figured in the killing Wednesday morning of Clyde Barrow and Bonnie Barker, Dallas outlaws. Left to right above are Clyde Barrow, Bonnie Parker and Frank Hamer, former Texas ranger and at present special highway patrolman. Below, left to right, are Deputy Sheriffs Bob Alcorn and Ted Hinton of Dallas County. Other officers, not shown here, who took part in the shooting down of the pair were M. T. Gault, also a former Texas ranger and at present a special highway patrolman; Sheriff Henderson Jordan of Bienville Parish, Louisiana, and his deputy, Curtis Oakley.

Church Must Aid New Deal Because Taught by Christ

Praise for Program of Roosevelt Government Given Presbyterians

CLEVELAND, Ohio, May 23 (AP).—National leaders of the Presbyterian Church in the United States of America were told Wednesday night the new deal in the Government is based on the fundamental tenets of Christ himself. The speaker was Secretary of the Interior Harold L. Ickes.

Addressing a public meeting here sponsored by the church's general council, Ickes pictured the social objectives of Christianity and the new deal as being identical.

"Christ wanted men and women to live upright lives, but He also wanted them to have for each other understanding and good will and mutual helpfulness," the Secretary said. "He wished them to be good neighbors. He hated injustice with a righteous hatred. His life was a fight against oppression. This was the man who drove

See CHURCH on Page 4.

Small Industries Granted Millions Of Federal Credit

House Passes Bill, Now to Go to Conference With Senate

WASHINGTON, May 23 (UP).—Federal credits of $440,000,000 to grease the wheels of small industries were authorized by the House Wednesday.

The vote was 178 to 6.

RFC loans of $75,000,000 to cities to pay school teachers' salaries also were authorized.

The bill for these new recovery credits now goes to the conference with the Senate, which has authorized Federal Reserve Banks and the RFC to lend $700,000,000 to small business.

Dallas Deputy Tells Of Ending Long Chase

Bob Alcorn Says All He Has Done for Months Is Hunt for Bandits

BY BOB ALCORN, Dallas County Deputy Sheriff.

(Copyright, 1934, NANA, Inc.)

ARCADIA, La., May 23.—With other officers for ten months I've been trying to get Clyde and Bonnie, ten months when I did little else except look for them, hope I'd find them and get them dead or alive. Today we got them. They won't kill anyone else now. We got them as they came along the road. It was all over in a moment. Both of them were dead as their car nosed into a sandbank and came to a stop. They didn't even fire a shot but they had grabbed at their guns when our bullets knocked them over.

I began following Clyde and Bonnie last summer. I got reports they were here, there and yonder but always when the other officers and I got there they were gone. Only once last November we ran onto them near Dallas but they got away when we let them have it and they weren't even hit.

Since then I've been after them and for the last four weeks I've done nothing else, all over East and South Texas.

See ALCORN on Page 4.

Planes Complete 1,000-Mile Flight To Aid Newlywed

Surgeons Go Prepared to Help Appendicitis-Stricken Bridegroom

LOS ANGELES, Cal., May 23 (AP).—Roaring across the equator, two navy planes from Coco Solo, Canal Zone, Wednesday completed a 1,000-mile flight to Tagus Cove of the Galapagos Islands with medical aid for William Albert Robinson, Cambridge, Mass., textile engineer and explorer, stricken with appendicitis.

Safe landing of the planes was reported by the Mackay Radio Corporation in a message relayed from the lonely equatorial archipelago by a fishing trawler that for two days has been standing by the little thirty-two-foot, round-the-world ketch on which the explorer is confined with appendicitis.

Naval surgeons who flew from the Canal Zone at dawn Wednesday were prepared for an immediate operation.

Since Sunday night, in the most remote spot in the world from medical aid that such a drama has been enacted, Florence Crane Robinson, Chicago heiress and socially prominent bride, has maintained a vigil by the bunk of her distressed bridegroom in the tragic interruption of their romantic honeymoon that started last June when the little craft sailed from New York.

The quickly executed flight, accomplished with the aid of two destroyers which set out from Coco Solo ahead of the planes, was the response of the navy to the frantic appeal of Mrs. Robinson.

Quick action followed the relaying of the appeal to Washington Tuesday and the planes set out at 6:40 a. m. Wednesday.

Body of Naval Officer Found Beside Road

GREENSBURG, Kan., May 23 (AP).—The body of Lieut. Commander S. J. Trowbridge, naval physician slain last Saturday night, was found about fifteen miles northwest of here beside a little used road in Edwards County. The skull was crushed.

The body was not removed pending the arrival of Leo Hudgins, 24-year-old hitchhiker, who admitted to authorities at Marietta, Ok., Tuesday that he killed the naval officer during a drunken orgy. He said he struck Trowbridge on the head with a hammer after a quarrel precipitated by back-seat driving.

Elusive Dallas Desperadoes Shot to Death in Louisiana

Long Hunt Over Three States Is Ended as Six Officers Ambush Pair in Speeding Auto

BY J. R. BRADFIELD JR., Staff Correspondent of The News.

ARCADIA, La., May 23.—Volleys of lead from the guns of six ambuscaded officers brought swift death Wednesday morning to Clyde Barrow, notorious Dallas desperado, and Bonnie Parker, his woman companion down the trail of crime. The Dallas Deputy Sheriffs, Bob Alcorn and Ted Hinton; two former Texas rangers, Frank Hamer and M. T. Gault, who are members of the Texas highway patrol working under special orders to "Get Barrow;" Sheriff Henderson Jordan and Deputy Sheriff Curtis Oakley of Bienville Paris, comprised the posse which shot down the much-hunted pair on the highway eight miles from Gibsland at 9:15 a. m. Wednesday.

Not a shot was fired by either Barrow or Parker but the bandit was reaching down for his gun when the officers turned loose their deadly fusillade. The car careened to one side of the road as the man fell backward and the woman forward. Fearing the two might be stalling, the officers stepped out from their ambuscade and poured more bullets into the wrecked auto, but they were not needed. Both Barrow and Parker were dead. Their bodies were brought in later to an undertaking establishment here, which quickly was jammed by ever-growing crowds of people, all anxious to get a look at the notorious couple.

It was a long and hard trail that ended on a lonely road near the little Louisiana town of Gibsland. Alcorn and Hinton had been following the elusive desperadoes for many days. Their hunt had been all over Northern Louisiana and East Texas and had dipped into Mississippi and South Texas. The father of Henry Methyn, freed from a Texas prison farm with Raymond Hamilton by the daring Barrow, lives in this vicinity. The officers learned definitely that Clyde and Bonnie had traversed the Gibsland road a few days ago. They figured the two would return.

Find Perfect Ambush.

"We took a chance that they would come," Alcorn said. "We found a perfect ambush behind an embankment and took our places at 2 o'clock Wednesday morning. Sheriff Jordan had been tipped off that Clyde was planning to rob a bank at Arcadia. Hamer and Gault had information that led them to believe the pair would come this way. So we laid down and waited.

"Daylight came, but no desperadoes. At 9 o'clock we were about ready to give up, but while we were discussing whether to stay or leave, I glanced down the road and, some distance away, saw a car whizzing along that looked like the one we knew Barrow was driving.

"'That's Clyde, sure as the world,' I exclaimed, and we kept perfectly still and watched as it came over a

See BARROW-PARKER on Page 4.

Failure of Clyde To Pay for Guns' Delivery Is Fatal

Henchman, Caught by Officers, Gives Valuable Information

Special to The News.

LONGVIEW, Texas, May 23.—Clyde Barrow and Bonnie Parker, will-o'-the-wisp killers, whose sanguine trail was terminated in a blast of gunfire and death in a small and rural Louisiana town Wednesday, frequently moved in and out of Gregg County, but so far as is known their sorties into this sector were made as sociable calls on relatives and were bloodless.

In recent weeks there have been a number of developments along a far-flung East Texas and Louisiana front to indicate the capture or death of the elusive Barrow and Bonnie Parker, was imminent. Officers, grim-faced and heavily armed, have moved out of Longview on several occasions during recent weeks, following tips on the desperate pair. Those enforcers of the law were serious. They went to kill, capture or face the hazards of battles with Barrow and his woman.

A posse of officers, among them Charles Gant and Marvin Utzman, slipped quietly out of Longview Tuesday night, turning their automobiles toward Winnsboro where the Barrows had arranged for a clandestine meeting with a henchman, a man who had delivered guns and ammunition to them in a stolen automobile. That trip to a Barrow rendezvous, in a stolen Dallas machine, proved to be the man's undoing, and hardened his heart toward the outlaw pair which he previously had served as contact man and aid.

Gun Runner in Jail.

The man is in jail here now. He gave his name as J. A. Nichols, Dallas, and officers say he is facing eleven charges in Dallas. The trend of his conversation indicates he had connection with one of the greatest rings in Dallas' history. He was taken in custody earlier in the week by Deputies Marvin Utzman and Charles Gant at a Gladewater road cottage.

When officers told him Wednesday that Barrow and Bonnie had failed in their efforts to reach their guns—met the fate which they have so unrelent-

See GUN DELIVERER on Page 4.

Comrades Praise Men That Trapped Barrow and Parker

Job Done, Message Sent by Ex-Rangers, Now on Highway Patrol

From the Austin Bureau of The News.

AUSTIN, Texas, May 23.—Frank Hamer and B. M. Gault, two Austin men who played the principal roles in trailing and slaying Clyde Barrow and Bonnie Parker, are veteran officers and former members of the rangers. Hamer retired as ranger Captain when the Fergusons entered the Governor's office and was succeeded by his brother, D. E. Hamer. It was Frank Hamer and Gault who did the work and their comrades here are paying them tribute.

Hamer has ferreted out a number of noted crimes and has had many brushes with so-called bad men. He is about six feet three inches tall and does not wear the boots and accoutrements of other rangers. Gault is a smaller, spare man with benevolent features and as gentle as men get to be. No one would pick him as a fearless chaser of desperadoes, as he has been for many years.

Commissioned as Patrolmen.

Under recent commissions as patrolmen from the Highway Department, Hamer and Gault have been seeking the hiding places of Barrow and Bonnie, and they laid the trap that caught them. "The job is done," was the telephone message from Hamer to Capt. L. G. Phares, chief of the highway patrol. Phares has been almost sleepless in his efforts to have the Easter Sunday killers of his two patrolmen, H. D. Murphy and E. B. Wheeler, run down. It was Phares who put Hamer and Gault on the trail with instructions to go the limit. Phares chartered a plane and flew to Arcadia, La., when apprised of the deaths.

Rewards to Be Paid.

Since his retirement from the rangers Hamer has worked under private employment in a number of crime investigations and has others on his list now.

Phares had accumulated a fund of more than $4,000 to chase the slayers of the patrolmen and only a part of it has been spent. The remainder is expected to paid in rewards. The Governor offered a $500 reward and the Legislature tried to offer $1,000 each for Barrow and Raymond Hamilton, but the bill was defeated.

State Candidate Dies After Being Shot at Trinity

Rail Clerk Is Held as Treasurer Aspirant, E. R. Waller, Expires

HOUSTON, Texas, May 23 (AP).—Edward Rex Waller, 34, candidate for State Treasurer, who was shot in front of the postoffice at Trinity on Wednesday, died here at night. Waller was brought here aboard a train. He died as physicians prepared to operate on him.

Will Splettstoesser, a railroad clerk, surrendered to officers after the shooting. He was taken to Groveton, the county seat, to make bond.

Waller had been interested in politics for many years. At one time he was city manager at Goose Creek.

Splettstoesser was charged with assault to murder before Justice Bert Dunlap at Trinity. Sheriff Joseph S. Evans of Trinity County attributed the shooting to family trouble."

Arcadia Sheriff Tells How Barrow Drove Into Trap

Report That Outlaws Planned to Rob Bank Led to Ambuscade

BY SHERIFF HENDERSON JORDAN, Of Bienville Parish, Louisiana, Eyewitness to the slaying of Bonnie Parker and Clyde Barrow. (Written exclusively for Associated Press.)

ARCADIA, La., May 23.—I have been working on this case about six weeks. I received a tip Wednesday that Clyde Barrow and Bonnie Parker were coming through the lower part of Bienville Parish and going to the northern part of Natchitoches Parish. We began checking on this. I put an undercover man on this job. I had him stationed in Shreveport. Upon getting a tip that Barrow and Parker figured on robbing the First National Bank of Arcadia, I got in touch with Frank Hamer, ex-Captain of the Texas rangers, and R. F. Alcorn, Dallas County Deputy Sheriff, I had to get some one who knew Barrow and Parker personally in order not to make a mistake in shooting them if we found them.

Tuesday night I received a tip they

See SHERIFF on Page 4.

State Troopers Asked at Toledo To Quell Strike

Disorders at Autolite Plant Involve 4,500 Workers—Four Hurt

TOLEDO, Ohio, May 23 (AP).—Sheriff David Kreiger Wednesday night asked Gov. George White and Adjutant Gen. Frank D. Henderson to send State troops to Toledo to quell the Auto-Lite plant disorders.

Three thousand angry strike pickets any sympathizers held 1,500 day shift workmen at the plant virtual prisoners Wednesday evening as riots which started in the afternoon continued. Four persons were in hospitals.

Meanwhile State and Federal conciliators were working to bring about a truce in the strike of 1,900 automotive workers, which has been under way here for five weeks. The situation was complicated by a threat of a general strike in sympathy with the automotive workers. A third of the local unions in Toledo were reported to have voted in favor of the general strike.

Wednesday's rioting began shortly after 100 policemen arrived at the plant to protect day shift workers leaving the building.

News Behind the News

By PAUL MALLON (Copyright, 1934, by Paul Mallon)

Revolting Democratic Congressmen Creeping Back in Fold as Primaries Near

Sweet Harmony.

WASHINGTON, May 23.—You can not believe all you hear from Washington. As an instance, it now appears that the wrath of the administration will not descend, as advertised, upon the heads of all rebellious Democratic Congressmen.

Speaker Rainey has, in fact, quietly been striking names off his secret blacklist so fast that there are few left.

One of the names on it was that of a semi-Southern Democrat. Early in the session he was bitter against the Rainey-Byrnes leadership and frequently opposed Roosevelt legislation.

The other day he made a public statement of praise for Speaker Rainey and almost immediately he was appointed to a juicy position on the Democratic patronage committee.

Another Prodigal.

A Democrat from a Pacific Coast State fared even better. He was the No. 1 man on the original blacklist.

Recently he paid tribute to the gr-r-eat Rainey-Byrnes generalship in a speech from the floor. Soon thereafter Floor Leader Byrnes wrote him a letter strongly approving him for re-election.

Hoopla.

The backslapping has replaced backbiting so extensively that Mr. Rainey recently appeared in the sound movie news reels with a first-term Democrat from Montana. Floor Leader Byrnes wrote another letter covering four pages of the Congressional Record (cost to the Government estimated at $55 per page), praising a Gulf States Democratic Congressman. A Texas Representative is using letters from both Rainey and Byrnes saying how good he is. In answer to an inquiry from the Middle West, Rainey also publicly approved a Congresswoman, although she had "opposed the administration on veterans' legislation."

Such tactics are extremely unusual in advance of the primaries. These Congressmen are not running for re-election yet, but only for renomination as Democrats.

The participation of Mr. Byrnes is even more extraordinary because he is chairman of the Democratic Congressional Campaign Committee, which keeps out of the primaries and acts only after Democratic nominations have been made.

Co-operation.

The reason for it is not hard to find.

When the House was in revolt on veterans' restorations, pay cuts and other matters, an impression was created by the party leaders that the revolters were going to be made to suffer. Aspiring young Democrats out through the country thought that afforded a splendid opportunity for them to get elected to Congress. They announced themselves in great numbers as opponents of sitting Congressmen on the ground that those now holding office did not stand with President Roosevelt.

As a result, the Congressmen have been running to Rainey and Byrnes on their hands and knees, asking for statements of approval.

When the bars were let down nearly all the wolves had to be given sheep's clothing.

Underlying it all is the fact that both the House and the Senate have a certain cameraderie and clublike atmosphere on the inside.

When misfortune befalls them they usually let bygones be bygones and sympathize and help each other.

Silver.

The silverites were not as enthusiastic about their new silver bill as they pretended, although it was exactly what Mr. Roosevelt promised them weeks ago.

Floor Leader Robinson picked Senator Key Pittman to introduce the bill in the Senate because Pittman has been the only silverite with whom the administration has worked closely. The final draft came from the Treasury and White House, where the administration worked it out in conference with all the silver group.

On silver enthusiast, in his despair, described it in the cloakroom as "a rimless zero." Another said: "It authorizes them to do something for silver when and if they want to."

Motives.

The reasons for such feelings are numerous. One is there are just as many different kinds of silverites as there are mosquitoes. Each likes a little different kind of meat. For instance, the main reason Senator Thomas has been so active for silver is that he wants to get that issue out of the way so we can have some real inflation.

Another reason is that the silverites doubt if the administration will carry out the flexible mandate of the act as enthusiastically as they would like. They noticed that the administration has lately placed stress on the international aspects of the program.

If they wait until they get an international silver agreement they will wait a long time. Otherwise they might be able to establish the 25 per cent silver base in thirty years.

Notes.

When S-2817 came up in the House last Monday Congressman Carter of California objected and the bill was blocked. It is the bill authorizing Congressmen to borrow from the farm credit administration and HOLC. If three Congressmen object the next time the bill comes up it will be killed.

Nothing will be done about the Darrow charges of malfeasance against the coal code authorities. The Government takes the position that, inasmuch as it will be a party to the price and marketing arrangement made by the code authorities, it can not prosecute even if it wanted to.

Among the industries on which Mr. Darrow is yet to report is oil.

The Darrow board was privately amazed at the public response to its recommendations. Members thought they did a splendid job.

For Fifty Years
A Daily Newspaper

THE EVENING GAZETTE

FULL LEASED WIRE TELEGRAPH NEWS SERVICE

WEATHER
Fair tonight, Tuesday; not quite so warm in extreme southwest tonight; slightly warmer Tuesday.

VOL. LIII NO. 174 — PRICE THREE CENTS — XENIA, OHIO, MONDAY, JULY 23, 1934 — EIGHT PAGES

DILLINGER DIED REACHING FOR GUN

DILLINGER CASE IS BLOODY WARNING TO GANGSTER MEMBERS

Attorney General Pleased; Drive For Others Going On

WASHINGTON, July 23.—John Dillinger's bullet-ridden body put bloody evidence before the eyes of gangsters today that U. S. agents, like the Northwest Mounted, get their man.

To the public went vivid assurance that the justice department means business in its drive against crime.

Criminals who scoffed at federal authority got their answer when a quick burst of bullets wiped out the nation's No. 1 public enemy as he walked from a Chicago theater lobby.

Hearty congratulations went from Attorney General Homer S. Cummings and Director Edgar Hoover of the justice division of investigation to the agents for a job well done.

But in the remorseless drive of the federal men against criminals, the end of Dillinger merely closed one chapter in an endless war on enemies of society.

The next move is the roundup of those few Dillinger associates who remain at large. One, Lester M. Gillis alias George (Baby Face) Nelson, is marked for a death such as Dillinger's the moment federal agents sight him.

The tactics which eventually cut down Dillinger after half a dozen narrow escapes are expected to get his associates in time.

The actual story of the how the justice department tracked down the most desperate outlaw of the midwest likely never will be told.

The sentiment of the department was expressed by Cummings, just before boarding a train for the West:

"The search for Dillinger had never been relaxed for a moment. He had escaped capture on several occasions by the narrowest of margins. The news tonight is exceedingly gratifying as well as reassuring."

Even in their hour of triumph, federal authorities were chary of details about the Dillinger hunt. Secrecy is the keynote of government operatives and an important factor in their success, Hoover believes. Even when a job has been completed there is much that is never revealed.

It is known, however, that about 100 agents have been concentrated on the Dillinger case.

They established that Dillinger had kept close to Chicago in recent months. He and his henchmen went separate ways when they narrowly escaped federal agents after the gun battle at Little Bohemia.

Although bank robberies from

(Continued On Page Five)

FARMER HURT WHEN TRUCK LEAVES ROAD

Forced Into Pole By Hit-Skip Driver

Wilfred Routzong, Fairfield Pike, four miles from Yellow Springs, suffered minor bruises when a livestock truck he was driving Friday night was crowded off the highway by another auto just north of Yellow Springs, the vehicle crashing into a telephone pole and snapping it. The truck was damaged considerably. Routzong did not procure the license number of the auto, which, he said, sped on without stopping.

Thomas Jacobs, residing south of Yellow Springs, escaped injury when his auto struck a pole Saturday afternoon in front of the John Birch oil station in Yellow Springs. Just a week ago Saturday the driver had a similar experience on a highway south of the village when he lost control of his car and it landed in a ditch. Then, as Saturday, he was unhurt.

STRIKE COLLAPSES

SAN FRANCISCO, July 23.—The million-dollar-a-day maritime strike on the Pacific Coast was collapsing on all sides today as striking longshoremen voted on acceptance of arbitration in the dispute which led to their walkout May 9.

TEMPERATURES YESTERDAY

(Up to 6 p. m.)

Cities	Low	High
Boston	68	78
Chicago	82	102
Cleveland	74	88
Denver	64	84
Des Moines	80	104
Los Angeles	62	80
Miami, Fla.	74	90
New Orleans	78	94
New York	72	88
Seattle	54	70
Xenia	85	106

Damaging Storms Sweep County

BUILDINGS SUFFER AS MINOR CYCLONE COMES WITH HEAVY RAINFALL

Trees And Service Poles Down In Many Sections; City In Darkness Sunday Night; Youth Burned By Electric Wire

Xenia residents were counting Monday the toll of a short-lived but destructive rain, electrical and windstorm, which broke over the city and vicinity at 9 o'clock Sunday night, disrupting electric service, crippling communication facilities, showering streets with limbs of trees and indirectly causing the serious injury of a youth who came in contact with a "live" wire.

Andrew Muterspaw, 19, of 223 N. Galloway St., was recovering from severe burns on the left wrist and right foot sustained at midnight Sunday while walking through his backyard, following the windstorm, when he came in contact with a "hot" wire. The youth touched a clothesline over which the wire was hanging after being blown down during the electrical storm earlier in the evening.

Although stunned temporarily, Muterspaw regained consciousness later at his home, according to Dr. Marshall Best, attending physician.

Accompanied by wind of high velocity, the storm drenched Xenia with a heavy twenty-minute rainfall and put a temporary crimp in the prolonged heat wave climaxed Sunday afternoon when temperatures rang the bell at 106 degrees. This established a new season's and presumably a new all-time high summer record. The mercury had reached 105 degrees Saturday, eclipsing the previous year's maximum on June 29 by three degrees.

The storm which hit Xenia came as the aftermath of a miniature cyclone which swept over a district five miles southeast of this city Saturday night blowing down telephone poles, uprooting trees and damaging barns and farm residences.

Damage wrought by Sunday night's storm was particularly severe in the northern section of the city.

Greene County Fair Board officials estimated $1,000 damage, insured, was caused by high wind and falling trees at the fairgrounds, on Fairground Road.

Between twenty-five and thirty trees were uprooted or broken off in various parts of the grounds. An open cattle shelter valued at $500 was blown down completely, the

(Continued on Page Three)

DILLINGER AND GIRL WHOSE PHOTO HE CARRIED

John Dillinger

EVELYN FRECHETTE

15 PERISH IN BUS FIRE

Fear Mounting Toll As Rescuers Search Charred Hulk; Sunday Excursion Ends In Tragedy On Hill

OSSINING, N. Y., July 23.—Searchers of the charred hulk of a bus that was a flaming coffin for at least fifteen persons, feared an even greater death list today as they sifted ashes for evidence of human cremation.

Fifty men, women and children were in the blazing bus that careened down a steep hill within sight of Sing Sing prison, and plunged over a forty-foot embankment. It was an end to a Sunday holiday excursion. Authorities feared many of the charred remains would never be identified.

Nearly a score of the surviving passengers were in hospitals. Three of these are not expected to live.

Throughout the night hysterical women and grief-stricken men visited morgues and hospitals attempting to identify masses of charred bones as relatives or friends. It was feared the death toll might reach seventeen or eighteen.

All the victims were members or friends of the Brooklyn Democratic League. They were on their way to Sing Sing to see their baseball team play a convict nine. A gay Sunday excursion at its start, the party transformed with tragic suddenness into a terror-stricken group watching relatives screaming and dying in the mobile pyre.

The fire spread from the bus to the lumber yard into which it fell, destroyed virtually the entire yard, then spread to a dock in the Hudson River and swept nineteen boats.

Preliminary check showed that brakes on the antiquated bus were defective. Survivors said that sev-

(Continued On Page Five)

EXTREME HEAT CLAIMS HEAVY TOLL IN STATE

Water Famine Looms; Slight Relief Is Predicted

COLUMBUS, July 23. — Ohio faced a severe water shortage today as temperatures soared to the 100-degree mark for the third successive day. Many persons died of heat prostration, or drowned in an attempt to escape the heat. Hundreds were in hospitals, recovering from the effects of the three-day heat wave.

Weather bureaus predicted relief today, as a gradual breaking up of the torrid areas begins. Temperatures will be above normal this week, according to predictions.

Severe electrical storms hit scattered sections of the state over the week-end. Thousands of dollars damage was done to crops and homes. Hail beat down crops withered by a scorching sun, and lightning started fires in many homes. A high wind whipped the roofs off many barns and farm buildings.

City officials at Springfield and Lima issued orders for conservation of water. At Springfield, city firemen ordered an immediate stop in use of water when a fire alarm is sounded.

At least eleven persons were dead as a result of the intense heat. Two drownings were reported today.

MYSTERY WOMAN GAVE "TIP"

CHICAGO, July 23—A mysterious "woman in red" led federal agents to the theater where they killed John Dillinger last night, one report said today.

Melvin L. Purvis, head of the Federal Bureau of Investigation, would neither confirm nor deny this story of how the nation's master investigators finally get a trap that caught Dillinger.

Purvis admitted that some unnamed person would be eligible for the Dillinger reward; he acknowledged that someone far removed from the ranks of federal agents and police supplied the tip that led to Dillinger's death, but he refused to confirm that this person was a woman.

STATE AUTO CLUBS PLAN CONVENTION

CEDAR POINT, July 23.—The Ohio State Automobile Association will hold its 33rd annual convention at Cedar Point, opening on Friday and closing on Saturday.

Sixty-two automobile clubs throughout the state will be represented, according to Fred H. Caley, secretary of the Cleveland automobile club and chairman of the legislative and convention committees.

NRA's Fate Is In Doubt; May Affect Votes

Think Johnson Favors Permanency; Would Need Legislature

By CHARLES P. STEWART
Central Press Staff Writer

WASHINGTON, July 23.—NRA's fate is a subject for anyone who enjoys guessing, to guess on.

General Hugh S. Johnson, by what he said just before leaving for the west coast, clouded the institution's future to such an extent that one person's guess is worth about as much as another's.

Hugh Johnson

The nub of business' conclusion from the general's remarks unmistakably is to the effect that their author believes NRA should be continued as a permanency. Otherwise there would be no point in transferring its management, as he suggests, from his own one-man control into the hands of a commission. That is to say, the general, while badly worn out by his work thus far, nevertheless considers himself equal to remaining on the job until next mid-June, when (unless its lease of life is extended in the meantime) NRA automatically will evaporate, under the terms of the law which created it. The task, however, the general holds, is too much for a single individual to carry on indefinitely. Assuming, then, a prolongation of the set-up into eternity, he argues that the matter of providing it with a board of directors, instead of just one lone director, should be attended to promptly.

* * *

The general's reasoning seems to be sound, on the theory that NRA

(Continued on Page Four)

JOHN DILLINGER HAD RAPID RISE TO TOP OF UNDERWORLD

Less than four months as the leader of the nation's most notorious gang of criminals earned John Dillinger the police listing as America's public enemy No. 1.

His leadership of a gang that included several escaped convicts extended from his liberation from Lima, O., jail to his capture in Tucson, Ariz., on Jan. 25.

During that period the Dillinger gang was reputed to have obtained more than $200,000 in a dozen or more Middle Western bank robberies. At least three police officers were slain by the gang.

Dillinger was born on an Indiana farm near Mooresville thirty-one years ago. His youth was spent in school and doing farm work.

"Fell into Bad Company"

He left the farm, where his 70-year-old father still lives, at the age of 20. By his own account he "fell into bad company." His career of crime, so far as police records show, began in the summer of 1924. Dillinger and a companion waylaid Frank Morgan, 65-year-old grocer, and beat him severely during a robbery attempt. He was arrested, convicted and sentenced to two to fourteen years in the Indiana state reformatory.

During his stay there Dillinger was far from a model prisoner. He was punished repeatedly for infractions of prison rules. He tried twice to escape. After serving four years of his sentence he was paroled in 1928.

There was no record of how Dillinger spent his next few months, but in 1929 he was arrested for the robbery of a grocery store in Grovetown, Ind. On July 16, 1929, he was sentenced to six to ten years in the state prison at Michigan City.

Met Bandit Gang

In the Michigan City prison Dillinger met the men he later was to lead in a bloody campaign of ban-

(Continued On Page Five)

FRAUD CHARGED IN GOVERNMENT SUIT

WILMINGTON, Del., July 23.—Sensational charges of wholesale fraud and embezzlement were made in U. S. District Court today against twenty-eight firms and officials formerly connected with the activities of the now defunct Federal Farm Board.

The charges were contained in a 43-page bill of complaint filed in connection with the $1,129,533,000 damage suit instituted by and on behalf of the United States government and Robert A. Gilchrist, of Philadelphia, as co-plaintiffs.

STORM HITS OSBORN AND FAIRFIELD AND DAMAGE TOLL HEAVY

Garages, Trees, Poles Leveled By Severe Windstorm

A heavy downpour of rain and hail accompanied a wind storm of tornadic proportions which hit the Osborn and Fairfield vicinity late Saturday afternoon, causing widespread property damage, uprooted buildings, blew down garages, trees, telephone and high tension wire poles and mowed down corn fields. No injuries were reported.

Hundreds of windows in private homes and business places were shattered by the hail and high wind. The twin cities were without lights and electric power for several hours. The storm, which swooped down at 4 p. m., lasting twenty minutes, also interrupted transportation on the Cincinnati and Lake Erie Railroad Co. snapping power lines.

Several box cars on a Big Four Railroad siding were blown down the rails by the terrific wind, crashing through switches and reaching the main line. Trains were delayed until the cars could be moved back on the siding.

Main and Second Sts. in Fairfield were virtually impassable after trees toppled on each side of the streets. The roof of the Bath Twp. consolidated High School was torn partly off, as was the roof on the pavilion at the abandoned dog racing plant near Fairfield.

Fields of corn in the vicinity were flattened by the wind and then shredded into bits by the hail, causing a total loss.

ADMITS MAIL THEFT

FINDLAY, O., July 23.—Leedal Ingle, 22, Kenton, has confessed the theft of two sacks of mail from a New York Central Railroad train at a station here. Sheriff Lyle Harvitt said today. He will be turned over to federal authorities.

"SHOT ME TOO AND I'M MAD," SAYS WOMAN

By MRS. ETTA NATELSKI
(As told to the United Press)

CHICAGO, July 23—They shot John Dillinger and they shot me, too.

I'm not very badly hurt, but I'm pretty mad.

Last evening my husband, Jacob, suggested that we go for a walk because it was so hot in our apartment. Lillian, my daughter, came along, too.

We were walking along Lincoln Avenue, talking about the heat like everybody else. As we came to the Biograph Theater, I noticed the picture was "Manhattan Melodrama". I turned to my husband and said:

"I'd like to see that picture."

Just then some shots were fired. It sounded to me like there were only two of them. I felt a burning sensation in my leg. I said to my husband:

"Jake, I think I'm shot!"

He grabbed me and I began to feel faint. We were right at the entrance to an alley next to the theatre. I saw a man fall. He was bleeding.

I thought I saw a woman run down the alley. I couldn't be sure. People began running from all directions. They started to crowd in on us and I guess I fainted.

FEDERAL AGENTS END CAREER OF GANGSTER IN HAIL OF BULLETS

America's No. 1 Public Enemy Died As He Lived—With Woman On Each Arm; Fell Into Ambush Laid Outside Chicago Theater

CHICAGO, July 23.—A stiffening corpse in the county morgue and a muddied pool of blood in the filth of an alley was all that was left today of John Dillinger, arch criminal of modern times.

Dillinger died as he lived—in a hail of bullets and a welter of blood.

He died at 10:40 o'clock last night with a smile on his lips and a woman on each arm. Twelve federal agents and five policemen, shooting through a crowd of men, women and children, dropped the little desperado as he left a motion picture theatre six blocks off the famous gold coast.

Three bullets ended the career that started with the escape of ten convicts from the Michigan City, Ind., state prison, continued with murder of Sheriff Sarber at Lima, O., brought death to fourteen men and was climaxed by Dillinger's "toy gun" escape from the Crown Point, Ind., jail.

Dillinger spotted the ambush almost as the officers located him in the after theater crowd.

He yanked at a tiny .38 pocket automatic—a favorite small but powerful gun of gangsters.

Pistols of the law crashed in a deafening fusillade. Men, women and children nearby screamed and trampled each other in flight. Two .45 caliber slugs smashed into the outlaw's chest. He whirled. He stumbled. His arms flailed aloft. Another slug burned into the back of his neck, crashed through his head and came out over his right eye.

Two women, crowded into the field of fire fell with bullet wounds. Mrs. Theresa Paulus was shot in the hip; Mrs. Etta Natelski in the leg.

Stumbling, his eyes already glazing, Dillinger dove clear through the line of guns, rocked a hundred feet to an alley and fell dead.

He died there—the man who had squandered hundreds of thousands of stolen dollars—in the muck of his own blood and the dirt of a dark alley.

His two woman companions, the last of an ever changing stream of feminine favorites, abandoned him at the first sign of danger and escaped.

In the morgue was found their justification. Carefully cased in the back of their escort's watch was the photograph of another woman, Marion Evelyn Frechette, half breed Indian girl who went to prison because she aided him.

Ironically, Dillinger just had seen on the silver screen within the Biograph Theater a career almost paralleling his own. He had watched another criminal walk to the electric chair—had seen prison lights dim under the pull of a death dealing load—had thought, perhaps, of the fate awaiting him if he ever was captured.

The picture was "Manhattan Melodrama," pointing in breathless action the moral that crime never pays. To Dillinger it was a warning he could not read.

Dillinger's face had been lifted by means of plastic surgery in an effort to avoid recognition, according to Melvin H. Purvis, the federal government's chief manhunt-

(Continued On Page Five)

THREE ESCAPE TEXAS PRISON DEATH HOUSE

Convict Killed, Three Wounded In Daring Jail Break

HUNTSVILLE, Tex., July 23.—Three embryonic John Dillingers—vicious killers all—roamed the southwest today. They escaped from the death house of state prison in a daring break yesterday that resulted in the death of a convict and the wounding of two convicts and a guard.

All three were awaiting electrocution. Most desperate was John Hamilton, member of the Clyde Barrow-Bonnie Parker gang, a bank robber and murderer the other were Joe Palmer and "Blackie" Thompson.

William "Whitey" Walker, member of the Thompson gang, was dead.

Wounded were Charles Fraser and Roy Johnson, convicts, and H. E. George, a guard. Fraser was in a critical condition; the others slightly injured.

Highways in Texas, Oklahoma and Kansas were blockaded as peace officers sought to cut off escape of the desperate criminals.

The escape was breath-taking. Lee Braswell, a guard taking food

(Continued On Page Five)

SARBER PLEASED TO LEARN OF SLAYING

LIMA, O., July 23—News of Dillinger's death was greeted here with varied comment.

Sheriff Donald Sarber, whose father Jesse Sarber was slain by the gang that delivered the notorious outlaw from the jail here, said: "I am very much elated at the killing of Dillinger. My only regret is that I was not there to help do the job."

Judge Emmit E. Everett, who sentenced Harry Pierpont and Charles Makley to the electric chair for the killing of Sheriff Sarber said: "All I care to say is that that's the end of that kind of life."

MANUFACTURER DIES

WASHINGTON C. H., O., July 23—Funeral services were being arranged today for M. J. Hagerty, 73, shoe manufacturer, who died at his home here following a brief illness. His widow and four sons survive.

PEACE ENDS IN COPPER STRIKE

Violence Flares In Montana Area

BUTTE, Mont., July 23.—Seared by fire and wracked by violence, Butte today sat atop dynamite.

After nearly three months of comparative peace, the strike of 5,000 copper miners and smeltermen was strafed with serious trouble.

A week-end of disorders was climaxed shortly after midnight by burning of a portion of a mine yard.

It came after two other mine fires, an explosion, mob stonings and gunfire.

Threat of a general strike and martial law followed on the heels of the violence.

LEARN PAL IS DEAD

COLUMBUS, O., July 23.—Harry Pierpont and Charles Makley, Dillinger gangsters under sentences to electrocution at Ohio penitentiary, today heard the news of the death of their former chief without emotion and predicted they would leave the penitentiary soon—"feet first."

TODAY IN THE GAZETTE

——If all the children born in the United States for 2,065 days were killed—

——Then perhaps you would have a better idea of the magnitude of the loss of life in the World War; 8,538,000 of the pick of the world's best manhood.

——Now, twenty years later, we will realize the real story of why those 8,538,000 died. From records of the great war now available, Clark Kinnaird has prepared the new picture feature starting in THE GAZETTE

——"The World War Twenty Years Ago Today" is made up of the best of 100,000 war pictures, arranged in sequence so that they tell a graphic chronological story of the greatest drama in 1900 years.

——Younger readers, especially, will like this photo feature starting today.

SPECIAL EXTRA EDITION

DOCK MEN VOTE ON STRIKE END

Only Los Angeles Newspaper With All Leading News Services—Associated Press, International News, United Press, Dow - Jones

LOS ANGELES EVENING HERALD AND Express
AN INDEPENDENT NEWSPAPER

Reg. U. S. Pat. Office. Copyright, 1934, by Evening Herald Publishing Company
The Evening Herald and Express Grows Just Like Los Angeles

LATEST NEWS

WEATHER FORECAST
Los Angeles and Vicinity—Fair tonight and Tuesday with overcast in the morning; seasonable temperatures and humidity; gentle winds.

VOL. LXIV THREE CENTS Hotels and Trains Five Cents MONDAY, JULY 23, 1934 Two Sections Section A THREE CENTS NO. 102

DILLINGER LED TO DEATH BY GIRL IN RED DRESS

ARBITRATION PLAN TO BE APPROVED, FORECAST

Port Strikers May Be Back on Jobs by Wednesday If Proposal Carries

SAN FRANCISCO, July 23.—Three passengers, the conductor and motorman of a Market Street Railway car jumped to safety today, when a car, out of control, sped down a steep grade and finally jumped the track. The rails had been greased, presumably by persons in sympathy with the 2000 trolleymen who were still on strike for shorter hours. Over the week-end rocks were hurled through car windows and platform men beaten up.

By Associated Press

SAN FRANCISCO, July 23.—Striking Pacific Coast longshoremen, whose 76-day-old dispute flared to a climax with the sympathetic mass walkout of union labor here, start balloting today on whether to accept arbitration of all issues.

Along the coast, representatives of President Roosevelt's natinal longshore board sped by airplane during the night to deliver ballots at the various ports and supervise the voting.

The 15,000 ballots prepared by the board were spread from Seattle to San Diego as details of the election, backed by the authority of the federal government, were hurried by Dr. Louis Bloch, secretary of the President's board.

Dr. Bloch said the result of the election should be known by tomorrow night at the latest. If the arbitration proposal carries, as predicted by even admitted extremist leaders of the strikers, the

(CONTINUED ON PAGE ELEVEN)

Dillinger Made 'Oriental' By Disguise Operations

By International News Service

CHICAGO, July 23.—John Dillinger's facial operations completely disguised the infamous desperado.

Two long strips of skin were removed from his cheeks, just forward of the ears. The operation drew his skin taught and gave him an oriental appearance.

As he lay on the sidewalk after being shot and killed by federal agents a small boy looked at his face and cried to his father:

"Oh, dad! The man is a Chinaman."

Dillinger had dyed his sandy hair a jet black and wore scholarly gold-rimmed glasses.

His fingerprints taken after he was dead, disclosed that he had attempted to mar them by the use of acid.

DEATH TOLL OF HEAT IN EAST UP TO 275

By Associated Press

CHICAGO, July 23.—The heat wave extended its sway over the sun-scourged nation today, raising the total of lives lost to at least 275.

With even more severe temperatures predicted, all sections paid—the cities with lives, the country with livestock, ravaged crops and failing water supplies.

A survey of drouth damage from the Mississippi to the Rocky mountains showed thousands of cattle lost, thousands more given up at forced sales, and crop losses placed at hundreds of millions of dollars.

Millions of persons, who found relief at the lakes and seashores over the weekend, came back today to baked pavements and steaming sidewalks.

In the heart of the nation, hardest hit of all, the mercury hovered about the 100 mark yesterday and official forecasts told of an indefinite continuance of the hot, dry spell.

The highest temperature reported yesterday was 107 in Aurora, Ill. Springfield, Ill., sweltered at 105, Minneapolis 104, St. Louis 102, Omaha and Chicago 101.

The heaviest loss of lives was in Missouri, where 76 have died from the heat. Illinois has forfeited 66 lives, Nebraska 41, Ohio 15, Kansas 12, Iowa and Minnesota 11 and Texas 10.

The east was favored with a cool breeze in the fourth day of its siege yesterday, holding the maximum temperature in New York to 89, but the weather bureau said warmer temperatures may be expected in the next few days. The mountain states were cooler after general showers.

DRAGGED BY STREET CAR

SAN FRANCISCO, July 23.—(I.N.S.)—Dragged beneath a street car for two blocks, Raymond Collins, 31, barber, was near death today. The motorman of the car was unable to explain the accident.

Evelyn Frechette's Picture Found in Dillinger's Watch

By Associated Press

CHICAGO, July 23.—John Dillinger carried Evelyn Frechette's picture to the end.

Officers found it in his watch.

Evelyn, part Indian girl, is now in prison for harboring the desperado whose sweetheart she was.

Sky Overcast but No Rain Forecast; Fair for Tonight

Though the sky remained overcast through the morning, fair weather was forecast by the government's meteorologist for tonight and tomorrow.

Again tomorrow morning skies will be cloudy, but there should be no rain, excepting in the mountains, where showers were predicted for this afternoon.

Temperatures will remain virtually unchanged, the weather man said. It was 81 at the highest point yesterday and 65 degrees at dawn this morning.

Out of season sprinkles of rain fell in scattered sections yesterday, the heaviest reported fall being at Ontario, where .01 of an inch was recorded.

More Liquidation In Stocks; Rails Again Weakest

By International News Service

NEW YORK, July 23.—Liquidation was resumed in the stock market today after a dull and relatively steady first hour. Strength in grains was ignored.

Rails were again the weak spots, and carried the others along. Atchison lost a point.

Heavy selling in Commonwealth & Southern developed in the utilities, which sold down to around their lows of the year.

Rails showed little support as the session wore on and this added further unsettlement to the rest of the list. United States Steel was heavily sold and broke its low for the year.

IDENTITY OF 'TIP' GIRL IS GUARDED

Pal of Slain Officer Traps Killer Through His Girl Friend

By International News Service

CHICAGO, July 23.—A double-crossing "girl friend" led John Dillinger, public enemy No. 1, to his death last night, it was revealed today.

The girl, dressed in a red dress, is being guarded in a loop hotel by federal men, and her identity will never be known if federal agents can keep it secret.

It was this "girl friend" and the perseverance of a uniformed police sergeant of the East Chicago police department that finally trapped the killer.

PARTNER OF VICTIM

The uniformed Policeman was Sergt. Martin Zarkovitch, who was the partner of Officer Pat O'Malley, who had been murdered by Dillinger.

Zarkovitch had obtained leave of absence from the East Chicago police force with the announced intention of capturing Dillinger.

He lingered around saloons in northern Indiana and finally a man intimated while intoxicated that he knew where Dillinger was hiding out.

This informant, in turn, took Zarkovitch to a girl who admitted she knew Dillinger and saw him at times.

Zarkovitch played on the man and the girl, pointing out that there was $15,000 reward for turning Dillinger in to the authorities, and that that was a lot of money these days.

CONTACTS OFFICER

Sunday afternoon the girl got in touch with Zarkovitch and told him that Dillinger would go to the movie "Manhattan Melodrama" some time that evening.

Zarkovitch, in turn, gave his in-

(CONTINUED ON PAGE NINE)

Herald-Express Special Features

TRAIL OF CRIMES ENDED

John Dillinger, above, America's Public Enemy No. 1, is dead today, his unprecedented trail of murders and robberies ended by the guns of justice. He was shot and killed by federal agents when he emerged from watching a gangster film in a little Chicago theater last night.

Here is Melvin H. Purvis, chief of the Chicago office of the department of justice, who laid the trap for Dillinger after receiving the tip the outlaw was going to be at the theater.

'BABY FACE' NELSON HUNTED AS NEW PUBLIC ENEMY NO. 1

By International News Service

WASHINGTON, July 23.—George ("Baby Face") Nelson, notorious killer, bank robber and all around bad man, succeeds John Dillinger as "public enemy No. 1," so far as the department of justice is concerned.

The smooth-faced Nelson, who shot to death W. Carter Baum, a department of justice agent, when he and Dillinger blasted their way out of Spider Lake, Wis., last spring, now becomes the most wanted man by federal agents.

J. Edgar Hoover, director of the department's bureau of investigation, so designated Nelson today, while still glowing over the success-

(CONTINUED ON PAGE SEVEN)

WOMEN COMPANIONS HELD AS DESPERADO KILLED BY FEDERALS

By International News Service

CHICAGO, July 23.—Two girl companions, who attended the movies last night with John Dillinger, today were reported in custody of federal agents. Melvin Purvis, chief of the federal bureau of investigation here, refused to reveal the names of the two girls or even to admit definitely that they were in his custody.

By JACK LAIT
International News Service Staff Correspondent
Copyright, 1934, by International News Service

CHICAGO, July 23.—John Dillinger, ace bad man of the world, got his last night—two slugs through his heart and one through his head.

He was tough and he was shrewd, but he wasn't as tough or as shrewd as the federals, who never close a case until the end. It took 27 men, under the head of the Chicago bureau, to close Dillinger's case. And their strength came out of his weakness—a woman.

Dillinger was put on the spot by a tip-off that came to Melvin H. Purvis, chief of the Chicago office of the department of justice. He had waited long. And when it came, Purvis acted, calmly, cooly and with such deadly efficiency that the killer who never gave a man a chance didn't have a chance.

TWO WOMEN COMPANIONS OF DESPERADO ESCAPE BULLETS

It was Sunday. But Uncle Sam doesn't observe any NRA. He works a seven-day week.

And on this sultry Sunday, Purvis, knowing precisely what to expect and what to do, organized his phalanx of 22 government agents and five East Chicago, Ind., police, and surrounded a little third-run, 15-cent movie house, the Biograph, on the near north side.

Purvis knew just when Dillinger would arrive, and he knew that two women, one wearing a red dress, would arrive at the same time.

These women must not be confused with two who were shot when Dillinger was shot. The slightly wounded victims were respectable residents of the neighborhood. The other two women were not shot. They were the ones who turned him up, led him into range of the gunfire, put the finger on him definitely, and disappeared.

EVERY AVENUE OF ESCAPE CUT OFF BY FEDERAL AGENTS

Purvis placed his men, covering every possible move Dillinger could possibly make. He himself stood in the tiny lobby of the theater. Dillinger entered at about 7:30. He wanted to see a film about a big-time killer, "Manhattan Melodrama." Near him as he entered were two women. Many men and women were entering at that time. The cashier says

(CONTINUED ON PAGE EIGHT)

Minnesota Weather
Fair today, frost morning; Saturday fair and warmer.
Detailed report on Page 14.

St. Paul Pioneer Press

Goering The Splendid
Prussia's premier and his astounding uniforms inspire guffaws in Germany, says the Interpreter. Editorial Page.

VOL. 81. NO. 236. Full Leased Wire Service of the Associated Press. ST. PAUL, MINN., FRIDAY, AUGUST 24, 1934. Complete Service of The United Press. c PRICE THREE CENTS IN ST. PAUL.

HOMER VAN METER KILLED BY POLICE HERE; WOMAN FRIEND LEADS TO TIP-OFF

F.-L. WOMEN ASK OUSTER OF PARTY NOMINEE

Demand That Gunderson Give Mrs. Naplin Court Clerk Place on Ballot.

DECISION SLATED TUESDAY

All Support Welcome, Olson Says; Republicans Lay Campaign Plans.

By C. D. JOHNSTON.

In the face of exhortations by Governor Olson and other party leaders to forget patronage, ticket and platform differences, and unite for "the most vicious campaign attack in our history," a group of Farmer-Labor women threw their party's State Central committee into an uproar Thursday by demanding that a duly nominated candidate be shelved and a woman independent supported in his place.

The attack was directed at O. E. Gunderson, St. Paul city employe, who although not a Farmer-Laborite, according to their charges, filed for clerk of the Supreme Court on the Farmer-Labor ticket and won the party's nomination at the primaries over State Senator Laura E. Naplin of Thief River Falls, who had been indorsed by the party's state convention at the insistence of the women's group.

While the Farmer-Labor Central committee concluded an otherwise harmonious meeting and launched plans for a co-ordinated and concentrated state campaign, the Republican State Executive committee mapped its campaign at a meeting in the Pioneer building.

The committee ignored the new "voters' fusion" proposal of the United Minnesota Voters, and announced it had "nothing to add to Chairman Thomas M. McCabe's statement about fusion, and will go down the line with an aggressive

(Please Turn to Page 2, Col. 1.)

Woman in Line of Fire Tells Story of Police Pursuit of Van Meter and His Death

MRS. STEDJE.

Observed Gangster Closely as He Ran Past Her, Noting He Was Well-Dressed; First Thought Was of Her Children as Shooting Began.

Mrs. Andrew Stedje, 476 Jay street, is the woman who was in the line of fire between police and Homer Van Meter just before the mobsman was shot down.

By MRS. ANDREW STEDJE.

If you had told me two mihutes before the shooting happened that I was going to see a dangerous gangster shot down, I wouldn't have believed you.

I was walking down University avenue toward Marion street. Just as I got to the southeast corner, I heard a couple of shots across the street. I turned around and saw a man running across University avenue, carrying a straw hat in his hand.

He passed right in front of me, going toward Aurora avenue. Then two men, with sawed-off shotguns, who had followed him across the street, rushed past me, too. They were in regular clothes, so I figured they must be deputy sheriffs.

Anxious Over Children.

The first man—I didn't know he was Van Meter then—got to the middle of the block between University and Aurora, and then he turned left into the alley. The other two men followed. My two young children were playing around the neighborhood and I was afraid they might be near, so I followed, too.

Just as the two men with guns got to the entrance to the alley they began shooting. I couldn't say how many times. Then I saw the first man down on one knee in an open space down the alley. I couldn't tell whether he had a gun or not, I was so excited.

The two men shot a couple more times and then the first man crumpled up and his hat rolled away. While he was lying there the two men fired several more shots at him. He didn't move when the men who killed him bent over him.

I never saw a crowd gather so quick. The policemen—as I found out later they were—put the man's hat over his face. There was blood spattered all over. I couldn't look at him. I went home quickly, to find out if my children were there.

Took Wrong Alley.

The man either got rattled or didn't know the neighborhood when he turned into that alley, because it's a blind alley. If he had turned right he might have got away. But then he would have come right by my back yard, and believe me, I wouldn't want a Dillinger gangster near my house!

The dead man was well-dressed. He had on black and white shoes, a dark-blue suit, a white shirt and was carrying a straw hat. It's funny, but I noticed all that when he ran past me.

How did I feel? Well, I was so excited, I was shaking all over. I went home and sat down for a while. Then I went over to the grocery store. When I passed by the alley on my way home—it must have been a half hour later—the body was still lying there and there were policemen all around.

BROWN DESCRIBES VAN METER BATTLE

Riddled Him With Bullets When He Opened Fire, Officer Relates.

Thomas A. Brown, former chief of police and now head of the police identification bureau, told in his own words how he and three other officers shot and killed Homer Van Meter, Dillinger mobster known as Public Enemy No. 2.

By THOMAS A. BROWN.
(Copyright, 1934 by the Associated Press.)

We riddled him with bullets when he opened up on us with his pistol, although we would have preferred to have taken him alive.

For two weeks we've had a line on Van Meter and we've been right on his trail all the time. At 5 o'clock Chief Cullen, Jeff Dittrich, Thomas McMahon and I jumped into an automobile and drove to University avenue. We had two machine guns and two shotguns with us.

At University avenue and Marion street we saw Van Meter walking along the street. He had a moustache, which he ordinarily does not have, but we recognized him. We took up positions nearby out of his vision.

Tom Brown.

As Van Meter came to the corner Chief Cullen and I, almost simultaneously, shouted a command for him to stop. He whipped out a pistol and fired twice. The bullets narrowly missed me.

Then all four of us opened up. I guess we fired about 50 shots in all. Van Meter whirled around and started to run toward the street. At that moment an elderly woman got in the line of fire between him and me. I, as well as the other three officers, had to stop shooting momentarily.

When the woman got out of our way all of us opened up again. I saw blood streaming from his left hand. We chased him almost a block and finally landed him in an alley. There he dropped. When we got to him he was dead. He had a pistol in his hand.

HOURLY TEMPERATURES

Hourly temperatures in St. Paul from 1 P. M. Thursday to 2 A. M. today as recorded on the Pioneer Press and Dispatch government tested thermometer were:

1 P. M.	58	8 P. M.	52
2 P. M.	57	9 P. M.	50
3 P. M.	55	10 P. M.	48
4 P. M.	54	11 P. M.	46
5 P. M.	54	12 M.	45
6 P. M.	54	1 A. M.	45
7 P. M.	53	2 A. M.	44

FROST PREDICTED TODAY, WITH SATURDAY WARMER

Frost was predicted for Minnesota this morning in the government weather forecast as the mercury in St. Paul dropped to 44 degrees at 2 A. M. today, only 12 degrees above freezing.

Clear skies and a northwest wind were expected to drop the temperature to 40 degrees before morning, with the probability of frost in low areas. Saturday will be generally fair and warmer, the forecast stated.

CUT IN WHEAT ACREAGE EASED BY 5 PER CENT

Farm Administration Sets Curtailment at 10 Per Cent Instead of This Year's 15.

SEEKS TO AVOID SHORTAGE

Decision Will Mean Increase of 2,575,000 Acres by Co-Operating Farmers.

Washington, Aug. 23.—(AP)—The farm administration tonight announced a curtailment of 10 per cent in the basic wheat acreage in 1935 for farmers co-operating in production control plans, instead of the 15 per cent required this year.

The change from the 15 per cent reduction was regarded by officials as a partial approach to the goal of adjusting supplies to normal domestic consumption plus whatever exports may be available.

In arriving at the decision, the administration compromised between an effort to guard against political criticism resulting from this year's curtailment in the light of drouth damage, and an effort to avoid repetition of surpluses with consequent low prices.

Officials also believe that some reduction by co-operating farmers is necessary to compensate for increased plantings by non-co-operators next year. The latter may be led by present high prices to increase their acreage.

Surplus Nearly Gone.

Last year's excessive surplus has been practically eliminated by this year's drouth. The lack of rain cut the probable crop to 491 million bushels and it is the aim of the administration to bring supplies up to and possibly above the normal carryover.

This year's supply is estimated at 781 million bushels, 290 million bushels of which is the present carryover. With normal domestic consumption of 625 million bushels the carryover next July is estimated at 156 million bushels.

It is felt that in the future the carryover should be about 200 million bushels to guard against future short crops in drouth years.

A return to normal weather next year probably would result in production of about 775 million bushels on the 62 million acres which would be planted under the proposed 1935 reduction. About 59,500,000 acres were planted during the past growing season under the 15 per cent curtailment.

2,575,000 Acre Increase.

Of the total base acreage, co-operating farmers control 51,500,000 acres and reduced their plantings to about 43,775,000. Since the modification of planting restrictions applies only to this area the relaxation will mean an increase of about 2,575,000 acres by co-operating producers.

No change will be made in the processing tax of 30 cents a bushel and farmers will receive benefit payments of 28 cents a bushel on that part of their crop which went into domestic consumption during the base period, 1928-32. Of the remaining 2 cents one will be held in reserve for possible continuation of subsidized exports in the same manner as under the North Pacific Emergency Wheat Export association during the past year. The other pays for administration.

GENE TUNNEY CONSIDERS OFFER OF NRA POSITION

Montreal, Aug. 23.—(AP)—Gene Tunney, former heavyweight boxing champion of the world, said here today he was considering an offer from General Hugh Johnson of an appointment to the NRA administration.

The former titleholder declined to say, however, in what capacity he would serve if he accepted the general's offer.

He said he was in Montreal on private business, having motored up from a Maine resort, and intended to return to Maine immediately.

Today's Editorials
Page 6.

Roper's Reassurance
To business.

Again the "Backyard Site"
For still another state office building.

To Extend Credit Unions
The Federal government enters this field of credit.

How Currency Depreciation Works
When all play the same game.

Idle Factories Again
The proposal to operate them with unemployed.

Dillinger Henchman Fires Twice When Surprised by Chief Cullen and 3 Officers

THE GUNMAN WHO PAID

WHERE DEATH CAME

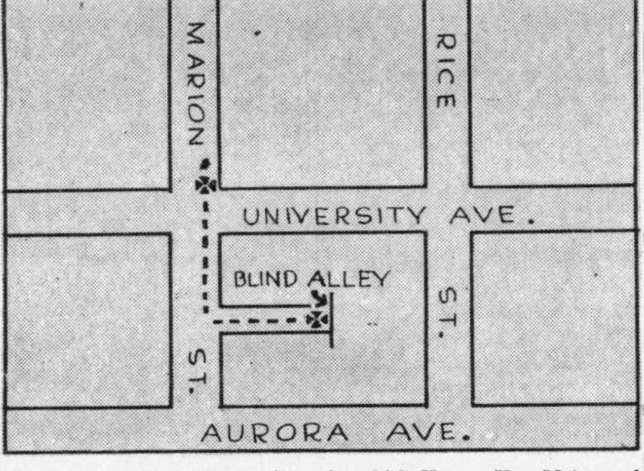

The map shows the territory in which Homer Van Meter, pal of the slain John Dillinger, was shot to death late Thursday by police. The upper cross indicates the northeast corner of University avenue and Marion street, where police ordered Van Meter to halt. On the southeast corner he was momentarily shielded by Mrs. Andrew Stedje, 476 Jay street, a passerby. The lower cross indicates the space in a blind alley where the desperado met his death.

Machine and Shotgun Fire Cuts Down Gunman as He Runs to Alley Near University and Marion After Getting Momentary Protection by Fleeing Toward Pedestrian; Trail Followed for 3 Weeks.

ONLY 2 OF DILLINGER GANG LEADERS STILL AT LARGE, 5 HAVING MET DEATH

Homer Van Meter, notorious desperado and Dillinger henchman, was shot and killed by St. Paul police at 5:12 P. M. Thursday near University avenue and Marion street.

Surprised as he stood on the street corner, Van Meter fired two shots at officers, then ran half a block into a blind alley where he went down under a withering blast from police shotguns and machine guns.

Five slugs pierced the gunman's chest, one reaching his heart. Both hands were ripped by bullets, his chin was crushed by another and he had several more wounds in the head.

Police Chief Frank Cullen led three detectives who ambushed and killed Van Meter. The chief announced later that police had "had a line" on the Dillinger lieutenant and knew of his presence in St. Paul for the past three weeks.

Van Meter, like three other Dillinger gangsters including the Indiana desperado himself, was led to his death by a woman, although she did not herself "put him on the spot."

Chief Cullen refused to disclose the source of his information that Van Meter was in St. Paul, but the Pioneer Press learned that it came through relatives of a woman with whom the outlaw associated here.

RELATIVES BECAME SUSPICIOUS.

The relatives became suspicious of the woman's new "boy friend" and went to police about three weeks ago. The police investigation disclosed Van Meter's identity and officers had been on his trail ever since.

Chief Cullen said his men had found several of Van Meter's hideouts here and on different occasions had planted men for him, but each time the outlaw had evaded them. He refused to say where the hideouts were.

The slaying of Van Meter leaves only two leaders of the Dillinger gang still at liberty—George (Baby Face) Nelson, Public Enemy No. 1, and John Hamilton. Chief Cullen said his information indicates that neither of the two was with Van Meter here.

Police, however, were still searching early today for two automobiles kept here by Van Meter, one a Packard and the other a smaller car, hoping the machines might furnish a clue to the whereabouts of other Dillinger mobsters.

Crime Does NOT Pay

The search for Van Meter was carried on during the three weeks with the utmost secrecy, not even Department of Justice agents, who also were hunting the outlaw, or other police officers outside the four who finally shot him, being informed of the gunman's presence in St. Paul.

Working with Chief Cullen in the investigation and shooting which climaxed it were Detectives Jeff Dittrich, Thomas McMahon and Thomas A. Brown, superintendent of the department of identification and former chief.

POLICE RECEIVE TIP AT 5 P. M.

The "tip" that Van Meter was at University avenue and Marion street was received at 5 P. M. and Chief Cullen and the three detectives left the Public Safety building immediately in the chief's car, carrying two shotguns and two machine guns.

Approaching University avenue on Marion street from the north, they recognized Van Meter strolling toward the corner on University avenue from the east. The four officers left their machine and headed toward the corner on foot, keeping close to the buildings so the gunman would not see them until he reached the corner.

Brown and Cullen were in front, armed with shotguns, and Dittrich and McMahon behind with machine guns. As Van Meter reached the corner and paused, Brown and Cullen were less than twenty feet away and both shouted simultaneously:

"Stick 'em up."

Instead of obeying, Van Meter whipped an automatic pistol from his waistband and fired two shots,

(Please Turn to Page 3, Col. 2.)

MACHINE GUNS PROVE THEIR VALUE

For the first time since the Pioneer Press and Dispatch police equipment campaign last May, St. Paul police had an opportunity Thursday to use their new machine guns in an affray with a major criminal.

Two of the weapons used in the killing of Homer Van Meter were part of the equipment purchased with the $1,839.19 contributed to the newspaper fund by public-spirited citizens.

The campaign was launched April 6, six days after John Dillinger, now dead, shot his way out of a Lexington avenue apartment house.

Cullen Balks at Talking Of Success in Big Test

Admits, However, "We Had to Do Some Straight Shooting."

A genuine Irishman even to the cob pipe, Frank Cullen, who became chief of St. Paul police by virtue of a sort of "compromise," puffed clouds of acrid smoke Thursday night as reporters pressed him for details of the killing of Homer Van Meter in which he took a leading part.

But he could not be persuaded to talk much. Perhaps he feared he might be accused of bragging. Anyway, he was fully at ease and there was just a trace of a twinkle in his eye as he admitted that "we had to do some straight shooting".

Chief Cullen.

Cullen, a middle-aged former detective lieutenant, who grew up in the police department from the rating of a plain pavement pounder, met his first big test in a way that brought smiles aplenty from his admirers within the department.

Cullen became chief after H. E. Warren, new public safety commis-

(Please Turn to Page 2, Col. 3.)

PIERPONT, MAKLEY TOLD OF PAL'S END

Neither Comments Directly on Killing on Hearing News in Ohio Prison.

Columbus, Ohio, Aug. 23.—(AP)—Again to two erstwhile members of the John Dillinger gang came the news tonight that one of their pals had been killed by the law.

A guard walked down the corridor of death row and informed Harry Pierpont and Charles Makley that Homer Van Meter had been shot to death by St. Paul police.

Both Pierpont and Makley were convicted of the slaying of Sheriff Jess Sarber of Allen county, Ohio, last October, in delivering John Dillinger from jail to a period of spectacular freedom. Sentenced to die July 13, they now are awaiting an Ohio Supreme court decision on their appeals for a new trial.

The pair were silent for a moment after the guard told them of Van Meter's end.

Then Makley called to Pierpont: "What do you think of that, Pete?"

Pierpont's answer was:

"It seems they're getting nice to us."

The statement was interpreted by prison officials to refer to the act of informing them.

Cubs Lose; Drop to 3d Place as Cards Win

Details in Sports Pages

Herald and Examiner (Chicago)

54TH YEAR No. 90 Registered in U. S. Patent Office. TWO PARTS C★ X SATURDAY, AUG[illegible]5, 1934 TWO CENTS IN CHICAGO AND SUBURBS ELSEWHERE THREE CENTS

2 CENTS METROPOLITAN EDITION

ORDER GUNMAN NELSON SLAIN

U. S. Issues 22 Millions for Teachers

Today

War—How Soon? Scorpion and Black Widow. 'A Mate, Not a Playmate.' Waiting to Be Killed.

—BY ARTHUR BRISBANE—

© 1934, King Features Syndicate, Inc.

PLENTY OF interest and excitement in today's news. British pounds, compared with French francs, fell to the lowest point ever reached. France predicts early "devaluation of American currency," official cutting-down of the value of the dollar, as the French cut down the value of their franc, from 100 centimes (worth 20 cents) to 20 centimes (worth 4 cents).

If we should imitate that here our dollars would officially be worth twenty cents each, instead of one hundred cents. That would take some adjustment, but whether you cheapen money by reducing the number of cents in the dollar or by reducing the dollar's actual value makes little difference.

Recently Mussolini said, "War, when it comes, will come like a flash," but he did not expect it soon. Now he expects it "at any moment," tells Italians it is their duty "to become warlike," and declares that war would have broken out after the Dollfuss murder had he not sent Italian troops to the Austrian border.

Russia begins to use "plain language" with Japan.

Japan is warned to "cease aggression and free Russian railroad men that have been seized."

And Moscow warns Tokyo to "make all necessary inferences," the inferences in this case being that if Tokyo does not behave there will be some shooting and bomb throwing.

Something disagreeable may come of that Japanese-Russian situation, although it would be foolish to let it come.

With all respect for the courage, determination and fighting ability of Japan, it must be said that Japan could not conquer the Russia of today, now organized and closely united. It is also probable that Russian airmen could and would destroy the chief Japanese cities with bombs, and burn up combustible Japanese towns and villages with fire bombs.

Japan and Russia should be interested in the battle between a big scorpion and a small spider, "black widow," one of the deadliest of insects.

The battle had been going on for forty-four hours yesterday afternoon, in the corner of a garage at Long Beach, Cal.

The "black widow," with a bite known to kill human beings, acts with intelligence and speed, spinning her web around the scorpion, while waiting for a chance to sting. With her web she has made one of the scorpion's pincers useless, and, at last accounts, was trying to enwrap the scorpion's sting.

She had, with her web, lifted the scorpion, three times her size, three inches off the floor.

The difference in size between the "black widow" spider and the scorpion is about the same as the difference between Japan and Russia.

Nazis have issued "Ten Marriage Commandments for Germans," emphasizing the commandment: "Seek a mate, not a playmate."

That would not suit marrying American youth. Imagine marrying a girl that could not dance the tango or play jazz music.

Young Germans are reminded that each of them will be, some day, "the ancestor of German Nordics, a great responsibility."

They are warned to marry for love, but with good judgment, and are told, "Never marry the one good person in a bad family," lest the family deficiencies crop out in their children.

Nature's old commandment, to "marry the person you like, and then make the best of it," is probably the best rule. At least, it has improved the race.

Two men were waiting to be killed by electricity in Kentucky. One, Will Chaney, received two shocks. A third shock called for by the doctor was not forthcoming; the death chair apparatus had broken down. Fortunately, Chaney was dead.

George W. Tincher, obliged to wait for death one hour and fifteen minutes while the electric chair was repaired, had killed a man in a bank holdup.

While Tincher was waiting to be killed, "a Negro chorus sang spirituals, gathered outside the death house."

What would a man think of, listening to the spirituals and the tinkering of the death chair mechanic? Tincher was philosophical: "I'm ready to go any time; it doesn't matter."

Mr. Capone's lawyer still protests against moving his famous client from Atlanta to the government's prison for "bad men" on Alcatraz, rocky island just inside the Golden Gate of San Francisco.

You sympathize with the lawyer, his prosperous client suddenly whisked to a point three thousand miles away.

Capone is said to be indignant because the warden of Alcatraz plans to "keep him away from all contact with his former underworld associates."

He and the other alleged "bad men" will be isolated, no baseball club, not even a radio. Well may

Turn to Page 4, Column 1.

14,000 HERE TO GET BACK PAY MONDAY

Jones Hands McCahey RFC Check in Washington Ceremony; New Fund for Clerks

Monday will be the long-awaited $22,300,000 payday for Chicago public school teachers.

President James B. McCahey of the school board made this promise yesterday in the Washington office of Chairman Jesse Jones of the Reconstruction Finance Corporation when a check for $22,365,983.56—one of the largest ever written—was presented to him.

McCahey said:

"The teachers have been patient for many months. We have used every means available to speed the closing of the loan.

"There will be no delay in distributing the pay checks. They will be available Monday."

14,000 TO GET PAY.

This means that, day after tomorrow, the 14,000 teachers who have seven months' back pay coming to them will be able to go to the pay office in the City State Bank Building at 130 N. Wells st., show their identification slips and get their money.

The 3,000 school board civil service workers, who have eight months' pay, aggregating $4,000,000, coming to them, will be able to get their money at the same place at the same time. Funds were raised by tax warrant sales.

McCahey's receipt of the big check was purely perfunctory. He gave it back soon afterward so it could be delivered by the government to Chicago's city treasurer today, for deposit to the school board account.

BOARD GETS INTEREST.

Of the sum covered by the check, $65,983.56 represents four weeks' interest, accrued before the bonds were pledged to the RFC. It amounts, actually to a refund on interest which has been charged against the school board before the money was received.

As soon as the school board is notified today that the money is on deposit to its account, it will turn over the $22,300,000 in 4½ per cent twenty-year bonds, which the RFC is taking as partial security. To be turned over, at the same time, is the mortgage on $35,000,000 in noneducational school property; pledged as additional collateral.

FILE DOCUMENTS.

Copies of the mortgage, leaseholds and other documents will be filed Monday with the Cook County recorder of deeds, Jones said.

The bonds will be delivered to the Chicago Federal Reserve Bank to the RFC account. Trustee of the bonds will be the First National Bank; of the mortgage, the Continental Illinois National Bank & Trust Company.

SIX-MONTH FIGHT.

Closing of the loan comes six months after the passage of the Sabath amendment to the loans to industries act, authorizing RFC loans to any school district posting adequate security.

The Chicago application is and probably will remain the only one made under the Sabath amendment, Jones declared.

THE WEATHER

CHICAGO AND VICINITY—Generally fair and continued cool, moderate winds mostly northerly. Outlook for Sunday: Probably fair and somewhat warmer.

UPPER LAKES—Fresh west to northwest winds on Superior and moderate winds mostly north to northwest on Michigan and Huron, generally fair, except some cloudiness on Superior.

LOWER LAKES—Moderate northwest winds; generally fair.

ILLINOIS AND INDIANA—Generally fair.

LOWER MICHIGAN—Generally fair.

UPPER MICHIGAN—Partly cloudy; not much change in temperature.

WISCONSIN—Fair.

IOWA—Probably fair and slightly warmer.

SWEETHEART

MARIE MARION CONFORTI—*No. 1 girl friend of the slain Homer Van Meter.*

WINDS KEEPING MERCURY DOWN

Reminder that Winter is not far away was given Chicago yesterday as frost-chilled winds from Minnesota and Wisconsin swept into the city and held temperatures in the sixties throughout the day.

Shivery breezes will continue today, the weather bureau reports, but by tomorrow shifting winds will bring a Sunday somewhat warmer.

Reporting freezing temperatures and frost in Minnesota and points in North Dakota, Chief Forecaster C. A. Donnel said:

"It is normal to have cool as well as warm spells during the Summer. There is nothing to worry about as far as an early Winter is concerned."

Donnel said that the cool wave will work itself through the Ohio valley and the East and Southwest today. Yesterday it was confined to the great central plain states.

Pope Indorses Aid in Chaco Dispute

VATICAN CITY, Aug. 24.—(I.N.S.)—Pope Pius today indorsed the initiative of the archbishops of Buenos Aires, Rio De Janeiro, Santiago and Lima in their efforts to bring about settlement of the Chaco dispute before opening of the Eucharistic Congress in Buenos Aires. The Pontiff expressed hope the appeal would result in sympathetic action by the Presidents of Bolivia and Paraguay, long in conflict over Chaco boundaries.

POLICE TRAIL DILLINGER AID AFTER KILLING

Money Belt Found on Van Meter's Body Gives Clue; Women Open Way for Hunt

ST. PAUL, Aug. 24.—Hot on the trail of George ("Baby Face") Nelson, successor to John Dillinger as head of his kill-crazy band of bank robbers, St. Paul police today struck out in three directions in an endeavor to exterminate the surviving members of Dillinger's gang.

A money belt found on the body of Homer van Meter, Nelson's ally who met death in a hail of police bullets here yesterday, and information supplied by the dead gangster's sweetheart, provided the police with two valuable clues.

Prompted by this new information, police asked Department of Justice agents in Chicago to renew their search for Nelson in Chicago and to find and arrest Marie Conforti, 21, olive-skinned beauty and Dillinger moll.

Acting on the same information, Chief of Police Frank Cullen and Detective Thomas Brown, who shot it out with Van Meter yesterday, today left hurriedly for an unannounced destination out of town.

'SHOOT TO KILL.'

Both the police of St. Paul and the agents of the federal government were under orders to take no chances should they encounter Nelson or other survivors of the Dillinger gang. The general command from their chiefs was:

"Shoot to kill!"

The search for John Hamilton, another Dillinger confederate, was relaxed somewhat when rumors continued to circulate that Hamilton is dead.

It was learned that federal agents during the past week have been searching swamp lands in Dakota County, Minnesota, and Pierce County, Wisconsin, for Hamilton's body.

DEATH REPORTED.

One report was that Hamilton was killed April 22 when the Dillinger gang made its getaway from Mercer, Wis., killing a federal agent and a CCC worker. Another report stated he was killed when he endeavored to cross the Minnesota boundary line and was met by a hail of bullets.

But Samuel P. Crowley, temporarily in charge of the bureau of

Turn to Page 2, Column 2.

'Daddy' Browning Called as Witness

NEW YORK, Aug. 24.—(I.N.S.)—A subpoena was issued today by Magistrate Goldstein ordering Edward W. (Daddy) Browning to appear as a witness in a petty larceny case against Samuel Benson, a former rent collector for Browning's real estate firm. Browning has been in a hospital since June 24.

Mrs. Whitehouse Granted Divorce; Charges Cruelty

Mrs. Lucille Douglas Whitehouse of 70 E. Walton place won an uncontested divorce yesterday from Howard D. Whitehouse, broker, whom she wed about a year ago after W. A. S. Douglas, her former husband, struck Whitehouse at a fashionable party.

Because reconciliation efforts have been in progress for several weeks, Superior Judge Sabath informed Mrs. Whitehouse's attorney that he would not sign the decree for three days. The judge hopes, he said, that a rapprochement may yet be effected.

Mrs. Whitehouse charged cruelty. Whitehouse had indicated at earlier hearings that he might ask alimony, but no statement of what, if any, settlement had been made was available yesterday.

The scene of the Whitehouse-Douglas incident was the Quatz Arts Ball, opening "Streets of Paris" at the fair in 1933. The then Mrs. Douglas was attending with Whitehouse, having effected an agreed separation with her husband because, as he said, their social outlooks differed.

Douglas, veteran of the Boer and world wars, is a newspaper and magazine writer.

Plane Reported Used in $51,000 Payroll Robbery

Bandits Force Mail Truck to Curb; Seize Sacks; Ship Circles Above.

BUTLER, Pa., Aug. 24.—(AP)—Apparently taking their signals from a circling airplane, three holdup men today pounced upon an unarmed mail truck driver, robbed him of a $51,000 payroll and escaped by auto.

The robbery took place not far from the Butler postoffice.

Maxwell C. Lackey, 28, driver, was en route to nearby Lyndora with payrolls of the Standard Steel Car Company and the American Rolling Mill plants. The robbers, in two automobiles, forced him to the curb.

SEIZE 3 MAIL SACKS.

Two bandits, wearing colored glasses, jumped on the running board and forced Lackey to lie down while they took three of the four bags of registered mail.

The robbers abandoned one of their automobiles and escaped in the other. Police believe the robbers met the plane at a planned spot outside the city and climbed aboard with their haul.

GEORGIA BANDITS ESCAPE.

ROME, Ga., Aug. 24.—(AP)—Bandits with a submachine gun today obtained $9,785 in the holdup of two bank messengers transporting a weekly payroll of the Tubize Chatillon Rayon Mill from the National City Bank. Joe Palmer, cashier of the bank, and Raymond Ford, bank employe, were in the car. Palmer said the payroll was insured. As the bandits raced toward East Rome officers fired three times at the machine. At Lindale, five miles south of here, officers fired on them again and they turned back toward Rome.

Austrian Leader in Plot Ends Life

VIENNA, Aug. 24.—(I.N.S.)—Karl Pogrzebaz, one of the leaders of the Austrian agrarian party, committed suicide by drinking poison today as the government aired charges of an alleged new Nazi conspiracy. Pogrzebaz and several other members of the Agrarian party, including Herr Bachinger, former minister of agriculture, and Deputy Dewagy were arrested on conspiracy charges.

Brunette Chosen Queen of Illinois

SPRINGFIELD, Ill., Aug. 24.—(I.N.S.) Miss Irene Bachman, 18, of Marion, a brunette, today was selected from thirty-five other beauties as the 1934 Country Life Queen of Illinois. Miss Bachman, 5 feet and 3 inches tall and weighing 107 pounds, was crowned by last year's winner—Roma Breimer, Dixon.

'What I Knew About Dillinger'

Evelyn Frechette, sloe-eyed, part-Indian beauty, has written the story of her adventures with the slain outlaw. Evelyn was Dillinger's sweetheart; she traveled with him in those days when the gangster lived on borrowed time; she is in jail now because she shielded him. She knows the real story!

Starting Next Monday in The Herald and Examiner

NASH DIGS UP A LAW TO HOLD TAX MILLIONS

Action Threatens to Paralyze Government; Legal Experts Take Issue With Treasurer

Startled by The Herald and Examiner's disclosures that County Treasurer Thomas D. Nash is withholding over thirty millions of tax money due the various governmental agencies, taxpayers yesterday received another shock when the treasurer unearthed an amendment to the revenue laws on which he bases his right to withhold the sixteen millions of taxes paid under protest.

County Treasurer Nash claimed that he has the right to withhold all taxes paid under protest in their entirety until a court has decided on the validity of the tax levied.

It was pointed out that if tax protests should become general the treasurer under his interpretation of the law could withhold the greater part of all taxes paid, and that government would became paralyzed for want of funds.

EXPERTS TAKE ISSUE.

Legal experts thoroughly versed in tax matters, however, took issue with the county treasurer by pointing out that the amendment to the tax laws on which he relies to keep his grip on the golden hoard in his custody has been superseded by another provision.

Under that section of the revenue law, taxpayers who file protests against their tax bills must specify distinctly the part of the tax to which they object, and the county treasurer may only detain that portion of the tax specifically objected to.

REMOVES LEGAL GROUNDS.

That section, it was pointed out, entirely cuts away the legal grounds on which County Treasurer Nash attempts to base his refusal to loosen his hold on the sixteen millions of protested tax money he has in his possession, and for which the governmental agencies in city and county are clamoring.

The section which deprives the

Turn to Page 4, Column 4.

Hayes Denounces Communism Spread

ASTORIA, Ore., Aug. 24.—(I.N.S.)—Advocating universal service in time of war for manpower and industry and denouncing the spread of Communism in the United States, Edward A. Hayes, national commander of the American Legion, addressed the annual convention of the Oregon department here today. Hayes said a tentative statement on the "Red menace," care of disabled veterans and universal wartime service is being considered.

Nation Watches as Chicago Busses Run Without Blue Eagle

Johnson to Stay With NRA; Work Curtailed.

RIFT DENIED

Refutes Reported 'Break' With Richberg.

WASHINGTON, Aug. 24.—(U.S.)—President Roosevelt said today Gen. Hugh S. Johnson will remain as recovery administrator during the interim period in which legislation is drafted for continuing those parts of the recovery act which are to be made permanent.

Saying a great many objectives of the act would be sought to be continued beyond the expiration date on June 16, 1935, the President specifically mentioned prohibition against child labor and unfair industrial practices, and provisions for maximum hours of labor.

HOLDS CONFERENCES.

Emphasizing that reorganization of NRA is still in the formative state, the President said he would confer with Johnson on the subject at Hyde Park after the administrator concludes his two weeks' vacation.

Today the President conferred separately with his recovery administrator and the chairman of his industrial emergency committee—both trusted advisers in the administration campaign to lead the country out of the depression.

ADMIT MISUNDERSTANDING.

Both Johnson and Richberg admitted misunderstandings, but denied there had been a "break" between them. Johnson said:

"The only controversy has been over the time for the reorganized setup to go into effect."

Richberg declared:

"We may have differences, but

Turn to Page 2, Column 1.

Volume of Traffic Normal, Says Ritchie.

CRUCIAL TEST

Drop in Patronage Claimed by Union.

Eyes of the nation turned on Chicago yesterday as the city became a laboratory and its bus-riding citizens experimental subjects in the first great test of the power and prestige of the National Recovery Administration.

Stripped of their Blue Eagles, busses of the Chicago Motor Coach Company kept their regular schedules following a break between the NRA and John A. Ritchie, president of the company, over the discharge of twenty-five employes.

What would be the reaction of the riding public to the withdrawal of the NRA insignia?

CLAIMS NORMAL TRAFFIC.

Ritchie claimed that business was going on as usual, that informal reports from division superintendents indicated there was no falling off of traffic because of the loss of the Blue Eagles. By 8 o'clock this morning, cashiers will make their reports, and officials will have an accurate gauge of public opinion.

Officials of Local 1022 of the Amalgamated Association of Street, Electric Railway and Motor Coach Employes, whose members are on strike, asserted that there was an appreciable loss of patronage on the busses as a result of Gen. Hugh Johnson's order recalling the company's insignia.

Unbiased observers differed. Some were of the opinion that traffic seemed lighter; others believed busloads normal. But none had figures to support his belief.

SEND REPRESENTATIVE.

Officials of the international association, in conference in Detroit, decided to have a representative in Chicago today to consult with members of the Chicago street car, elevated and bus locals on the possibility of a strike in sympathy with the bus drivers.

Before such a strike, which would almost completely paralyze the city's transportation facilities, can be called, permission must be given by the international officers, and the matter submitted to the vote of members. The representative will be empowered to give the officers' decision.

By Ritchie's orders, the Blue

Dall Named Head of Stock Committee

NEW YORK, Aug. 24.—(I.N.S.)—Curtis B. Dall, former son-in-law of President Roosevelt, today was named chairman of one of the thirteen committees appointed by the Association of Stock Exchange Firms in connection with the broadening of that organization's activities. Dall will head the committee on legal and tax problems.

Croons Turn to Croaks in Mexican Radio Strike

MEXICO, D. F., Aug. 24.—(AP)—Crooners' croons turned to croaks and sopranos frequently slipped from high C right off the air tonight as Mexico's unique strike went on and on and on.

Tortured by the odors of food cooking outside and harassed by crowds of demonstrators, radio station XEAL's hunger strikers—striking, they say, for back pay—nevertheless assured the public they were still going strong.

Outside, alert Red Cross employes waited beside their tent, ready to give first aid treatment.

As the virtually exhausted group of thirty announcers and artists neared their eightieth foodless hour several outsiders, amateur performers socially prominent, and one blind fiddler drove out to the station atop Mixcoac Hill to relieve the strikers at the microphone.

While the weaker ones bound their heads to relieve giddiness, the stronger carried on with music, songs and speeches. Outside steadily increasing crowds of curious gathered, and among these the vendors of tortillas, tacos, frijoles and other Mexican staples did a thriving business.

The strikers charge that the Ericsson Telephone Company, which they assert owns the station, has refused to pay them back wages. The company denies steadfastly having any financial interest in XEAL.

The Philadelphia Inquirer

PUBLIC LEDGER

To Place a Want-Ad in THE INQUIRER PHONE AD-TAKER
Rittenhouse 5000—Broad 5000

VOL. 211, NO. 83 — Published daily and Sunday. Entered as second-class matter at the Postoffice in Philadelphia under Act of March 3, 1879 — PHILADELPHIA, FRIDAY MORNING, SEPTEMBER 21, 1934 — Copyright, 1934, by The Philadelphia Inquirer Co. — WEATHER—Fair — a b d — TWO CENTS

LINDBERGH KIDNAPPING CASE SOLVED

MEDIATORS ASK BOARD OF 3 TO SETTLE STRIKE

Winant Group Asks Textile Workers to End Walkout on Basis of Report's Recommendations

Roosevelt Lauds Data; Plan Would Ban Stretch-out Till Feb., 1935; New Body Would Rule on All Disputes

WASHINGTON, Sept. 20 (A. P.).—The President's Mediation Board today recommended the creation of an impartial Textile Labor Relations Board of three to handle disputes in the textile industry.

It also recommended a study by the Labor Department and Federal Trade Commission aimed at the determination of whether the industry can "support an equal or greater number of employees at higher wages."

The suggestion was made that regulation of the stretchout—much complained of practice of increasing the machine load of individual workers—be left to the special board. Such increases would be definitely banned until Feb., 1935.

With reference to differentials between the code minimum and the wages of skilled workers, the board recommended a Labor Department study in advance of a decision.

Ask End of Strike

"We therefore earnestly hope," the board said in transmitting the report to President Roosevelt, "that the United Textile Workers will call off the strike on the basis of these recommendations.

"At the same time we request the employers in the industry to take

Continued on Page 20, Column 5

LEGISLATURE ENDS AFTER FIGHT OVER SESSION PAY ITEM

Assembly Finally Votes $500 Salary; Pinchot Signs Relief Bills

By JOHN M. CUMMINGS

HARRISBURG, Sept. 20.—The special session of the General Assembly adjourned sine die at 2.30 o'clock today (3.30 Philadelphia time) after a Senate-House deadlock had been broken by adoption of conference report fixing $500 as the compensation of each lawmaker for services rendered on the seven Legislative days they were at the Capitol.

Since late last night, when the Legislature passed finally the eight bills covering the $20,000,000 taxless relief program sponsored by the Republican majority, there had been staged behind the scenes conflict revolving around the amount of salary that should be accepted. The law fixes $500 as compensation for a special session, but not a few members felt that on account of

Continued on Page 6, Column 1

The Victim-- --The Suspect

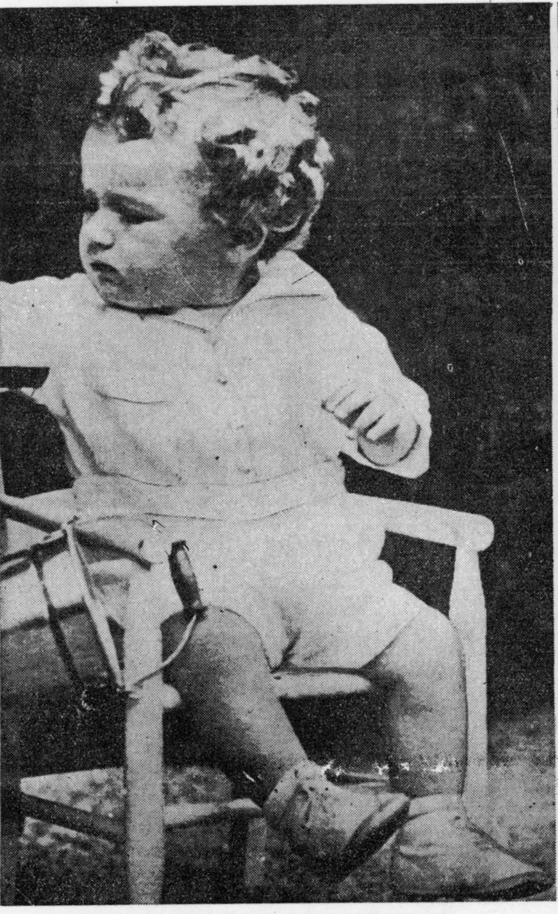

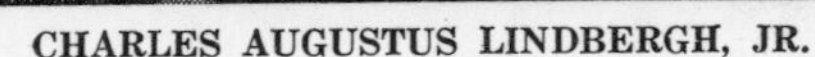

CHARLES AUGUSTUS LINDBERGH, JR.

BERNARD RICHARD HAUPTMANN

RAINBOW SPEEDS FROM BEHIND TO WIN 3RD CUP RACE

Passes Endeavour on Homeward Journey After Trailing at Half-way Mark by More Than 6 Minutes; No Contest Today

By WILLIAM H. TAYLOR

Special to The Inquirer.

NEWPORT, R. I., Sept. 20.—Rainbow, the Vanderbilt syndicate's hope for the defense of the America's Cup, won her first race in the cup series today from T. O. M. Sopwith's Endeavour, staging a comeback after being apparently a badly beaten boat for the third time. The series score now stands two races for Endeavour and one for Rainbow, with four victories by one boat necessary to settle the match.

The race was another of those demonstrations which Harold Vanderbilt and Rainbow have given of their ability to come through in the pinches. Endeavour utterly outsailed the American boat on the 15-mile run down wind before a light easterly to round the buoy 6 minutes 39 seconds ahead of the American boat, but on the way home Rainbow gained 2 minutes and 5 seconds to lead at the finish by 3 minutes 26 seconds.

Endeavour still looked like a fast boat, but a badly-setting Genoa jib, a bit of bad luck and two tacks

Continued on Page 24, Column 4

BLOOD ON HANDERCHIEF CLUE TO MISSING CHILD

Nashville Girl Kidnapped, Police Head Believes

NASHVILLE, Tenn., Sept. 20 (A. P.).—A blood-stained handkerchief bearing the initial "D" and what appear to be blood stains on the street near 6-year-old Dorothy Distelhurst's home, spurred police today in their efforts to solve the child's disappearance.

Police Inspector Eugene Dillard held the opinion that Dorothy had been put into a car and driven away from the neighborhood, but he said it was without supporting clues.

CAPTAIN DESERTED BRIDGE AFTER S.O.S. ALAGNA TESTIFIES

Radio Man Says Skipper Ignored Pleas to Send for Help

NEW YORK, Sept. 20 (A. P.).—The Federal Board, investigating the Morro Castle disaster today heard First Assistant Radio Operator George I. Alagna charge that Acting Captain W. F. Warms ordered an S. O. S. sent from the burning ship only after "strong pleading" on Alagna's fifth trip to the ship's bridge for instructions.

Alagna described conditions on the bridge as "unintelligible and confused." He said Capt. Warms "just kept pacing" and he had to follow him about and then doubted if the captain recognized him.

The man at the wheel, Alagna tes-

Continued on Page 4, Column 1

LINDBERGHS KNEW "BREAK" WAS NEAR; SILENT IN SECLUSION

Couple May Fly Back to New York; Whereabouts Unknown

LOS ANGELES, Sept. 20 (A. P.).—Colonel and Mrs. Charles A. Lindbergh secluded themselves even from their hosts here today while reports were circulated the famous couple knew in advance the kidnap case arrest was expected in New York.

They were nowhere to be reached when news flashed out of New York and Washington at the arrest, and the suggestion of investigators that it would solve the mystery of the kidnapping and death two and a half years ago of the Lindbergh's first born son.

A close friend, one of their hosts, said today they would have nothing to say save to authorities about the kidnapping arrest, and intimated they were preparing to fly back to

Continued on Page 12, Column 2

In The Inquirer Today

209 Help Wanted and Situation Wanted Ads in Today's Inquirer: "Want-Ad Headquarters"

SPEEDY TRIAL OF HAUPTMANN SOUGHT IN N. J.

Federal Kidnapping Act Not Applicable, But Lindbergh Suspect May Face Murder Death Law of State

WASHINGTON, Sept. 20 (A. P.).—Swift moves to prosecute Bernard Hauptmann in a New York State Court on a charge of kidnapping and murder in the case of Charles A. Lindbergh, Jr., were indicated tonight by Attorney General Cummings.

Obviously pleased at the capture of the suspect, a German alien, after 30 months of unrelenting search by Federal agents and police, the Attorney General explained the trial could not be held in a Federal Court.

The Federal kidnapping statute—known as the Lindbergh law—would not be effective in this case, Cummings told reporters, because of its enactment after the abduction of the child.

State Has "Death Law"

"New Jersey has a law, enacted in 1931, that provides a maximum of life imprisonment for kidnapping," he said.

"That State has a death penalty for first degree murder—murder that is premeditated. Its statute calls for life imprisonment for second degree murder."

The Attorney General explained

Continued on Page 3, Column 3

CALIFORNIA DEMOCRATS ADOPT SINCLAIR'S PLAN

State Convention Backs "EPIC" Program; Conservatives Beaten

SACRAMENTO, Calif., Sept. 20 (A. P.).—Upton Sinclair's "EPIC" plan which won him the Democratic nomination for Governor of California was incorporated virtually in full in the platform adopted today by the Democratic State convention.

Conservative opposition was routed.

PROOFS TO 'JAFSIE' IN DEAL ON RANSOM NOW TRAP SUSPECT

Clothing of Baby Shown to Agents Indicates "Right Gang" Took Cash

That there is full justification for the belief that the man arrested in New York yesterday may give information definitely solving the mystery of the kidnapping of Charles A. Lindbergh, Jr., is evidenced by facts made public more than two years ago.

When Dr. John F. "Jafsie" Condon, finally handed $50,000 over a cemetery wall to the man whom he supposed to be an agent of the real

Continued on Page 13, Column 5

THE WEATHER

Early forecast: Fair and slightly warmer.

Sun rises. 6.46 A.M. Sets 7.00 P.M.
Moon rises. 6.00 P.M. Sets 4.46 A.M.

Other Weather Reports on Page 2

ALIEN HELD, IDENTIFIED; CASH FOUND

Bernard R. Hauptmann, German, Arrested in N. Y. After He Tries to Pass Gold Note; $13,750 Ransom Recovered; Suspect Recognized by Taxi Driver; Viewed by "Jafsie"

(Copyright, 1934, The Associated Press)

NEW YORK, Sept. 20.—In swift, dramatic moves in the Lindbergh kidnapping case, police announced the arrest of Bernard Richard Hauptmann, a German alien, the finding of part of the ransom money and declared a solution of the greatest mystery of modern time was assured.

Police Commissioner John F. O'Ryan, announcing $13,750 of the $50,000 ransom money paid for the baby, later found dead, was found in Hauptmann's cellar in the Bronx, was asked:

"In your opinion, does this solve the Lindbergh kidnapping?"

O'Ryan conferred for a few minutes with J. Edgar Hoover, head of the Bureau of Investigation of the Department of Justice, and said:

"Yes, it will."

After the announcement of the arrest, Commissioner O'Ryan said Hauptmann was identified positively as the recipient of the ransom money in the cemetery.

The identification was made by "witnesses," O'Ryan said. This was taken to mean Dr. John F. Condon, "Jafsie," had seen the prisoner and had made the identification.

Hauptmann, placed in the prisoners' line-up later, was also identified by John Perrone, Bronx taxi driver, as the man who, two days after "Jafsie" advertised himself as the Lindbergh negotiator, gave him a dollar to deliver a note to the Condon home.

Hauptmann was in line with other prisoners. Perrone was led in.

"Pick up the man who handed you that note," Perrone was told.

Without hesitation, the taxi driver tapped Hauptmann on the shoulder.

"This is the man," he said.

Shortly after 6 P. M. O'Ryan, Assistant Chief Inspector Sweeney, Inspector Lyons and other police officials ran down the corridor and left the station.

At that time the prisoner was whisked from a room, where he had been seen by Dr. Condon and at least 20 detectives.

After an afternoon filled with sensational rumors that the "break" long awaited had come, O'Ryan emerged from secret conferences with Hoover and others at the Greenwich police station and issued this terse statement:

"We have in custody the man who received the ransom money. He is Bernard Richard Hauptmann, of 1279 E. 222nd st., the Bronx. He is an alien who came to this country as a stowaway 11 years ago."

Among those at the police station was the man of many missions in the long hunt, Dr. Con-

CONTINUED ON PAGE 2, COLUMN 1

Baseball Results

AMERICAN LEAGUE

Athletics, 6; Chicago, 5.
Cleveland, 6; Washington, 1.
New York, 11; Detroit, 7.
St. Louis, 4; Boston, 3.

NATIONAL LEAGUE

Phillies, 9; Chicago, 7.
Brooklyn, 2; Pittsburgh, 1.
New York, 4; Cincinnati, 3.
St. Louis, 4; Boston, 1 (first game).
St. Louis, 1; Boston, 0 (second game).

Weather Forecast
Fair tonight. Tuesday fair, slowly rising temperature in south and east portion of state.

EAST LIVERPOOL REVIEW

Complete News Coverage of Wellsville, Midland, Chester and Newell

HOME EDITION

ESTABLISHED: The Tribune 1876 The Review 1879 | The Associated Press, United Press International News Service | EAST LIVERPOOL, OHIO, MONDAY, OCTOBER 22, 1934. | TWENTY-SIX PAGES | TWO CENTS

SEARCH COUNTY FOR BANDIT FLOYD; PURVIS AND U. S. AGENTS SPREAD NET

Government Squad Concentrates in Wellsville, East Liverpool and Dillonvale To Track Slayer.

SEEK RICHETTI CUSTODY

Wellsville Authorities Unwilling To Release Desperado Prisoner Except On Federal Warrant.

Twenty-five state police were en route to Wellsville this afternoon to lend such assistance as they may in the search for Floyd.

Melvin H. Purvis, chief of the bureau of investigation for the department of justice in the Chicago area, with a dozen picked men from the Cincinnati, Cleveland and Pittsburgh bureaus, are at work in Wellsville, East Liverpool, Lisbon, Dillonvale and adjacent communities today, bent on finding Charles (Pretty Boy) Floyd.

They are convinced that Adam Richetti's companion in two encounters with Wellsville police and posses of citizens Saturday is Floyd and not James Warren of Toledo as Richetti told Chief of Police Fultz at Wellsville.

Mr. Purvis and some of his men came to East Liverpool and Wellsville by airplane from Cincinnati late Sunday night and immediately identified Richetti at the Wellsville jail as one of the trigger-man suspects in the Kansas City union station massacre of June, 1933.

Mr. Purvis requested Chief Fultz to turn Richetti over to him so that the federal investigation might be rapidly advanced but the chief declined to do so for the present.

County Awaits Federal Warrant

In conference with Mayor William H. Daugherty, Chief Fultz and County Prosecutor George Lafferty in Wellsville Sunday night Mr. Purvis endeavored to prevail upon them to release Richetti to him.

He was advised that Richetti would be surrendered only upon presentation of a federal warrant. Such warrant undoubtedly will be issued by federal authorities with little delay.

"We have had information for some months that Richetti was one of the participants in the Kansas City massacre," Mr. Purvis told The Review early this morning. "Two weeks ago we received definite proof of that fact. We have, of course, been searching for him for many months. Tonight I made a formal demand upon the chief of police of Wellsville for custody of Richetti and he refused to turn over the prisoner.

"Meantime, we shall continue our concentrated effort to find 'Pretty Boy' Floyd."

Mr. Purvis heard from George McMullin, whose automobile the fugitive commandeered, that Floyd—if indeed it is Floyd—was bleeding profusely from a bullet wound in the stomach. McMullin had the impression that the gunman lost possibly two pints of blood while riding in his car. If that is true, Mr. Purvis reasons, Floyd probably is not far away. He may be dead or dying in the woods or some other hideout.

Richetti Relative In Dillonvale

Richetti has a half-brother living in Dillonvale, west of Steubenville. Richetti's familiarity with this section of Ohio and the probability that he and Floyd were able to find friends with whom they might hide provides ample reason for their presence in this part of the country. Presumably they made their way from Missouri into Ohio during the past 10 days and have been hiding out in this area since.

Bloodstains were found on the cushions of the two motor cars commandeered by the man presumed to be Floyd, clearly indicating he was badly wounded.

Since Floyd made his getaway from the police and posse at Spence's Woods Saturday afternoon there have been no reports of other automobile holdups or of any cars commandeered. Floyd was afoot. He was wounded. He could not have gotten far away. He is either in the vicinity, still endeavoring to avoid capture or is "under cover" with his own or Richetti's friends.

Richetti Wanted On Several Charges

Chief Purvis said Richetti is wanted on several charges, the most important the Kansas City massacre. Other charges against Richetti include violation of the national motor vehicle theft act and an attempt to deliver a federal prisoner.

Floyd's criminal record gives the following information: He is 26 years old, 5 feet 8½ inches tall, weight 155 pounds, hair dark, eyes gray, complexion medium, scars—a vaccination and a tattoo. He was arrested as Charles Arthur Floyd in St. Louis, Sept. 16, 1925, on a charge of highway robbery, arrested as Charles Floyd in St. Louis on a charge of robbery and received a sentence in Jefferson City prison Dec. 18, 1925, arrested March 9, 1929, at Kansas City and held for investigation arrested May 6, 1929, at Kansas City on a charge of vagrancy and suspicion of highway robbery but released the next day, arrested at Pueblo, Colorado, May 9, 1929, on a charge of vagrancy and sentenced to serve 60 days in jail, arrested as Frank Mitchell at Akron, O., March 8, 1930, for investigation, arrested under the name of Charles Arthur Floyd at Toledo, May 20, 1930, on a charge of suspicion, sentenced to Ohio penitentiary to serve from 12 to 15 years on a charge of bank robbery at Sylvania, O., November 24, 1930, and escaped en route to prison.

Wanted For Five Missouri Murders

Floyd is wanted in connection with the murder of Otto Reed, chief of police of McAlester, Okla., William J. Grooms and Frank E. Hermanson, police officers of Kansas City, Raymond J. Caffery, special agent of the department of justice and their prisoner, Frank Nash, at the Kansas City Union station June 17, 1933.

Police in Canton, Akron and Steubenville are on the lookout for Floyd. He is said to have a girl friend living in Canton.

SUGAR CONTROL UPHELD

WASHINGTON, Oct. 22.—Justice Jennings Bailey of the District of Columbia supreme court today upheld the constitutionality of the sugar control act which had been attacked by Hawaiian growers.

Local Temperatures

Sunday, noon, 70; Sunday, 6 p. m., 67; Sunday, midnight, 52; today, 6 a. m., 54; today, noon, 52; maximum, 70; minimum, 52; precipitation, none.

3 HURT IN PENNSY WRECK

PITTSBURGH, Oct. 22—Pennsylvania police today investigated the cause of the wreck of Indianapolis section of the American Limited en route from St. Louis to New York last night 15 miles southwest of Pittsburgh. Two trainmen and a passenger were injured.

CAPTURED OUTLAW RICHETTI AND CHIEF OF POLICE FULTZ AT THE JAIL

ADAM RICHETTI, GUNMAN — CHIEF JOHN H. FULTZ

16 DEAD LEFT BY STORM ON PACIFIC COAST

By The Associated Press.

SEATTLE, Wash. Oct. 22—An October storm, lashing at the coast of Washington and Oregon, today left at least 16 dead today and a huge shipping and property loss in its wake.

The gales, which reached a recorded velocity of 83 miles an hour, had subsided, but two flooded cities, damaged shipping, wrecked buildings, power and communication line tangles, debris-strewn areas—and the death list—remained.

Striking with fury shortly after daybreak yesterday, the storm swept over this region all day, subsiding only after nightfall.

Harbor Cities Suffer

The waters of high tide flooded the business section and a large part of the residential sections of both Grays harbor cities, Aberdeen and Hoquiam.

With six feet of water at South Aberdeen, residents were either rescued by police in small boats, or remained marooned until the water fell. More than half the houses in Hoquiam were flooded.

At the height of the gale, the steamship Floridian sent out SOS messages from the mouth of the Columbia, the Trans-Pacific liner, President Madison swerved from its mooring here to crush against two other vessels and sink the small steamer Harvester, and the Tacoma-Seattle boat, Virginia was

(Continued On Page 3)

Directs Hunt

Melvin H. Purvis

PURVIS GOT DILLINGER; HE'S NOW OUT ON FLOYD'S TRAIL

Government's Ace Quietly Determined in His Job Tracking Down Criminals.

Melvin H. Purvis, alert, poised, is the Philo Vance of real life, a master detective for the United States government.

As chief of the bureau of investigation for the department of justice in Chicago his has been a busy life for the past year, but you'd never know it or hear it from him.

He has handled hundreds of routine investigations but the Dillinger case absorbed him mainly for many months. He was determined to get the arch criminal, bank bandit, slayer of policemen, fugitive from prison.

His months of determined search were rewarded. He found Dillinger and on the night of Sunday, July 22 saved the government the inconvenience delay and cost of trying the desperado in court. With a picked squad of men he trailed Dillinger to a small neighborhood theater in Chicago, Dillinger tried to make his getaway. He reached for a gun, the federal agents beat him to the draw and Dillinger was a dead man.

Newspapermen say it was Purvis' own bullet that found the mark first but officially there is no record.

A week ago Purvis and his men were searching for Mrs. Alice Speed

(Continued On Page 3)

KANSAS CITY ANXIOUS TO GET RICHETTI

By The Associated Press.

KANSAS CITY, Oct. 22.—The capture of Adam Richetti, companion of Charles (Pretty Boy) Floyd, southwest outlaw, set legal machinery in motion to bring the man before a federal grand jury which today started an investigation of the Union station murders here in June, 1933.

Richetti and Floyd have been named by the government as two of the three gunmen who unloosed a stream of lead which felled four officers and three federal prisoners in the Union station slaying.

R. B. Nathan, in charge of the bureau of investigation here, said a formal charge would be placed against the 32-year-old Richetti so he could be brought here to appear before the grand jury.

Positive of Identification

"Richetti is a murderer and we propose to make him pay the extreme penalty for his part in the station massacre," Sheriff Thomas B. Bash said. "Our identification of him as one of the killers at the station is so positive that our case against him is ironclad."

The third accused killer is Verne C. Miller, former South Dakota sheriff, who later was found slain near Detroit.

The Union station shootings climaxed an alleged attempt on the part of the three gunmen to liberate Frank Nash, an escaped convict and a friend of Miller's, who was being taken from Hot Springs, Ark., where he was apprehended, to the federal penitentiary at Leavenworth. Nash was believed to have been killed accidentally.

Link Politics and Crime

The officers slain were Otto Reed, chief of police at McAlester,

(Continued On Page 3)

FULTZ BRAVES BULLET HAIL TO NAB OUTLAW

Chief of Police John H. Fultz of Wellsville Saturday braved the bullets of two of America's public enemies to capture Adam Richetti and direct city, county and federal operatives to the new trail of Charles (Pretty Boy) Floyd.

Despite a wound in the right ankle, where one of Floyd's bullets struck him, Fultz engaged in a running pistol battle with the Oklahoma outlaw and his confederate in the Kountz avenue hollow, where the two men sought a hideout.

Twenty-nine shots were fired at Fultz by the two outlaws, members of the posse said, but Lady Luck with with him, for he escaped with a slight scratch.

He emptied the chambers of his revolvers and reloaded as he stood between the fire of Floyd, atop a hill, and Richetti, in the valley. But he refused to give ground, and finally forced "Pretty Boy's" pal to surrender.

Fultz, notwithstanding 48 hours' continuous duty, stayed on the job today, in the hope that he may clean up his task by aiding in the capture of the west's most desperate gunman since the death of John Dillinger.

Library Exhibit to Be Open This Week

The historical exhibit on the second floor of the Carnegie Public library which was one of the features in connection with East Liverpool's centennial celebration here week before last, will remain open to the public every day this week between the hours of 3 and 5 and 7 and 9 p. m.

FORMER STATE LINE KILLER PAL OF FLOYD

Willis Miller, 28, State line desperado, who was shot and killed by a Bowling Green policeman on April 16, 1931, was a "pal" of "Pretty Boy" Floyd, notorious "public enemy," for whom a county-wide search is being made by Wellsville police, county authorities, state highway patrolmen and Federal agents today.

Miller, alleged slayer of his elder brother "Alabama Joe" Miller in the "Hell's Half Acres," as the hillside territory along the Ohio-Pennsylvania border was known, was in company with Floyd and two girl companions in Bowling Green when Miller was killed in a gun battle with Patrolman Ralph Castner, fatally wounded in the battle.

Suspected in Store

The quartet visited a Bowling Green store to purchase clothing for the girls and when the clerk became suspicious of their actions the police were notified. Chief of Police Carl Galliher and Patrolman Castner found Miller, Floyd and their girl companions walking in a down-town street. The officers ordered the four to put their hands into the air. Miller and Floyd answered with gun fire.

Castner fell wounded and Chief Galliher fell to the street, firing at the gunmen. Miller was killed and one of the girls. Beulah Baird, 21 of Kansas City, was wounded. The other girl, Rose Baird, 23, also of Kansas City was captured, but "Pretty Boy" escaped in an auto.

(Continued On Page 3)

He is Hunted

Charles "Pretty Boy" Floyd

Wellsville Police and Posses Race to Fredericktown, Spence's Woods In "Pretty Boy" Hunt.

FULTZ, 2 OTHERS SHOT

Two Motorists Are Forced to Drive Oklahoma Outlaw in Wild Flight Over Highways.

Chief Fultz at 2 p. m. today refused to surrender Adam Richetti to Sheriff Thomas Bash of Kansas City, or to Melvin H. Purvis, chief of the Chicago bureau of investigation for the department of justice.

Sheriff Bash and S. P. Cowley, secret service investigator, arrived at noon from Kansas City. Accompanied by Purvis they went at once to Wellsville, conferring for an hour with Chief Fultz and Mayor Daugherty.

"I will not turn the man over unless he is indicted by a federal grand jury and unless Governor White orders his extradition," said Chief Fultz.

The hunt for Charles (Pretty Boy) Floyd, Oklahoma desperado-killer, believed wounded and hiding in southern Columbiana county, centered in Fredericktown and Spence's woods, near Lisbon today as department of justice operatives under Melvin H. Purvis, Wellsville police officials, Sheriff Ballantine's force and citizen posses united to track him down.

Adam Richetti, 26, Floyd's suspected accomplice in the Kansas City massacres of June 1933, is held under an augmented armed guard at the Wellsville jail.

Richetti and the fugitive believed to be Floyd were accosted by Wellsville police and a citizen posse, under Chief John H. Fultz Saturday in Kountz avenue, Wellsville. A gunfight ensued. Chief Fultz was slightly wounded. Special Patrolman Grover Potts was wounded, shot in the left shoulder.

Chief Fultz took Richetti prisoner. Richetti's companion fled, commandeered the automobile of George McMullin of East Liverpool and forced McMullin to drive.

Florist Wounded In Second Battle

Several hours later the fugitive, assumed to be Floyd, although Richetti insists he was James Warren of Toledo, engaged in a second gun battle with deputy sheriffs and a posse at Spence's wood. James Baum, 60, Wellsville florist, was wounded in the right leg by a citizen's bullet.

The fugitive had commandeered Baum's automobile when McMullin's ran out of gas and forced Baum to drive him.

Chief Fultz, Patrolman Potts and William Irwin identified rogue's gallery pictures of Richetti and Floyd at Wellsville Sunday night. Richetti admitted his own identity when confronted with fingerprints.

A Wellsville posse raced to Fredericktown after Laird Manurse, Buckeye avenue, Wellsville, Negro, reported a man who resembled the fugitive came out of the woods about 5:30 this morning and asked him for a "lift" to East Palestine in his truck.

Manurse told him the truck had broken down and the suspect immediately started to walk along the Fredericktown-East Palestine highway.

Meanwhile, about 100 citizens in a posse aiding police, together with the sheriff's force searched Spence's woods.

Machine Gun Found By Chief

Chief Fultz found a Thompson sub-machine gun in the Kountz avenue hollow hideout Sunday. He said the two men used automatic revolvers in the encounters Saturday.

Wellsville police assigned 12 guards, with rifles, as a precaution against a possible jail delivery on the part of Floyd or members of his gang. This action was taken as four men, with two machine guns, were reported to have been seen in an automobile Sunday.

McMullin said the stranger stopped him and offered him $10 for auto hire. He knew nothing of the gun battle and accepted the passenger.

The fugitive had scarcely entered the car when McMullin discovered he had been wounded and was bleeding freely. He gave McMullin no choice but to drive him, though by this time McMullin realized there was something strange about the situation.

McMullin said Floyd, or the fugitive if other than Floyd, showed him two wounds, one in the abdomen and the other in the back.

Richetti talked freely in his cell, but denied Floyd was with him. He said his companion was James Warren of Toledo, whom he met seven years ago in the Oklahoma oil fields.

"I only met him (Floyd) once in my life," Richetti said. "That was about a year ago."

Richetti Held Pending Warrant

He denied participating in the Kansas City crime.

Asked if he had readily admitted his identity, Richetti said: "What else could I do. They brought my fingerprints along. I couldn't say anything else."

Richetti is held on a charge of shooting with intent to kill Chief Fultz.

H. F. Snyder, of the Cincinnati division of the Pinkerton detective agency, also joined the investigators.

Cooperating with Wellsville police are Sheriffs Frank Ballantine of Lisbon and Ray Long of Steubenville, while police officials of East Liverpool, Youngstown and Alliance as well as state police from Warren, Salem and Bridgeport assisted.

Chief Fultz was certain of Floyd's identity from photographs.

"I could not be mistaken," said he. "I was not more than 15 feet from him."

Potts and Erwin confirmed the identification.

Gunfire Menaces Chief and Posse

Sequentially, events leading up to the sensational disclosure that the prisoner is Richetti and that the fugitive probably is Floyd are as follows:

Wellsville police received a call from Lon Isreal, who lives east of Silver's switch in the Wellsville-East Liverpool road, shortly before 1 p. m. Saturday, asking an investigation of the suspicious actions of two men in the neighborhood.

Chief Fultz, accompanied by Special Patrolman Grover Potts and William Erwin, responded and was met by Richetti and the man presumed to be Floyd. Richetti stood in the hollow, Floyd on a hill somewhat apart.

"Stick 'em up!" Floyd ordered, as Chief Fultz approached.

(Continued On Page 3)

EXTRA EAST LIVERPOOL REVIEW EXTRA

Complete News Coverage of Wellsville, Midland, Chester and Newell

ESTABLISHED: The Tribune 1876 The Review 1879 | The Associated Press, United Press International News Service | EAST LIVERPOOL, OHIO, MONDAY, OCTOBER 22, 1934. | TWO CENTS

FLOYD SHOT DOWN BY POLICE AND FEDERAL AGENTS

Charles (Pretty Boy) Floyd was shot down and killed just before 5 o'clock this afternoon by policemen under Chief of Police Hugh J. McDermott and federal agents at the Conkle farm on the Sprucevale road, seven miles north of East Liverpool.

Floyd was cornered, tried to flee and was shot down, all of the policemen and agents firing simultaneously.

Floyd's body was brought to the Sturgis funeral home in East Liverpool.

He was identified beyond doubt by Chief McDermott and by Melvin H. Purvis, chief of the federal agents on duty in the all-day search for the Oklahoma bandit.

The policemen and federal agents found Floyd trying to hide behind a corn crib.

He was armed with two automatic revolvers. He made no attempt to use his guns but started to run over a hill. Police and federal agents gave chase and fired approximately fifty shots.

Floyd fell instantly, dying within a few minutes. His last words were "I'm Floyd . . ."

Besides Chief McDermott and Mr. Purvis patrolmen in the searching squad were Patrolmen Chester Smith, Herman Roth and Raymond Montgomery, as well as three other department of justice agents.

All fired as Floyd tried to escape.

His body contains a dozen wounds.

KANSAS CITY SEEKS RICHETTI'S CUSTODY

Twenty-five state police were en route to Wellsville this afternoon to lend such assistance as they may in the search for Floyd.

Melvin H. Purvis, chief of the bureau of investigation for the department of justice in the Chicago area, with a dozen picked men from the Cincinnati, Cleveland and Pittsburgh bureaus, are at work in Wellsville, East Liverpool, Lisbon, Dillonvale and adjacent communities today, bent on finding Charles (Pretty Boy) Floyd.

They are convinced that Adam Richetti's companion in two encounters with Wellsville police and posses of citizens Saturday is Floyd and not James Warren of Toledo as Richetti told Chief of Police Fultz at Wellsville.

Mr. Purvis and some of his men came to East Liverpool and Wellsville by airplane from Cincinnati late Sunday night and immediately identified Richetti at the Wellsville jail as one of the trigger-man suspects in the Kansas City union station massacre of June, 1933.

Mr. Purvis requested Chief Fultz to turn Richetti over to him so that the federal investigation might be rapidly advanced but the chief declined to do so for the present.

County Awaits Federal Warrant

In conference with Mayor William H. Daugherty, Chief Fultz and County Prosecutor George Lafferty in Wellsville Sunday night Mr. Purvis endeavored to prevail upon them to release Richetti to him.

He was advised that Richetti would be surrendered only upon presentation of a federal warrant. Such warrant undoubtedly will be issued by federal authorities with little delay.

"We have had information for some months that Richetti was one of the participants in the Kansas City massacre," Mr. Purvis told The Review early this morning. "Two weeks ago we received definite proof of that fact. We have, of course, been searching for him for many months. Tonight I made a formal demand upon the chief of police of Wellsville for custody of Richetti and he refused to turn over the prisoner.

"Meantime, we shall continue our concentrated effort to find 'Pretty Boy' Floyd."

Mr. Purvis heard from George McMullin, whose automobile the fugitive commandeered, that Floyd—if indeed it is Floyd—was bleeding profusely from a bullet wound in the stomach. McMullin had the impression that the gunman lost possibly two pints of blood while riding in his car. If that is true, Mr. Purvis reasons, Floyd probably is not far away. He may be dead or dying in the woods or some other hideout.

Richetti Relative In Dillonvale

Richetti has a half-brother living in Dillonvale, west of Steubenville. Richetti's familiarity with this section of Ohio and the probability that he and Floyd were able to find friends with whom they might hide provides ample reason for their presence in this part of the country. Presumably they made their way from Missouri into Ohio during the past 10 days and have been hiding out in this area since.

Bloodstains were found on the cushions of the two motor cars commandeered by the man presumed to be Floyd, clearly indicating he was badly wounded.

Since Floyd made his getaway from the police and posse at Spence's woods Saturday afternoon there have been no reports of other automobile holdups or of any cars commandeered. Floyd was afoot. He was wounded. He could not have gotten far away. He is either in the vicinity, still endeavoring to avoid capture or is "under cover" with his own or Richetti's friends.

Richetti Wanted On Several Charges

Chief Purvis said Richetti is wanted on several charges, the most important the Kansas City massacre. Other charges against Richetti include violation of the national motor vehicle theft act and an attempt to deliver a federal prisoner.

Floyd's criminal record gives the following information:

He is 26 years old, 5 feet 8½ inches tall, weight 155 pounds, hair dark, eyes gray, complexion medium, scars—a vaccination and a tattoo. He was arrested as Charles Arthur Floyd in St. Louis, Sept. 16, 1925, on a charge of highway robbery, arrested as Charles Floyd in St. Louis on a charge of robbery and received a sentence in Jefferson City prison Dec. 18, 1925, arrested March 9, 1929, at Kansas City and held for investigation arrested May 6, 1929, at Kansas City on a charge of vagrancy and suspicion of highway robbery but released the next day, arrested at Pueblo, Colorado, May 9, 1929, on a charge of vagrancy and sentenced to serve 60 days in jail, arrested as Frank Mitchell at Akron, O., March 8, 1930, for investigation, arrested under the name of Charles Arthur Floyd at Toledo, May 20, 1930, on a charge of suspicion, sentenced to Ohio penitentiary to serve from 12 to 15 years on a charge of bank robbery at Sylvania, O., November 24, 1930, and escaped en route to prison.

Wanted For Five Missouri Murders

Floyd is wanted in connection with the murder of Otto Reed, chief of police of McAlester, Okla., William J. Grooms and Frank E. Hermanson, police officers of Kansas City, Raymond J. Caffery, special agent of the department of justice and their prisoner, Frank Nash, at the Kansas City Union station June 17, 1933.

Police in Canton, Akron and Steubenville are on the lookout for Floyd. He is said to have a girl friend living in Canton.

His Latest Picture

Charles "Pretty Boy" Floyd

FULTZ BRAVES BULLET HAIL

Chief of Police John H. Fultz of Wellsville Saturday braved the bullets of two of America's public enemies to capture Adam Richetti and direct city, county and federal operatives to the new trail of Charles (Pretty Boy) Floyd.

Despite a wound in the right ankle, where one of Floyd's bullets struck him, Fultz engaged in a running pistol battle with the Oklahoma outlaw and his confederate in the Kountz avenue hollow, where the two men sought a hideout.

Twenty-nine shots were fired at Fultz by the two outlaws, members of the posse said, but Lady Luck with with him, for he escaped with a slight scratch.

He emptied the chambers of his revolvers and reloaded as he stood between the fire of Floyd, atop a hill, and Richetti, in the valley. But he refused to give ground, and finally forced "Pretty Boy's" pal to surrender.

Fultz, notwithstanding 48 hours' continuous duty, stayed on the job today, in the hope that he may clean up his task by aiding in the capture of the west's most desperate gunman since the death of John Dillinger.

Got His Man

Melvin H. Purvis

Floyd As He Looked Two Years Ago.

Uncle Sam's bloodhounds, Secret Service operatives, are hot on the trail

FORMER STATE LINE KILLER PAL OF FLOYD

Willis Miller, 28, State line desperado, who was shot and killed by a Bowling Green policeman on April 16, 1931, was a "pal" of "Pretty Boy" Floyd, notorious "public enemy," for whom a county-wide search is being made by Wellsville police, county authorities, state highway patrolmen and Federal agents today.

Miller, alleged slayer of his elder brother "Alabama Joe" Miller in the "Hell's Half Acres," as the hillside territory along the Ohio-Pennsylvania border was known, was in company with Floyd and two girl companions in Bowling Green when Miller was killed in a gun battle with Patrolman Ralph Castner, fatally wounded in the battle.

Suspected in Store

The quartet visited a Bowling Green store to purchase clothing for the girls and when the clerk became suspicious of their actions the police were notified.

Castner fell wounded and Chief Galliher fell to the street, firing at the gunmen. Miller was killed and one of the girls. Beulah Baird, 21 of Kansas City, was wounded. The other girl, Rose Baird, 23, also of Kansas City was captured, but "Pretty Boy" escaped in an auto.

(Continued On Page 3)

16 DEAD LEFT BY STORM ON PACIFIC COAST

By The Associated Press.

SEATTLE, Wash. Oct. 22—An October storm, lashing at the coast of Washington and Oregon, today left at least 16 dead today and a huge shipping and property loss in its wake.

The gales, which reached a recorded velocity of 83 miles an hour, had subsided, but two flooded cities, damaged shipping, wrecked buildings, power and communication line tangles, debris-strewn areas—and the death list—remained.

Striking with fury shortly after daybreak yesterday, the storm swept over this region all day, subsiding only after nightfall.

Harbor Cities Suffer

The waters of high tide flooded the business section and a large part of the residential sections of both Grays harbor cities, Aberdeen and Hoquiam.

At the height of the gale, the steamship Floridian sent out SOS messages from the mouth of the Columbia, the Trans-Pacific liner, President Madison swerved from its mooring here to crush against two other vessels and sink the small steamer Harvester, and the Tacoma-Seattle boat, Virginia was

(Continued On Page 3)

THREE WOUNDED IN GUN BATTLES

Chief Fultz at 2 p. m. today refused to surrender Adam Richetti to Sheriff Thomas Bash of Kansas City, or to Melvin H. Purvis, chief of the Chicago bureau of investigation for the department of justice.

Sheriff Bash and S. P. Cowley, secret service investigator, arrived at noon from Kansas City. Accompanied by Purvis they went at once to Wellsville, conferring for an hour with Chief Fultz and Mayor Daugherty.

"I will not turn the man over unless he is indicted by a federal grand jury and unless Governor White orders his extradition," said Chief Fultz.

The hunt for Charles (Pretty Boy) Floyd, Oklahoma desperado-killer, believed wounded and hiding in southern Columbiana county, centered in Fredericktown and Spence's woods, near Lisbon today as department of justice operatives under Melvin H. Purvis, Wellsville police officials, Sheriff Ballantine's force and citizen posses united to track him down.

Adam Richetti, 26, Floyd's suspected accomplice in the Kansas City massacres of June 1933, is held under an augmented armed guard at the Wellsville jail.

Richetti and the fugitive believed to be Floyd were accosted by Wellsville police and a citizen posse, under Chief John H. Fultz Saturday in Kountz avenue, Wellsville. A gunfight ensued. Chief Fultz was slightly wounded. Special Patrolman Grover Potts was wounded, shot in the left shoulder.

Chief Fultz took Richetti prisoner. Richetti's companion fled, commandeered the automobile of George McMullin of East Liverpool and forced McMullin to drive.

Florist Wounded In Second Battle

Several hours later the fugitive, assumed to be Floyd, although Richetti insists he was James Warren of Toledo, engaged in a second gun battle with deputy sheriffs and a posse at Spence's wood. James Baum, 60, Wellsville florist, was wounded in the right leg by a citizen's bullet.

The fugitive had commandeered Baum's automobile when McMullin's ran out of gas and forced Baum to drive him.

Chief Fultz, Patrolman Potts and William Irwin identified rogue's gallery pictures of Richetti and Floyd at Wellsville Sunday night. Richetti admitted his own identity when confronted with fingerprints.

A Wellsville posse raced to Fredericktown after Laird Manurse, Buckeye avenue, Wellsville, Negro, reported a man who resembled the fugitive came out of the woods about 5:30 this morning and asked him for a "lift" to East Palestine in his truck.

Manurse told him the truck had broken down and the suspect immediately started to walk along the Fredericktown-East Palestine highway.

Meanwhile, about 100 citizens in a posse aiding police, together with the sheriff's force searched Spence's woods.

Machine Gun Found By Chief

Chief Fultz found a Thompson sub-machine gun in the Kountz avenue hollow hideout Sunday. He said the two men used automatic revolvers in the encounters Saturday.

Wellsville police assigned 12 guards, with rifles, as a precaution against a possible jail delivery on the part of Floyd or members of his gang. This action was taken as four men, with two machine guns, were reported to have been seen in an automobile Sunday.

McMullin said the stranger stopped him and offered him $10 for auto hire. He knew nothing of the gun battle and accepted the passenger.

The fugitive had scarcely entered the car when McMullin discovered he had been wounded and was bleeding freely. He gave McMullin no choice but to drive him, though by this time McMullin realized there was something strange about the situation.

McMullin said Floyd, or the fugitive if other than Floyd, showed him two wounds, one in the abdomen and the other in the back.

Richetti talked freely in his cell, but denied Floyd was with him. He said his companion was James Warren of Toledo, whom he met seven years ago in the Oklahoma oil fields.

"I only met him (Floyd) once in my life," Richetti said. "That was about a year ago."

Richetti Held Pending Warrant

He denied participating in the Kansas City crime.

Asked if he had readily admitted his identity, Richetti said:

"What else could I do. They brought my fingerprints along. I couldn't say anything else."

Richetti is held on a charge of shooting with intent to kill Chief Fultz.

Chief Fultz was certain of Floyd's identity from photographs.

"I could not be mistaken," said he. "I was not more than 15 feet from him."

Potts and Erwin confirmed the identification.

Gunfire Menaces Chief and Posse

Sequentially, events leading up to the sensational disclosure that the prisoner is Richetti and that the fugitive probably is Floyd are as follows:

Wellsville police received a call from Lon Isreal, who lives east of Silver's switch in the Wellsville-East Liverpool road, shortly before 1 p. m. Saturday, asking an investigation of the suspicious actions of two men in the neighborhood.

Chief Fultz, accompanied by Special Patrolman Grover Potts and William Erwin, responded and was met by Richetti and the man presumed to be Floyd. Richetti stood in the hollow, Floyd on a hill somewhat apart.

"Stick 'em up!" Floyd ordered, as Chief Fultz approached.

(Continued On Page 3)

Herald and Examiner

Chicago

54TH YEAR No. 172 — Registered in U. S. Patent Office. — FOUR PARTS — THURSDAY, NOVEMBER 29, 1934 — TWO CENTS IN CHICAGO AND SUBURBS — ELSEWHERE THREE CENTS

DYING U. S. AGENTS KILL 'BABY FACE' IN BATTLE!

Today

Let Us Be Thankful.
Farewell, Baby Face.
Many Fine Plans.
Happy Grizzly Mother.

—BY ARTHUR BRISBANE—

THANKSGIVING finds the nation with many causes for thankfulness.

Crime has been discouraged, and noticeably, on the very day before Thanksgiving.

The hungry are fed, billions of public money are spent to give work and wages.

We have plenty of everything, *more than enough*, and lack only brains to organize distribution.

We are not at war, *not in the league of nations*. We are all alive, and have learned useful lessons.

So let us be thankful.

Crime really does not pay as a profession. Mr. Dillinger knows it. Uncle Sam's agents killed him with many bullets not long ago.

"Baby Face" Nelson, one of the very able bandits, who postponed his death for some time, also knows it if he knows anything. To express disapproval of Dillinger's killing, he killed two federal agents. The next day, which was yesterday, he was found dead, pierced by ten bullets—a complete killing.

Also "Dutch" Schultz suspects that crime is not what he thought it was. When Washington casually mentioned a desire to get that "Public Enemy No. 1," Mr. Schultz scornfully remarked: "Come and get me."

Then he heard that federal agents, looking for him, were prepared to "say it with bullets," whereupon he hurried in, saying: "Here I am; take me."

Even a criminal looks upon the automatic or submachine gun as a blot on civilization when the other man holds it.

Senator Pat Harrison, head of the Senate finance committee and fresh from a talk with President Roosevelt, reports a "shoot the works" program for Congress, including among other things:

Payment of the bonus to *needy* soldiers.

Loosening up credit to help private business.

Old age pensions for the needy over 65.

No tax increases unless to preserve government credit.

A fair-sized public works program, with low cost housing, subsistence homesteads, road building, slum clearance.

The dollar to stay as it is, no attempt to "stabilize" it to oblige foreign countries or worried "best minds."

All of it is interesting and important, *BUT* why not help private business by giving veterans their two billion two hundred million dollars to spend NOW?

They would spend, wisely and at once, and it would cost the government exactly the paper that the money would be printed on, no more.

Why worry about taxes to help government "credit"? What's the matter with its credit? We are off "the gold" and have more gold than any other nation. We can print beautiful paper money that the whole world will take gladly; we can even buy gold with it, and diamonds, rubies, sapphires and pearls, foreign titles for our daughters. Is not that good money? Why not spend what we need to spend, pay veterans the money that must be paid to them eventually, and let them spend that, stop worrying, and "let the other man worry." There is nothing the matter with us except that we don't know how to DISTRIBUTE, and we are learning.

Mrs. Louise Menzoine, New York lady visiting Tallahassee, Fla., has a baby weighing twenty-one ounces, fed with an eye-dropper, crying when hungry.

That baby seems small, but what a wonderful thing if all babies could weigh as little, for the relief of human mothers! A thousand-pound grizzly bear mother bears a cub weighing less than that Florida baby. The cub is born during the mother's Winter sleep. She does not even know about it. It finds its own way to the dining car, all alone, in the dark. Wonderful nature!

A ten-pound baby for a ninety-pound human mother and a sixteen-ounce baby for a thousand-pound grizzly bear seems like overdoing

Turn to Page 6, Column 4.

MARINA AND DUKE MOBBED BY THRONGS

Thousands Block Royal Car's Path; Couple on Way to Look at Gifts; Marry Today

LONDON, Nov. 28.—(I.N.S.) — An admiring crowd of many thousands which had gathered outside of Buckingham Palace crashed through police lines and mobbed an automobile taking the Duke of Kent and his bride-to-be, Princess Marina, out to a party at St. James Palace today. They will be married tomorrow.

Cheering madly, the crowd staged a demonstration such as seldom is seen in England. The royal car was surrounded and the road was so jammed the vehicle was compelled to halt for some time until mounted police could clear the way.

A second demonstration, almost as great, developed when Queen Mary left for the party.

Ceremonies to Take Place on Schedule.

Fog crept high over London today, threatening to take just a little of the shine off the wedding.

But fog or no fog, the wedding and the processions leading to Westminster Abbey will be carried out on clocklike schedule, the lord chamberlain, who is responsible for arrangements, announced from Buckingham Palace.

The announcement was made to quiet the qualms of thousands who had paid $50 up for seats or even window peeping space along the route of the wedding procession. Telephones in the palace buzzed busily all morning with anxious queries as to whether the processions might be cancelled if the fog continues.

Duke and Marina Spend Busy Day.

The air ministry and the weather bureau joined in the joyful prediction that the chances of the fog's

Turn to Page 2, Column 3.

UNCLE SAM GOT HIM, AFTER ALL

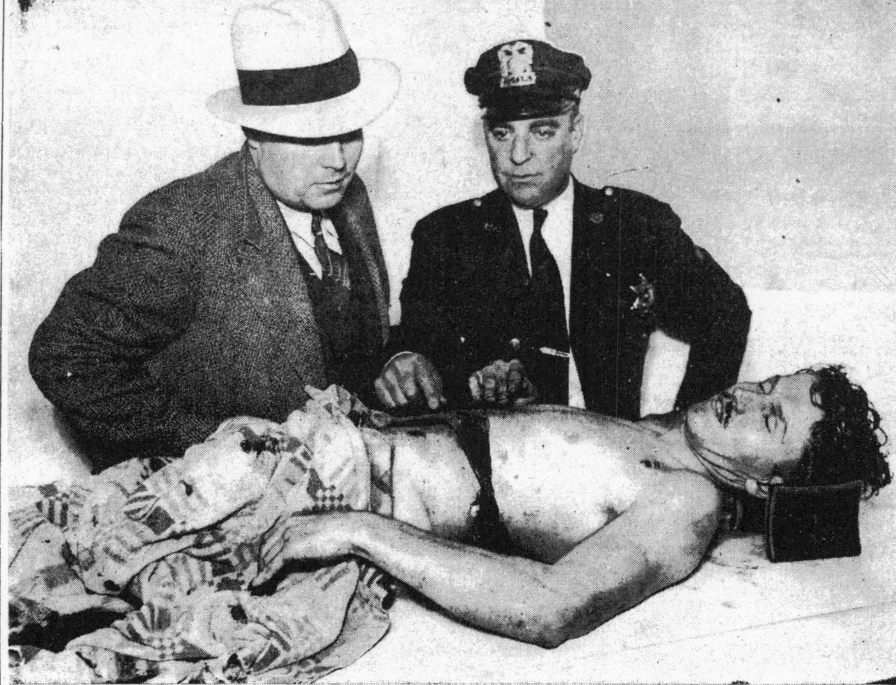

JUSTICE COLLECTS—"Baby Face" Nelson, until the day before yesterday Public Enemy No. 1, shown on a slab in a Niles Center morgue with the men who found his bullet-riddled body. They are Capt. A. C. Stollberg, left, and William Manderick. A blood-soaked handkerchief is shown across Nelson.—Herald and Examiner photo.

BODY FOUND ON PRAIRIE; RIDDLED BY HEAVY SLUGS; NEW U.S. MEN PURSUE GANG

Tip Given Chicago Undertaker by Unknown Gangster; Search Lasts Hours; Karpis New 'Top Man' of Gang

They got their man.

Lying with a twisted smile on his face, George ("Baby Face") Nelson, the nation's Public Enemy No. 1, was found dead yesterday in a Niles Center prairie.

He was killed by ten submachine gun and shotgun slugs poured into his body by Inspector Samuel P. Cowley and Special Agent Herman E. Hollis of the Department of Justice, who paid with their lives to blot him out.

The gunman companion of Nelson and the blond woman believed to be Nelson's wife, Mrs. Helen M. Gillis, carted the dying gunman away in the government automobile, after the savage gun battle Tuesday on the outskirts of Barrington.

Body Between Curb and Sidewalk on Niles Center Road.

He died on their hands, and his body, stripped nude and covered with a worn automobile blanket, was laid out between the curb and the sidewalk at Long av. and Niles Center rd. on the prairie a mile and a half west of Niles Center.

Dr. J. G. Frost, coroner's physician, said that a slug which entered the left side of the abdomen and coursed through to go out the right side caused death by internal hemorrhage. The course of the bullet was three inches deep at its furthest point.

Rigor mortis indicated that death occurred at about 6:25 a. m., Dr. Frost said, when he finished examining the body ten hours later. The physician said:

"Nelson was a slight man, but muscular. In a muscular man, rigor mortis begins setting in immediately after death."

A rude bandage made of two handkerchiefs bound together, pressing a wad of material that looked like stuffing from a mattress to a bullet wound in the abdomen, had failed to stop the flow of blood. Six more shots were in the left leg and two more in the right leg.

Because first notification of the gunman's death was received from Nelson's man companion by a Chicago undertaker, Philip Sadowski, 1845 N. Hermitage av., the great combined manhunt for Nelson's man and woman confederates centered on the Northwest Side.

Sweep Whole Section to Uncover Fugitives.

Government men and city detectives were sweeping through the whole section seeking a lead that will bring the capture of this pair that participated in the murder of Cowley and Hollis.

At the same time, Sheriff Lester Tiffany of Lake County, directing government agents, was concentrating on Lake Bluff and surrounding towns.

Sheriff Lester Edinger of McHenry County, at the head of a searching party of 500 men, was combing the resort country near Fox Lack, where, for the last two months, federal operatives had sought Nelson's hideout.

Nelson's wife was believed accompanied by either Alvin ("Bo") Karpis, Nelson's successor as the nation's No. 1 public enemy, or by a minor politician of the territory around Antioch, Ill., who last served as a policeman, but, since his discharge, is believed to have cast his lot with gangsters.

It was also considered possible that the man with Mrs. Gillis might be John Hamilton, notorious Dillinger gangster, who has been rumored dead and secretly buried in an unmarked grave, but who is still believed alive by the govern-

Turn to Page 6, Column 6.

POLICE LINK DEATH OF GIRLS AND COUPLE

CARLISLE, Pa., Nov. 28.—(AP)—Tracing a winding trail more than halfway across Pennsylvania, police tonight were "convinced" that the mysterious deaths of three little girls and an adult couple were linked, but the problem of identity seemed as baffling as when the quest began.

The five bodies were found Saturday, the girls nestled between blankets in a thicket southwest of Carlisle and the man and woman near Duncansville, 100 miles farther west.

Police said the man killed his companion and then himself with a small rifle, but the cause of the children's deaths is less positive.

Mrs. Anna Dill, who operates a tourist camp at South Langhorne, said she believed the children stayed at her place with a man and woman from November 19 to 21.

The couple gave the name of Mr. and Mrs. J. C. Malone of Vallejo, Cal., and they had a blue car with California license plates. The blue car found had no tags. Police traced the car's serial number to Seattle, Wash.

Horner to Spend Holiday at Mansion

SPRINGFIELD, Ill., Nov. 28.—(I.N.S.)—Governor Henry Horner will spend Thanksgiving Day at the executive mansion with relatives. His two brothers and several cousins will be there for Thanksgiving dinner, he said.

Nelson Big-Hearted Boy to His Mother

Just a great-hearted chap who was always taking the blame for others' sins, and who wouldn't hurt any one except in self-defense.

That was George ("Baby Face") Nelson as he was pictured yesterday by his mother, Mrs. Helen Gillis of 5516 S. Marshfield av. Stunned, but not altogether surprised, by his death, she said:

"He was not the terrible person he was painted. He was awfully kind, and he'd never harm anybody except to protect himself. After all, self-preservation is the first law of nature."

HUNTED ALL HIS LIFE.

She said he was hunted all his life by police because he used to take the blame for the things done by his boyhood pals. She added:

"He wasn't the kind who'd squeal. I tried to get him away from those boys.

"When prohibition came he began selling liquor and the police were always shaking him down. When they'd demand money he didn't have, he'd have to go out and get it.

"It's not true that he was in St. Charles reformatory three times. He was there only once, and he was a model boy there."

ALWAYS "BOYS' BOY."

She said that, as a youth, he was always a "boys' boy," and Nelson's sister, Mrs. Juliette Fitzsimmons, interposed:

"Yes, and since he's been grown up he's been a one-woman man. He always stuck to his wife and she always stuck to him."

Corroborating this, Mrs. Gillis added:

"And his wife will always be welcome here. Not only that, we can and want to take care of the child (Arlene, 4)."

Nelson also has a son, 5, living with a sister in Bremerton, Wash.

Mrs. Fitzsimmons' husband, Robert, a bookkeeper, observed:

"They killed a better man than he ever killed."

PLAN SIMPLE BURIAL.

News of the death had reached the family over the radio, but, believing it might be a false report and that they would be detained if they appeared at the police station, they telephoned the federal men and verified it, asking if they could claim the body.

Burial will be private and simple, they said.

And Mrs. Gillis summed up her feelings in these words:

"I'm still proud he was my son."

LATEST RACES

BAY MEADOWS

FIFTH RACE.

Seth's Hope	7.60	3.80	3.60
Rome Vennie		4.00	3.40
Sweet Chariot			6.80

SIXTH RACE.

King Caress........	5.40	3.00	3.00
Likipuu		3.80	3.60
Gallentia			4.00

SEVENTH RACE.

Gabbo	6.40	4.00	4.00
Wirt G. Bowman...		15.80	9.60
War Over			6.00

Result of earlier races will be found in the sports pages.

KARPIS GIVEN 'HIGH RANK' AS U.S. ENEMY NO. 1

Alvin Karpis, Chicago-born killer, kidnaper and jailbird, is the new public enemy No. 1.

He is the object of a nation-wide search begun yesterday even before the death of George ("Baby Face") Nelson was known, for police believe that he was Nelson's companion in the duel to death with federal agents at Barrington.

WANTED FOR KIDNAPING.

Karpis, with Arthur ("Doc") Barker, another Chicago criminal, has been sought by federal officers for nearly a year as the kidnaper of Edward G. Bremer, wealthy St. Paul brewer, for whose safe return Karpis and Barker are said to have collected $200,000.

Karpis moved up to the doubtful distinction of the nation's No. 1 bad man through the death of John Dil-

Turn to Page 6, Column 5.

THE WEATHER

CHICAGO AND VICINITY—Increasing cloudiness, rain at night, continued cool; moderate northwest winds, becoming southeast Thursday.

The following temperature readings were recorded from 3 a. m. yesterday:

3 a. m..54	8 a. m..48	1 p. m..43
4 a. m..52	9 a. m..48	2 p. m..44
5 a. m..51	10 a. m..48	3 p. m..44
6 a. m..48	11 a. m..48	4 p. m..44
7 a. m..48	12 noon .47	5 p. m..43

ILLINOIS—Increasing cloudiness, showers and somewhat warmer in west portions in afternoon.

INDIANA—Partly cloudy; colder in east portion.

LOWER MICHIGAN—Partly cloudy, colder.

WISCONSIN—Partly cloudy; colder.

MISSOURI—Showers; warmer.

IOWA—Rain in east and south, rain or snow in northwest portion, somewhat warmer in east and south.

THE WEATHER
Today: Fair, slightly colder
Tomorrow: Fair
Temperatures Yesterday: Max., 40; Min., 28
Detailed Report on Page 40

NEW YORK Herald Tribune

CITY EDITION

VOL. XCIV No. 32,170 (Copyright, 1934, New York Tribune Inc.) FRIDAY, DECEMBER 14, 1934 *** TWO CENTS In Greater New York | THREE CENTS Within 200 Miles | FOUR CENTS Elsewhere

Tons of Food Lying Idle While Needy Go Hungry, City Investigators Told

8 Million Lbs. of Potatoes Frozen in Warehouses, Veal Stacked for Lack of Cutters, Aldermen Hear

8,000 Relief Tickets Disappear Monthly

T.E.R.A., Blamed for Not Co-operating, Issues Denial; Mayor Hits System; Hodson's Hands Tied

The revelation that while thousands of families are crying for food surplus supplies of potatoes, cabbages, canned beef and veal shipped here by the Federal Emergency Relief Administration are lying in warehouses was brought out yesterday by the Aldermanic committee investigating the administration of relief by the Department of Welfare.

Enough potatoes to feed the entire population of the city for a day—1,400,000 pounds—had frozen in a corrugated iron storehouse in Brooklyn, it was testified, and another 7,000,000 pounds, a supply sufficient to feed the city's population for a week, are believed to be in the same condition.

Local Officials Blame T. E. R. A.

Officials of the local relief administration blamed lack of co-ordination between the local authorities and the Temporary Emergency Relief Administration, the state agency which distributes the supplies obtained from the Federal government, for the delay in distributing the foodstuffs to the needy of the city.

Chief among the disclosures were: Some 1,400,000 pounds of potatoes, delivered in the sub-freezing weather of the last few days, had frozen in the iron warehouse in Seventh Street, between Second and Third Avenues, Brooklyn. Another 7,000,000 pounds stored in a stone warehouse in Jay Street, Brooklyn, probably were in the same condition. The total monetary loss was put at $65,000.

No investigation had been made by the local relief administration to ascertain why 8,000 to 10,000 relief tickets were not turned in monthly for collection.

Some 9,000,000 pounds of cabbage had been shipped to New York by the Federal relief authorities, although the city administration had asked for but 300,000 pounds. When protest was made to the T. E. R. A., officials of that agency suggested that the surplus be converted into sauerkraut. The local agency contended it had neither the authority nor the facilities to make the conversion.

Over the protest of the local agency, 4,000,000 cans of roast beef were shipped to New York. A million cans are still stacked on city piers.

About 11,000,000 pounds of veal have been lying in the Bronx Terminal Market, the local administration being unable to distribute it because it lacked machines for cutting the meat. Six machines were delivered to the local administration yesterday, but it was discovered that they were not the type requested. The machines were purchased by the T. E. R. A.

T. E. R. A. Asks U. S. Inquiry

Samuel B. Barrows, director of the Federal Surplus Division of the T. E. R. A., last night branded the charges as "wholly unfounded and absurd."

"Since Federal surplus foods are purchased by the Federal Surplus Relief Corporation," he added, "and then allotted to the various states the T. E. R. A. asks that Mr. Harry Hopkins and those to whom the T. E. R. A. is responsible for proper care of the foods, make an investigation of the present methods of handling the foods. The T. E. R. A. would welcome such an investigation by qualified judges on food distribution."

Commissioner William Hodson, of the Department of Welfare, who is in charge of the local administration of relief, confessed that he did not know, until the Aldermanic committee brought the fact to light that between 8,000 and 10,000 food tickets fail to

(Continued on page fourteen)

British to Use Autogyro To Spot War Artillery

From the Herald Tribune Bureau
Copyright, 1934, New York Tribune Inc.

LONDON, Dec. 13.—Captive "sausage" balloons, universally used for spotting artillery in the World War, are to be replaced in the British army by autogyros, it was announced today.

The windmill plane is said to be easier to camouflage than the captive balloon and in addition to being able to stand still in the air, can fly away with sufficient speed to offer some chance of escape from hostile aircraft.

Smith Is Made Decency Legion Head by Hayes

Ex-Governor and 14 Laymen on Council to Advise Clergy on Film Crusade

Cardinal Hayes has appointed Alfred E. Smith as chairman of the new Legion of Decency Council of the Roman Catholic Archdiocese of New York. The announcement was made yesterday at the Cardinal's residence, 452 Madison Avenue, by his private secretary, the Rev. John J. Casey.

As chairman of the council, the former Governor will preside over a group of fourteen leading Catholic laymen. He and his council will advise the clergy of the archdiocese in their drive against indecent motion pictures, particularly with a view of gaining the co-operation of local motion-picture producers and distributors.

All counties in the archdiocese will be represented on the council. Members of the council are:

MANHATTAN

JAMES A. FARRELL, former president of the United States Steel Corporation.
GEORGE MACDONALD, Papal marquis.
JOHN P. O'BRIEN, former Mayor of New York.
MORGAN J. O'BRIEN, lawyer.
MARTIN QUIGLEY, publisher of "The Motion Picture Herald and The Motion Picture Daily."
JOHN J. RASKOB, former chairman of the Democratic National Committee.
ALFRED TALLEY, former judge of the Court of General Sessions.

THE BRONX

JAMES DONNELLY.

RICHMOND

WILLIAM T. PETHERSTON, former justice of the Court of Special Sessions.

WESTCHESTER

JUSTICE WILLIAM F. BLEAKLEY, of the Supreme Court.

DUTCHESS AND PUTNAM

JOHN E. MACK, of Poughkeepsie, former Supreme Court Justice.

ORANGE AND ROCKLAND

ARTHUR O'LEARY.

SULLIVAN

GEORGE COOK.

ULSTER

JAMES DWYER.

No crusade for a clean-up in the legitimate theater is being contemplated.

(Continued on page forty-two)

Chinese Reds Slay Two U.S. Missionaries

Mr. and Mrs. J. C. Stam, of Paterson, Seized Last Week; Fate of 3-Months Baby Is Still a Mystery

By Victor Keen
From the Herald Tribune Bureau
Copyright, 1934, New York Tribune Inc.

SHANGHAI, Dec. 13.—The slaying of Mr. and Mrs. John C. Stam, American missionaries, who, with their daughter of three months, were captured last week by Communist soldiers in southern Anhwei Province, was reported to the China Inland Mission headquarters here today.

The bodies of the young couple, who had been married only fourteen months, were discovered near Miaoshao village, about thirteen miles from Tsingteh, according to a telegram sent by the Governor of Anhwei. The message made no mention of the baby's fate.

The Stams, who were both twenty-seven years old, had recently returned to their missionary station at Tsingteh on assurances of the provincial authorities that the district was safe. The Communist band of about 3,000 which captured them was believed to be a remnant of Red forces scattered during the Chinese government's anti-Communist campaign in Kiangsi Province.

Mr. Stam was a native of Paterson, N. J. Mrs. Stam was born in Tsinan, capital of Shantung Province, the daughter of Dr. and Mrs. Charles E. Scott, attached to the Presbyterian mission there. Dr. Scott is a professor at Tsinan Christian University. He and his wife were formerly residents of Holyoke, Mass.

United States Legation to Act

WASHINGTON, Dec. 13 (AP).—William Phillips, Under Secretary of State, said today that the American Legation in China would make every effort to bring about the capture and execution of the bandits who murdered Mr. and Mrs. Stam.

The Chinese government, Mr. Phillips told reporters, had acted promptly when robbers recently shot and killed Dr. James H. Ingram, American medical missionary, in the Western Hills, near Peiping. Mr. Phillips declined to say whether the United States would make any claim for indemnity against the Chinese government.

Killed Before Chance to Pay Ransom

SHANGHAI, Dec. 14 (Friday) (UP).—Fear for the safety of the Rev. Erwin A. Kofield, American mission-

(Continued on page five)

Summary of Today's News

Grace Budd's Kidnaper-Slayer Leads Police to Child's '28 Grave

Associated Press photos
Albert H. Fish leaving Police Headquarters yesterday. Inset, Grace Budd

Mild-Mannered Father of Six, 65, Trapped by Letters Written to Girl's Parents, Admits Butchering; Victim's Head Found in Westchester

Albert H. Fish, a mild-mannered, stoop-shouldered little man sixty-five years old, was arrested yesterday and admitted to the police, they said, that he was the abductor of Grace Budd, who was ten years old when she vanished on June 3, 1928, from her home in the basement of 406 West Fifteenth Street.

He had taken the child, Fish said, to an unoccupied house near the Saw Mill River Parkway in the town of Greenburg, Westchester County, on the outskirts of Elmsford, strangled her, dismembered her body with a cleaver, saw and butcher knife which he had taken along, and had hidden the head in the woods near the house.

The head was found last night by New York policemen and state troopers at a spot pointed out to them by their prisoner, and a search was begun for the rest of the body.

Fish was brought back to New York, accused of abduction and homicide. He will be arranged today in Jefferson Market Police Court. He is married, and his wife and six children live in Astoria, Queens.

Aske by the police, who professed to be astonished at the cool account of murder given to them by their composed prisoner, why he had conceived and carried out such a crime, Fish remarked quietly that he guessed it was just "my blood lust." He said he was glad he had made his statement.

"It makes my conscience feel better," he said. "I'm glad I told everything."

It was his conscience, he said, which impelled him to write anonymous letters which the parents of the Budd child have received at intervals in the last six years, some of them, it is said, containing revolting details of the crime. It was through these letters that Detective William King, who had been on the case since the abduction of the girl, traced Fish and arrested him yesterday afternoon at 200 East Fifty-second Street, where he had had a room until November 11.

The police were lucky in having a sample of the kidnaper's writing early in the case. He had visited the Budds originally in response to an adver-

(Continued on page ten)

9-Point Attack Mapped to Cut Crime in Nation

600 Experts End Conference at Capital to Push Program of Wide Scope

From the Herald Tribune Bureau

WASHINGTON, Dec. 13.—The National Conference on Crime, called by President Roosevelt and Attorney General Homer S. Cummings to find methods of making more effective war on lawlessness, concluded its sessions here today with adoption of a nine-point program designed at least as a new approach to the handling of the problem.

The specific recommendations, reduced from a list of 110 resolutions placed before the conference, were accepted with virtual unanimity by 600-odd delegates.

Throughout the four days of discussion, in which experts in all lines were heard, and down to the closing session, addressed by Attorney General Cummings tonight, there was evidence of realization that only the surface had been scratched. The problem confronting them, they knew, apparently was epitomized by Professor Thorstein Sellin, of the University of Pennsylvania, when he estimated today that at a minimum estimate serious crime cases in the United States in 1933 numbered 1,300,000, and "for three-fourths of these crimes no one had been brought to justice."

Briefly the resolutions, read by Scott Loftin, president of the American Bar Association, proposed:

The crime conference be made a continuing organization with meetings biennially or oftener.

Establishment of a national scientific and educational center in Washington to train enforcement officers.

A strengthening of the law enforcement agencies of cities and states, leaving the major part of crime suppression in local hands.

The development of youth training through Federal and state co-operation in educational, vocational and recreational opportunities.

Condemnation of the use of un-

(Continued on page thirteen)

Boy Has a Close Shave Swallowing Razor Blade

Doctors All Set to Operate, Nature Saves Them Trouble

SOUTH SHIELDS, England, Dec. 13 (CP).—John George Hunter, ten years old, was playing with a safety razor blade in school today. He swallowed it.

John George told his teacher, who thought the boy was telling a tale, but sent him home with a companion. On the way the boy confided in a policeman, who hurried him to the infirmary. Sure enough, the X-ray revealed the blade in John George's stomach.

While doctors made careful preparations for a most difficult operation, John George became sick at his stomach. Up came the blade. Amazed doctors and nurses called it a miracle.

Borah and Nye Demand Republicans Reorganize For Leveling of Wealth

Arms Inquiry Hears Baruch Is Not Its Rival

But Nye Still Fears That Roosevelt Plans to Sidetrack Profits Investigation; Incomes Listed

By Ernest K. Lindley

WASHINGTON, Dec. 13.—President Roosevelt sought today to mollify the members of the Senate Munitions Committee who viewed his creation yesterday of a War Profits Committee under the chairmanship of Bernard M. Baruch as an attempt to stifle or sidetrack their investigation.

The President's chosen instrument of pacification was Senator Bennett C. Clark, Democrat, of Missouri, who happened to have an appointment with the President on another subject. On leaving the White House Senator Clark said:

"Mr. Roosevelt told me he expected his War Profits Committee to co-operate with our Senate committee, and vice versa. I see no basis for conflict between the two committees. We are trying our best to get something done and welcome aid."

There were no indications, however, that the President would easily succeed in effecting a reconciliation. His abrupt action yesterday put the members of the committee on their guard. Active Democratic members of the committee are known to be as suspicious of the President's motives, as are Senator Gerald P. Nye, chairman of the investigation, and Senator Arthur H. Vandenberg, Republicans.

While Mr. Baruch has a strong following among conservative Democrats in the Senate, he is regarded as a friend of big business by most of the liberals in the Senate. General Hugh S. Johnson, former National Recovery Administrator, who was brought back into the Administration fold as Mr. Baruch's assistant in the drafting of the President's program, succeeded in alienating both liberals and conservatives during his work as National Recovery Administrator.

The charges made or implied by Senators Nye and Vandenberg that the President was trying to head off the Senate investigation were buttressed by Senator Nye today with the disclosure that the committee's appropriation of $50,000 will be exhausted by the present series of hearings ending December 21. The committee was counting on obtaining an additional grant of funds from Congress within a few days after the opening of the session on January 3. What they profess to be afraid of is that the President will present his own plan for "taking the profit out of war" shortly after Congress convenes and attempt to use the large Democratic majorities to drive it through at once without waiting for the committee to finish its work and reach its own conclusions.

The committee today made public lists of huge corporation profits and large individual incomes reported in the United States during the World

(Continued on page twelve)

Farley Hails 2 'Victors;' 1 Lost, 2d Did Not Run

BOSTON, Dec. 13 (UP).—Either James A. Farley, chairman of the Democratic National Committee, has made a faux pas, or some one has perpetrated a hoax. John F. Daly, Cambridge lawyer, and James A. Bruin, Mayor of Lowell, both received notes today congratulating them on their "election" as Middlesex County District Attorney. The letters bore Washington postmarks, the stationery was that of the Democratic National Press Bureau, and the signature purported to be that of the Postmaster General. Mr. Daly lost the Democratic nomination to Mr. Bruin, and Mr. Bruin was defeated in the election by Warren L. Bishop, Republican incumbent by 31,000 votes.

Plan New Court To Pass on Civil Issues With U.S.

Senator Logan, Bar Group Prepare Bill to Meet New-Deal Law Criticisms

By Theodore C. Wallen

WASHINGTON, Dec. 13.—A court of administrative justice to determine civil controversies between citizens and their government was planned in legislation taking form today in conferences of Senator M. M. Logan, Democrat, of Kentucky, and a special committee of the American Bar Association. Mr. Logan is a former Chief Justice of Kentucky.

Designed to meet the situation criticized by the Supreme Court, the new court would take jurisdiction in disputes started by administrative orders which have the force of law, though not passed by Congress. It would also take over the functions of the United States Court of Claims and the Court of Customs and Patent Appeals.

Composed of fifteen judges appointed by the President, the new court also would supplant the Circuit Court of Appeals as the appellate body for the Board of Tax Appeals. The clerk of the new court would be made the repository for all executive orders and administrative rules and regulations. In that capacity he would be required to compile and publish all such decrees in the same manner that acts of Congress are handled.

The proposed legislation was one of two comprehensive plans announced following President Roosevelt's assertion that steps were being taken to

(Continued on page forty)

Lawyers Hot, Official Cold While Mail Burns

Letters a Sacrifice on Altar of Anti-Tampering Law

A small fire developed yesterday in the bottom of the mail chute in the Supreme Court Building, Joralemon and Fulton Streets, Brooklyn, and while a crowd of lawyers were imploring building attendants to open the mail box so they could rescue their correspondence, John McLinden, the superintendent, remained firm in his belief that no one might tamper with the property of the Federal government.

Dense clouds of smoke filled the lobby of the building just before noon. The fire was quickly traced to the mail box, and McLinden went into conference with Patrolman Charles Walsh. The lawyers offered a legal opinion that water should be poured in through the mail drop to extinguish the fire, while other bystanders contended that the best way was to close all vents in the chute and smother the blaze. McLinden restrained every one, and said that in no event would the box be touched until a mechanic from the postoffice should arrive.

While the lawyers continued to wail, McLinden remained courteously firm. Finally a postman and a mechanic appeared. They unlocked the box and scraped about thirty charred letters and a mass of burnt paper scraps from the box. The lawyers asked to have their letters returned to them, but this the postman declined to do, explaining that once mail had been deposited in a chute or a mail box, the government was its custodian, and neither snow nor rain nor heat nor gloom of night interfered with its swift delivery.

After an investigation, the mechanic said the fire had been started by a cigarette.

Realty Dealer Own Ice Breaker In Rescuing Girl, 4, From Pond

Special to the Herald Tribune

NEW ROCHELLE, N. Y., Dec. 13.—L. Franklin van Zelm, real estate dealer in New Rochelle, who lives at 17 Wilmot Road, rescued a four-year-old girl who had fallen through the ice of a pond on his property just before noon today. Mr. Van Zelm, who saw the child by the merest chance as he was looking from an upstairs window of his house, sprinted seventy-five yards to the pond in his shirt sleeves and acted as his own ice breaker as he waded, scrambled and swam forty feet through the cold water to reach her.

The child is Nancy Collins, one of the two children of Mr. and Mrs. Daniel C. Collins, of 21 Lord Kitchener Road, about five minutes' walk from Mr. Van Zelm's pond. This morning Nancy and two playmates, whose names were not revealed, walked to the pond and inspected longingly the crisp ice which had formed during the recent cold spell. Finally Nancy told her friends that she was going to walk on it.

She tentatively put her foot on the ice, then jumped eagerly near shore. It held, and she walked toward the center of the pond, which covers about a quarter of an acre.

When she was half way across the pond the ice cracked suddenly directly under her feet. She fell into the water, her waterproof playsuit supporting her slightly. The other children, not quite sure of what had happened but vaguely frightened, ran away to their nurse.

About this time Mr. Van Zelm was looking from the window. He owns twelve mallard ducks, of which he is very fond. Recently he took them to a sanctuary to protect them from the bitter weather. He saw the dark spot in a patch of broken ice and thought for a moment it might be a homesick mallard come back to the pond. Then he shouted to his wife: "Some one's fallen in the pond!"

After he brought the child back to the house he telephoned to New Rochelle police headquarters for doctors and an emergency squad. Nancy was unconscious when he brought her in, so Mrs. Van Zelm and a friend rolled her across a clothes hamper. Then they applied methods of artificial respiration. When the police arrived, an inhalator was used on Nancy until she was breathing normal. She was taken to New Rochelle Hospital, where her condition today was reported as good.

Mr. van Zelm, a former cartoonist for "The Evening World" and the King Features Syndicate, was quite hoarse tonight, and would not leave the vicinity of his own fireplace, even to accept congratulations of the neighbors.

Mr. Collins is employed as an engineer by the Western Electric Company in New York.

Both Appeal for Young Leadership, Rebuilding 'From Ground Up' at Meeting Called by Mellen

Insist Party Shed Wall St. 'Ball, Chain'

Idahoan Attacks Policies of Fletcher, Hilles; Asks War on Monopolies and New Deal Price Fixing

Senator William E. Borah, of Idaho, and Senator Gerald P. Nye, of North Dakota, addressing a mass meeting under the auspices of the New York County Republican Committee last night, demanded a revitalized Republican party under new leadership and with a program of redistribution of wealth. Both drove directly at the cautious leadership of the past and at past Republican policies which they charged had operated for the benefit of the few rather than the welfare of the many. Both predicted that unless those policies were changed the Republican party might as well fold up and go out of business.

Their addresses were delivered in Mecca Temple, 130 West Fifty-sixth Street, at the invitation of Chase Mellen jr., president of the New York County Republican Committee.

Assails Fletcher and Hilles

Rallying young Republicans throughout the country to organize for a leftward movement in the Republican party, Senator Borah derided both Henry P. Fletcher, chairman of the Republican National Committee, and Charles D. Hilles, National Committeeman from New York. The Senator had had recent clashes with them in the public prints. Many of the audience of several thousand laughed and cheered as the Idaho militant released his shafts against Mr. Fletcher and Mr. Hilles. Others were stony faced and silent.

Mr. Hilles sat on the platform almost under Senator Borah's left elbow. He listened complacently.

The addresses of the two outstanding Progressive Republican Senators—both severe critics of President Roosevelt's N. R. A. and other policies—were the first in a series which Mr. Mellen has arranged in a campaign to "liberalize" his organization. The meeting followed a Republican legislative conference in Utica on Wednesday, when Melvin C. Eaton, Republican state chairman, demanded that new and younger leadership take charge of the Assembly minority. Mr. Eaton made a brief address.

Both Senator Borah and Senator Nye suggested a number of policies which they thought the Republican party should pursue in order to rehabilitate itself.

Assails Code Handicaps

Foremost among Senator Borah's suggestions was an effort to free small business from the handicaps imposed by the blue-agle codes. Equally, he assailed the power of monopolies to fix prices arbitrarily and declared that that power in this country was greater than any power ever exercised by the czars.

"The driving power in politics for years to come, I venture to believe," Senator Borah explained, "will come from labor, from the producer, from small business and from the millions who have, through no fault of their own been stripped of their life savings and opportunity.

"If out of all this is to come orderly and constitutional government, there must also come a system and a body of laws insuring a wholly different distribution of the wealth of our country."

Would Replace Old Leaders

As to party leadership, Senator Borah said if the present leadership could not see the necessity of such changes there was only one thing to do, and that was to begin replacement of leadership, starting at the bottom with county and state organizations.

These remarks were directed at Mr. Fletcher, who has refused to acquiesce in Senator Borah's demand that he resign, and to Mr. Hilles, who recently criticized Senator Borah's efforts to reorganize the party. The Idaho Senator mentioned them by name.

"It is evident from these statements," Senator Borah said, "that there is only one thing for those who believe in reorganization to do, and that is to begin to organize in the different counties and states.

"The Young Republicans are very generally organized into clubs in the different states. These will serve as the beginning of state-wide organizations. . . . I have, and have had from the beginning, just one purpose, and that is to bring this issue to the front

Tides at the Beaches Today
High 6:48 A.M. 7:09 P.M.
Low 12:17A.M. 12:59P.M.

The Florida Times-Union

News from Every Section of the State. Complete Stock and Bond Market Reports. All Sports Events Covered in Detail.

Weather for Florida
Generally fair Thursday.
Full report on Page 18.

VOLUME LXX—70th YEAR | JACKSONVILLE, FLORIDA, THURSDAY, JANUARY 17, 1935. | SINGLE COPY—5 CENTS, DAILY; 10 CENTS, SUNDAY

Two Wanted in Bremer Hunt Killed in Florida

Convicts Seize Prison Board Members as Hostages; Beat San Quentin Warden and Flee

Four Desperate Criminals Kidnap Six Men from Luncheon at Penitentiary, Overawe Guards and Speed Away in Auto.

ALL CAUGHT, 1 SHOT AFTER TENSE PURSUIT

Felons Surrender 54 Miles from Prison After First Holding Officers at Bay With Withering Gun Fire

BULLETIN

SAN QUENTIN, Calif., Jan. 16, (AP)—Rudolph Straight, leader of four convicts who staged a sensational escape from San Quentin Prison today, died late tonight of wounds received in the gun battle with officers.

SAN QUENTIN, Calif., Jan 16, (AP)—Four San Quentin prison convicts slugged Warden James B. Holohan and kidnaped six men to escape today, only to be recaptured.

Two tense hours of pursuit and battle ended in the serious wounding of one convict, the surrender of three others, and the wounding of two hostages.

The break—most amazing in the history of crowded San Quentin—came as members of the State board of prison terms and paroles gathered for luncheon in Warden Holohan's residence.

The four convicts strode in, brandishing guns.

"Stand up, all of you!" their leader commanded.

Holohan refused to surrender and was promptly slugged unconscious by swinging guns. He was left lying in a pool of blood.

Quickly the prisoners seized C. Sykes, San Francisco contractor and board chairman, later shot; Warren Atherton, Stockton attorney; Joseph Stephens, Sacramento banker, wounded slightly, and Mark E. Noon, the board's secretary.

Guard Lieut. Harry Jones and Sergt. C. L. Doose fell into the convict-made cul de sac, surrendering at pistol point.

Two State automobiles in front of the warden's residence served for the getaway. Holding the board officials in one car and forcing the guards to ride on the running boards, the convicts sped toward the back gate.

Noon was forced to give the signal to guards to allow them to pass.

Car Speeds West.

The car sped westward through San Rafael to the Redwood Highway and then to the north—the only avenue of escape from the grim walls housing the largest prison population in the United States, 6000 men.

Most of the Northern California officialdom soon was on the trail.

Warden Holohan suffered a fractured skull. His physician said he might survive.

Sykes was shot in the hip and an operation at a Santa Rosa hospital disclosed that a 10 cent piece had saved his life by deflecting the bullet.

Stephens was wounded slightly in the abdomen.

The convicts were led by Rudolph Straight, 35, "bad boy" who previously had made two desperate attempts to escape. Unconfirmed reports said Straight was the fugitive who had been shot. He apparently had three confederates.

They were named as Alex McKay, 28; Joe Cristy, 26, and Fred Alenders, 27.

The felons surrendered to county and State officers at Valley Ford, 54 miles from the prison.

Running through two barricades across the highway, they got to Novato, about 10 miles north of the prison, where pursuing police overtook them.

The convicts then cut loose with withering gunfire that held the officers off while they fled northward again.

Thousands of officers were on the trail but they were doubly hampered by the use of the captive officials as hostages and by reports that the convicts had dressed in the clothing of their captives.

District Attorney Albert E. Bagshaw of Marin County told of the last stand of the desperadoes.

"Undersheriff Ed Blum and I received a call about the escape," he said. "We at once attempted to block the road but before we could do so the convicts came by.

"Shots were exchanged at Tomales and Constable John Bones shot a tire of the fleeing machine.

"Driving at high speed, we followed the convicts for eleven miles.

"They kept firing and bullets spattered through the windshield of one of the pursuing cars.

"Rubber began to tear away from the wheel of their car and when they jumped out and let the machine race away. It crashed into a nearby garage and was wrecked.

Flee Into Creamery.

"The convicts fled inside the creamery and shot at its attendant.

Continued on Page 2

Biplane Ends Non-Stop Hop To Canal Zone

Delayed By Winds, Makes 2000-Mile Flight in 25 Hours.

WASHINGTON, Jan. 16, (AP)—Held back by unfavorable winds, the giant Navy biplane XP2H-1 landed at Coco Solo, Canal Zone, at 4:50 P. M. (Eastern Standard Time) today, after a 2,000 mile non-stop flight from Norfolk, Va.

Exactly 25 hours had elapsed from the take-off when Lieutenant J. S. Thach, commander and pilot, brought the giant ship to an easy landing in the water off the air base near Christobal, Panama. The report sent back to the Navy Department head was that head winds had prevented holding the normal speed of 90 miles an hour.

The trip was without incident throughout, and Navy officials expressed no alarm when nothing was heard from the plane from 3 P. M., when it was 160 miles from its destination, until the wireless was received announcing the landing. With Lieutenant Thach were Lieutenant C. E. Giese, co-pilot, and six enlisted men.

Officials, saying this was the first single flight of its kind undertaken, recalled that a squadron of six planes last Summer made a non-stop hop from Norfolk to Coco Solo without incident.

The XP2H-1, a four motored biplane, will be assigned under Rear Admiral A. W. Johnson, commander of the base aircraft force, who recently came to the Canal Zone from the West Coast on the aircraft tender Wright.

Officials said plans were being considered to send the plane up the West Coast to join the main United States fleet.

The plane's route took it down the Eastern seaboard to Key West, Fla., and thence across Cuba. It passed over Mariel, a small town west of Havana, at 6 o'clock this morning. The last part of the journey was across the Caribbean Sea over 700 miles of open water.

Portland Theatre Damaged By Bomb

PORTLAND, Maine, Jan. 16, (AP)—A bomb exploded in the Casco theatre here early today partially wrecking the interior and causing damage estimated by Manager Fred C. Stone as "roughly $1,500."

The explosion awakened guests in a nearby hotel, many of whom dashed to the lobbies, fearing the blast had occurred in the hotel itself.

Police Capt. Harry B. Powers said the bomb was concealed behind a fire extinguisher in the theatre's second floor, just off the balcony in a corner adjoining the projection booth.

Every window in the theatre was shattered. Plaster and laths were torn from walls and ceilings in both the upper and lower lobbies. The Casco theatre is in the heart of downtown Portland. Stone could give no reason for the bombing.

Still Hunted

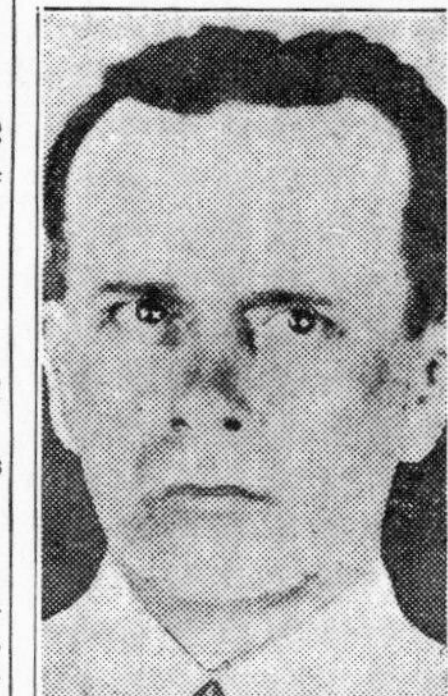

Top, Arthur (Doc) Barker, brother of Fred Barker, slain in Ocklawaha yesterday together with his mother, "Ma" Barker by Federal agents. Below, Alvin Karpis. Both of these men are still being hunted by the government as the real brains of the gang that kidnaped Edward G. Bremer, St. Paul banker.

U. S. to Press Wide Hunt for Gang Leaders

Arthur Barker and Alvin Karpis Regarded as Real Chieftains.

WASHINGTON, Jan. 16, (AP)—Orders went out from the Justice Department tonight to press the already intensive hunt for Alvin Karpis and Arthur (Doc) Barker.

Bullets which sprayed from the guns of Federal agents today at Oklawaha, Florida, killed Barker's mother and brother, Fred. But Arthur and Karpis were regarded as the real leaders of the gang which kidnaped Edward G. Bremer, St. Paul banker, last Winter.

The clash today between Federal officers and the Barkers was the first definite indication the Department of Justice was close upon the one criminal organization left virtually intact as far as personnel is concerned.

Dillinger, "Pretty Boy" Floyd and

Continued on Page 7.

World Court Entry Urged By Roosevelt

Bristling Opposition Drive Opens in Senate Following President's Message.

WASHINGTON, Jan. 16, (AP)—A burst of opposition oratory, asserting that the United States was moving toward entry into the League of Nations, today greeted in the Senate a special message from President Roosevelt urging American adherence to the World Court.

In a 22-line message, one of the briefest by a Chief Executive on a major subject, Mr. Roosevelt joined his predecessor Presidents—Harding, Coolidge, and Hoover—in advocating adherence of the three protocols now pending "in such a form as not to defeat or to delay the objective of adherence."

Almost immediately a bristling opposition drive began. Senator Hiram Johnson of California, ordinarily the President's strongest supporter in minority ranks, took the floor to flay the ratification resolution as "the first step" toward America entering the League of Nations.

With a biting sarcasm that kept the well-filled floor and galleries in rapt attention, the fighting Californian ripped into the court resolution as an effort to "meddle and muddle in the hysterical internationalism that Europe has and that Europe never will get rid of."

So vehement were his words that old observers recalled the League of Nations fight that split the Senate 15 years ago.

Called Non-Partisn.

In his message, read just before, the President had asserted the "movement to make international justice practicable and serviceable is not subject to partisan considerations"

The Executive pointed out both Republican and Democratic platforms for years have urged a "court of justice to which nations might voluntarily bring their disputes for judicial decision," and added:

"The sovereignty of the United States will be in no way diminished or jeopardized by such action. At this period in international relationships, when every act is of moment to the future of world peace, the United States has an opportunity once more to throw its weight into the scale in favor of peace"

Democratic leaders felt the message would swing several doubtful votes for ratification. They have never had any doubt of ratification, however, if a final vote can be reached.

Johnson disagreed strenuously that the move would be in the interest of peace. He contended America would just be involving itself in foreign politics in violaton of her traditional policy of isolation and that ultimate membership in the league would result "as surely as night follows day."

He asserted an effort was now afoot by Senator Pope (D Idaho), to get the United States into the league and said he had heard that the State Department was assisting Pope in writing his resolution.

Pope denied this, saying he had never consulted the State Department on the subject.

Calling attention that because this was the twenty-first birthday of his eldest grandson the day was just as significant to him as it was to Sheppard (D Texas), who spoke for a return of prohibition in his usual anniversary address, Johnson fairly shouted:

"I don't want any son or grandson of mine sent to work in China in a fight there over something between China and Japan.

"Why take the risk? Why join for the sake of peace, when there is no peace. I have never yet heard of a creditor submitting his questions to the judgment of his debtors. Now is the most unpropitious time to join the League Court."

Arguing America had more pres-

Continued on Page 2

Kidnaper Trail Leads from St. Paul to Florida

Edward G. Bremer, young St. Paul, Minn., banker, kidnaped a year ago and later ransomed for $200,000, is shown at the left, above. Search for the kidnapers, pushed by Federal agents, in the intervening months, was climaxed by yesterday's gun battle in Ocklawaha, when one of the alleged gangsters, Fred Barker, and "Ma" Barker, his mother, were slain. In the center, above, appears Adolph Bremer, wealthy St. Paul brewer, father of the kidnap victim. At the right, is Walter Magee, friend of the younger Bremer, who received ransom note, and later delivered the currency which resulted in the banker's release. The home in St. Paul, to which Bremer was returning after carrying his young daughter to school, when he was kidnaped, is shown in top panel.

State Ready to Bare Details Of Finding Lindbergh's Baby As Experts End Testimony

Four More Witnesses Positive Hauptmann Wrote Ransom Notes, They Tell Jury.

FLEMINGTON, N. J., Jan. 16, (AP) Bruno Hauptmann's murder trial was pushed tonight toward a grim word picture of Baby Lindbergh's hidden grave as prosecutors, with the positive opinions of eight experts, capped their accusation of Bruno as the ransom writer.

Thus the State, intent on sending the glum carpenter to the electric chair, is ready to show how Col. Charles A. Lindbergh's first born son lay buried in a thicket while Hauptmann allegedly wrote 14 lying letters and snatched the $50,000 ransom in a Bronx cemetery.

A negro laborer, William Allen, stumbled across the baby's shallow grave on May 12, 1932, more than two months after he was stolen from his Hopewell home a few miles away.

He will testify and then the body, found faced down, its skull horribly fractured, will be identified.

Since the defense has announced it will not dispute the identification, State's attorneys said it would not be necessary to recall Col. Lindbergh or the nurse, Betty Gow, to the stand. Both saw the body in a morgue before it was cremated.

Other witnesses will testify concerning the autopsy that fixed the cause of death. Then the State may proceed with evidence concerning the preparation of the ransom bills at the Morgan Bank in New York and the story of how the tell-tale notes began to appear in circulation five days after the ransom was paid.

The State says Bruno stole the baby from his nursery. Fell from a ladder with him and killed him in the fall.

Then, it claims, he callously stripped the sleeping suit from the body to use in bargaining for the ransom and buried his ghastly burden in the thicket, across the Hunterdon County line near Mount Rose, N. J.

The State's tedious handwriting testimony was completed at the trial's adjournment today after four more experts had called Bruno the author of all 14 notes.

Positive in their identification, they were just as sure in refuting defense insinuations that Hauptmann's handwriting was used as a disguise for somebody else.

The defense has made it plain it expects to name Isador Fisch, Hauptmann's dead alibi man, as that somebody else.

Fisch, frail little furrier, went to Germany to die. Before he sailed Hauptmann says, he left a shoe-box in which Bruno allegedly found more than $14,000 in ransom bills.

That was the carpenter's story when officers found the money hid-

Continued on Page 2

Three Killed, Four Wounded In Gun Battles

Sheriff, Cashier, Bandit Die in Fights After Raid on Bank.

LA SALLE, Ill., Jan. 16, (AP)—A gallant sheriff, a brave bank cashier and a bank robber died and three men and a boy were wounded today in a series of gun battles that raged through three counties.

Three pitched engagements, fought with guerrilla savagery by 65 participants, occurred along a 30-mile line as a quartet of gangsters sought to blast their way to freedom after they had been beaten back in an attempt to loot the Leonore (Ill.) State Bank.

The lives of Charles Bundy, 54, the bank official, and Sheriff Glenn Axline of Marshall County were snuffed out by the gunmen's bullets.

Melvin Leis, alias David Leech of Rockford, committed suicide a moment before his confederates were captured by a sharp shooting posse on a farm near McNabb, Ill.

Deputy Sheriff Reinis Brown of Marshall County; Charles Seipp, member of the La Salle County board of supervisors; Norbert Maas, 13-year-old Leonore lad; and one

Continued on Page 2

Woman Gives Graphic Account Of Gun Battle at Ocklawaha

By FLORIAN WOOD
(Copyright, 1935, by The Associated Press)

OCKLAWAHA, Jan. 16, (AP)—Mrs. A. F. Westberry, who lives across the street from the scene of a six-hour machine gun battle in which Federal agents killed Fred Barker and his mother, sought in connection with the Bremer kidnaping, lived a life-time in a few hours today.

Here is the vividly described account of what she saw and did during the withering fire:

"It was like war.

"I was suddenly awakened by guns firing. I got out of bed and as I stood up, some bullets came through the closed door between my bed room and dining room and hit the head of my bed. I was frightened.

"I managed to get to the door and cracked it open. Some more bullets came through the window and hit the facing of the door above my head.

Escaped Through Window.

"By that time there was plenty of firing. I went around by the wall and looked out of a window. The yard was full of men. I never saw so many.

"They were running all around the place. There were about five or six in my front yard. From Mr. Bradford's house across the road there was a lot of shooting. I could see streaks of fire from the guns.

"I could see the blazes from the men's guns on the outside, too. There was a lot of rapid firing like machine guns.

"After looking awhile, I felt my way back into the bedroom. It was just getting light. My daughter was in her bed.

"'What is it, mamma?' she asked me.

"'They are shooting,' I said.

"I broke open the back window of our room and told her we had to get out. About that time some more bullets came smacking through the dining room window and hit the wall.

"My daughter and I climbed through the window and got down on the ground. We were going to run to my neighbor's house about 50 yards back of our house.

"The house from which the bullets were coming was only about a hundred feet in front of my house.

Shot At, While Running.

"As we lay down on the ground for a moment we heard the firing coming louder. We got up and started to run to Mrs. Rex's house. As we ran some men yelled at us to stop. We almost tripped and fell in the deep grass but we did not stop.

"They began shooting at us. I learned later it was the Federal men. We kept on running and they kept on yelling and shooting. They must have shot at us two dozen times. They didn't know who we were. It was still a little dark.

"They did not hit us. We finally got to Mrs. Rex's house. She was awake. We got inside and went to a window.

"It was getting lighter now and we could see the men outside. It was about a hundred yards or less to the house from which the men

Continued on Page 7

SUMMARY OF THE NEWS

War Veteran Director of Lengthy Hunt

E. J. Connelley, Cincinnati, Handled Agents in Florida Gun-Fight.

WASHINGTON, Jan. 16, (AP)—A stocky, 38-year-old Federal agent, known throughout the service for his tenacity, led the 15 Government officers who killed two of the Barker gang today and were pursuing the leaders of the criminal band, tonight.

E. J. Connelley, war veteran, is in charge of the Cincinnati office of the Division of Investigation. He has had 15 years of service and has detailed knowledge of the Barker mob's personnel and their activities.

Connelley helped in laying a trap for Alvin Karpis and Arthur (Doc) Barker, criminal leaders in Cleveland, Ohio, last September. The trap failed but Connelley and his men kept working.

The death of Fred Barker, brother of Arthur, and his mother after the fierce battle in Ocklawaha, Fla., today resulted. The reckoning for Karpis and Arthur Barker, officials here hoped, may not be far away.

Connelley, who hails from Columbus, Ohio, was second in command of the 40 agents rushed to the Louisville area in October, when Mrs. Alice Speed Stoll, social leader, was abducted for a $50,000 ransom.

The Florida encounter today was regarded by the department as having done much to crack the last of the powerful roving gangs left. With the Dillinger, and Floyd groups broken, efforts have been directed principally at the Karpis-Barker syndicate.

"Ma" Barker was credited with authorship of a variety of schemes which have brought around $500,000 into the coffers of the gang.

Other than that, Department agents would give no details of her background.

Connelley has served as agent in charge of the New York and Chicago offices of the Division of Investigation. He is married and the father of two children.

He was a first lieutenant during the war.

Townsend Pension Plan in Congress

WASHINGTON, Jan. 16, (UP)—The Townsend plan reached Congress today, with its promise of $200 a month for all over 60. Rep. John Steven McGroarty (Id. Calif.) dropped it in a day ahead of President Roosevelt's long-range program for economic security, due tomorrow.

Dr. Francis E. Townsend, the 68-year-old country doctor who originated the plan, was present for the event and joined with McGroarty in a press conference.

Federal Men Slay Barker And Mother

Both Had Been Sought for $200,000 St. Paul Kidnaping; Found in Ocklawaha Hideout.

BATTLE CLIMAXES LONG HUNT FOR MOB

Officers "Shoot It Out" With Pair; Fired Upon After Calling for Surrender.

(Copyright, 1935, By The Associated Press).

OCKLAWAHA, Jan. 16, (AP)—Federal agents trapped two suspects in the Edward G. Bremer kidnaping in their Florida hide-out here today, killed them—Mrs. Kate (Ma) Barker and her son Fred—in a six hour machine gun battle and then began tearing apart the bullet spattered house in a search for some of the $200,000 ransom money.

The bodies of the mother and son were taken to Ocala, the nearby county seat, and placed in a morgue. An inquest was set for tomorrow morning. Machine guns were found beside each other.

The agents said they found four $1,000 bills on Fred Barker's body but declined to say if they found any money in the house, the garage and the large yard all of which they searched thoroughly using flashlights after nightfall. No one was permitted inside the yard.

Believed Spreading Net.

Agents presumably were spreading a relentless net for other members of the gang believed to be hiding in Florida. Some were known to be en route to Tampa and Miami, following clues.

They were told by Willie Woodbury, negro cook, that the house here had been a rendezvous for members of the underworold during the Barker occupancy. A man, said to have left the place last night, was believed to be Alvin Karpis, also sought for the Bremer kidnaping.

A couple known as "Mr. and Mrs. T. C. Blackburn," departed Sunday night and their destination was said to have been Miami. Blackburn, the cook said, was Barker's brother.

Residents of this small town said Fred Barker was lavish in his use of money during his stay here. Often he bought commodities costing small amounts and paid for them with large bills without waiting for his change, some persons said.

The Barkers' house here, residents said, had a radio which was turned on all day long, daily, and their two automobiles also were equipped with radios.

Machine Guns By Bodies.

Reports at first were that two men and a woman died in the withering shower of lead from Government machine guns, which led to the belief one of the men was Alvin Karpis, also hunted in the Bremer abduction. Later it was established only Barker and his mother were occupants of the handsome home on Lake Weir.

Machine guns were found beside the bodies of both victims. "Machine Gun" Kate and her son didn't have any intention of being taken alive.

Barker was 32 years old and his mother 55.

Last of Major Mobs.

Having already disposed of most of the notorious Dillinger and "Pretty Boy" Floyd gangs, agents had been hunting the Barkers for some time. On clues, they had come to Florida.

The Barker-Karpis gang has been described as the last of the free-running mobs at large in the United States. It was reported in Chicago that Arthur (Doc) Barker, brother of Fred, had been in Federal custody there for a week but Division of Investigation officers denied the story, published in The Evening American.

At the time of the Bremer kidnaping, Department of Justice men named "Doc" Barker and Karpis as those responsible for the kidnaping. The brewer was kidnaped January 17 1934. He was taken from St. Paul and released February 7 near

Continued on Page 7

Will Rogers Says—

WASHINGTON, D. C., Jan. 16.—I flew in here away in the middle of last night with a female co-pilot, she is the only one in existence on a regular organized line, from Cleveland to Washington and she was O. K.

Well I get in here and what do you think I find this Senate arguing over? The world court. Now I don't want to split the party, but the world court is the deadest thing in this country outside of prohibition. It's all right to fix the world, but you better get your own smoke house full of meat first.

Yours,

WILL.

'HOSTILE VALLEY' —By— Ben Ames Williams STARTS TOMORROW

Only Morning Paper in Chicago With All the Leading News Services—Associated Press, International News and Universal

Chicago Herald and Examiner

2 CENTS METROPOLITAN EDITION

54TH YEAR No. 217. Registered in U. S. Patent Office. TWO PARTS CXXX MONDAY, JANUARY 21, 1935 TWO CENTS IN CHICAGO AND SUBURBS ELSEWHERE THREE CENTS

KARPIS IN FIERCE GUN BATTLE! ESCAPES WITH PAL; WOMAN SHOT

Belgians Moving to Block German Putsch in Malmedy

Nazis Seek Return of Two Districts Lost in War.

PROTEST NEAR

League Expected to Receive Plea From Brussels.

BRUSSELS, Belgium, Jan. 20.—(A.P.) — Gendarmerie reinforcements were rushed to the cantons of Eupen and Malmedy today and a number of agitators for the return of the section to Germany were arrested.

The possibility of Belgium's protesting directly to Berlin or lodging a complaint with the league of nations concerning the re-invigorated campaign of the German sympathizers was seen in political circles today.

Nazi sympathizers, inspired by the result of last Sunday's Saar plebiscite which returned the basin to Germany, paraded several days ago to make plain their desire to have the cantons reannexed to the fatherland. They were taken from Germany under the Versailles treaty.

Nazis Driving East

By Karl H. von Wiegand.

(Copyright, 1935, Universal Service Inc.)

BERLIN, Jan. 20.—"Attention, eyes east!"

As if this command were sounded throughout the country, Germany with startling promptness and military precision was wheeled from the western battleground, swinging eastward.

Flushed by the victory in the Saar and lured by "drang nach osten" and Hitler's programmatic "Germany's future lies in the East," other territorial problems are rapidly coming to the surface.

The Nazi propaganda guns, so successful in the Saar, are being turned on the eastern front where political strategy is being concentrated.

EYES TURN TO DANZIG.

Danzig and Memel, it is hoped, will be under Hitler's swastika banner next Fall.

Sean Lester, the league of nations' Irish governor of Danzig, has voiced at Geneva "serious apprehension of Nazi activities for Danzig."

Some high Polish circles already have "written off" Danzig to Germany. An authoritative source

Turn to Page 2, Column 4.

Saar's Fires of Red Flags

Communist Offices Raided by Nazis.

SWASTIKAS FLY

Hitlerites March in Streets in Uniform.

SAARBRUECKEN, Saar Basin Territory, Jan. 20.—(A.P.)—Bonfires of red flags were being lighted throughout the Saar today by Nazis engaged in sweeping out Communist and Socialist centers from the territory.

All flags, banners and insignia found in workers' welfare centers and Socialist and Communist headquarters were burned while local Nazis dashed about singing the "Horst Wessel" and "Deutschland Ueber Alles."

Abundant anti-Nazi propaganda pamphlets used during the preplebiscite campaign added fuel to the flames.

NAZIS SEIZE CENTERS.

Virtually all welfare centers have been taken over by the Nazis, unaided by the police, and swastika flags hoisted over them. Nazi units in some districts held meetings in former "red" buildings now completely in their possession.

The property will be confiscated, Socialists fear, without recompense.

DEFY BAN ON UNIFORMS.

Nearly complete black shirt uniforms are appearing on the streets, although the governing commission has not lifted its prohibition on uniforms. Groups of storm troopers and well-disciplined boys walk the streets singing spiritedly. Sometimes they are accompanied by bands.

Newspapers, now all Nazi, proclaimed "liquidation all along the line" of Socialism.

The flow of refugees to France slackened today, only 200 persons taking their leave.

Church Destroyed by Fire; Five Hurt

EAST NEWARK, N. J., Jan. 20. (AP)—Fire destroyed St. Anthony's Roman Catholic Church today and spread through the rectory to an adjoining two-family dwelling. Damage was estimated at $35,000. Five firemen were slightly injured.

HAUPTMANN TO CALL HIMSELF FISCH 'STOOGE'

Lindy Defendant Will Place All Blame on 'Ghost' of Case; Prepares for Trip to Stand

By Damon Runyon.

(Copyright, 1935, Universal Service, Inc.)

FLEMINGTON, N. J., Jan. 20.—That Bruno Hauptmann was a "stooge" for the dead Isidor Fisch in stock market speculation will be Hauptmann's defense for any "sudden wealth" that the examination of his brokerage accounts discloses.

The defense will assert that Hauptmann was acting for his further partner, the man Hauptmann says left the Lindbergh ransom money with him, and who was often seen with Hauptmann in a New York broker's office, according to one of the state's own witnesses last week at the trial of Hauptmann for the slaying of the Lindbergh baby.

All Transactions in Captive's Name.

This witness, Edward C. Mulligan, said that Fisch and Hauptmann seemed to meet in his office by appointment, though Fisch had no account there, and all the stock transactions were in Hauptmann's name.

Edward J. Reilly, chief counsel for Hauptmann, asked the witness if it would not have been possible for Hauptmann to have been acting for Fisch without the brokerage house knowing it, and the witness said it would.

The state claims the brokerage accounts will show a considerable

Turn to Page 2, Column 1.

Ex-Candidate for Governor Arrested

NEW YORK, Jan. 20.—(AP)—A man booked as Nelson B. Clark, held here on a charge of receiving stolen goods, told police today he once was a candidate for governor of Massachusetts. He was arrested after four alleged companions slew a policeman here.

Carol's Ex-Wife Spikes Engagement

FLORENCE, Italy, Jan. 20.—(AP)—Former Queen Helen of Roumania today denied the truth of rumors published in London that she was engaged to marry a prince of the house of Colunna.

From Altar to Police Showup

GROOM'S FATE

Police Burst In on Wedding to Seize Him

From his wedding to the Sunday detective bureau showup!

Police who arrested a bridegroom on the steps of the church where the ceremony was performed yesterday took him to the W. North av. station for questioning in an automobile larceny case and had to play host to the entire bridal party.

Bruno Austin, 26, and Marie Brenko, 18, of 2332 Augusta blvd. were married at the Russian Holy Trinity Cathedral, 1121 N. Leavitt st, by Arch-Priest S. Snegiress. It was a colorful and popular wedding with 300 guests present. The bride, attended by six bridesmaids, wore a twenty-foot lace veil born by two tiny pages.

INTERRUPT FAREWELLS.

Into the glad goodbyes, the rice and the confetti and an old shoe or two—for the luck that wasn't there—burst two squads of police. They surrounded the guests and the bridal party and from their midst plucked the bridegroom.

Bruno Austin, 26, of 6969 Oakdale av., and Marie Brenko, 18, of 2332 Augusta blvd., were married at the Russian Holy Trinity Cathedral, 1121 N. Leavitt st., by Archpriest S. Snegiress. It was a colorful wedding with 300 guests present. The bride, attended by six bridesmaids, wore a twenty-foot lace veil borne by two tiny pages.

Bundling the bridegroom into a police wagon, the officers drove off—to be followed by a weeping bride, an angry best-man, bewildered parents and curious bridesmaids. At the station house the brand new Mrs. Austin threw herself into her husband's arms, crying:

"They can't take you away from me."

SENT TO SHOWUP.

But they did. It seems that Austin has forfeited bonds in an automobile larceny case. He was removed to the detective bureau in time to take his place in the regular weekly showup.

Meanwhile the disconsolate bride, her long veil hanging over her arm, was persuaded to go home with her parents.

Expect Decision on Mooney Today

WASHINGTON, Jan. 20.—(I.N.S.)—The Supreme Court is expected to announce its decision tomorrow on the petition of Thomas Mooney for a review of his charge he was convicted on perjured testimony. Mooney was sentenced to life imprisonment in connection with the bombing of the San Francisco preparedness day parade.

Marshal Pilsudski Ill, Berlin Hears

BERLIN, Jan. 20.—(AP)—Reports reached Berlin today that Marshal Joseph Pilsudski, the Polish dictator, is ill. They came from military quarters in Warsaw, but several credible circles here pointed out that Pilsudski, who reputedly receives no officials except when in perfect health, has conferred recently with several statesmen.

SUB-ZERO WAVE RACING ON CITY; BRINGING SNOW

Mountain and Plains States Deep in Drifts; Frigid Zone Extends Far South as Texas

Temperatures in the path of the cold wave advancing on Chicago yesterday were:

Battleford, Sask.	–54	Soda Springs, Cal.	–16
Havre, Mont.	–32	No. Platte, Neb.	–12
Helena, Mont.	–28	Sioux City, Ia.	–12
Devil's Lake, N.D.	–28	Norton, Kan.	–11
Spokane, Wash.	–22	Charles City, Ia.	–10
Cheyenne, Wyo.	–22	Omaha, Neb.	– 8
Valentine, Neb.	–18	Minneapolis	– 8
Ainsworth, Neb.	–19	Des Moines	– 2

Although Chicago experienced a mild 40-degree temperature yesterday, the coldest wave of the year, accompanied by snow, was due to greet Chicagoans this morning, the weather bureau warned last night.

Although several days behind Forecaster W. P. Day's schedule, it had advanced last evening as far as Moline, where temperatures fell suddenly to 17 degrees.

EVEN COLDER TONIGHT.

Mr. Day predicted that the mercury would drop to between 5 and 10 degrees below zero Monday night—a record here for 1935, since two degrees above zero on New Year's Day has been the coldest to date.

Driven by a fresh, strong wind, the cold snap placed all the country between here and the Yukon under Winter's thralldom. It left in its wake drifts of thirty to fifty feet in the Sierras and eastern Oregon, while Portage County, Wis., first midwestern section to receive a visit from the wave, had twenty-one inches of snow.

COLD FOR SEVERAL DAYS.

Forecaster Day could see nothing but cold weather ahead for several days. He said there might not be relief for a week.

Only a zone of tropical air, blown up by a sustaining wind from the Gulf, held off the cold wave during the last few days, said Mr. Day, who had predicted its arrival earlier in the week.

Temperatures were to drop steadily, Mr. Day said, as the cold moved in and took command. Already zero temperatures were reported all over western Wisconsin and Missouri.

WAVE SPREADS SOUTH.

The forecaster said that the wave extended as far south as Amarillo, Tex., where the temperature fell in twenty-four hours from 54 to 17, and he predicted that it would rush eastward to cover the whole country between the Rockies and Atlantic seaboard by the end of the week.

Mr. Day said that although blizzards were raging over the plains states, the wind here would not be strong enough to bring blizzard conditions, but that there would be a steady fall.

BREMER KIDNAP HOUSE

U. S. FINDS DEN IN BENSENVILLE; BANKER HELD THERE 23 DAYS

Death Penalty Possible

The house where for twenty-three days a year ago Edward G. Bremer, St. Paul banker and brewer, was imprisoned until he bought his release with $200,000 ransom from Alvin Karpis and Arthur Barker was located by Department of Justice agents yesterday in suburban Bensenville, northwest of Chicago.

It was learned that the government had arrested the owner of the house, who rented it to the Karpis-Barker gang and that he will be taken to St. Paul in an effort to identify Barker, who is in custody there, before the grand jury acts today or tomorrow.

DEATH PENALTY POSSIBLE.

By establishing the location of the hideout as in Illinois, authorities now will be able to indict Barker and Karpis, his sole surviving confederate, under the Lindbergh law, which makes a death sentence possible for kidnapers convicted of transporting their captive over state lines.

Government officials would not state whether Bremer came here to identify the house.

Karpis, after his narrow escape with Harry Campbell at Atlantic City yesterday, was expected to head for a Chicago hideout, and the Department of Justice, warning Chicago police to be on the lookout, had three hideouts in the city and two outside under surveillance, as well as the homes of Karpis' mother and two sisters here.

The government notified police that the fugitives might be in a green sedan bearing New Jersey 1935 license A-3073 or in a black sedan with white wall tires. The message ended:

"Caution should be used in approaching, and, if identified, shoot first and talk afterward."

BARKER CALLED INFORMER.

Barker, captured here January 8, the same night that a confederate, Russell Gibson was shot and killed in a federal raid on an apartment at 3920 Pine Grove av., was reported to have given government agents the information that led to the Florida slaying last Wednesday of his own mother, Kate Barker, and his brother, Fred.

Implicated in the Bremer kidnaping, they were surrounded at Lake Weir by agents led by Special Agent E. J. Connelly of Chicago, and killed when they refused to surrender. Karpis also was supposedly betrayed by Barker. He had left the Barkers' Florida cottage after a visit of several weeks just before government forces arrived.

8,000 WOMEN PLAN STRIKE

Preparations were made yesterday by the International Ladies' Garment Workers' Union for a strike this week in twenty-two Chicago cotton garment manufacturing concerns for refusal to agree to "collective bargaining" with Local 75 of the union.

David Dubinsky, international president of the union, met at the Morrison Hotel with Morris Bialis, manager of the Chicago joint board of the organization; M. A. Goldstein, secretary-treasurer, and Meyer Bernstein, chairman, and gave his sanction to the strike. The date of the strike will not be announced in advance.

There was a ray of hope that the strike may be averted. Dubinsky said that the manufacturers would be given one more chance to meet the union in conference this week. Previous attempts of the union to get the manufacturers to meet its representatives met with failure.

The strike would directly affect 8,000 garment workers and throw an additional 2,000 employes of the factories out of work, according to Mr. Bialis.

FRENCH BLOCS IN GUN BATTLE

CHARTRES, France, Jan. 20.—(AP)—A gun battle between nationalists and leftists in which one was shot in the foot terrorized street crowds here today.

Thirty shots were exchanged when members of the anti-Fascist "common front" mobbed the "patriotic youths" as the latter started back to Paris after attending a meeting of their organization.

The fighting started in Horse Market Square where the leftists had gathered in counter-demonstration against the nationalist meeting. Heavy forces of mobile guards stepped in and dispersed the crowds.

Police at Amiens broke up a forbidden parade of 3,500 "common front" members.

Clothes Take Fire; Burns Kill Woman

Mrs. Josephine De Francisco, 51, of 52 W. Thirty-seventh st., Steger, died in the St. James Hospital, Chicago Heights, yesterday of burns suffered December 27, when her dress caught fire from a stove in her home. She was standing with her back to the stove warming herself when her clothes ignited. Her screams awoke her son, Nicholas, 21, who smothered the flames with an overcoat.

ENEMY NO. 1 SHOOTS WAY OUT OF TRAP

Girl Companions Taken in Hotel at Atlantic City; Hundreds Join in Big Manhunt

(Copyright, 1935, by the Associated Press.)

ATLANTIC CITY, N. J., Jan. 20. — Alvin Karpis, America's "public enemy number 1", blazed his way with spitting machine gun fire early today from a police trap laid for him in a small hotel.

With Harry Campbell, another hunted Midwestern gangster, he shouted defiance to the police command to surrender, fired on the police, stole a motor car, tried to rescue two women companions from police and then, with guns roaring, sped away.

One policeman narrowly escaped death when a bullet pierced his cap.

Agents Say Campbell May be Wounded.

The Department of Justice, broadcasting an alarm, said there was some likelihood Campbell was wounded, and he might not have been able to get out of Atlantic City.

One of the two women, Dolores Delaney, described as "Karpis' girl," was slightly wounded in the leg. The other woman was identified as Louise Campbell, wife of Harry. One of the women was reported awaiting the birth of a child.

The latter, police say, also is identified as Winona Burdette of Tulsa, Okla. Both women are in their early twenties and attractive.

Tip Comes From Police in Florida.

The tip that led to the trap for Karpis, wanted for the Edward Bremer kidnaping in St. Paul, in which a $200,000 ransom was paid, came from Florida police. It told Atlantic City officers to watch for a car bearing a Florida license, and to be careful, as the passengers were "two bad men."

The Atlantic City police found

A $500,000 HEIRESS!

Girl Born to Donnelley Widow; Gets Half Father's Estate

KANSAS CITY, Jan. 20.—(AP)—A baby girl—heir to approximately $500,000—was born in New York today to Mrs. Paul F. Donnelly, widow of a wealthy Kansas City business man, friends here were advised.

Mr. Donnelly died September 7 in Hartford, Conn.

Under an agreement, one half his estate of nearly $1,000,000, amassed in the women's dress business in association with his former wife, now Mrs. James A. Reed, will go to the child. The other half will be divided among the 24-year-old widow and eight members of her husband's family.

Mr. Donnelly married Miss Virginia George, a former actress, in Florida in February, 1933, after he and Mrs. Nell Quinlan Donnelly were divorced here. The first Mrs. Donnelly later was married to Senator Reed of Missouri.

Seek to Re-indict 'Schultz' for Tax

ALBANY, Jan. 20.—(I.N.S.)—Arthur ("Dutch Schultz") Flegenheimer, who is hoping to evade his federal indictment in New York for tax evasion because he lives in the Albany internal revenue district, may be re-indicted here, it was indicated today by Assistant Attorney General John H. McEvers.

LATE RACE RESULTS

CALIENTE RESULTS.

FIRST RACE.			
Bens Hope	11.20	5.60	3.00
Moon Face		7.60	3.60
Dirigible			2.60
SECOND RACE.			
Susie Price	39.60	9.40	5.20
Wise Baby		3.00	2.80
Nite Rap			3.80
THIRD RACE.			
Ima Dreamer	5.20	3.00	2.60
Threat		4.00	4.40
Enthusiastic Edward			5.60
FOURTH RACE.			
Plum Shot	8.40	4.40	3.40
Honuapo		3.80	2.80
Ygnacio			5.00
FIFTH RACE.			
Lady Riaf	56.40	30.00	9.00
Brown Bank		5.20	3.20
Star Royal			3.00
SIXTH RACE.			
Carol Hills	14.80	5.40	3.00
Platinum Blonde		3.20	2.40
Opium			3.20
SEVENTH RACE.			
Dispeller	14.80	7.00	4.60
Gabbo		5.00	3.00
Crap Shooter			3.60
EIGHTH RACE.			
Sausalito	10.60	5.20	4.00
Suitor		5.00	3.40
Canny Scot			4.80
NINTH RACE.			
Bud Brooms	9.60	4.80	2.40
Lucky Jack		3.40	3.20
Cloiwald			2.40

THE WEATHER

CHICAGO AND VICINITY—Probably snow in morning; severe cold wave, temperature near zero.

LAKE MICHIGAN—Strong north to northwest winds; snow.

ILLINOIS—Snow probably in morning; severe cold wave.

INDIANA—Severe cold wave.

WISCONSIN—Partly cloudy and cold.

MISSOURI—Partly cloudy and cold.

IOWA—Probably fair and cold.

LOWER MICHIGAN—Snow; moderate cold wave.

UPPER MICHIGAN—Probably snow in morning; severe cold wave.

Culloden Wins Seventh Race at Santa Anita Track

COMPLETE SPORTS

Herald and Examiner

54TH YEAR No. 220. Registered in U. S. Patent Office. TWO PARTS C★ ...AY, JANUARY 24, 1935 TWO CENTS IN CHICAGO AND SUBURBS ELSEWHERE THREE CENTS

2 CENTS METROPOLITAN EDITION

MASSACRE CONFESSION PUTS CAPONE IN SHADOW OF CHAIR!

Today

The News Reel Tells Cool in Chicago. Crime Goes On. Real World Flight.

—BY ARTHUR BRISBANE—

CHICAGO, Jan. 23.—This ought to interest Washington. In Chicago talking pictures, Senator Joseph Robinson of Arkansas appears speaking in favor of the United States going into the world court. Audiences remain silent, a few hiss.

Then, as Universal Service tells you, Senator Hiram Johnson of California appears on the same screen, telling why America should NOT become entangled in the world court or any other European complication, and "THE AUDIENCE LET LOOSE A THUNDER OF APPLAUSE IN APPROVAL OF HIS STAND."

What happens in Chicago theaters would happen in any American boarding house, farm house, restaurant or street car, and President Roosevelt, who wants to do what the people want, and senators that are planning to vote foolishly should know it.

Brisk, stimulating air in Chicago this morning, one below zero. Sixteen below is predicted.

You meet all sorts of weather in the short run from the Pacific Coast.

Warm weather, with people bathing, in Los Angeles, ten degrees below zero at Gallup, New Mexico; warm sunshine at Dodge City, Kas.; one below zero here.

Kansas has abandoned its ancient specialty of complaining, and is almost cheerful.

The government is pouring money into the laps of farmers, in various ways. Beef yesterday sold at twelve dollars and fifty cents a hundred on the hoof, highest price since 1930.

Pork sells above eight dollars. It was selling for three dollars not long ago. The farmers' turn has come.

It is interesting to read about those savage nomads, Assai Imara tribesmen, fighting along the border of Ethiopia and French Somaliland, with "short, sharp cutlasses, and 1874 model rifles," fighting with wildly beating tom-toms to encourage them.

The fighters recently murdered twenty members of the French colony, including the French administrator. France is sending a few airplanes that will quiet the tom-toms.

Those tom-tom beating savages that recognize no law and no ruler could learn something among the gangsters of Chicago and other big American cities.

The Chicago American this afternoon publishes details of the "St. Valentine's Day Massacre," when seven racketeers were lined up, faces to the wall, by rival gangsters and shot dead. That wholesale killing in a bootleg-racketeer war is mild compared with a story told here in court yesterday.

Albert Semple related details of a killing paid for and far more dangerous to society than any crime of professional gangsters. Semple, indicted for murder, turned

Turn to Page 2, Column 2.

LEGISLATORS VOTE AGAINST LEAGUE COURT

State Representatives Hurl Warning at Washington; Crush Effort to Shelve Issue

By Harold Polland.

SPRINGFIELD, Ill., Jan. 23.—A ringing appeal to keep the United States out of the league of nations court was adopted today by the House of Representatives of the Illinois General Assembly.

All efforts to delay consideration of the resolution by sending it to a committee were crushed. In a wave of indignation, born of the fact that early action at Washington favoring adherence was feared, Democrats joined with Republicans in sweeping the state's formal protest to victory and speeding it to the Senate.

OBJECTORS ARE DOWNED.

In vain did a few powerful administration Democrats — vowing their personal opposition to entering the back door of the league of nations—urge that the matter go over. Some even pleaded that they were "on the spot." With the knowledge that the people of the state were behind them, having voted three times against the proposal, the advocates of immediate action took the bit in their teeth.

By a vote of 71 to 25 they downed a motion to table a motion to suspend the rules. Then, with a whooping viva voce vote which no one dared challenge with a request for a roll call, they adopted the resolution.

The resolution is directed to President Roosevelt, Vice President Garner, the United States Senate and Senators James Hamilton Lewis and William H. Dieterich of Illinois.

DEMOCRATS SPLIT.

The only objections to immediate consideration came from Democrats, but on the showdown nineteen Democrats joined with fifty-two Republicans in defeating the effort at delay. All twenty-five negative votes were Democratic.

Advocates of quick adoption of the protest insisted that an emerg-

Turn to Page 5, Column 1.

THE WEATHER

FOR CHICAGO AND VICINITY—Fair with rising temperature in afternoon; fresh northwest winds becoming moderate southwest.

The following temperature readings were recorded from 3 a. m. yesterday:

3 a. m.	7	9:40 a. m.	-1	4 p. m.	3
4 a. m.	5	10 a. m.	1	5 p. m.	1
5 a. m.	4	11 a. m.	2	6 p. m.	0
6 a. m.	3	12 Noon	3	7 p. m.	-2
7 a. m.	2	1 p. m.	4	8 p. m.	-3
8 a. m.	1	2 p. m.	4		
9 a. m.	0	3 p. m.	3		

LAKE MICHIGAN—Fresh northerly winds, diminishing and becoming moderate southwest; partly cloudy.

An advisory storm warning has been issued for Lake Michigan.

ILLINOIS—Fair, with slowly rising temperature in afternoon.

INDIANA—Fair, with slowly rising temperature, except in extreme southeast portion.

LOWER MICHIGAN—Partly cloudy, not so cold in west and north portions.

WISCONSIN—Fair; not so cold.

MISSOURI—Fair, with slowly rising temperature.

IOWA—Fair and warmer.

Rob U. S. Mail of $129,000

SEIZE CASH

Driver Kidnaped by Five Robbers; Escape

FALL RIVER, Mass., Jan. 23.—(A.P.)—In the largest mail robbery in the history of New England, five bandits armed with machine guns and pistols today held up a United States mail truck and escaped with $129,000 in currency.

FALL RIVER, Mass., Jan. 23.—(AP)—In the largest mail robbery in the history of New England, five bandits armed with machine guns and pistols today held up a United States mail truck and escaped with $129,000 in currency.

Apparently following a carefully prepared plan, a sedan cut ahead of the small truck, forcing it to stop. Two of the sedan's four occupants leaped aboard the truck.

DRIVER TIED UP.

Herbert B. Reid, 43, who was taking registered mail from a railroad station to the postoffice, was forced into the sedan, bound and blindfolded.

The truck then was convoyed by the sedan to South Somerset, two and a half miles away, where a fifth member of the gang waited in another car. The truck was driven to a back road.

TAKE KEY AWAY

Reid was forced to surrender the key to the truck compartment. The loot was tossed into the waiting automobile and the five sped away.

Reid succeeded in freeing himself and hailed a passing motorist.

The Postoffice Department immediately offered rewards totaling $10,000 for the five robbers.

Infanta and Her Prince Sail for U.S.

SOUTHAMPTON, England, Jan. 23.—(I.N.S.) — Prince Alessandro Torlonia, his bride, the Infanta Beatriz of Spain, and Sir Malcolm Campbell, British speed ace, were among the notables who sailed for the United States today aboard the Aquitania.

Gov. Murphy Sails to Visit Roosevelt

MANILA, P. I., Jan. 23.—(I.N.S.) —Governor General Frank Murphy today sailed for the United States and a conference with President Roosevelt regarding the freedom of the islands.

C. J. Neumeier Gets U. S. Housing Post

WASHINGTON, Jan. 23—(I.N.S.) —Chester J. Neumeier of Minneapolis today was appointed associate of the Federal Housing Administration for Minnesota.

Senators Confirm Katharine Lenroot

WASHINGTON, Jan. 23.—(I.N.S.) —The Senate today confirmed appointment of Katharine F. Lenroot of Wisconsin, as chief of the children's bureau, department of labor.

SCIENTIST TIES KIDNAP LADDER TO HAUPTMANN

Forestry Expert Demonstrates in Court; Marks Match Those on Criminal's Lumber

By Damon Runyon.

FLEMINGTON, N. J., Jan. 23.—One of the most astonishing tales of scientific detective work ever related as fact or fiction is poured into the ears of the amazed jurors in the Lindbergh baby murder trial of Bruno Hauptmann today, as the state virtually closes its case by apparently keeping its promise to "wrap the kidnap ladder around Hauptmann's neck."

This tale, told by a bald, mild-looking, middle-aged man from the woods of Wisconsin, a middle-aged expert for the federal government named Arthur Koehler, puts the greatest fictional exploits of Sherlock Holmes in the shade.

Makes Plane Marks Like Those on Ladder.

Using Judge Trenchard's rostrum as a work bench, Koehler takes one of Hauptmann's carpenter planes and planes a slab of wood before the eyes of the jury and the spectators in the snow-bound courtroom. Then he demonstrates to the jury how the plane marks on the wood are the same as those left by the plane that fashioned the kidnap ladder.

He almost falls over as he puts his weight behind a big push at the plane to make sure he slices off a good sized shaving, and at this, Hauptmann, watching him intently with the sunken eyes, gives

Turn to Page 7, Column 1.

Now U.S. Can Build Navy! Says McAdoo

ROME, Jan. 23.—(AP)—W. G. McAdoo, en route home from the Far East, said today he was pleased that Japan had denounced the Washington naval treaty "because this will enable the United States to build the navy of which she has a need." He arrived in good health after a seven-day airplane journey from Singapore.

LATEST RACES

SANTA ANITA

FIFTH RACE.

Cold Water	29.20	13.20	6.20
The Bailiff		4.60	3.80
Blondella			4.80

SIXTH RACE.

Arson	6.80	4.20	3.20
Major Lanphier		4.80	3.40
Storm			3.80

SEVENTH RACE.

Culloden	21.40	10.00	6.80
Eighth Pole		5.60	3.80
Tut Tut			5.00

Other Race Results in Sports Pages.

NORTH POLE ON WAY HERE; -16 LIKELY TODAY

Hope for Lake Wind to Break Cold; 73 Below in Canada; Gales Lash Atlantic Coast

It will be 12 to 16 degrees below zero at breakfast time, the weather man said last night—

If Lake Michigan, Chicago's refrigeration plant in the Summer and heater in the Winter, doesn't come to the rescue. And the lake may do it.

WARMER TOMORROW.

Anyway, the cold isn't going to last, and there isn't another cold wave in sight, after this one passes. Today, according to Forecaster W. P. Day, the temperature should climb to 10 or 15 above, or even more, and tomorrow will be warmer still.

In Ontario they'd be in their shirt sleeves in weather like this. It was 73 below yesterday at Iroquois Falls and 62 below at White River.

Eveleth, Minn., was the coldest spot in the United States, at 51 below. The Twin Cities reported 30 below, Duluth 38 below.

SEVEN DIE HERE.

The minimum here was 1 below, at 9:40 a. m. Several fires were blamed upon overheated stoves and furnaces. The cold wave toll here rose to seven when an unidentified man about 60 was found dead from cold at 507 W. North av., and William Kelly, a legless man living at 263 Alexander st., was found frozen to death at Eighteenth and Federal streets.

Hundreds of refugees, forced from their homes in northwest Mississippi and western Tennessee by flood waters of the Mississippi River, hovered in makeshift quarters.

New U.S. Destroyer Dale Is Launched

NEW YORK, Jan. 23.—(I.N.S.)—The newest U. S. navy destroyer—the Dale—was christened with champagne today by Mrs. Edward C. Dale, wife of the great-grandson of Richard Dale, first lieutenant under Admiral John Paul Jones, naval hero of the American revolution.

ASKS U. S. TO SEVER RUSSIAN RELATIONS

WASHINGTON, Jan. 23.—(I.N.S.) A resolution calling for abrogation of diplomatic relations with Soviet Russia was introduced in the Senate late today by Senator Barbour of New Jersey, Republican.

Barbour declared Russia has failed to keep her promise to stop the dissemination of subversive propaganda in America and said that projected trade stimulation between the two nations "has proved a delusion."

Bolton Names Six as Slayers of 7

Enemy No. 1 Again?

BLAMED FOR MASSACRE—Al Capone, former Chicago gang lord, now in prison, who ordered the Moran mob "wiped out," according to the confession of Byron Bolton yesterday.

'Public Enemy No. 1' in Captive's Story to U. S. Agents.

BALK LIBERTY

Ten-Year Term of Tax Evader Would Be Extended.

Through the purported confession of Byron Bolton that he and five others perpetrated Chicago's ghastliest crime—the St. Valentine's Day massacre of 1929—federal officials yesterday were said to be hopeful of pinning those seven murders on Al Capone, America's Public Enemy No. 1.

This, if successful, would take Capone from Alcatraz, where he is serving eleven years for income tax evasion, and head him toward the electric chair.

Names Five as Fellow Killers.

Bolton, arrested January 10 at 3920 Pine Grove av. in the federal raid that brought death to Russell Gibson, named as his fellow-killers:

Murray Humphreys, now-imprisoned successor of Capone.

Gus Winkler, former North Side gambling boss, killed a year ago.

Fred ("Killer") Burke, now serving a life term in Michigan

Turn to Page 4, Column 1.

Broker Charged With Embezzling $50,000

Charges that he embezzled $50,000 from a trust fund for the children of the late Mrs. Louise S. Schmidt, widow of a soap manufacturer, were made yesterday in a warrant issued against Otto C. Kraemer, a broker living at 827 S. Prospect av., Park Ridge, by Judge Matthew D. Hartigan in the Felony Court.

After Mrs. Schmidt foreclosed a mortgage on a garage at 1622 N. Wells st., the money was paid to Kraemer, who was supposed to put it in the trust fund, the charges read. Beneficiaries of the fund are Franklin R. Schmidt of 2923 Nelson st., now operating the soap works; Mrs. Louise Steiner of 2761 Windsor av., and Misses Elizabeth B. and Rose L. Schmidt of 2600 Windsor avenue.

Kraemer, the Schmidt children charge, had induced their mother to let him put the money in a trust fund for them prior to her death in 1930. Having received no income, they say, they asked him for the money on October 25.

While state's attorney's police were searching for him, Kraemer was reached by telephone. He said that the facts as stated by the Schmidts are not true and that he would immediately consult his attorney concerning his legal status.

'HOSTILE VALLEY'—Ben Ames Williams' Wonder Story of 1935— START IT TODAY PAGE 6

THE BALTIMORE NEWS
and The Baltimore Post
The Largest Daily Circulation in the Entire South

The Only Newspaper in Maryland with Four Great Newspaper Services — Associated Press, International News Service, Universal Service and United Press.

VOL. CXXVII.—NO. 111. Entered as second-class matter at Baltimore Postoffice. Copyright, 1935, by American Newspapers, Inc. TUESDAY EVENING, SEPTEMBER 10, 1935 PRICE 2 CENTS

THE WEATHER
Generally fair tonight and Wednesday, slightly colder tonight with the lowest temperature in the suburbs about 50 degrees and 55 in the center of the city; warmer Wednesday

MEAN TEMPERATURES.

Baltimore.....	74	Chicago.......	64
Atlanta.......	82	Omaha.........	62
Boston........	59	Los Angeles...	68
New York......	71	Salt Lake City.	68
Portland, Maine	64	Seattle.......	63
Washington...	75	New Orleans...	79

Duce Orders 20,000,000 To Mobilize

HUEY LONG DIES OF BULLET WOUND

Today

A Dreadful Crime.
Senator Long's New Book.
W. E. Holler Announces.
Bathtub Danger.

By Arthur Brisbane

ALL Americans sympathize deeply with Senator Long's widow and children. Those that have disagreed with Senator Long's political views will regret, perhaps more than others, his death.

Senator Long, who with only good reason had predicted an attempt to assassinate him, was a man who fought in the open, said what he thought, in the Senate and elsewhere.

In a country where speech and opinion are not hampered, and the ballot box is the final arbiter, there should be no trace of government "tempered by assassination."

Three Presidents of the United States have been murdered—Lincoln, Garfield, McKinley—and murderous attempts have been made upon the late Theodore Roosevelt and President Franklin D. Roosevelt.

The conclusion is that the Secret Service which protects our Presidents, or private bodyguards, such as usually accompanied Senator Long, cannot be relied on to thwart the assassin's plan.

Dr. Carl A. Weiss, Jr., who shot down Senator Long, was instantly killed by the Senator's bodyguards. Examination of his body showed 30 bullet holes in front, 29 in the back and 2 in the head, but the sub-machine guns and bodyguard could not protect Senator Long.

Universal Service sends information that Senator Huey Long, just before his assassination, had completed a new book, called "My First Days in the White House." Many throughout the country ask themselves what effect, if any, the death of Huey Long will have upon the 1936 election.

In his "My First Days in the White House" Senator Long is said to discuss frankly important political personalities—Senators Borah, Couzens and various members of the Cabinet. All politicians will be intensely interested in the details of the book.

In the book "President Long" allows farm organizations to appoint the Secretary of Agriculture, picks a Postmaster General from the regular postal service, names former Governor Alfred E. Smith Director of the Budget, with Cabinet rank.

He has John D. Rockefeller, Jr., and Winthrop W. Aldrich, head of the Chase National Bank, assisting him in drafting a plan for a redistribution of wealth. That will surprise many and sell well. It will be illustrated with caricatures of public persons, including one of Senator Long.

W. E. Holler, vice-president of Chevrolet Motor Company, announces ninety-nine thousand and eighteen new Chevrolet cars and trucks sold in August, twenty-four thousand nine hundred and seventy-nine more than in July—an all-time record for August.

That is good news for Mr. Holler, Mr. Knudsen and also Alfred P. Sloan, Jr., who runs General Motors; also good news for the rest of the country. The sale of automobiles is the most reliable gauge of increasing business and prosperity. And every family that gets a new automobile is, for that reason, a happier family.

Within a few days two women, one past sixty, the other seventy years old, have been found dead in their bathtubs, apparently drowned. The slippery surface of a porcelain tub is dangerous for older persons. They should observe the greatest care. A slip, the head striking the edge of the tub, can easily cause unconsciousness, followed by drowning.

Rubber factories should make and extensively advertise rubber mats for the bottom of bathtubs, with a suction arrangement to prevent slipping.

Stealing gas from an electric gasoline pump in Chicago, thieves broke the pump, flooding streets and alleys six inches deep with 16,000 gallons of gasoline. A stray spark or match would have cost many lives.

Gasoline storage below ground to avoid risk, prevent evaporation of gas and diminish lightning risks would be desirable.

Before the arrival of the automobile gasoline had practically no value and was a by-product in petroleum processing. On one occasion a great quantity of gasoline, "to get rid of it," was dumped into a Pennsylvania stream. It floated. Live coals from a locomotive passing over a bridge set fire to it. The bridge and many houses were destroyed.

DUCE ORDERS 20 MILLIONS TO MOBILIZE

Calls for One-Day Turnout Of All Fascist Strength; Test for Quick Rise to Arms

(Copyright, 1935, by United Press.)

ROME, Sept. 10.—Premier Benito Mussolini today prepared for any eventually in Europe by ordering a trial mobilization for the near future of the full force, civil and military, of the nation—some 20,000,000 men, boys and girls.

It was admitted that the mobilization order would be issued as the Italian expeditionary force crossed the Ethiopian frontier in Africa.

By Associated Press.

ROME, Sept. 10.—Premier Mussolini today ordered a nation-wide one-day mobilization of all the Fascist forces of Italy. The mobilization will test the nation's ability to spring to arms at a moment's notice.

The order involves 2,000,000 members of the Fascist party and 650,000 young Fascists between eighteen and twenty-one. They will be accompanied by 4,000,000 Fascist boys.

SIRENS, BELLS

The order set no date of the mobilization, but announced that it would be proclaimed by sirens and church bells.

Fascists living abroad are required to telegraph the secretary of the party.

Mobilization will be held in Italy's colonies.

REVIEWS GUARD

Il Duce today reviewed several thousand young Fascists, members of the Avanguardisti, and told them:

"You are more than a hope. You are a certainty. To whom is the right of battle reserved?"

"To us!" the youth answered in a tremendous shout.

HITLER SUPPORTS ITALY

Adolf Hitier's assurance of collaboration with Italy on a basis of "reciprocal comprehension of the vital necessities of the two peoples," was accepted in informed circles to mean support of Italy's expan-

Continued on Page 6, Column 1.

Treasury Balance

WASHINGTON, Sept. 10—(U. P.). Government expenses and receipts for the current fiscal year to September 7, compared with last year:

	This Year.	Last Year.
Expenses.	$1,372,754,267.52	$1,095,527,307.48
Receipts...	642,202,200.96	623,153,203.96
Deficit...	$730,552,066.56	$472,374,103.52
Cash bal.	$1,469,995,983.14	$2,112,765,264.64

Temperatures

Midnight ..	64	6 A. M....	60
1 A. M....	64	7 A. M....	61
2 A. M....	63	8 A. M....	63
3 A. M....	62	9 A. M....	66
4 A. M....	62	10 A. M....	68
5 A. M....	61		

"Watch Your Step" read the sign over Senator Huey Long's head as he boarded the train in Washington at the close of the Congressional session, en route to New Orleans and home. He did "watch his step," but not closely enough and met death in the corridor of the 33-story Louisiana Capitol Building from the bullet fired from an assassin's pistol. His guards, caught napping for just one fatal instant, then sprang into action and mowed down the killer, Dr. Carl A. Weiss, with slugs from their guns. Picture from International News Photograph Service.

POLITICAL FOES BLAMED BY COPELAND; STATE FUNERAL PLANNED

By International News Service.

NEW YORK, Sept. 10.—The charge that Senator Huey Long was assassinated indirectly by Louisiana political enemies was made today by Senator Royal S. Copeland, New York Democrat. Copeland said he was convinced Long's slayer had been keyed to murder pitch by Long's foes.

(Copyright, 1935, by Associated Press.)

BATON ROUGE, La., Sept. 10.—Senator Huey P. Long, the farm youth who wanted to make "every man a king" and gained unprecedented power in Louisiana, died today, the victim of an assassin. He was forty-two years old.

The political "dictator" of Louisiana and possible Presidential candidate next year, died at 5.06 A. M., Eastern standard time. His family and close political associates were at his bedside.

His death left his powerful political machine, which controls practically every office in the State, without a directing head. There is no "dictator" to take his place.

FOES TAKE COURAGE

While his leaders held conferences to decide what steps to take, the Senator's death gave courage to his opponents, whose split into several factions had aided Long's ascent to power.

Friends and enemies alike expressed regret at his death, the sole topic of conversation in every Baton Rouge household. Many intimate with the Senator showed marks of tears.

Fourteen members of the One Hundred and Forty-first Field Artillery, Louisiana National Guard, from New Orleans under Capt. Edward P. Benezech, were ordered here as a guard of honor. Later a company of infantry here received a like assignment.

ENDS LONG VIGIL

The widow, who married him 22 years ago after her alibi testimony saved him from charges in a shooting scrape, was led dry-eyed from Our Lady of the Lake Hospital. She had been at his bedside in constant vigil since Sunday night.

A "gunshot wound in the abdomen" was officially given as the cause of the Senator's death by Dr. E. L. Sanderson, who said there were "not necessarily" any complications.

Dr. G. S. Long, a brother of the Senator, was

Turn Over.

THE WEATHER
Fair, colder; moderate to fresh northwest winds.
High tides at 1:15 a. m. and 1:23 p. m.
Light all vehicles at :10 p. m.

DAILY RECORD

Copyright, 1935, by Northeastern Publishing Co., 5 Winthrop Square, Boston.
BOSTON'S HOME PICTURE NEWSPAPER
Entered as second class mail matter at Boston, Mass., under the Acts of March 3, 1879.

FINAL EDITION

Vol. 244, No. 100 32 Pages Boston, Thursday, October 24, 1935 PRICE TWO CENTS

DUTCH SCHULTZ SHOT DOWN!

DYING IN GANG WAR; FIVE PALS WOUNDED

Newark, N. J., Oct. 23 (AP)—Gang guns blazed tonight in a vicious outburst of racketeering rivalry, and Arthur "Dutch Schultz" Flegenheimer and three lieutenants fell on two fronts.

SCHULTZ IN 1925

SCHULTZ IN 1935

International News Photo

Schultz was critically wounded, his lungs punctured and a bullet lodged near the heart, and two henchmen were shot down in a Newark tavern.

A third member of the gang dropped in a hail of bullets that struck a subway barber shop refuge he sought near crowded 47th st. and Seventh ave. in New York at almost the same time.

Police definitely linked the shootings with the Brooklyn hatchet-torch killing early today of Louis "Pretty Louie" Amberg, the seventh to die in recent weeks during a New York gang war over control of petty rackets.

Deputy Chief Inspector Francis J. Kear, commanding detectives in Manhattan, began a hunt for Charles "Lucky Charlie" Luciano, whom he accused of having set a "zero hour" to extirpate the Schultz legions.

Kear said Luciano nominaly owned a chain of cabarets but he described him as "the most powerful gangster in Manhattan."

He said he believed Luciano conceived the

Continued on Page 2, Column 4

DAILY NEWS

Copyright 1935 by News Syndicate Co., Inc. Reg. U. S. Pat. Off.
NEW YORK'S PICTURE NEWSPAPER
Entered as 2nd class matter, Post Office, New York, N. Y.

Vol. 17. No. 103 | 72 Pages | New York, Thursday, October 24, 1935★ | 2 Cents IN CITY LIMITS | 3 CENTS Elsewhere

SCHULTZ, 5 PALS SHOT

One Dead; Times Sq. Guns Fell 2

Story on Page 2

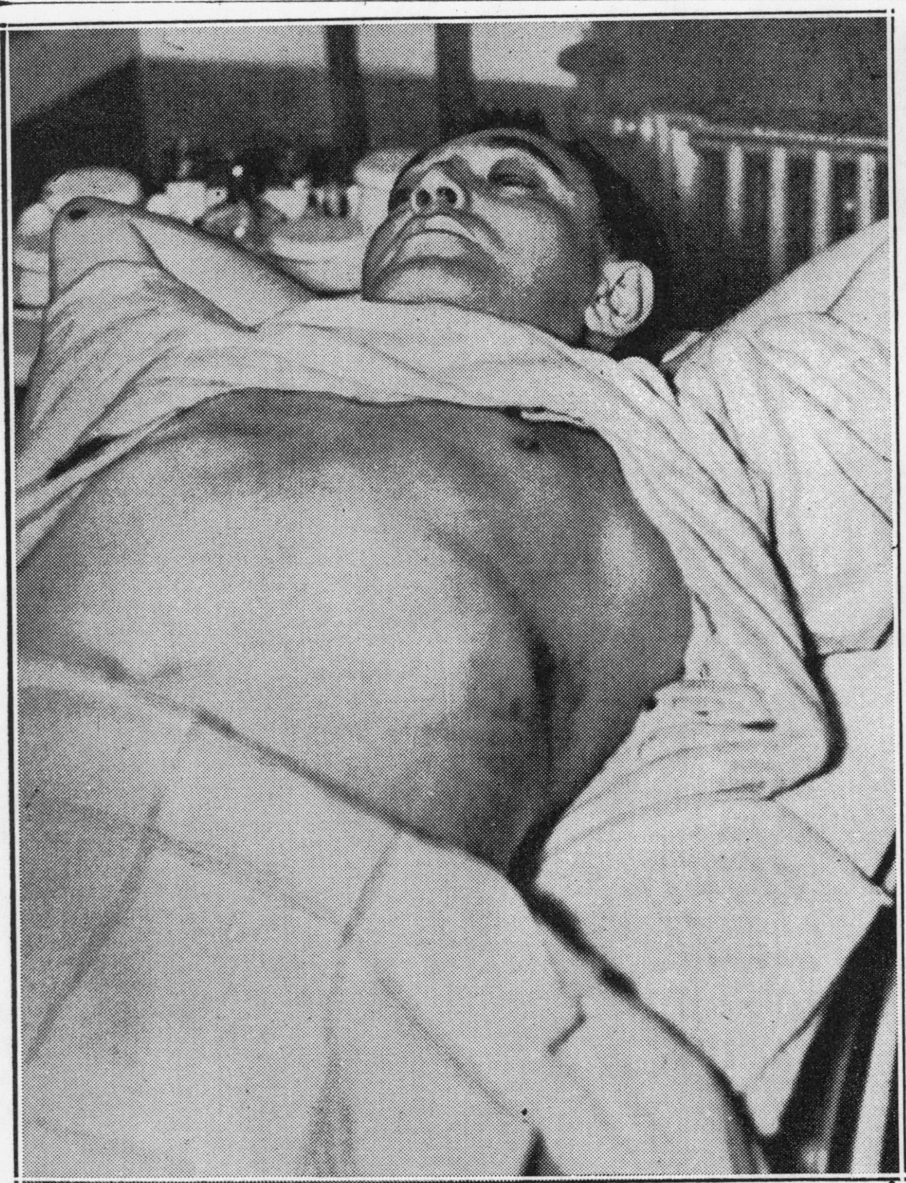

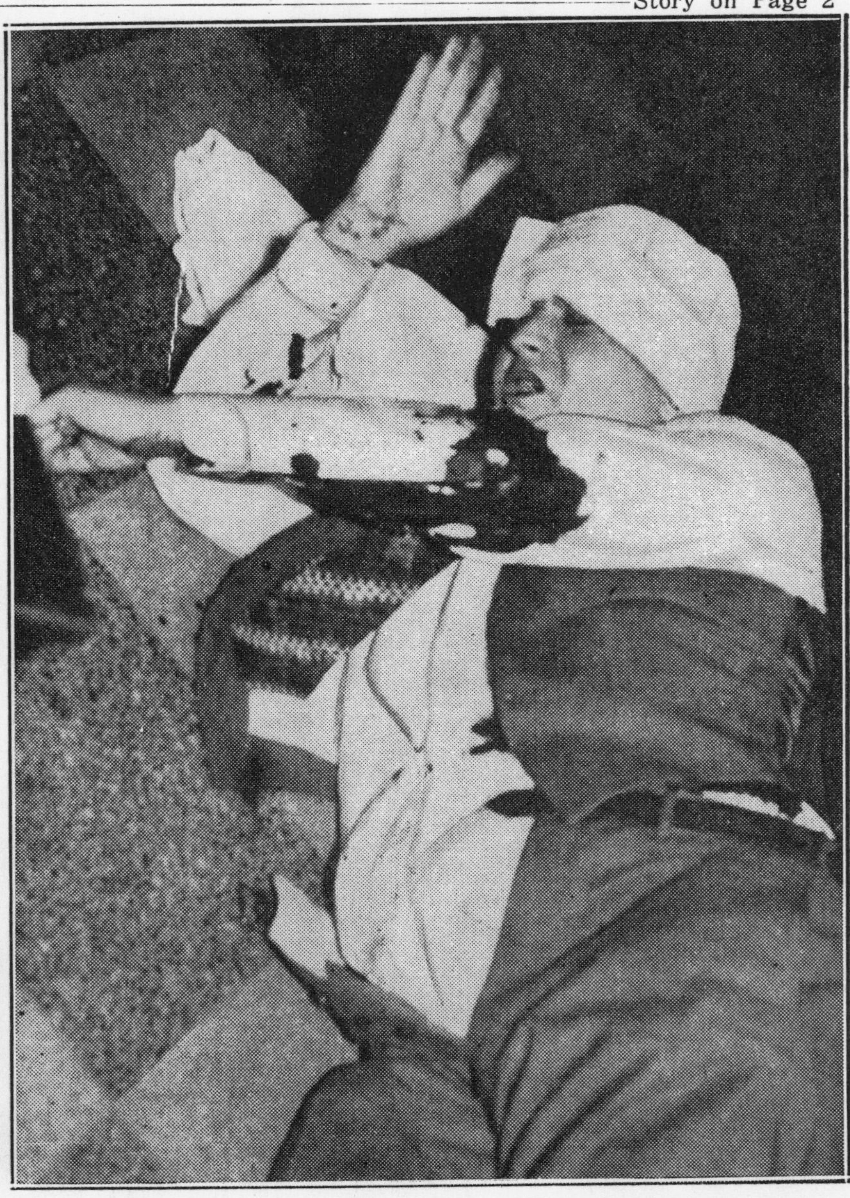

(NEWS photo by Mourer, © 1935 by News Syndicate Co., Inc.)
EXCLUSIVE PICTURE OF DUTCH SCHULTZ, semi-conscious on bed in Newark City Hospital last night after he was mowed down by machine gunners while in Newark bierstube.

(NEWS photo by Brown, © 1935 by News Syndicate Co., Inc.)
ANOTHER EXCLUSIVE PICTURE—SCHULTZ AID DROPPED IN TIMES SQUARE.—Camera mirrors agony on face of Sammy Gold, shot down in barber shop shortly after Dutch was wounded.

Underworld War Victims—More Pictures Pages 36, 37, Back Page

2 CENTS PAY NO MORE!

Chicago Daily Tribune

THE WORLD'S GREATEST NEWSPAPER

FINAL ★ ★

VOLUME XCV.—NO. 40 C [REG. U. S. PAT. OFFICE. COPYRIGHT 1936 BY THE CHICAGO TRIBUNE.] SATURDAY, FEBRUARY 15, 1936.—30 PAGES THIS PAPER CONSISTS OF TWO SECTIONS—SECTION ONE PRICE TWO CENTS IN CHICAGO AND SUBURBS ELSEWHERE THREE CENTS

'MACHINE GUN' M'GURN SLAIN

TOWNSEND PLAN SPONSORS FACE CONGRESS QUIZ

Backers Accused of Pocketing Cash.

[Chicago Tribune Press Service.]

Washington, D. C., Feb. 14.—[Special.]—A congressional investigation of the promotional methods used by leaders of the Townsend old age pension plan seemed certain today after Representative C. Lester Bell [Dem., Mo.], charged before the house rules committee that promoters of the plan were pocketing hundreds of thousands of dollars contributed by aged persons.

The committee will meet again next Monday to hear more testimony before deciding upon a resolution authorizing the speaker to appoint a committee of seven members to conduct an inquiry into what Bell termed "the old age pension racket." But it was reported that the committee's mind is made up and the investigation will be ordered.

Leaders of Scheme Assailed.

Dr. Francis E. Townsend and Robert E. Clements, co-leaders of the program which calls for legislation giving $200 a month to every person more than 60 years old, were singled out for attack by Bell. He also named Dr. F. E. Pope, head of the National Old Age Pension association, as another who, he charged, was enriching himself at the expense of old persons believing in the plan. Pope, Bell declared, served a term in prison for using the mails to defraud.

"Townsend, Clements, and Townsend's brother, a porter in a Los Angeles hotel, incorporated Old Age Revolving Pensions, Ltd.," Bell told the committee. "The first two also own the National Townsend Weekly and have got $200,000 each from this publication."

Everything Costs Money.

Bell detailed the many methods used by the Townsend organization to raise money from members. The amounts were small but numerous, he said. A 25 cent initiation fee is charged each member, and he or she pays 10 cents a month dues. Townsend buttons are sold at 10 cents each, photographs of Townsend may be purchased for from 50 cents to $5. Medallions at $1, auto stickers at 10 cents, copies of the Townsend bill at 25 cents, "Question and Answer" books at 25 cents, are sold by the tens of thousands to members, he declared.

In addition, dinners, raffles, barbecues, and rummage sales are held, the proceeds of which go to swell the Townsend war chest, Bell testified. Merchants are forced to put photographs of Townsend in their display windows or be subject to boycott by members, he said.

High Pressure Used.

Meetings are held "under high pressure religious fervor" at which the aged members sing "Onward Townsend Soldiers!" Radio pleas are made for donations, and membership in the National legion, inner shrine of the Townsend organization, involves dues of from $1 to $10 a month.

"I am not giving the names until an investigation can furnish unquestioned proof," Bell said, "but I understand that four men high in command of the organization are alien communists and one was repeatedly indicted for crimes."

People Are Deluded.

Representative Phil Ferguson [Dem., Okla.] joined Bell in his denunciation of the various old age pension plans.

"In the Townsend Weekly they are deluding people into believing that congress is about to enact their plan," he said. "I do not know a single congressman who is in favor of the $200 a month payments."

The estimated cost of the Townsend plan, if enacted into law, would be 24 billions annually, Bell said, an average of $800 a family, which would "fall largely on the poor."

If You Think You Have Trouble, Read This One

Tulsa, Okla., Feb. 14.—(AP)—Vest Terry's wife went to a hospital for an operation Wednesday.

Thursday his mother became critically ill at Noel, Mo.

Soon after he left for there in an automobile the city engineering department announced he had been dropped from the pay roll.

Near Chelsea, Okla., Terry's car was wrecked, injuring himself and his brother.

NEWS SUMMARY of The Tribune

[And Historical Scrap Book.]

Saturday, February 15, 1936.

Average net paid circulation
JANUARY, 1936
THE CHICAGO TRIBUNE
DAILY in excess of 800,000

LIBERTY LEAGUE ASSAILS BLACK'S LOBBY SNOOPING

Calls Questionnaires Illegal.

[Chicago Tribune Press Service.]

Washington, D. C., Feb. 14.—[Special.]—The American Liberty league tonight declared war on the senate lobby committee which is turning its attention from investigation of utility lobbying to cracking down on individuals and organizations fighting the New Deal. The league challenged the right of the committee to compel answer under oath to questionnaires sent out to individuals and groups suspected of anti-New Deal sentiments by the committee.

The league declared that it had been advised by counsel the committee, of which Senator Hugo L. Black [Dem., Ala.] is chairman and guiding spirit, has no power to compel answers to the questionnaires. It charged Black's effort is an obvious attempt to intimidate the citizenry and punish those opposed to New Deal principles.

Chairman Black promptly replied that it was "a little difficult to believe that the league would attempt to intimidate or coerce its own members to keep their mouths shut until the du Ponts say they can talk."

Thousands Get Questionnaire.

The questionnaire was considered remarkable even for such an inquisitorial group as the Black committee, which through a horde of spies, investigators, and undercover men is spreading terror in every quarter from which emanates administration criticism.

It was sent to several thousand individuals and groups, including the Liberty league, the Crusaders, the Sentinels of the Republic, the American Federation of Investors, the New York State Economic council, the National Association of Manufacturers, and American Taxpayers' league.

It calls on the recipient to list the names of all corporations, partnerships and organizations with which he is affiliated in any way. Although principally aimed at ferreting out anti-New Deal organizations the questionnaire would compel revelation of all investments and business enterprises.

Calls Course Illegal.

"The effort of the senate committee is an obvious attempt to intimidate citizens in the exercise of their constitutional rights of free speech and of petitioning the government," the league said. "These rights may be employed through group action as well as by individuals acting alone. The constitution expressly prohibits the congress from enacting any law impairing or abridging such rights."

The league said that it was created for the purposes of disseminating information on constitutional issues and it is not even remotely engaged in lobbying activities which might come under the scrutiny of the committee. It pointed out that "certain organizations were conspicuously omitted" from the questionnaire. In this the league was believed to be referring to the American Federation of Labor lobby, the bonus lobby and Father Coughlin's Union for Social Justice lobby, among others.

Voluntarily Files Report.

The league added that although it is not subject to the corrupt practices act it voluntarily filed with the clerk of the house of representatives

[Continued on page 8, column 4.]

EMPLOYES' ENTRANCE

CLOSED TO AMERICAN YOUTH.

Gains in Unity of Time Shown by Geographer

Dr. William H. Haas, professor of geography and geology at Northwestern university, pointed out yesterday how peoples all over the world have abandoned artificial adjustment of time standards to meridians and, wherever possible, have adopted a single time standard for convenience and national unity.

"Countries with a limited east-west extent rarely divide into time belts," he said, citing Spain, France, Norway, the Union of South Africa, Venezuela, India and many others. "The unity of the country through the use of the same time seems everywhere to have more weight than the arbitrary limits."

Study for ICC Hearing.

Dr. Haas made these statements to City Corporation Counsel Barnet Hodes after he was interviewed by members of the research division of the city law department. The department is making a study of eastern standard time, effective in Chicago March 1, in preparation for a hearing before the interstate commerce commission on Feb. 24.

The city has asked the commission to extend the western limits of the eastern standard time zone, as applied to railroads and other common carriers, to include Chicago.

Dr. Haas said he regarded as "unfortunate" the division of the central western industrial section of the United States and the eastern financial section into two time belts.

Line Moves Steadily West.

"When I was a boy," he recalled, "Pittsburgh was the division point for time. Gradually the line has moved west, until now practically all business of the industrial section of the country is in the eastern time belt except Chicago."

There is nothing sacred in time zone limits, the geographer added, and the whole purpose of time zones has always hinged on the convenience of commercial intercourse.

"As a stockholder in the Public Service company, I suppose I ought to vote against the change," Dr. Haas remarked, "because less electricity for lighting purposes will be used in Chicago after March 1. On the other hand, business undoubtedly will gain enough from the change to counteract such a loss."

Secretary Swanson, Ill of Pleurisy, Resting Well

Washington, D. C., Feb. 14.—Secretary Swanson, ill of pleurisy at the Naval hospital, was reported "holding his own" late today. A bulletin said he was resting comfortably.

ALFONSO'S SON TAKES TURN FOR THE WORSE; FEAR DEATH IS NEAR

HAVANA, Feb. 14.—The count of Covadonga was reported in a critical condition tonight and hope for his recovery was considered slight in some quarters.

The former crown prince of Spain took a sudden turn for the worse this morning. After another internal hemorrhage he was given two blood transfusions and regular injections of blood were made. A Swiss nurse furnished the blood.

The count suffers from hemophilia. This ailment has deterred physicians in their treatment of an abscess on the leg. Physicians early in the week had expressed the belief the count was out of danger.

POLICE LOOK INTO HIS WOES; NOW HE'S LOOKING OUT

A telephone caller with an unsteady voice complained to the Sheffield police last night that he had lost all his money in a handbook at the Rex hotel, 3120 North Ashland avenue. Police investigated and found no evidence of a handbook. Then the telephone caller reported to the station again and a squad was sent to a drug store at Lincoln and Belmont avenues, to which the phone call had been traced.

There the policemen found Howard Wubben, 26 years old, 4208 Kenmore avenue, a Works Progress administration laborer, who was hugging a bottle of gin. Police said he boasted that it was his third bottle of the day.

Wubben was taken to his home, where his wife, Josephine, said her husband had spent his last three WPA pay checks to buy liquor. Wubben was charged with disorderly conduct and locked up.

FLAMES DAMAGE PAPER PLANT ON KINZIE STREET

Fire for which a 4-11 alarm was sounded early this morning swept the basement and lower floor of the five story building at 230 West Kinzie street, occupied by the Odman Corporation of Illinois, manufacturers of paper products.

The fire started in the basement and spread to the first floor before firemen arrived. By that time smoke was pouring from the windows of all the floors, which were filled with paper, twine and cartons which are the company's principal products. Fire Commissioner Michael J. Corrigan expressed the belief that the flames would be held to the first floor. Earlier he estimated damage at $10,000.

Low Cost Clinic Will Stay Open Despite Court

The Illinois Supreme court yesterday handed down a decision holding [1] that a corporation is incapable of practicing medicine legally in Illinois, and [2] that the United Medical Service, Inc., which has a low cost clinic at 23 East Jackson boulevard, is a corporation engaged in medical practice.

Dr. Joseph G. Berkowitz, founder and president of the service, said that he and his associates were not disturbed by the court's ruling. He said the clinic would remain in existence.

"We will first ask for a rehearing and may carry the matter to the Supreme Court of the United States," he asserted. "We expected an adverse ruling and if it stands the clinic will be reorganized as a partnership. We believe this would be acceptable to the courts."

Affirms McKinley Order.

The Supreme court's ruling was made in an affirmation of an order by Judge Michael L. McKinley of the Cook County Superior court, directing the United Medical Service to cease practice.

Attorneys said that the ruling was the first in which the Supreme court had ruled on the invalidity of corporate medical practice, although it had previously been held that corporations cannot practice law. The justices in their decision held that it was a "well established rule that the state may deny corporations the right to practice professions and insist upon the personal obligations of individual practitioners."

May Affect Other Clinics.

It was uncertain whether the decision would outlaw other institutions like the Public Health institute and the clinics of the University of Chicago and Northwestern university. Legal experts asserted that the phraseology of the court would have to be closely studied before a guess could be hazarded.

The suit against the United Medical Service was brought by Attorney General Otto Kerner at the request of the Chicago Medical society. It was the contention of Dr. Berkowitz that his organization was not practicing medicine and that individual service was given patients by individual doctors, all of whom were qualified under the law.

To speed up the decision, attorneys for both sides submitted a stipulated set of facts and after Judge McKinley entered his order the United Medical Service took an appeal.

Capone Chief Shot Down in Bowling Alley

(Pictures on back page.)

"Machine Gun Jack" McGurn, notorious gangster who once swaggered in the train of Al Capone, was shot to death by three assassins early this morning in a bowling alley at 805 Milwaukee avenue. A dozen persons saw him killed.

With two companions McGurn entered the place only a short time before he was slain. The trio removed their coats and were preparing to bowl on the second alley when there was a sudden loud outcry. It came from one of three men who had followed the old Capone lieutenant into the place and was standing behind him at the head of the alley.

"Everybody stand still," was the cry. "Move and you die."

Guns Blaze; McGurn Dies.

As the witnesses looked on, spellbound, shots cracked. Each of the three men, grouped in a little semicircle about McGurn, participated in the firing. A bullet crashed into his head. Another plowed into his back.

As he fell, instantly dead, on the smooth wood of the alley the killers slowly backed toward the stairway [the alleys are on the second floor], dropped their weapons into their overcoat pockets, and fled to the street.

The spectators of the fast moving drama were themselves galvanized into action. They, too, fled to the street. When the police arrived only William Alosio, 1121 West Huron street, proprietor of the place, which is known as the Avenue Recreation rooms, was left. He it was who told the story of the slaying.

Yell Is Murder Signal.

"McGurn was choosing a ball to bowl with," Alosio said, "when that yell went up. The men knew what they were doing. They didn't miss. But it all happened so quickly I can't remember much about it."

Yesterday was the anniversary of the St. Valentine day massacre, one of the most sensational crimes in American history. On Feb. 14, 1929, seven members of the north side gang headed by George [Bugs] Moran, an enemy of Capone in the booze and vice rackets, were lined up against the wall of a garage at 2122 North Clark street and were all machine gunned to death.

Reminded of Massacre.

There were at times reports that McGurn was implicated in that shooting. Most investigators discredited this, however. That some one wished to remind McGurn of Valentine's day was proved by the discovery of a comic lithograph that was left with Alosio for him some time yesterday. It depicted a couple in scanty clothing, with a little jingle under it which read:

"You've lost your job, you've lost your dough;
Things still could be worse, you know—
At least you haven't lost your trousers."

The slain man's overcoat and suit coat were found on a bench near the bowling alleys. They contained no

[Continued on page 2, column 5.]

THE WEATHER

SATURDAY, FEBRUARY 15, 1936.

Sunrise, 6:46; sunset, 5:23. Moon rises at 1:50 a. m. tomorrow. Mars and Saturn are evening stars; Venus and Jupiter are morning stars.

Chicago and vicinity—Mostly cloudy Saturday, followed by snow by night and on Sunday; continued cold; moderate northwest to northeast winds Saturday.

Illinois—Cloudy Saturday, followed by snow before night; Sunday snow; not so cold Saturday night, otherwise continued cold.

TRIBUNE BAROMETER.

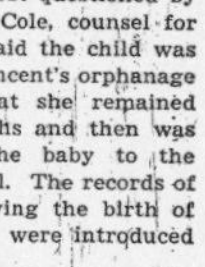

TEMPERATURES IN CHICAGO

MAXIMUM, 3 A. M. 28
MINIMUM, 2 A. M. .... —4

3 a. m.	28	Noon	17	8 p. m.	3
4 a. m.	27	1 p. m.	17	9 p. m.	1
5 a. m.	26	2 p. m.	15	Unofficial—	
6 a. m.	26	3 p. m.	12	10 p. m.	0
7 a. m.	26	4 p. m.	10	11 p. m.	—1
8 a. m.	23	5 p. m.	8	Midnight	—2
9 a. m.	24	6 p. m.	5	1 a. m.	—3
10 a. m.	20	7 p. m.	5	2 a. m.	—4
11 a. m.	19				

For 24 hours ended 7 p. m. Feb. 14:

Mean temperature, 18; normal, 26; deficiency for February, 212 degrees; deficiency since Jan. 1, 359 degrees.

Precipitation, trace; deficiency since Feb. 1, .26 of an inch; total since Jan. 1, 2.47 inches; deficiency since Jan. 1, .52 of an inch.

Highest wind velocity, 20 miles an hour, from the west, at 11:33 a. m.

Barometer, 7 a. m., 29.63; 7 p. m., 30.07.

Feb. 15, 1935:

Maximum temperature, 43; minimum, 32; mean, 38; cloudy, precipitation, .16 of an inch.

[Official weather table on page 25.]

GIVE ME MY SON! UNWED MOTHER PLEADS IN COURT

Battles Doctor for Baby's Custody.

(Pictures on back page.)

Miss Margaret Mann sat on the witness stand yesterday and related her claim that she is the mother of a 3 year old boy for whose possession she is fighting.

Before crowds that thronged a courtroom on the ninth floor of the county building and overflowed into the corridors, a dramatic scene was enacted as Miss Mann, who is 24 years old, declared that the child was born to her May 19, 1932. She refused to name the father.

Then Dr. Gordon Mordoff, 49 years old, a Wilmette physician, took the witness stand. He denied Miss Mann's claim that she is the boy's mother. He asserted the child was born on Sept. 2, 1932, to his wife, Madge, who died last Monday. He said he is the father.

Central Figure Is Unconcerned.

In the midst of all this legal turmoil the boy whose parentage is disputed sat happily in the courtroom and drew pictures on a pad. Whether he is Gordon Mordoff III., as the doctor claims, or Reginald Arthur Mann, as Miss Mann insists, the child was unconcerned. Pleasantly conscious of the commotion about him, he was entirely unaware of its relation to his fate.

At the conclusion of the hearing Superior Judge Rudolph F. Desort, who took an active part in the questioning of Miss Mann, reserved decision. Temporarily he awarded custody of the boy to the doctor.

Judge Considers Scientific Tests.

The judge said he might order lie detector tests to determine the truth of the stories told by Dr. Mordoff and Miss Mann. He also stated that he might direct blood tests for Miss Mann, the doctor, and the child. According to scientists, these blood tests are not conclusive but might aid in ascertaining the boy's parentage.

Judge Desort has jurisdiction of the case because a separate maintenance suit brought by Mrs. Mordoff against her husband and pending at the time of her death has the legal effect of making the child a ward of the court. In her suit Mrs. Mordoff charged infidelity and cruelty. When the parentage hearing began yesterday Attorney Edwin Robson, representing Miss Mann, filed an intervening petition in the suit to protect his client's alleged right to the boy's custody.

Conceals the Other Parent.

Before Miss Mann took the stand Attorney Robson told the court that she agreed to testify on the condition that she should not have to name the father of the child. Judge Desort ruled she would not have to disclose the father's identity.

There was a craning of necks in the courtroom crowd as Miss Mann walked to the stand. A slim, attractive brunette, she was clad in a tight fitting hat and a dark brown coat with a fur collar. She told her story in a low voice, pausing frequently from the stress of emotion.

Her eyes were ever on the boy, sitting a few yards away from her. He smiled at her, but gave no indication he knew who she was. The boy has been with Dr. Mordoff most of his short life.

Recounts Birth in Orphanage.

Miss Mann was first questioned by Attorney Harry X. Cole, counsel for Dr. Mordoff. She said the child was born to her in St. Vincent's orphanage in Chicago and that she remained there for two months and then was transferred with the baby to the Cook county hospital. The records of the orphanage showing the birth of a boy to Miss Mann were introduced in evidence.

The questioning by Attorney Cole proceeded:

Q.—Under what name was he registered? A.—Reginald Arthur Mann.

Q.—How did you come to take the child to the Mordoff home? A.—I read Mrs. Mordoff's ad. [Miss Mann stated on Thursday that Mrs. Mordoff advertised in a newspaper that she would board a child.]

Q.—Did you take the baby there? A.—Yes, but my mother [Mrs. Laura Mann] made the arrangements. I was working at the time.

Q.—Did you talk to Dr. Mordoff at the time you put the baby in his home? A.—I did not.

Q.—To whom did you pay the $5

Today

(Registered U. S. Patent Office.)

One War Over?
Dr. Eckener Smiles.
Nature's Savagery.
If Man Bit Monkey.

By Arthur Brisbane

ITALY says Ethiopia's "King of Kings" will soon abdicate, perhaps accepting in exchange for his throne a pension that would make him comfortable in Bagdad, where his ancestors may have lived, or in Paris, which he knows and likes well.

Abdication would be wise. Beaten kings are not popular, or even safe, among barbarous tribes. They beat their idols and kill their witch doctors in a prolonged drought. Haile Selassie's abdication, ending one war, might soon be followed by another, in the Far East, where Russia, with Mongolians, is fighting Japan's Manchukoans.

That might bring another "Big War."

Dr. Eckener, commander of the new giant Zeppelin, displeased the Nazis by his attitude in the recent election. His name is to be omitted from publicity connected with his airship. Dr. Eckener, now guiding his big ship over the ocean to Brazil, can smile at that, as others have done.

The Netherlands Synagogue excommunicated the great Jewish philosopher, Spinoza, because they did not like his views, and he declined to obey the order to lie down on the threshold of the synagogue and let the congregation walk over him. The excommunication text, published by Sir Frederick Pollock in his "Life of Spinoza," signed by the "great men" of the synagogue, solemnly declares that Spinoza's name must never again be mentioned among men. It *has* been mentioned, and only Spinoza's greatness has kept their names alive.

Colley Cibber wrote truly:

"The aspiring youth that fired
the Ephesian dome
Outlives in fame that pious
fool that raised it."

That youth set fire to Diana's Temple to make his name live. It was decreed that that name, Herostratus, should never be mentioned, yet every schoolboy learns it and knows very little about the builders of the temple, except that Croesus contributed some cows made of pure gold to decorate it.

The great Maimonides, or "Rambam," as many little boys call him, did not suffer in his reputation when the great synagogue of Lisbon excommunicated him. It is not easy to kill fame.

If superstition still ruled the world, Americans would think Divine power offended, after seven years of depression, followed by nature's recent wild outbreaks—floods, dust storms, hurricanes.

Now comes a tornado in Georgia, cutting a swath three blocks wide through the city of Cordele, killing many. The wide path of destruction extended for seven miles. Hurricane power was felt in other places, at Concord, N. C.; near Athens, in Northern Georgia; at Gordo, Ala., and many other places.

That the destruction was not willed by Divine power is proved by the fact that buildings destroyed included two public schools, and among the dead was Mrs. Mimms, wife of a Baptist preacher.

Another reminder of "news," as defined by "Doc" Wood, Charles A. Dana's city editor, who said:

"If a dog bites a man, that is NOT news. If a man bites a dog, that IS news."

New York police are hunting a man bitten by a monkey while the man was stealing $345 from the monkey's owner. The "faithful simian" provides an interesting small news item. If the man had bitten the monkey, that would have been *real* news.

Sentiment plays its part in modern, practical life. In New York city, Alexander Schirger's wife died of pneumonia. Two minutes later his body was found in the courtyard below his apartment window.

Alfred Dupre told Miss Thornton, a high-school girl, that if she would not marry him he would kill himself. She knew young men were expected to say that—did not take it seriously.

Rejected, he went away, came back, drank poison and died at her feet. With youth, *today* is everything.

Another who decided that life was not worth while was found at 4 o'clock in the morning, hanged by a rope fastened to the steel framework of New York's high Manhattan Bridge. No last letter; none was necessary. His pockets held a briar pipe, with just enough tobacco for one more smoke; a knife, spectacles and scissors.

THE WEATHER

Clear to partly cloudy tonight and tomorrow; colder tonight with lowest around 25 degrees.

MEAN TEMPERATURES

Baltimore	46	Chicago	28
Atlanta	62	Omaha	20
Boston	36	Los Angeles	58
New York	42	Salt Lake City	30
Portland, Me.	35	Seattle	42
Washington	47	New Orleans	70

THE BALTIMORE NEWS-POST

AN INDEPENDENT NEWSPAPER

The Largest Daily Circulation in the Entire South

EXTRA

VOL. CXXVIII.—NO. 129. Copyright, 1936, by Hearst Consolidated Publications, Inc. Entered as second-class matter at Baltimore Postoffice. FRIDAY EVENING, APRIL 3, 1936 PRICE 2 CENTS

BRUNO DIES FAILS TO TALK

TRENTON, N. J., April 3.—Bruno Richard Hauptmann died in the electric chair here tonight, paying with his life, after being granted three postponements, for the kidnap murder of Baby Charles Augustus Lindbergh. His head shaved and trouser legs slit for the contact with the electrodes, he walked to the chair of doom accompanied by the Rev. John Goorley, prison chaplain, and the Rev. John Matthiesen, his own spiritual adviser. Swiftly the straps were adjusted and the voices of the clerics were heard softly in prayer. At a pre-arranged signal the switch was thrown and Hauptmann's body lurched forward, then sank back. A second time the dynamo hummed. A stethoscope was applied. He was pronounced dead. The law had avenged the murder of Baby Lindbergh.

BABY LINDBERGH KIDNAPING BEGAN GREATEST MANHUNT WORLD HAS KNOWN

By United Press.

HOPEWELL, N. J., April 3.—The day and night of the first of March in 1932 was bleak and cold in the Sourland mountain region and a gusty wind whipped through the forests back of the big white stone mansion three miles from the small town of Hopewell, N. J.

Inside the home, comfortable and warm, the world's most widely publicized baby, Charles Augustus Lindbergh, Jr., spent the day like any other normal infant of the age of seventeen months.

In fact this secluded spot had been selected by the child's famous parents for the precise purpose of giving him a normal life by shielding him from a maudlin public that insisted on interrupting the private lives of the Lindberghs.

Present in the house as a dreary dusk drew near were the child, its mother, Anne Morrow Lindbergh, and the regular household staff.

3 House Servants

The staff was composed of an English butler, Oliver Whatley, his wife, Elsie, who was the cook, and Betty Gow, attractive brunette nursemaid.

Earlier in the day Miss Gow had been at the Englewood home of the child's grandmother, Mrs. Dwight Morrow, and it had been planned to take young Lindy there, too.

But the baby was suffering from a slight cold; plans were changed and Miss Gow was called to the Lindbergh residence near Hopewell.

At 7 P. M. Mrs. Lindbergh and Miss Gow took the youngster to the nursery and saw that he was bundled warmly into his bed.

Miss Gow made the rounds of the windows, closing shutters. There was one, warped by the weather, that could not be locked. She struggled with it unsuccessfully, then turned out the lights and went out of the room.

Lindy Returns

At 8.15 Colonel Lindbergh arrived unexpectedly from New York. He was scheduled to have made an address at New York University but he had become engrossed in business problems and had forgotten the engagement.

At 8.30 Whatley announced dinner and the Colonel and his wife sat down to eat.

The meal finished Mrs. Lindbergh went upstairs to prepare to retire. The colonel went to his study to work over some papers.

The stage now was set for the first move in a crime that was to shake the world and to cause more universal public interest than any other of modern days.

Heard Noise

At approximately 9.30 Colonel Lindbergh heard what he described as a "rather sharp crack," He didn't pay any attention to it for the whistling wind was breaking branches from trees outside.

At 10 o'clock, nursemaid Gow, ready to go to bed, took one last look into the nursery.

The baby wasn't in its bed. The nursemaid hurried to Mrs. Lindbergh's quarters, found that he wasn't there either and asked if it might be that Colonel Lindbergh had taken him downstairs.

"You had better ask Colonel Lindbergh," said Mrs. Lindbergh.

At the nursemaid's question, Lindbergh threw his papers aside and dashed upstairs, his long legs taking two steps at a time.

A hasty search revealed what the Lindberghs and Betty Gow

Continued on Page 5, Column 1.

BRUNO RICHARD HAUPTMANN

By JAMES L. KILGALLEN

International News Service Staff Correspondent.

TRENTON, N. J., April 3.—Without uttering a word and with a wistful smile on his pallid face, Bruno Richard Hauptmann went to his death in the electric chair here tonight, paying the supreme penalty for the murder of the Lindbergh baby.

As Hauptmann shuffled into the brilliantly lit execution chamber, with its high whitewashed walls, he glanced to his right at the witnesses and a sad smile flitted across his deathly pale face.

His lips twitched as if he wanted to say something but all he did was smile faintly.

His spiritual adviser, the Rev. John Matthiesen, was reading prayers in German from a Bible. The room was as silent as a tomb except for the droning of the minister.

PUT INTO CHAIR

Hauptmann was quickly propelled by the guards to the queer contraption known as "the chair."

In the flash of an eye he was in.

The doomed man's right trousers leg had been slit from knee to ankle and his bare flesh stood out. He wore a grayish-blue shirt, open at thethroat, and brown trousers.

His head was shaven. He looked so much different than he did when he was on trial inFlemington.

The old familiar TIC (involuntary flutter) of his eye was there as they put him in the chair. It was his only sign of nervousness.

He had come through the yellow door to the left at 8.39 P. M. He was accompanied by his two spiritual ad-

Continued on Page 2, Column 1.

Vera Stretz Freed In Gebhardt Death

By International News Service.

NEW YORK, April 3—Blonde Vera Stretz was acquitted early tonight of the slaying of Dr. Fritz Gebhardt, her married lover.

WEATHER

Fair tonight and Sunday, heavy frost tonight, somewhat warmer Sunday.

Hour	6	7	8	9	10	11	12	1	2
Temp'ture	37	37	38	39	40	41	42	43	

(Further Weather Details on Page 20.)

Complete Wire Service of United Press and International News Service

Vol. 37, No. 54 Home Edition St. Paul, Minn., Saturday, May 2, 1936 Three Cents

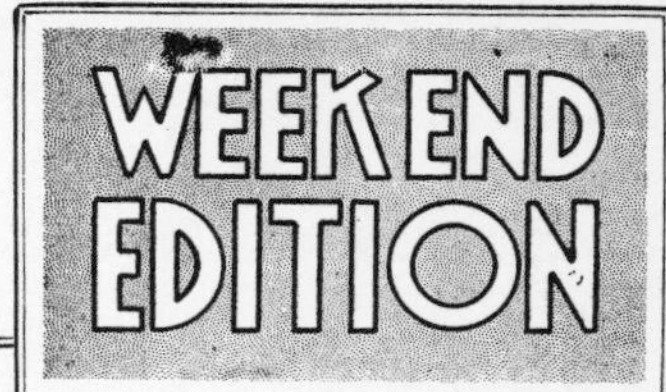

G-MEN JAIL KARPIS HERE AFTER NIGHT PLANE DASH

Drama Marks Capture And Landing Here

Nation's Leading Mobster Arrives Two Weeks After Feds Break Open Hamm Kidnaping.

Two weeks to the day after Uncle Sam's crack G-men smashed the $100,000 William Hamm, Jr., kidnaping case wide open and laid it at the door of the Barker-Karpis mob, Alvin Karpis, diminutive coleader of the gang, today faced the battering questions of G-men in the same locked room where two weeks ago he was named as the leader of the snatch mob.

In a quick, dramatic capture in New Orleans, and an equally dramatic and speedy dash northward, Karpis, wanted not only for the Hamm and Edward G. Bremer kidnapings, but for murder and bank robbery, joined the notorious company of underworld captives who have fallen beneath the department of justice's relentless drive on crime.

Same G-Men.

He was taken by the same G-men who have added to their gallery of captives such names as John Dillinger, Charles (Pretty Boy) Floyd, Kate (M) Barker, her sons, Fred and Arthur (Doc), George (Machine Gun) Kelly, George (Baby Face) Nelson, and dozens of others—some dead, some in prison.

Karpis, a price of $7,000 on his head and the most hunted criminal in G-men annals with the exception of Dillinger, was taken in New Orleans Friday night by a corps of G-men headed by J. Edgar Hoover, head of the intrepid corps that has put the underworld on the run. But Mr. Hoover, in an interview here today, declared that the capture of Karpis will not cost the government a cent of the reward.

Traced To Apartment.

Although G-men stepped in and captured Karpis, the Lindbergh law with its death penalty does not apply in either the Hamm or Bremer kidnapings because both occurred before enactment of the statute.

Through mysterious channels, the G-men learned Thursday that the man they wanted, who had been a phantom to them since Jan. 1, 1935, when he shot his way out of a trap at Atlantic City, was living in an apartment house on Canal st. in New Orleans.

Early Friday, the department of justice chartered a twin-motored Douglas transport plane from the Transcontinental and Western Air at Newark, N. J., airport. Hoover, who was in New York when the information was received, flew in it to Washington, where several of his lieutenants joined him. The plane then proceeded to New Orleans, arriving only a short time before the capture.

Agents Assembled.

Meanwhile, orders had gone to G-men stationed in cities near New Orleans and when Hoover arrived 20 agents, armed with sawed-off shotguns, revolvers and submachine guns, were assembled in the department of justice offices in the federal building there.

Little time was wasted. Hoover gave each man an assignment. Then all got into several cars and approached the apartment building from several directions. Each agent took up his pre-arranged post, under cover but instantly available.

Surrounded And Pinned.

Less than an hour after the trap was set, Karpis came strolling out and crossed the sidewalk to his automobile at the curb. In a flash, G-men surrounded him and had his arms pinned to his side. He couldn't have resisted if he had wanted.

Other agents went to action at once. They went to the Karpis apartment and, after a struggle, arrested a handsome 22-year-old girl, whose identity the agents still are concealing, and Fred Hunter, a suspected bank robber.

Karpis and the girl had lived in the apartment as Mr. and Mrs. Edward O'Hara since April 10, when Karpis is believed to have first come to New Orleans. Karpis had made at least two mysterious automobile trips since then. Returning from one, he was accompanied by Hunter. Federal men believe that he had come to a distant city, and, with Hunter, participated in a hold-up. Federal agents suspected him of using New Orleans as a base for a number of robberies.

"Federal agents, as usual, kept secret the source of the information that led to Karpis' arrest, but it was held authoritatively that a gossipy automobile salesman, Clarence Pucheu, known to his clients and

(Continued on Page 2, Col. 2.)

HOOVER, KARPIS FINALLY GET INTO SAME PICTURE

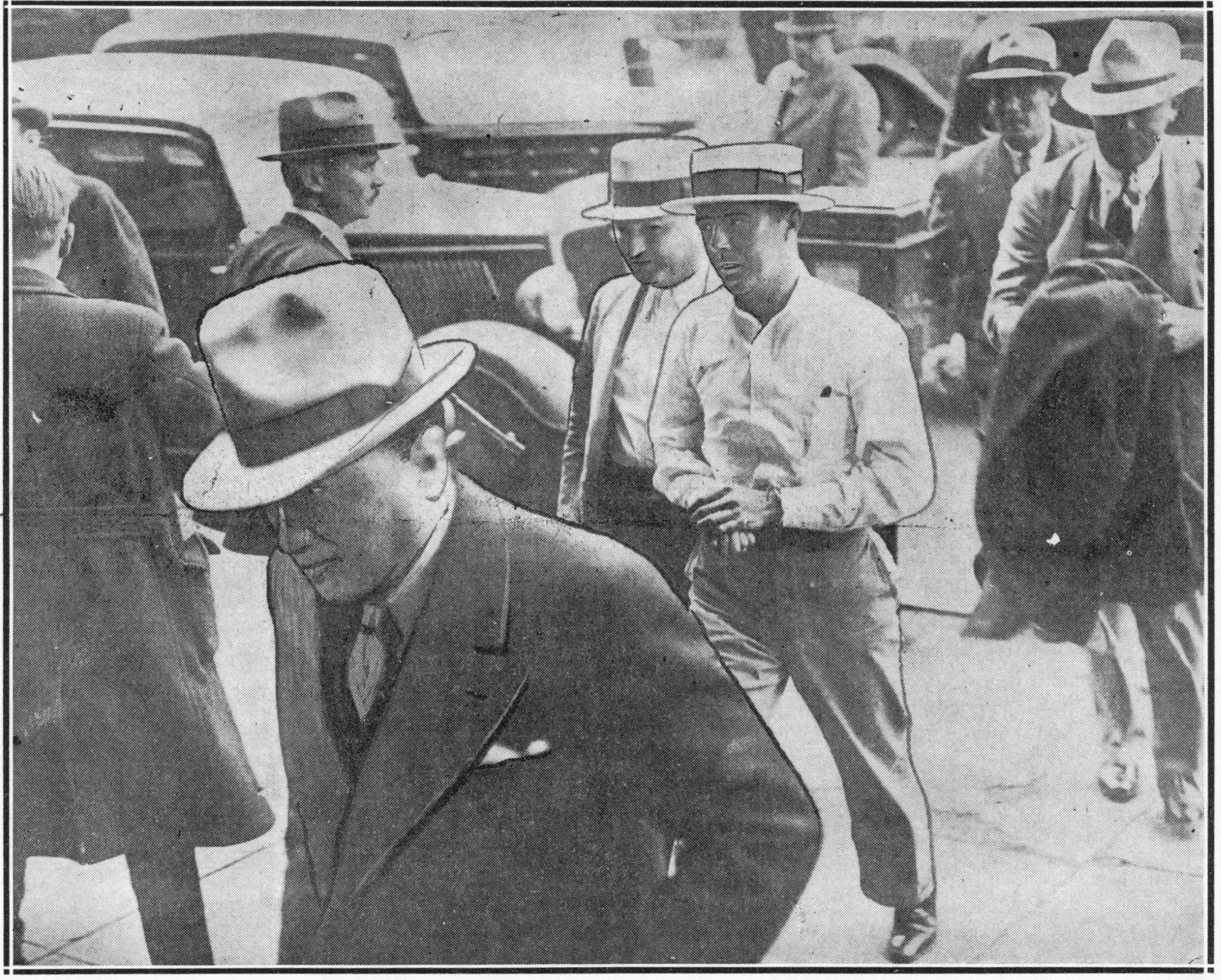

—Daily News Photo.

Here's what Uncle Sam's G-men have been wishing they could see for the past two years—ALVIN KARPIS, public enemy No. 1, and J. EDGAR HOOVER, chief of the nation's G-men in the same picture. It was taken just as Karpis, hands crossed and mancled and under heavy guard, was brought to the federal building from the airport, where he landed at 8:45 a. m. today after his capture Friday night in New Orleans. The photograph taken by a Daily News staff cameraman at the 5th st. entrance of the federal courts building, shows Karpis in the center, straw-hatted, coatless and wearing a deep southern tan, which soon will change to a prison pallor. Hoover, serving as advance guard to clear the way, is shown in the foregound.

No. 1 Enemy Brought By No. 1 Sleuth

Alvin Returns In Chains To Scene Of Alleged $300,000 Kidnaping Exploits.

The nation's two "No. 1" men came to St. Paul today.

One was Alvin Karpis, public enemy No. 1, since the steel-jacketed death in Chicago of John Dillinger—straw-hatted, coatless, manacled, a bewildered bellhop in appearance—returning to his "summer playground" to answer to charges of kidnaping William Hamm, Jr., and Edward G. Bremer.

The other was J. Edgar Hoover, G-man No. 1—stern-visaged, jutting-jawed, fierce-haired—a Roman conquering hero of modern times—demonstrating to the world, and to congressional inquisitors in particular, that the division of investigation, United States department of justice, always gets its man.

Has Armed Escort.

Not exactly arm in arm (when they entered the federal courts building after a speedy trip by automobile from the municipal airport Mr. Hoover led the way and Karpis was surrounded by a veritable arsenal of quick-firing small arms manned by determined federal agents) they arrived in the city in a specially-chartered airplane which had flown over night from New Orleans, where Karpis was captured Friday night.

For hours, from 2 a. m. on, a small army of federal agents and a larger army of newspaper reporters and photographers had waited at the municipal airport for their arrival.

For hours vagrant storms, roaming the central states, sneered at flying schedules and cameramen's flashlights; and not until 7:30 a. m. was it definitely learned that the plane had left Kansas City at 5:30 a. m. and would arrive in St. Paul "about 8:30."

Takes No Chances.

Travelers on two commercial transport planes were startled at the reception they received; thronging newsmen, camera-armed; racing automobiles bristling with firearms; awed airport attendants delaying normal activities until given "clearance" by the G-men who had "taken over" the entire field.

In charge of the force of about 15 federal agents of the St. Paul division, Chief Agent Clinton W. Stein took no chances on an upset of his plans for safe delivery of Karpis to the bureau of investigation offices.

Hour after hour the motors of the waiting high-powered government cars idled and the heads of waiting federal agents nodded sleepily. Toward breakfast time two men were released to "promote" coffee for themselves and the rest.

Guardsmen On Hand.

Finally the huge dual-motored plane for which all were waiting roared over the field. Newsmen scurried to and fro seeking places of vantage and waited nowhere. The huge doors of the hangar of the 109th aero squadron, Minnesota national guard, slid open and a crew of militiamen under command of Maj. Ray S. Miller took charge of the mechanical end of the reception for the two "No. 1" men.

The 14-passenger Douglas "skyliner" landed smoothly, taxied gracefully to the hangar—and was wheeled in backwards after Mr. Stein had gone to the plane door and held a brief consultation with someone inside. The someone was not visible to spectators. Newsmen jumped to the conclusion it was Mr. Hoover, for, immediately following, as the plane was being trundled in, all reporters and photographers were politely but firmly "shooshed" out of the building by the federal men. Submachine gun muzzles nudged the slow ones.

National guardsmen lowered the hangar doors after the federal agents' cars had purred inside.

Bars Camera Squad.

"Sorry, boys," said Mr. Stein. "There'll be no pictures for several days. We want to 'alk to him first."

The last glimpse had by the newsmen of the to-be-famous plane was one of shotguns and tommy guns protruding their noses out of windows, of the smiling Transcontinental Western Airways pilot and the cheerily grinning copilot who had braved a dozen storms and strange airlanes to bring their notable cargo to the city.

Through unsuspecting crowds on downtown streets the 35-mile-an-hour parade of victors and vanquished sped their way.

Photographers There First.

They were greeted at the federal courts building, 5th st. entrance, by the same army of newsmen—who had traveled 45 miles an hour to get there first.

The first car debouched a group of

(Continued On Page 2, Col. 1.)

Plan To Enlarge Upper End Of Harriet Island

Changes in the harbor line of the Mississippi river on the upstream end of Harriet island to increase its size as part of a WPA improvement program will be discussed at a public hearing in the council chamber at 2 p. m. May 14. The hearing is called by Maj. Dwight F. Johns, United States army engineer, on the application of the city of St. Paul to the war department for the revision of the harbor line.

Public Aid Official On Pension Errand

Miss Jane Hoey, Washington, director of the bureau of public assistance, will arrive Monday for a conference with state old-age pension officials on difficulties the Minnesota pension system is encountering. The situation in Aitkin county, which has declined to participate in pension payments because of lack of funds, will be discussed and delays in investigating and approving pension applications in Hennepin and Ramsey counties considered.

Will Urges Suicides.

NEW YORK, May 2.—(UP)—The will of Giuseppe Gallo left each of his four children 5 cents and requested them to "use same to purchase a piece of rope in the hope that each will strangle himself or herself with said rope."

'POLITICS PUBLIC FOE NO. 1.'—HOOVER

* *

Chief G-Man Says "Karpis Folded Up Like A Yellow Rat"

Alvin Karpis, two weeks ago branded by the United States government as the nation's most desperate public enemy, "folded up like the yellow rat he is" when captured by G-men.

Not one cent of the $7,000 in rewards offered by the federal government for information leading to his arrest will be paid because there was no "betrayal" of him by gangsters or other persons.

His statement relative to the nonpayment of rewards set at rest rumors that Mrs. John Meyer, who rented Karpis an apartment in New Orleans April 10, and Clarence (Duke) Pucheu, automobile salesman who sold him a car, might have been the "tipsters" who furnished the G-men with information which lead to his arrest.

Succeeding Karpis today as "Public Enemy No. 1" is "Old Man Politics."

Brief "Yes" and "No."

Weary, but with sparkling dark-brown eyes boring into those of his newspaper questioners, J. Edgar Hoover, chief of the nation's G-men, today shot back a rapid-fire of answers to a barrage of questions concerning the arrest of Karpis, the next step in the government's program of "cleaning house" on the nation's criminals, and the progress of the warfare on gangland in general.

Seated in a comfortable chair in the St. Paul offices of the division of investigation, United States department of justice, "for the first rest in five days," he answered most questions with a brief "yes" or "no," refused pointblank to answer some, and at times volunteered remarks.

Investigation of the Hamm and Bremer kidnapings, he said, has not ended with the capture of Karpis "nor will it end with the eventual capture of Harry Campbell (still a fugitive)," and, "indications are that several more individuals will be involved in both snatchings."

"Quit Cold."

"The man who said he would never be captured alive folded up like the yellow rat he is, and the rest of gangdom is, at heart," Mr. Hoover said.

"Stammering, stuttering, shaking as though he had palsy, the man upon whom you newspapermen bestowed the title of 'Public Enemy No. 1' quit cold, as all the others have.

"Who will replace him as Public Enemy No. 1? We, we don't rank the yellow rats. It is you newspapermen who do that for us. But if you want to know whom I rank as Public Enemy No. 1 today, it is Old Man Politics."

Karpis may have been coleader of the now extinct Barker-Karpis gang, but to Mr. Hoover the fugitive Harry Campbell is the "man with the brains."

"Karpis reminds me of Dillinger and George (Machine Gun) Kelly. (Kelly is serving life at Alcatraz prison for the Charles Urschel kidnaping.) They talked a lot, but each had to follow the master mind of their respective chief aids," Mr. Hoover said.

"Dillinger had his John Hamilton, Kelly his Harvey Bailey, and Karpis his Campbell. We're still after Campbell, and eventually we'll get him.

Planned Several Days.

"We (the federal agents) were in New Orleans for several days before the capture, about 5:15 p. m. Friday. We executed the plan we had had for several days, when the capture was made.

"We knew Karpis had been a frequent visitor at the home of Fred Hunter and the woman we now know as Ruth. Our cars and men (he would not say how many of either) surrounded the place, and Karpis had no chance.

"The three had just left their apartment at 3343 Canal st. and had entered their car when our car stationed in front of the driveway pulled up. Before Karpis could reach for the rifle alongside of him the agents in the car poked their guns at him and without a murmur of protest Karpis and Mr. and Mrs. Hunter stepped out of the car with their hands above their heads.

"Karpis stuttered and stammered. "'You are Mr. Hoover. I recognize you from a sailfish picture I saw of you in a Florida paper,' Karpis said."

Karpis Congratulates.

Later, on the plane ride to St. Paul, Karpis congratulated him on the fine catch shown in that picture. Also, on the way back, he read with interest at St. Louis a copy of a newspaper carrying the story of his capture and, alongside on the same page, the story of a Detroit bank robbery.

"'I know you fellows will be my alibi witnesses on that job," he laughed.

Karpis, Mr. Hoover said, had had his face "lifted" and his fingertips mutilated, "but not enough in either case to make identification impossible or even difficult." In the operations, two scars were removed from his ears, and lobes cut in the ears.

"Karpis is wanted for a third kidnaping job," Mr. Hoover said. "When

(Continued On Page 2, Col. 4.)

Zioncheck Arrested For 3d Time In 2 Weeks

SHALLOTTE, N. C., May 2.—(INS)—Rep. Marion A. (Barney Oldfield) Zioncheck, playboy legislator from the state of Washington, was arrested for speeding 70 miles an hour on the coastal highway near here today.

This marks the third time in exactly two weeks that Zioncheck, who married Rubye Nix a few days ago in the capital, has fallen into the toils of the law.

Sheriff Jasper A. Russ nabbed the speeding honeymooners a few moments after hearing via radio that Zioncheck had forfeited $200 bail, furnished by a bondsman following the congressman's last brush with the authorities in Alexandria, Va.

Zioncheck was assessed a small fine and released.

Gen. Hagood Takes Comamnd.

CHICAGO, May 2.—(UP)—Maj. Gen. Johnson Hagood assumed command of the 6th corps area second army today, relieving Maj. Gen. Frank McCoy.

Snow At Duluth.

DULUTH, May 2.—(UP)—Snowfall here today, added to heavy rains of Friday, to flood scores of basements and several streets

Heavy Frost Predicted

Cover up those plants in the yard tonight, because there'll be heavy frost, the weatherman warned. It will be fair tonight and Sunday and "somewhat warmer" Sunday, he said.

The net paid circulation for May exceeded
Daily---1,600,000
Sunday-2,800,000

DAILY  NEWS

NEW YORK'S PICTURE NEWSPAPER

FINAL ★★★

Copyright 1936 by News Syndicate Co., Inc. Reg. U. S. Pat. Off.

Entered as 2nd class matter, Post Office, New York, N. Y.

Vol. 17. No. 298 | 48 Pages | New York, Monday, June 8, 1936★ | 2 Cents IN CITY LIMITS | 3 CENTS Elsewhere

LUCIANO AND 8 FOUND GUILTY

All Face Life in Prison

Story on Page 3

(NEWS foto)

G. O. P. KEYNOTER.—Polishing up keynote speech, Senator Frederick Steiwer of Oregon rests in his hotel room for a big tomorrow, when G. O. P. convention opens. In pre-convention activity, Steiwer is spoken of as Vice Presidential possibility.

—Story on page 2; other pictures on pages 24 and 25.

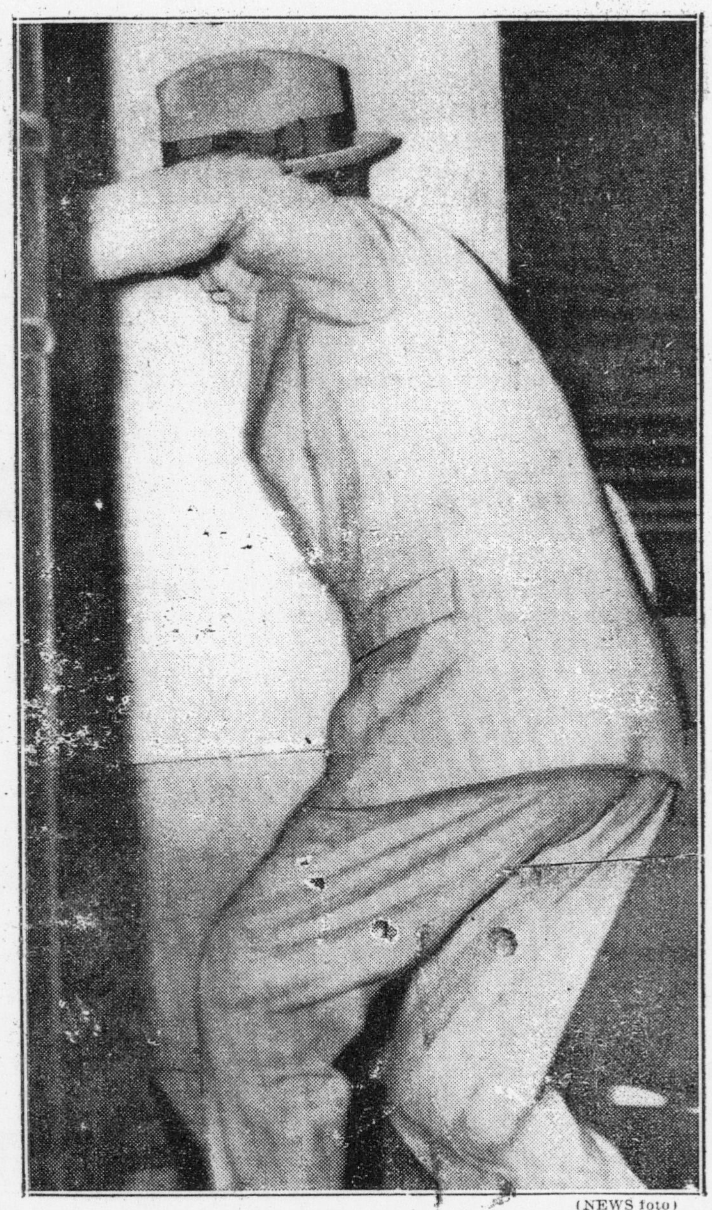

(NEWS foto)

LUCKY'S LUCK RUNS OUT.—Charles (Lucky) Luciano enters police van at Manhattan Supreme Court early yesterday after a blue-ribbon jury found him and his eight vice co-lords guilty of compulsory prostitution. Verdict will probably mean life imprisonment for Luciano. He and others, including four who pleaded guilty, will be sentenced June 18. *—Story on page 3.*

EXTRA!

COMPARATIVE TEMPERATURES	High	Low		High	Low
San Francisco	63	52	Denver	48	30
San Jose	63	46	Salt Lake	42	28
Los Angeles	74	54	New York	40	32
Seattle	52	46	Chicago	34	32
Honolulu	80	70	New Orleans	74	58

San Francisco Chronicle

THE CITY'S ONLY HOME-OWNED NEWSPAPER

Chronicle Home Carrier Service

If for any reason your Chronicle is not received please call City Circulation Department, phone DOuglas 1414, before 10 a. m. daily and 11 a. m. Sunday, and your Chronicle will be delivered promptly.

Weather Partly Cloudy and Cool Complete Weather Report on Page 31

FOUNDED 1865—VOL. CLI, NO. 155 .CCC* SAN FRANCISCO, FRIDAY, DECEMBER 17, 1937 DAILY 5 CENTS, SUNDAY 10 CENTS: DAILY AND SUNDAY PER WEEK 30c

TWO CONVICTS FLEE FROM ALCATRAZ ISLE

Refugees Fleeing Panay Fired On, Hull Asserts

U. S. Will Back Stern Demands With Denunciation of Attack on Imperiled Fugitives

WASHINGTON, Dec. 16 (AP)—The United States stiffened its attitude toward the sinking of the gunboat Panay upon the arrival of official information today that the vessel was machine-gunned by surface craft as well as attacked by airplanes.

Secretary of State Hull announced that, as a result, supplementary representations were being made to Japan through the American Ambassador, Joseph C. Grew.

He said that on the basis of partial official dispatches, he was able to confirm press dispatches that the Panay was machine-gunned by Japanese army motor boats.

Officials said Hull had additional information, as follows:

While survivors were escaping from the sinking Panay, airplanes dived and machine-gunned the small boats from an extremely low altitude, wounding two persons.

Bullet holes later were found in the Panay's outboard motor sampan.

Before the Panay sank, some Japanese military boarded the Panay and stayed there five minutes, although the American colors were flying and the nationality of the boat was easily discernible.

Hull said the charges would be presented by Ambassador Grew to the Japanese government to "confirm, elaborate and support" the allegations and demands already made in a formal note.

SEEK TO AVERT DANGER

Striving to prevent the Panay incident from slipping into more dangerous waters, State Department officials said they were awaiting direct, eye-witness reports from Commander Hughes of the Panay and Secretary Atcheson of the American Embassy in China.

These two are on their way to Shanghai and the report probably will not arrive before tomorrow.

State Department officials did not hide their feeling that the official message mentioned by Hull had given the situation a more serious aspect.

Many persons here felt the message indicated that the "manifest mistake" excuse in the Japanese note could not be validated.

GOVERNMENT HELPLESS

Officials said this did not necessarily imply knowledge and deliberation on the part of the Tokyo government, since the Japanese military organization in China seemed to operate on its own responsibility, subject only to the high command in Tokyo, which in turn was subject to the Emperor and not to the civil government.

The aggravation of the Panay affair may delay the Japanese reply to Secretary Hull's demands for apology, indemnification and guarantees several days.

It was felt at the State Department that Japan would wait until the United States had presented the additional information shortly forthcoming and until Tokyo had received a full report of the incident from its own officials.

The State Department acknowledged that the recall of Japanese Rear Admiral Teizo Mitsunami, in charge of naval air operations on the Yangtze, was a gesture in the right direction. What the department is chiefly interested in, however, is securing adequate guarantees for the future.

Citizenship Renounced By Barbara

(Picture on Page 19)

NEW YORK, Dec. 16 (AP)—Countess Haugwitz-Reventlow, the former Barbara Hutton, renounced her American citizenship yesterday, the law firm of White & Case announced late today.

The countess, who inherited a sizeable chunk of the Woolworth five-and-ten-cent store millions, sailed for Europe last night after a one-day visit here.

She had arrived in New York on the Europa, ostensibly to spend Christmas with her father, Franklyn Hutton. Her appearance here was unexpected and her departure just as sudden.

EMPLOYES STRIKE

Yesterday she went before Federal Judge Bondy and went through the formality of attesting her renunciation.

It was only a few hours after she sailed that employes in three Woolworth stores in New York city struck.

The strikers sent the following message to the countess this afternoon:

"Make a Santa Claus possible for 5000 Woolworth workers. Will you

(Continued on Page 18, Col. 5)

Bingham Condition Is Called 'Serious'

BALTIMORE, Dec. 16 (AP)—Robert W. Bingham, Ambassador to Great Britain is in a "serious but not critical" condition, authorities at Johns Hopkins Hospital said today.

Physicians said he had spent a comfortable night and is "feeling better than yesterday."

Hoover Urges Plan to End Business Ills

Former President Offers Alternative to New Deal's Planned Economy

CHICAGO, Dec. 16 (AP)—Herbert Hoover offered the broad outline of an alternative to the new deal's "planned economy" tonight.

The former President opined the recession need not be serious, attributed current uncertainties to Administration policies and called for the moulding of a social and economic system embracing these points in a prepared address before the Economic Club of Chicago:

"First: The main anchor of our civilization must be intellectual and spiritual liberty. Ideas, invention, initiative, enterprise and leadership spring best from free men and women. The only economic system which will not limit or destroy these forces of progress is private enterprise.

HOPE OF SECURITY

"Second: In the operation of the economic system there is but one hope of increased security, of increased standards of living, and of greater opportunity. That is to drive every new invention, every machine, every improvement, every elimination of waste unceasingly for the reduction of costs and the maximum production that can be consumed.

"By these means we sell goods cheaper. More people can buy. And thereby we have higher wages, more jobs and more new enterprise. New industries and new articles add

(Continued on Page 18, Col. 6)

Santa Claus Smiles On Youth in Need

By CAROLYN ANSPACHER

Christmas seemed very near yesterday. There was a nip in the air, a crispness that made the world feel new and gay and unbelievably young.

People smiled at one another as they jostled toward groaning department store counters, and everywhere were sprigs of holly and prim little wreaths made of sweet-smelling pine and fir.

And in a San Francisco office a slim blond youth smiled, too, and knew suddenly a great inner warmth that touched his heart into brightness.

GREAT MOMENT

Loneliness fell from him like a mantle in one breathless ecstatic moment, for in that moment he not only found Christmas but also the actuating force that has given the holiday life for nearly 2000 years.

James found the realization of his dreams yesterday — dreams valued at millions but calling for only $120 as a starter.

The story of this boy appeared in The Chronicle yesterday morning under the heading of Case No. 31 on the Neediest Families list. Less than one hour after it was read, a kindly San Francisco couple, who have no children of their own, signified their intention of sponsoring this unhappy lad and promptly contributed $120 to insure his future success.

Charles Hugh Singleton, manager of the Engineers' Club here, and Mrs. Singleton read James' story as they sat at breakfast.

YOUNGSTER BATTLING FATES

To them there was infinite pathos in the picture of this youngster battling the fates in this effort to support himself and his widowed mother.

"We have no children of our own," Singleton said. "And we felt that by assuming this small responsibility to give James his chance in life we would find compensation for that."

Because of the kindness and generosity of Mr. and Mrs. Singleton 17-year-old James will be able to gain his education more quickly and his joy will find reflection in the weary, tear-filled eyes of his mother.

HEARTENING GESTURE

Another heartening gesture came from San Francisco's City Hall, where Mayor Rossi paused long enough in the execution of his official duties to send the following letter to The Chronicle:

"I have been following with intense interest The Chronicle's very splendid campaign in behalf of San Francisco's needy families," the letter read.

"It seems to me that this campaign is an outstanding one, since it cannot help but do that for which it is intended, namely, give permanent relief and point the way to rehabilitation of those whom misfortune has struck.

"As you know, there is no government nor city in the world rich enough to provide for all such cases. Private enterprises and private organizations must step in.

MONETARY ASSISTANCE

"This The Chronicle has done in an outstanding manner, and it is with pleasure and regret that I enclose a small check toward your cause, pleasure that I am able in a small way to assist, and regret that the calls upon me throughout the year, and particularly at Christmas, prevent a larger donation.

"I wish you success in your under-

(Continued on Page 18, Col. 2)

Escape at Prison

Theodore Cole

One of the Two Felons Who Disappeared at Alcatraz Yesterday.

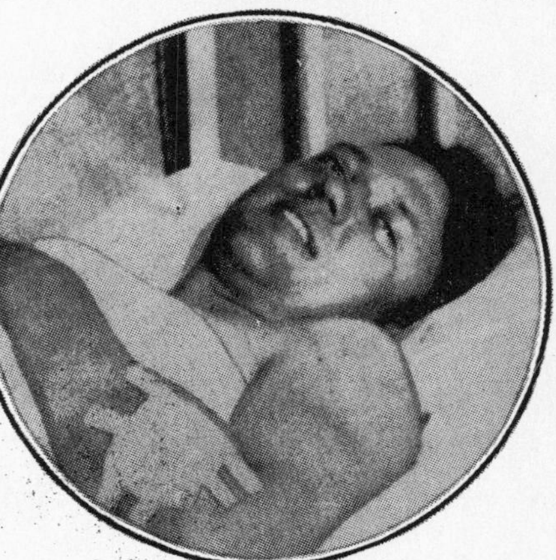

Ralph Roe

Picture Taken in 1933, When He was Wounded.

THE WEATHER

THE fog was so thick in San Francisco yesterday the weather man stood for half an hour in front of a mirror before he discovered he was not looking out of a window.

Off Pt. Reyes the Government fog cutter broke a blade and had to return to Hunter's Point. Fog drifted into the Presidio and so obscured visibility that several army rifles were found walking their posts without the sentries.

Shortly after noon a postcard was received from the lookout at Pt. Reyes. He reported continued fair and mild weather in this area and five more wild geese headed southwest. Off the Berkeley yacht harbor several hundred mud hens moored inshore, unable to find their customary fishing grounds.

Mrs. Hal Montgomery, 969 Bush street, got a real break.

"There's no fog at all here," she reported.

Her house had been overlooked by the FCA—the Fog Control Administration.

Algic Sailors Convicted on Mutiny Charge

BALTIMORE, Md., Dec. 16 (AP)—Fourteen members of the crew of the S. S. Algic were found guilty today by a Federal Court jury on charges of mutiny in a foreign port.

The case grew out of a sit-down demonstration by the defendants while the ship was in Montevideo, Uruguay, and involved the right of American foreign steamen to strike while in a foreign port.

FACE HEAVY PENALTIES

The jury returned verdicts of guilty on two indictments, charging revolt and conspiracy to disobey orders. Maximum penalties under each statute are a fine of $1000 or five years' imprisonment, or both.

Federal Judge W. Calvin Chestnut renewed bail of $500 each for the defendants, pending a motion for a new trial.

The verdict came after United States District Attorney Bernard J. Flynn demanded positive action to prevent bloody disorders in the American merchant marine.

WARNING GIVEN

"The defense has said that there was no bloodshed on the Algic," Flynn said. "The Government does

(Continued on Page 18, Col. 4)

Desperate Felons Elude Guards on Fog Bound Rock

Theodore Cole, Kidnaper, and Ralph Roe, Robber, Missing at Midday Checkup; Warden Leads Search

Two long-term convicts escaped from fog-shrouded Alcatraz Island Federal Penitentiary yesterday to become the object of the most intensive man-hunt in recent California history. It was the first escape from the supposedly escape-proof Federal prison.

The men, Theodore Cole, 23, Oklahoma kidnaper serving 50 years, and Ralph Roe, Oklahoma robber serving 99 years, were missing at the midday checkup and it was believed they had escaped over a stockade, hidden from the eyes of guards by the dense tule fog.

After a thorough search of the island, Warden James A. Johnston at 6 p. m. expressed the belief the men were "off the island," having jumped in the bay to chance a successful swim ashore.

Escape Discovered at 1:30 p. m.

The escape was first discovered at 1:30 p. m., when Warden Johnston completed an inspection of the prison and noted the absence of the two men. They had been working in the tire repair shop and broken glass in the rear was sighted. The window had been jimmied.

Additional news of the Alcatraz situation on Pages 2 and 17.

Despite the dense fog, the two men were traced to a gateway, over which they may have dropped 10 to 15 feet to make their way to the shore of the island.

After the Coast Guard had been summoned, it was declared no boats of a suspicious nature had been seen in the vicinity of the island, although it was possible a small craft had slipped through under the blanket of fog to pick up the two fugitives.

Coast Guard officials reported it would have been impossible for the men to swim long in the strong ebb tide that would have carried them out the Golden Gate within a few minutes.

Believes Boat Escape Unlikely

The warden declared he did not believe the men had sufficiently powerful outside contacts to have arranged the escape, and he believed it unlikely they escaped by speedboat.

Despite the warden's statement, some observers believed the convicts would not have been so foolhardy as to attempt the escape without outside assistance.

The warden advanced the theory the two might have "horned in" on the escape plan of some other "big shots" who could have arranged to have the necessary funds put up for the boat and other details. He thought they might have learned of another escape plot and have jumped the gate to take advantage of the arrangements of others.

As hours advanced and no trace of the two was found on the island, it became more and more apparent they had succeeded in leaving "the rock."

Six Coast Guard boats and the San Francisco police boat D. A. White were rushed to the island to patrol the rocky shore and cruise that area of the bay. All-point police bulletins, covering the entire bay area, ordered a special watch along waterfronts and the bay shore.

Search Centers on Island

For hours the search centered on the 12-acre island itself as it was believed the men might still be hidden, awaiting nightfall to slip into the bay and swim for shore.

Should the two desperadoes succeed in eluding the network of officers on boats and ashore, it would be the first successful escape from "The Rock" since it became the Federal prison for worst offenders, and the island's escape-proof tradition would be shattered.

Escape Had Been Long Planned

Officials believed the escape had been long planned, the pair waiting for such a day as yesterday when the fog was so

(Continued on Page 17, Col. 3)

Mystery Blasts Jar West Side; 3 Hurt

Shaking the ground like an artillery barrage and blowing manhole covers and flames high into the air, a series of mysterious explosions early yesterday terrorized residents of a two-mile area along Cicero av. from Haddon av. to Harrison st.

Hundreds fled from their homes in night clothing. Despite the flying manhole covers, however, only three persons were injured.

CAUSE SOUGHT.

Although five agencies, including the board of health, were searching for the cause of the blasts, Dr. Robert Black, acting health board head, said last night that the cause had not been determined. Theories as to the cause included:

Ignition of sewer gas by a fire in a building at Chicago and Cicero avs.

Gas from a leaky main entering the sewer. This was denied by the Peoples Gas Company after an investigation.

Accumulation of fumes from cleaning fluid dumped into sewers, or from gasoline dumped into sewers by "alley mechanics."

Possibility that a cigaret tossed into a sewer may have ignited sewer gas.

FULTON ST. IS CENTER.

Fire Marshal Frank Teboreck said the area affected by the blasts was bounded on the north by Haddon av., on the south by Harrison st., on the west by Lamon av. and on the east by Kilpatrick av., with the force of the explosions centering at Fulton st. and Cicero av.

Police estimated 100 manhole covers were blown off.

The most serious area of damage was along Cicero av. from Madison st. to Chicago av.

The injured:

David Biggerstaff, 22, of 320 N. Lamon av., knocked down by one explosion at Fulton st. and Cicero av.

Mrs. Mary Kopystynski, 43, burned on the head when a sheet of flame shot up through the wall of her frame house at 641 N. Cicero av.

Bernard Waegelein, 29, of 2930 N. Kilpatrick av., cut on the left thumb when his automobile was hurled into the air and turned around in front of 4941 W. Chicago av. One of his tire rims was blown half a block away.

GROCERIES JUMBLED.

Windows in a small grocery which the Kopystynskis operate in the front part of their home were broken, shelves were blown down and the stock was hopelessly jumbled.

Biggerstaff was found unconscious in the street by James Gaughan of 224 N. Cicero av.

Many store windows on Cicero av. were broken. In the 4900 block in Ferdinand st., an explosion blew a hole ten feet wide and six feet deep in the parkway. Telephone service was disrupted.

SCORES of manhole covers, like this one at Washington blvd. and Lamon av., were hurled into the air by the West Side explosions.

MISSING WOMAN FOUND IN LAGOON

Thet body of Mrs. Agnes Triner, 35, who disappeared from her home at 1920 S. Fifty-seventh av., Cicero, Saturday night, was taken from the Columbus Park lagoon by Fillmore police yesterday. On the shore, police found her purse, with a paper inside bearing her name and address. The body was identified by her husband, Rudolph.

Decorators' Party

The annual Spring party of the Illinois Chapter, American Institute of Decorators, will be at the Fortnightly Club tomorrow night. A one-act play, "Do It This Way," by Harold S. Darling, a member, will be given by decorators and actors. Miss Mabel Schamberg is president of the chapter.

Crashes Kill 4; Youth Dies in Flaming Auto

One man was burned to death and four other men and two girls were injured when an automobile crowded with young people collided with another at Lake st. and Mill road, Elmhurst, early yesterday.

Two men were killed in other Sunday motor accidents. Alvin Ott of 101 E. Ash st., Lombard, was killed in the Elmhurst accident. He was riding with Richard Kufer, 23, of 137 S. Stewart av., Lombard. Kufer was burned. Both men were WPA workers.

TRAPPED BY FLAMES.

The second car was driven by Milton Schrieber, 19, of 7442 N. Rockwell st. Coming east on Lake st. it crashed into Kufer's car at the intersection. Kufer's car turned over and burst into flames, trapping Ott within it.

In Schrieber's car were Miss Genevieve Birr, 19, of 42 N. Main st., Lombard, and Miss Loretta Wilke of 137 Edgewood av., Lombard, both of whom were burned. With them were three other young men, Abe Berzon, 18, of 4741 Monticello av.; Phillip Strom, 4822 Kenmore av., and Bud Lodall, 5250 Spaulding av. Berzon and Lodall were in the hospital.

AUTO HITS POLE.

Edward Barman, 48, of 5400 Montrose av., was killed when his car swerved across North av. at Twenty-first st. and struck a light pole and a hydrant.

Kenneth Grant, 28, of 712 Mulford st., Evanston died soon after a car turned over four times in McCormick road near Dempster st., Niles Center.

Miss Harriett Merrifield, 27, of 1010 Cherry st., Winnetka, his companion, was in a serious condition at St. Francis Hospital.

Merle Johnson, 22, of Howard st., driver of the car, and Miss Rae Merrifield, 21, Harriet's sister, were also injured.

Pay Averages Told

WASHINGTON, April 30.—(AP)—The social security board reported today that the 1937 average wage of women who have federal old age pension accounts was $525, that of men, $1,027.

Moran and Parker Guilty in Forgery; Face Year in Jail

George ("Bugs") Moran and Frank Parker, former airplane bootlegger, were found guilty last night of conspiring to make and distribute fraudulent checks.

Moran, erstwhile gang leader, and Parker, however, were convicted only on a misdemeanor count in the indictment against them and face maximum terms of a year in the county jail and fines of $2,000.

The jury in Judge Fardy's court returned its verdict, dodging possible felony counts on which Parker and Moran might have been sent to prison, at 10:30 last night, after twenty-five and a half hours' deliberation.

FREE CO-DEFENDANTS.

Their co-defendants, Daniel Driscoll, Frank Hicketts and Robert Sexton, were found not guilty.

Attorneys for Moran and Parker announced they would move for a new trial this morning.

They were accused of conspiring to forge $62,000 in counterfeit American Express Company travelers' checks.

CONVICTED BY U. S.

Parker, Moran and Hicketts were acquitted of a similar charge January 20 in Judge Fardy's court.

Assistant State's Attorney Robert Wright asked the jury to impose the maximum punishment of one to five years in the penitentiary and a $2,000 fine on Hicketts, Parker and Moran, but recommended lighter punishment for the other defendants.

During the trial, Parker was guarded in court by a federal agents, since he was found guilty in federal court two weeks ago on a charge of conspiring to possess and pass counterfeit money.

FDR 'TELECAST' FROM N. Y. FAIR

NEW YORK, April 30.—(AP)—Popular television in America, for years a fantasy of dreamers and a problem for scientists, was realized today. President Roosevelt and other guests at the World's Fair inaugural were among the subjects telecast to homes and radio stores as far as fifty miles away.

PEEVED . . .

GRACE MOORE, songstress. ". . . Never . . . another picture."

Grace Moore Paves Way to Film Feud

PORTLAND, Ore., April 30.—(I.N.S.)—The makings of another Hollywood feud were launched today when Grace Moore, beautiful star of the operatic stage and screen, wired her studio bosses this message:

"Have just seen 'Broadway Serenade' and never want to do another picture in Hollywood."

Miss Moore took time off from her concert tour of the Northwest to see the Jeanette McDonald picture at a Portland theater.

"Everything in it is 'One Night of Love' all over—only done in atrociously bad taste," bristled the silver-voiced star.

"One Night of Love" introduced the Metropolitan soprano to the films and it was hailed as a noteworthy example of operatic art in motion pictures.

Miss Moore, who climbed from obscurity in a small Tennessee town to eminence in the operatic firmament, revealed she had received a film offer to do Noel Coward's "Conversation Piece" and the telegram was her answer.

RIOT VETERANS MEET

Capt. Frank Tyrell (left) and George Roycroft.

The Haymarket Riot Veterans' Association, composed of policemen who participated in the bloody Haymarket riot May 4, 1886, held its fifty-third annual meeting yesterday in the Desplaines st. station.

Capt. Frank P. Tyrrell, 81, of 643 S. Clarence av., Oak Park, president of the association for the last thirty years, rapped for order and called the roll.

The only answer was from George Roycroft, 92, of 3304 Schubert av. Tyrrell and Roycroft are the only survivors among the 176 original members.

Then they strolled to the scene of the riot, an alley just north of 153 N. Desplaines st., where a bomb, hurled at an anarchist meeting, killed eight policemen and injured seventy-four others.

HOLLYWOOD PLAYBOY LINKED TO MURDER RING

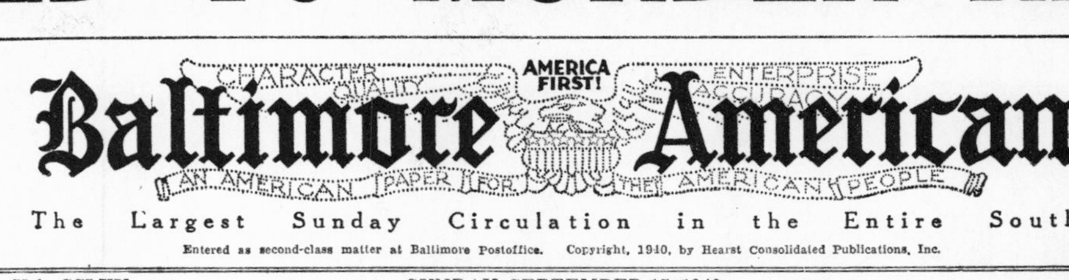

The Largest Sunday Circulation in the Entire South

Entered as second-class matter at Baltimore Postoffice. Copyright, 1940, by Hearst Consolidated Publications, Inc.

Est. 1773 Vol. CCLXV. SUNDAY, SEPTEMBER 15, 1940 PRICE 10 CENTS

G. O. P. In Drive To Wrest House Control From New Deal

BEN SIEGEL AND EVELYN MITTELMAN, A "MURDER, INC." WITNESS
After she talked in New York police in Hollywood found Siegel in an attic.

THE $250,000 MANSION, WHERE SIEGEL ENTERTAINED FILM NOTABLES AT LAVISH PARTIES
The police found enough hidden stairways and secret panels to turn Fu Manchu green with envy.

HARRY SEGAL
Also indicted.

AL TANNENBAUM GETS THE JITTERS
Watched the liquidation of "Big Greenie."

ABE RELES
He elected to "sing."

Hollywood Playboy Linked To Murder

Entertained Film Stars With Lavish Parties

By Universal Service.

LOS ANGELES, Sept. 14.—Hollywood is very sour on handsome strangers these days. For another rich "glamour boy" has turned out wrong.

His name is Ben Siegel, and up to a few weeks ago, he was on the best of terms with many a member of the gayer celebrity—set.

It was something to be invited to one of the many lavish parties he staged in his 35-room, $250,000 mansion in fashionable Holmsby Hills.

But it won't be any more. For the free-spending Ben has been revealed, through the medium of a murder indictment, as "Bugsy" Siegel, formerly a small-time Eastern hoodlum.

More recently he was alleged key figure in the sinister "Murder, Inc."—an aggregation of professional killers who have confessed to slaying of sixty-odd citizens between here and New York city.

Siegel is charged with being one of five men who engineered and carried out a typical gangland execution in Hollywood, last Thanksgiving Day.

BIG GREENIE'S CRIME.

The victim was one Harry (Big Greenie) Greenberg, New York mobster.

His crime was threatening to tell what he knew about Louis ("Lepke") Buchalter and other members of the coast-to-coast murder ring.

Indicted with Siegel were Buchalter, Harry (Champ) Segal, a friend, but not a relative of "Bugsy"; Emanuel (Mendy) Weiss, a Lepke lieutenant, and Frank Carbo, prize fight promoter and manager.

STILL HAS MONEY.

However, even though the indictment washed most of the glamour off Siegel, it hasn't dislodged him from his position as a man of wealth.

Coming here as a virtual unknown some six years ago, "Bugsy" has since accumulated, not only a host of prominent acquaintances, but a fortune estimated at $1,000,000.

District Attorney Buron Fitts hopes to bring out the extent to

Continued on Page 8, Column 1

Amateur Diver Aids Fishermen

NORRIS, Tenn., Sept. 14.—Whenever fishermen lose their false teeth or other articles pertinent to their well-being in TVA's Norris lake, they call for Barton Jones, Jr.

Barton, sixteen, has made out of odds and ends diving equipment which will permit him to descend to a depth of 70 feet although he has gone down only about 55.

Hog Ends Chase By Catching Fox

SHEPHERDSTOWN, W. Va., Sept. 14—(A. P.).—Mrs. Robert Gano, feeding her chickens, noticed a large red fox near the pen. She set out after the fox with a broom and chased it into the hog pen.

The startled hog gave one look and then seized the fox in its jaws. The chase ended right there.

U. S. Takes Olympe's Prints

ONE OF THE first members of the film colony to step up for fingerprinting when the U. S. Government started registering all aliens was Olympe Bradna, French-born movie star. She is shown here with George Comey, at the Beverly Hills postoffice, about to make her mark on the official form.

U. S. Dive Bomber Fastest In World

NEW YORK, Sept. 14—(I. N. S.).—New dive-bombers, capable of releasing almost three-quarters of a ton of explosives while plummeting earthward at speeds in excess of 370 miles an hour, are being produced today at the Republic Aviation Corporation plant at Farmingdale, Long Island.

The plane is the Guardsman dive-bomber, which company officials claim is the most heavily armed, fastest and most versatile two-place fighting plane in the world.

The plane is a new version of the design created by Major Alexander de Seversky.

The three-quarter ton bomb load the plane carries includes one projectile weighing 750 pounds and six 100-pound wing bombs.

A special displacing mechanism permits accurate release of the big fuselage bomb, while the plane is zooming earthward in a vertical dive. A cradle mechanism prevents the released bomb from hitting the propeller.

ROOM FOR MORE GUNS.

Two thirty-caliber rapid-firing guns synchronized to fire through the propeller and a flexible thirty-caliber gun mounted in the rear cockpit on a turret make up the armament of the plane.

Potentially, the plane has even more armament power. There are implacements in the wings for two rapid-firing cannons.

There is also room on each wing for thirty-caliber machine guns that could spray bullets on troops while the ship was diving.

PURSUIT-INTERCEPTER.

The low wing plane becomes an effective pursuit-intercepter when the heavy bombs have been released.

It is an all-metal plane powered with twin-row Wasp engines of more than 1,000 horsepower.

The crafts maximum cruising range of 1,800 miles is exceedingly long for a single-engined fighter. When the ship is free of her heavy bomb load it can climb 3,000 feet a minute and has a service ceiling of 30,000 feet above sea level.

Stork Pays Visit To Two Sisters

WALHALLA, S. C., Sept. 14—(A. P.).—Married to brothers, Mrs. Clarence Hawkins and Mrs. Cooper Hawkins, sisters, gave birth to daughters on the same day.

PARTY NEEDS 54-SEAT GAIN TO RULE BODY

Continuation of Swing to Republicanism Seen Likely in Balloting For Representatives

By SANFORD E. STANTON

WASHINGTON, Sept. 14—(U. S.).—More than 45,000,000 men and women will go to the polls Tuesday, November 5, to elect a President of the United States.

But of equal importance—and perhaps more from the viewpoint of national policy as it will be shaped by the next Congress—will be the election of 32 Senators and 435 members of the House of Representatives.

For eight years the Democratic party has controlled both Houses of Congress.

Until two years ago, the Republican minority had been so numerically overwhelmed that its voice, to all intents and purposes, was silenced.

Only a political miracle can change the control of the Senate. No one expects it to happen.

DIFFERENT IN HOUSE.

But in the House of Representatives the situation is different. That is the big political battleground of the year.

Of the 435 members of the House, 261 are Democrats, 164 Republicans, two Progressives, one Farmer-Labor and one American Labor. There are six vacancies.

The resurgence of the minority began in 1938 when the Republicans gained more than 90 seats.

The trend to the Republicans and away from the New Deal continued to show itself in 1939 where vacancies in Congress were to be filled in "off-year" elections.

Every indication now points to a continuation of the swing to Re-

Continued on Page 2, Column 7

Southern Leader Was Blitz Expert

MEMPHIS, Tenn., Sept. 14—(I. N. S.)—Hitler's blitzkrieg tactics may be devastating but they aren't new.

In the War between the States, Confederate General Nathan Bedford Forrest, daring cavalry raider whose troops harassed every Yankee encampment in the mid-South, was a member of the strike-first school.

His philosophy was:

"Git thar fustest with the mostest men."

Lately, however, Mrs. Mary Forrest Bradley, his only living granddaughter, has contested the validity of this backwoodsy, ungrammatical phrase.

SEIPNEP HOLDS HOPE FOR HAY FEVER VICTIMS

More baffling than many graver respiratory afflictions Hay Fever, at last is being conquered by science—Malady No Joke.

WHERE ARE GLAMOUR GIRLS OF YESTERYEAR?

Transient quality of Broadway fame is emphasized by plight of once highest paid showgirl who is now destitute.

NEXT SUNDAY!

GUARDSMEN FILL U. S. ARMY CAMPS

Mystering of peace-time army leaves thousands of "One-Year Jobs" open. Record of nation's militia replete with heroism.

CAMPAIGN BUTTON SALE CLUE TO ELECTION

History of badge-making shows symbols have played key role in Presidential campaign for more han a century.

3 CENTS PAY NO MORE!

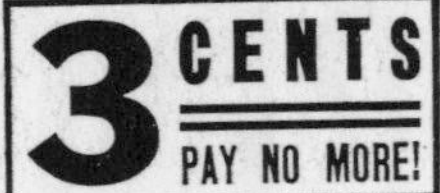

Chicago Daily Tribune

THE WORLD'S GREATEST NEWSPAPER

FINAL **

VOLUME CII.—NO. 68 C [REG. U. S. PAT. OFFICE, COPYRIGHT 1943 BY THE CHICAGO TRIBUNE.] SATURDAY, MARCH 20, 1943.—34 PAGES THIS PAPER CONSISTS OF TWO SECTIONS—SECTION ONE PRICE THREE CENTS

NITTI KILLS HIMSELF!

CITY SHATTERS POMP TO WAVE AT MME. CHIANG

Tumult Greets First Lady of China.

BY MARCIA WINN.

(Pictures on page 8.)

A pale, fragile little woman whose name, Mei-ling, means Beautiful Life, stood calmly at the balustrade in Union station yesterday.

Below her hung the American flag with the red flag of the Chinese republic on either side. Above her hung an avenue of flags of the allied nations fighting the axis. Beside her, looming like Gulliver, stood Edward J. Kelly, mayor of Chicago, extending a silver key.

Around them were dignitaries of the city and state, from Gov. Green down. Below them was a station filled with rapt, upturned faces, above which hands waved the flag of China.

"Typical of Democracy."

Mayor Kelly smiled as he looked down and extended the key. His voice, only occasionally booming thru the tumult, was saying, "Chicago . . . typifies . . . democracy. You, Mme. Chiang, belong here . . . because you, above all, typify . . . that ideal. Here . . . heart of America . . . our heart . . . to you."

Mme. Chiang Kai-shek, wife of the generalissimo of China, transferred her sable muff to the hand that held a great bouquet of roses. Her long Chinese dress of navy blue, profusely embroidered with flowers of yellow and blue and white, trailed beneath her sable coat. She smiled, a smile that irradiated her face and shot her butterfly-wing eyebrows upward, took the great key, and said in a little, warm voice that matched her size and face:

"It opens the door to a great heart. I thank you."

Begins Four Day Reception.

So began Chicago's four day reception to the woman whose name symbolizes to the world the valor of beleaguered China. It, like Mme. Chiang's appearance in the late afternoon at a reception in the Drake hotel tendered by Consul Gen. Chang-Chen, was brief [story of the reception on page 10]. Brief also will be her subsequent appearances, for her precarious health rides far below her indomitable spirit, and, as a Chinese official explained, "we must care for it as we would a precious piece of eggshell porcelain."

Today she will make no public appearance. Tomorrow she will make a brief visit to Chinatown at 5 p. m. and speak at the On Leong temple, in Wentworth avenue near Cermak road. In the interims she will rest, conserving her strength for the mass-meeting in the Chicago stadium Monday night at which she will continue her lone crusade of furthering in America the understanding her China requires.

Mme. Chiang and her entourage of 30 are staying in the Drake hotel, and half an hour after she had the key to Chicago in her scarlet-tipped fingers, she was in bed in her suite under the care of three nurses for an enforced rest of five hours.

Brave Men Go Limp.

And no wonder. Brave, stalwart men emerged from that first reception limp as dishrags. It wasn't supposed to be that way. It never is. But it always is.

Extreme precaution had been taken to guard Mme. Chiang's arrival. Only a few were supposed to come, and all officials, including 150 Chinese from the Chinese community here and nine surrounding states. Seventy uniformed policemen, four policewomen, a detachment of military police, railroad police, secret service men, and heavy ropes staking off a lane were to have obviated any crushing.

But the time of her arrival got out and a great crowd was on hand.

Those permitted to go out to the train shed when her five car special train, a section of the Pennsylvania railroad's Broadway Limited, pulled in, were carefully detailed: Mayor Kelly, Gov. Green, Silas H. Strawn [chairman of the citizens' welcoming committee], the Chinese consul general, Miss Florence Tom [who was

[Continued on page 10, column 2.]

NEWS SUMMARY OF THE TRIBUNE

(And Historical Scrapbook)

Saturday, March 20, 1943

THE WEATHER

SATURDAY, MARCH 20, 1943.

Sunrise, 6:54. Sunset, 7:03. Moonset, 7 a. m. tomorrow. Mars and Mercury are morning stars. Venus is the evening star. Saturn and Jupiter are night luminaries.

CHICAGO AND VICINITY: Colder, strong winds in forenoon, diminishing in afternoon and evening.

ILLINOIS: Colder; strong winds north today.

TEMPERATURES IN CHICAGO

For 24 hours ended 2 a. m. March 20:

3 a.m...31	9 a.m..32	3 p.m...37	9 p.m..26
4 a.m...31	10 a.m..33	4 p.m..*38	10 p.m..26
5 a.m...31	11 a.m..33	5 p.m...36	11 p.m..25
6 a.m...31	Noon...34	6 p.m...33	Midn't..24
7 a.m...31	1 p.m..36	7 p.m...30	1 a.m.†23
8 a.m...32	2 p.m..36	8 p.m...27	2 a.m..23

*High. †Low.

For 24 hours ended at 7:30 p. m. March 19:

Mean temperature, 33 degrees: normal, 36; March deficiency, 114; deficiency since Jan. 1, 20.

Precipitation, .30 of an inch; March excess, 1.06 inches; excess since Jan. 1, .52 of an inch.

Highest wind velocity, 35 miles per hour.

Relative humidity at 7:30 a. m., 93 per cent; at 1:30 p. m., 94 per cent; at 7:30 p. m., 77 per cent.

[Official weather report on page 14.]

Total average net paid circulation

FEBRUARY, 1943

DAILY in excess of 940,000

THE CHICAGO TRIBUNE

M'KIBBIN HALTS TALK TILL LADY GETS LAST WORD

Remarks on City Tax Set Off Debate.

BY RITA FITZPATRICK.

(Picture on page 8.)

George B. McKibbin tripped up Mayor Kelly in one of his campaign assertions that the city is solvent and "owes not a dollar" yesterday afternoon and caused a verbal free-for-all among the members of the Women's Civic council of the Chicago area, meeting in the Palmer House. The Republican nominee for mayor spoke immediately after Kelly, who had sandwiched in a few moments away from his duties as host to the city's distinguished guest, Mme. Chiang Kai-shek.

His head lowered to see where he was going, the mayor had bumped into his opponent as he stepped off the platform and for one of the few times in the campaign had shaken McKibbin's outstretched hand.

Rates Mean Nothing, He Says.

In a brief extemporaneous speech Mayor Kelly had asserted that the city had all its debts paid, and it was solvent and that its securities were demand all over the country. He contended also, amid the polite groans of some of the women, that taxes were lower than when he assumed the office 10 years ago and maintained that "present tax rates don't mean anything."

"I'm sure the mayor spoke inadvertently when he said the city was out of debt," McKibbin stated. "I think he forgot to mention that some $27,000,000 in tax anticipation warrants are outstanding against 1942 taxes. He also neglected to say that 11 years' taxes have been collected in 10 years and that the rate has gone up 60 per cent."

From the back row of the meeting room one avid woman Democrat shouted, "Speak for yourself and let the mayor alone." The remark started a flurry of comments on all sides, during which McKibbin waited patiently.

Then Every One Talks.

"Can't you take it?" "Does the truth hurt?" were remarks hurled at the heckler. The uproar came to an embarrassed pause when one intrepid Republican rose and reminded the assembly that they were "ladies" and had the privilege of taking their private politics home and to the polls.

"I am only trying to state the issues in the campaign," McKibbin explained, "and the tax problem is one of them. Another is the present coöperation between politics and crime in Chicago.

"If all the legitimate voters will go to the polls on April 6, by their very numbers they will overwhelm the Kelly machine and inaugurate a new era of honest and efficient government for Chicago and end forever the misrule to which our city has had to submit for the last 10 years."

Mayor Kelly did not hear McKibbin's remarks. The mayor's hurried exit had marked McKibbin's entrance. The mayor assured the women that the city now was in a better condition, financially and otherwise, than it had been in years.

Rests on Experience.

"I admit that I made some mistakes during the 10 years I have been mayor," he said, "but I feel that if I were working for a large industrial concern, they would forget those mistakes and keep me on as head of their business. Chicago is a big business and no one in the city hall is a miracle man. But the city is not sick, financially or otherwise.

The mayor stated that he had a great respect for McKibbin, a former neighbor of his, and that even if he possessed facts critical of McKibbin he would refuse to deal in any personalities in the campaign.

"I am not here to warp any one's mind," he explained. "Any one has a right to run for the office of mayor. I am not saying that I can do any more than any other man, but I do say that I have had the experience and the political finesse to handle the city council and all those with whom I came in contact."

[News of Mayor Kelly's and McKibbin's other political activity yesterday will be found on page 5.]

THE SCHEMERS

FIND FIRST HUSBAND OF WALLY SLASHED IN CALIFORNIA HOME

Santa Monica, Cal., March 19 [Special].—Earl Winfield Spencer, four times married, former husband of Mrs. David Windsor, was in the Long Beach naval hospital tonight suffering from a two inch knife slash in his upper left chest wall.

Spencer, 49 years old, a former lieutenant commander who retired from active duty in the navy four years ago, was noncommittal about the manner in which he received the injury. He explained only that he had "fallen against a knife."

Dr. Edison Bacon, Santa Monica physician, said he was summoned to the Spencer residence early yesterday by the former naval officer's fourth wife, Mrs. Lillian Margaret Spencer. The doctor said he found Spencer in a weakened condition lying on the floor covered with a pair of blankets. Mrs. Spencer said she found her husband lying on the kitchen floor when she returned from a brief absence.

Spencer was divorced in 1927 by Wallis Warfield of Baltimore, to whom he was married 25 years ago. She later married Ernest Simpson of New York and was divorced from him in London in 1936. Mrs. Simpson married Windsor, now governor of the Bahamas, after he abdicated as king of England.

M'ARTHUR PLANES SINK JAP SUB IN ATTACK AT NIGHT

ALLIED HDQ. IN AUSTRALIA, March 20 [Saturday] —(AP).— Gen. Douglas MacArthur's planes destroyed a Japanese submarine at Lae, New Guinea, an allied communique said today.

"In a night attack our aircraft surprised an enemy submarine discharging cargo in the harbor, destroying it with four direct hits," the communique said.

Allied raids for the second straight day extended over a huge area in the enemy's island held perimeter north of Australia.

An airdrome at Koepang in Dutch Timor was bombed, and a lugger was strafed at Semata Island in the Banda sea northwest of Australia. To the northeast five enemy invasion points were bombed, including Gasmata, Arawe, and Cape Gloucester in the New Britain area, and Lorengau in the Admiralty Islands.

Eighteen Japanese bombers escorted by 32 fighters struck back at one allied position at Porlock harbor, 50 miles south of recaptured Buna in New Guinea, shortly after noon yesterday. Dropping 70 bombs the enemy damaged the wharf and a launch.

Winchell Air Attack Riles Navy Mothers

Indignation among local navy personnel and the Navy Mothers' Club of Chicago which developed here after Walter Winchell's radio accusation March 14 that the mothers' organization had "adopted" an alleged pro-Nazi and draft evader, has resulted in a protest to the federal officials in Washington, D. C.

In his broadcast the New York gossip columnist declared in staccato accents that the navy mothers' club was "mothering" the Utopian post-war plannings of Joseph E. McWilliams, whose seditious activities have been probed by a federal grand jury and who was arrested in 1942 on a charge of draft evasion.

Charging that McWilliams had "practically been adopted by a group of Chicago navy mothers," the columnist implied that the women's clubrooms at 335 North Michigan avenue were frequented by McWilliams for the purpose of promoting sale of printed matter touting his post-war doctrines.

Advocates Big Loan.

This matter was in the form of a pamphlet advocating a 78 billion dollar bond issue at the close of the war and a gift of $7,800 in bonds to each of the 10 million service men. It sold for 50 cents. A "Post-War Bulletin" was also on sale for 25 cents.

In linking McWilliams' name to their organization, the navy mothers declare that Winchell, as is his wont, had again given a half truth to the public, which the mothers declare libeled their patriotic organization and impugned the unselfish motives that govern their activities.

What Winchell apparently didn't know and didn't bother to find out, according to the mothers, was that upon learning McWilliams' questionable background, the club immediately notified naval intelligence officers of McWilliams' presence and activities in Chicago and also told the federal bureau of investigation of McWilliams' doings and operations.

Club Aids Investigation.

Nor did Winchell know, apparently, that the club officials were requested to permit McWilliams' visits to the mothers' club offices to continue so that a thoro and secret investigation of his activities and of his pamphlets might be effected by naval intelligence and other governmental authorities.

All military intelligence services aided by the navy mothers were studying the texts and doctrines of McWilliams' publications before Winchell made the inquiry public, and surveillance of McWilliams had been intensified for a month before the date of the broadcast, naval officers said last night.

The Navy Mothers Club of Chicago, which is not associated with the Navy Mothers Club of America, has 700 members and has been stoutly supported in its work for sailors by all the navy's personnel stationed here.

Navy men last night declared that Winchell, who was placed on the inactive list for attacks broadcast against congressmen while a naval lieutenant commander, was guilty of reckless behavior in his March 14 broadcast.

PUT 1,000 POLICEMEN ON TRAIL OF MUGGER GANGS IN NEW YORK

New York, March 19 [Special].—Approximately 1,000 extra patrolmen, plain clothes operatives, and detectives, the largest detail in the city's history, tonight were thrown into the campaign against "muggers" who, working in gangs, beat, slash, or shoot their victims before robbing them. The reënforcements were sent to Harlem and Brooklyn, where the outbreak of "mugging" has been most severe.

The attacks have reached such proportions that extra details of policemen in Central park question any person found there after 10 p. m. Pedestrians on Fifth avenue have not escaped, however, and attacks have been made in the vicinity of some of the largest and best known hotels.

District Attorney Thomas C. Hughes said that in Brooklyn "the fear of law abiding people of many sections has become so great that they will not leave their homes after sundown."

The increased vigilance follows a series of mugging attacks and stabbings, including assault on a young night club singer, an attack on the son of a minister, and the stabbing of a white youth by three Negroes since Sunday.

Reports of these attacks have been made public, but civic leaders in recent days have charged that police have not reported all "mugging" cases. In one such case last Sunday in which the victim was a British naval officer, the information was withheld.

REAL AMERICAN TOLD TO LEARN ARMY LANGUAGE

Long Beach, Cal., March 19 (AP).—Rookie Pvt. Owen Keams presented a problem at the air transport command ferry division. Keams is a Navajo Indian from Arizona. He doesn't speak or understand English. No one at the base speaks or understands Navajo. Officers solved the problem. Keams will have to learn English.

GANG CHIEF DIES BY GUN AFTER U. S. JURY CHARGE

INDICTMENT OF 9 REPORTED ONLY FIRST OF SERIES

BY CHARLES LEAVELLE.

The nine indictments returned by a New York federal grand jury yesterday in the $2,500,000 shakedown of four major motion picture producers and 42,000 members of the International Alliance of Theatrical Stage Employés mark only the beginning of a government drive to smash gangster control of legitimate enterprises.

Within the next few weeks the same New York grand jury is expected to return two dozen or more additional indictments, naming labor leaders, politicians, attorneys, and other silent partners of the Nitti-Ricca-Campagna gangsters who seized IATSE and kindred unions.

Cases were built simultaneously against the gangsters and their shadowy henchmen by United States Atty. Mathias F. Correa of New York, and his first assistant, Boris Kostelanetz, who is an accountant as well as a prosecutor.

Others Under Scrutiny.

Under their scrutiny is a Chicago attorney whose knowledge of legal technicalities was invaluable in the gigantic shakedown of moviedom's owners and workers. On their list of wrongdoers is a former union organizer who has boosted himself into control of one of Hollywood's largest casting bureaus.

Labor leaders who looked the other way while their unions were seized and enslaved, and politicians whose influence smoothed the way for the racketeers, are expected to face trial along with the Capone-Nitti wrecking crew. And even these additional indictments will mark only a beginning.

Within 30 days, United States Atty. J. Albert Woll of Chicago will launch an investigation designed to penetrate beyond the gangster phalanx and into the ranks of business and professional men heretofore regarded as legitimate and above suspicion.

Simultaneously, the treasury department at Washington, which has been supplied with copies of all evidence and testimony adduced in the New York investigation, will inaugurate a series of income tax prosecutions, naming Chicagoans, New Yorkers, and Californians as defendants.

Al Capone's Fate Cited.

Convictions under the income tax laws have sent to the federal penitentiary many Chicago outlaws of the prohibition era who had come to be regarded as immune to state law enforcement. Even the powerful Al Capone fell before the agents of the treasury and spent more than eight years in Alcatraz.

The indictments returned in New York yesterday name nine men, seven of them Chicago gangsters. The indictments charge mail fraud and violation of the anti-racketeering laws. The first, containing three counts of mail fraud and one of conspiracy, covers the alleged shakedown of the IATSE's 42,000 members.

This was accomplished, the government charges, thru a 2 per cent special assessment on the wages and salaries of the IATSE rank and file, supposedly for use in promoting the union's interests and defending it against activities of the CIO. The law was violated, it is charged, when checks representing payments to special operatives were mailed to Chi-

[Continued on page 7, column 5.]

AT LAST! AN UNKNOWN WORKER GETS CHANCE TO MAKE BIG SPLASH

Portland, Ore., March 19 (AP).—The woman who wraps the bottles which are rapped against the ships at launchings is going to launch a ship. Mrs. J. H. Melvin, Portland, weaves the net containers, spending three days on each.

The net must be woven strong enough to hold the bottle, but not strong enough to cushion the shock and prevent a good smash.

Mrs. Melvin will christen a subchaser Monday. "It used to make me sick to see all my work ruined in an instant," Mrs. Melvin said. "Now I only hope I break the bottle."

3 Trainmen Look On as Racketeer Fires 3 Shots.

RICH SOURCE OF GRAFT.

How the gangsters moved in on Chicago's cleaning and dyeing industry, extracting a lucrative toll of graft, is told in today's installment of gangster control of many businesses in Chicago. Turn to page 7.] Other stories on Nitti are on page 6.]

BY CARL WIEGMAN.

(Pictures on page 8.)

Frank (The Enforcer) Nitti, successor to Al Capone as the chief of Chicago gangland, shot and killed himself yesterday afternoon.

He ended his life sprawled against a fence beside the Illinois Central tracks near Harlem avenue and Cermak road in North Riverside, less than a mile from his pretentious home at 712 Selbourne road in Riverside. A small revolver was in his right hand.

By his suicide, the first such death of a big time Chicago gangster, Nitti cheated the government, which indicted him and six Chicago associates in New York yesterday as members of a ring which extorted more than two million dollars from movie executives and their union employes.

Shortly before his suicide an attorney telephoned the United States marshal's office and made arrangements to surrender Nitti today on the indictment, which was returned in New York.

Inquest at 11 Today.

Last night Nitti's body was in the county morgue, where an inquest will be held at 11 a. m. today.

Three men watched Nitti die. A freight train was passing the spot he had chosen as the death scene. Members of the crew saw him fire the fatal shot and heard his dying gasp. Unaware that the dead man was the notorious Frank Nitti, they reported the shooting to police and rode on with their train.

Chief of Police Allen Rose of North Riverside hurried to the place. He found Nitti lying on his back, his head against the post of a fence. Two bullets had passed thru his brown felt hat. One bullet, which entered behind his right ear, had lodged in the top of his skull.

Trainmen Tell Story.

The story of Nitti's suicide was told by the three members of the freight train crew. They are L. M. Barnett, 1911 South Hamlin avenue, switchman; William F. Seebauer, 3206 48th court, Cicero, conductor, and E. H. Moran, 1329 52d court, Cicero, switchman.

All three of the witnesses said they saw Nitti staggering along the tracks, as if he were drunk, before he shot himself. Coroner's physicians who examined the body said they would not be able to determine whether Nitti was intoxicated until they completed a chemical analysis.

"It was around 3 o'clock and we were backing the train south, the caboose in front," said Barnett. "The crossing at Cermak road is unprotected, so we stopped to flag down traffic. Then I got back

[Continued on page 6, column 1.]

SUNDAY NEWS
Copr. 1944 by News Syndicate Co. Inc NEW YORK'S PICTURE NEWSPAPER Trade Mark Reg. U. S. Pat. Off

5 CENTS PAY NO MORE

Vol. 23. No. 45 New York, Sunday, March 5, 1944★ 76 Main+28 Brooklyn+4 Kings+12 Comic+32 Coloroto Pages

LEPKE, 2 PALS DIE IN CHAIR AT SING SING

Story on Page 3

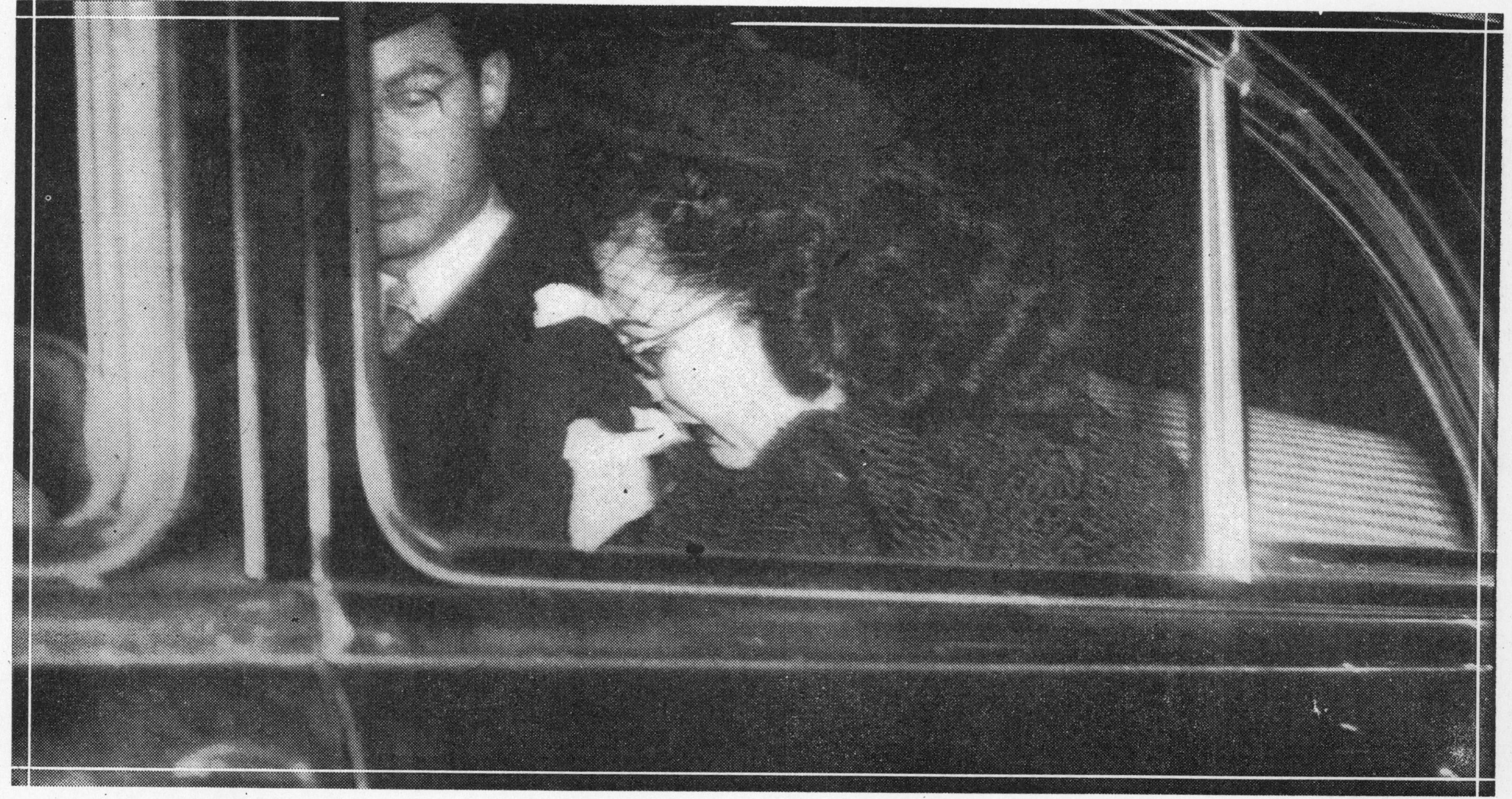

(NEWS foto)

Her Last Visit. Sobbing hysterically, Mrs. Betty Buchalter leaves the gates of Sing Sing after her final farewell visit with the doomed lord of the underworld less than two hours before he died. Until the last minute she fought to make him talk. Lepke, his face inscrutable, entered the death chamber at 11:13. He was pronounced dead at 11:16. Louis Capone and Emanuel (Mendy) Weiss preceded him to the chair.

—Story on page 3

Indiana Train Wreck; Fear Many Die

COMPLETE

RACES

Reg. U. S. Pat. Off.
Examiner Telephone RIchmond 1212

Examiner Building, 1111 S. Broadway

VOL. XLIV—NO. 48 LOS ANGELES, TUESDAY, JANUARY 28, 1947 PCC Two Sections—Part I—FIVE CENTS

SURRENDER OF BLACK DAHLIA'S KILLER AWAITED BY POLICE

Inside Story of Decision to Use A-Bomb

Action Saved Many Lives, Stimson Says

Only Two Explosives on Hand at Time

NEW YORK, Jan. 27.—(I N S) — Atomic bombs dropped on Hiroshima and Nagasaki to force Japan's unconditional surrender were the only two such bombs the United States had ready for such use.

That disclosure and many other inside facts relating to the momentous decision to atom-bomb Japan are contained in an article by former Secretary of War Henry Stimson.

It was released today by Harper's Magazine.

Stimson declares that use of the bomb saved countless Japanese as well as American lives that would have been lost in the planned invasion of Japan.

He says that intensified ordinary bombing of Japan had been planned to take place through summer and fall of 1945. That was "to be followed on November 1 by an invasion of the southern island of Kyushu . . . followed in turn by an invasion of the main island of Honshu in the spring of 1946."

MILLION LIVES—

"The total U. S. military and naval force involved in this grand design," Stimson continues, "was of the order of 5,000,000 men. . . . We estimated that if we should be forced to carry this plan to its conclusion, the major fighting would not end until the latter part of 1946, at the earliest.

"I was informed that such operations might be expected to cost over a million casualties, to American forces alone . . . enemy casualties would be much larger than our own."

Thus Stimson indicates that had the decision not been reached to use the atomic bomb against Japan, the war in the Far East might have raged on into 1947 with huge casualties on both sides.

As Secretary of War, Stimson was more closely associated with the development and decisions

(Continued on Page 2, Cols. 7-8)

World Court Rule on Atomic Violators Urged

By Rose McKee
Staff Correspondent International News Service

WASHINGTON, Jan. 27.—Senator McMahon (Democrat), Connecticut, proposed today that the United Nations solve the veto dispute blocking international agreement on atomic energy by giving the world court jurisdiction over violators of the rules.

McMahon, a member of the Senate atomic committee, declared on the Senate floor that his proposal would pave the way for an early agreement, provided Russia is sincere in its desire to outlaw the atomic bomb.

URGES HASTE—

He asserted that haste in reaching an international agreement on atomic energy control is imperative. The Senator said that other countries soon may have atomic bombs.

Even now, he said, Russia is probably "busily at work behind the Urals constructing an atomic fission plant."

Earlier, Senator Millikin (Republican), Colorado, stated that the American Atomic Energy Commission was ignoring the intent of Congress by failing to keep the military authorities fully informed of commission plans and actions.

'CLOSED DOOR' HIT—

Millikin told David Lilienthal, commission chairman-nominee, that the military liaison committee could not keep abreast of the work of the domestic commission unless it was represented at sessions.

Senate President Vandenberg (Republican), Michigan, agreed with Millikin. Vandenberg declared that "there must not be a single closed door anywhere" if the military and a joint congressional committee are to keep a check on the commission's work.

The Senators made their ob-

(Continued on Page 2, Column 5)

INDIANA TRAIN WRECK; FEAR MANY KILLED

Pennsylvania Rail Cars Leave Tracks on Way to Chicago

WALTON, IND., Jan. 27.—(AP)—Three persons were known dead tonight and other dead were believed in the wreckage of the Pennsylvania railroad's "Union" passenger train from Cincinnati to Chicago after it left its tracks in this north central Indiana town of 800.

LOGANSPORT, Ind., Jan. 27.—(AP)—Pennsylvania Railroad officials reported "a bad wreck" tonight near Walton, Ind., between Logansport and Kokomo.

All available ambulances and doctors in Logansport were ordered to the scene.

State police headquarters in Indianapolis said Kokomo city police received a report that "several persons were killed and injured."

A Pennsylvania spokesman at Columbus said he believed train No. 907 from Columbus had been added to No. 207 at Richmond, Ind. He had no additional information regarding the wreck.

DERAILED—

Harry Hirst, division operator in Pennsylvania Railroad offices here, said the train was No. 207 from Cincinnati to Chicago, a passenger train carrying additional passengers from a Columbus (Ohio) connect.

"We haye no information except that we received word at 6:08 p. m. (CST) that there had been a wreck at Walton," Hirst said. "We have men en route to the scene."

In Chicago, the Pennsylvania's passenger agent said he learned from Logansport that the locomotive was derailed, but remained upright, but he had no information as to whether any coaches left the rails or whether any passengers or crew members were killed or injured.

The Indiana state police post at West Lafayette, which covers the area of the wreck, said it had four units on their way to Walton after receiving a report of "a bad bad passenger train wreck."

The post said it expected to establish two-way radio communication shortly with its squad cars.

Are These From Killer?

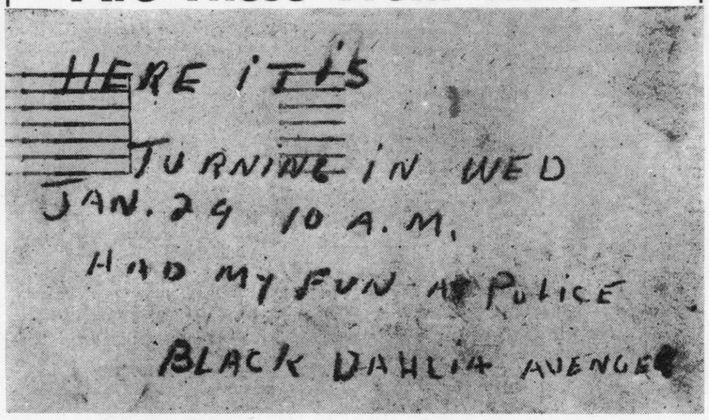

HERE IT IS
TURNING IN WED
JAN. 29 10 A. M.
HAD MY FUN AT POLICE
BLACK DAHLIA AVENGER

FROM 'AVENGER'—This note was received by Examiner Sunday. The "avenger" said he was "turning in" tomorrow. A previous note to Examiner said there would be a "letter to follow."

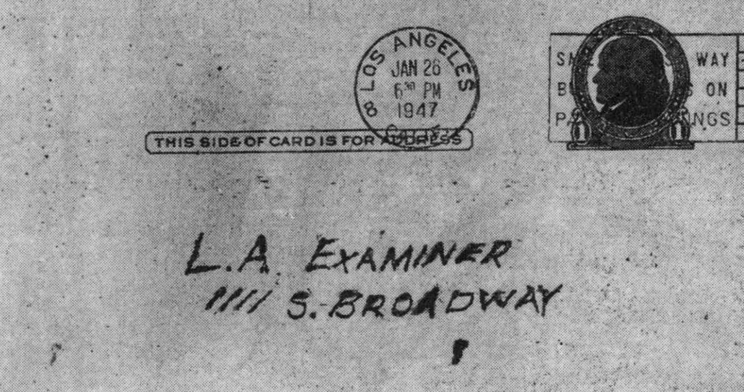

SLAYER'S CARD?—On the back of this postcard addressed to the Examiner was the "Black Dahlia Avenger's" note. Officials are standing by—is this a real offer or a taunt?

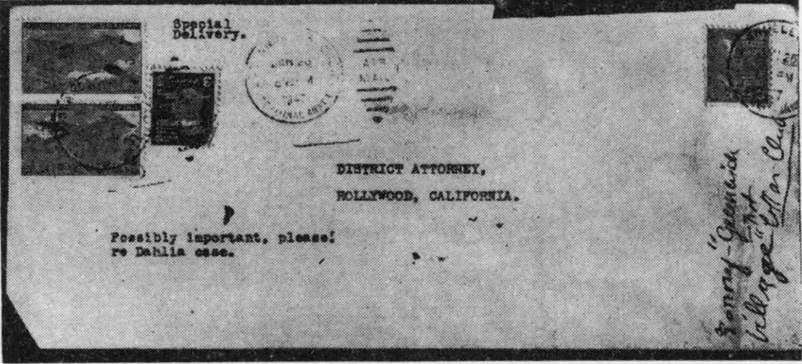

ANOTHER NOTE—This envelope to the District Attorney reportedly contained description of the night club incident involving the slain Elizabeth Short a day or two before the crime. Typed on front of envelope is message, "Possibly important, please! re Dahlia case."

Card Rouses Hope Slayer Will Appear

'Turning In Wed.,' Says Second Message to Examiner

Detectives and scientific experts yesterday tensely awaited the next move of the person professing to be the killer of Elizabeth Short.

In a postcard sent to the Los Angeles Examiner Sunday this person said:

"Here it is. Turning in Wed. Jan. 29 10 a. m. Had my fun at police."

The card, signed "Black Dahlia Avenger," was believed to be either a genuine offer of surrender or another taunting gesture in a game of "hare and hounds" apparently being played by the professed killer.

On Friday this person sent the Examiner items from the slain girl's purse. The items, which included her black address book, were in an envelope marked "Letter to Follow."

The postcard received by the Examiner Sunday is believed to be the "letter to follow."

Two More Letters Received

Two more letters, immediately recognized as not coming from the same person, were received by investigators yesterday.

One, intercepted in Pasadena by postal inspectors, said:

"Dahlia killer cracking—wants terms."

The other, addressed to the District Attorney and reported to be from a woman describing a night club incident involving "The Black Dahlia" a day or two before her murder, was unsigned.

In analyzing the postcard sent the Examiner, detectives and their scientific aides based their belief that a surrender was being contemplated on the words "Turning in Wed. Jan. 29 10 a. m."

The possibility that this was a genuine intention lay in the fact that the message on the postcard was printed. This indicated the writer was willing to risk possible identification.

The previous communication, with the items from Miss Short's purse, was built from words clipped from newspapers.

Ready to Surrender

If the killer no longer fears identification then he or she must be ready to surrender, investigators reasoned.

The opening words, "Here it is," were inter-

Navy Spending on San Diego Aqueduct Charged Illegal

WASHINGTON, Jan. 27.—(AP)—Comptroller General Lindsay Warren informed Congress today the Navy is illegally spending money to build a $14,500,000 aqueduct at San Diego.

Warren stated the "contract and expenditures of Federal funds are considered to be in violation of the law."

The aqueduct connects the Colorado River aqueduct of the Southern California Metropolitan Water District, near the San Jacinto tunnel in Riverside County, with the San Vicente reservoir in San Diego County.

The War Powers Acts, Warren's report to Congress said, "provide no authority for the use of Navy appropriations for the construction of the San Diego aqueduct."

Engle Urges End to Gold Trade Ban

WASHINGTON, Jan. 27.—(AP)—Representative Engle (Republican), California, proposed today that the Government ban on gold trading be abolished.

He introduced a bill to permit the purchase, sale, or trade, on the open market, of "gold in any form" for "any purpose whatsoever."

Gasperi, Red Chief End Italy Parleys

ROME, Jan. 27.—(AP)—A conference between Premier-designate Alcide de Gasperi and Communist Leader Palmiro Togliatti about Italy's week-old cabinet crisis ended this afternoon with both voicing optimism.

Argentine Envoy and Franco Meet

MADRID, Jan. 27.—(AP)—Pedro Radio, new Argentine ambassador, was escorted by a troop of mounted Spanish Moorish guards to the national palace today to present his credentials. He spent two hours with Generalissimo Francisco Franco.

Russ Ambassador Expected in Athens

ATHENS, Jan. 27.—(AP)—Constantine Rodianov, Soviet ambassador to Greece who was recalled to Moscow a few days before the Greek plebiscite, is expected to return to Athens today to resume his post, the Russian embassy announced.

213 Crimes Here in Day; Thefts at Top, Total 92

In the last 24 hours 213 crimes were committed in Los Angeles. They were:

92 thefts
56 burglaries
19 robberies
16 assaults with deadly weapons
4 morals offenses
2 attacks on women
1 attempted attack
23 automobiles stolen

JAN CIECHANOWSKI

DEFEAT IN VICTORY

By Jan Ciechanowski

CHAPTER ONE

This is the first of eight installments on "Defeat in Victory," by Jan Ciechanowski, the inside diplomatic story of the betrayal of Poland. The author is the former Polish ambassador to the United States and writes of behind-the-scenes conversations and conferences with the greatest authority. This condensation of his book shows the pattern of power politics and how Great Britain and this country have cynically yielded to Soviet Russia in abandoning principles for appeasement.

I left London on February 5, 1941, with my wife and two younger sons (my eldest son, John, was already in the Polish army in Scotland) and proceeded to Washington via Lisbon.

And now, here I was in the United States, once more given the opportunity of representing Poland as ambassador. In my first interview with President Roosevelt, he had encouraged me to do my utmost, to be active, to feel free in my work for Poland, for Europe, and the Allied cause.

As I studied the Washington political scene in the spring of 1941 and talked at length with Secretary of State Hull, Undersecretary of State Sumner Welles, James C. Dunn and Loy Henderson of the State Department, as well as with political and press personalities, I gained the impres-

(Continued on Page 14.)

CHARACTER QUALITY AMERICA FIRST! ENTERPRISE ACCURACY

Los Angeles Examiner

AN AMERICAN PAPER FOR THE AMERICAN PEOPLE — THE GREAT NEWSPAPER OF THE GREAT SOUTHWEST

Reg. U.S. Pat. Off

Examiner Telephone Richmond 1212 — Giant of Journalism — Examiner Building, 1111 S. Broadway

VOL. XLIV—NO. 193 LOS ANGELES, SUNDAY, JUNE 22, 1947 CC Six Sections—Part One—PRICE 15 CENTS IN CALIFORNIA (20 CENTS ELSEWHERE)

World Praises Mexico's Vivisection Ban

Illustrated Article on Page 16.

LABOR VETO FILIBUSTER ENDS

HINT SIEGEL SLAIN BY OWN MOB

Hotel Losses Put 'Bugsy' 'In Bad' With Syndicate

Pressure on L.A. Bookies Bared

Benjamin (Bugsy) Siegel, gang chieftain who was "rubbed out" Friday night in a Beverly Hills mansion, had enemies among both his allies and his rivals, police learned yesterday, as they pressed the search for his slayer.

His multi-million-dollar losses with the Flamingo Hotel in Las Vegas put him in bad with "The Mob"—a nationwide syndicate with headquarters in New York.

For 18 months he had been putting the pressure on Los Angeles bookmakers, forcing them to take his horse racing information service instead of rival services, or to pay for two services.

WIDE CHOICE——

Police had a wide choice of suspects from which to select the man — possibly an imported killer—who stood outside the window at 810 North Linden drive and riddled Siegel's body with bullets.

Nine empty .30 caliber cartridges were found on the driveway outside the window. They would fit a quick-firing automatic carbine.

Neighbors heard the burst of shots and a light car roared away a moment later.

Police measurements indicated the killer stood 14 feet from Siegel, who was seated on a couch. The bullets whizzed past Allen Smiley, business associate of Siegel, two of them piercing the shoulder of his coat.

Smiley was in "protective custody" at Beverly Hills po-

(Continued on Page 2, Cols. 6-8)

SLAIN—Benjamin (Bugsy) Siegel, 42, nation's number one gangster, who was "rubbed out" Friday night in typical gangland fashion.

ABSENT—Virginia Hill, in whose Beverly Hills home Benjamin (Bugsy) Siegel was slain. Miss Hill is reported to be in Europe.

894 Crimes in Week in Los Angeles

During last week 894 crimes were committed in Los Angeles. They were:

362 Thefts.
249 Burglaries.
75 Robberies.
67 Assaults with deadly weapons.
16 Morals offenses.
109 Automobiles stolen.
4 Attacks on women.
8 Attempted attacks on women.
1 Kidnaping.
3 Assaults and batteries.

HELSINKI WINS OLYMPIC SITE

STOCKHOLM, June 21.—(INS)—The International Olympic Committee chose Finland's capital of Helsinki today as the site of the 1952 Olympic summer games.

Oslo, capital of Norway, was chosen for the winter games in 1952. Helsinki received 15 votes on the second ballot as the summer games choice. Los Angeles received four votes.

Finnish citizens were jubilant. The only drawback is the country's housing shortage. If necessary, some Helsinki residents will be sent into the countryside during the games to make room for visitors.

OFFER EXPENSES——

Prior to the vote several American cities had signified agreement to an unprecedented request that they pay the traveling expenses of all European teams if chosen.

City Will Honor John Paul Jones

"He gave our Navy its earliest traditions of heroism and victory."

To the man, whose sarcophagus at the United States Naval Academy bears those words, Los Angeles will join in paying honor Sunday, July 6.

Celebrations, nation-wide, will mark the 200th anniversary of the birth of John Paul Jones.

In this area the observance will center at the United States Naval Base, Terminal Island.

Here, from 1 p. m. to 4:30 p. m. July 6, the base and all its facilities will be open to the public, with opportunities to inspect modern cruisers, a destroyer and a submarine, to visit the naval shipyard, see displays of up-to-date naval equipment and a contrasting exhibit of naval material of John Paul Jones' own days, and to make a boat tour of the harbor.

Directing plans for the observance are Vice Admiral Walter S. DeLany, commander of battleships and cruisers of the Pacific Fleet; Rear Admiral Paul S. Hendren, commander of the naval base, representing Rear Admiral Oscar S. Badger, commanding the 11th Naval District; Mayor Herbert Lewis of Long Beach, Acting Mayor George H. Moore of Los Angeles, David Hearst and R. A. Carrington Jr., publisher of the Examiner.

Navy ships open to visitors will include the heavy cruisers Los Angeles and Bremerton, the light cruisers Pasadena and Astoria, Admiral DeLany's flagship, the cruiser Helena; the destroyer Wedderburn and the submarine Sawfish.

The Helena will be berthed at the shipyard, and the other cruisers will be reached by small boats which will leave on regular schedules from the Terminal Island landing.

The Wedderburn and the Sawfish will be at the docks. On the way to the cruisers, visitors will make a harbor tour.

In Stark Center patio at the Terminal Island base will be a display of guided missiles, naval guns and other equipment and other modern material.

PUNJAB MOBS RIOTING OVER PARTITION VOTE

Fires Cast Smoke Pall Over Lahore; Death Toll at 71

NEW DELHI, June 21.—(AP)—Rioting mobs killed at least 16 persons and set fires that cast a smoke pall over Lahore today as legislators from all parts of Punjab province poured into the capital city to vote on partition.

The new outbreaks in the Punjab, along with rioting near Lucknow in the United Provinces, brought to 71 the death toll in two days of communal rioting in India.

The legislators attended meetings of the Moslem League, Sikh and Congress Parties prior to Monday's session of the assembly, when they were expected to decide to split the province into sections which will join Hindustan and Pakistan, the separate Hindu and Moslem states to be created in India.

SIKH DEMANDS——

Yesterday the Bengal provincial legislature voted for partition. The situation in the Punjab is complicated by a Sikh minority which is making militant demands for a homeland of its own.

The legislative actions constitute the first preliminaries under the plan of Viceroy Lord Mountbatten for setting up the two separate states, which are scheduled to become commonwealth dominions about August 15.

During today's rioting a bomb was tossed into a crowded vegetable market, killing five persons outright and wounding 40 more. The Mayo hospital said it had 16 dead and 60 wounded.

25 BLAZES——

The mobs fired upon each other, and in turn were fired upon by police trying to disperse them. Fire fighting brigades sped through the streets in efforts to put down at least 25 separate blazes.

Police and military patrols, heavily armed with machine guns, swept through the city in an effort to restore peace. The rioting did not extend to the fashionable Mall, where quiet prevailed.

Yesterday in Amritsar, holy city of the Sikhs in Punjab province, five persons were killed and 25 were injured in a bomb throwing battle.

From Lucknow, capital of the United Provinces, came word that 50 persons were killed and scores hurt in fighting between landholders and tenants in a village near the capital.

Troops and police were rushed into the area and a 24-hour curfew imposed.

With tension running high leaders of the major parties in the Punjab agreed upon a secret vote in Monday's assembly, with no speeches, shouting of slogans or demonstrations.

Heavy police and military guards will surround the assembly building.

Senate Will Vote on Bill Tomorrow

—Von Wiegand Interview:—

Gen. Holder Sees U.S. Undefeatable

'But Only Miracle Can Save Germany From Reds,' He Says

By Karl H. von Wiegand

Dean of American Foreign Correspondents

Written Expressly for the Hearst Newspapers

FRANKFURT, June 21.—"Only a miracle can save Germany from Communism and from being drawn—indeed, driven—into the waiting and beckoning arms of Soviet Russia.

"That miracle, let me add, will have to occur soon—very soon."

Colonel General Franz Halder, former chief of the German general staff, told me that today following a chance meeting in an eye clinic at Marburg University.

General Halder continued:

"In the great struggle between the civilizations of the East and West headed by Soviet Russia and America, Germany is a helpless pawn, but also may be the key in Central Europe whose turning in one or the other direction can be of influence in the final decision.

Key to Decisive Victory Over Reds

"America's atomic bomb alone, powerful as it is, will not be the decisive weapon in a war between America and Soviet Russia.

"Far more powerful than your atomic bomb to assure Soviet defeat in such a conflict would be the political *'centrifugal forces'* that are within that vast realm of Communism, if they could be released.

"I say this to you as one who can modestly claim to be something of a specialist on Soviet Russia and as a German general who was far into Russia, who was dismissed as chief of the general staff of the German army for opposing Hitler's views, strategy and orders, later imprisoned by him and whose life and that of my wife was saved in the Dachau concentration camp by the arrival of American forces."

General Halder spoke with great earnestness as he voiced his thoughts on an East-West conflict. He said:

"In such a war between America and Russia—the only remaining two world powers that emerged out of World War II—Western Europe, militarily speaking, would be only a forefield for you on the European continent.

U.S. Soil Comparatively Safe

"You may have some cities destroyed, or partly destroyed, by atomic weapons and long-range rocket missiles, but if you take the necessary measures and make proper preparations the United States, relatively speaking, will be safe and should be, I might say, undefeatable.

"The fact that Western Europe would be your forefield of operations on land and by air and that

(Continued on Page 6, Cols. 1-6.)

Democrats Fear Defeat

WASHINGTON, June 21.—(INS)—The Senate agreed today to vote on President Truman's veto of the labor bill at 3 p. m. (EDT) Monday, thus ending the filibuster.

WASHINGTON, June 21.—(AP)—Open filibuster thwarted Republican supporters of the Taft-Hartley Labor Bill from pushing it to final passage over President Truman's veto today, but they counted victory certain in the end.

Democratic leaders conceded they probably will be unable to muster their full strength on the test, which strategists of both sides said could come at any time and probably would develop Monday.

Yet, through a continuous Senate session already past the 24-hour mark and still going strong, a game but groggy group of last-ditch foes of the measure kept up the talk that prevented the vote.

RELAY——

Senator Morse (Republican), Oregon, weary and hoarse after more than seven straight hours on his feet, acknowledged that he and others were running a filibuster—"not a filibuster to prevent a vote," he said, but "a filibuster to assure unlimited debate in the Senate."

Senators Murray (Democrat), Montana, and Olin Johnston (Democrat), South Carolina, stood by to relieve him when he should have to sit down at last.

Morse had taken up the ball from Senator Taylor (Democrat), Idaho, at 5:30 a. m. (EST), and as he talked throughout the morning and into the afternoon he refused to concede that the President's supporters were defeated.

"It is true, of course," he said, leaning wearily against

Typhoon to Hit Coast of China

MANILA, June 21.—(AP)—U. S. naval weather observers said today a typhoon first sighted east of the Philippines was expected to strike the southeast coast of China in the Pamoy-Foochow area about midnight, Manila time.

The weathermen said late reports placed the typhoon about 150 miles southeast of Amoy.

England Suffers Potato Shortage

LONDON, June 21.—(INS)—London and cities of southeast ern England were struck today by the worst potato shortage in living memory.

Urge Housing Aid

SACRAMENTO, June 21.—(AP)—The Senate has adopted an Assembly joint resolution memorializing Congress to enact legislation to alleviate the housing shortage.

Fire Hitts La Havre

LE HAVRE, June 21.—(INS)—A fire broke out today in A Le Havre warehouse containing 6000 bales of American cotton.

Police were investigating the possibility of sabotage.

EXTRA

CHARACTER QUALITY · AMERICA FIRST! · ENTERPRISE ACCURACY

Los Angeles Examiner

AN AMERICAN PAPER FOR THE AMERICAN PEOPLE · THE GREAT NEWSPAPER OF THE GREAT SOUTHWEST

(Reg. U. S. Pat. Off.)

Examiner Building, 1111 S. Broadway, Zone 54 · Examiner Telephone Richmond 1212

·9 A·M· FINAL

VOL. XLVI—NO. 221 · LOS ANGELES, WEDNESDAY, JULY 20, 1949 · S · Two Sections—Part I—SEVEN CENTS

MICKY COHEN SHOT

Boys, 3, Blamed in Baby Killing

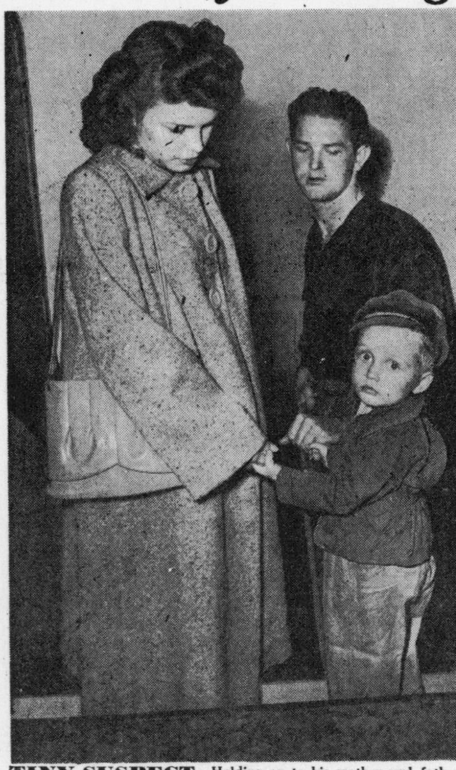

TINY SUSPECT—Holding on to his mother and father is little Garrie Hayes, one of two 3 year old boys blamed for beating his baby sister, Trudy, age 2 months, to death. Shown with him are his mother and father, Mrs. Wilma Jean Hayes and John Hayes. —Los Angeles Examiner photo.

Beaten and bitten by her 3-year-old brother and another boy the same age, according to police reports, Trudy Hayes, 2 months, died last night at General Hospital.

She was found lying unconscious on the floor at her home, 711 West Third street, by her father, John Hayes.

Juvenile Officers said she suffered a possible skull fracture and superficial bites over her body during rough play by her brother, Garrie, and his friend, Raymond Carr Jr., who lives at that address.

IN CRIB——

Hayes told officers that Trudy was in her crib when he left the apartment to buy cigarets. The infant's mother, Mrs. Wilma Jean Hayes, was working in a downtown store at the time.

He carried the infant to the Carr boy's apartment where the boy's grandmother, Mrs. Marie Carr, revived her before she was taken to the hospital. She died shortly afterward.

Juvenile authorities were puzzled as to what action to take with the two boys, because of their extreme youth.

Lieutenant C. E. McNamara, night commander at Georgia Street Juvenile Hall, said it was hard to attach responsibility to any act of children that young.

"They are even too young for psychiatric examination," he said.

No immediate action will be taken, he added, with any future move up to the Coroner's jury or the Juvenile Court.

Mrs. Mary Jean Carr, mother of little Raymond, said she could not see how the children could have reached Trudy.

"Both the boys would have difficulty reaching into the crib, let alone lifting Trudy out," she exclaimed.

Partial Rent Decontrol for Roomers Voted

Decontrol of rents on hotel, motel and rooming house rooms out of which "permanent guests" have moved voluntarily, was authorized yesterday by the City Council.

The ordinance which was passed specifically prohibits landlords from harassing such tenants as a means of forcing them to move.

Councilman Ed J. Davenport and Edward R. Roybal voted against the measure.

BANDIT KILLS MAN AND WIFE IN L.A. STORE

Tall Gunman Fires Bullet Through Heads of Couple

NORTH HOLLYWOOD, July 19.—A bandit tonight shot the proprietor of a market and his wife, killing them both instantly, during a holdup of the store at 11119 Burbank boulevard.

The victims were Jay Greene, 36, and his wife, Dorothy, 35.

Detectives R. S. Ingham and W. G. Von Platan learned from one of two witnesses that the gunman, tall and heavily built, shot Mrs. Greene when her husband told her to refuse the gunman's demand for money.

"He came in and said to Mrs. Greene, 'this is a stickup. Give me the money,'" according to the witness, Clinton Durham, 11260 Cumpston avenue.

"Her husband yelled to his wife, *'don't do it!'*"

Mrs. Greene said: "Don't shoot, I'll give you the money," and started to reach down behind the counter for it, Durham said.

The bandit apparently thought she was reaching for a gun and shot her through the head.

Scooping up an undetermined amount of money from the cash register, the killer turned to flee out the door. Greene tried to grab him and the bandit whirled on him and shot him through the head.

Then the holdup man escaped.

Greene was wearing a holster containing a pistol, but made no attempt to use it, Durham added.

The other witness was John C. Hann, 11127 Emelita street, who clerked for the Greenes. He was in the rear of the store.

Beery's Ex-Wife to Ask Million From Estate

Claims ranging up to possible $1,000,000 will be filed against the estate of the late Wallace Beery by his divorced wife, Rita, the Examiner learned last night.

Mrs. Beery will contend the gruff-voiced film star defrauded her in a property settlement incorporated in her 1939 Nevada divorce.

Beery then gave her $100,000, assertedly claiming he was worth only $200,000.

Since the actor's death last April, his executors already have found $800,000 in cash and certified checks—payable to him—in addition to rich property holdings and securities.

California's community property law makes husband and wife joint owners of each other's assets.

Citing Beery's income records and heavy taxes during the war years, Mrs. Beery will contend he could not possibly have amassed such wealth in the past 10 years alone. His will left his estate equally to Carol Ann, his adopted daughter, his brother, Will, and nephew, Noah Beery, Jr.

Gang Chieftain, 3 Others Blasted

Henchman, Bodyguard and Woman Also Felled by Bullets

Gangland guns early today mowed down Gambler Mickey Cohen as he stood outside a Sunset Strip restaurant.

The underworld leader was critically wounded by a shotgun blast through the right shoulder.

Also critically wounded by the barrage of shots were Harry Cooper, an agent of the Attorney General's office who had been assigned to "bodyguard" Cohen, and a Cohen henchman, Neddie Herbert.

Shortly before 4 a. m., Cohen and a party of friends came out of Sherry's Restaurant, 9039 Sunset boulevard, and were standing on the sidewalk in front.

Without warning, a fusillade of blasts roared from behind a signboard across the street, felling the three men and also wounding a woman in the party, Dee David.

Others in the party, who dropped to the ground and escaped unhurt, were Cohen Henchmen Frank Niccoli and Johnny Stomponato.

Niccoli said he saw the assailants at the time of the shooting, but in the confusion did not see how they made their escape.

"There were at least six of them," Niccoli said, "and I think more than that, but I don't know how many."

One Bodyguard Uninjured

Cohen and Cooper, the latter with two slugs through the stomach, were driven to Hollywood Receiving Hospital by Niccoli.

Herbert and Miss David, 27, a friend of Niccoli, were taken to Citizens Emergency Hospital. Herbert had been wounded in the side, arm, foot and wrist, and Miss David in the back. Both were in serious condition.

Uninjured was another "bodyguard," Sergeant D. L. Murray, assigned from Chief of Detectives Thad Brown's office to accompany Cohen along with Cooper.

Cohen, questioned at the hospital, professed complete ignorance of the identity of his assailants or the reason for the murder attempt.

"I'm completely in the dark," Cohen said.

The shooting came only a few hours after disclosure in the Examiner that Attorney General Fred Howser had asked the police, the district attorney and the Sheriff's office to "lay off" Cohen.

It was in this disclosure that the Examiner revealed Howser had assigned Cooper to accompany Cohen and act in the dual capacity of "investigator and bodyguard."

Asks End of Shadowing

The "lay off" request was made by Ralph Davis, chief investigator for the attorney general.

Davis personally made the request to Leo Stanley, chief of the district attorney's investigation bureau; Deputy Chief Thad Brown, commanding police detectives, and Inspector Gordon Bowers of the Sheriff's office.

He asked that they stop their continual shadowing of Cohen and his men for "at least two weeks."

Stanley Brown and Bowers said their respective offices would co-operate with Howser.

Davis further informed them Cooper would be with Cohen at all times and that Cooper was armed.

Attorney General Howser, reached by the Examiner, said:

"It is true I have asked the police, sheriff and district attorney to lay off Cohen. It is true I have an armed agent with him.

"All I can say at this time is this—I am making a widespread investigation which requires these moves. The investigation makes it imperative that Cohen be left alone by these other officers and that my man be with him."

Police officers, deputy sheriffs and district attorney's investigators have been shadowing Cohen and his men for some time, stopping them nightly for search and questioning.

FIRM BACKING OF U. N. VOWED BY PRESIDENT

Nation Assumes Responsibility to Outlaw Wars, He Asserts

By Robert G. Nixon
Staff Correspondent International News Service

CHICAGO, July 19.—President Truman, in a militant speech, declared tonight the United States must assume the leadership of the world's democracies to guarantee a force sufficient to assure peace.

The Chief Executive, in an off-the-cuff talk to a Shriner's dinner, declared:

"It's absolutely necessary that we assume the leadership of the democracies of the world so that there will be enough force to assure the peace of the world."

The President said that this nation will put its full strength behind the United Nations as a militant force for peace, adding:

"We have assumed the responsibility for peace in the world—it is necessary that we assumed that responsibility."

Earlier, Mr. Truman declared that **"tensions and conflicts appear to be increasing"** behind the Iron Curtain and that free nations can win the **"battle for men's minds"** without war.

The President said in a nationwide radio address that world Communism **"may have temporary triumphs, but in the long run it must either destroy itself or abandon its attempt to force other nations into its pattern."**

President Truman delivered his earlier address before 60,000 in Chicago's Soldier Field. The occasion was the diamond jubilee of the Shrine organization—of which the Chief Executive is himself a high-ranking member from Ararat Temple in Kansas City, Mo.

In his address, the President asserted that people are wrong who contend that war is inevitable between **"the nations which are devoted to our concept of international organization and the concept which now bears the name of Communism."**

Finland's Crops Damaged by Frost

HELSINKI, Finland, July 19.—(AP)—A devastating frost swept northern Finland for two nights causing extensive damage to rye and potato crops.

Temperatures Will Stay Up for Week End

Temperatures slightly above normal are expected for the week end, the U. S. Weather Bureau forecast yesterday.

There will be some night and morning fog near the coast during the remainder of the week, but otherwise mostly clear weather.

Maximum temperature in Los Angeles yesterday—85 degrees—was a repeat of Monday's high. Minimum was down a degreee to 64.

High today will be near 84.

Politics Blocks Statehood Bills

Effort to Force Vote on Alaska Proposal Due Today

By RAY RICHARDS
Los Angeles Examiner Washington Bureau

WASHINGTON, July 19.—Cheap partisan politics, and that alone, is preventing action at this session of Congress on bills for Hawaiian and Alaskan statehood.

The blame for delay in legislation which would bring national military security, a warning to aggressors against Pacific aggression, and a vast degree of increased prosperity, falls equally on the leadership of both parties in Congress.

Statehood for traditionally Democratic Alaska would give the Democratic Party two additional Senators and one Congressman.

Statehood for traditionally Republican Hawaii would give the Republican Party two additional Senators and two Congressmen.

The Democratic leadership in the House has been trying to bring up the Alaska statehood bill first and alone, but the Republican leaders have so far blocked the move successfully.

Representative Adolph J. Sabath, the old administration wheelhorse from Illinois, chairman of the House rules committee, will make his next attempt tomorrow to take the Alaska bill out of the committee to the floor.

Neither Measure Faces Vote

His opponent in the committee, Representative Leo E. Allen, also of Illinois, the top-ranking Republican member, said it will be contested unless the Hawaii statehood bill goes to the floor at the same time.

It is likely neither measure will be reported out, for Sabath tried the same plan a week ago and lost through Republican parliamentary moves.

The Senate and House rules committees have been called the most powerful in Congress, holding life and death powers over all legislation.

After other committees have reported measures favorably, the rules committees decide those that actually will come up in Senate and House for debate and final vote.

The Republican majority of the House rules committee in the last session of Congress reported out the Hawaiian measure, not the Alaskan. It passed the House but died as the Senate adjourned without acting on it.

Republican chiefs are willing for the Alaska and Hawaii statehood bills to come up simultaneously, but the Democratic leaders say no—the Republican Party would have a one-congressman advantage if both bills were passed.

So the measures stay in the committee, while

Index of Today's Features

Fair and Cold
BOSTON AND VICINITY—Fair today and tonight. Highest temperature near 30 degrees. Tides: High—11:46 A. M. Low—5:32 A. M., 6:09 P. M. Sunrise—7:09. Sunset—4:41. Full report on Page 2.

THE BOSTON HERALD

Robert S. Al. Anti-Truman Group Organizing Fight PAGE 14

VOL. CCVIII, NO. 19 BOSTON, THURSDAY, JANUARY 19, 1950—THIRTY-FOUR PAGES FIVE CENTS

HUGE HOLDUP PINNED TO LOCAL GANG

'Inside' Aid, Possession of Master Key Vital Links in Staging $1,500,000 Job; Big Rewards Spur Army of Sleuths

DURING INVESTIGATION ON THE $1,500,000 ROBBERY of Brink's, Inc., crowds of curious (left) gathered around the scene on Prince street, North End. At right, William Manter (left), Brink's employe who was in the company garage at the time of the robbery, talks to Police Capt. Francis M. Tiernan.

By ARTHUR STRATTON

One of Boston's own gangs, with "inside" help, staged the $1,500,000 Brink's robbery, police officials declared last night as the nation's top-flight investigators, spurred on by a potential $150,000 reward, converged on a jittery city.

Supt. Edward W. Fallon left no doubt his detectives, working with those of the state police and with agents of the FBI, had obtained evidence that the biggest cash haul in American crime was made possible through assistance from one or more persons thoroughly familiar with the express company's North End garage and money depot.

City Has Bad Case of Jitters

"We know now there is no doubt it was an inside job," said this official tersely at 9 o'clock last night after a methodical, painstaking probe of available clues over the first 24-hour period.

Meanwhile, the community demonstrated unmistakably that the skillful execution of a crime of such magnitude in Boston at 7 o'clock Tuesday evening had given it a severe case of raw, jittery nerves.

(Continued on Page Seventeen)

Luckman Resigns In Row on Policy

CHARLES LUCKMAN

Lever Chiefs Hail Move To N. Y. City

Charles Luckman's resignation as president of Lever Brothers Company was announced in New York yesterday, 49 days after Luckman moved the company's headquarters from Cambridge to New York.

Directors of the British and Dutch parent companies of Lever Brothers said the resignation stemmed from "a disagreement as to the future policy of the American company which they were unable to resolve."

Savings Seen

They hailed the execution and organization of the move from Cambridge, said it would save the company money and added that they concurred in it completely.

The announcement was made by Sir Geoffrey Heyworth, chairman of Lever Brothers & Unilever, Ltd., of Great Britain, and Paul Rykens, chairman of Lever Brothers & Unilever, N. V., The Netherlands.

Neither they nor Luckman would explain the nature of the disagreement. The 40-year-old executive, who has frequently been called "the wonder-boy of American business," had this comment, however:

"My relationship with Lever Brothers, and the directors of Unilever, has been a source of pleasure and satisfaction to me. Our inability to remove a basic disagreement

(Continued on Page Seven)

LEWIS SUED IN T-H TEST

Pickets Close More Mines in 7 States

By LOUIS STARK
[Boston Herald-N. Y. Times Dispatch]

WASHINGTON, Jan. 18—The government today sued to compel John L. Lewis and the United Mine Workers of America to restore normal coal production, in a move to end both the union-ordered three-day week and the total cessation of work by 90,000 soft coal miners.

NLRB Sets Hearing

Acting on a petition filed in the federal district court on behalf of Robert N. Denham, head of the independent office of general counsel, National Labor Relations Board, Judge Richmond Keech set Jan. 26 at 10 A. M. as a date for hearings.

The hearing will determine the outcome of Denham's action, filed under the Taft-Hartley Act. He is seeking a temporary injunction requiring theminers to work a normal week pending hearings before the National Labor Relations Board.

The NLRB promptly set Feb. 7 for the charges of unfair labor prac-

(Continued on Page Four)

Modern Answer To 'Where Is My Wandering Girl?'

For an hour last night, Malden police cars and two fire trucks with searchlights hunted for Claire Garrant, 4, daughter of Mr. and Mrs. Harry L. Garrant.

Claire disappeared about 6 P. M., from her home at 165 Linden avenue. The searchers hunted along the shores of Spot Pond brook.

While the search was on, the children of Mr. and Mrs. Ralph Hayes of 175 Linden avenue, next door, were sitting on the living room floor in the dark watching a television show. At 7 P. M., Mrs. Hayes turned up the lights and found an extra child among the spectators.

It was Claire. She had come in with the Hayes children when they were called, gone upstairs with them when Mrs. Hayes sent them to wash their hands and faces, and then watched the show.

SENATE VOTES OLEO TAX END

Foes' Maneuver Seen Doom of Civil Rights

By HAROLD B. HINTON
[Boston Herald-N. Y. Times Dispatch]

WASHINGTON, Jan. 18—The Senate adopted today, with only minor changes, the bill to repeal taxes on oleomargarine which the House passed last year. The vote on final passage was 56 to 16.

Langer Hard Foe

Before it was finally passed and sent to conference with the House, however, a combination of several Republicans with almost the solid Democratic majority of the Senate beat off three moves to couple "civil rights" legislation with the bill, and another amendment to write into it a repealer of most of the wartime "luxury" taxes on such things as furs, transportation, electric bulbs, etc.

Sen. Langer (R-ND), pressed all through the day for the adoption of his "civil rights" amendments. First, his anti-lynching amendment was tabled, 60 to 20. Then he called up his amendment to prohibit the collection of poll taxes as a condition to voting in a federal election, and it was tabled 59 to 17.

Toward the end of the afternoon, angered by repeated administration assertions that his amendments were offered not in the hope of securing their passage but merely for the purpose of killing the repeal of the oleomargarine tax, Langer suddenly moved to call up the fair-employment-practices bill which has already been reported to the Senate calendar.

He had intended to offer it, like the anti-poll-tax and anti-lynching amendments, as changes to the oleomargarine bill, but his new ma-

(Continued on Page Two)

GOP Acts to Delay Vote on Rules Issue

Move Adds to FEPC Confusion

By C. P. TRUSSELL
[Boston Herald-N. Y. Times Dispatch]

WASHINGTON, Jan. 18—House Republicans moved as a body late today to nullify a suddenly made agreement by the Democratic leadership for a voting showdown this week on whether the committee on rules should be restored its old powers to block administration legislation from floor consideration.

Chairman Outvoted

This threw in to further confusion the tangle into which the House has been precipitated, not only by the rules committee issue but by the bill designed to create a Fair Employment Practice Commission. This is the most controversial pending measure of President Truman's civil rights program.

On Jan. 3, 1949, as the 81st Congress convened, the House voted, 275-142, to draw the teeth of the rules committee by providing that any measure it bottled up for 21 days could be called up for floor action. Rep. Cox (D., Ga.), ranking Democrat on the rules body, is sponsor of a resolution which would rescind that action.

It was this measure which Democratic leadership decided this morning would be put before the House Friday. Yesterday the rules body voted, 7-2, to take the resolution out of the hands of Rep. Sabath of Illinois, the chairman, and let Cox put it to a House test today or later.

Against this background developments came today in rapid and

(Continued on Page Ten)

Gen. Vaughan Is Rebuked by Senate Group

WASHINGTON, Jan. 18 (AP)—Democrats and Republicans on a Senate investigating committee joined today in rebuking Maj. Gen. Harry H. Vaughan, President Truman's military aide, for accepting seven home freezers as gifts for himself and high-ranking friends.

The committee said that, except for the President and his family, any public official who gets something for nothing from persons doing business with the government does so because those making the gift hope he will reciprocate in some way.

Reason for Gift

"If he stops and thinks for a moment," said the group's unanimous report on its inquiry last year, "he will realize that probably he is not getting the gift because the donor likes the color of his eyes or is genuinely concerned with his household needs."

Vaughan told the committee last fall there was nothing improper about his accepting the freezers as gifts from the head of the Albert Verley Company, a Chicago perfume concern.

The committee received testimony that the gifts were made to the President's aide about the time the Verley Company was trying to get State Department clearance to send

Continued on Page Four)

HOLDUPS HERE NET 2 MILLION

'Carnival of Crime' For Year Reviewed

By W. E. PLAYFAIR

Boston's "carnival of crime" has imposed a price of upwards of $2,000,000 in the past year, it was estimated last night.

While Tuesday's $1,500,000 holdup of Brink's Inc., was the most costly in the city's history and set a new cash record in robberies, scores of lesser armed thefts swelled the year's inglorious total.

Hotel Holdups

High on the list was Monday morning's holdup at the Hotel Statler, when three masked bandits got away with $47,000 in cash, checks and vouchers.

It was the second major hotel robbery within three months. Oct. 6, last, two gunmen held up a paymaster and guard at the Copley Plaza in broad daylight and got away with $12,000 in payroll money.

Earlier in the year, on April 29, three masked men had held up employes of the Copley Square Hotel, taking $15,000 in payroll and hotel receipts.

Third biggest robbery of the year, after Brink's, Inc., and the Statler, was staged Aug. 22, when three men hijacked an armored truck in front of St. Mary's Church, Brookline, stole the $40,000 it was carrying, and abandoned it.

Included in the long list of crimes, which included payroll holdups and robberies of chain stores, liquor stores and other business establishments, were the following:

April 4—Robbery of $5945 from Hotel and Railroad News Company, 19 Reed street, Roxbury.

May 21—Three gunmen, disguised as white-clad employes, held up an Arlington chain store, kid-

(Continued on Page Sixteen)

Holdup-Happy City Bursts with Clues

By JOHN O'CONNOR

Boston, host city to the nation's championship robbery, was not exactly proud of this distinction yesterday, but possibly its inhabitants could be pardoned for asking each other: "What has Fort Knox got that we haven't got?"

And that went for everybody. The general public was just about ga-ga, with elderly women calling the police and newspapers to pass along their theories, most of which were a bit involved. As for the police, they were fuming and harassed, naturally.

Newspapers and radio reports of the $1,500,000 strike were not out very long before the city took a jittery turn. Pretty soon came an alarm that the a couple of Back Bay hotels had been stuck up. Then it was the Coca-Cola plant.

Sleuths Scour Brink's for Clues

By PAUL GIGUERE

The second floor of the Brink's garage on narrow Prince street, North End, where nine men escaped with about $1,500,000, became a crime laboratory yesterday.

Detectives from the Boston police department, insurance companies, the state and Brink's, scurried about the premises interviewing employes, employing magnifying glasses and dusting liberally with finger print powder.

What they uncovered remained a mystery.

Nothing Left Undone

Still more mysterious was the crawling movement of a vast underworld network of "police informers" from whom a worthwhile tip may come in response to reward offers totalling about $175,000.

The hold-up scene bristled with guns yesterday. If security measures were not fool-proof the night of the hold-up, there was nothing left undone yesterday.

Reporters were kept in a small front entryway. An armed guard sat nearby, grim with suspicion.

(Continued on Page Seventeen)

Myron C. Taylor, Ambassador To Vatican Since 1939, Resigns

Long Opposed By Protestants

WASHINGTON, Jan. 19 (AP)—Myron C. Taylor today resigned as special presidential ambassador to the Vatican, a post which has been frequently under Protestant fire during the past 10 years.

Taylor himself is an Episcopalian. He was first appointed as personal envoy to the Pope by the late President Franklin D. Roosevelt in December, 1939, and was continued in that role by President Truman.

Truman Regrets

The White House, in announcing that Mr. Truman accepted the resignation with "deep regret," gave no immediate indication whether a successor would be appointed.

As a possible clue in that direction, it was recalled that Mr. Truman told a news conference in mid-1946 that Taylor would continue to serve as liaison between the White House and the Vatican until the

(Continued on Page Ten)

MYRON C. TAYLOR
Resigns Post at Vatican

Today's Herald

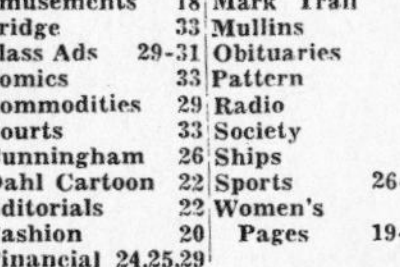

GANGS KNEW BRINK'S A 'PUSHOVER'

By PAUL STEVENS

A former convict told state police yesterday that he had known the Brink's set-up in Boston was a "pushover" for a long time.

Picked up for questioning along with a dozen other ex-convicts and parolees, he said it had been common talk in the underworld that Brink's could "easily be knocked off."

He said he was surprised that a robbery similar to the bold hold-up of Tuesday night that netted gunmen $1,500,000 at the armored car firm's garage in the North End hadn't taken place earlier.

All Have Alibis

Meanwhile, the state police were busy answering telephone calls and chasing down "tips" on the whereabouts of the nine men who featured in America's greatest robbery.

One such "tip" seemed so promising that seven troopers and two detectives were sent to investigate its validity. A telephone call had come in from a man who had said the bandits were hiding out in a cabin on Chestnut Hill between Millville and Mendon.

When the police arrived at the cabin, they found it was the home of the tipster, Morris Atchson. Atchson was alone. Police locked him up in the state police barracks at Grafton on a charge of drunkenness.

All the resources of the state police had been thrown into the "battle of wits" with the bandits. Capt. Joseph C. Crescio, supervisor of the state police, said he had 40 detectives and 350 uniformed men working on the case.

One of the state police lieutenants theorized that the bandits were "still in Boston."

Police to Study 'Holdup' Mask Found in Lowell

A rubber, hood-type mask of the kind used by the six bandits in the $1,500,000 Brink's robbery was found in Lowell late last night and brought to Boston.

A Lowell resident disclosed that a man with whom he said he had a "nodding acquaintance," borrowed the mask from him Monday and returned it to him last night. Capt. John D. Ahern planned to have the mask brought to Boston and shown to the Brink's employes held up for possible identification.

What Happens When an 'AA' Falls Off Wagon; Disappointed? See Oursler Parable—Page 4

5¢

MILD

Cloudy and warmer tonight; low 32. Mild with light rain Sunday, turning colder by night. High 45. Monday outlook, fair and colder. Sunrise 7:12, sunset 4:54.

10 p.m....26	6 a.m....26	10 a.m....31	2 p.m....40
Midnight...26	7 a.m....25	11 a.m....34	3 p.m....41
2 a.m....26	8 a.m....26	Noon......37	4 p.m....39
4 a.m....26	9 a.m....27	1 p.m....38	5 p.m....38

(U.S. official weather report.)

CHICAGO DAILY NEWS

☆ An Independent Newspaper ★

75TH YEAR—17 SATURDAY, JANUARY 21, 1950. 20 PAGES 5 CENTS

MARKETS

ALGER HISS CONVICTED; FACES TEN YEARS, FINE

Whittaker Chambers, who had testified that Hiss gave him secret papers for a Soviet spy ring.

[Associated Press Wirephoto.]

Alger Hiss and his wife, Priscilla, walk to the U.S. Courthouse in New York's Foley Square where the jurors in the Hiss perjury trial found him guilty Saturday.

[Associated Press Wirephoto.]

'Red Herring Cooked': Velde

WASHINGTON —(UP)— Rep. Velde (R., Ill.), a member of the House un-American activities committee, commented Saturday that Alger Hiss' perjury conviction "cooks President Truman's 'Red herring' and I hope he enjoys eating it."

"Red herring" was the expression used by Mr. Truman to describe the committee's investigation involving Hiss and others during the Republican-controlled 80th Congress.

Only Possible Verdict--- Chambers

WESTMINSTER, Md. —(AP)— Whittaker Chambers said of the conviction of Alger Hiss Saturday:

"I don't see how any other verdict was possible."

The self-confessed ex-Communist spy, whose testimony helped convict the former State Department aide of perjury, added:

"I hope the American people will realize the debt they owe to this jury, Mr. Murphy and the tireless and splendid efforts of the FBI."

Thomas F. Murphy, assistant U.S. attorney, was the chief prosecutor at the New York trial.

Chambers exhibited little interest in the case as he went about his farm chores Saturday while the jurors were deliberating.

Jurors Out Nearly a Day

Decide He Lied on Theft Of Secrets, Seeing Chambers

BY EDWIN A. LAHEY
Staff Writer

NEW YORK—Alger Hiss was found guilty on both counts of perjury Saturday afternoon.

The jury returned its verdict at 2:45 p.m. (1:45 p.m. Chicago time) nearly 24 hours after it began its deliberations.

The jury spent actually 9 hours and 13 minutes on deliberation.

Neither the defendant nor his wife, Priscilla, lost any of their icy calm as the forewoman of the jury, Mrs. Ada Condell, announced the verdict.

There was elation among government attorneys and FBI agents, who had begun to worry that they were up against another hung jury in the strange Hiss case.

There had been no sign of anything but confusion among the jurors as late as 12:50 p.m., when they were taken to lunch.

But they knocked on the door of the jury room to announce that they were in agreement only 30 minutes after they had returned from lunch.

Hiss, former State Department official, and the adviser of President Roosevelt at the Yalta conference, faces a maximum prison term of 10 years and a fine of $4,000.

The first count of the indictment against Hiss charged that he lied in denying that he had delivered stolen State Department documents in 1938 to Whittaker Chambers, former member of a Communist espionage ring.

The second count charged that Hiss lied again when he told the grand jury that he had never seen Chambers after Jan. 1, 1937.

* * *

THERE WAS a gasp in the courtroom when the foreman, in a low voice, said that the jurors had found the defendant guilty on both counts.

Defense Attorney Claude B. Cross, stunned by defeat, arose and asked that Federal Judge Henry W. Goddard have the jury polled.

A clerk then began asking the eight women and four men if this was their verdict. Each one gravely answered that it was.

The jurors on Saturday morning asked to be advised again on the meaning of reasonable doubt, "acceptable" corroborative evidence, and circumstantial evidence.

Judge Goddard spent 10 minutes reading sections of his in-

Turn to Page 3, Column 1.

Hiss Tells Wife: 'Keep Your Chin Up'

NEW YORK —(UP)— Alger Hiss and his wife Priscilla pushed out of the courtroom immediately after the verdict finding him guilty of perjury. They hurried across the corridor to the defense counsel rooms.

Hiss blinked his eyes slowly. As they entered the counsel room and the door swung shut, they embraced.

* * *

JUDGE HENRY W. Goddard set Wednesday for sentencing. Meanwhile Hiss was permitted to go free under his $5,000 bail.

In the elevator as they left the building, Hiss told his wife: "Keep your chin up."

As he left the courthouse, his arm was linked with that of his wife, who had sat beside him at both trials. Mrs. Hiss' face was flushed, and she bit her lip.

Hiss was pale, but composed.

"I have no comment to make," he said.

Hiss' attorney, Claude B. Cross, announced that "you can certainly say the case will be appealed."

Today's Chuckle

Of all the labor-saving devices invented for women none has ever been so popular as a husband with money.

PHOENIX FLAME.

ALCOHOLICS ANONYMOUS

What About the AA Who Skids Again After a Few Weeks?

The Erring Brother Comes Back Eventually, Statistics Indicate

At the request of readers the Daily News will continue for several more days this series of articles on Alcoholics Anonymous in Chicago. The articles are by a staff member who writes with the insight of one who has been a member of Alcoholics Anonymous (and dry) for nearly 10 years. The Chicago AA office is at 123 W. Madison st., telephone FInancial 6-1475.

What about the erring brother in Alcoholics Anonymous?

Consistently since the foundation of Alcoholics Anonymous in mid-1935, the group says these averages have held:

Fifty per cent of those who enter voluntarily, and with no psychotic complications, cease and desist from drinking then and there.

Another 25 per cent have some trouble before they achieve sobriety.

"They kick it around for a while," the group observes.

At first the group thought the other 25 per cent was lost, but as the years have gone on, the AAs have changed their mind about this 25 per cent.

"They come back," the AAs say, "if they live."

* * *

HERE'S THE story of a man who "kicked it around for eight months."

"I came into AA through the connivance of my wife and a friend, who also is in La Salle Street. I wasn't having much fun with my drinking, but nothing better occurred to me.

"First meeting I went to I heard a couple of speakers tell stories that set my few remaining hairs bolt upright.

"One was a nice-looking fellow, said he was an automobile

Turn to Page 2, Column 1

2 Flood-Blocked Roads Reopened

The Chicago Motor Club said Saturday the gradual recession of floodwaters along the Wabash and Ohio rivers has permitted reopening of the following roads:

U.S. 41 from Vincennes, Ind., to Emison, Ind.

Ill. Rt. 13 at Murphysboro, Ill.

Race Results

AT HIALEAH

7—Liberty Road 8.70 5.50 4.10
Chips Down 9.30 5.60
Shadow Shot 4.60

AT SUNSHINE

7—Adlibit 13.40 7.00 5.20
Raking 13.20 9.90
St. Jock 6.50

AT FAIR GROUNDS

6—Play Toy
Hypostyle
Photo for third.

AT SANTA ANITA

2—Holly Camp 19.80 10.00 7.50
Harza 7.00 5.30
Power Stroke 22.60

Today . . . In The Daily News

Jury Weighs Fate Of Tucker, Aides

BULLETIN

The Preston Tucker trial jury began its sixth hour of deliberation shortly before 4 p.m. Saturday. Through the afternoon there was no hint of the trend of the deliberations.

A federal trial jury deliberated the fate of Preston Tucker and seven associates Saturday.

The automobile promotion fraud case went to the jury at 10:55 a.m.

Judge Walter J. La Buy instructed the jury for an hour. He told the jurors the principal question was whether the defendants intended fraud.

* * *

"THE FACT that a defendant failed to mass-produce automobiles is not in itself proof of fraud," he said. "You are to decide the question of the good faith of any defendant."

The judge told the jurors each defendant must be considered separately.

Tucker's wife and mother were in the courtroom.

* * *

IN FINAL argument Friday, prosecutors and defense counsel summed up the case.

U.S. Attorney Otto Kerner Jr. and Lawrence J. Miller, assistant, reviewed the $28,000,000 collapse.

Miller pointed out that Tucker Corporation had made only 32 hand-assembled cars.

He said:

"It doesn't make any difference what their intent was when they started out. They made misrepresentations of what they had. Read the pack of lies in their ads and remember what they had and what they didn't have in the way of an auto."

The defendants are charged with conspiracy, fraud and violation of the regulations of the Securities and Exchange Commission.

* * *

THE EIGHT, and the maximum penalties that could be given them in the event of conviction, are:

—Tucker, corporation president, 155 years in prison and $60,000 fine.

—Floyd D. Cerf, broker who underwrote the stock issue, 155 years and $60,000 fine.

—Fred Rockelman, executive vice-president, 155 years and $60,000 fine.

—Robert Pierce, treasurer, 155 years and $60,000 fine.

—Harold Karsten, alias Abe Karatz, a co-promotor, 155 years and $60,000 fine.

—Mitchell Dulian, sales manager, 115 years and $48,000 fine.

—Otis Radford, treasurer, 95 years and $36,000 fine.

—Cliff Knoble, advertising manager, 75 years and $32,000 fine.

Bulletins

WASHINGTON—(UP)—President Truman Saturday urged Congress to "rectify" immediately the House's action in turning down his request for $60,000,000 in economic aid for Korea.

The President said, "I shall take up this matter with congressional leaders and urge upon them the need for immediate action in order that important foreign policy interests of this country may be properly safeguarded."

* * *

Obscene literature and gadgets valued at $1,500 were confiscated by police juvenile bureau officers Saturday in a raid on the Division Sales Co., 3224 Roosevelt rd. Morton Marks, 27, of 1135 N. Leclaire av., head of the firm, was charged with possession of indecent and obscene items.

* * *

WASHINGTON —(UP)— President Truman's fair employment practices legislation will not be brought up in the House Monday, Speaker Sam Rayburn announced Saturday. Rayburn's plans meant that the next chance the House will have to debate the controversial FEPC bill will be Feb. 13.

* * *

Vernon Seymour, 24, late Saturday was found guilty in Criminal Court of the murder of Herman Engelhard, 79, during a robbery, April 29, 1948, in Engelhard's home at 3261 Cottage Grove av. Seymour was sentenced to 50 years in prison.

ANNIVERSARY
Warren G. Harding, 29th President, was born, 1865

THE WASHINGTON OBSERVER

ERROR OF OPINION IS TO BE TOLERATED WHEN REASON IS LEFT FREE TO COMBAT IT

WEATHER
Scattered showers, cooler today; Friday considerably cooler

Established September 18, 1871—No. 18938—Price Five Cents | WASHINGTON, PA., THURSDAY MORNING, NOVEMBER 2, 1950 | Associated Press Wire and Feature Service — Phone 4010

Truman Assassination Fails; Guards Shoot Puerto Ricans

U. S. Regiment Is Encircled By Red Force

Chinese-North Korean Troops Trap Unit Of First Cavalry In Attack

SEOUL, Thursday, Nov. 2.—(AP)—Rocket-firing Chinese and North Korean troops today pressed attacks which have encircled an American regiment and forced other units to retreat in northwestern Korea.

Utilizing a new weapon—82 millimeter rockets— the revitalized Reds struck on the left flank of an American armored column which pushed up the west coast to within 15 air miles of the Manchurian border. This was a four-mile advance since yesterday.

A U. S. First Army Corps spokesman called the situation serious. The attacks put U. S. First Cavalry elements and four South Korean divisions—the First, Sixth, Seventh and Eighth—on the defensive. One thousand Reds on horseback were in the attacking forces.

One battalion of South Koreans has been surrounded for four days. Another group of regiment strength was cut off last night but broke free today.

For the first time, a U. S. First Corps spokesman admitted that "Chinese troops" were attacking in the northwest.

Corps officers cautiously added they were "not sure whether Chinese troops form the bulk of enemy forces which have thrown the United Nations off balance for the moment."

High American officers previously had acknowledged a Chinese Red regiment was in action in northeastern Korea. South Korean officers have insisted at least two Chinese Red divisions were in battle there.

The surrounded American regiment, a unit of the U. S. First Cavalry Division, was in the Unsan area on the east flank of a U. S. armored spearhead which drove west 13 miles yesterday to within 19 air miles of the Manchurian border.

Other First Cavalry elements moved up to the aid of the encircled regiment.

Division hetdquarters said the situation was "too confused" to say exactly how far the American and South Korean units had been forced to retreat.

The enemy blows rained down on U. S. First Cavalry and South Korean forces in the Unsan area, about 30 miles east of one of two 24th Infantry Division columns pounding for the border.

So close was the fighting that the First Cavalry Division lost several mortars, which the Reds turned on the Americans. The spokesman said the South Koreans lost heavily in men and equipment.

The blow followed four days of determined attacks by Communist forces, including considerable numbers of Chinese.

The U. S. 24th Division's spearhead nearest the border moved ahead as Russian-made jet fighter planes made their debut in support of Red forces. Six jet planes fought inconclusively with slower, propeller-driven Mustangs, then broke off the engagement.

East of Unsan on the curving, 250-mile front, North Korean and Chinese Reds put up spotty resistance. While they struck fiercely in some places, they vanished at other points. They dropped out of sight for no apparent reason before South Koreans on the north central front. And they attacked the U. S. Seventh Division without success in the northeast.

On the northwest, a column of the U. S. 24th Division thrust to Charyongwan, 19 air miles south-east of the border at its nearest point and 22 air miles southeast of Sinuiju. Sinuiju is just across the Yalu river from the Manchurian city of Antung, where the Chinese Reds maintain a large air base.

Sinuiju's own air field was say-

(Continued on Page 2, Column 3)

Pedestrian Is Killed By Truck

Clarence Tocci Is Badly Hurt In Crash

A pedestrian was killed and a motorist critically injured in two accidents on Route 19, north, Wednesday night.

State Police reported William James, 82, of Washington, R. D. 2, was instantly killed when struck by a tractor-trailer unit as he walked along the highway, three miles north of Washington, at 7:20 p.m.

Police said the truck was operated by Virgil Graley, 32, Charleston, W. Va., driving for the Nelson Transfer & Storage Company, Charleston, who was traveling south.

James, it was reported, was walking north on the left side, facing traffic, and suddenly wandered into the path of the truck. Graley told troopers he swerved to the left and the tractor missed James, but the right front corner of the trailer hit the man, fracturing his skull. Graley was ordered to furnish $500 bond by Coroner L. C. Gray for his release pending a coroner's inquest.

The other accident occurred shortly after 5 p.m. in the dip at Thompsonville when a Jeep truck driven by Clarence Tocci, 47, of 136 Church street, city, plunged over a guard rail, hit a bridge abutment and dropped fully 25 feet down to the Thompsonville road running under the bridge.

Tocci, local barber and operator of Club 40 road house, was en route to Washington when he was

(Continued on Page 2, Column 6)

Flames Destroy Interior Of StoragePlace

City Mission, Washington Ice Co. Suffer Losses

Fire gutted a large warehouse of the Washington Ice Company, 275 Meadow avenue, last night and roaring flames for a time threatened to engulf the adjoining buildings.

Completely destroyed by the fast spreading flames was a 40x75 foot brick building owned by the Ice Company and rented as a storage place by Washington City Mission.

At the left of the building, in the rear is the Litle Lumber Company and on the right other buildings of the Ice Company. Both were in danger for several hours by the far reaching flames and sparks, as well s possible collapse of the walls of the warehouse.

The daily ice storage room adjoins the warehouse building but damage was reported neglible by an engineer of the company. The engine room, freezer floor and locker plant were not reached by the flames or heat. Manager S. H. Hoch said not even a degree of temperature was lost in the food lockers.

City Fireman James Marshall, 59, of 28 Jefferson street, was treated at Washington Hospital for second degree burns of the left arm received when burning timber fell on him.

Fire Chief L. A. Loar said no cause of the fire could be determined last night.

The fire, which was reported to City Fireman at 8:30 p. m. was discovered by an unidentified man as he walked along the railroad tracks at the rear of the building. He called to Paul George, engineer, at the ice company who was pulling ice from molds.

The warehouse, filled with furniture, bedding and clothing donated to the City Mission, was quickly a mass of flames from top to bottom. The building, formerly used by the ice company as an ice storage plant, was approximately 65 feet high but had no floors.

The walls, reported to be lined with insulating cork eight inches thick, confined the flames within the walls and caused them to shoot upward.

The roaring fire could be seen in many parts of the city. Smoke and sparks spread over a wide area.

The City's new aerial truck was

(Continued on Page 2, Column 7)

Flames Leaping Above Building

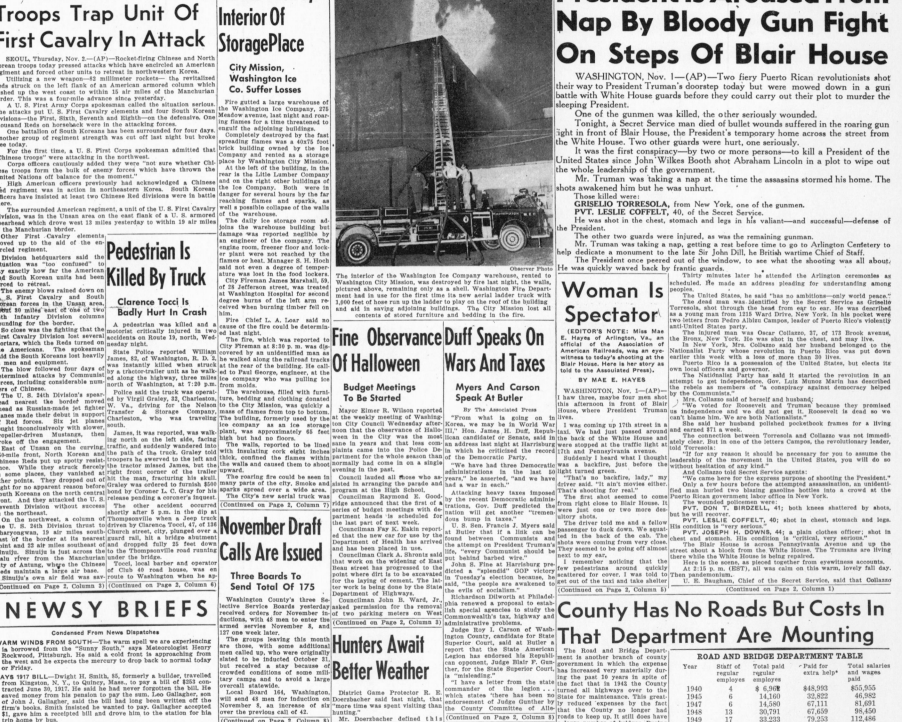

Observer Photo

The interior of the Washington Ice Company warehouse, rented to Washington City Mission, was destroyed by fire last night, the walls, pictured above, remaining only as a shell. Washington Fire Department had in use for the first time its new aerial ladder truck with 1,000 feet of hose run up the ladder to play on the roof of the building and aid in saving adjoining buildings. The City Mission lost all contents of stored furniture and bedding in the fire.

Fine Observance Of Halloween

Budget Meetings To Be Started

Mayor Elmer R. Wilson reported at the weekly meeting of Washington City Council Wednesday afternoon that the observance of Halloween in the City was the most sane in years and that less complaints came into the Police Department for the whole season than normally had come in on a single evening in the past.

Council lauded all those who assisted in arranging the parade and program at the High School.

Councilman Raymond E. Goodridge announced that the first of a series of budget meetings with department heads is scheduled for the last part of next week.

Councilman Fay K. Eakin reported that the new car for use by the Department of Health has arrived and has been placed in use.

Councilman Clark A. Shrontz said that work on the widening of East Beau street has progressed to the point where dirt is to be excavated for the laying of cement. The latter work is being done by the State Department of Highways.

Councilman John B. Ward, Jr., asked permission for the removal of two parking meters on West

(Continued on Page 2, Column 3)

Duff Speaks On Wars And Taxes

Myers And Carson Speak At Butler

By The Associated Press

"From what is going on in Korea, we may be in World War III," Hon. James H. Duff, Republican candidate for Senate, said in an address last night at Harrisburg in which he criticized the record of the Democratic Party.

"We have had three Democratic administrations in the last 50 years," he asserted, "and we have had a war in each."

Attacking heavy taxes imposed by the recent Democratic administrations, Gov. Duff predicted the nation will get another "tremendous bump in taxes."

U. S. Sen. Francis J. Myers said at Butler that if a link can be found between Communists and the attempt on President Truman's life, "every Communist should be put behind barbed wire."

John S. Fine at Harrisburg predicted a "splendid" GOP victory in Tuesday's election because, he said, "the people are awakened to the evils of socialism."

Richardson Dilworth at Philadelphia renewed a proposal to establish special agencies to study the Commonwealth's tax, highway and administrative problems.

Judge Roy I. Carson of Washington County, candidate for State Superior Court, said at Butler a report that the State American Legion has endorsed his Republican opponent, Judge Blair F. Gunther, for the State Superior Court, is "misleading."

"I have a letter from the state commander of the legion . . . which states 'there has been no endorsement of Judge Gunther by the County Committee of Alle-

(Continued on Page 2, Column 8)

November Draft Calls Are Issued

Three Boards To Send Total Of 175

Washington County's three Selective Service Boards yesterday received orders for November inductions, with 48 men to enter the armed services November 8, and 127 one week later.

The groups leaving this month are those, with some additional men called up, who were originally slated to be inducted October 31, but received a stay because of crowded conditions of some military camps and to avoid a large overcall statewide.

Local Board 164, Washington, will send 48 men for induction on November 8, an increase of six over the previous call of 42.

(Continued on Page 2, Column 8)

Hunters Await Better Weather

District Game Protector R. E. Doerzbacher said last night, that "more time was spent visiting than hunting."

Mr. Doerzbacher defined this statement by saying that the warm weather and dry ground discouraged many hunters from going into the fields. He estimated that about one half as many hunters as originally expected were in action.

However, the kill of pheasants was especially good, the Game Protector said. He reported seeing many nice, heavy birds which were for the most part accounted for by men with dogs.

Hunting conditions were average, he reported, with nothing unusual happening due to the weather and the consequent lack of interest.

Most of the hunters that were out were active between 9-11 a.m. and 2:30-5 p.m., he stated

But the highlight of the day was the fact that no hunters were injured due to hunting accidents, the Game Protector reported.

Two Polling Places Changed

Two polling place changes have been approved by the Washington County Commmissioners for the General Election to be held Tuesday, November 7, 1950.

The changes are:

North Franklin Township: Second Precinct from Lincoln Hill School to George Barbour residence.

Smith Township: First Precinct from Slovan School to Fireman's Hall, Slovan, Pa.

Lie Is Given Three-Year Term

NEW YORK, Nov. 1.—(AP)—The U. N. Assembly today gave Secretary-General Trygve Lie three more years in office and a big vote of confidence. It overrode repeated Soviet warnings that Moscow will ignore Lie and refuse to deal with him.

The final vote on extending Lie's term to Feb. 2, 1954, was 46 to 5 with seven abstentions. The Russian bloc alone voted against him.

(Continued on Page 2, Column 4)

NEWSY BRIEFS

Condensed From News Dispatches

WARM WINDS FROM SOUTH—The warm spell we are experiencing is borrowed from the "Sunny South," says Meteorologist Henry Rockwood, Pittsburgh. He said a cold front is approaching from the west and he expects the mercury to drop back to normal today or Friday.

PAYS 1917 BILL—Dwight H. Smith, 85, formerly a builder, travelled from Kingston, N. Y., to Quincy, Mass., to pay a bill of $253 contracted June 30, 1917. He said he had never forgotten the bill. He saved money from his pension to pay the sum. Leo Gallagher, son of John J. Gallagher, said the bill had long been written off the firm's books. Smith insisted he wanted to pay. Gallagher accepted $1, gave him a receipted bill and drove him to the station for his trip home by bus.

EXECUTIVE BOARD TO DECIDE—About 6,000 of the 13,000 workers employed at the East Pittsburgh plant of Westinghouse Electric Corp. voted yesterday to let their executive committee decide whether they shall strike. About 2,600 workers are already out but some began returning to work after the mass meeting ended.

STRIKE AT BETHLEHEM PLANT—About 11,000 of the 17,000 workers employed at the Lackawanna, N. Y., plant of the Bethlehem Steel Corp. were idled yesterday by a "wildcat strike." It started with 1,000 leaving their jobs because the company refused to reinstate a dismissed employe.

SOME COME TO "PREY"—The following sign is displayed in a hallway, near a cloak room of the Trinity Episcopal Church, Tulsa, Okla.: "Please do not leave hats or coats here unless attendant is on duty. Thieves sometimes come into the church to prey."

28TH DIVISION BAND WINS—The snappy 28th Division Band won first place in a contest sponsored by the American Legion of Bicknel, Ind. The musicians were not aware that they were competing when they performed.

"NO PROGRESS"—Another "no progress" meeting was held by publishers and striking mailers in Pittsburgh yesterday. No further meetings are scheduled but representatives of both groups are subject to call.

President Is Aroused From Nap By Bloody Gun Fight On Steps Of Blair House

WASHINGTON, Nov. 1—(AP)—Two fiery Puerto Rican revolutionists shot their way to President Truman's doorstep today but were mowed down in a gun battle with White House guards before they could carry out their plot to murder the sleeping President.

One of the gunmen was killed, the other seriously wounded.

Tonight, a Secret Service man died of bullet wounds suffered in the roaring gun fight in front of Blair House, the President's temporary home across the street from the White House. Two other guards were hurt, one seriously.

It was the first conspiracy—by two or more persons—to kill a President of the United States since John Wilkes Booth shot Abraham Lincoln in a plot to wipe out the whole leadership of the government.

Mr. Truman was taking a nap at the time the assassins stormed his home. The shots awakened him but he was unhurt.

Those killed were:

GRISELIO TORRESOLA, from New York, one of the gunmen.

PVT. LESLIE COFFELT, 40, of the Secret Service.

He was shot in the chest, stomach and legs in his valiant—and successful—defense of the President.

The other two guards were injured, as was the remaining gunman.

Mr. Truman was taking a nap, getting a rest before time to go to Arlington Cemetery to help dedicate a monument to the late Sir John Dill, he British wartime Chief of Staff.

The President once peered out of the window, to see what the shooting was all about. He was quickly waved back by frantic guards.

Thirty minutes later he attended the Arlington ceremonies as scheduled. He made an address pleading for understanding among peoples.

The United States, he said "has no ambitions—only world peace."

The dead man was identified by the Secret Service as Griselio Torresola, shot through the head from ear to ear. He was described as a young man from 1215 Ward Drive, New York. In his pocket were two letters from Pedro Albizu Campos, leader of Puerto Rico's violently anti-United States party.

The injured man was Oscar Collazzo, 37, of 173 Brook avenue, the Bronx, New York. He was shot in the chest, and may live.

In New York, Mrs. Collazzo said her husband belonged to the Nationalist Party whose revolution in Puerto Rico was put down earlier this week with a loss of more than 30 lives.

Puerto Rico is a possession of the United States, but elects its own local officers and governor.

The Nationalist Party has said it started the revolution in an attempt to get independence. Gov. Luiz Munoz Marin has described the rebels as members of "a conspiracy against democracy helped by the Communists."

Mrs. Collazzo said of herself and husband:

"We voted for Roosevelt and Truman because they promised us independence and we did not get it. Roosevelt is dead so we can't blame him. We are both Nationalists."

She said her husband polished pocketbook frames for a living and earned $71 a week.

The connection between Torresola and Collazzo was not immediately clear. But in one of the letters Campos, the revolutionary leader, told Torresola:

"If for any reason it should be necessary for you to assume the leadership of the movement in the United States, you will do so without hesitation of any kind."

And Collazzo told Secret Service agents:

"We came here for the express purpose of shooting the President."

Only a few hours before the attempted assassination, an unidentified man hurled two blazing gasoline bottles into a crowd at the Puerto Rican government labor office in New York.

The wounded policemen were:

PVT. DON T. BIRDZELL, 41; both knees shattered by shots, but he will recover.

PVT. LESLIE COFFELT, 40; shot in chest, stomach and legs. His condition is "very serious."

PVT. JOSEPH H. DOWNS, 44; a plain clothes officer; shot in chest and stomach. His condition is "critical, very serious."

The Blair House is across Pennsylvania Avenue and up the street about a block from the White House. The Trumans are living there while the White House is being repaired.

Here is the scene, as pieced together from eyewitness accounts.

At 2:15 p. m. (EST), all was calm on this warm, lovely fall day. Then pandemonium.

U. E. Baugham, Chief of the Secret Service, said that Collazzo

(Continued on Page 2, Column 1)

Woman Is Spectator

(EDITOR'S NOTE: Miss Mae E. Hayes of Arlington, Va., an official of the Association of American Railroads, was an eyewitness to today's shooting at the Blair House. Here is her story as told to the Assouiated Press).

BY MAE E. HAYES

WASHINGTON, Nov. 1—(AP)—I haw three, maybe four men shot this afternoon in front of Blair House, where President Truman lives.

I was coming up 17th street in a taxi. We had just passed around the back of the White House and were stopped at the traffic light at 17th and Pennsylvania avenue.

Suddenly I heard what I thought was a backfire, just before the light turned green.

"That's no backfire, lady," my driver said. "It ain't movies either. That's shooting for real."

The first shot seemed to come from right close to Blair House. It were just one or two more desultory shots.

The driver told me and a fellow passenger to duck down. We squatted in the back of the cab. The shots were coming from very close. They seemed to be going off almost next to my ear.

I remember noticing that the few pedestrians around quickly scattered for cover. I was told to get out of the taxi and take shelter

(Continued on Page 2, Column 5)

County Has No Roads But Costs In That Department Are Mounting

ROAD AND BRIDGE DEPARTMENT TABLE

Year	Staff of regular employes	Total paid regular employes	Paid for extra help*	Total salaries and wages paid
1940	4	$ 6,962	$48,993	$55,955
1945	6	14,160	32,822	46,982
1947	6	14,580	67,111	81,691
1948	13	30,791	67,659	98,450
1949	17	33,233	79,253	112,486

*Includes labor in maintenance of roads and bridges.

The county turned all highways over to the State for maintenance in 1943.

The Road and Bridge Department is another branch of county government in which the expense has increased very materially during the past 10 years in spite of the fact that in 1943 the County turned all highways over to the State for maintenance. This greatly reduced expenses by the fact that the County no longer had roads to keep up. It still does have a large number of bridges. During the years since 1943 it has been necessary to spend large sums in replacing and repairing bridges washed out by floods and in painting and repairing bridges over the Monongahela River.

In 1940 the total expense of this department was $55,955, but ten years later it had just doubled, $112,486. In 1940 there were four employes who received a total of $6,962, but $48,993 was paid for extra help, including the labor for maintenance of highways and bridges. One employe received between $1,200 and $1,399; one between $1,400 and $1,599 one between $1,600 and $1,799; one between $2,400 and $2,599.

By 1945 the total expense of this department was reduced to $46,982 or $8,973 less than in 1940. This was due to the fact that the State had taken over the roads in 1943, and there had been no great amount necessary by reason of bridge maintenance. Yet the number of regular employes had been increased to six and they received a total of $14,160. The sum of $32,822 was paid for extra help, which included labor in bridge maintenance. It is evident that during this period there was no serious bridge loss by floods. One employe received between $1,600 and $1,799; one between $1,800 and $1,999; one between $2,200 and $2,399; one between $2,400 and $2,599; two between $3,000 and $3,199.

In 1947 the number of regular employes remained at six, who received a total of $14,580. It is evident that some serious bridge loss occurred that year or repairs were necessary to the river bridges, for the total paid for extra help amounted to $67,111, making a total of $81,691 for the year. Two employes received $1,800 and $1,999; one between $2,200 and $2,399; one between $2,400 and $2,599; one between $2,600 and $2,799; one between $3,000 and $3,199.

The next year, 1948, the expenses

(Continued on Page 2, Column 2)

The Journal's FDR Letter —Is It a Forgery?

See Page 2

LATEST RACING RESULTS, SPORTS NEWS

New York Post

Re-entered as 2d-class matter Nov. 22, 1949, at the Post Office at New York, N. Y., under the act of March 3, 1879

THREE SECTIONS | Rain. | NEW YORK, TUESDAY, MARCH 13, 1951 | Volume 150, No. 98. | 64 PAGES

COSTELLO DEFIES PROBE

FRANK COSTELLO

Move Hinted To Deport Him

Story on Page 3

LATE CITY EDITION

New Haven Evening Register.

WITH SUNDAY MORNING EDITION

THE WEATHER
Tonight: Cloudy, Drizzle
Tomorrow: Mostly Cloudy
Detailed Report and Tides on Page 2

VOLUME CIX NUMBER 77 | NEW HAVEN 3, CONN., MONDAY, MARCH 19, 1951 | 32 PAGES | FOUR CENTS Delivered By Carrier 27 Cents Per Week

O'DWYER QUESTIONED ON MURDER, INC.

U. N. Patrols Close To 38th Parallel

NEW ATTEMPT MADE TO FREE MRS. FURINO

Court Gets Plea Again For Woman Jailed in Absentee Vote Case

Another attempt is being made to free Mrs. Anna C. Furino, 45, of 370 Blatchley Avenue, from the New Haven County Jail before her three-month sentence for conspiring to submit forged absentee ballots in last November's election expires April 7.

Vincent Villano, as counsel for Mrs. Furino, today submitted a petition for Mrs. Furino's freedom to Superior Court. It will be referred to Superior Court Judge Kenneth Wynne, who imposed the sentence, and he will set a date for hearing the petition. A similar application was rejected by Judge Wynne following a hearing February 9.

Petition Outlined

The reasons outlined by Villano in his second petition are similar to those listed in the first. It is claimed that the continued incarceration of Mrs. Furino might result in a physical or nervous breakdown. It is argued also that Mrs. Furino should be free to work for the support of her six children. The petition states the income of the family is not sufficient to maintain the group with Mrs. Furino's contribution stopped.

First Petition

In denying the first petition for Mrs. Furino's release, Judge Wynne declared: "No one goes to jail and feels happy about it. She doesn't want to stay in jail. I don't blame her. I'm sorry for her."

Mrs. Furino, wife of the operator of a grocery store, was one of four 27th Ward Republican workers sent to jail by Judge Wynne on January 23 for infractions of regulations pertaining to absentee ballots.

POLICE PROBE $1,000 BREAK, TWO 'MUGGINGS'

Six Cases of Liquor Included in Loot From West Rock Avenue Home

Burglars took nearly $1,000 worth of loot at the home of John M. Chapnick, well known attorney at 53 West Rock Avenue during the weekend, but were unable to open a safe in the house.

Police are also investigating two new "muggings." A New Haven Hospital physician was knocked unconscious in one of these.

The Chapnick home was entered while the attorney and his wife were away on a weekend trip. Detective Lawrence Ruggerio said the burglars forced a side window, and then proceeded to ransack the rooms of the house.

Liquor Taken

Chapnick said the burglars took six or seven cases of liquor, quantities of women's apparel and linens, and some perfume and canned food. They knocked the lock off a bedroom safe, but were unable to open the door.

Dr. Harrison O'Connor, of 789 Howard Avenue, a member of the resident surgical house staff at New Haven Hospital, was knocked unconscious and robbed of $12 and personal papers in Cedar Street, between Davenport and Congress Avenues, late Saturday night.

Dr. O'Connor told Detective Sgt. Leon Vaillancourt that two men grabbed him and forced him into a driveway between the Boardman and Brady Buildings. One man held his arms, and the other struck him in the face.

The physician regained consciousness about 10 minutes later. He was treated in the emergency room of New Haven Hospital.

Five Arrested

Five youths were arrested yesterday, in connection with the investigation into the mugging of Frank Barbiero, of 27 Downing Street, in Congress Avenue, near Commerce Street, late Saturday.

They were identified as Anthony L. Gaudino, 19, of 322 Lafayette Street, charged with theft and breach of the peace, and Anthony M. Carrano, 17, of 440 Howard Avenue; Andrew P. D'Ambrosio, 20, of 160 Columbus Avenue; Alphonse DeSimone, 19, of 78½ Hill Street, and Robert Rourke, 19, of 276 Cedar

(Please Turn to Page 2)

Slapped By Sailor

Air Force Maj. Gen David M. Schlatter (above) was slapped and "arrested" as a "Communist" by a sailor in Honolulu, Hawaii. The sailor, Edward C. Burt, 26, of Hibbing, Minn., said he thought the General asked him to join the Communist Party when he asked Burt and several other men if they were satisfied with their jobs and asked them to join his outfit. Both were in civilian clothes when incident took place.

AUTO MISHAPS CAUSE INJURY TO SEVEN HERE

Spectacular Crash at Bellevue Rd., Dyer St. Involves Five Cars

Seven persons were injured in automobile accidents here this morning and yesterday.

Mrs. Lottie Snaider, 73, of 99 Oak Street, suffered head and arm injuries when she was hit by a car at Congress Avenue and Cedar Street shortly before 6 o'clock this morning. She is reported in good condition at New Haven Hospital, however.

Police said the car was driven by Howard M. Cohen, 22, of 44 Redfield Street, who was arrested on a reckless driving charge.

Spectacular Crash

One youth was slightly hurt in a spectacular accident at Bellevue Road and Dyer Street shortly before 5 P. M. yesterday, in which five automobiles, four of them 1950 models, were damaged.

Patrolman Nicholas Civitello reported that a car driven by Harry B. Zemel, 18, of 350 Shelton Avenue, went out of control as he was turning from Bellevue Road into Dyer Street. Zebel's car then struck two cars on one side of the street, swerved over to the opposite side, where it crashed into another pair of 1950 autos, and then overturned.

(Please Turn to Page 2)

ALLIES SET UP HOLDING LINE 17 MILES AWAY

South Korean Troops Swim Chilly Hongchon River to Pursue Reds

Tokyo, March 19—(AP)—Allied patrols probed within a few miles of the 38th Parallel in Korea today.

Strong U. S. Eighth Army forces set up a holding line only 17 miles south of that politically sensitive boundary.

The Army, breaking a three-day silence, announced "holding elements are 17 miles from the 38th Parallel at five points." It did not locate the points and said it would not. Holding elements presumably are capable of holding their ground against heavy attack.

The brief announcement said patrols were operating "miles north" of the five points and in all other sectors. It did not say how many miles.

Swim River

South Korean troops swam the chilly Hongchon River in Central Korea in pursuit of Communist forces pulling back toward the Parallel.

The Republic of Korea (ROK) soldiers were spearheading the central front drive of the U. S. Eighth Army.

"There was no stopping those ROK troops," said a military spokesman. They swam the cold river rather than wait for boats to ferry them across in the northward drive. "They were just a lot of eager beavers."

The same ROK troops trapped and annihilated a Chinese Communist battalion Sunday.

The ROKs faded back when they first met the Reds. But they sent strong patrols out in a flanking movement until they were north of the Chinese. Then they smashed the Reds simultaneously from the front and rear.

American liaison officers with the South Koreans counted 231 dead Chinese after the battle.

The ROKS captured a battery of 75-mm. howitzers, several mortars and rifles, and large quantities of ammunition.

It was the first action of any size along the Korean front in 83 hours.

Parallel 38, which cuts across Korea about in the center, has been the arbitrary dividing line between Communist North and Republican

(Please Turn to Page 2)

'Korean Youngsters Give Troops Trolley Ride In Seoul

Willing Korean youngsters give GIs and newsmen a "trolley" ride as Third Division troops occupy the almost deserted South Korean capital of Seoul. In the foreground wearing dark glasses is Associated Press staff correspondent Jim Becker. (AP)

Tells How Gangs Work In 'Troops'

Senate Probers Told Underworld Has Own Courts—Anastasia Called Brooklyn 'Troop' Leader—Ex-Mayor Clashes With Tobey on Reles Death Testimony — Committee Invites Dewey to Appear

New York, March 19—(AP)—Former Mayor William O'Dwyer told the Senate Crime Committee today the underworld had its own court system that meted out death sentences to violators of the gangland code.

O'Dwyer, now Ambassador to Mexico, described it as "a judicial set-up—a kangaroo court where they held trials, usually at night."

"We also found," he said, "that in certain sections of the country, there were men who carried out the orders of these courts, and there would be only one order—death, execution."

O'Dwyer said in many sections of the country "they had troops under one man who had authority to direct those troops."

"Albert Anastasia was the one who had authority to order the Brooklyn troops," he said.

Anastasia was a suspect in a slaying attributed to Murder, Inc., Brooklyn crime syndicate. Anastasia escaped prosecution after the death of Abe Reles, a witness, in a mysterious plunge from a Coney Island hotel window in 1941.

Asked who was chairman of the board of directors in the underworld syndicate, O'Dwyer said:

"It was rather a combination. There was no chief man in charge, a combination, an alliance."

Clashes With Senator Tobey

O'Dwyer told his story of the virtual nation-wide Murder, Inc., after a sharp encounter with Sen. Charles W. Tobey (R-N. H.).

The former mayor was smiling and poised as he took the witness stand after a voluntary trip here from Mexico City. He was dressed in a natty blue, pencil-stripe suit and blue and white tie.

But beads of perspiration appeared on his forehead under the warm moving picture and television camera lights and at times his voice broke. He took frequent drinks of water.

The bitter exchange with Tobey came after the senator said O'Dwyer's version of Reles' death varied from that of a previous witness, Frank C. Bals, a former deputy police commissioner.

O'Dwyer defended Bals' record as a police officer, but Tobey described Bals as a "a flat tire" whom O'Dwyer was attempting to defend.

O'Dwyer, obviously angry, declared he was entitled to a respectful hearing. A brief recess was called, then the former mayor returned with his story of the underworld court system.

Discussing the underworld crime syndicate that dispensed death sentences, O'Dwyer said the Brooklyn "troop" was involved in deaths in east New York, Nassau County on Long Island, Newark, N. J., and Los Angeles.

Tells of 'Pay-offs'

He said that by agreement among the underworlds in various cities "the little fellows" who actually did the murdering were "rewarded with pinball concessions, houses of prostitution and other certain unlawful activities."

O'Dwyer said he obtained this information, while he was district attorney in Brooklyn, from Reles shortly before Reles died.

The underworld trials, he said, dealt with "any violation of jurisdiction of rules and regulations and it was also found that these meetings were held all over the country.

(Please Turn to Page 3)

SIX NATIONS INITIAL PLAN OF SCHUMAN

West Europe States Join in Program of Pooling Coal and Steel

Paris, March 19—(AP)—Six nations of Western Europe today initialled the Schuman Plan for pooling most of their coal and steel.

The agreement, coming after nine months of negotiations, constituted one of the most ambitious economic proposals made in Europe in this Century.

The plan for an international control of West Europe's major resources was initialled at noon today at the French Foreign Ministry by technical experts of the six nations—France, Italy, Belgium, Luxembourg, The Netherlands and West Germany.

French Foreign Minister Robert Schuman proposed last May to put nearly two-thirds of free Europe's

(Please Turn to Page 2)

Woman Plunges From Window At Costello's Residence

New York, March 19—(AP)—A woman plunged today from a fourth floor window of the fashionable Central Park West apartment house where gambler Frank Costello lives.

She was identified as Mrs. Roslyn Lewis, about 30 years old, of New York City. She was taken to Roosevelt Hospital in critical condition.

Mrs. Lewis, who was visiting relatives in the apartment house, was said by police to have been depressed over the death of her husband a year ago. Her body was found in a rear court yard at 11:45 A. M. (E. S. T.).

Costello, a principal witness at the current hearings of the Kefauver Senate Crime Committee, lives on the 31st floor of the apartment house at 115 Central Park West.

Rowe Demands Charges Against Him Be Dropped

RFC Director Denies Senate Investigators' Accusations Linking Him to Influence Ring With White House Contacts—Fails to Mention Dunham Episode

Washington, March 19—(AP)—RFC Director C. Edward Rowe demanded today that Senate investigators withdraw their charges linking him to an influence ring with alleged White House contacts.

Rowe denied the accusations in a prepared statement to the Fulbright Subcommittee. His written reply made no mention of sworn testimony that he had tried to make a fellow Reconstruction Finance Corporation (RFC) director "the goat" of the inquiry.

Director Walter L. Dunham had told the subcommittee on March 8 that Rowe urged him to resign his post under circumstances that would make Dunham "the goat" of charges the RFC had yielded to an influence ring in making government loans.

Says He's Clear

Rowe told the banking subcommittee, headed by Senator Fulbright (D-Ark.), he is entitled to a finding "that an exhaustive investigation of my conduct proves I have acted in a perfectly ethical and legal manner."

The subcommittee, in a report to the Senate last month, had made much of Rowe's friendship with men the group named as members of an influence ring. It also had cited a loan to a firm in which Rowe is a large stockholder as evidence that he had benefitted from favoritism. The loan was made and paid off not long before Rowe joined the RFC board October 3, 1950.

"Not one of you gentlemen, I am sure," Rowe said in his statement, "wants to be guilty of maligning a person by innuendo, garbled and distorted reports, or half truths."

Another director, Walter E. Cosgriff, in a statement prepared for the subcommittee, declared he has seen no evidence of an influence ring operating around RFC since he took office last October 12. He said

Wants Name Cleared

C. EDWARD ROWE

he considers the other board members to be "honest and capable" men. The subcommittee has never criticized Cosgriff.

Cosgriff said:

"It is impossible, of course, for me to be able to say what may have happened at some time prior to my association with the corporation, but it is my firm conviction that if an influence ring did exist or other improper political activities went on at some prior date, nothing of this nature has been active in the recent months since my association on the

(Please Turn to Page 3)

GRAU LINKED TO THEFT OF CUBAN FUNDS

Regime of Ex-President Accused of $40 Million Misappropriations

Havana, Cuba, March 19—(AP)—Two-time Cuban President Ramon Grau San Martin stood accused today of "principal responsibility" in the alleged theft or misappropriation of more than $40,000,000 of Government money.

Judge Federico Justiniani, after many months investigation of charges that Grau's regime mishandled more than $174,000,000 in Government funds, over the weekend indicted the former president and 10 close associates during his 1944-48 presidential term on charges of criminal responsibility.

Grau was not ordered to prison because he twice had occupied the presidential chair, the first time from September 10, 1933, until January 15, 1934. He was required to post pond to cover civil responsibility on the $40,000,000, however.

No Comment

No comment was immediately forthcoming from Grau on the indictment. In the past he and his followers have denied the accusations, terming them maneuvers by their political opponents. Grau and Cuba's present president, Carlos Prio Socarras, had been friends for many years but split in a political dispute after Prio took office in 1948.

Grau's former Minister of Edu-

(Please Turn to Page 2)

Tehran Student Shoots Ex-Education Minister

Young Moslem, Caught Cheating on Exam, Wounds Dr. Zanganeh, Friend of Late Premier—Communist Tie-up With Attack Sought

Tehran, Iran, March 19—(AP)—Dr. Abdul Hamid Zanganeh, former education minister and close friend of the late Premier Ali Razmara, was shot and wounded by a student he had caught cheating on an examination. A Communist tie-up with the attack also was sought.

Police arrested the gunman, a young Moslem divinity student at the University of Tehran, and began an investigation to determine whether he was a member of the Communist Tudeh Party—the bitter enemy of Zanganeh.

The 46-year-old educator, president of the university law faculty, had been the target of frequent Leftist student demonstrations in the past two years.

The shooting occurred on the university steps.

Police also sought to determine if the students, Nusratullah Abdul Hossein Qumi was linked with Fadayan Islam, the fanatic Moslem group from whose ranks came the gunman who assassinated Premier Razmara March 7.

Zanganeh, however, had not been involved in the oil nationalization dispute which was responsible for the premier's death.

Failed to Fire

A witness to the shooting today said Qumi pointed the gun at Zanganeh's head but it failed to fire. He then chased him around an automobile in front of the building and shot him once in the small of his back.

At the hospital a doctor said the bullet had been removed and Zanganeh's condition was fair.

Zanganeh during his first tenure as education minister, in 1949 and 1950, introduced a drastic press law which the Parliament passed after an attempt to assassinate Shah Mohammed Reza Pahlevi.

The law, since repealed, provided for the jailing of editors and sus-

(Please Turn to Page 2)

Today's Register

Field Under Fire In Contempt Case

Washington, March 19—(AP)—A Government prosecutor today challenged the good faith of Frederick Vanderbilt Field in refusing to answer questions during a probe of Communist-in-Government charges.

Field, a New York millionaire, is on trial in Federal Court on contempt of Congress charges growing out of his appearance before a Senate Foreign Relations Subcommittee last April 28.

Assistant U. S. Attorney William Hitz conceded Field, in refusing to answer 32 questions, claimed replies might tend to incriminate him.

But Hitz insisted that Field was "picking and choosing" what questions he wanted to answer and had no "reasonable and honest fear" of being prosecuted for answering.

Hitz pointed out in his opening statement that Field voluntarily testified before the Senate group that he had never been a Soviet espionage agent. Accordingly, Hitz told Judge T. Alan Goldsborough "he couldn't claim that as one of his fears."

Hitz described Field as "a man of great wealth who has expended it freely over a long period of time for Communist-front organizations at least."

"We say he did not have good faith when he made that claim (possible self incrimination)," Hitz told Judge Goldsborough.

Goldsborough is hearing the case without a jury.

Field, 45, faces a 32-count indictment based on his refusal to answer questions put to him at the Senate inquiry.

In his testimony then Field, a great grandson of Comdr. Cornelius Vanderbilt, denied (1) that he had ever served as a Soviet agent, and (2) that he had ever called Owen Lattimore a Communist. Both these allegations had been made by Louis Budenz during the subcommittee's inquiry into charges by Senator McCarthy (R-Wis.) of Communist infiltration of the State Department.

But for the most part Field refused to answer questions. He said he was relying on his constitutional privilege against possible self-incrimination.

Thus the legal issue is the same as in eight of nine contempts of Congress cases tried here in recent weeks: Did the witness properly invoke his privilege under the Fifth Amendment against possible self-incrimination?

In five cases, judges ruled that witnesses did and acquitted them. In two cases where possible self-incrimination figured there have been convictions. Two other cases are awaiting decisions. All involved witnesses before various congressional committees.

Only Earl Browder, former No. 1 American Communist, failed to

(Please Turn to Page 2)

U.S. Weather Forecast
FOG—DRIZZLE
(Details on Page 2)

4c in N. Y. C.
5c Elsewhere

Vol. 29. No. 127. NEW YORK 17, N. Y., TUESDAY, NOVEMBER 18, 1952 CO FINAL EDITION ★

U. S. MOVES TO BOUNCE LUCHESE

Bare De Sapio Draft Deferment; He Blasts Committee Tactics

Stories on Page 3

Joseph (Socks) Lanza . . . knew "biggies."

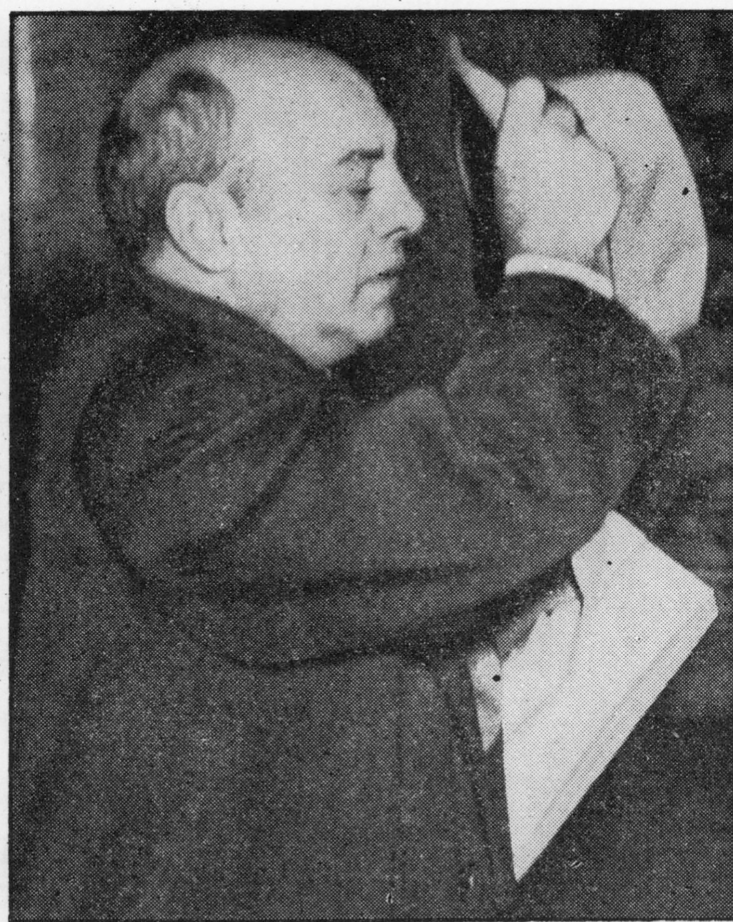

(Mirror Photos by Dan McElleney)

PROBE SPOTLIGHT BROUGHT 'EM OUT . . .

Frank De Stasio, a worker in East Side's 8th A.D., ducks photographers as he appears before State Crime Commission. He admitted "kicking back" to his club secretary half of his $240-a-month pay as a Municipal Court Justice's clerk. At left, notorious Joseph (Socks) Lanza sickly grins as he enters, to state that after Robert V. Santangelo offered him a job, Santangelo got dual party backing for Municipal Court Justice. At right, Tammany chief Carmine DeSapio is another arrival. *(Other Photos, Page 3)*

Carmine DeSapio . . . Tammany chief's angry.

If It's News and True It's Here

New Haven Journal-Courier

And New Haven Times

Weather Today
Sunny And Warm
U. S. Weather Report on Page 2
High Tide 6:25 A. M. and 6:54 P. M.

VOL. CLXXXVII, NO. 145 MEMBER ASSOCIATED PRESS NEW HAVEN, CONN., SATURDAY MORNING, JUNE 20, 1953 AN INDEPENDENT PAPER FIVE CENTS 30c Per Week Home Delivered

Rosenbergs Die In Electric Chair

Two U. S. Judges Here Refused To Aid A-Spies

Last Ditch Appeal For Stay Rejected

U. S. Appeals Court Justices, Visited By Counsel For Rosenbergs, Study Pleas But Refuse To Bar Executions.

The case of condemned atom spies Julius and Ethel Rosenberg reached into New Haven yesterday afternoon, only four hours before the two met death in Sing Sing Prison's electric chair.

Judges Thomas W. Swan and Jerome Frank of the Second Federal Circuit Court of Appeals which heard the matter before it went to the Supreme Court in Washington, were asked by lawyers to issue stays of execution. Pleas made to both were denied.

After the Supreme Court in Washington by a six-to-three decision at noon, revoked Justice Douglas' stay of execution, defense attorneys made their futile final try by appealing another point to the Circuit Court. A stay would have kept the Rosenbergs alive while the matter was considered. Other appeals were made both in Washington and in New York.

No Written Opinions

Neither Judge Swan nor Judge Frank gave written opinions on the requests made to them. It was learned they based their decisions on the Supreme Court ruling that the case doesn't warrant further litigation. They told the Rosenberg lawyers, it is said, they saw no substantial question to be argued.

Judge Swan gave the attorneys a brief hearing in his chambers in the Post Office Building before denying their request. He then accompanied them to Judge Frank's home where the latter jurist also gave a brief hearing before issuing his denial.

32 New Homes Are Planned In West Haven

Plans for the erection of 32 new homes in West Haven were disclosed at a meeting held by the Board of Selectmen last night.

The new homes, to be constructed on 80-foot lots, will be built by the Elm City Construction Co., of which Fausto Bertolini is president. The proposed project is located in an undeveloped area off Meloy Road, north of Saw Mill Road.

The selectmen approved of the plans submitted at the meeting under the provisions that the building firm install storm water drainage systems, sidewalks and curbs. Town Engineer John F. Lynch, board members said, would be asked to look over the proposed area and make any recommendations that he may deem necessary.

President Bertolini told the board that they have made no decision

(Continued on Page 3)

City Police Union Raps Pension Plan

Fearful that the proposed pension adjustment will jeopardize the future salaries and pensions of active policemen, the New Haven Police Union, Local 530, AFL, has issued a bulletin opposing the referendum question for the special election on Monday.

Through this action, the Police Union joins the Board of Finance and the Taxpayers Research Council in condemning the pension bill, which can be passed by a simple majority of those voting.

If passed the trustees of the Policemen's Relief Fund will be immediately ordered to increase the pension for 123 policemen and continue to do so to an amount equal to 50 per cent of the salary paid in 1955, or, in the future, to that of a regular member of the force of the same grade as that held by the pensioner at the time of his retirement.

The bill provides for the 123 only. It does not provide equal benefits for policemen retired since January 1, 1952, and it makes no provision for pensions for widows, firemen or other city employes.

Met Wednesday

The Police Union executive committee met Wednesday night to study the bill and as a result issued a long bulletin opposing the bill and setting forth the reasons for so doing.

Considering the "continuously adjusting" phase of the proposed pension plan, Shaw called attention

(Continued on Page 2)

G.O.P. Leader Arrested In Parking Row

A local political leader, a member of the City of New Haven Board of Assessors, was arrested on four counts, stemming from a traffic violation, Thursday night, it was learned yesterday.

According to a report by Foot Patrolman Alfred Marrone, Benjamin Levine of 165 Dwight Street, became abusive following his arrest. Marrone's report quoted Levine as saying "he knew someone and that he would have my badge taken from me."

Marrone said he noticed a car parked in a no parking zone in Chapel Street between Orange and Church Streets. He said he asked the operator, Levine, to move it, at which point the man became abusive.

Brought to Police Headquarters, Levine was charged with obstructing traffic, refusing to obey an officer, abusing an officer and resisting arrest.

A member of the Board of Assessors for a number of years, Levine is also Republican chairman of the 21st Ward and a member of the Republican Town Committee. He was chief moderator here, in the recent presidential election.

CAR HITS POLE

Milford, June 20—Police said a 23-year-old Broad Street man struck and shattered a utility pole at Cooper and East Broadway at about 12:45 A. M. Authorities at Milford Hospital said Frank Lee is under treatment for a possible fractured jaw.

33 Sworn In As Republican Registrars

Few Changes Made In Party's 1951 List—Rosien Officiates.

Republican Registrar of Voters Victor Rosien swore in 33 Republican assistant registrars this week. There are a few changes from last year's list. Registrars are:

Peter Usus, 76 Grove Street, Ward 1; Morris Greenberg, 13 Spruce St., Ward 2; Cecil Svirsky, 254 Orchard Street, Ward 3; Joseph D'Andrea, 746 Legion Avenue, Ward 4; Louis Bettigole, 32 Gilbert Street, Ward 5.

Also: Vincent Sanacata, 62 Arch Street, Ward 6; Anthony Romano, 127 Carlisle Street, Ward 7; Frank J. Ferreno, 494 Howard Avenue, Ward 8; Ralph Luciano, 146 Greenwich Avenue, Ward 9; Dominic Vitolo, 22 Brown Street, Ward 10; Pasquale Celotto, 107 Wallace Street, Ward 11; Julius Rescigno, 191 Franklin Street, Ward 12; Julius Spier, 145 Bradley Street, Ward 13.

And: Edward Fink, 153 Foster Street, Ward 14; Le Roy Brown, Ward 15; Norman Eddy, 752 Dixwell Avenue, Ward 16; Fred McFarlan, 276 West Hazel Street, Ward 17; Anthony DiPalmi, 257 Highland Street, Ward 18; George Cross, 52 Foote Street, Ward 19; John J. Fallon, 62 Winchester Avenue, Ward 20; Albert A. Seretny, 80 Howe Street, Ward 21; Robert Weiss, 20 Platt Street, Ward 22; Thomas Bloor, 222 Norton Street, Ward 23; Joseph Carrano, 834 Elm Street, Ward 24; Arthur Rappa, 8 Woolsey Street, Ward 25.

Wesley J. O'Brien, 47 Downing Street, Ward 26; Augustus Gilligan, 462 Poplar Street, Ward 27; John Flanagan, 41 Lombard Street, Ward 28; David A. Harper, 1028 Whalley Avenue, Ward 29; Lloyd Crapo, 1029 Whalley Avenue, Ward 29B; John H. Davidson, 55 Ramsdell Street, Ward 29C; William H. Beebe, 257 West Rock Avenue, Ward 30; John T. Kimberly, 130 West Rock Avenue, Ward 30B; John Leonard Priest, 80 Clifton Street, Ward 31, Anthony Marino, 143 Beacon Avenue, Ward 32; Burton C. Clarkson, 115 Morris Avenue, Ward 33.

Sports Highlights

YESTERDAY'S RESULTS

American League

Detroit 3, New York 2.
Cleveland 4, Washington 2.
Boston 4, St. Louis 1.
Chicago 5, Philadelphia 2.

National League

Chicago 11-1, Brooklyn 8-7.
St. Louis 10, Pittsburgh 2.
New York 15, Milwaukee 1.
Philadelphia 10, Cincinnati 3.

Sport Headlines

—Eddie Compo Denies He Will Quit Ring
—Sports Editor Bill Ahern Tells Story About "A Kid"

Full Details On Pages 6 & 7

Spy Drama Of Rosenbergs Ends In Execution

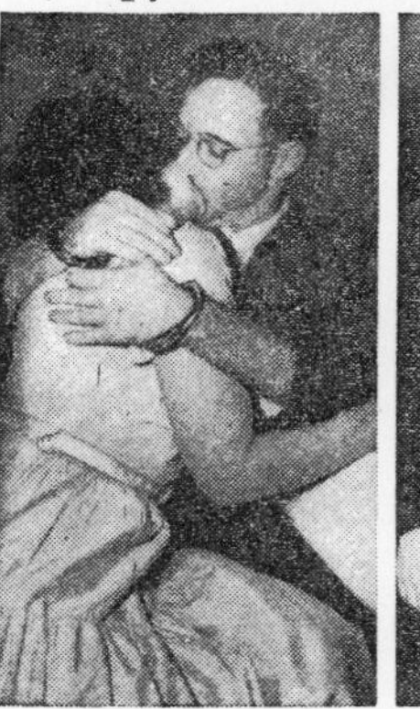

Julius and Ethel Rosenberg, atom spy team whose stay of execution was set aside yesterday by the Supreme Court, are shown in New York in stages of arraignment and trial. Left, Julius kisses his wife in prison van in September, 1950; center, they arrive at Federal Court during trial in March, 1951; right, they are separated by wire screen as they head for jail following conviction in March, 1951. They have been separated for two years in Sing Sing prison. (AP)

Reds Demand Recovery Of Freed POWs

Indefinite Recess In Armistice Talks Also Sought.

Munsan, Saturday, June 20—(AP)—Communists today demanded immediate recovery of 25,000 North Korean prisoners of war freed on order of President Rhee and asked for an indefinite recess in the Korean armistice negotiations.

Their demand was made in a plenary truce session at Panmunjom in a strongly worded protest which charged that the United Nations Command "deliberately connived with Rhee to free the prisoners."

"The United Nations must bear the serious responsibility for this incident," said the Communist protest. It was signed by North Korean Marshal Kim Il Sung and Red Chinese Gen. Peng Teh-Huai.

Talks To Continue

The Red protest did not break off the armistice talks. But it dealt a telling blow to the prospects of a few days ago for an immediate truce.

South Korean guards acting on Rhee's orders permitted and aided mass breakouts Thursday and Friday from six big stockades. The government urged the entire South Korean population to help the prisoners make good their escape.

President Eisenhower rebuked Rhee. World opinion mounted against the fiery South Korean leader who had abruptly and arbitrarily confronted the truce talks with a new crisis.

(Continued on Page 3)

House Approves Foreign Aid Bill

Strong Democratic Support Gives Eisenhower Vote Of Confidence — More Than Dozen Attempts To Cut Funds Beaten Down.

Washington, June 19—(AP)—Strong Democratic support gave President Eisenhower a vote of confidence today when the House approved without change a $4,998,732,500 foreign aid program for the coming year.

The roll call vote on final passage was 280 to 108.

The measure now goes to the Senate.

Democratic votes enabled G.O.P. leaders to beat down more than a dozen attempts to cut the bill up to half a billion dollars. Almost all of these amendments were offered by Republicans, and half of the Republicans present supported proposed major reductions.

Test Of Confidence

Rep. Vorys (R-Ohio), leading the administration fight, had called the bill a test of congressional confidence in the President's foreign policy.

The House sustained cuts of 476 million dollars made by the Foreign Affairs Committee in the President's "minimum" budget for the year beginning July 1.

Despite strong appeals by leaders of both parties to support the President, two efforts were made to cut the whole program by half a billion dollars. Other amendments proposed eliminating military aid to Yugoslavia, Spain, Portugal and Japan.

The House sustained an administration-opposed committee amendment withholding more than one billion dollars of aid for Europe until the European Defense Community and its international Army are set up.

Appropriations Vote Later

The measure only sets a ceiling. Today's stormy all-day session indicated the administration

(Continued on Page 3)

Gas Prices To Be Raised On Monday

Cost Of Domestic Fuels Also To Be Increased.

The retail price of gasoline will be increased as much as eight-tenths of a cent per gallon for certain brands in the New Haven area beginning Monday.

Joseph Wehner, plant manager of the Esso plant here, said regular and premium gasoline prices at the Esso stations will be raised by that much next week. Domestic range oils will cost six-tenths of a cent per gallon more next week, he added.

Wehner said the price of crude oil from the wells has been increased and the added cost is being passed along to the consumer. Less than two weeks ago there had been a slight rise in the price of gasoline.

Several other gasoline distributors in the area last night indicated they will fall in line with the price

(Continued on Page 3)

Freedom-Bound Youngsters Mob Their Teacher

Vacation-bound youngsters in the first grade at Seth Haley School, South Street in West Haven, mob pretty teacher Miss Greta Cina (center) as the last class ends and the whole, wonderful free summer stretches before them. Getting in a good departing 'smack' is Bobby Tellier, as his home room pupils surge close.

20 Are Hurt In Warehouse Blast In Texas

Fort Worth, Texas, June 19—(AP)—A warehouse jammed with fireworks blew up today in a brilliant spout of flames and four thunderclap roars, injuring about 20 persons and damaging at least 100 nearby homes.

No one was killed in the noontime blast. Only two of the injured were in a serious condition.

Numerous Blazes Started

Crackling fireworks spewed more than 150 feet across the busy four-lane Jacksboro highway, starting numerous blazes in the drought-dry countryside on the northwest outskirts of the city. Then the wind whipped the smoke and flames back toward residential areas. Sparks carried as far as 18 miles to the north to start pasture fires.

Intense heat and a series of smaller blasts hampered fire-fighting and rescue operations.

(Continued on Page 3)

Germans Raid Reds' Office; Officials Flee

Berlin, June 20—(AP)—A crowd of 2,000 Germans, aroused by events in East Germany, raided a Communist (Socialist Unity) Party office in the U. S. sector late today and forced several Red officials to flee through a back door.

Furniture, propaganda publications and pictures of Stalin and Communist East German leaders were thrown in the street and burned. West Berlin police reported they made no arrests.

The outburst developed as a wave of arrests by the Communist people's police spurred rebellious East Germans back to work.

Tension Increases

Tension increased tonight when Communist police shot a West Berlin businessman as he unwittingly stepped into Soviet territory near Potsdamer Platz.

The victim, Karl Wilhelm Kin-

(Continued on Page 3)

Legal Moves Fail To Save 2 A-Spies

No Demonstration Outside Walls Of Sing Sing Prison—Police Stop Mass Meeting Of 5,000 In New York City.

Ossining, N. Y., June 19—(AP)—Julius and Ethel Rosenberg, silent and without emotion, died in the electric chair tonight for betraying atomic bomb secrets to Russia.

Julius, treading firmly and unsupported by guards, entered the Sing Sing death chamber first, at 7:04 P. M. (EST), as a chaplain intoned the 23d psalm by his side. Two minutes later he was pronounced dead.

His wife was then led in, at 7:11, and she was dead at 7:16, just 15 minutes before the last rays of the setting sun betokened the start of the Hebrew sabbath.

Their deaths ended a frenzied day of dramatic legal moves after the Supreme Court had voided a stay of execution previously granted by Associate Justice William O. Douglas.

There was no demonstration outside the walls of the grim fortress prison on the banks of the Hudson River, but 30 miles away in New York City, the Rosenberg's home, police stopped a mass meeting of 5,000 persons as a hysterical wave of screaming and shouting arose as the hour of execution arrived.

The Rosenbergs were the first civilians in American history to die for espionage.

Nine Appeals By Lawyers

The day's dramatic efforts to save the couple—there were nine appeals by lawyers to jurists in Washington, New York and New Haven for stays after the Supreme Court acted—were climaxed as President Eisenhower rejected a plea for clemency with a sharply worded statement.

"I can only say," said Eisenhower, "that by immeasurably increasing the chances of atomic war, the Rosenbergs may have condemned to death tens of millions of innocent people all over the world."

As the Rosenbergs, their final reprieve gone, entered the death chamber, their two sons, Michael, 10, and Robert, 6, were being cared for by family friends at Toms River, N. J., 100 miles away.

Although their last day had been filled with stormy excitement outside for their supporters, there was but a single, small moment of drama within. Ever since they were convicted, the Rosenbergs displayed stoical calm.

Mouth Seems Twisted

But as Ethel, a short, plumpish woman of 37, stood before the electric chair in a shapeless green patterned dress and slippers, her small mouth seemed twisted, though none could say if it was a smile or sneer.

She took one step, then turned suddenly toward Mrs. Helen Evans, prison matron, who had walked to the chamber with her. Mrs. Rosenberg pulled Mrs. Evans to her and they kissed.

Visibly affected, the matron quickly left the room with Mrs. Lucy Many, a telephone operator who had also accompanied Mrs. Rosenberg.

Mrs. Rosenberg sat down calmly and her arms dropped limply on the chair sides. She winced slightly as the electrode helmet was attached to her clipped head and the restraining thongs were fitted in place. The other electrode was connected to her bare right leg.

Low Rasping Rattle

Then a long moment, followed by a low rasping rattle as the execution switch was thrown. Her hands

(Continued on Page 2)

Death Comes Quickly For Doomed Couple

Rosenbergs Emotionless As They Go To Deaths At Sing Sing.

Ossining, N. Y., June 19—(AP)—Atom spies Julius and Ethel Rosenberg died tonight in Sing Sing's electric chair.

The first to die was Julius Rosenberg, who was pronounced dead at 7:06 P. M. (EST). Ethel Rosenberg followed her husband and was pronounced dead at 7:16 P. M. Neither husband nor wife said anything before they died.

They were the first civilians in American history to be executed for espionage. They were convicted of betraying American atomic secrets to Russia.

The electrocutions took place after a suspense-packed 24-hour delay while the Supreme Court studied and rejected a fifth appeal in the case.

Julius died after three jolts. He was placed in the chair at 7:04 P. M. and was pronounced dead two and three-quarter minutes later.

Silent Unto Death

His wife, however, required five jolts, and the time was four and one-half minutes.

The pair, who maintained an unemotional front throughout the day, went to their deaths a day after their 14th wedding anniversary and a few minutes before start of the Hebrew Sabbath.

As Mrs. Rosenberg entered the death chamber she was accompanied by Mrs. Helen Evans, prison matron, and Mrs. Lucy Many, a telephone operator.

Mrs. Rosenberg turned just before she was placed in the electric chair, drew Mrs. Evans toward her and they kissed. The matron was visibly affected. She quickly turned and, with Mrs. Many, left the chamber. The Rosenbergs displayed no emotion whatever.

At 7 P. M. (EST) the voice of Rabbi Irving Koslowe could be heard in the corridor leading to the death chamber. He was intoning the 23rd Psalm, "The Lord is my Shepherd; I shall not want. Though I walk in the shadow of death, I shall fear no evil." The rabbi was in his rabbinical robe.

Rosenberg, wearing dark brown

(Continued on Page 2)

Hill To Name Survey Group On Expressway

Bridgeport, June 19—(AP)—Connecticut's highway commissioner said today he hopes "in about three weeks" to suggest the name of a nationally-known engineering firm to undertake a cost and toll-traffic survey in connection with the proposed $213,000,000 cross-state expressway.

Commissioner G. Albert Hill, who said preliminary work on the expressway project was being pressed by his department, estimated that some four months will be required for the surveys set up by law.

Must Approve Selection

Under the law authorizing construction of the 125-mile artery from Greenwich to Danielson on a revenue bond basis, a special bond com-

(Continued on Page 2)

Today's Index

If It's News and True It's Here

New Haven Journal-Courier

And New Haven Times

Weather Today
Cloudy And Colder
U. S. Weather Report on Page 3
High Tide 8:16 A. M. and 9:12 P. M.

VOL. CLXXXVIII, NO. 51 | AN INDEPENDENT PAPER | NEW HAVEN, CONN., TUESDAY MORNING, MARCH 2, 1954 | ★★ MEMBER ASSOCIATED PRESS | FIVE CENTS | Home Delivered 30c Per Week

FANATICS WOUND FIVE SOLONS

Trio Seized After Wounding Five Congressmen

These two pictures show two of the Puerto Ricans in custody yesterday after members of House of Representatives in Washington were fired on from House gallery. At left is woman who identified herself as Lolita Lebron. She said that she was a Puerto Rican, and as she was hustled through the crowd, shouted, "Freedom for Puerto Rico." At the left is Andres Cordero, who was arrested along with Lolita Lebron and a man named Rafael Miranda, for shooting a volley into House chambers. Five Congressmen were wounded. (AP Wirephoto)

Bentley And Jensen Undergo Emergency Washington Surgery

4 Puerto Ricans Held In $100,000 Bond After Wild Shooting In House Chamber — Rep. Bentley Fights For Life — Arrest In Hartford Tied To Case

WASHINGTON, March 1 (AP)—Four fanatics seated in the House gallery today suddenly shouted, "Free Puerto Rico!" waved their flag, and then fired at least 20 wild pistol shots that wounded five congressmen.

One congressman, Alvin M. Bentley (R-Mich.), was so seriously wounded that he was given only an even chance of survival.

Dr. Charles White, who helped operate on Bentley said:

"The operation was a success. Bentley has a 50-50 chance. He is now in the hands of the Lord."

Another congressman had a shoulder wound, and three were hit in the leg.

Three Seized On Spot

Two gunmen and their woman companion, Puerto Ricans from New York City, were seized on the spot. Police Chief Robert V. Murray said tonight that they have confessed the shooting, and have implicated a fourth.

The wounded congressmen:

Bentley, 35, hit in the left side below the heart. The bullet went on through, and came out the right side.

Ben F. Jensen (R-Iowa), 61, struck in the left shoulder.

Clifford Davis (D-Tenn), 56, shot through the upper calf of his right leg.

Kenneth A. Roberts (D-Ala), 41, bullet struck left leg while he was seated. It entered above the knee and came out below.

George H. Fallon (D-Md), 51, shot in the hip.

Police identified the Puerto Ricans as members of the Nationalist party of Puerto Rico. Two other members of the party tried to assassinate President Truman in 1950.

Admit Shooting

Police Chief Murray said these three had admitted the shooting:

Mrs. Lolita Lebron, 34, of 315 W. 94th St., New York City. Murray said she has just been divorced.

Rafael Concel Miranda, 25, of 120 1st St., New York City.

Andres Figueroa Cordero, 29, of 108 E. 103rd St., New York City.

Edgar E. Scott, deputy chief of detectives, said that Mrs. Lebron had said Irving Flores, 27, of 108 E. 103rd St., New York City, also was a member of the group. But Scott said Flores had not admitted he was present at the shooting.

"Flores ducked out in the confusion," Scott said, "but we have a witness (Mrs. Lebron) to his participation."

Held In $100,000 Bonds

The four were arraigned before U. S. Commissioner Cyril S. Lawrence tonight and held in bonds of $100,000 each to cover charges of felonious assault with intent to kill.

The U. S. attorney for the District of Columbia, Leo A. Rover, told Lawrence two of the five congressmen are in very serious condition and that there was a grave possibility one or both might die.

Three other persons who had been taken into custody were still being held without any charge being filed against them.

Murray talked for a long time with Lolita Lebron. He said he's convinced the four are from the same group which tried to assassinate Truman.

"Dangerous Group"

"They're a dangerous group of people," Murray said. "They are fanatics and it's going to be a hard situation to deal with."

Murray said Mrs. Lebron said they had no special targets, that "they were just shooting at random to attract attention to their cause."

Later, in an interview, Mrs. Lebron said the shooting was timed to coincide with the opening of the inter-American conference in Caracas, Venezuela, today. She said it would dramatize "the problem of colonialism."

She said the shooting was to 'bring the attention of the people to the plight of Puerto Rico. It is a country that is not free."

"Did you shoot to kill or wound?" newsmen asked.

"Not to kill," she said. The shooting, she added, "was my idea. It was the idea of four of us. I feel I did something for my country." Mrs. Lebron, a native of Lares, Puerto Rico, said members of the Puerto Rican colony in New

(Continued on Page 8)

A complete layout of latest news pictures on the Washington shooting of five Congressmen will be found on Page 8.

Puerto Rican, 24, Held In Hartford After Ike Threat

The case of a 24-year-old Puerto Rican who declared in Hartford yesterday that he planned to "kill President Eisenhower" is scheduled to go before a Federal Grand Jury here today.

Pedro S. Orozco, 24, was arrested in Hartford yesterday afternoon about the same time that gunfire from a small group of Puerto Ricand wounded five Congressmen in the House of Representatives in Washington, D. C.

Held Under $50,000

Orozco, described as a Puerto Rican leader in Hartford, was taken before U. S. Commissioner Benedict M. Holden there. He was ordered held under $50,000 for the grand jury. Bond earlier had been set at $15,000.

Det. Capt. Joseph P. McDonald of Hartford Police notified Secret Service agents after Policeman Otto H. Felie reported that Orozco threatened to kill the president after he had been fingerprinted at police headquarters on a charge of non-support.

McDonald said Orozco was testifying in Hartford Police Court in another case when he was picked up by Probation Officer Richard Fleming on the non-support accusation.

Threat on President

Taken to the cell block in the police station for fingerprinting, Orozco objected and, according to McDonald, said he was "going to kill the president," a threat he

(Continued on Page 3)

Coroner Says W. H. Slaying Was Planned

Calls Crime Deliberate, Malicious And Premeditated.

Coroner James J Corrigan ruled yesterday that the November 21 fatal shooting of Mrs. Dorothy Kennedy in West Haven was "malicious, deliberate, and premeditated."

He held Harold D Rogers, 45, of 704 Orchard Street, "criminally responsible for the death."

The coroner held 'that the shooting and death" of Mrs. Kennedy, 41, of 22 Abigail Street Woodmont, Milford, "were part of a preconceived plan and design; that they were committed during the perpetration of the crime of robbery."

Discounts Claim

Corrigan, in his findings, took note of Rogers' claim to have

(Continued on Page 2)

Today's Index

Ruling Asked On Attorneys Serving City

A resolution requesting Corporation Counsel George W. Crawford to give a written opinion as to the legality of the appointments of the three assistant corporation counsels was introduced to the Board of Aldermen last night by Minority Leader Henry J. DeVita, 32 Ward Republican.

DeVita said Mayor Richard C. Lee did not give the assistant corporation counsels any rank, as required in Section 15 of the City Charter, when he appointed them. He also doubted that the three assistants "can reecive payment out of the City Budget without any designation as to their correct and proper rank."

Minority Spokesman

Speaking for the minority group, DeVita said "we feel that these appointments are not in accord

(Continued on Page 3)

Rafael Miranda third of group charged with firing on members of House of Representatives from gallery is shown as Capitol police rushed him from House. Police say that Miranda and his co-conspirators are members of the Nationalist Independence Party in Puerto Rico. The same group was blamed for an attempted assassination of President Truman in 1950. (AP Wirephoto)

Security In House Impotent, Rep. Cretella Tells Courier

Representative Albert W. Cretella told a Journal-Courier reporter in a telephone interview from Washington last night that security measures in the House of Representatives in Washington are "completely impotent."

Cretella, who was in a committee meeting considering postal affairs, said he rushed to the floor of the House when he heard the House bell signals ringing. "The hearing room was about 20 feet from the floor," he said. "I heard five bells, which was somewhat unusual, and hurried onto the floor."

He said that the shooting had stopped when he arrived, and that he saw Representative Jensen (R-Iowa) and Representative Bentley (R-Mich.) on the house floor. "There was a pool of blood around Jensen," he said.

Cretella said that the only rule concerning visitors in the House gallery was "no cameras." He said that visitors are not searched. "This group got in with Lugers," he said.

(Continued on Page 2)

Record Budget Presented To Milford Council

(Special to The Journal-Courier)

MILFORD, March 1 — A record high budget of $4,336,980.92, which is expected to call for at least a two-mill tax rate increase, was presented to the Town Council tonight by Town Manager John J. Desmond.

This budget is $524,090.50 greater than the current budget. It covers the period from July 1, 1954, to June 30, 1955.

The largest single increase is in the Department of Education's budget of $1,844,196.46, an increase of $244,196.46 over the current figure. The Board of Education has requested an appropriation of $2,037,521.85.

Desmond explained that the education budget had been cut by deleting an item of $193,325.39, which

(Continued on Page 2)

Board Eases Parking Ban In State St.

A reduction of three hours on the parking ban in the Elm-State Street area, the appointment of 33 men as supernumerary policemen and the retirement of three veteran members of the department were all approved at a Board of Police Commissioners meeting yesterday.

The parking ban, which was put into effect last December and raised protests from merchants in the area at the last meeting that it was resulting in a loss of 50 percent in their businesses, was cut three hours from 12 noon to 9 P M. to 12 noon to 6 P.M.

Reduced to Six Hours

The restriction calls for no parking on the south side of Elm Street from Church to State Streets, and on the west side of State Street from Elm Street to Crown Street. It was

(Continued on Page 2)

Atomic Device Exploded In Pacific Tests

Brief Announcement Of Blast Does Not Give Details.

WASHINGTON, March 1 (AP)—The government tersely announced today that an "atomic device" has been exploded in the mid-Pacific in the first of a new series of tests widely heralded to include a hydrogen bomb blast.

The scene of the latest explosion was in the general vicinity of Eniwetok Atoll, in the Marshall Islands, where the first hydrogen device was detonated in 1952.

Airtight Secrecy

Matching the airtight secrecy surrounding the current tests, today's brief announcement said merely:

"Lewis L. Strauss, chairman of the U. S. Atomic Energy Commission, announced today that Joint Task Force 7 has detonated an atomic device at the AEC's Pacific proving ground in the Marshall Islands.

"This detonation was the first in a series of tests."

No other details were given.

The commission and the Defense Department announced Jan. 8 that the new tests would "carry out a further phase of a continuing series of weapons tests of all categories."

As recently as Feb. 17, President

(Continued on Page 2)

Railroad Man Is Killed By Freight Train

Brakeman Victim Of Cedar Hill Yards Accident.

A 29-year old brakeman for the New Haven Railroad was killed here last night when he was struck and run over by two freight cars in the Cedar Hill yards.

Dead on arrival at New Haven Hospital was Donald Post of 28 Carmel Street. Acting Medical Examiner Dr. Sterling Taylor said the cause of death was "amputation of both legs."

Hit By Two Cars

A railroad spokesman said Post was struck by the two cars which were being "humped" onto Track 5. "Humping" is a railroad expression for the switching of cars onto different tracks for route purposes.

Post, an employe of the railroad since 1944, was a brakeman for a freight train on Track 3 which was being made up for a run to Maybrook, N. Y. The railroad spokesman said Post was apparently standing on Track 5 but could not give any details of how the accident occurred.

Trains being "humped," the spokesman pointed out, are not run by locomotive but are rolled by gravity onto the designated tracks. The Division superintendent's office will continue the investigation today.

Post was removed to New Haven Hospital by Flanagan ambulance and was pronounced dead on arrival at 7:05 P. M. Funeral arrangements are incomplete.

Dulles Revokes McLeod Power To Hire, Fire

Wailes Is Placed In Personnel Post In State Department.

WASHINGTON, March 1 (AP) — R. W. Scott McLeod today lost the hiring-firing authority he had called "inseparable" from his security duties at the State Department.

A department announcement said Secretary Dulles had ordered McLeod relieved of personnel matters at once. He remains in charge of security and consular affairs.

Edward T. Wailes, assistant secretary for administration, was placed in charge of personnel. The change, besides the power to hire and fire, involves a shift of 277 workers in the personnel office.

Center Of Political Storm

McLeod was the center of a political storm less than three weeks ago. He made five speeches for the Republican National Committee despite outcries, mainly from Democrats in Congress, that a security officer had no business in partisan politics.

The "Lincoln Day" speaking tour was frowned on by the Civil Service Commission. It ruled McLeod was subject to the Hatch Act barring federal workers from political activity.

However, the commission said it had no jurisdiction in McLeod's case. The State Department legal office held he was exempt from the act because his pay, $1,500 a year, and status are equivalent to that of an assistant secretary, an exempt job.

Study Continuing

Henry Suydam, State Department press officer, told newsmen the shift of power was in line with a recommendation by a non-par-

(Continued on Page 3)

Lee Attacked For Promises In Campaign

Minority Leader Henry J. DeVita, 32d Ward Republican, last night attacked Mayor Richard C Lee's annual message, in which he attacked the fiscal practices of the past administration, and the attack was immediately termed "sour grapes" by Majority Leader John N. Reynolds, Democrat of the 20th Ward.

DeVita made his attack at the monthly meeting of the Board of Aldermen and scored the Mayor for not including the plans for a new City Hall in an outline of his views on the job he expects to do in the next 23 months. DeVita also declared there was no need for an administrative assistant to the mayor, in his opinion.

(Continued on Page 3)

CLEVELAND — Partly cloudy today, increasing cloudiness tonight. Expected high today 34, low tonight 20. See Page 23.

CLEVELAND PLAIN DEALER FINAL

113TH YEAR—NO 356 Entered as Second Class Matter Post Office, under Act of March 3, 1879. CLEVELAND, WEDNESDAY MORNING, DECEMBER 22, 1954 40 PAGES MAin 1-4500 SEVEN CENTS

SHEPPARD GUILTY, GETS LIFE; INNOCENT, DOCTOR INSISTS

QUAKE DAMAGES WEST COAST TOWN, TOSSES MAN TO DEATH IN POOL

Quick Guide to Today's Plain Dealer

Appearing on inside pages of the Cleveland Plain Dealer, Wednesday, December 22, 1954

Score Injured; Damage Exceeds Million in Temblor

EUREKA, Cal., Dec. 21—(AP)—This northern California lumber port city and logging towns around it were violently shaken just before noon by a two-minute rolling earthquake that caused one death.

At least 20 persons were slightly injured. The damage exceeded a million dollars.

The sudden shock at 11:57 a. m. P. S. T. (2:57 p. m., E. S. T.) hurled Carl Wilkerson, 42, into a lumber mill pond while he was eating lunch. He drowned.

Mrs. James Walsh, wife of a dentist, who had just given birth to a baby in Eureka's St. Joseph Hospital, rolled three feet across the delivery room floor on a table. Her new-born baby son spun in his bassinette in another direction. The stool shot out from under the attending surgeon, Dr. Ted W. Loring, who "thought the whole hospital was coming down."

Nearly Gulped By Creek

Two boys, James Linier, 12, and Larry Devore, 13, who were trout fishing near Blue Lake, said they narrowly escaped being "swallowed up." They said the shallow creek in which they were wading parted to make a trench a foot wide and three feet deep.

Miss Iola Kennedy, an elevator operator, was trapped for more than an hour between the first and second floors of Eureka's Commercial Building when the temblor shut off power.

In West Eureka, the quake caused an earth crack eight inches wide and five feet deep. U. S. Highway 101 buckled between Eureka and Arcata.

Bottles, cans and goods in stores of a six-block area in downtown Eureka were dumped on the floors; walls cracked; and the area was roped off.

Eureka's old City Hall and the Humboldt County Courthouse were so severely damaged that they had to be evacuated.

Radiators were ripped from

(Continued on Page 7, Column 2)

A-Weapons Will Guard West Europe

BY PHIL G. GOULDING
Plain Dealer Bureau

WASHINGTON, Dec. 21—Secretary of State John Foster Dulles predicted today that atomic weapons gradually will replace conventional arms in the defense of western Europe.

The secretary emphasized that he was talking about "tactical" weapons, used in the field to deter armed aggression, and not "strategic" arms employed for mass destructive purposes.

At his first news conference since returning from the NATO council meeting in Paris, Dulles said each nation would have to decide whether to use atomic weapons for the latter purpose.

Dulles said, as have other high officials, that Russia had not altered its basic policy of world domination. There has been a shift from the cooing dove to hard talk, he added, but no change in the ultimate goal of the Soviet.

In a statement issued at the beginning of his conference, the secretary commented on the communique summarizing results of the NATO conference, specifically the approval of the military committee's report.

(Continued on Page 2, Column 3)

DEATH URGED BY AT LEAST ONE WOMAN

Jurors Fail to Keep Score on Number of Ballots; Hurry to Homes

BY SANFORD WATZMAN

Jurors in the Sheppard case balloted "so many, so many times" they did not keep a running score and at least one woman held out for an electric chair verdict before an agreement was reached, it was learned last night.

One member of the panel, Mrs. Luella Williams, was asked whether much time was spent in argument with those who might have favored an acquital. She answered no.

Then she refused to reply to the next question, which was: "Did you mostly consider the degree of murder that you thought the defendant guilty of?"

Get Police Escort

Like the four other women and seven men on the jury, Mrs. Williams returned to her home after five grueling days of deliberations, keeping all but a few of the secrets they had discussed in more than 39 hours of jury action.

Besieged by reporters, the jurors got a police escort from the courtroom to their rooms at Hotel Carter, where they picked up their belongings. They went there in four taxis, with squad cars leading the convoy and others bringing up the rear.

They paused only once to speak to newsmen before parting company with each other. That was in their bailiff's room at the hotel, where a few newspaper representatives were admitted after several minutes of frantic persuasion.

Foreman Speaks

James C. Bird, their foreman, spoke for the group. He said they had agreed not to discuss the case because it had not yet been heard in the higher courts.

He issued this brief verbal statement and refused to amplify it:

"After hearing Mr. (Defense Chief Wiliam J.) Corrigan request a new trial we felt that in

(Continued on Page 8, Column 3)

Mississippi Votes Law to Continue Separate Schools

JACKSON, Miss., Dec. 21—(AP)—Mississippi voters apparently gave a more than two to one stamp of approval today to a constitutional amendment designed to continue school segregation.

Returning from 1,067 of 1,825 precincts gave 74,572 votes for the amendment and 30,236 against.

The precincts counted were from all areas of the state and included both city and rural areas.

The amendment, similar to those approved already by Georgia and South Carolina, gives the legislature standby authority to abolish the public school system and subsidize private schools to continue separate Negro and White school systems.

It was designed to bypass the U.S. Supreme Court ruling banning segregation in public schools.

SEES JAP-RED TRADE

TOKYO, Wednesday, Dec. 22—(AP)—Prime Minister Ichiro Hatoyama told the diet yesterday he was confident Japan could trade with Russia and Red China and still enjoy close relations with the United States.

AP Photo

CONVICTED AS MURDERER. Dr. Samuel H. Sheppard, 30, was found guilty of bludgeoning his wife, Marilyn, to death by a seven-man, five-woman jury.

MAYOR SATISFIED VERDICT IS JUST

Praises Police; McArthur Says 'Justice Prevailed'

Mayor Anthony J. Celebrezze, the man responsible for Cleveland police taking full charge of the Sheppard murder case, is completely satisfied with the verdict of second-degree murder.

"I feel," Cleveland's mayor said last night, "that the defendant received a fair trial and that the verdict is justified by the evidence presented.

"I especially would like to commend the Cleveland police department for its fine work in investigating the murder and in preparing the case for trial."

Similar satisfaction was expressed by Deputy Inspector James E. McArthur, Cleveland detective chief who spearheaded the probe.

"Justice prevailed," McArthur asserted. "I am satisfied with the verdict.

"I would also like to convey my appreciation of the sacrifices

(Continued on Page 11, Column 4)

BODY IS FOUND IN LAKE

Boy at Play Notifies Police; Man Unidentified

The body of an unidentified man was found yesterday frozen in shore ice in Lake Erie near Harborview Drive N. W.

Paul Smith, 14, of 1314 W. 114th Street, who was playing along the shore, found the body and called police.

An examination was to be made today to determine how long the man had been in the water and the cause of death.

Dr. Sam Elated, Then Shattered by Verdict

BY JOHN G. BLAIR

*"We, the jury * * * do find the defendant * * * not guilty of murder in the first degree * * *"*

For a fleeting moment, Dr. Samuel H. Sheppard thought he had been freed late yesterday.

He opened his eyes, which he had closed waiting for the verdict. His features lightened and there was a hint of elation around his full lips as he unclenched his teeth.

*"But, guilty of murder in the second degree * * *"*

Judge Edward Blythin's words came crashing down on the defendant seated expectantly at the trial table.

Mouth Falls Open

Dr. Sam's mouth fell open, and he gasped audibly.

There was a look of stunned disbelief . . . it could not be true . . . but it was.

Dr. Sam stared hard at the jurors, who had just crushed his hopes of reunion with his family and resumption of his career.

William H. Corrigan, one of Dr. Sam's defense attorneys, leaned forward and clasped his hand on Dr. Sam's left shoulder.

Dr. Sam wet his lips repeatedly.

Still staring at the jurors, Dr. Sam started shaking his handsome head back and forth.

Corrigan Stands Up

He closed his eyes and clasped his hands before him as through the heavy silence he heard his defense chief, William J. Corrigan, scrape his chair back and inform the court that he would like to file a motion for a new trial.

"* * * sometime after Christmas * * *," Corrigan suggested for the hearing on the motion.

Sometime after Christmas—the words must have repeated themselves over and over in Dr.

(Continued on Page 11, Column 3)

HURT IN GARAGE BLAST

Employee Critically Burned in Explosion of Wash Gasoline

James Watkins, 423, of 2421 E. 63d Street, was severely burned last night when a can of gasoline exploded as he was cleaning auto parts at the Pure Oil Station, 6303 Quincy Avenue S. E.

He is in critical condition at St. Luke's Hospital with severe burns over half his body. Damage to the service station was set at $600.

A spark from a heater was believed to have ignited the fuel.

SEA STILL TOSSING 31

CALAIS, France, Dec. 21—(AP)—The 31 passengers aboard the helpless French ferryboat Cote D'Azur settled down for their second night of buffeting by rough seas off the French coast.

Just 3 More Shopping Days to Christmas

Downtown store hours: Today and tomorrow, 10 a. m. to 9 p. m.; Friday, 10 a. m. to 5 p. m.

SECOND-DEGREE VERDICT COMES IN 102 HOURS

BY TODD SIMON

The jury found Dr. Samuel H. Sheppard guilty of second-degree murder of his wife, Marilyn, yesterday at 4:12 p. m.

Shaken but able to give a 31-word "I am not guilty" speech, the boy-faced osteopath was promptly sentenced to "life" in the Ohio Penitentiary. In 10 years he could be paroled.

That is the inescapable punishment brought on by the jurors' agreement, reached after they had considered the evidence 39 hours and 23 minutes. They had been out some 102 hours in all.

Common Pleas Judge Edward Blythin

Full Page of Sheppard Case Pictures on Page 40

meted out that penalty over the objections of Dr. Sam's chief counsel, William J. Corrigan.

"Why sentence him now, before I file a motion for a new trial?" protested Corrigan. "Oh, go ahead. It's just indicative of the whole thing."

Corrigan Shouts

Corrigan tried to talk to two jurors. Court was still going on. He got called down for it.

"I object to the way this whole case was tried!" he shouted. But he moved away from the jury box and apologized at last to the judge.

And his white-faced client, who will be 31 on Dec. 29, was taken handcuffed upstairs to his fourth-floor County Jail cell. That has been his home almost constantly since he was arrested July 30.

He threw one last, terrible look back at the jury that had branded him a brutal murderer. His eyes burned in an angry scowl. Up to now he had turned only a prayerful or interested face toward the jurors.

He will not be shipped off to prison for a while. Corrigan got a stay of execution.

That staves off the ride to Columbus while Corrigan argues for a second chance in court at 9:30 a. m. on Dec. 30, files an appeal and maybe a plea to let Dr. Sam out on bail.

One long, firm buzz signaled the end of the jury's marathon debate over the dim, wood-paneled court, where the case ground along for nine weeks and three days. Twelve minutes after 4.

Bailiff Nervous

Bailiff Edgar Francis went up. One could tell it meant a verdict. Francis' hand trembled and he fumbled for seconds, trying to get his key into the lock of the judge's office door.

Twenty-six minutes of unbearable tension then, before Judge Blythin got the verdict and read it:

"We the jury, being duly impaneled and sworn, do find the defendant, Samuel H. Sheppard, not guilty of murder in the first degree * * *"

There was the smallest pause—gasps. Sam's eyes flew open.

"* * * but guilty of murder in the second degree. Signed James C. Bird, foreman."

Dr. Sam's jaw fell. The faces of his brothers, Drs. Richard and Steve, began flushing fiery red.

Corrigan asked in a steady voice for the usual recheck. He showed no sign then of disappointment in this monumental courtroom defeat.

Judge Blythin polled the jury: "Is this your verdict?" The bailiff read off each name. All answered "Yes" or "Yes, sir."

That meant that the seven men and five women decided it was Dr. Sam who beat out the life of Marilyn Sheppard "maliciously and purposely," but not "deliberately and of premeditated malice," which is first-degree murder, on July 4 as she lay in her bed.

The next climax: Dr. Sam's speech.

"Sam Sheppard, will you come up here, please?" said the judge.

(Continued on Page 15, Column 2)

The 'HAPPY' PILLS Are They?

Start This Series Today on Page 4

LATEST RACING RESULTS

5¢ IN NEW YORK CITY AND SUBURBS

10¢ ELSEWHERE IN THE U. S. A.

New York Post

Re-entered as 2nd class matter Nov. 22, 1949, at the Post Office at New York under the Act of March 3, 1879.

THREE SECTIONS 72 PAGES | NEW YORK, TUESDAY, JANUARY 22, 1957 | Cloudy | Volume 156 No. 55

Caught After 16 Years

BOMBER TALKING

GEORGE METESKY
Associated Press Wirephoto

Story on Page 3

Basilio Beats Robinson—Details in Sports Section

THE WEATHER
Today: Partly cloudy and cool; mostly fair at night.
Tomorrow: Fair and pleasant.
Temperatures Yesterday: Max. 74.3; Min. 60.9
Today's Probable Range: Max., 68; Min., 58.
Humidity at 3 P. M. Yesterday: 70%
Expected Humidity This Afternoon: 50-60%
Report, Maps—Sec. 2 Page 10

NEW YORK Herald Tribune

A European Edition Is Published Daily in Paris

Late City Edition

117th Year VOL. CXVII NO. 40,490 230 West 41st Street, New York 36, N. Y. Telephone PEnnsylvania 6-4000 TUESDAY, SEPTEMBER 24, 1957 10c in areas 100 miles from New York City FIVE CENTS

Eisenhower Warns: Peace or Troops, After Mob Riots at Little Rock School

Associated Press wirephotos

LITTLE ROCK VIOLENCE—While nine Negro youngsters were being spirited into Central High yesterday, mob was busy attacking Negro reporter Alex Wilson (above).

President Sees Peril In World Inflation

Tells Fund Governors That Price Rises Can Bring a Depression

By Joseph R. Slevin

WASHINGTON, Sept. 23 — President Eisenhower today said inflation is a worldwide phenomenon that threatens sound economic growth and must be halted.

He told the boards of governors of the International Monetary Fund and the International Bank for Reconstruction and Development that the attainment of higher living standards must go hand in hand with the preservation of stable prices.

Mr. Eisenhower spoke as the financial officials began a five-day annual meeting and he warned that inflation is the most important problem that they will consider.

"Wise and courageous leaders in every land are sounding a call to their fellow citizens to join in the defense of their currencies," Mr. Eisenhower said.

He contended that the call "must be heeded" for inflation destroys savings and can bring a depression in its wake.

Mr. Eisenhower sounded a theme that will be repeated again and again during this week's meeting. The delegates to the I.M.F.-I.B.R.D. session are deeply concerned about inflation and about the impact that rising prices are having upon the value of major currencies such as the pound sterling.

Peter Thorneycroft, Britain's Chancellor of the Exchequer, is preparing to tell the governors tomorrow that the United Kingdom is determined to maintain the pound's current $2.80 par value. He will call attention to a fresh series of anti-inflationary credit restrictions that he announced in London last Thursday.

The I. M. F. said in an annual report to the governors today that the worldwide inflationary movement has been caused chiefly by a capital goods boom. The I. M. F. contended that investment demands have outstripped the available supply of savings with the result that prices and interest rates have risen in country after country.

Most of the I. M. F. and I. B. R. D. governors are either Continued on page 18, column 5

U. N. Assembly Urged To Stop ICBM Race

By John Molleson

UNITED NATIONS, N. Y., Sept. 23.—John G. Diefenbaker, Prime Minister of Canada, today proposed that the present General Assembly try to break the disarmament deadlock.

"The danger of a secret and surprise attack," he said, "has been multiplied with the potential development of the intercontinental ballistic missile." This "new and terrible weapon" has given a "somber urgency" to the work of the twelfth Assembly, he asserted.

Russia has already announced the launching of one of the multi-stage rockets. But "experience has taught us that no country possesses a monopoly of any device," Mr. Diefenbaker said, "and the day will not long be distant when there will be armories of these rockets."

The world's budget for arms and mobilization of man power now totals $85,000,000,000 each year, he said, and "action is demanded" to halt this spending on an atomic arms race. Quantity production of ballistic missiles would mean that the world had entered "another era ... an even more frightening and awful time to contemplate than the one we know," he said.

Japan today asked the Assembly to consider a resolution suspending nuclear-test explosions. Russia has already made the request. Mr. Diefenbaker reminded the delegates that Western proposals for a one-year suspension would be conditional on a convention on disarmament. "To some persons a ban on atomic tests has become a sort of panacea," he said. These people have lost sight of the fact that a suspension of tests will not stop the stockpiling of nuclear weapons, he added.

The "only way" to end the Continued on page 8, column 2

5 Survivors From Bark Picked Up

U. S. Freighter Reports Rescue

By Walter Hamshar

The freighter Saxon of the Isbrandtsen Company yesterday picked up five survivors of the German bark Pamir from a small lifeboat in which five other crewmen had perished before rescue came on the stormy Atlantic.

The survivors reported that twenty-five other men had successfully launched a lifeboat before the four-masted square-rigger foundered Sunday night. The story told by the exhausted men was the first report that the steel-hulled sailing ship had remained afloat any length of time after sending a distress call Saturday that she was in danger of sinking after losing her sails and taking a 45-degree list in hurricane winds.

Lights and flares spotted yesterday by sea and air rescue craft raised hopes that other survivors may be picked up when visibility in the storm-swept area improves. The Coast Guard reported that the cutter Absecon and at least ten merchant ships were continuing the search that began Saturday.

Capt. Lars Bjotvedt of the Continued on page 8, column 3

INDEX

TANGLE TOWNS See Page 4 Sec. 3

Eisenhower Texts

By a Staff Correspondent

NEWPORT, R. I., Sept. 23.—The texts of President Eisenhower's proclamation at 7 o'clock tonight and his statement at 5 p. m. on the Little Rock situation follow:

Proclamation

OBSTRUCTION OF JUSTICE IN THE STATE OF ARKANSAS:
By the President of the United States of America,
A PROCLAMATION

Whereas certain persons in the State of Arkansas, individually and in unlawful assemblages, combinations, and conspiracies, have willfully obstructed the enforcement of orders of the United States District Court for the Eastern District of Arkansas with respect to matters relating to enrollment and attendance at public schools, particularly at Central High School, located in Little Rock school district, Little Rock, Ark.; and

Whereas such willful obstruction hinders the execution of the laws of that state and of the United States, and makes it impracticable to enforce such laws by ordinary course of judicial proceedings; and

Whereas such obstruction of justice constitutes a denial of the equal protection of the laws secured by the Constitution of the United States and impedes the course of justice under those laws;

Now, therefore, I, Dwight D. Eisenhower, President of the United States, under and by virtue of the authority vested in me by the Constitution and the statutes of the United States, including Chapter 15 of Title 10 of the United States Code, particularly Sections 333 and 334, do command all persons engaged in such obstruction of justice to cease and desist therefrom and to disperse forthwith.

In witness thereof, I have hereunto set my hand and caused the seal of the United States of America to be affixed.

Done at the City of Newport, R. I., this twenty-third day of September in the Year of Our Lord 1957 and in the independence of the United States the 182d year.

DWIGHT D. EISENHOWER.

Statement

I want to make several things very clear in connection with the disgraceful occurrences of today at Central High School in the city of Little Rock. They are:

1. The Federal law and orders of a United States District Court implementing that law cannot be flouted with impunity by any individual or any mob of extremists.

2. I will use the full power of the United States, including whatever force may be necessary, to prevent any obstruction of the law and to carry out the orders of the Federal court.

3. Of course, every right-thinking citizen will hope that the American sense of justice and fair play will prevail in this case. It will be a sad day for this country—both at home and abroad—if school children can safely attend their classes only under the protection of armed guards.

4. I repeat my expressed confidence that the citizens of Little Rock and of Arkansas will respect the law and will not countenance violations of law and order by extremists.

Reds' Big Wolf Hunt Flops: Costs $23,781, Bags 3 Deer

By B. J. Cutler

From Herald Tribune Bureau

MOSCOW, Sept. 23.—It is more than 4,000 miles from Magadan in the Soviet Far East to Moscow, but some people here think they can hear the raucous laughter of Siberian wolves.

The hilarity has been caused by what was perhaps the most expensive and least successful wolf hunt in history.

The satirical magazine "Krokodil" said today that comrades on the Magadan Agricultural Board decided to free the collective farm from wolves by shooting them from airplanes.

After seventy-one hours of flying, the purchase of guns, the hire of skilled hunters, the payment to them of salaries, commission and bonuses, the expedition turned in a bill for 95,124 rubles ($23,781 at the official rate of exchange). The hunters reported they had scored three probable hits on the wolves and had shot three deer by mistake.

"The wolves," remarked "Krokodil" unhappily, "being very proud of the high cost of their skins, are stepping up their attacks on the local deer."

In School 3 Hours, 9 Negroes Withdrawn

They Slip In as Little Rock Mob Turns to Attack Negro Newsmen

By Walter Lister Jr.

LITTLE ROCK, Ark., Sept. 23.—Hysteria overcame law and order today as the Mayor and School Superintendent withdrew nine Negro pupils shortly before noon to appease a shouting, lunging mob of 800 white supremacists outside Central High School.

Mrs. L. C. Bates, president of the Arkansas branch of the National Association for the Advancement of Colored People, said tonight that President Eisenhower's pledge of the "full power of the United States" to enforce the law is "gratifying and a step forward." But, she added, "a little more assurance will be necessary" before the students go back to school.

The six girls and three boys had slipped in a side door at about 9 o'clock while virtually all of the 200 demonstrators near the school entrance were attacking and chasing four Negro newsmen. The Negro students' admission had been blocked for three weeks by armed National Guardsmen on orders from Gov. Orval Faubus.

"Did they get in?" a woman gasped.

"They're in now," a man told her.

"Oh my God!" the woman screamed and pushed her hands through her hair.

The mob, in two separate sections, was restrained, with gradually lessening effectiveness, by eighty city police, half the force, backed up by fifty state troopers. More than 100 white pupils left classes during Continued on page 14, column 3

Faubus Says U. S. Can't Use Troops

Unless He Asks For Them First

By Earl Mazo

SEA ISLAND, Ga., Sept. 23.—Gov. Orval Faubus tonight challenged President Eisenhower's right and power to "use force" to uphold a Federal Court order directing the integration of a Little Rock high school.

In the wake of Mr. Eisenhower's statement today from Newport, R. I., the Arkansas Governor insisted the Constitution and American laws state "the forces of the Federal government cannot be employed, except on the request of the Governor of a sovereign state."

Gov. Faubus made it clear he has no intention of asking for Federal help.

On the contrary, he insisted that he and Lt. Gov. Nathan Gordon have the power and the will to "maintain peace and Continued on page 17, column 1

Quits Police, Gets Mob Gifts

Special to the Herald Tribune

LITTLE ROCK, Ark., Sept. 23.—Most of the city police remained poker-faced during disorders here today. But one patrolman, Thomas Dunaway, an ex-prizefighter, unpinned his badge, threw it down and stalked away.

A gas-station attendant passed his hat to collect money for the ex-policeman. When last seen he had a fat collection of bills, including some fives and tens.

President Orders Mob To 'Desist'

Can Act Today If Disobeyed

By Edwin Holden

NEWPORT, R. I., Sept. 23.—President Eisenhower tonight issued a proclamation which cleared the legal road for the possible calling out of Federal troops to prevent any further violence in the Little Rock, Ark., school integration situation.

Mr. Eisenhower, who late in the afternoon had issued a statement saying that he would use the "full power of the United States, including whatever force may be necessary" to back up the law, in tonight's proclamation commanded all persons engaged in obstruction at Little Rock to "cease and desist."

Little Rock Rioting

The President's statement and proclamation followed hours of violence at Little Rock, during which nine Negro pupils were first spirited into Central High School and then withdrawn after three hours when disorders outside contin[ued].

If today's violence sh[ould be] repeated tomorrow in Li[ttle] Rock, it would thus constit[ute] violation of the Presid[ent's] "cease and desist" order and Federal troops could then be employed to enforce the Federal court's orders for integration.

James C. Hagerty, White House press secretary, said the signing of the proclamation does not necessarily mean Fe[deral] Continued on page 10, column 4

Integration News Inside

The Mob in Action: Scene Outside School

By Charles N. Quinn

LITTLE ROCK, Ark., Sept. 23.—"Here they come! Here come the niggers!"

When the cry went up, just two minutes after a buzzer signaled the opening of classes at 8:45 a. m. at Central High School today, a seething crowd of men and women swiftly turned into a frenzied, many-armed brute.

The sullen gathering of 200 persons, held back by police barricades, had been waiting at the intersection of Park Ave. and 16th St. at the southeast corner of the school. The Negro pupils had not yet arrived. The crowd, which had been assembling since before 6 a. m., was impatient. A larger group stood two blocks away behind barricades at 14th St.

The cry, "Here come the niggers," called attention to four men, one carrying a press camera, who advanced along 16th St. toward the school. They were newsmen, here ostensibly to cover the integration at Central High. At that time, unknown to the mob as it swirled toward the four Negroes, two cars pulled up at the side entrance of the school on 16th St., only a few hundred feet away, and nine young Negroes walked unmolested and unnoticed into the school.

Shouting, several white men moved toward the four Negro adults. One colored man had a weak, almost sick smile on his face and he was turned aside by three or four burly white men. The Negroes tried to move around the whites, then turned back.

Not satisfied, the whites began shoving and pushing to hurry the intruders along. Then they kicked. A woman screamed. A man wearing a metal construction-worker's helmet jumped on the back of the Negro holding the camera, and Continued on page 15, column 2

EXTRA

LATEST RACING

10¢

New York Post

Re-entered as 2nd class matter Nov. 22. 1949. at the Post Office at New York under the Act of March 3. 1879.

THREE SECTIONS 96 PAGES | NEW YORK, FRIDAY, OCTOBER 25, 1957 | Cloudy | Volume 156 No. 289

MURDER INC. BOSS SLAIN

Albert Anastasia, one-time executioner for Murder Inc., was shot to death by two masked men today in the barber shop of the Park Sheraton Hotel, 56th St. and Seventh Av. See Pages 2 and 3.

Al Anastasia Shot in Midtown Hotel

FOOTNOTES TO THE BRITISH REPORT:

By Max Lerner

Magazine Page 4

Is There a Homosexual Menace?

LATEST RACING

10¢

New York Post

©1957 New York Post Corporation
Re-entered as 2nd class matter Nov. 22 1949, at the Post Office at New York under the Act of March 3, 1879

THREE SECTIONS 96 PAGES | NEW YORK, FRIDAY, NOVEMBER 15, 1957 | Cooler | Volume 156 No. 307

THE MOB MEETS

Police rounded up Vito Genovese and 64 other mobsters convening in an upstate village. No charges—all were let go.

Cops Seize 65 Hoods —New Killings Feared

Story on Page 3

EXTRA

NAB SLAYER OF 10

Shot in Running Gun Battle

8 STAR LATEST SPORTS

LOS ANGELES EVENING
HERALD EXPRESS
International News Service Associated Press United Press Dow-Jones

VOL. LXXXVII | Four Sections Section A | 1111 So. Broadway, L. A., 54 Phone RI. 8-4141 | WEDNESDAY, JANUARY 29, 1958 | 8-R | NO. 265

Ruckus in Cafe

Hit by Cohen, Waiter Charges

(Photo on A-10)

Mickey Cohen was accused of threatening the life of a Hollywood waiter at the Villa Capri, top Hollywood night spot, early today after the former gambling kingpin and two muscled bodyguards assertedly clobbered the victim.

Among those at the party for singer Sammy Davis jr., where the alleged incident occurred, were singer Frank Sinatra, comedian Ernie Kovaks, his wife, Edie Adams; orchestra leader Spike Jones and his wife, songstress Helen Greco; actress Shirley MacLaine and her husband, Steve Parker.

Earlier police reports that actress Lauren Bacall and actor Robert Mitchum were present were unfounded.

Arthur M. Black, 30, the alleged victim, told police:

"I brushed against someone and the next thing I knew he ripped the pocket off my shirt and hit me in the mouth."

Cohen answered:

"This waiter pushed me and I told him not to ever push me again. I probably would have hit him if I had had a chance. Every waiter in town respects me. They take care of me and I take care of them."

Officers at Hollywood Police Station, where Black lodged a formal complaint, asked the city attorney to take action against Cohen.

Deputy City Attorney Perry Thomas said a hearing on a misdemeanor battery charge would be held Feb. 6.

The waiter, who refused to give police his address "for fear of reprisal," said he was

(Continued on Page 5, Col. 1)

Special Features

Latest Sports

Race Results

AT SANTA ANITA

1 Curtsy 8.50, 3.80, 3.10; Snow Bug 3.30, 2.80; Lil. Hour 10.30
2 Gunsmith 102.20,47.10,21.30;IverHigh 9.70,5.90;LeftyLee 4.60
3 F.Scribendi 4.80,3.20,2.50; CraftyPrty 3.90,3.20; E.Drums 4.20

FOURTH—Six fur., 4 yrs. up, claiming. Purse $4500:

Scratched—One T. Tony, E. Read, S. Gamble, K. Julien.

(For tomorrow's Santa Anita race selections and other races, see sport pages.)

Coroner Admits Secrecy on Death

Police Not Told Baby Killed by 'Overdose'

Los Angeles County Coroner Theodore J. Curphey admitted today that he personally ordered his office not to notify police of the unnatural death of a 4-month-old baby girl last Jan. 10.

The infant, Margaret Harrison, died at the UCLA Medical Center. Autopsy surgeon Dr. Robert Stone said death was caused by an inadevertent overdose of medicine administered to the child because of a heart condition.

A coroner's office form relating to the death and subsequent medical examination bore the notation: "Non police report as per Dr. Curphey."

The coroner's report stated that the fatal dose of medication was prepared according to instruc-

(Continued on Page 5, Col. 3)

Campanella Life Story In Herald

• THE CAMPANELLA STORY—Colorful highlights, background and anecdotes of this famous Los Angeles Dodger catcher will start tomorrow in a three-part series by Dave Anderson in the Herald-Express. Anderson's keen knowledge of "Campy's" career makes this a "must" for all baseball readers.

In today's Herald-Express, Page D-2, Bill Corum, noted sports authority, has a human interest story on Campanella, while George T. Davis' column quotes Leo Durocher on what a credit to baseball "Campy" has been.

Fog Grips Southland

(U. S. Weather, Tides, C-5)

A record-breaking fog—it held the Southland in its grip for nearly 15 hours—paralyzed land, sea and air traffic last night and today, and brought cooler weather.

The zero-zero fog held the temperature to 59 after a low 51.

The area may get occasional rain Thursday and again Monday, with snow at the 5000-foot level.

Downtown motorists and public vehicles burned headlights until 11 a. m., to pierce the fog.

Gunsmith in 'Hundred Dollar' Win at 'Anita

The sixth "hundred dollar" winner at Santa Anita, Gunsmith, stunned this afternoon's crowd of 21,000 by paying $102.20, with apprentice Chloy Cunnington aboard. Gunsmith was up in the last strides to beat Over High and Lefty Lee.

Other three-figure upsetters at the meet have been Marcador, $128.20; Read the Mail, $124.10; Papa Taj, $113.30; Ballywit, $105.69, and Doshay, $103.40, in that order of payoff.

'THE RED DOG KILLER' OF NEBRASKA IS CAPTURED IN WYOMING
Charles Starkweather, 19, Accused of 10 Slayings, Is Shown With Carol Fugate—She Says He Held Her as Captive Since Monday

—Associated Press Wirephoto

WHERE THREE MORE VICTIMS OF MAD KILLER WERE FOUND SLAIN
Bodies of Mr. and Mrs. C. Lauer Ward and Elderly Maid Found in This Dwelling in Fashionable Section of South Lincoln, Neb. (Other Photo, A-10)

High Winds Delay 'Jupiter'

CAPE CANAVERAL, Fla., Jan. 29 (AP)—Hurricane-force winds in upper altitudes made uncertain today the time when the army will fire its Jupiter-C satellite launching vehicle.

The Air Force Weather Central reported high-level winds of 140 miles an hour. Winds of such velocity could topple the rocket.

On the ground, winds of 20 to 30 miles an hour were forecast this afternoon and there was a chance of even higher winds in squalls along this portion of the Florida coast.

Strict secrecy has been maintained in official circles about the army's firing plans, but it has been generally expected that the attempt would be made this week. In earlier speculation, today or tomorrow had been set as

(Continued on Page 4, Col. 4)

End Murder Rampage of Youth, 19

DOUGLAS, Wyo., Jan. 29 (AP)—Charles Starkweather, 19, sought as the "Red Dog" killer in a wave of Nebraska slayings, was captured five miles west of Douglas this afternoon.

Starkweather was wounded in a gun battle with a deputy sheriff.

Officers said the body of a man was found near this eastern Wyoming town. He was not immediately identified nor was the cause of death learned at once but he was believed to be the tenth victim of Starkweather.

Deputy Sheriff Bill Romer identified the man as Starkweather, accused as the slayer of nine persons in the last two days in Nebraska. Romer notified the sheriff's office in Casper that a girl was with Starkweather.

Ken Sackett, an official of the State Department of Revnue at Casper, Wyo., told the patrol here that Caril Fugate, Starkweather's 14-year-old girl friend, also was in custody. He said she broke away from Starkweather during the capture and reached deputies safely.

The girl said she had been held by Starkweather as a captive since they left Lincoln Monday. She said she feared he was "going to take me to Washington state and kill me."

At Lincoln at least 200 combat veterans of the Nebraska National Guard had been ordered to join forces of officers in the all-out search for red-haired, 19-year-old Starkweather.

The latest victims in Lincoln were a businessman, his wife and their maid whose home was on a garbage collecting route manned by Starkweather until he began his spree of bloodletting a few days ago.

Officers said Starkweather was driving a black

(Continued on Page 4, Col. 3)

Backs Pitchess as Successor

Sheriff Biscailuz Will Retire Dec. 1

Sheriff Eugene Biscailuz today officially announced his retirement from office at the conclusion of his term next Dec. 1 due to provisions of the Retirement Act, and declared he will support Undersheriff Peter J. Pitchess as his successor.

In a statement issued by Biscailuz, the veteran peace officer, said:

"I have served in the Sheriff's Office of Los Angeles County for over 51 years. I have been elected Sheriff for six terms and have served a total of 26 years as Sheriff.

"My present term expires Dec. 1 next. I will not be a candidate to succeed myself due to restrictions in the Retirement Laws. I am deeply grateful for the great trust given me by the citizens of Los Angeles County.

"The voters will either nom-

(Continued on Page 4, Col. 6)

Report 5 Killed In Blast at Texas Refinery

PORT ARTHUR, Texas, Jan. 29 (UP)—Police reported today that an accident, probably an explosion, killed five persons at the Texas Company refinery.

Police said about eight other persons were injured. Details were nit immediately available, police said.

EXTRA

DAUGHTER KILLS LANA TURNER'S BOY FRIEND

8 STAR LATEST SPORTS

THE SATURDAY PICTORIAL
LOS ANGELES EVENING
HERALD EXPRESS
International News Service Associated Press United Press Dow-Jones

VOL. LXXXVIII | Three Sections Section A | 1111 So. Broadway, L. A., 54 Phone RI. 8-4141 | SATURDAY, APRIL 5, 1958 | 8-R | 10 Cents 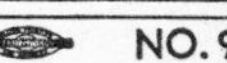 | NO. 9

Why She Killed Stompanato

Cheryl's Own Story

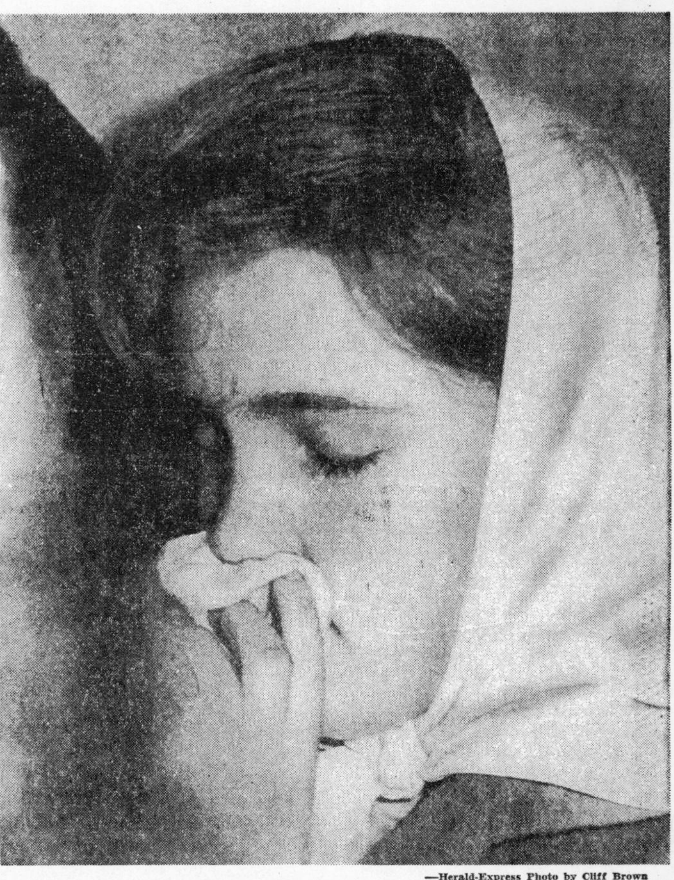

—Herald-Express Photo by Cliff Brown

SOME OF THE SHOCK LEAVES CHERYL CRANE—NOW SHE CAN CRY
Shortly Before Photo Was Taken, Lana's Daughter Said, 'At Least Mama Is Able to Cry. I Can't'... And Then She Did

Film Actress in Tears

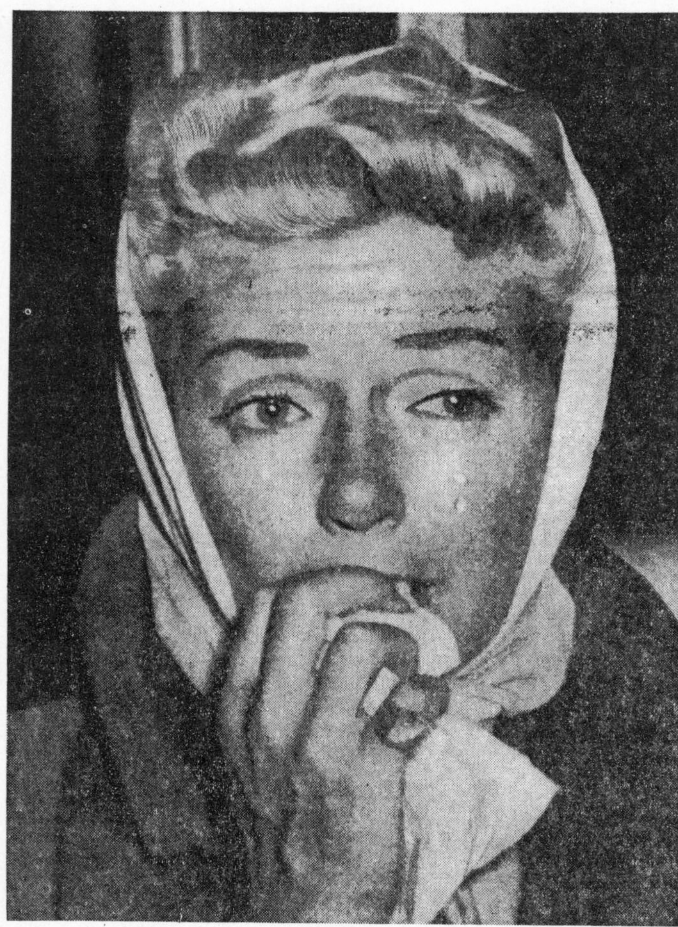

—Herald-Express Photo by Frank Rutherford

LANA TURNER DAZED AFTER SEEING DAUGHTER KILL BOY FRIEND
Famous Actress Weeps Hysterically, Says She Couldn't Believe What She Saw When Daughter Plunged Knife Into Johnny Stompanato

Bracelet on Slain Stompanato Tells Star's Love for Him

(Other Photos and Stories on A-2 and A-3)

"Daddy John, my sweet love, this remembers a piece of my heart which will be with you always, and remember, Guido, my life for you all time. Lanita."

Such was the inscription on a gold bracelet found today on the body of Johnny Stompanato, underworld 'Adonis' and sweetheart of film star Lana Turner who was slain last night by the actress' 14-year-old daughter, Cheryl.

The shy teenager ended the former Mickey Cohen bodyguard's life with an eight-inch butcher knife last night in the bedroom of Miss Turner's Beverly Hills home.

Stompanato's death was a tragic climax, police said, to a bitter quarrel between Miss Turner and the handsome mobster which raged from Cheryl's room to that of her mother.

A horrified Miss Turner viewed the slaying.

Police, although declining to discuss it at length, hinted that Stompanato may have been blackmailing the blonde actress.

"She very definitely tried to break off the relationship with Stompanato," a detective said. "Stompanato didn't want it that way and they quarreled."

On several occasions, Miss Turner told detectives, Stompanato had beaten her and once threatened her with "exposure."

"I did it to protect my mother," Cheryl sobbed as she recounted details of the slaying for Beverly Hills Police Chief Clinton H. Anderson before being transferred to Juvenile Hall.

The personable, dark-haired Stompanato, Miss Turner's attentive companion on many recent dates, died from the effects of one stab wound, inflicted by Cheryl with an eight-inch-blade butcher knife, so new it still bore the price tag.

The fatal thrust, which buried Cheryl's weapon to the hilt in Stompanato's abdomen, came after she assertedly heard him tell her mother:

Knife Finds Its Mark

"I'll get you if it takes a day, a week, or a year. I'll cut your face up. I'll stomp you. And if I can't do it myself, I'll find somebody who will—that's my business."

Believing the pronouncement an immediate threat to her mother's life, Cheryl said she hastened downstairs, picked up the knife and returned to Miss Turner's room.

"You don't have to take that, mother," the stately teenager reportedly announced.

It was then the knife found its mark.

Stompanato's athletic frame toppled, almost as

(Continued on Page 2, Col. 4)

Following is Cheryl Crane's own story of how she killed Johnny Stompanato, the boy friend of her mother, Lana Turner, as quoted by Beverly Hills police officers:

By CHERYL CRANE
(Daughter of Lana Turner)

I did it to protect my mother.

I was scared to death he was going to kill her.

He threatened to cut and maim mother if she broke up with him. I heard him yell:

"I'll get you if it takes a day, a week or a year. I'll cut you up. I'll stomp on you and if I can't do it myself I'll find someone who can."

I went downstairs and got the knife. I came back and told mother:

"You don't have to take that Mama."

Then I jabbed the knife with all my might.

I wish I were like my mother. At least she is able to cry. I can't.

TELLS ARGUMENTS

I came home last night from Ojai for Easter vacation. I had heard my mother and him arguing before. Arguments broke out again last night.

I was in my room talking to mother when he came in and began yelling at her. She told him:

"I told you I don't want

(Continued on Page 2, Col. 8)

Stormy Easter For L.A.

Easter Sunrise services, and the later Easter parades will be marred by a storm expected to hit Southern California late tonight and continue tomorrow, bringing from one to two inches of rain.

The rain will be moderate to heavy, the bureau said, and will be accompanied by winds. High temperature today was 64 degrees.

Can't Believe Stompanato Dead

Cohen Thought Pal Was to Wed Lana

By RAY PARKER

Johnny Stompanato's fatal knifing at the hands of Lana Turner's schoolgirl daughter today brought cries of anguish mixed with incredulity from his ex-boss and closest friend, Mickey Cohen.

Cohen was near tears as he identified the body of his former bodyguard at the County Morgue.

"I don't like the whole thing," he shouted. "There's a lot of unanswered questions about how Johnny was killed. I'm going to find some of those answers —no matter what happens."

Later, the ex-gang boss calmed and told reporters he had broken the news of Stompanato's death to his bodyguard's stepmother and brother, Carmen, in Woodstock, Ill.

"They requested me to see Lana and Steve Crane (Cheryl's father) and find out everything about how Johnny died," Cohen said.

He said Mrs. John Stompanato sr., and the brother,

(Continued on P. ? Cols. 2-3)

Deputies Aid Birth of L.A. Baby in Auto

It was quiet in East Los Angeles early this morning when deputies Robert Gordon and Wesley Paulus were suddenly flagged down by a passing car at 3rd st. and Mednick st.

The deputies pulled over and stepped out to investigate.

In the car they found Anulfo Rodriquez and his wife, Dorothy, 24, of 2228 Kelborn st., S. San Gabriel.

Minutes later the four were joined by a 7 pound, 8 ounce baby girl, brought into the world by the two deputies.

Mrs. Rodriquez was rushed to Angeles Emergency Hospital where she and the baby were reported in excellent condition.

Councilwoman Wyman Mother Of Daughter

A daughter was born today to Councilwoman Rosalind Weiner Wyman and her husband, attorney Eugene L. Wyman. The baby weighed 8 pounds 4½ ounces.

Mrs. Wyman was elected to the Los Angeles City Council five years ago at the age of 22.

Launch 7th Atlas ICBM at Cape

CAPE CANAVERAL, Fla., April 5 (AP)—The Air Force launched its seventh Atlas ICBM at noon today.

The giant missile took off in a cloud of white steam and great flash of flame.

Special Features

Bonus Bucks Special, B-6

(For today's race results see page A-9.)

WEATHER
Partly cloudy, warm tonight and Sunday.
High expected today 88
Low expected Sunday 64
High expected Sunday 88

THE MACON NEWS

Vol. 75, No. 269 | Leased Wire Service AP and UPI | TODAY'S NEWS TODAY | P. O. Box 1016, Macon, Ga. Saturday Afternoon, September 26, 1959 | 12 PAGES—PRICE: 5 CENTS

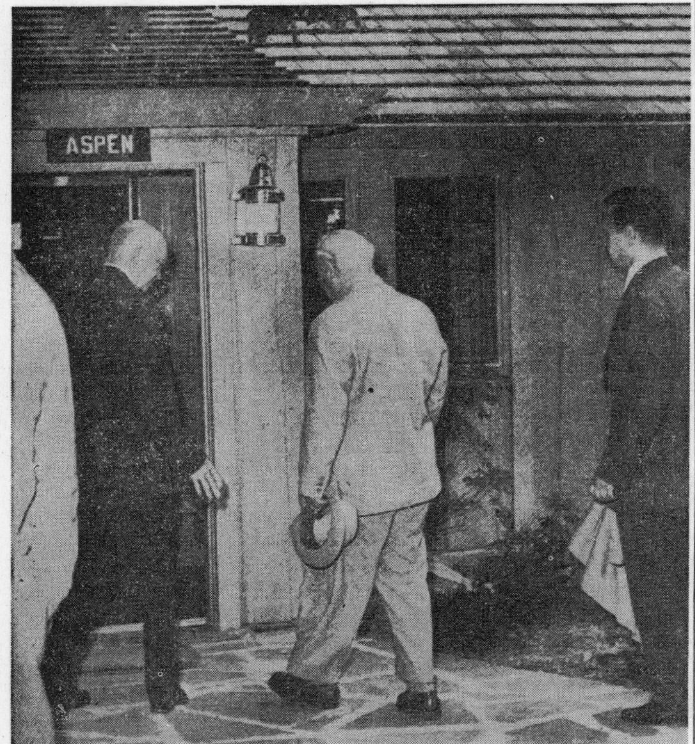

ESCORTS PREMIER — President Eisenhower ushers Soviet Premier Khrushchev into Aspen Lodge at Camp David, the presidential hideaway in the Catoctin Mountains, to start their talks on world problems. Man at right is interpreter Oleg Troyanovsky. [AP Photofax.]

Mob Kingpin, Woman Shot To Death In Auto

Little Augie Pisano, Beauty Queen Killed

NEW YORK, (AP) — Underworld kingpin Anthony (Little Augie Pisano) Carfano, 62, and a married beauty queen were shot to death Friday night in a flashy black Cadillac in a quietly substantial Queens neighborhood.

Carfano, the pudgy Prohibition era henchman of Al Capone and long-time buddy of Frank Costello, and Janice Drake, 32, who was married to comedian Allan Drake, were shot from the rear of the gangsters's swanky car. In 1943, as Janice Hansen, she won a Palisades Park beauty contest. She was Miss New Jersey of 1944.

The auto, apparently moving at the time, veered onto a curb in the Jackson Heights section of Queens about a half mile from LaGuardia Field.

Neighbors told police they saw two men flee from the car after they heard shots. No weapon was found. Carfano was shot twice in the back of the head and once in his left cheek. Mrs. Drake, the mother of a 13 - year - old boy, Michael, was shot in the neck and in the right temple.

* * *

Carfano, short and pot-bellied, wore a dark blue silk suit. His pockets were stuffed with money. Mrs. Drake, who was linked with another murder seven years ago, wore a smart blue cocktail dress and a mink stole. Police said been seen earlier at a hotel near LaGuardia.

Police said two weapons were used—.32 and .38 caliber revolvers. Carfano's trousers pockets bulged with $1,500 in 50- and 100-dollar bills and $433 in smaller bills. He was identified from his auto license.

Mrs. Drake, who lived at 63-60 102nd Street, Forest Hills, Queens, was identified from labels in her clothes. In 1952 she was questioned in connection with the slaying of playboy dress manufacturer Nat Nelson. She was released after she told police she had dated Nelson the night before his death.

Her husband, who had been appearing at the Lotus Club in Washington with singer Tony Martin, was notified of Mrs. Drake's death and was en route to New York.

* * *

Carfano, who lived in a palatial mansion in Long Beach, on Long Island, was a familiar name in underworld investigations for the past 35 years.

During Prohibition, he was a kingpin in bootlegging operations in Brooklyn and a top lieutenant of Capone. When his operations were raided, however, Little Augie was the man who wasn't there. Usually, he was in Florida.

In 1933, he was tried and acquitted in connection with the slaying of Det. Sgt. James Knight during an attempted theft in Union City, N.J. Several years later, there were reports that Little Augie had shifted his operational quarters to Springfield, Mass.

After Costello was wounded in the lobby of his Manhattan hotel by a gunshot, Little Augie was questioned and released.

In 1955 Sol Cilento, a former secretary-treasurer of the AFL Distillers Union, George Scalise, a Brooklyn labor racketeer, and Little Augie were indicted on bribery charges in connection with a union welfare fund racket.

Louis B. Saperstein, a Newark, N.J., broker, through whom the three allegedly channeled a welfare fund's insurance business had been sentenced for contempt of court for refusing to testify before the grand jury that indictchanged his mind and appeared before the grnd jury tht indicted Little Augie and the other two.

Several months later, the bribery indictment was dismissed because of a legal technicality.

LITTLE AUGIE
Former Capone Aide

10 Navy Airmen Rescued at Sea After Ditching

Pacific Operation Goes Like Clockwork

SEATTLE, Wash. (AP) — Ten wet and weary Navy airmen were plucked unharmed from the tossing Pacific Ocean early today, nearly 12 hours after they had ditched their twin-engined patrol plane.

A massive rescue operation went like clockwork, despite foul weather, darkness, fog and the fliers' position — 110 miles off the mouth of the Columbia River.

The ten, crammed into a pair of well-outfitted rubber liferafts, were pulled to safety aboard the Coast Guard cutter Locoma from Astoria, Ore. The freighter Olympic Pioneer had reached the scene only moments before and stood by as the men were hauled from the sea at 12:50 a.m., PST.

Hovering above were four Navy and Coast Guard planes, their powerful searchlights cutting through a heavy overcast onto the drama enfolding below.

* * *

The cutter radioed Coast Guard headquarters here that the airmen, three officers and seven enlisted men, were in good condition but suffering from exposure and exhaustion. None was injured in the ditching or durisg the tricky transfer from the liferafts to the cutter.

The freighter, which had changed course toward the fliers while en route up the coast to Seattle, was allowed to proceed after a "well done" from the Coast Guard.

Rescue operations moved into full speed as soon as the P5M patrol plane radioed an SOS that one of its two engines was afire. The craft, a Marlin, was on a routine coastal patrol from Whidbey Island, Wash., Naval Air Station.

The plane steadily lost altitude as its pilot, Lt. James B. Henson, 27, of Pearcy, Ark., fought desperately to make it to land. Henson finally sent word he had to ditch, radioed his position and the craft slapped down.

* * *

It remained afloat long enough for the men to clamber aboard the rafts, which are equipped with food, water, radios, flares, radar reflectors, paddles and foul weather canopies.

The downed men radioed at one time that they were okay. "We're wet, that's all," they told the aircraft circling above them.

The 10 were identified by officials at the Whidbey Island station as Henson, Lt. [JG] Donald T. McClosky, 26, co-pilot, Belleville, N. J.; Lt. [JG] Walter E. White Jr., 25, navigator, Havertown, Pa.; Chief Aviation Machinists' Mate Jack Bostick, 34, Hoffman, N. C.; Aviation Machinists' Mate [1C] Clarence R. Hart, 34, San Gabriel, Calif.; Aviation Electronics Technician [2C] Daniel R. Coleman, 22, Verdale, Minn.; Aviation Technician [3C] Billy L. Watson, 28, Chula Vista, Calif.; Aviation Ordnanceman [2C] Edmond H. Erland, 22, Canby, Ore.; Aviation Airman Ronald J. Eberle, 21, Maple Valley, Wash., and Aviation Structural Mechanic [3C] Richard V. Coesens, 22, Burlington, Wash.

BANDARANAIKE
Victim of Assassin

Prime Minister Of Ceylon Dies Of Gun Wounds

COLOMBO, Ceylon [AP] — Prime Minister Solomon Bandaranaike 60, died today from an assassin's bullets — apparent victim of the struggle between Eastern and Western ways which swept him into power 3½ years ago.

The frail champion of Asian neutralism succumbed almost on the eve of a visit to the United States, which only a few months ago he termed Asia's best friend.

Wijayananda Dahanayake, 57, a politician from Bandaranaike's cabinet, was sworn in as the new prime minister. Dahanayake in the past has ranged the political spectrum from revolutionary red to conservative blue.

His most recent exploit was to force the resignation of Marxist ministers of food and industries from the cabinet.

British - educated Bandaranaike failed to survive a five-hour operation to remove three bullets which pierced his liver, spleen and arm.

* * *

Gov. Gen. Sir Oliver Goonetilleke, one of Britain's last remaining links with Ceylon, proclaimed a state of emergency on the island until the uncertain political situation is clarified.

On his deathbed, the mild-mannered Prime Minister forgave his accused assassin — a professed Buddhist medical monk, who whipped out a revolver and fired as Bandaranaike bowed in reverence to him.

The monk and another man clad in saffron monk's robes had called at the Prime Minister's private bungalow in a luxurious Colombo residential area Friday morning.

The gunman reportedly was angered by the Prime Minister's refusal to go all the way in shidding Western ways in favor of ancient Eastern medical techniques known as "Ayurveda."

* * *

The assassin was shot by a sentry while trying to flee and was captured. He identified himself at the hospital as Talduwa Sovarama, 43, a specialist in Eastern style medicine. He was being guarded in the hospital ward by 35 policemen.

Police today seized a Buddhist monk, G. Pannasekera Thero of Colombo, who was accused of being with the gunman. Police questioned several monks throughout the night in an effort to determine the motive.

* * *

Ayurvedic medicine men, who favor hot compresses, massages and secret herb formulas handed down from father to son, have practiced in Ceylon for 2,000 years. In recent years they gained stature as a political power.

Ayurvedic supporters along with the Buddhist clergy and teachers were among the three influential groups who boosted Bandaranaike to power in 1956.

The Buddhist clergy pressed him to declare Ceylon a Buddhist state. Bandaranaike, raised an Anglican, embraced Buddhism but refused to bow to the monks' demands.

Steel Talks Site May Be Switched

USW President McDonald Declares He's Through Talking in New York

NEW YORK, (AP) — The steel industry's top negotiator in the 74-day-old strike says he's ready to resume talks here Monday. But Steelworkers President David J. McDonald says he's through talking in New York.

Chief Federal Mediator Joseph F. Finnegan plans to meet during the weekend in Washington with Secretary of Labor James P. Mitchell to review the stalemate. Finnegan indicated the talks might be shifted from New York when they resume, but he didn't say where.

McDonald broke off the negotiations here Friday, calling the sessions a "farcical filibuster." He said he would resume only when management offers something "worthy of consideration by self-respecting steel workers."

Chief industry negotiator R. Conrad Cooper said: "We hope that the union will reconsider its position and join with us then in a renewed effort to break the deadlock. This [New York] has been our agreed seat of negotiations. We plan to be here. We want to bargain and we want to reach an agreement."

* * *

Asked if the union would resume talks if the government requests it, McDonald said: "We have never resisted a call of our government. But we see no sense in coming back to New York City. The seat of the government is in Washington. The seat of the steel industry is in Pittsburgh."

The break-off might speed any decision by President Eisenhower to invoke the Taft-Hartley Act. Under an emergency provision of the law, the President could obtain an injunction that would require the striking steel workers to return to their jobs for 80 days for fact-finding and cooling off.

McDonald left the door open to the possibility of resumed negotiations Monday in some city other than New York if the companies have some kind of economic offer to make.

* * *

Asked what he would do if the government requests that the talks take place elsewhere, Cooper commented: "We will meet any request we have when we have it."

The White House has declined comment on the break-off.

The strike, which started July 14, has idled more than 500,000 steelworkers and thousands of workers in related industries. The union is seeking unspecified wage increases. But management has argued that wage increases would result in an increase in the price of steel and further inflation. The union says the wage increases should come from steel profits.

Mitchell has said he would recommend that the President use Taft-Hartley emergency measures if the strike extends into October and creates a national emergency.

President, Premier Start Cold War Talks

GETTYSBURG, Pa., (AP) — President Eisenhower and Soviet Prime Minister Nikita S. Khrushchev today began a problem-by-problem debate of critical cold war issues.

The second round of their historic discussions began in Eisenhower's hideaway on a mountaintop surrounded by low-hanging clouds.

Meeting in Eisenhower's lodge Aspen at Camp David in Maryland's Catoctin Mountains, the two leaders could see only a few yards through the picture window of their conference room.

The critical East-West dispute over the future of West Berlin as well as the broader problem of divided Germany had a high priority on the agenda of the day's session.

* * *

Eisenhower and Khrushchev, who began their talks early Friday night after a helicopter flight from Washington to Camp David, met for the first time this morning at the breakfast table and immediately "began their informal conversations."

This start on the day's work—with the world watching for the results to be announced Sunday—was reported to newsmen at the Gettysburg press center by Mrs. Anne Wheaton of the White House press office.

Press secretary James C. Hagerty and Asst. Secretary of State Andrew H. Burney arranged a full report on the morning session around midday.

The Khrushchev - Eisenhower breakfast talk reportedly lasted an hour or less in the living room of Aspen lodge.

Vice President Richard M. Nixon arrived by automobile at Camp David at 9:45 a.m. EDT, to join in the talks.

The Vice President originally had planned to travel from Washington by helicopter, but had to switch to an automobile because of a heavy fog shrouding Camp David.

* * *

Eisenhower and Khrushchev will come to grips at their conference with cold war problems that have kept the world in turmoil and periodically threatened nuclear disaster for more than a decade.

Agreement on a solution for any one of these bitterly disputed issues, ranging from Berlin to Laos, was ruled out in the course of the brief two-man summit conference. But both men are looking for some new approach to further East-West negotiations.

But the American and Soviet leaders were reported near accord on measures for greater U.S.-Soviet cooperation in several fields of peaceful enterprise, including atomic energy for power production.

Such accords, if actually worked out in the mountain hideaway, could prove to be the first steps toward truce in the cold war. Yet American officials, deeply suspicious of Khrushchev's true aims, refrained from any optimistic forecasts.

The conference began Friday night after Eisenhower and Khrushchev flew to the Catoctin Mountain camp by helicopter from the White house, 65 miles away. Their first talk lasted about three hours.

From this they turned today to debate of the Berlin crisis, disarmament, Laos, and the threat of U.S. bases near the Soviet Union versus the threat of forward Soviet forces in eastern Europe.

Chairman John A. McCone of the U.S. Atomic Energy Commission was expected to take part. He and his Soviet opposite number, V. A. Emelyanov, have already laid the groundwork for an Eisenhower - Khrushchev agreement on an exchange of information about development of atomic power plants—a potential new venture in Soviet-American cooperation. Visits of scientists working on the peaceful uses of atomic energy may also be arranged.

Much spadework is also reported on expanding exchanges of visits between the United States and the Soviet Union by experts in education, industry and medicine.

If Eisenhower and Khrushchev can make any headway at all in their discussions of the critical Berlin dispute, the Camp David meeting may also produce a recommendation to Britain and France that a new meeting of the Big Four foreign ministers on Berlin should be called in the next few months.

The tumult and shouting of Khrushchev's American tour was temporarily suspended about 6 o'clock Friday night when the Soviet Premier stepped across the threshold of Aspen Lodge and into the quiet of its oak paneled living room.

He will reappear on the public stage Sunday afternoon, following conclusion of the Camp David talks. He is scheduled to hold an hour-long Washington news conference and make a subsequent hour-long television speech prior to his departure for Moscow Sunday night.

But Khrushchev the traveling quip-maker got in a few last licks before Khrushchev the diplomat took over at Camp David.

As Eisenhower and he stood at the lodge door posing for photographs, Eisenhower said of the busy, crowding photographers: "I'm glad they don't shoot."

"It's lucky," Khrushchev rejoined with a chuckle, "that Mr. Garst is not here. If he were he would try to organize this his own way."

The reference was to Roswell Garst, the farmer who was Khrushchev's host near Coon Rapids, Iowa, three days ago. The crush of newsmen on the farm was so great that Garst at one time fought a running battle with kicks and corn stocks against onrushing photographers.

Mrs. K Friendly In Talk With Ladies of Press

WASHINGTON [AP] — Nina Khrushchev, in her first formal news conference, showed her wits were every bit as sharp as her famous husband's and her temper considerably more even.

Mrs. Khrushchev met with women reporters Friday in the living room of Blair House. She carefully answered every question thrown at her and never once lost he good humor that has characterized her throughout the state visit.

True, there were no barbed queries or hot potatoes tossed. But Mrs. Khrushchev seized on several innocuous questions to drive home some of the differences in Soviet and American customs.

The news conference itself, for instance, was a brand new experience, and she admitted some trepidation at the outset. "We don't have that custom," she said. "We do not believe the habit of reporting in the press things that are mostly of social interest."

Was it a painful experience? "No, but we are not accustomed to it."

* * *

She was asked how she spent her time at home, was it mostly housework or charity work? She quickly replied:

"I don't do any charity work. In our country, all that is your country requires charity, collection of funds and so on—the state takes care of all that."

Dressed in a white and grey figured dress, Mrs. Khrushchev met the press in a room that might be a museum of Americana. Portraits of Daniel Webster, Gen. George C. Marhsall and of several American Presidents looked down from the walls.

Although she knows some English, she spoke in Russian through an interpreter. The entire tone of the meeting was pleasant. She produced some nice-sounding generalities about American - Soviet relations, and she cleared up some of the personal history of the Khrushchev family.

The almost complete lack of this kind of information in official biographies of the Khrushchevs had puzzled many American reporters who were used to public officials living in goldfish bowls.

She first met Khrushchev at Stalino in the early 20's, she said, while she was teaching an adult education class and he was studying mining and engineering. They were married in 1924.

She said Khrushchev's first wife died in a famine. There were two children by that first marriage, Julia, and a son, Leonid, a pilot killed in combat in World War II.

She is the mother of the other three Khrushchev children, Rada, 29, Sergei, 24, and Yelena, 21, a Moscow University student who did not come along on the trip.

"Wives of our prominent officials," she said in answer to a question, "have no official duties to perform in our country. Most of the wives of our prominent officials work. I used to work too."

Inside The News

The nip-and-tuck race for the National League pennant could be settled in favor of Los Angeles today, or it could be prolonged through Sunday's final games. Full details of this exciting climax to the regular baseball season will be found on Page 12.

* * *

Educators believe that going back to school would help some adults get rid of their tensions. For the reasons why, see Page 4.

Woman Killed In Twiggs Crash

JEFFERSONVILLE — An accident on a Twiggs County road killed one woman and slightly injured two other persons early this morning, Twiggs County Sheriff W. Earl Hamrick reported.

The dead woman was identified as Mrs. Isabell Rucker, 31, of 150 L Street, Apartment 318, Atlanta. The driver of the car was identified as Henry Stokes, 43, of 2747 Santa Barbara Drive, Atlanta. Both were Negroes. They were accompanied by another woman of Atlanta whose name was not available.

Stokes was charged with traveling at high speed and not having the vehicle under control, according to State Patrol records, and was released on bond. The accident occurred 12 miles south of Jeffersonville on the Longstreet Road. The car, traveling at a high rate of speed, turned over after rounding a curve. The dead woman was thrown out and the vehicle landed on her abdomen, officers said.

The group was en route from Atlanta to attend an Eastern Star convention in Savannah. Stokes took the wrong road coming out of Macon and was en route to U. S. 80 at the time of the accident, patrolmen said.

The accident was investigated by Sheriff Hamrick, Sgt. B. S. Snipes, and Trooper Hooks of the Dublin Patrol station.

Weather To Be Cloudy and Warm

Partly cloudy and warm weather will continue in the Macon area tonight and Sunday, according to the U. S. Weather Bureau station at Cochran Field.

Today's high temperature was expected to be about 88 degrees, with a low of 64 degrees forecast for Sunday morning. Sunday's high is expetced to be 88 degrees again.

Scientists Say Research Indicates Cigaret Smoking May Be Aid to Health

BIRMINGHAM, England, [UPI] — A team of Birmingham University scientists today reported smoking—especially a pack or more a day—may help health.

The scientists, led by Dr. Thomas McKeown, said research indicated cigaret smoking keeps blood pressure down. They said a survey of 1,000 men over 60 years of age revealed that life-long non-smokers had the highest blood pressures.

McKeown and his fellow scientists reported chain smokers had the lowest blood pressures among the men interviewed. These were men smoking 20 or more cigarets a day.

Pipe smokers generally registered blood pressures between the non-smokers and the chain smokers.

McKeown's report said consumption of alcoholic beverages tended to raise blood pressure. However he said drinking does not raise blood pressure to the extent that smoking lowers it.

The doctors said the highest blood pressures of all came from those men who didn't smoke but did drink.

DEATHS

Robert L. White of Danville.
Mrs. J. T. Dunaway Sr., of Unadilla Route 1.
Mrs. E. P. Griffin of Perry.
Mrs. Adah Youngblood of Milledgeville.
Mrs. Myrtle G. Simmons of Atlanta.
Mrs. Robert H. Waldrep of Macon.
John T. Barnes of Macon.
Thomas Bledsoe of Pinehurst Route 1.
Col. Wilhelm Parry Kennard of Macon.

CLOSE CONVERSATION — Sen. Herman Talmadge, Georgia Democrat, whispers a remark that brings a smile from Sen. John McClellan [D-Ark] at a dinner meeting of Associated Industries of Georgia in Atlanta Friday night. Talmadge introduced McClellan, who made the principal speech. McClellan told the businessmen more remedial labor legislation may be necessary. [AP Photofax.]

Keeping Up With Khrushchev

WASHINGTON (AP)—Here is Premier Nikita Khrushchev's schedule for the remainder of his visits [Eastern Daylight]:

Today—At Camp David.

Schedule for Sunday:

Noon — Departure from Camp David.

1:30 p.m.—Arrives at Soviet embassy here.

2 p.m.—Luncheon at embassy.

4-5 p.m.—Holds news conference at the embassy.

6-7 p.m.—Delivers nation-wide television address from NBC studio.

7:30 p.m.—Dines privately.

10 p.m.—Departs for Moscow from Andrews Air Force Base.

The Cleveland Press

The Newspaper That Serves Its Readers

NO. 25746 — CLEVELAND, MONDAY, NOVEMBER 2, 1959 — Phone MAin 3-1111

Home ★★★ 46 Pages — 10 Cents

I GOT QUESTIONS AND ANSWERS, SAYS VAN DOREN; LIED TO JURY

CHARLES VAN DOREN says he followed script on his TV quiz appearances. (UPI Telephoto)

By ROBERT CRATER, *Press Washington Writer*

WASHINGTON — Charles Van Doren told House investigators today that the 14 shows on which he won fame and fortune on TV's "21" were rigged.

He said he was supplied with the questions and some of the answers before each appearance. He confessed that he even followed a script to make the program "more interesting."

"I was almost able to convince myself that it did not matter what I was doing," the former quiz king said. "I was getting more money than I had ever dreamed of having."

Van Doren, who won $129,000 on the program, appeared before a House investigating committee under subpena.

He had earlier claimed he had received no help and so had told the New York Grand Jury when it investigated rigged TV shows.

Today Van Doren admitted he had lied to the jury. He said he earlier had claimed innocence on instructions from the National Broadcasting Co. which threatened to void his $50,000-a-year contract unless he did so.

"I would give almost anything I have to reverse the course of my life in the last few years," he read from a statement before making his confession.

"I have learned a lot about good and evil. They are not always what they seem. I have deceived my friends and I have millions of them."

Van Doren said the questions and some of the answers were supplied by Albert Freedman, producer of "21."

He said Freedman explained the show was "merely entertainment and giving help to contestants was a common practice."

The 33-year-old Columbia University English instructor said that "foolishly and wrongly" after "an intense moral struggle" he persuaded himself to go along.

"I was like a child who had a problem and believed it would go away," he said.

The youthful quiz figure, who has been suspended from his NBC job, made a frank and open confession. His admission that he had lied to a grand jury left him open to be prosecuted under a perjury charge.

Recalling how he became interested in the quiz programs, he said he sought to go on "Tic Tac Dough," a

Turn to Page 4, Column 1

AF Jet Hits House, Kills 2 Children

By Press State Service

DAYTON—A million-dollar F-104-Starfighter jet plane crashed into a home near here today, killing two children and their mother.

The plane crashed into the rural home of Mr. and Mrs. John H. Shoup. It crumbled the brick structure and set it afire.

Neighbors said the Shoup's children, Marie Lynn, 12, and Lori, 2, inside the house were killed. They said Mrs. Shoup was outside of the house at the time, walking toward the garage. Her clothing caught fire. A neighbor doused the flames.

The pilot, Maj. James W. Bradbury, 34, bailed out of the supersonic plane before it crashed. He was not injured.

The jet, one of the world's fastest, was from the Wright-Patterson Air Force Base here.

The base public information officer said the pilot parachuted from the jet at about 4000 feet. The Starfighter has flown at speeds of 1400 mph and at altitudes above 90,000 feet.

Suede Shoes Trip Fake Doctor in Maternity Ward

NEW YORK —(UPI)—Police arrested Walter Weichel, 40, a former convict, for impersonating a maternity doctor and examining patients in a New York hospital.

A man answering Weichel's description had visited the hospital twice last month and had examined maternity patients.

His description had been circulated to the hospital staff after complaints of patients. He didn't look or act like a doctor—he wore suede shoes, the patients said.

Last night, one of the regular hospital doctors took a look at a man in a white smock, noticed the suede shoes and called police.

Police said Weichel, who was charged with assault, used the name Dr. Potter. He had recently completed a 10-year prison term for burglary.

IF WINTER COMES

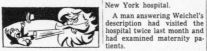

Partly cloudy and colder tonight with occasional snow flurries, low 30. Mostly sunny and a little warmer tomorrow. High 45 to 49.

Winds on the lake diminishing to 20 to 25 mph tonight. West to northwest 15 mph

FIVE-DAY FORECAST: Temperatures will average 4 to 8 degrees below normal. Normal high is 55. A little warmer about Wednesday, turning colder Thursday or Friday. Precipitation averaging one to three-tenths of an inch with a few showers or snow flurries late tomorrow or Wednesday and possibly Friday or Saturday.

Temperatures

	Airport	Press
Midnight	43	45
2 a. m.	46	48
4 a. m.	44	46
6 a. m.	41	43
8 a. m.	40	41
10 a. m.	39	42
*Noon	40	43

*Unofficial

Yesterday

High	54	56
Low	43	45

Weather Map on Page 44

Bishop Defies Ban, Preaches in E. Berlin

BERLIN—(UPI) — Lutheran Bishop Otto Dibelius defied a Communist ban yesterday and entered East Berlin to preach in the jampacked Marien Church.

Bishop Dibelius was ordered by the Commuinsts to stay out of East Berlin — he already had been barred from the Soviet Zone. And he has been asked to recant his statement that East Germany is a godless state to which no Christian owes allegiances.

Vote for Charter, Hotel on Mall and Celebrezze

AN EDITORIAL

Of all the decisions the voters will make at tomorrow's election, the most important are these:

The County Charter.

The Mall hotel.

The mayor's race in Cleveland.

The results in these races will have a tremendous impact on both the immediate and long-range future of this community.

In these races, The Press believes the sound decisions are these:

FOR the County Charter—

BECAUSE it would replace the county's weak, century-old ox-cart government with one capable of dealing with modern problems.

BECAUSE it would in time place under community-wide direction those things such as water, sewage and transportation which have no relation to individual city and village lines.

BECAUSE it would leave to local direction those things like police and fire protection, zoning and schools which give Cleveland and each suburb its own individual character and personality.

FOR the Mall hotel—

BECAUSE of the jobs it would create, and the cash it would bring into the city treasury (at least $265,000 a year, which is a factual answer to the "giveaway" charges the opposition is tossing around so recklessly).

BECAUSE it would occupy only a small portion of the Mall, and would bring life and excitement to this downtown beauty spot which is now almost deserted.

BECAUSE it would spur other tax-paying downtown development, and give Cleveland a chance to keep up with the other great cities of America.

FOR Anthony J. Celebrezze for mayor—

BECAUSE he has been a conscientious, tireless and effective mayor.

BECAUSE he knows so overwhelmingly much more about the city and its problems than his opponents.

BECAUSE the city has made great strides during his administration, while keeping one of the lowest tax rates of any major city in the country.

(For a summary of Press choices in all major races in tomorrow's election, see Page 10.)

440,000 Expected to Vote Tomorrow

By RICHARD L. MAHER, *Politics Editor*

More than 60% of Cuyahoga County's 681,694 registered electors are expected to go to the polls tomorrow to select their municipal officials, pass on a county charter and on scores of state, county and local issues.

Election officials peg the possible vote at 440,000, evenly divided between the city and the suburban areas.

For the first time in the county's voting history, suburban registration exceeds that of Cleveland proper. In the city there are 338,258 eligible voters; in the suburbs, 343,438.

As the voters go to the county's 2348 polling places, 50 special deputy election inspectors will be on duty throughout the county—though principally in city precincts—to preserve order, prevent disturbances, advise election officials and enforce the law.

"There is to be no electioneering in the booths or inside the prescribed lines,"

Turn to Page 2, Column 4

LAKE ERIE ROARED that winter is approaching today. This mountainous wave was caught by the camera of Press Photographer Clayton Knipper from the Lake Shore Country Club.

Cold Snap Brings Preview of Winter

A winter preview, complete with snow flurries and high winds, swooped down on Greater Cleveland from Canada today.

Weatherman Bob Matanick warned of the coldest night of the season coming up—a low of 30. It'll be a bit warmer tomorrow and Wednesday, he said, but for the next five days temperatures will average four to eight degrees below the normal high of 55 and low of 39.

Lake Erie was whipped with gale winds that reached 46 mph at the water-intake crib and 40 mph at the lakefront weather station atop The Press Bldg. at E. Ninth St. and Lakeside Ave.

Snow flurries and showers of snow pellets were reported in downtown Cleveland, at Cleveland Hopkins Airport, in South Euclid and in Cleveland Heights early in the day.

East Siders can expect more snow flurries tonight, Matanick said.

He predicted slightly warmer weather for voters tomorrow. It'll be mostly sunny, he said, with temperatures in the mid 40's.

Winds will die down, too, Matanick said. Last night's big blow darkened some homes in Cleveland Heights, Euclid, South Euclid, Maple Heights and Lakewood. Tumbled trees and wires interrupted power supplies in these areas.

Girl, 17, Killed by Falling Oak

EPHRATA, Pa. — (UPI) — A giant oak tree, rotting at the roots, toppled on three girls yesterday, killing one and seriously injuring the others.

The victim, Ella Weaver Nolt, 17, of Ephrata, was among eight girls and two boys gathered along the Conestoga Creek watching preparations for a mass baptism.

7th Annual Book Fair for Boys and Girls

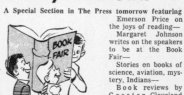

A Special Section in The Press tomorrow featuring

Emerson Price on the joys of reading—

Margaret Johnson writes on the speakers to be at the Book Fair—

Stories on books of science, aviation, mystery, Indians—

Book reviews by Greater Cleveland boys and girls—

All of this and more in The Press Children's Books Section Tomorrow!

IN THE PRESS

Gas Blast Perils Northern Ohio Area

By Press State Service

NORTH JACKSON—A thundering blast rocked western Mahoning County early today.

The explosion was reported in a natural gas line at an East Ohio Gas Co. substation on New Rd., south of here. (North Jacksson is between Warren and Salem, about 13 miles west of Youngstown).

The explosion ripped out a 40-foot section of pipe and blasted a hole 60 feet and 100 feet wide in an open field.

For a time thousands of families in the area were imperiled by escaping gas. No one was reported injured.

Residents said gas fumes hovered over the area for two hours.

An East Ohio spokesman said gas flow through the line hurriedly was cut off at nearby Newton Falls.

The company representative said service to homes in the area was not disrupted.

A deputy sheriff reported the explosion was in a 15-inch, 600-pound pressure transmission line.

Frightened residents in a 20-mile area, awakened by the blast that shook homes and rattled windows, at first blamed it on jets from Youngstown Air Force Base cracking the sonic barrier.

"It made a terrific noise," said a resident in Canfield, 10 miles away. "The boom seemed to hang in the air for several minutes. It woke up the entire town."

Deputies re-routed traffic on Rt. 18 and other highways in the blast area until the danger from escaping gas was eliminated.

Senator to Tour

WASHINGTON—(UPI)— Sen. Olin D. Johnston (D., S. C.), will leave Wednesday for a European tour.

WEATHER
Clear tonight, low near 60. Tomorrow: fair and continued warm.
FROM THE WEATHER BUREAU

New York Post

©1961 New York Post Corporation
Re-entered as 2nd class matter Nov. 22, 1949, at the Post Office at New York under Act of March 3, 1879.

Vol. 160 No. 276 NEW YORK, TUESDAY, OCTOBER 10, 1961 10 Cents

BLUE ★★★★ FINAL

Quiz 13, Nab Guns In Raid on Gallo HQ

Berra Hints He's Quitting

Yankee star Yogi Berra—aboard train for New York with wife after World Series—hints he'll retire as an active player but would consider managing in the majors. **See Ike Gellis' story on Page 74.**

DA: We Nipped A Massacre

Police raided the headquarters of Brooklyn's Gallo gang today "because we heard they were going to war and we didn't want a St. Valentine's Day massacre here," Asst. DA Benjamin Schmier said.

Lawrence Gallo and 11 henchmen were picked up at Gallo headquarters, 51 President St., while Joe Gallo was followed to Greenwich Village and seized at 20 W. Eighth St.

The St. Valentine's Day massacre occurred on Feb. 14, 1929, in Chicago, when seven members of the George (Bugs) Moran gang were lined up against a garage wall and machine-gunned to death by members of the Al Capone mob. **Earlier story on Page 4.**

Gromyko: Peace 'Possible'

London, Oct. 10 (Reuters)—Soviet Foreign Minister Gromyko flew in here today for talks with British government leaders and said there is "a possibility" of a peaceful settlement of the East-West crisis over Berlin and Germany.

Gromyko, flying home to Moscow after talks with President Kennedy last Friday in Washington, stopped off here for 24 hours for a meeting with Prime Minister Macmillan and British Foreign Secretary Lord Home.

Gromyko said he felt President Kennedy "realizes that Germany—we call it the question of the German peace treaty—is the most important and acute at present.

"My definite opinion is that he agrees with this," Gromyko said.

FINAL ★★★★ 5¢ **New York Mirror**

WEATHER: Sunny, warm, with high in low 80s.

Vol. 40, No. 99 WEDNESDAY, OCTOBER 16, 1963

Valachi Sings Here Today

STORY ON PAGE 3

Probe Copter Tragedy Harry Black, Civil Aeronautics Board inspector, scrutinizes portion of rotorblade from helicopter which crashed after takeoff at Idlewild, killing six. The prop had flown off the copter and damaged a hangar roof 3200 feet from the takeoff site. Rotorblade phase is "a high focus of our investigation," a CAB official said.

(Mirror Photo by Dennis Bur[illegible])

Johnson Takes Nation's Helm, Pages 4 and 5

The Dallas Morning News

John F. Kennedy Life History, Pages 16 and 17

VOL. 115—NO. 54 TELEPHONE: Riverside 7-4611 DALLAS, TEXAS, SATURDAY, NOVEMBER 23, 1963—50 PAGES IN 4 SECTIONS ★★★★ PRICE 5 CENTS

KENNEDY SLAIN ON DALLAS STREET

★ ★ ★ ★ ★ ★ ★ ★ ★ ★ ★ ★ ★ ★ ★ ★

JOHNSON BECOMES PRESIDENT

Receives Oath on Aircraft

By ROBERT E. BASKIN
Washington Bureau of The News

In a solemn and sorrowful hour, with a nation mourning its dead President, Lyndon B. Johnson Friday took the oath of office as the 36th chief executive of the United States.

Following custom, the oath-taking took place quickly—only an hour and a half after the assassination of President Kennedy.

Federal Judge Sarah T. Hughes of Dallas administered the oath in a hurriedly arranged ceremony at 2:39 p.m. aboard Air Force 1, the presidential plane that brought Kennedy on his ill-fated Texas trip and on which his body was taken back to Washington.

Mrs. Johnson and Mrs. Kennedy, her stocking still flecked with blood from the assassination, flanked the vice-president as he raised his right hand in the forward compartment of the presidential jetliner at Love Field. About 25 White House staff members and friends were present as Johnson intoned the familiar oath:

"I do solemnly swear that I will perform the duties of President of the United States to the best of my ability, and defend, protect and preserve the Constitution of the United States."

The 55-year-old Johnson, the first Texan ever to become President, turned and kissed his wife on the cheek, giving her shoulders a squeeze. Then he put his arm around Mrs. Kennedy, kissing her gently on her right cheek.

Mrs. Kennedy, in tears, was wearing the same bright pink suit she wore on the fatal ride, a ride in which she had been wildly acclaimed by friendly, cheering crowds in Dallas before rifle shots rang out and the President collapsed in the seat of the car beside her.

Johnson had deliberately delayed the ceremony to give Kennedy's widow time to compose herself for one of the gruelling aspects of her husband's assassination.

CONTINUED ON PAGE 15

Lyndon B. Johnson

Gov. Connally Resting Well

By MIKE QUINN

Gov. John Connally — felled Friday by a sniper's bullet in the back—rested in "quite satisfactory" condition late Friday night at Parkland Hospital following nearly four hours of surgery in the afternoon.

An aide for the governor reported at 10:30 p.m. that the governor was asleep and resting comfortably following the incident which claimed President Kennedy's life.

Meanwhile, Dr. Tom Shires, chief of surgeons at University of Texas Southwestern Medical School, said Connally barely missed a fatal wound:

"After consulting with Mrs. Connally and others on the scene, the consensus is that the governor was quite fortunate that he turned to see what happened to the President. If he had not turned to his right, there is a good chance he probably would have been shot through the heart—as it was, the bullet caused a tangential wound."

Dr. Shires rushed to Dallas by Air Force jet after word of the shooting was flashed.

Connally was operated on by Dr. Robert R. Shaw, thoracic

CONTINUED ON PAGE 2.

Impact Shattering To World Capitals

By the Associated Press

Word of President Kennedy's assassination struck the world's capitals wjth shattering impact, leaving heads of state and the man in the street stunned and grief-stricken.

While messages of condolence poured into the White House from presidents, premiers and crowned heads, the littie people of many lands reacted with numbed disbelief.

Pubs in London and cafes in Paris fell silent, as the news came over radio and television.

IN MOSCOW, a Russian girl walked weeping along the street.

At U.N. headquarters in New York, delegates of 11 nations bowed their heads in a moment of silence.

In Buenos Aires, newspapers sounded sirens reserved for news of the utmost gravity.

Britain's Prime Minister Douglas-Home sent condolences, and Sir Winston Churchill branded the slaying a monstrous act.

"The loss to the United States and to the world is incalculable," Sir Winston declared. "Those who come after Mr. Kennedy must strive the more to achieve the ideals of world peace and human happiness and dignity to which his presidency was dedicated."

Douglas-Home issued this terse statement:

"The Prime Minister has learned with the most profound shock and horror of the death

CONTINUED ON PAGE 2.

Pro-Communist Charged With Act

A sniper shot and killed President John F. Kennedy on the streets of Dallas Friday. A 24-year-old pro-Communist who once tried to defect to Russia was charged with the murder shortly before midnight.

Kennedy was shot about 12:20 p.m. Friday at the foot of Elm Street as the Presidential car entered the approach to the Triple Underpass. The President died in a sixth-floor surgery room at Parkland Hospital about 1 p.m., though doctors said there was no chance for him to live when he reached the hospital.

Within two hours, Vice-President Lyndon Johnson was sworn in as the nation's 36th President inside the presidential plane before departing for Washington.

The gunman also seriously wounded Texas Gov. John Connally, who was riding with the President.

Four Hours in Surgery

Connally spent four hours on an operating table, but his condition was reported as "quite satisfactory" at midnight.

The assassin, firing from the sixth floor of the Texas School Book Depository Building near the Triple Underpass sent a Mauser 6.5 rifle bullet smashing into the President's head.

An hour after the President died, police hauled the 24-year-old suspect, Lee Harvey Oswald, out of an Oak Cliff movie house.

He had worked for a short time at the depository, and police had encountered him while searching the building shortly after the assassination. They turned him loose when he was identified as an employe but put out a pickup order on him when he failed to report for a work roll call.

He also was accused of killing a Dallas policeman, J. D. Tippit, whose body was found during the vast manhunt for the President's assassin.

Oswald, who has an extensive pro-Communist background, four years ago renounced his American citizenship in Russia and tried to become a Russian citizen. Later, he returned to this country.

Friendly Crowd Cheered Kennedy

Shockingly, the President was shot after driving the length of Main Street through a crowd termed the largest and friendliest of his 2-day Texas visit. It was a good-natured crowd that surged out from the curbs almost against the swiftly moving presidential car. The protective bubble had been removed from the official convertible.

Mrs. Connally, who occupied one of the two jump seats in the car, turned to the President a few moments before and remarked, "You can't say Dallas wasn't friendly to you."

At Fort Worth, Kennedy had just delivered one of the most well-received speeches of his ca-

CONTINUED ON PAGE 2.

FUNERAL FOR PRESIDENT WILL BE HELD ON MONDAY

WASHINGTON (AP)—President Kennedy's funeral will be held Monday at St. Matthews Roman Catholic Cathedral, the White House announced Friday night.

The body of the slain President will lie in repose at the White House Saturday and will lie in state in the rotunda of the Capitol on Sunday and Monday.

The President's body will be taken a couple of miles to the cathedral at 11 a.m. (EST) Monday. There, Richard Cardinal Cushing, Archbishop of Boston and close friend of the Kennedy family, will celebrate a pontifical requiem Mass at noon.

Acting White House Press Secretary Andrew T. Hatcher said he did not know where Kennedy will be buried. There has been one report, still unconfirmed, that burial would be in the family plot in Brookline, Mass.

The President's body will be moved from the White House in an official cortege to the Capitol rotunda at 1 p.m. Sunday. This ceremony will be attended by members of the

CONTINUED ON PAGE 12.

John F. Kennedy

GRAY CLOUDS WENT AWAY

Day Began as Auspiciously As Any in Kennedy's Career

(Robert E. Baskin, chief of the Washington Bureau of The News, was one of four persons representing the world press in the motorcade which resulted in the President's assassination. This is his account of what happened.)

By ROBERT E. BASKIN
Washington Bureau of The News

It was a day that started as auspiciously as any in the career of John F. Kennedy.

When we boarded the Presidential jetliner, Air Force One, at Fort Worth at midmorning, the White House party was in high spirits. The Fort Worth welcome had been a tremendous one. Shortly before the 15-minute flight to Love Field, ugly gray clouds were swept away by a brisk breeze. The sun was out, and the Texas sky was a vivid blue.

President and Mrs. Kennedy, she strikingly attired in a pink suit with a pert matching hat, made an instant hit at Love Field as they shook hands with hundreds of persons along the fence line.

Then the last journey began. The big open Lincoln car moved out smoothly, carrying Mr. and Mrs. Kennedy and Gov. John Connally and his wife, Nellie.

Three cars back was the press pool car, in which three other newspapermen and I rode. Just ahead of us were Dallas Mayor and Mrs. Earle Cabell and Rep. Ray Roberts of McKinney.

Malcolm Kilduff, assistant presidential press secretary, was with us, and as we moved into the heart of the city Kilduff expressed elation over the friendly nature of the welcome and the great outpouring of people.

Everyone in the press car agreed it was one of the most cordial receptions the President had received in quite a while.

Buoyed by the cheers of the multitudes on Main Street, our motorcade moved on past the courthouse. Then came the approach to the Triple Underpass, with the leading cars picking up speed as the crowd thinned out somewhat. Over to our right loomed the gaunt structure labeled the Texas State School Book Depositary.

It was 12:30 p.m.

The sharp crack of a rifle rang out. But at that moment we couldn't believe it was just that. "What the hell was that?" someone in our car asked.

Then there were two more shots—measured carefully.

We saw people along the street diving for the ground.

CONTINUED ON PAGE 2.

SUNDAY NEWS

NEW YORK'S PICTURE NEWSPAPER®

20¢

Vol. 43. No. 46 Copr. 1964 News Syndicate Co. Inc. New York, N.Y. 10017, Sunday, March 15, 1964★ WEATHER: Mostly fair, windy, mild.

DOOMED

(UPI Telefoto)

Jack Ruby hears Judge Joe B. Brown read verdict: "Guilty, with malice." Jury sentenced him to die in chair.

Story on page 3; other pictures in centerfold

COLD
Windy with Flurries
High 16-20: Low 3-7
Map and Details on Page D-7.

HOURLY TEMPERATURES

10 p.m. 13	2 a.m. 11	6 p.m. [illegible]
11 p.m. 13	3 p.m. 24	7 p.m. 17
12 mid. 12	4 p.m. 23	8 p.m. 17
1 a.m. 12	5 p.m. 22	9 p.m. 15

V

Detroit Free Press

METRO FINAL ★★★ Ten Cents

Vol. 134—No. 293 On Guard for 133 Years Monday, February 22, 1965

Malcolm X Is Slain At Rally in New York

Tough Mazey Thin-Skinned On Bank Flop

Plans to Change UAW Policy on Investments

Merger talk dominates lobbies at AFL-CIO council. Page 3A.

BY ROBERT E. HOYT
Free Press Labor Writer

MIAMI BEACH — UAW Secretary-Treasurer Emil Mazey is a rough, blunt man who rarely has had to apologize to anyone.

Perhaps that's why he has taken so hard the publicity growing out of the failure of two national banks in which auto worker strike fund money was invested.

Emil Mazey

Mazey has been vacationing in Florida and is here for the winter, meeting of the AFL-CIO executive council.

"You'd think I was the only guy who made this mistake," Mazey said.

Though assuming responsibility for subordinates, Mazey publicly has taken the blame. If he had it to do over, however, he wouldn't have made the investments. As he said: "My hindsight is 20-20."

Still, Mazey feels the investment was a reasonable one, when you consider that there were 271 others in the nation—savings and loan associations, credit unions, banks, foundations, insurance companies and corporations — which made the same mistake.

The UAW had $3 million in certificates of deposit in the San Francisco National Bank and another $50,000 in the Brighton National Bank in Colorado when they were closed last month by the Federal Government's comptroller of the currency, James J. Saxon.

The San Francisco failure was the largest in the country since 1935.

Mazy feels that news stories and editorials on the failure have singled out him and the UAW and ignored the other investors. He is sensitive about his reputation—he has been regarded for years in the union as a watchdog who won't part with a cent without justification.

Hoyt

Close associates in the UAW say they've never known Mazey to be so affected by anything in his 18 years as UAW secretary-treasurer. His attitude confirms their judgment.

"I just had to get away for a while," Mazey said, referring to his vacation.

"That's the trouble with trying to be an executive," he said. "I used to go over all these details myself, then everybody insisted I was trying to do too much. You let someone else handle something—and you end up with a $3 million headache."

Has Some Changes in Mind

Mazey admits it's like locking the barn door after the horse has escaped, but he has some changes in mind.

"For one thing," he said, "I'm making up a form to be filled out for all new investments—it'll show how long a bank has been in existence, what its assets and its loans are and how much of the total loans is backed up by security."

Mazey also wants to add an investment counselor to his staff.

"We've had a policy," he explained, "of trying to hire men from the shop to take staff jobs. Maybe it's been a mistake. Until very recently I had a 25-man auditing staff without one CPA."

"I can understand how we made this mistake," he said. "Investment is a relatively new business for us. We had nothing to invest until I persuaded the union that we had to build a strike fund in 1955. But I don't understand how these other institutions could make the mistake. This is their business. They had up to $1.5 million in one case in this bank."

Trying to Salvage Part

Mazey has been meeting with the other San Francisco investors to see what can be done to save as much as possible of the $3 million. "I asked some of these guys," he said, "why they guessed wrong. All they say is: 'We don't know.' "

There's no way of knowing—at this point—how much,

Turn to Page 2A, Column 1

Partying with Lynda Bird

AP Photo

GUEST OF HONOR at an after-theater Broadway party was Lynda Bird Johnson, daughter of the President. Carol Channing (right) showed Lynda (second from right) around the Rainbow Room atop the RCA Building. Others (left to right) are Beatrice Lillie, Sally Ann Howes, Barbra Streisand.

Accused Gunman Wounded

How Malcolm X's background led to his hatred. Page 7C.

From AP, UPI and New York Times

NEW YORK—Malcolm X, the Negro leader who formed his own black nationalist group after feuding with the Black Muslims, was fatally shot Sunday moments after one of his followers described him as "a man who would give his life for you."

* * *

MALCOLM WAS SHOT more than five times while addressing a rally of 500 of his followers. The rally was turned into a panic by the shooting.

Police charged a 22-year-old Negro, Thomas Hagan, with firing the fatal shots. Hagan, shot in the leg in the melee that followed the assassination, was held in the prison ward of Bellevue Hospital.

Police Capt. Paul Glaser said Hagan killed Malcolm with a sawed-off, double-barrelled shotgun, and was then shot by one of Malcolm's followers, Reuben Francis.

Police said three weapons had been fired at the scene—a .38 caliber revolver, a .45 caliber revolver and a sawed-off shotgun.

Hagan was shot in the left thigh. His left leg was broken, apparently from kicks. Police said he had been beaten by members of the audience immediately after the shooting.

Two others persons were wounded in a hail of gunfire while Malcolm was addressing his Organization of Afro-American Unity in Harlem's Audubon Ballroom.

The wounded men, described by police as spectators, also had been shot. They were identified as William Harris, wounded seriously in the abdomen, and William Parker, shot in the foot.

Hagan was wrestled to the sidewalk outside the ballroom by followers of Malcolm, who preached black supremacy over whites and advocated that Negroes arm themselves to protect their rights.

AP Photo

Malcolm X met a violent death

Malcolm, who had charged that the Muslims had plotted against his life, was removed on a stretcher to the Columbia-Presbyterian Medical Center two blocks away and rushed into the emergency operating room.

* * *

A MEDICAL CENTER spokesman later said: "The person you know as Malcolm X is dead."

He said Malcolm died of more than five gunshot wounds.

"The wounds were centered in his chest and I believe one was in his cheek," the spokesman said.

Police blamed the assissination on the Balck Muslims.

Shortly after the slaying, while police were swooping down on Muslims here and rushing them to police headquarters for questioning, police received a report that six Malcolm X followers had left for Chicago by various routes to attack Elijah Muhammad, the Black Muslim chieftan.

Chicago police were notified and ordered patrols in the area of Muhammad's residence to "pay some extra attention" to his mansion.

It was 3 p.m. when Malcolm rose to address his audience.

One of his followers took the rostrum and told the audience: "Malcolm is a man who would give his life for you. There aren't many men who would lay

Turn to Page 2A, Column 3

Khanh Quits After Ouster, Ending New Revolt Threat

U.S. general helped prevent bloodshed in Viet coup. See Page 5C.

From UPI and AP

SAIGON — (UPI) — Lt. Gen. Nguyen Khanh formally announced his resignation Monday as commander in chief of the South Vietnamese armed forces.

Khanh made the announcement by telephone from a seldom-used mountain airfield where his plane landed after running low on fuel.

There was speculation Khanh was trying to flee the country when his plane put down at the military airstrip at Da Lat, 150 miles northeast of Saigon.

A spokesman for the South Vietnamese Armed Forces Council said Khanh telephoned to say that he was resigning and giving up in his bid to remain in power.

Shortly after receiving the call, the Armed Forces Council sent three members to Da Lat to negotiate with Khanh the terms of his surrender.

Earlier Monday Khanh refused to accept his ouster as head of the armed forces and called on all nine army division commanders to remain loyal to him.

Gen. Nguyen Khanh
Bows to generals

* * *

KHANH WAS ousted from power Sunday night by South Vietnam's military leaders. A decree broadcast by Saigon radio said he had been replaced temporarily by Maj. Gen Tran Van Minh, a Catholic who is chief of staff of the armed forces.

Khanh's military opponents said the former commander will have to leave the country.

"It is up to him, but he has to leave Vietnam," air force commander Nguyen Cao Ky said.

Meanwhile, U.S. intelligence officers theorized that seaborne shipments of Communist arms and ammunition to the Viet Cong in South Vietnam have been going on for a long time.

American experts still sorted through the gigantic cache of Communist arms and ammunition seized in the coastal jungle Friday after a camouflaged mystery ship was destroyed off Thy Hoa, 240 miles northeast of Saigon.

The arms, ammunition and documents taken from the sunken hull bore markings showing that they had originally come from the Soviet Union, Communist China, Bulgaria, Czechoslovakia and Japan.

Missing U.S. Flier Shot Down in Laos

DA NANG, Vietnam — (AP) — U.S. Air Force Maj. Robert Ronca, of Norristown, Pa., listed officially as missing in action, was shot down in Laos and his plane crashed into a hill, it was learned here Sunday.

Ronca, regarded as one of the best U.S. jet pilots at this South Vietnam base, went down over Sam Neau Province in the Communist-held section of northern Laos Friday.

The Communist Pathet Lao claimed to have shot down four U.S. jets over Laos Friday, a Peking radio broadcast said. U.S. planes have been flying missions against the Pathet Lao since May. The planes also have been bombing Communist supply routes through Laos from North Vietnam to South Vietnam.

Burma Seizes Rebel Dynamite

RANGOON, Burma — (AP) — A consignment of dynamite was seized by a combined Burmese-Thai police party at Maesod, on the Thai side of the Burma-Thai border, according to Sunday press reports.

They said the dynamite was on a bus bound for the Karen guerillas, most militant of Burma's ethnic rebel groups.

'Cut My Salary Or I'll Resign'

MINEOLA, N.Y.—(AP)—Laura Davis went to see her bosses last week about an adjustment in her county salary and set off a furor that's still going strong.

On the face of it, her situation would not be too unusual, except that Miss Davis asked that her salary be reduced $7,000 a year.

In fact, the 42-year-old Miss Davis said that unless the salary is reduced she wants no part of her new post as deputy elections commissioner in Nassau County.

* * *

"I UNDERSTOOD when I accepted the post that it paid $10,500 a year," Miss Davis explained. "Then, just as I was about to go to the commission headquarters last Monday to be sworn in, I learned the salary had been upped to $17,500 a year.

"I told the commission that unless they drop it to its original figure, they can keep the job. I want out.

"I know what my work is worth. I was willing to accept a moderate increase over what I have earned in the last six years as research director for the Nassau County Democratic Committee.

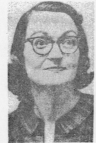

"But this—$7,000—is outlandish. I wouldn't accept it."

Laura Davis

Killing Stirs Fear Of Muslim War

New York Times Service

NEW YORK—The murder of Malcolm X is an apparent example of the mounting pattern of violence in the Black Muslim movement.

In the last six months at least two Muslim defectors have been beaten in Boston and one has been shot. Kenneth Morton died of injuries sustained in a beating, and Benjamin Brown, a New York corrections officer, was shot in January.

* * *

THE MOST publicized attack was upon Leon 4X Ameer, a ranking Muslim official, in a Boston hotel lobby.

Ameer, who did not renounce the movement until after a second beating, warned Sunday of more violence between Negro factions, and upon whites, in the wake of Malcolm's death.

Leon Ameer

Ameer said "open warfare triggered by maximum retaliation for Malcolm" would be only the first order of business.

Ameer, 31, who left the movement last month, was once Malcolm's bodyguard in New York and press secretary for Muhammad Ali (boxer Cassius Clay).

"If the white power structure thinks this is all going to be just another case of colored killing off other colored and they're going to sit back safely and watch it happen, they're in for a terrible surprise," Ameer said.

Ameer said Malcolm X told him he was preparing to offer evidence of financial links between Elijah Muhammad, the Muslim leader, and the Ku Klux Klan and other rightist groups.

Malcolm A Forlorn Visitor Here

Malcolm X hardly resembled a fiery Black Nationalist leader when he spoke last Sunday in Detroit's Ford Auditorium.

He looked forlorn and a little confused.

His New York home had been bombed early that morning. All the clothing he was able to salvage from the flames was a rumpled gray suit that hung loosely on his lanky frame.

He had played hide-and-seek with reporters most of the day. The doors to the Green Room, backstage at the auditorium, were closed to the press before he appeared.

Spokesmen said he was under heavy sedation.

The speaking engagement, sponsored by the Afro-American Broadcasting Co., had drawn only about 400 people. But they gave him a noisy, standing ovation when he appeared at 11 p.m., nearly three hours after the scheduled time for his speech.

He spoke for more than an hour, stumbling badly at times in his pronunciation and slurring many words. It was a rambling address condemning Negro reliance on nonviolent methods to win the fight for equality.

He had praise for the Moslem religion and President Nasser of Egypt and criticism of Christianity and the late President Kennedy.

The audience, about 85 per cent Negro, ate it up. He was frequently interrupted by cheering and applause.

He was warmly applauded again when he finished. He

Turn to Page 2A, Column 1

Special On the Inside

It's Your Money

Borrowing on life insurance is a handy source of cash but should be done with care, warns Nancy Lowe. See Family Financing, Page 7B.

The American Paper for Americans

Chicago Tribune

THE WORLD'S GREATEST NEWSPAPER

SPORTS ★★★ | FINAL

119th YEAR—No. 211 FRIDAY, JULY 30, 1965 64 PAGES, 4 SECTIONS 10c

UPHOLD HOFFA CONVICTION

TRIED TO FIX JURY, APPEALS JUDGES AGREE

Plea to Supreme Court Expected

Cincinnati, July 29 (UPI)—The 6th United States Circuit Court of Appeals today unanimously affirmed an 8-year prison sentence imposed upon James R. Hoffa, president of the International Teamsters union, for attempting to bribe members of a jury.

Hoffa

The convictions of three other men in the same case also were affirmed.

The court's order sending the labor leader to prison will be effective within 20 days unless Hoffa makes his expected appeal to the United States Supreme court.

Hoffa was convicted in Chattanooga, Tenn., Feb. 12, 1964, on charges of trying to influence a jury trying him on another charge in Nashville, two years earlier.

Slapped at Kennedy

Hoffa in his appeal said that he was innocent and that the federal government under Sen. Robert Kennedy [D., N. Y.] was out to "get" him when Kennedy as attorney general uncovered the evidence that led to his indictment.

Hoffa was reported in Washington when the court announced its decision affirming his prison sentence and a $10,000 fine.

The appeals court in upholding the conviction overruled 16 points Hoffa had raised to support his claim that he did not receive a fair trial in Chattanooga.

No Doubt on Tampering

The court said, "There can be no question but that endeavors were made to tamper or bribe, not merely one juror, but at least three other jurors."

There was ample evidence, the three-judge court said, of "large scale endeavors at juror tampering" which it said came about from "instigation, careful planning and agreement in which Hoffa was an active participant."

The government had produced detailed testimony by witnesses of two efforts to bribe members

[Continued on page 2, col. 3]

Pentagon Plan: 3,000,000 GIs

Johnson to Sign Medicare Today at Truman Site

Plans to Confer with Former President

Washington, July 29 (AP) — President Johnson will fly to Missouri tomorrow and sign the medicare bill in the presence of former President Truman who unsuccessfully sponsored similar legislation 20 years ago.

Johnson will sign the 133-page bill in the auditorium of the Truman library at Independence, Mo. He will fly from Washington to Kansas City and then drive to Independence for the ceremony and a meeting with Truman.

Wished to Visit Him

Horace Busby, a special assistant to Johnson, said the President "has been wanting for some time to visit personally with President Truman" and now had the opportunity.

He said that Johnson and Truman will talk about a variety of topics, ranging from agricultural programs to civil rights, at a private conference after the bill is signed.

"President Truman is looking forward to this visit tomorrow and seeing his friends from Washington," Busby reported. Some members of Congress will accompany the President.

No Word on Plans

There was no immediate word on whether Johnson would return to Washington from Missouri, fly to his Texas ranch for the week-end, or go elsewhere.

On Nov. 19, 1945, Truman sent a special message to Congress dealing with national health needs. He made five major proposals, and all except the medicare plan were adopted.

Truman's proposal for prepayment of medical costs thru social security actually was somewhat broader than the measure passed by Congress this week.

HOUSE-SENATE GROUP AGREES ON VOTE BILL

BY JOSEPH HEARST

[Chicago Tribune Press Service]

Washington, July 29—House and Senate conferees today agreed on a voting rights bill that does not ban the poll tax and which would enfranchise Spanish-speaking Puerto Ricans in New York.

Rep. Emanuel Celler [D., N. Y.], head of the House conferees, said the bill represented a compromise he believes will be acceptable to all. Sen. Philip A. Hart [D., Mich.] called it a sound solution.

Celler said the conference report will be filed in the House Monday and that he expects the House to act on the bill Tuesday. Hart said it was possible the Senate would act Tuesday.

Urged by Johnson

Celler, when asked how the conferees agreed in 30 minutes today on the compromise after breaking up in complete disagreement three days ago, said it is essential to get the bill out as quickly as possible to avoid violence.

He said the Leadership Conference on Civil Rights, composed of numerous civil rights organizations, approved the compromise. President Johnson, he said, is vitally interested, and wants the bill to come out of Congress as quickly as possible.

Similar to Bill

The agreement of the House representatives to recede from the House position that the poll tax, collected in four states as a precondition to voting in state and local elections, be banned by statute was particularly pleasing to Rep. William M. McCulloch [R., O.], ranking minority member of the judiciary committee.

McCulloch said the compromise, which states that Congress finds the poll tax discriminates against voters of

[Continued on page 2, col. 6]

OUT OF THE FRYING PAN...?

MAP 330,000 BUILDUP OF YANKS IN UNIFORM

101st Greeted by Taylor Before He Leaves Viet

(Pictures on back page)

SAIGON, Viet Nam [Friday] July 30 (UPI)—Outgoing Ambassador Maxwell D. Taylor said good-by to South Viet Nam today just hours after welcoming the 101st airborne division and his soldier-son to the war-torn country.

"We will carry thru to our objective," he said shortly before boarding President Johnson's personal plane for a flight to Hawaii. Taylor will spend a few days resting and conferring with defense department officials in Honolulu before continuing to Washington.

"With our Vietnamese friends we have the men, the equipment, and the spirit to carry thru," he said. "I don't see how anyone could doubt it in view of the decision of President Johnson announced just 48 hours ago."

Arrives in August

From now until Ambassador-Designate Henry Cabot Lodge arrives in mid-August, the United States embassy here will be run by Deputy Ambassador U. Alexis Johnson. Taylor was ambassador to Viet Nam for one year.

Taylor, World War II commander of the Screaming Eagles of the 101st division, welcomed the division to Viet Nam yesterday. He talked briefly with his son, Capt. Thomas Taylor, 30, one of the first members of the 101st to arrive.

The 101st came ashore at Cam Ranh bay, 180 miles northeast of Saigon, to take up defensive positions around United States army engineers building a coastal stronghold and air base in the area.

Westmoreland at Beach

Taylor, who led the 101st thru the battles of Normandy and Bastogne, told the division's successors they would meet "an enemy who is shrewd . . . in a new war, a new kind of war."

Gen. William C. Westmoreland, commander of American forces in Viet Nam, accompanied Taylor to the beach. Westmoreland also is a former commander of the division. The

[Continued on page 2, col. 1]

Work on Orders Sending More Men to War

BY WILLIAM ANDERSON

(Picture on back page)

[Chicago Tribune Press Service]

Washington, July 29—The Pentagon was making plans today to increase active duty military strength by at least 330,000 persons, THE CHICAGO TRIBUNE learned.

The planners are still setting up a time schedule for an increase raising to 3 million from 2,700,000 the number of Americans in uniform.

They are also working on new orders for additional military units to be sent to Viet Nam as soon as bases of operation can be established and the logistical support pipelines welded together.

Expect September Call

It is expected that the next major group of troops—beyond the 50,000 increase announced yesterday by President Johnson—will be called to the front in September.

Johnson said in public that the American commanders would get what they need, and in private high administration sources said flatly there was no doubt that additional troops would be required—and sent.

Estimates of how many will eventually be needed—short of more direct involvement by North Viet Nam and Red China—usually center around the figure of 500,000.

Meanwhile, combat operations of United States forces against the communist insurgents will sharply increase. The army today was loading its 1st cavalry [air mobile] division at Fort Benning, Ga., to go to Viet Nam, and expressed high hopes that the division would be able to pin down a large number of the Viet Cong guerrillas.

Copter Pilots Experienced

Altho never tested as a division under fire, the 1st has a high percentage of helicopter pilots with combat experience in Viet Nam, and is specially designed to use the wingless craft to move large numbers of troops at high speeds over rough terrain.

The American center of new activity is to be in the highlands of Viet Nam. Major communist forces have moved there from the delta region, have broken roads, rails and communications, and seized control of at least 50 provincial capitals and other cities.

Plea for Billion Expected

The war plans seem to call for Americans to take over the battle role, while the South Vietnamese army of 550,000 will conduct more and more actions to secure and hold areas. There are plans for the South Vietnamese to increase their pacification program in civilian villages which the Communists have dominated for years.

Many of the specific details—such as what units are to

[Continued on page 2, col. 1]

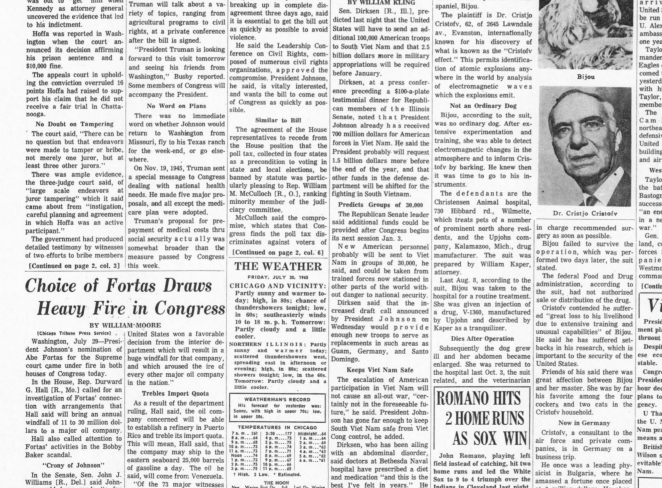

DIRKSEN SEES HUGE VIET COST

Says 100,000 More Men Will Be Used

BY WILLIAM KLING

Sen. Dirksen [R., Ill.], predicted last night that the United States will have to send an additional 100,000 American troops to South Viet Nam and that 2.5 billion dollars more in military appropriations will be required before January.

Dirksen, at a press conference preceding a $100-a-plate testimonial dinner for Republican members of the Illinois Senate, noted that President Johnson already has received 700 million dollars for American forces in Viet Nam. He said the President probably will request 1.5 billion dollars more before the end of the year, and that other funds in the defense department will be shifted for the fighting in South Vietnam.

Predicts Groups of 30,000

The Republican Senate leader said additional funds could be provided after Congress begins its next session Jan. 3.

New American personnel probably will be sent to Viet Nam in groups of 30,000, he said, and could be taken from trained forces now stationed in other parts of the world without danger to national security.

Dirksen said that the increased draft call announced by President Johnson on Wednesday would provide enough new troops to serve as replacements in such areas as Guam, Germany, and Santo Domingo.

Keeps Viet Nam Safe

The escalation of American participation in Viet Nam will not cause an all-out war, "certainly not in the foreseeable future," he said. President Johnson has gone far enough to keep South Viet Nam safe from Viet Cong control, he added.

Dirksen, who has been ailing with an abdominal disorder, said doctors at Bethesda Naval hospital have prescribed a diet and medication "and this is the best I've felt in years." He blamed the disorder on his heavy work schedule and erratic eating habits.

In his dinner speech, Dirksen said that the Johnson administration's record already has raised numerous issues that Republicans can use in the 1968 Presidential campaign.

Specifically, Dirksen said, they are the shaky conditions

[Continued on page 2, col. 2]

Sues for 10 Million in Death of His Dog

BY JOHN OSWALD

A scientist filed suit in Circuit court yesterday asking 10 million dollars damages for the death of his 4-year-old cocker spaniel, Bijou.

Bijou

The plaintiff is Dr. Cristjo Cristofv, 62, of 2645 Lawndale av., Evanston, internationally known for his discovery of what is known as the "Cristofv effect." This permits identification of atomic explosions anywhere in the world by analysis of electromagnetic waves which the explosions emit.

Not an Ordinary Dog

Bijou, according to the suit, was no ordinary dog. After extensive experimentation and training, she was able to detect electromagnetic changes in the atmosphere and to inform Cristofv by barking. He knew then it was time to go to his instruments.

Dr. Cristjo Cristofv

The defendants are the Christensen Animal hospital, 730 Hibbard rd., Wilmette, which treats pets of a number of prominent north shore residents, and the Upjohn company, Kalamazoo, Mich., drug manufacturer. The suit was prepared by William Kaper, attorney.

Last Aug. 8, according to the suit, Bijou was taken to the hospital for a routine treatment. She was given an injection of a drug, V-1360, manufactured by Upjohn and described by Kaper as a tranquilizer.

Dies After Operation

Subsequently the dog grew ill and her abdomen became enlarged. She was returned to the hospital last Oct. 3, the suit related, and the veterinarian in charge recommended surgery as soon as possible.

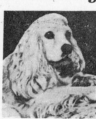

Bijou failed to survive the operation, which was performed two days later, the suit stated.

The federal Food and Drug administration, according to the suit, had not authorized sale or distribution of the drug.

Cristofv contended he suffered "great loss to his livelihood due to extensive training and unusual capabilities" of Bijou. He said he has suffered setbacks in his research, which is important to the security of the United States.

Friends of his said there was great affection between Bijou and her master. She was by far his favorite among the four cockers and two cats in the Cristofv household.

Now in Germany

Cristofv, a consultant to the air force and private companies, is in Germany on a business trip.

He once was a leading physicist in Bulgaria, where he amassed a fortune once placed at 6 million dollars. He abandoned this after World War II to escape the Communists, and became an American citizen in 1962.

Cristofv has continued to work on other applications of his discovery, which also permits identification of other types of major explosions.

A spokesman for the animal hospital declined comment on the suit.

ROMANO HITS 2 HOME RUNS AS SOX WIN

John Romano, playing left field instead of catching, hit two home runs and led the White Sox to 9 to 4 triumph over the Indians in Cleveland last night. This ended a road trip which brought nine defeats in 11 games.

Ron Santo led off the 12th inning with his 22d home run to give the Cubs a 2 to 1 victory in Wrigley field yesterday, but the New York Mets won the opening game of the double header, 14 to 0, with the aid of six Chicago errors.

[Details in Sports Section]

Choice of Fortas Draws Heavy Fire in Congress

BY WILLIAM MOORE

[Chicago Tribune Press Service]

Washington, July 29—President Johnson's nomination of Abe Fortas for the Supreme court came under fire in both houses of Congress today.

In the House, Rep. Durward G. Hall [R., Mo.] called for an investigation of Fortas' connection with arrangements that Hall said will bring an annual windfall of 11 to 30 million dollars to a major oil company.

Hall also called attention to Fortas' activities in the Bobby Baker scandal.

"Crony of Johnson"

In the Senate, Sen. John J. Williams [R., Del.] said Johnson could have made "a far wiser choice" and read an editorial saying that Fortas was chosen because he is a crony of Johnson.

Challenging Johnson's assertion that he looked all over the country to find the best man for the job, Williams said:

"It is quite obvious that he did not look beyond his inner circle of friends."

"A few weeks ago," Hall said, "a major oil company in the United States won a favorable decision from the interior department which will result in a huge windfall for that company, and which aroused the ire of every other major oil company in the nation."

Trebles Import Quota

As a result of the department ruling, Hall said, the oil company concerned will be able to establish a refinery in Puerto Rico and treble its import quota. This will mean, Hall said, that the company may ship to the eastern seaboard 25,000 barrels of gasoline a day. The oil he said, will come from Venezuela.

"Of the 73 major witnesses before the interior department," Hall said, "71 were strongly opposed to permitting this special dispensation in favor of one firm. It has been estimated that the windfall will total from 11 to 30 million dollars a year.

"Two men had a vital part in this decision. One of them was Abe Fortas, who acted as

[Continued on page 2, col. 5]

THE WEATHER

FRIDAY, JULY 30, 1965

CHICAGO AND VICINITY: Partly sunny and warmer today; high, in 80s; chance of thundershowers tonight; low, in 60s; southeasterly winds 10 to 18 m. p. h. Tomorrow: Partly cloudy and a little cooler.

NORTHERN ILLINOIS: Partly sunny and warmer today; scattered thundershowers west, spreading east in afternoon or evening; high, in 80s; scattered showers tonight; low, in the 60s. Tomorrow: Partly cloudy and a little cooler.

WEATHERMAN'S RECORD

His forecast for yesterday was: Sunny, with high in upper 70s; low, in upper 50s.

TEMPERATURES IN CHICAGO

7 a. m. ‡61	3:30 †77	Midnight 64
8 a. m. 64	4 p. m. 75	1 a. m. 64
9 a. m. 68	5 p. m. 75	2 a. m. 64
10 a. m. 73	6 p. m. 74	3 a. m. *63
11 a. m. 73	7 p. m. 71	4 a. m. *63
Noon 74	8 p. m. 69	5 a. m. *62
1 p. m. 73	9 p. m. 67	6 a. m. *61
2 p. m. 75	10 p. m. 66	
3 p. m. 75	11 p. m. 65	

† High. ‡ Low. * Estimated.

THE MOON

New	Waxing	First Qu.	Full	Last Qu.	Waning
July 28	J.29-Aug.2	Aug.3	Aug.12	Aug.19	Aug.20-25

Sunrise, 5:42. Sunset, 8:11. Moonset, 10:07 p. m. Morning stars: Jupiter and Saturn. Evening stars: Venus and Mars.

For 24 hours ended 1 a. m., July 30:

Mean temperature, 67 degrees; normal, 76; month's deficiency, 77; year's deficiency, 254.

Relative humidity, 7 a. m., 87 per cent; 1 p. m., 55; 7 p. m., 59.

Precipitation, none; month's total, 4.24 inches; July normal, 3.37 inches; year's total, 22.10 inches; excess thru June 30, .82 inch.

Highest wind velocity, 15 m. p. h. at 10:52 a. m. from northwest.

Barometer, 7 a. m., 30.14; 7 p. m., 30.13.

[Map and other reports on page 10]

Viet Crisis

President Johnson's reinforcement plan hailed and denounced thruout world. Page 5

Despite war, South Vietnamese economy is described as stable. Page 5

Congressional sources say that President Johnson, in an 11th hour decision Tuesday, canceled plans to declare state of emergency. Page 7

U Thant, secretary general of the U. N., vows to pursue Viet Nam peace attempts with all the means at his disposal. Page 7

British Prime Minister Harold Wilson supports but regrets "inevitable" U. S. buildup in Viet Nam. Page 7

The Cost of War

Fighting in Viet Nam has cost the lives of more than 530 United States service men since 1961. More than 250 additional men have died there from other causes. For the first time The Tribune has obtained a list of the casualties of all the American military services engaged there. The list begins on page 15.

The American Paper for Americans

Chicago Tribune

THE WORLD'S GREATEST NEWSPAPER

CITY ★ | FINAL

119th YEAR—No. 154 ®© 1966 Chicago Tribune

FRIDAY, JUNE 3, 1966 ★ 68 PAGES, 6 SECTIONS 10c

ATTACK GIANCANA RULING

Gemini Gets 'Go' for Today

FBI ARRESTS 14 IN INDIANA GAMING RAIDS

Estimate Profit at 6 Million

The Federal Bureau of Investigation arrested 14 persons last night and dispersed nearly 150 patrons of a crime syndicate gambling empire established in northern Indiana by Cicero gamblers.

The raids on three major gambling locations were staged by 60 FBI agents from the Chicago and Indianapolis divisions.

The raids struck at what was described by federal investigators as a 6-million-dollar-a-year gambling operation which derived its profits from the steel making centers of northern Indiana. This is in the rackets sanctuary of two mobsters, Anthony Pinelli and Gaetano [Tommy] Morgano.

100 Patrons Flee

The largest center hit in the FBI investigation, which resulted from TRIBUNE stories more than a year ago, was Forsythe Recreation-Billiards, 4610 Indianapolis blvd., East Chicago. More than 100 patrons fled into the streets as FBI agents battered down the doors.

Federal agents said the main room was devoted to drinking and card playing while a rear room was given to betting on day and night racing.

The Forsythe club was described as a 24-hour-a-day operation.

Gamblers Arrested

The key persons arrested, all identified as former Cicero gamblers who moved their operation to Indiana because of repeated FBI raids, are:

John Fezekas, 54, of 561 Ingraham st., Calumet City; Eugene [Gino] Izzi, 42, of 13323 Commercial av.; and Leo Kronberg, 67, of 5480 Cornell av.

Agents also arrested as a Forsythe club gambler, Carl Karchmer, 50, of 7834 Coles av., Chicago. He was seized in his home.

Equipment Also Seized

Others arrested at the Forsythe were William S. Ramer, 65, of 4725 Todd av., East Chicago; Samuel Murat, 64, of 4624 Magoon st., East Chicago; and Michael Karris, 63, of 4601 Indianapolis blvd., East Chicago.

Agents said that lottery tickets, cards, and dice were seized in the club.

Investigators estimated the monthly intake of the Forsythe club at $300,000.

The betting in the two other locations raided was estimated at more than $100,000 each.

They are the Four Aces Rec-

[Continued on page 4, col. 3]

'Objects' Circle Space Garage; Create Mystery

Astronauts Told to Take a Close Look at Them

BY WILLIAM ANDERSON

(Picture on back page)

[Chicago Tribune Press Service]

Cape Kennedy, Fla., June 2—A space garage, surrounded by flying objects, circled the earth tonight as preparations moved ahead for Astronauts Thomas P. Stafford and Eugene A. Cernan to start chasing it at 8:39 a. m. Chicago time tomorrow.

The plan is to park inside the garage after a complicated rendezvous attempt, but there was some mystery involving the pieces floating around the garage. The astronauts have been told to take a close look at the target spacecraft before any decision is made to go inside.

Complicates the Mission

The target was blasted off a pad here yesterday. On the way up signals showed that a protective cover failed to come off. The pieces indicated that the cover came off in space, complicating and adding some unknown and potentially dangerous aspects to the mission of Gemini 9.

Christopher C. Kraft Jr., a flight director, said the air force had spotted by radar from 10 to 12 pieces around the 10-foot long target vehicle.

"Your guess may be as good as ours as to what the pieces are," he said.

The spacecraft and pieces, along with part of the Atlas boosting device, are flying at speeds in excess of 17,000 miles an hour about 185 miles above the earth.

Don't Want to Guess

Officials said they wouldn't want to guess whether the shroud was on or off, but they did tell of revised plans created by the doubt. Kraft then said if the shroud had come only "partly unglued," he would want Cernan to stay

[Continued on page 5, col. 2]

144 PICTURES OF MOON SENT BY SURVEYOR

(Pictures on back page)

Pasadena, Cal., June 2 (UPI)—Surveyor 1, which planted the American flag on the moon, blazed a trail for space pioneers today by sending back 144 pictures in contrast to the few sent in a 48-hour span last February by Russia's Luna 9.

Welsh

Space scientists exulted over the feat of the first-try success of Surveyor as a forerunner to American astronauts landing in the same arid Sea of Storms by 1969 and strolling over the dusty flat terrain shown by the first pictures.

Flag Cost 23 Cents

A four-by-six-inch flag, purchased for 23 cents at drug store, was furled in a section

FIRST PICTURES

First photos transmitted from Surveyor space craft after moon landing are on page 10.

of structural tubing of the three-legged robot.

The accomplishment of the pinpoint soft landing by the 10-foot high 620-pound robot was seen by millions of American television watchers, including some behind the iron curtain, shared in seeing pictures transmitted by the swivel-eyed camera of Surveyor.

In contrast, Luna 9 was two-feet high, weighed 220 pounds and sent back only 27 pictures before its storage batteries failed. Surveyor, built by Hughes Aircraft company, is equipped with solar panels that provide battery power from the sun and can function for an unlimited time.

"It's not getting there first

[Continued on page 10, col. 1]

THE LOST COMPASS

ARN'T WE GOING AROUND IN CIRCLES, LYNDON?
"THERE IS NO SUBSTITUTE FOR VICTORY" —GEN. MACARTHUR
VIET NAM BOG
JOHNSON'S "WAR OF CONTAINMENT"
HOLLAND
© 1966 by The Chicago Tribune

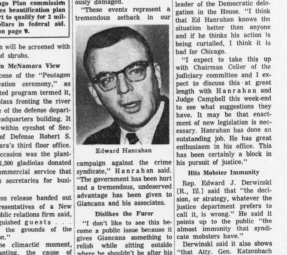

WATERS RETIRING AS ARMY CHIEF IN PACIFIC AREA

Washington, June 2 (AP)—President Johnson announced today the retirement Sept. 1 of Gen. John K. Waters as commander in chief of the army in the Pacific and the selection of Gen. Dwight E. Beach to replace him. Beach now is commander in chief of United Nations and United States forces in Korea. The Pacific army command headquarters is in Honolulu.

The replacement of Waters by Beach led to two other appointments: Lt. Gen. Charles H. Bonesteel III is being nominated to the grade of general and will succeed Beach. Bonesteel is director of special studies in the office of the army chief of staff and senior army member of the military staff committee of the United Nations. To replace him, Johnson selected Lt. Gen. John L. Throckmorton, now chief of the army's office of reserve components.

The president said that Lt. Gen. Vernon P. Mock, deputy chief of staff for military operations, is being reassigned and his position will go to Maj. Gen. Harry J. Lemley Jr., now commandant of the army command and general staff college at Fort Leavenworth, Kas. Lemley is being nominated for lieutenant general.

Brass Digs for Sake of Pentagon's Beauty

Washington, June 2 (AP)—Beautification came to the Pentagon today with a big brass band and lots of brass dutifully planting gladiola bulbs.

The secretary of the army, three generals, and an assistant secretary of defense took turns wielding a shiny spade and digging holes—not very expertly—in a flower bed. In the background, a blue-clad army band played "America the Beautiful" in soft, soothing tones.

"Everyone's Business"

It was all done in the name of Mrs. Lyndon B. Johnson's campaign to beautify Washington. But Mrs. Johnson wasn't there. She sent Mrs. Katie Louchheim of her "committee for a more beautiful capital."

Mrs. Louchheim proclaimed, "We have learned from Mrs. Johnson that beauty is everyone's business."

Pentagon officials, whose main business is war, evidently had gotten Mrs. Johnson's message.

For Stanley R. Resor, secretary of the army, took the microphone to announce that acres of barren parking lots surrounding the squat, unlovely

CITY SEEKS FUNDS

Chicago Plan commission approves beautification plan in effort to qualify for 2 million dollars in federal aid. Story on page 9.

Pentagon will be screened with trees and shrubs.

Within McNamara View

The scene of the "Pentagon beautification ceremony," as the printed program termed it, was a plaza fronting the river entrance of the defense department headquarters building. It is well within eyeshot of Secretary of Defense Robert S. McNamara's third floor office.

The occasion was the planting of 1,500 gladiolas donated by a commercial service that provides secretaries for businesses.

A press release handed out by representatives of a New York public relations firm said, "Distinguished guests . . . studded the grounds of the Pentagon."

At the climactic moment, the planting, the cause of beautification was set back by two army photographers who trampled on the flower bed in their eagerness to take a picture of the event.

CONGRESSMEN STUDY MOBSTER LAW NEEDS

Hanrahan Vow: He Won't Quit War on Gang

BY ROBERT WIEDRICH

Edward V. Hanrahan, the United States attorney, told his critics yesterday that he will not resign and intends to keep fighting the Chicago crime syndicate with every tool at his command.

"I'm going to stay in office and fight organized crime," Hanrahan said. "No one is going to force me out of this office. If I didn't think that I could perform the functions of this office effectively, I would not be in it."

Slaps Back at Critics

Hanrahan struck back at high justice department officials in Washington who had twice overruled his plan to seek the indictment of Sam [Momo] Giancana, the mob's operating boss, for the obstruction of justice and criminal contempt.

The prosecutor said that because of the controversy over the Washington decision to drop further action against Giancana, the government's fight against the mob had been seriously damaged.

"These events represent a tremendous setback in our

Edward Hanrahan

campaign against the crime syndicate," Hanrahan said. "The government has been hurt and a tremendous, undeserved advantage has been given to Giancana and his associates.

Dislikes the Furor

"I don't like to see this become a public issue because it gives Giancana something to relish while sitting outside where he shouldn't be after his kind of conduct."

Hanrahan referred to the re-

[Continued on page 2, col. 1]

Speak in Praise of Judge and U. S. Attorney

JUSTICE DEPARTMENT NEEDS A LAWYER

See editorial on page 8

BY PHILIP WARDEN

[Chicago Tribune Press Service]

Washington, June 2—Members of Congress from Chicago today deplored the action of the justice department in dropping charges against Sam [Momo] Giancana, boss of the Chicago crime syndicate.

They said they intended to discuss the legal issues with Chairman Emanuel Celler [D., N. Y.] of the House judiciary committee and to seek legislation if new laws are needed.

They spoke in highest terms of the ability and devotion of Edward V. Hanrahan, the United States attorney in Chicago, and of Chief Judge William J. Campbell of federal District court.

Called Bad for Chicago

"I am disappointed that Atty. Gen. Nicholas Katzenbach has taken this position," said Rep. Dan Rostenkowski [D., Ill.] leader of the Democratic delegation in the House. "I think that Ed Hanrahan knows the situation better than anyone and if he thinks his action is being curtailed, I think it is bad for Chicago.

"I expect to take this up with Chairman Celler of the judiciary committee and I expect to discuss this at great length with Hanrahan and Judge Campbell this week-end to see what suggestions they have. It may be that enactment of new legislation is necessary. Hanrahan has done an outstanding job. He has great enthusiasm in his office. This has been certainly a block in his pursuit of justice."

Hits Mobster Immunity

Rep. Edward J. Derwinski [R., Ill.] said that "the decision, or strategy, whatever the justice department prefers to call it, is wrong." He said it points up to the public "the almost immunity that syndicate mobsters have."

Derwinski said it also shows "that Atty. Gen. Katzenbach is more interested in anti-trust actions and the harassment of

[Continued on page 4, col. 3]

Find Evidence of Cancer Virus

Discovery Called Milestone in Research

BY RONALD KOTULAK

Scientists from Columbia university reported yesterday the first evidence indicating that a virus may be responsible for causing a common type of human cancer.

The announcement is considered a milestone in cancer research. No one has ever been able to find the exact cause of cancer in humans altho many investigators believe that viruses are responsible.

"A disease generally cannot be cured until you know what causes it, and these findings may open the door for the prevention of cancer thru the development of vaccines," said Dr. John K. Lattimer, head of the department of urology at Columbia.

Pathologist Explains

The results were reported at the 61st annual meeting of the American Urological association in the Palmer House by Dr. Myron Tannebaum, a pathologist in Columbia's urology department.

He reported that virus-like particles were observed in normal cells adjacent to cancer cells in the prostate gland and that the cells containing the virus particles were multiplying as fast as cancer tissue.

At a press conference called to explain the findings, Dr. Lattimer said that the virus-like particles found in the human prostate cells looked exactly like a virus known to cause kidney cancer in frogs.

The particles had the same size, shape, and structure of the known cancer-causing virus called the Lucke virus.

First Link to Humans

A number of viruses are known to cause different cancers in animals, but researchers have so far failed to definitely show this relationship with human cancers.

"The findings are definite that these virus-like particles exist and that the cells containing them are multiplying like cancer cells," Dr. Lattimer said.

"Because of these two facts, it is extremely likely that the virus-like particles are responsible for causing cancer in the prostate gland."

The findings are based on a year-and-a-half-long study in which 7,000 samples of prostate tissue were taken from more than 100 persons.

Powerful Microscope

Dr. Lattimer said that the virus-like particles were found in a large proportion of the tissue of persons who had prostate cancer.

The ability to identify the tiny particles was made possible by the use of a powerful electron microscope which magnified the interior of cells 80,000 times.

Dr. Lattimer said that none of the particles were found in cancerous tissue. It was observed in apparently healthy tissue adjoining the tumor. Examination of cells beyond the tumor area did not turn up any of the particles, he said.

This observation opens the possibility that the virus may be infectious and that once it causes a cell to become abnormal it moves on to infect other cells, he explained.

Investigators at Columbia are now attempting to isolate

[Continued on page 2, col. 4]

YANKS BEAT SOX, 5 TO 3; CUBS LOSE

The New York Yankees scored four runs in the fourth inning off Tommy John last night in Comiskey park and went on to defeat the White Sox, 5 to 3, before only 8,650 in a twilight game.

The Cubs scored two runs in the ninth inning, but still lost their third game in a row to the Philadelphia Phillies, 5 to 4, in Philadelphia. It was the Cubs' fifth loss in six games on their road trip.

[Details in Sports Section]

THE WEATHER

FRIDAY, JUNE 3, 1966

CHICAGO AND VICINITY: Considerable cloudiness and warm today with showers likely; high, in lower 80s; chance of showers tonight; low, near 60. Tomorrow: Partly cloudy with chance of showers and little temperature change.

NORTHERN ILLINOIS: Mostly cloudy and warm today with showers and thundershowers likely; high, 78 to 86; chance of showers with little temperature change tonight and tomorrow; low tonight, 56 to 62.

WEATHERMAN'S RECORD

His forecast for yesterday was: Sunny; high, in 70s; low, in 50s.

TEMPERATURES IN CHICAGO

3 a. m.	48	Noon	71	7 p. m.	75
4 a. m.	47	1 p. m.	73	8 p. m.	71
5 a. m.	47	2 p. m.	75	9 p. m.	68
6 a. m.	†46	3 p. m.	77	10 p. m.	66
7 a. m.	52	4 p. m.	75	11 p. m.	64
8 a. m.	56	5 p. m.	77	Midnight	*63
9 a. m.	61	5:15	†78	1 a. m.	*62
10 a. m.	65	6 p. m.	77	2 a. m.	*60
11 a. m.	69				

*Estimated. †High. ‡Low.

THE MOON

Full	Last Qu.	Waning	New	Waxing	First Qu.
June 3	June 10	June 11-17	June 18	June 19-24	June 25

Sunrise, 5:18. Sunset, 8:20. Moonrise, 9:11 p. m. Morning stars: Venus and Saturn. Evening star: Jupiter.

For 24 hours ended 7 p. m. June 2: Mean temperature, 62 degrees; normal, 67; month's deficiency, 15; year's deficiency, 262.

Relative humidity, 7 a. m., 54 per cent; 1 p. m., 30; 7 p. m., 23.

Precipitation, none; June normal, 4.07 inches; year's total 16.39 inches; excess thru May 31, 3.42 inches.

Highest wind velocity, 12 m. p. h. at 5:53 p. m. from south southwest.

Barometer, 7 a. m., 30.23; 7 p. m., 30.07.

[Map and other reports on page 6]

U. S. CONVICTS HAIR STYLIST IN DOPE PLOT

Hartford, Conn., June 2 (UPI)—A federal court jury today convicted James J. Miller, 39, a hairdresser, of conspiracy in connection with an international heroin-smuggling ring. The panel of 10 men and two women deliberated more than an hour before returning the verdict before District Judge M. Joseph Blumenfeld.

Miller, of Orange, Conn., who faces a possible maximum sentence of 20 years in prison, was accused of being a go-between for a gang of Montreal heroin runners whose operation was smashed in 1963 when a courier was seized in Laredo, Tex. A courier, Joseph M. Caron, 36, was the government's key witness. He identified Miller as the man to whom he relayed 52 pounds of heroin at a motel in Bridgeport in 1963.

Caron's wife, Ida, 33, corroborated her husband's testimony. She accompanied her husband on some of his runs and was seized with him in Texas. Caron is serving a 10-year sentence for his part in the narcotics running.

Rap Story Hanrahan Misled U. S. Judge

Charges that Edward V. Hanrahan, the United States attorney, deliberately misled the chief federal judge in a grand jury investigation of political ties with the crime syndicate were branded false last night here and in Washington.

Fred M. Vinson Jr., chief of the justice department's criminal division, said that he had never accused Hanrahan of deceiving Chief Judge William J. Campbell of federal District court and that, in fact, he had no information that Hanrahan had ever told Campbell he lacked evidence against three 1st ward Democratic political figures.

Hanrahan Issues challenge

Meanwhile, Hanrahan vehemently denied the accusation, adding:

"I defy anyone to document it. If anyone has evidence, let them bring it before Judge Campbell and ask that I be cited before him as an officer of the court.

"The last thing that I would do is to mislead a federal judge. I did not mislead Judge

Daley Praise

Mayor Daley yesterday praised United States Atty. Edward V. Hanrahan and Chief Judge William J. Campbell of federal District court, but he declined to take sides in the Sam [Momo] Giancana case "because I don't know enough of the facts." He said Hanrahan is "an outstanding lawyer, and his reputation for integrity, ability, honesty, and courage is unequaled. Judge Campbell," he said, "is one of the outstanding jurists in the federal court system."

Campbell and anyone who says so is a liar."

Judge Campbell said that he, too, was shocked at the charge.

"I have every confidence in the statements of Mr. Hanrahan," Judge Campbell said. "I accept his word."

The three politicians involved in the investigation are John D'Arco, 1st ward Democratic committeeman and for-

[Continued on page 2, col. 4]

Weather
WARMER
Report on Page 2

264 Pages, 28 Comics
2 Magazines

Sunday BOSTON Advertiser

Sunday, July 17, 1966

Phone Liberty 2-4000

4-STAR
★★★★
Edition

20c Within 15 Miles
25c Beyond

NAME KILLER OF 8 NURSES

CHICAGO POLICE issued a wanted circular for Richard B. Speck, 25, in connection with the massacre of eight student nurses. Nurse Corazon Amurao, who escaped killer, identified this picture of Speck as being the man. Police said "identification is positive based on fingerprints found in dormitory and on file with FBI." See how closely photograph above resembles sketch on page 3 which was made from survivor's description.

UPI Telephoto

Hunt Man, 25; Was Identified By His Prints

Surviving Nurse Picked Out Photograph From FBI Files

CHICAGO (AP)—A nationwide manhunt is under way for a seaman who has been named as the mass slayer of eight nurses Thursday in a Chicago town house.

Police Supt. O. W. Wilson said Saturday fingerprints lifted at the bloodstained, disarrayed town house led to the identification of Richard B. Speck, 25, white.

Speck is also known by the aliases of Richard Franklin Lindberg and Richard Benjamin Speck. Speck's physical appearance is almost a perfect match to the description given police Friday by the lone survivor of the massacre, Corazon Amurao, 23.

Speck is 6 feet, 1 inch, 160 pounds, has brown blond hair, worn slightly longer than a crew cut, and blue eyes.

Wilson said Speck was seen in Chicago as late as 9 p.m. Friday. He was registered at a hotel on North Dearborn st.

"He may have left the city after seeing in the newspapers what was virtually a portrait of him."

Clinching Print From Door

Wilson said 32 of Speck's fingerprints were found in the South Side town house where Chicago's most horrible crime occurred.

The fingerprint that identified Speck, Wilson said, was taken from the door of the bedroom where the six student nurses and two exchange Filipino nurses were tied before being led to their strangling and stabbing deaths.

Wilson said Speck has several tattos. One reads: "Born to raise hell."

One on his upper arm is a drawing of hat and goggles and a tattoo of a dagger and sickle is on his right forearm.

A nationwide FBI "stop order" was flashed as soon as Miss Amurao viewed the photograph of Speck from FBI files. Chief of Detectives Otto Kreuzer said the FBI rushed Speck's record, photograph and fingerprints via messenger and airplane as soon as his identity was determined.

Wilson said Speck had a record of arrests in Texas. He was arrested for disturbing the peace in 1959, and later was arrested in Dallas on a charge of

Turn to Page 14, Col. 1

• *Surviving nurse's dramatic story to police that led to identification of suspect in massacre — on Page 3.*

The Dallas Morning News

Vol. 117—No. 307 | Phone RI 7-4611 | Dallas, Texas, Wednesday, August 3, 1966 | 4 Sections ★★★★ | Price 10 Cents

Last Hours of Charles Whitman

Tortured Mind Held Plan of Terror

By H. D. QUIGG

AUSTIN, Texas (UPI)—The moon rose full and fat. Just at dusk, 7:25 p.m., it hung—pale harbinger of things that happen in full-moon time—just above the horizon due east of the little brick house.

It was Sunday evening, hot, clear. Inside the 1-story, 33-by-24-foot house, the probability is that a young man sat writing a note. His vision of the moonrise and the simultaneous sunset glow was blocked by similar little houses to the east and west of him.

NOR, if he had gone out onto the yellowing grassy front lawn, parted in the middle by a cement walkway, would the terrain have let him glimpse the colonnaded top of the 307-foot tower of the University of Texas. But he must have been thinking of it.

And specifically, he must have had in mind the observation platform, 280 feet high, under the Corinthian-columned bell tower—students call it "the Greek outhouse." The Westminster chimes strike the quarters and the hour from the time decreed by the gear that runs the four mammoth Roman-numeral clock faces below the bell assembly.

The little brick house is about three miles south of the tower that is the Austin landmark. Its neatly kept, modestly furnished interior was home to Mr. and Mrs. Charles Joseph Whitman.

About an hour before the Sunday moonrise, a neighbor saw the 6-foot, 198-pound Whitman, 25, walk with a man-and-wife couple to the bell-tinkling truck of the Bluebird Ice Cream Co. in front of the Whitman home and buy ice cream.

Later, Mr. and Mrs. Lawrence Fuess of Dallas, close friends of the Whitmans, said they dropped by the little house in Austin Sunday about dusk. Whitman, the honor student and honor Scout, was writing what appeared to be a letter. He was relaxed, seemed "more calm than usual."

BUT the honor student had a plan. How long he had it in the back of his crewcut blond head, no one knows. It is for the psychiatrists to say how long he had had mass terror—launched from the observation tower—coddled and nurtured in his tortured brain.

He had been under mental strain. One of the notes he left said he had gone to a psychiatrist for two hours but never returned. He had had extreme headaches—and in the last three months had taken three large bottles of aspirin-type pills. He didn't know it, but a tumor was growing in his brain. An autopsy report disclosed that.

But an Austin psychiatrist, Dr. David Wade, said: "The man must have been carrying a paranoid psychosis for a long time and suddenly lost all ability to control his behavior. His arsenal itself would indicate he had unsure feelings prompted by delusions of persecution."

And so he sat printing out a note that was found later on the bed in his house. He said he was going to pick up his wife, Kathleen, 23, at work (at Southwestern Bell Telephone Co.), and kill her. "I loved her dearly," he wrote, but he wanted to "save her from the embarrassment" of what he was going to do.

Her body was found—after his sniping spree of Monday—in their little house, dead of stab wounds in the mid-chest, in bed and nude.

At half past midnight Monday, Whitman started a 2-page note, part typed and part handwritten (he timed the note on its face). He said he killed his mother: "If there is a heaven, she is in heaven; but if there is no heaven, she's at least out of her misery."

THE MOTHER, Mrs. C. A. Whitman, was found shot to death in her penthouse apartment at 1212 Guadalupe St., a few blocks from the tower. Whitman had picked up his wife at work some time after 9:30 p.m. Sunday, but it was unclear which one was killed first.

At 3 a.m. Monday, he wrote that "Now both are dead," and he stopped typing, noting that friends earlier had interrupted him. He resumed writing in longhand, saying he loved his mother and wife but hated his father "with a passion."

Now, he prepared for the trek to the tower. His late-model Chevrolet came out of its garage at the side of the back yard and along the drive beside the little house. He drove about five miles to a shopping center department store. It was between 9:30 and 10 a.m., a police check showed, that he purchased on credit a 12-gauge shotgun.

He drove home and sawed off both barrel and stock of the shotgun. Then he loaded his car with the fantastic cargo to which Dr. Wade later referred in reference to his mental state.

He was going to the tower, and in his mind he was going to stay a while. Into a trunk-size footlocker he loaded:

TWO CANS of pork and beans, a can of spiced meat, two cans of Vienna sausage, a can of fruit cocktail, cans of sliced pineapple, peanuts, beef ravioli, a vacuum bottle of coffee and six boxes of raisins.

Among other personal items were spray deodorant, a can of charcoal lighter, a roll of toilet paper, a wash game bag, dark glasses and a lantern-type flashlight.

Also a clock, matches, adhesive tape, cigarette lighter, various types of brushes, screwdriver, binoculars, four flashlight batteries, several hundred feet of nylon rope, a long extension cord, about 25 feet of additional electrical wiring, a Stillson wrench . . .

And two pairs of gloves, a canteen, an old service knapsack, a 3-gallon jug of water and a 3-gallon jug of gasoline.

On top of the footlocker, underneath a blanket, he put: The new sawed-off automatic shotgun, a .35-caliber Remington pump rifle, a 6-millimeter Remington bolt-action rifle with a 4-power scope, a .30-caliber M1 carbine, a .25-caliber Galesi-Brascia pistol, a 9-millimeter Luger and a .357 Smith & Wesson magnum pistol—plus three hunting knives of various sizes, one pocket knife, and probably 600 to 700 rounds of ammunition.

In the footlocker after the sniping spree, police found more than 500 rounds of unfired ammunition of various calibers. Police said some of his shots carried 350-400 yards from the tower to Guadalupe Street two blocks west.

IN ADDITION to the seven guns on the roof, police found in the Whitman home a pair of matched .22-caliber derringers, a .410-gauge shotgun and a .25-20 Winchester rifle.

Into the car also, he loaded a new-looking, bluish, 2-wheel dolly, the 2-handle push type of hand truck used to move heavy things. Then, methodically, he got a permit to park in the loading zone at the northwest corner of the tower. The car was found there later.

Sometime after 11 a.m., he wheeled the dolly and its load into the tower hallway. He had on an olive drab flight jacket, and he told receptionist Vera Palmer that he was a workman. Mrs. Palmer held the self-service elevator door for him. Onto it he went. When he returned about two hours later, he was a gun-riddled corpse.

He took the elevator to its 27th floor top. Then he struggled up three flights of stairs, jerking the dolly after him, to what is regarded as the 28th floor, about 280 feet above ground.

Halfway up the stairs, he met a family of four tourists from Texarkana, Texas, who were on their way down with a relative from Austin. He killed two of them and wounded two others.

Then, at the entrance to the observation deck, he encountered receptionist Edna Townsley, 51, and shot her. Mrs. Townsley died later.

AT THAT POINT he moved onto the observation tower walk-around. He barricaded the entrance with the dolly and stashed his arsenal on the walk, sweating in the sunlight that heated the tower floor to far over 100 degrees.

He stationed himself on the south side, beneath the VI on the tower clock. The staircase and observation deck reception desk are painted pale green. The walkway is paved with red tile, and its stone parapet came nearly chest-high on Whitman.

To the south, he could see, 12 blocks away, the dome of the State Capitol and the Colorado River, snaking east. To the west, the first low rolling ridges of the Hill Country, purple in the distance, where 65 miles away is located President Johnson's LBJ Ranch.

Below, the university was a sea of beauty—red tile roofs and white stone and cement walkways and malls, with bright green grass along the malls and on the roof gardens of the Humanities Research Center on the third floor of the main building.

He raised a rifle, aimed and fired. It was about 11:44 a.m. Within seconds a young boy had been shot off his bicycle as he passed the Hemphill Book Store, near the white garbage pail lettered "Help Keep Our Campus Clean," on Guadalupe Street.

Now he was operating. Police were called at 11:52 a.m. The air shuddered with siren shrieks. The running and ducking police found the bullets whe-e-wing down from the tower — the gun barks never coming at machine-gun speed but never more than 2- to 3-minute intervals.

WHITMAN STARTED on the south side, overlooking the concrete south mall that leads down to the pretentious Littlefield Fountain, with its clutch of bronze stallions rearing out of its waters. There, two blocks away from the tower, several people were hit. On Guadalupe Street, shots hit the doorways of the 1-story college-gathering businesses. Blood soon stained the 20-foot-wide sidewalks.

On the sidewalk of Inner Campus Drive, which cuts across the south mall between the tower and the fountain, a girl cried: "Help me; somebody help me!"

She fell. The boy with her bent over her. Another shot rang. He fell on top of the girl. Paul Sonntag, 18, and his girl friend, Claudia Rutt, 18, died together.

Watching the wild scene from a corner of the third floor of a nearby building, UPI correspondent James T. Young saw Whitman ducking, bobbing from parapet to parapet, and finally taking refuge behind the stone wall as the police fire grew heavier. Then the sniper began to fire through the portholes.

FOR ABOUT 10 minutes after Whitman started firing, the walls of the university and the sidewalk along the "Drag" remained crowded. At first, the killer had his choice of targets.

By 15 minutes past noon police had cornered off the campus. Students were cowering behind trees, buildings, a flagpole, and Whitman had to settle for firing on those whose curiosity exceeded their common sense, those few who blundered out unknowingly, the brave who tried to rescue the fallen and the police who tried to reach him and still his guns.

He fired approximately 100 rounds in the 80 minutes, sometimes in quick bursts which made the police suspect he had one or more companions, sometimes pausing as long as three minutes between shots.

Most of the wounded were struck in the first half hour. There were an estimated 15 dead, dying or wounded lying on the ground by that time.

WHEN POLICE who closed in on him and shot him dead finally announced the end at 1:22 p.m., at least 30 had been wounded, and 13 killed or mortally wounded by the sniper.

The final shotgun blast was fired into Whitman's badly wounded and twitching body by city Policeman Ramiro Martinez, who already had emptied the six shells from his service revolver at the sniper.

Martinez entered the observation deck by kicking down the dolly that blocked the door. He later recalled:

"I just said a prayer, gave my life to God and plunged out the door."

On Tuesday, an epilog came in the statement of Dr. Maurice D. Heatly of the Student Health Center. The staff psychiatrist said Whitman was referred to him for private consultation last March 29, was told to come back the next week, but never came.

He quoted Whitman as saying at one time that he was "thinking about going up to the tower with a deer rifle and start shooting people."

"THE REAL precipitating factor for this initial visit after being on campus for several years," said Dr. Heatly, "seemed to stem from separation of his parents some 30 days prior to the visit.

"The youth said his father had averaged calling every 48 hours for several weeks, petitioning him to persuade his mother to return to him."

He said the youth displayed hostility toward his father and said he had no intention of trying to get his mother to return.

Paul Crume's

Big D

As you may have noticed, I sneaked out for a short vacation while nobody was looking, and I discovered that this sort of thing is almost more than the human spirit can stand.

A kind of cosmic conspiracy exists to keep me from taking a vacation anyway. For four years I had been attempting every summer to take some time off, but a job that had to be done immediately developed or a family emergency came up. It always seemed easier just to go on with the daily routine.

This year, I decided, would be different. Whatever the fates might do against me, I would prevail in taking a vacation. Faced with this stern attitude, the fates seemed for awhile to quail.

Then I took the family car to the garage. It had been missing a little when it was cold, but mainly I wanted a check on some brake linings that had 35,000 miles on them.

"This is a cranky old car," I told the garage man, "but it is a good one. I have never been out a dime on maintenance."

This is the kind of statement that the unwary human being is always betrayed into making, and it always backfires. An hour or so later, the mechanic telephoned and said the brake linings were okay.

"But your shocks are gone," he said. "And a seal is broken. Your transmission fluid is leaking, and we'd better do a universal joint check."

We had intended to leave the next day, but it seemed wise to wait while the garage did a crash repair job. The mechanic got everything done except attending to the small miss when the engine was cold. He said to drive the car by next morning, and he would fix that. Probably a minor job of tuning, he said.

Early next morning we drove the car by and he checked it out and said wuh-oh.

"There is water in the cylinder," he said. "It means there is a leak in the cooling system. I hope it is not a cylinder head."

It wasn't the head, only a gasket, but we put off the trip another couple of days.

Finally, we loaded up the trunk and took off. It was gratifying to know that all these defects in the car had been detected before it broke down somewhere in the Great American Desert around Albuquerque. It ran beautifully. Then, midway between Dallas and Fort Worth, a frightful red light warned us that the engine had overheated. We limped back home.

The radiator was stopped up. The mechanic had to disassemble the cooling system and clean it out.

We finally departed about a week late. It may have been the longest departure in history.

You would have thought that was all the trouble we could have, but while crossing the malpais in New Mexico, the lady at our house who does most of the driving got a couple of chunks of lava in her eye and had to go to the hospital in the middle of the night.

This is the reason I'm going along with whatever the fates want to do in the future. I don't think my constitution can stand another vacation.

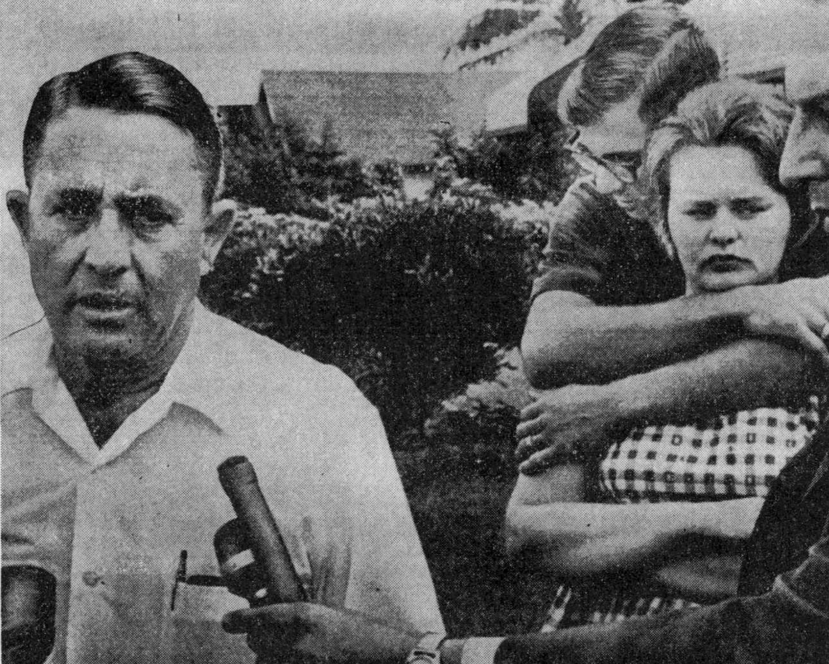

—Associated Press Wirephoto.

Charles A. Whitman Jr., father of Austin sniper, met with the press in front of his home in Lake Worth, Fla. His son, Patrick, 21, and wife, Patricia, 20, are watching in the background.

Austin Surgeon Discovers Sniper Had Brain Tumor

By LEE JONES

AUSTIN, Texas (AP) — Investigators were told Tuesday Charles Joseph Whitman suffered from a possibly agonizing brain tumor and revealed four months ago that he thought of shooting people from a perch on the University of Texas Tower.

Police seeking the cause of a homicidal outburst which left the 25-year-old ex-Marine and 15 others dead, plus 31 wounded, received this information from a surgeon and a psychiatrist.

The tumor, about the size of a pecan, was found in Whitman's brain during an autopsy.

Justice of the Peace Jerry Dellana said the examining surgeon, Dr. C. DeChenar, expressed the opinion that Whitman's tumor may have "caused intense pain—headaches — that could have indirectly caused or contributed to his actions." He stressed that the tumor did not "have anything to do with the part of the brain that affected logical thinking."

Meanwhile Dr. Maurice Dean Heatly, a University of Texas psychiatrist, said at a news conference Whitman told him about visions of sniping from the tower with a high-powered gun.

DR. HEATLY said Whitman, a student at the university, ranged from "overt hostility" to weeping during an appointment they had on March 29. He said he asked Whitman to return for a further interview in a week, but that the student never came back.

Dr. Heatly said Whitman was a troubled personality, vastly different from the "good guy" neighbors, classmates and friends supposed him to be.

The psychiatrist added that Whitman admitted "having overwhelming periods of hostility with a very minimum of provocation."

Explaining why no action was taken when Whitman failed to continue his psychiatrist interviews, Dr. Charles LeMaistre, the university vice-chancellor said:

"Dr. Heatly's conclusion on March 29 that there was no indication at that time that Whitman was a danger to either himself or the community was consistent with the impressions of his teachers, his employer and his associates."

Before and during the hours that police say Whitman killed his wife and mother, he wrote three notes, leaving them with their bodies.

Police Chief Robert A. Miles, who gave reporters this information, said that on the advice of legal authorities he had decided against making the text of the notes public.

The climax to the murderous drama took place on the observation deck of the tower.

Along with other policemen, officer Ramiro Martinez, 29, who had been relaxing on his day off, sped to the tower in response to word that a man was shooting at people.

Related stories, pictures on Pages 6-11A.

Martinez said Tuesday he accompanied officers Houston McCoy and Jerry Day and Allen Crum, a civilian volunteer, in an elevator to the 26th floor.

The young policeman said he and Crum advanced up a flight of stairs leading to the observation deck. With McCoy and Day following, they pushed open a door leading to the floor Whitman was firing from.

"I SAW WHITMAN pointing the rifle in the direction that Crum was coming," Martinez said. "I shot him the first time and he jerked up and fired the carbine. I kept firing and he kept trembling and couldn't bring his rifle down."

Martinez said McCoy then ran up and pumped two rounds into Whitman from a shotgun.

"The guy was still flopping," Martinez continued. "I grabbed the shotgun and I ran at him and shot at the same time."

"I dropped my gun and started shaking," he said.

The battle of an hour and a half was over.

The count of dead mounted during the day as Whitman carefully picked off officers, students, visitors and a reporter.

Spectators and police sought to reach the wounded and the dead, but Whitman's accuracy was so deadly that finally armored trucks were called to pick up the victims.

Not until the fight ended did officers find the body of his mother and wife in separate apartments.

Notes left with their bodies indicated he killed his mother a half hour after midnight and his wife at 3 a.m.

He then hauled a footlocker filled with weapons, ammunition, food and water by elevator and steps to the observation deck of the tower. There he killed the woman custodian of the tower and a woman and one of her two nephews who were sightseeing. The second child was wounded.

THEN, UNDER the disturbing pressures he discussed in his notes, he "decided to fight it out alone."

In his mother's apartment was a note, police reported, which said he killed her to "relieve her of her suffering, that he didn't want her embarrassed by all of this."

Whitman added to a note, police said:

"12:30 a.m.—Mother already dead.

"3 o'clock—Wife and mother both dead."

It was 11 a.m.—after purchase of the shotgun—that he took his footlocker to the tower's elevator on a workman's cart and rode as high as the elevator goes. He then dragged the cart up four short flights of stairs to the observation platform.

Solvent Explosion Kills 2 Missilemen

MIAMI, Fla. (AP)—Two missilemen were killed when a solvent they used to clean walls exploded in the administration building of a missile site at North Key Largo.

They were Spec. 4 Samuel W. Littlejohn, 26, of El Paso, and Pfc. Carl Osborne, 18, of Mascot, Tenn. They died Friday in a Miami hospital, it was disclosed Tuesday.

The Index

Braniff Plans Airport Facility

Braniff International Airways has announced plans to build an 8-million-dollar passenger terminal at Dallas Love Field. Love Field.

Story on Page 8B.

U.S. Weather Bureau forecast:

Dallas and Vicinity: Clear to partly cloudy and warm. High Wednesday in mid-90s; low Thursday morning in the upper 70s. Tuesday's high: 91.

Complete weather on Page 18D.

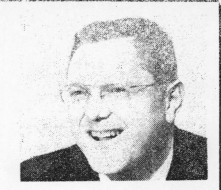

WEATHER
Mostly cloudy, mild, 55-60.
Tomorrow: Partly cloudy, 60.
SUNSET: 4:37 PM
SUNRISE TOMORROW: 6:45 AM

New York Post

Vol. 166 No. 2 | NEW YORK, THURSDAY, NOVEMBER 17, 1966 | 10 Cents

HOME EDITION BRONX
60c WEEKLY HOME DELIVERED

WHY THE JURY FREED DR. SAM

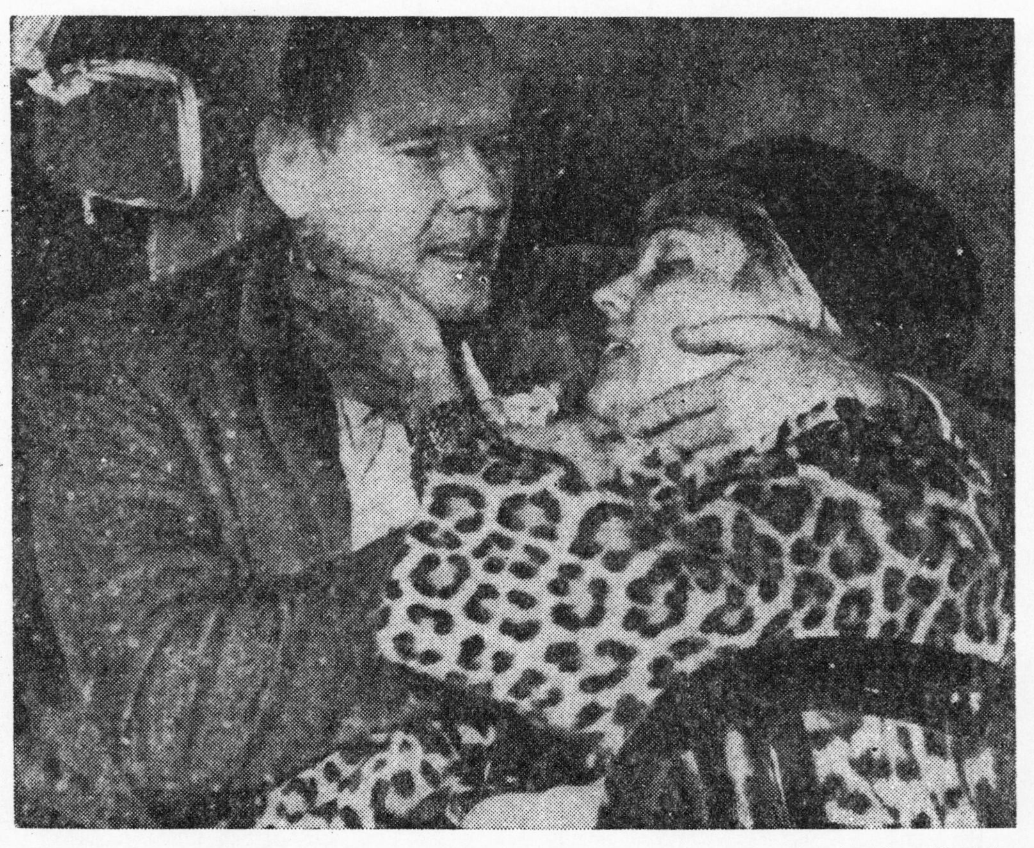

Associated Press Wirephoto

After the verdict: Ariane and Sam. Story on Page 5.

Lindsay's Shakeup: More To Come

Story on Page 2

Secrets Of Albert DeSalvo's Lust Told In His Own Words

NATIONAL

INFORMER

TRUTHFUL NEWS OF ALL FACTS OF LIFE

SPECIAL

15c

50c In Europe

Vol. 11 — No. 22 May 28, 1967

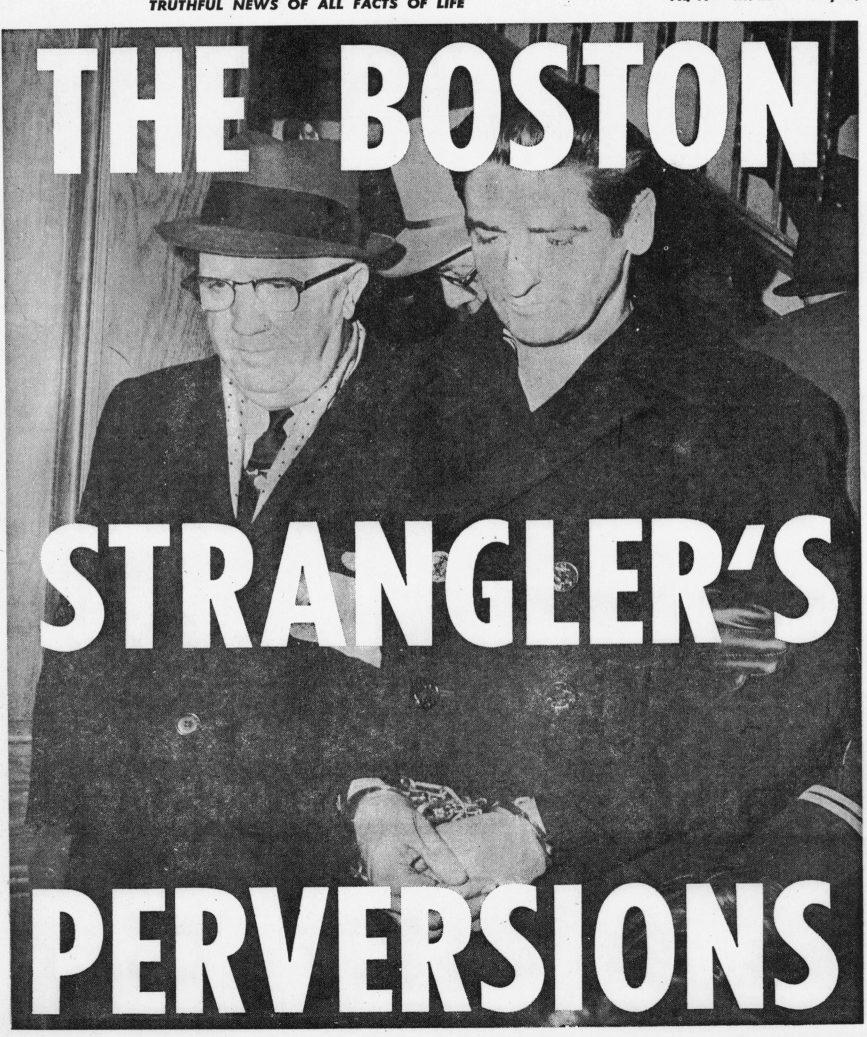

THE BOSTON STRANGLER'S PERVERSIONS

WEATHER
Clear and cool tonight.
(Details on Page 6A)

The Detroit News

FINAL EDITION

TUESDAY, JULY 25, 1967 — 94th YEAR, NO. 337 — THE HOME NEWSPAPER — 2 SECTIONS — 10 CENTS

Snipers Prolong Emergency; Death Toll Climbs to 23

Detroit's racial outbreak, costliest in the nation's history, today had settled into vicious guerilla warfare that sent the death toll to 23, including a Detroit fireman, and put the city under virtual martial law.

At least six policemen were wounded, two critically, during the night as the crackle of sniper fire echoed across the city from out Grand River almost to Grosse Pointe.

Describing Detroit as a city "out of control," President Johnson in a midnight television appearance sent 1,800 crack regular Army paratroopers into the city.

THEIR ADVANCE ELEMENTS took positions on the city's east side, scene of some of the most vicious sniping shortly before dawn. The troops were bivouacked at Southeastern and Eastern High Schools.

Another 2,900 remained in readiness at Selfridge Air Force Base, Mt. Clemens:

President Johnson's order also placed the 8,000 national guardsmen already on duty here under federal control.

Firebombing arsonists roamed the city again, and flames in dozens of areas reddened the sky. By daybreak the number of fires reported since early Sunday was more than 800.

All businesses and retail stores were given permission to reopen today by Cyrus Vance, former deputy defense secretary and now President Johnson's personal emissary.

Vance made the recommendation at 7 a.m. after a predawn tour of the city and a conference with Gov. Romney and Mayor Cavanagh.

City, state and federal offices also were authorized to reopen. City and county officials began notifying employes to come to work today.

However, Romney said his state of emergency proclamation remains in effect and that all gasoline stations, bars and theaters will remain closed. The 9 p.m. to 5:30 a.m. curfew remains in effect, Romney said.

The ban on gas stations was viewed as a possible deterrent to "business as usual." The world's motor capital was rapidly running out of gasoline for its cars.

STUNNED CITY OFFICIALS no longer attempted to put a price tag on the destruction but it had soared far past yesterday's estimate of $150 million.

"The fact of the matter is that law and order have broken down in Detroit," said President Johnson in his midnight television statement explaining why he was sending the Army paratroopers and federalizing the Michigan National Guard.

"I am sure the American people will realize that I take this action with the greatest regret — and only because of the clear, unmistakable and undisputed evidence that Gov. Romney and the local officials have been unable to bring the situation under control," Mr. Johnson said.

Declaring that the federal government should not

(Concluded on Page 8A)

- News Photo by Craig Wellman

U.S. Troops Move Into Detroit On President Johnson's Orders to Combat Rioting

Grim Johnson Orders In Troops

(Text of TV Speech and Proclamation on Page 19A)

By ERIC LUDVIGSEN
Detroit News Washington Bureau

WASHINGTON — In a dramatic nationwide telecast moments after midnight today, President Johnson grimly announced to the nation that he had sent U.S. Army paratroopers for riot duty in Detroit's stricken city center.

Mr. Johnson said:

"I am sure the American people will realize that I take this action with the greatest regret—and only because of the clear, unmistakable and undisputed evidence that Gov. Romney and the local officials have been unable to bring the situation under control."

IN THE SOLEMN, seven-minute, softly spoken statement, the President added:

"Law enforcement is a local matter. It is the responsibility of local officials and the governors of the respective states. The federal. government should not intervene — except in extraordinary circumstances.

"The fact of the matter, however, is that law and order have broken down in Detroit."

Mr. Johnson seemed bent on making the record show as clearly as possible that Romney, a possible Republican presidential candidate next year, had failed to establish law and order.

Mr. Johnson at one point said the federal government had acted because it had been "called upon by the governor and presented with proof of his inability to restore order."

IN HIS MESSAGE, Mr. Johnson mentioned seven times that Romney had initiated the action by requesting the troops. The President stressed the federal government had to respond "since it was called upon by the governor of the state and presented with proof of his inability to restore order."

The statement followed by half an hour the issuance of a presidential proclamation and an executive order, commanding rioters to "cease and desist," and authorizing Secretary of Defense Robert S. McNamara to quell the riots by force.

The orders allowed McNamara to federalize the 8,000 Michigan national guardsmen already in the city, and to employ two brigades of airborne troops airlifted to Selfridge Air Force Base earlier yesterday.

The President thus acceded to pleas from Romney, Mayor Cavanagh and Senator Robert P. Griffin, Michigan Republican, although he stressed that it was only the inability of local officials to contain the rioting that forced his hand.

The Michigan officials had appealed an earlier decision to hold the troops outside the city on an hour-to-hour basis. That decision was made by Mr. Johnson's personal representative on the scene, Cyrus K. Vance, former deputy secretary of defense, now in private law practice in New York.

As he read the statement before the television cameras in the floodlit White House little theater, Mr. Johnson was flanked by five of the nation's highest-ranking military and law enforcement officials.

In attendance were McNamara; U.S. Atty. Gen. Ramsey Clark; Army Secretary Stanley Resor; Gen. Harold K. Johnson, Army chief of staff; and FBI Director J. Edgar Hoover.

The President conferred with the five shortly before the telecast, though Clark and McNamara had been in and out of the White House all day, relaying reports from Detroit to the President.

"Pillage, looting, murder and arson have nothing to do with civil rights," the President said in soft but determined tones.

"They are criminal conduct. The federal government in the circumstances here presented has no alternative but to respond, since it was called upon by the governor of the state, and presented with proof of his inability to restore order."

AFTER MEETINGS between Vance and local officials last evening, Johnson said the "initial report was that it then appeared that the situation might be controlled without bringing the federal troops from Selfridge Air Force Base to Detroit."

But about 10:30 p.m., the President said, Vance and Lt. Gen. John L. Throckmorton, commander of the paratroopers, phoned him to say that federal intervention was "imperative."

"They described the situation in considerable detail," the President said, "and submitted as the unanimous judgement of all concerned that the situation was totally beyond

See PRESIDENT—Page 4A

'I Saw Sniper Slay Fireman'

(Pictures on Page 4A)

By JAMES L. KERWIN
Detroit News Staff Writer

A sniper's bullet killed Detroit Fire Fighter Carl E. Smith before my eyes.

Detroit News photographer Ted Gladwell and I were with eight police officers and guardsman — and Smith — pinned down by sniper fire last night outside a fire station at Mack and St. Jean.

The siege continued for two hours before it ended as suddenly as it had started, and Smith lay dead on the pavement.

The bullets seemed to come from nowhere.

That's the terrifying thing about a concealed sniper under darkness. No one knows who may be the next victim.

GLADWELL AND I, on assignment in the riot area, stumbled on the scene in a News' car just as the gunfire erupted.

Bullets shattered windows in surrounding buildings and chipped the cement near our car.

We stopped the car and ducked below the windows. Then, under a protective barrage by policemen and guardsmen, we crawled out of the line of fire.

A drunk who nearly lurched into the line of the sniper's fire was shoved to safety.

The fire station was one of the busiest in attempting to quell flames sweeping across the lower east side. In fact, Smith, a fireman for five years, had been transferred from a safer fire station.

But about 11 p.m. the Mack-St. Jean fire house came under fire. They broadcast for help. Two scout cars filled with eight patrolmen and Guardsmen road to the scene and engaged in battle with the concealed sniper.

FRANTIC PLEAS went out over emergency radios:

"We're running low on ammo!" Get some help in here."

Above their heads the sniper shattered a street light—a near miss.

After a fretful wait, other police units moved into the area, screeching through the intersection with lights out.

"Don't fire at those windows, damn it," snapped a young National Guard sergeant. The guardsman didn't want onlookers struck by wild rounds.

"You people get out of the way or you'll get shot," he shouted.

Policemen, guardsmen and frightened newsmen anxiously scanned the tops of the buildings at the intersection and the windows from which the shots were coming.

There would be a loud "pow" —much like those spectacular fireworks of the Freedom Festival earlier this month — and everyone crouched closer to the buildings or the lamp post.

THE RETURN FIRE was deafening.

"Go easy or you'll be hitting your own buddies," cautioned a helmeted policeman.

Guardsmen and police officers, fearing they were being silhouetted, began shooting out street lights.

Fire equipment crept slowly from the besieged quarters with headlights out.

Smith was still inside but was hustled into a scout car.

When a state trooper dashed across the street to blast out a light, the fireman jumped from the car, saying he wanted to get to his "rig," still back in the firehouse.

SMITH DASHED for the curb, dodged as guardsmen and newsmen looked on, and tried to duck behind a white trash barrel.

A shot cracked and the young fireman fell hard on the curb.

A policeman ran across the street and pounced on top of him to shield Smith. Another policeman drove The News car over him as a shield.

Guardsmen and police rattled off a terrific round of fire, but it was too late—Smith was dead and the sniper had vanished.

Eventually, when firing ceased, an ambulance arrived and removed the body.

Then police moved on to seek out other snipers.

Pontiac Rioting Leaves 2 Dead

Detroit News Metropolitan Bureau

Negroes rioted in Pontiac last night, and two of them were shot and killed by store owners.

One of the owners, Rep. Arthur J. Law, Pontiac Democrat, was being questioned in the fatal shooting of a 17-year-old youth.

In Mt. Clemens, Negroes heckled and stoned firemen and roamed briefly through the city's north side. But they were quickly dispersed. There was no shooting.

There also was trouble in Grand Rapids and Flint.

THE PONTIAC riot began about 10 p.m., when bands of Negroes—most of them youths —began breaking windows of stores on Orchard Lake road south of the city's main business district. They also set fires with Molotov cocktails.

But Pontiac police — reinforced by police from several neighboring communities and by State Police—kept the rioters moving and largely prevented wholesale looting.

By 2:30 a.m., 52 persons had been arrested, and police thought the trouble was diminishing.

But a half hour later, shooting broke out in the largely Negro south side of the city, and the first death occurred.

Police said Bobby Reeves, a 25-year-old Pontiac Negro, was shot and killed by Joe Guzman, a store owner. Guzman told police that he fired at a car which had pulled up to his grocery store, and from which someone had pitched out a Molotov cocktail.

POLICE SAID a car they believe to be the same one dropped Reeves a short time later at the emergency entrance to Pontiac General Hospital, where he was found by attendants and pronounced dead of a gunshot wound.

The second fatal shooting was at Law's grocery store, 200 Earlmoor.

Authorities said Law, once mayor of Pontiac, and his son, Charles, 27, both fired shotguns from the store after someone had thrown a trash can through the front window.

One of the charges struck and killed Alfred Taylor, 17, a Negro, of Pontiac.

An assistant Oakland County prosecutor, who took a statement from Law, said it had not been determined whether Law's shot or his son's killed the Taylor youth.

Pontiac Patrolman Santiago Surna was struck in the neck by shotgun pellets fired from a rooftop in the Negro section.

(Concluded on Page 4A)

The Riot Picture

Dead—23.
Total injuries—more than 500.
Injured by gunshot—22.
Fires—837.
Stores looted—over 1,500.
Damage—over $150 million.
Arrests—1,876.
Injured Detroit police—37.
Injured State Police—3.
Injured soldiers—6.
Injured firemen—17.

•

Other Riot Stories, Pictures:

Section A — Pages 2, 4, 5, 7, 8, 9, 10, 13, 17, 18, 19, 24
Section B — Pages 7, 8, 18

Today's Index

JULY
23 24 25 26 27 28 29
30 31
AUGUST
1 2 3 4 5
6 7 8 9 10 11 12
13 14 15 16 17 18

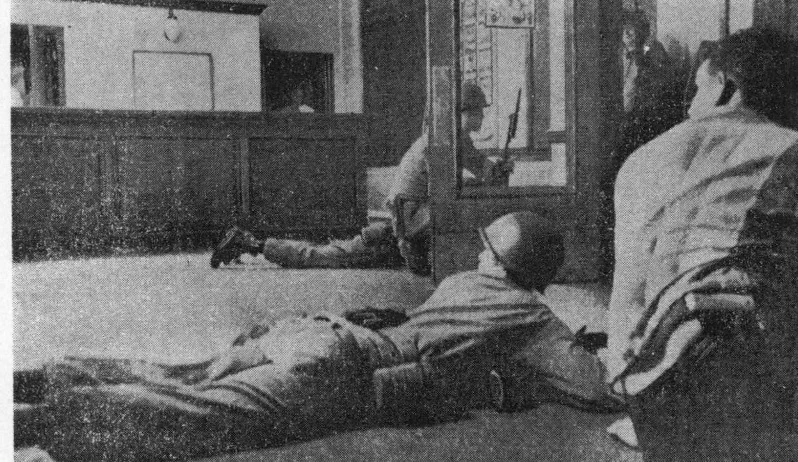

POLICE STATION UNDER FIRE — National guardsmen hit the floor as shots ring out at the McGraw Police Station. The snipers fled before guardsmen returned the fire. No one was hurt

FINAL **THE COMMERCIAL APPEAL** FINAL

129th YEAR—No. 96 ***** MEMPHIS, TENN., FRIDAY MORNING, APRIL 5, 1968 60 PAGES PRICE 10 CENTS

DR. KING IS SLAIN BY SNIPER

Looting, Arson Touched Off By Death

GUARDSMEN RETURN; CURFEW IS ORDERED

By RICHARD LENTZ

Looting, arson and shooting began minutes after the death of Dr. Martin Luther King Jr. lates last night and in hours Tennessee National Guardsmen arrived to take over street patrols in riot-torn Memphis.

Negroes began swarming into streets, smashing windows and setting fires shortly after the announcement of the civil rights leader's death at 7 p.m.

As the news of Dr. King's slaying flashed, Negroes clashed with police as far away as Miami, in Jackson, Miss., and in Nashville, where another 4,000 guardsmen were called out to keep the peace.

In Memphis, police had arrested 80 persons, including two juveniles and two women by 1 a.m. There were at least 28 persons reported hurt and a steady flow of injured was being treated at hospitals.

No one had been reported killed in the turmoil.

The most seriously injured person was Ellis Tate of 88 West Utah, whom police said was shot while looting. He was in critical condition at John Gaston Hospital.

Officers said he fired at officers with a rifle when they came into a liquor store he was looting. They returned his fire and he was hit.

A 24-hour general curfew was ordered last night, with travel allowed only for emergency or health reasons. Schools, shops and businesses were ordered closed. The curfew will remain in effect indefinitely.

At the biggest fire of the night, policemen armed with submachine guns and riot guns guarded firemen who were battling flames that arched 100 feet into the air at O. W. Ferrell Co. at 1001 North Second Street.

Within minutes, 14 pieces of fire equipment were on the scene. There were no incidents.

Black smoke from burning barrels of tar and piles of roofing at the building supplies company rolled over the area.

Earlier, piles of boxes 20 feet high had been set on fire behind Leone's Liberty Cash Crocery at 485 Vance. The flames were endangering an apartment complex and firemen after burning through live electrical wires. The fire was put out in minutes after Deptuy Fire Chief R. F. Doyle shouted "Knock It down, knock it down. Let's get out of here."

Tennessee Highway Patrolmen were reported moving in force toward Memphis to supplement police and guardsmen. More than 200 of the state police were sent into Memphis when violence erupted March 28.

Arkansas Gov. Winthrop Rockefeller sent state troopers to Memphis to observe the rioting. Last week he ordered 175 Arkansas guardsmen called for duty in West Memphis.

Officials said firemen from Station One answered eight calls in 20 minutes at one point during the night.

A store on Firestone Boulevard was burned so completely it could not be immediately identified.

First elements of Guardsmen reported no trouble as they cautiously patrolled Memphis streets last night. Three artillery batteries were committed to the city and nine patrols of 16 guardsmen each were deployed on streets.

A spokesman in the governor's office said Governor Buford Ellingtons also was in contact with United States Atty. Gen. Ramsey Clark, presumably to discuss the availability of federal troops for use in Memphis.

A straight line to Washington was kept open last night at Police Headquarters at Second and Adams.

Just minutes after Dr. King died, city offices began receiving telephone threats against the life of Mayor Henry Loeb, who was traveling by car to the University of Mississippi for a speech. Notified of the death and outbreak of violence and looting, Mayor Loeb quickly returned to City Hall here.

Governor Ellington, who had ordered the 4,000 Guardsmen into Memphis March 28 after an outbreak of looting and rioting during a march led by Dr. King, said "I can fully appreciate the feelings and emotions which this crime has aroused.

"But for the b e n e f i t of everyone, all of our citizens must exercise caution a n d good judgment."

The c u r f e w immediately closed all liquor stores and establishments selling beer, firearms or ammunition, as it did last Thursday.

Shooting began at 7:17 p.m. when shots were reported in the vicinity of Tillman and Johnson.

The worst sniping appeared to be in the Springdale-Howell area, where two police officers were reported wounded at 8:30 by a gunman shooting from around the corner of a building. At 9:20, police cars were still under fire in the same area.

Condition of the two wounded policemen was not immediately known. They were hit by glass when their squad car windshield was shot out.

Fire and Police Director Frank Holloman said, "Rioting and looting is rampant" in the city.

Mr. Holloman, listening to calls from police radio bands and reports from the field, said his 35 tactical units had the situation fairly well under control by about 9:15 p.m. and looting and other violent incidents had subsided somewhat.

"Remain off the streets, keep your children at home and remain calm," he said. "We are doing everything we can do. I call upon all citizens of Memphis . . . to cooperate fully with officers as they do

(Continued on Page 3)

WARSAW REGIME RAPPED

More Voice In Government For People Asked

WARSAW, April 4. —(UPI) — A pro-government Roman Catholic newspaper Thursday criticized the all-powerful ruling Communist coalition for not allowing the people more voice in government and called for more democracy in Poland's socialist system.

The attack by Slowo Powszechne against the Communist-dominated National Unity Front was mild but considered surprising. The editorial came in the midst of a wave of dismissals of high-ranking government officials and followed student demands for reforms and more freedom.

Two more officials were sacked during the day —Daniel Kac, chairman of the Office of State Economic Reserves, and Welhelm Billig, the government plenipotentiary for the use of nuclear energy. It brought to 22 the number of high officials removed since the shakeup began in the wake of student demonstrations.

Most of those dismissed have been Jews. It was not known whether Kac or Billig were Jewish.

Polish Jews have been blamed for helping stir student unrest.

Firemen Battle Blaze At Ferrell Lumber Co. At 1001 North Second —Staff Photo by Sam Melhorn

An Editorial—

Memphis Needs Calm

THE assassination of Dr. Martin Luther King in Memphis was a cowardly action. It was a tragedy for Memphis.

The need now is for the community to remain calm and restrained despite the increased tensions which this action has caused. As President Johnson said, all America must "reject blind violence," and "search their hearts."

All citizens should keep in mind that this was the deed of an individual who in some warped-minded way thought he could bring an end to a complex problem with a simple, primitive action.

THE death of Dr. King does not solve any problems in Memphis or in the nation. Indeed, it aggravates the existing problems and makes more urgent the need for settlement of the Memphis dispute that precipitated the assassination. Mayor Loeb and the City Council must move swiftly to that end now.

This is not a time for discussion of the provocations which lay behind this action. Murder has been done. Swift apprehension of the killer and just punishment must follow.

To many who were not aware of the angry forces which have been tearing away at the structure of this community in recent weeks, this should bring understanding. There should be no further divisive actions which we all would certainly regret. Rather, this should serve as an example of what such racial rending causes, and should result in solidifying of sentiment in the community more than ever before.

IT IS time now that those of us in all circumstances and of all attitudes realize in the shock of this emotional action that somehow our difficulties and apparent differences must be resolved without further violence and bloodshed.

Hate has produced its ultimate product at the ultimate price.

THE Commercial Appeal is aware that all law enforcement agencies are doing their utmost to apprehend the killer, but we also realize that information from any source could be helpful. Therefore, The Commercial Appeal offers a reward of $25,000 for information leading to the arrest and conviction of the person or persons responsible for this monstrous crime.

Open Housing Voted

LANSING, Mich., April 4. — (AP) — The Michigan Senate Thursday approved a controversial open housing bill 22-14 after turning down two substitutes for the administration-backed measure. The senators also defeated amendments to provide for a public referendum on the issue and exempt individual home owners.

On The Inside Pages—

Humphrey Comes Close

VICE PRESIDENT Hubert Humphrey comes very close to announcing his candidacy for the Democratic presidential nomination. —Page 14.

HOWARD HUGHES, who has spent 125 million dollars in Las Vegas in one year, buys 480 acres of gold and silver mining land. —Page 32.

SPORTS

PIRATES MUST BE rated a contender but Tim McCarver rates them out as a winner. —Page 27.

* * *

TELEPHONES:

NEWS AND GENERAL ..526-8811
CLASSIFIED ADS 526-8892
CIRCULATION 525-7801
SPORTS SCORES 525-8651

* * *

Today's 60-page editions of The Commercial Appeal include a 12-page tabloid section for Woolco, featuring an Easter Parade of Values.

The Weather

U.S. DEPARTMENT OF COMMERCE

FOR MEMPHIS and vicinity — Fair through Saturday. Cool today and tonight and a little warmer Saturday. High today about 58, winds northwesterly 6 to 12 miles per hour. Low Friday night near 34, with chance of frost.

Sunrise 5:42; sunset 6:25

FIVE-DAY OUTLOOK

Temperatures two to six degrees below normal. Normal high 69, low 48. Warmer over weekend, turning cooler again early next week. Rainfall will average near one inch with chance of locally heavier amounts. Thundershowers most likely near the first of the week.

YESTERDAY'S REPORT

High, 72 degrees at midnight.

Low 44 degrees at midnight.

Mean (midway between high and low), 58. Normal mean for date, 57.

HOURLY READINGS

4 a.m.	70	4 p.m.	57
6 a.m.	70	6 p.m.	55
8 a.m.	64	8 p.m.	50
10 a.m.	57	10 p.m.	46
Noon	59	12 p.m.	44
2 p.m.	59	2 a.m.	42

Temperature 7 a.m., 69; 7 p.m., 53.
Precipitation at Airport, .19.
Dewpoint (condensation temperature) at midnight, 30; barometer reading at midnight 30.13 rising.
Precipitation Jan. 1-April 3, 15.98 inches, which is .36 inches below normal.

A YEAR AGO YESTERDAY

Maximum temperature, 79; minimum, 46; rainfall, none.
Precipitation Jan. 1-April 4, 9.21 inches, which was 7.30 inches below normal.

(Map, Forecast on Page 35)

First Lady Ends Visit

WASHINGTON, April 4. — (AP) — Mrs. Lyndon B. Johnson returned Thursday from two days spent at Mar-a-Lago, the Palm Beach, Fla., home of Mrs. Marjorie Merriweather Post. The First Lady flew back in Mrs. Post's private plane. She plans to leave early Friday for a five-day tour of Texas with 40 foreign editors.

Dr. Martin Luther King

Rights And Political Leaders Voice Anguish, Shock, Grief

Johnson Speaks For Saddened Nation And Condemns Violence—Some Express Fear Of Increased Terrorism

From Our Press Services

The nation's civil rights and political leaders reacted with anguish, shock and grief last night at the slaying of Dr. Martin Luther King Jr. in Memphis.

There also was fear that the slaying could lead to more violence.

President Johnson spoke of an "America shocked and saddened" by the assassination as he condemned violence, lawlessness and divisiveness.

The President appeared in the doorway of the White House offices, stern-faced and spoke on all television and radio networks.

"I ask every American citizen," he said, "to reject the blind violence that has struck down Dr. King, who lived by nonviolence."

The President urged prayers for peace and understanding in the land and said:

"We can achieve nothing by lawlessness and divisiveness among the American people."

He said he hopes all Americans would s e a r c h their hearts.

Vice President Hubert H. Humphrey said the slaying "brings shame to our country. An apostle of nonviolence has been the victim of violence."

The vice president said, however, that his death will bring new strength to the cause he fought for.

Former Vice President Richard M. Nixon sent a telegram to Mrs. King, which said: "Dr. King's death is a great personal tragedy for everyone who knew him and a great tragedy for the nation. "Mrs. Nixon joines me in sympathy and prayers for you and your family in this terrible ordeal."

New York Mayor John V. Lindsay: "The people of our city of every race, I am sure, will join hands in paying tribute to him. Our greatest tribute to him will be to bear ourselves as he would want us to — with dignity and prayer."

Senator Wayne Morse (D-Ore.), said Dr. King's death is "one of the saddest tragedies to befall the nation" and warned that the shooting will add to "a very serious domestic crisis. It's going to increase marching across our country."

Fred Meely, a spokesman for the militant Student Non-Violent Coordinating Committee, said, "There is no real comment that we can make. Everybody knows what happened and everybody knows why it happened and the black people in this country know what they have to do about it. That's all I have to say."

Tennessee Gov. Buford Ellington sent a telegram to Dr. King's widow saying he was "deeply s a d d e n e d and shocked" by the shooting.

Representative Dan Kuykendall (R-Tenn.) in Washington said:

"This dastardly, cowardly act on the part of this unknown person is of great grief to me and, I know, to my city. This is an example of how violence breeds violence. Let's hope and pray that the action and

(Continued on Page 12)

Intensive Manhunt Is Quickly Mounted

President Johnson's Plane Is Reported En Route To Memphis; State Guard Alerted

By JOHN MEANS

A sniper shot and killed Dr. Martin Luther King last night as he stood on the balcony of a downtown hotel.

The most intensive manhunt in the city's history was touched off minutes after the shooting

Violence broke out in Memphis, Nashville, Birmingham, Miami, Raleigh, Washington, New York and other cities as news of the assassination swept the nation.

National leaders, including President Lyndon Johnson, and aides close to the slain 39-year-old Nobel Peace Prize winner, urged the nation to stand calm and avoid violence.

The entire nation was tense.

It was learned early this morning that Air Force One — the President's plane — had left Washington. It may be en route to Memphis.

There was no confirmation that the President was aboard.

The slaying of Dr. King brought Tennessee National Guardsmen back into Memphis. The entire 11,000 men in the state guard were on alert early today.

Memphis was placed under a tight, 24-hour curfew by Mayor Henry Loeb.

All schools will be closed today. Parents were urged to keep their children at home.

A rifle bullet slammed into Dr. King's jaw and neck at 6:01 p.m.

He died in the emergency room at St. Joseph Hospital at 7:05 p.m.

King, the foremost American civil rights leader, was alone on the second-floor walk of the Lorraine Hotel at 406 Mulberry when the bullet struck.

A young white man is believed to have fired the fatal shot from a nearby building.

Looters and vandals roamed the streets despite the imposition of a tight curfew. Shooting was widespread. National Guardsmen were rushed to the North Memphis area of Springdale and Howell after bullets blasted the windshield out of a police car near there.

Police — estimated at more than 150 — descended on the south Memphis hotel, sealed off the area, and almost immediately broadcast a description of the sniper: a while male, 30 to 32 years old, 5 feet, 10 inches tall, about 165 pounds, dark to sandy hair, medium build, ruddy complexion as if he worked outside, wearing a black suit and white shirt.

Frank R. Ahlgren, editor of The Commercial Appeal, announced that the newspaper will pay a $25,000 reward for information leading to the arrest and conviction of Dr. King's assassin.

Dr. King returned to Memphis Wednesday morning to map plans for another downtown march — scheduled for next Monday — in support of the city's striking sanitation workers. He had spent part of the day yesterday awaiting reports from his attorneys, who were in Federal Judge Bailey Brown's courtroom asking that a temporary restraining order against the proposed march be lifted.

The injunction was obtained by the city after Dr. King's first march broke out in violence downtown, brought the National Guard to the city in strength and seriously damaged the Negro leader's reputation for nonviolence. For the first time in his career, he had been present during violence, and it was this picture he was planning to dispel with the march next Monday.

Mayor Loeb declared today, tomorrow and Sunday as days of mourning, and said all flags in the city would be lowered "with appropriate observances."

All ministers, priests and rabbis in the Memphis area have been asked to meet at 10 a.m. today at St. Mary's Cathedral (Episcopal).

Frank Holloman, fire and police director, who took personal command of the murder investigation minutes after the shooting, said "every resource" of city, county, state and federal law enforcement agencies "is committed and dedicated to identifying and apprehending the person or persons responsible."

Mayor Loeb ordered a tight curfew, much stricter than the one imposed after last week's rioting. "All movement is restricted except for health or emergency reasons," the order said.

A few minutes after the shooting, police reported a high-speed chase in which a blue Pontiac was being pursued by a white Mustang out the Austin Peay Highway. Shots were reported fired between the two cars. A white Mustang, seen near the scene of the slaying, was still being sought by police early today.

Officials of Dr. King's Southern Christian L e a d e r s h i p Conference, some of whom were standing near him on the narrow balcony of the hotel when he was shot, continued to urge his nonviolent teachings. His chief lieutenant, Dr. Ralph Abernathy, went to the Mason Temple last night to address a gathering of Dr. King's followers.

"Let us live for what he died for," Dr. Abernathy told the mourning group. "If we respect his leadership, if we appreciate the service that he rendered, then we must do all in our power to carry forth the work that is incomplete.

"If a riot or violence would erupt in Memphis tonight, Dr. King in Heaven would not be pleased."

A few had other ideas. "He died for us, and we're going to die for him," a young man shouted.

Early Friday morning, Mr. Holloman said police believe the murder weapon was a 30-caliber, pump-action Remington rifle equipped with a telescopic sight. Such a weapon was among those stolen Tuesday night from Dowdle Sporting Goods Co. at 2896 Walnut Grove Road.

"The distance over which the bullet traveled before it struck Dr. King was 205 feet, 3 inches, at a down angle," Mr. Holloman said.

He also detailed "other evidence . . . that may help us identify the assassin. The shot was fired from the window of a common bathroom at the end of the hall on the east side of the building at 420 South Main. The suspect checked into the boarding house between 3 and 3:30 p.m. His room was close to the bathroom. The suspect was a white man, 6 feet tall, about 165-175 pounds, between 26 and 32 years of age."

"We do know he bought a pair of binoculars this (Thursday) afternoon in Memphis . . . The man was seen to run from the 420 South Main building and discard the gun and a suitcase at 424 South Main. He simply faded. Nobody saw him get in the car, but a white Mustang was seen to flee the area.

"The evidence we now have indicates that only one man was physically in the area (the bathroom)."

Mr. Holloman would not reveal where the binoculars were purchased, and said he did not know if the name used by the sniper is his real one.

The gun found at the Main street address was turned over to the FBI for ballistics tests. Mr. Holloman said his office is "working closely with the FBI" on other aspects of the investigation.

The former FBI officer also said the investigation was "impaired by the riot situation which developed almost immediately."

"The bullet knocked him off his feet," said the Rev. Jesse Jackson, executive staff member of SCLC. "It sounded like

(Continued on Page 12)

BOSTON HERALD TRAVELER

THE WEATHER — FAIR, MILD (PAGE 2) — WEDNESDAY, JUNE 5, 1968 — FIFTY-SIX PAGES — HA 6-3000 TEN CENTS

EXTRA

Bob Kennedy Shot in Calif.

Wounded After Victory, Condition Critical

He Won--Then Tragedy

LOS ANGELES — Robert F. Kennedy turned the Democratic presidential primary race around yesterday with a smashing victory over Eugene J. McCarthy in the California primary.

Projection of returns from a tidal wave of votes, a record 72-plus per cent of those eligible in the most critical of the tests between the two men, indicated Kennedy might even take a majority in a three-man contest.

(Continued on Page Twenty-six)

By W. J. McCARTHY

LOS ANGELES—Robert F. Kennedy, brother of assassinated President John F. Kennedy, was shot early today in his Ambassador Hotel headquarters minutes after he had thanked his workers for his apparent California primary victory.

First reports were that Kennedy was shot in the hip in the kitchen of the hotel. As he lay on the floor, he had blood on his face, but his eyes were open.

Kennedy said to persons who clustered around him, "Will you please move back and give me some air?"

Four shots were fired, according to those taking part in the victory celebration at the downtown Los Angeles hotel.

One of the shots struck an American Broadcasting Company associate director, William Weisel, in the hand.

Los Angeles police seized a man and hustled him away. It was not known immediately whether he was suspected of the shootings.

Kennedy and Smith were taken to the Central Receiving Hospital, not far from the hotel.

Before he was taken from the hotel kitchen on a stretcher, Kennedy complained of pains in his back of head and neck.

Later reports made clear that the gunfire broke out as Kennedy was pushing his way through the crowd in the

(Continued on Page Two)

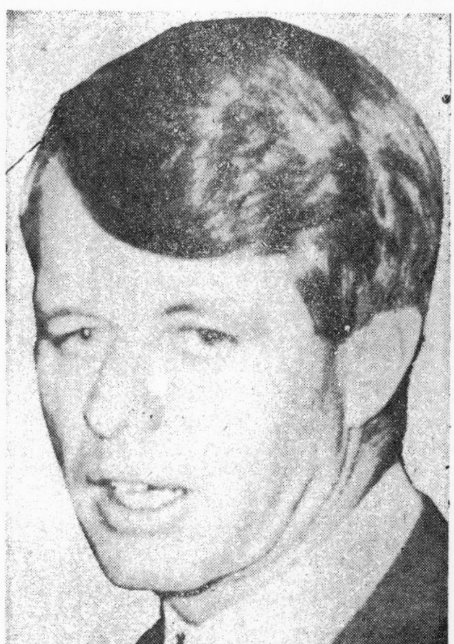

SEN. ROBERT KENNEDY

LATE BRIEFS

At Senator Eugene McCarthy's headquarters in the Beverly Hilton, the Minnesota Senator asked all those gathered in the ballroom to say a silent prayer for Kennedy.

McCarthy urged them to then go home to say more prayers in their own way.

One of the witnesses said the man who was captured after Kennedy was shot "was yelling something about saving the country or something. What he said was something like, 'I did it for my country.'"

Senator Kennedy was given the last rites of the Catholic church in the hospital at 1 a.m.

Doctors at Central Receiving Hospital in Los Angeles said Senator Kennedy's condition was critical.

Less than an hour after the shooting, Kennedy was transferred from Central Receiving Hospital to the nearby Hospital of Good Samaritan.

Ann Gargan to Notify RFK's Parents in Morning

By FRANK FALACCI

HYANNIS PORT — The waterfront mansion of Ambassador Joseph P. Kennedy was quiet las night when the eldest son of the Kennedy clan was shot in alifornia.

Joseph P. Kennedy, Mrs. Rose Kennedy and their neice, Ann Gargen, were asleep at 3:15 a.m. when first word came over the wires and television.

She was awakened by a telephone call from a news service. Seconds after she hung up, Send. Edward M. Kennedy called to notify the family of Robert's condition. At that time he was uncertain of his brother's condition.

MRS. JOSEPH KENNEDY

He told her that Stephen Smith was not wounded but was accompanying Robert to the hospital. z

She said she would not awaken either of the parents to tell them.

However, Mrs. Kennedy is an early riser who usually attends the 7 a.m. Mass at St. Francis Xavier Church. She would be told when she wakes.

Joseph P. Kennedy would be told in the morning. "if he can take it," she said.

This is the third time that Miss Gargan has had the burden of informing the parents of a family tragedy. The first was the plane crash in Northampton, Mass., that hospitalized Sen. Kennedy for months and the second was the Assassination of President Kennedy.

Artillery Duel in Violent Outburst

Israeli Jets Attack In Clash with Jordan

By THE ASSOCIATED PRESS

Israeli jet fighters attacked Jordan yesterday while Israeli and Jordanian ground gunners traded thunderous artillery barrages like those of the six-day 1967 Middle East war that began a year ago Wednesday.

Jordanian and Israeli accounts of casualties, damage and how the fighting started varied widely. With the shooting dragging on past nightfall, ambassadors of the two countries took up an exchange of charges at the United Nations in New York.

Officials in Jordan said the Israelis fired first in "a surprise attack." Israeli spokesmen said the attack across the Jordan River was in reply to the shelling of four Israeli farm cooperatives.

"We hope that this will teach Jordan the lesson once and for all that the shelling of settlements and army positions is taboo," Maj. Gen. Haim Bar-Lev, Israel's chief of staff, told a newsman.

Israeli Ambassador Yosef Tekoah said at the United Nations three farm people were killed and five wounded in "a large-scale Jordanian assault." He said it became necessary "to order Israeli aircraft to take action in self-defense to silence the sources of fire."

Muhammad H. el-Farra, Jordan's U.N. ambassador, said 30 persons were killed, 60 wounded and raging forest fires set off near the Jordanian city of Irbid, south of the Sea of Galilee.

(Continued on Page Four)

Allies Intercept Reds, Kill 250 In Fierce Battles

By RICHARD V. OLIVER

SAIGON—U. S. and South Vietnamese infantry intercepted two large forces of Communist troops advancing on Saigon and killed an estimated 250 of them in fierce battles, military spokesmen reported yesterday. In one clash Vietcong used a wounded GI as bait to cut down methodically fellow infantrymen coming to his aid.

The biggest battle, in the Mekong Delta southwest of the capital, proved costly to the Americans. Spokesmen said 36 U. S. soldiers were killed and 62 wounded in the fighting between U. S. 9th Division soldiers and a battalion of Vietcong. "More than 200" Communists were killed in the same battle, the spokesmen said.

(Continued on Page Eleven)

Shot Fired at Bank Teller

Three Gunmen Grab $108,000

By TOM MURRAY and CHARLES LEVERONI

HANOVER — Three gunmen wearing flesh colored Halloween masks yesterday robbed the Rockland Trust Co. branch bank in the Tedeschi Shopping Center and escaped with $108,000.

One held a gun at the head of Thomas F. Reagan of Rockland, head teller, and fired a shot past his ear when he delayed in opening a safe.

The money had been set aside for a pickup by a Brink's armored truck which arrived an hour after the robbery.

Reagan protested he couldn't open the safe.

"You're a liar," the bandit shouted.

He pushed Reagan into some shelves and as Reagan was bent over, fired a shot by his right ear. The bullet smashed through a trash barrel and imbedded itself in a wall near the floor.

Reagan opened the safe, the bandit scooped up the money and threw Reagan into a door as he fled with his companion to the waiting car.

Reagan, three girl tellers and two customers were in the bank when two gunmen entered. One carried a pistol and the other

(Continued on Page Fourteen)

Two Pour Paint on Draft Files

By EARL MARCHAND

A young man and woman, described as "hippie types," yesterday poured two quarts of black paint over some 700 Selective Service records in an 11th floor office of the Custom House.

The FBI has launched an intensive investigation to apprehend the pair, who pulled off their act with precision and left the building untouched.

The Massachusetts Selective Service director, Col. Paul Feeney, said yesterday that the damaged records would result in "closer surveillance at local (Selective Service) boards throughout the state."

Col. Feeney said that 500 were the records of 1-As already examined, and the others of 1-As

(Continued on Page Twelve)

He Grows Vegetables at Bridgewater

Inmate Pleads to Stay

By BOB CREAMER

One of Bridgewater's "forgotten men," illegally held in maximum security for nearly half his 62 years, told a judge yesterday he'd rather not leave, at least not until the vegetable growing season is over.

But the plea for more time made by the inmate, Willis M. Stone, was denied by Judge Allan M. Hale because the man's "best interests would not be served if he remains" at Bridgewater.

The judge, sitting in a unique session of Plymouth Superior Court on Ward B of the hospital's unit for the criminally insane, ordered Stone transfered to Taunton State Hospital.

Stone works his own garden at Bridgewater and what he grows he can sell to employes there and make as much as $60. That's why, he explained, he'd just as soon remain through fall.

On Oct. 15, 1935, Stone entered old Charlestown Prison to serve 4 to 8 years for robbery. Two years later he was transfered to Bridgewater. His prison term expired on Oct. 14, 1943. But nothing happened to Stone. He remained in maximum security and nobody ever paid any attention to him until yesterday.

Stone is still mentally ill, Dr. Lawrence Barrows, a Bridgewater psychiatrist said, but his "prognosis is quite good" and there's a chance that someday he might work in a garden as a free man.

(Continued on Page Nineteen)

JUDGE ALLAN HALE

LAWRENCE BARROWS

LBJ Urges Russia Aid World Peace

By MERRIMAN SMITH

GLASSBORO, N.J.—President Johnson, returning to the college town where he and Soviet Premier Alexei Kosygin kindled the "spirit of Hollybush" a year ago, made a new plea to Russia yesterday for world peace—including an offer to discuss disarmament.

The road to peace, the President told the graduating class at Glassboro State College, "is far less rocky when the world's two greatest powers—the United States and the Soviet Union —are willing to travel part way together."

Standing only 200 yards from Hollybush, the college president's home where he and Kosygin

(Continued on Page Ten)

Warhol Assailant Loses Cool

By IRA RIFKIN

NEW YORK — The man-hating actress-playwright who shot and critically wounded "Pop" art and movie pioneer Andy Warhol lost her cool in court yesterday and shouted "I didn't do it for nothing."

While the artist's assailant, Valerie Solanas, was being arraigned for attempted murder and possession of a dangerous weapon, Warhol fought for his life at Columbus Hospital. Physicians said he showed some improvement and had slightly better than a 50-50 chance for survival.

Miss Solanas, 28-year-old star of Warhol's recent film, "I, A Man," indicated to Criminal Court Judge David Getzoff that the 36-year-old Pasha of the pop art movement had tried to stop her from getting a play she had written published or produced because he had first claim on it.

"It was reported in the papers that I shot Andy because he wouldn't produce my play, but it was for the opposite reason," she shouted. "He had a legal claim on my work. It is not often I shoot somebody. I didn't do it for nothing."

Miss Solanas had to be pulled from the courtroom after Getzoff put the arraignment over for 24 hours to allow time for a preliminary psychiatric examination "in view of the defendant's conduct." He appointed a legal aid attorney to represent her over her protestations that she intended to "defend myself."

(Continued on Page Fifty-six)

INDEX

"All the News That's Fit to Print"

The New York Times

LATE CITY EDITION

Weather: Cloudy, showers likely today. Clearing tonight, fair tomorrow. Temp. range: today 80-70. Saturday 85-69. Temp.-Hum. Index yesterday 76. Complete U.S. report on Page 79.

SECTION ONE

VOL. CXVIII....No. 40,741

NEW YORK, SUNDAY, AUGUST 10, 1969

60¢ beyond 50-mile zone from New York City, except Long Island. 75¢ beyond 200-mile radius. Higher in air delivery cities.

50 CENTS

LINDSAY PRAISES NIXON PROPOSAL ON WELFARE AID

Calls It 'Most Important Step in Field in Generation,' but Believes City Is Slighted

WILL HELP DRAFT BILL

Mayor Says He Will Use Role to Seek a 'Fair Share' of Tax Relief for Residents

By MAURICE CARROLL

Mayor Lindsay praised President Nixon's welfare proposals yesterday as "the most important step forward by the Federal Government in this field in a generation," but said there was not enough money in the plan for New York City.

He estimated that the city would get $20-million a year more as a result of the proposed welfare changes. The current city budget forecasts that New York City will spend $1.5-billion this year on one million welfare recipients.

The Mayor said that he had been "invited by the White House to assist in the final drafting of this legislation" and that he would seek a "fair share of tax relief" for the city.

Mr. Lindsay, who had been sent an advance text of the President's speech, sat with six aides in his Gracie Mansion office watching Mr. Nixon on television Friday night as he made his proposals to overhaul the present Federal welfare systems.

A 'Critical Point'

The group stayed up until 2:30 A.M., reshaping drafts of reaction statements that had been prepared by the staff of Mitchell I. Ginsberg, the city's Human Resources Administrator. They met again at breakfast at 8:15 to decide on the final language.

Although praising the thrust of the President's program, Mr. Lindsay said in his statement that it had failed to "relieve the unfair burden of welfare on local taxpayers."

"On this critical point, the program for welfare reform is very disappointing for New York City," he said. "The President's proposal will distribute over $3-billion nationally, but of that amount the plan would give New York City only $20-million—less than 1 per cent for the relief of local tax contributions to welfare. The President's plan fails completely to correct the present inequities in the distribution of Federal welfare assistance."

Mr. Ginsberg, in a separate statement, noted that city offi-

Continued on Page 33, Column 1

F.P.C. ASKS CON ED TO DISCUSS PLANS

Washington Meeting Set Up for Information Purposes

By PAUL L. MONTGOMERY

The staff of the Federal Power Commission has invited representatives of the Consolidated Edison Company to a meeting in Washington next Wednesday to discuss the utility's power shortage and its plans for the rest of the summer.

An official of the commission's Bureau of Power said in Washington yesterday that the meeting was "not an investigation, just a request for information." A Con Edison spokesman said the utility would cooperate fully.

The commission has been monitoring Con Edison operations since Monday, when it was disclosed that the breakdown of a one-million-kilowatt generator in the utility's Ravenswood plant had brought its capacity down dangerously close to the city's total demand for power during peak periods.

The F.P.C. official said yesterday that Wednesday's meeting was simply "an effort to enlighten the staff so that we can advise the commissioners."

He described the discussion

Continued on Page 40, Column 1

Actress Is Among 5 Slain At Home in Beverly Hills

Sharon Tate, 2d Woman and 3 Men Victims—Suspect Is Seized

By STEVEN V. ROBERTS

Special to The New York Times

LOS ANGELES, Aug. 9—Five persons, including the actress Sharon Tate, were found this morning brutally murdered in a home in a secluded area of Beverly Hills.

The home, perched on a wooded hillside overlooking the city of Los Angeles, was being rented by Miss Tate and her husband, Roman Polanski, the movie director, who was in London at the time writing a script for a new movie.

The other victims were identified as Jay Sebring, a men's hair stylist well known in Hollywood social circles; Voyteck Frykowski a Polish film director said to be a close friend of Mr. Polanski's; Mr. Frykowski's girl friend, Abigail Folger, a member of the Folger coffee family, and a fifth man who remained unidentified.

The police arrested William Garretson, a 19-year-old caretaker, and charged him with suspected murder. Mr. Garretson was asleep in a small cottage near the main house of the property when the police arrived this morning.

The Los Angeles coroner, Thomas Noguchi, told a news conference that there was no evidence that a party had taken place or that narcotics had been used. He said that no murder weapon had been found. He also said that there was no

Continued on Page 63, Column 4

Associated Press

Sharon Tate

Marine Report Predicted Race Unrest Before Killing

By E. W. KENWORTHY

Special to The New York Times

WASHINGTON, Aug. 9—Three months before a white marine was killed as a result of a racial clash at Camp Lejeune, N. C., a committee of seven officers warned the camp's commanding general that "an explosive situation of major proportions has been created and continues to be aggravated."

In a report and proposed statement of policy, which was obtained by The New York Times, the committee laid the

Text of committee's report will be found on Page 67.

blame for the tense situation in large measure on officers of the Second Marine Division.

"The lack of informed, courageous leadership in dealing with racial matters is widening the gulf of misunderstanding between the races," the Ad Hoc Committee on Equal Treatment and Opportunity told the commanding officer, Maj. Gen. Edwin B. Wheeler, who has since been assigned to Vietnam on a normal rotation.

In its report, the committee stated that there had been "a general lack of compliance on the part of officers and noncommissioned officers with the existing policies, either by in-

Continued on Page 67, Column 1

PROTESTANTS GIVE ON A LOCAL BASIS

National Programs Suffer First Cutback in Funds Since Depression Days

The national programs of the major Protestant churches are suffering their first cutback in funds since the Depression.

A study of the budgets of the country's large Protestant denominations and the National Council of Churches discloses that although total donations to churches continue to increase slightly, church members are beginning to keep a higher proportion of their contributions at the local level.

The new pattern has important implications for American Protestantism because it constitutes a reversal of the massive build-up of large national bureaucracies that has characterized Protestant religious life for the last two decades.

One probable effect, according to Protestant leaders, will be significant changes in the pattern of church involvement in social action. The national agencies that are now being forced to cut back on expenses have poured millions of dollars into such controversial areas as civil rights, community organization and the peace movement.

Some Key Aspects

According to church leaders, the following key developments are emerging from the serious decline in financial support of Protestantism's national administrative and policymaking organizations:

¶National budgets are being cut back on existing social-action programs, staffs are being reduced and experiments in new forms of activism are being eliminated.

¶The national bodies are reshaping their roles as planners and administrators and are becoming consultants on social-action projects increasingly being initiated and administered on the local church level.

¶In part, such decentralization is the apparent result of a backlash among conservative local congregations against the liberal policies of the national denominations and the National Council of Churches in such areas as race and opposition to

Continued on Page 64, Column 2

ROBERT LEHMAN, FINANCIER, DEAD

Robert Lehman

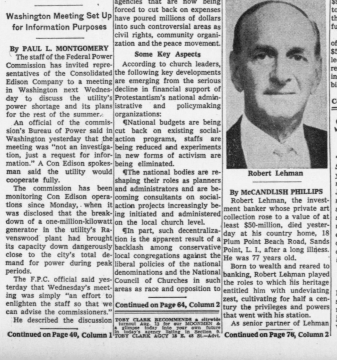

By McCANDLISH PHILLIPS

Robert Lehman, the investment banker whose private art collection rose to a value of at least $50-million, died yesterday at his country home, 18 Plum Point Beach Road, Sands Point, L. I., after a long illness. He was 77 years old.

Born to wealth and reared to banking, Robert Lehman played the roles to which his heritage entitled him with undeviating zest, cultivating for half a century the privileges and powers that went with his station.

As senior partner of Lehman

Continued on Page 76, Column 2

A TREASURY AIDE HINTS HOUSE CUT TAXES TOO MUCH

Cohen Finds Improvements but Criticizes Provisions Aiding Individuals Only

By EILEEN SHANAHAN

Special to The New York Times

WASHINGTON, Aug. 9 — A high Treasury official hinted today that the Administration thought the tax reductions voted by the House of Representatives on Thursday might be too big.

Assistant Secretary of the Treasury Edwin S. Cohen dropped the hint in a speech he had prepared for delivery to a meeting in Dallas of the Section on Taxation of the American Bar Association. Advance copies of his text were made available by his office here.

The tax bill, as a whole, "provides major improvements in the tax structure," Mr. Cohen said.

But he had a number of complaints about the measure, in addition to voicing fear that it might offer more tax reduction than the Federal budget could stand.

Among the other defects, as the Treasury views the bill, are the following:

¶Its emphasis on tax reduction for individuals, to the exclusion of corporations.

¶Its treatment of the oil industry and other mining industries.

¶Its provisions involving real estate.

Cites Additional Relief

Mr. Cohen made only one brief mention of the possibility that the Administration might seek a cutback in the amount of tax relief the House voted.

His specific reference was to the $2.4-billion annually in additional tax relief that was hastily added to the bill last week. This relief was added after it was discovered that the bill, as originally reported by the Ways and Means Committee, would have provided little, if any, tax reduction for home-owning families in the $7,000-to-$12,000 income bracket.

This additional cut, on top of the $6.8-billion already in the bill, "will have to be considered carefully in the light of budgetary needs for 1971 and subsequent years," Mr. Cohen said.

Mr. Cohen did not indicate whether the Administration might seek simple removal of the last-minute additional tax reduction or an entirely different approach to cutting taxes that would spread the cuts more evenly than the committee's original bill.

Total Cut $9.2-Billion

The bill contains a complex group of tax reduction provisions, including a special allowance for low income families, an increase in the standard deduction and cuts in tax rates.

Mr. Cohen noted that individuals would get all of the $9.2-billion in tax relief, the total expected by 1972 when all the bill's relief provisions are fully in effect.

But the tax reform provisions of the bill would raise about $5-billion in increased tax collections from those who currently enjoy some preferences in the tax law, and all but $1.3-billion of this will come from

Continued on Page 37, Column 1

Nixon Picks a Woman to Head Maritime Commission

United Press International

President Nixon with Mrs. Helen Delich Bentley yesterday at conference in White House

Special to The New York Times

WASHINGTON, Aug. 9—President Nixon announced today that he would nominate Mrs. Helen Delich Bentley, maritime editor of The Baltimore Sun, as a member and chairman of the Federal Maritime Commission. It was the President's first selection of a woman to head a Federal regulatory agency. Mrs. Bentley and Mrs. Virginia Mae Brown, chairman of the Interstate Commerce Commission, would be the highest-ranking women in the Government. Mrs. Brown was appointed to the I.C.C. in March, 1964, by President Johnson. She became chairman last Jan. 1. The commission elected her to the rotating post on the basis of length of service. The 45-year-old Mrs. Bentley would succeed John Harllee, a retired Navy rear admiral, in the $40,000-

Continued on Page 30, Column 2

DIVERS HUNT BODY IN BERET SPY CASE

May Quit Search Today for Vietnamese Agent Linked to Inquiry on Americans

By JAMES P. STERBA

Special to The New York Times

CAUDA, South Vietnam, Aug. 9—Three United States Navy vessels have been searching intensively off the coast here for a canvas bag believed to contain the body of a slain Vietnamese intelligence agent.

The agent's death has been linked with the current investigation involving eight United States soldiers of the Special Forces, or Green Berets, who face possible charges of murder and conspiracy to commit murder.

Canvas Bag Sought

About 40 Navy divers, working under officers of the Central Intelligence Agency and the Army's Criminal Investigation Division have been scouring the mud and sand bottom off Nhatrang harbor in vain for the canvas bag tied to steel tire rims containing the body, qualified informants disclosed here.

Navy officers said that the search, by vessels that specialize in undersea salvage and rescue operations, would be abandoned tomorrow.

Several crew members of the ships said the case was apparently the one that led on July 21 to the sudden replacement of Col. Robert B. Rheault as commander of the Fifth Special Forces group here. The colonel is among the eight

Continued on Page 16, Column 2

Laird Backs Senate Curb On Chemical War Agents

By WARREN WEAVER Jr.

Special to The New York Times

WASHINGTON, Aug. 9—A Senate campaign to curb the Pentagon's chemical and biological warfare programs won the endorsement today of the Secretary of Defense, Melvin R. Laird. It appeared to be a case of the Defense Department's acknowledging the inevitable.

An amendment containing numerous restrictions on the development, transportation and use of chemical and biological agents had already been scheduled for a vote in the Senate on Monday as debate on the military procurement authorization bill continued.

Approval Considered Certain

Approval of the amendment is considered all but certain.

Although the Senate sustained the Administration's Safeguard missile defense program by a single vote last week, there has been a rising movement among liberal Senators of both parties to subject the Pentagon to closer scrutiny on the cost and substance of its programs.

Senator Mike Mansfield, the Democratic floor leader, predicted early yesterday that this latest restriction on the military would be approved. Later in the day, Senator John C. Stennis, chairman of the Armed Services Committee, agreed and said he was "inclined to support" the amendment.

Secretary Laird said that defense officials, including Dr. John S. Foster Jr., director of defense research and engineering, had been "working with the Senators in drafting the

Continued on Page 29, Column 1

DECREE BY LISBON CURBS OPPONENTS

Caetano Government Bans Committees Organized for National Elections

Special to The New York Times

LISBON, Aug. 9—The Portuguese Government today banned all election campaign committees except those that already have official recognition.

The ban, published in the Official Bulletin, was considered a major blow to the opposition, which has been organizing committees throughout the country for the forthcoming National Assembly election.

At the request of the Ministry of the Interior, Attorney General Manuel Maria Gonçalves presented a lengthy report declaring the committees illicit and warning that the leaders and members of the committees would be subject to sanctions for "subversive activities."

The Government's political machinery, known as the National Union, has been actively and openly preparing for elections since the beginning of the year. The opposition, which is

Continued on Page 2, Column 5

FRANCE PREPARES TO EASE EFFECTS OF DEVALUATION

Cabinet Members Confer on Common Market Talks Tomorrow in Belgium

FOOD PRICES KEY ISSUE

Costs Expected to Increase by 2 or 3 Per Cent—Austerity Studied

By CLYDE H. FARNSWORTH

Special to The New York Times

PARIS, Aug. 9—The French Government laid plans today to mitigate effects on food prices of her devaluation of the franc and to shift her productive resources to export markets.

Official sources calculated devaluation would bring additional increases in the cost of living of 2 to 3 per cent, lifting the annual rate of inflation to nearly 10 per cent.

This is about twice the rate in the United States and four times the rate in West Germany.

It is in the price, and eventually the export sector, that the success of the devaluation—to 18.004 United States cents from 20.255 cents — will be judged. Some French economic experts were doubtful about the prospects.

No Planned Recession

Cabinet officials met to devise a strategy for a key meeting in Brussels on Monday, which is to determine moves in food prices. They also discussed a new austerity program that will be formally presented to the full cabinet on Aug. 28.

President Pompidou has promised "vigorous and rigorous" measures to reduce home demand, thereby channeling more of France's output to foreign markets. But he has rejected the idea of engineering a recession, which would mean "unbearable sacrifices."

On Monday France will ask the Common Market's Council of Ministers in Brussels to reduce the value of the unit of account that is the standard for pegging common farm prices in the European Economic Community.

Unlikely to Agree

The unit of account is now one American dollar. Under the Community's regulations, prices for French farmers rise in francs by the amount of the devaluation, if there is no change in the unit of account. The higher farm prices inevitably mean higher consumer food prices.

This enormously inflationary burden could be eliminated if France's partners agree to reduce the unit of account by 12.5 per cent, but there is little likelihood of this. The farmers in the other five Common Market countries — Italy, West

Continued on Page 2, Column 5

Soviet Defector Tells How Secret Police Used Him

The following article, "Russian Writers and the Secret Police," is by the 39-year-old Soviet author who received asylum in Britain on July 30, saying that he could no longer work under repression and censorship. He describes the surveillance directed against him, and his enforced role in overseeing other prominent writers. He also tells of his long yearning to go abroad.

By ANATOLY KUZNETSOV

©1969 The Daily Telegraph, London

It is a frightful story that I have to tell. Sometimes it seems to me as though it never happened, that it was just a nightmare. If only that were true.

The Soviet system remains firmly in power in Russia only thanks to an exceptionally powerful apparatus of oppression and primarily thanks to what has been called at various times the Cheka, the G.P.U., the N.K.V.D., the M.G.B. and K.G.B. In other words, the secret police, or the Soviet Gestapo.

Everybody knows that the number of people murdered by the secret police runs into many millions. But when we come to reckon the number of people who are terrorized and deformed by them, then we have to include the whole population of the Soviet Union. The K.G.B.'s tentacles reach, like cancerous growths, into every branch of life in Russia. And in particular into the world of Soviet literature.

I do not know a single writer in Russia who has not had some connection with the K.G.B. This connection can be one of three different kinds.

The first kind: You collaborate enthusiastically with the K.G.B. In that case you have every chance of prospering.

The second kind: You acknowledge your duty toward the K.G.B., but you refuse to collaborate directly. In that case you are deprived of a great deal, and in particular of the prospect of traveling abroad.

The third kind: You brush aside all advances made by the K.G.B. and enter into conflict with them. In that case your works are not published and you may even find yourself in a concentration camp.

How all this works out in practice I shall explain by reference to my own experience. As a matter of fact a similar story could be told by any Russian writer who is even slightly known. But they are there, and they want to live, and so they keep quiet.

In August, 1951, I was preparing for the first time in my life to travel abroad, to France. I had been included in a delegation of writers. It was a most impressive ex-

Continued on Page 24, Column 3

Today's Sections

Index to Subjects

SUMMER BONUS: Two Book Digests

The Peter Principle — The No. 1 Best-Seller | **Theft of the Nation** — The Mafia Story

Both Continue Today in the Magazine

WEATHER
Sunny, 80s.
Tomorrow: Fair, 80s.
SUNSET: 8:01 PM
SUNRISE TOMORROW: 6:02 AM

New York Post

© 1969 New York Post Corporation RR

Vol. 168 No. 225 — NEW YORK, MONDAY, AUGUST 11, 1969 — 10 Cents, 15c Beyond 50-mile Zone

LATE CITY
Over the Counter Stocks Scratches

Two More Murders

DID TATE KILLER STRIKE AGAIN?

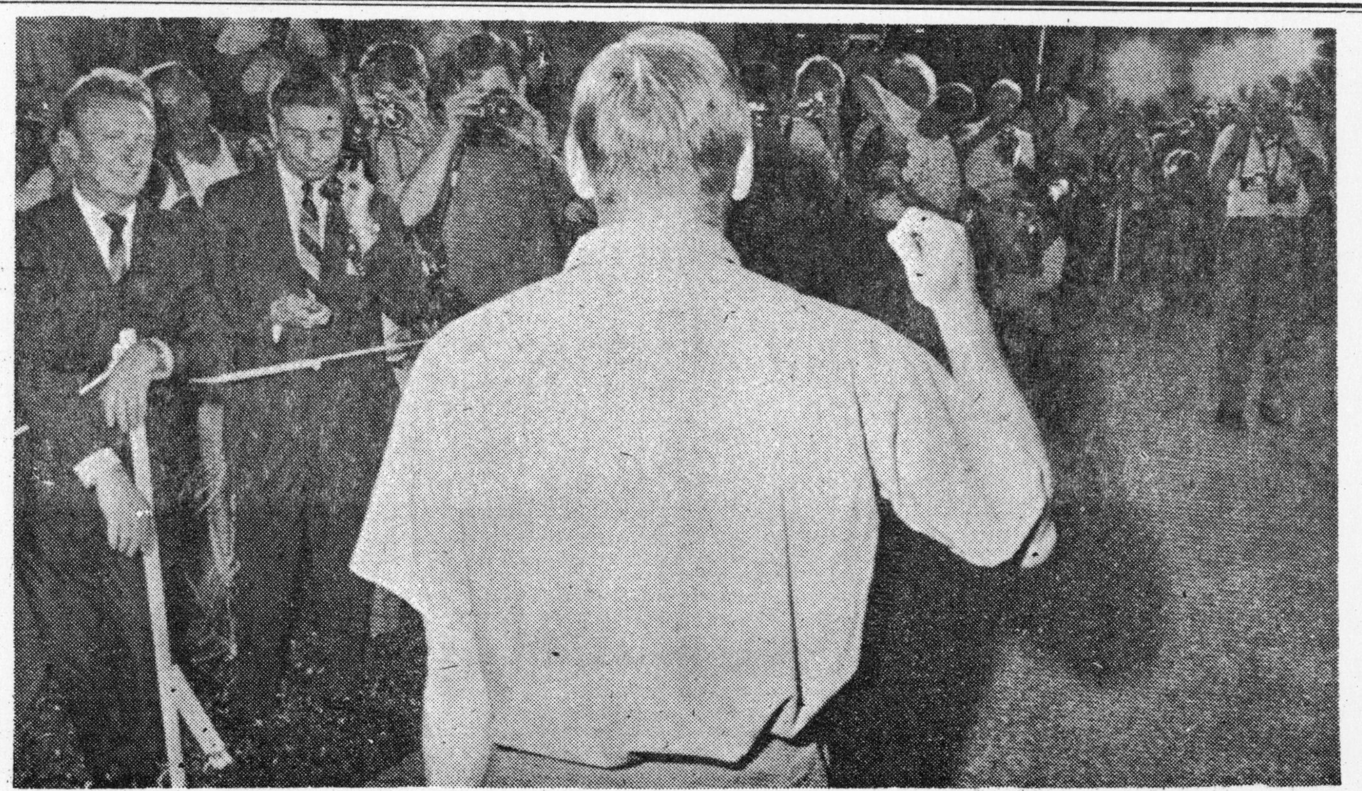

Associated Press Wirephoto

ALL THE WAY HOME: Neil Armstrong, first man on the moon, faces reporters after release from 17-day quarantine in Houston with fellow Apollo 11 astronauts Edwin Aldrin and Michael Collins. Story on Page 5.

LOS ANGELES — Police today sought the slayer of seven persons instead of five after a man and woman were found murdered in a style similar to Saturday's bizarre massacre of actress Sharon Tate and four others.

The two new victims, tentatively identified as Mr. and Mrs. Leno A. LaBianca, were found stabbed repeatedly in their fashionable Hollywood home only five miles from Miss Tate's $200-000 rented house.

"There is a similarity, but whether it's the same suspect or a copycat we just don't know," said Police Sgt. Bryce Houchin.

One similarity was immediately apparent. The words "death to pigs" were reported scrawled in blood on the LaBiancas' refrigerator door. On Miss Tate's front door the word "pig" had been written in blood.

In another parallel, LaBianca's head was wrapped

Continued on Page 3

Colts' Hinton Says Waiting Worth It

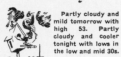

Cloudy

Partly cloudy and mild tomorrow with high 53. Partly cloudy and cooler tonight with lows in the low and mid 30s.

The News American

BALTIMORE MARYLAND

Baltimore, Monday, December 8, 1969 — 97th Year—No. 29 — 10 Cents

***

300 Police Surround Panthers In L. A.; 3 Officers Wounded

Special Report

Colts' Hinton Says Waiting Was Worth It

● Baltimore Colt wide receiver Eddie Hinton gives News American readers an exclusive account of the 17-17 tie against the Detroit Lions at the Stadium.

By EDDIE HINTON

Baltimore Colts

I waited almost an entire rookie season to do the job the Colts expect of me but believe me, it was worth the wait.

HINTON

It's difficult to get excited over the fact that we came away from the Lions with a tie instead of a victory but it beats losing.

Catching the football is my stock in trade. Things didn't work out at the running back position I was used at earlier in the season, but here's what I felt after yesterday's game.

My job is receiving and that's satisfaction enough when you contribute. In practice you work and work for the chance to play, but it can get discouraging after a while.

I felt the College All-Star Game workouts set me back in my work with the Colts. But that's no excuse. I simply found out there is a lot to learn in professional football playing.

Dick LeBeau of the Lions, the man who defended on me, was a lesson in experience. I consider myself a fast runner, but speed alone doesn't do it.

BEATING LeBEAU FOR THE touchdown that put us ahead 17-14 was not as easy as the game film shows. I had to set LeBeau up for my outside curl-takeoff pattern by making inside moves on him, even on running plays.

You learn best in the National Football League by doing, the same as most other things in life.

The Lions were playing a strict man-to-man defense. I got advice from Jimmy Orr and Ray Perkins on how to work against LeBeau and what to expect from him.

Jim and Ray worked with me all week, but

Turn to Page 7C, Column 3

Mathias Asks War Resolution Repeal

SEN. McC MATHIAS

WASHINGTON, Dec. 8 — (AP)—Sen. Charles McC. Mathias proposed today that Congress repeal the Gulf of Tonkin resolution, prod Saigon toward reform, and endorse President Nixon's "plan for accelerated withdrawal of all American forces from South Vietnam."

The Maryland Republican advocated those steps as part of a foreign policy resolution aimed at "clearing away the debris of cold war dogmas."

In a speech prepared for the Senate, Mathias proposed repeal of a package of past congressional resolutions he said were "interpreted as relinquishing broad authority to the executive to intervene militarily around the world."

MATHIAS CALLED the Tonkin measure, cited by former President Lyndon B. Johnson as authority for the step up in U.S. involvement in Vietnam, as "the most questionable of all."

He said the resolution, which followed claims of North Vietnamese attacks on U.S. ships in the Gulf of Tonkin, "apparently authorized an overwhelming and substantially ineffectual extension of the Vietnam War into the North through bombing . . .

"As long as the resolution remains on the books, it may be interpreted as authorizing further attacks. Yet American public opinion would not accept such a drastic step nor would the Congress acquiesce in it."

Mathias said in his speech "we discover that in a very real sense, the war has Vietnamized American diplomacy," explaining:

"THIS IS NO criticism of our present leaders. They are the inheritors and victims, not creators, of this Asian thralldom . . ."

In addition, Mathias said a state of national emergency dating from Dec. 16, 1950, during the Korean War, should be declared at an end.

The Mathias resolution would have Congress declare support for Mr. Nixon's efforts at a political solution in Vietnam, and for the Administration's troop withdrawal program.

"No plan for American military withdrawal will end the war," he noted, "unless the present South Vietnam government adopts a plan for its own political withdrawal," Mathias said.

JOHN STENNIS, chairman of the Senate Armed Services Committee, wants President Nixon to appoint an independent commission to investigate the alleged My Lai massacre in Vietnam. (Story on Page 5A.)

Group's Hq. Raid Target

LOS ANGELES, Dec. 8 — (AP) — Black Panthers barricaded their main headquarters and exchanged gunfire with police today. Three officers were wounded as a task force of 300 surrounded headquarters. About three hours after the pre-dawn police raid started officers issued an ultimatum: Come out with your hands up or we'll come in.

The deadline passed with only one man following the instructions.

Grenades weer tossed at police about 20 minutes after the surrender deadline.

POLICE SAID they understood at least four others were inside the building, a former store located across from the street from Wrigley Field, the former baseball park. The area is mostly Negro.

Police made no immediate move on the building.

Sgt. Dan Cook, a police spokesman, said the pre-dawn raids were not connected with recent Black Panther confrontations with police in other areas around the nation.

He said simultaneous raids were ordered to serve warrants on two persons after authorities received information machine-guns and other weapons were stored at the main headquarters —located about four miles from downtown Los Angeles—and two other Panther-occupied locations.

POLICE DESCRIBED the two other buildings as "secured."

The wounded officers were in the task force around the main headquarters.

Cook said he was not sure what type of grenades were tossed at police.

He said the building was sandbagged at doors and windows. Those inside, he said, appeared

Turn to Page 2A, Column 5

Violence Unit Backs Obedience

WASHINGTON, Dec. 9 — (AP)—A bare majority of the National Violence Commission —publicly divided for the first time—condemned today the use of massive civil disobedience as a tactic to change the law.

A six-member minority of the commission—including its two Negroes—contended that the tactic, when practiced without violence, is perhaps the only effective means of overturning unjust laws.

The commission divided over the kinds of disobedience—restaurant sit-ins and violation of segregation laws—that led to enactment of major civil rights legislation in the 1960s.

SPEAKING FOR the seven-man majority, Houston Attorney Leon Jaworski said its views were a direct result of those instances of disobedience.

"We suggest," the majority said, "that if on good faith the constitutionality of a statue, ordinance or a court decree is

Turn to Page 2A, Column 7

Russ Talk Peace Pact With Bonn

MOSCOW, Dec. 9—(AP)—West Germany and the Soviet Union today began talks on a formal agreement to renounce the use of force against each other.

Soviet Foreign Minister Andrei Gromyko and West German Ambassador Helmut Allardt opened the negotiations at the Foreign Ministry, an official German source reported.

With the opening of today's talks, the Soviet Union now is engaged in negotiations with the three countries that until recently have been its favorite propaganda targets — Communist China, the United States and West Germany.

U. S.-SOVIET talks on the limitation of strategic weaponry are under way in Helsinki and Soviet-Chinese negotiations on border problems are in progress in Peking.

Allardt is expected to remain chief of the West German delegation at the Moscow talks but Gromyko probably will step down

Turn to Page 5A, Column 3

170 Reds Killed Near Cambodia

SAIGON, Dec. 8—(AP)—American air cavalrymen and airmen dogging North Vietnamese troops along a 100-mile stretch of the Cambodian border north of Saigon killed 170 in a dozen clashes over the weekend, military spokesmen said today.

Much of the attacking was done by rocket-firing helicopter gunships, dive-bombers and artillery, and as a result, U.S. casualties were held to three killed and 18 wounded, the spokesman said.

The heaviest action occurred in War Zone C, 58 miles northwest of Saigon, and near the Bu Dop Special Forces camp 88 miles north of Saigon.

OFFICIAL SOURCES said the North Vietnamese were trying to protect the infiltration corridors from Cambodia, and several fights were triggered by enemy fire on scout helicopters flying at treetop level.

There were no reports of any helicopters being shot down.

About 40 American B52 bombers attacked North Vietnamese base camps and gun positions along the Cambodian border during the night, unloading more than 1,000 tons of explosives.

The targets were 4½ miles northeast of the Bu Dop camp and within two miles of the Cambodian border.

THE CAMP HAS been the target of sporadic shelling for more than a month. Five rockets hit the camp's airstrip yesterday, killing six Vietnamese and wounding 12 as they waited for helicopters.

"Light" American casualties also were reported.

Despite the shelling, no ma-

Turn to Page 5A, Column 2

8,800 More GIs Head Home

SAIGON, Dec. 8—(UPI)—U. S. headquarters said today 8,800 GIs have left Vietnam in addition to the 60,000 involved in President Nixon's pullout program, reducing American troop strength to its lowest level in 25 months.

The troop strength report said 4,300 U.S. servicemen left the war zone last week to drop the number of GIs in Vietnam to 475,200, fewest since November, 1967.

IT MEANT THE number of war zone GIs is 8,800 lower than the 484,000 ceiling authorized by President Nixon once his two-phase withdrawal of 60,000 men is completed by Dec. 15.

Those 8,800 troops left the war zone at the end of their tours of duty and were not replaced.

A spokesman for the U.S. Command issued this statement in answer to speculation that the withdrawal of American troops was continuing past the 60,000 mark without an announcement from the White House:

"This decline in strength below the authorized 484,000 results from a temporary slowdown in the replacement flow and does not represent an additional redeployment increment."

President Nixon was to hold a nationally televised news conference tonight amid reports he might be ready to announce a further troop cutback from Vietnam.

WHITE HOUSE press secretary Ronald L. Ziegler said today Mr.

Turn to Page 5A, Column 3

Cautious TV Analysis To Follow Nixon Talk

NEW YORK, Dec. 8—(AP)—President Nixon's televised news conference tonight will be his first scheduled television appearance since Vice President Spiro T. Agnew's attack on TV news analysis that followed Mr. Nixon's speech on Vietnam Nov. 3.

CBS said it plans several minutes of summation and analysis by Eric Sevareid and Roger Mudd after the conference, which begins at 9 p.m.

NBC said John Chancellor will offer a brief summary.

ABC said it will have a brief summary if the news conference ends before 9.30 p.m. to fill out the half hour. If it runs more than a half hour, the network will go directly to regular programming.

After the last Presidential news conference Sept. 26, CBS had about four minutes of analysis, which 200 of its 203 stations carried. ABC and NBC had brief summaries.

CBS president Frank Stanton said last week that one affiliate station had notified him it would no longer carry network analysis after Presidential speeches.

Agnew had charged that network commentators, following the speech with "instant" analysis, made difficult an objective evaluation of Mr. Nixon's remarks.

Inside Today

Today's News American 3 Sections

● Did you know that despite a hog cholera epidemic on the Eastern Shore there's no danger to humans, even if they eat the diseased pork? Louis Azrael does, along with other answers to readers' questions. Page 7B.

● Most businesses that get into a jam and lose money can blame it on poor management, an industrial trouble shooter said in an address at Ft. Holabird. The Federal Log, Page 6A.

● Columbia is very hush-hush about its new movie which started a riot at a sneak preview. And Director Bill Wyler is in trouble over the film's violence, Dorothy Manners writes on Page 5B.

Maryland's only newspaper with all the great news and photo services: Associated Press, United Press International, AP Wirephoto, UPI Telephoto, Hearst Headline Service, Chicago Daily News Wire Service, London Daily Express Wire Service.

For All Departments—PLaza 2-1212

Asian Flu KOs Italy

ROME, Dec. 8—(AP)—With one quarter of Italy's 54 million citizens stricken in a Hong Kong flu epidemic, the healthy are trying to ward off the bug with extra clothing, vitamin C pills and nips of cognac.

Today's Chuckle

Middle-age spread: Too many nights round the table.

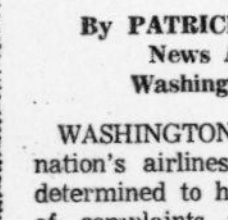

Shopping Days Until Christmas

See Christmas Gift Spotter in Today's Classified Section

Air Travel Crisis---Part 2

Friendly Sky—In Name Only

By PATRICK J. SLOYAN
News American
Washington Bureau

● Frustration and delay beset many of the 170 million persons who use America's air systems. In this second of a series of five articles on the air travel crisis, Patrick J. Sloyan of The New American Washington Bureau tells how the airlines are grappling with the gripes from passengers and complaints from homeowners who live near airports.

WASHINGTON, Dec. 8 — The nation's airlines sometimes seem determined to handle the upsurge of complaints about service by bombing the passengers — with liquor.

What was the first thing the TWA captain did last month when his jetliner was hijacked by a rifle-carrying Marine destined for Rome? "He was very cool," said one passenger. "He said booze on the house."

An Eastern Airline hostess sloshed coffee on a soldier in one recent flight. She rushed to the galley and back — with a towel and a miniature of scotch.

Whether it is a delay in take-off or landing, the solution always seems to call for a belt for the passenger. Perhaps they will forget. But they don't.

FRUSTRATION, delay and even exhaustion that besets many of the 170 million who travel on this country's sagging air system each year has produced growing hostility against the airlines and airports.

Americans living near airports are venting their anger in the courts and sometimes in the streets. In Boston, for example, Logan-bound jets glide over heavily populated neighborhoods causing conversations to stop

Turn to Page 5A, Column 1

Alert TV $weepstake$ Fan Sees Santa---Turn to Page 4A

VOL. 16 — NO 28 JANUARY 26, 1970 ★★★ 15¢

Hushed Up By Authorities:

NAMES OF 9 HOLLYWOOD STARS MARKED FOR DEATH BY SHARON TATE'S MURDERERS

LEADER OF ACCUSED TATE killers, Charles Manson has been taken into custody and will face trial along with other members of his hippie cult

U.S. Army Deserters Reveal:

More Vietnam Massacres Covered Up By Pentagon

The Weather

Today — Considerable cloudiness, high near 40. Tuesday—Cloudy, cool, chance of rain. Probability of precipitation 20% today and tonight. Temperature range: Today, 28-39. Yesterday, 23-36. Details, Page B9.

The Washington Post

Times Herald

FINAL

64 Pages — 4 Sections

93d Year ···· No. 73 MONDAY, FEBRUARY 16, 1970 Phone 223-6000 Circulation 223-6100 Classified 223-6200 10c

Enemy Battalion Overrun

Saigon Troops Kill 145 Reds Near Danang

LANDING ZONE BALDY, Vietnam, Feb. 15 (AP) — Allied military sources reported an enemy sapper battalion was virtually wiped out today by a government armored brigade.

By nightfall, spokesmen said, 145 of the specially trained enemy soldiers had been killed and 12 captured as South Vietnamese armor overran their concealed foxholes and bunkers in rice paddy dikes 18 miles south of Danang.

Four miles away, government militiamen reported killing 37 more enemy soldiers, possibly stragglers from the big fight.

The enemy dead included the battalion commander, his executive officer and a company commander; another company commander and a political officer were captured, the spokesmen said.

Sunday's action ended five days of fighting in the area that cost the enemy 280 dead and 36 captured, military sources said. South Vietnamese losses were put at 23 killed and 70 wounded during the period. No U.S. casualties have been reported.

"This day we are certain we destroyed that battalion," said Col. Than Hoa Hiep, commander of the South Vietnamese 1st Armored Brigade.

Government losses were put at four killed and 26 wounded in the bitter fighting Sunday near the Lyly River east of Highway 1.

Hiep said the enemy battalion consisted of 150 to 200 men, most of them North Vietnamese.

See VIETNAM, A16, Col. 1

By Associated Press & United Press International

Federal Judge Julius J. Hoffman, left, sentenced "Chicago Seven" defendant Jerry Rubin, center, and defense attorney William M. Kunstler for contempt.

Chicago 7, Lawyers Face Jail

Kunstler Gets 4-Year Term For Contempt

By William Chapman
Washington Post Staff Writer

CHICAGO, Feb. 15 — A defense lawyer in the Chicago conspiracy trial was sentenced to more than four years in prison today for contempt of court.

Judge Julius J. Hoffman cited William M. Kunstler for 24 different items of contempt during the long trial and said, "I have never heard a lawyer say to a judge the things you have said to me."

Another defense lawyer, Leonard Weinglass, was sentenced to more than 20 months for contempt. The sentences for both attorneys were stayed by the judge until May so they will be free to defend the seven men whom they represent in the case.

But three more defendants were sentenced for contempt and taken promptly to jail today. The four others were sentenced and jailed yesterday.

The jury, meanwhile, finished its second day of deliberation at 9 p.m. CST without a verdict. Deliberations will continue Monday morning.

Tonight, Weinglass offered the defense's first words of optimism about the possible verdict. He observed that the jury had been out some time and said that indicated to him a growing possibility of acquittal or a hung jury.

He said he originally had been "very pessimistic" because "they were being tried under a difficult law . . . by a judge who gave us no latitude."

The sentence against Kunstler, a veteran of many civil rights suits, was the longest one imposed during the trial and may set a precedent. The total time was four years and 13 days.

In a highly unusual statement from the bench, Hoffman declared that behavior such as Kunstler's encourages crime in the United States.

Hoffman acknowledged that he was about to make an "unorthodox" comment and then said:

"We hear lots about crime in this country. There is a lot of crime . . . I am one of those who believes that the fact crime is on the increase is due in large part to the fact that waiting in the wings are lawyers willing to go beyond their professional responsibilities in the defense of clients."

See TRIAL, A9, Col. 5

9 Churches in U.S. Outline Unity Plan

By Betty Medsger
Washington Post Staff Writer

Details of a plan that would put one-third of America's Protestants in a single church—the Church of Christ Uniting—were made public yesterday.

The result of eight years of deliberation by the Consultation on Church Union, the plan would unite nine denominations and leave the door open for other Christian bodies to become part of the 25-million-member church.

The new union, however, is unlikely to be a reality in less than 10 years.

The plan must go through study periods and then legislative action by the members of the Consultation: African Methodist Episcopal Church, African Methodist Episcopal Zion Church, Christian Church (Disciples of Christ), Christian Methodist Episcopal Church, Episcopal Church, Presbyterian Church in the United States (Southern), United Church of Christ, United Methodist Church and United Presbyterian Church in the USA.

In the proposal that will go to the member churches for study, bishops would be the chief executive officials at various levels in the church, including the office of presiding bishop at the national level.

The plan stresses that in all areas of the new church, in both lay and ordained leadership, "all minority races, various age groups, and men and women shall participate fully."

In an unexpected move, the plan permits women bishops. None of the churches in the Consultation that now have bishops has ever had a woman bishop.

The first presiding bishop of the church, as called for in the plan of union, would be black.

Five of the churches in the consultation now have bishops. All these bishops will retain their rank in the new church, according to the plan. Additional bishops will be elected from all participating churches as needed.

See UNITE, A2, Col. 1

Dominican Jet With 102 Falls in Sea

From News Dispatches

SANTO DOMINGO, Feb. 16 (Monday)—A Dominican Airways DC-9 jetliner bound for San Juan, Puerto Rico, crashed into the Caribbean last night on take-off, apparently killing the 102 passengers and crewmembers aboard.

Rescue officials and the Dominican Navy said there were no survivors. Baggage and clothing were picked up floating in the water some five miles off shore.

Airline officials said the passengers included former world lightweight boxing champion Carlos "Teo" Cruz, who held the crown in 1968, his wife and two children. He planned to fight in Paris next week in a comeback bid.

Officials also said the wife and daughter of former Dominican president Antonio Imbert Barreras, who headed the government in 1965, were aboard.

Also listed on the plane were 12 members of a women's volleyball team from Puerto Rico.

AP said none of the passengers were from the United States mainland, but UPI said the list included four North Americans along with a number of Puerto Ricans, Dominicans, Peruvians, an Argentinian and a Belgian.

The control tower at Punta Caucedo airport, 15 miles from Santo Domingo, said the plane took off normally for the 250-mile flight to San Juan. Then the pilot radioed that he was losing power in one engine and was trying to return.

The plane hit the water a few miles from shore. Dominican helicopters and boats searched for survivors. The airport is bounded by flat fields, but most of its flights take off over the ocean.

Israel Opens Big Oil Pipeline Meant to Supplant Suez Canal

By Louis B. Fleming
Los Angeles Times

JERUSALEM, Feb. 15—Oil has started to flow through Israel's new 42-inch pipeline from Eilat on the Gulf of Aqaba to Ashkelon on the Mediterranean, consummating Israel's ultimate challenge to the Suez Canal, according to informed sources here.

The 160-mile line eventually will have a capacity of 60 million tons a year, about one-third the tonage carried by tankers through the canal in its last full year of operation before the 1967 war.

A foreign oil journal reported that oil already has been loaded at Ashkelon, but this has not been confirmed here. A correspondent last Wednesday saw no ships at the Ashkelon loading facility.

Egyptians Failed

Completion of the pipeline came shortly after Egyptian plans for a rival line west of the Suez Canal had collapsed.

It is understood that the warfare along the canal had prevented surveys by engineers from the European consortium of Italian, British, French and German companies that had agreed to build the Egyptian line.

Opening of the pipeline followed by a fortnight the visit to Eilat of Israel's first large tanker, the Zim line's Nivi, a 121,000-ton Swedish-built ship.

Two additional tankers, each of 250,000 tons, will soon be in service. Orders for three more are under consideration.

These ships would ply between ports east of Suez through the Red Sea and Gulf of Aqaba, to feed the pipeline.

Plan to Sell Oil

The oil will exceed the domestic needs of Israel, whose officials are confident they can sell the surplus to Southern European customers. The price will be higher than for oil brought from the Persian Gulf directly in supertankers, but many Southern European ports cannot handle such ships.

Eilat is ideally suited to large tankers because the Gulf of Aqaba shoreline is almost sheer.

But the sabotaging of four Israeli ships at Eilat in recent months by Egyptian frogmen has raised anxiety about the security of the port. It is only three miles from the Jordanian port of Aqaba.

The new pipeline will augment an existing small line that links Eilat with Haifa.

Haifa will remain the principal oil-refining center for Israel, according to recent announcements here. Haifa has a refining capacity of close to six million tons a year. A new refinery will be completed in three years at Ashdod, the southern Israeli port about 12 miles north of Ashkelon, terminus of the new pipeline. It will have a capacity of nearly three million tons a year.

Israel is not expected to announce the source of the petroleum for the new line or the customers for the oil because of the threat of secondary boycotts by the Arab states.

See ISRAEL, A5, Col. 6

Policing the Polluters: The Puget Sound Fight

By George C. Wilson
Washington Post Staff Writer

"If you really want to understand why President Nixon wants more power to clean up the waterways," said a veteran pollution fighter, "then go study the record of Puget Sound."

The Sound — as anybody who has seen it even briefly knows—is a breathtakingly beautiful waterway setting off the house-spotted hills of Washington State.

But—like so many other lakes, rivers and bays in the United States—Puget Sound is infected with the poisons of people and industry.

The salmon and trout fishermen in the Pacific Northwest know this. So do the men who go after the crabs, scallops and oysters in the Sound. And the weekend swimmers, sailors and beachcombers know it, too.

Knowing about pollution and proving it exists, however, are two very different things when it comes to "the law." Former Gov. Albert Rosellini found this out when he tried to crack down on polluters.

In 1961, he asked the federal government to come into Washington State to help him with the cleanup. Only five governors have seen fit to invite such aid since the Water Pollution Control Act was enacted in 1956.

See PUGET, A4, Col. 1

Oil spilled from Greek tanker spreads in Tampa Bay. Page A3.

Soviet Economic Ills Spurring Dissidents

By Anthony Astrachan
Washington Post Foreign Service

MOSCOW, Feb. 15—An underground letter circulating here says the Soviets have lost both the moon and the economic races because they live in an imaginary world. Some observers see it as the latest political consequence of the country's economic troubles.

The letter calls for free discussion as the only cure.

It bears the typed signature "Sakharov." Hence a few observers attributed it to physicist Andrei Sakharov, who caused a sensation in 1968 with a 10,000-word samizdat (self-published) document that urged cooperation and eventual convergence between American and Soviet societies.

Others were sure it was not by that same Sakharov because it mentions competition rather than cooperation. Also its prose style and format are different; it is typed in several copies on thin paper.

There was no way of authenticating it. In the past, samizdat letters by political dissidents have called for free discussion, but none recently has dealt with economies. One Russian who has seen it reportedly said, "Even if it's not by the same Sakharov, it's still a fascinating document."

This and other possible political consequences of the economic problems have been the subject of speculation in Moscow. The speculation begins with the plenary meeting of the Central Committee of the Communist Party, held in December just before the budget and fiscal session of the Supreme Soviet.

Party leader Brezhnev gave a report at that plenum which has since been the subject of secret discussions at all levels of the party. This is standard practice in Communist countries.

See SOVIET, A16, Col. 4

Students Plan Antiwar Rallies

A conference of 3,000 students has voted to support a "spring offensive" against the Vietnam war from April 13 to 18.

The vote came during a two-day meeting sponsored by the Student Mobilization Committee at Case Western Reserve University in Cleveland.

Details on Page A3

By Ken Feil—The Washington Post

Many in the crowd of more than 3,800 stand on seats and spill out in the aisle as "Sly and the Family Stone" perform.

Rock Fans Rock Constitution Hall; 100 Crash Gate, 3,800 Wait 5 Hours

By Paul Hodge
Washington Post Staff Writer

A delay of almost five hours in the start of a rock music concert at Constitution Hall last night, coupled with a crowd of 1,000 luckless ticket-seekers left out in the cold, created a situation that had police worried until the music started.

With the hall filled to its 3,811 capacity, 100 of the crowd outside pushed past doormen shortly after 7 p.m., the time the concert of "Sly and The Family Stone" was to begin.

At about the same time others on the outside began pelting the building with rocks and broke about a dozen small windows in the doors on either side of the hall. There was no immediate estimate of the damage.

Police arrested 18 persons, 12 adults and six juveniles, on charges ranging from disorderly conduct and unlawful entry to destruction of property and assault on a police officer.

A spokesman for "Sly and the Family Stone" blamed the delay on a late airplane departure from New York. The group finally appeared on stage at 11:50 p.m. and was greeted by a chorus of boos and cheers from the still-full house.

George Peterson, a student at Georgetown University, said he has seen the group three times before. They have been "almost this late every time," he said.

Sylvester "Sly" Stewart, a member of the group, apologized to the audience and said, "I know exactly how you feel. It's unfortunate. We'll play as long as they let us play."

However, Sly and his group left the stage 40 minutes later and the concert was over. The crowd left quietly and dispersed quickly, but many expressed displeasure with the brevity of the affair.

Police had their hands full from the time the concert was scheduled to begin and the time it actually did start.

Initially, 50 policemen arrived and began ejecting gate crashers. A call for reinforcements brought the total of policemen on the scene to 80, including 25 from other police districts and 16 from the special operations division, which normally would be operatin in high-crime areas of the c

Shortly after 9 p.m., a group never identified audience—and whose the management s couldn't rememb played on the st for a short time About an hou audience wa 15 mi mu s

in memoriam

Allison Krause	Jeffrey Glenn Miller	Sandra Lee Scheuer	William K. Schroeder
19-year-old freshman from Pittsburgh, Pa.	20, of Plainview, N.Y. Antiwar activist at Mich. State University before transferring to Kent.	20-year-old speech-therapy major of Youngstown, Ohio.	19-year-old sophomore of Lorain, Ohio. Psychology major attending Kent on ROTC scholarship.

Honor the Kent martyrs — build giant antiwar demonstrations Memorial Day

— see page 12 —

Eyewitness report of Kent massacre

By MIKE YORK and FRED KIRSCH
Special to The Militant

(The authors are both students at Kent State University. Mike York, 28, is a veteran, working on a federal grant studying transportation. He is married and a staff assistant. Fred Kirsch, 22, is a junior in psychology.)

KENT, Ohio, May 5—Four students were murdered at Kent State University yesterday, and several wounded when National Guardsmen opened fire without warning.

It was cold-blooded murder. We narrowly missed getting killed ourselves.

The students had been protesting President Nixon's escalation of the war into Cambodia and the bombing of North Vietnam.

The day of the massacre there had been an impromptu call for a student strike at Kent.

The statement from the National Guard that they started shooting in response to sniping is untrue. It was a one-sided shootout.

We were caught with hundreds of other students near a parking lot when suddenly a line of Guardsmen turned toward us, knelt down, aimed—almost as if by an order.

Briefly, the events leading up to the bloodshed were this:

On Friday noon, May 1, there was a rally of about 2,000 to bury a copy of the Constitution. It was in response to Nixon's speech escalating the war. A serviceman with a silver star and a bronze star burned his discharge papers. Later the Black United Students held a rally.

That evening the Guard was brought in.

Saturday night a crowd of several thousand burned down the ROTC building. When ROTC burned, the Guardsmen had orders to shoot anyone who cut firehoses.

On Monday, May 4, we both went down to the Commons, an open field, at noon.

Someone climbed up on the base of a liberty bell and said, "It's time to strike. It's time to strike."

An Army jeep pulled up. There were four men, three Guardsmen and one state trooper in it. The trooper had a bullhorn. He said, "Please leave the area. Please leave the area. This is an illegal gathering. Leave, before someone is hurt."

A few students—no more than a handful—were heaving rocks. Thousands of students were in the area.

A group of Guardsmen approached. Before we knew it, we saw tear gas cannisters in the midst of us. People started running.

"Walk, walk," people shouted. The students walked. It was an orderly retreat.

Several truckloads of Guardsmen pulled up, got out, formed a single line, fixed their bayonets, put on tear gas masks and started

(Continued on page 12)

Student holds head in anguish as she views body of one of slain Kent State Four

The American Paper for Americans

Chicago Tribune

THE WORLD'S GREATEST NEWSPAPER

SPORTS ★★★★ FINAL

124th YEAR—No. 287 © 1970 Chicago Tribune WEDNESDAY, OCTOBER 14, 1970 ☆☆☆ 92 PAGES, 6 SECTIONS 10c

FBI ARRESTS ANGELA DAVIS

Canada-Red China Tie

Ottawa Cuts Its Relations with Formosa

BY EUGENE GRIFFIN
[Chief of Canada Bureau]
[Chicago Tribune Press Service]

OTTAWA, Ont., Oct. 13—Canada today announced the immediate establishment of diplomatic relations with Red China, a move at odds with American policy. It also announced an immediate break in relations with Nationalist China.

The recognition of the Communist regime in Peking has been a goal of Prime Minister Pierre Trudeau. He made his aim known in one of his first statements after he took office in 1968, and the discussions have been carried out for nearly two years in Stockholm.

"I am pleased to announce the successful conclusion of our discussions," Mitchell Sharp, secretary of state for external affairs, told the House of Commons.

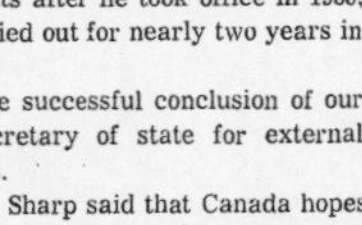

Sharp said that Canada hopes to have an embassy in operation in Peking within three months. Canadian officials are leaving for Peking soon to prepare for diplomatic and trade operations. The two countries plan to exchange ambassadors within six months.

Canada Changes Position

At the beginning of the negotiations, the Trudeau government said that it would not recognize Peking at the price of breaking relations with Nationalist China. This position was dropped when Peking would recognize Canada on no other terms. Red China insists that the Nationalist Chinese

Mitchell Sharp . . . announces change

island of Formosa is part of the territory of mainland China.

"The Chinese government reaffirms that Taiwan [Chinese name for Formosa] is an inalienable part of the territory of the People's Republic of China," according to a statement agreed upon by Canada and Peking. "The Canadian

OUR WAYWARD ALLIES
See the editorial page

government takes note of this position of the Chinese government.

"The Canadian government recognizes the government of the People's Republic of China as the sole legal government of China."

Agree to Make Break

Sharp told Parliament that the Canadian government and Formosa had agreed on the impossibility of continuing diplomatic relations after Canada recognized Peking. He said steps had been taken by both Canada and Formosa to end formal relations with the announcement of Canadian recognition of Red China.

Robert L. Stanfield, the Conservative opposition leader, said he objected to breaking relations with Formosa altho he said it would be right to establish relations with Peking under proper conditions.

"It is not appropriate to accept as a condition the withdrawal of recognition of the

[Continued on page 2, col. 1]

Trudeau Hardens on Kidnap

BY EUGENE GRIFFIN
[Chief of Canada Bureau]
[Chicago Tribune Press Service]

OTTAWA, Ont., Oct. 13—Prime Minister Pierre Trudeau said today that it is more important for society to protect itself against terrorist blackmail than to worry about civil rights.

"There's a lot of bleeding hearts around that just don't like to see people with helmets and guns," he snapped at reporters questioning him about the use of troops to guard against terrorist action in Ottawa. "All I can say is, 'Go on and bleed.'"

"It's more important to keep law and order in society than to be worried about weak-kneed people who don't like the looks of an army."

Protect Top Officials

The troops were called last night to protect political figures, foreign diplomats and government buildings against the Quebec Liberation Front, which kidnaped James R. Cross, a British diplomat, and Pierre Laporte, the Quebec minister of labor, last week in Montreal.

The front threatened to kill Cross and Laporte and to conduct other kidnapings unless the government frees 23 terrorist prisoners from Quebec jails, flies them to Cuba or Algeria and meets other demands.

Radio station CHLN, in Trois-Rivieres on the St. Lawrence between Montreal and Quebec City, received a second statement late today, setting a new deadline of noon tomorrow for the front demands to be met.

Breaks Off Talks

In Montreal tonight, Robert Lemieux, the lawyer for the front, broke off talks with a representative of the Quebec government. He said the government refused to meet the front's demands.

He said the government insists that the separatists guarantee the safety of Cross and Laporte before it will discuss the front's demands.

Trudeau said in the House of Commons today that Ottawa and the Quebec governments were in agreement that "the only thing that has to be done now is to insure thru negotiations that a mechanism be established for the release of Cross and Laporte."

Trudeau has been maintained a hard line in dealing with the kidnapers. Few observers here

[Continued on page 2, col. 1]

GETTING HARDER TO IGNORE

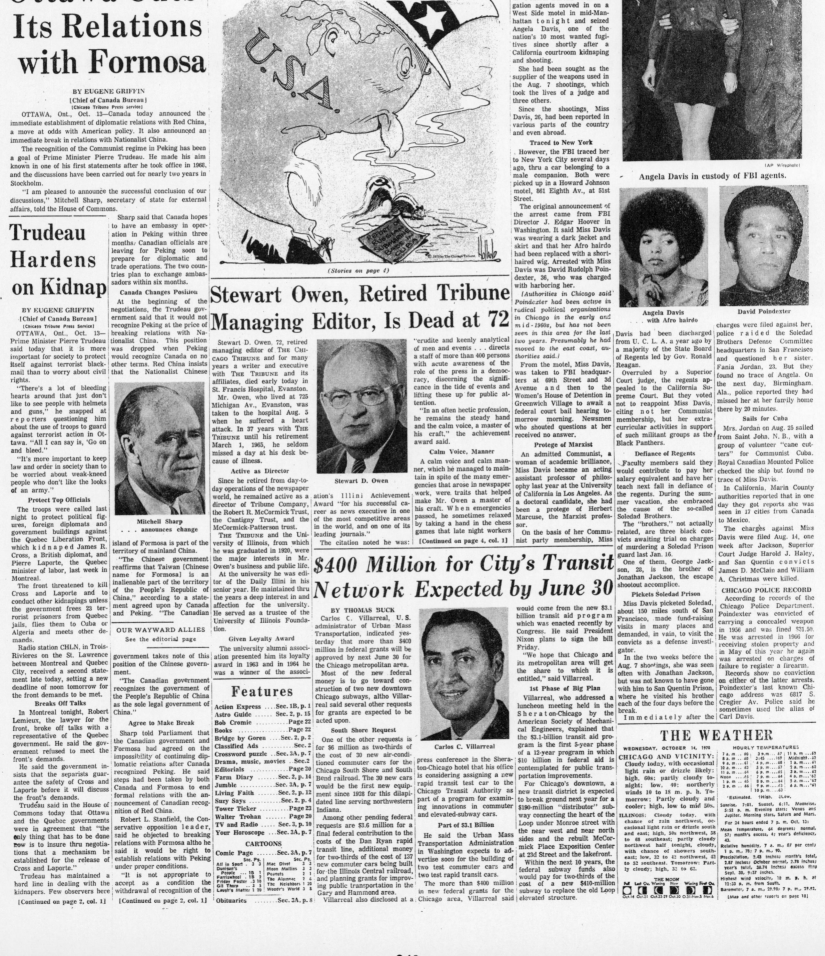

(Stories on page 4)

Stewart Owen, Retired Tribune Managing Editor, Is Dead at 72

Stewart D. Owen, 72, retired managing editor of THE CHICAGO TRIBUNE and for many years a writer and executive with THE TRIBUNE and its affiliates, died early today in St. Francis Hospital, Evanston.

Mr. Owen, who lived at 725 Michigan Av., Evanston, was taken to the hospital Aug. 5 when he suffered a heart attack. In 37 years with THE TRIBUNE until his retirement March 1, 1965, he seldom missed a day at his desk because of illness.

Active as Director

Since he retired from day-to-day operations of the newspaper world, he remained active as a director of Tribune Company, the Robert R. McCormick Trust, the Cantigny Trust, and the McCormick-Patterson trust.

THE TRIBUNE and the University of Illinois, from which he was graduated in 1920, were the major interests in Mr. Owen's business and public life.

At the university he was editor of the Daily Illini in his senior year. He maintained thru the years a deep interest in and affection for the university. He served as a trustee of the University of Illinois Foundation.

Given Loyalty Award

The university alumni association presented him its loyalty award in 1963 and in 1964 he was a winner of the association's Illini Achievement Award "for his successful career as news executive in one of the most competitive areas in the world, and on one of its leading journals."

Stewart D. Owen

The citation noted he was: "erudite and keenly analytical of men and events . . . directs a staff of more than 400 persons with acute awareness of the role of the press in a democracy, discerning the significance in the tide of events and lifting these up for public attention.

"In an often hectic profession, he remains the steady hand and the calm voice, a master of his craft," the achievement award said.

Calm Voice, Manner

A calm voice and calm manner, which he managed to maintain in spite of the many emergencies that arose in newspaper work, were traits that helped make Mr. Owen a master of his craft. When emergencies passed, he sometimes relaxed by taking a hand in the chess games that late night workers

[Continued on page 4, col. 1]

Features

$400 Million for City's Transit Network Expected by June 30

BY THOMAS BUCK

Carlos C. Villarreal, U. S. administrator of Urban Mass Transportation, indicated yesterday that more than $400 million in federal grants will be approved by next June 30 for the Chicago metropolitan area.

Most of the new federal money is to go toward construction of two new downtown Chicago subways, altho Villarreal said several other requests for grants are expected to be acted upon.

South Shore Request

One of the other requests is for $6 million as two-thirds of the cost of 30 new air-conditioned commuter cars for the Chicago South Shore and South Bend railroad. The 30 new cars would be the first new equipment since 1928 for this dilapidated line serving northwestern Indiana.

Among other pending federal requests are $3.6 million for a final federal contribution to the costs of the Dan Ryan rapid transit line, additional money for two-thirds of the cost of 137 new commuter cars being built for the Illinois Central railroad, and planning grants for improving public transportation in the Gary and Hammond area.

Villarreal also disclosed at a press conference in the Sheraton-Chicago hotel that his office is considering assigning a new rapid transit test car to the Chicago Transit Authority as part of a program for examining innovations in commuter and elevated-subway cars.

Carlos C. Villarreal

Part of $3.1 Billion

He said the Urban Mass Transportation Administration in Washington expects to advertise soon for the building of two test commuter cars and two test rapid transit cars.

The more than $400 million in new federal grants for the Chicago area, Villarreal said would come from the new $3.1 billion transit aid program which was enacted recently by Congress. He said President Nixon plans to sign the bill Friday.

"We hope that Chicago and its metropolitan area will get the share to which it is entitled," said Villarreal.

1st Phase of Big Plan

Villarreal, who addressed a luncheon meeting held in the Sheraton-Chicago by the American Society of Mechanical Engineers, explained that the $3.1-billion transit aid program is the first 5-year phase of a 12-year program in which $10 billion in federal aid is contemplated for public transportation improvements.

For Chicago's downtown, a new transit district is expected to break ground next year for a $190-million "distributor" subway connecting the heart of the Loop under Monroe street with the near west and near north sides and the rebuilt McCormick Place Exposition Center at 23d Street and the lakefront.

Within the next 10 years, the federal subway funds also would pay for two-thirds of the cost of a new $410-million subway to replace the old Loop elevated structure.

Fugitive Found in N.Y. Motel

NEW YORK, Oct. 13 (AP)—Federal Bureau of Investigation agents moved in on a West Side motel in mid-Manhattan tonight and seized Angela Davis, one of the nation's 10 most wanted fugitives since shortly after a California courtroom kidnaping and shooting.

She had been sought as the supplier of the weapons used in the Aug. 7 shootings, which took the lives of a judge and three others.

Since the shootings, Miss Davis, 26, had been reported in various parts of the country and even abroad.

Traced to New York

However, the FBI traced her to New York City several days ago, thru a car belonging to a male companion. Both were picked up in a Howard Johnson motel, 861 Eighth Av., at 51st Street.

The original announcement of the arrest came from FBI Director J. Edgar Hoover in Washington. It said Miss Davis was wearing a dark jacket and skirt and that her Afro hairdo had been replaced with a short-haired wig. Arrested with Miss Davis was David Rudolph Poindexter, 36, who was charged with harboring her.

[Authorities in Chicago said Poindexter had been active in radical political organizations in Chicago in the early and mid-1960s, but has not been seen in this area for the last two years. Presumably he had moved to the east coast, authorities said.]

From the motel, Miss Davis, was taken to FBI headquarters at 69th Street and 3d Avenue and then to the Women's House of Detention in Greenwich Village to await a federal court bail hearing tomorrow morning. Newsmen who shouted questions at her received no answer.

Protege of Marxist

An admitted Communist, a woman of academic brilliance, Miss Davis became an acting assistant professor of philosophy last year at the University of California in Los Angeles. As a doctoral candidate, she had been a protege of Herbert Marcuse, the Marxist professor.

On the basis of her Communist party membership, Miss Davis had been discharged from U. C. L. A. a year ago by a majority of the State Board of Regents led by Gov. Ronald Reagan.

Overruled by a Superior Court judge, the regents appealed to the California Supreme Court. But they voted not to reappoint Miss Davis, citing not her Communist membership, but her extra-curricular activities in support of such militant groups as the Black Panthers.

Defiance of Regents

Faculty members said they would contribute to pay her salary equivalent and have her teach next fall in defiance of the regents. During the summer vacation, she embraced the cause of the so-called Soledad Brothers.

The "brothers," not actually related, are three black convicts awaiting trial on charges of murdering a Soledad Prison guard last Jan. 16.

One of them, George Jackson, 28, is the brother of Jonathan Jackson, the escape shootout accomplice.

Pickets Soledad Prison

Miss Davis picketed Soledad, about 150 miles south of San Francisco, made fund-raising visits in many places and demanded, in vain, to visit the convicts as a defense investigator.

In the two weeks before the Aug. 7 shootings, she was seen often with Jonathan Jackson, but was not known to have gone with him to San Quentin Prison, where he visited his brother each of the four days before the break.

Immediately after the charges were filed against her, police raided the Soledad Brothers Defense Committee headquarters in San Francisco and questioned her sister, Fania Jordan, 23. But they found no trace of Angela. On the next day, Birmingham, Ala., police reported they had missed her at her family home there by 20 minutes.

Sails for Cuba

Mrs. Jordan on Aug. 25 sailed from Saint John, N. B., with a group of volunteer "cane cutters" for Communist Cuba. Royal Canadian Mounted Police checked the ship but found no trace of Miss Davis.

In California, Marin County authorities reported that in one day they got reports she was seen in 17 cities from Canada to Mexico.

The charges against Miss Davis were filed Aug. 14, one week after Jackson, Superior Court Judge Harold J. Haley, and San Quentin convicts James D. McClain and William A. Christmas were killed.

CHICAGO POLICE RECORD

According to records of the Chicago Police Department, Poindexter was convicted of carrying a concealed weapon in 1956 and was fined $31.50. He was arrested in 1966 for receiving stolen property and in May of this year he again was arrested on charges of failure to register a firearm.

Records show no conviction on either of the latter arrests. Poindexter's last known Chicago address was 6817 S. Cregier Av. Police said he sometimes used the alias of Carl Davis.

[AP Wirephoto]

Angela Davis in custody of FBI agents.

Angela Davis . . . with Afro hairdo

David Poindexter

THE WEATHER

WEDNESDAY, OCTOBER 14, 1970

CHICAGO AND VICINITY: Cloudy today, with occasional light rain or drizzle likely; high, 60s; partly cloudy tonight; low, 40; northerly winds 10 to 18 m. p. h. Tomorrow: Partly cloudy and cooler; high, low to mid 50s.

ILLINOIS: Cloudy today, with chance of rain northwest, occasional light rain or drizzle south and east; high, 50s northwest, 58 to 68 southeast; partly cloudy northwest half tonight, cloudy, with chance of showers southeast; low, 32 to 42 northwest, 42 to 52 southeast. Tomorrow: Partly cloudy; high, 52 to 62.

THE MOON

Full	Last Qu.	Waning	New	Waxing	First Qu.
Oct.14	Oct.21	Oct.22-29	Oct.30	O.31-Nov.5	Nov.6

HOURLY TEMPERATURES

7 a. m.	60	3 p. m.	67	11 p. m.	62
8 a. m.	60	3:45	†69	Midnight	62
9 a. m.	61	4 p. m.	68	1 a. m.	61
10 a. m.	63	5 p. m.	67	2 a. m.	60
11 a. m.	64	6 p. m.	65	3 a. m.	62
Noon	65	7 p. m.	64	4 a. m.	*62
1 p. m.	65	8 p. m.	64	5 a. m.	*62
2 p. m.	66	9 p. m.	63	6 a. m.	*61
		10 p. m.	63		

*Estimated. †High. ‡Low.

Sunrise, 7:01. Sunset, 6:11. Moonrise, 5:52 p. m. Evening stars: Venus and Jupiter. Morning stars, Saturn and Mars.

For 24 hours ended 7 p. m. Oct. 13:

Mean temperature, 64 degrees; normal, 57; month's excess, 4; year's deficiency, 43.

Relative humidity, 7 a. m., 87 per cent; 1 p. m., 78; 7 p. m., 90.

Precipitation, 2.43 inches; month's total, 2.87 inches; October normal, 2.78 inches; year's total, 38.74 inches; excess thru Sept. 30, 9.57 inches.

Highest wind velocity, 10 m. p. h. at 12:33 p. m. from South.

Barometer, 7 a. m., 29.98; 7 p. m., 29.92.

[Map and other reports on page 18]

Calley Found Guilty of Murder

Court-Martial Jury Returns Verdict in My Lai Massacre

FT. BENNING, Ga. (AP) — Lt. William Calley was convicted Monday of the premeditated murder of 22 Vietnamese civilians at My Lai three years ago. He is the first American veteran of Vietnam to be held responsible in the My Lai massacre.

Calley stood ramrod straight as the verdict was read, then did an about face. He was flanked by his military and civilian lawyers.

A half-hour after the verdict was announced, military police escorted him to the post stockade. "Take my word for it, the boy's crushed," his civilian attorney, George Latimer said, as they left the courtroom.

He was placed in quarters separate from those of enlisted men, and will be returned to the courtroom at 9 a.m. today when the sentencing phase of the court-martial begins.

Calley was convicted of killing one person at a trail intersection, 20 at a ditch where he admitted firing six or eight bullets, of the death of a man in white and of assault on a child believed to be about 2-years-old.

He had been charged with the deaths of 102 Vietnamese men, women and children.

Calley was notified that a verdict was ready by an Army officer who went to his bachelor apartment on the post. "They're finally ready," he said. He was tense when he arrived at the courtroom, but smiled at newsmen.

"We're with you Calley" shouted a young blonde teenager in the crowd of about 100 persons who watched Calley escorted to the two-room cell at the stockade.

Capt. Ernest Medina, Calley's superior officer at My Lai who also faces court-martial on murder charges, could not be reached for comment at Ft. McPherson in Atlanta. His military counsel, Capt. Mark Kadish, said Medina would have no statement until today. At that time, Kadish said, Medina would issue a statement from the Boston office of his civilian attorney, F. Lee Bailey.

To convict Calley, the jury needed only the concurrence of four of the six members of the panel. In civilian cases, the verdict must be unanimous.

But in the sentencing phase, it will require the vote of all six members for the death sentence. And the agreement of five members is needed for a life sentence.

The jury members remained sequestered for the sentencing phase and no one was permitted to question them about how the voting went during the lengthy deliberations.

Once Calley had been taken away, Latimer was asked if Calley expected the verdict.

"I don't think so," said the Salt Lake City lawyer who once served as a judge on the U.S. Military Court of Appeals. "I didn't expect it."

While there can be no hung jury in the verdict deliberations, there is the possibility of irreconcilable differences in the sentence phase. Should that happen, the jury is permitted, under stringent rules, to modify the verdict.

Calley, 27, took the verdict and then snapped a salute to the jury foreman, Col. Clifford Ford, 53, the only officer on the jury who is not a veteran of Vietnam.

After the verdict, Calley was escorted out of the courthouse at 5:03 p.m. and taken in a military vehicle to the stockade about a half-mile away. There he occupied a separate officer's cell of two rooms. While not occupied by a prisoner, it is used as a chaplain's office.

Lt. Calley being led to post stockade after verdict.

Manson Jury Votes Death

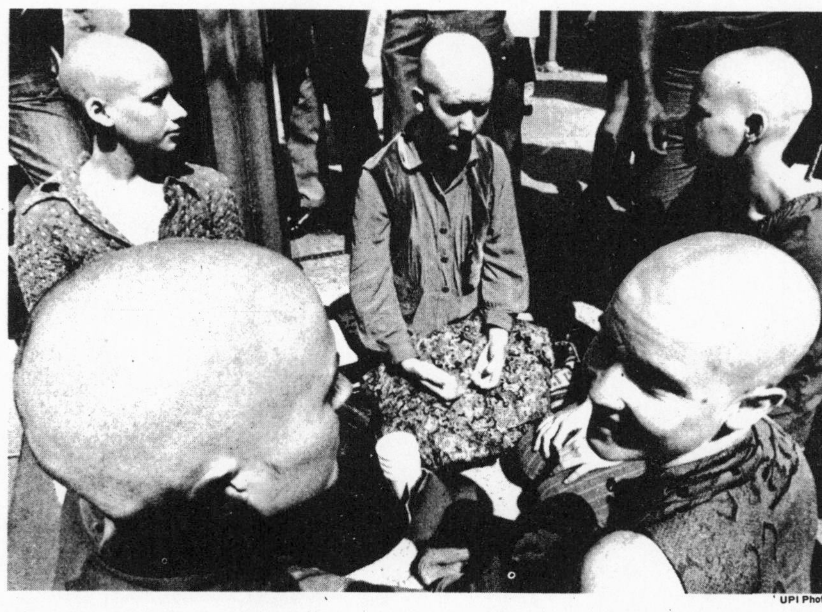

UPI Photo

These followers of Charles Manson have threatened to set themselves afire if their idol is sentenced to death. They have maintained a vigil outside the Los Angeles Hall of Justice since the trial began. With heads completely shaved, they apparently are imitating Manson, who cut his hair short last week. Clockwise from upper left, they are Cappy, Kathy, Mary, Sandra Goode and Brenda.

The Sacramento Union

Oldest Daily In the West ★ ★ It's Tuesday, March 30, 1971 10¢

Girl Hitchhikers' Ride With Terror

By BILL CROSBY
Sacramento Union Staff Writer

A 16-year-old Sacramento girl Monday recalled a day and night of terror during which she and a girl friend were kidnaped and raped and the other girl was murdered.

Marjorie Meyers was obviously upset as she related what happened between the time she and Charleyce Whalen, 17, were picked up as they hitchhiked on Arden Way Saturday morning.

"We've hitchhiked hundreds of times" Miss Meyer said, "but I'll never do it again. Never."

The girls were threatened with guns and driven to San Francisco by two men who later were arrested on charges of kidnap, rape, of being ex-convicts with guns, possession of narcotics and furnishing narcotics to minors.

One of the men, Bernard Joseph Mora, 35, who escaped from the Sacramento County Jail last November, also was charged with the murder of Miss Whalen, whose bullet-riddled body was found beside a dirt road in Half Moon Bay late Saturday night.

Police Chiet Fred Ceranski said it was

Please See Page A2, Col. 1

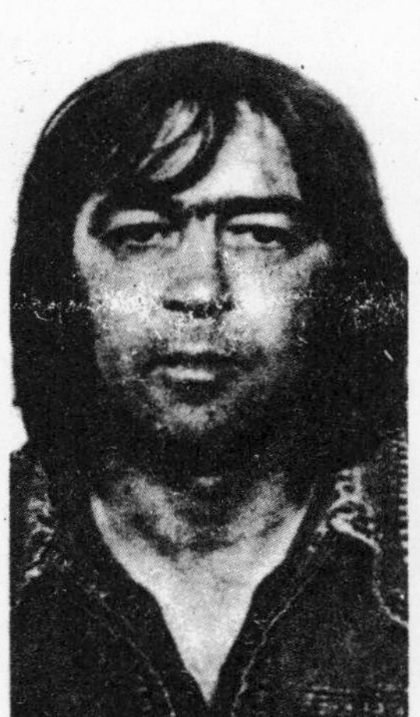

Lawrence Fontes Jr.

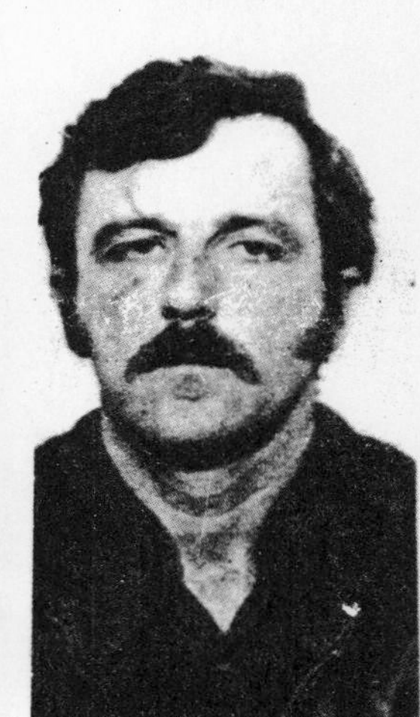

Bernard J. Mora

Good Morning!

The brighter side

MENLO PARK (UPI) — Skydiver John Erickson has made 34 successful jumps without parachute trouble, but he had some Sunday. His chute opened while he was riding a motorcycle home from a jump and yanked him off the bike.

Growers adamant

SALINAS — Representatives of 200 Salinas and Imperial Valley produce growers agreed Monday to fight any move to switch their Teamster Union contracts to Cesar Chavez' United Farm Workers Organizing Committee.

Worth repeating

Duty is what one expects from others.

—Oscar Wilde

Fair and windy

Sacramento and vicinity: Mostly fair though windy this afternoon. High near 70, low 43. Sierra: Mostly fair. Lake Tahoe: High 45, low 25. Details, Page D-10.

For highway conditions, call 445-0120.

On the inside

Phone: 442-7811 Classified: 444-5555

121st Year, Volume 142, No. 12 36 Pages, 4 Sections

301 Capitol Mall, Sacramento, Calif., 95812

Jury Votes Death For Manson, Girls

LOS ANGELES (AP) — A jury — acting after the defendants were ejected for angry shouts — Monday decreed death in San Quentin Prison's gas chamber for Charles Manson and three women followers convicted of the savage murders of movie actress Sharon Tate and six others.

When the jury came to court in late afternoon, after less than two full days of deliberations, Manson, 36, shouted before any of the penalties were announced:

"I don't see how you can get by with this. You don't have no authority over me. You're not nearly as good as me. This is not the people's courtroom."

After the judge ordered him out the three women codefendants, their long hair cropped close to their heads for the occasion, spoke out.

"You've all judged yourselves," said Patricia Krenwinkel, 23. "It's gonna come down hard," cried Susan Atkins, 22, "Lock your doors. Protect your kids." After that the judge ordered her out and she shouted: "Remove yourself from the face of the earth. You're all fools."

Leslie Van Houten, 21, was ushered out last after muttering, "You've all just judged yourselves."

Defense attorneys appeared shaken by the death penalties. They had asked the jurors for "the gift of life" for the defendants. Women jurors looked tearful and the foreman wiped his eyes after the verdicts.

The judge has the power to reduce the death penalty to life imprisonment.

The action climaxed a nine-month, two-part trial tabbed the longest such criminal proceeding in California and perhaps the nation.

The same seven men and five women who convicted the four of first-degree murder and conspiracy last Jan. 25 chose the death penalty over the only alternative, life imprisonment with the possibility of parole after seven years.

As the first of the women's death sentences were read, two women jurors ap-

Please See Page A9 Col. 1

Two Rescued 3 Days After Ship Sinking

NEW YORK (AP) — The Coast Guard reported that two life-jacketed survivors were snatched from the sea Monday nearly three days after their ship went down off Cape Hatteras, N.C. One of the men was reported in serious condition.

The Coast Guard said it planned to drop Air Force paramedics to the Texaco Nebraska, which picked up the men. They were identified by Texaco officials as Jorge Martinez of Honduras and Gard A. Morgan of New Orleans.

The Texaco Nebraska was taking part in an intensified air sea search in 13-foot seas for those missing from the 44-man crew of the lost tanker Texaco Oklahoma.

A Texaco spokesman said the search would continue through the night.

Late Monday night the Coast Guard cutter Escanaba sighted three apparently lifeless bodies floating 180 miles off Cape Hatteras, N.C.

Court Battle

Two Estates Fighting For Almost $10,000

By MIKE OTTEN
Sacramento Union Staff Writer

The estates of two murder victims are battling each other in Sacramento County Superior Court for the right to nearly $10,000 in $100 bills.

The ingredients in the unusual court trial would "make a great subject for a novel," said Judge Irving H. Perluss as he finished hearing evidence Monday.

They include international drug trafficking, the murder of an alleged narcotic wholesaler in London and the murder of a Sacramento pool hall owner.

Billie Crawford, 43, contends the money was stolen from her father, Palmer Pinckney, 71, who was fatally shot Jan. 24, 1968, as he exchanged shots with robbers in his home at 2643 21st Ave.

Rae Nelle Harmening Stanpfl, now 23, contends the money came from Thomas Scott Ezelle's wholesale drug business in which he allegedly parlayed $200 into a $10,000 bankroll in San Francisco's Haight-Ashbury district.

Ezelle, according to attorney James Ford, who represents his estate, was stabbed to death at the age of 20 on Jan. 21, 1970, in London over narcotics dealings.

The money — $9,722.40 of which $9,600 was in $100 bills — was seized by Sacramento police March 23 after Mrs. Stanpfl's mother called police.

The money was in a large brown paper bag which also contained marijuana, LSD

Please See Page A2, Col. 1

Nixon Order

Wage-Price Curbs On Building Industry

SAN CLEMENTE (AP) — President Nixon set up a cooperative wage-price system of restraints Monday for the inflation-plagued construction industry, tying any wage boosts generally to an average of about 6 per cent a year.

He reported: "Contractors and labor leaders have indicated their willingness to coooperate with the government in fair measures to achieve greater wage and price stability."

In a companion move, Nixon reinstated the Davis-Bacon Act, which he had suspended Feb. 23. It calls for payment of union-scale wages on federal government building projects.

Nixon said success of the wage-price system will rest largely "on the mutual understanding of labor and management in an industry whose future is now being undermined by its own excessess."

Nixon signed an executive order at the Western White House setting up the complex mechanism. It includes craft-by-craft boards in the construction industry to determine whether future negotiated wage agreements fall under a set of criteria that aims to restore a pattern of wage increase that existed during the years 1961-1968.

That level, Secretary of Labor James D. Hodgson said, is somewhere around 6 per cent a year, compared to the construction industry's 1970 average wage increases of better than 18 per cent for a single year and an average in the first three months in 1971 of 16.5 per cent.

A 12-member review committee will look over all construction industry collective bargaining agreements negotiated henceforth. They will determine whether the wage sections fall within the criteria that will be worked out by the craft union-management boards.

Nixon's suspension of the Davis-Bacon Act, Hodgson said, was mainly responsible for getting the industry and the unions to agree to the self-enforcing plan.

4,500 Sign Petitions

Yolo Pay Raise Protested

Special to The Union

WOODLAND — Officials of the Yolo County Taxpayers Association said Monday about 4,500 signatures have been collected protesting the action of county supervisors raising their own pay March 1.

Directors of the association said 200 volunteers signed up about 4,500 registered voters in only 15 days.

The association is demanding that supervisors rescind action increasing their annual pay from $7,800 to $9,300, or place the issue before Yolo County voters.

They need 3,068 signatures, or 10 per cent of the registered voters in Yolo County, to block the action. Supervisors have indicated that if the association is successful, they will call a special election.

A spokesman for the association said Monday that "4,500 signatures are in hand." But as the work day ended, the signatures had not been turned over to the county clerk for verification.

The association has until 5 p.m. Wednesday to turn in the signatures.

The association has contended that voters were misled about state Proposition 12 during the last election and were under the impression that the action of county supervisors seeking pay increases would be put to a popular vote.

On March 1, the supervisors voted themselves a $1,500 annual raise, retroactive to Jan. 1. Neighboring Sacramento County supervisors voted themselves pay raises from $10,800 annually to $13,200, and an additional boost next January to $15,000. No group has protested the action in Sacramento County.

If the association is successful when petition signatures are checked against voter registrations, the supervisors must either rescind their action or call an election not sooner than 60 days and not later than 120 days.

CLOSING STOCK PRICES

Pages 64-66

WEATHER

Tonight: Rain, wind, around 70.
Tomorrow: Cloudy, high 60s.
Seasonable Thursday.
SUNSET: 8:15 PM
SUNRISE TOMORROW: 5:30 AM

New York Post

FOUNDED 1801. THE OLDEST CONTINUOUSLY PUBLISHED DAILY IN THE UNITED STATES.

Vol. 170 No. 161 | NEW YORK, TUESDAY, MAY 25, 1971 | 15 Cents

Post Photo by Arthur Pomerantz

A cop flicks away a tear as McCoy Jones, 11, bears up bravely at the funeral of his father, slain Patrolman Waverly Jones, today.

SEALE CHARGES DROPPED

NEW HAVEN (AP)—A Superior Court judge today dismissed murder-kidnap charges against Black Panther Chairman Bobby Seale and a local Panther leader on grounds that an unbiased jury would be impossible to select.

The decision came just 24 hours after a jury had reported it could not reach a verdict in the case, and the judge had declared a mistrial.

"The state has put its best foot forward," said Judge Harold V. Mulvey.

Seale's co-defendant Mrs. Erica Huggins, was mobbed by Panther supporters as she left the courtroom. Seale remained in custody, awaiting posting of bail on his four-year

Continued on Page 4

Dragnet Tightens On Cop Killers

By Cy Egan

A police dragnet in the ambush murders of two Harlem policemen tightened today as several possible suspects remained at large.

A source close to the investigation revealed that "several suspects continue to be checked" because detectives have so far been unable to locate them.

Several names have been given police both by informers and through special phone numbers set up by police to receive information in the shootings.

Detectives still have been unable to track down a number of them who fit the general description of the two killers.

Meantime, the police were reported accumulating information on the whereabouts of the suspects.

While it was explained that anyone pointed out to police remains a suspect, it said that the names of those being sought now remained high on the priority list because police couldn't locate them.

At first identified as a "prime suspect," but subsequently cleared of any connection with the shootings was Leroy King, 23.

A brief flurry came in the investigation with the arrest of two Black Panther Party figures on weapons possession charges, but police offi-

Continued on Page 3

Draft Foes Lose Test

WASHINGTON (AP)—The Senate today rejected, 52-21, legislation that would have forbidden the use of draftees on combat assignments in Southeast Asia.

Opponents, led by Sen. John C. Stennis (D-Miss.), said the amendment would have crippled efforts to attract more volunteers into the Army.

Instead of enlisting, Stennis said, men would have waited for induction, knowing it carried a guarantee against combat as-

Continued on Page 3

ON THE INSIDE

MORE $2 LOTTERY WINNERS Page 28

THE ISRAELIS: Founders & Sons

By Amos Elon • Digest of the Best-Seller Continues on Page 33

WEATHER
Chance of rain, 90-95.
Tonight: Rain, 70-75.
Tomorrow: Partly sunny, less humid, 85-90.
Fair Saturday.
SUNSET: 8:31 PM
SUNRISE TOMORROW: 5:29 AM

New York Post

FOUNDED 1801. THE OLDEST CONTINUOUSLY PUBLISHED DAILY IN THE UNITED STATES.

Vol. 170 No. 192 | NEW YORK, THURSDAY, JULY 1, 1971 | 15 Cents

Associated Press Wirephoto

Daniel Ellsberg, right, who leaked the Pentagon Papers, arrives at Harvard Law School to get a report on the Supreme Court decision permitting publication of the documents. With him is his lawyer, Leonard B. Boudin.

Pentagon Papers —The Lid Is Off

By Dick Belsky

It was President Kennedy—not Johnson—who first raised the stakes in Vietnam and passed up the best opportunity to quit the war, newspapers resuming publication of the secret Pentagon study said today.

The New York Times, in a 12-page report following yesterday's Supreme Court go-ahead decision, said Kennedy and his advisers considered defeat unthinkable and began the first in a series of steps that led to the 1965 escalation by President Johnson.

Meanwhile, The Washington Post speculated on the fumbled chance for peace, saying that Kennedy Administration officials apparently feared a "neutralist" end to the war as much as a Communist takeover.

"The Pentagon's study . . . concludes," the Times said, "that . . . Kennedy transformed the 'limited risk gamble' of the Eisenhower Administration into a 'broad commitment' to prevent Commu-

Continued on Page 2

ON THE INSIDE

New Angle In Shooting Of Colombo

By Cy Egan

The investigation into the shooting of Joseph Colombo Sr. focused today on the possibility that black revolutionaries were behind the attempt to kill the reputed underworld boss last Monday.

The search for links between the would-be assassin, Jerome Johnson, 24, and black militants was stepped up after the Bronx home of an alleged narcotics kingpin was bombed by the same black revolutionary group that claimed credit for the Colombo shooting.

Colombo remained in critical condition and in a coma at Roosevelt Hospital, where he was rushed with head and other wounds after the shooting. He was gunned down at Columbus Circle just prior to a rally of the Italian-American Civil Rights League, of which he is founder.

In telephone calls to news agencies shortly before and after the pipe bomb exploded last night outside the apartment of Frank Townsend, 30, at 1040 Gerard Av., a spokesman for the Black Revolutionary Assault Team announced:

"We just bombed the home of Frank Townsend. We dislike a two-bit hoodlum who peddles dope and we're the same people who shot Joe Colombo."

Townsend, a black ex-C. W. Post College basketball star, is under indictment stemming from his arrest last March 26 on charges of possession of more than $1.5 million worth of heroin. Authorities called him "a kingpin in a wholesale organization that supplies heroin to pushers all over the city."

The Black Revolutionary Assault Team mentioned no specific motive when it claimed responsibility for the Colombo shooting. It had announced that it was responsible for the shooting in a telephone call to news agencies right after the guns went off on Monday.

But the Brooklyn underworld family reputedly headed by Colombo has been linked by authorities at various times to narcotics trafficking —target of intense resentment among militants in the black community.

Chief of Detectives Albert A. Seedman, who is

Continued on Page 4

Cong Make New Offer In Paris

By Michael Goldsmith

PARIS (AP)—The Viet Cong submitted a new seven-point peace plan today offering to release all prisoners taken by the Communists in the Vietnam war if the U.S. agrees to withdraw all its forces by the end of the year.

The plan calls for the gradual release of the prisoners simultaneously with the American withdrawal.

The plan was outlined at the 119th weekly session of the Vietnam peace talks by the Viet Cong foreign minister, Mrs. Nguyen Thi Binh.

Basic conditions for ending the war were unchanged from all previous Communist proposals submitted to the long-deadlocked conference. They were total and unconditional withdrawal of all American forces and es-

Continued on Page 2

"All the News That's Fit to Print"

The New York Times

LATE CITY EDITION

Weather: Showers likely today and tonight. Partly cloudy tomorrow. Temp. range: today 63-75; Tuesday 60-75. Full U.S. report on Page 94.

VOL. CXXI. No. 41,738

NEW YORK, WEDNESDAY, MAY 3, 1972

15 CENTS

Story of Joe Gallo's Murder: 5 in Colombo Gang Implicated

Informant, in Fear, Goes to the F.B.I.

Suspects Abandon Hideout in Nyack

By NICHOLAS GAGE

An associate of the Mafia family of Joseph A. Colombo Sr. has turned himself in to the Federal Bureau of Investigation and said that he and four other men carried out the killing of Joseph Gallo on April 7, according to law-enforcement officials.

An investigation by The New York Times has established that the informant, who is now in police custody, is Joseph Luparelli, a close associate of Joseph Yacovelli, now the acting head of the Colombo family and the man who officials believe sanctioned the Gallo murder.

The officials said that over the last three weeks Luparelli had given Federal authorities and the New York police the following account of the events surrounding the shooting of Gallo, a Colombo rival, at Umberto's Clam House on Mulberry Street:

At about 4:30 A.M. on April 7, Luparelli happened to be sitting at the clam bar in Umberto's with a friend. Ten minutes later Joseph Gallo, who was celebrating his 43d birthday, entered with a jovial group—his bride of three weeks, her 10-year-old daughter, Gallo's sister, his bodyguard Peter Diapoulas, 42, and the latter's date.

The New York Times

Joseph Yacovelli after he appeared in the Brooklyn Federal Court last year.

When he saw Gallo, who for several months had been marked for execution by the Colombo family, Luparelli dropped his spoon and hurried out of the restaurant.

He walked two blocks to another restaurant nearby frequented by Colombo men. Luparelli asked for Yacovelli, acting head of the family since Colombo was gravely wounded last year at a Columbus Circle rally of the Italian-American Civil Rights League. He was told that Yacovelli was not around.

Then Luparelli related what he had seen to Philip Gambino, a Colombo man, and Carmine Di Biase, a former member of the family of the late Vito Genovese who had reportedly shifted to the Colombo group.

The two of them telephoned Yacovelli and were told to arm themselves, according to Luparelli. Gambino and Di Biase left the restaurant briefly and returned about 5:15 with several guns.

Luparelli, two men believed to be brothers whom Luparelli has not as yet identified, Gambino and Di Biase then drove two cars down Mulberry Street and parked not far from Umberto's. One of the cars was to serve as a "crash" car to intercept any car that tried to thwart the getaway.

All but one of the five entered Umberto's through the back door. Luparelli says he stayed at the wheel of one of the cars.

As the four gunmen casually

Continued on Page 39, Column 1

Yoichi Okamoto/Rapho Guillumette

J. Edgar Hoover

J. Edgar Hoover, 77, Dies; Will Lie in State in Capitol

By FRED P. GRAHAM
Special to The New York Times

WASHINGTON, May 2—J. Edgar Hoover, who directed the Federal Bureau of Investigation for 48 years and built it into a dominant and controversial force in American law enforcement, died during the night from the effects of high blood pressure.

Mr. Hoover, who at 77 years of age still held the F.B.I. firmly within his control, died in his bedroom after working a full day in his office yesterday. He was found by his housekeeper at 8:30 this morning, slumped on the floor beside his bed.

His home is near Rock Creek Park in the northwest section of Washington.

Dr. James L. Luke, Washington's Medical Examiner, attributed the death to "hypertensive cardio-vascular disease." He said that Mr. Hoover had been suffering from a heart ailment for some time but gave no details.

He said that death could have been caused by heart failure associated with high blood pressure, but that no autopsy would be performed because the death was known to be due to natural causes.

Acting Attorney General Richard G. Kleindienst announced the death at 11 A.M., after F.B.I. offices around the world had been given the news and reports of it began to circulate here. Congress promptly voted its permission for his body to lie in state in the Capitol Rotunda—an honor accorded to only 21 persons before, of whom eight were Presidents or former Presidents.

Mr. Hoover's body will be taken to the Rotunda tomorrow morning and will lie in state until shortly before the funeral Thursday. Arrangements for the funeral were incomplete today, but it was learned that President Nixon would deliver the eulogy at 11 A.M. Thursday at the National Presbyterian

Continued on Page 53, Column 1

BASES NEAR HUE ATTACKED; SOUTH VIETNAMESE TROOPS FLEE QUANGTRI IN DISORDER

Retreat Leaves Small Unit Of Marines Facing Enemy

By SYDNEY H. SCHANBERG
Special to The New York Times

HUE, South Vietnam, May 2—Thousands of panicking South Vietnamese soldiers—most of whom did not appear to have made much contact with the advancing North Vietnamese—fled in confusion from Quangtri Province today, streaming south down Route 1 like a rabble out of control.

Commandeering civilian vehicles at rifle point, feigning nonexistent injuries, carrying away C rations but not their ammunition, and hurling rocks at Western news photographers taking pictures of their flight, the Government troops of the Third Infantry Division ran from the fighting in one of the biggest retreats of the war.

No one tried to stop them: their officers were running too.

The battlefront north of Hue was thus left solely to a brigade of a few thousand South Vietnamese marines.

The Third Division had fallen back before, at the beginning of the enemy offensive a month ago, but the commander, Brig. Gen. Vu Van Giai, had managed to scrape it together again and put it back on the line around Quangtri until yesterday.

But today, according to American advisers, virtually the entire division—about 10,000 infantrymen plus 1,000 rangers—was in rout, not even stopping at the checkpoints where military policemen were supposed to halt runaways and turn them around.

It was the force that was supposed to have defended the city of Quangtri, which was abandoned yesterday and which had been the northernmost town held by the Government.

There does not seem to be much now between the North Vietnamese and their next and more important objective,

Continued on Page 20, Column 4

NEW ASSAULT DUE

U.S. General Expects Enemy Step-Up in Next Few Days

By HENRY KAMM
Special to The New York Times

SAIGON, South Vietnam, Wednesday, May 3—With the city of Quangtri lost, two South Vietnamese fire bases on the approaches to the former imperial capital of Hue were reported under enemy attack yesterday.

Hue itself, 32 miles southeast of the fallen capital of Quangtri Province, was bracing for a North Vietnamese onslaught.

Serious attacks could be expected in the next few days, newsmen in Hue were told last night by Brig. Gen. Thomas W. Bowen, senior adviser to the regional commander. United States intelligence sources estimated that it would take the enemy forces six to eight days to prepare for the assault.

Artillery Batters Base

United States military sources said last night that Fire Base Nancy, the northernmost position held by the South Vietnamese and their last one in Quangtri Province, was battered by enemy artillery. [United Press International, quoting officers in the field, said enemy soldiers attacking with the support of tanks had seized part of the outpost.]

The base, which is 20 miles northwest of Hue, lies a little west of Route 1, South Vietnam's main north-south highway, and on the boundary between Quangtri and Thuathien Provinces. Hue is the capital of Thuathien Province.

Heightening the threat to Hue, North Vietnamese troops nearing the city from the southwest reportedly struck at Fire Base Birmingham, 13 miles from the city. The base was subjected to heavy artillery fire.

[Meanwhile, the United States aircraft carrier Midway arrived off Vietnam to help support South Vietnamese forces, The Associated Press reported. With her arrival, the United States had five carriers operating in the area for the first time in the war.]

In the center of South Vietnam, Landing Zone English, the last Government position in the northern part of the coastal province of Binhdinh, was reportedly abandoned last night after several days of heavy enemy pressure. American advisers were evacuated from the base Monday, indicating that the base had been effectively written off.

American military sources reported that South Vietnam's 40th Infantry Regiment pulled out of Landing Zone English, north of the fallen district town

Continued on Page 20, Column 1

Pessimism in Saigon

Army's Inability to Defend the South Puts Government in a Perilous Stage

By CRAIG R. WHITNEY
Special to The New York Times

SAIGON, South Vietnam, May 2—The loss of South Vietnam's northernmost province and the collapse of two of its combat divisions in the last week have brought the Government of President Nguyen Van Thieu to a perilous stage.

News Analysis

Both American and Vietnamese officials here and elsewhere are deeply pessimistic — for the first time in years — about the country's prospects of pulling through.

The growing consensus among Americans here is that the South Vietnamese armed forces, in their country's hour of greatest danger, have unexpectedly proved unequal to the task of defending it. The principal reason is that the commanders, never before tested so rigorously, are not spurring the troops to resist the three-front North Vietnamese onslaught with the vigor and determination that would be required to repel rather than stalemate it.

Vietnamese observers in Hue described the scene in the former imperial capital today as "an agony," with the streets full of soldiers running aimlessly about.

The road from Hue south to Danang, Vietnam's second largest city, is jammed with refugees and with soldiers who appear to be deserters, trying to make their way to safety.

A senior American official in Danang said tonight that the

Continued on Page 21, Column 3

Washington Aides, Discouraged, Hint At Wider Bombings

By WILLIAM BEECHER
Special to The New York Times

WASHINGTON, May 2 — Administration officials tried publicly today to put a brave face on their reaction to news of the battle in South Vietnam, but throughout the Government there were widespread signs of growing pessimism.

Well-placed sources in the Nixon Administration hinted that unless the promise of positive results emerged later this week from public or secret peace talks, the United States would soon resume heavy bombing in the Hanoi and Haiphong areas of North Vietnam.

As officials at the White House, the State Department and the Defense Department studied reports of enemy advances in the south, there were these developments:

¶Pentagon officials said American field commanders were being given increasing latitude in conducting air strikes in the southern part of North Vietnam.

¶Diplomatic and Government

Continued on Page 20, Column 7

Humphrey Indiana Victor; Jackson Quits Primaries

Wallace Defeat Narrow

By SETH S. KING
Special to The New York Times

INDIANAPOLIS, May 2—Senator Hubert H. Humphrey of Minnesota won a narrow victory tonight over Gov. George C. Wallace of Alabama in the Indiana Presidential primary.

The Senator's edge in the statewide total, plus a lead in five Congressional Districts, indicated that he would have 49 of Indiana's 76 first-ballot votes at the Democratic National Convention. Mr. Wallace was leading in six districts, which would give him 27 delegates.

With 88 per cent of 4,480 precincts reporting, the tally was:

Humphrey ...286,850 (47%)
Wallace 255,593 (41%)
Muskie 74,307 (12%)

In the Alabama primary today, Governor Wallace appeared to be assured of winning the majority of the state's 29 delegates. In the District of Columbia, a favorite-son slate pledged to the Rev. Walter E. Fauntroy won at least 13 of the district's 15 Democratic delegate votes [Details, Page 32.]

In Indiana, the Alabama Governor's percentage of the total

Continued on Page 32, Column 1

Race in Ohio Is Close

By DOUGLAS E. KNEELAND
Special to The New York Times

COLUMBUS, Ohio, Wednesday, May 3—Senators Hubert H. Humphrey of Minnesota and George McGovern of South Dakota were locked in a tight race early today in the Ohio Presidential primary.

Senator Henry M. Jackson of Washington, who was trailing badly, announced shortly before midnight that, while he would remain a candidate, he would campaign in no more primaries. [Details on Page 32.]

There was no Presidential preference vote as such, but 38 of the 153 Democratic delegates were selected at large, providing a measure of popular sentiment statewide. The voter turnout was large.

With 5,592 of the 12,648 precincts reporting, the tally on at-large slates was:

Humphrey ...188,467 (41%)
McGovern ...174,589 (38%)
Muskie 45,796 (10%)
Jackson 37,789 (8%)
McCarthy 10,950 (2%)

Far behind were Senator Edmund S. Muskie of Maine, who had withdrawn from active campaigning, and former Senator Eugene J. McCarthy of

Continued on Page 32, Column 4

24 POLICE INDICTED IN A BRIBERY CASE

Accused of Taking $250,000 Annually in Brooklyn to Protect Gamblers

By MORRIS KAPLAN

Three police sergeants, 20 patrolmen and one patrolwoman were arrested and suspended from the Police Department yesterday after they were indicted and accused of taking a quarter of a million dollars annually in payoffs to protect gamblers linked to the Mafia.

The arrests under what was called the largest single indictment ever handed up here against members of the police force followed by a day the suicide of a police lieutenant who was also under investigation in the case. He shot himself in the head in a rented hotel room.

The lieutenant, Fletcher Hueston, had been second in command of the Public Morals Squad of the 13th Division in Brooklyn — the unit to which each of the individuals named in the indictment had been assigned during some portion of the last 18 months.

Deputy Police Commissioner William P. McCarthy indicated that additional investigations were being made in several of the 17 other public morals units. At least two policemen and possibly some gamblers were used as undercover agents in the investigation, police sources said.

The Knapp Commission's

Continued on Page 51, Column 1

Canada Announces Plans To Curb Foreign Business

By JAY WALZ
Special to The New York Times

OTTAWA, May 2—Canada announced her long-awaited plans today to tighten controls over take-overs of Canadian businesses by foreign interests. Under proposed legislation, which is expected to pass, the Government would screen take-overs involving Canadian businesses worth $250,000 or more and whose annual revenues exceeded $3-million.

A prospective buyer would be judged on the basis of

Text of minister's statement is printed on Page 74.

Cabinet-level findings that his purchase "will result in significant benefit to Canada."

"Our policy," Revenue Minister Herbert E. Gray told the House of Commons "is designed to insure that this country continues to develop as rapidly as possible in a way which is consistent with Canadian needs and aspirations and which safeguards our vital interests."

Mr. Gray's statement summarized the Government's decision to hold a closer rein on the country's industrial development. Over the last 40 years industry has fallen increasingly into the hands of foreign investors and managers, mostly Americans.

Attending legislation was immediately criticized by the Government's Political Opponents. They maintained that a plan to oversee foreign take-overs was not enough to meet the challenge to Canada's control of her economy.

Jean-Luc Pepin, Industry Minister who would administer the program under the proposed law, said at a news conference that the plan should be considered in the context of existing laws—on taxation, investment and Canadian-content. The proposal, he suggest-

Continued on Page 74, Column 2

5 Dead, 77 Missing In Idaho Mine Fire

By The Associated Press

KELLOGG, Idaho, May 2 — Fire swept through the nation's deepest and richest silver mine today, killing at least five miners and leaving 77 unaccounted for in the rugged hills of northern Idaho.

Wallace Wilson, vice president of the Sunshine Silver Mine, said only five bodies had been counted and that company officials did not know the condition of the 77 missing men. He said 108 men were brought from the mine after the fire started.

Mr. Wilson held out hope for the missing miners. "There is fresh air as well as smoke-filled areas," he said.

Officials said an electrical failure may have been the cause of the fire.

Miners from other mines in

Continued on Page 22, Column 1

Bill to Stop Forest Hills Project Gets Final Passage in Assembly

By ALFONSO A. NARVAEZ
Special to The New York Times

ALBANY, May 2—The Assembly gave final passage today to a bill designed to kill the controversial Forest Hills low-income housing project.

The bill, passed by a vote of 101 to 35, provides that where projects planned by a housing authority have not progressed beyond the foundation stage within five years of the approval by the local legislative body they would have to be resubmitted for review and further determination as to their approval or disapproval.

The bill takes effect immediately. However, it provides that it is deemed to have been in effect since Sept. 1, 1971. The Forest Hills project was approved in the latter part of 1966, putting it within the five-year provision of the bill.

If the Forest Hills issue comes before the Board of Estimate the board is expected to vote it down and kill the plan for three 24-story buildings on the site in the middle-class community.

In other action, the Senate voted to amend the State Constitution to permit the legalization of new forms of gambling that are now illicit. The measure now goes to the Assembly, where the sponsors are hopeful of passage.

In another action, the Assembly Codes Committee released a bill to repeal the state's liberalized abortion law, even though Governor Rockefeller has said he would veto it. (Details on Page 18.)

The housing bill now goes to the Governor, who has not indicated what action he will take. However, during a news conference in March he noted that he was against scatter-site housing, which places low-income projects in the heart of middle income areas. The Governor said that he favored rehabilitating deteriorating communities to provide areas where integrated living could be accomplished.

"I think myself for the long pull that you would avoid exactly the kind of conflict which exists now," the Governor said at that time. "The community is faced with a very unfortunate, intense situation and I can't believe this is going

Continued on Page 17, Column 1

NEWS INDEX

Associated Press

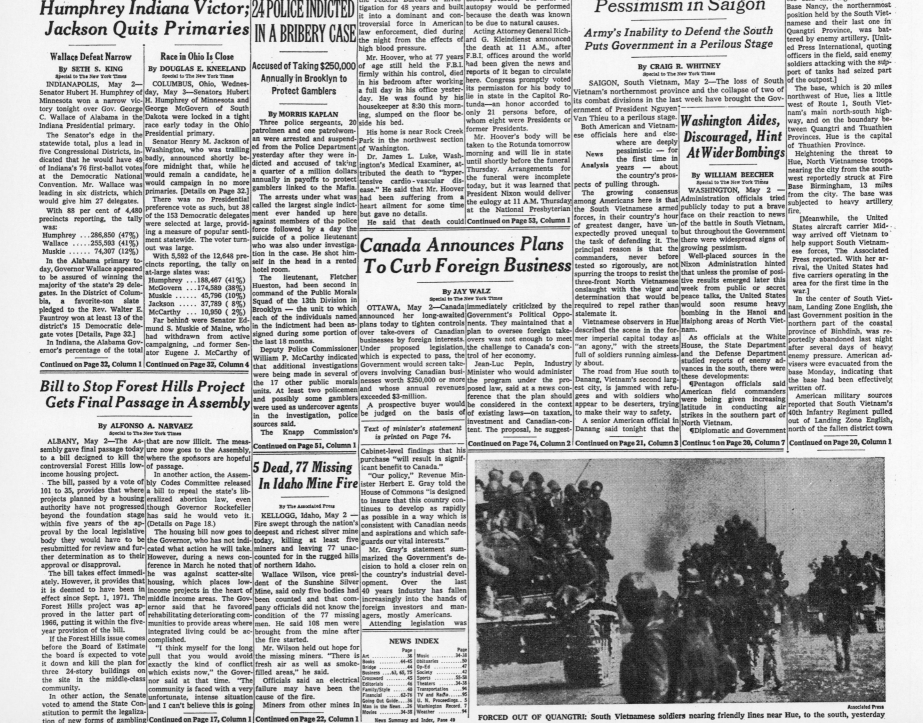

FORCED OUT OF QUANGTRI: South Vietnamese soldiers nearing friendly lines near Hue, to the south, yesterday

The Weather

Today—Variable cloudiness, with a 40 per cent chance of rain decreasing to 20 per cent tonight, high in 70s, low in 50s. Wednesday—Fair, high in the 70s. Temp. range: Today, 58-74; Yesterday, 61-73. Details, C5.

The Washington Post

Times Herald

FINAL

72 Pages—4 Sections

95th Year ···· No. 163 TUESDAY, MAY 16, 1972 Phone 223-6000 Classified 223-6200 Circulation 223-6100 15c Beyond Washington, Maryland and Virginia 10c

Wallace Is Shot, Legs Paralyzed; Suspect Seized at Laurel Rally

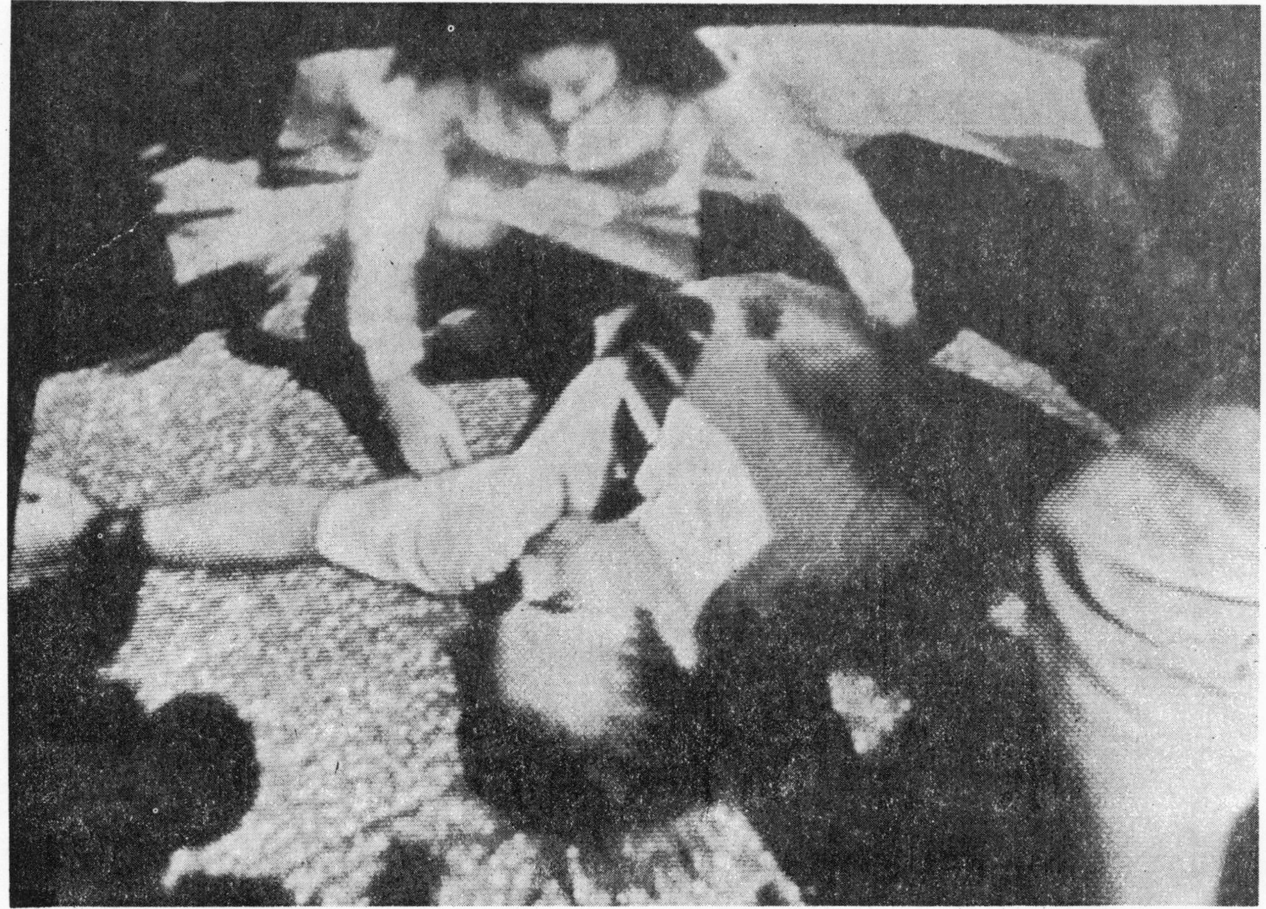

CBS News

Cornelia Wallace bends over her husband in Laurel just after he was shot. Dark smudge on Wallace's shirt locates wound.

Gunman Wounds 3 Others in Party

By William Greider
Washington Post Staff Writer

A young assailant dressed in red, white and blue shot Gov. George C. Wallace of Alabama yesterday in the midst of a Laurel campaign rally, leaving him paralyzed in both legs.

Surrounded by a crowd of 1,000, the 52-year-old governor was shot at close range following his speech at the Laurel Shopping Center, about 14 miles northeast of Washington.

Wallace, campaigning in his third bid for the presidency, was hit in the chest and stomach by two bullets that caused four or five wounds.

At 2:15 a.m., a spokesman for Holy Cross Hospital in Silver Spring said the governor was "awake and alert" in the recovery room. "At this point, his progress is satisfactory," the spokesman said.

At 11 p.m., after five hours surgery, his wife told a press conference that, though he is seriously injured, "I feel very optimistic about him and you know his nature. He didn't earn the title of 'Fighting Little Judge' for nothing . . ."

Mrs. Wallace said he was conscious through the ordeal, except while under surgery, and remains in good spirits. "I feel very good that he is alive and he has a sound heart and sound brain . . . I couldn't thank God more for that," she said.

Three persons traveling with Wallace were also wounded in the shooting.

Police immediately arrested a blond young man identified as Arthur Herman Bremer, a 21-year-old bus boy and janitor from Milwaukee, Wis. He was charged by state authorities with four counts of assault with intent to murder and was arraigned in Baltimore on two federal charges. One of the federal charges was interfering with the civil rights of a candidate for federal office, a provision of the 1968 Civil Rights Act. The Wallace second charge was for assaulting a federal officer; one of the four people shot at the rally was Secret Service officer.

According to Prince George's County police, no other persons are being sought and there is no evidence that other persons are involved.

First reports said that Wallace campaign materials and pornography were found in Bremer's Milwaukee apartment, but interviews with his family and friends produced no clear picture of his political leanings.

Bremer was in the rally audience, dressed in a red, white and blue shirt and socks, wearing a Wallace cam-

See WALLACE, A12, Col. 1

Milwaukee Man Held As Suspect

By Richard M. Cohen
Washington Post Staff Writer

A 21-year-old Milwaukee man, described by aquaintances as a loner with a fondness for pornography, was charged last night and early this morning with the shooting of Gov. George C. Wallace.

The man was identified by federal and Maryland authorities as Arthur Herman Bremer of 2433 W. Michigan St., Apt. 9, Milwaukee. Maryland and Prince George's County police each said there was no evidence that more than one person was involved in the shooting. Col. John W. Rhoads. acting Prince George's police chief, said no other persons were being sought.

Bremer was first charged with four counts of assault with intent to murder by Prince George's County State's Attorney Arthur A. Marshall Jr. while Bremer was being held in Prince George's General Hospital in Cheverly under heavy guard, sometime between 7 p.m. and 9 p.m. He was taken to the hospital, Marshall said, for observation.

Earlier, Marshall said, Bremer had been treated for four cuts on the back of his head, apparently suffered in the scuffle with the crowd or the police who arrested Bremer following the shooting at a Wallace rally in Laurel about 4 p.m.

Bremer was charged with four counts on the state charges because three other people were shot in addition to Wallace.

Shortly before 10 p.m., Bremer was transferred secretly from Prince George's Hospital to the federal courthouse in Baltimore in a motorcade of five sedans. Witnesses in Baltimore said the five cars pulled up at the courthouse, where the Post Office is also located, at

See SUSPECT, A13, Col. 5

Associated Press

Arthur Herman Bremer ducks beside agent in car taking him to a Baltimore court.

Slug Lodged Near Spine Of Governor

By Stuart Auerbach and Jon Katz
Washington Post Staff Writers

Alabama Gov. George C. Wallace underwent nearly five hours of surgery at Holy Cross Hospital in Silver Spring last night, and doctors announced the governor is paralyzed in both legs.

"He is paralyzed in both extremities," said Dr. James G. Arnold, a neurosurgeon with the University of Maryland who operated on Wallace. Shortly before midnight, he said the governor's chances of regaining use of his legs cannot be predicted yet, "but the outlook is not favorable."

Wallace "has a bullet lodged in the spinal canal at the level of the first lumbar (lower back) vertebrae," Dr. Arnold said. He said that when Wallace's "general condition warrants it, we will operate to remove the bullet."

A doctor at the hospital said the reason the bullet wasn't removed from Wallace's spine was that his system couldn't tolerate any more surgery. He said five to seven pints of blood were lost during the operation, all of which were replaced. He said the blood was lost from damage to the large intestine.

According to a doctor at the hospital, there were four or five wounds caused by two bullets.

One bullet went through the lower edge of Wallace's right thorax and lodged near the spinal column, below the last rib in the chest. The doctors pulled out the first bullet in the stomach but left in the bullet next to the spinal column.

That bullet caused the paralysis below the hips, but the doctors said they were not sure if this paralysis was permanent or temporay.

They said, We expect a good recovery." They added it is hard to tell how much

See HOSPITAL, A12, Col. 6

Campaign Thrown in Disarray

Results to Be Distorted

By Haynes Johnson
Washington Post Staff Writer

Once again a gunman's bullet has disrupted the American policial process and thrown a critical presidential campaign into disarray.

Like the earlier shots that felled the Kennedys and Martin Luther King Jr. the bullets that struck George Corley Wallace of Alabama yesterday in Maryland have irrevocably altered the politics of this presidential year.

His shooting will overshadow the actions of every other candidate from now until the November election. And once again it forces forward onto the center stage the most disturbing of all American issues—violence.

After more than a decade of prominence on the American scene, George Wallace yesterday stood on the verge of gaining one of his greatest political triumphs.

He was favored to win presidential primaries in both Maryland and Michigan today in states that have gone Democratic in the last three presidential elections.

Now no one will ever know to what extent the ballots to be cast are affected by this new American tragedy.

If Wallace survives, as did Theodore Roosevelt when he was shot during a campaign speech in 1912, he is likely to receive

See IMPACT, A13, Col. 1

Friends, Foes Shocked

By Stephen Green
Washington Post Staff Writer

Shock and sorrow from Democratic and Republican leaders as well as ordinary citizens followed the shooting in Laurel yesterday of Alabama Gov. George C. Wallace.

"Oh my God," said Sen. Hubert Humphrey (D-Minn.), Wallace's chief opponent in today's Maryland primary as he received news of the shooting from two Secret Service men who whispered in his ear while he spoke at a day-care center in Baltimore.

"All I can say is that it is a sad business. It's getting so you don't know what's going to happen in our country any more in politics," Humphrey said as he suspended campaigning and went to Holy Cross Hospital in Silver Spring where Wallace was hospitalized.

At the hospital, Humphrey, spent an hour with Mrs. Wallace. "What I've heard is encouraging. The governor has a lot of fight in him and he's showing it now. Thank God, it's not fatal," Humphrey told reporters.

"I'm totally shocked by this savage act," said Sen. George S. McGovern (D-S.D.) at the Kalamazoo, Mich, airport. McGovern is competing against Wallace in that state's primary, which also will be held today.

See REACT, A14, Col. 1

South Vietnamese Recapture Firebase

Aiming to Spoil Attack on Hue

By Lee Lescaze
Washington Post Foreign Service

SAIGON, May 16 (Tuesday) — South Vietnamese troops recaptured a firebase southwest of Hue Monday that had been taken by the Communists on the eve of their seizure of Quangtri Province.

The South Vietnamese action was the second attempt by government troops to push out from the defensive perimeter around Hue which they formed after the loss of Quangtri Province May 1.

Like the one-day Marine sweep into southern Quangtri Province Saturday, the retaking of Firebase Bastogne by 1st Division soldiers Monday does not appear to be an effort to permanently take back territory from the North Vietnamese, but is designed to spoil future enemy plans — principally the expected North Vietnamese attack on Hue, 12 miles northeast of Bastogne.

North Vietnamese battle plans are generally drawn up well in advance and followed as closely as possible, allied

See INDOCHINA, A14, Col. 5

'Vietnam Legacy'

The third in George C. Wilson's series "Vietnam Legacy—The People" will appear on Wednesday.

Rogers: Soviet Clash Unlikely

By Murrey Marder
Washington Post Staff Writer

Secretary of State William P. Rogers expressed confidence yesterday that there will be no "damaging confrontation" with the Soviet Union over the mining of North Vietnam's harbors, which he said is likely to be "a turning point" in the war.

None of the dire predictions about "catastrophic" consequences of the President's decision "have come to pass," Rogers told a Senate Appropriations subcommittee.

With President Nixon preparing to go to the Soviet Union this weekend, said Rogers, "it is not the time to be critical. There will be plenty of time to criticize the President in July and August and September."

Rogers voice rose sharply in defense of the President when subcommittee Chairman William Proxmire (D-Wis.) questioned the May 8 order to plant mines in the waters of North Vietnam. Rogers first claimed, and Proxmire challenged the contention, that "Vietnamization is working."

If Vietnamization is working, Proxmire countered, "why is this extraordinary kind of lethal and dangerous confrontation necessary . . .

See ROGERS, A15, Col. 1

'Gun Still Firing' as Bystander Wrestled Suspect to the Ground

By Lawrence Meyer
Washington Post Staff Writer

"My husband said "Shake his hand, honey.' I said, 'I already have, but I'll do it again.'" Mabel Speigle, a Laurel housewife, shook George Wallace's hand a second time.

"The gun brushed my left shoulder and my husband's right," she recalled hours later. "I saw the dark-colored gun. I saw the hand. I saw it firing.

"Other people said it sounded like firecrackers, but it sounded to me like an atomic bomb it was so loud."

Mrs. Speigle's husband, Ross, a 46-year-old crane operator, said he acted "on instinct."

"I just climbed up on this man. I throwed my legs around him, grabbed by the head and down we went. The gun was still firing when we took him down," Speigle said. Another man, whom Speigle could not identify, helped him wrestle the suspect to the ground.

"I had my hands on his head, I had my legs around him," Speigle said. "When we hit the asphalt, I just held his head down as hard as I could. I picked it up and slammed it down a couple of times.

"The funny thing was, his hand brushed by me and my wife. I thought he just wanted to shake hands. Where the gun came from, I don't know, but he had it.

"I was afraid for my wife and my mother-in-law. I was afraid for everyone there. When you're in a situation like that, you just act on instinct. You do what you can do," Speigle said.

Although Speigle said he thought the suspect had dark hair, his wife said she was certain the man had light hair. She said she noticed him standing behind her when she turned around during Wallace's speech to see the reaction of her friends. "I thought he was for Gov. Wallace," she said, "because when we would applaud, he would applaud. It just shocked me. I'm still in a state of shock."

"All the News That's Fit to Print"

The New York Times

CITY EDITION

Weather: Partly sunny today; cool tonight. Fair and milder tomorrow. Temp. range: today 54-68; Wed. 58-75. Additional details on Page 82.

VOL. CXXIII... No. 42,264 — NEW YORK, THURSDAY, OCTOBER 11, 1973 — Higher newsstand price in air delivery cities M 15 CENTS

AGNEW QUITS VICE PRESIDENCY AND ADMITS TAX EVASION IN '67; NIXON CONSULTS ON SUCCESSOR

U.S. Believes Moscow Is Resupplying Arabs by Airlift

Soviet Could Spur Move to Aid Israel

By JOHN W. FINNEY

Special to The New York Times

WASHINGTON, Oct. 10—Administration officials said today that they believed the Soviet Union was airlifting military equipment to resupply the forces of Egypt and Syria.

The State Department said that if the Russians were in fact engaged in a huge resupply effort, this 'would 'put a "new face" in the Middle-East conflict. Speaking for the department, Robert J. McCloskey said, however, that he was "not in a position to confirm that any of this is taking place at this time."

But other officials, apparently acting upon instructions laid down by the State Department, readily volunteered information. They did so, however, on a basis that precluded their identification.

The fact that officials who until today had been extremely reluctant to discuss any detail of the Middle East war were now willing to talk openly about indications of a Soviet resupply effort prompted immediate speculations that the Nixon Administration might be laying the groundwork for resupplying the forces of Israel.

The exact nature of the reported Soviet airlift remains unclear, United States officials said. All that is known, according to officials, is that in the last day or so, an unusually large number of Soviet transports have been observed landing at Egyptian and Syrian airports. The presumption is that the planes are carying military equipment.

The airlift, officials reported, was being staged primarily from Hungary, with the planes flying south over the Mediterrean. Diplomatic sources reported that about 30 planes had been observed landing at Syrian airports since yesterday afternoon. The number landing at Egyptian airports was not disclosed.

Diplomatic sources reported that Israel had already approached the United States

Continued on Page 18, Column 1

A 10-Mile Egyptian Gain

By HENRY TANNER

Special to The New York Times

IN THE SINAI PENINSULA, Oct. 10 — Egyptian soldiers, tanks and equipment are continuing to pour across the Suez Canal, a group of Western correspondents confirmed from the battle area today.

On a three-and-half-mile tour into the Sinai Peninsula, this correspondent also saw evidence that Egyptian forces had reached positions 10 miles or more east of the canal in some parts of the sector.

[In the air war the Egyptans said they had shot down six more Israeli planes. Egyptan aircraft were said to have attacked Israeli command headquarters, units and administrative installations on the northern Sinai coast.]

The Egyptian soldiers in the area toured by the correspondents were in high spirits, often jubilant, and seemed oblivious to Israeli artillery shells bursting near them.

"Don't worry, God is with us!" one of three young soldiers shouted laughingly to the correspondents, who ducked for cover when a shell burst too close for comfort. The Egyptians remained where they were, standing atop a ridge.

Shells fell every few moments but caused no casualties during a half-hour visit to the particular sector. An Egyptian officer said they were from an Israeli battery 15 miles away that was trying to hit a military bridge.

More than 50 trucks interspersed with antiaircraft guns were lined up in open country on the west bank, waiting for their turn to cross the canal. Waved onto the bridge by a young soldier with a yellow flag, they moved quickly, often with three or four vehicles on the bridge simultaneously.

On one truck two young soldiers were dancing. Others clapped their hands rhythmically.

The elation and excitement of returning to Egyptian territory occupied for more than six years by Israel was everywhere.

The loose boards and pontoons that made up the bridge

Continued on Page 18, Column 5

Israel Claiming Heights

By CHARLES MOHR

Special to The New York Times

TEL AVIV, Thursday, Oct. 11—Israel said last night that the Syrian Army on the Golan heights had been driven back to the 1967 cease-fire line, but Israeli forces fighting the Egyptians clearly seemed to have suspended a counterattack aimed at pushing them from the eastern bank of the Suez Canal.

A highly informed source said that Israel estimated the Egyptian invasion force at five divisions, which could be close to 75,000 men. The force, he said, crossed with about 600 tanks and 300 to 400 of these may still be operational.

[The Iraqi command announced that its air and ground forces had joined the war against Israel and were taking "an active part" in the fighting on both fronts. Page 17.]

The Israeli Air Force bombed two air fields in the Nile delta as well as a naval headquarters, fuel installation and power plant in Syria in a day of slackening air action.

Premier Golda Meir, in an address to the nation on the religious holiday of Euccouth, the Feast of Tabernacles, said she had no doubt that the war would end in victory but she added that "it may take more than six days."

"But I am glad," she said, "I am happy to say today that the heights are in our hands, the settlers are returning to

Continued on Page 19, Column 3

CONGRESS TO VOTE

Opposition Indicated if Choice Is Possible 1976 Candidate

By CHRISTOPHER LYDON

Special to The New York Times

WASHINGTON, Oct. 10—President Nixon began his search today for a successor to Vice President Agnew amid indications that he will face stiff resistance from Congress if he chooses anyone who might qualify as a strong Republican candidate in 1976.

The Senate majority leader, Mike Mansfield, Democrat of Montana, said the choice of either John B. Connally, the former Treasury Secretary and Texas Governor, or Governor Ronald Reagan of California—both presumed contenders for the Republican Presidential nomination in 1976— would provoke a fight from Seiate Democrats.

Similar warnings had come from Democratic leaders in the House.

Quick Action Indicated

Mr. Nixon's first moves today indicated that he wished to move quickly but with some show of bipartisan consultation.

"President Nixon intends to move expeditiously in selecting a nominee and he trusts the Congress will then act promtly to consider the nomination," Ronald L. Ziegler, the President's Press Secretary, announced shortly after word that the President had accepted Mr. Agnew's resignation spread through the White House.

Mr. Nixon then began meeting with Congressional leaders of both parties and with George Bush, the Republican party chairman, to reach an understanding on the procedures he will follow in selecting a Vice President acceptable to both houses of Congress.

Under the 25th Amendment, ratified in 1967, when there is a vacancy in the office of Vice President the President must appoint a person to fill the

Continued on Page 34, Column 2

Associated Press

Spiro T. Agnew speaking to reporters after appearing at court in Baltimore yesterday

Agnew Plea Ends 65 Days Of Insisting on Innocence

By BEN A. FRANKLIN

Special to The New York Times

BALTIMORE, Oct. 10—Vice President Agnew ended today 65 days of defiant insistence that he was innocent of any wrongdoing by pleading no contest to a charge of cheating the Government of $13,551.47 on his Federal income tax payment for 1967, his first year as Governor of Maryland. Then he resigned his Federal office.

Richardson, Agnew and Judge Hoffman's remarks, Page 35.

At a dramatic, surprise appearance here before United States District Court Judge Walter E. Hoffman after two days of secret negotiations, Mr. Agnew was confronted in open court by Attorney General Elliot L. Richardson.

The Attorney General said in a prepared statement that the Government's evidence against the former Vice President went far beyond the six-year-old tax violation. But he said that "critical national interests"—the avoidance of the "serious and permanent scars" upon the nation that would have been inflicted by months or years of a criminal prosecution of a sitting Vice President, together with the new and allied dispute over newsmen's sources—justified the agreement with Mr. Agnew. Judge Hoffman then approved the agreement.

Under it, Mr. Agnew in a 40-minute court appearance waived all his rights as a defendant—the right to be indicted and to an arraignment—and was sentenced on the spot to pay $10,000 fine and to three years of probation. He was admonished by Judge Hoffman to violate no state or Federal laws on pain of having his avoidance of a prison term reconsidered.

A long list of other charges, involving perhaps $100,000 in payoffs by Maryland contrac-

Continued on Page 35, Column 1

EVIDENCE SHOWS GIFTS TO AGNEW

Cites Requests and Receipt of Over $100,000—Denial Also Entered in Record

By ANTONY RIPLEY

Special to The New York Times

BALTIMORE, Oct. 10—Spiro T. Agnew, in three elective offices including the Vice Presidency, asked for and accepted cash payments totaling more than $100,000, according to the evidence gathered against him by the United States Attorneys in Baltimore.

That evidence, denied by Mr. Agnew, was entered by Attorney General Elliott L. Richardson in Federal District Court today as part of the agreement between the Justice Department and Mr. Agnew's lawyers.

U.S. Attorney's papers in Agnew Case, Pages 36 and 37.

It became a permanent part of the record in the case, along with Mr. Agnew's denial and other terms of the agreement that included his resignation and a plea of no contest to a tax charge.

The 40-page document told of

Continued on Page 37, Column 7

Mets Win, Take Pennant And Enter World Series

By JOSEPH DURSO

The New York Mets completed their six-week odyssey from last place to the National League pennant yesterday when they overpowered the favored Cincinnati Reds, 7-2, in a tumultuous game that rocked and almost ruined Shea Stadium.

In a riotous scene that brought back memories of their "miracle" of 1969, they decided the issue with four runs in the fith inning of a 2-2 game.

But then, in a swirling scene, thousands of persons in the crowd of 50,323 stormed the field after delaying the game in the ninth inning and clawed huge chunks of fence, sod and fixtures from the arena.

Professional sports may have had more clamorous moments. But New York baseball has had none since the Mets won the World Series four years ago after eight seasons as the comic relief of the leagues.

Their rise this summer carried them from medical history to baseball history, and their public responded yesterday by mobbing Willie Mays, Pete Rose and the 340 police officers struggling to prevent panic.

Repairs on the stadium were started immediately after the crowd had dispersed shortly after 5 o'clock, while the Mets celebrated their victory in champagne and prepared for the next milestone.

They will open the World Series on Saturday in the home park of the Oakland A's or Baltimore Orioles, who will decide the American League pennant this after-

Continued on Page 61, Column 4

NEWS INDEX

I.R.S. Sees Nothing to Prevent New Tax Cases Against Agnew

By EILEEN SHANAHAN

Special to The New York Times

WASHINGTON, Oct. 10—Former Vice President Agnew's plea of "no contest" today in the income-tax evasion case against him could mark only the beginning of difficulties for him with the Internal Revenue Service.

An official spokesman for Internal Revenue said that so far as the Agency is aware, there was nothing in the agreement leading to Mr. Agnew's resignation that would prohibit Internal Revenue from attempting to collect taxes on every payment to Mr. Agnew that could be documented as having been made but not reported on his tax returns.

The charge of tax-evasion to which Mr. Agnew pleaded "nolo contendere" involved $29,500. But a document released by the Justice Department detailing the evidence against the former Vice President alleges payments from contractors and others totaling as much as $100,000. The precise figure is not clear, because some of the allegations of illegal payments are stated in terms of percentages of the value of construction contracts awarded, and the figures for the contracts themselves are not given.

The Internal Revenue spokesman said, however, that it was common in tax-evasion cases fo a charge of criminal tax-evasion to be made involving a

Continued on Page 33, Column 3

Judge Orders Fine, 3 Years' Probation

By JAMES M. NAUGHTON

Special to The New York Times

WASHINGTON, Oct. 10—Vice President Agnew resigned today under an agreement with the Department of Justice to admit evasion of Federal income taxes and avoid imprisonment.

The stunning development, ending a Federal grand jury investigation of Mr. Agnew in Baltimore and probably terminating his political career, shocked his closest associates and precipitated an immediate search by President Nixon for a successor.

"I hereby resign the office of Vice President of the United States, effective immediately," Mr. Agnew declared in a formal statement delivered at 2:05 P.M. to Secretary of State Kissinger, as provided in the Succession Act of 1792.

Minutes later, Mr. Agnew stood before United States District Judge Walter E. Hoffman in a Baltimore courtroom and, his hands trembling, read from a statement in which he pleaded nolo contendere, or no contest, to a Government charge that he had failed to report $29,500 of income received in 1967, when he was Governor of Maryland. Such a plea, while not an admission of guilt, subjects a defendant to a judgment of conviction on the charge.

"I admit that I did receive payments during the year 1967 which were not expended for political purposes and that, therefore, these payments were income taxable to me in that year and that I so knew," the nation's 39th Vice President told the stilled courtroom.

Richardson Makes Leniency Plea

Judge Hoffman sentenced Mr. Agnew to three years probation and fined him $10,000. The judge declared from the bench that he would have sent Mr. Agnew to prison had not attorney general Elliot L. Richardson personally interceded arguing that "leniency is justified."

In his dramatic courtroom statement, Mr. Agnew declared that he was innocent of any other wrongdoing but that it would "seriously prejudice the national interest" to involve himself in a protracted struggle before the courts or Congress.

Mr. Agnew also cited the national interest in a letter to President Nixon saying that he was resigning.

"I respect your decision," the President wrote to Mr. Agnew in a "Dear Ted" letter made public by the White House. The letter hailed Mr. Agnew for "courage and candor," praised his patriotism and dedication, and expressed Mr. Nixon's "great sense of personal loss." But it agreed

Continued on Page 33, Column 1

Agnew-Nixon Exchange

October 10, 1973

Dear Mr. President:

As you are aware, the accusations against me cannot be resolved without a long, divisive and debilitating struggle in the Congress and in the courts. I have concluded that, painful as it is to me and to my family, it is in the best interests of the nation that I relinquish the Vice Presidency.

Accordingly, I have today resigned the office of Vice President of the United States. A copy of the instrument of resignation is enclosed.

It has been a privilege to serve with you. May I express to the American people, through you, my deep gratitude for their confidence in twice electing me to Vice President.

Sincerely,
SPIRO T. AGNEW

October 10, 1973.

Dear Ted:

The most difficult decisions are often those that are the most personal, and I know your decision to resign as Vice President has been as difficult as any facing a man in public life could be. Your departure from the Administration leaves me with a great sense of personal loss. You have been a valued associate throughout these nearly five years that we have served together. However, I respect your decision, and I also respect the concern for the national interest that led you to conclude that a resolution of the matter in this way, rather than through an extended battle in the courts and the Congress, was advisable in order to prevent a protracted period of national division and uncertainty.

As Vice President, you have addressed the great issues of our times with courage and candor. Your strong patriotism, and your profound dedication to the welfare of the nation, have been an inspiration to all who have served with you as well as to millions of others throughout the country.

I have been deeply saddened by this whole course of events, and I hope that you and your family will be sustained in the days ahead by a well-justified pride in all that you have contributed to the nation by your years of service as Vice President.

Sincerely,
RICHARD NIXON

$500 Lucky Losers Bonus Number Today on Page 16A

Sunday, November 18, 1973 Our 201st Year—No. 90

The Weather
Partly cloudy today. Highs in the 50s.

FINAL
35c

'I'm Not a Crook,' Nixon Says

JOHN F. KENNEDY: 1917-63

John F. Kennedy: 10 Years Later

- News American reporter Rich Hollander interviewed some people who knew Jack Kennedy personally, including the late president's old prep school roommate who remained a close friend right up to the tragedy in Dallas. His account is on the cover of Showcase.
- Michael Olesker recalls what it was like on Nov. 22, 1963 and ponders what has happened to the nation since. His report is also in today's Showcase.
- President Kennedy's two children, Caroline and John-John, remain remarkably unscarred by the nightmare in Dallas. Story on Page 3A.
- Many doubts persist on the Dallas assassination. Could it have been a conspiracy? Are there unanswered questions to the Warren Report. See dispatch on Page 3A.
- City Councilman Robert J. Fitzpatrick reminisces about his meeting with Lee Harvey Oswald a few months before Kennedy's assassination. See Blaine Taylor's account in Extra magazine.

Fuel Crisis Seen Eliminating Jobs

• More energy stories on Pages 2A, 25A, 1C and 3C.

By DAVID AHEARN
News American Bureau

ANNAPOLIS — The energy crisis will cost virtually every Maryland household some economic loss. And it will cost some Marylanders their jobs.

It will be more expensive to keep warm, to drive cars and to do many things we take for granted. And some thing taken for granted will disappear.

What will the fuel shortage cost you?

It will vary from person to person, household to household.

A top state official dealing with the crisis, gubernatorial aide Thomas Downs, said no precise figure ever could be devised to show the total economic loss — but there will be a loss.

Soon, many Marylanders who have not taken seriously the warnings from President Nixon and Gov. Mandel are going to find out the hard way just how serious the crisis is.

A report predicting dimensions of the loss statewide is being prepared now by State Comptroller Louis L. Goldstein. He won't have it ready for about two weeks.

But The News American has been able to gain a comprehensive picture of the economic loss Marylanders face, a picture drawn during interviews with state officials.

The problem is broken down into three main areas — higher costs of driving cars, higher costs of heating homes, and the chilling effect the energy shortage will have on Maryland's economy — causing a rise in unemployment. This is the picture:

CARS — It's the end of the road for the American love affair with sexy autos.

Gasoline prices are rising and will increase much more in coming months. The black gold flowing into your gas tank will be pumped at 14K rates.

Turn to Page 25A, Column 1

City Lists Fuel Crisis Priorities

By DREW MARCKS

Recreational programs and City Hall operations would be the first to be closed by the city government in the next few weeks if energy shortages threaten the health and safety of the poor.

Offering a glimpse at an energy conservation contingency program that will be presented to Mayor Schaefer soon, aides indicated that after recreational programs, decentralized operations such as the Health Department would be curtailed next.

Police, education, penal, hospital and fire services would remain open regardless of the energy situation, according to the plan.

Mayor Schaefer's energy policy adviser William Sykes explained that city departments and agencies are being categorized to determine those that:

- Can be closed down and cause a minimum of inconvenience to the community, such as recreation facilities.
- Can be closed down and create a moderate degree of inconvenience, such as certain health department facilities.
- Must remain open at all

Turn To Page 20A, Col. 1

BRAVING WIND, ARSONIST — Fire fighters worked to control fires that broke out in a group of three-story buildings in the 300 block S. Charles St. late Saturday. The blaze was another in a series of fires which have struck harbor area warehouses slated for demolition. Arson investigators said they are questioning a suspect in connection with the fire. Story on Page 1C.

—News American Photo by Bill Perry.

He Vows To Restore Confidence

News American Wire Services

ORLANDO, Fla. — "I'm not a crook," President Nixon told the nation Saturday night —not in Watergate, in his personal finances or in any of the other charges of scandal that confront his administration.

For more than an hour in a nationally televised appearance before The Associated Press Managing Editors Association, Nixon denied wrongdoing and said time and again that he is telling the truth.

He vowed to work for as long as he is physically able at the job to which he was elected twice, and said he will strive "to restore confidence in the White House and in the President."

"It is a big job, but I think it can be done, and I intend to do it," Nixon said.

At another point, he said, "I want to be remembered as a President who did his best to bring peace . . . prosperity . . . a contribution in the energy field . . . the environment field . . . and who did his best when his own campaign got out of hand to see that nobody else's campaign gets out of hand."

Only briefly did the discussion turn from the scandals to other matters, notably gasoline rationing which the President said he does not want imposed.

It was in a discussion of personal finances that Nixon made this dramatic statement, after specifically alerting his television audience to what was coming:

"I've made my mistakes but in all my years of public life I have never profited from public service. I have earned every cent. And in all of my years of public life I have never obstructed justice.

"People have got to know whether or not their President is a crook," he said. "Well, I'm not a crook. I earned everything I've got."

The scene was the Ballroom

Turn to Page 19A Col. 1.

Israel Building Canal Span

By Associated Press

Israel was pushing thousands of tons of dirt into the Suez Canal Saturday to build a land bridge across the closed waterway, newsmen reported.

Meanwhile, diplomatic efforts were reported under way by Romania and the United Nations to get Syria and Israel to agree to a consolidation of the ceasefire. Syria reportedly took the initiative in proposing one of the plans.

One report on the Suez Canal bridge construction came from Associated Press photographer Spartago Bodini. He said he saw Israeli bulldozers working rapidly on both banks of the canal.

Correspondents traveling near the area north of the Great Bitter Lake said work was going on to span the 200-yard-wide waterway with the first permanent structure in its history.

Reporters were not allowed to approach the new bridge, and it was not known if the Israelis were using cement to reinforce the structure. Egypt said earlier it was studying such a report, and that if it were true, it would constitute a serious violation of the ceasefire.

At the United Nations, officials said Syria had proposed a ceasefire consolidation and that UN Undersecretary-General Roberto Guyer discussed the plan in Tel Aviv with Premier Golda Meir.

The plan reportedly includes an exchange of prisoners, withdrawal of Israeli forces from two positions on Mt. Hermon in Israeli occupied Syrian territory, and Israeli consent to the return of 15,000 Syrians to their homes in the war zone.

Syria accepted a UN ceasefire in the October war, but unlike Egypt, has not agreed to a prisoner exchange or to other points beyond a halt in fighting.

UN truce observers reported Saturday there had been two outbreaks of Syrian artillery fire Friday below Mt. Hermon, one lasting two hours and the other only a few minutes.

Along the Israeli-Egyptian ceasefire line, observers reported nearly an hour of Israeli small-arms fire, and that in a separate action, Egyptian troops moved 725 feet from their positions.

The other effort toward an Israeli-Syrian truce was reported from Beirut, Lebanon, where diplomatic sources said two top-level Romanian diplomats were visiting Arab capitals to propose a Middle East peace plan.

5 Die in Athens Student Riots

ATHENS — (AP) — The Greek capital fell silent Saturday night under a martial law curfew imposed after street clashes between soldiers and students left five dead and more than 300 injured.

Restaurants and bars closed. Foreign tourists stayed in their hotels. All incoming and outgoing airline flights were canceled at Athens streets dropped to a Athens airport. Traffic on trickle.

Scores of buses with their tires slit and windows broken sat in the streets where they had been taken over by rioters and used as barricades. Litter covered most of the main avenues and fires smoldered. Overturned cars blocked streets.

President George Papadopoulos, strong man in the military-backed regime, said the bloody street fighting had created "a dangerously explosive situation."

The uprising was the most serious challenge to his rule since he and a group of fellow colonels seized power in April 1967 and suspended democracy.

He told the nation is a brief radio address that the antigovernment demonstrations proved there was a "conspiracy against democracy and factors supporting inemployment. tion."

Papadopoulos reinstated martial law and slapped the curfew on Athens after soldiers and police smashed their way into Athens Polytechnic Institute to quell student demonstrators demanding the overthrow of his government.

The military intervention had been expected since antigovernment protests reached their peak Friday after a four-day sit-in at the Polytechnic Institute. Student demonstrations on and off campus had drawn more than 10,000 each night, bringing Athens to a virtual standstill.

Late Friday night, the students switched their demands from academic liberties. They began calling for overthrow of the regime, chanting anti-American slogans and demanding expulsion of Americans and Greek withdrawal from the North Atlantic Treaty Organization.

Their protests spread to the streets and riots flared in downtown Athens for six hours. In the early morning, soldiers behind tanks and armored personnel carriers crashed through a gate and ended the occupation of the institute.

Editor's Report

Time to Get Tough

By WILLIAM RANDOLPH HEARST JR.
Editor-in-Chief, The Hearst Newspapers

HONG KONG—A funny thing happened to me this week on my way to Peking. I was ready and willing, even eager to visit the ancient capital for an on-the-spot report of Henry Kissinger's talks with the Chinese Communist leaders, but my People's Republic of China visa was conspicuous by its absence.

Although applied for through the State Department and the Chinese liaison mission in Washington several weeks ago, the visa has failed to materialize.

W. R. HEARST JR.

I could have gone with the secretary of state as the representative of our Hearst newspapers, but I think I did right in giving my place on the Kissinger plane to our capable young State Department correspondent, John Wallach, who by now is probably back in Washington.

I am inclined to think the Kissinger cyclone left the Chinese Red rulers so breathless they did not want any aftermath questioning by American

Turn to Page 2A, Column 1

Jackpot Puzzle Worth $2,100, See Page 34A

SHOPPING DAYS UNTIL CHRISTMAS

See The Gift Spotter In Today's Classified Section.

Your Life Tomorrow

Housing Quality Seen Key to City's Future Well-Being

By J. WILLIAM JOYNES

If any single factor can be called the key to Baltimore's future well-being, it's housing.

The quality of housing has a bearing on nearly everything. It touches the lives of everyone. It affects, for good or bad, the status of crime, race relations and racial progress, education, health, jobs, transportation.

What's going to happen in the years ahead?

The keystone problem in housing has been, is and will be economic.

A single dwelling, let alone a group of them, is an economic can of worms —the

What can you expect in the foreseeable future? Will you be able to drive your car to work—or, for that matter, to the beach? What about taxes? Will they get worse? Will you have more leisure time and, if you do, how will you spend it? How will the races get along? Will there be plenty of good jobs? Can the public schools do a decent job of educating your children?

In a series of articles scheduled for consecutive Sundays, staff writers of the News American are exploring these questions. Previous articles have dealt with the future of health care and crime. Today and tomorrow—housing.

availability of land, the cost of that land, the complexities of financing, the role of city, state and federal government, union procedures, building codes, taxes, utilities, insurance, maintenance, management, many other things.

The future does not look rosy. The Nixon administration has cut off funds for public housing, and virtually ended the supply of federal mortgage money.

Investors are shying away from buying and rehabilitating houses in the city, particularly in the inner city. Many savings and loan associations will not handle a mortgage under $10,000, and some will not even consider a mortgage in the city.

Thus, it may be a long time until Baltimoreans who need houses most will be able to buy. And the time for some may be never.

Still, Baltimore has much going for it — more than most major cities. The consensus is that the city's Department of Housing and Community Development is doing an effective job. There are plenty of sound neighborhoods, and plenty of sound buildings.

Baltimore's housing stock, to use the word of the housing experts, is sound, too; more than half the city's housing is in good shape, making it relatively easy to rehabilitate. Indeed, a major trend, especially in the public housing sector, is toward the "recycling" of existing houses rather than the construction of developments.

Says an architect: "With the brick row house, you've got something to start with. You can slide a new house inside, and you have a much better house than many new ones."

There are plans which could drastically change the housing situation as it now exists, even the willingness to lend money for home-buying in the city.

Dr. Jack S. Fisher, director of Johns Hopkins University's Center for Metropolitan Planning and Research, says that no one really knows the answers, at least not all of

Turn to Page 3A, Column 1

Latest On British Vote
Page 2

Mackell Case Goes to Jury
Page 2

Market Down At the Close
Final Prices, Pages 58-60

WEATHER
Tonight: Clear, 30s.
Tomorrow: Partly sunny, 40-45.
Sunday: Mild, chance of rain.
Air: Acceptable
SUNSET: 6:47
SUNRISE TOMORROW: 7:29

New York Post

FOUNDED 1801. THE OLDEST CONTINUOUSLY PUBLISHED DAILY IN THE UNITED STATES.

Vol. 173 No. 88 | NEW YORK, FRIDAY, MARCH 1, 1974 | 15 Cents

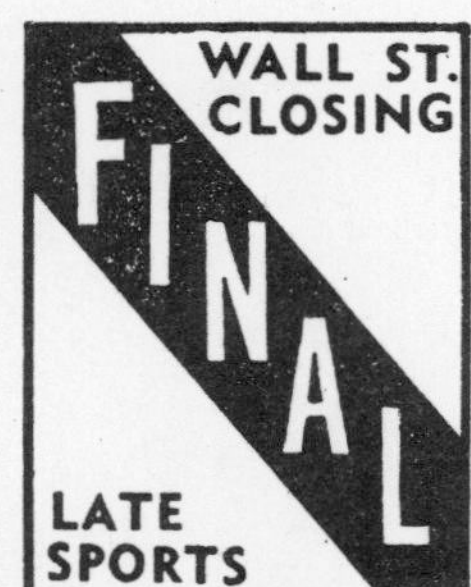

7 WATERGATE INDICTMENTS

JOHN N. MITCHELL

H. R. HALDEMAN

CHARLES W. COLSON

JOHN EHRLICHMAN

Secret Report on Nixon?

Stories on Pages 4 and 5

WEEKEND EDITION

ROOTS
FROM THE BEST-SELLER
BY ALEX HALEY

Carter's Theologians
3 WHO INSPIRED HIM

Milton Friedman
A NOBEL FOR ECONOMICS

SLIPOUT TV SECTION • ENTERTAINMENT SECTION • MAGAZINE SECTION

WEATHER
Sunny, 50s.
Tonight: Clear, 40s.
Tomorrow: Fair, 50s.
Fair Monday.
SUNRISE TOMORROW: 7:09
SUNSET: 6:15

New York Post

FOUNDED 1801. THE OLDEST CONTINUOUSLY PUBLISHED DAILY IN THE UNITED STATES.

Vol. 175
No. 282

NEW YORK, SATURDAY, OCTOBER 16, 1976

25 Cents

GAMBINO HEIR: A BONANNO MAN

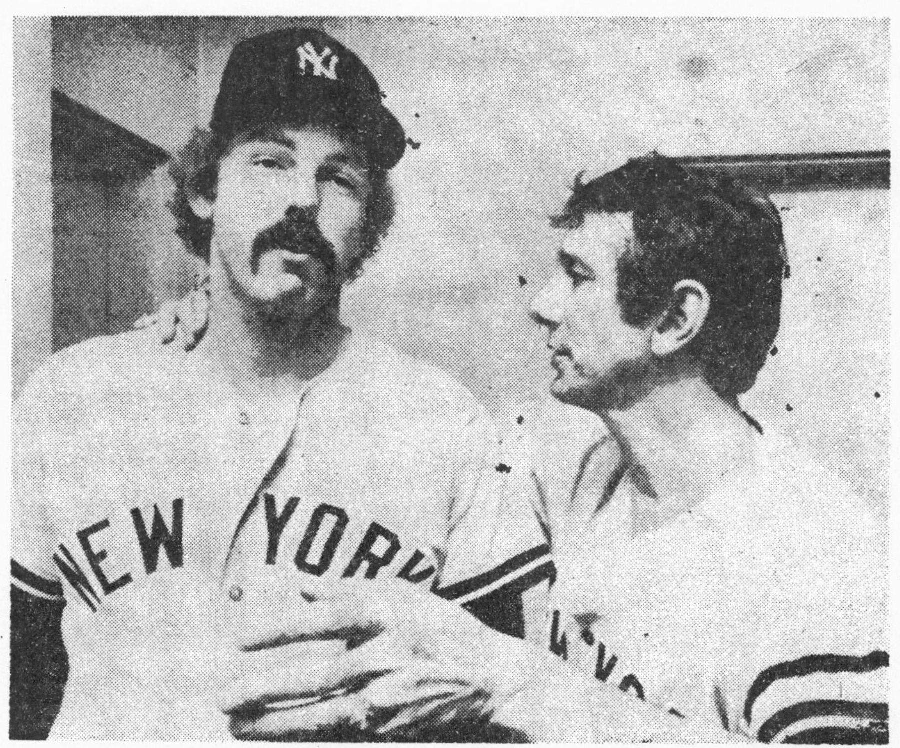

Associated Press Wirephoto

THE STARTER: Yankee hurler Doyle Alexander (left) who'll pitch the opening World Series game against the Reds today, looks confident as he poses in the Cincinnati clubhouse with manager Billy Martin. See Maury Allen and Henry Hecht on the Back Page.

By Carl J. Pelleck and William T. Slattery

Carmine (Lilo) Galente, head of the Joe Bonanno crime family, appeared certain today to take over as kingpin of all mob activities here following the death of Carlo Gambino.

Law enforcement authorities predicted that the accession of Galente would be swift and bloodless.

However, Galente, who has spent nearly half his life in jail, won't get control of the vast riches of Gambino or his mob family, and won't—at least for now—have the nationwide clout of the small, quiet Gambino—known as the boss of bosses.

But with his ties to Canadian mob bosses, he will be a dominant national figure, and is expected to lead the five families here back into an active place in the drug traffic.

The new head of the Gambino family will probably be the underboss, Aniello (O'Neil) Dellacroce.

Authorities say Gambino had maneuvered the mob away from its once-dominant drug role after several top leaders were

Continued on Page 3

Ford & Carter Loved It

From Combined Services

President Ford thanked Sen. Bob Dole for an "anniversary present" — the vice presidential candidate's showing on last night's TV debate.

Jimmy Carter thought his running-mate came out on top. "I'm just glad I'm not running against you," he told Sen. Walter Mondale after the debate in Houston concluded.

Neither Ford nor Carter, both in the Midwest on the campaign trail today, was handed any new issues in last night's 75-minute debate, the first ever between vice presidential aspirants.

The confrontation was sharper and more pungent than the two Ford-Carter debates, but each candidate for the second spot stuck to the issues raised by the top of his ticket.

Ford, who was celebrating his 28th wedding anniversary, told Dole "you've done a fine job . . . I'm very proud of you."

Carter, heaping praise on Mondale, said "I've never been so sure of my choice" of a running-mate. "You did a superb job."

The Debate and the Candidates: Page 4.

Carter, Artis Convicted Again

N.J. Jury Rules They Killed 3 in 1966

News photo by Clarence Davis

John Artis and Rubin (Hurricane) Carter outside court yesterday.

By PATRICK CLARK and ROGER WITHERSPOON

Former boxer Rubin (Hurricane) Carter and John Artis were convicted for a second time last night on charges that the two shot and killed three persons in a Paterson, N.J., bar in June 1966.

After a second trial that lasted 32 days, the jury of eight men and four women deliberated seven hours before returning the guilty verdict to Passaic County (N.J.) Court Judge Bruno L. Leopizzi at 9 p.m.

The retrial was ordered after the New Jersey Supreme Court threw out an earlier conviction on the ground that evidence had been withheld in the first trial.

Carter and Artis sat impassively at the defense table with their hands folded, staring straight ahead, as foreman Helen T. LaRocco took six minutes to read the verdict.

None of the jurors looked at the defendants. Several friends of the defendants burst into tears.

After thanking the jurors and ordering them not to speak to reporters, the judge ordered Carter and Artis remanded to Passaic County Jail pending sentencing Feb. 2.

The jurors were told by the trial judge in his charge yesterday that if they idd not accept the credibility of the state's key witness, they should find the defendants innocent.

Judge Bruno L. Leopizzi said there must be an identification of the murderers before a person can be convicted of committing a murder. "If you do not believe that the identification of Rubin Carter and John Artis was made accurately, and unmistakably then you must find the defendants not guilty.

The jury began its deliberations at 11:45 a.m.

Passaic County Prosecutor Burrell Ives Humphreys objected to the judge's statement that "the entire case rests on the identification of Alfred Bello," the only witness to place Carter and Artis at the scene. Humphreys said there were five other points to the state's case "whoch would warrant a conviction without the eyewitness identification, despite the fact that they are circumstantial."

Bello's Various Versions

Bello, a convicted thief, told the jury that on the morning of June 17, 1966, he had been robbing a factory across the street from the Lafayette Bar & Grill in Paterson. Bello said that he saw Carter and Artis coming out of the bar, carrying a shotgun and a revolver.

Over the 10-year interim, Bello charged his story five times under oath, and he has given other versions which were introduced during the trial.

State to Run City Medicaid

By HUGH WYATT

The state has moved to seize control of the city's Medicaid program, it was learned yesterday. The city has run the program since its inception about a decade ago.

Under federal law, the United States Department of Health, Education and Welfare awards a Medicaid contract to the state, which in turn makes an agreement with the city. The state can void its agreement with the city whenever it so decides.

The state's move will have a strong impact on the fiscal operations of the city's Health Department, which oversees Medicaid operations here.

As part of the state's plan, an estimated $2.5 million a year used until now by the city for investigation and en forcement will be transferred tothe state Health and Social Services departments. Only about $300,000 will remain with the city for minor functions.

The state will monitor all medical institutions receiving Medicaid funds. These include the so-called Medicaid mills and out-patient departments at proprietary, voluntary and municipal hospitals.

The takeover decision was disclosed in a personal letter, dated Dec. 20, from State Health Commissioner Robert Whalen to City Health Commissioner Lowell E. Bellin, who is leaving at the end of the month to become a professor of public health administration at Columbia University.

"Based on the decision to reduce fragmentation, and based on my review of your program, we will no longer fund your department as of Dec. 31," Whalen wrote. "The investigation and enforcement activities presently being performed under the Medicaid contract

(Continued on page 76, col. 3)

Ulasewicz Has a Pie (In Face) for Lunch

By STEWART AIN and HARRY STATHOS

A parade of Watergate stars, including John Dean, John Ehrlichman and Herbert Kalmbach, testified here yesterday at the tax-evasion trial of Watergate "bagman" Anthony Ulasewicz, whose day was not brightened when he was hit by a pie during a lunch break.

Ulasewicz, 59, who told the Senate Watergate committee in 1973 that he had paid $200,000 in hush money to members of the Watergate break-in team, is charged with understating his income by $41,000 — in payments from the White House — in 1971 and 1972.

Kalmbach, one-time attorney of former President Nixon, told a Federal Court jury in Brooklyn that he had paid Ulasewicz $3,000 a month in cash for his services to the Nixon White House.

Kalmbach testified that he had given Ulasewicz a secret assignment after the Watergate break-in to pay money to the families of those arrested, to defray the cost of their lawyers' fees.

The pie-throwing incident occurred shortly before 1 p.m. Ulasewicz, a former New York City cop, had just walked out the front door of the courthouse, at 225 Cadman Plaza East, with his lawyer, John Sutter, and was being interviewed by reporters when a young man threw a coconut cream pie at him. The pie hit him on the side of his neck and splattered one side of his face.

The pie-thrower ran into a nearby park and escaped. Later, a man who identified himself as Aron Kay, 27, called the press office in the courthouse and said he had thrown the pie.

"We are sick and tired of people like Ulasewicz, who are still in the government," he said. "This is just the beginning. We're planning bigger things for the inauguration."

In his opening statement, Assistant

(Continued on page 76, col. 4)

News photo by Leonard Detrick

Anthony Ulasewicz cleans up the cream pie before lunch yesterday.

DAILY NEWS

NEW YORK'S PICTURE NEWSPAPER®

15¢

Vol. 58. No. 177 New York, N.Y. 10017, Tuesday, January 18, 1977* Cold and windy, 3-17. Details p. 59

WITNESS' STORY OF EXECUTION

Gary's Last Words: Let's Do It; Said He Was Sorry for Crimes

UPI Photo

This is the view one of the five executioners had yesterday morning as he fired a 30-30 rifle at Gary Mark Gilmore. —*Stories p. 3; other pics back page*

Sorensen Withdraws As CIA Pick

Page 2

Record Cold Ties Up Rails; N.J. Gas Crisis

Page 2

TODAY
Partly Cloudy, 85-90
TONIGHT
Partly Cloudy, low 70s
TOMORROW
Sunny, 90s
Details, page 2
TV: PAGE 34

NEW YORK POST

THURSDAY, AUGUST 11, 1977 25 CENTS Vol. 176, No. 225 R

METRO
TODAY'S RACING

DAILY PAID CIRCULATION 2D QUARTER 1977 609,390

CAUGHT!

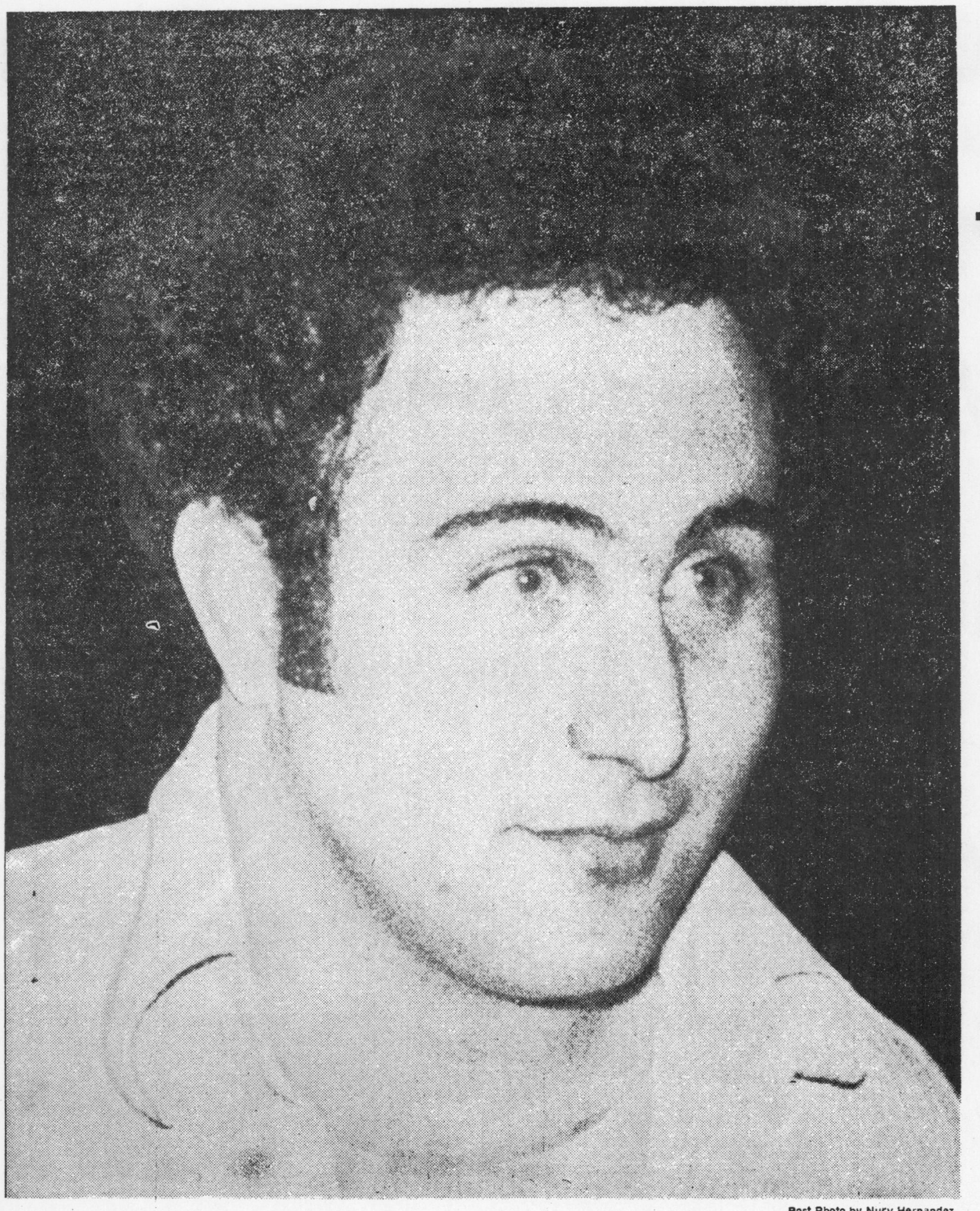

Post Photo by Nury Hernandez

Son of Sam was on way to kill again

'I wanted to go out in a blaze of glory'

By CARL J. PELLECK

The man police say is the Son of Sam was on his way to claim more victims when he walked into the arms of waiting detectives.

David Berkowitz, 24, had already written a letter—his third—addressed to Suffolk County and New York police and the press. He was going to leave it alongside his latest victim. It had no stamp on it.

In questioning after his arrest last night, Berkowitz said he hadn't quite made up his mind whether to stalk his next victims in Riverdale or in the Hamptons.

And he told police that he wanted to "go out in a blaze of glory" because he felt the cops were closing in on him. Sources said the letter made a similar claim.

'DID IT FOR SAM'

A pleasant-looking, slightly chubby young man, Berkowitz remained calm throughout the many hours of questioning at Police Headquarters.

He gave no reason why he started his killing spree on July 29, 1976 other than "I was doing it for Sam . . . Sam can do anything . . . I was driven to do it by Sam."

He gave cops the answer they had long been seeking: Sam is a man who lives in a building behind Berkowitz' Yonkers apartment house.

He identified the man as Sam Carr of 316 Warburton Av.

When Berkowitz was grabbed, he had the dreaded .44-caliber pistol with him. He had two dozen extra bullets in a brown paper bag he had

Continued on Page 4

Full coverage: Pages 2, 3, 4, 5, 7, 32, 33.

DAILY NEWS
NEW YORK, SUNDAY, JULY 15, 1979
★ Vol. 59. No. 11 50 cents

As Galante died

20 MOB BOSSES HAILED SLAYING

Page 3

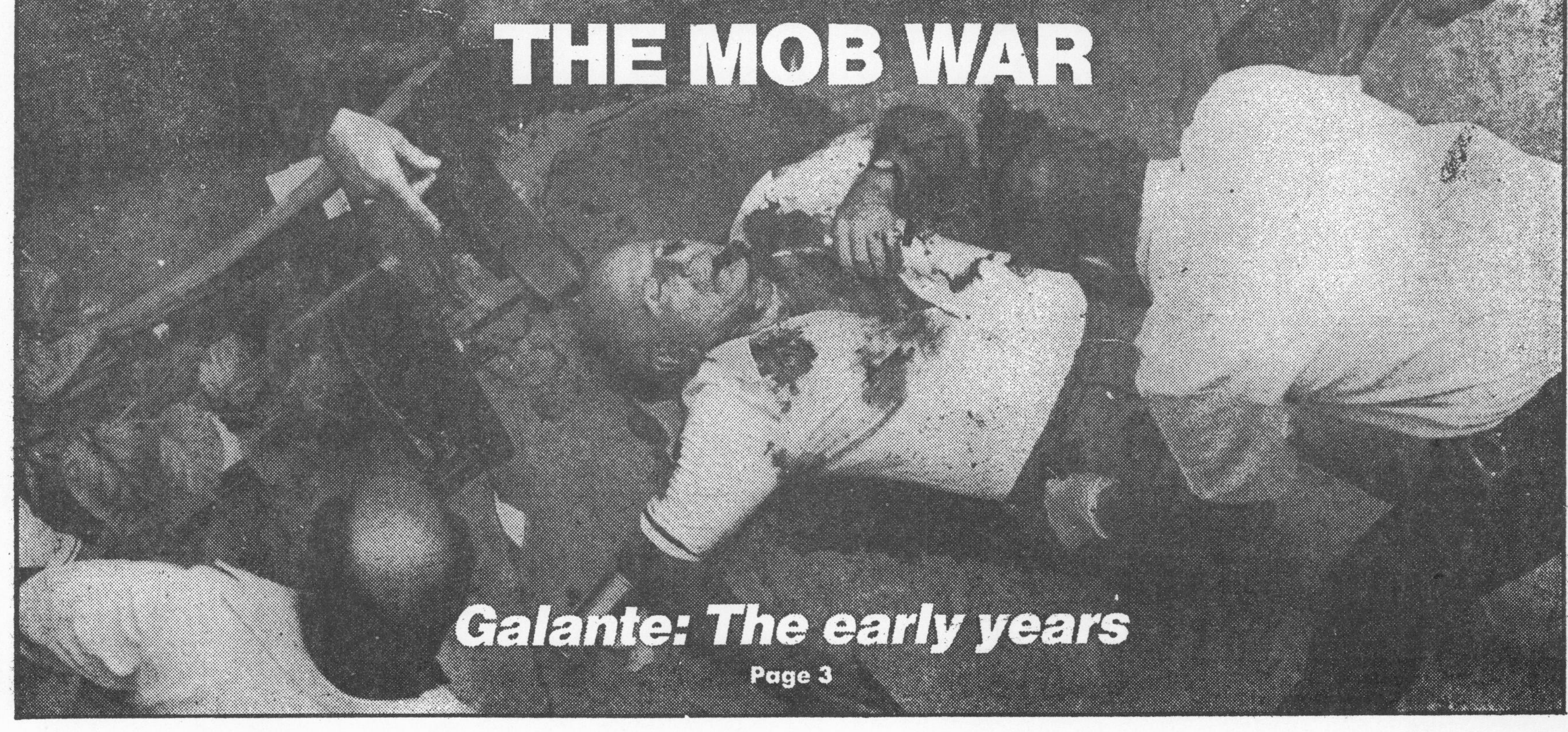
THE MOB WAR
Galante: The early years
Page 3

Synthetic fuels: Will they save us? P. 5

Chicago Tribune

5 Star Final ★★★★★

Thursday, March 13, 1980

133d Year—No. 73 © 1980 Chicago Tribune

8 Sections 20¢

Gacy found guilty

Jury turns down insanity defense

In Business

Mortgage interest raised to 16.25% by First Federal

First Federal Savings and Loan of Chicago raised its basic mortgage interest rate to 16.25 per cent Wednesday, becoming the first major association here to go over 16 per cent.

Column 1

'Ugly Arab' stereotype under attack

Israel lobby, television blamed for racial slurs

By John Maclean

Chicago Tribune Press Service

WASHINGTON—When Boston Mayor Kevin White wanted to express outrage over the sale of a chunk of Massachusetts' cultural heritage to outlanders, he reached for a handy verbal club.

Losing the Gilbert Stuart portraits of George and Martha Washington to the nation's capital, he said, would be "like the Louvre selling the Mona Lisa to the Arabs." For those who think any slur against the capital city is a slur worth making, hold on a moment.

White's remark received wide attention, particularly from the National Association of Arab Americans. They protested. It was not equating Arabs and Washingtonians that worried them, but rather the casual assumption that Arabs are culturally unworthy.

"Consider whether you would have substituted the word 'Jews' for Arabs, and you will begin to realize that too few people are sensitive to negative stereotyping of Arabs," the NAAA wrote White.

WHITE REPLIED: "You are correct in calling me to task. It was a thoughtless, insensitive remark, inappropriate to the occasion. You have my apology and assurance that it will not happen again."

Few would have been so gracious as White. In fact, many Arab-Americans believe they are among the last of the nation's minorities about whom racial slurs are acceptable.

They cite the FBI's Abscam operation as only the most notorious example of an "ugly Arab" image in the American mind. They give various reasons for the negative stereotyping, ranging from a campaign by the pro-Israeli lobby to the lack of Arab-American writers in the entertainment industry.

Since the FBI's acronym became public knowledge, Arab and Arab-American spokesmen have condemned it as a slur, the State Department has apologized, and a group of Arab-Americans has begun formation of an anti-defamation league.

JAMES ABOUREZK, the former South Dakota senator turned legal counsel for clients including the government of Iran, blames pro-Israeli forces for creating the ugly Arab image. Abourezk is organizing an Arab anti-defamation

Continued on page 4, col. 1

Weather

CHICAGO AND VICINITY: Thursday: Snow or flurries ending; northerly winds 10 to 20 miles [16 to 32 kilometers] an hour; high 37 F [3 C]. Thursday night: Clear; low 24 F [-4 C]. Friday: Mostly sunny; high 43 F [6 C]. Map and other reports on page 14, Sec. 3.

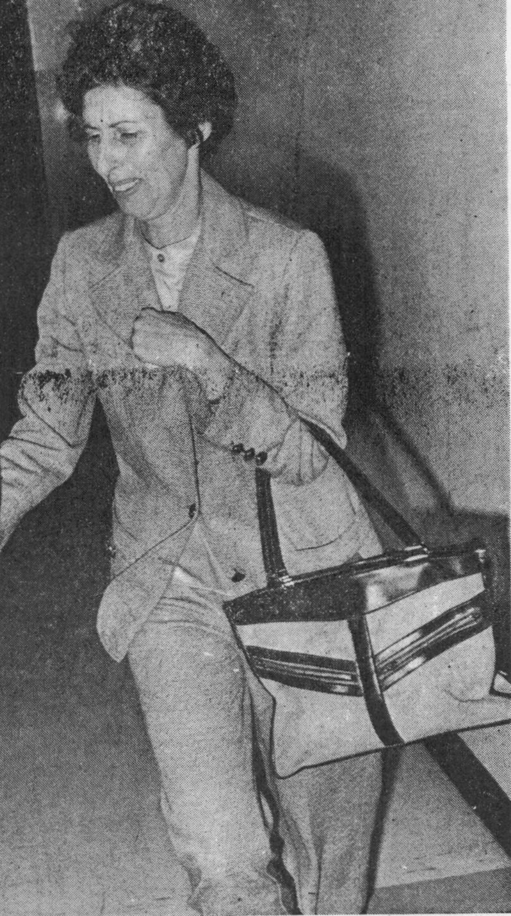

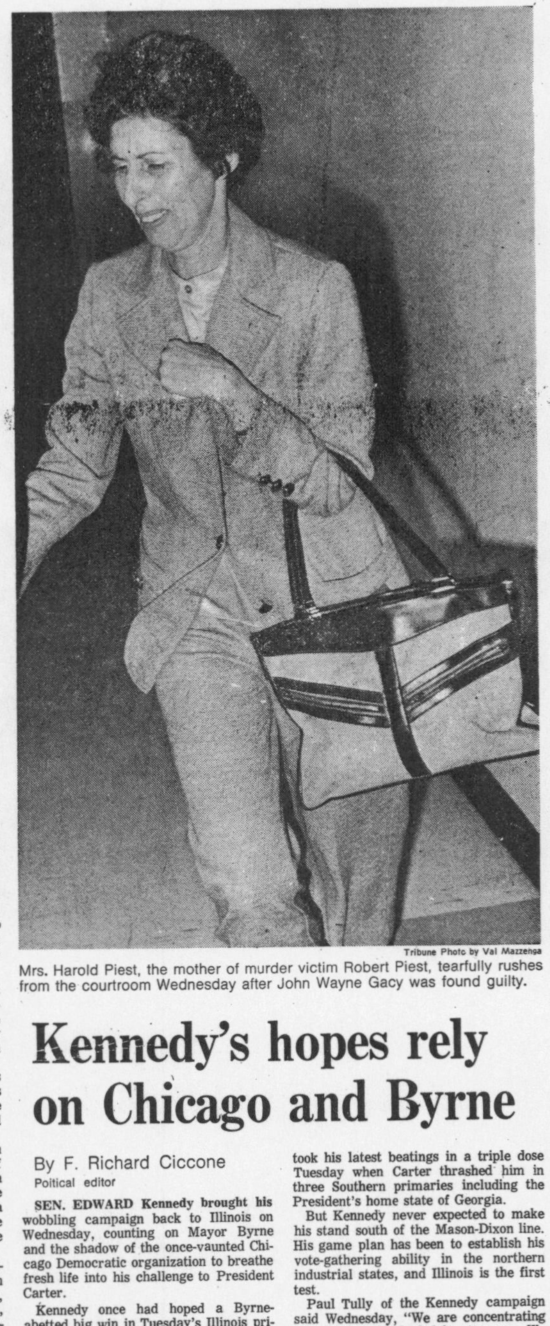

Tribune Photo by Val Mazzenga

Mrs. Harold Piest, the mother of murder victim Robert Piest, tearfully rushes from the courtroom Wednesday after John Wayne Gacy was found guilty.

Convicted of all 33 murders

By Jane Fritsch

A JURY deliberated for less than two hours Wednesday before convicting John Gacy of murdering 33 young men and boys—a conviction unparalleled in the nation's history.

Gacy, 37, a self-employed building contractor, sat expressionless in a leather chair as the court clerk read the litany of guilty verdicts to a packed and hushed courtroom.

Moments earlier, when Gacy was led into the courtroom, he said to the sheriff's deputies guarding him, "Cheer up boys. Keep a straight face."

After the verdicts were read, which rejected a strong insanity plea by the defense, Gacy smiled and winked at a deputy, then strolled calmly out of the courtroom.

RELATIVES OF the victims, warned earlier by Judge Louis B. Garippo that they should keep their emotions in check, cried quietly. Some held hands as they awaited the verdicts in the tension-filled courtroom.

They smiled their relief as the clerk announced the first verdict: "We, the jury, find John Gacy guilty of the murder of Robert Piest." The reading was repeated another 32 times, using the names of the other 21 victims who have been identified and police case numbers for those who remain anonymous.

"They got a good jury. Oh, I love those people," exclaimed a tearful Bessie Stapleton, whose son, Sam, disappeared in 1976. His body was later unearthed in the crawlspace under Gacy's home.

Garippo ordered the jury of seven men and five women to return to court Thursday at 1:30 p.m. for the start of a hearing on whether Gacy should be sentenced to death.

Gacy could be given the death penalty because he committed multiple murders and because he committed a murder during a forcible felony by taking indecent liberties with a minor and committing deviate sexual assault before he strangled 15-year-old Piest.

THE JURY FOUND Gacy guilty of the two sex charges Wednesday, in addition to the 33 murders.

"This was the right verdict," chief prosecutor William Kunkle Jr. said. "There was never any doubt about his guilt or sanity. I was gratified that it was returned so quickly."

Kunkle said it will be "up to the defense [Thursday] to show why Gacy should not receive the death penalty."

State's Atty. Bernard Carey, who was present when the verdicts were read, said, "The fact that the jury returned the verdicts so quickly showed that they feel he deserves to pay for his crimes."

CAREY SAID the quick verdict could be an indication that the jury will sentence Gacy to death.

"He certainly qualifies for the death penalty," Carey said. "If he doesn't, who does?"

The five-week trial ended Wednesday with a dramatic flourish when Kunkle, in his final argument, flung the photographs of the 22 identified victims onto the hatch to the crawlspace, which had been placed on the courtroom floor about 6 feet from the jury box.

"Don't show sympathy. Don't show pity," Kunkle thundered. "Show justice. Show the same sympathy and pity this man showed when he took those lives and put them there."

Kunkle then stunned the hushed courtroom when he threw the pictures into the hatch and they resounded with a thud.

"YOU DON'T have the power to change the fact," the prosecutor said. "But you can control the future for this villain.

"You can do justice for the people of the State of Illinois. You represent the people of the State of Illinois. If you allow this evil man to walk the earth, then God help us all."

Defense attorneys Sam Amirante and Robert Motta brushed past reporters after the verdicts were announced and said they had no comment. They had hoped to convince the jury that Gacy was a "madman" who was not guilty of the crimes because he was insane.

Kunkle attacked that defense as a "sham" Wednesday and implored the jury to reject "the high-blown theories" of the psychoanalysts who testified for the defense.

WHETHER GACY was sane at the times of the murders had been the only real issue in the case since the first of 26 bodies was unearthed in the crawlspace on Dec. 21, 1978. Three other bodies were found buried elsewhere on Gacy's property at 8213 W. Summerdale Av. in Norwood Park Township. Four

Continued on page 14, col. 5

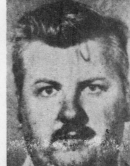

John Wayne Gacy

The victims . . .

Pictures of the 22 victims who have been identified in the Gacy case and pictures from the Criminal Courts Building, scene of the trial, are on the back page of Sec. 4.

. . . the relatives

After hearing the guilty verdict on TV, John Godzik, father of one of the victims who is confined to his home because of emphysema, said, "I'd probably kill him (John Gacy) myself—with my bare hands—if I'd been there." His wife, Eugenia, who regularly attended the trial, said, "I tell you, the (electric) chair is almost too good for him." Story on page 3.

Kennedy's hopes rely on Chicago and Byrne

By F. Richard Ciccone

Political editor

SEN. EDWARD Kennedy brought his wobbling campaign back to Illinois on Wednesday, counting on Mayor Byrne and the shadow of the once-vaunted Chicago Democratic organization to breathe fresh life into his challenge to President Carter.

Kennedy once had hoped a Byrne-abetted big win in Tuesday's Illinois primary would cripple Carter's re-election plans. But the polls and the pols indicate Kennedy has little chance to overtake Carter in the popularity contest and must concentrate on collecting a sufficient number of the 152 delegates to salvage his campaign.

Mayor Byrne already has pledged that her loyalists will elect all 49 delegates alloted to the city of Chicago, but various party committeemen are doubtful they can do much to help Kennedy in the "beauty contest" part of the election.

President Carter's men in Illinois are working hardest at trying not to laugh out loud because they think they will sweep the preferential contest and win the lion's share of delegates.

KENNEDY ARRIVED late Wednesday for five days of campaigning. He took his latest beatings in a triple dose Tuesday when Carter thrashed him in three Southern primaries including the President's home state of Georgia.

But Kennedy never expected to make his stand south of the Mason-Dixon line. His game plan has been to establish his vote-gathering ability in the northern industrial states, and Illinois is the first test.

Paul Tully of the Kennedy campaign said Wednesday, "We are concentrating heavily on individual delegate races. We have a long way to go on the beauty contest.

"We think the delegate races will be a lot tighter than a popularity contest," Tully added.

CARTER'S ILLINOIS campaign director Larry Hansen said, "Illinois is neither Georgia nor Massachusetts. At stake are 152 delegates. It's terribly important."

Kennedy's only triumph in the early primary battles came two weeks ago in his native Massachusetts, and he trails Carter in delegates by a 283-141 count, with 1,667 needed to win the nomination.

Although the popularity contest does not have any relevance to the selection of delegates, which are chosen in each of the state's 24 congressional districts,

Continued on page 5, col. 1

CAMPAIGN '80

- William Scott's numbers have always been impressive—on election night—but a different set of numbers might end his career. Page 12.
- Mayor Byrne gets mixed reports from Democratic ward committeemen on Kennedy's chances in Tuesday's primary. Page 12.
- John Anderson drew cheers that drowned out the hisses of abortion opponents at Wheaton College Wednesday. Page 12.
- Former President Gerald Ford, sounding very much like a candidate, told a GOP fund-raiser that "Carter must go" and that the nation "is in deep, deep trouble." Page 14.
- George Bush and Sen. Edward Kennedy lost three Southern primaries Tuesday, making next week's Illinois vote crucial to their dwindling chances for the presidential nomination. Page 5.

Bush to go on offensive in Illinois primary fight

By Jon Margolis

THE REPUBLICAN presidential candidates prepared for a final, and perhaps contentious, stretch run to Tuesday's Illinois primary with underdog George Bush reportedly ready to come out swinging at surprise front-runner John Anderson.

Knowledgeable Bush campaign aides said Wednesday that their candidate, weakened by losses in three Southern primaries this week, would sharpen his attacks on both Anderson and Ronald Reagan.

Bush reportedly was set to concentrate his attack on Anderson, the Rockford congressman who now leads in the polls in his home state and threatens to supplant Bush as the major alternative to Reagan.

BUSH AIDES SAID the former United Nations Ambassador would try to paint Anderson as a liberal outside the mainstream of the Republican Party and disloyal to the party. They said Bush would mention specifically Anderson's refusal to disavow entirely all plans to run as an independent this year, as well as a statement he made last month that he would vote for a Democrat, even Sen. Edward Kennedy [D., Mass.], over Reagan.

One Bush source said there was a personal as well as political motive to the planned criticism. "Not only is Anderson liberal," the aide said, "he's thin-skinned. We'll see if we can make his self-righteousness show."

Bush also is likely to criticize Reagan for being "inexperienced" and for "proposing solutions based on the past," one Bush worker said.

BUSH'S STRATEGY appears to be aimed at reviving his own candidacy and at showing enough forcefulness to give former President Gerald Ford pause about entering the Republican race.

But the strategy contains risks. In the past, Bush has often seemed unnatural as an attacker, and on several occasions he has rejected the advice of his aides to criticize his opponents.

In fact, some of his top advisers remained uncertain that he would follow the attack plan at Thursday's debate in the Continental Plaza Hotel. "He'd better," one said.

Furthermore, Anderson and Reagan have both shown themselves to be quick on the uptake in debate, and anyone enters into tough combat with them at his own risk.

THE DEBATE promises to be livelier

Continued on page 14, col. 1

EXTRA • EXTRA

TODAY
Chance of showers, 45-50
TONIGHT
Rain, 35-40
TOMORROW
Partial clearing, 40-45
Details, Page 2

NEW YORK POST

METRO
TODAY'S RACING

TV listings: P. 63

TUESDAY, DECEMBER 9, 1980 25 CENTS ★ R

© 1980 News Group Publications Inc Vol. 180, No. 2
AMERICA'S FASTEST-GROWING NEWSPAPER

AVERAGE DAILY SALES EXCEED 700,000

JOHN LENNON SHOT DEAD

JOHN LENNON
The 40-year-old ex-Beatle was shot and killed late last night in front of his home on the Upper West Side.

Gunned down by 'screwball' outside home as wife Yoko watches in horror

DRAMATIC COVERAGE: PAGES 2, 3, 4, 5, 31, 32, 33

THE ASSASSINATION ATTEMPT: A SPECIAL REPORT

The Dallas Morning News

Texas' Leading Newspaper ©The Dallas Morning News, 1981 | Dallas, Texas, Tuesday, March 31, 1981 | 25 Cents

PRESIDENT SHOT

Suspect once lived in Highland Park

Associated Press

Secret Service agents shove President Reagan into the presidential limousine after he was shot in the left side outside a Washington hotel Monday afternoon.

Hinckley recalled as quiet

By Allen Pusey
Staff Writer of The News

John Warnock Hinckley Jr. was the kind of Highland Park youngster old friends have trouble recollecting: a line and a half in his senior yearbook, some lawns mowed with his brother, a gentle, easy-going smile.

His past is the quintessential obscurity of the upper middle-class. But acquaintances will have no trouble remembering John Hinckley in Highland Park now.

Hinckley, who attended Armstrong Elementary School and Highland Park Middle School and Highland Park High School, is said to have wounded four people early Monday afternoon — including the president of the United States.

But for the people who witnessed his sturdy, uneventful upbringing, light-years of change would have been needed to connect the sleepy-eyed boy in Spanish class with the young man they saw being wrestled by U.S. Secret Service agents to the ground on evening news videotapes.

"He just kind of blended in with everybody. He wasn't outstanding, but he wasn't a troublemaker or anything like that," said a boyhood friend, Bill Griffith, of Mobile, Ala.:

But while his youth was a blend of sports and clubs and activity, each year seemed to draw him a bit more into himself.

"You name the activity, he was in it," Griffith said. There was Indian Guides, Cub Scouts and YMCA football, he said. "But as he got on up to junior high, he didn't get into any activities."

His father, John W. (Jack) Hinckley Sr., directed an oil company, Hinckley Oil. His older sister, Diane, was a cheerleader at Southern Methodist University. His older brother, Scott, a Vanderbilt graduate, runs Hinckley Oil — renamed Vanderbilt Resources Corp in Denver, Colo.

They are described as doers, joiners and extroverts, but John is pictured as being turned inward.

Hinckley's Highland Park senior yearbook reflects his only activities as Spanish Club, Rodeo Club and Students in Government.

"I just vaguely remember the kid

See SUSPECT'S FAMILY on Page 2A.

Associated Press

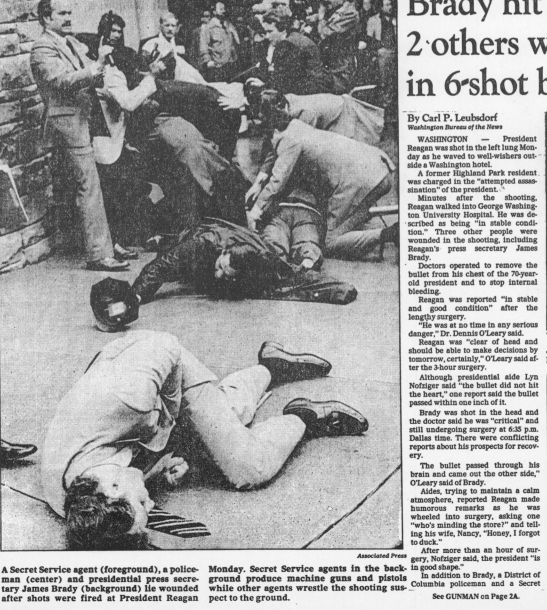

A Secret Service agent (foreground), a policeman (center) and presidential press secretary James Brady (background) lie wounded after shots were fired at President Reagan Monday. Secret Service agents in the background produce machine guns and pistols while other agents wrestle the shooting suspect to the ground.

Brady hit in head, 2 others wounded in 6-shot barrage

By Carl P. Leubsdorf
Washington Bureau of the News

WASHINGTON — President Reagan was shot in the left lung Monday as he waved to well-wishers outside a Washington hotel.

A former Highland Park resident was charged in the "attempted assassination" of the president.

Minutes after the shooting, Reagan walked into George Washington University Hospital. He was described as being "in stable condition." Three other people were wounded in the shooting, including Reagan's press secretary James Brady.

Doctors operated to remove the bullet from his chest of the 70-year-old president and to stop internal bleeding.

Reagan was reported "in stable and good condition" after the lengthy surgery.

"He was at no time in any serious danger," Dr. Dennis O'Leary said.

Reagan was "clear of head and should be able to make decisions by tomorrow, certainly," O'Leary said after the 3-hour surgery.

Although presidential aide Lyn Nofziger said "the bullet did not hit the heart," one report said the bullet passed within one inch of it.

Brady was shot in the head and the doctor said he was "critical" and still undergoing surgery at 6:35 p.m. Dallas time. There were conflicting reports about his prospects for recovery.

The bullet passed through his brain and came out the other side," O'Leary said of Brady.

Aides, trying to maintain a calm atmosphere, reported Reagan made humorous remarks as he was wheeled into surgery, asking one "who's minding the store?" and telling his wife, Nancy, "Honey, I forgot to duck."

After more than an hour of surgery, Nofziger said, the president "is in good shape."

In addition to Brady, a District of Columbia policeman and a Secret

See GUNMAN on Page 2A.

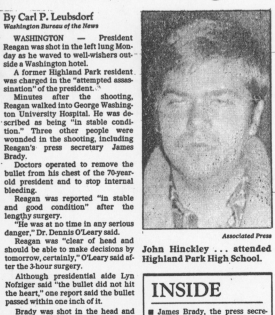

Associated Press

John Hinckley ... attended Highland Park High School.

INSIDE

4 STAR ★ ★ ★ ★ FINAL

DAILY NEWS

.35¢ NEW YORK'S PICTURE NEWSPAPER® Tuesday, November 18, 1986

PERSICO GETS 39 YRS. IN JAIL

Story on page 3

UNITED IN GRIEF IN AN UNEASY PEACE

TRUCE Mayor Koch and PBA President Phil Caruso are separated by (from left) Police Commissioner Benjamin Ward, Controller Harrison Goldin and Chief of Department Robert Johnson at funeral services for Police Officer Kenton Britt, killed in an auto crash last week, at Brooklyn church yesterday. Meanwhile, details of hotly contested plans for police transfers remained unsettled. **Page 18**

Koch warns taxi drivers as protest drones on

Page 5

"All the News That's Fit to Print"

The New York Times

Late Edition

New York: Today, some sun and clouds, warmer. High 42-47. Tonight, cloudy. Low 34-40. Tomorrow, cloudy, showers developing. High 44-49. Yesterday: High 39, low 28. Details on page 52.

VOL.CXXXVII . . . No. 47,358 NEW YORK, SATURDAY, DECEMBER 19, 1987 50 cents beyond 75 miles from New York City, except on Long Island. 30 CENTS

BOESKY SENTENCED TO 3 YEARS IN JAIL IN INSIDER SCANDAL

BUT NO FINE IS IMPOSED

Giuliani Praises Prison Term, Calling It Major Deterrent to White-Collar Crime

By JAMES STERNGOLD

Ivan F. Boesky, once among the financial world's most powerful speculators and now a symbol of Wall Street's excesses, was sentenced yesterday to three years in prison for conspiring to file false stock trading records.

The 50-year-old Mr. Boesky, trim and steady as he stood before Federal District Judge Morris E. Lasker, had sipped water nervously and tugged at the knot of his dark blue tie throughout the proceedings, but showed no emotion in response to the sentence.

According to records kept by the United States Attorney's office in Manhattan, the three-year term is the third longest to have been imposed in a case related to insider trading. Mr. Boesky had faced a maximum penalty of five years in jail and a $250,000 fine.

In Line With Expectations

The United States Attorney, Rudolph W. Giuliani, expressed satisfaction with the sentence. Other lawyers and Wall Street officials said it was somewhat lenient but in line with their expectations. Mr. Giuliani called the three-year prison term "a heavy sentence," emphasizing its importance to deterring white-collar crime. He said it was "well deserved and very well balanced."

Mr. Boesky, who was given 90 days, or until March 24, to surrender and begin serving his sentence, did not comment after yesterday's hearing. His attorney, Leon Silverman, would only say that Mr. Boesky "accepts the court's decision." He continued, "He must now pick up the remnants and try to get on with the business of living a constructive and useful life."

Record $100 Million Paid

A year ago, Mr. Boesky settled civil insider trading charges, paying a record $100 million. He had been charged with illegally earning more than $50 million by trading with inside information he bought from Dennis B. Levine, a former investment banker who pleaded guilty to criminal charges earlier and is now in prison.

Mr. Boesky subsequently disclosed that he additionally earned more than $30 million by illegally trading with inside information sold to him for $700,000 by Martin A. Siegel, once one of Wall Street's top corporate merger specialists. Mr. Siegel has pleaded guilty to criminal charges and is awaiting sentencing.

Last April, Mr. Boesky pleaded guilty to the single felony count, at that time one of the most important devel-

Continued on Page 39, Column 1

The New York Times/Keith Meyers

Ivan F. Boesky, second from left, being escorted by Federal marshals as he left court after sentencing.

CONTRA AID SNAGS BUDGET PACKAGE

Reagan Adds Two Conditions for Support on Spending

By JONATHAN FUERBRINGER

Special to The New York Times

WASHINGTON, Dec. 18 — President Reagan today threatened to veto legislation needed to put this year's budget compromise into effect if it does not contain support he considers "adequate" to sustain the Nicaraguan rebels as a fighting force into February.

In a meeting with Republican leaders, the President also specified two other conditions for his approval of the two bills needed to put into effect the budget agreement reached last month by Congress and the White House.

He said he would veto the measures if they did not include all of the provisions of the budget agreement. The President objected to a provision renewing a Federal requirement that television and radio stations offer reasonable time for opposing views on public issues, so as to assure fairness.

Referring to the broadcasting rule, aid to the contras and conformity to the budget compromise, Marlin Fitzwater, the White House spokesman, said, "These are three very important items to us."

In defiance of this veto threat, the House and Senate conferees tonight included the broadcast-fairness rule in one of two key bills. Senate conferees voted, 12 to 10, to accept the provision, which had been included in legislation approved by the House. Opponents of

Continued on Page 33, Column 1

Court Backs Treatment of Woman Held Under Koch Homeless Plan

By KIRK JOHNSON

A sharply divided appeals court yesterday upheld New York City's involuntary hospitalization of Joyce Brown, a 40-year-old homeless woman whose case has become a test of the city's powers to remove disturbed homeless people from the streets.

The 3-to-2 decision by the Appellate Division of State Supreme Court in Manhattan said Miss Brown, who lived for more than a year near a warm air vent on Second Avenue near 65th Street, was mentally ill and a danger to herself and others.

The court said a trial judge who last month ordered Miss Brown released had erred by placing too much emphasis on her own testimony, and not enough on the psychiatrists who had treated her.

"Although we deplore, with our fellow New Yorkers, the tragedy of the homeless in this city, their plight is not the issue in this case," wrote Justice David Ross in the 41-page majority ruling, which attorneys for Miss Brown said would be appealed. The issue, the court said, was narrow: whether Miss Brown, a former secretary from New Jersey, was mentally ill to an extent that her release would pose an immediate danger to herself or society.

In the language of the decision and in that of the accompanying minority dissent, the panel also provided a broad-brush picture of the terms of the debate over the homeless in New York.

Divided on Key Questions

The court was deeply divided on key questions such as when a verbally abusive, dirty and disheveled person passes beyond the point of a nuisance to the level of a danger or menace. And in a city like New York, where both sides agreed that a person could draw an assault from others through abusive language in the street, how to define when people become a danger to themselves.

Mayor Koch, under whose program Miss Brown was picked up, said the

Continued on Page 30, Column 4

Stronger Dollar Propels Stocks Sharply Higher

Dow Extends Advance With a Gain of 50.90

By LAWRENCE J. De MARIA

Stock prices rose sharply in heavy trading yesterday, extending Wall Street's latest rally to two weeks.

Traders said strength in the dollar enabled the stock market to overcome its concern over yesterday's expiration of three types of investments related to stocks or stock indexes.

Many people on Wall Street attributed the dollar's turnaround, and the subsequent strength in the stock and bond markets, to remarks made yesterday by the chairman of the Federal Reserve, Alan Greenspan. In his first comprehensive review of economic issues since taking office in August, Mr. Greenspan told Congress that the nation's recent $17.6 billion record October trade deficit was an aberration and that the deficit figures might improve. [Page 37.]

Policy-Coordination Statement

Traders said the dollar was also helped by speculation that officials of the United States and six other industrial nations might soon make a statement on coordinating their economic and currency policies.

Inflation fears have also subsided, particularly as oil prices have declined following the discord among OPEC members in Vienna several days ago. Yesterday, the Government reported that consumer prices in November had risen only three-tenths of 1 percent, a figure that analysts said suggested inflation would remain subdued in the coming months. [Page 37.]

The Dow Jones industrial average jumped 50.90 points, or 2.64 percent, yesterday to close at 1,975.30. The Dow, made up of stocks of 30 of the nation's premier corporations, gained a record 108.26 points for the week, surpassing last week's 100.30-point gain.

'A Pretty Good Week'

"We wound up with a pretty good week," said Robert N. Gordon, president of the Twenty-First Securities Corporation.

The Dow is now 236.5 points, or 13.6 percent, above the level of Oct. 19, when the key blue-chip indicator plunged a record 508 points and set off a global financial crisis. During the October decline, the Dow, which peaked at

Continued on Page 41, Column 5

TEXACO REPORTED TO REACH ACCORD ON PENNZOIL SUIT

$3 BILLION PAYMENT SEEN

Additional $2.5 Billion Would Go to Pay Off Creditors in Biggest Bankruptcy

By STEPHEN LABATON

A tumultuous four-year legal battle that pitted the Pennzoil Company against the giant Texaco Inc. was brought to a conclusion last night when Texaco agreed in principle to give Pennzoil $3 billion, a lawyer for Texaco said.

An additional amount, about $2.5 billion, would be paid to Texaco's creditors to bring the company out of bankruptcy, the lawyer, David Boies, said.

A Pennzoil spokesman, Robert Harper, said the company would neither confirm nor deny that an agreement had been reached between the companies. "We're not commenting," he said. Calls to Pennzoil's chairman, J. Hugh Liedtke, were not returned.

Icahn Informed

Carl C. Icahn, chairman of Trans World Airlines Inc. and Texaco's largest shareholder, said he had been informed by Texaco executives that a settlement in principle had been reached and that only a few small issues remained to be worked out before an official statement would be made by Texaco and Pennzoil.

The agreement settles a case in which a jury awarded the largest judgment in American history. The accord will also allow Texaco, the nation's third-largest oil company, to emerge from bankruptcy in the next few months.

It also marks the closing chapter of an acrimonious corporate feud that began almost four years ago as a contracts dispute. The fight has been punctuated by thousands of hours of fruitless negotiations, legal wranglings, dashed hopes and charges by executives of both companies accusing the other side of greed, arrogance and duplicity.

The dispute dates to January 1984, when Texaco acquired the Getty Oil Company for $10.1 billion. Pennzoil, a Houston-based company that thought it had previously reached a binding agreement to buy three-sevenths of Getty, sued Texaco for interference of contract.

Huge Bond Required

In 1985, after a trial that lasted more than four months, a Texas jury awarded Pennzoil $10.53 billion, plus interest, in damages.

Texaco, saying that it could not put up a bond in that amount, which was required by Texas law during the appeal process, filed for protection from its creditors on April 12 of this year.

The filing made Texaco the largest company ever to enter bankruptcy proceedings. The Federal trustee supervising the bankruptcy, Harry Jones, then appointed committees to represent the interests of Texaco's shareholders and creditors.

Last night, Texaco's 14-member board held a telephone-conference call and approved the most important details of the settlement, Mr. Boies said. The two companies are expected to an-

Continued on Page 44, Column 3

British Press Freedom Erodes Under Thatcher, Critics Say

By HOWELL RAINES

Special to The New York Times

LONDON, Dec. 18 — The Thatcher Government's legal actions against newspapers and broadcasters have resulted in a significant erosion of freedom of the press in Britain in 1987, in the view of journalists, civil libertarians and the handful of politicians interested in the issue.

Throughout the year, the Government pursued its efforts to inhibit British publication of and news reporting about "Spycatcher," an account of misconduct in the British security services by Peter Wright, a former intelligence agent.

At the same time, in less publicized cases, it has used the Police and Criminal Evidence Act to look for evidence in the news and photo libraries of newspapers, and it has turned to another restrictive statute to try to compel a financial reporter to serve as a police informant in an insider trading case.

These actions are among nine areas of legal activity directed against the press that have been identified by the Press Council, an ombudsman group financed by the newspaper industry. "With all these, Britain is sinking further into that league of nations where press freedom is barely understood, let alone protected," said Kenneth Morgan, director of the council.

Experts differ on whether the rash of litigation represents a coordinated Government effort to bring the press to heel. But they agree that the plight of the financial journalist, Jeremy Warner of The Independent, illustrates the fragility of press freedom in Britain and the vulnerability of journalists to Government pressure in this country.

Mr. Warner could become the first British journalist in 25 years to go to jail to protect a source of information if he continues to refuse to tell police inspectors how he got information about purported insider trading by civil ser-

Continued on Page 5, Column 1

Karsh, Ottawa/Woodfin Camp

Yourcenar Dead at 84

Marguerite Yourcenar, the author and the first woman named to the Académie Française, died at her home in Maine. Page 34.

Agence France-Presse

A Marriage Raises Political Questions in Pakistan

Benazir Bhutto, the opposition leader, with her husband, Asif Ali Zardari, after their wedding yesterday in Karachi. Many wondered whether the marriage would help or hinder her political movement. Page 4.

Key Jobs in Military Off Limits for AIDS-Infected

By ROBERT PEAR

Special to The New York Times

WASHINGTON, Dec. 18 — Officials of the Defense Department said today that military personnel infected with the AIDS virus were being removed from sensitive, stressful jobs because of new evidence that the virus could impair mental function, even in people who show no overt symptoms of the disease.

The officials acknowledged that some people infected with the virus suffered no neurological impairment. But they said they had no way to distinguish reliably between those who would and those who would not.

The policy is certain to cause wide debate and concern because of the possibility that it could be used to justify mandatory testing of people in stressful civilian occupations, and removal of AIDS virus carriers from such jobs. While more than 48,000 Americans have developed AIDS, experts estimate that a million to a million and a half have been infected with the virus.

Dr. Peter J. Fischinger, AIDS coordinator for the United States Public Health Service, and Dr. Anthony S. Fauci, one of the Government's top experts on AIDS, said not enough scientific data were available on neurological effects of AIDS infections to know whether civilian employers should follow the example of the military.

Dr. Fauci warned against any precipitate measures to require testing for infection with the AIDS virus or to dismiss infected employees.

Civil rights advocates criticized the military policy on the ground that it stigmatized an entire group without cause, rather than focusing only on individuals who actually showed signs of

Continued on Page 33, Column 1

INSIDE

Hospitalization Is Upheld

A New York State appeals court ruled that a homeless woman picked up under the Mayor's new program is mentally ill and may be hospitalized involuntarily. Page 11.

Chess Duel Continues

The final game of the world chess championship adjourned, with analysts saying either player could win when play resumes today. Page 14.

No Longer the Helpmate

In growing numbers, wives of college presidents are pursuing careers instead of devoting themselves entirely to their husbands' careers. Page 8.

House Reprimands Member

Austin J. Murphy of Pennsylvania was reprimanded by a vote of 324 to 68 for acts that included having someone else vote for him. Page 8.

News Summary, Page 2

SPORTS FINAL

WEDNESDAY, JANUARY 25, 1989 / Partly sunny, cold, upper 30s today; cloudy, low 30s tonight / Details, Page 2 R 40¢ in New York City 50¢ elsewhere

WHAT, ME WORRY?

Grinning godfather: 'I'll beat this case'

A jolly John Gotti shares a few comical words with his driver outside Manhattan Supreme Court yesterday. Pages 4 & 5.

DEATH PENALTY MAY BE BACK IN N.Y. Page Two

SOBBING BUNDY DRAGGED TO CHAIR

Mass murderer executed for killing of 12-year-old

By BILL HOFFMANN

Mass murderer Theodore Bundy — who confessed to beating, strangling and choking 20 women to death — was dragged from his cell and executed in Florida's electric chair yesterday.

The 42-year-old law-school dropout was electrocuted at 7:06 a.m., ending one of the darkest, most chilling chapters in the history of American crime.

Witnesses said Bundy's trademark cockiness and boasting swagger were gone as he spent his final hours in prayer and occasional tears in a Florida State Prison cell.

The remorseful killer placed two farewell calls to his mother, Louise, who told him: "You'll always be my precious son."

"He sounds very much at peace with himself," she told reporters.

At 4:50 a.m., Bundy was offered a last meal consisting of steak, eggs, hash browns, toast, juice and coffee. But he refused to eat.

Forty minutes later, a prison barber shaved his head and right leg where electrodes would be attached.

> ***"I'd like you to give my love to my family and friends."***
>
> TED BUNDY'S LAST WORDS

Then, at 7 a.m., prison officials told Bundy, "It's time," and tried to move him out.

But he resisted and prison officials had to physically drag him from his cell, WCBS radio reported. Then Bundy regained his composure.

"He was quiet, subdued, docile. He did not struggle when he was led to the chair," Bob Macmaster, a prison spokesman who witnessed his death, told The Post.

Accompanied by a handful of prison officials, guards and a minister, Bundy — not wearing handcuffs — walked 30 feet down the dimly lit death row to the electrocution chamber.

When he saw the 66-year-old wooden electric chair — nicknamed "Ole Sparky" — Bundy's composure changed once again. His blue eyes widened and he became apprehensive, frightened and "pale white."

He was told to sit down, was strapped in with arm, leg and chin restraints, and "wired" for electricity.

Asked if he had any final words, Bundy whispered to his lawyer, James Coleman, and minister, the Rev. Fred Lawrence: "Jim and Fred, I'd like you to give my love to my family and friends."

T-SHIRT VIGIL: *Many cheered outside prison.*

Associated Press

SHE WAS LUCKY: *Little did Carol Bartholomew of Salt Lake City know she was washing dishes with serial killer Ted Bundy in this 1974 photograph.*

A black hood was placed over his face and an anonymous executioner — a woman who was paid $150 for the job — turned on the power at 7:06 a.m.

Some 2,000 volts raced through his body.

"There was a slight arching of his back and clenching of his hands," said Macmaster.

The juice was turned off 60 seconds later. At 7:16 a.m., Bundy was declared dead.

His body was placed in a white hearse and driven past hundreds of curious onlookers. Some cheered and lit firecrackers and screamed, "Burn, Bundy, Burn!"

Bundy was executed for the 1978 rape-murder of Kimberly Leach, 12, whose corpse was found in an abandoned Florida pigsty.

But authorities say he was responsible for as many as 36 grisly murders in four Western states and Florida.

In the days before his execution, he confessed to 20 of them.

Bundy was the subject of several books and a TV movie, "The Deliberate Stranger."

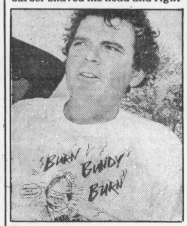

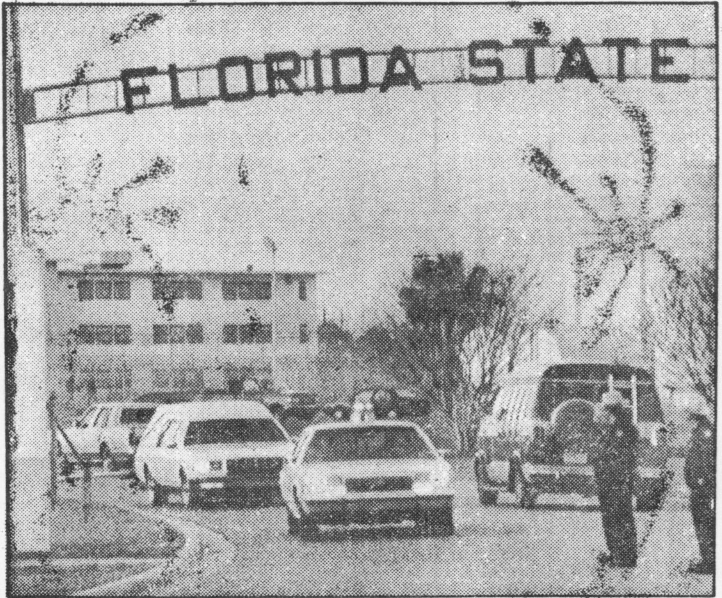

Associated Press

BUNDY'S BODY REMOVED: *Executed serial killer Ted Bundy's body is taken from prison in a white hearse.*

Hahn's ex-pastor cops surprise guilty plea

By CHRIS McKENNA

ALBANY — Jessica Hahn's flamboyant ex-pastor — facing 57 years in jail for tax evasion and potentially embarrassing testimony from Hahn herself — copped a plea yesterday to reduced charges.

"He's a wimp," said a tearful and shaking Hahn minutes after the Rev. Gene Profeta entered a surprise guilty plea to two counts of his 18-count indictment.

"Rev. Profeta was my idol. But he couldn't say, 'Hey, I made a mistake,' " Hahn said.

Hahn, 29, Profeta's former church secretary and lover, was to testify yesterday in a pre-trial bid to uphold two witness-tampering charges against the pompadoured preacher.

"I thank God it didn't get to that — for my family's sake. For no other reason except my family's sake," she said.

In fact, insiders said it was Hahn's expected testimony about Atlantic City gambling junkets and lavish gifts — all allegedly paid with money skimmed from Profeta's Full Gospel Tabernacle church — that finally convinced the preacher to make a deal.

"I just knew him the best," Hahn said of her role as star prosecution witness.

During a pre-trial hearing Monday, a state investigator testified officials agreed to drop probes into tax evasion and cocaine use by Hahn in exchange for her testimony.

Hahn had admitted to state investigators that she independently had "extorted" $12,000 from former PTL leader Jim Bakker — who she alleges raped her in 1980 — and spent more than half that money on cocaine.

As part of his plea bargain, Profeta, 52, who admitted that he evaded $13,000 in back taxes between 1984 and 1986, will spend as little as four months in jail.

He also agreed to repay the taxes, plus $15,000 in penalties and a $5,000 fine.

Profeta, nicknamed the "Pistol-Packin' Preacher" because he's licensed to carry handguns, will never be able to do that again because state law bars convicted felons from owning or carrying weapons.

He was also ordered by state Supreme Court Justice Joseph Harris to stay away from Hahn.

Prosecutors also agreed to drop tax fraud charges against Profeta's wife, Glenda, 44.

"It was the best way to end this matter and for him to get on with his life," Profeta's lawyer, John Gross, said of the plea bargain.

After entering his plea, Profeta — dressed in a gray suit and black shirt — paused just long enough to shake Harris' hand before quickly leaving.

He wouldn't comment to reporters about the proceedings.

LILCO's $700M Property Tax Suit Goes to Trial

Page 7

1940 50TH YEAR 1990

Newsday

THE LONG ISLAND NEWSPAPER

MONDAY, MARCH 26, 1990 • NASSAU 35¢

SOCIAL CLUB TRAGEDY

Arson Kills 87 in Bronx

Man Held; Motive Called Lover's Revenge

Newsday / Susan Farley

Happy Land club, where authorities said a man, angry at being spurned by a woman, set blaze in doorway. It was the city's worst fire since 1911.

Coverage Begins on Page 3

'Crumb' dunked over $3,800 cookie money

By TIMOTHY McDARRAH

A Long Island man was arrested yesterday for allegedly milking the Girl Scouts out of $3,800 in cookie money.

Daniel Guinan of Levittown was arraigned last night on grand-larceny charges.

Nassau County police said Guinan's wife, Carol, handed him $3,864 cash in March after leading last winter's cookie drive for her 11-year-old daughter's troop, No. 3041 in Levittown.

Guinan, later dubbed the Cookie Monster by some of the youngsters, was supposed to write a check to the Girl Scouts of Nassau County.

He wrote the check, all right — but on a closed account, and pocketed the cash, police said.

"Like any business who gets a bad check, we contacted him and went through the usual series of steps when these things happen," Trish Hughes, a spokeswoman for the Scouts, told The Post. "But we never received a penny from him."

A man who answered the phone at the Guinan residence said it was "probably a mistake" that the check was written on a closed account.

But a police spokesman said: "It happened back in March and they haven't been able to get the money from him. That doesn't look like a mistake to me."

Hughes said all the customers who bought cookies from the troop got what they ordered, and the girls received their prizes.

"Based on how many boxes they sell, the girls earned everything from sweatshirts to cameras," Hughes said.

She said the Scouts organization had covered the costs of the girls' prizes and still hoped to recover the allegedly stolen money from Guinan.

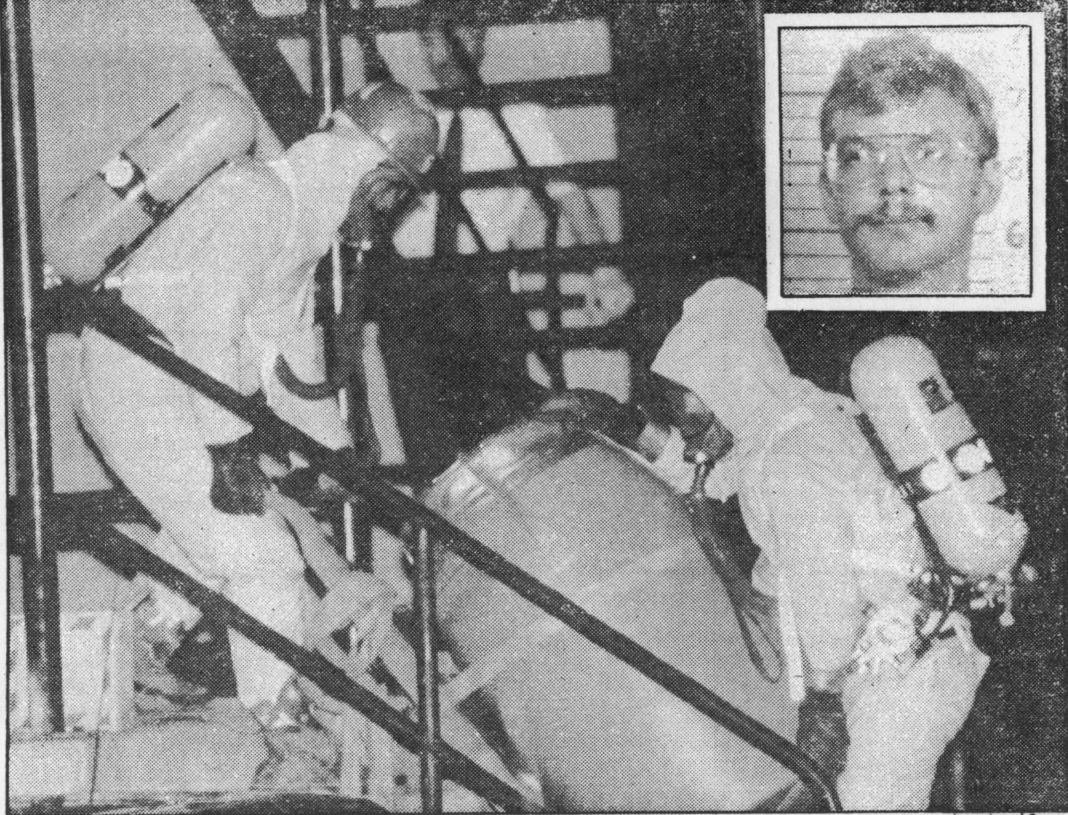
Associated Press

GRISLY JOB *Milwaukee cops in protective suits remove a barrel of body parts from the apartment of Jeffrey Dahmer (inset), where as many as 15 people may have been slain.*

LITTLE BODY SHOP OF HORRORS

Wis. man held as dismembered victims are found

MILWAUKEE (AP) — As many as 15 dismembered human bodies were found yesterday in an apartment after a man fled the building and told police he was handcuffed and threatened with a knife, authorities said.

Police went to the dingy, fly-infested apartment and found boxes filled with body parts, a refrigerator containing three human heads, and a dresser brimming with photographs and drawings of mutilated bodies.

Police arrested the apartment's tenant, whom they identified as Jeffrey Dahmer.

Neighbors had complained of a stench for up to a year, and yesterday a hazardous-materials team wore yellow rubber suits and breathed from air tanks while removing boxes from the apartment.

Some neighbors told police they had heard the sound of sawing from the apartment at all hours.

Ella Vickers, 31, who lives next door to the Oxford Apartments where the body parts were found, said: "We've been smelling odors for weeks, but we thought it was a dead animal or something like that. We had no idea it was humans."

Police Chief Phillip Arreola said there were many victims, most of them male and of various races. He did not specify the number. One officer, speaking anonymously, said there may have been 15 victims.

Arreola said it was too early to determine if the killings were sexually motivated.

Authorities did not reveal the identity of the man who fled the apartment.

Rolf Mueller, one of the patrolmen who made the discovery, said the officers were overpowered by the stench.

"You think you've seen it all out here, and then something like this happens," said Mueller.

Arreola said the bodies were found after a man in handcuffs flagged down a patrol car and said he had escaped from the apartment.

Police said Dahmer was originally from Medina, Ohio, and had been in Milwaukee several years. Records show he has a 1988 conviction for second-degree sexual assault for offering a 13-year-old boy $50 to pose nude.

The apartment complex is just a few blocks from the Marquette University campus.

Regents set to duck condom issue

By CHRIS McKENNA
Post Correspondent

ALBANY — The Board of Regents appeared ready to turn its back on the state's Catholic bishops yesterday by refusing to take a stand on New York City's controversial condom-distribution plan.

The board, which sets education policy for the entire state, was urged by the New York Catholic Conference, the bishops' lobby group here, to pull rank on city schools Chancellor Joseph Fernandez and overturn the plan, which is aimed at fighting the spread of AIDS.

But sources both inside and outside the board predicted that the Regents would once again

SOBOL

FERNANDEZ

duck the issue and give Fernandez a green light to set his own condom policy.

"After they have a massive debate over morality, they are going to go for local control," said a source close to the board.

"It's the safest way out for them."

That move, backed by state education Commissioner Thomas Sobol, is expected to spark bitter and lengthy debate among the Regents, many of whom are pushing for the ban, or an alternative parental-consent requirement.

"The only way to fight AIDS is to teach abstinence," said Regents board member Willard Genrich of Buffalo, a condom opponent who said he still hopes to sway his colleagues to ban the Fernandez plan.

"The city Board [of Education] is not promoting abstinence. They are promoting sexual activity"

KILLEEN DAILY HERALD

Serving The Central Texas Metroplex Of Killeen, Fort Hood, Copperas Cove, Harker Heights And Nolanville

VOLUME 39, Number 286 | PUBLISHED EVERY MORNING | KILLEEN, TEXAS 76540 | THURSDAY, OCTOBER 17, 1991 | DAILY 25¢ • SUNDAY $1.00

GUNMAN KILLS 22

Herald Photo by Lee Schexnaider

SHATTERED — Justice of the Peace Robert Stubblefield, far left, walks away from the broken window Wednesday where a truck plowed into Luby's Cafeteria in Killeen before its driver opened fire in the restaurant, killing 22 people. Police investigators, from left, Joe Galiano, Lt. Rick Morrarty and Sgt. Mike Keefe stand near the window where the truck entered.

Suicide Finishes Killer's Rampage

From Staff Reports

A gunman rammed a pickup through a large window at Luby's Cafeteria in Killeen during the noon rush hour Wednesday and opened fire with a semiautomatic handgun, killing 22 people and wounding 18 others. After police officers closed in and wounded the gunman, he retreated into a restroom and killed himself with a shot to the head.

It was the worst mass murder by gunfire in U.S. history.

Witnesses who survived the massacre said the pickup crashed through the window on the south side of the restaurant near the front entrance of the building, hitting several diners as it entered. The tragedy began about 12:40 p.m.

Survivors said the man, later identified as George "Jo" Hennard, 35, of Belton shouted and then opened fire while still seated in the truck. He then opened the truck door, got out and walked through the restaurant shooting people with a semiautomatic handgun. He carried several ammunition clips and was able to quickly reload after expending each clip.

According to employees of the popular cafeteria, the dining room was packed with well over 100 customers, many of whom had brought their bosses for Bosses' Day luncheons. When the firing began, customers and Luby's employees scattered, according to survivors' accounts.

Eddie Sanchez, 31, had just arrived at the cafeteria when the gunman crashed into the cafeteria front.

"He smashed into the window. A lady flew to the right, and a man flew to the left and there was another man, I guess he pushed him with his truck. The man was laying there, and he shot the man that was looking up at him, then he shot the other man.

"I was standing at the window when he crashed in," he said. "And when he stepped out of the car and shot the first man, I paused for a second, and he shot the second person ... then he turned around and fired at me ... that's when I ran back to the back (of the restaurant)."

Sanchez said the shooter stood by the truck and fired an entire clip after crashing into the building.

He said the gunman also shot at people who had taken cover on the ground.

Sanchez said he had dropped someone off at the restaurant when the truck crashed through

(See RAMPAGE, Page 2-A.)

Realtors Say Belton Man Acted Strangely

Shocked, Horrified Neighbors Recall Suspect Was Standoffish But Friendly

By THOM MATHEWS
Herald Staff Writer

BELTON — Shocked and horrified neighbors of George Hennard describe the mass murder suspect as a standoffish but friendly fellow who kept to himself most of the time, appearing outside on occasion to mow the yard of his divorced parents' posh Colonial home in Belton.

But a realtor who once showed the home to prospective buyers described him as a non-stop talker who left the impression that he was mentally disturbed.

Hennard, 35, lived alone in his parents' four-bedroom, three-bath, 3,500-square-foot two-story red-brick home at 301 E. 14th St. in Belton. The home and grounds cover almost a city block in an older but well-kept neighborhood of much smaller homes.

Miss Myrtle Hander, a retired accountant who lives directly across the street from the Hennard home, referred to her neighbor as Jo. She said she seldom talked with the sandy-haired man except to exchange greetings.

Miss Hander said the last time she saw Hennard was Tuesday afternoon when he and she took in their garbage cans. They did not speak to each other, she said.

She said her neighbor's father, Dr. George Hennard, is an orthopedic surgeon in Houston. She said the younger Hennard was known as Jo because he and his father shared the same name and people would sometimes confuse them.

Dr. Hennard, she said, formerly practiced in the Temple-Belton area but moved to Houston when he and his wife, Jeanna Hennard, divorced in 1983 or 1984. She said the couple lived in the house for about 12 years.

Mrs. Hennard now lives in Las Vegas, Nev., Miss Hander said, and hasn't returned to the Belton residence in months. Miss Hander said Hennard has a sister, Deseree Hennard, in Killeen and another married sister who resides in Austin.

Miss Hander said she understood the young Hennard was a merchant seaman or employee of the U.S. Coast Guard.

Miss Hander said the tall, slim and swarthy Hennard had lived in the 50-year-old six-columned house for about three years and is not married as far as she knows.

She said he was maintaining the property until it sold. Sale price of the house and 137- by 232-foot lot is listed in the Temple-Belton real estate multi-list book for $137,500.

Miss Hander said Hennard last summer restored a storm-damaged brick fence that encloses a swimming pool in the back yard and was constantly puttering about the home.

Miss Hander said she was shocked to hear Hennard was the suspect in the

(See SUSPECT, Page 3-A.)

'Am I Going To Die? I Just Held My Breath'

By SUSAN ROBINSON-HESTER
Special To The Herald

▪ AN EYEWITNESS ACCOUNT

Is this really happening?

Will I ever see my girls again? Will I see my husband? Am I going to die?

I just held my breath.

The gunshots seemed to ring out for hours, even though it lasted only a matter of minutes.

Moments before the shooting began, we were finishing our lunch at Luby's cafeteria, having a good time and giving gifts to our boss for Bosses' Day.

The good time was quickly shattered by the sound of breaking glass as a blue pickup came crashing through the front windows about 12:40 Wednesday afternoon.

Before it was over, our boss, James Swift, lay bleeding from a gunshot wound.

Mr. Swift, the director of KISD's Chapter 1/Bilingual/Adult Ed Program, survived the shooting. Two of his staff members did not.

One sat right across the table from me at lunch. I was just talking to her when we heard the truck crash through the window.

After the ordeal was over and we were sure it was safe to get up, I grabbed her leg and shook it. I called out her name, but she didn't respond. I didn't realize how close the bullets came to me until that moment.

The truck was completely inside the building when it came to a stop, and it would've kept going if something hadn't forced it to stop. I don't know what it was.

I saw a glimpse of the gunman's head. He began shooting and yelling. "Look at what Belton's done to me," he screamed.

The next thing I knew, I was on the floor ... as was everyone around me.

My face was pressed as far into the carpet as possible. I was getting as low to the ground as I could. I was trying to hide from him ... even though I knew I

(See EYEWITNESS, Page 4-A.)

Forecast: Mostly Clear

Index

Weather

High Today	upper 80s
Low Tonight	low 60s
Winds	Southerly, 10-15 mph
Chance Of Rain	10 percent
High Yesterday	82
Low Yesterday	48
Rainfall (past 24 hrs.)	none
Sunset Tonight	6:55
Sunrise Tomorrow	7:34

Founders Of Retreat Earn Mayborn Honor

By LINDA A. COX
Herald Staff Writer

TEMPLE — A "work of noble note" was recognized Wednesday with the presentation of the first Frank W. Mayborn Humanitarian Award to Daurice and Jim Bowmer of Temple.

The award was established recently by Sue Mayborn, president of the Killeen Daily Herald and editor and publisher of the Temple Daily Telegram, in honor of her late husband, Frank W. Mayborn, who died in 1987. It will be given periodically to a Central Texas resident whose deed or deeds during the preceding year conferred the greatest lasting benefit upon the area.

"This award is not an effort to honor Frank, but an effort to encourage the caring, participation and leadership that his life personified," said Mrs. Mayborn at a luncheon held Wednesday at the Frank W. Mayborn Civic and Convention Center in Temple.

The Bowmers were selected from among 26 nominees for the award by a committee of the board of directors of the two sponsoring newspapers. Announcing the recipients at Wednesday's luncheon was Temple attorney William R. Courtney.

Courtney counted the Bowmers among Bell County's many citizens who, "motivated solely by love and compassion," make Central Texas a better place.

"They (the Bowmers) have conceived and performed a work of noble note," said Courtney, referring to the Peaceable Kingdom Retreat for Children near the Bowmer ranch on the banks of the Lampasas River in West Bell County.

Several years ago, the Bowmers created the Central Texas Natural Laboratory at their ranch. They also donated land for the Peaceable Kingdom Baptist Church.

After their infant grandson died of a heart problem, and two other grandchildren developed childhood diabetes, the couple asked the Peaceable Kingdom Baptist Church to start the Peaceable

(See MAYBORN, Page 11-A.)

Herald Photo by Duane A. Laverty

HONORED HUMANITARIANS — Jim and Daurice Bowmer, winners of the 1991 Frank W. Mayborn Humanitarian Award, talk about their award following a luncheon Wednesday at the Frank W. Mayborn Civic Center in Temple. The Bowmers are the founders of the Peaceable Kingdom Retreat for chronically ill children near Youngsport.

Weather
Today: Snow flurries early, then variably cloudy. High 38. Low 26. Wind north 10-20 mph. **Sunday:** Mostly sunny. High 42. Wind 10-20 mph. **Yesterday:** Temp. range: 25-29. Wind chill: 10. Details on B2.

The Washington Post

Sections
A News/Editorials
B Metro/Obituaries
C Business/Religion
D Style/Television
E, F Real Estate/Comics
G Sports/Classified
Today's Contents: *Page A2*

116th Year ... No. 84 · SATURDAY, FEBRUARY 27, 1993 · A · Prices May Vary in Areas Outside Metropolitan Washington (See Box on A4) 25¢

At Least 7 Die, 500 Hurt as Explosion Rips Garage Under World Trade Center

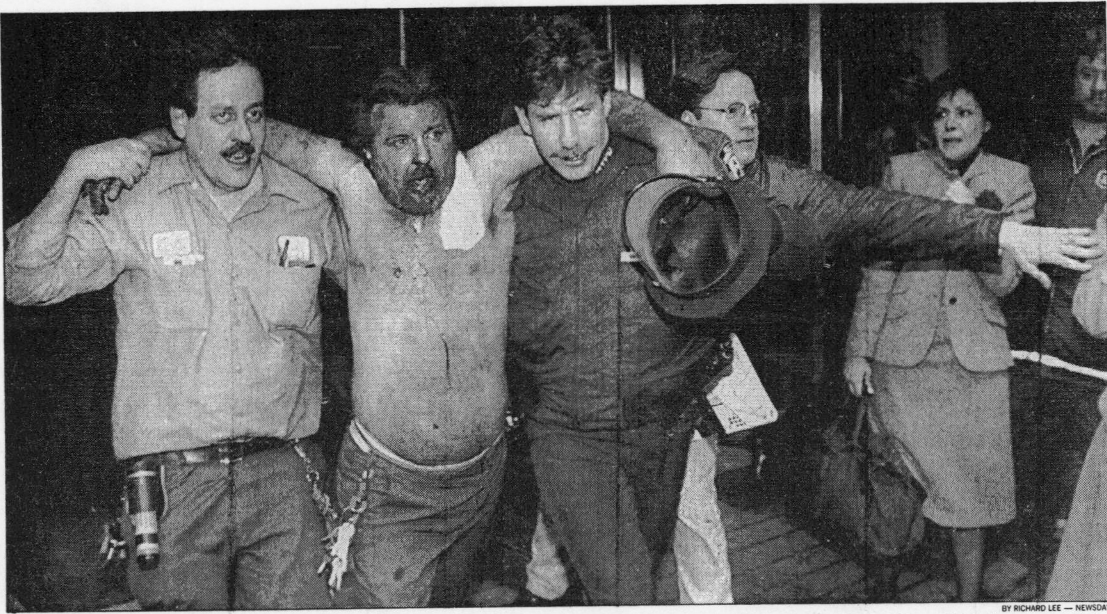

BY RICHARD LEE — NEWSDAY

Rescue workers carry an injured man out of New York's World Trade Center after an explosion that officials suspect was caused by a bomb. More than 500 injuries were reported.

Bomb Suspected In Midday Blast; Thousands Flee

By Malcolm Gladwell
Washington Post Staff Writer

NEW YORK, Feb. 26—An explosion, possibly caused by a bomb, ripped through a hotel parking garage beneath the World Trade Center this afternoon, killing at least seven people, injuring more than 500 and causing a frantic midday evacuation of tens of thousands of workers from the complex's twin towers.

The blast at 12:17 p.m. left a crater measuring at least 100-by-100 feet in the three-story garage, scattering concrete debris throughout an adjacent commuter-rail station and filling all 110 stories of one tower with smoke within minutes.

Authorities here said tonight that they had not determined the cause of the blast, although they said it was "possible" that it was caused by a bomb.

"I heard a boom," said Shannon Murphy, 24, who works for an accounting firm on the 101st floor of One World Trade Center. "It felt like thunder up there. You always feel it when it's windy. But this was different. I felt the floor move . . . . Within five minutes, there was smoke on our floor."

In Washington, John C. Killorin, spokesman for the Bureau of Alcohol, Tobacco and Firearms (BATF), said, "We are suspicious of what happened" and "are going to investigate it as a bombing." He said authorities are aware that "key evidence as to what happened is under rubble." No one, he said, "has the evidence in hand to say it was a bombing."

FBI bomb technicians and a special BATF team of explosives experts and forensic technicians were sent here tonight.

After New York Gov. Mario M. Cuomo (D) and Mayor David N. Dinkins (D) spoke late today with President Clinton about the explosion, White House press secretary Dee Dee Myers said New York authorities "have reason to believe it was a bomb but are not definite."

New York Police Commissioner Raymond W. Kelly said police received at least seven calls, apparently from different people, saying they were responsible for the blast after it occurred. "To the best of our knowledge," he said, "there were no calls before" the blast.

A federal law enforcement official speaking on condition of anonymity said at least nine such phone calls had been logged and that the first came within an hour after the explosion to a nonemergency police number. There were several reports that one caller used the phrase "Serbian Liberation Front," but U.S. officials said they knew of no such organization.

In an interview with reporters, Cuomo said he had been told that one caller identified himself as represent-

See NEW YORK, A14, Col. 1

Descending the Stairwell Into a Smoky Hell

'People Were Screaming, Crying, Coughing. That Was the Worst,' Broker Recounts

By Jay Mathews and Julia Preston
Washington Post Staff Writers

NEW YORK, Feb. 26—The group of young trainee stockbrokers had endured two spasms of mindless, smoke-induced panic on their 108-floor journey down the stifling stairwell in One World Trade Center today. But at the 30th floor, just when the air seemed to freshen and relief seemed near, the lights failed, and they plunged into a black hell.

"Many people lost it then," said Robert Rose, 24, a Californian. "You couldn't see a thing. People were screaming, crying, coughing. That was the worst."

Michael Kaiser, who had been attending a meeting on the 55th floor, said he started down the stairs but ran into a "traffic jam" of people, a "gridlock" of humanity in the pitch-black of the stairwells.

He and the others with him then took refuge in a suite of offices on the 51st floor. "The smoke was thick and it was black and it was everywhere," Kaiser said, and with "people just on the verge of starting to really panic," they smashed six or seven windows in the skyscraper so they could breathe.

By 3 p.m. firefighters appeared, he said, and escorted them with flashlights on a half-hour trek down 51 flights to an exit and safety.

Far below, in the underground shopping arcade that is one of lower Manhattan's brightest and busiest scenes, Wall Street Journal reporter Warren Getler stepped from a subway train into a confusing jumble of terrified, ash-covered workers and frantic pedestrians.

There was a petrochemical smell in the air, as if everyone had just imbibed a pint of gasoline at lunch, different but just as frightening as the scent of burnt wood that gushed from the fatal King's Cross subway fire he covered in London in November 1987.

Getler said that he tried to talk to one man, bleeding from his nostrils as he was

See SCENE, A15, Col. 1

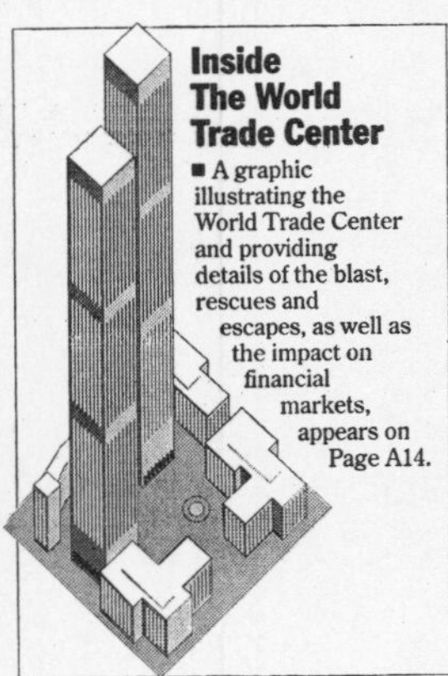

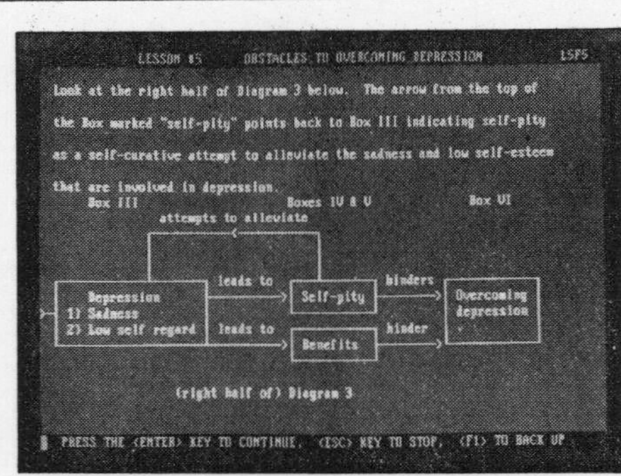

Psychiatrist Kenneth Colby has developed this interactive program for treating depression. It costs $200 and requires only a home computer.

The Computer Couch

Psychiatry's New Technological Tools

By Megan Rosenfeld
Washington Post Staff Writer

The voice is chirpy and girly, with a teenager's rushed diction. She sounds like someone offering you a great deal on a fantastic home tanning bed or amazing aluminum siding. She sounds ready to send a demonstrator to your home this very minute, to take your charge card number and ship within seven to 10 days.

But she is not selling any of that.

Hello! You have reached Psych-line, where you can receive counseling or advice over the phone. . . . You can talk privately and confidentially in the comfort of your own environment with experienced and licensed counselors, and you will control the length of your call. If you are experiencing depression, anxiety, if you need advice on a specific problem, or would like to discuss a concern in greater depth—whatever your situation—Psych-line is here for you.

Psych-line is just one of the modern technologies affecting the practice of psychotherapy, one more way to examine the id, the odd or the meaning of life. There is no indication that vast numbers of therapists are tossing out their couches, but according to those employing these new methods, these are the waves of the future.

Computer programs, videohookups, anonymous telephone calls—the technology available in the therapeutic marketplace varies from faddish to serious, from profit-oriented to altruistic. Their proponents say these methods can provide help that is quicker and cheaper, and as effective for

See THERAPY, A12, Col. 1

Kessler Asked To Remain as Head of FDA

Healy Announces Resignation at NIH

By David Brown
and Boyce Rensberger
Washington Post Staff Writers

David A. Kessler, the aggressive administrator of the Food and Drug Administration appointed by President George Bush, has been asked to retain his position in the Clinton administration. But Bush appointee Bernadine P. Healy, controversial head of the National Institutes of Health, announced her resignation yesterday.

Kessler, 41, whose activist leadership of the FDA over the last two years has won high praise from consumer-rights groups, accepted an offer from the Clinton administration to stay on.

Healy, 48, whose two-year tenure as the first woman director of NIH was marked by several bold and widely debated innovations, said she will leave her job in June to return to the Cleveland Clinic Foundation where she practiced cardiology before assuming the NIH post.

Like Healy, Kessler had offered his resignation after President Clinton's electoral victory. But privately Kessler made it clear that he felt work remained to be done in his effort to reinvigorate an agency that critics charged had become lethargic and scandal-ridden over the previous decade or more.

When Kessler, who has degrees in medicine and law, took up his post in late 1990, morale at the FDA was low. Many believed that it had been years since the agency

See KESSLER, A4, Col. 1

Clinton Spells Out Free Trade Pledge

President to Demand 'New Responsibility' From Other Major Powers

By Ann Devroy and Peter Behr
Washington Post Staff Writers

President Clinton yesterday laid out a broad blueprint for an American leadership role in global commerce. He vowed to help the nation "compete not retreat" abroad and made a broad commitment to free trade, but warned that unfair trade practices by foreign countries will get stern scrutiny from the new administration.

The address, the president's first international policy speech, used as its starting point Clinton's new economic package, calling it an effort by the United States to "get its own house in order." What follows, he said, will be the exercise of U.S. leadership to put into better order the rules and practices of global commerce. "If we set a new direction at home, we can set a new direction for the world," he said.

Clinton's blueprint did not differ significantly from a global economic speech President George Bush might have given, with the exception of a sharper edge against protectionism by U.S. trading partners, an issue with strong resonance among Democrats.

Carla A. Hills, Bush's special trade negotiator, called it "a very good speech and very welcome" because of fears at home and abroad that a "lack of clear statements" on Clinton's trade views was allowing protectionist voices to dominate.

■ ***Progress on deadlocked trade issues may be blocked by the uneven global recovery.*** *Page A9*

BY RICH LIPSKI—THE WASHINGTON POST

In his speech at American University, Clinton promised to make trade a "priority element" of U.S. national security.

The address offered no specifics on brewing trade battles and irritations—such as the recent verbal jousts over whether the Airbus, produced by a European airplane consortium, is unfairly subsidized. The major significance of yesterday's speech appeared to lay in its

See PRESIDENT, A8, Col. 1

INSIDE

'Monster' Tax Backed
■ A 'monster cigarette tax' of up to $2 a pack to pay for health care is said to have the support of key Clinton administration departments.
NATION, *Page A4*

Snow Goes Easy
■ Yesterday's snowstorm was gentle enough to create a minimum of disruptions and, for area youngsters, a maximum of fun.
METRO, *Page B1*

Dulles Access Road
■ The chairman of the regional airport review board says the Dulles Access Road was designed to serve the airport and should not be opened to car pools.
METRO, *Page B1*

First American Sold To Charlotte Bank
■ First Union Corp. of Charlotte, N.C., said yesterday that it will buy First American Bancorp's D.C. area banks for $453 million, ending two years of trouble for First American over revelations of its illegal ownership by the Bank of Credit and Commerce International. First Union will become the second-largest bank in the Washington area.
BUSINESS, *Page C1*

Weather
Today: Increasingly cloudy, breezy. High 74. Low 56. Wind east 8-16 mph.
Friday: Mostly cloudy, breezy, showers, thunderstorm possible. High 68. Low 56. Wind 10-20 mph.
Yesterday: Temp. range: 57-90.
AQI: Moderate-60. Details on Page C2.

The Washington Post

FINAL
Inside: **The Weekly, Classified, Washington Home**
Today's Contents on Page A2

118TH YEAR ···· No. 136 THURSDAY, APRIL 20, 1995 Prices May Vary in Areas Outside Metropolitan Washington (See Box on A4) 25¢

Bomb Kills Dozens in Oklahoma Federal Building

More Than 200 Missing; Children at Day Care Among Victims in Apparent Terrorist Attack

'This Is Your Nightmare Come True'

Preschoolers' Facility Within Yards of Blast

By Thomas Heath
Washington Post Staff Writer

OKLAHOMA CITY, April 19—As he walked the halls of St. Anthony's Hospital here, the Rev. George Young tried to explain to 4-year-old Katie, cradled in his arms in a bloody jumper, why her little sister died under a pile of rubble.

"She was very introspective about it all," Young said.

Katie was one of the lucky ones who survived the explosion that rocked the federal building today. She was in the building because it was home not just to federal agencies such as the Social Security Administration and the DEA, but also to a day-care center serving children of federal workers and families from the community. The powerful bomb that went off this morning exploded in a car parked just yards away from the second-floor room where the 30 or so children believed to be at the center were about to eat breakfast.

Authorities tonight said they had found 12 bodies of children from the day-care center but held out little hope of finding many survivors, given the location of the bomb.

If the bomb had gone off a little later, during the playtime, the story might have been different. Many children might have survived because the playground is on the opposite side of the building, where it was shielded from the bomb's blast.

Instead, the bomb literally wiped out "America's Kids," as the center was known. Rescue workers who searched for victims reported a horrific scene of mangled and decapitated bodies and toys scattered in the rubble. At another day-care center at a YMCA across the street, many children were injured but there were no known fatalities.

"This is your nightmare come true," said Ron Phelps, chaplain at Children's Hospital, where about a dozen of the injured children were taken.

Children's, St. Anthony's and Baptist Hospitals were flooded with calls from distraught and anxious parents hoping that their children were among the survivors.

Doloris Watson, a telephone company service representative, had delivered P.J. Allen, her 20-month-old grandson, to the day-care center this morning. When she heard the explosion, she got off her truck and ran back to the federal building.

"I saw a puff of smoke and I said, 'Oh, it can't be,'" she said.

By the time she got to the building, however, there was no sign of her

See CHILDREN, A26, Col. 1

ASSOCIATED PRESS PHOTOS

A rescue worker passes an injured child to a firefighter outside the structure where bomb exploded. The building housed a day-care center.

By Sue Anne Pressley
Washington Post Staff Writer

OKLAHOMA CITY, April 19—An apparent terrorist car bomb exploded outside a federal office building here today, collapsing the north face of the nine-story concrete building, injuring hundreds of workers, and killing at least 31, including 12 children who attended a day-care center on the second floor. Local officials said they feared that the toll would rise quickly because by early evening more than half of the estimated 550 people who worked in the building were still unaccounted for.

Assistant Fire Chief John Hansen said rescue workers had seen "many more fatalities in the building that we are working around" while searching for survivors. He added, "The death toll could really skyrocket" when they begin removing corpses.

The bombing, described by authorities as the deadliest terrorist attack ever on U.S. soil, occurred in the most unlikely of targets—this heartland capital city of 440,000 that residents once jokingly described as "the town where nothing much ever happens." It occurred shortly after 9 a.m. Central time, when employees were settling down to their work day at the Alfred P. Murrah Federal Building and when the maximum number of people were going in and out of the structure.

The explosion quickly turned the placid, tree-shaded downtown into a scene more reminiscent of the aftermath of bombings in Beirut or Tel Aviv. Workers staggered out of stairwells, blood dripping into their eyes. A woman moaned on the ground, part of her leg apparently missing from the blast. Employees at buildings blocks away reported being thrown from their chairs, windows were shattered, and residents who live 30 miles from downtown reported feeling the powerful vibrations of the blast. Everywhere around the city, people stood in stunned silence, not believing what they had just seen and heard, not comprehending how anyone could have done such a thing.

"Obviously, no amateur did this," said Gov. Frank A. Keating (R). "Whoever did this was an animal."

The building itself was so damaged that simply searching for survivors became a long, perilous task that stretched throughout the day and into the night. The entire front portion appeared to be excavated, as if it had been hit with a wrecking ball many times—cables stringing down over the sides, steel reinforcements visible, portions of offices still recognizable. Debris from the blast formed a pile two stories high in front of the building, cascading all the way across the street and into a parking lot. The explosion itself blasted a crater eight feet deep and 20 feet in diameter that was filled with rubble.

Tonight, the First Christian Church on 36th Street also doubled as the Family Assistance Center, the sad place where relatives came to bring pictures of their missing loved ones, to tell about birthmarks and scars and other things that might help to identify them. At 11 p.m., 100 people still waited here, holding a quiet prayer vigil and listening to television reports that told them nothing.

Antonio Cooper and his wife, Renee, were still trying to find their 6-month-old son, Antonio Jr., who was enrolled in the day-care center and is still unaccounted for. They held a picture of him, dressed up in a bow tie and grinning broadly. "He is a playful boy," Cooper said, as the boy's mother cried at his side. They said they would wait all night for news.

"This is a sad place to be," said Richard Dugger, an agent of the Oklahoma medical examiner's office who was helping. "Tomorrow

See OKLAHOMA, A25, Col. 1

Clinton Condemns 'Evil Cowards' for Blast

President Launches Massive Federal Probe; Attorney General Cites Death Penalty

By Pierre Thomas and Ann Devroy
Washington Post Staff Writers

President Clinton vowed yesterday to bring to justice the "evil cowards" responsible for the devastating explosion in Oklahoma City, launching a massive probe into a bombing that officials said had all the characteristics of a terrorist attack.

The sophistication of the attack, believed to be the product of a car or truck bomb, and the choice of a federal building as the target made it very likely that terrorists carried out the assault, administration and federal law enforcement officials said.

Clinton and Attorney General Janet Reno, in afternoon news conferences, stopped short of saying terrorists carried out the bombing but hinted strongly that they suspected as much. U.S. intelligence agencies were "tickling every source worldwide" in probing whether a foreign government was behind the attack, a senior official said.

"I will not allow the people of this country to be intimidated," Clinton said. "Let there be no room for doubt: We will find the people who did this. When we do, justice will be swift, certain and severe."

Echoing Clinton's remarks, Reno said the perpetrators, once found and convicted, would face the death penalty.

More than 100 FBI and Treasury agents and support personnel were dispatched to Oklahoma City from locations across the nation. Officials said they were pursuing three basic theories about who staged the bombing: Muslim radicals similar to those convicted of staging the World Trade Center bombing in New York two years ago; extremists who hate the federal government, including white supremacists active in western states; or people seeking vengeance for the bloody federal assault

See SECURITY, A24, Col. 3

Behind firefighter, wrecked vehicles and tons of debris from blown-out building.

Court Allows Anonymous Campaign Fliers

By Joan Biskupic
Washington Post Staff Writer

In an opinion celebrating the American tradition of pamphleteers, the Supreme Court ruled yesterday that states cannot require people to sign leaflets and other campaign literature.

The court by 7 to 2 rejected an Ohio statute—similar to those in many states—that required election literature to contain the name and address of the person responsible for it. The court majority broadly endorsed robust and free political speech and said the right to remain anonymous is part of the First Amendment's free speech guarantee.

"Under our Constitution, anonymous pamphleteering is not a pernicious, fraudulent practice, but an honorable tradition of advocacy and of dissent," Justice John Paul Stevens wrote for the court. "Anonymity is a shield from the tyranny of the majority."

Stevens's opinion was laced with references to anonymous literature and political speech, including the Federalist Papers, which were published under the name Publius. He compared anonymous political speech to "the secret ballot, the hard-won

See COURT, A9, Col. 1

D.C. Council Completes a Budget Unbalancing Act

By Howard Schneider
and David A. Vise
Washington Post Staff Writers

The D.C. Council approved an unbalanced city budget early yesterday that promises tough financial decisions in the future but departs little from a spending plan initially proposed by Mayor Marion Barry and roundly criticized by Congress as too generous.

In 10 hours of debate that ended about 5 a.m., council members talked about getting tough with city workers, killing low-priority programs such as the D.C. School of Law and using newly won power over public school spending to start cutting waste.

But in the end, they did none of those things, instead choosing to break a $3.25 billion spending limit Congress imposed on the city and producing a $3.5 billion plan that even on paper includes a deficit.

The law school was left hanging by a thread; the Board of Education escaped without major budget surgery; and municipal unions were spared a 12 percent wage cut. The cut will be replaced with a hodgepodge of furlough days and other concessions designed to save the same amount of money. Even police officers—who never reached an agreement with the city and recently disrupted a council meeting to protest the pay cut—were granted a reprieve.

The council did reinstate a $40 million property tax cut that has been the focus of political acrimony since December. Council supporters have approved it five times, and a coalition of opponents led by Barry has blocked it four; it now is attached to a piece of legislation that will be extremely difficult for Barry to veto.

Council members also laid the groundwork for a five-year government spending plan that they said will address tough problems such as reducing the city work force and cutting services.

But otherwise it was a night of shifting majorities, conflicting votes

See DISTRICT, A22, Col. 1

▪ ***The D.C. Council has moved to toughen standards for teachers despite the union's opposition.*** ***Page C1***

Barry's Choice to Head New Convention Center Withdraws

By Hamil R. Harris and Vernon Loeb
Washington Post Staff Writers

D.C. Mayor Marion Barry's nominee to oversee construction of a new downtown convention center withdrew his name from consideration yesterday after a key D.C. Council member voiced concern about his financial dealings, including links to a businessman who helped renovate Barry's home.

Phinis Jones, 47, a Southeast Washington businessman and political activist, sent Barry a letter late yesterday afternoon withdrawing his nomination as chairman of the Washington Convention Center Authority "with much regret" in the face of "recent allegations that have been made about me" that "are without merit and unsubstantiated."

Council member Charlene Drew Jarvis (D-Ward 4) said earlier in the day that she had informed Barry that Jones's nomination would not be confirmed by the Economic Development Committee, of which she is chairwoman, "because there is controversy, and I do not want the new, expanded convention center to begin with any controversy."

The controversy, Jarvis said, centers on "as-yet-unsubstantiated allegations" concerning Jones's role in helping Washington businessman Yong Yun secure a $17.6 million city lease for a building Yun has constructed on Martin Luther King Jr. Avenue SE. The city began paying Yun in February even though the building is still empty. Yun's ties to Barry have become the focus of a federal investigation.

In an interview with The Washington Post shortly before Jones withdrew yesterday, his attorney, Wayne R. Cohen, confirmed that Jones has several links to Yun. Jones worked as a paid consultant to Yun to help him obtain the lease. Later, Jones recommended that Yun pay $100,000 to a taxpayer-funded organization, East of the River Community Development, for its help in obtaining the lease. Three years later, Jones became the group's chairman.

Cohen also acknowledged that Jones is selling a building he owns to the organization for $179,900.

Court records show that Jones and his largest business have failed to pay more than $200,000 in

See JONES, A18, Col. 1

INSIDE

Whitewater Probe
▪ The Whitewater counsel is looking into whether a box of papers was removed from Vincent Foster's office the day after his suicide.
NATION, *Page A3*

Iran's Plans
▪ Iran's president said his government has made no decision to seek nuclear weapons but will continue nuclear research programs.
WORLD, *Page A29*

Shrinking Deficit
▪ The trade deficit dropped by 24.6 percent in February, partly due to lowering demand for consumer goods.
BUSINESS, *Page B10*

USAir Cuts Loss
▪ USAir reported a first-quarter loss of $96.9 million, $100 million less than its loss during the same period last year.
BUSINESS, *Page B10*

Los Angeles Times

CIRCULATION: 1,058,498 DAILY / 1,457,583 SUNDAY

WEDNESDAY, OCTOBER 4, 1995

COPYRIGHT 1995/THE TIMES MIRROR COMPANY/CC†/102 PAGES

DAILY 50¢ DESIGNATED AREAS HIGHER

Simpson Not Guilty

Drama Ends 474 Days After Arrest

Case Had Many Holes, Juror Says

■ **Panel:** Group agreed with forensic expert Lee that there was 'something wrong' with prosecution's evidence, he reports. Opportunities for contamination are cited.

By EDWARD J. BOYER and ELAINE WOO
TIMES STAFF WRITERS

In the end, what swayed them wasn't the impassioned rhetoric of Johnnie L. Cochran Jr. or the calmer but no less dramatic appeals of Marcia Clark.

They didn't buy the prosecution's so-called mountain of evidence, from a barking dog to DNA. They didn't buy the motive, a husband exploding in jealous, murderous rage.

And the race card, played so brazenly in the defense team's blistering attacks on former LAPD Detective Mark Fuhrman, rated "barely a blip" for the most part on their mental radar screens.

In the end, said Lionel (Lon) Cryer—the juror who will long be remembered for his raised-fist salute to O.J. Simpson at the close of the fractious and unpredictable murder trial—what mattered was what wasn't there, the holes he said jurors kept finding in the prosecution case.

"It was garbage in, garbage out," Cryer, known as the juror in seat No. 6, said Tuesday about the prosecution's evidence. "There was a problem with what was being presented to [prosecutors] for testing from LAPD. We felt there were a lot of opportunities for either contamination of evidence, samples being mixed or stored together."

That summed up the panel's "whole mode of thinking" very soon after the 10 women and two men entered the deliberations room Monday morning, Cryer said in an exclusive interview with The Times. As they walked into that room on the ninth floor of the Downtown courthouse, Cryer said, the words of noted forensic pathologist Dr. Henry Lee, whom Cryer said the jury viewed as "the most credible witness" of all, reverberated in their ears.

Lee, Cryer recounted, said, "There is something wrong here."

"He had a lot of impact on a lot of people. A lot of people were in agreement that there was some-

Please see JURY, A4

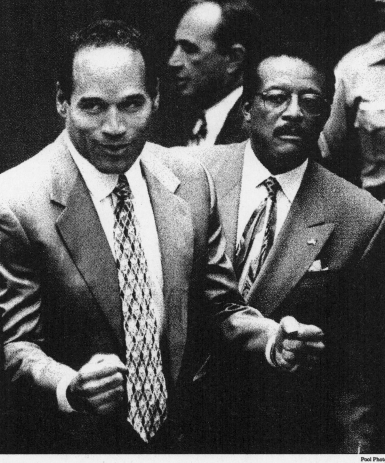

Pool Photo

O.J. Simpson clenches his fists in victory as verdicts are read. At right is attorney Johnnie L. Cochran Jr.

■ **Verdicts:** The ex-football star expresses gratitude and returns to his Brentwood estate where friends and family celebrate. Relatives of the victims react with pain and grim silence to the jurors' decision.

By JIM NEWTON, TIMES STAFF WRITER

Bringing one of history's most riveting courtroom dramas to a stunning climax, O.J. Simpson was acquitted of two counts of murder Tuesday, verdicts that set the football Hall of Famer free 474 days after he was arrested and charged with a brutal double homicide.

At 11:16 a.m., Simpson returned home to his Brentwood estate, embracing his longtime friend Al Cowlings in the same driveway where the two were arrested on June 17, 1994. As night fell, crowds of well-wishers and detractors gathered beyond police barricades while the Simpson entourage partied inside the famous home.

Within hours of the verdicts—broadcast live and bringing businesses across the country to a temporary standstill—family members of the victims retreated in grief, and the first of the anonymous jurors emerged to give The Times an interview in which he dismissed the prosecution's physical evidence as "garbage in, garbage out."

While jurors scattered to their homes, prosecutors, defense lawyers and family members of the victims and defendant gathered in an extraordinary series of news conferences.

In a statement read by his eldest son during one of the media sessions, Simpson expressed relief, gratitude and a commitment to finding whoever murdered his ex-wife Nicole Brown Simpson and her friend Ronald Lyle Goldman.

"I am relieved that this part of the incredible nightmare that occurred on June 12, 1994, is over with," Simpson said. "My first obligation is to my young children, who will be raised in the way that Nicole and I had always planned."

Simpson vowed to pursue "as my primary goal in life" the killer or killers responsible for the murders, concluding: "I only hope someday that—despite every prejudicial thing that has been said about me publicly, both in and out of the courtroom—people will come to understand and believe that I would not, could not and did not kill anyone."

After 266 days of sequestration at the Inter-Continental Hotel in Downtown Los Angeles, jurors deliberated a mere three hours before accepting Simpson's contention that the charges against him were unproven.

Their verdicts, which were delivered in a courtroom so tense that some spectators trembled visibly in anticipation, united jurors and Simpson in a strangely triumphant moment.

Simpson smiled thinly and mouthed the words "thank you" as the not guilty verdicts were read. Two jurors smiled back. Another, Lionel (Lon) Cryer, raised his left fist in a salute toward Simpson as the panel left the courtroom.

Please see SIMPSON, A10

Miscalculations, Bad Luck Hurt Prosecution

By HENRY WEINSTEIN, MAURA DOLAN and TIM RUTTEN
TIMES STAFF WRITERS

On the morning of her final argument in O.J. Simpson's double murder trial, Deputy Dist. Atty. Marcia Clark stepped onto the elevator outside her 18th-floor office in the Downtown Criminal Courts Building and began the usual, halting nine-floor ride down to Judge Lance A. Ito's high-security courtroom.

As she clutched a brace of green loose-leaf notebooks tightly to her chest, Clark turned to a reporter and asked, "Do you think the jurors

NEWS ANALYSIS

are interested in what I have to say?" With each syllable, the concern in her voice seemed to deepen until it filled the tiny space like a cloud.

In fact, that dark pall of doubt had cast its anxious shadow across the Simpson prosecution from the start. So, even though she argued her case from atop what she repeatedly called a "mountain of evidence," Clark and her colleagues

Please see EXPERTS, A12

Half of Americans Disagree With Verdict

■ **Times Poll:** Many cite race as key factor in trial.

By CATHLEEN DECKER and SHERYL STOLBERG
TIMES STAFF WRITERS

Across the nation, the verdict rendered by the jury in the O.J. Simpson case was met with disapproval by a plurality of Americans, who also felt strongly that justice was not served and whose confidence in the criminal justice system has plummeted as a result.

A national Los Angeles Times poll conducted Tuesday also found that Americans overwhelmingly believe that race loomed large as

Please see POLL, A11

Views on the Verdicts

In a nationwide Times poll, the response to the jury's finding:

Agree 41%

Disagree 50%

Don't know 9%

Source: Los Angeles Times Poll

Los Angeles Times

■ **Reaction:** High-voltage joy, angry denouncements.

By JOHN L. MITCHELL and JEFF LEEDS
TIMES STAFF WRITER

For a tingling instant, the city stopped—its freeways nearly empty, sidewalks clear, the day's business put on hold as people gathered silently before their televisions.

Then out came all the emotions generated during a trial that mesmerized the world, a high-voltage discharge of jubilation and outrage, relief and sorrow. No urban violence accompanied Tuesday's not guilty verdicts in the O.J. Simpson trial, but there were plenty of

Please see REACTION, A7

More Coverage

■ **NEW LEADER**—Defense attorney Johnnie L. Cochran Jr. has emerged as a black leader. **A3**

■ **SHARP WORDS**—Simpson lawyer Robert L. Shapiro trades barbs with co-counsels in separate TV interviews. **A3**

■ **LAPD SHOCKED**—The acquittal of O.J. Simpson stuns the LAPD. **A8**

■ **THREE VIEWS**—Columnists Robert A. Jones, Al Martinez and Lynell George give their insights on the Simpson case. **B1**

■ **DIVIDED REACTION**—Opinions across America are sharply split, mostly along racial lines. **B2**

■ **Additional coverage:** A3-A13, A18, D2

Simpson Is Free, but Can He Regain His Life and Image?

■ **Aftermath:** He faces civil suits and possible custody battle. But his far greater fame may carry a high price.

By ALAN ABRAHAMSON and TONY PERRY
TIMES STAFF WRITERS

O.J. Simpson has regained his freedom, but at what price?

A man acquitted of murder hears the cell door open, but usually the next thing he hears is the sound of doors closing—doors to opportunity, to approval, to old friends.

For one who once seemed to imbibe his legendary popularity like strong drink, for whom charm was a passport across every sort of border, the sound of such doors closing could easily become a kind of dirge.

Simpson, in essence, faces the possibility of becoming, if not a man without a country, a man without the country he once knew—and something worse, a kind of exile in his own life.

It was a possibility the former football star seemed to envision in an eerily prophetic passage from the letter he left behind when he fled arrest in June, 1994: "No matter what the outcome, people will look and point," wrote the man who once basked in the applause of thousands.

During last week's final arguments, defense attorney F. Lee Bailey mused that, even if Simpson were to be acquitted, he would spend the rest of his life defending himself from those who believe that wealth and luck had allowed him to evade the consequences of

Please see FUTURE, A12

INSIDE TODAY'S TIMES

SPENDING BILL VETOED

President Clinton refused to sign a bill that allows for $2.1 billion in congressional spending. It was the third veto of his presidency. **A22**

GANG KILLINGS SOAR

Analysis of gang killings in Los Angeles County charts a sharp rise in such murders, which were 43% of all homicides last year. **B3**

DISASTER FOR DODGERS

The Cincinnati Reds scored four runs in the first inning and went on to beat the Dodgers, 7-2, in the first game of their NL playoff series. **C1**

WEATHER: Mostly clear and warm today and Thursday with gusty canyon winds. Civic Center low/high: 66/96. Details: B7

■ TOP OF THE NEWS ON A2

A Corner Is Turned in Lives of 3 Families

■ **Relatives:** Some emerge exultant. Others wonder how they will go on.

Through it all, Kim Goldman was sure of this one thing: No pain could ever match the grief that swamped her life when her big brother, Ron, was murdered on a warm spring night nearly 16 months ago.

But then came Tuesday.

At 10:07 a.m., as she huddled in her seat in Department 103 of the Los Angeles County Criminal Courts Building, Kim Goldman heard the unfathomable: The accused killer was not guilty, jurors declared. He would go free at once.

Exultant, O.J. Simpson clenched his fists in victory—liberated. Nearby, his relatives flashed smiles of deep relief and cried tears of joy, while the parents of his

Please see FAMILIES, A6

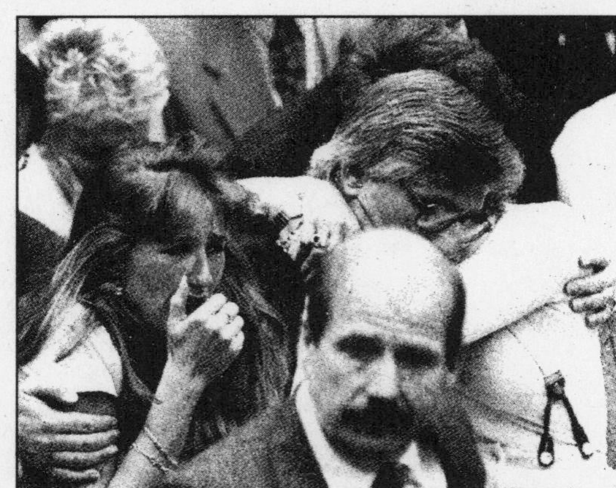

Pool Photo

Upon hearing the verdicts, Kim Goldman weeps while Fred Goldman is hugged by his wife Patti. In foreground is Detective Tom Lange.

"All the News That's Fit to Print"

The New York Times

Late Edition

New York: **Today,** early shower then brightening skies. High 48. **Tonight,** partly cloudy. Low 35. **Tomorrow,** partly sunny. High 47. **Yesterday,** high 57, low 40. Details, page D16.

VOL.CXLV . . . . No. 50,388 NEW YORK, FRIDAY, APRIL 5, 1996 — $1 beyond the greater New York metropolitan area. — 60 CENTS

Reuters

A NATO helicopter hovers over the wreckage of the military jet that carried the Secretary of Commerce and American business executives.

Plane Crash in Croatia Silenced A Big Player in Capital Debates

By DAVID E. SANGER

WASHINGTON, April 4 — When Ronald H. Brown died on a hillside near Dubrovnik, Croatia, on Wednesday, he was in the thick of three battles here that touched the divergent roles he played in Washington.

The first was a continuing struggle within the Administration — sometimes still heated three years after it began — over the degree to which the nation's commercial interests should drive its foreign policy agenda.

As Commerce Secretary, Mr. Brown often argued fiercely for what he called "commercial diplomacy," the use of America's clout abroad to create jobs at home, a stark counterpoint to the "high diplomacy" of the cold war. But there was always resistance, and many wonder whether, without Mr. Brown's high-profile circuiting of the globe, that approach will prove a permanent legacy of the Clinton Administration, or whether it could slowly dissolve.

His second battle was to save the Commerce Department from a Republican-dominated Congress that viewed it as a ripe target for disassembly or outright abolition. With his trademark passion, Mr. Brown called this "unilateral disarmament" in the face of Japanese and European competition, and was winning the argument. But without him, many in the Administration said today, the issue is bound to arise again.

And the third battle centered on Mr. Brown's true passion in life: politics. His death deprives the Clinton Administration of its most visible black Cabinet member and its bridge to black voters, even though some prominent blacks were concerned that Mr. Brown was a bit too much of an insider, too interested in compromise. Mr. Brown was just beginning to try again to work the

Continued on Page A13, Column 5

Bad Equipment Tied to Crash, Perry Suggests

By R. W. APPLE Jr.

WASHINGTON, April 4 — Defense Secretary William J. Perry suggested today that malfunctioning instruments may have caused the crash of an Air Force jet that took the life of Commerce Secretary Ronald H. Brown and at least 32 others in Croatia on Wednesday.

Returning from a trip to Egypt, Mr. Perry told reporters on his plane, "It was a classic sort of accident that good instrumentation should be able to prevent."

He did not specify whether he was referring to instruments on the ground or in the plane. Mr. Brown's plane, a military version of the Boeing 737, smashed into a mountain near Dubrovnik, the storied port on the Adriatic Sea.

More than 36 hours after the crash, it was still not clear how many passengers were aboard, though it was evident there were no survivors. After rescue teams searched all Wednesday night and all day today, hampered by fog and rain, Miomir Zuzul, the Croatian Ambassador to the United States, said they had discovered 33 bodies. The Pentagon used the same figure.

But the plane's manifest, issued by the State Department, listed 35 people: Mr. Brown and 11 Commerce Department aides, including Charles F. Meissner, Assistant Secretary for International Trade, whose wife, Doris, heads the Immigration and

Continued on Page A12, Column 3

COMMUNISTS LOOK TO THE SOVIET ERA IN THEIR PLATFORM

A DRAFT LAW IS PREPARED

Moscow Party Would Curtail Free-Market Reforms if It Wins Back Power

By MICHAEL R. GORDON

MOSCOW, April 4 — In a stark expression of what they hope to achieve if they take back power, Communist members of Parliament have prepared a draft law that calls for heavy state intervention in the economy.

The proposed law would curtail pro-market reforms and rejects some key measures Russia has adopted at the insistence of the International Monetary Fund, which recently granted Russia a $10.1 billion loan.

Some aspects of the bill, which has not yet been made public, read like an evocation of the worker's paradise promised by the Bolsheviks 70 years ago: guaranteed employment, cheap apartments and controls on the price of consumer goods.

It would even restore a State Planning Committee, an echo of the Gosplan agency that controlled virtually every facet of economic life in the old Soviet Union.

Prepared by a leading Communist policy team, the plan may yet be modified as the election team of Gennadi A. Zyuganov tries to mold it into a platform that can be sold to non-Communists as well as the party's rank and file.

Trying to strike a pragmatic note, Yuri D. Maslyukov, the Communist chairman of the Parliament's Committee for Economic Policy, said the draft law was just one possible proposal.

"I won't criticize it in this particular case," he said in an interview. "I think this proposal is premature."

But ardent Communists, who constitute much of Mr. Zyuganov's constituency, said the plan was needed to restore social protections and pull Russian industry out of a state of "crisis."

Oleg V. Malyarov, one of the advisers who worked on the draft law, said it could serve as "the specific embodiment" of Mr. Zyuganov's promises.

And though the Communists are debating among themselves how far and how fast to push, much of the draft law appears to reflect a broad consensus within the party about how to overhaul Russia's economy.

The draft law comes at a time of rising political expectations among the Communists. A copy of the draft law — "Urgent Measures to Take Russia

Continued on Page A10, Column 4

Suspect Arraigned on One Bomb Count

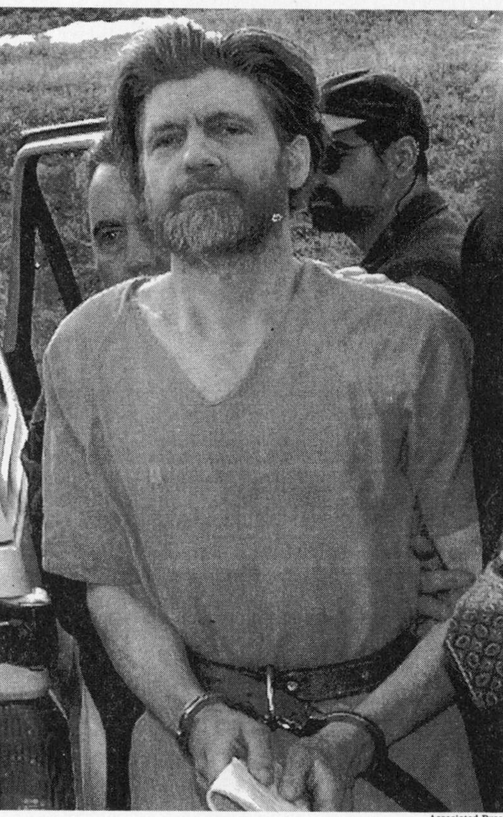

Associated Press

Theodore J. Kaczynski ignored shouted questions as he was escorted into the Federal courthouse in Helena, Mont.

Search of Cabin Yields Lethal Ingredients

By TIMOTHY EGAN

HELENA, Mont., April 4 — Theodore J. Kaczynski, the onetime university professor taken into custody on Wednesday as a suspect in the Unabom case, was arraigned here today on a single felony charge of possessing bomb components and was held without bail.

The arraignment followed a search in which, Federal authorities said, they found evidence that Mr. Kaczynski had turned his one-room mountain cabin, 50 miles to the northwest near the town of Lincoln, into a virtual bomb laboratory.

When the 53-year-old suspect was brought into the Lewis and Clark County jail here on Wednesday evening, his hair was matted and his stained jeans were badly torn, as if from the scuffle that he had had with the Federal agents who had seized him at the cabin earlier in the day. By this morning, at his arraignment, he was dressed in orange jailhouse overalls, and he seemed confident, a bit of a smirk on his face as he glanced around the courtroom.

Just beforehand, as Mr. Kaczynski was taken into the Federal courthouse here, he ignored shouts from reporters asking him whether he was the Unabomber, the mail-bomb terrorist who has killed 3 people and injured 23 others from coast to coast in the last 18 years.

The Government did not charge Mr. Kaczynski today with any crimes specifically relating to the Unabom case, and indeed Federal officials have not publicly said that they consider him to be the serial bomber.

But it is not unusual for a suspect regarded as dangerous to be held on a relatively modest charge while Federal prosecutors build a larger case against him, and investigators privately said they were certain that Mr. Kaczynski was the Unabomber, a conviction apparently bolstered by the results of the intensive search at his 10-by-12-foot cabin.

The F.B.I. affidavit that was the basis of the charge brought today against Mr. Kaczynski (pronounced kah-SIN-skee) listed an extensive array of bomb parts and bomb-making manuals that Federal agents said had been found at the cabin. And law-enforcement officials said in interviews tonight that the bomb materials matched fragments from the Unabomber's devices almost precisely in terms of chemicals and techniques.

Government officials also said tonight that the agents had discovered at the cabin the manual typewriter believed to have been used to type the Unabomber's 35,000-word mani-

Continued on Page A24, Column 4

Long and Twisting Trail Led To Unabom Suspect's Arrest

By DAVID JOHNSTON

WASHINGTON, April 4 — The tip came the way the F.B.I. had long expected, from a family member with misgivings. But the search for the man investigators believe is the Unabomber still had months to go before the suspect was arrested on Wednesday, as his deeply torn family struggled with its loyalties and then as an elite team of agents stood vigil for weeks in the Montana snows.

And even now the case is far from finished, postal inspectors and other law-enforcement officials said today. With the arrest of Theodore J. Kaczynski in Montana, hundreds of agents, held back in recent weeks for fear of somehow tipping their hand to a fugitive who had eluded them for nearly 18 years, are now fanning out to airports, bus stations, homeless shelters and universities nationwide. They are trying to fill the many blanks in the life of Mr. Kaczynski, a Harvard-educated recluse.

The tip that led to the arrest arrived in a similarly mysterious fashion, investigators said today. When Mr. Kaczynski's brother, David, of Schenectady, N.Y., first approached the Federal Bureau of Investigation early this year, his initial contact was through an intermediary.

As described by Federal officials supervising the investigation, David Kaczynski, who had also attended Harvard and who in 1971 helped his brother buy the Montana property, grew suspicious late last year that his brother might be the author of the Unabomber's published 35,000-word manifesto.

David Kaczynski combed old family papers, finding what he feared might exist, copies of some letters dating to the 1970's that were written by his brother to newspapers protesting the abuses of technology. The sentiments were disturbingly reminiscent of what he thought he had read in the Unabomber manuscript.

But it was not until January that a lawyer for the family telephoned the F.B.I. in Washington.

"The lawyer was nervous," one official recalled. The lawyer described the situation without reveal-

Continued on Page A25, Column 6

Burst Main Points to a Wider Pipe Problem

By PAM BELLUCK

A huge water main break in Astoria, Queens, in January was caused by defective pipe, city officials said yesterday, and tests show that the problem extends far beyond the intersection where the main burst. A significant part of the 8,900-foot-long pipe is of equally poor quality, the officials said, and would have to be replaced or repaired at a possible cost of several million dollars.

The flaw in the pipe — brittle steel that ruptured after it was in use for only five months — could have been caught if the city had required the manufacturer to perform a special test, city officials acknowledged. The test is not routine and not required under industry standards, experts said, but has been recommended for 10 years under certain conditions, some of which occurred in Astoria.

The problem with the steel in the Astoria pipe is considered so serious that city officials say they will test much of the other steel pipe installed across the city in the last decade. That may include waterlines in Manhattan that were replaced under Columbus Avenue, 14th Street and the 79th Street transverse in Central Park during recent construction.

The city has not yet determined who is at fault for the defective pipe, David Golub, a spokesman for the city's Department of Environmental Protection, said, adding that the department was investigating to determine if the steel supplier, the pipe manufacturer or any other companies involved in the project could be legally liable.

But from now on, Mr. Golub said, all steel pipe will be tested to determine how brittle it is, or its "fracture toughness," before it is installed.

"We learned about something only

Continued on Page B6, Column 1

John Sotomayor/The New York Times

Officials say defective steel water pipe could extend far beyond this section that ruptured in January in Astoria, Queens.

INSIDE

Pact on Drug Prices Blocked

A judge has thrown out a $408.9 million settlement of a price-fixing lawsuit brought by pharmacies against big drug makers. Page D1.

Uphill Campaign for Rao

Prime Minister P. V. Narasimha Rao has opened his re-election campaign in India, by apologizing for not being somebody else. Page A3.

City Official Helped Group Win Contract

Last April, when a Queens social-services organization was trying to gain a multimillion-dollar contract with the city, it sent an unusual salesman to the city agency that was evaluating competing bids.

The salesman, it turned out, was a city official himself, and he had already been offered a job with the private group seeking the contract.

The presentation by the official, Albert J. Farina, on behalf of the Hellenic American Neighborhood Action Committee appears to have violated city conflict-of-interest rules, which generally prohibit city workers from lobbying city agencies on matters in which they have a financial interest. And the disclosure of his role is the latest problem to arise from the city's dealings with the Queens group, whose $43 million contracts to monitor welfare recipients were canceled last week by Mayor Rudolph W. Giuliani.

Article, page B1.

Study Recommends The Yankees Move To a West Side Site

By RICHARD SANDOMIR

A consulting firm's recommendation that the Yankees move from the Bronx to the West Side of Manhattan was based on the conclusion that a new ball park along the Hudson River would produce a significant increase in attendance, higher prices for luxury seats and an enhanced image for New York City.

The report, jointly commissioned by the city, the state and the Yankees, studied four options, including renovating the current Yankee Stadium, but came down solidly in favor of a West Side stadium with a retractable domed roof that could be used for baseball, football, concerts and conventions. The cost for such a stadium would be $1.06 billion, it said.

Although he has insisted that he wants the team to remain in the South Bronx, Mayor Rudolph W. Giuliani has pitched the West Side site as the most attractive lure to keep the Yankees from relocating to New Jersey, and the best way to avoid a repetition of the Dodgers' move from Brooklyn to Los Angeles in 1958.

The Yankees' lease in the Bronx expires in 2002, and the team's principal owner, George M. Steinbrenner 3d, has made it clear that he is dissatisfied with the team's 73-year-old home in the South Bronx, complaining about security, parking,

Continued on Page B4, Column 1

NEWS SUMMARY A2

Parcells may cost Jets No. 1 pick

PAGE 100

Special Playoff Guide

12 PAGES OF MATCHUPS & SCOUTING REPORTS IN SPORTS

Arnold Palmer has cancer

PAGE 3

NEW YORK POST

SUNDAY LATE CITY FINAL

SUNDAY, JANUARY 12, 1997 / Sunny & windy, 35 / Weather: Page 63 ★★ http://www.nypostonline.com/ • • • • 50¢

JonBenet Ramsey, just a few months before she was brutally strangled.

Dave Sartin

Was murdered 6-year-old a victim of pageants that turn girls into sexual targets?

TRAGIC LITTLE BEAUTY

FULL REPORT, MORE PICTURES: PAGES 4 & 5

State Liquor Authority: Tipsy watchdog

DAY ONE OF NEW POST PROBE: PAGES 12-13